Microsoft®

Office 2007

Introductory Concepts and Techniques

Windows Vista Edition

Gary B. Shelly

Thomas J. Cashman

Misty E. Vermaat

Contributing Authors

Steven G. Forsythe

Mary Z. Last

Philip J. Pratt

Jeffrey J. Quasney

Susan L. Sebok

Jeffrey J. Webb

THOMSON

COURSE TECHNOLOGY™

THOMSON COURSE TECHNOLOGY   25 THOMSON PLACE   BOSTON MA 02210

 SHELLY CASHMAN SERIES®

Australia • Canada • Denmark • Japan • Mexico • New Zealand • Philippines • Puerto Rico • Singapore • South Africa • Spain • United Kingdom • United States

Microsoft Office 2007
Introductory Concepts and Techniques, Windows Vista Edition

Gary B. Shelly

Thomas J. Cashman

Misty E. Vermaat

Executive Editor
Alexandra Arnold

Senior Product Managers
Reed Curry, Mali Jones

Product Manager
Heather Hawkins

Associate Product Manager
Klenda Martinez

Editorial Assistant
Jon Farnham

Senior Marketing Manager
Joy Stark-Vancs

Marketing Coordinator
Julie Schuster

Print Buyer
Julio Esperas

Director of Production
Patty Stephan

Lead Production Editor
Matthew Hutchinson

Production Editors
**Cathie DiMassa,
Jill Klaffky, Phillipa Lehar**

Developmental Editors
**Jill Batistick, Amanda Brodkin,
Laurie Brown, Lyn Markowicz**

Proofreaders
**John Bosco,
Kim Kosmatka**

Indexer
Rich Carlson

QA Manuscript Reviewers
**John Freitas, Serge Palladino,
Chris Scriver, Danielle Shaw,
Marianne Snow, Teresa Storch**

Art Director
Bruce Bond

Cover and Text Design
Joel Sadagursky

Cover Photo
Jon Chomitz

Compositor
GEX Publishing Services

Printer
Banta Menasha

softcover binding:
ISBN-13: 978-1-4239-1228-6
ISBN-10: 1-4239-1228-4

softcover-spiral binding:
ISBN-13: 978-1-4239-1230-9
ISBN-10: 1-4239-1230-6

hardcover-spiral binding:
ISBN-13: 978-1-4239-1231-6
ISBN-10: 1-4239-1231-4

Microsoft® Office 2007
Introductory Concepts and Techniques
Windows Vista Edition

Contents

Preface xiv
To the Student xxiv

Essential Introduction to Computers
Objectives **COM 1**
What Is a Computer? **COM 2**
What Does a Computer Do? **COM 3**
Why Is a Computer so Powerful? **COM 4**
How Does a Computer Know What to Do? **COM 4**
What Are the Components of a Computer? **COM 4**
Input Devices **COM 5**
  The Keyboard COM 5
  The Mouse COM 7
System Unit **COM 8**
  Processor COM 8
  Memory COM 8
Output Devices **COM 9**
  Printers COM 9
  Display Devices COM 10
Storage Devices **COM 11**
  Magnetic Disks COM 11
  Optical Disks COM 14
  Tape COM 16
  Miniature Mobile Storage Media COM 16
Communications Devices **COM 18**
Computer Software **COM 18**
  System Software COM 18
  Application Software COM 19
Networks and the Internet **COM 20**
  The Internet COM 21
  The World Wide Web COM 21
  Electronic Commerce COM 23
How to Purchase a Personal Computer **COM 24**
How to Purchase a Desktop Computer **COM 25**
How to Purchase a Notebook Computer **COM 32**
How to Purchase a Tablet PC **COM 35**
How to Purchase a Personal Mobile Device **COM 37**
Learn It Online **COM 39**
Case Studies **COM 39**
Index **COM 40**
Photo Credits **COM 40**

Microsoft **Windows Vista**

CHAPTER ONE
Introduction to Windows Vista
Objectives **WIN 1**
What Is an Operating System? **WIN 2**
  Overview WIN 2
  What Is a User Interface? WIN 3
Windows Vista **WIN 4**
Windows Vista Operating System Editions **WIN 5**
  Windows Vista Basic Interface and Windows Aero WIN 5
  Starting Windows Vista WIN 7
  Logging On to the Computer WIN 8
  To Log On to the Computer WIN 8
The Windows Vista Desktop **WIN 9**
  To Close the Welcome Center Window WIN 10
  To Add a Gadget to the Windows Sidebar WIN 10
  To Remove a Gadget from the Windows Sidebar WIN 12
  To Display the Start Menu WIN 13
  To Scroll Using Scroll Arrows, the Scroll Bar, and the
    Scroll Box WIN 15
  To Add an Icon to the Desktop WIN 16
  To Open a Window Using a Desktop Icon WIN 18
  Folder Windows WIN 18
  To Minimize and Redisplay a Window WIN 19
  To Maximize and Restore a Window WIN 20
  To Close a Window WIN 21
  To Open a Window Using the Start Menu WIN 21
  To Move a Window by Dragging WIN 22
  To Expand the Folders List WIN 22
  To Size a Window by Dragging WIN 23
  To Collapse the Folders List WIN 24
  To Delete a Desktop Icon by Right-Dragging WIN 25
  Summary of Mouse and Windows Operations WIN 26
The Keyboard and Keyboard Shortcuts **WIN 26**
Starting an Application Program **WIN 27**
  What Is Internet Explorer? WIN 27
  To Start an Application Using the Start Menu WIN 27
Uniform Resource Locator (URL) **WIN 28**
Browsing the World Wide Web **WIN 29**
  To Browse the Web by Entering a URL WIN 30
  To Open a Link in a New Tab WIN 31

To Switch Between Tabs WIN 33
To Close a Tab WIN 33
Working with Folders **WIN 34**
To Work with Folders WIN 34
Using a Hierarchical Format to Organize Files
  and Folders WIN 36
Removable Media and Network Drives WIN 37
To Plug a USB Flash Drive into a USB Port WIN 38
Naming a Folder WIN 38
To Create a Folder on a Removable Drive WIN 39
Downloading a Hierarchy of Folders into the
  Freshman Folder WIN 40
To Expand a Drive WIN 42
To Collapse a Folder WIN 43
To Display the Contents of a Folder WIN 44
Creating a Document and Folder Using WordPad **WIN 44**
To Start WordPad Using the Start Search Box WIN 45
To Type Text WIN 47
To Save a WordPad Document in a New Folder WIN 47
To Verify the Contents of a Folder WIN 52
File Management **WIN 52**
To Copy a File by Right-Dragging WIN 52
To Display the Contents of a Folder WIN 54
To Rename a File WIN 55
To Delete a File by Right-Clicking WIN 56
To Close Expanded Folders WIN 57
Using Help and Support **WIN 58**
To Start Windows Help and Support WIN 58
To Browse for Help Topics in Windows Basics WIN 60
To Search for Help Topics Using the Table of
  Contents WIN 62
Logging Off and Turning Off the Computer **WIN 64**
To Log Off the Computer WIN 64
To Turn Off the Computer WIN 66
Chapter Summary **WIN 66**
Learn It Online **WIN 67**
In the Lab **WIN 68**

Microsoft Office **Word 2007**

CHAPTER ONE
Creating and Editing a Word Document

Objectives **WD 1**
What Is Microsoft Office Word 2007? **WD 2**
Project — Document with a Picture **WD 2**
Overview WD 4
Starting Word **WD 4**
To Start Word WD 5
The Word Window **WD 6**
Document Window WD 6
Ribbon WD 7
Mini Toolbar and Shortcut Menus WD 9
Quick Access Toolbar WD 10
Office Button WD 11
Key Tips WD 12
Entering Text **WD 12**
To Type Text WD 13

To Display Formatting Marks WD 14
Wordwrap WD 14
To Wordwrap Text as You Type WD 15
To Insert a Blank Line WD 15
Spelling and Grammar Check WD 16
To Check Spelling and Grammar as You Type WD 16
Saving the Project **WD 18**
To Save a Document WD 19
Formatting Paragraphs and Characters in a
  Document **WD 22**
Fonts, Font Sizes, Styles, and Themes WD 23
To Apply Styles WD 24
To Center a Paragraph WD 26
Formatting Single Versus Multiple Paragraphs
  and Characters WD 26
To Select a Line WD 27
To Change the Font Size of Selected Text WD 28
To Change the Font of Selected Text WD 29
To Select Multiple Paragraphs WD 30
To Bullet a List of Paragraphs WD 32
To Undo and Redo an Action WD 32
To Select a Group of Words WD 33
To Bold Text WD 34
To Underline a Word WD 35
To Italicize Text WD 36
Document Formats WD 36
To Change the Style Set WD 37
To Change Theme Colors WD 39
To Change Theme Fonts WD 39
Inserting and Formatting a Picture in a Word
  Document **WD 40**
To Insert a Picture WD 41
Scrolling WD 43
To Apply a Picture Style WD 44
To Change a Picture Border Color WD 45
To Zoom the Document WD 45
To Resize a Graphic WD 46
Enhancing the Page **WD 48**
To Add a Page Border WD 48
To Change Spacing Above and
  Below Paragraphs WD 50
Changing Document Properties and
  Saving Again **WD 50**
To Change Document Properties WD 51
To Save an Existing Document with the Same
  File Name WD 53
Printing a Document **WD 53**
To Print a Document WD 54
Quitting Word **WD 55**
To Quit Word with One Document Open WD 55
Starting Word and Opening a Document **WD 55**
To Open a Document from Word WD 56
Correcting Errors **WD 57**
Types of Changes Made to Documents WD 57
To Insert Text in an Existing Document WD 58
Deleting Text from an Existing Document WD 59
To Select a Word and Delete It WD 59
Closing the Entire Document WD 59
Word Help **WD 60**
To Search for Word Help WD 60

Contents

Chapter Summary **WD 62**
Learn It Online **WD 63**
Apply Your Knowledge **WD 63**
Extend Your Knowledge **WD 65**
Make It Right **WD 66**
In the Lab **WD 67**
Cases and Places **WD 71**

CHAPTER TWO
Creating a Research Paper
Objectives **WD 73**
Introduction **WD 74**
Project — Research Paper **WD 74**
Overview WD 74
MLA Documentation Style WD 76
Changing Document Settings **WD 77**
Adjusting Line and Paragraph Spacing WD 78
To Double-Space Text WD 78
To Remove Space after a Paragraph WD 79
Headers and Footers WD 79
To Switch to the Header WD 80
To Right-Align a Paragraph WD 81
To Insert a Page Number WD 82
To Close the Header WD 83
Typing the Research Paper Text **WD 83**
To Click and Type WD 85
Shortcut Keys WD 86
To Display the Rulers WD 87
To First-Line Indent Paragraphs WD 88
To Create a Quick Style WD 90
To AutoCorrect as You Type WD 91
To Use the AutoCorrect Options Button WD 92
To Create an AutoCorrect Entry WD 93
The AutoCorrect Dialog Box WD 94
Citations WD 94
To Change the Bibliography Style WD 95
To Insert a Citation and Create Its Source WD 96
To Edit a Citation WD 98
Footnotes WD 99
To Insert a Footnote Reference Mark WD 100
To Insert a Citation Placeholder WD 101
Footnote Text Style WD 102
To Modify a Style Using a Shortcut Menu WD 102
To Edit a Source WD 104
Working with Footnotes and Endnotes WD 106
To Count Words WD 107
Automatic Page Breaks WD 107
Creating an Alphabetical Works Cited Page **WD 111**
To Page Break Manually WD 112
To Create the Bibliographical List WD 113
To Modify a Style Using the Styles Task Pane WD 114
To Create a Hanging Indent WD 116
To Modify a Source and Update the
    Bibliographical List WD 117
Proofing and Revising the Research Paper **WD 118**
To Use the Select Browse Object Menu WD 118
Moving Text WD 119

To Select a Sentence WD 120
Selecting Text WD 120
To Move Selected Text WD 121
To Display the Paste Options Menu WD 122
To Find and Replace Text WD 123
Find and Replace Dialog Box WD 124
To Find and Insert a Synonym WD 124
To Check Spelling and Grammar at Once WD 125
The Main and Custom Dictionaries WD 127
To Use the Research Task Pane to Look Up
    Information WD 128
Research Task Pane Options WD 129
To Print Document Properties and then
    the Document WD 130
Chapter Summary **WD 132**
Learn It Online **WD 133**
Apply Your Knowledge **WD 133**
Extend Your Knowledge **WD 135**
Make It Right **WD 136**
In the Lab **WD 138**
Cases and Places **WD 143**

CHAPTER THREE
Creating a Cover Letter and a Resume
Objectives **WD 145**
Introduction **WD 146**
Project — Cover Letter and Resume **WD 146**
Overview WD 146
Creating a Letterhead **WD 149**
Mini Toolbar WD 151
To Use the Grow Font Button to Increase
    Font Size WD 151
To Color Text WD 152
To Insert Clip Art WD 153
To Resize a Graphic Using the Size Dialog Box WD 155
To Recolor a Graphic WD 156
To Set a Transparent Color in a Graphic WD 157
Using Tab Stops to Align Text WD 158
To Set Custom Tab Stops Using the Tabs
    Dialog Box WD 158
Tab Stops WD 159
To Bottom Border a Paragraph WD 161
To Clear Formatting WD 162
AutoFormat As You Type WD 162
To Convert a Hyperlink to Regular Text WD 163
Creating a Cover Letter **WD 165**
To Set Custom Tab Stops Using the Ruler WD 167
To Insert the Current Date in a Document WD 168
To Create a Building Block WD 170
To Insert a Nonbreaking Space WD 171
To Insert a Building Block WD 172
Building Blocks vs. AutoCorrect WD 172
Tables WD 173
To Insert an Empty Table WD 173
To Enter Data in a Table WD 174
To Apply a Table Style WD 176
To Resize Table Columns to Fit Table Contents WD 177

Selecting Table Contents | WD 178
To Select a Table | WD 179
Adding and Deleting Table Rows | WD 180
To Bullet a List as You Type | WD 180
Using a Template to Create a Resume | **WD 183**
To Use a Template | WD 183
Resume Template | WD 185
To Delete Rows | WD 186
To Modify Text in a Content Control | WD 187
Copying and Pasting | WD 188
To Switch from One Open Document to
  Another | WD 189
To Copy Items to the Office Clipboard | WD 189
To Paste from the Office Clipboard | WD 191
Paste Options Button | WD 192
To Delete Text and Lines | WD 193
To Zoom the Document | WD 193
To Enter a Line Break | WD 194
To Indent a Paragraph | WD 196
To Insert a Building Block Using the Quick Parts
  Gallery | WD 198
To Sort Paragraphs | WD 200
To Print Preview a Document | WD 201
Addressing and Printing Envelopes and
  Mailing Labels | **WD 203**
To Address and Print an Envelope | WD 203
Envelopes and Labels | WD 204
Chapter Summary | **WD 204**
Learn It Online | **WD 205**
Apply Your Knowledge | **WD 205**
Extend Your Knowledge | **WD 206**
Make It Right | **WD 208**
In the Lab | **WD 209**
Cases and Places | **WD 213**

WEB FEATURE
Creating a Web Page Using Word
Objectives | **WD 215**
Web Feature Introduction | **WD 216**
Project — Web Page | **WD 216**
Overview | WD 216
Saving a Word Document as a Web Page | **WD 218**
To Save a Word Document as a Web Page | WD 218
Saving to a Web Server | WD 219
Formatting a Web Page | **WD 220**
To Format Text as a Hyperlink | WD 220
To Add a Background Color | WD 221
To Add a Pattern Fill Effect to a Background | WD 222
Testing the Web Page | **WD 222**
To Test the Web Page in a Web Browser | WD 223
Feature Summary | **WD 223**
In the Lab | **WD 224**

Microsoft Office Excel 2007

CHAPTER ONE
Creating a Worksheet and an Embedded Chart

Objectives | **EX 1**
What Is Microsoft Office Excel 2007? | **EX 2**
Project — Worksheet with an Embedded Chart | **EX 2**
Overview | EX 4
Starting Excel | **EX 6**
To Start Excel | EX 6
The Excel Workbook | **EX 7**
The Worksheet | EX 7
Worksheet Window | **EX 9**
Status Bar | EX 9
Ribbon | EX 9
Formula Bar | EX 12
Mini Toolbar and Shortcut Menus | EX 12
Quick Access Toolbar | EX 13
Office Button | EX 14
Key Tips | EX 15
Selecting a Cell | **EX 15**
Entering Text | **EX 15**
To Enter the Worksheet Titles | EX 17
Entering Text in a Cell | EX 18
Correcting a Mistake while Typing | EX 19
AutoCorrect | EX 19
To Enter Column Titles | EX 19
To Enter Row Titles | EX 21
Entering Numbers | **EX 22**
To Enter Numbers | EX 23
Calculating a Sum | **EX 24**
To Sum a Column of Numbers | EX 25
Using the Fill Handle to Copy a Cell to
  Adjacent Cells | **EX 26**
To Copy a Cell to Adjacent Cells in a Row | EX 27
To Determine Multiple Totals at the Same Time | EX 28
Saving the Project | **EX 29**
To Save a Workbook | EX 30
Formatting the Worksheet | **EX 33**
Font Type, Style, Size, and Color | EX 34
To Change a Cell Style | EX 35
To Change the Font Type | EX 36
To Bold a Cell | EX 38
To Increase the Font Size of a Cell Entry | EX 38
To Change the Font Color of a Cell Entry | EX 39
To Center Cell Entries across Columns by
  Merging Cells | EX 40
To Format Column Titles and the Total Row | EX 42
To Format Numbers in the Worksheet | EX 44
To Adjust the Column Width | EX 46
Using the Name Box to Select a Cell | **EX 47**
To Use the Name Box to Select a Cell | EX 47
Other Ways to Select Cells | EX 48

Adding a 3-D Clustered Column Chart to the Worksheet **EX 49**
To Add a 3-D Clustered Column Chart to the Worksheet EX 50
Changing Document Properties and Saving Again **EX 54**
To Change Document Properties EX 55
To Save an Existing Workbook with the Same File Name EX 56
Printing a Worksheet **EX 57**
To Print a Worksheet EX 58
Quitting Excel **EX 59**
To Quit Excel with One Workbook Open EX 59
Starting Excel and Opening a Workbook **EX 60**
To Open a Workbook from Excel EX 60
AutoCalculate **EX 62**
To Use the AutoCalculate Area to Determine a Maximum EX 62
Correcting Errors **EX 63**
Correcting Errors while You Are Typing Data into a Cell EX 63
Correcting Errors after Entering Data into a Cell EX 63
Undoing the Last Cell Entry EX 65
Clearing a Cell or Range of Cells EX 66
Clearing the Entire Worksheet EX 66
Excel Help **EX 67**
To Search for Excel Help EX 67
Chapter Summary **EX 69**
Learn It Online **EX 70**
Apply Your Knowledge **EX 70**
Extend Your Knowledge **EX 72**
Make It Right **EX 73**
In the Lab **EX 74**
Cases and Places **EX 79**

CHAPTER TWO
Formulas, Functions, Formatting, and Web Queries
Objectives **EX 81**
Introduction **EX 82**
Project — Worksheet with Formulas, Functions, and Web Queries **EX 82**
Overview EX 84
Entering the Titles and Numbers into the Worksheet **EX 87**
Entering Formulas **EX 90**
To Enter a Formula Using the Keyboard EX 91
Arithmetic Operations EX 92
Order of Operations EX 92
To Enter Formulas Using Point Mode EX 93
To Copy Formulas Using the Fill Handle EX 95
Smart Tags and Option Buttons EX 96
Using the AVERAGE, MAX, and MIN Functions **EX 98**
To Determine the Average of a Range of Numbers Using the Keyboard and Mouse EX 99
To Determine the Highest Number in a Range of Numbers Using the Insert Function Box EX 101

To Determine the Lowest Number in a Range of Numbers Using the Sum Menu EX 102
To Copy a Range of Cells across Columns to an Adjacent Range Using the Fill Handle EX 104
Verifying Formulas Using Range Finder **EX 106**
To Verify a Formula Using Range Finder EX 106
Formatting the Worksheet **EX 107**
To Change the Workbook Theme EX 109
To Change the Background Color and Apply a Box Border to the Worksheet Title and Subtitle EX 110
To Center Data in Cells and Format Dates EX 113
Formatting Numbers Using the Ribbon EX 114
To Apply an Accounting Style Format and Comma Style Format Using the Ribbon EX 115
To Apply a Currency Style Format with a Floating Dollar Sign Using the Format Cells Dialog Box EX 116
To Apply a Percent Style Format and Use the Increase Decimal Button EX 118
Conditional Formatting EX 118
To Apply Conditional Formatting EX 119
Conditional Formatting Operators EX 121
Changing the Widths of Columns and Heights of Rows EX 122
To Change the Widths of Columns EX 122
To Change the Heights of Rows EX 125
Checking Spelling **EX 127**
To Check Spelling on the Worksheet EX 127
Additional Spell Checker Considerations EX 129
Preparing to Print the Worksheet **EX 129**
To Change the Worksheet's Margins, Header, and Orientation in Page Layout View EX 130
Previewing and Printing the Worksheet **EX 132**
To Preview and Print a Worksheet EX 132
To Print a Section of the Worksheet EX 134
Displaying and Printing the Formulas Version of the Worksheet **EX 135**
To Display the Formulas in the Worksheet and Fit the Printout on One Page EX 136
Importing External Data from a Web Source Using a Web Query **EX 137**
To Import Data from a Web Source Using a Web Query EX 138
Changing the Worksheet Names **EX 140**
To Change the Worksheet Names EX 141
E-Mailing a Workbook from within Excel **EX 142**
To E-Mail a Workbook from within Excel EX 142
Chapter Summary **EX 143**
Learn It Online **EX 144**
Apply Your Knowledge **EX 145**
Extend Your Knowledge **EX 147**
Make It Right **EX 148**
In the Lab **EX 149**
Cases and Places **EX 156**

CHAPTER THREE
What-If Analysis, Charting, and Working with Large Worksheets

Objectives	**EX 161**
Introduction	**EX 162**
Project — Financial Projection Worksheet with What-If Analysis and Chart	**EX 162**
Overview	EX 165
Rotating Text and Using the Fill Handle to Create a Series	**EX 168**
To Rotate Text and Use the Fill Handle to Create a Series of Month Names	EX 169
Using the Auto Fill Options Menu	EX 171
To Increase Column Widths and Enter Row Titles	EX 173
Copying a Range of Cells to a Nonadjacent Destination Area	**EX 174**
To Copy a Range of Cells to a Nonadjacent Destination Area	EX 175
Using the Paste Options Menu	EX 176
Using Drag and Drop to Move or Copy Cells	EX 177
Using Cut and Paste to Move Cells	EX 177
Inserting and Deleting Cells in a Worksheet	**EX 177**
To Insert a Row	EX 177
Inserting Columns	EX 179
Inserting Single Cells or a Range of Cells	EX 179
Deleting Columns and Rows	EX 180
Deleting Individual Cells or a Range of Cells	EX 180
Entering Numbers with Format Symbols	**EX 180**
To Enter Numbers with Format Symbols	EX 181
Freezing Worksheet Titles	**EX 181**
To Freeze Column and Row Titles	EX 182
Displaying a System Date	**EX 183**
To Enter and Format the System Date	EX 185
Absolute versus Relative Addressing	**EX 186**
To Enter a Formula Containing Absolute Cell References	EX 187
Making Decisions — The IF Function	**EX 189**
To Enter an IF Function	EX 190
To Copy Formulas with Absolute Cell References Using the Fill Handle	EX 192
Nested Forms of the IF Function	EX 195
Formatting the Worksheet	**EX 195**
To Assign Formats to Nonadjacent Ranges	EX 196
To Format the Worksheet Titles	EX 199
Copying a Cell's Format Using the Format Painter Button	**EX 201**
To Copy a Cell's Format Using the Format Painter Button	EX 201
Adding a 3-D Pie Chart to the Workbook	**EX 204**
To Draw a 3-D Pie Chart on a Separate Chart Sheet	EX 205
To Insert a Chart Title and Data Labels	EX 206
To Rotate the 3-D Pie Chart	EX 209
To Apply a 3-D Format to the Pie Chart	EX 211
To Explode the 3-D Pie Chart and Change the Color of a Slice	EX 213
Renaming and Reordering the Sheets and Coloring Their Tabs	**EX 216**
To Rename and Reorder the Sheets and Color Their Tabs	EX 216
Checking Spelling, Saving, Previewing, and Printing the Workbook	**EX 218**
Changing the View of the Worksheet	**EX 220**
To Shrink and Magnify the View of a Worksheet or Chart	EX 220
To Split a Window into Panes	EX 222
What-If Analysis	**EX 223**
To Analyze Data in a Worksheet by Changing Values	EX 224
To Goal Seek	EX 225
Goal Seeking	EX 227
Chapter Summary	**EX 228**
Learn It Online	**EX 229**
Apply Your Knowledge	**EX 229**
Extend Your Knowledge	**EX 230**
Make It Right	**EX 232**
In the Lab	**EX 233**
Cases and Places	**EX 245**

WEB FEATURE
Creating Web Pages Using Excel

Objectives	**EX 249**
Web Feature Introduction	**EX 250**
Project — Workbook with Chart Saved as a Web Page	**EX 251**
Overview	EX 252
Using Web Page Preview and Saving an Excel Workbook as a Web Page	**EX 252**
To Add a Button to the Quick Access Toolbar	EX 252
To Preview the Web Page	EX 255
To Save an Excel Workbook as a Web Page in a Newly Created Folder	EX 256
Saving Workbooks as Web Pages	EX 258
File Management Tools in Excel	EX 259
To View and Manipulate the Web Page Using a Browser	EX 260
Feature Summary	**EX 261**
In the Lab	**EX 262**

Microsoft Office Access 2007

CHAPTER ONE
Creating and Using a Database

Objectives	**AC 1**
What Is Microsoft Office Access 2007?	**AC 2**
Project — Database Creation	**AC 3**
Overview	AC 4
Designing a Database	**AC 6**
Database Requirements	AC 6
Naming Tables and Fields	AC 8
Identifying the Tables	AC 8
Determining the Primary Keys	AC 8
Determining Additional Fields	AC 8

Determining and Implementing Relationships
    Between the Tables AC 9
Determining Data Types for the Fields AC 9
Identifying and Removing Redundancy AC 10
Starting Access **AC 12**
    To Start Access AC 12
Creating a Database **AC 13**
    To Create a Database AC 14
The Access Window **AC 17**
    Navigation Pane and Access Work Area AC 18
    Ribbon AC 19
    Mini Toolbar and Shortcut Menus AC 21
    Quick Access Toolbar AC 22
    Office Button AC 22
    Key Tips AC 23
Creating a Table **AC 23**
    To Define the Fields in a Table AC 24
    Making Changes to the Structure AC 26
    To Save a Table AC 27
    To Change the Primary Key AC 28
    To Add Records to a Table AC 30
    Making Changes to the Data AC 34
    AutoCorrect AC 34
    To Close a Table AC 35
Quitting Access **AC 35**
Starting Access and Opening a Database **AC 36**
    To Open a Database from Access AC 37
    To Add Additional Records to a Table AC 38
Previewing and Printing the Contents of a Table **AC 40**
    To Preview and Print the Contents of a Table AC 41
Creating Additional Tables **AC 44**
    To Create an Additional Table AC 44
    To Modify the Primary Key and Field Properties AC 46
    To Add Records to an Additional Table AC 49
Creating a Report **AC 50**
    To Create a Report AC 51
Using a Form to View Data **AC 57**
    To Create a Split Form AC 57
    To Use a Split Form AC 58
Changing Document Properties **AC 60**
    To Change Database Properties AC 60
Access Help **AC 61**
    To Search for Access Help AC 62
Chapter Summary **AC 63**
Learn It Online **AC 64**
Apply Your Knowledge **AC 64**
Extend Your Knowledge **AC 65**
Make It Right **AC 66**
In the Lab **AC 67**
Cases and Places **AC 71**

CHAPTER TWO
Querying a Database
Objectives **AC 73**
Introduction **AC 74**
Project — Querying a Database **AC 74**
    Overview AC 76
Starting Access **AC 77**

Creating Queries **AC 78**
    To Use the Simple Query Wizard to Create
        a Query AC 78
    Using Queries AC 80
    To Use a Criterion in a Query AC 81
    To Create a Query in Design View AC 83
    To Add Fields to the Design Grid AC 85
Entering Criteria **AC 85**
    To Use Text Data in a Criterion AC 86
    To Use a Wildcard AC 87
    To Use Criteria for a Field Not Included in the
        Results AC 88
    Creating a Parameter Query AC 89
    To Create a Parameter Query AC 90
    To Save a Query AC 91
    To Use a Saved Query AC 92
    To Use a Number in a Criterion AC 93
    To Use a Comparison Operator in a Criterion AC 94
    Using Compound Criteria AC 95
    To Use a Compound Criterion Involving AND AC 95
    To Use a Compound Criterion Involving OR AC 96
Sorting **AC 97**
    To Clear the Design Grid AC 98
    To Sort Data in a Query AC 98
    To Omit Duplicates AC 100
    To Sort on Multiple Keys AC 101
    To Create a Top-Values Query AC 102
Joining Tables **AC 103**
    To Join Tables AC 105
    To Save the Query AC 107
    To Change Join Properties AC 108
    To Create a Report Involving a Join AC 109
    To Restrict the Records in a Join AC 112
Calculations **AC 113**
    To Use a Calculated Field in a Query AC 113
    To Change a Caption AC 116
    Calculating Statistics AC 117
    To Calculate Statistics AC 118
    To Use Criteria in Calculating Statistics AC 120
    To Use Grouping AC 121
Crosstab Queries **AC 122**
    To Create a Crosstab Query AC 123
    To Customize the Navigation Pane AC 126
Chapter Summary **AC 127**
Learn It Online **AC 128**
Apply Your Knowledge **AC 128**
Extend Your Knowledge **AC 129**
Make It Right **AC 130**
In the Lab **AC 131**
Cases and Places **AC 135**

CHAPTER THREE
Maintaining a Database
Objectives **AC 137**
Introduction **AC 138**
Project — Maintaining a Database **AC 138**
    Overview AC 139
Starting Access **AC 140**

Updating Records — AC 141
Adding Records — AC 141
To Create a Simple Form — AC 142
To Use a Form to Add Records — AC 144
To Search for a Record — AC 145
To Update the Contents of a Record — AC 147
To Delete a Record — AC 148
Filtering Records — AC 148
To Use Filter By Selection — AC 149
To Toggle a Filter — AC 151
To Use a Common Filter — AC 152
To Use Filter By Form — AC 153
To Use Advanced Filter/Sort — AC 155
Filters and Queries — AC 156
Changing the Database Structure — AC 156
To Add a New Field — AC 157
To Create a Lookup Field — AC 158
Mass Changes — AC 162
To Use an Update Query — AC 162
To Use a Delete Query — AC 163
Validation Rules — AC 165
To Specify a Required Field — AC 166
To Specify a Range — AC 166
To Specify a Default Value — AC 167
To Specify a Collection of Allowable Values — AC 167
To Specify a Format — AC 168
To Save the Validation Rules, Default Values, and Formats — AC 169
Updating a Table that Contains Validation Rules — AC 169
To Use a Lookup Field — AC 172
To Use a Multivalued Lookup Field — AC 173
To Resize a Column in a Datasheet — AC 175
To Include Totals in a Datasheet — AC 176
To Remove Totals from a Datasheet — AC 178
Changing the Appearance of a Datasheet — AC 178
To Change Gridlines in a Datasheet — AC 179
To Change the Colors and Font in a Datasheet — AC 180
Using the Datasheet Formatting Dialog Box — AC 181
Multivalued Field in Queries — AC 181
To Query a Multivalued Field Showing Multiple Values on a Single Row — AC 182
To Query a Multivalued Field Showing Multiple Values on Multiple Rows — AC 183
Referential Integrity — AC 185
To Specify Referential Integrity — AC 186
Effect of Referential Integrity — AC 189
To Use a Subdatasheet — AC 190
Ordering Records — AC 192
To Use the Ascending Button to Order Records — AC 192
Special Database Operations — AC 192
Backup and Recovery — AC 193
Compacting and Repairing a Database — AC 193
Additional Operations — AC 194
Chapter Summary — AC 195
Learn It Online — AC 196
Apply Your Knowledge — AC 196
Extend Your Knowledge — AC 197
Make It Right — AC 198
In the Lab — AC 199
Cases and Places — AC 203

INTEGRATION FEATURE
Sharing Data Among Applications
Objectives — AC 205
Integration Feature Introduction — AC 206
Project — Sharing Data Among Applications — AC 206
Overview — AC 209
Starting Access — AC 210
Importing or Linking Data from Other Applications to Access — AC 211
To Import an Excel Worksheet — AC 212
Using the Access Table — AC 215
Linking versus Importing — AC 216
The Linked Table Manager — AC 216
Importing from or Linking to Data in Another Access Database — AC 217
Text Files — AC 218
Using Saved Import Steps — AC 219
Exporting Data from Access to Other Applications — AC 220
To Export Data to Excel — AC 221
To Publish a Report — AC 225
Using Saved Export Steps — AC 225
XML — AC 226
To Export XML Data — AC 226
To Import XML Data — AC 228
Feature Summary — AC 230
In the Lab — AC 230

Microsoft Office PowerPoint 2007

CHAPTER ONE
Creating and Editing a Presentation

Objectives — PPT 1
What Is Microsoft Office PowerPoint 2007? — PPT 2
Project — Presentation with Bulleted Lists — PPT 3
Overview — PPT 4
Starting PowerPoint — PPT 5
To Start PowerPoint — PPT 5
The PowerPoint Window — PPT 6
PowerPoint Window — PPT 6
PowerPoint Views — PPT 8
Ribbon — PPT 8
Mini Toolbar and Shortcut Menus — PPT 11
Quick Access Toolbar — PPT 13
Office Button — PPT 14
Key Tips — PPT 15
Choosing a Document Theme — PPT 16
To Choose a Document Theme — PPT 16
Creating a Title Slide — PPT 18
To Enter the Presentation Title — PPT 18
Correcting a Mistake When Typing — PPT 19
Paragraphs — PPT 19
To Enter the Presentation Subtitle Paragraph — PPT 20
Formatting Characters in a Presentation — PPT 21
Fonts and Font Styles — PPT 21
To Select a Paragraph — PPT 21
To Italicize Text — PPT 22

To Select Multiple Paragraphs .... PPT 22
To Change the Text Color .... PPT 23
To Select a Group of Words .... PPT 24
To Increase Font Size .... PPT 24
To Bold Text .... PPT 25
To Decrease the Title Slide Title Text Font Size ...... PPT 25
Saving the Project .... **PPT 26**
To Save a Presentation .... PPT 27
Adding a New Slide to a Presentation .... **PPT 29**
To Add a New Text Slide with a Bulleted List .... PPT 29
**Creating a Text Slide with a Single-Level
  Bulleted List** .... **PPT 31**
To Enter a Slide Title .... PPT 31
To Select a Text Placeholder .... PPT 31
To Type a Single-Level Bulleted List .... PPT 32
**Creating a Text Slide with a Multi-Level
  Bulleted List** .... **PPT 33**
To Add a New Slide and Enter a Slide Title .... PPT 33
To Type a Multi-Level Bulleted List .... PPT 34
To Create a Third-Level Paragraph .... PPT 37
Ending a Slide Show with a Closing Slide ...... **PPT 40**
To Duplicate a Slide .... PPT 40
To Arrange a Slide .... PPT 41
To Delete All Text in a Placeholder .... PPT 42
**Changing Document Properties and
  Saving Again** .... **PPT 43**
To Change Document Properties .... PPT 44
To Save an Existing Presentation with the
  Same File Name .... PPT 45
Moving to Another Slide in Normal View .... **PPT 46**
To Use the Scroll Box on the Slide Pane to
  Move to Another Slide .... PPT 47
Viewing the Presentation in Slide Show View .. **PPT 48**
To Start Slide Show View .... PPT 49
To Move Manually through Slides in a
  Slide Show .... PPT 50
To Display the Pop-Up Menu and Go to a
  Specific Slide .... PPT 51
To Use the Pop-Up Menu to End a Slide Show ...... PPT 52
Quitting PowerPoint .... **PPT 52**
To Quit PowerPoint with One Document Open ...... PPT 53
**Starting PowerPoint and Opening a
  Presentation** .... **PPT 53**
To Open a Presentation from PowerPoint .... PPT 54
Checking a Presentation for Spelling Errors ... **PPT 55**
To Check Spelling .... PPT 56
Correcting Errors .... **PPT 58**
Types of Corrections Made to Presentations .... PPT 58
Deleting Text .... PPT 58
Replacing Text in an Existing Slide .... PPT 59
Displaying a Presentation in Grayscale .... **PPT 59**
To Display a Presentation in Grayscale .... PPT 59
Printing a Presentation .... **PPT 61**
To Print a Presentation .... PPT 61
Making a Transparency .... PPT 62
PowerPoint Help .... **PPT 63**
To Search for PowerPoint Help .... PPT 63
Chapter Summary .... **PPT 65**
Learn It Online .... **PPT 66**

Apply Your Knowledge .... **PPT 66**
Extend Your Knowledge .... **PPT 67**
Make It Right .... **PPT 68**
In the Lab .... **PPT 69**
Cases and Places .... **PPT 78**

CHAPTER TWO
**Creating a Presentation with Illustrations
and Shapes**
Objectives .... **PPT 81**
Introduction .... **PPT 82**
**Project — Presentation with Illustrations
  and a Shape** .... **PPT 82**
Overview .... PPT 82
Starting PowerPoint .... **PPT 84**
Creating Slides from a Blank Presentation ..... **PPT 85**
To Choose a Background Style .... PPT 89
Changing Views to Review a Presentation ...... **PPT 90**
To Change the View to Slide Sorter View .... PPT 91
To Change the View to Normal View .... PPT 91
Changing Layouts .... **PPT 92**
To Change the Slide Layout to Two Content .... PPT 92
Inserting Clip Art and Photographs into Slides .. **PPT 95**
The Clip Art Task Pane .... PPT 95
To Insert a Clip from the Clip Organizer
  into a Content Placeholder .... PPT 96
Photographs and the Clip Organizer .... PPT 97
To Insert a Photograph from a File into a Slide ..... PPT 99
Resizing Clip Art and Photographs .... **PPT 101**
To Resize Clip Art .... PPT 101
To Delete a Placeholder .... PPT 104
To Move Clips .... PPT 105
Formatting Title and Content Text .... **PPT 106**
To Format Title Text Using Quick Styles .... PPT 106
To Change the Heading Font .... PPT 109
To Shadow Text .... PPT 110
To Change Font Color .... PPT 110
Format Painter .... PPT 111
To Format Slide 3 Text Using the Format Painter ... PPT 112
Adding and Formatting a Shape .... **PPT 115**
To Add a Shape .... PPT 116
To Resize a Shape .... PPT 117
To Add Text to a Shape .... PPT 119
To Format Shape Text and Add a Shape
  Quick Style .... PPT 119
To Delete a Placeholder .... PPT 121
Adding a Transition .... **PPT 122**
To Add a Transition between Slides .... PPT 122
**Printing a Presentation as an Outline and
  Handouts** .... **PPT 126**
To Preview and Print an Outline .... PPT 126
Saving and Quitting PowerPoint .... PPT 130
Chapter Summary .... **PPT 131**
Learn It Online .... **PPT 132**
Apply Your Knowledge .... **PPT 132**
Extend Your Knowledge .... **PPT 134**
Make It Right .... **PPT 135**
In the Lab .... **PPT 136**
Cases and Places .... **PPT 142**

WEB FEATURE
Creating Web Pages Using PowerPoint
Objectives	**PPT 145**
Web Feature Introduction	**PPT 146**
Project — Web Page	**PPT 146**
Overview	PPT 146
Using Web Page Preview and Saving a	
PowerPoint Presentation as a Web Page	**PPT 146**
To Add a Button to the Quick Access Toolbar	PPT 148
To Preview the Web Page	PPT 151
Web Page Format Options	PPT 152
To Save a PowerPoint Presentation as a	
Web Page in a Newly Created Folder	PPT 153
Saving Presentations as Web Pages	PPT 154
File Management Tools in PowerPoint	PPT 155
To View the Web Page Using a Browser	PPT 156
Feature Summary	**PPT 157**
In the Lab	**PPT 158**

Microsoft Office Outlook 2007

CHAPTER ONE
Managing E-Mail and Contacts with Outlook
Objectives	**OUT 1**
What Is Microsoft Office Outlook 2007?	**OUT 2**
Project — Communicating Over the Internet	**OUT 3**
Overview	OUT 4
Starting and Customizing Outlook	**OUT 5**
To Start and Customize Outlook	OUT 5
The Inbox — Microsoft Outlook Window	**OUT 7**
Working with Incoming Messages	**OUT 10**
To Open (Read) an E-Mail Message	OUT 10
Ribbon	OUT 11
Quick Access Toolbar	OUT 12
Office Button	OUT 13
Key Tips	OUT 14
To Close an E-Mail Message	OUT 15
To Print an E-Mail Message	OUT 15
To Reply to an E-Mail Message	OUT 16
New Message Ribbon	OUT 18
Message Formats	OUT 19
To Change Message Formats	OUT 19
To Forward an E-Mail Message	OUT 20
To Delete an E-Mail Message	OUT 21
To View a File Attachment	OUT 22
Working with Outgoing Messages	**OUT 23**
To Create and Insert an E-Mail Signature	OUT 24
E-Mail Signatures for Multiple Accounts	OUT 27
New Mail Messages	OUT 27
To Compose an E-Mail Message	OUT 27
To Format an E-Mail Message	OUT 29
To Attach a File to an E-Mail Message and	
Send the Message	OUT 31
Organizing E-Mail Messages	**OUT 33**
To Categorize E-Mail Messages	OUT 33
To Flag E-Mail Messages	OUT 34
To Sort E-Mail Messages by Category Color	OUT 35
To Create and Apply a View Filter	OUT 36
E-Mail Message Options	OUT 38
To Set Message Importance, Sensitivity,	
and Delivery Options in a Single Message	OUT 38
To Change the Default Level of Importance	
and Sensitivity	OUT 40
Search Folders	OUT 43
Using Contacts	**OUT 44**
To Create a Personal Folder	OUT 44
To Create a Contact List	OUT 47
To Change the View and Sort the Contact List	OUT 49
To Find a Contact	OUT 50
To Organize Contacts	OUT 51
To Display the Contacts in a Category	OUT 52
To Preview and Print the Contact List	OUT 53
To Use the Contact List to Address an E-Mail	
Message	OUT 55
To Create a Distribution List	OUT 58
Saving Outlook Information in Different	
Formats	OUT 59
To Save a Contact List as a Text File and	
Display it in WordPad	OUT 60
Tracking Activities	OUT 61
To Track Activities for a Contact	OUT 62
Outlook Help	**OUT 62**
To Search for Outlook Help	OUT 63
Chapter Summary	**OUT 65**
Learn It Online	**OUT 66**
Apply Your Knowledge	**OUT 66**
Extend Your Knowledge	**OUT 67**
Make It Right	**OUT 67**
In the Lab	**OUT 69**
Cases and Places	**OUT 72**

Microsoft Integration 2007

CHAPTER ONE
Integrating Office 2007 Applications and the World Wide Web
Objectives	**INT 1**
Introduction	**INT 2**
Project — Integrating Office 2007 Applications	
and the World Wide Web	**INT 2**
Overview	INT 3
Adding Hyperlinks to a Word Document	**INT 6**
To Insert a Table into a Word Document	INT 8
To Remove the Table Border, View Gridlines,	
and AutoFit the Table Contents	INT 9
To Insert Text for Hyperlinks	INT 11
To Create a Hyperlink to PowerPoint Web Pages	INT 11
Embedding an Excel Chart into a Word Document	**INT 13**
To Embed an Excel Chart into a Word Document	INT 14
Copy Methods	INT 16
To Change the Size of an Embedded Object	INT 17

**Viewing the Word Document in Your Browser
and Saving It as a Web Page** **INT 19**
To Add a Button to the Quick Access Toolbar INT 19
To Preview the Web Page INT 22
Creating a PowerPoint Presentation Web Page **INT 23**
To Insert a Hyperlink into a PowerPoint
Presentation INT 25
Using Hyperlinks in PowerPoint INT 27
Creating a Web Page from an Access Report **INT 28**
To Create a Report Using the Report Wizard INT 29
To Add a Hyperlink to a Report and Change
the Text Background Color INT 32
To Save the Report and View It in Your Browser INT 36
Testing the Web Site **INT 38**
Chapter Summary **INT 40**
Learn It Online **INT 40**
In the Lab **INT 41**
Cases and Places **INT 46**

Appendices

APPENDIX A
Project Planning Guidelines

Using Project Planning Guidelines **APP 1**
Determine the Project's Purpose APP 1
Analyze your Audience APP 1
Gather Possible Content APP 2
Determine What Content to Present to your
Audience APP 2
Summary **APP 2**

APPENDIX B
Introduction to Microsoft Office 2007

What Is Microsoft Office 2007? **APP 3**
Office 2007 and the Internet, World Wide Web,
and Intranets APP 4
Online Collaboration Using Office APP 4
Using Microsoft Office 2007 **APP 4**
Microsoft Office Word 2007 APP 4
Microsoft Office Excel 2007 APP 5
Microsoft Office Access 2007 APP 5
Microsoft Office PowerPoint 2007 APP 6
Microsoft Office Publisher 2007 APP 6
Microsoft Office Outlook 2007 APP 6
Microsoft Office 2007 Help **APP 7**
Collaboration and SharePoint **APP 7**

APPENDIX C
Microsoft Office 2007 Help

Using Microsoft Office Help **APP 9**
To Open the Word Help Window APP 10
The Word Help Window **APP 11**
Search Features APP 11
Toolbar Buttons APP 12
Searching Word Help **APP 13**
To Obtain Help Using the Type Words
to Search for Text Box APP 13
To Obtain Help Using the Help Links APP 15
To Obtain Help Using the Help Table
of Contents APP 16
Obtaining Help while Working in Word **APP 17**
Use Help **APP 18**

APPENDIX D
Publishing Office 2007 Web Pages to a Web Server

Using Web Folders to Publish Office 2007
Web Pages APP 19
Using FTP to Publish Office 2007 Web Pages APP 20

APPENDIX E
Customizing Microsoft Office 2007

Changing Screen Resolution **APP 21**
To Change the Screen Resolution APP 21
Screen Resolution and the Appearance of the
Ribbon in Office 2007 Programs APP 24
Customizing the Word Window **APP 25**
To Minimize the Ribbon in Word APP 25
Customizing and Resetting the Quick Access
Toolbar APP 26
To Change the Location of the Quick Access
Toolbar APP 26
To Add Commands to the Quick Access
Toolbar Using the Customize Quick
Access Toolbar Menu APP 27
To Add Commands to the Quick Access
Toolbar Using the Shortcut Menu APP 28
To Add Commands to the Quick Access
Toolbar using Word Options APP 29
To Remove a Command from the Quick
Access Toolbar APP 32
To Reset the Quick Access Toolbar APP 33
Changing the Word Color Scheme **APP 34**
To Change the Word Color Scheme APP 34

APPENDIX F
Steps for the Windows XP User

For the XP User of this Book **APP 35**
To Start Word APP 35
To Save a Document APP 36
To Open a Document from Word APP 38

APPENDIX G
Microsoft Business Certification Program

**What Is the Microsoft Business Certification
Program?** **APP 40**
What Is the Microsoft Certified Application
Specialist Certification? APP 40
What Is the Microsoft Certified Application
Professional Certification? APP 40

Index **IND 1**

Quick Reference Summary **QR 1**

Preface

The Shelly Cashman Series® offers the finest textbooks in computer education. We are proud of the fact that our series of Microsoft Office 4.3, Microsoft Office 95, Microsoft Office 97, Microsoft Office 2000, Microsoft Office XP, and Microsoft Office 2003 textbooks have been the most widely used books in education. With each new edition of our Office books, we have made significant improvements based on the software and comments made by instructors and students.

Microsoft Office 2007 contains more changes in the user interface and feature set than all other previous versions combined. Recognizing that the new features and functionality of Microsoft Office 2007 would impact the way that students are taught skills, the Shelly Cashman Series development team carefully reviewed our pedagogy and analyzed its effectiveness in teaching today's Office student. An extensive customer survey produced results confirming what the series is best known for: its step-by-step, screen-by-screen instructions, its project-oriented approach, and the quality of its content.

We learned, though, that students entering computer courses today are different than students taking these classes just a few years ago. Students today read less, but need to retain more. They need not only to be able to perform skills, but to retain those skills and know how to apply them to different settings. Today's students need to be continually engaged and challenged to retain what they're learning.

As a result, we've renewed our commitment to focusing on the user and how they learn best. This commitment is reflected in every change we've made to our Office 2007 books.

Objectives of This Textbook

Microsoft Office 2007: Introductory Concepts and Techniques, Windows Vista Edition is intended for a course that includes an introduction to Office 2007. No experience with a computer is assumed, and no mathematics beyond the high school freshman level is required. The objectives of this book are:

- To teach the fundamentals of Microsoft Office Word 2007, Microsoft Office Excel 2007, Microsoft Office Access 2007, Microsoft Office PowerPoint 2007, Microsoft Office Outlook 2007, and Microsoft Windows Vista

- To expose students to practical examples of the computer as a useful tool

- To acquaint students with the proper procedures to create documents, worksheets, databases, and presentations suitable for coursework, professional purposes, and personal use

- To help students discover the underlying functionality of Office 2007 so they can become more productive

- To develop an exercise-oriented approach that allows learning by doing

The Shelly Cashman Approach

Features of the Shelly Cashman Series Microsoft Office 2007 books include:

- **Project Orientation** Each chapter in the book presents a project with a practical problem and complete solution in an easy-to-understand approach.

- **Plan Ahead Boxes** The project orientation is enhanced by the inclusion of Plan Ahead boxes. These new features prepare students to create successful projects by encouraging them to think strategically about what they are trying to accomplish before they begin working.

- **Step-by-Step, Screen-by-Screen Instructions** Each of the tasks required to complete a project is clearly identified throughout the chapter. Now, the step-by-step instructions provide a context beyond point-and-click. Each step explains why students are performing a task, or the result of performing a certain action. Found on the screens accompanying each step, call-outs give students the information they need to know when they need to know it. Now, we've used color to distinguish the content in the call-outs. The Explanatory call-outs (in black) summarize what is happening on the screen and the Navigational call-outs (in red) show students where to click.

- **Q&A** Found within many of the step-by-step sequences, Q&As raise the kinds of questions students may ask when working through a step sequence and provide answers about what they are doing, why they are doing it, and how that task might be approached differently.

- **Experimental Steps** These new steps, within our step-by-step instructions, encourage students to explore, experiment, and take advantage of the features of the Office 2007 new user interface. These steps are not necessary to complete the projects, but are designed to increase the confidence with the software and build problem-solving skills.

- **Thoroughly Tested Projects** Unparalleled quality is ensured because every screen in the book is produced by the author only after performing a step, and then each project must pass Thomson Course Technology's Quality Assurance program.

- **Other Ways Boxes and Quick Reference Summary** The Other Ways boxes displayed at the end of most of the step-by-step sequences specify the other ways to do the task completed in the steps. Thus, the steps and the Other Ways box make a comprehensive reference unit. A Quick Reference Summary at the end of the book contains all of the tasks presented in the chapters, and all ways identified of accomplishing the tasks.

- **BTW** These marginal annotations provide background information, tips, and answers to common questions that complement the topics covered, adding depth and perspective to the learning process.

- **Integration of the World Wide Web** The World Wide Web is integrated into the Office 2007 learning experience by (1) BTW annotations that send students to Web sites for up-to-date information and alternative approaches to tasks; (2) a Microsoft Business Certification Program Web page so students can prepare for the certification examinations; (3) a Quick Reference Summary Web page that summarizes the ways to complete tasks (mouse, Ribbon, shortcut menu, and keyboard); and (4) the Learn It Online section at the end of each chapter, which has chapter reinforcement exercises, learning games, and other types of student activities.

- **End-of-Chapter Student Activities** Extensive student activities at the end of each chapter provide the student with plenty of opportunities to reinforce the materials learned in the chapter through hands-on assignments. Several new types of activities have been added that challenge the student in new ways to expand their knowledge, and to apply their new skills to a project with personal relevance.

Q&A

What is a maximized window?

A maximized window fills the entire screen. When you maximize a window, the Maximize button changes to a Restore Down button.

Other Ways

1. Click Italic button on Mini toolbar
2. Right-click selected text, click Font on shortcut menu, click Font tab, click Italic in Font style list, click OK button
3. Click Font Dialog Box Launcher, click Font tab, click Italic in Font style list, click OK button
4. Press CTRL+I

BTW

Minimizing the Ribbon
If you want to minimize the Ribbon, right-click the Ribbon and then click Minimize the Ribbon on the shortcut menu, double-click the active tab, or press CTRL+F1. To restore a minimized Ribbon, right-click the Ribbon and then click Minimize the Ribbon on the shortcut menu, double-click any top-level tab, or press CTRL+F1. To use commands on a minimized Ribbon, click the top-level tab.

Organization of This Textbook

Microsoft Office 2007: Introductory Concepts and Techniques, Windows Vista Edition consists of a brief introduction to computers, a chapter that introduces Microsoft Windows Vista, three chapters each on Microsoft Office Word 2007, Microsoft Office Excel 2007, and Microsoft Office Access 2007, two chapters on Microsoft Office PowerPoint 2007, four special features emphasizing Web-related topics, one project on Microsoft Office Outlook 2007, one chapter on integrating Office 2007 programs and the World Wide Web, seven appendices and a Quick Reference Summary.

End-of-Chapter Student Activities

A notable strength of the Shelly Cashman Series Microsoft Office 2007 books is the extensive student activities at the end of each chapter. Well-structured student activities can make the difference between students merely participating in a class and students retaining the information they learn. The activities in the Shelly Cashman Series Office books include the following.

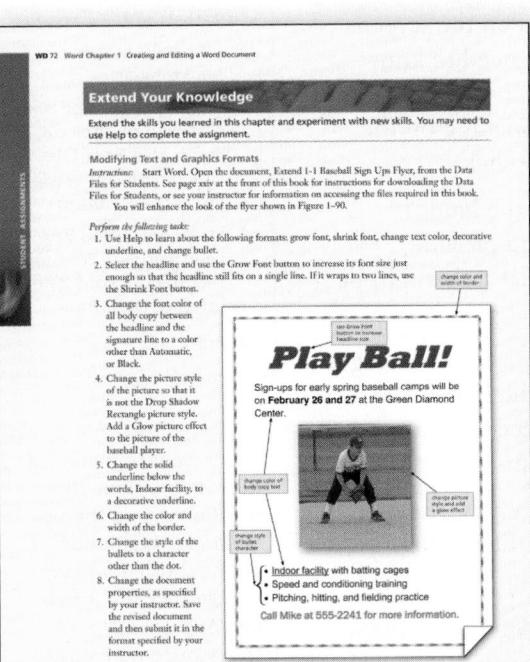

CHAPTER SUMMARY A concluding paragraph, followed by a listing of the tasks completed within a chapter together with the pages on which the step-by-step, screen-by-screen explanations appear.

LEARN IT ONLINE Every chapter features a Learn It Online section that is comprised of six exercises. These exercises include True/False, Multiple Choice, Short Answer, Flash Cards, Practice Test, and Learning Games.

APPLY YOUR KNOWLEDGE This exercise usually requires students to open and manipulate a file from the Data Files that parallels the activities learned in the chapter. To obtain a copy of the Data Files for Students, follow the instructions on the inside back cover of this text.

EXTEND YOUR KNOWLEDGE This exercise allows students to extend and expand on the skills learned within the chapter.

MAKE IT RIGHT This exercise requires students to analyze a document, identify errors and issues, and correct those errors and issues using skills learned in the chapter.

IN THE LAB Three all new in-depth assignments per chapter require students to utilize the chapter concepts and techniques to solve problems on a computer.

CASES AND PLACES Five unique real-world case-study situations, including Make It Personal, an open-ended project that relates to student's personal lives, and one small-group activity.

Instructor Resources CD-ROM

The Shelly Cashman Series is dedicated to providing you with all of the tools you need to make your class a success. Information about all supplementary materials is available through your Thomson Course Technology representative or by calling one of the following telephone numbers: Colleges, Universities, and Continuing Ed departments, 1-800-648-7450; High Schools, 1-800-824-5179; and Career Colleges, Business, Government, Library and Resellers, 1-800-477-3692.

The Instructor Resources CD-ROM for this textbook include both teaching and testing aids. The contents of each item on the Instructor Resources CD-ROM (ISBN 1-4239-1226-8) are described on the following pages.

INSTRUCTOR'S MANUAL The Instructor's Manual consists of Microsoft Word files, which include chapter objectives, lecture notes, teaching tips, classroom activities, lab activities, quick quizzes, figures and boxed elements summarized in the chapters, and a glossary page. The new format of the Instructor's Manual will allow you to map through every chapter easily.

LECTURE SUCCESS SYSTEM The Lecture Success System consists of intermediate files that correspond to certain figures in the book, allowing you to step through the creation of a project in a chapter during a lecture without entering large amounts of data.

SYLLABUS Sample syllabi, which can be customized easily to a course, are included. The syllabi cover policies, class and lab assignments and exams, and procedural information.

FIGURE FILES Illustrations for every figure in the textbook are available in electronic form. Use this ancillary to present a slide show in lecture or to print transparencies for use in lecture with an overhead projector. If you have a personal computer and LCD device, this ancillary can be an effective tool for presenting lectures.

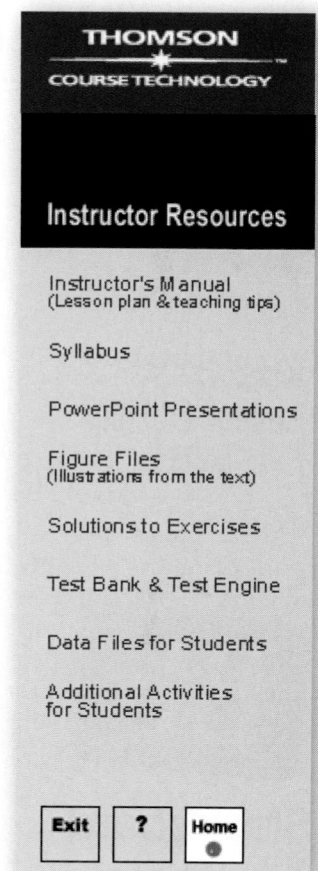

POWERPOINT PRESENTATIONS PowerPoint Presentations is a multimedia lecture presentation system that provides slides for each chapter. Presentations are based on chapter objectives. Use this presentation system to present well-organized lectures that are both interesting and knowledge based. PowerPoint Presentations provides consistent coverage at schools that use multiple lecturers.

SOLUTIONS TO EXERCISES Solutions are included for the end-of-chapter exercises, as well as the Chapter Reinforcement exercises. Rubrics and annotated solution files, as described below, are also included.

RUBRICS AND ANNOTATED SOLUTION FILES The grading rubrics provide a customizable framework for assigning point values to the laboratory exercises. Annotated solution files that correspond to the grading rubrics make it easy for you to compare students' results with the correct solutions whether you receive their homework as hard copy or via e-mail.

TEST BANK & TEST ENGINE In the ExamView test bank, you will find our standard question types (40 multiple-choice, 25 true/false, 20 completion) and new objective-based question types (5 modified multiple-choice, 5 modified true/false and 10 matching). Critical Thinking questions are also included (3 essays and 2 cases with 2 questions each) totaling the test bank to 112 questions for every chapter with page number references, and when appropriate, figure references. A version of the test bank you can print also is included. The test bank comes with a copy of the test engine, ExamView, the ultimate tool for your objective-based testing needs. ExamView is a state-of-the-art test builder that is easy to use. ExamView enables you to create paper-, LAN-, or Web-based tests from test banks designed specifically for your Thomson Course Technology textbook. Utilize the ultra-efficient QuickTest Wizard to create tests in less than five minutes by taking advantage of Thomson Course Technology's question banks, or customize your own exams from scratch.

LAB TESTS/TEST OUT The Lab Tests/Test Out exercises parallel the In the Lab assignments and are supplied for the purpose of testing students in the laboratory on the material covered in the chapter or testing students out of the course.

DATA FILES FOR STUDENTS All the files that are required by students to complete the exercises are included. You can distribute the files on the Instructor Resources CD-ROM to your students over a network, or you can have them follow the instructions on the inside back cover of this book to obtain a copy of the Data Files for Students.

ADDITIONAL ACTIVITIES FOR STUDENTS These additional activities consist of Chapter Reinforcement Exercises, which are true/false, multiple-choice, and short answer questions that help students gain confidence in the material learned.

Assessment & Training Solutions
SAM 2007

SAM 2007 helps bridge the gap between the classroom and the real world by allowing students to train and test on important computer skills in an active, hands-on environment.

SAM 2007's easy-to-use system includes powerful interactive exams, training or projects on critical applications such as Word, Excel, Access, PowerPoint, Outlook, Windows, the Internet, and much more. SAM simulates the application environment, allowing students to demonstrate their knowledge and think through the skills by performing real-world tasks.

Designed to be used with the Shelly Cashman series, SAM 2007 includes built-in page references so students can print helpful study guides that match the Shelly Cashman series textbooks used in class. Powerful administrative options allow instructors to schedule exams and assignments, secure tests, and run reports with almost limitless flexibility.

Student Edition Labs

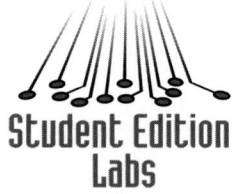

Our Web-based interactive labs help students master hundreds of computer concepts, including input and output devices, file management and desktop applications, computer ethics, virus protection, and much more. Featuring up-to-the-minute content, eye-popping graphics, and rich animation, the highly interactive Student Edition Labs offer students an alternative way to learn through dynamic observation, step-by-step practice, and challenging review questions.

Online Content

Blackboard is the leading distance learning solution provider and class-management platform today. Thomson Course Technology has partnered with Blackboard to bring you premium online content. Instructors: Content for use with *Microsoft Office 2007: Introductory Concepts and Techniques, Windows Vista Edition* is available in a Blackboard Course Cartridge and may include topic reviews, case projects, review questions, test banks, practice tests, custom syllabi, and more.

Thomson Course Technology also has solutions for several other learning management systems. Please visit http://www.course.com today to see what's available for this title.

Workbook for Microsoft Office 2007: Introductory Concepts and Techniques

This highly popular supplement (ISBN 1-4188-4335-0) includes a variety of activities that help students recall, review, and master the concepts presented. The Workbook complements the end-of-chapter material with an outline; a self-test consisting of true/false, multiple-choice, short answer, and matching questions; and activities calculated to help students develop a deeper understanding of the information presented.

CourseCasts Learning on the Go. Always Available...Always Relevant.

Want to keep up with the latest technology trends relevant to you? Visit our site to find a library of podcasts, CourseCasts, featuring a "CourseCast of the Week," and download them to your portable media player at http://coursecasts.course.com.

Our fast-paced world is driven by technology. You know because you are an active participant — always on the go, always keeping up with technological trends, and always learning new ways to embrace technology to power your life.

Ken Baldauf, a faculty member of the Florida State University (FSU) Computer Science Department, is responsible for teaching technology classes to thousands of FSU students each year. He knows what you know; he knows what you want to learn. He is also an expert in the latest technology and will sort through and aggregate the most pertinent news and information so you can spend your time enjoying technology, rather than trying to figure it out.

Visit us at http://coursecasts.course.com to learn on the go!

CourseNotes

Course Technology's CourseNotes are six-panel quick reference cards that reinforce the most important and widely used features of a software application in a visual and user-friendly format. CourseNotes will serve as a great reference tool during and after the student completes the course. CourseNotes for Microsoft Office 2007, Word 2007, Excel 2007, Access 2007, PowerPoint 2007, Windows Vista, and more are available now!

To the Student . . . Getting the Most Out of Your Book

Welcome to *Microsoft Office 2007: Introductory Concepts and Techniques, Windows Vista Edition.* You can save yourself a lot of time and gain a better understanding of the Office 2007 programs if you spend a few minutes reviewing the figures and callouts in this section.

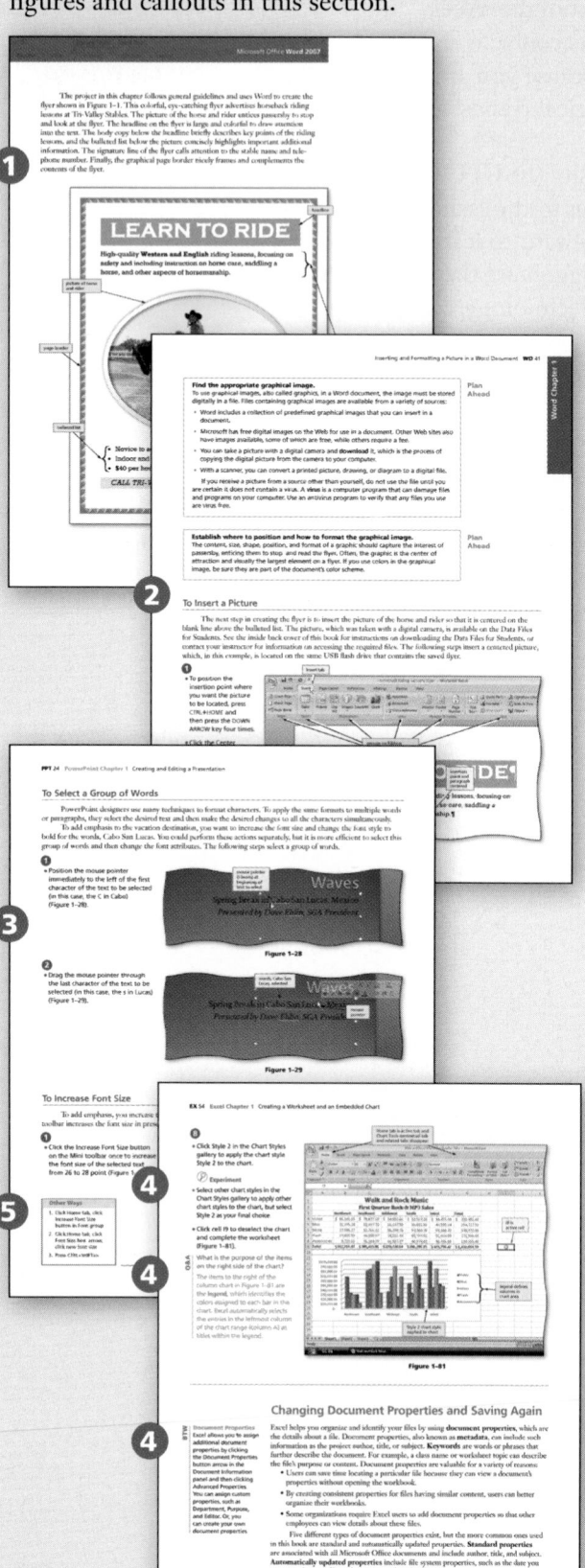

1 PROJECT ORIENTATION
Each chapter's project presents a practical problem and shows the solution in the first figure of the chapter. The project orientation lets you see firsthand how problems are solved from start to finish using application software and computers.

2 PROJECT PLANNING GUIDELINES AND PLAN AHEAD BOXES
Overall planning guidelines at the beginning of a chapter and Plan Ahead boxes throughout encourage you to think critically about how to accomplish the next goal before you actually begin working.

3 CONSISTENT STEP-BY-STEP, SCREEN-BY-SCREEN PRESENTATION
Chapter solutions are built using a step-by-step, screen-by-screen approach. This pedagogy allows you to build the solution on a computer as you read through the chapter. Generally, each step includes an explanation that indicates the result of the step.

4 MORE THAN JUST STEP-BY-STEP
BTW annotations in the margins of the book, Q&As in the steps, and substantive text in the paragraphs provide background information, tips, and answers to common questions that complement the topics covered, adding depth and perspective. When you finish with this book, you will be ready to use the Office programs to solve problems on your own. Experimental steps provide you with opportunities to step out on your own to try features of the programs, and pick up right where you left off in the chapter.

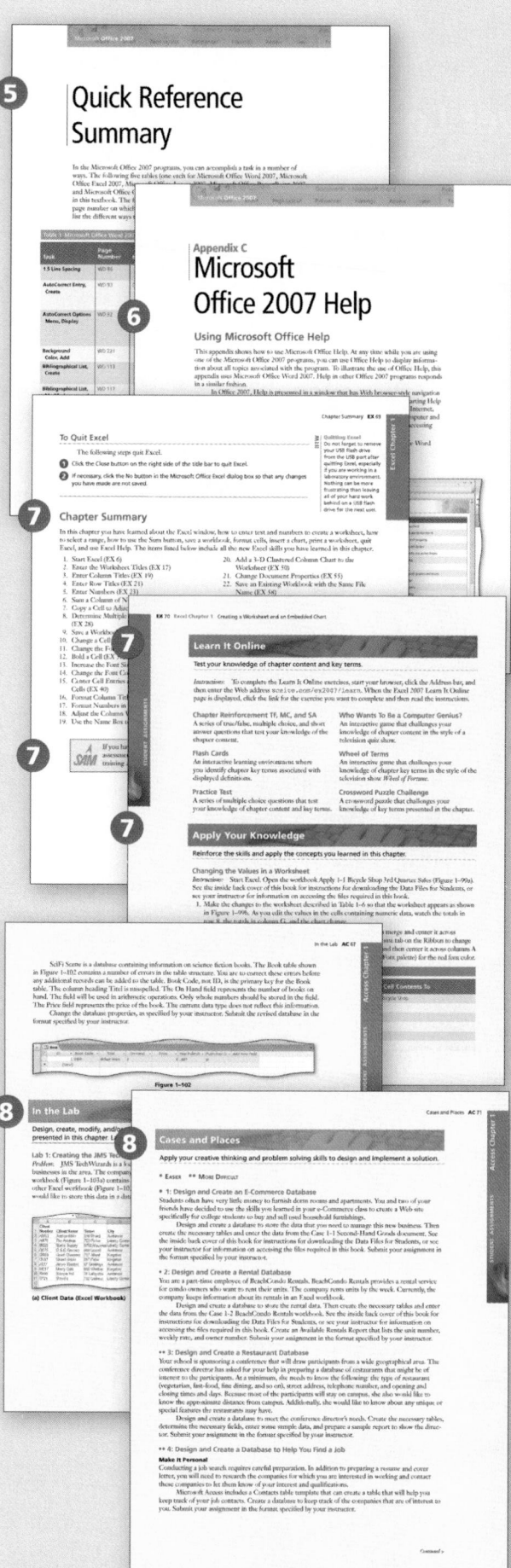

5 OTHER WAYS BOXES AND QUICK REFERENCE SUMMARY
Other Ways boxes that follow many of the step sequences and a Quick Reference Summary at the back of the book explain the other ways to complete the task presented, such as using the mouse, Ribbon, shortcut menu, and keyboard.

6 EMPHASIS ON GETTING HELP WHEN YOU NEED IT
The first project of each application and Appendix C show you how to use all the elements of Office Help. Being able to answer your own questions will increase your productivity and reduce your frustrations by minimizing the time it takes to learn how to complete a task.

7 REVIEW, REINFORCEMENT, AND EXTENSION
After you successfully step through a project in a chapter, a section titled Chapter Summary identifies the tasks with which you should be familiar. Terms you should know for test purposes are bold in the text. The SAM Training feature provides the opportunity for addional reinforcement on important skills covered in each chapter. The Learn It Online section at the end of each chapter offers reinforcement in the form of review questions, learning games, and practice tests. Also included are exercises that require you to extend your learning beyond the book.

8 LABORATORY EXERCISES
If you really want to learn how to use the programs, then you must design and implement solutions to problems on your own. Every chapter concludes with several carefully developed laboratory assignments that increase in complexity.

Preface

About Our New Cover Look

Learning styles of students have changed, but the Shelly Cashman Series' dedication to their success has remained steadfast for over 30 years. We are committed to continually updating our approach and content to reflect the way today's students learn and experience new technology.

This focus on the user is reflected in our bold new cover design, which features photographs of real students using the Shelly Cashman Series in their courses. Each book features a different user, reflecting the many ages, experiences, and backgrounds of all of the students learning with our books. When you use the Shelly Cashman Series, you can be assured that you are learning computer skills using the most effective courseware available.

We would like to thank the administration and faculty at the participating schools for their help in making our vision a reality. Most of all, we'd like to thank the wonderful students from all over the world who learn from our texts and now appear on our covers.

Microsoft Office 2007

ESSENTIAL
Introduction to Computers

and How to Purchase a Personal Computer

OBJECTIVES

After completing this material, you will be able to:

1. Define the term computer and discuss the four basic computer operations: input, processing, output, and storage

2. Define data and information

3. Explain the principal components of the computer and their use

4. Describe the use of magnetic disks, USB flash drives, and other storage media

5. Discuss computer software and explain the difference between system software and application software

6. Identify several types of personal computer application software

7. Discuss computer communications channels and equipment and the Internet and World Wide Web

8. Define e-commerce

9. Explain how to purchase a personal computer

C omputers are everywhere: at work, at school, and at home. In the workplace, employees use computers to create correspondence such as e-mail, memos, and letters; calculate payroll; track inventory; and generate invoices. At school, teachers use computers to assist with classroom instruction. Students complete assignments and do research on computers. At home, people spend hours of leisure time on the computer. They play games, communicate with friends and relatives using e-mail, purchase goods online, chat in chat rooms, listen to music, watch videos and movies, read books and magazines, research genealogy, compose music and videos, retouch photographs, and plan vacations. At work, at school, and at home, computers are helping people do their work faster, more accurately, and in some cases, in ways that previously would not have been possible.

WEB LINK

Computers

For more information, visit scsite.com/ic7/ weblink and then click Computers.

WHAT IS A COMPUTER?

A **computer** is an electronic device, operating under the control of instructions stored in its own memory, that can accept data (input), process the data according to specified rules (process), produce results (output), and store the results (storage) for future use. Generally, the term is used to describe a collection of hardware components that function together as a system. An example of common hardware components that make up a personal computer is shown in Figure 1.

FIGURE 1   Common computer hardware components.

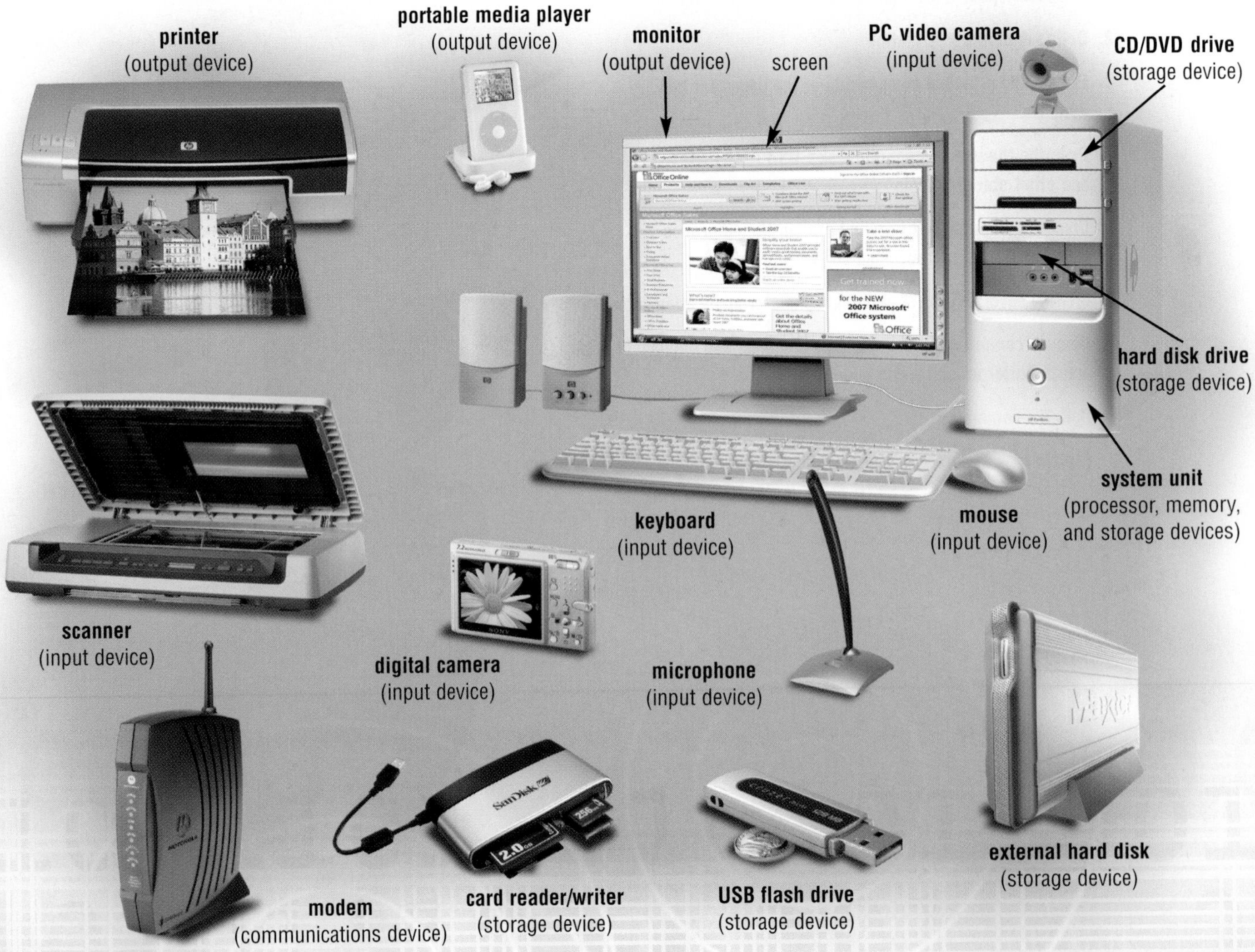

printer
(output device)

portable media player
(output device)

monitor
(output device)   screen

PC video camera
(input device)

CD/DVD drive
(storage device)

hard disk drive
(storage device)

system unit
(processor, memory,
and storage devices)

keyboard
(input device)

mouse
(input device)

scanner
(input device)

digital camera
(input device)

microphone
(input device)

external hard disk
(storage device)

modem
(communications device)

card reader/writer
(storage device)

USB flash drive
(storage device)

WHAT DOES A COMPUTER DO?

WEB LINK

Information

For more information, visit scsite.com/ic7/ weblink and then click Information.

Computers perform four basic operations — input, process, output, and storage. These operations comprise the **information processing cycle**. Collectively, these operations change data into information and store it for future use.

All computer processing requires data. **Data** is a collection of unprocessed items, which can include text, numbers, images, audio, and video. Computers manipulate data to create information. **Information** conveys meaning and is useful to one or more people. During the output operation, the information that has been created is put into some form, such as a printed report, or it can be written on computer storage for future use. As shown in Figure 2, a computer processes several data items to produce a grade report.

People who use the computer directly or use the information it provides are called **computer users**, **end users**, or sometimes, just **users**.

DATA

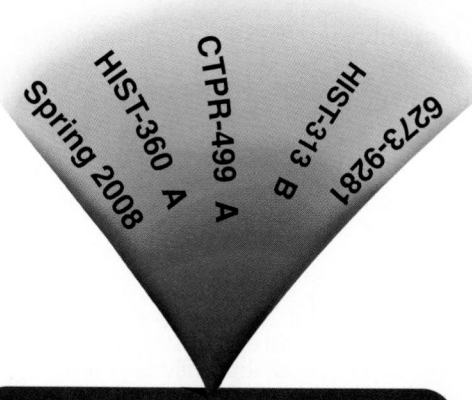

FIGURE 2 A computer processes data into information. In this example, the student identification number, semester, course codes, and course grades all represent data. The computer processes the data to produce the grade report (information).

PROCESSES

- Computes each course's grade points by multiplying the credits earned by the grade value (i.e., 4.0 * 3.0 = 12.00)
- Organizes data
- Sums all credits attempted, credits earned, and grade points (10.00, 10.00, and 36.00)
- Divides total grade points by credits earned to compute term GPA (3.60)

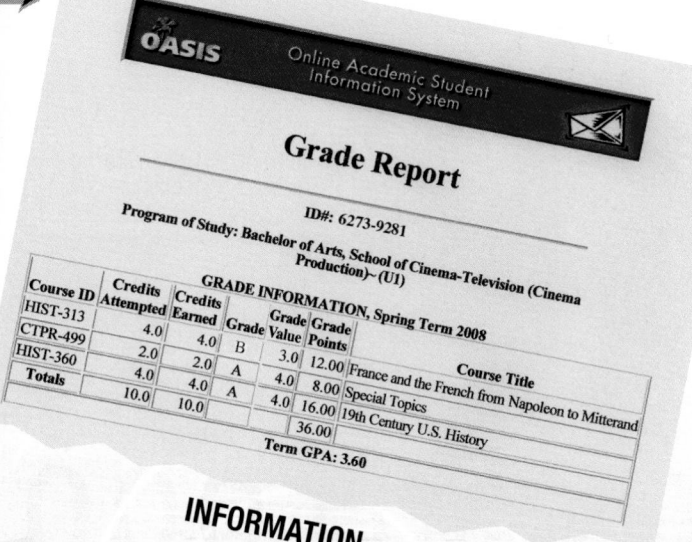

INFORMATION

WEB LINK

Computer Programs

For more information, visit scsite.com/ic7/ weblink and then click Computer Programs.

WHY IS A COMPUTER SO POWERFUL?

A computer derives its power from its capability to perform the information processing cycle with amazing speed, reliability (low failure rate), and accuracy; its capacity to store huge amounts of data and information; and its ability to communicate with other computers.

HOW DOES A COMPUTER KNOW WHAT TO DO?

For a computer to perform operations, it must be given a detailed set of instructions that tells it exactly what to do. These instructions are called a **computer program**, or **software**. Before processing for a specific job begins, the computer program corresponding to that job is stored in the computer. Once the program is stored, the computer can begin to operate by executing the program's first instruction. The computer executes one program instruction after another until the job is complete.

WHAT ARE THE COMPONENTS OF A COMPUTER?

To understand how computers process data into information, you need to examine the primary components of the computer. The six primary components of a computer are input devices, the processor (control unit and arithmetic/logic unit), memory, output devices, storage devices, and communications devices. The processor, memory, and storage devices are housed in a box-like case called the **system unit**. Figure 3 shows the flow of data, information, and instructions between the first five components mentioned. The following sections describe these primary components.

FIGURE 3   Most devices connected to the computer communicate with the processor to carry out a task. When a user starts a program, for example, its instructions transfer from a storage device to memory. Data needed by programs enters memory either from an input device or a storage device. The control unit interprets and executes instructions in memory and the ALU performs calculations on the data in memory. Resulting information is stored in memory, from which it can be sent to an output device or a storage device for future access, as needed.

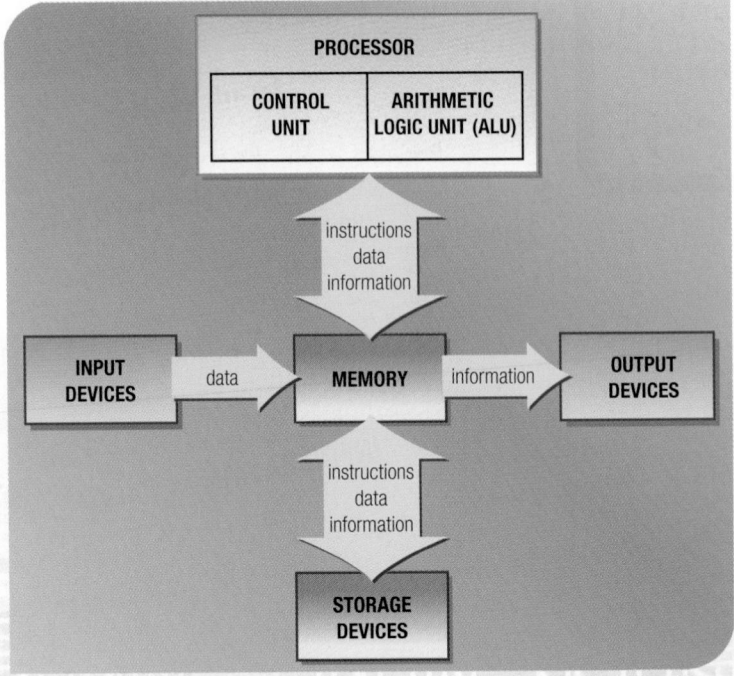

INPUT DEVICES

WEB LINK
Input Devices
For more information, visit scsite.com/ic7/ weblink and then click Input Devices.

An **input device** is any hardware component that allows you to enter data, programs, commands, and user responses into a computer. Depending on your particular application and requirements, the input device you use may vary. Popular input devices include the keyboard, mouse, digital camera, scanner, and microphone. The two primary input devices used are the keyboard and the mouse. This section discusses both of these input devices.

The Keyboard

A **keyboard** is an input device that contains keys you press to enter data into the computer. A desktop computer keyboard (Figure 4) typically has 101 to 105 keys. Keyboards for smaller computers, such as notebooks, contain fewer keys. A computer keyboard includes keys that allow you to type letters of the alphabet, numbers, spaces, punctuation marks, and other symbols such as the dollar sign ($) and asterisk (*). A keyboard also contains other keys that allow you to enter data and instructions into the computer.

FIGURE 4   On a desktop computer keyboard, you type using keys in the typing area and on the numeric keypad.

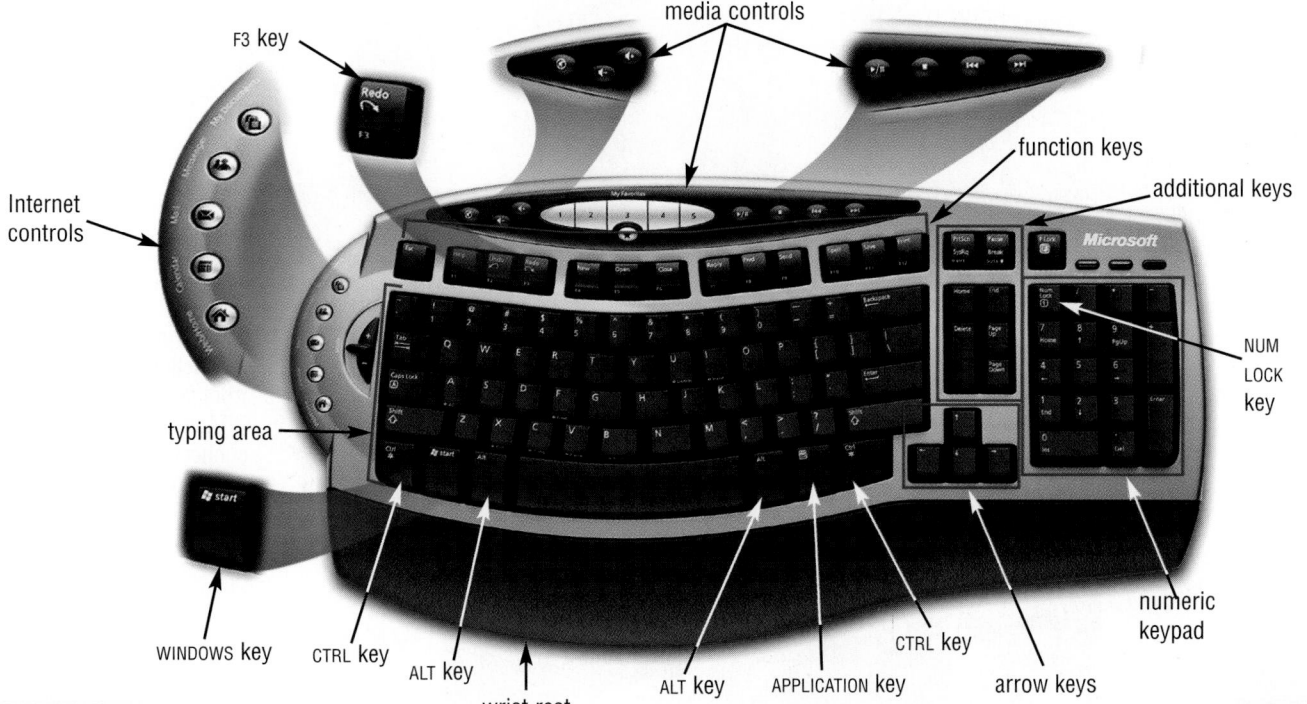

Most handheld computers, such as smart phones, PDAs, and Tablet PCs, use a variety of alternatives for entering data and instructions (Figure 5). One of the more popular handheld computer input devices is the stylus. A **stylus** is a small metal or plastic device that looks like a ballpoint pen, but uses pressure instead of ink to write, draw, or make selections.

Smart phones often include a digital camera so users can send pictures and videos to others (Figure 6).

FIGURE 5   Users enter data and instructions into a PDA using a variety of techniques.

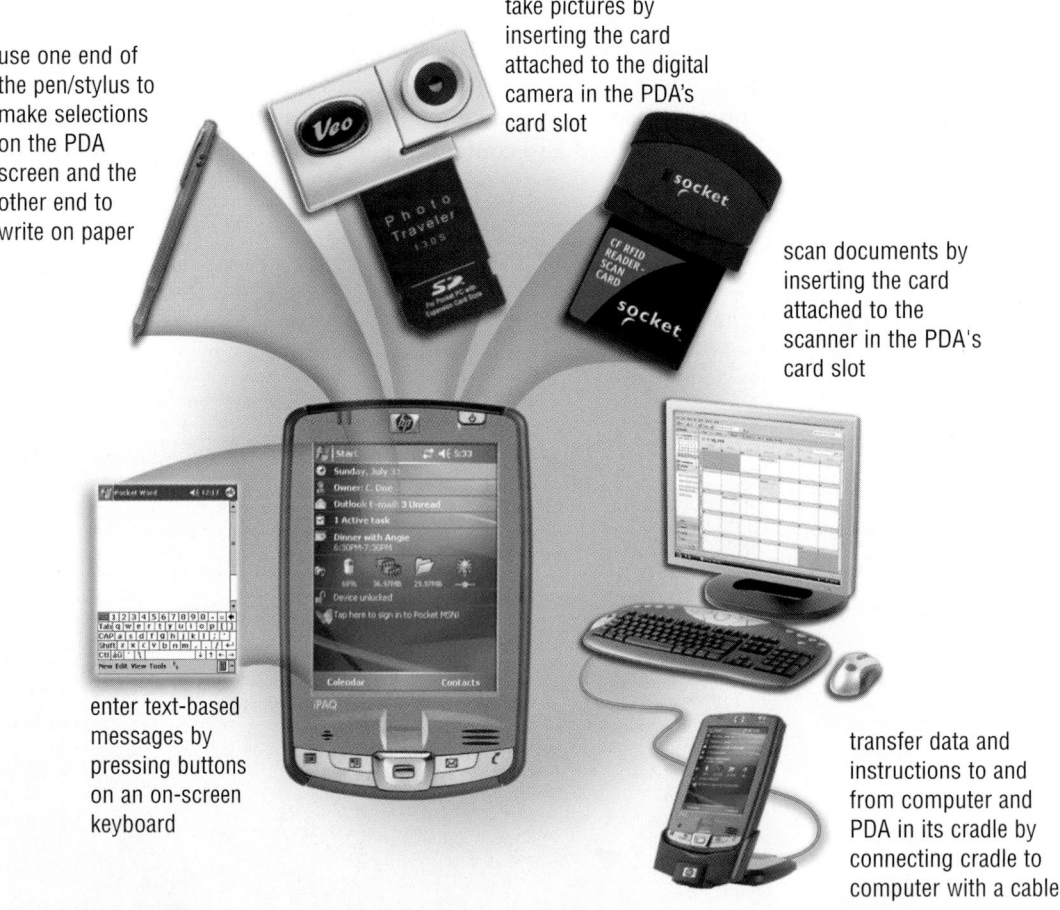

use one end of the pen/stylus to make selections on the PDA screen and the other end to write on paper

take pictures by inserting the card attached to the digital camera in the PDA's card slot

scan documents by inserting the card attached to the scanner in the PDA's card slot

enter text-based messages by pressing buttons on an on-screen keyboard

transfer data and instructions to and from computer and PDA in its cradle by connecting cradle to computer with a cable

FIGURE 6   Many smart phones include a digital camera so users can send pictures and videos to others.

The Mouse

A **mouse** (Figure 7) is a pointing device that fits comfortably under the palm of your hand. With a mouse, you control the movement of the **pointer**, often called the **mouse pointer**, on the screen and make selections from the screen. A mouse has one to five buttons. The bottom of a mouse is flat and contains a mechanism (ball, optical sensor, or laser sensor) that detects movement of the mouse.

Most notebook computers come with a touchpad, a small, flat, rectangular pointing device near the keyboard that allows you to move the pointer by sliding a fingertip on the surface of the pad (Figure 8). Notice in Figure 8 that the notebook computer has the keyboard built into the unit.

FIGURE 7   A laser mouse (a) uses a laser sensor to detect movement of the mouse. It also includes buttons you push with your thumb to navigate forward and backward through Web pages. A media mouse (b) also includes buttons to control media presentations.

(a) laser mouse   (b) optical media mouse

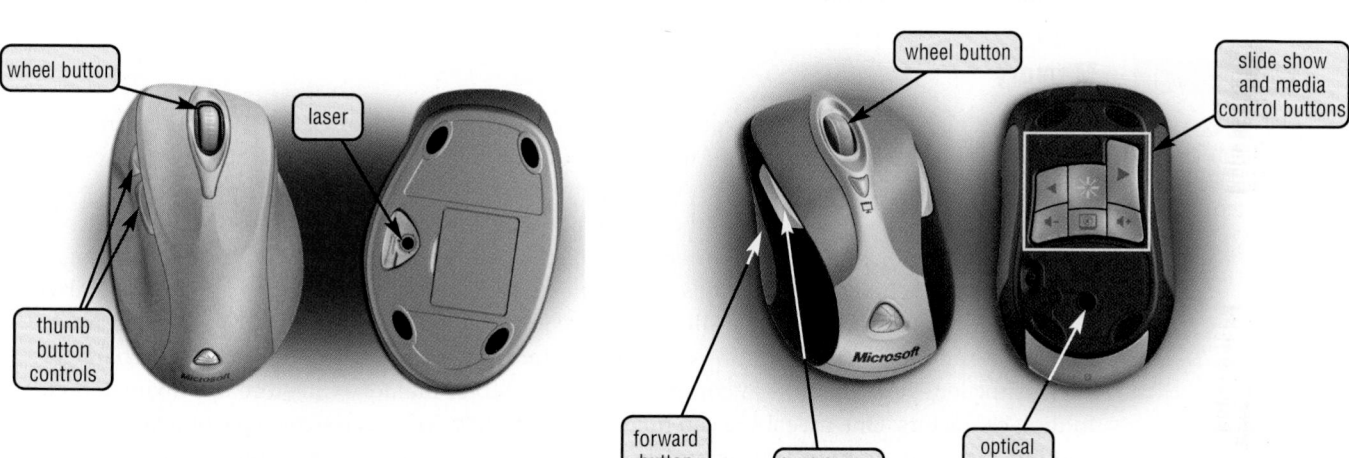

FIGURE 8   Most notebook computers have a touchpad that allows a user to control the movement of the pointer.

SYSTEM UNIT

The **system unit** (Figure 9) is a case that contains electronic components of the computer used to process data. System units are available in a variety of shapes and sizes. The case of the system unit, also called the chassis, is made of metal or plastic and protects the internal electronic parts from damage. The **motherboard**, sometimes called a system board, is the main circuit board of the system unit. Many electronic components attach to the motherboard, such as the processor, memory, and expansion slots. The sound card and video card shown in Figure 9 are examples of adapter cards, which allow a user to enhance the computer system with add-on products.

Processor

The **processor** (bottom right in Figure 9), also called the **central processing unit** (**CPU**), interprets and carries out the basic instructions that operate a computer. The processor is made up of the control unit and arithmetic/ logic unit (Figure 3 on page COM 4). The **control unit** interprets the instructions. The **arithmetic/logic unit** performs the logical and arithmetic processes. High-end processors contain over 200 million transistors and are capable of performing some operations 10 million times in a tenth of a second, or in the time it takes to blink your eye.

Memory

Memory, also called **random access memory**, or **RAM**, consists of electronic components that temporarily store instructions waiting to be executed by the processor, data needed by those instructions, and the results of processed data (information). Memory consists of chips on a memory module (lower left of Figure 9) that fits in a slot on the motherboard in the system unit.

The amount of memory in computers typically is measured in kilobytes, megabytes, or gigabytes. One **kilobyte** (**K or KB**) equals approximately 1,000 memory locations and one **megabyte** (**MB**) equals approximately one million memory locations. One **gigabyte** (**GB**) equals approximately one billion memory locations. A **memory location**, or **byte**, usually stores one character such as the letter A. Therefore, a computer with 512 MB of memory can store approximately 512 million characters. One megabyte can hold approximately 500 letter-size pages of text information and one gigabyte can hold approximately 500,000 letter-size pages of text information.

WEB LINK

Processor

For more information, visit scsite.com/ic7/ weblink and then click Processor.

WEB LINK

Memory

For more information, visit scsite.com/ic7/ weblink and then click Memory.

drive bays

sound card

video card

power supply

memory

(intel)
Core 2 Duo

processor

FIGURE 9 The system unit on a typical personal computer consists of numerous electronic components, some of which are shown in this figure. The sound card and video card are two types of adapter cards.

OUTPUT DEVICES

Output devices make the information resulting from processing available for use. The output from computers can be presented in many forms, such as a printed report or displaying it on a screen. When a computer is used for processing tasks such as word processing, spreadsheets, or database management, the two output devices more commonly used are the printer and a display device.

Printers

Printers used with computers are impact or nonimpact. An **impact printer** prints by striking an inked ribbon against the paper. One type of impact printer used with personal computers is the dot-matrix printer (Figure 10).

Nonimpact printers, such as ink-jet printers (Figure 11) and laser printers (Figure 12), form characters by means other than striking a ribbon against paper. One advantage of using a nonimpact printer is that it can print higher-quality text and graphics than an impact printer, such as the dot-matrix. Nonimpact printers also do a better job of printing different fonts, are quieter, and can print in color. The popular and affordable ink-jet printer forms a character or graphic by using a nozzle that sprays tiny drops of ink onto the page.

Ink-jet printers produce text and graphics in both black and white and color on a variety of paper types and sizes. Some ink-jet printers, called **photo printers**, produce photo-quality pictures and are ideal for home or small-business use. The speed of an ink-jet printer is measured by the number of pages per minute (ppm) it can print. Most ink-jet printers print from 6 to 33 pages per minute. Graphics and colors print at the slower rate.

A laser printer (Figure 12) is a high-speed, high-quality nonimpact printer that employs copier-machine technology. It converts data from the computer into a beam of light that is focused on a photoconductor drum, forming the images to be printed. Laser printers can cost from a couple hundred dollars to a few thousand dollars for the home and small office user, to hundreds of thousands of dollars for large business users. Generally, the more expensive the laser printer, the more pages it can print per minute.

FIGURE 10
A dot-matrix printer is capable of handling wide paper and printing multipart forms. It produces printed images when tiny pins strike an inked ribbon.

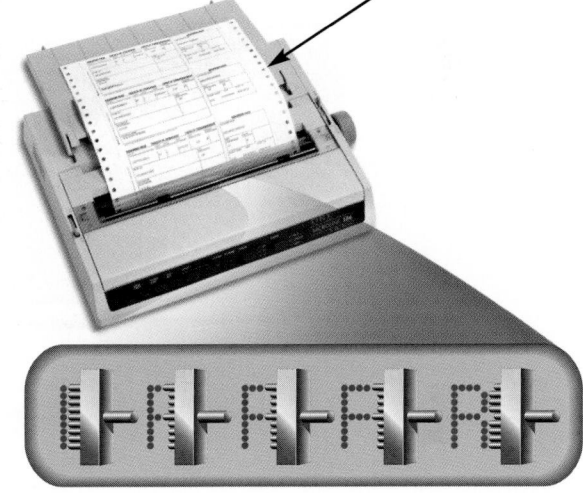

continuous-form paper

FIGURE 11   Ink-jet printers are a popular type of color printer used in the home. Many photo printers, which can produce photo-lab quality pictures, use ink-jet technology.

FIGURE 12   Laser printers, which are available in both black and white and color, are used with personal computers, as well as larger computers.

color laser printer

WEB LINK

Output Devices

For more information, visit scsite.com/ic7/ weblink and then click Output Devices.

Display Devices

A **display device** is an output device that visually conveys text, graphics, and video information. A **monitor** is a display device that is packaged as a separate unit. Two basic types of monitors are the **flat panel monitor** and CRT. The **LCD monitor**, the most popular type of flat panel monitor, shown on the left in Figure 13, uses a liquid display crystal, similar to a digital watch, to produce images on the screen. Flat panel monitors take up much less desk space and have gained significant popularity over the past few years. The television-like **CRT** (**cathode ray tube**) monitor is shown on the right in Figure 13. The surface of the screen of either a CRT monitor or LCD monitor is composed of individual picture elements called **pixels**. A screen set to a resolution of 800 x 600 pixels has a total of 480,000 pixels. Each pixel can be illuminated to form parts of a character or graphic shape on the screen.

Mobile computers such as notebook computers and Tablet PCs, and mobile device such as PDAs, portable media players, and smart phones, have built-in LCD screens (Figure 14).

FIGURE 13   The flat-panel LCD monitor (left), and the CRT monitor (right) are used with desktop computers. The LCD monitor is thin, lightweight, and far more popular today than the CRT monitor.

FIGURE 14   Notebook computers, Tablet PCs, ultra personal computers, portable media players, and most PDAs and smart phones have color LCD screens.

notebook computer

Tablet PC

ultra personal computer

portable media player

smart phone

PDA

STORAGE DEVICES

A **storage device** is used to store instructions, data, and information when they are not being used in memory. Four common types of storage devices, sometimes called storage media, are magnetic disks, optical discs, tape, and miniature mobile storage media. Figure 15 shows how different types of storage media and memory compare in terms of relative speeds and uses.

Magnetic Disks

Magnetic disks use magnetic particles to store items such as data, instructions, and information on a disk's surface. Before any data can be read from or written on a magnetic disk, the disk must be formatted. **Formatting** is the process of dividing the disk into tracks and sectors (Figure 16), so the computer can locate the data, instructions, and information on the disk. A **track** is a narrow recording band that forms a full circle on the surface of the disk. The disk's storage locations consist of pie-shaped sections, which break the tracks into small arcs called **sectors**. On a magnetic disk, a sector typically stores up to 512 bytes of data.

Two types of magnetic disks are floppy disks and hard disks. Some are portable, others are not. **Portable storage medium** means you can remove the medium from one computer and carry it to another computer. The following sections discuss specific types of magnetic disks.

FIGURE 15 Comparison of different types of storage media and memory in terms of relative speed and uses. Memory is faster than storage, but is expensive and not practical for all storage requirements. Storage is less expensive but is slower than memory.

		Stores...
Memory	Memory (most RAM)	Items waiting to be interpreted and executed by the processor
Storage	Hard Disk	Operating system, application software, user data and information, including pictures, music, and videos
	Flash Memory Cards and USB Flash Drives	Digital pictures or files to be transported
	CDs and DVDs	Software, backups, movies, music
	Tape	Backups
	Floppy Disk	Small files to be transported

faster transfer rates → *slower transfer rates*

FIGURE 16 Tracks form circles on the surface of a magnetic disk. The disk's storage locations are divided into pie-shaped sections, which break the tracks into small arcs called sectors.

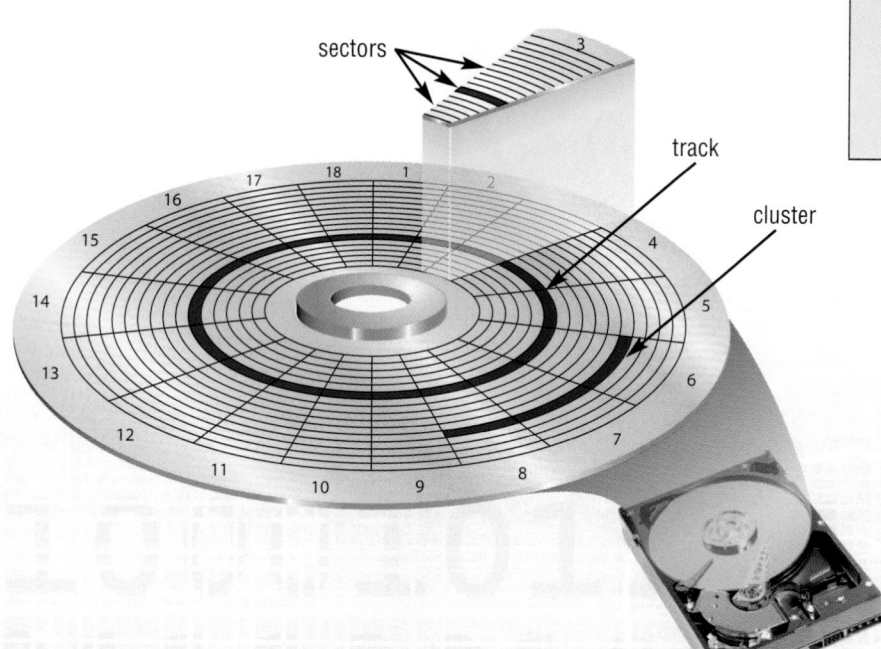

sectors

track

cluster

WEB LINK

Hard Disks

For more information,
visit scsite.com/ic7/
weblink and then click
Hard Disks.

HARD DISKS   A **hard disk**, also called a hard disk drive, is a storage device that contains one or more inflexible, circular platters that magnetically store data, instructions, and information. Home users store documents, spreadsheets, presentations, databases, e-mail messages, Web pages, digital photographs, music, videos, and software on hard disks. The data on hard disks is recorded on a series of tracks located on one or more platters. The tracks are divided into sectors when the disk is formatted. Figure 17 shows how a hard disk works. The hard disk platters spin at a high rate of speed, typically 5,400 to 15,000 revolutions per minute. When reading data from the disk, the read head senses the magnetic spots that are recorded on the disk along the various tracks and transfers that data to memory. When writing, the data is transferred from memory and is stored as magnetic spots on the tracks on the recording surface of one or more of the disk platters.

When reading or writing, the read/write heads on a hard disk drive do not actually touch the surface of the disk. The distance between the read/write heads and the platters is about two millionths of one inch. This close clearance means that dirt, dust, smoke, or other particles could cause a **head crash**, when a read/write head touches a platter, usually resulting in loss of data or sometimes the entire drive. Although current hard disks are sealed tightly to keep out contaminants, head crashes do occasionally occur. Thus, it is crucial that you back up your hard disk regularly. A **backup** is a duplicate of a file, program, or disk that you can use in case the original is lost, damaged, or destroyed.

The number of platters permanently mounted on the spindle of a hard disk varies. On most drives, each surface of the platter can be used to store data. Thus, if a hard disk drive uses one

FIGURE 17 How a hard disk works.

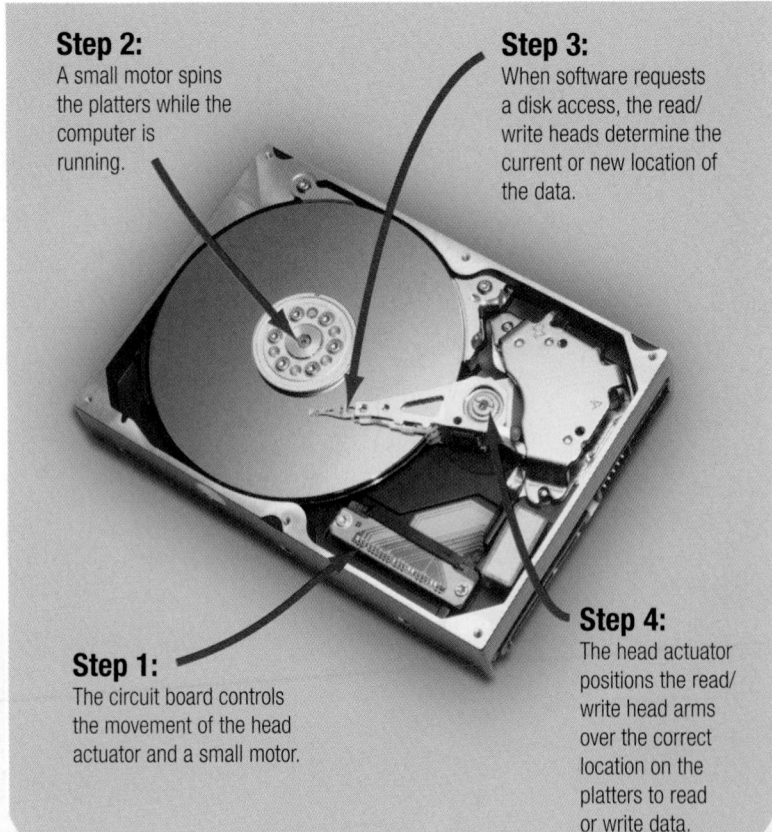

Step 2:
A small motor spins the platters while the computer is running.

Step 3:
When software requests a disk access, the read/write heads determine the current or new location of the data.

Step 1:
The circuit board controls the movement of the head actuator and a small motor.

Step 4:
The head actuator positions the read/write head arms over the correct location on the platters to read or write data.

platter, two surfaces are available for data. If the drive uses two platters, four sets of read/write heads read and record data from the four surfaces. Storage capacities of internally mounted fixed disks for personal computers range from 10 GB to more than 750 GB.

The system unit on most desktop and notebook computers contains at least one hard disk. Although hard disks are available in removable cartridge form, most hard disks cannot be removed from the computer.

FLOPPY DISKS   Another older form of magnetic storage is the **floppy disk**, or **diskette**, an inexpensive portable storage medium (Figure 18a). The most widely used floppy disk is 3.5 inches wide and typically can store up to 1.44 megabytes of data, or 1,474,560 characters. Although the exterior of the 3.5-inch disk is not floppy, users still refer to them as floppy disks. Floppy disks are not as widely used as they were 15 years ago because of their low storage capacity.

A **floppy disk drive** is a device that can read from and write on a floppy disk. Floppy disk drives are either built into the system unit (Figure 18a) or are external to the system unit and connected to the computer via a cable (Figure 18b).

Data stored on a floppy disk must be retrieved and placed into memory to be processed. The time required to access and retrieve data is called the **access time**. The access time for floppy disks varies from about 175 milliseconds to approximately 300 milliseconds (one millisecond equals 1/1000 of a second). On average, data stored in a single sector on a floppy disk can be retrieved in approximately 1/15 to 1/3 of a second.

FIGURE 18   On a personal computer, you insert and remove a floppy disk from a floppy disk drive.

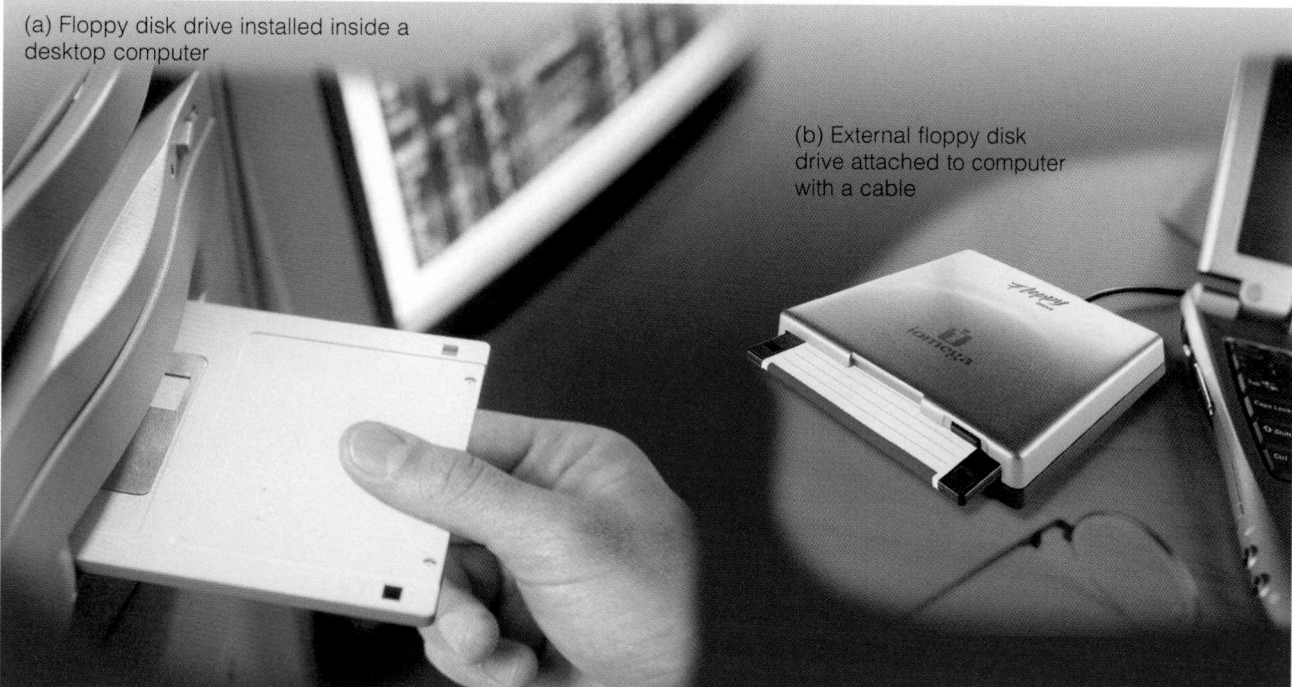

(a) Floppy disk drive installed inside a desktop computer

(b) External floppy disk drive attached to computer with a cable

WEB LINK

CDs

For more information, visit scsite.com/ic7/ weblink and then click CDs.

Optical Discs

An optical disc is a portable storage medium that consists of a flat, round, portable disc made of metal, plastic, and lacquer that is written and read by a laser. Optical discs used in personal computers are 4.75 inches in diameter and less than 1/20 of an inch thick. Nearly every personal computer today has some type of optical disc drive installed in a drive bay. On these drives, you push a button to slide the tray out, insert the disc, and then push the same button to close the tray (Figure 19).

Many different formats of optical discs exist today. These include CD-ROM, CD-R, CD-RW, DVD-ROM, DVD-R, DVD+R, DVD-RW, DVD+RW, and DVD+RAM. Figure 21 on the next page identifies each of these optical disc formats and specifies whether a user can read from the disc, write on the disc, and/or erase the disc.

A **CD-ROM** (compact disc read-only memory) is a type of optical disc that users can read but not write on (record) or erase — hence, the name read-only. A typical CD-ROM holds from 650 MB to 1 GB of data, instructions, and information. Software manufacturers often distribute their programs using CD-ROMs.

To read a CD-ROM, insert the disc in a **CD-ROM drive** or a CD-ROM player. Because audio CDs and CD-ROMs use the same laser technology, you may be able to use a CD-ROM drive to listen to an audio CD while working on the computer. Some music companies, however, configure their CDs so the music will not play on a computer. They do this to protect themselves from customers illegally copying and sharing the music.

Push the button to slide out the tray.

Insert the disc, label side up.

Push the same button to close the tray.

FIGURE 19   On optical disc drives, you push a button to slide out a tray, insert the disc, and then push the same button to close the tray.

A **CD-R** (compact disc-recordable) is an optical disc onto which you can record your own items such as text, graphics, and audio. With a CD-R, you can write on part of the disc at one time and another part at a later time. Once you have recorded the CD-R, you can read from it as many times as you wish. You can write on each part only one time, and you cannot erase the disc's contents. Most CD-ROM drives can read a CD-R.

A **CD-RW** (compact disc-rewriteable) is an erasable optical disc you can write on multiple times. A CD-RW overcomes the major disadvantage of CD-R discs, which is that you can write on them only once. With CD-RWs, the disc acts like a floppy or hard disk, allowing you to write and rewrite data, instructions, and information onto it multiple times.

Although CDs have large storage capacities, even a CD cannot hold many of today's complex programs. Some software, for example, is sold on five or more CDs. To meet these tremendous storage requirements, some software companies have moved from CDs to the larger DVDs — a technology that can be used to store large amounts of text and even videos (Figure 20).

OPTICAL DISC FORMATS

Optical Disc	Read	Write	Erase
 CD-ROM	Y	N	N
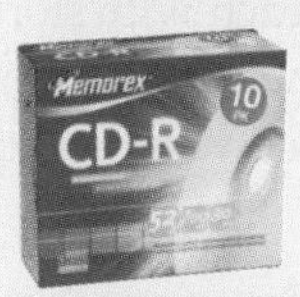 CD-R	Y	Y	N
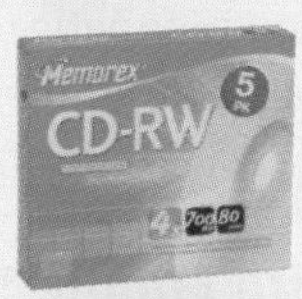 CD-RW	Y	Y	Y
 DVD-ROM BD-ROM HD DVD-ROM	Y	N	N
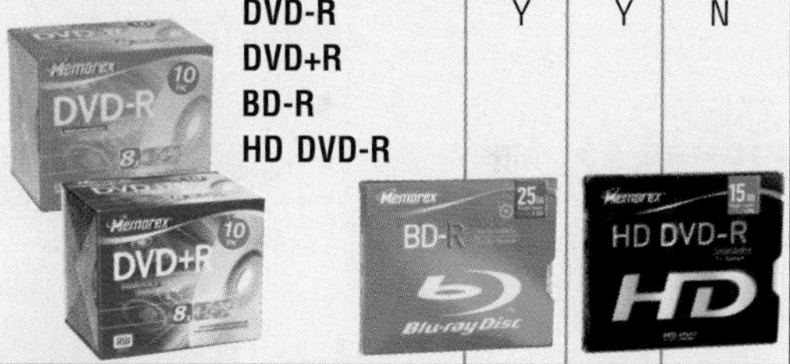 DVD-R DVD+R BD-R HD DVD-R	Y	Y	N
 DVD-RW DVD+RW DVD+RAM BD-RE HD DVD-RW	Y	Y	Y

FIGURE 20   A DVD is an extremely high-capacity optical disc.

FIGURE 21   Manufacturers sell CD-ROM and DVD-ROM media prerecorded (written) with audio, video, and software. Users cannot change the contents of these discs. Users, however, can purchase the other formats of CDs and DVDs as blank media and record (write) their own data, instructions, and information on these discs.

A **DVD-ROM** (digital versatile disk-read-only memory) is a very high-capacity optical disc capable of storing from 4.7 GB to 17 GB — more than enough to hold a telephone book containing every resident in the United States. As with the CD-ROM format, you cannot write on an optical disc that uses the DVD-ROM format. You can only read from it. To read a DVD-ROM, you need a **DVD-ROM drive**. Most DVD-ROM drives can also read CDs.

DVD-R and **DVD+R** are competing DVD-recordable formats, each with up to 4.7 GB storage capacity. Both allow users to write on the disc once and read (play) it many times. Two newer, more expensive DVD-recordable formats are **Blu-ray (BD-ROM)** and **HD DVD**, with higher quality and more capacity than standard DVDs. **DVD-RW**, **DVD+RW**, and **DVD+RAM** are competing DVD formats, each with storage capacities up to 4.7 GB per side, that allow users to erase and write (record) many times. **BD-RE** and **HD DVD-RW** are competing higher-capacity rewriteable DVD formats. To write to a DVD, you need a recordable or rewriteable DVD-ROM drive.

Tape

Tape is a magnetically coated ribbon of plastic housed in a tape cartridge (Figure 22) capable of storing large amounts of data and information at a low cost. A **tape drive** is used to read from and write on a tape. Tape is primarily used for long-term storage and backup.

Miniature Mobile Storage Media

Miniature mobile storage media are rewriteable media usually in the form of a flash memory card, USB flash drive, or a smart card. Miniature mobile storage media allow mobile users to transport digital images, music, or documents easily to and from computers and other devices (Figure 23).

FIGURE 22   A tape drive and a tape cartridge.

FIGURE 23   Many types of computers and devices use miniature mobile storage media.

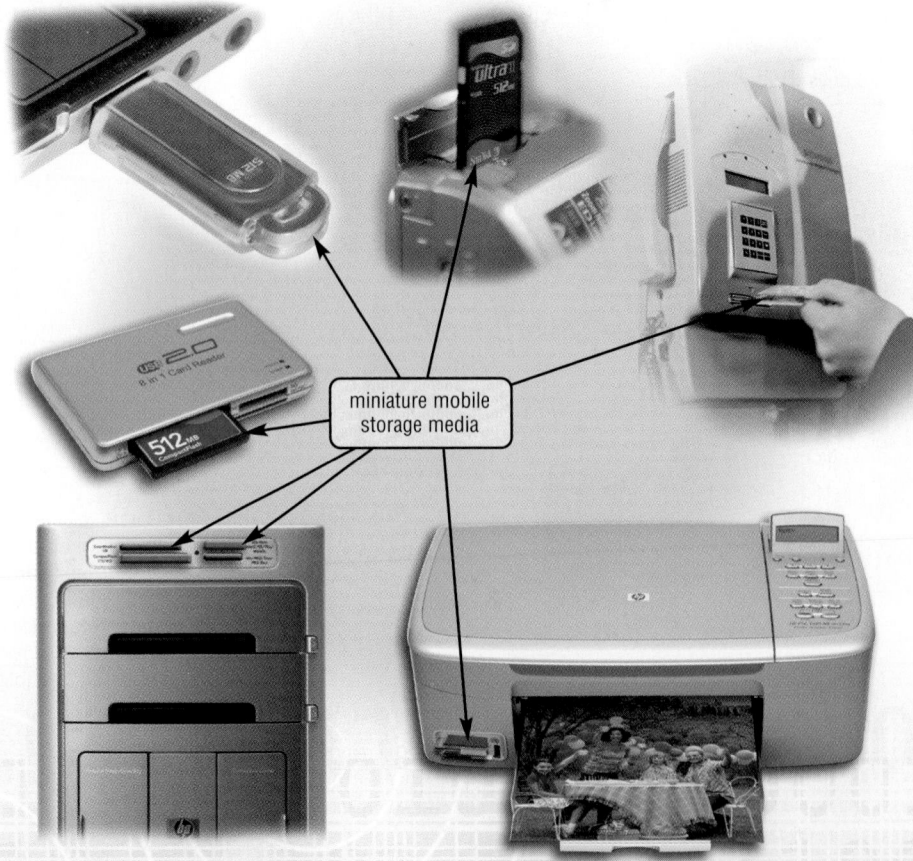

miniature mobile storage media

Flash memory cards are solid-state media, which means they consist entirely of electronics (chips, wires, etc.) and contain no moving parts. Common types of flash memory include CompactFlash (CF), Secure Digital (SD), xD Picture Card, and Memory Stick (Figure 24).

A **USB flash drive** (Figure 25), sometimes called a pen drive or thumb drive, is a flash memory storage device that plugs into a USB port on a computer or mobile device. USB flash drives are the portable storage media of choice among users today, making the floppy disk nearly obsolete, because they are small, lightweight, and have such large storage capacities. Capacities typically range from 32 MB to 64 GB.

VARIOUS FLASH MEMORY CARDS

Media Name	Storage Capacity	Use
CompactFlash 	64 MB to 16 GB	Digital cameras, PDAs, smart phones, photo printers, portable media players, notebook computers, desktop computers
Secure Digital 	64 MB to 4 GB	Digital cameras, digital video cameras, PDAs, smart phones, photo printers, portable media players
xD Picture Card 	64 MB to 2 GB	Digital cameras, photo printers
Memory Stick 	256 MB to 4 GB	Digital cameras, digital video cameras, PDAs, photo printers, smart phones, handheld game consoles, notebook computers
Memory Stick PRO Duo 	128 MB to 4 GB	Digital cameras, smart phones, handheld game consoles

FIGURE 24
A variety of flash memory cards.

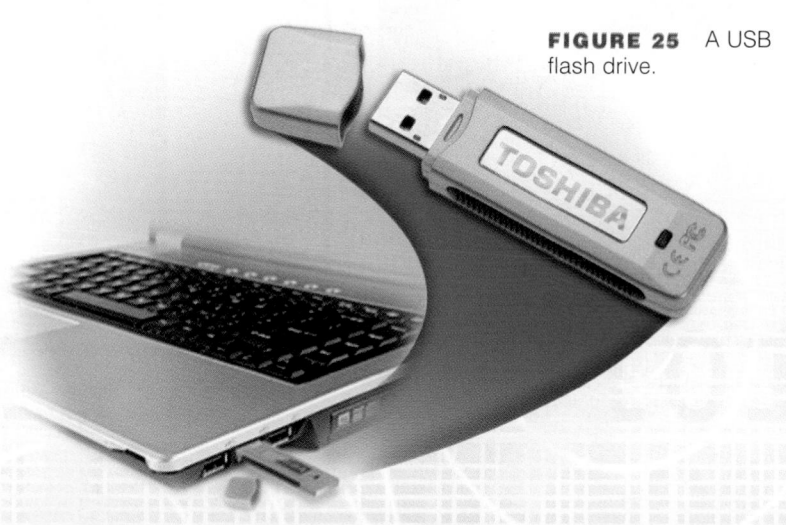

FIGURE 25 A USB flash drive.

A **smart card**, which is similar in size to a credit card or ATM card, stores data on a thin microprocessor embedded in the card. When you insert the smart card in a specialized card reader, the information on the card is read and, if necessary, updated (Figure 26). Uses of smart cards include storing medical records, tracking customer purchases, storing a prepaid amount of money, and authenticating users, such as for Internet purchases.

COMMUNICATIONS DEVICES

A **communications device** is a hardware component that enables a computer to send (transmit) and receive data, instructions, and information to and from one or more computers. A widely used communications device is the telephone or cable modem (Figure 1 on page COM 2).

Communications occur over **transmission media** such as telephone lines, cables, cellular radio networks, and satellites. Some transmission media, such as satellites and cellular radio networks, are **wireless**, which means they have no physical lines or wires. People around the world use computers and communications devices to communicate with each other using one or more transmission media.

COMPUTER SOFTWARE

Computer software is the key to productive use of computers. With the correct software, a computer can become a valuable tool. Software can be categorized into two types: system software and application software.

WEB LINK

Operating Systems

For more information, visit scsite.com/ic7/ weblink and then click Operating Systems.

System Software

System software consists of programs to control the operations of computer equipment. An important part of system software is a set of programs called the operating system. Instructions in the **operating system** tell the computer how to perform the functions of loading, storing, and executing an application program and how to transfer data. For a computer to operate, an operating system must be stored in the computer's memory. When a computer is turned on, the operating system is loaded into the computer's memory from auxiliary storage. This process is called **booting**.

Today, most computers use an operating system that has a **graphical user interface (GUI)** that provides visual cues such as icon symbols to help the user. Each **icon** represents an application such as word processing, or a file or document where data is stored. Microsoft Windows Vista (Figure 27) and Windows XP, Apple Mac OS X, and Linux are four popular personal computer operating systems.

FIGURE 26   A smart card and smart card reader.

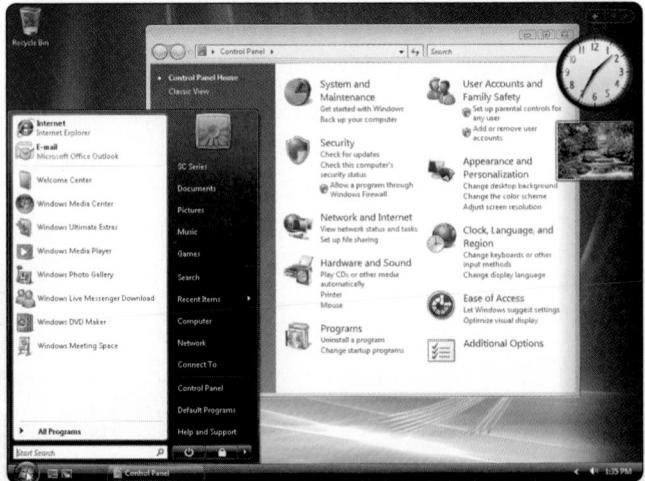

FIGURE 27   A graphical user interface, such as Microsoft Windows Vista, makes the computer easier to use.

Application Software

Application software consists of programs designed to make users more productive and/or assist them with personal tasks. Some widely used application software includes Web browsers, personal information managers, project management, accounting, computer-aided design, desktop publishing, paint/image editing, audio and video editing, multimedia authoring, Web page authoring, personal finance, legal, tax preparation, home design/landscaping, educational, reference, and entertainment (games, simulations, etc.). Often, application software is available for purchase from a Web site or store that sells computer products (Figure 28).

Personal computer users regularly use application software. Some of the more commonly used applications are word processing, electronic spreadsheet, database, and presentation graphics.

WORD PROCESSING   **Word processing software** (Figure 29) is used to create, edit, format, and print documents. A key advantage of word processing software is that users easily can make changes in documents, such as correcting spelling; changing margins; and adding, deleting, or relocating entire paragraphs. These changes would be difficult and time consuming to make using manual methods such as a typewriter. With a word processor, documents can be printed quickly and accurately and easily stored on a disk for future use. Word processing software is oriented toward working with text, but word processing packages also support features that enable users to manipulate numeric data and utilize graphics.

SPREADSHEET   **Electronic spreadsheet software** (Figure 30) allows the user to add, subtract, and perform user-defined calculations on rows and columns of numbers. These numbers can be changed, and the spreadsheet quickly recalculates the new results. Electronic spreadsheet software eliminates the tedious recalculations required with manual methods. Spreadsheet information frequently is converted into a graphic form, such as charts. Graphics capabilities now are included in most spreadsheet packages.

WEB LINK

Word Processing Software

For more information, visit scsite.com/ic7/ weblink and then click Word Processing Software.

WEB LINK

Spreadsheet Software

For more information, visit scsite.com/ic7/ weblink and then click Spreadsheet Software.

FIGURE 28 Stores that sell computer products have shelves stocked with software for sale.

FIGURE 29 Word processing software is used to create letters, memos, newsletters, and other documents.

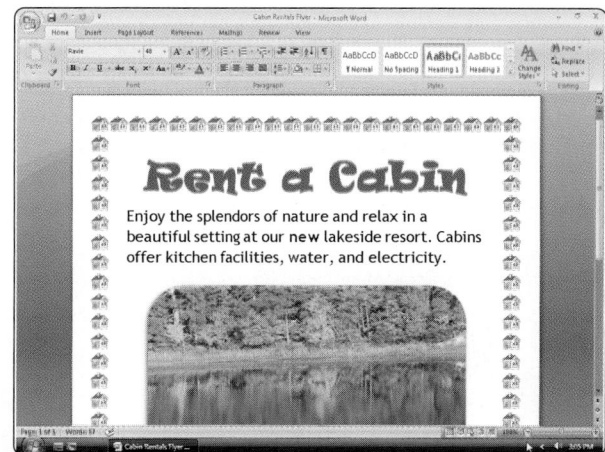

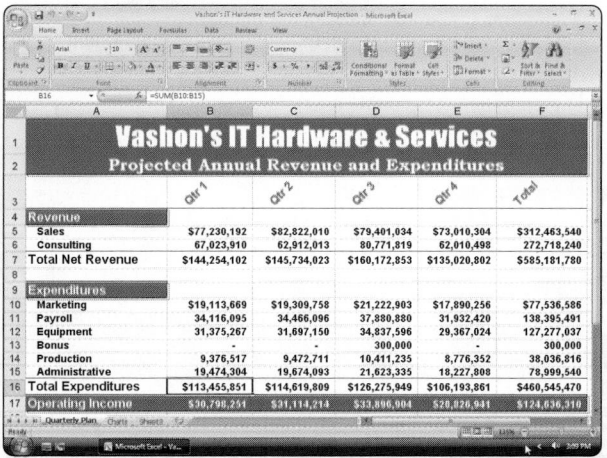

FIGURE 30 Electronic spreadsheet software frequently is used by people who work with numbers. The user enters the data and the formulas to be used on the data, and the computer calculates the results.

DATABASE   Database software (Figure 31) allows the user to enter, retrieve, and update data in an organized and efficient manner. These software packages have flexible inquiry and reporting capabilities that let users access the data in different ways and create custom reports that include some or all of the information in the database.

PRESENTATION GRAPHICS   Presentation graphics software (Figure 32) allows the user to create slides for use in a presentation to a group. Using special projection devices, the slides are projected directly from the computer.

NETWORKS AND THE INTERNET

A **network** is a collection of computers and devices connected together, often wirelessly, via communications devices and transmission media. When a computer connects to a network, it is **online**.

Networks allow users to share resources, such as hardware, software, data, and information. Sharing resources saves time and money. For example, instead of purchasing one printer for every computer in a company, the firm can connect a single printer and all computers via a network (Figure 33); the network enables all of the computers to access the same printer.

Most business computers are networked together. These networks can be relatively small or quite extensive. A network that connects computers in a limited geographic area, such as a school computer laboratory, office, or group of buildings, is called a **local area network** (**LAN**). A network that covers a large geographical area, such as one that connects the district offices of a national corporation, is called a **wide area network** (**WAN**) (Figure 34).

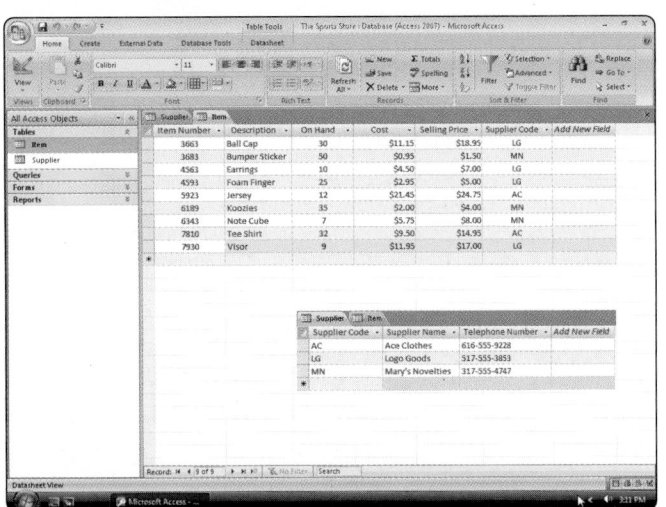

FIGURE 31   Database software allows the user to enter, retrieve, and update data in an organized and efficient manner.

FIGURE 32   Presentation graphics software allows the user to produce professional-looking presentations.

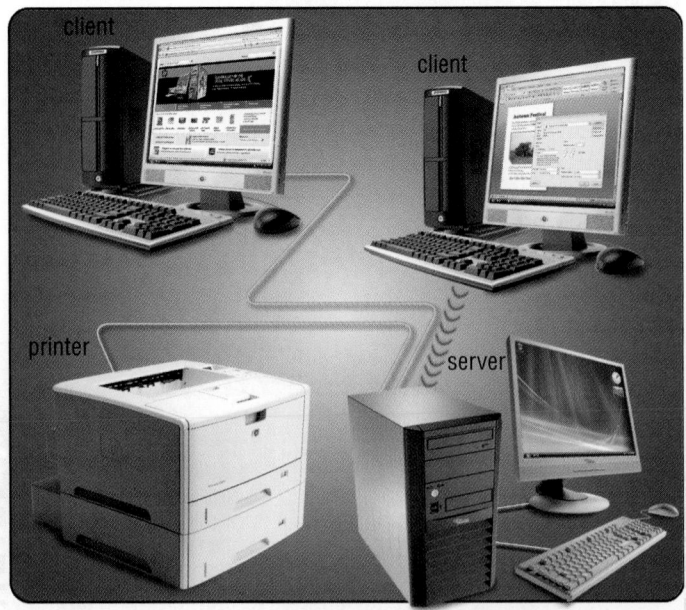

FIGURE 33   The local area network (LAN) enables two or more separate computers to share the same printer.

The Internet

The world's largest network is the **Internet**, which is a worldwide collection of networks that connects millions of businesses, government agencies, educational institutions, and individuals. With an abundance of resources and data accessible via the Internet, more than 1 billion people around the world use the Internet for a variety of reasons, including the following:

- Communicating with and meeting other people
- Accessing a wealth of information, news, and research findings
- Shopping for goods and services
- Banking and investing
- Accessing sources of entertainment and leisure, such as online games, music, videos, books and magazines

Most users connect to the Internet through a regional or national ISP, an online service provider, or a wireless Internet service provider. An **ISP (Internet service provider)** is an organization, such as a cable company or telephone company, that supplies connections to the Internet for a monthly fee. Earthlink and AT&T Worldnet are examples of national ISPs. Like an ISP, an **online service provider (OSP)** provides access to the Internet, but it also provides a variety of other specialized content and services such as news, weather, financial data, e-mail, games, and more. Two popular online services are America Online (AOL) and The Microsoft Network (MSN). A **wireless Internet service provider** (WISP) is a company that provides wireless Internet access to computers and mobile devices such as smart phones and PDAs. Boingo Wireless and Cingular Wireless are examples of WISPs.

WEB LINK

World Wide Web

For more information, visit scsite.com/ic7/ weblink and then click World Wide Web.

The World Wide Web

One of the more popular segments of the Internet is the **World Wide Web**, also called the **Web**, which contains billions of documents called Web pages. A **Web page** can contain text, graphics, audio, and video, and has built-in connections, or links, to other Web documents. Figure 35 on the next page shows different types of Web pages found on the World Wide Web today. Web pages are stored on computers throughout the world. A **Web site** is a related collection of Web pages. Visitors to a Web site access and view Web pages using a software program called a **Web browser**. A Web page has a unique address, called a **Uniform Resource Locator (URL)**.

FIGURE 34   A wide area network (WAN) can be quite large and complex, connecting users in district offices around the world.

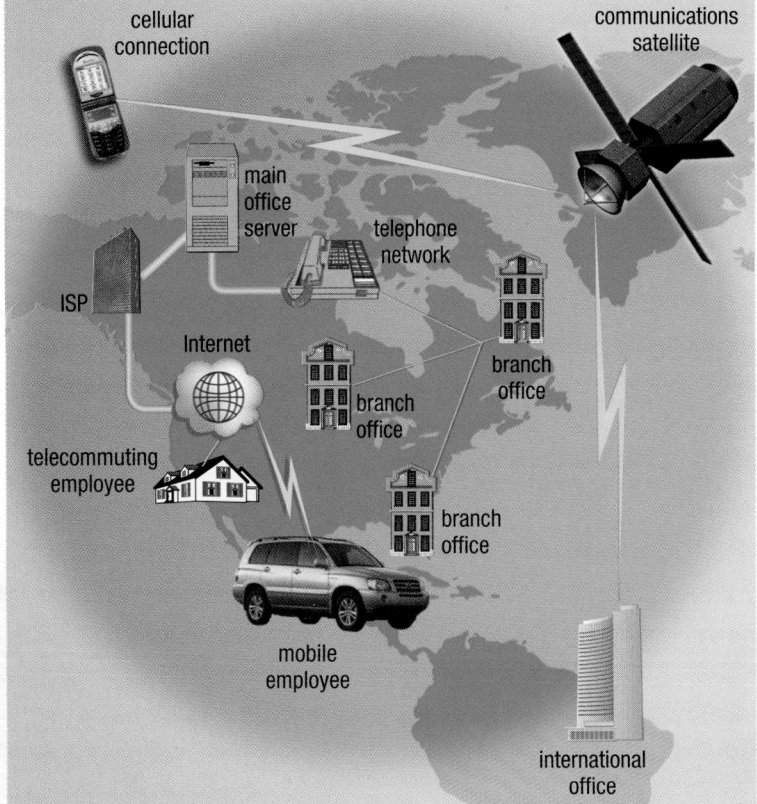

FIGURE 35 Types of Web sites.

As shown in Figure 36, a URL consists of a protocol, a domain name, sometimes the path to a specific Web page or location in a Web page, and the Web page name. Most Web page URLs begin with **http://**, which stands for **hypertext transfer protocol**, the communications standard used to transfer pages on the Web. The domain name identifies the Web site, which is stored on a Web server. A **Web server** is a computer that delivers (serves) requested Web pages.

Electronic Commerce

When you conduct business activities online, you are participating in electronic commerce, also known as **e-commerce**. Some people use the term m-commerce (mobile commerce) to identify e-commerce that uses mobile devices. These commercial activities include shopping, investing, and any other venture that represents a business transaction. Today, three types of e-commerce exist. **Business to consumer (B2C)** involves the sale of goods to the general public. **Consumer to consumer (C2C)** involves one consumer selling directly to another. **Business to business (B2B)** provides goods and services to other businesses.

WEB LINK

E-Commerce

For more information, visit scsite.com/ic7/ weblink and then click E-Commerce.

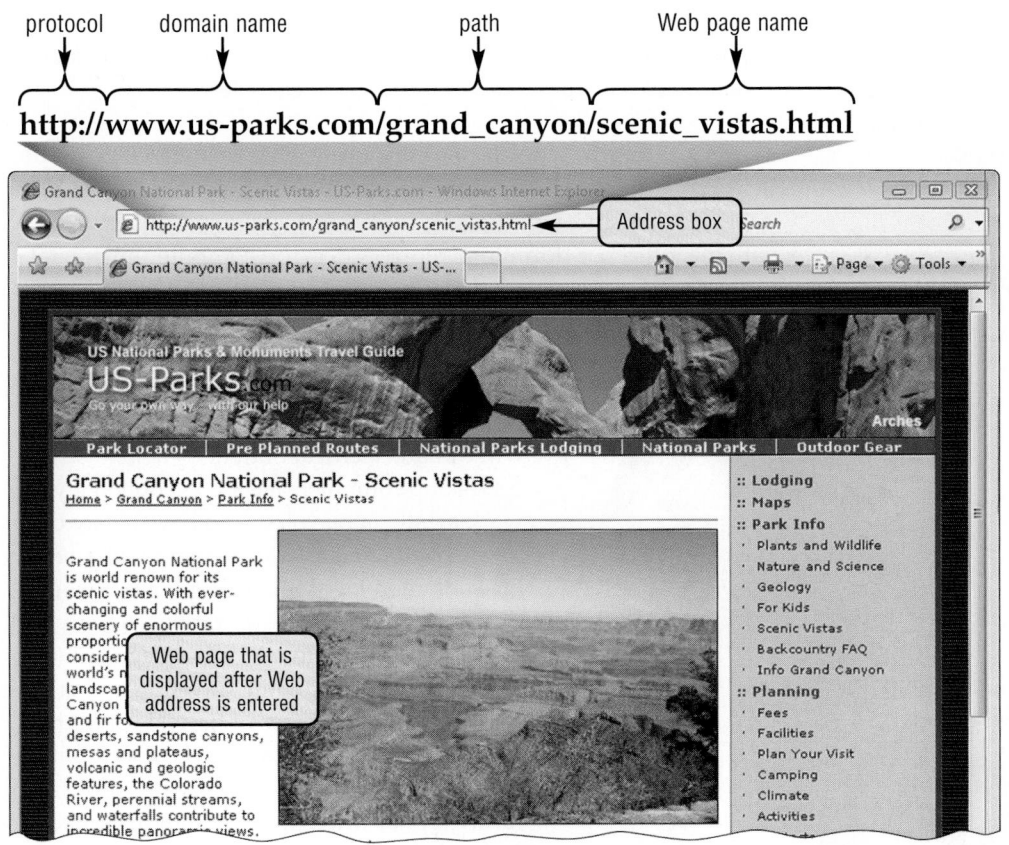

FIGURE 36   After entering the Web address http://www.us-parks.com/grand_canyon/scenic_vistas.html in the Address box, this Web page at the US National Parks Travel Guide Web site is displayed.

How to Purchase a Personal Computer

(a) desktop computer

(b) mobile computer (notebook computer or Tablet PC)

Should I buy a desktop or mobile computer or personal mobile device?

For what purposes will I use the computer?

Should the computer I buy be compatible with the computers at school or work?

At some point, perhaps while you are taking this course, you may decide to buy a personal computer. The decision is an important one and will require an investment of both time and money. Like many buyers, you may have little computer experience and find yourself unsure of how to proceed. You can get started by talking to your friends, coworkers, and instructors about their computers. What type of computers did they buy? Why? For what purposes do they use their computers? You also should answer the following three questions to help narrow your choices to a specific computer type, before reading this guide. At the end of this guide, you'll also find tips on purchasing PDAs, smart phones, portable media players, and other personal mobile devices such as handheld navigation devices and game consoles.

1 **Do you want a desktop computer or mobile computer?**
A desktop computer (Figure 37a) is designed as a stationary device that sits on or below a desk or table in a location such as a home, office, or dormitory room. A desktop computer must be plugged in an electrical outlet to operate. A mobile computer, such as a notebook computer or Tablet PC (Figure 37b), is smaller than a desktop computer, more portable, and has a battery that allows you to operate it for a period without an electrical outlet.

Desktop computers are a good option if you work mostly in one place and have plenty of space in your work area. Desktop computers generally give you more performance for your money.

Increasingly, more corporations are buying mobile computers to take advantage of their portability to work while traveling and at home. The past disadvantages of mobile computers, such as lower processor speeds, poor-quality monitors, weight, short battery life, and significantly higher prices, have all but disappeared. Today, hard drive speed, capacity, processor speed, and graphics capability in notebook computers are equal to, if not better than, desktop computers.

If you are thinking of using a mobile computer to take notes in class or in business meetings, then consider a Tablet PC with handwriting and drawing capabilities. Typically, note-taking involves writing text notes and drawing charts,

FIGURE 37

schematics, and other illustrations. By allowing you to write and draw directly on the screen with a digital pen, a Tablet PC eliminates the distracting sound of the notebook keyboard tapping and allows you to capture drawings. Some notebook computers can convert to Tablet PCs.

Mobile computers used to have several drawbacks, including the lack of high-end capabilities. Today's high-end notebook computers include most of the capabilities of a good desktop computer. Manufacturers have made great strides in improving durability and battery life. Most notebook computers are 1.5 to 2 inches thick and weigh less than 10 pounds, making them very portable and easy to carry.

 For what purposes will you use the computer?
Having a general idea of the purposes for which you want to use your computer will help you decide on the type of computer to buy. At this point in your research, it is not necessary to know the exact application software titles or version numbers you might want to use. Knowing that you plan to use the computer primarily to create word processing, spreadsheet, database, and presentation documents, however, will point you in the direction of a desktop or notebook computer. If you want the portability of a smart phone or PDA, but you need more computing power, then a Tablet PC may be the best alternative. You also must consider that some application software runs only on a Mac, while others run only on a PC with the Windows operating system. Still other software may run only on a PC running the UNIX or Linux operating system.

Should the computer be compatible with the computers at school or work?
If you plan to bring work home, telecommute, or take distance education courses, then you should purchase a computer that is compatible with those at school or work.

Compatibility is primarily a software issue. If your computer runs the same operating system version, such as Microsoft Windows Vista, and the same application software, such as Microsoft Office, then your computer will be able to read documents created at school or work and vice versa. Incompatible hardware can become an issue if you plan to connect directly to a school or office network using a cable or wireless technology. You usually can obtain the minimum system requirements from the Information Technology department at your school or workplace.

After evaluating the answers to these three questions, you should have a general idea of how you plan to use your computer and the type of computer you want to buy. Once you have decided on the type of computer you want, you can follow the guidelines presented in this guide to help

you purchase a specific computer, along with software, peripherals, and other accessories.

Many of the desktop computer guidelines presented also apply to the purchase of a notebook computer and a Tablet PC. Later in this guide, sections on purchasing a notebook computer or Tablet PC address additional considerations specific to those computer types.

This guide concentrates on recommendations for purchasing a desktop computer or mobile computer.

HOW TO PURCHASE A DESKTOP COMPUTER

Once you have decided that a desktop computer is most suited to your computing needs, the next step is to determine specific software, hardware, peripheral devices, and services to purchase, as well as where to buy the computer.

Determine the specific software you want to use on your computer.
Before deciding to purchase software, be sure it contains the features necessary for the tasks you want to perform. Rely on the computer users in whom you have confidence to help you decide on the software to use. The minimum requirements of the software you select may determine the operating system (Microsoft Windows Vista, Linux, UNIX, Mac OS X) you need. If you have decided to use a particular operating system that does not support software you want to use, you may be able to purchase similar software from other manufacturers.

Many Web sites and trade magazines, such as those listed in Figure 38 on the next page, provide reviews of software products. These Web sites frequently have articles that rate computers and software on cost, performance, and support.

Your hardware requirements depend on the minimum requirements of the software you will run on your computer.

Some software requires more memory and disk space than others, as well as additional input, output, and storage devices. For example, suppose you want to run software that can copy one CD's or DVD's contents directly to another CD or DVD, without first copying the data to your hard disk. To support that, you should consider a desktop computer or a high-end notebook computer, because the computer will need two CD or DVD drives: one that reads from a CD or DVD, and one that reads from and writes on a CD or DVD. If you plan to run software that allows your computer to work as an entertainment system, then you will need a CD or DVD drive, quality speakers, and an upgraded sound card.

Type of Computer	Web Site	Web Address
PC	CNET Shopper	shopper.cnet.com
	PC World Magazine	pcworld.com
	BYTE Magazine	byte.com
	PC Magazine	pcmag.com
	Yahoo! Computers	computers.yahoo.com
	MSN Shopping	shopping.msn.com
	Dave's Guide to Buying a Home Computer	css.msu.edu/PC-Guide
Mac	Macworld Magazine	macworld.com
	Apple	apple.com
	Switch to Mac Campaign	apple.com/switch

For an updated list of hardware and software reviews and their Web site addresses, visit scsite.com/ic7/buyers.

FIGURE 38 Hardware and software reviews.

2 **Know the System Requirements of the Operating System.**

After deciding what software you want to run on your new computer, you need to determine the operating system you want to use. If, however, you purchase a new computer, chances are it will have the latest version of your preferred operating system (Windows Vista, Linux, UNIX, Mac OS X). Figure 39 lists the minimum computer requirements of Windows Vista versions.

Windows Vista Versions	Minimum Computer Requirements
Windows Vista Home Basic	• 800 MHz processor • 512 MB of RAM • DirectX 9 capable graphics processor
Windows Vista Home Premium **Windows Vista Ultimate** **Windows Vista Business** **Windows Vista Enterprise**	• 1 GHz processor • 1 GB of RAM • DirectX 9 capable graphics Windows Vista Enterprise • 40 GB of hard disk capacity (15 GB free space) • DVD-ROM drive • Audio output capability • Internet access capability

FIGURE 39 Hardware requirements for Windows Vista.

3 **Look for bundled software.**

When you purchase a computer, it may come bundled with software. Some sellers even let you choose which software you want. Remember, however, that bundled software has value only if you would have purchased the software even if it had not come with the computer. At the very least, you probably will want word processing software and a browser to access the Internet. If you need additional applications, such as a spreadsheet, a database, or presentation graphics, consider purchasing Microsoft Works, Microsoft Office, OpenOffice.org, or Sun StarOffice, which include several programs at a reduced price.

4 **Avoid buying the least powerful computer available.**

Once you know the application software you want to use, you then can consider the following important criteria about the computer's components: (1) processor speed, (2) size and types of memory (RAM) and storage, (3) types of input/output devices, (4) types of ports and adapter cards, and (5) types of communications devices. You also need to consider if the computer is upgradeable and to what extent you are able to upgrade. For example, all manufacturers limit the amount of memory you can add. The information in Figures 40 and 41 can help you determine what system components are best for you. Figure 40 (on COM 27 to COM 28) outlines considerations for specific hardware components. Figure 41 (on page COM 29) provides a Base Components worksheet that lists PC recommendations for each category of user discussed in this book: Home User, Small Office/Home Office User, Mobile User, Power User, and Large Business User. In the worksheet, the Home User category is divided into two groups: Application Home User and Game Home User. The Mobile User recommendations list criteria for a notebook computer, but do not include the PDA or Tablet PC options.

Computer technology changes rapidly, meaning a computer that seems powerful enough today may not serve your computing needs in a few years. In fact, studies show that many users regret not buying a more powerful computer. To avoid this, plan to buy a computer that will last you for two to three years. You can help delay obsolescence by purchasing the fastest processor, the most memory, and the largest hard disk you can afford. If you must buy a less powerful computer, be sure you can upgrade it with additional memory, components, and peripheral devices as your computer requirements grow.

5 **Consider upgrades to the mouse, keyboard, monitor, printer, microphone, and speakers.**

You use these peripheral devices to interact with your computer, so you should make sure they are up to your standards. Review the peripheral devices listed in Figure 40 on pages COM 27 to COM 28 and then visit both local computer dealers and large retail stores to test the computers on display. Ask the salesperson what input and output devices would be best for you and whether you should upgrade beyond what comes standard. Consider purchasing a wireless keyboard and wireless mouse to eliminate bothersome wires on your desktop. A few extra dollars spent on these components when you initially purchase a computer can extend its usefulness by years.

CD/DVD Drives: Most computers come with a CD-RW drive. A CD-RW drive allows you to create your own custom data CDs for data backup or data transfer purposes. It also will allow you to store and share video files, digital photos, and other large files with other people who have access to a CD-ROM drive. An even better alternative is to upgrade to a DVD±RW combination drive. It allows you to read DVDs and CDs and to write data on (burn) a DVD or CD. A DVD has a capacity of at least 4.7 GB versus the 650 MB capacity of a CD. An HD DVD has a minimum capacity of 45 GB.

Card Reader/Writer: A card reader/writer is useful for transferring data directly to and from a removable flash memory card, such as the ones used in your camera or audio player. Make sure the card reader/writer can read from and write on the flash memory cards that you use.

Digital Camera: Consider an inexpensive point-and-shoot digital camera. They are small enough to carry around, usually operate automatically in terms of lighting and focus, and contain storage cards for storing photographs. A 5-megapixel camera with a 512 MB storage card is fine for creating images for use on the Web or to send via e-mail.

Digital Video Capture Device: A digital video capture device allows you to connect your computer to a camcorder or VCR and record, edit, manage, and then write video back on a VCR tape, a CD, or a DVD. To create quality video (true 30 frames per second, full-sized TV), the digital video capture device should have a USB 2.0 or FireWire port. You also will need sufficient storage: an hour of data on a VCR tape takes up about 5 GB of disk storage.

External Hard Disk: An external hard disk can serve many purposes: it can serve as extra storage for your computer, provide a way to store and transport large files or large quantities of files, and provide security by allowing you to keep all of your data on the external disk without leaving any data on the computer. External hard disks can be purchased with the same amount of capacity as any internal disk. If you are going to use it as a backup to your internal hard disk, you should purchase an external hard drive with at least as much capacity as your internal hard disk.

Hard Disk: It is recommended that you buy a computer with 60 to 80 GB if your primary interests are browsing the Web and using e-mail and Office suite-type applications; 80 to 100 GB if you also want to edit digital photographs; 100 to 200 GB if you plan to edit digital video or manipulate large audio files even occasionally; and 200 to 500 GB if you will edit digital video, movies, or photography often; store audio files and music; or consider yourself to be a power user. It also is recommended that you use Serial ATA (SATA) as opposed to Parallel ATA (PATA). SATA has many advantages over PATA, including support for Plug and Play devices.

Joystick/Wheel: If you use your computer to play games, then you will want to purchase a joystick or a wheel. These devices, especially the more expensive ones, provide for realistic game play with force feedback, programmable buttons, and specialized levers and wheels.

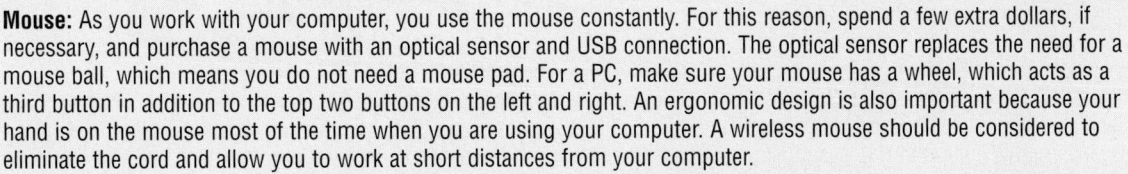

Keyboard: The keyboard is one of the more important devices used to communicate with the computer. For this reason, make sure the keyboard you purchase has 101 to 105 keys, is comfortable and easy to use, and has a USB connection. A wireless keyboard should be considered, especially if you have a small desk area.

Microphone: If you plan to record audio or use speech recognition to enter text and commands, then purchase a close-talk headset with gain adjustment support.

Modem: Most computers come with a modem so that you can use your telephone line to access the Internet. Some modems also have fax capabilities. Your modem should be rated at 56 Kbps.

Monitor: The monitor is where you will view documents, read e-mail messages, and view pictures. A minimum of a 17" screen is recommended, but if you are planning to use your computer for graphic design or game playing, then you may want to purchase a 19" or 21" monitor. The LCD flat panel monitor should be considered, especially if space is an issue.

Mouse: As you work with your computer, you use the mouse constantly. For this reason, spend a few extra dollars, if necessary, and purchase a mouse with an optical sensor and USB connection. The optical sensor replaces the need for a mouse ball, which means you do not need a mouse pad. For a PC, make sure your mouse has a wheel, which acts as a third button in addition to the top two buttons on the left and right. An ergonomic design is also important because your hand is on the mouse most of the time when you are using your computer. A wireless mouse should be considered to eliminate the cord and allow you to work at short distances from your computer.

FIGURE 40 Hardware guidelines.

(continued next page)

(continued from previous page)

Ports: Depending on how you are using your computer, you may need anywhere from 4 to 10 USB 2.0 ports. USB 2.0 ports have become the connection of choice in the computer industry. They offer an easy way to connect peripheral devices such as printers, digital cameras, portable media players, etc. Many computers intended for home or professional audio/video use have built-in FireWire ports. Most personal computers come with a minimum of six USB 2.0 ports and two FireWire ports.

Port Hub Expander: If you plan to connect several peripheral devices to your computer at the same time, then you need to be concerned with the number of ports available on your computer. If your computer does not have enough ports, then you should purchase a port hub expander. A port hub expander plugs into a single FireWire port or USB port and gives several additional ports.

Printer: Your two basic printer choices are ink-jet and laser. Color ink-jet printers cost on average between $50 and $300. Laser printers cost from $200 to $2,000. In general, the cheaper the printer, the lower the resolution and speed, and the more often you are required to change the ink cartridge or toner. Laser printers print faster and with a higher quality than an ink-jet, and their toner on average costs less. If you want color, then go with a high-end ink-jet printer to ensure quality of print. Duty cycle (the number of pages you expect to print each month) also should be a determining factor. If your duty cycle is on the low end — hundreds of pages per month — then stay with a high-end ink-jet printer, rather than purchasing a laser printer. If you plan to print photographs taken with a digital camera, then you should purchase a photo printer. A photo printer is a dye-sublimation printer or an ink-jet printer with higher resolution and features that allow you to print quality photographs.

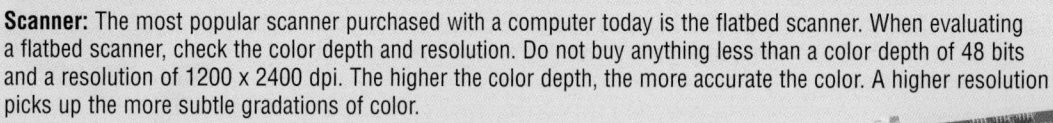

Processor: For a PC, an Intel Core 2 Duo processor at 2.66 GHz is more than enough processor power for application home and small office/home office users. Game home, large business, and power users should upgrade to faster processors.

RAM: RAM plays a vital role in the speed of your computer. Make sure the computer you purchase has at least 512 MB of RAM. If you have extra money to invest in your computer, then consider increasing the RAM to 1 GB or more. The extra money for RAM will be well spent.

Scanner: The most popular scanner purchased with a computer today is the flatbed scanner. When evaluating a flatbed scanner, check the color depth and resolution. Do not buy anything less than a color depth of 48 bits and a resolution of 1200 x 2400 dpi. The higher the color depth, the more accurate the color. A higher resolution picks up the more subtle gradations of color.

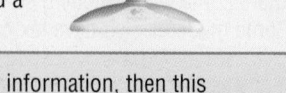

Sound Card: Many computers come with a standard sound card that supports Dolby 5.1 surround and is capable of recording and playing digital audio. Make sure it is suitable in the event you decide to use your computer as an entertainment or gaming system.

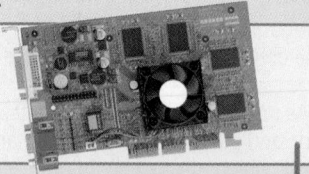

Speakers: Once you have a good sound card, quality speakers and a separate subwoofer that amplifies the bass frequencies of the speakers can turn your computer into a premium stereo system.

PC Video Camera: A PC video camera is a small camera used to capture and display live video (in some cases with sound), primarily on a Web page. You also can capture, edit, and share video and still photos. The camera sits on your monitor or desk. Recommended minimum specifications include 640 x 480 resolution, a video with a rate of 30 frames per second, and a USB 2.0 or FireWire port.

USB Flash Drive: If you work on different computers and need access to the same data and information, then this portable miniature mobile storage device is ideal. USB flash drive capacity varies from 16 MB to 4 GB.

Video Card: Most standard video cards satisfy the monitor display needs of application home and small office users. If you are a game home user or a graphic designer, you will want to upgrade to a higher quality video card. The higher refresh rates will further enhance the display of games, graphics, and movies.

Wireless LAN Access Point: A Wireless LAN Access Point allows you to network several computers, so they can share files and access the Internet through a single cable modem or DSL connection. Each device that you connect requires a wireless card. A Wireless LAN Access Point can offer a range of operations up to several hundred feet, so be sure the device has a high-powered antenna.

BASE COMPONENTS

	Application Home User	Game Home User	Small Office/Home Office User	Mobile User	Large Business User	Power User
HARDWARE						
Processor	Intel Core 2 Duo at 2.66 GHz	Intel Core 2 Duo at 2.93 GHz	Intel Core 2 Duo at 2.93 GHz	Intel Core 2 Duo at 2.33 GHz	Intel Core 2 Duo at 2.66 GHz	Intel Core 2 Extreme
RAM	512 MB	4 GB	1 GB	1 GB	1 GB	2 GB
Cache	512 KB L2	512 KB L2	512 KB L2	512 KB L2	512 KB L2	2 MB L3
Hard Disk	250 GB	300 GB	500 GB	100 GB	500 GB	1.5 TB
LCD Flat Panel	17" or 19"	21"	19" or 21"	17" Wide Display	19" of 21"	23"
Video Card	256 MB	512 MB	256 MB	256 MB	256 MB	256 MB
CD/DVD Bay 1	CD-RW	Blue-ray or HD DVD reader/writer	CD-RW	CD-RW/DVD	CD-RW	Blue-ray or HD DVD reader/writer
CD/DVD Bay 2	DVD+RW	DVD+RW	DVD+RW	DVD+RW	DVD+RW	DVD+RW
Printer	Color Ink-Jet	Color Ink-Jet	18 ppm Laser	Portable Ink-Jet	50 ppm Laser	10 ppm Color Laser
PC Video Camera	Yes	Yes	Yes	Yes	Yes	Yes
Fax/Modem	Yes	Yes	Yes	Yes	Yes	Yes
Microphone	Close-Talk Headset With Gain Adjustment	Close-Talk Headset With Gain Adjustment	Close-Talk Headset With Gain Adjustment	Close-Talk Headset With Gain Adjustment	Close-Talk Headset With Gain Adjustment	Close-Talk Headset With Gain Adjustment
Speakers	5.1 Dolby Surround	5.1 Dolby Surround	5.1 Dolby Surround	Stereo	5.1 Dolby Surround	5.1 Dolby Surround
Pointing Device	IntelliMouse or Optical Mouse	Laser Mouse and Joystick	IntelliMouse or Optical Mouse	Touchpad or Pointing Stick and Laser Mouse	IntelliMouse or Optical Mouse	IntelliMouse or Laser Mouse and Joystick
Keyboard	Yes	Yes	Yes	Built-In	Yes	Yes
Backup Disk/Tape Drive	External or Removable Hard Disk	External or Removable Hard Disk	External or Removable Hard Disk	External or Removable Hard Disk	Tape Drive	External or Removable Hard Disk
USB Flash Drive	256 MB	512 MB	512 MB	512 MB	4 GB	2 GB
Sound Card	Sound Blaster Compatible	Sound Blaster Audigy 2	Sound Blaster Compatible	Built-In	Sound Blaster Compatible	Sound Blaster Audigy 2
Network Card	Yes	Yes	Yes	Yes	Yes	Yes
TV-Out Connector	Yes	Yes	Yes	Yes	Yes	Yes
USB 2.0 Port	6	8	6	4	9	10
FireWire Port	2	2	2	1	2	2
SOFTWARE						
Operating System	Windows Vista Home Basic	Windows Vista Home Premium	Windows Vista Business	Windows Vista Business	Windows Vista Enterprise	Windows Vista Ultimate
Application Suite	Office Standard 2007	Office Standard 2007	Office Small Business 2007	Office Small Business 2007	Office Professional 2007	Office Professional 2007
Antivirus	Yes, 12-Mo. Subscription	Yes, 12-Mo. Subscription	Yes, 12-Mo. Subscription	Yes, 12-Mo. Subscription	Yes, 12-Mo. Subscription	Yes, 12-Mo. Subscription
Internet Access	Cable, DSL, or Dial-up	Cable or DSL	Cable or DSL	Wireless or Dial-up	LAN/WAN (T1/T3)	Cable or DSL
OTHER						
Surge Protector	Yes	Yes	Yes	Portable	Yes	Yes
Warranty	3-Year Limited, 1-Year Next Business Day On-Site Service	3-Year Limited, 1-Year Next Business Day On-Site Service	3-year On-Site Service	3-Year Limited, 1-Year Next Business Day On-Site Service	3-year On-Site Service	3-year On-Site Service
Other		Wheel	Postage Printer	Docking Station Carrying Case Fingerprint Scanner Portable Data Projector		Graphics Tablet Plotter or Large-Format Printer

Optional Components for all Categories	
802.11g Wireless Card	Graphics Tablet
Bluetooth Enabled	Portable Media Player
Biometric Input Device	IrDA Port
Card Reader/Writer	Multifunction Peripheral
Digital Camera	Photo Printer
Digital Video Capture Device	Port Hub Expander
Digital Video Camera	Portable Data Projector
Dual-Monitor Support with Second Monitor	Scanner
Ergonomic Keyboard	TV/FM Tuner
External Hard Disk	Uninterruptible Power Supply

FIGURE 41 Base desktop and mobile computer components and optional components. A copy of the Base Components worksheet is part of the Data Files for Students. To obtain a copy of the Data Files for Students, see the inside back cover of this book for instructions.

⑥ Determine whether you want to use telephone lines or broadband (cable or DSL) to access the Internet.

If your computer has a modem, then you can access the Internet using a standard telephone line. Ordinarily, you call a local or toll-free 800 number to connect to an ISP (see Guideline 7 on the next page). Using a dial-up Internet connection is relatively inexpensive but slow.

DSL and cable connections provide much faster Internet connections, which are ideal if you want faster file download speeds for software, digital photos, and music. As you would expect, they also are more expensive. DSL, which is available through local telephone companies, also may require that you subscribe to an ISP. Cable is available through your local cable television provider and some online service providers (OSPs). If you get cable, then you would not use a separate Internet service provider or online service provider.

7 **If you are using a dial-up or wireless connection to connect to the Internet, then select an ISP or OSP.**

You can access the Internet via telephone lines in one of two ways: an ISP or an OSP. Both provide Internet access for a monthly fee that ranges from $6 to $25. Local ISPs offer Internet access to users in a limited geographic region, through local telephone numbers. National ISPs provide access for users nationwide (including mobile users), through local and toll-free telephone numbers and cable. Because of their size, national ISPs generally offer more services and have a larger technical support staff than local ISPs. OSPs furnish Internet access as well as members-only features for users nationwide. Figure 42 lists several national ISPs and OSPs. Before you choose an ISP or OSP, compare such features as the number of access hours, monthly fees, available services (e-mail, Web page hosting, chat), and reliability.

Company	Service	Web Address
America Online	OSP	aol.com
AT&T Worldnet	ISP	www.att.net
Comcast	OSP	comcast.net
CompuServe	OSP	compuserve.com
EarthLink	ISP	earthlink.net
Juno	OSP	juno.com
NetZero	OSP	netzero.com
MSN	OSP	msn.com
Prodigy	ISP/OSP	myhome.prodigy.net

For an updated list of national ISPs and OSPs and their Web site addresses, visit scsite.com/ic7/buyers.

FIGURE 42   National ISPs and OSPs.

8 **Use a worksheet to compare computers, services, and other considerations.**

You can use a separate sheet of paper to take notes on each vendor's computer and then summarize the information on a worksheet, such as the one shown in Figure 43. You can use Figure 43 to compare prices for either a PC or a Mac. Most companies advertise a price for a base computer that includes components housed in the system unit (processor, RAM, sound card, video card), disk drives (hard disk, CD-ROM, CD-RW, DVD-ROM, and DVD6RW), a keyboard, mouse, monitor, printer, speakers, and modem. Be aware, however, that some advertisements list prices for computers with only some of these components. Monitors and printers, for example, often are not included in a base computer's price. Depending on how you plan to use the computer, you may want to invest in additional or more powerful components. When you are comparing the prices of computers, make sure you are comparing identical or similar configurations.

PC or MAC Cost Comparison Worksheet

Dealers list prices for computers with most of these components (instead of listing individual component costs). Some dealers do not supply a monitor. Some dealers offer significant discounts, but you must subscribe to an Internet service for a specified period to receive the dicounted price. To compare computers, enter overall system price at top and enter a 0 (zero) for components included in the system cost. For any additional components not covered in the system price, enter the cost in the appropriate cells.

Items to Purchase	Desired System (PC)	Desired System (Mac)	Local Dealer #1	Local Dealer #2	Online Dealer #1	Online Dealer #2	Comments
OVERALL SYSTEM							
Overall System Price	< $2,000	< $2,000					
HARDWARE							
Processor	Intel Core 2 Duo	Intel Core 2 Duo					
RAM	1 GB	1 GB					
Cache	256 KB L2	256 KB L2					
Hard Disk	250 GB	250 GB					
Monitor/LCD Flat Panel	20 Inch	20 Inch					
Video Card	256 MB	256 MB					
USB Flash Drive	1 GB	1 GB					
CD/DVD Bay 1	CD-RW	DVD±RW					
CD/DVD Bay 2	DVD±RW	NA					
Speakers	Dolby 5.1 Surround	Dolby 5.1 Surround					
Sound Card	Sound Blaster Compatible	Sound Blaster Compatible					
USB 2.0 Port	6	6					
FireWire Port	2	2					
Network Card	Yes	Yes					
Fax/Modem	56 Kbps	56 Kbps					
Keyboard	Standard	Apple Pro Keyboard					
Pointing Device	IntelliMouse	Intellimouse or Apple Pro Mouse					
Microphone	Close-Talk Headset with Gain Adjustment	Close-Talk Headset with Gain Adjustment					
Printer	Color Ink-Jet	Color Ink-Jet					
SOFTWARE							
Operating System	Windows Vista Ultimate	Mac OS X					
Application Software	Office 2007 Small Business	Office 2007 for Mac					
Antivirus	Yes - 12 Mo. Subscription	Yes - 12 Mo. Subscription					
OTHER							
Card Reader							
Digital Camera	5-Megapixel	5-Megapixel					
Internet Connection	1-Year Subscription	1-Year Subscription					
Joystick	Yes	Yes					
PC Video Camera	With Microphone	With Microphone					
Port Hub Expander							
Scanner							
Surge Protector							
Warranty	3-Year On-Site Service	3-Year On-Site Service					
Wireless Card	Internal	Internal					
Wireless LAN Access Point	LinkSys	Apple AirPort					
Total Cost			$ -	$ -	$ -	$ -	

FIGURE 43   A worksheet is an effective tool for summarizing and comparing components and prices of different computer vendors. A copy of the Computer Cost Comparison Worksheet is part of the Data Files for Students. To obtain a copy of the Data Files for Students, see the inside back cover of this book for instructions.

9 **If you are buying a new computer, you have several purchasing options: buying from your school bookstore, a local computer dealer, a local large retail store, or ordering by mail via telephone or the Web.**

Each purchasing option has certain advantages. Many college bookstores, for example, sign exclusive pricing agreements with computer manufacturers and, thus, can offer student discounts. Local dealers and local large retail stores, however, more easily can provide hands-on support. Mail-order companies that sell computers by telephone or online via the Web (Figure 44) often provide the lowest prices, but extend less personal service. Some major mail-order companies, however, have started to provide next-business-day, on-site services. A credit card usually is required to buy from a mail-order company. Figure 45 lists some of the more popular mail-order companies and their Web site addresses.

10 **If you are buying a used computer, stay with name brands such as Dell, Gateway, Hewlett-Packard, and Apple.**

Although brand-name equipment can cost more, most brand-name computers have longer, more comprehensive warranties, are better supported, and have more authorized centers for repair services. As with new computers, you can purchase a used computer from local computer dealers, local large retail stores, or mail order via the telephone or the Web. Classified ads and used computer sellers offer additional outlets for purchasing used computers. Figure 46 lists several major used computer brokers and their Web site addresses.

11 **If you have a computer and are upgrading to a new one, then consider selling or trading in the old one.**

If you are a replacement buyer, your older computer still may have value. If you cannot sell the computer through the classified ads, via a Web site, or to a friend, then ask if the computer dealer will buy your old computer. An increasing number of companies are taking trade-ins, but do not expect too much money for your old computer. Other companies offer free disposal of your old PC.

12 **Be aware of hidden costs.**

Before purchasing, be sure to consider any additional costs associated with buying a computer, such as an additional telephone line, a cable or DSL modem, an uninterruptible power supply (UPS), computer furniture, a USB flash drive, paper, and computer training classes you may want to take. Depending on where you buy your computer, the seller may be willing to include some or all of these in the computer purchase price.

Type of Computer	Company	Web Address
PC	CNET Shopper	shopper.cnet.com
	Hewlett-Packard	hp.com
	CompUSA	compusa.com
	TigerDirect	tigerdirect.com
	Dell	dell.com
	Gateway	gateway.com
Macintosh	Apple Computer	store.apple.com
	ClubMac	clubmac.com
	MacConnection	macconnection.com
	PC & MacExchange	macx.com

For an updated list of mail-order computer companies and their Web site addresses, visit scsite.com/ic7/buyers.

FIGURE 45 Computer mail-order companies.

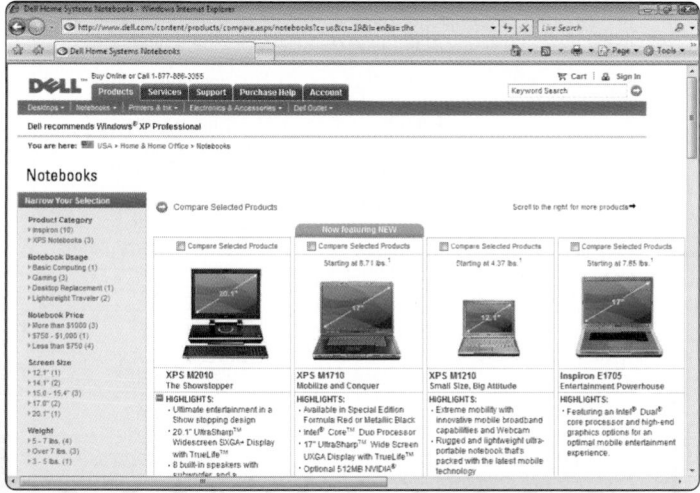

FIGURE 44 Mail-order companies, such as Dell, sell computers online.

Company	Web Address
Amazon.com	amazon.com
TECHAGAIN	techagain.com
American Computer Express	americancomputerex.com
U.S. Computer Exchange	usce.org
eBay	ebay.com

For an updated list of used computer mail-order companies and their Web site addresses, visit scsite.com/ic7/buyers.

FIGURE 46 Used computer mail-order companies.

13 **Consider more than just price.**

The lowest-cost computer may not be the best long-term buy. Consider such intangibles as the vendor's time in business, the vendor's regard for quality, and the vendor's reputation for support. If you need to upgrade your computer often, you may want to consider a leasing arrangement, in which you pay monthly lease fees, but can upgrade or add on to your computer as your equipment needs change. No matter what type of buyer you are, insist on a 30-day, no-questions-asked return policy on your computer.

14 **Avoid restocking fees.**

Some companies charge a restocking fee of 10 to 20 percent as part of their money-back return policy. In some cases, no restocking fee for hardware is applied, but it is applied for software. Ask about the existence and terms of any restocking policies before you buy.

15 **Use a credit card to purchase your new computer.**

Many credit cards offer purchase protection and extended warranty benefits that cover you in case of loss of or damage to purchased goods. Paying by credit card also gives you time to install and use the computer before you have to pay for it. Finally, if you are dissatisfied with the computer and are unable to reach an agreement with the seller, paying by credit card gives you certain rights regarding withholding payment until the dispute is resolved. Check your credit card terms for specific details.

15 **Consider purchasing an extended warranty or service plan.**

If you use your computer for business or require fast resolution to major computer problems, consider purchasing an extended warranty or a service plan through a local dealer or third-party company. Most extended warranties cover the repair and replacement of computer components beyond the standard warranty. Most service plans ensure that your technical support calls receive priority response from technicians. You also can purchase an on-site service plan that states that a technician will come to your home, work, or school within 24 hours. If your computer includes a warranty and service agreement for a year or less, think about extending the service for two or three years when you buy the computer.

HOW TO PURCHASE A NOTEBOOK COMPUTER

If you need computing capability when you travel or to use in lectures or meetings, you may find a notebook computer to be an appropriate choice. The guidelines mentioned in the previous section also apply to the purchase of a notebook computer. The following are additional considerations unique to notebook computers.

1 **Purchase a notebook computer with a sufficiently large active-matrix screen.**

Active-matrix screens display high-quality color that is viewable from all angles. Less expensive, passive-matrix screens sometimes are difficult to see in low-light conditions and cannot be viewed from an angle. Notebook computers typically come with a 12.1-inch, 13.3-inch, 14.1-inch, 15.4-inch, or 17-inch display. For most users, a 14.1-inch display is satisfactory. If you intend to use your notebook computer as a desktop computer replacement, however, you may opt for a 15.7-inch or 17-inch display. Dell offers a notebook computer with a 20.1-inch display that looks like a briefcase when closed. Notebook computers with these larger displays weigh seven to ten pounds, however, so if you travel a lot and portability is essential, you might want a lighter computer with a smaller display. The lightest notebook computers, which weigh less than 3 pounds, are equipped with a 12.1-inch display. Regardless of size, the resolution of the display should be at least 1024 × 768 pixels. To compare the monitor size on various notebook computers, visit the company Web sites in Figure 47.

CENTURY COMPUTERS
Performance Guarantee
(See reverse for terms & conditions of this contract)

Invoice #: 1984409   Effective Date: 10/12/07
Invoice Date: 10/12/07   Expiration Date: 10/12/10

Customer Name: Leon, Richard   System & Serial Numbers
Date: 10/12/07   IMB computer
Address: 1123 Roxbury   S/N: US759290C
       Sycamore, IL 60178
Day phone: (815) 555-0303
Evening Phone: (728) 555-0203

John Smith
Print Name of Century's Authorized Signature   _10/12/07_
                     Date

Type of Notebook	Company	Web Address
PC	Acer	global.acer.com
	Dell	dell.com
	Fujitsu	fujitsu.com
	Gateway	gateway.com
	Hewlett-Packard	hp.com
	Lenovo	lenovo.com/us/en/
	NEC	nec.com
	Sony	sony.com
	Toshiba	toshiba.com
Mac	Apple	apple.com

For an updated list of companies and their Web site addresses, visit scsite.com/ic7/buyers.

FIGURE 47 Companies that sell notebook computers.

2   Experiment with different keyboards and pointing devices.

Notebook computer keyboards are far less standardized than those for desktop computers. Some notebook computers, for example, have wide wrist rests, while others have none, and keyboard layouts on notebook computers often vary. Notebook computers also use a range of pointing devices, including pointing sticks, touchpads, and trackballs. Before you purchase a notebook computer, try various types of keyboard and pointing devices to determine which is easiest for you to use. Regardless of the pointing device you select, you also may want to purchase a regular mouse to use when you are working at a desk or other large surface.

3   Make sure the notebook computer you purchase has a CD and/or DVD drive.

Most notebook computers come with a CD and/or a DVD drive. Although DVD drives are slightly more expensive, they allow you to play CDs and DVD movies using your notebook computer and a headset.

4   If necessary, upgrade the processor, memory, and disk storage at the time of purchase.

As with a desktop computer, upgrading your notebook computer's memory and disk storage usually is less expensive at the time of initial purchase. Some disk storage is custom designed for notebook computer manufacturers, meaning an upgrade might not be available in the future. If you are purchasing a lightweight notebook computer, then it should include at least an Intel Core Duo processor, 512 MB RAM, and 80 GB of storage.

5   The availability of built-in ports and a port extender on a notebook computer is important.

A notebook computer does not have a lot of room to add adapter cards. If you know the purpose for which you plan to use your notebook computer, then you can determine the ports you will need. Most notebooks come with common ports, such as a mouse port, IrDA port, serial port, parallel port, video port, a FireWire port, and multiple USB ports. If you plan to connect your notebook computer to a TV, however, then you will need a PCtoTV port. If you want to connect to networks at school or in various offices via a network cable, make sure the notebook computer you purchase has a network port. If your notebook computer does not come with a network port, then you will have to purchase an external network card that slides into an expansion slot in your notebook computer, as well as a network cable. While newer portable media players connect to a USB port, older ones require a FireWire port.

6   If you plan to use your notebook computer for note-taking at school or in meetings, consider a notebook computer that converts to a Tablet PC.

Some computer manufacturers have developed convertible notebook computers that allow the screen to rotate 180 degrees on a central hinge and then fold down to cover the keyboard and become a Tablet PC (Figure 48). You then can use a stylus to enter text or drawings into the computer by writing on the screen. Some notebook computers have wide screens for better viewing and editing, and some even have a screen on top of the unit in addition to the regular screen.

FIGURE 48   The HP Compaq tc4200 Tablet PC converts to a notebook computer.

7   Purchase a notebook computer with a built-in wireless network connection.

A wireless network connection (Bluetooth, Wi-Fi a/b/g, WiMAX, etc.) can be useful when you travel or as part of a home network. Increasingly more airports, hotels, and cafes have wireless networks that allow you to connect to the Internet. Many users today are setting up wireless home networks. With a wireless home network, the desktop computer functions as the server, and your notebook computer can access the desktop computer from any location in the house to share files and hardware, such as a printer, and browse the Web. Most home wireless networks allow connections from distances of 150 to 800 feet.

8   If you are going to use your notebook computer for long periods without access to an electrical outlet, purchase a second battery.

The trend among notebook computer users today is power and size over battery life, and notebook computer manufacturers have picked up on this. Many notebook computer users today are willing to give up longer battery life for a larger screen, faster processor, and more storage. In addition, some manufacturers typically sell the notebook with the lowest capacity battery. For this reason, you need to be careful in choosing a notebook computer if you plan to use it without access to electrical outlets for long periods, such as an airplane flight. You also might want to purchase a second battery as a backup. If you anticipate running your notebook computer on batteries frequently, choose a computer that uses lithium-ion batteries, which last longer than nickel cadmium or nickel hydride batteries.

9 Purchase a well-padded and well-designed carrying case.

An amply padded carrying case will protect your notebook computer from the bumps it will receive while traveling. A well-designed carrying case will have room for accessories such as spare CDs and DVDs, a user manual, pens, and paperwork (Figure 49).

FIGURE 49 A well-designed notebook computer carrying case.

10 If you travel overseas, obtain a set of electrical and telephone adapters.

Different countries use different outlets for electrical and telephone connections. Several manufacturers sell sets of adapters that will work in most countries.

11 If you plan to connect your notebook computer to a video projector, make sure the notebook computer is compatible with the video projector.

You should check, for example, to be sure that your notebook computer will allow you to display an image on the computer screen and projection device at the same time (Figure 50). Also, ensure that your notebook computer has the ports required to connect to the video projector. You also may consider purchasing a notebook computer with a built-in video camera for videoconferencing purposes.

12 For improved security, consider a fingerprint scanner.

More than half a million notebook computers are stolen or lost each year. If you have critical information stored on your notebook computer, then consider purchasing one with a fingerprint scanner (Figure 51) to protect the data if your computer is stolen or lost. Fingerprint security offers a level of protection that extends well beyond the standard password protection. If your notebook computer is stolen, the odds of recovering it improve dramatically with anti-theft tracking software. Manufacturers claim recovery rates of 90 percent or more for notebook computers using their product.

FIGURE 51 Fingerprint scanner technology offers greater security than passwords.

FIGURE 50 A notebook computer connected to a video projector projects the image displayed on the screen.

HOW TO PURCHASE A TABLET PC

The Tablet PC (Figure 52) combines the mobility features of a traditional notebook computer with the simplicity of pencil and paper, because you can create and save Office-type documents by writing and drawing directly on the screen with a digital pen. Tablet PCs use the Windows Tablet Technology in Windows Vista operating system. A notebook computer and a Tablet PC have many similarities. For this reason, if you are considering purchasing a Tablet PC, review the guidelines for purchasing a notebook computer, as well as the guidelines below.

FIGURE 52 The lightweight Tablet PC, with its handwriting capabilities, is the latest addition to the family of mobile computers.

 Make sure the Tablet PC fits your mobile computing needs.

The Tablet PC is not for every mobile user. If you find yourself in need of a computer in class or you are spending more time in meetings than in your office, then the Tablet PC may be the answer. Before you invest money in a Tablet PC, however, determine the programs you plan to use on it. You should not buy a Tablet PC simply because it is an interesting type of computer. For additional information on the Tablet PC, visit the Web sites listed in Figure 53. You may have to

Company	Web Address
Fujitsu	fujitsu.com
Hewlett-Packard	hp.com
Microsoft	microsoft.com/windowsxp/tabletpc
ViewSonic	viewsonic.com
For an updated list of companies and their Web site addresses, visit scsite.com/ic7/buyers.	

FIGURE 53 Companies involved with Tablet PCs and their Web sites.

use the search capabilities on the home page of the companies listed to locate information about the Tablet PC.

 Decide whether you want a convertible or pure Tablet PC.

Convertible Tablet PCs have an attached keyboard and look like a notebook computer. You rotate the screen and lay it flat against the computer for note-taking. The pure Tablet PCs are slim and lightweight, weighing less than four pounds. They have the capability of easily docking at a desktop to gain access to a large monitor, keyboard, and mouse. If you spend a lot of time attending lectures or meetings, then the pure Tablet PC is ideal. Acceptable specifications for a Tablet PC are shown in Figure 54.

TABLET PC SPECIFICATIONS

Dimensions	12" × 9" × 1.2"
Weight	Less than 5 Pounds
Processor	Pentium M Processor at 2 GHz
RAM	1 GB
Hard Disk	60 GB
Display	12.1" TFT
Digitizer	Electromagnetic Digitizer
Battery	6-Cell High Capacity Lithium-Ion
USB	3
FireWire	1
Docking Station	Grab and Go with CD-ROM, Keyboard, and Mouse
Bluetooth Port	Yes
Wireless	802.11a/b/g Card
Network Card	10/100 Ethernet
Modem	56 Kbps
Speakers	Internal
Microphone	Internal
Operating System	Windows Vista
Application Software	Office Small Business Edition
Antivirus Software	Yes – 12 Month Subscription
Warranty	1-Year Limited Warranty Parts and Labor

FIGURE 54 Tablet PC specifications.

 Be sure the weight and dimensions are conducive to portability.

The weight and dimensions of the Tablet PC are important because you carry it around like a notepad. The Tablet PC you buy should weigh four pounds or less. Its dimensions should be approximately 12 inches by 9 inches by 1.2 inches.

4 **Port availability, battery life, and durability are even more important with a Tablet PC than they are with a notebook computer.**

Make sure the Tablet PC you purchase has the ports required for the applications you plan to run. As with any mobile computer, battery life is important especially if you plan to use your Tablet PC for long periods without access to an electrical outlet. A Tablet PC must be durable because if you use it the way it was designed to be used, then you will be handling it much like you handle a pad of paper.

5 **Experiment with different models of the Tablet PC to find the digital pen that works best for you.**

The key to making use of the Tablet PC is to be comfortable with its handwriting capabilities and on-screen keyboard. Not only is the digital pen used to write on the screen (Figure 55), you also use it to make gestures to complete tasks, in a manner similar to the way you use a mouse. Figure 56 compares the standard point-and-click of a mouse with the gestures made with a digital pen. Other gestures with the digital pen replicate some of the commonly used keys on a keyboard.

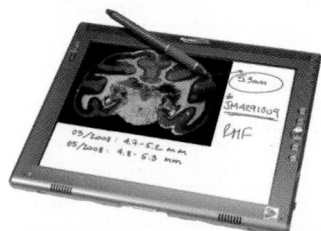

FIGURE 55 A Tablet PC lets you handwrite notes and draw on the screen using a digital pen.

Mouse Unit	Digital Pen
Point	Point
Click	Tap
Double-click	Double-tap
Right-click	Tap and hold
Click and drag	Drag

FIGURE 56 Standard point-and-click of a mouse compared with the gestures made with a digital pen.

6 **Check out the comfort level of handwriting in different positions.**

You should be able to handwrite on a Tablet PC with your hand resting on the screen. You also should be able to handwrite holding the Tablet PC in one hand, as well as with it sitting in your lap.

7 **Make sure the LCD display device has a resolution high enough to take advantage of Microsoft's ClearType technologies.**

Tablet PCs use a digitizer under a standard 10.4-inch motion-sensitive LCD display to make the digital ink on the screen look like real ink on paper. To ensure you get the maximum benefits from the new ClearType technology, make sure the LCD display has a resolution of 800 × 600 in landscape mode and a 600 × 800 in portrait mode.

8 **Test the built-in Tablet PC microphone and speakers.**

Although most application software, including Microsoft Office, recognizes human speech, it is important that the Tablet PC's built-in microphone operates at an acceptable level. If the microphone is not to your liking, you may want to purchase a close-talk headset with your Tablet PC. Increasingly more users are sending information as audio files, rather than relying solely on text. For this reason, you also should check the speakers on the Tablet PC to make sure they meet your standards.

9 **Consider a Tablet PC with a built-in PC video camera.**

A PC video camera adds streaming video and still photography capabilities to your Tablet PC, while still allowing you to take notes in lectures or meetings.

10 **Review the docking capabilities of the Tablet PC.**

The Tablet Technology in Windows Vista operating system supports a grab-and-go form of docking, so you can pick up and take a docked Tablet PC with you, just as you would pick up a notepad on your way to a meeting (Figure 57).

11 **Wireless access to the Internet and your e-mail is essential with a Tablet PC.**

Make sure the Tablet PC has wireless networking (Bluetooth, Wi-Fi a/b/g, WiMAX, etc.), so you can access the Internet and your e-mail anytime and anywhere. Your Tablet PC also should include standard network connections, such as dial-up and Ethernet connections.

FIGURE 57 A Tablet PC docked to create a desktop computer with the Tablet PC as the monitor.

12 **Review available accessories to purchase with your Tablet PC.**

Tablet PC accessories include docking stations, mouse units, keyboards, security cables, additional memory and storage, protective handgrips, screen protectors, and various types of digital pens.

HOW TO PURCHASE A PERSONAL MOBILE DEVICE

Whether you choose a PDA, smart phone, ultra personal computer, or portable media player, handheld navigation device, or handheld game console depends on where, when, and how you will use the device. If you need to stay organized and in touch when on the go, then a smart phone or ultra personal computer may be the right choice. Choose a handheld navigation device if you often need directions or information about your surroundings. If you plan to relax and play games, then a handheld game console may be right for you. Busy professionals who are on the move often carry more than one personal mobile device.

This section lists guidelines you should consider when purchasing a PDA, smart phone, ultra personal computer, portable media player, handheld navigation device, or handheld game console. You also should visit the Web sites listed in Figure 58 on the next page to gather more information about the type of personal mobile device that best suits your computing needs.

1 Determine the programs you plan to run on your device.

All PDAs and most smart phones can handle basic organizer-type software such as a calendar, address book, and notepad. Portable media players and handheld navigation devices usually have the fewest programs available to run on them. Ultra personal computers usually have the most number of programs available because the devices can run almost any personal computer software. The availability of other software depends on the operating system you choose. The depth and breadth of software for the Palm OS is significant, with more than 20,000 basic programs and more than 600 wireless programs. Devices that run Windows-based operating systems, such as Windows Mobile may have fewer programs available, but the operating system and application software are similar to those with which you are familiar, such as Word and Excel. When choosing a handheld game console, consider whether your favorite games are available for the device. Consider if you want extras on the device, such as the capability of playing media files.

2 Consider how much you want to pay.

The price of a personal mobile device can range from $100 to more than $2,000, depending on its capabilities. Some Palm OS devices are at the lower end of the cost spectrum, and ultra personal computers often are at the higher end. A PDA will be less expensive than a smart phone with a similar configuration. For the latest prices, capabilities, and accessories, visit the Web sites listed in Figure 58.

3 Determine whether you need wireless access to the Internet and e-mail or mobile telephone capabilities with your device.

Smart phones often give you access to e-mail and other data and Internet services. Some PDAs, smart phones, ultra personal computers, and handheld game consoles include wireless networking capability to allow you to connect to the Internet wirelessly. These wireless features and services allow users to access real-time information from anywhere to help make decisions while on the go. Most portable media players do not include the capability to access Internet services.

4 For wireless devices, determine how and where you will use the service.

When purchasing a wireless device, you must subscribe to a wireless service. Determine if the wireless network (carrier) you choose has service in the area where you plan to use the device. Some networks have high-speed data networks only in certain areas, such as large cities or business districts. Also, a few carriers allow you to use your device in other countries.

When purchasing a smart phone, determine if you plan to use the device more as a phone, PDA, or wireless data device. Some smart phones, such as those based on the Pocket PC Phone edition or the Palm OS, are geared more for use as a PDA and have a PDA form factor. Other smart phones, such as those based on Microsoft Smartphone or Symbian operating systems, mainly are phone devices that include robust PDA functionality. Research in Motion Blackberry-based smart phones include robust data features that are oriented to accessing e-mail and wireless data services.

5 Make sure your device has enough memory and storage.

Memory (RAM) is not a major issue with low-end devices with monochrome displays and basic organizer functions. Memory is a major issue, however, for high-end devices that have color displays and wireless features. Without enough memory, the performance level of your device will drop dramatically. If you plan to purchase a high-end device running the Palm OS operating system, the device should have at least 32 MB of RAM. If you plan to purchase a high-end device running the Windows Mobile operating system, the PDA should have at least 64 MB of RAM. An ultra personal computer can have 512 MB of RAM or more while a handheld navigation device may have over 2 GB of flash memory.

An ultra personal computer can have 512 MB of RAM or more while a handheld navigation device may have over 2 GB of flash memory.

Many personal mobile devices include a hard disk for storage. Portable media players, ultra personal computers, and some smart phones include hard disks to store media and other data. Consider how much media and other data you need to store on your device. The hard disk size may range from 4 GB to more than 80 GB.

6 **Practice with the touch screen, handwriting recognition, and built-in keyboard before deciding on a model.**

To enter data into a PDA, smart phone, and some ultra personal computers and handheld game consoles, you use a pen-like stylus to handwrite on the screen or a keyboard. The keyboard either slides out or is mounted on the front of the device. With handwriting recognition, the device translates the handwriting into a computerized font. You also can use the stylus as a pointing device to select items on the screen and enter data by tapping on an on-screen keyboard. By practicing data entry before buying a device, you can learn if one device may be easier for you to use than another. You also can buy third-party software to improve a device's handwriting recognition.

7 **Decide whether you want a color display.**

PDAs, ultra personal computers, some handheld navigation devices, and some handheld game consoles usually come with a color display that supports as many as 65,536 colors. Smart phones also have the option for color displays. Having a color display does result in greater on-screen detail, but it also requires more memory and uses more power. Resolution also influences the quality of the display.

8 **Compare battery life.**

Any mobile device is good only if it has the power required to run. For example, smart phones with monochrome screens typically have a much longer battery life than Pocket PC devices with color screens. The use of wireless networking will shorten battery time considerably. To help alleviate this problem, most devices have incorporated rechargeable batteries that can be recharged by placing the device in a cradle or connecting it to a charger.

9 **Seriously consider the importance of ergonomics.**

Will you put the device in your pocket, a carrying case, or wear it on your belt? How does it feel in your hand? Will you use it indoors or outdoors? Many screens are unreadable outdoors. Do you need extra ruggedness, such as would be required in construction, in a plant, or in a warehouse? A smart phone with a PDA form factor may be larger than a typical PDA. A smart phone with a phone form factor may be smaller, but have fewer capabilities.

10 **Check out the accessories.**

Determine which accessories you want for your personal mobile device. Accessories include carrying cases, portable mini- and full-sized keyboards, removable storage, modems, synchronization cradles and cables, car chargers, wireless communications, global positioning system modules, digital camera modules, expansion cards, dashboard mounts, replacement styli, headsets, microphones, and more.

11 **Decide whether you want additional functionality.**

In general, off-the-shelf Microsoft operating system-based devices have broader functionality than devices with other operating systems. For example, voice-recording capability, e-book players, and media players are standard on most Windows Mobile devices. If you are leaning towards a Palm OS device and want these additional functions, you may need to purchase additional software or expansion modules to add them later. Determine whether your employer permits devices with cameras on the premises, and if not, do not consider devices with cameras. Some handheld game consoles include the capability to access the Web. High-end handheld navigation devices may include destination information, such as information about restaurants and points of interest, an e-book reader, a media player, and currency converter.

12 **Determine whether synchronization of data with other devices or personal computers is important.**

Most devices include a cradle that connects to the USB or serial port on your computer so you can synchronize data on your device with your desktop or notebook computer. Increasingly more devices are Bluetooth and/or wireless networking enabled, which gives them the capability of synchronizing wirelessly. Many devices today also have an infrared port that allows you to synchronize data with any device that has a similar infrared port, including desktop and notebook computers or other personal mobile devices.

Web Site	Web Address
CNET Shopper	shopper.cnet.com
iPod	ipod.com
Palm	palm.com
Microsoft	windowsmobile.com pocketpc.com microsoft.com/smartphone
Oqo	oqo.com
MobileTechReview	pdabuyersguide.com
Nintendo	nintendo.com/channel/ds
Research in Motion	rim.com
Garmin	garmin.com
Symbian	symbian.com
Wireless Developer Network	wirelessdevnet.com
Sharp	www.myzaurus.com

For an updated list of reviews and information about personal mobile devices and their Web addresses, visit scsite.com/ic7/pda.

FIGURE 58 Web site reviews and information about personal mobile devices.

Learn It Online

INSTRUCTIONS

To complete the Learn It Online exercises, start your browser, click the address bar, and then enter the Web address scsite.com/ic7/learn. When the Essential Introduction to Computers Learn It Online page is displayed, click the link for the exercise you want to complete and then read the instructions.

(1) Chapter Reinforcement TF, MC, and SA

A series of true/false, multiple choice, and short answer questions that test your knowledge of the chapter content.

(2) Flash Cards

An interactive learning environment where you identify key terms associated with displayed definitions.

(3) Practice Test

A series of multiple choice questions that test your knowledge of chapter content and key terms.

(4) Who Wants To Be a Computer Genius?

An interactive game that challenges your knowledge of chapter content in the style of a television quiz show.

(5) Wheel of Terms

An interactive game that challenges your knowledge of chapter key terms in the style of the television show *Wheel of Fortune*.

(6) Crossword Puzzle Challenge

A crossword puzzle that challenges your knowledge of key terms presented in the chapter.

Case Studies

1. Computers are ubiquitous. Watching television, driving a car, using a charge card, ordering fast food, and the more obvious activity of typing a term paper on a personal computer, all involve interaction with computers. Make a list of every computer you can recall that you encountered over the past week (be careful not to limit yourself just to the computers you see). Consider how each computer is used. How were the tasks the computers performed done before computers existed? Write a brief report and submit it to your instructor.

2. The Internet has had a tremendous impact on business. For some businesses, that influence has not been positive. For example, surveys suggest that as a growing number of people make their own travel plans online, travel agents are seeing fewer customers. Use the Web and/or printed media to research businesses that have been affected negatively by the Internet. What effect has the Internet had? How can the business compete with the Internet? Write a brief report and submit it to your instructor.

3. People use personal computers for many reasons – for work, for school, for entertainment, and much more. What are your main reasons for using a personal computer? With these in mind, research your ideal personal computer system using one or more local computer stores or online computer Web sites. Create a list of the hardware and software that would be included, the cost of each item, the total cost for the entire system, and your main reasons for using this computer system.

4. Today the functional lines between personal mobile devices seem blurred. Your cell phone has a digital camera; your PDA has wireless Internet access and plays digital music; and your game console plays videos. These are examples of technological convergence, a process in which separate technologies merge in single products. Write a brief report on how your favorite personal mobile device is an example of convergence, listing the various technologies that it uses.

INDEX

access points, wireless, COM 27
active-matrix screens, COM 32
adapters for overseas computer use, COM 34
application software, COM 19–20
arithmetic/logic unit, COM 8

backups, COM 12
Base Components worksheet, COM 29
batteries for computers, COM 33, COM 38
booting process, COM 18
browsers, Web, COM 21
bytes, COM 8

cable, broadband, COM 29
cameras, digital, COM 2, COM 6, COM 27
card readers/writers, COM 2, COM 27
CD/DVD drives, COM 2, COM 27
CD-ROM, CD-R, CD-RW discs, COM 14
commerce, electronic, COM 23
communication devices, COM 18–20
computers
    See also specific type
    components of, COM 2, COM 4
    operations of, COM 3
    PC vs. Mac, COM 30
    purchasing. See purchasing
consumer-to-consumer (C2C)
    e-commerce, COM 23
control unit, COM 8
CPU (central processing unit), COM 8

data
    described, COM 3
    synchronization, COM 39
database software, COM 20
desktop computers, COM 24–32
devices
    See also specific device
    communication, COM 18–20
    display, COM 10
    input, output, COM 5–10
    storage, COM 11–18
digital cameras, COM 2, COM 6, COM 27
digital pens, COM 36
discs, optical, COM 14–16
disks, storage, COM 2, COM 11–13

display devices, COM 10
drives
    CD/DVD, COM 2, COM 27
    CD-ROM, COM 14
    DVD-ROM, COM 16
    floppy disk, COM 13
    hard disk, COM 2
    USB flash, COM 2, COM 17
DVD-ROM media, COM 15–16

electronic commerce (e-commerce), COM 23
electronic spreadsheet software, COM 19
ergonomics, COM 38
external hard disks, COM 2, COM 27

fingerprint scanners, COM 34
flash memory, COM 17
flat panel monitors, COM 10
floppy disks, COM 13
formatting magnetic disks, COM 11

gigabyte (GB), COM 8

hard disks/drives, COM 12–13, COM 27
HD DVDs, COM 16

impact printers, COM 9
information, processing cycle, COM 3, COM 4
ink-jet printers, COM 9
input device types, COM 5–7
Internet, and networks, COM 20–23
ISPs (Internet service providers), COM 21, COM 30

joystick/wheel devices, COM 27

keyboards, COM 2, COM 5, COM 27, COM 33

LAN (local area networks), COM 20, COM 27
LAN access points, COM 27
LCD monitor, COM 10

Mac computers vs. PCs, COM 30
magnetic disks, COM 11
megabyte (MB), COM 8

memory
    cards, COM 17
    computer, COM 8, COM 26
    on personal mobile devices, COM 37–38
    and storage devices, COM 11
microphones, COM 2, COM 26, COM 27, COM 36
miniature mobile storage media, COM 16
mobile computers, COM 24–25
modems, COM 2, COM 27, COM 29
monitors, COM 2, COM 10, COM 26, COM 27
motherboard, COM 8
mouse, COM 26, COM 27

networks and the Internet, COM 20–23
notebook computers, COM 7, COM 32–34

online
    computers, COM 20
    service providers (OSPs), COM 21, COM 30
operating systems, COM 18, COM 25, COM 26
optical discs, COM 14–16
OSPs (online service providers), COM 21, COM 30
output device types, COM 9–10

PC video cameras, COM 2, COM 28
PCs vs. Macs, COM 30
PDAs (personal digital assistants), COM 6, COM 37
personal computers, COM 24–25
personal mobile devices, COM 37–39
photo printers, COM 9
pointer, mouse, COM 7
portable storage medium, COM 11
ports, COM 33, COM 36
power supply, notebook computers, COM 33
presentation graphics software, COM 20
printers, COM 2, COM 9, COM 26
programs, COM 3–4
purchasing
    computers generally, COM 24–25, COM 31
    desktop computers, COM 25–32

notebook computers, COM 32–34
    personal mobile devices, COM 37–39
    tablet PCs, COM 35–36

reviews of software products, COM 25–26

scanners, COM 2, COM 28, COM 34
screens (monitors), COM 2, COM 32
security, fingerprint scanners, COM 34
servers, Web, COM 23
smart phones, cards, COM 6, COM 18
software, COM 3, COM 4
    types of, COM 19–20
    product reviews, COM 25–26
speakers, computer, COM 26, COM 36
storage device types, COM 11–18
synchronization of data, COM 39
system software, COM 18
system units, COM 2, COM 4, COM 8

tablet PCs, COM 24–25, COM 35–36
tape, tape drives, COM 15–16
touch screens, COM 38
touchpads, COM 7
transmission media, COM 18

URLs (Uniform Resource Locators), COM 21, COM 22
USB flash drives, COM 2, COM 17

video cameras, COM 2, COM 27, COM 36
video cards, COM 27
Vista operating system, COM 26

Web browsers, pages, servers, COM 21–23
WANs (wide area networks), COM 20–21
wireless
    Internet service providers (WISPs), COM 21
    LAN access points, COM 27
    media, COM 18
    synchronization of data, COM 39
    tablet PC access, COM 36
worksheet, Base Components, COM 29
World Wide Web, COM 21

PHOTO CREDITS

Opener: Courtesy of SanDisk Corporation, © Medioimages / Alamy, Courtesy of Intel Corporation, Courtesy of Intel Corporation, Courtesy of Advanced Micro Devices, Inc, Courtesy of Microsoft Corporation, Courtesy of Hewlett-Packard Company, Courtesy of Sony Electronics Inc, Courtesy of Acer America Corp, Courtesy of Microsoft Corporation; Figure 1 Courtesy of Hewlett-Packard Company, Courtesy of D-Link Systems, Courtesy of Logitech, Inc, Courtesy of Maxtor, Courtesy of Hewlett-Packard Company, Courtesy of Sandisk Corporation, Courtesy of SanDisk Corporation, Courtesy of Motorola, Courtesy of Sony Electronics Inc, Courtesy of Hewlett-Packard Company, © David Young-Wolff/Photo Edit; Figure 2 © Bill Aron / PhotoEdit ; Figure 4 Courtesy of Microsoft Corporation; Figure 5 Courtesy of Veo Intl, Courtesy of Socket Communications Inc, © Gustaf Brundin/istockphoto.com, Courtesy of Hewlett-Packard Company; Figure 6 © Kaluzny-Thatcher/Getty Images; Figure 7 Courtesy of Microsoft Corporation, Courtesy of Microsoft Corporation; Figure 8 © Yo/Getty Images; Figure 9 Courtesy of Intel Corporation, Courtesy of Hewlett-Packard Company, Courtesy of SMART Modular Technologies, Inc. © 2002, Courtesy of Creative Labs, Inc. Copyright © 2003 Creative Technology Ltd. (SOUND BLASTER AUDIGY 2S). All rights reserved, Courtesy of Matrox Graphics Inc; Figure 10 Courtesy of Oki Data Amercas, Inc; Figure 11 Courtesy of Hewlett-Packard Company, Courtesy of Xerox Corporation, Courtesy of Epson America, Inc; Figure 12 Courtesy of Xerox Corporation; Figure 13 Courtesy of Hewlett-Packard Company, Courtesy of NEC-Mitsubishi Electronics Display of America Inc; Figure 14 Courtesy of Acer America Corp, Image courtesy of TabletKiosk, Courtesy of Archos, Courtesy of Nokia, Courtesy of Palm, Inc; Figure 17 Courtesy of Maxtor Corporation; Figure 18 © Masterfile (Royalty Free Div.) www.masterfile.com, Photo Courtesy of Iomega Corporation. Copyright (c) 2005 Iomega Corporation. All Rights Reserved. Zip is a registered trademark in the United States and/or other countries. Iomega, the sylized "i" logo and product images are property of Iomega Corporation in the United States and/or other countries; Figure 19 © Gary Herrington Photography; Figure 20 © 2005 Dell Inc. All Rights Reserved, Courtesy of DeLorme; Figure 21 Courtesy of Merriam-Webster Inc, Courtesy of Memorex Products, Inc, Courtesy of DeLorme; Figure 22 Courtesy of Sony Electronics Inc; Figure 23 Sam Lee/istockphoto.com, © Marianna Day Massey/ZUMA/Corbis, Courtesy of Hewlett-Packard Company, Courtesy of Hewlett-Packard Company, Scrambled/istockphoto.com; Figure 24 Courtesy of SanDisk Corporation; Figure 25 Toshiba America Information Systems, Inc; Figure 26 ITAR-TASS/Alexander Bundin /Landov; Figure 28 ©Mark Richards / Photo Edit ; Figure 33 Courtesy of Hewlett-Packard Company, Courtesy of Fujitsu Siemens Computers; Figure 37 Courtesy of Hewlett-Packard Company, Courtesy of Wacom, © Darrin Klimek/Getty Images; Figure 40 Courtesy of Hewlett-Packard Company, Courtesy of SanDisk Corporation, Courtesy of Hewlett-Packard Company, Courtesy of Avid Technology, Courtesy of Seagate Technology, Courtesy of Hewlett-Packard Company, Courtesy of Logitech, Courtesy of Microsoft Corporation, Courtesy of Zoom Technologies Inc, Courtesy of ViewSonic Corporation, Courtesy of Microsoft Corporation, Courtesy of Hewlett-Packard Company, Courtesy of Hewlett-Packard Company, Courtesy of Intel Corporation, Courtesy of Kingston Technology, Courtesy of UMAX, Courtesy of Logitech, Courtesy of Logitech, Courtesy of SanDisk Corporation, Courtesy of 3Com Corporation, Courtesy of D-Link Corporation/D-Link Systems, Inc; Figure 48 PRNewsFoto/Mindjet LLC; Figure 49 Courtesy of Fujitsu-Siemens Computers; Figure 50 Courtesy of InFocus Corporation; Figure 51 © Digital Archive Japan / Alamy; Figure 52 © Patrick Olear / PhotoEdit; Figure 55 Courtesy of Motion Computing; Figure 57 Courtesy of Motion Computing.

1 | Introduction to Windows Vista

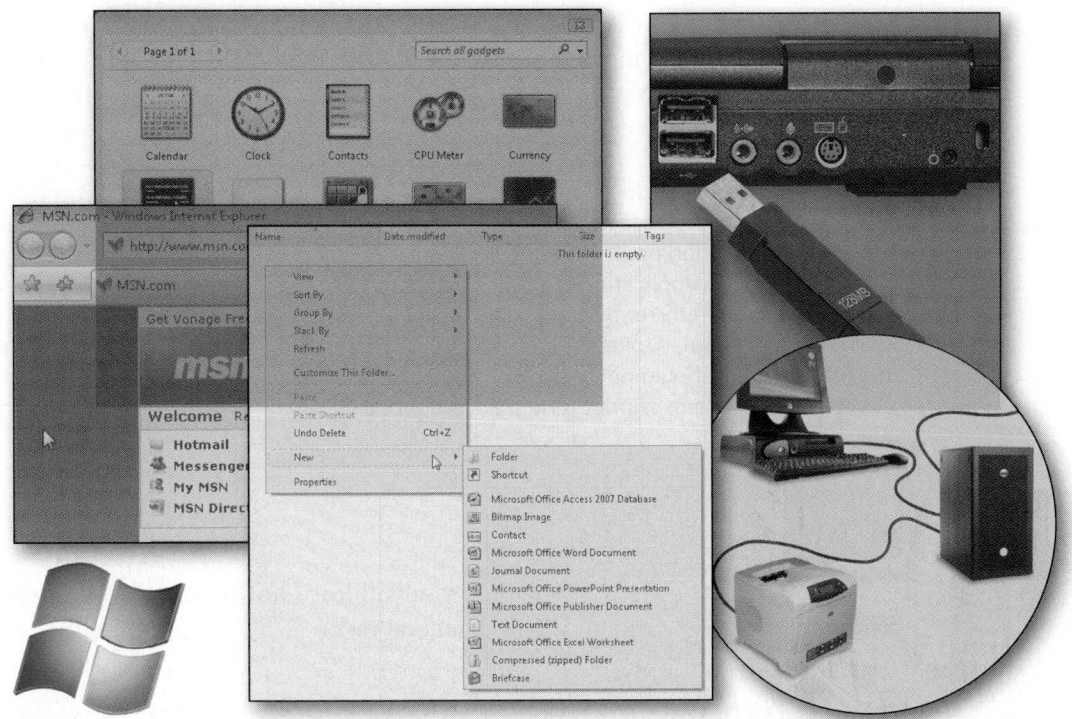

Objectives

You will have mastered the material in this chapter when you can:

- Start Windows Vista, log on to the computer, and identify the objects on the desktop

- Customize the Windows Sidebar with Gadgets

- Perform basic mouse operations

- Display the Start menu and start an application program

- Open, minimize, maximize, restore, move, size, scroll, and close a window

- Display drive and folder contents

- Create a folder in Folder Windows and WordPad

- Browse the Web using Windows Internet Explorer 7.0, a URL, and tabbed browsing

- Download folders from scsite.com

- Copy, move, rename, and delete files

- Search for files using a word or phrase in the file or by name

- Use Windows Help and Support

- Log off from the computer and turn it off

1 | Introduction to Windows Vista

What Is an Operating System?

An **operating system** is the set of computer instructions, called a computer program, that controls the allocation of computer hardware such as memory, disk devices, printers, and CD and DVD drives, and provides the capability for you to communicate with the computer. The most popular and widely used operating systems is **Microsoft Windows**. **Microsoft Windows Vista** is the newest version of Microsoft Windows. Windows Vista allows you to communicate with and control the computer.

Project Planning Guidelines

Working with an operating system requires a basic knowledge of how to start the operating system, log on and log off the computer, and identify the objects on the Windows Vista desktop. As a starting point, you must be familiar with the Start menu and its commands, and be able to start an application. You should be able to personalize the operating system to allow you to work more efficiently. You will want to know how to manipulate windows as well as create a folder, display folder contents, recognize a disk drive, and download information from the Internet. You should be able to copy, move, rename, delete, and search for files. If you encounter a problem, Windows Help and Support is available to answer any questions you may have.

Overview

As you read through this chapter, you will learn how to use the Windows Vista operating system by performing these general tasks:

- Start the Windows Vista operating system.
- Log on to the computer.
- Perform basic mouse operations.
- Add and Remove a gadget to the Windows Sidebar.
- Open the Start menu and start an application program.
- Add and delete icons on the desktop.
- Open, minimize, maximize, restore, move, size, scroll, and close a window.
- Display drive and folder contents.
- Create folders and download folders from the Internet.
- Copy, move, rename, delete, and search for files.
- Use Help and Support.
- Log off and turn off the computer.

What Is a User Interface?

A **user interface** is the combination of hardware and software that you use to communicate with and control the computer. Through the user interface, you are able to make selections on the computer, request information from the computer, and respond to messages displayed by the computer.

Hardware and software together form the user interface. Among the hardware devices associated with a user interface are the monitor, keyboard, and mouse (Figure 1–1). The **monitor** displays messages and provides information. You respond by entering data in the form of a command or other response using an input device such as a **keyboard** or **mouse**.

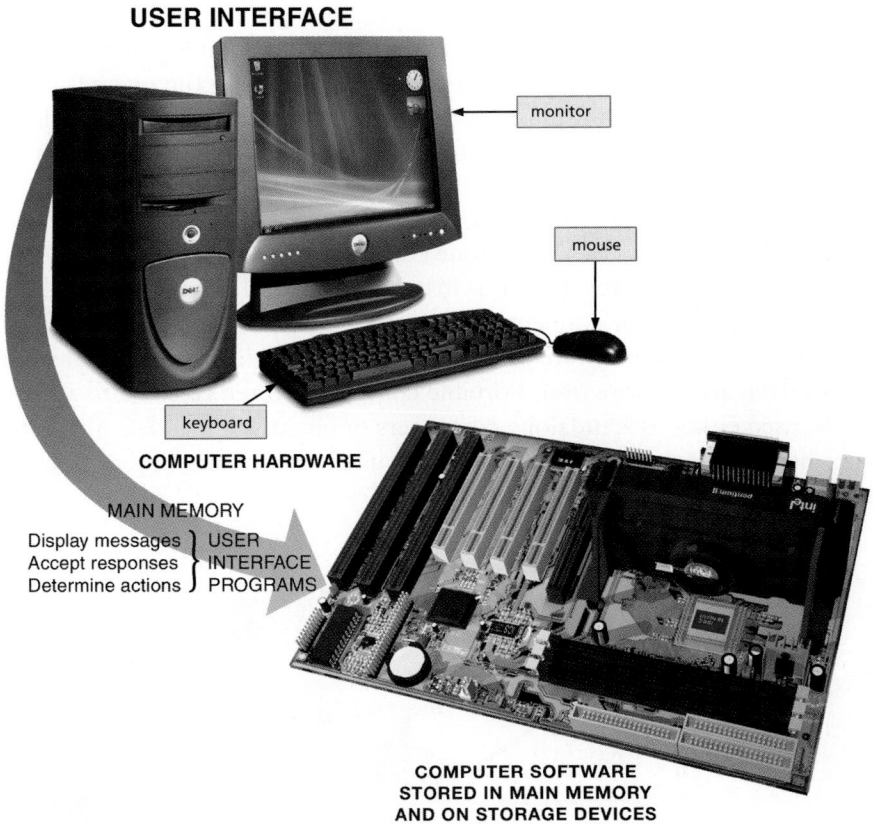

Figure 1–1

The computer software associated with the user interface consists of the programs that engage you in dialogue. The computer software determines the messages you receive, the manner in which you should respond, and the actions that occur based on your responses.

The goal of an effective user interface is to be **user-friendly**, which means the software can be used easily by individuals with limited training. A **graphical user interface**, or **GUI** (pronounced gooey), is a user interface that displays graphics in addition to text when it communicates with the user.

To communicate with the operating system, you can use a mouse. A **mouse** is a pointing device used with Windows Vista that may be attached to the computer by a cable or may be wireless.

Many common tasks, such as logging on to the computer or logging off, are performed by pointing to an item and then clicking the item. **Point** means you move the mouse across a flat surface until the mouse pointer on the monitor rests on the item of choice. As you move the mouse across a flat surface, the optical sensor on the underside of the mouse senses the movement of the mouse, and the mouse pointer moves across the computer desktop in the same direction. In Office 2007, you can point to buttons on the Ribbon in a window and observe a live preview of the effect of selecting that button.

Click means you press and release the primary mouse button, which in most cases is the left mouse button. In most cases, you must point to an item before you click it.

Windows Vista

The Windows Vista operating system simplifies the process of working with documents and applications by transferring data between documents, organizing the manner in which you interact with the computer, and using the computer to access information on the Internet or an intranet. Windows Vista is used to run **application programs**, which are programs that perform a specific function such as word processing.

In business, Windows Vista is commonly used on standalone computers, client computers, and portable computers. A standalone computer is not part of a computer network, and has access only to software that is installed on it, and hardware directly connected to it. A **client** is a computer connected to a server. A **server** is a computer that controls access to the hardware and software on a network and provides a centralized storage area for programs, data, and information. Portable computers, often referred to as laptop computers, can be used either as standalone computers or clients. Figure 1–2 illustrates a simple computer network consisting of a server, three client computers, and a laser printer connected to the server.

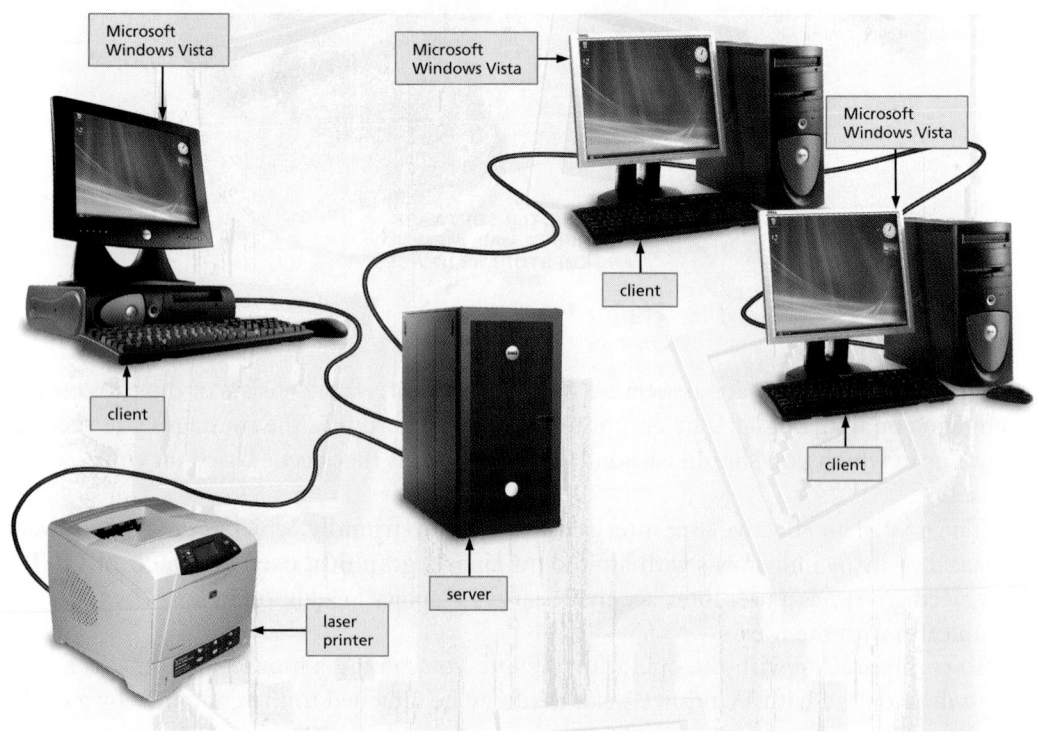

Figure 1–2

Windows Vista Operating System Editions

The Windows Vista operating systems is available in five editions: Windows Vista Home Basic, Windows Vista Home Premium, Windows Vista Business, Windows Vista Ultimate, and Windows Vista Enterprise. Windows Vista Ultimate (called **Windows Vista** for the rest of the chapter) is an operating system that performs every function necessary for you to communicate with and use the computer. The five editions of Windows Vista are described in Table 1–1.

Table 1–1 Windows Vista Editions	
Edition	**Description**
Windows Vista Home Basic	This edition is easy to set up and maintain, provides security and parental controls, allows access to e-mail, simplifies searching for pictures and music, and allows the creation of simple documents.
Windows Vista Home Premium Edition	This edition is designed for individuals who have a home desktop or mobile PC. The built-in Windows Media Center allows you to watch and record television, play video games, listen to music, and burn and play CDs and DVDs.
Windows Vista Business Edition	This edition is the first operating system designed specifically for the needs of small and mid-sized businesses. Features include keeping PCs up-to-date and running smoothly, as well as powerful ways to find, organize, and share information on the road or in the office. Additional features include Windows Tablet PC capability, PC-to-PC synchronization, Domain Join, Group Policy support, and Encrypting File System.
Windows Vista Ultimate Edition	This edition, the most complete edition of the five, contains the most advanced capabilities, and is the choice of individuals who want the power, security, and mobility needed for work and the entertainment features desired for fun. The edition includes support for Windows Tablet and Touch Technology, Windows SideShow, Windows Mobility Center, Windows DreamScene, and Windows BitLocker Secure Online Key storage.
Windows Vista Enterprise	This edition was designed to help global organizations and enterprises with complex IT infrastructures to lower IT costs, reduce risk, and stay connected. This edition is only available to Volume License customers who have PCs covered by Microsoft Software Assurance. Windows BitLocker Drive Encryption is used to help prevent sensitive data and intellectual property from being lost or stolen.

Windows Vista Basic Interface and Windows Aero

Windows Vista offers two different GUIs, depending on your hardware configuration. Computers with up to 1 GB of RAM work with the Windows Vista Basic interface (Figure 1–3a). Computers with more than 1 GB of RAM can work also with the Windows Aero interface (Figure 1–3b), which provides an enhanced visual experience designed for Windows Vista, including additional navigation options, and animation. Windows Aero features a transparent glass design with subtle window animations and new window colors. The Windows Vista Business, Windows Vista Enterprise, Windows Vista Home Premium, and Windows Vista Ultimate editions have the ability to use Windows Aero. In this chapter, all figures were created on a computer using the Windows Vista Basic interface.

(a)

(b)

Figure 1–3

Starting Windows Vista

It is not an unusual occurrence for multiple people to use the same computer in a work, educational, recreational, or home setting. Windows Vista uses User Accounts to organize the resources that are made available to a person when they use the computer. A **user account** identifies to Windows Vista which resources a person can use when using the computer. Associated with a user account is a **user name**, which identifies the person to Windows Vista, and a **password**, a string of letters, numbers, and special characters, which is used to restrict access to a user account's resources to only those who know the password. In Windows Vista, you can choose a picture to associated with your user name as well.

In a work or school environment your user name and password may be set up for you automatically. Usually, you are given the option to reset the password to something that only you know. A good password is important for ensuring the security and privacy of your work. When you turn on the computer, an introductory black screen consisting of a progress bar and copyright message (© Microsoft Corporation) are displayed. After a short time, the Windows Vista logo and Welcome screen are displayed on the desktop (Figure 1–4).

Plan Ahead

Determine a user name and password.

Before logging on to the computer, you must have a unique user name and password.

1. Choose a user name that is unique and non-offensive. Your user name may be automatically set for you in a work or educational setting.

2. Choose a password that no one could guess. Do not use any part of your first or last name, your spouse's or child's name, telephone number, street address, license plate number, Social Security number, and so on.

3. Be sure your password is at least six characters long, mixed with letters and numbers.

4. Protect your password. Change your password frequently and do not disclose it to anyone or write it on a slip of paper kept near the computer. E-mail and telemarketing scams often ask you to disclose a password, so be wary, if you did not initiate the inquiry or telephone call.

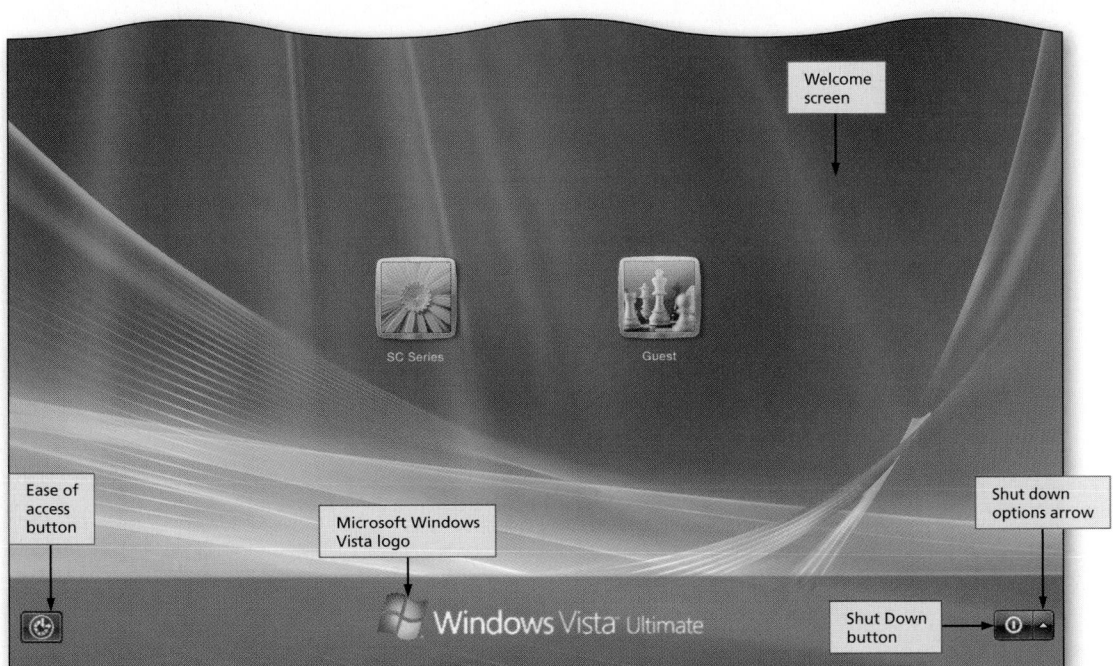

Figure 1–4

The **Welcome screen** shows the user names of every computer user on the computer. Clicking the user name or picture begins the process of logging on to the computer. The list of user names on your computer will be different.

At the bottom of the Welcome screen is the Ease of access button, Windows Vista logo, and a Shut down button. Clicking the **Ease of access button** displays the Ease of Access Center. The Ease of Access Center provides access to tools you can use to optimize your computer to accomodate the needs of the mobility, hearing and vision impaired. To the right of the Ease of access button is the Windows Vista logo. Located in the lower corner of the Welcome screen is the **Shut down button**. Clicking this button shuts down Windows Vista and the computer. To the right of the Shut down button is the **Shut down options arrow**, which provides access to a menu containing 3 commands, Restart, Sleep, and Shut Down.

The **Restart command** closes open programs, shuts down Windows Vista, and then restarts Windows Vista, and displays the Welcome screen. The **Sleep command** waits for Windows Vista to save your work and then turns off the fans and hard disk. To wake the computer from the Sleep state, press the Power button or lift the laptop cover, and log on to the computer. The **Shut Down command** shuts down and turns off the computer.

Logging On to the Computer

After starting Windows Vista, you must log on to the computer. **Logging on** to the computer opens your user account and makes the computer available for use.

If you are using a computer to step through the project in this chapter and you want your screen to match the figures in this book, you should change your screen's resolution to 1024 × 768. For information about how to change a computer's resolution, read Appendix E.

To Log On to the Computer

The following steps illustrate how to log on to the computer. In this chapter, the user name SC Series is used in the figures.

1

• Click your user name on the Welcome screen to display the password text box.

Q&A

What is a text box?

A text box is a rectangular area in which you can enter text.

• Type your password in the password text box as shown in Figure 1–5.

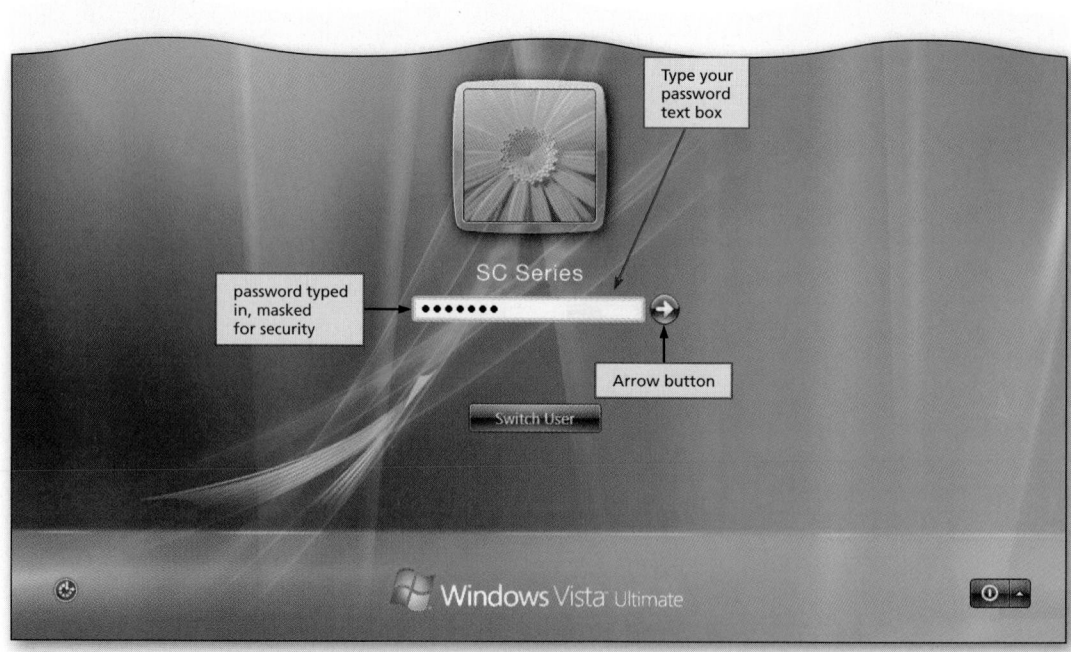

Figure 1–5

2

• Click the arrow button to log on to the computer to display the Welcome Center window and Windows Sidebar on the Windows Vista desktop (Figure 1–6).

Q&A

What is displayed on the desktop when I log on to the computer?

The Recycle Bin icon, Welcome Center, Windows Sidebar, and taskbar are displayed on the desktop.

Q&A

What if the Computer displays a different desktop design?

Windows Vista offers many standard desktop backgrounds, so any background is fine. The background design shown in Figure 1–6 is called img24.

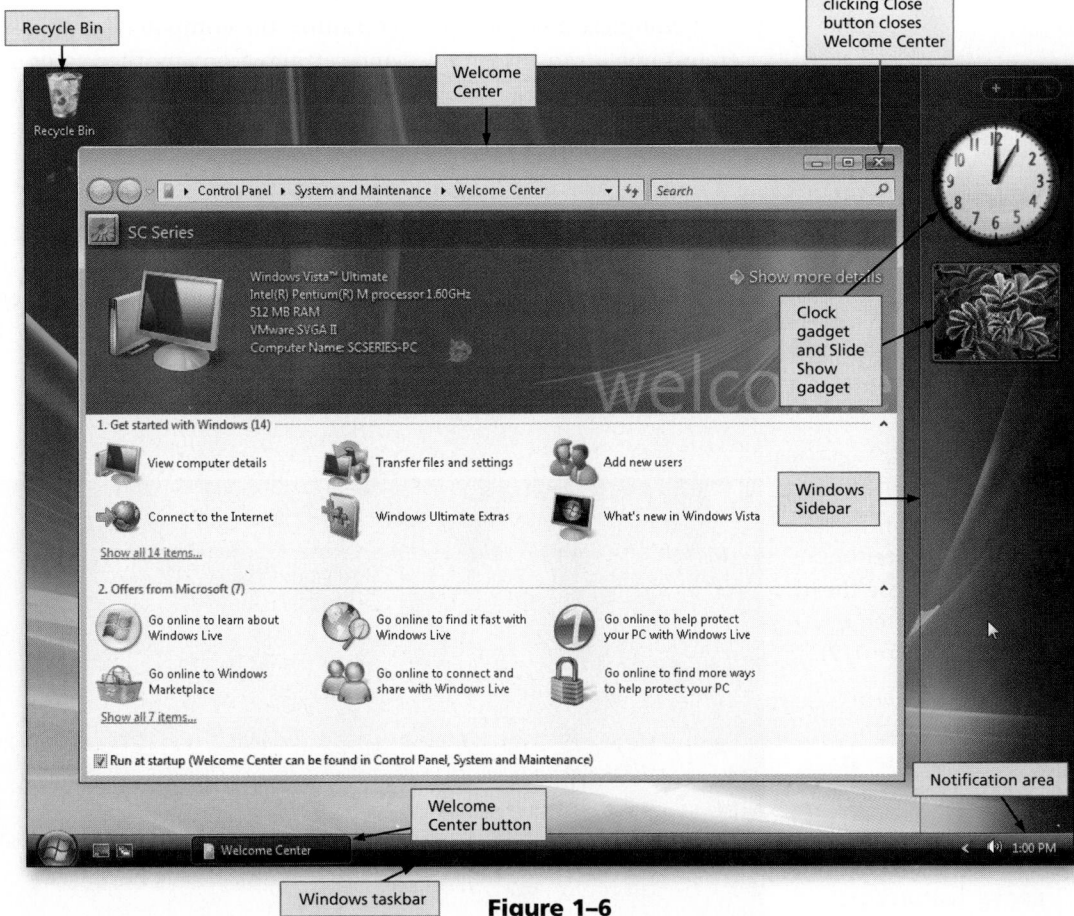

Figure 1–6

The Windows Vista Desktop

The Windows Vista desktop is similar to a real physical desktop. It is the main work area when you are logged into Windows Vista. When you open a program, it appears on the desktop. Some items are on the desktop by default. For instance, the **Recycle Bin**, the location of files that have been deleted, sits on the desktop by default. You can customize your desktop so that programs and files you use often are out on your desktop and easily accessible.

Also on the Windows Vista desktop is the Windows Sidebar. The **Windows Sidebar** is a long, vertical strip on the right edge of the desktop that holds mini-programs called gadgets (Figure 1–6). A **gadget** is a mini-program that provides continuously updated information, such as current weather information, news updates, traffic information, and Internet radio streams. You can customize your Sidebar to hold gadgets that you choose.

Across the bottom of the Windows Vista desktop is the Windows Taskbar (Figure 1–6). The Windows Taskbar contains the Start button, which you use to access programs, files, folders, and settings on your computer. It also shows you which programs are currently running on your computer, by displaying a button per program.

In addition, the Windows Vista desktop may contain the Welcome Center Window. The **Welcome Center** is displayed when the computer is used for the first time and allows you to complete a set of tasks to optimize the computer. The tasks may include adding user accounts, transferring files and settings from another computer, and connecting to the Internet.

To Close the Welcome Center Window

The Welcome Center window is displayed when you launch Windows Vista for the first time, and subsequently unless you turn it off. If the Welcome Center window is displayed, you can close it prior to beginning any other operations using Windows Vista. This provides you with a clear desktop with which to work. The following step illustrates how to close the Welcome Center window.

- Click the Close button in the top right corner of the Welcome Center window to close the Welcome Center window (Figure 1–7).

Q&A

Are there other ways to access the Welcome Center if it doesn't appear at startup?

Yes. The Welcome Center features are available in the Control Panel under System and Maintenance.

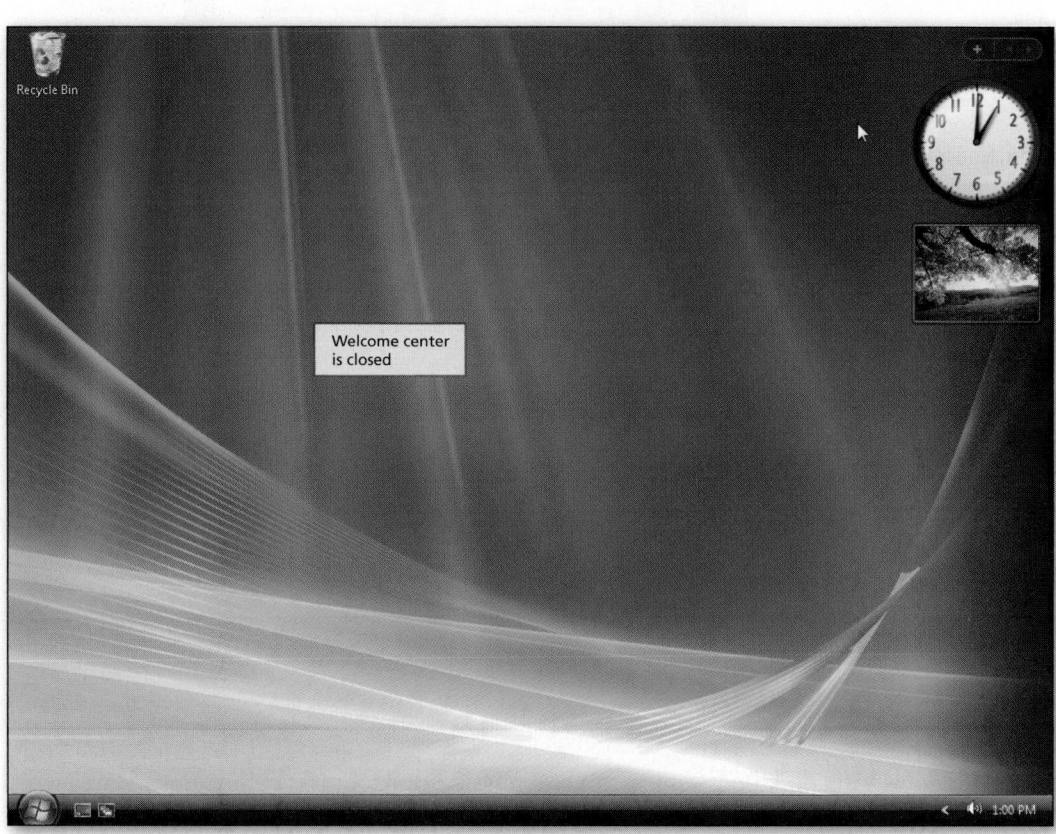

Figure 1–7

To Add a Gadget to the Windows Sidebar

When you start Windows Vista, some gadgets are attached to the Windows Sidebar. There are many additional gadgets that can be added according to personal preference. Gadgets can be found in the **Gadget Gallery**, which is a collection of gadgets. To use gadgets, they must be added to the Windows Sidebar. One method to add a gadget to the Windows Sidebar is to double-click the gadget in the Gadget Gallery. **Double-click** means you quickly press and release the left mouse button twice without moving the mouse. The steps on the following page illustrate how to open the Gadget Gallery and add a gadget to the Windows Sidebar.

1

- Click the Add Gadgets button to open the Gadget Gallery on the desktop. (Figure 1–8).

Where can I find additional gadgets?

You can find more gadgets on the www.microsoft.com website by searching for "sidebar gadgets".

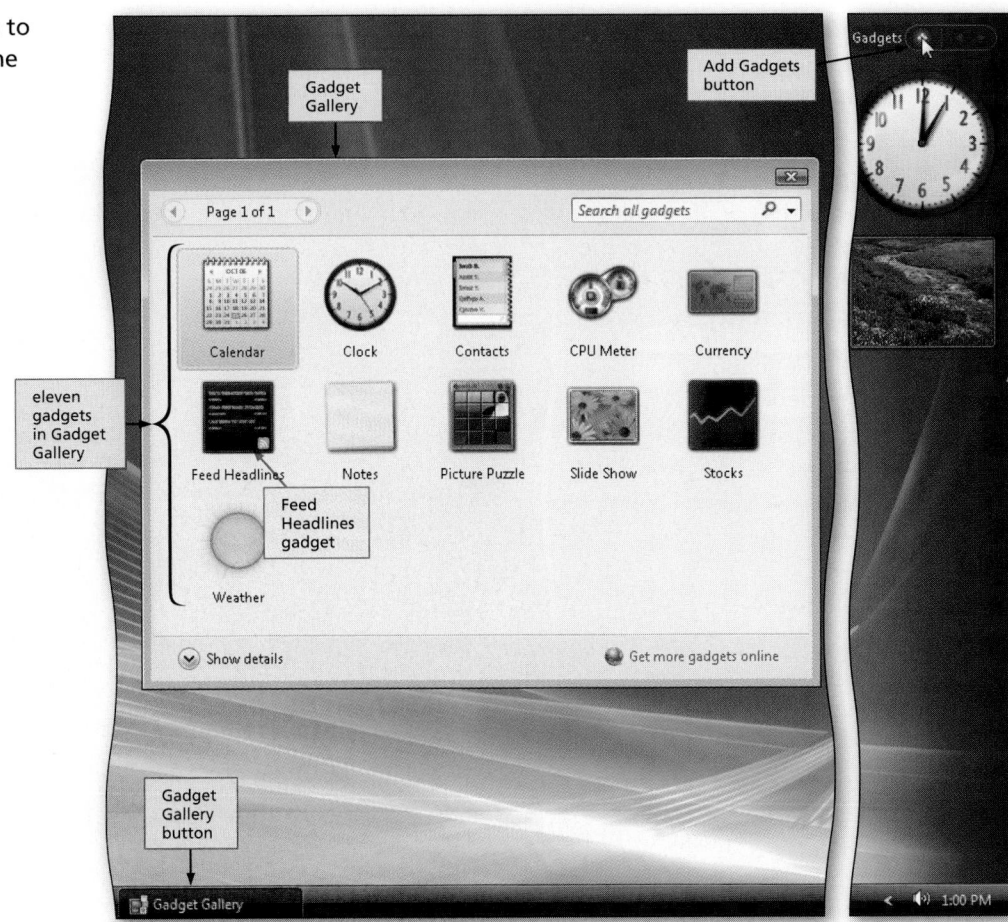

Figure 1–8

2

- Double-click the Feed Headlines gadget in the Gadget Gallery to add the gadget to the top of the Windows Sidebar and display frequently updated headlines (Figure 1–9).

3

- Click the Close button to close the Gadget Gallery.

Q&A

Can I customize the Windows Sidebar?

Yes. You can select which gadgets you want to add or remove, add multiple instances of a particular gadget, and detach one or more gadgets from the Sidebar and place them on the desktop

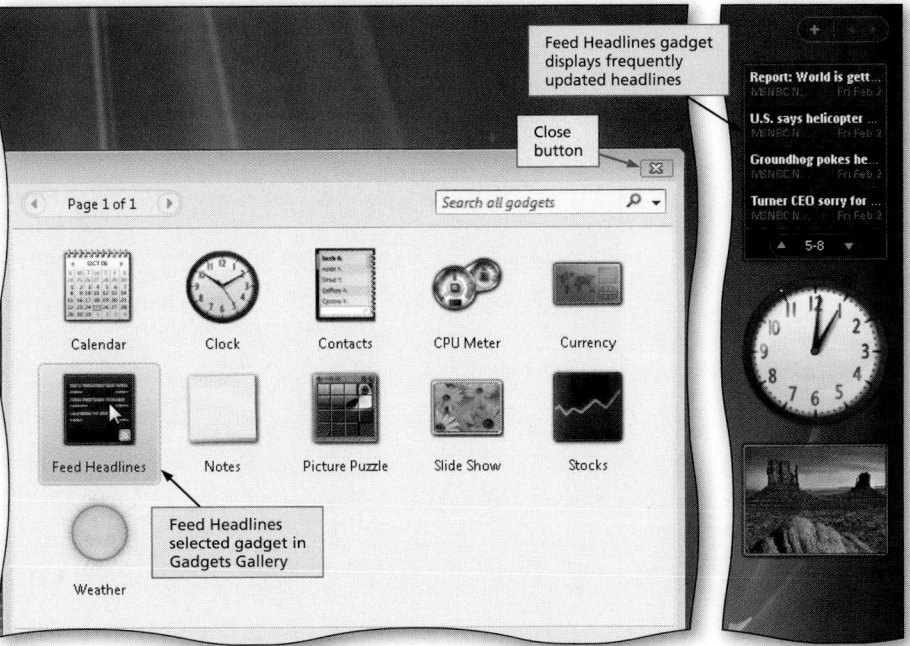

Figure 1–9

To Remove a Gadget from the Windows Sidebar

In addition to adding gadgets to the Windows Sidebar, you may want to customize the desktop by removing one or more gadgets from the sidebar. The following step illustrates how to remove a gadget from the Windows Sidebar.

- Point to the Feed Headlines gadget to make the Close button visible. (Figure 1–10).

- Click the Close button to remove the Feed Headlines gadget from the Windows Sidebar.

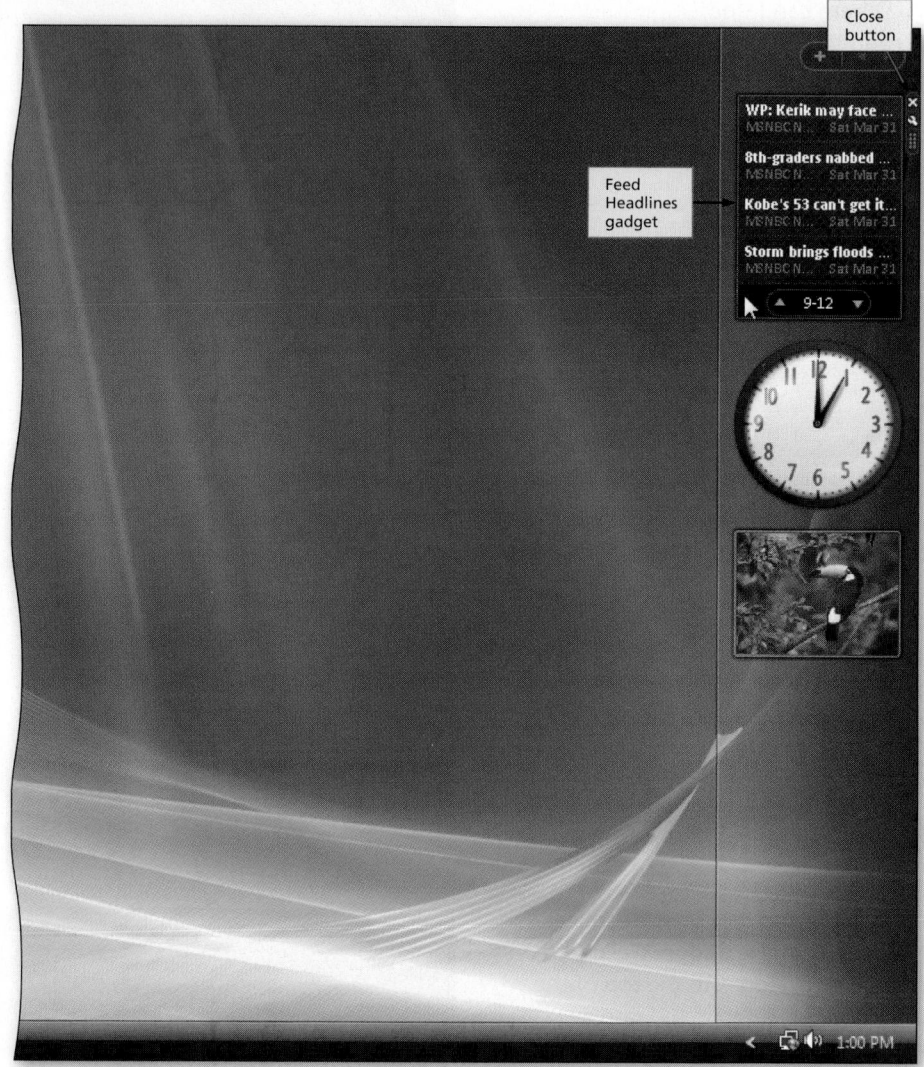

Figure 1–10

Other Ways

1. Right-click gadget, click Close Gadget

To Open the Start Menu

A **menu** is a list of related items, including folders, programs, and commands. Each **command** on a menu performs a specific action, such as searching for files or obtaining Help. The **Start menu** allows you to access programs and files on the computer and contains commands that allow you to connect to and browse the Internet, start an e-mail program, start application programs, store and search for documents, customize the computer, and obtain Help on thousands of topics. The Start menu contains the All Programs command, Search box, and right pane. The following steps open the Start menu, display the All Programs list, and then display the Accessories list.

1

• Click the Start button on the Windows Vista taskbar to open the Start menu (Figure 1–11).

Q&A

What are the various sections on the Start menu?

The left pane contains the pinned items list, frequently used programs list, All Programs command, and the Search box. The right pane contains the computer user name and illustration, list links, Power button, Lock this computer button, and Lock menu arrow.

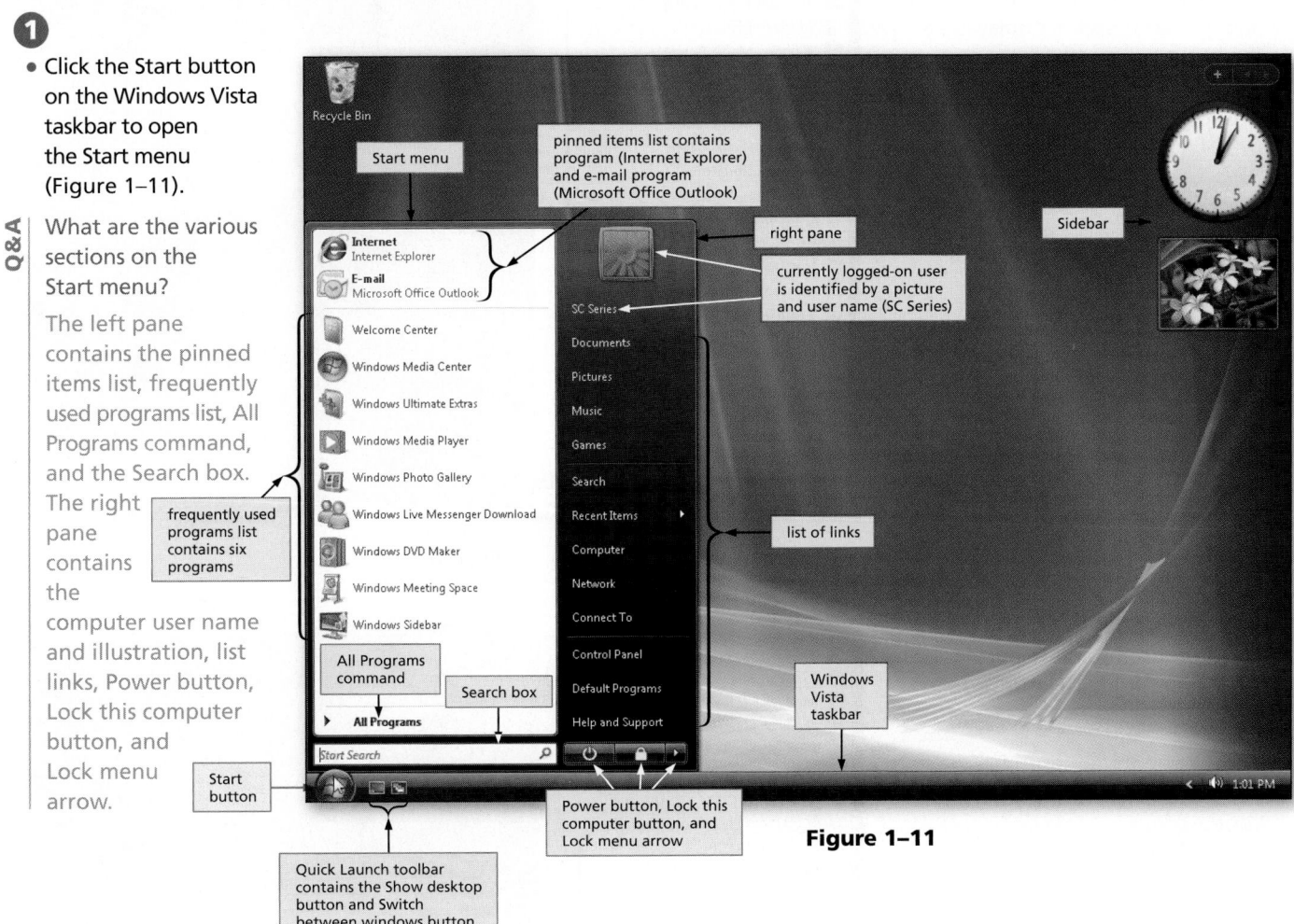

Figure 1–11

2

- Point to All Programs at the bottom of the left pane on the Start menu to display the All Programs list (Figure 1–12).

Q&A What happens when you point to All Programs on the Start menu?

The All Programs list is displayed and the word Back is displayed at the bottom of the All Programs list.

Figure 1–12

3

- Click Accessories to expand the list of programs and folders in the Accessories folder (Figure 1–13).

Q&A What are Accessories?

Accessories are application programs that accomplish a variety of tasks commonly required on a computer. For example, the Accessories programs include Calculator, Notepad, Paint, etc.

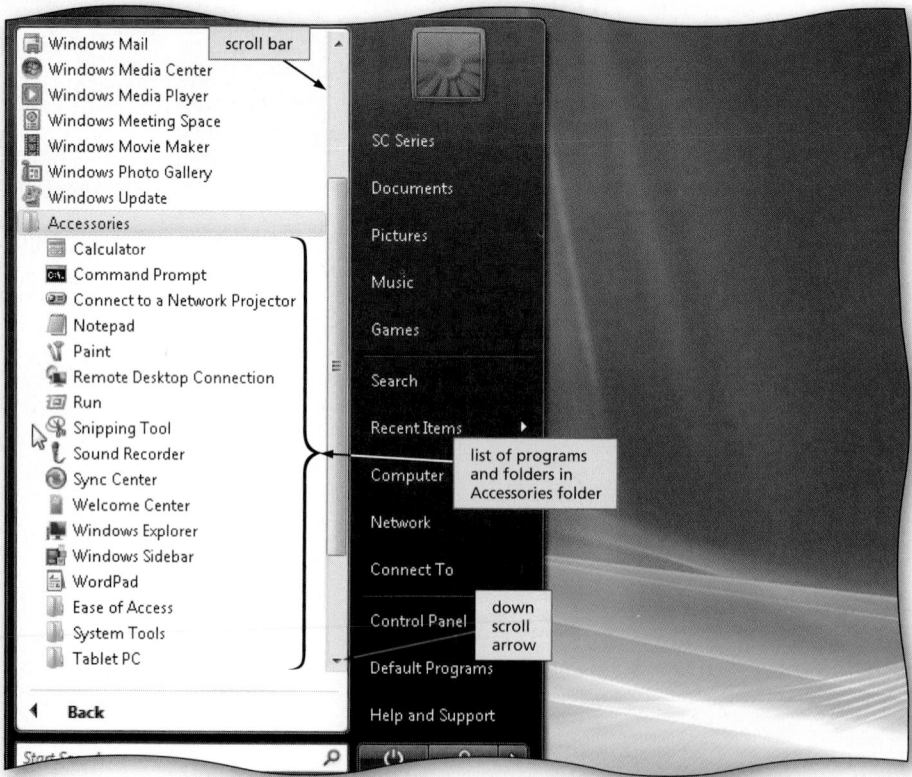

Figure 1–13

To Scroll Using Scroll Arrows, the Scroll Bar, and the Scroll Box

A **scroll bar** is a bar that displays when the contents of an area may not be completely visible. A vertical scroll bar contains an **up scroll arrow**, a **down scroll arrow**, and a **scroll box** that enables you to view areas that currently are not visible. In Figure 1–14, a vertical scroll bar displays along the right side of the All Programs list. Scrolling can be accomplished in three ways: (1) click the scroll arrows; (2) click the scroll bar; and (3) drag the scroll box. **Drag** means you point to an item, hold down the left mouse button, move the item to the desired location, and then release the left mouse button. The following steps scroll the items in the All Programs list.

1

- Click the down scroll arrow on the vertical scroll bar to display additional folders at the bottom of the All Programs list (Figure 1–14). You may need to click more than once to get to the bottom of the All Programs list.

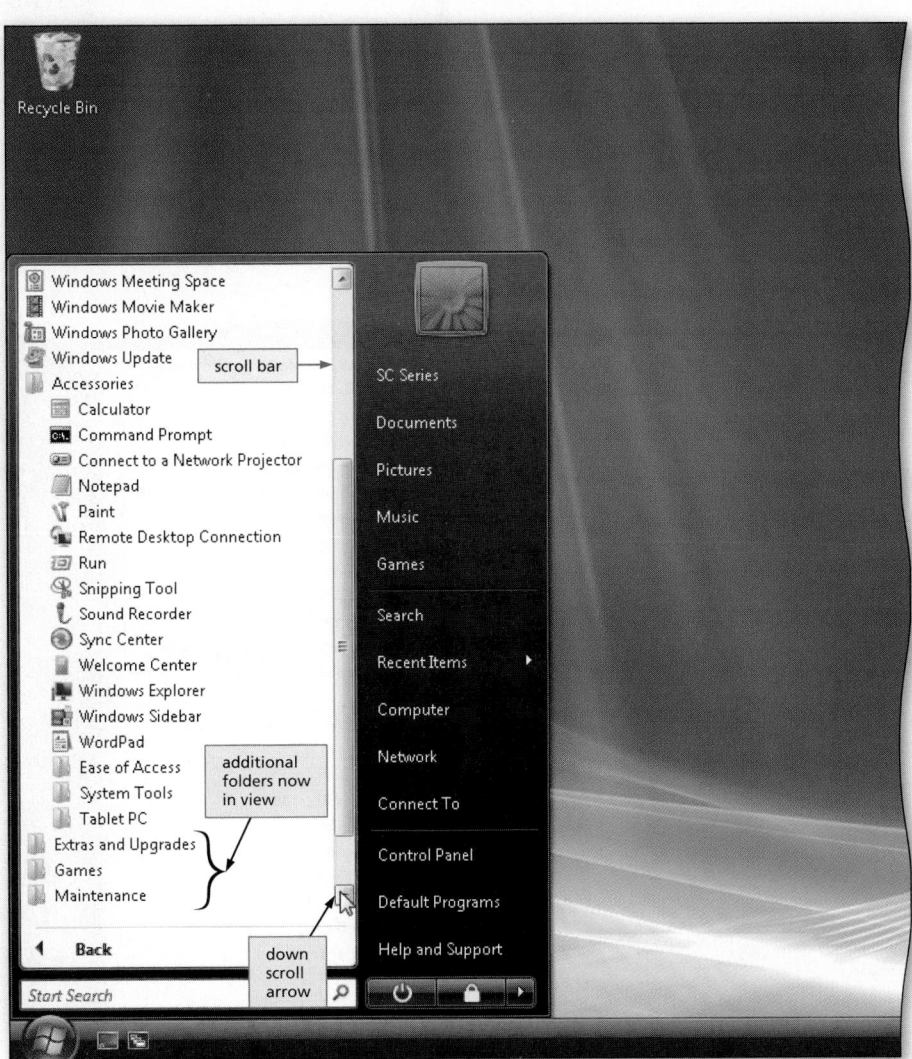

Figure 1–14

- Click the scroll bar above the scroll box to move the scroll box to the top of the scroll bar and display the top of the All Programs list (Figure 1–15).

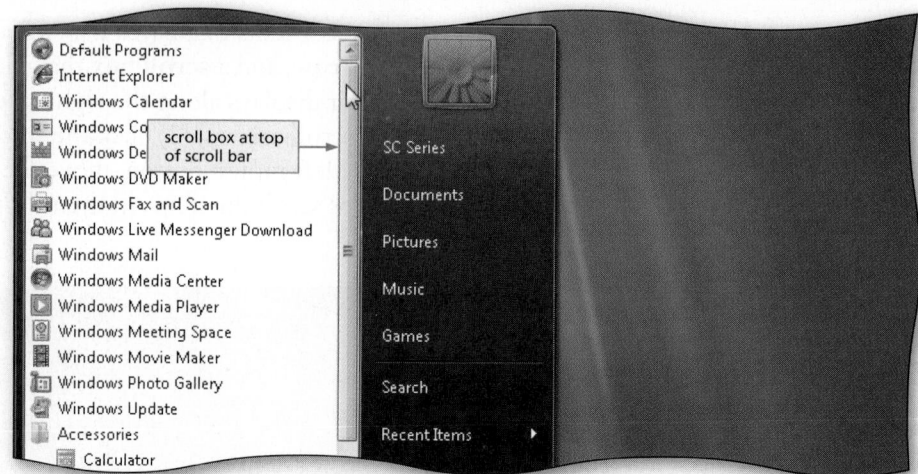

Figure 1–15

- Drag the scroll box down the scroll bar until the scroll box is about halfway down the scroll bar (Figure 1–16).

- Click an open area on the desktop to close the Start menu.

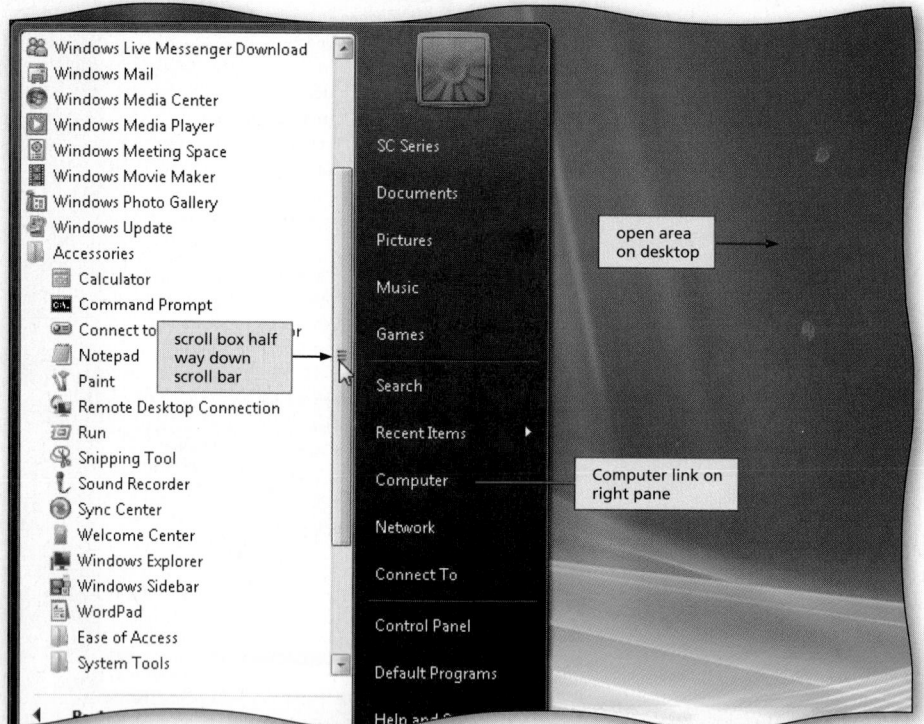

Figure 1–16

To Add an Icon to the Desktop

In addition to gadgets, you may want to add icons to the desktop. An **icon** is a picture that represents a file, folder, object, or program. For example, you may want to add the Computer icon to the desktop so you can view the contents of the computer folder without having to use the Start menu. The steps on the following page add the Computer icon to the desktop.

1

- Click the Start button to open the Start menu.

- Right-click Computer on the right pane to select the Computer link and display a shortcut menu (Figure 1–17).

 Q&A

What is a shortcut menu?

A shortcut menu appears when you right-click an object and includes commands specifically for use with the object clicked.

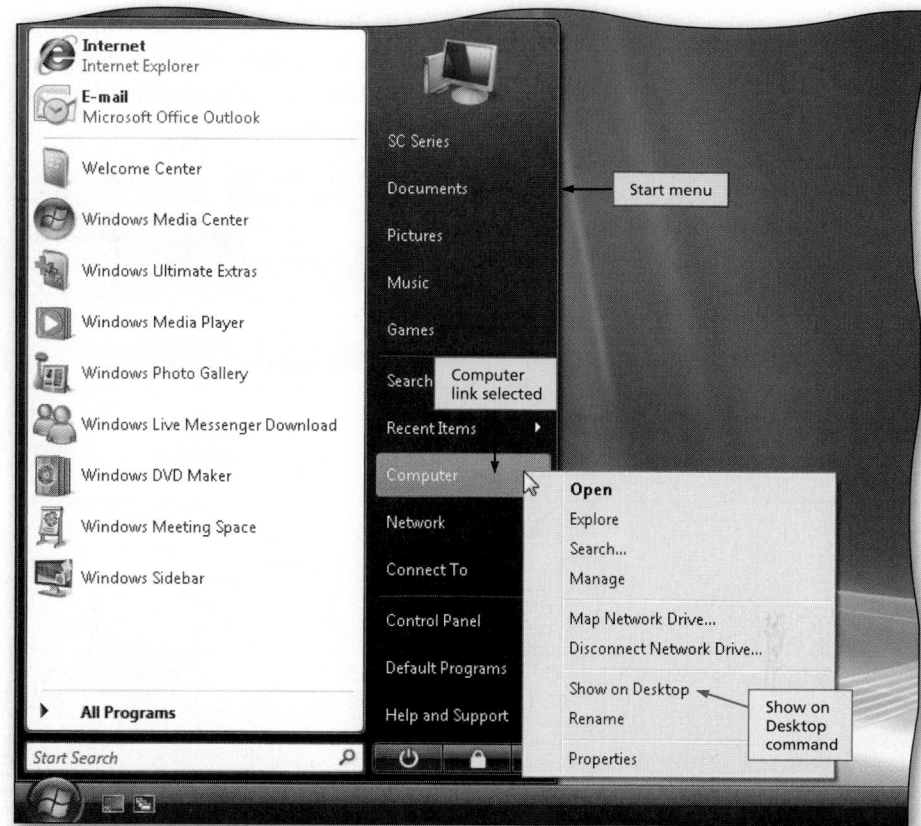

Figure 1–17

2

- Click Show on Desktop to close the shortcut menu and display the Computer icon on the desktop (Figure 1–18).

 Q&A

Why should I use a shortcut menu?

A shortcut menu speeds up your work and adds flexibility to your interaction with the computer by making often used items available in multiple locations.

3

- Click an open area on the desktop to close the Start menu.

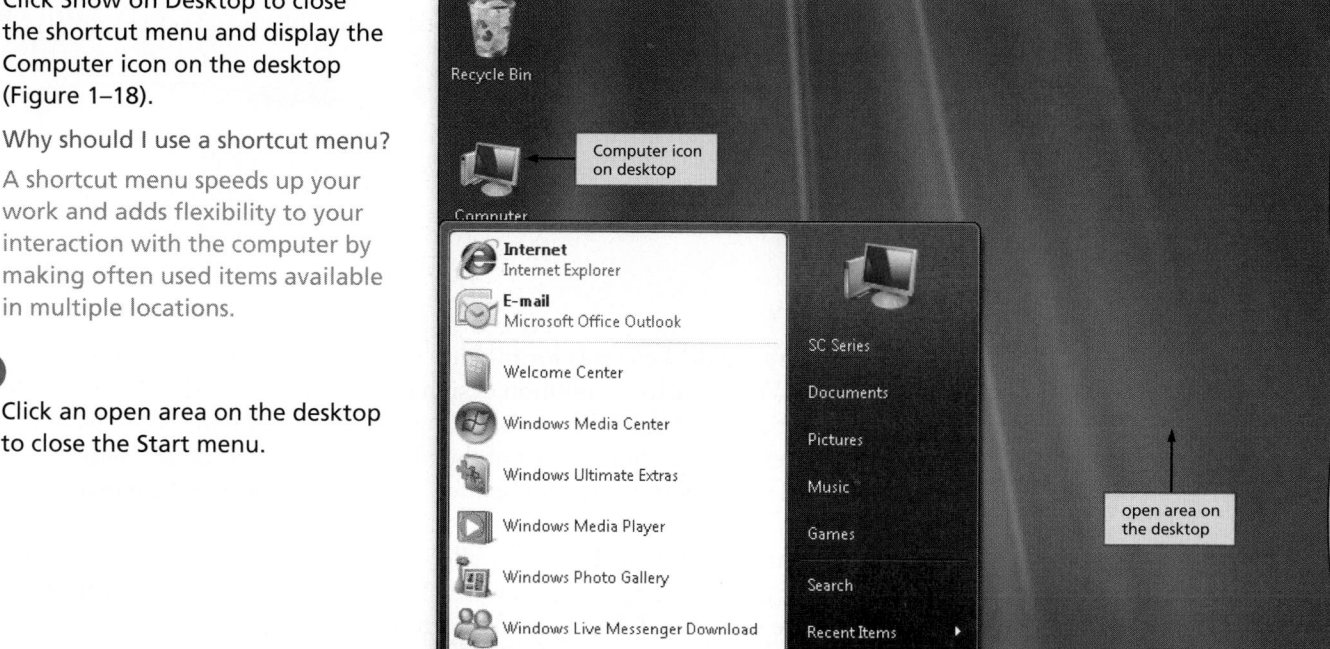

Figure 1–18

To Open a Window Using a Desktop Icon

When an icon, like the Computer icon, is displayed on the desktop, you can use the icon to open the application or window it represents. One method for opening a window with a desktop icon is to double-click the icon. The following step opens the Computer window on the desktop by double-clicking the Computer icon on the desktop.

1

• Double-click the Computer icon on the desktop to open the Computer window (Figure 1–19).

Q&A

What does the Computer window allow me to do?

The Computer window allows you to view the contents of the computer.

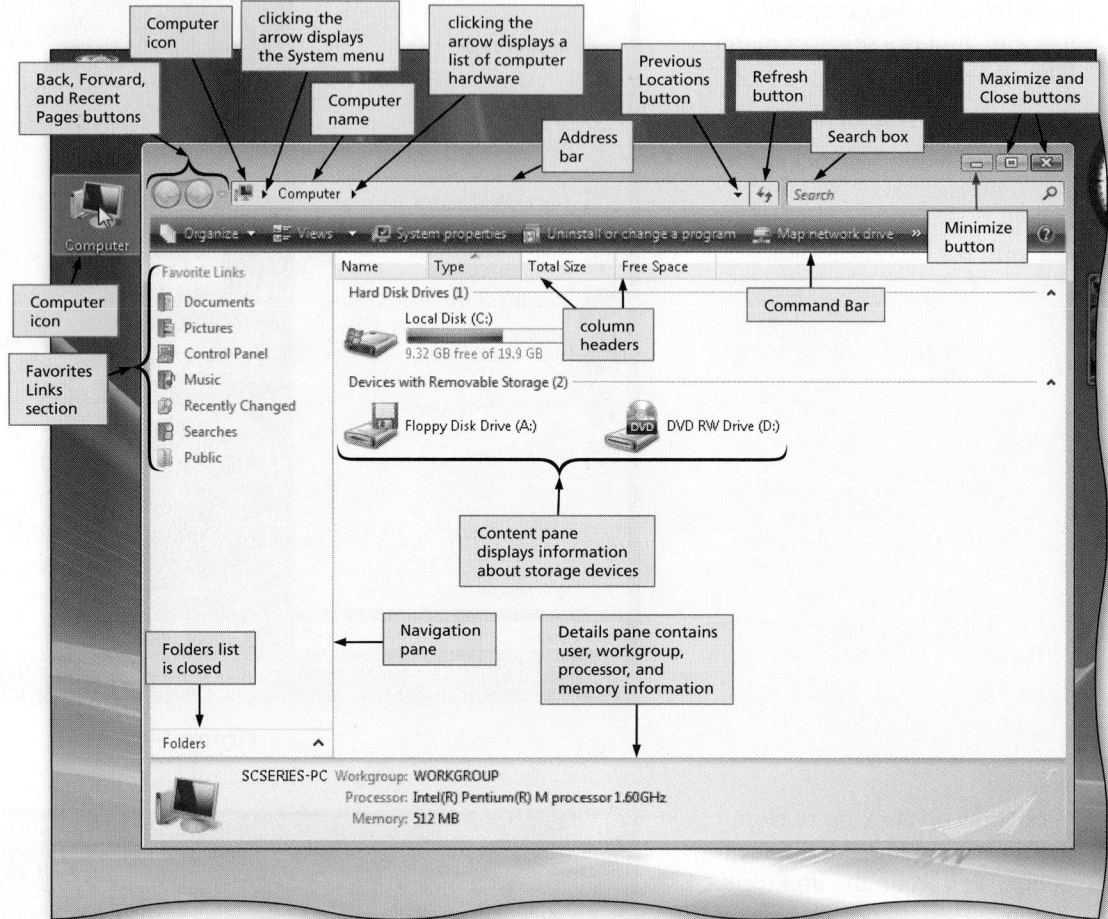

Figure 1–19

Other Ways

1. Right-click desktop icon, click Open on shortcut menu
2. Press WINDOWS+E

Folder Windows

Folder windows are the key tools for finding, viewing, and managing information on the computer. Folder Windows have common design elements, illustrated in Figure 1–19. The three buttons to the left of the **Address bar** allow you to navigate the contents of the left pane and view recent pages. On the right of the title bar are the Minimize button, Maximize button, and Close button that can be used to specify the size of the window or close the window.

The two right arrows in the Address bar allow you to visit different locations on the computer and display a list of computer hardware. The **Previous Locations button** saves the locations you have visited and displays the locations using computer path names.

The **Refresh button** at the end of the Address bar refreshes the contents of the right pane of the Computer window. The **Search box** to the right of the Address bar contains the dimmed word, Search. You can type a term into the Search box for a list of files, folders, shortcuts, and such containing that term within the location you are searching.

The **Command Bar** contains five buttons used to accomplish various tasks on the computer related to organizing and managing the contents of the open window. The area below the Command Bar contains the Navigation pane and four column headers (Name, Type, Total Size, and Free Space) on the right. The **Navigation pane** on the left contains the Favorite Links section and the Folders list. The **Favorite Links list** contains your documents, pictures, music files, and more.

Four **column headers** displayed in the right pane allow you to sort and group the entries below the column header.

To Minimize and Redisplay a Window

Two buttons on the title bar, the Minimize button and the Maximize button, allow you to control the way a window is displayed on the desktop. The following steps minimize and then redisplay the Computer window.

1

- Click the Minimize button on the title bar of the Computer window to minimize the Computer window (Figure 1–20).

Q&A What happens to the Computer window when I click the Minimize button?

The Computer window is still available, but it is no longer the active window. It collapses down to a non-recessed, light gray and black button on the task bar.

Figure 1–20

2

- Click the Computer button on the taskbar to display the Computer window (Figure 1–21).

Q&A Why does the Computer button on the taskbar change?

The button changes to reflect the status of the Computer window. A recessed button indicates that the Computer window is active on the screen. A non-recessed button indicates that the Computer window is not active, but is open.

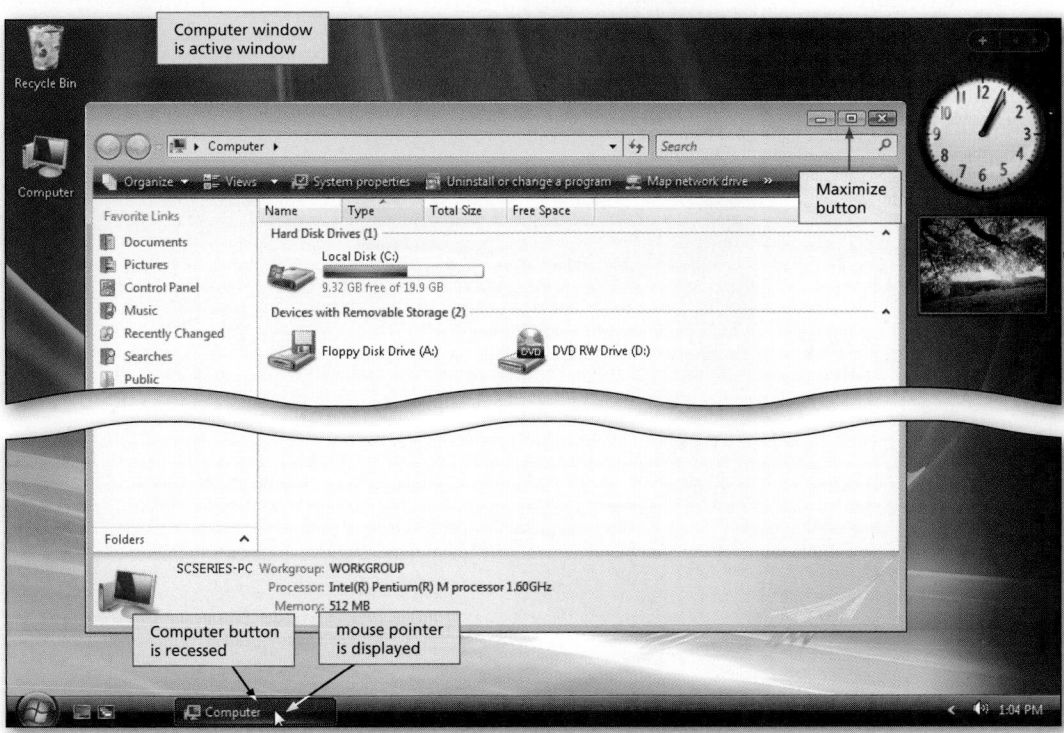

Figure 1–21

Other Ways

1. Right-click title bar, click Minimize, on taskbar click taskbar button

2. Press WINDOWS+M, press WINDOWS+SHIFT+M

To Maximize and Restore a Window

Sometimes information shown in a window is not completely visible. One method of displaying more contents in a window is to enlarge the window using the **Maximize button**, so the window fills the entire screen. If a window is filling the entire screen and you want to see part of the desktop, you can use the **Restore** button to return the window to its previous state. The following steps maximize and restore the Computer window.

- Click the Maximize button on the title bar of the Computer window to maximize the Computer window (Figure 1–22).

Q&A

When a window is maximized, can you also minimize it?

Yes. Click the Minimize button to minimize the window.

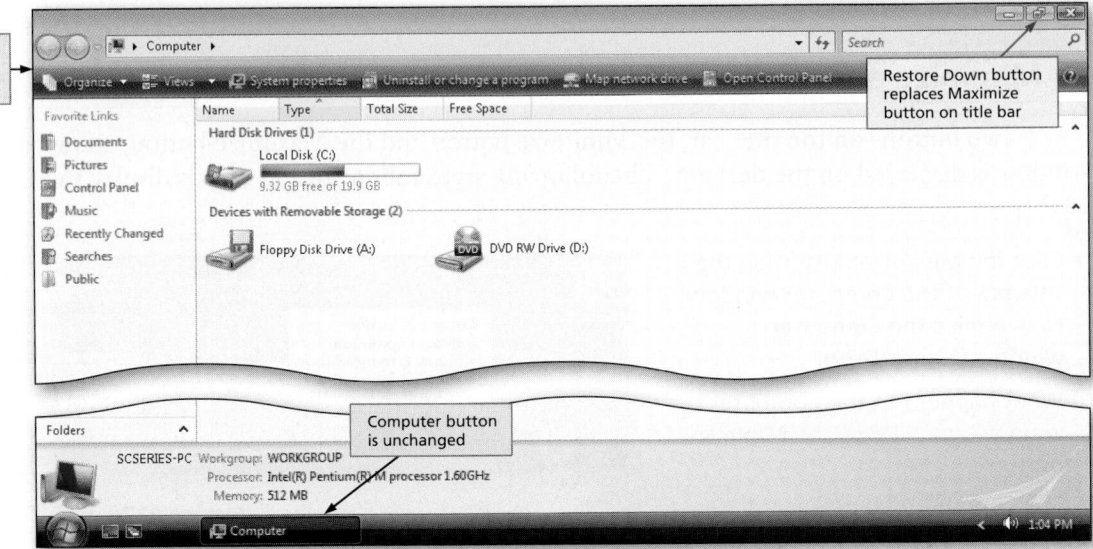

Figure 1–22

- Click the Restore Down button on the title bar of the Computer window to return the Computer window to its previous size (Figure 1–23).

Q&A

What happens to the Restore Down button when I click it?

The Maximize button replaces the Restore Down button on the title bar.

Other Ways

1. Right-click title bar, click Maximize, right-click title bar, click Restore
2. Double-click title bar, double-click title bar

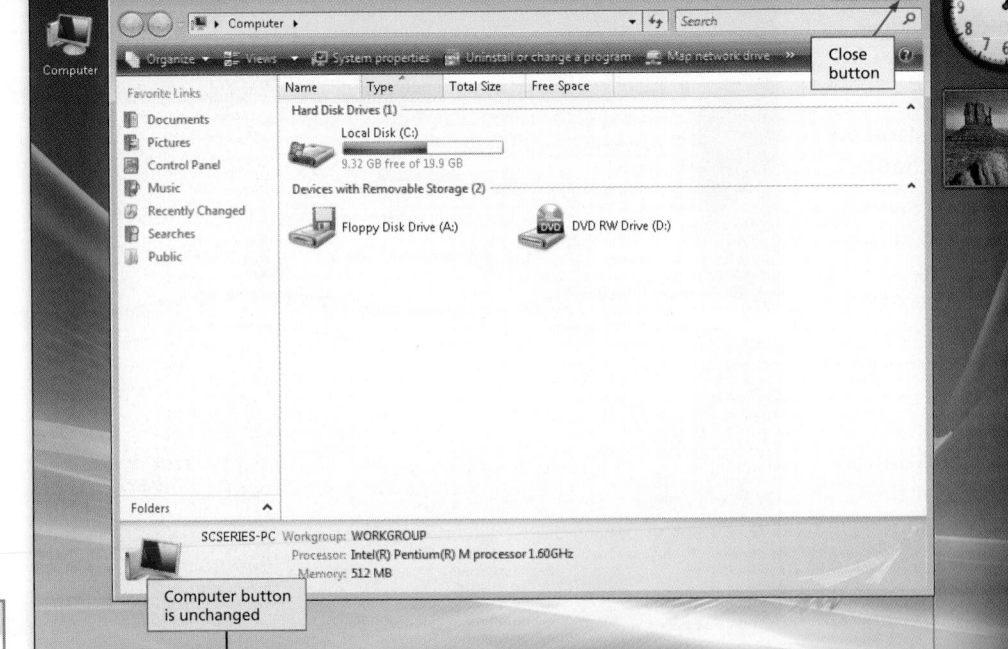

Figure 1–23

To Close a Window

You can click the **Close button** on the title bar of a window to close the window and remove the taskbar button from the Windows taskbar. The following step closes the Computer window.

- Click the Close button on the title bar of the Computer window to close the Computer window (Figure 1–24).

Q&A What happens to the Computer window when I click the Close button?

The Computer window closes and the Computer button no longer is displayed in the taskbar button area.

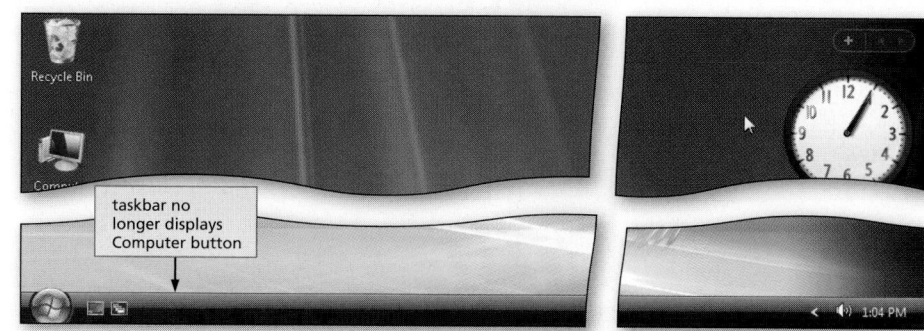

taskbar no longer displays Computer button

Figure 1–24

Other Ways

1. Right-click title bar, click Close
2. Press ALT+F4

To Open a Window Using the Start Menu

Previously, you opened the Computer window by double-clicking the Computer icon on the desktop. Another method of opening a window and viewing the contents of the window is to click a link on the Start menu. The **Pictures folder** is a convenient location to store your digital pictures, view and share your pictures, and edit pictures. The following steps open the Pictures window using the Pictures link on the Start menu.

- Open the Start menu (Figure 1–25).

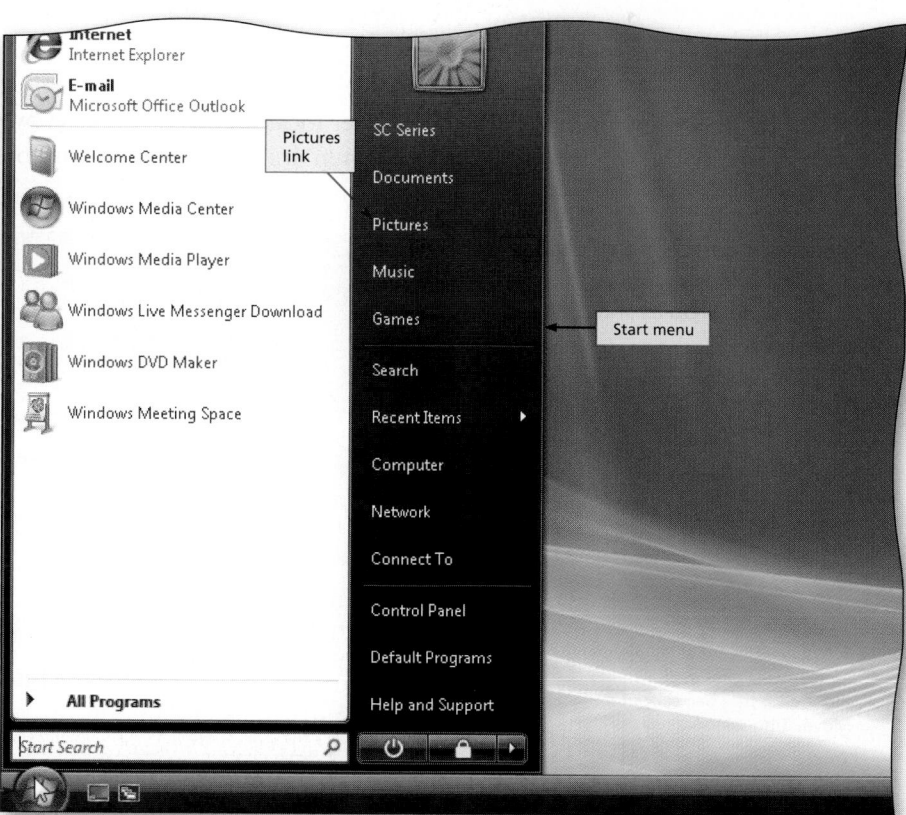

Figure 1–25

- Click Pictures on the Start menu to open the Pictures window (Figure 1–26).

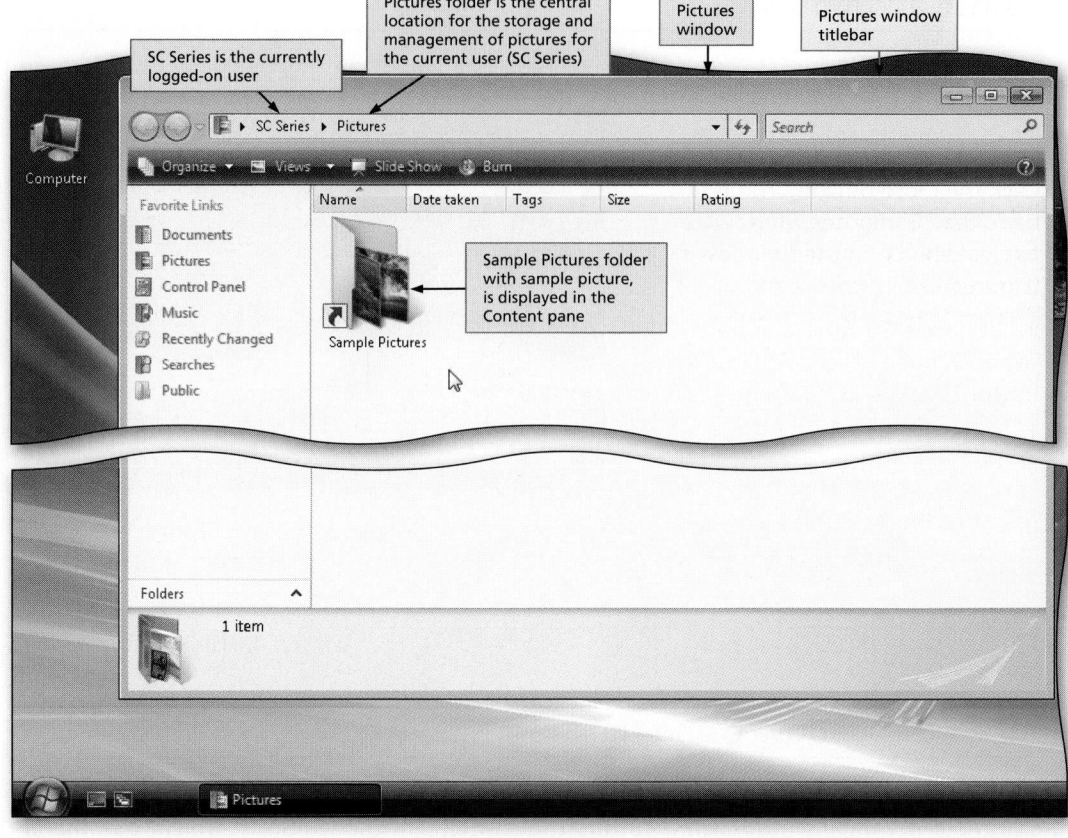

Figure 1–26

Other Ways

1. Click Start button, right-click Pictures, click Open

To Move a Window by Dragging

You can move any open window to another location on the desktop by pointing to the title bar of the window and then dragging the window. The following step drags the Pictures window to the top of the desktop.

- Drag the Pictures window title bar so the window moves to the top of the desktop as shown in Figure 1–27.

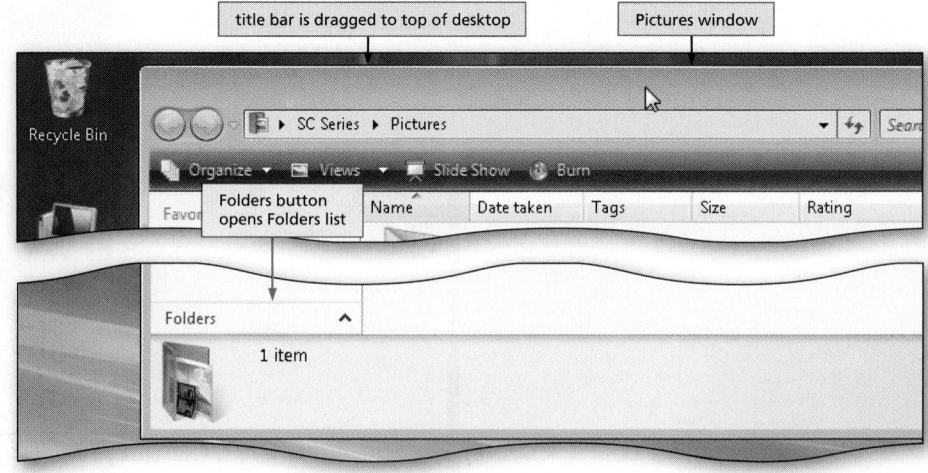

Figure 1–27

Other Ways

1. Right-click title bar, click Move, drag window

To Expand the Folders List

The Folders list in the Pictures window is collapsed and an up arrow appears to the right of the Folders name (see Figure 1–27 on the previous page). Clicking the up arrow or the Folders button expands the Folders list and reveals the contents of the Folders list. The following step expands the Folders list in the Pictures window.

1

- Click the Folders button to expand the Folders list in the Navigation pane of the Pictures window (Figure 1–28).

Q&A What is shown in the Folders list?

The Folders list displays a hierarchical structure of files, folders, and drives on the computer.

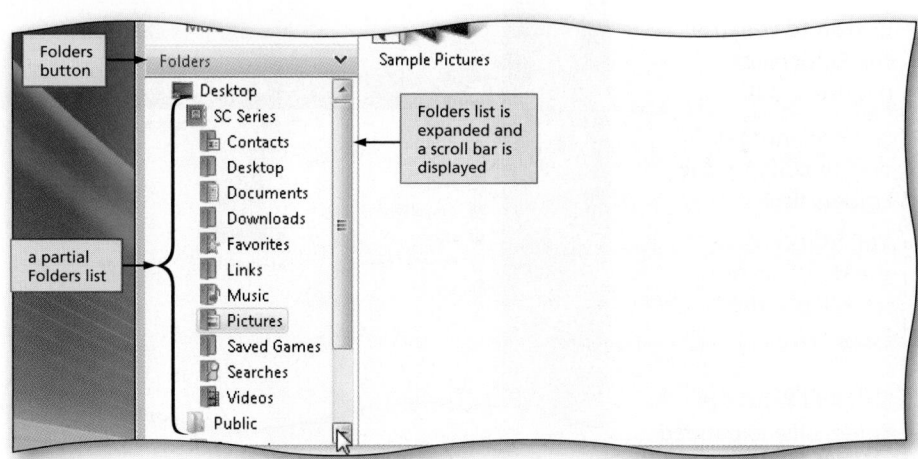

Figure 1–28

To Size a Window by Dragging

You can resize any open window to a more desirable size by pointing to one of the outside borders of the window and then dragging the window in or out. The following steps drag the bottom border of the Pictures window downward to enlarge the window until the contents of the Folders list is visible.

1

- Point to the bottom border of the Pictures window until the mouse pointer changes to a two-headed arrow.

- Drag the bottom border downward until the entire contents of the Folders list are visible and the scroll bar no longer appears (Figure 1–29).

Q&A Can I drag anything else to enlarge or shrink the window?

You can drag the left, right, and top borders and any window corner.

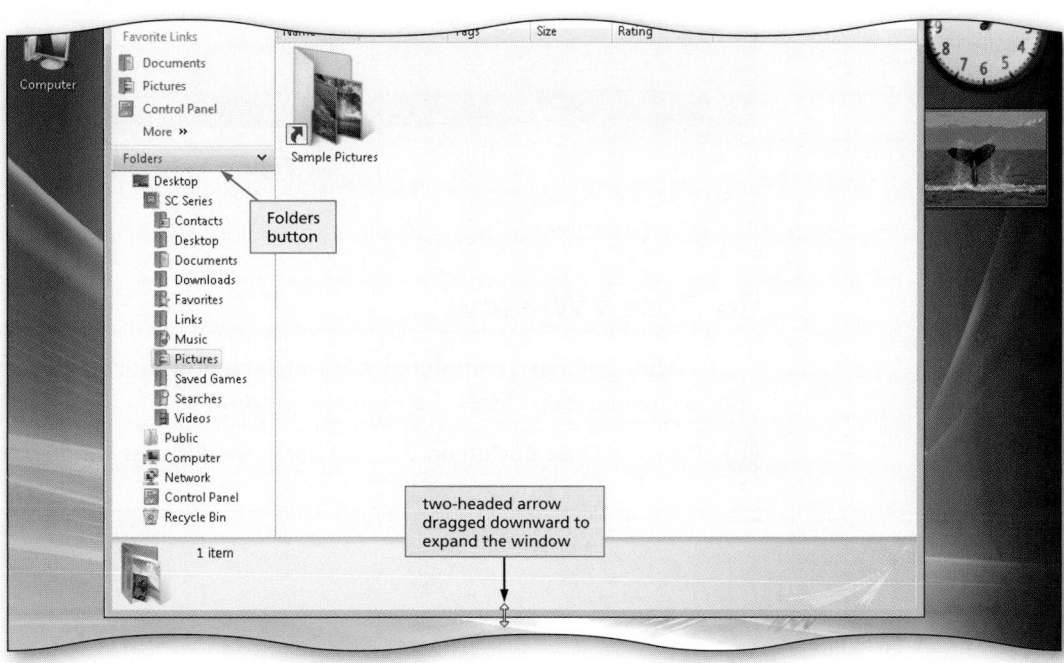

Figure 1–29

To Collapse the Folders List

When the Folders list is expanded, a down arrow is displayed. In the following step, you will collapse the list by clicking the Folders button.

- Click the Folders button to collapse the Folders list (Figure 1–30).

Q&A Is there another way to collapse the Folders list?

Yes. You can click the down arrow to collapse the Folders list.

Q&A Should I keep the Folders list expanded or collapsed?

If you need to use the contents within the Folders list, it is handy to keep the Folders list expanded. You can collapse the Folders list when the information is not needed.

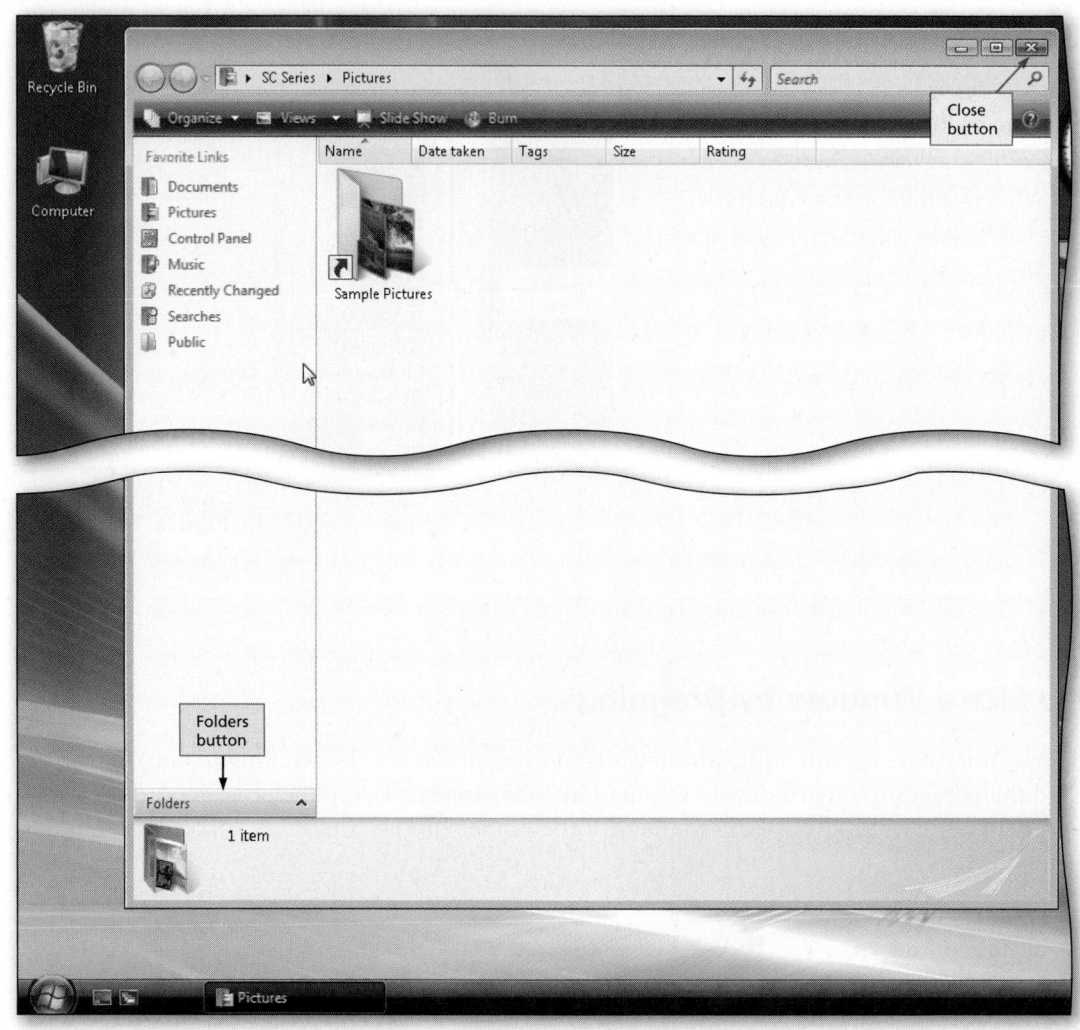

Figure 1–30

To Close a Window

After you have completed work in a window, normally you will close the window. The following step closes the Pictures window.

1 Click the Close button on the title bar in the Pictures window to close the Pictures window.

To Delete a Desktop Icon by Right-Dragging

Sometimes, you will want to remove an icon from the desktop. One method of deleting an icon from the desktop is to right-drag the icon to the Recycle Bin icon on the desktop. **Right-drag** means you point to an item, hold down the right mouse button, move the item to the desired location, and then release the right mouse button. When you right-drag an object, a shortcut menu is displayed. The shortcut menu contains commands specifically for use with the object being dragged. The following steps delete the Computer icon by right-dragging the icon to the Recycle Bin icon. A **dialog box** is displayed whenever Windows Vista needs to supply information to you or wants you to enter information or select among several options. The Confirm Delete dialog box is used in the following steps.

- Point to the Computer icon on the desktop, hold down the right mouse button, drag the Computer icon over the Recycle Bin icon, and then release the right mouse button to display a shortcut menu (Figure 1–31).

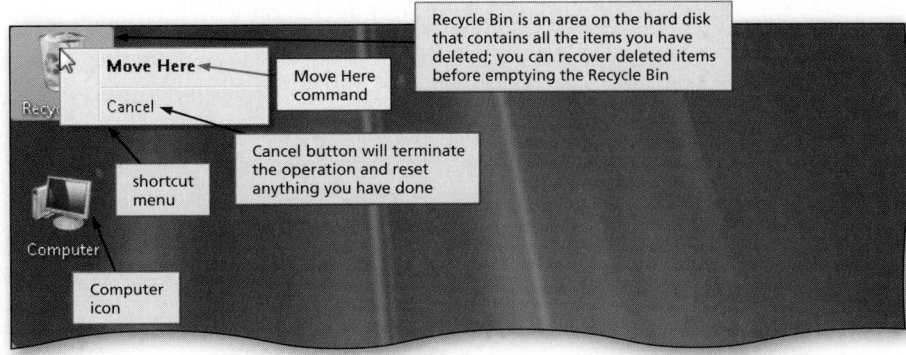

Figure 1–31

- Click Move Here on the shortcut menu to close the shortcut menu and display the Confirm Delete dialog box (Figure 1–32).

Q&A
Why should I right-drag instead of simply dragging?

Although you can move icons by dragging with the primary (left) mouse button and by right-dragging with the secondary (right) mouse button, it is strongly suggested you right-drag because a shortcut menu appears and, in most cases, you can specify the exact operation you want to occur. When you drag using the left mouse button, a default operation takes place and that operation may not be the operation you intended to perform.

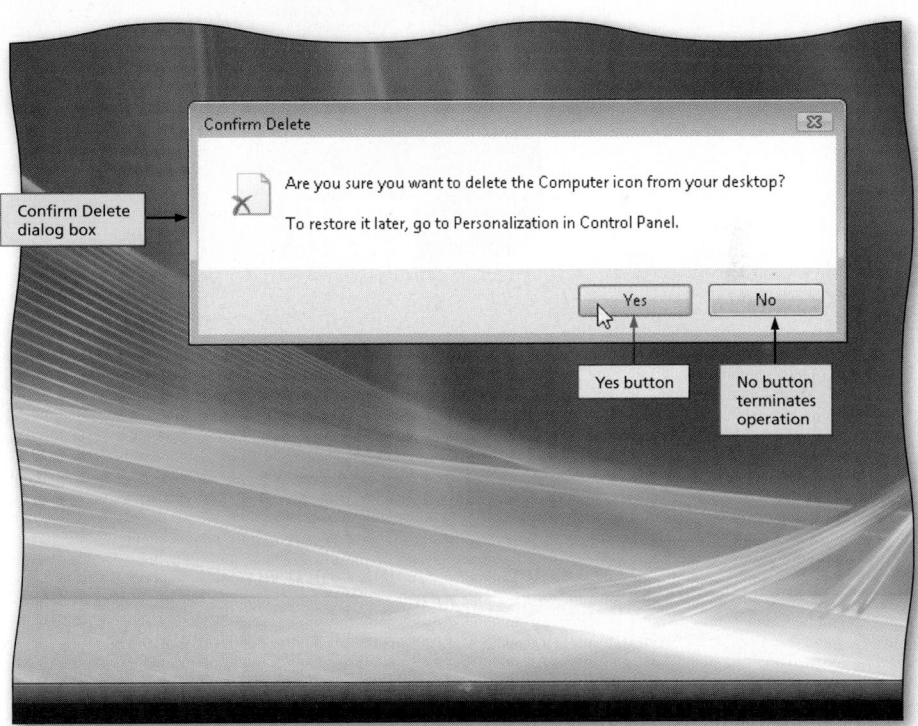

Figure 1–32

- Click the Yes button to delete the Computer icon and close the Confirm Delete dialog box.

Other Ways
1. Drag icon to Recycle Bin, click Yes button
2. Right-click icon, click Delete, click Yes button

Summary of Mouse and Windows Operations

You have seen how to use the mouse to point, click, right-click, double-click, drag, and right-drag in order to accomplish certain tasks on the desktop. The use of a mouse is an important skill when using Windows Vista. In addition, you have learned how to move around and use windows on the Windows Vista desktop.

The Keyboard and Keyboard Shortcuts

The **keyboard** is an input device on which you manually key in, or type, data. Figure 1–33 illustrates the rechargeable Wireless Entertainment Desktop 8000 keyboard designed for use with Microsoft Office and the Internet. Keyboards can be basic input devices, or in the case of the keyboard illustrated, can serve other purposes, such as providing USB ports for plugging in hardware, and specialized buttons such as the Windows Gadget button, which allow access to certain Windows Vista features at the touch of a button.

Figure 1–33

Many tasks you accomplish with a mouse can also be accomplished using a keyboard. To perform tasks using the keyboard, you must understand the notation used to identify which keys to press. This notation is used throughout Windows Vista to identify a **keyboard shortcut**.

Keyboard shortcuts consist of (1) pressing a single key (such as press the F1 key); or (2) pressing and holding down one key and pressing a second key, as shown by two key names separated by a plus sign (such as press CTRL+ESC). For example, to obtain help about Windows Vista, you can press the F1 key and to open the Start menu, hold down the CTRL key and then press the ESC key (press CRTL+ESC).

Starting an Application Program

One of the basic tasks you can perform using Windows Vista is starting an application program. A **program** is a set of computer instructions that carries out a task on the computer. An **application program** is a set of specific computer instructions that is designed to allow you to accomplish a particular task. For example, a **word processing program** is an application program that allows you to create written documents; a **presentation graphics program** is an application program that allows you to create graphic presentations for display on a computer; and a **Web browser program** is an application program that allows you to search for and display **Web pages**, documents designed to be viewed using a Web browser.

The **default Web browser program** (Internet Explorer) appears in the pinned items list on the Start menu shown in Figure 1–34. Because the default **Web browser** is selected during the installation of the Windows Vista operating system, the default Web browser on your computer may be different. In addition, you can easily select another Web browser as the default Web browser. Another frequently used Web browser program is **Mozilla Firefox**.

What Is Internet Explorer?

Internet Explorer is a **Web browsing program** that allows you to search for and view Web pages, save pages you find for use in the future, maintain a list of the pages you visit, send and receive e-mail messages, and edit Web pages. The Internet Explorer application program is included with the Windows Vista operating system software and Microsoft Office software, or you can download it from the Internet.

To Start an Application Using the Start Menu

A common activity performed on a computer is starting an application program to accomplish specific tasks. You can start an application program by using the Start menu. To illustrate the use of the Start menu to start an application program, the following steps start Internet Explorer using the Internet command on the Start menu.

1
- Open the Start menu (Figure 1–34).

Q&A
Is Internet Explorer included in the All Programs list?

Yes. All application programs stored on the computer are listed on the All Programs list. Internet Explorer also is on the pinned items list because it is used often, but you can start Internet Explorer from the All Programs list as well.

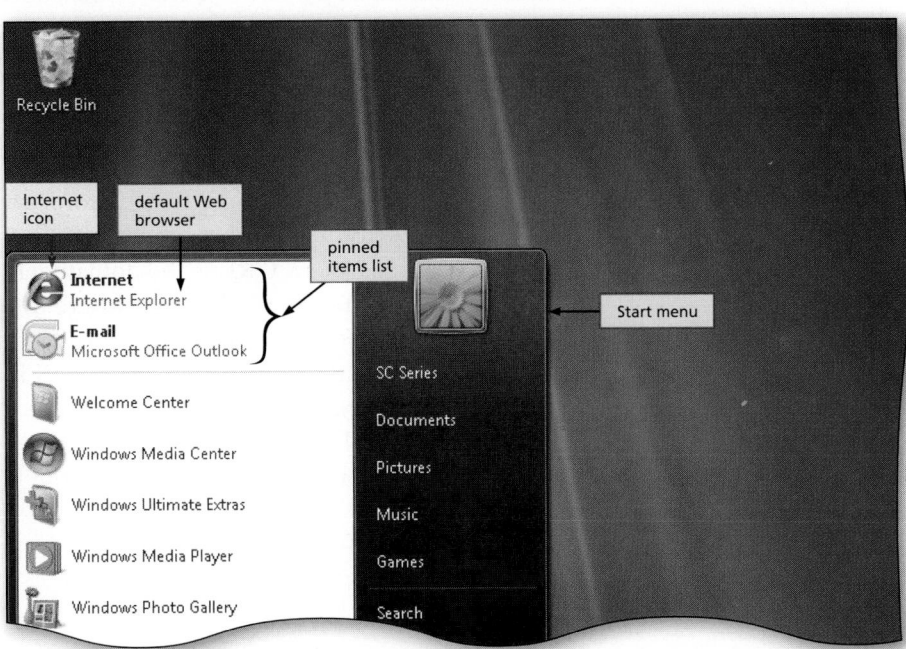

Figure 1–34

②

- Click the Internet icon in the pinned items list on the Start menu to start Windows Internet Explorer (Figure 1–35).

Q&A

What is displayed in the Windows Internet Explorer window?

A title bar, Address bar, Standard toolbar, Instant Search box, scroll bar, status bar, and display area where pages from the World Wide Web display.

Figure 1–35

Other Ways

1. Click Start button, point to All Programs, click Internet Explorer

BTW

Web Sites
A collection of related Web pages on a computer is called a **Web site**. The MSN.com Web page shown in Figure 1–35 is the first Web page you see when you access the MSN.com Web site and is, therefore, referred to as a **home page**, or **start page**.

Uniform Resource Locator (URL)

A **Uniform Resource Locator (URL)** is the address on the World Wide Web where a Web page is located. It often is composed of three parts (Figure 1–36 on page WIN 29). The first part is the **protocol**. A protocol is a set of rules. Most Web pages use the Hypertext Transfer Protocol. **Hypertext Transfer Protocol (HTTP)** describes the rules used to transmit Web pages electronically over the Internet. You enter the protocol in lowercase as http followed by a colon and two forward slashes (http://). If you do not begin a URL with a protocol, Internet Explorer will assume it is http, and automatically will append http:// to the front of the URL.

The second part of a URL is the domain name. The **domain name** is the Internet address of the computer on the Internet where the Web page is located. The domain name in the URL in Figure 1–36 on the next page is www.scsite.com.

The last part of the domain name (com in Figure 1–36 on the next page) indicates the type of organization that owns the Web site. Table 1–2 shows some types of organizations and their extensions. In addition to the 14 domain name extensions listed in the table, there are country specific extensions, such as .uk for the United Kingdom and .dk for Denmark.

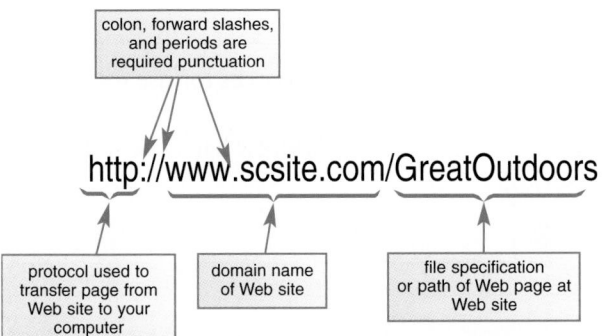

Figure 1–36

Table 1–2 Organizations and their Domain Name Extensions			
Organization	**Extension**	**Organization**	**Extension**
Commercial	.com	aviation	.aero
Educational	.edu	businesses	.biz
Government	.gov	co-operatives	.coop
Military	.mil	general	.info
Major network support	.net	museums	.museum
Organizations not covered above	.org	individuals	.name
International	.int	professionals	.pro

The optional third part of a URL is the file specification of the Web page. The **file specification** includes the file name and possibly a directory or folder name. This information is called the **path**. If no file specification of a Web page is specified in the URL, a default Web page is displayed.

Browsing the World Wide Web

One method to browse the World Wide Web is to find URLs that identify interesting Web sites in magazines or newspapers, on television, from friends, or even from just browsing the Web. URLs of well-known companies and organizations usually contain the company's name and institution's name. For example, ibm.com is the IBM Corporation URL, and umich.edu is the URL for the University of Michigan.

When you find a URL of a Web page you want to visit, enter the URL into the Address bar. The following steps show how to view a Web site provided by Thomson Course Technology and visit the Web page titled SC Site – Shelly Cashman Series Student Resources Web site, which contains student resources for use with Shelly Cashman Series textbooks. The URL for the SC Site – Shelly Cashman Series Student Resources Web site is:

www.scsite.com

You are not required to provide the leading http:// protocol when initially typing the URL in the Address bar. Internet Explorer will insert http:// and assume the www automatically, if you do not supply it.

To Browse the Web by Entering a URL

The SC Site — Shelly Cashman Series Student Resources Web site contains student resources for use with Shelly Cashman Series textbooks. The URL for this Web page is www.scsite.com.

When you find the URL of a Web page you want to visit, enter the URL into the Address bar. The following steps show how to display the Web page from the Shelly Cashman Series.

- Click the Address bar to select the URL in the Address bar (Figure 1–37).

Q&A

What happens when I click the Address bar?

Internet Explorer selects the URL in the Address bar and the mouse pointer changes to an I-beam.

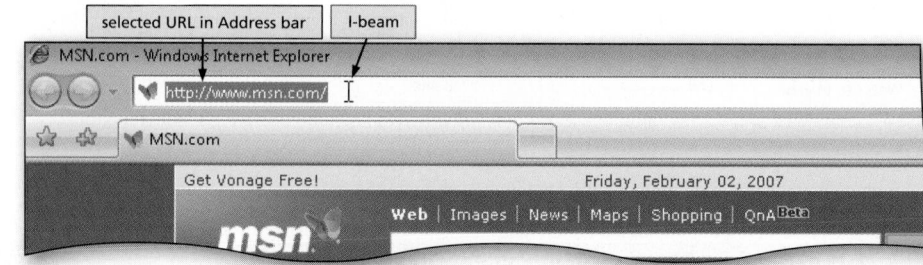

Figure 1–37

- Type www.scsite.com in the Address bar to display the new URL in the Address bar (Figure 1–38).

Q&A

Must I type www. in the URL?

No. If you type scsite.com, Internet Explorer automatically will add www.

Figure 1–38

- Click the Go to button to display the SC Site –Shelly Cashman Series Student Resources Web site (Figure 1–39).

Q&A

The Go to button changes after I click it. Why?

When you type the URL, the button changes to the Go to button. After the page is displayed, the button changes to the Refresh button. When you click the Refresh button, the Web page is downloaded again from the Web server, resulting in the most up-to-date version of the page being displayed.

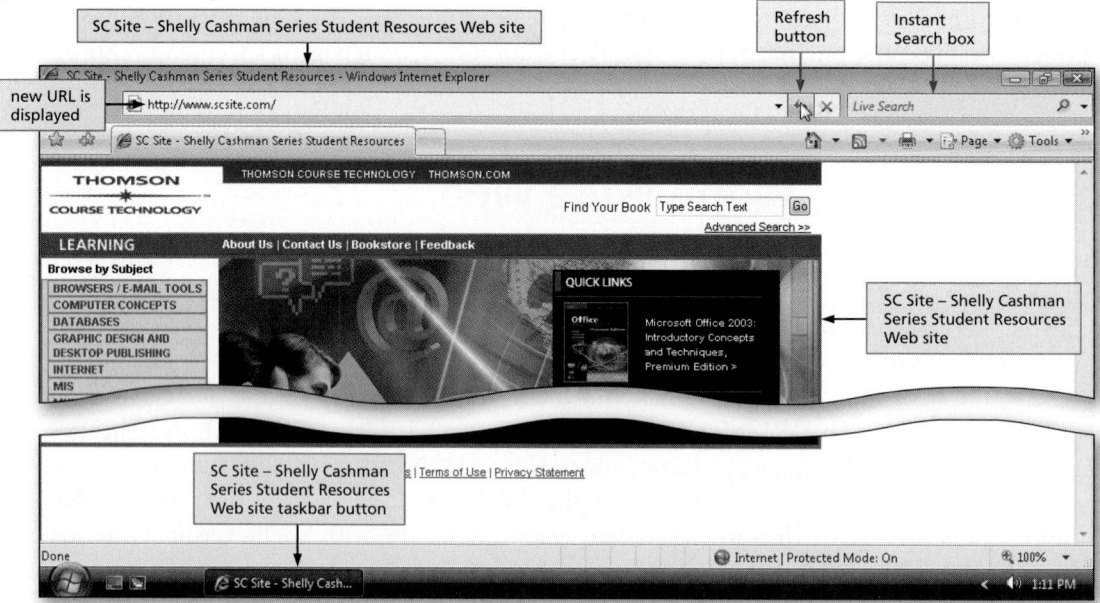

Figure 1–39

To Open a Link in a New Tab

You can view multiple Web pages in a single window using tabbed pages. A **tabbed page** consists of a tab in the Internet Explorer window and the associated Web page. When you start Internet Explorer only one tab is displayed, but you can open as many tabbed pages as you want. The following steps use the Instant Search box and the Course Technology – Shelly Cashman Series link to open a Web page on a new tabbed page.

1

- Click the Instant Search box and type `Shelly Cashman Series` in the Instant Search box (Figure 1–40).

Q&A What is an Instant Search box?

It is a text box in which you can type a term which then can be searched for by a Search engine. Internet Explorer provides an Instant Search box in the upper right corner of the window.

Search button

SC Site - Shelly Cashman Series Student Resources Web site tab

Shelly Cashman Series typed in Instant Search box

Figure 1–40

2

- Click the Search button to the right of the Instant Search box to display the results of the Web search (Figure 1–41).

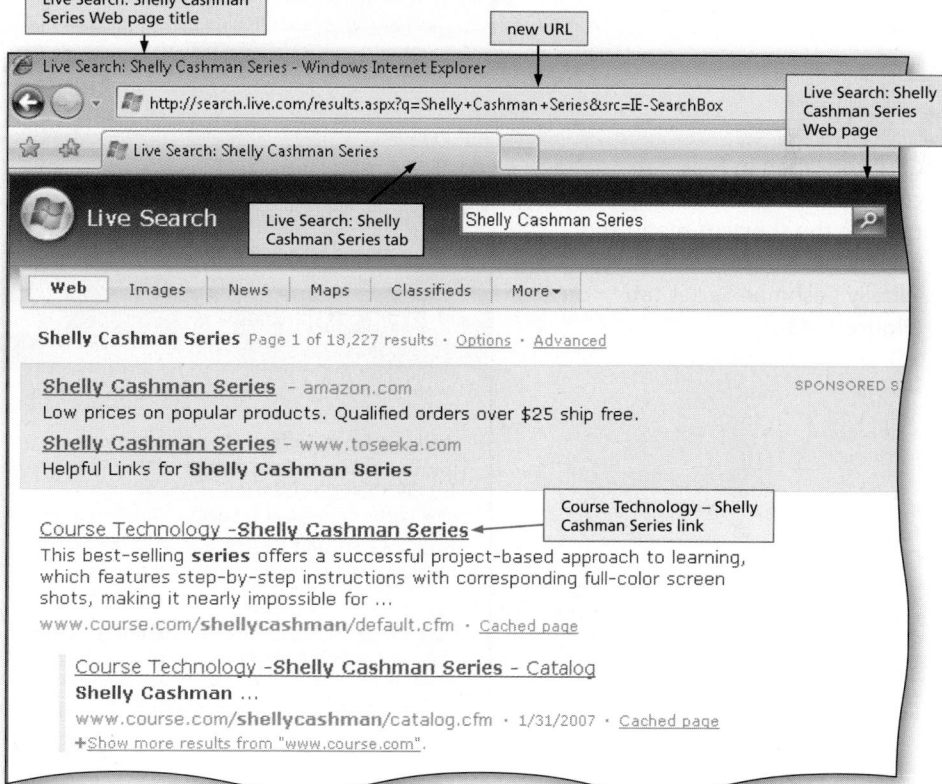

Live Search: Shelly Cashman Series Web page title

new URL

Live Search: Shelly Cashman Series Web page

Live Search: Shelly Cashman Series tab

Course Technology – Shelly Cashman Series link

Figure 1–41

3

- If necessary, scroll to view the Course Technology –Shelly Cashman Series link.

- Right-click the Course Technology –Shelly Cashman Series link to display a shortcut menu (Figure 1–42).

Q&A

What happens when I just click a link?

The Web page will open on the same tabbed page as the search results and will replace the search results page.

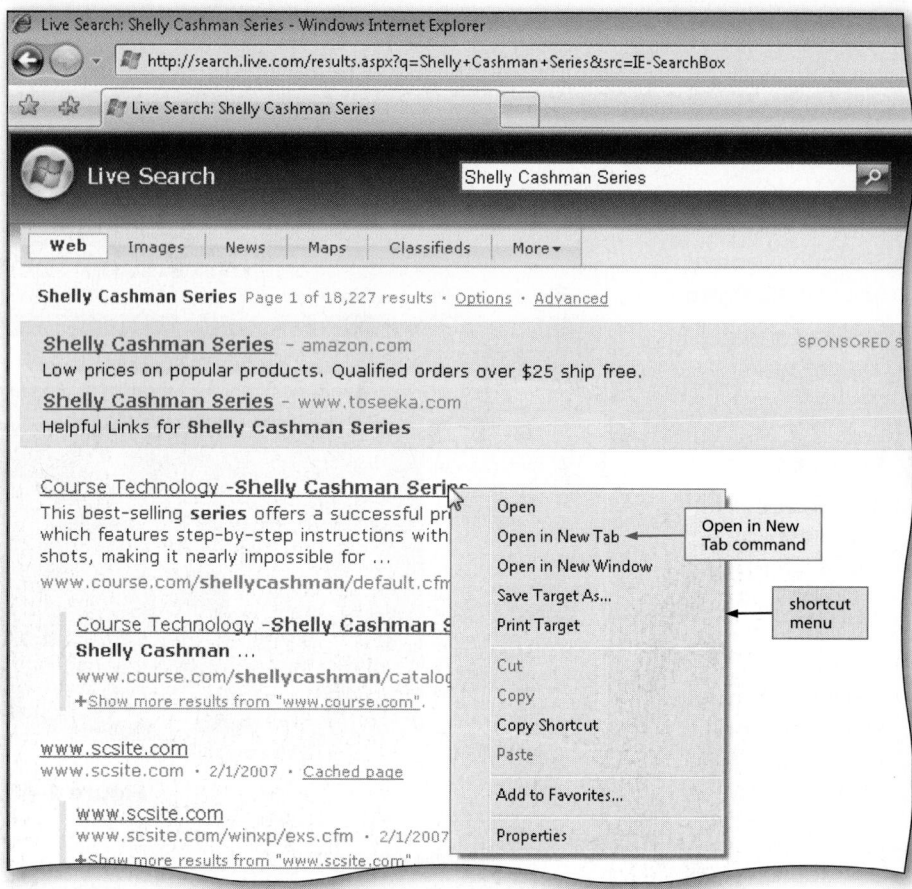

Figure 1–42

4

- Click the Open in New Tab command on the shortcut menu to close the shortcut menu and display the Course Technology –Shelly Cashman Series tab (Figure 1–43).

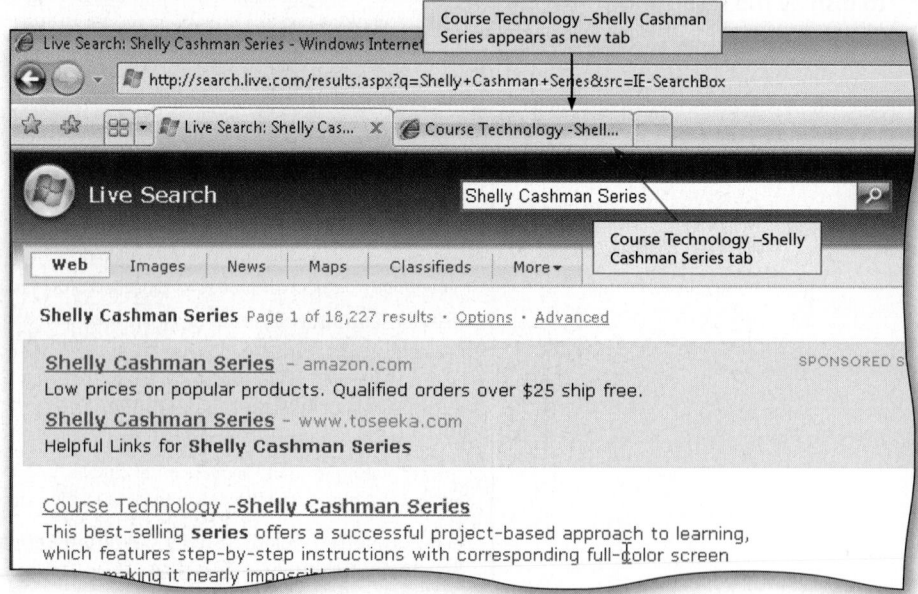

Figure 1–43

Other Ways

1. While holding down CTRL, click link

To Switch Between Tabs

You can display the contents of any tabbed page by clicking the tab, as shown in the following step which activates the Course Technology –Shelly Cashman Series tab.

1
- Click the Course Technology –Shelly Cashman Series tab to activate the tab and display The Shelly Cashman Series® Web page in the display area (Figure 1–44).

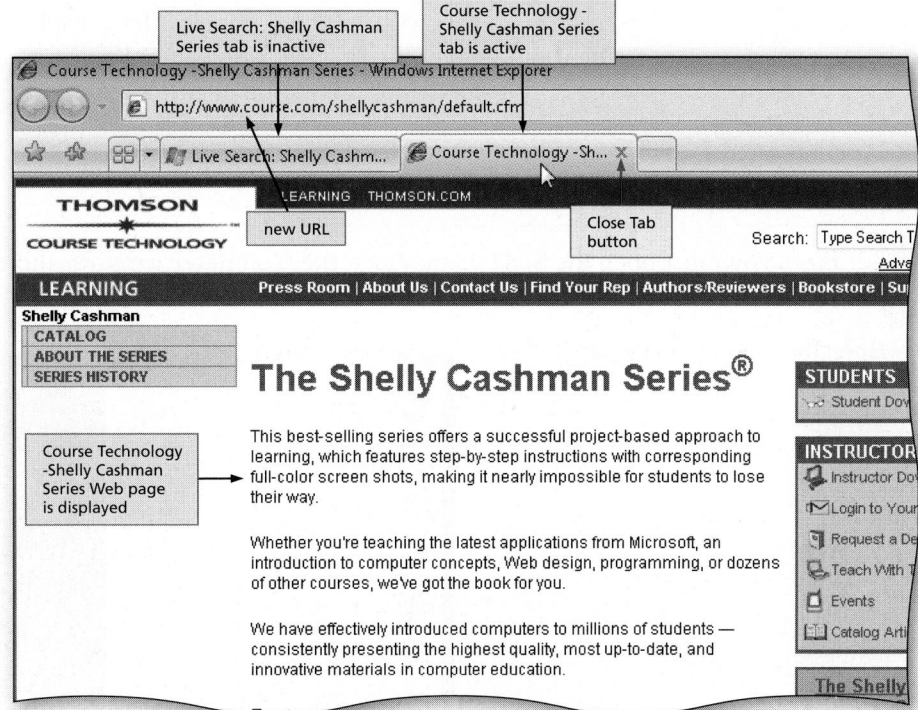

Figure 1–44

Other Ways
1. Press CTRL+TAB, press CTRL+TAB 2. Press CTRL+2, press CTRL+1

To Close a Tab

You can keep as many tabbed pages open as necessary. If you no longer have a need for the tabbed page to be open, you can close the tab using the following steps.

1
- Click the Close Tab button in the Course Technology –Shelly Cashman Series tab to close the Course Technology –Shelly Cashman Series tab (Figure 1–45).

2
- Click the Close button on the title bar to close the Live Search: Shelly Cashman Series - Windows Internet Explorer window.

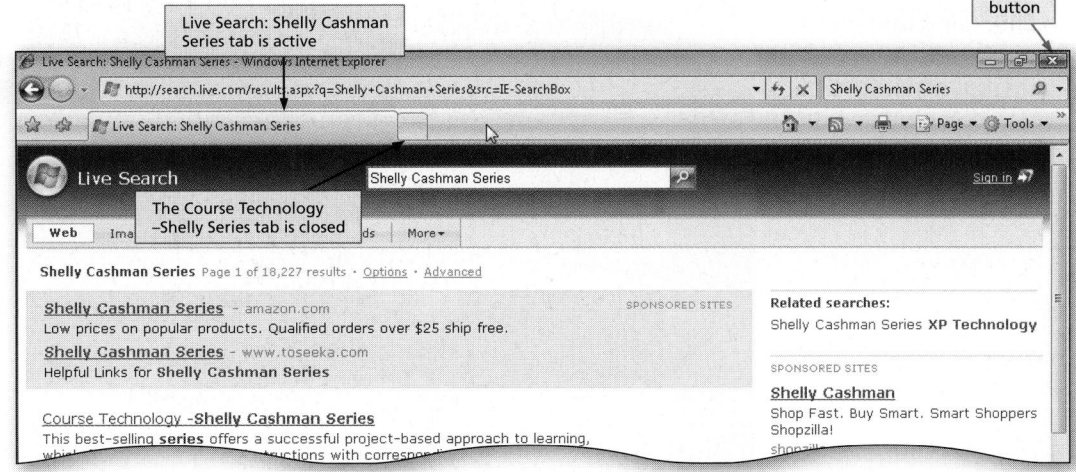

Figure 1–45

Working with Folders

The steps below allow you to view the contents of the computer, the hierarchy of drives and folders on the computer, and the files and folders in each folder. In this section, you will expand and collapse drives and folders, display drive and folder contents, create a new folder, copy a file between folders, and rename and then delete a file. These are common operations that you should understand how to perform.

To Work with Folders

First, you must open the Start menu, open the Computer window, and then maximize the window.

1

- Open the Start menu (Figure 1–46).

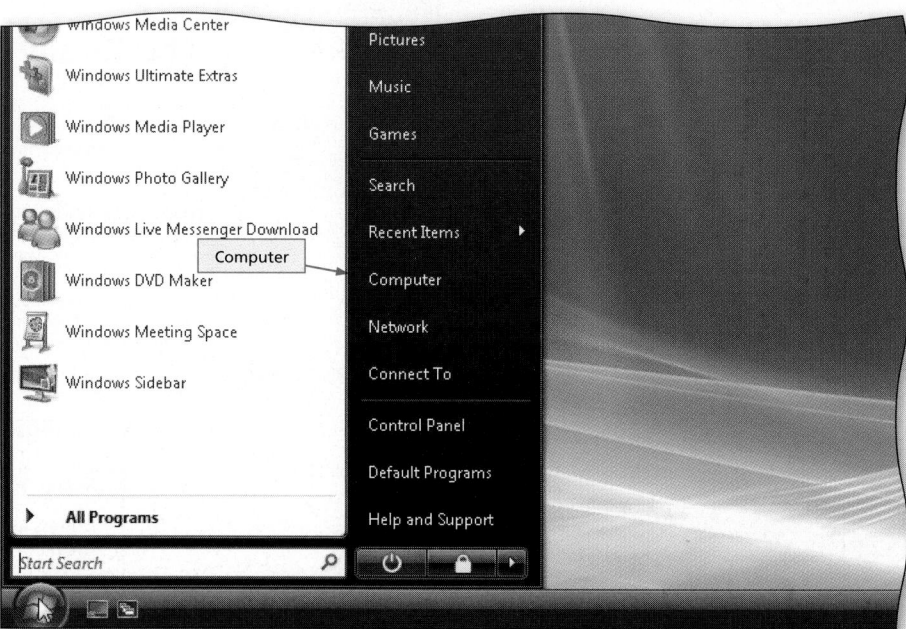

Figure 1–46

2

- Click Computer on the Start menu to display the Computer window (Figure 1–47).

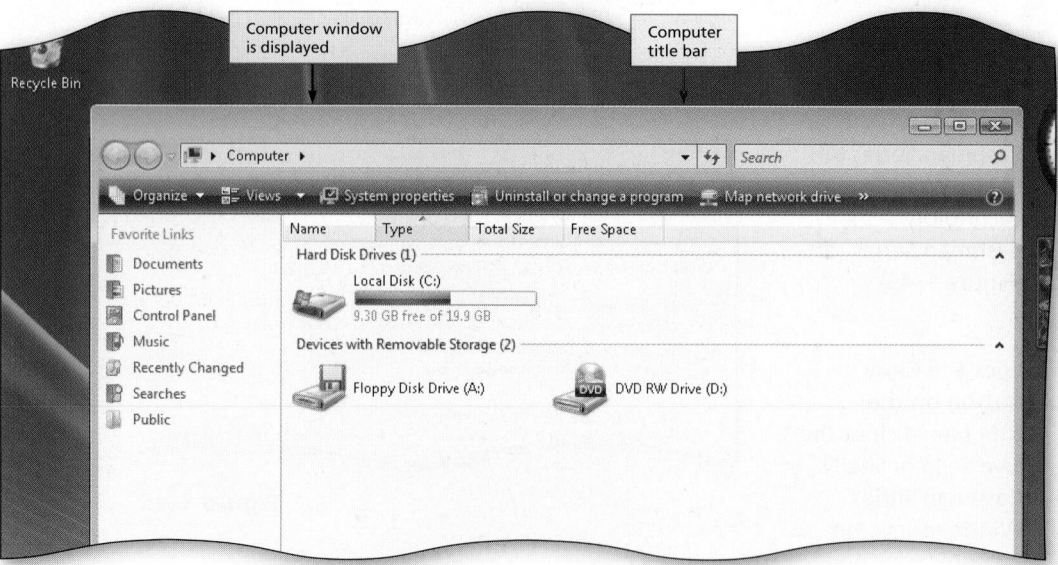

Figure 1–47

3

- If necessary, double-click the Computer title bar to maximize the Computer window.

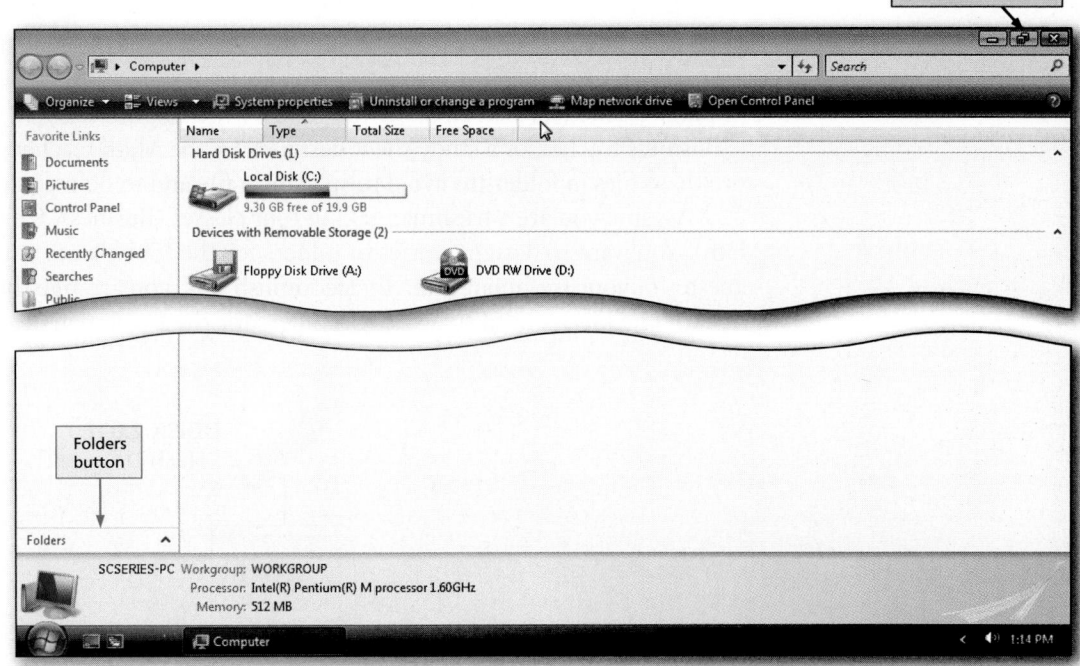

Figure 1–48

4

- If necessary, click the Folders button to display the Folders list (Figure 1–49).

Q&A

Is it possible to display my folders and drives in the right pane differently than what is shown in Figure 1–49?

You can display files and folders in the right pane in several different views. Currently, the drives and folders in the right pane are displayed in Tiles view.

Experiment

- Click a black arrow in the Folders list and observe the changes in the window. Then click the resulting white arrow to return the window to its previous state. Do the same for another black arrow and resulting white arrow.

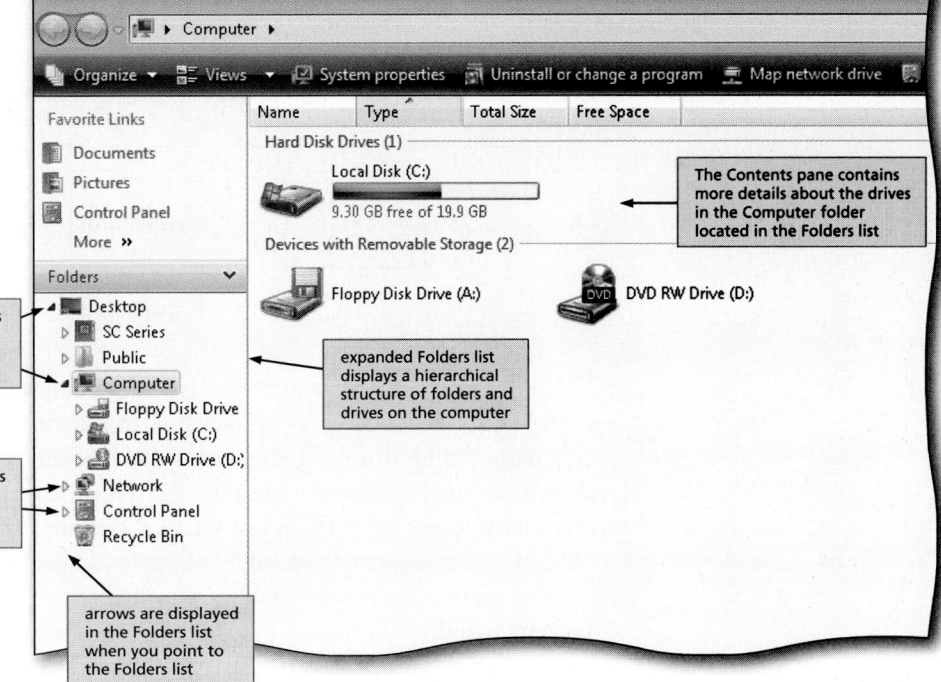

Figure 1–49

Other Ways
1. Click Start button, right-click Computer, click Explore on shortcut menu
2. Press WINDOWS+E

Using a Hierarchical Format to Organize Files and Folders

Besides navigating drives and folder, you also need to be able to create and organize the files and folders on the computer. A file may contain a spreadsheet assignment given by the computer teacher, a research paper assigned by the English teacher, an electronic quiz given by the Business teacher, or a study sheet designed by the Math teacher. You should organize and store these files in folders to avoid misplacing a file and to help you quickly find a file.

Assume you are a freshman taking four classes (Business, Computer, English, and Math). You want to design a series of folders for the four classes you are taking in the first semester of your freshman year. To accomplish this, you arrange the folders in a **hierarchical format**. The hierarchical structure of folders for the Freshman year is shown in Figure 1–50.

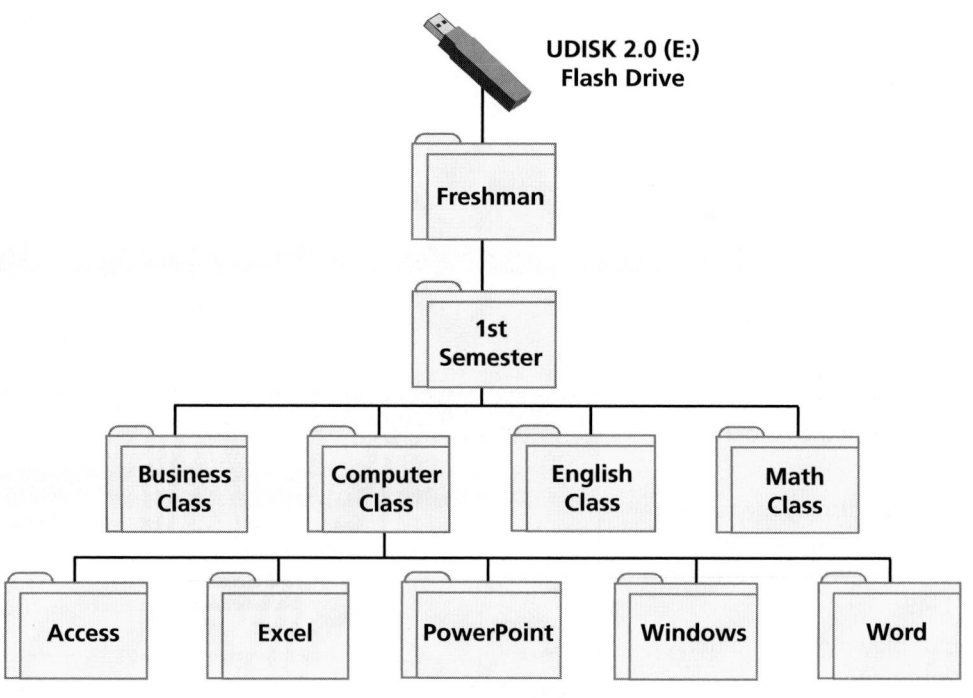

Figure 1–50

The hierarchy contains five levels. The first level contains the storage device, in this case a flash drive. Windows Vista identifies the storage device with a letter, and, in some cases, a name. In Figure 1–50, the flash drive is identified as UDISK 2.0 (E:). The second level contains the Freshman folder, the third level contains the 1st Semester folder, the fourth level contains four folders (Business Class, Computer Class, English Class, and Math Class), and the fifth level contains five folders (Access, Excel, PowerPoint, Windows, and Word).

The vertical and horizontal lines in the hierarchy chart form a pathway that allows you to navigate to a drive or folder. Each pathway is a means of navigation to a specific location on a computer or network. A **path** consists of a drive letter (preceded by a drive name when necessary) and colon, to identify the storage device, and one or more folder names. Each drive or folder in the hierarchy chart has a corresponding path. When you click a drive or folder icon in the Folders list, the corresponding path appears in the Address bar. Table 1–3 contains examples of paths and their corresponding drives and folders. These paths are referred to as **breadcrumb trails**, showing you where the current page or folder is in the hierarchy.

When the hierarchy in Figure 1–50 is created, the UDISK 2.0 (E:) drive is said "to contain" the Freshman folder, the Freshman folder is said "to contain" the 1st Semester folder, and so on. In addition, this hierarchy can easily be expanded to include folders from the Sophomore, Junior, and Senior years and any additional semesters.

Table 1–3 Paths and Corresponding Drives and Folders

Path	Drive and Folder
Computer ► UDISK 2.0 (E:)	Drive E (UDISK 2.0 (E:))
Computer ► UDISK 2.0 (E:) ► Freshman	Freshman folder on drive E
Computer ► UDISK 2.0 (E:) ► Freshman ► 1st Semester	1st Semester folder in Freshman folder on drive E
Computer ► UDISK 2.0 (E:) ► Freshman ► 1st Semester ► Computer Class ► Word	Word folder in Computer Class folder in 1st Semester folder in Freshman folder on drive E

Removable Media and Network Drives

Types of removable media such as USB flash drives are ideal for storing files and folders on a computer. A **USB flash drive**, sometimes called a **keychain drive**, is a flash memory storage device that plugs into a USB port on a computer. A **USB port**, short for universal serial bus port, can be found on most computers. USB flash drives, like the one shown in Figure 1–51, are convenient for mobile users because they are small and lightweight enough to be transported on a keychain or in a pocket.

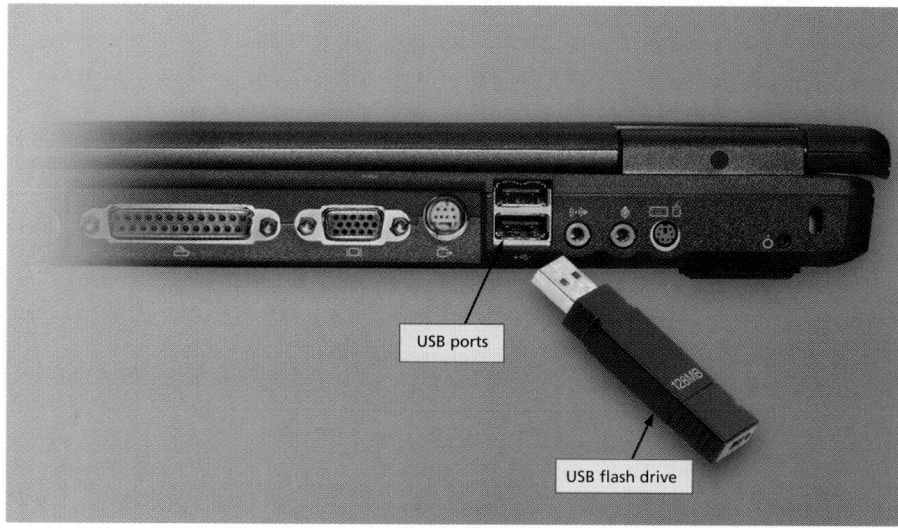

USB ports

USB flash drive

Figure 1–51

Instead of a USB drive, you might use files stored on a network drive. A **network** is a collection of computers and devices connected together for the purpose of sharing information between computer users. In some cases, students might be required to store their files on a network drive found on the school's computer network. A **network drive** is a storage device that is connected to the server on the computer network. A **server** controls access to the hardware, software, and other resources on the network and provides a centralized storage area for programs, data, and information. If student files reside on the network drive on the school's network, files may be accessed from a school computer, or from a personal computer with permission from the school. Ask your teacher if the school requires you to use a network drive.

To Plug a USB Flash Drive into a USB Port

Although other removable media may be used for storage, the USB flash drive is one of the more popular drives. To store files and folders on the USB flash drive, you must plug the USB flash drive into a USB port on the computer. After you do, the flash drive window is displayed on the desktop. The removable media drive name on your computer may be different. The following step plugs a USB flash drive into a USB port.

1

- Plug the USB flash drive into a USB port on the computer to display the UDISK 2.0 (E:) window (Figure 1–52).

 What does UDISK 2.0 (E:) mean?

UDISK 2.0 is the name of a particular type of USB drive. (E:) is the drive letter assigned by Windows Vista to your removable drive. The name and drive letter of your USB drive might be different.

2

- Close the UDISK 2.0 (E:) window.

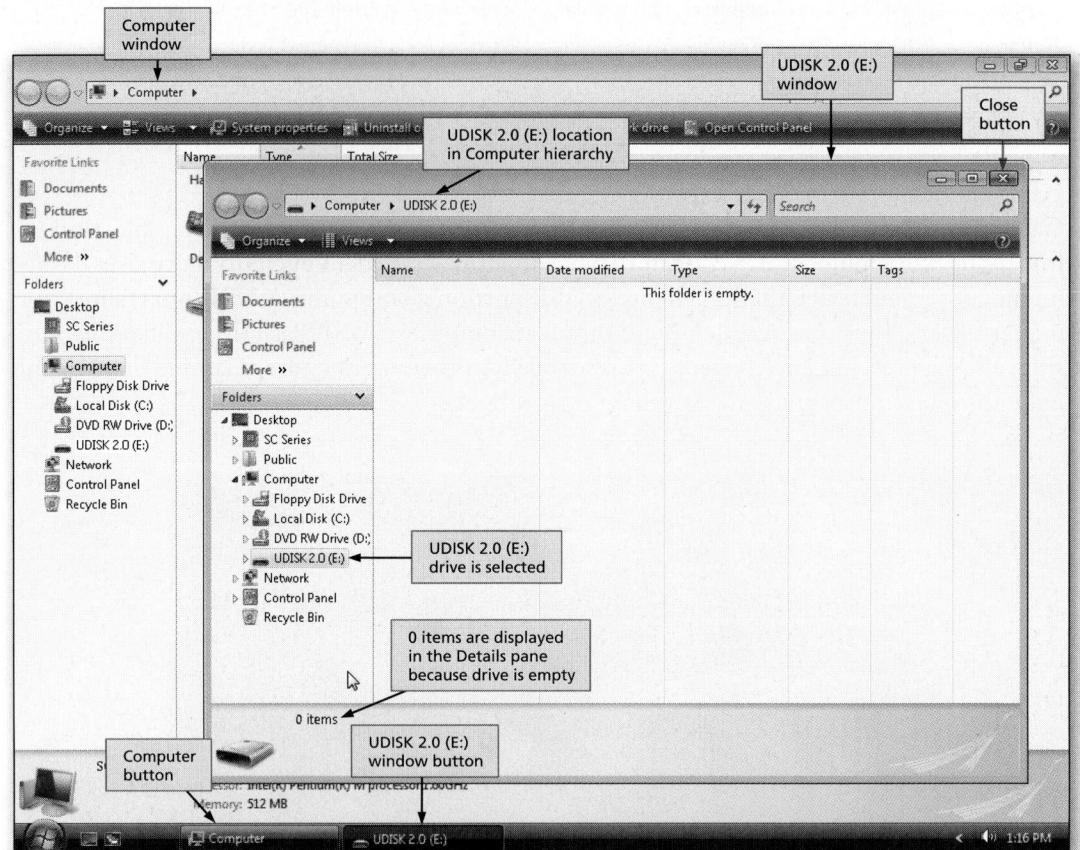

Figure 1–52

Naming a Folder

When you create a folder, such as the Freshman folder in Figure 1–50 on page 36, you must name the folder. A folder name should describe the folder and its contents. A folder name can contain up to 255 characters, including spaces. Any uppercase or lowercase character is valid when creating a folder name, except a backslash (\), slash (/), colon (:), asterisk (*), question mark (?), quotation marks (''), less than symbol (<), greater than symbol (>), or vertical bar (|). Folder names cannot be CON, AUX, COM1, COM2, COM3, COM4, LPT1, LPT2, LPT3, PRN, or NUL. The same rules for naming folders also apply to naming files.

To Create a Folder on a Removable Drive

To create a folder on a removable drive, you must open the UDISK 2.0 (E:) drive and then create the folder in the right pane. The following steps create the Freshman folder on the UDISK 2.0 (E:) drive.

1

- Double-click the UDISK 2.0 (E:) icon in the Folders list to open it.

- Right-click an open area of the right pane to display a shortcut menu.

- Point to New on the shortcut menu to display the New submenu (Figure 1–53).

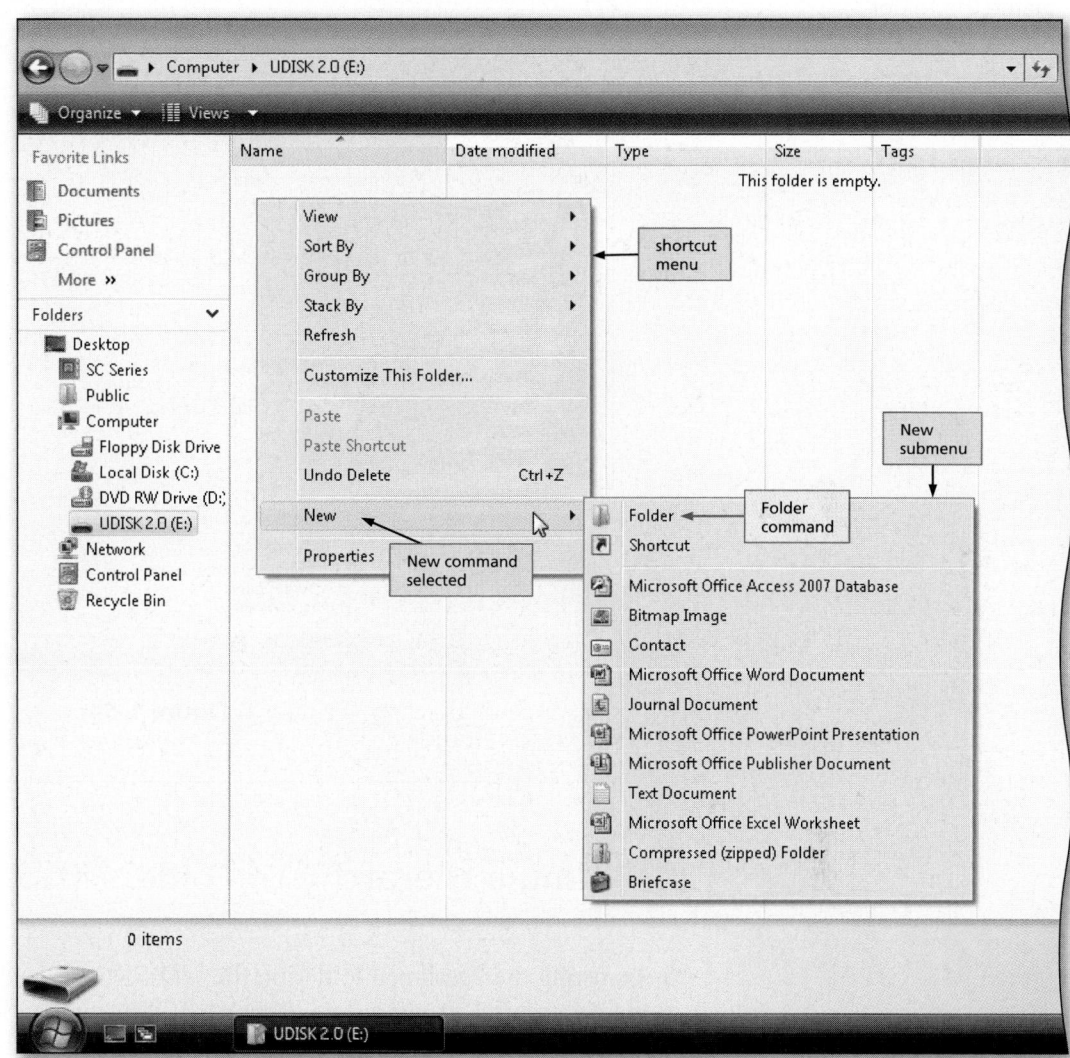

Figure 1–53

2
- Click Folder on the New submenu to display the new Folder icon.

- Type `Freshman` in the text box to name the folder.

- Press the ENTER key to create the Freshman folder on the UDISK 2.0 (E:) drive (Figure 1–54).

Q&A What happens when I press the ENTER key?

The Freshman folder is displayed in the File list, which contains the folder name, date modified, and file folder type.

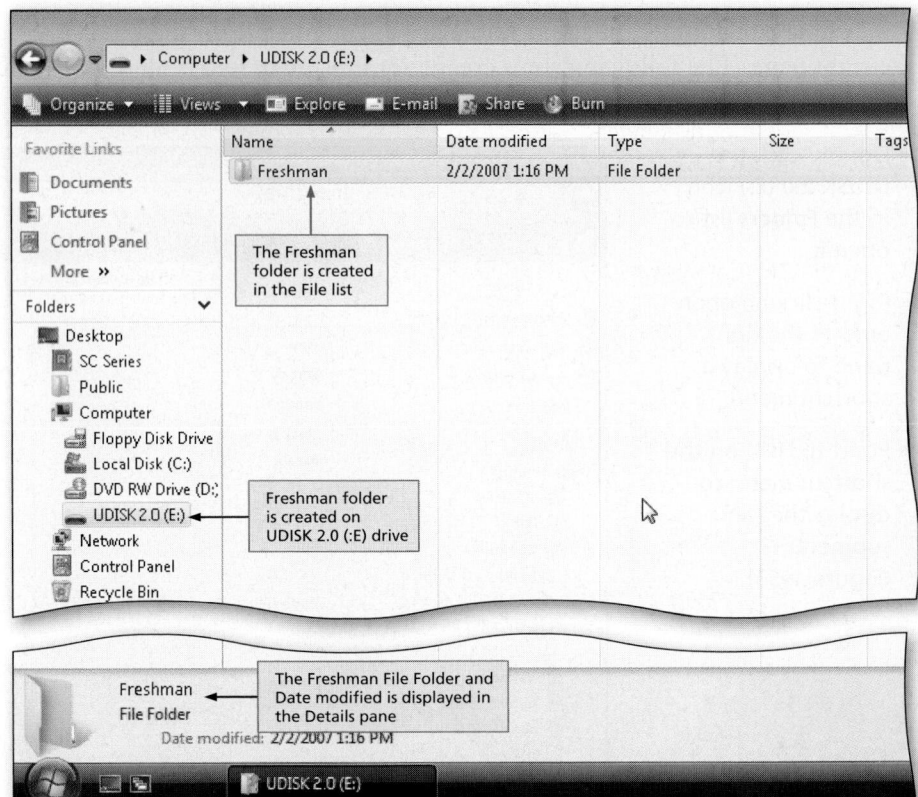

Figure 1–54

Downloading a Hierarchy of Folders into the Freshman Folder

After creating the Freshman folder on the UDISK 2.0 (E:) drive, the remaining folders in the hierarchical structure (see Figure 1–50), starting with the 1st Semester folder, should be downloaded to the Freshman folder. **Downloading** is the process of a computer receiving information, such as a set of files or folders from a Web site, from a server on the Internet. To make the task of creating the folders easier, the folders have been created and stored in a hierarchical structure on the SC Site - Shelly Cashman Series Student Resources Web site.

To Download a Hierarchy of Folders into the Freshman Folder

The following steps download the folders in the hierarchical structure into the Freshman folder.

1. Start Internet Explorer by clicking the Start button on the taskbar and then clicking Internet on the Start menu.

2. Click the Address box on the Address bar, type `scsite.com` in the Address box, and then click the Go button.

3 When the SC Site - Shelly Cashman Series Student Resources Web site is displayed, use the Browse by Subject navigation bar, click Office Suites, and then click Microsoft Office 2007.

4 In the center of the screen, locate your textbook and click the title (for example, Microsoft Office 2007: Introductory Concepts and Techniques, Windows Vista Edition).

5 Scroll down to display the Data Files for Students (Windows) area and then click the Windows Vista Chapter 1 Data Files link.

6 When the File Download – Security Warning dialog box is displayed, click the Run button.

7 When the Internet Explorer – Security Warning dialog box is displayed, click the Run button.

8 When the WinZip Self-Extractor dialog box is displayed, type the removable media drive letter of your removable media drive followed by a colon, backslash, and folder name (Freshman) (for example, E:\Freshman).

9 Click the Unzip button.

10 When Windows displays the WinZip Self-Extractor dialog box, click the OK button.

11 Click the Close button in the WinZip Self-Extractor dialog box.

12 Click the Close button in the SC Site – Shelly Cashman Series Student Resources Web site window (Figure 1–55).

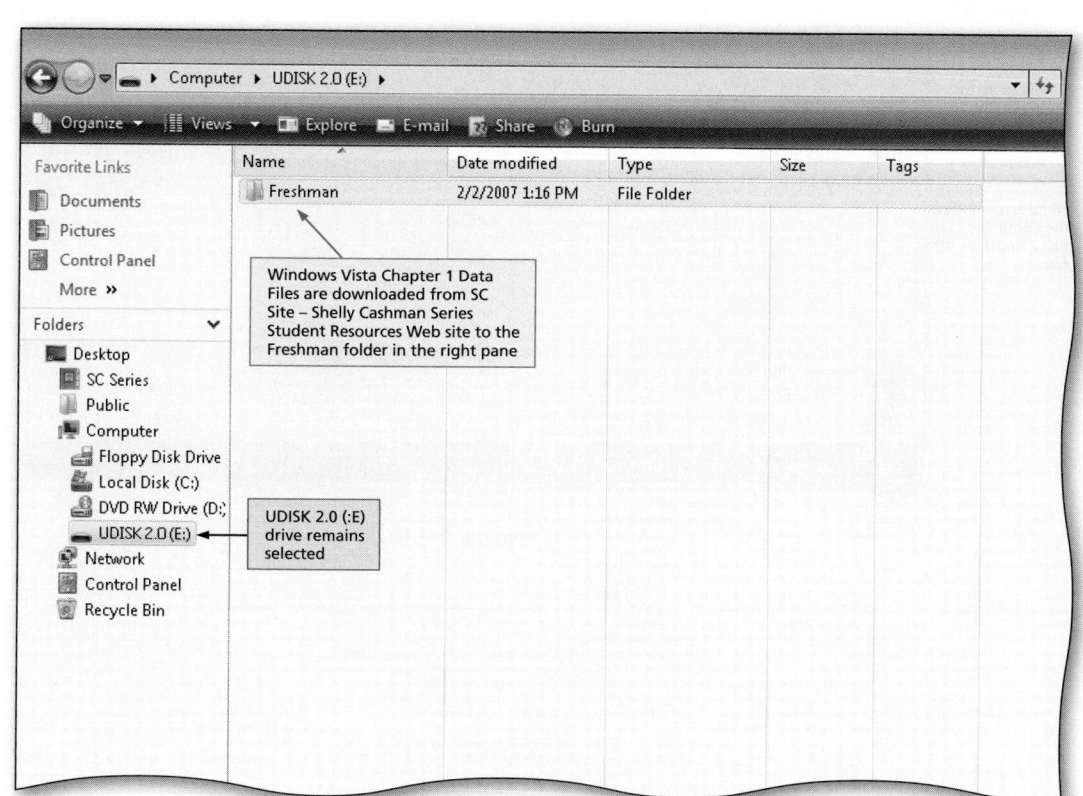

Figure 1–55

To Expand a Drive

Folder Windows display the hierarchy of items in the Folders list and the contents of drives and folders in the right pane. You might want to expand a drive to view its contents in the Folders list. The following step expands a drive.

- Point to any item in the Folders list to display arrows, and then click the white arrow to the left of the UDISK 2.0 (E:) icon in the Folders list to display the Freshman folder.

Q&A

Why are there black arrows and white arrows in the Folders list?

The black arrows represent folders and drives that contain other folders that have been expanded to show their contents. The white arrows represent folders and drives that contain other folders that have not been expanded.

- Click the white arrow next to the Freshman folder, and then click the white arrow next to the 1st Semester folder to display its contents (Figure 1–56).

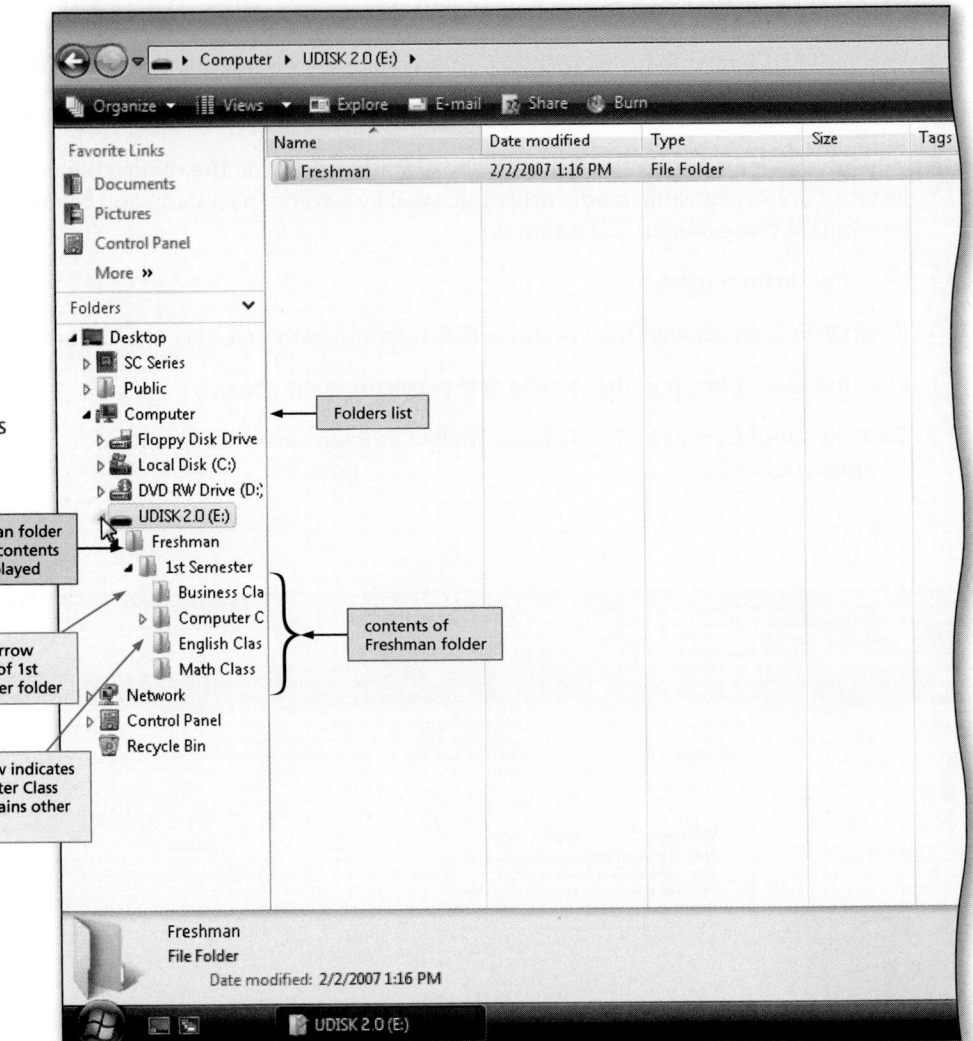

Figure 1–56

Other Ways
1. Double-click drive icon in Folders list
2. Select drive to expand using ARROW keys, press RIGHT ARROW on keyboard
3. Select drive to expand, press RIGHT ARROW

To Collapse a Folder

When a black arrow is displayed to the left of a folder icon in the Folders list, the folder is expanded and shows all the folders it contains. The following step collapses the 1st Semester folder.

1

● Click the black arrow to the left of the 1st Semester folder icon in the Folders list to collapse the 1st Semester folder (Figure 1–57).

Q&A

Why is the 1st Semester folder indented below the Freshman folder in the Folders list?

The folder is indented below the Freshman icon to show that the folder is contained within the Freshman folder.

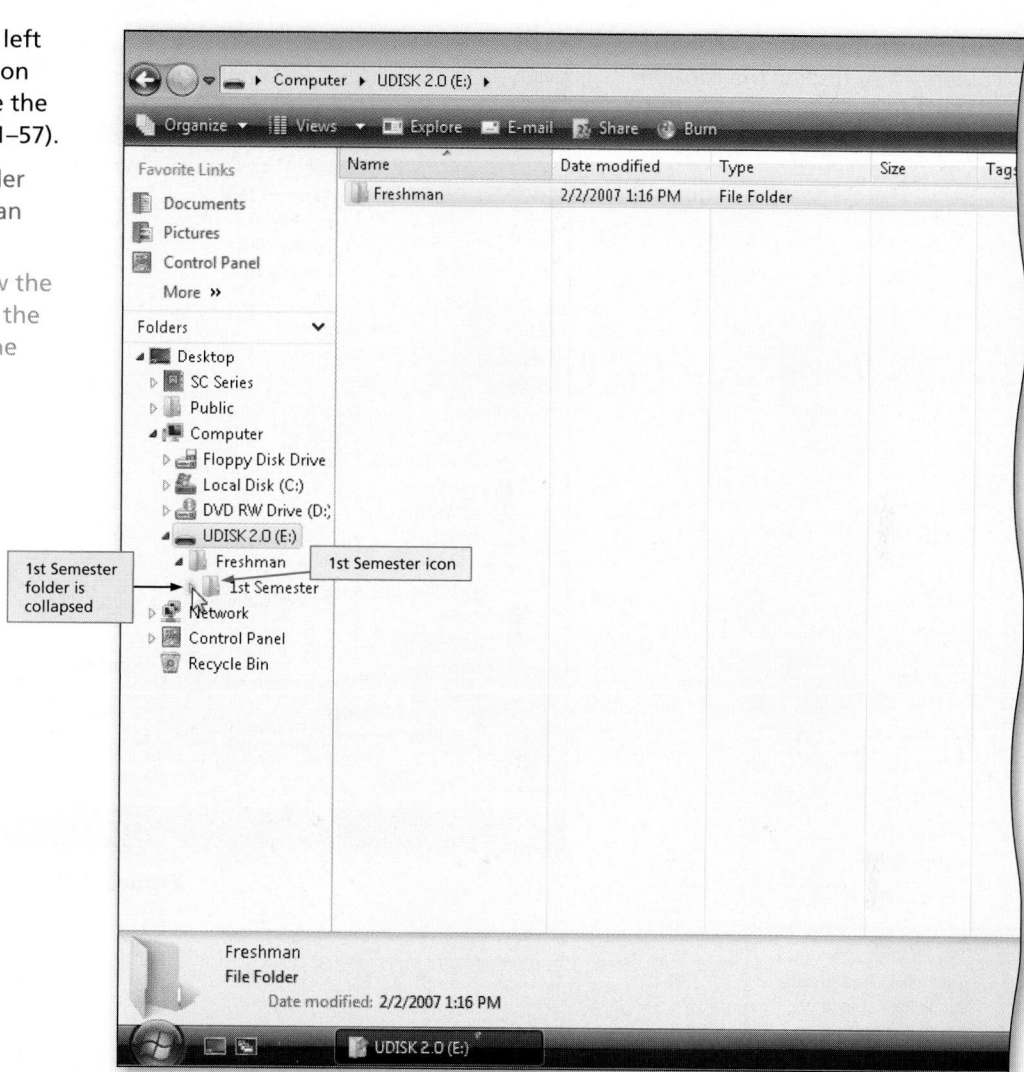

Figure 1–57

Other Ways

1. Double-click folder icon in Folders list
2. Select folder to collapse using ARROW keys, press LEFT ARROW on keyboard
3. Select folder to collapse, press LEFT ARROW

To Display the Contents of a Folder

Clicking a folder icon in the Folders list displays the contents of the drive or folder in the File list and displays the path in the Address bar. The following step displays the contents of the 1st Semester folder.

1

- Click the 1st Semester icon in the Folders list to display the contents of the 1st Semester folder in the File list (Figure 1–58).

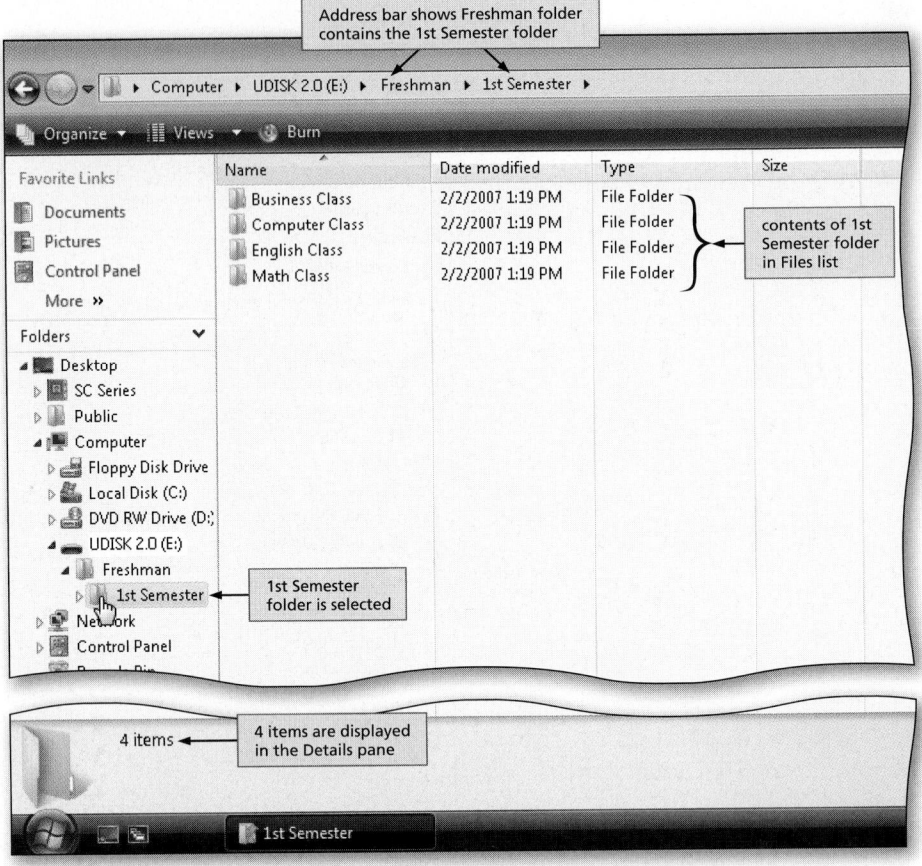

Figure 1–58

Other Ways

1. Right-click 1st Semester icon, click Explore on shortcut menu

Creating a Document and Folder Using WordPad

The Freshman folder was created in the UDISK 2.0 (E:) drive when you downloaded the files. You also can create a folder anytime you save a file in a Windows application. For example, you can use WordPad to create a document and then save the new document in a folder. **WordPad** is a word processing program included with Windows Vista that allows you to create a limited variety of personal and business documents.

As one of the programs in the Accessories list, one method to start the WordPad application is to display the Start menu, click All Programs, click Accessories, and click WordPad in the Accessories list.

An easier method to start WordPad is to use the Start Search box on the Start menu. The **Start Search** box allows you to find a specific application, file, e-mail, or Internet favorite by typing the first few letters in the Start Search box at the bottom of the Start menu.

To Start WordPad Using the Start Search Box

Assume you want to create a WordPad document that lists your homework for Friday, April 11. The first step is to start the WordPad application using the Start Search box. The following steps find and then start WordPad based on using the Start Search box at the bottom of the Start menu.

1

• Open the Start menu.

• Type w (the first letter in the WordPad name) in the Start Search box on the Start menu to display a list of programs, favorites, and history (Figure 1–59).

Q&A What is displayed on the Start menu when I type the letter w?

A list of programs, favorites, and history. The WordPad program does not appear yet. As you type the entire program name, fewer selections remain in the list until you find your selection or no items match your search term.

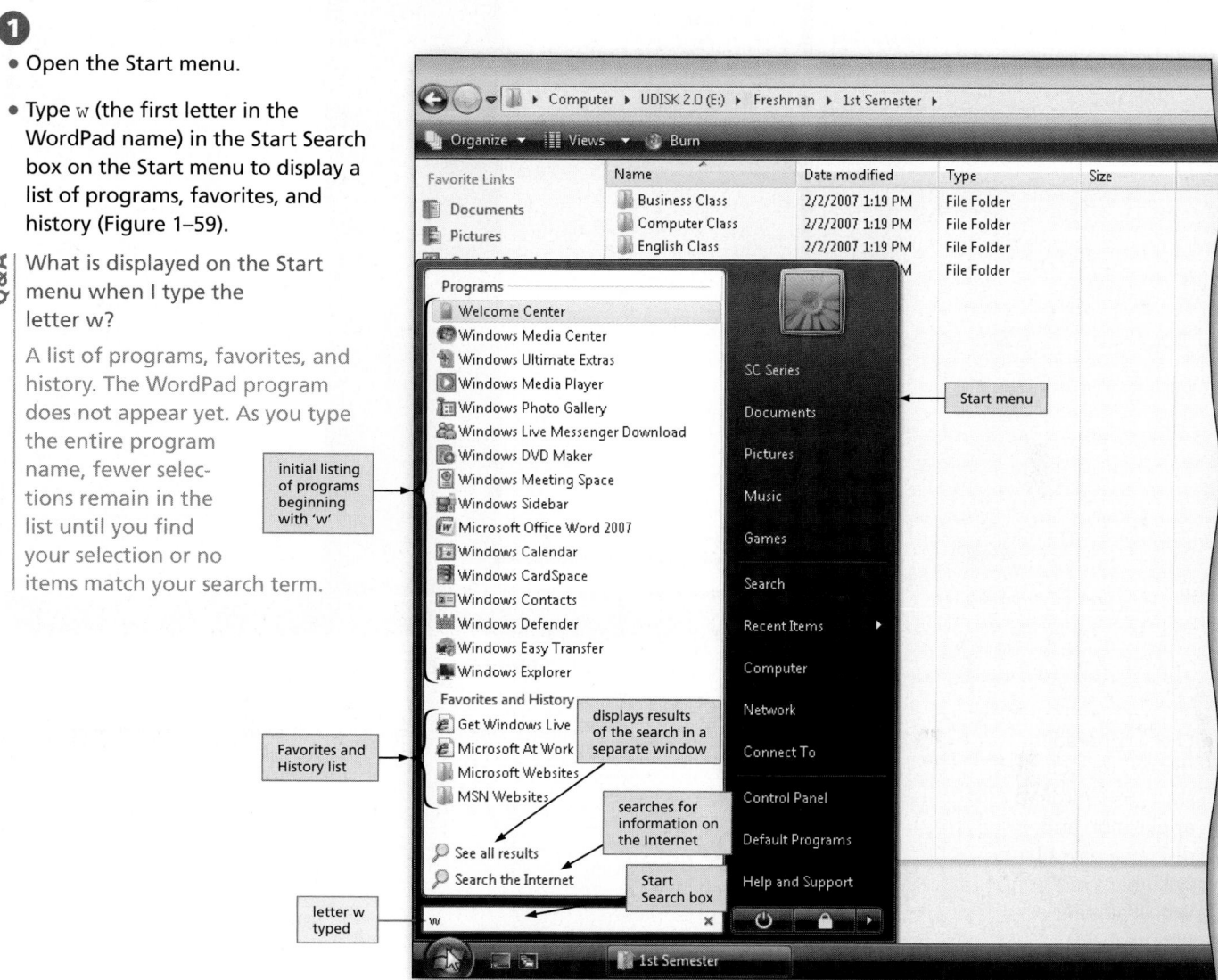

Figure 1–59

- Type the letter o (the second letter in the WordPad name) in the Start Search box on the Start menu to display a list of programs, favorites, history, and files (Figure 1–60).

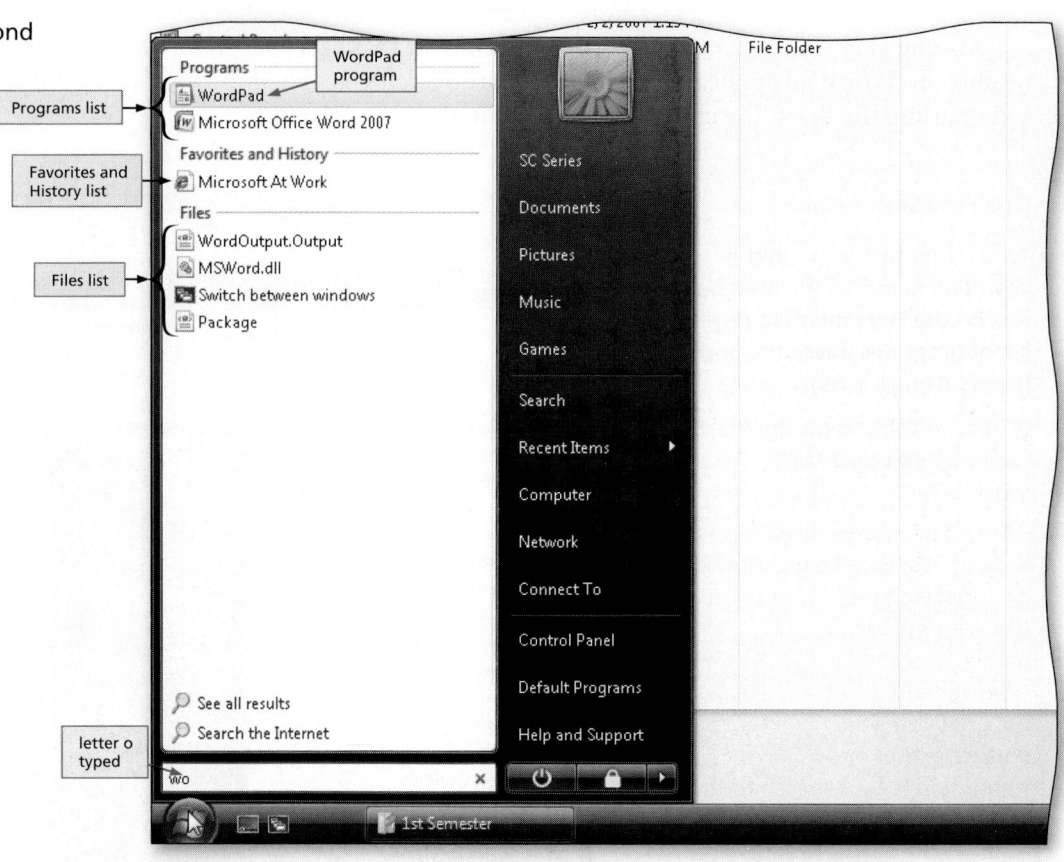

Figure 1–60

- Click WordPad in the Programs list to start the WordPad application and display a new blank document in the WordPad window (Figure 1–61).

- If the WordPad window is not maximized, click the Maximize button on the title bar to maximize the window.

Q&A

Could I continue typing the remainder of the letters in the WordPad name?

Yes. To start the program you still need to click WordPad in the Programs list to start the WordPad application.

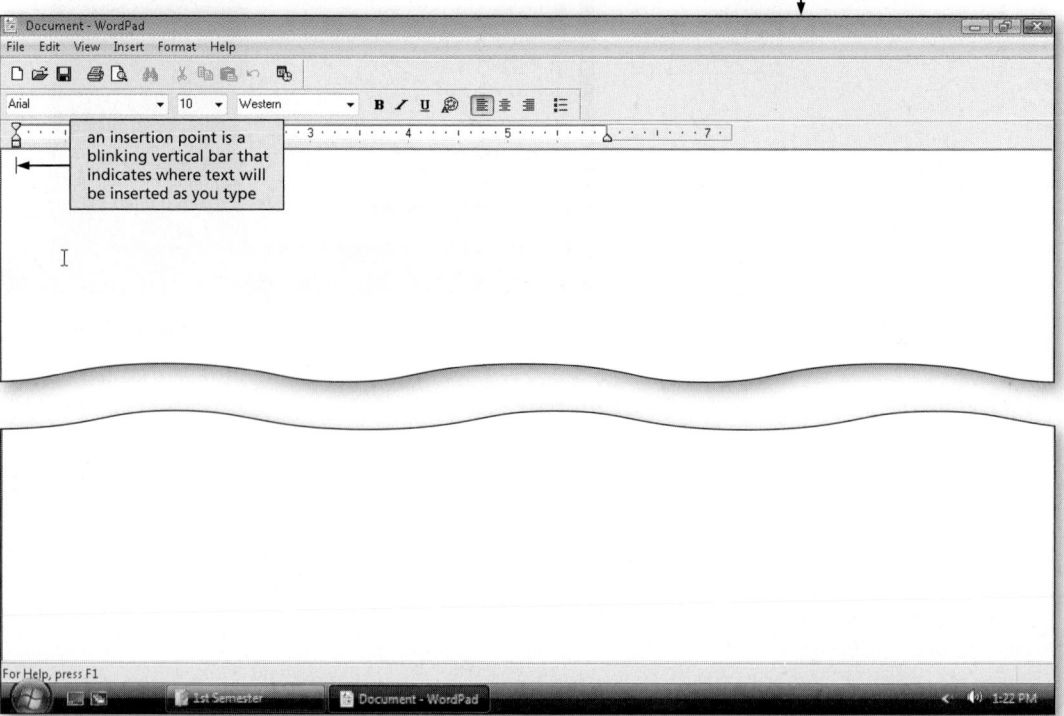

Figure 1–61

To Type Text

After starting WordPad, you can enter the text for a new document. To enter text in the document, you type on the keyboard. The following steps enter text in the new WordPad document.

- Type `Friday, April 11` and then press the ENTER key twice.

- Type `Finish - The Bike Delivers Data Base` and then press the ENTER key.

- Type `Read - Next Project` and then press the ENTER key (Figure 1–62).

Q&A

What if I make an error while typing?

You can press the BACKSPACE key to delete the error and then retype the text correctly.

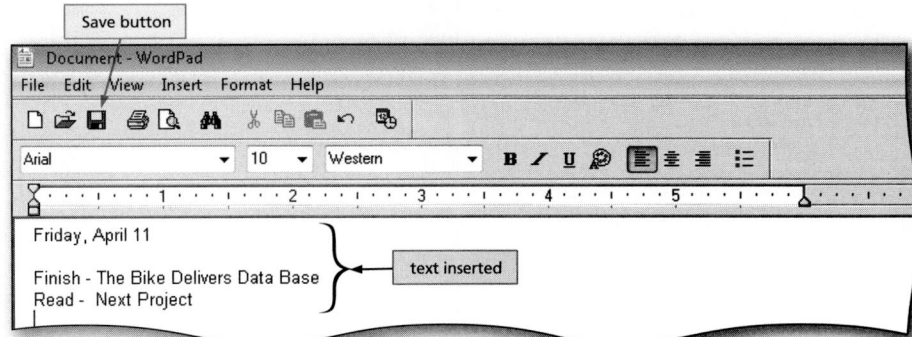

Figure 1–62

To Save a WordPad Document in a New Folder

After typing the text of a WordPad document, you can create a folder in which to save the document, and then save the document in the created folder. The following steps save the new document in a created folder named Homework, with a name of Friday, April 11. The Homework folder is created within the Computer Class folder (see the hierarchy in Figure 1–50 on page 36).

1

- Click the Save button on the Standard toolbar to display the Save As dialog box.

- If necessary, double-click the Save As dialog box title bar to maximize the Save As dialog box (Figure 1–63).

Q&A

Why is the Document file name selected in the File name text box?

It is selected in the File name text box as the default file name.

You can change the default file name by immediately typing the new name.

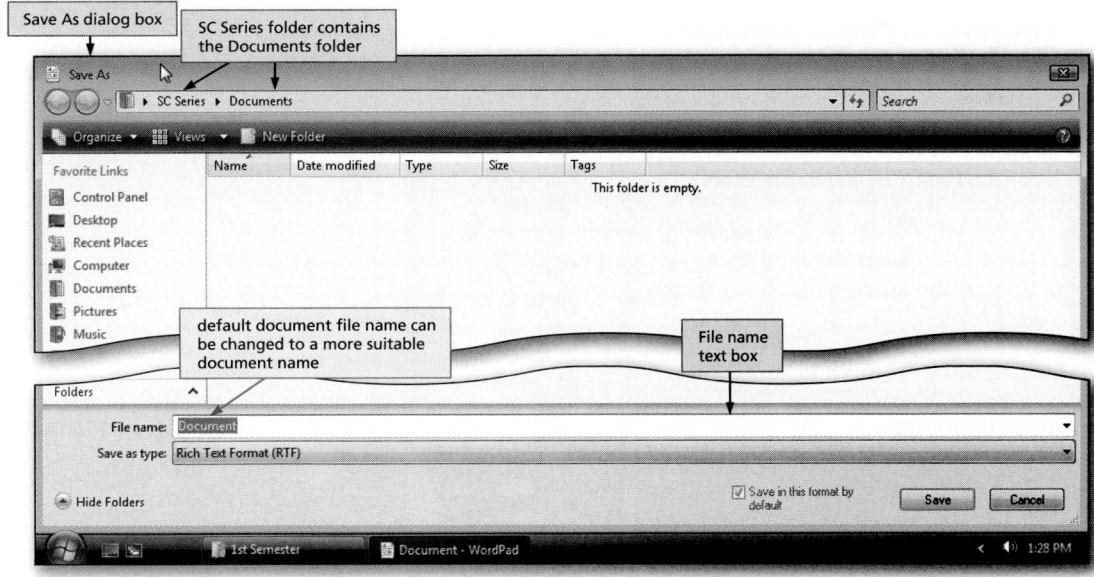

Figure 1–63

2

- Type Friday, April 11 in the File name text box. Do not press the ENTER key after typing the file name (Figure 1–64).

Q&A

What happens if I press the ENTER key after typing the file name?

If you press the ENTER key, the Save As dialog box closes and the file is saved in the Documents folder. If you want to save the file in a folder other than the Documents folder, you must select the desired folder.

Q&A

What if the Navigation pane does not appear in the Save As dialog box?

Click the Browse Folders button.

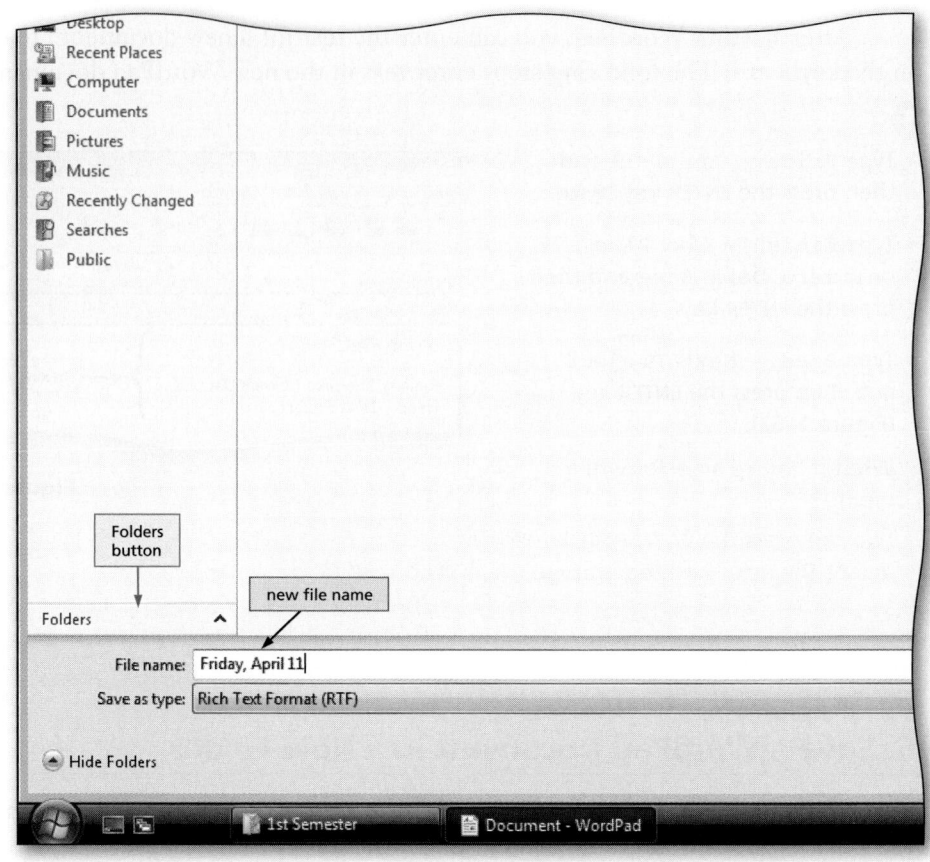

Figure 1–64

3

- If necessary, click the Folders button to expand the Folders list.

- Click the white arrow next to the Computer icon in the Folders list to display a list of available disks and drives (Figure 1–65).

Q&A

What if I don't see the white arrows in the Folders list?

To display both the white and black arrows, point to any item in the Folders list.

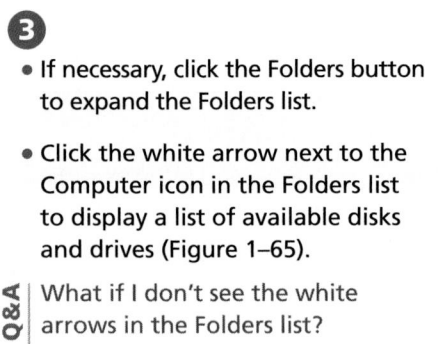

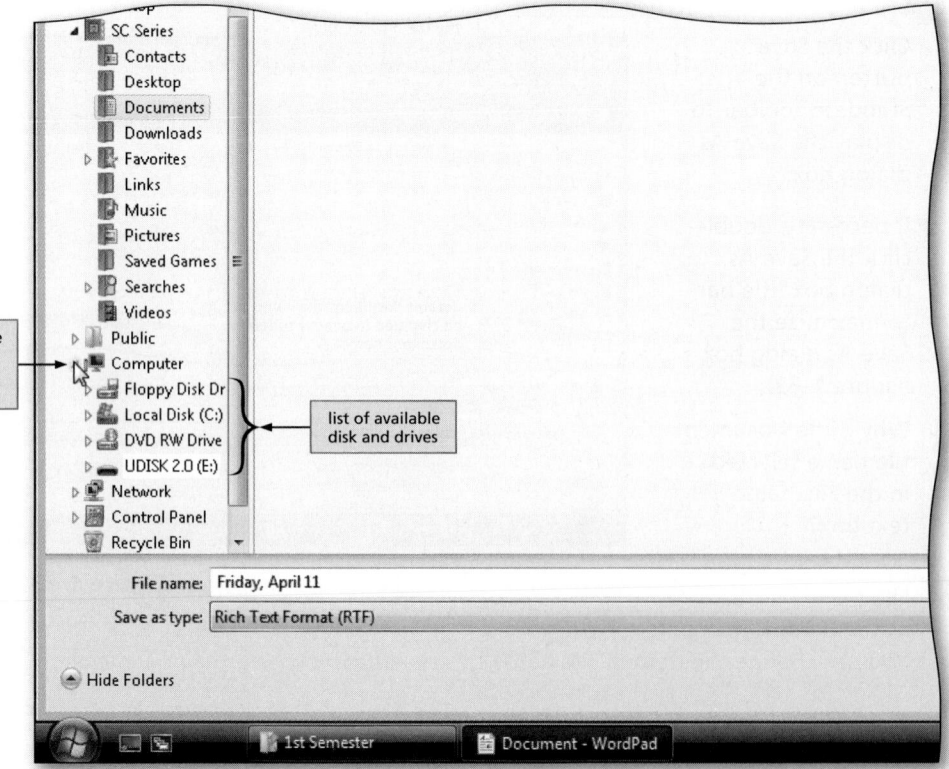

Figure 1–65

4

- Click UDISK 2.0 (E:) in the Folders list to display the contents of the UDISK 2.0 (E:) folder in the File list (Figure 1–66).

Q&A

Is it OK if my list of drives and folders is different from the one in Figure 1–66?

Yes. Folders and drives can be unique for each computer.

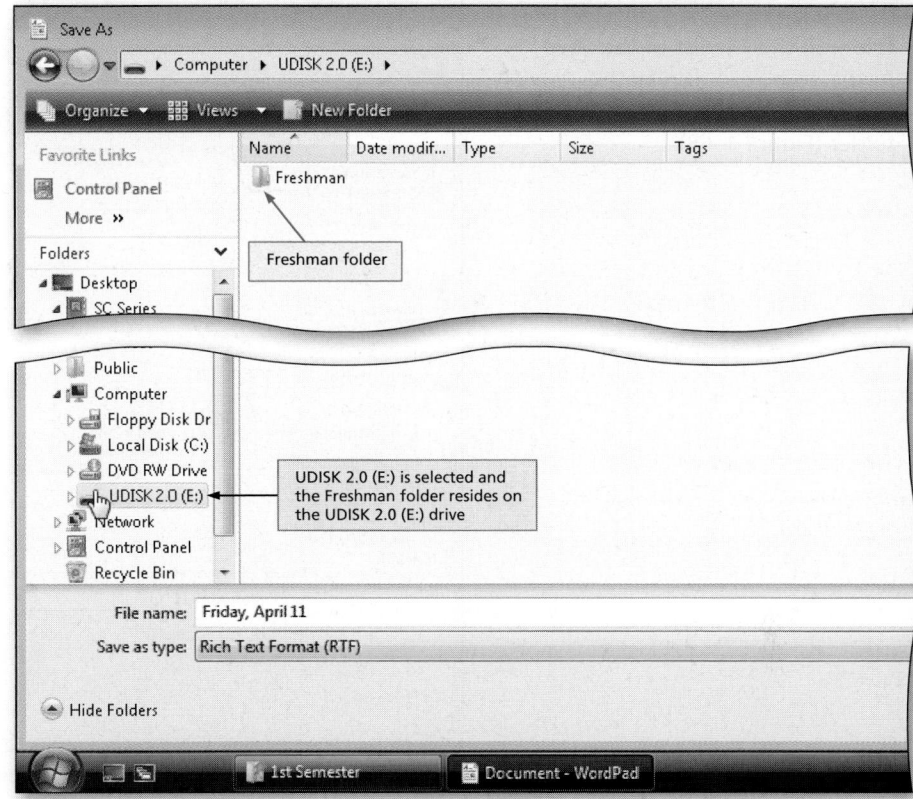

Figure 1–66

5

- Double-click the Freshman folder in the File list of the Save As dialog box to display the 1st Semester folder in the File list (Figure 1–67).

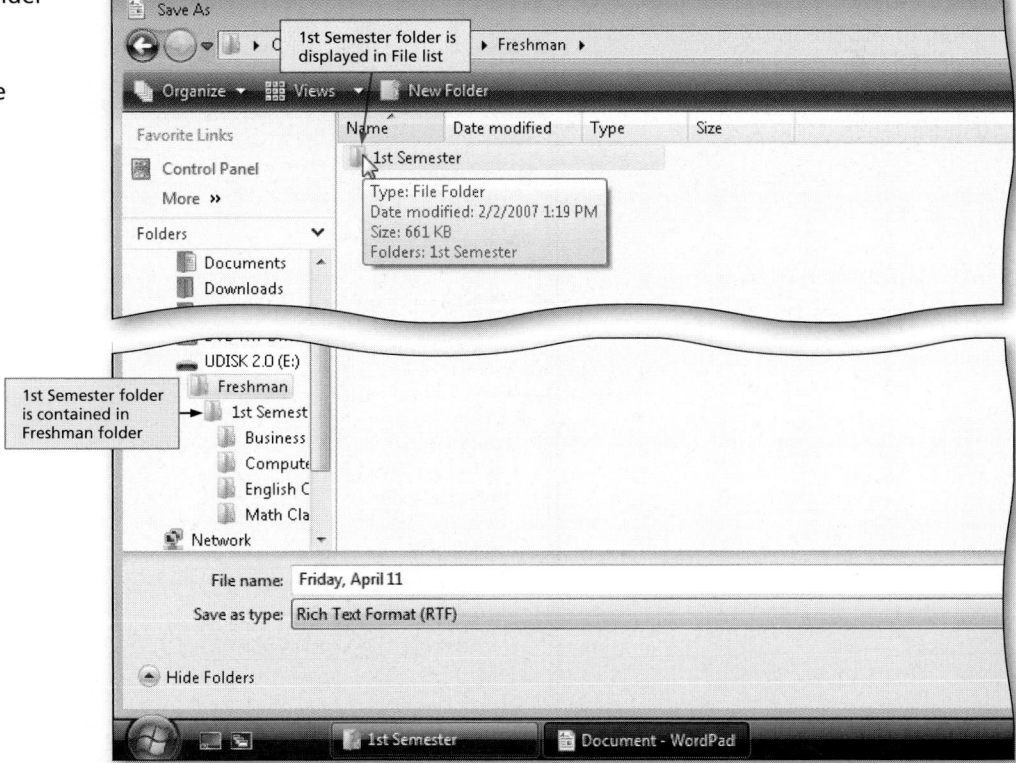

Figure 1–67

6

• Double-click the 1st Semester folder in the File list of the Save As dialog box to display the contents of the 1st Semester folder (Figure 1–68)

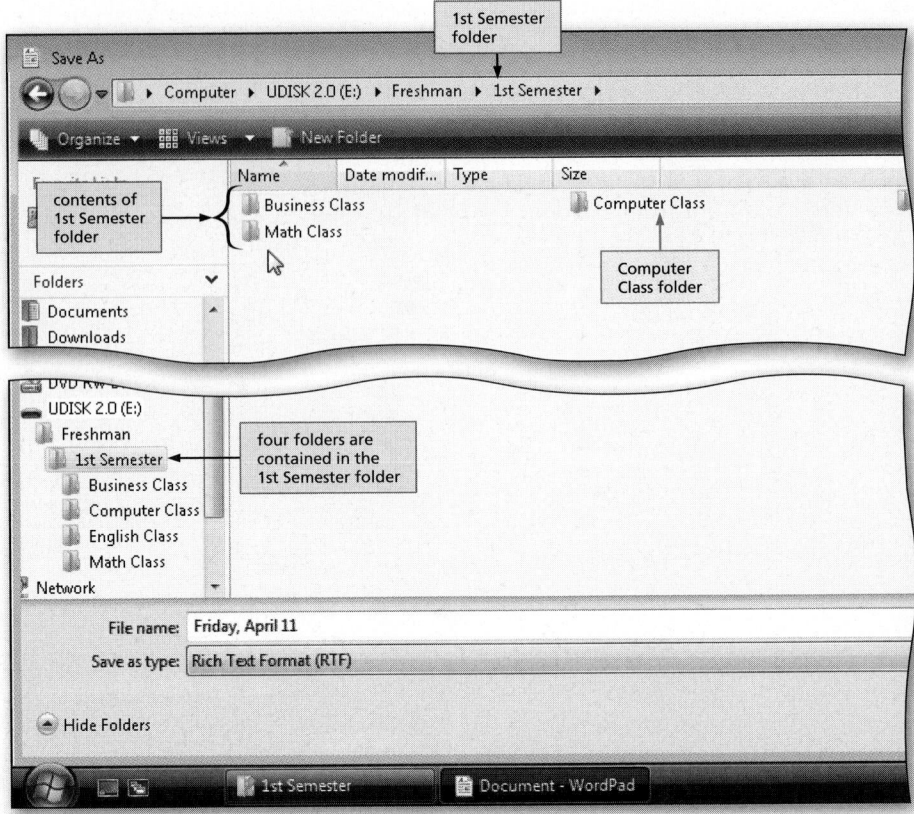

Figure 1–68

7

• Double-click the Computer Class folder in the File list of the Save As dialog box to display the contents of the Computer Class folder (Figure 1–69).

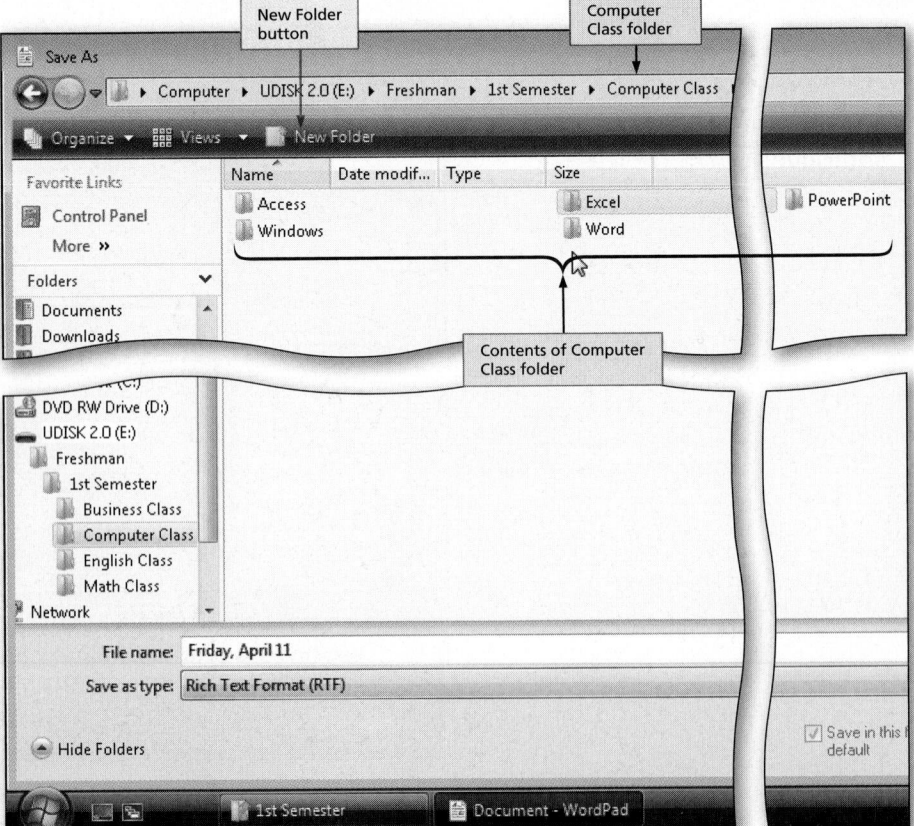

Figure 1–69

8

- Click the New Folder button on the Save As dialog toolbar to create a new folder within the Computer Class folder.

- Type `Homework` as the name of the folder and then press the ENTER key (Figure 1–70).

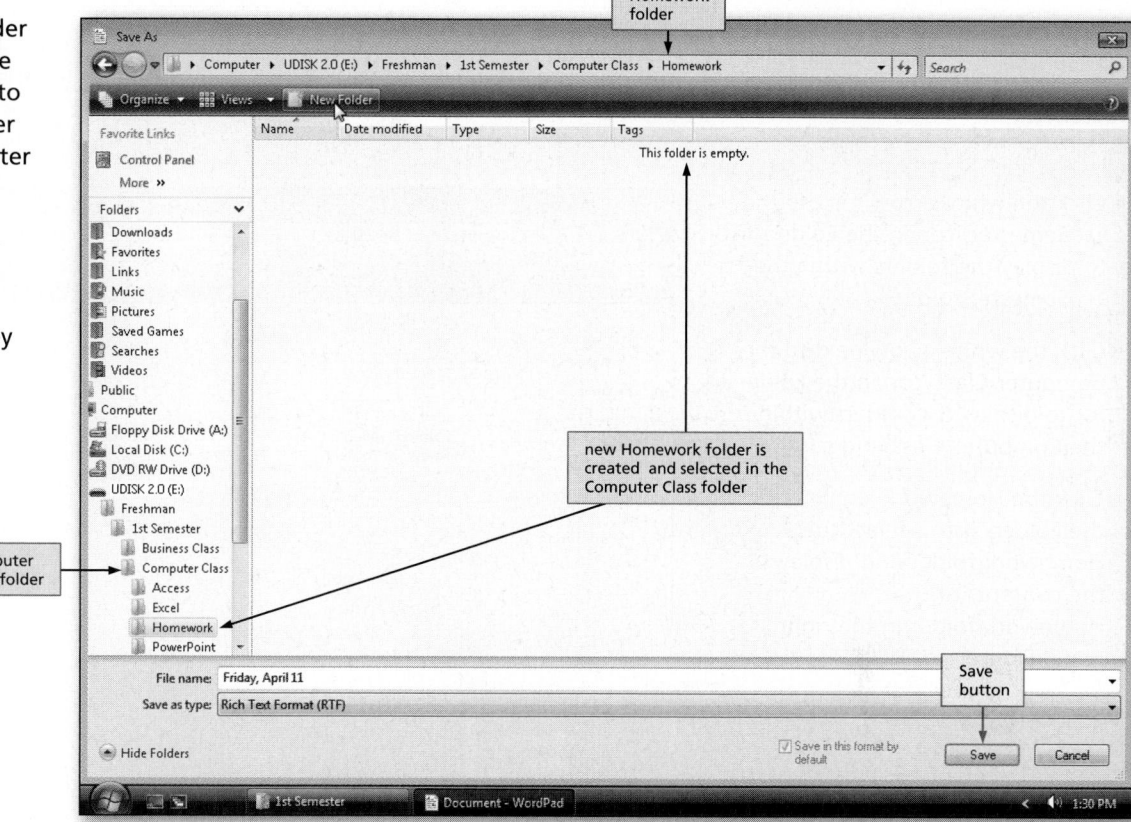

Figure 1–70

9

- Click the Save button in the Save As dialog box to save the Friday, April 11 document to its new location in the Homework folder (Figure 1–71).

- Click the Close button in the Friday, April 11 - WordPad window to close the window.

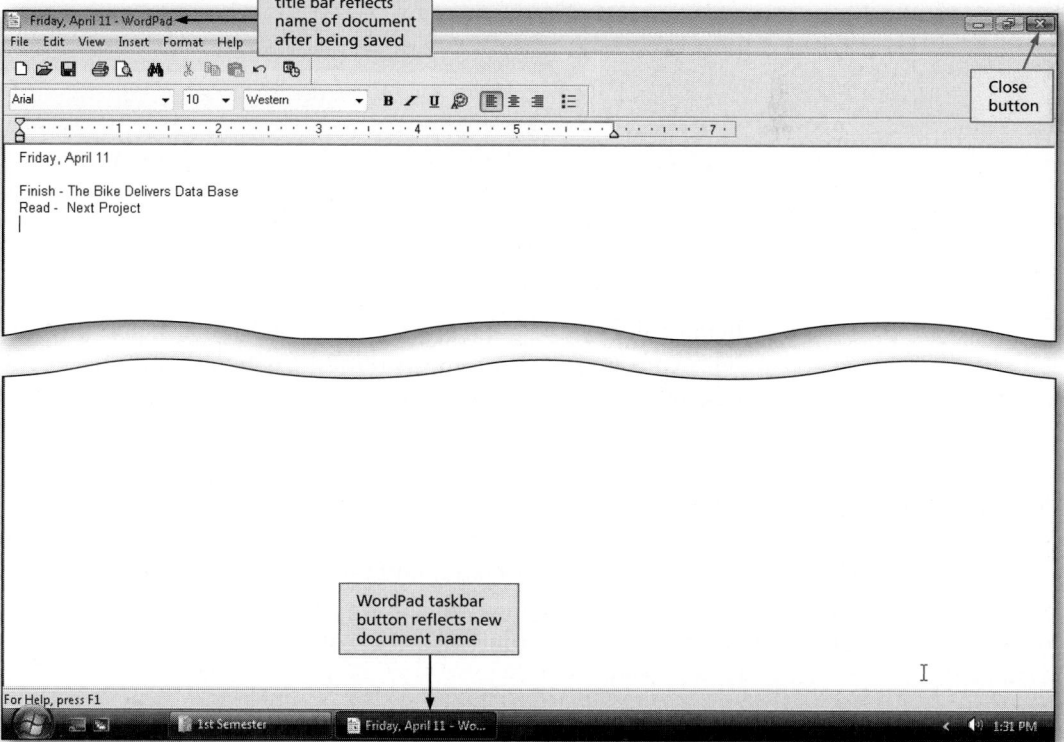

Figure 1–71

To Verify the Contents of a Folder

After saving the Friday, April 11 document in the Homework folder, you can verify that the document was correctly saved in the Homework folder. The following step verifies the Homework folder contains the Friday, April 11 document.

- Click the white arrow next to the 1st Semester icon in the Folders list to display the folders within the 1st Semester folder.

- Click the white arrow next to the Computer Class icon in the Folders list to display the folders within the Computer Class folder.

- Click the Homework icon in the Folders list to select the Homework folder and display the contents of the Homework folder in the right pane (Figure 1–72).

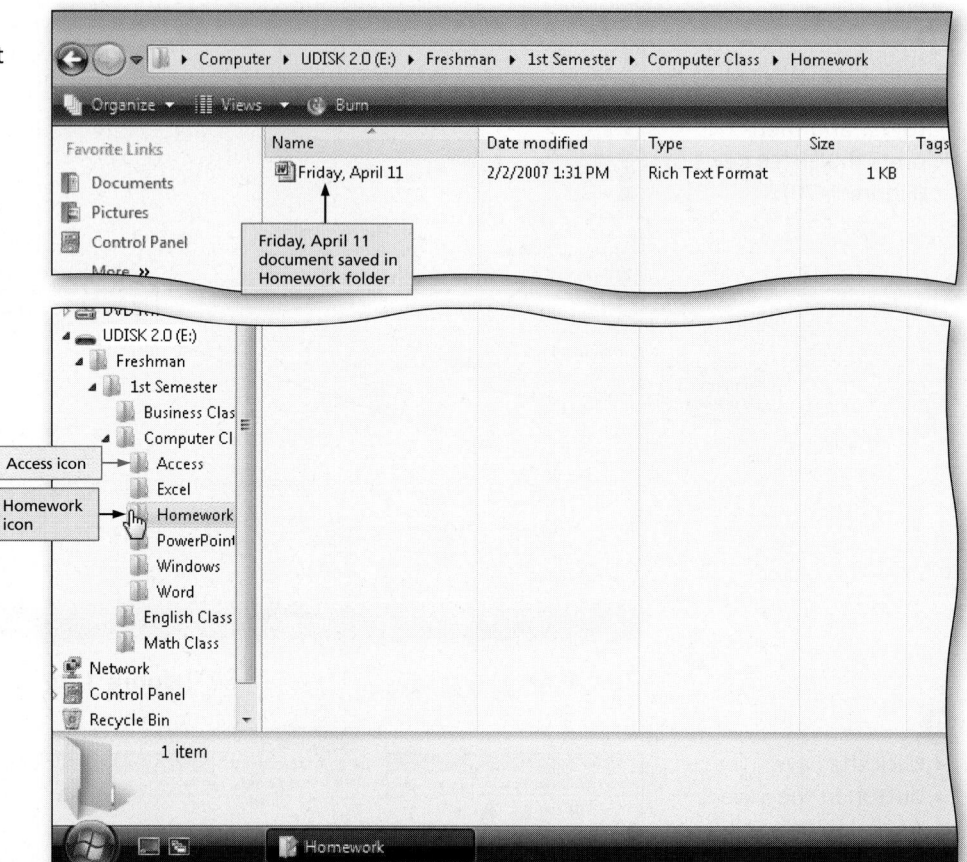

Figure 1–72

File Management

Being able to manage the files on the computer is one of the most important computer skills you can have. **File management** includes copying, moving, renaming, and deleting files and folders on the computer.

To Copy a File by Right-Dragging

When copying files, the drive and folder containing the files to be copied are called the **source drive** and **source folder**, respectively. The drive and folder to which the files are copied are called the **destination drive** and **destination folder**, respectively. The Access folder contains two Access database files (SciFi Scene and The Bike Delivers).

The following steps on the next page show one method of copying files - right-drag a file icon from the right pane to a folder or drive icon in the Folders list. The following steps on the next page copy the The Bike Delivers file from the Access folder (source folder) to the Homework (destination folder). The UDISK 2.0 (E:) drive is both the source drive and the destination drive.

1

- Click the Access folder in the Folders list to select the Access folder and display its contents in the right pane (Figure 1–73).

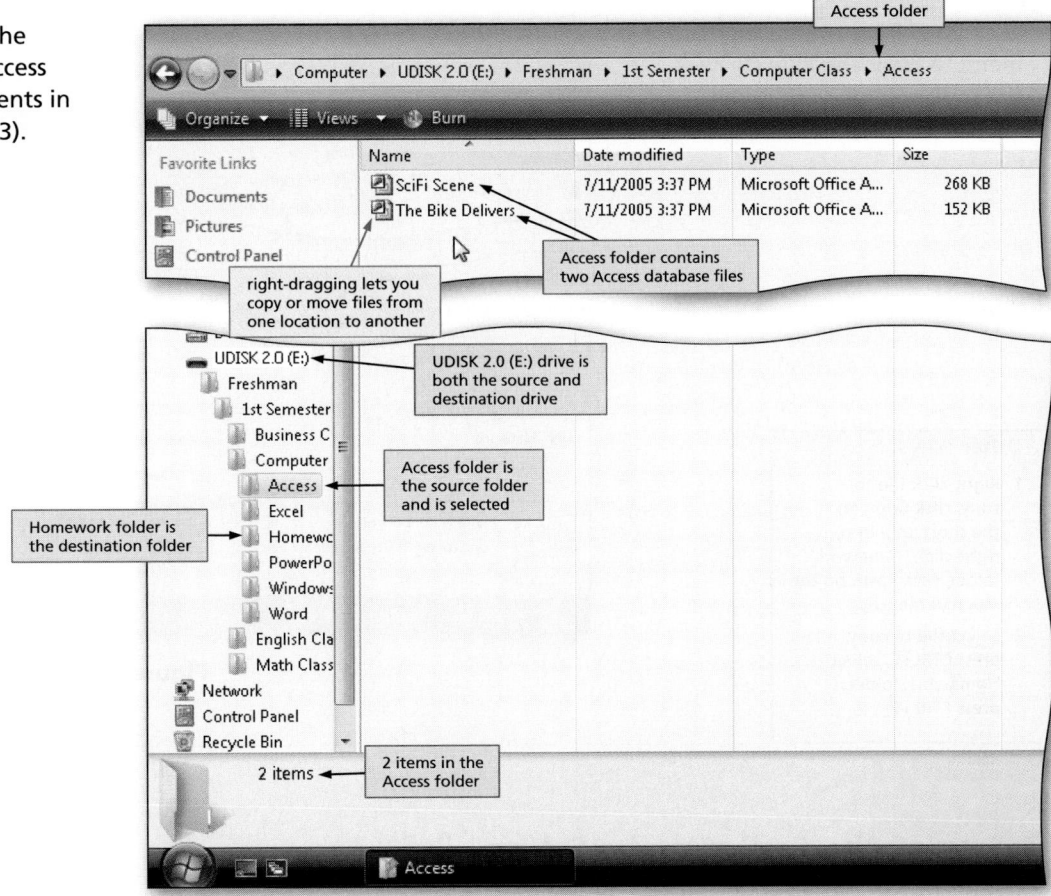

Figure 1–73

2

- Right-drag the The Bike Delivers icon from the right pane onto the Homework folder icon in the Folders list to open the shortcut menu (Figure 1–74).

Q&A

What should I do if I right-drag a file to the wrong folder?

Click Cancel on the shortcut menu, and then right-drag the file to the correct folder.

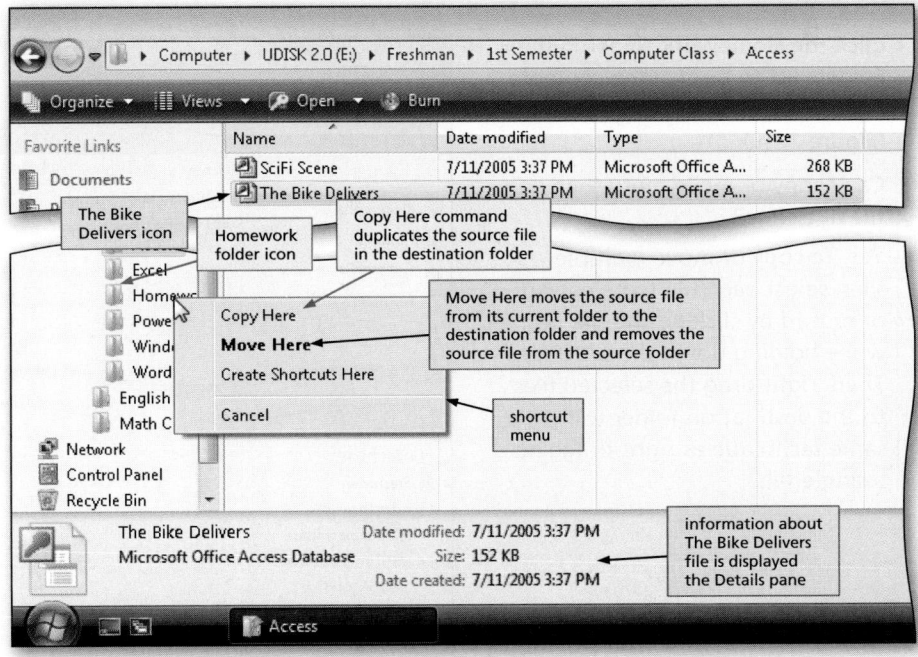

Figure 1–74

- Click Copy Here on the shortcut menu to copy The Bike Delivers file to the Homework folder.

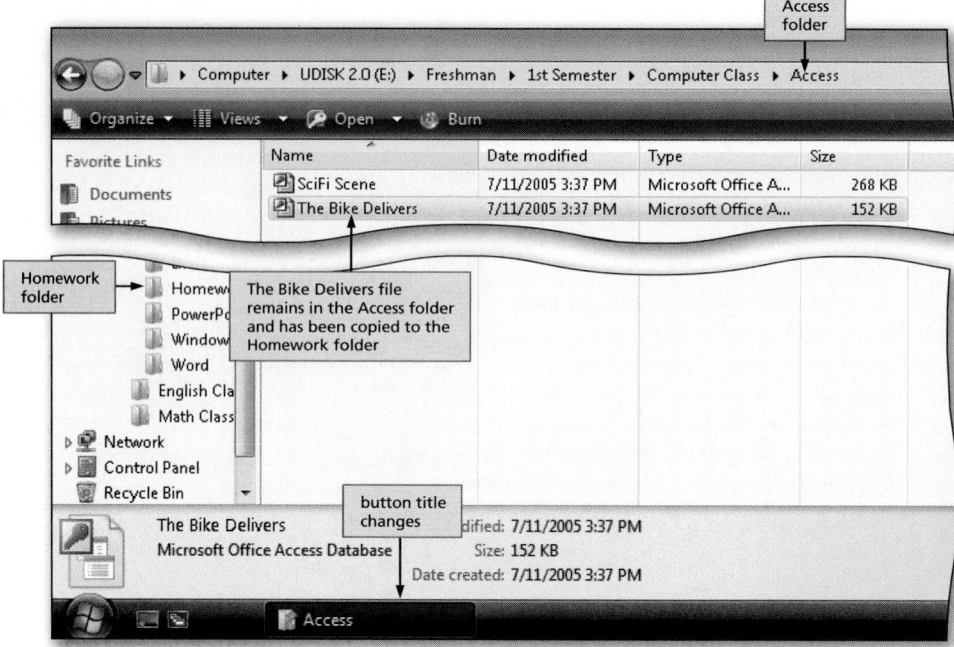

Figure 1–75

Other Ways

1. Right-click file to copy, click Copy on the shortcut menu, right-click Homework folder, click Paste on the shortcut menu

2. Select file to copy, press CTRL+C, select Homework folder, press CTRL+V

To Display the Contents of a Folder

After copying a file, you might want to examine the folder or drive where the file was copied to ensure it was copied properly. The following step displays the contents of the Homework folder.

- Click the Homework folder in the Folders list to display the contents of the Homework folder (Figure 1–76).

Q&A

Can I copy or move more than one file at a time?

Yes. To copy or move multiple files, select each file to be copied or moved by clicking the file icon while holding down the CTRL key. Then, right-drag the selected files to the destination folder using the same technique as right-dragging a single file.

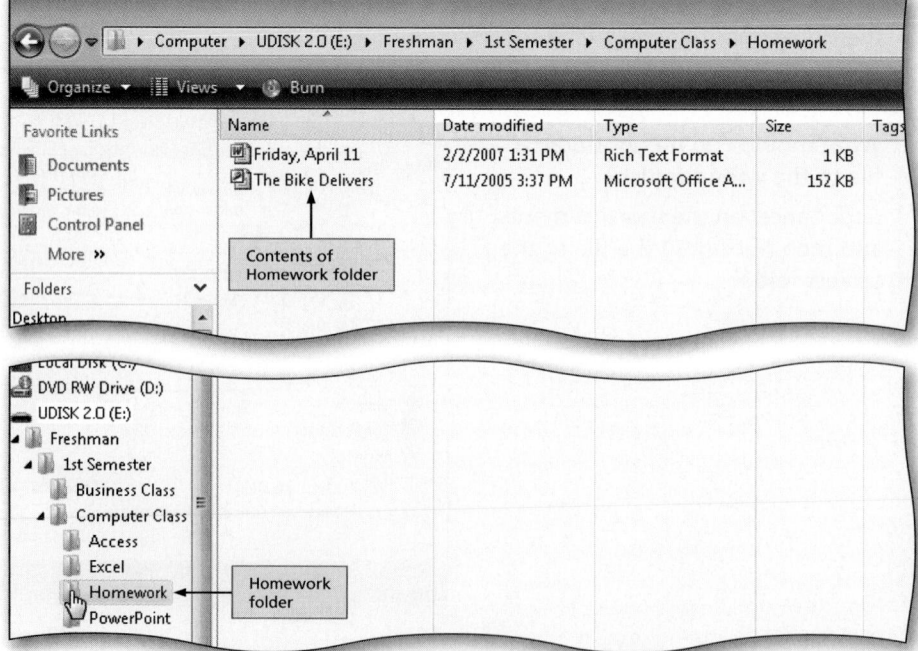

Figure 1–76

To Rename a File

In some circumstances, you may want to rename a file or a folder. This could occur when you want to distinguish a file in one folder or drive from a copy, or if you decide you need a better name to identify a file. The Word folder in Figure 1–77 contains the three Word documents (Barn and Silo, Fall Harvest, and Lake at Sunset). In this case, you decide to change the Fall Harvest name to Great Fall Harvest. The following steps change the name of the Fall Harvest file in the Word folder to Great Fall Harvest.

1
- Click the Word folder in the left pane to display the three files it contains in the right pane.

- Right-click the Fall Harvest icon in the right pane to select the Fall Harvest icon and display a shortcut menu (Figure 1–77).

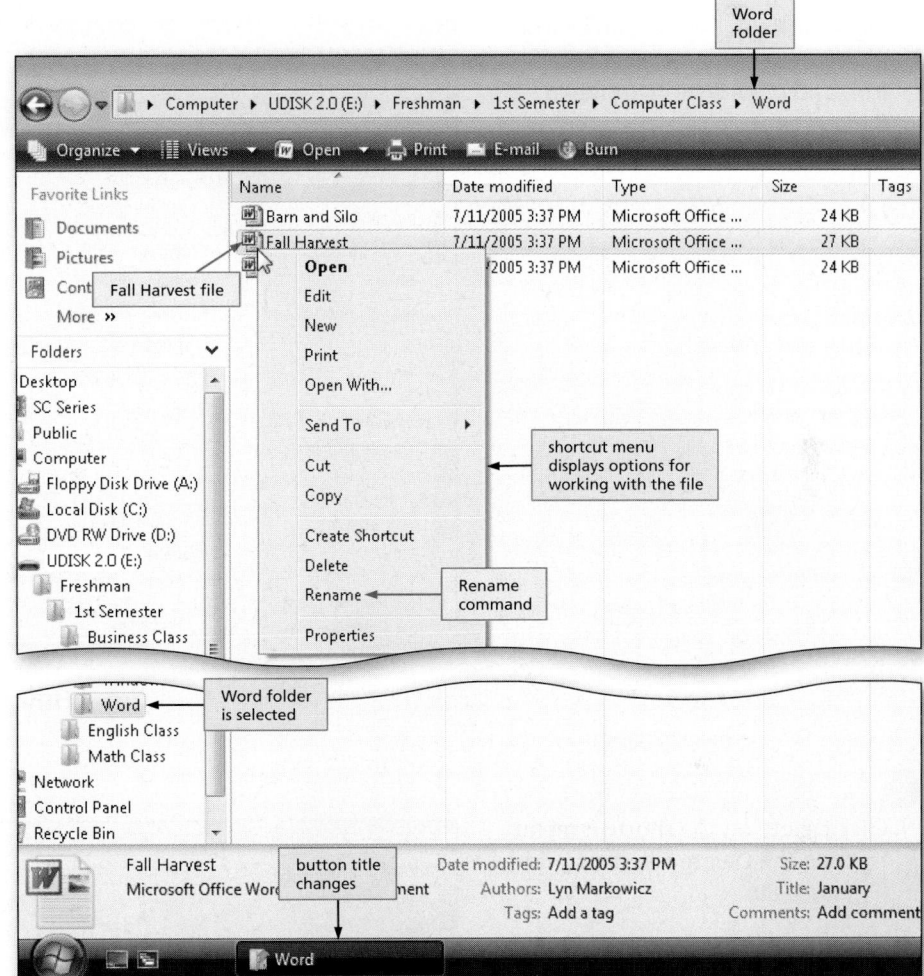

Figure 1–77

2
- Click Rename on the shortcut menu to select the file name for renaming.

- Type `Great Fall Harvest` and then press the ENTER key (Figure 1–78).

Q&A Are there any risks to renaming files that are located on the hard disk?

If you inadvertently rename a file that is associated with certain programs, the programs may not be able to find the file and, therefore, may not execute properly. Always use caution when renaming files.

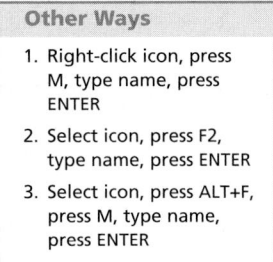

Other Ways

1. Right-click icon, press M, type name, press ENTER

2. Select icon, press F2, type name, press ENTER

3. Select icon, press ALT+F, press M, type name, press ENTER

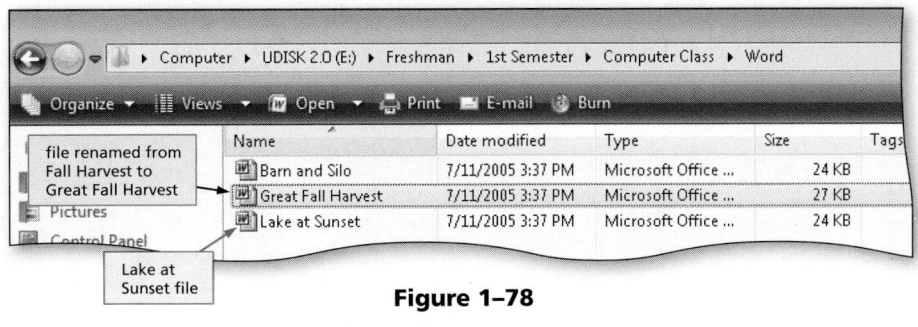

Figure 1–78

To Delete a File by Right-Clicking

A final task you may want to perform is to delete a file. Exercise extreme caution when deleting a file or files. When you delete a file from a hard drive, the deleted file is stored in the Recycle Bin where you can recover it until you empty the Recycle Bin. If you delete a file from removable media, the file is gone permanently once you delete it. The following steps delete the Lake at Sunset file.

- Right-click the Lake at Sunset icon in the right pane to select the icon and open a shortcut menu (Figure 1–79).

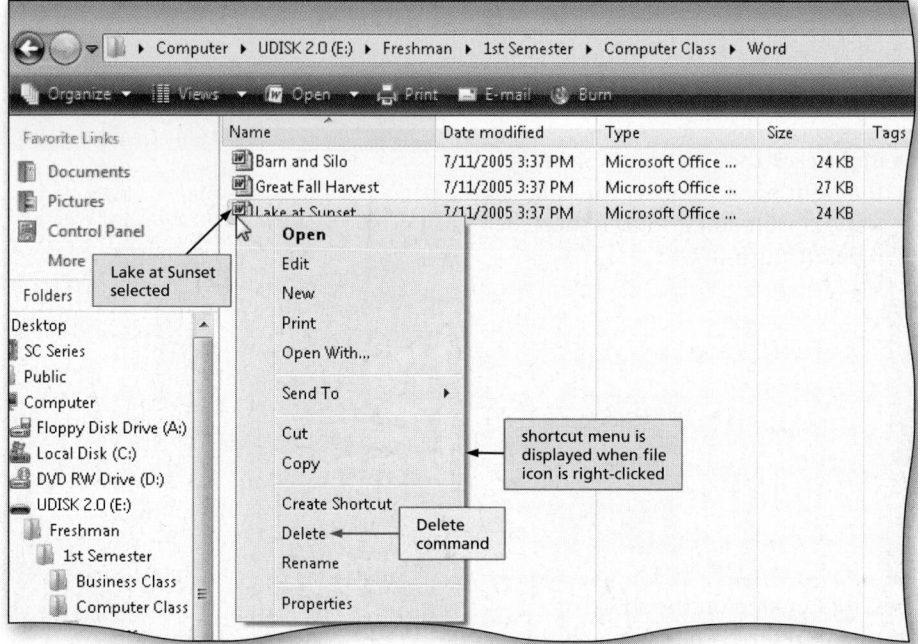

Figure 1–79

- Click Delete on the shortcut menu to open the Delete File dialog box (Figure 1–80).

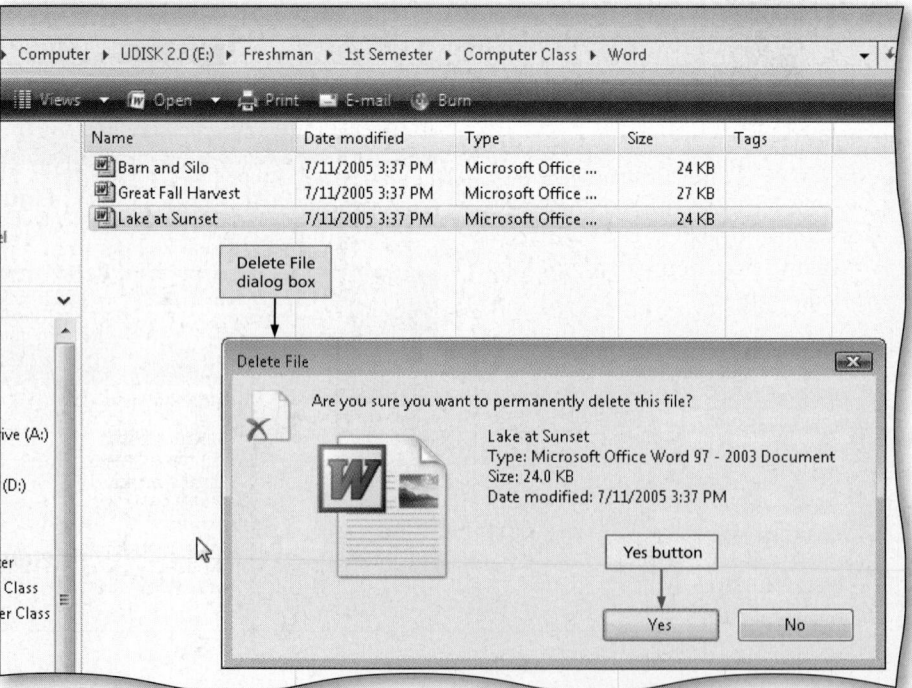

Figure 1–80

❸

- Click the Yes button in the Delete File dialog box to remove the Lake at Sunset file (Figure 1–81).

Q&A Can I use this same technique to delete a folder?

Yes. Right-click the folder and then click Delete on the shortcut menu. When you delete a folder, all the files and folders contained in the folder you are deleting, together with any files and folders on lower hierarchical levels, are deleted as well.

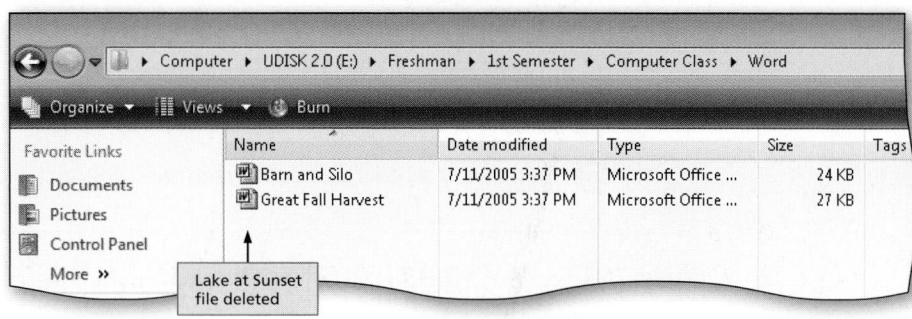

Figure 1–81

To Close Expanded Folders

Sometimes, after you have completed work with expanded folders, you will want to close the expanded folders while still leaving the Word window open. The following steps close the Computer Class folder, 1st Semester folder, Freshman folder, and UDISK 2.0 (E:) drive.

❶

- Click the black arrow to the left of the Computer Class folder in the Folders list to collapse the Computer Class folder (Figure 1–82).

❷

- Click the black arrow to the left of the 1st Semester folder to collapse the folder.

- Click the black arrow to the left of the Freshman folder to collapse the folder.

- Click the black arrow to the left of the UDISK 2.0 (E:) drive to collapse the drive.

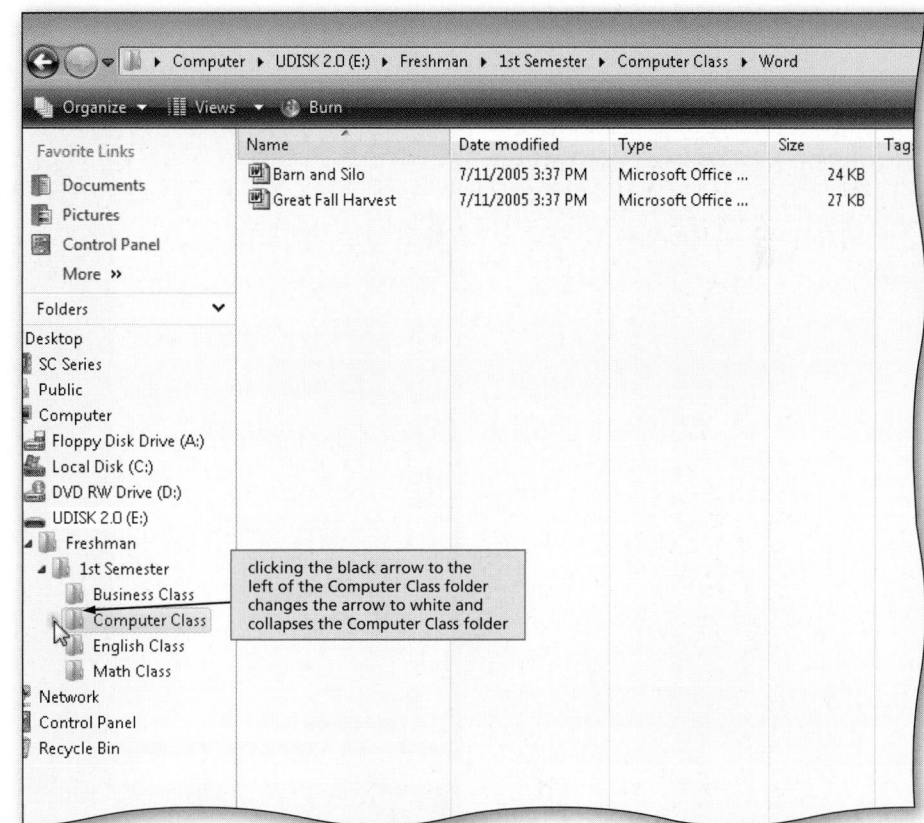

Figure 1–82

To Close the Computer Window

When you have finished working, you can close the Folders list and close the Computer window. The following steps close the Computer window.

1 Click the Close button on the Computer window title bar to close the Computer window.

2 Remove the USB flash drive from the USB port.

Using Help and Support

One of the more powerful Windows Vista features is Windows Help and Support. **Windows Help and Support** is available when using Windows Vista, or when using any application program running under Windows Vista. It contains answers to many questions you may ask with respect to the Windows Vista operating system.

To Start Windows Help and Support

Before you can access the Windows Help and Support services, you must start Help and Support. One method of starting Help and Support uses the Start menu. The following steps start Help and Support.

• Open the Start menu (Figure 1–83).

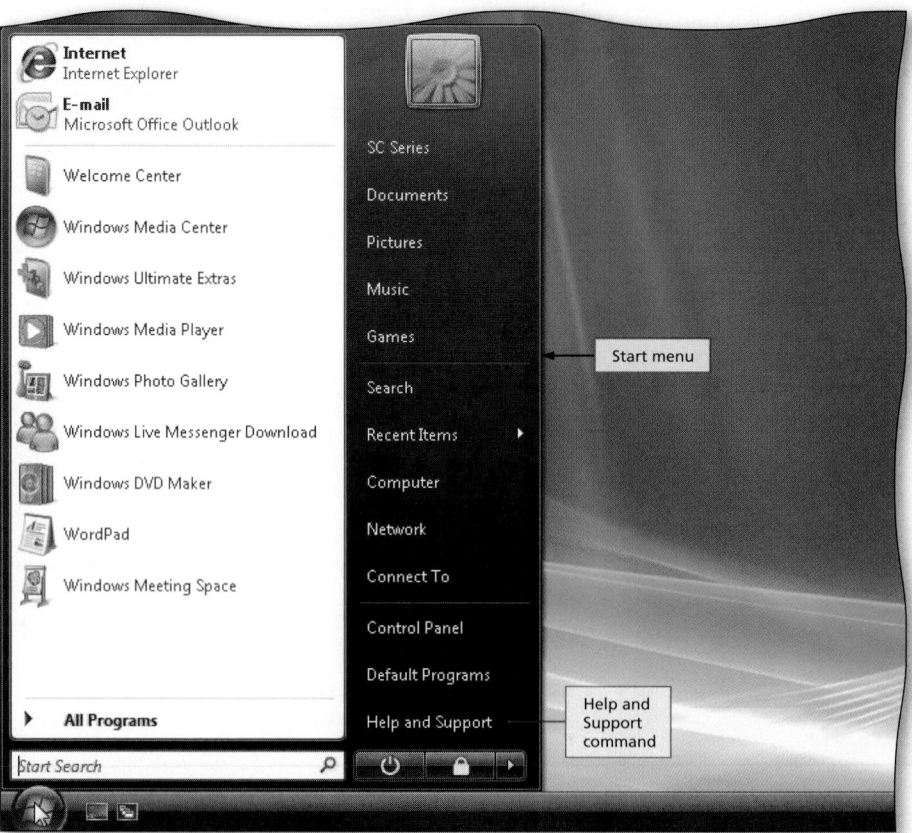

Figure 1–83

2

- Click Help and Support to display the Windows Help and Support window.

- If necessary, click the Maximize button on the Windows Help and Support title bar to maximize the Windows Help and Support window (Figure 1–84).

Q&A

What does Windows Help and Support contain?

Windows Help and Support contains a title bar, navigation toolbar, Find an answer area, Ask someone area, and Information from Microsoft area

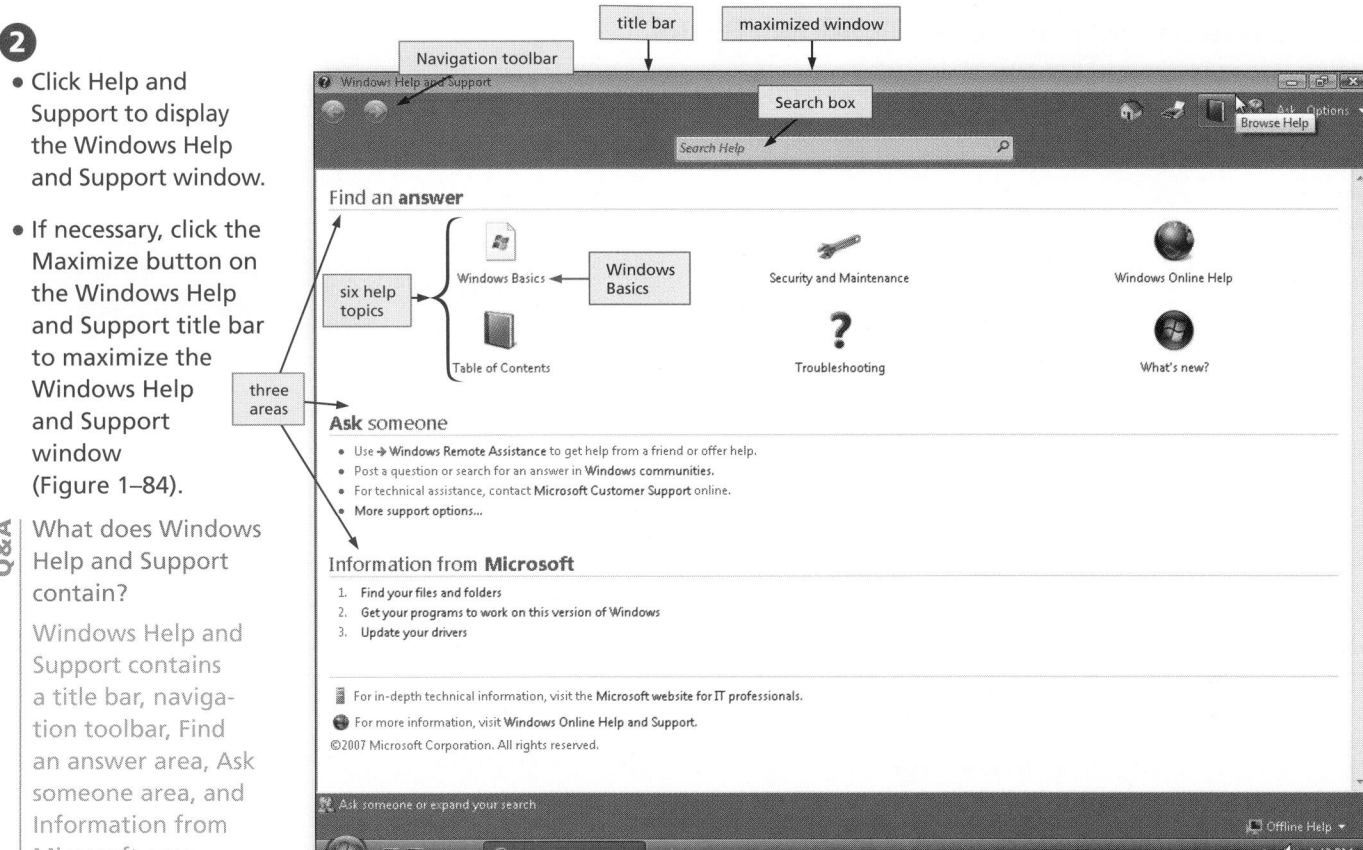

Figure 1–84

Table 1–4 shows the content areas in the Windows Help and Support Center.

Other Ways

1. Press CTRL+ESC, press RIGHT ARROW, press UP ARROW, Press ENTER

2. Press WINDOWS+F1

Table 1–4 Windows Help and Support Center Content Areas

Area	Function
Find an answer	Area contains six Help topics: Windows Basics, Table of Contents, Security and Maintenance, Troubleshooting, Windows Online Help, and What's new? Clicking a category displays a list of subcategories and Help topics related to the category.
Ask someone	Area contains Windows Remote Assistance allowing you to get help from a friend or offer help, post a question or search for an answer in Windows communities, get technical assistance from Microsoft Customer Support online. Clicking the More support options link allows you to search the Knowledge Base, get in-depth technical information from Microsoft Website for IT professionals, and Windows Online Help and Support.
Information from Microsoft	Area contains links to Find your files and folders, Get your programs to work on this version of Windows, and Update your drives.

To Browse for Help Topics in Windows Basics

After starting Windows Help and Support, the next action is to find the Help topic in which you are interested. The following steps use the 'Find an answer' area in the Windows Help and Support Center to find a Help topic that describes how to use the Windows Help and Support Center.

- Click Windows Basics in the 'Find an answer' area to display the Windows Basics: all topics heading (Figure 1–85).

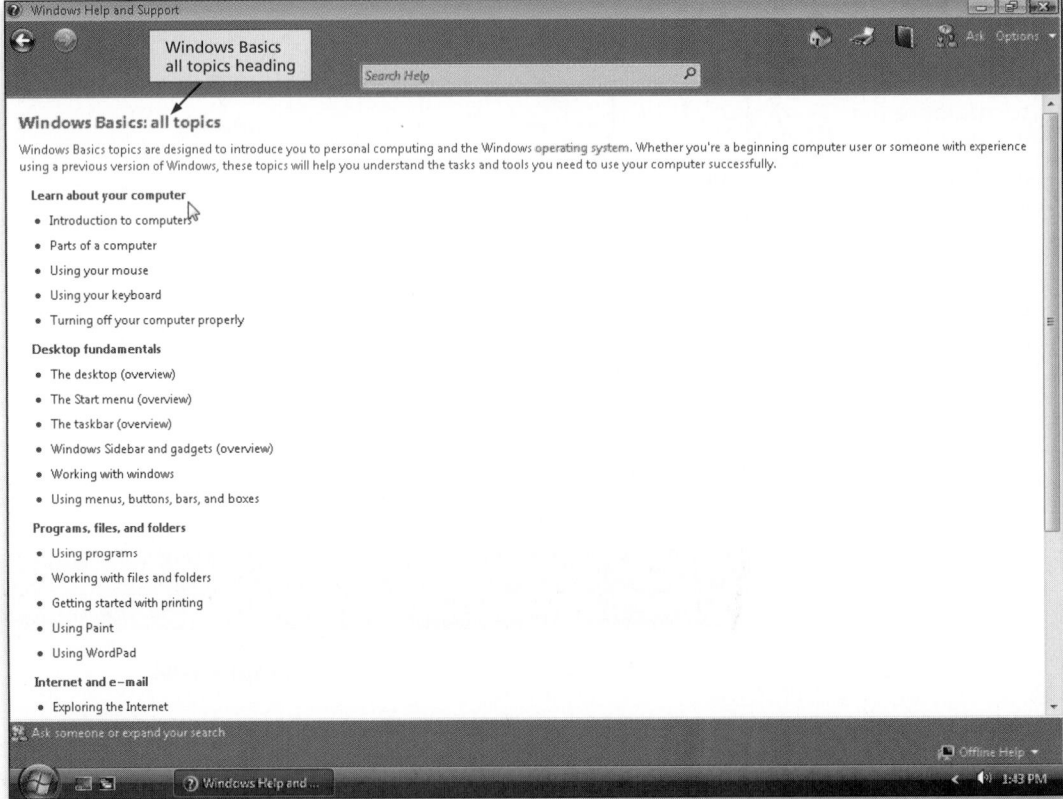

Figure 1–85

- Scroll down to view Getting help topic (Figure 1–86).

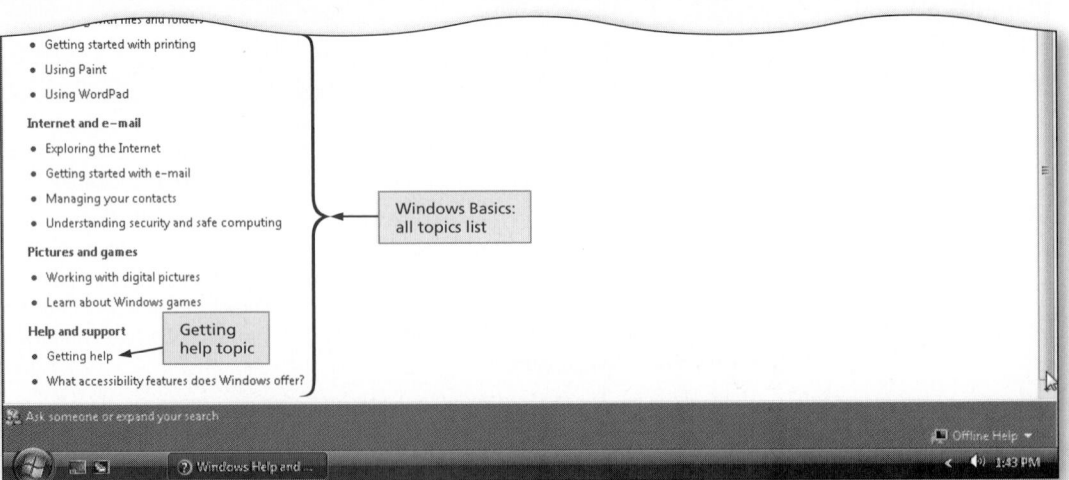

Figure 1–86

3
- Click the Getting help topic (Figure 1–87).

- Read the information in the Getting help topic.

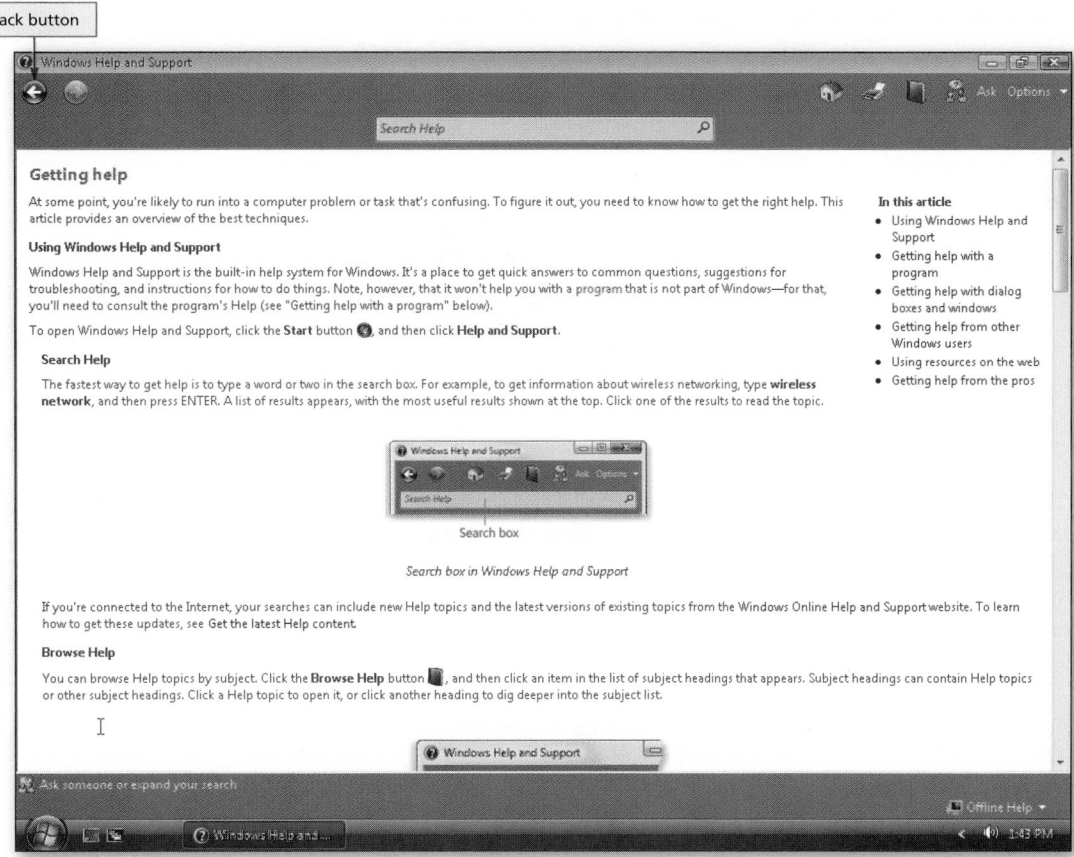

Figure 1–87

4
- Click the Back button on the Navigation toolbar two times to return to the Find an answer area (Figure 1–88).

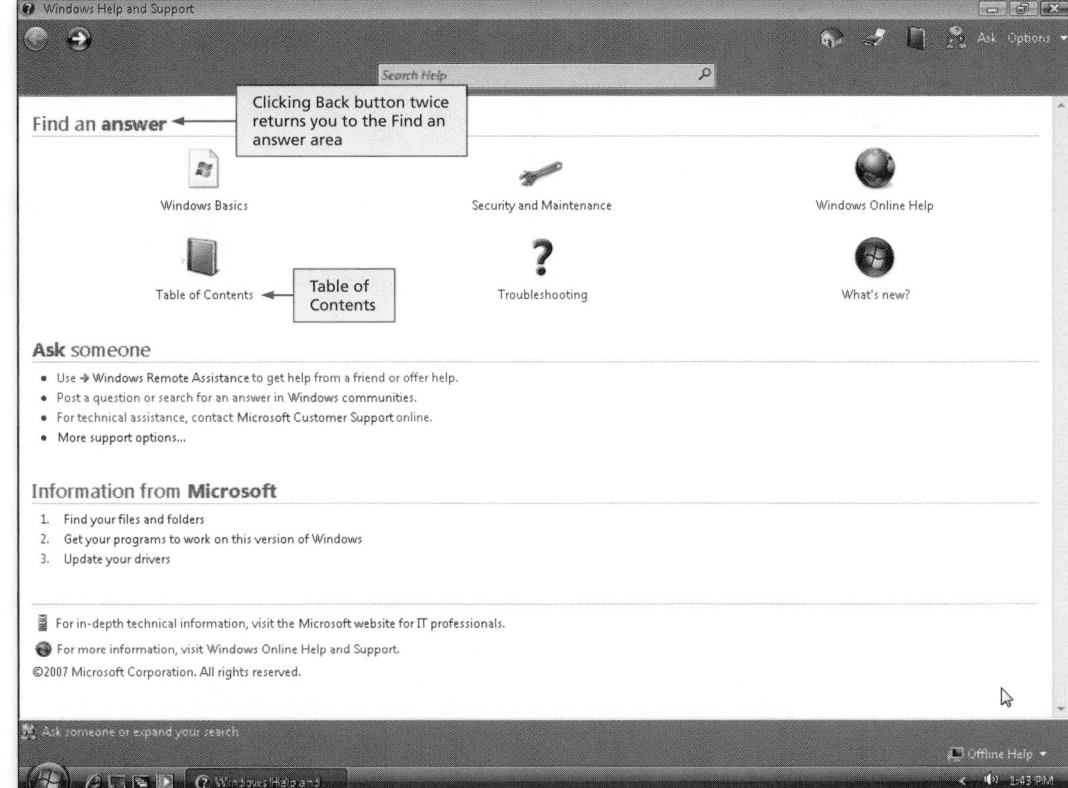

Figure 1–88

To Search for Help Topics Using the Table of Contents

A second method of finding answers to your questions about Windows Vista is to use the Table of Contents. The **Table of Contents** contains a list of entries, each of which references one or more Help topics. The following steps obtain help and information about what you need to set up a home network.

- Click the Table of Contents link in the Find an answer area to display the Table of Contents (Figure 1–89).

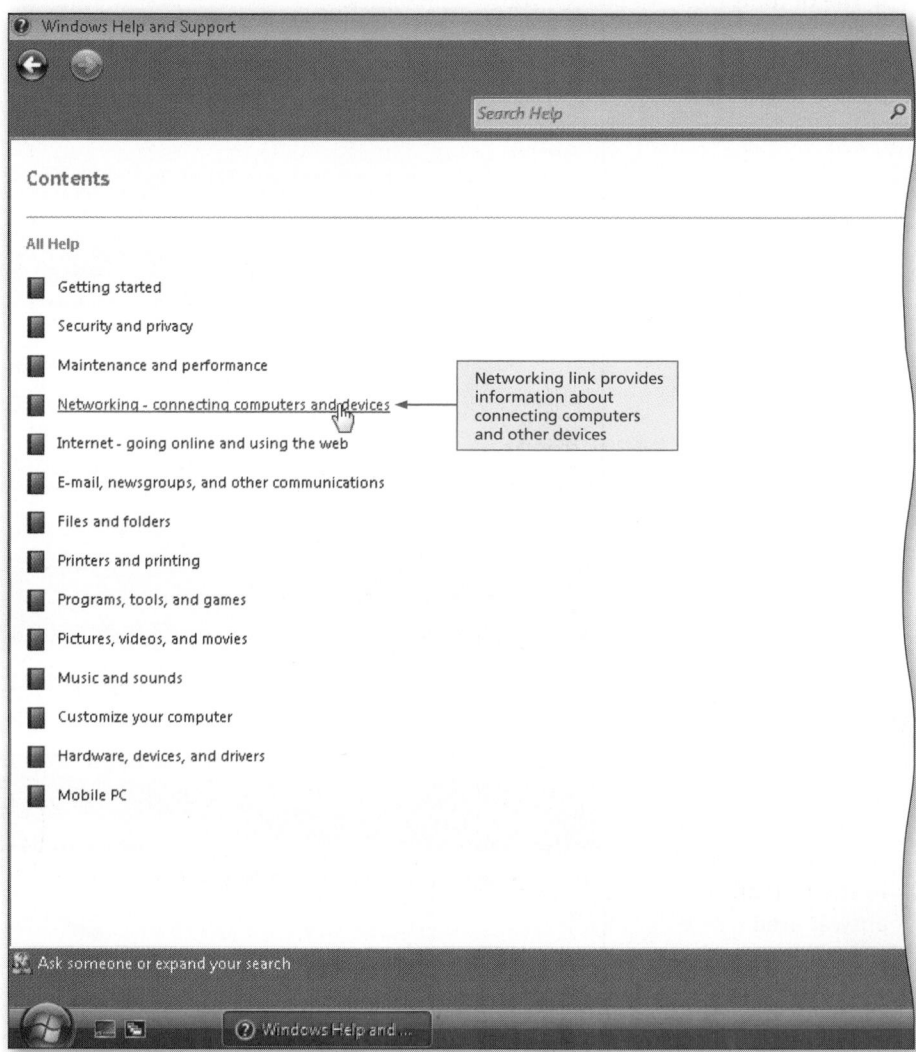

Figure 1–89

2

- Click the 'Networking – connecting computers and devices' link in the Contents area (Figure 1–90).

Q&A

What happens if the topic I am interested in is not included in the table of contents?

Type the term into the Search Help text box in the Windows Help and Support window, and then press ENTER to find information about your topic.

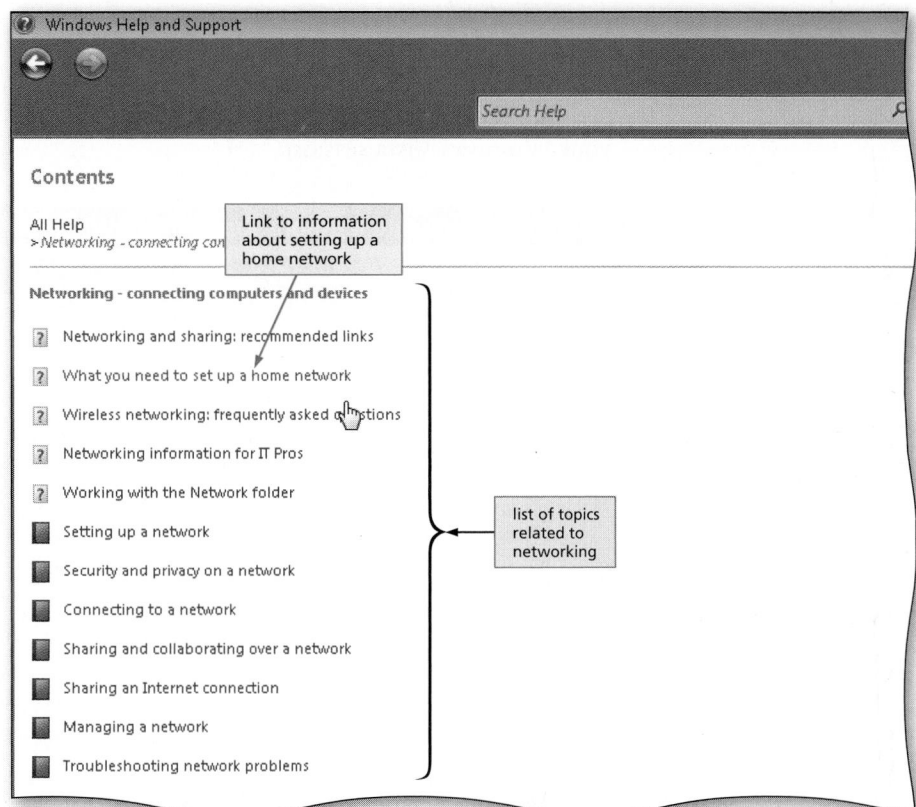

Figure 1–90

3

- Click the 'What you need to set up a home network' link (Figure 1–91).

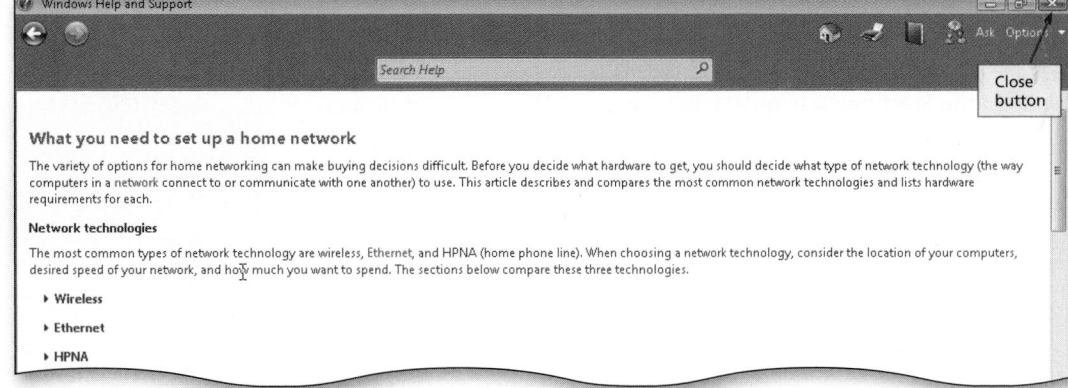

Figure 1–91

To Close Windows Help and Support

The following step shows how to close Windows Help and Support.

1 Click the Close button on the title bar of the Windows Help and Support window to close the Windows Help and Support window.

Logging Off and Turning Off the Computer

After completing your work with Windows Vista, you should close your user account by logging off the computer. In addition to logging off, there are several options available for ending your Windows Vista session. Table 1–5 illustrates the various options for ending your Windows Vista session.

Table 1–5 Options and Methods for Ending a Windows Vista Session	
Option	**Method**
Switch User	Click the Start button, point to the arrow next to the Lock button, and then click Switch User to keep your programs running in the background (but inaccessible until you log on again), which can allow another user to log on.
Log Off	Click the Start button, point to the arrow next to the Lock button, and then click Log Off to close all your programs but leave the computer running so that another user can log on.
Lock	Click the Start button, and then click the Lock button to deny anyone except those you have authorized access to log on to the computer.
Restart	Click the Start button, point to the arrow next to the Lock button, and then click Restart to shut down and then restart the computer.
Sleep	Click the Start button, click the Sleep button, wait for Windows to save your work, and then power down to a hibernating state.
Shut Down	Click the Start button, point to the arrow next to the Lock button, and then click Shut Down to close all your programs and turn off the computer.

To Log Off the Computer

Logging off the computer closes any open applications, allows you to save any unsaved documents, ends the Windows Vista session, and makes the computer available for other users. The following steps log off the computer.

• Open the Start menu (Figure 1–92).

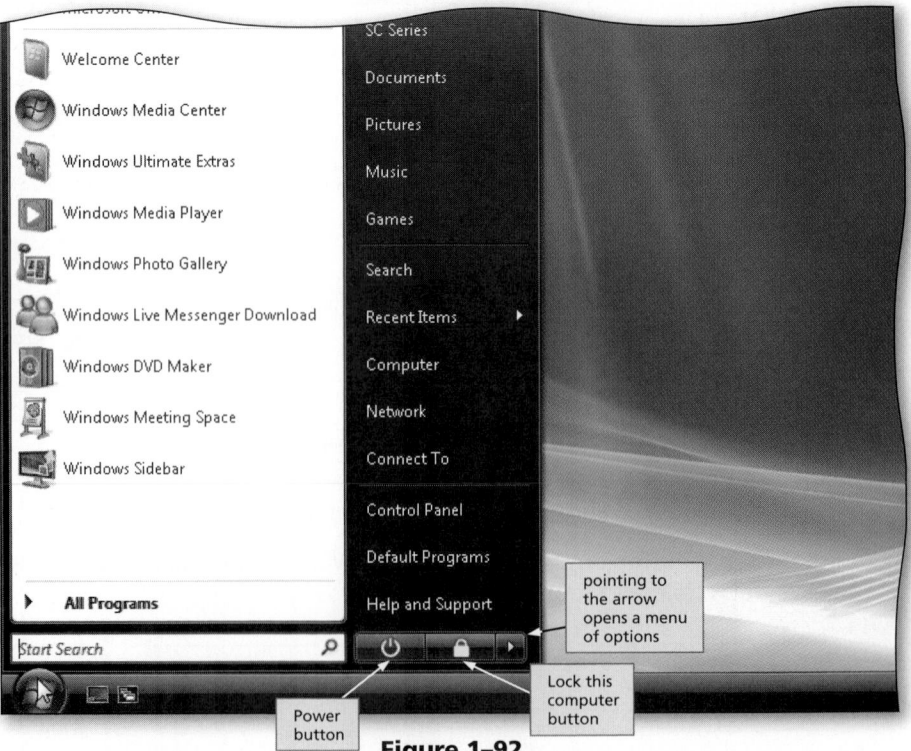

Figure 1–92

2

- Point to the arrow to the right of the 'Lock this computer' button to display a menu. (Figure 1–93).

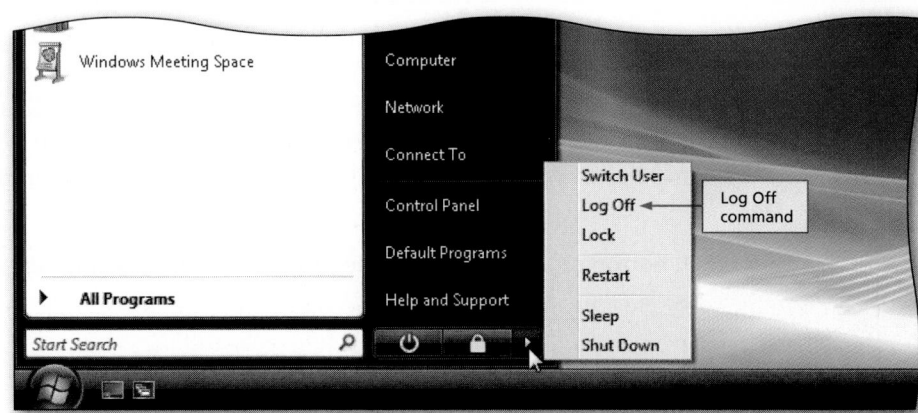

Figure 1–93

3

- Click the Log Off command, and then wait for Windows Vista to prompt you to save any unsaved and log off (Figure 1–94).

 Q&A

Why should I log off the computer?

It is important to log off the computer so you do not lose your work. Some users of Windows Vista have turned off their computers without following the log off procedure only to find data they lost data thought they had stored on disk.

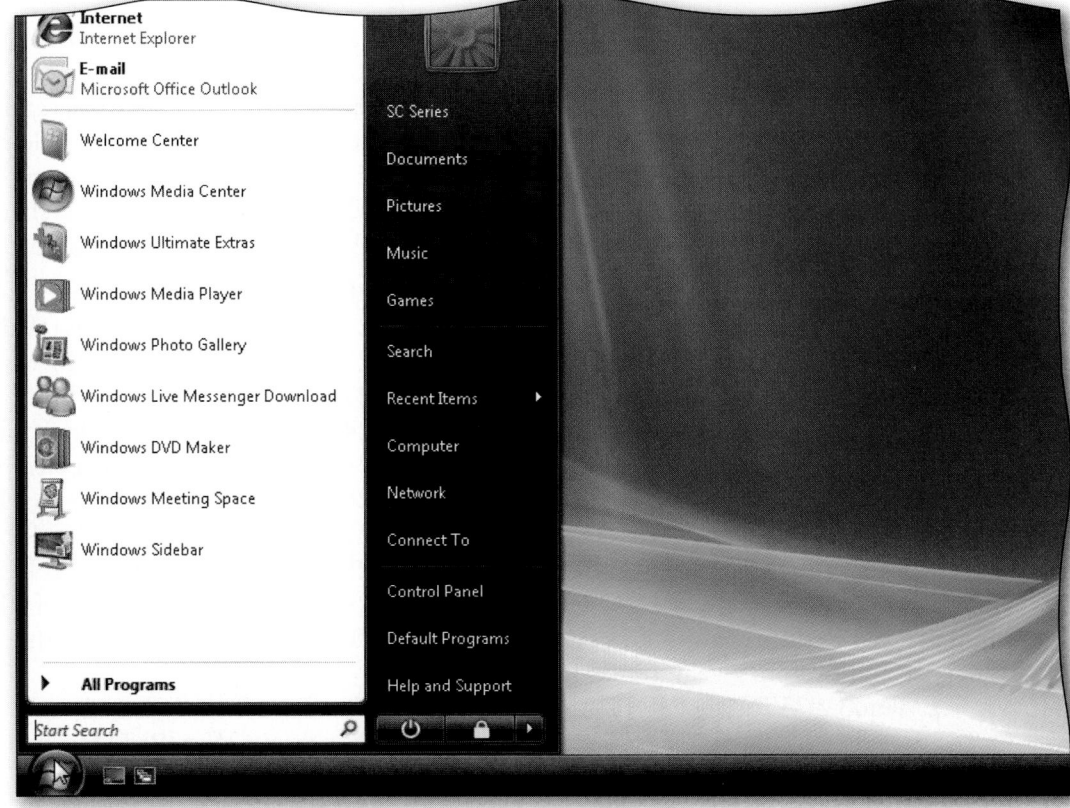

Figure 1–94

To Turn Off the Computer

After logging off, you also may want to shut down the computer using the Shut down button or the Shut down options arrow in the lower corner of the Welcome screen. Clicking the left button shuts down your computer, and clicking the right button displays a menu containing three commands (Restart, Sleep, and Shut Down) that can be used to restart the computer, put the computer into sleep mode, and shut down the computer). The following step turns off the computer. If you are not sure about turning off the computer, simply read the step.

- Click the Shut down button on the Welcome screen to shut down the computer.

Other Ways
1. Press ALT+F4, press the down arrow, select Shut Down, press OK

Chapter Summary

In this chapter you have learned about the Windows Vista graphical interface. You started Windows Vista, learned the components of the desktop and the six mouse operations. You opened, closed, moved, resized, minimized, maximized, and scrolled a window. You used Folder Windows to expand and collapse drives and folders, display drive and folder contents, create a folder, copy a file between folders, and rename and then delete a file. You used Internet Explorer to browse using a URL and tabs. You learned about the hierarchical format, removable media flash drives, and you used WordPad to type and save a document in a newly created folder. You searched for files using a word or phrase in the file or by name, you obtained help about using Windows Vista, and shut down Windows Vista.

1. Log On to the Computer (WIN 8)
2. Close the Welcome Center Window (WIN 10)
3. Add a Gadget to the Windows Sidebar (WIN 10)
4. Remove a Gadget from the Windows Sidebar (WIN 12)
5. Open the Start Menu (WIN 13)
6. Scroll Using Scroll Arrows, the Scroll Bar, and the Scroll Box (WIN 15)
7. Add an Icon to the Desktop (WIN 16)
8. Open a Window Using the Desktop Icon (WIN 18)
9. Minimize and Redisplay a Window (WIN 19)
10. Maximize and Restore a Window (WIN 20)
11. Close a Window (WIN 21, WIN 24)
12. Open a Window Using the Start Menu (WIN 21)
13. Move a Window by Dragging (WIN 22)
14. Expand the Folders List (WIN 23)
15. Size a Window by Dragging (WIN 23)
16. Collapse the Folders List (WIN 24)
17. Delete a Desktop Icon by Right-Dragging (WIN 25)
18. Start an Application Using the Start Menu (WIN 27)
19. Browse the Web by Entering a URL (WIN 30)
20. Open a Link in a New Tab (WIN 31)
21. Switch Between Tabs (WIN 33)
22. Close a Tab (WIN 33)
23. Work with Folders (WIN 34)
24. Plug a USB Flash Drive into a USB Port (WIN 38)
25. Create a Folder on a Removable Drive (WIN 39)
26. Download a Hierarchy of Folders (WIN 40)
27. Expand a Drive (WIN 42)
28. Collapse a Folder (WIN 43)
29. Display the Contents of a Folder (WIN 44)
30. Start WordPad Using the Start Search Box (WIN 45)
31. Type Text (WIN 47)
32. Save a WordPad Document in a New Folder (WIN 47)
33. Verify the Contents of a Folder (WIN 52)
34. Copy a File by Right-Dragging (WIN 52)
35. Display the Contents of a Folder (WIN 54)
36. Rename a File (WIN 55)
37. Delete a File by Right-Clicking (WIN 56)
38. Close Expanded Folders (WIN 57)
39. Start Windows Help and Support (WIN 58)

40. Browse for Help Topics in Windows Basics (WIN 60)
41. Search for Help Topics Using the Table of Contents (WIN 62)
42. Close Windows Help and Support (WIN 63)
43. Log Off from the Computer (WIN 64)
44. Turn Off the Computer (WIN 66)

 If you have a SAM user profile, you may have access to hands-on instruction, practice, and assessment. Log in to your SAM account (http://sam2007.course.com) to launch any assigned training activities or exams that relate to the skills covered in this chapter.

Learn It Online

Test your knowledge of chapter content and key terms.

Instructions: To complete the Learn It Online exercises, start your browser, click the Address bar, and then enter the Web address scsite.com/winvista2007/learn. When the Windows Learn It Online page is displayed, click the link for the exercise you want to complete and then read the instructions.

Chapter Reinforcement TF, MC, and SA

A series of true/false, multiple choice, and short answer questions that test your knowledge of the chapter content.

Flash Cards

An interactive learning environment where you identify chapter key terms associated with displayed definitions.

Practice Test

A series of multiple choice questions that test your knowledge of chapter content and key terms.

Who Wants To Be a Computer Genius?

An interactive game that challenges your knowledge of chapter content in the style of a television quiz show.

Wheel of Terms

An interactive game that challenges your knowledge of chapter key terms in the style of the television show *Wheel of Fortune*.

Crossword Puzzle Challenge

A crossword puzzle that challenges your knowledge of key terms presented in the chapter.

In the Lab

Using the guidelines, concepts, and skills presented in this chapter, complete the following Labs.

Lab 1: Windows Vista Demos

Instructions: Use a computer to perform the following tasks.

Part 1: Windows Vista Demos

1. If necessary, start Windows Vista and then log on to the computer.
2. Click the Start button and then click Help and Support on the Start menu.
3. If necessary, maximize the Windows Help and Support window.
4. Click What's new? in the 'Find an answer' area in the Windows Help and Support window.

Part 2: What's New in Windows Vista?

1. In the Searching and organizing area, click the 'Demo: Working with files and folders' link, and then click the 'Watch the demo' link. As you watch the demo, answer the questions below.

   a. The Start menu provides access to several folders. What are the three folders mentioned?

   _____

   b. How do you create a new folder?

   _____

   c. If you use a folder frequently, where should you put the folder?

   _____

2. Click the Back button below the Windows Help and Support title to return to the What's new in Windows Vista heading.

Part 3: What's New in Security?

1. In the Security area, click the green arrow to the left of the 'Click to open the Security Center' link. Answer the questions below.

   a. What are the four security essentials shown in the Windows Security Center.

   b. Close the Windows Security Center.

   c. In the Security area, click the 'Demo: Security basics' link and then click the Read the transcript' link.

   d. What's the quickest way to check your computer's security status and fix security problems.

   _____

   e. What does a firewall do?

   _____

   f. What does it mean when all the lights in the Security Center are green?

   _____

2. Click the Back button below the Windows Help and Support title to return to the 'What's new in Windows Vista Ultimate' page.

Part 4: What's New in Parental Controls?

1. Scroll down to view the Parental Controls area.

   a. In the Parental Controls area, click the 'What can I control with Parental Controls?' link.

   b. What can I do with Parental Controls?

   _____

   _____

c. After setting up Parental Controls, how can a parent keep a record of a child's computer activity?

_____

2. Click the Back button below the Windows Help and Support title to view the topics in the Windows and Help Support window.

Part 5: What's New in the Pictures Area?

1. Scroll down the Windows Help and Support window to view the Pictures area.

   a. In the Pictures area, click the 'Working with digital pictures' link.

   b. What are the two main ways to import pictures?

   _____

   _____

2. Click the Back button below the Windows Help and Support title to view the topics in the Windows Help and Support window.

Part 6: What's New in the Mobile PC Features Area?

1. If necessary, scroll to view the Mobile PC features area, click the Using Windows Mobility Center link. Answer the following question.

   a. How do you open the Mobility Center?

   _____

   _____

2. Click the Close button in the Windows Help and Support window.

In the Lab

Lab 2: Internet Explorer

Instructions: Use a computer to perform the following tasks.

1. Start Windows Vista and connect to the Internet.

2. Right-click the Start button on the taskbar, click Explore on the shortcut menu, and then maximize the Start Menu window.

3. If necessary, open the Folders list so the Start Menu and Programs icons are visible.

4. Click the Programs icon in the Start Menu folder.

5. Double-click the Internet Explorer shortcut icon in the Contents pane to start the Internet Explorer application. What is the URL of the Web page that appears in the Address bar in the Windows Internet Explorer window? _____

6. Click the URL in the Address bar in the Windows Internet Explorer window to select it. Type scsite.com and then press the ENTER key.

7. If necessary, scroll the Web page to display the Browse by Subject navigation bar containing the subject categories. Clicking a subject category displays the book titles in that category.

8. Click Operating Systems in the Browse by Subject navigation bar.

9. Click the Windows Vista link.

10. Right-click the first Windows Vista textbook cover image on the Web page, click Save Picture As on the shortcut menu, type Windows Vista Cover in the File name box, and then click the Save button in the Save Picture dialog box to save the image in the Pictures folder.

Continued >

In the Lab *continued*

11. Click the Close button in the Windows Internet Explorer window.

12. If necessary, scroll to the top of the Folders list to make the drive (C:) icon visible.

13. Click the black arrow to the left of the drive (C:) icon.

14. Click the Documents folder name in the Favorites Links list.

15. Click the Pictures folder name in the Folders list.

16. Right-click the Windows Vista Cover icon and then click Properties on the shortcut menu.

    a.   What type of file is the Windows Vista Cover file? _____

    b.   When was the file last modified? _____

    c.   With what application does this file open? _____

17. Click the Cancel button in the Windows Vista Cover Properties dialog box.

18. If necessary, click the Close button in the Auto Play window.

19. Insert a USB flash drive into your computer.

19. Right-drag the Windows Vista Cover icon to the USB flash drive icon in the Folders list. Click Move Here on the shortcut menu. Click the USB flash drive icon in the Folders list.

    a.   Is the Windows Vista Cover file stored on the USB flash drive? _____

20. Click the Close button in the USB flash drive window.

In the Lab

Lab 3: Getting Help

Instructions: Use a computer to perform the following tasks.

Part 1: Using Windows Basics to Get Help

1. If necessary, start Windows Vista and then log on to the computer.

2. Click the Start button and then click Help and Support on the Start menu.

3. If necessary, maximize the Windows Help and Support window.

4. Click Windows Basics icon in the 'Find an answer' area.

5. Click the 'Turning off your computer properly' link. Why are there two different looking Power buttons?

_____

_____

6. Click the Back button in the upper-left corner of the Windows Help and Support window.

Part 2: Using Desktop Fundamentals to Get Help

1. Look in the Desktop fundamentals area and identify the three parts of the desktop.

_____

2. Click the 'Getting started with printing' link. List the three types of printers shown in the Getting started with printing area.

_____

3. Click the Back button in the upper-left corner of the Windows Help and Support window.

4. If necessary, scroll to view the Getting help topic under the 'Help and support' heading. Click the Getting help link. List the eight ways to get help.

_____

_____

5. Click the Back button twice in the upper-left corner of the Windows Help and Support window.

Part 3:   Using Table of Contents to Get Help

1. Click the Table of Contents icon in the 'Find an answer' area.

2. Click the 'E-mail, newsgroups, and other communications' link. List six communication options.

_____

_____

3. Click Newsgroups in the Contents list.

4. Click the 'What are newsgroups?' in the Contents list.

5. Describe what a newsgroup is.

_____

_____

6. Click the Back button four times in the upper-left corner of the Windows Help and Support window.

Part 4:   Using Security and Maintenance to Get Help

1. Click the Security and Maintenance link in the 'Find an answer' area.

2. What does Windows Defender prevent?

_____

3. What's so important about Back up and Restore?

_____

_____

4. Click the Back button in the upper-left corner of the Windows Help and Support window.

Part 5:   Using Troubleshooting to Get Help

1. Click the Troubleshooting icon in the 'Find an answer' area.

2. Click the Connect to the Internet link under the 'Using the web' heading.

3. Click the 'What do I need to connect to the Internet?' link.

4. What do you use to connect to the Internet?

_____

5. Click the Back button three times in the upper-left corner of the Windows Help and Support.

Part 6:   Using Windows Online Help to Get Help

1. Click Windows the Online Help icon in the 'Find an answer' area to open Internet Explorer to the Windows Vista: Help and How-to window.

2. Click the 'Music and sounds' icon.

3. What can you do in the Music and sounds area in the Windows Help and How-to Web site?

_____

_____

4. Close the Windows Vista: Help Music window, and then close the Windows Help and Support window.

In the Lab

Lab 4: Downloading the Word 2007 Chapters 1–3 Data Files

Instructions: Use the SC Site—Shelly Cashman Series Student Resources Web site to download the Word 2007 Chapters 1–3 Data Files into the Word folder.

Part 1: Plug the USB Flash Drive into the USB Port

1. If necessary, launch Windows Vista and log on to the computer.

2. Plug the USB flash drive into the USB port on the computer. The UDISK 2.0 (E:) window should display on the desktop and should contain the Freshman folder.

3. If the Freshman folder does not display in the UDISK 2.0 (E:) window, follow the steps in Chapter One to create the hierarchy of folders shown in Figure 1–50 on page WIN 36.

Part 2: Download the Word 2007 Chapters 1-3 Data Files into the Word Folder

1. Start Internet Explorer by clicking the Start button on the taskbar and then clicking Internet on the Start menu.

2. Click the Address box on the Address bar, type `scsite.com` in the Address box, and then click the Go button.

3. When the SC Site — Shelly Cashman Series Student Resources Web site is displayed, use the Browse by Subject navigation bar, click Office Suites, and then click Microsoft Office 2007.

4. In the center of the screen, locate your textbook, and then click the title (for example, Microsoft Office 2007: Introductory Concepts and Techniques, Windows Vista Edition).

5. When the page for your textbook displays, click the Word Chapters 1–3 Data Files link (You may need to scroll down the page).

6. When the File Download – Security Warning dialog box is displayed, click the Run button.

7. When the Internet Explorer – Security Warning dialog box is displayed, click the Run button.

8. When the WinZip Self-Extractor dialog box displays, click the Browse button.

9. Click the plus sign to the left of the removable drive, click the plus sign to the left of the Freshman folder, click the plus sign to the left of the 1st Semester folder, click the plus sign to the left of the Computer Class folder, and then click the Word folder.

10. Click the OK button in the Browse for Folder dialog box.

11. Click the Unzip button in the WinZip Self-Extractor dialog box.

12. When a smaller WinZip Self-Extractor dialog box appears, click the OK button.

13. Click the Close button in the WinZip Self-Extractor dialog box.

14. Click the Close button in the SC Site — Shelly Cashman Series Student Resources Web site window.

15. Verify the Word 2007 Chapters 1–3 Data Files folder is contain in the Word folder.

16. Close the Word window. Unplug the USB flash drive from the USB port.

1 | Creating and Editing a Word Document

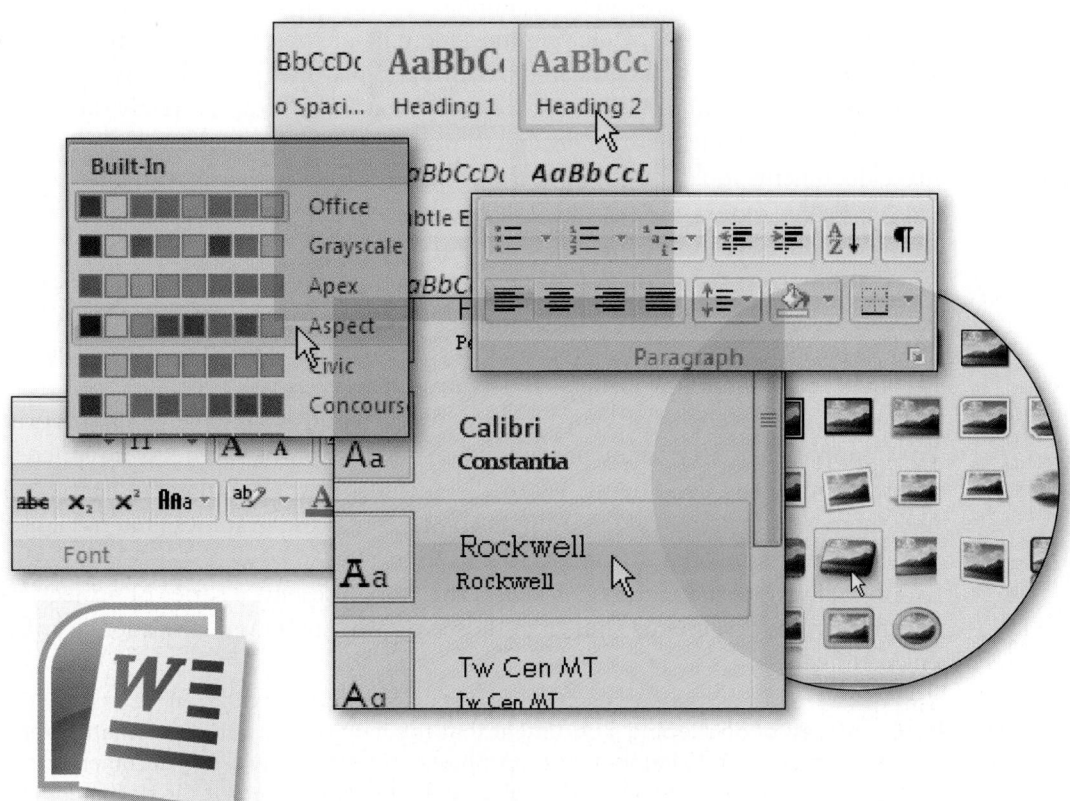

Objectives

You will have mastered the material in this chapter when you can:

- Start and quit Word
- Describe the Word window
- Enter text in a document
- Check spelling as you type
- Save a document
- Format text, paragraphs, and document elements
- Undo and redo commands or actions

- Insert a picture and format it
- Print a document
- Change document properties
- Open a document
- Correct errors in a document
- Use Word's Help

1 | Creating and Editing a Word Document

What Is Microsoft Office Word 2007?

Microsoft Office Word 2007 is a full-featured word processing program that allows you to create professional-looking documents and revise them easily. A document is a printed or electronic medium people use to communicate with others. With Word, you can develop many types of documents, including flyers, letters, memos, resumes, reports, fax cover sheets, mailing labels, and newsletters. Word also provides tools that enable you to create Web pages. From within Word, you can place these Web pages directly on a Web server.

Word has many features designed to simplify the production of documents and make documents look visually appealing. Using Word, you easily can change the shape, size, and color of text. You can include borders, shading, tables, images, pictures, charts, and Web addresses in documents.

While you are typing, Word performs many tasks automatically. For example, Word detects and corrects spelling and grammar errors in several languages. Word's thesaurus allows you to add variety and precision to your writing. Word also can format text, such as headings, lists, fractions, borders, and Web addresses, as you type.

This latest version of Word has many new features to make you more productive. For example, Word has many predefined text and graphical elements designed to assist you with preparing documents. Word also includes new charting and diagramming tools; uses themes so that you can coordinate colors, fonts, and graphics; and has a tool that enables you to convert a document to a PDF format.

To illustrate the features of Word, this book presents a series of projects that use Word to create documents similar to those you will encounter in academic and business environments.

Project Planning Guidelines

The process of developing a document that communicates specific information requires careful analysis and planning. As a starting point, establish why the document is needed. Once the purpose is determined, analyze the intended readers of the document and their unique needs. Then, gather information about the topic and decide what to include in the document. Finally, determine the document design and style that will be most successful at delivering the message. Details of these guidelines are provided in Appendix A. In addition, each project in this book provides practical applications of these planning considerations.

Project — Document with a Picture

To advertise a sale, promote a business, publicize an event, or convey a message to the community, you may want to create a flyer and post it in a public location. Libraries, schools, churches, grocery stores, and other places often provide bulletin boards or windows for flyers. These flyers announce personal items for sale or rent (car, boat, apartment); garage or block sales; services being offered (animal care, housecleaning, lessons); membership, sponsorship, or donation requests (club, church, charity); and other messages. Flyers are an inexpensive means of reaching the community, yet many go unnoticed because they are designed poorly.

The project in this chapter follows general guidelines and uses Word to create the flyer shown in Figure 1–1. This colorful, eye-catching flyer advertises horseback riding lessons at Tri-Valley Stables. The picture of the horse and rider entices passersby to stop and look at the flyer. The headline on the flyer is large and colorful to draw attention into the text. The body copy below the headline briefly describes key points of the riding lessons, and the bulleted list below the picture concisely highlights important additional information. The signature line of the flyer calls attention to the stable name and tele- phone number. Finally, the graphical page border nicely frames and complements the contents of the flyer.

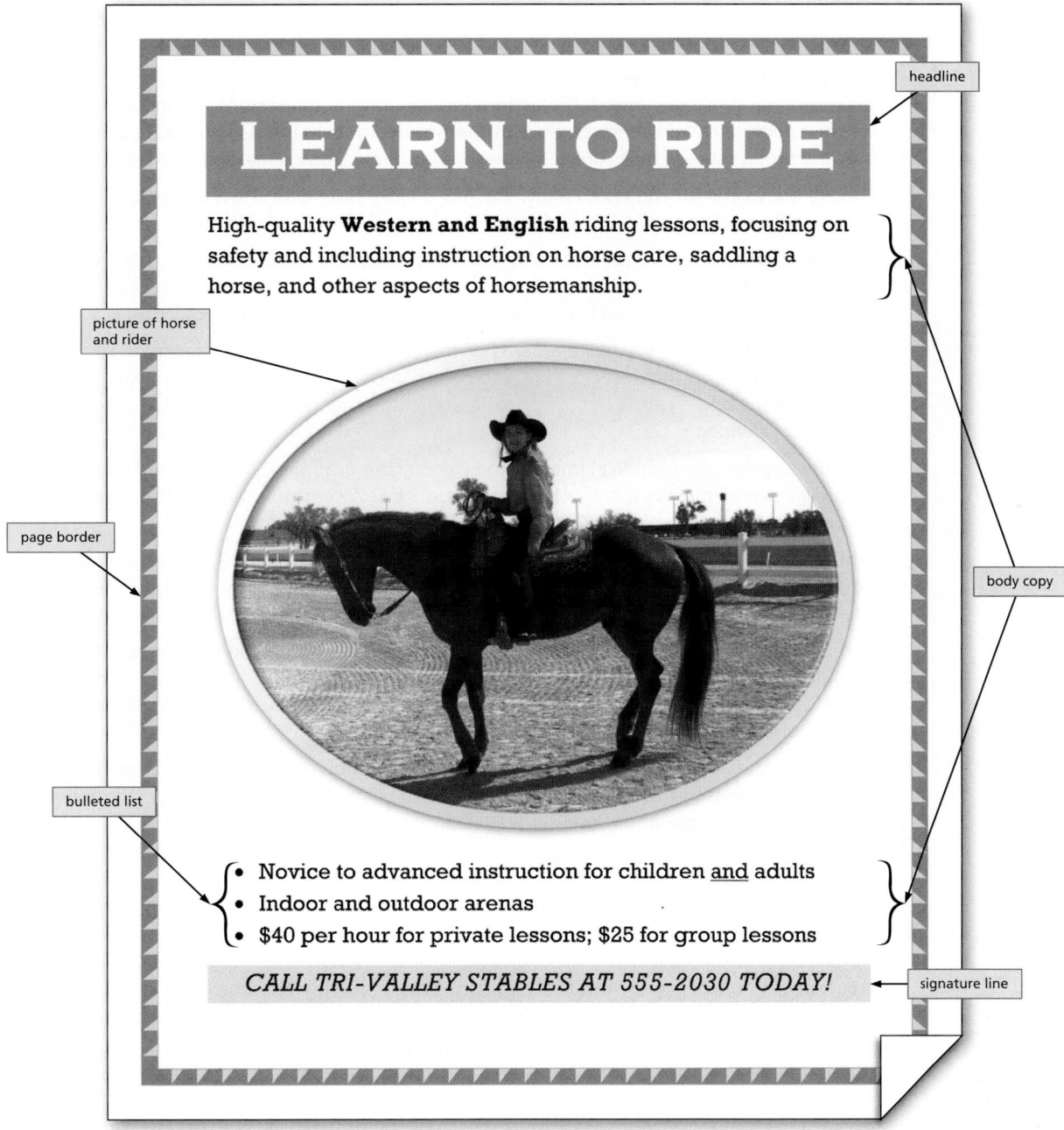

Figure 1–1

Overview

As you read this chapter, you will learn how to create the flyer shown in Figure 1–1 on the previous page by performing these general tasks:

- Enter text in the document.
- Save the document.
- Format the text in the document.
- Insert a picture in the document.
- Format the picture.
- Add a border to the page.
- Print the document.

**Plan
Ahead**

General Project Guidelines

When creating a Word document, the actions you perform and decisions you make will affect the appearance and characteristics of the finished document. As you create a flyer, such as the project shown in Figure 1–1, you should follow these general guidelines:

1. **Choose the words for the text.** Follow the *less is more* principle. The less text, the more likely the flyer will be read. Use as few words as possible to make a point.

2. **Determine where to save the flyer.** You can store a document permanently, or **save** it, on a variety of storage media including a hard disk, USB flash drive, or CD. You also can indicate a specific location on the storage media for saving the document.

3. **Identify how to format various elements of the text.** The overall appearance of a document significantly affects its ability to communicate clearly. Examples of how you can modify the appearance, or **format**, of text include changing its shape, size, color, and position on the page.

4. **Find the appropriate graphical image.** An eye-catching graphical image should convey the flyer's overall message. It could show a product, service, result, or benefit, or visually convey a message that is not expressed easily with words.

5. **Establish where to position and how to format the graphical image.** The position and format of the graphical image should grab the attention of passersby and draw them into reading the flyer.

6. **Determine whether the flyer needs a page border, and if so, its style and format.** A graphical, color-coordinated page border can further draw attention to a flyer and nicely frame its contents. Be careful, however, that a page border does not make the flyer look too cluttered.

When necessary, more specific details concerning the above guidelines are presented at appropriate points in the chapter. The chapter also will identify the actions performed and decisions made regarding these guidelines during the creation of the flyer shown in Figure 1–1.

Starting Word

If you are using a computer to step through the project in this chapter and you want your screen to match the figures in this book, you should change your screen's resolution to 1024 × 768. For information about how to change a computer's resolution, read Appendix E.

Note: If you are using Windows XP, see Appendix F for alternate steps.

To Start Word

The following steps, which assume Windows Vista is running, start Word based on a typical installation. You may need to ask your instructor how to start Word for your computer.

1

- Click the Start button on the Windows Vista taskbar to display the Start menu.

- Click All Programs at the bottom of the left pane on the Start menu to display the All Programs list.

- Click Microsoft Office in the All Programs list to display the Microsoft Office list (Figure 1–2).

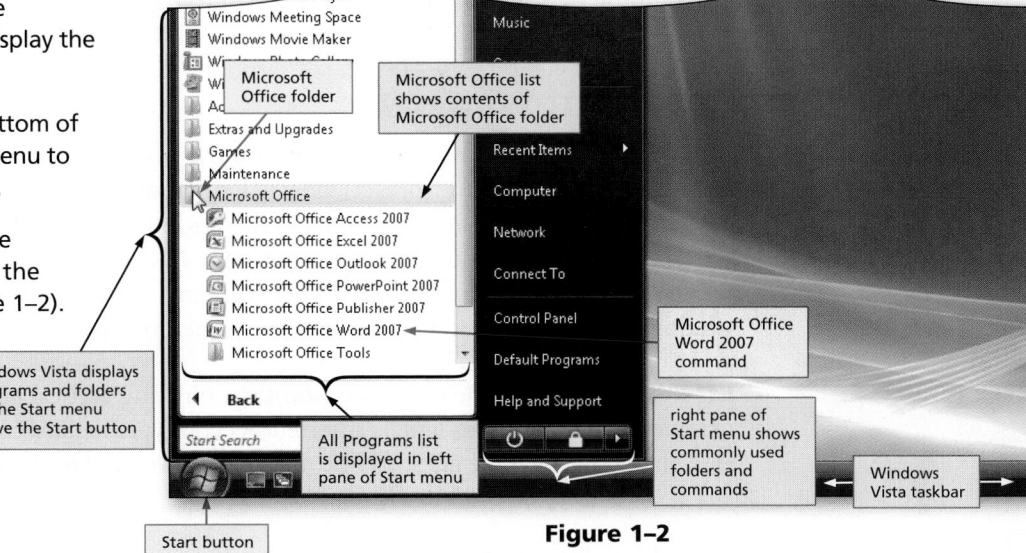

Figure 1–2

2

- Click Microsoft Office Word 2007 to start Word and display a new blank document in the Word window (Figure 1–3).

- If the Word window is not maximized, click the Maximize button next to the Close button on its title bar to maximize the window.

Q&A What is a maximized window?

A maximized window fills the entire screen. When you maximize a window, the Maximize button changes to a Restore Down button.

3

- If the Print Layout button is not selected, click it so that your screen layout matches Figure 1–3.

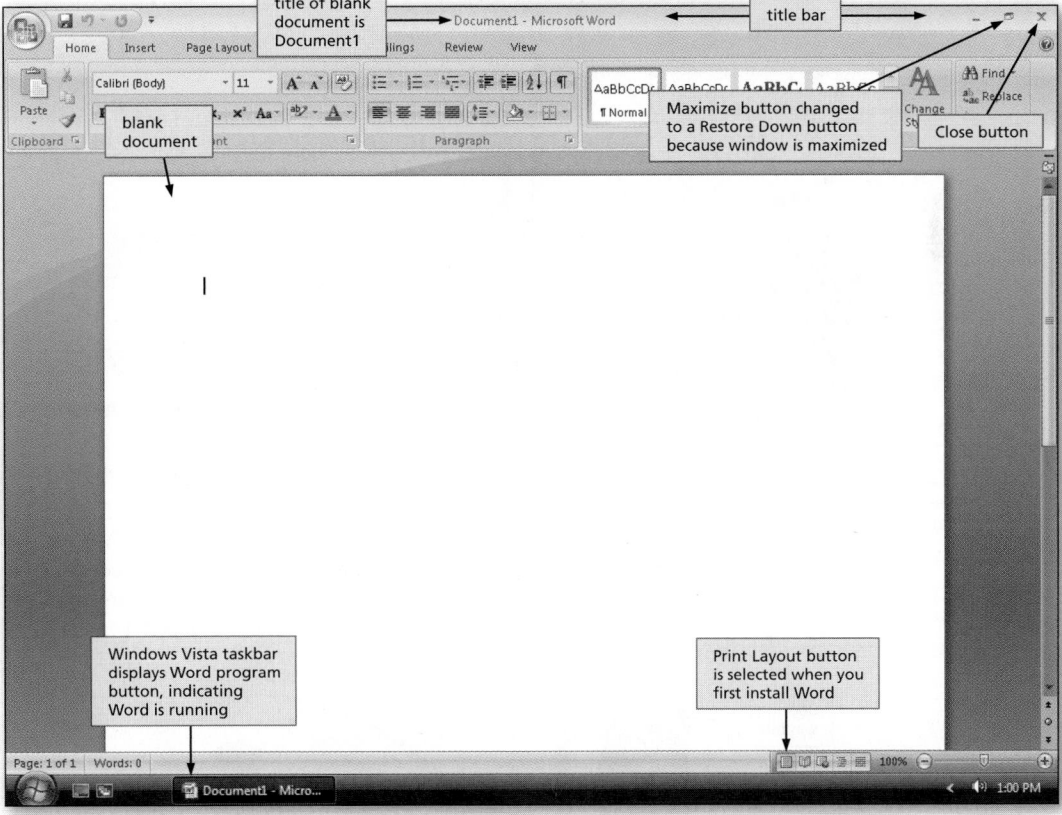

Figure 1–3

Other Ways
1. Double-click Word icon on desktop, if one is present   2. Click Microsoft Office Word 2007 on Start menu

The Word Window

The Word window consists of a variety of components to make your work more efficient and documents more professional. These include the document window, Ribbon, Mini toolbar and shortcut menus, Quick Access Toolbar, and Office Button. Some of these components are common to other Microsoft Office 2007 programs; others are unique to Word.

Document Window

You view a portion of a document on the screen through a **document window** (Figure 1–4). The default (preset) view is **Print Layout view**, which shows the document on a mock sheet of paper in the document window.

The Word document window in Figure 1–4 contains an insertion point, mouse pointer, scroll bar, and status bar. Other elements that may appear in the document window are discussed later in this and subsequent chapters.

Insertion Point   The **insertion point** is a blinking vertical bar that indicates where text, graphics, and other items will be inserted. As you type, the insertion point moves to the right, and when you reach the end of a line, it moves downward to the beginning of the next line.

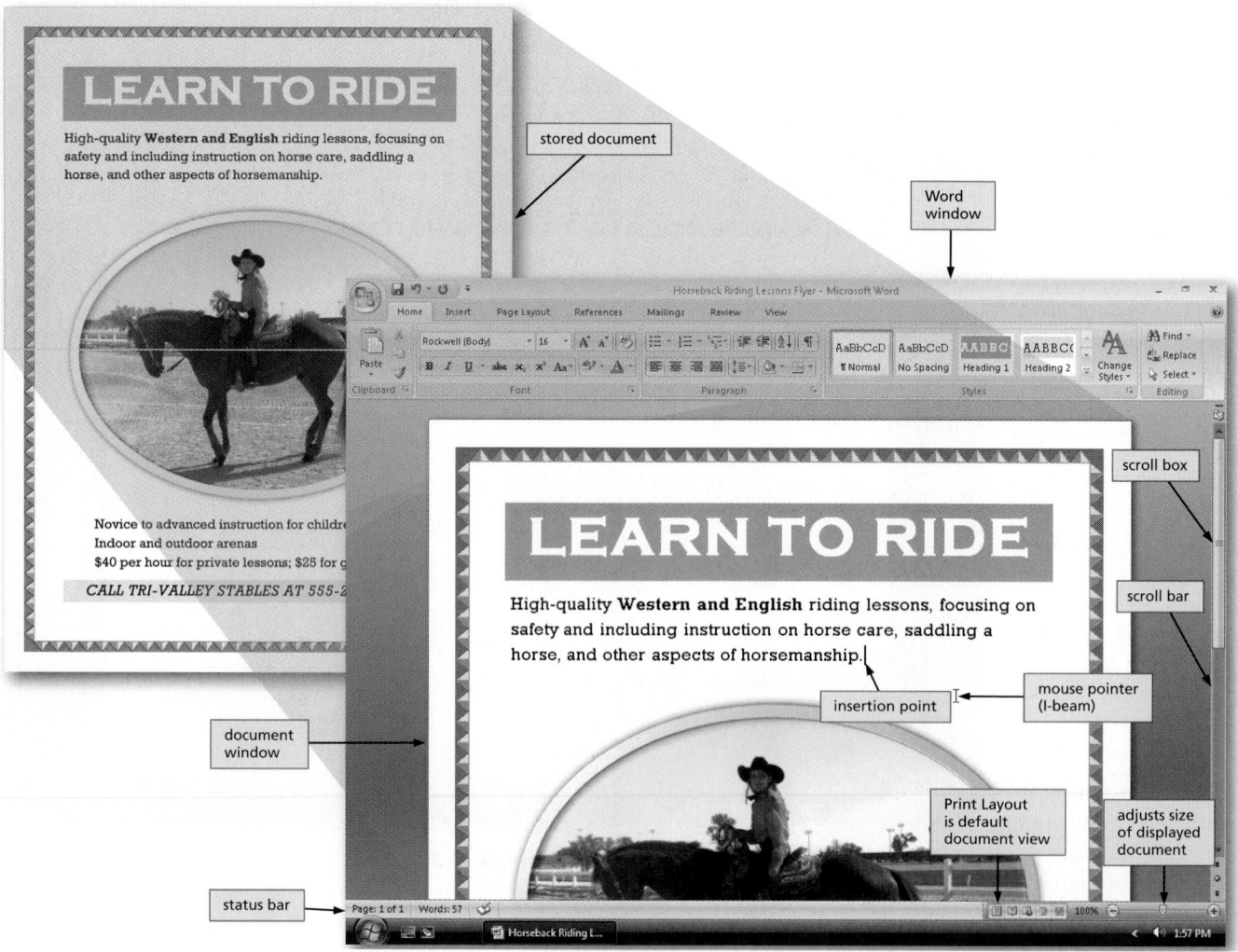

Figure 1–4

Mouse Pointer   The **mouse pointer** becomes different shapes depending on the task you are performing in Word and the pointer's location on the screen. The mouse pointer in Figure 1–4 is the shape of an I-beam.

Scroll Bar   You use a **scroll bar** to display different portions of a document in the document window. At the right edge of the document window is a vertical scroll bar. If a document is too wide to fit in the document window, a horizontal scroll bar also appears at the bottom of the document window. On a scroll bar, the position of the **scroll box** reflects the location of the portion of the document that is displayed in the document window. A **scroll arrow** is located at each end of a scroll bar. To scroll through, or display different portions of the document in the document window, you can click a scroll arrow or drag the scroll box.

Status Bar   The **status bar**, located at the bottom of the document window above the Windows Vista taskbar, presents information about the document, the progress of current tasks, and the status of certain commands and keys; it also provides controls for viewing the document. As you type text or perform certain commands, various indicators and buttons may appear on the status bar.

The left edge of the status bar in Figure 1–4 shows the current page followed by the total number of pages in the document, the number of words in the document, and a button to check spelling and grammar. Toward the right edge are buttons and controls you can use to change the view of a document and adjust the size of the displayed document.

Ribbon

The **Ribbon**, located near the top of the Word window, is the control center in Word (Figure 1–5a). The Ribbon provides easy, central access to the tasks you perform while creating a document. The Ribbon consists of tabs, groups, and commands. Each **tab** surrounds a collection of groups, and each group contains related commands.

When you start Word, the Ribbon displays seven top-level tabs: Home, Insert, Page Layout, References, Mailings, Review, and View. The **Home tab**, called the primary tab, contains the more frequently used commands. To display a different tab on the Ribbon, click the top-level tab. That is, to display the Insert tab, click Insert on the Ribbon. To return to the Home tab, click Home on the Ribbon. The tab currently displayed is called the **active tab**.

To display more of the document in the document window, some users prefer to minimize the Ribbon, which hides the groups on the Ribbon and displays only the top-level tabs (Figure 1–5b). To use commands on a minimized Ribbon, click the top-level tab.

BTW

Minimizing the Ribbon
If you want to minimize the Ribbon, right-click the Ribbon and then click Minimize the Ribbon on the shortcut menu, double-click the active tab, or press CTRL+F1. To restore a minimized Ribbon, right-click the Ribbon and then click Minimize the Ribbon on the shortcut menu, double-click any top-level tab, or press CTRL+F1. To use commands on a minimized Ribbon, click the top-level tab.

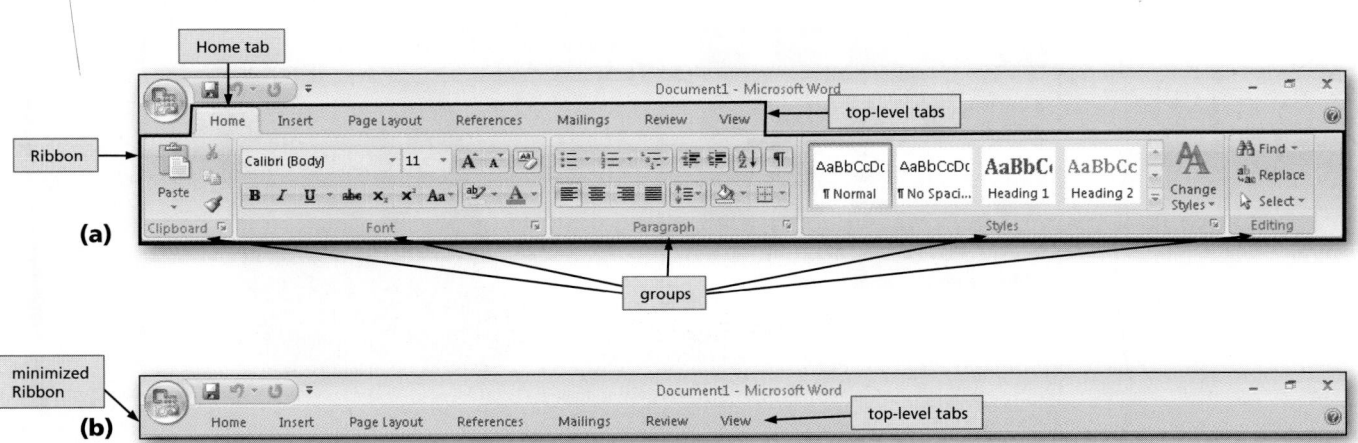

Figure 1–5

Each time you start Word, the Ribbon appears the same way it did the last time you used Word. The chapters in this book, however, begin with the Ribbon appearing as it did at the initial installation of the software. If you are stepping through this chapter on a computer and you want your Ribbon to match the figures in this book, read Appendix E.

In addition to the top-level tabs, Word displays other tabs, called **contextual tabs**, when you perform certain tasks or work with objects such as pictures or tables. If you insert a picture in the document, for example, the Picture Tools tab and its related subordinate Format tab appear (Figure 1–6). When you are finished working with the picture, the Picture Tools and Format tabs disappear from the Ribbon. Word determines when contextual tabs should appear and disappear based on tasks you perform. Some contextual tabs, such as the Table Tools tab, have more than one related subordinate tab.

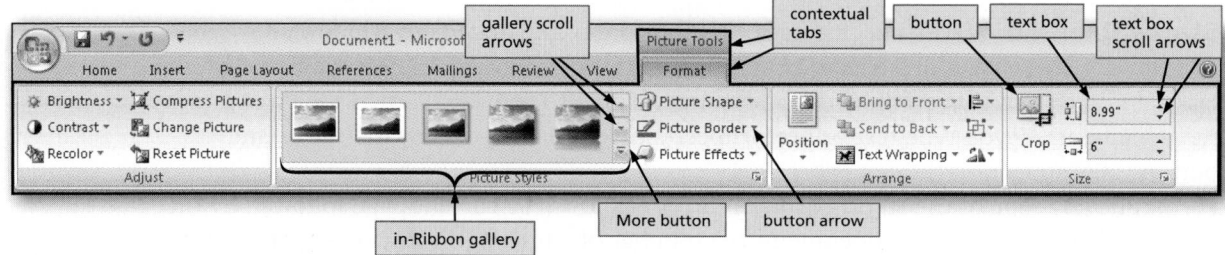

Figure 1–6

Commands on the Ribbon include buttons, boxes (text boxes, check boxes, etc.), and galleries (Figure 1–6). A **gallery** is a set of choices, often graphical, arranged in a grid or in a list. You can scroll through choices on an in-Ribbon gallery by clicking the gallery's scroll arrows. Or, you can click a gallery's More button to view more gallery options on the screen at a time. Some buttons and boxes have arrows that, when clicked, also display a gallery; others always cause a gallery to be displayed when clicked. Most galleries support **live preview**, which is a feature that allows you to point to a gallery choice and see its effect in the document — without actually selecting the choice (Figure 1–7).

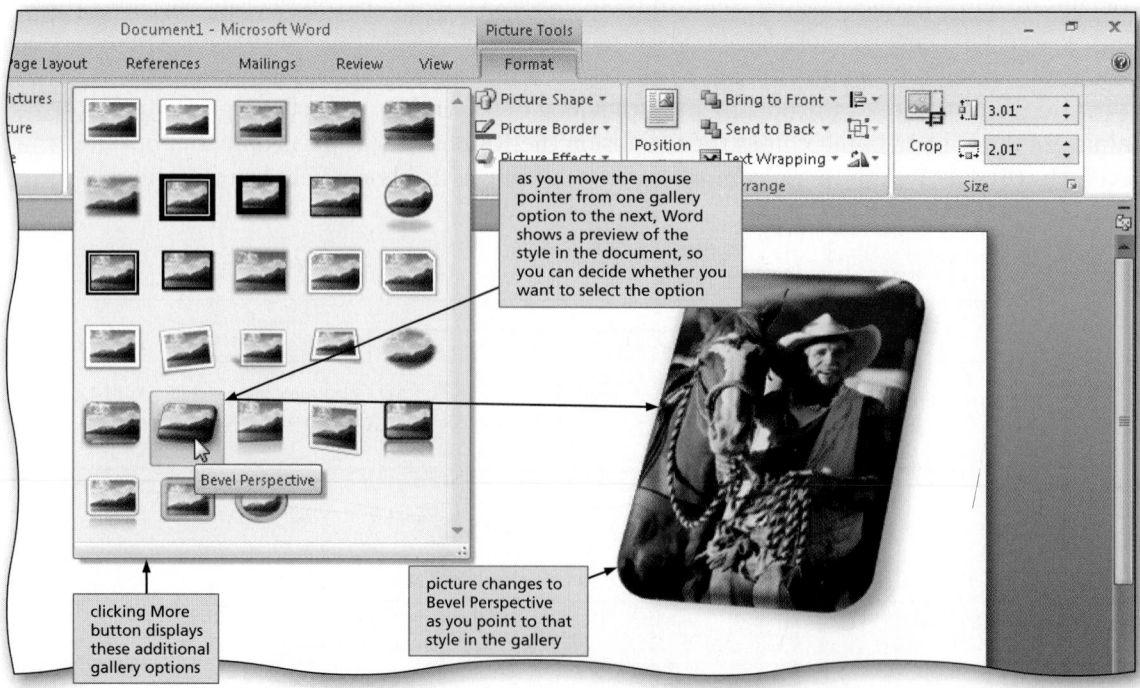

Figure 1–7

Some commands on the Ribbon display an image to help you remember their function. When you point to a command on the Ribbon, all or part of the command glows in shades of yellow and orange, and an Enhanced ScreenTip appears on the screen. An **Enhanced ScreenTip** is an on-screen note that provides the name of the command, available keyboard shortcut(s), a description of the command, and sometimes instructions for how to obtain help about the command (Figure 1–8). Enhanced ScreenTips are more detailed than a typical ScreenTip, which usually only displays the name of the command.

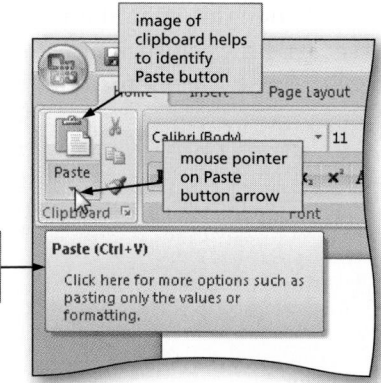

Figure 1–8

The lower-right corner of some groups on the Ribbon has a small arrow, called a **Dialog Box Launcher**, that when clicked, displays a dialog box or a task pane with additional options for the group (Figure 1–9). When presented with a dialog box, you make selections and must close the dialog box before returning to the document. A **task pane**, by contrast, is a window that can remain open and visible while you work in the document.

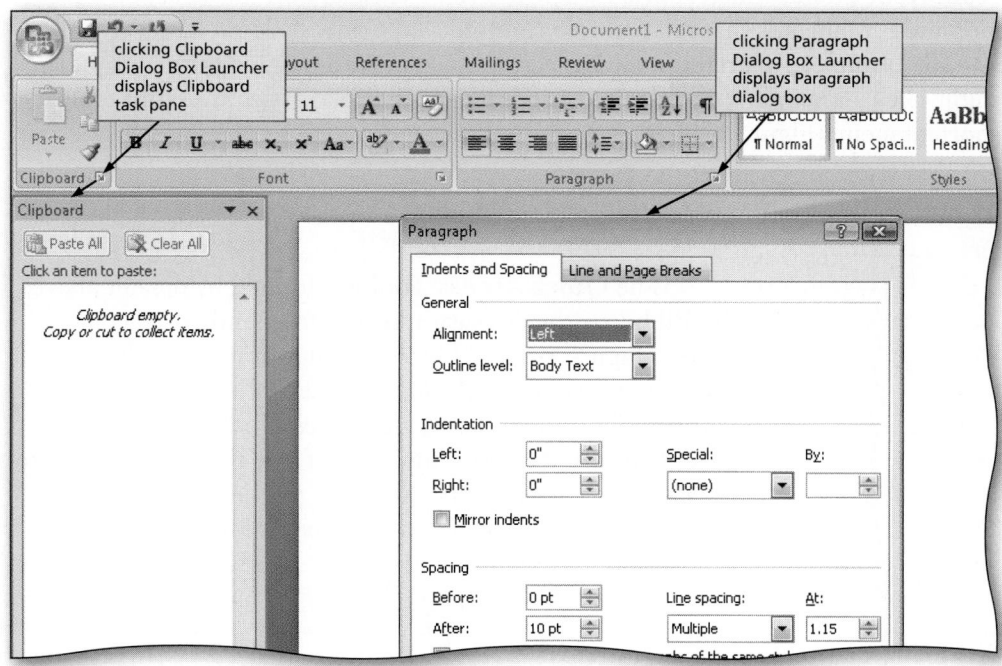

Figure 1–9

Mini Toolbar and Shortcut Menus

The **Mini toolbar**, which appears automatically based on tasks you perform, contains commands related to changing the appearance of text in a document. All commands on the Mini toolbar also exist on the Ribbon. The purpose of the Mini toolbar is to minimize mouse movement. For example, if you want to use a command that currently is not displayed on the active tab, you can use the command on the Mini toolbar — instead of switching to a different tab to use the command.

When the Mini toolbar appears, it initially is transparent (Figure 1–10a). If you do not use the transparent Mini toolbar, it disappears from the screen. To use the Mini toolbar, move the mouse pointer into the toolbar, which causes the Mini toolbar to change from a transparent to bright appearance (Figure 1–10b).

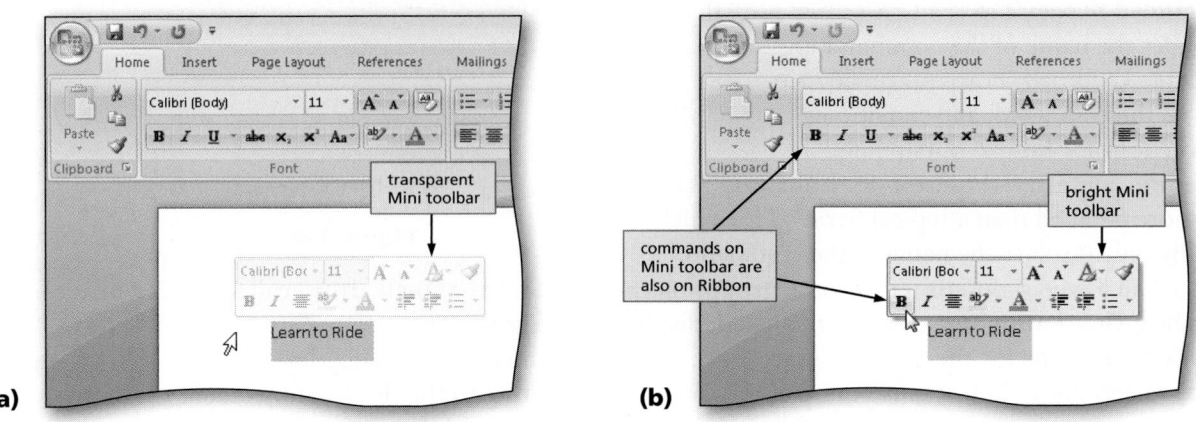

Figure 1–10

A **shortcut menu**, which appears when you right-click an object, is a list of frequently used commands that relate to the right-clicked object. When you right-click a scroll bar, for example, a shortcut menu appears with commands related to the scroll bar. If you right-click an item in the document window, Word displays both the Mini toolbar and a shortcut menu (Figure 1–11).

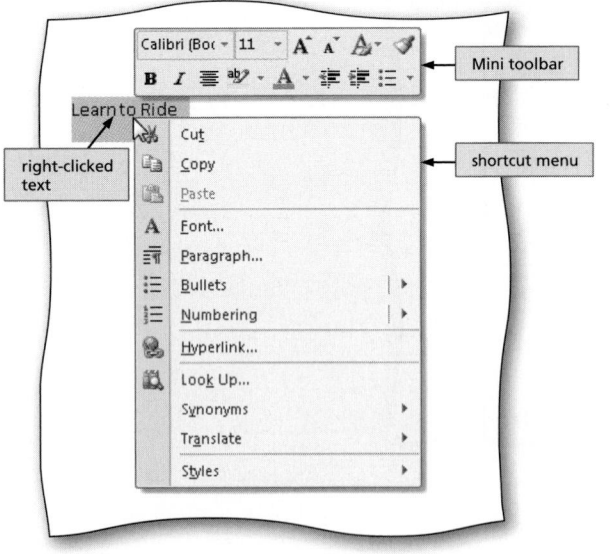

Figure 1–11

Quick Access Toolbar

The **Quick Access Toolbar**, located by default above the Ribbon, provides easy access to frequently used commands (Figure 1–12a). The commands on the Quick Access Toolbar always are available, regardless of the task you are performing. Initially, the Quick Access Toolbar contains the Save, Undo, and Redo commands. If you click the Customize Quick Access Toolbar button, Word provides a list of commands you quickly can add to and remove from the Quick Access Toolbar (Figure 1–12b).

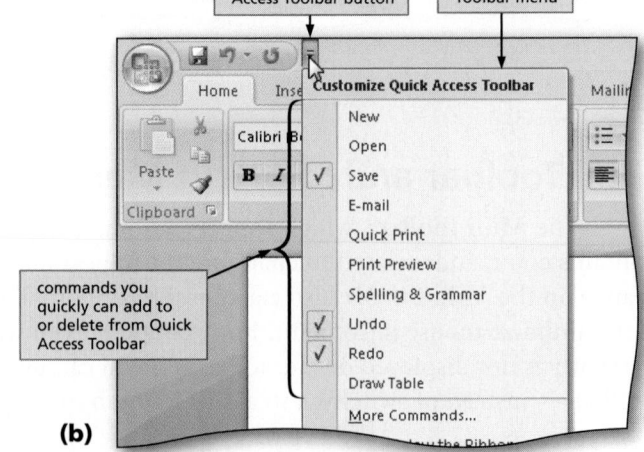

Figure 1–12

You also can add other commands to or delete commands from the Quick Access Toolbar so that it contains the commands you use most often. As you add commands to the Quick Access Toolbar, its commands may interfere with the document title on the title bar. For this reason, Word provides an option of displaying the Quick Access Toolbar below the Ribbon (Figure 1–13).

Each time you start Word, the Quick Access Toolbar appears the same way it did the last time you used Word. The chapters in this book, however, begin with the Quick Access Toolbar appearing as it did at the initial installation of the software. If you are stepping through this chapter on a computer and you want your Quick Access Toolbar to match the figures in this book, you should reset your Quick Access Toolbar. For more information about how to reset the Quick Access Toolbar, read Appendix E.

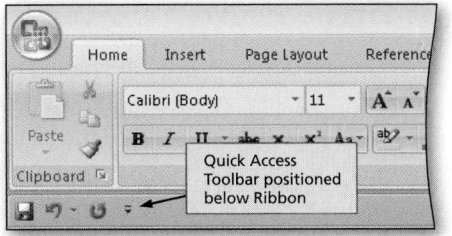

Figure 1–13

BTW

Quick Access Toolbar Commands
To add a Ribbon command to the Quick Access Toolbar, right-click the command on the Ribbon and then click Add to Quick Access Toolbar on the shortcut menu. To delete a command from the Quick Access Toolbar, right-click the command on the Quick Access Toolbar and then click Remove from Quick Access Toolbar on the shortcut menu. To display the Quick Access Toolbar below the Ribbon, right-click the Quick Access Toolbar and then click Show Quick Access Toolbar Below the Ribbon on the shortcut menu.

Office Button

While the Ribbon is a control center for creating documents, the **Office Button** is a central location for managing and sharing documents. When you click the Office Button, located in the upper-left corner of the window, Word displays the Office Button menu (Figure 1–14a). A **menu** contains a list of commands.

When you click the New, Open, Save As, and Print commands on the Office Button menu, Word displays a dialog box with additional options. The Save As, Print, Prepare, Send, and Publish commands have an arrow to their right. If you point to this arrow, Word displays a **submenu**, which is a list of additional commands associated with the selected command (Figure 1–14b). For the Prepare, Send, and Publish commands that do not display a dialog box when clicked, you can point either to the command or the arrow to display the submenu.

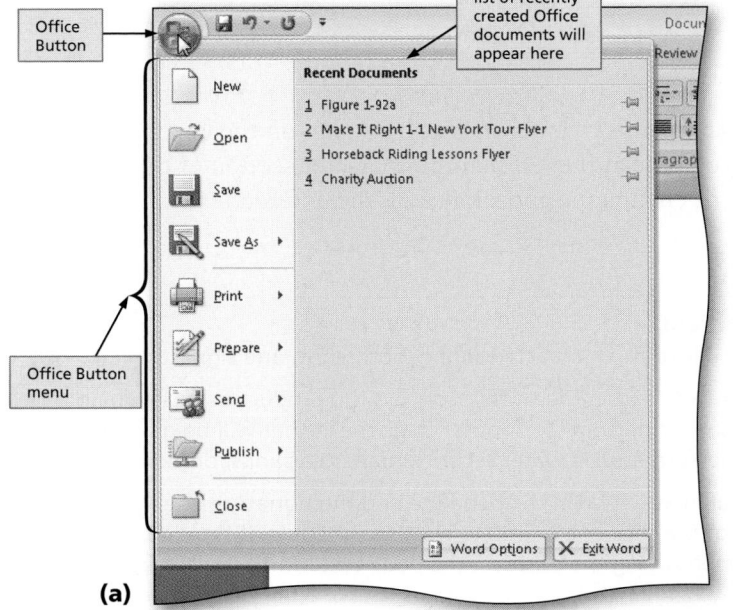

(a)

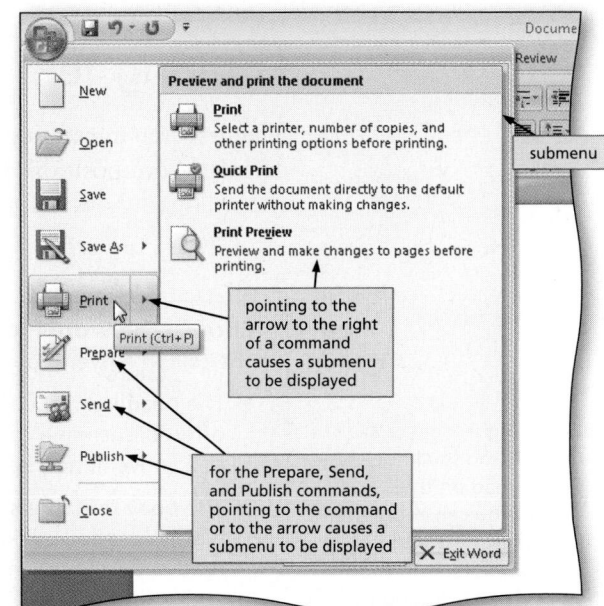

(b)

Figure 1–14

Key Tips

If you prefer using the keyboard instead of the mouse, you can press the ALT key on the keyboard to display a **Key Tip badge**, or keyboard code icon, for certain commands (Figure 1–15). To select a command using the keyboard, press its displayed code letter, or **Key Tip**. When you press a Key Tip, additional Key Tips related to the selected command may appear. For example, to select the New command on the Office Button menu, press the ALT key, then press the F key, and then press the N key.

To remove the Key Tip badges from the screen, press the ALT key or the ESC key until all Key Tip badges disappear, or click the mouse anywhere in the Word window.

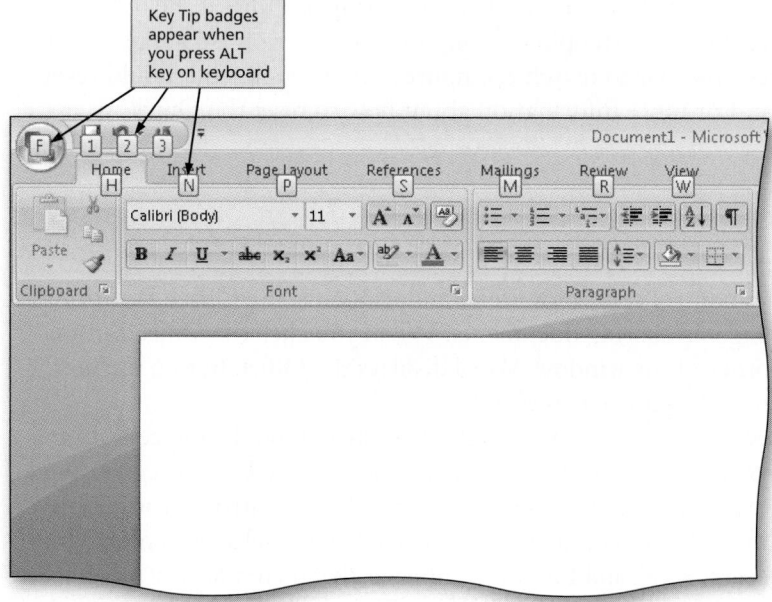

Figure 1–15

Entering Text

The first step in creating a document is to enter its text by typing on the keyboard. By default, Word positions text you type at the left margin. In a later section of this chapter, you will learn how to format, or change the appearance of, the entered text.

Plan Ahead

Choose the words for the text.
The text in a flyer is organized into three areas: headline, body copy, and signature line.

- The headline is the first line of text on the flyer. It conveys the product or service being offered, such as a car for sale or personal lessons, or the benefit that will be gained, such as a convenience, better performance, greater security, higher earnings, or more comfort.

- The body text consists of all text between the headline and the signature line. This text highlights the key points of the message in as few words as possible. It should be easy to read and follow. While emphasizing the positive, the body text must be realistic, truthful, and believable.

- The signature line, which is the last line of text on the flyer, contains contact information or identifies a call to action.

To Type Text

To begin creating the flyer in this chapter, you type the headline in the document window. The following steps type this first line of text in the document.

 1

- **Type** Learn to Ride **as the headline (Figure 1–16).**

Q&A What if I make an error while typing?

You can press the **BACKSPACE** key until you have deleted the text in error and then retype the text correctly.

Q&A Why did the Spelling and Grammar Check icon appear on the status bar?

When you begin typing text, the **Spelling and Grammar Check icon** appears on the status bar with an animated pencil writing on paper that indicates Word is checking for spelling and grammar errors. When you stop typing, the pencil changes to a blue check mark (no errors) or a red X (potential errors found). Word flags potential errors in the document with a red or green wavy underline. Later, this chapter shows how to fix flagged errors.

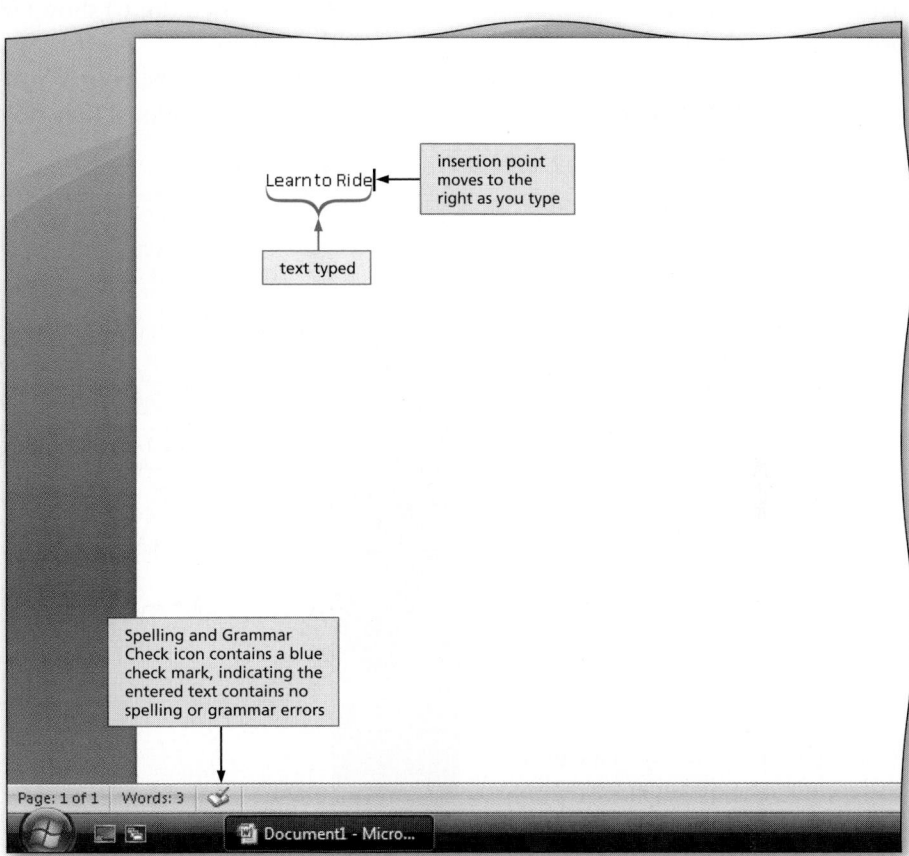

Figure 1–16

 2

- **Press the ENTER key to move the insertion point to the beginning of the next line (Figure 1–17).**

 Q&A Why did blank space appear between the headline and the insertion point?

Each time you press the ENTER key, Word creates a new paragraph and inserts blank space between the two paragraphs. Later in this chapter, you will learn how to adjust the spacing between paragraphs.

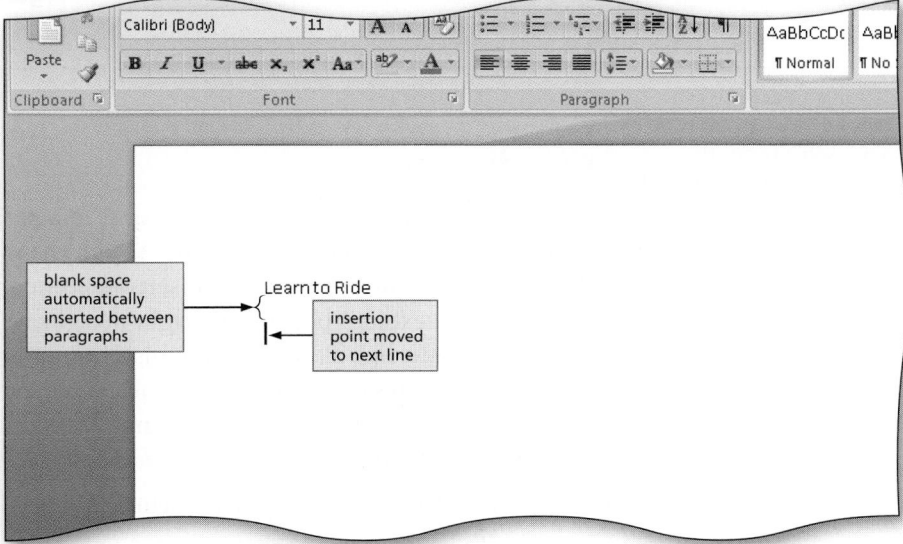

Figure 1–17

To Display Formatting Marks

To indicate where in a document you press the ENTER key or SPACEBAR, you may find it helpful to display formatting marks. A **formatting mark**, sometimes called a **nonprinting character**, is a character that Word displays on the screen but is not visible on a printed document. For example, the paragraph mark (¶) is a formatting mark that indicates where you pressed the ENTER key. A raised dot (·) shows where you pressed the SPACEBAR. Other formatting marks are discussed as they appear on the screen.

Depending on settings made during previous Word sessions, your Word screen already may display formatting marks (Figure 1–18). The following step displays formatting marks, if they do not show already on the screen.

1

- If necessary, click Home on the Ribbon to display the Home tab.

- If it is not selected already, click the Show/Hide ¶ button on the Home tab to display formatting marks on the screen (Figure 1–18).

Q&A

What if I do not want formatting marks to show on the screen?

If you feel the formatting marks clutter the screen, you can hide them by clicking the Show/Hide ¶ button again. It is recommended that you display formatting marks so that you visually can identify when you press the ENTER key, SPACEBAR, and other keys associated with nonprinting characters; therefore, the document windows presented in this book show the formatting marks.

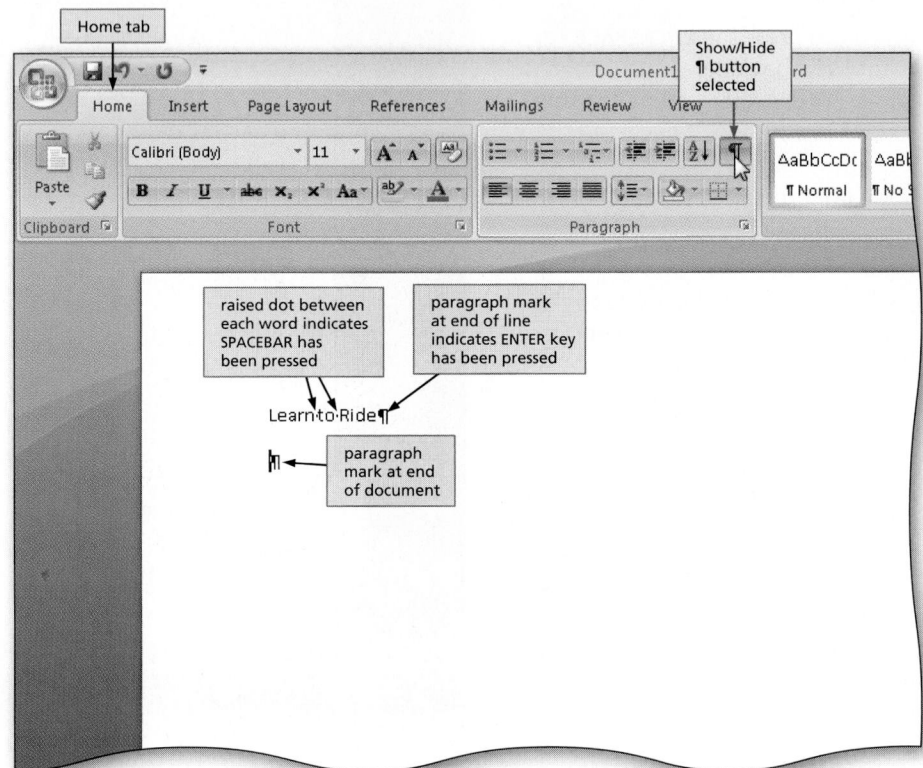

Figure 1–18

Other Ways

1. Press CTRL+SHIFT+*

Wordwrap

Wordwrap allows you to type words in a paragraph continually without pressing the ENTER key at the end of each line. When the insertion point reaches the right margin, Word automatically positions the insertion point at the beginning of the next line. As you type, if a word extends beyond the right margin, Word also automatically positions that word on the next line along with the insertion point.

Word creates a new paragraph each time you press the ENTER key. Thus, as you type text in the document window, do not press the ENTER key when the insertion point reaches the right margin. Instead, press the ENTER key only in these circumstances:

1. To insert blank lines in a document
2. To begin a new paragraph
3. To terminate a short line of text and advance to the next line
4. To respond to questions or prompts in Word dialog boxes, task panes, and other on-screen objects

To Wordwrap Text as You Type

The next step in creating the flyer is to type the body copy. The following step wordwraps the text in the body copy.

- **Type** High-quality Western and English riding lessons, focusing on safety and including instruction on horse care, saddling a horse, and other aspects of horsemanship.

Q&A

Why does my document wrap on different words?

Differences in wordwrap relate to the printer used by your computer. That is, the printer controls where wordwrap occurs for each line in your document. Thus, it is possible that the same document could wordwrap differently if printed on different printers.

- Press the ENTER key to position the insertion point on the next line in the document (Figure 1–19).

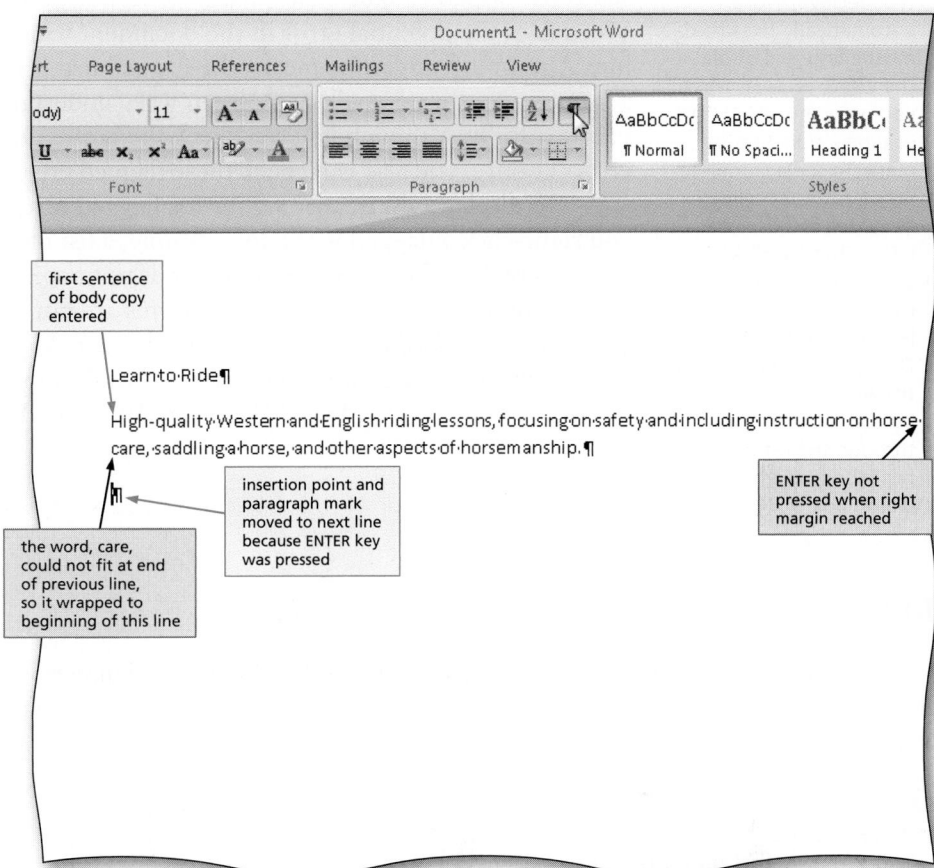

Figure 1–19

To Insert a Blank Line

In the flyer, the picture of the horse and rider should be positioned below the paragraph just entered. The picture will be inserted after all text is entered and formatted. Thus, you will leave a blank line in the document for the picture. To enter a blank line in a document, press the ENTER key without typing any text on the line. The following step inserts one blank line below the first paragraph of body copy.

- Press the ENTER key to insert a blank line in the document (Figure 1–20).

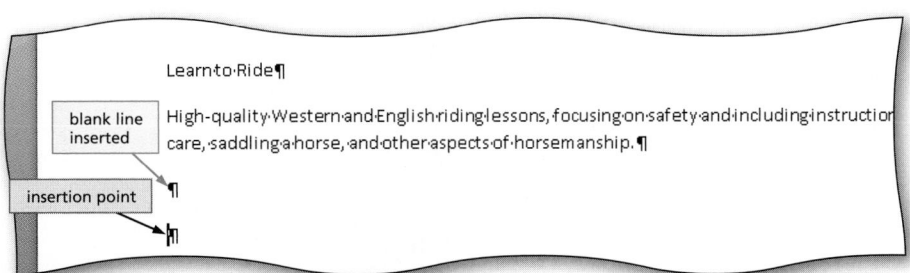

Figure 1–20

BTW

Automatic Spelling Correction

As you type, Word automatically corrects some misspelled words. For example, if you type recieve, Word automatically fixes the misspelling and displays the word, receive, when you press the SPACEBAR or type a punctuation mark. To see a complete list of automatically corrected words, click Office Button, click the Word Options button, click Proofing in the left pane of the Word Options dialog box, click the AutoCorrect Options button, and then scroll through the list of words near the bottom of the dialog box.

Spelling and Grammar Check

As you type text in a document, Word checks your typing for possible spelling and grammar errors. If all of the words you have typed are in Word's dictionary and your grammar is correct, as mentioned earlier, the Spelling and Grammar Check icon on the status bar displays a blue check mark. Otherwise, the icon shows a red X. In this case, Word flags the potential error in the document window with a red or green wavy underline. A red wavy underline means the flagged text is not in Word's dictionary (because it is a proper name or misspelled). A green wavy underline indicates the text may be incorrect grammatically. Although you can check the entire document for spelling and grammar errors at once, you also can check these flagged errors as they appear on the screen.

To display a list of corrections for flagged text, right-click the flagged text. When you right-click a flagged word, for example, a list of suggested spelling corrections appears on the screen. A flagged word, however, is not necessarily misspelled. For example, many names, abbreviations, and specialized terms are not in Word's main dictionary. In these cases, you tell Word to ignore the flagged word. As you type, Word also detects duplicate words while checking for spelling errors. For example, if your document contains the phrase, to the the store, Word places a red wavy underline below the second occurrence of the word, the.

To Check Spelling and Grammar as You Type

In the following steps, the word, instruction, has been misspelled intentionally as intrution to illustrate Word's check spelling as you type feature. If you are doing this project on a computer, your flyer may contain other misspelled words, depending on the accuracy of your typing.

- **Type** Novice to advanced intrution **and then press the** SPACEBAR (Figure 1–21).

Q&A

What if Word does not flag my spelling and grammar errors with wavy underlines?

To verify that the check spelling and grammar as you type features are enabled, click the Office Button and then click the Word Options button. When the Word Options dialog box is displayed, click Proofing, and then ensure the 'Check spelling as you type' and 'Mark grammar errors as you type' check boxes have check marks. Also ensure the 'Hide spelling errors in this document only' and 'Hide grammar errors in this document only' check boxes do not have check marks. Click the OK button.

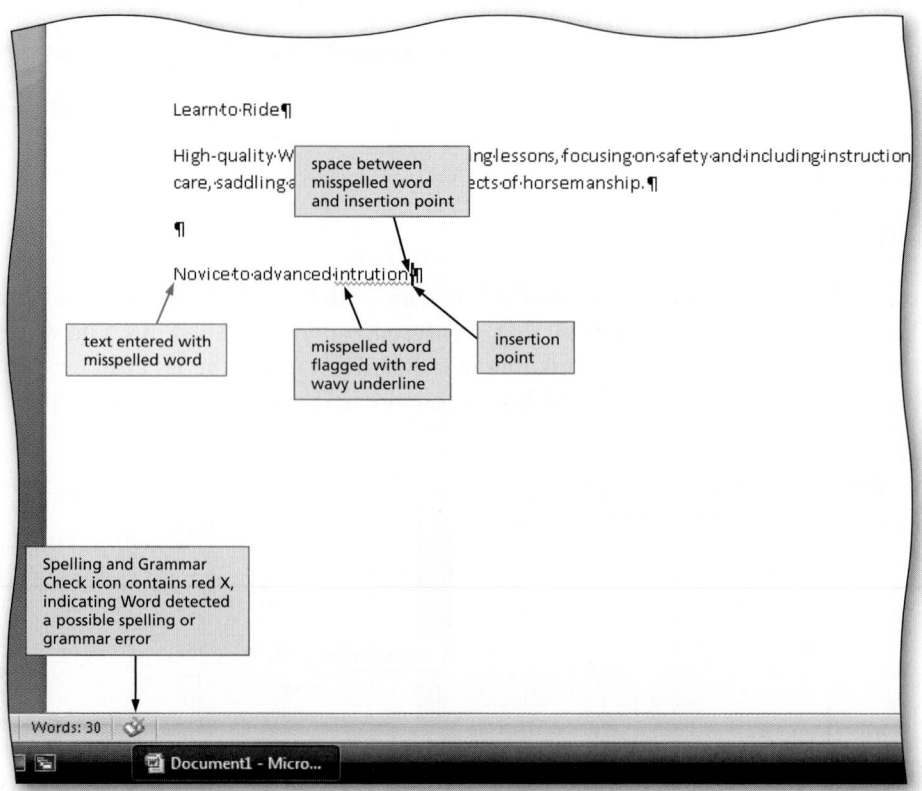

Figure 1–21

- Right-click the flagged word (intrution, in this case) to display a shortcut menu that includes a list of suggested spelling corrections for the flagged word (Figure 1–22).

Q&A

What if, when I right-click the misspelled word, my desired correction is not in the list on the shortcut menu?

You can click outside the shortcut menu to close the menu and then retype the correct word, or you can click Spelling on the shortcut menu to display the Spelling dialog box. Chapter 2 discusses the Spelling dialog box.

Q&A

What if a flagged word actually is, for example, a proper name and spelled correctly?

Right-click it and then click Ignore All on the shortcut menu to instruct Word not to flag future occurrences of the same word.

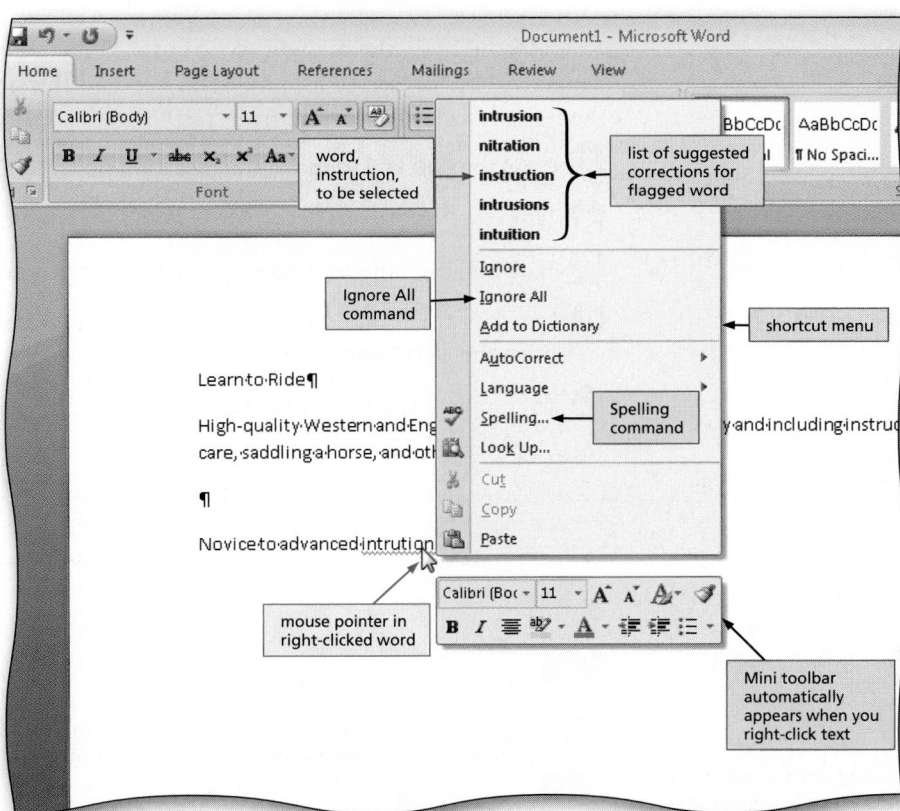

Figure 1–22

- Click instruction on the shortcut menu to replace the misspelled word in the document (intrution) with the word, instruction (Figure 1–23).

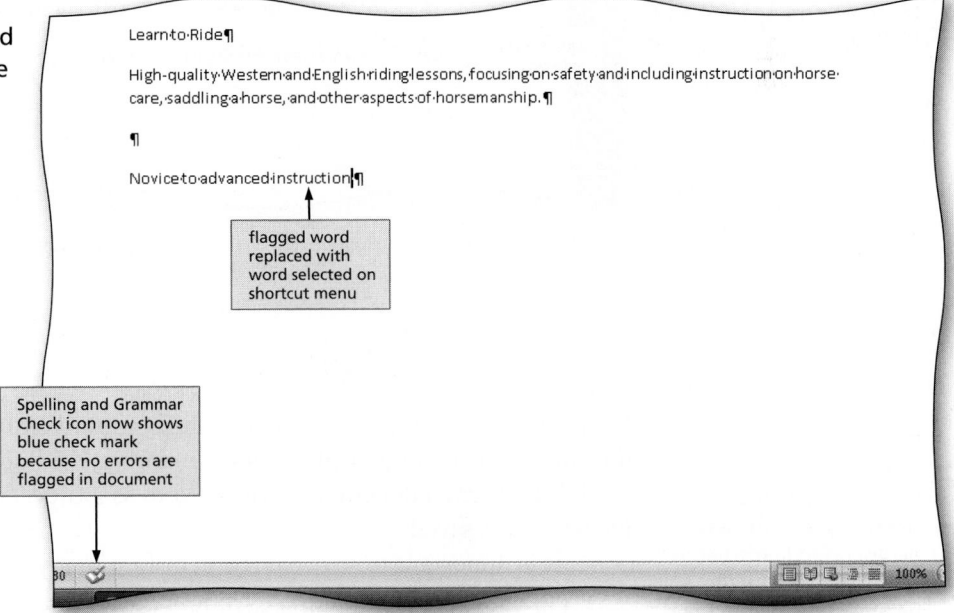

Figure 1–23

Other Ways

1. Click Spelling and Grammar Check icon on status bar, click correct word on shortcut menu

To Enter More Text

In the flyer, the text yet to be entered includes the remainder of the body copy, which will be formatted as a bulleted list, and the signature line. The following steps enter the remainder of text in the flyer.

1 Press the END key to move the insertion point to the end of the current line.

2 Type `for children and adults` and then press the ENTER key.

3 Type `Indoor and outdoor arenas` and then press the ENTER key.

4 Type `$40 per hour for private lessons; $25 for group lessons` and then press the ENTER key.

5 To complete the text in the flyer, type `Call Tri-Valley Stables at 555-2030 today!` (Figure 1–24).

Character Widths
Many word processing documents use variable character fonts, where some characters are wider than others; for example, the letter w takes up more space than the letter i.

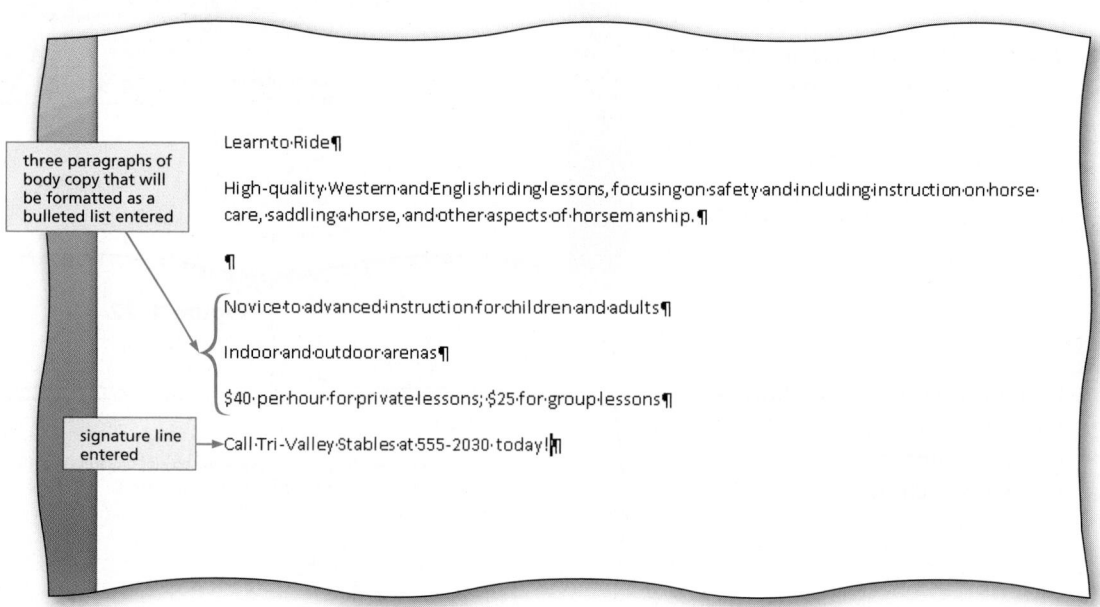

Figure 1–24

Saving the Project

File Type
Depending on your Windows Vista settings, the file type .docx may be displayed immediately to the right of the file name after you save the file. The file type .docx is a Word 2007 document. Previous versions of Word had a file type of .doc.

While you are creating a document, the computer stores it in memory. When you save a document, the computer places it on a storage medium such as a USB flash drive, CD, or hard disk. A saved document is referred to as a **file**. A **file name** is the name assigned to a file when it is saved.

It is important to save a document frequently for the following reasons:

• The document in memory will be lost if the computer is turned off or you lose electrical power while Word is open.

• If you run out of time before completing your project, you may finish your document at a future time without starting over.

<table>
<tr><td>

Determine where to save the document.
When saving a document, you must decide which storage medium to use.

• If you always work on the same computer and have no need to transport your projects to a different location, then your computer's hard disk will suffice as a storage location. It is a good idea, however, to save a backup copy of your projects on a separate medium in case the file becomes corrupted or the computer's hard disk fails.

• If you plan to work on your projects in various locations or on multiple computers, then you should save your projects on a portable medium, such as a USB flash drive or CD. The projects in this book use a USB flash drive, which saves files quickly and reliably and can be reused. CDs are easily portable and serve as good backups for the final versions of projects because they generally can save files only one time.

</td><td>

Plan Ahead

</td></tr>
</table>

To Save a Document

You have performed many tasks while creating this project and do not want to risk losing the work completed thus far. Accordingly, you should save the document. The following steps save a document on a USB flash drive using the file name, Horseback Riding Lessons Flyer.

Note: If you are using Windows XP, see Appendix F for alternate steps.

1

• With a USB flash drive connected to one of the computer's USB ports, click the Save button on the Quick Access Toolbar to display the Save As dialog box (Figure 1–25).

• If the Navigation pane is not displayed in the Save As dialog box, click the Browse Folders button to expand the dialog box.

• If a Folders list is displayed below the Folders button, click the Folders button to remove the Folders list.

Q&A

Do I have to save to a USB flash drive?

No. You can save to any device or folder. A **folder** is a specific location on a storage medium. You can save to the default folder or a different folder. You also can create your own folders, which is explained later in this book.

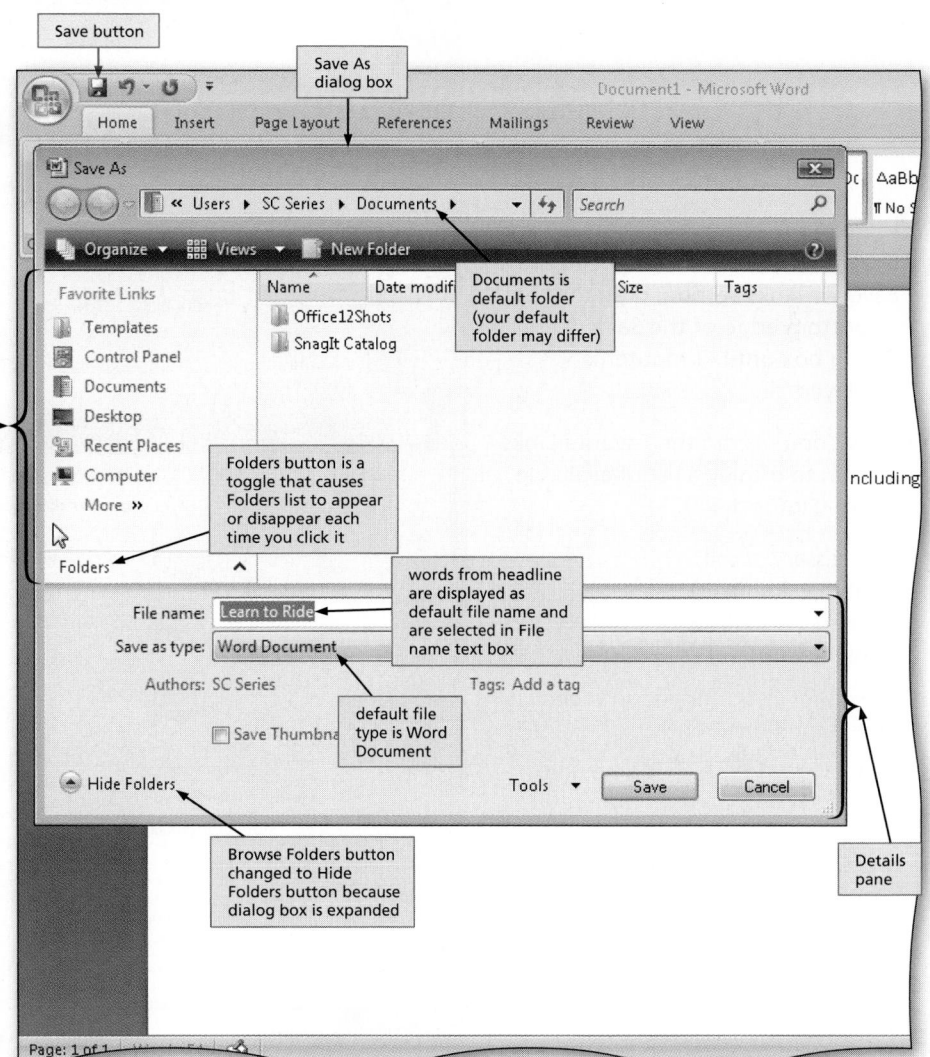

Figure 1–25

2

- Type `Horseback Riding Lessons Flyer` in the File name text box to change the file name. Do not press the ENTER key after typing the file name (Figure 1–26).

Q&A

What characters can I use in a file name?

A file name can have a maximum of 260 characters, including spaces. The only invalid characters are the backslash (\\), slash (/), colon (:), asterisk (*), question mark (?), quotation mark ("), less than symbol (<), greater than symbol (>), and vertical bar (|).

Q&A

What are file properties and tags?

File properties contain information about a file such as the the file name, author name, date the file was modified, and tags. A tag is a file property that contains a word or phrase about a file. You can organize and locate files based on their file properties.

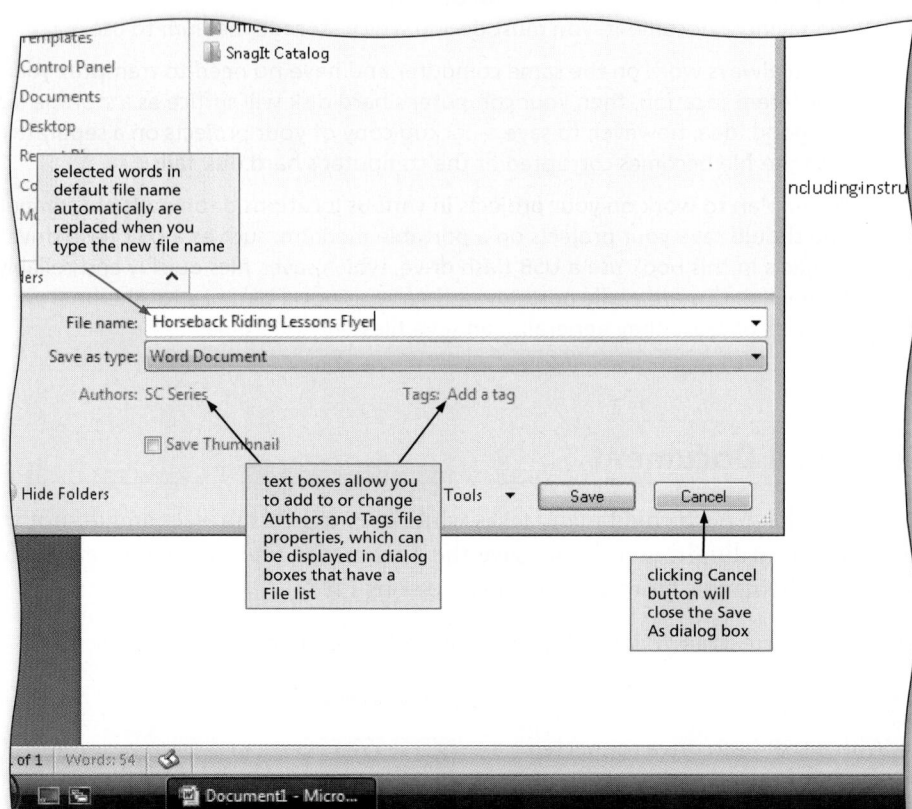

Figure 1–26

3

- If Computer is not displayed in the Favorite Links section, drag the top or bottom edge of the Save As dialog box until Computer is displayed.

- Click Computer in the Favorite Links section to display a list of available drives (Figure 1–27).

- If necessary, scroll until UDISK 2.0 (E:) appears in the list of available drives.

Q&A

Why is my list of drives arranged and named differently?

The size of the Save As dialog box and your computer's configuration determine how the list is displayed and how the drives are named.

Q&A

How do I save the file if I am not using a USB flash drive?

Use the same process, but select your desired save location in the Favorite Links section.

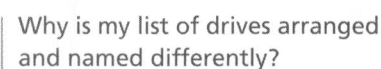

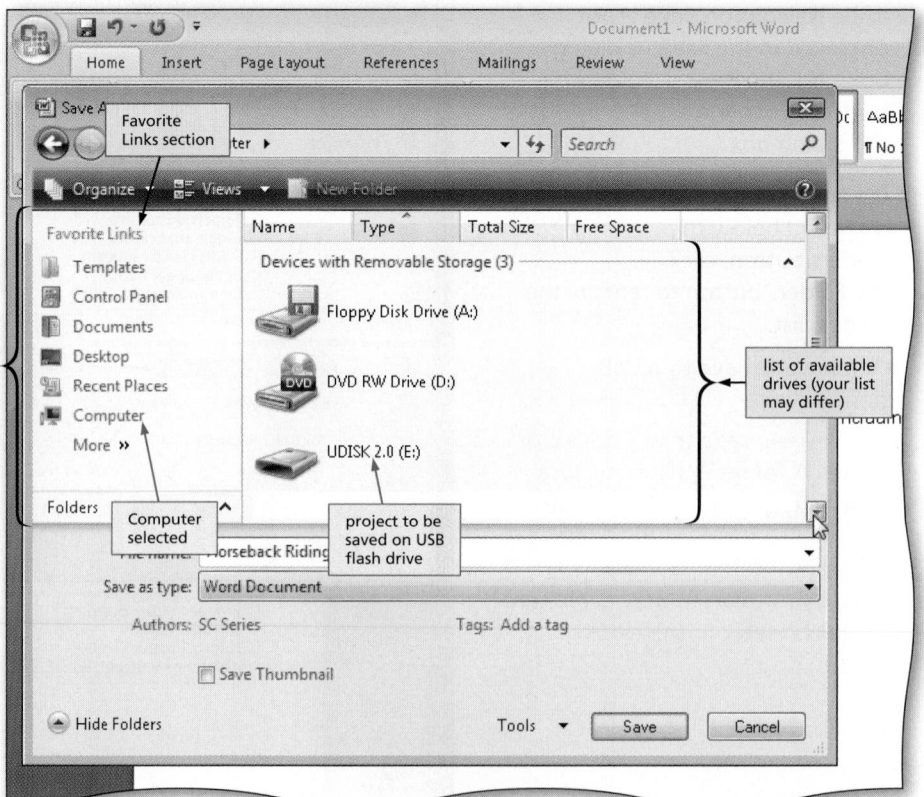

Figure 1–27

- Double-click UDISK 2.0 (E:) in the Computer list to select the USB flash drive, Drive E in this case, as the new save location (Figure 1–28).

Q&A

What if my USB flash drive has a different name or letter?

It is very likely that your USB flash drive will have a different name and drive letter and be connected to a different port. Verify the device in your Computer list is correct.

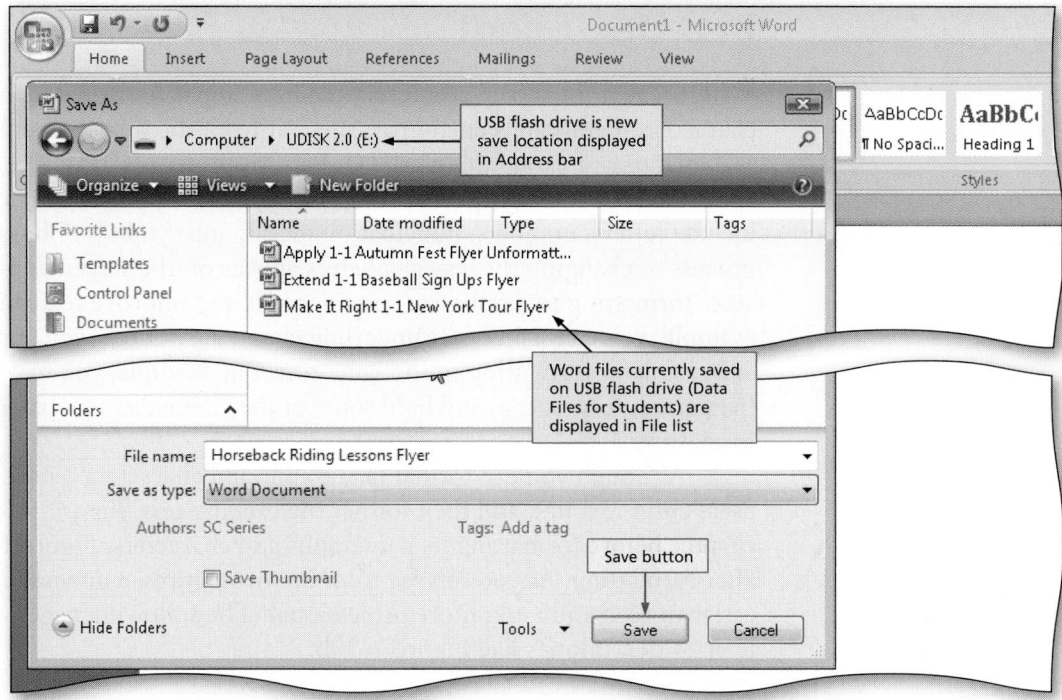

Figure 1–28

- Click the Save button in the Save As dialog box to save the document on the USB flash drive with the file name, Horseback Riding Lessons Flyer (Figure 1–29).

Q&A

How do I know that the project is saved?

While Word is saving your file, it briefly displays a message on the status bar indicating the amount of the file saved. In addition, your USB drive may have a light that flashes during the save process.

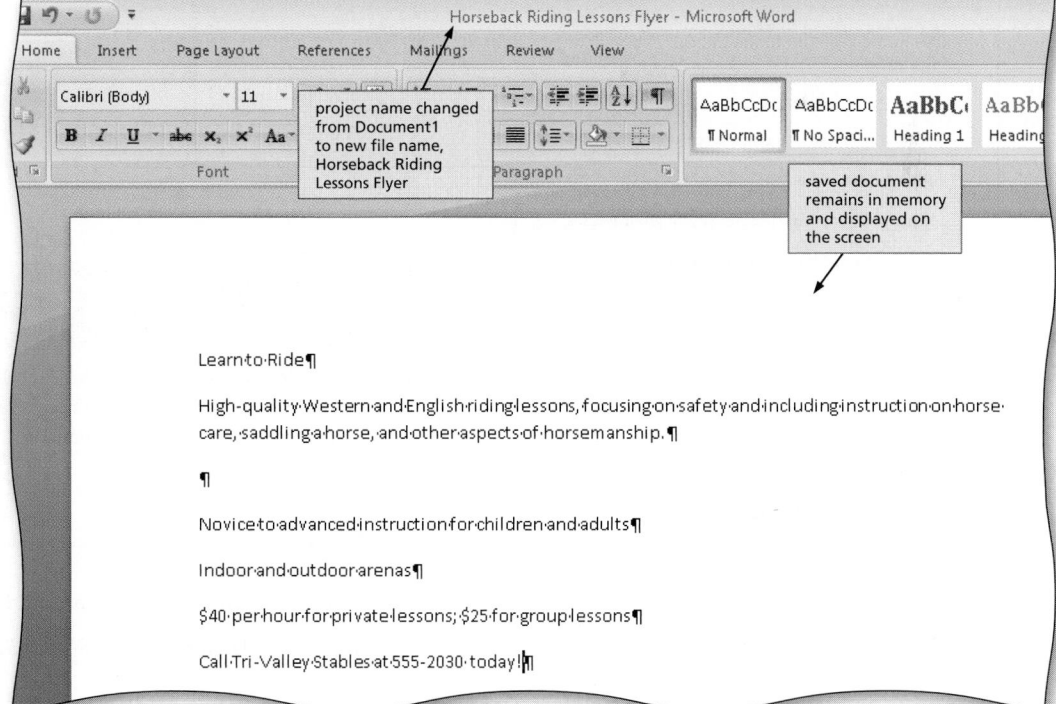

Figure 1–29

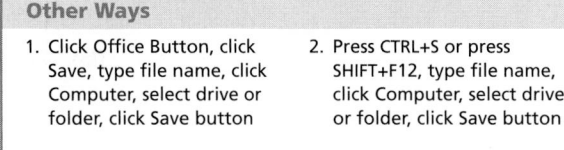

Other Ways

1. Click Office Button, click Save, type file name, click Computer, select drive or folder, click Save button

2. Press CTRL+S or press SHIFT+F12, type file name, click Computer, select drive or folder, click Save button

Formatting Paragraphs and Characters in a Document

With the text for the flyer entered, the next step is to format its paragraphs and characters. Paragraphs encompass the text from the first character in a paragraph up to and including a paragraph mark (¶). **Paragraph formatting** is the process of changing the appearance of a paragraph. For example, you can center or indent a paragraph. Characters include letters, numbers, punctuation marks, and symbols. **Character formatting** is the process of changing the way characters appear on the screen and in print. You use character formatting to emphasize certain words and improve readability of a document. For example, you can italicize or underline characters. Often, you apply both paragraph and character formatting to the same text. For example, you may center a paragraph (paragraph formatting) and bold some of the characters in a paragraph (character formatting).

Although you can format paragraphs and characters before you type, many Word users enter text first and then format the existing text. Figure 1–30a shows the flyer in this chapter before formatting its paragraphs and characters. Figure 1–30b shows the flyer after formatting. As you can see from the two figures, a document that is formatted is easier to read and looks more professional. The following pages discuss how to format the flyer so that it looks like Figure 1–30b.

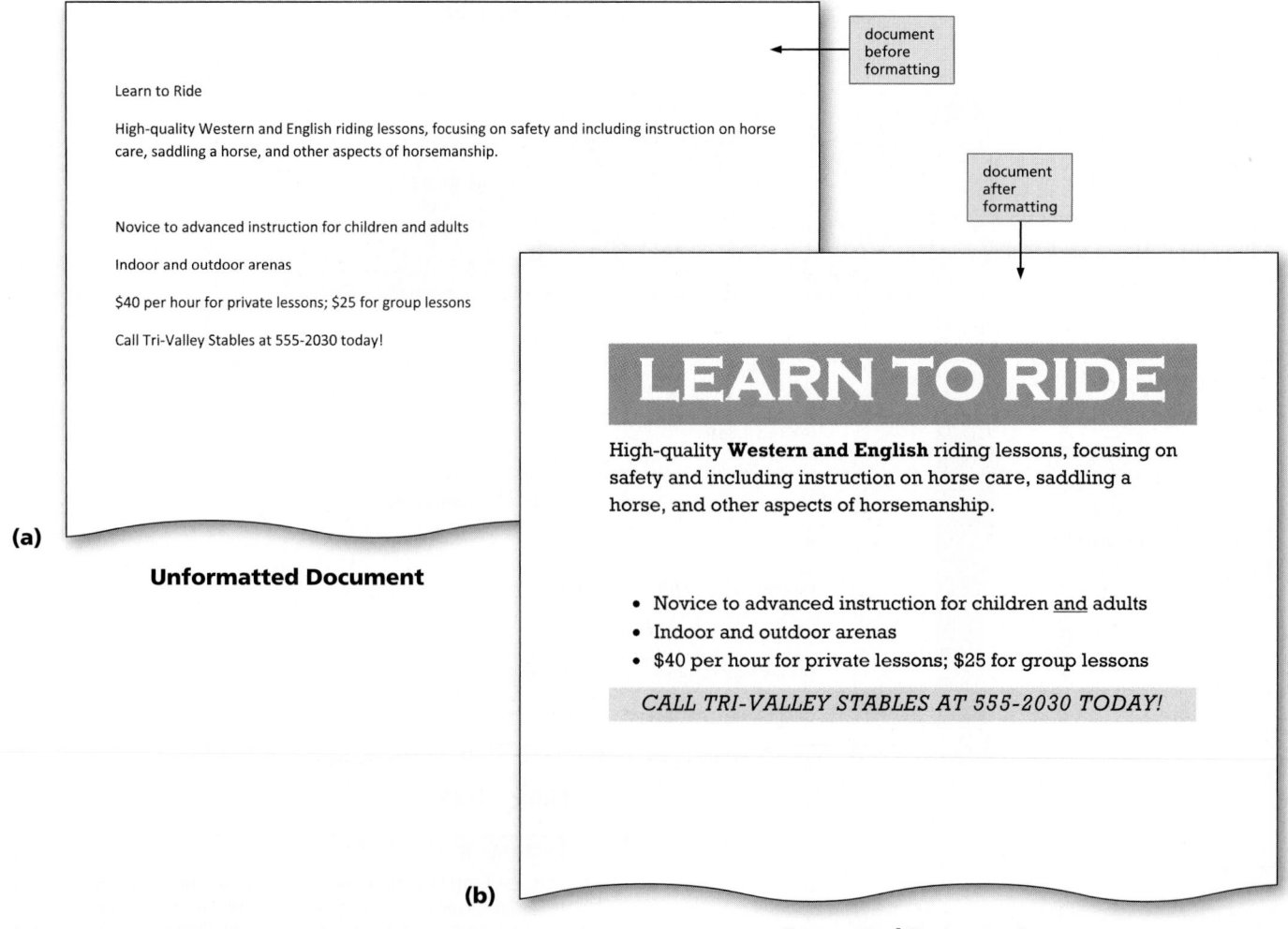

(a) **Unformatted Document**

(b) **Formatted Document**

Figure 1–30

Fonts, Font Sizes, Styles, and Themes

Characters that appear on the screen are a specific shape and size. The **font**, or typeface, defines the appearance and shape of the letters, numbers, and special characters. In Word, the default font usually is Calibri (Figure 1–31 on the next page). You can leave characters in the default font or change them to a different font. **Font size** specifies the size of the characters and is determined by a measurement system called points. A single **point** is about 1/72 of one inch in height. The default font size in Word typically is 11 (Figure 1–31). A character with a font size of 11 is about 11/72 or a little less than 1/6 of one inch in height. You can increase or decrease the font size of characters in a document.

When you create a document, Word formats the text using a particular style. A **style** is a named group of formatting characteristics, including font and font size. The default style in Word is called the **Normal style**, which most likely uses 11-point Calibri font. If you do not specify a style for text you type, Word applies the Normal style to the text. In addition to the Normal style, Word has many other built-in, or predefined, styles that you can use to format text. You also can create your own styles. Styles make it easy to apply many formats at once to text. After you apply a style to text, you easily can modify the text to include additional formats. You also can modify the style.

To assist you with coordinating colors and fonts and other formats, Word uses document themes. A document **theme** is a set of unified formats for fonts, colors, and graphics. The default theme fonts are Cambria for headings and Calibri for body text (Figure 1–31). Word includes a variety of document themes. By changing the document theme, you quickly give your document a new look. You also can define your own document themes.

Identify how to format various elements of the text.
By formatting the characters and paragraphs in a document, you can improve its overall appearance. In a flyer, consider the following formatting suggestions.

- **Increase the font size of characters.** Flyers usually are posted on a bulletin board or in a window. Thus, the font size should be as large as possible so that passersby easily can read the flyer. To give the headline more impact, its font size should be larger than the font size of the text in the body copy. If possible, make the font size of the signature line larger than the body copy but smaller than the headline.

- **Change the font of characters.** Use fonts that are easy to read. Try to use only two different fonts in a flyer, for example, one for the headline and the other for all other text. Too many fonts can make the flyer visually confusing.

- **Change paragraph alignment.** The default alignment for paragraphs in a document is **left-aligned**, that is, flush at the left margin of the document with uneven right edges. Consider changing the alignment of some of the paragraphs to add interest and variety to the flyer.

- **Highlight key paragraphs with bullets.** A **bullet** is a dot or other symbol positioned at the beginning of a paragraph. Use bullets to highlight important paragraphs in a flyer.

- **Emphasize important words.** To call attention to certain words or lines, you can underline them, italicize them, or bold them. Use these formats sparingly, however, because overuse will minimize their effect and make the flyer look too busy.

- **Use color.** Use colors that complement each other and convey the meaning of the flyer. Vary colors in terms of hue and brightness. Headline colors, for example, can be bold and bright. Signature lines should stand out more than body copy but less than headlines. Keep in mind that too many colors can detract from the flyer and make it difficult to read.

Plan Ahead

To Apply Styles

In the flyer, you want the headline and the signature line to be emphasized more than the other text. Word provides heading styles designed to emphasize this type of text. The first step in formatting the flyer is to apply the Heading 1 style to the headline and the Heading 2 style to the signature line. The default Heading 1 style is a 14-point Cambria bold font. The default Heading 2 style is a 13-point Cambria bold font. The default theme color scheme uses shades of blue for headings.

To apply a style to a paragraph, you first position the insertion point in the paragraph and then apply the style. The following steps apply heading styles to paragraphs.

- Press CTRL+HOME (that is, press and hold down the CTRL key, press the HOME key, and then release both keys) to position the insertion point at the top of the document (Figure 1–31).

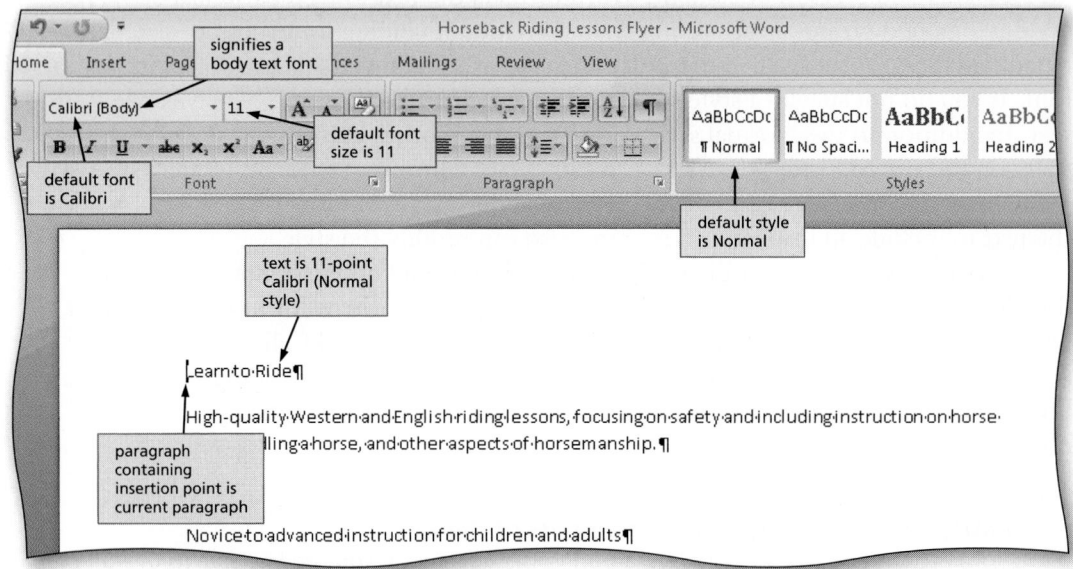

Figure 1–31

- Point to Heading 1 in the Styles gallery to display a live preview in the document of the Heading 1 style (Figure 1–32).

Q&A

What happens if I move the mouse pointer?

If you move the mouse pointer away from the gallery, the text containing the insertion point returns to the Normal style.

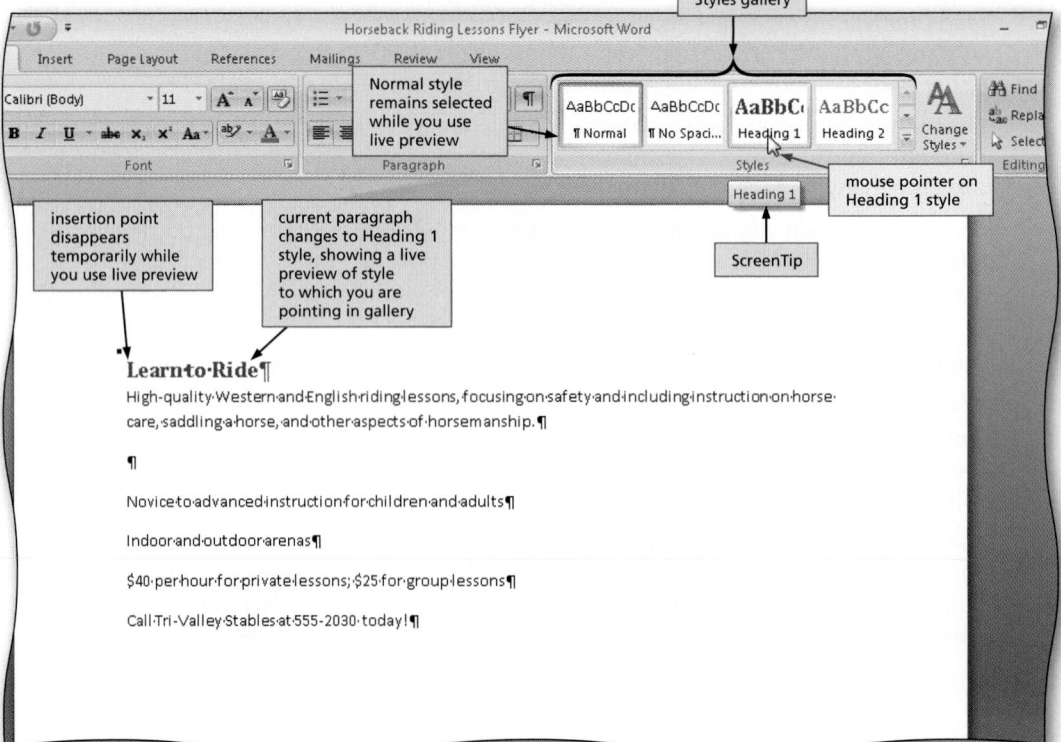

Figure 1–32

3

- Click Heading 1 in the Styles gallery to apply the Heading 1 style to the headline (Figure 1–33).

Why did a square appear on the screen near the left edge of the headline?

The square is a nonprinting character, like the paragraph mark, that indicates text to its right has a special paragraph format applied to it.

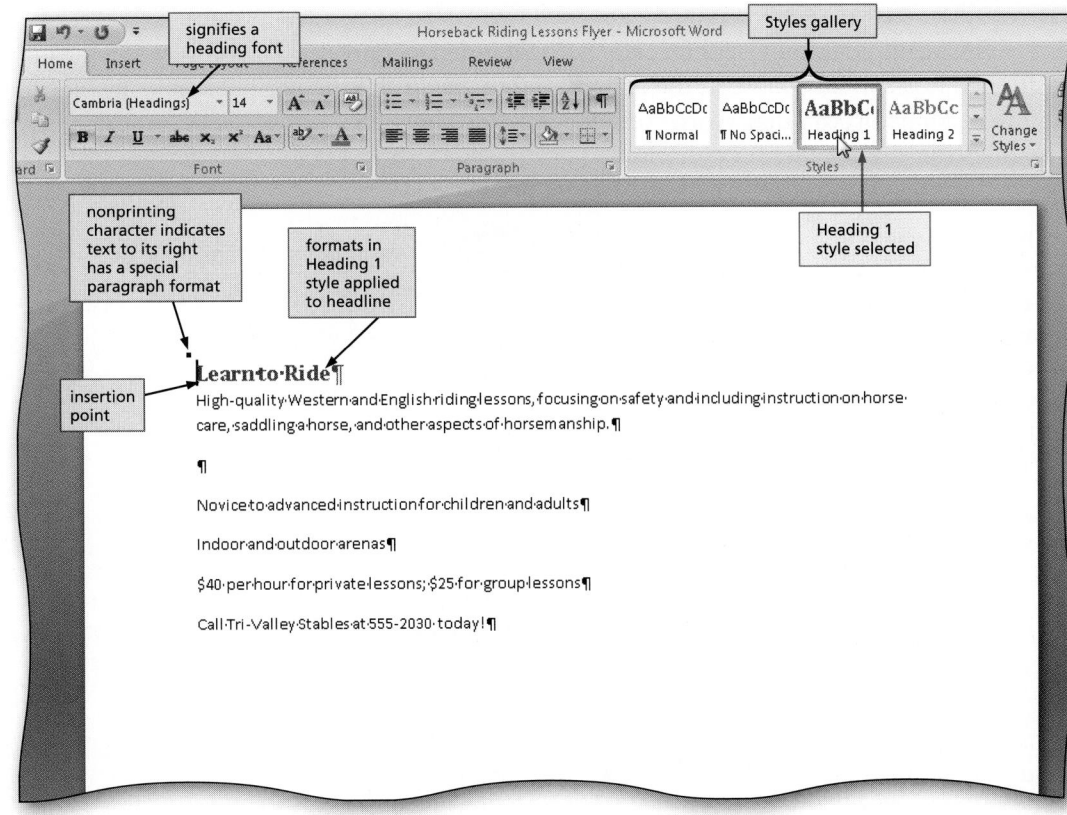

Figure 1–33

4

- Press CTRL+END (that is, press and hold down the CTRL key, press the END key, and then release both keys) to position the insertion point at the end of the document.

- Click Heading 2 in the Styles gallery to apply the Heading 2 style to the signature line (Figure 1–34).

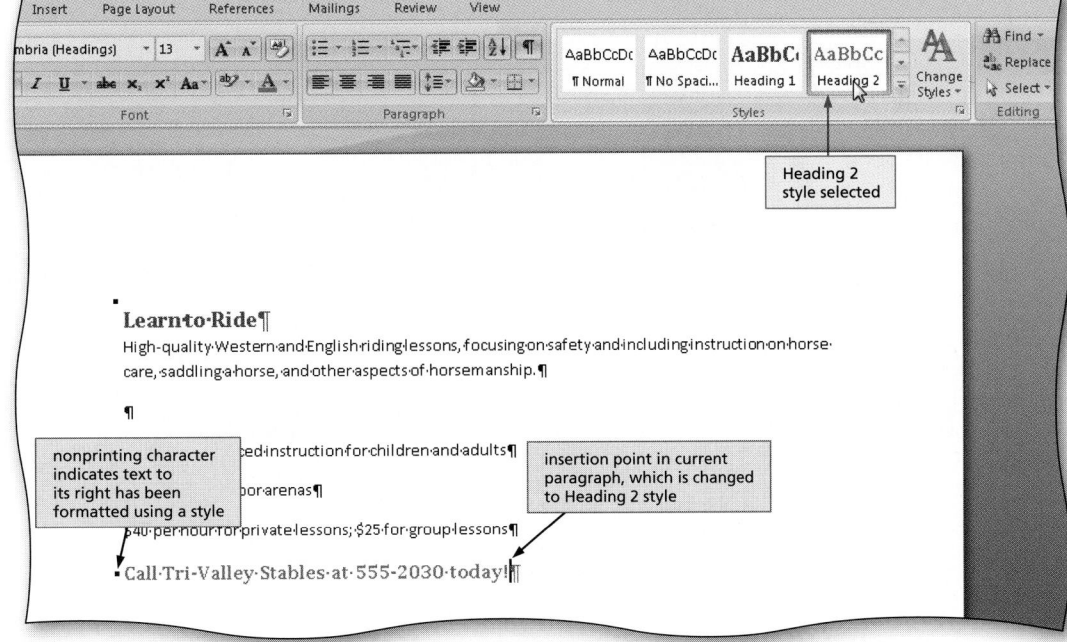

Figure 1–34

Other Ways	
1. Click Styles Dialog Box Launcher, click desired style in Styles task pane	2. Press CTRL+SHIFT+S, click Style Name box arrow in Apply Styles task pane, click desired style in list

To Center a Paragraph

The headline in the flyer currently is left-aligned (Figure 1–35). You want the headline to be **centered**, that is, positioned horizontally between the left and right margins on the page. Thus, you will center the paragraph containing the headline. Recall that Word considers a single short line of text, such as the three-word headline, a paragraph. The following steps center a paragraph.

- Click somewhere in the paragraph to be centered (in this case, the headline) to position the insertion point in the paragraph to be formatted (Figure 1–35).

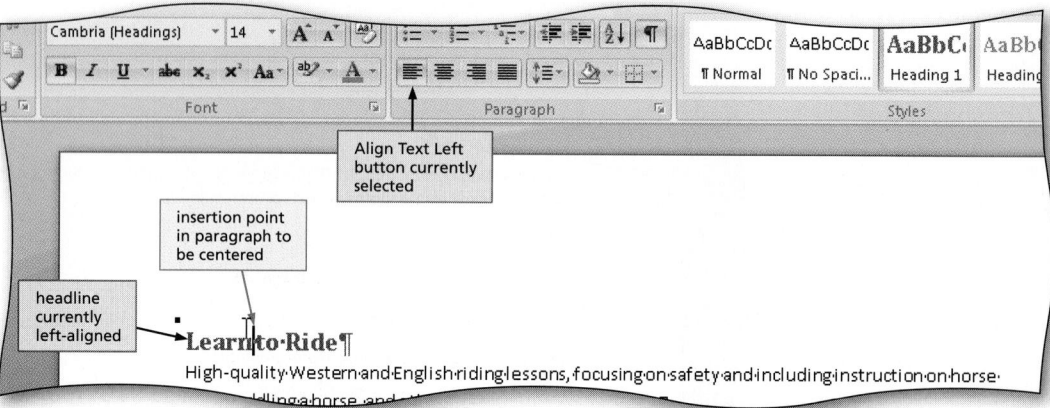

Figure 1–35

- Click the Center button on the Home tab to center the headline (Figure 1–36).

Q&A

What if I want to return the paragraph to left-aligned?

Click the Align Text Left button on the Home tab.

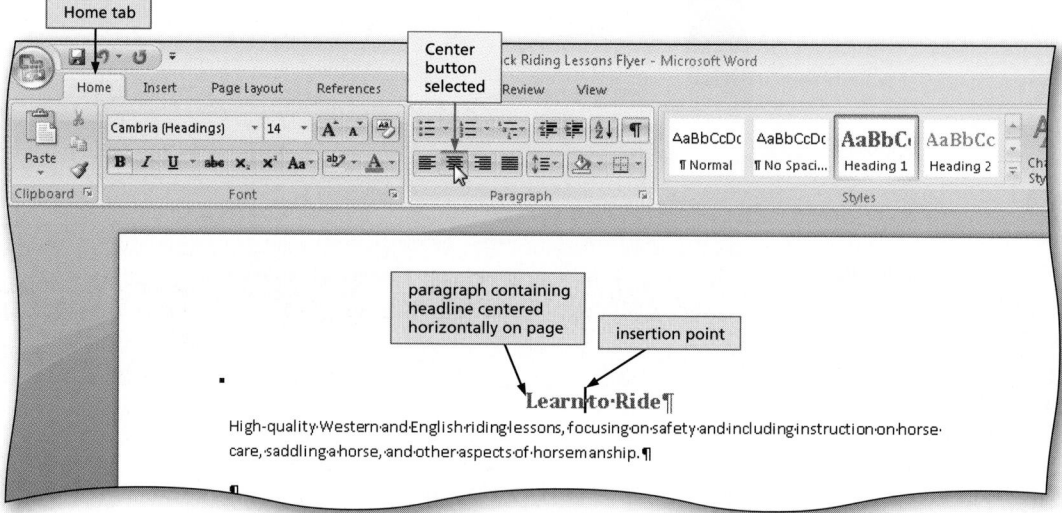

Figure 1–36

Other Ways		
1. Right-click paragraph, click Center button on Mini toolbar	2. Right-click paragraph, click Paragraph on shortcut menu, click Indents and Spacing tab, click Alignment box arrow, click Centered, click OK button	3. Click Paragraph Dialog Box Launcher, click Indents and Spacing tab, click Alignment box arrow, click Centered, click OK button 4. Press CTRL+E

Formatting Single Versus Multiple Paragraphs and Characters

As shown in the previous pages, to format a single paragraph, simply move the insertion point in the paragraph and then format the paragraph. Likewise, to format a single word, position the insertion point in the word and then format the word.

To format *multiple* paragraphs or words, however, you first must select the paragraphs or words you want to format and then format the selection. If your screen normally displays dark letters on a light background, which is the default setting in Word, then selected text displays light letters on a dark background.

To Select a Line

The font size of characters in the Heading 1 style, 14 point, is too small for passersby to read in the headline of the flyer. To increase the font size of the characters in the headline, you must first select the line of text containing the headline. The following steps select a line.

- Move the mouse pointer to the left of the line to be selected (in this case, the headline) until the mouse pointer changes to a right-pointing block arrow (Figure 1–37).

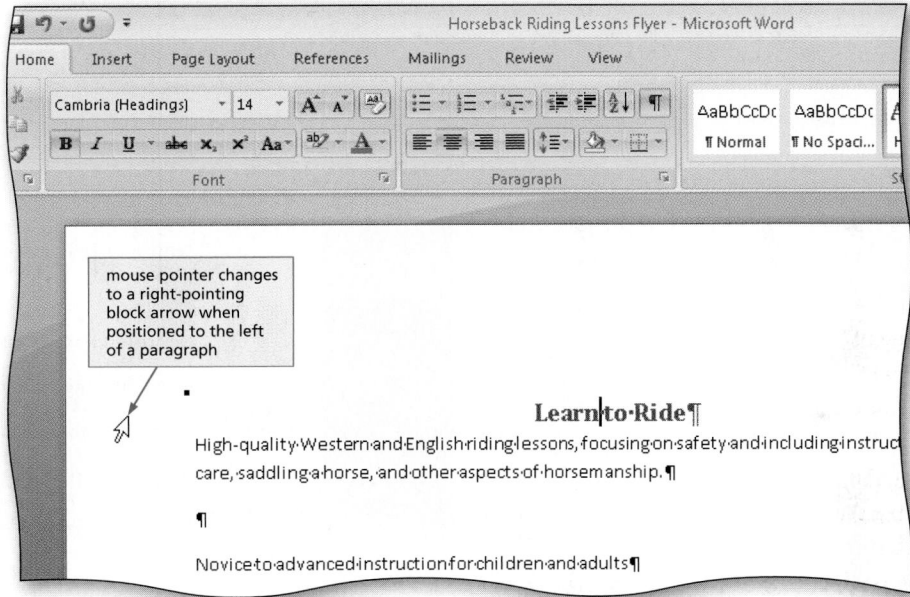

Figure 1–37

- While the mouse pointer is a right-pointing block arrow, click the mouse to select the entire line to the right of the mouse pointer (Figure 1–38).

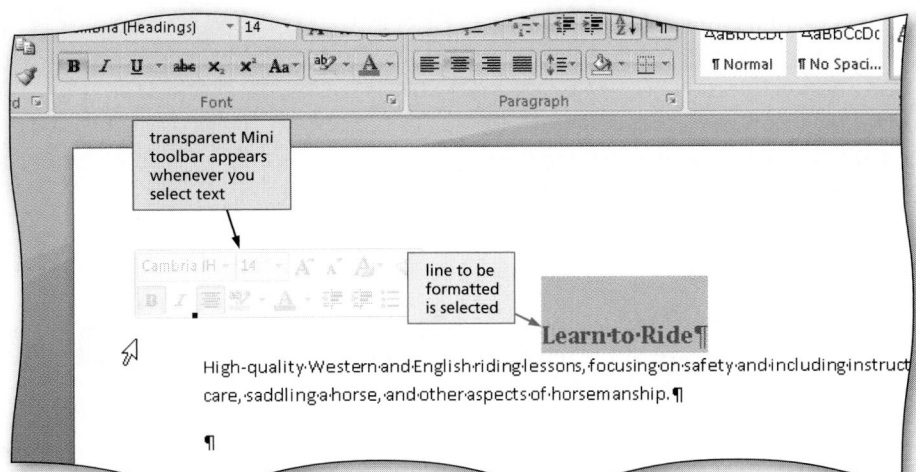

Figure 1–38

Other Ways	
1. Drag mouse through line	2. With insertion point at beginning of desired line, press SHIFT+DOWN ARROW

To Change the Font Size of Selected Text

The next step is to increase the font size of the characters in the selected headline. You would like the headline to be as large as possible and still fit on a single line, which in this case is 48 point. The following steps increase the font size of the headline from 14 to 48 point.

- With the text selected, click the Font Size box arrow on the Home tab to display the Font Size gallery (Figure 1–39).

Q&A

Why are the font sizes in my Font Size gallery different from those in Figure 1–39?

Font sizes may vary depending on the current font and your printer driver.

Q&A

What happened to the Mini toolbar?

The Mini toolbar disappears if you do not use it. These steps use the Font Size box arrow on the Home tab instead of the Font Size box arrow on the Mini toolbar. If a command exists both on the currently displayed tab and the Mini toolbar, this book uses the command on the tab. When the command is not on the currently displayed tab, the Mini toolbar is used.

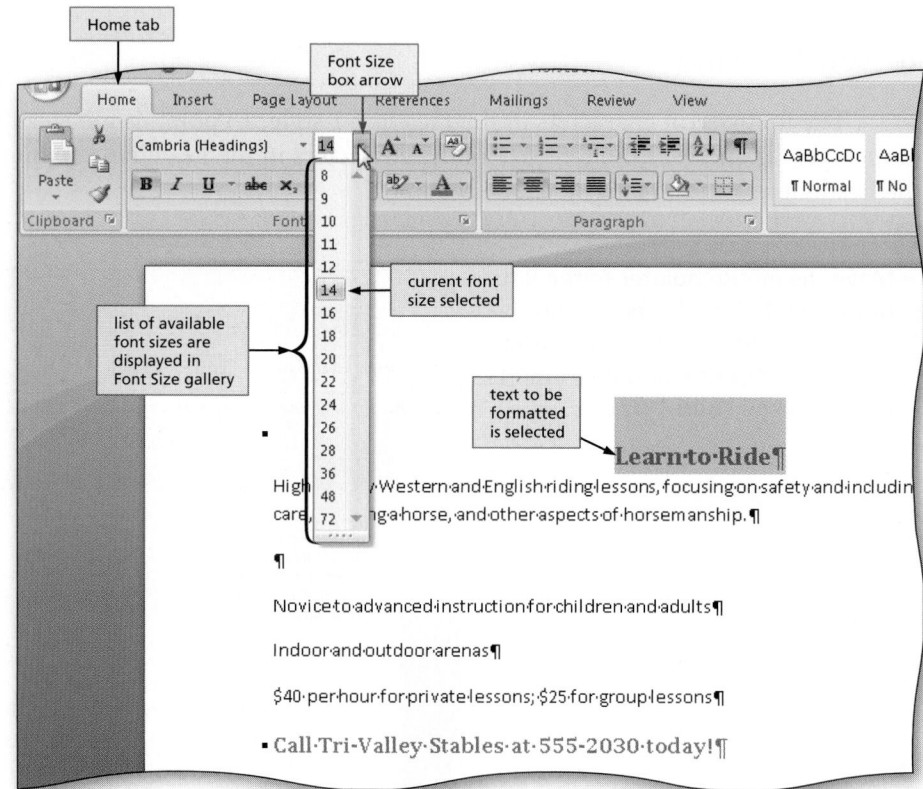

Figure 1–39

- Point to 48 in the Font Size gallery to display a live preview of the headline at 48 point (Figure 1–40).

Experiment

- Point to various font sizes in the Font Size gallery and watch the font size of the headline change in the document window.

- Click 48 in the Font Size gallery to increase the font size of the selected text to 48.

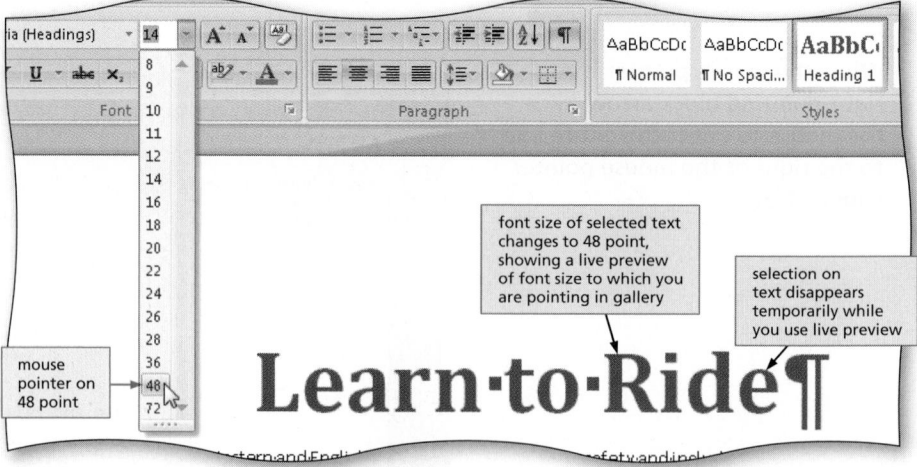

Figure 1–40

Other Ways

1. Click Font Size box arrow on Mini toolbar, click desired font size in Font Size gallery

2. Right-click selected text, click Font on shortcut menu, click Font tab, select desired font size in Size list, click OK button

3. Click Font Dialog Box Launcher, click Font tab, select desired font size in Size list, click OK button

4. Press CTRL+SHIFT+P, click Font tab, select desired font size in Size list, click OK button

To Change the Font of Selected Text

As mentioned earlier, the default Heading 1 style uses the font called Cambria. Word, however, provides many other fonts to add variety to your documents. To draw more attention to the headline, you change its font so it differs from the font of other text in the flyer. The following steps change the font from Cambria to Copperplate Gothic Bold.

1

- With the text selected, click the Font box arrow on the Home tab to display the Font gallery (Figure 1–41).

Q&A

Will the fonts in my Font gallery be the same as those in Figure 1–41?

Your list of available fonts may differ, depending on the type of printer you are using.

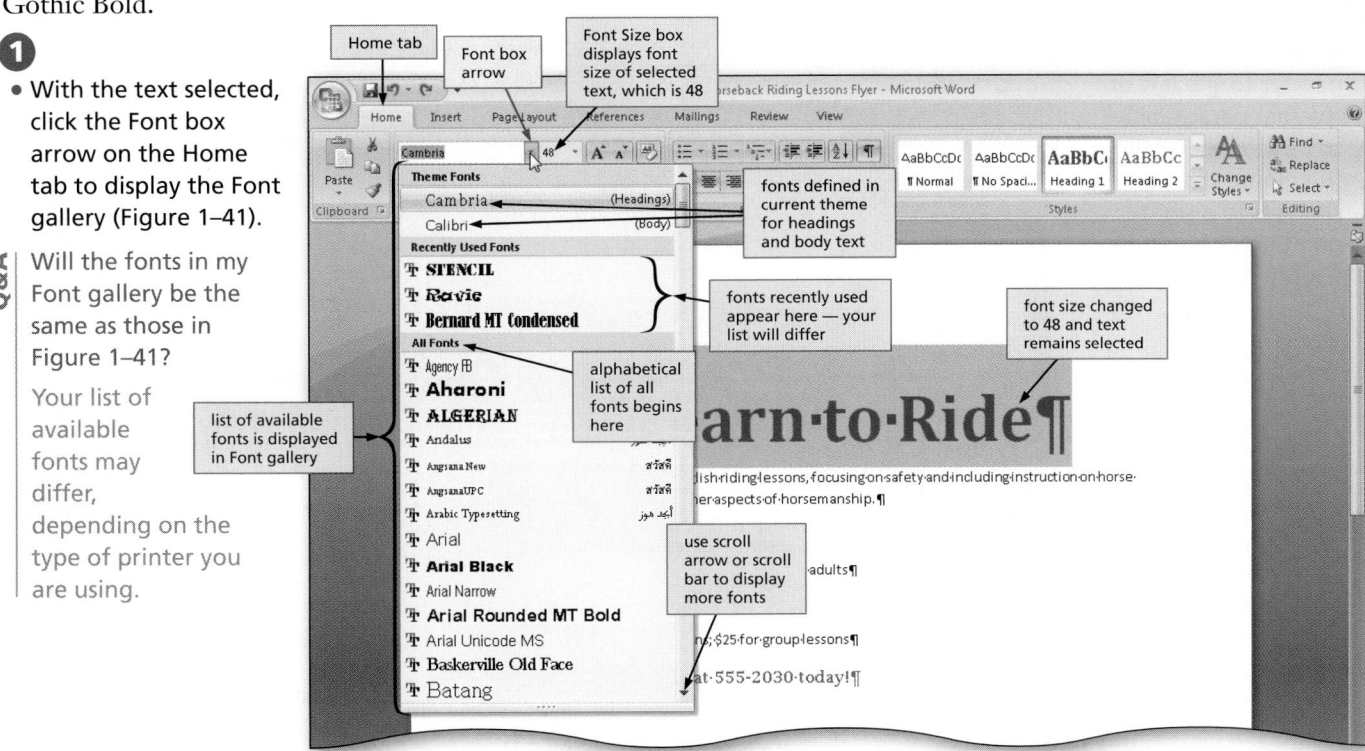

Figure 1–41

2

- Scroll through the Font gallery, if necessary, and then point to Copperplate Gothic Bold (or a similar font) to display a live preview of the headline in Copperplate Gothic Bold font (Figure 1–42).

 **Experiment**

- Point to various fonts in the Font gallery and watch the font of the headline change in the document window.

3

- Click Copperplate Gothic Bold (or a similar font) to change the font of the selected text to Copperplate Gothic Bold.

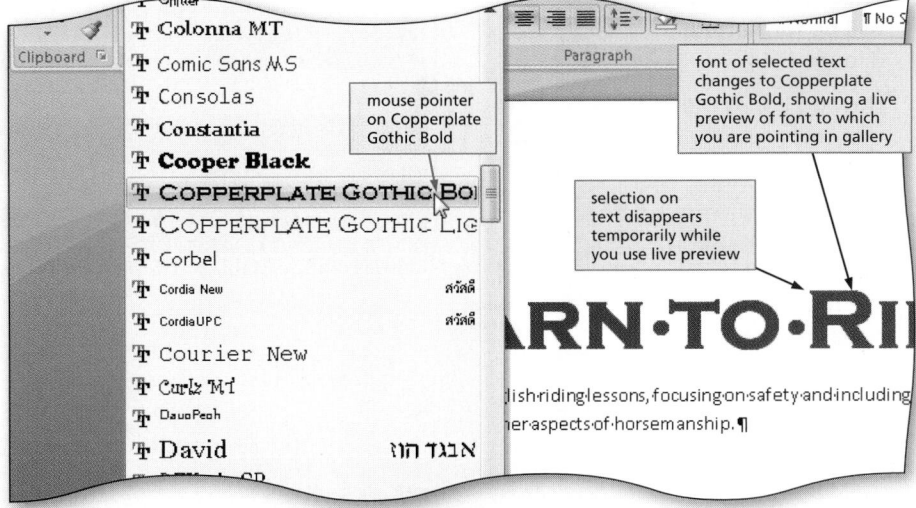

Figure 1–42

Other Ways

1. Click Font box arrow on Mini toolbar, click desired font in Font gallery

2. Right-click selected text, click Font on shortcut menu, click

   Font tab, select desired font in Font list, click OK button

3. Click Font Dialog Box Launcher, click Font tab, select desired font in Font list, click OK button

4. Press CTRL+SHIFT+F, click Font tab, select desired font in the Font list, click OK button

To Select Multiple Paragraphs

The next formatting step in creating the flyer is to increase the font size of the characters between the headline and the signature line so that they are easier to read from a distance. To change the font size of the characters in multiple lines, you first must select all the lines to be formatted. The following steps select multiple lines.

1

• Move the mouse pointer to the left of the first paragraph to be selected until the mouse pointer changes to a right-pointing block arrow (Figure 1–43).

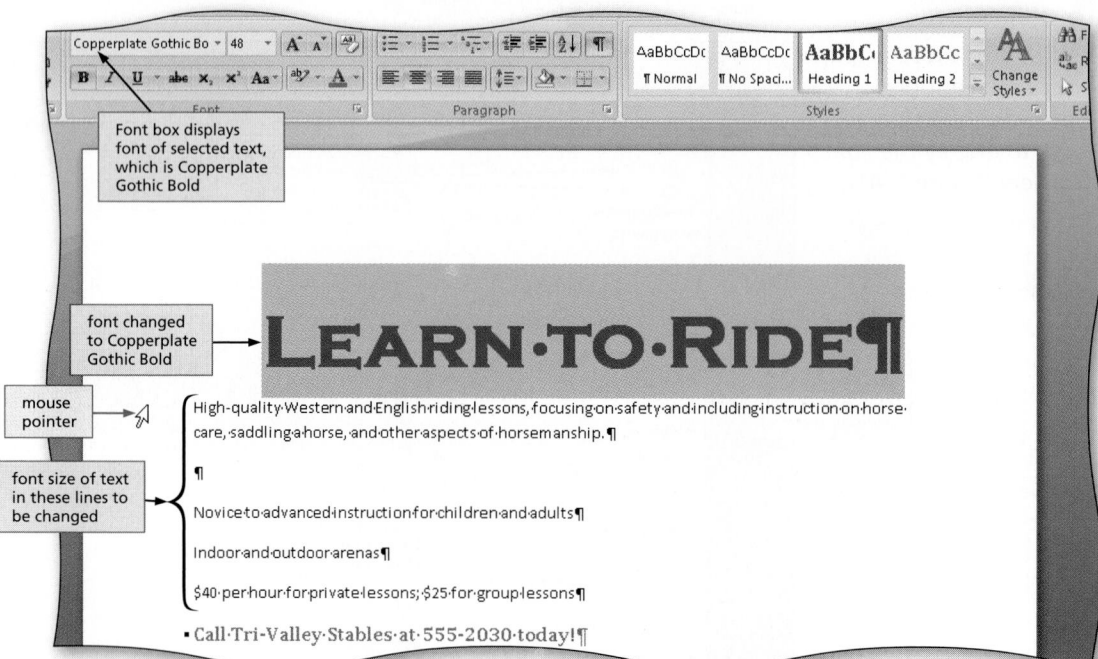

Figure 1–43

2

• Drag downward to select all lines that will be formatted (Figure 1–44).

Q&A

How do I *drag* the mouse?

Dragging is the process of holding down the mouse button while moving the mouse and then releasing the mouse button.

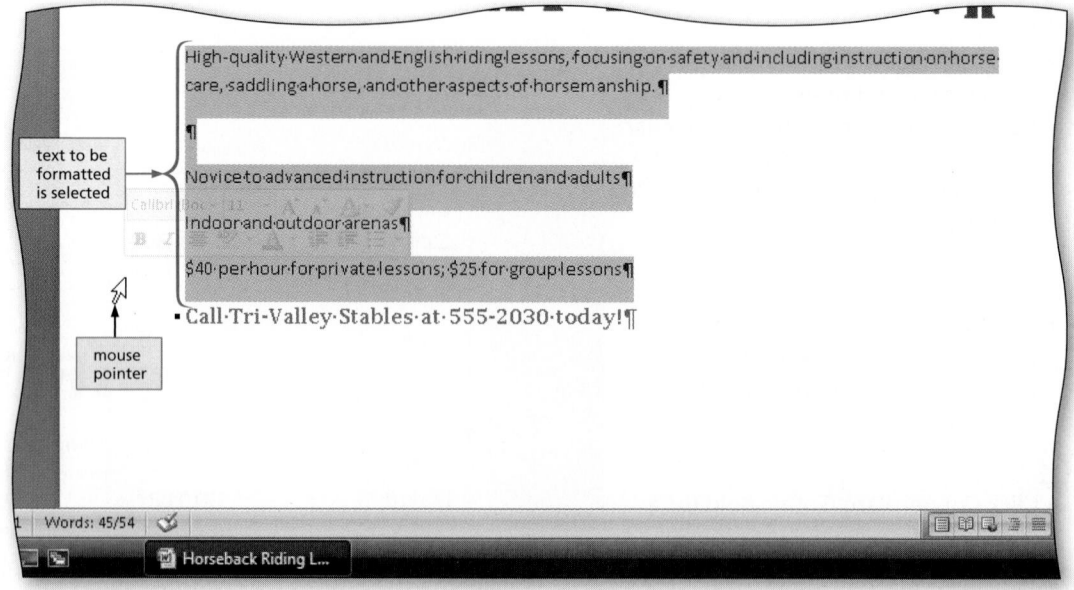

Figure 1–44

Other Ways

1. With insertion point at beginning of desired line, press SHIFT+DOWN ARROW repeatedly until all lines are selected

To Change the Font Size of Selected Text

The characters between the headline and the signature line in the flyer currently are 11 point. To make them easier to read from a distance, this flyer uses 16 point for these characters. The following steps change the font size of the selected text.

1 With the text selected, click the Font Size box arrow on the Home tab to display the Font Size gallery.

2 Click 16 in the Font Size gallery to increase the font size of the selected text to 16.

To Format a Line

In the flyer, the signature line is to be centered to match the paragraph alignment of the headline. Also, its text should have a font size larger than the rest of the body copy. The following steps center the line and increase its font size to 18.

1 Click somewhere in the paragraph to be centered (in this case, the signature line) to position the insertion point in the paragraph to be formatted.

2 Click the Center button on the Home tab to center the signature line.

3 Move the mouse pointer to the left of the line to be selected (in this case, the signature line) until the mouse pointer changes to a right-pointing block arrow and then click to select the line.

4 With the signature line selected, click the Font Size box arrow on the Home tab and then click 18 in the Font Size gallery to increase the font size of the selected text to 18 (Figure 1–45).

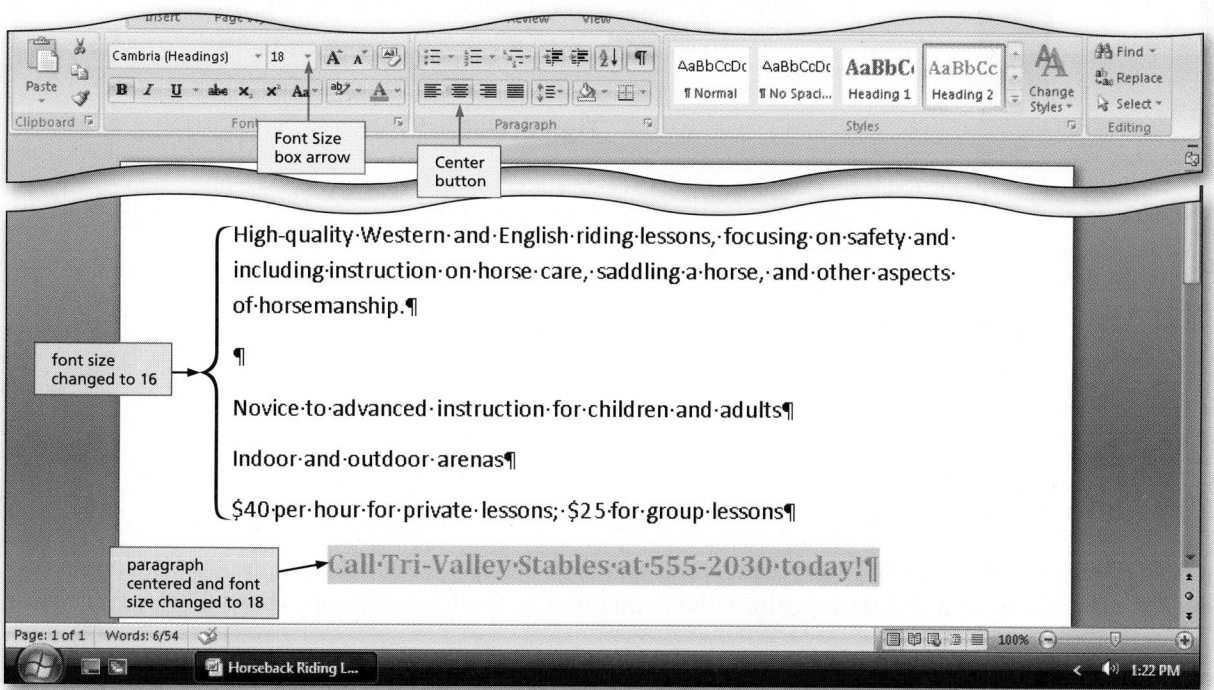

Figure 1–45

To Bullet a List of Paragraphs

The next step is to format the three important points above the signature line in the flyer as a bulleted list. A **bulleted list** is a series of paragraphs, each beginning with a bullet character. The three lines each end with a paragraph mark because you pressed the ENTER key at the end of each line. Thus, these three lines actually are three separate paragraphs.

To format a list of paragraphs with bullets, you first must select all the lines in the paragraphs. The following steps bullet a list of paragraphs.

- Move the mouse pointer to the left of the first paragraph to be selected until the mouse pointer changes to a right-pointing block arrow.

- Drag downward until all paragraphs (lines) that will be formatted with a bullet character are selected.

2

- Click the Bullets button on the Home tab to place a bullet character at the beginning of each selected paragraph (Figure 1–46).

Q&A

How do I remove bullets from a list or paragraph?

Select the list or paragraph and click the Bullets button again.

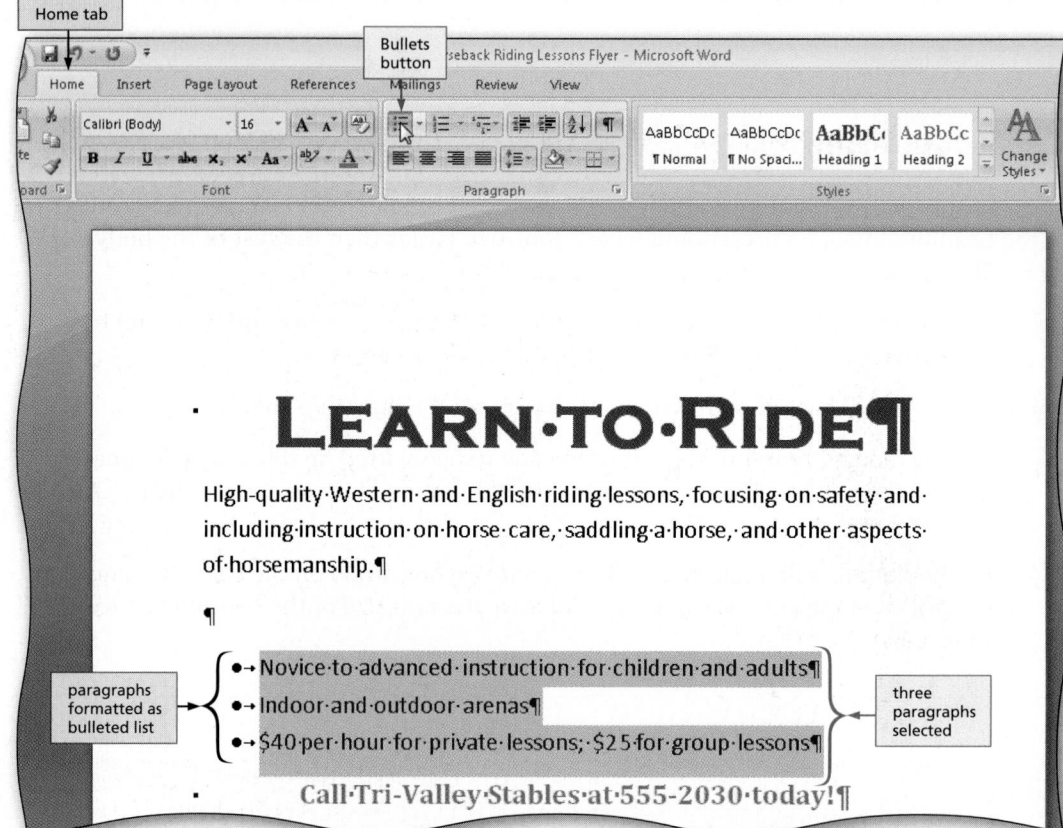

Figure 1–46

Other Ways

1. Right-click selected paragraphs, click Bullets button on Mini toolbar

2. Right-click selected paragraphs, point to Bullets on shortcut menu, click desired bullet style

To Undo and Redo an Action

Word provides a means of canceling your recent command(s) or action(s). For example, if you format text incorrectly, you can undo the format and try it again. When you point to the Undo button, Word displays the action you can undo as part of the ScreenTip.

If, after you undo an action, you decide you did not want to perform the undo, you can redo the undone action. Word does not allow you to undo or redo some actions, such as saving or printing a document. The next steps undo the bullet format just applied and then redo the bullet format.

1

- Click the Undo button on the Quick Access Toolbar to remove the bullets from the selected paragraphs (Figure 1–47).

2

- Click the Redo button on the Quick Access Toolbar to place a bullet character at the beginning of each selected paragraph again (shown in Figure 1–46).

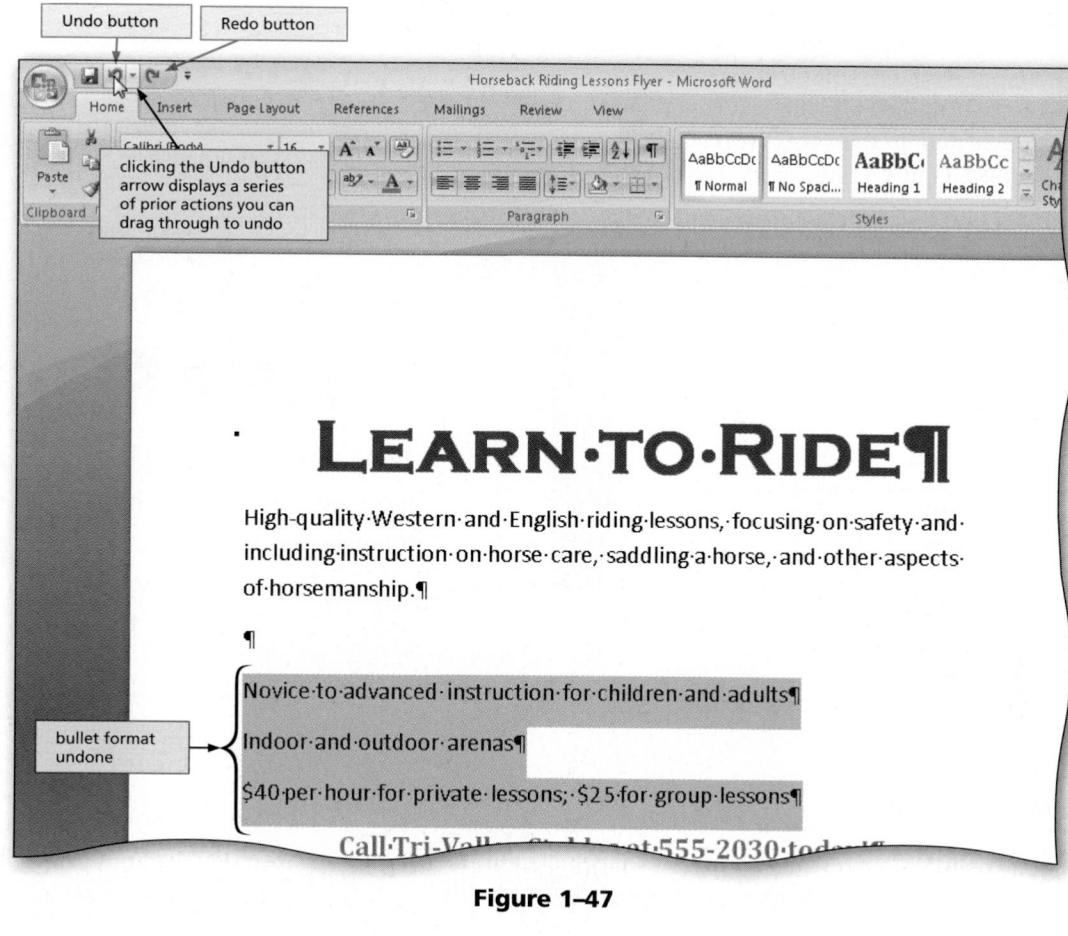

Figure 1–47

Other Ways

1. Press CTRL+Z; press CTRL+Y

To Select a Group of Words

To emphasize the types of riding lessons, Western and English, these words are bold in the flyer. To format a group of words, you first must select them. The following steps select a group of words.

1

- Position the mouse pointer immediately to the left of the first character of the text to be selected, in this case, the W in Western (Figure 1–48).

Q&A

Why did the shape of the mouse pointer change?

The mouse pointer's shape is an I-beam when positioned in unselected text in the document window.

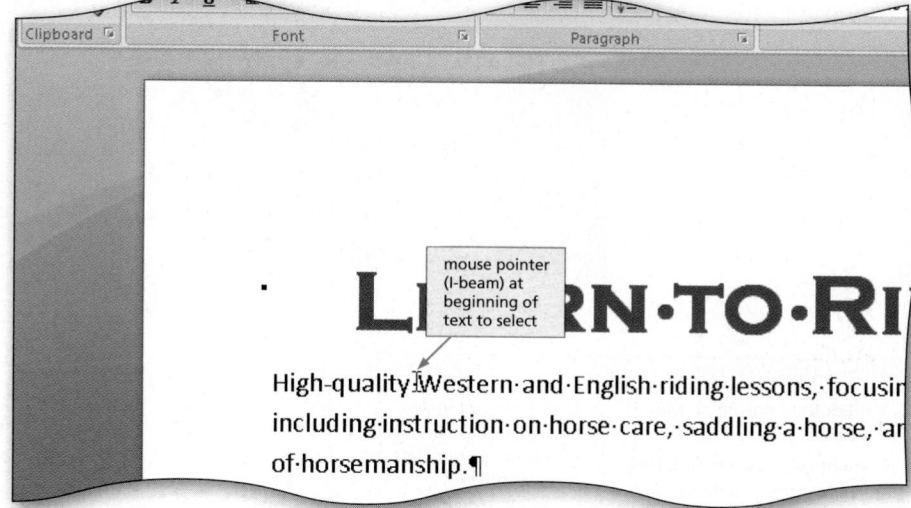

Figure 1–48

②

- Drag the mouse pointer through the last character of the text to be selected, in this case, the h in English (Figure 1–49).

Q&A

Why did the mouse pointer shape change again?

When the mouse pointer is positioned in selected text, its shape is a left-pointing block arrow.

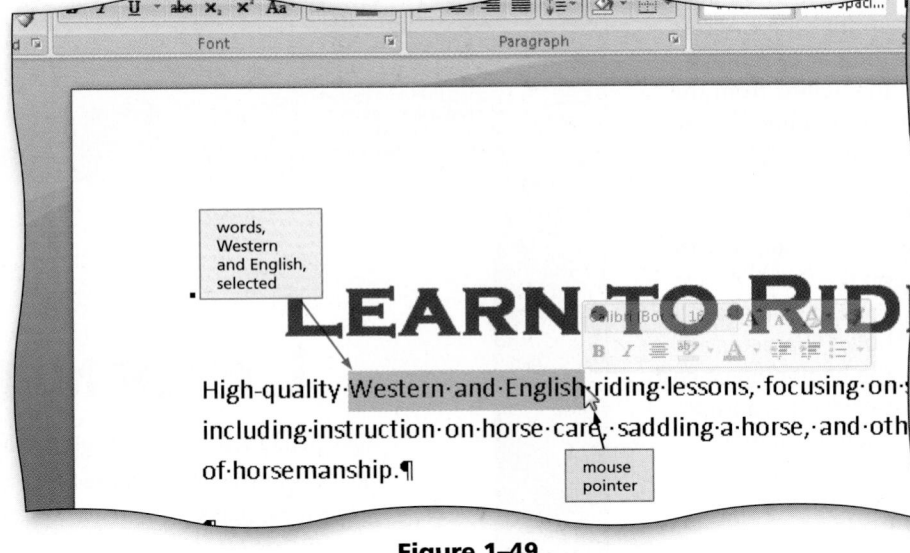

Figure 1–49

Other Ways

1. With insertion point at beginning of first word in group, press CTRL+SHIFT+RIGHT ARROW repeatedly until all words are selected

To Bold Text

Bold characters display somewhat thicker and darker than those that are not bold. The following step formats the selected words, Western and English, as bold.

①

- With the text selected, click the Bold button on the Home tab to format the selected text in bold (Figure 1–50).

Q&A

How would I remove a bold format?

You would click the Bold button a second time, or you immediately could click the Undo button on the Quick Access Toolbar.

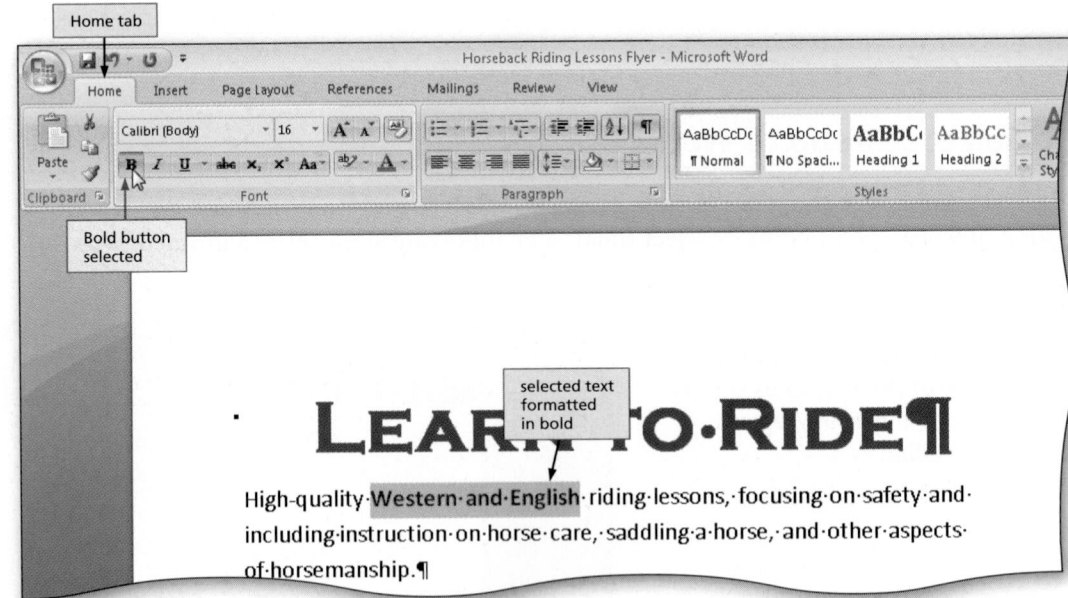

Figure 1–50

Other Ways

1. Click Bold button on Mini toolbar

2. Right-click selected text, click Font on shortcut menu, click Font tab, click Bold in Font style list, click OK button

3. Click Font Dialog Box Launcher, click Font tab, click Bold in Font style list, click OK button

4. Press CTRL+B

To Underline a Word

As with bold text, underlines are used to emphasize or draw attention to specific text. **Underlined** text prints with an underscore (_) below each character. In the flyer, the word, and, in the first bulleted paragraph is emphasized with an underline.

As with a single paragraph, if you want to format a single word, you do not need to select the word. Simply position the insertion point somewhere in the word and apply the desired format. The following step formats a word with an underline.

1

- Click somewhere in the word to be underlined (and, in this case).

- Click the Underline button on the Home tab to underline the word containing the insertion point (Figure 1–51).

Q&A How would I remove an underline?

You would click the Underline button a second time, or you immediately could click the Undo button on the Quick Access Toolbar.

Q&A Are other types of underlines available?

In addition to the basic solid underline shown in Figure 1–51, Word has many decorative underlines, such as double underlines, dotted underlines, and wavy underlines. You can access the decorative underlines and also change the color of an underline through the Underline gallery.

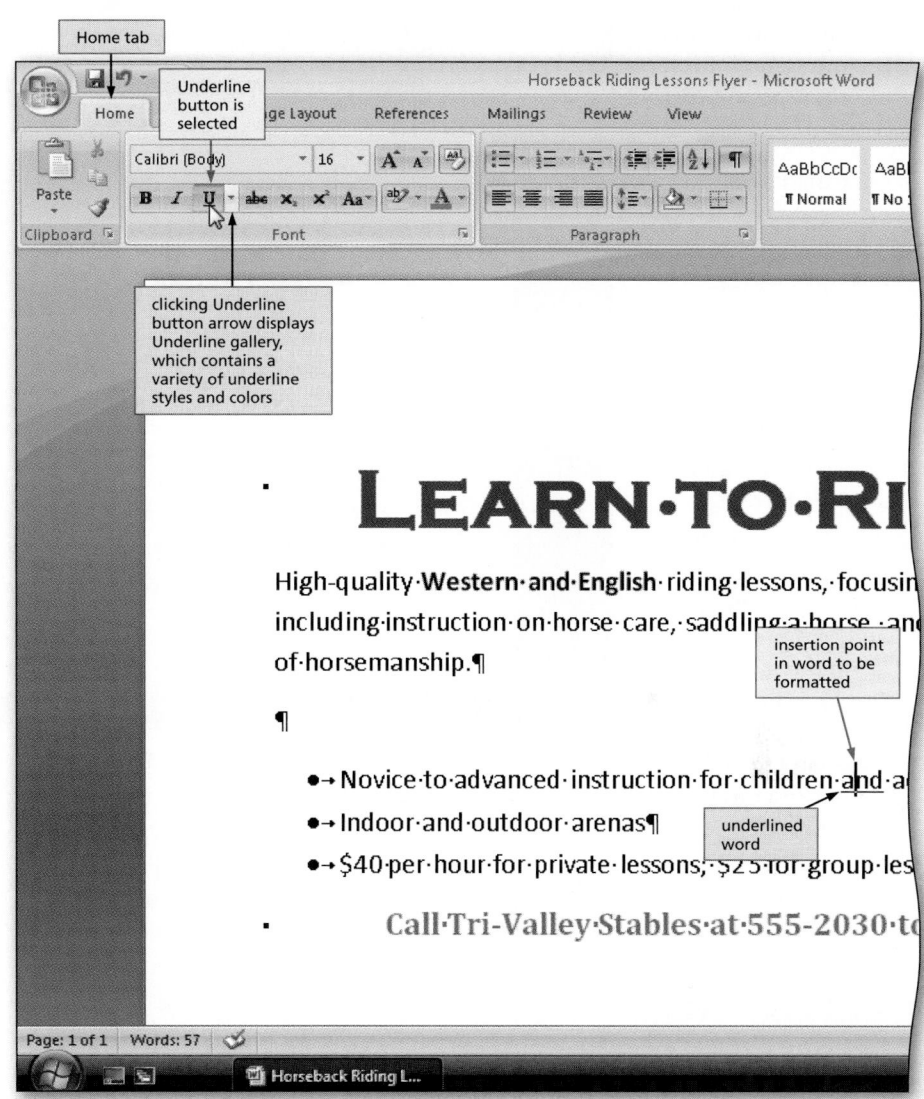

Figure 1–51

Other Ways

1. Right-click text, click Font on shortcut menu, click Font tab, click Underline style box arrow, click desired underline style, click OK button

2. Click Font Dialog Box Launcher, click Font tab, click Underline style box arrow, click desired underline style, click OK button

3. Press CTRL+U

To Italicize Text

To further emphasize the signature line, this line is italicized in the flyer. **Italicized** text has a slanted appearance. The following steps select the text and then italicize it.

- Point to the left of the line to be selected (in this case, the signature line) and click when the mouse pointer is a right-pointing block arrow.

- Click the Italic button on the Home tab to italicize the selected text.

- Click inside the selected text to remove the selection (Figure 1–52).

Q&A
How would I remove an italic format?

You would click the Italic button a second time, or you immediately could click the Undo button on the Quick Access Toolbar.

Q&A
How can I tell what formatting has been applied to text?

The selected buttons and boxes on the Home tab show formatting characteristics of the location of the insertion point. With the insertion point in the signature line, the Home tab shows these formats: 18-point Cambria bold italic font, centered paragraph, and Heading 2 style.

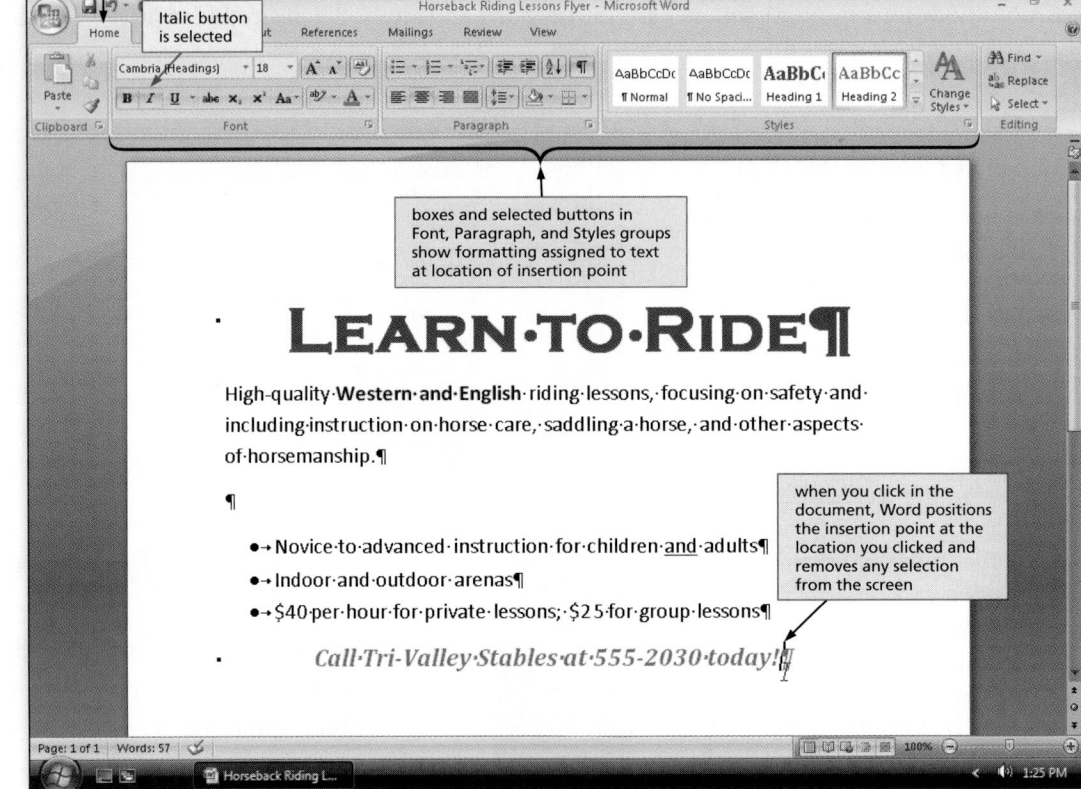

Figure 1–52

Other Ways

1. Click Italic button on Mini toolbar
2. Right-click selected text, click Font on shortcut menu, click Font tab, click Italic in Font style list, click OK button
3. Click Font Dialog Box Launcher, click Font tab, click Italic in Font style list, click OK button
4. Press CTRL+I

Document Formats

One advantage of using styles to format text is that you easily can change the formats of styles and themes in your document to give it a different or new look. Recall that a style is a named group of formatting characteristics and a theme is a set of unified formats for fonts, colors, and graphics. In Word, you can change the style set, theme colors, and theme fonts.

- The predefined styles in the Styles gallery, such as Heading 1 and Heading 2, each known as a **Quick Style**, are part of a style set. A **style set** consists of a group of frequently used styles formatted so they look pleasing when used together. When you change the style set, formats assigned to each Quick Style also change.

- Each **color scheme** in a theme identifies 12 complementary colors for text, background, accents, and links in a document. With more than 20 predefined color schemes, Word provides a simple way to select colors that work well together.
- Each theme has a **font set** that defines formats for two fonts: one for headings and another for body text. In Word, you can select from more than 20 predefined coordinated font sets to give the document's text a new look.

Plan Ahead

Use color.

When choosing color, associate the meaning of color to your message:

- Red expresses danger, power, or energy, and often is associated with sports or physical exertion.
- Brown represents simplicity, honesty, and dependability.
- Orange denotes success, victory, creativity, and enthusiasm.
- Yellow suggests sunshine, happiness, hope, liveliness, and intelligence.
- Green symbolizes growth, healthiness, harmony, blooming, and healing, and often is associated with safety or money.
- Blue indicates integrity, trust, importance, confidence, and stability.
- Purple represents wealth, power, comfort, extravagance, magic, mystery, and spirituality.
- White stands for purity, goodness, cleanliness, precision, and perfection.
- Black suggests authority, strength, elegance, power, and prestige.
- Gray conveys neutrality and thus often is found in backgrounds and other effects.

To Change the Style Set

To symbolize perfection and precision in the flyer, the characters in the headline are white. The style set, called Modern, formats Heading 1 characters in white. It also formats the Heading 1 and Heading 2 styles in all capital letters and places a background color around the paragraphs, which further emphasize the headline and signature line in the flyer. Thus, you will change the style set from Default to Modern. The following steps change a style set.

- Click the Change Styles button on the Home tab to display the Change Styles menu (Figure 1–53).

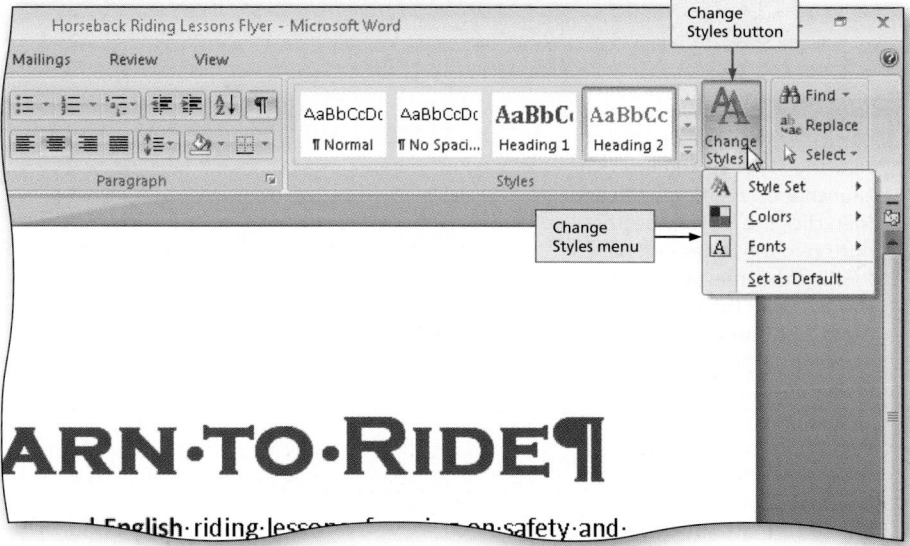

Figure 1–53

2

- Point to Style Set on the Change Styles menu to display the Style Set gallery.

- Point to Modern in the Style Set gallery to display a live preview of the formats associated with the Modern style set (Figure 1–54).

 Experiment

- Point to various style sets in the Style Set gallery and watch the formats of the styled text change in the document window.

3

- Click Modern in the Style Set gallery to change the document style set to Modern.

Q&A What if I want to return to the original style set?

You would click the Change Styles button, click Style Set on the Change Styles menu, and then click Default in the Style Set gallery, or you could click the Undo button on the Quick Access Toolbar.

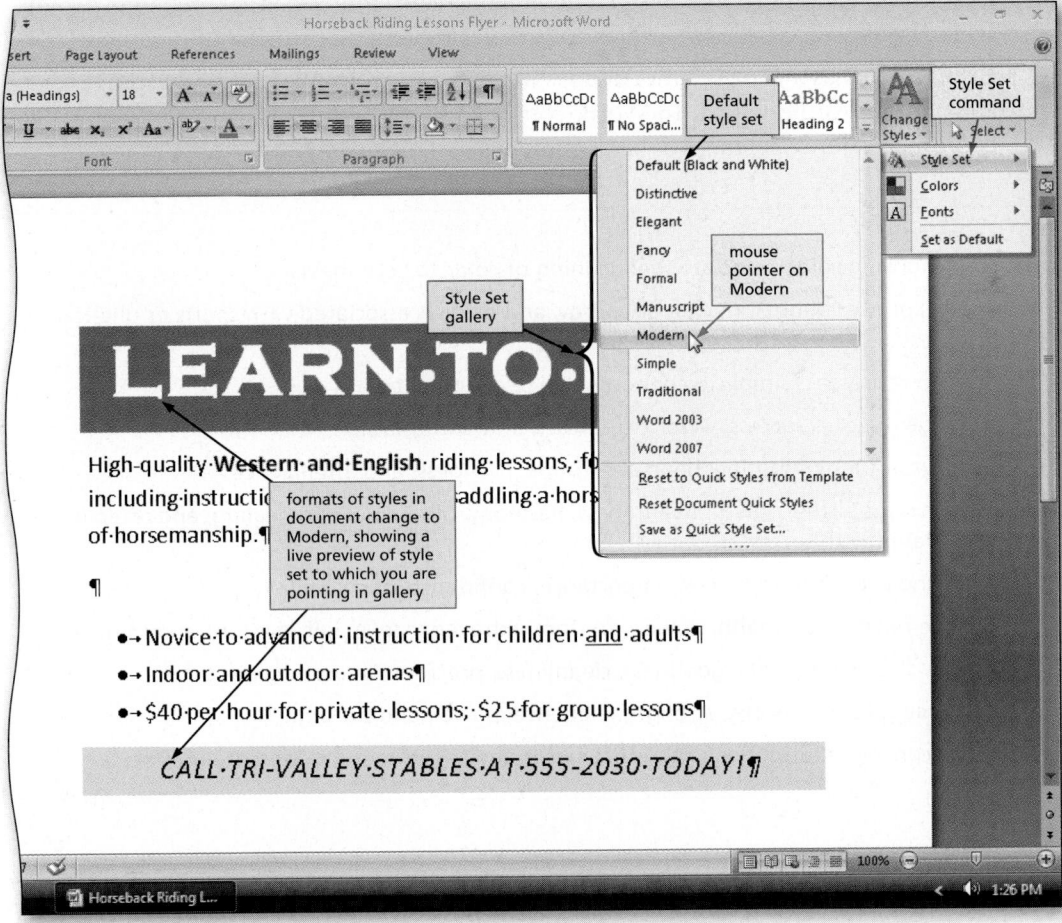

Figure 1–54

BTW

Style Formats
To see the formats assigned to a particular style in a document, click the Styles Dialog Box Launcher on the Home tab and then click the Style Inspector button in the Styles task pane. Position the insertion point in the style and then point to the Paragraph formatting or Text level formatting areas in the Style Inspector task pane to display an Enhanced ScreenTip describing formats assigned to the location of the insertion point. You also can click the Reveal Formatting button in the Style Inspector to display the Reveal Formatting task pane.

To Change Theme Colors

To suggest enthusiasm, success, and honesty, the background colors around the headline and signature line paragraphs in the flyer use shades of orange and brown. In Word, the color scheme called Aspect uses these colors. Thus, you will change the color scheme to Aspect. The following steps change theme colors.

1

- Click the Change Styles button on the Home tab to display the Change Styles menu.

- Point to Colors on the Change Styles menu to display the Colors gallery.

- Point to Aspect in the Colors gallery to display a live preview of the Aspect color scheme (Figure 1–55).

 Experiment

- Point to various color schemes in the Colors gallery and watch the paragraph background colors change in the document window.

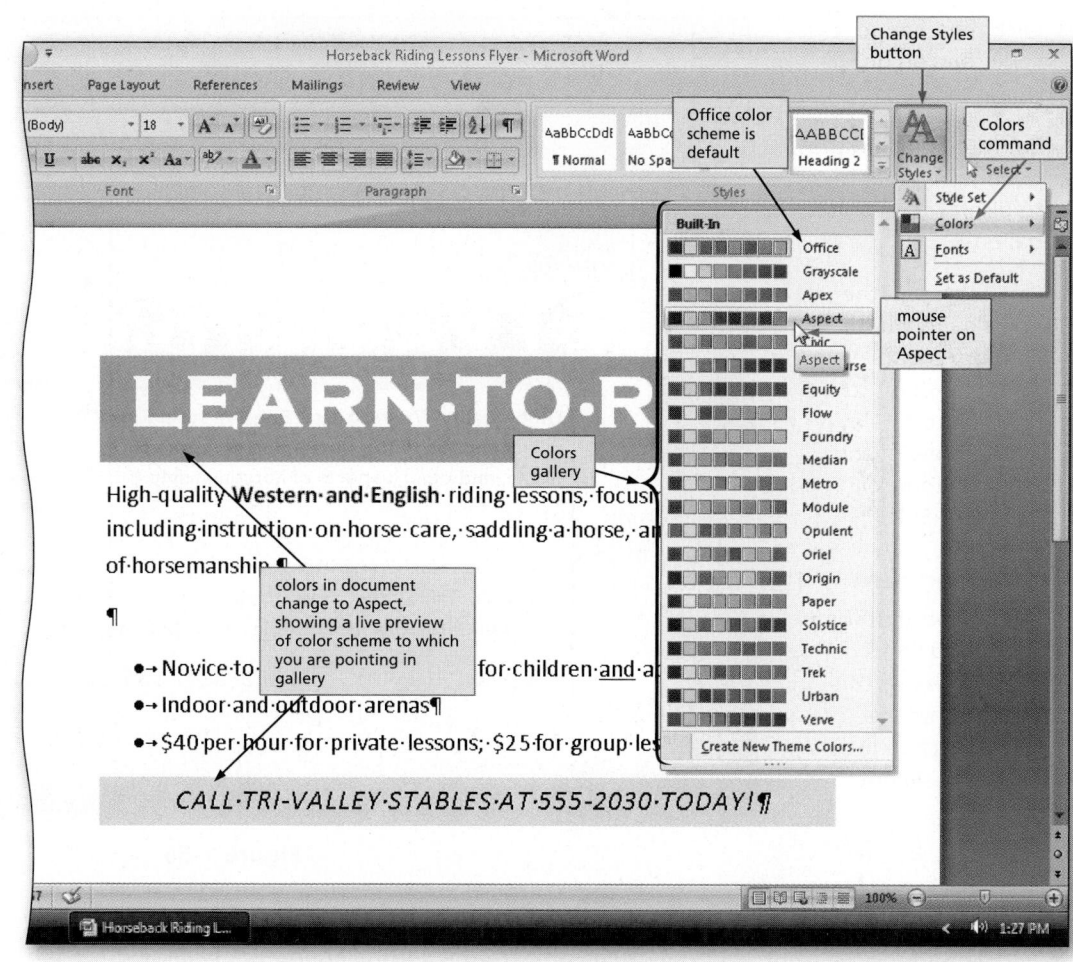

Figure 1–55

2

- Click Aspect in the Colors gallery to change the document theme colors to Aspect.

Q&A

What if I want to return to the original color scheme?

You would click the Change Styles button, click Colors on the Change Styles menu, and then click Office in the Colors gallery.

Other Ways

1. Click Theme Colors button arrow on Page Layout tab, select desired color scheme

To Change Theme Fonts

Earlier in this chapter, you changed the font of the headline to Copperplate Gothic Bold. In this flyer, all text below the headline should be the Rockwell font, instead of the Calibri font, because it better matches the western tone of the flyer. Thus, the next step is to change the current font set, which is called Office, to a font set called Foundry, which uses the Rockwell font for headings and body text.

If you previously changed a font using buttons on the Ribbon or Mini toolbar, Word will not alter those when you change the font set because changes to the font set are not applied to fonts changed individually. This means the font headline in the flyer will stay as Copperplate Gothic Bold when you change the font set. The following steps change the font set to Foundry.

- Click the Change Styles button on the Home tab.

- Point to Fonts on the Change Styles menu to display the Fonts gallery.

- Scroll through the Fonts gallery until Foundry is displayed and then point to Foundry to display a live preview of the Foundry font set (Figure 1–56).

🔍 **Experiment**

- Point to various font sets in the Fonts gallery and watch the fonts below the headline change in the document window.

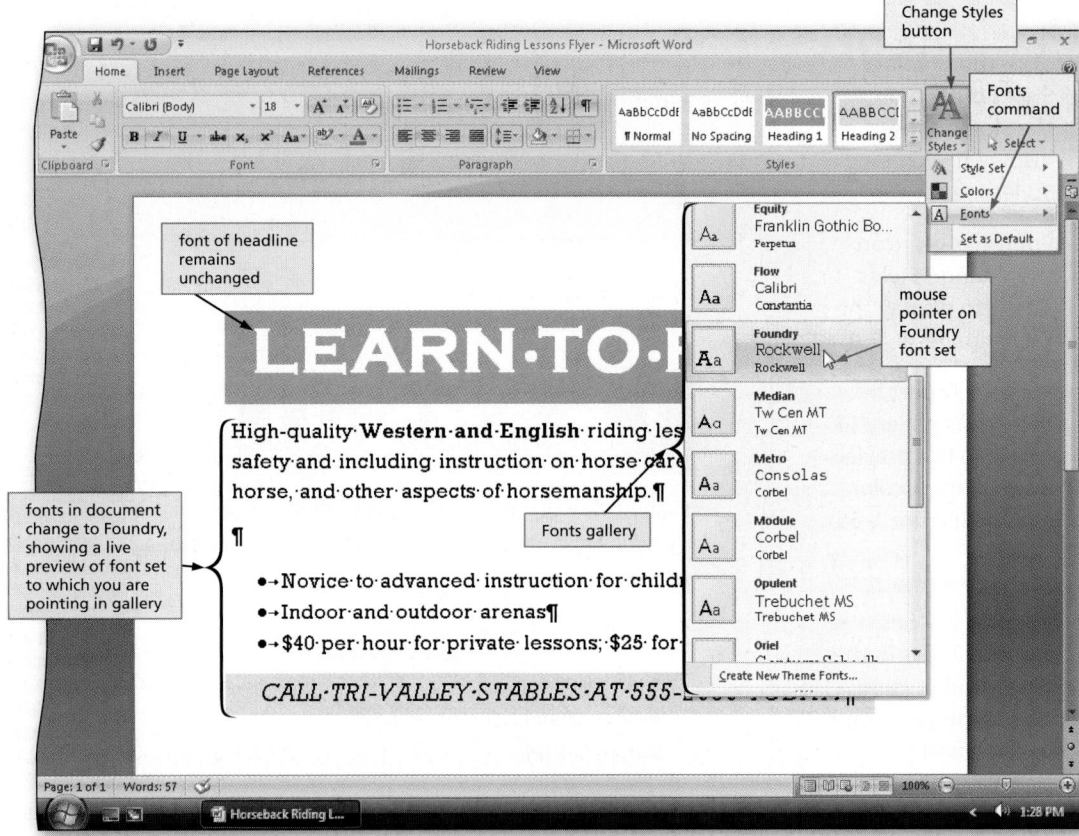

Figure 1–56

- Click Foundry in the Fonts gallery to change the document theme fonts to Foundry.

Q&A

What if I want to return to the original font set?

You would click the Change Styles button, click Fonts on the Change Styles menu, and then click Office in the Fonts gallery.

Other Ways

1. Click Theme Fonts button arrow on Page Layout tab, select desired font set

Inserting and Formatting a Picture in a Word Document

With the text formatted in the flyer, the next step is to insert a picture in the flyer and format the picture. Flyers usually contain graphical images, such as a picture, to attract the attention of passersby.

Note: If you are using Windows XP, see Appendix F for alternate steps.

Plan
Ahead

Find the appropriate graphical image.
To use graphical images, also called graphics, in a Word document, the image must be stored digitally in a file. Files containing graphical images are available from a variety of sources:

- Word includes a collection of predefined graphical images that you can insert in a document.

- Microsoft has free digital images on the Web for use in a document. Other Web sites also have images available, some of which are free, while others require a fee.

- You can take a picture with a digital camera and **download** it, which is the process of copying the digital picture from the camera to your computer.

- With a scanner, you can convert a printed picture, drawing, or diagram to a digital file.

   If you receive a picture from a source other than yourself, do not use the file until you are certain it does not contain a virus. A **virus** is a computer program that can damage files and programs on your computer. Use an antivirus program to verify that any files you use are virus free.

Plan
Ahead

Establish where to position and how to format the graphical image.
The content, size, shape, position, and format of a graphic should capture the interest of passersby, enticing them to stop and read the flyer. Often, the graphic is the center of attraction and visually the largest element on a flyer. If you use colors in the graphical image, be sure they are part of the document's color scheme.

To Insert a Picture

The next step in creating the flyer is to insert the picture of the horse and rider so that it is centered on the blank line above the bulleted list. The picture, which was taken with a digital camera, is available on the Data Files for Students. See the inside back cover of this book for instructions on downloading the Data Files for Students, or contact your instructor for information about accessing the required files. The following steps insert a centered picture, which, in this example, is located on the same USB flash drive that contains the saved flyer.

- To position the insertion point where you want the picture to be located, press CTRL+HOME and then press the DOWN ARROW key four times.

- Click the Center button on the Home tab to center the paragraph that will contain the picture.

- Click Insert on the Ribbon to display the Insert tab (Figure 1–57).

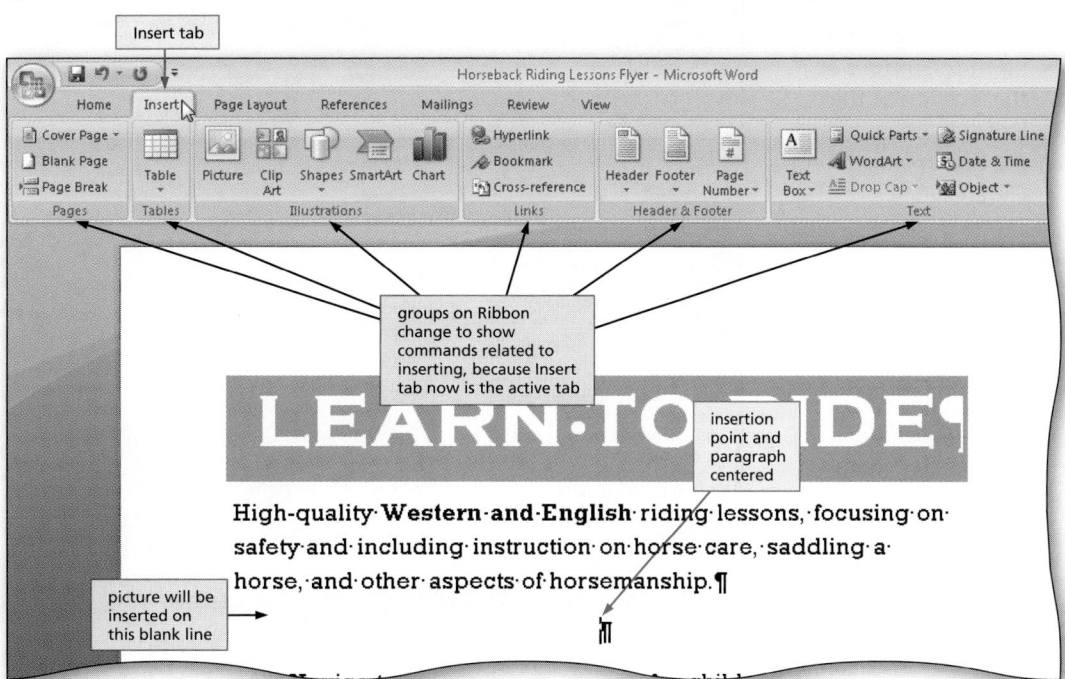

Figure 1–57

2

- With your USB flash drive connected to one of the computer's USB ports, click the Insert Picture from File button on the Insert tab to display the Insert Picture dialog box.

- If the Folders list is displayed below the Folders button, click the Folders button to remove the Folders list.

- If necessary, click Computer in the Favorite Links section and then scroll until UDISK 2.0 (E:) appears in the list of available drives.

- Double-click UDISK 2.0 (E:) to select the USB flash drive, Drive E in this case, as the device that contains the picture.

- Click Horse and Rider to select the file name (Figure 1–58).

Q&A What if the picture is not on a USB flash drive?

Use the same process, but select the device containing the picture in the Favorite Links section.

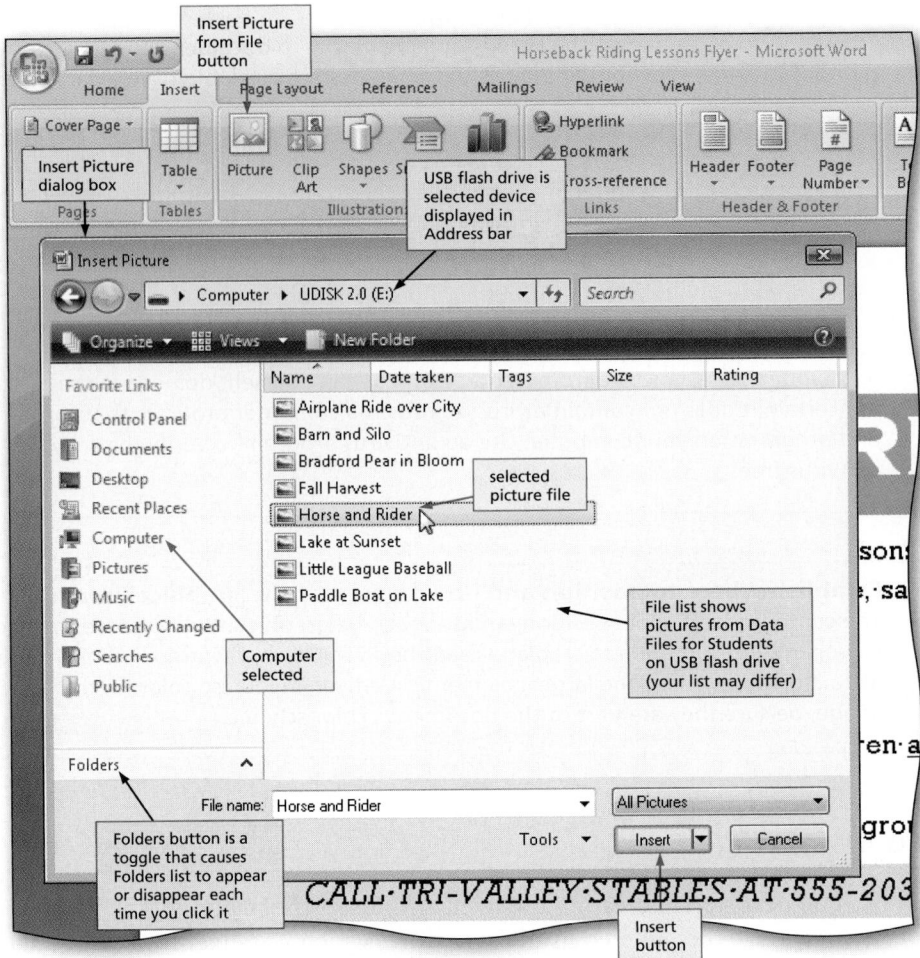

Figure 1–58

3

- Click the Insert button in the dialog box to insert the picture at the location of the insertion point in the document (Figure 1–59).

Q&A What are the symbols around the picture?

A selected graphic appears surrounded by a **selection rectangle**, which has small squares and circles, called **sizing handles**, at each corner and middle location.

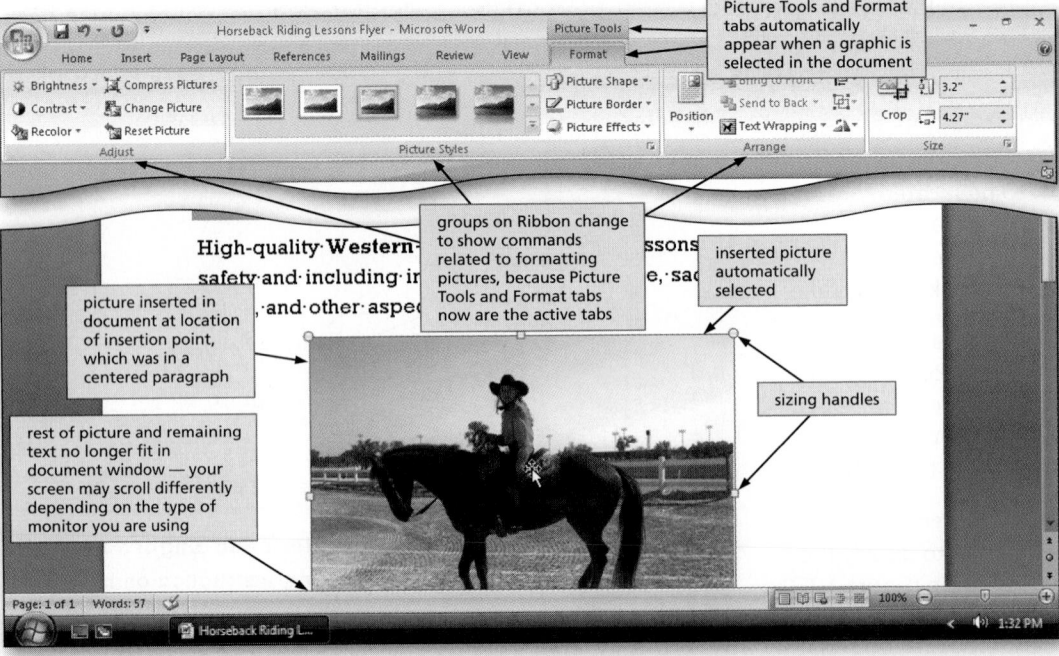

Figure 1–59

Scrolling

As mentioned at the beginning of this chapter, you view only a portion of a document on the screen through the document window. At some point when you type text or insert graphics, Word will **scroll** the top or bottom portion of the document off the screen. Although you cannot see the text and graphics once they scroll off the screen, they remain in the document.

As shown in Figure 1–59, when you insert the picture in the flyer, the text and graphics are too long to fit in the document window. Thus, to see the bottom of the flyer, you will need to scroll downward.

You may use either the mouse or the keyboard to scroll to a different location in a document. With the mouse, you can use the scroll arrows or the scroll box on the scroll bar to display a different portion of the document in the document window, and then click the mouse to move the insertion point to that location. Table 1–1 explains various techniques for using the scroll bar to scroll vertically with the mouse.

BTW

Minimize Wrist Injury
Computer users frequently switch between the keyboard and the mouse during a word processing session; such switching strains the wrist. To help prevent wrist injury, minimize switching. For instance, if your fingers already are on the keyboard, use keyboard keys to scroll. If your hand already is on the mouse, use the mouse to scroll.

Table 1–1 Using the Scroll Bar to Scroll with the Mouse

SCROLL DIRECTION	MOUSE ACTION
Up	Drag the scroll box upward.
Down	Drag the scroll box downward.
Up one screen	Click anywhere above the scroll box on the vertical scroll bar.
Down one screen	Click anywhere below the scroll box on the vertical scroll bar.
Up one line	Click the scroll arrow at the top of the vertical scroll bar.
Down one line	Click the scroll arrow at the bottom of the vertical scroll bar.

When you use the keyboard to scroll, the insertion point automatically moves when you press the appropriate keys. Table 1–2 outlines various techniques to scroll through a document using the keyboard, some of which you have seen used in this chapter.

Table 1–2 Scrolling with the Keyboard

SCROLL DIRECTION	KEY(S) TO PRESS
Left one character	LEFT ARROW
Right one character	RIGHT ARROW
Left one word	CTRL+LEFT ARROW
Right one word	CTRL+RIGHT ARROW
Up one line	UP ARROW
Down one line	DOWN ARROW
To end of line	END
To beginning of line	HOME
Up one paragraph	CTRL+UP ARROW
Down one paragraph	CTRL+DOWN ARROW
Up one screen	PAGE UP
Down one screen	PAGE DOWN
To top of document window	ALT+CTRL+PAGE UP
To bottom of document window	ALT+CTRL+PAGE DOWN
To beginning of document	CTRL+HOME
To end of document	CTRL+END

To Apply a Picture Style

Earlier in this chapter, you applied the heading styles to the headline and signature line in the flyer. Word also provides styles for pictures, allowing you easily to change the basic rectangle format to a more visually appealing style. Word provides a gallery of more than 25 picture styles, which include a variety of shapes, angles, borders, and reflections. The flyer in this chapter uses an oval picture style that has a border around its edges. The following steps apply a picture style to the picture in the flyer.

1

- Click the down scroll arrow on the vertical scroll bar as many times as necessary until the entire picture is displayed in the document window (Figure 1–60).

Q&A What if the Picture Tools and Format tabs no longer are displayed on my Ribbon?

Double-click the picture to display the Picture Tools and Format tabs.

Figure 1–60

2

- Click the More button in the Picture Styles gallery, which shows more gallery options.

- Point to Metal Oval in the Picture Styles gallery to display a live preview of that style applied to the picture in the document (Figure 1–61).

Experiment

- Point to various picture styles in the Picture Styles gallery and watch the format of the picture change in the document window.

3

- Click Metal Oval in the Picture Styles gallery to apply the selected style to the picture.

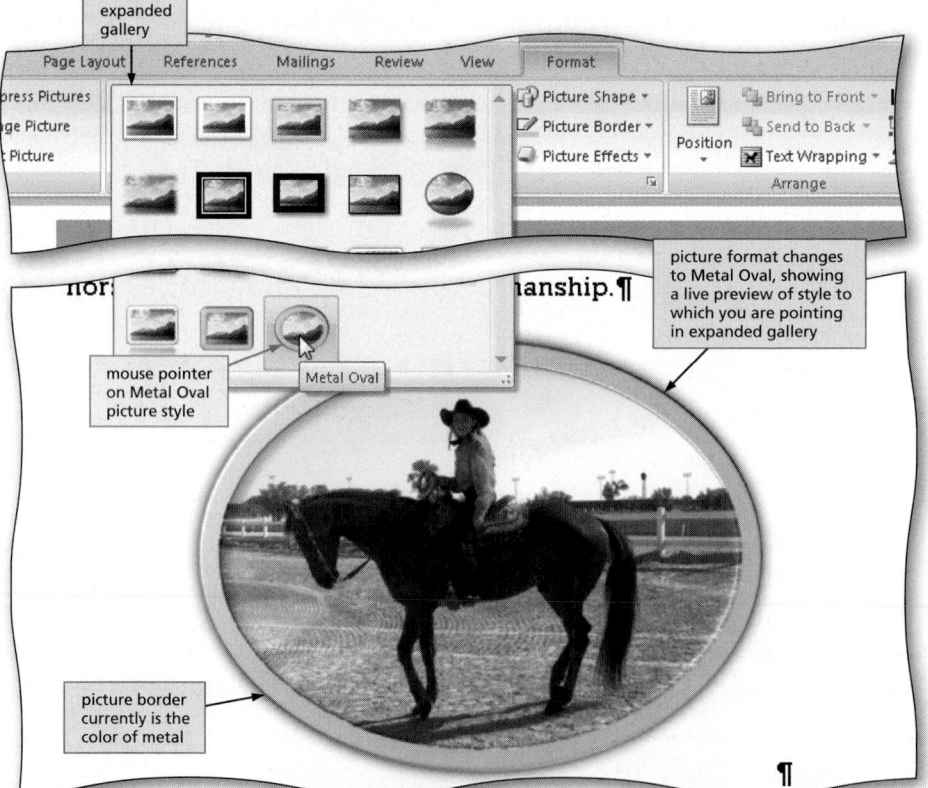

Figure 1–61

To Change a Picture Border Color

The flyer in this chapter has a tan border around the picture. Earlier in this chapter, you changed the color scheme to Aspect. To coordinate the border color with the other colors in the document, you will use a shade of tan in Aspect color scheme for the picture border. Any color galleries you display show colors defined in this current color scheme. The following steps change the picture border color.

1

- Click the Picture Border button arrow on the Format tab to display the Picture Border gallery.

Q&A What if the Picture Tools and Format tabs no longer are displayed on my Ribbon?

Double-click the picture to display the Picture Tools and Format tabs.

- Point to Tan, Background 2 (third theme color from left in the first row) in the Picture Border gallery to display a live preview of that border color on the picture (Figure 1–62).

 Experiment

- Point to various colors in the Picture Border gallery and watch the border color on the picture change in the document window.

2

- Click Tan, Background 2 in the Picture Styles gallery to change the picture border color.

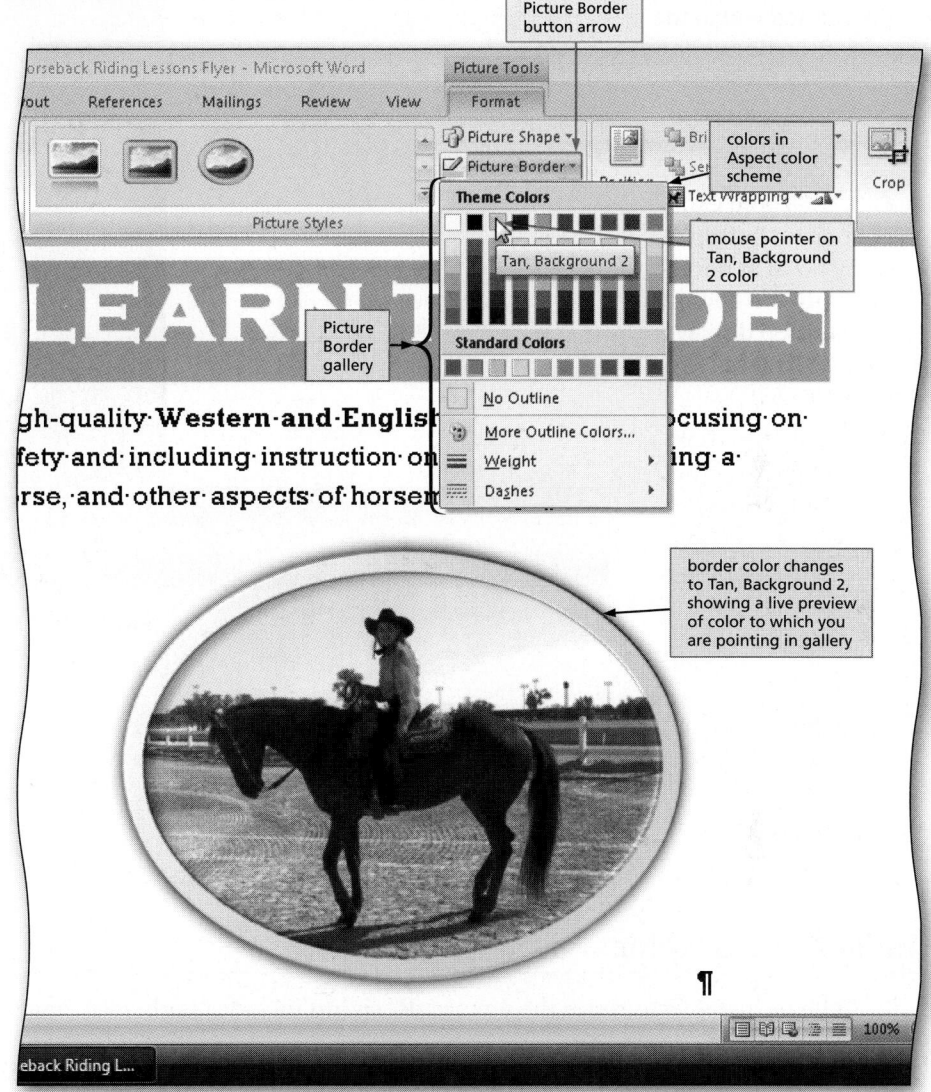

Figure 1–62

To Zoom the Document

The next step in formatting the picture is to resize it. Specifically, you will increase the size of the picture. You do not want it so large, however, that it causes the flyer text to flow to a second page. You can change the zoom so that you can see the entire document on the screen at once. Seeing the entire document at once helps you determine the appropriate size of the picture. The steps on the next page zoom the document.

① Experiment

- Repeatedly click the Zoom Out and Zoom In buttons on the status bar and watch the size of the document change in the document window.

②

- Click the Zoom Out or Zoom In button as many times as necessary until the Zoom level button displays 50% on its face (Figure 1–63).

Q&A If I change the zoom percentage, will the document print differently?

Changing the zoom has no effect on the printed document.

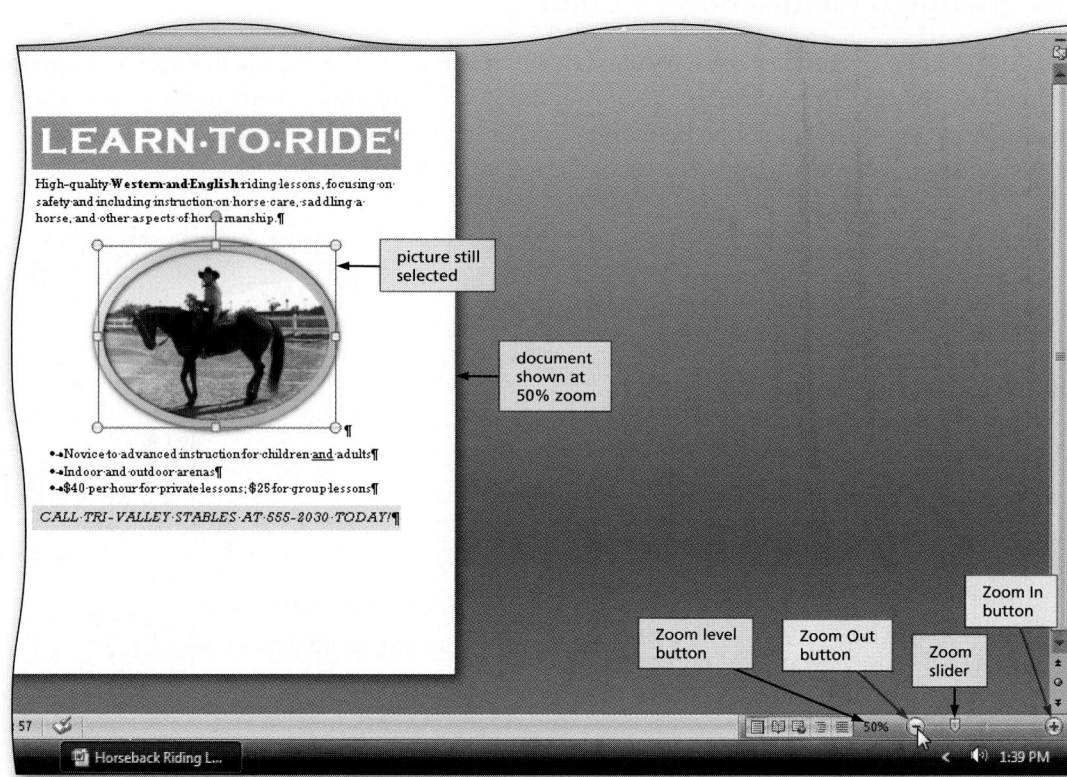

Figure 1–63

Other Ways		
1. Drag Zoom slider on status bar	2. Click Zoom level button on status bar, select desired zoom percent or type, click OK button	3. Click Zoom button on View tab, select desired zoom percent or type, click OK button

To Resize a Graphic

The next step is to resize the picture. **Resizing** includes both enlarging and reducing the size of a graphic. The picture in the flyer should be as large as possible, without causing any flyer text to flow to a second page.

With the entire document displaying in the document window, you will be able to see how the resized graphic will look on the entire page. The following steps resize a selected graphic.

①

- With the graphic still selected, point to the upper-right corner sizing handle on the picture so that the mouse pointer shape changes to a two-headed arrow (Figure 1–64).

Q&A What if my graphic (picture) is not selected?

To select a graphic, click it.

Figure 1–64

• Drag the sizing handle diagonally outward until the crosshair mouse pointer is positioned approximately as shown in Figure 1–65.

3

• Release the mouse button to resize the graphic.

Q&A What if the graphic is the wrong size?

Repeat Steps 1, 2, and 3.

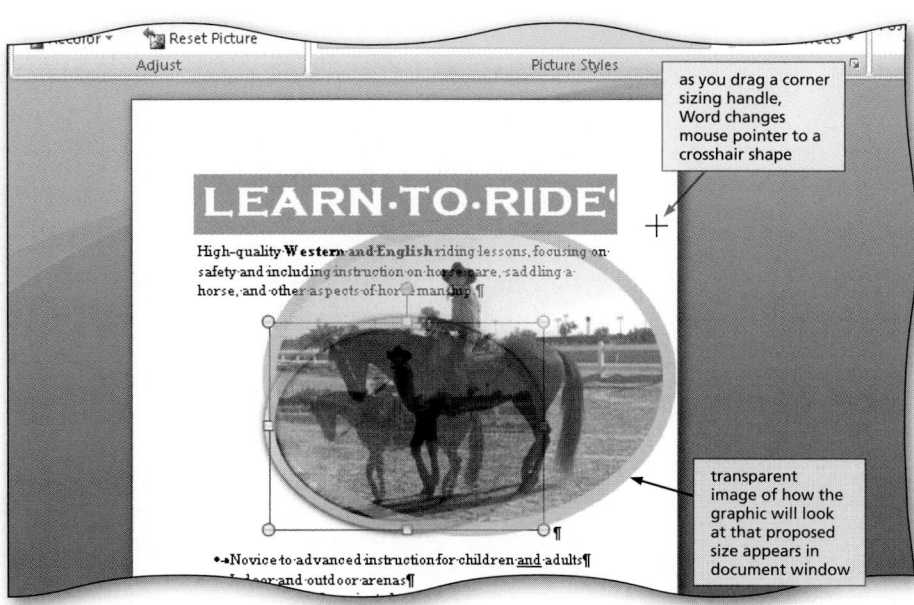

Figure 1–65

4

• Click outside the graphic to deselect it (Figure 1–66).

Q&A What happened to the Picture Tools and Format tabs?

When you click outside of a graphic or press a key to scroll through a document, Word deselects the graphic and removes the Picture Tools and Format tabs from the screen.

Q&A What if I want to return a graphic to its original size and start again?

With the graphic selected, click the Size Dialog Box Launcher on the Format tab to display the Size dialog box, click the Size tab, click the Reset button, and then click the Close button.

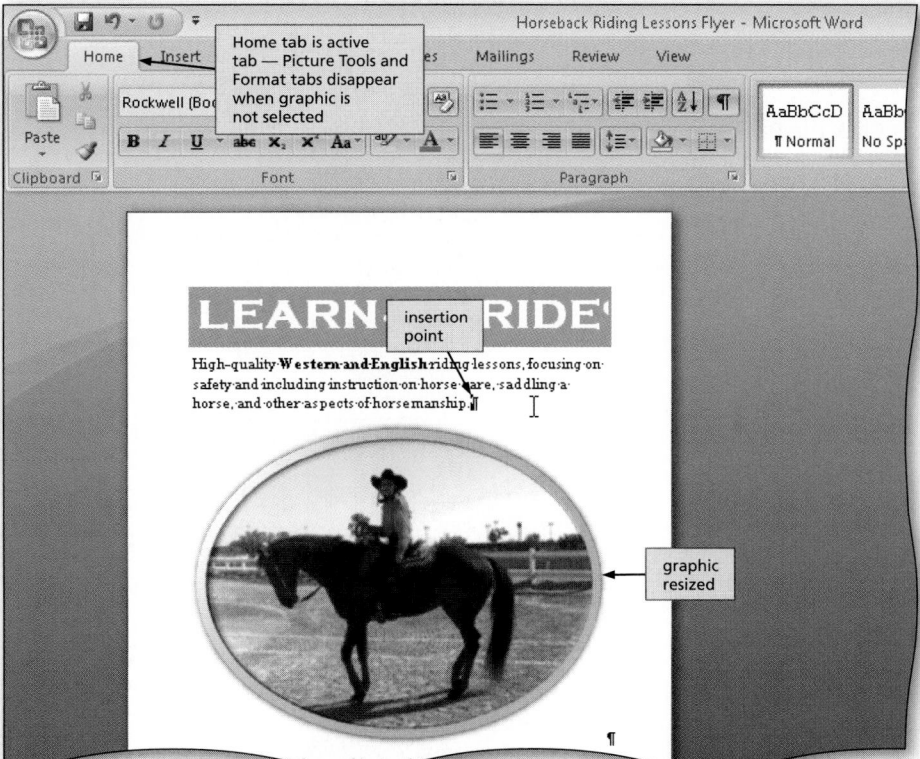

Figure 1–66

Other Ways
1. Enter graphic height and width in Shape Height and Shape Width text boxes in Size group on Format tab in Picture Tools tab	2. Click Size Dialog Box Launcher on Format tab in Picture Tools tab, click Size tab, enter desired height and width values in text boxes, click Close button

Enhancing the Page

With the text and graphics entered and formatted, the next step is to look at the page as a whole and determine if it looks finished in its current state. As you review the page, answer these questions:

- Does it need a page border to frame its contents, or would a page border make it look too busy?
- Is the spacing between paragraphs and graphics on the page adequate? Do any sections of text or graphics look as if they are positioned too closely to the items above or below them?

You determine that a graphical, color-coordinated border would enhance the flyer. You also notice that the flyer would look more proportionate if it had a little more space below the headline and above the graphic. The following pages make these enhancements to the flyer.

To Add a Page Border

In Word, you can add a border around the perimeter of an entire page. In this flyer, you add a graphical border that uses a shade of brown from the Aspect color scheme. The following steps add a graphical page border.

- Click Page Layout on the Ribbon to display the Page Layout tab.
- Click the Page Borders button on the Page Layout tab to display the Borders and Shading dialog box (Figure 1–67).

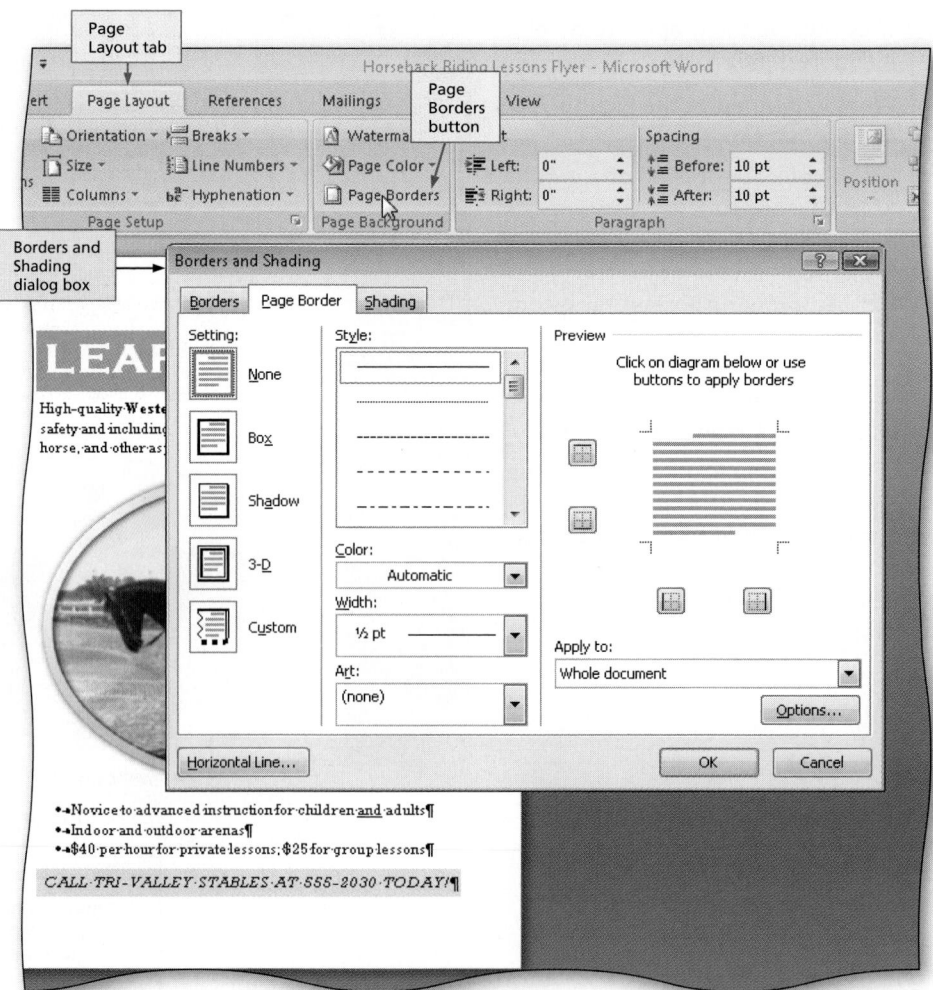

Figure 1–67

- Click the Art box arrow to display the Art gallery.

- Click the down scroll arrow in the Art gallery until the art border shown in Figure 1–68 appears.

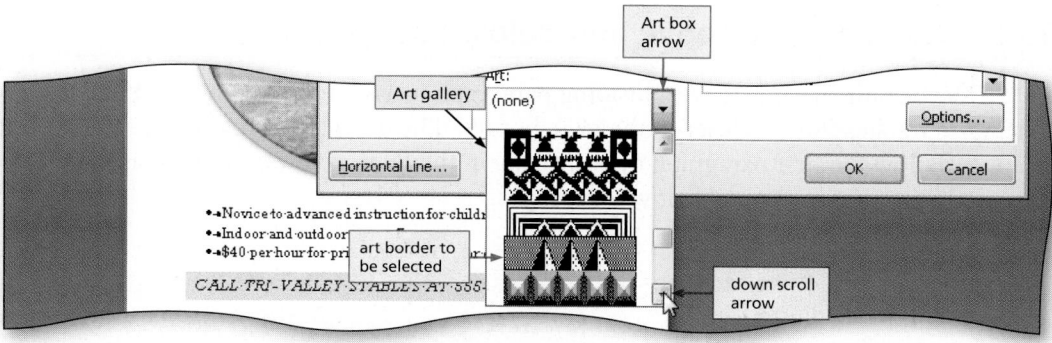

Figure 1–68

❸

- Click the art border shown in Figure 1–68 to display a preview of the selection in the Preview area of the dialog box.

- Click the Color box arrow to display a Color gallery (Figure 1–69).

Q&A Do I have to use an art border?

No. You can select a solid or decorative line in the Style list.

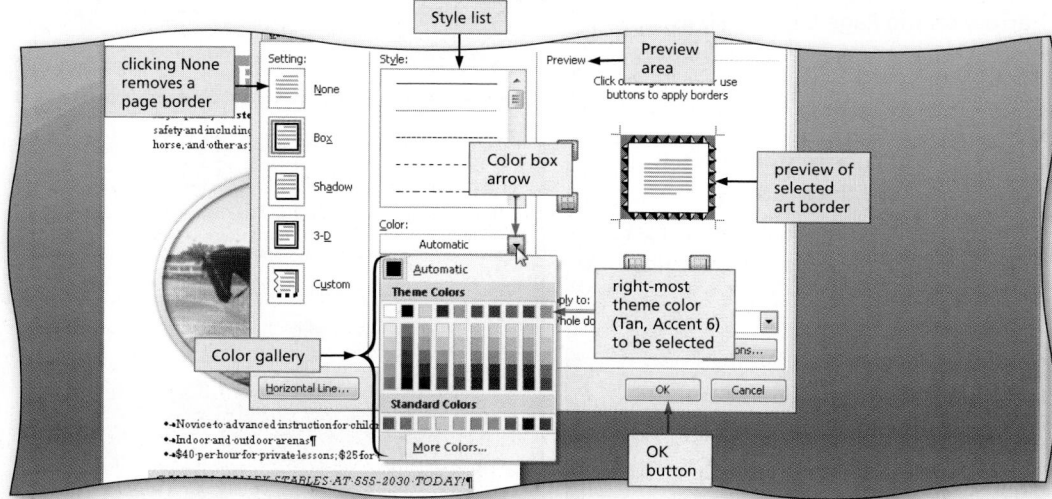

Figure 1–69

Q&A Can I add color to every border type?

You can color all of the line styles and many of the art borders.

❹

- Click the right-most theme color (Tan, Accent 6) in the Color gallery to display a preview of the selection in the Preview area.

- Click the OK button to add the border to the page (Figure 1–70).

Q&A What if I wanted to remove the border?

Click None in the Setting list in the Borders and Shading dialog box.

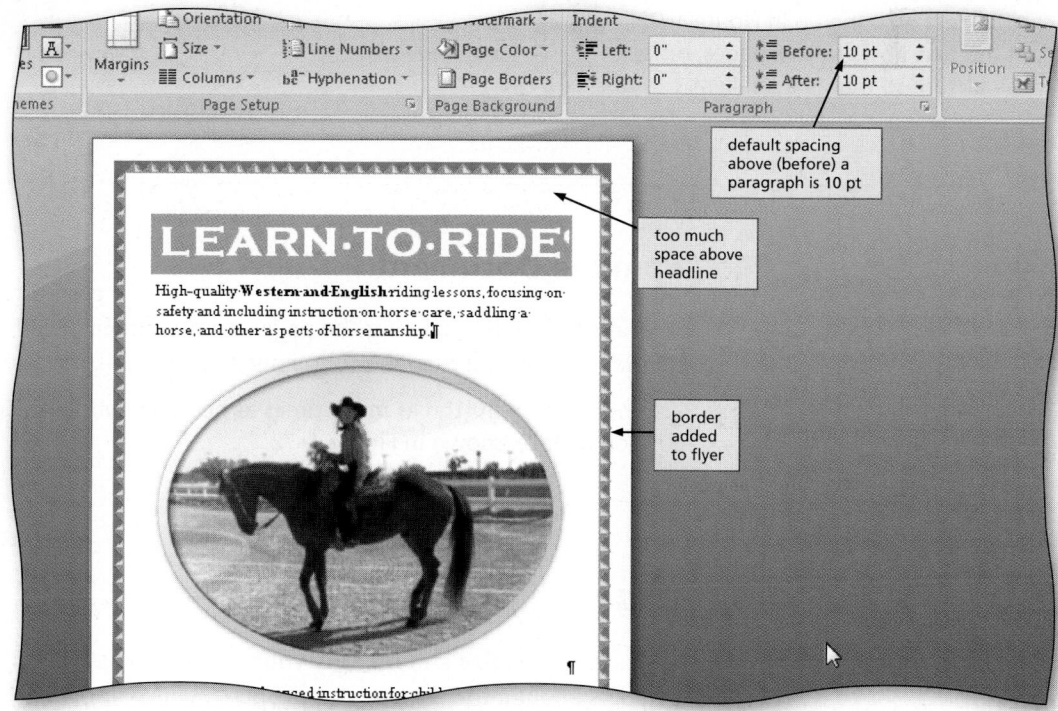

Figure 1–70

To Change Spacing Above and Below Paragraphs

The default spacing above a heading paragraph in Word is 10 points. In the flyer, you want to remove this spacing so the headline is closer to the page border. The default spacing below (after) a body text paragraph is 0 points. Below the first paragraph of body copy in the flyer, you want to increase this space. The following steps change the spacing above and below paragraphs.

- Position the insertion point in the paragraph to be adjusted, in this case, the headline.

- Click the Spacing Before box down arrow on the Page Layout tab as many times as necessary until 0 pt is displayed in the Spacing Before text box (Figure 1–71).

Why is a blank space still between the border and the headline?

The space is a result of Word's preset left, right, top, and bottom margins and other settings.

- Position the insertion point in the paragraph below the headline.

- Click the Spacing After box up arrow on the Page Layout tab as many times as necessary until 24 pt is displayed in the Spacing After text box, shown in Figure 1–72. (If the text flows to two pages, resize the picture so that it is smaller.)

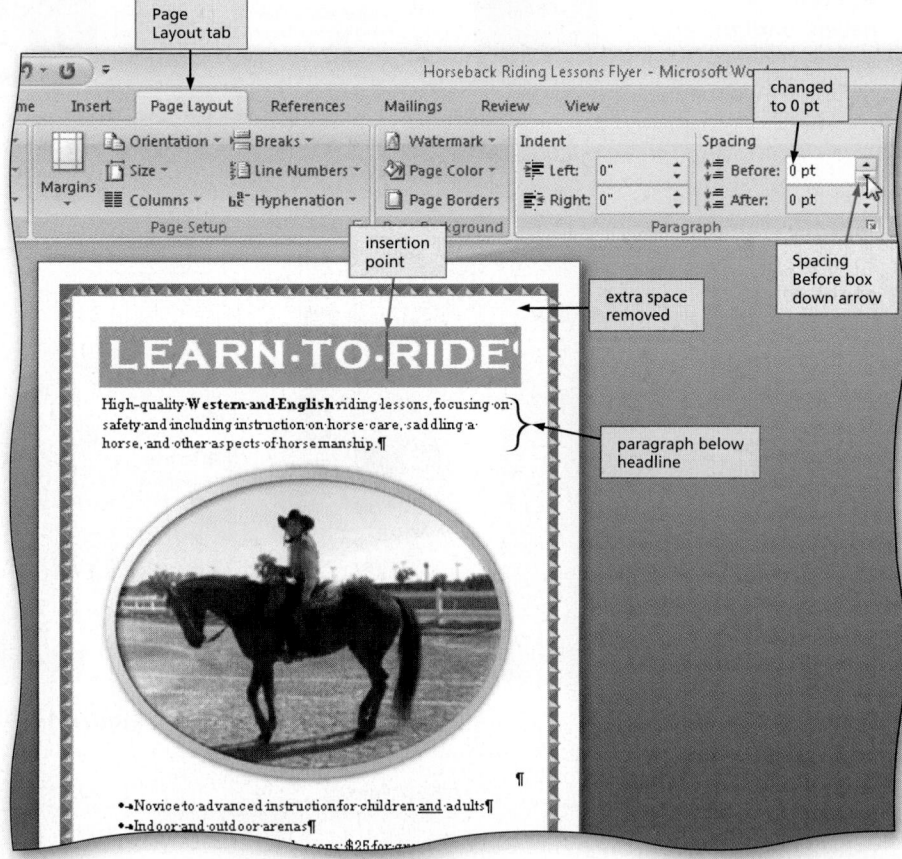

Figure 1–71

To Zoom the Document

You are finished enhancing the page and no longer need to view the entire page in the document window. Thus, the following step changes the zoom back to 100 percent.

1 Click the Zoom In button as many times as necessary until the Zoom level button displays 100% on its face, shown in Figure 1–72.

Changing Document Properties and Saving Again

Word helps you organize and identify your files by using **document properties**, which are the details about a file. Document properties, also known as **metadata**, can include such information as the project author, title, or subject. **Keywords** are words or phrases that further describe the document. For example, a class name or document topic can describe the file's purpose or content.

Document properties are valuable for a variety of reasons:

- Users can save time locating a particular file because they can view a document's properties without opening the document.

- By creating consistent properties for files having similar content, users can better organize their documents.

- Some organizations require Word users to add document properties so that other employees can view details about these files.

Five different types of document properties exist, but the more common ones used in this book are standard and automatically updated properties. **Standard properties** are associated with all Microsoft Office documents and include author, title, and subject. **Automatically updated properties** include file system properties, such as the date you create or change a file, and statistics, such as the file size.

BTW

Printing Document Properties
To print document properties, click the Office Button to display the Office Button menu, point to Print on the Office Button menu to display the Print submenu, click Print on the Print submenu to display the Print dialog box, click the Print what box arrow, click Document properties to instruct Word to print the document properties instead of the document, and then click the OK button.

To Change Document Properties

The **Document Information Panel** contains areas where you can view and enter document properties. You can view and change information in this panel at any time while you are creating a document. Before saving the flyer again, you want to add your name and course information as document properties. The following steps use the Document Information Panel to change document properties.

1

- Click the Office Button to display the Office Button menu.

- Point to Prepare on the Office Button menu to display the Prepare submenu (Figure 1–72).

Q&A

What other types of actions besides changing properties can you take to prepare a document for distribution?

The Prepare submenu provides commands related to sharing a document with others, such as allowing or restricting people to view and modify your document, checking to see if your document will open in earlier versions of Word, and searching for hidden personal information.

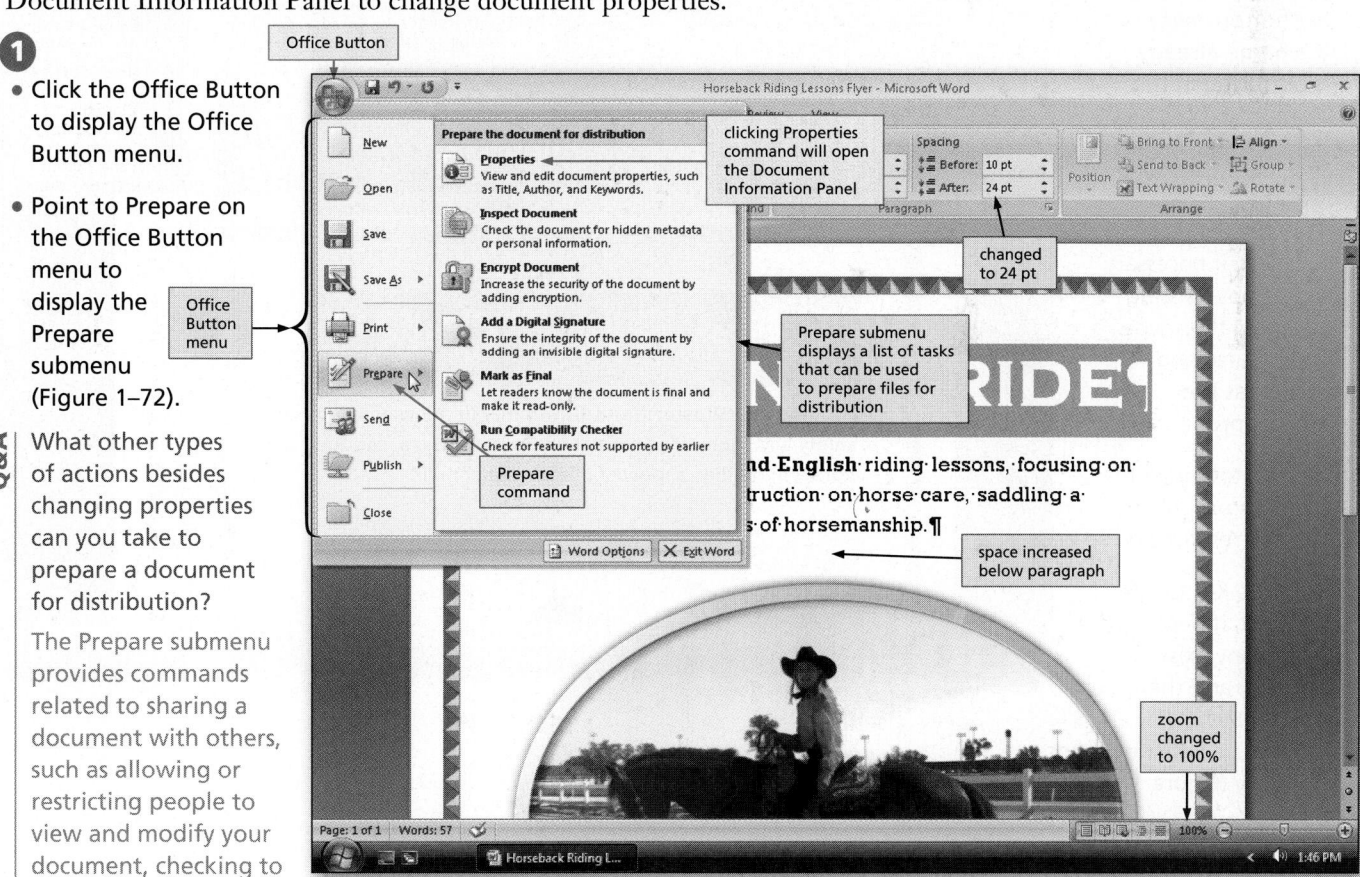

Figure 1–72

2

- Click Properties on the Prepare submenu to display the Document Information Panel (Figure 1–73).

Why are some of the document properties in my Document Information Panel already filled in?

The person who installed Microsoft Office 2007 on your computer or network may have set or customized the properties.

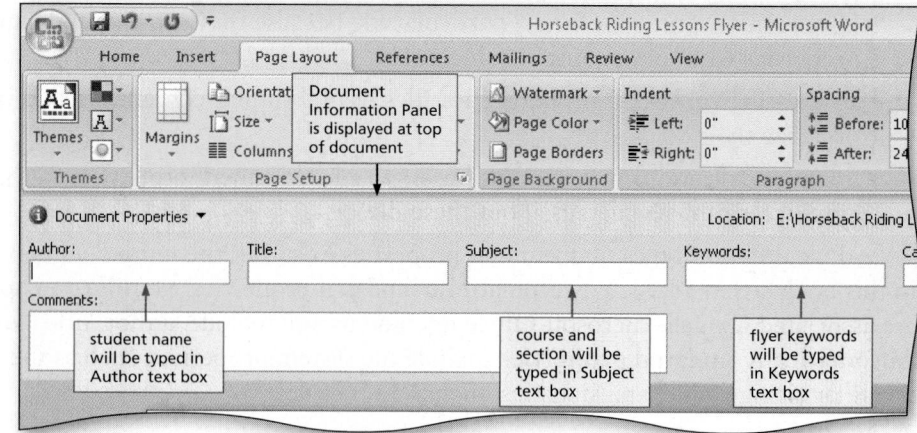

Figure 1–73

3

- Click the Author text box, if necessary, and then type your name as the Author property. If a name already is displayed in the Author text box, delete it before typing your name.

- Click the Subject text box, if necessary delete any existing text, and then type your course and section as the Subject property.

- If an AutoComplete dialog box appears, click its Yes button.

- Click the Keywords text box, if necessary delete any existing text, and then type `Tri-Valley Stables` as the Keywords property (Figure 1–74).

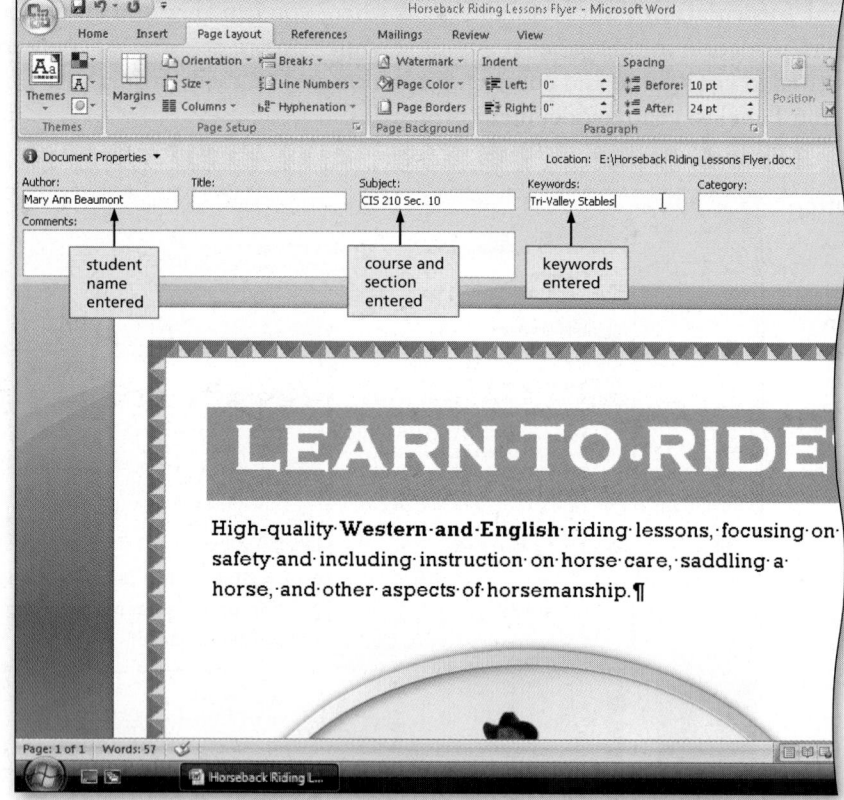
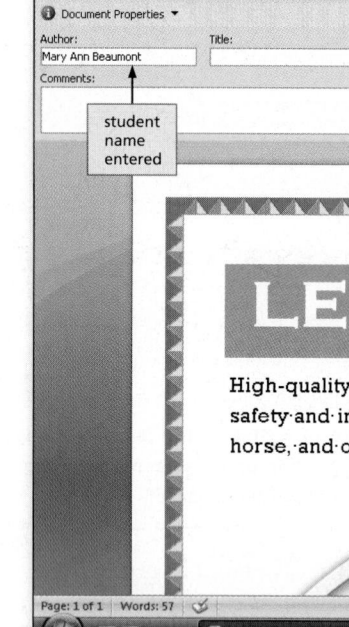
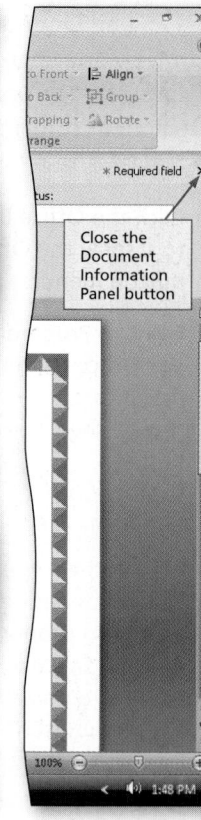

Figure 1–74

What types of document properties does Word collect automatically?

Word records such details as how long you worked at creating your project, how many times you revised the document, and what fonts and themes are used.

4

- Click the Close the Document Information Panel button so that the Document Information Panel no longer is displayed.

To Save an Existing Document with the Same File Name

Saving frequently cannot be overemphasized. You have made several modifications to the document since you saved it earlier in the chapter. When you first saved the document, you clicked the Save button on the Quick Access Toolbar, the Save As dialog box appeared, and you entered the file name, Horseback Riding Lessons Flyer. If you want to use the same file name to save the changes made to the document, you again click the Save button on the Quick Access Toolbar. The following step saves the document again.

1

• Click the Save button on the Quick Access Toolbar to overwrite the previous Horseback Riding Lessons Flyer file on the USB flash drive (Figure 1–75).

Why did the Save As dialog box not appear?

Word overwrites the document using the settings specified the first time you saved the document. To save the file with a different file name or on different media, display the Save As dialog box by clicking the Office Button and then clicking Save As on the Office Button menu. Then, fill in the Save As dialog box as described in Steps 2 through 5 on pages WD 20 and WD 21.

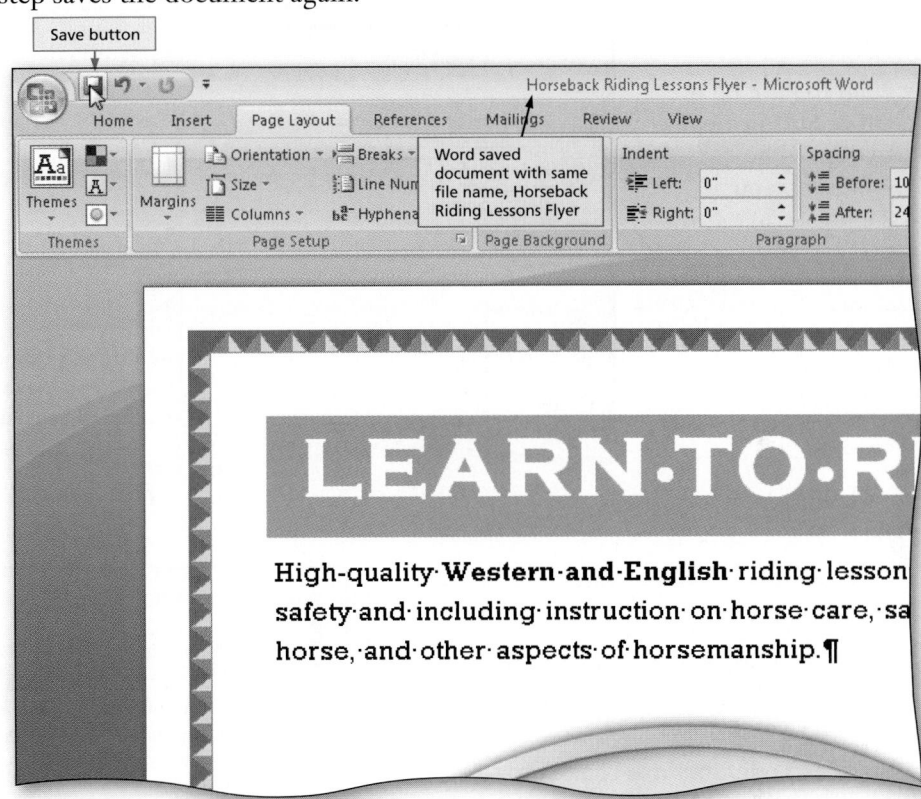

Figure 1–75

Other Ways

1. Press CTRL+S or press SHIFT+F12

Printing a Document

After you create a document, you often want to print it. A printed version of the document is called a **hard copy** or **printout**.

Printed copies of your document can be useful for the following reasons:

• Many people prefer proofreading a hard copy of the document rather than viewing it on the screen to check for errors and readability.

• Hard copies can serve as reference material if your storage medium is lost or becomes corrupted and you need to re-create the document.

It is a good practice to save a document before printing it, in the event you experience difficulties with the printer.

BTW

Conserving Ink and Toner

You can instruct Word to print draft quality documents to conserve ink or toner by clicking the Office Button, clicking the Word Options button, clicking Advanced in the left pane of the Word Options dialog box, scrolling to the Print area, placing a check mark in the 'Use draft quality' check box, and then clicking the OK button. To print the document with these settings, click the Office Button, point to Print, and then click Quick Print.

To Print a Document

   With the completed document saved, you may want to print it. The following steps print the contents of the saved Horseback Riding Lessons Flyer project.

1

- Click the Office Button to display the Office Button menu.

- Point to Print on the Office Button menu to display the Print submenu (Figure 1–76).

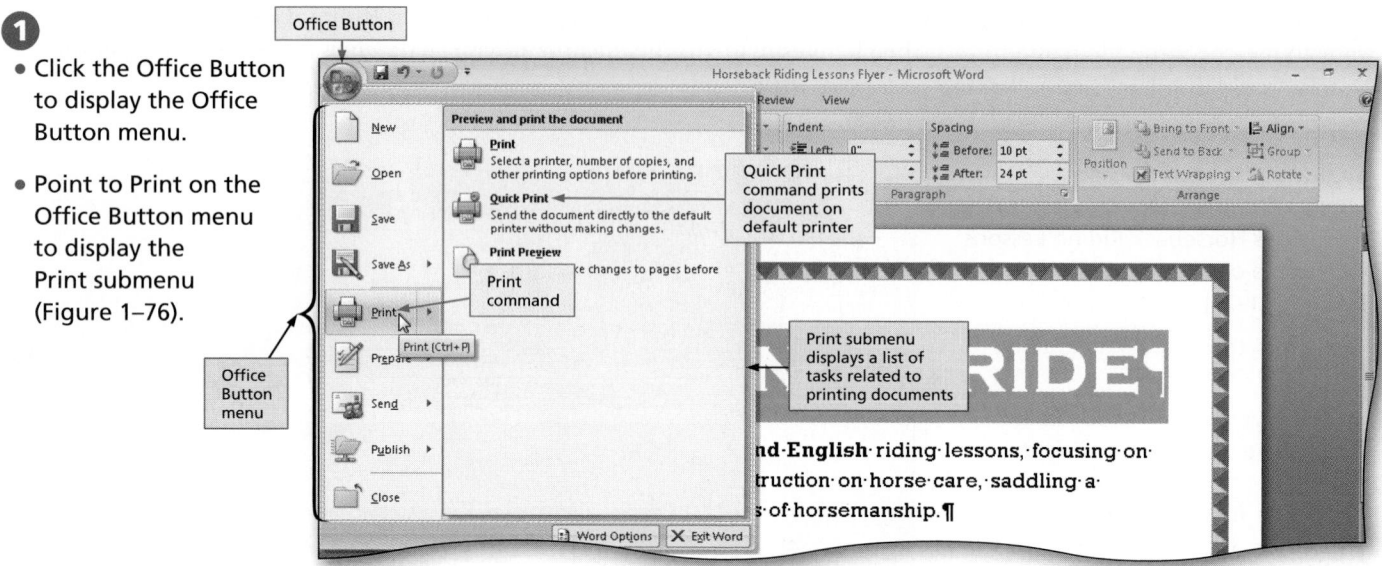

Figure 1–76

2

- Click Quick Print on the Print submenu to print the document.

- When the printer stops, retrieve the hard copy of the Horseback Riding Lessons Flyer (Figures 1–77).

Q&A How can I print multiple copies of my document other than issuing the Quick Print command twice?

Click the Office Button, point to Print on the Office Button menu, click Print on the Print submenu, increase the number in the Number of copies box, and then click the OK button.

Q&A Do I have to wait until my document is complete to print it?

No, you can follow these steps to print a document at any time while you are creating it.

BTW **Printed Borders**
If one or more of your borders do not print, click the Page Borders button on the Page Layout tab, click the Options button in the dialog box, click the Measure from box arrow and click Text, change the four text boxes to 15 pt, and then click the OK button in each dialog box. Try printing the document again. If the borders still do not print, adjust the text boxes in the dialog box to a number smaller than 15 point.

Figure 1–77

Other Ways

1. Press CTRL+P, press ENTER

Quitting Word

When you quit Word, if you have made changes to a document since the last time the file was saved, Word displays a dialog box asking if you want to save the changes you made to the file before it closes that window. The dialog box contains three buttons with these resulting actions: the Yes button saves the changes and then quits Word; the No button quits Word without saving changes; and the Cancel button closes the dialog box and redisplays the document without saving the changes.

If no changes have been made to an open document since the last time the file was saved, Word will close the window without displaying a dialog box.

To Quit Word with One Document Open

You saved the document prior to printing and did not make any changes to the project. The Horseback Riding Lessons Flyer project now is complete, and you are ready to quit Word. When one Word document is open, the following steps quit Word.

1
- Point to the Close button on the right side of the Word title bar (Figure 1–78).

2
- Click the Close button to quit Word.

Q&A
What if I have more than one Word document open?

You would click the Close button for each open document. When you click the last open document's Close button, Word also quits. As an alternative, you could click the Office Button and then click the Exit Word button on the Office Button menu, which closes all open Word documents and then quits Word.

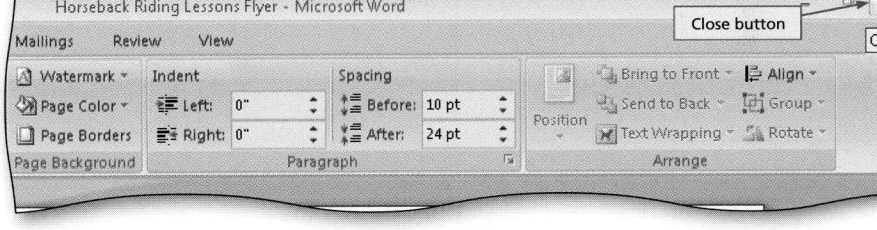

Figure 1–78

Other Ways

1. Double-click Office Button
2. With multiple documents open, click Office Button, click Exit Word on Office Button menu
3. Right-click Microsoft Word button on Windows Vista taskbar, click Close on shortcut menu
4. Press ALT+F4

Starting Word and Opening a Document

Once you have created and saved a document, you may need to retrieve it from your storage medium. For example, you might want to revise the document or reprint it. Opening a document requires that Word is running on your computer.

To Start Word

The following steps, which assume Windows Vista is running, start Word.

1 Click the Start button on the Windows Vista taskbar to display the Start menu.

2 Click All Programs at the bottom of the left pane on the Start menu to display the All Programs list and then click Microsoft Office in the All Programs list to display the Microsoft Office list.

3 Click Microsoft Office Word 2007 in the Microsoft Office list to start Word and display a new blank document in the Word window.

4 If the Word window is not maximized, click the Maximize button on its title bar to maximize the window.

Note: If you are using Windows XP, see Appendix F for alternate steps.

To Open a Document from Word

Earlier in this chapter you saved your project on a USB flash drive using the file name, Horseback Riding Lessons Flyer. The following steps open the Horseback Riding Lessons Flyer file from the USB flash drive.

1

• With your USB flash drive connected to one of the computer's USB ports, click the Office Button to display the Office Button menu (Figure 1–79).

Q&A What files are shown in the Recent Documents list?

Word displays the most recently opened document file names in this list. If the name of the file you want to open appears in the Recent Documents list, you could click it to open the file.

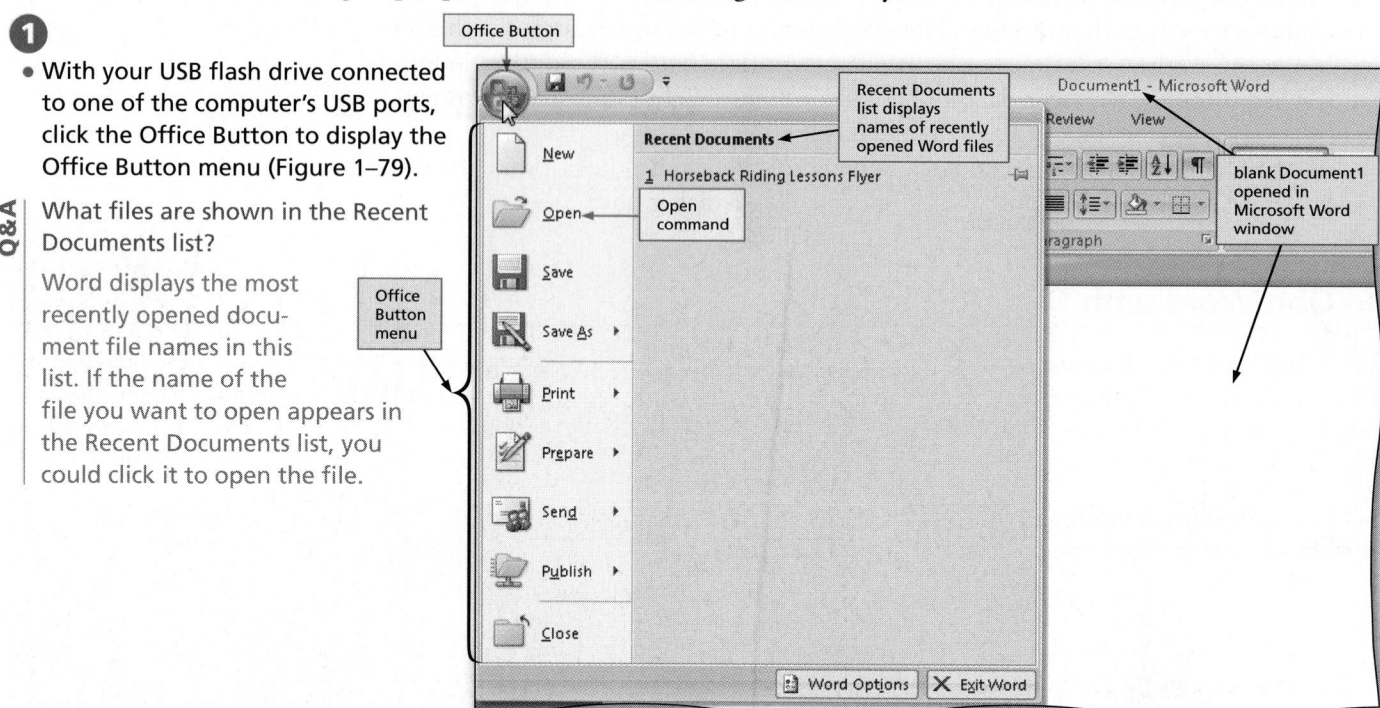

Figure 1–79

2

• Click Open on the Office Button menu to display the Open dialog box.

• If the Folders list is displayed below the Folders button, click the Folders button to remove the Folders list.

• If necessary, click Computer in the Favorite Links section and then scroll until UDISK 2.0 (E:) appears in the list of available drives.

• Double-click UDISK 2.0 (E:) to select the USB flash drive, Drive E in this case, as the new open location.

• Click Horseback Riding Lessons Flyer to select the file name (Figure 1–80).

Q&A How do I open the file if I am not using a USB flash drive?

Use the same process, but be certain to select your device in the Computer list.

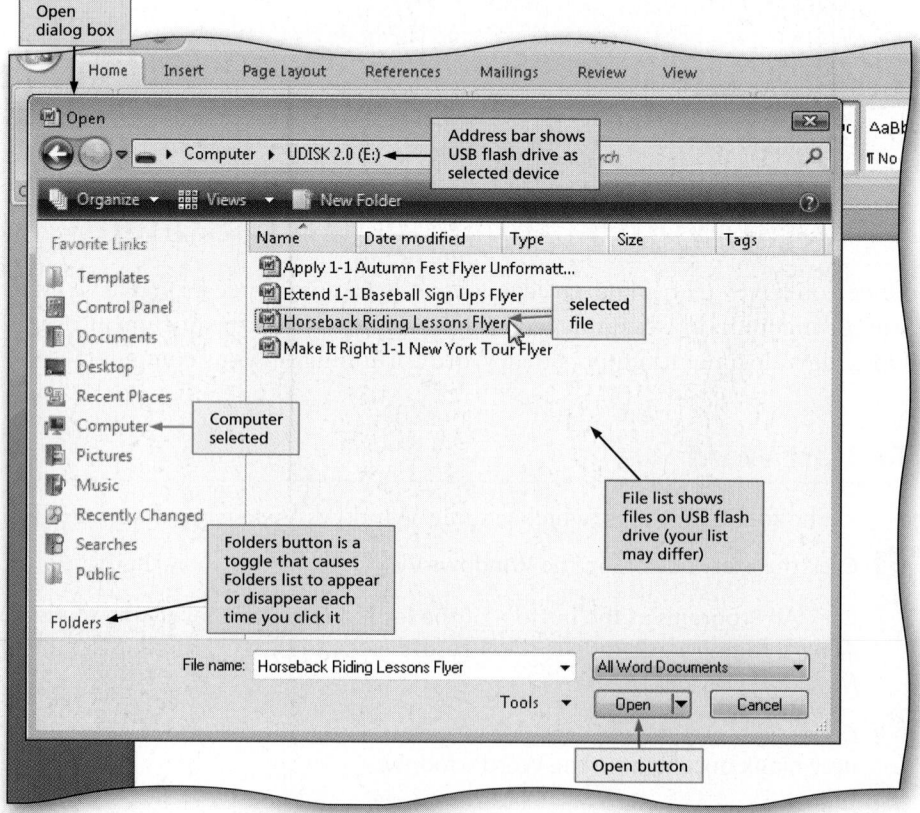

Figure 1–80

3

- Click the Open button to open the selected file and display the Horseback Riding Lessons Flyer document in the Word window (Figure 1–81).

Q&A

Why is the Word icon and document name on the Windows Vista taskbar?

When you open a Word file, a Word program button is displayed on the taskbar. The button in Figure 1–81 contains an ellipsis because some of its contents do not fit in the allotted button space. If you point to a program button, its entire contents appear in a ScreenTip, which in this case would be the file name followed by the program name.

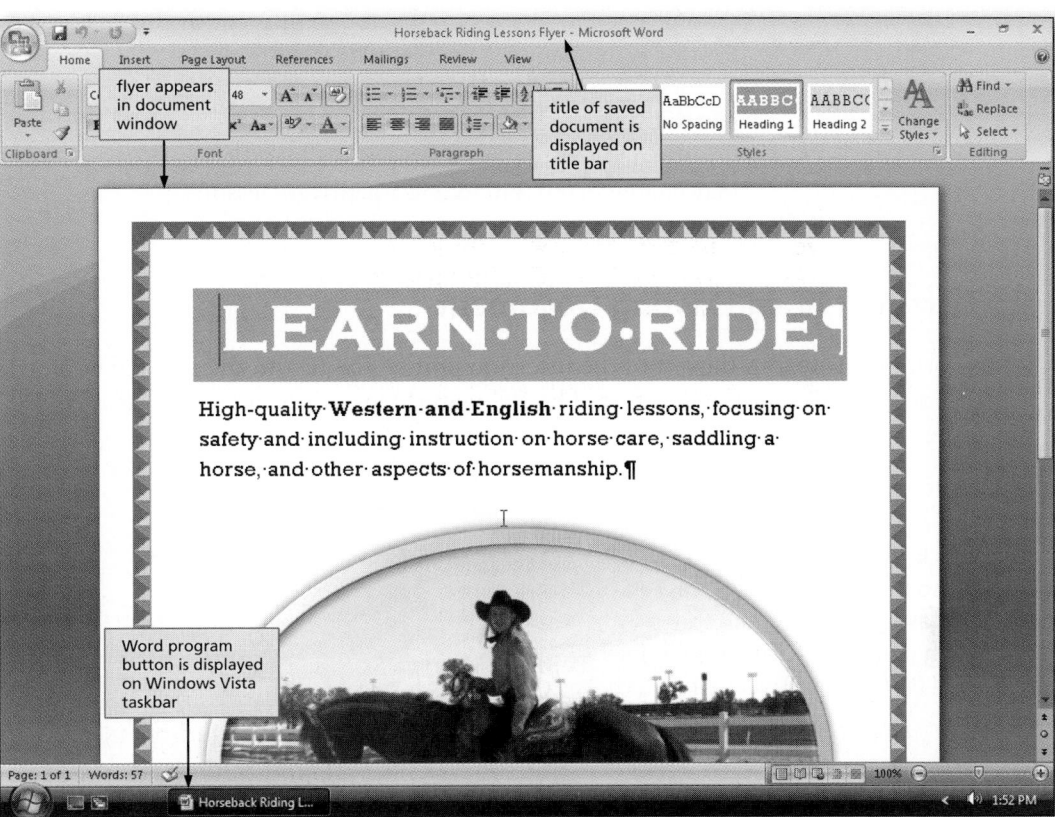

Figure 1–81

Other Ways

1. Click Office Button, click file name in Recent Documents list
2. Press CTRL+O, select file name, press ENTER

Correcting Errors

After creating a document, you often will find you must make changes to it. For example, the document may contain an error, or new circumstances may require you to add text to the document.

Types of Changes Made to Documents

The types of changes made to documents normally fall into one of the three following categories: additions, deletions, or modifications.

Additions Additional words, sentences, or paragraphs may be required in a document. Additions occur when you omit text from a document and want to insert it later. For example, additional types of riding lessons may be offered.

BTW

Print Preview
You can preview a document before printing it by clicking the Office Button, pointing to Print, and then clicking Print Preview. When finished previewing the document, click the Close Print Preview button.

Deletions Sometimes, text in a document is incorrect or is no longer needed. For example, group lessons might not be offered. In this case, you would delete the words, $25 for group lessons, from the flyer.

Modifications If an error is made in a document or changes take place that affect the document, you might have to revise a word(s) in the text. For example, the fee per hour may change from $40 to $50 for private lessons.

To Insert Text in an Existing Document

Word inserts text to the left of the insertion point. The text to the right of the insertion point moves to the right and downward to fit the new text. The following steps insert the word, various, to the left of the word, aspects, in the flyer.

- Scroll through the document and then click to the left of the location of text to be inserted (in this case, the a in aspects) to position the insertion point where text should be inserted (Figure 1–82).

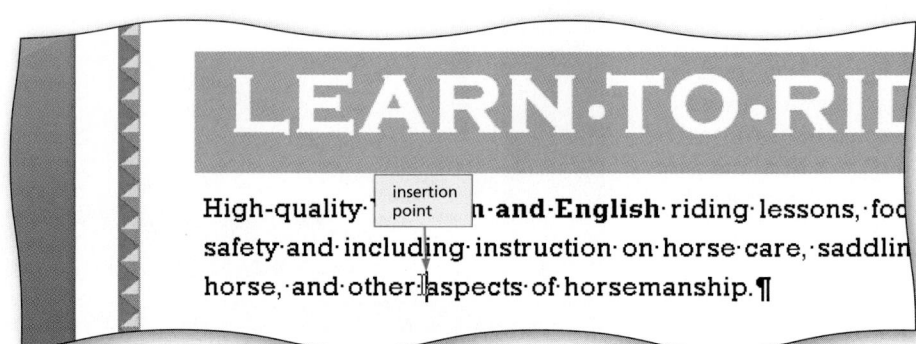

Figure 1–82

- Type various and then press the SPACEBAR to insert the word, various, to the left of the insertion point (Figure 1–83).

Q&A

Why did the text move to the right as I typed?

In Word, the default typing mode is **insert mode**, which means as you type a character, Word moves all the characters to the right of the typed character one position to the right.

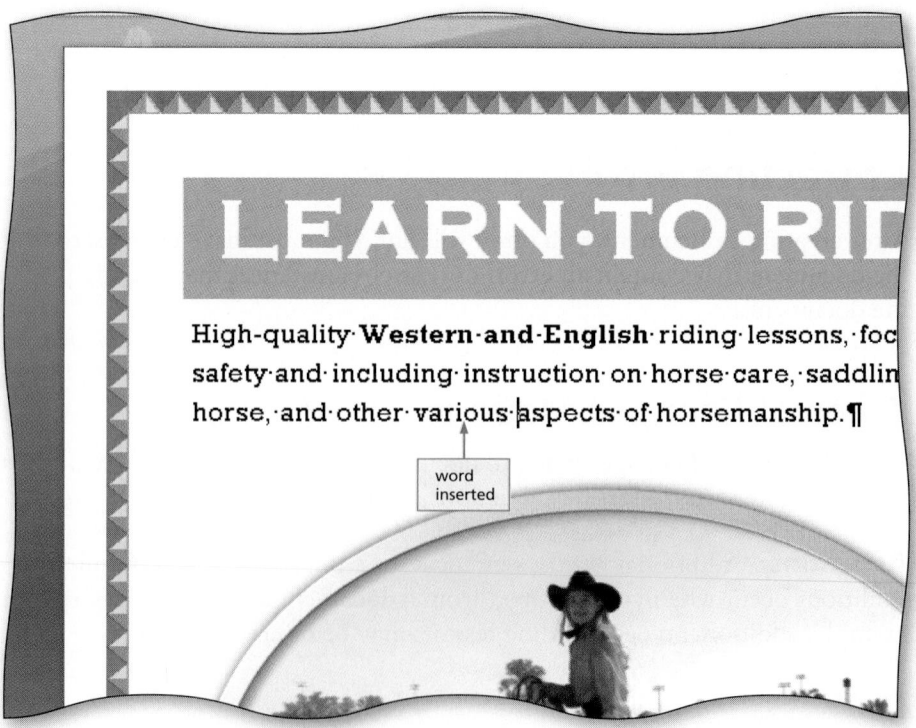

Figure 1–83

Deleting Text from an Existing Document

It is not unusual to type incorrect characters or words in a document. As discussed earlier in this chapter, you can click the Undo button on the Quick Access Toolbar to immediately undo a command or action — this includes typing. Word also provides other methods of correcting typing errors.

To delete an incorrect character in a document, simply click next to the incorrect character and then press the BACKSPACE key to erase to the left of the insertion point, or press the DELETE key to erase to the right of the insertion point.

To Select a Word and Delete It

To delete a word or phrase, you first must select the word or phrase. The following steps select the word, various, that was just added in the previous steps and then delete the selection.

- Position the mouse pointer somewhere in the word to be selected (in this case, various), as shown in Figure 1–84.

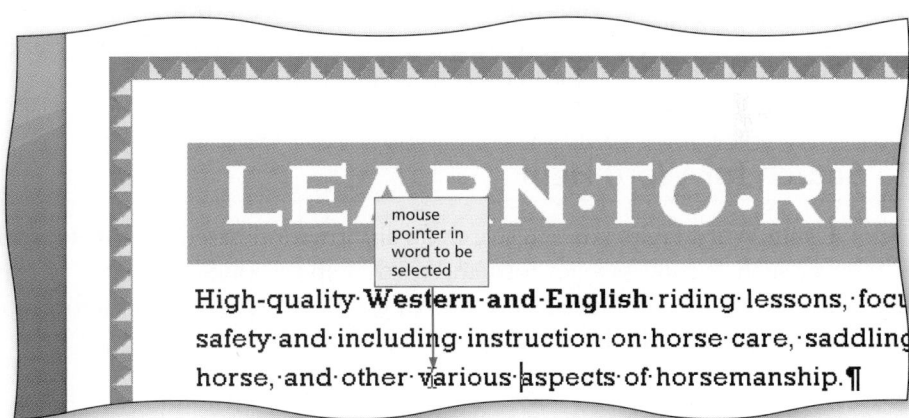

Figure 1–84

- Double-click the word to select it (Figure 1–85).

- With the text selected, press the DELETE key to delete the selected text (shown in Figure 1–82).

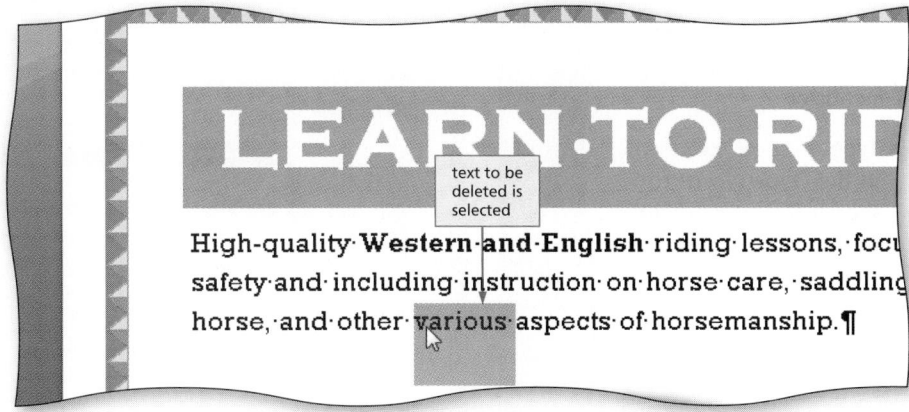

Figure 1–85

Closing the Entire Document

Sometimes, everything goes wrong. If this happens, you may want to close the document entirely and start over with a new document. You also may want to close a document when you are finished with it so you can begin your next document. If you wanted to close a document, you would use the steps on the next page.

To Close the Entire Document and Start Over

1. Click the Office Button and then click Close.

2. If Word displays a dialog box, click the No button to ignore the changes since the last time you saved the document.

3. Click the Office Button and then click New on the Office Button menu. When Word displays the New Document dialog box, click Blank document and then click the Create button.

Word Help

At any time while using Word, you can find answers to questions and display information about various topics through **Word Help**. Used properly, this form of assistance can increase your productivity and reduce your frustrations by minimizing the time you spend learning how to use Word.

This section introduces you to Word Help. Additional information about using Word Help is available in Appendix C.

To Search for Word Help

Using Word Help, you can search for information based on phrases such as save a document or format text, or key terms such as copy, save, or format. Word Help responds with a list of search results displayed as links to a variety of resources. The following steps, which use Word Help to search for information about selecting text, assume you are connected to the Internet.

1

- Click the Microsoft Office Word Help button near the upper-right corner of the Word window to open the Word Help window.

- Type select text in the 'Type words to search for' text box at the top of the Word Help window (Figure 1–86).

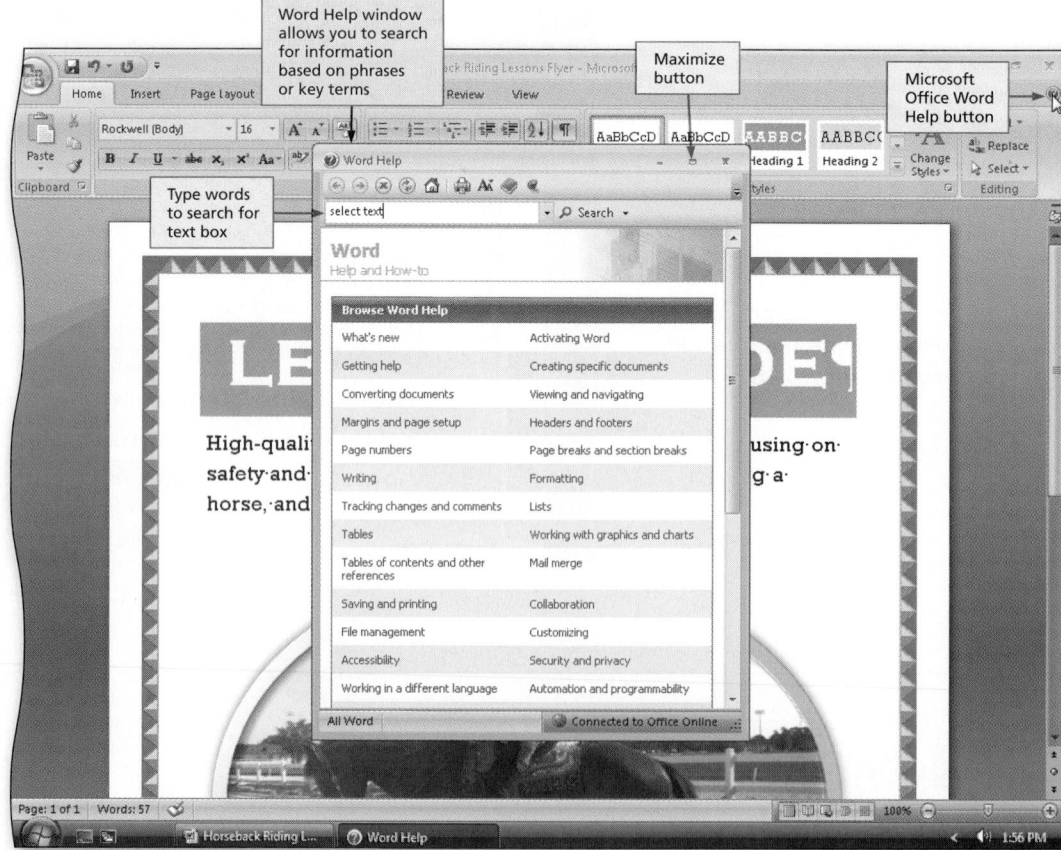

Figure 1–86

2

- Press the ENTER key to display the search results.

- Click the Maximize button on the Word Help window title bar to maximize the Help window (Figure 1–87).

Q&A Where is the Word window with the Horseback Riding Lessons Flyer document?

Word is open in the background, but the Word Help window is overlaid on top of the Word window. When the Word Help window is closed, the document will reappear.

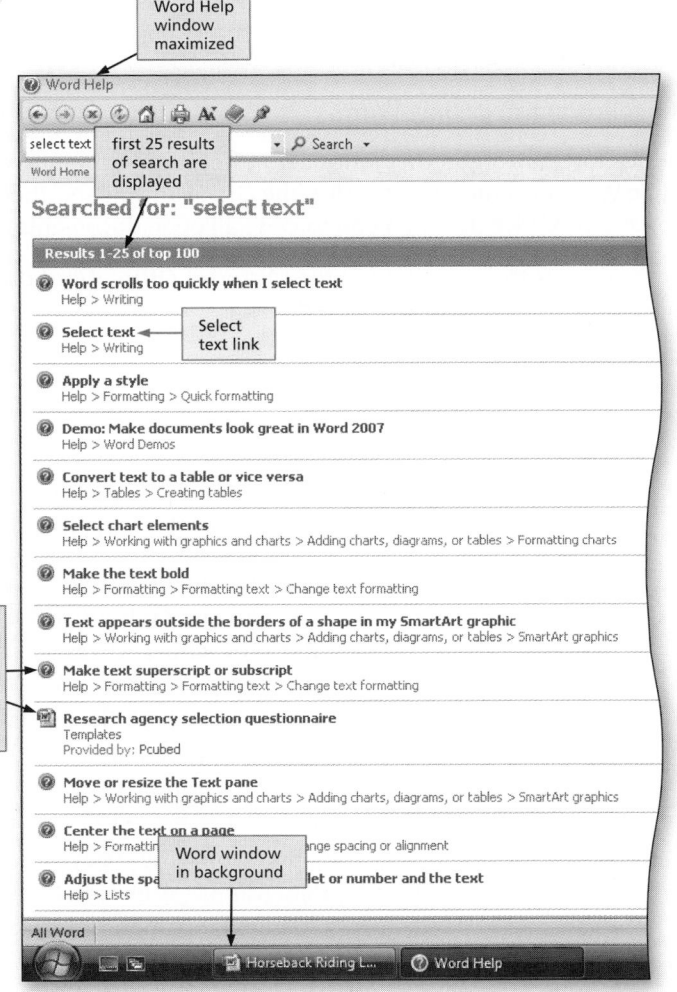

Figure 1–87

3

- Click the Select text link to display information about selecting text (Figure 1–88).

Q&A What is the purpose of the buttons at the top of the Word Help window?

Use the buttons in the upper-left corner of the Word Help window to navigate through Help, change the display, show the Word Help table of contents, and print the contents of the window.

4

- Click the Close button on the Word Help window title bar to close the Word Help window and redisplay the Word window.

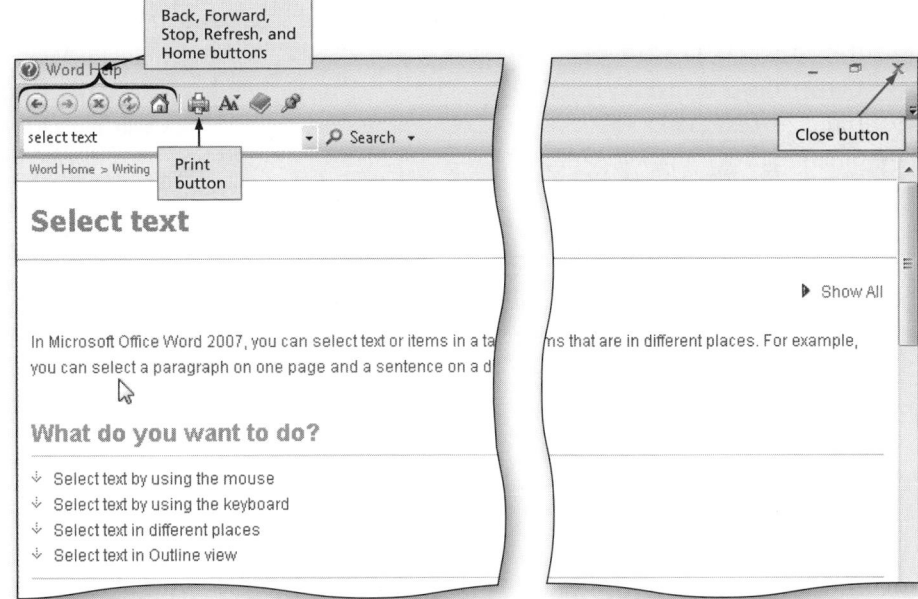

Figure 1–88

Other Ways
1. Press F1

BTW

Quick Reference
For a table that lists how to complete the tasks covered in this book using the mouse, Ribbon, shortcut menu, and keyboard, see the Quick Reference Summary at the back of this book, or visit the Word 2007 Quick Reference Web page (scsite.com/wd2007/qr).

To Quit Word

The following steps quit Word.

1 Click the Close button on the right side of the title bar to quit Word; or if you have multiple Word documents open, click the Office Button and then click the Exit Word button on the Office Button menu to close all open documents and quit Word.

2 If necessary, click the No button in the Microsoft Office Word dialog box so that any changes you have made are not saved.

Chapter Summary

In this chapter you have learned how to enter text in a document, format text, insert a picture, format a picture, add a page border, and print a document. The items listed below include all the new Word skills you have learned in this chapter.

1. Start Word (WD 5)
2. Type Text (WD 13)
3. Display Formatting Marks (WD 14)
4. Wordwrap Text as You Type (WD 15)
5. Insert a Blank Line (WD 15)
6. Check Spelling and Grammar as You Type (WD 16)
7. Save a Document (WD 19)
8. Apply Styles (WD 24)
9. Center a Paragraph (WD 26)
10. Select a Line (WD 27)
11. Change the Font Size of Selected Text (WD 28)
12. Change the Font of Selected Text (WD 29)
13. Select Multiple Paragraphs (WD 30)
14. Bullet a List of Paragraphs (WD 32)
15. Undo and Redo an Action (WD 32)
16. Select a Group of Words (WD 33)
17. Bold Text (WD 34)
18. Underline a Word (WD 35)
19. Italicize Text (WD 36)
20. Change the Style Set (WD 37)
21. Change Theme Colors (WD 39)
22. Change Theme Fonts (WD 39)
23. Insert a Picture (WD 41)
24. Apply a Picture Style (WD 44)
25. Change a Picture Border Color (WD 45)
26. Zoom the Document (WD 45)
27. Resize a Graphic (WD 46)
28. Add a Page Border (WD 48)
29. Change Spacing Above and Below Paragraphs (WD 50)
30. Change Document Properties (WD 51)
31. Save an Existing Document with the Same File Name (WD 53)
32. Print a Document (WD 54)
33. Quit Word with One Document Open (WD 55)
34. Open a Document from Word (WD 56)
35. Insert Text in an Existing Document (WD 58)
36. Select a Word and Delete It (WD 59)
37. Close the Entire Document and Start Over (WD 60)
38. Search for Word Help (WD 60)

If you have a SAM user profile, you may have access to hands-on instruction, practice, and assessment. Log in to your SAM account (http://sam2007.course.com) to launch any assigned training activities or exams that relate to the skills covered in this chapter.

BTW

Certification
The Microsoft Certified Application Specialist (MCAS) program provides an opportunity for you to obtain a valuable industry credential – proof that you have the Word 2007 skills required by employers. For more information, see Appendix G or visit the Word 2007 Certification Web page (scsite.com/wd2007/cert).

Learn It Online

Test your knowledge of chapter content and key terms.

Instructions: To complete the Learn It Online exercises, start your browser, click the Address bar, and then enter the Web address `scsite.com/wd2007/learn`. When the Word 2007 Learn It Online page is displayed, click the link for the exercise you want to complete and then read the instructions.

Chapter Reinforcement TF, MC, and SA
A series of true/false, multiple choice, and short answer questions that test your knowledge of the chapter content.

Flash Cards
An interactive learning environment where you identify chapter key terms associated with displayed definitions.

Practice Test
A series of multiple choice questions that test your knowledge of chapter content and key terms.

Who Wants To Be a Computer Genius?
An interactive game that challenges your knowledge of chapter content in the style of a television quiz show.

Wheel of Terms
An interactive game that challenges your knowledge of chapter key terms in the style of the television show *Wheel of Fortune*.

Crossword Puzzle Challenge
A crossword puzzle that challenges your knowledge of key terms presented in the chapter.

Apply Your Knowledge

Reinforce the skills and apply the concepts you learned in this chapter.

Modifying Text and Formatting a Document
Instructions: Start Word. Open the document, Apply 1-1 Autumn Fest Flyer Unformatted, from the Data Files for Students. See the inside back cover of this book for instructions on downloading the Data Files for Students, or contact your instructor for information about accessing the required files.

The document you open is an unformatted flyer. You are to modify text, format paragraphs and characters, and insert a picture in the flyer.

Perform the following tasks:

1. Delete the word, entire, in the sentence of body copy below the headline.

2. Insert the word, Creek, between the text, Honey Farm, in the sentence of body copy below the headline. The sentence should end: …Honey Creek Farm.

3. At the end of the signature line, change the period to an exclamation point. The sentence should end: …This Year's Fest!

4. Apply the Heading 1 style to the headline. Apply the Heading 2 style to the signature line.

5. Center the headline and the signature line.

6. Change the font and font size of the headline to 48-point Cooper Black, or a similar font.

7. Change the font size of body copy between the headline and the signature line to 22 point.

8. Change the font size of the signature line to 28 point.

9. Bullet the three lines (paragraphs) of text above the signature line.

10. Bold the text, October 4 and 5.

Continued >

Apply Your Knowledge *continued*

11. Underline the word, and, in the first bulleted paragraph.

12. Italicize the text in the signature line.

13. Change the theme colors to the Civic color scheme.

14. Change the theme fonts to the Opulent font set.

15. Change the zoom to 50 percent so the entire page is visible in the document window.

16. Change the spacing before the headline paragraph to 0 point. Change the spacing after the headline paragraph to 12 point.

17. Insert the picture of the combine centered on the blank line above the bulleted list. The picture is called Fall Harvest and is available on the Data Files for Students. Apply the Snip Diagonal Corner, White picture style to the inserted picture. Change the color of the picture border to Orange, Accent 6.

18. The entire flyer now should fit on a single page. If it flows to two pages, resize the picture or decrease spacing before and after paragraphs until the entire flyer text fits on a single page.

19. Enter the text, Honey Creek, as the keywords. Change the other document properties, as specified by your instructor.

20. Click the Office Button and then click Save As. Save the document using the file name, Apply 1-1 Autumn Fest Flyer Formatted.

21. Position the Quick Access Toolbar below the Ribbon. Save the document again by clicking the Save button. Reposition the Quick Access Toolbar above the Ribbon.

22. Submit the revised document, shown in Figure 1–89, in the format specified by your instructor.

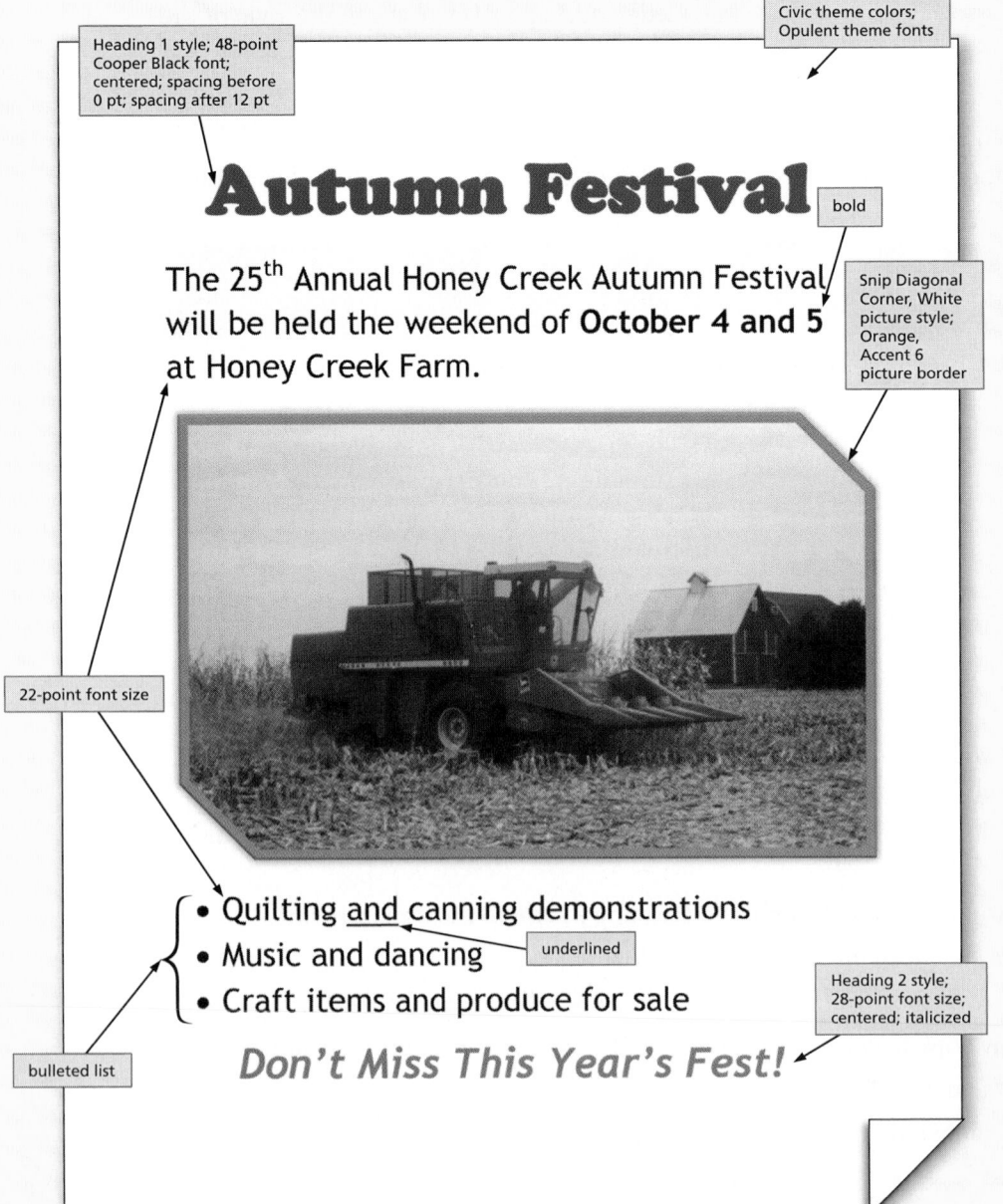

Heading 1 style; 48-point Cooper Black font; centered; spacing before 0 pt; spacing after 12 pt

Civic theme colors; Opulent theme fonts

bold

Snip Diagonal Corner, White picture style; Orange, Accent 6 picture border

22-point font size

underlined

bulleted list

Heading 2 style; 28-point font size; centered; italicized

Figure 1–89

Extend Your Knowledge

Extend the skills you learned in this chapter and experiment with new skills. You may need to use Help to complete the assignment.

Modifying Text and Graphics Formats

Instructions: Start Word. Open the document, Extend 1-1 Baseball Sign Ups Flyer, from the Data Files for Students. See the inside back cover of this book for instructions on downloading the Data Files for Students, or contact your instructor for information about accessing the required files.

You will enhance the look of the flyer shown in Figure 1–90.

Perform the following tasks:

1. Use Help to learn about the following formats: grow font, shrink font, change text color, decorative underline, and change bullet.

2. Select the headline and use the Grow Font button to increase its font size just enough so that the headline still fits on a single line. If it wraps to two lines, use the Shrink Font button.

3. Change the font color of all body copy between the headline and the signature line to a color other than Automatic, or Black.

4. Change the picture style of the picture so that it is not the Drop Shadow Rectangle picture style. Add a Glow picture effect to the picture of the baseball player.

5. Change the solid underline below the words, Indoor facility, to a decorative underline.

6. Change the color and width of the border.

7. Change the style of the bullets to a character other than the dot.

8. Change the document properties, including keywords, as specified by your instructor. Save the revised document with a new file name and then submit it in the format specified by your instructor.

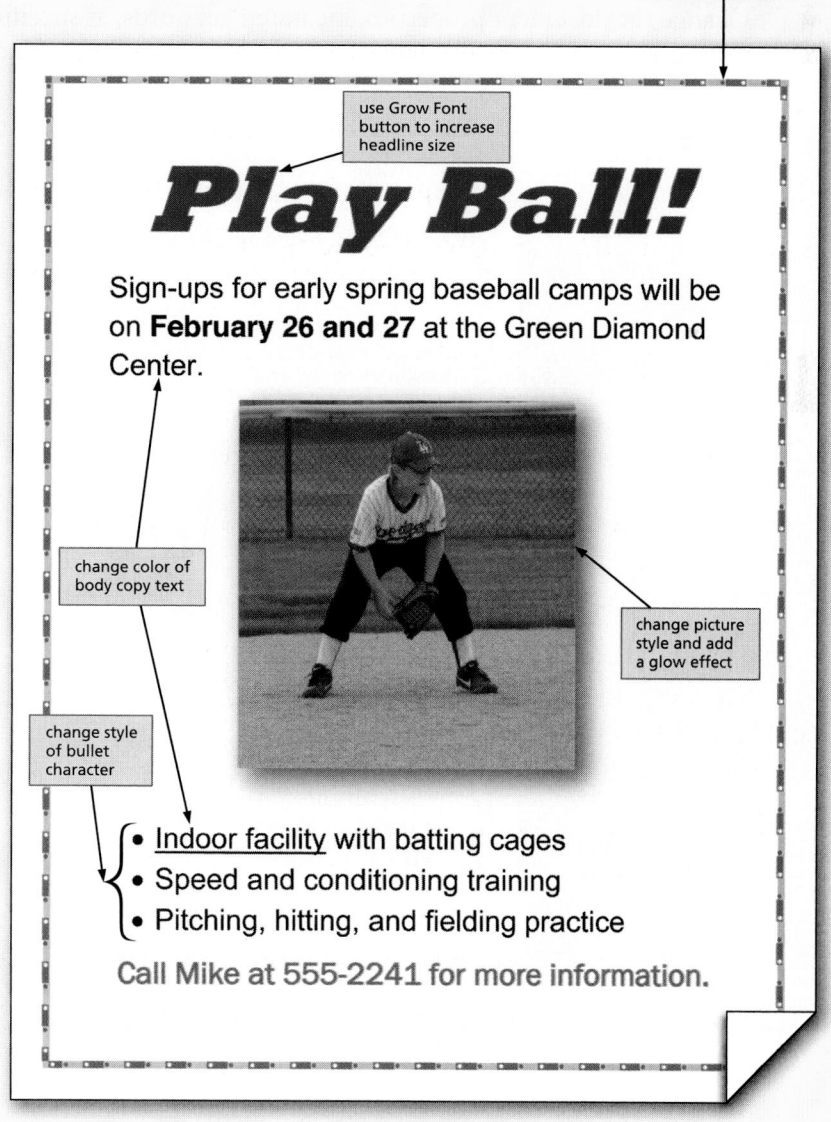

change color and width of border

use Grow Font button to increase headline size

change color of body copy text

change picture style and add a glow effect

change style of bullet character

Figure 1–90

Make It Right

Analyze a document and correct all errors and/or improve the design.

Correcting Spelling and Grammar Errors

Instructions: Start Word. Open the document, Make It Right 1-1 New York Tour Flyer, from the Data Files for Students. See the inside back cover of this book for instructions on downloading the Data Files for Students, or contact your instructor for information on accessing the required files.

The document is a flyer that contains spelling and grammar errors, as shown in Figure 1–91. You are to correct each spelling (red wavy underline) and grammar error (green wavy underline) by right-clicking the flagged text and then clicking the appropriate correction on the shortcut menu. If your screen does not display the wavy underlines, click the Office Button and then click the Word Options button. When the Word Options dialog box is displayed, click Proofing, be sure the 'Hide spelling errors in this document only' and 'Hide grammar errors in this document only' check boxes do not have check marks, and then click the OK button. If your screen still does not display the wavy underlines, redisplay the Word Options dialog box, click Proofing, and then click the Recheck Document button.

Change the document properties, including keywords, as specified by your instructor. Save the revised document with a new file name and then submit it in the format specified by your instructor.

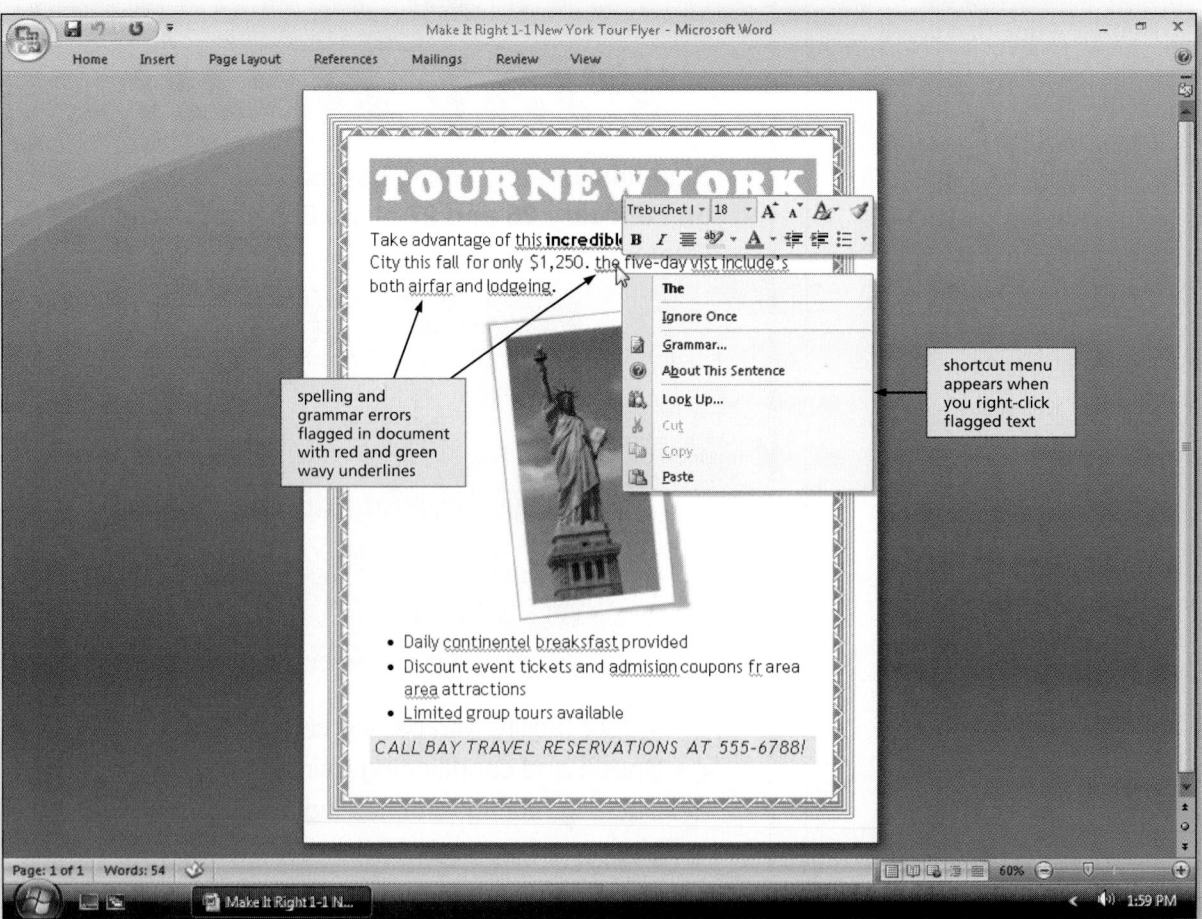

Figure 1–91

In the Lab

Design and/or create a document using the guidelines, concepts, and skills presented in this chapter. Labs are listed in order of increasing difficulty.

Lab 1: Creating a Flyer with a Picture

Problem: You work part-time at Scenic Air. Your boss has asked you to prepare a flyer that advertises aerial tours over the city of Campton. First, you prepare the unformatted flyer shown in Figure 1–92a, and then you format it so that it looks like Figure 1–92b on the next page. *Hint:* Remember, if you make a mistake while formatting the flyer, you can click the Undo button on the Quick Access Toolbar to undo your last action.

Instructions: Perform the following tasks:

1. Display formatting marks on the screen.
2. Type the flyer text, unformatted, as shown in Figure 1–92a. If Word flags any misspelled words as you type, check the spelling of these words and correct them.
3. Save the document on a USB flash drive using the file name, Lab 1-1 Airplane Rides Flyer.
4. Apply the Heading 1 style to the headline. Apply the Heading 2 style to the signature line.
5. Center the headline and the signature line.
6. Change the font and font size of the headline to 48-point Arial Rounded MT Bold, or a similar font.
7. Change the font size of body copy between the headline and the signature line to 22 point.
8. Change the font size of the signature line to 28 point.
9. Bullet the three lines (paragraphs) of text above the signature line.
10. Bold the text, change your view.
11. Italicize the word, aerial.

Airplane Rides

Gain an entirely new vision of Campton by taking an aerial tour. Visitor or local, business or pleasure, the trip will change your view of the city.

Pilots are licensed and experienced

15-, 30-, or 60-minute tours available during daylight hours

Individual and group rates

Call Scenic Air at 555-9883!

Figure 1–92a

Continued >

STUDENT ASSIGNMENTS

In the Lab *continued*

12. Underline the word, and, in the first bulleted paragraph.

13. Change the style set to Formal.

14. Change the theme fonts to the Metro font set.

15. Change the zoom to 50 percent so the entire page is visible in the document window.

16. Change the spacing before the headline to 0 point. Change the spacing after the first paragraph of body copy to 0 point. Change the spacing before the first bulleted paragraph to 12 point.

17. Insert the picture on the blank line above the bulleted list. The picture is called Airplane Ride over City and is available on the Data Files for Students. Apply the Relaxed Perspective, White picture style to the inserted picture.

18. The entire flyer should fit on a single page. If it flows to two pages, resize the picture or decrease spacing before and after paragraphs until the entire flyer text fits on a single page.

19. Change the document properties, including keywords, as specified by your instructor.

20. Save the flyer again with the same file name.

21. Submit the document, shown in Figure 1–92b, in the format specified by your instructor.

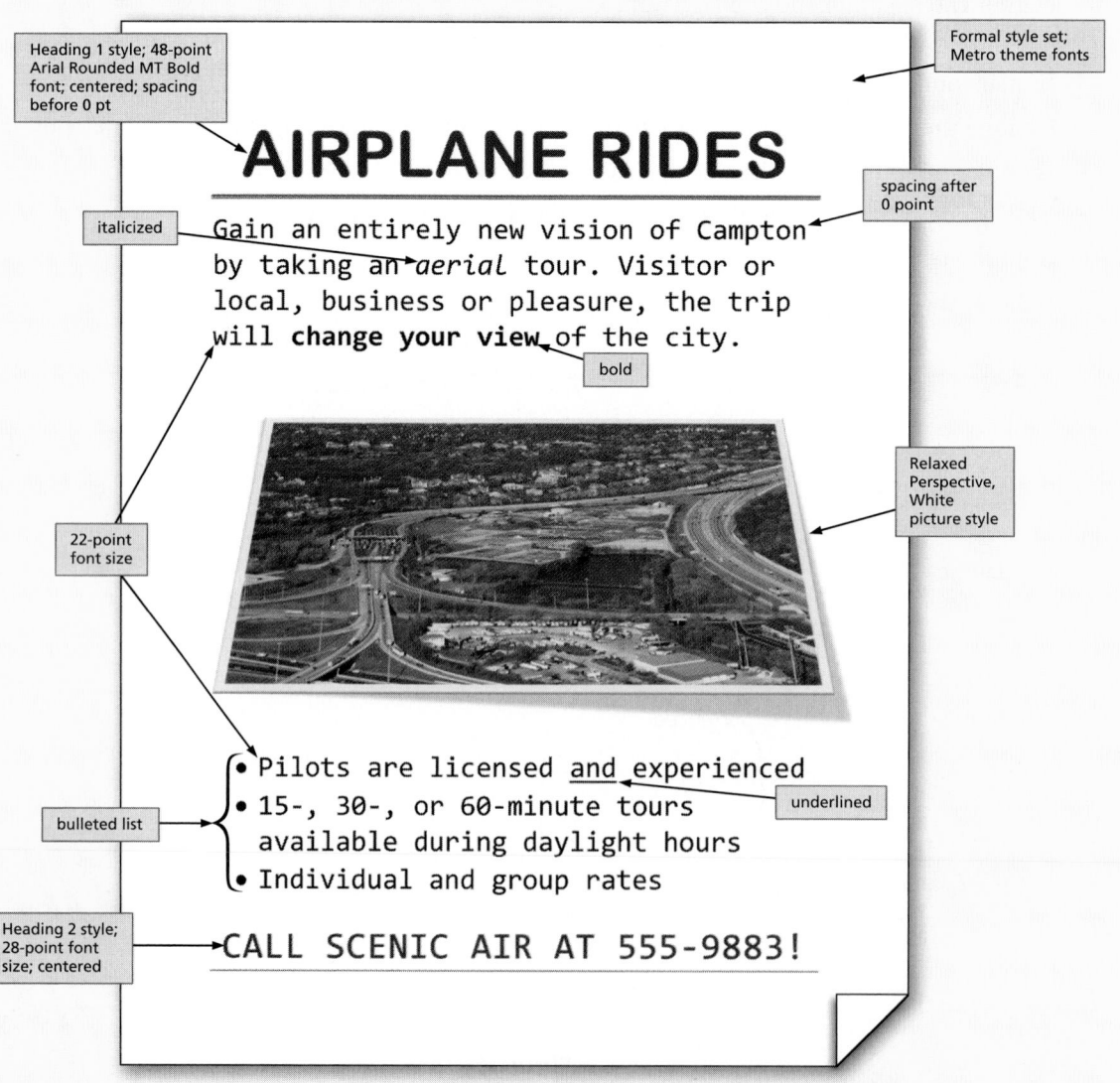

Figure 1–92b

In the Lab

Lab 2: Creating a Flyer with a Picture and a Border

Problem: Your boss at Danvers Nursery has asked you to prepare a flyer that promotes its expanded greenhouses and grounds. You prepare the flyer shown in Figure 1–93. *Hint:* Remember, if you make a mistake while formatting the flyer, you can click the Undo button on the Quick Access Toolbar to undo your last action.

Instructions: Perform the following tasks:

1. Display formatting marks on the screen.

2. Type the flyer text, unformatted. If Word flags any misspelled words as you type, check the spelling of these words and correct them.

3. Save the document on a USB flash drive using the file name, Lab 1-2 Nursery Expansion Flyer.

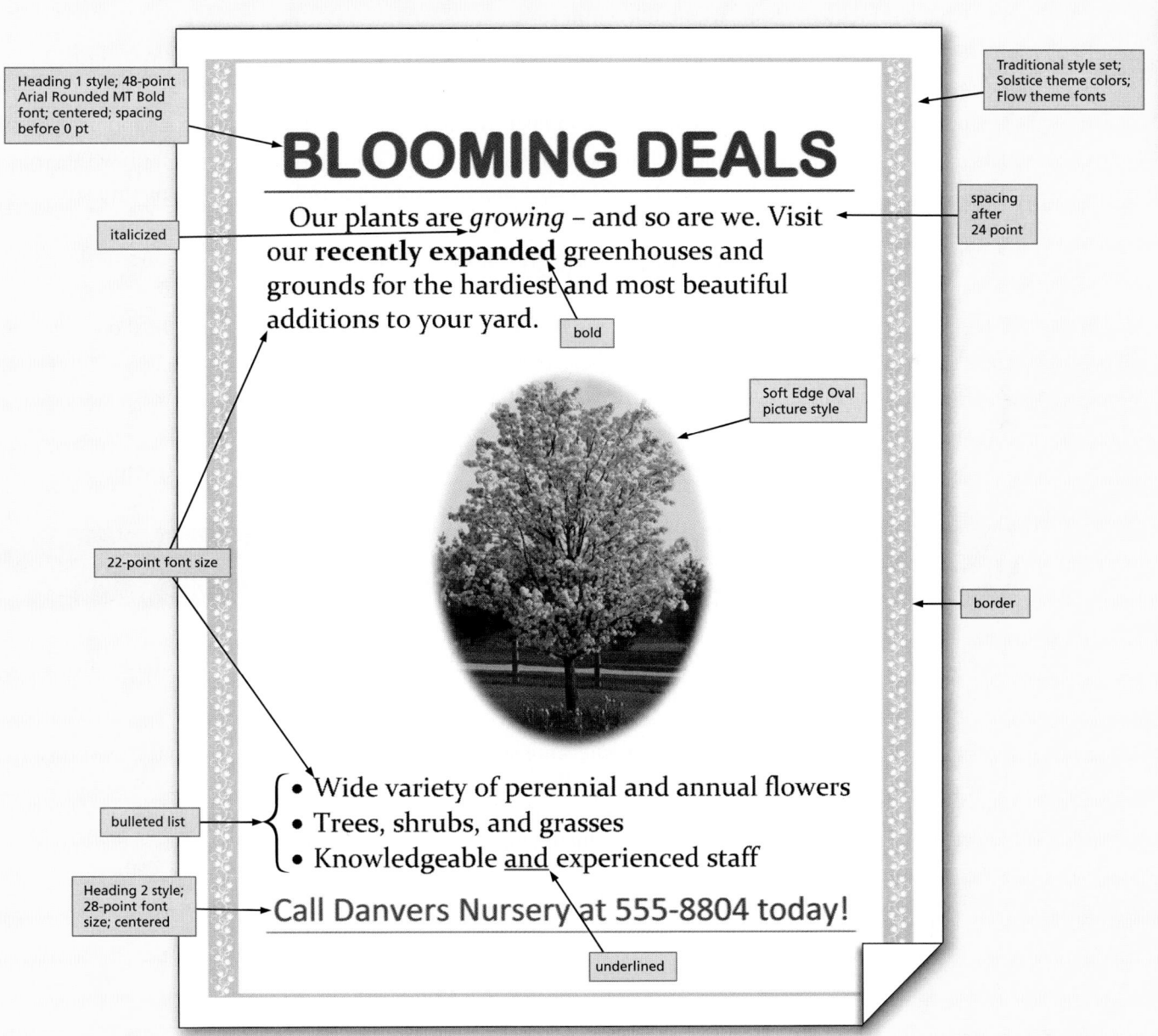

Heading 1 style; 48-point Arial Rounded MT Bold font; centered; spacing before 0 pt

Traditional style set; Solstice theme colors; Flow theme fonts

italicized

spacing after 24 point

bold

Soft Edge Oval picture style

22-point font size

border

bulleted list

Heading 2 style; 28-point font size; centered

underlined

BLOOMING DEALS

Our plants are *growing* – and so are we. Visit our **recently expanded** greenhouses and grounds for the hardiest and most beautiful additions to your yard.

- Wide variety of perennial and annual flowers
- Trees, shrubs, and grasses
- Knowledgeable <u>and</u> experienced staff

Call Danvers Nursery at 555-8804 today!

Figure 1–93

Continued >

In the Lab *continued*

4. Apply the Heading 1 style to the headline. Apply the Heading 2 style to the signature line.

5. Center the headline and the signature line.

6. Change the font and font size of the headline to 48-point Arial Rounded MT Bold, or a similar font.

7. Change the font size of body copy between the headline and the signature line to 22 point.

8. Change the font size of the signature line to 28 point.

9. Bullet the three lines (paragraphs) of text above the signature line.

10. Italicize the word, growing.

11. Bold the text, recently expanded.

12. Underline the word, and, in the third bulleted paragraph.

13. Change the style set to Traditional.

14. Change the theme colors to the Solstice color scheme.

15. Change the theme fonts to the Flow font set.

16. Change the zoom to 50 percent so the entire page is visible in the document window.

17. Change the spacing before the headline to 0 point. Change the spacing after the first paragraph of body copy to 24 point. Change the spacing before the first bulleted paragraph to 12 point.

18. Insert the picture on the blank line above the bulleted list. The picture is called Bradford Pear in Bloom and is available on the Data Files for Students. Apply the Soft Edge Oval picture style to the inserted picture.

19. The entire flyer should fit on a single page. If it flows to two pages, resize the picture or decrease spacing before and after paragraphs until the entire flyer text fits on a single page.

20. Add the graphic border, shown in Figure 1–93 on the previous page (about one-third down in the Art gallery). Change the color of the border to Tan, Background 2.

21. Change the document properties, including keywords, as specified by your instructor.

22. Save the flyer again with the same file name.

23. Submit the document, shown in Figure 1–93, in the format specified by your instructor.

In the Lab

Lab 3: Creating a Flyer with a Picture and Resized Border Art

Problem: Your neighbor has asked you to prepare a flyer that promotes her cabin rental business. You prepare the flyer shown in Figure 1–94.

Instructions: Enter the text in the flyer, checking spelling as you type, and then format it as shown in Figure 1–94. The picture to be inserted is called Paddle Boat on Lake and is available on the Data Files for Students. After adding the page border, reduce the point size of its width so that the border is not so predominant on the page. Change the document properties, including keywords, as specified by your instructor. Save the document on a USB flash drive using the file name, Lab 1-3 Cabin Rentals Flyer. Submit the document, shown in Figure 1–94, in the format specified by your instructor.

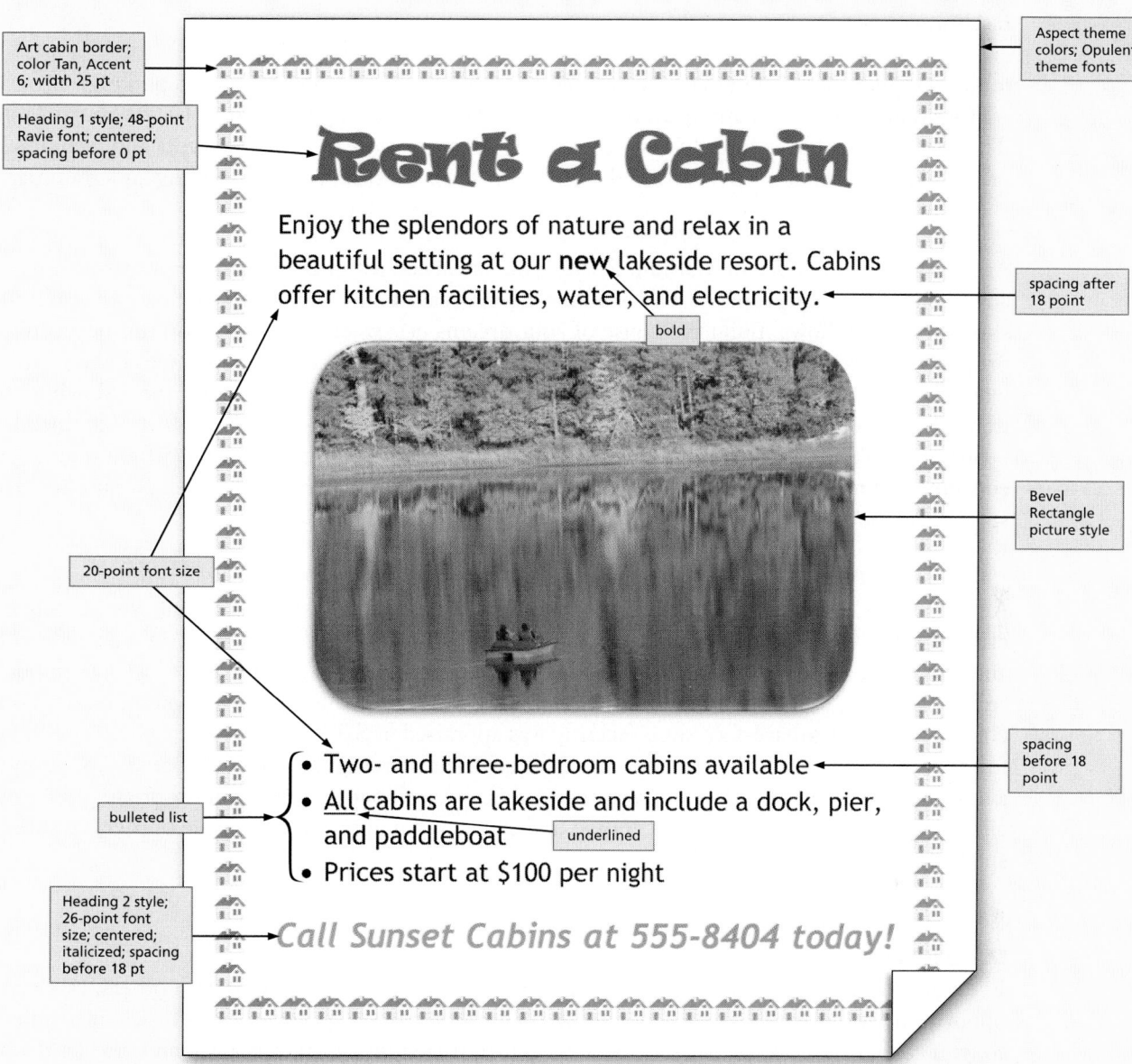

The following callouts appear in the figure:

- Art cabin border; color Tan, Accent 6; width 25 pt
- Heading 1 style; 48-point Ravie font; centered; spacing before 0 pt
- 20-point font size
- bulleted list
- Heading 2 style; 26-point font size; centered; italicized; spacing before 18 pt
- Aspect theme colors; Opulent theme fonts
- spacing after 18 point
- Bevel Rectangle picture style
- spacing before 18 point
- bold
- underlined

Figure content:

Rent a Cabin

Enjoy the splendors of nature and relax in a beautiful setting at our **new** lakeside resort. Cabins offer kitchen facilities, water, and electricity.

- Two- and three-bedroom cabins available
- All cabins are lakeside and include a dock, pier, and paddleboat
- Prices start at $100 per night

Call Sunset Cabins at 555-8404 today!

Figure 1–94

Cases and Places

Apply your creative thinking and problem solving skills to design and implement a solution.

● EASIER   ●● MORE DIFFICULT

● 1: Design and Create a Grand Reopening Flyer

Your friend owns the Craft Barn, a large, year-round craft fair. She recently has renovated and remodeled the facility and is planning a grand reopening. She has asked you to create a flyer advertising this fact. The flyer should contain the following headline: Craft Barn. The first paragraph of text below the headline should read: Pick up a jar of homemade jam or a handcrafted gift at the completely remodeled and renovated Craft Barn, located at 8701 County Road 300 West. Insert the photograph named, Barn and Silo, which is available on the Data Files for Students. The bullet items

Continued >

Cases and Places *continued*

under the photograph should read as follows: first bullet – Expanded and paved parking; second bullet – More than 150 booths; and third bullet – Open Monday through Saturday, 10:00 a.m. to 7:00 p.m. The last line should read: Call 555-5709 for more information! Use the concepts and techniques presented in this chapter to create and format this flyer. Be sure to check spelling and grammar.

• 2: Design and Create a Property Advertisement Flyer

As a part-time employee of Markum Realty, you have been assigned the task of preparing a flyer advertising lakefront property. The headline should read: Lakefront Lot. The first paragraph of text should read as follows: Build the house of your dreams or a weekend getaway on this beautiful lakeside property located on the north side of Lake Pleasant. Insert the photograph named, Lake at Sunset, which is available on the Data Files for Students. Below the photograph, insert the following bullet items: first bullet — City sewer and water available; second bullet – Lot size 110 × 300; third bullet – List price $65,000. The last line should read: Call Markum Realty at 555-0995 for a tour! Use the concepts and techniques presented in this chapter to create and format this flyer. Be sure to check spelling and grammar.

•• 3: Design and Create a Flyer for the Sale of a Business

After 25 years, your Uncle Mitch has decided to sell his ice cream shop and wants you to help him create a sales flyer. The shop is in a choice location at the corner of 135th and Main Street and has an established customer base. The building has an adjacent, paved parking lot, as well as an outdoor seating area. He wants to sell the store and all its contents, including the equipment, tables, booths, and chairs. The 1200-square-foot shop recently was appraised at $200,000, and your uncle is willing to sell for cash or on contract. Use the concepts and techniques presented in this chapter to create and format a sales flyer. Include a headline, descriptive body copy, a signature line, an appropriate photograph or clip art image, a bulleted list, a decorative underline, and if appropriate, a page border. Be sure to check spelling and grammar in the flyer.

•• 4: Design and Create a Flyer that Advertises You

Make It Personal

Everyone has at least one skill, talent, or special capability, which if shared with others, can lead to opportunity for growth, experience, and personal reward. Perhaps you play a musical instrument. If so, you could offer lessons. Maybe you are a skilled carpenter or other tradesman who could advertise your services. If you speak a second language, you could offer tutoring. Budding athletes might harbor a desire to pass on their knowledge by coaching a youth sports team. You may have a special knack for singing, sewing, knitting, photography, typing, housecleaning, or pet care. Carefully consider your own personal capabilities, skills, and talents and then use the concepts and techniques presented in this chapter to create a flyer advertising a service you can provide. Include a headline, descriptive body copy, a signature line, an appropriate photograph or clip art image, a bulleted list, a decorative underline, and if appropriate, a page border. Be sure to check spelling and grammar in the flyer.

•• 5: Redesign and Enhance a Poorly Designed Flyer

Working Together

Public locations, such as stores, schools, and libraries, have bulletin boards or windows for people to post flyers. Often, these bulletin boards or windows have so many flyers that some go unnoticed. Locate a posted flyer on a bulletin board or window that you think might be overlooked. Copy the text from the flyer and distribute it to each team member. Each member then independently should use this text, together with the techniques presented in this chapter, to create a flyer that would be more likely to catch the attention of passersby. Be sure to check spelling and grammar. As a group, critique each flyer and have team members redesign their flyer based on the group's recommendations. Hand in each team member's original and final flyers.

2 | Creating a Research Paper

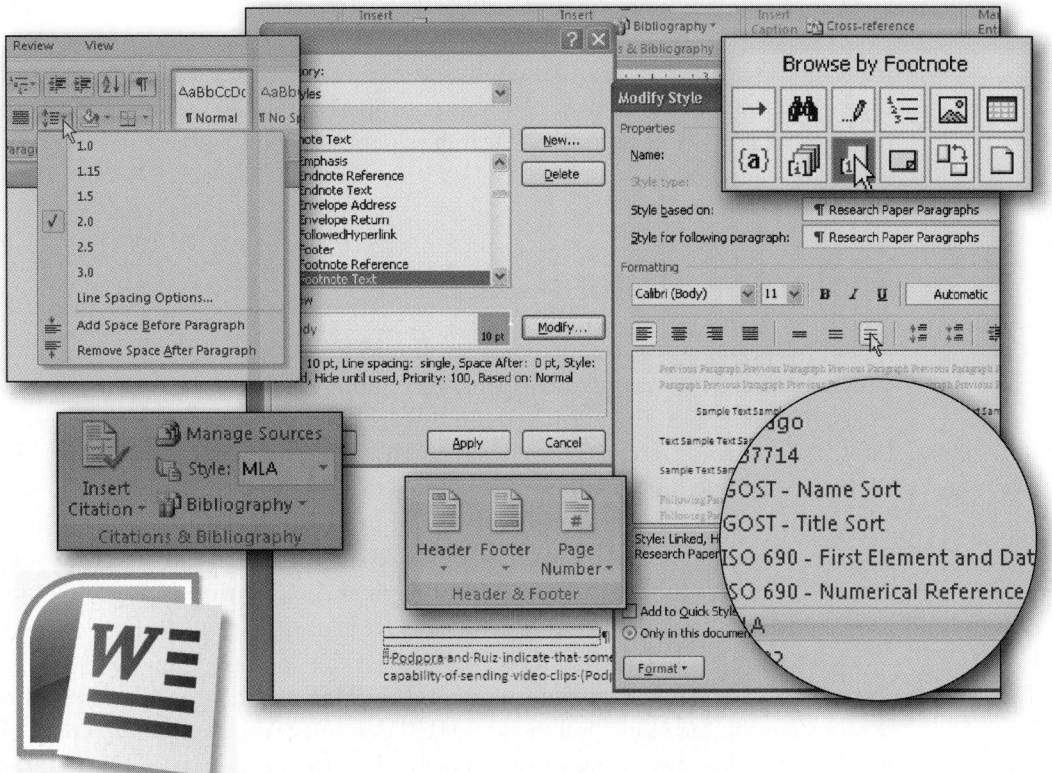

Objectives

You will have mastered the material in this chapter when you can:

- Describe the MLA documentation style for research papers

- Change line and paragraph spacing in a document

- Use a header to number pages of a document

- Apply formatting using shortcut keys

- Modify paragraph indentation

- Create and modify styles

- Insert and edit citations and their sources

- Add a footnote to a document

- Insert a manual page break

- Create a bibliographical list of sources

- Move text

- Find and replace text

- Use the Research task pane to look up information

2 | Creating a Research Paper

Introduction

In both academic and business environments, you will be asked to write reports. Business reports range from proposals to cost justifications to five-year plans to research findings. Academic reports focus mostly on research findings. A **research paper** is a document you can use to communicate the results of research findings. To write a research paper, you learn about a particular topic from a variety of sources (research), organize your ideas from the research results, and then present relevant facts and/or opinions that support the topic. Your final research paper combines properly credited outside information along with personal insights. Thus, no two research papers — even if about the same topic — will or should be the same.

Project — Research Paper

When preparing a research paper, you should follow a standard documentation style that defines the rules for creating the paper and crediting sources. A variety of documentation styles exists, depending on the nature of the research paper. Each style requires the same basic information; the differences in styles relate to requirements for presenting the information. For example, one documentation style uses the term bibliography for the list of sources, whereas another uses references, and yet a third prefers the title works cited. Two popular documentation styles for research papers are the **Modern Language Association of America (MLA)** and **American Psychological Association (APA)** styles. This chapter uses the MLA documentation style because it is used in a wide range of disciplines.

The project in this chapter follows research paper guidelines and uses Word to create the short research paper shown in Figure 2–1. This paper, which discusses three types of wireless communications, follows the MLA documentation style. Each page contains a page number. The first two pages present the heading (name, course, and date information), paper title, an introduction with a thesis statement, details that support the thesis, and a conclusion. This section of the paper also includes references to research sources. The third page contains a detailed, alphabetical list of the sources used in the research paper.

Overview

As you read through this chapter, you will learn how to create the research paper shown in Figure 2–1 by performing these general tasks:

- Change the document settings.
- Type the research paper.
- Save the research paper.
- Create an alphabetical list of sources.
- Proof and revise the research paper.
- Print the research paper.

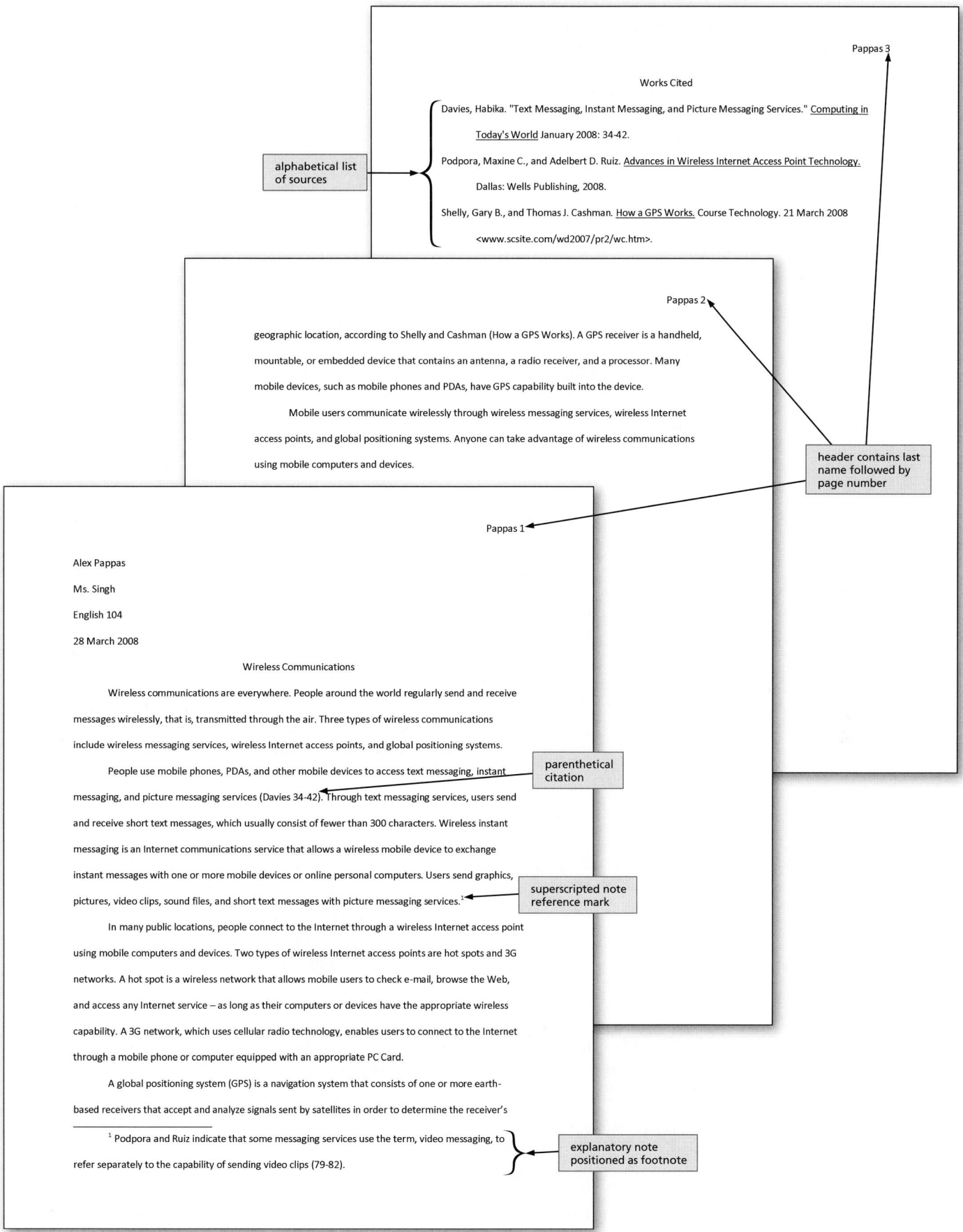

Pappas 3

Works Cited

Davies, Habika. "Text Messaging, Instant Messaging, and Picture Messaging Services." Computing in

Today's World January 2008: 34-42.

alphabetical list of sources

Podpora, Maxine C., and Adelbert D. Ruiz. Advances in Wireless Internet Access Point Technology.

Dallas: Wells Publishing, 2008.

Shelly, Gary B., and Thomas J. Cashman. How a GPS Works. Course Technology. 21 March 2008

<www.scsite.com/wd2007/pr2/wc.htm>.

Pappas 2

geographic location, according to Shelly and Cashman (How a GPS Works). A GPS receiver is a handheld,

mountable, or embedded device that contains an antenna, a radio receiver, and a processor. Many

mobile devices, such as mobile phones and PDAs, have GPS capability built into the device.

Mobile users communicate wirelessly through wireless messaging services, wireless Internet

access points, and global positioning systems. Anyone can take advantage of wireless communications

using mobile computers and devices.

header contains last name followed by page number

Pappas 1

Alex Pappas

Ms. Singh

English 104

28 March 2008

Wireless Communications

Wireless communications are everywhere. People around the world regularly send and receive

messages wirelessly, that is, transmitted through the air. Three types of wireless communications

include wireless messaging services, wireless Internet access points, and global positioning systems.

People use mobile phones, PDAs, and other mobile devices to access text messaging, instant

parenthetical citation

messaging, and picture messaging services (Davies 34-42). Through text messaging services, users send

and receive short text messages, which usually consist of fewer than 300 characters. Wireless instant

messaging is an Internet communications service that allows a wireless mobile device to exchange

instant messages with one or more mobile devices or online personal computers. Users send graphics,

pictures, video clips, sound files, and short text messages with picture messaging services.[1]

superscripted note reference mark

In many public locations, people connect to the Internet through a wireless Internet access point

using mobile computers and devices. Two types of wireless Internet access points are hot spots and 3G

networks. A hot spot is a wireless network that allows mobile users to check e-mail, browse the Web,

and access any Internet service – as long as their computers or devices have the appropriate wireless

capability. A 3G network, which uses cellular radio technology, enables users to connect to the Internet

through a mobile phone or computer equipped with an appropriate PC Card.

A global positioning system (GPS) is a navigation system that consists of one or more earth-

based receivers that accept and analyze signals sent by satellites in order to determine the receiver's

[1] Podpora and Ruiz indicate that some messaging services use the term, video messaging, to

refer separately to the capability of sending video clips (79-82).

explanatory note positioned as footnote

Figure 2–1

Plan
Ahead

General Project Guidelines

When creating a Word document, the actions you perform and decisions you make will affect the appearance and characteristics of the finished document. As you create a research paper, such as the project shown in Figure 2–1 on the previous page, you should follow these general guidelines:

1. **Select a topic.** Spend time brainstorming ideas for a topic. Choose one you find interesting. For shorter papers, narrow down the scope of the topic; for longer papers, broaden the scope. Identify a tentative thesis statement, which is a sentence describing the paper's subject matter.

2. **Research the topic and take notes.** Gather credible, relevant information about the topic that supports the thesis statement. Sources of research include books, magazines, news-papers, and the Internet. As you record facts and ideas, list details about the source: title, author, place of publication, publisher, date of publication, etc. When taking notes, be careful not to **plagiarize**. That is, do not use someone else's work and claim it to be your own. If you copy information directly, place it in quotation marks and identify its source.

3. **Organize your ideas.** Classify your notes into related concepts. Make an outline from the categories of notes. In the outline, identify all main ideas and supporting details.

4. **Write the first draft, referencing sources.** From the outline, compose the paper. Every research paper should include an introduction containing the thesis statement, supporting details, and a conclusion. Follow the guidelines identified in the required documentation style. Reference all sources of information.

5. **Create the list of sources.** Using the formats specified in the required documentation style, completely list all sources referenced in the body of the research paper in alphabetical order.

6. **Proofread and revise the paper.** If possible, proofread the paper with a fresh set of eyes, that is, at least one to two days after completing the first draft. Proofreading involves reading the paper with the intent of identifying errors (spelling, grammar, etc.) and looking for ways to improve the paper (wording, transitions, flow, etc.). Try reading the paper out loud, which helps to identify unclear or awkward wording. Ask someone else to proofread the paper and give you suggestions for improvements.

When necessary, more specific details concerning the above guidelines are presented at appropriate points in the chapter. The chapter also will identify the actions performed and decisions made regarding these guidelines during the creation of the research paper shown in Figure 2–1.

BTW

APA Documentation Style

In the APA style, a separate title page is required instead of placing name and course information on the paper's first page. Double-space all pages of the paper with 1.5" top, bottom, left, and right margins. Indent the first word of each paragraph .5" from the left margin. In the upper-right margin of each page, including the title page, place a running head that consists of the page number double-spaced below a brief summary of the paper title.

MLA Documentation Style

The research paper in this project follows the guidelines presented by the MLA. To follow the MLA style, double-space text on all pages of the paper using one-inch top, bottom, left, and right margins. Indent the first word of each paragraph one-half inch from the left margin. At the right margin of each page, place a page number one-half inch from the top margin. On each page, precede the page number by your last name.

The MLA style does not require a title page. Instead, place your name and course information in a block at the left margin beginning one inch from the top of the page. Center the title one double-space below your name and course information.

In the text of the paper, place author references in parentheses with the page number(s) of the referenced information. The MLA style uses in-text **parenthetical citations** instead of noting each source at the bottom of the page or at the end of the paper. In the MLA style, notes are used only for optional explanatory notes.

If used, explanatory notes elaborate on points discussed in the paper. Use a super-script (raised number) to signal that an explanatory note exists, and also to sequence the notes. Position explanatory notes either at the bottom of the page as footnotes or at the end of the paper as endnotes. Indent the first line of each explanatory note one-half inch from the left margin. Place one space following the superscripted number before beginning the note text. Double-space the note text. At the end of the note text, you may list bibliographic information for further reference.

The MLA style uses the term **works cited** to refer to the bibliographic list of sources at the end of the paper. The works cited page alphabetically lists sources that are referenced directly in the paper. Place the list of sources on a separate numbered page. Center the title, Works Cited, one inch from the top margin. Double-space all lines. Begin the first line of each source at the left margin, indenting subsequent lines of the same source one-half inch from the left margin. List each source by the author's last name, or, if the author's name is not available, by the title of the source. Underline or italicize the title of each source.

Changing Document Settings

The MLA documentation style defines some global formats that apply to the entire research paper. Some of these formats are the default in Word. For example, the default left, right, top, and bottom margin settings in Word are one inch, which meets the MLA style. You will modify, however, the paragraph and line spacing and header formats as required by the MLA style.

After starting Word, the following pages adjust line and paragraph spacing and define a header for the current document.

To Start Word

If you are using a computer to step through the project in this chapter and you want your screens to match the figures in this book, you should change your computer's resolution to 1024 × 768. For information about how to change a computer's resolution, read Appendix E.

The following steps, which assume Windows Vista is running, start Word based on a typical installation. You may need to ask your instructor how to start Word for your computer.

Note: If you are using Windows XP, see Appendix F for alternate steps.

1 Click the Start button on the Windows Vista taskbar to display the Start menu and then click All Programs at the bottom of the left pane on the Start menu to display the All Programs list.

2 Click Microsoft Office in the All Programs list to display the Microsoft Office list and then click Microsoft Office Word 2007 to start Word and display a new blank document in the Word window.

3 If the Word window is not maximized, click the Maximize button next to the Close button on its title bar to maximize the window.

4 If the Print Layout button is not selected, click it so that your screen layout matches Figure 2–2 on the next page.

5 If your zoom percent is not 100, click the Zoom Out or Zoom In button as many times as necessary until the Zoom level button displays 100% on its face.

To Display Formatting Marks

As discussed in Chapter 1, it is helpful to display formatting marks that indicate where in the document you pressed the ENTER key, SPACEBAR, and other keys. The following step displays formatting marks.

1 If necessary, click Home on the Ribbon to display the Home tab. If the Show/Hide ¶ button on the Home tab is not selected already, click it to display formatting marks on the screen.

BTW

Line Spacing
If the top of a set of characters or a graphical image is chopped off, then line spacing may be set to Exactly. To remedy the problem, change line spacing to 1.0, 1.15, 1.5, 2.0, 2.5, 3.0, or At least (in the Paragraph dialog box), all of which accommodate the largest font or image.

Adjusting Line and Paragraph Spacing

Line spacing is the amount of vertical space between lines of text in a paragraph. **Paragraph spacing** is the amount of space above and below a paragraph. By default, the Normal style places 10 points of blank space after each paragraph and inserts a vertical space equal to 1.15 lines between each line of text. It also automatically adjusts line height to accommodate various font sizes and graphics.

The MLA documentation style requires that you **double-space** the entire research paper. That is, the amount of vertical space between each line of text and above and below paragraphs should be equal to one blank line. The next sets of steps adjust line spacing and paragraph spacing according to the MLA documentation style.

To Double-Space Text

To double-space the lines in the research paper, change the line spacing to 2.0. The following steps change line spacing to double.

1

- Click the Line spacing button on the Home tab to display the Line spacing gallery (Figure 2–2).

Q&A

What do the numbers in the Line spacing gallery represent?

The default line spacing is 1.15 lines. The options 1.0, 2.0, and 3.0 set line spacing to single, double, and triple, respectively. Similarly, the 1.5 and 2.5 options set line spacing to 1.5 and 2.5 lines. All these options adjust line spacing automatically to accommodate the largest font or graphic on a line.

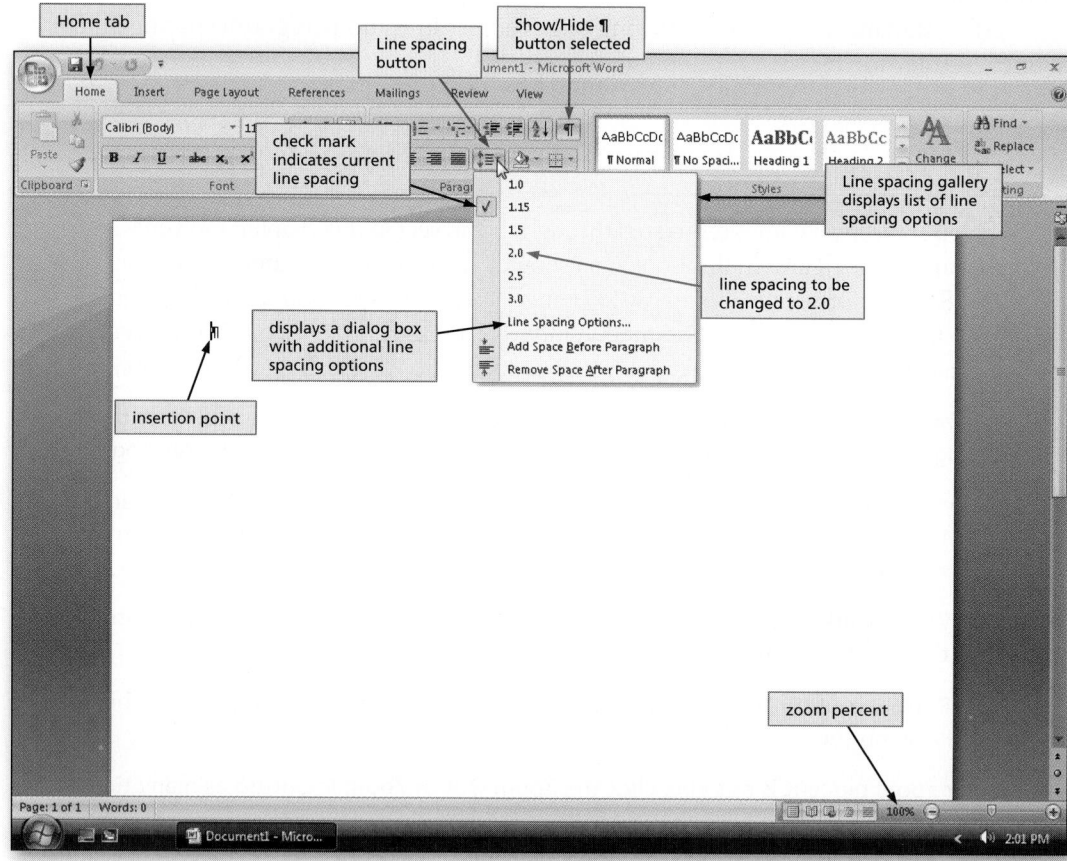

Figure 2–2

2

- Click 2.0 in the Line spacing gallery to change the line spacing to double at the location of the insertion point.

Q&A

Can I change the line spacing of existing text?

Yes. Select the text first and then change the line spacing as described in these steps.

Other Ways
1. Right-click paragraph, click Paragraph on shortcut menu, click Indents and Spacing tab, click Line spacing box arrow, click Double, click OK button
2. Click Paragraph Dialog Box Launcher, click Indents and Spacing tab, click Line spacing box arrow, click Double, click OK button
3. Press CTRL+2

To Remove Space after a Paragraph

The research paper should not have additional blank space after each paragraph. The following steps remove space after a paragraph.

- Click the Line spacing button on the Home tab to display the Line spacing gallery (Figure 2–3).

- Click Remove Space After Paragraph in the Line spacing gallery so that no blank space appears after a paragraph.

Q&A

Can I remove space after existing paragraphs?

Yes. Select the paragraphs first and then remove the space as described in these steps.

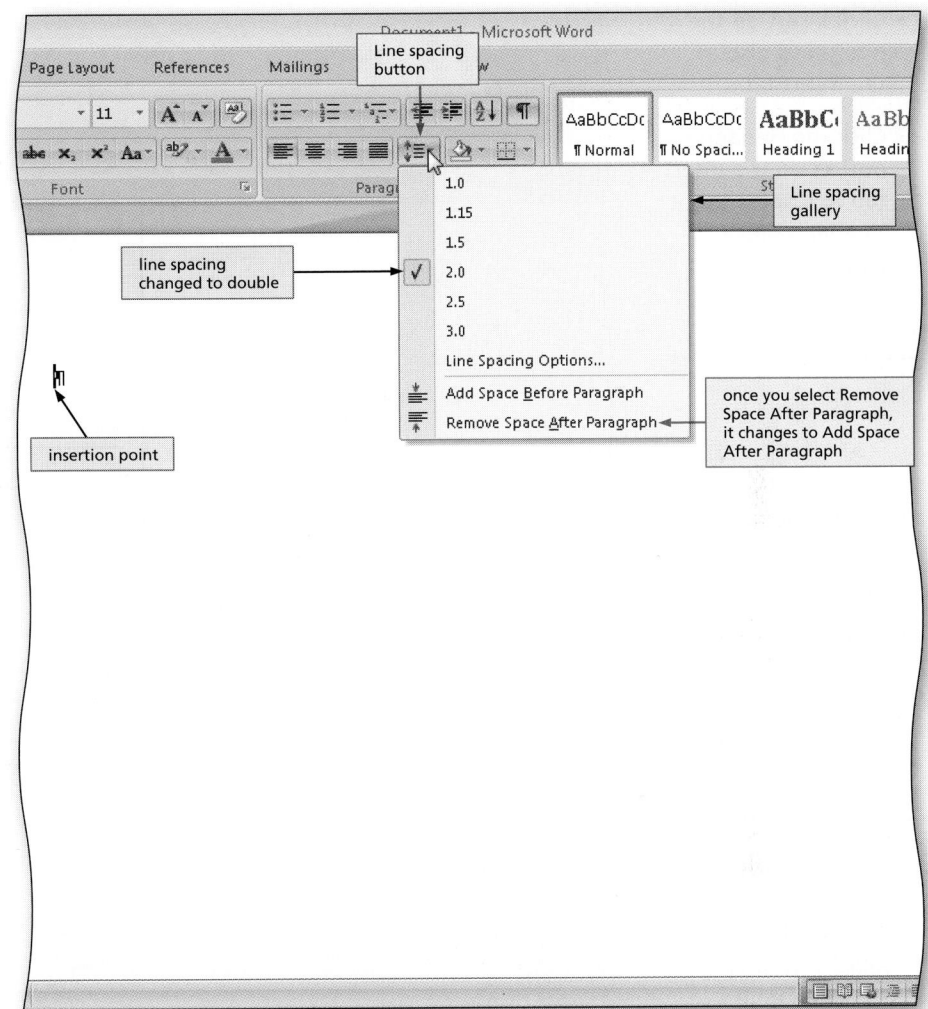

Figure 2–3

Other Ways

1. Click Spacing After box arrow on Page Layout tab until 0 pt is displayed
2. Right-click paragraph, click Paragraph on shortcut menu, click Indents and Spacing tab, click Spacing After box arrow until 0 pt is displayed, click OK button
3. Click Paragraph Dialog Box Launcher, click Indents and Spacing tab, click Spacing After box arrow until 0 pt is displayed, click OK button

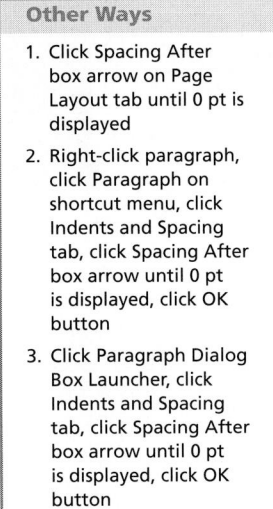

Headers and Footers

A **header** is text and graphics that print at the top of each page in a document. Similarly, a **footer** is text and graphics that print at the bottom of every page. In Word, headers print in the top margin one-half inch from the top of every page, and footers print in the bottom margin one-half inch from the bottom of each page, which meets the MLA style. In addition to text and graphics, headers and footers can include document information such as the page number, current date, current time, and author's name.

In this research paper, you are to precede the page number with your last name placed one-half inch from the upper-right edge of each page. The procedures on the following pages enter your name and the page number in the header, as specified by the MLA style.

To Switch to the Header

To enter text in the header, you instruct Word to edit the header. The following steps switch from editing the document text to editing the header.

1

- Click Insert on the Ribbon to display the Insert tab.

- Click the Header button on the Insert tab to display the Header gallery (Figure 2–4).

Q&A Can I use a built-in header for this research paper?

None of the built-in headers adhere to the MLA style. Thus, you enter your own header contents, instead of using a built-in header, for this research paper.

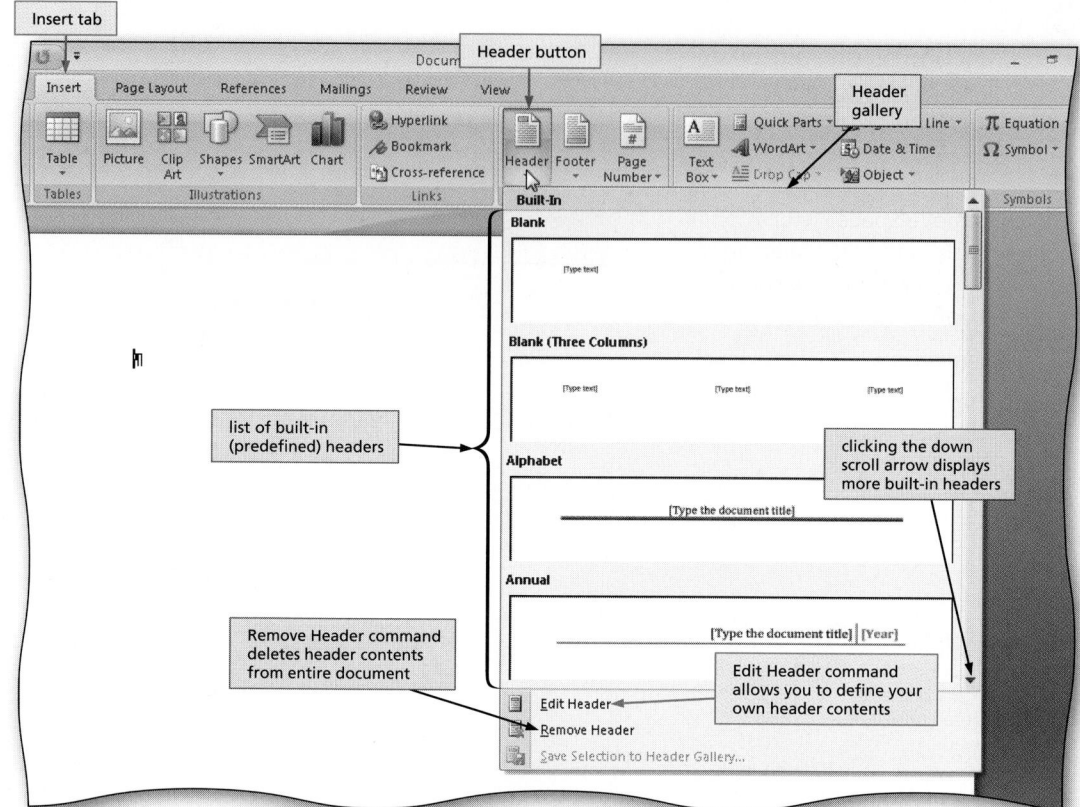

Figure 2–4

2

 Experiment

- Click the down scroll arrow in the Header gallery to see the available built-in headers.

3

- Click Edit Header in the Header gallery to switch from the document text to the header, which allows you to edit the contents of the header (Figure 2–5).

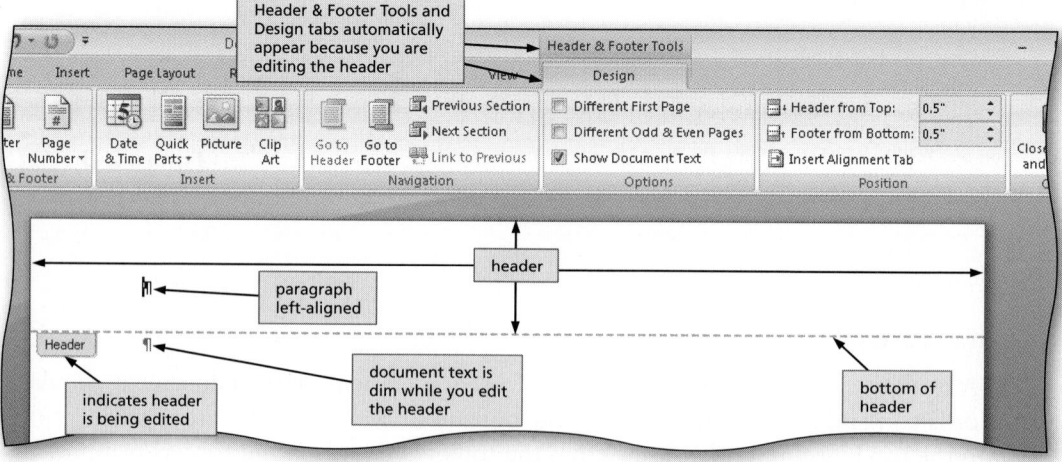

Figure 2–5

Q&A How do I remove the Header & Footer Tools and Design tabs from the Ribbon?

When you are finished editing the header, you will close it, which removes the Header & Footer Tools tabs.

Other Ways

1. Double-click dimmed header

To Right-Align a Paragraph

The paragraph in the header currently is left-aligned (Figure 2–5). Your last name and the page number should print **right-aligned**, that is, at the right margin. The following step right-aligns a paragraph.

1

- Click Home on the Ribbon to display the Home tab.

- Click the Align Text Right button on the Home tab to right-align the paragraph in the header (Figure 2–6).

Q&A

What if I wanted to return the paragraph to left-aligned?

Click the Align Text Right button again, or click the Align Text Left button.

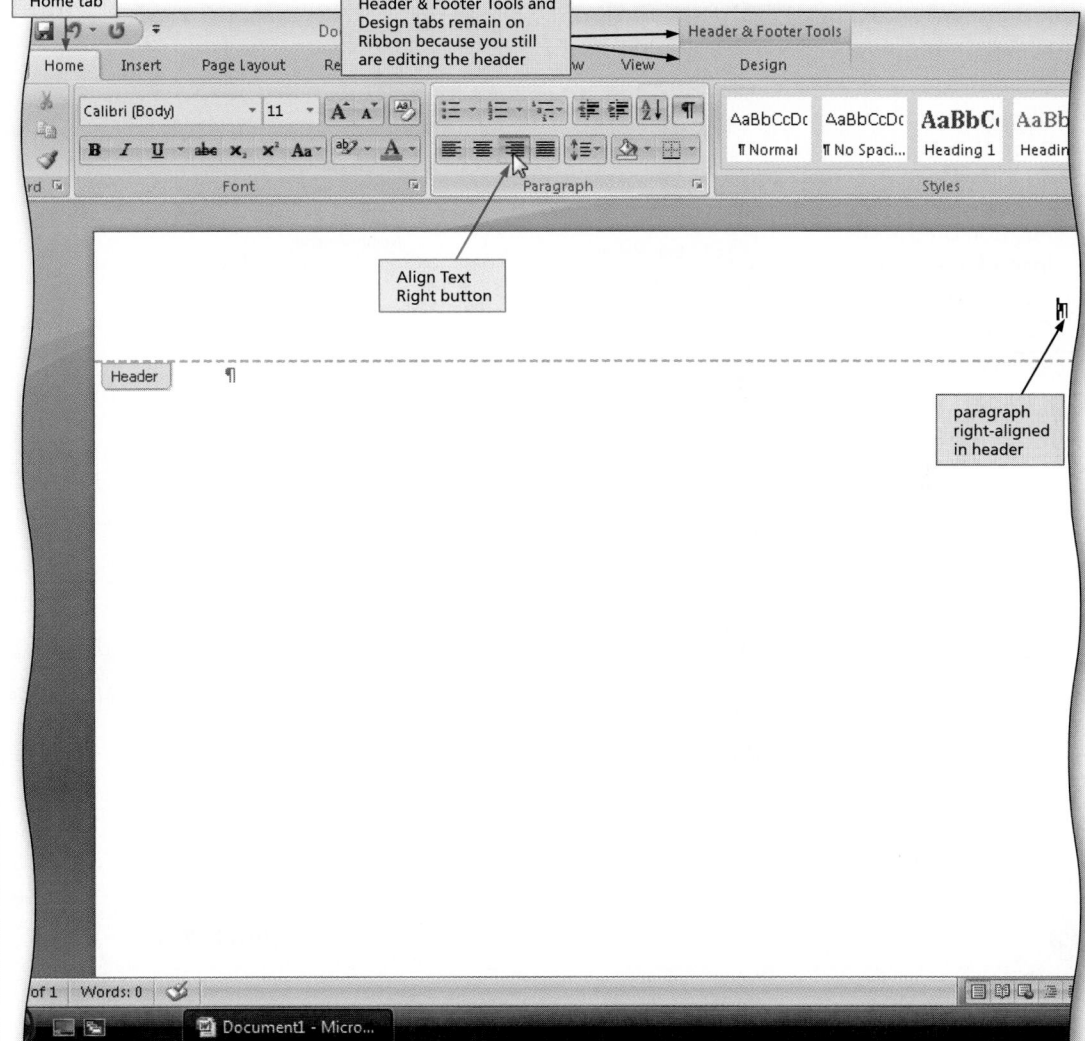

Figure 2–6

Other Ways

1. Right-click paragraph, click Paragraph on shortcut menu, click Indents and Spacing tab, click Alignment box arrow, click Right, click OK button

2. Click Paragraph Dialog Box Launcher, click Indents and Spacing tab, click Alignment box arrow, click Right, click OK button

3. Press CTRL+R

To Enter Text

The following steps enter your last name right-aligned in the header area.

1 Click Design on the Ribbon to display the Design tab.

2 Type Pappas and then press the SPACEBAR to enter the last name in the header.

BTW

Footers

If you wanted to create a footer, you would click the Footer button on the Insert tab and then select the desired built-in footer or click Edit Footer to create a customized footer.

To Insert a Page Number

The next task is to insert the current page number in the header. The following steps insert a page number at the location of the insertion point.

1

- Click the Insert Page Number button on the Design tab to display the Insert Page Number menu.

- Point to Current Position on the Insert Page Number menu to display the Current Position gallery (Figure 2–7).

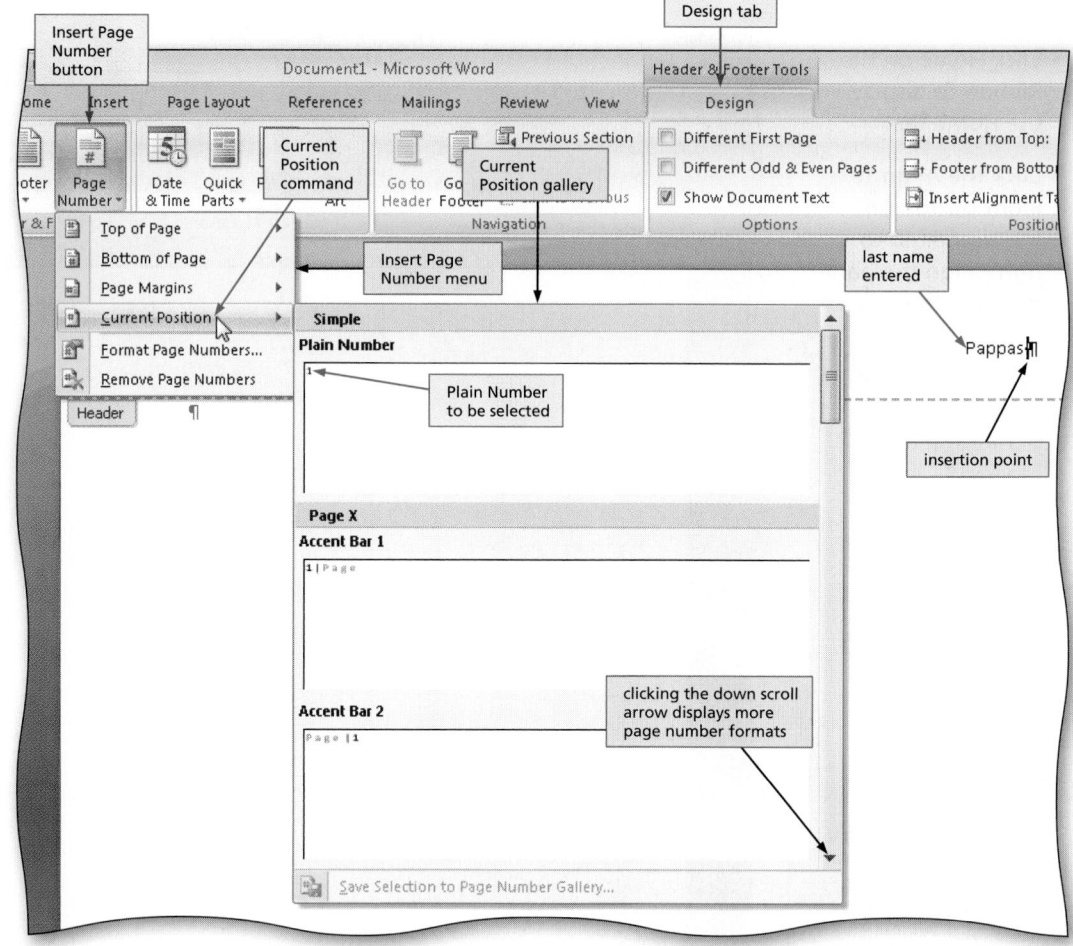

Figure 2–7

2

 Experiment

- Click the down scroll arrow in the Current Position gallery to see the available page number formats.

3

- If necessary, scroll to the top of the Current Position gallery. Click Plain Number in the Current Position gallery to insert an unformatted page number at the location of the insertion point (Figure 2–8).

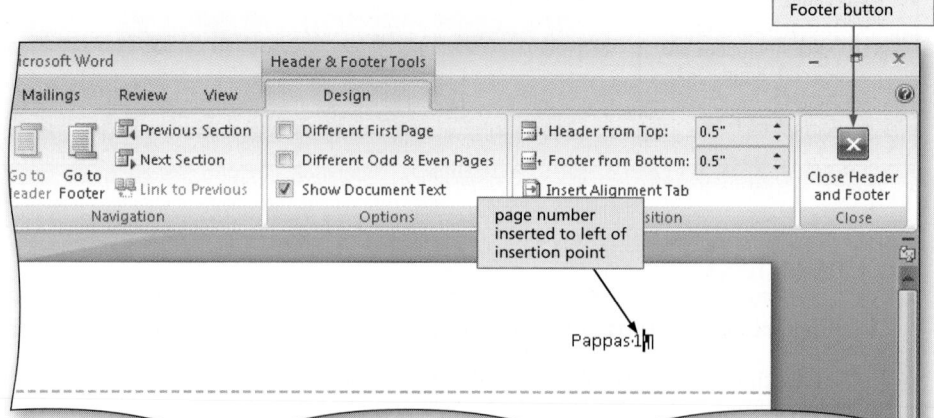

Figure 2–8

Other Ways

1. Click Insert Page Number button on Insert tab

2. Click Quick Parts button on Insert tab or on Design tab on Header & Footer Tools tab, click Field on Quick Parts menu, select Page in Field names list, click OK button

To Close the Header

You are finished entering text in the header. Thus, the next task is to switch back to the document text. The following step closes the header.

1

- Click the Close Header and Footer button on the Design tab (shown in Figure 2–8) to close the header and switch back to the document text (Figure 2–9).

Q&A

How do I make changes to existing header text?

Switch to the header using the steps described on page WD 80, edit the header as you would edit text in the document window, and then switch back to the document text.

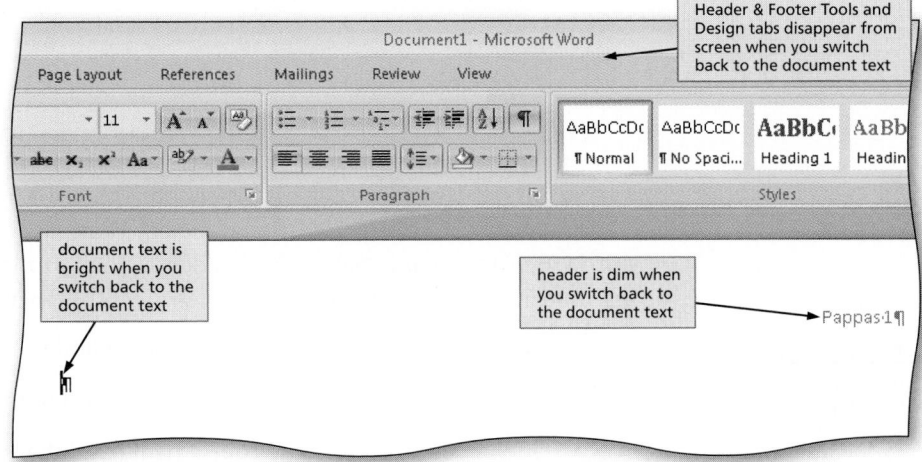

Figure 2–9

Other Ways

1. Double-click dimmed document text

Typing the Research Paper Text

The text of the research paper in this chapter encompasses the first two pages of the paper. You will type the text of the research paper and then modify it later in the chapter, so that it matches Figure 2–1 on page WD 75.

Plan Ahead

Write the first draft, referencing sources.
As you write the first draft of your research paper, be sure it includes the proper components, uses credible sources, and does not contain any plagiarism.

- **Include an introduction, body, and conclusion.** The first paragraph of the paper introduces the topic and captures the reader's attention. The body, which follows the introduction, consists of several paragraphs that support the topic. The conclusion summarizes the main points in the body and restates the topic.

- **Evaluate sources for authority, currency, and accuracy.** Be especially wary of information obtained from the Web. Any person, company, or organization can publish a Web page on the Internet. Ask yourself these questions about the source:

  - Authority: Does a reputable institution or group support the source? Is the information presented without bias? Are the author's credentials listed and verifiable?

  - Currency: Is the information up to date? Are dates of sources listed? What is the last date revised or updated?

  - Accuracy: Is the information free of errors? Is it verifiable? Are the sources clearly identified?

- **Acknowledge all sources of information; do not plagiarize.** Not only is plagiarism unethical, but it is considered an academic crime that can have severe punishments such as failing a course or being expelled from school.

  When you summarize, paraphrase (rewrite information in your own words), present facts, give statistics, quote exact words, or show a map, chart, or other graphical image, you

(continued)

<table>
<tr><td>

Plan Ahead

</td><td>

(continued)

must acknowledge the source. Information that commonly is known or accessible to the audience constitutes common knowledge and does not need to be acknowledged. If, however, you question whether certain information is common knowledge, you should document it — just to be safe.

</td></tr>
</table>

To Enter Name and Course Information

As discussed earlier in this chapter, the MLA style does not require a separate title page for research papers. Instead, place your name and course information in a block at the top of the page, below the header, at the left margin. The following steps enter the name and course information in the research paper.

1 Type `Alex Pappas` as the student name and then press the ENTER key.

2 Type `Ms. Singh` as the instructor name and then press the ENTER key.

3 Type `English 104` as the course name and then press the ENTER key.

4 Type `28 March 2008` as the paper due date and then press the ENTER key (Figure 2–10).

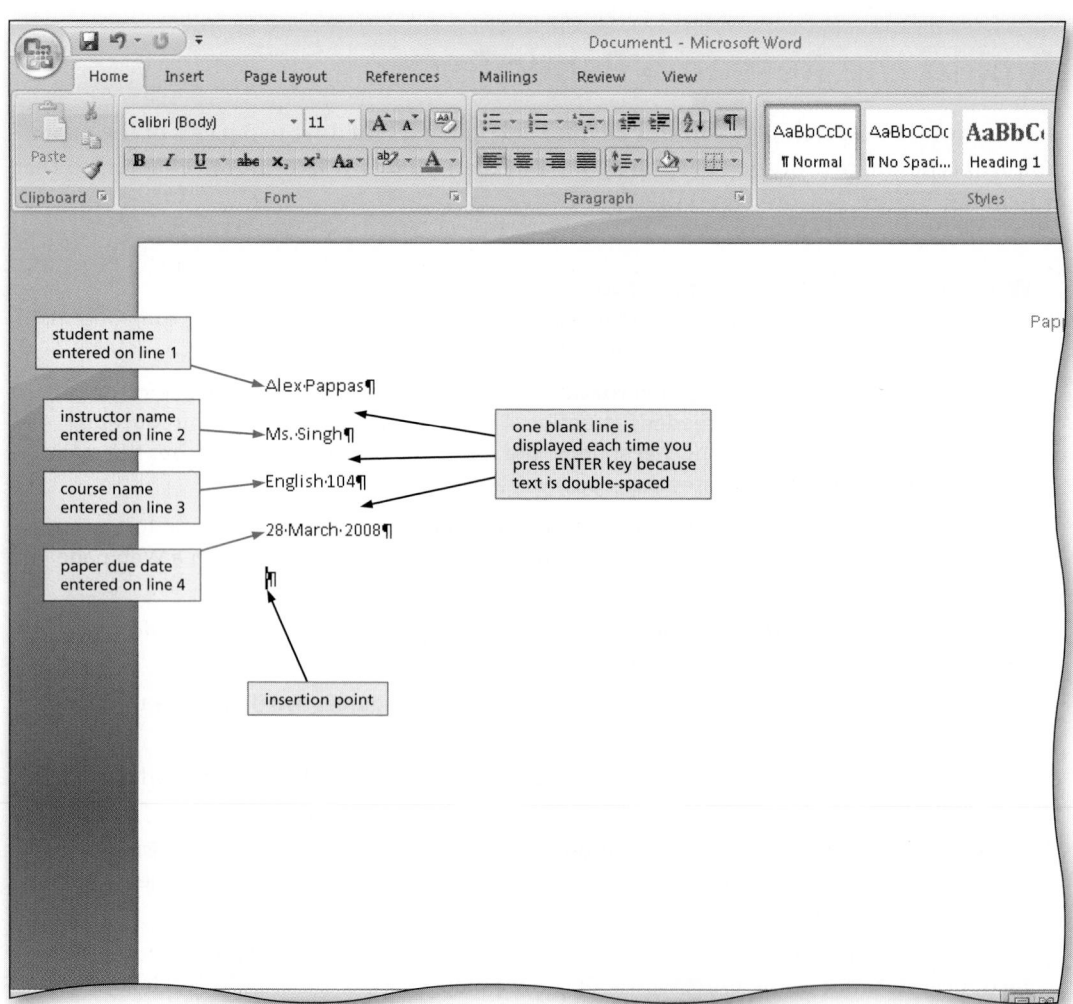

Figure 2–10

To Click and Type

The next step is to enter the title of the research paper centered between the page margins. In Chapter 1, you used the Center button on the Home tab to center text and graphics. As an alternative, you can use **Click and Type** to format and enter text, graphics, and other items. To use Click and Type, you double-click a blank area of the document window. Word automatically formats the item you enter according to the location where you just double-clicked. The following steps use Click and Type to center and then type the title of the research paper.

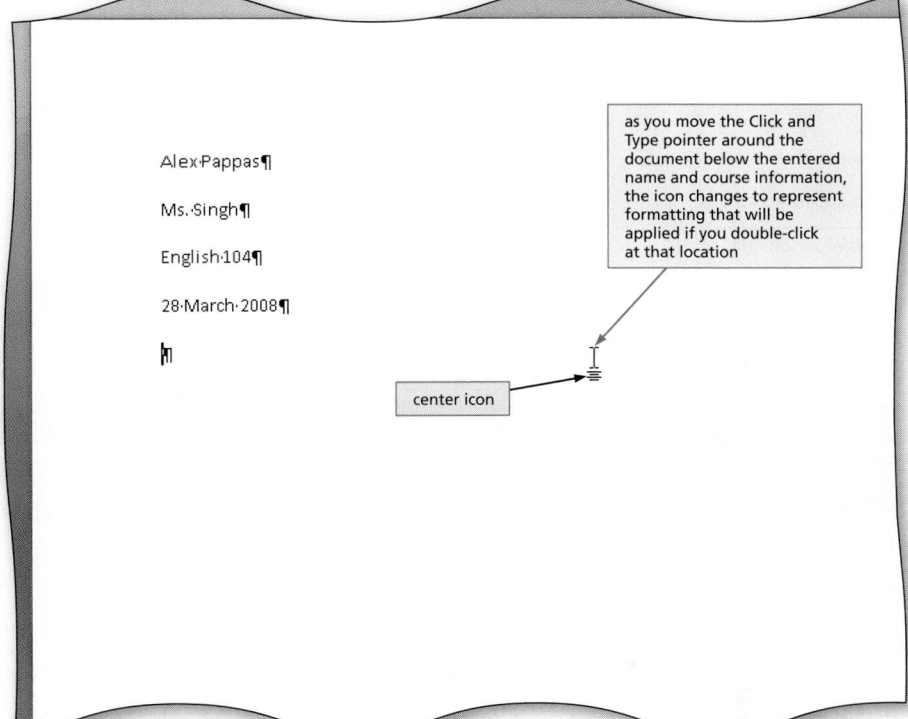

Experiment

- Move the mouse pointer around the document below the entered name and course information and observe the various icons that appear with the I-beam.

2

- Position the mouse pointer in the center of the document at the approximate location for the research paper title until a center icon appears below the I-beam (Figure 2–11).

Q&A What are the other icons that appear in the Click and Type pointer?

A left-align icon appears to the right of the I-beam when the Click and Type pointer is in certain locations on the left side of the document window. A right-align icon appears to the left of the icon when the Click and Type pointer is in certain locations on the right side of the document window.

3

- Double-click to center the paragraph mark and insertion point between the left and right margins.

- Type Wireless Communications as the paper title and then press the ENTER key (Figure 2–12).

Alex·Pappas¶

Ms.·Singh¶

English·104¶

28·March·2008¶

as you move the Click and Type pointer around the document below the entered name and course information, the icon changes to represent formatting that will be applied if you double-click at that location

center icon

Figure 2–11

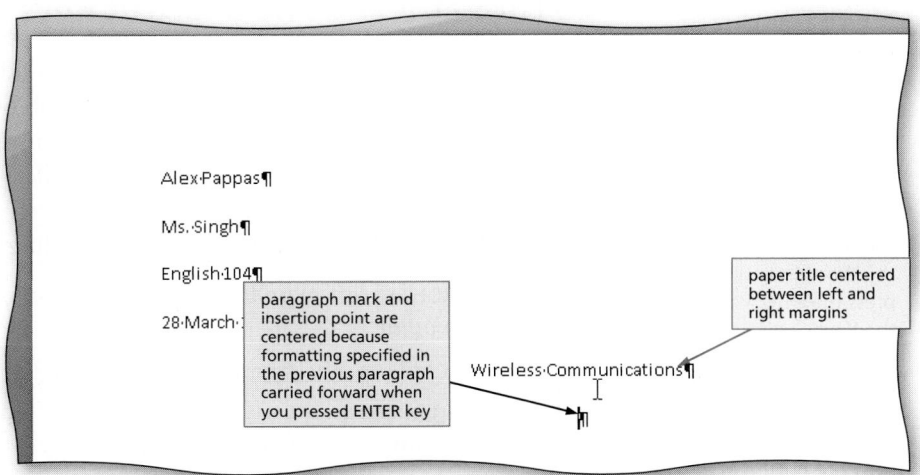

Alex·Pappas¶

Ms.·Singh¶

English·104¶

28·March·

paragraph mark and insertion point are centered because formatting specified in the previous paragraph carried forward when you pressed ENTER key

paper title centered between left and right margins

Wireless·Communications¶

Figure 2–12

Shortcut Keys

Word has many shortcut keys for your convenience while typing. Table 2–1 lists the common shortcut keys for formatting characters. Table 2–2 lists common shortcut keys for formatting paragraphs.

Table 2–1 Shortcut Keys for Formatting Characters

Character Formatting Task	Shortcut Keys	Character Formatting Task	Shortcut Keys
All capital letters	CTRL+SHIFT+A	Italic	CTRL+I
Bold	CTRL+B	Remove character formatting (plain text)	CTRL+SPACEBAR
Case of letters	SHIFT+F3	Small uppercase letters	CTRL+SHIFT+K
Decrease font size	CTRL+SHIFT+<	Subscript	CTRL+EQUAL SIGN
Decrease font size 1 point	CTRL+[	Superscript	CTRL+SHIFT+PLUS SIGN
Double-underline	CTRL+SHIFT+D	Underline	CTRL+U
Increase font size	CTRL+SHIFT+>	Underline words, not spaces	CTRL+SHIFT+W
Increase font size 1 point	CTRL+]		

Table 2–2 Shortcut Keys for Formatting Paragraphs

Paragraph Formatting	Shortcut Keys	Paragraph Formatting	Shortcut Keys
1.5 line spacing	CTRL+5	Justify paragraph	CTRL+J
Add/remove one line above paragraph	CTRL+0 (ZERO)	Left-align paragraph	CTRL+L
Center paragraph	CTRL+E	Remove hanging indent	CTRL+SHIFT+T
Decrease paragraph indent	CTRL+SHIFT+M	Remove paragraph formatting	CTRL+Q
Double-space lines	CTRL+2	Right-align paragraph	CTRL+R
Hanging indent	CTRL+T	Single-space lines	CTRL+1
Increase paragraph indent	CTRL+M		

BTW

Shortcut Keys
To print a complete list of shortcut keys in Word, click the Microsoft Office Word Help button near the upper-right corner of the Word window, type shortcut keys in the 'Type words to search for' text box at the top of the Word Help window, press the ENTER key, click the Keyboard shortcuts for Microsoft Office Word link, click the Show All link in the upper-right corner of the Help window, click the Print button in the Help window, and then click the Print button in the Print dialog box.

To Format Text Using Shortcut Keys

The paragraphs below the paper title should be left-aligned, instead of centered. Thus, the next step is to left-align the paragraph below the paper title. When your fingers are already on the keyboard, you may prefer using **shortcut keys**, or keyboard key combinations, to format text as you type it. The following step left-aligns a paragraph using the shortcut keys CTRL+L. (Recall from Chapter 1 that a notation such as CTRL+L means to press the letter l on the keyboard while holding down the CTRL key.)

1 Press CTRL+L to left-align the current paragraph, that is, the paragraph containing the insertion point.

Q&A Why would I use a keyboard shortcut, instead of the Ribbon, to format text?

Switching between the mouse and the keyboard takes time. If your hands are already on the keyboard, use a keyboard shortcut. If your hand is on the mouse, use the Ribbon.

To Save a Document

You have performed many tasks while creating the research paper and do not want to risk losing the work completed thus far. Accordingly, you should save the document. For a detailed example of the procedure summarized below, refer to pages WD 19 through WD 21 in Chapter 1.

Note: If you are using Windows XP, see Appendix F for alternate steps.

1 With a USB flash drive connected to one of the computer's USB ports, click the Save button on the Quick Access Toolbar to display the Save As dialog box.

2 Type `Wireless Communications Paper` in the File name text box to change the file name.

3 If Computer is not displayed in the Favorite Links section, drag the top or bottom edge of the Save As dialog box until Computer is displayed. Click Computer in the Favorite Links section and then double-click your USB flash drive in the list of available drives.

4 Click the Save button in the Save As dialog box to save the document on the USB flash drive with the file name, Wireless Communications Paper.

To Display the Rulers

According to the MLA style, the first line of each paragraph in the research paper is to be indented one-half inch from the left margin. Although you can use a dialog box to indent paragraphs, Word provides a quicker way through the **horizontal ruler**. This ruler displays at the top edge of the document window just below the Ribbon. Word also provides a **vertical ruler** that displays along the left edge of the Word window. The following steps display the rulers.

Experiment

- Repeatedly click the View Ruler button on the vertical scroll bar to see the how this button is used to both show and hide the rulers.

- If the rulers are not displayed, click the View Ruler button on the vertical scroll bar because you want to use the ruler to indent paragraphs (Figure 2–13).

Q&A
Can I use the rulers for other tasks?

In addition to indenting paragraphs, you can use the rulers to set tab stops, change page margins, and adjust column widths.

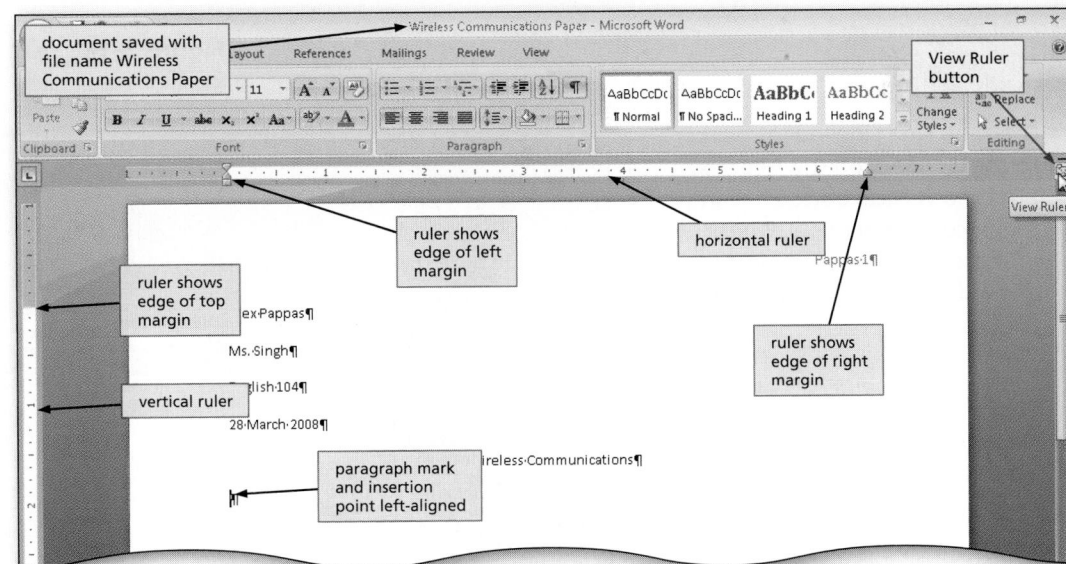

Figure 2–13

Other Ways

1. Click View Ruler check box on View tab

To First-Line Indent Paragraphs

The first line of each paragraph in the research paper is to be indented one-half inch from the left margin. You can use the horizontal ruler, usually simply called the **ruler**, to indent just the first line of a paragraph, called **first-line indent**.

The left margin on the ruler contains two triangles above a square. The **First Line Indent marker** is the top triangle at the 0" mark on the ruler (Figure 2–14). The bottom triangle is discussed later in this chapter. The small square at the 0" mark is the Left Indent marker. The **Left Indent marker** allows you to change the entire left margin, whereas the First Line Indent marker indents only the first line of the paragraph. The following steps first-line indent paragraphs in the research paper.

- With the insertion point on the paragraph mark below the research paper title, point to the First Line Indent marker on the ruler (Figure 2–14).

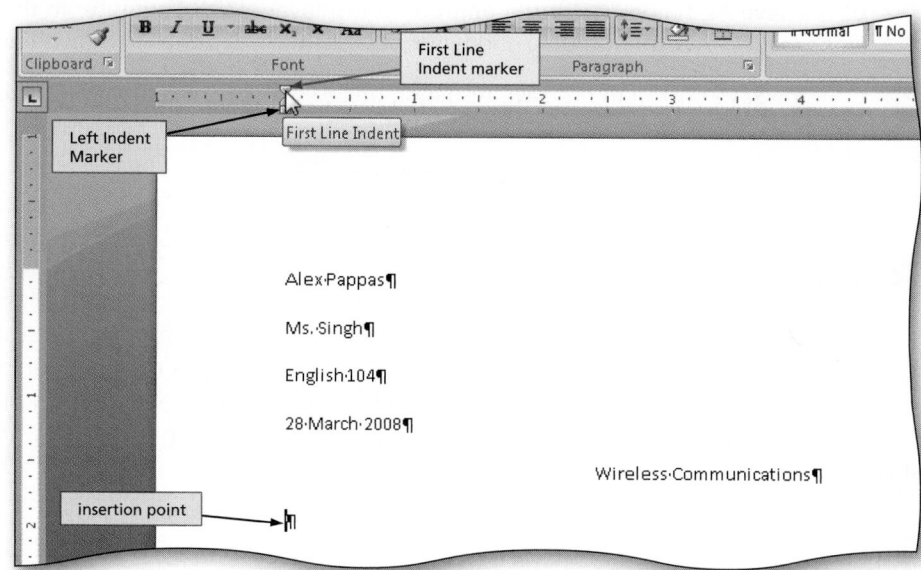

Figure 2–14

- Drag the First Line Indent marker to the .5" mark on the ruler to display a vertical dotted line in the document window, which indicates the proposed location of the first line of the paragraph (Figure 2–15).

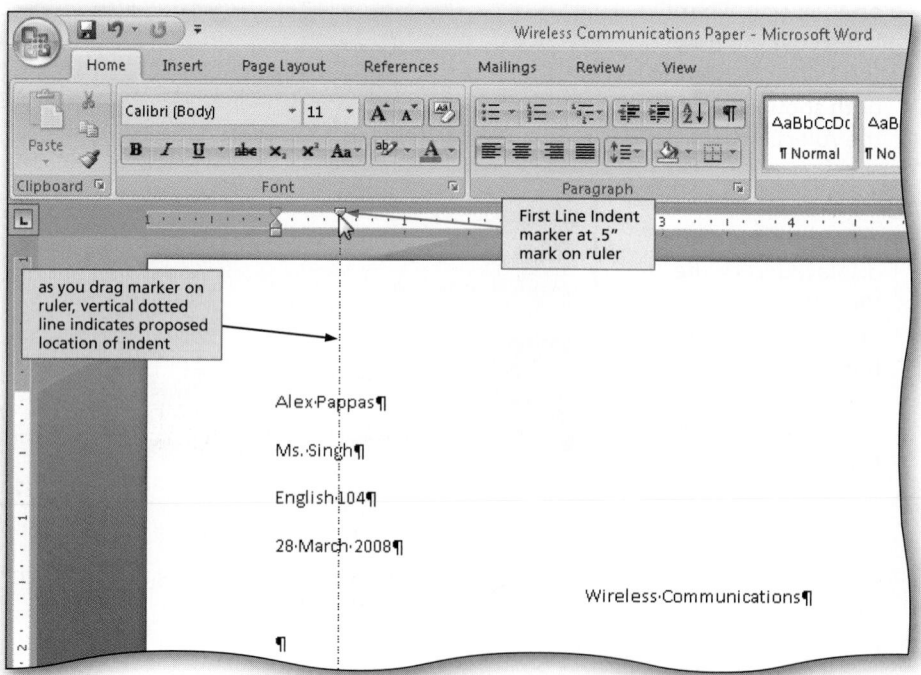

Figure 2–15

3

- Release the mouse button to place the First Line Indent marker at the .5" mark on the ruler, or one-half inch from the left margin (Figure 2–16).

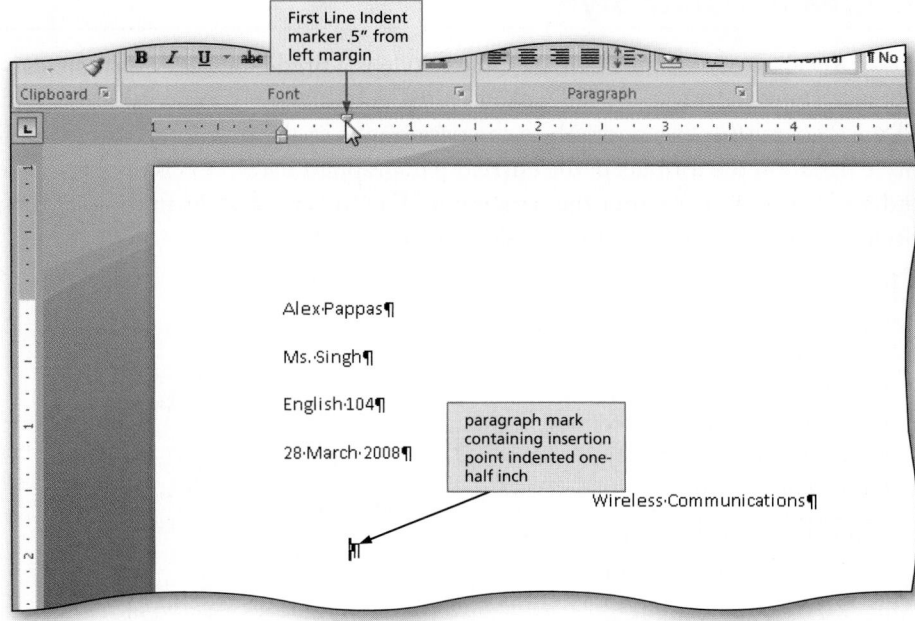

Figure 2–16

4

- Type Wireless communications are everywhere. People around the world regularly send and receive messages wirelessly, that is, transmitted through the air. and notice that Word automatically indented the first line of the paragraph by one-half inch (Figure 2–17).

Will I have to set first-line indent for each paragraph in the paper?

No. Each time you press the ENTER key, paragraph formatting in the previous paragraph carries forward to the next paragraph. Thus, once you set the first-line indent, its format carries forward automatically to each subsequent paragraph you type.

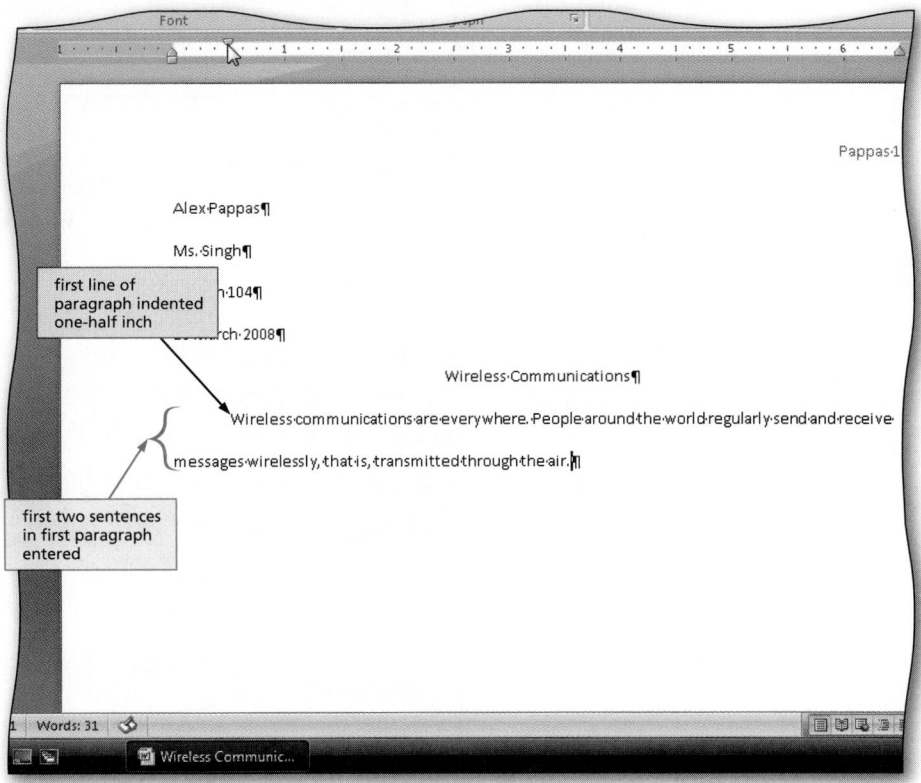

Figure 2–17

Other Ways

1. Right-click paragraph, click Paragraph on shortcut menu, click Indents and Spacing tab, click Special box arrow, click First line, click OK button
2. Click Paragraph Dialog Box Launcher, click Indents and Spacing tab, click Special box arrow, click First line, click OK button
3. Press TAB key at beginning of paragraph

To Create a Quick Style

Recall from Chapter 1 that a Quick Style is a predefined style that appears in the Styles gallery on the Ribbon. You use styles in the Styles gallery to apply defined formats to text. Later in this chapter, you will apply the formats of the research paper paragraph to the paragraphs in the footnote. To accomplish this task, you can create a Quick Style based on the formats in the current paragraph. That is, text is double-spaced with the first line of the paragraph indented and no space after the paragraph. The following steps first select the paragraph and then create a Quick Style based on the formats in the selected paragraph.

- Position the mouse pointer in the paragraph below the title and then triple-click; that is, press the mouse button three times in rapid succession, to select the paragraph.

- Right-click the selected paragraph to display a shortcut menu.

- Point to Styles on the shortcut menu to display the Styles submenu (Figure 2–18).

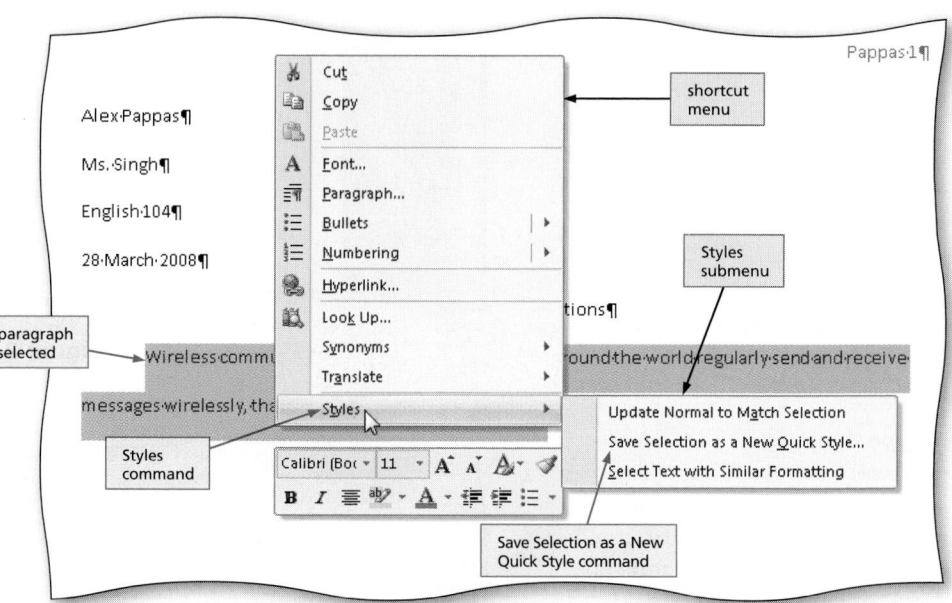

Figure 2–18

- Click Save Selection as a New Quick Style on the Styles submenu to display the Create New Style from Formatting dialog box.

- Type `Research Paper Paragraphs` in the Name text box (Figure 2–19).

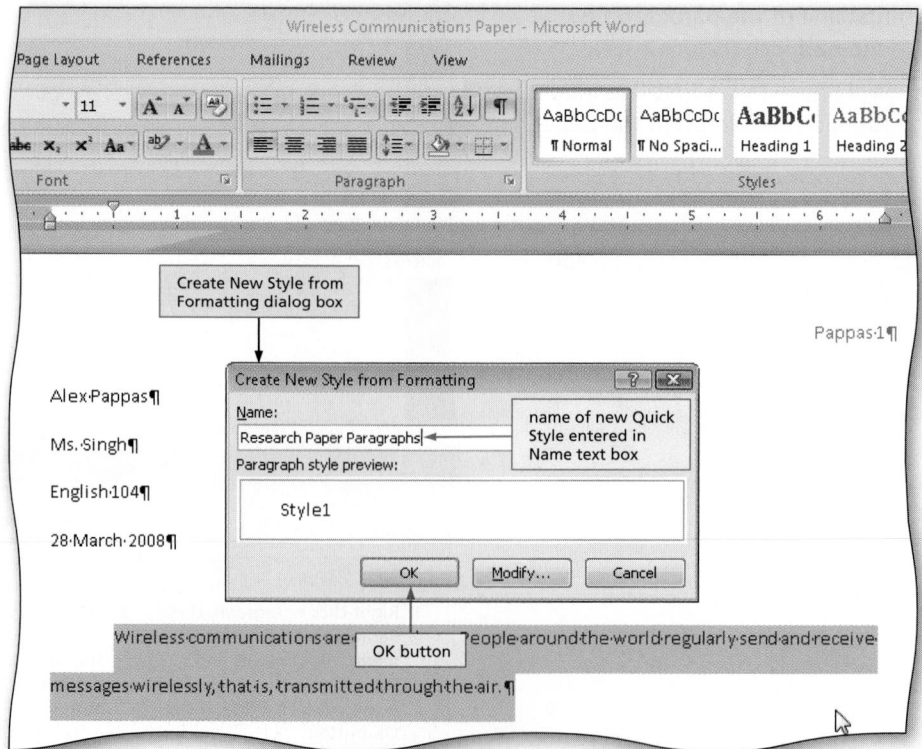

Figure 2–19

3

- Click the OK button to create the new Quick Style and add it to the Styles gallery (Figure 2–20).

Q&A How can I see the formats assigned to a Quick Style?

Click the Styles Dialog Box Launcher. When the Styles task pane appears, position the mouse pointer on any style to display its formats in a ScreenTip. When finished, click the Close button in the task pane.

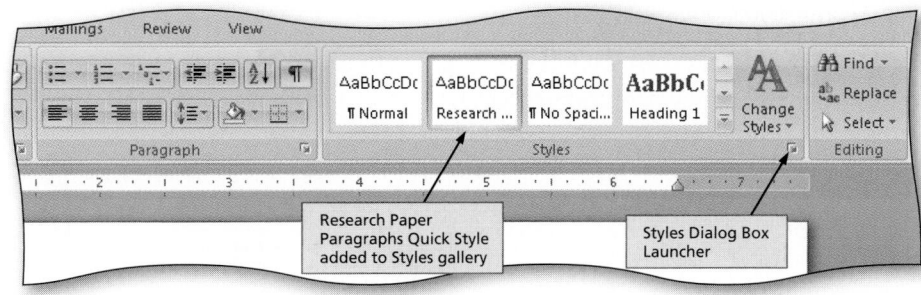

Research Paper Paragraphs Quick Style added to Styles gallery

Styles Dialog Box Launcher

Figure 2–20

Other Ways

1. Click More button in Styles gallery on Home tab, click Save Selection as a New Quick Style, enter name of new Quick Style, click OK button

To AutoCorrect as You Type

As you type, you may make typing, spelling, capitalization, or grammar errors. For this reason, Word provides an **AutoCorrect** feature that automatically corrects these kinds of errors as you type them in the document. For example, if you type the text ahve, Word automatically changes it to the correct spelling, have, when you press the SPACEBAR or a punctuation mark key such as a period or comma.

Word has predefined many commonly misspelled words, which it automatically corrects for you. In the following steps, the word wireless is misspelled intentionally as wreless to illustrate the AutoCorrect as you type feature.

1

- Press CTRL+END to move the insertion point to the end of the document.

- Press the SPACEBAR.

- Type the beginning of the next sentence, misspelling the word, wireless, as follows: Three types of wireless communications include wireless messaging services, wreless (Figure 2–21).

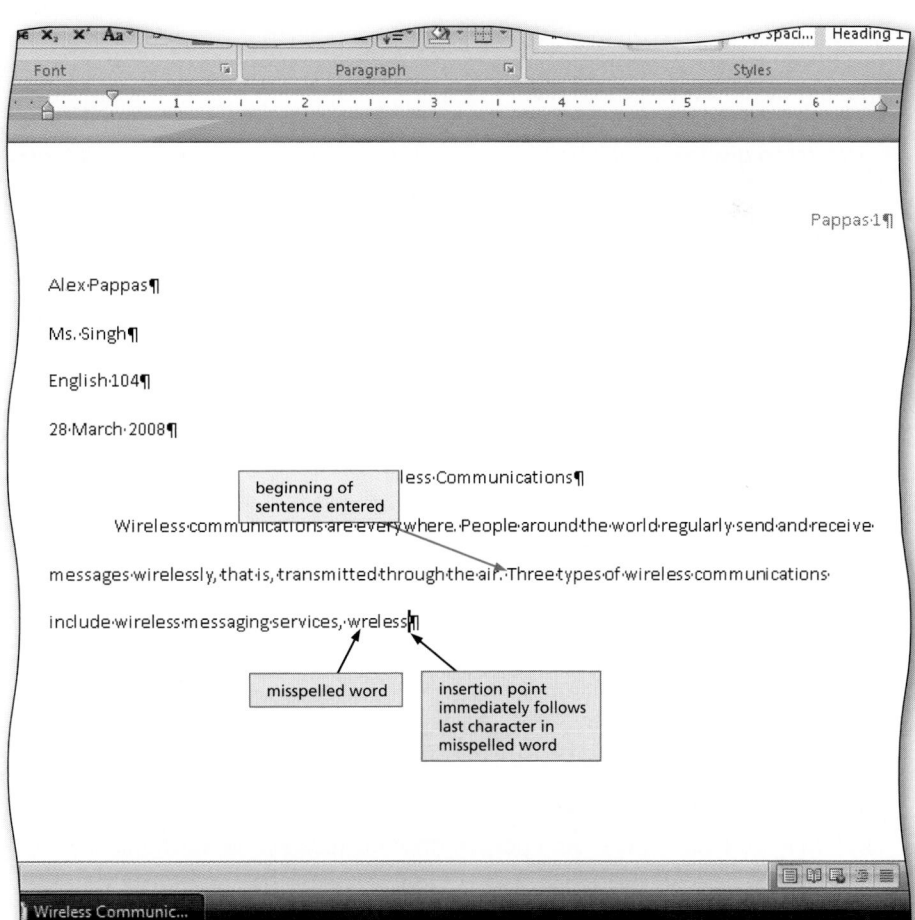

beginning of sentence entered

misspelled word

insertion point immediately follows last character in misspelled word

Figure 2–21

2

- Press the SPACEBAR and watch Word automatically correct the misspelled word.

- Type the rest of the sentence (Figure 2–22): `Internet access points, and global positioning systems.`

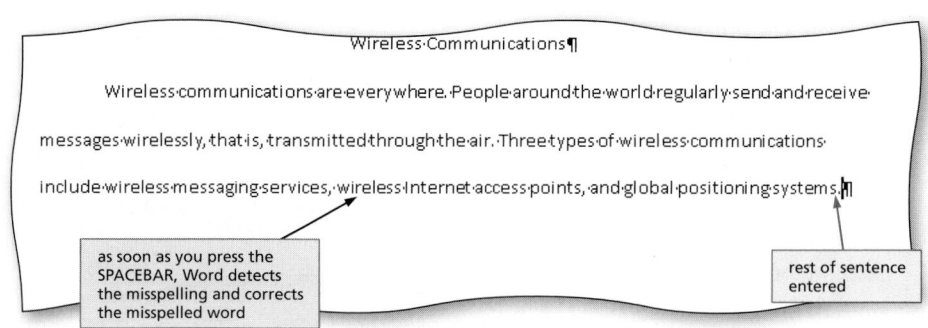

Figure 2–22

To Use the AutoCorrect Options Button

When you position the mouse pointer on text that Word automatically corrected, a small blue box appears below the text. If you point to the small blue box, Word displays the AutoCorrect Options button. When you click the **AutoCorrect Options button**, Word displays a menu that allows you to undo a correction or change how Word handles future automatic corrections of this type. The following steps illustrate the AutoCorrect Options button and menu.

1

- Position the mouse pointer in the text automatically corrected by Word (in this case, the word wireless) to display a small blue box below the automatically corrected word (Figure 2–23).

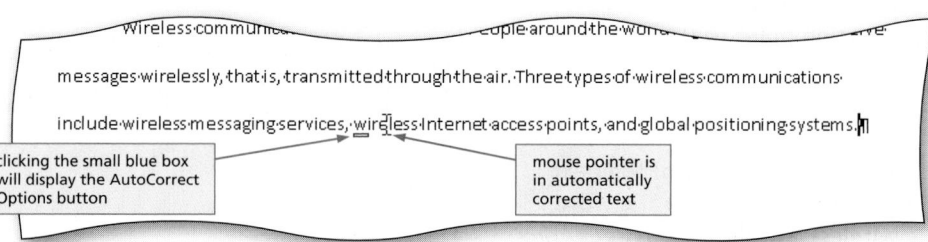

Figure 2–23

2

- Point to the small blue box to display the AutoCorrect Options button.

- Click the AutoCorrect Options button to display the AutoCorrect Options menu (Figure 2–24).

- Press the ESCAPE key to remove the AutoCorrect Options menu from the screen.

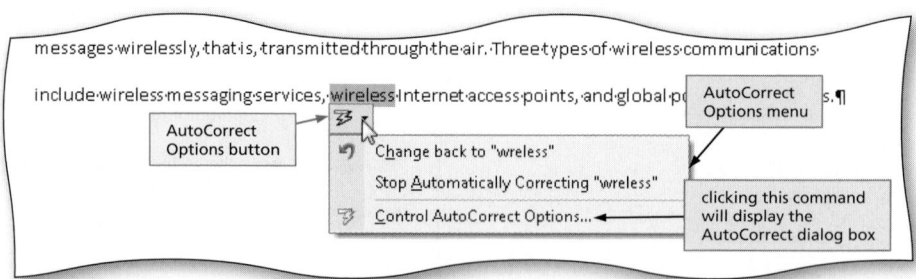

Figure 2–24

Q&A

Do I need to remove the AutoCorrect Options button from the screen?

No. When you move the mouse pointer, the AutoCorrect Options button will disappear from the screen. If, for some reason, you wanted to remove the AutoCorrect Options button from the screen, you could press the ESCAPE key a second time.

To Create an AutoCorrect Entry

In addition to the predefined list of AutoCorrect spelling, capitalization, and grammar errors, you can create your own AutoCorrect entries to add to the list. For example, if you tend to type the word mobile as moble, you should create an AutoCorrect entry for it. The following steps create an AutoCorrect entry.

- Click the Office Button to display the Office Button menu (Figure 2–25).

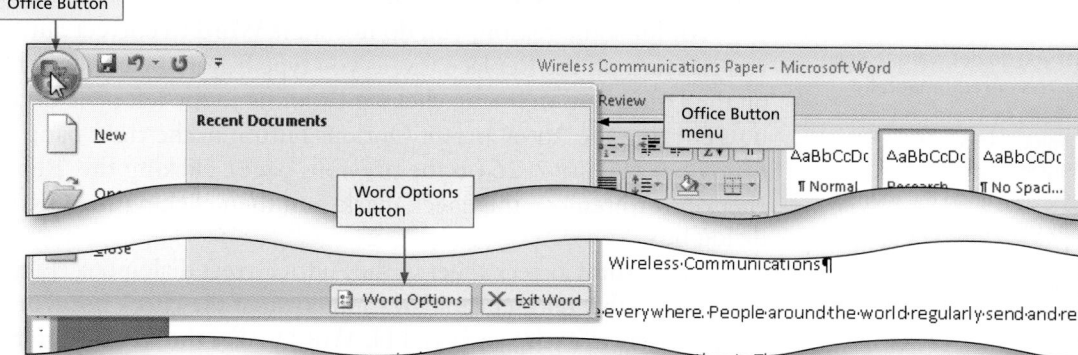

Figure 2–25

- Click the Word Options button on the Office Button menu to display the Word Options dialog box.

- Click Proofing in the left pane to display proofing options in the right pane.

- Click the AutoCorrect Options button in the right pane to display the AutoCorrect dialog box.

- When Word displays the AutoCorrect dialog box, type `moble` in the Replace text box.

- Press the TAB key and then type `mobile` in the With text box (Figure 2–26).

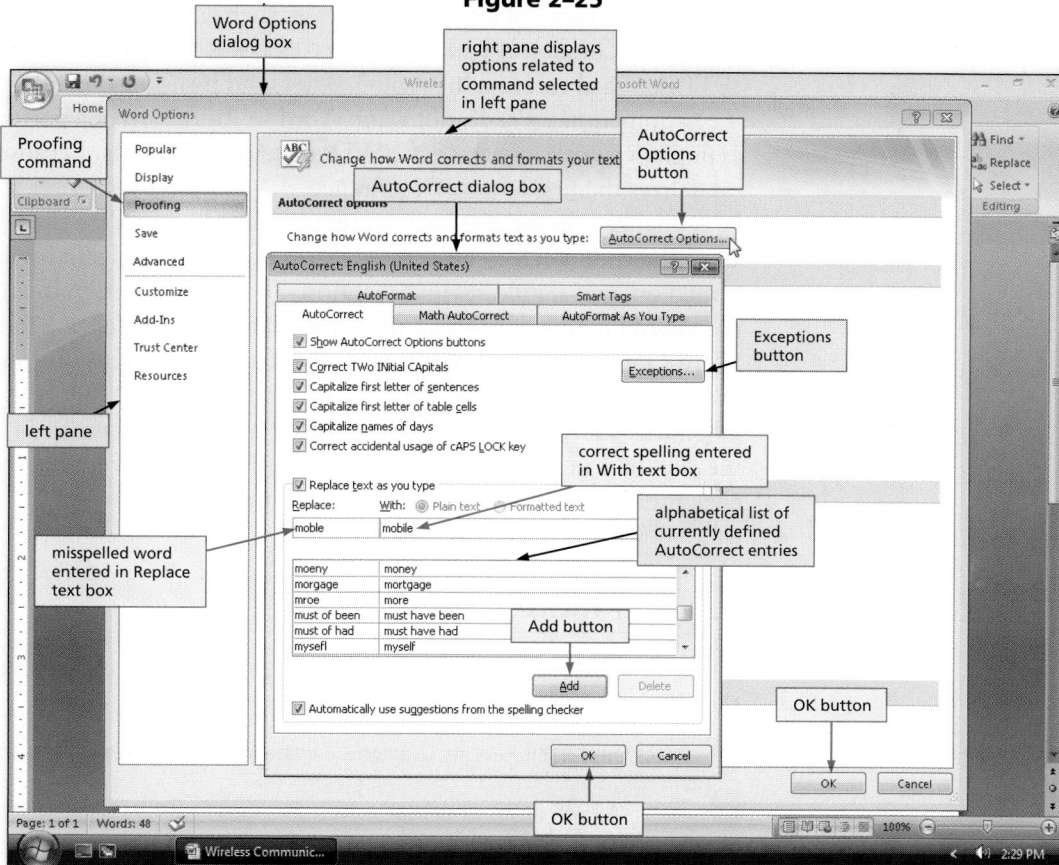

Figure 2–26

- Click the Add button in the AutoCorrect dialog box. (If your dialog box displays a Replace button instead, click it and then click the Yes button in the Microsoft Office Word dialog box.)

- Click the OK button to add the entry alphabetically to the list of words to correct automatically as you type.

- Click the OK button in the Word Options dialog box.

The AutoCorrect Dialog Box

In addition to creating AutoCorrect entries for words you commonly misspell or mistype, you can create entries for abbreviations, codes, and so on. For example, you could create an AutoCorrect entry for asap, indicating that Word should replace this text with the phrase, as soon as possible.

If, for some reason, you do not want Word to correct automatically as you type, you can turn off the Replace text as you type feature by clicking the Word Options button on the Office Button menu, clicking Proofing in the left pane of the Word Options dialog box, clicking the AutoCorrect Options button in the right pane of the Word Options dialog box (Figure 2–26 on the previous page), clicking the 'Replace text as you type' check box to remove the check mark, and then clicking the OK button in each open dialog box.

The AutoCorrect sheet in the AutoCorrect dialog box (Figure 2–26) contains other check boxes that correct capitalization errors if the check boxes are selected. If you type two capital letters in a row, such as TH, Word makes the second letter lowercase, Th. If you begin a sentence with a lowercase letter, Word capitalizes the first letter of the sentence. If you type the name of a day in lowercase, such as tuesday, Word capitalizes the first letter of the day, Tuesday. If you leave the CAPS LOCK key on and begin a new sentence, such as aFTER, Word corrects the typing, After, and turns off the CAPS LOCK key.

Sometimes you do not want Word to AutoCorrect a particular word or phrase. For example, you may use the code WD. in your documents. Because Word automatically capitalizes the first letter of a sentence, the character you enter following the period will be capitalized (in the previous sentence, it would capitalize the letter i in the word, in). To allow the code WD. to be entered into a document and still leave the AutoCorrect feature turned on, you should set an exception. To set an exception to an AutoCorrect rule, click the Word Options button on the Office Button menu, click Proofing in the left pane of the Word Options dialog box, click the AutoCorrect Options button in the right pane of the Word Options dialog box, click the Exceptions button (Figure 2–26), click the appropriate tab in the AutoCorrect Exceptions dialog box, type the exception entry in the text box, click the Add button, click the Close button in the AutoCorrect Exceptions dialog box, and then click the OK button in each of the remaining dialog boxes.

BTW

Automatic Corrections
If you do not want to keep a change automatically made by Word and you immediately notice the automatic correction, you can undo the change by clicking the Undo button on the Quick Access Toolbar or pressing CTRL+Z. You also can undo a correction through the AutoCorrect Options button, which was shown on page WD 92.

To Enter More Text

The next step is to continue typing text in the research paper up to the location of the citation.

1 Press the ENTER key, so that you can begin typing the text in the second paragraph.

2 Type `People use mobile phones, PDAs, and other mobile devices to access text messaging, instant messaging, and picture messaging services` and then press the SPACEBAR.

Citations

Both the MLA and APA guidelines suggest the use of in-text parenthetical citations (placed at the end of a sentence), instead of footnoting each source of material in a paper. These parenthetical acknowledgments guide the reader to the end of the paper for complete information about the source.

**Plan
Ahead**

Reference all sources.
During your research, be sure to record essential publication information about each of your sources. Following is a sample list of types of required information.

- Book: full name of author(s), complete title of book, edition (if available), volume (if available), publication city, publication year

- Magazine: full name of author(s), complete title of article, magazine title, date of magazine, page numbers of article

- Web site: full name of author(s), title of Web site, date viewed, Web address

Word provides tools to assist you with inserting citations in a paper and later generating a list of sources from the citations. With a documentation style selected, Word automatically formats the citations and list of sources. The process for adding citations in Word is as follows:

1. Modify the documentation style, if necessary.
2. Insert a citation placeholder.
3. Enter the source information for the citation.

You can combine Steps 2 and 3, where you insert the citation placeholder and enter the source information at once. Or, you can insert the citation placeholder as you write and then enter the source information for the citation at a later time. While entering the research paper in this chapter, you will use both methods.

To Change the Bibliography Style

The first step in inserting a citation is to be sure the citations and sources will be formatted using the correct documentation style, called the bibliography style in Word. The following steps change the specified documentation style.

1

- Click References on the Ribbon to display the References tab.

- Click the Bibliography Style box arrow on the References tab to display a gallery of predefined documentation styles (Figure 2–27).

2

- Click MLA in the Bibliography Style gallery to change the documentation style to MLA.

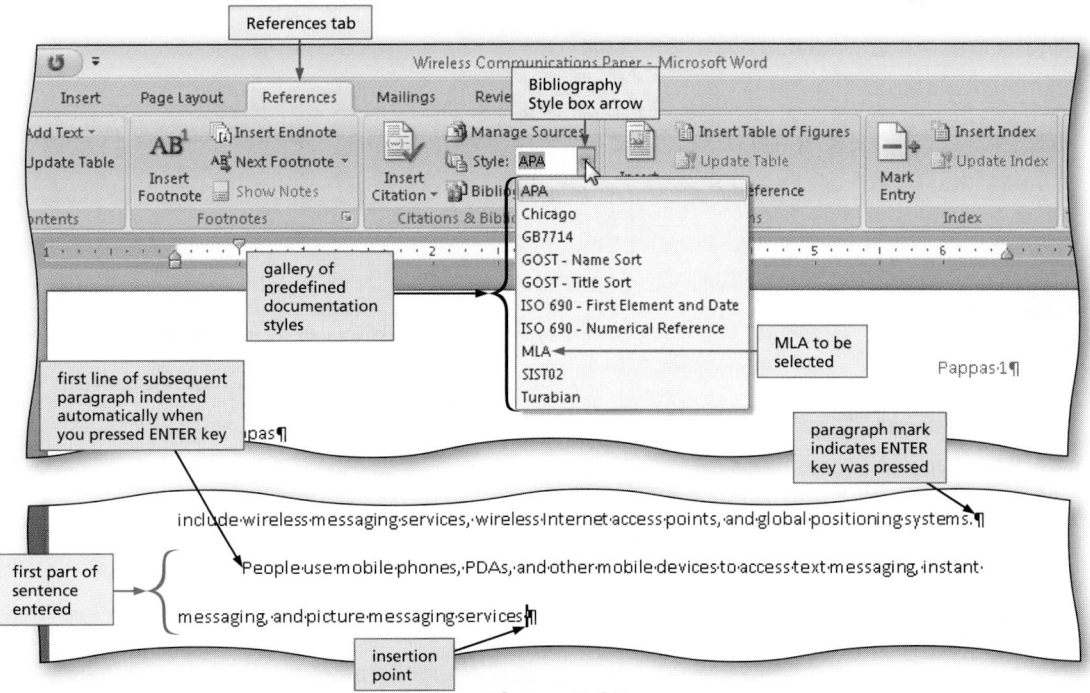

Figure 2–27

To Insert a Citation and Create Its Source

With the documentation style selected, the next task is to insert a citation placeholder and enter the source information. You can accomplish these steps at once by instructing Word to add a new source. The following steps add a new source for a magazine (periodical) article.

- Click the Insert Citation button on the References tab to display the Insert Citation menu (Figure 2–28).

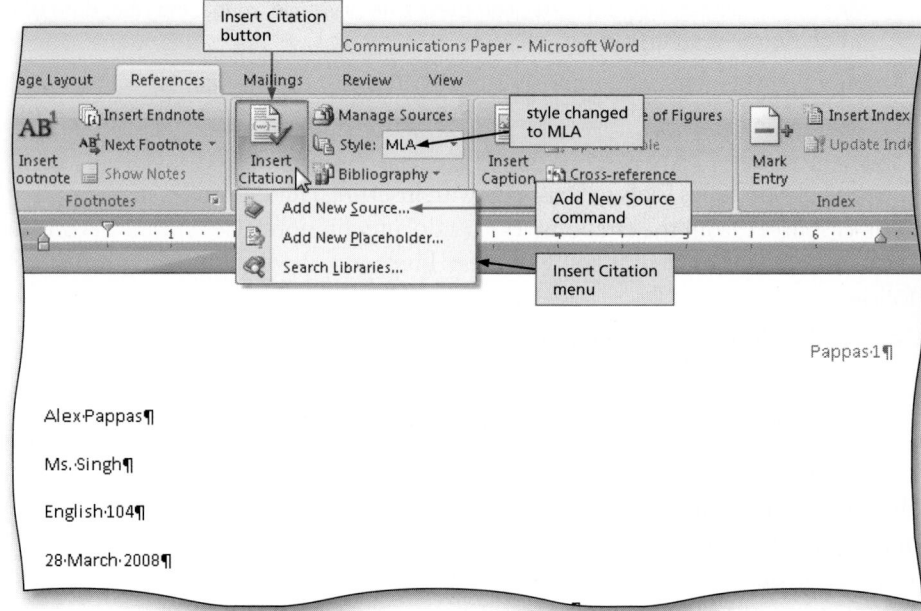

Figure 2–28

- Click Add New Source on the Insert Citation menu to display the Create Source dialog box (Figure 2–29).

Q&A

What are the Bibliography Fields in the Create Source dialog box?

A **field** is a placeholder for data whose contents can change. You enter data in some fields; Word supplies data for others. In this case, you enter the contents of the fields for a particular source, for example, the author name in the Author field.

Experiment

- Click the Type of Source box arrow and then click one of the source types in the list, so that you can see how the list of fields changes to reflect the source type you selected.

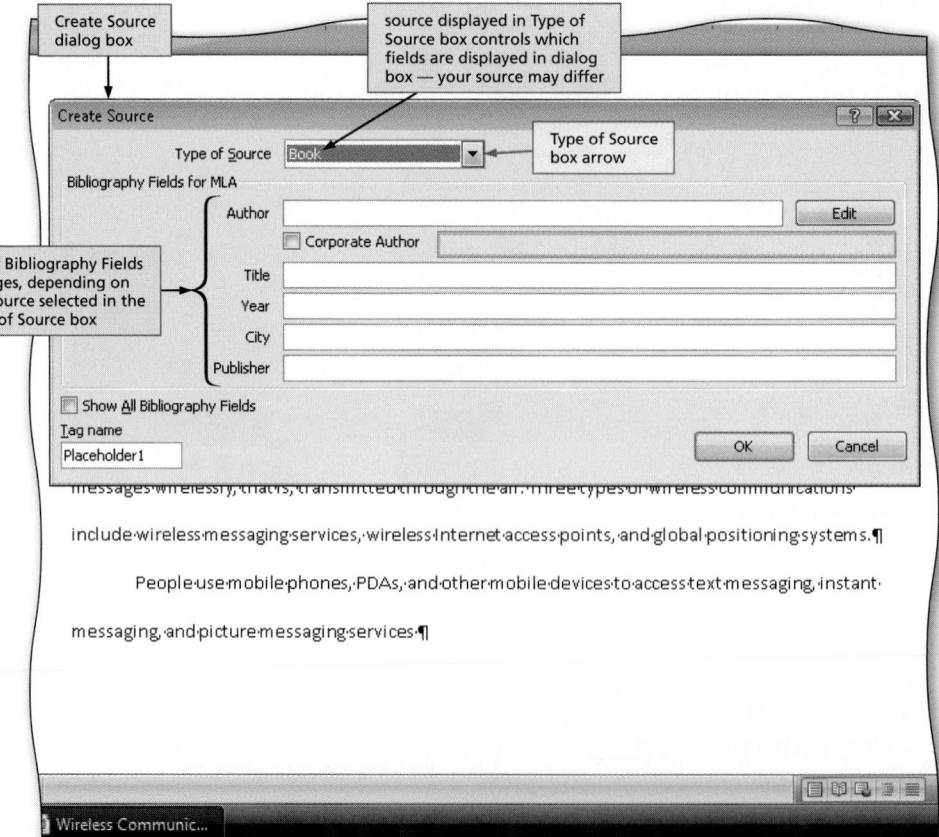

Figure 2–29

3

- If necessary, click the Type of Source box arrow and then click Article in a Periodical, so that the list shows fields required for a magazine (periodical).

- Click the Author text box. Type Davies, Habika as the author.

- Click the Title text box. Type Text Messaging, Instant Messaging, and Picture Messaging as the article title.

- Press the TAB key and then type Computing in Today's World as the periodical title.

- Press the TAB key and then type 2008 as the year.

- Press the TAB key and then type January as the month.

- Press the TAB key twice and then type 34-42 as the pages (Figure 2–30).

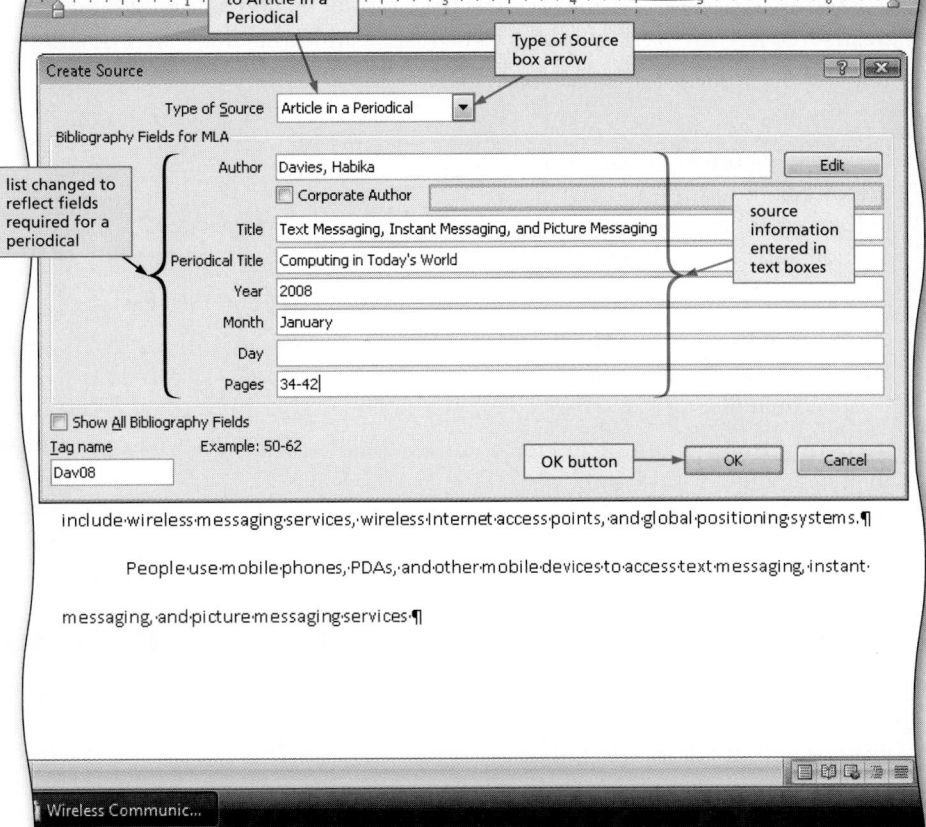

Figure 2–30

4

- Click the OK button to close the dialog box, create the source, and insert the citation in the document at the location of the insertion point (Figure 2–31).

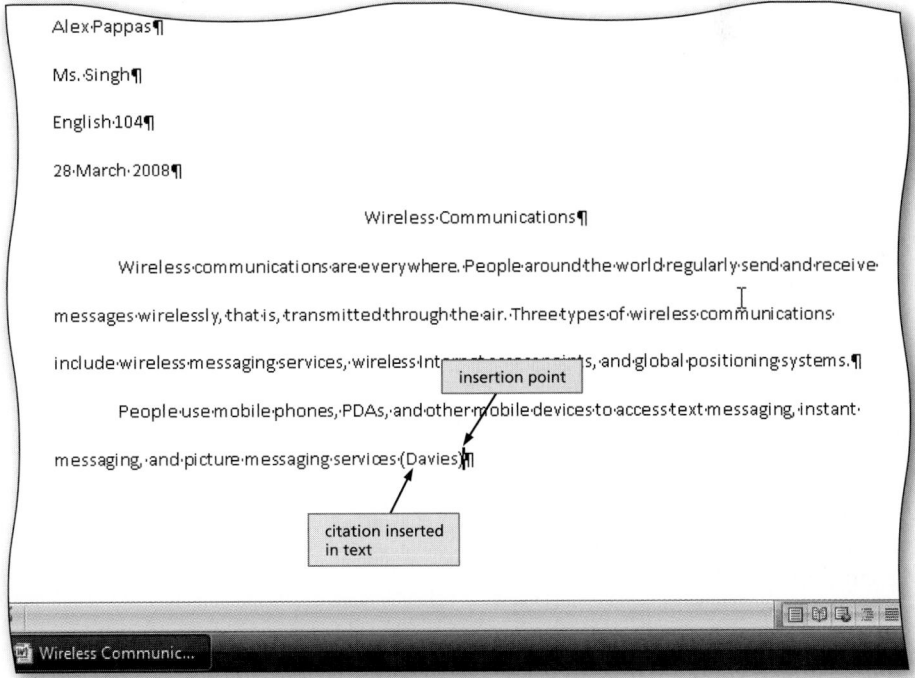

Figure 2–31

To Edit a Citation

In the MLA style, if a source has page numbers, you should include them in the citation. Thus, Word provides a means to enter the page numbers to be displayed in the citation. The following steps edit a citation, so that the page numbers appear in it.

- Click somewhere in the citation to be edited, in this case somewhere in (Davies), which selects the citation and displays the Citation Options box arrow.

- Click the Citation Options box arrow to display the Citation Options menu (Figure 2–32).

Q&A

What is the purpose of the tab to the left of the selected citation?

If, for some reason, you wanted to move a citation to a different location in the document, you would select it and then drag the citation tab to the desired location.

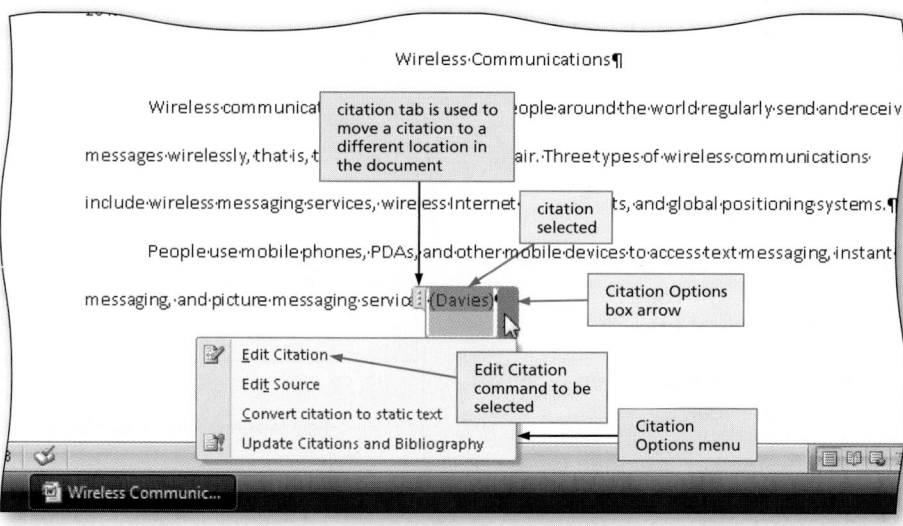

Figure 2–32

- Click Edit Citation on the Citation Options menu to display the Edit Citation dialog box.

- Type 34–42 in the Pages text box (Figure 2–33).

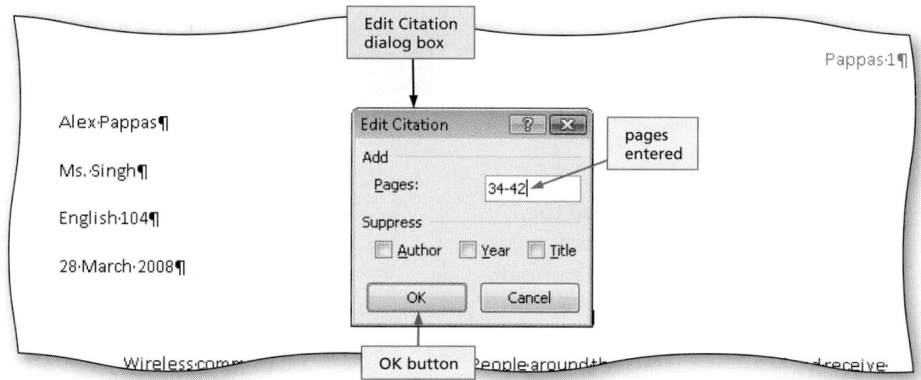

Figure 2–33

3

- Click the OK button to close the dialog box and add the page numbers to the citation in the document (Figure 2–34).

4

- Press the END key to move the insertion point to the end of the line, which also deselects the citation.

- Press the PERIOD key to end the sentence.

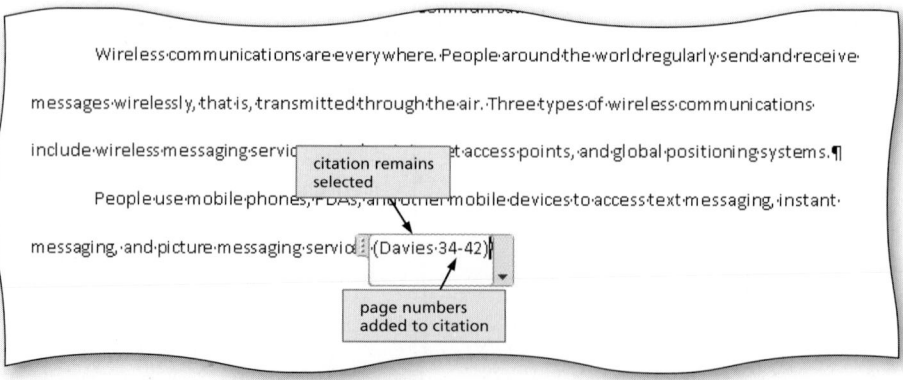

Figure 2–34

To Enter More Text

The next step is to continue typing text in the research paper up to the location of the footnote.

1 Press the SPACEBAR.

2 Type these three sentences (Figure 2–35): `Through text messaging services, users send and receive short text messages, which usually consist of fewer than 300 characters. Wireless instant messaging is an Internet communications service that allows a wireless mobile device to exchange instant messages with one or more mobile devices or online personal computers. Users send graphics, pictures, video clips, sound files, and short text messages with picture messaging services.`

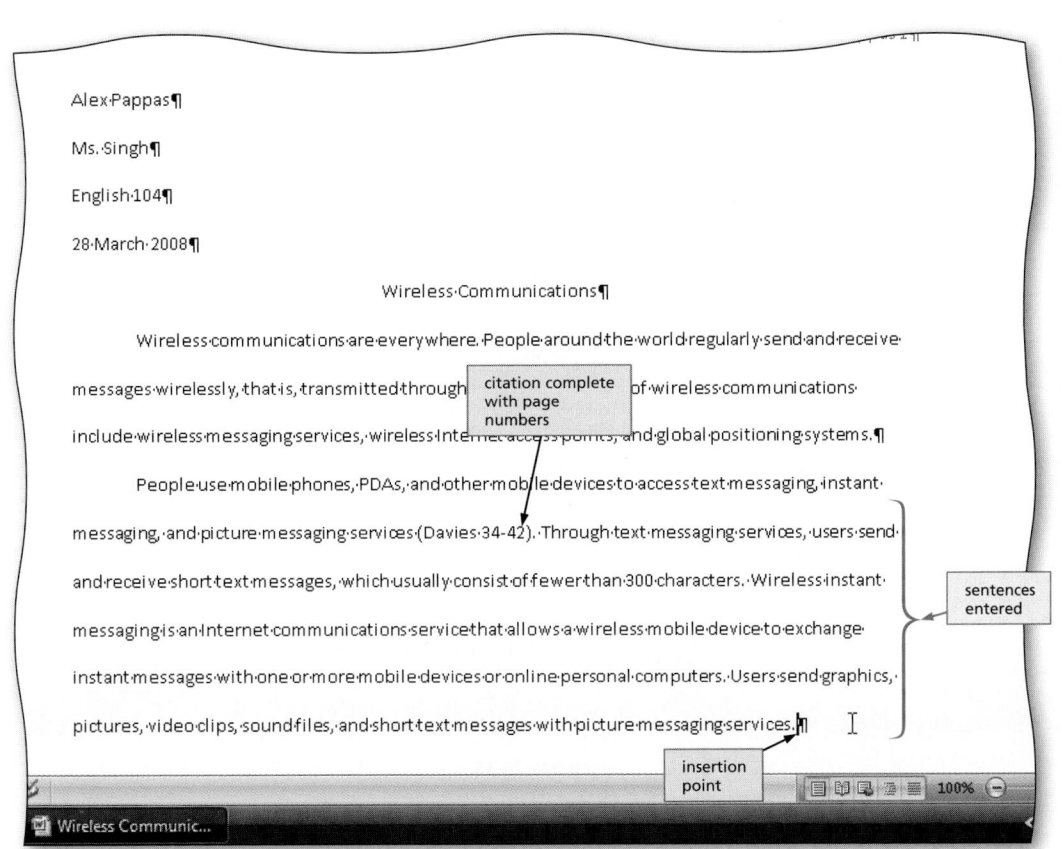

Figure 2–35

BTW

Edit a Source
To edit a source, click somewhere in the citation, click the Citation Options box arrow, and then click Edit Source on the Citation Options menu to display the Edit Source dialog box (which resembles the Create Source dialog box). Make necessary changes and then click the OK button.

Footnotes

As discussed earlier in this chapter, explanatory notes are optional in the MLA documentation style. They are used primarily to elaborate on points discussed in the body of a research paper. The MLA style specifies that a superscript (raised number) be used for a **note reference mark** to signal that an explanatory note exists either at the bottom of the page as a **footnote** or at the end of the document as an **endnote**.

In Word, **note text** can be any length and format. Word automatically numbers notes sequentially by placing a note reference mark in the body of the document and also to the left of the note text. If you insert, rearrange, or remove notes, Word renumbers any subsequent note reference marks according to their new sequence in the document.

To Insert a Footnote Reference Mark

The following step inserts a footnote reference mark in the document at the location of the insertion point and also at the location where the footnote text will be typed.

1

- With the insertion point positioned as shown in Figure 2–35 on the previous page, click the Insert Footnote button on the References tab to display a note reference mark (a superscripted 1) in two places: (1) in the document window at the location of the insertion point and (2) at the bottom of the page where the footnote will be positioned, just below a separator line (Figure 2–36).

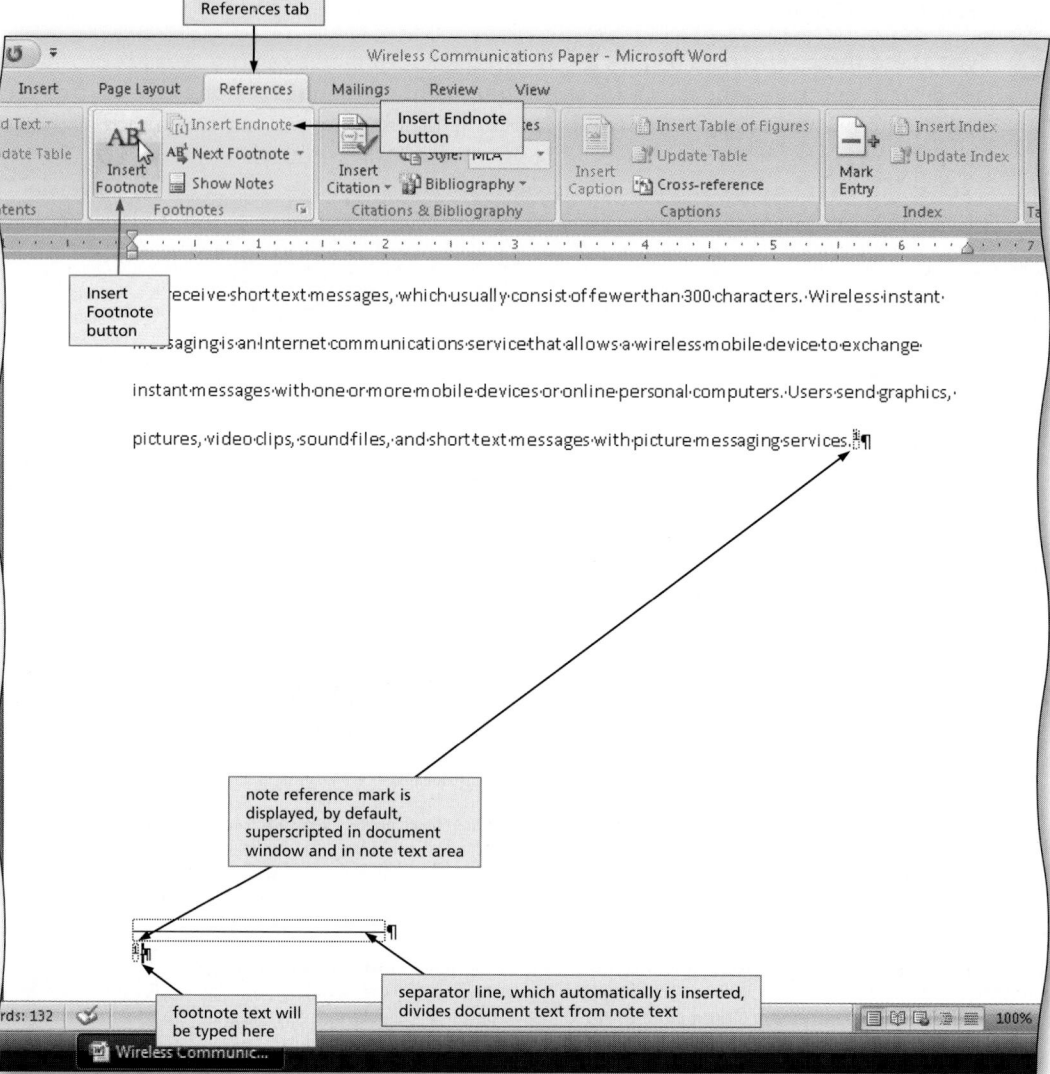

Figure 2–36

What if I wanted explanatory notes to be positioned as endnotes instead of as footnotes?

You would click the Insert Endnote button on the References tab, which places the separator line and the endnote text at the end of the document, instead of the bottom of the page containing the reference.

Other Ways

1. Press CTRL+ALT+F

To Enter Footnote Text

The next step is to type the footnote text to the right of the note reference mark below the separator line.

1 Type the footnote text up to the citation: `Podpora and Ruiz indicate that some messaging services use the term, video messaging, to refer separately to the capability of sending video clips` **and then press the SPACEBAR.**

To Insert a Citation Placeholder

Earlier in this chapter, you inserted a citation and its source at once. Sometimes, you may not have the source information readily available and would prefer entering it at a later time.

In the footnote, you will insert a placeholder for the citation and enter the source information later. The following steps insert a citation placeholder.

1

• With the insertion point positioned as shown in Figure 2–37, click the Insert Citation button on the References tab to display the Insert Citation menu (Figure 2–37).

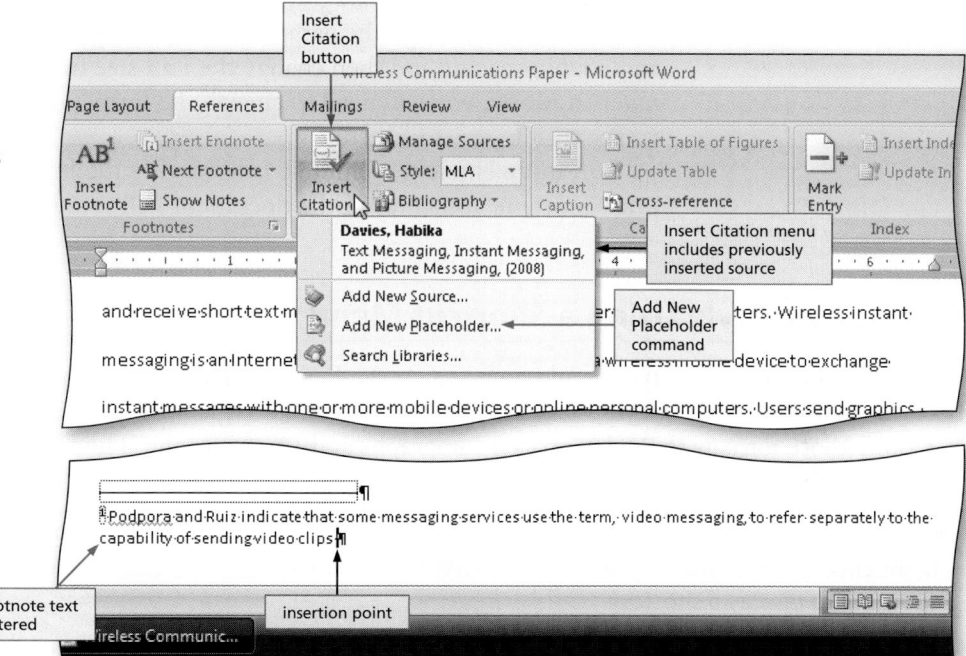

Figure 2–37

2

• Click Add New Placeholder on the Insert Citation menu to display the Placeholder Name dialog box.

• Type Podpora as the tag name for the source (Figure 2–38).

Q&A

What is a tag name?

A tag name is an identifier that links a citation to a source. Word automatically creates a tag name when you enter a source. When you create a citation placeholder, enter a meaningful tag name, which will appear in the citation placeholder until you edit the source.

3

• Click the OK button to close the dialog box and insert the tag name in the citation placeholder.

• Press the PERIOD key to end the sentence.

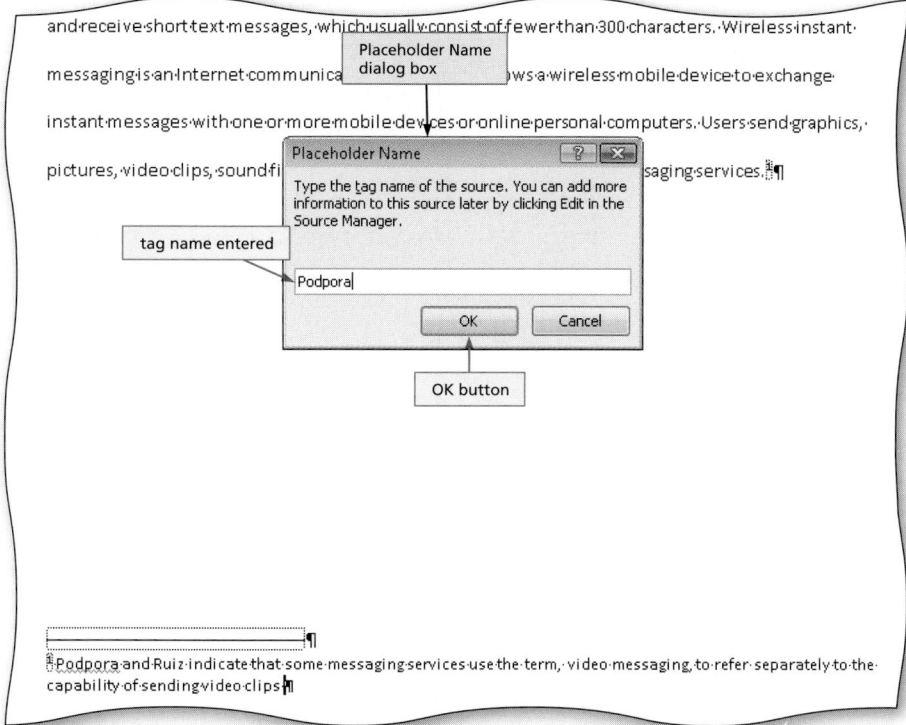

Figure 2–38

Footnote Text Style

When you insert a footnote, Word formats it using the Footnote Text style, which does not adhere to the MLA documentation style. For example, notice in Figure 2–38 on the previous page that the footnote text is single-spaced, left-aligned, and a smaller font size than the text in the research paper. According to the MLA style, notes should be formatted like all other paragraphs in the paper.

You could change the paragraph formatting of the footnote text to first-line indent and double-spacing and then change the font size from 10 to 11 point. If you use this technique, however, you will need to change the format of the footnote text for each footnote you enter into the document.

A more efficient technique is to modify the format of the Footnote Text style so that every footnote you enter in the document will use the formats defined in this style.

To Modify a Style Using a Shortcut Menu

The Footnote Text style should be based on the Research Paper Paragraphs style defined earlier in this chapter. Because the Footnote Text style specifically set paragraphs to single-spaced and the font size to 10 point, you will need to modify those formats to double-spaced paragraphs and 11-point font. The following steps modify the Footnote Text style.

- Right-click the note text in the footnote to display a shortcut menu related to footnotes (Figure 2–39).

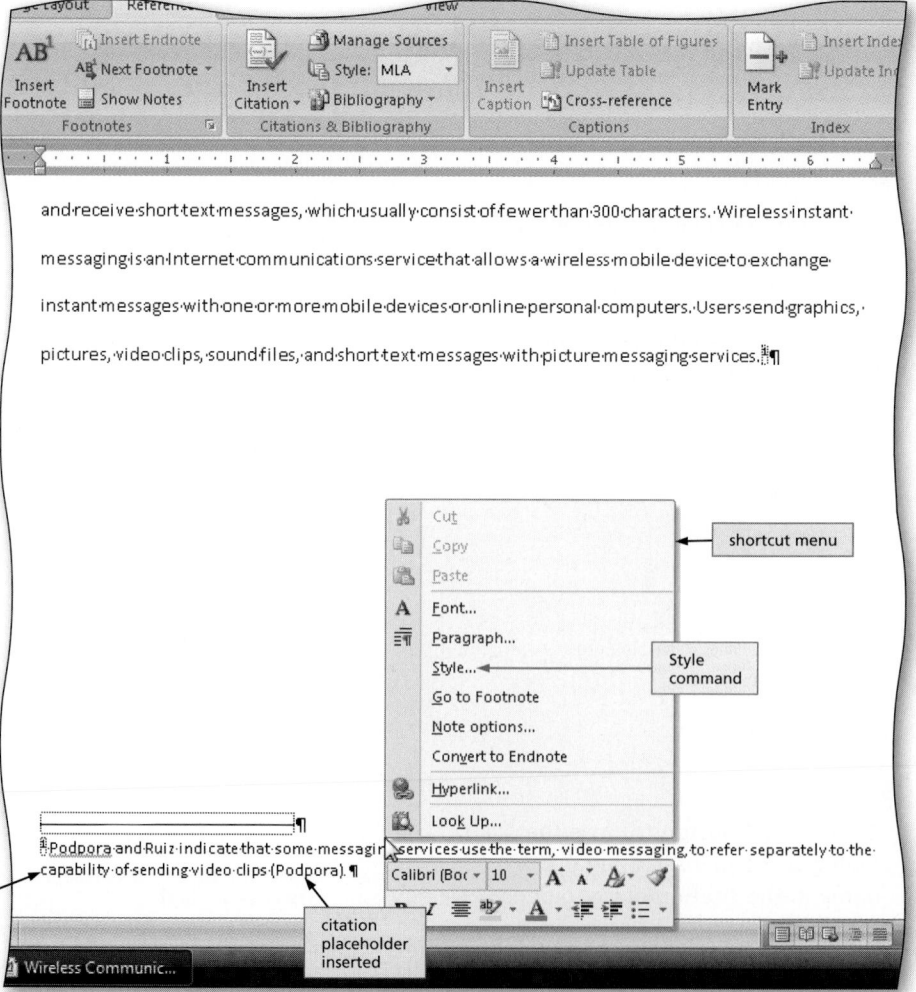

Figure 2–39

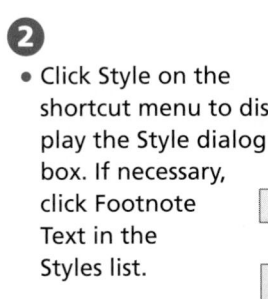

- Click Style on the shortcut menu to display the Style dialog box. If necessary, click Footnote Text in the Styles list.

- Click the Modify button in the Style dialog box to display the Modify Style dialog box.

- Click the 'Style based on' box arrow and then click Research Paper Paragraphs so that the Footnote Text style is based on the Research Paper Paragraphs style.

- Click the 'Style for following paragraph' box arrow and then scroll to and click Research Paper Paragraphs so that the additional footnote paragraphs are based on the Research Paper Paragraphs style.

- Click the Font Size box arrow and then click 11 in the Font Size list to change the font size to 11.

- Click the Double Space button to set the line spacing to double (Figure 2–40).

Figure 2–40

③

- Click the OK button in the Modify Style dialog box to close the dialog box.

- Click the Apply button in the Style dialog box to apply the style changes to the footnote text (Figure 2–41).

Q&A Will all footnotes use this modified style?

Yes. Any future footnotes entered in the document will use an 11-point font with the paragraphs first-line indented and double-spaced.

Figure 2–41

Other Ways
1. Click Styles Dialog Box Launcher, click Footnote Text in list, click Footnote Text box arrow, click Modify, change settings, click OK button 2. Click Styles Dialog Box Launcher, click Manage Styles button, scroll to Footnote Text and then select it, click Modify button, change settings, click OK button in each dialog box

To Edit a Source

When you typed the footnote text for this research paper, you inserted a citation placeholder for the source. You now have the source information and are ready to enter it. The following steps edit the source.

- Click somewhere in the citation placeholder to be edited, in this case (Podpora), to select the citation placeholder.

- Click the Citation Options box arrow to display the Citation Options menu (Figure 2–42).

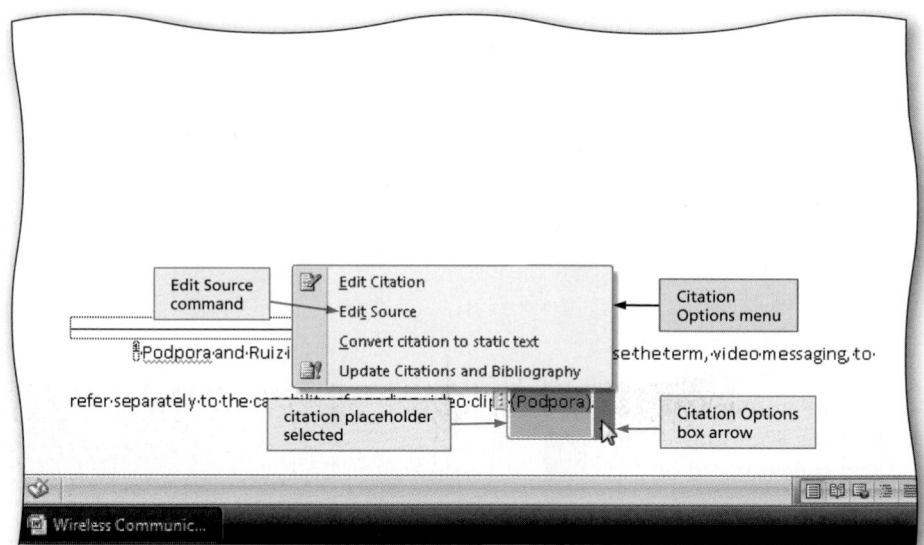

Figure 2–42

- Click Edit Source on the Citation Options menu to display the Edit Source dialog box.

- If necessary, click the Type of Source box arrow and then click Book, so that the list shows fields required for a book.

- Click the Author text box. Type Podpora, Maxine C., and Adelbert D. Ruiz as the author.

- Click the Title text box. Type Advances in Wireless Internet Access Point Technology as the book title.

- Press the TAB key and then type 2008 as the year.

- Press the TAB key and then type Dallas as the city.

- Press the TAB key and then type Wells Publishing as the publisher (Figure 2–43).

- Click the OK button to close the dialog box and create the source.

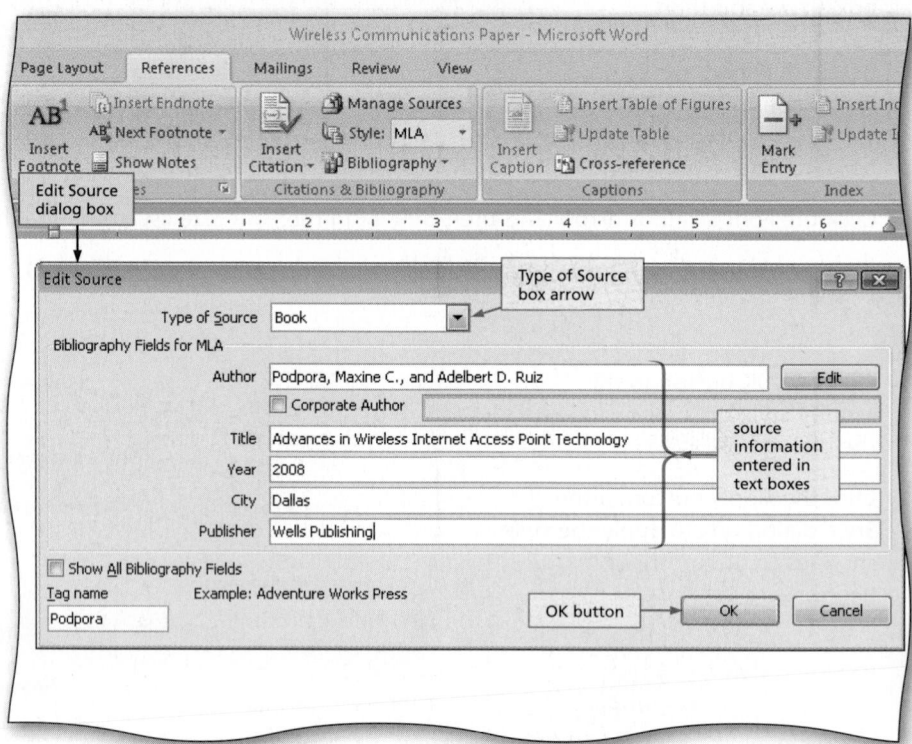

Figure 2–43

Other Ways

1. Click Manage Sources button on References tab, click placeholder source in Current List, click Edit button

To Edit a Citation

In the MLA style, if you reference the author's name in the text, you should not list it again in the parenthetical citation. Instead, just list the page number in the citation. The following steps edit the citation, suppressing the author but displaying the page numbers.

1 If necessary, click somewhere in the citation to be edited, in this case (Podpora), to select the citation and display the Citation Options box arrow.

2 Click the Citation Options box arrow to display the Citation Options menu.

3 Click Edit Citation on the Citation Options menu to display the Edit Citation dialog box.

4 Type 79-82 in the Pages text box.

5 Click the Author check box to place a check mark in it (Figure 2–44).

6 Click the OK button to close the dialog box, remove the author name from the citation in the footnote, and add page numbers to the citation.

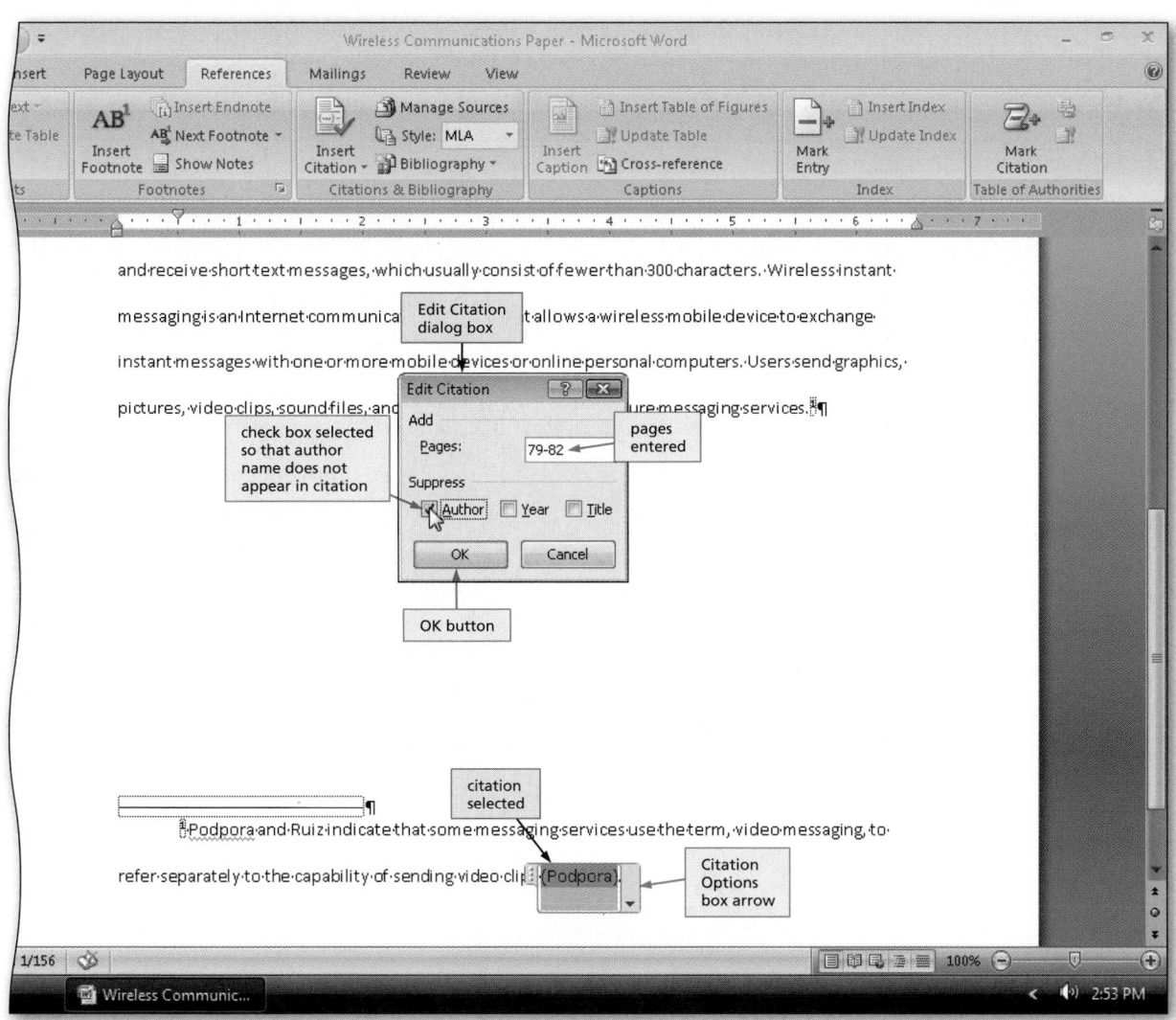

Figure 2–44

Working with Footnotes and Endnotes

You edit footnote text just as you edit any other text in the document. To delete or move a note reference mark, however, you must be in the document text (not in the footnote text).

To delete a note, select the note reference mark in the document text (not in the footnote text) by dragging through the note reference mark and then click the Cut button on the Home tab. Another way to delete a note is to click immediately to the right of the note reference mark in the document text and then press the BACKSPACE key twice, or click immediately to the left of the note reference mark in the document text and then press the DELETE key twice.

To move a note to a different location in a document, select the note reference mark in the document text (not in the footnote text), click the Cut button on the Home tab, click the location where you want to move the note, and then click the Paste button on the Home tab. When you move or delete notes, Word automatically renumbers any remaining notes in the correct sequence.

If you position the mouse pointer on the note reference mark, the note text displays above the note reference mark as a ScreenTip. To remove the ScreenTip, move the mouse pointer.

If, for some reason, you wanted to change the format of note reference marks in footnotes or endnotes (i.e., from 1, 2, 3, to A, B, C), you would click the Footnotes Dialog Box Launcher to display the Footnote and Endnote dialog box, click the Number format box arrow, click the desired number format in the list, and then click the OK button.

If, for some reason, you wanted to convert footnotes to endnotes, you would click the Footnotes Dialog Box Launcher to display the Footnote and Endnote dialog box, click the Convert button, make sure the 'Convert all footnotes to endnotes' option button is selected, click the OK button, and then click the Close button in the Footnote and Endnote dialog box.

To Enter More Text

The next step is to continue typing text in the body of the research paper.

1 Position the insertion point after the note reference mark in the document, and then press the ENTER key.

2 Type the third paragraph of the research paper (Figure 2–45): `In many public locations, people connect to the Internet through a wireless Internet access point using mobile computers and devices. Two types of wireless Internet access points are hot spots and 3-G networks. A 3-G network, which uses cellular radio technology, enables users to connect to the Internet through a mobile phone or computer equipped with an appropriate PC Card. A hot spot is a wireless network that allows mobile users to check e-mail, browse the Web, and access any Internet service - as long as their computers or devices have the proper wireless capability.`

BTW

Spacing after Punctuation
Because word processing documents use variable character fonts, it often is difficult to determine in a printed document how many times someone has pressed the SPACEBAR between sentences. The rule is to press the SPACEBAR only once after periods, colons, and other punctuation marks.

To Count Words

Often when you write papers, you are required to compose the papers with a minimum number of words. The minimum requirement for the research paper in this chapter is 325 words. You can look on the status bar and see the total number of words thus far in a document. For example, Figure 2–45 shows the research paper has 250 words, but you are not sure if that count includes the words in your footnote. The following steps display the Word Count dialog box, so that you can verify whether the footnote text is included in the count.

1

- Click the Word Count indicator on the status bar to display the Word Count dialog box.

- If necessary, place a check mark in the 'Include textboxes, footnotes and endnotes' check box (Figure 2-45).

Q&A Why do the statistics in my Word Count dialog box differ from Figure 2–45?

Depending on the accuracy of your typing, your statistics may differ.

2

- Click the Close button to close the dialog box.

Q&A Can I display statistics for just a section of the document?

Yes. Select the section and then click the Word Count indicator on the status bar to display statistics about the selected text.

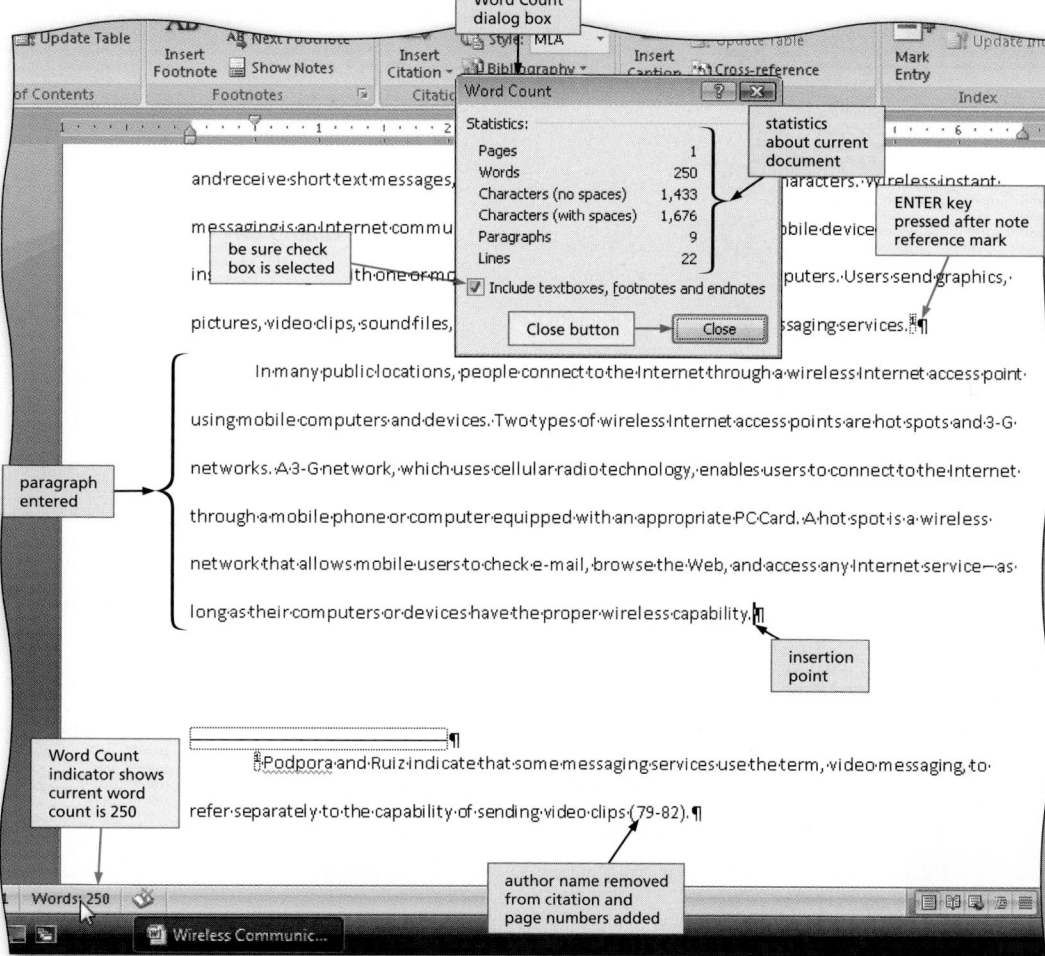

Figure 2–45

Other Ways

1. Click Word Count button on Review tab
2. Press CTRL+SHIFT+G

Automatic Page Breaks

As you type documents that exceed one page, Word automatically inserts page breaks, called **automatic page breaks** or **soft page breaks**, when it determines the text has filled one page according to paper size, margin settings, line spacing, and other settings. If you add text, delete text, or modify text on a page, Word recomputes the location of automatic page breaks and adjusts them accordingly.

Word performs page recomputation between the keystrokes, that is, in between the pauses in your typing. Thus, Word refers to the automatic page break task as **background repagination**. The steps on the next page illustrate Word's automatic page break feature.

To Enter More Text and Insert a Citation Placeholder

The next task is to type the fourth paragraph in the body of the research paper.

1 With the insertion point positioned at the end of the third paragraph as shown in Figure 2–45 on the previous page, press the ENTER key. Type the fourth paragraph of the research paper (Figure 2–46): `A global positioning system (GPS) is a navigation system that consists of one or more earth-based receivers that accept and analyze signals sent by satellites in order to determine the receiver's geographic location, according to Shelly and Cashman` and then press the SPACEBAR.

2 Click the Insert Citation button on the References tab to display the Insert Citation menu. Click Add New Placeholder on the Insert Citation menu to display the Placeholder Name dialog box.

3 Type `Shelly` as the tag name for the source.

4 Click the OK button to close the dialog box and insert the tag name in the citation placeholder.

5 Press the PERIOD key to end the sentence. Press the SPACEBAR. Type `A GPS receiver is a handheld, mountable, or embedded device that contains an antenna, a radio receiver, and a processor. Many mobile devices, such as mobile phones and PDAs, have GPS capability built into the device.`

6 Press the ENTER key.

BTW

Page Break Locations
As you type, your page break may occur at different locations depending on Word settings and the type of printer connected to the computer.

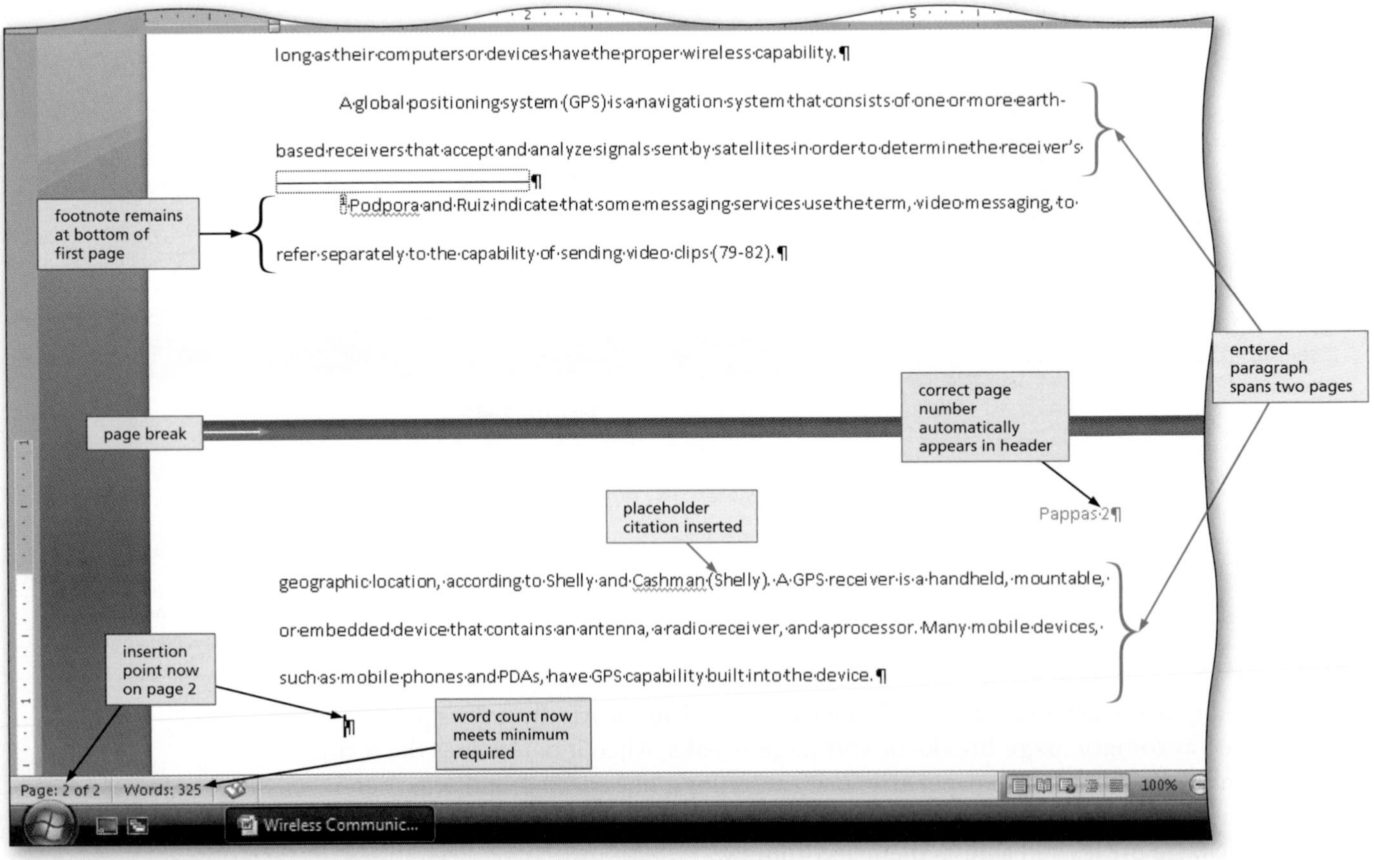

Figure 2–46

To Edit a Source

When you typed the fourth paragraph of the research paper, you inserted a citation placeholder, Shelly, for the source. You now have the source information, which is for a Web site, and are ready to enter it. The following steps edit the source for the Shelly citation placeholder.

1 Click somewhere in the citation placeholder to be edited, in this case (Shelly), to select the citation placeholder.

2 Click the Citation Options box arrow to display the Citation Options menu.

3 Click Edit Source on the Citation Options menu to display the Edit Source dialog box.

4 If necessary, click the Type of Source box arrow; scroll to and then click Web site, so that the list shows fields required for a Web site.

5 Place a check mark in the Show All Bibliography Fields check box to display more fields related to Web sites.

6 Click the Author text box. Type `Shelly, Gary B., and Thomas J. Cashman` as the author.

7 Click the Name of Web Page text box. Type `How a GPS Works` as the Web page title.

8 Click the Production Company text box. Type `Course Technology` as the production company.

9 Click the Year Accessed text box. Type `2008` as the year.

10 Press the TAB key and then type `March` as the month accessed.

Q&A What if some of the text boxes disappear as I enter the Web site fields?

With the Show All Bibliography Fields check box selected, all Web site fields may not be able to be displayed in the dialog box at the same time. In this case, some may scroll up.

11 Press the TAB key and then type `21` as the day accessed.

12 Press the TAB key and then type `www.scsite.com/wd2007/pr2/wc.htm` as the URL (Figure 2–47).

13 Click the OK button to close the dialog box and create the source.

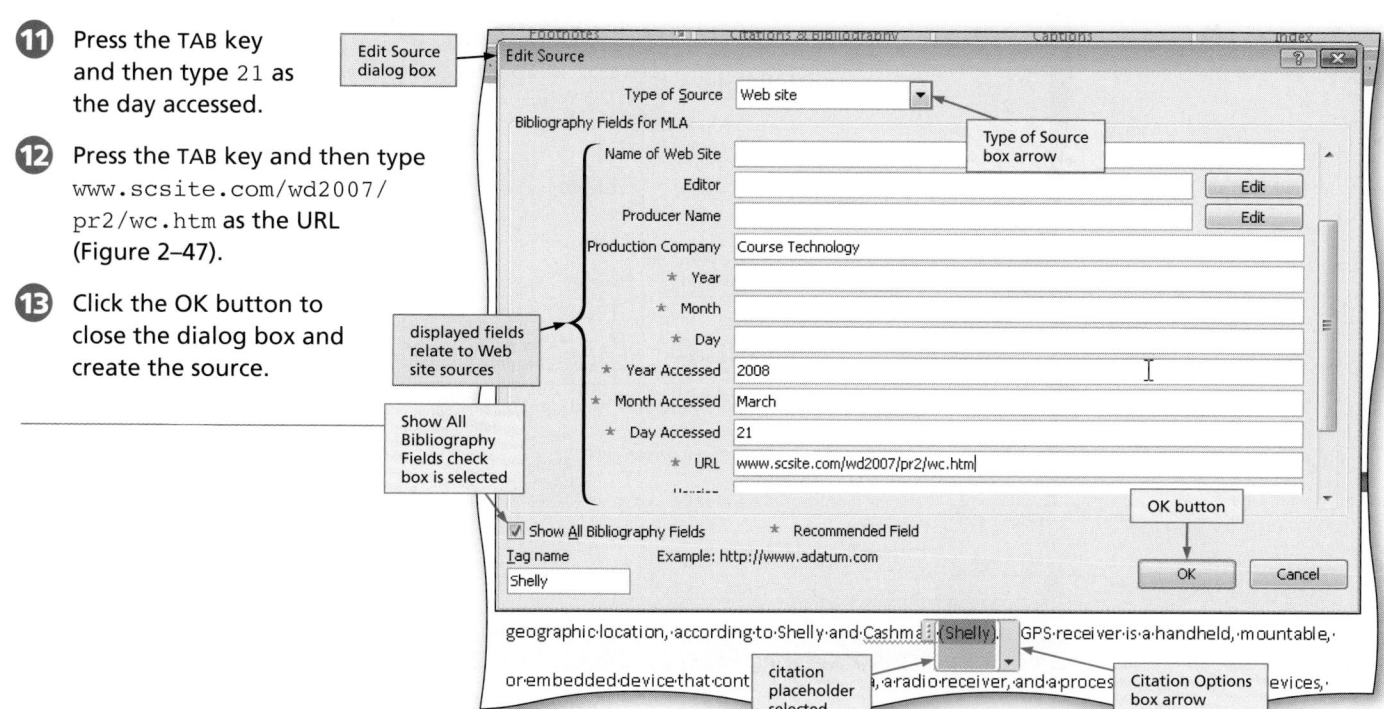

Figure 2–47

To Edit a Citation

As mentioned earlier, if you reference the author's name in the text, you should not list it again in the parenthetical citation. For Web site citations, when you suppress the author's name, the citation shows the Web site name because page numbers do not apply. The following steps edit the citation, suppressing the author and displaying the name of the Web site instead.

1 If necessary, click somewhere in the citation to be edited, in this case (Shelly), to select the citation and display the Citation Options box arrow.

2 Click the Citation Options box arrow and then click Edit Citation on the Citation Options menu to display the Edit Citation dialog box.

3 Click the Author check box to place a check mark in it (Figure 2–48).

4 Click the OK button to close the dialog box, remove the author name from the citation, and show the name of the Web site in the citation.

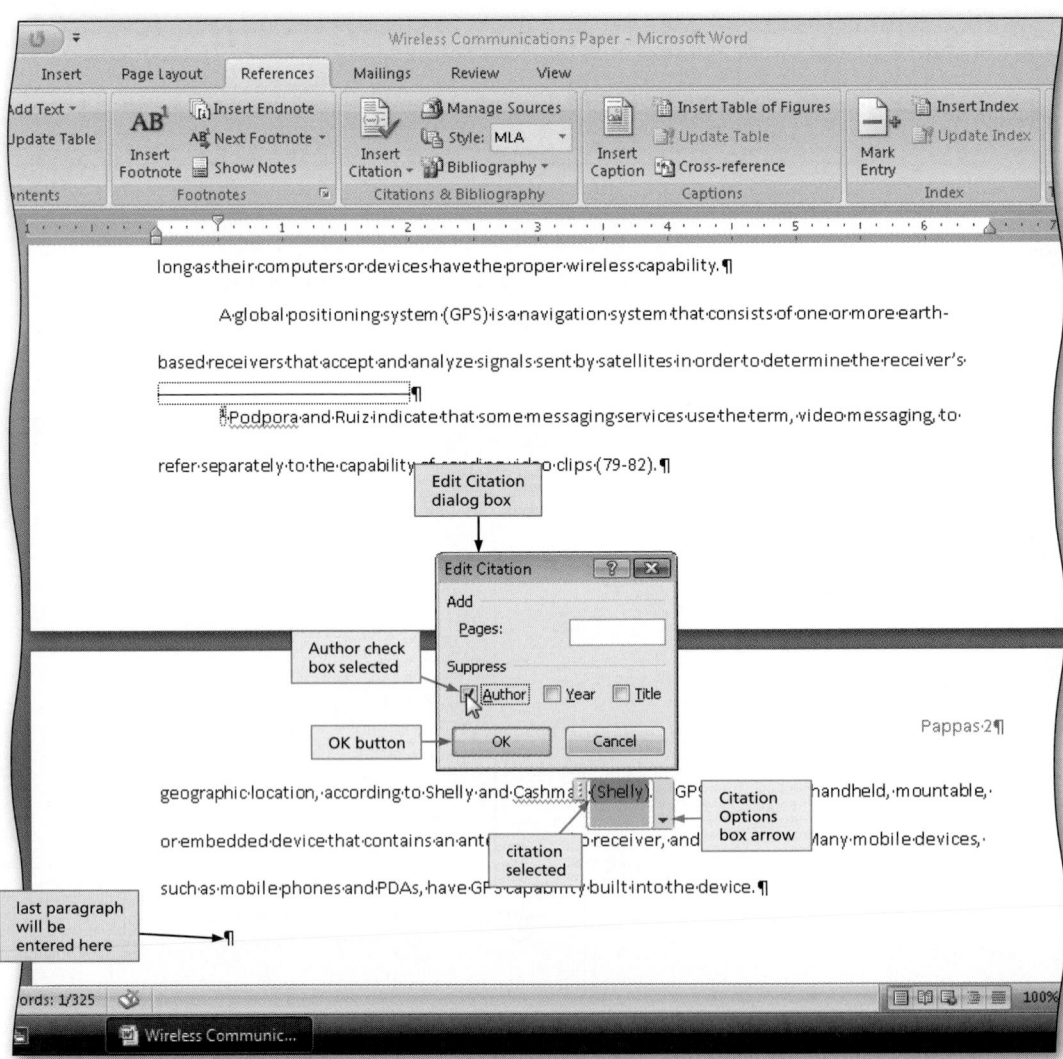

Figure 2–48

To Enter More Text

The next step is to type the last paragraph of text in the research paper.

1 Position the insertion point on the paragraph mark below the fourth paragraph in the research paper (Figure 2–48).

2 Type the last paragraph of the research paper (Figure 2–49):
Mobile users
communicate
wirelessly
through
wireless
messaging services, wireless Internet access points, and global positioning systems. Anyone can take advantage of wireless communications using mobile computers and devices.

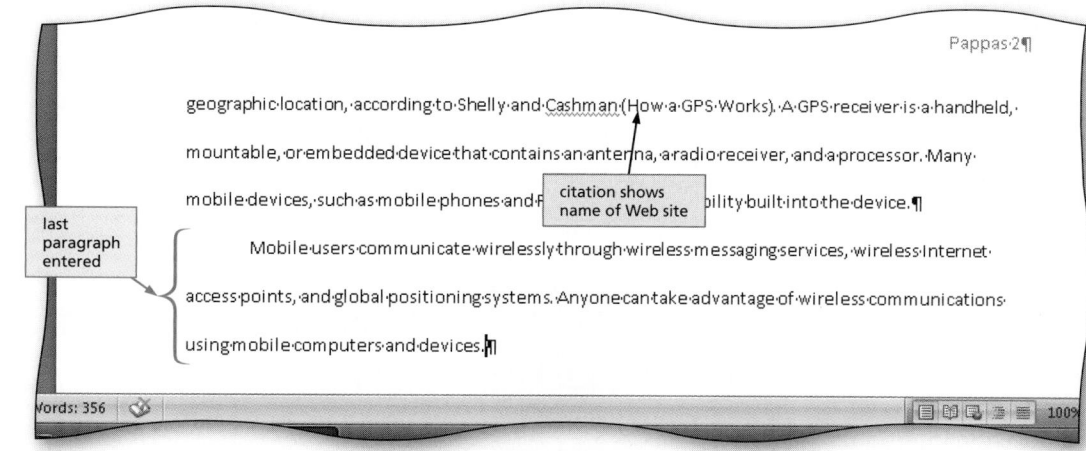

Figure 2–49

To Save an Existing Document with the Same File Name

You have made several edits to the research paper since you last saved it. Thus, you should save it again. The following step saves the document again.

1 Click the Save button on the Quick Access Toolbar to overwrite the previous Wireless Communications Paper file on the USB flash drive.

Creating an Alphabetical Works Cited Page

According to the MLA style, the **works cited page** is a list of sources that are referenced directly in a research paper. You place the list on a separate numbered page with the title, Works Cited, centered one inch from the top margin. The works are to be alphabetized by the author's last name or, if the work has no author, by the work's title. The first line of each entry begins at the left margin. Indent subsequent lines of the same entry one-half inch from the left margin.

Create the list of sources.
A **bibliography** is an alphabetical list of sources referenced in a paper. Whereas the text of the research paper contains brief references to the source (the citations), the bibliography lists all publication information about the source. Documentation styles differ significantly in their guidelines for preparing a bibliography. Each style identifies formats for various sources including books, magazines, pamphlets, newspapers, Web sites, television programs, paintings, maps, advertisements, letters, memos, and much more. You can find information about various styles and their guidelines in printed style guides and on the Web.

Plan Ahead

To Page Break Manually

The works cited are to be displayed on a separate numbered page. Thus, you must insert a manual page break following the body of the research paper so that the list of sources is displayed on a separate page. A **manual page break**, or **hard page break**, is one that you force into the document at a specific location.

Word never moves or adjusts manual page breaks; however, Word adjusts any automatic page breaks that follow a manual page break. Word inserts manual page breaks immediately above the location of the insertion point. The following step inserts a manual page break after the text of the research paper.

- With the insertion point at the end of the text of the research paper (Figure 2-49 on the previous page), press the ENTER key.

- Then, press CTRL+ENTER to insert a manual page break immediately above the insertion point and position the insertion point immediately below the manual page break (Figure 2–50).

- Scroll to position the top of the third page closer to the ruler.

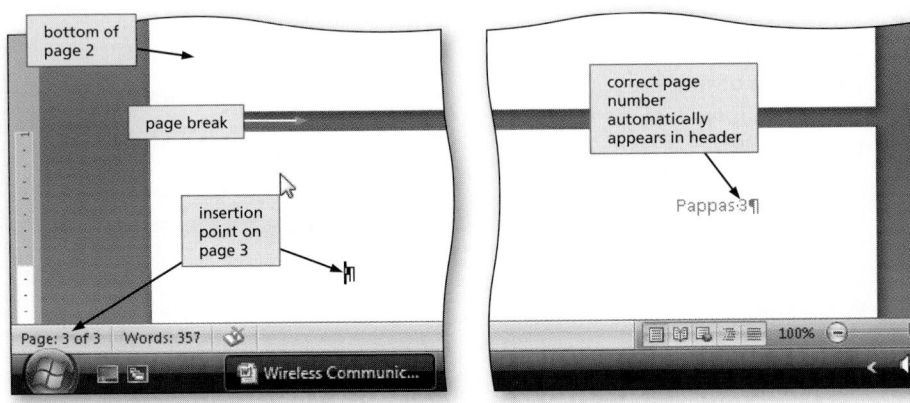

Figure 2–50

Other Ways
1. Click Page Break button on Insert tab

To Center the Title of the Works Cited Page

The works cited title is to be centered between the margins of the paper. If you simply issue the Center command, the title will not be centered properly. Instead, it will be one-half inch to the right of the center point because earlier you set first-line indent at one-half inch. Recall that Word is indenting the first line of every paragraph one-half inch.

To properly center the title of the works cited page, you must move the First Line Indent marker back to the left margin before centering the paragraph.

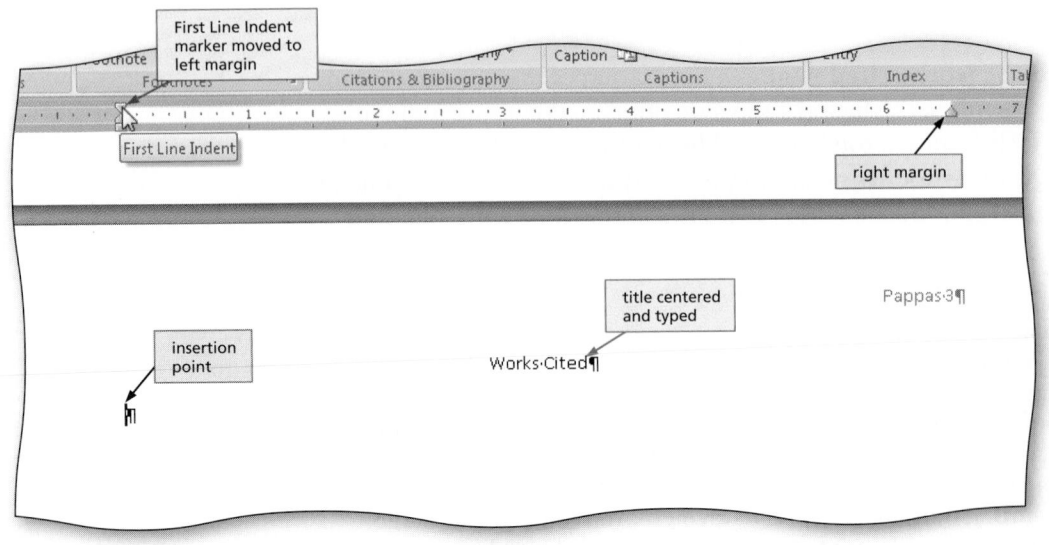

Figure 2–51

1️⃣ Drag the First Line Indent marker to the 0" mark on the ruler, which is at the left margin, to remove the first-line indent setting.

2️⃣ Press CTRL+E to center the paragraph mark.

3️⃣ Type Works Cited as the title.

4️⃣ Press the ENTER key.

5️⃣ Press CTRL+L to left-align the paragraph mark (Figure 2–51).

To Create the Bibliographical List

While typing the research paper, you created several citations and their sources. Word can format the list of sources and alphabetize them in a **bibliographical list**, saving you time looking up style guidelines. That is, Word will create a bibliographical list with each element of the source placed in its correct position with proper formatting and punctuation, according to the specified style. For example, in this research paper, the book source will list, in this order, the author name(s), book title, publisher city, publishing company name, and publication year with the book title underlined and the correct punctuation between each element according to the MLA style. The following steps create a MLA formatted bibliographical list from the sources previously entered.

1

- With the insertion point positioned as shown in Figure 2–52, click the Bibliography button on the References tab to display the Bibliography gallery (Figure 2–52).

Q&A Will I select Works Cited from the Bibliography gallery?

No. The title it inserts is not formatted according to the MLA style. Thus, you will use the Insert Bibliography command instead.

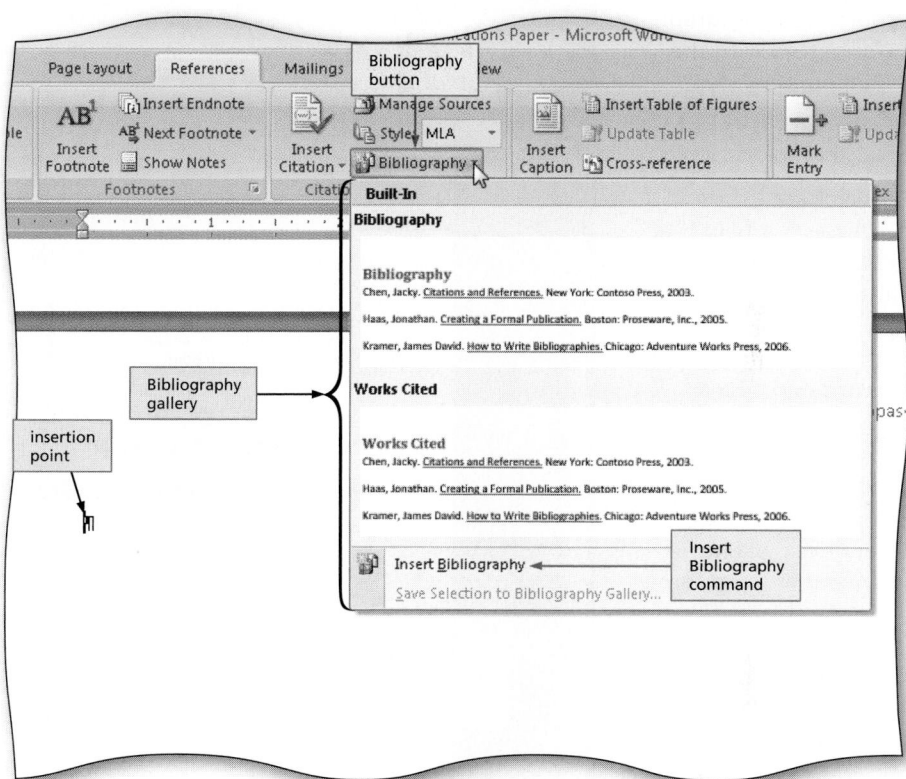

Figure 2–52

2

- Click Insert Bibliography in the Bibliography gallery to insert a list of sources at the location of the insertion point.

- If necessary, scroll to display the entire list of sources in the document window (Figure 2–53).

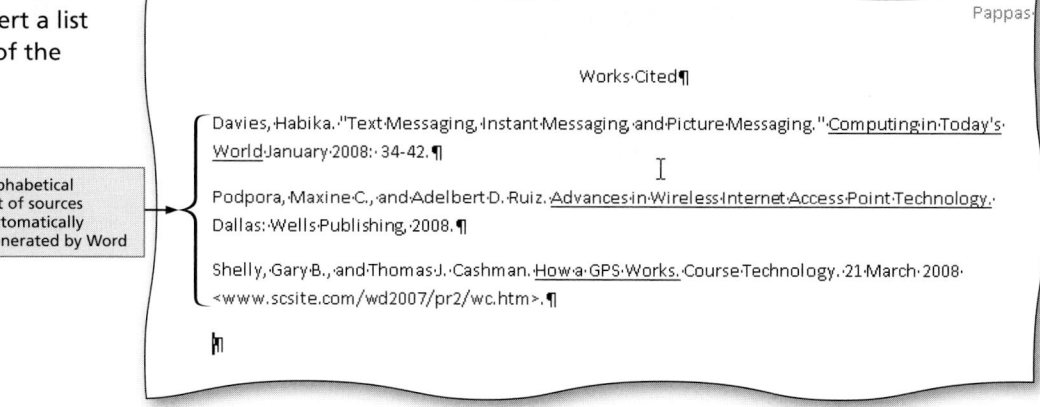

Figure 2–53

To Modify a Style Using the Styles Task Pane

Although the format within each entry in the bibliographical list meets the MLA style, the paragraph formatting does not. Currently, entries are based on the Normal style, which does not have the correct line or paragraph spacing. Thus, you will modify the style so that it is based on the No Spacing style (no blank space before or after a paragraph) and change its line spacing to double. The following steps modify the Bibliography style.

1

- Click somewhere in the list of sources to position the insertion point in a paragraph formatted with the Bibliography style.

Q&A Why did the list of sources turn gray?

The entire list of sources is a field that Word automatically updates each time you make a change to one of the sources. Word, by default, shades fields gray on the screen to help you identify them. The gray shading, however, will not appear in the printed document.

- Click Home on the Ribbon to display the Home tab.

- Click the Styles Dialog Box Launcher to display the Styles task pane.

- If necessary, scroll to Bibliography in the Styles task pane. Click Bibliography to select it, if necessary, and then click its box arrow to display the Bibliography menu (Figure 2–54).

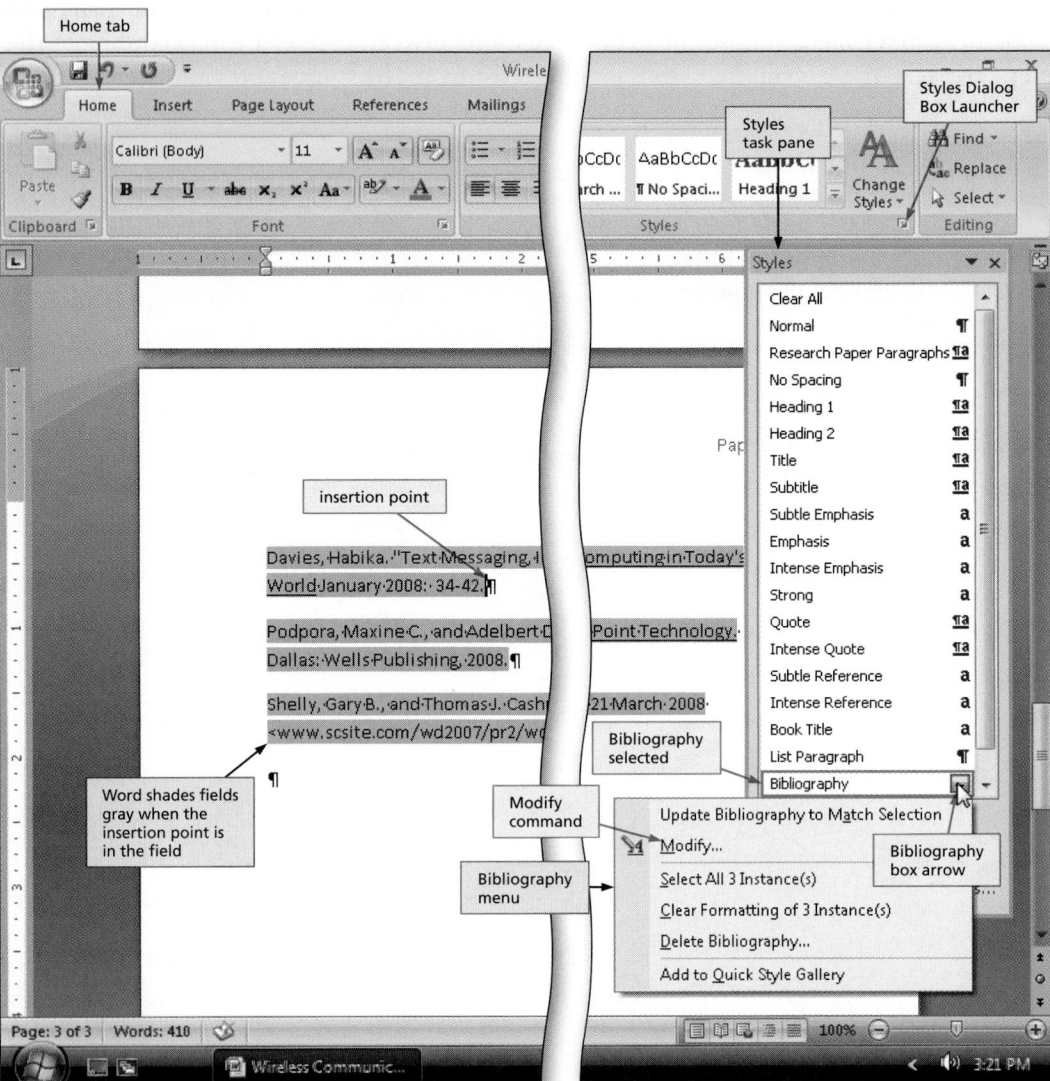

Figure 2–54

2

- Click Modify on the Bibliography menu to display the Modify Style dialog box.

- Click the 'Style based on' box arrow and then click No Spacing to base the Bibliography style on the No Spacing style.

- Click the 'Style for following paragraph' box arrow and then click No Spacing to base additional bibliographical paragraphs on the No Spacing style.

- Click the Double Space button to set the line spacing to double.

- Place a check mark in the Automatically update check box so that any future changes you make to the bibliographical paragraphs will update the Bibliography style automatically (Figure 2–55).

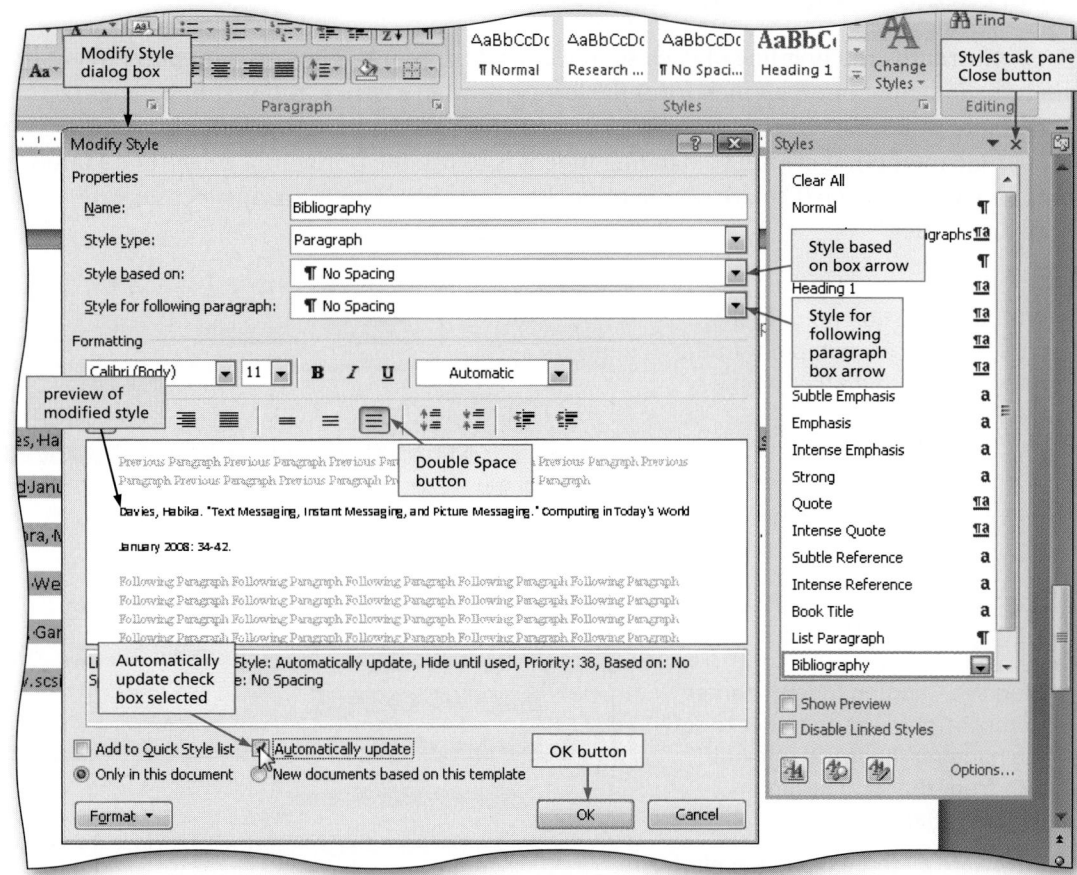

Figure 2–55

3

- Click the OK button in the Modify Style dialog box to close the dialog box and apply the style changes to the paragraphs in the document.

- Click the Close button on the Styles task pane title bar to close the task pane (Figure 2–56).

Other Ways

1. Click Styles Dialog Box Launcher, click Manage Styles button, scroll to style and then select it, click Modify button, change settings, click OK button in each dialog box

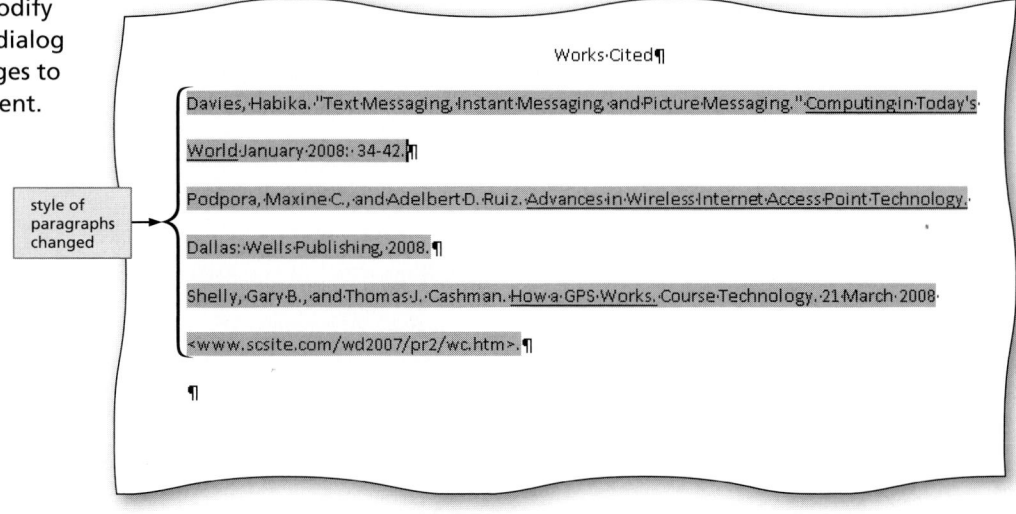

Figure 2–56

To Create a Hanging Indent

Currently, the first line of each source entry begins at the left margin. Subsequent lines in the same paragraph are to be indented one-half inch from the left margin. In essence, the first line hangs to the left of the rest of the paragraph; thus, this type of paragraph formatting is called a **hanging indent**.

One method of creating a hanging indent is to use the horizontal ruler. The **Hanging Indent marker** is the bottom triangle at the 0" mark on the ruler (Figure 2–57). The following steps create a hanging indent using the horizontal ruler.

- With the insertion point in the paragraph to format, point to the Hanging Indent marker on the ruler (Figure 2–57).

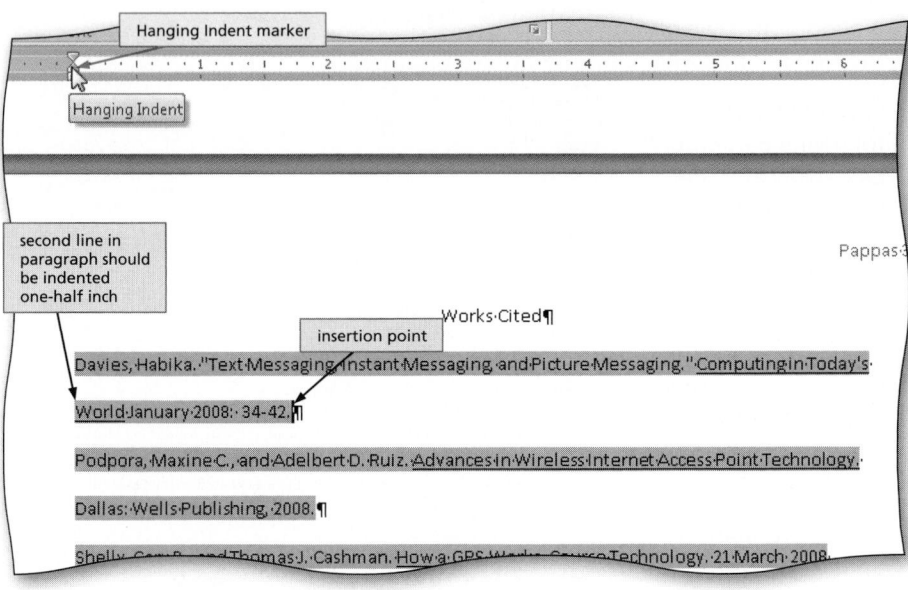

Figure 2–57

- Drag the Hanging Indent marker to the .5" mark on the ruler to set the hanging indent to one-half inch from the left margin (Figure 2–58).

Q&A

Why were all three bibliographical paragraphs formatted with a hanging indent?

When you make a change to a paragraph based on the Bibliography style, the style is updated and all paragraphs based on that style also change because you selected the Automatically update check box in the Modify Style dialog box (shown in Figure 2–55 on the previous page).

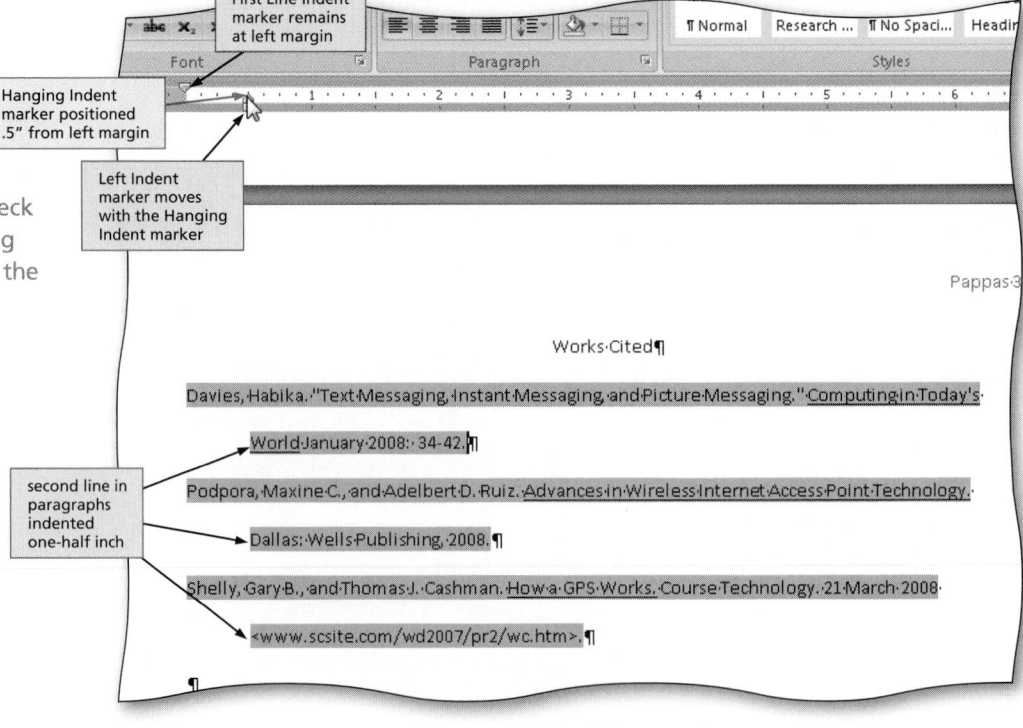

Figure 2–58

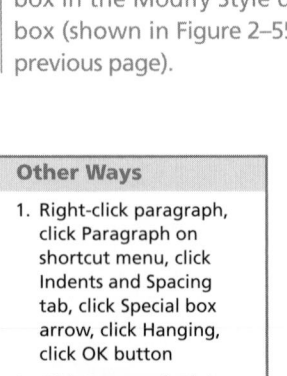

Other Ways

1. Right-click paragraph, click Paragraph on shortcut menu, click Indents and Spacing tab, click Special box arrow, click Hanging, click OK button
2. Click Paragraph Dialog Box Launcher, click Indents and Spacing tab, click Special box arrow, click Hanging, click OK button
3. Press CTRL+T

To Modify a Source and Update the Bibliographical List

If you modify the contents of any source, the list of sources automatically updates because the list is a field. The following steps modify the title of the magazine article.

- Click References on the Ribbon to display the References tab.

- Click the Manage Sources button on the References tab to display the Source Manager dialog box.

- Click the source you wish to edit in the Current List.

- Click the Edit button to display the Edit Source dialog box.

- In the Title text box, add the word, Services, to the end of the title (Figure 2–59).

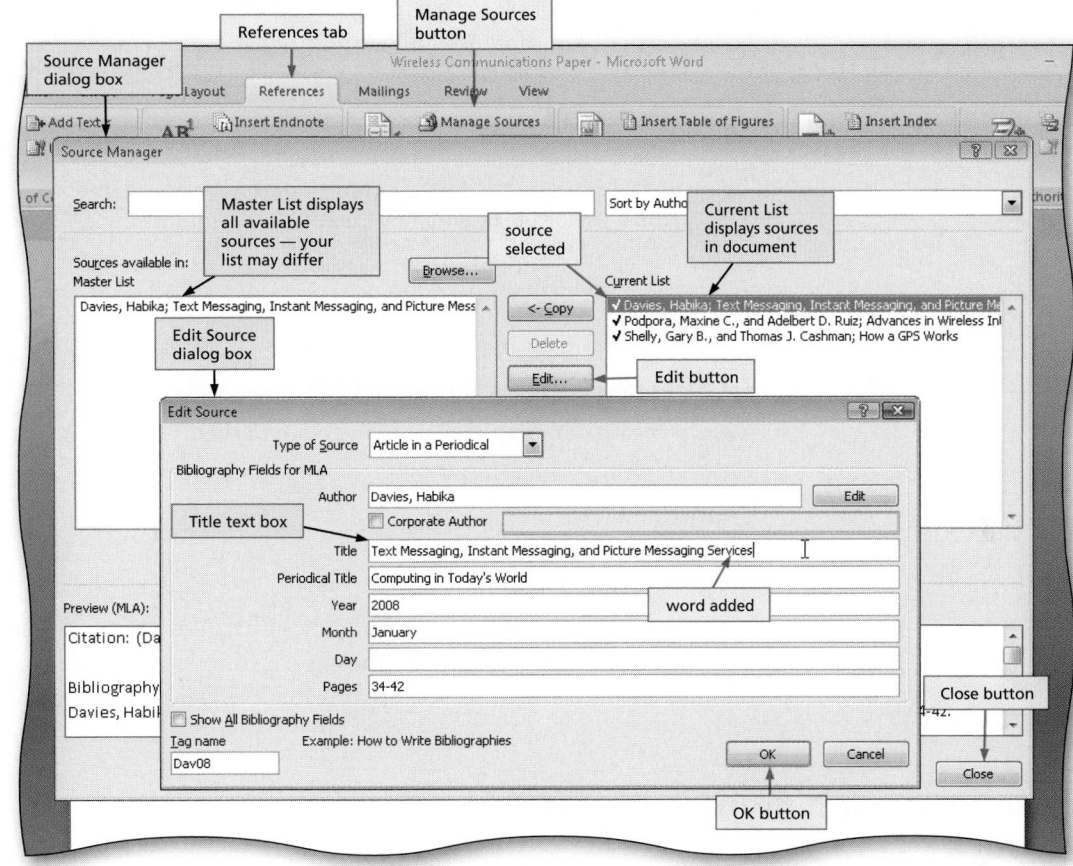

Figure 2–59

- Click the OK button to close the Edit Source dialog box.

- If a Microsoft Office Word dialog box appears, click its Yes button to update all occurrences of the source.

- Click the Close button in the Source Manager dialog box to update the list of sources in the document (Figure 2–60).

Q&A What if the list of sources in the document does not update automatically?

Click in the list of sources and then press the F9 key, which is the shortcut key to update a field.

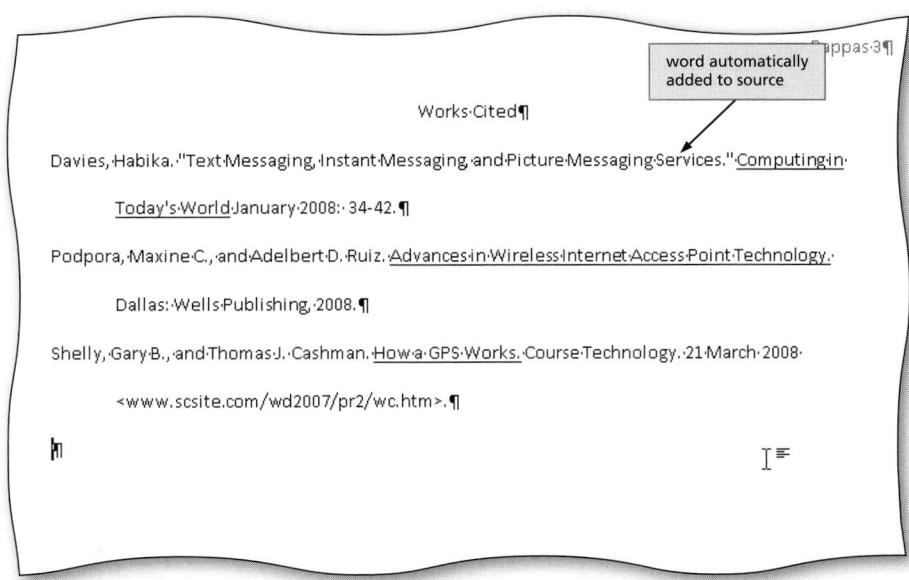

Figure 2–60

Proofing and Revising the Research Paper

As discussed in Chapter 1, once you complete a document, you might find it necessary to make changes to it. Before submitting a paper to be graded, you should proofread it. While **proofreading**, you look for grammatical errors and spelling errors. You want to be sure the transitions between sentences flow smoothly and the sentences themselves make sense.

Plan Ahead

Proofread and revise the paper.

As you proofread the paper, look for ways to improve it. Check all grammar, spelling, and punctuation. Be sure the text is logical and transitions are smooth. Where necessary, add text, delete text, reword text, and move text to different locations. Ask yourself these questions:

- Does the title suggest the topic?
- Is the thesis clear?
- Is the purpose of the paper clear?
- Does the paper have an introduction, body, and conclusion?
- Does each paragraph in the body relate to the thesis?
- Is the conclusion effective?
- Are all sources acknowledged?

To assist you with the proofreading effort, Word provides several tools. You can go to a specific location in a document, move text, find and replace text, insert a synonym, check spelling and grammar, and look up information. The following pages discuss these tools.

To Use the Select Browse Object Menu

Often, you would like to bring a certain page, footnote, or other object into view in the document window. To accomplish this, you could scroll through the document to find a desired page, footnote, or item. Instead of scrolling through the document, however, you can use Word to go to a specific location via the Select Browse Object menu. The following steps display the footnote in the research paper using the Select Browse Object menu.

- Click the Select Browse Object button on the vertical scroll bar to display the Select Browse Object menu and then position the mouse pointer on the Browse by Footnote icon (Figure 2–61).

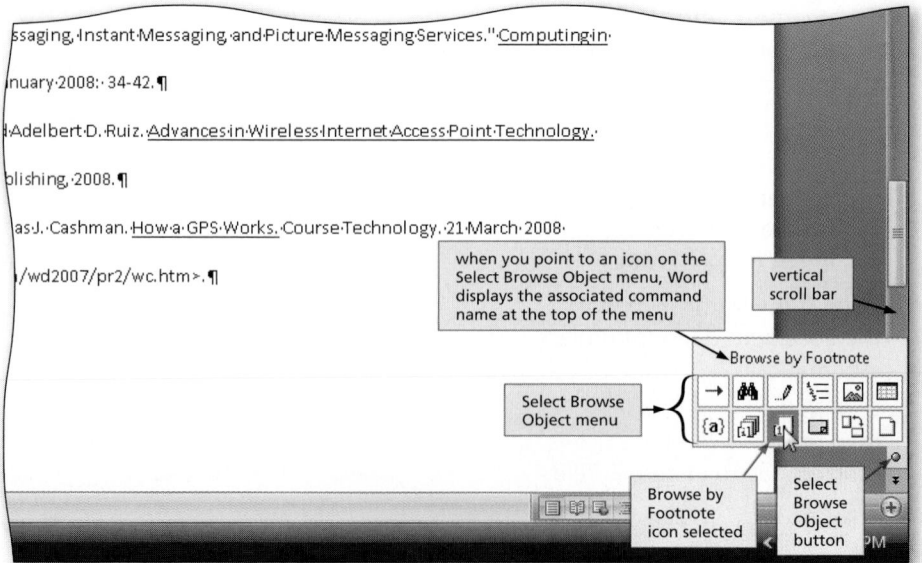

Figure 2–61

2

- Click the Browse by Footnote icon to set the browse object to footnotes.

- Position the mouse pointer on the Previous Footnote button on the vertical scroll bar (Figure 2–62).

Did the function of the button change?

Yes. By default, it is the Previous Page button. Depending on the icon you click on the Select Browse Object menu, the function of the buttons above and below the Select Browse Object button on the vertical scroll bar changes.

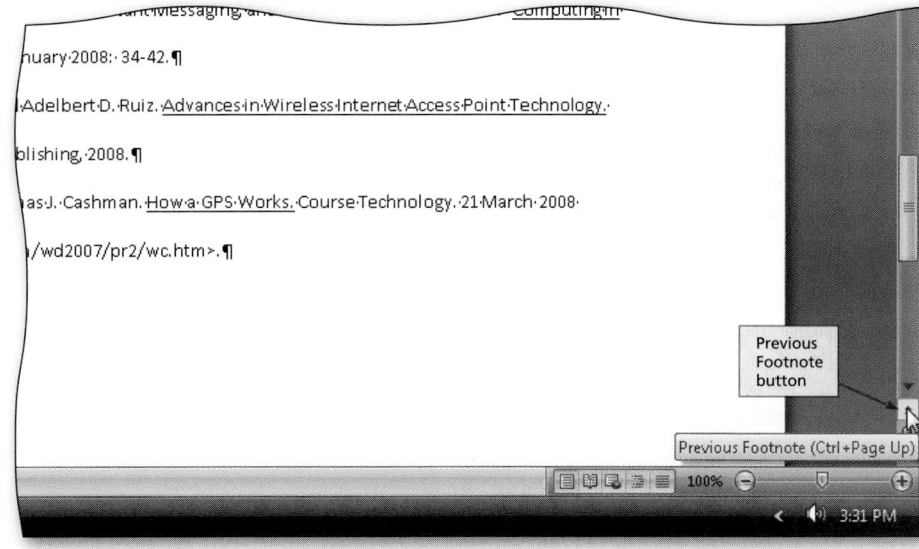

Figure 2–62

3

- Click the Previous Footnote button to display the footnote reference mark in the document window (Figure 2–63).

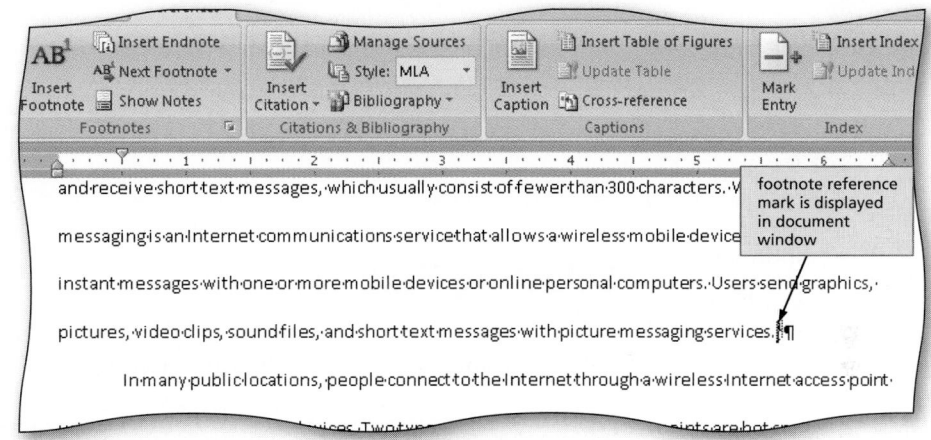

Figure 2–63

Other Ways

1. Click Page Number indicator on status bar, click desired object in Go to what list, type desired object number in Enter object number text box, click Go To button

2. Press ALT+CTRL+HOME

Moving Text

While proofreading the research paper, you realize that text in the third paragraph would flow better if the third sentence were moved to the end of the paragraph.

To move text, such as words, characters, sentences, or paragraphs, you first select the text to be moved and then use drag-and-drop editing or the cut-and-paste technique to move the selected text. With **drag-and-drop editing**, you drag the selected item to the new location and then insert, or *drop*, it there. **Cutting** involves removing the selected item from the document and then placing it on the Clipboard. The **Clipboard** is a temporary Windows storage area. **Pasting** is the process of copying an item from the Clipboard into the document at the location of the insertion point.

When moving text a long distance or between application programs, use the Clipboard task pane to cut and paste. When moving text a short distance, the drag-and-drop technique is more efficient. Thus, the steps on the following pages demonstrate drag-and-drop editing.

To Select a Sentence

To drag-and-drop a sentence in the research paper, you first must select the sentence. The following step selects a sentence.

- Position the mouse pointer in the sentence to be moved (shown in Figure 2–64).

- Press and hold down the CTRL key. While holding down the CTRL key, click the sentence to select the entire sentence.

- Release the CTRL key.

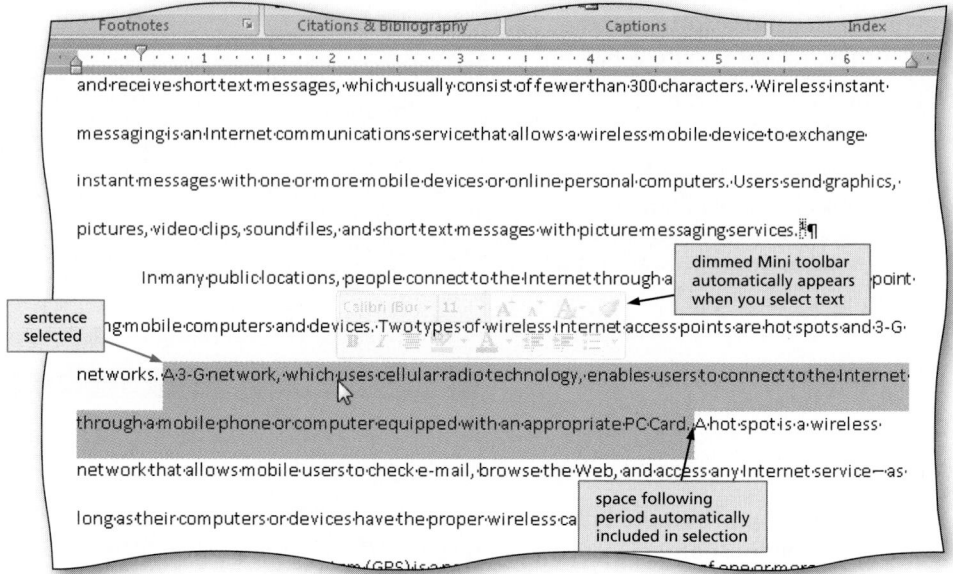

and receive short text messages, which usually consist of fewer than 300 characters. Wireless instant messaging is an Internet communications service that allows a wireless mobile device to exchange instant messages with one or more mobile devices or online personal computers. Users send graphics, pictures, video clips, sound files, and short text messages with picture messaging services.¶

In many public locations, people connect to the Internet through a [...] point
[dimmed Mini toolbar automatically appears when you select text]

[sentence selected]

...ng mobile computers and devices. Two types of wireless Internet access points are hot spots and 3-G networks. A 3-G network, which uses cellular radio technology, enables users to connect to the Internet through a mobile phone or computer equipped with an appropriate PC Card. A hot spot is a wireless network that allows mobile users to check e-mail, browse the Web, and access any Internet service—as long as their computers or devices have the proper wireless ca [space following period automatically included in selection]

Figure 2–64

Other Ways

1. Drag through the sentence
2. With insertion point at beginning of sentence, press CTRL+SHIFT+RIGHT ARROW until sentence is selected

Selecting Text

In the previous steps and throughout Chapters 1 and 2, you have selected text. Table 2–3 summarizes the techniques used to select various items with the mouse.

BTW

Selecting Nonadjacent Items
In Word, you can select nonadjacent items, that is, items not next to each other. This is helpful when you are formatting multiple items the same way. To select nonadjacent items (text or graphics), do the following: select the first item, such as a word or paragraph, as usual. Press and hold down the CTRL key. While holding down the CTRL key, select any additional items.

Table 2–3 Techniques for Selecting Items with the Mouse	
Item To Select	**Mouse Action**
Block of text	Click at beginning of selection, scroll to end of selection, position mouse pointer at end of selection, hold down SHIFT key and then click; or drag through the text
Character(s)	Drag through character(s)
Document	Move mouse to left of text until mouse pointer changes to a right-pointing block arrow and then triple-click
Graphic	Click the graphic
Line	Move mouse to left of line until mouse pointer changes to a right-pointing block arrow and then click
Lines	Move mouse to left of first line until mouse pointer changes to a right-pointing block arrow and then drag up or down
Paragraph	Triple-click paragraph; or move mouse to left of paragraph until mouse pointer changes to a right-pointing block arrow and then double-click
Paragraphs	Move mouse to left of paragraph until mouse pointer changes to a right-pointing block arrow, double-click, and then drag up or down
Sentence	Press and hold down CTRL key and then click sentence
Word	Double-click the word
Words	Drag through words

To Move Selected Text

With the sentence to be moved selected, you can use drag-and-drop editing to move it. You should be sure that drag-and-drop editing is enabled by clicking the Word Options button on the Office Button menu, clicking Advanced in the left pane of the Word Options dialog box, verifying the 'Allow text to be dragged and dropped' check box is selected, and then clicking the OK button.

The following steps move the selected sentence so that it becomes the last sentence in the paragraph.

- With the mouse pointer in the selected text, press and hold down the mouse button (Figure 2–65).

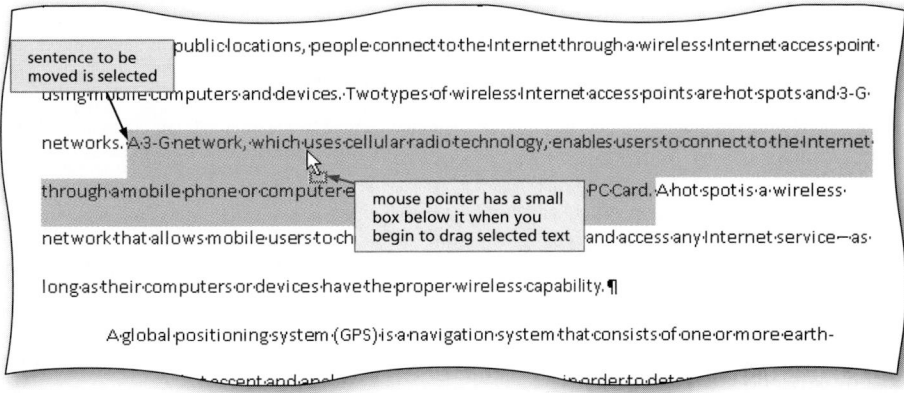

Figure 2–65

- Drag the mouse pointer to the location where the selected text is to be moved, as shown in Figure 2–66.

- Release the mouse button to move the selected text to the location of the mouse pointer.

- Click outside the selected text to remove the selection (Figure 2–67).

Q&A What if I accidentally drag text to the wrong location?

Click the Undo button on the Quick Access Toolbar and try again.

Q&A Can I use drag-and-drop editing to move any selected item?

Yes, you can select words, sentences, phrases, and graphics and then use drag-and-drop editing to move them.

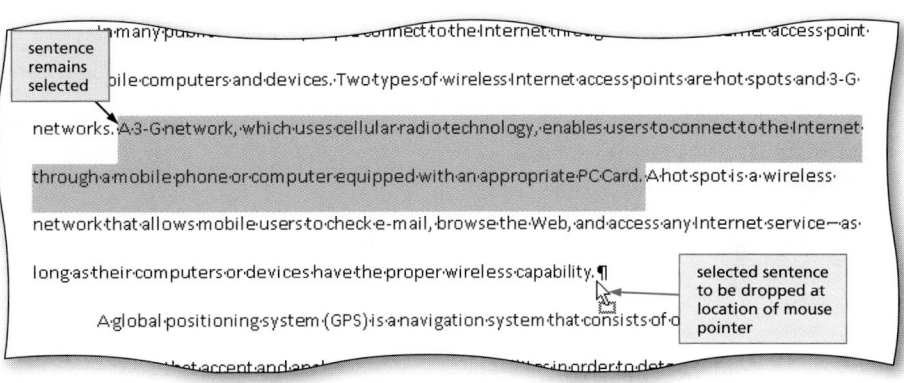

Figure 2–66

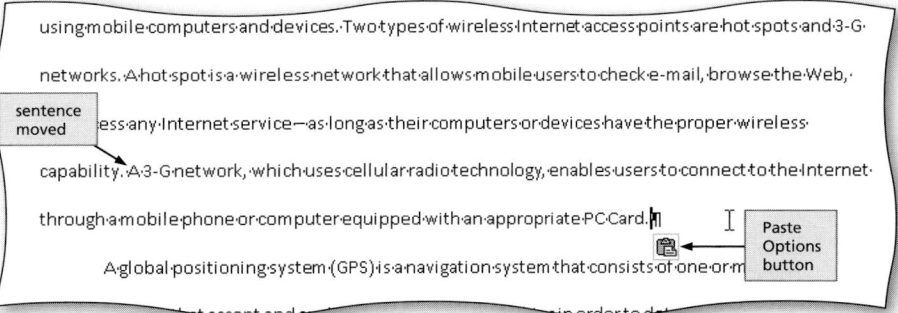

Figure 2–67

Other Ways

1. Click Cut button on Home tab, click where text is to be pasted, click Paste button on Home tab
2. Right-click selected text, click Cut on shortcut menu, right-click where text is to be pasted, click Paste on shortcut menu
3. Press CTRL+X, position insertion point where text is to be pasted, press CTRL+V

To Display the Paste Options Menu

When you drag-and-drop text, Word automatically displays a Paste Options button near the location of the drag-and-dropped text (Figure 2–67 on the previous page). If you click the **Paste Options button**, a menu appears that allows you to change the format of the item that was moved. The following steps display the Paste Options menu.

- Click the Paste Options button to display the Paste Options menu (Figure 2–68).

Q&A

What is the purpose of the commands on the Paste Options menu?

In general, the first command indicates the pasted text should look the same as it did in its original location. The second command formats the pasted text to match the rest of the text where it was pasted. The third command removes all formatting from the pasted text. The last command displays the Word Options dialog box.

- Press the ESCAPE key to remove the Paste Options menu from the window.

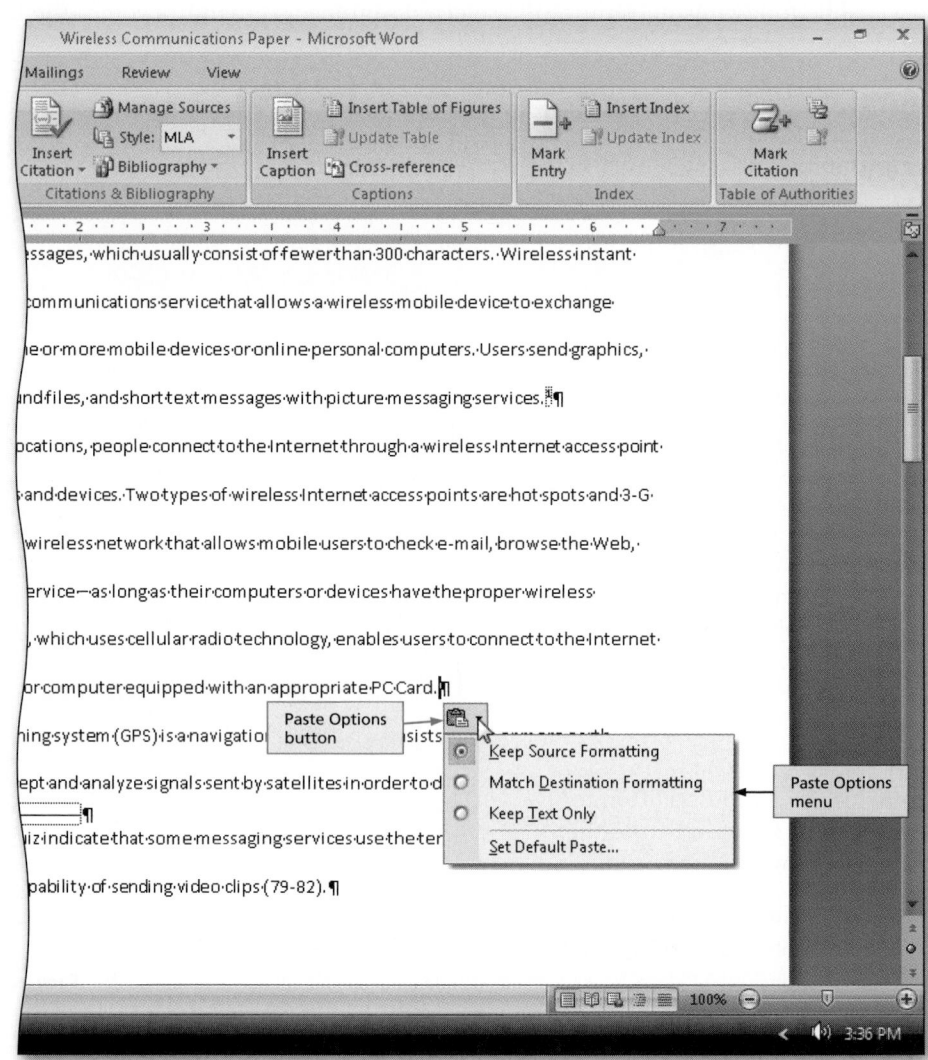

Figure 2–68

BTW

Dragging-and-Dropping
If you hold down the CTRL key while dragging a selected item, Word copies the item instead of moving it.

To Find and Replace Text

While proofreading the paper, you notice that you typed 3-G in the third paragraph (Figure 2–69). You prefer to use 3G, instead. Therefore, you need to change all occurrences of 3-G to 3G. To do this, you can use Word's find and replace feature, which automatically locates each occurrence of a word or phrase and then replaces it with specified text. The following steps use Find and Replace to replace all occurrences of 3-G with 3G.

1
- Click Home on the Ribbon to display the Home tab.

- Click the Replace button on the Home tab to display the Find and Replace dialog box.

- Type 3-G in the Find what text box.

- Press the TAB key. Type 3G in the Replace with text box (Figure 2–69).

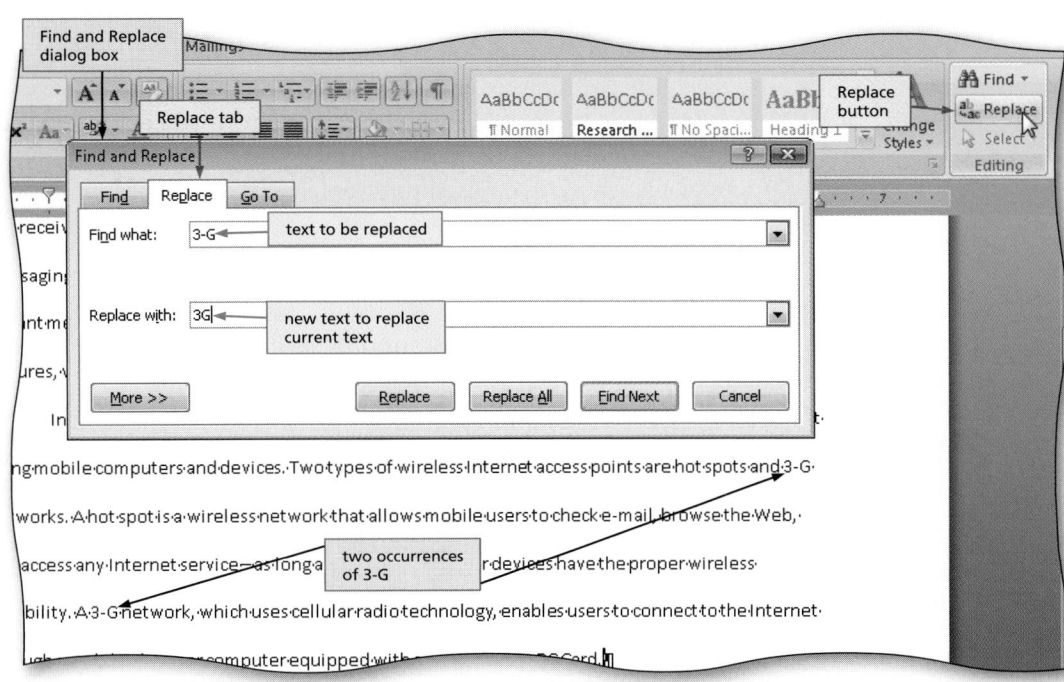

Figure 2–69

2
- Click the Replace All button in the Find and Replace dialog box to instruct Word to replace all occurrences of the Find what text with the Replace with text (Figure 2–70).

3
- Click the OK button in the Microsoft Office Word dialog box.

- Click the Close button in the Find and Replace dialog box.

Other Ways

1. Click Select Browse Object button on vertical scroll bar, click Find icon, click Replace tab
2. Click Page Number indicator on status bar, click Replace tab in dialog box
3. Press CTRL+H

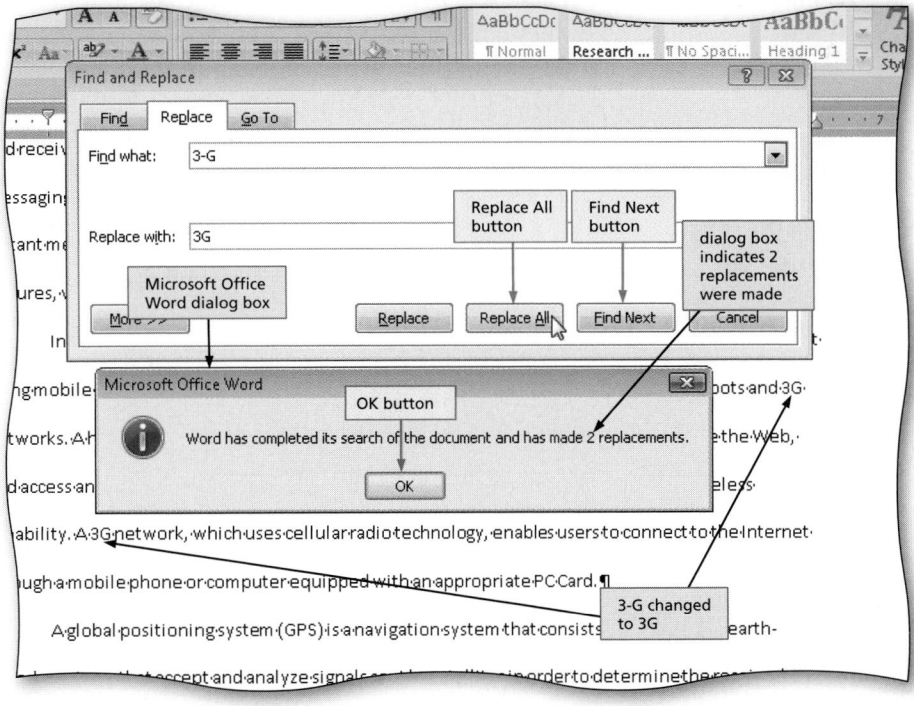

Figure 2–70

Find and Replace Dialog Box

The Replace All button in the Find and Replace dialog box replaces all occurrences of the Find what text with the Replace with text. In some cases, you may want to replace only certain occurrences of a word or phrase, not all of them. To instruct Word to confirm each change, click the Find Next button in the Find and Replace dialog box (Figure 2–70 on the previous page), instead of the Replace All button. When Word locates an occurrence of the text, it pauses and waits for you to click either the Replace button or the Find Next button. Clicking the Replace button changes the text; clicking the Find Next button instructs Word to disregard the replacement and look for the next occurrence of the Find what text.

If you accidentally replace the wrong text, you can undo a replacement by clicking the Undo button on the Standard toolbar. If you used the Replace All button, Word undoes all replacements. If you used the Replace button, Word undoes only the most recent replacement.

To Find Text

BTW

Finding Formatting
To search for formatting or a special character, click the More button in the Find dialog box. To find formatting, use the Format button in the Find dialog box. To find a special character, use the Special button.

Sometimes, you may want only to find text, instead of finding and replacing text. To search for just a single occurrence of text, you would follow these steps.

1. Click the Find button on the Home tab; or click the Select Browse Object button on the vertical scroll bar and then click the Find icon on the Select Browse Object menu; or click the page indicator on the status bar and then click the Find tab; or press CTRL+F.

2. Type the text to locate in the Find what text box and then click the Find Next button. To edit the text, click the Cancel button in the Find and Replace dialog box; to find the next occurrence of the text, click the Find Next button.

To Find and Insert a Synonym

When writing, you may discover that you used the same word in multiple locations or that a word you used was not quite appropriate. In these instances, you will want to look up a **synonym**, or a word similar in meaning, to the duplicate or inappropriate word. A **thesaurus** is a book of synonyms. Word provides synonyms and a thesaurus for your convenience.

In this project, you would like a synonym for the word, proper, in the third paragraph of the research paper. The following steps show how to find a suitable synonym.

- Locate and then right-click the word for which you want to find a synonym (in this case, proper) to display a shortcut menu related to the word you right-clicked.

- Point to Synonyms on the shortcut menu to display a list of synonyms for the word you right-clicked (Figure 2–71).

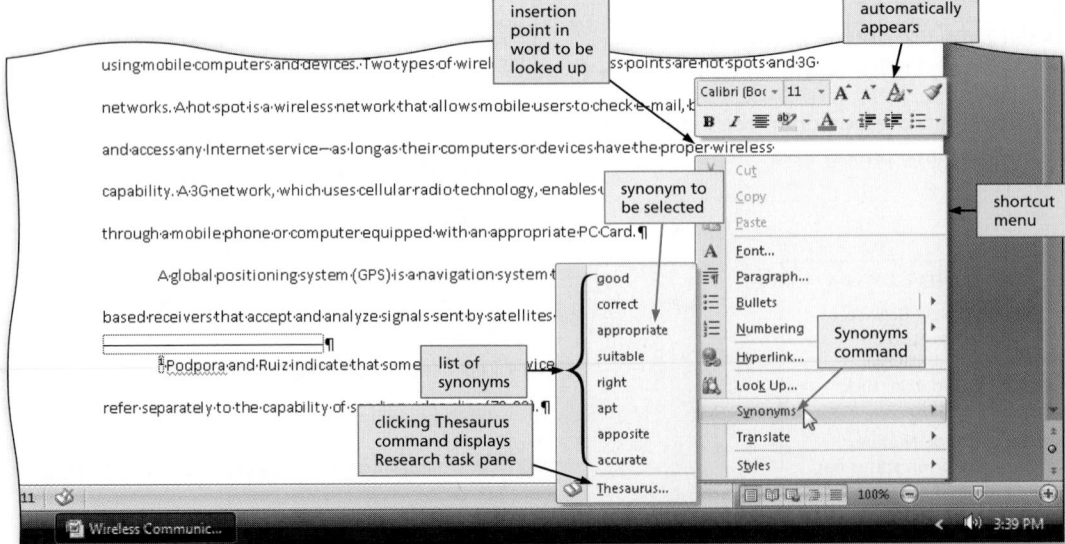

Figure 2–71

2

- Click the synonym you want (appropriate) on the Synonyms submenu to replace the word, proper, in the document with the word, appropriate (Figure 2–72).

Q&A

What if the synonyms list on the shortcut menu does not display a suitable word?

You can display the thesaurus in the Research task pane by clicking Thesaurus on the Synonyms submenu. The Research task pane displays a complete thesaurus, in which you can look up synonyms for various meanings of a word. You also can look up an **antonym**, or word with an opposite meaning. The Research task pane is discussed later in this chapter.

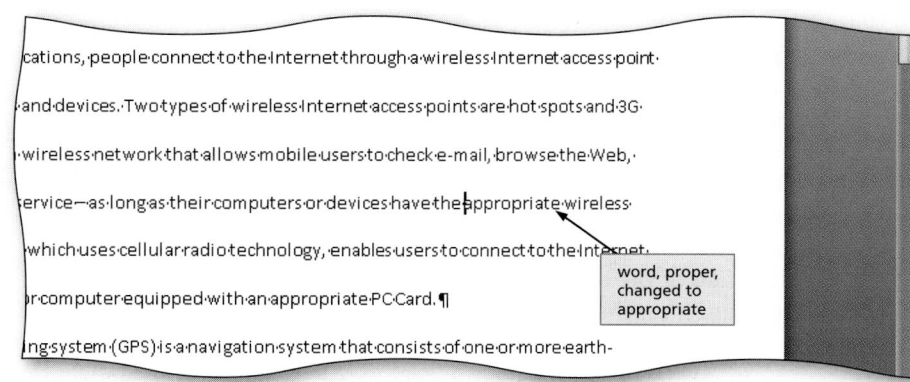

Figure 2–72

Other Ways	
1. Click Thesaurus on Review tab	2. Press SHIFT+F7

To Check Spelling and Grammar at Once

As discussed in Chapter 1, Word checks spelling and grammar as you type and places a wavy underline below possible spelling or grammar errors. Chapter 1 illustrated how to check these flagged words immediately. As an alternative, you can wait and check the entire document for spelling and grammar errors at once.

Note: In the following example the word, world, has been misspelled intentionally as wrld to illustrate the use of Word's check spelling and grammar at once feature. If you are completing this project on a personal computer, your research paper may contain different misspelled words, depending on the accuracy of your typing.

1

- Press CTRL+HOME because you want the spelling and grammar check to begin from the top of the document.

- Click Review on the Ribbon to display the Review tab.

- Click the Spelling & Grammar button on the Review tab to begin the spelling and grammar check at the location of the insertion point, which in this case, is at the beginning of the document (Figure 2–73).

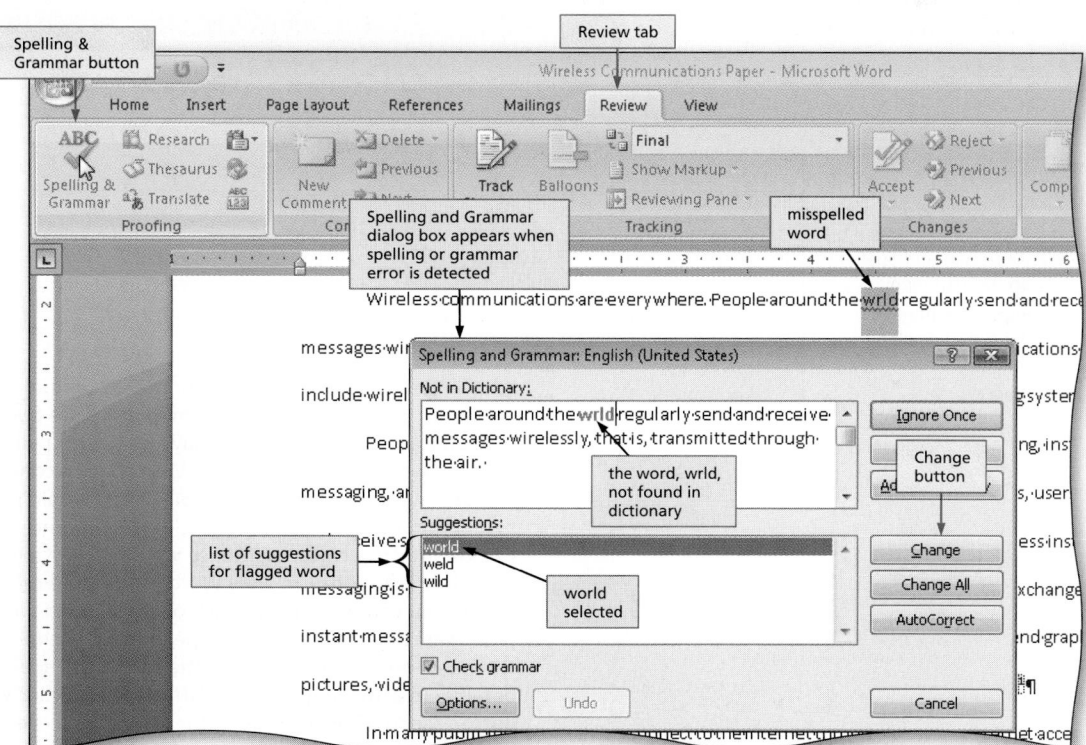

Figure 2–73

- With the word, world, selected in the Suggestions list, click the Change button in the Spelling and Grammar dialog box to change the flagged word, wrld, to the selected suggestion, world, and then continue the spelling and grammar check until the next error is identified or the end of the document is reached (Figure 2–74).

- Click the Ignore All button in the Spelling and Grammar dialog box to ignore this and future occurrences of the flagged proper noun and then continue the spelling and grammar check until the next error is identified or the end of the document is reached.

4

- When Word flags the proper noun, Podpora, click the Ignore All button.

- When the spelling and grammar check is finished and Word displays a dialog box, click its OK button.

Q&A
Can I check spelling of just a section of a document?

Yes, select the text before starting the spelling and grammar check.

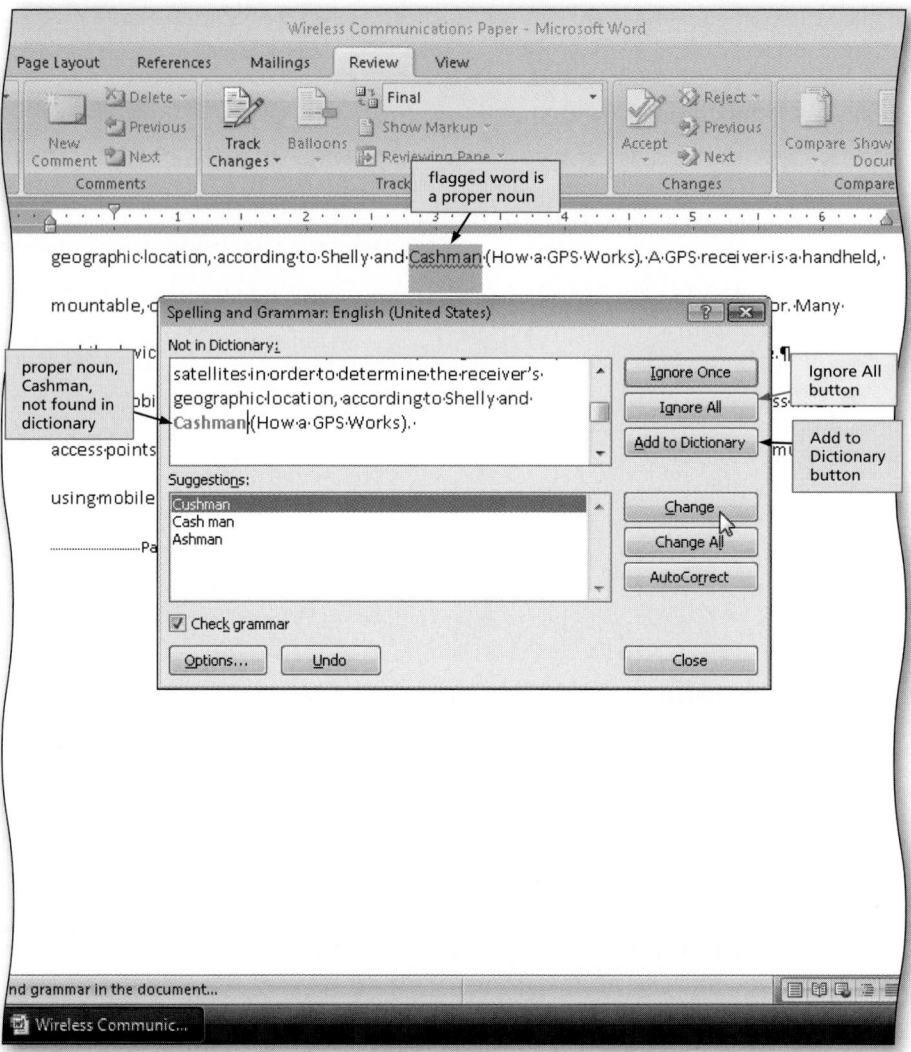

Figure 2–74

Other Ways

1. Click Spelling and Grammar Check icon on status bar, click Spelling on shortcut menu
2. Right-click flagged word, click Spelling on shortcut menu
3. Press F7

BTW

Contextual Spelling Errors
You can instruct Word to check for misuse of homophones and other types of contextual spelling errors. (Homophones are two or more words that are pronounced the same but that have different spellings or meanings, such as one and won.) With this feature, Word flags a contextual spelling error with a blue wavy underline. For example, Word would place a blue wavy underline below the words, one and knight, in this sentence: The team one the game last knight. (The correct sentence would be written as follows: The team won the game last night.) To view Word's suggested replacements for the flagged words, you could right-click each of the flagged words or start the spelling and grammar check by clicking the Spelling & Grammar button on the Review tab. On many installations of Word, the contextual spelling check is not activated by default. To activate it, click the Office Button, click Word Options on the Office Button menu, click Proofing in the left pane, place a check mark in the 'Use contextual spelling' check box, and then click the OK button.

The Main and Custom Dictionaries

As shown in the previous steps, Word may flag a proper noun as an error because the proper noun is not in its main dictionary. To prevent Word from flagging proper nouns as errors, you can add the proper nouns to the custom dictionary. To add a correctly spelled word to the custom dictionary, click the Add to Dictionary button in the Spelling and Grammar dialog box (Figure 2–74) or right-click the flagged word and then click Add to Dictionary on the shortcut menu. Once you have added a word to the custom dictionary, Word no longer will flag it as an error.

TO VIEW OR MODIFY ENTRIES IN A CUSTOM DICTIONARY

To view or modify the list of words in a custom dictionary, you would follow these steps.

1. Click the Office Button and then click the Word Options button.

2. Click Proofing in the left pane of the Word Options dialog box.

3. Click the Custom Dictionaries button.

4. When Word displays the Custom Dictionaries dialog box, place a check mark next to the dictionary name to view or modify. Click the Edit Word List button. (In this dialog box, you can add or delete entries to and from the selected custom dictionary.)

5. When finished viewing and/or modifying the list, click the OK button in the dialog box.

6. Click the OK button in the Custom Dictionaries dialog box.

7. If the 'Suggest from main dictionary only' check box is selected in the Word Options dialog box, remove the check mark. Click the OK button in the Word Options dialog box.

TO SET THE DEFAULT CUSTOM DICTIONARY

If you have multiple custom dictionaries, you can specify which one Word should use when checking spelling. To set the default custom dictionary, you would follow these steps.

1. Click the Office Button and then click the Word Options button.

2. Click Proofing in the left pane of the Word Options dialog box.

3. Click the Custom Dictionaries button.

4. When the Custom Dictionaries dialog box is displayed, place a check mark next to the desired dictionary name. Click the Change Default button.

5. Click the OK button in the Custom Dictionaries dialog box.

6. If the 'Suggest from main dictionary only' check box is selected in the Word Options dialog box, remove the check mark. Click the OK button in the Word Options dialog box.

To Use the Research Task Pane to Look Up Information

From within Word, you can search through various forms of reference information. Earlier, this chapter discussed the Research task pane with respect to looking up a synonym in a thesaurus. Other services available in the Research task pane include a dictionary and if you are connected to the Web, an encyclopedia, a search engine, and other Web sites that provide information such as stock quotes, news articles, and company profiles.

Assume you want to know more about the acronym, PDA. The following steps use the Research task pane to look up information about a word.

- Locate the word you want to look up.

- While holding down the ALT key, click the word you want to look up (in this case, PDAs) to open the Research task pane and display a dictionary entry for the ALT+CLICKED word. Release the ALT key (Figure 2–75).

- If the Research task pane does not display a dictionary entry for the ALT+CLICKED word, click the Search for box arrow and then click All Reference Books.

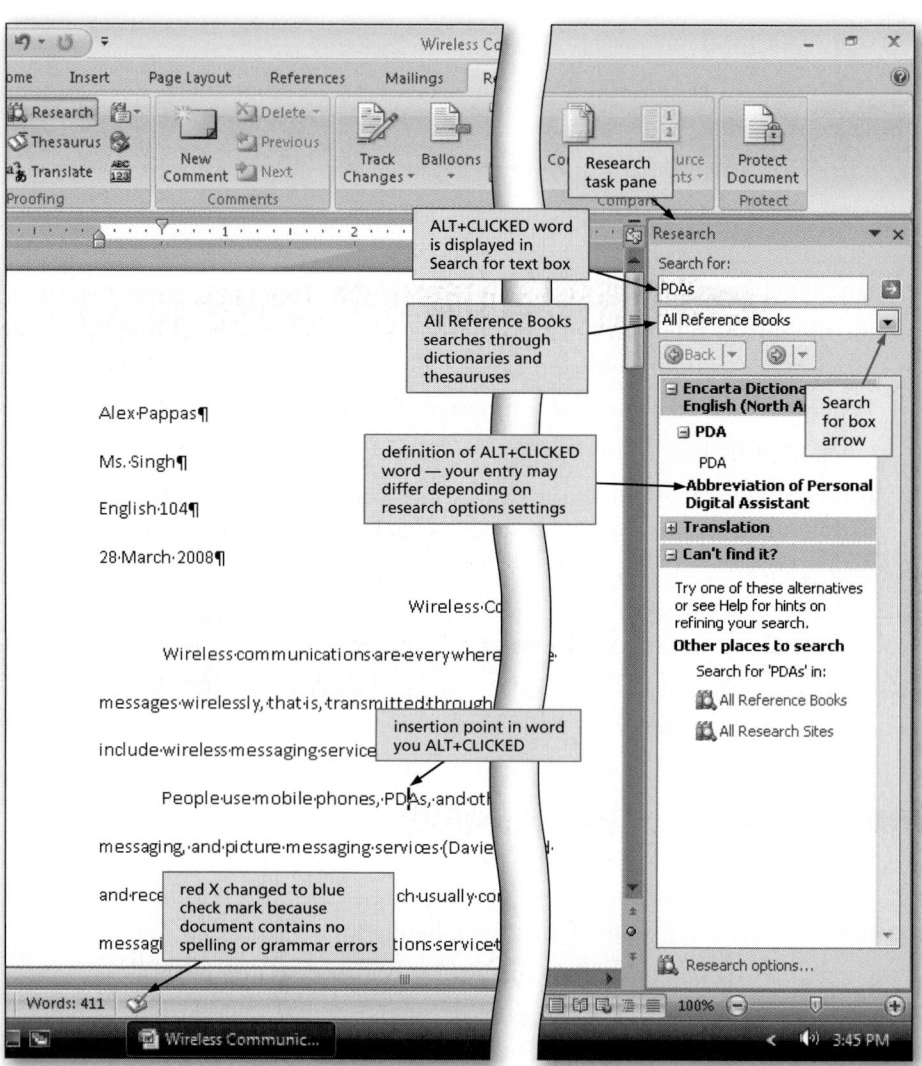

Figure 2–75

2
- Click the Search for box arrow and then click All Research Sites in the list to display Web sites with information about the ALT+CLICKED word (Figure 2–76).

Q&A Can I copy information from the Research task pane into my document?

Yes, you can use the Copy and Paste commands. When using Word to insert material from the Research task pane or any other online reference, however, be very careful not to plagiarize.

3
- Click the Close button in the Research task pane.

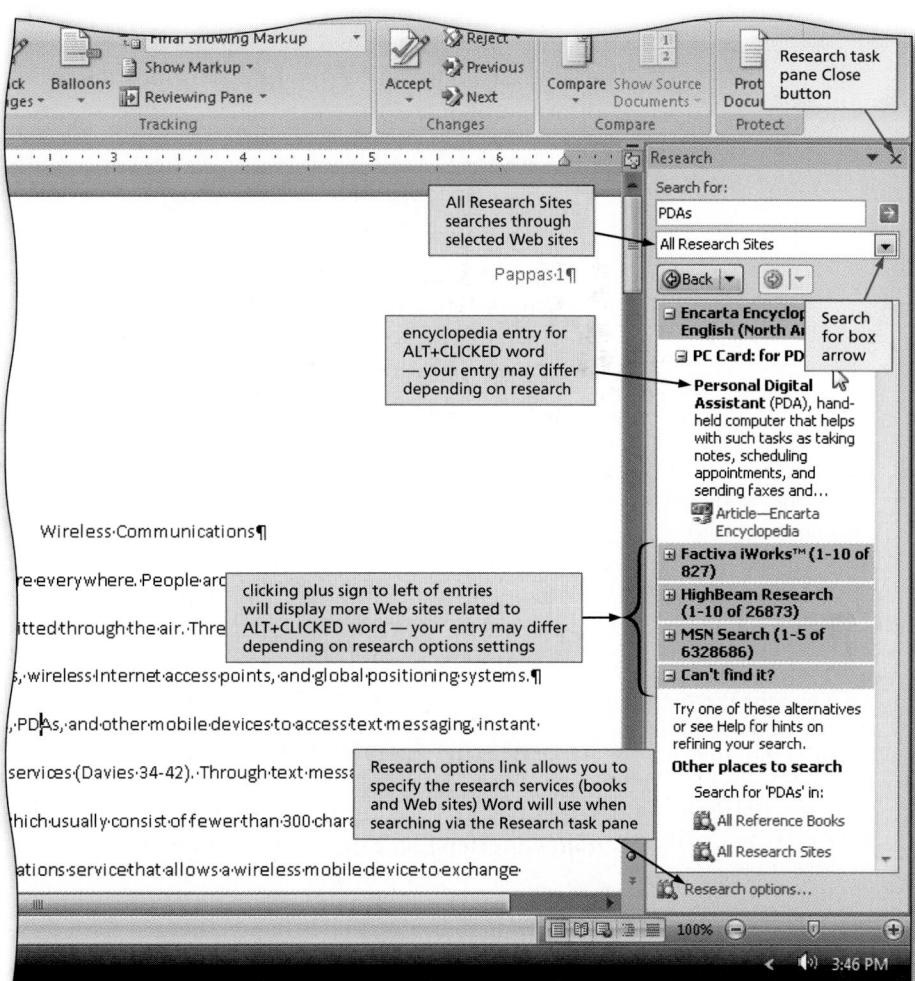

Figure 2–76

Other Ways

1. Click Research button on Review tab
2. Click Insert Citation button on References tab, click Search Libraries

Research Task Pane Options

When you install Word, it selects a series of services (reference books and Web sites) through which it searches when you use the Research task pane. You can view, modify, and update the list of services at any time.

Clicking the Research options link at the bottom of the Research task pane displays the Research Options dialog box, where you can view or modify the list of installed services. You can view information about any installed service by clicking the service in the list and then clicking the Properties button. To activate an installed service, click the check box to its left; likewise, to deactivate a service, remove the check mark. To add a particular Web site to the list, click the Add Services button, enter the Web address in the Address text box, and then click the Add button in the Add Services dialog box. To update or remove services, click the Update/Remove button, select the service in the list, click the Update (or Remove) button in the Update or Remove Services dialog box, and then click the Close button. You also can install parental controls through the Parental Control button in the Research Options dialog box, for example, if you want to restrict Web access from minor children who use Word.

To Change Document Properties

Before saving the research paper again, you want to add your name, course information, and some keywords as document properties. The following steps use the Document Information Panel to change document properties.

1 Click the Office Button to display the Office Button menu, point to Prepare on the Office Button menu, and then click Properties on the Prepare submenu to display the Document Information Panel.

2 Click the Author text box, if necessary, and then type your name as the Author property. If a name already is displayed in the Author text box, delete it before typing your name.

3 Click the Subject text box, if necessary delete any existing text, and then type your course and section as the Subject property.

4 Click the Keywords text box, if necessary delete any existing text, and then type `instant messaging, Internet access points, global positioning systems` as the Keywords property.

5 Click the Close the Document Information Panel button so that the Document Information Panel no longer is displayed.

BTW

Conserving Ink and Toner
You can instruct Word to print draft quality documents to conserve ink or toner by clicking the Office Button, clicking the Word Options button, clicking Advanced in the left pane of the Word Options dialog box, scrolling to the Print area, placing a check mark in the 'Use draft quality' check box, and then clicking the OK button. Click the Office Button, point to Print, and then click Quick Print.

To Save an Existing Document with the Same File Name

The document now is complete. You should save the research paper again. The following step saves the document again.

1 Click the Save button on the Quick Access Toolbar to overwrite the previous Wireless Communications Paper file on the USB flash drive.

To Print Document Properties and then the Document

With the document properties entered and the completed document saved, you may want to print the document properties along with the document. The following steps print the document properties, followed by the contents of the saved Wireless Communications Paper project.

1

• Click the Office Button to display the Office Button menu and then point to Print on the Office Button menu to display the Print submenu (Figure 2–77).

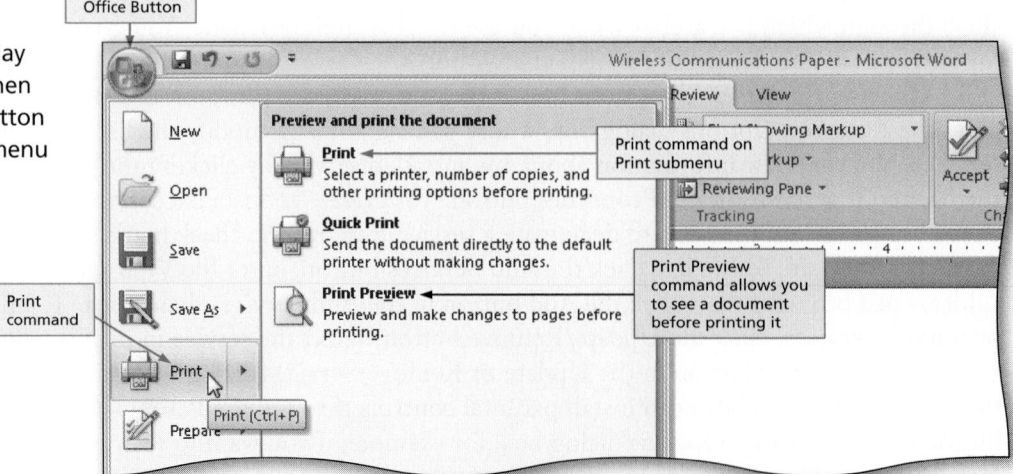

Figure 2–77

2

- Click Print on the Print submenu to display the Print dialog box.

- Click the Print what box arrow and then click Document properties to instruct Word to print the document properties instead of the document (Figure 2–78).

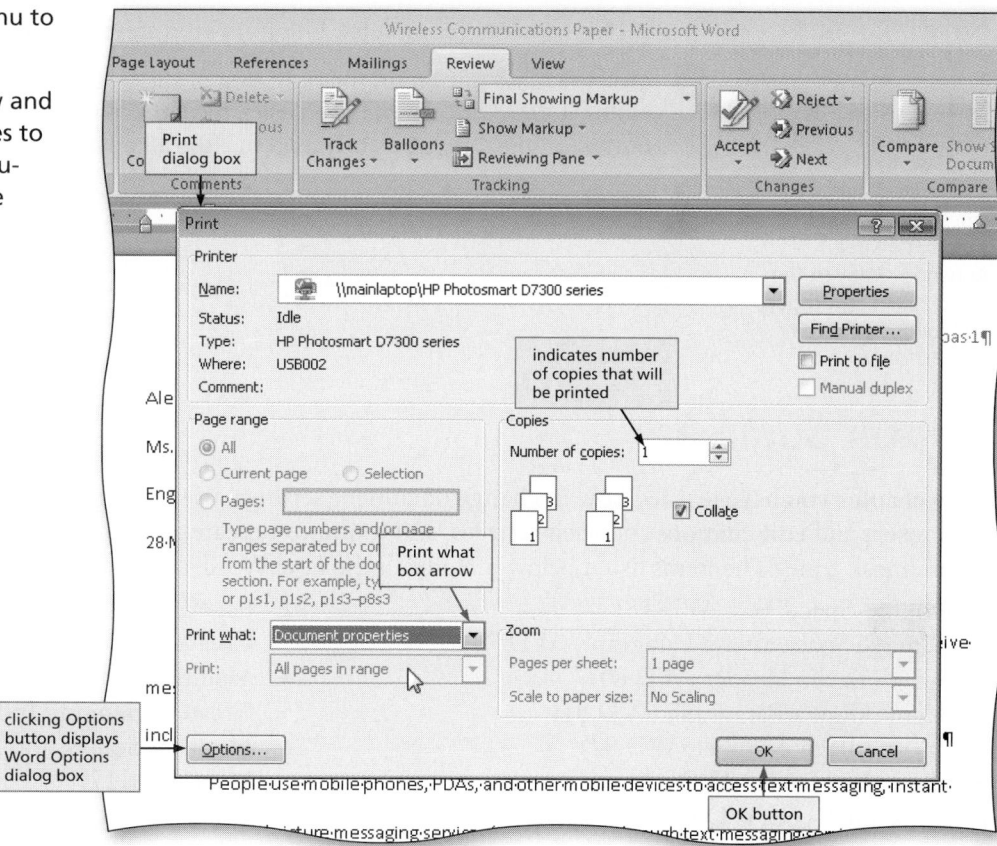

Figure 2–78

3

- Click the OK button to print the document properties (Figure 2–79).

4

- Click the Office Button again to display the Office Button menu, point to Print on the Office Button menu, and then click Quick Print on the Print submenu to print the research paper (shown in Figure 2–1 on page WD 75).

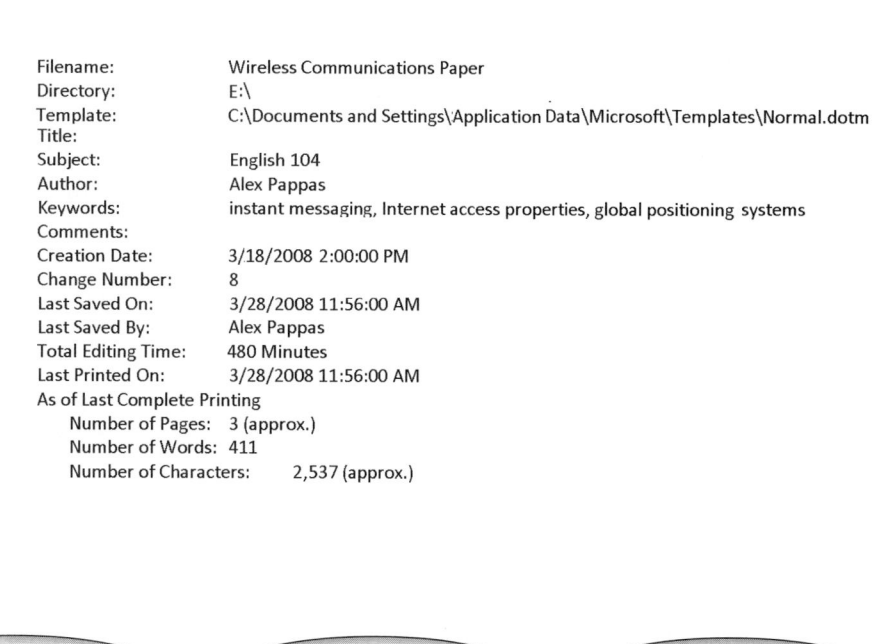

Filename:	Wireless Communications Paper
Directory:	E:\
Template:	C:\Documents and Settings\Application Data\Microsoft\Templates\Normal.dotm
Title:	
Subject:	English 104
Author:	Alex Pappas
Keywords:	instant messaging, Internet access properties, global positioning systems
Comments:	
Creation Date:	3/18/2008 2:00:00 PM
Change Number:	8
Last Saved On:	3/28/2008 11:56:00 AM
Last Saved By:	Alex Pappas
Total Editing Time:	480 Minutes
Last Printed On:	3/28/2008 11:56:00 AM

As of Last Complete Printing
    Number of Pages: 3 (approx.)
    Number of Words: 411
    Number of Characters: 2,537 (approx.)

printed document properties — your properties may differ, depending on settings

Figure 2–79

BTW

Certification
The Microsoft Certified Application Specialist (MCAS) program provides an opportunity for you to obtain a valuable industry credential — proof that you have the Word 2007 skills required by employers. For more information, see Appendix G or visit the Word 2007 Certification Web page (scsite.com/wd2007/cert).

To Quit Word

This project is complete. The following steps quit Word.

1 Click the Close button on the right side of the title bar to quit Word; or if you have multiple Word documents open, click the Office Button and then click the Exit Word button on the Office Button menu to close all open documents and quit Word.

2 If necessary, click the Yes button in the Microsoft Office Word dialog box so that any changes you have made are saved.

Chapter Summary

In this chapter you have learned how to change document settings, use headers to number pages, create and modify styles, insert and edit citations and their sources, add footnotes, create a bibliographical list of sources, and use the Research task pane. The items listed below include all the new Word skills you have learned in this chapter.

1. Double-Space Text (WD 78)
2. Remove Space after a Paragraph (WD 79)
3. Switch to the Header (WD 80)
4. Right-Align a Paragraph (WD 81)
5. Insert a Page Number (WD 82)
6. Close the Header (WD 83)
7. Click and Type (WD 85)
8. Display the Rulers (WD 87)
9. First-Line Indent Paragraphs (WD 88)
10. Create a Quick Style (WD 90)
11. AutoCorrect as You Type (WD 91)
12. Use the AutoCorrect Options Button (WD 92)
13. Create an AutoCorrect Entry (WD 93)
14. Change the Bibliography Style (WD 95)
15. Insert a Citation and Create Its Source (WD 96)
16. Edit a Citation (WD 98)
17. Insert a Footnote Reference Mark (WD 100)
18. Insert a Citation Placeholder (WD 101)
19. Modify a Style Using a Shortcut Menu (WD 102)
20. Edit a Source (WD 104)
21. Count Words (WD 107)
22. Page Break Manually (WD 112)
23. Create the Bibliographical List (WD 113)
24. Modify a Style Using the Styles Task Pane (WD 114)
25. Create a Hanging Indent (WD 116)
26. Modify a Source and Update the Bibliographical List (WD 117)
27. Use the Select Browse Object Menu (WD 118)
28. Select a Sentence (WD 120)
29. Move Selected Text (WD 121)
30. Display the Paste Options Menu (WD 122)
31. Find and Replace Text (WD 123)
32. Find Text (WD 124)
33. Find and Insert a Synonym (WD 124)
34. Check Spelling and Grammar at Once (WD 125)
35. View or Modify Entries in a Custom Dictionary (WD 127)
36. Set the Default Custom Dictionary (WD 127)
37. Use the Research Task Pane to Look Up Information (WD 128)
38. Print Document Properties and then the Document (WD 130)

If you have a SAM user profile, you may have access to hands-on instruction, practice, and assessment. Log in to your SAM account (http://sam2007.course.com) to launch any assigned training activities or exams that relate to the skills covered in this chapter.

BTW

Quick Reference
For a table that lists how to complete the tasks covered in this book using the mouse, Ribbon, shortcut menu, and keyboard, see the Quick Reference Summary at the back of this book, or visit the Word 2007 Quick Reference Web page (scsite.com/wd2007/qr).

Learn It Online

Test your knowledge of chapter content and key terms.

Instructions: To complete the Learn It Online exercises, start your browser, click the Address bar, and then enter the Web address scsite.com/wd2007/learn. When the Word 2007 Learn It Online page is displayed, click the link for the exercise you want to complete and then read the instructions.

Chapter Reinforcement TF, MC, and SA
A series of true/false, multiple choice, and short answer questions that test your knowledge of the chapter content.

Flash Cards
An interactive learning environment where you identify chapter key terms associated with displayed definitions.

Practice Test
A series of multiple choice questions that test your knowledge of chapter content and key terms.

Who Wants To Be a Computer Genius?
An interactive game that challenges your knowledge of chapter content in the style of a television quiz show.

Wheel of Terms
An interactive game that challenges your knowledge of chapter key terms in the style of the television show *Wheel of Fortune*.

Crossword Puzzle Challenge
A crossword puzzle that challenges your knowledge of key terms presented in the chapter.

Apply Your Knowledge

Reinforce the skills and apply the concepts you learned in this chapter.

Revising Text and Paragraphs in a Document

Instructions: Start Word. Open the document, Apply 2-1 Software Paragraphs Draft, from the Data Files for Students. See the inside back cover of this book for instructions on downloading the Data Files for Students, or contact your instructor for information about accessing the required files.

The document you open has a header and three paragraphs of text. You are to revise the document as follows: move a paragraph, move a word and change the format of the moved word, change paragraph indentation, change line spacing and paragraph spacing, replace all occurrences of a word with another word, and edit the header.

Perform the following tasks:

1. Select the last (third) paragraph. Use drag-and-drop editing to move this paragraph, so that it is the second paragraph in the document.

2. Select the underlined word, effectively, in the second sentence of the first paragraph. Use drag-and-drop editing to move the selected word, effectively, so that it follows the word, software, in the same sentence. Click the Paste Options button that displays to the right of the moved word, effectively. Remove the underline format from the moved sentence by clicking Keep Text Only on the shortcut menu.

3. Select the three paragraphs of text in the document.

4. Display the ruler, if necessary. With the paragraphs selected, use the ruler to indent the first line of the selected paragraphs one-half inch.

5. With the paragraphs still selected, change the line spacing of the selected paragraphs from single to double.

Continued >

Apply Your Knowledge *continued*

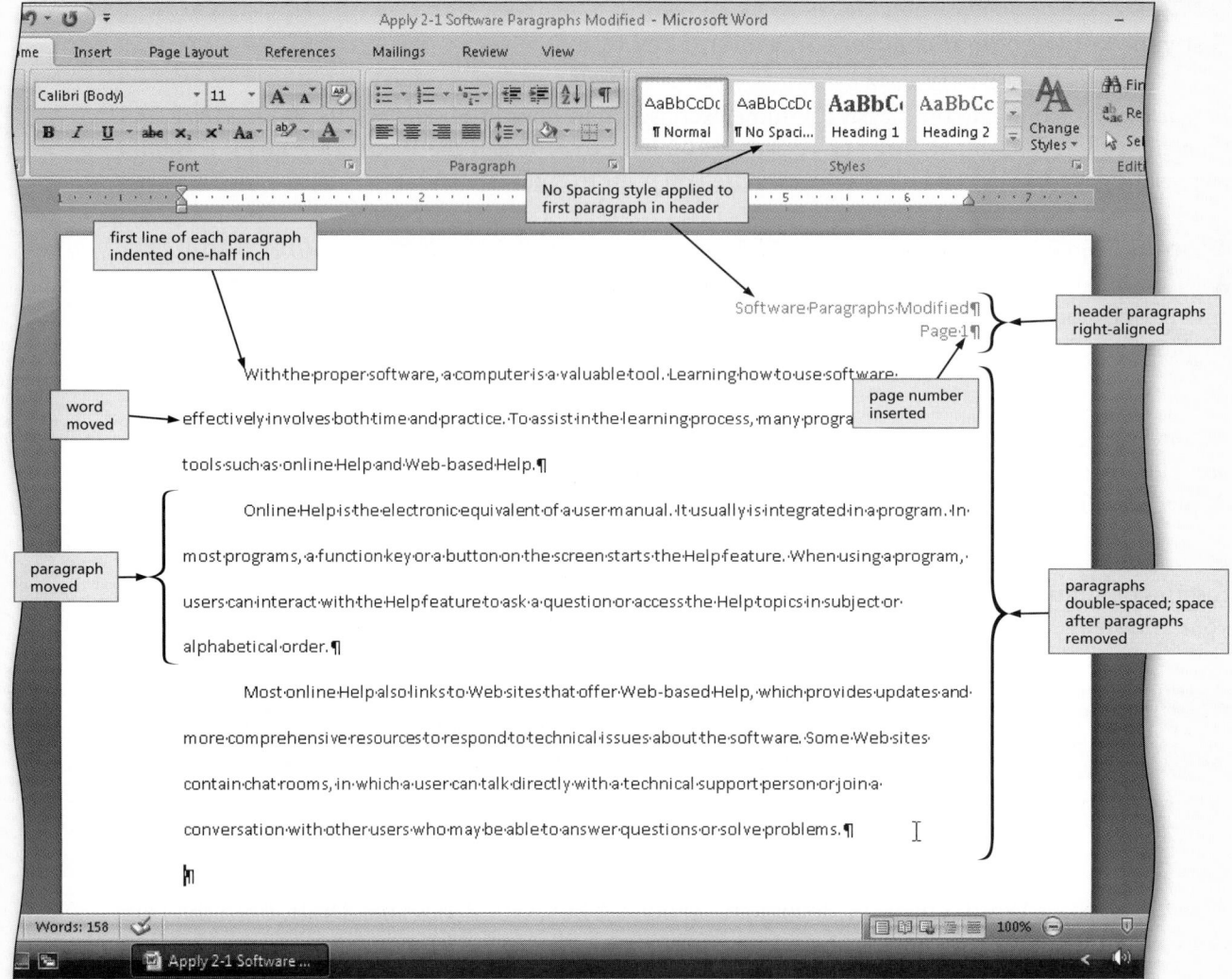

Figure 2–80

6. With the paragraphs still selected, use Line spacing box arrow to remove extra space below (after) the paragraphs. Click anywhere to remove the selection.

7. Use the Find and Replace dialog box to replace all occurrences of the word, Internet, with the word, Web. How many replacements were made?

8. Use the Find dialog box to locate the word, incorporated. Use Word's thesaurus to change the word, incorporated, to the word, integrated, in the first sentence of the second paragraph.

9. Switch to the header so that you can edit it. In the first line of the header, change the word, Draft, to the word, Modified, so that it reads: Software Paragraphs Modified. Change the first line of the header from the Normal style to the No Spacing style.

10. In the second line of the header, insert the page number (with no formatting) one space after the word, Page.

11. Change the alignment of both lines of text in the header from left-aligned to right-aligned. Switch back to the document text.

12. Change the document properties, as specified by your instructor.

13. Click the Office Button and then click Save As. Save the document using the file name, Apply 2-1 Software Paragraphs Modified.

14. Print the document properties and then print the revised document, shown in Figure 2–80.

15. Use the Research task pane to look up the definition of the word, online, in the first sentence of the second paragraph. Handwrite the COMPUTING definition of the word, online, on your printout.

16. Display the Research Options dialog box and on your printout, handwrite the currently active Reference Books, Research Sites, and Business and Financial Sites. If your instructor approves, activate one of the services.

Extend Your Knowledge

Extend the skills you learned in this chapter and experiment with new skills. You may need to use Help to complete the assignment.

Working with References and Proofing Tools

Instructions: Start Word. Open the document, Extend 2-1 Computing Options Paper Draft, from the Data Files for Students. See the inside back cover of this book for instructions on downloading the Data Files for Students, or contact your instructor for information on accessing the required files.

You will add another footnote to the paper, use the thesaurus, convert the document from MLA to APA style, convert the footnotes to endnotes, modify the Endnote Text style, change the format of the note reference marks, and translate the document to another language.

Perform the following tasks:

1. Insert a second footnote at an appropriate place in the research paper. Use the following footnote text: The Americans with Disabilities Act (ADA) requires any company with 15 or more employees to make reasonable attempts to accommodate the needs of physically challenged workers.

2. Use the Replace dialog box to find the word, imagine, in the document and then replace it with a word of your choice.

3. Save the document with a new file name and then print it. Select the entire document and then change the style of the citations and bibliography from MLA to APA. Save the APA version of the document with a new file name and then print it. Compare the two versions. Circle the differences between the two documents.

4. Convert the footnotes to endnotes.

5. Modify the Endnote Text style to 11-point Calibri font, double-spaced text with a first-line indent.

6. Change the format of the note reference marks to capital letters (A, B, etc.).

7. Save the revised document with endnotes with a new file name and then print it. On the printout with the endnotes, write the number of words, characters without spaces, characters with spaces, paragraphs, and lines in the document. Be sure to include endnote text in the statistics.

8. Translate the research paper into a language of your choice (Figure 2–81 on the next page) using the Translate button on the Review tab. Print the translated document.

Continued >

Extend Your Knowledge *continued*

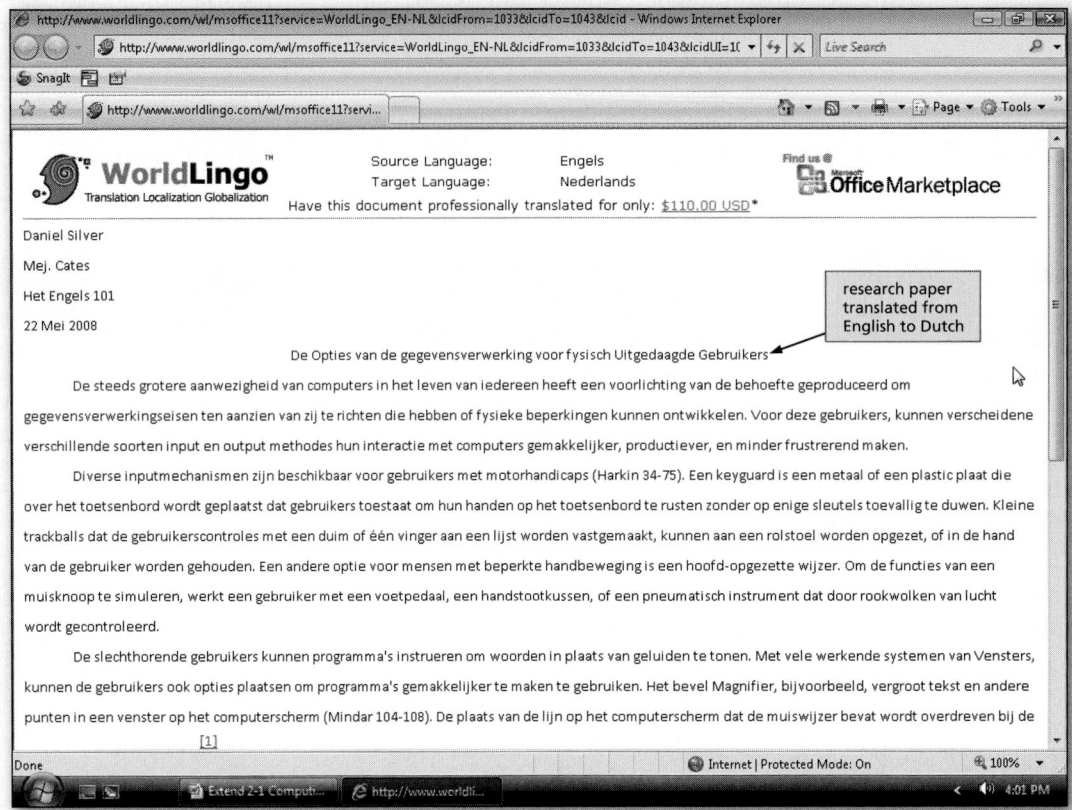

Figure 2–81

Make It Right

Analyze a document and correct all errors and/or improve the design.

Inserting Missing Elements in an MLA Style Research Paper

Instructions: Start Word. Open the document, Make It Right 2-1 Certification Paper Draft, from the Data Files for Students. See the inside back cover of this book for instructions on downloading the Data Files for Students, or contact your instructor for information on accessing the required files.

The document is a research paper that is missing several elements. You are to insert these missing elements, all formatted according to the MLA documentation style: header with a page number, heading (name, course, and date information), paper title, footnote, and source information for the first citation and the citation in the footnote.

Perform the following tasks:
1. Insert a header with a page number, heading (use your own information: name, course information, and date), and an appropriate paper title, all formatted according to the MLA style.
2. Use the Select Browse Object button to go to page 2. How many bibliographical entries currently are on the Works Cited page? You will create additional source entries in Steps 3 and 4.
3. The Otoole placeholder (tag name) is missing its source information (Figure 2–82). Use the following source information to edit the source: magazine article titled "Career Builders and Boosts," written by Sarah W. O'Toole, magazine name is *IT World and Certifications*, publication date is March 2008, article is on pages 88-93. Edit the citation so that it displays the author name and the page numbers.

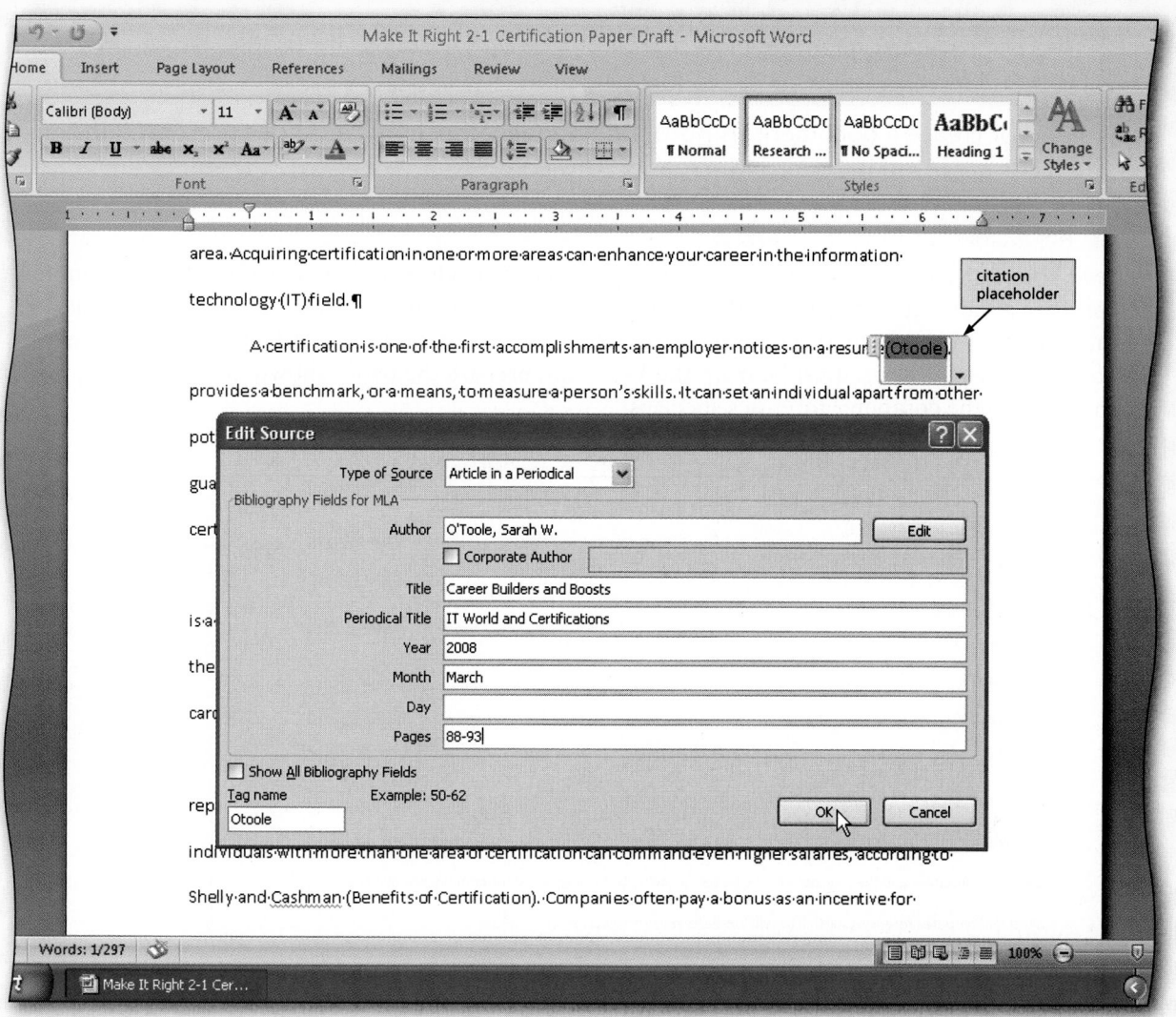

Figure 2–82

4. Insert the following footnote with the note reference at an appropriate place in the paper, formatted according to the MLA style: Debbins points out that, as an additional bonus, some certification training can be used for college credit. The citation for this footnote should be at the end of the footnote. The source information is as follows: book named *Preparing for the Future: IT Strategies*, authored by Floyd I. Debbins, published in 2008 at IT World Press in Chicago, pages 99-104. Edit the citation so that it displays only page numbers.

5. Use the Select Browse Object button to go to page 3. Be sure the bibliographical list on the Works Cited page contains all three entries. If necessary, use the F9 key to update the bibliographical list. Format the bibliographical paragraphs with a one-half inch hanging indent.

6. Modify the source of the book authored by Floyd I. Debbins, so that the publisher city is Boston instead of Chicago.

7. Use the Select Browse Object button to go to the footnote. Be sure the footnote is formatted properly.

8. Change the document properties, as specified by your instructor. Save the revised document with a new file name and then submit it in the format specified by your instructor.

In the Lab

Design and/or create a document using the guidelines, concepts, and skills presented in this chapter. Labs are listed in order of increasing difficulty.

Lab 1: Preparing a Short Research Paper

Problem: You are a college student currently enrolled in an introductory business class. Your assignment is to prepare a short research paper (300-350 words) about a computer-related job. The requirements are that the paper be presented according to the MLA documentation style and have three references. One of the three references must be from the Web. You prepare the paper shown in Figure 2–83, which discusses the computer forensics specialist.

Hankins 1

Mary Hankins

Mr. Habib

Business 102

14 March 2008

Computer Forensics Specialist

Computer forensics, also called digital forensics, network forensics, or cyberforensics, is a rapidly growing field that involves gathering and analyzing evidence from computers and networks. Because computers and the Internet are the fastest growing technology used for criminal activity, the need for computer forensics specialists will increase in years to come.

A computer forensics specialist examines computer media, programs, data, and log files on computers, servers, and networks. According to Shelly and Cashman (Computer Careers), many areas employ computer forensics specialists, including law enforcement, criminal prosecutors, military intelligence, insurance agencies, and information security departments in the private sector. A computer forensics specialist must have knowledge of the law, technical experience with many types of hardware and software products, superior communication skills, a willingness to learn and update skills, and a knack for problem solving.

When a problem occurs, it is the responsibility of the computer forensics specialist to carefully take several steps to identify and retrieve possible evidence that may exist on a suspect's computer. These steps include protecting the suspect's computer, discovering all files, recovering deleted files, revealing hidden files, accessing protected or encrypted files, analyzing all the data, and providing expert consultation and/or testimony as required (Reinman 52-58).

A computer forensics specialist must have knowledge of all aspects of the computer, from the operating system to computer architecture and hardware design. In the past, many computer forensics specialists were self-taught computer users. Today, extensive training, usually from several different

(a)

Figure 2–83

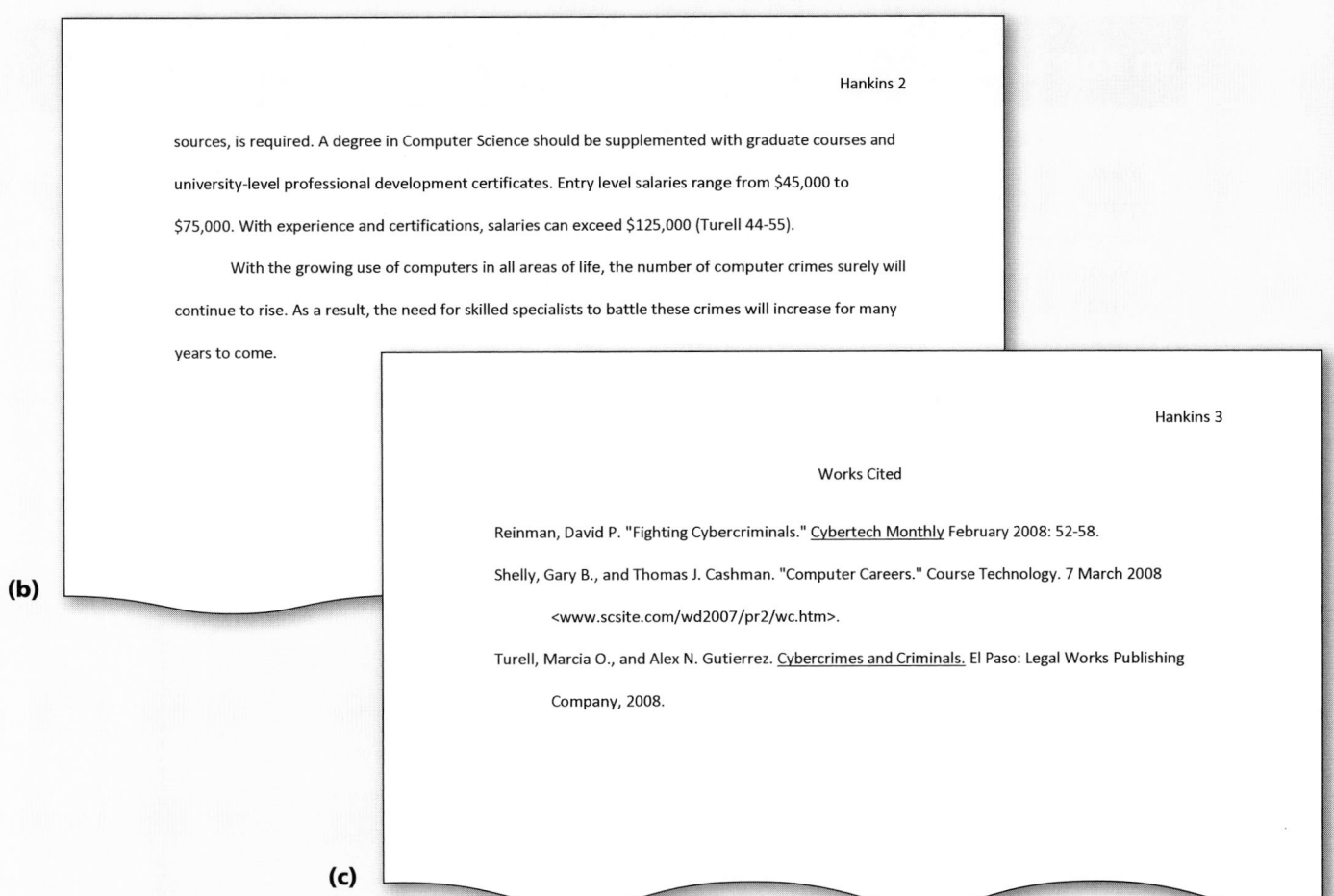

(b)

(c)

Figure 2–83 (continued)

Instructions: Perform the following tasks:

1. If necessary, display formatting marks on the screen.

2. Adjust line spacing to double.

3. Remove space below (after) paragraphs.

4. Create a header to number pages.

5. Type the name and course information at the left margin. Center and type the title.

6. Set first-line indent for paragraphs in the body of the research paper.

7. Create a Quick Style for the research paper paragraphs.

8. Type the research paper as shown in Figures 2–83a and 2–83b. Change the bibliography style to MLA. As you insert citations, enter their source information (shown in Figure 2–83c). Edit the citations so that they display according to Figures 2–83a and 2–83b.

9. At the end of the research paper text, press the ENTER key and then insert a manual page break so that the Works Cited page begins on a new page. Enter and format the works cited title (Figure 2–83c). Use Word to insert the bibliographical list (bibliography). Format the paragraphs in the list with a hanging indent.

10. Check the spelling and grammar of the paper at once.

11. Save the document on a USB flash drive using Lab 2-1 Computer Forensics Paper as the file name.

12. Print the research paper. Handwrite the number of words, paragraphs, and characters in the research paper above the title of your printed research paper.

In the Lab

Lab 2: Preparing a Research Report with a Footnote

Problem: You are a college student enrolled in an introductory English class. Your assignment is to prepare a short research paper in any area of interest to you. The requirements are that the paper be presented according to the MLA documentation style, contain at least one explanatory note positioned as a footnote, and have three references. One of the three references must be from the Internet. You prepare a paper about antivirus programs (Figure 2–84).

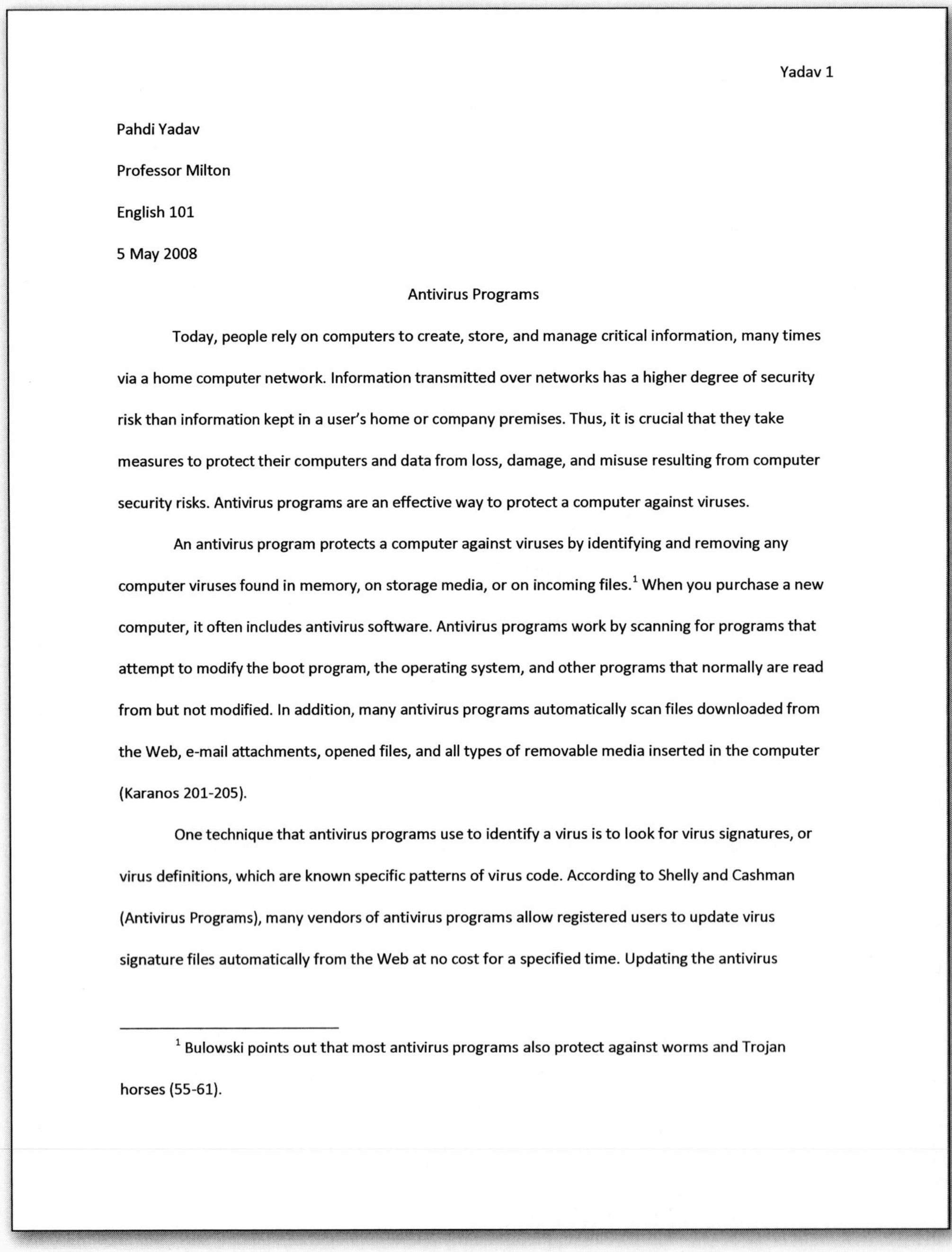

Yadav 1

Pahdi Yadav

Professor Milton

English 101

5 May 2008

Antivirus Programs

Today, people rely on computers to create, store, and manage critical information, many times via a home computer network. Information transmitted over networks has a higher degree of security risk than information kept in a user's home or company premises. Thus, it is crucial that they take measures to protect their computers and data from loss, damage, and misuse resulting from computer security risks. Antivirus programs are an effective way to protect a computer against viruses.

An antivirus program protects a computer against viruses by identifying and removing any computer viruses found in memory, on storage media, or on incoming files.[1] When you purchase a new computer, it often includes antivirus software. Antivirus programs work by scanning for programs that attempt to modify the boot program, the operating system, and other programs that normally are read from but not modified. In addition, many antivirus programs automatically scan files downloaded from the Web, e-mail attachments, opened files, and all types of removable media inserted in the computer (Karanos 201-205).

One technique that antivirus programs use to identify a virus is to look for virus signatures, or virus definitions, which are known specific patterns of virus code. According to Shelly and Cashman (Antivirus Programs), many vendors of antivirus programs allow registered users to update virus signature files automatically from the Web at no cost for a specified time. Updating the antivirus

_____

[1] Bulowski points out that most antivirus programs also protect against worms and Trojan horses (55-61).

(a)

Figure 2–84

Yadav 2

program's signature files regularly is important, because it will download any new virus definitions that

have been added since the last update.

Methods that guarantee a computer or network is safe from computer viruses simply do not

exist. Installing, updating, and using an antivirus program, though, is an effective technique to safeguard

your computer from loss.

(b)

Figure 2–84 (continued)

Instructions: Perform the following tasks:

1. Adjust line spacing to double and remove space below (after) paragraphs. Create a header to number pages. Type the name and course information at the left margin. Center and type the title. Set first-line indent for paragraphs in the body of the research paper. Create a Quick Style for the research paper paragraphs.

2. Type the research paper as shown in Figures 2–84a and 2–84b. Add the footnote as shown in Figure 2–84a. Change the Footnote Text style to the format specified in the MLA style. Change the bibliography style to MLA. As you insert citations, use the following source information:

   a. Type of Source: Periodical
      Author: Bulowski, Dana
      Title: Protection and Precaution: Keeping Your Computer Healthy
      Periodical Title: Computing Today
      Year: 2008
      Month: February
      Pages 55-61
   b. Type of Source: Book
      Author: Karanos, Hector
      Title: Internet Security
      Year: 2008
      City: Indianapolis
      Publisher: Citywide Cyber Press
   c. Type of Source: Web site
      Author: Shelly, Gary B., and Thomas J. Cashman
      Name of Web page: Antivirus Programs
      Production Company: Course Technology
      Year Accessed: 2008
      Month Accessed: February
      Day Accessed: 7
      URL: www.scsite.com/wd2007/pr2/wc.htm

3. At the end of the research paper text, press the ENTER key once and insert a manual page break so that the Works Cited page begins on a new page. Enter and format the works cited title. Use Word to insert the bibliographical list. Format the paragraphs in the list with a hanging indent.

4. Check the spelling and grammar of the paper.

5. Save the document on a USB flash drive using Lab 2-2 Antivirus Programs Paper as the file name.

6. Print the research paper. Handwrite the number of words, including the footnotes, in the research paper above the title of your printed research paper.

In the Lab

Lab 3: Composing a Research Paper from Notes

Problem: You have drafted the notes shown in Figure 2–85. Your assignment is to prepare a short research paper from these notes.

Home networks:
- Home users connect multiple computers and devices together in a home network.
- Home networking saves money and provides conveniences.
- Approximately 39 million homes have more than one computer.
- Many vendors offer home networking packages that include all the necessary hardware and software to network a home using wired or wireless techniques.

Three types of wired home networks: Ethernet, powerline cable, and phoneline (source: "Wired vs. Wireless Networks," an article on pages 24-29 in March 2008 issue of Modern Networking by Mark A. Travis).
- Traditional Ethernet networks require that each computer have built-in network capabilities or contain a network card, which connects to a central network hub or similar device with a physical cable. This may involve running cable through walls, ceilings, and floors in the house.
- The hardware and software of an Ethernet network can be difficult to configure for the average home user (source: a book called <u>Home Networking</u> by Frank A. Deakins, published at Current Press in New York in 2008).
- A phoneline network is an easy-to-install and inexpensive network that uses existing telephone lines in the home.
- A home powerline cable network is a network that uses the same lines that bring electricity into the house. This network requires no additional wiring.

Two types of wireless home networks: HomeRF and Wi-Fi (source: a Web site titled "Wired and Wireless Networks" by Gary B. Shelly and Thomas J. Cashman of Course Technology, viewed on April 23, 2008. Web address is www.scsite.com/wd2007/pr2/wc.htm).
- Wireless networks have the disadvantage of interference, because walls, ceilings, and other electrical devices such as cordless telephones and microwave ovens can disrupt wireless communications.
- A HomeRF (radio frequency) network uses radio waves, instead of cables, to transmit data.
- A Wi-Fi network sends signals over a wider distance than the Home RF network, which can be up to 1,500 feet in some configurations.

Figure 2–85

Instructions: Perform the following tasks:

1. Review the notes in Figure 2–85 and then rearrange and reword them. Embellish the paper as you deem necessary. Present the paper according to the MLA documentation style. Create an AutoCorrect entry that automatically corrects the spelling of the misspelled word, wird, to the correct spelling, wired. Add a footnote that refers the reader to the Web for more information. Enter citations and their sources as shown. Create the works cited page (bibliography) from the listed sources.

2. Check the spelling and grammar of the paper. Save the document on a USB flash drive using Lab 2-3 Home Networks Paper as the file name.

3. Use the Research task pane to look up a definition of a word in the paper. Copy and insert the definition into the document as a footnote. Be sure to quote the definition and cite the source.

4. Print the research paper. Handwrite the number of words, including the footnotes, in the research paper above the title of the printed research paper.

Cases and Places

Apply your creative thinking and problem solving skills to design and implement a solution.

• EASIER   •• MORE DIFFICULT

• 1: Create a Research Paper about Word Using the MLA Documentation Style

Chapter 1 of this book discussed the components of the Word window (pages WD 6 through 11). Using the material presented on those pages, write a short research paper (350–400 words) that describes the purpose and functionality of one or more of these components: document window, Ribbon, Mini toolbar and shortcut menus, Quick Access Toolbar, and Office Button. Use your textbook and Word Help as sources. Include at least two citations and one explanatory note positioned as a footnote. Add an AutoCorrect entry to correct a word you commonly mistype. Use the concepts and techniques presented in this chapter to format the paper according to the MLA documentation style. Check spelling and grammar of the finished paper.

•• 2: Create the Research Paper Presented in this Chapter Using the APA Documentation Style

As discussed in this chapter, two popular documentation styles for research papers are the Modern Language Association of America (MLA) and American Psychological Association (APA) styles. In this chapter, you created a research paper that followed guidelines of the MLA documentation style. Using the school library, this textbook, other textbooks, the Internet, magazines, or other sources, research the guidelines of the APA documentation style. Then, prepare the Wireless Communications Paper from this chapter following the guidelines of the APA documentation style. Use Figure 2–1 on page WD 75 as a starting point for the text and source information. Check spelling and grammar of the finished paper.

•• 3: Create a Research Paper that Compares Documentation Styles

This chapter discussed the requirements of the MLA documentation style. The American Psychological Association (APA) and the Chicago Manual of Style (CMS) are two other documentation styles supported by Word. Using the school library, this textbook, other textbooks, the Internet, magazines, or other sources, research the guidelines of the APA and CMS documentation styles to learn more about the differences among the MLA, APA, and CMS documentation styles. Using what you learn, write a short research paper (450-500 words) that compares the requirements and formats of the three documentation styles. Include at least two references and one explanatory note positioned as a footnote. Use the documentation style specified by your instructor to format the paper. Check spelling and grammar of the finished paper.

•• 4: Create a Research Paper about the Month You Were Born

Make It Personal

Did you ever wonder what world events took place during the month you were born (besides your birth)? For example, what happened with respect to politics, world affairs, and the economy? What made headline news? Were there any scientific breakthroughs? What was on television and at the box office? Were any famous people born? Did anyone famous die? What songs topped the charts? What was happening in the world of sports? Research the newsworthy events that took place during the month and year you were born (i.e., July 1981) by looking through newspapers, magazines, searching the Web, and/or interviewing family and friends. Write a short research paper (450-500 words) that summarizes your findings. Include at least two references and one explanatory note. Use the documentation style specified by your instructor to format the paper. Check spelling and grammar of the finished paper.

Continued >

Cases and Places *continued*

•• 5: Create a Research Paper about Spring Break Vacation Destinations

Working Together

With spring break just two months away, you and your fellow classmates are thinking about various spring break vacation destinations. Many options are available. Should you vacation close to home or travel across the country? Stay at a hotel, rent a condominium, or camp outdoors? Travel by car, train, or airplane? Book through a travel agent or the Web? Each team member is to research the attractions, accommodations, required transportation, and total cost of one spring break destination by looking through newspapers, magazines, searching the Web, and/or visiting a travel agency. Each team member is to write a minimum of 200 words summarizing his or her findings. Each team member also is to write at least one explanatory note and supply his or her source information for the citation and bibliography. Then, the team should meet as a group to compose a research paper that includes all team members' write-ups. Start by copying and pasting the text into a single document and then write an introduction and conclusion as a group. Use the documentation style specified by your instructor to format the paper. Check spelling and grammar of the finished paper. Set the default dictionary. If Word flags any of your last names as an error, add the name(s) to the custom dictionary. Hand in printouts of each team member's original write-up, as well as the final research paper.

3 | Creating a Cover Letter and a Resume

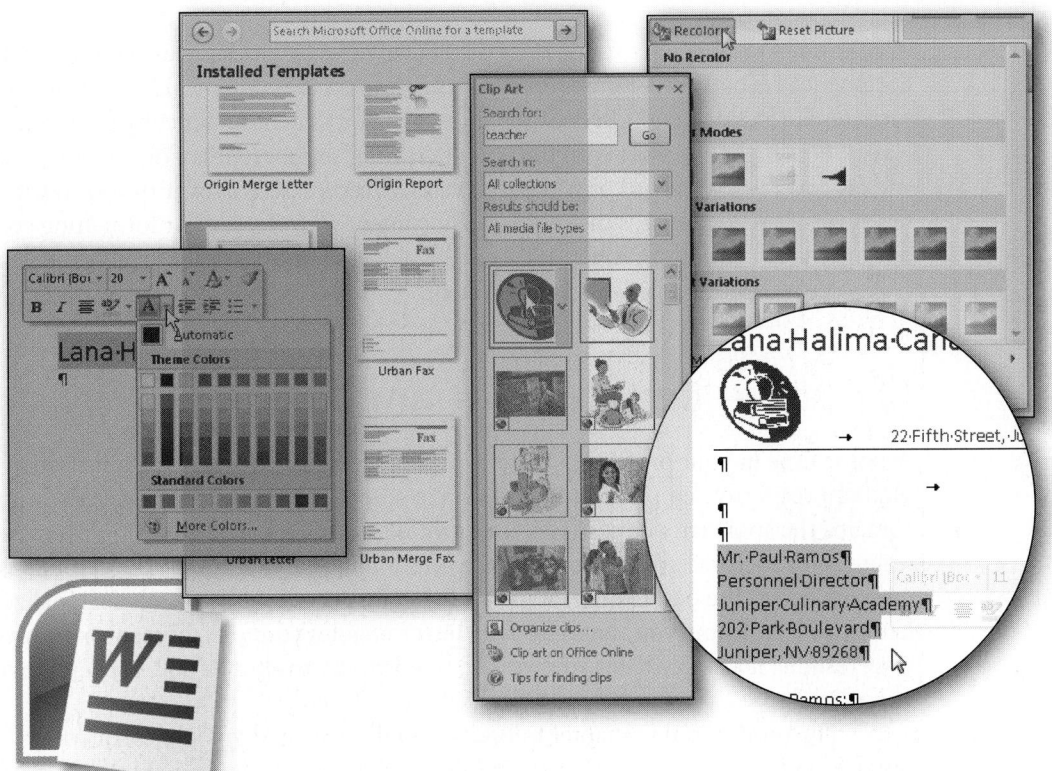

Objectives

You will have mastered the material in this chapter when you can:

- Format characters and paragraphs
- Insert and format clip art
- Set and use tab stops
- Identify the components of a business letter
- Insert the current date
- Create and insert a building block
- Insert a Word table, enter data in the table, and format the table
- Use a template to create a document

- Fill in a document template
- Copy and paste using the Office Clipboard
- Indent paragraphs
- Insert a Quick Part
- Sort a list
- Use print preview to view and print a document
- Address and print an envelope

3 | Creating a Cover Letter and a Resume

Introduction

In a business environment, people use documents to communicate with others. Business documents can include letters, memos, newsletters, proposals, and resumes. An effective business document clearly and concisely conveys its message and has a professional, organized appearance.

Some people prefer to use their own creative skills to design and compose business documents. Using Word, for example, you can develop the content and decide on the location of each item in a document. On occasion, however, you may have difficulty composing a particular type of document. To assist with the task of creating certain types of documents, such as resumes and fax cover letters, Word provides templates. A **template** is similar to a form with prewritten text; that is, Word prepares the requested document with text and/or formatting common to all documents of this nature. After Word creates a document from a template, you fill in the blanks or replace prewritten words in the document.

Project — Cover Letter and Resume

At some time in your professional life, you will prepare a cover letter along with a resume to send to prospective employers. In addition to some personal information, a **resume** usually contains the applicant's educational background and job experience. Employers review many resumes for each vacant position. Thus, you should design your resume carefully so that it presents you as the best candidate for the job. You also should attach a personalized cover letter to each resume you send. A **cover letter** enables you to elaborate on positive points in your resume; it also provides you with an opportunity to show a potential employer your writing skills.

The project in this chapter follows generally accepted guidelines for writing letters and resumes and uses Word to create the cover letter shown in Figure 3–1 and the resume shown in Figure 3–2 on page WD 148. The personalized cover letter to the prospective employer (Juniper Culinary Academy) includes a custom-made letterhead, as well as all essential business letter components. The resume for Lana Halima Canaan, a recent graduate of the culinary arts program, uses a Word template to present relevant information to a potential employer.

Overview

As you read through this chapter, you will learn how to create the cover letter and resume shown in Figures 3–1 and 3–2 by performing these general tasks:

- Design and compose a letterhead.
- Compose a cover letter.
- Print the cover letter.
- Use a template to create a resume.
- Print the resume.
- Address and print an envelope.

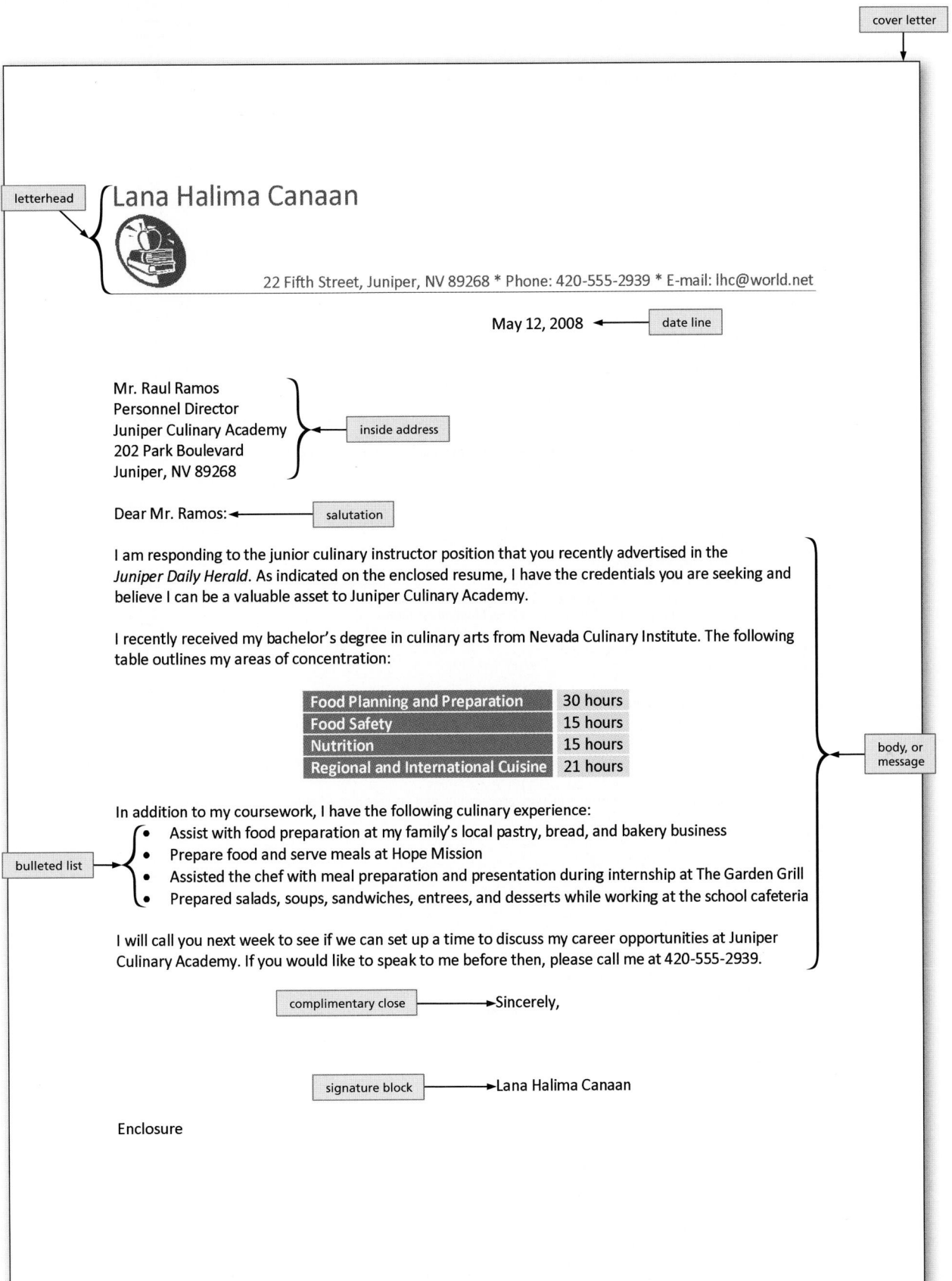

cover letter

letterhead

Lana Halima Canaan

22 Fifth Street, Juniper, NV 89268 * Phone: 420-555-2939 * E-mail: lhc@world.net

May 12, 2008 ← date line

Mr. Raul Ramos
Personnel Director
Juniper Culinary Academy ← inside address
202 Park Boulevard
Juniper, NV 89268

Dear Mr. Ramos: ← salutation

I am responding to the junior culinary instructor position that you recently advertised in the *Juniper Daily Herald*. As indicated on the enclosed resume, I have the credentials you are seeking and believe I can be a valuable asset to Juniper Culinary Academy.

I recently received my bachelor's degree in culinary arts from Nevada Culinary Institute. The following table outlines my areas of concentration:

Food Planning and Preparation	30 hours
Food Safety	15 hours
Nutrition	15 hours
Regional and International Cuisine	21 hours

body, or message

In addition to my coursework, I have the following culinary experience:

bulleted list

- Assist with food preparation at my family's local pastry, bread, and bakery business
- Prepare food and serve meals at Hope Mission
- Assisted the chef with meal preparation and presentation during internship at The Garden Grill
- Prepared salads, soups, sandwiches, entrees, and desserts while working at the school cafeteria

I will call you next week to see if we can set up a time to discuss my career opportunities at Juniper Culinary Academy. If you would like to speak to me before then, please call me at 420-555-2939.

complimentary close → Sincerely,

signature block → Lana Halima Canaan

Enclosure

Figure 3–1

resume

▶Lana Halima Canaan

22 Fifth Street, Juniper, NV 89268
Phone: 420-555-2939
E-mail: lhc@world.net

Objectives

To obtain a full-time culinary instructor position with a culinary academy, school, or institute in the Juniper area.

Education

B.S. Culinary Arts (Nevada Culinary Institute, May 2008)

- ▶ Dean's List, six semesters
- ▶ Moeller Nutrition Award, January 2008
- ▶ Marge Rae Outstanding Student Scholarship, 2006 – 2008
- ▶ Baker Food Preparation Contest, 1st Place, November 2008
- ▶ Areas of concentration:
  Food Planning and Preparation
  Food Safety
  Nutrition
  Regional and International Cuisine

Experience

Chef Intern (September 2006 – May 2008)
The Garden Grill (Juniper, NV)
Assisted chef with meal selection, preparation, and presentation. Assumed chef responsibilities during last semester of school.

Assistant Cook (September 2004 – August 2006)
Nevada Culinary Institute Cafeteria (Juniper, NV)
Planned meals for staff and students. Prepared salads, soups, sandwiches, entrees, and desserts.

Skills

- ▶ Culinary Arts Association
- ▶ National Honor Society
- ▶ Nevada Restaurant Federation
- ▶ Nutrition Services of America
- ▶ Student Government Association, President

Community Service

Prepare food and serve meals at Hope Mission every week.

Figure 3–2

Plan
Ahead

General Project Guidelines

When creating a Word document, the actions you perform and decisions you make will affect the appearance and characteristics of the finished document. As you create a cover letter and resume, such as the project shown in Figure 3–1 on page WD 147 and Figure 3–2, you should follow these general guidelines:

1. **Design a creative letterhead.** Use text, graphics, formats, and colors that reflect your personality or employment goals. Include your name, postal mailing address, and telephone number. If you have an e-mail address and Web address, include those as well.

2. **Compose an effective cover letter.** A finished business letter (i.e., cover letter) should look like a symmetrically framed picture with evenly spaced margins, all balanced below an attractive letterhead. A well-written, properly formatted cover letter presents solid evidence of your writing skills and provides insight into your personality. The content of a letter should contain proper grammar, correct spelling, logically constructed sentences, flowing paragraphs, and sound ideas. Be sure to proofread it carefully.

3. **Craft a successful resume.** Your resume should present, at a minimum, your contact information, objective, educational background, and work experience to a potential employer. It should honestly present all your positive points. As with the cover letter, the resume should be error free. Ask someone else to proofread your resume and give you suggestions for improvements.

When necessary, more specific details concerning the above guidelines are presented at appropriate points in the chapter. The chapter also will identify the actions performed and decisions made regarding these guidelines during the creation of the cover letter shown in Figure 3–1 and the resume shown in Figure 3–2.

Creating a Letterhead

In many businesses, letterhead is preprinted on stationery that everyone in the company uses for correspondence. For personal letters, the cost of preprinted letterhead can be high. An alternative is to create your own letterhead and save it in a file. At a later time, when you want to create a letter using the letterhead, simply open the letterhead file and then save the file with a new name to preserve the original letterhead file. The letterhead in this project (Figure 3–1), follows this process; that is, you design and create a letterhead and then save it in a file.

Plan
Ahead

Design a creative letterhead.

A letterhead often is the first section a reader notices on a letter. Thus, it is important your letterhead appropriately reflect the essence of the individual or business (i.e., formal, youthful, technical, etc.). The letterhead should leave ample room for the contents of the letter. When designing a letterhead, consider its contents, placement, and appearance.

- **Contents of letterhead.** A letterhead should contain these elements:
  - Complete legal name of the individual, group, or company
  - Complete mailing address: street address including building, room, suite number, or post office box, along with city, state, and postal code
  - Telephone number(s) and fax number, if one exists

  Many letterheads also include a Web address, e-mail address, and a logo or other image. If you use an image, select one that expresses your personality or goals.

(continued)

Plan Ahead

(continued)

- **Placement of elements in the letterhead.** Some letterheads center their elements across the top of the page. Others align some or all of the elements with the left or right margins. Sometimes, the elements are split between the top and bottom of the page. For example, a name and logo may be at the top of the page with the address at the bottom of the page.

- **Appearance of letterhead elements.** Use fonts that are easy to read. Give your name impact by making its font size larger than the rest of the text in the letterhead. For additional emphasis, consider formatting the name in bold or italic. Choose colors that complement each other and convey your goals or personality.

  When finished designing the letterhead, determine if a divider line would help to visually separate the letterhead from the text of the letter.

The following pages start Word, enter and format the text and graphics in the letterhead, shown in Figure 3–1 on page WD 147, and then save the personal letterhead file.

To Start Word and Display Formatting Marks

BTW

Normal Style
If your screen settings differ from Figure 3–3, it is possible the default settings in your Normal style have been changed. Normal style settings are saved in the normal.dotm file. To restore the original Normal style settings, quit Word and use Windows Explorer to locate the normal.dotm file (be sure that hidden files and folders are displayed, and include system and hidden files in your search). Rename the normal.dotm file to oldnormal.dotm file. After renaming the normal.dotm file, it no longer will exist as normal.dotm. The next time you start Word, it will recreate a normal .dotm file using the original default settings.

If you are using a computer to step through the project in this chapter and you want your screens to match the figures in this book, you should change your computer's resolution to 1024×768. For information about how to change a computer's resolution, read Appendix D.

The following steps start Word and display formatting marks.

1 Start Word. If necessary, maximize the Word window.

2 If the Print Layout button is not selected, click it so that your screen layout matches Figure 3–3.

3 If your zoom level is not 100%, change it to 100%.

4 If the Show/Hide ¶ button on the Home tab is not selected already, click it to display formatting marks on the screen.

To Apply a Quick Style

When you press the ENTER key in the letterhead, you want the insertion point to advance to the next line, with no blank space between the lines. Recall that, by default, the Normal style in Word places 10 points of blank space after each paragraph and inserts a blank space equal to 1.15 lines between each line of text. The No Spacing style, however, does not put any extra blank space between lines when you press the ENTER key. The following step applies the No Spacing style to the current paragraph.

1 Click No Spacing in the Styles gallery to apply the No Spacing style to the current paragraph.

To Change Theme Colors

Recall that Word provides document themes that contain a variety of color schemes to assist you in selecting complementary colors in a document. In your own letterhead, you would select a color scheme that reflects your personality or goals. This letterhead uses the Urban color scheme. The following steps change theme colors.

1 Click the Change Styles button on the Home tab to display the Change Styles menu, and then point to Colors on the Change Styles menu to display the Colors gallery.

2 Click Urban in the Colors gallery to change the document theme colors to Urban.

To Type Text

To begin creating the personal letterhead file in this chapter, type your name in the document window. The following step types this first line of text in the document.

1 Type Lana Halima Canaan **and then press the ENTER key.**

Q&A Why not type the name in all capital letters?

Studies show that all capital letters can be more difficult to read.

Mini Toolbar

Recall from Chapter 1 that the Mini toolbar, which automatically appears based on certain tasks you perform, contains commands related to changing the appearance of text in a document. All commands on the Mini toolbar also exist on the Ribbon.

When the Mini toolbar appears, it initially is transparent. If you do not use the transparent Mini toolbar, it disappears from the screen. To use the Mini toolbar, move the mouse pointer into the toolbar, which causes the Mini toolbar to change from a transparent to a bright appearance. The following steps illustrate the use of the Mini toolbar.

To Use the Grow Font Button to Increase Font Size

You want the font size of the name to be larger than the rest of the text in the letterhead. In previous chapters, you used the Font Size box arrow on the Home tab to change the font size of text. Word also provides a Grow Font button, which increases the font size of selected text each time you click the button. The following steps use the Grow Font button on the Mini toolbar to increase the font size of the name.

1

- Move the mouse pointer to the left of the line to be selected (in this case, the line containing your name) until the mouse pointer changes to a right-pointing block arrow, and then click the mouse to select the line (Figure 3–3).

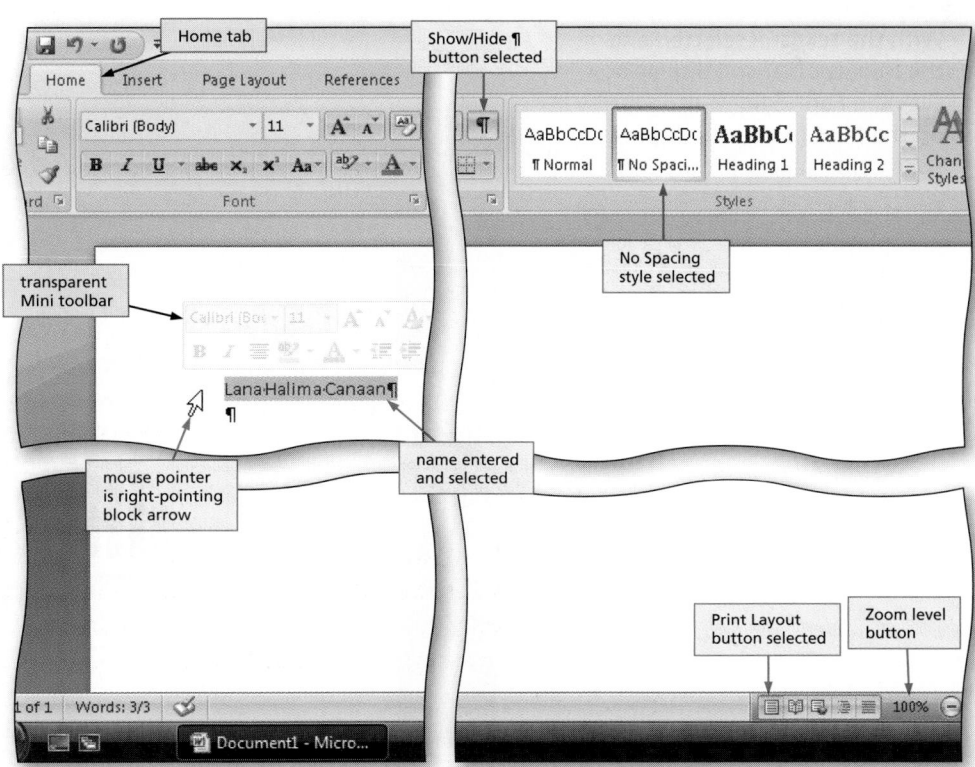

Figure 3–3

- Move the mouse pointer into the transparent Mini toolbar, so that it changes to a bright toolbar.

- Repeatedly click the Grow Font button on the Mini toolbar until the Font Size box displays 20, for 20 point (Figure 3–4).

Q&A

What if I click the Grow Font button too many times and make the font size too big?

Click the Shrink Font button until the desired font size is displayed.

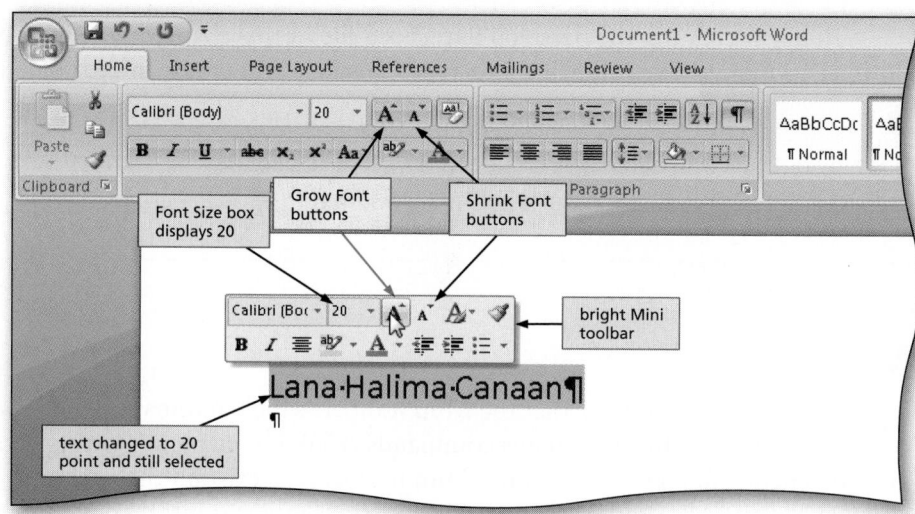

Figure 3–4

🔍 **Experiment**

- Repeatedly click the Grow Font and Shrink Font buttons on the Mini toolbar and watch the font size of the selected name change in the document window. When you have finished experimenting, set the font size to 20 point.

Other Ways

1. Click Grow Font button on Home tab

2. Press CTRL+>

To Color Text

The text in the letterhead is to be a shade of teal. The following steps change the color of the entered text.

- With the text still selected and the Mini toolbar still displaying, click the Font Color button arrow on the Mini toolbar to display the Font Color gallery (Figure 3–5).

Q&A

What if my Mini toolbar no longer is displayed?

Use the Font Color button arrow on the Home tab.

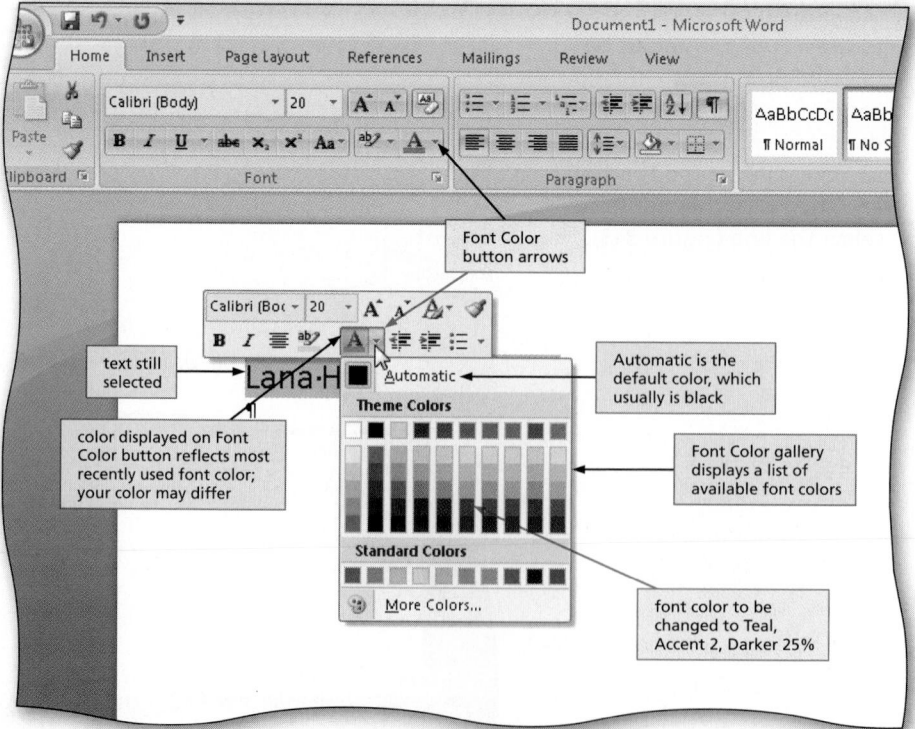

Figure 3–5

2

- Click Teal, Accent 2, Darker 25%, which is the sixth color in the fifth row in the Theme Colors area, to change the color of the selected text to a shade of teal.

- Click the paragraph mark below the name to deselect the text and position the insertion point on line 2 of the document (Figure 3–6).

Q&A How would I change the text color back to black?

If, for some reason, you wanted to change the text color back to black at this point, you would select the text, click the Font Color button arrow again, and then click Automatic in the Font Color gallery.

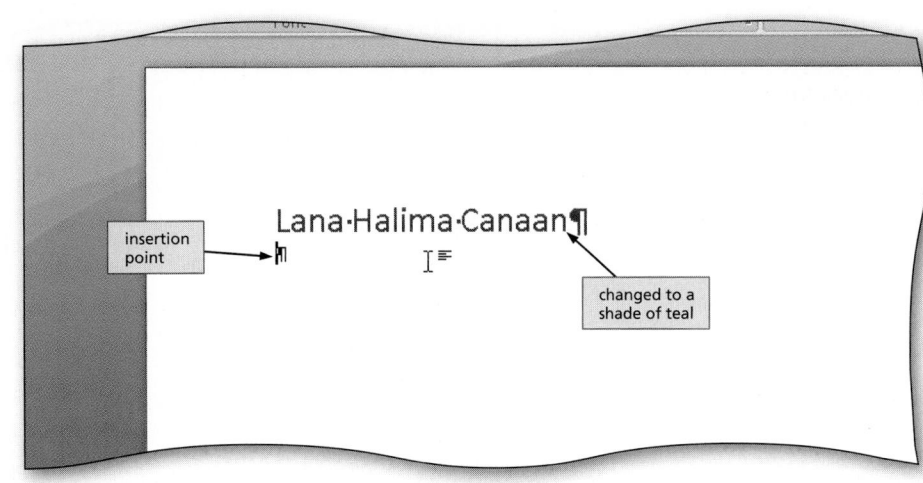

Figure 3–6

Other Ways		
1. Click the Font Color button arrow on Home tab, click desired color	2. Click Font Dialog Box Launcher, click Font tab, click Font color box arrow,	click desired color, click OK button

To Insert Clip Art

Files containing graphical images, or **graphics**, are available from a variety of sources. In Chapter 1, you inserted a digital picture taken with a digital camera in a document. In this project, you insert **clip art**, which is a predefined graphic. In the Microsoft Office programs, clip art is located in the **Clip Organizer**, which contains a collection of clip art, photographs, sounds, and videos.

The letterhead in this project contains clip art of an apple on a stack of books (Figure 3–1 on page WD 147), which represents Lana's desire to be an instructor. Thus, the next steps insert clip art on line 2 of the letterhead below the job seeker's name.

1

- With the insertion point on line 2 below the name, click Insert on the Ribbon to display the Insert tab.

- Click the Clip Art button on the Insert tab to display the Clip Art task pane.

Q&A What is a task pane?

A **task pane** is a separate window that enables you to carry out some Word tasks more efficiently.

- If the Search for text box displays text, drag through the text to select it.

- Type teacher in the Search for text box (Figure 3–7).

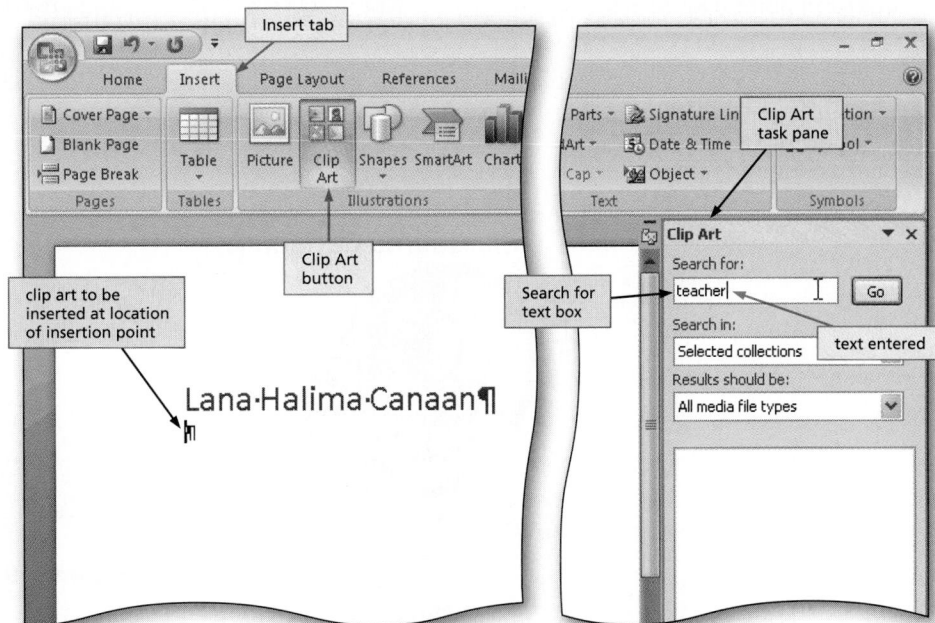

Figure 3–7

2

- Click the Go button to display a list of clips that match the description, teacher (Figure 3–8).

Q&A

Why is my list of clips different from Figure 3–8?

If you are connected to the Internet, the Clip Art task pane displays clips from the Web as well as those installed on your hard disk.

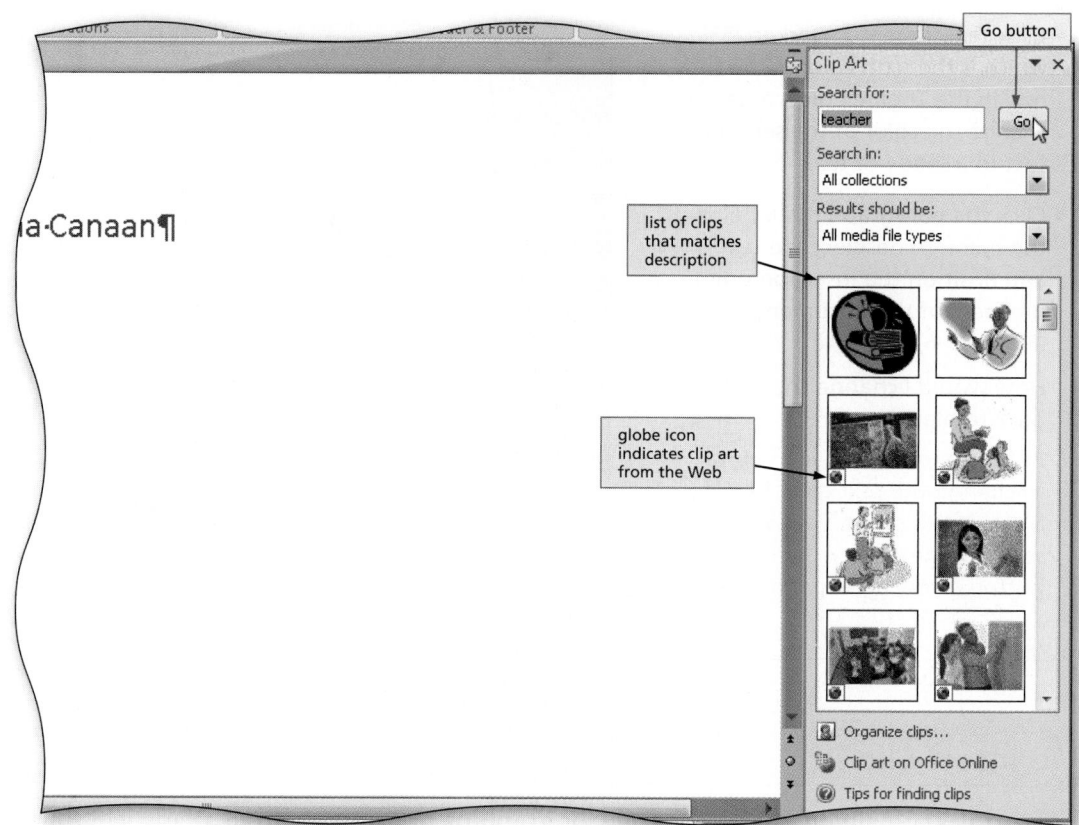

Figure 3–8

3

- Click the clip art of the apple on the stack of books to insert it in the document at the location of the insertion point (Figure 3–9).

4

- Click the Close button on the Clip Art task pane title bar to close the task pane.

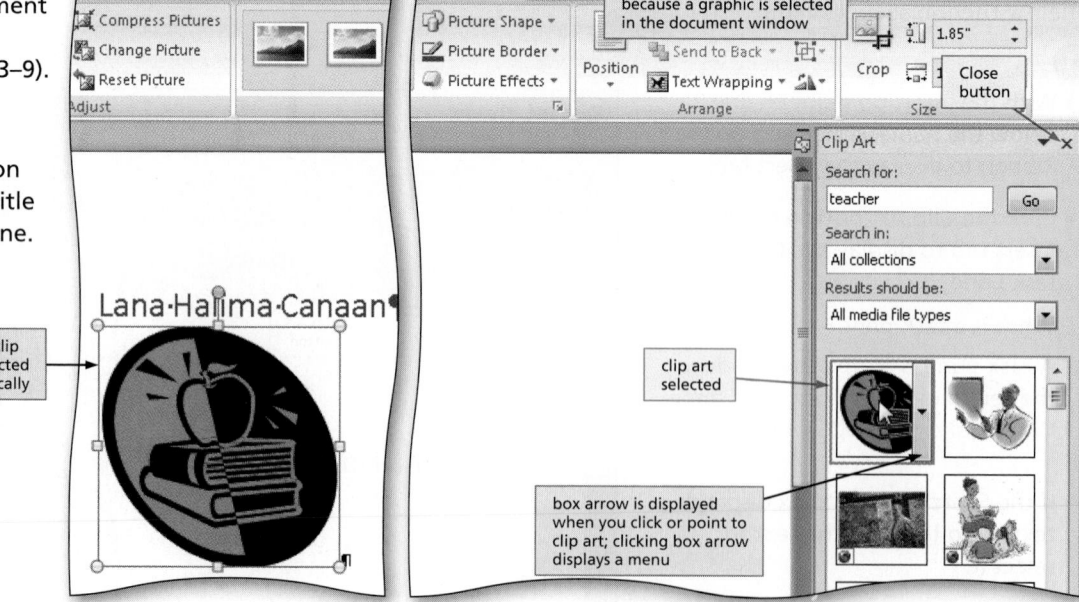

Figure 3–9

To Resize a Graphic Using the Size Dialog Box

In this project, the graphic is 35 percent of its original size. Instead of dragging the sizing handle to change the graphic's size, as you learned how to do in Chapter 1, you can use the Size dialog box to set exact size percentages. The following steps resize a graphic using the Size dialog box.

- With the graphic still selected, click the Size Dialog Box Launcher on the Format tab to display the Size dialog box (Figure 3–10).

Q&A

What if the Format tab is not the active tab on my Ribbon?

Double-click the graphic or click Format on the Ribbon to display the Format tab.

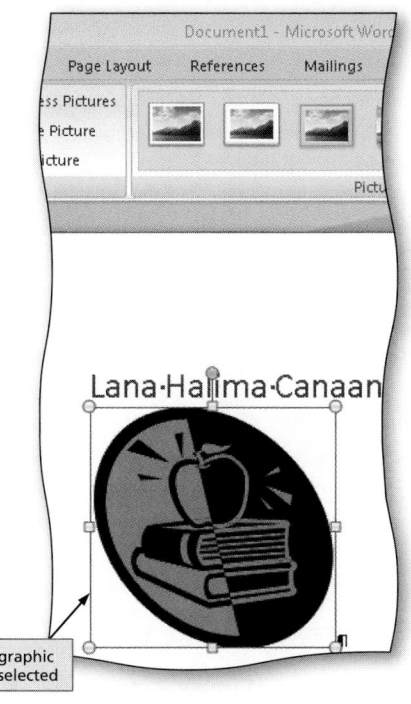
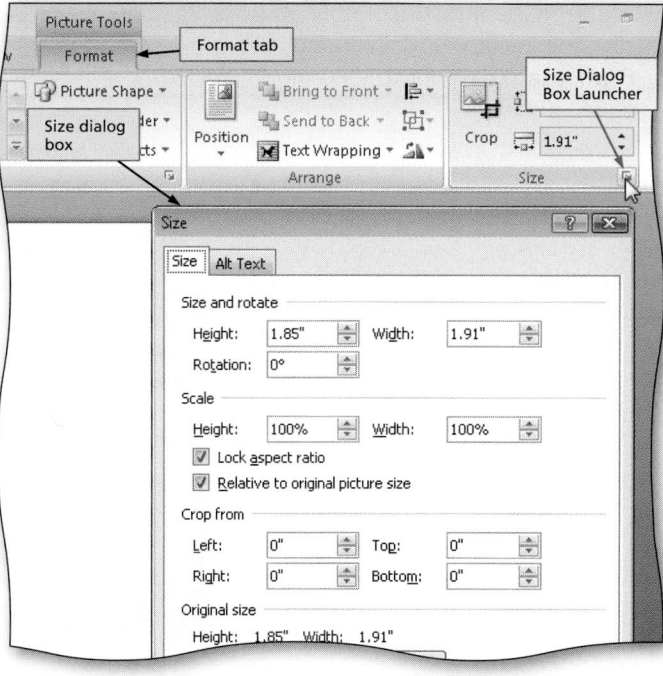

Figure 3–10

- In the Scale area, triple-click the Height text box to select it.

- Type 35 and then press the TAB key to display 35% in the Height and Width text boxes and resize the selected graphic to 35 percent of its original size (Figure 3–11).

Q&A

How do I know to use 35 percent for the resized graphic?

The larger graphic consumed too much room on the page. Try various percentages to determine the size that works best in the letterhead design.

❸

- Click the Close button in the Size dialog box to close the dialog box.

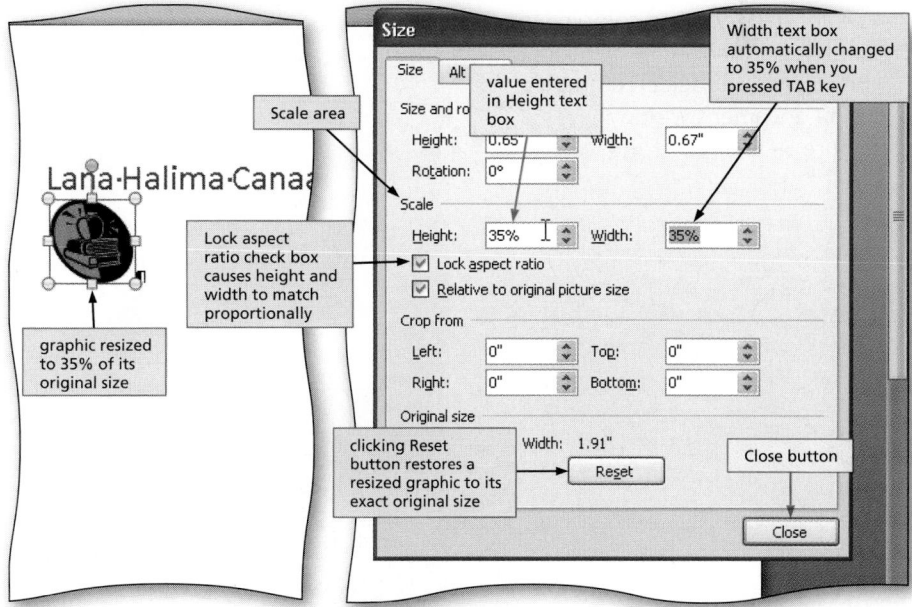

Figure 3–11

Other Ways
1. Right-click graphic, click Size on shortcut menu, click Size tab, enter Height and Width values, click Close button

To Recolor a Graphic

The clip art currently is bright red and black, which does not blend well with the current color scheme. In Word, you can change the color of a graphic. The following steps change the color of the graphic to a shade in the current color scheme.

- With the graphic still selected, click the Recolor button on the Format tab to display the Recolor gallery (Figure 3–12).

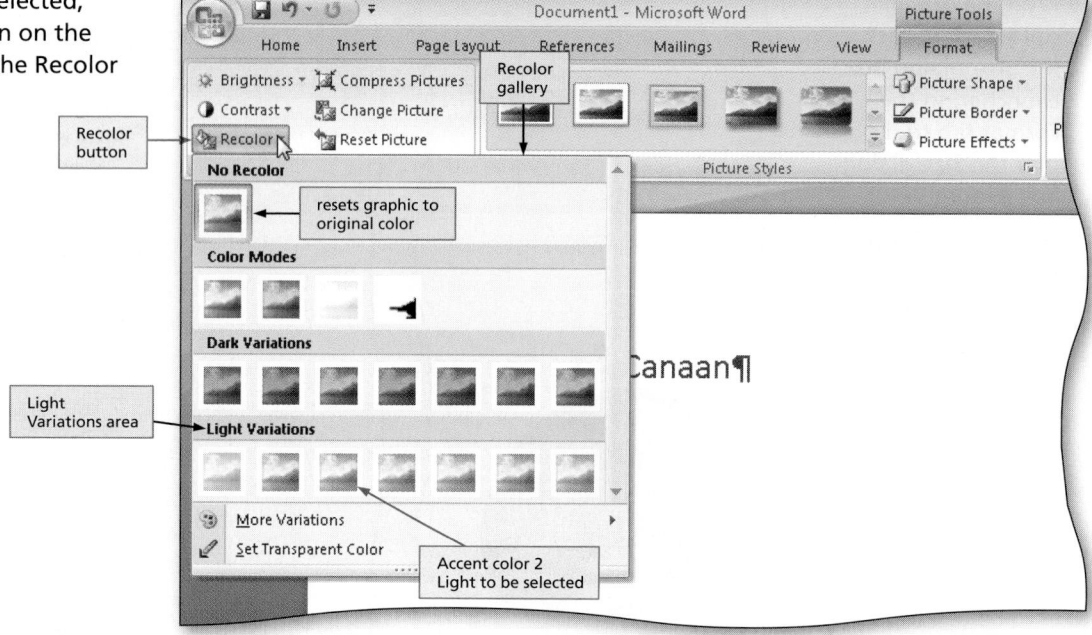

Figure 3–12

- Click Accent color 2 Light in the Recolor gallery (third color in Light Variations area) to change the color of the selected graphic in the document window (Figure 3–13).

Q&A

How would I change a graphic back to its original colors?

With the graphic selected, you would click the Reset Picture button on the Format tab or click No Recolor in the Recolor gallery.

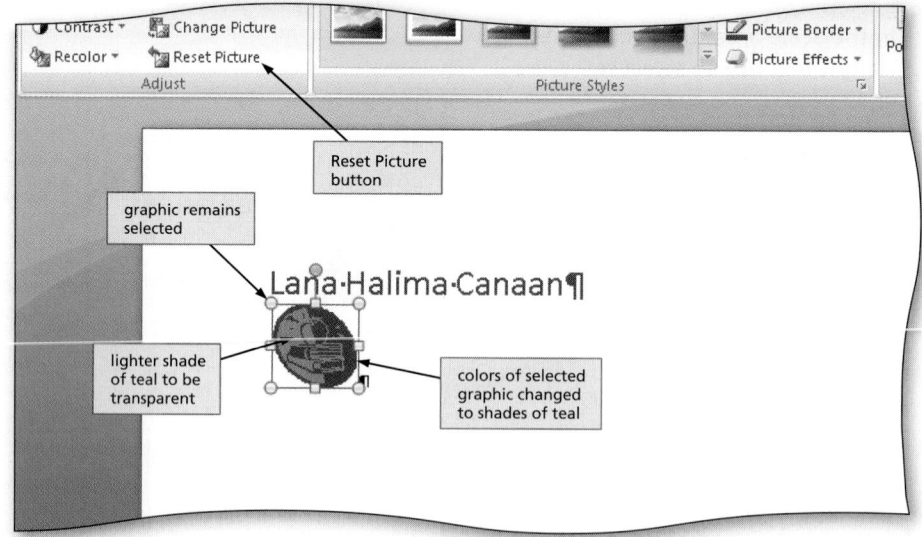

Figure 3–13

Other Ways

1. Right-click graphic, click Format Picture on shortcut menu, click Picture in left pane, click Recolor button, select color, click Close button

To Set a Transparent Color in a Graphic

Although the graphic now is the right color scheme, it is difficult to distinguish the objects in the graphic because they use shades of the same color. In Word, you can make one color in a graphic transparent, that is, remove the color. In this project, you make the lighter shades of teal in the graphic transparent, which results in a graphic that is teal and white — making the image easier to identify. The following steps set a transparent color in a graphic.

- With the graphic still selected, click the Recolor button on the Format tab to display the Recolor gallery (Figure 3–14).

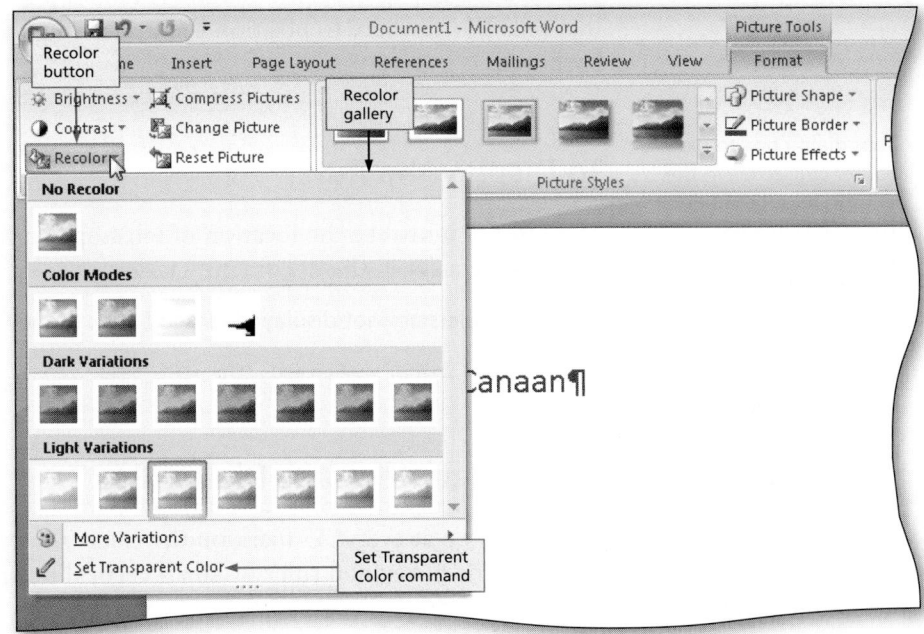

Figure 3–14

- Click Set Transparent Color in the Recolor gallery to display a pen mouse pointer in the document window.

- Position the pen mouse pointer in the graphic where you want to make the color transparent (Figure 3–15).

Figure 3–15

- Click the location in the graphic where you want the color to be transparent (Figure 3–16).

- Press the END key to deselect the graphic and move the insertion point to the end of the line, which is between the graphic and the paragraph mark.

Figure 3–16

Using Tab Stops to Align Text

In the letterhead, the graphic of the apple and the stack of books is left-aligned. The address, phone, and e-mail information in the letterhead is to be positioned at the right margin on the same line. In Word, a paragraph cannot be both left-aligned and right-aligned. If you click the Align Text Right button on the Ribbon, for example, the graphic will be right-aligned. To place text at the right margin of a left-aligned paragraph, you set a tab stop at the right margin. A **tab stop** is a location on the horizontal ruler that tells Word where to position the insertion point when you press the TAB key on the keyboard.

To Display the Ruler

You want to see the location of tab stops on the horizontal ruler. The following step displays the ruler in the document window.

 If the rulers are not displayed already, click the View Ruler button on the vertical scroll bar.

To Set Custom Tab Stops Using the Tabs Dialog Box

Word, by default, places a tab stop at every .5" mark on the ruler (shown in Figure 3–17). These default tab stops are indicated at the bottom of the horizontal ruler by small vertical tick marks. You also can set your own custom tab stops.

The next step in creating the letterhead for this project is to set a custom tab stop at the right margin, that is, at the 6.5" mark on the ruler, because you want the address, phone, and e-mail information at the right margin. One method of setting custom tab stops is to click the ruler at the desired location of the tab stop. You cannot click, however, at the right margin location. Thus, the following steps use the Tabs dialog box to set a custom tab stop.

1
- With the insertion point positioned between the paragraph mark and the graphic, click the Paragraph Dialog Box Launcher to display the Paragraph dialog box (Figure 3–17).

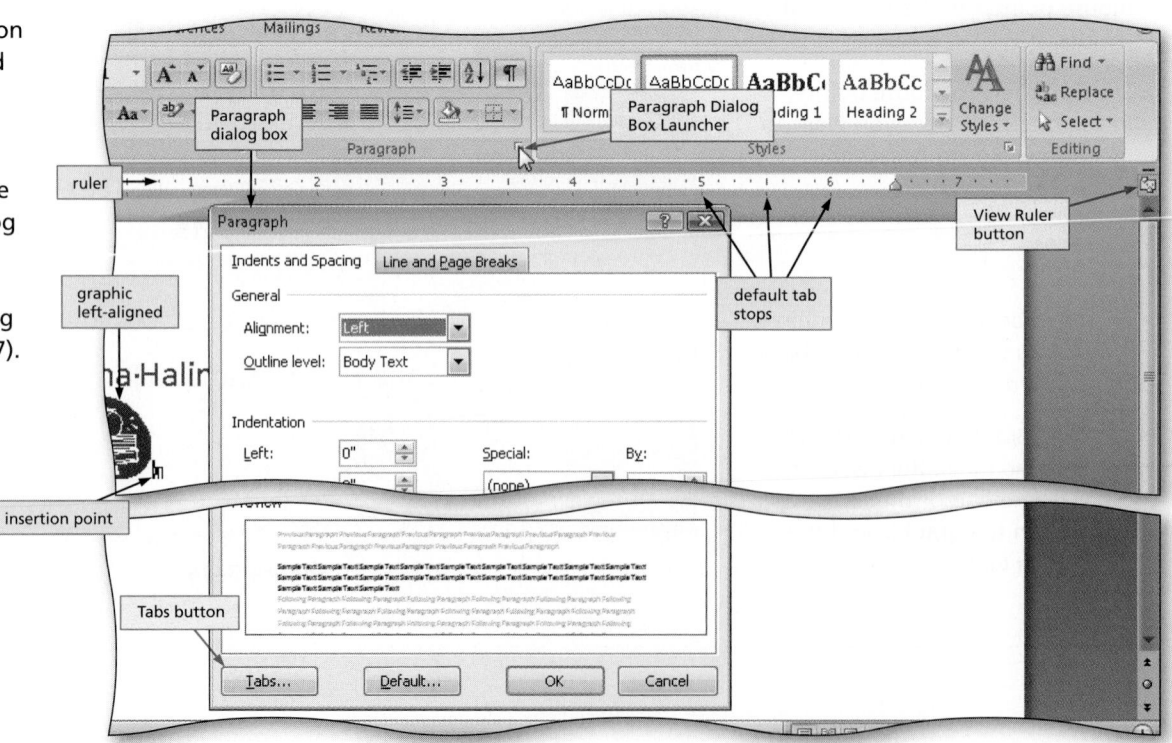

Figure 3–17

2

- Click the Tabs button in the Paragraph dialog box to display the Tabs dialog box.

- Type 6.5 in the Tab stop position text box.

- Click Right in the Alignment area to specify alignment for text at the tab stop (Figure 3–18).

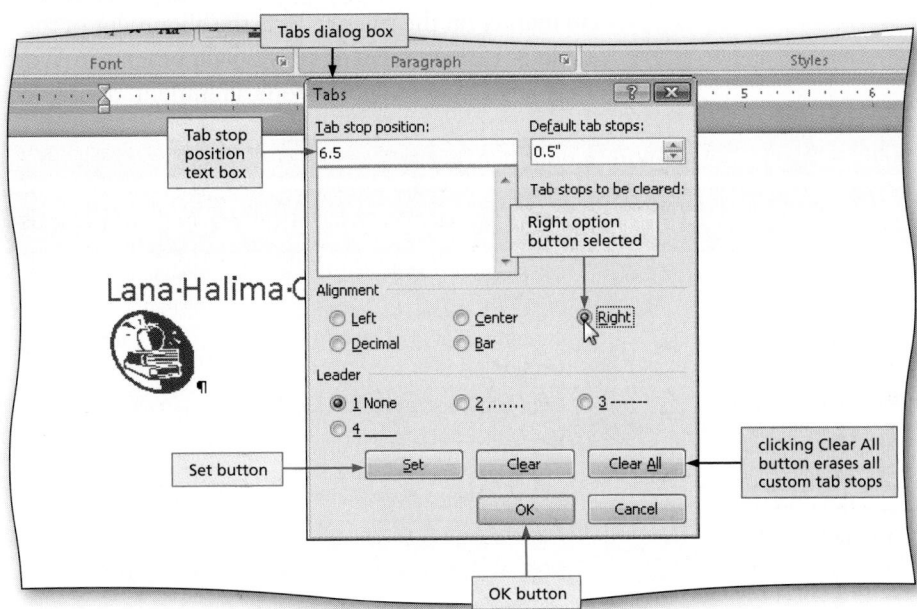

Figure 3–18

3

- Click the Set button in the Tabs dialog box to set a right-aligned custom tab stop.

- Click the OK button to place a right tab marker at the 6.5" mark on the ruler (Figure 3–19).

 What happened to all the default tab stops on the ruler?

When you set a custom tab stop, Word clears all default tab stops to the left of the newly set custom tab stop on the ruler.

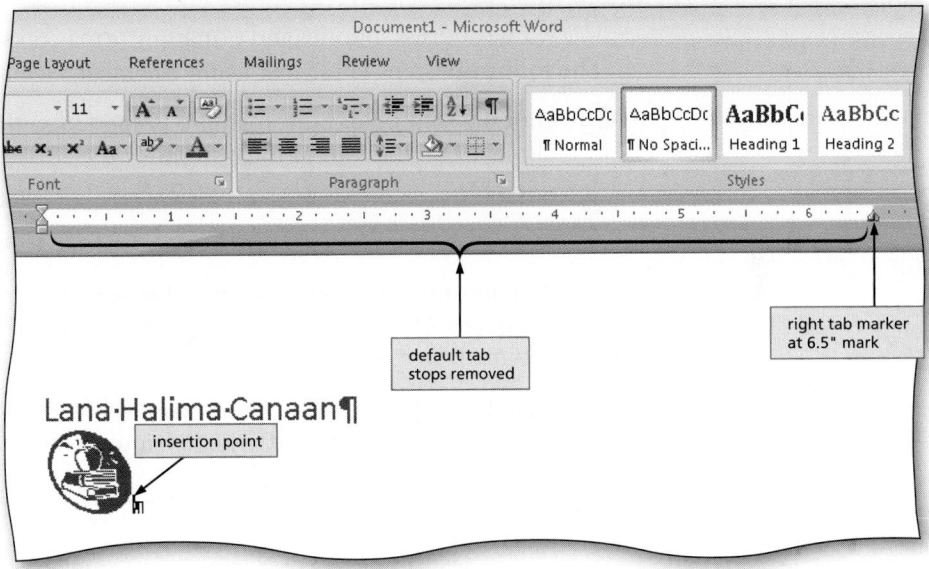

Figure 3–19

Other Ways

1. Right-click paragraph, click Paragraph on shortcut menu, click Tabs button

Tab Stops

Tab settings are a paragraph format. Thus, each time you press the ENTER key, any custom tab stops are carried forward to the next paragraph.

To move the insertion point from one tab stop to another, press the TAB key on the keyboard. When you press the TAB key, a **tab character** formatting mark appears in the empty space between the tab stops.

When you set a custom tab stop, you specify how the text will align at a tab stop. The tab marker on the ruler reflects the alignment of the characters at the location of the tab stop. Table 3–1 shows types of tab stop alignments in Word and their corresponding tab markers. To change an existing tab stop's alignment, double-click the tab marker on the ruler to display the Tabs dialog box (or display the Tabs dialog box as described in the steps on the previous page), click the tab stop position you wish to change, click the new alignment, and then click the OK button. You can remove an existing tab stop by clicking the tab stop position in the Tabs dialog box and then clicking the Clear button in the dialog box. To remove all tab stops, click the Clear All button in the Tabs dialog box.

Table 3–1 Types of Tab Stop Alignments

Tab Stop	Tab Marker	Result of Pressing TAB Key	Example
Left Tab	L	Left-aligns text at the location of the tab stop	toolbar ruler
Center Tab	⊥	Centers text at location of the tab stop	toolbar ruler
Right Tab	⌐	Right-aligns text at location of the tab stop	toolbar ruler
Decimal Tab	⊥	Aligns text on decimal point at location of the tab stop	45.72 223.75
Bar Tab	I	Aligns text at a bar character at the location of the tab stop	toolbar ruler

To Specify Font Color before Typing

The address, phone, and e-mail information should be the same color as the name. The following steps enter text using the most recently defined color.

1 Click the Font Color button on the Home tab so that the text you type will be the color displayed on the face of the button.

Q&A What if the color I want is not displayed on the face of the Font Color button?

Click the Font Color button arrow and then click the desired color in the Font Color gallery.

2 With the insertion point positioned between the graphic and the paragraph mark (as shown in Figure 3–19 on the previous page), press the TAB key to move the insertion point to the 6.5" mark on the ruler.

3 Type `22 Fifth Street, Juniper, NV 89268 * Phone: 420-555-2939 * E-mail: lhc@world.net` in the letterhead (Figure 3–20).

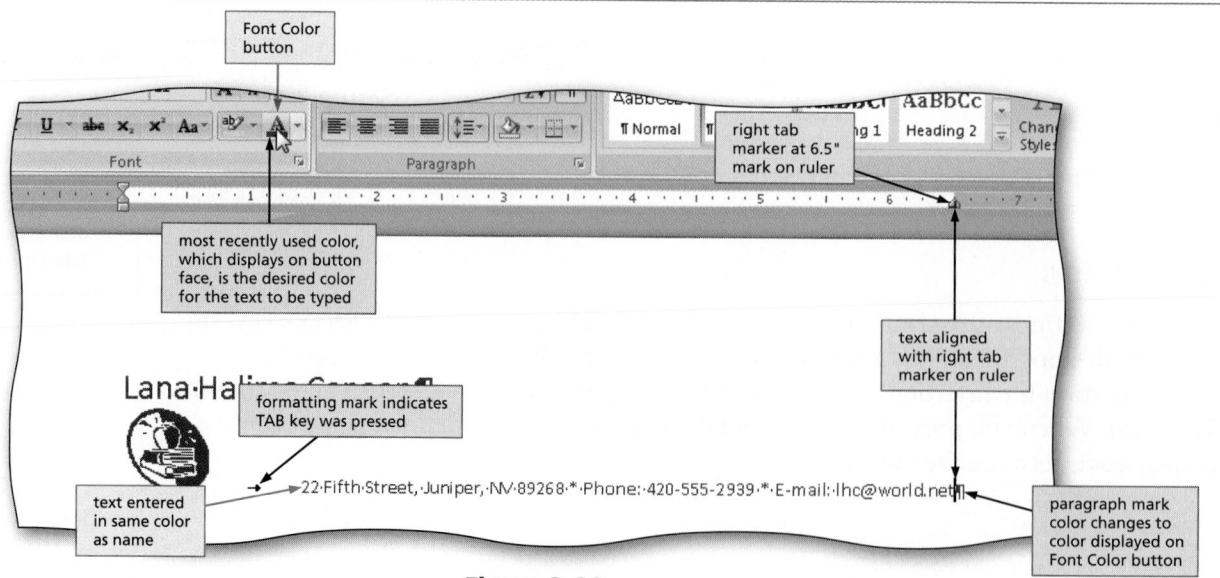

Figure 3–20

To Bottom Border a Paragraph

The letterhead in this project has a horizontal line that extends from the left margin to the right margin immediately below the address, phone, and e-mail information. In Word, you can draw a solid line, called a **border**, at any edge of a paragraph. That is, borders may be added above or below a paragraph, to the left or right of a paragraph, or in any combination of these sides. The following steps add a bottom border to the paragraph containing address, phone, and e-mail information.

1

- With the insertion point in the paragraph to border, click the Border button arrow on the Home tab to display the Border gallery (Figure 3–21).

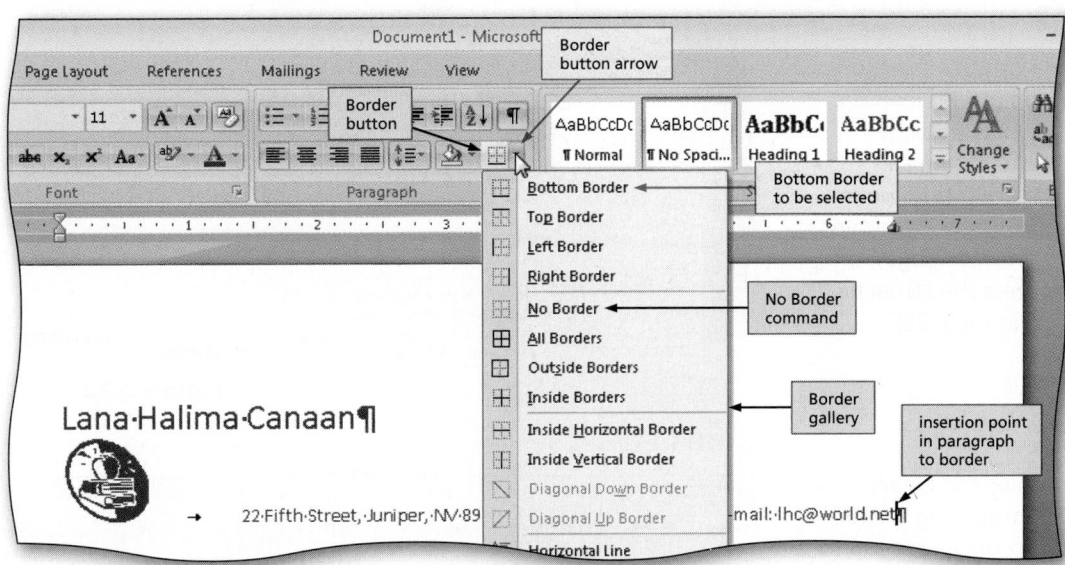

Figure 3–21

2

- Click Bottom Border in the Border gallery to place a border below the paragraph containing the insertion point (Figure 3–22).

 If the face of the Border button displays the border icon I want to use, can I click the Border button instead of using the Border button arrow?

Yes.

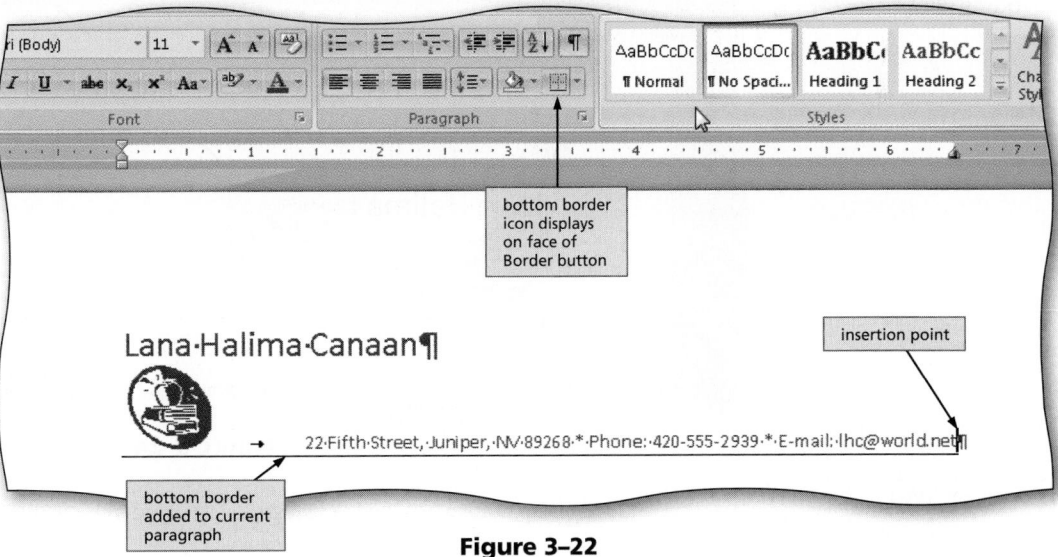

Figure 3–22

How would I remove an existing border from a paragraph?

If, for some reason, you wanted to remove a border from a paragraph, you would position the insertion point in the paragraph, click the Border button arrow on the Home tab, and then click No Border (Figure 3–21) in the Border gallery.

Other Ways

1. Click Page Borders on Page Layout tab, click Borders tab in Borders and Shading dialog box, select desired border, click OK button

To Clear Formatting

The next step is to position the insertion point below the letterhead, so that you can type the content of the letter. When you press the ENTER key at the end of a paragraph containing a border, Word moves the border forward to the next paragraph. It also retains all current settings. That is, the paragraph text will be teal and will have a bottom border. Instead, you want the paragraph and characters on the new line to use the Normal style: black font with no border. In Word, the term, **clear formatting**, refers to returning the formatting to the Normal style. The following steps clear formatting at the location of the insertion point.

- With the insertion point between the e-mail address and paragraph mark (as shown in Figure 3–22 on the previous page), press the ENTER key (Figure 3–23).

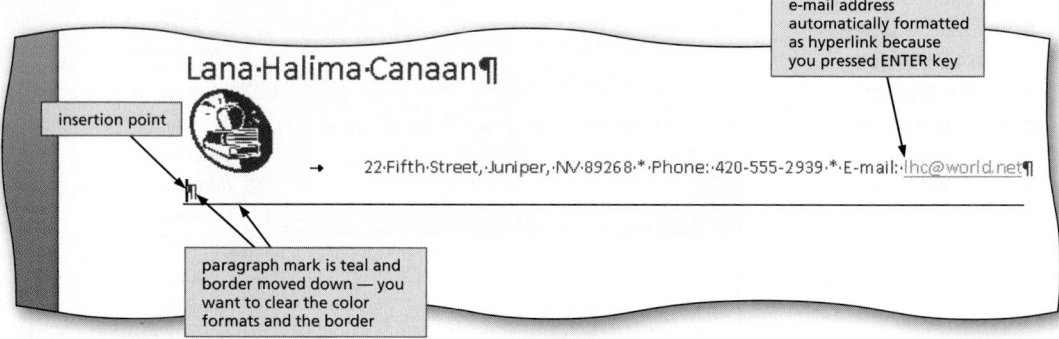

Figure 3–23

- Click the Clear Formatting button on the Home tab to apply the Normal style to the location of the insertion point (Figure 3–24).

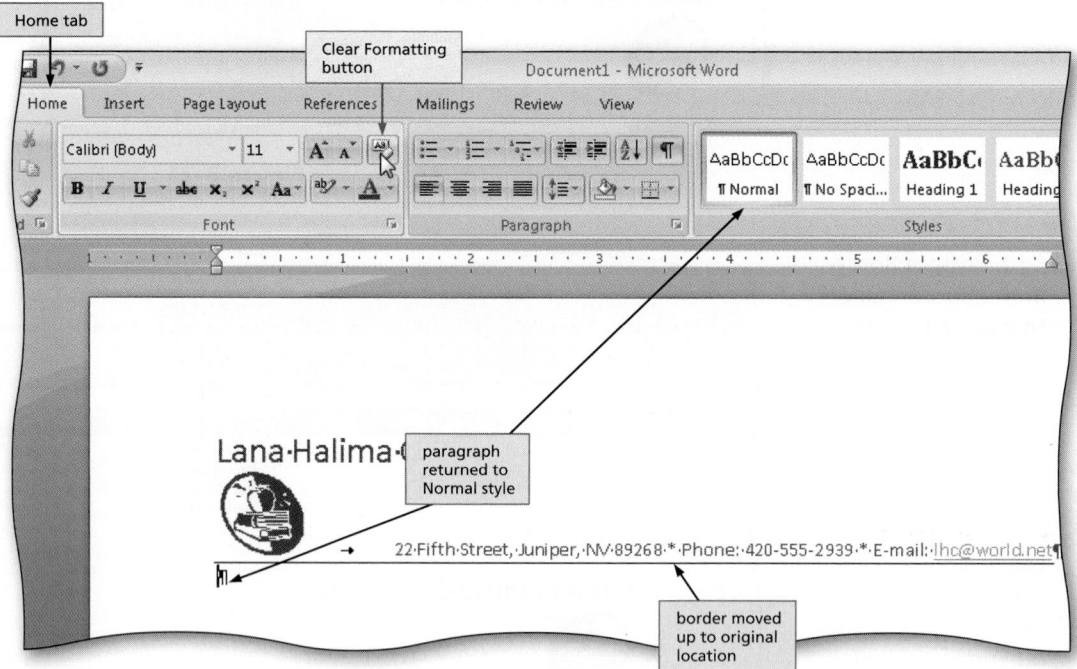

Figure 3–24

Other Ways

1. Click More button in Styles gallery on Home tab, click Clear Formatting
2. Click Styles Dialog Box Launcher, click Clear All in Styles task pane
3. Press CTRL+SPACEBAR, press CTRL+Q

AutoFormat As You Type

As you type text in a document, Word automatically formats it for you. For example, when you press the ENTER key or SPACEBAR after typing an e-mail address or Web address, Word automatically formats the address as a hyperlink, that is, colored blue and underlined. In Figure 3–23, Word formatted the e-mail address as a hyperlink because you pressed the ENTER key at the end of the line. Table 3–2 outlines commonly used AutoFormat As You Type options and their results.

Table 3–2 Commonly Used AutoFormat As You Type Options		
Typed Text	**AutoFormat Feature**	**Example**
Quotation marks or apostrophes	Changes straight quotation marks or apostrophes to curly ones	"the" becomes "the"
Text, a space, one hyphen, one or no spaces, text, space	Changes the hyphen to an en dash	ages 20 - 45 becomes ages 20 – 45
Text, two hyphens, text, space	Changes the two hyphens to an em dash	Two types--yellow and red becomes Two types—yellow and red
Web or e-mail address followed by SPACEBAR or ENTER key	Formats Web or e-mail address as a hyperlink	www.scsite.com becomes www.scsite.com
Three hyphens, underscores, equal signs, asterisks, tildes, or number signs and then ENTER key	Places a border above a paragraph	--- This line becomes _____ This line
Number followed by a period, hyphen, right parenthesis, or greater than sign and then a space or tab followed by text	Creates a numbered list when you press the SPACEBAR or TAB key	1. Word 2. Excel becomes 1. Word 2. Excel
Asterisk, hyphen, or greater than sign and then a space or tab followed by text	Creates a bulleted list when you press the SPACEBAR or TAB key	* Home tab * Insert tab becomes • Home tab • Insert tab
Fraction and then a space or hyphen	Condenses the fraction entry so that it consumes one space instead of three	1/2 becomes ½
Ordinal and then a space or hyphen	Makes part of the ordinal a superscript	3rd becomes 3rd

BTW

AutoFormat Settings
For an AutoFormat option to work as expected, it must be enabled. To check if an AutoFormat option is enabled, click the Office Button, click the Word Options button, click Proofing in the left pane, click the AutoCorrect Options button, click the AutoFormat As You Type tab, select the appropriate check boxes, and then click the OK button in each open dialog box.

To Convert a Hyperlink to Regular Text

The e-mail address in the letterhead should be formatted as regular text; that is, it should not be blue or underlined. Thus, the next step is to remove the hyperlink format from the e-mail address in the letterhead.

- Right-click the hyperlink (in this case, the e-mail address) to display the Mini toolbar and a shortcut menu (Figure 3–25).

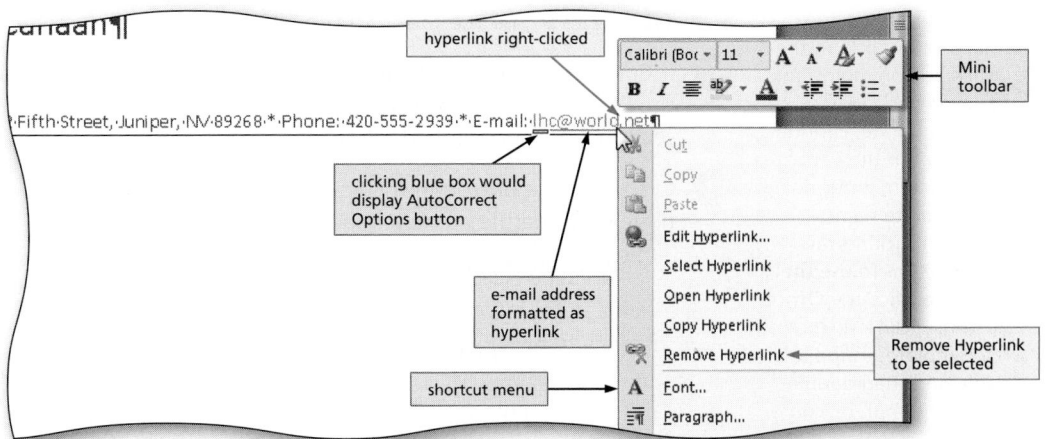

Figure 3–25

2

- Click Remove Hyperlink on the shortcut menu to remove the hyperlink format from the e-mail address.

- Position the insertion point on the paragraph mark below the border (Figure 3–26).

Q&A

Could I have used the AutoCorrect Options button instead of the Remove Hyperlink command?

Yes. Alternatively, you could have pointed to the small blue box at the beginning of the hyperlink, clicked the AutoCorrect Options button, and then clicked Undo Hyperlink on the AutoCorrect Options menu.

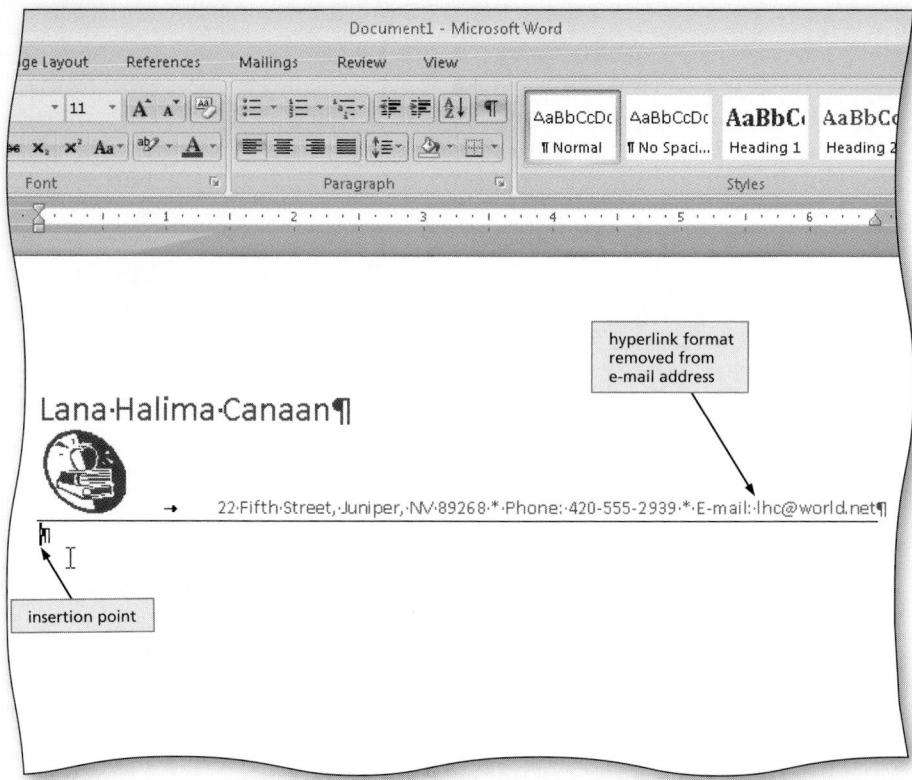

Figure 3–26

Other Ways

1. With insertion point in hyperlink, click Hyperlink button on Insert tab, click Remove Link button

To Save the Letterhead

The letterhead now is complete. Thus, you should save it in a file. For a detailed example of the procedure summarized below, refer to pages WD 19 through WD 21 in Chapter 1.

Note: If you are using Windows XP, see Appendix F for alternate steps.

1 With a USB flash drive connected to one of the computer's USB ports, click the Save button on the Quick Access Toolbar to display the Save As dialog box.

2 Type `Canaan Letterhead` in the File name text box to change the file name.

3 If Computer is not displayed in the Favorite Links section, drag the top or bottom edge of the Save As dialog box until Computer is displayed. Click Computer in the Favorite Links section and then select the USB flash drive.

4 Click the Save button in the Save As dialog box to save the document on the USB flash drive with the file name, Canaan Letterhead.

BTW

Saving a Template
As an alternative to saving the letterhead as a Word document, you could save it as a template by clicking the Office Button, pointing to Save As, clicking Word Template, clicking Templates in the Favorite Links section, entering the template name, and then clicking the Save button. To use the template, click the Office Button, click New, click My templates in the left pane, and then double-click the template icon or name.

Q&A

How can I keep reusing this same letterhead file for every letter I create?

If the letterhead file is not yet opened, you can instruct Word to create a new document window that contains the contents of an existing document. If the letterhead file is already opened, you can save the file with a new file name.

To Create a New File from an Existing File

If you wish to open a new document window that contains the contents of an existing file, you would follow these steps.

1. Click the Office Button and then click New to display the New Document dialog box.
2. Click 'New from existing' in the Templates area to display the New from Existing Document dialog box.
3. Locate and select the file from which you wish to create a new file.
4. Click the Create New button in the dialog box.

Creating a Cover Letter

You have created a letterhead for the cover letter. The next step is to compose the cover letter. The following pages use Word to compose a cover letter that contains a table and a bulleted list.

Plan Ahead

Compose an effective cover letter.
You always should send a personalized cover letter with a resume. The cover letter should highlight aspects of your background relevant to the position. To help you recall past achievements and activities, keep a personal file containing documents that outline your accomplishments.

A cover letter is a type of business letter. When composing a business letter, you need to be sure to include all essential elements and to decide which letter style to use.

- **Include all essential letter elements.** All business letters, including cover letters, contain the same basic elements. Essential business letter elements include the date line, inside address, message, and signature block (shown in Figure 3–1 on page WD 147).

- **Determine which letter style to use.** You can follow many different styles when creating business letters. A letter style specifies guidelines for the alignment and spacing of elements in the business letter.

To Save the Document with a New File Name

The current open file has the name Canaan Letterhead, which is the name of the personal letterhead. You want the letterhead to remain intact. Thus, the following steps save the document with a new file name.

1 With a USB flash drive connected to one of the computer's USB ports, click the Office Button to display the Office Button menu and then click Save As on the Office Button menu to display the Save As dialog box.

2 Type `Canaan Cover Letter` in the File name text box to change the file name.

3 If necessary, select the USB flash drive as the save location.

4 Click the Save button in the Save As dialog box to save the document on the USB flash drive with the file name, Canaan Cover Letter.

To Apply a Quick Style

When you press the ENTER key in the letter, you want the insertion point to advance to the next line, with no blank space between the lines. Recall that, by default, the Normal style in Word places 10 points of blank space after each paragraph and inserts a blank space equal to 1.15 lines between each line of text. The No Spacing style, however, does not put any blank space between lines when you press the ENTER key. Thus, the following step applies the No Spacing style to the current paragraph.

 With the insertion point on the paragraph mark below the border, click No Spacing in the Styles gallery to apply the No Spacing style to the current paragraph.

Plan Ahead

Include all essential letter elements.
Be sure to include all essential business letter elements, properly spaced, in your cover letter.

- The **date line**, which consists of the month, day, and year, is positioned two to six lines below the letterhead.

- The **inside address**, placed three to eight lines below the date line, usually contains the addressee's courtesy title plus full name, job title, business affiliation, and full geographical address.

- The **salutation**, if present, begins two lines below the last line of the inside address. If you do not know the recipient's name, avoid using the salutation "To whom it may concern" — it is impersonal. Instead, use the recipient's title in the salutation, e.g., Dear Personnel Director.

- The body of the letter, the **message**, begins two lines below the salutation. Within the message, paragraphs are single-spaced with one blank line between paragraphs.

- Two lines below the last line of the message, the **complimentary close** is displayed. Capitalize only the first word in a complimentary close.

- Type the **signature block** at least four blank lines below the complimentary close, allowing room for the author to sign his or her name.

Plan Ahead

Determine which letter style to use.
Three common business letter styles are the block, the modified block, and the modified semi-block. Each style specifies different alignments and indentations.

- In the block letter style, all components of the letter begin flush with the left margin.

- In the modified block letter style, the date, complimentary close, and signature block are positioned approximately one-half inch to the right of center or at the right margin. All other components of the letter begin flush with the left margin.

- In the modified semi-block letter style, the date, complimentary close, and signature block are centered, positioned approximately one-half inch to the right of center or at the right margin. The first line of each paragraph in the body of the letter is indented one-half to one inch from the left margin. All other components of the letter begin flush with the left margin.

The cover letter in this project follows the modified block style.

To Set Custom Tab Stops Using the Ruler

The first required element of the cover letter is the date line, which in this letter is to be positioned two lines below the letterhead. The date line contains the month, day, and year, and begins 3.5 inches from the left margin, which is approximately one-half inch to the right of center. Thus, you should set a custom tab stop at the 3.5" mark on the ruler. Earlier you used the Tabs dialog box to set a tab stop because you could not use the ruler to set a tab stop at the right margin. The following steps set a left-aligned tab stop using the ruler.

1

- With the insertion point on the paragraph mark below the border, press the ENTER key so that a blank line appears between the letterhead and the date line.

- If necessary, click the tab selector at the left edge of the horizontal ruler until it displays the Left Tab icon.

- Position the mouse pointer on the 3.5" mark on the ruler (Figure 3–27).

Q&A

What is the purpose of the tab selector?

Before using the ruler to set a tab stop, you must ensure the correct tab stop icon appears in the tab selector. Each time you click the tab selector, its icon changes. For a list of the types of tab stops, see Table 3–1 on page WD 160.

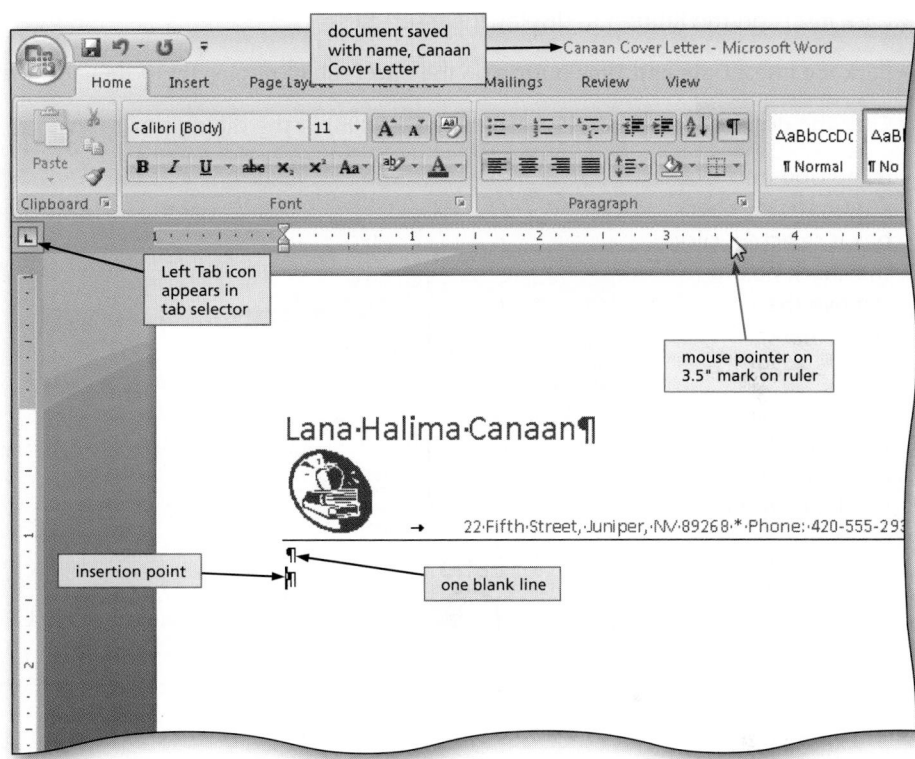

Figure 3–27

2

- Click the 3.5" mark on the ruler to place a left tab marker at that location on the ruler (Figure 3–28).

Q&A

What if I click the wrong location on the ruler?

You can move a custom tab stop by dragging the tab marker to the desired location on the ruler. Or, you can remove a custom tab stop by pointing to the tab marker on the ruler and then dragging the tab marker down and out of the ruler.

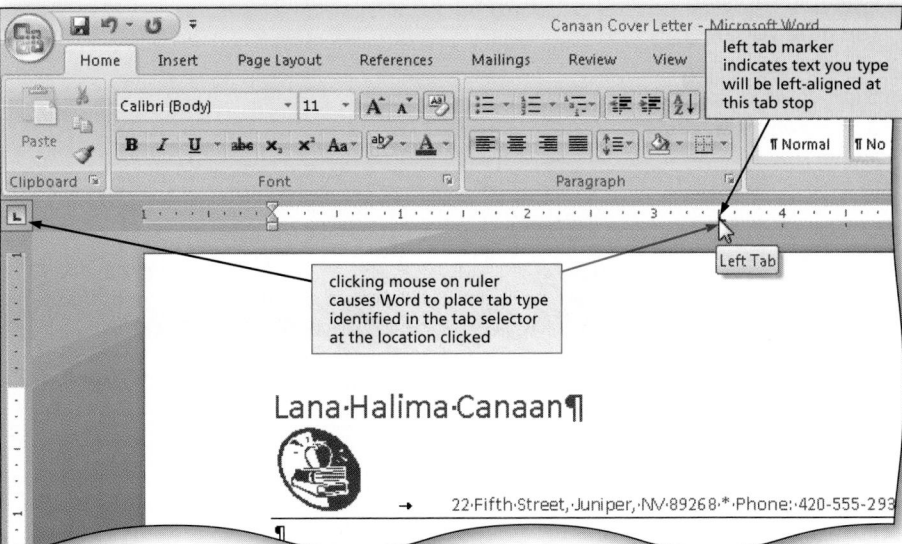

Figure 3–28

To Insert the Current Date in a Document

The next step is to enter the current date at the 3.5" tab stop in the document, as specified in the guidelines for a modified block style letter. Word provides a method of inserting a computer's system date in a document. The following steps insert the current date in the cover letter.

- Press the TAB key.

- Click Insert on the Ribbon to display the Insert tab.

- Click the Insert Date and Time button on the Insert tab to display the Date and Time dialog box.

- Click the desired format (in this case, May 12, 2008) in the dialog box.

- If the Update automatically check box is selected, click the check box to remove the check mark (Figure 3–29).

Q&A

Why should the Update automatically check box not be selected?

In this project, the date at the top of the letter should always show today's date. If, however, you wanted the date always to change to reflect the current computer date, for example showing the date you open or print the letter, then you would put a check mark in this check box.

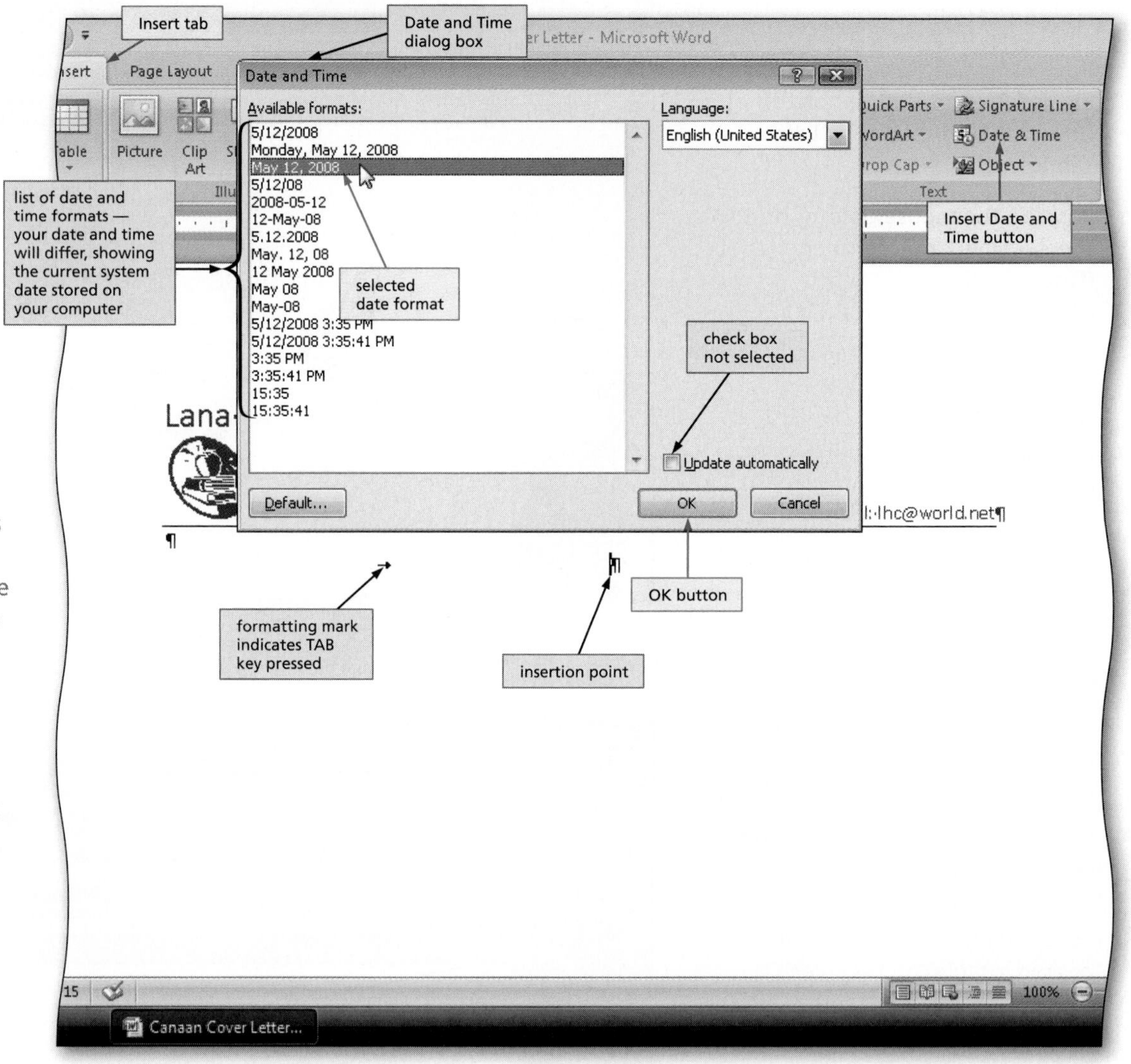

Figure 3–29

2

• Click the OK button to insert the current date at the location of the insertion point (Figure 3–30).

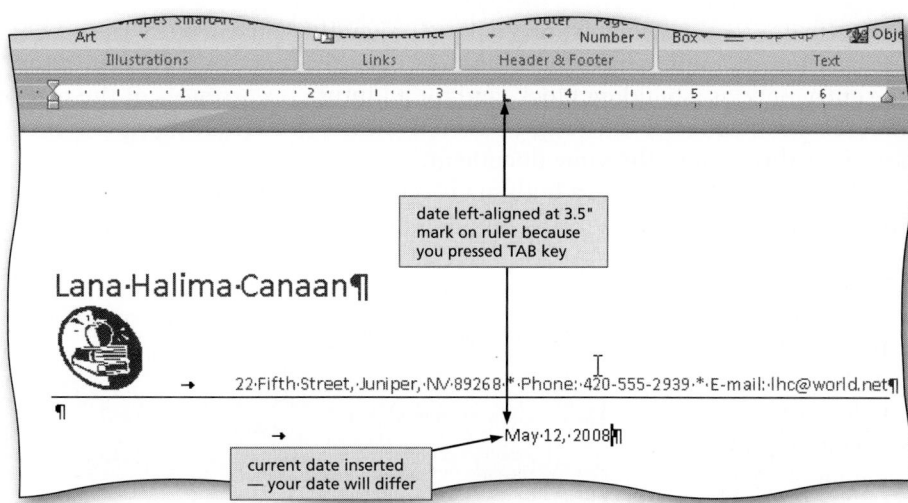

> date left-aligned at 3.5" mark on ruler because you pressed TAB key

> current date inserted — your date will differ

Figure 3–30

To Enter the Inside Address and Salutation

The next step in composing the cover letter is to type the inside address and salutation.

1 With the insertion point at the end of the date, press the ENTER key three times.

2 Type Mr. Raul Ramos and then press the ENTER key.

3 Type Personnel Director and then press the ENTER key.

4 Type Juniper Culinary Academy and then press the ENTER key.

5 Type 202 Park Boulevard and then press the ENTER key.

6 Type Juniper, NV 89268 and then press the ENTER key twice.

7 Type Dear Mr. Ramos and then press the COLON key (:) to complete the entries of the inside address and salutation (Figure 3–31).

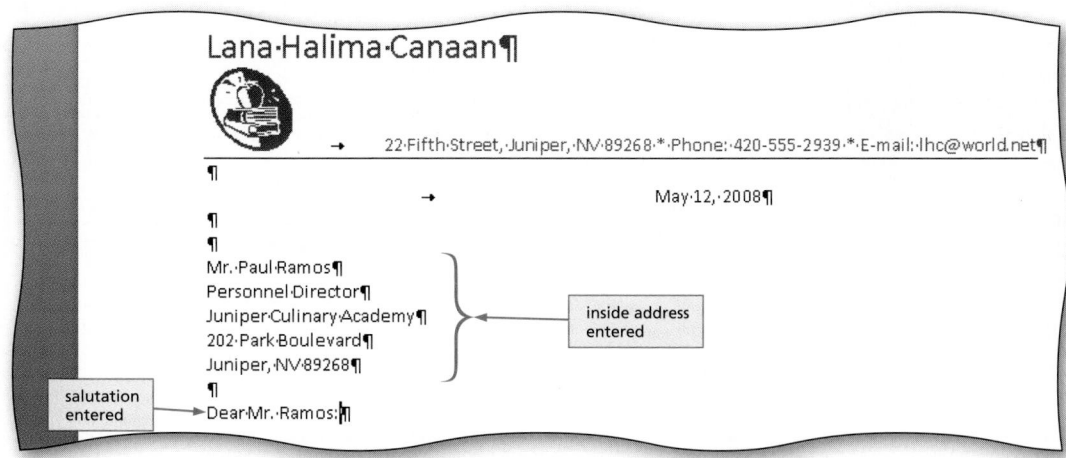

> inside address entered

> salutation entered

Figure 3–31

To Create a Building Block

If you use the same text or graphic frequently, you can store the text or graphic in a **building block** and then use the stored building block entry in the open document, as well as in future documents. That is, you can create the entry once as a building block, and for all future occurrences of the text or graphic, you can insert the building block as you need it. In this way, you avoid entering the text or graphics inconsistently or incorrectly in different locations throughout the same document.

The next steps create a building block for the prospective employer's name, Juniper Culinary Academy. Later in the chapter, you will insert the building block in the document instead of typing the employer's name.

1

- Select the text to be a building block, in this case, Juniper Culinary Academy. Do not select the paragraph mark at the end of the text.

Why is the paragraph mark not part of the building block?

Only select the paragraph mark if you want to store paragraph formatting, such as indentation and line spacing, as part of the building block.

- Click the Quick Parts button on the Insert tab to display the Quick Parts menu (Figure 3–32).

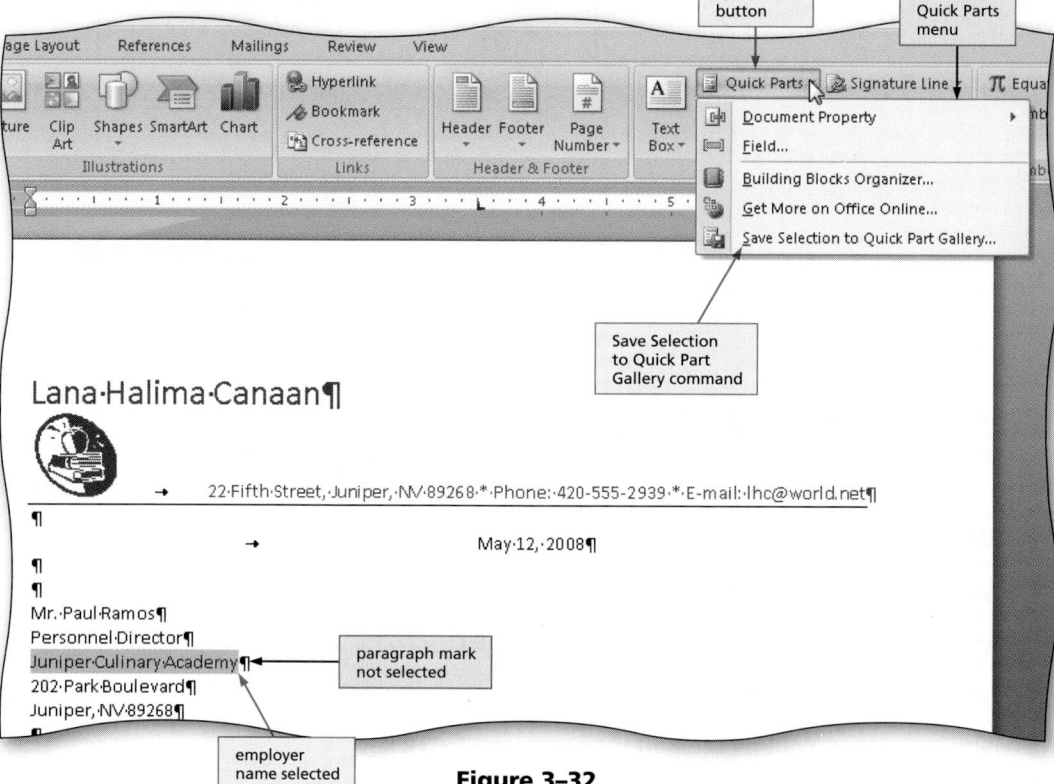

Figure 3–32

2

- Click Save Selection to Quick Part Gallery on the Quick Parts menu to display the Create New Building Block dialog box.

- Type jca in the Name text box to replace the proposed building block name (Juniper Culinary) with a shorter building block name (Figure 3–33).

3

- Click the OK button to store the building block entry and close the dialog box.

- If Word displays another dialog box, click the Yes button.

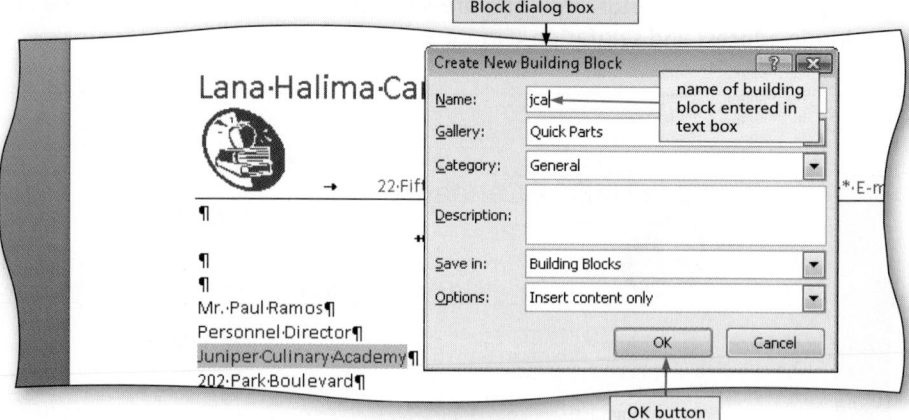

Figure 3–33

To Insert a Nonbreaking Space

Some compound words, such as proper nouns, dates, units of time and measure, abbreviations, and geographic destinations, should not be divided at the end of a line. These words either should fit as a unit at the end of a line or be wrapped together to the next line.

Word provides two special characters to assist with this task: nonbreaking space and nonbreaking hyphen. A **nonbreaking space** is a special space character that prevents two words from splitting if the first word falls at the end of a line. Similarly, a **nonbreaking hyphen** is a special type of hyphen that prevents two words separated by a hyphen from splitting at the end of a line.

The following steps insert a nonbreaking space between the words in the newspaper name.

- Click to the right of the colon in the salutation and then press the ENTER key twice to position the insertion point one blank line below the salutation.

- Type I am responding to the junior culinary instructor position that you recently advertised in the and then press the SPACEBAR.

- Press CTRL+I to turn on italics. Type Juniper as the first word in the newspaper name and then press CTRL+SHIFT+SPACEBAR to insert a nonbreaking space after the word, Juniper (Figure 3–34).

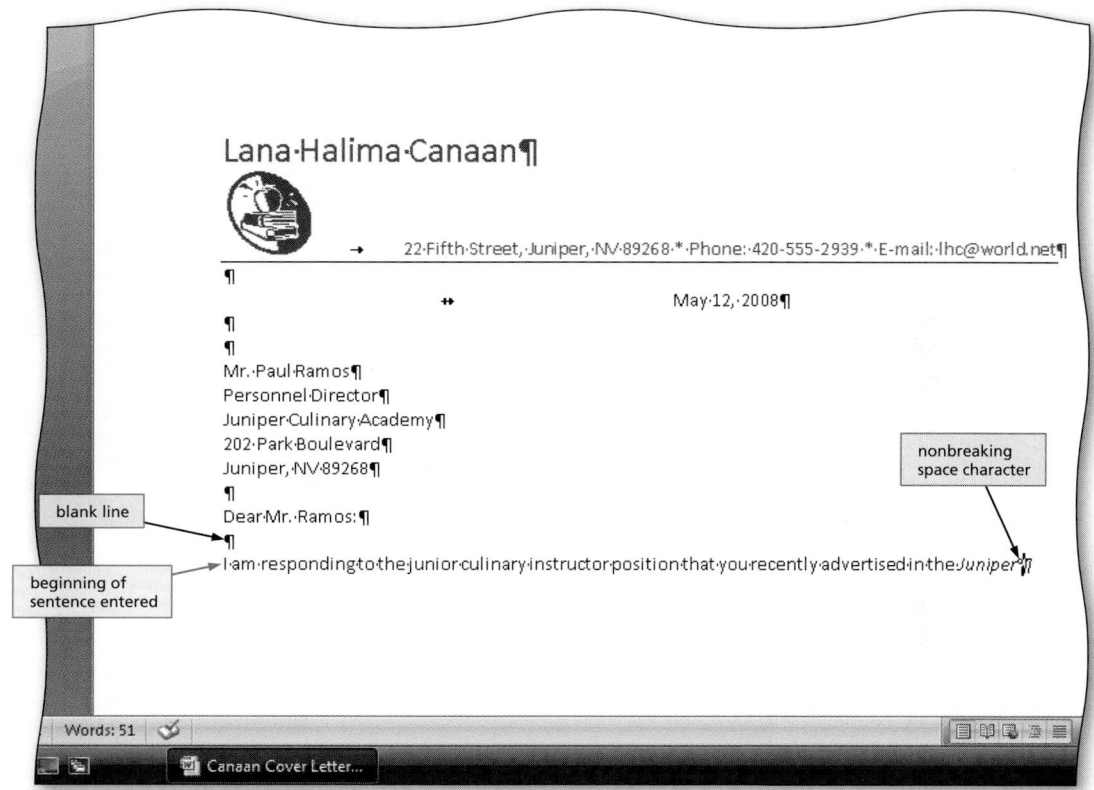

Figure 3–34

2

- Type Daily and then press CTRL+SHIFT+SPACEBAR to insert another nonbreaking space after the word, Daily.

- Type Herald and then press CTRL+I to turn off italics. Press the PERIOD key (Figure 3–35).

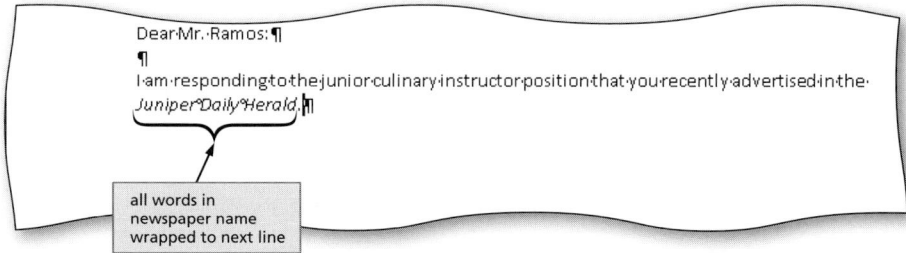

Figure 3–35

Other Ways
1. Click Symbol button on Insert tab, click More Symbols, click Special Characters tab, click   Nonbreaking Space in Character list, click Insert button, click Close button

To Insert a Building Block

At the end of the next sentence in the body of the cover letter, you want the prospective employer name, Juniper Culinary Academy, to be displayed. Recall that earlier in this chapter, you created a building block name of jca for Juniper Culinary Academy. Thus, you will type the building block name and then instruct Word to replace the building block name with the stored building block entry of Juniper Culinary Academy. The following steps insert a building block.

1

- Press the SPACEBAR. Type `As indicated on the enclosed resume, I have the credentials you are seeking and believe I can be a valuable asset to jca` as shown in Figure 3–36.

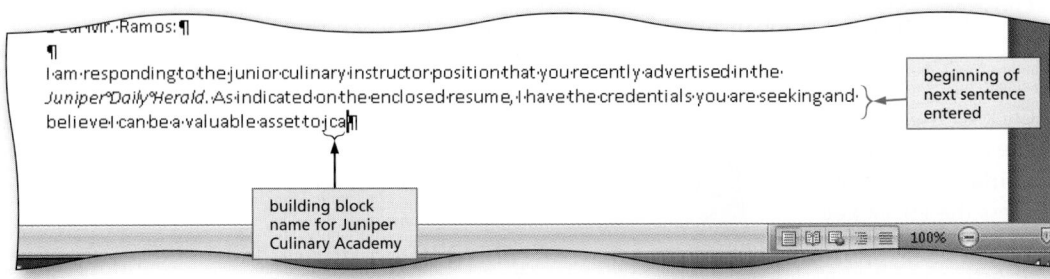

Figure 3–36

2

- Press the F3 key to instruct word to replace the building block name (jca) with the stored building block entry (Juniper Culinary Academy).
- Press the PERIOD key (Figure 3–37).

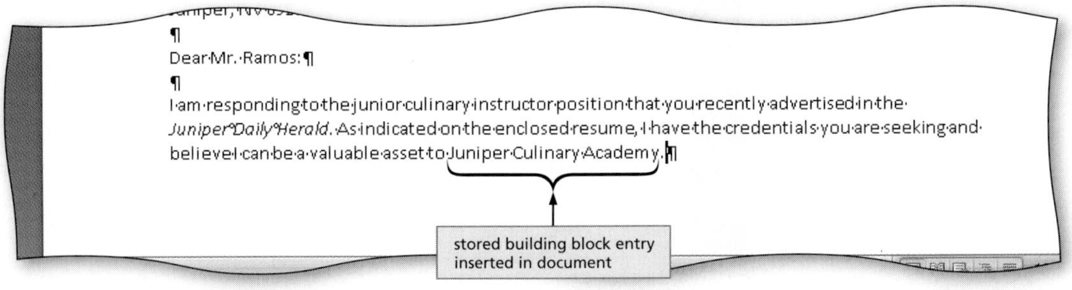

Figure 3–37

Other Ways

1. Click Quick Parts button on Insert tab, click desired building block

Building Blocks vs. AutoCorrect

In Project 2, you learned how to use the AutoCorrect feature, which enables you to insert and create AutoCorrect entries, similarly to how you created and inserted building blocks in this chapter. The difference between an AutoCorrect entry and a building block entry is that the AutoCorrect feature makes corrections for you automatically as soon as you press the SPACEBAR or type a punctuation mark, whereas you must instruct Word to insert a building block. That is, you enter the building block name and then press the F3 key, or click the Quick Parts button and select the building block from the list.

To Enter a Paragraph

The next step in creating the cover letter is to enter a paragraph of text.

1 Press the ENTER key twice to place a blank line between paragraphs, according to the guidelines of the modified block letter style.

BTW **Nonbreaking Hyphen**
If you wanted to insert a nonbreaking hyphen, you would press CTRL+SHIFT+HYPHEN.

2 Type I recently received my bachelor's degree in culinary arts from Nevada Culinary Institute. The following table outlines my areas of concentration:

3 Press the ENTER key twice.

Tables

The next step in composing the cover letter is to place a table listing the number of credit hours for areas of concentration (shown in Figure 3–1 on page WD 147). A Word **table** is a collection of rows and columns. The intersection of a row and a column is called a **cell**, and cells are filled with text.

The first step in creating a table is to insert an empty table into the document. When inserting a table, you must specify the total number of rows and columns required, which is called the **dimension** of the table. The table in this project has two columns. You often do not know the total number of rows in a table. Thus, many Word users create one row initially and then add more rows as needed. In Word, the first number in a dimension is the number of columns, and the second is the number of rows. For example, in Word, a 2×1 (pronounced "two by one") table consists of two columns and one row.

To Insert an Empty Table

The next step is to insert an empty table in the cover letter. The following steps insert a table with two columns and one row at the location of the insertion point.

1
- Click the Table button on the Insert tab to display the Table gallery.

Experiment
- Point to various cells on the grid to see a preview of the table in the document window.

2
- Position the mouse pointer on the cell in the first row and second column of the grid to preview the desired table dimension (Figure 3–38).

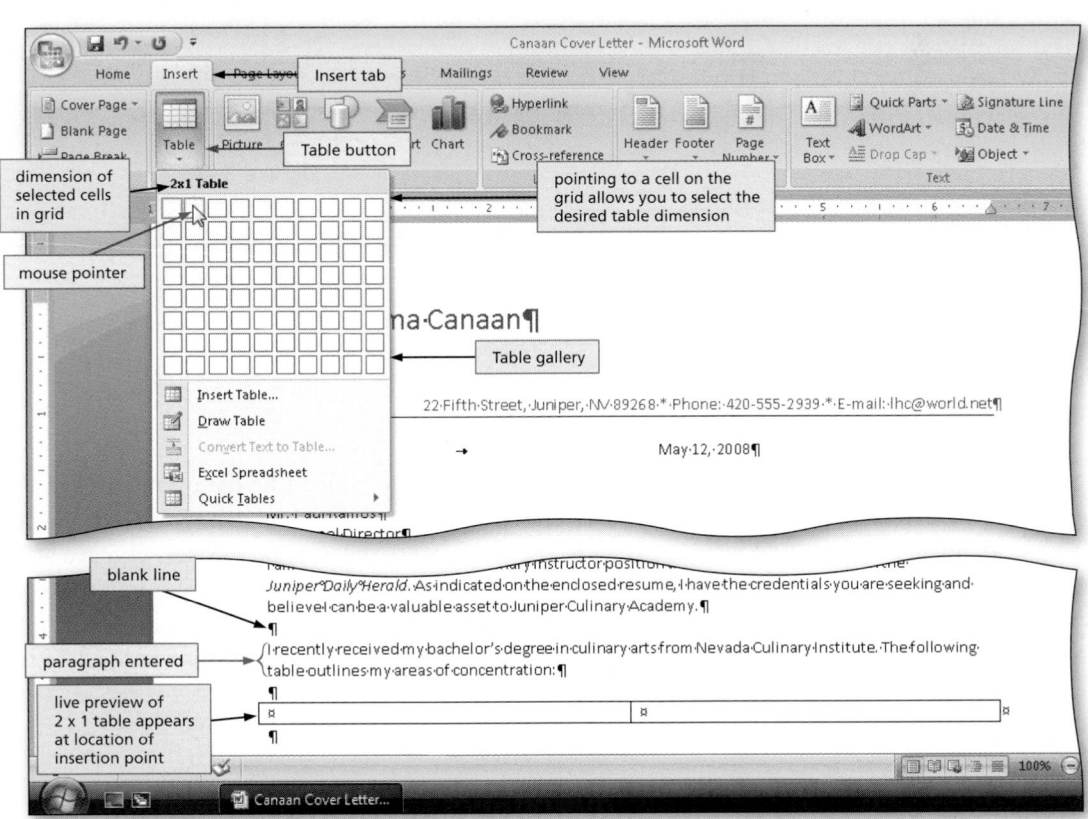

Figure 3–38

• Click the cell in the first row and second column of the grid to insert an empty table with one row and two columns in the document (Figure 3–39).

Q&A

What are the small circles in the table cells?

Each table cell has an **end-of-cell mark**, which is a formatting mark that assists you with selecting and formatting cells. Similarly, each row has an **end-of-row mark**, which you can use to add columns to the right of a table. Recall that formatting marks do not print on a hard copy. The end-of-cell marks currently are left-aligned, that is, positioned at the left edge of each cell.

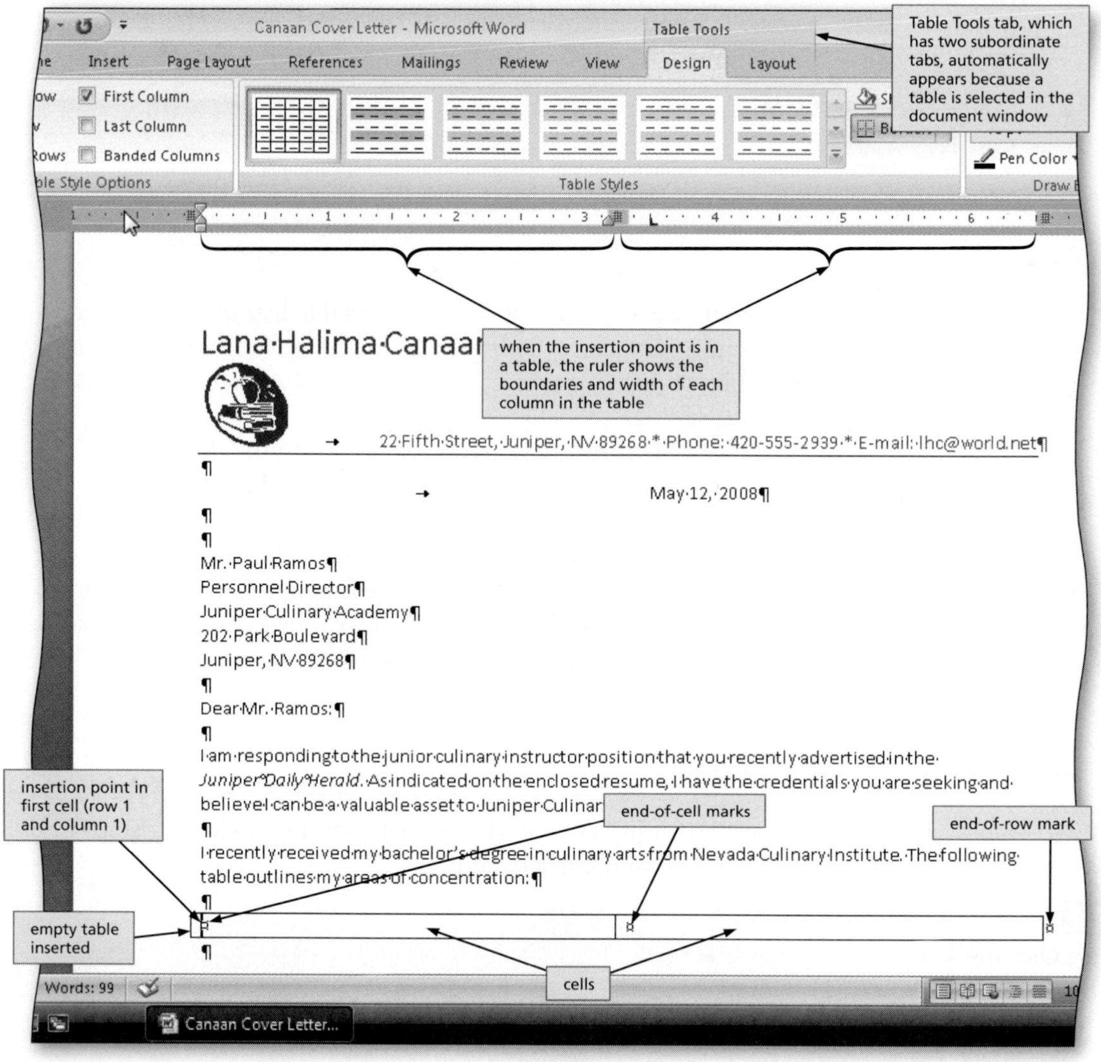

Canaan Cover Letter - Microsoft Word

Table Tools tab, which has two subordinate tabs, automatically appears because a table is selected in the document window

when the insertion point is in a table, the ruler shows the boundaries and width of each column in the table

insertion point in first cell (row 1 and column 1)

end-of-cell marks

end-of-row mark

empty table inserted

cells

Figure 3–39

Other Ways

1. Click Table on Insert tab, click Insert Table on Table gallery, enter number of columns and rows, click OK button

To Enter Data in a Table

The next step is to enter data in the cells of the empty table. The data you enter in a cell wordwraps just as text wordwraps between the margins of a document. To place data in a cell, you click the cell and then type.

To advance rightward from one cell to the next, press the TAB key. When you are at the rightmost cell in a row, press the TAB key to move to the first cell in the next row; do not press the ENTER key. The ENTER key is used to begin a new paragraph within a cell. One way to add new rows to a table is to press the TAB key when the insertion point is positioned in the bottom-right corner cell of the table. The next steps enter data in the table, adding rows as necessary.

1

• If necessary, scroll the table up in the document window.

• With the insertion point in the left cell of the table, type Food Planning and Preparation and then press the TAB key to advance the insertion point to the next cell.

• Type 30 hours and then press the TAB key to add a second row to the table and position the insertion point in the first column of the new row (Figure 3–40).

Q&A

How do I edit cell contents if I make a mistake?

Click in the cell and then correct the entry.

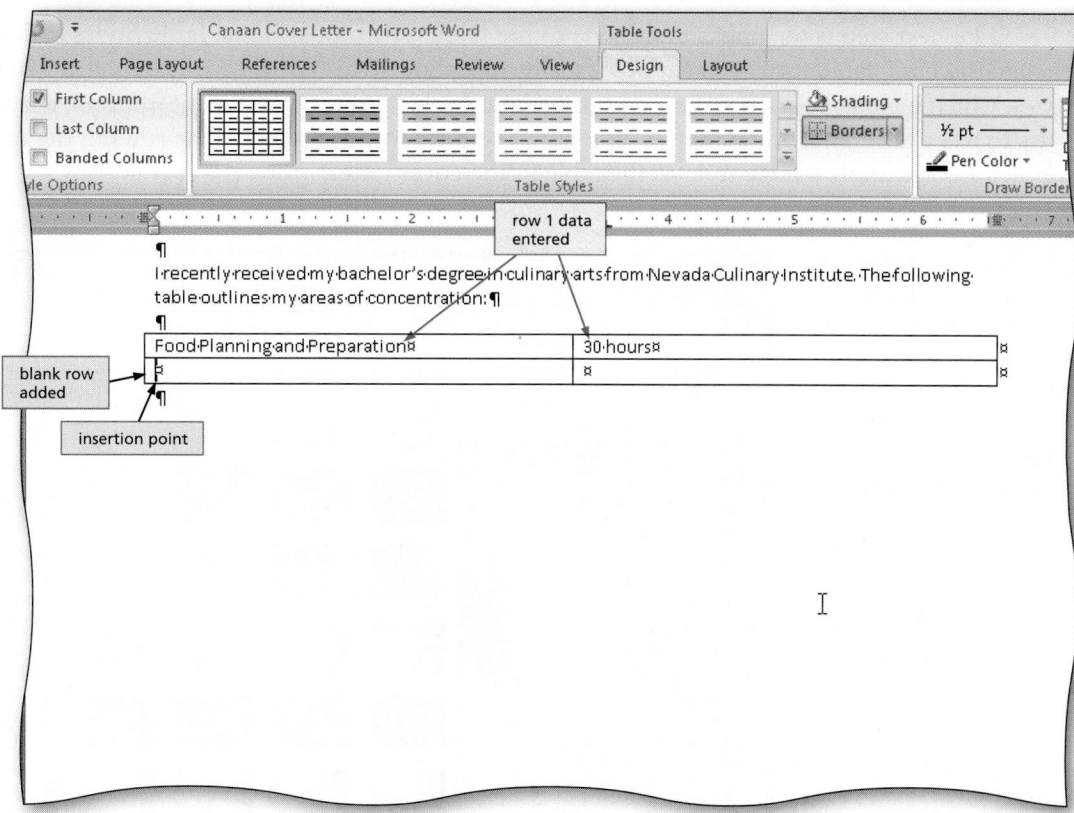

Figure 3–40

2

• Type Food Safety and then press the TAB key. Type 15 hours and then press the TAB key.

• Type Nutrition and then press the TAB key. Type 15 hours and then press the TAB key.

• Type Regional and International Cuisine and then press the TAB key. Type 21 hours to complete the entries in the table (Figure 3–41).

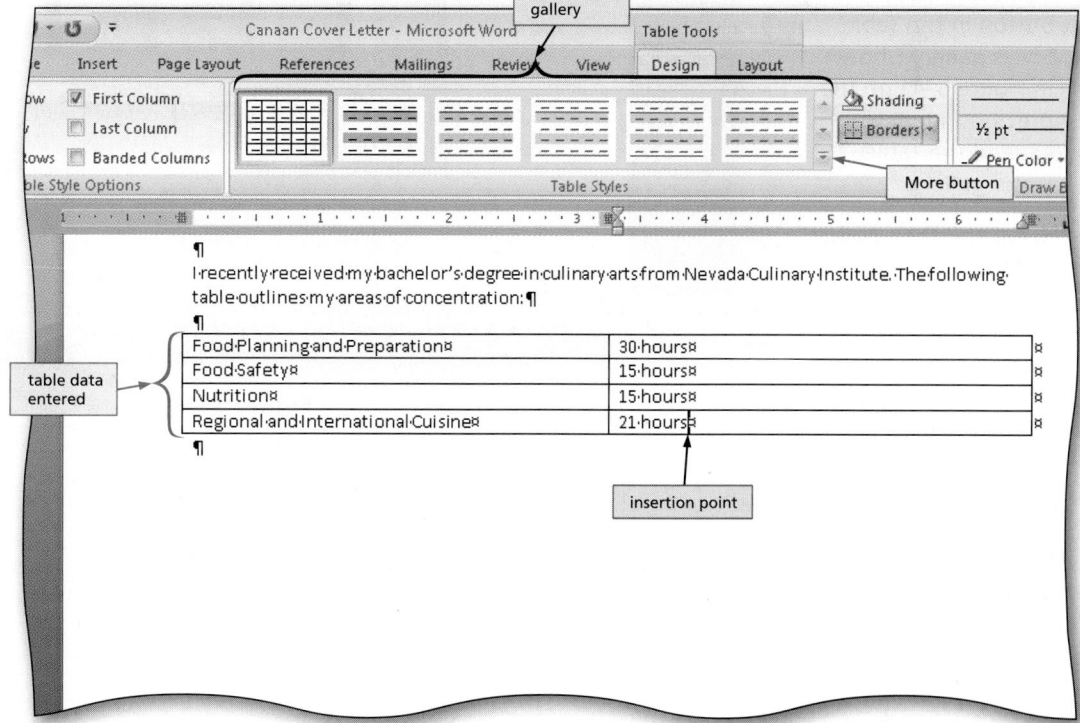

Figure 3–41

To Apply a Table Style

The next step is to apply a table style to the table. Word provides a Table Styles gallery, allowing you to change the basic table format to a more visually appealing style. Word provides a gallery of more than 90 table styles, which include a variety of colors and shading. In this project, you do not want the heading rows or alternating rows to use a different format; that is, you want the formatting applied to the rows in the table to be the same. The following steps apply a table style to the table in the cover letter.

1

- With the insertion point in the table, remove the check marks from the Header Row and Banded Rows check boxes on the Design tab so that all rows in the table will be formatted the same.

Q&A

What if the Design tab in the Table Tools tab no longer is the active tab?

Click in the table and then click Design on the Ribbon.

2

- Click the More button in the Table Styles gallery (shown in Figure 3–41 on the previous page) to expand the Table Styles gallery.

- Scroll and then point to Medium Grid 3 - Accent 2 in the Table Styles gallery to display a live preview of that style applied to the table in the document (Figure 3–42).

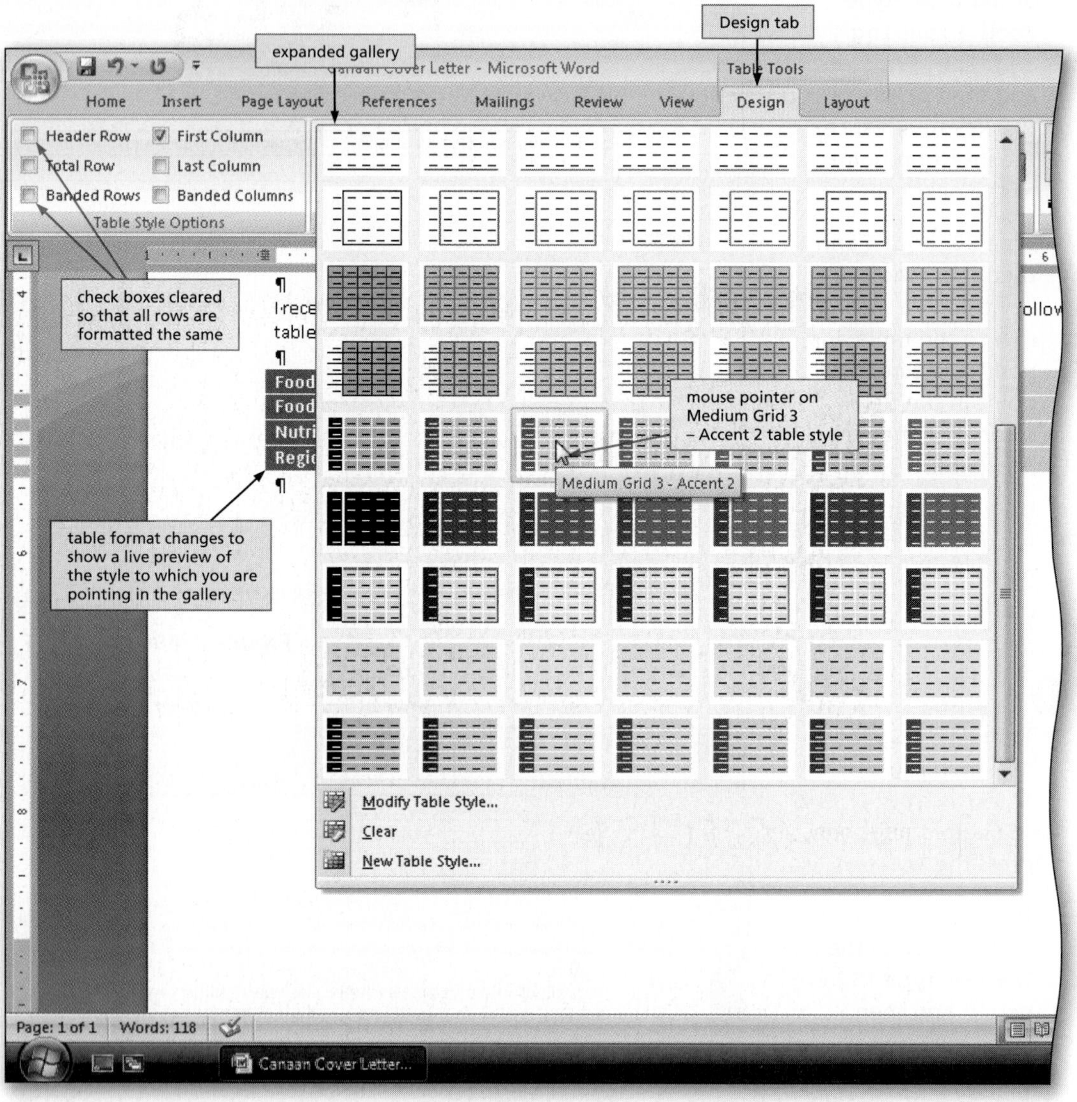

Figure 3–42

Experiment

- Point to various table styles in the Table Styles gallery and watch the format of the table change in the document window.

3

- Click Medium Grid 3 - Accent 2 in the Table Styles gallery to apply the selected style to the table (Figure 3–43).

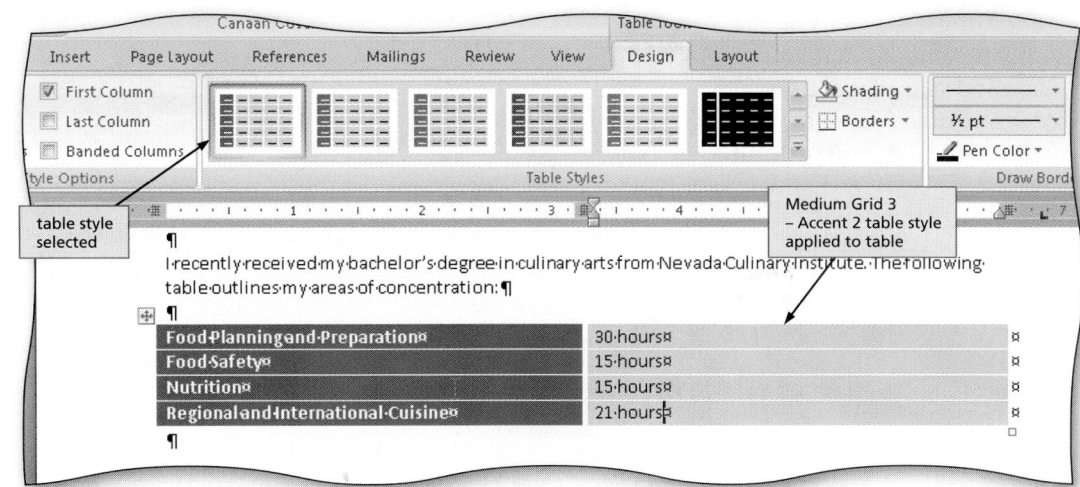

Figure 3–43

To Resize Table Columns to Fit Table Contents

The table in this project currently extends from the left margin to the right margin of the document. You want each column only to be as wide as the longest entry in the table. That is, the first column must be wide enough to accommodate the words, Regional and International Cuisine, and the second column should be only as wide as the hours entered. The following steps instruct Word to fit the width of the columns to the contents of the table automatically.

1

- With the insertion point in the table, click Layout on the Ribbon to display the Layout tab.

- Click the AutoFit button on the Layout tab to display the AutoFit menu (Figure 3–44).

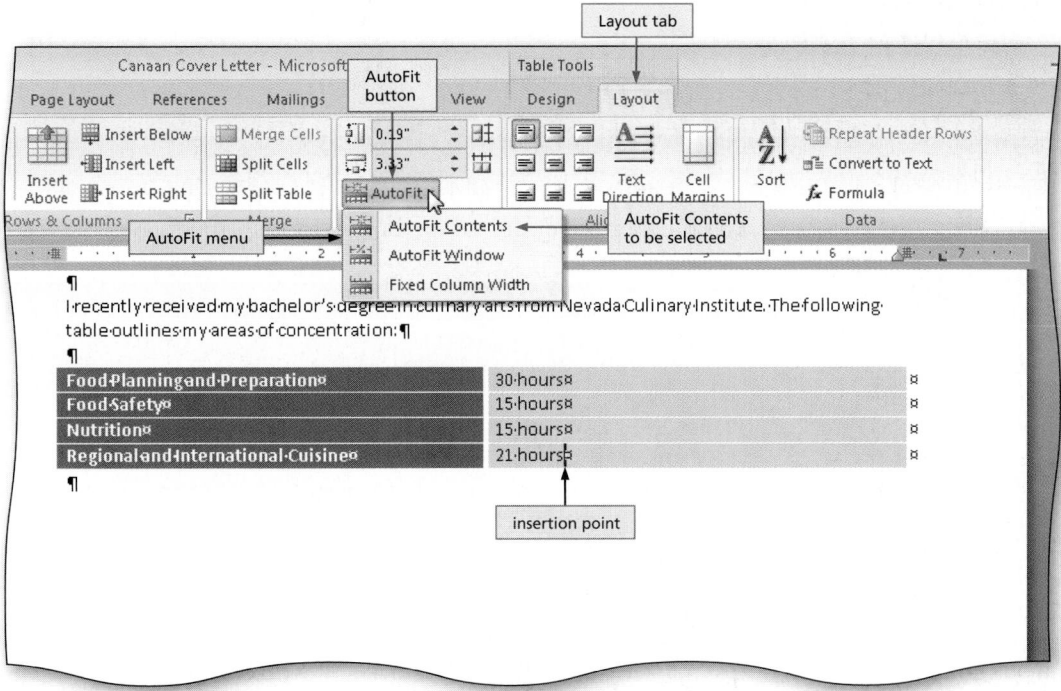

Figure 3–44

2

- Click AutoFit Contents on the AutoFit menu, so that Word automatically adjusts the widths of the columns based on the text in the table (Figure 3–45).

Q&A

Can I resize columns manually?

Yes, you can drag a **column boundary**, the border to the right of a column, until the column is the desired width. Similarly, you can resize a row by dragging the **row boundary**, the border at the bottom of a row, until the row is the desired height. You also can resize the entire table by dragging the **table resize handle**, which is a small square that appears when you point to a corner of the table (shown in Figure 3–46).

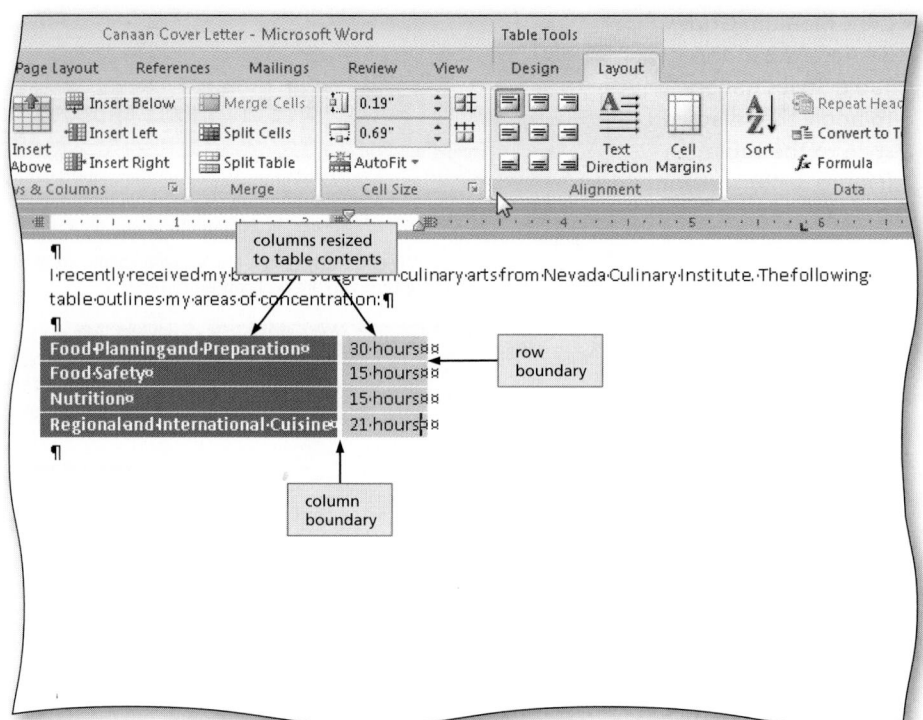

Figure 3–45

Other Ways

1. Right-click table, point to AutoFit on shortcut menu, click AutoFit to Contents
2. Double-click column boundary

Selecting Table Contents

When working with tables, you may need to select the contents of cells, rows, columns, or the entire table. Table 3–3 identifies ways to select various items in a table.

Table 3–3 Selecting Items in a Table

Item to Select	Action
Cell	Click left edge of cell
Column	Click border at top of column
Multiple cells, rows, or columns adjacent to one another	Drag through cells, rows, or columns
Multiple cells, rows, or columns not adjacent to one another	Select first cell, row, or column and then hold down CTRL key while selecting next cell, row, or column
Next cell	Press TAB key
Previous cell	Press SHIFT+TAB
Row	Click to left of row
Table	Click table move handle

BTW

Tab Character

In a table, the TAB key advances the insertion point from one cell to the next in a table. To insert a tab character in a cell, you must press CTRL+TAB.

To Select a Table

When you first create a table, it is left-aligned, that is, flush with the left margin. In this cover letter, the table should be centered. To center a table, you first select the entire table.

- Position the mouse pointer in the table so that the table move handle appears.

- Click the table move handle to select the entire table (Figure 3–46).

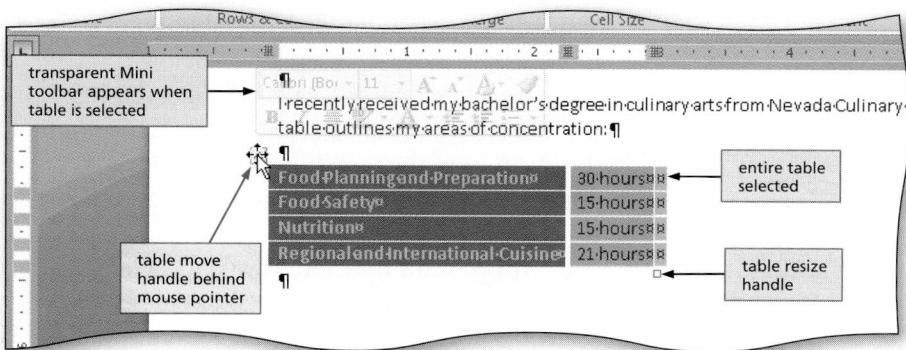

Figure 3–46

Other Ways

1. Click Select button on Layout tab, click Select Table on Select menu

To Center a Selected Table

The following steps center the selected table between the margins.

1. Move the mouse pointer into the Mini toolbar, so that the toolbar changes to a bright toolbar.

2. Click the Center button on the Mini toolbar to center the selected table between the left and right margins (Figure 3–47).

Q&A When should I use the Mini toolbar versus the Ribbon?

If the command you want to use is not on the currently displayed tab on the Ribbon and it is available on the Mini toolbar, use the Mini toolbar instead of switching to a different tab. This technique minimizes mouse movement.

Q&A How would I center the contents of the table cells instead of the entire table?

If you wanted to center the contents of the cells, you would select the cells by dragging through them and then click the Center button.

BTW

Tables
For simple tables, such as the one just created, Word users often select the table dimension in the grid to create the table. For more complex tables, such as one with a varying number of columns per row, Word has a Draw Table feature that allows users to draw a table in the document using a pencil pointer. To use this feature, click Table on the Insert tab and then click Draw Table.

Figure 3–47

Adding and Deleting Table Rows

As discussed in the previous steps, you can add a row to the end of a table by positioning the insertion point in the bottom-right corner cell and then pressing the TAB key. You also can add rows to a table by clicking the Insert Rows Above button or Insert Rows Below button on the Layout tab to insert a row above or below the location of the insertion point in the table. Similarly, you can right-click the table, point to Insert on the shortcut menu, and then click Insert Rows Above or Insert Rows Below.

To add columns to a table, click the Insert Columns to the Left button or Insert Columns to the Right button on the Layout tab to insert a column to the left or right of the location of the insertion point in the table. Similarly, you can right-click the table, point to Insert on the shortcut menu, and then click Insert Columns to the Left or Insert Columns to the Right.

If you want to delete row(s) or delete column(s) from a table, position the insertion point in the row(s) or column(s) to delete, click the Delete button on the Layout tab, and then click Delete Rows or Delete Columns. Or, select the row or column to delete, right-click the selection, and then click Delete Rows or Delete Columns on the shortcut menu.

To delete the contents of a cell, select the cell contents by pointing to the left edge of a cell and clicking when the mouse pointer changes direction, and then press the DELETE key. You also can drag and drop or cut and paste the contents of cells.

BTW

Table Rows and Columns
To change the width of a column to an exact measurement, hold down the ALT key while dragging markers on the ruler. Or, enter values in the Table Row Height and Table Column Width text boxes on the Layout tab.

To Add More Text

The next step is to add more text below the table.

1 Position the insertion point on the paragraph mark below the table and then press the ENTER key.

2 Type `In addition to my coursework, I have the following culinary experience:` and then press the ENTER key.

To Bullet a List as You Type

In Chapter 1, you learned how to apply bullets to existing paragraphs. If you know before you type that a list should be bulleted, you can use Word's AutoFormat As You Type feature to bullet the paragraphs as you type them (Table 3–2 on page WD 163). The following steps add bullets to a list as you type.

• Press the ASTERISK key (*) as the first character on the line (Figure 3–48).

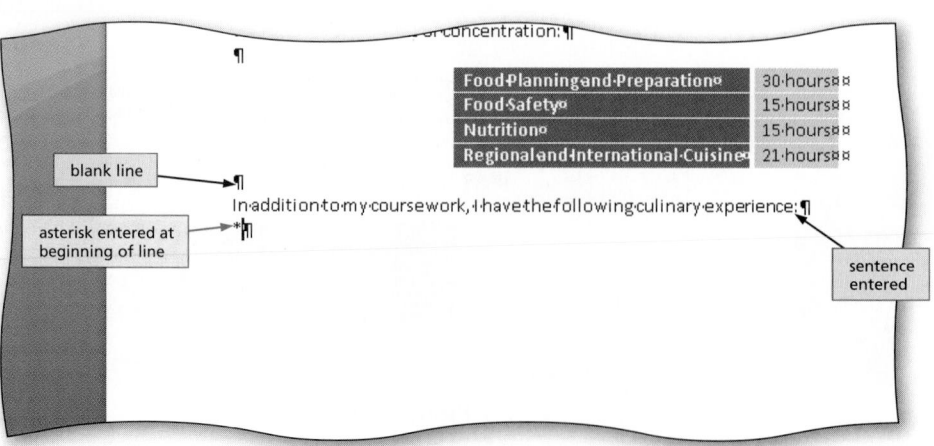

Figure 3–48

2

- Press the SPACEBAR to convert the asterisk to a bullet character.

What if I did not want the asterisk converted to a bullet character?

You would undo the AutoFormat by clicking the Undo button, or by clicking the AutoCorrect Options button and then clicking Undo Automatic Bullets on the AutoCorrect Options menu, or by clicking the Bullets button on the Home tab.

- **Type** Assist with food preparation at my family's local pastry, bread, and bakery business as the first bulleted item.

- Press the ENTER key to place another bullet character at the beginning of the next line (Figure 3–49).

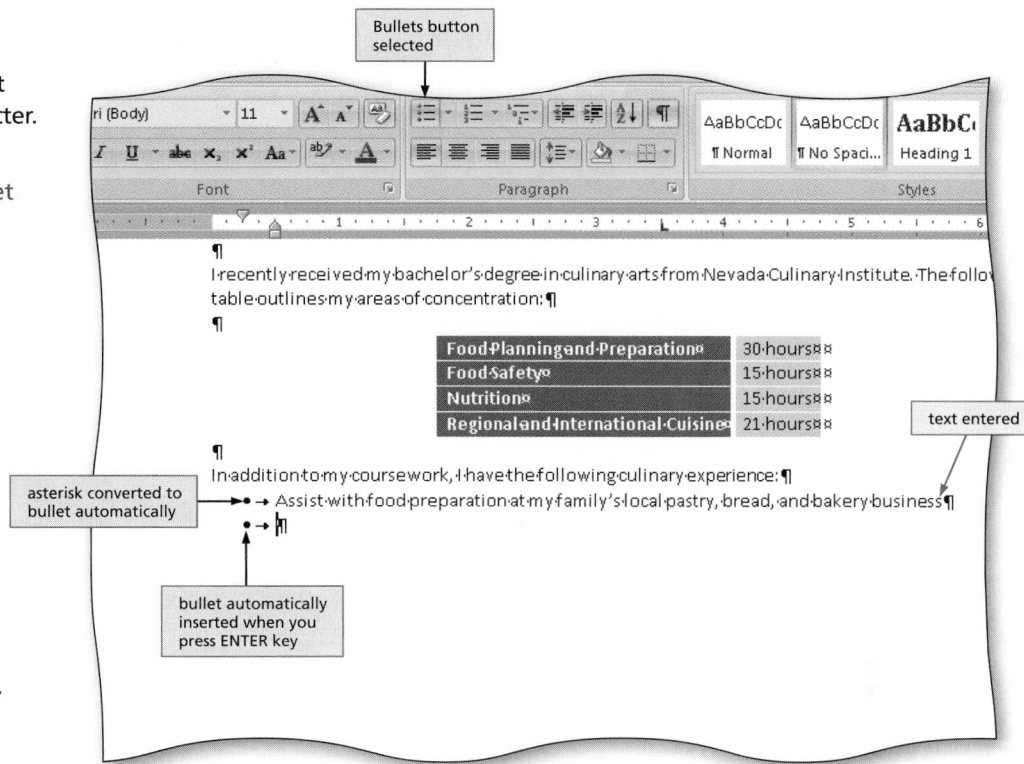

Figure 3–49

3

- **Type** Prepare food and serve meals at Hope Mission and then press the ENTER key.

- **Type** Assisted the chef with meal preparation and presentation during internship at The Garden Grill and then press the ENTER key.

- **Type** Prepared salads, soups, sandwiches, entrees, and desserts while working at the school cafeteria and then press the ENTER key.

- Press the ENTER key to turn off automatic bullets as you type (Figure 3–50).

Why did automatic bullets stop?

When you press the ENTER key without entering any text after the automatic bullet character, Word turns off the automatic bullets feature.

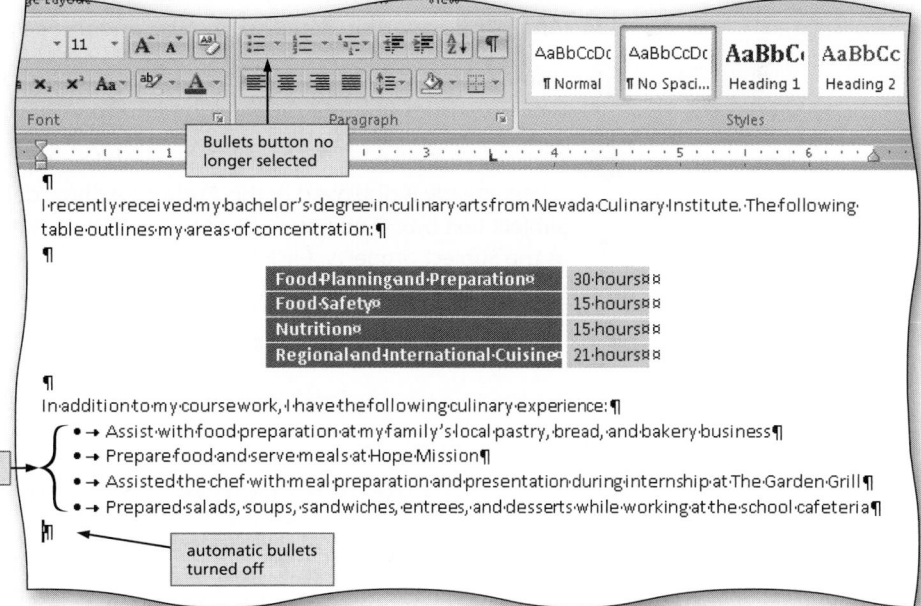

Figure 3–50

Other Ways
1. Click Bullets button on Home tab
2. Right-click paragraph to be bulleted, click bullets button on Mini toolbar
3. Right-click paragraph to be bulleted, point to Bullets on shortcut menu, click desired bullet style

To Enter the Remainder of the Cover Letter

The next step is to enter the remainder of the cover letter.

1 Press the ENTER key and then type the paragraph shown in Figure 3–51, making certain you use the building block name, jca, to insert the employer name.

2 Press the ENTER key twice. Press the TAB key. Type Sincerely and then press the COMMA key.

3 Press the ENTER key four times. Press the TAB key. Type Lana Halima Canaan and then press the ENTER key twice. Type Enclosure as the final text in the cover letter (Figure 3–51).

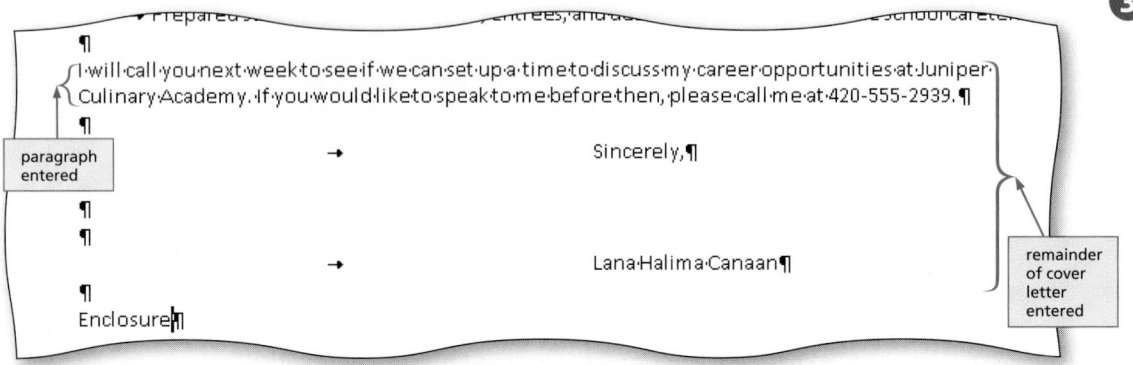

Figure 3–51

To Change Document Properties

Before saving the research paper again, you want to add your name, course and section, and some keywords as document properties. The following steps use the Document Information Panel to change document properties.

1 Display the Office Button menu, point to Prepare on the Office Button menu, and then click Properties on the Prepare submenu to display the Document Information Panel.

2 Click the Author text box, if necessary, and then type your name as the Author property. If a name already is displayed in the Author text box, delete it before typing your name. Click the Subject text box, if necessary delete any existing text, and then type your course and section as the Subject property. Click the Keywords text box, if necessary delete any existing text, and then type Cover Letter as the Keywords property.

3 Close the Document Information Panel.

BTW

Conserving Ink and Toner
You can instruct Word to print draft quality documents to conserve ink or toner by clicking the Office Button, clicking the Word Options button, clicking Advanced in the left pane of the Word Options dialog box, scrolling to the Print area, placing a check mark in the 'Use draft quality' check box, and then clicking the OK button. Click the Office Button, point to Print, and then click Quick Print.

To Save an Existing Document and Print It

The document now is complete. You should save the cover letter again. The following steps save the document again and then print it. Do not close the Canaan Cover Letter file. You will use it again later in this chapter to copy the address, phone, and e-mail information to the resume.

1 Click the Save button on the Quick Access Toolbar to overwrite the previous Canaan Cover Letter file on the USB flash drive.

2 Display the Office Button menu, point to Print, and then click Quick Print to print the cover letter (shown in Figure 3–1 on page WD 147).

Using a Template to Create a Resume

The next step in this project is to create the resume (Figure 3–2 on page WD 148). Although you could compose a resume in a blank document window, this chapter shows instead how to use a template, where Word formats the resume with appropriate headings and spacing. You customize the resume created by the template by filling in blanks and by selecting and replacing text.

Craft a successful resume.

Two types of resumes are the chronological resume and the functional resume. A chronological resume sequences information by time, with the most recent listed first. This type of resume highlights a job seeker's job continuity and growth. A functional resume groups information by skills and accomplishments. This resume emphasizes a job seeker's experience and qualifications in specialized areas. Some resumes use a combination of the two formats. For an entry-level job search, experts recommend a chronological resume or a combination of the two types of resumes.

When creating your resume, be sure to include necessary information and present it appropriately. Keep descriptions short and concise, using action words and bulleted lists.

- **Include necessary information.** Your resume should include contact information, a clearly written objective, educational background, and experience. Use your complete legal name and mailing address, along with phone number and e-mail address, if one exists. Other sections you might consider including are organizations, recognitions and awards, and skills. Do not include your social security number, marital status, age, height, weight, gender, physical appearance, health, citizenship, previous pay rates, reasons for leaving a prior job, current date, high-school information (if you are a college graduate), and references. Employers assume you will give references, if asked, and this information simply clutters a resume.

- **Present your resume appropriately.** For printed resumes, use a high-quality ink-jet or laser printer to print your resume (and cover letter) on standard letter-size white or ivory paper. Consider using paper that contains cotton fibers for a professional look. Select envelopes that are the same quality and grade as the paper. If you e-mail the resume, consider that the potential employer may not have the same software you used to create the resume and thus may not be able to open it up. As an alternative, you could save the file in a format, such as a PDF, that can be viewed with a reader program. Many job seekers also post their resume on the Web.

To Use a Template

Word installs a variety of templates for letters, fax cover sheets, reports, and resumes on your hard disk. The templates are grouped in five styles: Equity, Median, Oriel, Origin, and Urban. The templates in each style use similar formatting, themes, etc., enabling users to create a set of documents that complement one another. In this chapter, you will create a resume from the template in the Origin style. The following steps create a new document based on a template.

1
- Display the Office Button menu (Figure 3–52).

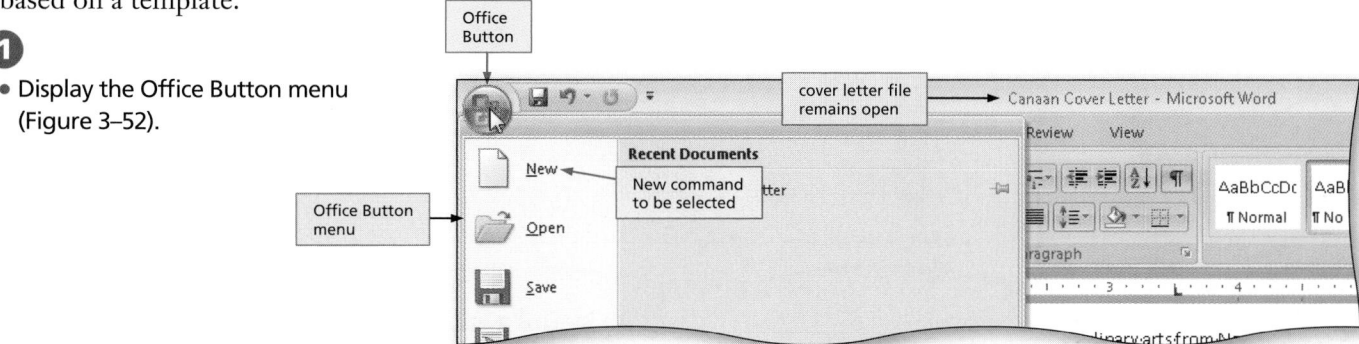

Figure 3–52

2

- Click New on the Office Button menu to display the New Document dialog box.

- Click Installed Templates in the Templates area to display the list of templates on the hard disk.

🔍 Experiment

- Click various installed templates in the Installed Templates list and watch the preview of the template display at the right edge of the dialog box.

3

- Scroll through the Installed Templates list and then click Origin Resume to select it (Figure 3–53).

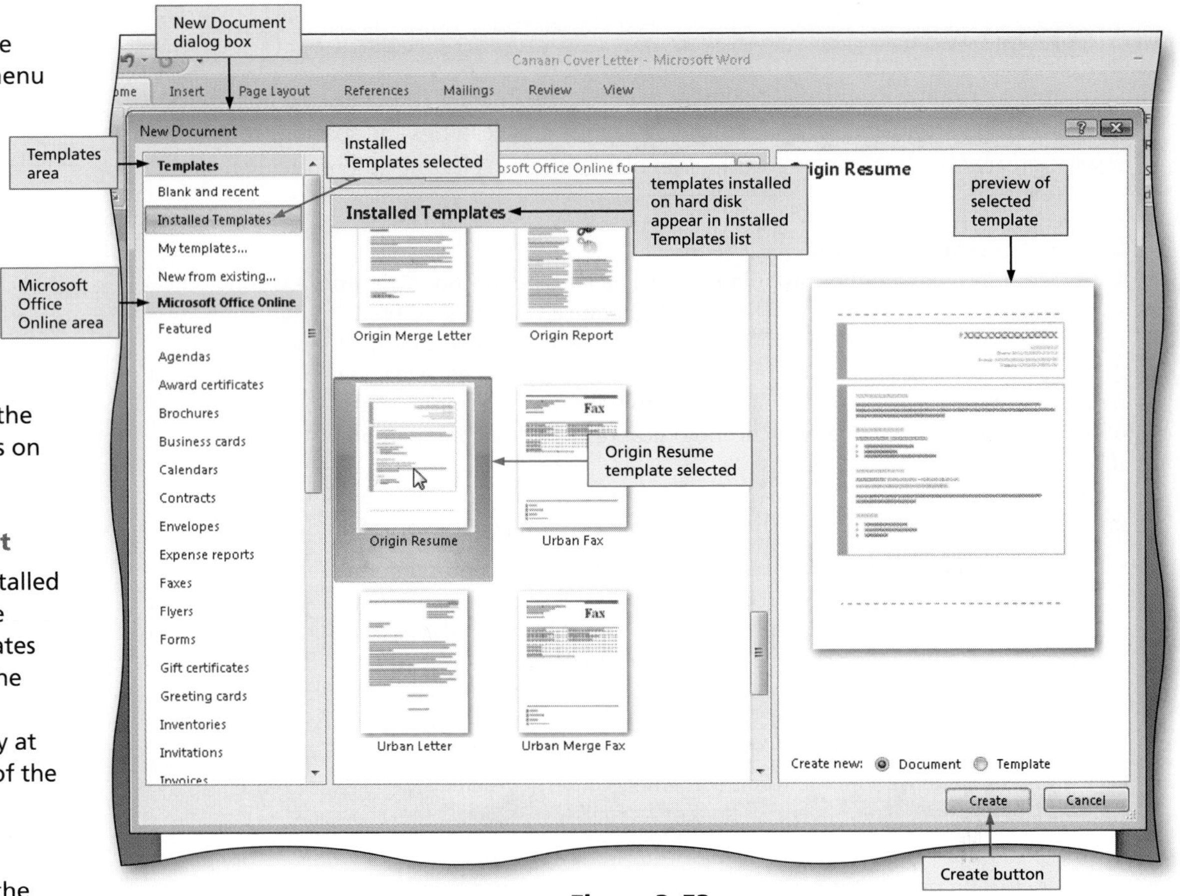

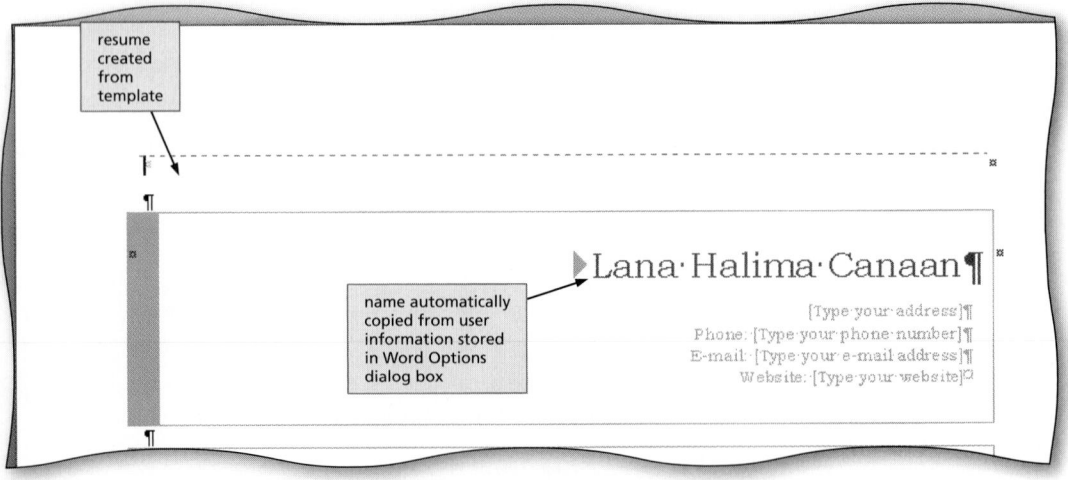

Figure 3–53

Q&A | How do I access a template on the Web?

If you are connected to the Internet when you click the desired template in the Microsoft Office Online area of the New Document dialog box, Word automatically displays templates from the Microsoft Office Online Web page that you can download.

4

- Click the Create button to create a new document based on the selected template (Figure 3–54).

resume created from template

name automatically copied from user information stored in Word Options dialog box

▶Lana·Halima·Canaan¶

[Type·your·address]¶
Phone:·[Type·your·phone·number]¶
E-mail:·[Type·your·e-mail·address]¶
Website:·[Type·your·website]□

Figure 3–54

To Print the Resume

To see the entire resume created by the resume template, print the document shown in the Word window.

1 Ready the printer. Display the Office Button menu, point to Print, and then click Quick Print to print the resume created from the template (Figure 3–55).

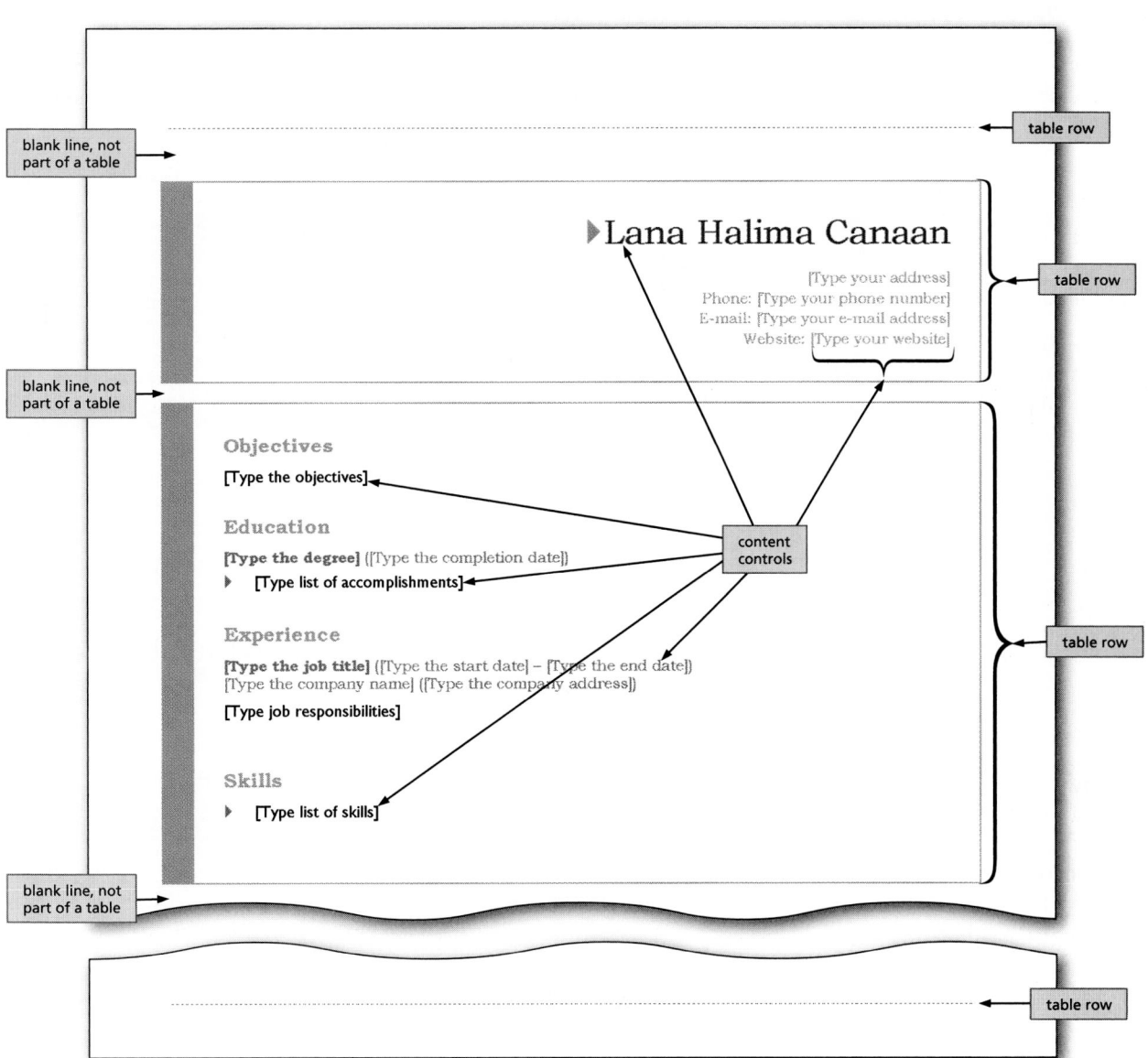

Figure 3–55

Resume Template

The resume created from the template, shown in Figure 3–55, consists of four individual tables, each with one row and one column. The first and last tables contain a decorative blue line; the second table contains the labels and content controls for the job seeker's contact information; and the third table contains labels and content controls for the Objectives, Education, Experience, and Skills sections of the resume. A **content control** contains instructions for filling areas of the template. To select a content control, you click it. As soon as you begin typing in the selected content control, your typing replaces the instruction in the control. Thus, you do not need to delete the selection before you begin typing.

The next step is to personalize the resume. The following pages personalize the resume created by the resume template.

To Delete Rows

The first and last rows of the resume created from the template contain a decorative line. The resume in this project deletes those rows to provide more space for the contents of the resume. The following steps delete the first and last rows on the resume.

- With the insertion point at the top of the document, click Layout on the Ribbon to display the Layout tab.

- Click the Delete button on the Layout tab to display the Delete menu (Figure 3–56).

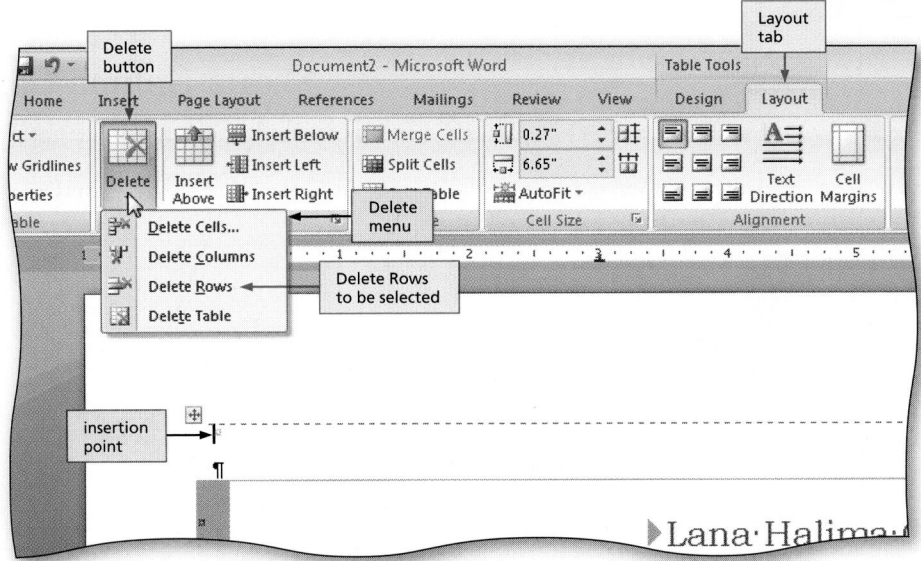

Figure 3–56

- Click Delete Rows on the Delete menu to delete the row containing the insertion point (Figure 3–57).

Q&A

What happened to the Table Tools tab on the Ribbon?

It is a contextual tab that appears only when the insertion point is in a table. With the row deleted, the insertion point is above the table row containing contact information.

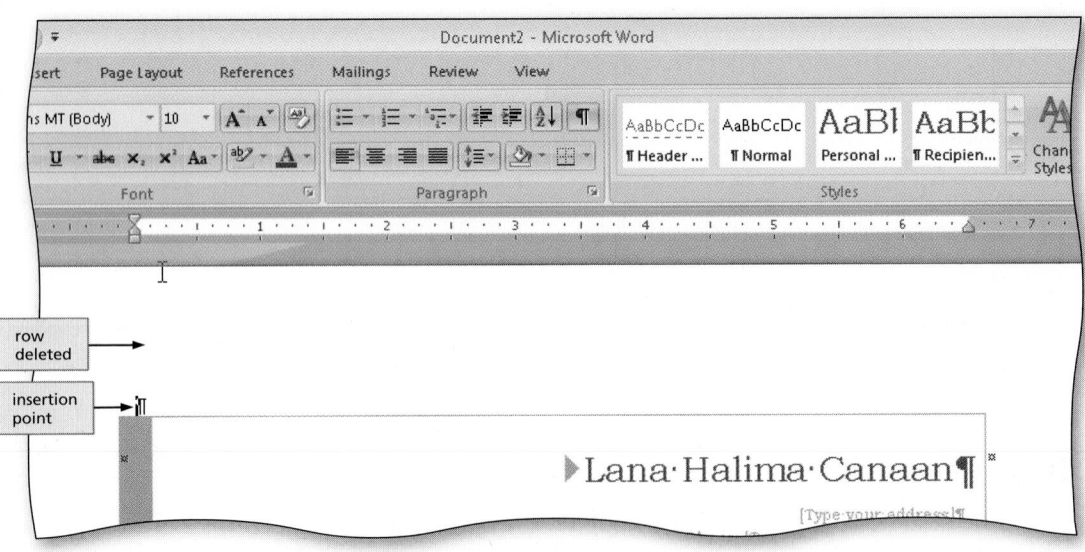

Figure 3–57

3

- Press CTRL+END and then press the DOWN ARROW key to position the insertion point at the bottom of the document in the last row.

- Click Layout on the Ribbon to display the Layout tab.

- Click the Delete button on the Layout tab to display the Delete menu (Figure 3–58).

4

- Click Delete Rows on the Delete menu to delete the row containing the insertion point.

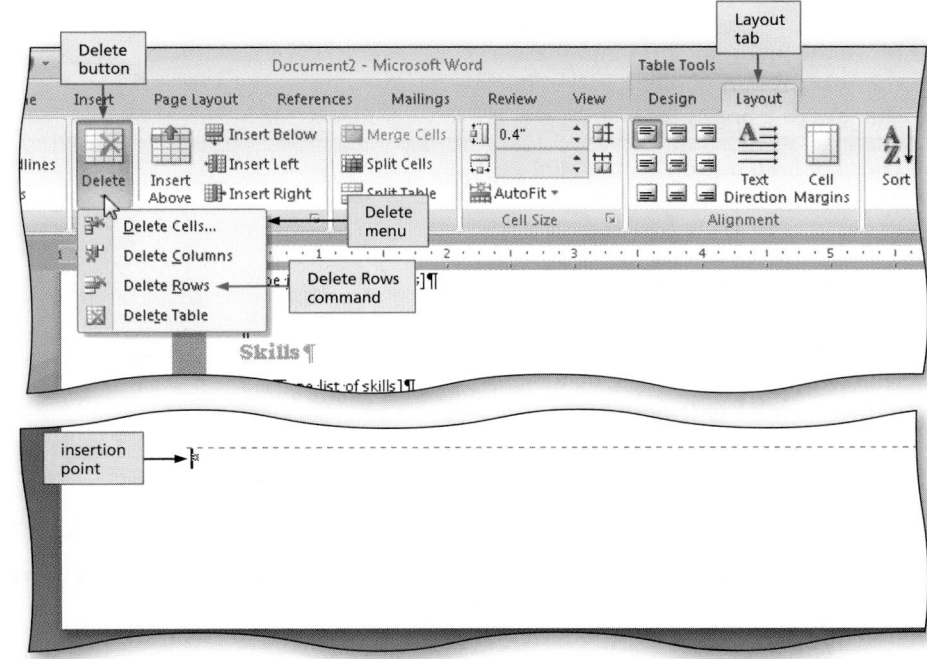

Figure 3–58

To Modify Text in a Content Control

The next step is to select text that the template inserted in the resume and replace it with personal information. The name area on your resume may contain a name, which Word copied from the Word Options dialog box, or it may contain the instruction, Type your name. This content control should contain your name. In this project, the name is bold to give it more emphasis on the resume. It also uses the same color as the name on the cover letter.

The following steps modify the text in the content control that contains the job seeker's name.

1

- Press CTRL+HOME to position the insertion point at the top of the document.

- Click the name content control to select it (if it already contains a name, instead of the instruction, Type name here, drag through the name to select it). Then, type Lana Halima Canaan as the name.

- Triple-click the name content control to select its contents, so that you can format the name (Figure 3–59).

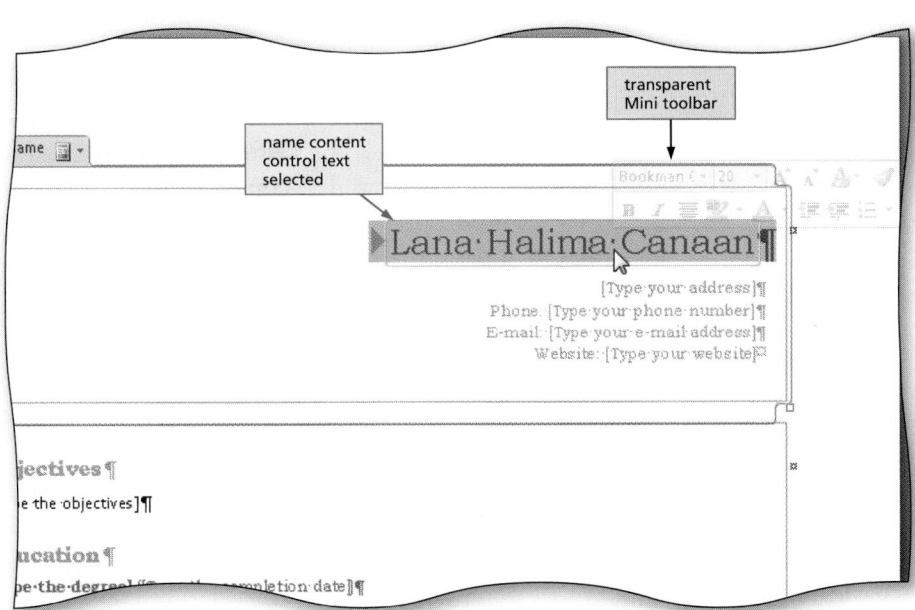

Figure 3–59

2

- Move the mouse pointer into the transparent Mini toolbar, so that it changes to a bright toolbar.

- Click the Bold button on the Mini toolbar to bold the selected name.

- Click the Font Color button on the Mini toolbar to change the font color of the selected name to the most recently used font color, which was the color of the name in the cover letter (Figure 3–60).

Instead of using buttons on the Mini toolbar, can I use the Bold and Font Color buttons on the Home tab?

Yes.

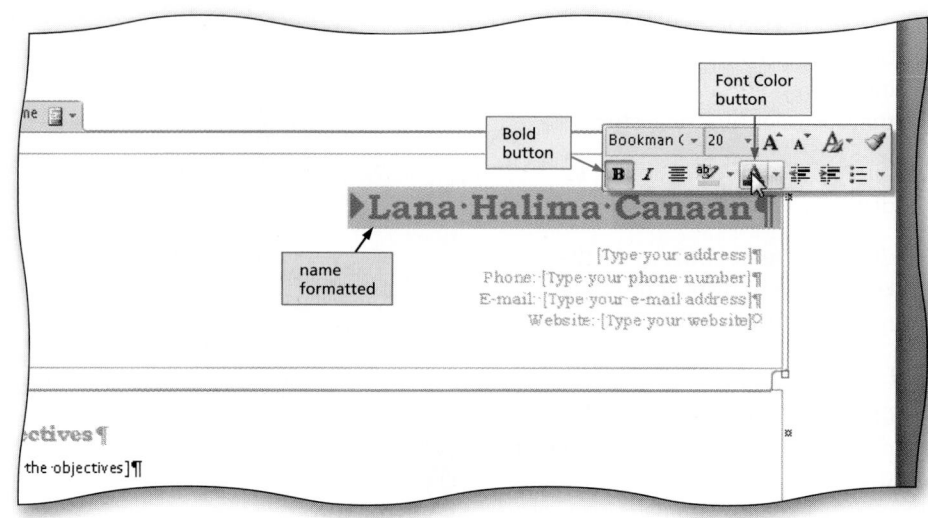

Figure 3–60

BTW

Windows Vista Taskbar
If your Windows Vista taskbar does not display a separate program button for each open Word document (as shown in Figure 3–61), click the Office Button, click the Word Options button, click Advanced in the left pane, scroll to the Display area in the right pane, place a check mark in the Show all windows in the Taskbar check box, and then click the OK button.

To Save the Resume

You have completed several tasks on the resume. Thus, you should save it in a file.

1 Click the Save button on the Quick Access Toolbar.

2 Save the file on your USB flash drive using `Canaan Resume` as the file name.

BTW

Clipboard
The Windows Clipboard, which can hold only one item at a time, is not the same as the Office Clipboard. When you collect multiple items on the Office Clipboard, however, the last copied item is copied to the Windows Clipboard as well. When you clear the Office Clipboard, the Windows Clipboard also is cleared.

Copying and Pasting

The next step in personalizing the resume is to enter the address, phone, and e-mail information in the content controls. One way to enter this information in the resume is to type it. Recall, however, that you already typed this information in the cover letter. Thus, a timesaving alternative would be to use the Office Clipboard to copy it from the cover letter to the resume. The **Office Clipboard** is a temporary storage area that holds up to 24 items (text or graphics) copied from any Office program.

Through the Office Clipboard, you can copy multiple items from any Office document and then paste them into the same or another Office document by following these general guidelines:

1. Items are copied *from* a **source document**. If the source document is not the active document, display it in the document window.

2. Display the Office Clipboard task pane and then copy items from the source document to the Office Clipboard.

3. Items are copied *to* a **destination document**. If the destination document is not the active document, display the destination document in the document window.

4. Paste items from the Office Clipboard to the destination document.

The following pages use these guidelines to copy the address, phone, and e-mail information from the letterhead to the resume.

To Switch from One Open Document to Another

The step below switches from the open resume document to the open cover letter document, which is the source document in this case.

- Click the Canaan Cover Letter - Microsoft Word program button on the Windows Vista taskbar to switch from the resume document to the cover letter document (Figure 3–61).

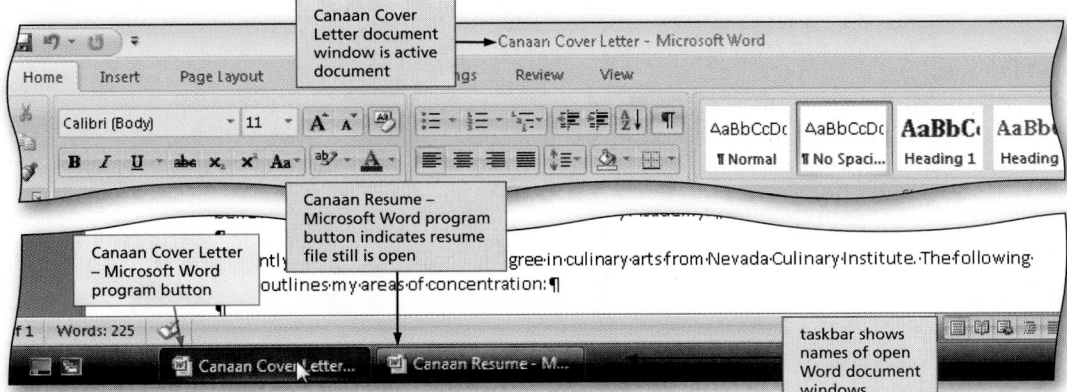

Figure 3–61

Other Ways
1. Click Switch Windows button on View tab, click document name   2. Press ALT+TAB

To Copy Items to the Office Clipboard

You can copy multiple items to the Office Clipboard through the Clipboard task pane and then paste them later. The following steps copy three items from the source document, the Canaan Cover Letter document, to the Office Clipboard.

- If necessary, scroll to the top of the cover letter, so that the items to be copied are visible in the document window.

- Click the Clipboard Dialog Box Launcher on the Home tab to display the Clipboard task pane.

- If the Office Clipboard in the Clipboard task pane is not empty, click the Clear All button in the Clipboard task pane (Figure 3–62).

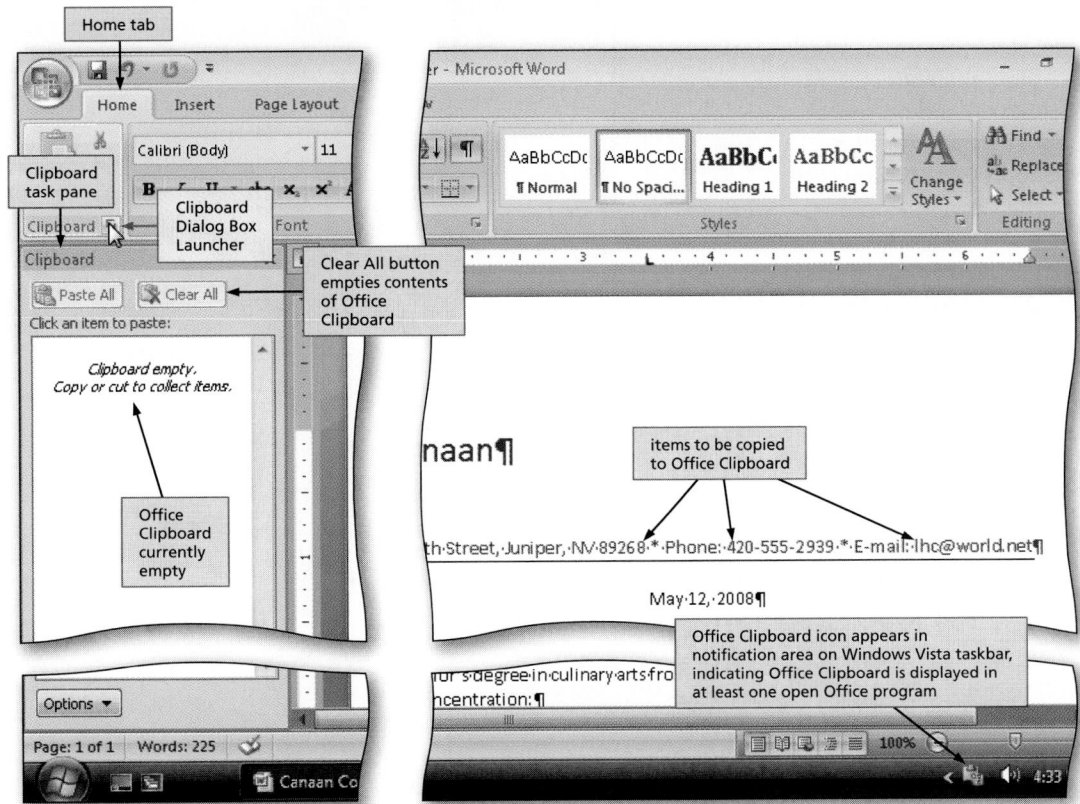

Figure 3–62

- In the cover letter, select the address, 22 Fifth Street, Juniper, NV 89268, which is the first item to be copied. Do not include the spaces to the right and left of the address.

- Click the Copy button on the Home tab to copy the selection to the Office Clipboard (Figure 3–63).

Q&A Does the copied item always display in its entirety in the Office Clipboard?

No. If the entry is too long, only the first portion is displayed.

Q&A What appears in the Office Clipboard if I copy a graphic instead of text?

A thumbnail of the copied graphic is displayed.

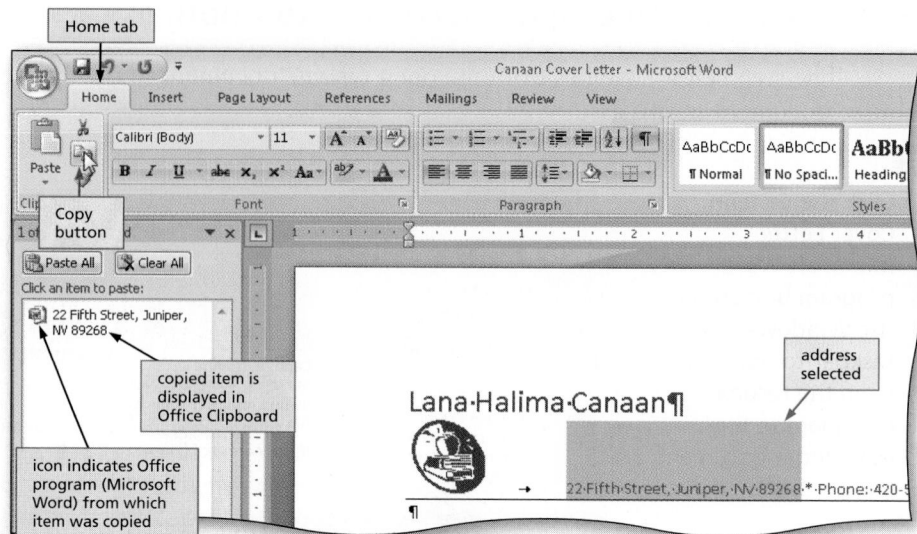

Figure 3–63

- Select the phone number (just the number, not the word Phone: and no spaces before or after the number) and then click the Copy button on the Home tab to copy the selection to the Office Clipboard.

- Select the e-mail address (just the e-mail address, not the word E-mail: and no spaces before or after the address) and then click the Copy button on the Home tab to copy the selection to the Office Clipboard (Figure 3–64).

Q&A What if I copy more than the maximum 24 items allowed in the Office Clipboard?

When you copy a 25th item, Word deletes the first item to make room for the new item.

Q&A Can I delete an item from the Office Clipboard?

Yes. Point to the item in the gallery, click the box arrow to the right of the item, and then click Delete.

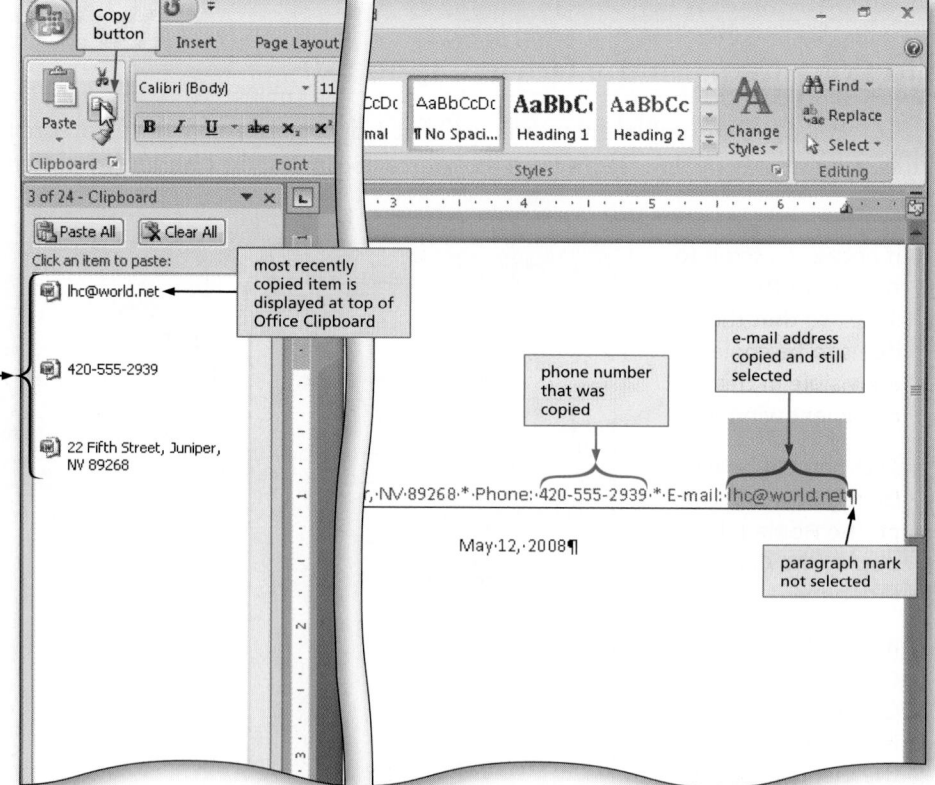

Figure 3–64

Other Ways	
1. With Clipboard task pane displayed, right-click selected item, click Copy on shortcut menu	2. With Clipboard task pane displayed and item to copy selected, press CTRL+C

To Paste from the Office Clipboard

The next step is to paste the copied items (the address, phone, and e-mail information) into the destination document, in this case, the resume document. Recall that the address, phone, and e-mail address are part of content controls in the resume.

The following steps paste the address, phone, and e-mail information from the Office Clipboard into the resume.

1

- Click the Canaan Resume - Microsoft Word program button on the Windows Vista taskbar to display the resume document.

Q&A
Does the destination document have to be a different document?

No. The source and destination documents can be the same document.

- If the Clipboard task pane is not displayed on the screen, click the Clipboard Dialog Box Launcher on the Home tab to display the Clipboard task pane.

- Click the content control in the resume with the instruction, Type your address, to select it (Figure 3–65).

Q&A
What is the function of the Paste All button?

It pastes all items in a row, without any characters between them, at the location of the insertion point or selection.

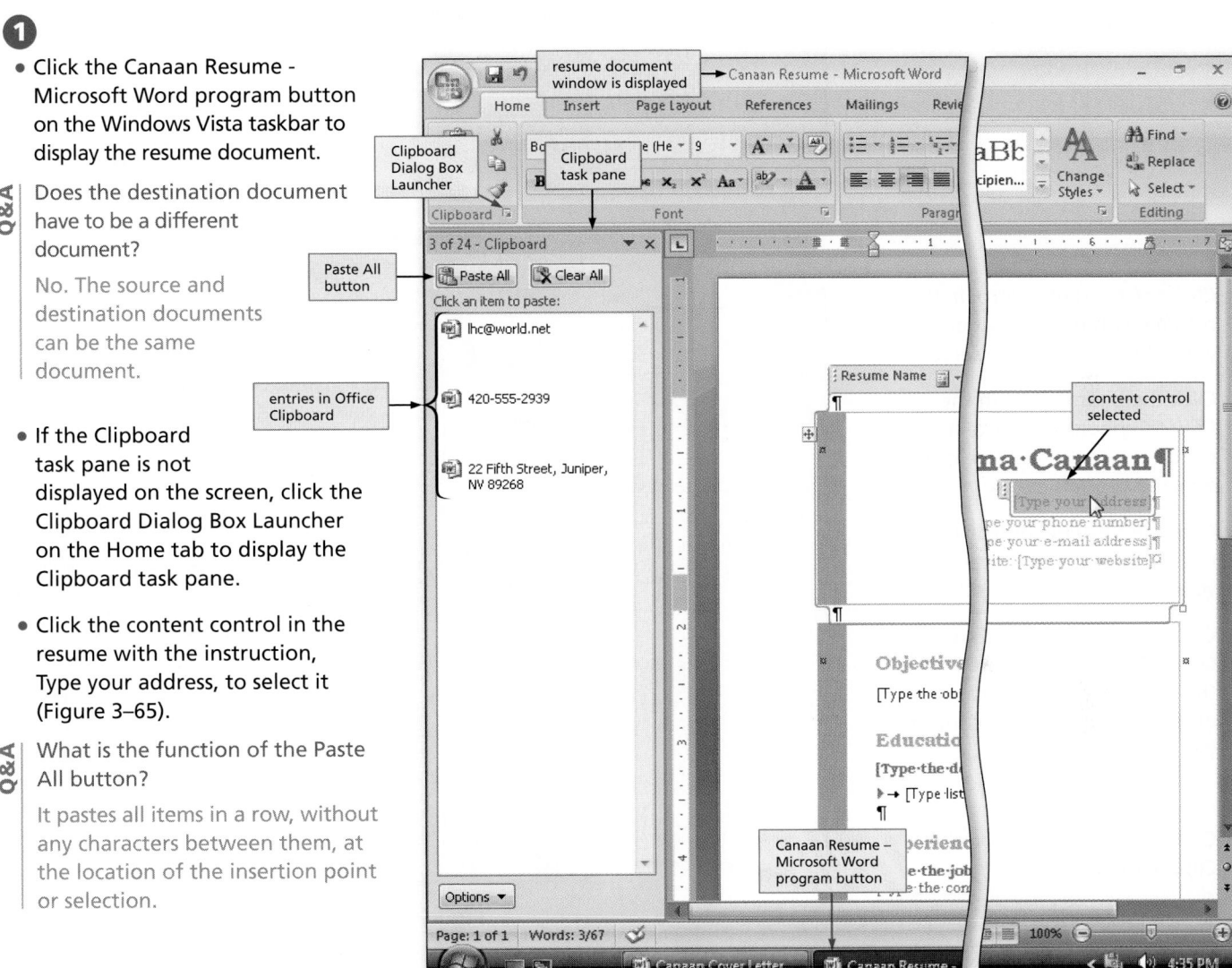

Figure 3–65

2

- Click the address entry in the Office Clipboard to paste it in the document at the location of the selected content control (Figure 3–66).

Q&A

Are the contents of the Office Clipboard erased when you paste?

No.

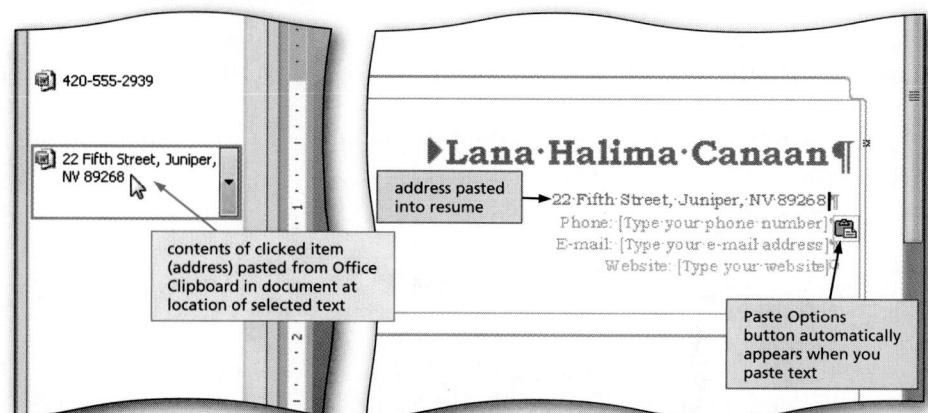

Figure 3–66

3

- Click the content control in the resume with the instruction, Type your phone number, to select it.

- Click the phone entry in the Office Clipboard to paste it in the document at the location of the selected content control.

- Click the content control in the resume with the instruction, Type your e-mail address, to select it.

- Click the e-mail entry in the Office Clipboard to paste it in the document at the location of the selected content control (Figure 3–67).

4

- Click the Close button on the Clipboard task pane title bar.

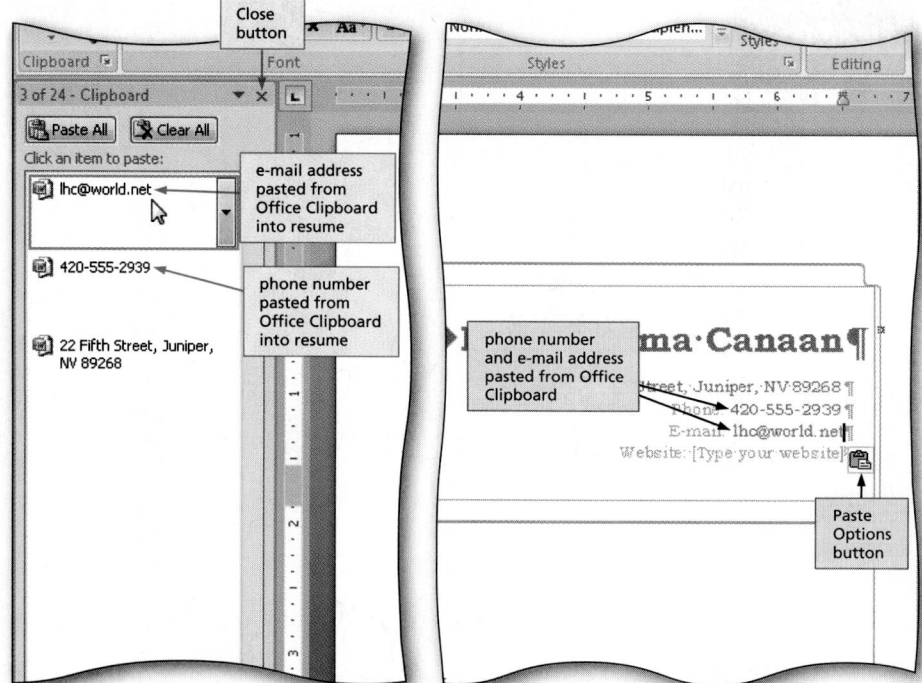

Figure 3–67

Other Ways

1. With Clipboard task pane displayed, right-click selected item, click Paste on shortcut menu

2. With Clipboard task pane displayed, press CTRL+V

Paste Options Button

When you paste items into a document, Word automatically displays the Paste Options button on the screen. The Paste Options button allows you to change the format of pasted items. For example, you can instruct Word to format the pasted text the same as the text from where it was copied or format it the same as the text to where it was pasted. You also can have Word remove all extra non-text characters that were pasted. For example, if you included a paragraph mark when copying at the end of a line in the address of the resume, the Paste Options button allows you to remove the paragraph mark from the pasted text.

To Change Font Color

The phone and e-mail labels should be the same color as the other contact information. Currently, they are a shade different from each other. The following steps change text color to the most recently used color.

1 Drag through the text, Phone:, to select it. Move the mouse pointer into the transparent Mini toolbar, so that it changes to a bright toolbar. Click the Font Color button on the Mini toolbar to change the color of the Phone: label to the color displayed on the button.

2 Drag through the text, E-mail:, to select it. Move the mouse pointer into the transparent Mini toolbar, so that it changes to a bright toolbar. Click the Font Color button on the Mini toolbar to change the color of the E-mail: label.

To Delete Text and Lines

You do not have a Web address. Thus, the Website content control, its corresponding label, and the line should be deleted. The following steps delete text.

1
- Drag through the text to be deleted, as shown in Figure 3–68.

2
- Press the DELETE key to delete the label and content control.

- Press the UP ARROW key to position the insertion point at the end of the e-mail address.

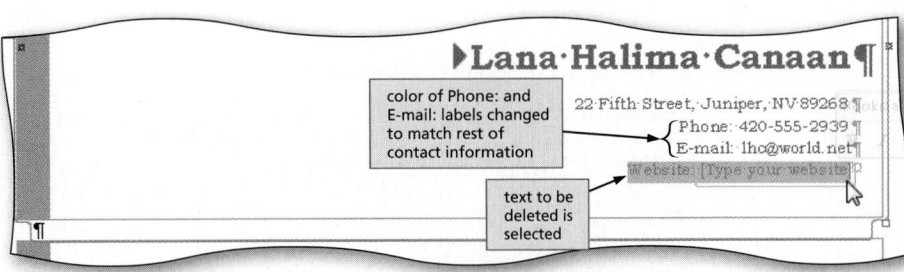

Figure 3–68

- Press the DELETE key to delete the extra paragraph mark and line below the e-mail address.

Other Ways
1. With text selected, click Cut button on Home tab   2. Right-click selected text, click Cut on shortcut menu   3. With text selected, press CTRL+X

To Zoom the Document

The text in the resume is a little small for you to read. The following step changes the zoom to 110 percent.

1 Use the Zoom slider to change the zoom to 110% (Figure 3–69).

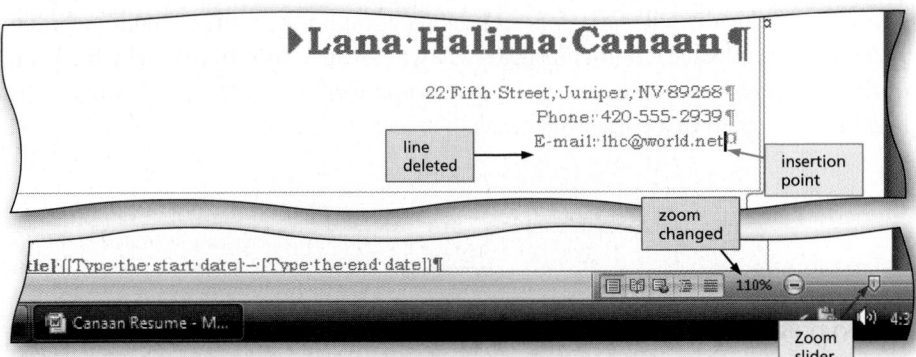

Figure 3–69

To Enter More Text in Content Controls

The next step is to select content controls in the resume and replace their instructions with personal information. The following steps enter text in the Objectives and some of the Education sections of the resume.

1 Scroll to position the Objectives section near the top of the document window. In the Objectives section of the resume, click the content control with the instruction, Type the objectives. Type `To obtain a full-time culinary instructor position with a culinary academy, school, or institute in the Juniper area.`

2 In the Education section of the resume, click the content control with the instruction, Type the degree. Type `B.S. Culinary Arts` and then click the content control with the instruction, Type the completion date.

3 Type `Nevada Culinary Institute, May 2008` and then click the content control with the instruction, Type list of accomplishments. Type `Dean's List, six semesters` and then press the ENTER key. Type `Moeller Nutrition Award, January 2008` and then press the ENTER key. Type `Marge Rae Outstanding Student Scholarship, 2006 - 2008` and then press the ENTER key. Type `Baker Food Preparation Contest, 1st Place, November 2008` (Figure 3–70).

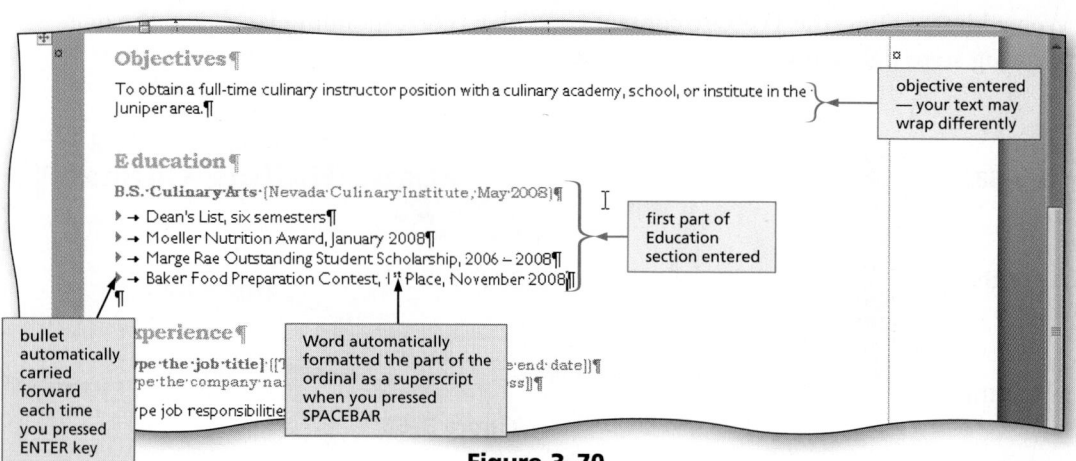

Figure 3–70

To Enter a Line Break

The next step in personalizing the resume is to enter the areas of concentration in the education section. You want only the first line that says, Areas of concentration:, to begin with a bullet. If you press the ENTER key on subsequent lines, Word automatically will carry forward the paragraph formatting, which includes the bullet. Thus, you will not press the ENTER key between each line. Instead, you will create a **line break**, which advances the insertion point to the beginning of the next physical line, ignoring any paragraph formatting. The following steps enter the areas of concentration using a line break, instead of a paragraph break, between each line.

- Press the ENTER key.

- Type `Areas of concentration:` and then press SHIFT+ENTER to insert a line break character and move the insertion point to the beginning of the next physical line (Figure 3–71).

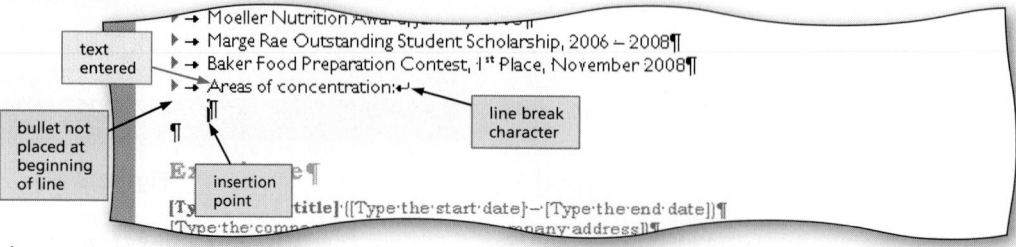

Figure 3–71

2

- Type Food Planning and Preparation and then press SHIFT+ENTER.

- Type Food Safety and then press SHIFT+ENTER.

- Type Nutrition and then press SHIFT+ENTER.

- Type Regional and International Cuisine as the last entry. Do not press SHIFT+ENTER at the end of this line (Figure 3–72).

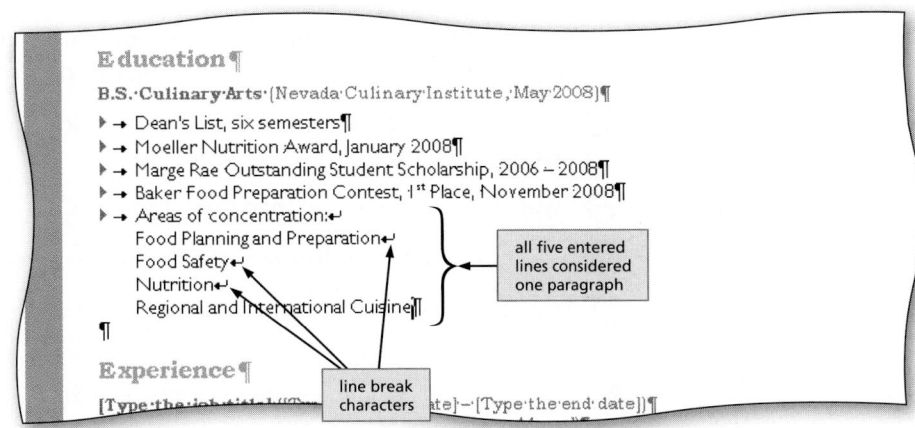

Figure 3–72

BTW

Line Break Character
Line break characters do not print. A line break character is a formatting mark that indicates a line break at the end of the line.

To Change Spacing Below Paragraphs

The blank paragraph below the Education section has spacing after (below) of 6 point. You do not want space below this paragraph because you want enough room for all the resume text. The following steps change the spacing after to 0 point.

1 Position the insertion point in the paragraph to be adjusted, in this case, the paragraph mark below the Education section on the resume.

2 Display the Page Layout tab.

3 Click the Spacing After box down arrow on the Page Layout tab as many times as necessary until 0 pt is displayed in the Spacing After text box (Figure 3–73).

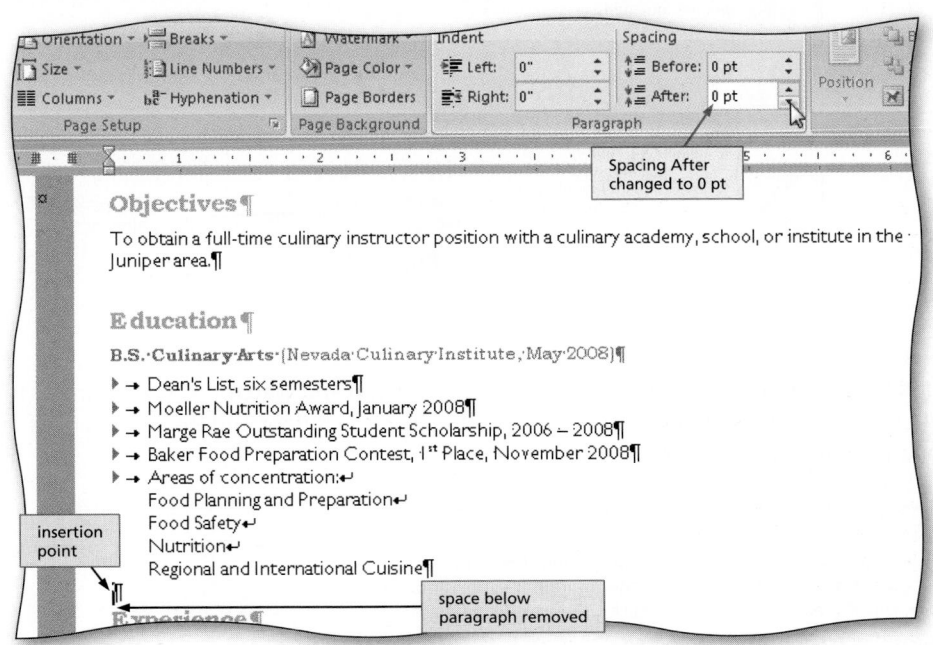

Figure 3–73

To Enter More Text in Content Controls

The next step is to select content controls in the Experience section of the resume and replace their instructions with personalized information.

1 In the Experience section of the resume, click the content control with the instruction, Type the job title.

2 Type `Chef Intern` and then bold the text, Chef Intern.

3 Click the content control with the instruction, Type the start date.

4 Type `September 2006` and then click the content control with the instruction, Type the end date.

5 Type `May 2008` and then click the content control with the instruction, Type the company name.

6 Type `The Garden Grill` and then click the content control with the instruction, Type the company address.

7 Type `Juniper, NV` as the company address.

To Indent a Paragraph

In the resume, the lines below the job title that contain the company name and job responsibilities are to be indented, so that the job titles are easier to see. The following step indents the left edge of a paragraph.

1

- Display the Home tab.

- With the insertion point in the paragraph to indent, click the Increase Indent button on the Home tab to indent the paragraph one-half inch (Figure 3–74).

Q&A

Why did the paragraph indent one-half inch?

Each time you click the Increase Indent button, the current paragraph indents one-half inch. Similarly, when you click the Decrease Indent button, the paragraph decreases the indent by one-half inch.

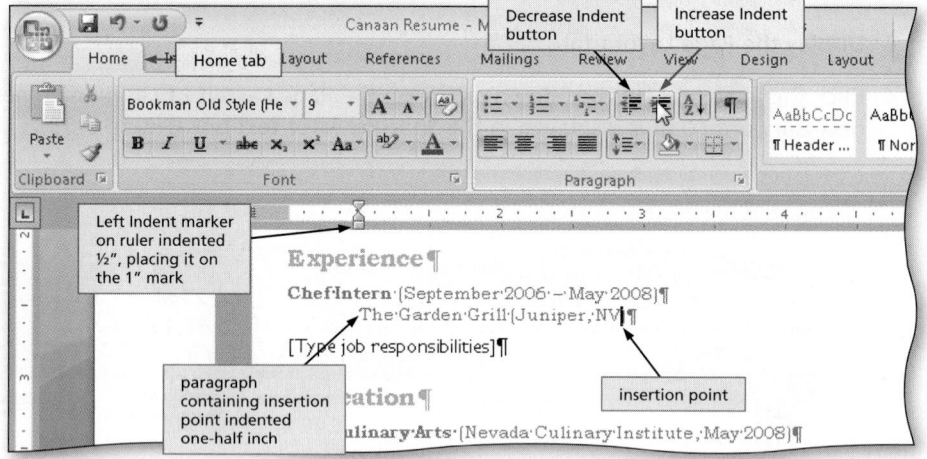

Figure 3–74

Experiment

- Repeatedly click the Increase Indent and Decrease Indent buttons on the Home tab and watch the left indent of the current paragraph change. When you have finished experimenting, use the Increase Indent and Decrease Indent buttons to set the left margin to the one-inch mark on the ruler.

Other Ways

1. Drag Left Indent marker on ruler

2. Enter value in Indent Left text box on Page Layout tab

3. Click Paragraph Dialog Box Launcher on Home tab, click

Indents and Spacing sheet, set indentation in Left text box, click OK button

4. Right-click text, click Paragraph on shortcut menu, click Indents

and Spacing sheet, set indentation in Left text box, click OK button

5. Press CTRL+M

To Change Spacing Below Paragraphs

The next step is to remove the blank space below the company name paragraph, so that the company name and job description paragraphs are closer together. The following steps change the spacing after to 0 point.

1 Display the Page Layout tab.

2 With the insertion point in the paragraph to be adjusted, as shown in Figure 3–74, click the Spacing After box down arrow on the Page Layout tab as many times as necessary until 0 pt is displayed in the Spacing After text box.

To Enter and Format More Text in Content Controls

The next step is to select the job responsibilities content control in the Experience section of the resume and replace its instructions with personal information.

1 In the Experience section of the resume, click the content control with the instruction, Type job responsibilities.

2 Type Assisted chef with meal selection, preparation, and presentation. Assumed chef responsibilities during last semester of school.

3 With the insertion point in the paragraph to be adjusted, in this case, the job responsibilities paragraph, click the Spacing After box down arrow on the Page Layout tab as many times as necessary until 6 pt is displayed in the Spacing After text box.

4 Display the Home tab.

5 Click the Increase Indent button on the Home tab to indent the paragraph one-half inch (Figure 3–75).

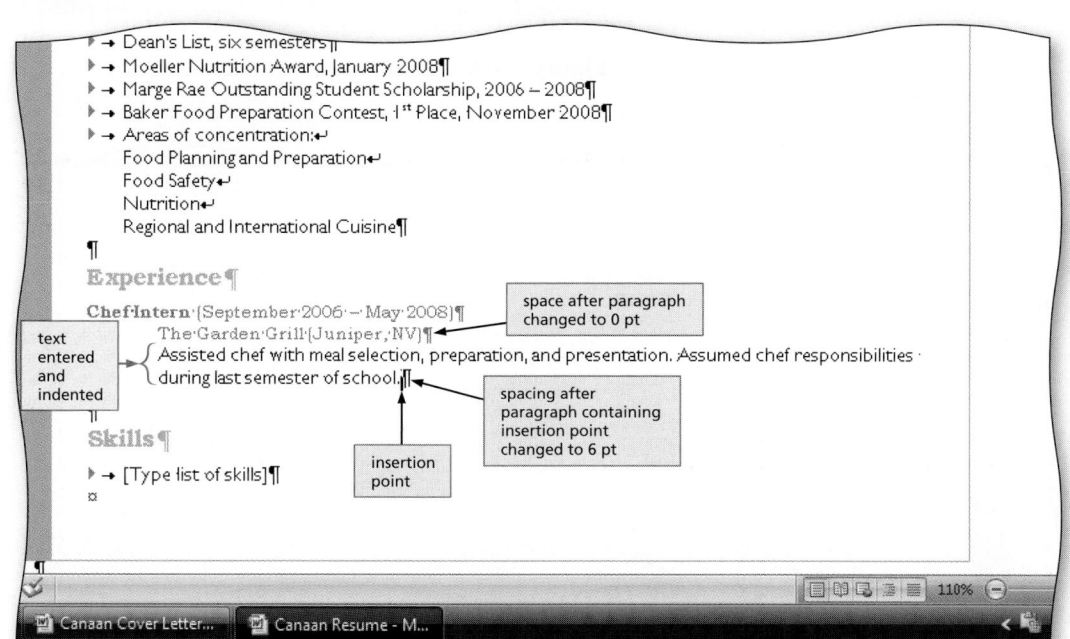

Figure 3–75

To Insert a Building Block Using the Quick Parts Gallery

In this resume, the Experience section contains two jobs. The template, however, inserted content controls for only one job. Word has defined the sections and subsections of the resume in the building blocks, which you can insert in the document. In this case, you want to insert the Experience Subsection building block. The following steps insert a building block.

- Scroll to display the Experience section at the top of the document window.

- Position the insertion point on the paragraph mark below the first job entry.

- Display the Insert tab.

- Click the Quick Parts button on the Insert tab and then scroll through the Quick Parts gallery until Experience Subsection is displayed (Figure 3–76).

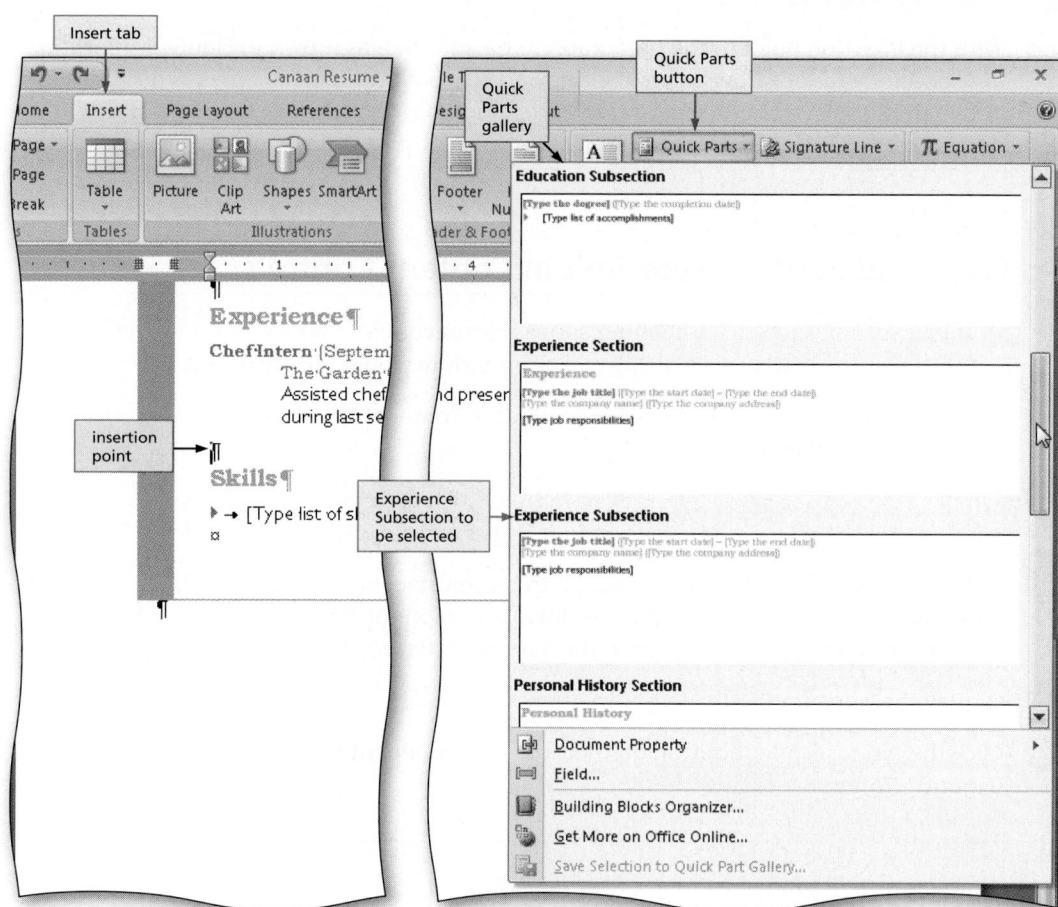

Figure 3–76

- Click Experience Subsection in the Quick Parts gallery to insert the building block in the document at the location of the insertion point.

- Press the DELETE key to remove the extra paragraph mark inserted with the building block (Figure 3–77).

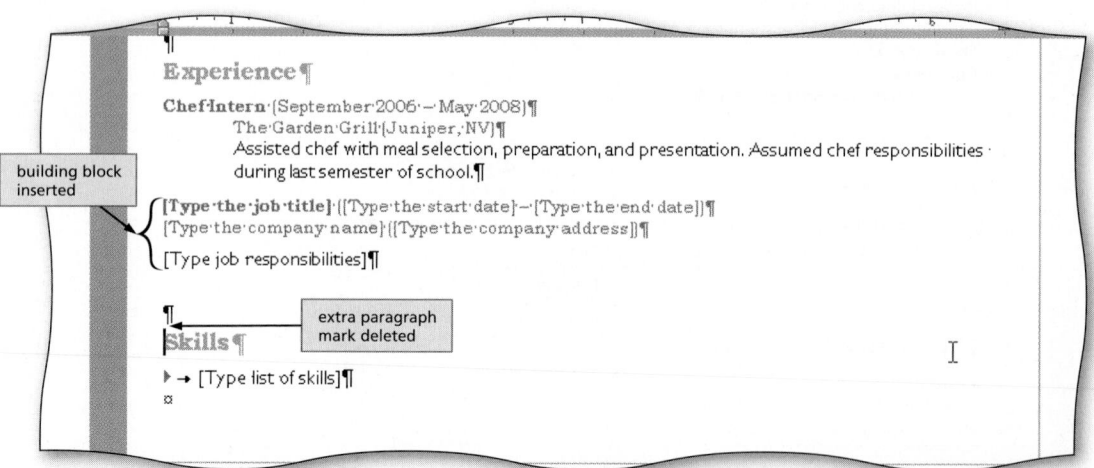

Figure 3–77

To Enter and Format the Experience Subsection and the Skills Section

The next step is to select content controls in the Experience Subsection building block just inserted and the Skills section in the resume and replace the instructions with personal information.

1 Enter `Assistant Cook` as the job title and then bold the job title. Enter `September 2004` as the start date. Enter `August 2006` as the end date. Enter `Nevada Culinary Institute Cafeteria` as the company name. Enter `Juniper, NV` as the company address.

2 Display the Home tab. With the insertion point in the paragraph to indent (company address line), click the Increase Indent button on the Home tab to indent the paragraph one-half inch.

3 Display the Page Layout tab. With the insertion point in the paragraph to be adjusted (company address line), change the Spacing After to 0 point.

4 Enter this text for the job responsibilities: `Planned meals for staff and students. Prepared salads, soups, sandwiches, entrees, and desserts.`

5 With the insertion point in the paragraph to be adjusted, in this case, the job responsibilities paragraph, change Spacing After to 0 point.

6 Display the Home tab. Click the Increase Indent button on the Home tab to indent the paragraph one-half inch.

7 In the Skills section, click the content control with the instruction, Type list of skills, to select it. Type `National Honor Society` and then press the ENTER key. Type `Culinary Arts Association` and then press the ENTER key. Type `Nutrition Services of America` and then press the ENTER key. Type `Student Government Association, President` and then press the ENTER key. Enter `Nevada Restaurant Federation` as the last skill (Figure 3–78).

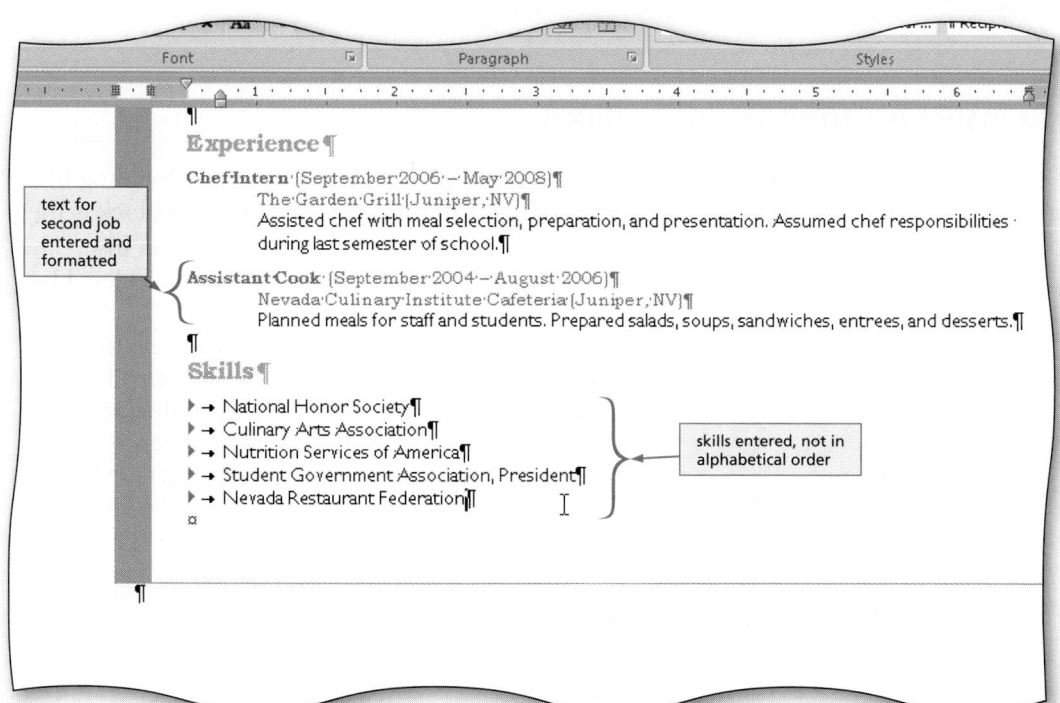

Figure 3–78

To Sort Paragraphs

The next step is to alphabetize the paragraphs in the Skills section of the resume. In Word, you can arrange paragraphs in alphabetic, numeric, or date order based on the first character in each paragraph. Ordering characters in this manner is called **sorting**. The following steps sort paragraphs.

1

- Drag through the paragraphs to be sorted, in this case, the list of skills.

- Click the Sort button on the Home tab to display the Sort Text dialog box (Figure 3–79).

Q&A What does ascending mean?

Ascending means to sort in alphabetic, numeric or earliest-to-latest date order.

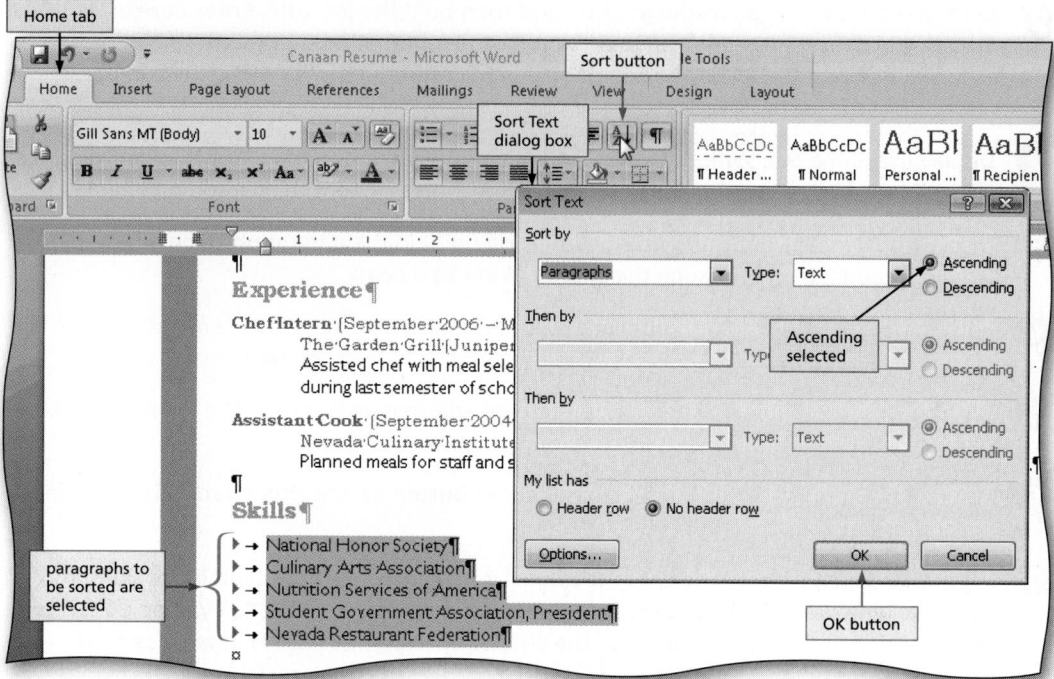

Figure 3–79

2

- Click the OK button to close the dialog box and instruct Word to alphabetize the selected paragraphs.

To Insert Another Building Block

The last section of the resume is the Community Service section. No building block exists for this section; however, the format of the Reference Section building block is the same format you would like for the Community Service section. Thus, you will insert the Reference Section building block and modify its text. The following steps insert a building block.

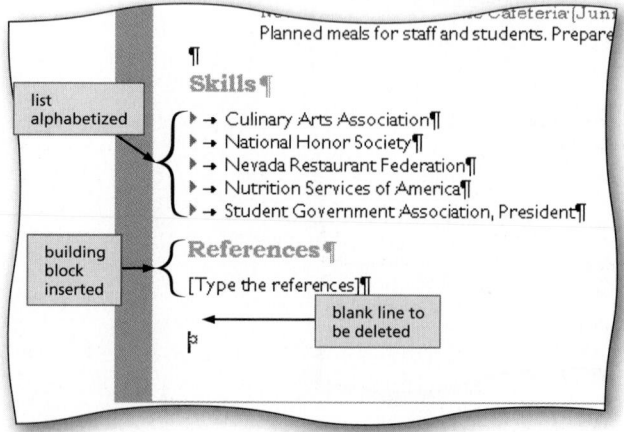

1 Position the insertion point on the line below the Skills section on the resume. Display the Insert tab. Click the Quick Parts button on the Insert tab and then scroll through the Quick Parts gallery until Reference Section is displayed. Click Reference Section to insert the building block in the document at the location of the insertion point (Figure 3–80).

2 Press the BACKSPACE key to remove the extra blank line inserted with the building block.

Figure 3–80

To Enter and Format the Community Service Section

The next step is to select content controls in the section just inserted in the resume and replace its instructions with community service information.

1 Change the title, References, to Community Service.

2 Display the Page Layout tab. With the insertion point in the paragraph to be adjusted (Community Service heading), change the Spacing Before to 12 point.

3 In the last content control, type Prepare food and serve meals at Hope Mission every week.

4 With the insertion point in the paragraph to be adjusted, in this case, the community services paragraph, change Spacing After to 0 point (Figure 3–81).

5 If the document flows to a second page, reduce the space after internal paragraphs so that it fits on a single page.

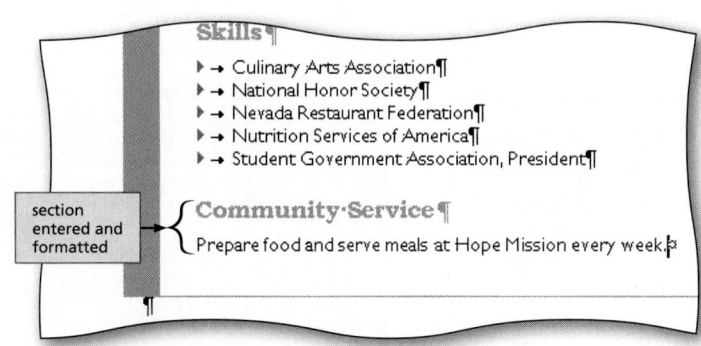

Figure 3–81

To Change Theme Colors

The cover letter created earlier in this chapter used the Urban color scheme. Because you will be mailing the resume along with the cover letter, you decide also to use the Urban color scheme for the resume. The following step changes theme colors.

1 Display the Home tab. Click the Change Styles button on the Home tab, point to Colors on the Change Styles menu, and then click Urban in the Colors gallery to change the document theme colors to Urban.

To Print Preview a Document

To see exactly how a document will look when you print it, you could display it in print preview. **Print preview** displays the entire document in reduced size on the Word screen. In print preview, you can edit and format text, adjust margins, view multiple pages, reduce the document to fit on a single page, and print the document. The following steps view and print the resume in print preview.

1

• Click the Office Button and then point to Print on the Office Button menu (Figure 3–82).

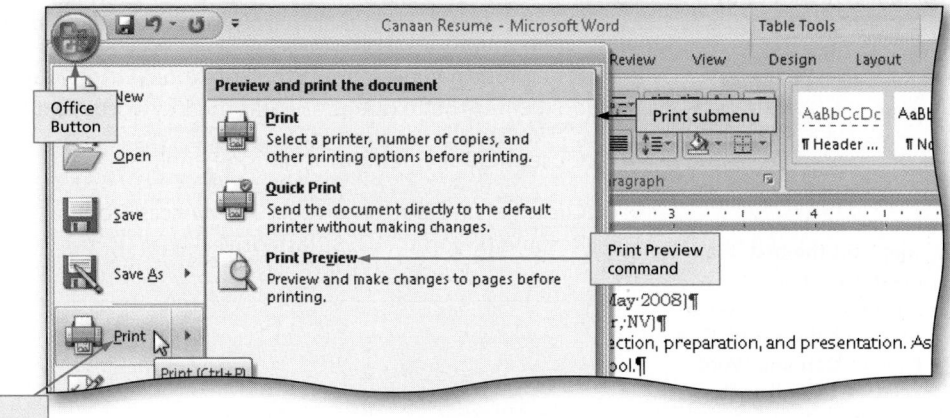

Figure 3–82

2

- Click Print Preview on the Print submenu to display the document in print preview (Figure 3–83).

- If necessary, click the One Page button on the Print Preview tab to display the document as one readable page in the window.

- Click the Print button on the Print Preview tab and then click the OK button in the Print dialog box to print the resume, as shown in Figure 3–2 on page WD 148.

- Click the Close Print Preview button on the Print Preview tab to redisplay the resume in the document window.

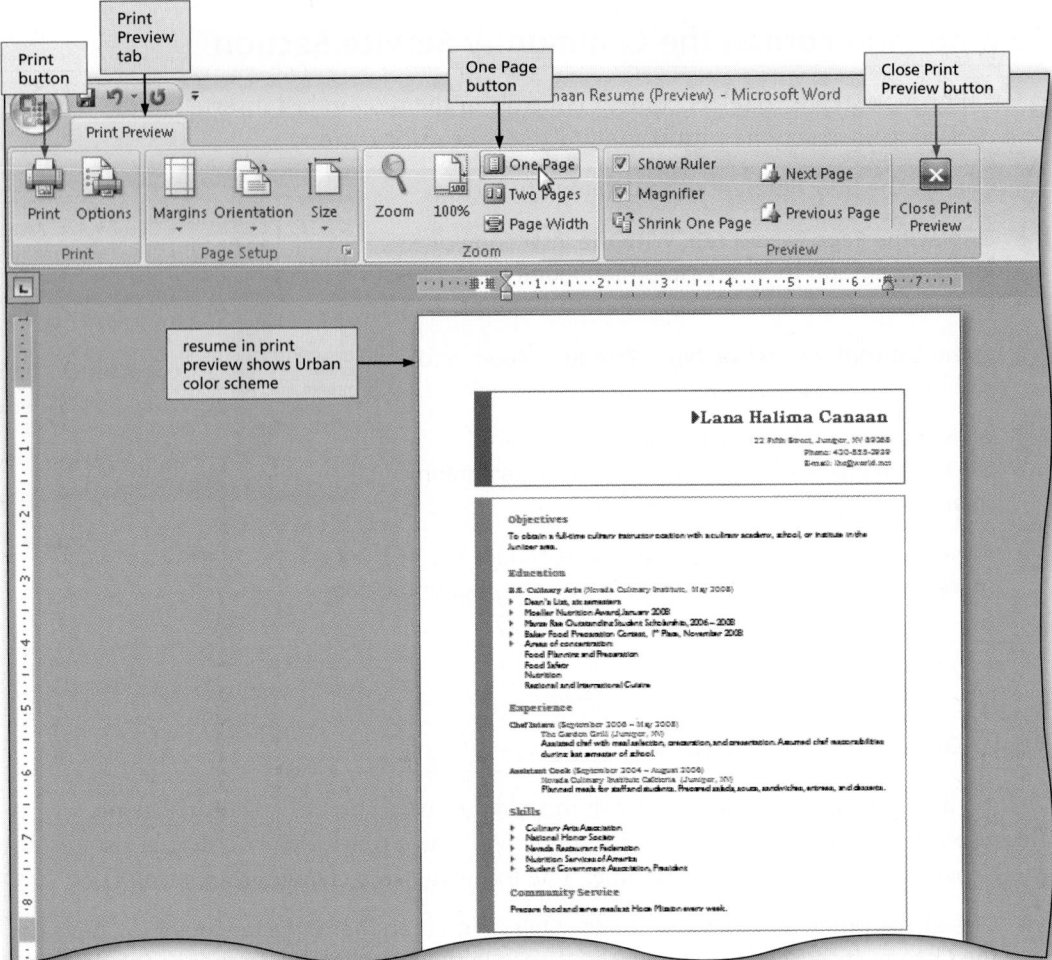

Figure 3–83

Print Preview
If you want to display two pages in print preview, click the Two Pages button on the Print Preview tab. With the Magnifier check box on the Print Preview tab selected, you can click in the document to zoom in or out. Magnifying a page does not affect the printed document. To edit a document, remove the check mark from the Magnifier check box and then edit the text. If a document spills onto a second page by a line or two, click the Shrink One Page button and Word will try to fit all content on a single page.

To Change Document Properties and Save Again

Before saving the resume a final time, you want to add your name, course and section, and some keywords as document properties. The following steps use the Document Information Panel to change document properties and then save the document again.

1 Display the Office Button menu, point to Prepare on the Office Button menu, and then click Properties on the Prepare submenu to display the Document Information Panel.

2 Enter your name in the Author text box. Enter your course and section in the Subject text box. Enter the text, Resume, in the Keywords text box.

3 Close the Document Information Panel.

4 Click the Save button on the Quick Access Toolbar to overwrite the previous Canaan Resume file on the USB flash drive.

Addressing and Printing Envelopes and Mailing Labels

BTW | **Quick Reference**
For a table that lists how to complete the tasks covered in this book using the mouse, Ribbon, shortcut menu, and keyboard, see the Quick Reference Summary at the back of this book, or visit the Word 2007 Quick Reference Web page (scsite.com/wd2007/qr).

With Word, you can print address information on an envelope or on a mailing label. Computer-printed addresses look more professional than handwritten ones. Thus, the following steps address and print an envelope.

To Address and Print an Envelope

- Switch to the cover letter by clicking its program button on the Windows Vista taskbar.

- Close the Clipboard task pane.

- Scroll through the cover letter to display the inside address in the document window.

- Drag through the inside address to select it (Figure 3–84).

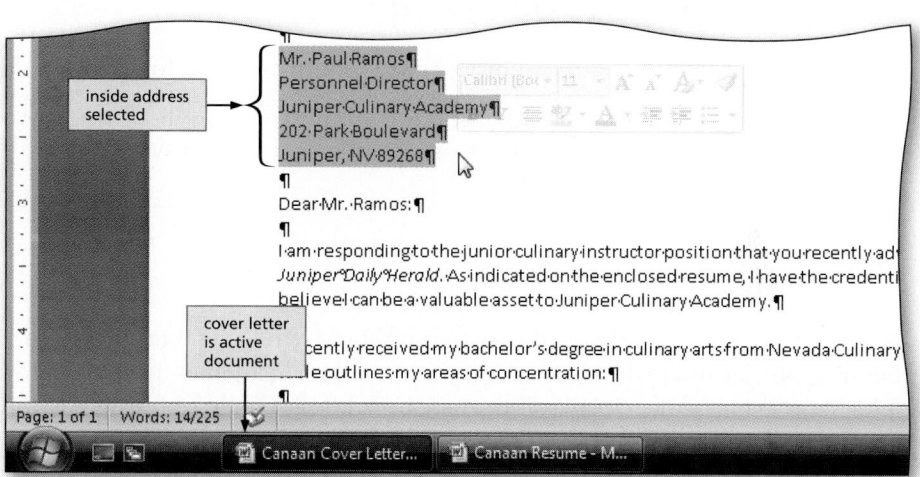

Figure 3–84

2

- Click Mailings on the Ribbon to display the Mailings tab.

- Click the Create Envelopes button on the Mailings tab to display the Envelopes and Labels dialog box.

- If necessary, click the Envelopes tab in the dialog box.

- Click the Return address text box.

- Type Lana Halima Canaan and then press the ENTER key.

- Type 22 Fifth Street and then press the ENTER key.

- Type Juniper, NV 89268 (Figure 3–85).

- Insert an envelope in your printer, as shown in the Feed area of the dialog box (your Feed area may be different depending on your printer).

- Click the Print button in the Envelopes and Labels dialog box to print the envelope.

- If a dialog box is displayed, click the No button.

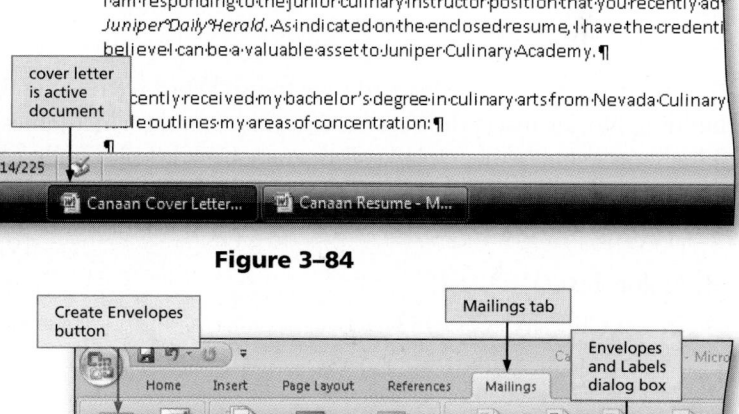
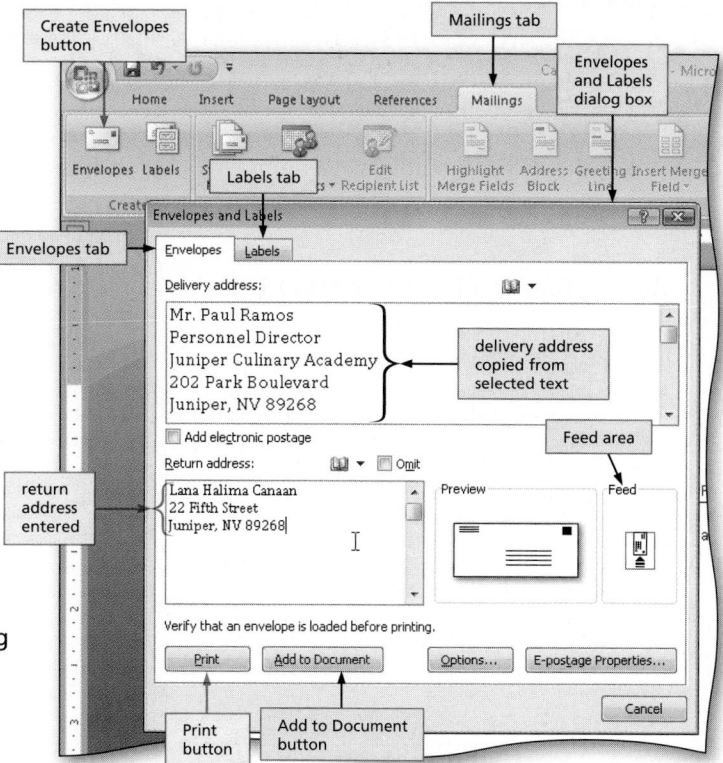

Figure 3–85

BTW

Certification
The Microsoft Certified Application Specialist (MCAS) program provides an opportunity for you to obtain a valuable industry credential — proof that you have the Word 2007 skills required by employers. For more information, see Appendix G or visit the Word 2007 Certification Web page (scsite.com/wd2007/cert).

Envelopes and Labels

Instead of printing the envelope immediately, you can add it to the document by clicking the Add to Document button in the Envelopes and Labels dialog box. To specify a different envelope or label type (identified by a number on the box of envelopes or labels), click the Options button in the Envelopes and Labels dialog box.

Instead of printing an envelope, you can print a mailing label. To do this, click the Labels tab in the Envelopes and Labels dialog box (Figure 3–85 on the previous page). Type the delivery address in the Address box. To print the same address on all labels on the page, click Full page of the same label. Click the Print button in the dialog box.

To Quit Word

This project is complete. The following step quits Word.

 Click the Office Button and then click the Exit Word button on the Office Button menu to close all open documents and quit Word.

Chapter Summary

In this chapter, you have learned how to use Word to insert and format clip art, set and use tab stops, create and insert building blocks, insert the current date, insert and format tables, use print preview, copy and paste, and use templates. The items listed below include all the new Word skills you have learned in this chapter.

1. Use the Grow Font Button to Increase Font Size (WD 151)
2. Color Text (WD 152)
3. Insert Clip Art (WD 153)
4. Resize a Graphic Using the Size Dialog Box (WD 155)
5. Recolor a Graphic (WD 156)
6. Set a Transparent Color in a Graphic (WD 157)
7. Set Custom Tab Stops Using the Tabs Dialog Box (WD 158)
8. Bottom Border a Paragraph (WD 161)
9. Clear Formatting (WD 162)
10. Convert a Hyperlink to Regular Text (WD 163)
11. Create a New File from an Existing File (WD 165)
12. Set Custom Tab Stops Using the Ruler (WD 167)
13. Insert the Current Date in a Document (WD 168)
14. Create a Building Block (WD 170)
15. Insert a Nonbreaking Space (WD 171)
16. Insert a Building Block (WD 172)
17. Insert an Empty Table (WD 173)
18. Enter Data in a Table (WD 175)
19. Apply a Table Style (WD 176)
20. Resize Table Columns to Fit Table Contents (WD 177)
21. Bullet a List as You Type (WD 180)
22. Use a Template (WD 183)
23. Delete Rows (WD 186)
24. Modify Text in a Content Control (WD 187)
25. Switch from One Open Document to Another (WD 189)
26. Copy Items to the Office Clipboard (WD 189)
27. Paste from the Office Clipboard (WD 191)
28. Delete Text and Lines (WD 193)
29. Enter a Line Break (WD 194)
30. Indent a Paragraph (WD 196)
31. Insert a Building Block Using the Quick Parts Gallery (WD 198)
32. Sort Paragraphs (WD 200)
33. Print Preview a Document (WD 201)
34. Address and Print an Envelope (WD 203)

Learn It Online

Test your knowledge of chapter content and key terms.

Instructions: To complete the Learn It Online exercises, start your browser, click the Address bar, and then enter the Web address scsite.com/wd2007/learn. When the Word 2007 Learn It Online page is displayed, click the link for the exercise you want to complete and then read the instructions.

Chapter Reinforcement TF, MC, and SA
A series of true/false, multiple choice, and short answer questions that test your knowledge of the chapter content.

Flash Cards
An interactive learning environment where you identify chapter key terms associated with displayed definitions.

Practice Test
A series of multiple choice questions that test your knowledge of chapter content and key terms.

Who Wants To Be a Computer Genius?
An interactive game that challenges your knowledge of chapter content in the style of a television quiz show.

Wheel of Terms
An interactive game that challenges your knowledge of chapter key terms in the style of the television show *Wheel of Fortune*.

Crossword Puzzle Challenge
A crossword puzzle that challenges your knowledge of key terms presented in the chapter.

Apply Your Knowledge

Reinforce the skills and apply the concepts you learned in this chapter.

Working with Tabs and a Table
Instructions: Start Word. Open the document, Apply 3-1 Expenses Table Draft, from the Data Files for Students. See the inside back cover of this book for instructions on downloading the Data Files for Students, or contact your instructor for information about accessing the required files.

The document is a Word table that you are to edit and format. The revised table is shown in Figure 3–86.

Monthly Club Expenses

	January	February	March	April
Decorations	170.88	129.72	74.43	167.85
Postage	65.90	62.90	40.19	69.91
Computer Supplies	17.29	18.50	72.50	19.12
Paper Supplies	46.57	41.67	38.82	48.70
Food/Beverages	122.04	99.88	55.43	100.00
Hall Rental	120.00	120.00	120.00	120.00
Total	542.68	472.67	401.37	525.58

Figure 3–86

Continued >

Apply Your Knowledge *continued*

Perform the following tasks:

1. In the line containing the table title, Monthly Club Expenses, remove the tab stop at the 1" mark on the ruler.

2. Set a centered tab at the 3.25" mark on the ruler.

3. Bold the characters in the title. Increase their font size to 14. Change their color to Red, Accent 2, Darker 25%.

4. Add a new row to the bottom of the table. In the first cell of the new row, type Total as the entry. Enter these values in the next three cells: January – 542.68; February – 472.67; April – 525.58.

5. Delete the row containing the Duplicating Fees expenses.

6. Insert a column between the February and April columns. Fill in the column as follows: Column Title – March; Decorations – 74.43; Postage – 40.19; Computer Supplies – 72.50; Paper Supplies – 38.82; Food/Beverages – 55.43; Hall Rental – 120.00; Total – 401.37.

7. In the Design tab, remove the check mark from the Banded Rows check box. Place a check mark in the Total Row check box. The three check boxes that should have check marks are Header Row, Total Row, and First Column. Apply the Medium Grid 3 - Accent 1 style to the table.

8. Make all columns as wide as their contents (AutoFit Contents).

9. Center the table between the left and right margins of the page.

10. Change the document properties, as specified by your instructor.

11. Click the Office Button and then click Save As. Save the document using the file name, Apply 3-1 Expenses Table Modified.

12. Print the document properties.

13. Print the revised table, shown in Figure 3–86.

Extend Your Knowledge

Extend the skills you learned in this chapter and experiment with new skills. You may need to use Help to complete the assignment.

Working with Pictures, Symbols, Borders, and Tables

Instructions: Start Word. Open the document, Extend 3-1 Club Letter Draft, from the Data Files for Students. See the inside back cover of this book for instructions on downloading the Data Files for Students, or contact your instructor for information about accessing the required files.

You will flip the clip art, insert symbols, add a decorative border, add totals to the table, modify the table style, and print mailing labels.

Perform the following tasks:

1. Use Help to learn about rotating objects, inserting symbols, working with borders, entering formulas, and printing mailing labels.

2. Flip the image in the letterhead horizontally so that the fruit faces toward the middle of the letter instead of toward the margin.

3. In the letterhead, replace the asterisk characters that separate the address, phone, and e-mail information with a symbol in one of the Wingdings fonts (Figure 3–87).

4. Remove the bottom border in the letterhead. Add a new bottom border that has a color and style different from the default Word border.

5. Add a row to the bottom of the table with a label indicating it contains totals. For each of the columns, use the Formula button on the Layout tab to sum the contents of the column. Write down the formula that Word uses to sum the contents of a column. Add a column to the right of the table with a label indicating it contains totals. For each of the rows, use a formula to sum the row. Write down the formula that Word uses to sum the contents of a row.

6. Change the table style. One at a time, select and deselect each check box in the Table Style Options group. Write down the function of each check box: Header Row, Total Row, Banded Rows, First Column, Last Column, and Banded Columns. Select the check boxes you prefer for the table.

7. Change the document properties, as specified by your instructor. Save the revised document using a new file name and then submit it in the format specified by your instructor.

8. Print a single mailing label for the letter.

9. Print a full page of mailing labels, each containing the address shown in Figure 3-87.

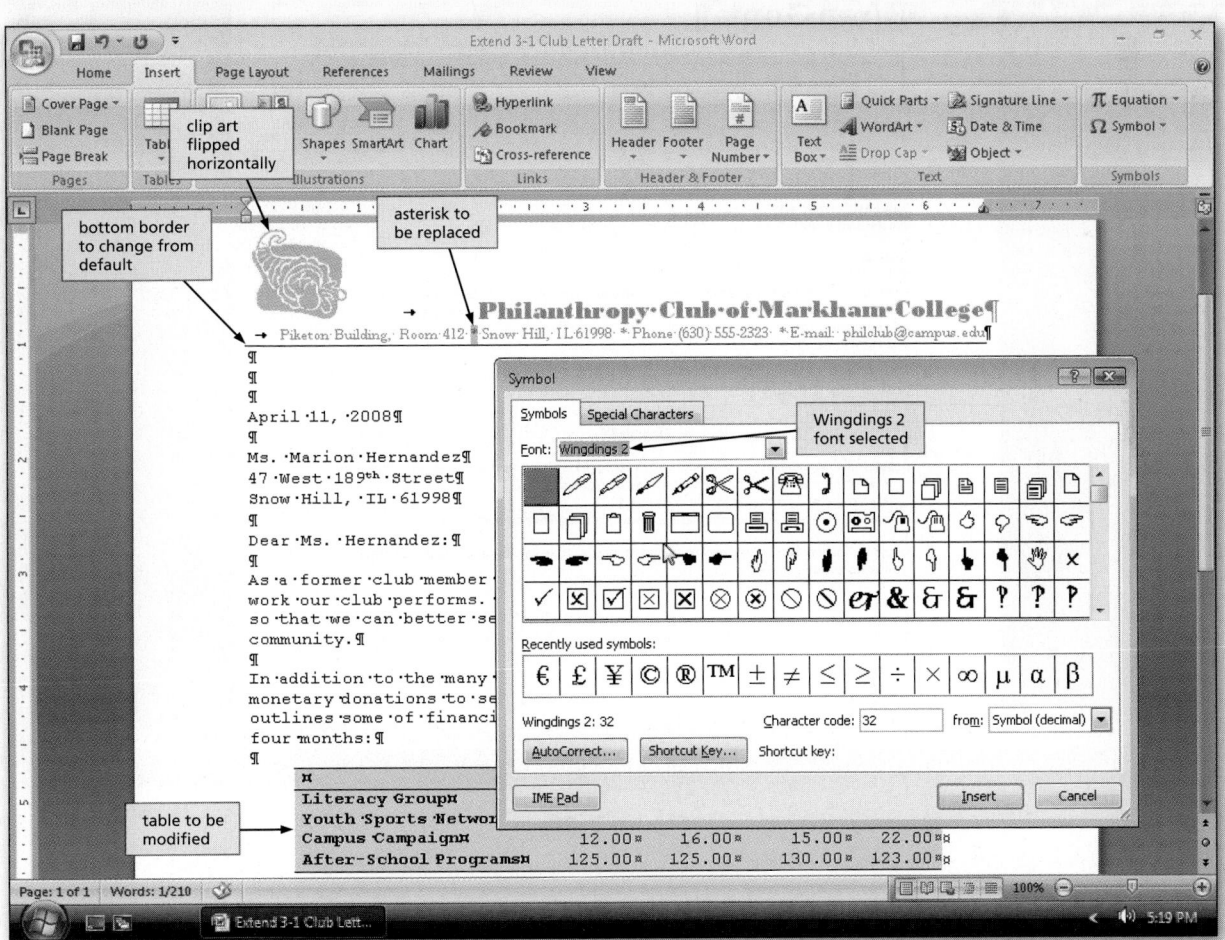

Figure 3–87

Make It Right

Analyze a document and correct all errors and/or improve the design.

Formatting a Business Letter

Instructions: Start Word. Open the document, Make It Right 3-1 Cover Letter Draft, from the Data Files for Students. See the inside back cover of this book for instructions about downloading the Data Files for Students, or contact your instructor for information on accessing the required files.

The document is a cover letter that is missing elements and formatted incorrectly (Figure 3–88). You are to insert and format clip art in the letterhead, change the color of the text and graphic, change the letter style from block to modified block, sort a list, and format the table.

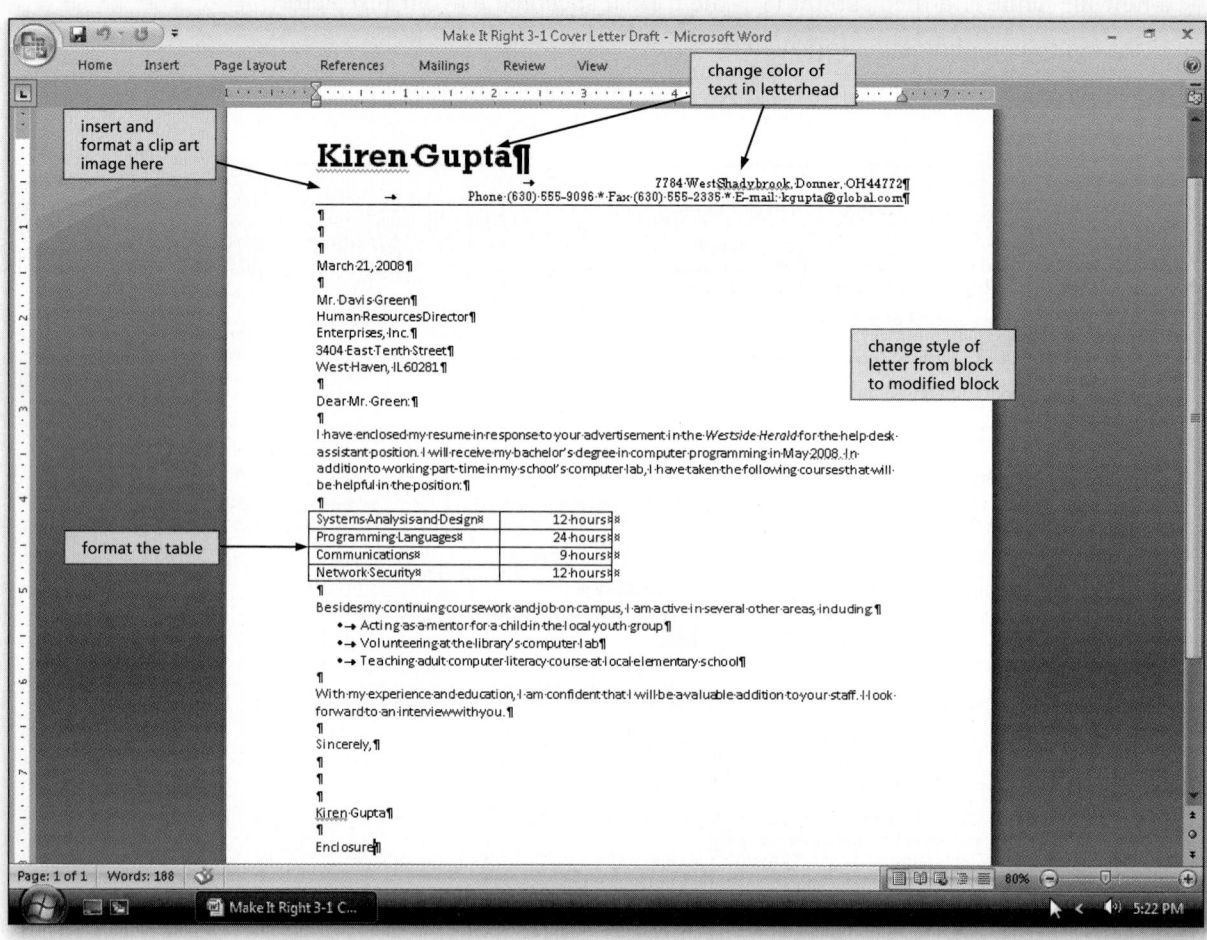

Figure 3–88

Perform the following tasks:

1. Locate and insert an appropriate clip art image. If you have access to the Internet, use one from the Web. Resize the graphic, if necessary.

2. Change the color of the text in the letterhead. Recolor the graphic to match the color of the text. Format one color in the graphic as transparent.

3. The letter currently is the block letter style. It should be the modified block letter style. Format the appropriate paragraphs by setting custom tab stops and then positioning those paragraphs at the tab stops. Be sure to position the insertion point in the paragraph before setting the tab stop.

4. Sort the paragraphs in the bulleted list.

5. Center the table. Apply a table style of your choice. Resize the table columns to fit the contents of the cells.

6. Change the document properties, as specified by your instructor. Save the revised document using a new file name and then submit it in the format specified by your instructor.

In the Lab

Design and/or create a document using the guidelines, concepts, and skills presented in this chapter. Labs are listed in order of increasing difficulty.

Lab 1: Creating a Cover Letter with a Table

Problem: You are a student at Norson Central College. Graduation is approaching quickly and you would like a part-time job while furthering your studies. Thus, you prepare the cover letter shown in Figure 3–89.

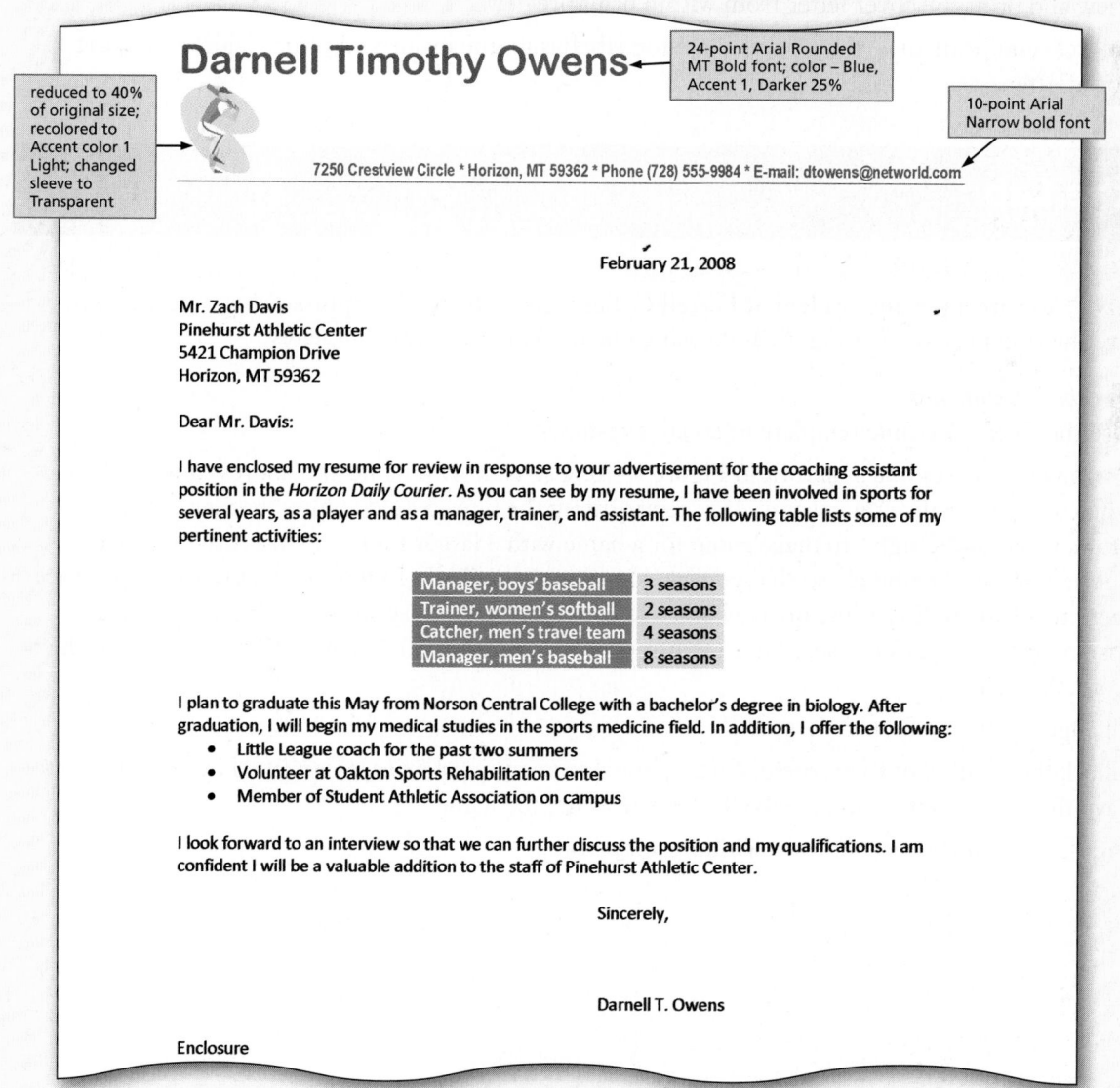

Figure 3–89

Continued >

STUDENT ASSIGNMENTS

In the Lab *continued*

Perform the following tasks:

1. Create the letterhead shown at the top of Figure 3–89 on the previous page. Insert the clip art image and then resize and format it as indicated in the figure. Remove the hyperlink format from the e-mail address. If necessary, clear formatting after entering the bottom border. Save the letterhead with the file name, Lab 3-1 Owens Letterhead.

2. Create the letter shown in Figure 3–89. Set a tab stop at the 3.5" mark on the ruler for the date line, complimentary close, and signature block. Insert the current date. After entering the inside address, create a building block for Pinehurst Athletic Center and insert the building block whenever you have to enter the company name. Insert nonbreaking space characters in the newspaper name. Insert and center the table. Format the table using the Medium Grid 3 - Accent 1 table style. Select only the First Column check box in the Table Style Options group. Adjust the column widths so that they are as wide as the contents of the cells. Bullet the list as you type it.

3. Check the spelling of the letter. Change the document properties, as specified by your instructor. Save the letter with Lab 3-1 Owens Cover Letter as the file name.

4. View and print the cover letter from within print preview.

5. Address and print an envelope and a mailing label using the inside and return addresses in the cover letter.

In the Lab

Lab 2: Creating a Resume from a Template

Problem: You are a nursing student at Ferrell College. As graduation is approaching quickly, you prepare the resume shown in Figure 3–90 using one of Word's resume templates.

Perform the following tasks:

1. Use the Equity Resume template to create a resume.

2. Personalize the resume as shown in Figure 3–90. Use your own name and address information when you personalize the resume. If necessary, drag the blue-dotted column border to the right of the name to the right, to make room for a name with a larger font size. Insert the Experience Subsection building block, so that you can enter the second job. Indent the text in the Experience section as shown. Enter line break characters between the job responsibility lines. Adjust line spacing in the Experience section, so that it matches Figure 3–90. Change the title, Skills, to the word, Activities.

3. Change the theme fonts to Aspect.

4. Check the spelling of the resume. Change the document properties, as specified by your instructor. Save the resume with Lab 3-2 Marsh Resume as the file name.

5. View and print the resume from within print preview.

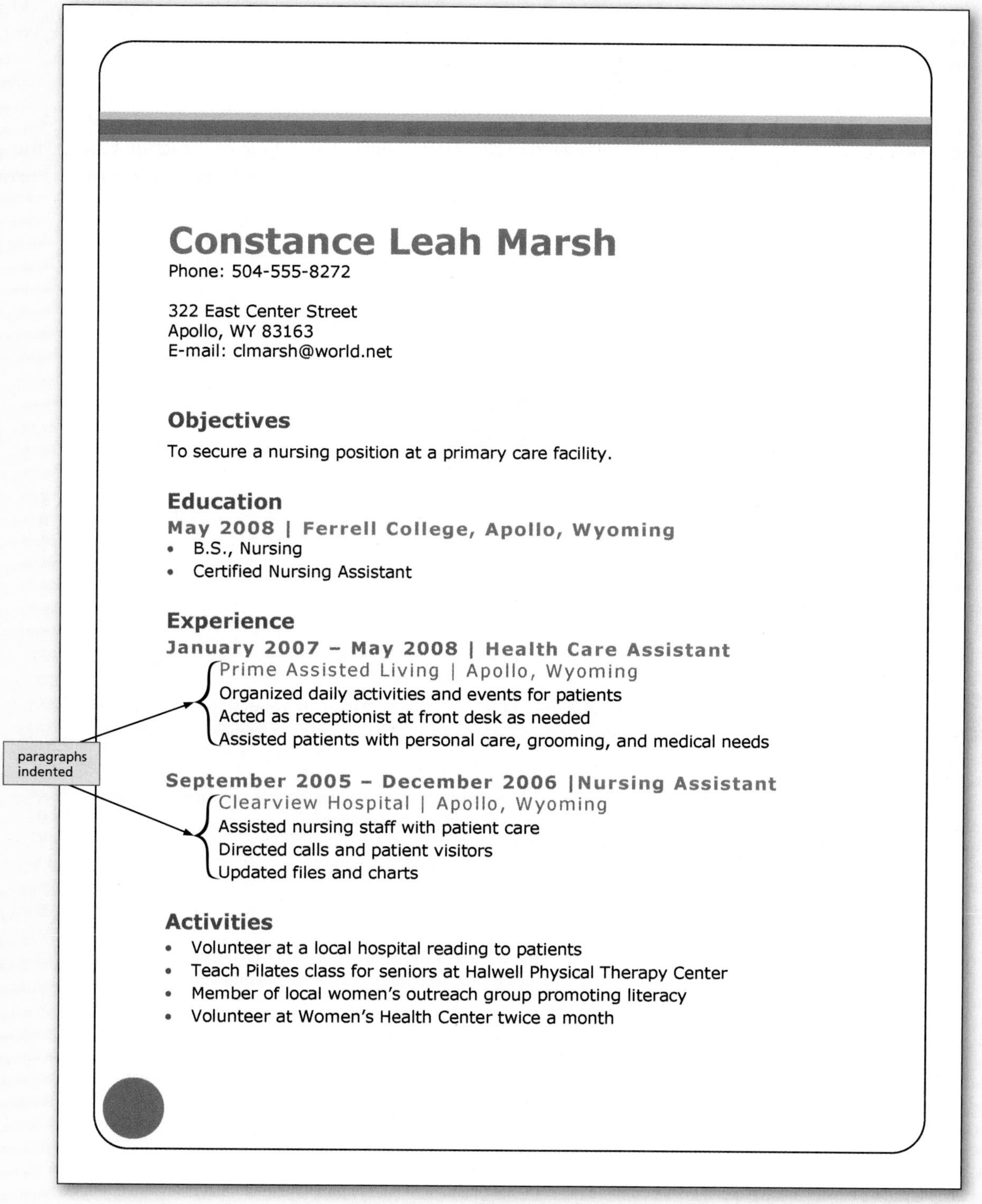

Constance Leah Marsh
Phone: 504-555-8272

322 East Center Street
Apollo, WY 83163
E-mail: clmarsh@world.net

Objectives
To secure a nursing position at a primary care facility.

Education
May 2008 | Ferrell College, Apollo, Wyoming
- B.S., Nursing
- Certified Nursing Assistant

Experience
January 2007 – May 2008 | Health Care Assistant
Prime Assisted Living | Apollo, Wyoming
Organized daily activities and events for patients
Acted as receptionist at front desk as needed
Assisted patients with personal care, grooming, and medical needs

September 2005 – December 2006 |Nursing Assistant
Clearview Hospital | Apollo, Wyoming
Assisted nursing staff with patient care
Directed calls and patient visitors
Updated files and charts

paragraphs indented

Activities
- Volunteer at a local hospital reading to patients
- Teach Pilates class for seniors at Halwell Physical Therapy Center
- Member of local women's outreach group promoting literacy
- Volunteer at Women's Health Center twice a month

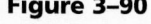

Figure 3–90

In the Lab

Lab 3: Creating a Letter

Problem: You are a president of the Parents Educational Organization for the local high school. The organization currently is taking nominations for outstanding teacher award and you write thank-you letters to nominators, also asking them for donations.

Instructions: Prepare the letter shown in Figure 3–91. Follow the guidelines in the modified semi-block letter style. Use proper spacing between elements of the letter. Check the spelling of the letter. Change the document properties, as specified by your instructor. Save the letter with Lab 3-3 Ling Letter as the file name.

Kim S. Ling
Parents Educational Organization
99 Ohio Avenue, Harrust, NH 03891
(317) 555-1865 * E-mail: ksling@net.com

February 14, 2008

Ms. Laura Ennis
74 MacEnroe Court
Fairview, IN 46142

Dear Ms. Ennis:

Thank you for your recent nomination of Mr. Serensi from Bakersville North High School for our outstanding teacher award. He will be pleased that you believe he was a great influence in your decision to become a teacher.

In addition to the honor of being selected outstanding teacher, we present our candidates with a monetary gift. They use the funds for future classroom needs, including:
- Reading materials to be kept in the classroom
- Emergency funds to assist students in need of supplies
- Supplies for additional projects to be determined by teacher
- Guest author and speaker visits

If you are interested in donating to this worthy cause, please contact me via e-mail or telephone. All donors' names are engraved on a plaque on display in the school auditorium. Listed in the table below are the donation levels.

Donation Level	Donation Amount
Gold	$500
Silver	$250
Bronze	$100

Again, we thank you for your interest in our project.

Yours truly,

Kim Ling
President

Figure 3–91

Cases and Places

Apply your creative thinking and problem solving skills to design and implement a solution.

● EASIER   ●● MORE DIFFICULT

● 1: Create a Fax Cover Sheet from a Template

Your boss has asked you to send a fax that includes a fax cover sheet. In the New Document dialog box, click Installed Templates in the Templates pane and then click Equity Fax in the Installed Templates list. Click in each area to enter the following information in the fax cover sheet: the fax is from your boss, Max Henreich; the fax should go to Shirelle Bradley; her fax number is (317) 555-0922; the fax contains three pages; and the phone is (317) 555-1350. Use today's date for the date. The Re: area should contain the following text: Site visit materials. Leave the CC: field blank. The For Review check box should be checked, and your boss wants the following comment on the cover sheet: Here are the notes for tomorrow's site visit.

● 2: Create this Chapter's Resume Using a Different Template

Information can look and be perceived completely differently simply by virtue of the way it is presented. Take the resume created in this chapter and create it using a different template. For example, try the Equity, Median, Oreil, or Urban Resume template in the Installed Templates list. Make sure each section of the resume in this chapter is presented in the new document. You may need to rename or delete sections and add building blocks. Open the resume you created in this chapter and use the copy and paste commands to simplify entering the text. Select a theme you like best for the finished resume.

●● 3: Create a Memo Using a Template from the Web

As assistant director of programs at a local park, you are responsible for soliciting ideas from employees regarding future programs and activities. In the New Document dialog box, click Memos in the Microsoft Office Online area to create a memo. Select a template you like. Use the following information to complete the memo: the memo should go to all staff members; the meeting will be held in room A42 on March 14, 2008 at 3:00 p.m.; attendees should be prepared to discuss their ideas for spring and summer activities; and attendance is mandatory. Mention that if anyone is to be on vacation or unavailable, he or she should contact you prior to the meeting to arrange for submission of activities lists.

●● 4: Create Your Resume and Cover Letter for a Potential Job

Make It Personal

Assume you are graduating this semester and need to find a job immediately after graduation. Check a local newspaper or online employment source to find an advertisement for a job relating to your major or a job for which you believe you are qualified. Use the techniques you learned in this chapter to create your resume and a cover letter. Tailor your cover letter and your resume to fit the job description. Make sure you include an objective, education, and work experience section. Also include any other pertinent sections. Use the copy and paste commands on the Office Clipboard to copy your name and address information from one document to the other.

Continued >

STUDENT ASSIGNMENTS

Cases and Places *continued*

●● 5: Create Documents Using Templates from the Web

Working Together

As active members of your school's Travel and Leisure Club, you have been assigned the task of publicizing the club's upcoming activities and soliciting new memberships. Assign each team member one of the following tasks: create a calendar listing various club activities for a three-month period, including any scheduled trips, parties, or meetings; design an award or certificate for excellence or other recognition presented to your club by another campus group; compose a letter of thanks from a past member; and create an invitation to join the Travel and Leisure Club. Visit Microsoft Office Online to obtain templates for awards and certificates, calendars, and invitations. Then, as a group, write a cover letter soliciting memberships and listing the reasons why students should join the club. Include a table or bulleted list similar to those used in this chapter. Make the package attractive and eye-catching.

Web Feature

Creating a Web Page Using Word

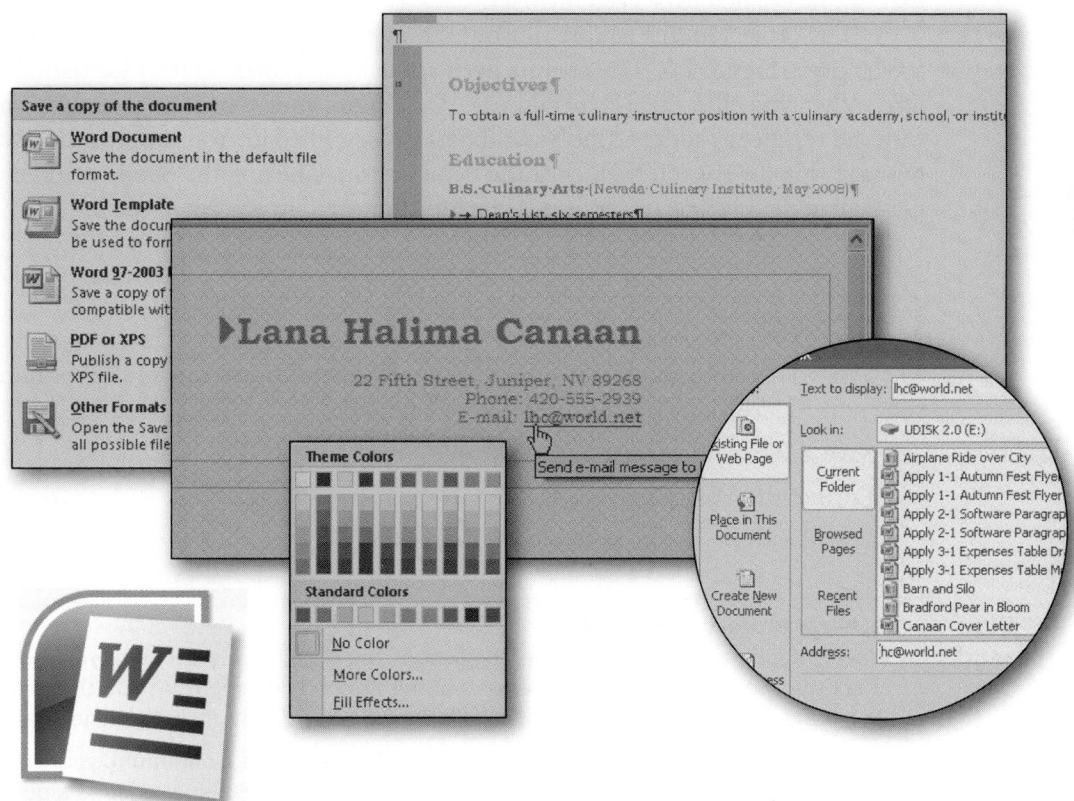

Objectives

You will have mastered the material in this feature when you can:

- Save a Word document as a Web page

- Insert a hyperlink

- Add a background color with a pattern

- Use Windows Explorer to view a Web page

Web Feature Introduction

Many people have personal Web pages, allowing them to share personal information with users around the world. Job seekers often post their resume on the Web so that potential employers can search for and view their resumes online. With Word, you easily can save any existing document as a Web page. You then can post your Web page to a Web server.

Project — Web Page

Personal Web pages contain text, documents, images, links, videos, and audio. If you have created a document using an Office program, such as Word, you can save it in a format that can be opened by a Web browser.

The project in this feature illustrates how to save the resume created in Chapter 3 as a Web page (Figure 1a). The resume itself contains an e-mail address formatted as a hyperlink. When you click the e-mail address, Word starts your e-mail program automatically with the recipient's address (lhc@world.net) already filled in. You simply type a subject and message (Figure 1b) and then click the Send button. Clicking the Send button places the message in the Outbox or sends it if you are connected to an e-mail server.

Overview

As you read through this feature, you will learn how to create the resume Web page shown in Figure 1a by performing these general tasks:

- Save a Word document as a Web page.
- Format the Web page.
- Use Windows Explorer to view a Web page.

Plan Ahead

General Project Guidelines

When creating a resume Web page, the actions you perform and decisions you make will affect the appearance and characteristics of the finished document. As you create a resume Web page, such as the project shown in Figure 1a, you should follow these general guidelines:

1. **Craft a successful resume.** Your resume should present, at a minimum, your contact information, objective, educational background, and work experience to a potential employer. It should honestly present all your positive points. Ask someone else to proofread your resume and give you suggestions for improvements.

2. **Create a resume Web page from your resume Word document.** Save the Word document as a Web page. Improve the usability of the resume Web page by making your e-mail address a link to an e-mail program. Enhance the look of the Web page by adding, for example, a background color. Be sure to test your finished Web page document in at least one browser program to be sure it looks and works as you intended.

3. **Publish your resume Web page.** Once you have created a Web page, you can publish it. **Publishing** is the process of making a Web page available to others on a network, such as the Internet or a company's intranet. In Word, you can publish a Web page by saving it to a Web server or to an FTP site. Many Internet access providers offer storage space on their Web servers at no cost to their subscribers. The procedures for using Microsoft Office to publish a Web page are discussed in Appendix D.

This Web Feature focuses on the second guideline, identifying the actions you perform and the decisions you make during the creation of the resume Web page shown in Figure 1a.

BTW

Planning a Resume Web Page
Chapter 3 presented details about the first guideline in the Plan Ahead, and Appendix D presents details about the third guideline.

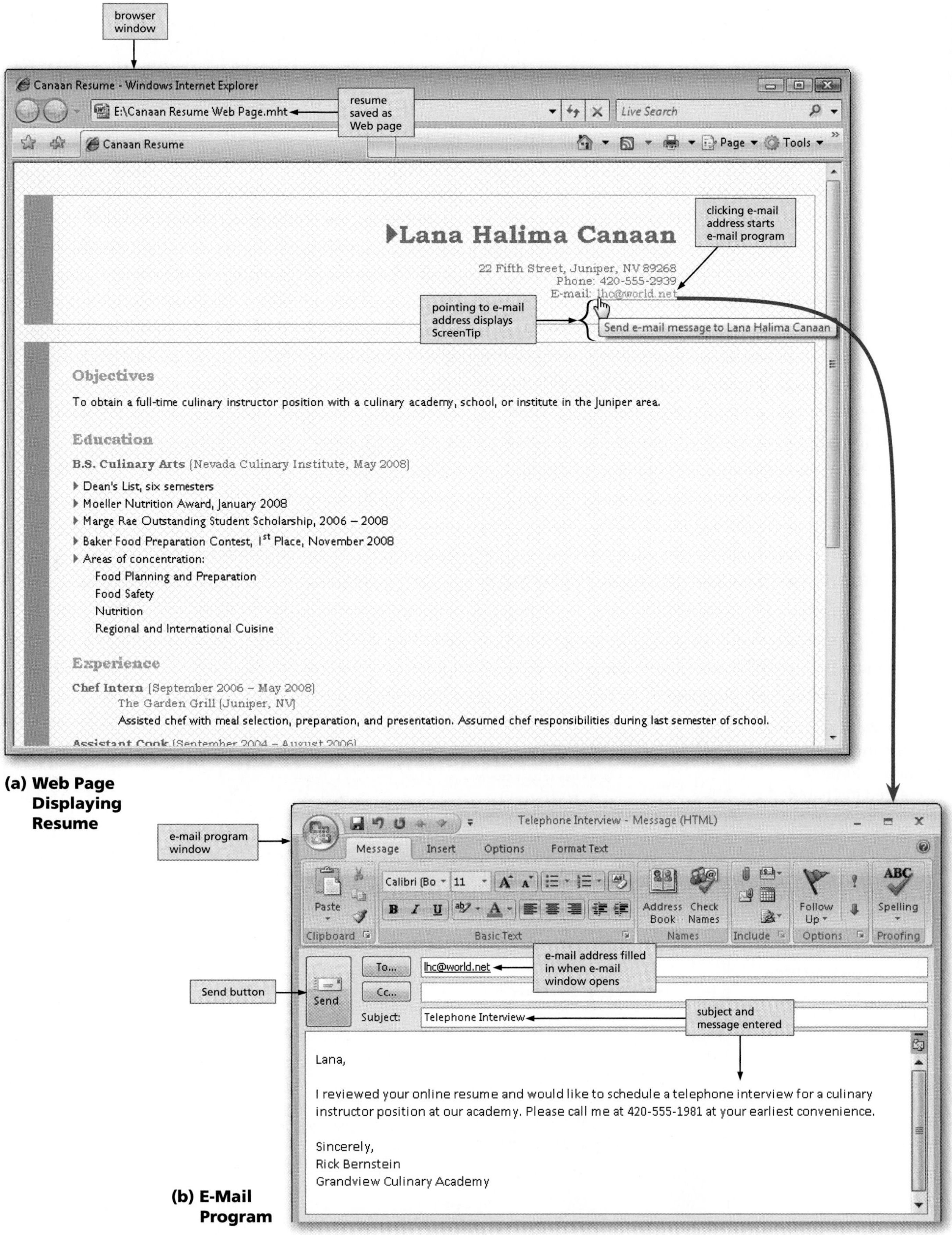

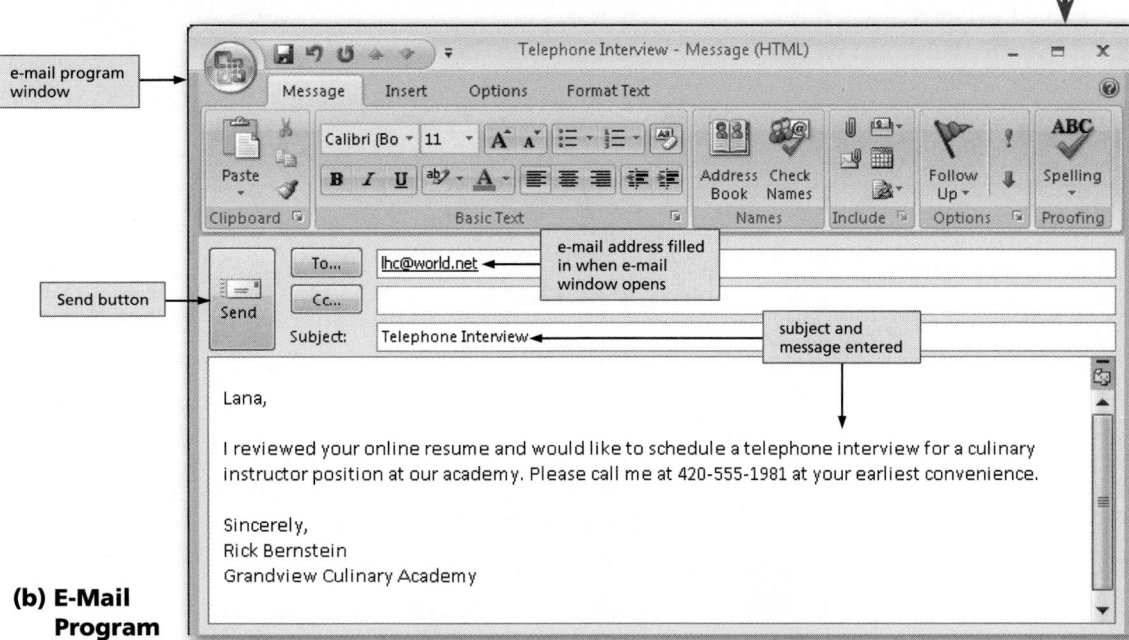

browser window

Canaan Resume - Windows Internet Explorer

E:\Canaan Resume Web Page.mht

resume saved as Web page

Live Search

Canaan Resume

Page ▾ Tools ▾

▶**Lana Halima Canaan**

clicking e-mail address starts e-mail program

22 Fifth Street, Juniper, NV 89268
Phone: 420-555-2939
E-mail: lhc@world.net

pointing to e-mail address displays ScreenTip

Send e-mail message to Lana Halima Canaan

Objectives

To obtain a full-time culinary instructor position with a culinary academy, school, or institute in the Juniper area.

Education

B.S. Culinary Arts (Nevada Culinary Institute, May 2008)

▶ Dean's List, six semesters
▶ Moeller Nutrition Award, January 2008
▶ Marge Rae Outstanding Student Scholarship, 2006 – 2008
▶ Baker Food Preparation Contest, 1st Place, November 2008
▶ Areas of concentration:
    Food Planning and Preparation
    Food Safety
    Nutrition
    Regional and International Cuisine

Experience

Chef Intern (September 2006 – May 2008)
    The Garden Grill (Juniper, NV)
    Assisted chef with meal selection, preparation, and presentation. Assumed chef responsibilities during last semester of school.

Assistant Cook (September 2004 – August 2006)

(a) Web Page Displaying Resume

e-mail program window

Telephone Interview - Message (HTML)

Message   Insert   Options   Format Text

Calibri (Bo ▾ 11

Paste

Clipboard

B I U

Basic Text

Address Check
Book   Names

Names

Follow
Up ▾

Options

ABC

Spelling

Proofing

Send button

Send

To...

Cc...

Subject:

lhc@world.net

Telephone Interview

e-mail address filled in when e-mail window opens

subject and message entered

Lana,

I reviewed your online resume and would like to schedule a telephone interview for a culinary instructor position at our academy. Please call me at 420-555-1981 at your earliest convenience.

Sincerely,
Rick Bernstein
Grandview Culinary Academy

(b) E-Mail Program

Figure 1

Saving a Word Document as a Web Page

Once you have created a Word document, you can save it as a Web page so that it can be published and then viewed in a Web browser, such as Internet Explorer. When you save a file as a Web page, Word converts the contents of the document into **HTML** (hypertext markup language), which is a language that browsers can interpret. Some of Word's formatting features are not supported by Web pages. Thus, your Web page may look slightly different from the original Word document.

When saving a document as a Web page, you have three choices in Word:

- The **single file Web page format** saves all of the components of the Web page in a single file that has an .mht extension. This format is particularly useful for e-mailing documents in HTML format.

- The **Web Page format** saves some of the components of the Web page in a folder, separate from the Web page. This format is useful if you need access to the individual components, such as images, that make up the Web page.

- The **filtered Web Page format** saves the file in Web page format and then reduces the size of the file by removing specific Microsoft Office formats. This format is useful if you want to speed up the time it takes to download a Web page that contains many graphics, video, audio, or animations.

The Web page in this feature uses the single file Web page format.

BTW

Saving as a Web Page
Because you might not have access to a Web server, the Web page you create in this feature is saved on a USB flash drive rather than to a Web server.

To Save a Word Document as a Web Page

The following steps save the resume created in Chapter 3 as a Web page. If you are stepping through this feature on a computer, you will need the resume document named Canaan Resume that was created in Chapter 3. (If you did not create the resume, see your instructor for a copy of it.)

1
- Start Word and then open the file named Canaan Resume created in Chapter 3.

2
- With the resume file open in the document window, click the Office Button and then point to Save As on the Office Button menu to display the Save As submenu (Figure 2).

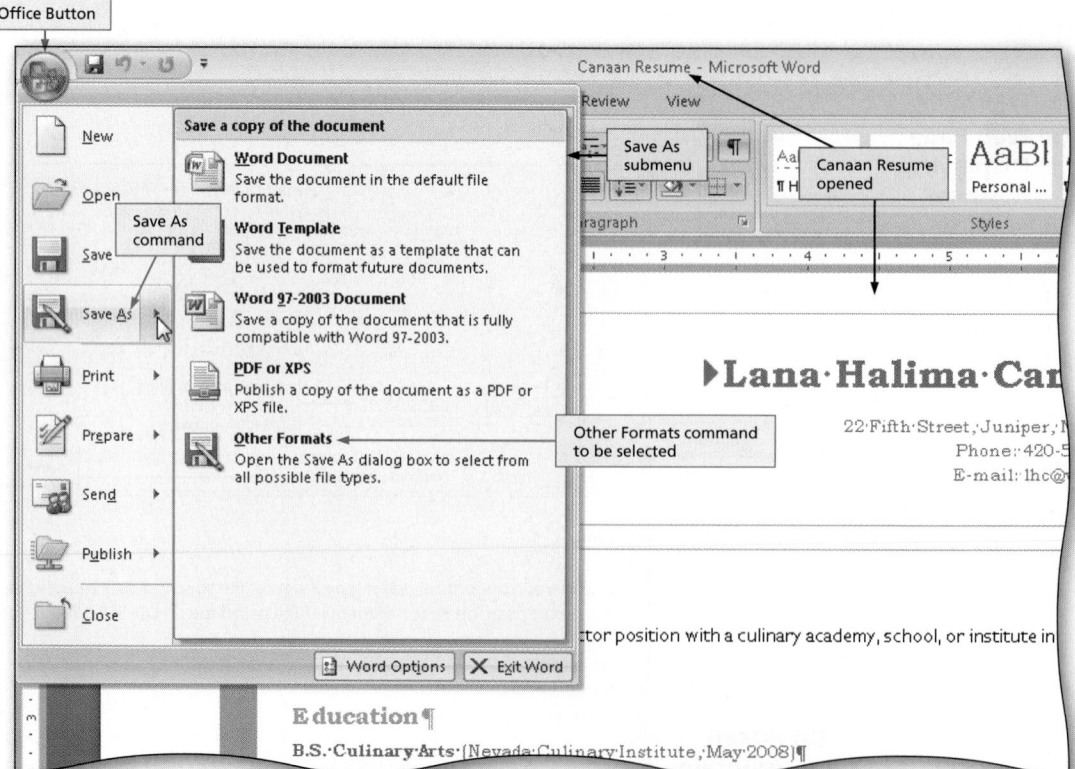

Figure 2

3

- Click Other Formats on the Save As submenu to display the Save As dialog box.

- Type Canaan Resume Web Page in the File name text box to change the file name. If necessary, change the Save location to UDISK 2.0 (E:). (Your USB flash drive may have a different name and letter.)

- Click the Save as type box arrow and then click Single File Web Page.

- Click the Change Title button to display the Set Page Title dialog box.

- Type Canaan Resume in the Page title text box (Figure 3).

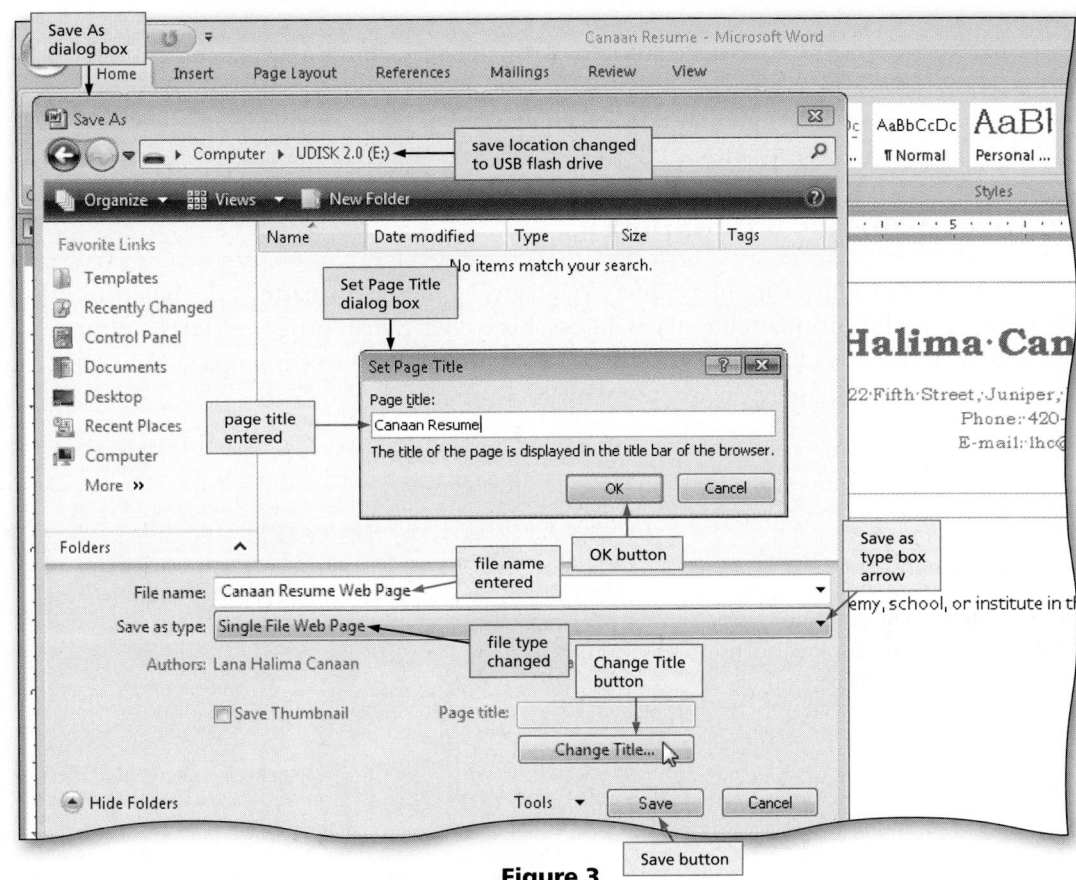

Figure 3

4

- Click the OK button in the Set Page Title dialog box.

- Click the Save button in the Save As dialog box to save the resume as a Web page and display it in the document window (Figure 4). (If Word displays a dialog box about compatibility with Web browsers, click the Continue button in the dialog box.)

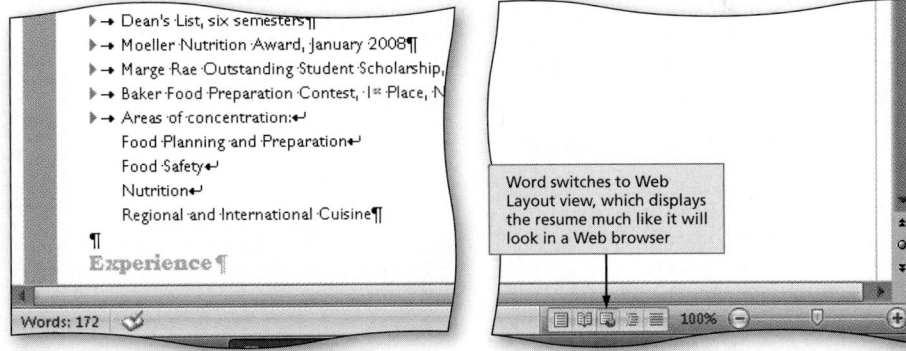

Figure 4

Other Ways

1. Press F12

Saving to a Web Server

If you have access to and can save files to a Web server, then you can save the Web page directly to the Web server by clicking the appropriate network location in the File list in the Save As dialog box. If you have access to a Web server that allows you to save to an FTP site, then you can save to the FTP site by selecting the site below FTP locations in the File list in the Save As dialog box. To learn more about saving Web pages to a Web server or FTP site using Microsoft Office programs, refer to Appendix D.

Formatting a Web Page

In this feature, the e-mail address on the Canaan Resume Web page is formatted as a hyperlink. Also, the background color of the Web page is blue. The following sections modify the Web page to include these enhancements.

To Format Text as a Hyperlink

The e-mail address in the resume Web page should be formatted as a hyperlink. When a Web page visitor clicks the hyperlink-formatted e-mail address, his or her e-mail program starts automatically and displays an e-mail window with the e-mail address already filled in (shown in Figure 1b on page WD 217). The following steps format the e-mail address as a hyperlink.

- Select the e-mail address (lhc@world.net, in this case).

- Display the Insert tab.

- Click the Insert Hyperlink button on the Insert tab to display the Insert Hyperlink dialog box (Figure 5).

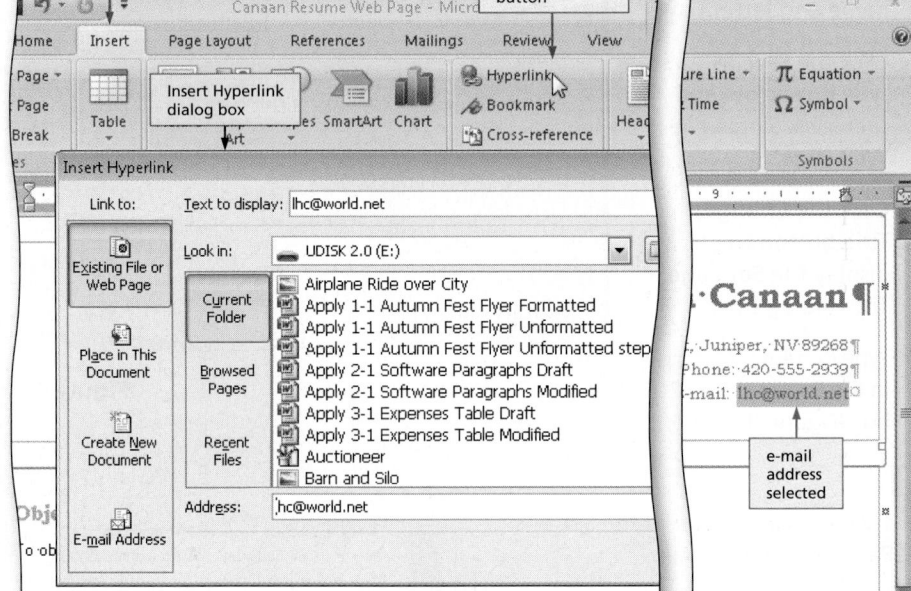

Figure 5

2

- Click E-mail Address in the Link to bar so that the dialog box displays e-mail address settings instead of Web page settings.

- In the 'Text to display' text box, if necessary, type lhc@world.net, which specifies the text that shows on the screen for the hyperlink.

- Click the E-mail address text box and then type lhc@world.net to specify the e-mail address that the Web browser uses when a user clicks the hyperlink.

- Click the ScreenTip button to display the Set Hyperlink ScreenTip dialog box.

- In the text box, type Send e-mail message to Lana Halima Canaan, which is the text that will be displayed when a user points to the hyperlink (Figure 6).

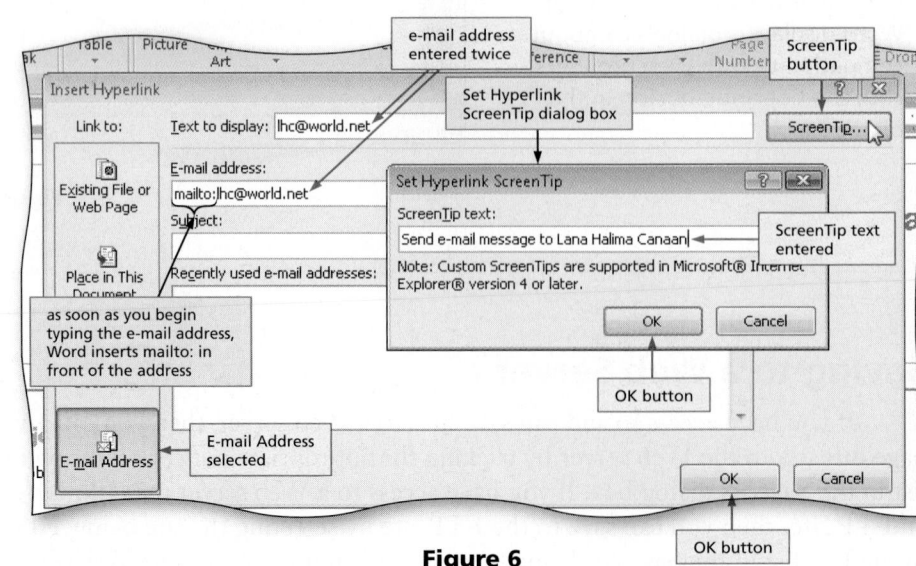

Figure 6

3

- Click the OK button in each dialog box to format the e-mail address as a hyperlink (Figure 7).

How do I know if the hyperlink works?

In Word, you can test the hyperlink by holding down the CTRL key while clicking the hyperlink. In this case, CTRL+clicking the e-mail address should open an e-mail window. If you need to make a change to the hyperlink, right-click it and then click Edit Hyperlink on the shortcut menu.

Figure 7

Other Ways
1. Right-click selected text, click Hyperlink on shortcut menu
2. Select text, press CTRL+K

To Add a Background Color

The next step is to add background color to the Web page so that it looks more eye-catching. Select a color that best represents your personality. This Web page uses a light shade of blue. The following steps add a background color.

1

- Display the Page Layout tab.

- Click the Page Color button on the Page Layout tab to display the Page Color gallery.

- Point to the sixth color in the second row (Ice Blue, Accent 2, Lighter 80%) to display a live preview of the background color (Figure 8).

Experiment

- Point to various colors in the Page Color gallery and watch the background color change in the document window.

2

- Click the sixth color in the second row to change the background color to a light shade of blue.

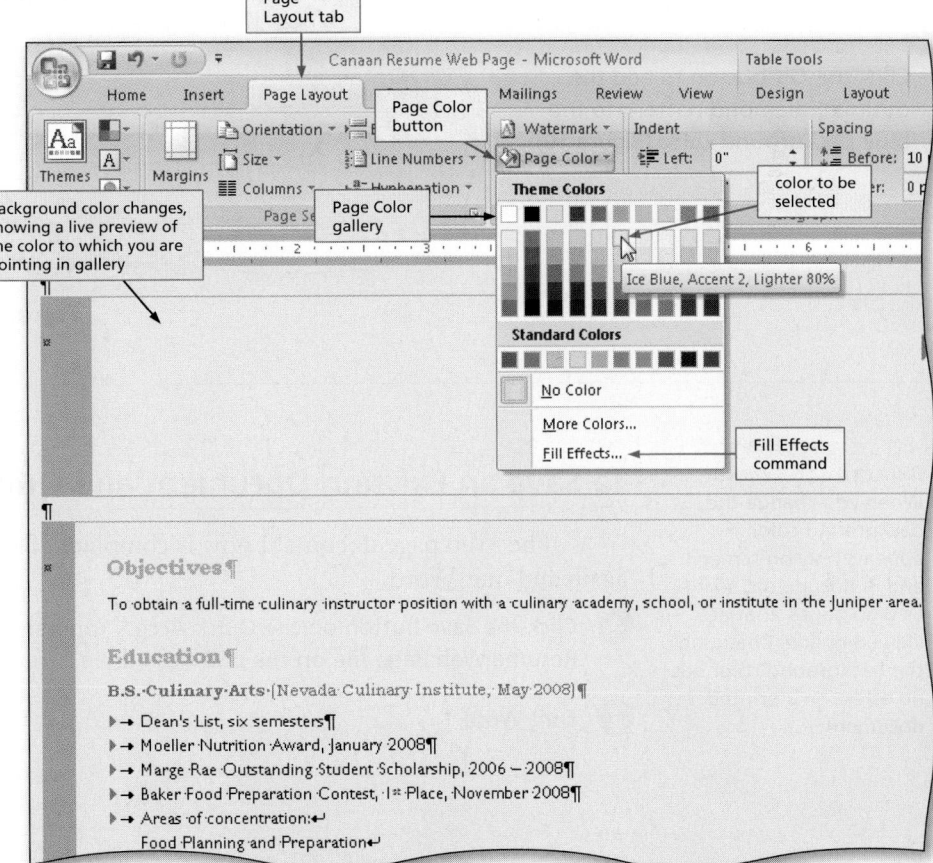

Figure 8

To Add a Pattern Fill Effect to a Background

When you changed the background color in the previous steps, Word placed a solid background color on the screen. For this resume Web page, the solid background color is a little too intense. To soften the background color, you can add patterns to it. The following steps add a pattern to the blue background.

- Click the Page Color button on the Page Layout tab (shown in Figure 8 on the previous page) to display the Page Color gallery again.

- Click Fill Effects in the Page Color gallery (shown in Figure 8) to display the Fill Effects dialog box.

- Click the Pattern tab to display the Pattern sheet in the dialog box.

- Click the Outlined diamond pattern (rightmost pattern in the fifth row) to select it (Figure 9).

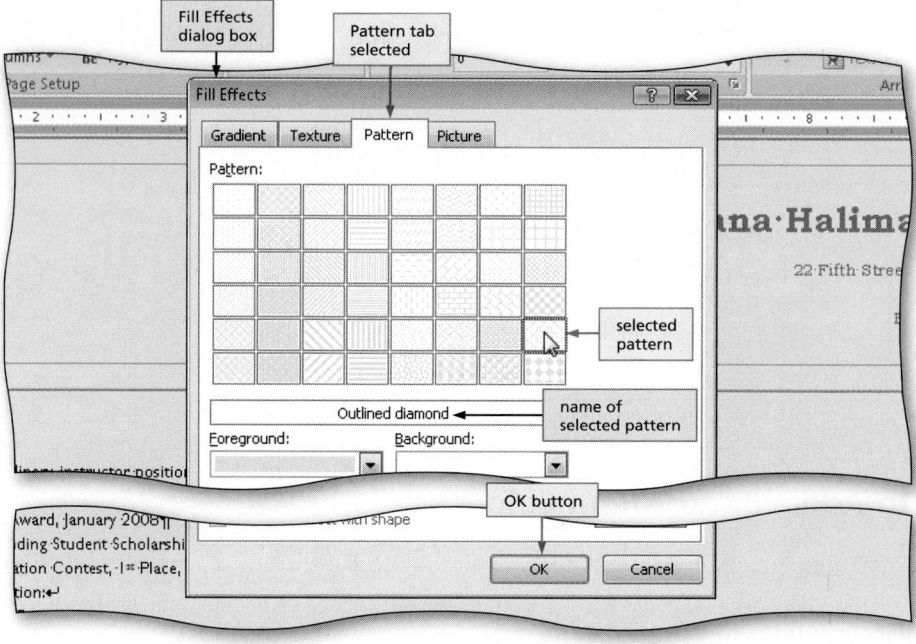

Figure 9

- Click the OK button to add the outlined diamond pattern to the blue background color (Figure 10).

Figure 10

BTW

Background Colors
When you change the background color, it appears only on-screen and in documents, such as Web pages, that are viewed online. Changing the background color has no effect on a printed document.

To Save an Existing Document and Quit Word

The Web page document now is complete. The following steps save the document again and quit Word.

1. Click the Save button on the Quick Access Toolbar to overwrite the previous Canaan Resume Web Page file on the USB flash drive.

2. Quit Word.

Testing the Web Page

After creating and saving a Web page, you will want to test it in at least one browser to be sure it looks and works the way you intended.

To Test the Web Page in a Web Browser

The following steps use Windows Explorer to display the resume Web page in the Internet Explorer Web browser.

1
- Click the Start button on the Windows Vista taskbar to display the Start menu.
- Click Computer on the Start menu to display the Computer window.
- If necessary, maximize the Computer window (Figure 11).

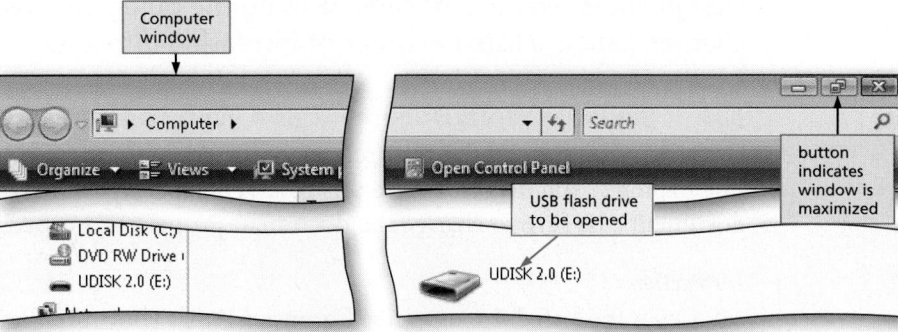

Figure 11

2
- Double-click the USB flash drive icon in the Computer window to display the contents of the USB flash drive (Figure 12).

3
- Double-click the file name, Canaan Resume Web Page, to start the Internet Explorer Web browser and display the file in the browser window (shown in Figure 1a on page WD 217).
- With the Web page document displaying in the Web browser, click the e-mail address link to ensure it displays the e-mail window, as shown in Figure 1b on page WD 217.

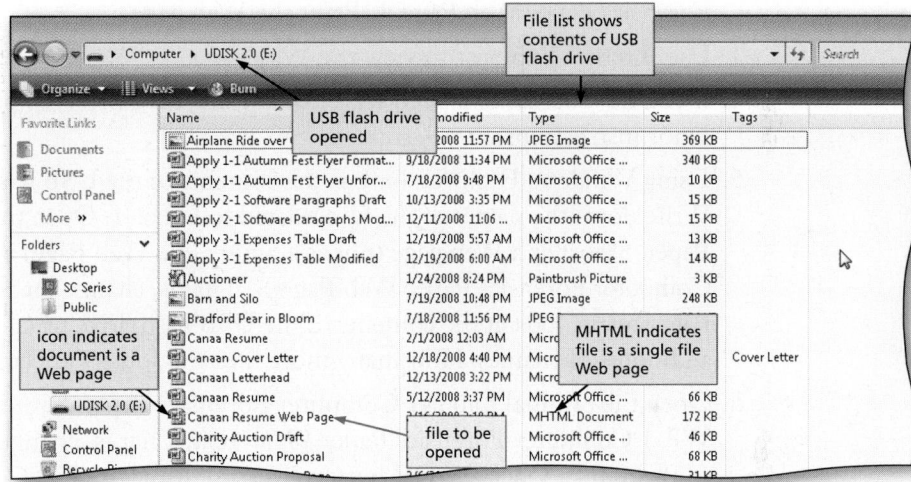

Figure 12

4
- Close all open windows.

BTW

Quick Reference
For a table that lists how to complete the tasks covered in this book using the mouse, Ribbon, shortcut menu, and keyboard, see the Quick Reference Summary at the back of this book, or visit the Word 2007 Quick Reference Web page (scsite.com/wd2007/qr).

Feature Summary

In this feature, you have learned how to save a Word document as a Web page, insert a hyperlink, add background color, and view a Web page. The items listed below include all the new Word skills you have learned in this feature.

1. Save a Word Document as a Web Page (WD 218)
2. Format Text as a Hyperlink (WD 220)
3. Add a Background Color (WD 221)
4. Add a Pattern Fill Effect to a Background (WD 222)
5. Test the Web Page in a Web Browser (WD 223)

 If you have a SAM user profile, you may have access to hands-on instruction, practice, and assessment. Log in to your SAM account (http://sam2007.course.com) to launch any assigned training activities or exams that relate to the skills covered in this feature.

In the Lab

Design and/or create a document using the guidelines, concepts, and skills presented in this chapter. Labs are listed in order of increasing difficulty.

Lab 1: Saving a Word Document as a Web Page and in Other Formats

Problem: You created the research paper shown in Figure 2-83 on pages WD 138 and WD 139 in Chapter 2. You decide to save this research paper in a variety of formats. For each of the saved documents, be sure to change the document properties, as specified by your instructor.

Instructions:

1. Open the Lab 2-1 Computer Forensics Paper shown in Figure 2-83. (If you did not create the research paper, see your instructor for a copy.)

2. Save the research paper as a single file Web page using the file name, Lab WF-1 Computer Forensics Paper Web Page A. Print the Web page.

3. Use Internet Explorer to view the Web page.

4. If you have access to a Web server or ftp site, save the Web page to the server or site (see Appendix D for instructions).

5. Using Windows Explorer, look at the contents of the USB flash drive containing the Web page. Write down the names of the files related to Lab 2-1. Open the original Lab 2-1 Computer Forensics Paper. Save it as a Web page (not as a Single File Web Page) using the file name, Lab WF-1 Computer Forensics Paper Web Page B. That is, change the file type in the Save as type box to Web Page. Again, look at the contents of the USB flash drive using Windows Explorer. Write down any additional file names. How many more files and folders are created by the Web Page format?

6. Open the original Lab 2-1 Computer Forensics Paper. Save it as plain text using the file name, Lab WF-1 Computer Forensics Paper Plain Text. That is, change the file type in the Save as type box to Plain Text. Click the OK button if Word displays a File Conversion dialog box. Open the plain text file. *Hint:* In the Open dialog box, click the Files of type box arrow and then click All Files. Write down the difference between the plain text file and the original file.

In the Lab

Lab 2: Creating a Web Page with a Hyperlink

Problem: You created the resume shown in Figure 3-90 on page WD 211 in Chapter 3. You decide to save it as a Web page with the e-mail address as a hyperlink.

Instructions:

1. Open the Lab 3-2 Marsh Resume shown in Figure 3-90. (If you did not create the resume, see your instructor for a copy.)

2. Save the resume as a single file Web page using the file name, Lab WF-2 Marsh Resume Web Page. Change the page title to Constance Marsh. Convert the e-mail address to a hyperlink. Apply the Orange, Accent 1, Lighter 80% background color to the document. Apply the Divot pattern fill effect to the background color. Change the document properties, as specified by your instructor. Save the resume Web page again. View the Web page in Internet Explorer. Test the e-mail address hyperlink. Print the Web page.

3. If you have access to a Web server or ftp site, save the Web page to the server or site (see Appendix D).

1 | Creating a Worksheet and an Embedded Chart

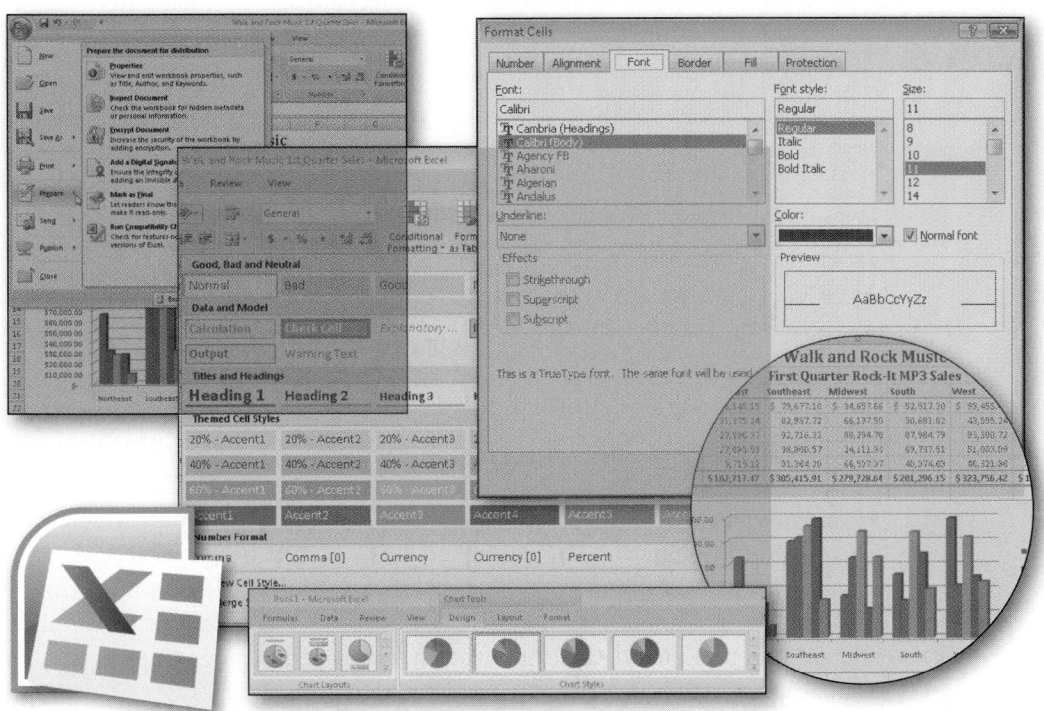

Objectives

You will have mastered the material in this chapter when you can:

- Start and quit Excel
- Describe the Excel worksheet
- Enter text and numbers
- Use the Sum button to sum a range of cells
- Copy the contents of a cell to a range of cells using the fill handle
- Save a workbook
- Format cells in a worksheet
- Create a 3-D Clustered Column chart

- Change document properties
- Save a workbook a second time using the same file name
- Print a worksheet
- Open a workbook
- Use the AutoCalculate area to determine statistics
- Correct errors on a worksheet
- Use Excel Help to answer questions

1 | Creating a Worksheet and an Embedded Chart

What Is Microsoft Office Excel 2007?

Microsoft Office Excel 2007 is a powerful spreadsheet program that allows users to organize data, complete calculations, make decisions, graph data, develop professional looking reports (Figure 1–1), publish organized data to the Web, and access real-time data from Web sites. The four major parts of Excel are:

- **Workbooks and Worksheets** Workbooks are a collection of worksheets. Worksheets allow users to enter, calculate, manipulate, and analyze data such as numbers and text. The terms worksheet and spreadsheet are interchangeable.

- **Charts** Excel can draw a variety of charts.

- **Tables** Tables organize and store data within worksheets. For example, once a user enters data into a worksheet, an Excel table can sort the data, search for specific data, and select data that satisfies defined criteria.

- **Web Support** Web support allows users to save Excel worksheets or parts of a worksheet in HTML format, so a user can view and manipulate the worksheet using a browser. Excel Web support also provides access to real-time data, such as stock quotes, using Web queries.

This latest version of Excel makes it much easier than in previous versions to perform common functions by introducing a new style of user interface. It also offers the capability of creating larger worksheets, improved formatting and printing, improved charting and table functionality, industry-standard XML support that simplifies the sharing of data within and outside an organization, improved business intelligence functionality, and the capability of performing complex tasks on a server.

In this chapter, you will create a worksheet that includes a chart. The data in the worksheet and chart includes sales data for several stores that a company owns and operates.

Project Planning Guidelines

The process of developing a worksheet that communicates specific information requires careful analysis and planning. As a starting point, establish why the worksheet is needed. Once the purpose is determined, analyze the intended users of the worksheet and their unique needs. Then, gather information about the topic and decide what to include in the worksheet. Finally, determine the worksheet design and style that will be most successful at delivering the message. Details of these guidelines are provided in Appendix A. In addition, each project developed in this book provides practical applications of these planning considerations.

Project — Worksheet with an Embedded Chart

The project in this chapter follows proper design guidelines and uses Excel to create the worksheet shown in Figure 1–1. The worksheet contains sales data for Walk and Rock Music stores. The Walk and Rock Music product line includes a variety of MP3 music players, called Rock-It MP3, including players that show pictures and video, as well as a complete line of headphones and other accessories. The company sells its products at kiosks in several malls throughout the United States. By concentrating its stores near colleges and universities and keeping the newest items in stock, the Walk and Rock Music stores quickly became trendy. As sales continued to grow in the past year, senior management requested an easy-to-read worksheet that shows product sales for the first quarter by region. In addition, they asked for a chart showing first quarter sales, because the president of the company likes to have a graphical representation of sales that allows him quickly to identify stronger and weaker product types by region.

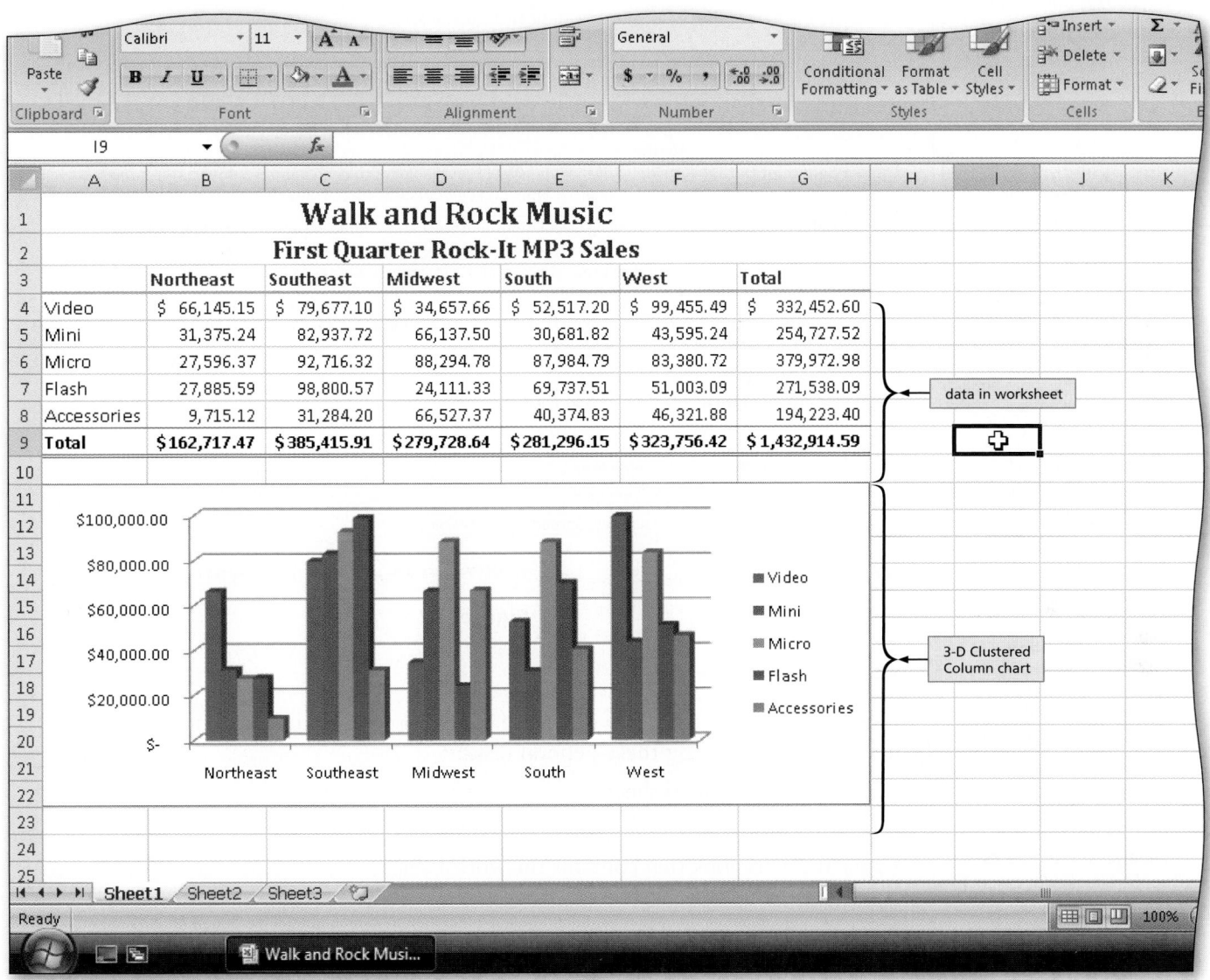

Figure 1–1

The first step in creating an effective worksheet is to make sure you understand what is required. The person or persons requesting the worksheet should supply their requirements in a requirements document. A **requirements document** includes a needs

BTW

Excel 2007 Features
With its what-if analysis tools, research capabilities, collaboration tools, streamlined user interface, smart tags, charting features, Web capabilities, hundreds of functions, and enhanced formatting capabilities, Excel 2007 is one of the easier and more powerful spreadsheet packages available.

statement, source of data, summary of calculations, and any other special requirements for the worksheet, such as charting and Web support. Figure 1–2 shows the requirements document for the new workbook to be created in this chapter.

requirements document →

REQUEST FOR NEW WORKBOOK

Date Submitted:	April 15, 2008
Submitted By:	Trisha Samuels
Worksheet Title:	Walk and Rock Music First Quarter Sales
Needs:	An easy-to-read worksheet that shows Walk and Rock Music's first quarter sales for each of our sales regions in which we operate (Northeast, Southeast, Midwest, South, West). The worksheet also should include total sales for each region, total sales for each product type, and total company sales for the first quarter.
Source of Data:	The data for the worksheet is available for the end of the first quarter from the chief financial officer (CFO) of Walk and Rock Music.
Calculations:	The following calculations must be made for the worksheet: (a) total first quarter sales for each of the five regions; (b) total first quarter sales for each of the five product types; and (c) total first quarter sales for the company.
Chart Requirements:	Below the data in the worksheet, construct a 3-D Clustered Column chart that compares the total sales for each region within each type of product.

Approvals

Approval Status:	X	Approved
		Rejected
Approved By:	Stan Maderbek	
Date:	April 22, 2008	
Assigned To:	J. Quasney, Spreadsheet Specialist	

Figure 1–2

BTW

Worksheet Development Cycle
Spreadsheet specialists do not sit down and start entering text, formulas, and data into a blank Excel worksheet as soon as they have a spreadsheet assignment. Instead, they follow an organized plan, or methodology, that breaks the development cycle into a series of tasks. The recommended methodology for creating worksheets includes: (1) analyze requirements (supplied in a requirements document); (2) design solution; (3) validate design; (4) implement design; (5) test solution; and (6) document solution.

Overview

As you read this chapter, you will learn how to create the worksheet shown in Figure 1–1 by performing these general tasks:

• Enter text in the worksheet
• Add totals to the worksheet
• Save the workbook that contains the worksheet
• Format the text in the worksheet
• Insert a chart in the worksheet
• Save the workbook a second time using the same file name
• Print the worksheet

Plan Ahead

General Project Guidelines
While creating an Excel worksheet, you need to make several decisions that will determine the appearance and characteristics of the finished worksheet. As you create the worksheet shown in Figure 1–1, you should follow these general guidelines:

1. **Select titles and subtitles for the worksheet.** Follow the *less is more* guideline. The less text in the titles and subtitles, the more impact the titles and subtitles will have. Use the fewest words possible to specify the information presented in the worksheet to the intended audience.

(continued)

sketch of worksheet →

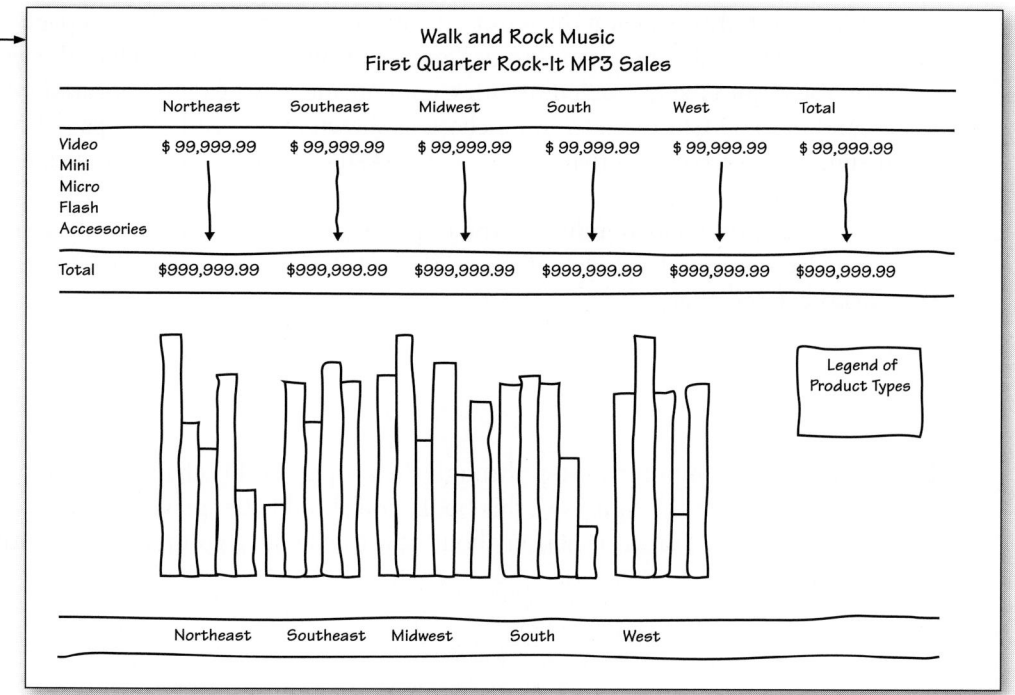

Figure 1–3

Plan Ahead

(continued)

2. **Determine the contents for rows and columns.** Rows typically contain information that is analogous to items in a list, such as the products sold by a company. Columns typically contain descriptive information about items in rows or contain information that helps to group the data in the worksheet, such as company regions.

3. **Determine the calculations that are needed.** You can decide to total data in a variety of ways, such as across rows or in columns. You also can include a grand total.

4. **Determine where to save the workbook.** You can store a workbook permanently, or **save** it, on a variety of storage media including a hard disk, USB flash drive, or CD. You also can indicate a specific location on the storage media for saving the workbook.

5. **Identify how to format various elements of the worksheet.** The overall appearance of a worksheet significantly affects its ability to communicate clearly. Examples of how you can modify the appearance, or **format**, of text include changing its shape, size, color, and position on the worksheet.

6. **Decide on the type of chart needed.** Excel includes the capability of creating many different types of charts, such as bar charts and pie charts. Each chart type relays a different message about the data in the worksheet. Choose a chart type that relays the message that you want to convey.

7. **Establish where to position and how to format the chart.** The position and format of the chart should command the attention of the intended audience. If possible, position the chart so that it prints with the worksheet data on a single page.

When necessary, more specific details concerning the above guidelines are presented at appropriate points in the chapter. The chapter also will identify the actions performed and decisions made regarding these guidelines during the creation of the worksheet shown in Figure 1–1 on page EX 3.

After carefully reviewing the requirements document (Figure 1–2 on page EX 4) and necessary decisions, the next step is to design a solution or draw a sketch of the worksheet based on the requirements, including titles, column and row headings, location of data values, and the 3-D Clustered Column chart, as shown in Figure 1–3 on page EX 5. The dollar signs, 9s, and commas that you see in the sketch of the worksheet indicate formatted numeric values.

With a good understanding of the requirements document, an understanding of the necessary decisions, and a sketch of the worksheet, the next step is to use Excel to create the worksheet and chart.

Starting Excel

If you are using a computer to step through the project in this chapter and you want your screen to match the figures in this book, you should change your computer's resolution to 1024 × 768. For information about how to change a computer's resolution, read Appendix E.

To Start Excel

The following steps, which assume Windows Vista is running, start Excel based on a typical installation of Microsoft Office on your computer. You may need to ask your instructor how to start Excel for your computer.

Note: If you are using Windows XP, see Appendix F for alternate steps.

1

- Click the Start button on the Windows Vista taskbar to display the Start menu.

- Click All Programs at the bottom of left pane on the the Start menu to display the All Programs list.

- Click Microsoft Office in the All Programs list to display the Microsoft Office list (Figure 1–4).

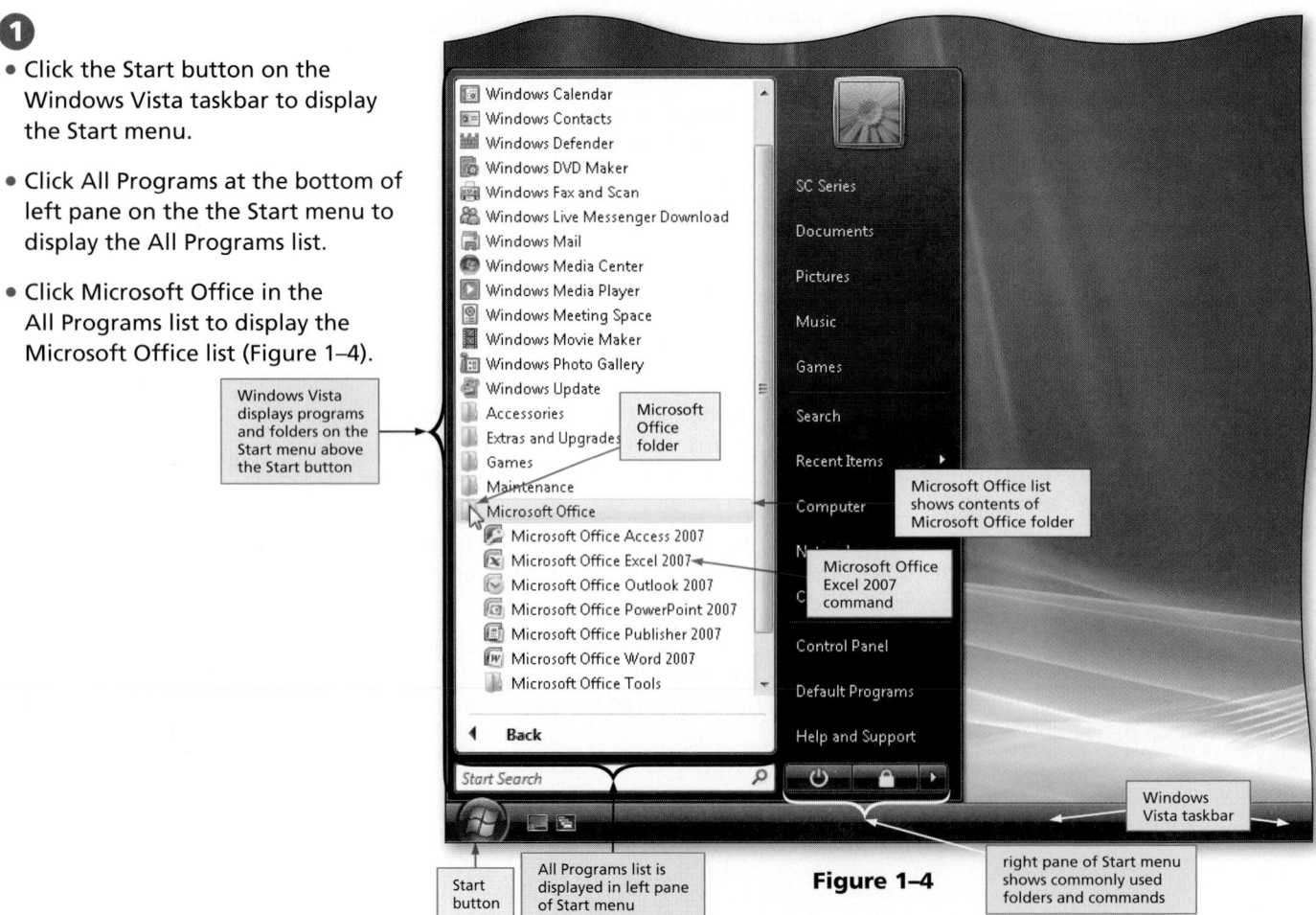

Figure 1–4

❷

- Click Microsoft Office Excel 2007 to start Excel and display a new blank workbook titled Book1 in the Excel window (Figure 1–5).

- If the Excel window is not maximized, click the Maximize button next to the Close button on its title bar to maximize the window.

- If the worksheet window in Excel is not maximized, click the Maximize button next to the Close button on its title bar to maximize the worksheet window within Excel.

Q&A

What is a maximized window?

A maximized window fills the entire screen. When you maximize a window, the Maximize button changes to a Restore Down button. When you restore a maximized window, the window returns to its previous size and the Restore Down button changes to a Maximize button.

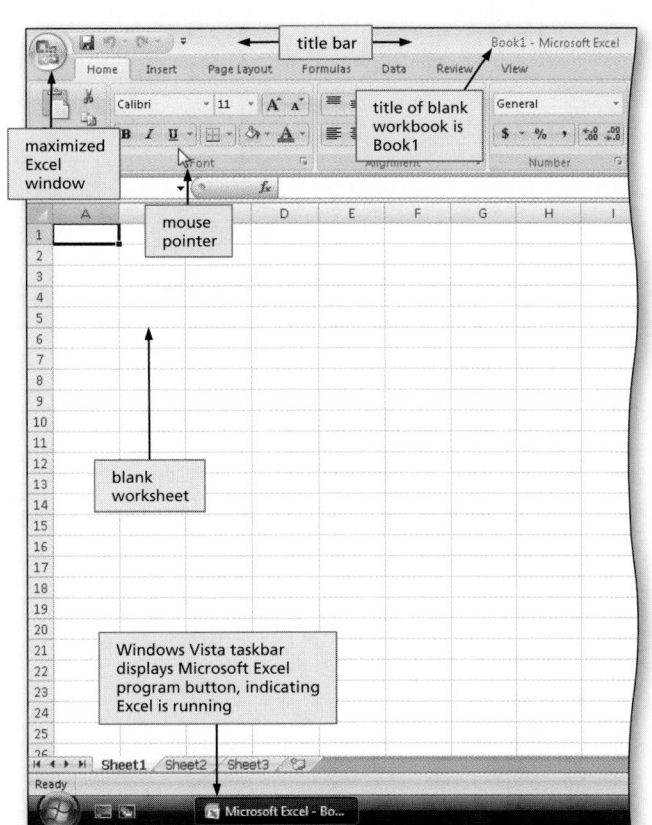
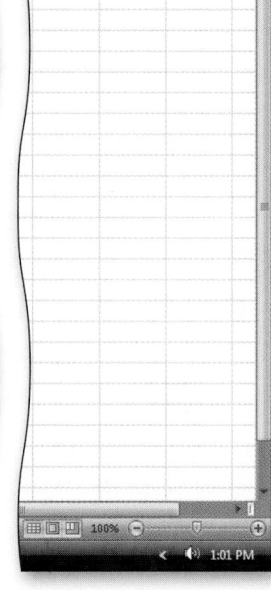

Figure 1–5

Other Ways

1. Double-click Excel 2007 icon on desktop, if one is present

2. Click Microsoft Office Excel 2007 on Start menu

The Excel Workbook

The Excel window consists of a variety of components to make your work more efficient and worksheets more professional. These include the document window, Ribbon, Mini toolbar and shortcut menus, Quick Access Toolbar, and Office Button. Some of these components are common to other Microsoft Office 2007 programs; others are unique to Excel.

When Excel starts, it creates a new blank workbook, called Book1. The **workbook** (Figure 1–6) is like a notebook. Inside the workbook are sheets, each of which is called a **worksheet**. Excel opens a new workbook with three worksheets.

If necessary, you can add additional worksheets as long as your computer has enough memory to accommodate them. Each worksheet has a sheet name that appears on a **sheet tab** at the bottom of the workbook. For example, Sheet1 is the name of the active worksheet displayed in the Book1 workbook. If you click the sheet tab labeled Sheet2, Excel displays the Sheet2 worksheet. The project in this chapter uses only the Sheet1 worksheet.

The Worksheet

The worksheet is organized into a rectangular grid containing vertical columns and horizontal rows. A column letter above the grid, also called the **column heading**, identifies each column. A row number on the left side of the grid, also called the **row heading**, identifies

BTW

Excel Help
Help with Excel is no further away than the Help button on the right side of the Ribbon. Click the Help button, type help in the 'Type words to search for' box, and then press the ENTER key. Excel responds with a list of topics you can click to learn about obtaining Help on any Excel-related topic. To find out what is new in Excel 2007, type what is new in Excel in the 'Type words to search for' box.

each row. With the screen resolution set to 1024 × 768 and the Excel window maximized, Excel displays 15 columns (A through O) and 25 rows (1 through 25) of the worksheet on the screen, as shown in Figure 1–6.

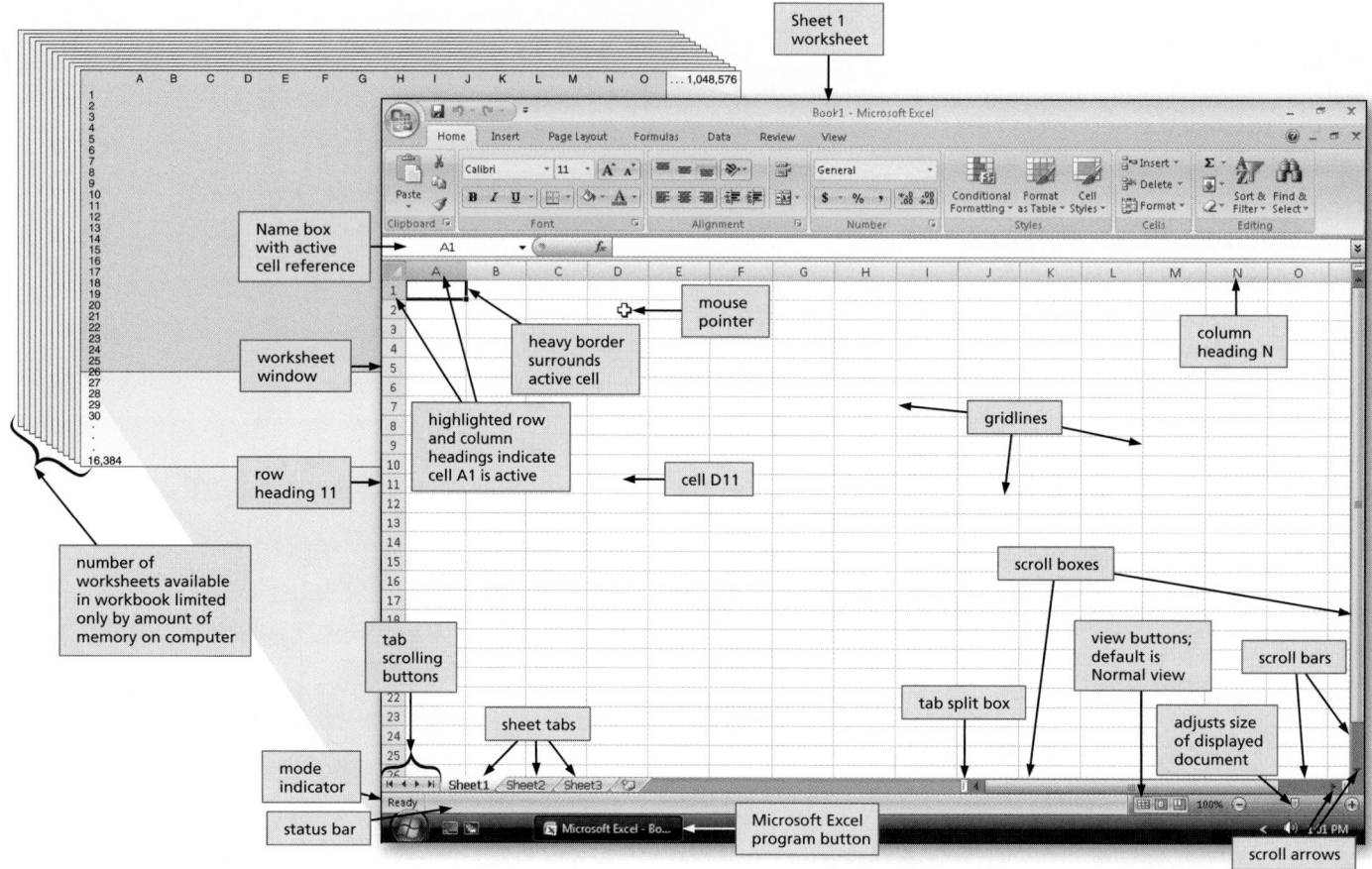

Figure 1–6

BTW

Worksheet Development
The key to developing a useful worksheet is careful planning. Careful planning can reduce your effort significantly and result in a worksheet that is accurate, easy to read, flexible, and useful. When analyzing a problem and designing a worksheet solution, you should follow these steps: (1) define the problem, including need, source of data, calculations, charting, and Web or special requirements; (2) design the worksheet; (3) enter the data and formulas; and (4) test the worksheet.

The intersection of each column and row is a cell. A **cell** is the basic unit of a worksheet into which you enter data. Each worksheet in a workbook has 16,384 columns and 1,048,576 rows for a total of 17,179,869,180 cells. Only a small fraction of the active worksheet appears on the screen at one time.

A cell is referred to by its unique address, or **cell reference**, which is the coordinates of the intersection of a column and a row. To identify a cell, specify the column letter first, followed by the row number. For example, cell reference D11 refers to the cell located at the intersection of column D and row 11 (Figure 1–6).

One cell on the worksheet, designated the **active cell**, is the one into which you can enter data. The active cell in Figure 1–6 is A1. The active cell is identified in three ways. First, a heavy border surrounds the cell; second, the active cell reference shows immediately above column A in the Name box; and third, the column heading A and row heading 1 are highlighted so it is easy to see which cell is active (Figure 1–6).

The horizontal and vertical lines on the worksheet itself are called **gridlines**. Gridlines make it easier to see and identify each cell in the worksheet. If desired, you can turn the gridlines off so they do not show on the worksheet, but it is recommended that you leave them on for now.

The mouse pointer in Figure 1–6 has the shape of a block plus sign. The mouse pointer appears as a block plus sign whenever it is located in a cell on the worksheet. Another common shape of the mouse pointer is the block arrow. The mouse pointer turns into the block arrow whenever you move it outside the worksheet or when you drag cell contents between rows or columns. The other mouse pointer shapes are described when they appear on the screen.

Worksheet Window

You view the portion of the worksheet displayed on the screen through a **worksheet window** (Figure 1–6). The default (preset) view is **normal view**. Below and to the right of the worksheet window are **scroll bars**, **scroll arrows**, and **scroll boxes** that you can use to move the worksheet window around to view different parts of the active worksheet. To the right of the sheet tabs at the bottom of the screen is the tab split box. You can drag the **tab split box** to increase or decrease the view of the sheet tabs (Figure 1–6). When you decrease the view of the sheet tabs, you increase the length of the horizontal scroll bar, and vice versa.

Status Bar

The status bar is located immediately above the Windows Vista taskbar at the bottom of the screen (Figure 1–6). The **status bar** presents information about the worksheet, the function of the button the mouse pointer is pointing to, or the mode of Excel. **Mode indicators**, such as Enter and Ready, appear on the status bar and specify the current mode of Excel. When the mode is **Ready**, Excel is ready to accept the next command or data entry. When the mode indicator reads **Enter**, Excel is in the process of accepting data through the keyboard into the active cell.

Keyboard indicators, such as Scroll Lock, show which toggle keys are engaged. Keyboard indicators appear to the right of the mode indicator. Toward the right edge of the status bar are buttons and controls you can use to change the view of a document and adjust the size of the displayed document.

Ribbon

The **Ribbon**, located near the top of the Excel window, is the control center in Excel (Figure 1–7a). The Ribbon provides easy, central access to the tasks you perform while creating a worksheet. The Ribbon consists of tabs, groups, and commands. Each **tab** surrounds a collection of groups, and each **group** contains related commands.

BTW

The Worksheet Size and Window
Excel's 16,384 columns and 1,048,576 rows make for a huge worksheet that – if you could imagine – takes up the entire side of a building to display in its entirety. Your computer screen, by comparison, is a small window that allows you to view only a minute area of the worksheet at one time. While you cannot see the entire worksheet, you can move the window over the worksheet to view any part of it.

BTW

Increasing the Viewing Area
You can increase the size of the Excel window or viewing area to show more of the worksheet. Two ways exist to increase what you can see in the viewing area: (1) on the View tab on the Ribbon, click Full Screen; and (2) change to a higher resolution. See Appendix E for information about how to change to a higher resolution.

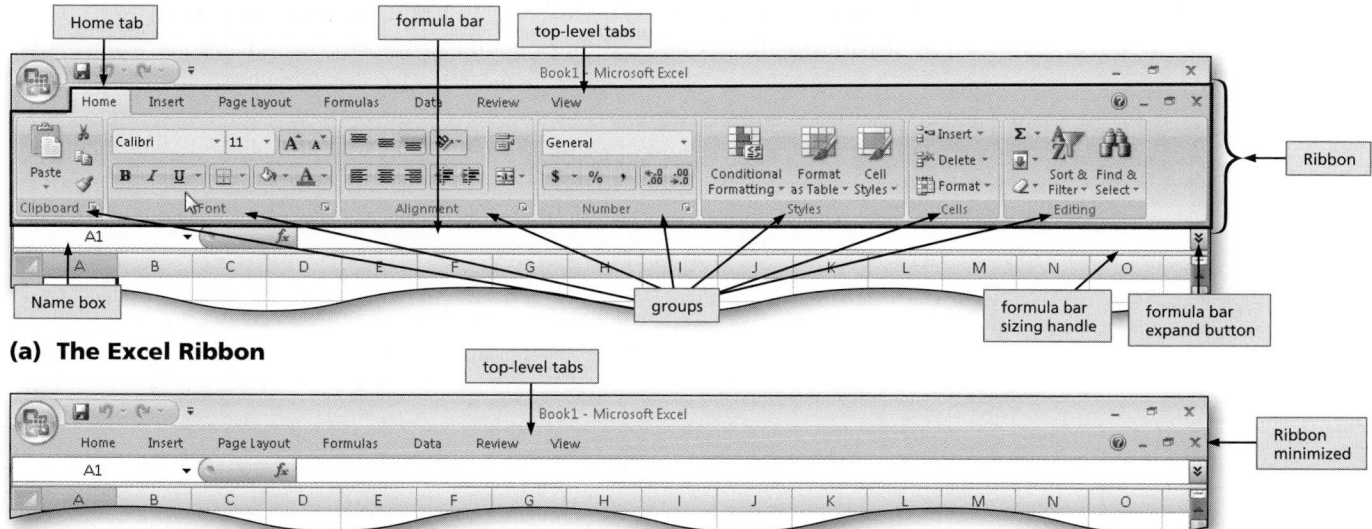

(a) The Excel Ribbon

(b) The Excel Ribbon Minimized

Figure 1–7

Minimizing the Ribbon
If you want to minimize the Ribbon, right-click the Ribbon and then click Minimize the Ribbon on the shortcut menu, double-click the active tab, or press CTRL+F1. To restore a minimized Ribbon, right-click the Ribbon and then click Minimize the Ribbon on the shortcut menu, double-click any top-level tab, or press CTRL+F1. To use commands on a minimized Ribbon, click the top-level tab.

When you start Excel, the Ribbon displays seven top-level tabs: Home, Insert, Page Layout, Formulas, Data, Review, and View. The **Home tab**, called the primary tab, contains groups with the more frequently used commands. To display a different tab on the Ribbon, click the top-level tab. That is, to display the Insert tab, click Insert on the Ribbon. To return to the Home tab, click Home on the Ribbon. The tab currently displayed is called the **active tab**.

To display more of the document in the document window, some users prefer to minimize the Ribbon, which hides the groups on the Ribbon and displays only the top-level tabs (Figure 1–7b). To use commands on a minimized Ribbon, click the top-level tab.

Each time you start Excel, the Ribbon appears the same way it did the last time you used Excel. The chapters in this book, however, begin with the Ribbon appearing as it did at the initial installation of the software. If you are stepping through this chapter on a computer and you want your Ribbon to match the figures in this book, read Appendix E.

In addition to the top-level tabs, Excel displays other tabs, called **contextual tabs**, when you perform certain tasks or work with objects such as charts or tables. If you insert a chart in the worksheet, for example, the Chart Tools tab and its related subordinate Design tab appear (Figure 1–8). When you are finished working with the chart, the Chart Tools and Design tabs disappear from the Ribbon. Excel determines when contextual tabs should appear and disappear, based on the tasks you perform.

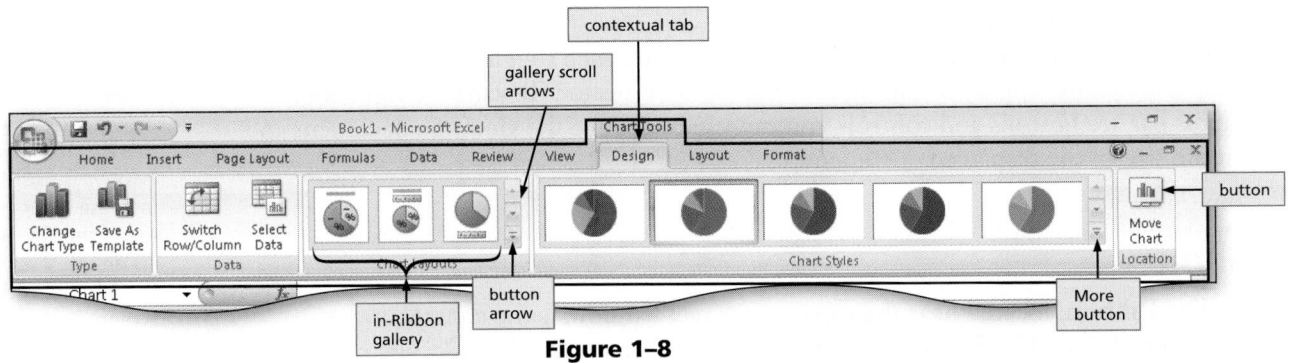

Figure 1–8

Ribbon commands include buttons, boxes (text boxes, check boxes, etc.), and galleries (Figure 1–8). A **gallery** is a set of choices, often graphical, arranged in a grid or in a list. You can scroll through choices on an in-Ribbon gallery by clicking the gallery's scroll arrows. An **in-Ribbon** gallery shows common gallery choices on the Ribbon rather than in a dropdown list. Or, you can click a gallery's More button to view more gallery options on the screen at a time. Some buttons and boxes have arrows that, when clicked, also display a gallery; others always cause a gallery to be displayed when clicked. Most galleries support **live preview**, which is a feature that allows you to point to a gallery choice and see its effect in the worksheet without actually selecting the choice (Figure 1–9).

Some commands on the Ribbon display an image to help you remember their function. When you point to a command on the Ribbon, all or part of the command glows in shades of yellow and orange, and an Enhanced ScreenTip appears on the screen. An **Enhanced ScreenTip** is an on-screen note that provides the name of the command, available keyboard shortcut(s), a description of the command, and sometimes instructions for how to obtain Help about the command (Figure 1–10). Enhanced ScreenTips are more detailed than a typical **ScreenTip**, which usually displays only the name of the command.

The lower-right corner of some groups on the Ribbon has a small arrow, called a **Dialog Box Launcher**, that when clicked displays a dialog box or a task pane (Figure 1–11). A **dialog box** contains additional commands and options for the group. When presented with a dialog box, you make selections and must close the dialog box before returning to the worksheet. A **task pane**, by contrast, is a window that contains additional commands and can stay open and visible while you work on the worksheet.

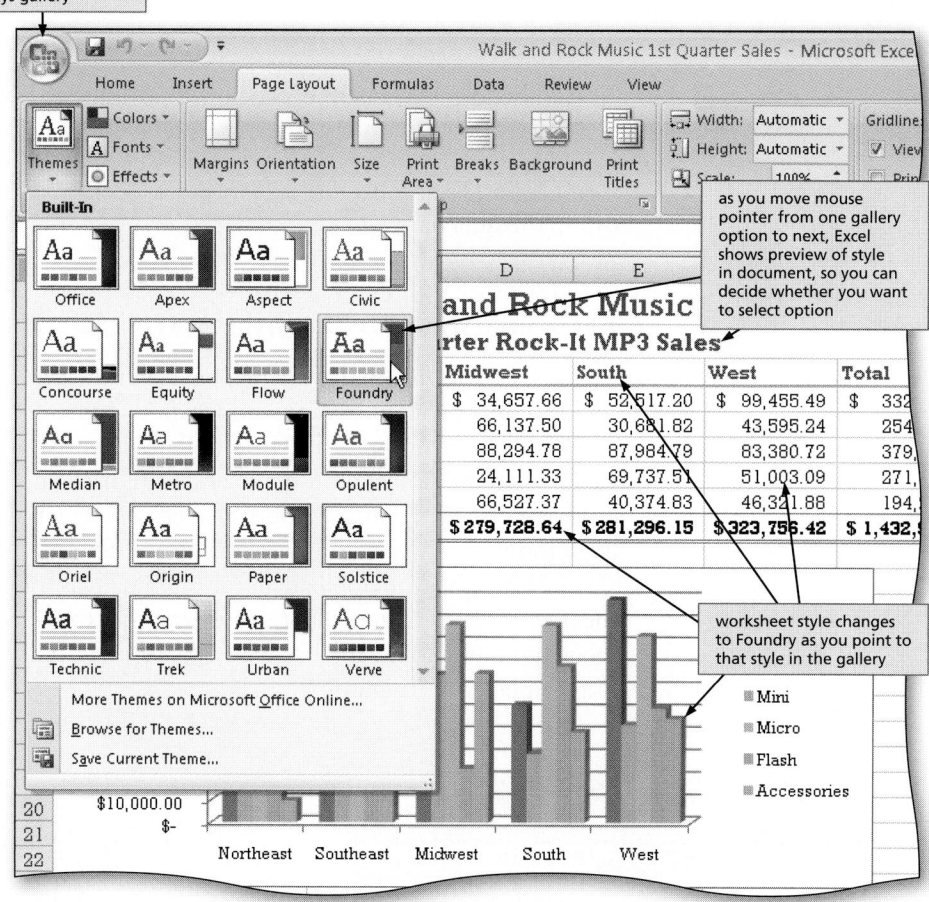

clicking Themes button displays gallery

as you move mouse pointer from one gallery option to next, Excel shows preview of style in document, so you can decide whether you want to select option

worksheet style changes to Foundry as you point to that style in the gallery

Figure 1–9

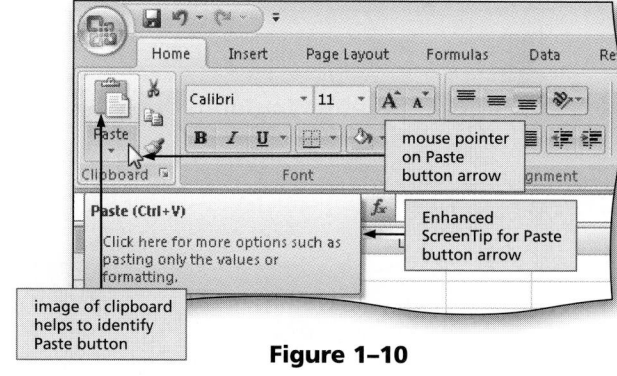

mouse pointer on Paste button arrow

Enhanced ScreenTip for Paste button arrow

image of clipboard helps to identify Paste button

Figure 1–10

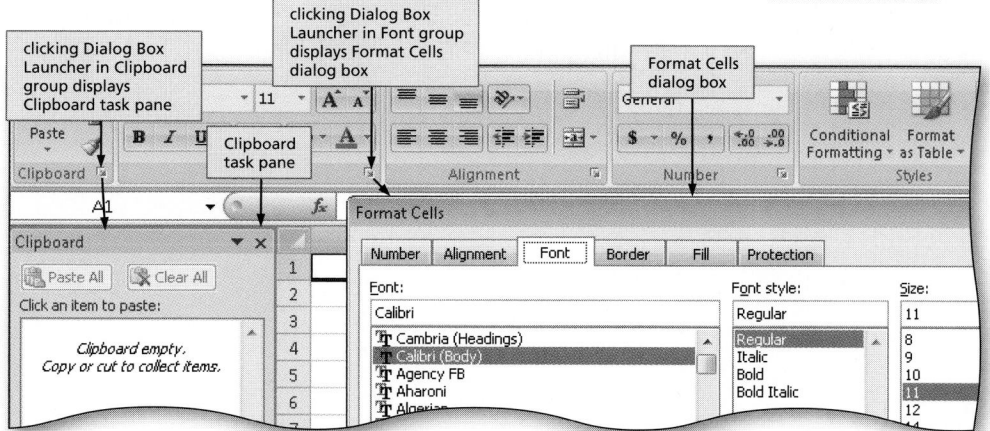

clicking Dialog Box Launcher in Clipboard group displays Clipboard task pane

clicking Dialog Box Launcher in Font group displays Format Cells dialog box

Format Cells dialog box

Clipboard task pane

Figure 1–11

Formula Bar

The formula bar appears below the Ribbon (Figure 1–12a). As you type, Excel displays the entry in the **formula bar**. You can make the formula bar larger by dragging the sizing handle (Figure 1–7) on the formula bar or clicking the expand button to the right of the formula bar. Excel also displays the active cell reference in the **Name box** on the left side of the formula bar.

Mini Toolbar and Shortcut Menus

The **Mini toolbar**, which appears automatically based on tasks you perform (such as selecting text), contains commands related to changing the appearance of text in a worksheet. All commands on the Mini toolbar also exist on the Ribbon. The purpose of the Mini toolbar is to minimize mouse movement. For example, if you want to format text using a command that currently is not displayed on the active tab, you can use the command on the Mini toolbar — instead of switching to a different tab to use the command.

When the Mini toolbar appears, it initially is transparent (Figure 1–12a). If you do not use the transparent Mini toolbar, it disappears from the screen. To use the Mini toolbar, move the mouse pointer into the toolbar, which causes the Mini toolbar to change from a transparent to bright appearance (Figure 1–12b).

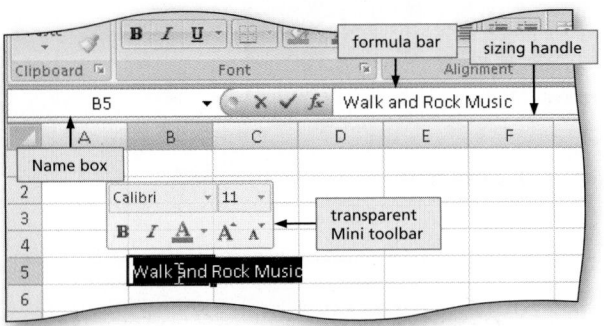

(a) Transparent Mini Toolbar

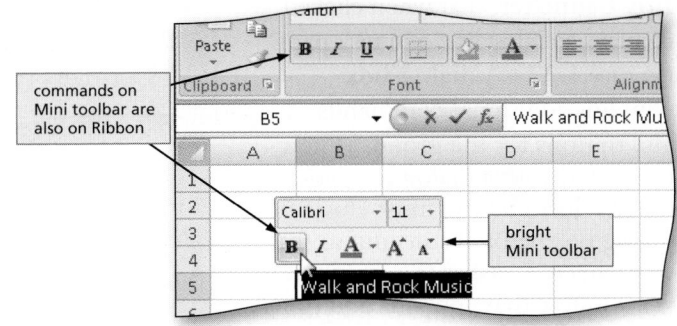

(b) Bright Mini Toolbar

Figure 1–12

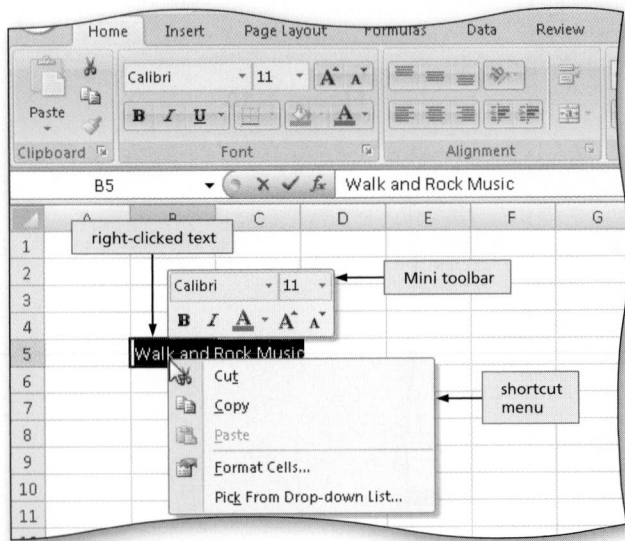

Figure 1–13

A **shortcut menu**, which appears when you right-click an object, is a list of frequently used commands that relate to the right-clicked object. If you right-click an item in the document window such as a cell, Excel displays both the Mini toolbar and a shortcut menu (Figure 1–13).

Quick Access Toolbar

The **Quick Access Toolbar**, located by default above the Ribbon, provides easy access to frequently used commands (Figure 1–14a). The commands on the Quick Access Toolbar always are available, regardless of the task you are performing. Initially, the Quick Access Toolbar contains the Save, Undo, and Redo buttons. If you click the Customize Quick Access Toolbar button, Excel provides a list of commands you quickly can add to and remove from the Quick Access Toolbar (Figure 1–14b).

You also can add other commands to or delete commands from the Quick Access Toolbar so that it contains the commands you use most often. As you add commands to the Quick Access Toolbar, its commands may interfere with the workbook title on the title bar. For this reason, Excel provides an option of displaying the Quick Access Toolbar below the Ribbon (Figure 1–14c).

BTW

Quick Access Toolbar Commands
To add a Ribbon command as a button to the Quick Access Toolbar, right-click the command on the Ribbon and then click Add to Quick Access Toolbar on the shortcut menu. To delete a button from the Quick Access Toolbar, right-click the button on the Quick Access Toolbar and then click Remove from Quick Access Toolbar on the shortcut menu. To display the Quick Access Toolbar below the Ribbon, right-click the Quick Access Toolbar and then click Show Quick Access Toolbar Below the Ribbon on the shortcut menu.

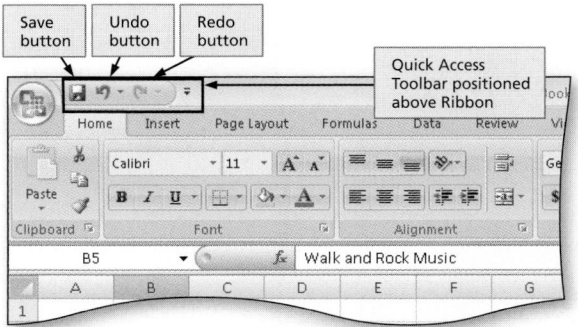

(a) Quick Access Toolbar above Ribbon

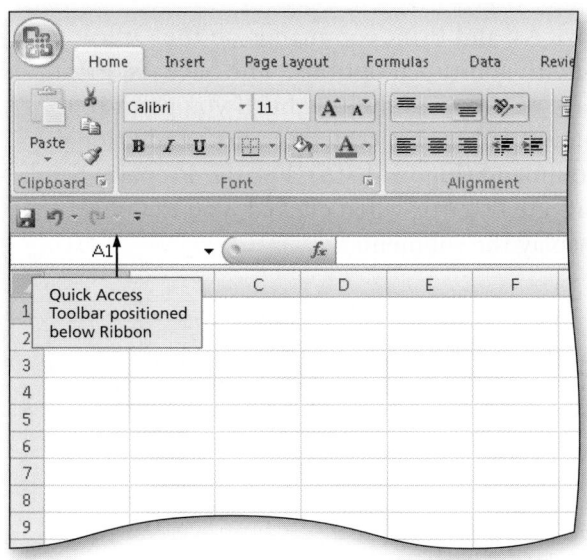

(c) Quick Access Toolbar below Ribbon

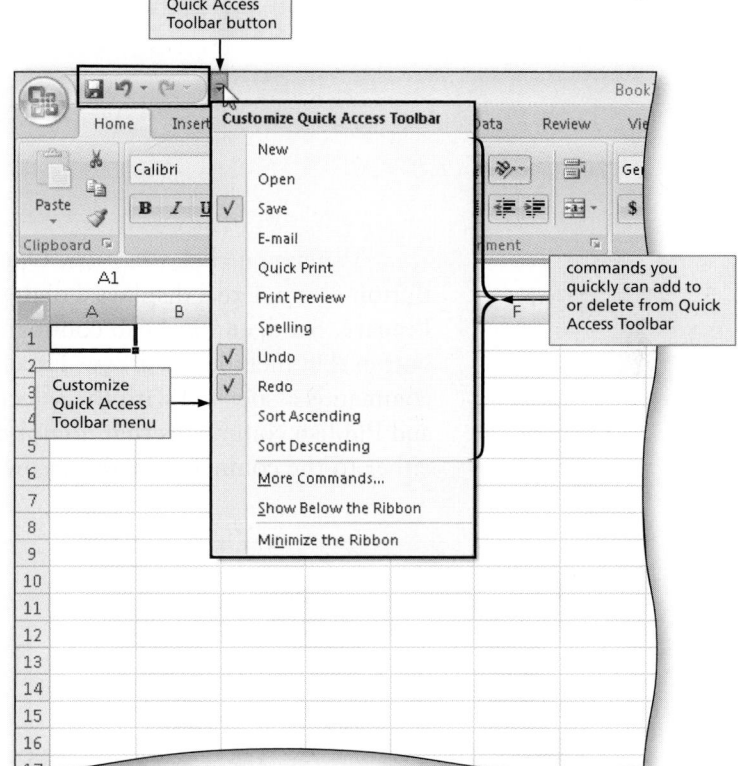

(b) Customize Quick Access Toolbar Menu

Figure 1–14

Each time you start Excel, the Quick Access Toolbar appears the same way it did the last time you used Excel. The chapters in this book, however, begin with the Quick Access Toolbar appearing as it did at the initial installation of the software. If you are stepping through this chapter on a computer and you want your Quick Access Toolbar to match the figures in this book, you should reset your Quick Access Toolbar. For more information about how to reset the Quick Access Toolbar, read Appendix E.

Office Button

While the Ribbon is a control center for creating worksheets, the **Office Button** is a central location for managing and sharing workbooks. When you click the Office Button, located in the upper-left corner of the window, Excel displays the Office Button menu (Figure 1–15). A **menu** contains a list of commands.

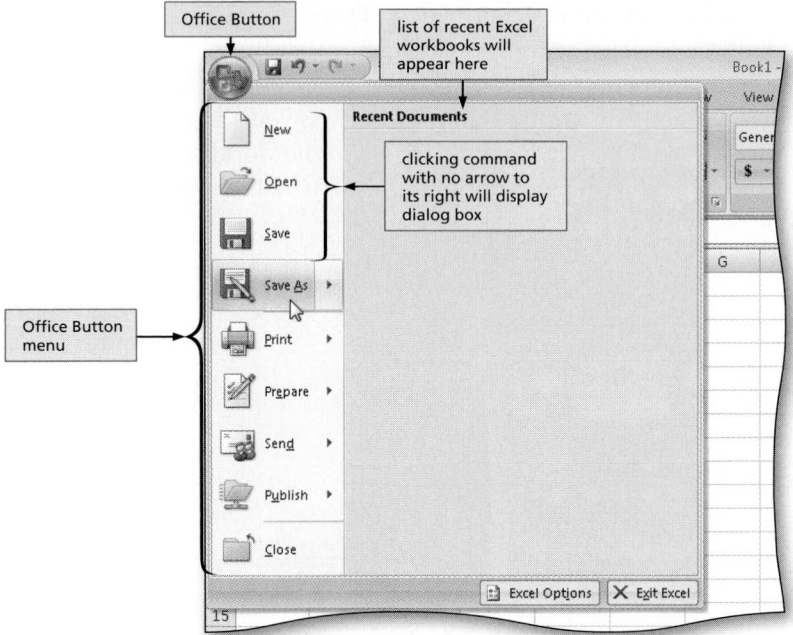

Figure 1–15

When you click the New, Open, Save As, and Print commands on the Office Button menu, Excel displays a dialog box with additional options. The Save As, Print, Prepare, Send, and Publish commands have an arrow to their right. If you point to a button that includes an arrow, Excel displays a **submenu**, which is a list of additional commands associated with the selected command (Figure 1–16). For the Prepare, Send, and Publish commands that do not display a dialog box when clicked, you can point either to the command or the arrow to display the submenu.

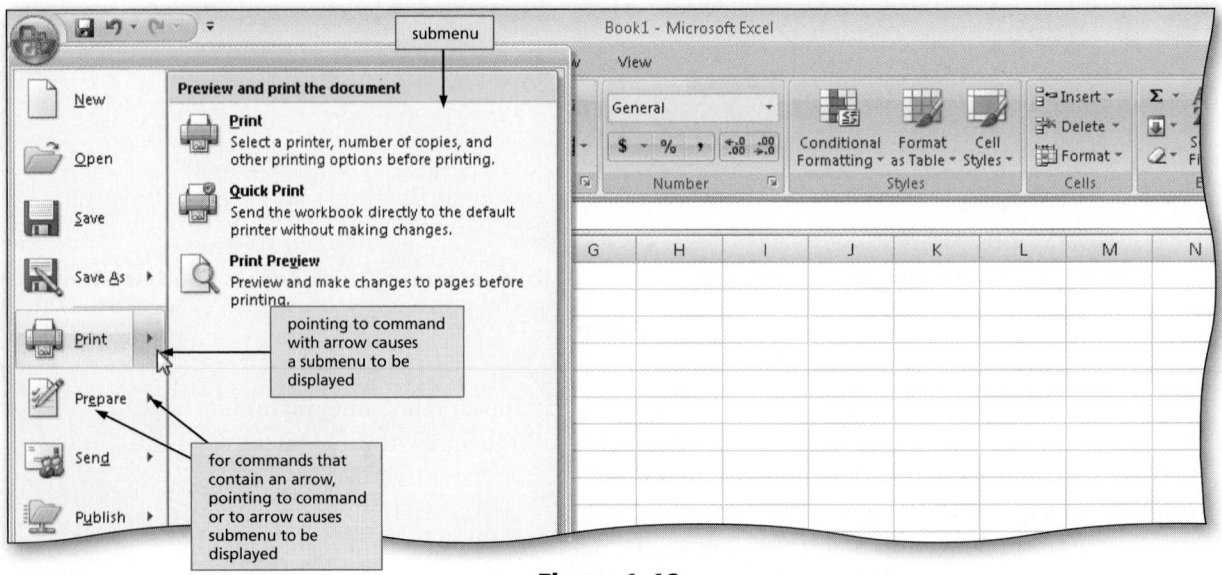

Figure 1–16

Key Tips

If you prefer using the keyboard, instead of the mouse, you can press the ALT key on the keyboard to display a **Key Tip badge**, or keyboard code icon, for certain commands (Figure 1–17). To select a command using the keyboard, press its displayed code letter, or **Key Tip**. When you press a Key Tip, additional Key Tips related to the selected command appear. For example, to select the New command on the Office Button menu, press the ALT key, then press the F key, then press the N key.

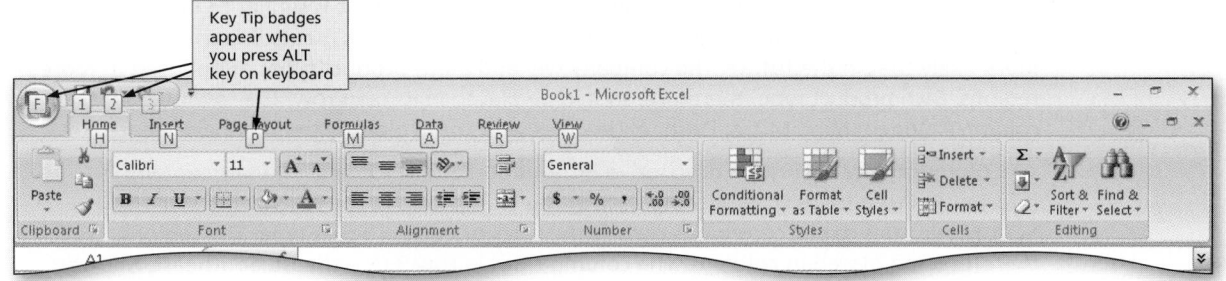

Figure 1–17

To remove the Key Tip badges from the screen, press the ALT key or the ESC key on the keyboard until all Key Tip badges disappear or click the mouse anywhere in the Excel window.

Selecting a Cell

To enter data into a cell, you first must select it. The easiest way **to select a cell** (make it active) is to use the mouse to move the block plus sign mouse pointer to the cell and then click.

An alternative method is to use the arrow keys that are located just to the right of the typewriter keys on the keyboard. An arrow key selects the cell adjacent to the active cell in the direction of the arrow on the key.

You know a cell is selected, or active, when a heavy border surrounds the cell and the active cell reference appears in the Name box on the left side of the formula bar. Excel also changes the active cell's column heading and row heading to a gold color.

Entering Text

In Excel, any set of characters containing a letter, hyphen (as in a telephone number), or space is considered text. **Text** is used to place titles, such as worksheet titles, column titles, and row titles, on the worksheet.

Plan Ahead	**Select titles and subtitles for the worksheet.**
	As previously stated, worksheet titles and subtitles should be as brief and meaningful as possible. As shown in Figure 1–18, the worksheet title, Walk and Rock Music, identifies the company for whom the worksheet is being created in Chapter 1. The worksheet subtitle, First Quarter Rock-It MP3 Sales, identifies the type of report.

Plan Ahead	**Determine the contents of rows and columns.**
	As previously mentioned, rows typically contain information that is similar to items in a list. For the Walk and Rock Music sales data, the list of product types meets this criterion. It is more likely that in the future, the company will add more product types as opposed to more regions. Each product type, therefore, should be placed in its own row. The row titles in column A (Video, Mini, Micro, Flash, Accessories, and Total) identify the numbers in each row.
	Columns typically contain descriptive information about items in rows or contain information that helps to group the data in the worksheet. In the case of the Walk and Rock Music sales data, the regions classify the sales of each product type. The regions, therefore, are placed in columns. The column titles in row 3 (Northeast, Southeast, Midwest, South, West, and Total) identify the numbers in each column.

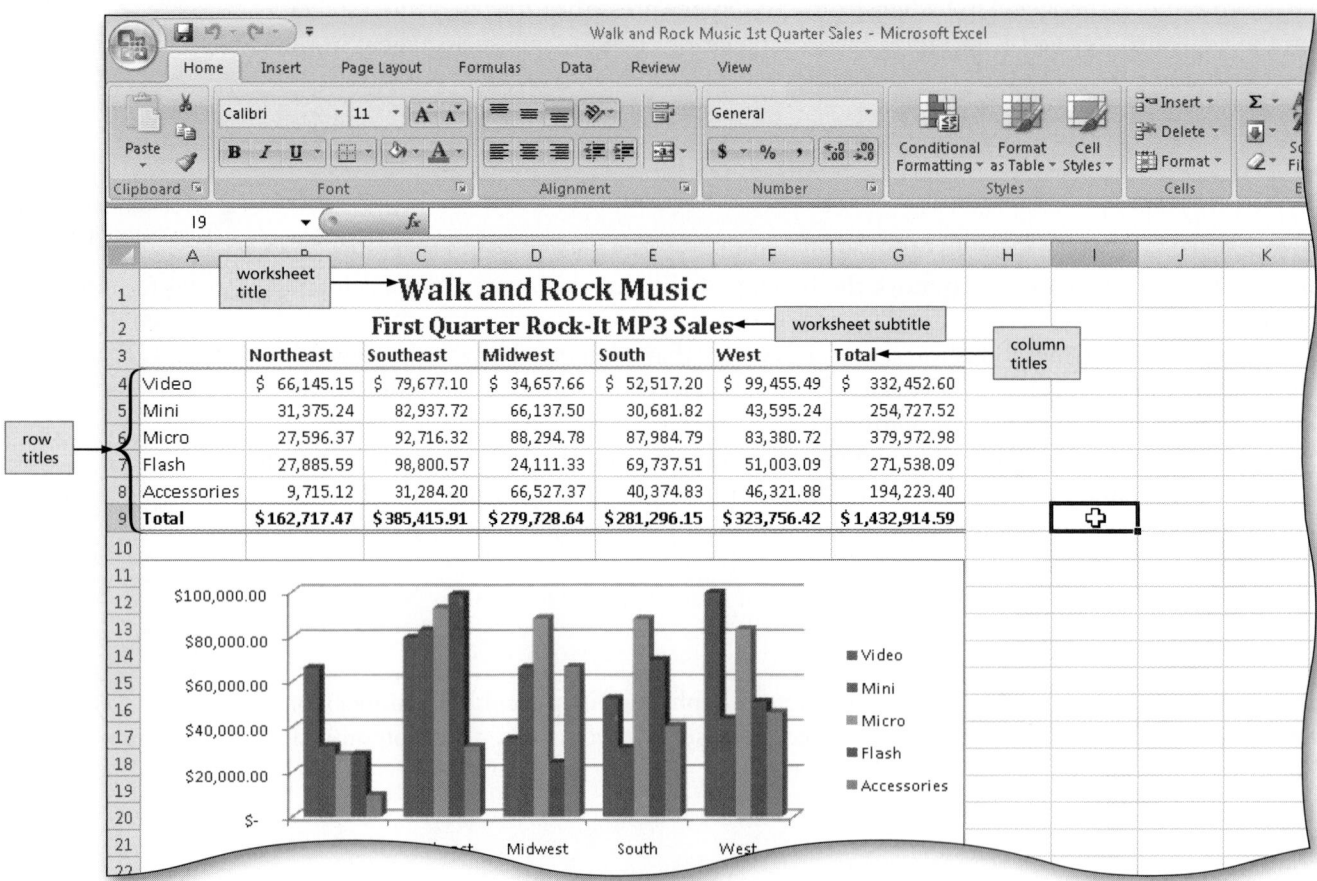

Figure 1–18

To Enter the Worksheet Titles

The following steps show how to enter the worksheet titles in cells A1 and A2. Later in this chapter, the worksheet titles will be formatted so they appear as shown in Figure 1–18.

 1

- Click cell A1 to make cell A1 the active cell (Figure 1–19).

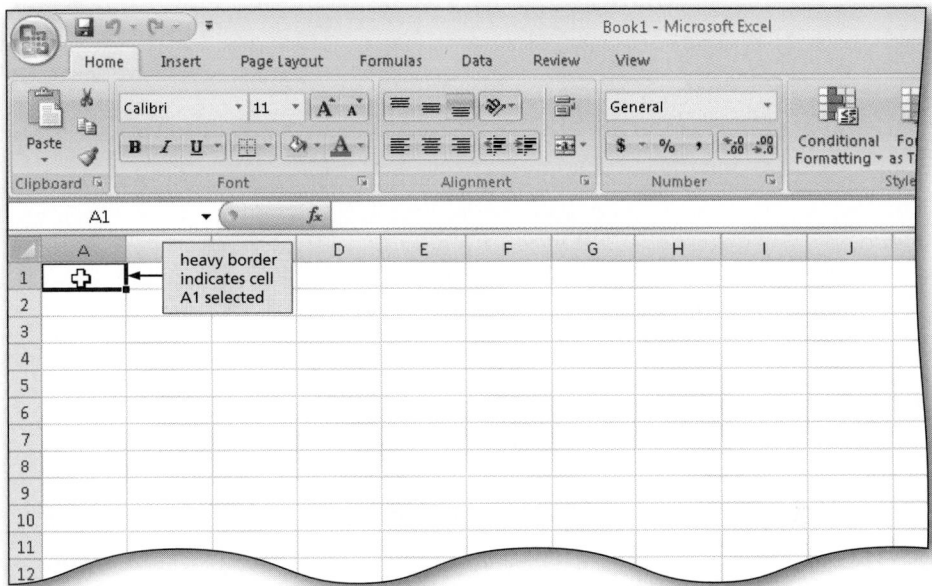

Figure 1–19

 2

- Type Walk and Rock Music in cell A1, and then point to the Enter box in the formula bar.

Q&A Why did the appearance of the formula bar change?

Excel displays the title in the formula bar and in cell A1. When you begin typing a cell entry, Excel displays two additional boxes in the formula bar: the Cancel box and the Enter box. Clicking the **Enter box** completes an entry. Clicking the **Cancel box** cancels an entry.

Q&A What is the vertical line in cell A1?

In Figure 1–20, the text in cell A1 is followed by the insertion point. The **insertion point** is a blinking vertical line that indicates where the next typed character will appear.

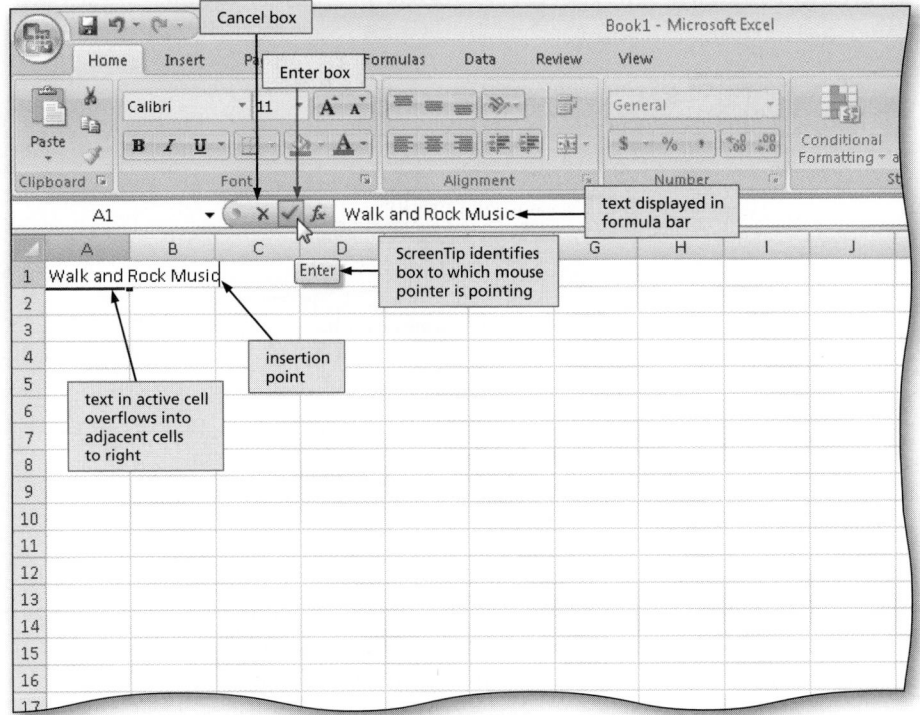

Figure 1–20

● Click the Enter box to complete the entry and enter the worksheet title in cell A1 (Figure 1–21).

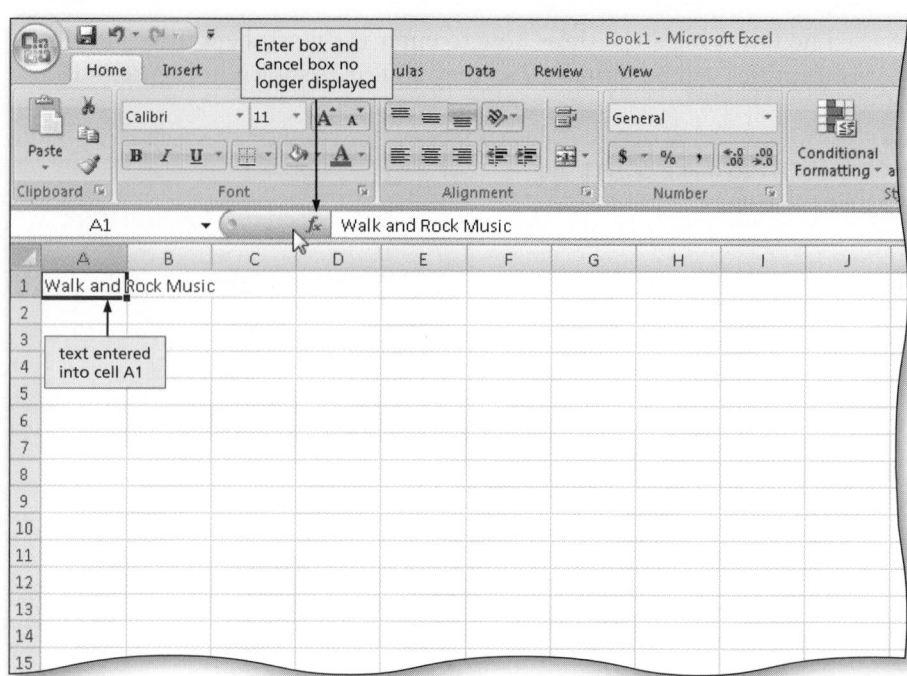

Figure 1–21

● Click cell A2 to select it.

● Type `First Quarter Rock-It MP3 Sales` as the cell entry.

● Click the Enter box to complete the entry and enter the worksheet subtitle in cell A2 (Figure 1–22).

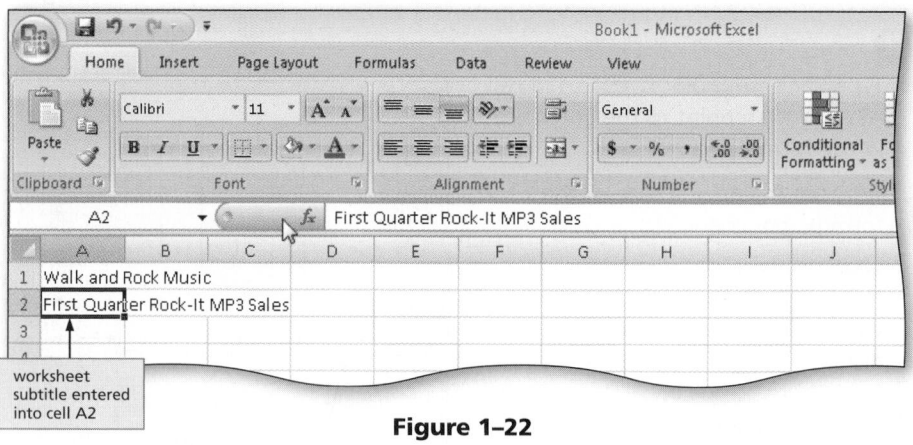

Figure 1–22

Other Ways

1. To complete entry, click any cell other than active cell
2. To complete entry, press ENTER key
3. To complete entry, press HOME, PAGE UP, PAGE DOWN, or END key
4. To complete entry, press UP, DOWN, LEFT, or RIGHT key.

Entering Text in a Cell

When you complete a text entry into a cell, a series of events occurs. First, Excel positions the text left-aligned in the cell. **Left-aligned** means the cell entry is positioned at the far left in the cell. Therefore, the W in the worksheet title, Walk and Rock Music, begins in the leftmost position of cell A1.

Second, when the text is longer than the width of a column, Excel displays the overflow characters in adjacent cells to the right as long as these adjacent cells contain no data. In Figure 1–22, the width of cell A1 is approximately nine characters. The text consists of 19 characters. Therefore, Excel displays the overflow characters from cell A1 in cells B1 and C1, because cells B1 and C1 are empty. If cell B1 contained data, Excel would hide the overflow characters, so that only the first nine characters in cell A1 would appear on the worksheet. Excel stores the overflow characters in cell A1 and displays them in the formula bar whenever cell A1 is the active cell.

Third, when you complete an entry by clicking the Enter box, the cell in which the text is entered remains the active cell.

Correcting a Mistake while Typing

If you type the wrong letter and notice the error before clicking the Enter box or pressing the ENTER key, use the BACKSPACE key to delete all the characters back to and including the incorrect letter. To cancel the entire entry before entering it into the cell, click the Cancel box in the formula bar or press the ESC key. If you see an error in a cell after entering the text, select the cell and retype the entry. Later in this chapter, additional error-correction techniques are discussed.

AutoCorrect

The **AutoCorrect feature** of Excel works behind the scenes, correcting common mistakes when you complete a text entry in a cell. AutoCorrect makes three types of corrections for you:

1. Corrects two initial capital letters by changing the second letter to lowercase.
2. Capitalizes the first letter in the names of days.
3. Replaces commonly misspelled words with their correct spelling. For example, it will change the misspelled word *recieve* to *receive* when you complete the entry. AutoCorrect will correct the spelling of hundreds of commonly misspelled words automatically.

To Enter Column Titles

To enter the column titles in row 3, select the appropriate cell and then enter the text. The following steps enter the column titles in row 3.

- Click cell B3 to make cell B3 the active cell (Figure 1–23).

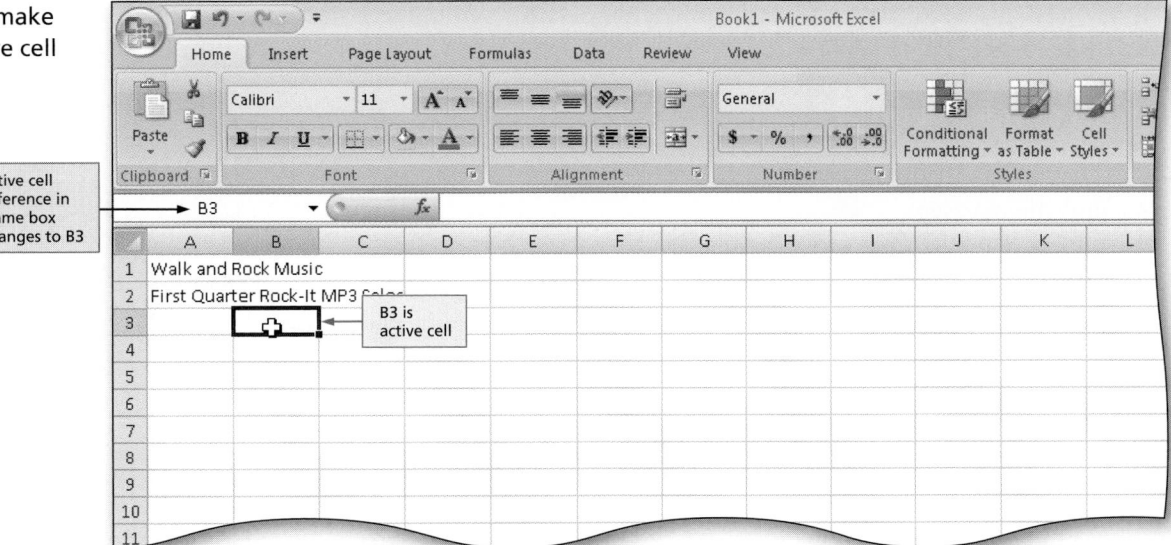

Figure 1–23

● Type Northeast in cell B3
(Figure 1–24).

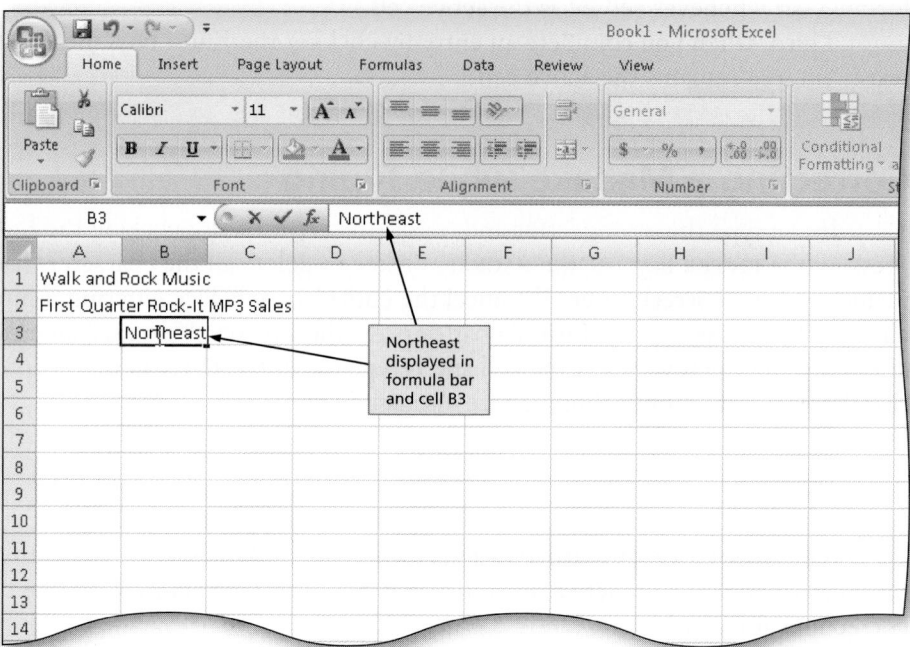

Figure 1–24

● Press the RIGHT
ARROW key to
enter the column title,
Northeast, in cell B3
and make cell C3
the active cell
(Figure 1–25).

Why is the RIGHT
ARROW key used to
complete the entry in
the cell?

If the next entry is in
an adjacent cell, use
the arrow keys to
complete the entry in a
cell. When you press an
arrow key to complete
an entry, the adjacent
cell in the direction of
the arrow (up, down,
left, or right) becomes
the active cell. If the
next entry is in a

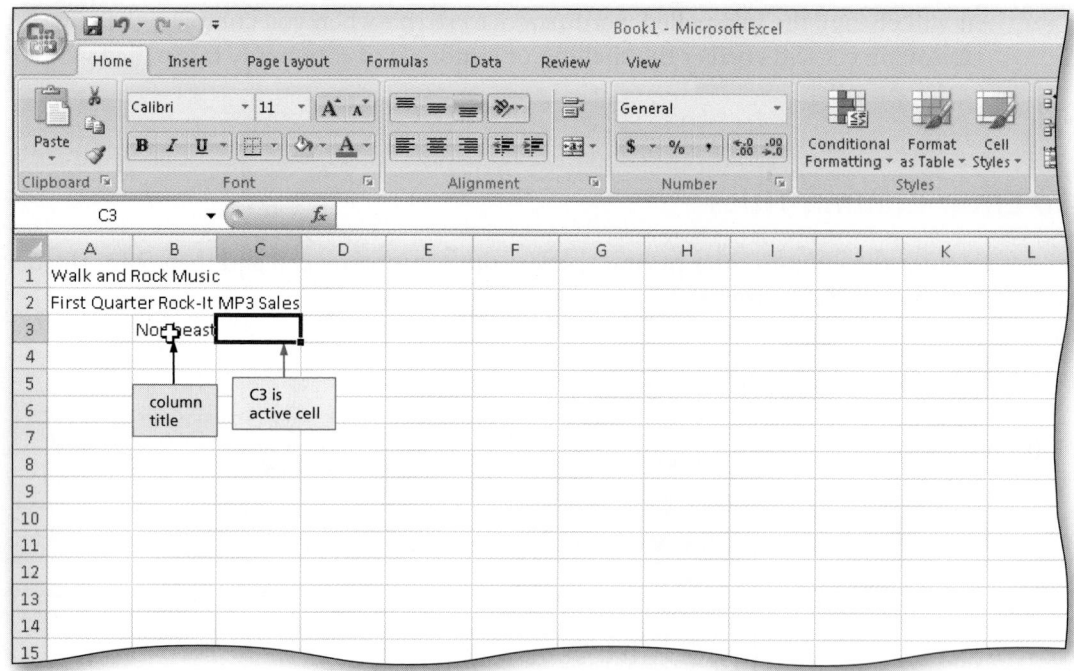

Figure 1–25

nonadjacent cell, complete an entry by clicking the next cell in which you plan to enter data.
You also can click the Enter box or press the ENTER key and then click the appropriate cell for
the next entry.

4

• Repeat Steps 2 and 3 to enter the remaining column titles in row 3; that is, enter Southeast in cell C3, Midwest in cell D3, South in cell E3, West in cell F3, and Total in cell G3 (complete the last entry in cell G3 by clicking the Enter box in the formula bar) (Figure 1–26).

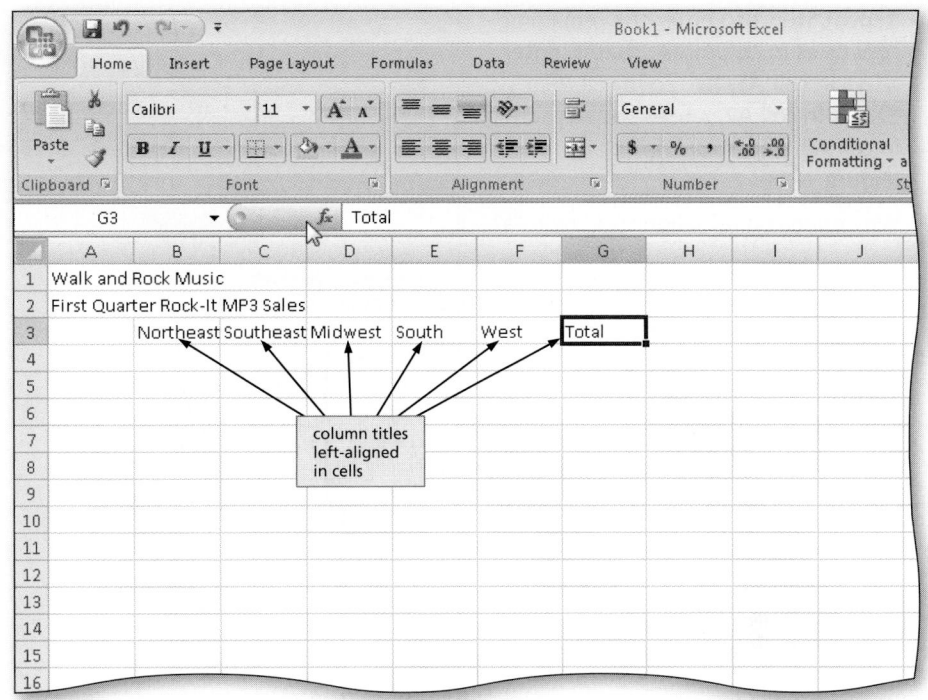

Figure 1–26

To Enter Row Titles

The next step in developing the worksheet for this project is to enter the row titles in column A. This process is similar to entering the column titles. The following steps enter the row titles in the worksheet.

1

• Click cell A4 to select it.

• Type Video and then press the DOWN ARROW key to enter the row title and make cell A5 the active cell (Figure 1–27).

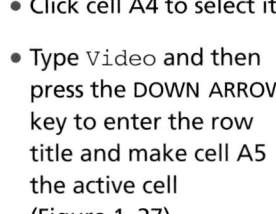

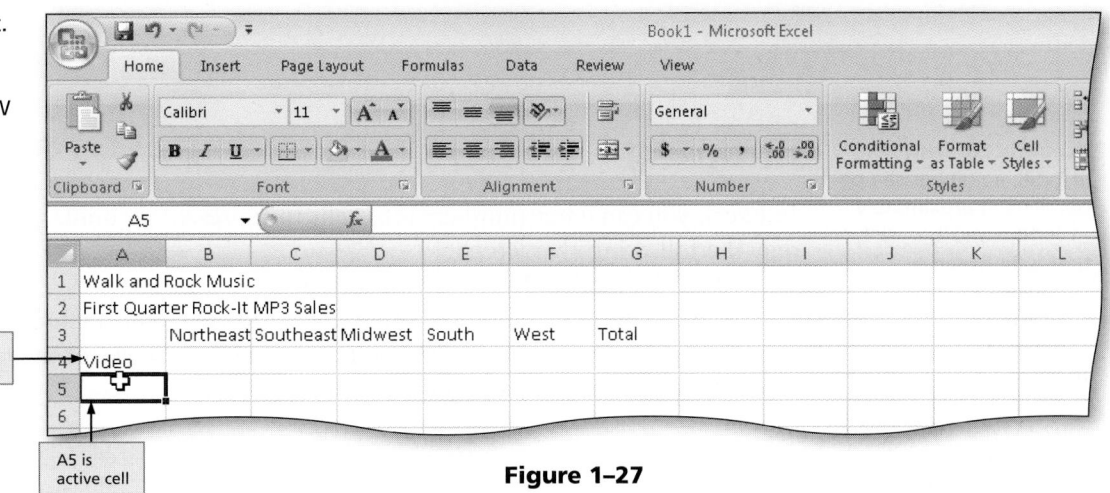

Figure 1–27

2

- Repeat Step 1 to enter the remaining row titles in column A; that is, enter Mini in cell A5, Micro in cell A6, Flash in cell A7, Accessories in cell A8, and Total in cell A9 (Figure 1–28).

Q&A

Why is the text left-aligned in the cells?

When you enter text, Excel automatically left-aligns the text in the cell. Excel treats any combination of numbers, spaces, and nonnumeric characters as text. For example, the following entries are text:

401AX21, 921-231, 619 321, 883XTY

You can change the text alignment in a cell by realigning it. Several alignment techniques are discussed later in the chapter.

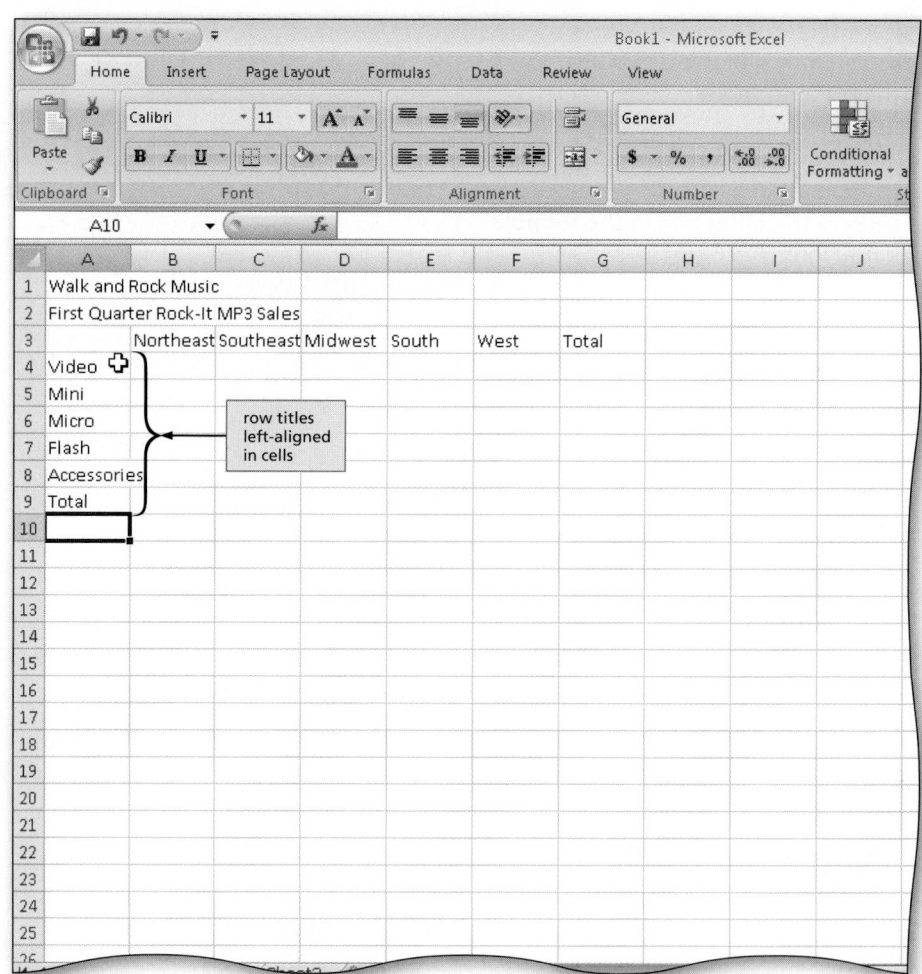

Figure 1–28

BTW

Numeric Limitations
In Excel, a number can be between approximately -1×10^{308} and 1×10^{308}, that is, between a negative 1 followed by 308 zeros and a positive 1 followed by 308 zeros. To enter a number such as 6,000,000,000,000,000, you can type 6,000,000,000,000,000, or you can type 6E15, which stands for 6×10^{15}.

Entering Numbers

In Excel, you can enter numbers into cells to represent amounts. A **number** can contain only the following characters:

0 1 2 3 4 5 6 7 8 9 + - ( ) , / . $ % E e

If a cell entry contains any other keyboard character (including spaces), Excel interprets the entry as text and treats it accordingly. The use of the special characters is explained when they are used in this book.

To Enter Numbers

The Walk and Rock Music First Quarter Rock-It MP3 Sales numbers used in Chapter 1 are summarized in Table 1–1. These numbers, which represent sales revenue for each of the product types and regions, must be entered in rows 4, 5, 6, 7, and 8.

Table 1–1 Walk and Rock Music First Quarter Rock-It MP3 Sales					
	Northeast	**Southeast**	**Midwest**	**South**	**West**
Video	66145.15	79677.10	34657.66	52517.20	99455.49
Mini	31375.24	82937.72	66137.50	30681.82	43595.24
Micro	27596.37	92716.32	88294.78	87984.79	83380.72
Flash	27885.59	98800.57	24111.33	69737.51	51003.09
Accessories	9715.12	31284.20	66527.37	40374.83	46321.88

The following steps enter the numbers in Table 1–1 one row at a time.

- Click cell B4.

- Type 66145.15 and then press the RIGHT ARROW key to enter the data in cell B4 and make cell C4 the active cell (Figure 1–29).

Q&A

Do I need to enter dollar signs, commas, or trailing zeros for the quarterly sales numbers?

You are not required to type dollar signs, commas, or trailing zeros. When you enter a dollar value that has cents, however, you must add the decimal point and the numbers representing the cents. Later in this chapter, the numbers will be formatted to use dollar signs, commas, and trailing zeros to improve the appearance and readability of the numbers.

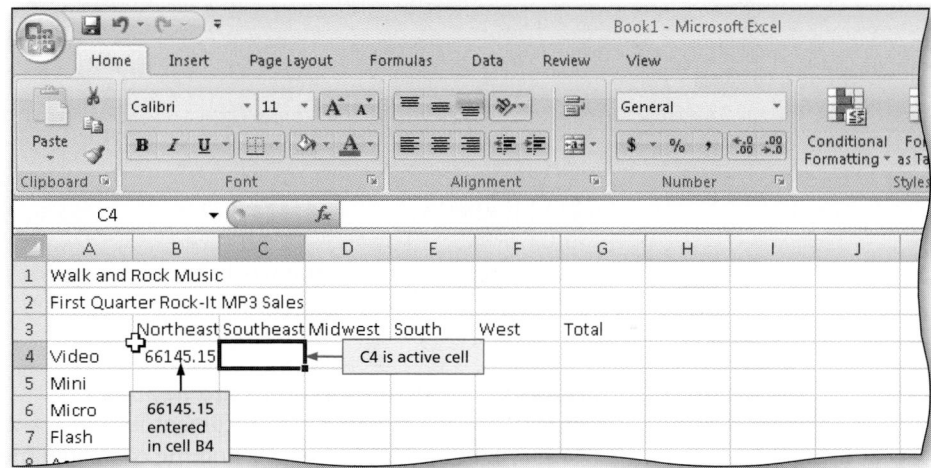

Figure 1–29

- Enter 79677.1 in cell C4, 34657.66 in cell D4, 52517.2 in cell E4, and 99455.49 in cell F4 (Figure 1–30).

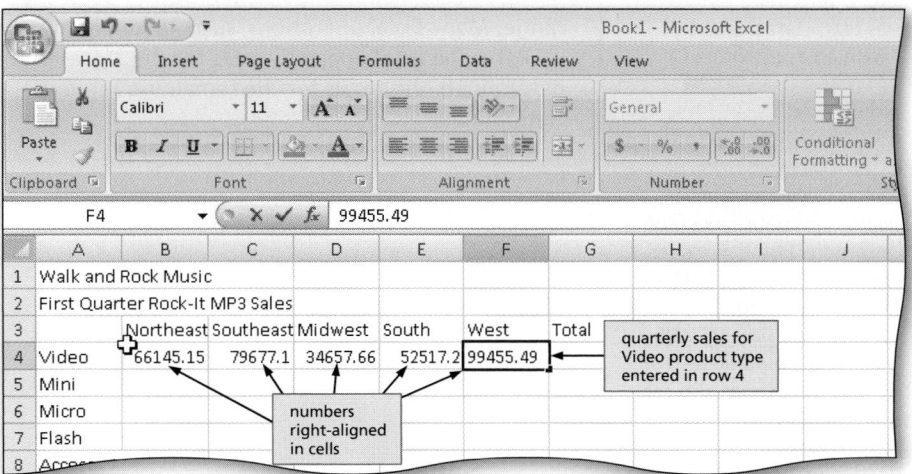

Figure 1–30

3

- Click cell B5.

- Enter the remaining first quarter sales numbers provided in Table 1–1 for each of the four remaining offerings in rows 5, 6, 7, and 8 to display the quarterly sales in the worksheet (Figure 1–31).

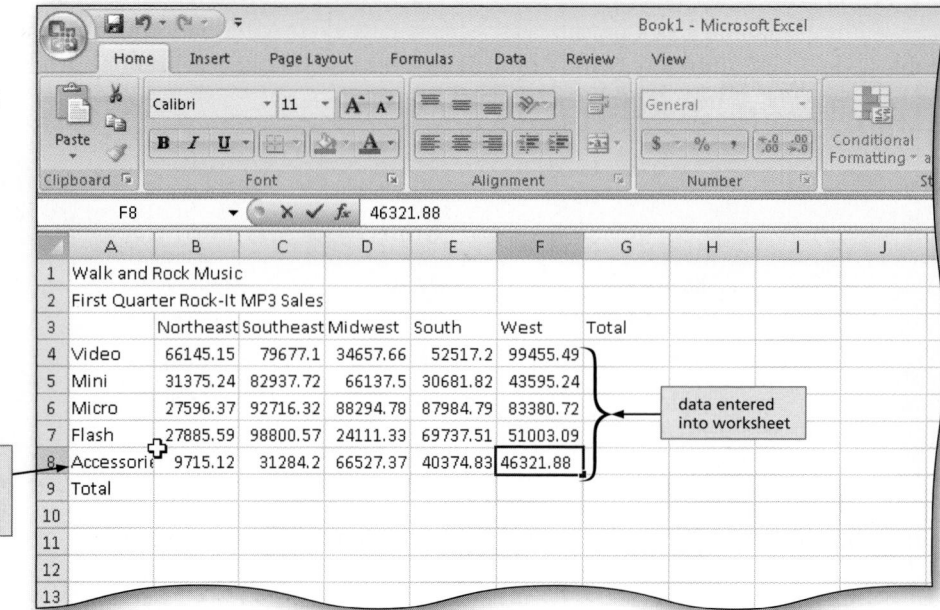

Figure 1–31

Calculating a Sum

The next step in creating the worksheet is to perform any necessary calculations, such as calculating the column and row totals.

Determine calculations that are needed.
As stated in the requirements document in Figure 1–2 on page EX 4, totals are required for each region, each product type, and the company. The first calculation is to determine the quarterly sales for the stores in the Northeast region in column B. To calculate this value in cell B9, Excel must add, or sum, the numbers in cells B4, B5, B6, B7, and B8. Excel's **SUM function**, which adds all of the numbers in a range of cells, provides a convenient means to accomplish this task.

A **range** is a series of two or more adjacent cells in a column or row or a rectangular group of cells. For example, the group of adjacent cells B4, B5, B6, B7, and B8 is called a range. Many Excel operations, such as summing numbers, take place on a range of cells.

After the total quarterly sales for the stores in the Northeast region in column B is determined, the totals for the remaining regions and totals for each product type will be determined.

BTW

Entering Numbers as Text
Sometimes, you will want Excel to treat numbers, such as Zip codes and telephone numbers, as text. To enter a number as text, start the entry with an apostrophe (').

BTW

Calculating Sums
Excel calculates sums for a variety of data types. For example, Boolean values, such as TRUE and FALSE, can be summed. Excel treats the value of TRUE as 1 and the value of FALSE as 0. Times also can be summed. For example, Excel treats the sum of 1:15 and 2:45 as 4:00.

To Sum a Column of Numbers

The following steps sum the numbers in column B.

1

- Click cell B9 to make it the active cell and then point to the Sum button on the Ribbon (Figure 1–32).

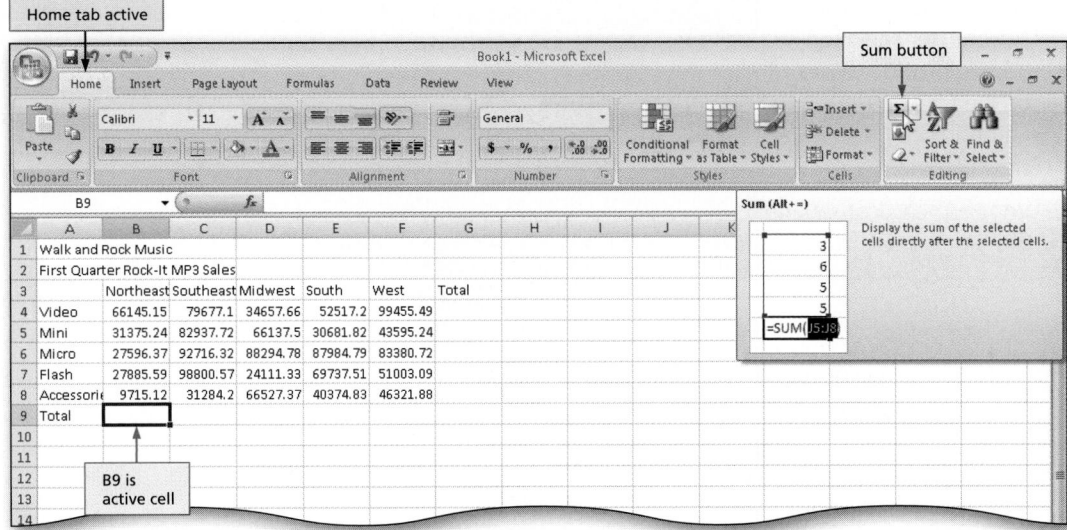

Figure 1–32

2

- Click the Sum button on the Ribbon to display =SUM(B4: B8) in the formula bar and in the active cell B9 (Figure 1–33).

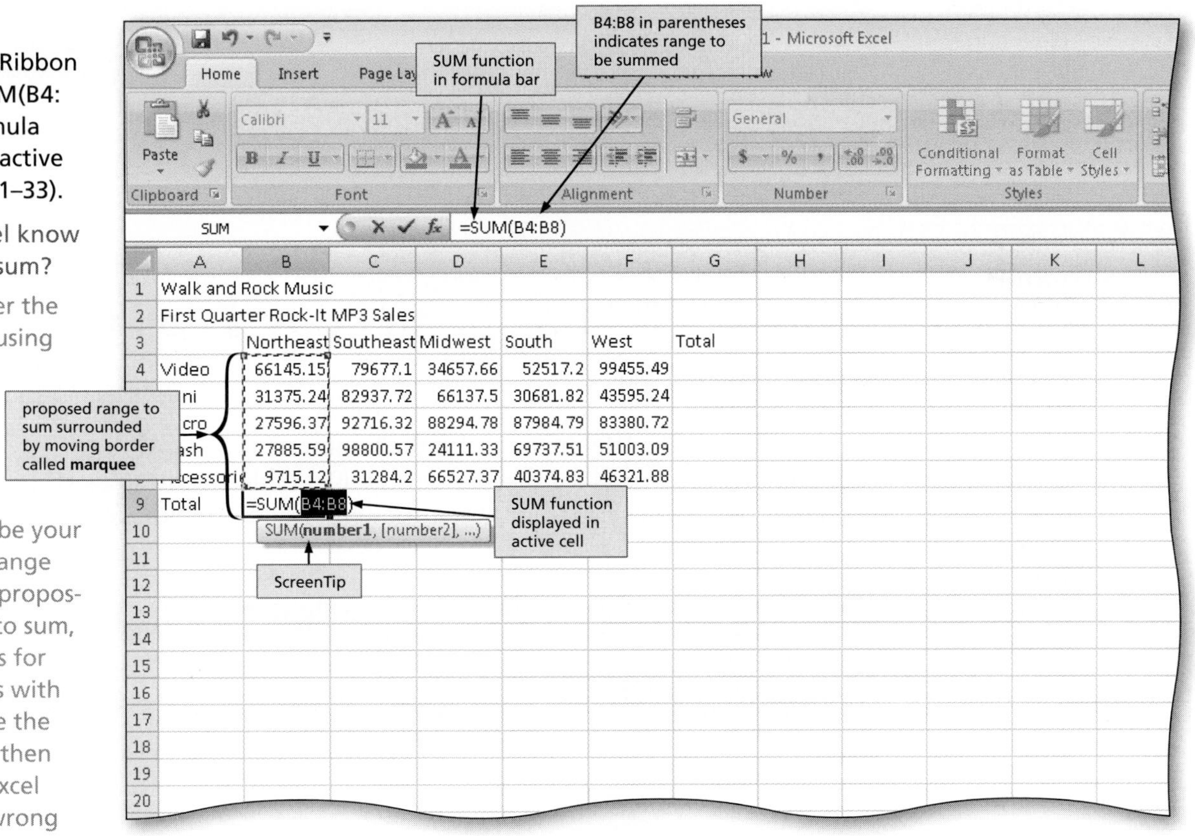

Q&A

How does Excel know which cells to sum?

When you enter the SUM function using the Sum button, Excel automatically selects what it considers to be your choice of the range to sum. When proposing the range to sum, Excel first looks for a range of cells with numbers above the active cell and then to the left. If Excel proposes the wrong range, you can correct it by dragging through the correct range before pressing the ENTER key. You also can enter the correct range by typing the beginning cell reference, a colon (:), and the ending cell reference.

Figure 1–33

3

- Click the Enter box in the formula bar to enter the sum of the first quarter sales for the five product types for the Northeast region in cell B9 (Figure 1-34).

Q&A

What is the purpose of the Sum button arrow?

If you click the Sum button arrow on the right side of the Sum button (Figure 1–34), Excel displays a list of often-used functions from which you can choose. The list includes functions that allow you to determine the average, the number of items in the selected range, the minimum value, or the maximum value of a range of numbers.

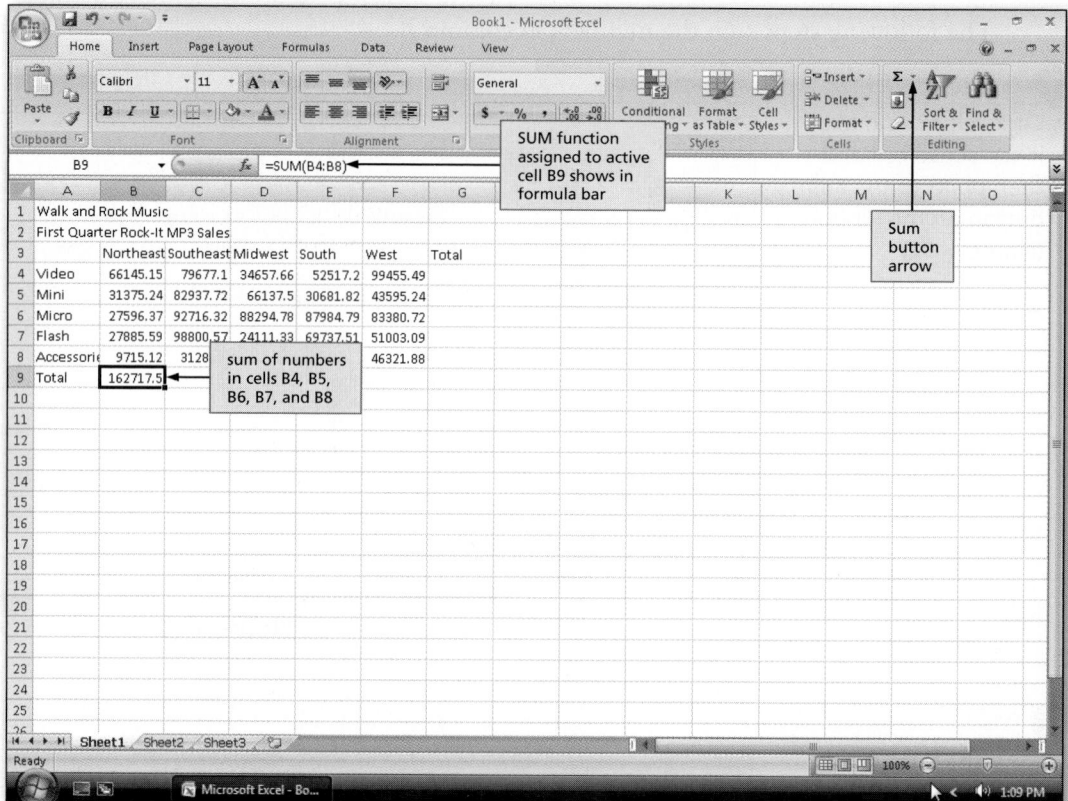

Figure 1–34

Other Ways

1. Click Insert Function button in formula bar, select SUM in Select a function list, click OK button, select range, click OK button
2. Click Sum button arrow on Ribbon, click More Functions, select SUM in Select a function list, click OK button, select range, click OK button
3. Type = s in cell, select SUM from list, select range
4. Press ALT + EQUAL SIGN (=) twice

Using the Fill Handle to Copy a Cell to Adjacent Cells

Excel also must calculate the totals for the Southeast in cell C9, the Midwest in cell D9, the South in cell E9, and for the West in cell F9. Table 1–2 illustrates the similarities between the entry in cell B9 and the entries required to sum the totals in cells C9, D9, E9, and F9.

Table 1–2 Sum Function Entries in Row 9		
Cell	**Sum Function Entries**	**Remark**
B9	=SUM(B4:B8)	Sums cells B4, B5, B6, B7, and B8
C9	=SUM(C4:C8)	Sums cells C4, C5, C6, C7, and C8
D9	=SUM(D4:D8)	Sums cells D4, D5, D6, D7, and D8
E9	=SUM(E4:E8)	Sums cells E4, E5, E6, E7, and E8
F9	=SUM(F4:F8)	Sums cells F4, F5, F6, F7, and F8

To place the SUM functions in cells C9, D9, E9, and F9, you could follow the same steps shown previously in Figures 1–32 through 1–34. A second, more efficient method is to copy the SUM function from cell B9 to the range C9:F9. The cell being copied is called the **source area** or **copy area**. The range of cells receiving the copy is called the **destination area** or **paste area**.

Although the SUM function entries in Table 1–2 are similar, they are not exact copies. The range in each SUM function entry uses cell references that are one column to the right of the previous column. When you copy cell references, Excel automatically adjusts them for each new position, resulting in the SUM function entries illustrated in Table 1–2. Each adjusted cell reference is called a **relative reference**.

To Copy a Cell to Adjacent Cells in a Row

The easiest way to copy the SUM formula from cell B9 to cells C9, D9, E9, and F9 is to use the fill handle. The **fill handle** is the small black square located in the lower-right corner of the heavy border around the active cell. The following steps use the fill handle to copy cell B9 to the adjacent cells C9:F9.

1
- With cell B9 active, point to the fill handle (Figure 1–35).

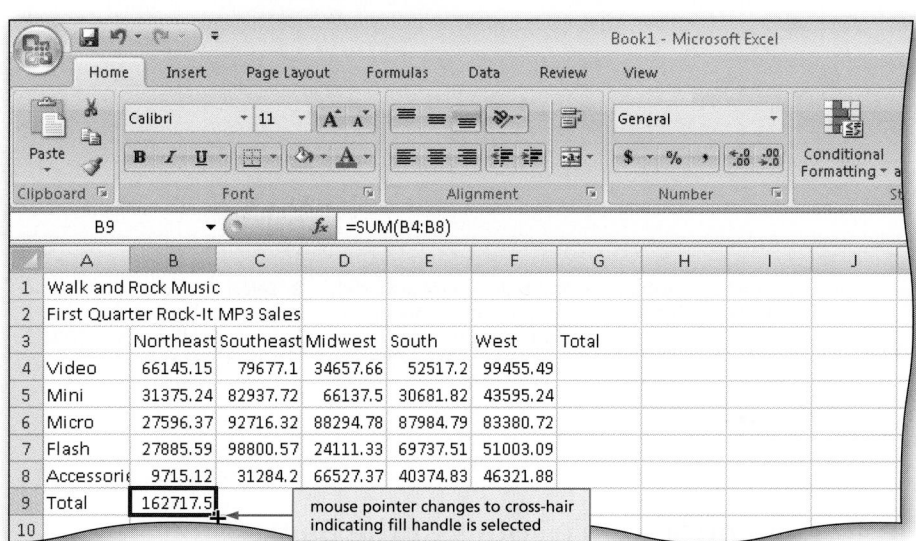

Figure 1–35

2
- Drag the fill handle to select the destination area, range C9:F9, to display a shaded border around the destination area, range C9:F9, and the source area, cell B9 (Figure 1–36). Do not release the mouse button.

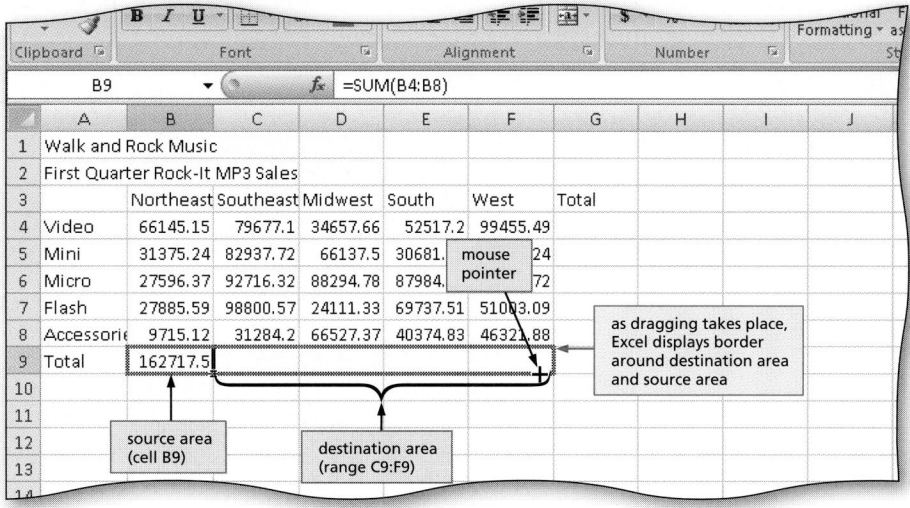

Figure 1–36

• Release the mouse button to copy the SUM function in cell B9 to the range C9:F9 (Figure 1–37) and calculate the sums in cells C9, D9, E9, and F9.

Q&A

What is the purpose of the Auto Fill Options button?

When you copy one range to another, Excel displays an Auto Fill Options button (Figure 1–37). The Auto Fill Options button allows you to choose whether you want to copy the values from the source area to the destination area with formatting, without formatting, or copy only the format. To view the available fill options, click the Auto Fill Options button. The Auto Fill Options button disappears when you begin another activity.

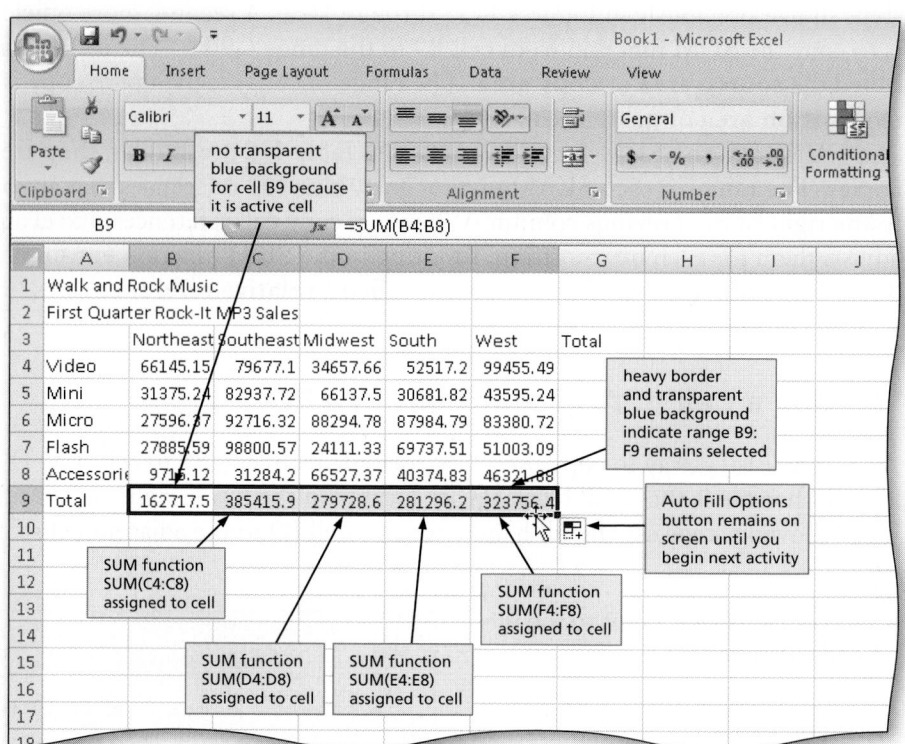

Figure 1–37

Other Ways
1. Select source area, click Copy button on Ribbon, select destination area, click Paste button on Ribbon	2. Right-click source area, click Copy on shortcut menu, right-click destination area, click Paste on shortcut menu	3. Select source area and then point to border of range; while holding down CTRL key, drag source area to destination area

To Determine Multiple Totals at the Same Time

The next step in building the worksheet is to determine the quarterly sales for each product type and total quarterly sales for the company in column G. To calculate these totals, you can use the SUM function much as it was used to total the quarterly sales by region in row 9. In this example, however, Excel will determine totals for all of the rows at the same time. The following steps illustrate this process.

• Click cell G4 to make it the active cell (Figure 1–38).

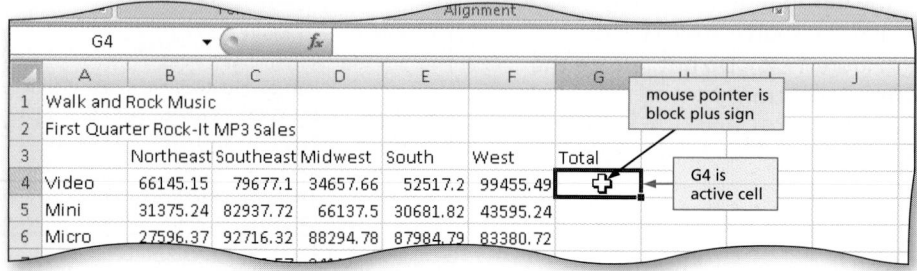

Figure 1–38

2

- With the mouse pointer in cell G4 and in the shape of a block plus sign, drag the mouse pointer down to cell G9 to highlight the range G4:G9 with a transparent view (Figure 1–39).

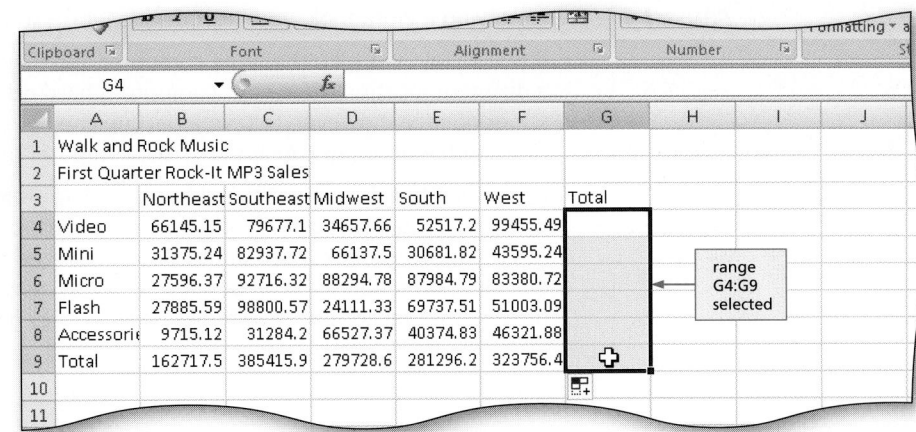

Figure 1–39

3

- Click the Sum button on the Ribbon to calculate and display the sums of the corresponding rows of sales in cells G4, G5, G6, G7, G8, and G9 (Figure 1–40).

4

- Select cell A10 to deselect the range G4:G9.

Q&A

Why does Excel create totals for each row?

If each cell in a selected range is next to a row of numbers, Excel assigns the SUM function to each cell when you click the Sum button.

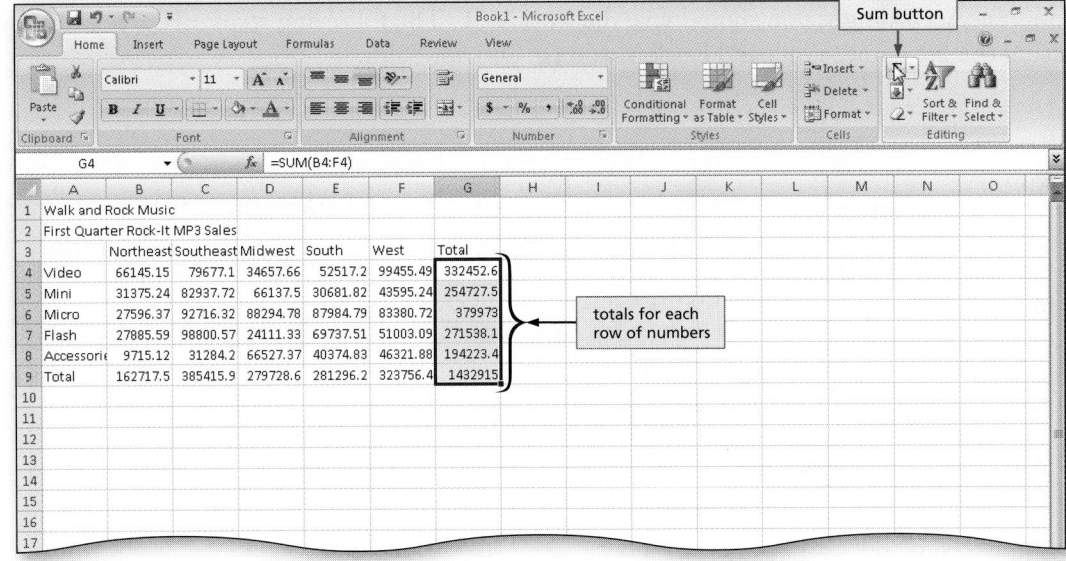

Figure 1–40

Saving the Project

While you are building a worksheet in a workbook, the computer stores it in memory. When you save a workbook, the computer places it on a storage medium such as a USB flash drive, CD, or hard disk. A saved workbook is referred to as a **file**. A **file name** is the name assigned to a file when it is saved. It is important to save the workbook frequently for the following reasons:

- The worksheet in memory will be lost if the computer is turned off or you lose electrical power while Excel is open.
- If you run out of time before completing your workbook, you may finish your worksheet at a future time without starting over.

BTW

Saving

Excel allows you to save a workbook in more than 30 different file formats. Choose the file format by clicking the 'Save as type' box arrow at the bottom of the Save As dialog box (Figure 1–41 on the next page). Excel Workbook is the default file format.

<table>
<tr><td>**Plan**
Ahead</td><td>**Determine where to save the workbook.**
When saving a workbook, you must decide which storage medium to use.

• If you always work on the same computer and have no need to transport your projects to a different location, then your computer's hard drive will suffice as a storage location. It is a good idea, however, to save a backup copy of your projects on a separate medium in case the file becomes corrupted or the computer's hard drive fails.

• If you plan to work on your workbooks in various locations or on multiple computers, then you should save your workbooks on a portable medium, such as a USB flash drive or CD. The workbooks used in this book are saved to a USB flash drive, which saves files quickly and reliably and can be reused. CDs are easily portable and serve as good backups for the final versions of workbooks because they generally can save files only one time.</td></tr>
</table>

To Save a Workbook

You have performed many tasks while creating this project and do not want to risk losing the work completed thus far. Accordingly, you should save the workbook. The following steps save a workbook on a USB flash drive using the file name, Walk and Rock Music 1st Quarter Sales.

Note: If you are using Windows XP, see Appendix F for alternate steps.

1

• With a USB flash drive connected to one of the computer's USB ports, click the Save button on the Quick Access Toolbar to display the Save As dialog box (Figure 1–41).

• If the Navigation pane is not displayed in the Save As dialog box, click the Browse Folders button to expand the dialog box.

• If a Folders list is displayed below the Folders button, click the Folders button to remove the Folders list.

Q&A
Do I have to save to a USB flash drive?

No. You can save to any device or folder. A **folder** is a specific location on a storage medium. You can save to the default folder or a different folder. You also can create your own folders, which is explained later in this book.

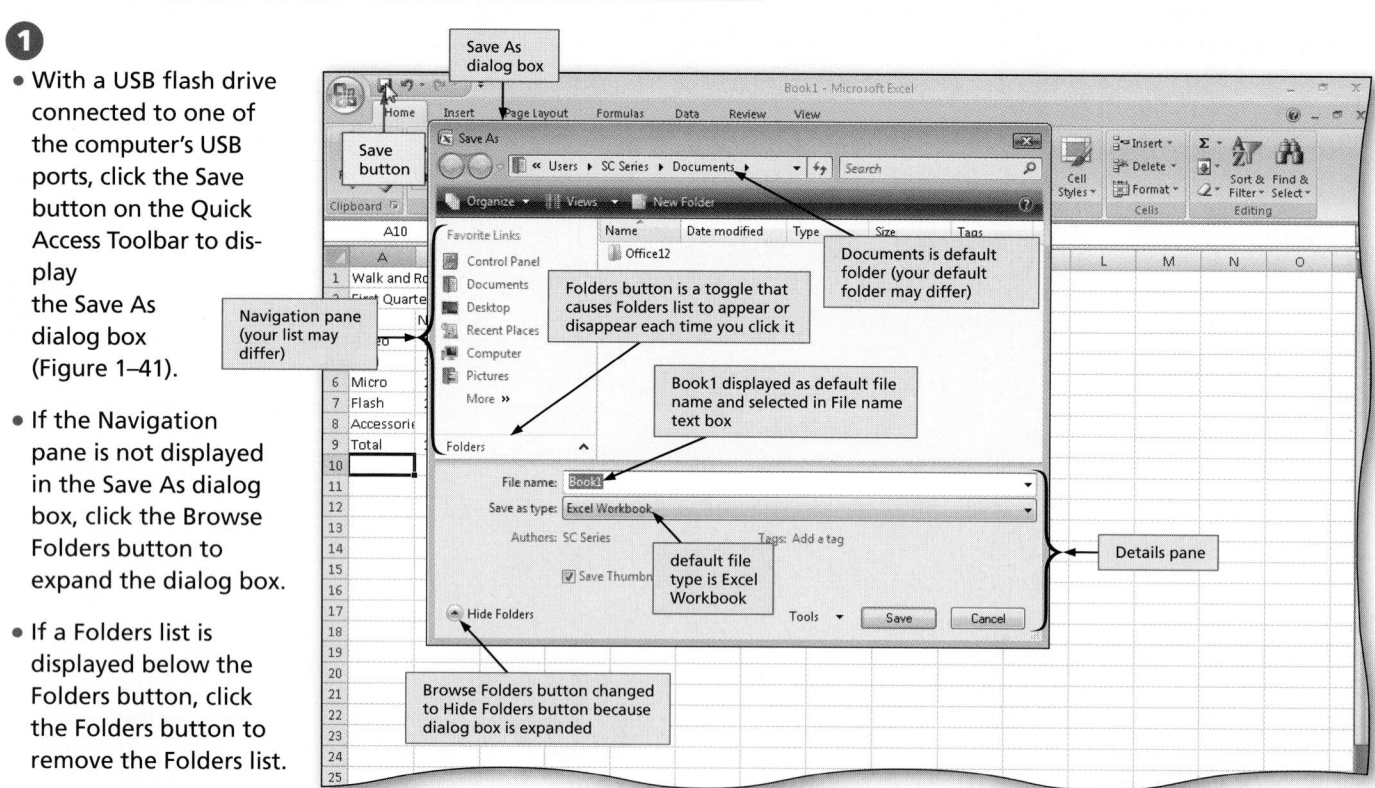

Figure 1–41

2

- Type Walk and Rock Music 1st Quarter Sales in the File name text box to change the file name. Do not press the ENTER key after typing the file name (Figure 1–42).

Q&A What characters can I use in a file name?

A file name can have a maximum of 255 characters, including spaces. The only invalid characters are the backslash (\), slash (/), colon (:), asterisk (*), question mark (?), quotation mark ("), less than symbol (<), greater than symbol (>), and vertical bar (|).

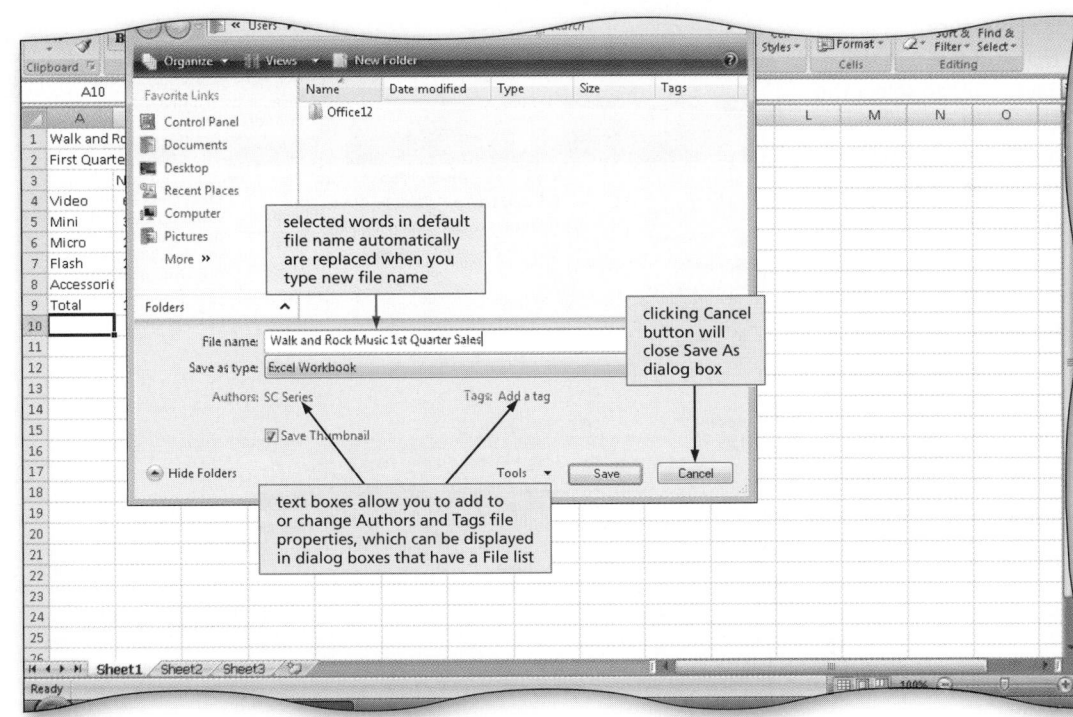

Figure 1–42

3

- If Computer is not displayed in the Favorite Links section, drag the top or bottom edge of the Save As dialog box until Computer is displayed.

- Click Computer in the Favorite Links section to display a list of available drives (Figure 1–43).

- If necessary, scroll until UDISK 2.0 (E :) appears in the list of available drives.

Q&A Why is my list of files, folders, and drives arranged and named differently from those shown in the figure?

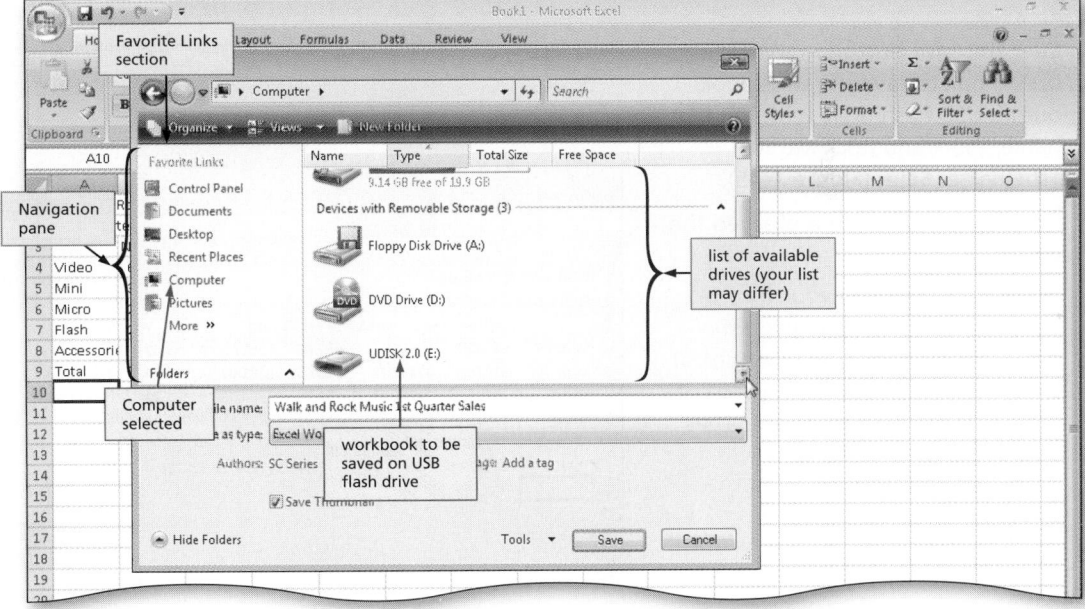

Figure 1–43

Your computer's configuration determines how the list of files and folders is displayed and how drives are named. You can change the save location by clicking links on the **Favorite Links section**.

Q&A How do I save the file if I am not using a USB flash drive?

Use the same process, but be certain to select your device in the list of available drives.

4

- Double-click UDISK 2.0 (E:) in the Save in list to select the USB flash drive, Drive E in this case, as the new save location (Figure 1–44).

Q&A What if my USB flash drive has a different name or letter?

It is very likely that your USB flash drive will have a different name and drive letter and be connected to a different port.

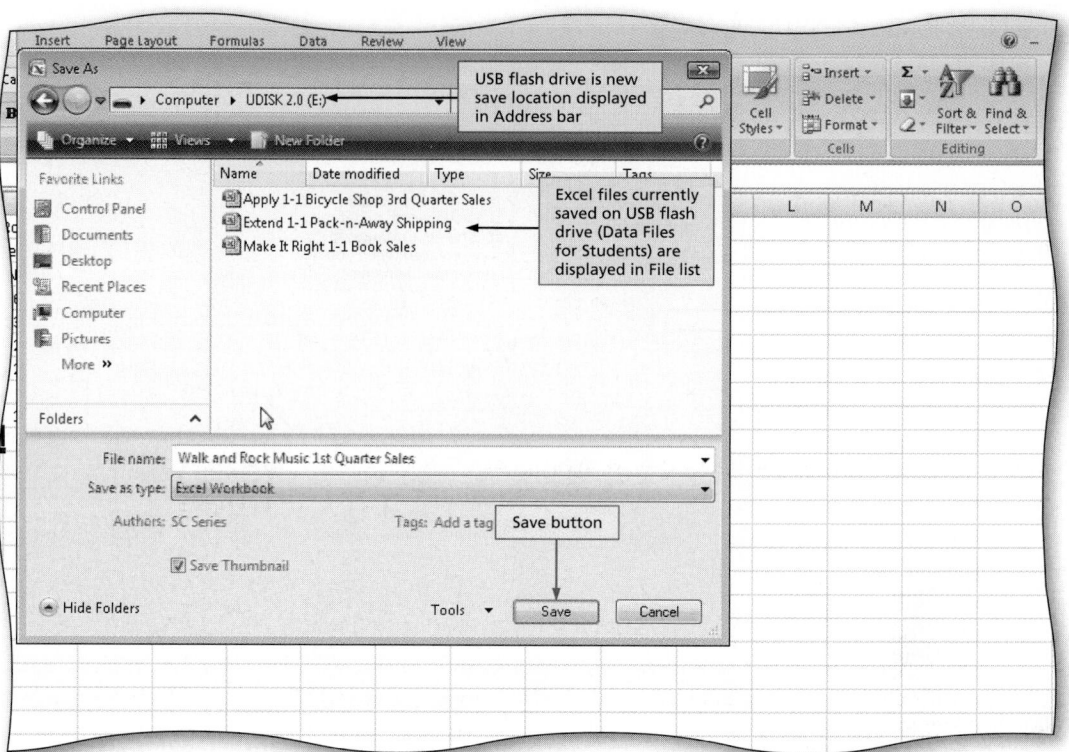

Figure 1–44

5

- Click the Save button in the Save As dialog box to save the workbook on the USB flash drive with the file name, Walk and Rock Music 1st Quarter Sales (Figure 1–45).

Q&A How do I know that Excel saved the workbook?

While Excel is saving your file, it briefly displays a message on the status bar indicating the amount of the file saved. In addition, your USB drive may have a light that flashes during the save process.

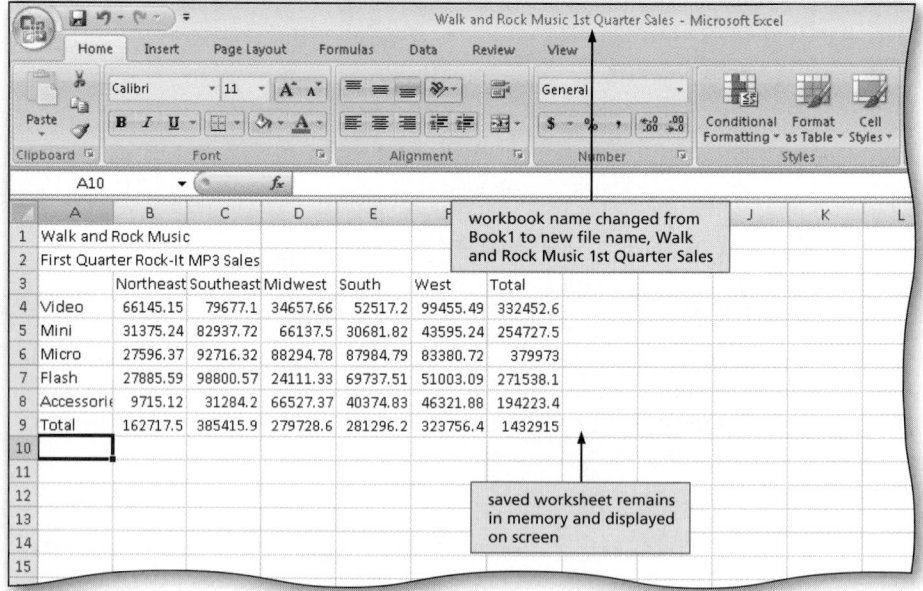

Figure 1–45

Other Ways

1. Click Office Button, click Save, type file name, select drive or folder, click Save button
2. Press CTRL+S or press SHIFT+F12, type file name, select drive or folder, click Save button

Formatting the Worksheet

The text, numeric entries, and functions for the worksheet now are complete. The next step is to format the worksheet. You **format** a worksheet to emphasize certain entries and make the worksheet easier to read and understand.

Figure 1–46a shows the worksheet before formatting. Figure 1–46b shows the worksheet after formatting. As you can see from the two figures, a worksheet that is formatted not only is easier to read but also looks more professional.

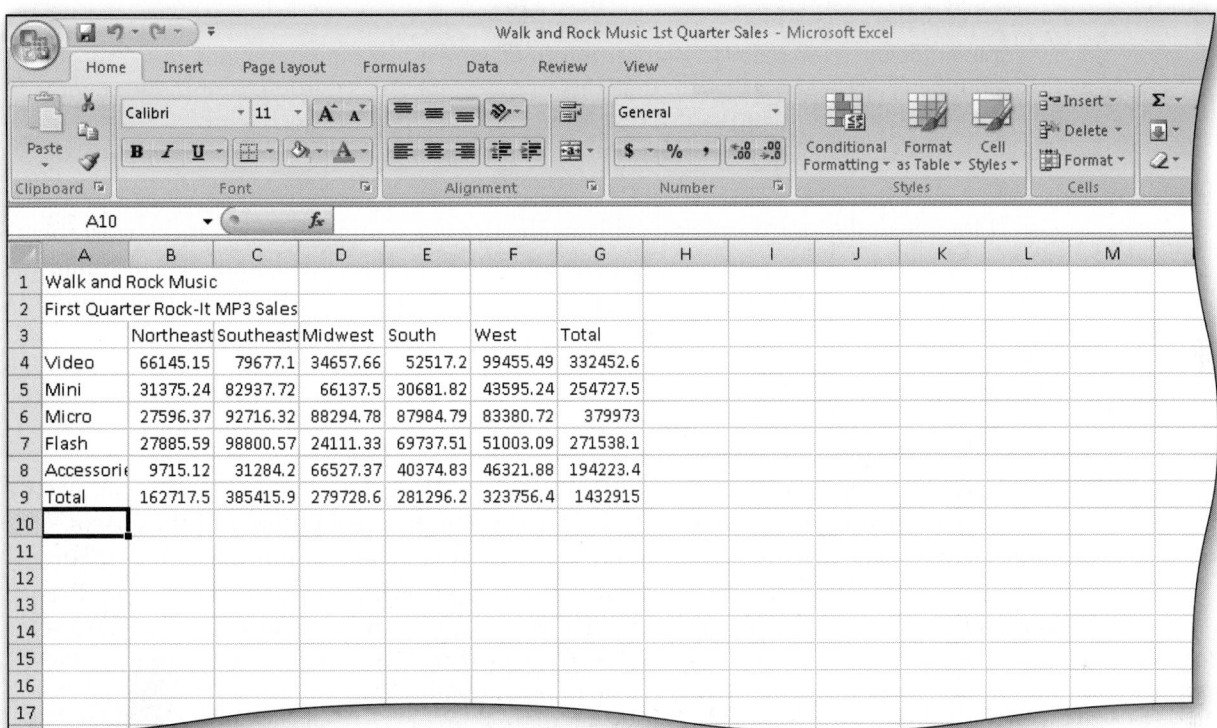

(a) Before Formatting

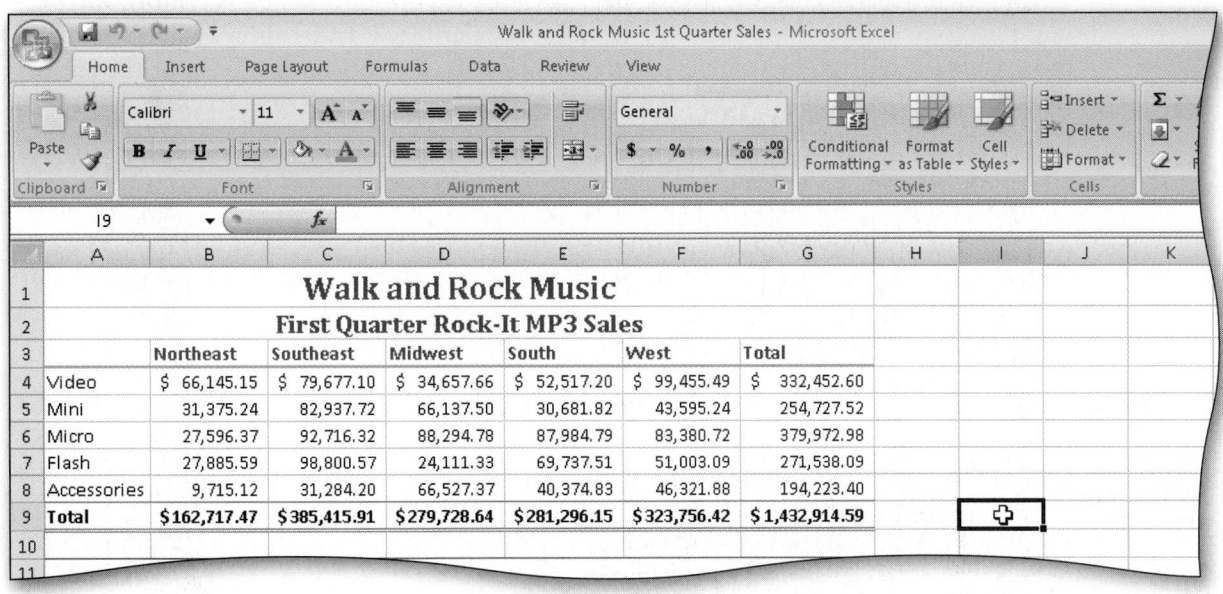

(b) After Formatting

Figure 1–46

**Plan
Ahead**

> **Identify how to format various elements of the worksheet.**
> To change the unformatted worksheet in Figure 1–46a to the formatted worksheet in Figure 1–46b, the following tasks must be completed:
>
> 1. Change the font type, change the font style to bold, increase the font size, and change the font color of the worksheet titles in cells A1 and A2. These changes make the worksheet title prominently display to the user and inform the user of the purpose of the worksheet.
>
> 2. Center the worksheet titles in cells A1 and A2 across columns A through G.
>
> 3. Format the body of the worksheet. The body of the worksheet, range A3:G9, includes the column titles, row titles, and numbers. Formatting the body of the worksheet changes the numbers to use a dollars-and-cents format, with dollar signs in the first row (row 4) and the total row (row 9); adds underlining that emphasizes portions of the worksheet; and modifies the column widths to make the text and numbers readable.

The remainder of this section explains the process required to format the worksheet. Although the format procedures are explained in the order described above, you should be aware that you could make these format changes in any order. Modifying the column widths, however, usually is done last.

BTW

Fonts
In general, use no more than two font types in a worksheet.

BTW

Fonts and Themes
Excel uses default recommended fonts based on the workbook's theme. A theme is a collection of fonts and color schemes. The default theme is named Office, and the two recommended fonts for the Office theme are Calibri and Cambria. Excel, however, allows you to apply any font to a cell or range as long as the font is installed on your computer.

Font Type, Style, Size, and Color

The characters that Excel displays on the screen are a specific font type, style, size, and color. The **font type**, or font face, defines the appearance and shape of the letters, numbers, and special characters. Examples of font types include Calibri, Cambria, Times New Roman, Arial, and Courier. **Font style** indicates how the characters are emphasized. Common font styles include regular, bold, underline, or italic. The **font size** specifies the size of the characters on the screen. Font size is gauged by a measurement system called points. A single point is about 1/72 of one inch in height. Thus, a character with a **point size** of 10 is about 10/72 of one inch in height. The **font color** defines the color of the characters. Excel can display characters in a wide variety of colors, including black, red, orange, and blue.

When Excel begins, the preset font type for the entire workbook is Calibri, with a font size, font style, and font color of 11-point regular black. Excel allows you to change the font characteristics in a single cell, a range of cells, the entire worksheet, or the entire workbook.

To Change a Cell Style

Excel includes the capability of changing several characteristics of a cell, such as font type, font size, and font color, all at once by assigning a predefined cell style to a cell. The following steps assign the Title cell style to the worksheet title in cell A1.

1

- Click cell A1 to make cell A1 the active cell.

- Click the Cell Styles button on the Ribbon to display the Cell Styles gallery (Figure 1–47).

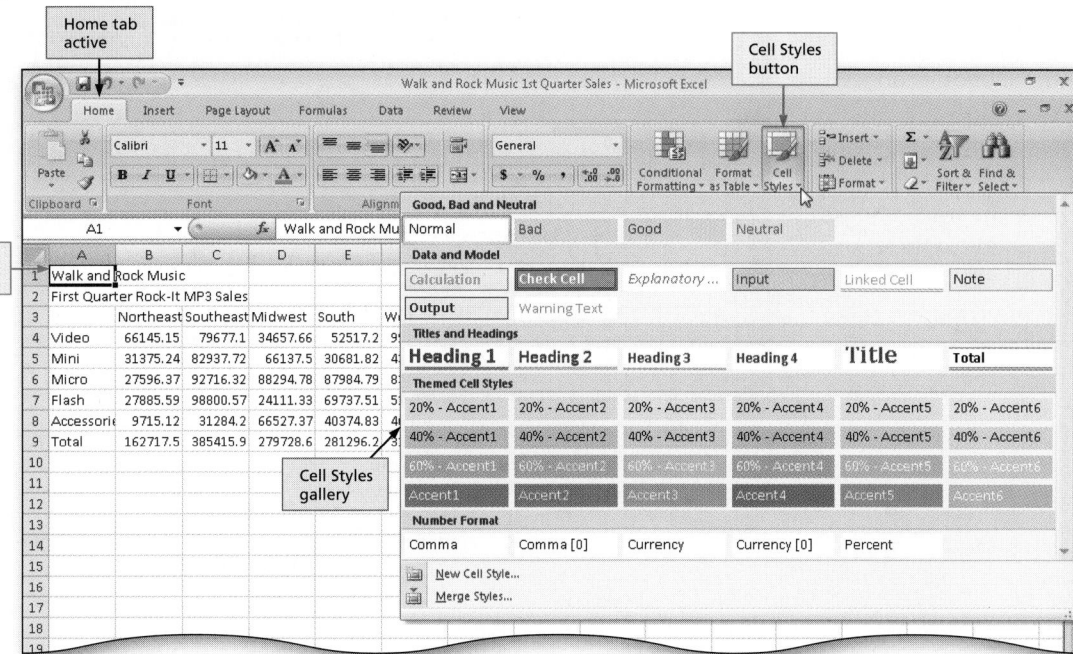

Figure 1–47

2

- Point to the Title cell style in the Titles and Headings area of the Cell Styles gallery to see a live preview of the cell style in cell A1 (Figure 1–48).

 Experiment

- Point to several other cell styles in the Cell Styles gallery to see a live preview of other cell styles in cell A1.

Q&A

Why does the font type, font size, and font color change in cell A1 when I point to it?

The change in cell A1 is a result of live preview. Live preview is a feature of Excel 2007 that allows you to preview cell styles as you point to them in the Cell Styles gallery.

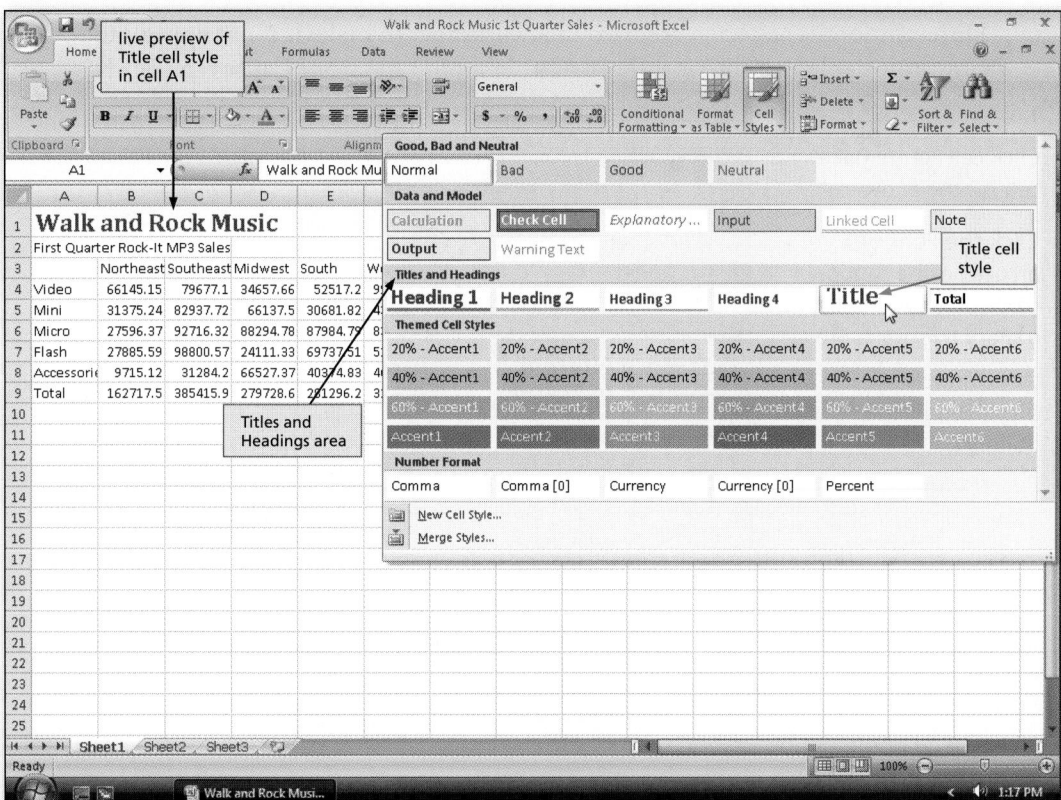

Figure 1–48

3

- Click the Title cell style to apply the cell style to cell A1 (Figure 1–49).

Why do several items in the Font group on the Ribbon change?

The changes to the Font box, Bold button, and Font Size box indicate the font changes applied to the active cell, cell A1, as a result of applying the Title cell style.

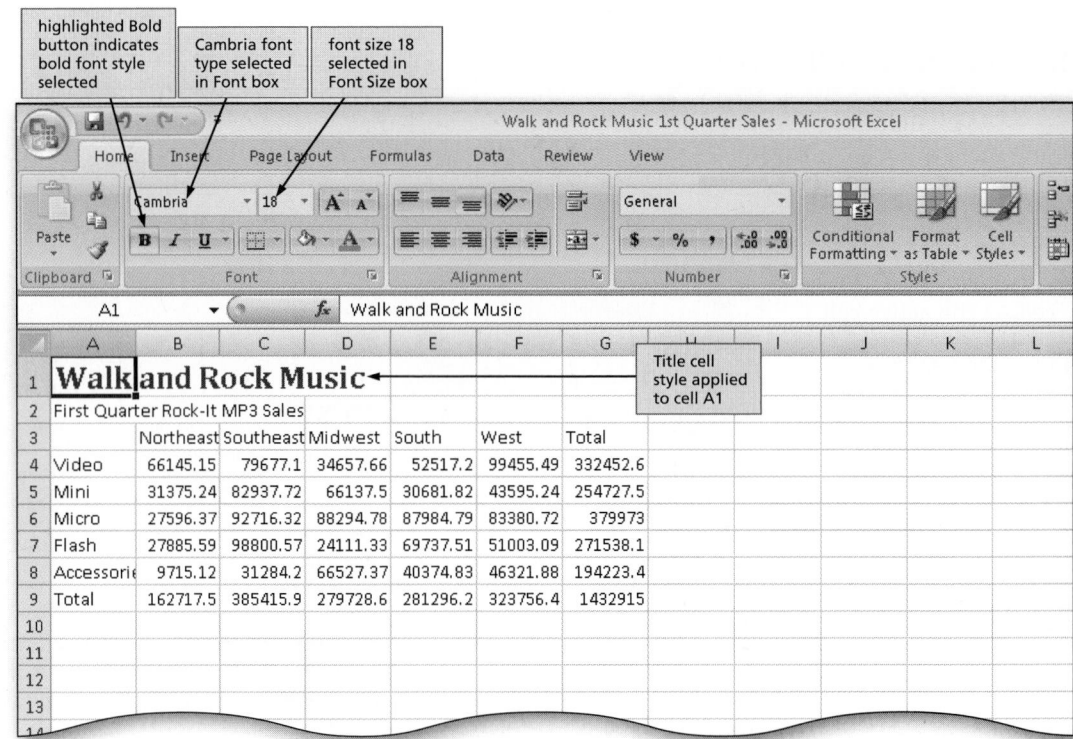

Figure 1–49

To Change the Font Type

Different font types often are used in a worksheet to make it more appealing to the reader. The following steps show how to change the worksheet subtitle's font type from Calibri to Cambria.

1

- Click cell A2 to make cell A2 the active cell.

- Click the Font box arrow on the Ribbon to display the Font gallery (Figure 1–50).

Which fonts are displayed in the Font gallery?

Because many applications supply additional font types beyond what comes with the Windows Vista operating system, the number of font types available on your computer will depend on the applications installed. This book uses only font types that come with the Windows Vista operating system and Microsoft Office.

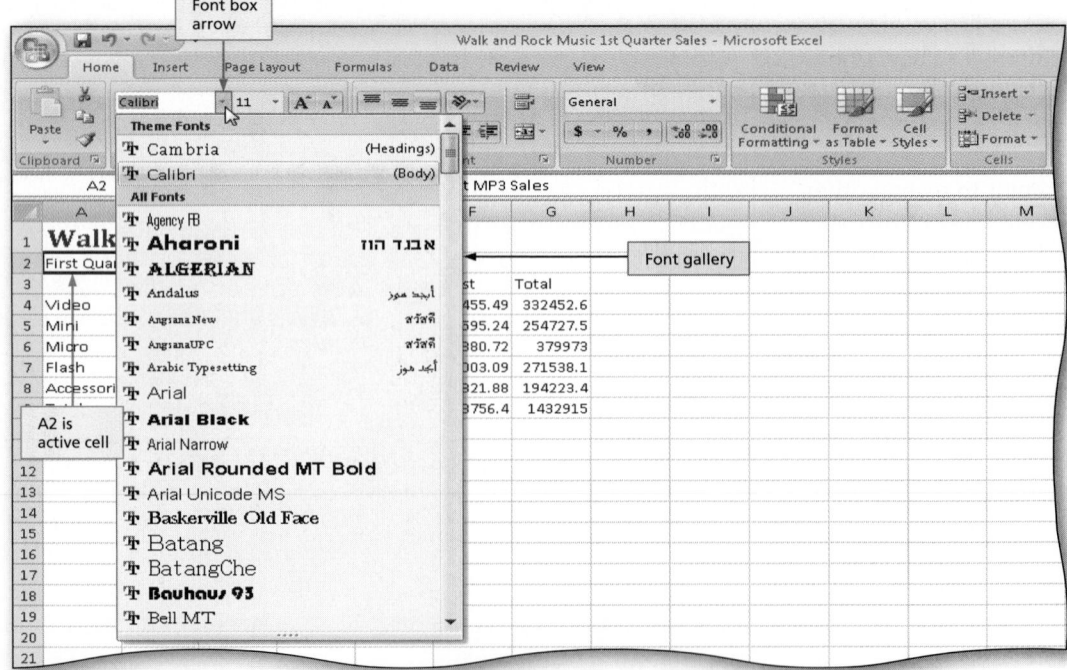

Figure 1–50

● Point to Cambria in the Theme Fonts area of the Font gallery to see a live preview of the Cambria font in cell A2 (Figure 1–51).

Experiment

● Point to several other fonts in the Font gallery to see a live preview of other fonts in cell A2.

What is the Theme Fonts area?

Excel applies the same default theme to any new workbook that you start. A **theme** is a collection of cell styles and other styles that have common characteristics, such as a color scheme and font type. The default theme for an Excel workbook is the Office theme. The Theme Fonts area of the Font gallery includes the fonts included in the default Office theme. Cambria is recommended for headings and Calibri is recommended for cells in the body of the worksheet (Figure 1–51).

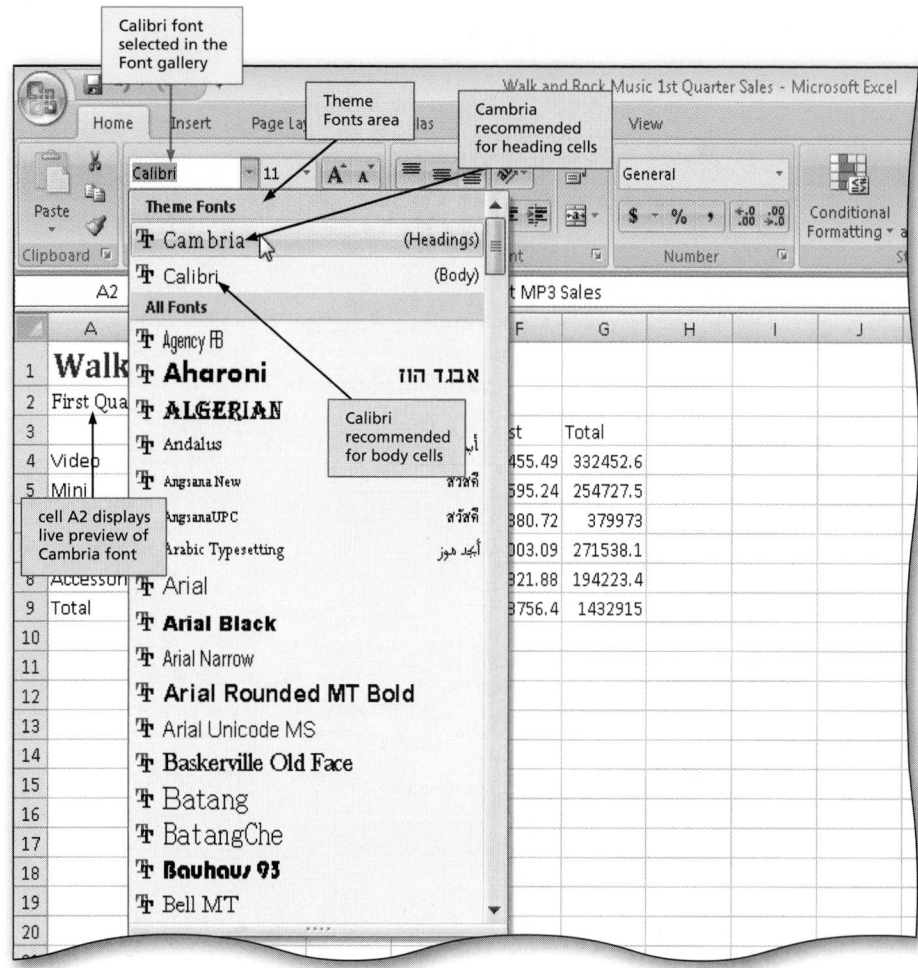

Figure 1–51

❸

● Click Cambria in the Theme Fonts area to change the font type of the worksheet subtitle in cell A2 from Calibri to Cambria (Figure 1–52).

Figure 1–52

Other Ways

1. Select font type from Font list on Mini toolbar

2. Right-click cell, click Format Cells on shortcut menu, click Font tab, click desired font type, click OK button

To Bold a Cell

You **bold** an entry in a cell to emphasize it or make it stand out from the rest of the worksheet. The following step shows how to bold the worksheet subtitle in cell A2.

1

• With cell A2 active, click the Bold button on the Ribbon to change the font style of the worksheet subtitle to bold (Figure 1–53).

Q&A

What if a cell already includes a bold style?

If you point to the Bold button and the active cell already is bold, then Excel displays the button with a transparent orange background.

Q&A

How do I remove the bold style from a cell?

Clicking the Bold button a second time removes the bold font style.

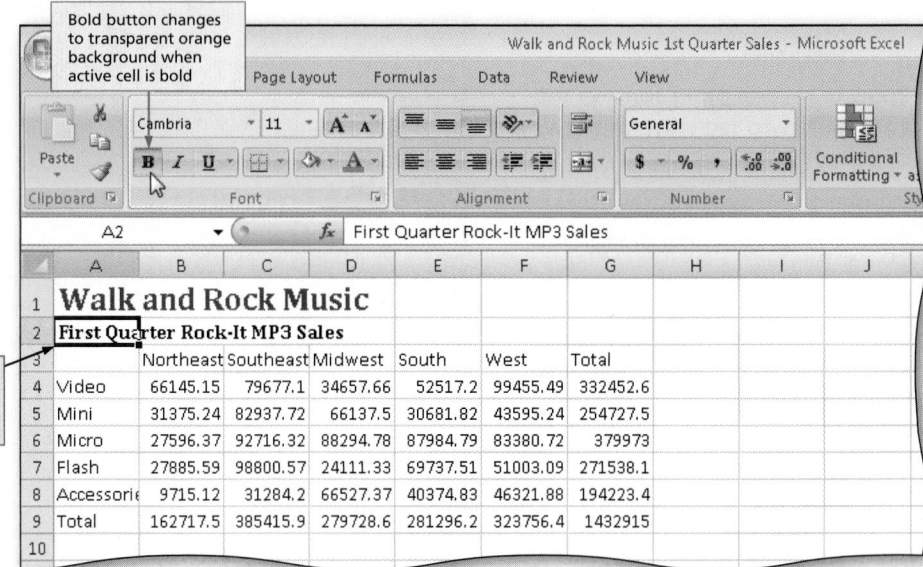

Figure 1–53

Other Ways

1. Click Bold button on Mini toolbar
2. Right-click cell, click Format Cells on shortcut menu, click Font tab, click Bold, click OK button
3. Press CTRL+B

To Increase the Font Size of a Cell Entry

Increasing the font size is the next step in formatting the worksheet subtitle. You increase the font size of a cell so the entry stands out and is easier to read. The following steps increase the font size of the worksheet subtitle in cell A2.

1

• With cell A2 selected, click the Font Size box arrow on the Ribbon to display the Font Size list.

• Point to 14 in the Font Size list to see a live preview of cell A2 with a font size of 14 (Figure 1–54).

Experiment

• Point to several other font sizes in the Font Size list to see a live preview of other font sizes in cell A2.

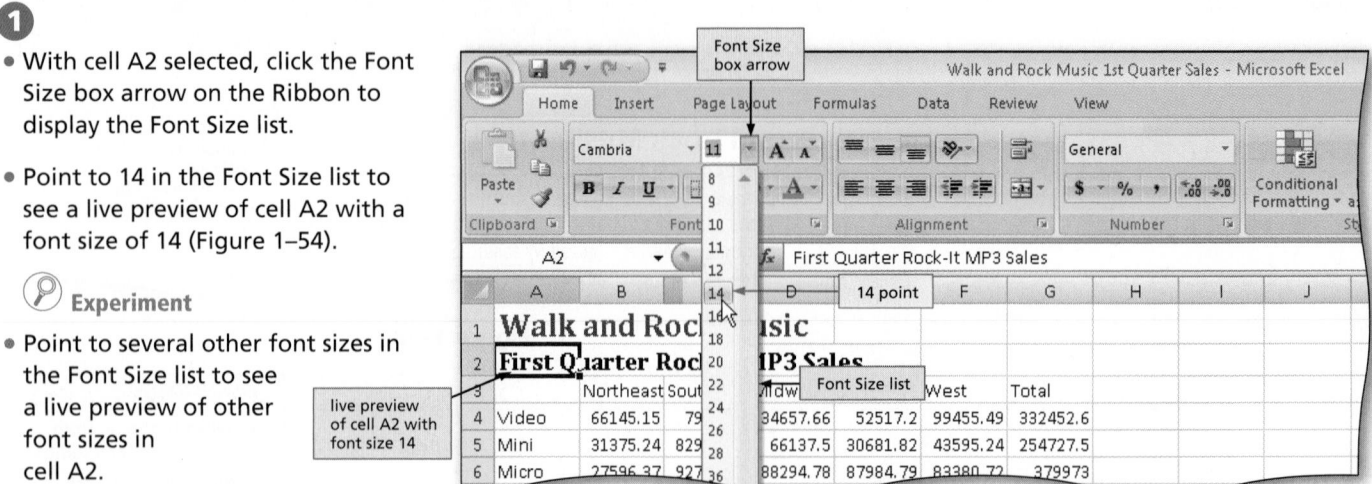

Figure 1–54

2

- Click 14 in the Font Size list to change the font in cell A2 from 11 point to 14 point (Figure 1–55).

Q&A Can I assign a font size that is not in the Font Size list?

Yes. An alternative to clicking a font size in the Font Size list is to click the Font Size box, type the font size, and then press the ENTER key. This procedure allows you to assign a font size not available in the Font Size list to a selected cell entry.

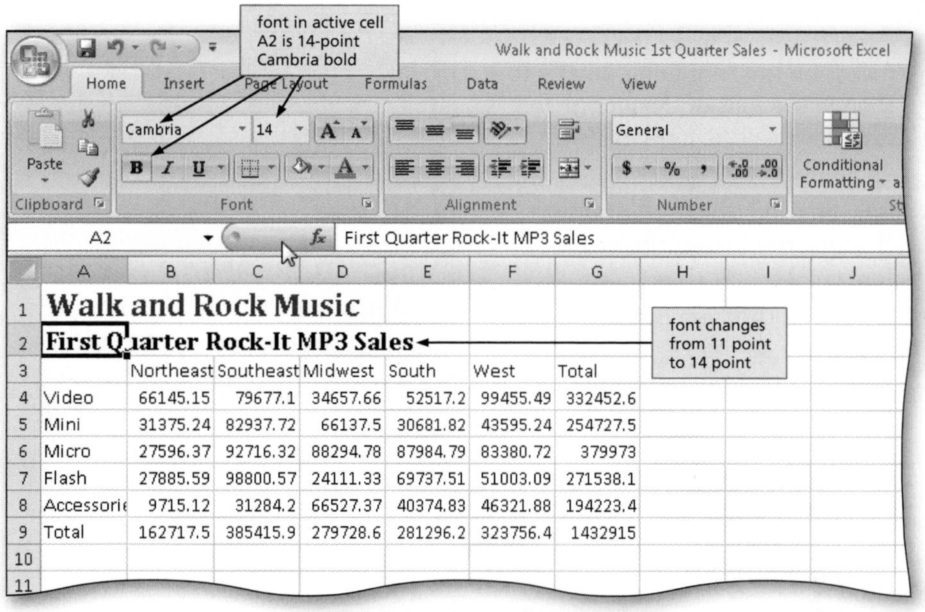

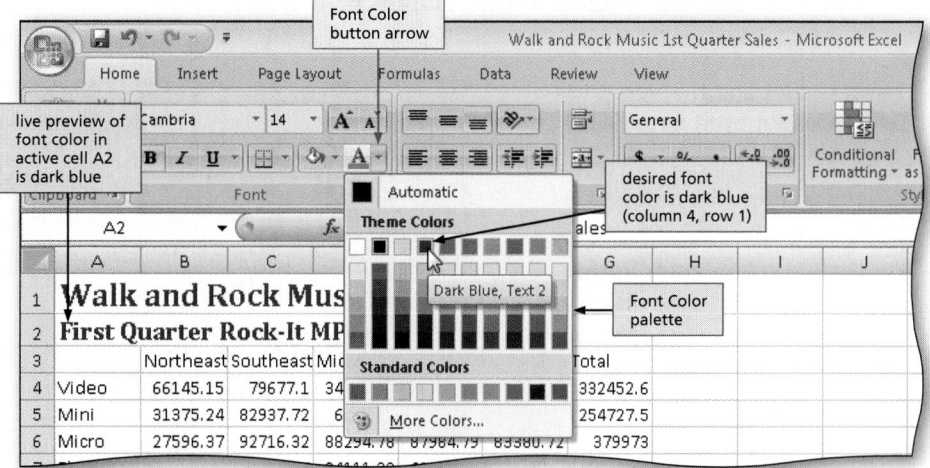

Figure 1–55

Other Ways

1. Click Increase Font Size button or Decrease Font Size button on Ribbon

2. Select font size from Font Size list on Mini toolbar

3. Right-click cell, click Format Cells on shortcut menu, click Font tab, select font size in Size box, click OK button

To Change the Font Color of a Cell Entry

The next step is to change the color of the font in cell A2 from black to dark blue. The following steps change the font color of a cell entry.

1

- With cell A2 selected, click the Font Color button arrow on the Ribbon to display the Font Color palette.

- Point to Dark Blue, Text 2 (dark blue color in column 4, row 1) in the Theme Colors area of the Font Color palette to see a live preview of the font color in cell A2 (Figure 1–56).

Experiment

- Point to several other colors in the Font Color palette to see a live preview of other font colors in cell A2.

Q&A Which colors does Excel make available on the Font Color palette?

Figure 1–56

You can choose from more than 60 different font colors on the Font Color palette (Figure 1–56). Your Font Color palette may have more or fewer colors, depending on color settings of your operating system. The Theme Colors area includes colors that are included in the current workbook's theme.

2

- Click Dark Blue, Text 2 (column 4, row 1) on the Font Color palette to change the font of the worksheet subtitle in cell A2 from black to dark blue (Figure 1–57).

Q&A

Why does the Font Color button change after I select the new font color?

When you choose a color on the Font Color palette, Excel changes the Font Color button on the Formatting toolbar to the chosen color. Thus, to change the font color of the cell entry in another cell to the same color, you need only to select the cell and then click the Font Color button.

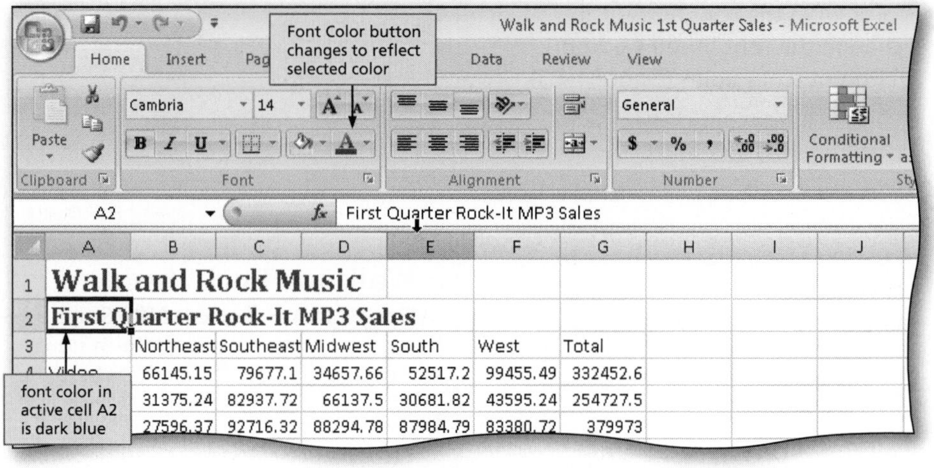

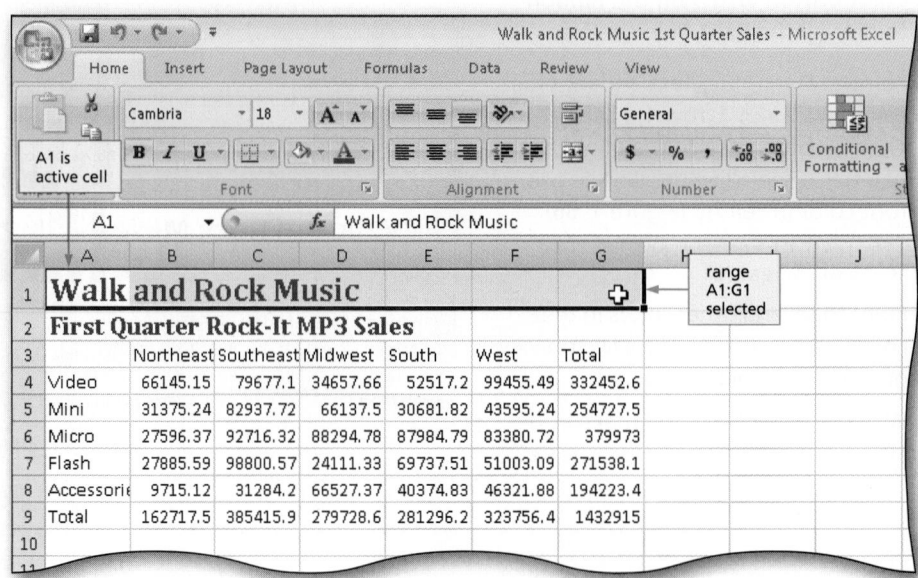

Figure 1–57

Other Ways

1. Select font color from Font Color list on Mini toolbar
2. Right-click cell, click Format Cells on shortcut menu, click Font tab, select color on Font Color palette, click OK button

To Center Cell Entries across Columns by Merging Cells

The final step in formatting the worksheet title and subtitle is to center them across columns A through G. Centering a title across the columns used in the body of the worksheet improves the worksheet's appearance. To do this, the seven cells in the range A1:G1 are combined, or merged, into a single cell that is the width of the columns in the body of the worksheet. The seven cells in the range A2:G2 also are merged in a similar manner. **Merging cells** involves creating a single cell by combining two or more selected cells. The following steps center the worksheet title and subtitle across columns by merging cells.

1

- Select cell A1 and then drag to cell G1 to highlight the range A1:G1 (Figure 1–58).

Q&A

What if a cell in the range B1:G1 contained data?

For the Merge & Center button to work properly, all the cells except the leftmost cell in the selected range must be empty.

Figure 1–58

2

- Click the Merge & Center button on the Ribbon to merge cells A1 through G1 and center the contents of cell A1 across columns A through G (Figure 1–59).

Q&A

What happened to cells B1 through G1?

After the merge, cells B1 through G1 no longer exist. Cell A1 now extends across columns A through G.

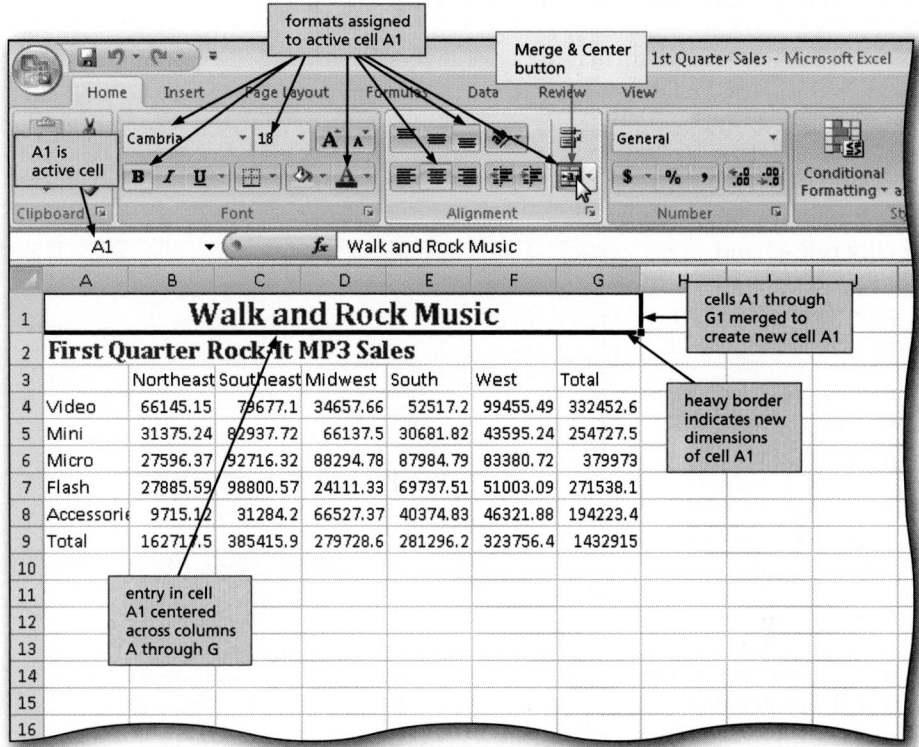

Figure 1–59

3

- Repeat Steps 1 and 2 to merge and center the worksheet subtitle across cells A2 through G2 (Figure 1–60).

Q&A

Are cells B1 through G1 and B2 through G2 lost forever?

No. The opposite of merging cells is **splitting a merged cell**. After you have merged multiple cells to create one merged cell, you can unmerge, or split, the merged cell to display the original cells on the worksheet. You split a merged cell by selecting it and clicking the Merge & Center button. For example, if you click the Merge & Center button a second time in Step 2, it will split the merged cell A1 to cells A1, B1, C1, D1, E1, F1, and G1.

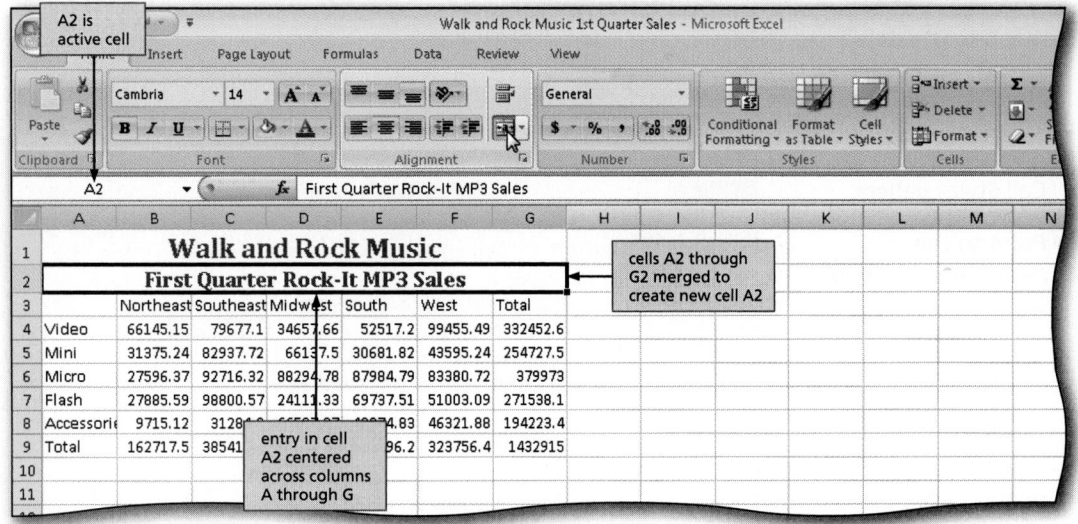

Figure 1–60

Other Ways
1. Right-click selection, click Merge & Center button on Mini toolbar
2. Right-click selection, click Format Cells on shortcut menu, click Alignment tab, select Center Across Selection in Horizontal list, click OK button

To Format Column Titles and the Total Row

The next step to format the worksheet is to format the column titles in row 3 and the total row, row 9. Column titles and the total row should be formatted so anyone who views the worksheet can quickly distinguish the column titles and total row from the data in the body of the worksheet. The following steps format the column titles and total row using cell styles in the default worksheet theme.

1

- Click cell A3 and then drag the mouse pointer to cell G3 to select the range A3:G3.

- Point to the Cell Styles button on the Ribbon (Figure 1–61).

Q&A

Why is cell A3 selected in the range for the column headings?

The style to be applied to the column headings includes an underline that will help to distinguish the column headings from the rest of the worksheet. Including cell A3 in the range ensures that the cell will include the underline, which is visually appealing and further helps to separate the data in the worksheet.

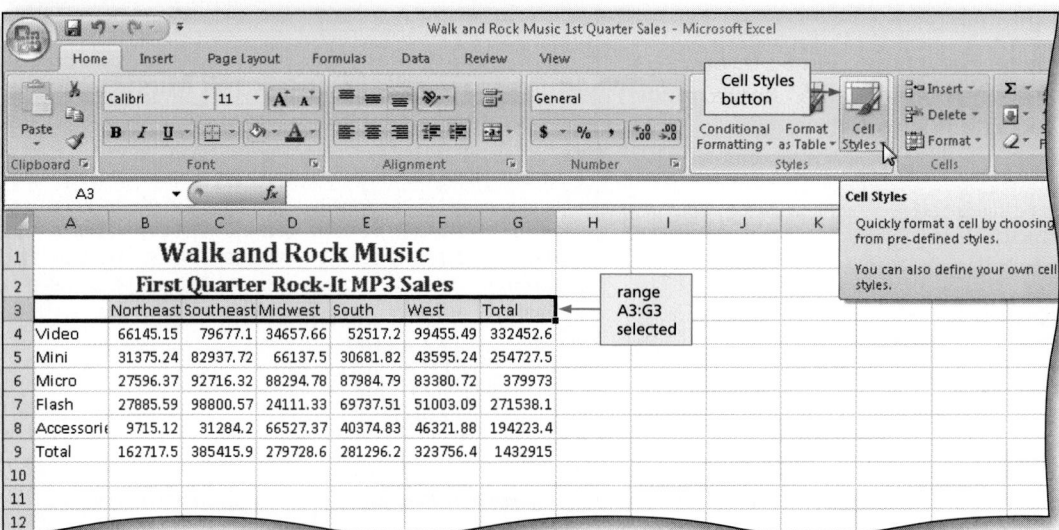

Figure 1–61

2

- Click the Cell Styles button to display the Cell Styles gallery.

- Point to the Heading 3 cell style in the Titles and Headings area of the Cell Styles gallery to see a live preview of the cell style in the range A3:G3 (Figure 1–62).

Experiment

- Point to other cell styles in the Titles and Headings area of the Cell Styles gallery to see a live preview of other cell styles in the range A3:G3.

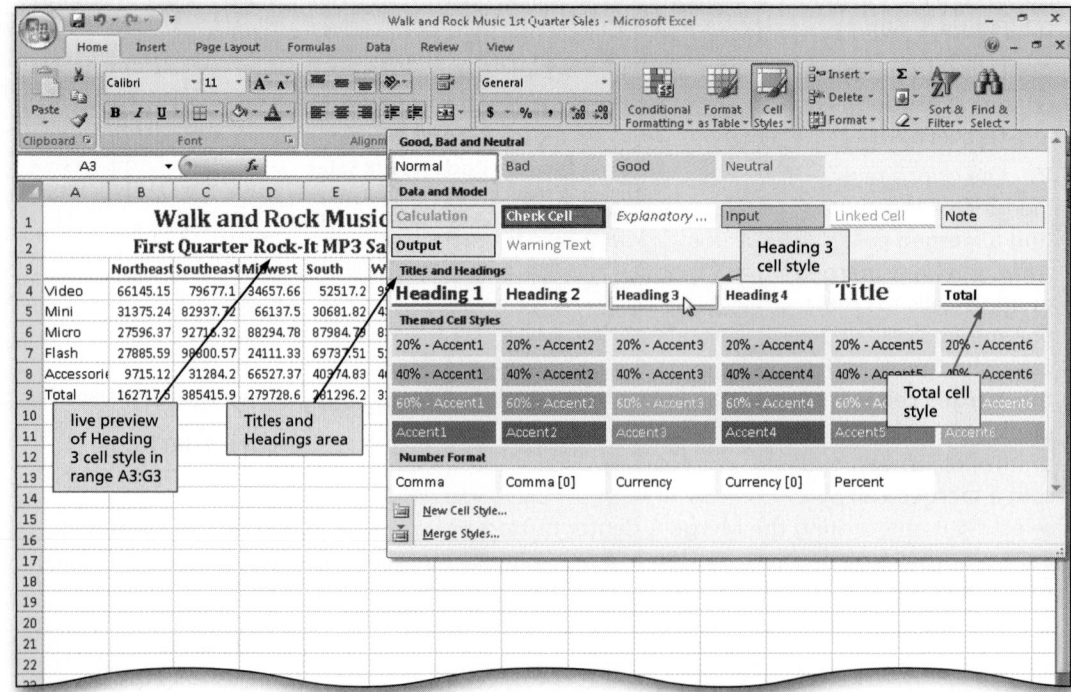

Figure 1–62

3

- Click the Heading 3 cell style to apply the cell style to the range A3:G3.

- Click cell A9 and then drag the mouse pointer to cell G9 to select the range A9:G9.

- Point to the Cell Styles button on the Ribbon (Figure 1–63).

Q&A

Why should I choose Heading 3 instead of another heading cell style?

Excel includes many types of headings, such as Heading 1 and Heading 2, because worksheets often include many levels of headings above columns. In the case of the worksheet created for this project, the Heading 3 title includes formatting that makes the column titles' font size smaller than the title and subtitle and makes the column titles stand out from the data in the body of the worksheet.

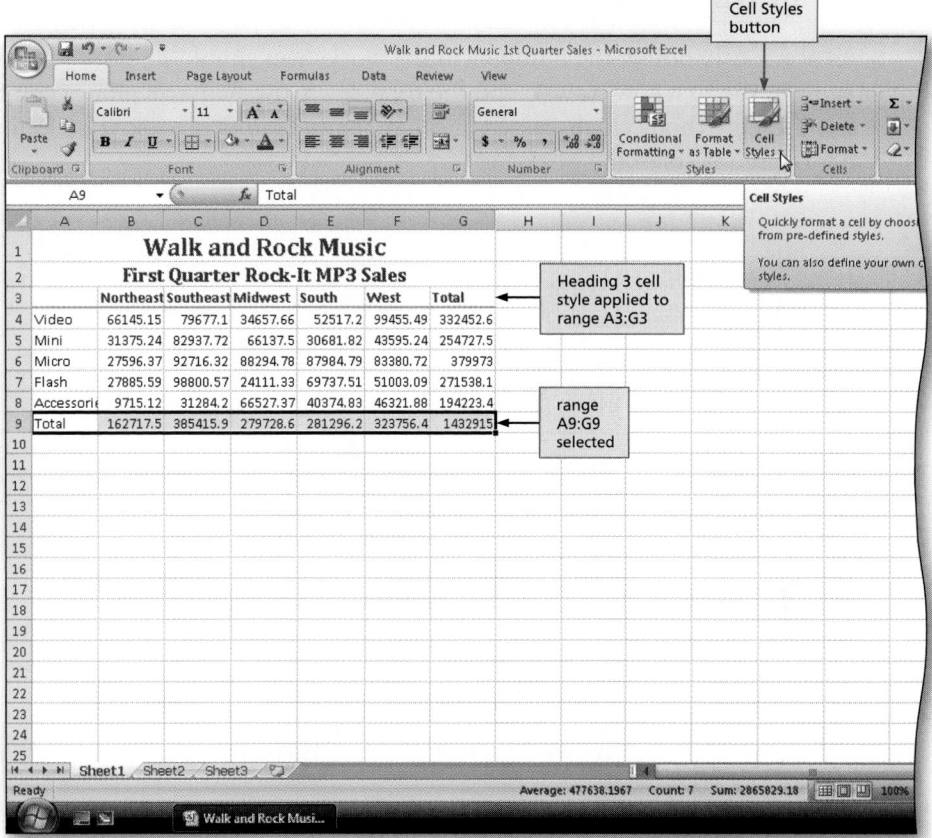

Figure 1–63

4

- Click the Cell Styles button on the Ribbon to display the Cell Styles gallery and then click the Total cell style in the Titles and Headings area to apply the Total cell style to the cells in the range A9:G9.

- Click cell A11 to select the cell (Figure 1–64).

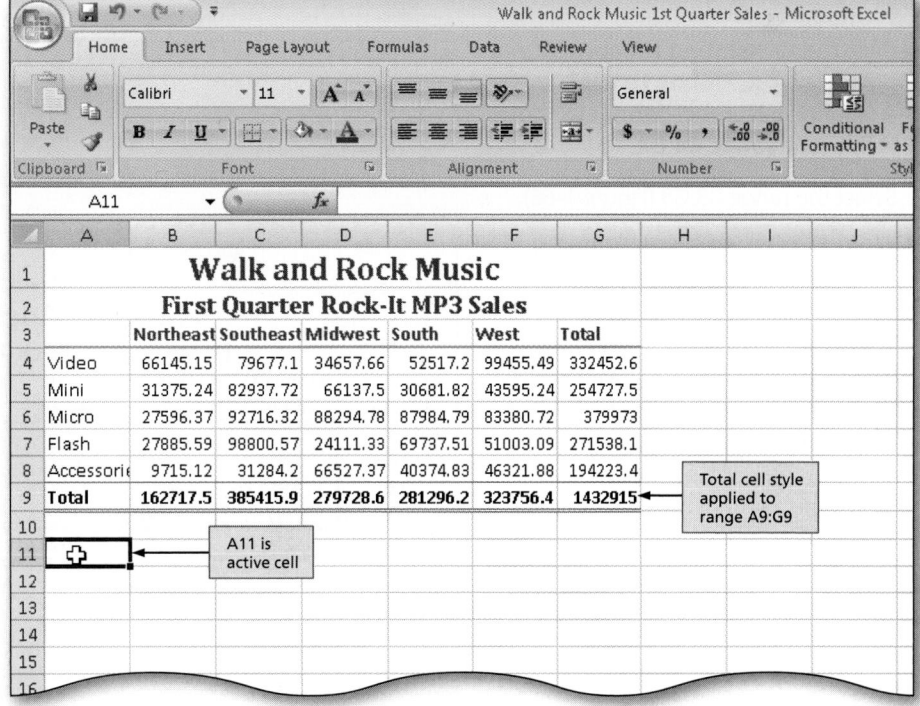

Figure 1–64

To Format Numbers in the Worksheet

As previously noted, the numbers in the worksheet should be formatted to use a dollar-and-cents format, with dollar signs in the first row (row 4) and the total row (row 9). Excel allows you to format numbers in a variety of ways, and these methods are discussed in other chapters in this book. The following steps use buttons on the Ribbon to format the numbers in the worksheet.

1

• Select cell B4 and drag the mouse pointer to cell G4 to select the range B4:G4.

• Point to the Accounting Number Format button on the Ribbon to display the Enhanced ScreenTip (Figure 1–65).

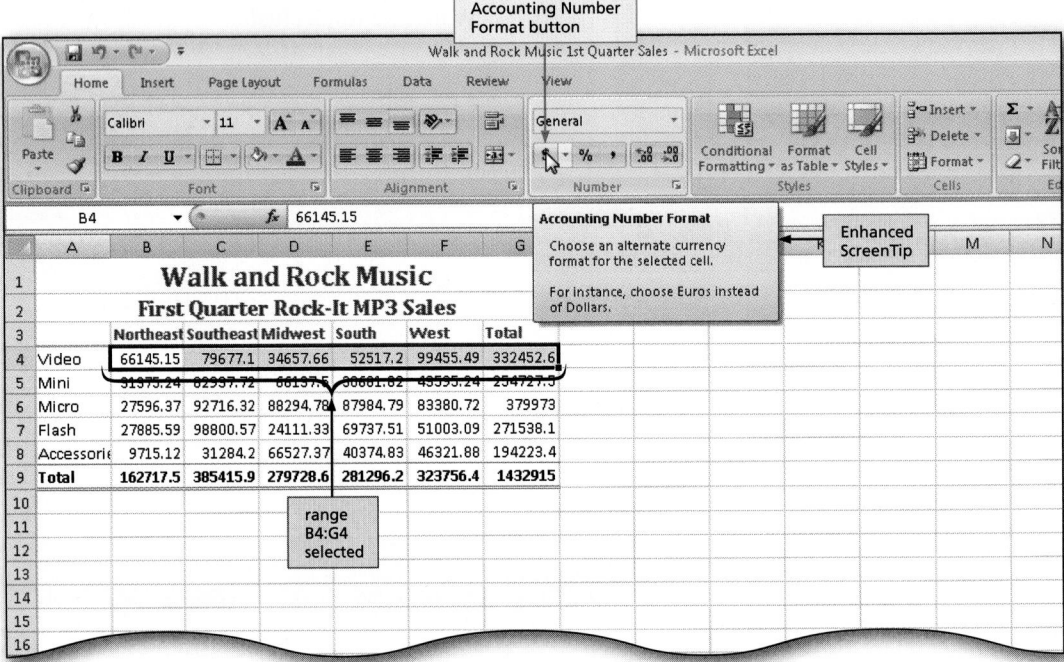

Figure 1–65

2

• Click the Accounting Number Format button on the Ribbon to apply the Accounting Number format to the cells in the range B4:G4.

• Select the range B5:G8 (Figure 1–66).

Q&A

What effect does the Accounting Number format have on the selected cells?

The Accounting Number format causes the cells to display with two decimal places so that decimal places in cells below the selected cells align vertically. Cell widths are automatically adjusted to accommodate the new formatting.

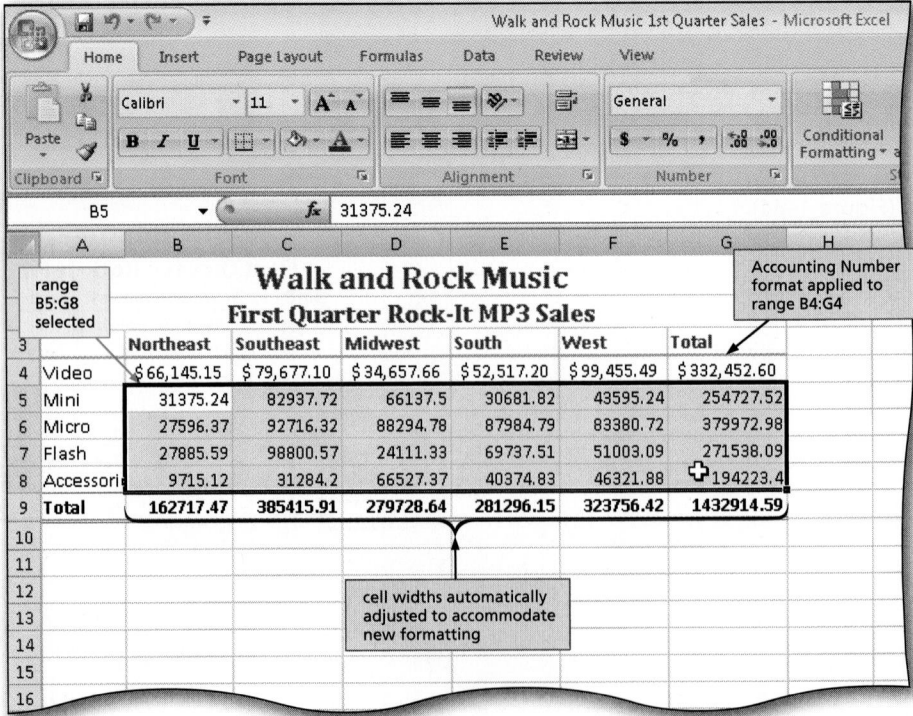

Figure 1–66

3

- Click the Comma Style button on the Ribbon to apply the Comma Style to the range B5:G8.

- Select the range B9:G9 (Figure 1–67).

Q&A

What effect does the Comma Style format have on the selected cells?

The Comma Style format causes the cells to display with two decimal places and commas as thousands separators.

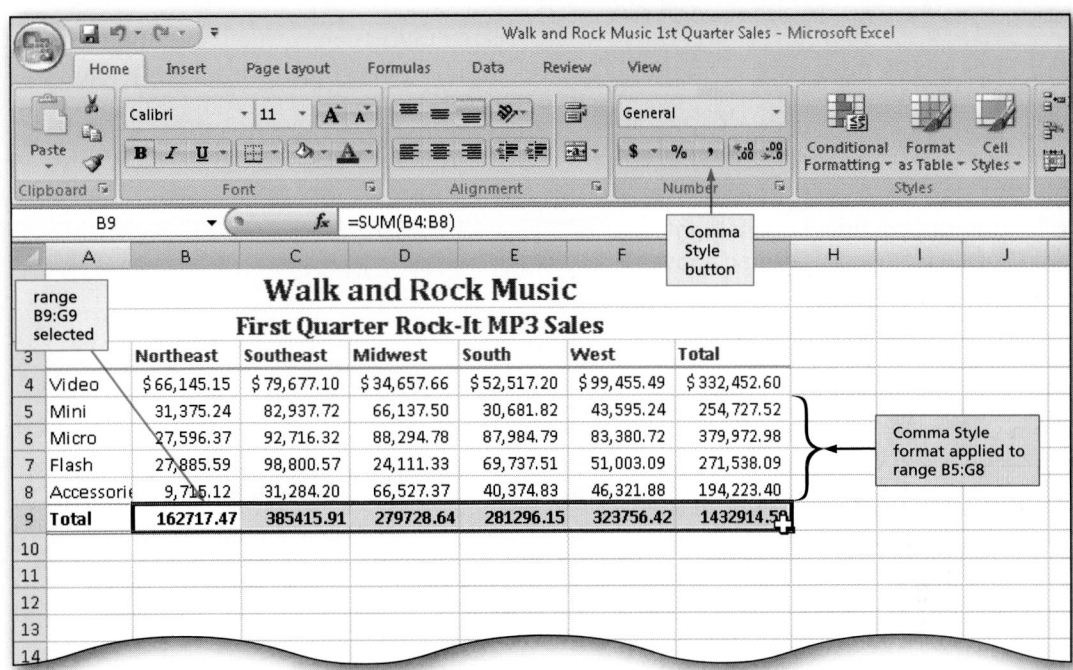

Figure 1–67

4

- Click the Accounting Number Format button on the Ribbon to apply the Accounting Number format to the cells in the range B9:G9.

- Select cell A11 (Figure 1-68).

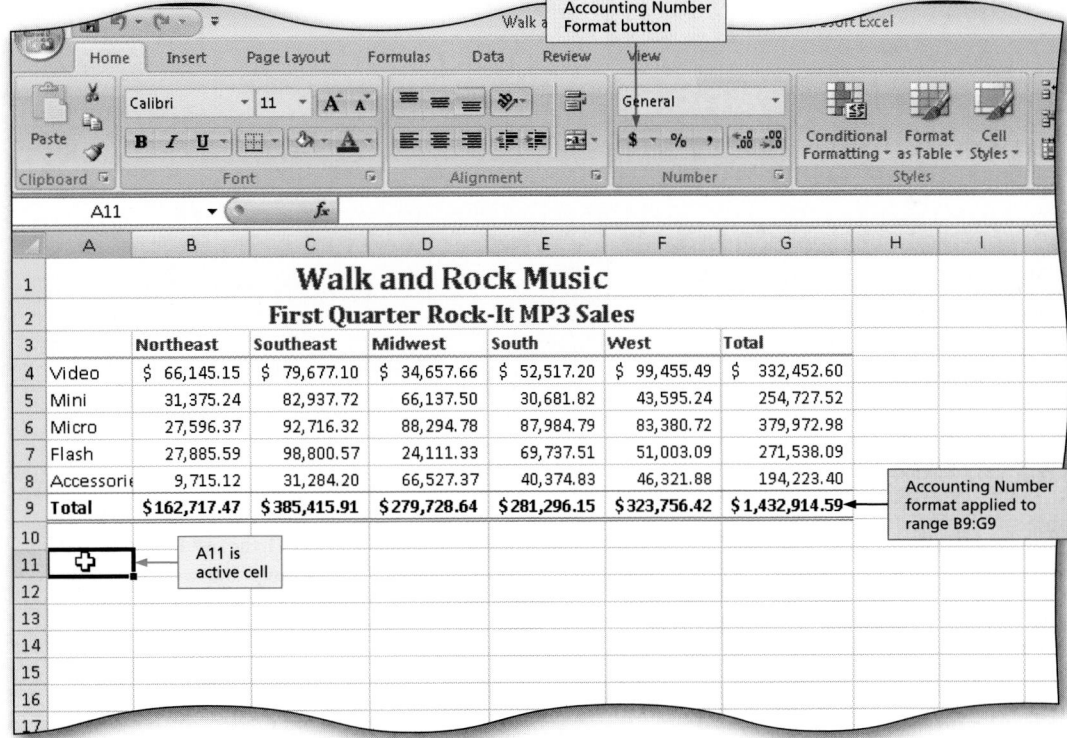

Figure 1–68

Other Ways
1. Click Accounting Number Format or Comma button on Mini toolbar	2. Right-click selection, click Format Cells on the shortcut menu, click Number tab, select Accounting in Category list or select Number and click Use 1000 Separator, click OK button

To Adjust the Column Width

The last step in formatting the worksheet is to adjust the width of column A so that the word Accessories in cell A8 is shown in its entirety in the cell. Excel includes several methods for adjusting cell widths and row heights, and these methods are discussed later in this book. The following steps adjust the width of column A so that the contents of cell A8 are displayed in the cell.

1

- Point to the boundary on the right side of the column A heading above row 1 to change the mouse pointer to a split double arrow (Figure 1–69).

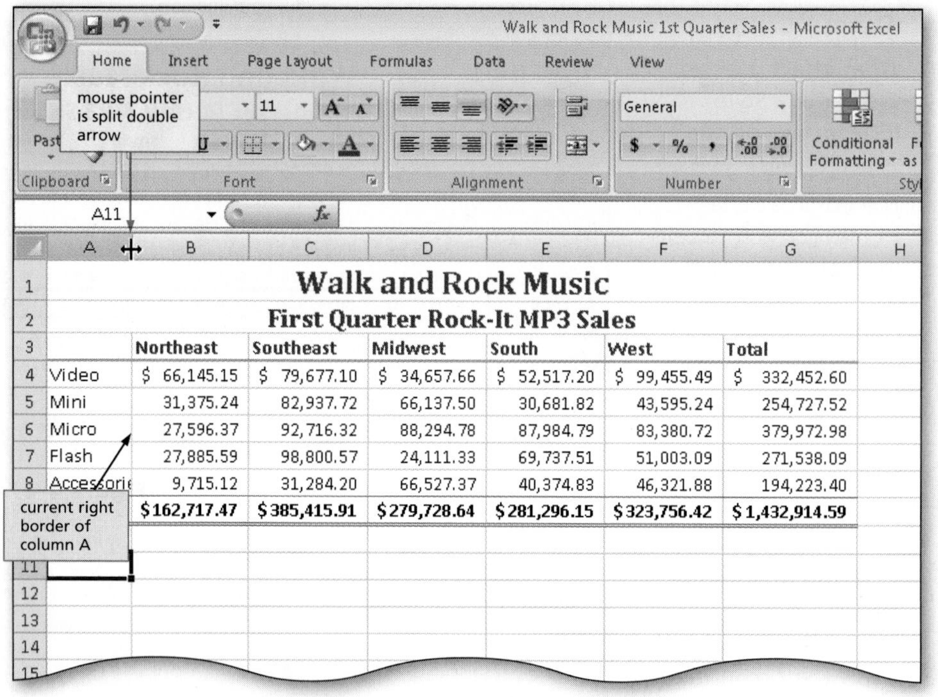

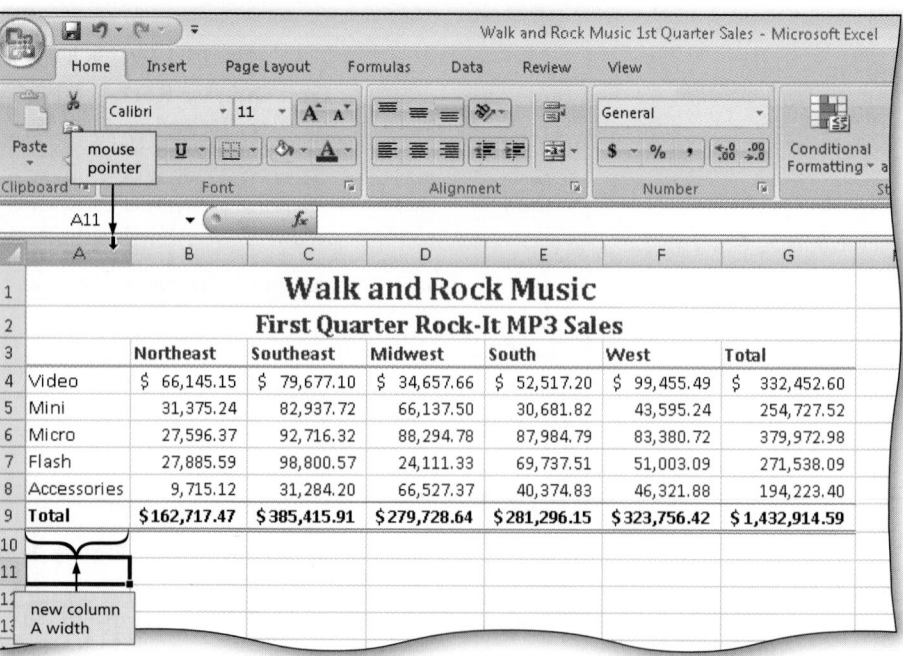

Figure 1–69

2

- Double-click on the boundary to adjust the width of column A to the width of the largest item in the column (Figure 1–70).

Q&A

What if none of the items in column A extended through the entire width of the column?

If all of the items in column A were shorter in length than the width of the column when you double-click the right side of the column A heading, then Excel still would adjust the column width to the largest item in the column. That is, Excel would reduce the width of the column to the largest item.

Figure 1–70

Using the Name Box to Select a Cell

The next step is to chart the quarterly sales for the five product types sold by the company. To create the chart, you must select the cell in the upper-left corner of the range to chart (cell A3). Rather than clicking cell A3 to select it, the next section describes how to use the Name box to select the cell.

To Use the Name Box to Select a Cell

As previously noted, the Name box is located on the left side of the formula bar. To select any cell, click the Name box and enter the cell reference of the cell you want to select. The following steps select cell A3.

1

- Click the Name box in the formula bar and then type a3 as the cell to select (Figure 1–71).

Q&A

Why is cell A11 still selected?

Even though cell A11 is the active cell, Excel displays the typed cell reference a3 in the Name box until you press the ENTER key.

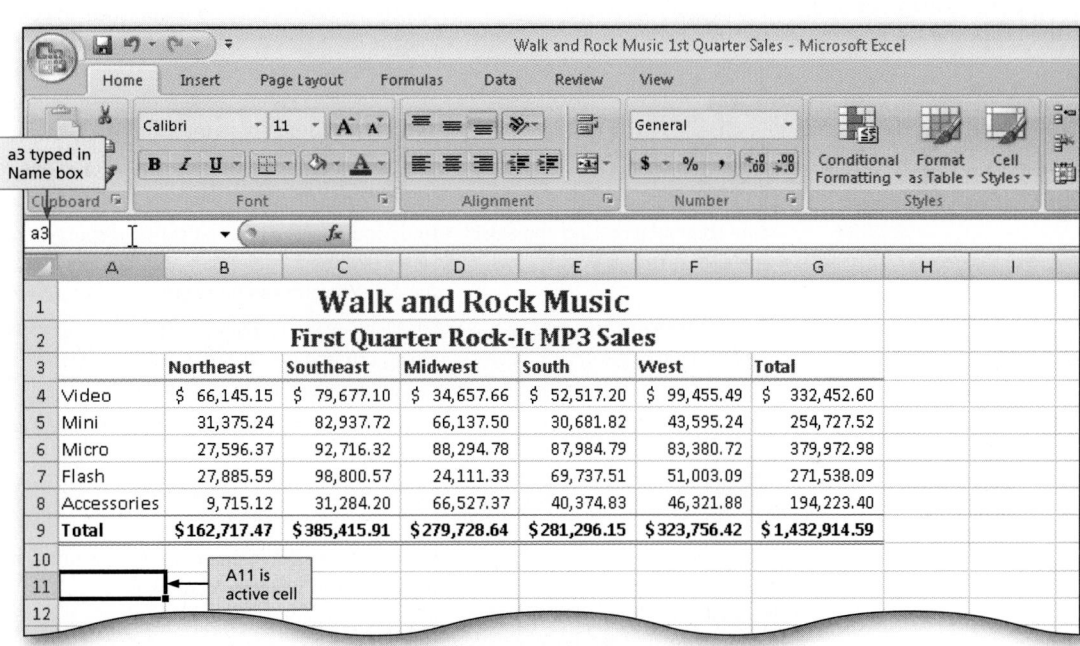

Figure 1–71

2

- Press the ENTER key to change the active cell from A11 to cell A3 (Figure 1–72).

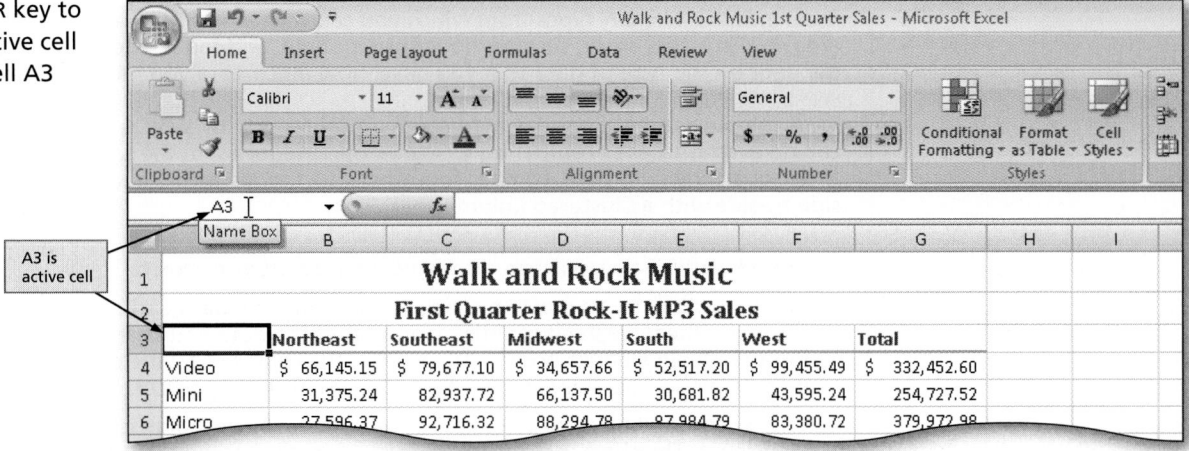

Figure 1–72

Other Ways to Select Cells

As you will see in later chapters, in addition to using the Name box to select any cell in a worksheet, you also can use it to assign names to a cell or range of cells. Excel supports several additional ways to select a cell, as summarized in Table 1–3.

BTW

Find & Select
You can find and select cells based on their content. Click the Find & Select button on the Home tab on the Ribbon. Then, click the Go To Special command. Choose your desired option in the Select area of the Go To Special dialog box and then click the OK button.

Table 1–3 Selecting Cells in Excel

Key, Box, or Command	Function
ALT+PAGE DOWN	Selects the cell one worksheet window to the right and moves the worksheet window accordingly.
ALT+PAGE UP	Selects the cell one worksheet window to the left and moves the worksheet window accordingly.
ARROW	Selects the adjacent cell in the direction of the arrow on the key.
CTRL+ARROW	Selects the border cell of the worksheet in combination with the arrow keys and moves the worksheet window accordingly. For example, to select the rightmost cell in the row that contains the active cell, press CTRL+RIGHT ARROW. You also can press the END key, release it, and then press the appropriate arrow key to accomplish the same task.
CTRL+HOME	Selects cell A1 or the cell one column and one row below and to the right of frozen titles and moves the worksheet window accordingly.
Find command on Find and Select menu or SHIFT+F5	Finds and selects a cell that contains specific contents that you enter in the Find dialog box. If necessary, Excel moves the worksheet window to display the cell. You also can press CTRL+F to display the Find dialog box.
Go To command on Find and Select menu or F5	Selects the cell that corresponds to the cell reference you enter in the Go To dialog box and moves the worksheet window accordingly. You also can press CTRL+G to display the Go To dialog box.
HOME	Selects the cell at the beginning of the row that contains the active cell and moves the worksheet window accordingly.
Name box	Selects the cell in the workbook that corresponds to the cell reference you enter in the Name box.
PAGE DOWN	Selects the cell down one worksheet window from the active cell and moves the worksheet window accordingly.
PAGE UP	Selects the cell up one worksheet window from the active cell and moves the worksheet window accordingly.

Plan Ahead

Decide on the type of chart needed.
Excel includes 11 chart types from which you can choose including column, line, pie, bar, area, X Y (scatter), stock, surface, doughnut, bubble, and radar. The type of chart you choose depends on the type of data that you have, how much data you have, and the message you want to convey.

A column chart is a good way to compare values side-by-side. A Clustered Column chart can go even further in comparing values across categories. In the case of the Walk and Rock Music quarterly sales data, comparisons of product types within each region can be made side-by-side with a Clustered Column chart.

Establish where to position and how to format the chart.

- When possible, try to position charts so that both the data and chart appear on the screen on the worksheet together and so that the data and chart can be printed in the most readable manner possible. By placing the chart below the data on the Walk and Rock Music 1st Quarter Sales worksheet, both of these goals are accomplished.

- When choosing/selecting colors for a chart, consider the color scheme of the rest of the worksheet. The chart should not present colors that are in stark contrast to the rest of the worksheet. If the chart will be printed in color, minimize the amount of dark colors on the chart so that the chart both prints quickly and preserves ink.

Adding a 3-D Clustered Column Chart to the Worksheet

As outlined in the requirements document in Figure 1–2 on page EX 4, the worksheet should include a 3-D Clustered Column chart to graphically represent quarterly sales for each product type that the company sells. The 3-D Clustered Column chart shown in Figure 1–73 is called an **embedded chart** because it is drawn on the same worksheet as the data.

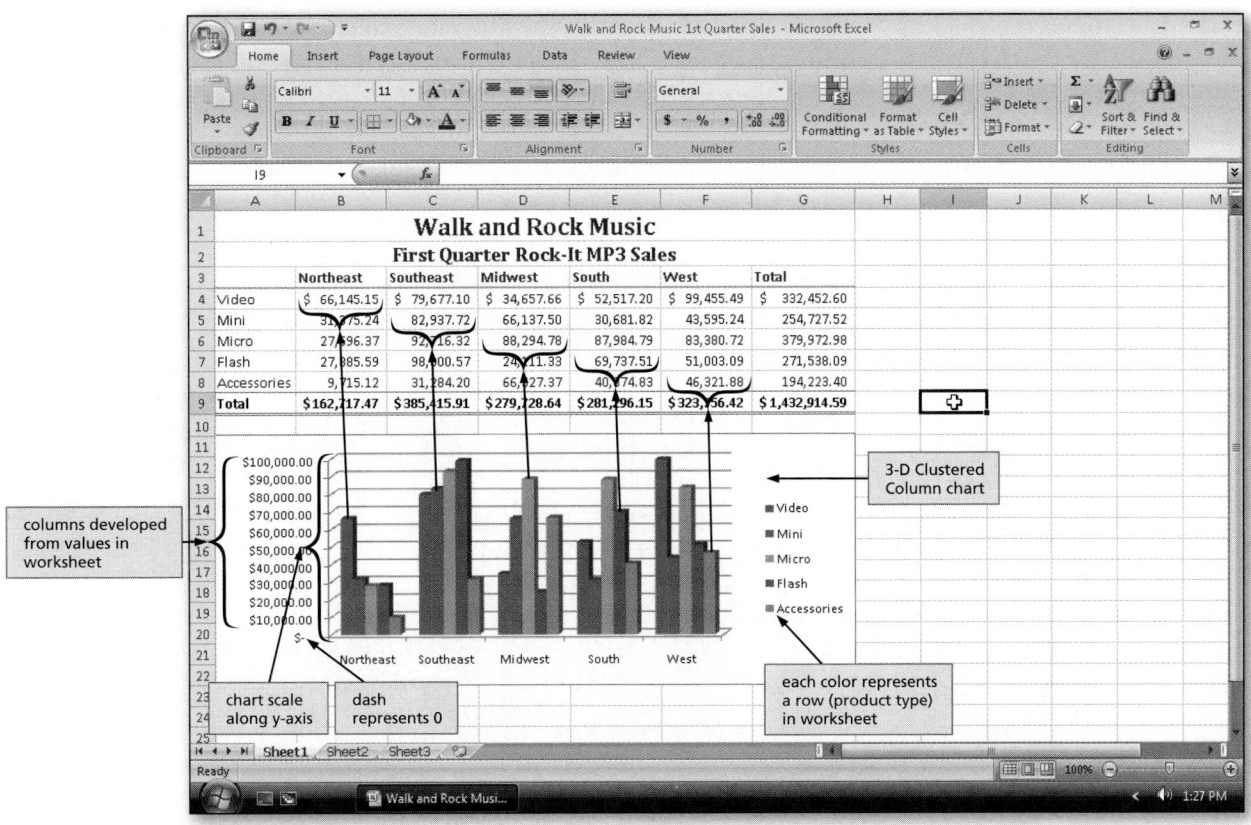

Figure 1–73

The chart uses different colored columns to represent sales for different product types. Each region uses the same color scheme for identifying product types, which allows for easy identification and comparison. For the Northeast sales region, for example, the dark blue column representing Video products shows quarterly sales of $66,145.15; for the Southeast sales region, the maroon column representing Mini products shows quarterly sales of $82,937.72; for the Midwest sales region, the pale green column representing Micro products shows quarterly sales of $88,294.78; for the South sales region, the violet column representing Flash products shows quarterly sales of $69,737.51; and for the West sales region, the light blue column representing Accessories shows quarterly sales of $46,321.88. Because the same color scheme is used in each region to represent the five product types, you easily can compare sales of product types among the sales regions. The totals from the worksheet are not represented, because the totals are not in the range specified for charting.

BTW

Cell Values and Charting
When you change a cell value on which a chart is dependent, Excel redraws the chart instantaneously, unless automatic recalculation is disabled. If automatic recalculation is disabled, then you must press the F9 key to redraw the chart. To enable or disable automatic recalculation, click the Calculations Options button on the Formulas tab on the Ribbon.

Excel derives the chart scale based on the values in the worksheet and then displays the scale along the vertical axis (also called the **y-axis** or **value axis**) of the chart. For example, no value in the range B4:F8 is less than 0 or greater than $100,000.00, so the scale ranges from 0 to $100,000.00. Excel also determines the $10,000.00 increments of the scale automatically. For the numbers along the y-axis, Excel uses a format that includes representing the 0 value with a dash (Figure 1–73 on the previous page).

To Add a 3-D Clustered Column Chart to the Worksheet

The commands to insert a chart are located on the Insert tab. With the range to chart selected, you click the Column button on the Ribbon to initiate drawing the chart. The area on the worksheet where the chart appears is called the chart location. As shown in Figure 1–73, the chart location in this worksheet is the range A11:G22, immediately below the worksheet data.

The following steps draw a 3-D Clustered Column chart that compares the quarterly sales by product type for the five sales regions.

- Click cell A3 and then drag the mouse pointer to the cell F8 to select the range A3:F8 (Figure 1–74).

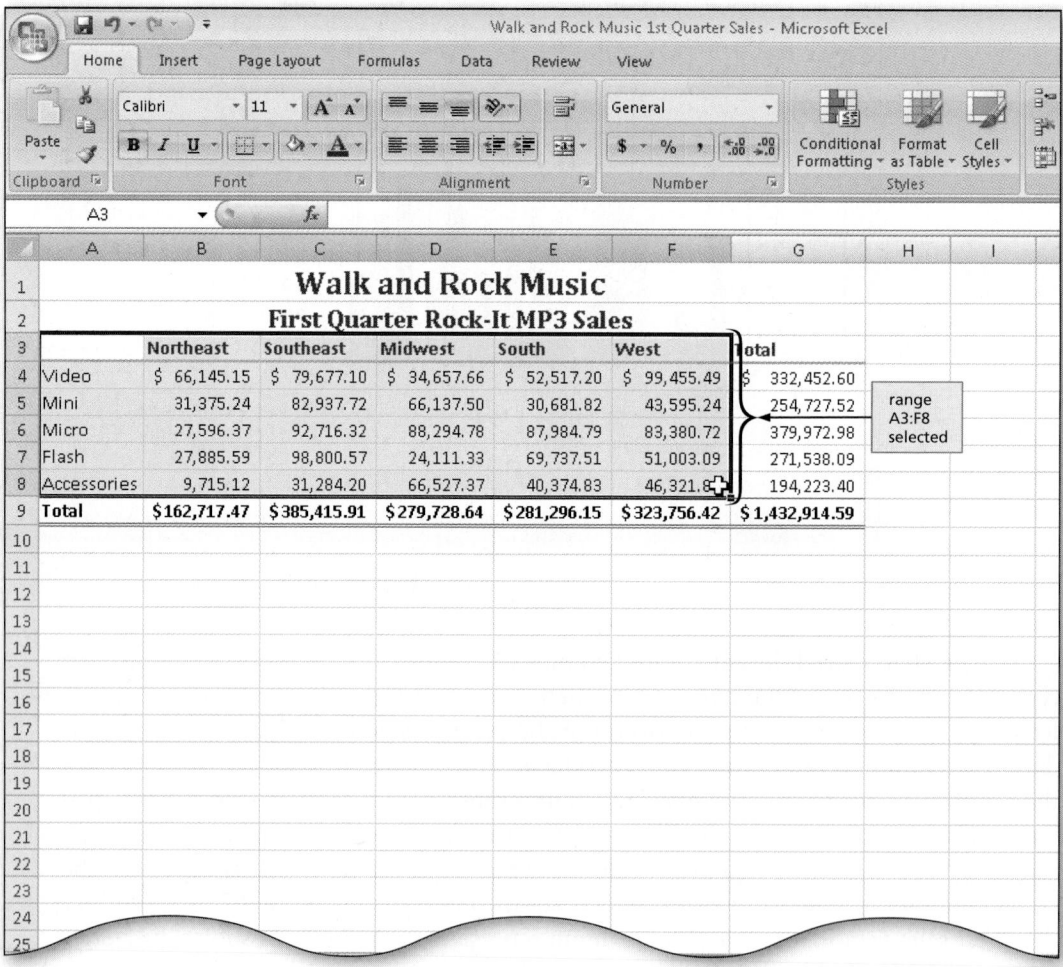

Figure 1–74

2

- Click the Insert tab to make the Insert tab the active tab (Figure 1–75).

Q&A

What tasks can I perform with the Insert tab?

The Insert tab includes commands that allow you to insert various objects, such as shapes, tables, illustrations, and charts, into a work-sheet. These objects will be discussed as they are used throughout this book.

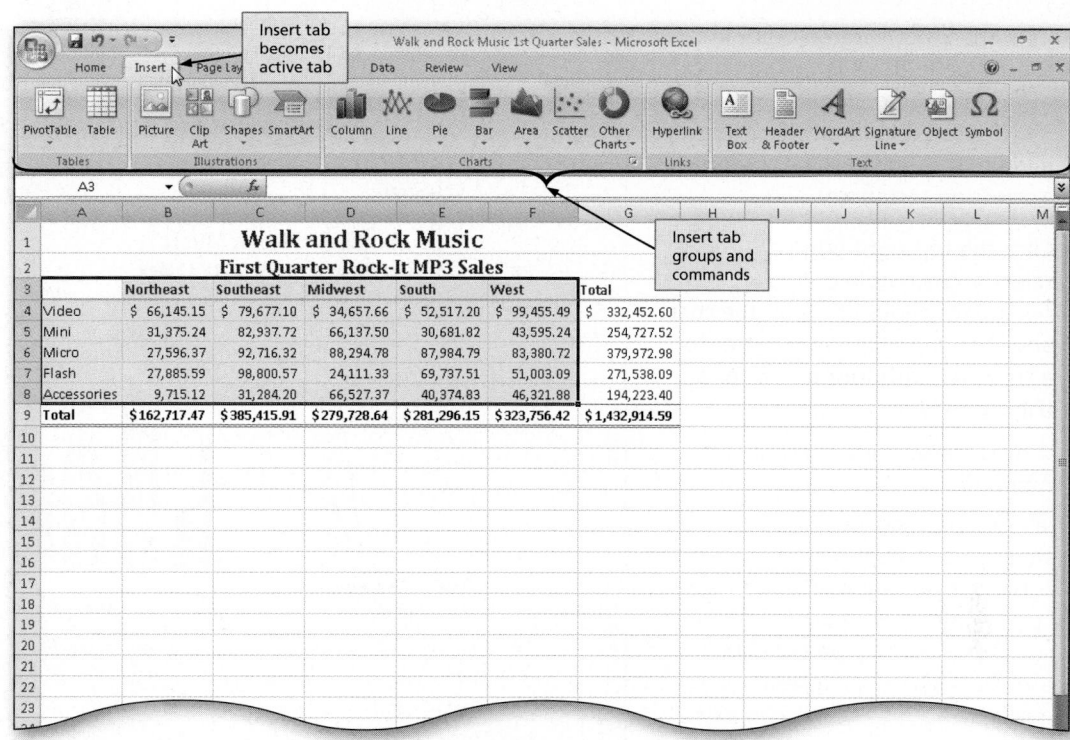

Figure 1–75

3

- Click the Column button on the Ribbon to display the Column gallery.

- Point to the 3-D Clustered Column chart type in the 3-D Column area of the Column gallery (Figure 1–76).

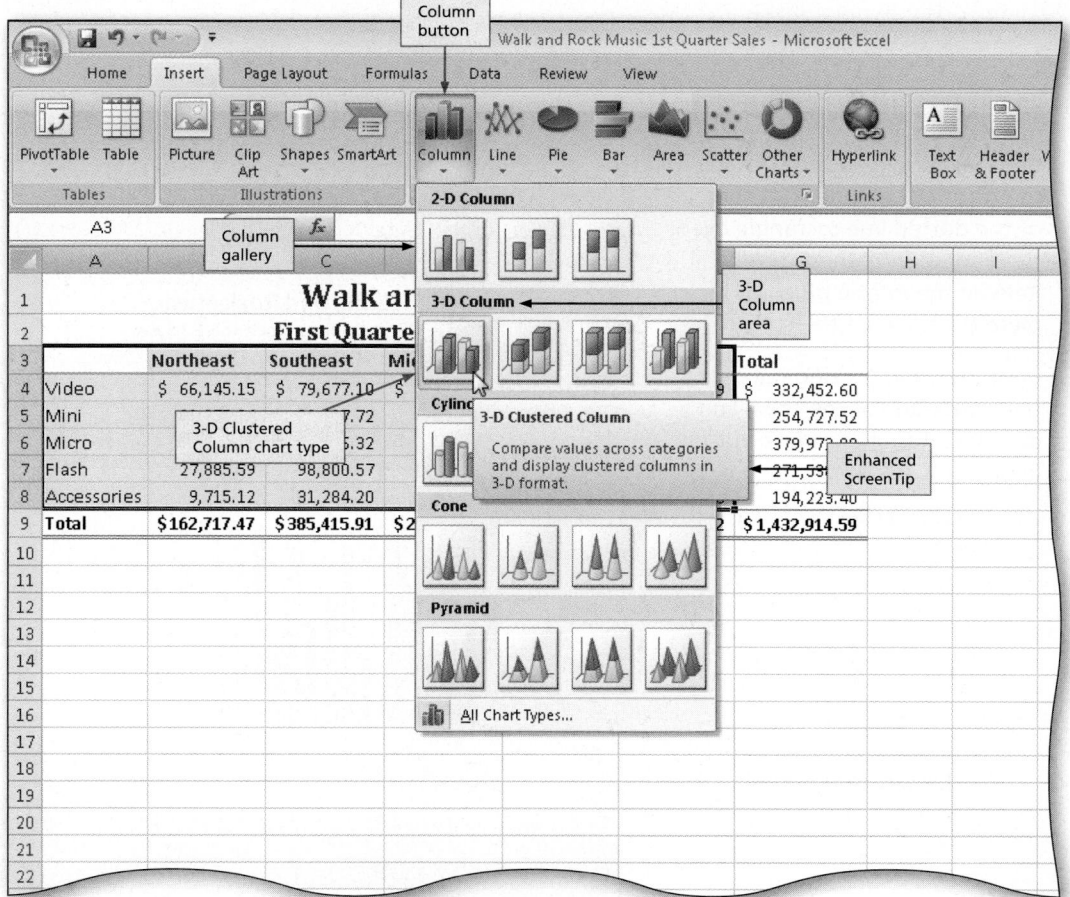

Figure 1–76

4

- Click the 3-D Clustered Column chart type in the 3-D Column area of the Column gallery to add a 3-D Clustered Column chart to the middle of the worksheet in a selection rectangle.

- Click the top-right edge of the selection rectangle but do not release the mouse to grab the chart and change the mouse pointer to a crosshair with four arrowheads (Figure 1–77).

Why is a new tab displayed on the Ribbon?

When you select objects such as shapes or charts, Excel displays contextual tabs that include special commands that are used to work with the type of object selected. Because a chart is selected, Excel displays the Chart Tools contextual tab. The three tabs below the Chart Tools contextual tab, Design, Layout, and Format, are tabs that include commands to work with charts.

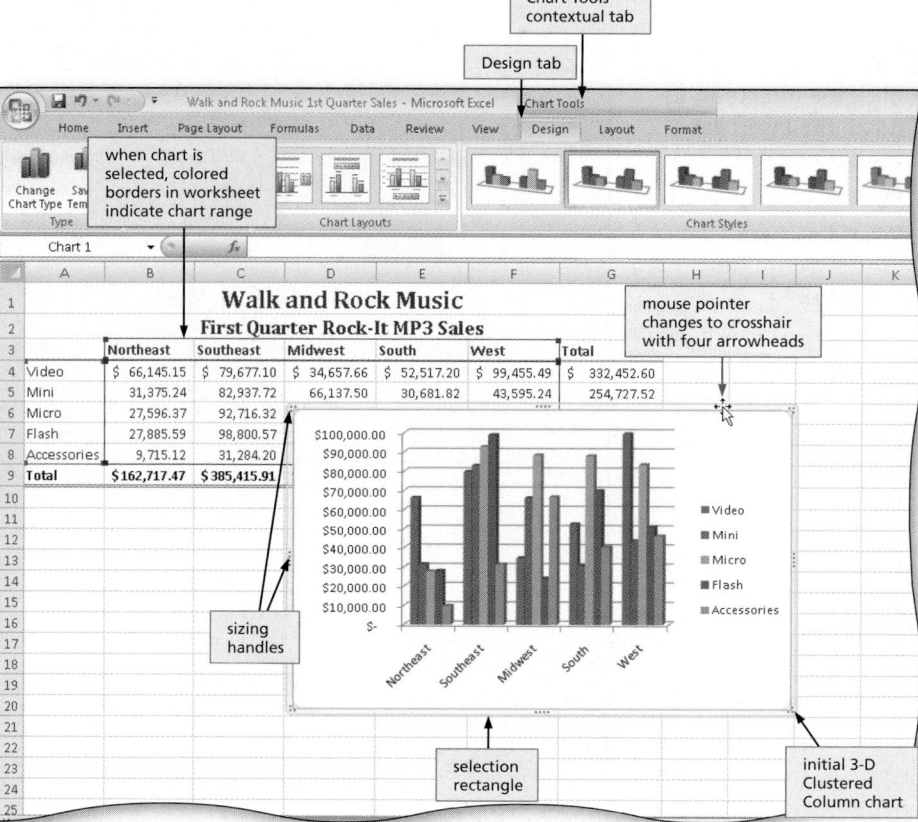

Figure 1–77

5

- Continue holding down the left mouse button while dragging the chart down and to the left to position the upper-left corner of the dotted line rectangle over the upper-left corner of cell A11. Release the mouse button to complete the move of the chart.

- Click the middle sizing handle on the right edge of the chart and do not release the mouse button (Figure 1–78).

How does Excel know how to create the chart?

Excel automatically selects the entries in the topmost row of the chart range (row 3) as the titles for the horizontal axis (also called the **x-axis** or **category axis**) and draws a column for each of the 25 cells in the range containing numbers.

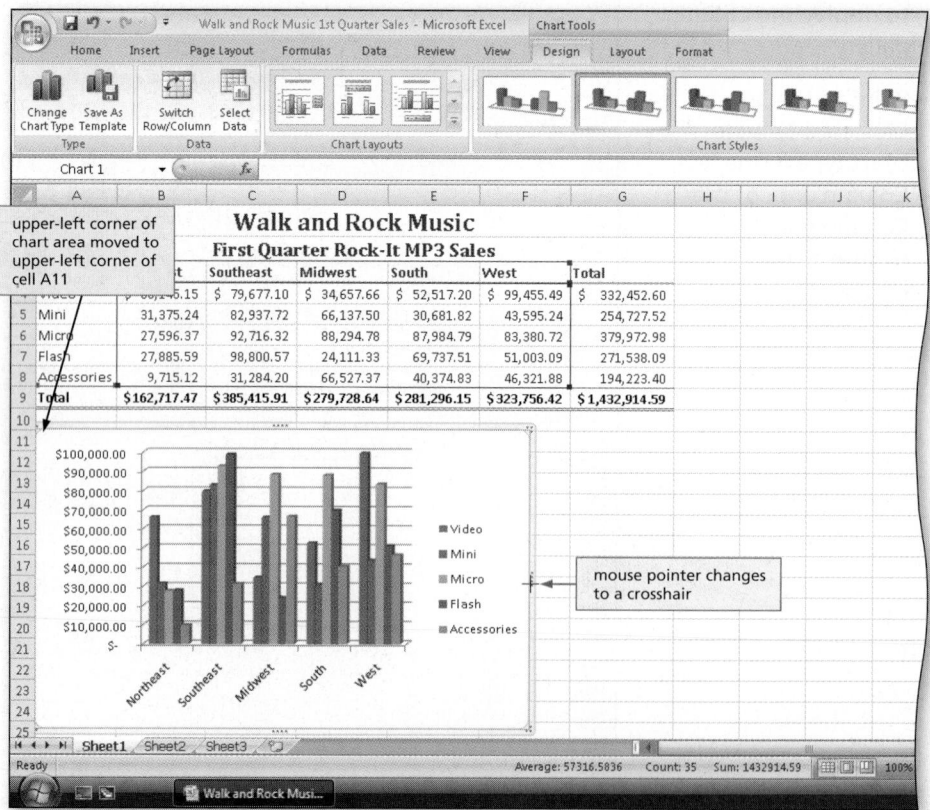

Figure 1–78

6

- While continuing to hold down the mouse button, press the ALT key and drag the right edge of the chart to the right edge of column G and then release the mouse button to resize the chart.

- Point to the middle sizing handle on the bottom edge of the selection rectangle and do not release the mouse button (Figure 1–79).

 Why should I hold the ALT key down while I resize a chart?

Holding down the ALT key while you drag a chart **snaps** (aligns) the edge of the chart area to the worksheet gridlines. If you do not hold down the ALT key, then you can place an edge of a chart in the middle of a column or row.

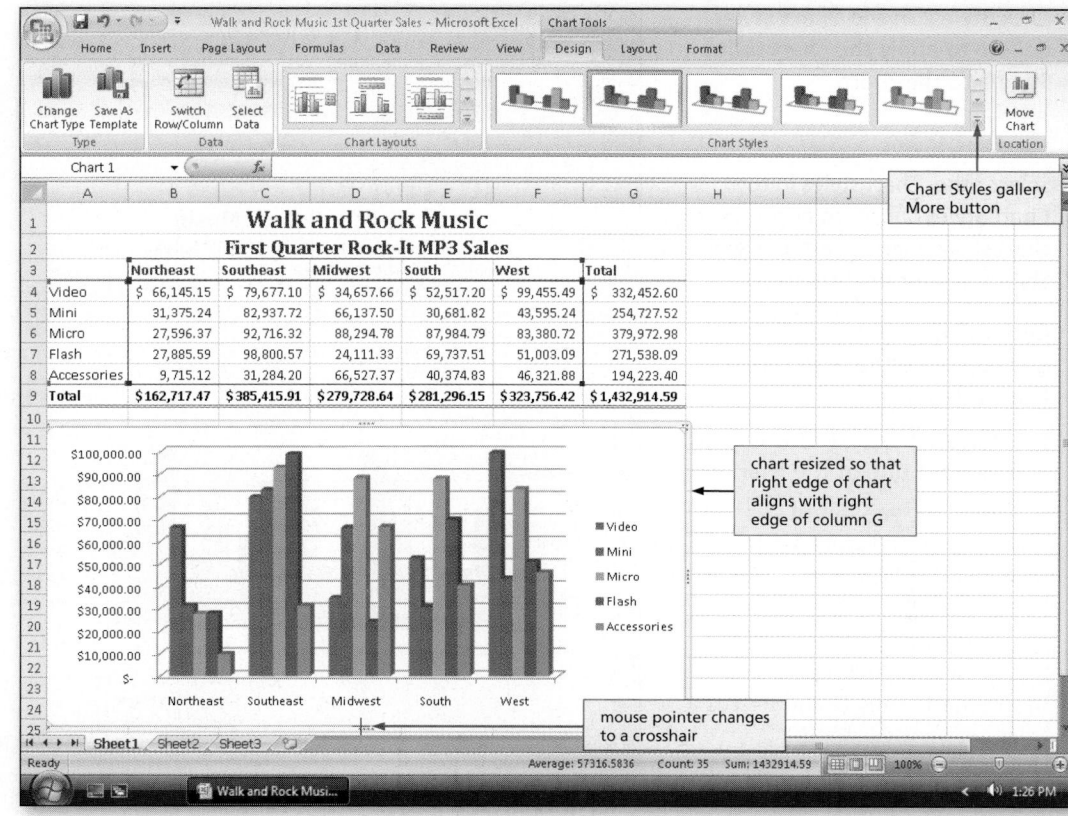

Figure 1–79

7

- While continuing to hold down the mouse button, press the ALT key and drag the bottom edge of the chart up to the bottom edge of row 22 and then release the mouse button to resize the chart.

- Click the More button in the Chart Styles gallery to expand the gallery and point to Style 2 in the gallery (column 2, row 1) (Figure 1–80).

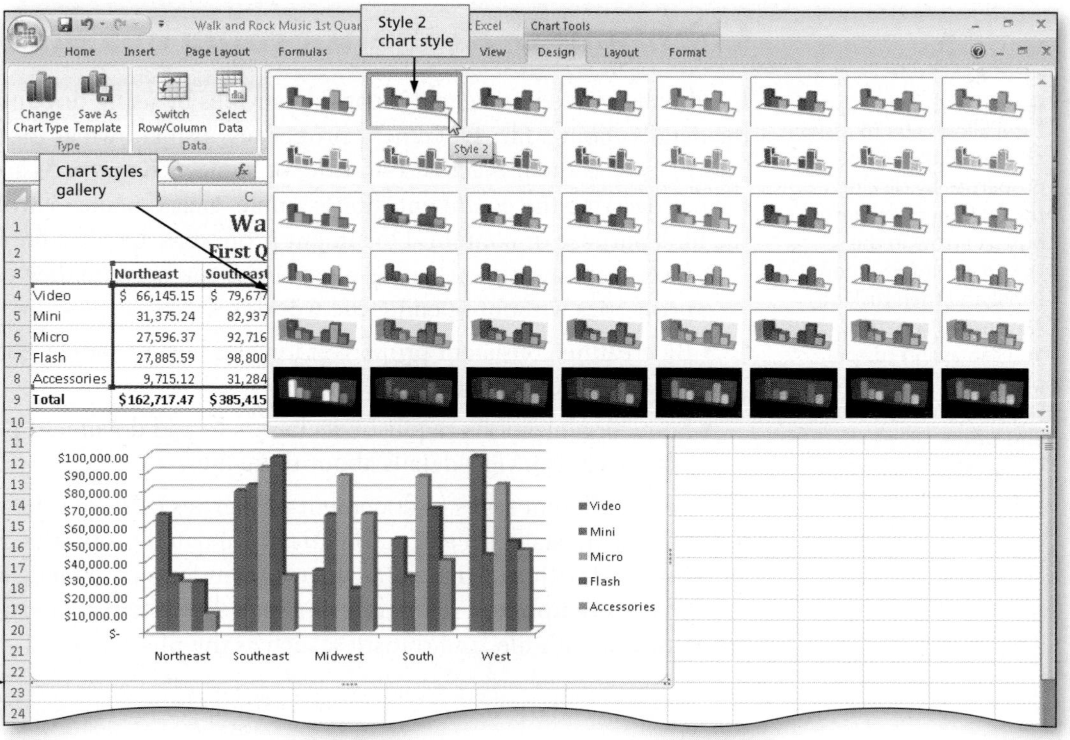

Figure 1–80

8

- Click Style 2 in the Chart Styles gallery to apply the chart style Style 2 to the chart.

Experiment

- Select other chart styles in the Chart Styles gallery to apply other chart styles to the chart, but select Style 2 as your final choice.

- Click cell I9 to deselect the chart and complete the worksheet (Figure 1–81).

Q&A

What is the purpose of the items on the right side of the chart?

The items to the right of the column chart in Figure 1–81 are the **legend**, which identifies the colors assigned to each bar in the chart. Excel automatically selects the entries in the leftmost column of the chart range (column A) as titles within the legend.

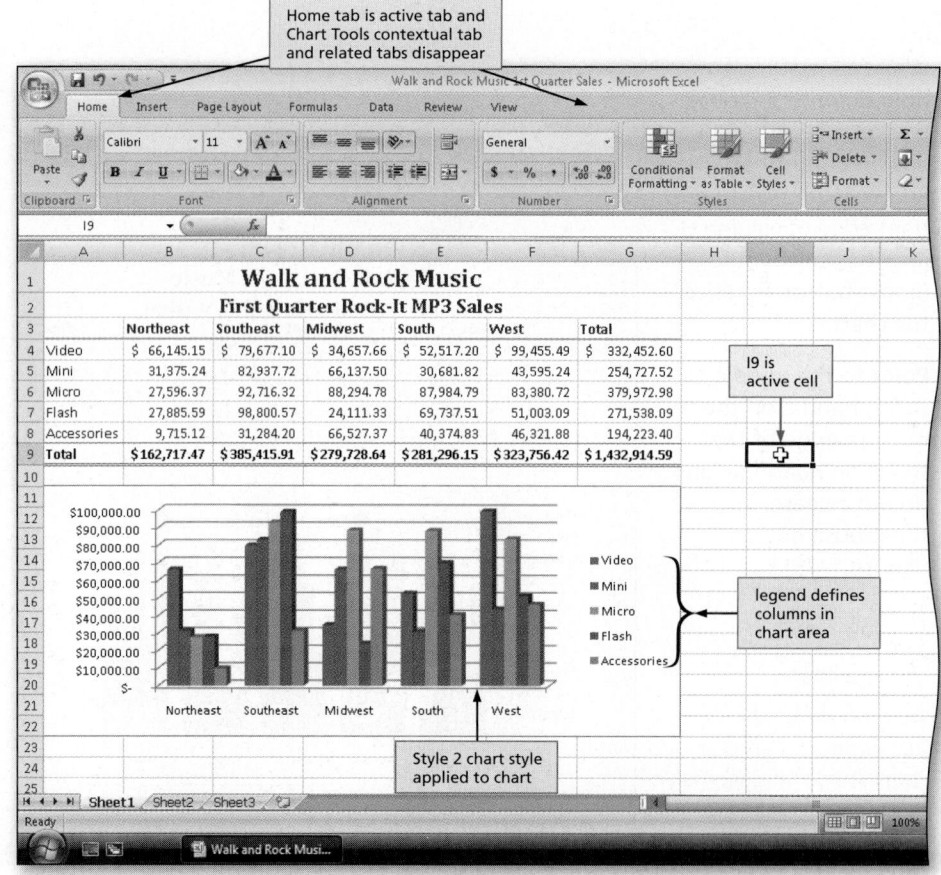

Figure 1–81

Changing Document Properties and Saving Again

BTW

Document Properties
Excel allows you to assign additional document properties by clicking the Document Properties button arrow in the Document Information Panel and then clicking Advanced Properties. You can assign custom properties, such as Department, Purpose, and Editor. Or, you can create your own document properties.

Excel helps you organize and identify your files by using **document properties**, which are the details about a file. Document properties, also known as **metadata**, can include such information as the project author, title, or subject. **Keywords** are words or phrases that further describe the document. For example, a class name or worksheet topic can describe the file's purpose or content. Document properties are valuable for a variety of reasons:

- Users can save time locating a particular file because they can view a document's properties without opening the workbook.

- By creating consistent properties for files having similar content, users can better organize their workbooks.

- Some organizations require Excel users to add document properties so that other employees can view details about these files.

Five different types of document properties exist, but the more common ones used in this book are standard and automatically updated properties. **Standard properties** are associated with all Microsoft Office documents and include author, title, and subject. **Automatically updated properties** include file system properties, such as the date you create or change a file, and statistics, such as the file size.

To Change Document Properties

The **Document Information Panel** contains areas where you can view and enter document properties. You can view and change information in this panel at any time while you are creating your workbook. Before saving the workbook again, you want to add your name and class name as document properties. The following steps use the Document Information Panel to change document properties.

- Click the Office Button to display the Office Button menu.

- Point to Prepare on the Office Button menu to display the Prepare submenu (Figure 1–82).

Q&A

What other types of actions besides changing properties can you take to prepare a document for distribution?

The Prepare submenu provides commands related to sharing a document with others, such as allowing or restricting people to view and modify your document, checking to see if your worksheet will work in earlier versions of Excel, and searching for hidden personal information.

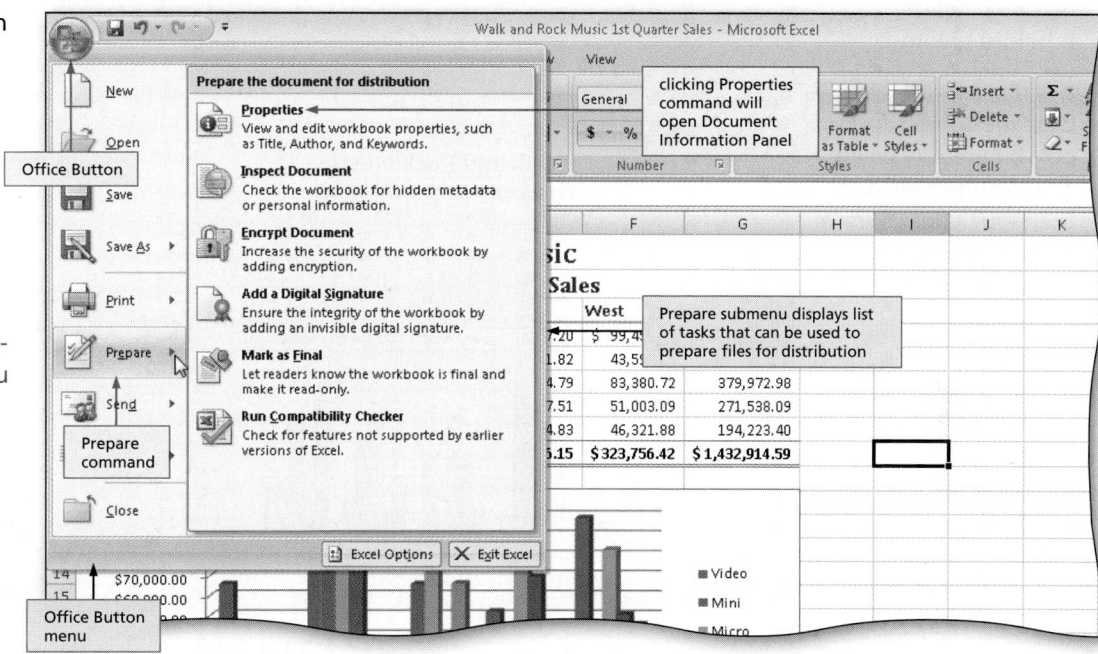

Figure 1–82

- Click Properties on the Prepare submenu to display the Document Information Panel (Figure 1–83).

Q&A

Why are some of the document properties in my Document Information Panel already filled in?

The person who installed Microsoft Office 2007 on your computer or network may have set or customized the properties.

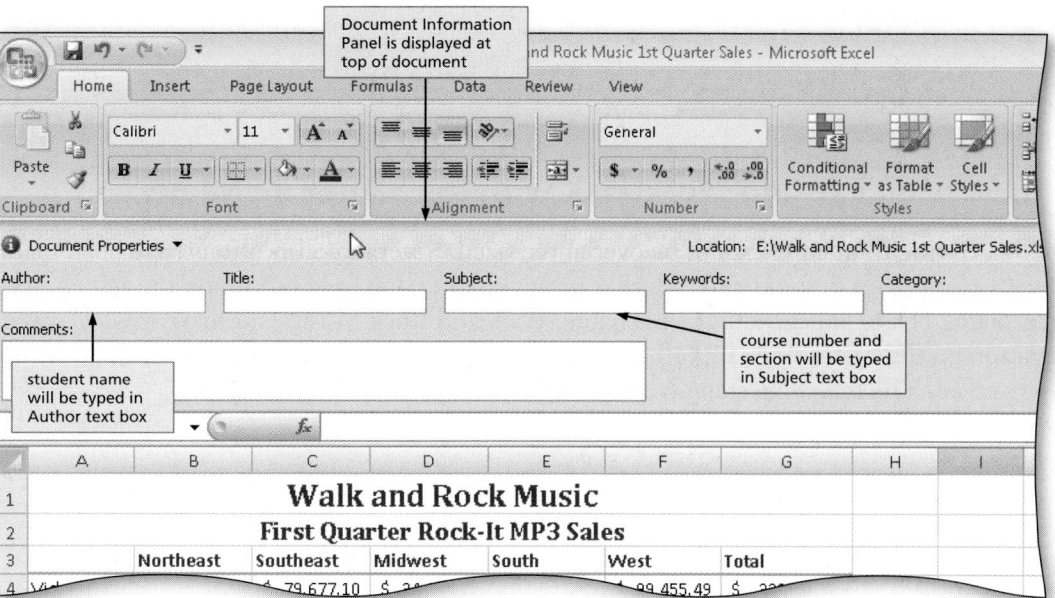

Figure 1–83

3

- Click the Author text box and then type your name as the Author property. If a name already is displayed in the Author text box, delete it before typing your name.

- Click the Subject text box, if necessary delete any existing text, and then type your course and section as the Subject property.

- Click the Keywords text box, if necessary delete any existing text, and then type First Quarter Rock-It MP3 Sales (Figure 1-84).

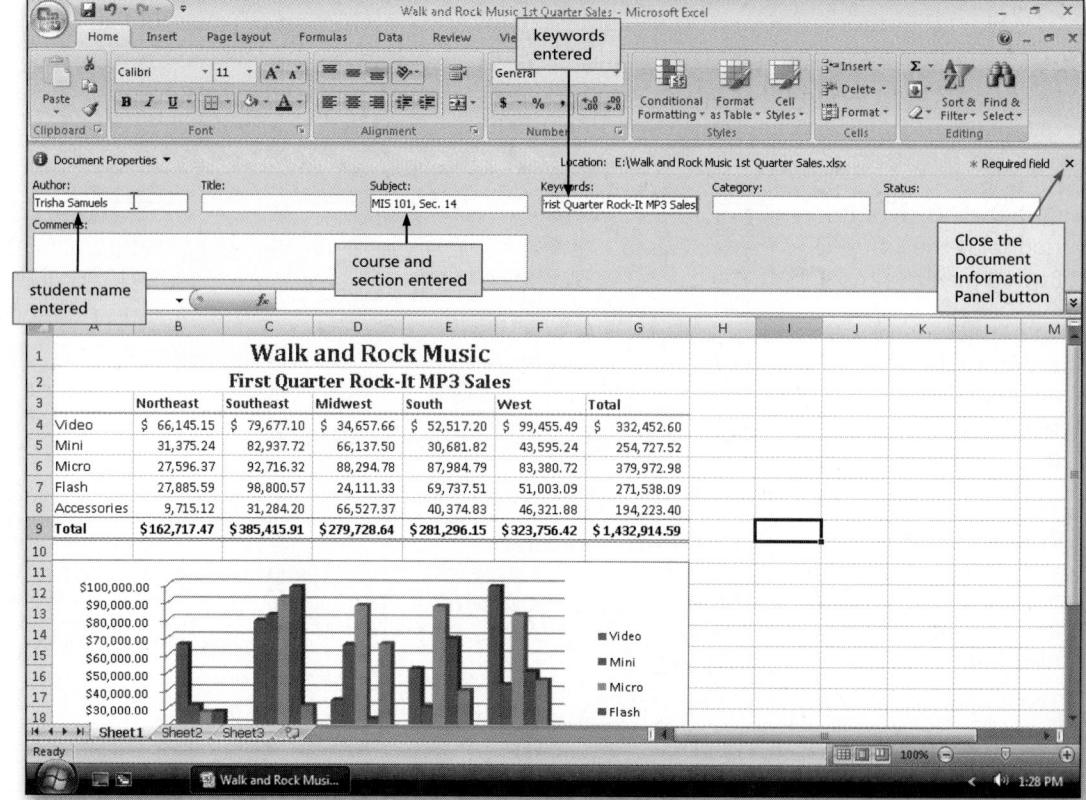

Figure 1–84

Q&A

What types of document properties does Excel collect automatically?

Excel records such details as how long you worked at creating your project, how many times you revised the document, and what fonts and themes are used.

4

- Click the Close the Document Information Panel button so that the Document Information Panel no longer is displayed.

To Save an Existing Workbook with the Same File Name

Saving frequently cannot be overemphasized. Several modifications have been made to the workbook since it was saved earlier in the chapter. Earlier in this chapter, the Save button on the Quick Access Toolbar caused the Save As dialog box to appear, and the file name, Walk and Rock Music 1st Quarter Sales, was entered. Clicking the Save button on the Quick Access Toolbar causes Excel to save the changes made to the workbook since the last time it was saved. The following step saves the workbook again.

1

- With your USB flash drive connected to one of the computer's USB ports, click the Save button on the Quick Access Toolbar to overwrite the previous Walk and Rock Music 1st Quarter Sales file on the USB flash drive (Figure 1–85).

Q&A

Why did the Save As dialog box not appear?

Excel overwrites the document using the settings specified the first time the document was saved. To save the file with a different file name or on different media, display the Save As dialog box by clicking the Office Button and then clicking Save As on the Office Button menu. Then, fill in the Save As dialog box as described in Steps 2 through 5 on pages EX 31 and EX 32.

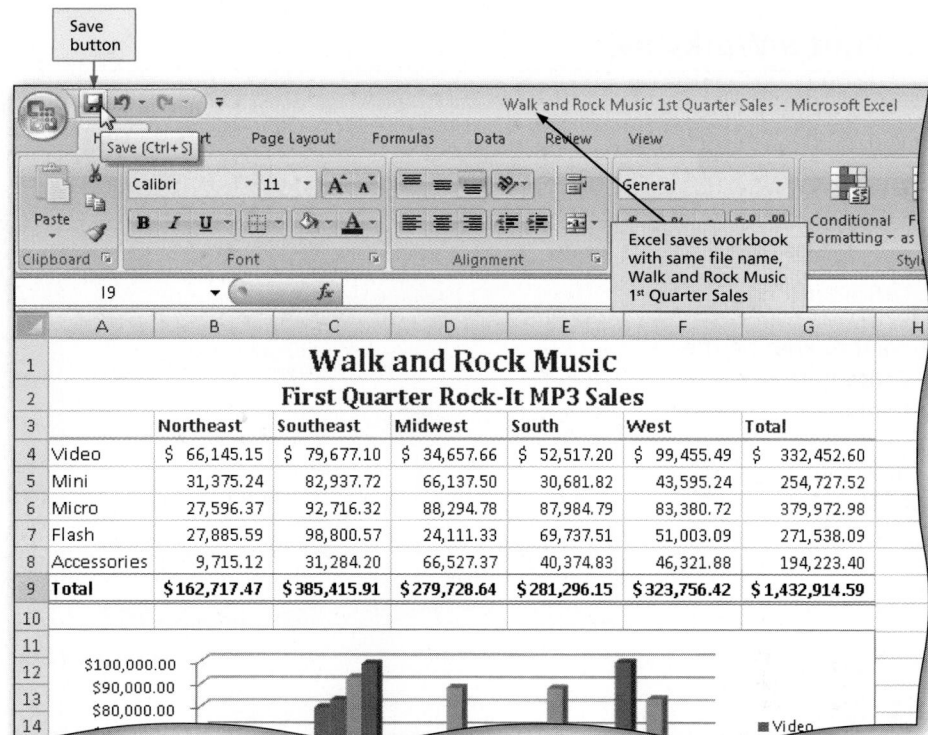

Figure 1–85

Other Ways

1. Press CTRL+S or press SHIFT+F12, press ENTER

Printing a Worksheet

After you create a worksheet, you often want to print it. A printed version of the worksheet is called a **hard copy** or **printout**. Printed copies of your worksheet can be useful for the following reasons:

- Many people prefer proofreading a hard copy of the worksheet rather than viewing the worksheet on the screen to check for errors and readability.
- Someone without computer access can view the worksheet's content.
- Copies can be distributed as handouts to people during a meeting or presentation.
- Hard copies can serve as reference material if your storage medium is lost or becomes corrupted and you need to recreate the worksheet.

It is a good practice to save a workbook before printing it, in the event you experience difficulties with the printer.

BTW

Conserving Ink and Toner

You can print a presentation in black and white to conserve ink or toner by clicking the Office Button, pointing to Print on the Office Button menu, and then clicking Print Preview on the Print submenu. Click the Page Setup button on the Print Preview tab, click the Sheet tab, and then click the Black and White check box in the Print area. Click the OK button to close the Page Setup dialog box. Click the Office Button, point to Print, and then click Quick Print.

To Print a Worksheet

With the completed worksheet saved, you may want to print it. The following steps print the worksheet in the saved Walk and Rock Music 1st Quarter Sales workbook.

- Click the Office Button to display the Office Button menu.

- Point to Print on the Office Button menu to display the Print submenu (Figure 1–86).

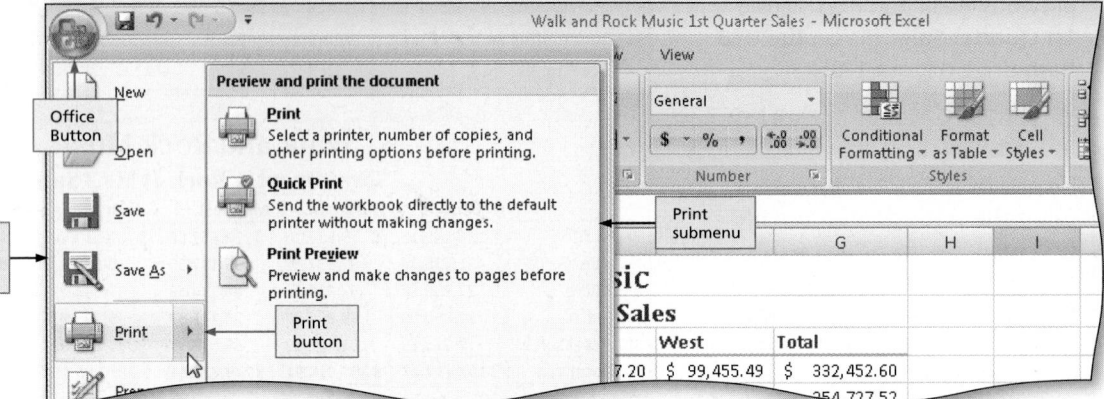

Figure 1–86

❷

- Click Quick Print on the Print submenu to print the document (Figure 1–87).

Q&A

Can I print my document in black and white to conserve ink or toner?

Yes. Click the Office Button and then click the Excel Options button on the Office Button menu. When the Excel Options dialog box is displayed, click Advanced, scroll to the Print area, place a check mark in the Use draft quality check box if it is displayed, and then click the OK button. Click the Office Button, point to Print, and then click Quick Print.

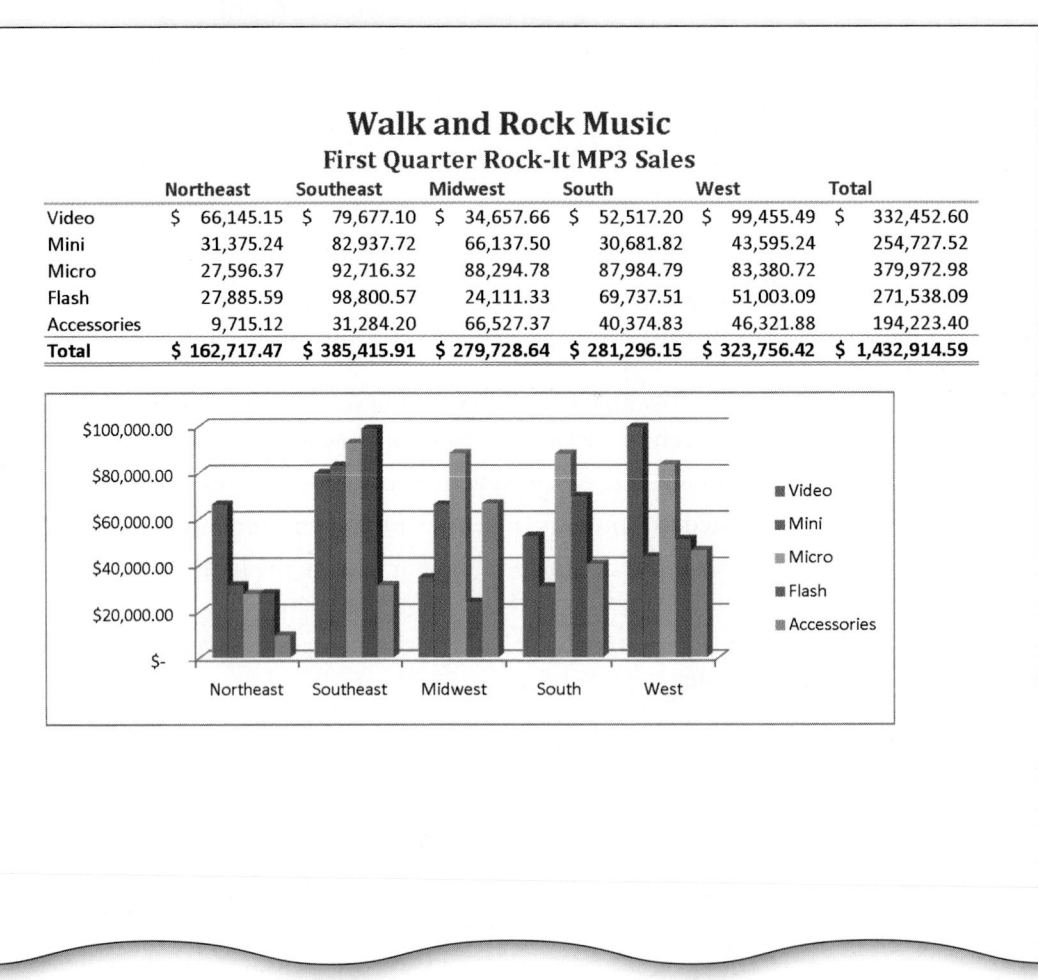

Figure 1–87

Other Ways

1. Press CTRL+P, press ENTER

Quitting Excel

When you quit Excel, if you have made changes to a workbook since the last time the file was saved, Excel displays a dialog box asking if you want to save the changes you made to the file before it closes that window. The dialog box contains three buttons with these resulting actions:

- Yes button — Saves the changes and then quits Excel
- No button — Quits Excel without saving changes
- Cancel button — Closes the dialog box and redisplays the worksheet without saving the changes

If no changes have been made to an open workbook since the last time the file was saved, Excel will close the window without displaying a dialog box.

To Quit Excel with One Workbook Open

The Walk and Rock 1st Quarter Sales worksheet is complete. The following steps quit Excel if only one workbook is open.

1

- Point to the Close button on the right side of the Excel title bar (Figure 1–88).

2

- Click the Close button to quit Excel.

Q&A What if I have more than one Excel workbook open?

You would click the Close button on the Excel title bar for each open workbook. When you click the Close button with the last workbook open, Excel also quits. As an alternative, you could click the Office Button and then click the Exit Excel button on the Office Button menu, which closes all open workbooks and then quits Excel.

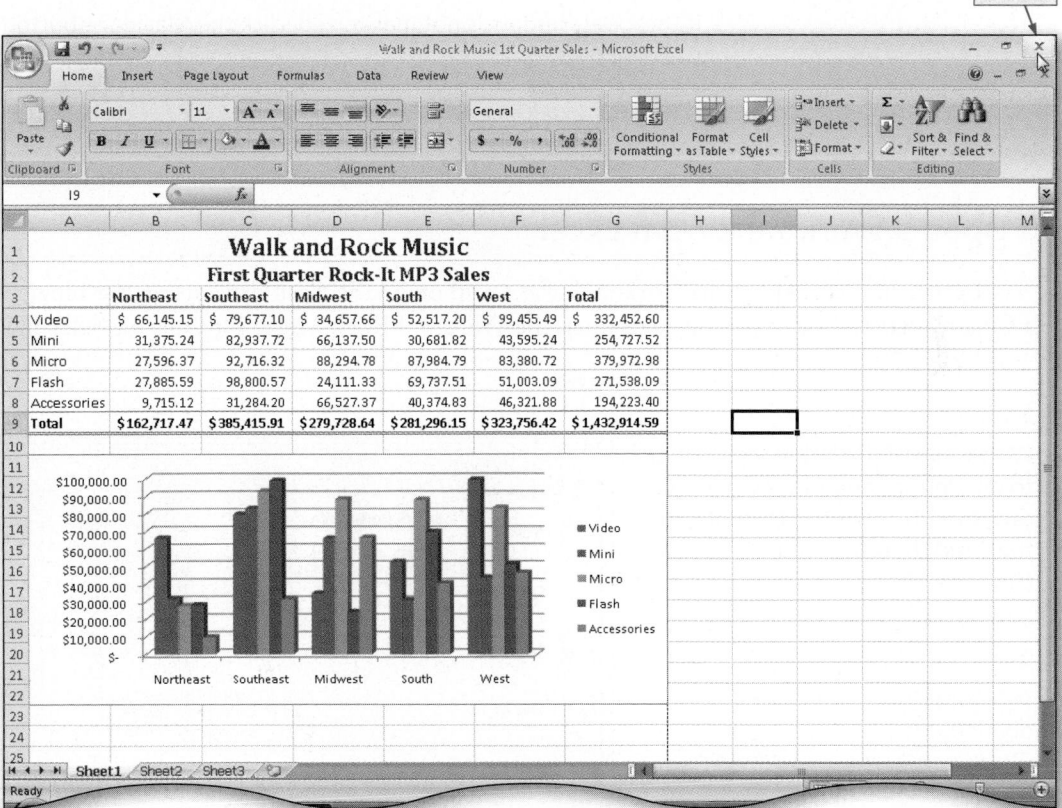

Close button

Figure 1–88

Other Ways
1. Double-click Office Button
2. With multiple workbooks open, click Office Button, click Exit Excel on Office Button menu
3. Right-click Microsoft Excel button on Windows Vista taskbar, click Close on shortcut menu
4. Press ALT+F4

BTW

Print Preview
You can preview the printout on your screen using the Print Preview command on the Print submenu (Figure 1–86 on page EX 58), make adjustments to the worksheet, and then print it only when it appears exactly as you want. Each time you preview rather than print, you save both ink and paper.

Starting Excel and Opening a Workbook

Once you have created and saved a workbook, you may need to retrieve it from your storage medium. For example, you might want to revise a worksheet or reprint it. Opening a workbook requires that Excel is running on your computer.

To Start Excel

The following steps, which assume Windows Vista is running, start Excel.

Note: If you are using Windows XP, please see Appendix F for alternate steps.

1 Click the Start button on the Windows Vista taskbar to display the Start menu.

2 Click All Programs at the bottom of the left pane on the Start menu to display the All Programs list and then click Microsoft Office in the All Programs list to display the Microsoft Office list.

3 Click Microsoft Office Excel 2007 in the Microsoft Office list to start Excel and display a new blank worksheet in the Excel window.

4 If the Excel window is not maximized, click the Maximize button on its title bar to maximize the window.

To Open a Workbook from Excel

Earlier in this chapter, the workbook was saved on a USB flash drive using the file name, Walk and Rock Music 1st Quarter Sales. The following steps open the Walk and Rock Music 1st Quarter Sales file from the USB flash drive.

1

- With your USB flash drive connected to one of the computer's USB ports, click the Office Button to display the Office Button menu (Figure 1–89).

Q&A

What files are shown in the Recent Documents list?

Excel displays the most recently opened document file names in this list. If the name of the file you want to open appears in the Recent Documents list, you could double-click it to open the file.

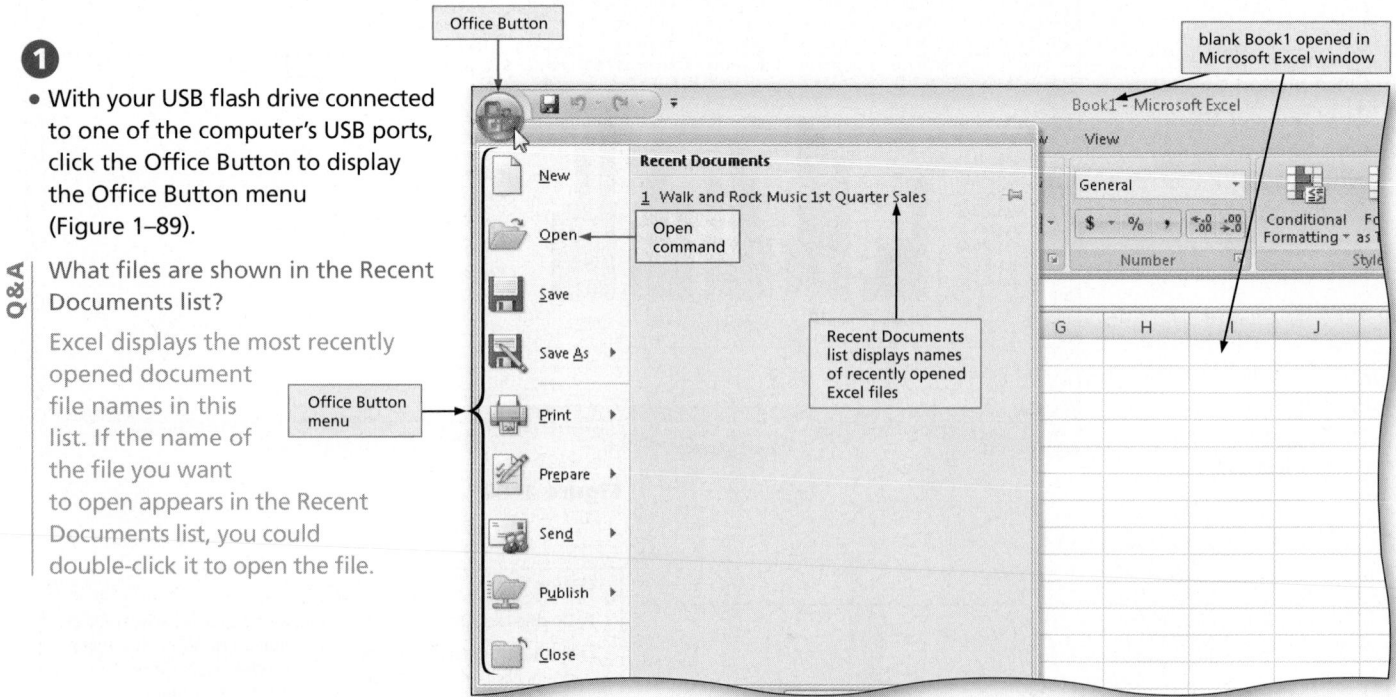

Figure 1–89

2

- Click Open on the Office Button menu to display the Open dialog box.

- If the Folders list is displayed below the Folders button, click the Folders button to remove the Folders list.

- If necessary, click Computer in the Favorite Links section and then scroll until UDISK 2.0 (E:) appears in the list of available drives.

- Double-click UDISK 2.0 (E:) to select the USB flash drive, Drive E in this case, as the new open location.

- Click Walk and Rock Music 1st Quarter Sales to select the file name (Figure 1–90).

Q&A

How do I open the file if I am not using a USB flash drive?

Use the same process, but be certain to select your device in the Computer list.

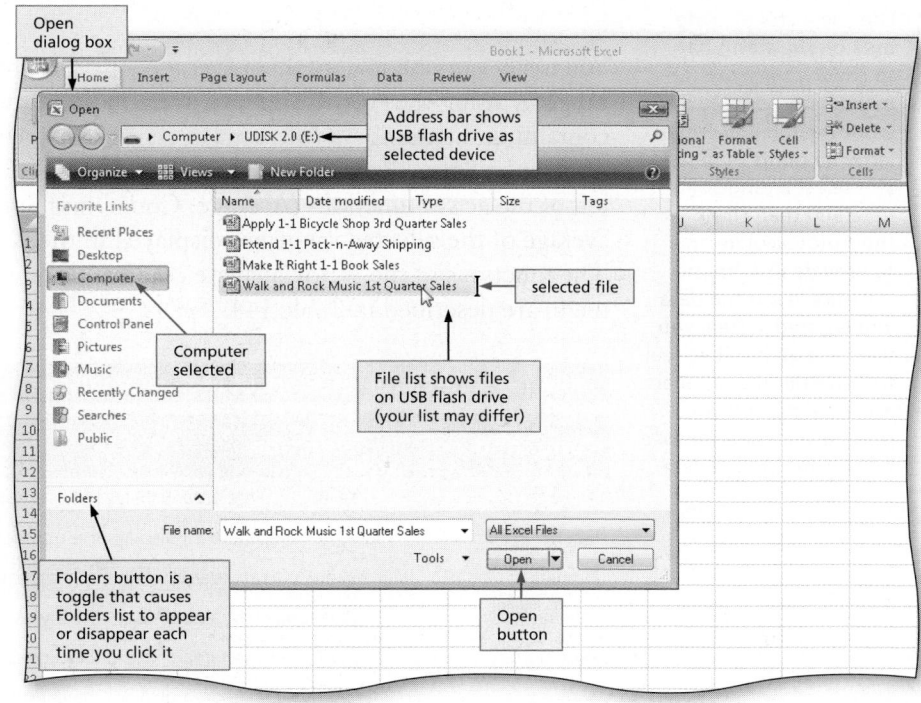

Figure 1–90

3

- Click the Open button to open the selected file and display the worksheet in the Excel window (Figure 1–91).

Q&A

Why do I see the Microsoft Excel icon and name on the Windows Vista taskbar?

When you open an Excel file, the application name (Microsoft Excel) is displayed on a selected button on the Windows Vista taskbar. If you point to this button, the file name also appears in a ScreenTip.

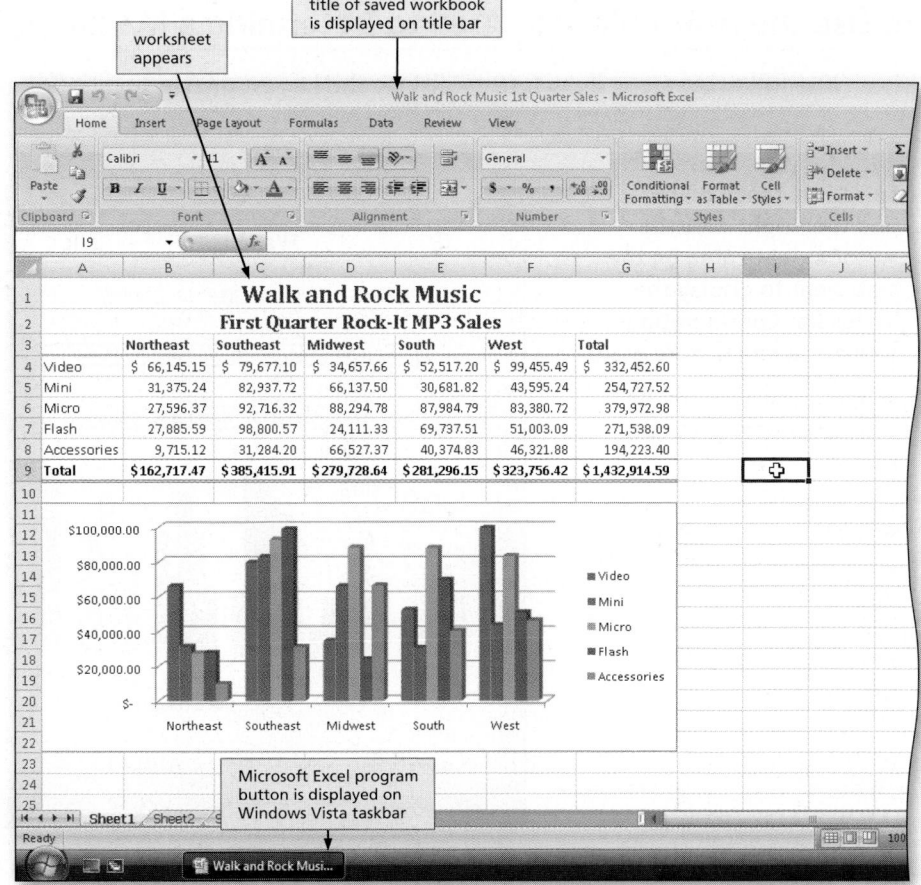

Figure 1–91

Other Ways

1. Click Office Button, double-click file name in Recent Documents list

2. Press CTRL+O, select file name, press ENTER

BTW

AutoCalculate
Use the AutoCalculate area on the status bar to check your work as you enter data in a worksheet. If you enter large amounts of data, you select a range of data and then check the AutoCalculate area to provide insight into statistics about the data you entered. Often, you will have an intuitive feel for whether the numbers are accurate or if you may have made a mistake while entering the data.

AutoCalculate

You easily can obtain a total, an average, or other information about the numbers in a range by using the **AutoCalculate area** on the status bar. First, select the range of cells containing the numbers you want to check. Next, right-click the AutoCalculate area to display the Status Bar Configuration shortcut menu (Figure 1–92). The check mark to the left of the active functions (Average, Count, and Sum) indicates that the sum, count, and average of the selected range are displayed in the AutoCalculate area on the status bar. The functions of the AutoCalculate commands on the Status Bar Configuration shortcut menu are described in Table 1–4.

Table 1–4 AutoCalculate Shortcut Menu Commands	
Command	**Function**
Average	AutoCalculate area displays the average of the numbers in the selected range
Count	AutoCalculate area displays the number of nonblank cells in the selected range
Numerical Count	AutoCalculate area displays the number of cells containing numbers in the selected range
Minimum	AutoCalculate area displays the lowest value in the selected range
Maximum	AutoCalculate area displays the highest value in the selected range
Sum	AutoCalculate area displays the sum of the numbers in the selected range

To Use the AutoCalculate Area to Determine a Maximum

The following steps show how to display the largest quarterly sales for any region for the Micro product type.

1

● Select the range B6:F6 and then right-click the AutoCalculate area on the status bar to display the Status Bar Configuration shortcut menu (Figure 1–92).

Q&A

What is displayed on the Status Bar Configuration shortcut menu?

This shortcut menu includes several commands that allow you to control the items displayed on the Customize Status Bar shortcut menu. The AutoCalculate area of the shortcut menu includes six commands as well as the result of the associated calculation on the right side of the menu.

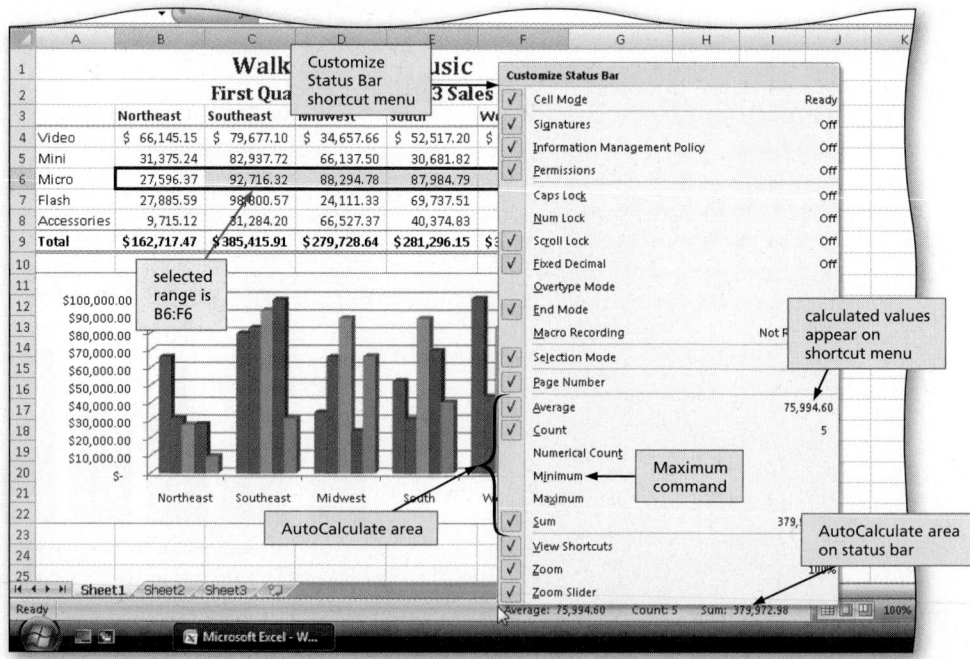

Figure 1–92

- Click Maximum on the shortcut menu to display the Maximum value in the range B6:F6 in the AutoCalculate area of the status bar.

- Click anywhere on the worksheet to cause the shortcut menu to disappear (Figure 1–93).

- Right-click the AutoCalculate area and then click Maximum on the shortcut menu to cause the Maximum value to no longer appear in the AutoCalculate area.

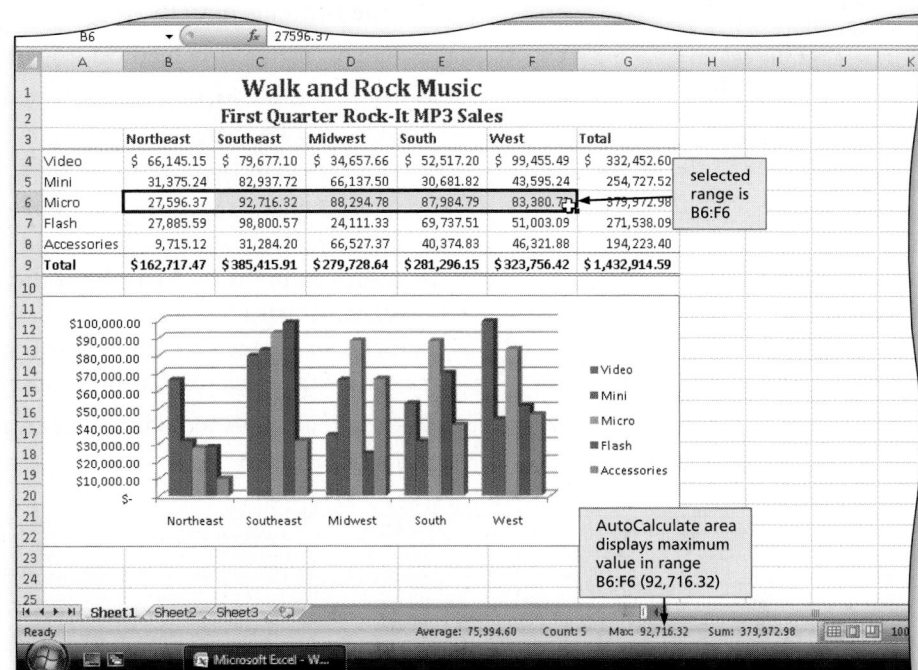

Figure 1–93

Correcting Errors

You can correct errors on a worksheet using one of several methods. The method you choose will depend on the extent of the error and whether you notice it while typing the data or after you have entered the incorrect data into the cell.

Correcting Errors while You Are Typing Data into a Cell

If you notice an error while you are typing data into a cell, press the BACKSPACE key to erase the incorrect characters and then type the correct characters. If the error is a major one, click the Cancel box in the formula bar or press the ESC key to erase the entire entry and then reenter the data from the beginning.

Correcting Errors after Entering Data into a Cell

If you find an error in the worksheet after entering the data, you can correct the error in one of two ways:

1. If the entry is short, select the cell, retype the entry correctly, and then click the Enter box or press the ENTER key. The new entry will replace the old entry.

2. If the entry in the cell is long and the errors are minor, using Edit mode may be a better choice than retyping the cell entry. Use the Edit mode as described below.

   a. Double-click the cell containing the error to switch Excel to Edit mode. In **Edit mode**, Excel displays the active cell entry in the formula bar and a flashing

BTW

In-Cell Editing
An alternative to double-clicking the cell to edit it is to select the cell and then press the F2 key.

insertion point in the active cell (Figure 1–94). With Excel in Edit mode, you can edit the contents directly in the cell — a procedure called **in-cell editing**.

b. Make changes using in-cell editing, as indicated below.

(1) To insert new characters between two characters, place the insertion point between the two characters and begin typing. Excel inserts the new characters at the location of the insertion point.

(2) To delete a character in the cell, move the insertion point to the left of the character you want to delete and then press the DELETE key or place the insertion point to the right of the character you want to delete and then press the BACKSPACE key. You also can use the mouse to drag through the character or adjacent characters you want to delete and then press the DELETE key or click the Cut button on the Home tab on the Ribbon.

(3) When you are finished editing an entry, click the Enter box or press the ENTER key.

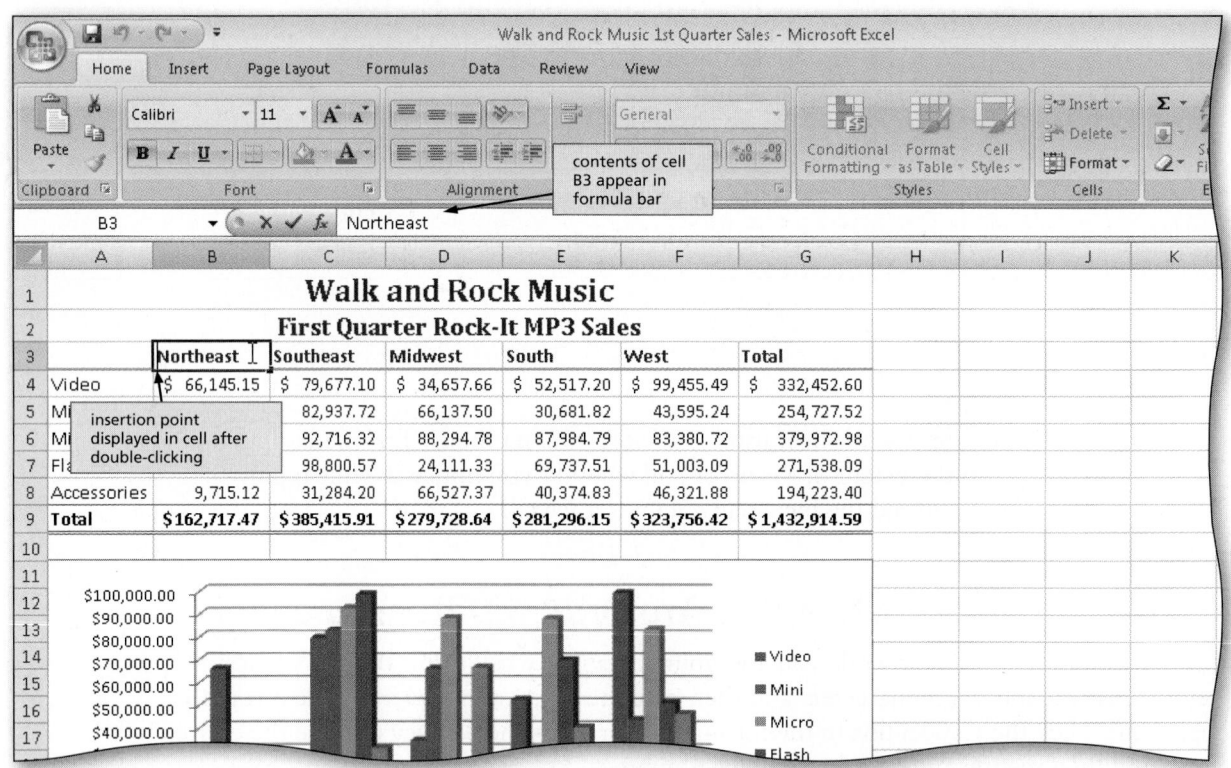

Figure 1–94

When Excel enters the Edit mode, the keyboard usually is in Insert mode. In **Insert mode**, as you type a character, Excel inserts the character and moves all characters to the right of the typed character one position to the right. You can change to Overtype mode by pressing the INSERT key. In **Overtype mode**, Excel overtypes, or replaces, the character to the right of the insertion point. The INSERT key toggles the keyboard between Insert mode and Overtype mode.

While in Edit mode, you may have reason to move the insertion point to various points in the cell, select portions of the data in the cell, or switch from inserting characters to overtyping characters. Table 1–5 summarizes the more common tasks used during in-cell editing.

BTW

Editing the Contents of a Cell
Rather than using in-cell editing, you can select the cell and then click the formula bar to edit the contents.

Table 1–5 Summary of In-Cell Editing Tasks

	Task	Mouse	Keyboard
1	Move the insertion point to the beginning of data in a cell.	Point to the left of the first character and click.	Press HOME
2	Move the insertion point to the end of data in a cell.	Point to the right of the last character and click.	Press END
3	Move the insertion point anywhere in a cell.	Point to the appropriate position and click the character.	Press RIGHT ARROW or LEFT ARROW
4	Highlight one or more adjacent characters.	Drag the mouse pointer through adjacent characters.	Press SHIFT+RIGHT ARROW or SHIFT+LEFT ARROW
5	Select all data in a cell.	Double-click the cell with the insertion point in the cell if there are no spaces in the data in the cell.	
6	Delete selected characters.	Click the Cut button on the Home tab on the Ribbon.	Press DELETE
7	Delete characters to the left of the insertion point.		Press BACKSPACE
8	Delete characters to the right of the insertion point.		Press DELETE
9	Toggle between Insert and Overtype modes.		Press INSERT

Undoing the Last Cell Entry

Excel provides the Undo command on the Quick Access Toolbar (Figure 1–95), which allows you to erase recent cell entries. Thus, if you enter incorrect data in a cell and notice it immediately, click the Undo button and Excel changes the cell entry to what it was prior to the incorrect data entry.

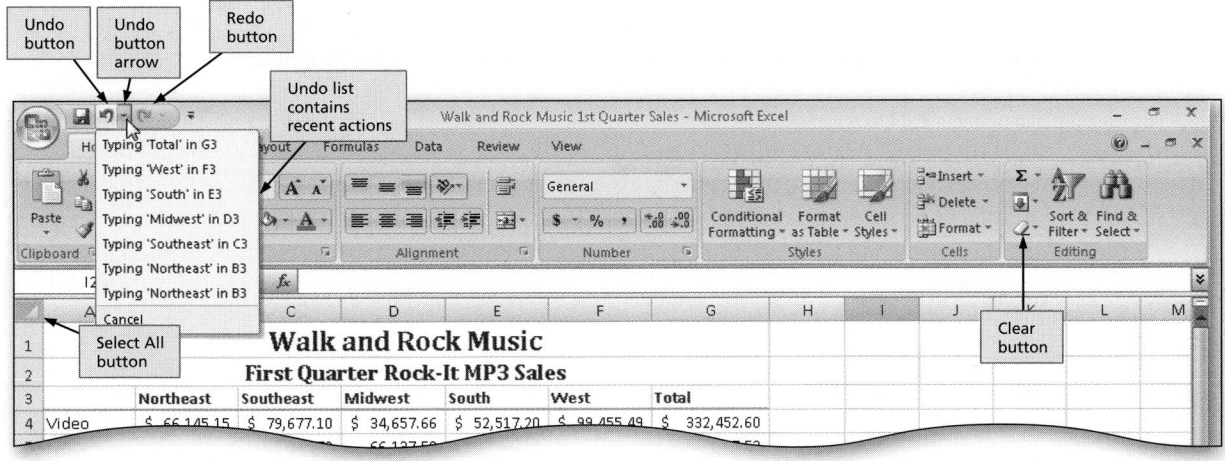

Figure 1–95

Excel remembers the last 100 actions you have completed. Thus, you can undo up to 100 previous actions by clicking the Undo button arrow to display the Undo list and then clicking the action to be undone (Figure 1–95). You can drag through several actions in the Undo list to undo all of them at once. If no actions are available for Excel to undo, then the Undo button is dimmed and inoperative.

The Redo button, next to the Undo button on the Quick Access Toolbar, allows you to repeat previous actions.

BTW

Quick Reference
For a table that lists how to complete the tasks covered in this book using the mouse, Ribbon, shortcut menu, and keyboard, see the Quick Reference Summary at the back of this book, or visit the Excel 2007 Quick Reference Web page (scsite.com/ex2007/qr).

BTW

Certification
The Microsoft Certified Application Specialist (MCAS) program provides an opportunity for you to obtain a valuable industry credential – proof that you have the Excel 2007 skills required by employers. For more information, see Appendix G or visit the Excel 2007 Certification Web page (scsite.com/ex2007/cert).

BTW

Getting Back to Normal
If you accidentally assign unwanted formats to a range of cells, you can use the Normal cell style selection in the Cell Styles gallery. Click Cell Styles on the Home tab on the Ribbon and then click Normal. Doing so changes the format to Normal style. To view the characteristics of the Normal style, right-click the style in the Cell Styles gallery and then click Modify, or press ALT+APOSTROPHE (').

Clearing a Cell or Range of Cells

If you enter data into the wrong cell or range of cells, you can erase, or clear, the data using one of the first four methods listed below. The fifth method clears the formatting from the selected cells.

To Clear Cell Entries Using the Fill Handle

1. Select the cell or range of cells and then point to the fill handle so the mouse pointer changes to a crosshair.
2. Drag the fill handle back into the selected cell or range until a shadow covers the cell or cells you want to erase. Release the mouse button.

To Clear Cell Entries Using the Shortcut Menu

1. Select the cell or range of cells to be cleared.
2. Right-click the selection.
3. Click Clear Contents on the shortcut menu.

To Clear Cell Entries Using the delete Key

1. Select the cell or range of cells to be cleared.
2. Press the DELETE key.

To Clear Cell Entries and Formatting Using the Clear Button

1. Select the cell or range of cells to be cleared.
2. Click the Clear button on the Home tab (Figure 1–95 on the previous page).
3. Click Clear Contents on the menu.

To Clear Formatting Using the Cell Styles Button

1. Select the cell or range of cells from which you want to remove the formatting.
2. Click the Cell Styles button on the Home tab and point to Normal.
3. Click Normal in the Live Preview Gallery.

The Clear button on the Home tab is the only command that clears both the cell entry and the cell formatting. As you are clearing cell entries, always remember that you should *never press the* SPACEBAR *to clear a cell*. Pressing the SPACEBAR enters a blank character. A blank character is text and is different from an empty cell, even though the cell may appear empty.

Clearing the Entire Worksheet

If required worksheet edits are extremely extensive, you may want to clear the entire worksheet and start over. To clear the worksheet or delete an embedded chart, use the following steps.

To Clear the Entire Worksheet

1. Click the Select All button on the worksheet (Figure 1–95).
2. Click the Clear button on the Home tab to delete both the entries and formats.

The Select All button selects the entire worksheet. Instead of clicking the Select All button, you also can press CTRL+A. To clear an unsaved workbook, click the workbook's Close Window button or click the Close command on the Office Button menu. Click the No button if the Microsoft Excel dialog box asks if you want to save changes. To start a new, blank workbook, click the New command on the Office Button menu.

To delete an embedded chart, complete the following steps.

TO DELETE AN EMBEDDED CHART

1. Click the chart to select it.
2. Press the DELETE key.

BTW

Excel Help
The best way to become familiar with Excel Help is to use it. Appendix C includes detailed information about Excel Help and exercises that will help you gain confidence in using it.

Excel Help

At any time while using Excel, you can find answers to questions and display information about various topics through **Excel Help**. This section introduces you to Excel Help.

To Search for Excel Help

Using Excel Help, you can search for information based on phrases such as save a workbook or format a chart, or key terms such as copy, save, or format. Excel Help responds with a list of search results displayed as links to a variety of resources. The following steps, which use Excel Help to search for information about formatting a chart, assume you are connected to the Internet.

- Click the Microsoft Office Excel Help button near the upper-right corner of the Excel window to open the Excel Help window.

- Type format a chart in the Type words to search for text box at the top of the Excel Help window (Figure 1–96).

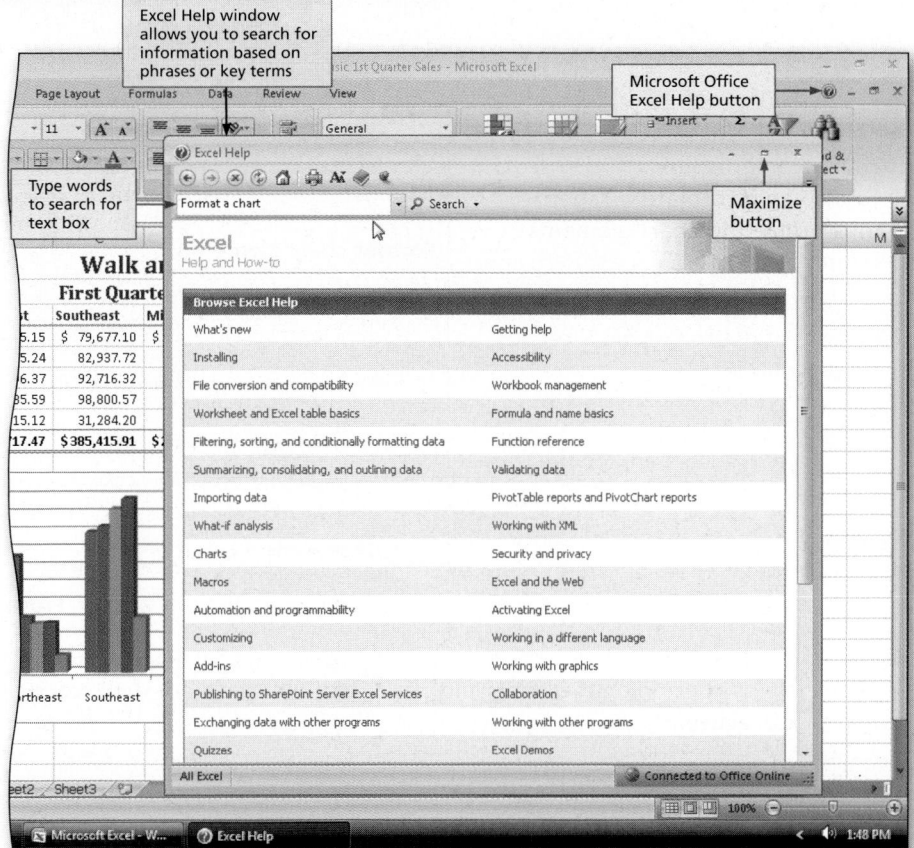

Figure 1–96

2

- Press the ENTER key to display the search results.

- Click the Maximize button on the Excel Help window title bar to maximize the Help window (Figure 1–97).

Q&A

Where is the Excel window with the Walk and Rock Music 1st Quarter Sales worksheet?

Excel is open in the background, but the Excel Help window is overlaid on top of the Microsoft Excel window. When the Excel Help window is closed, the worksheet will reappear.

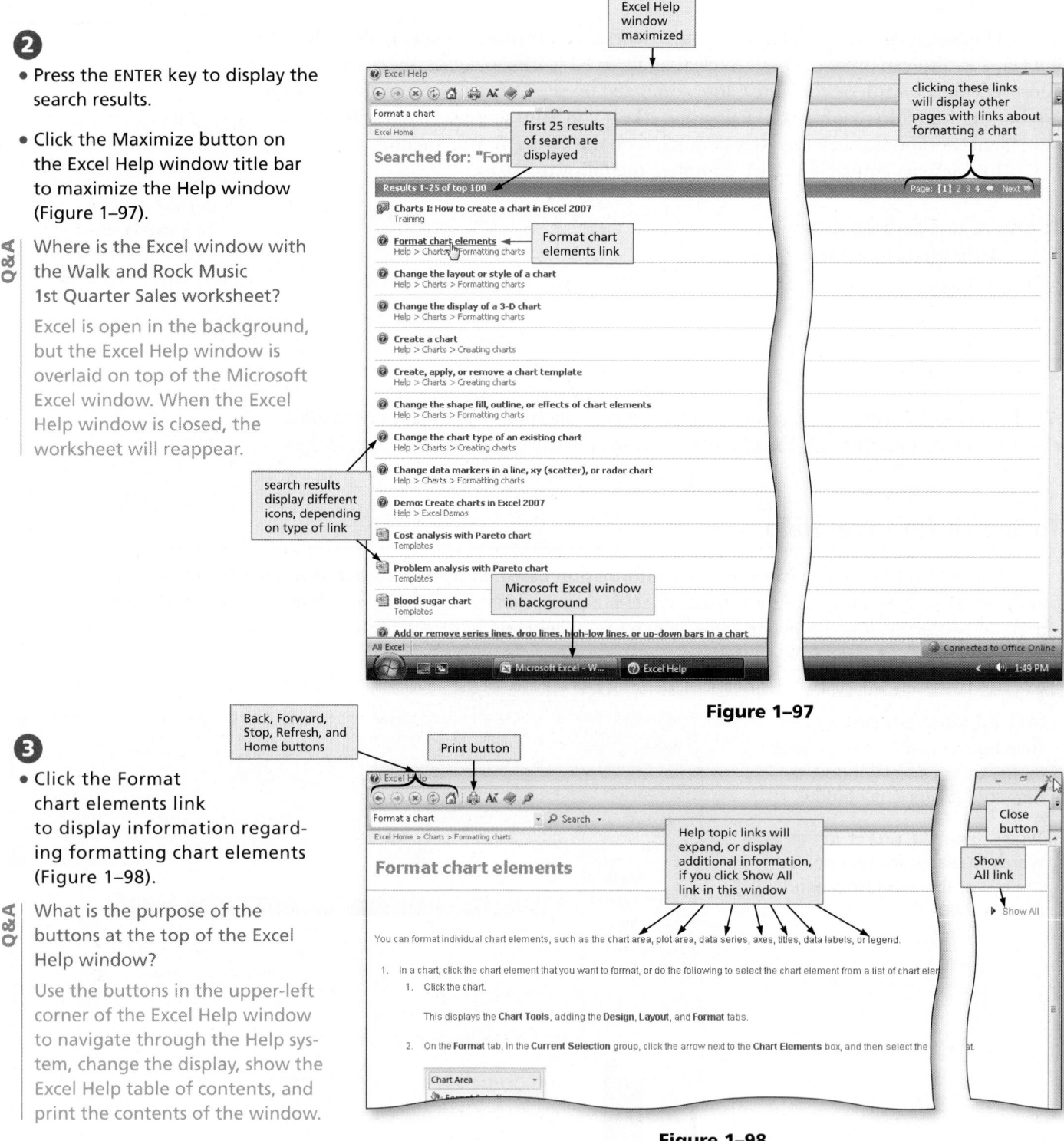

Figure 1–97

Figure 1–98

3

- Click the Format chart elements link to display information regarding formatting chart elements (Figure 1–98).

Q&A

What is the purpose of the buttons at the top of the Excel Help window?

Use the buttons in the upper-left corner of the Excel Help window to navigate through the Help system, change the display, show the Excel Help table of contents, and print the contents of the window.

4

- Click the Close button on the Excel Help window title bar to close the Excel Help window and make Excel active.

Other Ways
1. Press F1

To Quit Excel

The following steps quit Excel.

1 Click the Close button on the right side of the title bar to quit Excel; or if you have multiple Excel workbooks open, click the Office Button and then click the Exit Excel button on the Office Button menu to close all open workbooks and quit Excel.

2 If necessary, click the No button in the Microsoft Office Excel dialog box so that any changes you have made are not saved.

BTW | **Quitting Excel**
Do not forget to remove your USB flash drive from the USB port after quitting Excel, especially if you are working in a laboratory environment. Nothing can be more frustrating than leaving all of your hard work behind on a USB flash drive for the next user.

Chapter Summary

In this chapter you have learned about the Excel window, how to enter text and numbers to create a worksheet, how to select a range, how to use the Sum button, save a workbook, format cells, insert a chart, print a worksheet, quit Excel, and use Excel Help. The items listed below include all the new Excel skills you have learned in this chapter.

1. Start Excel (EX 6)
2. Enter the Worksheet Titles (EX 17)
3. Enter Column Titles (EX 19)
4. Enter Row Titles (EX 21)
5. Enter Numbers (EX 23)
6. Sum a Column of Numbers (EX 25)
7. Copy a Cell to Adjacent Cells in a Row (EX 27)
8. Determine Multiple Totals at the Same Time (EX 28)
9. Save a Workbook (EX 30)
10. Change a Cell Style (EX 35)
11. Change the Font Type (EX 36)
12. Bold a Cell (EX 38)
13. Increase the Font Size of a Cell Entry (EX 38)
14. Change the Font Color of a Cell Entry (EX 39)
15. Center Cell Entries across Columns by Merging Cells (EX 40)
16. Format Column Titles and the Total Row (EX 42)
17. Format Numbers in the Worksheet (EX 44)
18. Adjust the Column Width (EX 46)
19. Use the Name Box to Select a Cell (EX 47)
20. Add a 3-D Clustered Column Chart to the Worksheet (EX 50)
21. Change Document Properties (EX 55)
22. Save an Existing Workbook with the Same File Name (EX 58)
23. Print a Worksheet (EX 58)
24. Quit Excel with One Workbook Open (EX 59)
25. Open a Workbook from Excel (EX 60)
26. Use the AutoCalculate Area to Determine a Maximum (EX 62)
27. Clear Cell Entries Using the Fill Handle (EX 66)
28. Clear Cell Entries Using the Shortcut Menu (EX 66)
29. Clear Cell Entries Using the DELETE Key (EX 66)
30. Clear Cell Entries and Formatting Using the Clear Button (EX 66)
31. Clear Formatting Using the Cell Styles Button (EX 66)
32. Clear the Entire Worksheet (EX 66)
33. Delete an Embedded Chart (EX 67)
34. Search for Excel Help (EX 67)

If you have a SAM user profile, you may have access to hands-on instruction, practice, and assessment. Log in to your SAM account (http://sam2007.course.com) to launch any assigned training activities or exams that relate to the skills covered in this chapter.

Learn It Online

Test your knowledge of chapter content and key terms.

Instructions: To complete the Learn It Online exercises, start your browser, click the Address bar, and then enter the Web address scsite.com/ex2007/learn. When the Excel 2007 Learn It Online page is displayed, click the link for the exercise you want to complete and then read the instructions.

Chapter Reinforcement TF, MC, and SA

A series of true/false, multiple choice, and short answer questions that test your knowledge of the chapter content.

Flash Cards

An interactive learning environment where you identify chapter key terms associated with displayed definitions.

Practice Test

A series of multiple choice questions that test your knowledge of chapter content and key terms.

Who Wants To Be a Computer Genius?

An interactive game that challenges your knowledge of chapter content in the style of a television quiz show.

Wheel of Terms

An interactive game that challenges your knowledge of chapter key terms in the style of the television show *Wheel of Fortune*.

Crossword Puzzle Challenge

A crossword puzzle that challenges your knowledge of key terms presented in the chapter.

Apply Your Knowledge

Reinforce the skills and apply the concepts you learned in this chapter.

Changing the Values in a Worksheet

Instructions: Start Excel. Open the workbook Apply 1-1 Bicycle Shop 3rd Quarter Sales (Figure 1–99a). See the inside back cover of this book for instructions for downloading the Data Files for Students, or see your instructor for information on accessing the files required in this book.

1. Make the changes to the worksheet described in Table 1–6 so that the worksheet appears as shown in Figure 1–99b. As you edit the values in the cells containing numeric data, watch the totals in row 8, the totals in column G, and the chart change.

2. Change the worksheet title in cell A1 to the Title cell style and then merge and center it across columns A through G. Use commands in the Font group on the Home tab on the Ribbon to change the worksheet subtitle in cell A2 to 16-point Corbel red, bold font and then center it across columns A through G. Use the Accent 1 theme color (column 5, row 1 on the Font palette) for the red font color.

3. Update the document properties with your name, course number, and name for the workbook. Save the workbook using the file name, Apply 1-1 Spoke-Up Bicycle Shop 3rd Quarter Sales. Submit the assignment as requested by your instructor.

Table 1–6 New Worksheet Data	
Cell	**Change Cell Contents To**
A1	Spoke-Up Bicycle Shop
B4	11869.2
E4	9157.83
D6	5217.92
F6	6239.46
B7	3437.64

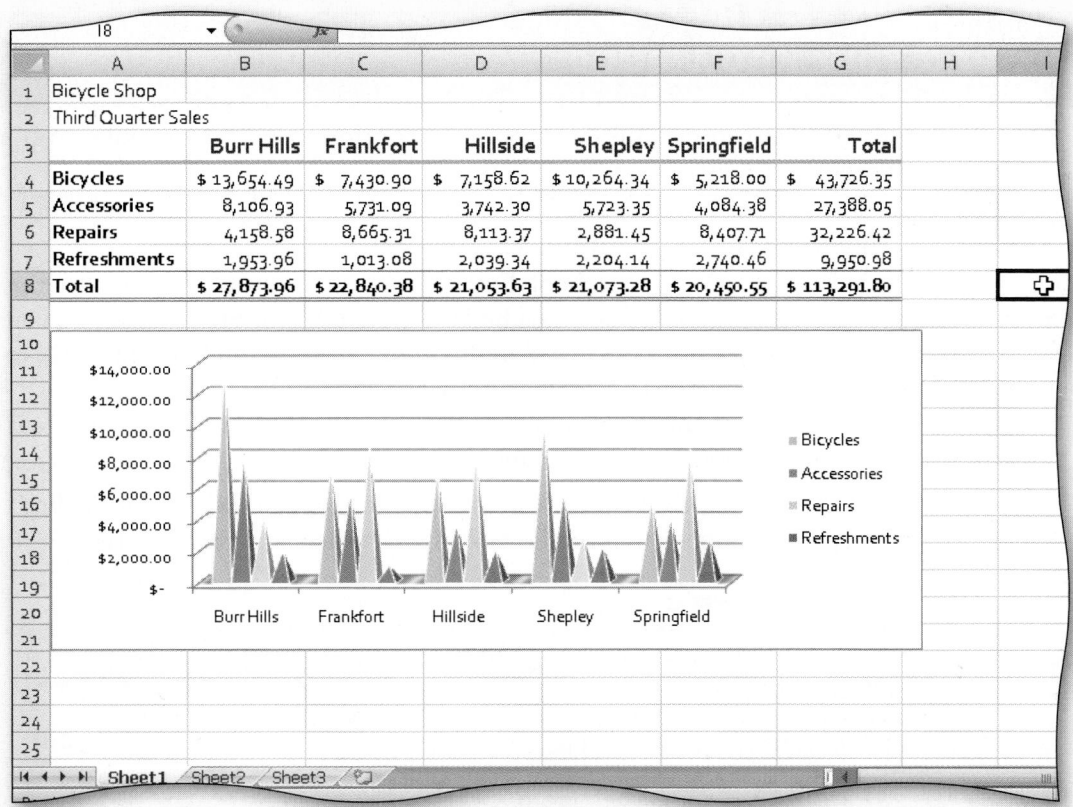

(a) Before

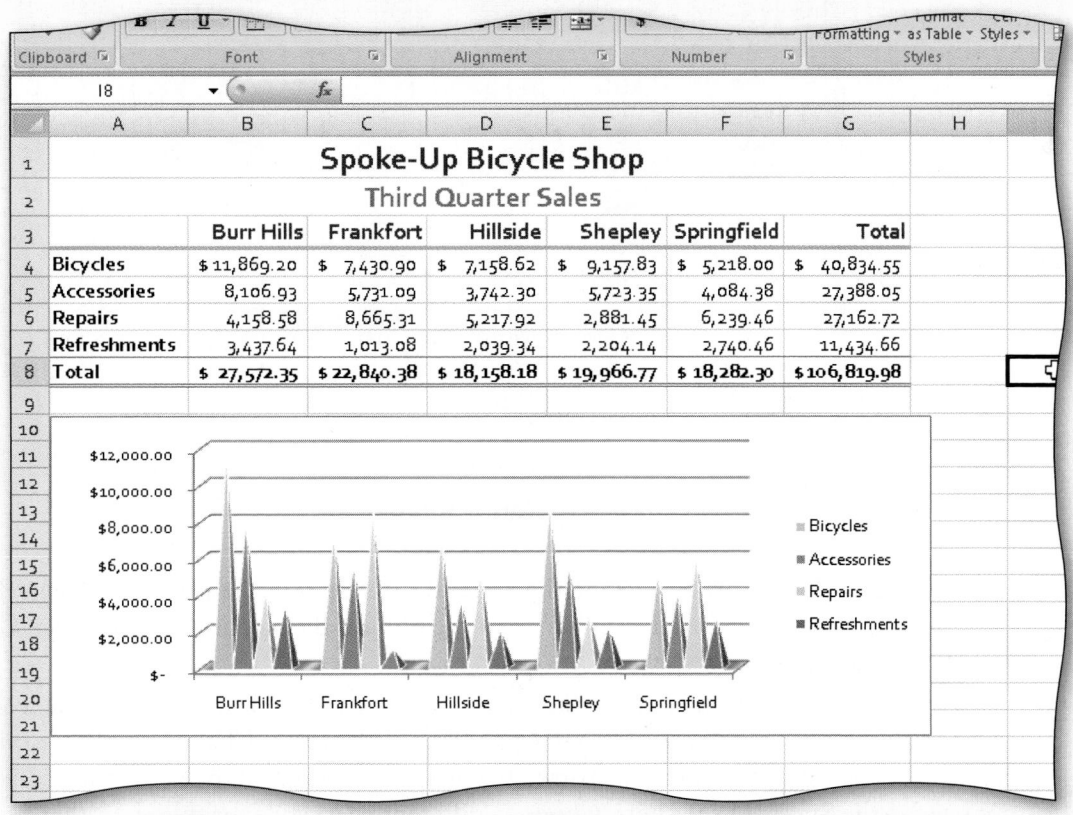

(b) After

Figure 1–99

Extend Your Knowledge

Extend the skills you learned in this chapter and experiment with new skills. You may need to use Help to complete the assignment.

Formatting Cells and Inserting Multiple Charts

Instructions: Start Excel. Open the workbook Extend 1-1 Pack-n-Away Shipping. See the inside back cover of this book for instructions for downloading the Data Files for Students, or see your instructor for information on accessing the files required in this book. Perform the following tasks to format cells in the worksheet and to add two charts to the worksheet.

1. Use the commands in the Font group on the Home tab on the Ribbon to change the font of the title in cell A1 to 24-point Arial, red; bold and subtitle of the worksheet to 16-point Arial Narrow, blue, bold.

2. Select the range A3:E8, click the Insert tab on the Ribbon, and then click the Dialog Box Launcher in the Charts group on the Ribbon to open the Insert Chart dialog box (Figure 1–100).

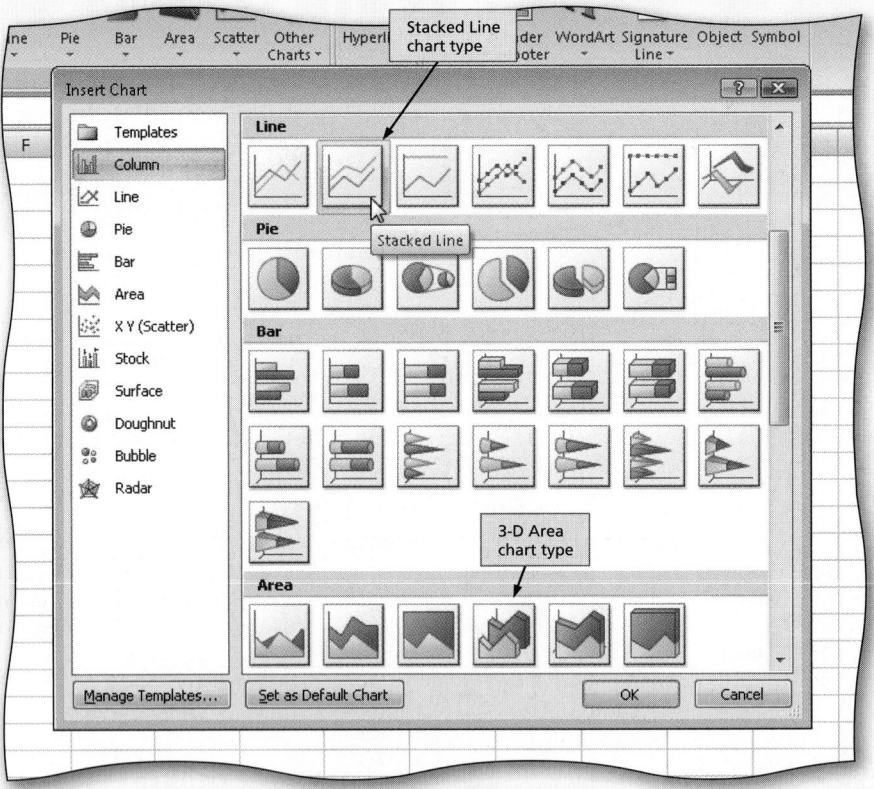

Figure 1–100

3. Insert a Stacked Line chart by clicking the Stacked Line chart in the gallery and then clicking the OK button. Move the chart either below or to the right of the data in the worksheet. Click the Design tab and apply a chart style to the chart.

4. With the same range selected, follow Step 3 above to insert a 3-D Area chart in the worksheet. You may need to use the scroll box on the right side of the Insert Chart dialog box to view the Area charts in the gallery. Move the chart either below or to the right of the data so that each chart does not overlap the Stacked Line chart. Choose a different chart style for this chart than the one you selected for the Stacked Line chart.

5. Resize each chart so that each snaps to the worksheet gridlines. Make certain that both charts are visible with the worksheet data without the need to scroll the worksheet.

6. Update the document properties with your name, course number, and name for the workbook.

7. Save the workbook using the file name, Extend 1-1 Pack-n-Away Shipping Charts. Submit the assignment as requested by your instructor.

Make It Right

Analyze a workbook and correct all errors and/or improve the design.

Correcting Formatting and Values in a Worksheet

Instructions: Start Excel. Open the workbook Make It Right 1-1 Book Sales. See the inside back cover of this book for instructions for downloading the Data Files for Students, or see your instructor for information on accessing the files required for this book. Correct the following formatting problems and data errors (Figure 1–101) in the worksheet, while keeping in mind the guidelines presented in this chapter.

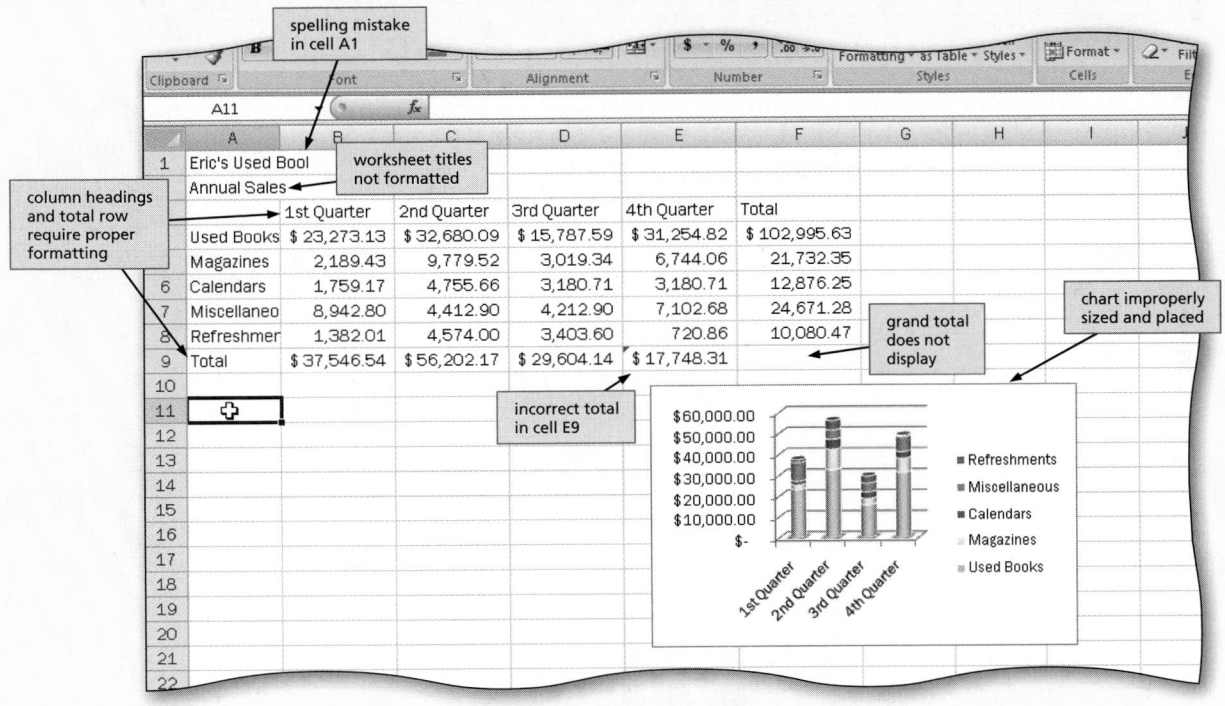

Figure 1–101

1. Merge and center the worksheet title and subtitle appropriately.

2. Format the worksheet title with a cell style appropriate for a worksheet title.

3. Format the subtitle using commands in the Font group on the Ribbon.

4. Correct the spelling mistake in cell A1 by changing Bool to Books.

5. Apply proper formatting to the column headers and total row.

Continued >

Make It Right *continued*

6. Adjust column sizes so that all data in each column is visible.

7. Use the SUM function to create the grand total for annual sales.

8. The SUM function in cell E9 does not sum all of the numbers in the column. Correct this error by editing the range for the SUM function in the cell.

9. Resize and move the chart so that it is below the worksheet data and does not extend past the right edge of the worksheet data. Be certain to snap the chart to the worksheet gridlines by holding down the ALT key as you resize the chart.

10. Update the document properties with your name, course number, and name for the workbook. Save the workbook using the file name, Make It Right 1-1 Eric's Used Books Annual Sales. Submit the assignment as requested by your instructor.

In the Lab

Design and/or create a workbook using the guidelines, concepts, and skills presented in this chapter. Labs 1, 2, and 3 are listed in order of increasing difficulty.

Lab 1: Annual Cost of Goods Worksheet

Problem: You work part-time as a spreadsheet specialist for Kona's Expresso Coffee, one of the up-and-coming coffee franchises in the United States. Your manager has asked you to develop an annual cost of goods analysis worksheet similar to the one shown in Figure 1–102.

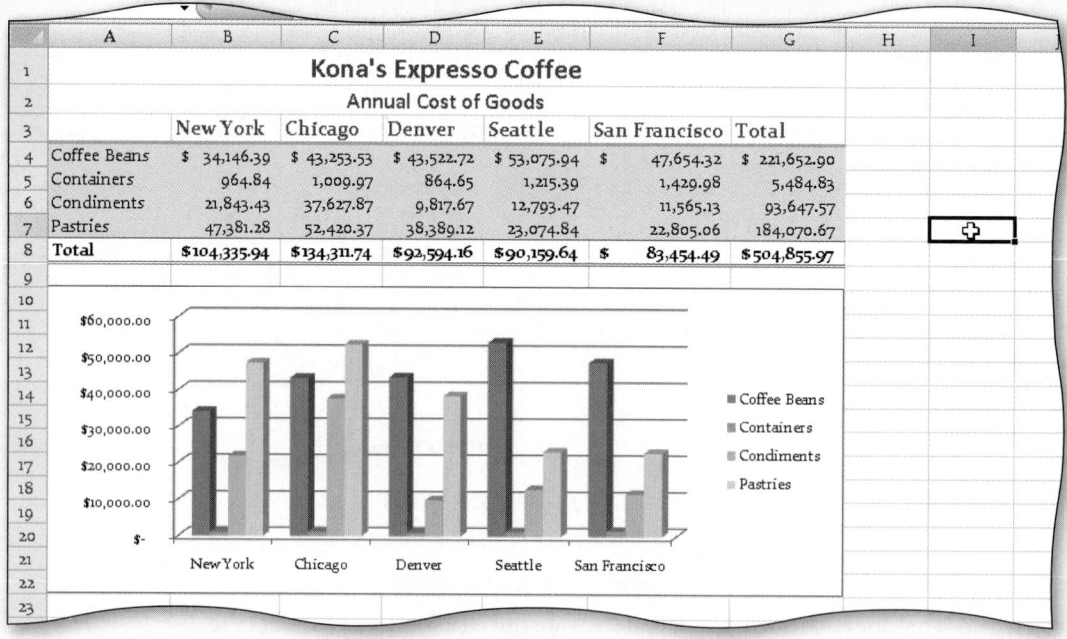

Figure 1–102

Instructions: Perform the following tasks.

1. Start Excel. Enter the worksheet title, Kona's Expresso Coffee, in cell A1 and the worksheet subtitle, Annual Cost of Goods, in cell A2. Beginning in row 3, enter the store locations, costs of goods, and supplies categories shown in Table 1–7.

Table 1–7 Kona's Expresso Coffee Annual Cost of Goods					
	New York	**Chicago**	**Denver**	**Seattle**	**San Franscisco**
Coffee Beans	34146.39	43253.53	43522.72	53075.94	47654.32
Containers	964.84	1009.97	864.65	1215.39	1429.98
Condiments	21843.43	37627.87	9817.67	12793.47	11565.13
Pastries	47381.28	52420.37	38389.12	23074.84	22805.06

2. Use the SUM function to determine the totals for each store location, type of supply, and company grand total.

3. Use Cell Styles in the Styles group on the Home tab on the Ribbon to format the worksheet title with the Title cell style. Center the title across columns A through G. Do not be concerned if the edges of the worksheet title are not displayed.

4. Use buttons in the Font group on the Home tab on the Ribbon to format the worksheet subtitle to 14-point Calibri dark blue, bold font, and center it across columns A through G.

5. Use Cell Styles in the Styles group on the Home tab on the Ribbon to format the range A3:G3 with the Heading 2 cell style, the range A4:G7 with the 20% - Accent1 cell style, and the range A8:G8 with the Total cell style. Use the buttons in the Number group on the Home tab on the Ribbon to apply the Accounting Number format to the range B4:G4 and the range B8:G8. Use the buttons in the Number group on the Home tab on the Ribbon to apply the Comma Style to the range B5:G7. Adjust any column widths to the widest text entry in each column.

6. Select the range A3:F7 and then insert a 3-D Clustered Column chart. Apply the Style 8 chart style to the chart. Move and resize the chart so that it appears in the range A10:G22. If the labels along the horizontal axis (x-axis) do not appear as shown in Figure 1-102, then drag the right side of the chart so that it is displayed in the range A10:H22.

7. Update the document properties with your name, course number, and name for the workbook.

8. Save the workbook using the file name Lab 1-1 Konas Expresso Coffee Annual Cost of Goods.

9. Print the worksheet.

10. Make the following two corrections to the sales amounts: $9,648.12 for Seattle Condiments (cell E6), $12,844.79 for Chicago Pastries (cell C7). After you enter the corrections, the company totals in cell G8 should equal $462,135.04.

11. Print the revised worksheet. Close the workbook without saving the changes. Submit the assignment as requested by your instructor.

In the Lab

Lab 2: Annual Sales Analysis Worksheet

Problem: As the chief accountant for Scissors Office Supply, Inc., you have been asked by the sales manager to create a worksheet to analyze the annual sales for the company by location and customer type category (Figure 1–103). The office locations and corresponding sales by customer type for the year are shown in Table 1–8.

Continued >

In the Lab *continued*

Instructions: Perform the following tasks.

1. Create the worksheet shown in Figure 1–103 using the data in Table 1–8.
2. Use the SUM function to determine totals sales for the four offices, the totals for each customer type, and the company total. Add column and row headings for the totals row and totals column, as appropriate.

Table 1–8 Scissors Office Supply Annual Sales				
	Boston	**Miami**	**St. Louis**	**Santa Fe**
Consumer	206348.81	113861.40	69854.13	242286.82
Small Business	235573.28	133511.24	199158.35	228365.51
Large Business	237317.55	234036.08	126519.10	111773.38
Government	178798.04	144548.80	135470.86	132599.75
Nonprofit	15180.63	28837.75	63924.48	21361.42

3. Format the worksheet title with the Title cell style and center it across columns A through F. Use the Font group on the Ribbon to format the worksheet subtitle to 16-point Cambria green, and bold font. Center the title across columns A through F.

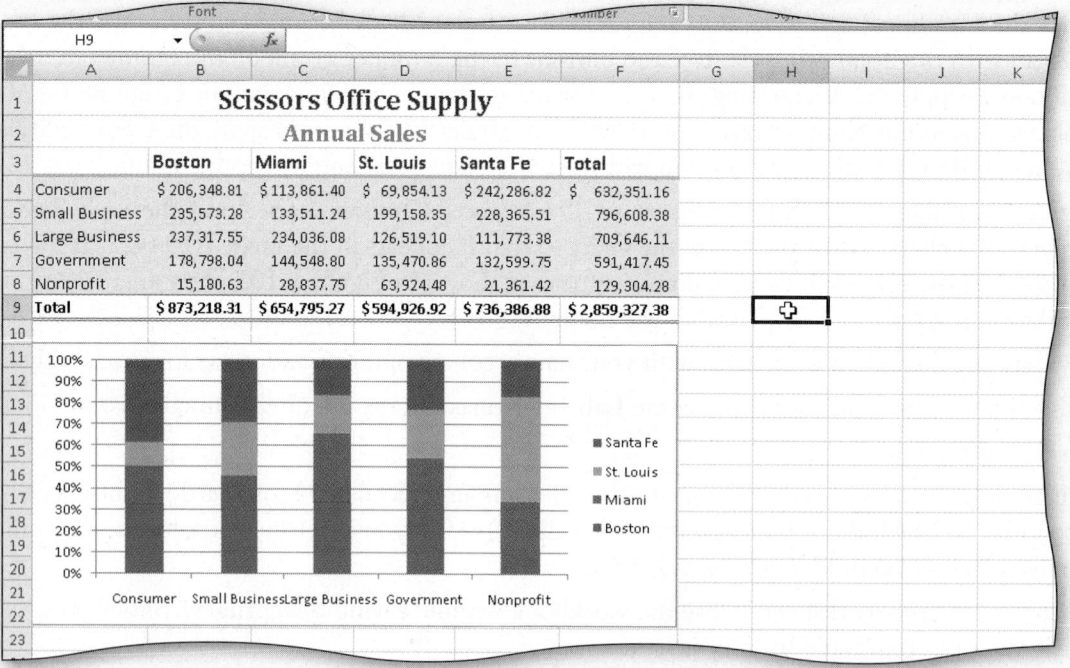

Figure 1–103

4. Format the range A3:F3 with the Heading 2 cell style, the range A4:F8 with the 20% - Accent3 cell style, and the range B9:F9 with the Total cell style. Use the Number group on the Ribbon to format cells B4:F4 and B9:F9 with the Accounting Number Format and cells B5:F8 with the Comma Style numeric format.

5. Chart the range A3:E8. Insert a 100% Stacked Column chart for the range A3:E8, as shown in Figure 1–103, by using the Column button on the Insert tab on the Ribbon. Use the chart location A11:F22.

6. Update the document properties with your name, course number, and name for the workbook.

7. Save the workbook using the file name, Lab 1-2 Scissors Office Supply Annual Sales. Print the worksheet.

8. Two corrections to the figures were sent in from the accounting department. The correct sales are $98,342.16 for Miami's annual Small Business sales (cell C5) and $48,933.75 for St. Louis's annual Nonprofit sales (cell D8). After you enter the two corrections, the company total in cell F9 should equal $2,809,167.57. Print the revised worksheet.

9. Use the Undo button to change the worksheet back to the original numbers in Table 1–8. Use the Redo button to change the worksheet back to the revised state.

10. Close Excel without saving the latest changes. Start Excel and open the workbook saved in Step 7. Double-click cell E6 and use in-cell editing to change the Santa Fe annual Large Business sales (cell E6) to $154,108.49. Write the company total in cell F9 at the top of the first printout. Click the Undo button.

11. Click cell A1 and then click the Merge & Center button to split cell A1 into cells A1, B1, C1, D1, E1, and F1. To merge the cells into one again, select the range A1:F1 and then click the Merge & Center button on the Home tab on the Ribbon.

12. Close the workbook without saving the changes. Submit the assignment as requested by your instructor.

In the Lab

Lab 3: College Cost and Financial Support Worksheet

Problem: Attending college is an expensive proposition and your resources are limited. To plan for your four-year college career, you have decided to organize your anticipated resources and costs in a worksheet. The data required to prepare your worksheet is shown in Table 1–9.

Table 1–9 College Cost and Resources

Cost	Freshman	Sophomore	Junior	Senior
Books	450.00	477.00	505.62	535.95
Room & Board	7500.00	7950.00	8427.00	8932.62
Tuition	8200.00	8692.00	9213.52	9766.33
Entertainment	1325.00	1404.50	1488.77	1578.10
Miscellaneous	950.00	1007.00	1067.42	1131.47
Clothes	725.00	768.50	814.61	863.49

Financial Support	Freshman	Sophomore	Junior	Senior
Job	3400.00	3604.00	3820.24	4049.45
Savings	4350.00	4611.00	4887.66	5180.92
Parents	4700.00	4982.00	5280.92	5597.78
Financial Aid	5500.00	5830.00	6179.80	6550.59
Other	1200.00	1272.00	1348.32	1429.22

Continued >

Instructions Part 1: Using the numbers in Table 1–9, create the worksheet shown in columns A through F in Figure 1–104. Format the worksheet title as Calibri 24-point bold red. Merge and center the worksheet title in cell A1 across columns A through F. Format the worksheet subtitles in cells A2 and A11 as Calibri 16-point bold green. Format the ranges A3:F3 and A12:F12 with the Heading 2 cell style, the ranges A4:F9 and A13:F17 with the 20% - Accent cell style, and the ranges A10:F10 and A18:F18 with the Total cell style.

Update the document properties, including the addition of at least one keyword to the properties, and save the workbook using the file name, Lab 1-3 Part 1 College Cost and Financial Support. Print the worksheet. Submit the assignment as requested by your instructor.

A20												
	A	B	C	D	E	F	G	H	I	J	K	L
1	**College Cost and Financial Support**											
2	Cost						Freshman Expenses					
3		Freshman	Sophomore	Junior	Senior	Total						
4	Books	$ 450.00	$ 477.00	$ 505.62	$ 535.95	$ 1,968.57				Books		
5	Room & Board	7,500.00	7,950.00	8,427.00	8,932.62	32,809.62				Room & Board		
6	Tuition	8,200.00	8,692.00	9,213.52	9,766.33	35,871.85				Tuition		
7	Entertainment	1,325.00	1,404.50	1,488.77	1,578.10	5,796.37				Entertainment		
8	Miscellaneous	950.00	1,007.00	1,067.42	1,131.47	4,155.89				Miscellaneous		
9	Clothes	725.00	768.50	814.61	863.49	3,171.60				Clothes		
10	Total	$19,150.00	$ 20,299.00	$21,516.94	$22,807.96	$83,773.90						
11	Financial Support						Freshman Financial Support					
12		Freshman	Sophomore	Junior	Senior	Total						
13	Job	$ 3,400.00	$ 3,604.00	$ 3,820.24	$ 4,049.45	$14,873.69				Job		
14	Savings	4,350.00	4,611.00	4,887.66	5,180.92	19,029.58				Savings		
15	Parents	4,700.00	4,982.00	5,280.92	5,597.78	20,560.70				Parents		
16	Financial Aid	5,500.00	5,830.00	6,179.80	6,550.59	24,060.39				Financial Aid		
17	Other	1,200.00	1,272.00	1,348.32	1,429.22	5,249.54				Other		
18	Total	$19,150.00	$ 20,299.00	$21,516.94	$22,807.96	$83,773.90						

Figure 1–104

After reviewing the numbers, you realize you need to increase manually each of the Junior-year expenses in column D by $600. Change the Junior-year expenses to reflect this change. Manually change the financial aid for the Junior year by the amount required to cover the increase in costs. The totals in cells F10 and F18 should equal $87,373.90. Print the worksheet. Close the workbook without saving changes.

Instructions Part 2: Open the workbook Lab 1-3 Part 1 College Cost and Financial Support and then save the workbook using the file name, Lab 1-3 Part 2 College Cost and Financial Support. Insert an Exploded pie in 3-D chart in the range G3:K10 to show the contribution of each category of cost for the Freshman year. Chart the range A4:B9 and apply the Style 8 chart style to the chart. Add the Pie chart title as shown in cell G2 in Figure 1–104. Insert an Exploded pie in 3-D chart in the range G12:K18 to show the contribution of each category of financial support for the Freshman year. Chart the range A13:B17 and apply the Style 8 chart style to the chart. Add the Pie chart title shown in cell G11 in Figure 1–104. Update the identification area with the exercise part number and save the workbook. Print the worksheet. Submit the assignment as requested by your instructor.

Instructions Part 3: Open the workbook Lab 1-3 Part 2 College Cost and Financial Support. Do not save the workbook in this part. A close inspection of Table 1–9 shows that both cost and financial support figures increase 6% each year. Use Excel Help to learn how to enter the data for the last three years using a formula and the Copy and Paste buttons on the Home tab on the Ribbon. For example, the formula to enter in cell C4 is =B4*1.06. Enter formulas to replace all the numbers in the range C4:E9 and C13:E17. If necessary, reformat the tables, as described in Part 1. The worksheet should appear as shown in Figure 1–104, except that some of the totals will be off by 0.01 due to rounding errors. Save the worksheet using the file name, Lab 1-3 Part 3 College Cost and Financial Support. Print the worksheet. Press CTRL+ACCENT MARK (`) to display the formulas. Print the formulas version. Submit the assignment as requested by your instructor. Close the workbook without saving changes.

Cases and Places

Apply your creative thinking and problem solving skills to design and implement a solution.

• EASIER   •• MORE DIFFICULT

• 1: Design and Create a Workbook to Analyze Yearly Sales

You are working as a summer intern for Hit-the-Road Mobile Services. Your manager has asked you to prepare a worksheet to help her analyze historical yearly sales by type of product (Table 1–10). Use the concepts and techniques presented in this chapter to create the worksheet and an embedded 3-D Clustered Column chart.

Table 1–10 Hit-the-Road Mobile Services Sales	2005	2006	2007	2008
Standard Mobile Phones	87598	99087	129791	188785
Camera Phones	71035	75909	96886	100512
Music Phones	65942	24923	34590	15696
Wireless PDAs	67604	58793	44483	35095
Satellite Radios	15161	27293	34763	43367
Headsets	9549	6264	2600	4048
Other Accessories	47963	108059	100025	62367

• 2: Design and Create a Worksheet and Chart to Analyze a Budget

To estimate the funds needed by your school's Environmental Club to make it through the upcoming year, you decide to create a budget for the club itemizing the expected quarterly expenses. The anticipated expenses are listed in Table 1–11. Use the concepts and techniques presented in this chapter to create the worksheet and an embedded 3-D Column chart using an appropriate chart style that compares the quarterly cost of each expense. Use the AutoCalculate area to determine the average amount spent per quarter on each expense. Manually insert the averages with appropriate titles in an empty area on the worksheet.

Table 1–11 Quarterly Environmental Club Budget	Jan – Mar	April – June	July – Sept	Oct – Dec
Meeting Room Rent	300	300	150	450
Copies and Supplies	390	725	325	640
Travel	450	755	275	850
Refreshments	105	85	215	155
Speaker Fees	200	200	0	500
Miscellaneous	125	110	75	215

Continued >

Cases and Places *continued*

• • 3: Create a 3-D Pie Chart to Analyze Quarterly Revenue

In-the-Villa DVD Rental is a DVD movie rental store. The owner of the store is trying to decide if it is feasible to hire more employees during certain times of the year. You have been asked to develop a worksheet totaling all the revenue received last year by quarter. The revenue per quarter is: Quarter 1, $52,699.23; Quarter 2, $111,244.32; Quarter 3, $70,905.03; and Quarter 4, $87,560.10. Create a 3-D Pie chart to illustrate quarterly revenue contribution by quarter. Use the AutoCalculate area to find the average, maximum, and minimum quarterly revenue and manually enter them and their corresponding identifiers in an empty area of the worksheet.

• • 4: Design and Create a Workbook to Analyze Your Field of Interest

Make It Personal

Based on your college major, area of interest, or career, use an Internet search engine or other research material to determine the total number of people employed in your chosen field of interest in the country over the past five years. For each year, break the yearly number down into two or more categories. For example, the number for each year can be broken into management and nonmanagement employees. Create an Excel worksheet that includes this data. Place the data in appropriate rows and columns for each year and category. Create totals for each row, totals for each column, and a grand total. Format the worksheet title, column headings, and data using the concepts presented in this chapter. Create a properly formatted Clustered Cone chart for the data and place it below the data in the worksheet. Make certain that years are on the X axis and number of employees is on the Y axis.

• • 5: Design and Create a Workbook to Analyze Your School

Working Together

Visit the registrar's office at your school and obtain data, such as age, gender, and full-time versus part-time status, for the students majoring in at least six different academic departments this semester. Have each member of your team divide the data into different categories. For example, separate the data by:

1. Age, divided into four different age groups

2. Gender, divided into male and female

3. Status, divided into full-time and part-time

After coordinating the data as a group, have each member independently use the concepts and techniques presented in this chapter to create a worksheet and appropriate chart to show the total students by characteristics by academic department. As a group, critique each worksheet and have each member modify his or her worksheet based on the group recommendations.

2 | Formulas, Functions, Formatting, and Web Queries

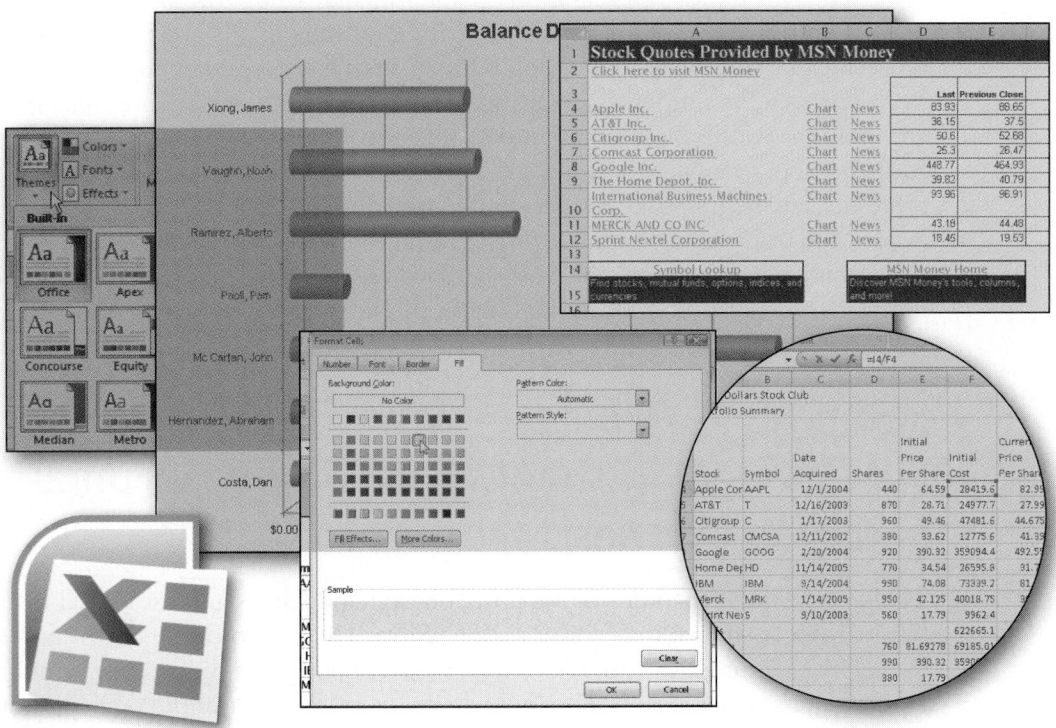

Objectives

You will have mastered the material in this chapter when you can:

- Enter formulas using the keyboard and Point mode
- Apply the AVERAGE, MAX, and MIN functions
- Verify a formula using Range Finder
- Apply a theme to a workbook
- Add conditional formatting to cells
- Change column width and row height
- Check the spelling of a worksheet

- Set margins, headers and footers in Page Layout View
- Preview and print versions of a worksheet
- Use a Web query to get real-time data from a Web site
- Rename sheets in a workbook
- E-mail the active workbook from within Excel

2 | Formulas, Functions, Formatting, and Web Queries

Introduction

In Chapter 1, you learned how to enter data, sum values, format the worksheet to make it easier to read, and draw a chart. You also learned about using Help and saving, printing, and opening a workbook. This chapter continues to highlight these topics and presents some new ones.

The new topics covered in this chapter include using formulas and functions to create a worksheet. A **function** is a prewritten formula that is built into Excel. Other new topics include smart tags and option buttons, verifying formulas, applying a theme to a worksheet, adding borders, formatting numbers and text, using conditional formatting, changing the widths of columns and heights of rows, spell checking, e-mailing from within an application, renaming worksheets, using alternative types of worksheet displays and printouts, and adding page headers and footers to a worksheet. One alternative worksheet display and printout shows the formulas in the worksheet, instead of the values. When you display the formulas in the worksheet, you see exactly what text, data, formulas, and functions you have entered into it. Finally, this chapter covers Web queries to obtain real-time data from a Web site.

Project — Worksheet with Formulas, Functions, and Web Queries

The project in the chapter follows proper design guidelines and uses Excel to create the two worksheets shown in Figure 2–1. The Silver Dollars Stock Club was started and is owned by a national academic fraternity, which pools contributions from a number of local chapters. Each local chapter contributes $150 per month; the money is then invested in the stock market for the benefit of the organization and as a tool to help members learn about investing. At the end of each month, the club's treasurer summarizes the club's financial status in a portfolio summary. This summary includes information such as the stocks owned by the club, the cost of the stocks to the club, and the gain or loss that the club has seen over time on the stock. As the complexity of the task of creating the summary increases, the treasurer wants to use Excel to create the monthly portfolio summary. The treasurer also sees an opportunity to use Excel's built-in capability to access real-time stock quotes over the Internet.

Recall that the first step in creating an effective worksheet is to make sure you understand what is required. The people who will use the worksheet usually provide requirements. The requirements document for the Silver Dollars Stock Club Portfolio Summary worksheet includes the following: needs, source of data, summary of calculations, Web requirements, and other facts about its development (Figure 2–2 on page EX 84). The real-time stock quotes (shown in Figure 2–1b) will be accessed via a Web query. The stock quotes will be returned to the active workbook on a separate worksheet. Microsoft determines the content and format of the Real-Time Stock Quotes worksheet.

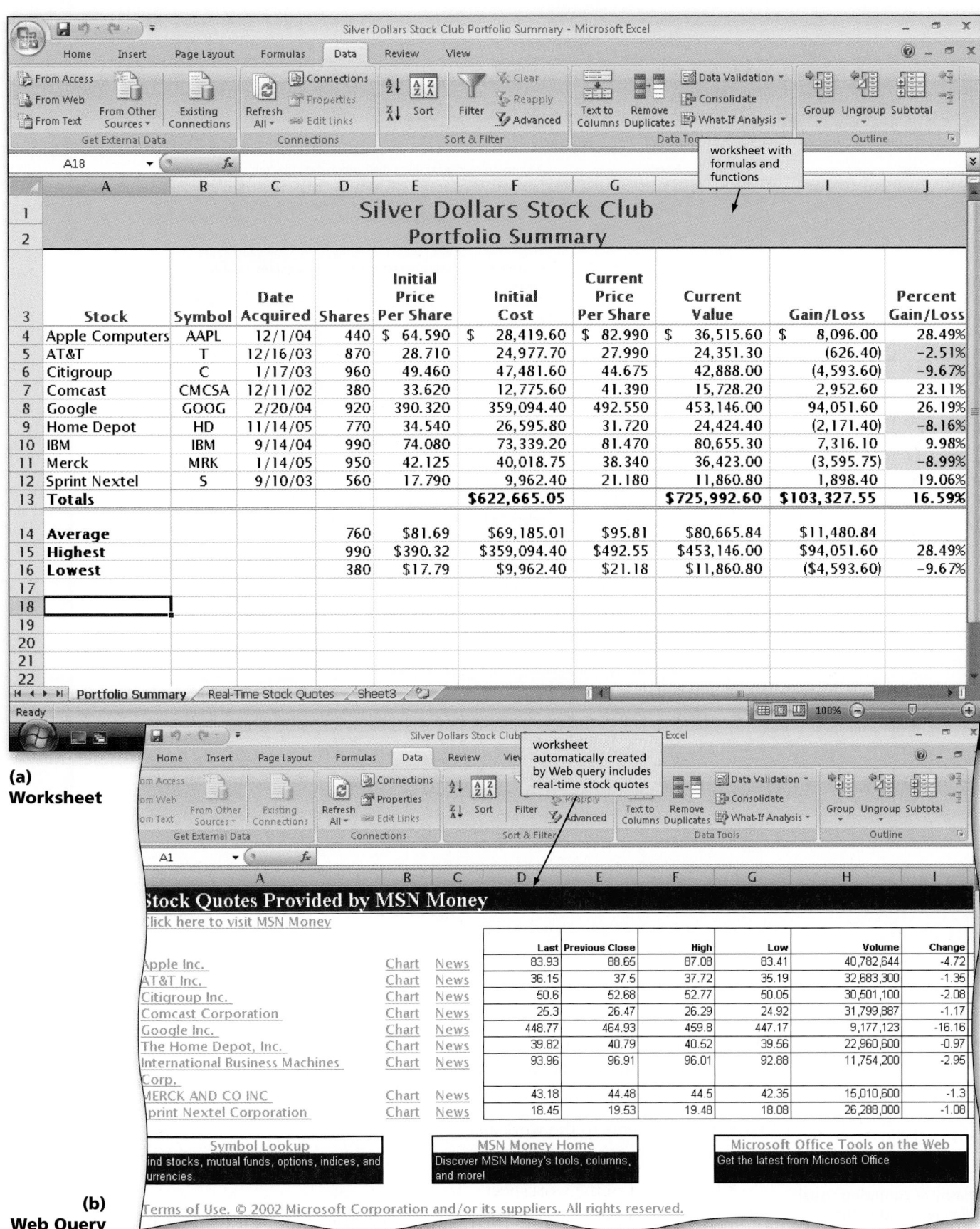

(a) Worksheet

(b) Web Query

Figure 2–1

REQUEST FOR NEW WORKSHEET

Date Submitted:	April 8, 2008
Submitted By:	Juan Castillo
Worksheet Title:	Silver Dollars Stock Club Portfolio Summary
Needs:	An easy-to-read worksheet that summarizes the club's investments (Figure 2-3). For each stock, the worksheet is to include the stock name, stock symbol, date acquired, shares, initial price per share, initial cost, current price per share, current value, gain/loss, and percent gain/loss. Also include totals and the average, highest value, and lowest value for each column of numbers. Use the import data capabilities of Excel to access real-time stock quotes using Web queries.
Source of Data:	The data supplied by Juan includes the stock names, symbols, dates acquired, number of shares, initial price per share, and current price per share. This data is shown in Table 2-1 on page EX 89.
Calculations:	The following calculations must be made for each of the stocks: 1. Initial Cost = Shares × Initial Price Per Share 2. Current Value = Shares × Current Price Per Share 3. Gain/Loss = Current Value − Initial Cost 4. Percent Gain/Loss = Gain/Loss / Initial Cost 5. Compute the totals for initial cost, current value, and gain/loss. 6. Use the AVERAGE function to determine the average for the number of shares, initial price per share, initial cost per share, current price per share, current value, and gain/loss. 7. Use the MAX and MIN functions to determine the highest and lowest values for the number of shares, initial price per share, initial cost per share, current price per share, current value, gain/loss, and percent gain/loss.
Web Requirements:	Use the Web query feature of Excel to get real-time stock quotes for the stocks owned by the Silver Dollars Stock Club.

Approvals

Approval Status:	X	Approved
		Rejected
Approved By:	Members of the Silver Dollars Stock Club	
Date:	April 15, 2008	
Assigned To:	J. Quasney, Spreadsheet Specialist	

Figure 2–2

BTW

Aesthetics versus Function
In designing a worksheet, functional considerations should come first, before visual aesthetics. The function, or purpose, of a worksheet is to provide a user with direct ways to accomplish tasks. Avoid the temptation to use flashy or confusing visual elements within the worksheet, unless they will help the user more easily complete a task.

Overview

As you read this chapter, you will learn how to create the worksheet shown in Figure 2–1 by performing these general tasks:

- Enter formulas and apply functions in the worksheet
- Add conditional formatting to the worksheet
- Apply a theme to the worksheet
- Work with the worksheet in Page Layout View
- Print a part of the worksheet
- Perform a Web query to get real-time data from a Web site and create a new worksheet
- E-mail the worksheet

Plan
Ahead

General Project Decisions

While creating an Excel worksheet, you need to make several decisions that will determine the appearance and characteristics of the finished worksheet. As you create the worksheet required to meet the requirements shown in Figure 2–2, you should follow these general guidelines:

1. **Plan the layout of the worksheet.** As discussed in Chapter 1 and shown in Figure 2–3, rows typically contain items analogous to items in a list. In the case of the stock club's data, the individual stocks serve this purpose and each stock should be placed in a row. As the club adds more stocks, the number of rows in the worksheet will increase. Information about each stock and associated calculations should appear in columns.

2. **Determine the necessary formulas and functions needed.** Values such as initial cost and current value are calculated from known values. The formulas for these calculations should be known in advance of creating the worksheet. Values such as the average, highest, and lowest values can be calculated using Excel functions as opposed to relying on complex formulas.

3. **Identify how to format various elements of the worksheet.** As discussed in Chapter 1 and shown in Figure 2–3, the appearance of the worksheet affects its ability to communicate clearly. Numeric data should be formatted in generally accepted formats, such as using commas as thousands separators and parentheses for negative values.

4. **Establish rules for conditional formatting.** Conditional formatting allows you to format a cell based on the contents of the cell. Decide under which circumstances you would like a cell to stand out from similar cells and determine in what way the cell will stand out. In the case of the Percent Gain/Loss column on the worksheet, placing a different background color in cells that show losses is an appropriate format for the column.

5. **Specify how the printed worksheet should appear.** When it is possible that a person will want to print a worksheet, care should be taken in the development of the worksheet to ensure that the contents can be printed in a readable manner. Excel prints worksheets in landscape or portrait orientation and margins can be adjusted to fit more or less data on each page. Headers and footers add an additional level of customization to the printed page.

(continued)

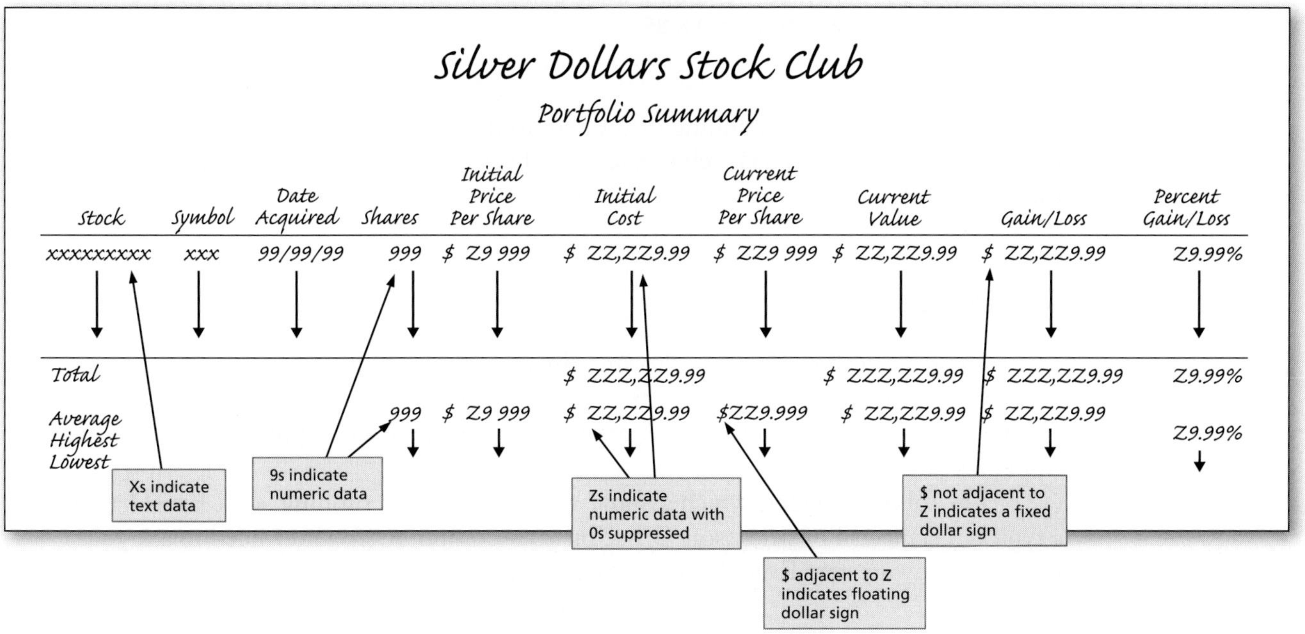

Figure 2–3

Plan Ahead

(continued)

6. **Gather information regarding the needed Web query.** You must also know what information the Web query requires in order for it to generate results that you can use in Excel.

7. **Choose names for the worksheets.** When a workbook includes multiple worksheets, each worksheet should be named. A good worksheet name is succinct, unique to the workbook, and meaningful to any user of the workbook.

In addition, using a sketch of the worksheet can help you visualize its design. The sketch for Silver Dollars Stock Club Portfolio Summary worksheet (Figure 2–3 on the previous page) includes a title, a subtitle, column and row headings, and the location of data values. It also uses specific characters to define the desired formatting for the worksheet as follows:

1. The row of Xs below the leftmost column defines the cell entries as text, such as stock names and stock symbols.

2. The rows of Zs and 9s with slashes, dollar signs, decimal points, commas, and percent signs in the remaining columns define the cell entries as numbers. The Zs indicate that the selected format should instruct Excel to suppress leading 0s. The 9s indicate that the selected format should instruct Excel to display any digits, including 0s.

3. The decimal point means that a decimal point should appear in the cell entry and indicates the number of decimal places to use.

4. The commas indicate that the selected format should instruct Excel to display a comma separator only if the number has enough digits to the left of the decimal point.

5. The slashes in the third column identify the cell entry as a date.

6. The dollar signs that are not adjacent to the Zs in the first row below the column headings and in the total row signify a fixed dollar sign. The dollar signs that are adjacent to the Zs below the total row signify a floating dollar sign, or one that appears next to the first significant digit.

7. The percent sign (%) in the far right column indicates a percent sign should appear after the number.

When necessary, more specific details concerning the above guidelines are presented at appropriate points in the chapter. The chapter also will identify the actions you perform and decisions made regarding these guidelines during the creation of the worksheet shown in Figure 2–3 on page EX 85.

With a good understanding of the requirements document, an understanding of the necessary decisions, and a sketch of the worksheet, the next step is to use Excel to create the worksheet.

To Start Excel

If you are using a computer to step through the project in this chapter and you want your screen to match the figures in this book, you should change your computer's resolution to 1024 × 768. For information about how to change a computer's resolution, read Appendix E.

The following steps, which assume Windows Vista is running, start Excel based on a typical installation of Microsoft Office on your computer. You may need to ask your instructor how to start Excel for your computer.

Note: If you are using Windows XP, see Appendix F for alternate steps.

1 Click the Start button on the Windows Vista taskbar to display the Start menu.

2 Point to All Programs at the bottom of the left pane on the Start menu to display the All Programs list.

3 Click Microsoft Office in the All Programs list to display the Microsoft Office list.

4 Click Microsoft Office Excel to start Excel and display a blank worksheet in the Excel window.

5 If the Excel window is not maximized, click the Maximize button next to the Close button on its title bar to maximize the window.

6 If the worksheet window in Excel is not maximized, click the Maximize button next to the Close button on its title bar to maximize the worksheet window within Excel.

BTW

Starting Excel
You can use a command-line switch to start Excel and control how it starts. First, click the Start button on the Windows Vista taskbar, and then click the Start Search box. Next, enter the complete path to Excel's application file including the switch (for example, C:\Program Files\Microsoft Office\ Office12\Excel.exe/e). The switch /e starts Excel without opening a new workbook; /i starts Excel with a maximized window; /p "folder" sets the active path to folder and ignores the default folder; /r "filename" opens filename in read-only mode; and /s starts Excel in safe mode.

Entering the Titles and Numbers into the Worksheet

The first step in creating the worksheet is to enter the titles and numbers into the worksheet.

To Enter the Worksheet Title and Subtitle

The following steps enter the worksheet title and subtitle into cells A1 and A2.

1 If necessary, select cell A1. Type `Silver Dollars Stock Club` in the cell and then press the DOWN ARROW key to enter the worksheet title in cell A1.

2 Type `Portfolio Summary` in cell A2 and then press the DOWN ARROW key to enter the worksheet subtitle in cell A2 (Figure 2–4 on page EX 89).

To Enter the Column Titles

The column titles in row 3 begin in cell A3 and extend through cell J3. The column titles in Figure 2–3 include multiple lines of text. To start a new line in a cell, press ALT+ENTER after each line, except for the last line, which is completed by clicking the Enter box, pressing the ENTER key, or pressing one of the arrow keys. When you see ALT+ENTER in a step, press the ENTER key while holding down the ALT key and then release both keys.

The stock names and the row titles Totals, Average, Highest, and Lowest in the leftmost column begin in cell A4 and continue down to cell A16. This data is entered into rows 4 through 12 of the worksheet. The remainder of this section explains the steps required to enter the column titles, stock data, and row titles as shown in Figure 2–4 on page EX 89 and then save the workbook.

1 With cell A3 selected, type `Stock` and then press the RIGHT ARROW key.

2 Type `Symbol` in cell B3 and then press the RIGHT ARROW key.

BTW

Wrapping Text
If you have a long text entry, such as a paragraph, you can instruct Excel to wrap the text in a cell, rather than pressing ALT+ENTER to end a line. To wrap text, right-click in the cell, click Format Cells on the shortcut menu, click the Alignment tab, click Wrap text, and then click OK. Excel will increase the height of the cell automatically so the additional lines will fit. If you want to control where each line ends in the cell, rather than letting Excel wrap based on the cell width, however, then you must end each line with ALT+ENTER.

3 In cell C3, type `Date` and then press ALT+ENTER. Type `Acquired` and then press the RIGHT ARROW key.

4 In cell D3, type `Shares` and then press the RIGHT ARROW key.

5 In cell E3, type `Initial` and then press ALT+ENTER. Type `Price` and then press ALT+ENTER. Type `Per Share` and then press the RIGHT ARROW key.

6 Type `Initial` in cell F3 and then press ALT+ENTER. Type `Cost` and then press the RIGHT ARROW key.

7 In cell G3, type `Current` and then press ALT+ENTER. Type `Price` and then press ALT+ENTER. Type `Per Share` and then press the RIGHT ARROW key.

8 Type `Current` in cell H3 and then press ALT+ENTER. Type `Value` and then press the RIGHT ARROW key.

9 In cell I3, type `Gain/Loss` and then press the RIGHT ARROW key.

10 In cell J3, type `Percent` and then press ALT+ENTER. Type `Gain/Loss`.

BTW

Two-Digit Years
When you enter a two-digit year value, Excel changes a two-digit year less than 30 to 20xx and a two-digit year of 30 and greater to 19xx. Use four-digit years to ensure that Excel interprets year values the way you intend, if necessary.

To Enter the Portfolio Summary Data

The portfolio summary data in Table 2–1 includes a purchase date for each stock. Excel considers a date to be a number and, therefore, it displays the date right-aligned in the cell. The following steps enter the portfolio summary data shown in Table 2–1.

1 Select cell A4, type `Apple Computers`, and then press the RIGHT ARROW key.

2 Type `AAPL` in cell B4 and then press the RIGHT ARROW key.

3 Type `12/1/04` in cell C4 and then press the RIGHT ARROW key.

4 Type `440` in cell D4 and then press the RIGHT ARROW key.

5 Type `64.59` in cell E4 and then click cell G4.

6 Type `82.99` in cell G4 and then click cell A5.

7 Enter the portfolio summary data in Table 2–1 for the eight remaining stocks in rows 5 through 12 (Figure 2–4).

BTW

Formatting a Worksheet
With early worksheet programs, users often skipped rows to improve the appearance of the worksheet. With Excel it is not necessary to skip rows because you can increase row heights to add white space between information.

To Enter the Row Titles

1 Select cell A13. Type `Totals` and then press the DOWN ARROW key. Type `Average` in cell A14 and then press the DOWN ARROW key.

2 Type `Highest` in cell A15 and then press the DOWN ARROW key. Type `Lowest` in cell A16 and then press the ENTER key. Select cell F4 (Figure 2–4).

Table 2–1 Silver Dollars Stock Club Portfolio Summary Data

Stock	Symbol	Date Acquired	Shares	Initial Price Per Share	Current Price Per Share
Apple Computers	AAPL	12/1/04	440	64.59	82.99
AT&T	T	12/16/03	870	28.71	27.99
Citigroup	C	1/17/03	960	49.46	44.675
Comcast	CMCSA	12/11/02	380	33.62	41.39
Google	GOOG	2/20/04	920	390.32	492.55
Home Depot	HD	11/14/05	770	34.54	31.72
IBM	IBM	9/14/04	990	74.08	81.47
Merck	MRK	1/14/05	950	42.125	38.34
Sprint Nextel	S	9/10/03	560	17.79	21.18

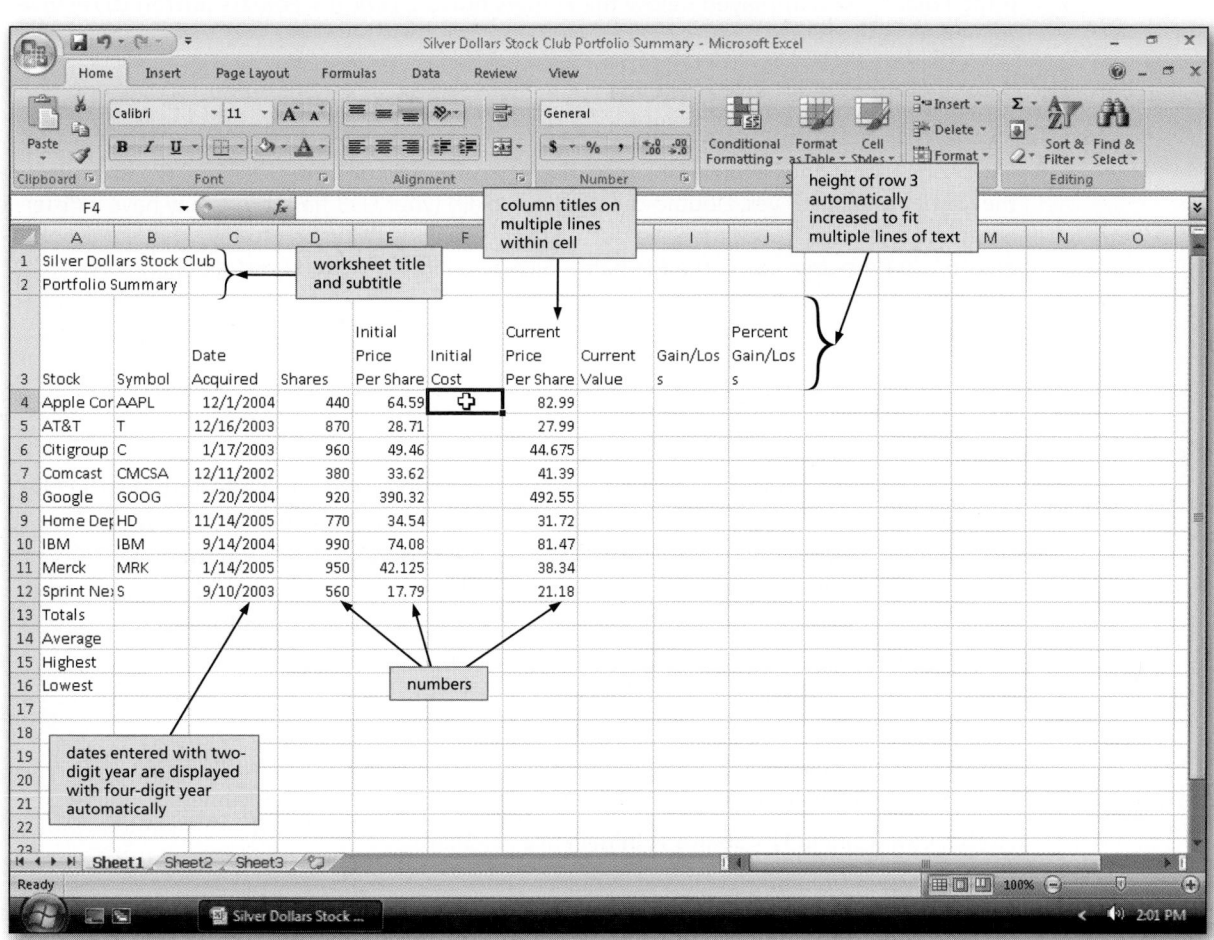

Figure 2–4

To Change Workbook Properties and Save the Workbook

With the data entered into the worksheet, the following steps save the workbook using the file name, Silver Dollars Stock Club Portfolio Summary. As you are building a workbook, it is a good idea to save it often so that you do not lose your work if the computer is turned off or if you lose electrical power. The first time you save a workbook, you should change the workbook properties.

BTW

Entering Numbers in a Range
An efficient way to enter data into a range of cells is to select a range and then enter the first number in the upper-left cell of the range. Excel responds by entering the value and moving the active cell selection down one cell. When you enter the last value in the first column, Excel moves the active cell selection to the top of the next column.

1 Click the Office Button, click Prepare on the Office Button menu, and then click Properties.

2 Update the document properties with your name and any other information required.

3 Click the Close button on the Document Properties pane.

Note: If you are using Windows XP, see Appendix F for alternate steps.

4 With a USB flash drive connected to one of the computer's USB ports, click the Save button on the Quick Access Toolbar.

5 When Excel displays the Save As dialog box, type `Silver Dollars Stock Club Portfolio Summary` in the File name text box.

6 If the Folders list is displayed below the Folders button, click the Folders button to remove the Folders list.

7 If Computer is not displayed in the Favorite Links section, drag the top or bottom edge of the Save As dialog box until Computer is displayed.

8 Click Computer in the Favorite Links section. If necessary, scroll until UDISK 2.0 (E:) appears in the list of available drives. Double-click UDISK 2.0 (E:) (your USB flash drive may have a different name and letter). Click the Save button in the Save As dialog box to save the workbook on the USB flash drive using the file name, Silver Dollars Stock Club Portfolio Summary.

Entering Formulas

One of the reasons Excel is such a valuable tool is that you can assign a **formula** to a cell and Excel will calculate the result. Consider, for example, what would happen if you had to multiply 440×64.59 and then manually enter the product, 28,419.60, in cell F4. Every time the values in cells D4 or E4 changed, you would have to recalculate the product and enter the new value in cell F4. By contrast, if you enter a formula in cell F4 to multiply the values in cells D4 and E4, Excel recalculates the product whenever new values are entered into those cells and displays the result in cell F4.

Plan Ahead

> **Determine the necessary formulas and functions needed.**
> The formulas needed in the worksheet are noted in the requirements document as follows:
>
> 1. Initial Cost (column F) = Shares × Initial Price Per Share
>
> 2. Current Value (column H) = Shares × Current Price Per Share
>
> 3. Gain/Loss (column I) = Current Value – Initial Cost
>
> 4. Percent Gain/Loss (column J) = Gain/Loss / Initial Cost
>
> The necessary functions to determine the average, highest, and lowest numbers are discussed shortly.

To Enter a Formula Using the Keyboard

The initial cost for each stock, which appears in column F, is equal to the number of shares in column D times the initial price per share in column E. Thus, the initial cost for Apple Computers in cell F4 is obtained by multiplying 440 (cell D4) by 64.59 (cell E4) or =D4*E4. The following steps enter the initial cost formula in cell F4 using the keyboard.

1

• With cell **F4** selected, type =d4*e4 in the cell to display the formula in the formula bar and in cell F4 and to display colored borders around the cells referenced in the formula (Figure 2–5).

Q&A

What is happening on the worksheet as I enter the formula?

The **equal sign** (=) preceding d4*e4 is an important part of the formula. It alerts Excel that you are entering a formula or function and not text. Because the most common error when entering a formula is to reference the wrong cell in a formula mistakenly, Excel colors the borders of the cells referenced in the formula. The coloring helps in the reviewing process to ensure the cell references are correct. The **asterisk** (*) following d4 is the arithmetic operator that directs Excel to perform the multiplication operation.

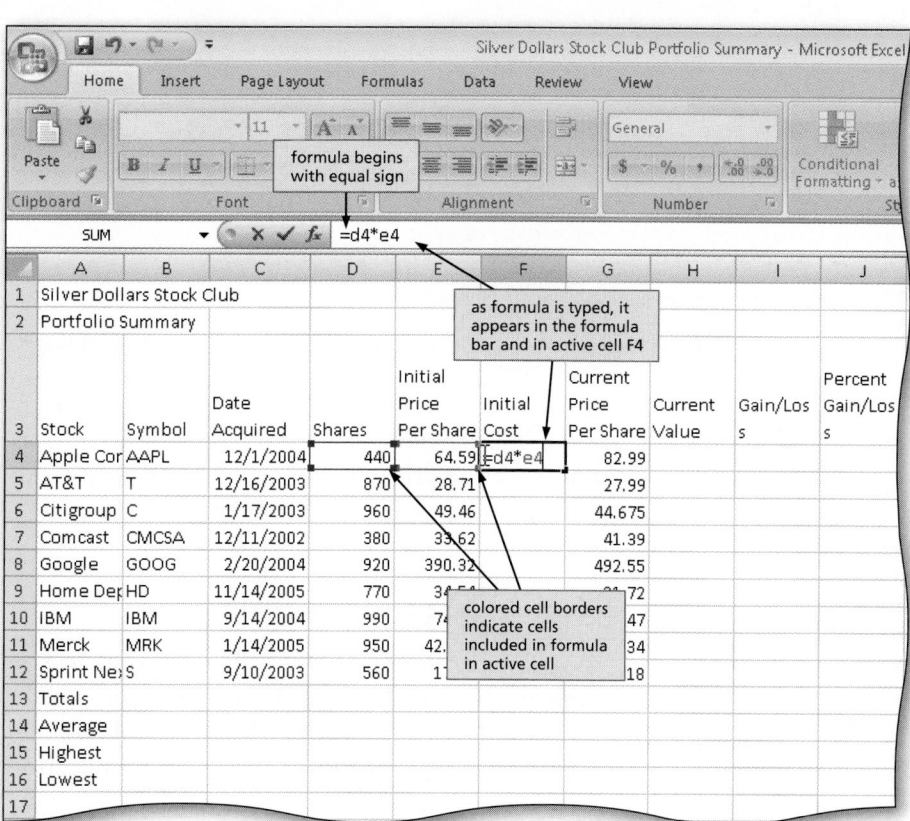

Figure 2–5

2

• Press the RIGHT ARROW key twice to complete the arithmetic operation indicated by the formula, display the result, 28419.6, and to select cell H4 (Figure 2–6).

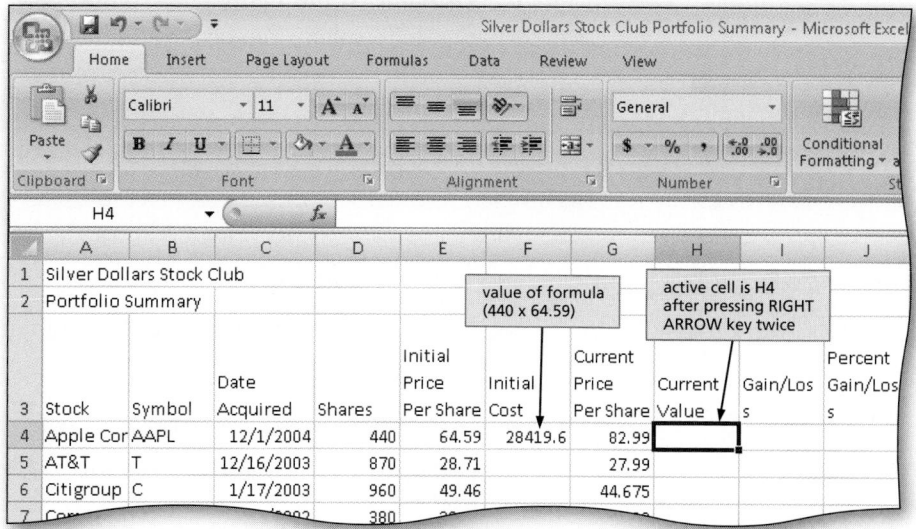

Figure 2–6

Arithmetic Operations

Table 2–2 describes multiplication and other valid Excel arithmetic operators.

Table 2–2 Summary of Arithmetic Operators

Arithmetic Operator	Meaning	Example of Usage	Meaning
–	Negation	–34	Negative 34
%	Percentage	=72%	Multiplies 72 by 0.01
^	Exponentiation	=4 ^ 6	Raises 4 to the sixth power
*	Multiplication	=22.6 * F4	Multiplies the contents of cell F4 by 22.6
/	Division	=C3 / C6	Divides the contents of cell C3 by the contents of cell C6
+	Addition	=7 + 3	Adds 7 and 3
–	Subtraction	=F12 – 22	Subtracts 22 from the contents of cell F12

BTW

Troubling Formulas
If Excel does not accept a formula, remove the equal sign from the left side and complete the entry as text. Later, after you have entered additional data or determined the error, reinsert the equal sign to change the text back to a formula and edit the formula as needed.

You can enter the cell references in formulas in uppercase or lowercase, and you can add spaces before and after arithmetic operators to make the formulas easier to read. The formula, =d4*e4, is the same as the formulas, =d4 * e4, =D4 * e4, or =D4 * E4.

Order of Operations

When more than one arithmetic operator is involved in a formula, Excel follows the same basic order of operations that you use in algebra. Moving from left to right in a formula, the **order of operations** is as follows: first negation (–), then all percentages (%), then all exponentiations (^), then all multiplications (*) and divisions (/), and finally, all additions (+) and subtractions (–).

You can use parentheses to override the order of operations. For example, if Excel follows the order of operations, 5 * 9 + 8 equals 53. If you use parentheses, however, to change the formula to 5 * (9 + 8), the result is 85, because the parentheses instruct Excel to add 9 and 8 before multiplying by 5. Table 2–3 illustrates several examples of valid Excel formulas and explains the order of operations.

Table 2–3 Examples of Excel Formulas

Formula	Meaning
=K12	Assigns the value in cell K12 to the active cell.
=10 + 4^2	Assigns the sum of 10 + 16 (or 26) to the active cell.
=3 * C20 or =C20 * 3 or =(3 * C20)	Assigns three times the contents of cell C20 to the active cell.
=50% * 12	Assigns the product of 0.50 times 12 (or 6) to the active cell.
– (H3 * Q30)	Assigns the negative value of the product of the values contained in cells H3 and Q30 to the active cell.
=12 * (N8 – O8)	Assigns the product of 12 times the difference between the values contained in cells N8 and O8 to the active cell.
=M9 / Z8 – C3 * Q19 + A3 ^ B3	Completes the following operations, from left to right: exponentiation (A3 ^ B3), then division (M9 / Z8), then multiplication (C3 * Q19), then subtraction (M9 / Z8) – (C3 * Q19), and finally addition (M9 / Z8 – C3 * Q19) + (A3 ^ B3). If cells A3 = 2, B3 = 4, C3 = 6, M9 = 3, Q19 = 4, and Z8 = 3, then Excel assigns the active cell the value 18; that is, 3 / 3 – 6 * 4 + 2 ^ 4 = -7.

To Enter Formulas Using Point Mode

The sketch of the worksheet in Figure 2–3 on page EX 85 calls for the current value, gain/loss, and percent gain/loss of each stock to appear in columns H, I, and J respectively. All three of these values are calculated using formulas in row 4:

Current Value (cell H4) = Shares $\times$ Current Price Per Share or =D4*G4

Gain/Loss (cell I4) = Current Value – Initial Cost or H4-F4

Percent Gain/Loss (cell J4) = Gain/Loss / Initial Cost or I4/F4

An alternative to entering the formulas in cells H4, I4, and J4 using the keyboard is to enter the formulas using the mouse and Point mode. **Point mode** allows you to select cells for use in a formula by using the mouse. The following steps enter formulas using Point mode.

1

- With cell H4 selected, type = (equal sign) to begin the formula and then click cell D4 to add a reference to cell D4 to the formula (Figure 2–7).

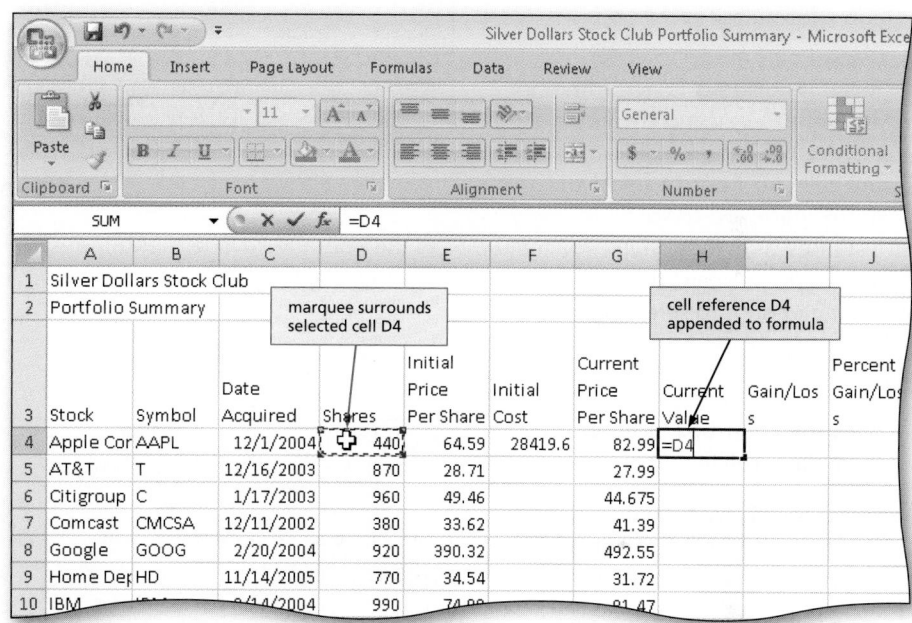

Figure 2–7

2

- Type * (asterisk) and then click cell G4 to add a multiplication operator and reference to cell G4 to the formula (Figure 2–8).

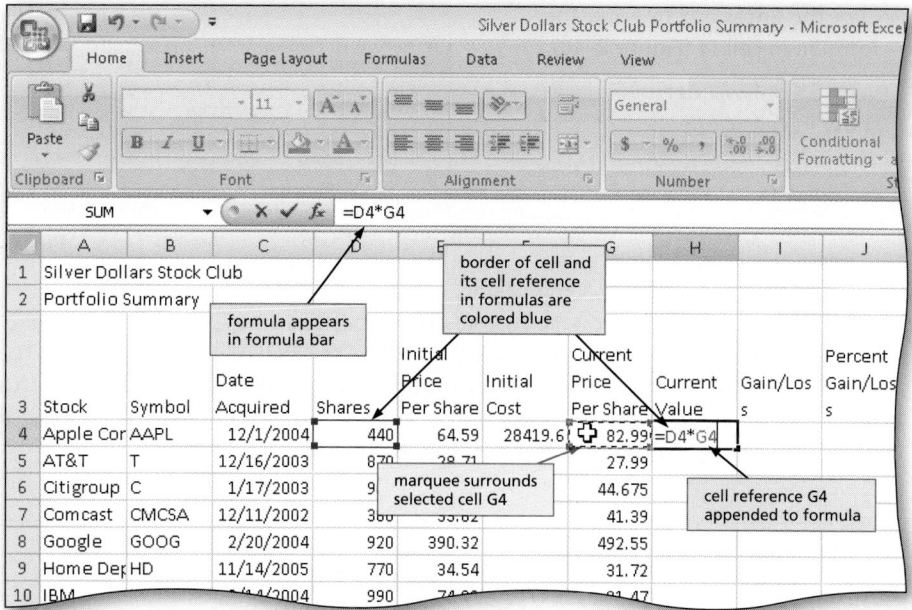

Figure 2–8

❸

- Click the Enter box and then click cell I4 to select cell I4.

- Type = (equal sign) and then click cell H4 to add a reference to cell H4 to the formula.

- Type – (minus sign) and then click cell F4 to add a subtraction operator and reference to cell F4 to the formula (Figure 2–9).

Q&A

When should I use Point mode to enter formulas?

Using Point mode to enter formulas often is faster and more accurate than using the keyboard to type the entire formula when the cell you want to select does not require you to scroll. In many instances, as in these steps, you may want to use both the keyboard and mouse when entering a formula in a cell. You can use the keyboard to begin the formula, for example, and then use the mouse to select a range of cells.

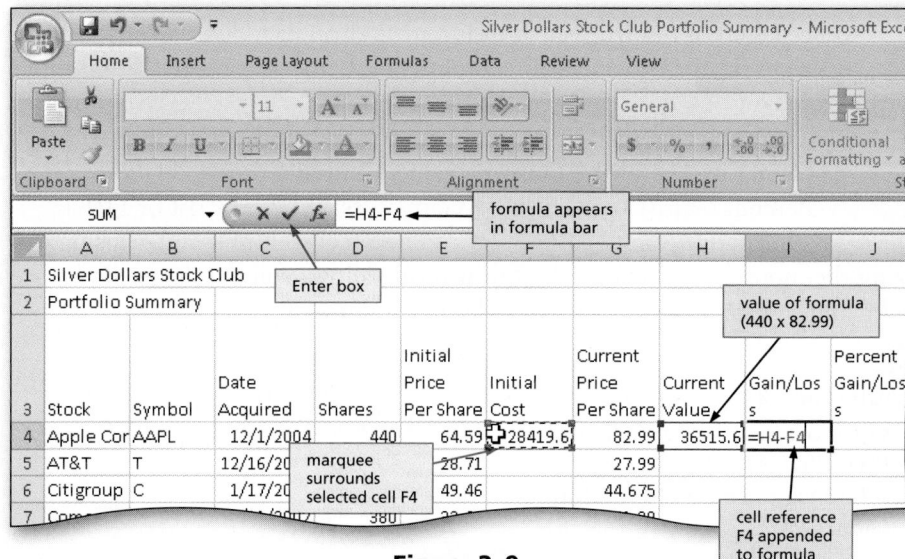

Figure 2–9

❹

- Click the Enter box to enter the formula in cell I4.

- Select cell J4. Type = (equal sign) and then click cell I4 to add a reference to cell I4 to the formula.

- Type / (forward slash) and then click cell F4 to add a reference to cell F4 to the formula.

- Click the Enter box to enter the formula in cell J4 (Figure 2–10).

Q&A

Why do only six decimal places show in cell J4?

The actual value assigned by Excel to cell J4 from the division operation in Step 4 is 0.284873819. While not all the decimal places appear in Figure 2–10, Excel maintains all of them for computational purposes. Thus, if referencing cell J4 in a formula, the value used for computational purposes is 0.284873819, not 0.284874. Excel displays the value in cell J4 as 0.284874 because the cell formatting is set to display only six digits after the decimal point. If you change the cell formatting of column J to display nine digits after the decimal point, then Excel displays the true value 0.284873819.

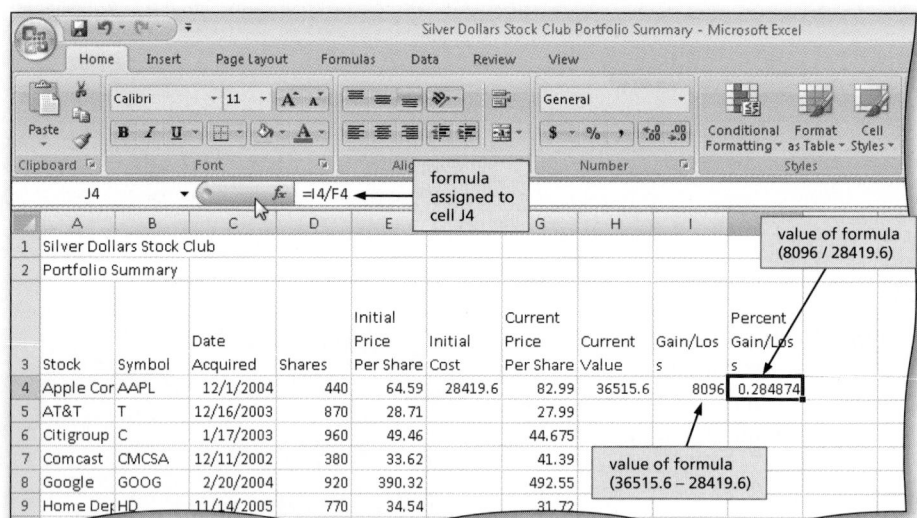

Figure 2–10

To Copy Formulas Using the Fill Handle

The four formulas for Apple Computers in cells F4, H4, I4, and J4 now are complete. You could enter the same four formulas one at a time for the eight remaining stocks. A much easier method of entering the formulas, however, is to select the formulas in row 4 and then use the fill handle to copy them through row 12. Recall from Chapter 1 that the fill handle is a small rectangle in the lower-right corner of the active cell or active range. The following steps copy the formulas using the fill handle.

- Select cell F4 and then point to the fill handle.

- Drag the fill handle down through cell F12 and continue to hold the mouse button to select the destination range (Figure 2–11).

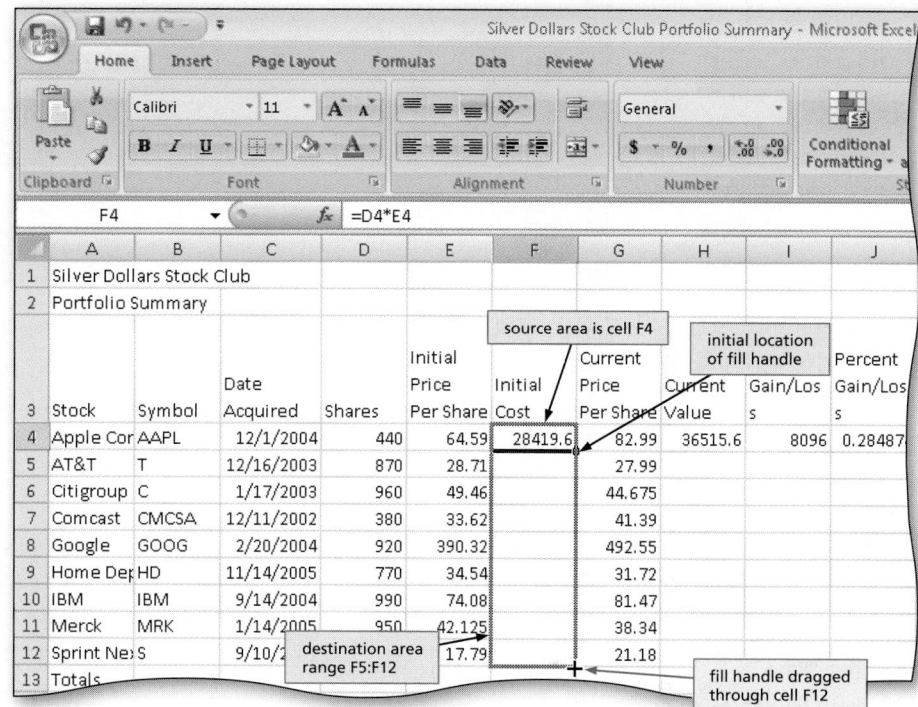

Figure 2–11

- Release the mouse button to copy the formula in cell F4 to the cells in the range F5:F12.

- Select the range H4:J4 and then point to the fill handle (Figure 2–12).

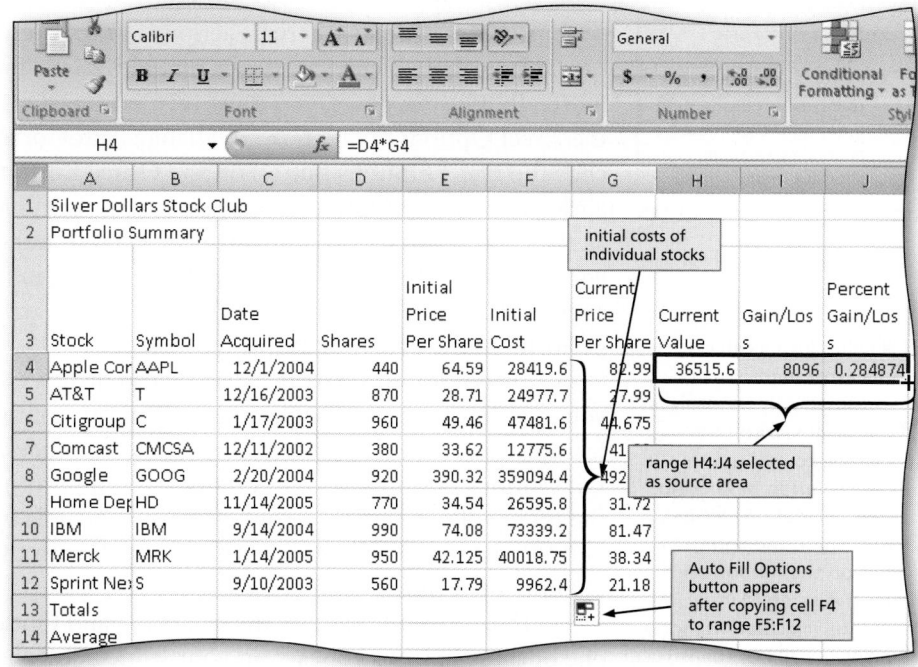

Figure 2–12

3

- Drag the fill handle down through the range H5:J12 to copy the three formulas =D4*G4 in cell H4, =H4-F4 in cell I4, and =I4/F4 in cell J4 to the range H5:J12 (Figure 2–13).

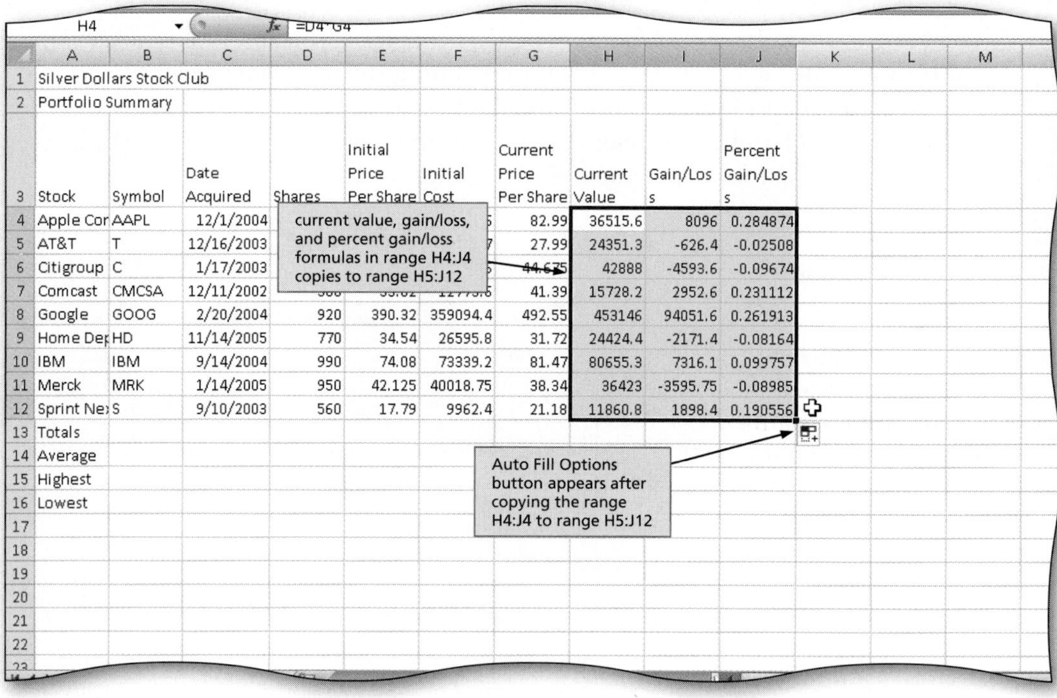

Q&A

How does Excel adjust the cell references in the formulas in the destination area?

Recall that when you copy a formula, Excel adjusts the cell references so the new formulas contain references corresponding to the new location and performs calculations using the appropriate

Figure 2–13

values. Thus, if you copy downward, Excel adjusts the row portion of cell references. If you copy across, then Excel adjusts the column portion of cell references. These cell references are called **relative cell references**.

Other Ways

1. Select source area, click Copy button on Ribbon, select destination area, click Paste button on Ribbon

2. Select source area, right-click copy area, click Copy on shortcut menu, select destination area, right-click paste area, click Paste on shortcut menu

BTW

Automatic Recalculation

Every time you enter a value into a cell in the worksheet, Excel automatically recalculates all formulas. You can change to manual recalculation by clicking the Calculation Options button on the Formulas tab on the Ribbon and then clicking Manual. In manual calculation mode, press the F9 key to instruct Excel to recalculate all formulas.

Smart Tags and Option Buttons

Excel can identify certain actions to take on specific data in workbooks using **smart tags**. Data labeled with smart tags includes dates, financial symbols, people's names, and more. To use smart tags, you must turn on smart tags using the AutoCorrect Options in the Excel Options dialog box. To change AutoCorrect options, click the Office Button, click the Excel Options button on the Office Button menu, point to Proofing, and then click AutoCorrect Options. Once smart tags are turned on, Excel places a small purple triangle, called a **smart tag indicator**, in a cell to indicate that a smart tag is available. When you move the insertion point over the smart tag indicator, the Smart Tag Actions button appears. Clicking the Smart Tag Actions button arrow produces a list of actions you can perform on the data in that specific cell.

In addition to smart tags, Excel also displays Options buttons in a workbook while you are working on it to indicate that you can complete an operation using automatic features such as AutoCorrect, Auto Fill, error checking, and others. For example, the Auto Fill Options button shown in Figure 2–13 appears after a fill operation, such as dragging the fill handle. When an error occurs in a formula in a cell, Excel displays the Trace Error button next to the cell and identifies the cell with the error by placing a green triangle in the upper left of the cell.

Table 2–4 summarizes the smart tag and Options buttons available in Excel. When one of these buttons appears on your worksheet, click the button arrow to produce the list of options for modifying the operation or to obtain additional information.

Table 2–4 Smart Tag and Options Buttons in Excel

Button	Name	Menu Function
	Auto Fill Options	Gives options for how to fill cells following a fill operation, such as dragging the fill handle.
	AutoCorrect Options	Undoes an automatic correction, stops future automatic corrections of this type, or causes Excel to display the AutoCorrect Options dialog box.
	Insert Options	Lists formatting options following an insertion of cells, rows, or columns.
	Paste Options	Specifies how moved or pasted items should appear (for example, with original formatting, without formatting, or with different formatting).
	Smart Tag Actions	Lists information options for a cell containing data recognized by Excel, such as a stock symbol.
	Trace Error	Lists error checking options following the assignment of an invalid formula to a cell.

To Determine Totals Using the Sum Button

The next step is to determine the totals in row 13 for the initial cost in column F, current value in column H, and gain/loss in column I. To determine the total initial cost in column F, the values in the range F4 through F12 must be summed. To do so, enter the function =sum(f4:f12) in cell F13 or select cell F13 and then click the Sum button on the Ribbon and then press the ENTER key. Recall that a function is a prewritten formula that is built into Excel. Similar SUM functions or the Sum button can be used in cells H13 and I13 to determine total current value and total gain/loss, respectively.

1 Select cell F13. Click the Sum button on the Ribbon and then click the Enter button.

2 Select the range H13:I13. Click the Sum button on the Ribbon to display the totals in row 13 as shown in Figure 2–14.

BTW

Selecting a Range
You can select a range using the keyboard. Press the F8 key and then use the arrow keys to select the desired range. After you are finished, make sure to press the F8 key to turn off the selection or you will continue to select ranges.

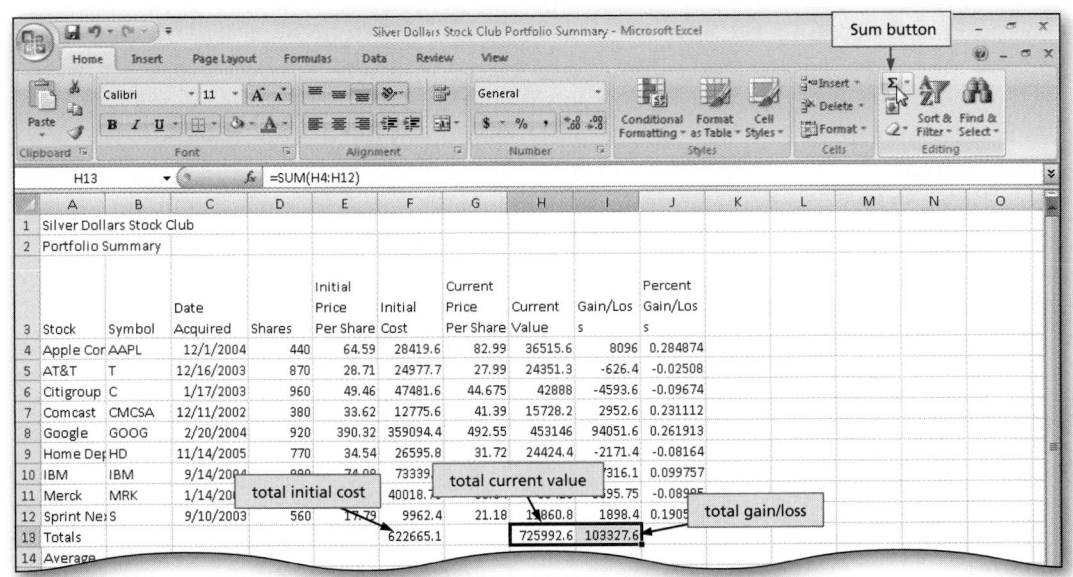

Figure 2–14

To Determine the Total Percent Gain/Loss

With the totals in row 13 determined, the next step is to copy the percent gain/loss formula in cell J12 to cell J13 as performed in the following steps.

1 Select cell J12 and then point to the fill handle.

2 Drag the fill handle down through cell J13 to copy the formula in cell J12 to cell J13 (Figure 2–15).

Q&A

Why was the formula I13/F13 not copied to cell J13 earlier?

The formula, I13/F13, was not copied to cell J13 when cell J4 was copied to the range J5:J12 because both cells involved in the computation (I13 and F13) were blank, or zero, at the time. A **blank cell** in Excel has a numerical value of zero, which would have resulted in an error message in cell J13. Once the totals were determined, both cells I13 and F13 (especially F13, because it is the divisor) had nonzero numerical values.

3	Stock	Symbol	Date Acquired	Shares	Initial Price Per Share	Initial Cost	Current Price Per Share	Current Value	Gain/Loss	Percent Gain/Loss
4	Apple Cor	AAPL	12/1/2004	440	64.59	28419.6	82.99	36515.6	8096	0.284874
5	AT&T	T	12/16/2003	870	28.71	24977.7	27.99	24351.3	-626.4	-0.02508
6	Citigroup	C	1/17/2003	960	49.46	47481.6	44.675	42888	-4593.6	-0.09674
7	Comcast	CMCSA	12/11/2002	380	33.62	12775.6	41.39	15728.2	2952.6	0.231112
8	Google	GOOG	2/20/2004	920	390.32	359094.4	492.55	453146	94051.6	0.261913
9	Home Dep	HD	11/14/2005	770	34.54	26595.8	31.72	24424.4	-2171.4	-0.08164
10	IBM	IBM	9/14/2004	990	74.08	73339.2	81.47	80655.3	7316.1	0.099757
11	Merck	MRK	1/14/2005	950	42.125	40018.75	38.34	36423	-3595.75	-0.08985
12	Sprint Nex	S	9/10/2003	560	17.79	9962.4	21.18	11860.8	1898.4	0.190556
13	Totals					622665.1		725992.6	103327.6	0.165944
14	Average									
15	Highest									
16	Lowest									

formula is =I12/F12

formula is =I13/F13

Auto Fill Options button appears after copying cell J12 to cell J13

Figure 2–15

Using the AVERAGE, MAX, and MIN Functions

The next step in creating the Silver Dollars Stock Club Portfolio Summary worksheet is to compute the average, highest value, and lowest value for the number of shares listed in the range D4:D12 using the AVERAGE, MAX, and MIN functions in the range D14:D16. Once the values are determined for column D, the entries can be copied across to the other columns.

Excel includes prewritten formulas called functions to help you compute these statistics. A **function** takes a value or values, performs an operation, and returns a result to the cell. The values that you use with a function are called **arguments**. All functions begin with an equal sign and include the arguments in parentheses after the function name. For example, in the function =AVERAGE(D4:D12), the function name is AVERAGE, and the argument is the range D4:D12.

With Excel, you can enter functions using one of five methods: (1) the keyboard or mouse; (2) the Insert Function box in the formula bar; (3) the Sum menu; (4) the AutoSum command on the Formulas tab on the Ribbon; and (5) the Name box area in the formula bar (Figure 2–16). The method you choose will depend on your typing skills and whether you can recall the function name and required arguments.

In the following pages, each of the first three methods will be used. The keyboard and mouse method will be used to determine the average number of shares (cell D14). The Insert Function button in the formula bar method will be used to determine the highest number of shares (cell D15). The Sum menu method will be used to determine the lowest number of shares (cell D16).

To Determine the Average of a Range of Numbers Using the Keyboard and Mouse

The **AVERAGE function** sums the numbers in the specified range and then divides the sum by the number of nonzero cells in the range. The following steps use the AVERAGE function to determine the average of the numbers in the range D4:D12.

1

- Select cell D14.

- Type =av in the cell to display the Formula AutoComplete list.

- Point to the AVERAGE function name (Figure 2–16).

Q&A

What is happening as I type?

As you type the equal sign followed by the characters in the name of a function, Excel displays the Formula AutoComplete list. This list contains those functions that alphabetically match the letters you have typed. Because you typed =av, Excel displays all the functions that begin with the letters av.

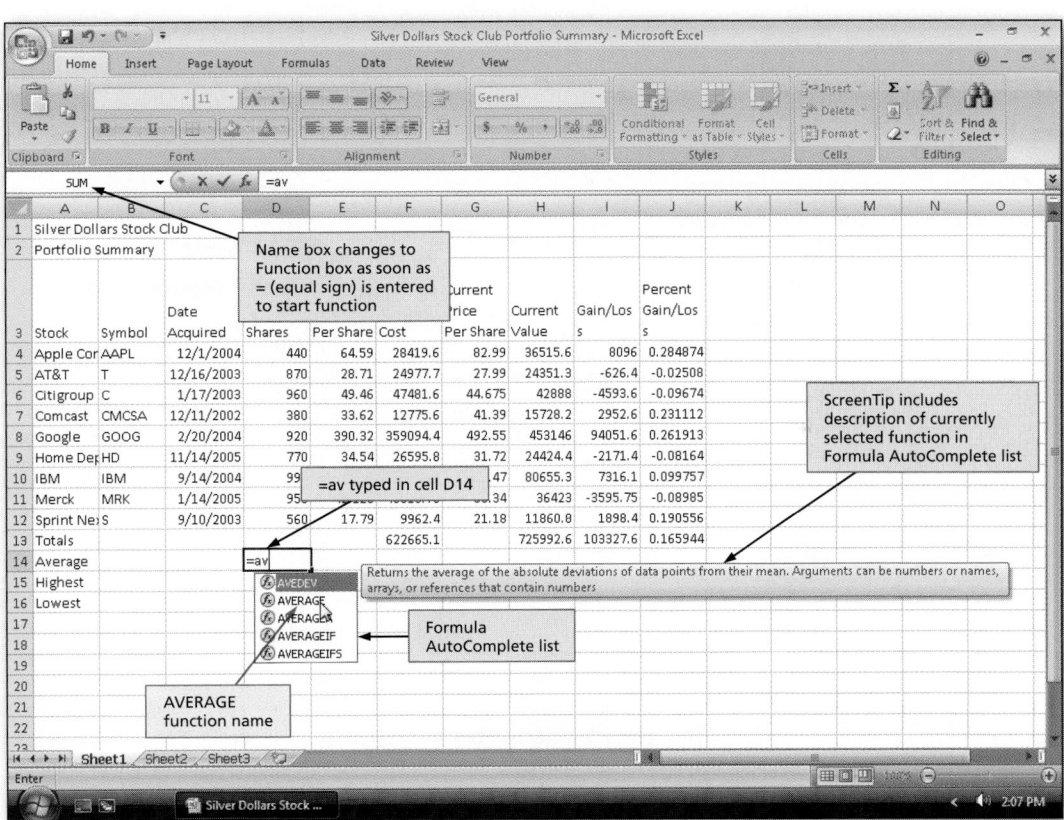

Figure 2–16

● Double-click AVERAGE in the Formula AutoComplete list to select the AVERAGE function.

● Select the range D4:D12 to insert the range as the argument to the AVERAGE function (Figure 2–17).

Q&A

As I drag, why does the function in cell D14 change?

When you click cell D4, Excel appends cell D4 to the left parenthesis in the formula bar and surrounds cell D4 with a marquee. When you begin dragging, Excel appends to the argument a colon (:) and the cell reference of the cell where the mouse pointer is located.

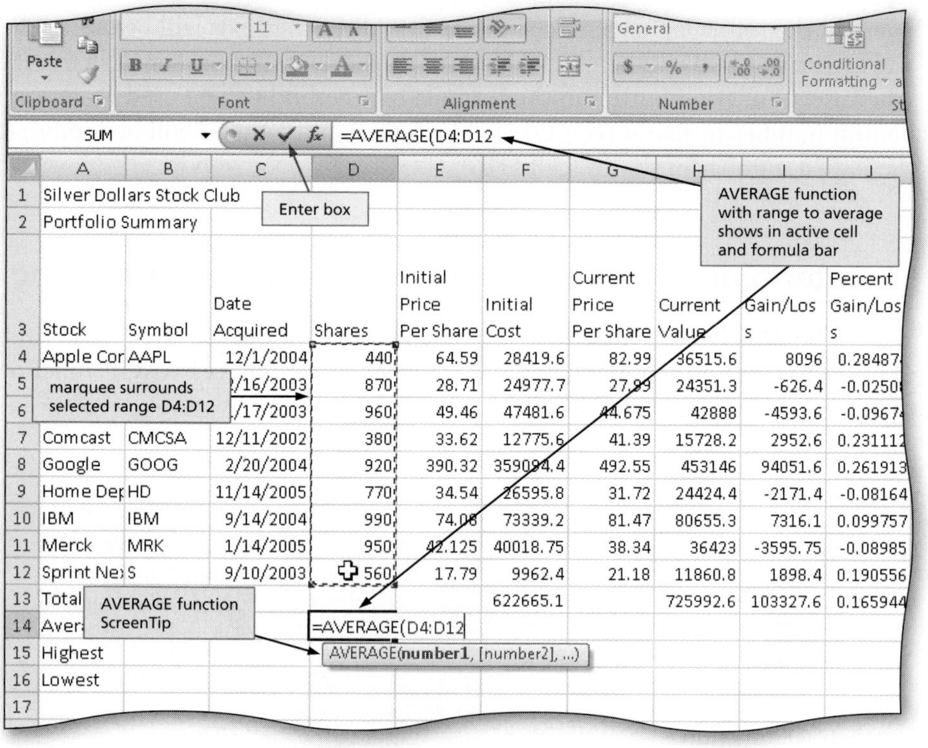

3

● Click the Enter box to compute the average of the nine numbers in the range D4:D12 and display the result in cell D14 (Figure 2–18).

Q&A

Can I use the arrow keys to complete the entry instead?

No. When you use Point mode you cannot use the arrow keys to complete the entry. While in Point mode, the arrow keys change the selected cell reference in the range you are selecting.

Q&A

What is the purpose of the parentheses in the function?

The AVERAGE function requires that the argument (in this case, the range D4:D12) be included within parentheses following the function name. Excel automatically appends the right parenthesis to complete the AVERAGE function when you click the Enter box or press the ENTER key.

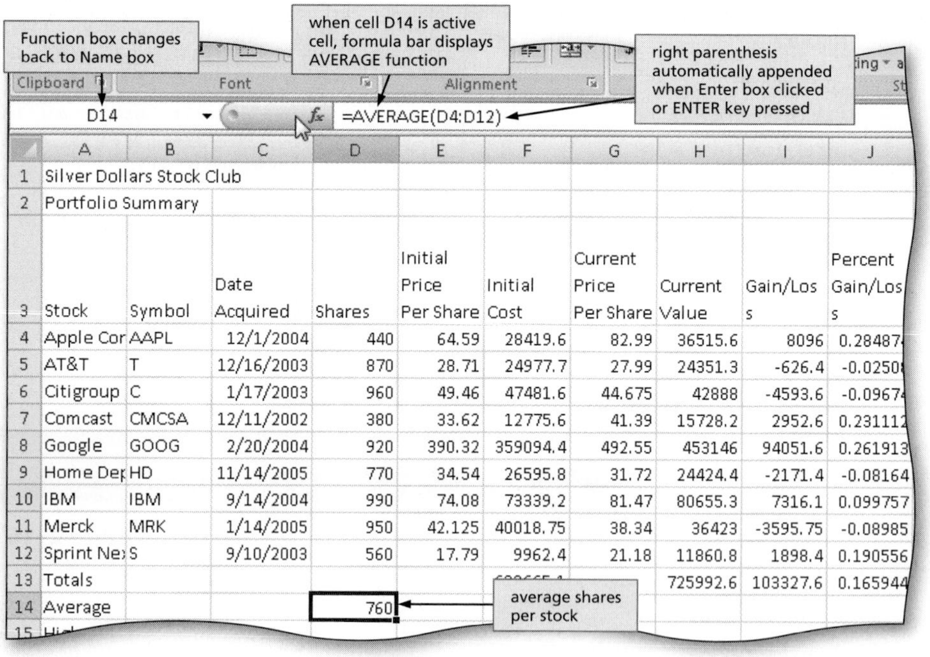

Figure 2–17

Figure 2–18

Other Ways

1. Click Insert Function box in formula bar, click AVERAGE function
2. Click Sum button arrow on Ribbon, click Average function
3. Click Formulas tab on Ribbon, click AutoSum button arrow, click Average function

To Determine the Highest Number in a Range of Numbers Using the Insert Function Box

The next step is to select cell D15 and determine the highest (maximum) number in the range D4:D12. Excel has a function called the **MAX function** that displays the highest value in a range. Although you could enter the MAX function using the keyboard and Point mode as described in the previous steps, an alternative method to entering the function is to use the Insert Function box in the formula bar, as performed in the following steps.

- Select cell D15.

- Click the Insert Function box in the formula bar to display the Insert Function dialog box.

- When Excel displays the Insert Function dialog box, click MAX in the 'Select a function' list (Figure 2–19).

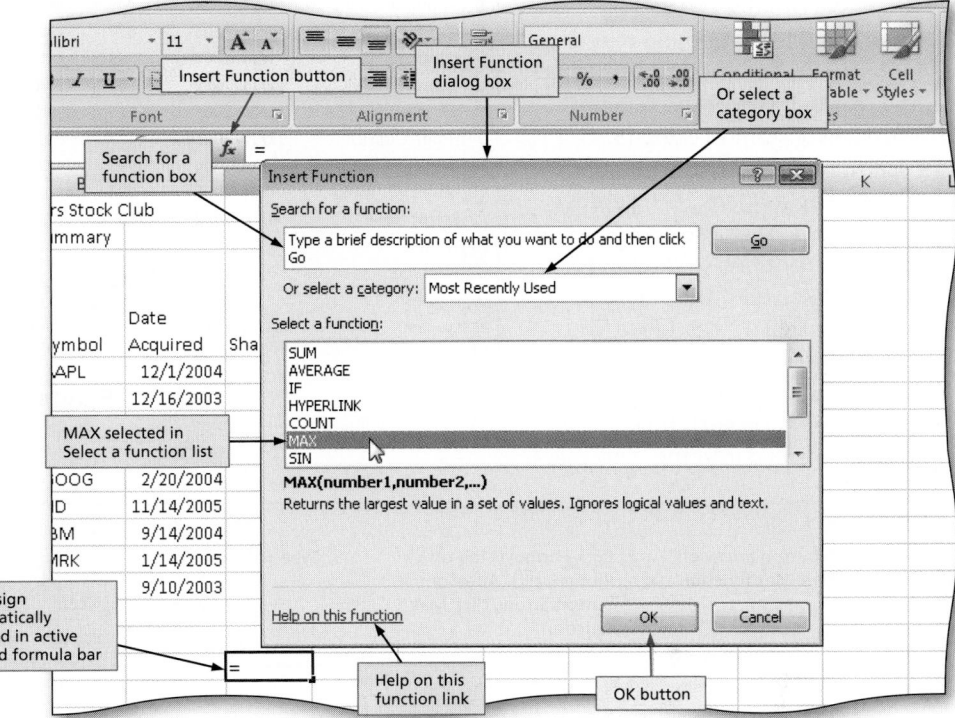

Figure 2–19

- Click the OK button.

- When Excel displays the Function Arguments dialog box, type d4:d12 in the Number1 box (Figure 2–20).

Q&A

Why did numbers appear in the Function Arguments dialog box?

As shown in Figure 2–20, Excel displays the value the MAX function will return to cell D15 in the Function Arguments dialog box. It also lists the first few numbers in the selected range, next to the Number1 box.

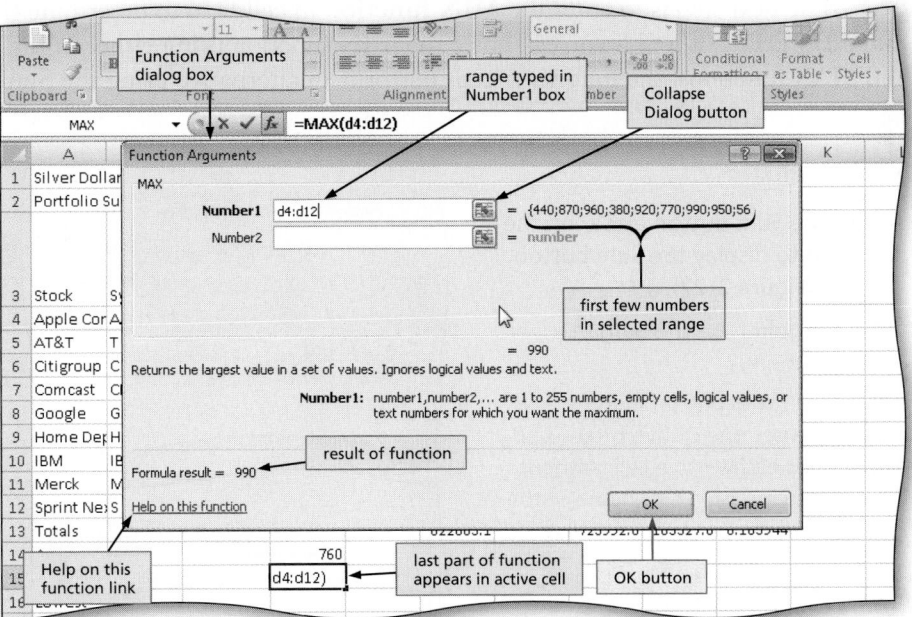

Figure 2–20

- Click the OK button to display the highest value in the range D4:D12 in cell D15 (Figure 2–21).

Q&A

Why should I not just enter the highest value that I see in the range D4:D12 in cell D15?

In this example, rather than entering the MAX function, you easily could scan the range D4:D12, determine that the highest number of shares is 990, and manually enter the number 990 as a constant in cell D15. Excel would display the number the same as in Figure 2–21. Because it contains a constant, however, Excel will continue to display 990 in cell D15, even if the values in the range D4:D12 change. If you use the MAX function, Excel will recalculate the highest value in the range D4:D9 each time a new value is entered into the worksheet.

D15 f_x =MAX(D4:D12)

MAX function determines highest value in range D4:D12

	A	B	C	D	E	F	G	H	I	J
1	Silver Dollars Stock Club									
2	Portfolio Summary									
3	Stock	Symbol	Date Acquired	Shares	Initial Price Per Share	Initial Cost	Current Price Per Share	Current Value	Gain/Loss	Percent Gain/Loss
4	Apple Cor	AAPL	12/1/2004	440	64.59	28419.6	82.99	36515.6	8096	0.28487
5	AT&T	T	12/16/2003	870	28.71	24977.7	27.99	24351.3	-626.4	-0.0250
6	Citigroup	C	1/17/2003	960	49.46	47481.6	44.675	42888	-4593.6	-0.0967
7	Comcast	CMCSA	12/11/2002	380	33.62	12775.6	41.39	15728.2	2952.6	0.231111
8	Google	GOOG	2/20/2004	920	390.32	359094.4	492.55	453146	94051.6	0.261913
9	Home Dep	HD	11/14/2005	770	34.54	26595.8	31.72	24424.4	-2171.4	-0.08164
10	IBM	IBM	9/14/2004	990	74.08	73339.2	81.47	80655.3	7316.1	0.099757
11	Merck	MRK	1/14/2005	950	42.125	40018.75	38.34	36423	-3595.75	-0.08985
12	Sprint Nex	S	9/10/2003	560	17.79	9962.4	21.18	11860.8	1898.4	0.190556
13	Totals					622665.1		725992.6	103327.6	0.165944
14	Average			760						
15	Highest			990						
16	Lowest									
17										

highest value in range D4:D12

Figure 2–21

Other Ways

1. Click Sum button arrow on Ribbon, click Max function
2. Click Formulas tab on Ribbon, click AutoSum button arrow, click Max function
3. Type =MAX in cell

To Determine the Lowest Number in a Range of Numbers Using the Sum Menu

The next step is to enter the **MIN function** in cell D16 to determine the lowest (minimum) number in the range D4:D12. Although you can enter the MIN function using either of the methods used to enter the AVERAGE and MAX functions, the following steps perform an alternative using the Sum button on the Ribbon.

- Select cell D16.

- Click the Sum button arrow on the Ribbon to display the Sum button menu (Figure 2–22).

Q&A

Why should I use the Sum button menu?

Using the Sum button menu allows you to enter one of five often-used functions easily into a cell, without having to memorize its name or the required arguments.

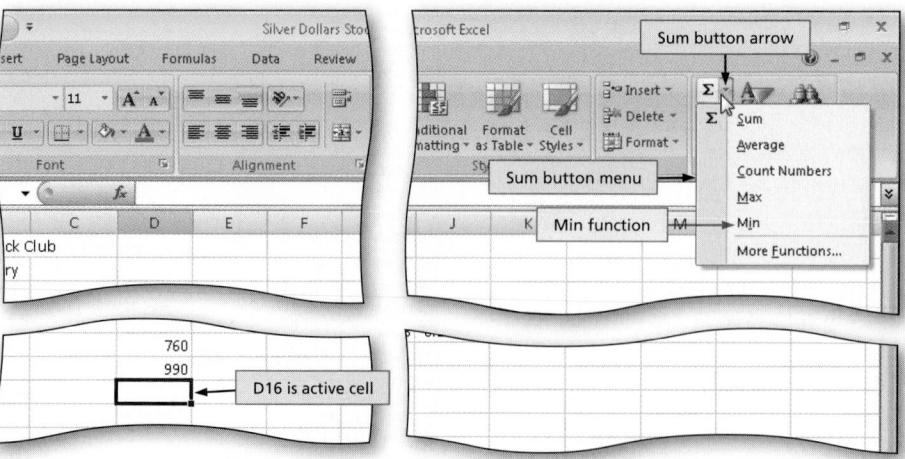

Figure 2–22

- Click Min to display the function =MIN(D14:D15) in the formula bar and in cell D16 (Figure 2–23).

Q&A

Why does Excel select the range D14:D15?

The range D14:D15 automatically selected by Excel is not correct. Excel attempts to guess which cells you want to include in the function by looking for adjacent ranges to the selected cell that contain numeric data.

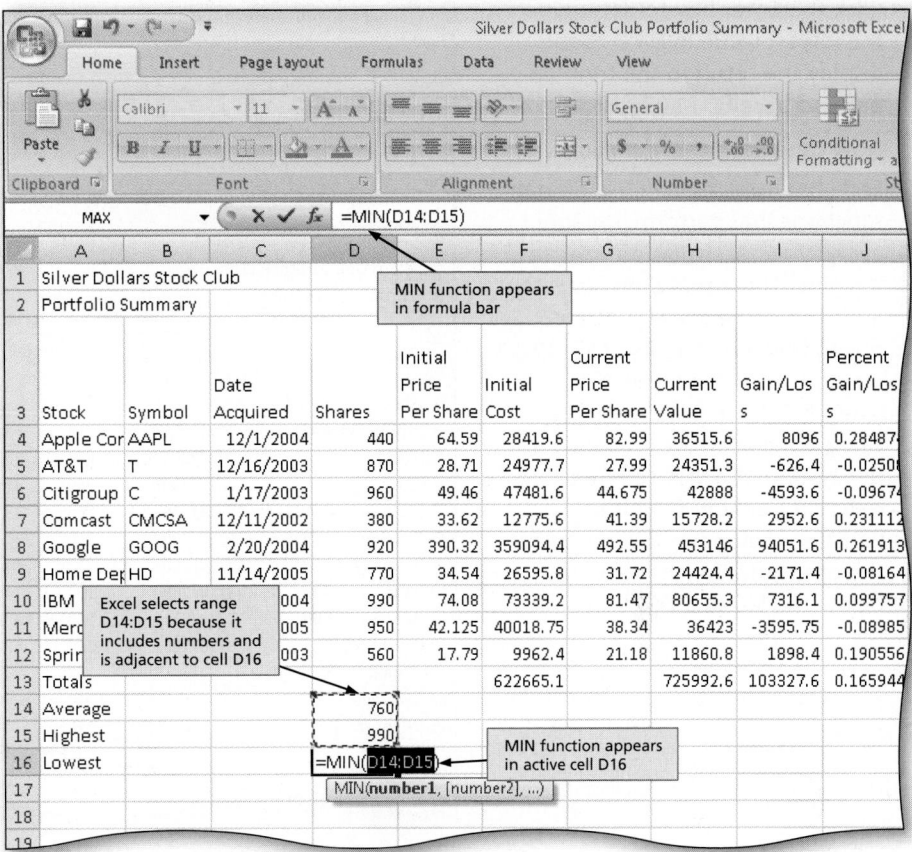

Figure 2–23

- Click cell D4 and then drag through cell D12 to display the function in the formula bar and in cell D14 with the new range (Figure 2–24).

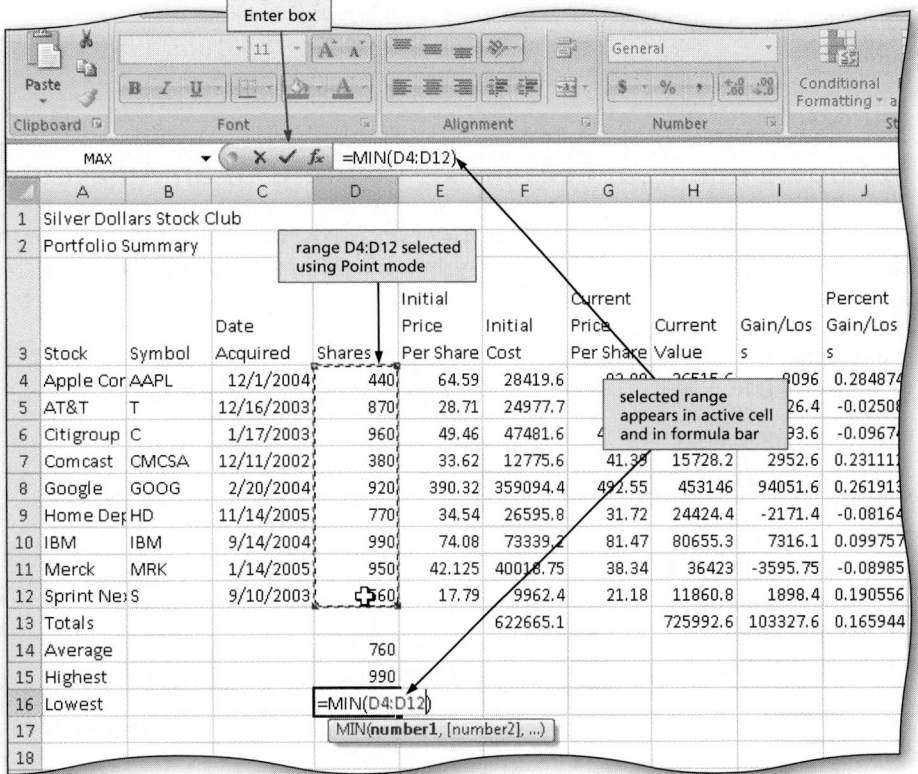

Figure 2–24

4

- Click the Enter box to determine the lowest value in D4:D12 and display the result in the formula bar and in cell D14 (Figure 2–25).

Q&A

How can I use other functions?

Excel has more than 400 additional functions that perform just about every type of calculation you can imagine. These functions are categorized in the Insert Function dialog box shown in Figure 2–19 on page EX 101. To view the categories, click the 'Or select a category' box arrow. To obtain a description of a selected function, select its name in the Insert Function dialog box. Excel displays the description of the function below the Select a function list in the dialog box.

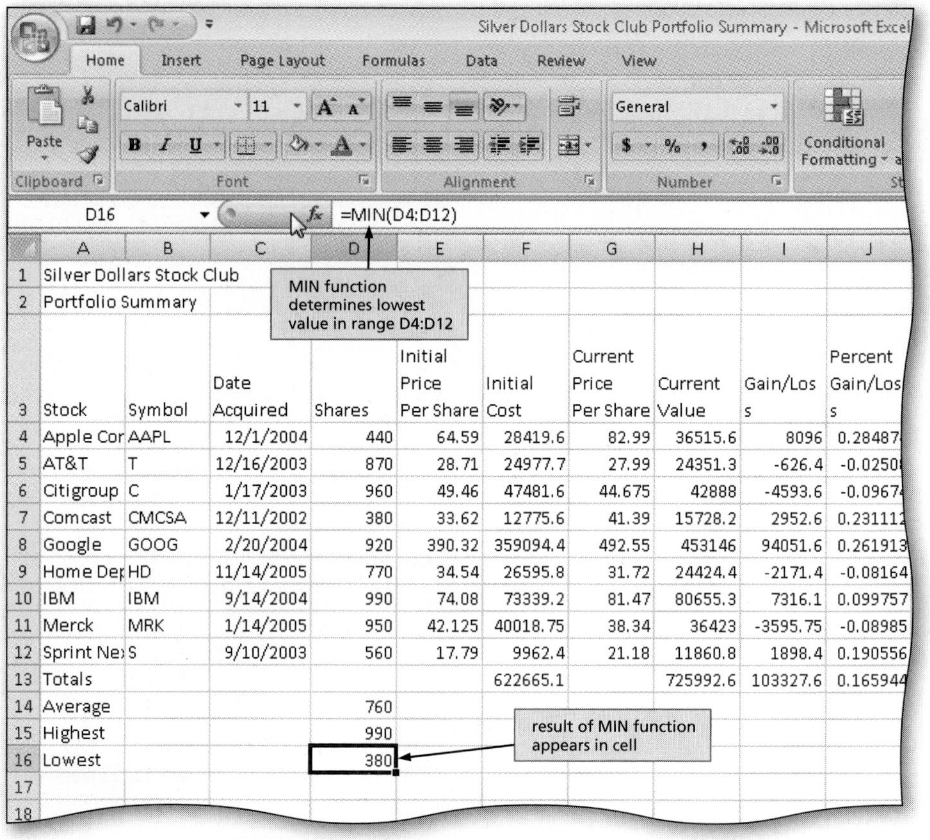

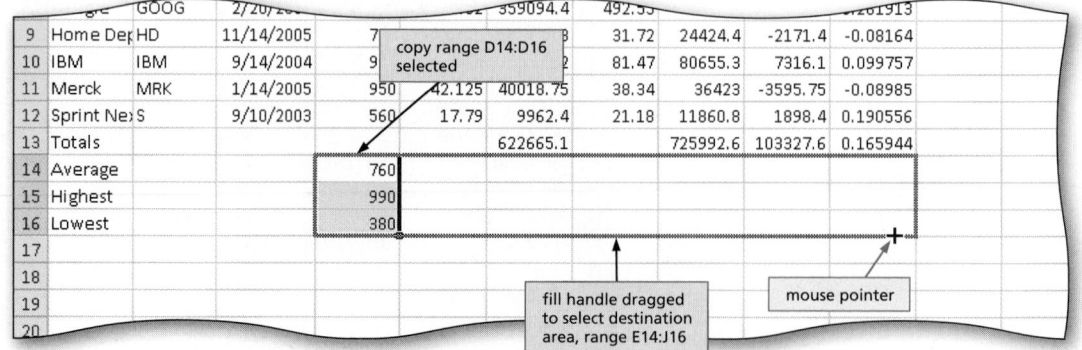

Figure 2–25

Other Ways
1. Click Insert Function box in formula bar, click MIN function	2. Click Formulas tab on Ribbon, click AutoSum button arrow, click Min function	3. Type =MIN in cell

To Copy a Range of Cells across Columns to an Adjacent Range Using the Fill Handle

The next step is to copy the AVERAGE, MAX, and MIN functions in the range D14:D16 to the adjacent range E14:J16. The following steps use the fill handle to copy the functions.

1

- Select the range D14:D16.

- Drag the fill handle in the lower-right corner of the selected range through cell J16 and continue to hold down the mouse button (Figure 2–26).

Figure 2–26

2

- Release the mouse button to copy the three functions to the range E14:J16 (Figure 2–27).

Q&A

How can I be sure that the function arguments are proper for the cells in range E14:J16?

Remember that Excel adjusts the cell references in the copied functions so each function refers to the range of numbers above it in the same column. Review the numbers in rows 14 through 16 in Figure 2–27. You should see that the functions in each column return the appropriate values, based on the numbers in rows 4 through 12 of that column.

Figure 2–27

3

- Select cell J14 and press the DELETE key to delete the average of the percent gain/loss (Figure 2–28).

Q&A

Why is the formula in cell J14 deleted?

The average of the percent gain/loss in cell J14 is deleted because an average of percentages of this type is mathematically invalid.

Other Ways

1. Select source area and point to border of range, while holding down CTRL key, drag source area to destination area

2. Select source area, on Ribbon click Copy button, select destination area, on Ribbon click Paste button

3. Right-click source area, click Copy on shortcut menu, right-click destination area, click Paste on shortcut menu

4. Select source area, press CTRL+C, select destination area, press CTRL+V

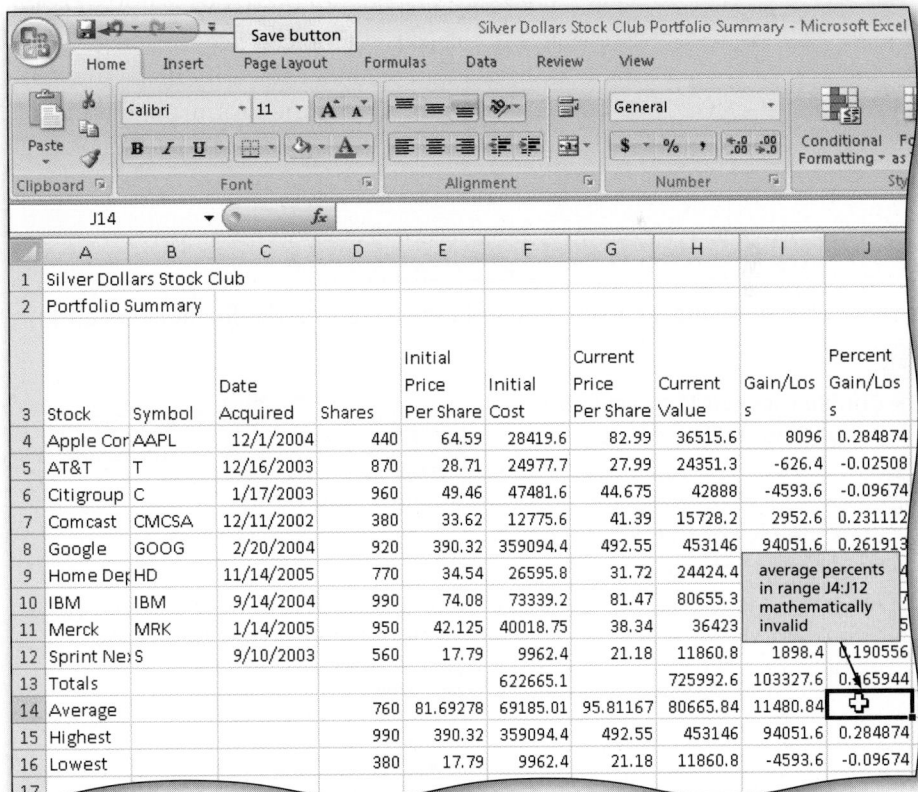

Figure 2–28

To Save a Workbook Using the Same File Name

Earlier in this project, an intermediate version of the workbook was saved using the file name, Silver Dollars Stock Club Portfolio Summary. The following step saves the workbook a second time using the same file name.

1 Click the Save button on the Quick Access Toolbar to save the workbook on the USB flash drive using the file name, Silver Dollars Stock Club Portfolio Summary.

Q&A

Why did Excel not display the Save As dialog box?

When you save a workbook a second time using the same file name, Excel will not display the Save As dialog box as it does the first time you save the workbook. Excel automatically stores the latest version of the workbook using the same file name, Silver Dollars Stock Club Portfolio Summary. You also can click Save on the Office Button menu or press SHIFT+F12 or CTRL+S to save a workbook again.

Verifying Formulas Using Range Finder

One of the more common mistakes made with Excel is to include a wrong cell reference in a formula. An easy way to verify that a formula references the cells you want it to reference is to use Excel's Range Finder. Use the **Range Finder** to check which cells are referenced in the formula assigned to the active cell. Range Finder allows you to make immediate changes to the cells referenced in a formula.

To use Range Finder to verify that a formula contains the intended cell references, double-click the cell with the formula you want to check. Excel responds by highlighting the cells referenced in the formula so you can check that the cell references are correct.

To Verify a Formula Using Range Finder

The following steps use Range Finder to check the formula in cell J4.

1
• Double-click cell J4 to activate Range Finder (Figure 2–29).

2
• Press the ESC key to quit Range Finder and then select cell A18.

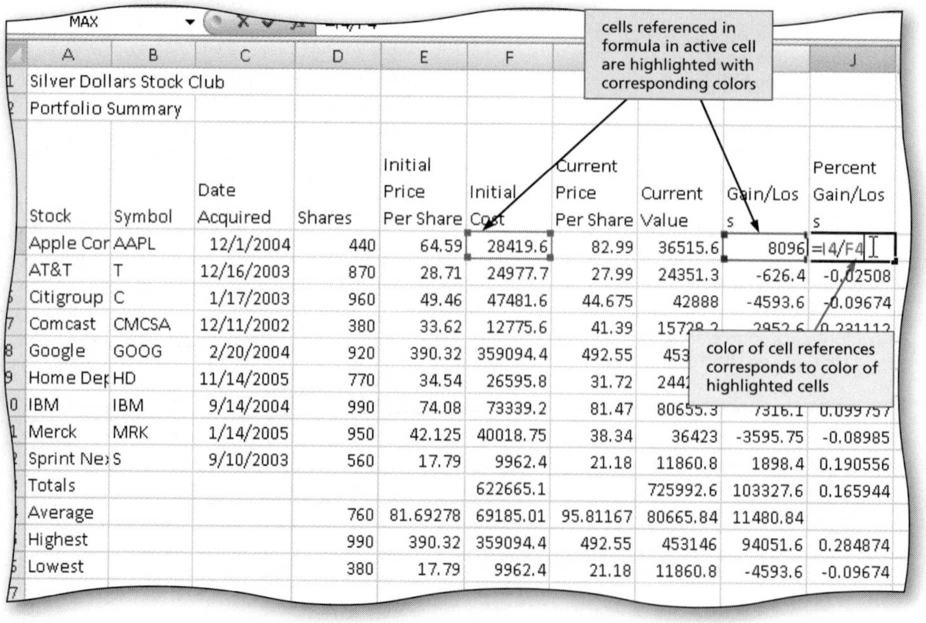

Figure 2–29

Formatting the Worksheet

Although the worksheet contains the appropriate data, formulas, and functions, the text and numbers need to be formatted to improve their appearance and readability.

In Chapter 1, cell styles were used to format much of the worksheet. This section describes how to change the unformatted worksheet in Figure 2–30a to the formatted worksheet in Figure 2–30b using a theme and other commands on the Ribbon. A **theme** is a predefined set of colors, fonts, chart styles, cell styles, and fill effects that can be applied to an entire workbook. Every new workbook that you create is assigned a default theme named Office. The colors and fonts that are used in the worksheet shown in Figure 2–30b are those that are associated with the Concourse theme.

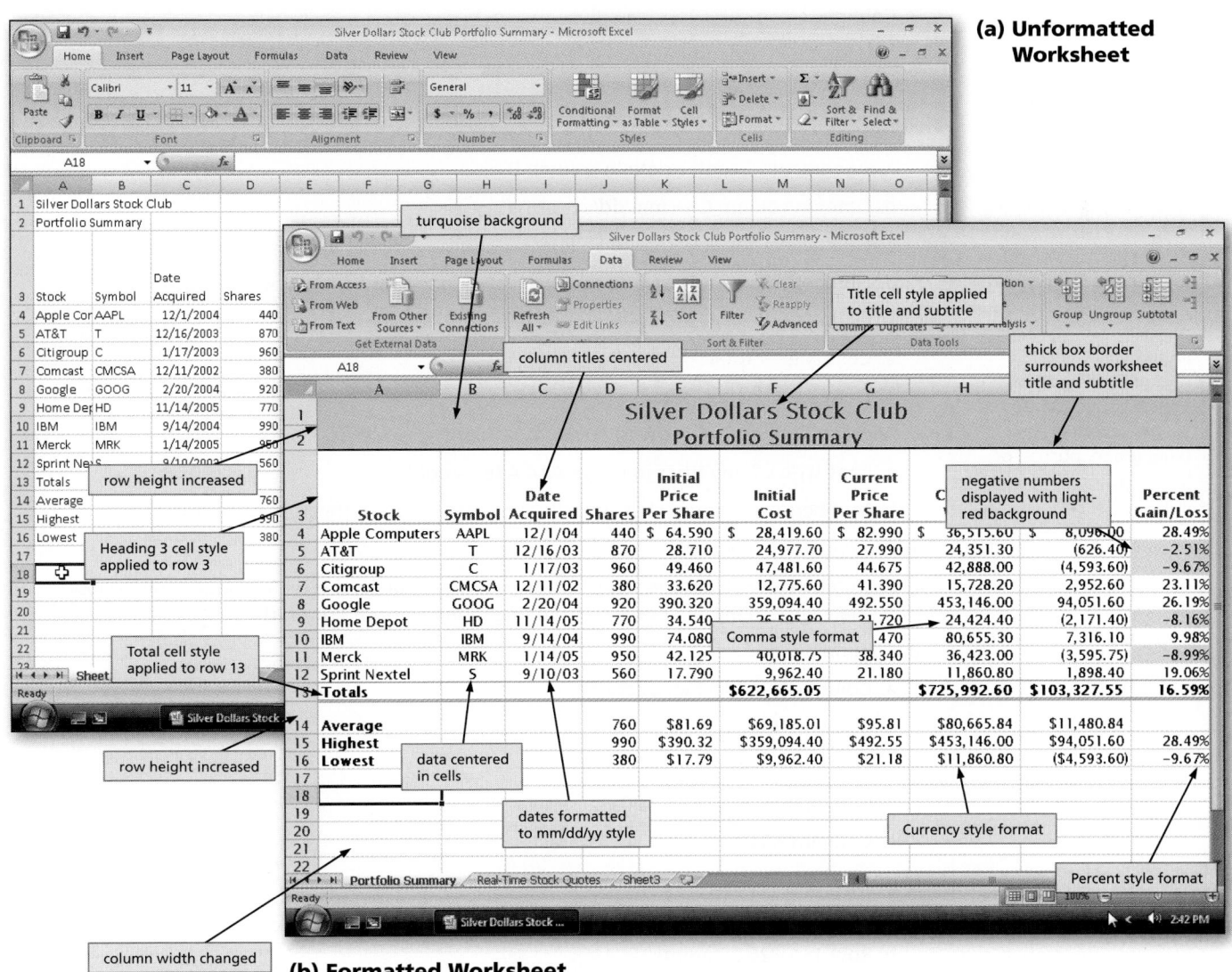

(a) Unformatted Worksheet

(b) Formatted Worksheet

Figure 2–30

Plan Ahead

Identify how to format various elements of the worksheet.
The following outlines the formatting suggested in the sketch of the worksheet in Figure 2–3 on page EX 85:

1. Workbook theme - Concourse

2. Worksheet title and subtitle

    a. Alignment — center across columns A through J

    b. Cell style —Title

    c. Font size — title 18; subtitle 16

    d. Background color (range A1:J2) — Turquoise Accent 1, Lighter 60%

    e. Border — thick box border around range A1:J2

3. Column titles

    a. Cell style — Heading 3

    b. Alignment — center

4. Data

    a. Alignment — center data in column B

    b. Dates in column C — mm/dd/yy format

    c. Numbers in top row (range E4:I4) — Accounting style

    d. Numbers below top row (range E5:I12) — Comma style and decimal places

5. Total line

    a. Cell style — Total

    b. Numbers — Accounting style

6. Average, Highest, and Lowest rows

    a. Font style of row titles in range A14:A16 — bold

    b. Numbers — Currency style with floating dollar sign in the range E14:I16

7. Percentages in column J

    a. Numbers — Percentage style with two decimal places; if a cell in range J4:J12 is less than zero, then cell appears with background color of light red

8. Column widths

    a. Column A — 14.11 characters

    b. Columns B and C — best fit

    c. Column D — 6.00 characters

    d. Column E, G, and J — 9.00 characters

    e. Columns F, H, and I — 12.67 characters

9. Row heights

    a. Row 3 — 60.00 points

    b. Row 14 — 26.25 points

    c. Remaining rows — default

To Change the Workbook Theme

The Concourse theme includes fonts and colors that provide the worksheet a professional and subtly colored appearance. The following steps change the workbook theme to the Concourse theme.

1

- Click the Page Layout tab on the Ribbon.

- Click the Themes button on the Ribbon to display the Theme gallery (Figure 2–31).

Experiment

- Point to several themes in the Theme gallery to see a live preview of the themes.

Q&A Why should I change the theme of a workbook?

A company or department may standardize on a specific theme so that all of their documents have a similar appearance. Similarly, an individual may want to have a theme that sets their work apart from others. Other Office applications, such as Word and PowerPoint, include the same themes included with Excel, meaning that all of your Microsoft Office documents can share a common theme.

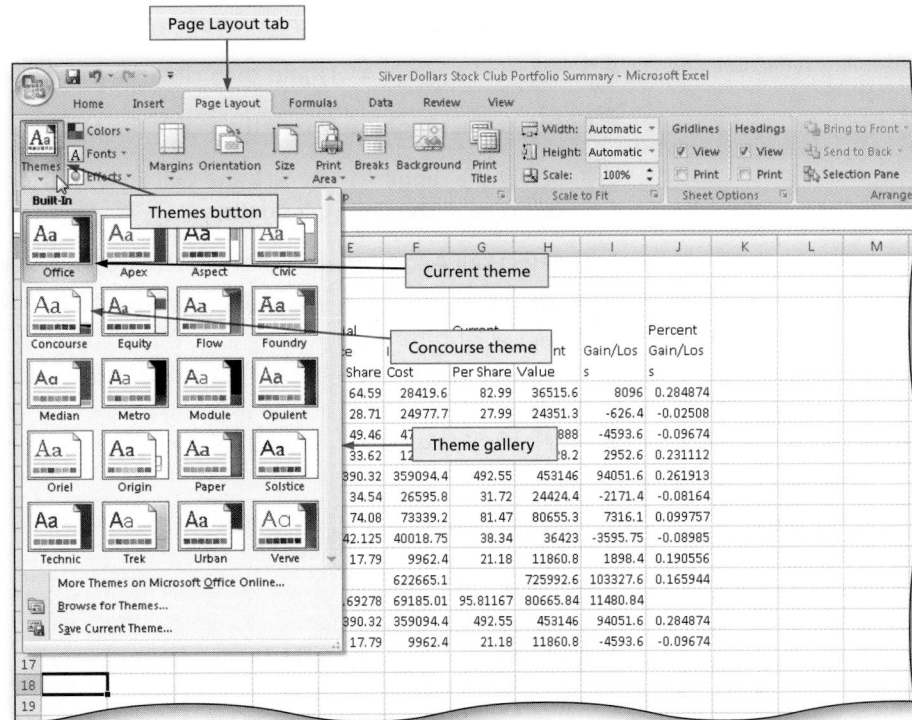

Figure 2–31

2

- Click Concourse in the Theme gallery to change the workbook theme to Concourse (Figure 2–32).

Q&A Why did the cells in the worksheet change?

The cells in the worksheet originally were formatted with the default font for the default Office theme. The default font for the Concourse theme is different than that of the default font for the Office theme and therefore changed on the worksheet when you changed the theme. If you had modified the font for any of the cells, those cells would not receive the default font for the Concourse theme.

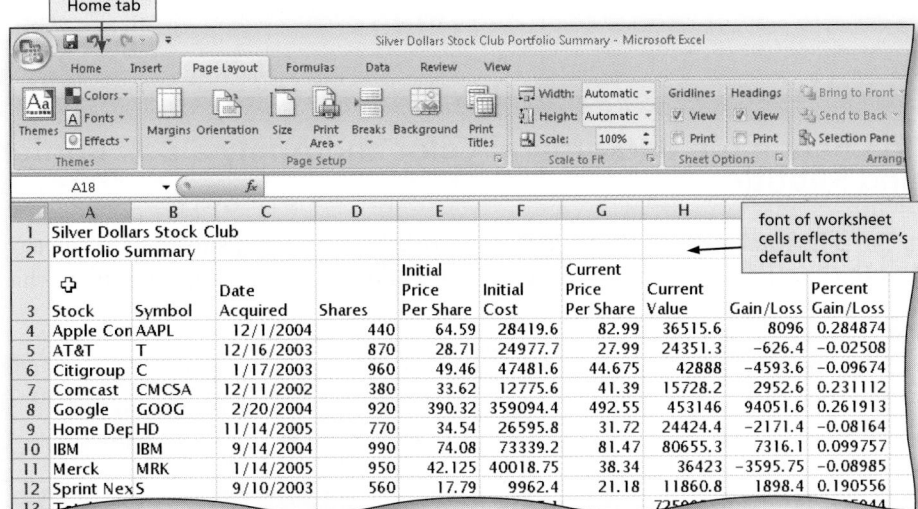

Figure 2–32

To Format the Worksheet Titles

The following steps merge and center the worksheet titles, apply the Title cells style to the worksheet titles, and decrease the font of the worksheet subtitle.

1 Click the Home tab on the Ribbon.

2 Select the range A1:J1 and then click the Merge & Center button on the Ribbon.

3 Select the range A2:J2 and then click the Merge & Center button on the Ribbon.

4 Select the range A1:A2, click the Cell Styles button on the Ribbon, and then click the Title cell style in the Cell Styles gallery.

5 Select cell A2 and then click the Decrease Font Size button on the Ribbon (Figure 2–33).

Q&A What is the effect of clicking the Decrease Font Size button?

When you click the Decrease Font Size button Excel assigns the next lowest font size in the Font Size gallery to the selected range. The Increase Font Size button works in a similar manner, but causes Excel to assign the next highest font size in the Font Size gallery to the selected range.

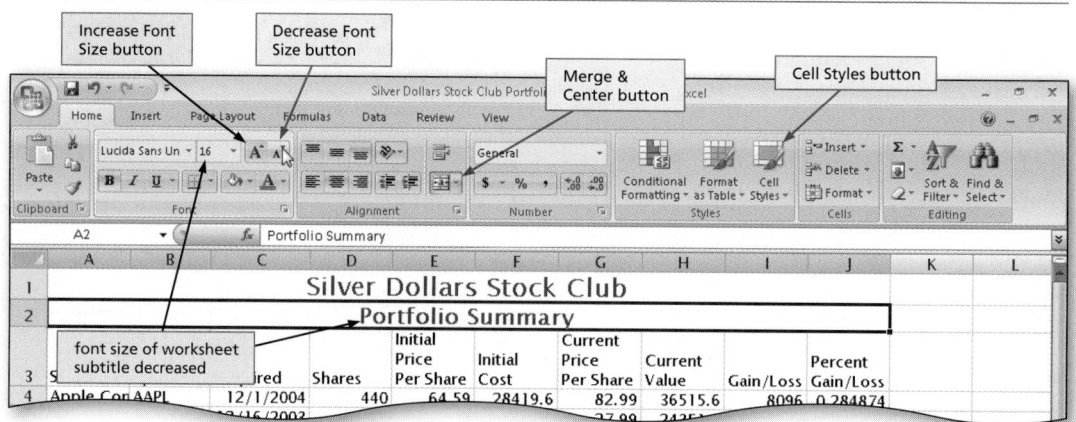

Figure 2–33

To Change the Background Color and Apply a Box Border to the Worksheet Title and Subtitle

The final formats assigned to the worksheet title and subtitle are the turquoise background color and thick box border (Figure 2–30b on page EX 107). The following steps complete the formatting of the worksheet titles.

- Select the range A1:A2 and then click the Fill Color button arrow on the Ribbon to display the Fill Color palette (Figure 2–34).

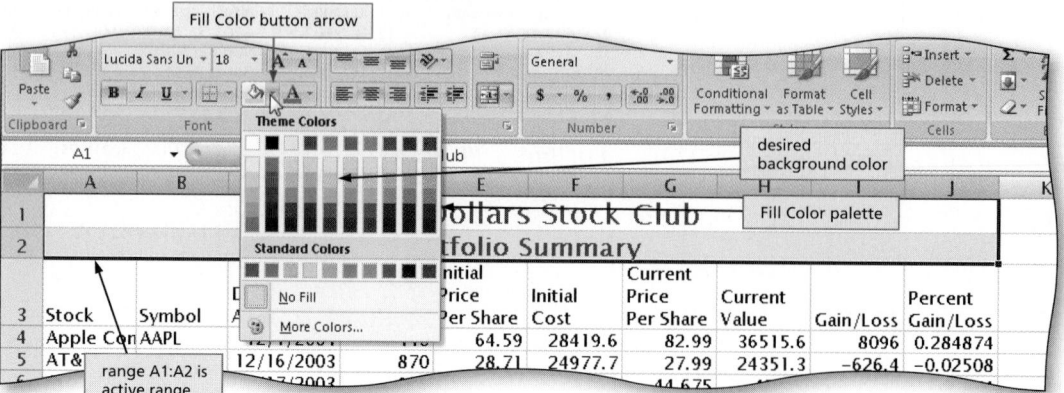

Figure 2–34

2

- Click Turquoise Accent 1, lighter 60% (column 5, row 3) on the Fill Color palette to change the background color of cells A1 and A2 from white to turquoise (Figure 2–35).

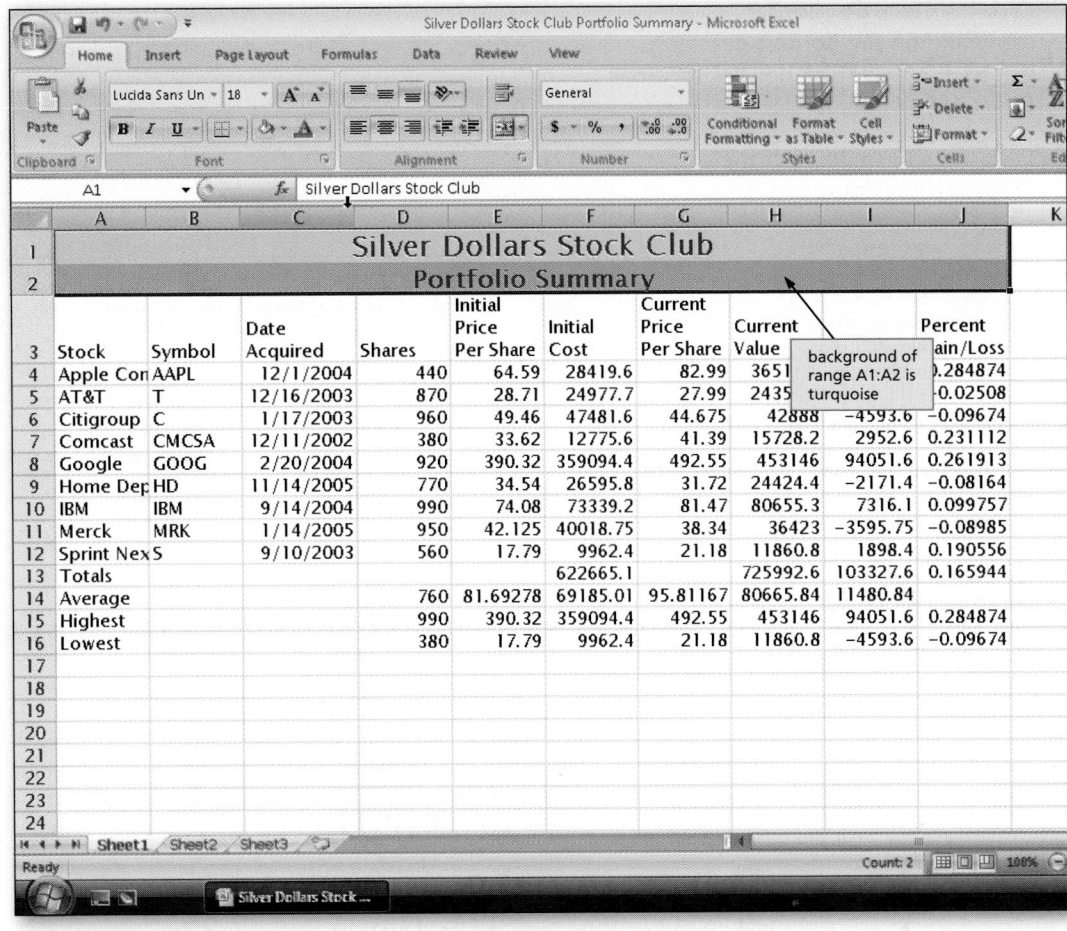

Figure 2–35

3

- Click the Borders button arrow on the Ribbon to display the Borders gallery (Figure 2–36).

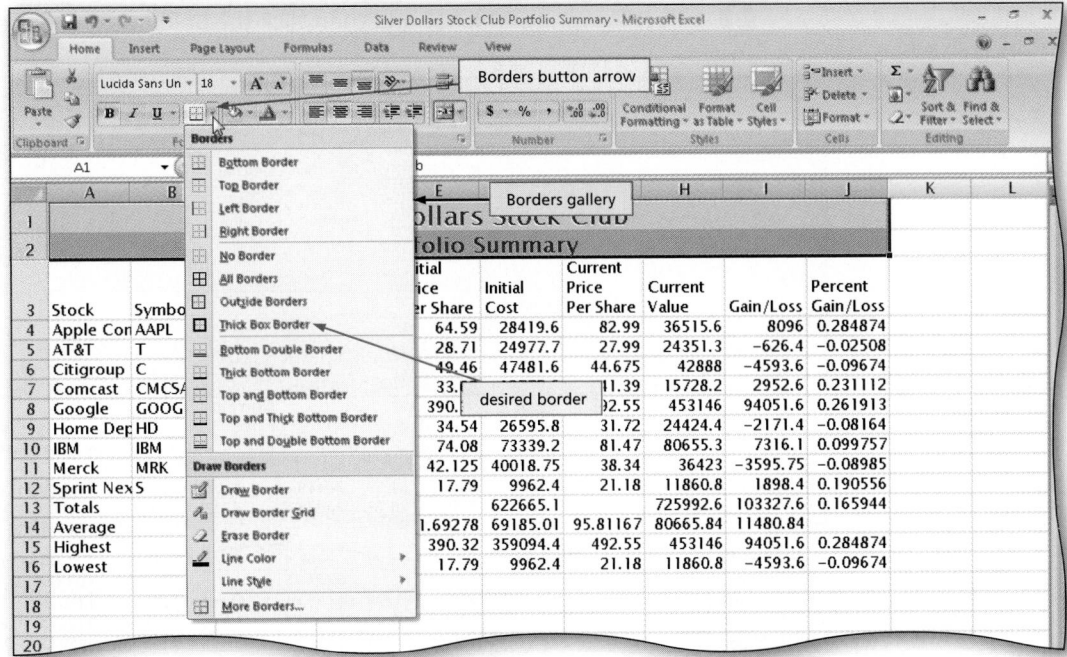

Figure 2–36

- Click the Thick Box Border command on the Borders gallery to display a thick box border around the range A1:A2.

- Click cell A18 to deselect the range A1:A2 (Figure 2–37).

Other Ways

1. On Ribbon click Format Cells Dialog Box Launcher, click appropriate tab, click desired format, click OK button

2. Right-click range, click Format Cells on shortcut menu, click appropriate tab, click desired format, click OK button

3. Press CTRL+1, click appropriate tab, click desired format, click OK button

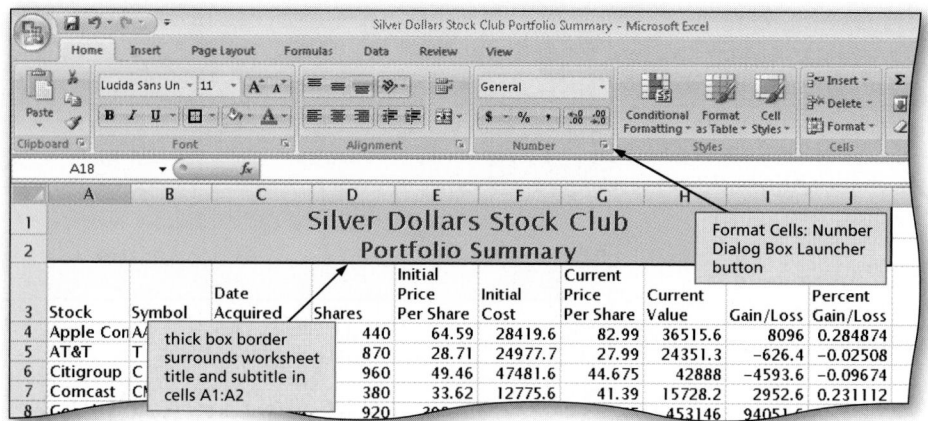

Figure 2–37

To Apply a Cell Style to the Column Headings and Format the Total Rows

As shown in Figure 2–30b on page EX 107, the column titles (row 3) have the Heading 3 cell style and the total row (row 13) has the Total cell style. The summary information headings in the range A14:A16 should be bold. The following steps assign these styles to row 3 and row 13 and the range A14:A16.

1. Select the range A3:J3.

2. Apply the Heading 3 cell style to the range A3:J3.

3. Apply the Total cell style to the range A13:J13.

4. Select the range A14:A16 and then click the Bold button on the Ribbon (Figure 2–38).

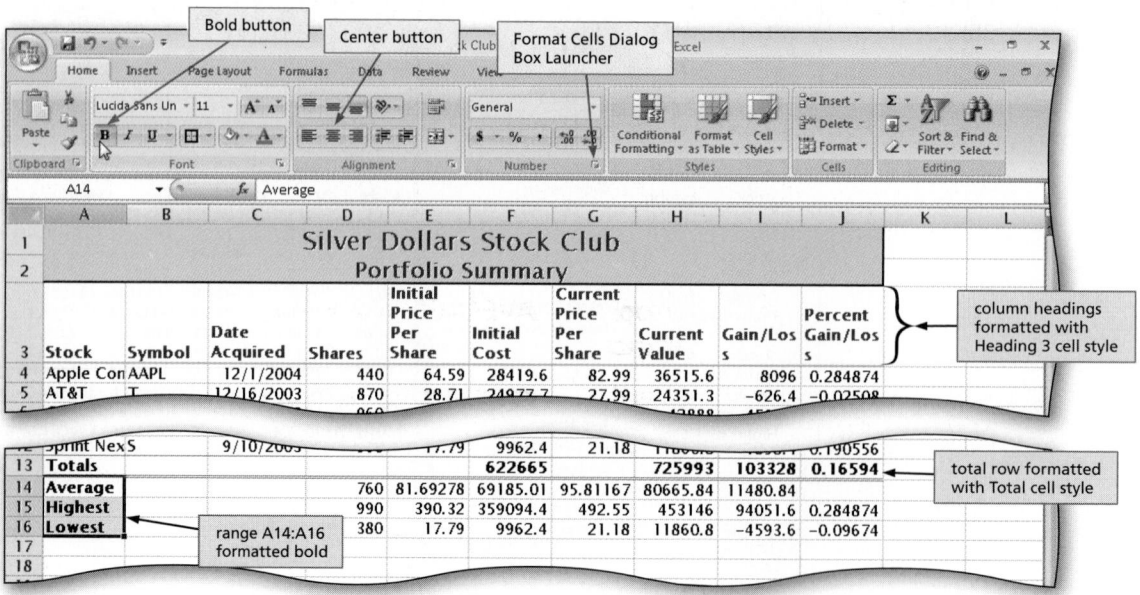

Figure 2–38

To Center Data in Cells and Format Dates

With the column titles and total rows formatted, the next step is to center the stock symbols in column B and format the dates in column C. If a cell entry is short, such as the stock symbols in column B, centering the entries within their respective columns improves the appearance of the worksheet. The following steps center the data in the range B4:B12 and format the dates in the range C4:C12.

- Select the range B4:B12 and then click the Center button on the Ribbon to center the data in the range B4:B12.

2

- Select the range C4:C12.

- Click the Format Cells: Number Dialog Box Launcher on the Ribbon to display the Format Cells dialog box.

- When Excel displays the Format Cells dialog box, if necessary click the Number tab, click Date in the Category list, and then click 3/14/01 in the Type list to choose the format for the range C4:C12 (Figure 2–39).

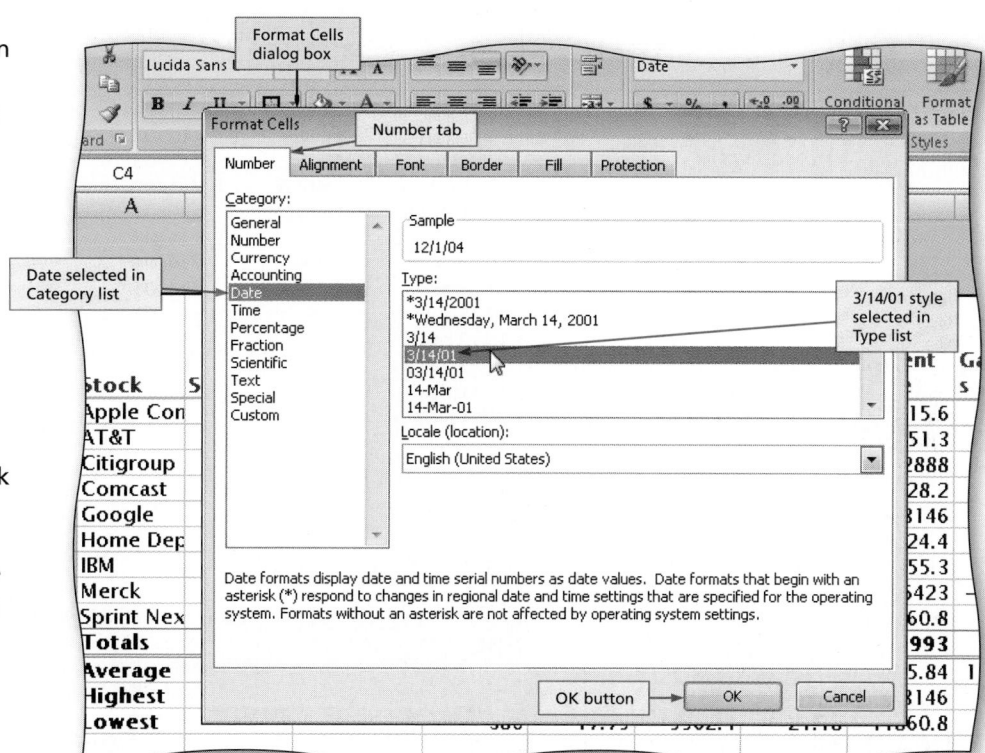

Figure 2–39

3

- Click the OK button to format the dates in column C using the date format style, mm/dd/yy.

- Select cell E4 to deselect the range C4:C13 (Figure 2–40).

Q&A

Can I format an entire column at once?

Yes. Rather than selecting the range B4:B12 in Step 1, you could have clicked the column B heading immediately above cell B1, and then clicked the Center button on the Ribbon. In this case, all cells in column B down to the last cell in the worksheet would have been formatted to use center alignment. This same procedure could have been used to format the dates in column C.

	E4		▼	f_x	64.59		
	A	B	C	D	E	F	G	H

Silver Dollars Stock Club
Portfolio Summary

	Stock	Symbol	Date Acquired	Shares	Initial Price Per Share	Initial Cost	Current Price Per Share	Currer Value
3	Stock	Symbol	Date Acquired	Shares	Initial Price Per Share	Initial Cost	Current Price Per Share	Currer Value
4	Apple Con	AAPL	12/1/04	440	64.59	28419.6	82.99	3651
5	AT&T	T	12/16/03	870	28.71	24977.7	27.99	2435
6	Citigroup	C	1/17/03	960	49.46	47481.6	44.675	428
7	Comcast	CMCSA	12/11/02	380	33.62	12775.6	41.39	15726
8	Google	GOOG	2/20/04	920	390.32	359094.4	492.55	4531
9	Home Dep	HD	11/14/05	770	34.54	26595.8	31.72	24424
10	IBM	IBM	9/14/04	990	74.08	73339.2	81.47	80655
11	Merck	MRK	1/14/05			018.75	38.34	3642
12	Sprint Nex	S	9/10/03			9962.4	21.18	11860
13	Totals					22665		7259
14	Average					185.01	95.81167	80665
15	Highest			990	390.32	359094.4	492.55	4531
16	Lowest			380	17.79	9962.4	21.18	1186

Excel displays dates in range C4:C12 using date style format, mm/dd/yy

Sheet1 / Sheet2 / Sheet3

Ready

Silver Dollars Stock ...

Figure 2–40

Other Ways

1. Right-click range, click Format Cells on shortcut menu, click appropriate tab, click desired format, click OK button

2. Press CTRL+1, click appropriate tab, click desired format, click OK button

Formatting Numbers Using the Ribbon

As shown in Figure 2–30b on page EX 107, the worksheet is formatted to resemble an accounting report. For example, in columns E through I, the numbers in the first row (row 4), the totals row (row 13), and the rows below the totals (rows 14 through 16) have dollar signs, while the remaining numbers (rows 5 through 12) in columns E through I do not.

To append a dollar sign to a number, you should use the Accounting number format. Excel displays numbers using the **Accounting number format** with a dollar sign to the left of the number, inserts a comma every three positions to the left of the decimal point, and displays numbers to the nearest cent (hundredths place). Clicking the Accounting Number Format button on the Ribbon assigns the desired Accounting number format. When you use the Accounting Number Format button to assign the Accounting number format, Excel displays a **fixed dollar sign** to the far left in the cell, often with spaces between it and the first digit. To assign a **floating dollar sign** that appears immediately to the left of the first digit with no spaces, use the Currency style in the Format Cells dialog box.

The Comma style format is used to instruct Excel to display numbers with commas and no dollar signs. The **Comma style format**, which can be assigned to a range of cells by clicking the Comma Style button on the Ribbon, inserts a comma every three positions to the left of the decimal point and causes numbers to be displayed to the nearest hundredths.

To Apply an Accounting Style Format and Comma Style Format Using the Ribbon

The following steps show how to assign formats using the Accounting Number Format button and the Comma Style button on the Ribbon.

- Select the range E4:I4.

- While holding down the CTRL key, select the ranges F13:I13.

- Click the Accounting Number Format button on the Ribbon (Figure 2–41) to apply the Accounting style format with fixed dollar signs to the nonadjacent ranges E4:I4 and F13:I13 (Figure 2–41).

Q&A

What is the effect of applying the Accounting style format?

The Accounting Number Format button assigns a fixed dollar sign to the numbers in the ranges E4:I4 and F13:I13. In each cell in these ranges, Excel displays the dollar sign to the far left with spaces between it and the first digit in the cell.

Figure 2–41

- Select the range E5:I12.

- Click the Comma Style button on the Ribbon to assign the Comma style format to the range E5:I12 (Figure 2–42).

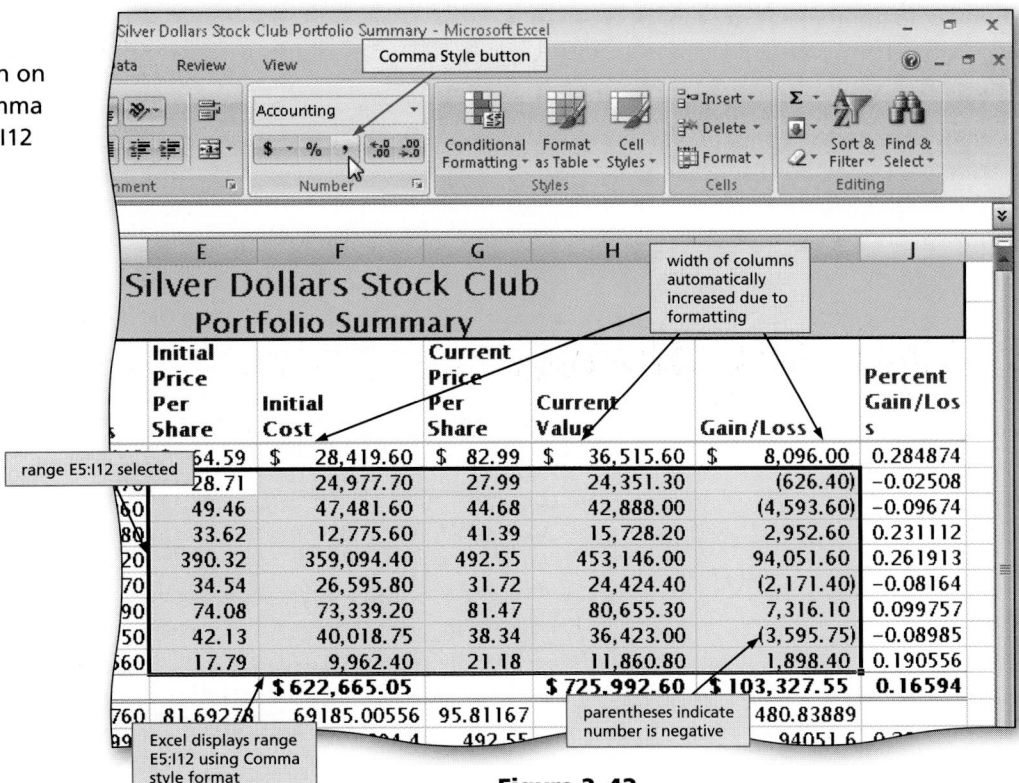

Figure 2–42

- Click cell E4.

- While holding down the CTRL key, select cell G4.

- Click the Increase Decimal button on the Ribbon to increase the number of decimal places displayed in cell E4 and G4.

- Select the range E5:E12. While holding down the CTRL key, select the range G5:G12.

- Click the Increase Decimal button on the Ribbon to increase the number of decimal places displayed in selected ranges (Figure 2–43).

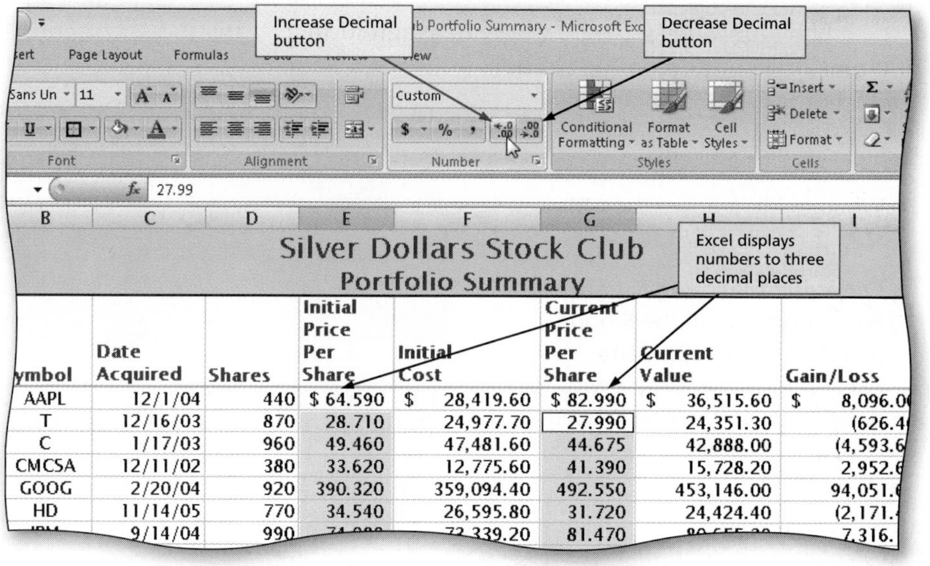

Q&A

What is the effect of clicking the Increase Decimal button?

The Increase Decimal button instructs Excel to display additional decimal places in a cell. Each time you click the Increase Decimal button, Excel adds a decimal place to the selected cell.

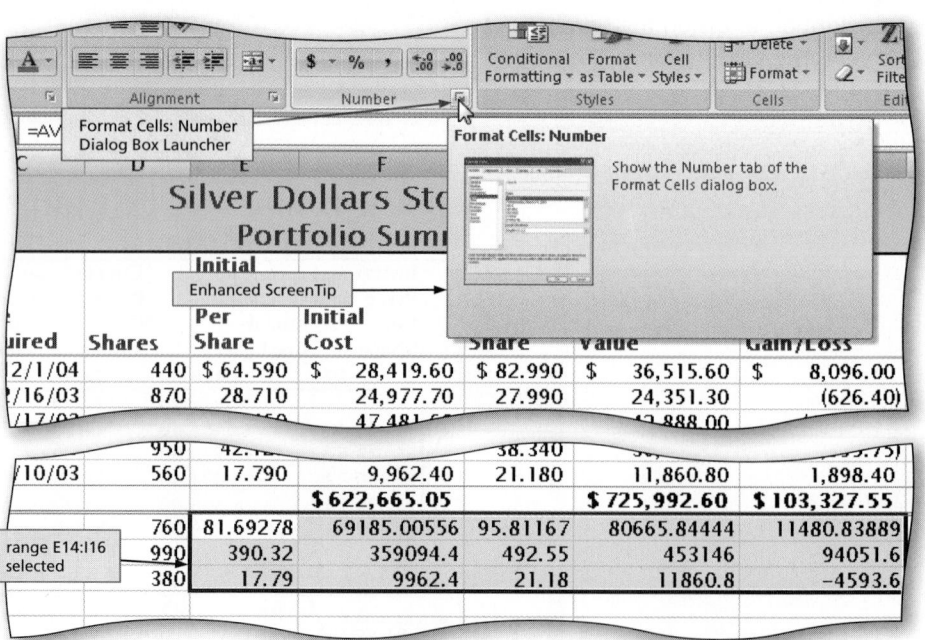

Figure 2–43

To Apply a Currency Style Format with a Floating Dollar Sign Using the Format Cells Dialog Box

The following steps use the Format Cells dialog box to apply the Currency style format with a floating dollar sign to the numbers in the ranges E14:I16.

1

- Select the range E14:I16 and then point to the Format Cells: Number Dialog Box Launcher on the Ribbon (Figure 2–44).

Figure 2–44

2

- Click the Format Cells: Number Dialog Box Launcher.

- If necessary, click the Number tab in the Format Cells dialog box.

- Click Currency in the Category list and then click the third style ($1,234.10) in the Negative numbers list (Figure 2–45).

Q&A How do I select the proper format?

You can choose from 12 categories of formats. Once you select a category, you can select the number of decimal places, whether or not a dollar sign should be displayed, and how negative numbers should appear. Selecting the appropriate negative numbers format is important, because doing so adds a space to the right of the number in order to align the numbers in the worksheet on the decimal points. Some of the available negative number formats do not align the numbers in the worksheet on the decimal points.

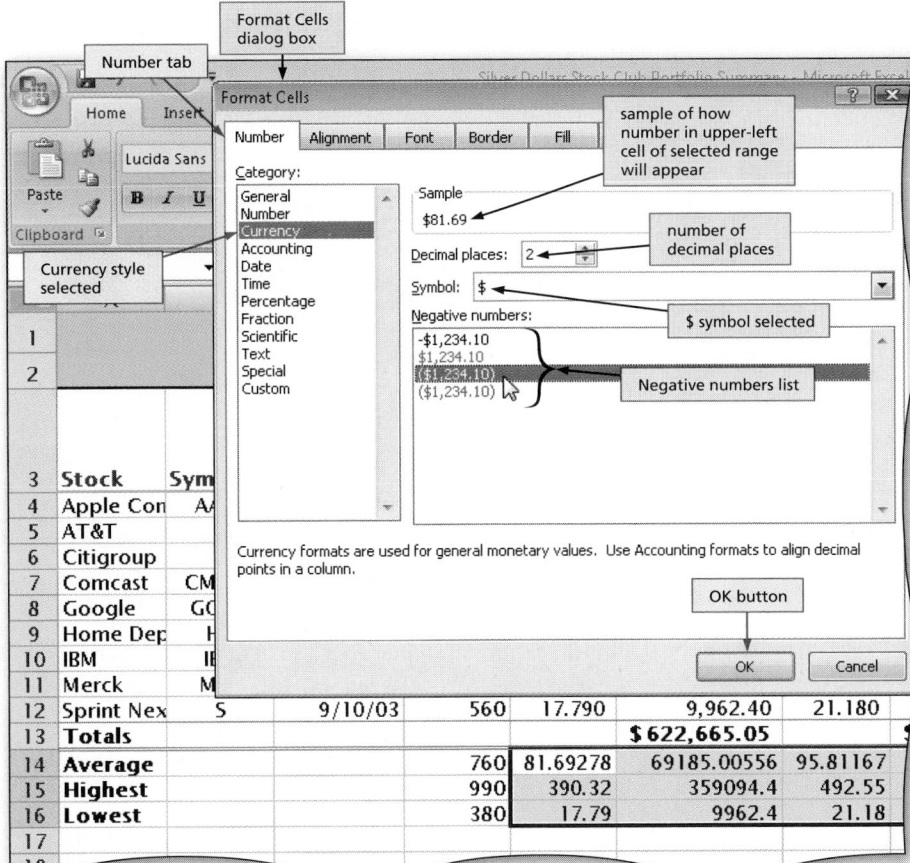

Figure 2–45

3

- Click the OK button to assign the Currency style format with a floating dollar sign to the range E14:I16 (Figure 2–46).

Q&A Should I click the Accounting Number Style button on the Ribbon or use the Format Cells dialog box?

Recall that a floating dollar sign always appears immediately to the left of the first digit, and the fixed dollar sign always appears on the left side of the cell. Cell E4, for example, has a fixed dollar sign, while cell E14 has a floating dollar sign. The Currency style was assigned to cell E14 using the Format Cells dialog box and the result is a floating dollar sign.

Figure 2–46

Other Ways

1. Press CTRL+1, click Number tab, click Currency in Category list, select format, click OK button

2. Press CTRL+SHIFT+ DOLLAR SIGN ($)

To Apply a Percent Style Format and Use the Increase Decimal Button

The next step is to format the percent gain/loss in column J. Currently, Excel displays the numbers in column J as a decimal fraction (for example, 0.284874 in cell J4). The following steps format the range J4:J16 to the Percent style format with two decimal places.

- Select the range J4:J16.

- Click the Percent Style button on the Ribbon to display the numbers in column J as a rounded whole percent.

Q&A

What is the result of clicking the Percent Style button?

The Percent Style button instructs Excel to display a value as a percentage, determined by multiplying the cell entry by 100, rounding the result to the nearest percent, and adding a percent sign. For example, when cell J4 is formatted using the Percent Style and Increase Decimal buttons, Excel displays the actual value 0.284874 as 28.49%.

- Click the Increase Decimal button on the Ribbon two times to display the numbers in column J with the Percent style format and two decimal places (Figure 2–47).

Figure 2–47

Other Ways

1. Right-click range, click Format Cells on shortcut menu, click Number tab, click Percentage in Category list, select format, click OK button

2. Press CTRL+1, click Number tab, click Percentage in Category list, select format, click OK button

3. Press CTRL+SHIFT+ PERCENT SIGN (%)

Conditional Formatting

The next step is to emphasize the negative percentages in column J by formatting them to appear with a tinted background. The Conditional Formatting button on the Ribbon will be used to complete this task.

Excel lets you apply formatting that appears only when the value in a cell meets conditions that you specify. This type of formatting is called **conditional formatting**. You can apply conditional formatting to a cell, a range of cells, the entire worksheet, or the entire workbook. Usually, you apply conditional formatting to a range of cells that contains values you want to highlight, if conditions warrant. For example, you can instruct Excel to change the color of the background of a cell if the value in the cell meets a condition, such as being less than 0 as shown in Figure 2–48.

A **condition**, which is made up of two values and a relational operator, is true or false for each cell in the range. If the condition is true, then Excel applies the formatting. If the condition is false, then Excel suppresses the formatting. What makes conditional formatting so powerful is that the cell's appearance can change as you enter new values in the worksheet.

To Apply Conditional Formatting

The following steps assign conditional formatting to the range J4:J12, so that any cell value less than zero will cause Excel to display the number in the cell with a light red background.

- Select the range J4:J12.

- Click the Conditional Formatting button on the Ribbon to display the Conditional Formatting gallery (Figure 2–48).

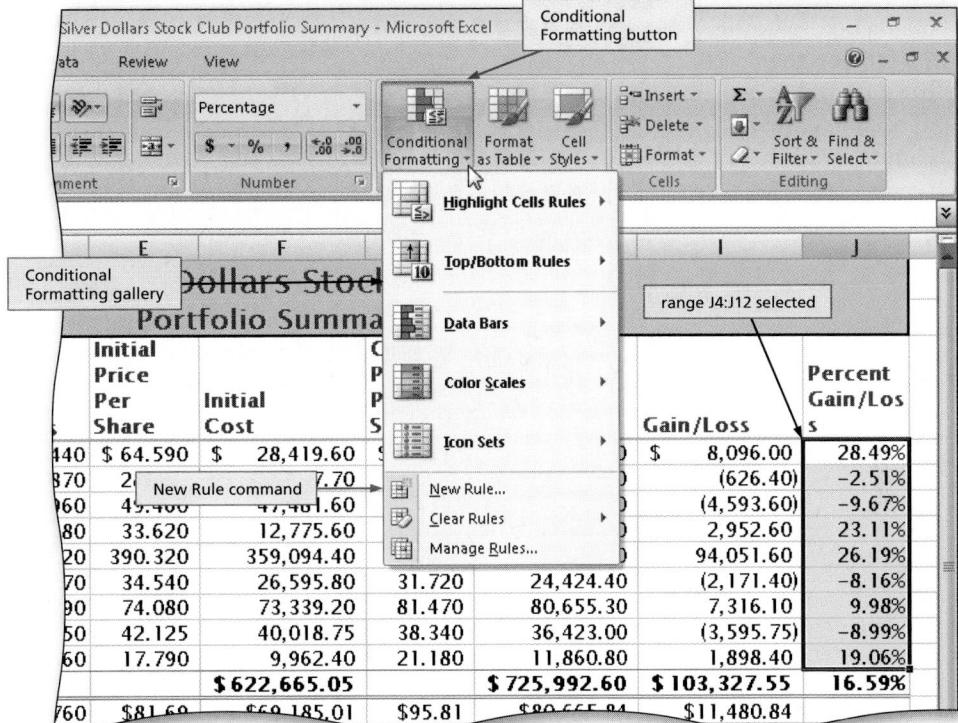

Figure 2–48

- Click New Rule in the Conditional Formatting gallery to display the New Formatting Rule dialog box.

- Click 'Format only cells that contain' in the Select a Rule Type area.

- In the Edit the Rule Description area, click the box arrow in the relational operator box (second text box) and then select less than.

- Type 0 (zero) in the rightmost box in the Edit the Rule Description area (Figure 2–49).

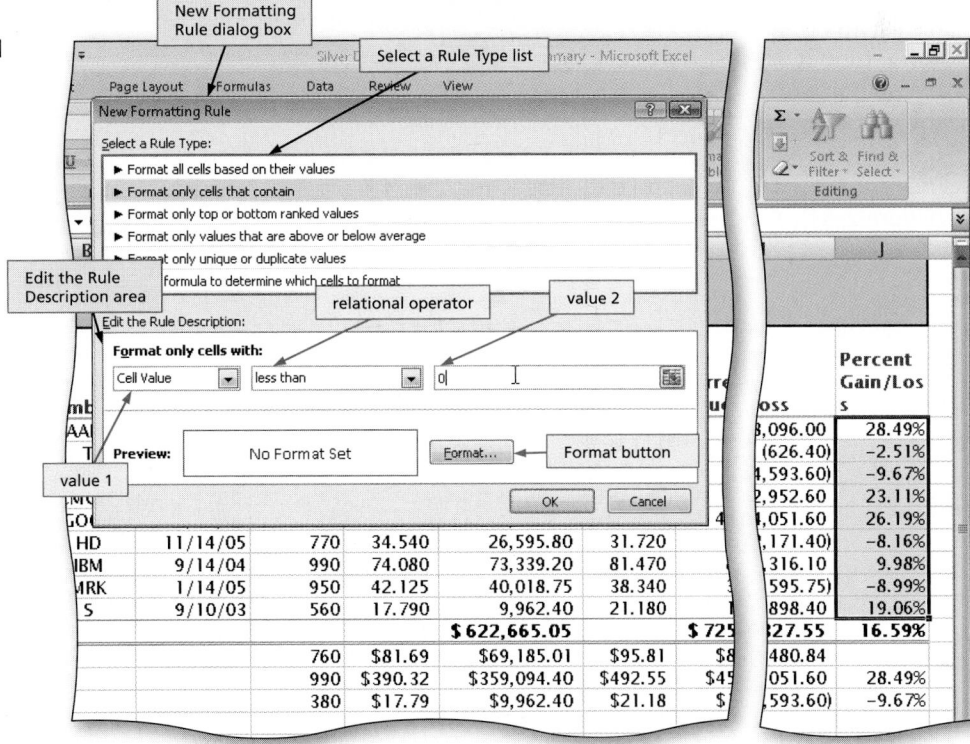

Figure 2–49

3

- Click the Format button.

- When Excel displays the Format Cells dialog box, click the Fill tab and then click the light red color in column 6, row 2 (Figure 2–50).

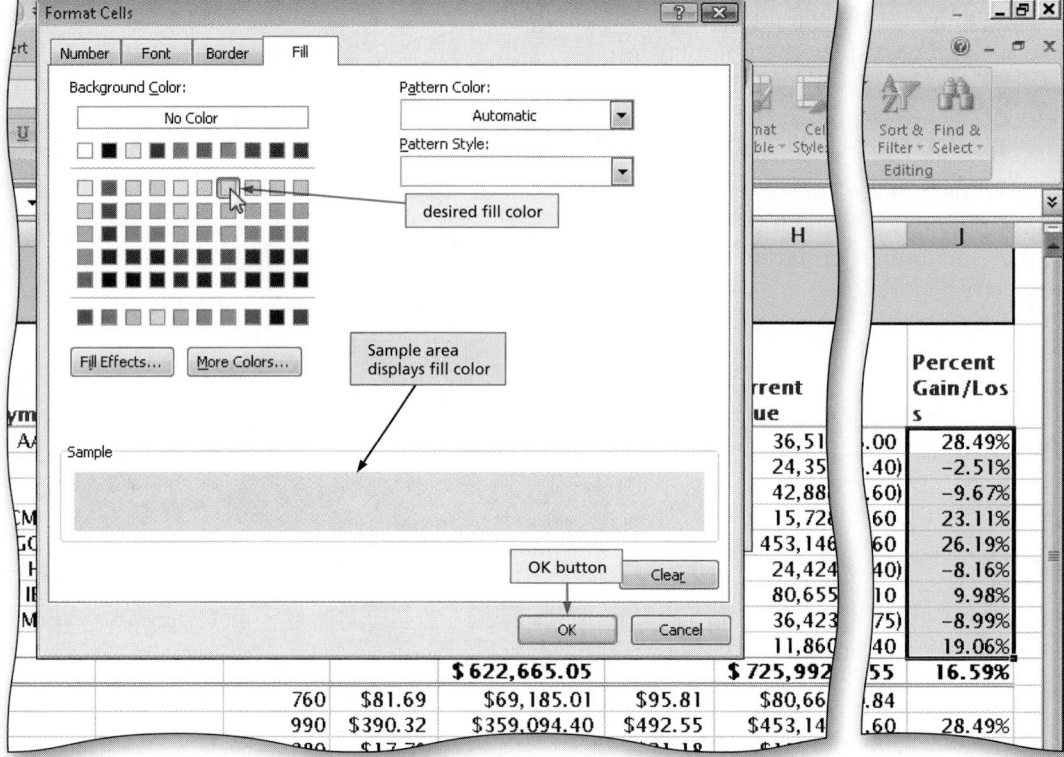

Figure 2–50

4

- Click the OK button to close the Format Cells dialog box and display the New Formatting Rule dialog box with the desired color displayed in the Preview box (Figure 2–51).

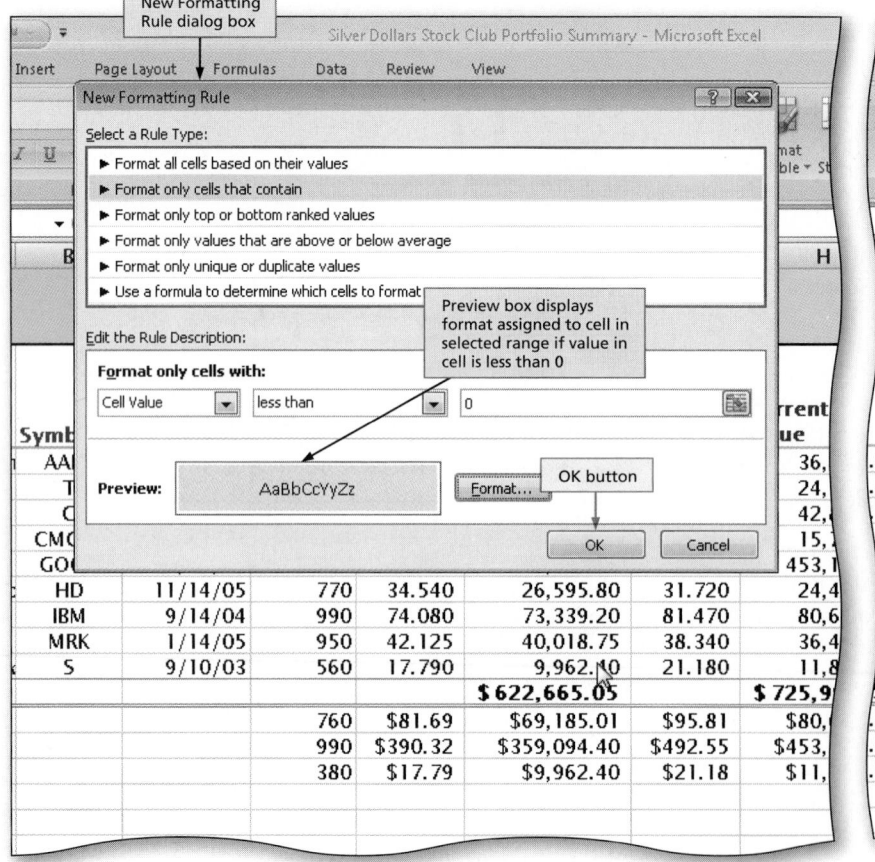

Figure 2–51

5

- Click the OK button to assign the conditional format to the range J4:J12.

- Click cell A18 to deselect the range J4:J12 (Figure 2–52).

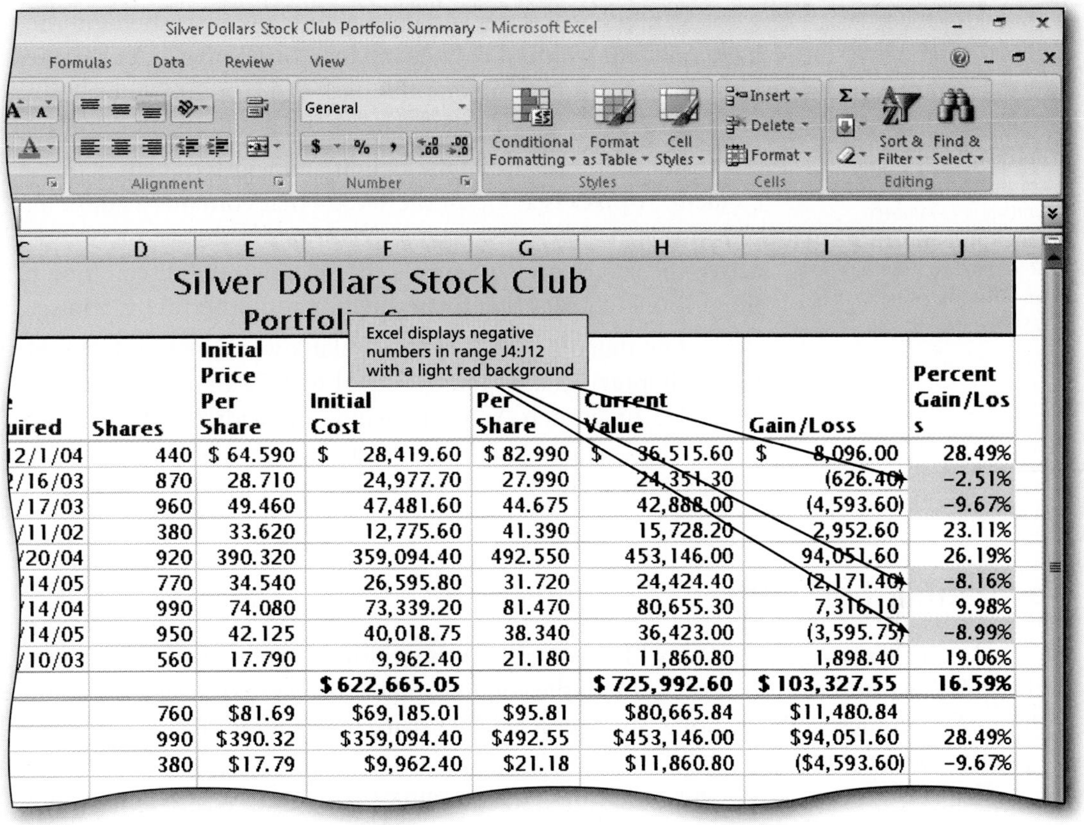

Figure 2–52

Conditional Formatting Operators

As shown in Figure 2–49 on page EX 119, the second text box in the New Formatting Rule dialog box allows you to select a relational operator, such as less than, to use in the condition. The eight different relational operators from which you can choose for conditional formatting in the New Formatting Rule dialog box are summarized in Table 2–5.

BTW

Conditional Formatting
You can assign any format to a cell, a range of cells, a worksheet, or an entire workbook conditionally. If the value of the cell changes and no longer meets the specified condition, Excel suppresses the conditional formatting.

Table 2–5 Summary of Conditional Formatting Relational Operators	
Relational Operator	**Description**
Between	Cell value is between two numbers
Not between	Cell value is not between two numbers
Equal to	Cell value is equal to a number
Not equal to	Cell value is not equal to a number
Greater than	Cell value is greater than a number
Less than	Cell value is less than a number
Greater than or equal to	Cell value is greater than or equal to a number
Less than or equal to	Cell value is less than or equal to a number

BTW

Hidden Columns
Trying to unhide a range of columns using the mouse can be frustrating. An alternative is to use the keyboard: select the columns to the right and left of the hidden columns and then press CTRL+SHIFT+) (RIGHT PARENTHESIS). To use the keyboard to hide a range of columns, press CTRL+0 (ZERO).

Changing the Widths of Columns and Heights of Rows

When Excel starts and displays a blank worksheet on the screen, all of the columns have a default width of 8.43 characters, or 64 pixels. A character is defined as a letter, number, symbol, or punctuation mark in 11-point Calibri font, the default font used by Excel. An average of 8.43 characters in 11-point Calibri font will fit in a cell.

Another measure of the height and width of cells is pixels, which is short for picture element. A **pixel** is a dot on the screen that contains a color. The size of the dot is based on your screen's resolution. At a common resolution of 1024 × 768, 1024 pixels appear across the screen and 768 pixels appear down the screen for a total of 786,432 pixels. It is these 786,432 pixels that form the font and other items you see on the screen.

The default row height in a blank worksheet is 15 points (or 20 pixels). Recall from Chapter 1 that a point is equal to 1/72 of an inch. Thus, 15 points is equal to about 1/5 of an inch. You can change the width of the columns or height of the rows at any time to make the worksheet easier to read or to ensure that Excel displays an entry properly in a cell.

To Change the Widths of Columns

When changing the column width, you can set the width manually or you can instruct Excel to size the column to best fit. **Best fit** means that the width of the column will be increased or decreased so the widest entry will fit in the column. Sometimes, you may prefer more or less white space in a column than best fit provides. Excel thus allows you to change column widths manually.

When the format you assign to a cell causes the entry to exceed the width of a column, Excel automatically changes the column width to best fit. If you do not assign a format to a cell or cells in a column, the column width will remain 8.43 characters. To set a column width to best fit, double-click the right boundary of the column heading above row 1.

The following steps change the column widths: column A to 14.11 characters; columns B and C to best fit; column D to 6.00 characters; columns E, G, and J to 9.00 characters; and columns F, H, and I to 12.67 characters.

1

- Point to the boundary on the right side of the column A heading above row 1.

- When the mouse pointer changes to a split double arrow, drag until the ScreenTip indicates Width: 14.11 (134 pixels). Do not release the mouse button (Figure 2–53).

Q&A

What happens if I change the column width to zero (0)?

If you decrease the column width to 0, the column is hidden. **Hiding cells** is a technique you can use to hide data that might not be relevant to a particular report or sensitive data that you do not want others to see. To instruct Excel to display a hidden column, position the mouse pointer to the right of the column heading boundary where the hidden column is located and then drag to the right.

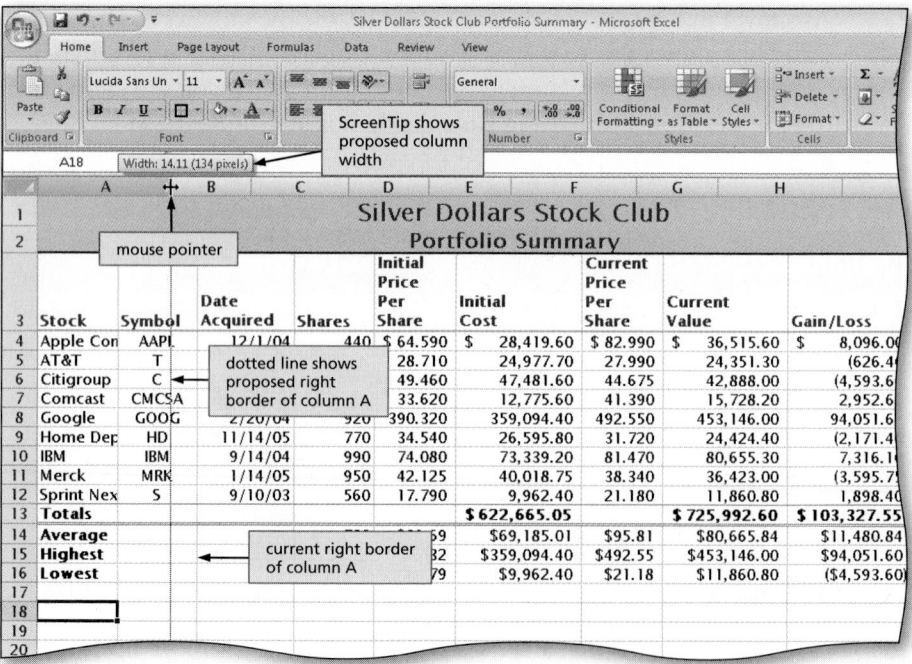

Figure 2–53

2

- Release the mouse button.

- Drag through column headings B and C above row 1.

- Point to the boundary on the right side of column heading C to cause the mouse pointer to become a split double arrow (Figure 2–54).

Q&A

What if I want to make a large change to the column width?

If you want to increase or decrease column width significantly, you can right-click a column heading and then use the Column Width command on the shortcut menu to change the column's width. To use this command, however, you must select one or more entire columns.

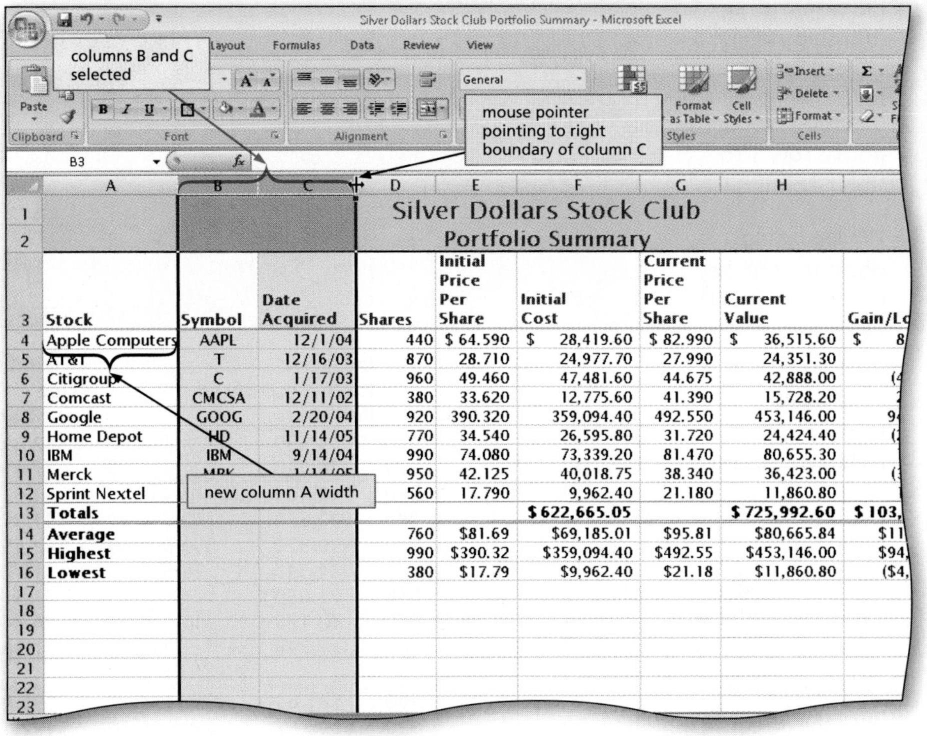

Figure 2–54

3

- Double-click the right boundary of column heading C to change the width of columns B and C to best fit.

- Click the column E heading above row 1.

- While holding down the CTRL key, click the column G heading and then the column J heading above row 1 so that columns E, G, and J are selected.

- If necessary, scroll the worksheet to the right so that the right border of column J is visible. Point to the boundary on the right side of the column J heading above row 1.

- Drag until the ScreenTip indicates Width: 9.00 (88 pixels). Do not release the mouse button (Figure 2–55).

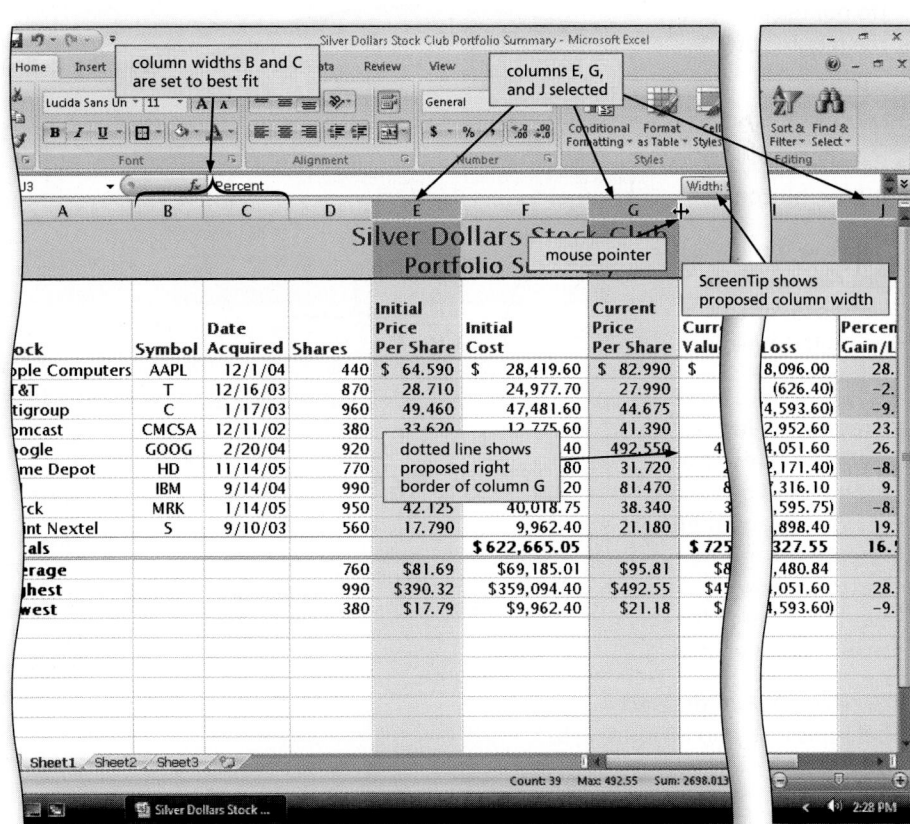

Figure 2–55

4

- Release the mouse button.

- Click the column F heading above row 1 to select column F.

- While holding down the CTRL key, click the column H heading and then the column I heading above row 1, to select columns F, H, and I.

- Point to the boundary on the right side of the column I heading above row 1.

- Drag to the left until the ScreenTip indicates Width: 12.67 (121 pixels). Do not release the mouse button (Figure 2–56).

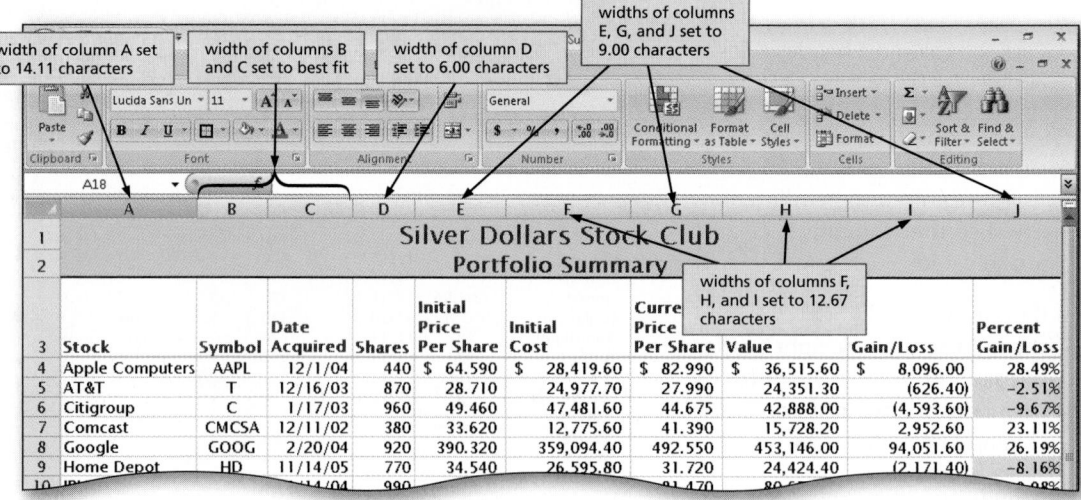

Figure 2–56

5

- Release the mouse button.

- Point to the boundary on the right side of the column D heading above row 1.

- Drag to the left until the ScreenTip indicates Width: 6.00 (61 pixels) and then release the mouse button to display the worksheet with the new column widths.

- Click cell A18 to deselect columns F, H, and I (Figure 2–57).

Figure 2–57

Other Ways

1. Right-click column heading or drag through multiple column headings and right-click, click Column Width on shortcut menu, enter desired column width, click OK button

2. Right-click column heading or drag through multiple column headings and right-click, click Format button on Ribbon, click Column Width in Format gallery, enter desired column width, click OK button

To Change the Heights of Rows

When you increase the font size of a cell entry, such as the title in cell A1, Excel automatically increases the row height to best fit so it can display the characters properly. Recall that Excel did this earlier when multiple lines were entered in a cell in row 3, and when the cell style of the worksheet title and subtitle was changed.

You also can increase or decrease the height of a row manually to improve the appearance of the worksheet. The following steps show how to improve the appearance of the worksheet by increasing the height of row 3 to 60.00 points, and increasing the height of row 14 to 26.25 points.

1

- Point to the boundary below row heading 3.

- Drag down until the ScreenTip indicates Height: 60.00 (80 pixels). Do not release the mouse button (Figure 2–58).

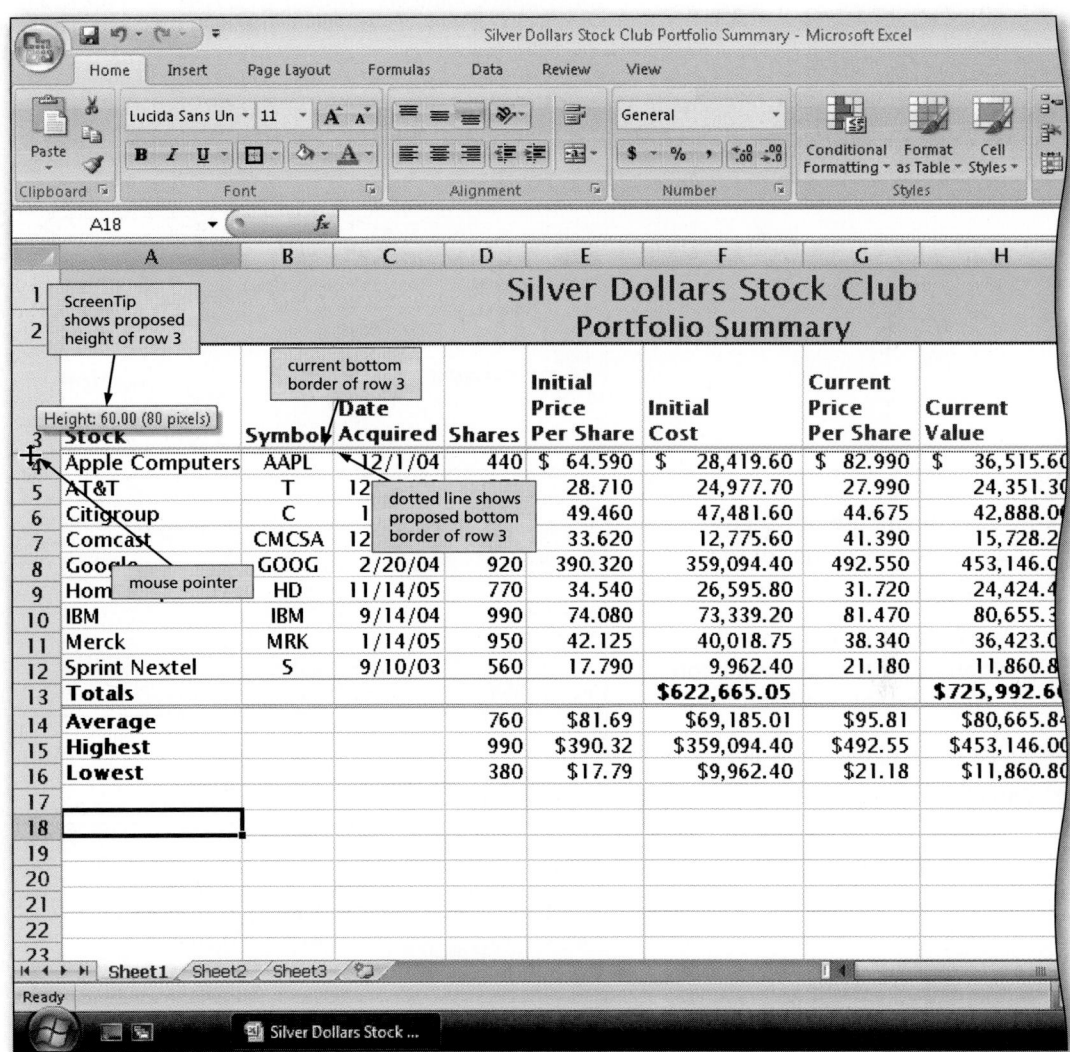

Figure 2–58

2

- Release the mouse button.

- Point to the boundary below row heading 14.

- Drag down until the ScreenTip indicates Height: 26.25 (35 pixels). Do not release the mouse button (Figure 2–59).

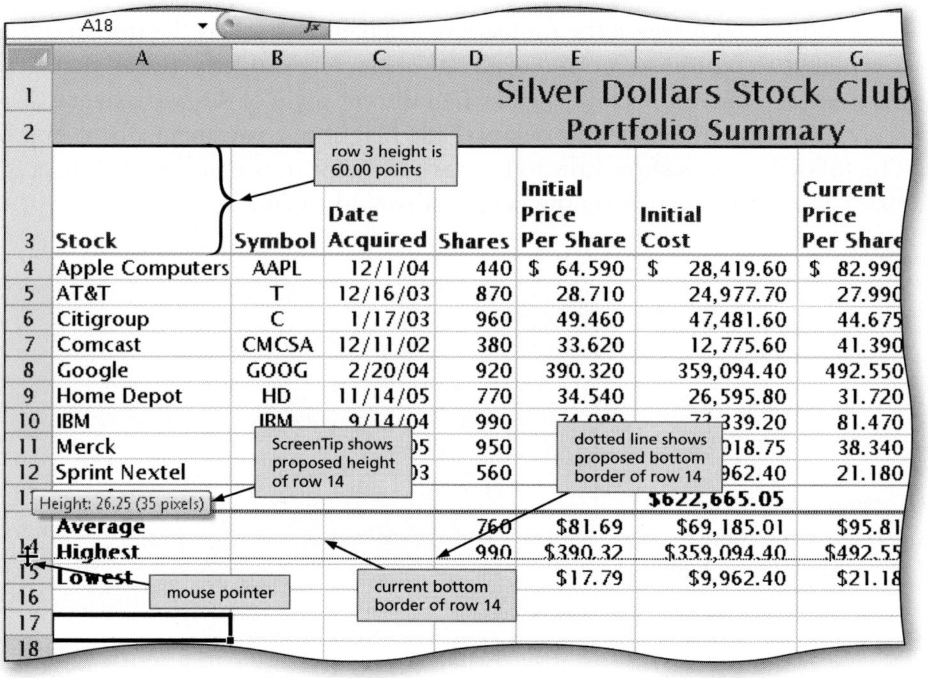

row 3 height is 60.00 points

ScreenTip shows proposed height of row 14

Height: 26.25 (35 pixels)

mouse pointer

dotted line shows proposed bottom border of row 14

current bottom border of row 14

Figure 2–59

3

- Release the mouse button to change the row height of row 14 to 26.25.

- Select cells A3:J3 and then click the Center button on the Ribbon to center the column headings.

- Select cell A18 (Figure 2–60).

Q&A

Can I hide a row?

Yes. As with column widths, when you decrease the row height to 0, the row is hidden. To instruct Excel to display a hidden row, position the mouse pointer just below the row heading boundary where the row is hidden and then drag down. To set a row height to best fit, double-click the bottom boundary of the row heading.

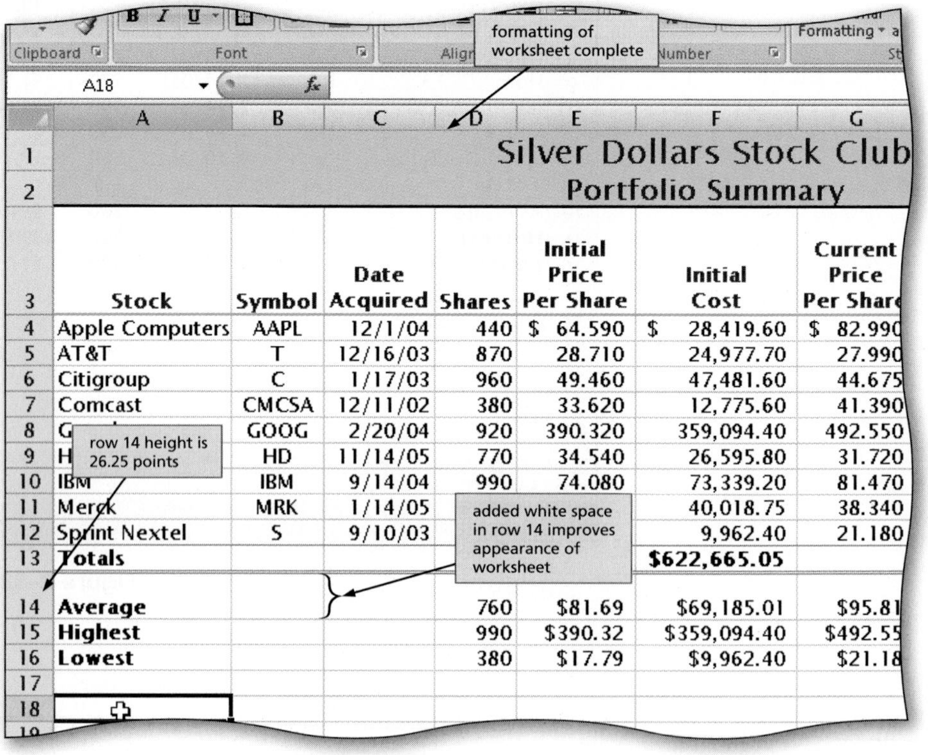

formatting of worksheet complete

Formatting

row 14 height is 26.25 points

added white space in row 14 improves appearance of worksheet

Figure 2–60

Other Ways

1. Right-click row heading or drag through multiple row headings and right-click, click Row Height on shortcut menu, enter desired row height, click OK button

Checking Spelling

Excel has a **spell checker** you can use to check the worksheet for spelling errors. The spell checker looks for spelling errors by comparing words on the worksheet against words contained in its standard dictionary. If you often use specialized terms that are not in the standard dictionary, you may want to add them to a custom dictionary using the Spelling dialog box.

When the spell checker finds a word that is not in either dictionary, it displays the word in the Spelling dialog box. You then can correct it if it is misspelled.

To Check Spelling on the Worksheet

To illustrate how Excel responds to a misspelled word, the word, Stock, in cell A3 is misspelled purposely as the word, Stcok, as shown in Figure 2–61.

1

- Click cell A3 and then type Stcok to misspell the word Stock.

- Click cell A1.

- Click the Review tab on the Ribbon.

- Click the Spelling button on the Ribbon to run the spell checker and display the misspelled word, Stcok, in the Spelling dialog box (Figure 2–61).

Q&A

What happens when the spell checker finds a misspelled word?

When the spell checker identifies that a cell contains a word not in its standard or custom dictionary, it selects that cell as the active cell and displays the Spelling dialog box. The Spelling dialog box (Figure 2–61) lists the word not found in the dictionary and a list of suggested corrections.

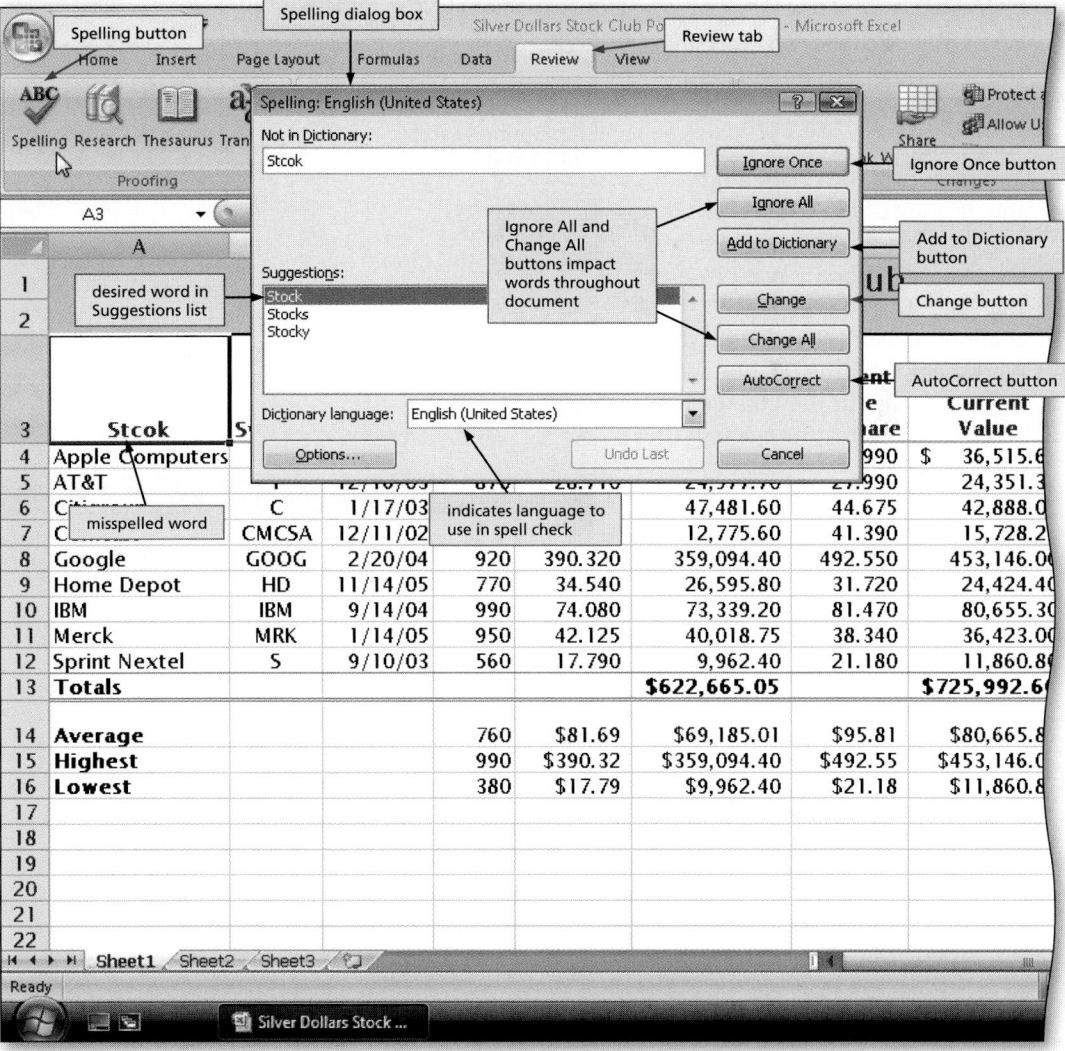

Figure 2–61

2

- With the word Stock highlighted in the Suggestions list, click the Change button to change the misspelled word, Stcok, to the correct word, Stock (Figure 2–62).

- If the Microsoft Office Excel dialog box is displayed, click the OK button.

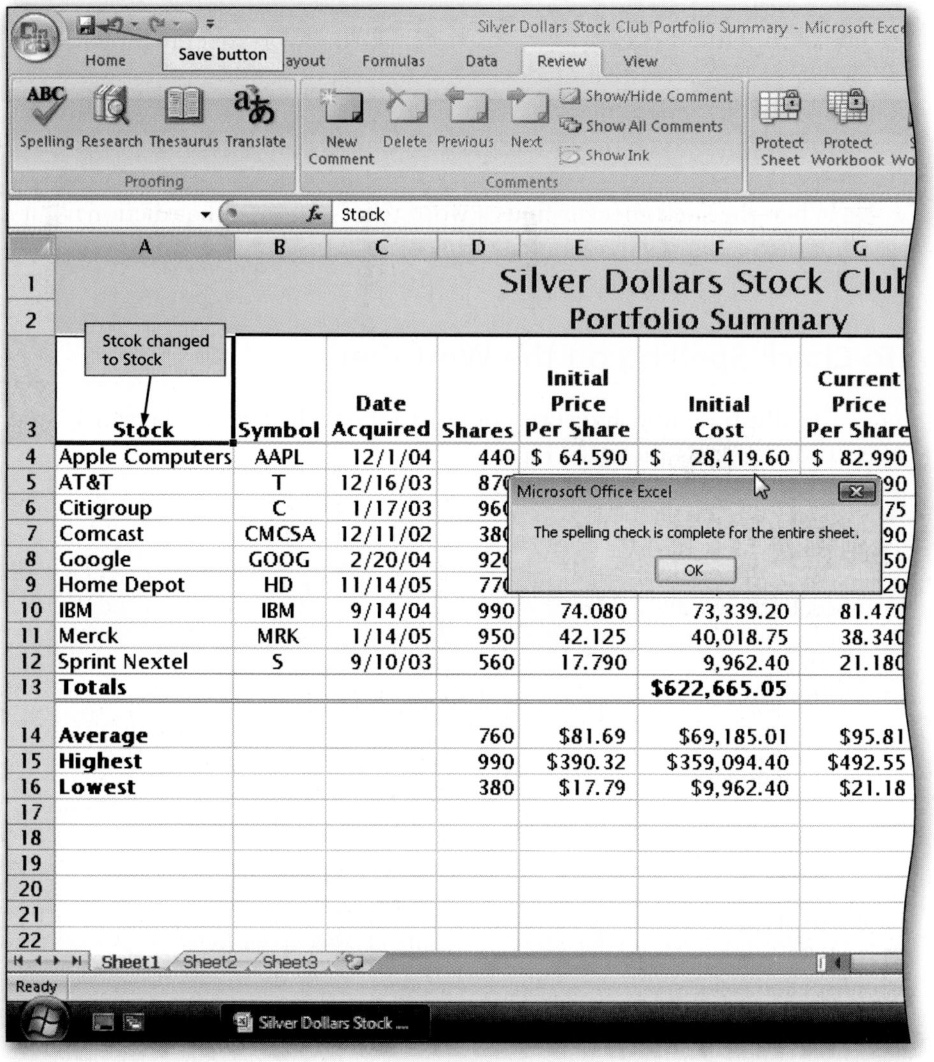

3

- Select cell A18.

- Click the Home tab on the Ribbon.

- Click the Save button on the Quick Access Toolbar to save the workbook.

Q&A

What other actions can I take in the Spelling dialog box?

If one of the words in the Suggestions list is correct, click it and then click the Change button. If none of the suggestions is correct, type the correct word in the Not in Dictionary text box and then click the Change button. To change the word throughout the worksheet, click the Change All button instead of the Change button. To skip correcting the word, click the Ignore Once button. To have Excel ignore the word for the remainder of the worksheet, click the Ignore All button.

Figure 2–62

Other Ways
1. Press F7

Additional Spell Checker Considerations

Consider these additional guidelines when using the spell checker:

- To check the spelling of the text in a single cell, double-click the cell to make the formula bar active and then click the Spelling button on the Review tab on the Ribbon.

- If you select a single cell so that the formula bar is not active and then start the spell checker, Excel checks the remainder of the worksheet, including notes and embedded charts.

- If you select a cell other than cell A1 before you start the spell checker, Excel will display a dialog box when the spell checker reaches the end of the worksheet, asking if you want to continue checking at the beginning.

- If you select a range of cells before starting the spell checker, Excel checks the spelling of the words only in the selected range.

- To check the spelling of all the sheets in a workbook, click Select All Sheets on the sheet tab shortcut menu and then start the spell checker. To instruct Excel to display the sheet tab shortcut menu, right-click any sheet tab.

- To add words to the dictionary such as your last name, click the Add to Dictionary button in the Spelling dialog box (Figure 2–61 on page EX 127) when Excel identifies the word as not in the dictionary.

- Click the AutoCorrect button (Figure 2–61) to add the misspelled word and the correct version of the word to the AutoCorrect list. For example, suppose you misspell the word, do, as the word, dox. When the spell checker displays the Spelling dialog box with the correct word, do, in the Change to box, click the AutoCorrect button. Then, anytime in the future that you type the word, dox, Excel automatically will change it to the word, do.

Preparing to Print the Worksheet

Excel allows for a great deal of customization in how a worksheet appears when printed. For example, the margins on the page can be adjusted. A header or footer can be added to each printed page as well. Excel also has the capability to work on the worksheet in Page Layout View. **Page Layout View** allows you to create or modify a worksheet while viewing how it will look in printed format. The default view that you have worked in up until this point in the book is called **Normal View**.

Specify how the printed worksheet should appear.
Before printing a worksheet, you should consider how the worksheet will appear when printed. In order to fit as much information on the printed page as possible, the margins of the worksheet should be set to a reasonably small width and height. The current Portfolio Summary worksheet will print on one page. If, however, the club added more data to the worksheet, then it may extend to multiple pages. It is, therefore, a good idea to add a page header to the worksheet that prints in the top margin of each page.

In Chapter 1, the worksheet was printed in **portrait orientation**, which means the printout is printed across the width of the page. **Landscape orientation** means the printout is printed across the length of the page. Landscape orientation is a good choice for the Silver Dollars Stock Club Portfolio Summary because the printed worksheet's width is greater than its length.

BTW

Spell Checking
While Excel's spell checker is a valuable tool, it is not infallible. You should proofread your workbook carefully by pointing to each word and saying it aloud as you point to it. Be mindful of misused words such as its and it's, through and though, and to and too. Nothing undermines a good impression more than a professional looking report with misspelled words.

BTW

Error Checking
Always take the time to check the formulas of a worksheet before submitting it to your supervisor. You can check formulas by clicking the Error Checking button on the Formulas tab on the Ribbon. You also should test the formulas by employing data that tests the limits of formulas. Experienced spreadsheet specialists spend as much time testing a workbook as they do creating it, before placing it into production.

Plan Ahead

BTW

Certification
The Microsoft Certified Application Specialist (MCAS) program provides an opportunity for you to obtain a valuable industry credential – proof that you have the Excel 2007 skills required by employers. For more information, see Appendix G or visit the Excel 2007 Certification Web page (scsite.com/ex2007/cert).

To Change the Worksheet's Margins, Header, and Orientation in Page Layout View

The following steps change to Page Layout View, narrow the margins of the worksheet, change the header of the worksheet, and set the orientation of the worksheet to landscape.

①

- Click the Page Layout View button on the status bar to view the worksheet in Page Layout View (Figure 2–63).

What are some key features of Page Layout View?

Page Layout View shows the worksheet divided into pages. A blue background separates each page. The white areas surrounding each page indicate the print margins. The top of each page includes a Header area, and the bottom of each page includes a Footer area. Page Layout View also includes a ruler at the top of the page that assists you in placing objects on the page, such as charts and pictures.

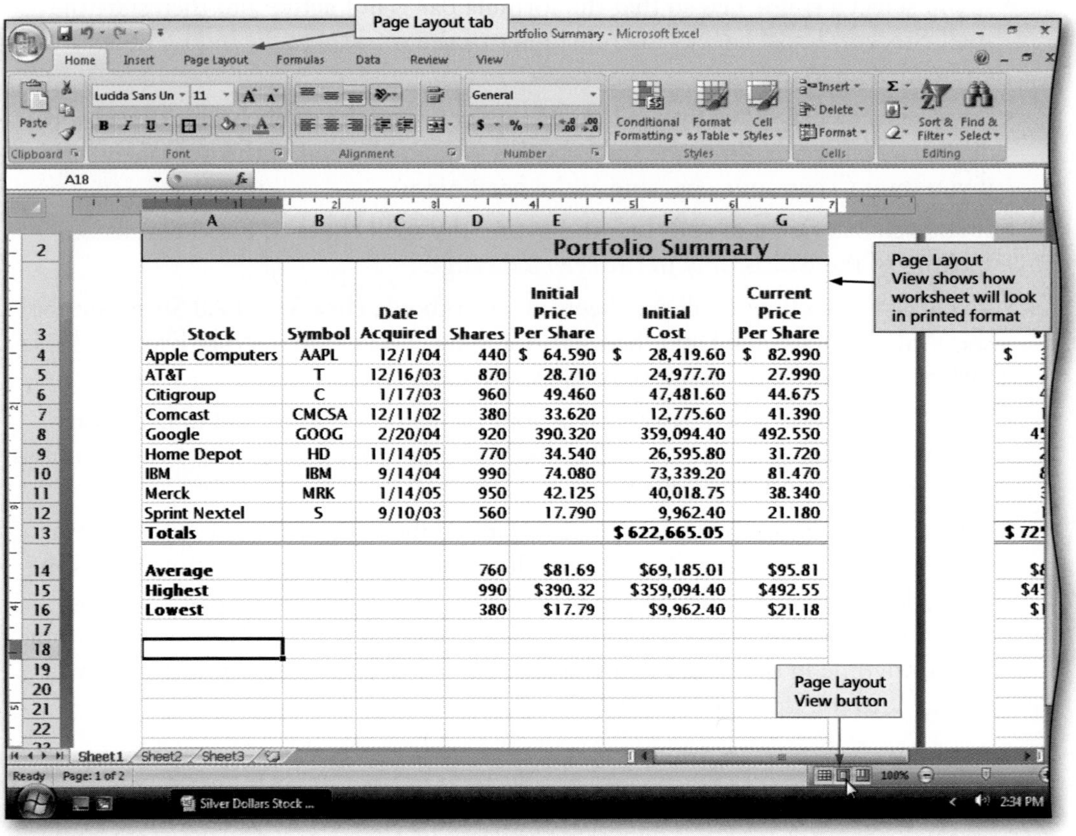

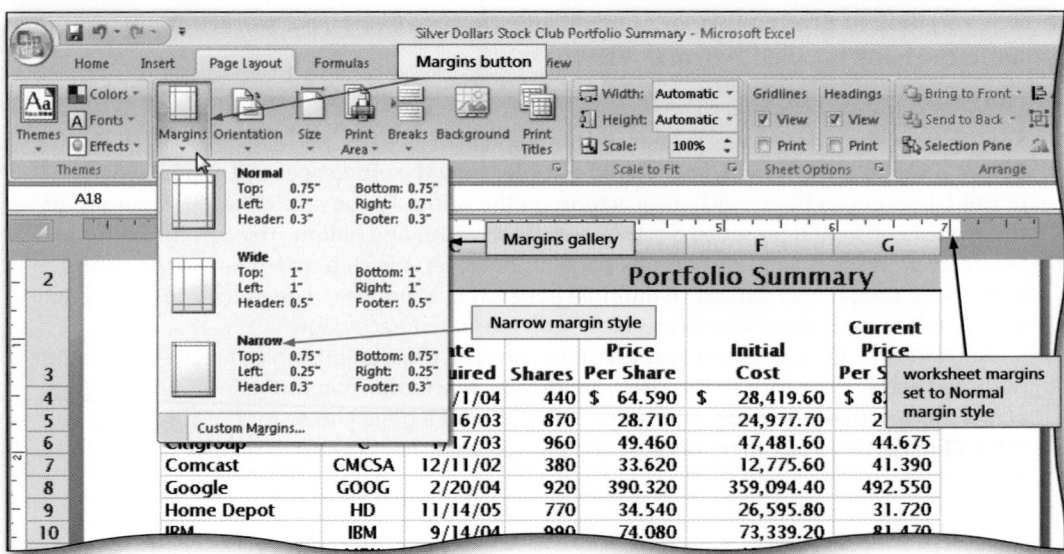

Figure 2–63

②

- Click the Page Layout tab on the Ribbon.

- Click the Margins button on the Ribbon to display the Margins gallery (Figure 2–64).

Figure 2–64

3

- Click Narrow in the Margins gallery to change the worksheet margins to the Narrow margin style.

- Drag the scroll bar on the right side of the worksheet to the top so that row 1 of the worksheet is displayed.

- Click above the worksheet title in cell A1 in the Header area.

- Type `Treasurer: Juan Castillo` and then press the ENTER key. Type `castillo_ juan37@hotmail. com` to complete the worksheet header (Figure 2–65).

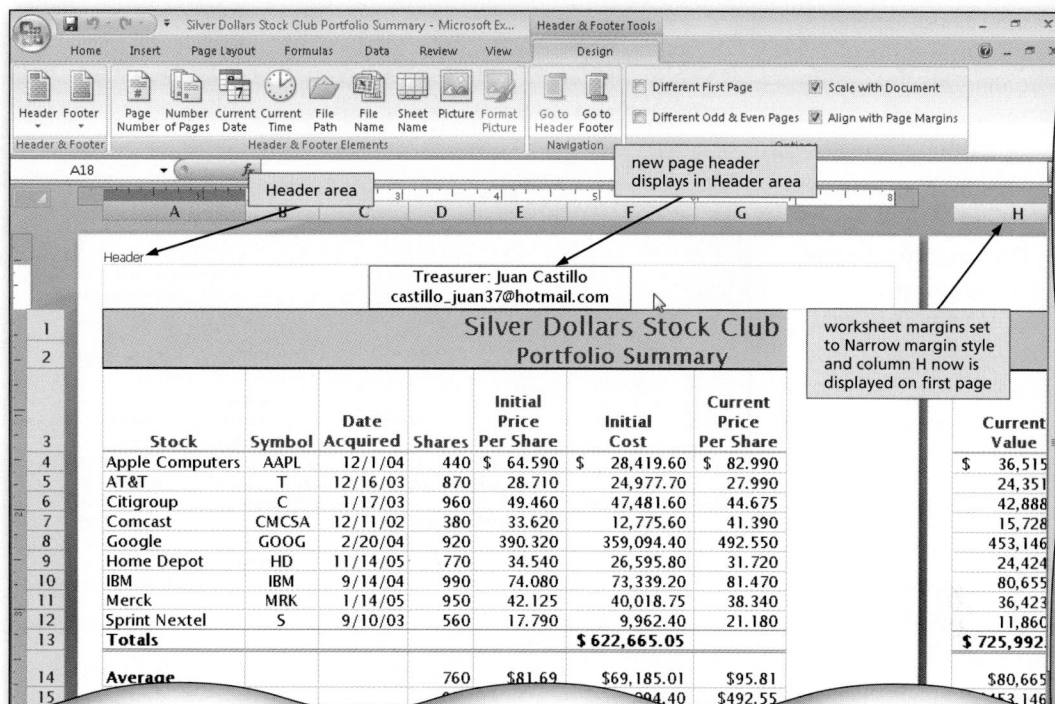

Figure 2–65

4

- Select cell B16 to deselect the header. Click the Orientation button on the Ribbon to display the Orientation gallery.

- Point to Landscape but do not click the mouse button (Figure 2–66).

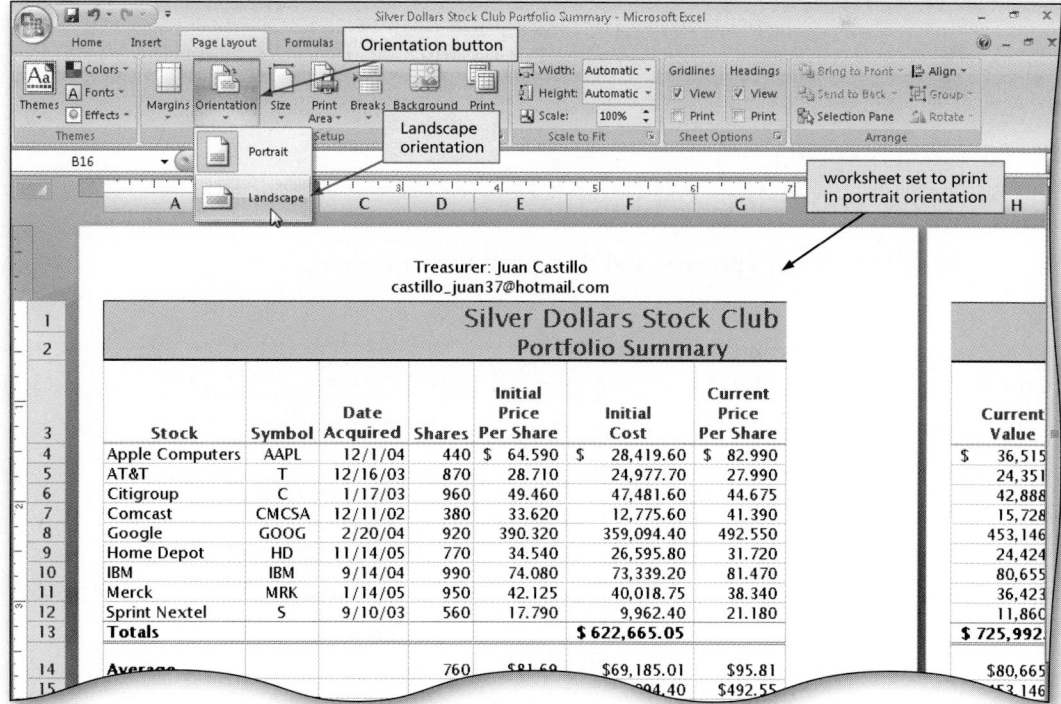

Figure 2–66

● Click Landscape in
the Orientation
gallery to change
the worksheet's
orientation to
landscape
(Figure 2–67).

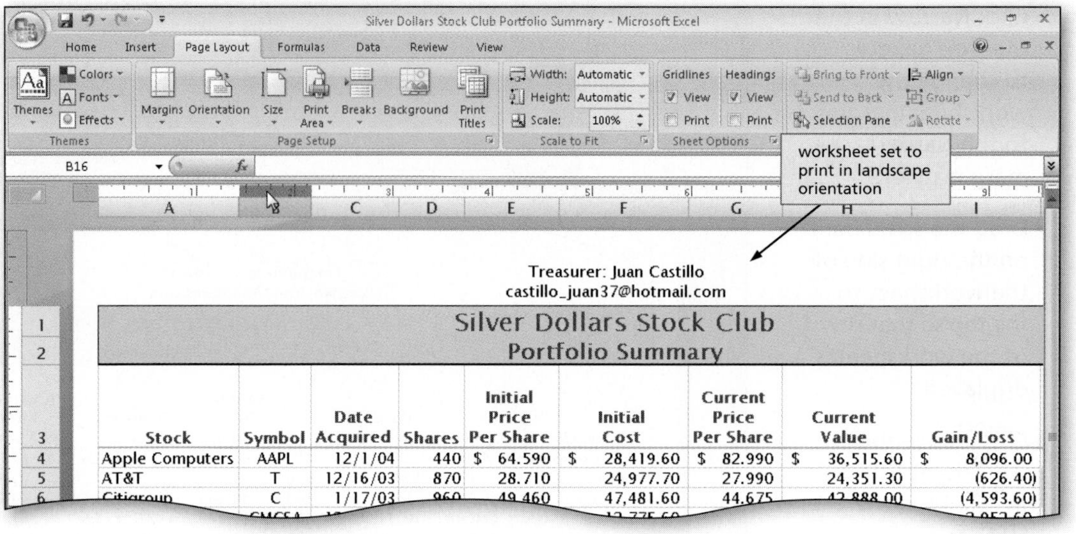

Q&A

Do I need to change
the orientation
every time I want to
print the
worksheet?

No. Once you change
the orientation and
save the workbook,
Excel will save the
orientation setting
for that workbook
until you change it.
When you open a new workbook, Excel sets the orientation to portrait.

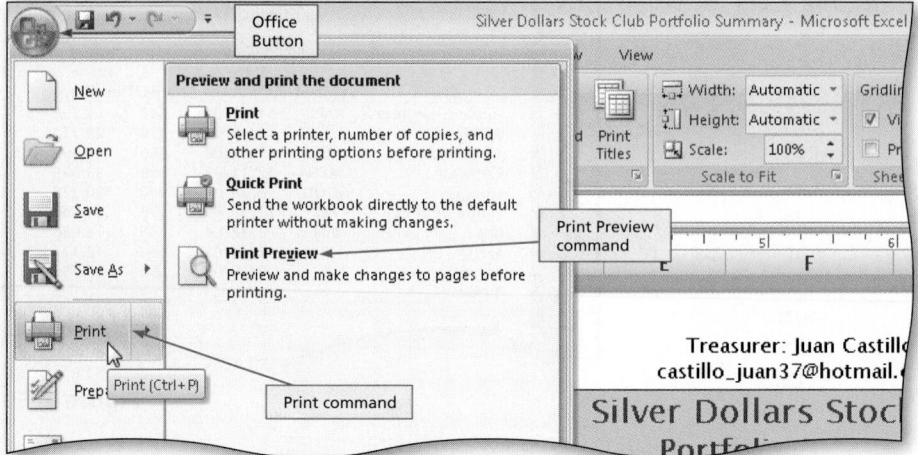

Figure 2–67

Other Ways

1. Click Page Layout tab
on Ribbon, click Page
Setup Dialog Box
Launcher, click Page
tab, click Portrait or
Landscape, click OK
button

Previewing and Printing the Worksheet

In Chapter 1, the worksheet was printed without first previewing it on the screen. By
previewing the worksheet, however, you see exactly how it will look without generating
a printout. Previewing a worksheet using the Print Preview command can save time,
paper, and the frustration of waiting for a printout only to discover it is not what you want.

To Preview and Print a Worksheet

The following steps preview and then print the worksheet.

● Click the Office Button and then
point to Print on the Office
Button menu to display the Print
submenu (Figure 2–68).

Figure 2–68

2

- Click Print Preview on the Print submenu to display a preview of the worksheet in landscape orientation (Figure 2–69).

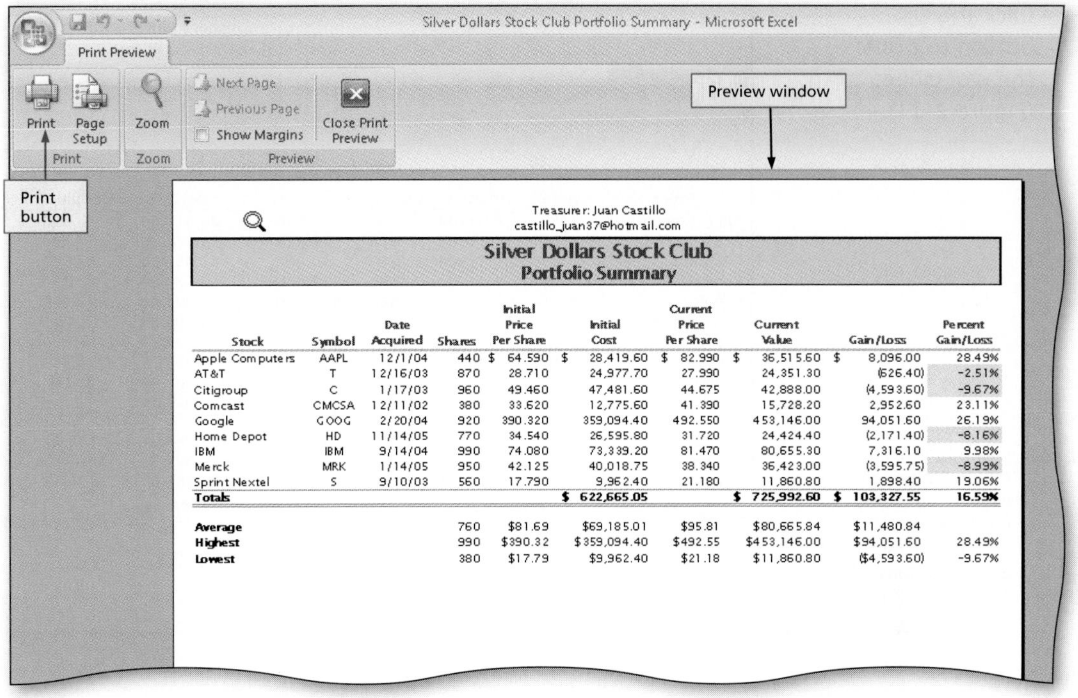

Q&A What is the purpose of the buttons in the Print Preview area?

The Print button displays the Print dialog box and allows you to print the worksheet. The Page Setup button displays the Page Setup dialog box. The Zoom button allows you to zoom in and out of the page displayed in the Preview window. You also can click the previewed page in the Preview window when the mouse pointer shape is a magnifying glass to carry out the function of the Zoom button.

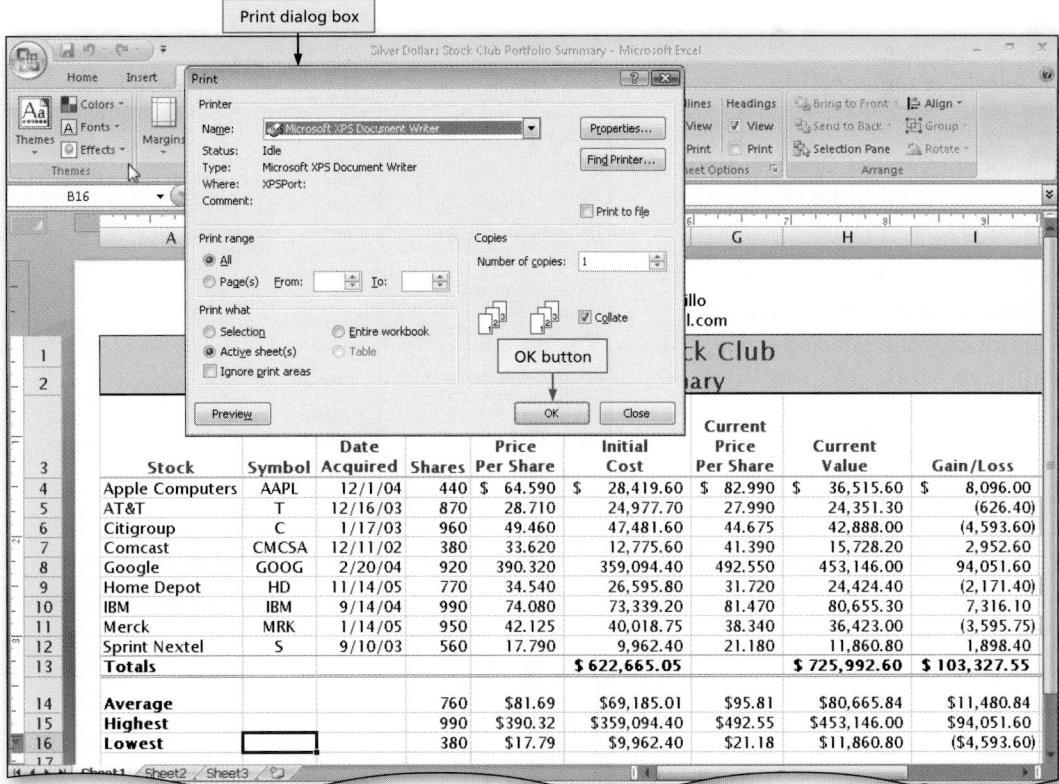

Figure 2–69

3

- Click the Print button to display the Print dialog box (Figure 2–70).

Q&A How can I use the Print dialog box?

When you click the Print command on the Print submenu of the Office Button menu or a Print button in a dialog box or Preview window, Excel displays the Print dialog box shown in Figure 2–70. Excel does not display the Print dialog box when you use the Print button on the Quick Access Toolbar, as was the case in Chapter 1. The Print dialog box allows you to select a printer, instruct Excel what to print, and indicate how many copies of the printout you want.

Figure 2–70

- Click the OK button to print the worksheet (Figure 2–71).

worksheet printed in landscape orientation

Treasurer: Juan Castillo
castillo_juan37@hotmail.com

Silver Dollars Stock Club
Portfolio Summary

Stock	Symbol	Date Aquired	Shares	Initial Price Per Share	Initial Cost	Current Price Per Share	Current Value	Gain/Loss
Apple Computers	AAPL	12/1/04	440	$ 64.590	$ 28,419.60	$ 82.990	$ 36,515.60	$ 8,096.00
AT&T	T	12/16/03	870	28.710	24,977.70	27.990	24,351.30	(626.40)
Citigroup	C	1/17/04	960	49.460	47,481.60	44.675	42,888.00	(4,593.60)
Comcast	CMCSA	2/11/02	380	33.620	12,775.60	41.390	15,728.20	2,952.60
Google	GOOG	2/20/04	920	390.320	359,094.40	492.550	453,146.00	94,051.60
Home Depot	HD	11/14/05	770	34.540	26,595.80	31.720	24,424.40	(2,171.40)
IBM	IBM	9/14/04	990	74.080	73,339.20	81.470	80,655.30	7,316.10
Merck	MRK	1/14/05	950	42.125	40,018.75	38.340	36,423.00	(3,595.75)
Sprint Nextel	S	9/10/03	560	17.790	9,962.40	21.180	11,860.80	1,898.40
Totals					$ 622,665.05		$ 725,992.60	$ 103,327.55
Average			760	$81.69	$69,185.01	$95.81	$80,665.84	$11,480.84
Highest			990	$390.32	$359,094.40	$492.55	$453,146.00	$94,051.60
Lowest			380	$17.79	$9,962.40	$21.18	$11,860.80	($4,593.60)

Figure 2–71

To Print a Section of the Worksheet

You might not always want to print the entire worksheet. You can print portions of the worksheet by selecting the range of cells to print and then clicking the Selection option button in the Print what area in the Print dialog box. The following steps print the range A3:F16.

- Select the range A3:F16.

- Click the Office Button and then click Print on the Office Button menu to display the Print dialog box.

- Click Selection in the Print what area to instruct Excel to print only the selected range (Figure 2–72).

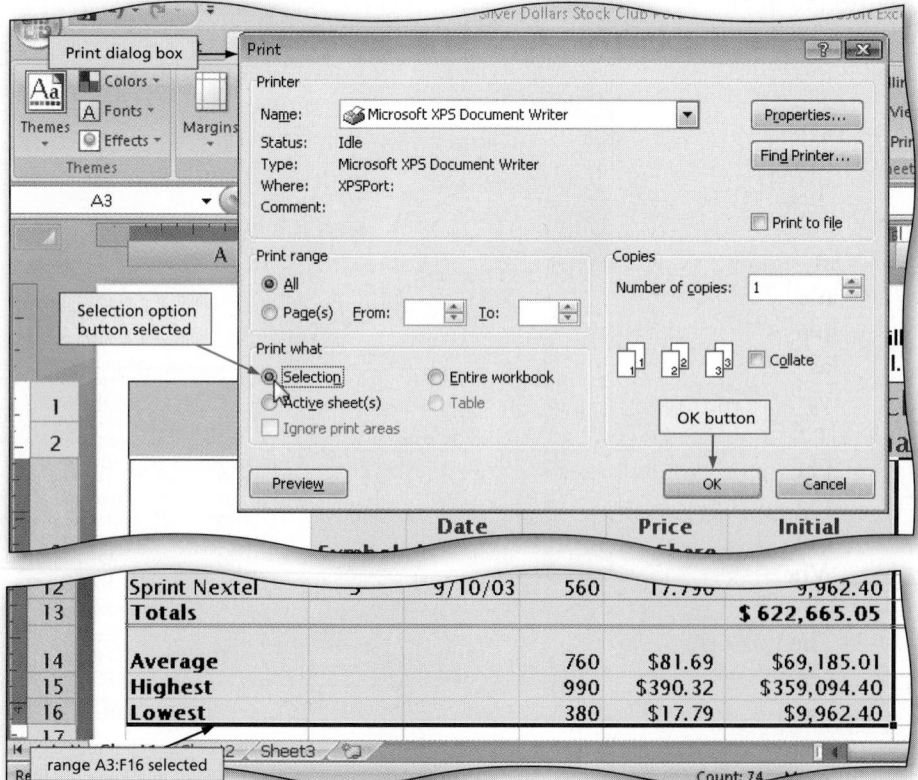

Figure 2–72

2

- Click the OK button to print the selected range of the worksheet on the printer (Figure 2–73).

- Click the Normal View button on the status bar.

- Click cell A18 to deselect the range A3:F13.

What are the options in the Print what area?

The Print what area of the Print dialog box includes four option buttons (Figure 2–72). As shown in the previous steps, the Selection option button instructs Excel to print the selected range. The Active sheet(s) option

	header prints				Treasurer: Juan Castillo		selected range prints
					castillo_juan37@hotmail.com		

Stock	Symbol	Date Acquired	Shares	Initial Price Per Share	Initial Cost
Apple Computers	AAPL	12/1/04	440	$ 64.590	$ 28,419.60
AT&T	T	12/16/03	870	28.710	24,977.70
Citigroup	C	1/17/04	960	49.460	47,481.60
Comcast	CMCSA	2/11/02	380	33.620	12,775.60
Google	GOOG	2/20/04	920	390.320	359,094.40
Home Depot	HD	11/14/05	770	34.540	26,595.80
IBM	IBM	9/14/04	990	74.080	73,339.20
Merck	MRK	1/14/05	950	42.125	40,018.75
Sprint Nextel	S	9/10/03	560	17.790	9,962.40
Totals					$ 622,665.05
Average			760	$81.69	$69,185.01
Highest			990	$390.32	$359,094.40
Lowest			380	$17.79	$9,962.40

Figure 2–73

button instructs Excel to print the active worksheet (the worksheet currently on the screen) or the selected worksheets. Finally, the Entire workbook option button instructs Excel to print all of the worksheets in the workbook.

Displaying and Printing the Formulas Version of the Worksheet

Thus far, you have been working with the **values version** of the worksheet, which shows the results of the formulas you have entered, rather than the actual formulas. Excel also can display and print the **formulas version** of the worksheet, which shows the actual formulas you have entered, rather than the resulting values. You can toggle between the values version and formulas version by holding down the CTRL key while pressing the ACCENT MARK (`) key, which is located to the left of the number 1 key on the keyboard.

The formulas version is useful for debugging a worksheet. **Debugging** is the process of finding and correcting errors in the worksheet. Viewing and printing the formulas version instead of the values version makes it easier to see any mistakes in the formulas.

When you change from the values version to the formulas version, Excel increases the width of the columns so the formulas and text do not overflow into adjacent cells on the right. The formulas version of the worksheet thus usually is significantly wider than the values version. To fit the wide printout on one page, you can use landscape orientation, which has already been selected for the workbook, and the Fit to option in the Page sheet in the Page Setup dialog box.

Other Ways

1. Select range, click Page Layout tab on Ribbon, click Print Area button, click Set Print Area, click Quick Print button on Quick Access Toolbar, click Print Area button, click Clear Print Area button

BTW

Values versus Formulas
When completing class assignments, do not enter numbers in cells that require formulas. Most instructors require their students to hand in both the values version and formulas version of the worksheet. The formulas version verifies that you entered formulas, rather than numbers, in formula-based cells.

To Display the Formulas in the Worksheet and Fit the Printout on One Page

The following steps change the view of the worksheet from the values version to the formulas version of the worksheet and then print the formulas version on one page.

 1

- Press CTRL+ACCENT MARK (`).

- When Excel displays the formulas version of the worksheet, click the right horizontal scroll arrow until column J appears to display the worksheet with formulas (Figure 2–74).

 2

- If necessary, click the Page Layout tab on the Ribbon and then click the Page Setup Dialog Box Launcher to display the Page Setup dialog box.

- If necessary, click Landscape to select it and then click Fit to in the Scaling area.

Figure 2–74

 3

- Click the Print button in the Page Setup dialog box to print the formulas in the worksheet on one page in landscape orientation (Figure 2–75).

- When Excel displays the Print dialog box, click the OK button.

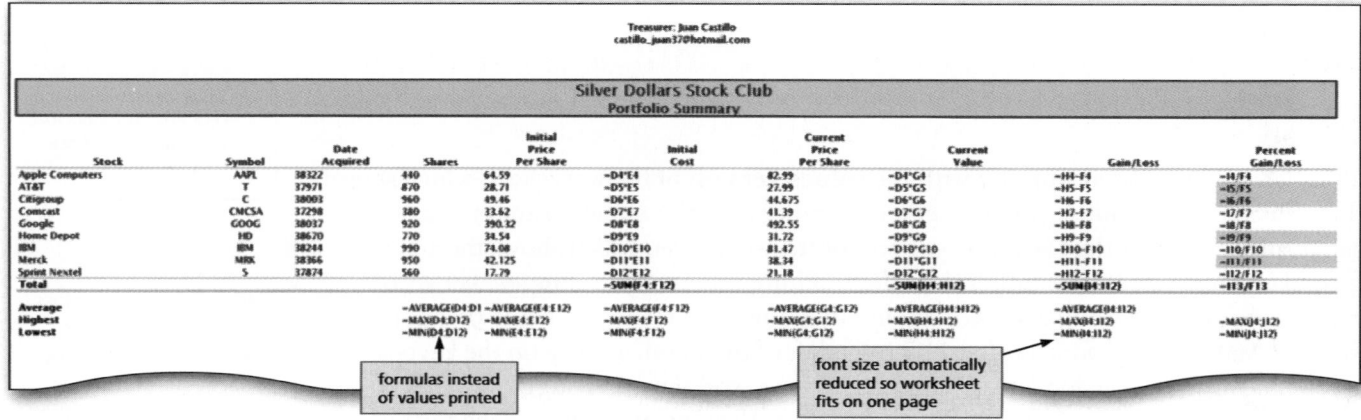

Figure 2–75

 4

- After viewing and printing the formulas version, press CTRL+ACCENT MARK (`) to instruct Excel to display the values version.

- Click the left horizontal scroll arrow until column A appears.

Other Ways

1. Click Show Formulas button on Formulas tab on Ribbon

To Change the Print Scaling Option Back to 100%

Depending on your printer, you may have to change the Print Scaling option back to 100% after using the Fit to option. The following steps reset the Print Scaling option so future worksheets print at 100%, instead of being resized to print on one page.

1 If necessary, click the Page Layout tab on the Ribbon and then click the Page Setup Dialog Box Launcher to display the Page Setup dialog box.

2 Click Adjust to in the Scaling area.

3 If necessary, type 100 in the Adjust to box.

4 Click the OK button to set the print scaling to normal.

5 Click the Home tab on the Ribbon.

Q&A | What is the purpose of the Adjust to box in the Page Setup dialog box?

The Adjust to box allows you to specify the percentage of reduction or enlargement in the printout of a worksheet. The default percentage is 100%. When you click the Fit to option, this percentage automatically changes to the percentage required to fit the printout on one page.

Importing External Data from a Web Source Using a Web Query

One of the major features of Excel is its capability of importing external data from Web sites. To import external data from a Web site, you must have access to the Internet. You then can import data stored on a Web site using a **Web query**. When you run a Web query, Excel imports the external data in the form of a worksheet. As described in Table 2–6, three Web queries are available when you first install Excel. All three Web queries relate to investment and stock market activities.

Table 2–6 Excel Web Queries	
Query	**External Data Returned**
MSN MoneyCentral Investor Currency Rates	Currency rates
MSN MoneyCentral Investor Major Indices	Major indices
MSN MoneyCentral Investor Stock Quotes	Up to 20 stocks of your choice

Gather information regarding the needed Web query.
As shown in Table 2–6, the MSN Money Central Investor Stock Quotes feature that is included with Excel allows you to retrieve information on up to 20 stocks of your choice. The Web query requires that you supply the stock symbols. The stock symbols are located in column B of the Portfolio Summary worksheet.

Plan Ahead

BTW | **Web Queries**
Most Excel specialists that build Web queries use the worksheet returned from the Web query as an engine to supply data to another worksheet in the workbook. With 3-D cell references, you can create a worksheet similar to the Silver Dollars Stock Club worksheet to feed the Web query stock symbols and get refreshed stock prices in return.

To Import Data from a Web Source Using a Web Query

Although you can have a Web query return data to a blank workbook, the following steps have the data for the nine stock symbols in column B of the Portfolio Summary worksheet returned to a blank worksheet in the Silver Dollars Stock Club Portfolio Summary workbook. The data returned by the stock-related Web queries is real time in the sense that it is no more than 20 minutes old during the business day.

- With the Silver Dollars Stock Club Portfolio Summary workbook open, click the Sheet2 tab at the bottom of the window.

- With cell A1 active, click the Data tab on the Ribbon, and then click the Existing Connections button to display the Existing Connections dialog box (Figure 2–76).

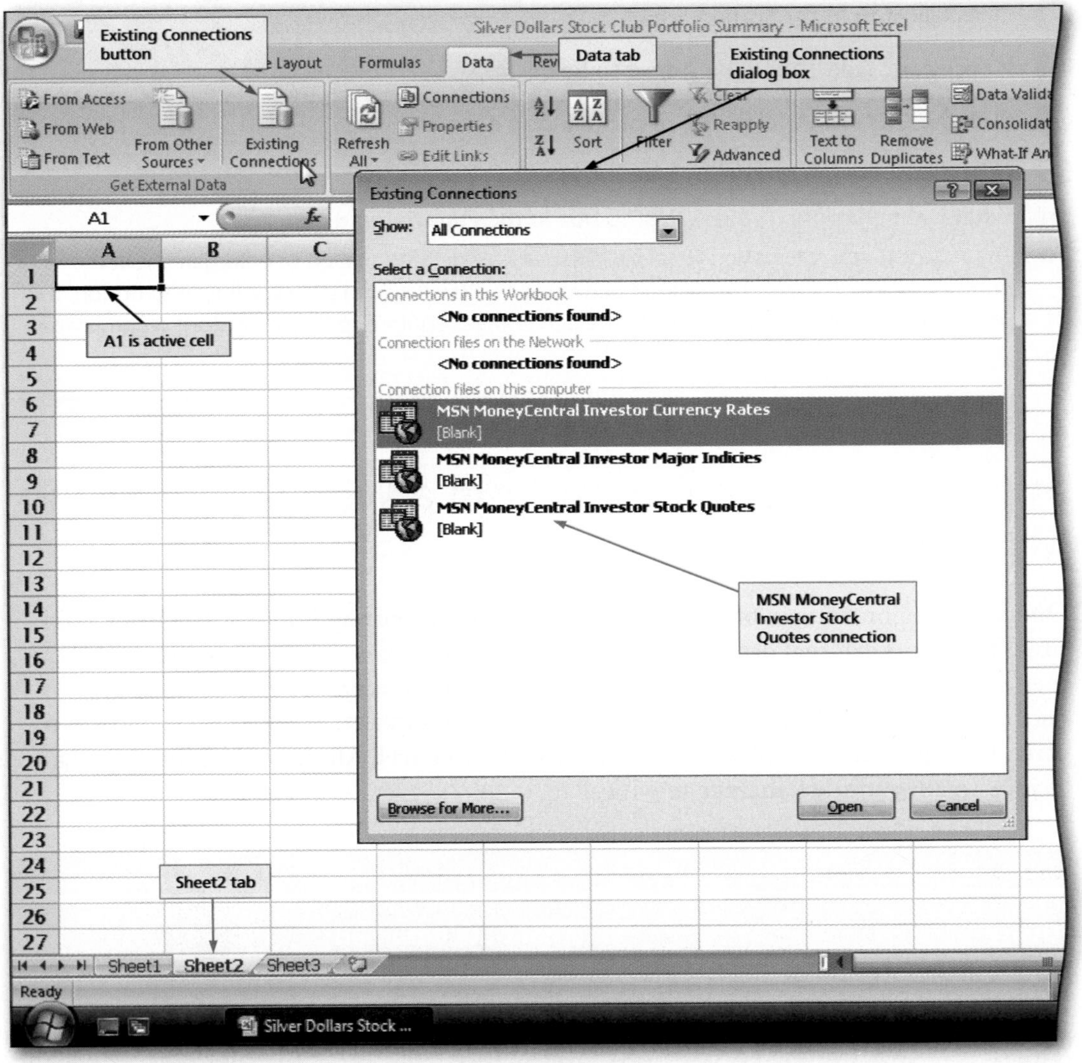

Figure 2–76

2

- Double-click MSN MoneyCentral Investor Stock Quotes to display the Import Data dialog box (Figure 2–77).

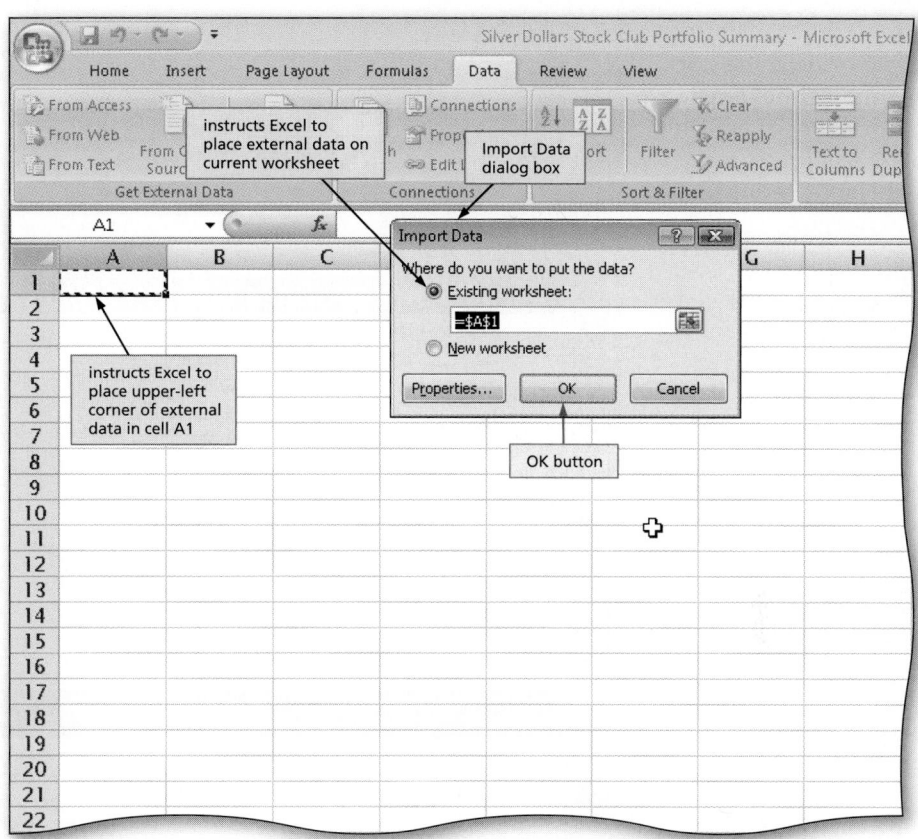

Figure 2–77

3

- Click the OK button.

- When Excel displays the Enter Parameter Value dialog box, type the nine stock symbols `aapl t c cmcsa goog hd ibm mrk s` in the text box.

- Click the 'Use this value/reference for future refreshes' check box to select it (Figure 2–78).

Q&A What is the purpose of clicking the check box?

Once Excel displays the worksheet, you can refresh the data as often as you want. To refresh the data for all the stocks, click the Refresh All button on the Data tab on the Ribbon. Because the 'Use this value/reference for future refreshes' check box was selected, Excel will continue to use the same stock symbols each time it refreshes.

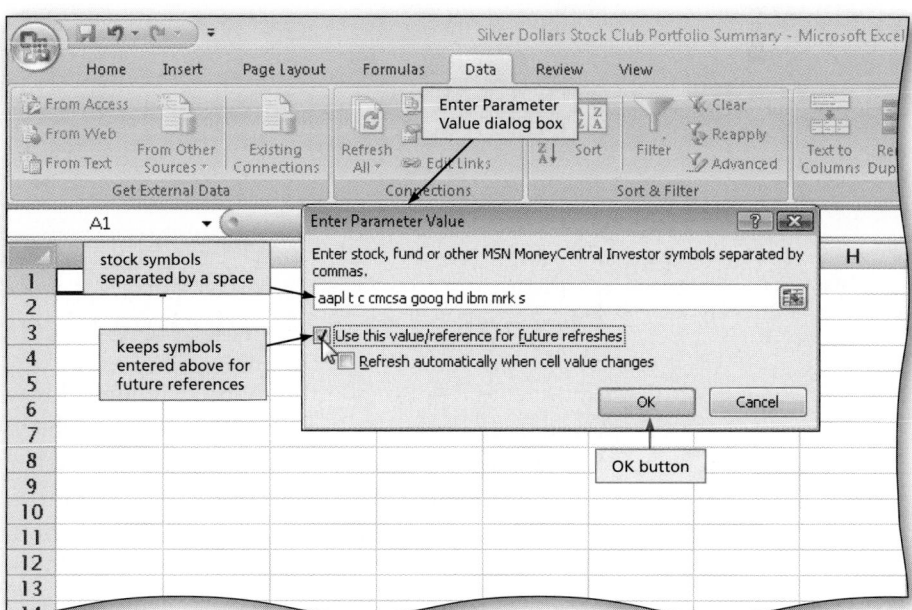

Figure 2–78

4

- Click the OK button to retrieve the stock quotes and display a new worksheet with the desired data (Figure 2–79).

Q&A

What composes the new worksheet?

As shown in Figure 2–79, Excel displays the data returned from the Web query in an organized, formatted worksheet, which has a worksheet title, column titles, and a row of data for each stock symbol entered. Other than the first column, which contains the stock name and stock symbol, you have no control over the remaining columns of data returned. The latest price of each stock appears in column D.

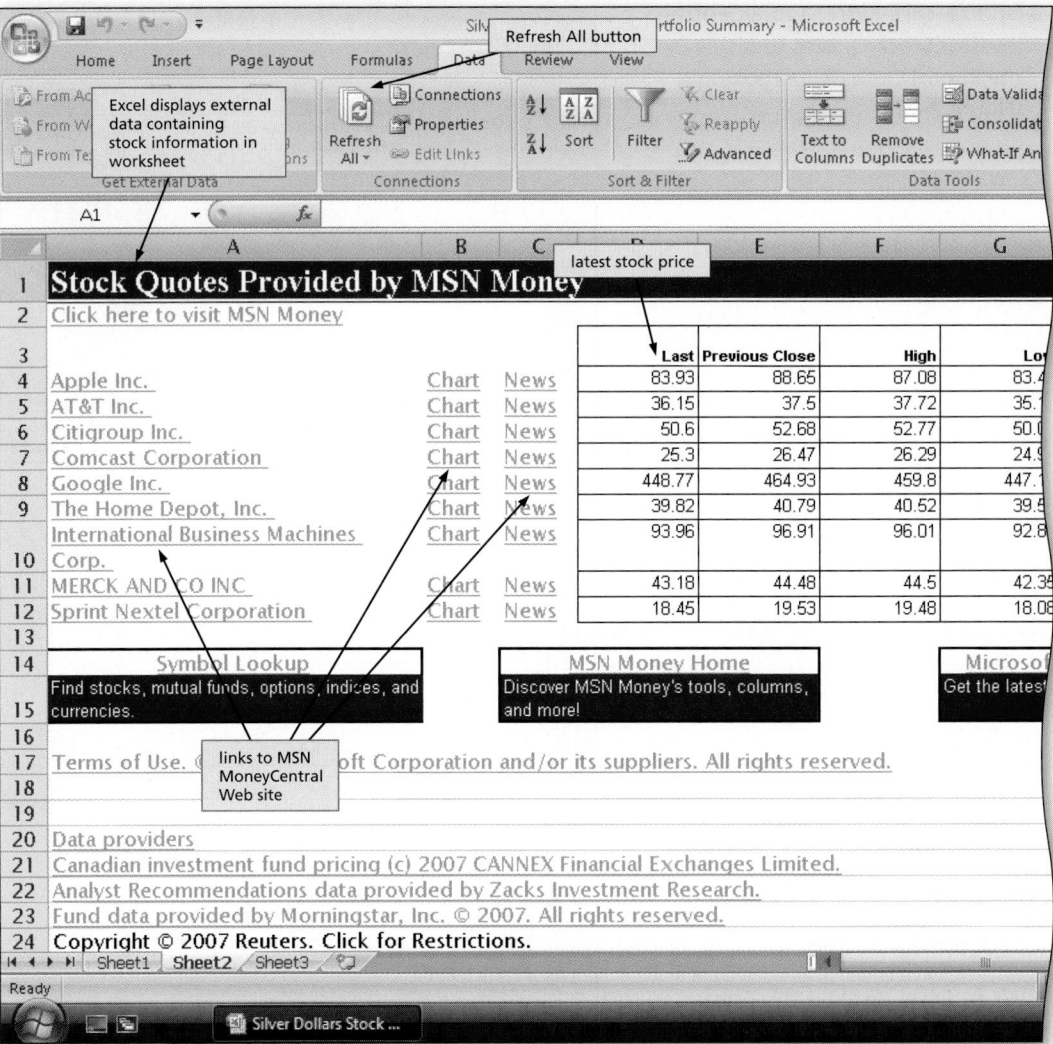

Figure 2–79

Other Ways

1. Press ALT+A, X, select data source

Changing the Worksheet Names

The sheet tabs at the bottom of the window allow you to view any worksheet in the workbook. You click the sheet tab of the worksheet you want to view in the Excel window. By default, Excel presets the names of the worksheets to Sheet1, Sheet2, and so on. The worksheet names become increasingly important as you move towards more sophisticated workbooks, especially workbooks in which you reference cells between worksheets.

Plan Ahead

Choose names for the worksheets.

Use simple, meaningful names for each worksheet. Name the first worksheet that includes the portfolio summary Portfolio Summary. The second worksheet that includes the stock quotes should be named Real-Time Stock Quotes to reflect its contents.

To Change the Worksheet Names

The following steps show how to rename worksheets by double-clicking the sheet tabs.

- Double-click the sheet tab labeled Sheet2 in the lower-left corner of the window.

- Type `Real-Time Stock Quotes` as the worksheet name and then press the ENTER key to display the new worksheet name on the sheet tab (Figure 2–80).

Q&A

What is the maximum length for a worksheet tab?

Worksheet names can be up to 31 characters (including spaces) in length. Longer worksheet names, however, mean that fewer sheet tabs will show. To view more sheet tabs, you can drag the tab split box (Figure 2–81) to the right. This will reduce the size of the scroll bar at the bottom of the screen. Double-click the tab split box to reset it to its normal position.

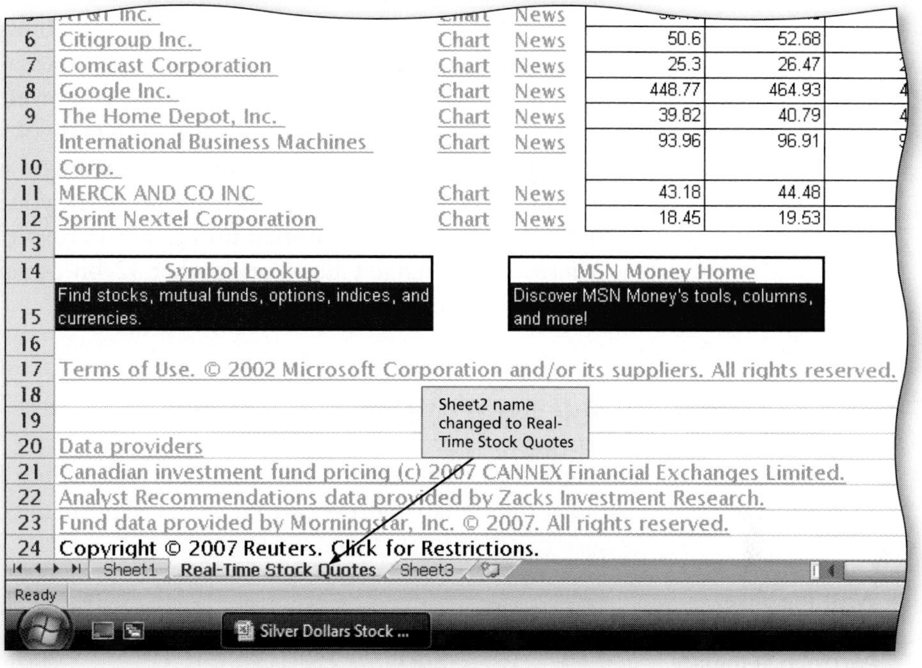

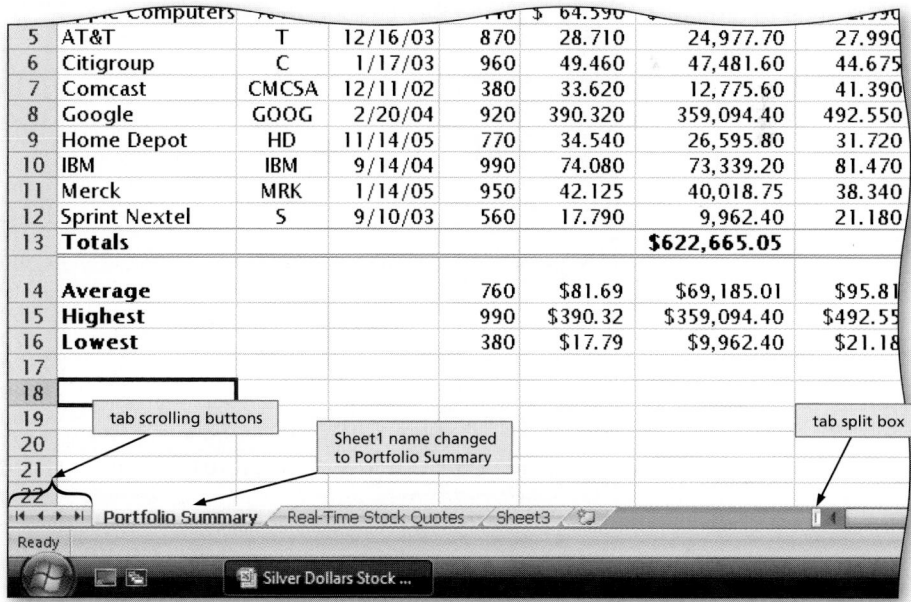

Figure 2–80

- Double-click the sheet tab labeled Sheet1 in the lower-left corner of the window.

- Type `Portfolio Summary` as the worksheet name and then press the ENTER key to change the name of the worksheet from Sheet 1 to Portfolio Summary (Figure 2–81).

Q&A

How can I quickly move between worksheet tabs?

You can use the tab scrolling buttons to the left of the sheet tabs (Figure 2–81) to move between worksheets. The leftmost and rightmost scroll buttons move to the first or last worksheet in the workbook. The two middle scroll buttons move one worksheet to the left or right.

Figure 2–81

- Click the Home tab on the Ribbon.

Obtaining an E-Mail Account
Several Web sites that allow you to sign up for free e-mail are available. Some choices are MSN Hotmail, Yahoo! Mail, and Google Gmail.

E-Mailing a Workbook from within Excel

The most popular service on the Internet is electronic mail, or **e-mail**, which is the electronic transmission of messages and files to and from other computers using the Internet. Using e-mail, you can converse with friends across the room or on another continent. One of the features of e-mail is the capability to attach Office files, such as Word documents or Excel workbooks, to an e-mail message and send it to a coworker. In the past, if you wanted to e-mail a workbook, you saved the workbook, closed the file, started your e-mail program, and then attached the workbook to the e-mail message before sending it. With Excel, you have the capability of e-mailing a worksheet or workbook directly from within Excel. For these steps to work properly, you must have an e-mail address and one of the following as your e-mail program: Microsoft Outlook, Microsoft Outlook Express, Microsoft Exchange Client, or another 32-bit e-mail program compatible with Messaging Application Programming Interface.

To E-Mail a Workbook from within Excel

The following steps show how to e-mail the Silver Dollars Stock Club Portfolio Summary workbook from within Excel to Juan Castillo at the e-mail address castillo_juan37@hotmail.com.

1

- With the Silver Dollars Stock Club Portfolio Summary workbook open, click the Office Button and then click Send to display the Send submenu (Figure 2–82).

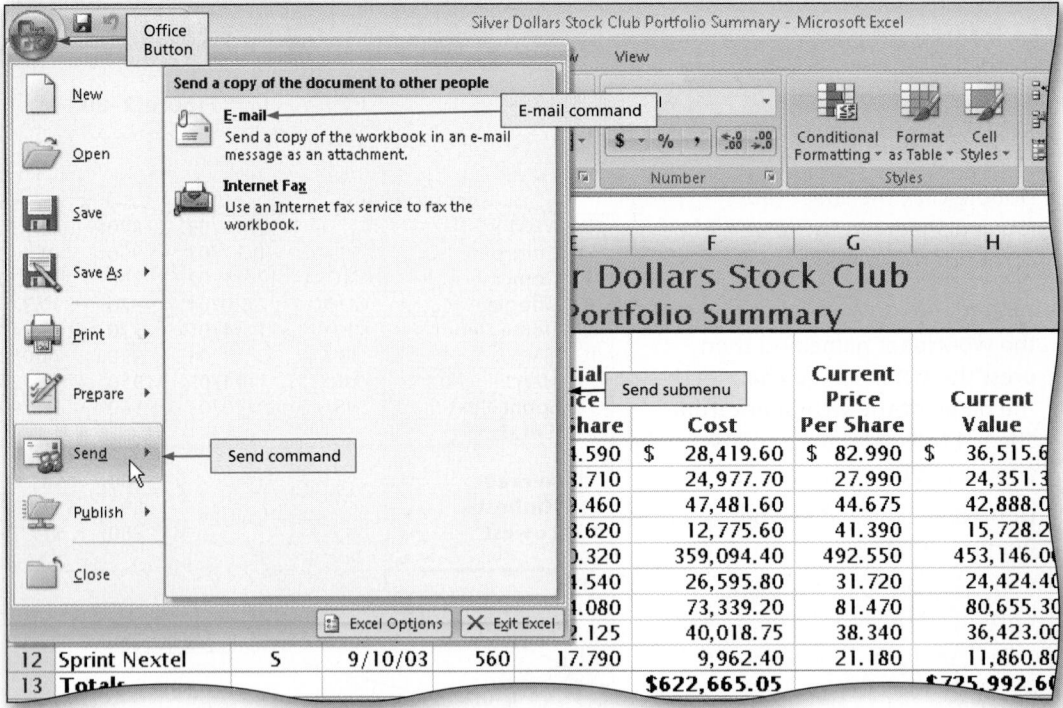

Figure 2–82

2

- Click E-mail on the Send submenu.

- When the e-mail Message window appears, type castillo_ juan37@hotmail. com in the To text box.

- Type the message shown in the message area in Figure 2–83.

3

- Click the Send button to send the e-mail with the attached workbook to castillo_juan37@ hotmail.com.

Q&A

How can the recipient use the attached workbook?

Because the workbook was sent as an attachment, Juan Castillo can double-click the attachment in the e-mail to open it in Excel, or he can save it on disk and then open it later.

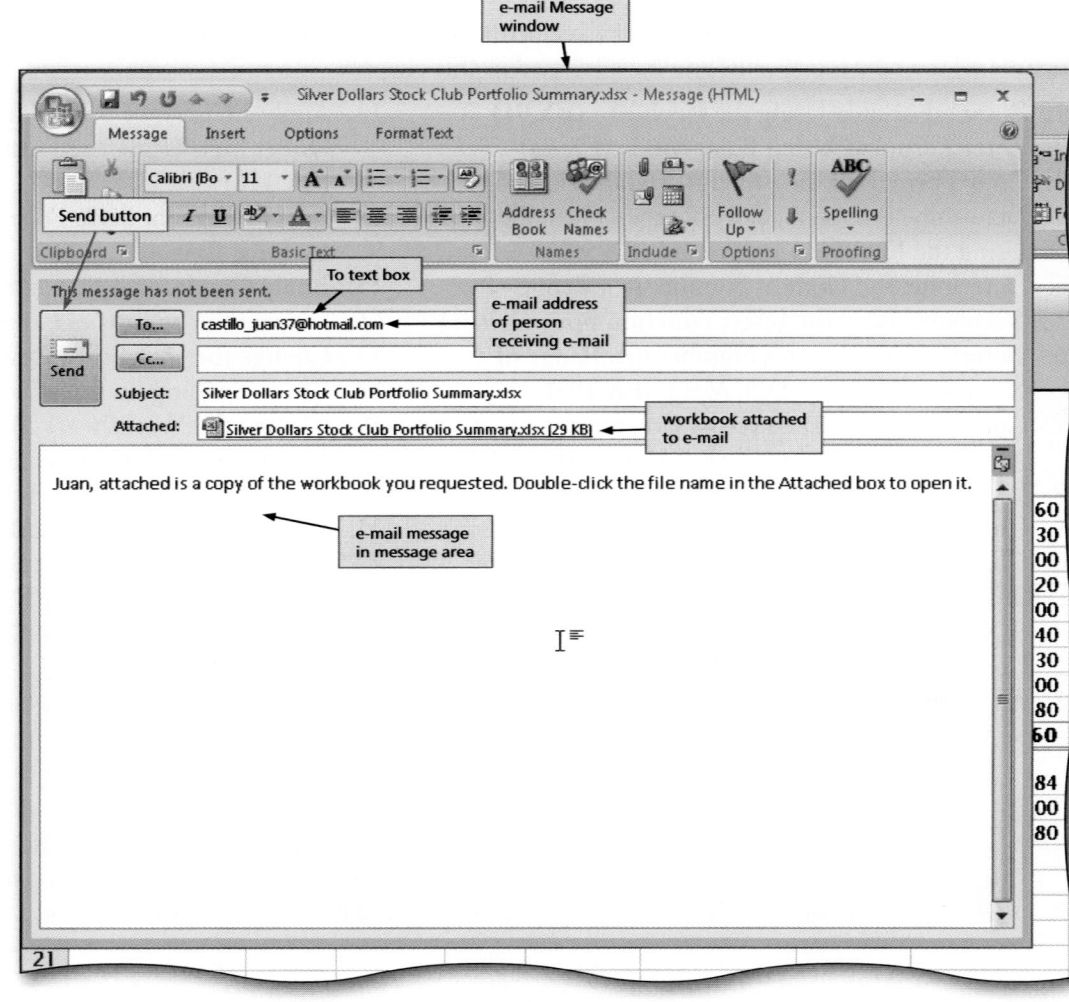

Figure 2–83

To Save the Workbook and Quit Excel

With the workbook complete and e-mailed, the following steps save the workbook and quit Excel.

1 Click the Save button on the Quick Access Toolbar.

2 Click the Close button on the upper-right corner of the title bar.

BTW

Quick Reference
For a table that lists how to complete the tasks covered in this book using the mouse, Ribbon, shortcut menu, and keyboard, see the Quick Reference Summary at the back of this book, or visit the Excel 2007 Quick Reference Web page (scsite.com/ex2007/qr).

Chapter Summary

In creating the Silver Dollars Stock Club Portfolio Summary workbook, you learned how to enter formulas, calculate an average, find the highest and lowest numbers in a range, verify formulas using Range Finder, draw borders, align text, format numbers, change column widths and row heights, and add conditional formatting to a range of numbers. In addition, you learned to spell check a worksheet, preview a worksheet, print a section of a worksheet, display and print the formulas version of the worksheet using the Fit to option, complete a Web query, rename sheet tabs, and send an e-mail directly from within Excel with the opened workbook as an attachment. The items listed below include all the new Excel skills you have learned in this chapter.

1. Enter a Formula Using the Keyboard (EX 91)
2. Enter Formulas Using Point Mode (EX 93)
3. Copy Formulas Using the Fill Handle (EX 95)
4. Determine the Average of a Range of Numbers Using the Keyboard and Mouse (EX 99)
5. Determine the Highest Number in a Range of Numbers Using the Insert Function Box (EX 101)
6. Determine the Lowest Number in a Range of Numbers Using the Sum Menu (EX 102)
7. Copy a Range of Cells across Columns to an Adjacent Range Using the Fill Handle (EX 104)
8. Verify a Formula Using Range Finder (EX 106)
9. Change the Workbook Theme (EX 109)
10. Change the Background Color and Apply a Box Border to the Worksheet Title and Subtitle (EX 110)
11. Center Data in Cells and Format Dates (EX 113)
12. Apply an Accounting Number Format and Comma Style Format Using the Ribbon (EX 115)
13. Apply a Currency Style Format with a Floating Dollar Sign Using the Format Cells Dialog Box (EX 116)
14. Apply a Percent Style Format and Use the Increase Decimal Button (EX 118)
15. Apply Conditional Formatting (EX 119)
16. Change the Widths of Columns (EX 122)
17. Change the Heights of Rows (EX 125)
18. Check Spelling on the Worksheet (EX 127)
19. Change the Worksheet's Margins, Header, and Orientation in Page Layout View (EX 130)
20. Preview and Print a Worksheet (EX 132)
21. Print a Section of the Worksheet (EX 134)
22. Display the Formulas in the Worksheet and Fit the Printout on One Page (EX 136)
23. Import Data from a Web Source Using a Web Query (EX 138)
24. Change the Worksheet Names (EX 141)
25. E-Mail a Workbook from within Excel (EX 142)

 If you have a SAM user profile, you may have access to hands-on instruction, practice, and assessment. Log in to your SAM account (http://sam2007.course.com) to launch any assigned training activities or exams that relate to the skills covered in this chapter.

Learn It Online

Learn It Online is a series of online student exercises that test your knowledge of chapter content and key terms.

Instructions: To complete the Learn It Online exercises, start your browser, click the Address bar, and then enter the Web address scsite.com/ex2007/learn. When the Excel 2007 Learn It Online page is displayed, click the link for the exercise you want to complete and then read the instructions.

Chapter Reinforcement TF, MC, and SA
A series of true/false, multiple choice, and short answer questions that test your knowledge of the chapter content.

Flash Cards
An interactive learning environment where you identify chapter key terms associated with displayed definitions.

Practice Test
A series of multiple choice questions that test your knowledge of chapter content and key terms.

Who Wants To Be a Computer Genius?
An interactive game that challenges your knowledge of chapter content in the style of a television quiz show.

Wheel of Terms
An interactive game that challenges your knowledge of chapter key terms in the style of the television show *Wheel of Fortune*.

Crossword Puzzle Challenge
A crossword puzzle that challenges your knowledge of key terms presented in the chapter.

Apply Your Knowledge

Reinforce the skills and apply the concepts you learned in this chapter.

Profit Analysis Worksheet

Instructions Part 1: Start Excel. Open the workbook Apply 2-1 Car-B-Clean Profit Analysis. See the inside back cover of this book for instructions for downloading the Data Files for Students or see your instructor for information on accessing the files required in this book. The purpose of this exercise is to open a partially completed workbook, enter formulas and functions, copy the formulas and functions, and then format the worksheet titles and numbers. As shown in Figure 2–84, the completed worksheet analyzes profits by product.

Item	Unit Cost	Unit Profit	Units Sold	Total Sales	Total Profit	% Total Profit
Brush	$ 5.84	$ 3.15	36,751	$ 330,391.49	$ 115,765.65	35.039%
Bucket	7.14	2.75	57,758	571,226.62	158,834.50	27.806%
Drying Cloth	3.52	1.17	42,555	199,582.95	49,789.35	24.947%
Duster	2.55	1.04	78,816	282,949.44	81,968.64	28.969%
Polish	7.19	7.80	57,758	865,792.42	450,512.40	52.035%
Soap	8.52	4.09	50,646	638,646.06	207,142.14	32.435%
Sponge	2.05	1.84	23,154	90,069.06	42,603.36	47.301%
Wax	10.15	7.44	53,099	934,011.41	395,056.56	42.297%
Vacuum	43.91	33.09	17,780	1,369,060.00	588,340.20	42.974%
Totals			418,317	$5,281,729.45	$2,090,012.80	39.571%
Lowest	$2.05	$1.04	17,780	$90,069.06	$42,603.36	24.947%
Highest	$43.91	$33.09	78,816	$1,369,060.00	$588,340.20	52.035%
Average	$10.10	$6.93	46,480	$586,858.83	$232,223.64	

Title: **Car–B–Clean Accessories** / Profit Analysis

Figure 2–84

Perform the following tasks.

1. Use the following formulas in cells E4, F4, and G4:

    Total Sales (cell E4) = Units Sold * (Unit Cost + Unit Profit) or =D4 * (B4 + C4)

    Total Profit (cell F4) = Units Sold * Unit Profit or = D4 * C4

    % Total Profit (cell G4) = Total Profit / Total Sales or = F4 / E4

    Use the fill handle to copy the three formulas in the range E4:G4 to the range E5:G12.

2. Determine totals for the units sold, total sales, and total profit in row 13. Copy cell G12 to G13 to assign the formula in cell G12 to G13 in the total line.

Continued >

3. In the range B14:B16, determine the lowest value, highest value, and average value, respectively, for the values in the range B4:B12. Use the fill handle to copy the three functions to the range C14:G16. Delete the average from cell G16, because an average of percentages of this type is mathematically invalid.

4. Format the worksheet as follows:

   a. change the workbook theme to Concourse by using the Themes button on the Page Layout tab on the Ribbon

   b. cell A1 — change to font size 24 with a green (column 6 of standard colors) background and white font color by using the buttons in the Font group on the Home tab on the Ribbon

   c. cell A2 — change to a green (column 6 of standard colors) background and white font color

   d. cells B4:C4, E4:F4, and E13:F13 — Accounting style format with two decimal places and fixed dollar signs (use the Accounting Style button on the Home tab on the Ribbon)

   e. cells B5:C12 and E5:F12 — Comma style format with two decimal places (use the Comma Style button on the Home tab on the Ribbon)

   f. cells D4:D16 — Comma style format with no decimal places

   g. cells G4:G15 — Percent style format with three decimal places

   h. cells B14:C16 and E14:F16 — Currency style format with floating dollar signs (use the Format Cells: Number Dialog Box Launcher on the Home tab on the Ribbon)

5. Switch to Page Layout View and enter your name, course, laboratory assignment number (Apply 2-1), date, and any other information requested by your instructor in the Header area. Preview and print the worksheet in landscape orientation. Change the document properties, as specified by your instructor. Save the workbook using the file name, Apply 2-1 Car-B-Clean Profit Analysis Complete in the format specified by your instructor.

6. Use Range Finder to verify the formula in cell F4.

7. Print the range A3:E16. Press CTRL+ACCENT MARK (`) to change the display from the values version of the worksheet to the formulas version. Print the formulas version in landscape orientation on one page (Figure 2–85) by using the Fit to option in the Page sheet in the Page Setup dialog box. Press CTRL+ACCENT MARK (`) to change the display of the worksheet back to the values version. Do not save the workbook. If requested, submit the three printouts to your instructor.

Instructions Part 2:

1. Do not save the workbook in this part. In column C, use the keyboard to add manually $1.00 to the profit of each product with a unit profit less than $7.00 and $3.00 to the profits of all other products. You should end up with $2,765,603.80 in cell F13.

2. Print the worksheet. Do not save the workbook. If requested, submit the revised workbook in the format specified by your instructor.

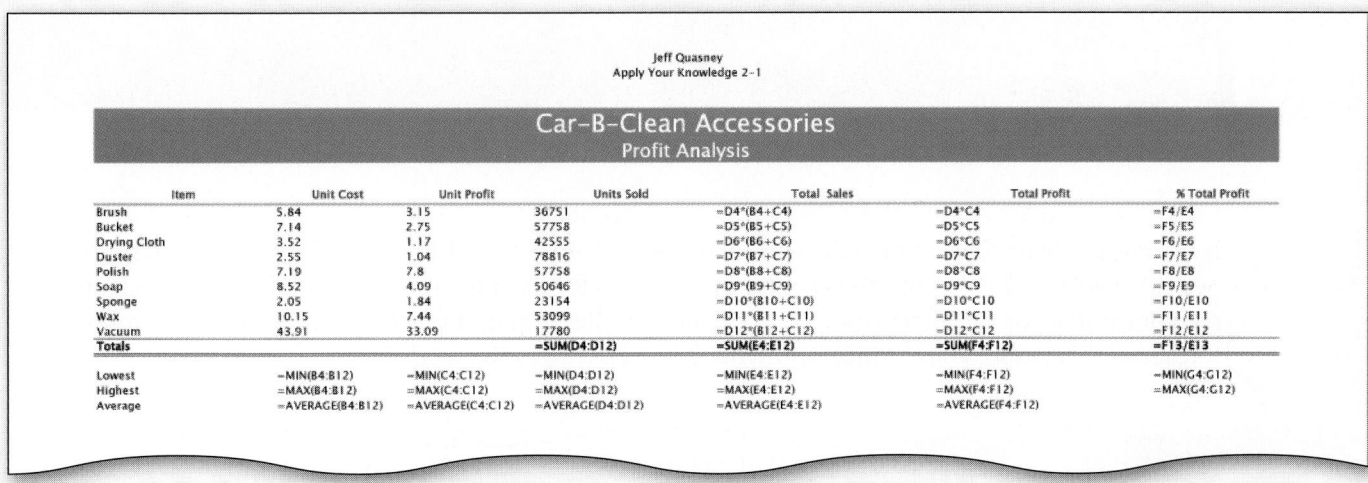

Jeff Quasney
Apply Your Knowledge 2-1

Car-B-Clean Accessories
Profit Analysis

Item	Unit Cost	Unit Profit	Units Sold	Total Sales	Total Profit	% Total Profit
Brush	5.84	3.15	36751	=D4*(B4+C4)	=D4*C4	=F4/E4
Bucket	7.14	2.75	57758	=D5*(B5+C5)	=D5*C5	=F5/E5
Drying Cloth	3.52	1.17	42555	=D6*(B6+C6)	=D6*C6	=F6/E6
Duster	2.55	1.04	78816	=D7*(B7+C7)	=D7*C7	=F7/E7
Polish	7.19	7.8	57758	=D8*(B8+C8)	=D8*C8	=F8/E8
Soap	8.52	4.09	50646	=D9*(B9+C9)	=D9*C9	=F9/E9
Sponge	2.05	1.84	23154	=D10*(B10+C10)	=D10*C10	=F10/E10
Wax	10.15	7.44	53099	=D11*(B11+C11)	=D11*C11	=F11/E11
Vacuum	43.91	33.09	17780	=D12*(B12+C12)	=D12*C12	=F12/E12
Totals			=SUM(D4:D12)	=SUM(E4:E12)	=SUM(F4:F12)	=F13/E13
Lowest	=MIN(B4:B12)	=MIN(C4:C12)	=MIN(D4:D12)	=MIN(E4:E12)	=MIN(F4:F12)	=MIN(G4:G12)
Highest	=MAX(B4:B12)	=MAX(C4:C12)	=MAX(D4:D12)	=MAX(E4:E12)	=MAX(F4:F12)	=MAX(G4:G12)
Average	=AVERAGE(B4:B12)	=AVERAGE(C4:C12)	=AVERAGE(D4:D12)	=AVERAGE(E4:E12)	=AVERAGE(F4:F12)	

Figure 2–85

Extend Your Knowledge

Extend the skills you learned in this chapter and experiment with new skills. You may need to use Help to complete the assignment.

Applying Conditional Formatting to Cells

Instructions: Start Excel. Open the workbook Extend 2-1 Biology 201 Midterm Scores. See the inside back cover of this book for instructions for downloading the Data Files for Students, or see your instructor for information on accessing the files required in this book. Perform the following tasks to apply new conditional formatting to the worksheet.

1. Select the range C4:C18. Click the Conditional Formatting button on the Home tab on the Ribbon and then select New Rule in the Conditional Formatting gallery. Select 'Format only top or bottom ranked values' in the Select a Rule Type area (Figure 2–86). Enter a value between 20 and 35 of your choosing in the text box in the Edit the Rule Description area and click the '% of the selected range' check box to select it. Click the Format button and choose a format to assign to this conditional format. Click the OK button in each dialog box to close the dialog boxes and view the worksheet.

2. With range C4:C18 selected, apply a conditional format to the range that highlights scores that are below average.

3. With range D4:D18 selected, apply a conditional format to the range that highlights any grade that is a D or an F.

4. With range B4:B18 selected, apply a conditional format to the range that uses a red color to highlight any duplicate student names.

5. Change the document properties, as specified by your instructor. Change the worksheet header with your name, course number, and other information requested by your instructor. Save the workbook using the file name, Extend 2-1 Biology 201 Midterm Scores Complete, and submit the revised workbook as specified by your instructor.

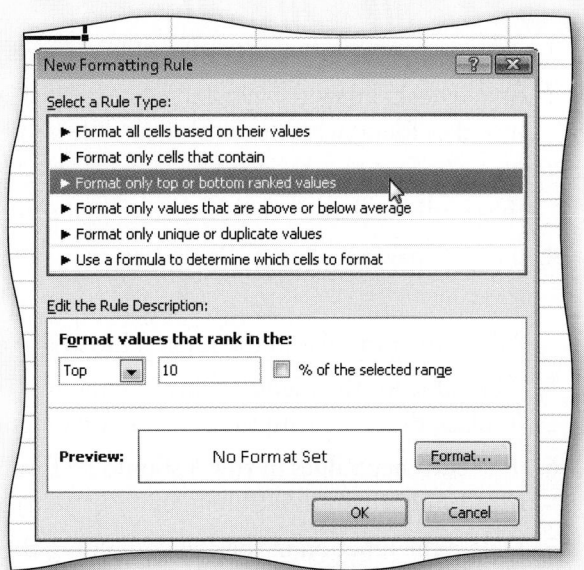

Figure 2–86

Make It Right

Analyze a workbook and correct all errors and/or improve the design.

Correcting Functions and Formulas in a Worksheet

Instructions: Start Excel. Open the workbook Make It Right 2-1 El Centro Diner Payroll Report. See the inside back cover of this book for instructions for downloading the Data Files for Students, or see your instructor for information on accessing the files required for this book. Correct the following formatting, function, and formula problems (Figure 2–87) in the worksheet.

	Employee	Dependents	Rate per Hour	Hours Worked	Gross Pay	Federal Tax	State Tax	Net Pay	% Taxes		
1				**El Centro Diner**							
2				**Payrol Report**							
4	Vincent Flores	1	$9.90	20.00	$198.00	$34.97	$7.92	$162.03	21.660%		
5	Wonda Jefferson	2	11.20	40.00	448.00	80.33	17.92	365.67	21.931%		
6	Anthony Sanchez	2	15.90	21.25	337.88	58.31	13.52	277.57	21.257%		
7	Alexa Martin	3	11.30	23.50	265.55	39.21	10.62	223.34	18.765%		
8	Maria Reyes	1	10.30	21.25	218.88	39.14	8.76	178.73	21.883%		
9	Lori Romanoff	2	10.75	40.00	430.00	76.73	17.20	351.27	21.845%		
10	Carmen Alvarez	1	12.60	21.50	270.90	49.55	10.84	220.35	22.289%		
11	Peter Lane	4	14.50	37.50	543.75	90.21	21.75	449.54	20.591%		
12	Claudi Moreno	1	16.00	33.00	528.00	100.97	21.12	426.03	23.122%		
13	Wayne Vargas	3	8.00	29.25	234.00	32.90	9.36	198.10	18.059%		
14	**Totals**			287.25	$3,474.95	$ 602.31	$ 139.00	$2,852.64	21.333%		
15	Average	1.8888889	$12.49	28.67	$360.11	$60.23	$13.90	$294.95	21.140%		
16	Highest	4	$16.00	40.00	$543.75	$100.97	$21.75	$449.54	23.122%		
17	Lowest	1	$8.00	20.00	$198.00	$32.90	$7.92	$162.03	18.059%		

Figure 2–87

1. Adjust the width of column B to 11.25 pixels so that the word in the column header does not wrap.

2. Spell check the worksheet and correct any spelling mistakes that are found, but ignore any spelling mistakes found with the worksheet title and the employee names.

3. The averages in several columns do not include the employee in row 13. Adjust the functions in these cells so that all employees are included in the calculation.

4. The net pay calculation should be:

    Net Pay = Gross Pay – (Federal Taxes + State Taxes)

    Adjust the formulas in the range H4:H13 so that the correct formula is used.

5. The value for the highest value in column C was entered as a number rather than as a function. Replace the value with the appropriate function.

6. The currency values in row 4 should be formatted with the Accounting Number Format button on the Home tab on the Ribbon. They are currently formatted with the Currency format.

7. Delete the function in the cell containing the average of % Taxes because it is mathematically invalid.

8. Change the document properties, as specified by your instructor. Change the worksheet header with your name, course number, and other information requested by your instructor. Save the workbook using the file name, Make It Right 2-1 El Centro Diner Payroll Report Corrected. Submit the revised workbook as specified by your instructor.

In the Lab

Create a workbook using the guidelines, concepts, and skills presented in this chapter. Labs are listed in order of increasing difficulty.

Lab 1: Sales Analysis Worksheet

Problem: You have been asked to build a sales analysis worksheet for Facade Importers that determines the sales quota and percentage of quota met for the sales representatives in Table 2–8. The desired worksheet is shown in Figure 2–88.

Table 2–8 Facade Importers Sales Data

Sales Representative	Sales Amount	Sales Return	Sales Quota
Polizzi, Bernard	591518	12638	765130
Li, Grace	895050	12015	776381
Volpe, Pamela	716502	18141	733309
Khan, Anwer	709672	22326	566940
Hudson, Emma	802525	11138	712222
Huerta, Teresa	885156	18721	778060

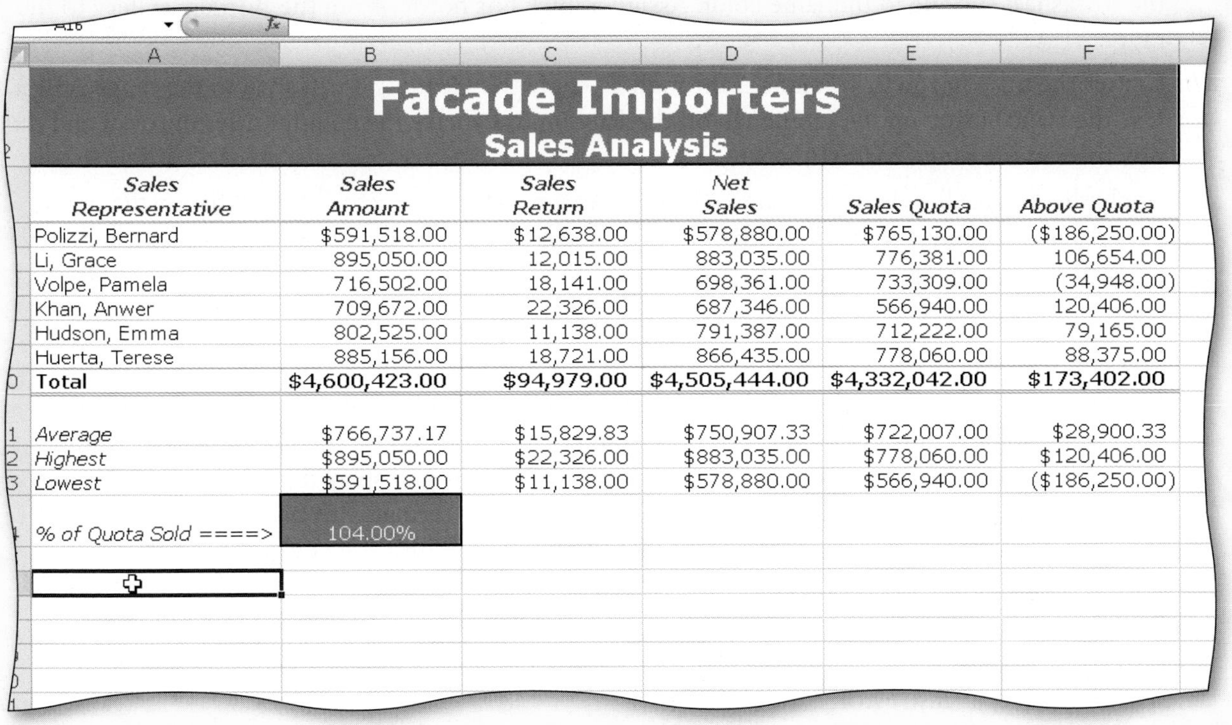

Facade Importers
Sales Analysis

Sales Representative	Sales Amount	Sales Return	Net Sales	Sales Quota	Above Quota
Polizzi, Bernard	$591,518.00	$12,638.00	$578,880.00	$765,130.00	($186,250.00)
Li, Grace	895,050.00	12,015.00	883,035.00	776,381.00	106,654.00
Volpe, Pamela	716,502.00	18,141.00	698,361.00	733,309.00	(34,948.00)
Khan, Anwer	709,672.00	22,326.00	687,346.00	566,940.00	120,406.00
Hudson, Emma	802,525.00	11,138.00	791,387.00	712,222.00	79,165.00
Huerta, Terese	885,156.00	18,721.00	866,435.00	778,060.00	88,375.00
Total	$4,600,423.00	$94,979.00	$4,505,444.00	$4,332,042.00	$173,402.00
Average	$766,737.17	$15,829.83	$750,907.33	$722,007.00	$28,900.33
Highest	$895,050.00	$22,326.00	$883,035.00	$778,060.00	$120,406.00
Lowest	$591,518.00	$11,138.00	$578,880.00	$566,940.00	($186,250.00)
% of Quota Sold ====>	104.00%				

Figure 2–88

Continued >

In the Lab *continued*

Instructions Part 1: Perform the following tasks to build the worksheet shown in Figure 2–88.

1. Apply the Aspect theme to the worksheet by using the Themes button on the Page Layout tab on the Ribbon.

2. Increase the width of column A to 19.00 points and the width of columns B through F to 13.50 points.

3. Enter the worksheet title `Facade Importers` in cell A1 and the worksheet subtitle `Sales Analysis` in cell A2. Enter the column titles in row 3 as shown in Figure 2–88. In row 3, use ALT+ENTER to start a new line in a cell.

4. Enter the sales data described in Table 2–8 in columns A, B, C, and E in rows 4 through 9. Enter the row titles in the range A10:A14 as shown in Figure 2–88 on the previous page.

5. Obtain the net sales in column D by subtracting the sales returns in column C from the sales amount in column B. Enter the formula in cell D4 and copy it to the range D5:D9.

6. Obtain the above quota amounts in column F by subtracting the sales quota in column E from the net sales in column D. Enter the formula in cell F4 and copy it to the range F5:F9.

7. Obtain the totals in row 10 by adding the column values for each salesperson. In the range B11:B13, use the AVERAGE, MAX, and MIN functions to determine the average, highest value, and lowest value in the range B4:B9. Copy the range B11:B13 to the range C11:F13.

8. Determine the percent of quota sold in cell B14 by dividing the total net sales amount in cell D10 by the total sales quota amount in cell E10. Center this value in the cell.

9. If necessary, click the Home tab on the Ribbon. One at a time, merge and center the worksheet title and subtitle across columns A through F. Select cells A1 and A2 and change the background color to red (column 2 in the Standard Colors area on the Fill Color palette). Apply the Title cell style to cells A1 and B1 by clicking the Cell Styles button on the Home tab on the Ribbon and clicking the Title cell style in the Titles and Headings area in the Cell Styles gallery. Change the worksheet title in cell A1 to 28-point white (column 1, row 1 on the Font Color gallery). Change the worksheet subtitle to the same color. Assign a thick box border from the Borders gallery to the range A1:A2.

10. Center the titles in row 3, columns A through F. Apply the Heading 3 cell style to the range A3:F3. Use the Italic button on the Home tab on the Ribbon to italicize the column titles in row 3 and the row titles in the range A10:A14.

11. Apply the Total cell style to the range A10:F10. Assign a thick box to cell B14. Change the background and font colors for cell B14 to the same colors applied to the worksheet title in Step 9.

12. Change the row heights of row 3 to 33.00 points and rows 11 and 14 to 30.00 points.

13. Select cell B14 and then click the Percent Style button on the Home tab on the Ribbon. Click the Increase Decimal button on the Ribbon twice to display the percent in cell B14 to hundredths.

14. Use the CTRL key to select the ranges B4:F4 and B10:F13. That is, select the range B4:F4 and then while holding down the CTRL key, select the range B10:F13. Use the Format Cells: Number Dialog Box Launcher button on the Home tab on the Ribbon to display the Format Cells dialog box to assign the selected ranges a Floating Dollar Sign style format with two decimal places and parentheses to represent negative numbers. Select the range B5:F9 and click the Comma Style button on the Home tab on the Ribbon.

15. Rename the sheet tab as Sales Analysis. Change the document properties, as specified by your instructor. Change the worksheet header with your name, course number, and other information requested by your instructor.

16. Save the workbook using the file name Lab 2-1 Part 1 Facade Importers Sales Analysis. Print the entire worksheet in landscape orientation. Print only the range A3:B10.

17. Display the formulas version by pressing CTRL+ACCENT MARK (`). Print the formulas version using the Fit to option button in the Scaling area on the Page tab in the Page Setup dialog box. After printing the worksheet, reset the Scaling option by selecting the Adjust to option button on the Page tab in the Page Setup dialog box and changing the percent value to 100%. Change the display from the formulas version to the values version by pressing CTRL+ACCENT MARK (`). Do not save the workbook.

18. Submit the assignment as specified by your instructor.

Instructions Part 2: Open the workbook created in Part 1 and save the workbook as Lab 2-1 Part 2 Facade Importers Sales Analysis. Manually decrement each of the six values in the net sales column by $10,000.00 until the percent of quota sold in cell B14 is below, yet as close as possible to, 100%. All six values in column E must be incremented the same number of times. The percent of quota sold in B14 should equal 99.85%. Update the worksheet header and save the workbook. Print the worksheet. Submit the assignment as specified by your instructor.

Instructions Part 3: Open the workbook created in Part 2 and then save the workbook as Lab 2-1 Part 3 Facade Importers Sales Analysis. With the percent of quota sold in cell B14 equal to 99.85% from Part 2, manually decrement each of the six values in the sales return column by $1,000.00 until the percent of quota sold in cell B14 is above, yet as close as possible to, 100%. Decrement all six values in column C the same number of times. Your worksheet is correct when the percent of quota sold in cell B14 is equal to 100.12%. Update the worksheet header and save the workbook. Print the worksheet. Submit the assignment as specified by your instructor.

In the Lab

Lab 2: Balance Due Worksheet

Problem: You are a spreadsheet intern for Jackson's Bright Ideas, a popular Denver-based light fixture store with outlets in major cities across the western United States. You have been asked to use Excel to generate a report (Figure 2–89) that summarizes the monthly balance due. A graphic breakdown of the data also is desired. The customer data in Table 2–9 is available for test purposes.

Table 2–9 Jackson's Bright Ideas Monthly Balance Due Data				
Customer	**Beginning Balance**	**Credits**	**Payments**	**Purchases**
Costa, Dan	160.68	18.70	99.33	68.28
Hernandez, Abraham	138.11	48.47	75.81	46.72
Mc Cartan, John	820.15	32.11	31.23	29.19
Paoli, Pam	167.35	59.32	52.91	33.90
Ramirez, Alberto	568.34	55.17	18.53	36.34
Vaughn, Noah	449.92	25.90	82.05	99.77
Xiong, James	390.73	48.12	19.35	92.13

Continued >

In the Lab *continued*

Instructions Part 1: Create a worksheet similar to the one shown in Figure 2–89. Include the five columns of customer data in Table 2–9 in the report, plus two additional columns to compute a service charge and a new balance for each customer. Assume no negative unpaid monthly balances.

	A	B	C	D	E	F	G	H
1			Jackson's Bright Ideas					
2			Monthly Balance Due Report					
3	Customer	Beginning Balance	Credits	Payments	Purchases	Service Charge	New Balance	
4	Costa, Dan	$160.68	$18.70	$99.33	$68.28	$1.17	$112.10	
5	Hernandez, Abraham	138.11	48.47	75.81	46.72	0.38	60.93	
6	Mc Cartan, John	820.15	32.11	31.23	29.19	20.81	806.81	
7	Paoli, Pam	167.35	59.32	52.91	33.90	1.52	90.54	
8	Ramirez, Alberto	568.34	55.17	18.53	36.34	13.60	544.58	
9	Vaughn, Noah	449.92	25.90	82.05	99.77	9.40	451.14	
10	Xiong, James	390.73	48.12	19.35	92.13	8.89	424.28	
11	**Totals**	$2,695.28	$287.79	$379.21	$406.33	$55.78	$2,490.39	
12	**Highest**	$820.15	$59.32	$99.33	$99.77	$20.81	$806.81	
13	**Lowest**	$138.11	$18.70	$18.53	$29.19	$0.38	$60.93	
14	**Average**	$385.04	$41.11	$54.17	$58.05	$7.97	$355.77	
15								
16								

Figure 2–89

Perform the following tasks:

1. Enter and format the worksheet title `Jackson's Bright Ideas` and worksheet subtitle `Monthly Balance Due Report` in cells A1 and A2. Change the theme of the worksheet to the Technic theme. Apply the Title cell style to cells A1 and A2. Change the font size in cell A1 to 28 points. One at a time, merge and center the worksheet title and subtitle across columns A through G. Change the background color of cells A1 and A2 to yellow (column 4 in the Standard Colors area in the Font Color palette). Draw a thick box border around the range A1:A2.

2. Change the width of column A to 20.00 characters. Change the widths of columns B through G to 12.00. Change the heights of row 3 to 36.00 and row 12 to 30.00 points.

3. Enter the column titles in row 3 and row titles in the range A11:A14 as shown in Figure 2–89. Center the column titles in the range A3:G3. Apply the Heading 3 cell style to the range A3:G3. Bold the titles in the range A11:A14. Apply the Total cell style to the range A11:G11. Change the font size of the cells in the range A3:G14 to 12 points.

4. Enter the data in Table 2–9 in the range A4:E10.

5. Use the following formulas to determine the service charge in column F and the new balance in column G for the first customer. Copy the two formulas down through the remaining customers.

   a. Service Charge (cell F4) = 2.75% * (Beginning Balance – Payments – Credits)
      or = 0.0275 * (B4 – D4 – C4)

   b. New Balance (G4) = Beginning Balance + Purchases – Credits – Payments + Service Charge
      or =B4 + E4 – C4 – D4 + F4

6. Determine the totals in row 11.

7. Determine the maximum, minimum, and average values in cells B12:B14 for the range B4:B10 and then copy the range B12:B14 to C12:G14.

8. Use the Format Cells command on the shortcut menu to format the numbers as follows: (a) assign the Currency style with a floating dollar sign to the cells containing numeric data in the ranges B4:G4 and B11:G14; and (b) assign the Comma style (currency with no dollar sign) to the range B5:G10.

9. Use conditional formatting to change the formatting to white font on a red background in any cell in the range C4:C10 that contains a value greater than 50.

10. Change the worksheet name from Sheet1 to Balance Due. Change the document properties, as specified by your instructor. Change the worksheet header with your name, course number, and other information requested by your instructor.

11. Spell check the worksheet. Preview and then print the worksheet in landscape orientation. Save the workbook using the file name, Lab 2-2 Part 1 Jackson's Bright Ideas Monthly Balance Due Report.

12. Print the range A3:D14. Print the formulas version on one page. Close the workbook without saving the changes. Submit the assignment as specified by your instructor.

Instructions Part 2: This part requires that a 3-D Bar chart with a cylindrical shape be inserted on a new worksheet in the workbook. If necessary, use Excel Help to obtain information on inserting a chart on a separate sheet in the workbook.

1. With the Lab 2-2 Part 1 Jackson's Bright Ideas Monthly Balance Due Report workbook open, save the workbook using the file name, Lab 2-2 Part 2 Jackson's Bright Ideas Monthly Balance Due Report. Draw the 3-D Bar chart with cylindrical shape showing each customer's total new balance as shown in Figure 2–90.

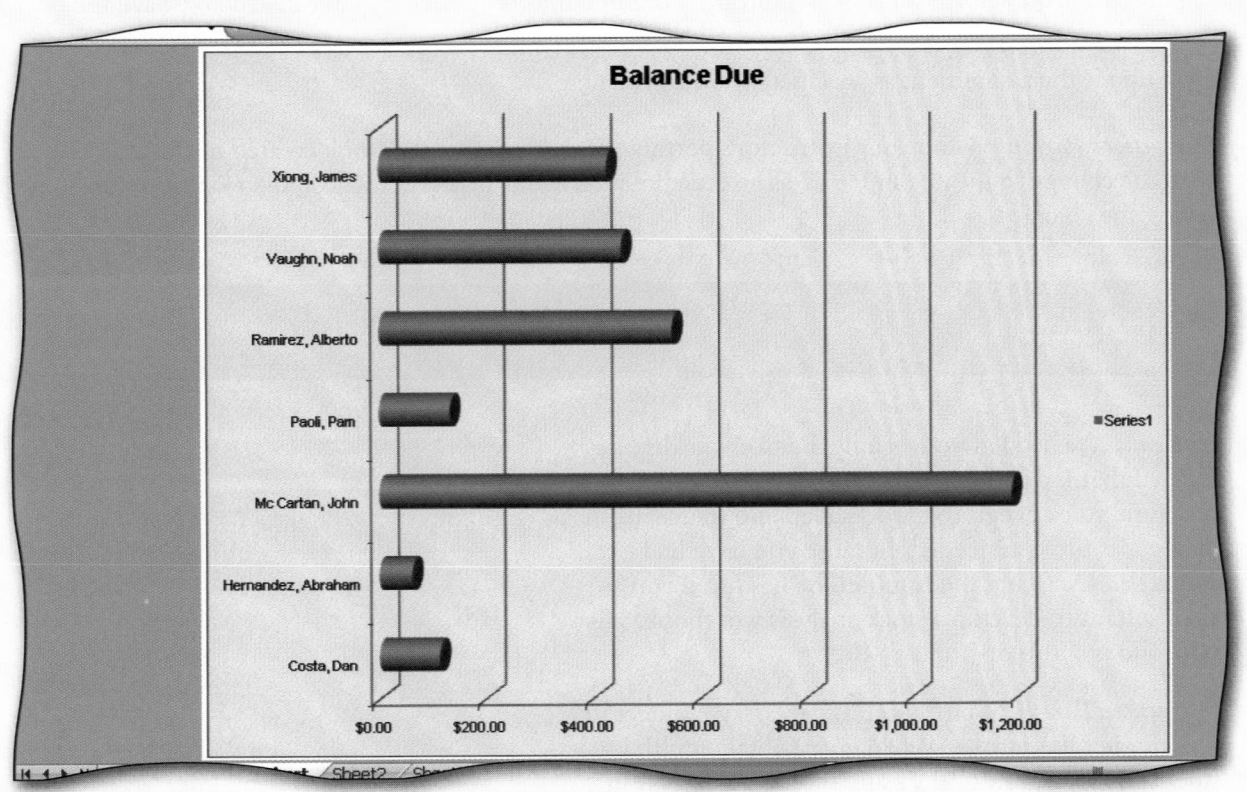

Figure 2–90

2. Use the CTRL key and mouse to select the nonadjacent chart ranges A4:A10 and G4:G10. That is, select the range A4:A10 and then while holding down the CTRL key, select the range G4:G10. The customer names in the range A4:A10 will identify the cylindrical bars, while the data series in the range G4:G10 will determine the length of the bars.

Continued >

In the Lab *continued*

3. Click the Insert tab on the Ribbon. Click the Bar button in the Charts group on the Ribbon and then select Clustered Horizontal Cylinder in the Cylinder area. When the chart is displayed on the worksheet, click the Move Chart button on the Ribbon. When the Move Chart dialog box appears, click New sheet and then type Bar Chart for the sheet name. Click the OK button.

4. When the chart is displayed on the new worksheet, click the chart area, which is a blank area near the edge of the chart, and then click the Format contextual tab. Click the Shape Fill button on the Ribbon and then select Gold, Accent 2, Lighter 80% in the gallery (column 6, row 2). Click the Layout contextual tab. Click the Chart Title button on the Ribbon and then select Above Chart in the Chart Title gallery. If necessary, use the scroll bar on the right side of the worksheet to scroll to the top of the chart. Click the edge of the chart title to select it and then type Balance Due as the chart title.

5. Drag the Balance Due tab at the bottom of the worksheet to the left of the Bar Chart tab to reorder the sheets in the workbook. Preview and print the chart.

6. Click the Balance Due sheet tab. Change the following purchases: customer John Mc Cartan to $406.58, and customer Pam Paoli to $74.99. The company also decided to change the service charge from 2.75% to 3.25% for all customers. After copying the adjusted formula in cell F4 to the range F5:F10, click the Auto Fill Options button and then click Fill without Formatting to maintain the original formatting in the range F5:F10. The total new balance in cell G11 should equal $2,919.01.

7. Select both sheets by holding down the SHIFT key and then clicking the Bar Chart tab. Preview and print the selected sheets. Submit the assignment as requested by your instructor. Save the workbook.

8. Submit the assignment as specified by your instructor.

Instructions Part 3: With your instructor's permission, e-mail the workbook created in this exercise with the changes indicated in Part 2 as an attachment to your instructor. Close the workbook without saving the changes.

In the Lab

Lab 3: Equity Web Queries

Problem: A friend of your family, Benson Yackley, has learned that Excel can connect to the Web, download real-time stock data into a worksheet, and then refresh the data as often as needed. Because you have had courses in Excel and the Internet, he has hired you as a consultant to develop a stock analysis workbook. His portfolio is shown in Table 2–10.

Instructions Part 1: Start Excel. If necessary, connect to the Internet. Perform a Web query to obtain multiple stock quotes (Figure 2–91), using the stock symbols in the second column of Table 2–10. Place the results of the Web query in a new worksheet. Rename the worksheet

Table 2–10 Benson Yackley's Stock Portfolio	
Company	**Stock Symbol**
Exxon Mobil	XOM
Dell	DELL
Hewlett-Packard	HPQ
Intel	INTC
MetLife	MET
PepsiCo	PEP

Real-Time Stock Quotes. Change the document properties, as specified by your instructor. Add a header with your name, course number, and other information requested by your instructor. Save the workbook using the file name, Lab 2-3 Part 1 Benson Yackley Equities Online. Preview and then print the worksheet in landscape orientation using the Fit to option.

Click the following links and print the Web page that appears in the browser window: Click here to visit MSN Money; Dell Inc.; Chart (to the right of MetLife, Inc.); and News (to the right of PepsiCo, Inc.). Submit the assignment as specified by your instructor.

			Last	Previous Close	High	Low	Volume	Change	% Change	52 Wk High	52 Wk Low	
4	ExxonMobil Corporation	Chart News	69.17	69.41	69.99	68.77	19,322,100	-0.24	-0.35%	71.22	54.5	411
5	Dell Inc.	Chart News	24.7	24.54	24.95	24.18	18,115,232	0.16	0.65%	33.22	18.95	56
6	Hewlett-Packard Company	Chart News	39.01	39.06	39.49	38.62	9,591,800	-0.05	-0.13%	39.15	25.53	106
7	Intel Corporation	Chart News	21.11	20.9	21.63	21.03	114,550,185	0.21	1.00%	27.49	16.75	121
8	MetLife, Inc.	Chart News	58.75	57.42	58.91	57.79	4,310,300	1.33	2.32%	58	47.02	44
9	PepsiCo, Inc.	Chart News	63.19	62.37	63.25	62.36	6,147,000	0.82	1.31%	65.99	56	103

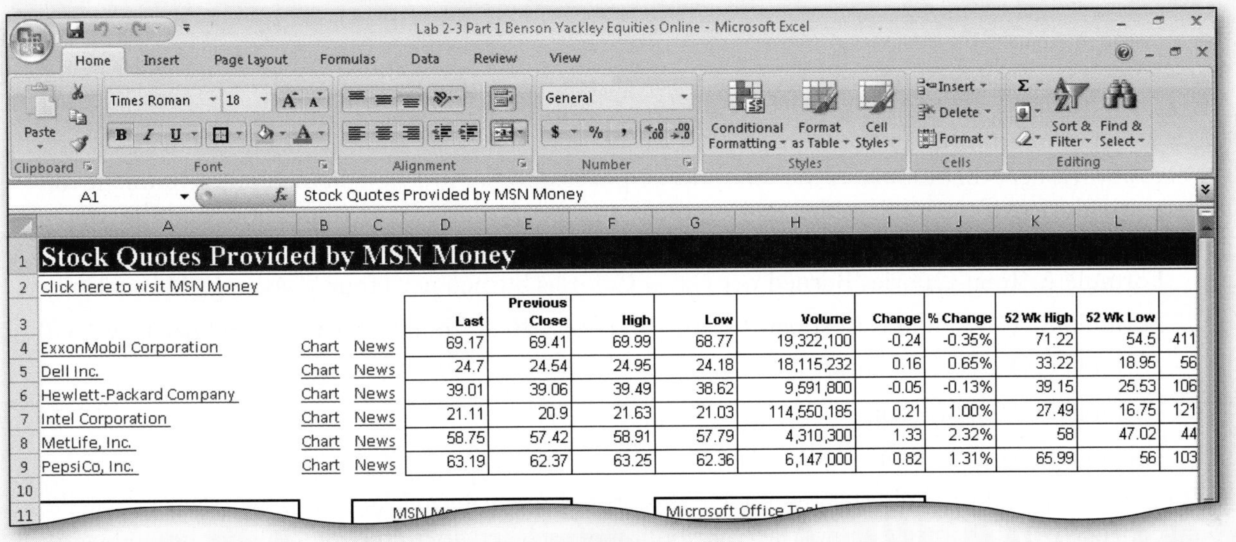

Figure 2–91

Instructions Part 2: While connected to the Internet and with the Lab 2-3 Benson Yackley Equities Online workbook open, create a worksheet listing the major indices and their current values on Sheet2 of the workbook (Figure 2–92). After clicking the Sheet2 tab, create the worksheet by double-clicking MSN MoneyCentral Investor Major Indices in the Existing Connections dialog box. The dialog box is displayed when you click the Existing Connections button on the Data tab on the Ribbon. Rename the worksheet Major Indices. Preview and then print the Major Indices worksheet in landscape orientation using the Fit to option. Save the workbook using the same file name as in Part 1. Submit the assignment as specified by your instructor.

			Last	Previous Close	High	Low	Volume	Change	% Change	52 Wk High	52 Wk Low
	DOW JONES INDUSTRIAL AVERAGE INDEX	Chart News	11992.68	11950.02	12049.03	11947.62	276,354,912	42.66	0.36%	11997.25	10193.45
5	DOW JONES COMPOSITE INDEX	Chart News	4030.49	4028.71	4068.22	4013.22	344,654,987	1.78	0.04%	4053.4	3346.66
	DOW JONES TRANSPORTATION AVERAGE INDEX	Chart News	4605.27	4648.65	4718.13	4574.62	44,944,975	-43.38	-0.93%	5013.67	3550.55
7	DOW JONES UTILITIES INDEX	Chart News	442.81	439.33	443.03	439.35	23,355,100	3.48	0.79%	443.49	378.95
8	$DAX (Invalid symbol)	??? ???	???	???	???	???	???	???	???	???	???
9	$FTSE (Invalid symbol)	??? ???	???	???	???	???	???	???	???	???	???
10	Hang Seng	Chart News	18048.09	18014.84	18048.09	17881.78	0	33.25	0.18%	0	0
	AMEX INTERACTIVE WEEK INTERNET INDEX	Chart News	186.5	187.51	188.97	186.09	0	-1.01	-0.54%	192.64	156.16
12	NASDAQ COMPOSITE INDEX	Chart News	2337.15	2344.95	2362.09	2330.49	2,091,566,611	-7.8	-0.33%	2375.54	2012.78
13	$NI225 (Invalid symbol)	??? ???	???	???	???	???	???	???	???	???	???
14	$CAC (Invalid symbol)	??? ???	???	???	???	???	???	???	???	???	???
	PHLX SEMICONDUCTOR SECTOR INDEX	Chart News	450.79	463.74	462.46	449.51	0	-12.95	-2.79%	559.6	384.28

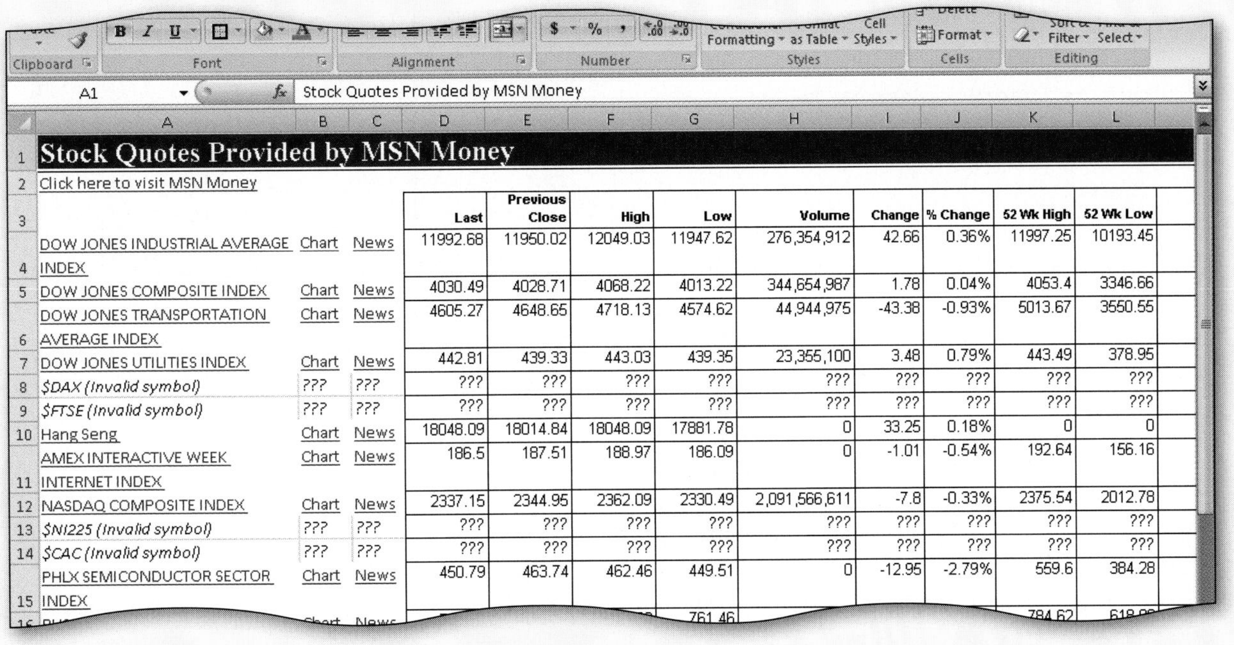

Figure 2–92

Cases and Places

Apply your creative thinking and problem solving skills to design and implement a solution.

● Easier ● ● More Difficult

● 1: Design and Create a Weight-Loss Plan Worksheet

As a summer intern working for Choose to Lose, a local weight-loss clinic, you have been asked to create a worksheet that estimates the monthly weight lost for an individual based on recommended average daily activities. You have been given the numbers of calories burned per hour and the average number of hours for each activity (Table 2–11). Use the following formulas:

Formula A: Total Calories Burned per Day = Calories burned per Hour × Average Hours Daily

Formula B: Total Pounds Lost per Month (30 days) = 30 × Total Calories Burned per Day / 3500

Formula C: Average function

Formula D: Max function

Formula E: Min function

Use the concepts and techniques presented in this project to create and format the worksheet. Include an embedded 3-D Pie chart that shows the contribution of each activity to the total calories burned per day. Use Microsoft Excel Help to create a professional looking 3-D Pie chart with title and data labels.

Table 2–11 Activities with Corresponding Calories Burned per Hour and Worksheet Layout				
Activity	**Calories Burned per Hour**	**Average Hours Daily**	**Total Calories Burned per Day**	**Total Pounds Lost per Month (30 Days)**
Aerobics class	450	0.50	Formula A	Formula B
Brisk walking	350	0.50		
House work	150	1.00		
Office work/sitting	120	6.00		
Sleeping	70	9.00		
Standing	105	2.00		
Swimming	290	0.50		
Tennis	315	0.25		
Walking	240	4.25		
Totals	—		—	—
Average	Formula C			
Highest	Formula D			
Lowest	Formula E			

• **2: Create a Profit Potential Worksheet**

You work part-time for Doze-Now, a retailer of sleep-related products. Your manager wants to know the profit potential of their inventory based on the categories of inventory in Table 2–12. Table 2–12 contains the format of the desired report. The required formulas are shown in Table 2–13. Use the concepts and techniques developed in this project to create and format the worksheet. Submit a printout of the values version and formulas version of the worksheet. The company just received a shipment of 175 additional comforters and 273 items of sleepwear. Update the appropriate cells in the Units on Hand column.

Table 2–12 Doze-Now Profit Potential Data and Worksheet Layout

Item	Units on Hand	Average Unit Cost	Total Cost	Average Unit Price	Total Value	Potential Profit
Comforters	216	46.52	Formula A	Formula B	Formula C	Formula D
Night lights	4,283	6.89				
Pillows	691	47.64				
Sleep sound machines	103	45.06				
Sleepwear	489	16.77				
Total	—		—	—	—	—
Average	Formula E					
Lowest	Formula F					
Highest	Formula G					

Table 2–13 Doze-Now Profit Potential Formulas

Formula A = Units on Hand * Average Unit Cost

Formula B = Average Unit Cost * (1 / (1 − .58))

Formula C = Units on Hand * Average Unit Price

Formula D = Total Value − Total Cost

Formula E = AVERAGE function

Formula F = MIN function

Formula G = MAX function

Continued >

STUDENT ASSIGNMENTS

Cases and Places *continued*

•• 3: Create a Fund-Raising Analysis Worksheet

You are the chairperson of the fund-raising committee for a local charity. You want to compare various fund-raising ideas to determine which will give you the best profit. The data obtained from six businesses about their products and the format of the desired report are shown in Table 2–14. The required formulas are shown in Table 2–15. Use the concepts and techniques presented in this project to create and format the worksheet.

Table 2–14 Fund-Raising Data and Worksheet Layout

Product	Company	Cost per Unit	Margin	Selling Price	Profit per 2000 Sales	Profit per 5000 Sales
Candles	Woodland Farms	$4.75	40%	Formula A	Formula B	Formula C
Candy	Polkandy	3.00	70%			
Coffee	Garcia Coffee	6.50	45%			
Cookie dough	Oh, Dough!	2.90	65%			
Flower bulbs	Early Bloom	2.40	50%			
T-shirts	Zed's Sports	5.75	42%			
Minimum		Formula D				
Maximum		Formula E				

Table 2–15 Band Fund-Raising Formulas

Formula A = Cost per Unit / (1 – Margin)

Formula B = 2000 * (Selling Price – Cost per Unit)

Formula C = 5000 *110% * (Selling Price – Cost per Unit)

Formula D = MIN function

Formula E = MAX function

•• 4: Design and Create a Projected Budget

Make It Personal

For the next six-month period, forecast your income for each month, your base expenditures for each month, and your special expenditures for each month. Base expenditures include expenses that occur each month, such as food and loan payments. Special expenditures include expenses that are out of the ordinary, such as the purchase of gifts, automobile insurance, and medical expenses. With this data, develop a worksheet calculating the amount of remaining money at the end of each month. You can determine this amount by subtracting both expenses from the anticipated income.

Include a total, average value, highest value, and lowest value for income, base expenditures, special expenditures, and remaining money. Use the concepts and techniques presented in this project to create and format the worksheet.

Create a 3-D Pie chart on a separate sheet illustrating the portion each month's special expenditures deducts from the total remaining money after all six months have passed. Use Microsoft Excel Help to create a professional looking 3-D Pie chart with title and data labels.

•• 5: Design and Create a Stock Analysis Worksheet

Working Together

Have each member of your team select six stocks — two bank stocks, two communications stocks, and two Internet stocks. Each member should submit the stock names, stock symbols, and an approximate six-month-old price. Create a worksheet that lists the stock names, symbols, price, and number of shares for each stock (use 350 shares as the number of shares for all stocks). Format the worksheet so that it has a professional appearance and is as informative as possible.

Have the group do research on the use of 3-D references, which is a reference to a range that spans two or more worksheets in a workbook (use Microsoft Excel Help). Use what the group learns to create a Web query on the Sheet2 worksheet by referencing the stock symbols on the Sheet1 worksheet. On the Sheet1 worksheet, change the cells that list current price per share numbers on the Sheet1 worksheet so that they use 3-D cell references that refer to the worksheet created by the Web query on the Sheet2 worksheet. Present your workbook and findings to the class.

3 What-If Analysis, Charting, and Working with Large Worksheets

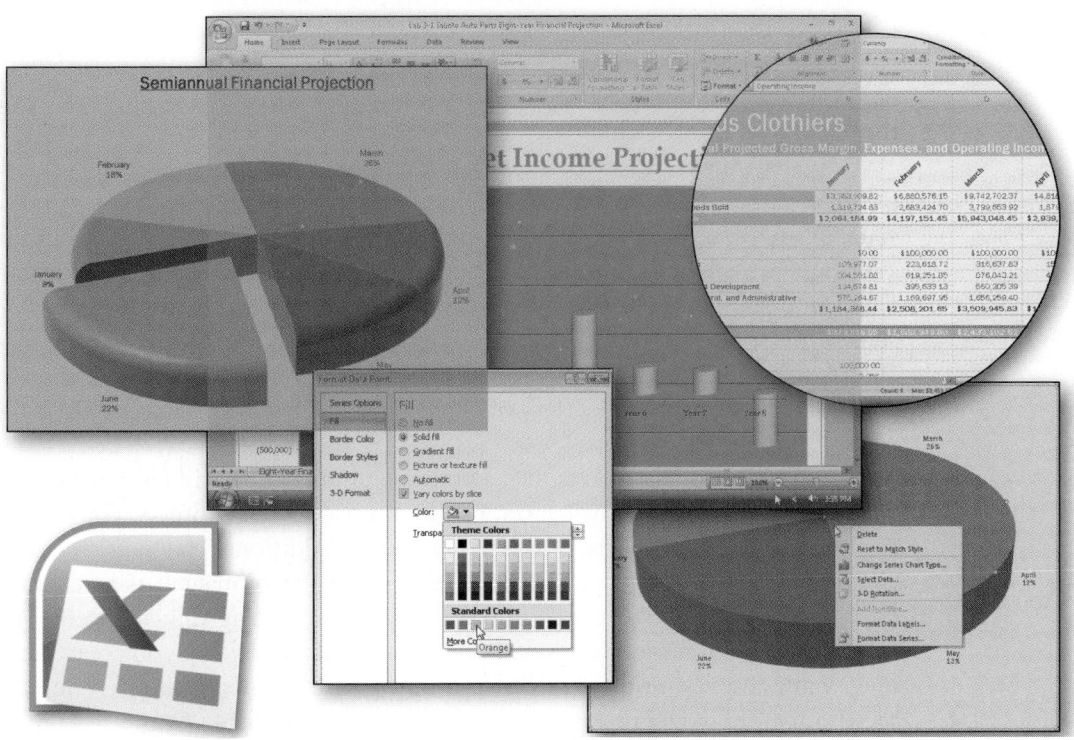

Objectives

You will have mastered the material in this chapter when you can:

- Rotate text in a cell
- Create a series of month names
- Copy, paste, insert, and delete cells
- Format numbers using format symbols
- Freeze and unfreeze titles
- Show and format the system date
- Use absolute cell references in a formula
- Use the IF function to perform a logical test

- Use the Format Painter button to format cells
- Create a 3-D Pie chart on a separate chart sheet
- Color and rearrange worksheet tabs
- Change the worksheet view
- Answer what-if questions
- Goal seek to answer what-if questions

3 | What-If Analysis, Charting, and Working with Large Worksheets

Introduction

Worksheets normally are much larger than those created in the previous chapters, often extending beyond the size of the window. Because you cannot see the entire worksheet on the screen at one time, working with a large worksheet sometimes can be frustrating. This chapter introduces several Excel commands that allow you to control what displays on the screen so you can view critical parts of a large worksheet at one time. One command lets you freeze the row and column titles so Excel always displays them on the screen. Another command splits the worksheet into separate window panes so you can view different parts of a worksheet on the screen at one time. Hiding the Ribbon will allow a larger portion of the worksheet to be visible.

When you set up a worksheet, you should use cell references in formulas whenever possible, rather than constant values. The use of a cell reference allows you to change a value in multiple formulas by changing the value in a single cell. The cell references in a formula are called assumptions. Assumptions are values in cells that you can change to determine new values for formulas. This chapter emphasizes the use of assumptions and shows how to use Excel to answer what-if questions such as, what happens to the semi-annual operating income if you decrease the marketing expenses assumption by 2%? Being able to analyze quickly the effect of changing values in a worksheet is an important skill in making business decisions.

This chapter also introduces you to techniques that will enhance your ability to create worksheets and draw charts. From your work in Chapter 1, you are aware of how easily you can create charts. This chapter covers additional charting techniques that allow you to convey your message in a dramatic pictorial fashion such as an exploded 3-D Pie chart. This chapter also covers other methods for entering values in cells, such as allowing Excel to enter values for you based on a pattern of values that you create, and formatting these values. In addition, you will learn how to use absolute cell references and how to use the IF function to assign a value to a cell based on a logical test.

Project — Financial Projection Worksheet with What-If Analysis and Chart

The project in the chapter follows proper design guidelines and uses Excel to create the worksheet and pie chart shown in Figure 3–1. Campus Clothiers manufactures and sells customized clothing to college students on campuses around the country. Each June and December, the director of finance and accounting submits a plan to the management team to show projected monthly revenues, costs of goods, gross margin, expenses, and operating income for the next six months. The director requires an easy-to-read worksheet that shows financial projections for the next six months. The worksheet should allow for quick analysis if projections for certain numbers change, such as the percentage of expenses allocated to marketing. In addition, a 3-D Pie chart is required that shows the projected operating income contribution for each of the six months.

Campus Clothiers

Semiannual Projected Gross Margin, Expenses, and Operating Income   11/5/2008

	January	February	March	April	May	June	Total
Sales	$3,383,909.82	$6,880,576.15	$9,742,702.37	$4,818,493.53	$4,566,722.63	$8,527,504.39	$37,919,908.89
Cost of Goods Sold	1,319,724.83	2,683,424.70	3,799,653.92	1,879,212.48	1,781,021.83	3,325,726.71	14,788,764.47
Gross Margin	**$2,064,184.99**	**$4,197,151.45**	**$5,943,048.45**	**$2,939,281.05**	**$2,785,700.80**	**$5,201,777.68**	**$23,131,144.42**
Expenses							
Bonus	$0.00	$100,000.00	$100,000.00	$100,000.00	$0.00	$100,000.00	$400,000.00
Commission	109,977.07	223,618.72	316,637.83	156,601.04	148,418.49	277,143.89	1,232,397.04
Marketing	304,551.88	619,251.85	876,843.21	433,664.42	411,005.04	767,475.40	3,412,791.80
Research and Development	194,574.81	395,633.13	560,205.39	277,063.38	262,586.55	490,331.50	2,180,394.76
Support, General, and Administrative	575,264.67	1,169,697.95	1,656,259.40	819,143.90	776,342.85	1,449,675.75	6,446,384.51
Total Expenses	**$1,184,368.44**	**$2,508,201.65**	**$3,509,945.83**	**$1,786,472.74**	**$1,598,352.92**	**$3,084,626.54**	**$13,671,968.11**
Operating Income	**$879,816.55**	**$1,688,949.80**	**$2,433,102.62**	**$1,152,808.32**	**$1,187,347.88**	**$2,117,151.14**	**$9,459,176.31**
What-if Assumptions							
Bonus	100,000.00						
Commission	3.25%						
Margin	61.00%						
Marketing	9.00%						
Research and Development	5.75%						
Revenue for Bonus	4,750,000.00						
Support, General, and Administrative	17.00%						

(a) Worksheet

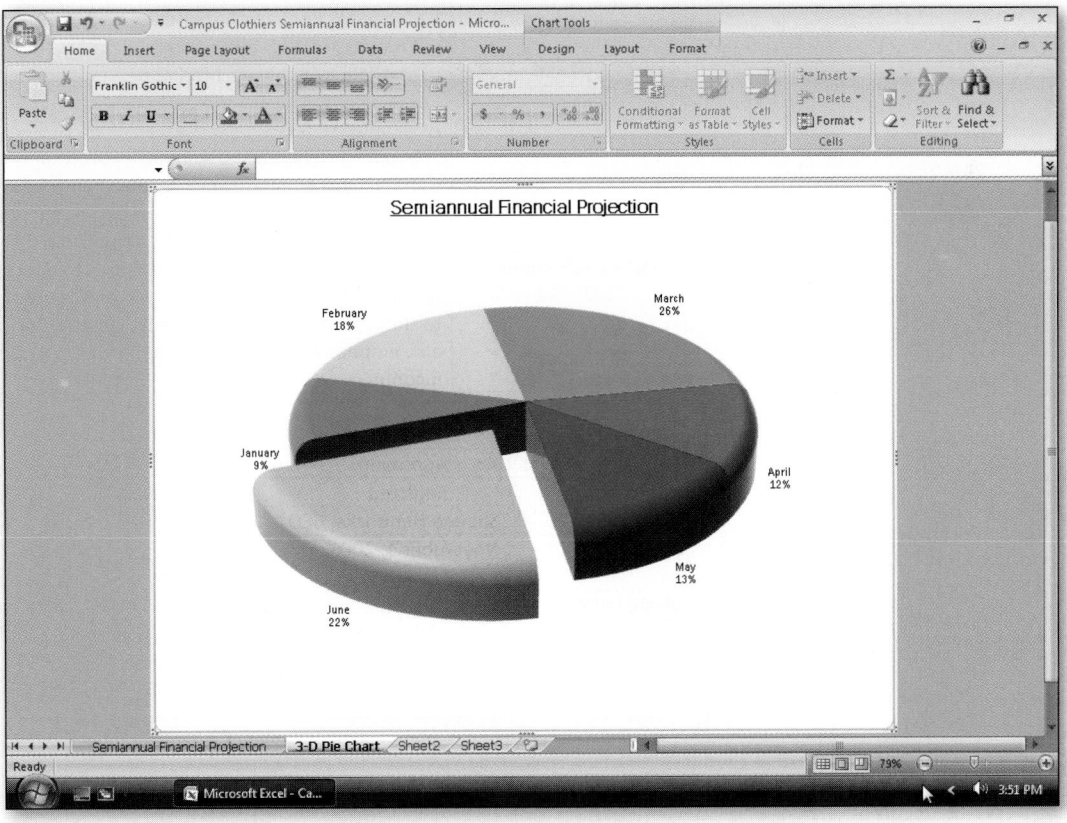

(b) 3-D Pie Chart

Figure 3–1

The requirements document for the Campus Clothiers Semiannual Financial Projection worksheet is shown in Figure 3–2. It includes the needs, source of data, summary of calculations, chart requirements, and other facts about its development.

REQUEST FOR NEW WORKBOOK

Date Submitted:	October 27, 2008
Submitted By:	Norm Armand
Worksheet Title:	Campus Clothiers Semiannual Projected Gross Margin, Expenses, and Operating Income
Needs:	The needs are: (1) a worksheet (Figure 3-3a) that shows Campus Clothiers's projected monthly sales, cost of goods, gross margin, expenses, and operating income for a six-month period; and (2) a 3-D Pie chart (Figure 3-3b) that shows the projected contribution of each month's operating income to the six-month period operating income.
Source of Data:	The data supplied by the Finance department includes projections of the monthly sales and expenses (Table 3-1) that are based on prior years. All the remaining numbers in the worksheet are determined from these 13 numbers using formulas.
Calculations:	The following calculations must be made for each month: 1. Cost of Goods = Sales − Sales * Margin 2. Gross Margin = Sales − Cost of Goods 3. Bonus Expense = $100,000.00 if the Sales exceeds the Revenue for Bonus; otherwise Bonus Expense = 0 4. Commission Expense = Commission Assumption * Sales 5. Marketing Expense = Marketing Assumption * Sales 6. Research and Development = Research and Development Assumption * Sales 7. Support, General, and Administrative Expense = Support, General, and Administrative Assumption * Sales 8. Total Expenses = Sum of Expenses 9. Operating Income = Gross Margin − Total Expenses
Chart Requirements:	A 3-D Pie chart is required on a separate sheet (Figure 3-3b) to show the contribution of each month's operating income to the six-month period operating income. The chart should also emphasize the month with the greatest operating income.

Approvals

Approval Status:	X	Approved
		Rejected
Approved By:		Shauna Hendricks, CFO
Date:		November 1, 2008
Assigned To:		J. Quasney, Spreadsheet Specialist

Figure 3–2

Overview

As you read this chapter, you will learn how to create the worksheet shown in Figure 3–1 by performing these general tasks:

- Create a series of month names

- Use absolute cell references in a formula

- Use the IF function to perform a logical test

- Use the Format Painter button to format cells

- Create a 3-D Pie chart on a separate chart sheet

- Answer what-if questions

- Manipulate large worksheets

Plan Ahead

General Project Decisions

While creating an Excel worksheet, you need to make several decisions that will determine the appearance and characteristics of the finished worksheet. As you create the worksheet required to meet the requirements shown in Figure 3–2, you should follow these general guidelines:

1. Plan the layout of the worksheet. The requirements state that six months are necessary in the worksheet. It is therefore sensible to place the months across columns so that the financial headings can be placed in rows. The what-if assumptions should not clutter the worksheet, but they should be placed in an easily located portion of the worksheet.

2. Determine the necessary formulas and functions needed. Except for the monthly sales numbers, the remaining numbers in the main portion of the worksheet are calculated based on the numbers in the what-if portion of the worksheet. The formulas are stated in the requirements document (Figure 3–2). The Bonus expense is included only if a certain condition is met. A function can check for the condition and include the bonus when necessary.

3. Identify how to format various elements of the worksheet. Sales and Expenses are two distinct categories of financial data and should be separated visually. Gross Margin and Total Expenses should stand out because they are subtotals. The Operating Income is the key piece of information being calculated in the worksheet and, therefore, should be formatted in such a manner as to draw the reader's attention. The what-if assumptions should be formatted in a manner which indicates that they are separate from the main area of the worksheet.

4. Specify how the chart should convey necessary information. The requirements document indicates that the chart should be a 3-D Pie chart and emphasize the month with the greatest operating income. A 3-D Pie chart is a good way to compare visually a small set of numbers. The month, which is emphasized, also should appear closer to the reader in order to draw the reader's attention.

5. Perform what-if analysis and goal seeking using the best techniques. What-if analysis allows you quickly to answer questions regarding various predictions. In Campus Clothiers Semiannual Financial Projection worksheet, the only cells that you should change when performing what-if analysis are those in the what-if portion of the worksheet. All other values in the worksheet, except for the projected sales, are calculated. Goal seeking allows you automatically to modify values in the what-if area of the worksheet based on a goal that you have for another cell in the worksheet.

(continued)

Plan Ahead

(continued)

In addition, using a sketch of the worksheet can help you visualize its design. The sketch of the worksheet (Figure 3-3a) consists of titles, column and row headings, location of data values, calculations, and a rough idea of the desired formatting. The sketch of the 3-D Pie chart (Figure 3–3b) shows the expected contribution of each month's operating income to the semiannual operating income. The projected monthly sales will be entered in row 4 of the worksheet. The assumptions will be entered below the operating income (Figure 3–3a). The projected monthly sales and the assumptions will be used to calculate the remaining numbers in the worksheet.

When necessary, more specific details concerning the above guidelines are presented at appropriate points in the chapter. The chapter also will identify the actions you perform and decisions made regarding these guidelines during the creation of the worksheet shown in Figure 3–1 on page EX 163.

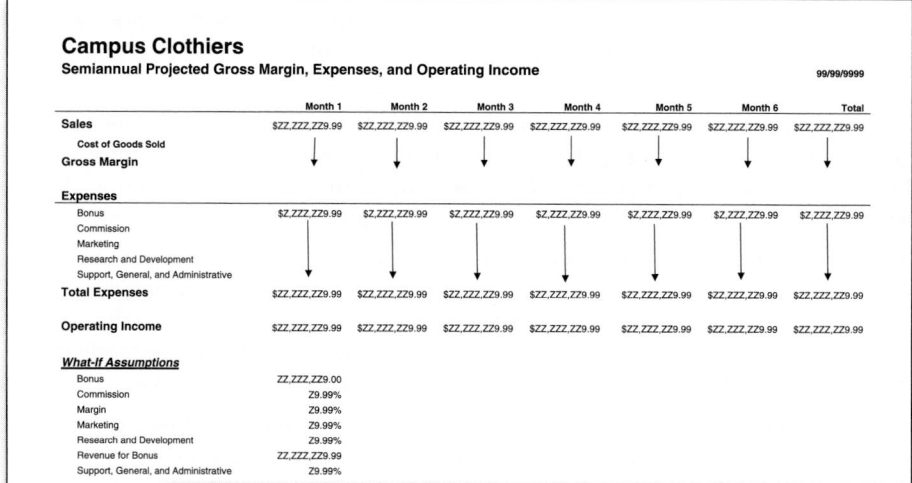

(a) Worksheet

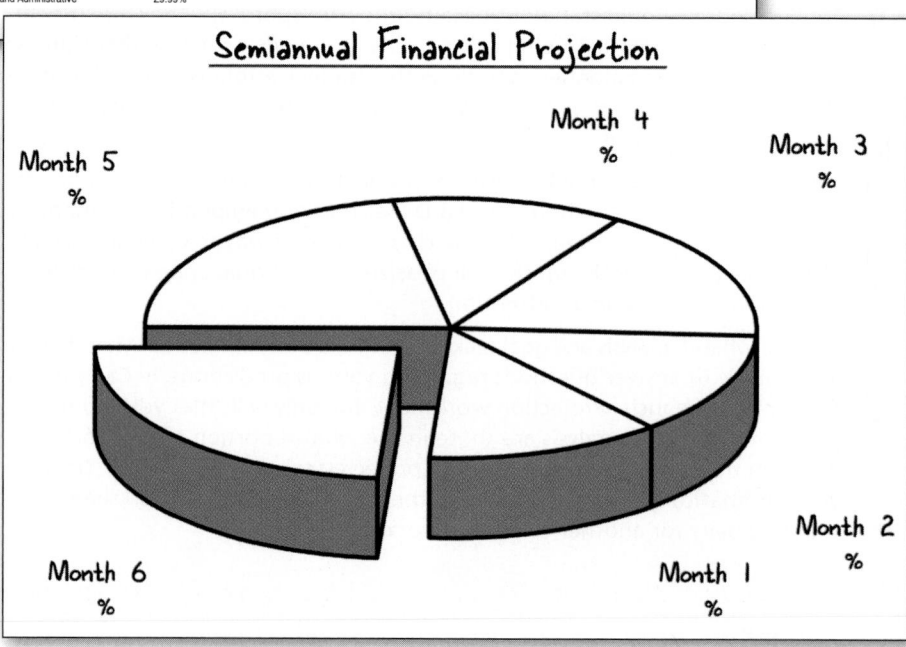

(b) 3-D Pie Chart

Figure 3–3

Excel Chapter 3

With a good understanding of the requirements document, an understanding of the necessary decisions, and a sketch of the worksheet, the next step is to use Excel to create the worksheet.

Table 3–1 Campus Clothiers Semiannual Financial Projections Data and What-If Assumptions	
Projected Monthly Total Net Revenues	
January	$3,383,909.82
February	6,880,576.15
March	9,742,702.37
April	4,818,493.53
May	4,566,722.63
June	8,527,504.39
What-If Assumptions	
Bonus	$100,000.00
Commission	3.25%
Margin	61.00%
Marketing	9.00%
Research and Development	5.75%
Revenue for Bonus	$4,750,000.00
Support, General, and Administrative	17.00%

To Start Excel

If you are using a computer to step through the project in this chapter and you want your screen to match the figures in this book, you should change your computer's resolution to 1024 × 768. For information about how to change a computer's resolution, see page APP 36 in Appendix E.

The following steps, which assume Windows Vista is running, start Excel based on a typical installation of Microsoft Office on your computer. You may need to ask your instructor how to start Excel for your computer.

Note: If you are using Windows XP, see Appendix F for alternate steps.

1 Click the Start button on the Windows Vista taskbar to display the Start menu.

2 Click All Programs at the bottom of the left pane on the Start menu to display the All Programs list.

3 Click Microsoft Office in the All Programs list to display the Microsoft Office list.

4 Click Microsoft Office Excel 2007 to start Excel and display a blank worksheet in the Excel window.

5 If the Excel window is not maximized, click the Maximize button next to the Close button on its title bar to maximize the window.

6 If the worksheet window in Excel is not maximized, click the Maximize button next to the Close button on its title bar to maximize the worksheet window within Excel.

To Enter the Worksheet Titles, Change Workbook Properties, Apply a Theme, and Save the Workbook

The worksheet contains two titles, one in cell A1 and another in cell A2. In the previous chapters, titles were centered across the worksheet. With large worksheets that extend beyond the size of a window, it is best to enter titles in the upper-left corner as shown in the sketch of the worksheet in Figure 3–3a. The following steps enter the worksheet titles and save the workbook.

1 Click cell A1 and then enter Campus Clothiers as the worksheet title.

2 Click cell A2 and then enter Semiannual Projected Gross Margin, Expenses, and Operating Income as the worksheet subtitle and then press the ENTER key.

3 Click the Office Button, click Prepare on the Office Button menu, and then click Properties.

4 Update the document properties with your name and any other relevant information.

5 Click the Close button in the Document Properties pane.

6 Apply the Trek theme to the worksheet by clicking the Themes button on the Page Layout tab on the Ribbon and then return to the Home tab on the Ribbon.

7 With a USB flash drive connected to one of the computer's USB ports, click the Save button on the Quick Access Toolbar.

8 When Excel displays the Save As dialog box, type Campus Clothiers Semiannual Financial Projection in the File name text box.

9 If the Folders list is displayed below the Folders button, click the Folders button to remove the Folders list.

10 If Computer is not displayed in the Favorite Links section, drag the top or bottom edge of the Save As dialog box until Computer is displayed.

11 Click Computer in the Favorite Links section. If necessary, scroll until UDISK 2.0 (E:) appears in the list of available drives. Double-click UDISK 2.0 (E:) (your USB flash drive may have a different name and letter). Click the Save button in the Save As dialog box to save the workbook.

Note: If you are using Windows XP, see Appendix F for alternate steps.

BTW

Rotating Text in a Cell
In Excel, you use the Alignment sheet of the Format Cells dialog box, as shown in Figure 3–5, to position data in a cell by centering, left-aligning, or right-aligning; indenting; aligning at the top, bottom, or center; and rotating. If you enter 90 in the Degrees box in the Orientation area, the text will appear vertically and read from bottom to top in the cell.

Rotating Text and Using the Fill Handle to Create a Series

The data on the worksheet, including month names and the What-If Assumptions section, now can be added to the worksheet.

Plan Ahead

> **Plan the layout of the worksheet.**
> The design of the worksheet calls specifically for only six months of data. Because there always will be only six months of data in the worksheet, the months should be placed across the top of the worksheet as column headings rather than as row headings. There are more data items regarding each month than there are months, and it is possible that more expense categories could be added in the future. A proper layout, therefore, includes placing the data items for each month as row headings. The What-If Assumptions section should be placed in an area of the worksheet that is easily accessible, yet does not impair the view of the main section of the worksheet. As shown in Figure 3–3a, the What-If Assumptions should be placed below the calculations in the worksheet.

When you first enter text, its angle is zero degrees (0°), and it reads from left to right in a cell. Text in a cell can be rotated counterclockwise by entering a number between 1° and 90° in the Alignment sheet in the Format Cells dialog box.

To Rotate Text and Use the Fill Handle to Create a Series of Month Names

Chapters 1 and 2 used the fill handle to copy a cell or a range of cells to adjacent cells. The fill handle also can be used to create a series of numbers, dates, or month names automatically. The following steps enter the month name, January, in cell B3; format cell B3 (including rotating the text); and then use the fill handle to enter the remaining month names in the range C3:G3.

- Select cell B3.

- Type January as the cell entry and then click the Enter box.

- Click the Format Cells: Alignment Dialog Box Launcher on the Ribbon to display the Format Cells dialog box (Figure 3–4).

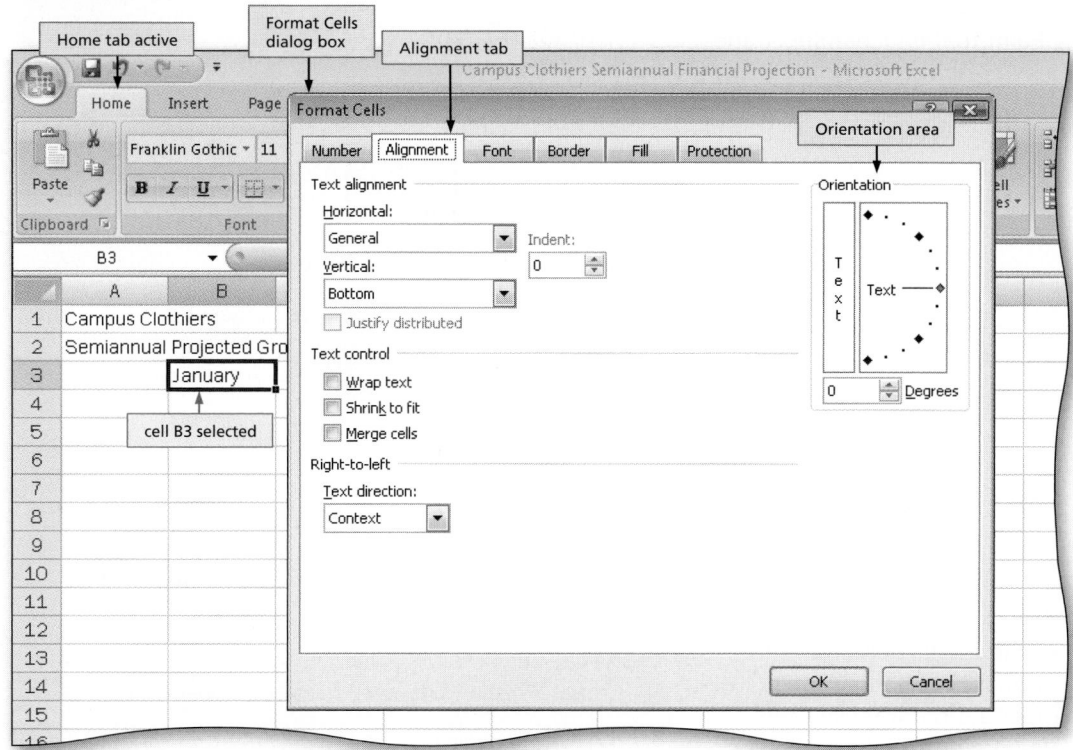

Figure 3–4

- Click the 45° point in the Orientation area to move the Text hand in the Orientation area to the 45° point and to display 45 in the Degrees box (Figure 3–5).

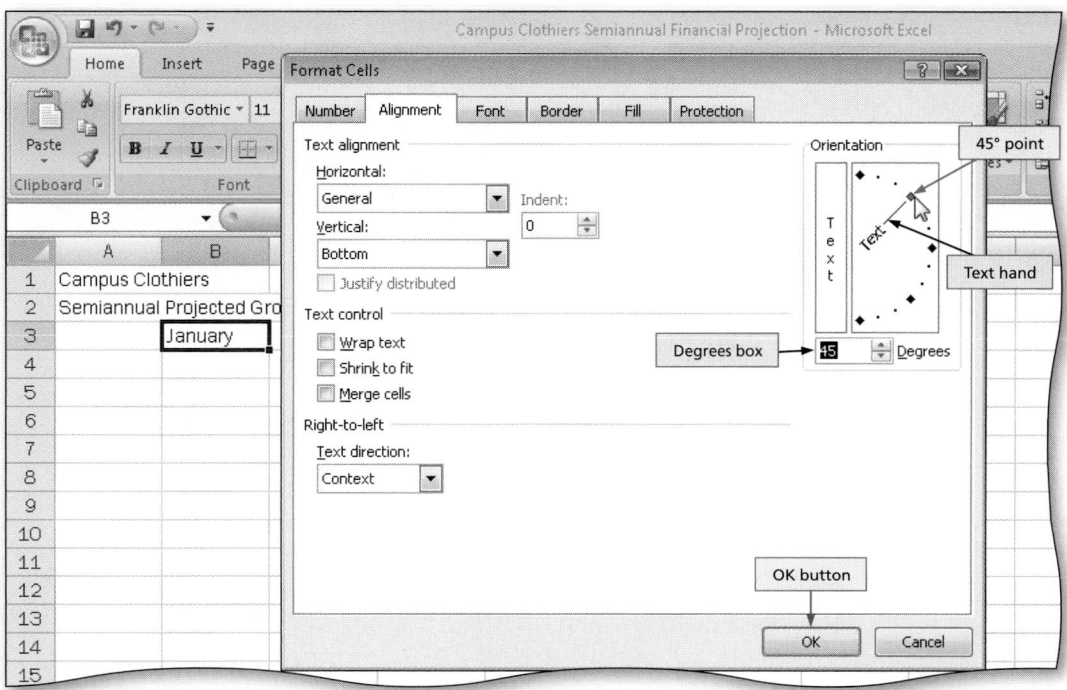

Figure 3–5

- Click the OK button to rotate the text in cell B3 at a 45° angle and automatically increase the height of row 3 to best fit the rotated text (Figure 3–6).

- Point to the fill handle on the lower-right corner of cell B3.

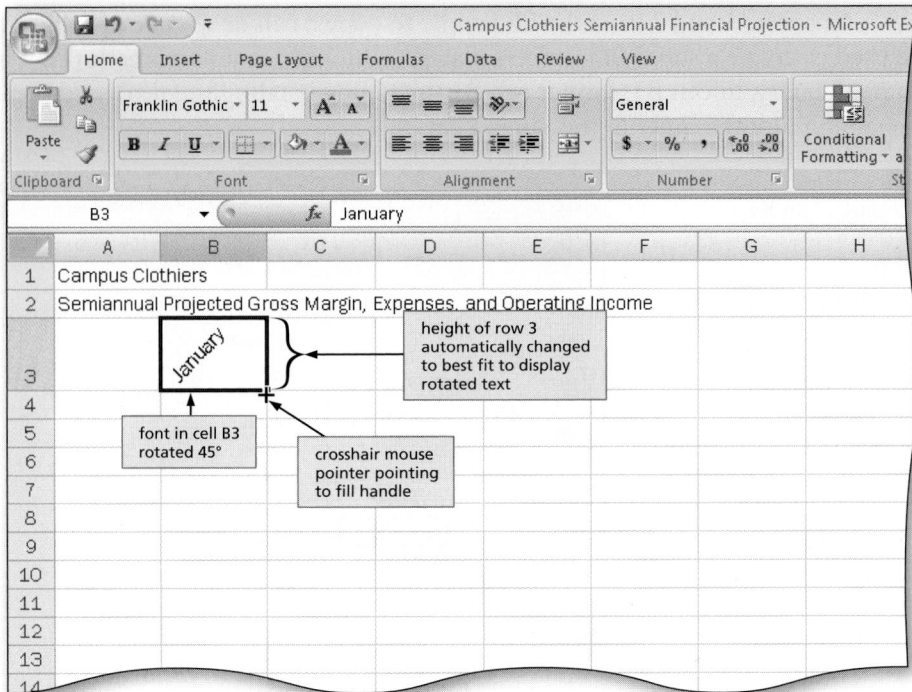

Figure 3–6

- Drag the fill handle to the right to select the range C3:G3. Do not release the mouse button (Figure 3–7).

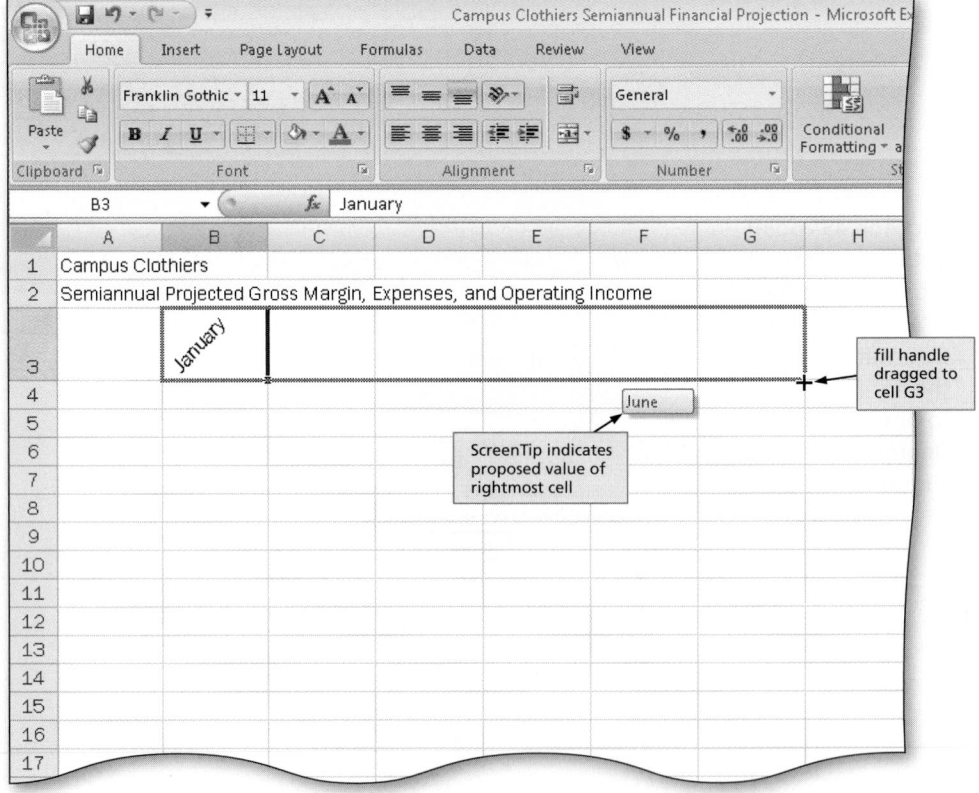

Figure 3–7

5

- Release the mouse button to create a month name series January through June in the range B3:G3 and copy the format in cell B3 to the range C3:G3.

- Click the Auto Fill Options button below the lower-right corner of the fill area to display the Auto Fill Options menu (Figure 3–8).

Q&A

What if I do not want to copy the format of cell B3 during the auto fill operation?

In addition to creating a series of values, dragging the fill handle instructs Excel to copy the format of cell B3 to the range C3:G3. With some fill operations, you may not want to copy the formats of the source cell or range to the destination cell or range. If this is the case, click the Auto Fill Options button after the range fills (Figure 3–8) and then select the option you desire on the Auto Fill Options menu.

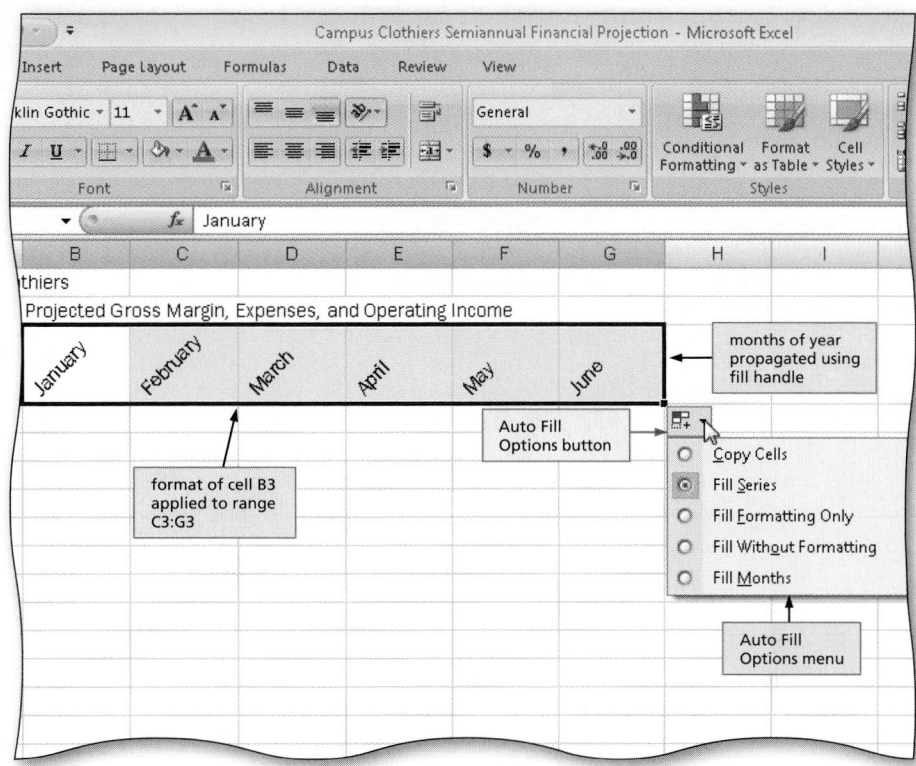

Figure 3–8

6

- Click the Auto Fill Options button to hide the Auto Fill Options menu.

- Click cell H3, type `Total`, and then press the RIGHT ARROW key.

Q&A

Why is the word Total automatically formatted with the Heading 3 cell style and 45° rotation?

Excel tries to save you time by automatically recognizing the adjacent cell format in cell G3 and applying it to cell H3. The Heading 3 cell style in cell G3 causes this action to occur.

Using the Auto Fill Options Menu

As shown in Figure 3–8, Fill Series is the default option that Excel uses to fill the area, which means it fills the destination area with a series, using the same formatting as the source area. If you choose another option on the Auto Fill Options menu, then Excel immediately changes the contents of the destination range. Following the use of the fill handle, the Auto Fill Options button remains active until you begin the next Excel operation. Table 3–2 summarizes the options on the Auto Fill Options menu.

Other Ways

1. Enter start month in cell, apply formatting, right-drag fill handle in direction to fill, click Fill Months on shortcut menu
2. Enter start month in cell, apply formatting, select range, click Fill button on Home tab on Ribbon, click Series, click AutoFill

BTW

The Mighty Fill Handle
If you drag the fill handle to the left or up, Excel will decrement the series rather than increment the series. To copy a word, such as January or Monday, which Excel might interpret as the start of a series, hold down the CTRL key while you drag the fill handle to a destination area. If you drag the fill handle back into the middle of a cell, Excel erases the contents.

Table 3–2 Options Available on the Auto Fill Options Menu

Auto Fill Option	Description
Copy Cells	Fill destination area with contents using format of source area. Do not create a series.
Fill Series	Fill destination area with series using format of source area. This option is the default.
Fill Formatting Only	Fill destination area using format of source area. No content is copied unless fill is series.
Fill Without Formatting	Fill destination area with contents, without the formatting of source area.
Fill Months	Fill destination area with series of months using format of source area. Same as Fill Series and shows as an option only if source area contains a month.

You can use the fill handle to create a series longer than the one shown in Figure 3–8. If you drag the fill handle past cell G3 in Step 4, Excel continues to increment the months and logically will repeat January, February, and so on, if you extend the range far enough to the right.

You can create several different types of series using the fill handle. Table 3–3 illustrates several examples. Notice in examples 4 through 7, 9, and 11 that, if you use the fill handle to create a series of numbers or nonsequential months, you must enter the first item in the series in one cell and the second item in the series in an adjacent cell. Next, select both cells and drag the fill handle through the destination area.

Table 3–3 Examples of Series Using the Fill Handle

Example	Contents of Cell(s) Copied Using the Fill Handle	Next Three Values of Extended Series
1	2:00	3:00, 4:00, 5:00
2	Qtr3	Qtr4, Qtr1, Qtr2
3	Quarter 1	Quarter 2, Quarter 3, Quarter 4
4	5-Jan, 5-Mar	5-May, 5-Jul, 5-Sep
5	2007, 2008	2009, 2010, 2011
6	1, 2	3, 4, 5
7	430, 410	390, 370, 350
8	Sun	Mon, Tue, Wed
9	Sunday, Tuesday	Thursday, Saturday, Monday
10	4th Section	5th Section, 6th Section, 7th Section
11	−205, −208	−211, −214, −217

To Increase Column Widths and Enter Row Titles

In Chapter 2, the column widths were increased after the values were entered into the worksheet. Sometimes, you may want to increase the column widths before you enter the values and, if necessary, adjust them later. The following steps increase the column widths and then enter the row titles in column A down to What-If Assumptions in cell A18.

- Move the mouse pointer to the boundary between column heading A and column heading B so that the mouse pointer changes to a split double arrow.

- Drag the mouse pointer to the right until the ScreenTip displays, Width: 35.00 (322 pixels). Do not release the mouse button (Figure 3–9).

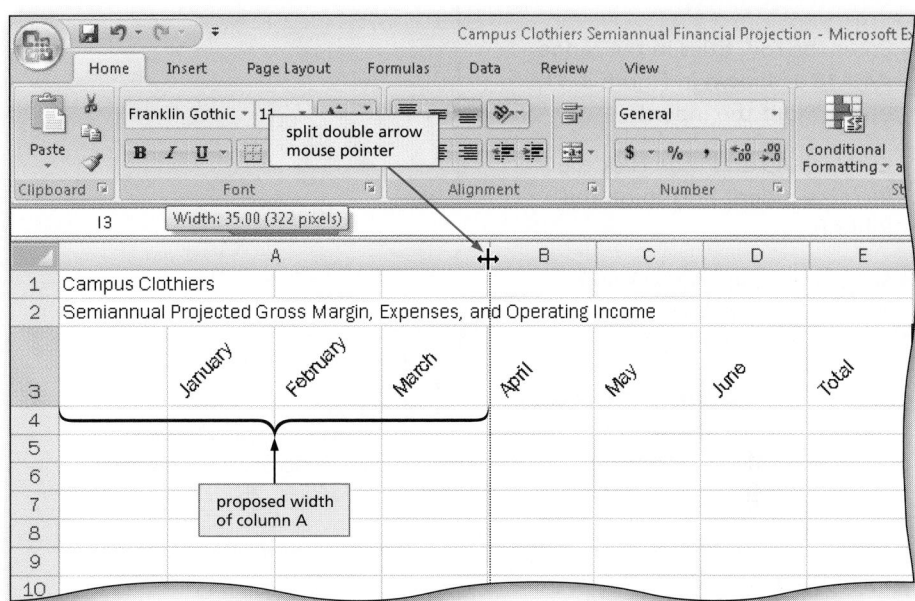

Figure 3–9

- Release the mouse button to change the width of column A.

- Click column heading B and then drag through column heading G to select columns B through G.

- Move the mouse pointer to the boundary between column headings B and C and then drag the mouse to the right until the ScreenTip displays, Width: 14.00 (133 pixels). Do not release the mouse button (Figure 3–10).

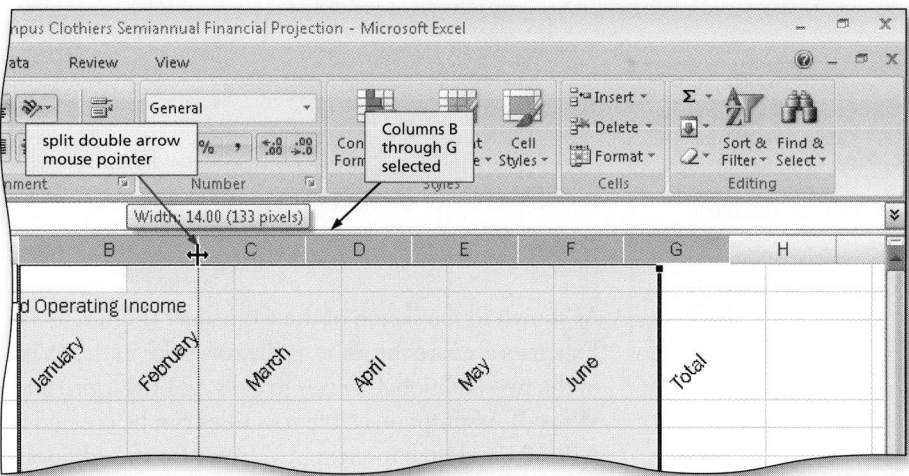

Figure 3–10

3

- Release the mouse button to change the width of columns B through G.

- Use the technique described in Step 1 to increase the width of column H to 15.00.

- Enter the row titles in the range A4:A18 as shown in Figure 3–11, but without the indents.

- Click cell A5 and then click the Increase Indent button on the Ribbon.

- Select the range A9:A13 and then click the Increase Indent button on the Ribbon.

- Click cell A19 to finish entering the row titles (Figure 3–11).

Q&A

What happens when I click the Increase Indent button?

The Increase Indent button indents the contents of a cell to the right by three spaces each time you click it. The Decrease Indent button decreases the indent by three spaces each time you click it.

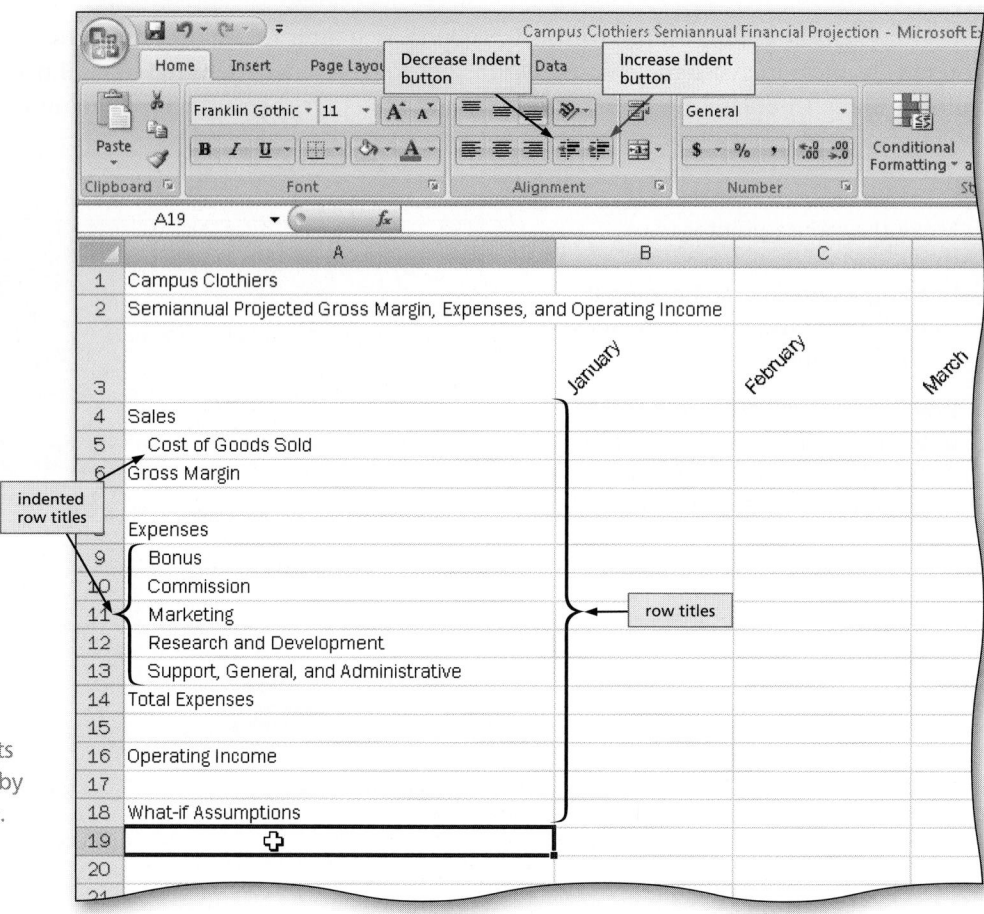

Figure 3–11

Other Ways

1. To indent, right-click range, click Format Cells on shortcut menu, click Alignment tab, click Left (Indent) in Horizontal list, type number of spaces to indent in Indent text box, click OK button

BTW

Fitting Entries in a Cell
An alternative to increasing the column widths or row heights is to shrink the characters in the cell to fit the current width of the column. To shrink to fit, click Format Cells: Alignment Dialog Box Launcher on the Ribbon, and click Shrink to fit in the Text control area. After shrinking entries to fit in a cell, consider using the Zoom slider on the status bar to make the entries more readable.

Copying a Range of Cells to a Nonadjacent Destination Area

As shown in the sketch of the worksheet (Figure 3–3a on page EX 166), the row titles in the Expenses area are the same as the row titles in the What-If Assumptions table, with the exception of the two additional entries in cells A21 (Margin) and A24 (Revenue for Bonus). Hence, the What-If Assumptions table row titles can be created by copying the range A9:A13 to the range A19:A23 and then inserting two rows for the additional entries in cells A21 and A24. The source area (range A9:A13) is not adjacent to the destination area (range A19:A23). The first two chapters used the fill handle to copy a source area to an adjacent destination area. To copy a source area to a nonadjacent destination area, however, you cannot use the fill handle.

A more versatile method of copying a source area is to use the Copy button and Paste button on the Home tab on the Ribbon. You can use these two buttons to copy a source area to an adjacent or nonadjacent destination area.

The Copy button copies the contents and format of the source area to the **Office Clipboard**, a reserved place in the computer's memory that allows you to collect text and graphic items from an Office document and then paste them into any Office document. The Copy command on the Edit menu or shortcut menu works the same as the Copy button. The Paste button copies the item from the Office Clipboard to the destination area.

To Copy a Range of Cells to a Nonadjacent Destination Area

The following steps use the Copy and Paste buttons to copy the range A9:A13 to the nonadjacent range A19:A23.

1

- Select the range A9:A13 and then click the Copy button on the Home tab on the Ribbon to copy the values and formats of the range A9:A13 to the Office Clipboard.

- Click cell A19, the top cell in the destination area (Figure 3–12).

Q&A

Why do I not need to select the entire destination area?

You are not required to select the entire destination area (range A19:A23) before clicking the Paste button. Excel needs to know only the upper-left cell of the destination area. In the case of a single column range, such as A19:A23, the top cell of the destination area (cell A19) also is the upper-left cell of the destination area.

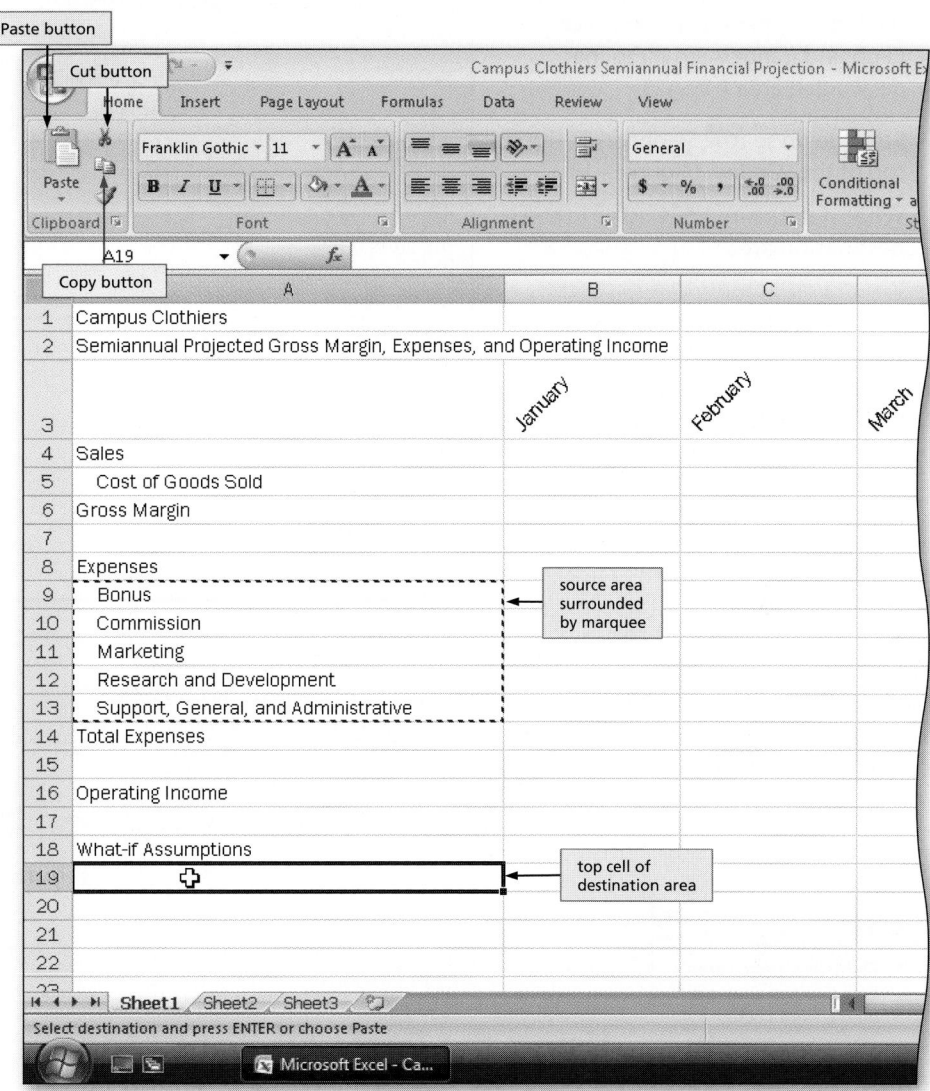

Figure 3–12

2
- Click the Paste button on the Ribbon to copy the values and formats of the last item placed on the Office Clipboard (range A9:A13) to the destination area A19:A23.

- Scroll down so row 5 appears at the top of the window (Figure 3–13).

Q&A

What if data already existed in the destination area?

When you complete a copy, the values and formats in the destination area are replaced with the values and formats of the source area. Any data contained in the destination area prior to the copy and paste is lost. If you accidentally delete valuable data, immediately click the Undo button on the Quick Access Toolbar.

3
- Press the ESC key to remove the marquee from the source area and disable the Paste button on the Ribbon.

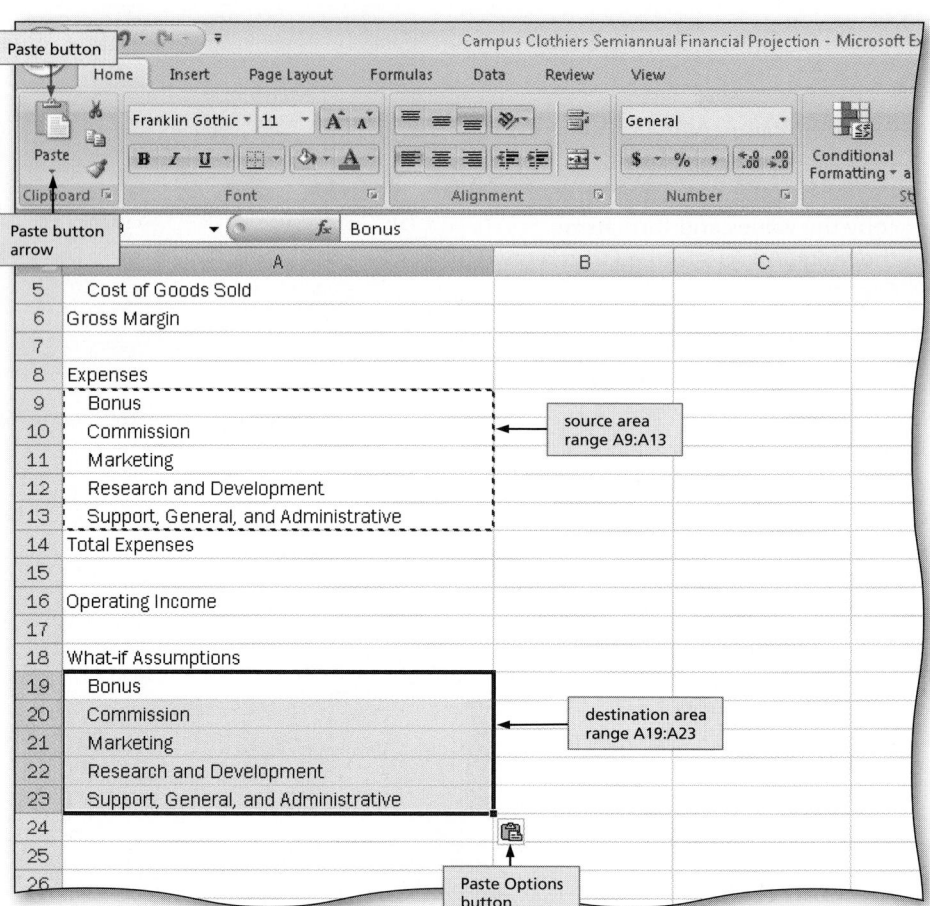

Figure 3–13

Other Ways

1. Right-click source area, click Copy on shortcut menu, right-click destination area, click Paste on shortcut menu
2. Select source area and point on border of range; while holding down CTRL key, drag source area to destination area
3. Select source area, press CTRL+C, select destination area, press CTRL+V

Using the Paste Options Menu

After the Paste button is clicked, Excel immediately displays the Paste Options button, as shown in Figure 3–13. If you click the Paste Options button arrow and select an option on the Paste Options menu, Excel modifies the most recent paste operation based on your selection. Table 3–4 summarizes the options available on the Paste Options menu.

Table 3–4 Options Available on the Paste Options Menu	
Paste Option	**Description**
Keep Source Formatting	Copy contents and format of source area. This option is the default.
Match Destination Formatting	Copy contents of source area, but not the format.
Values and Number Formatting	Copy contents and format of source area for numbers or formulas, but use format of destination area for text.
Keep Source Column Widths	Copy contents and format of source area. Change destination column widths to source column widths.
Formatting Only	Copy format of source area, but not the contents.
Link Cells	Copy contents and format and link cells so that a change to the cells in source area updates the corresponding cells in destination area.

The Paste button on the Ribbon (Figure 3–13) includes an arrow, which displays a list of advanced paste options (Paste, Paste Special, and Paste as Hyperlink). These options will be discussed when they are used.

An alternative to clicking the Paste button is to press the ENTER key. The ENTER key completes the paste operation, removes the marquee from the source area, and disables the Paste button so that you cannot paste the copied source area to other destination areas. The ENTER key was not used in the previous set of steps so that the capabilities of the Paste Options button could be discussed. The Paste Options button does not appear on the screen when you use the ENTER key to complete the paste operation.

Using Drag and Drop to Move or Copy Cells

You also can use the mouse to move or copy cells. First, you select the source area and point to the border of the cell or range. You know you are pointing to the border of the cell or range when the mouse pointer changes to a block arrow. To move the selected cell or cells, drag the selection to the destination area. To copy a selection, hold down the CTRL key while dragging the selection to the destination area. You know Excel is in copy mode when a small plus sign appears next to the block arrow mouse pointer. Be sure to release the mouse button before you release the CTRL key. Using the mouse to move or copy cells is called **drag and drop**.

Using Cut and Paste to Move Cells

Another way to move cells is to select them, click the Cut button on the Ribbon (Figure 3–12 on page EX 175) to remove them from the worksheet and copy them to the Office Clipboard, select the destination area, and then click the Paste button on the Ribbon or press the ENTER key. You also can use the Cut command on the shortcut menu, instead of the Cut button.

Inserting and Deleting Cells in a Worksheet

At any time while the worksheet is on the screen, you can insert cells to enter new data or delete cells to remove unwanted data. You can insert or delete individual cells; a range of cells, rows, columns; or entire worksheets.

To Insert a Row

The Insert command on the shortcut menu allows you to insert rows between rows that already contain data. According to the sketch of the worksheet in Figure 3–3a on page EX 166, two rows must be inserted in the What-If Assumptions table, one between Commission and Marketing for the Margin assumption and another between Research and Development and Support, General, and Administrative for the Revenue for Bonus assumption. The following steps accomplish the task of inserting the new rows into the worksheet.

BTW

Move It or Copy It
You may hear someone say, "Move it or copy it, it's all the same." No, it is not the same! When you move a cell, the data in the original location is cleared and the format is reset to the default. When you copy a cell, the data and format of the copy area remain intact. In short, you should copy cells to duplicate entries and move cells to rearrange entries.

BTW

Cutting
When you cut a cell or range of cells using the Cut command or Cut button, Excel copies the cells to the Office Clipboard, but does not remove the cells from the source area until you paste the cells in the destination area by clicking the Paste button or pressing the ENTER key. When you complete the paste, Excel clears the cell entry and its formats from the source area.

BTW

Inserting Multiple Rows
If you want to insert multiple rows, you have two choices. First, you can insert a single row by using the Insert command on the shortcut menu and then repeatedly press F4 to keep inserting rows. Alternatively, you can select any number of existing rows before inserting new rows. For instance, if you want to insert five rows, select five existing rows in the worksheet, right-click the rows, and then click Insert on the shortcut menu.

1

- Right-click row heading 21, the row below where you want to insert a row, to display the shortcut menu and the Mini toolbar (Figure 3–14).

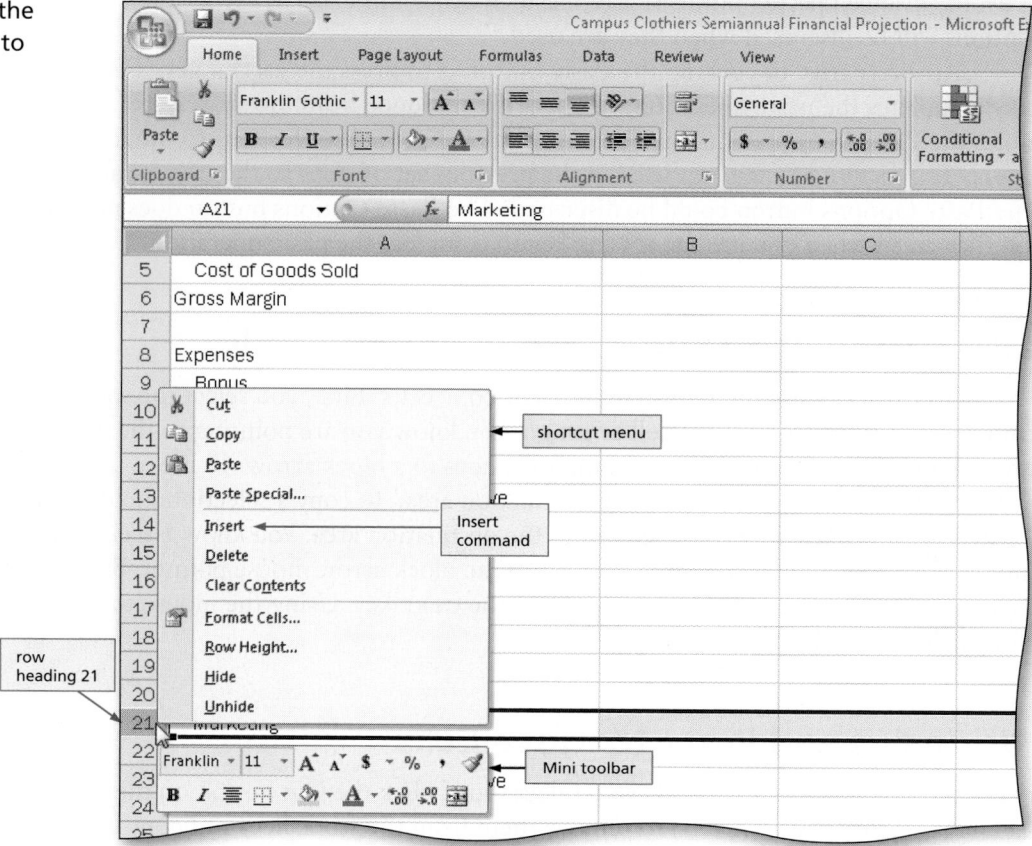

Figure 3–14

2

- Click Insert on the shortcut menu to insert a new row in the worksheet by shifting the selected row 21 and all rows below it down one row.

- Click cell A21 in the new row and then enter `Margin` as the row title (Figure 3–15).

Q&A

What is the resulting format of the new row?

The cells in the new row inherit the formats of the cells in the row above them. You can change this by clicking the Insert Options button that appears immediately above the inserted row. Following the insertion of a row, the Insert Options button lets you select from the following options: (1) Format Same As Above; (2) Format Same As Below; and (3) Clear Formatting. The Format Same as Above option is the default. The Insert Options button remains active until you begin the next Excel operation.

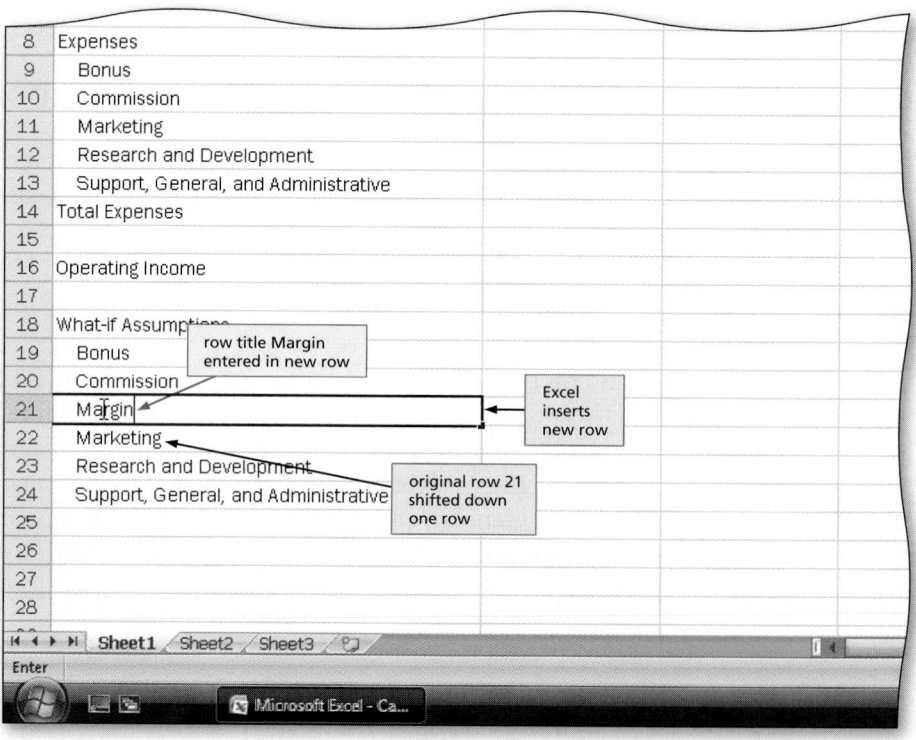

Figure 3–15

3

- Right-click row heading 24 and then click Insert on the shortcut menu to insert a new row in the worksheet.

- Click cell A24 in the new row and then enter Revenue for Bonus as the row title (Figure 3–16).

Q&A

What would happen if cells in the shifted rows are included in formulas?

If the rows that are shifted down include cell references in formulas located in the worksheet, Excel automatically adjusts the cell references in the formulas to their new locations. Thus, in Step 2, if a formula in the worksheet references a cell in row 21 before the insert, then the cell reference in the formula is adjusted to row 22 after the insert.

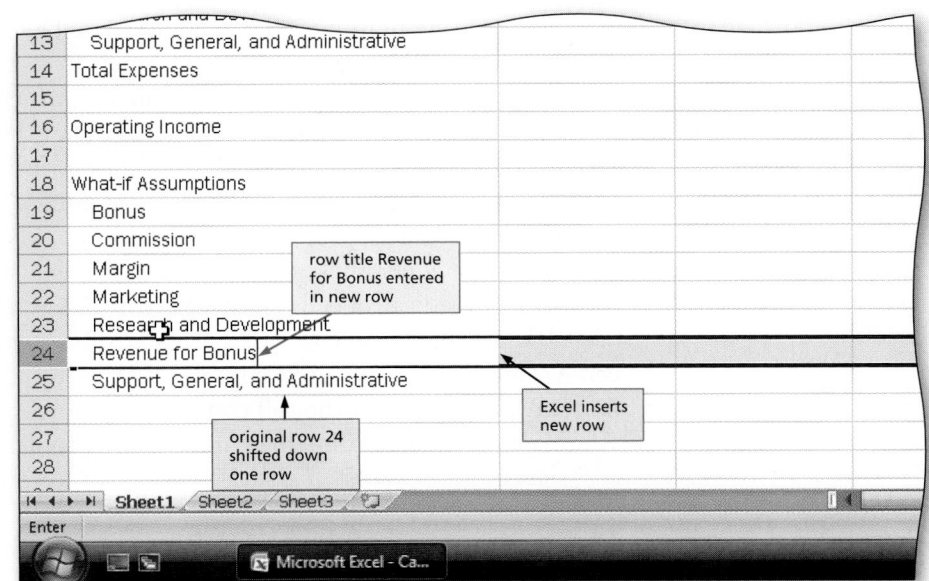

Figure 3–16

Other Ways

1. On Home tab on Ribbon, click Insert, click Insert Sheet Rows

2. Press CTRL+SHIFT+PLUS SIGN, click Entire Row, click OK button

Inserting Columns

You insert columns into a worksheet in the same way you insert rows. To insert columns, select one or more columns immediately to the right of where you want Excel to insert the new column or columns. Select the number of columns you want to insert. Next, click the Insert tab on the Ribbon and then click Insert Sheet Rows in the Insert gallery or click Insert on the shortcut menu. The Insert command on the shortcut menu requires that you select an entire column (or columns) to insert a column (or columns). Following the insertion of a column, Excel displays the Insert Options button, which allows you to modify the insertion in a fashion similar to that discussed earlier when inserting rows.

Inserting Single Cells or a Range of Cells

The Insert command on the shortcut menu or the Cells command on the Insert gallery of the Insert button on the Ribbon allows you to insert a single cell or a range of cells. You should be aware that if you shift a single cell or a range of cells, however, it no longer may be lined up with its associated cells. To ensure that the values in the worksheet do not get out of order, it is recommended that you insert only entire rows or entire columns. When you insert a single cell or a range of cells, Excel displays the Insert Options button so that you can change the format of the inserted cell, using options similar to those for inserting rows and columns.

BTW

Dragging Ranges
You can move and insert a selected cell or range between existing cells by holding down the SHIFT key while you drag the selection to the gridline where you want to insert. You also can copy and insert by holding down the CTRL+SHIFT keys while you drag the selection to the desired gridline.

BTW

The Insert Options Button
When you insert columns or rows, Excel only displays the Insert Options button if formats are assigned to the leftmost column or top row of the selection.

Deleting Columns and Rows

BTW

Ranges and Undo
Copying, deleting, inserting, and moving ranges of cells have the potential to render a worksheet useless. Carefully review these actions before continuing on to the next task. If you are not sure the action is correct, click the Undo button on the Quick Access Toolbar.

The Delete button on the Ribbon or the Delete command on the shortcut menu removes cells (including the data and format) from the worksheet. Deleting cells is not the same as clearing cells. The Clear command, which was described earlier in Chapter 1 on page EX 66, clears the data from the cells, but the cells remain in the worksheet. The Delete command removes the cells from the worksheet and shifts the remaining rows up (when you delete rows) or shifts the remaining columns to the left (when you delete columns). If formulas located in other cells reference cells in the deleted row or column, Excel does not adjust these cell references. Excel displays the error message **#REF!** in those cells to indicate a cell reference error. For example, if cell A7 contains the formula =A4+A5 and you delete row 5, Excel assigns the formula =A4+#REF! to cell A6 (originally cell A7) and displays the error message #REF! in cell A6. It also displays an Error Options button when you select the cell containing the error message #REF!, which allows you to select options to determine the nature of the problem.

Deleting Individual Cells or a Range of Cells

Although Excel allows you to delete an individual cell or range of cells, you should be aware that if you shift a cell or range of cells on the worksheet, it no longer may be lined up with its associated cells. For this reason, it is recommended that you delete only entire rows or entire columns.

Entering Numbers with Format Symbols

The next step in creating the Semiannual Financial Projection worksheet is to enter the what-if assumptions values in the range B19:B25. The numbers in the table can be entered and then formatted as in Chapters 1 and 2, or each one can be entered with format symbols. When a number is entered with a **format symbol**, Excel immediately displays it with the assigned format. Valid format symbols include the dollar sign ($), comma (,), and percent sign (%).

If you enter a whole number, it appears without any decimal places. If you enter a number with one or more decimal places and a format symbol, Excel displays the number with two decimal places. Table 3–5 illustrates several examples of numbers entered with format symbols. The number in parentheses in column 4 indicates the number of decimal places.

Table 3–5 Numbers Entered with Format Symbols			
Format Symbol	**Typed in Formula Bar**	**Displays in Cell**	**Comparable Format**
,	83,341	83,341	Comma (0)
	1,675.8	1,675.80	Comma (2)
$	$278	$278	Currency (0)
	$3818.54	$3,818.54	Currency (2)
	$45,612.3	$45,612.30	Currency (2)
%	23%	23%	Percent (0)
	97.50%	97.50%	Percent (2)
	39.833%	39.83%	Percent (2)

To Enter Numbers with Format Symbols

The following step enters the numbers in the What-If Assumptions table with format symbols.

1

• Enter 100,000.00 in cell B19, 3.25% in cell B20, 61.00% in cell B21, 9.00% in cell B22, 5.75% in cell B23, 4,750,000.00 in cell B24, and 17.00% in cell B25 to display the entries using a format based on the format symbols entered with the numbers (Figure 3–17).

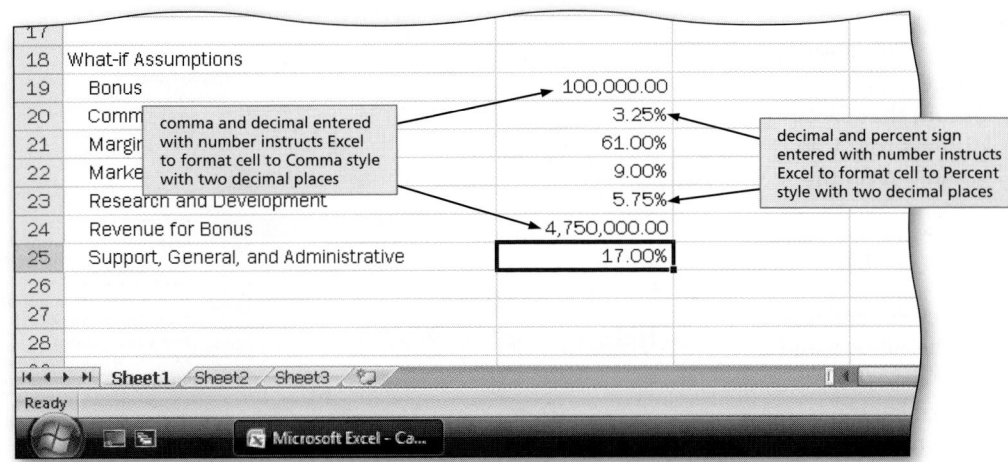

Figure 3–17

Other Ways
1. Right-click range, click Format Cells on shortcut menu, click Number tab, click category in Category list, [select desired format], click OK button
2. Press CTRL+1, click Number tab, click category in Category list, [select desired format], click OK button

Freezing Worksheet Titles

Freezing worksheet titles is a useful technique for viewing large worksheets that extend beyond the window. Normally, when you scroll down or to the right, the column titles in row 3 and the row titles in column A that define the numbers no longer appear on the screen. This makes it difficult to remember what the numbers in these rows and columns represent. To alleviate this problem, Excel allows you to **freeze the titles**, so that Excel displays the titles on the screen, no matter how far down or to the right you scroll.

BTW

Freezing Titles
If you want to freeze only column headings, select the appropriate cell in column A before you click the Freeze Panes button on the View tab on the Ribbon. If you only want to freeze row titles, then select the appropriate cell in row 1. To freeze both column headings and row titles, select the cell that is the intersection of the column and row titles before you click the Freeze Panes button on the View tab on the Ribbon.

To Freeze Column and Row Titles

The following steps use the Freeze Panes button on the View tab on the Ribbon to freeze the worksheet title and column titles in rows 1, 2, and 3, and the row titles in column A.

1

- Press CTRL+HOME to select cell A1 and ensure that Excel displays row 1 and column A on the screen.

- Select cell B4.

- Click the View tab on the Ribbon and then click the Freeze Panes button on the Ribbon to display the Freeze Panes gallery (Figure 3–18).

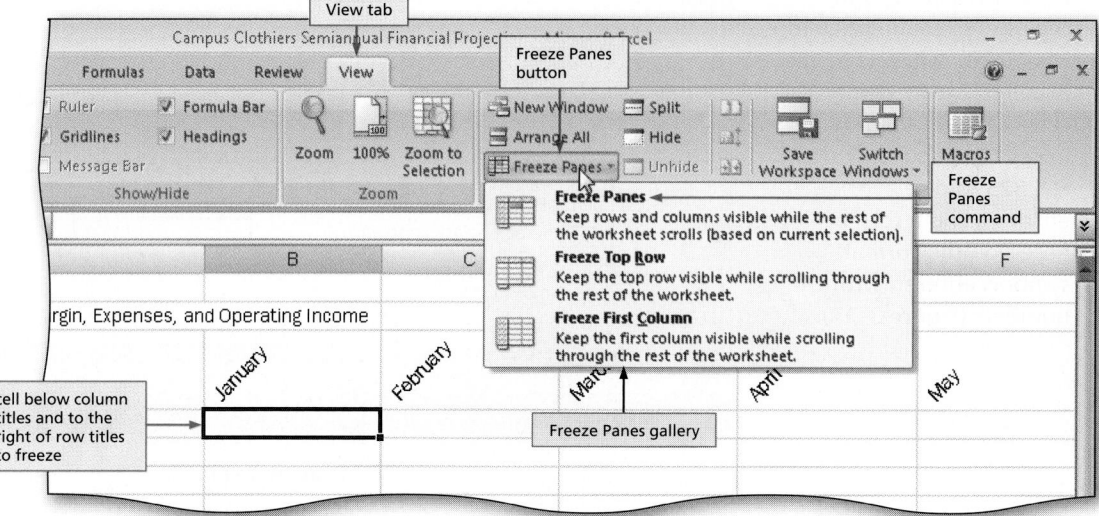

Figure 3–18

Q&A Why is cell A1 selected first?

Before freezing the titles, it is important that Excel displays cell A1 in the upper-left corner of the screen. For example, if cell B4 was selected without first selecting cell A1 to ensure Excel displays the upper-left corner of the screen, then Excel would freeze the titles and also hide rows 1 and 2. Excel thus would not be able to display rows 1 and 2 until they are unfrozen.

2

- Click Freeze Panes in the Freeze Panes gallery to freeze column A and rows 1 through 3 (Figure 3–19).

Q&A What happens after I click the Freeze Panes command?

Excel displays a thin black line on the right side of column A, indicating the split between the frozen row titles in column A and the rest of the worksheet. It also displays a thin black line below row 3, indicating the split between the frozen column titles in rows 1 through 3 and the rest of the worksheet (Figure 3–19).

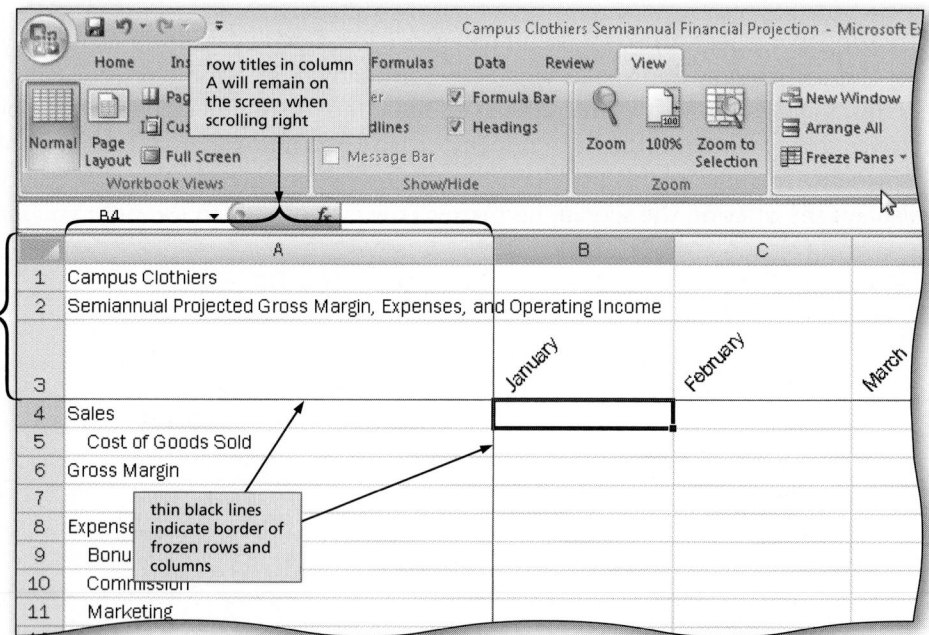

Figure 3–19

Other Ways

1. Press ALT+W, F

To Enter the Projected Monthly Sales

The following steps enter the projected monthly sales, listed earlier in Table 3–1 on page EX 167, in row 4 and compute the projected semiannual sales in cell H4.

1 If necessary, click the Home tab on the Ribbon.

2 Enter 3383909.82 in cell B4, 6880576.15 in cell C4, 9742702.37 in cell D4, 4818493.53 in cell E4, 4566722.63 in cell F4, and 8527504.39 in cell G4.

3 Click cell H4 and then click the Sum button on the Ribbon twice to total the semiannual sales in cell H4 (Figure 3–20).

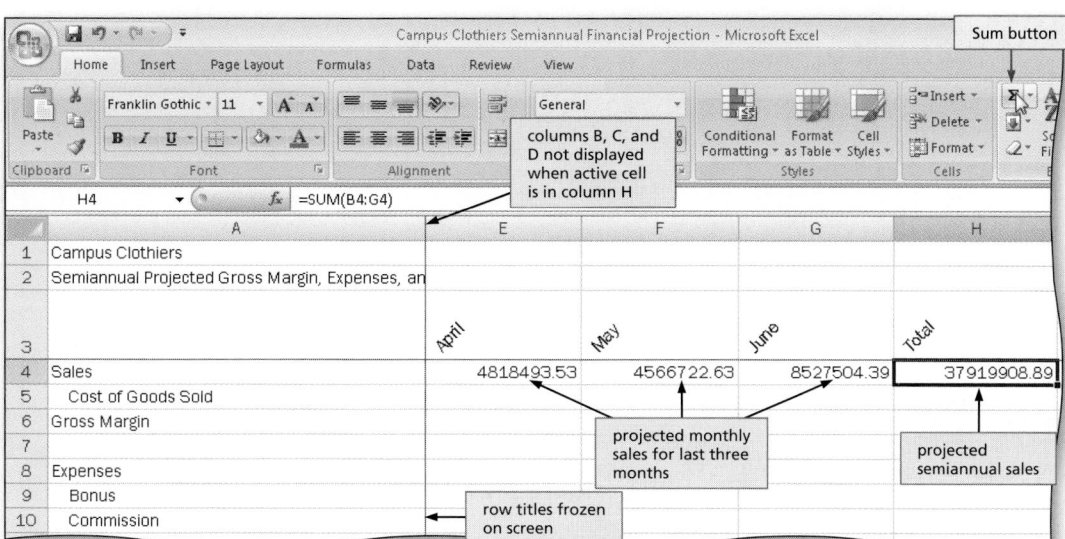

Figure 3–20

Displaying a System Date

The sketch of the worksheet in Figure 3–3a on page EX 166 includes a date stamp on the right side of the heading section. A **date stamp** shows the date a workbook, report, or other document was created or the period it represents. In business, a report often is meaningless without a date stamp. For example, if a printout of the worksheet in this chapter were distributed to the company's analysts, the date stamp would show when the six-month projections were made, as well as what period the report represents.

A simple way to create a date stamp is to use the NOW function to enter the system date tracked by your computer in a cell in the worksheet. The **NOW function** is one of 14 date and time functions available in Excel. When assigned to a cell, the NOW function returns a number that corresponds to the system date and time beginning with December 31, 1899. For example, January 1, 1900 equals 1, January 2, 1900 equals 2, and so on. Noon equals .5. Thus, noon on January 1, 1900 equals 1.5 and 6 P.M. on January 1, 1900 equals 1.75. If the computer's system date is set to the current date, which normally it is, then the date stamp is equivalent to the current date.

Excel automatically formats this number as a date, using the date and time format, mm/dd/yyyy hh:mm, where the first mm is the month, dd is the day of the month, yyyy is the year, hh is the hour of the day, and mm is the minutes past the hour.

To Enter and Format the System Date

The following steps enter the NOW function and change the format from mm/dd/yyyy hh:mm to mm/dd/yyyy.

- Click cell H2 and then click the Insert Function box in the formula bar.

- When Excel displays the Insert Function dialog box, click the 'Or select a category' box arrow, and then select Date & Time in the list.

- Scroll down in the Select a function list and then click NOW (Figure 3–21).

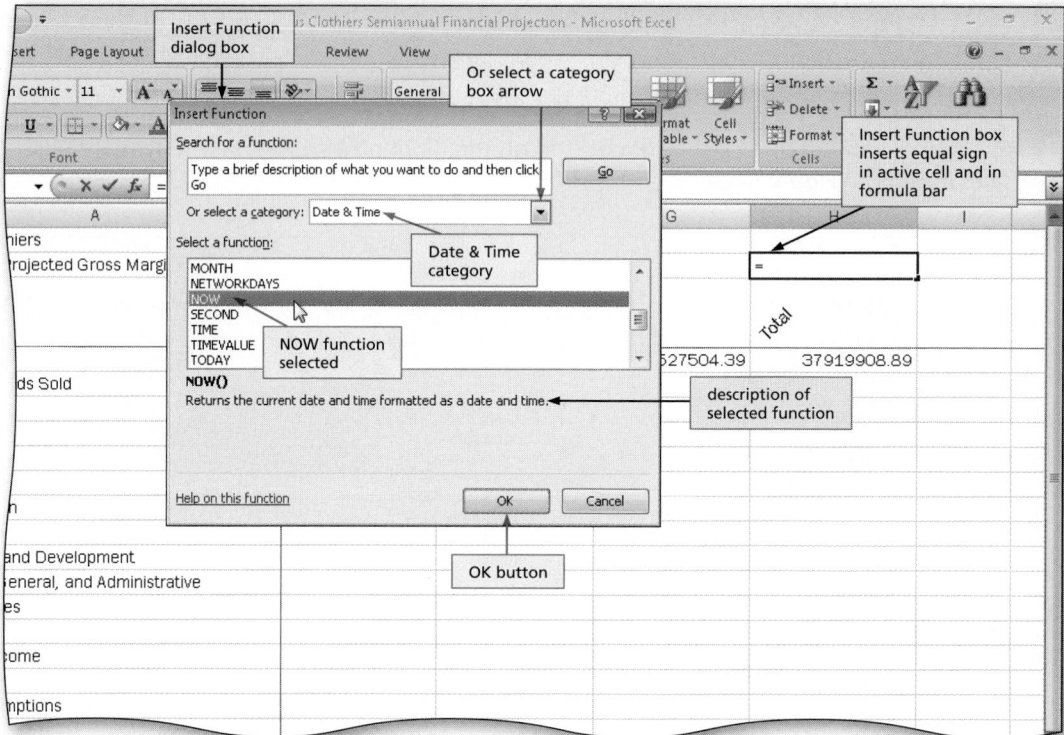

Figure 3–21

- Click the OK button.

- When Excel displays the Function Arguments dialog box, click the OK button to display the system date and time in cell H2, using the default date and time format mm/dd/yyyy hh:mm.

- Right-click cell H2 to display the shortcut menu (Figure 3–22).

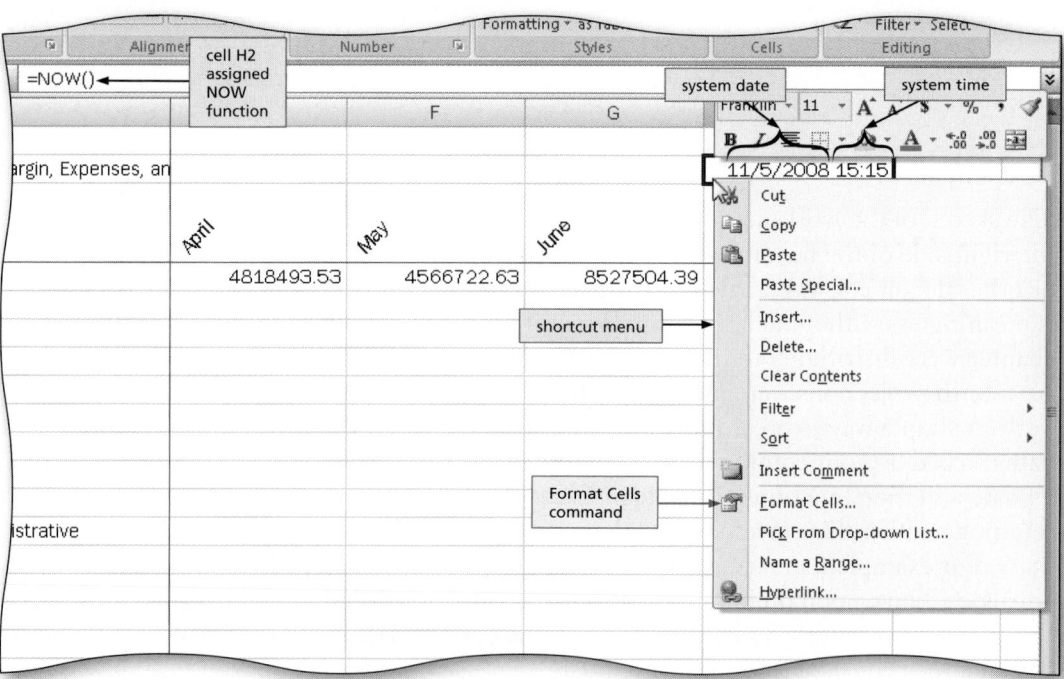

Figure 3–22

3

- Click Format Cells on the shortcut menu.

- When Excel displays the Format Cells dialog box, if necessary, click the Number tab.

- Click Date in the Category list. Scroll down in the Type list and then click 3/14/2001 to display a sample of the data in the active cell (H2) using the selected format in the Sample area (Figure 3–23).

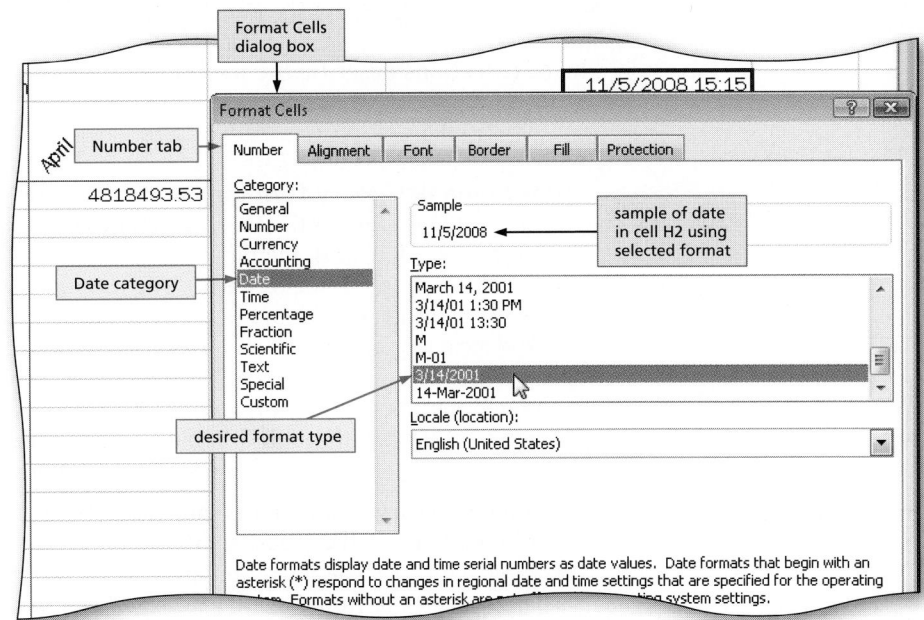

Figure 3–23

4

- Click the OK button in the Format Cells dialog box to display the system date in the form mm/dd/yyyy (Figure 3–24).

Q&A

How does Excel format a date?

In Figure 3–24, the date is displayed right-aligned in the cell because Excel treats a date as a number formatted to display as a date. If you assign the General format (Excel's default format for numbers) to a date in a cell, the date is displayed as a number with two decimal places. For example, if the system time and date is 6:00 PM on December 28, 2007 and the cell containing the NOW function is

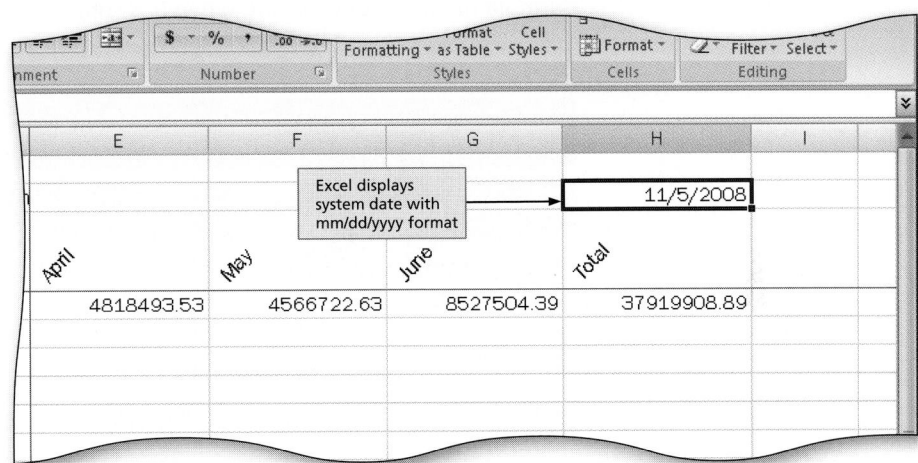

Figure 3–24

assigned the General format, then Excel displays the following number in the cell:

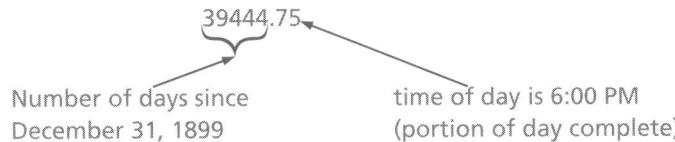

Number of days since December 31, 1899

time of day is 6:00 PM (portion of day complete)

The whole number portion of the number (39444) represents the number of days since December 31, 1899. The decimal portion of the number (.75) represents 6:00 PM as the time of day, at which point 3/4 of the day is complete. To assign the General format to a cell, click General in the Category list in the Format Cells dialog box (Figure 3–23).

Other Ways

1. On Formulas tab on Ribbon, click Date & Time, click NOW

2. Press CTRL+SEMICOLON (not a volatile date)

3. Press CTRL+SHIFT+# to format date to day-month-year

Absolute versus Relative Addressing

The next sections describe the formulas and functions needed to complete the calculations in the worksheet.

Determine necessary formulas and functions needed.
The next step is to enter the formulas that calculate the following values for January: cost of goods sold (cell B5), gross margin (cell B6), expenses (range B9:B13), total expenses (cell B14), and the operating income (cell B16). The formulas are based on the projected monthly sales in cell B4 and the assumptions in the range B19:B25.

The formulas for each column (month) are the same, except for the reference to the projected monthly sales in row 4, which varies according to the month (B4 for January, C4 for February, and so on). Thus, the formulas for January can be entered in column B and then copied to columns C through G. Table 3–6 shows the formulas for determining the January costs of goods, gross margin, expenses, total expenses, and operating income in column B.

If the formulas are entered as shown in Table 3–6 in column B for January and then copied to columns C through G (February through June) in the worksheet, Excel will adjust the cell references for each column automatically. Thus, after the copy, the February Commission expense in cell C10 would be =C4 * C20. While the cell reference C4 (February Sales) is correct, the cell reference C20 references an empty cell. The formula for cell C7 should read =C4 * B20, rather than =C4 * C20, because B20 references the Commission % value in the What-If Assumptions table. In this instance, a way is needed to keep a cell reference in a formula the same, or constant, when it is copied.

Table 3–6 Formulas for Determining Cost of Goods, Margin, Expenses, Total Expenses, and Operating Income for January

Cell	Row Title	Formula	Comment
B5	Cost of Goods Sold	=B4 * (1 − B21)	Sales times (1 minus Margin %)
B6	Gross Margin	= B4 − B5	Sales minus Cost of Goods
B9	Bonus	=IF(B4 >= B24, B19, 0)	Bonus equals value in B19 or 0
B10	Commission	=B4 * B20	Sales times Commission %
B11	Marketing	=B4 * B22	Sales times Marketing %
B12	Research and Development	=B4 * B23	Sales times Research and Development %
B13	Support, General, and Administrative	=B4 * B25	Sales times Support, General, and Administrative %
B14	Total Expenses	=SUM(B9:B13)	Sum of January Expenses
B16	Operating Income	=B6 − B14	Gross Margin minus Total Expense

To keep a cell reference constant when copying a formula or function, Excel uses a technique called absolute cell referencing. To specify an absolute cell reference in a formula, enter a dollar sign ($) before any column letters or row numbers you want to keep constant in formulas you plan to copy. For example, $B$20 is an absolute cell reference, while B20 is a relative cell reference. Both reference the same cell. The difference becomes apparent when they are copied to a destination area. A formula using the **absolute cell reference** $B$20 instructs Excel to keep the cell reference B20 constant (absolute) in the formula as it copies it to the destination area. A formula using the **relative cell reference** B20 instructs Excel to adjust the cell reference as it copies it to the destination area. A cell reference with only one dollar sign before either the column or the row is called a **mixed cell reference**. Table 3–7 gives some additional examples of absolute, relative, and mixed cell references.

Table 3–7 Examples of Absolute, Relative, and Mixed Cell References

Cell Reference	Type of Reference	Meaning
$B$20	Absolute cell reference	Both column and row references remain the same when you copy this cell, because the cell references are absolute.
B$20	Mixed reference	This cell reference is mixed. The column reference changes when you copy this cell to another column because it is relative. The row reference does not change because it is absolute.
$B20	Mixed reference	This cell reference is mixed. The column reference does not change because it is absolute. The row reference changes when you copy this cell reference to another row because it is relative.
B20	Relative cell reference	Both column and row references are relative. When copied to another cell, both the column and row in the cell reference are adjusted to reflect the new location.

To Enter a Formula Containing Absolute Cell References

The following steps enter the cost of goods formula = B4*(1 − $B$21) in cell B5 using Point mode. To enter an absolute cell reference, you can type the dollar sign ($) as part of the cell reference or enter it by pressing F4 with the insertion point in or to the right of the cell reference to change to absolute.

- Press CTRL+HOME and then click cell B5.

- Type = (equal sign), click cell B4, type *(1−b21 and then press F4 to change b21 from a relative cell reference to an absolute cell reference.

- Type) to complete the formula (Figure 3–25).

Q&A

Is an absolute reference required in this formula?

No, because a mixed cell reference could have been used. The formula in cell B4 will be copied across columns, rather than down rows. So, the formula entered in cell B4 in Step 1 could have been entered as =B4*(1-$B21), rather than =B4*(1-$B$21). That is, the formula could have included the mixed cell reference $B21, rather than the absolute cell reference $B$21. When you copy a formula across columns, the row does not change anyway. The key is to ensure that column B remains constant as you copy the formula across rows. To change the absolute cell reference to a mixed cell reference, continue to press the F4 key until you get the desired cell reference.

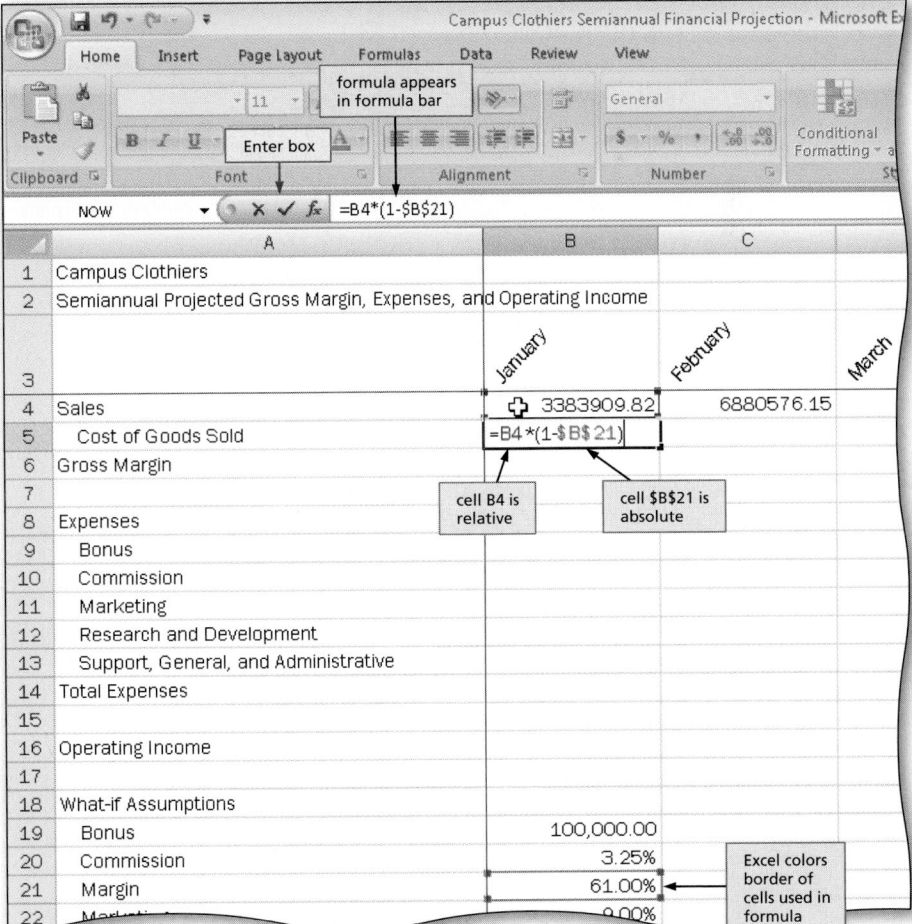

Figure 3–25

2

- Click the Enter box in the formula bar to display the result, 1319724.83, in cell B5, instead of the formula (Figure 3–26).

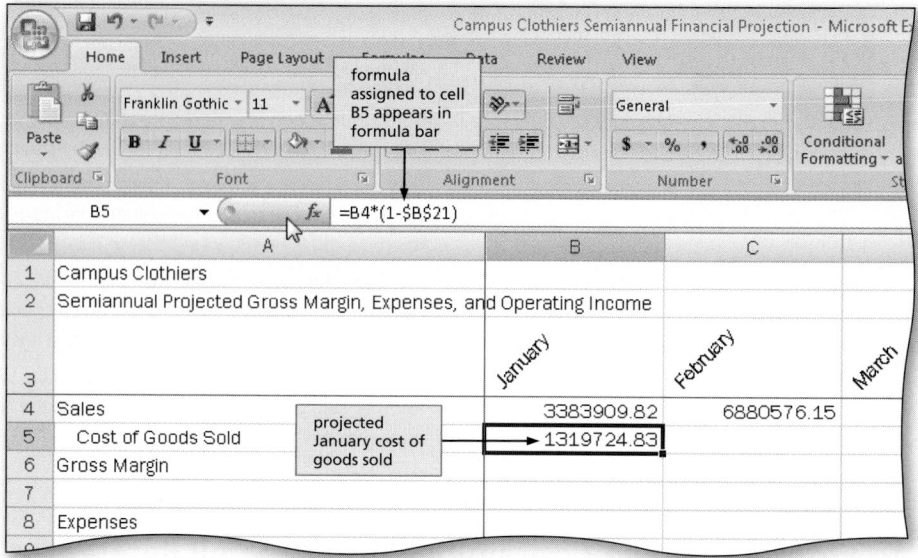

Figure 3–26

3

- Click cell B6, type = (equal sign), click cell B4, type − (minus sign), and then click cell B5.

- Click the Enter box in the formula bar to display the gross margin for January, 2064184.99, in cell B6 (Figure 3-27).

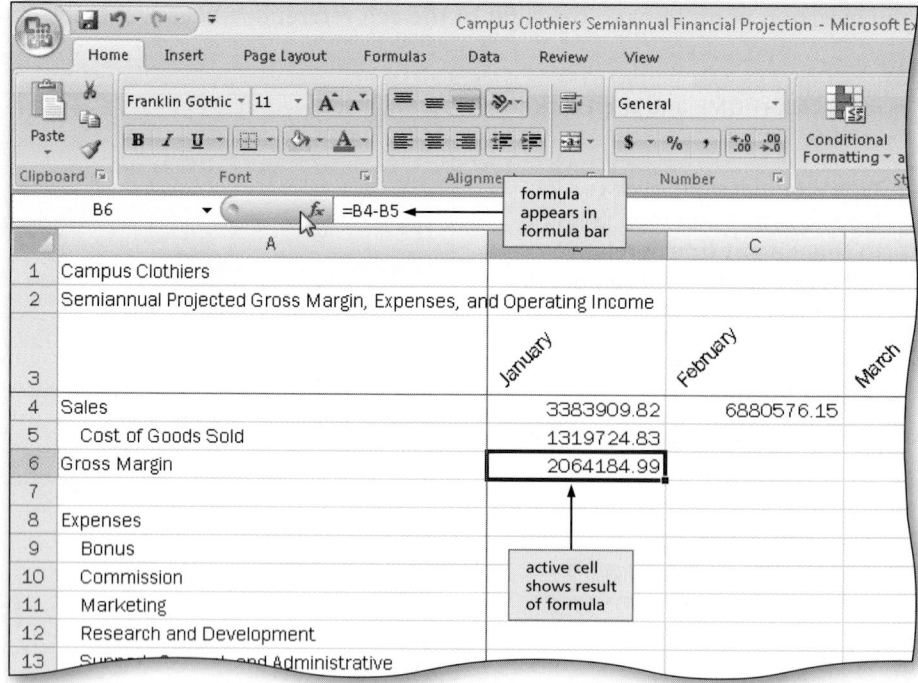

Figure 3–27

Making Decisions — The IF Function

According to the Request for New Workbook in Figure 3–2 on page EX 164, if the projected January sales in cell B4 is greater than or equal to the revenue for bonus in cell B24 (4,750,000.00), then the January bonus value in cell B9 is equal to the bonus value in cell B19 (100,000.00); otherwise, cell B9 is equal to 0. One way to assign the January bonus value in cell B9 is to check to see if the sales in cell B4 equal or exceed the revenue for bonus amount in cell B24 and, if so, then to enter 100,000.00 in cell B9. You can use this manual process for all six months by checking the values for the corresponding month.

Because the data in the worksheet changes each time a report is prepared or the figures are adjusted, however, it is preferable to have Excel assign the monthly bonus to the entries in the appropriate cells automatically. To do so, cell B9 must include a formula or function that displays 100,000.00 or 0.00 (zero), depending on whether the projected January sales in cell B4 is greater than, equal to, or less than the revenue for bonus value in cell B24.

The **IF function** is useful when you want to assign a value to a cell based on a logical test. For example, using the IF function, cell B9 can be assigned the following IF function:

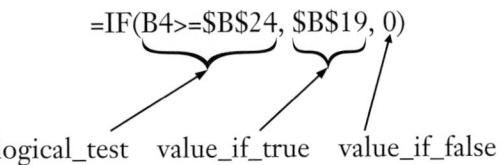

$$=IF(B4>=\$B\$24, \$B\$19, 0)$$

logical_test   value_if_true   value_if_false

The IF function instructs Excel that, if the projected January sales in cell B4 is greater than or equal to the revenue for bonus value in cell B24, then Excel should display the value 100000 in cell B19, in cell B9. If the projected January sales in cell B4 is less than the revenue for bonus value in cell B24, then Excel displays a 0 (zero) in cell B9.

The general form of the IF function is:

$$=IF(logical\_test, value\_if\_true, value\_if\_false)$$

The argument, logical_test, is made up of two expressions and a comparison operator. Each expression can be a cell reference, a number, text, a function, or a formula. Valid comparison operators, their meaning, and examples of their use in IF functions are shown in Table 3–8. The argument, value_if_true, is the value you want Excel to display in the cell when the logical test is true. The argument, value_if_false, is the value you want Excel to display in the cell when the logical test is false.

Table 3–8 Comparison Operators

Comparison Operator	Meaning	Example
=	Equal to	=IF(H7 = 0, J6 ^ H4, L9 + D3)
<	Less than	=IF(C34 * W3 < K7, $K$6, L33 - 5)
>	Greater than	=IF(MIN(K8:K12) > 75, 1, 0)
>=	Greater than or equal to	=IF(P8 >= $H$6, J7 / V4, 7.5)
<=	Less than or equal to	=IF(G7 - G2 <= 23, L$9, 35 / Q2)
<>	Not equal to	=IF(B1 <> 0, "No","Yes")

To Enter an IF Function

The following steps assign the IF function =IF(B4>=$B$24,$B$19,0) to cell B9. This IF function determines whether or not the worksheet assigns a bonus for January.

• Click cell B9. Type
=if(b4>=b24,
b19,0) in the cell
(Figure 3–28).

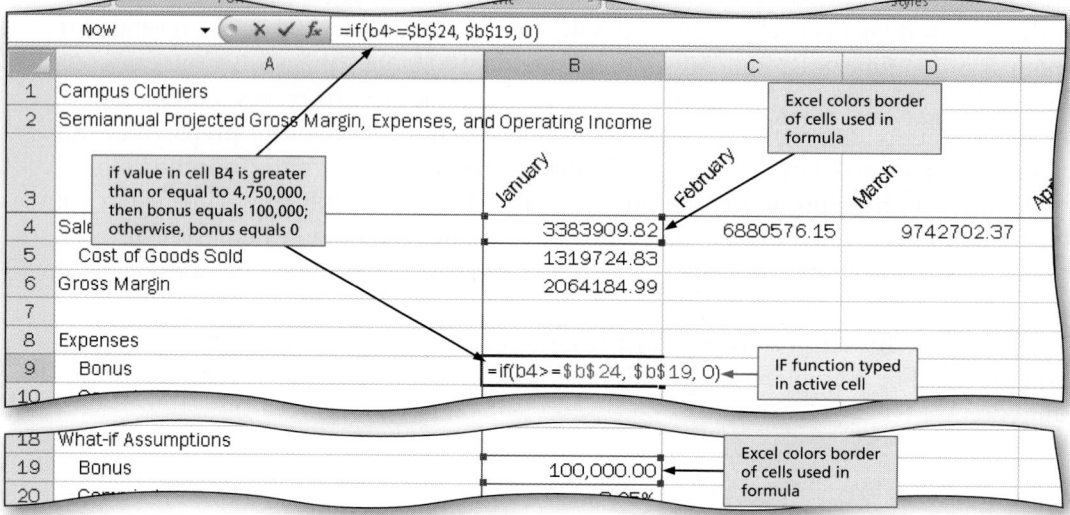

Figure 3–28

• Click the Enter box
in the formula bar
to display 0 in
cell B9 (Figure 3–29),
because the value in
cell B4 (3383909.82)
is less than the value
in cell B24 (4,750,000)
(Figure 3–29).

  Why does the value
0 display in cell B9?

The value that Excel
displays in cell B9
depends on the
values assigned to
cells B4, B19, and
B24. For example, if the value for January sales in cell B4 is reduced below 4,750,000.00, then
the IF function in cell B9 will cause Excel to display a 0. If you change the bonus in cell B19 from
100,000.00 to another number and the value in cell B4 is greater than or equal to the value in
cell B24, it will change the results in cell B9 as well. Finally, increasing the revenue for bonus
in cell B24 so that it is greater than the value in cell B4 will change the result in cell B9.

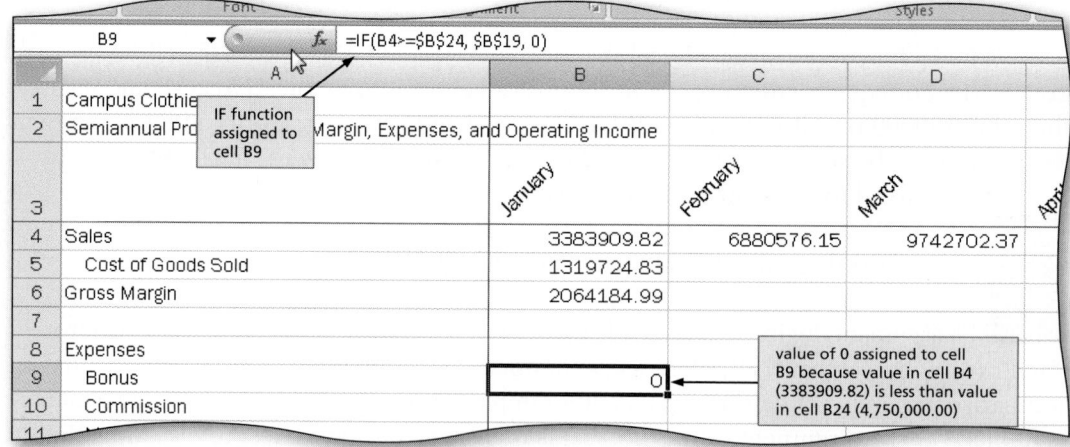

Figure 3–29

Other Ways

1. On Formulas tab on
   Ribbon, click Logical
   button, click IF

2. Click Insert Function
   box in formula bar, click
   Logical in 'Or select a
   category list', click IF
   in drop-down list, click
   OK button

To Enter the Remaining January Formulas

The January commission expense in cell B10 is equal to the sales in cell B4 times the commission assumption in cell B20 (3.25%). The January marketing expense in cell B11 is equal to the projected January sales in cell B4 times the marketing assumption in cell B22 (9.00%). Similar formulas determine the remaining January expenses in cells B12 and B13.

The total expenses value in cell B14 is equal to the sum of the expenses in the range B9:B13. The operating income in cell B16 is equal to the gross margin in cell B6 minus the total expenses in cell B14. The formulas are short, and therefore, they are typed in the following steps, rather than entered using Point mode.

BTW

Replacing a Formula with a Constant
You can replace a formula with its result so it remains constant. Do the following: (1) Click the cell with the formula; (2) press F2 or click in the formula bar; (3) press F9 to display the value in the formula bar; and (4) press the ENTER key.

1 Click cell B10. Type =b4*b20 and then press the DOWN ARROW key. Type =b4*b22 and then press the DOWN ARROW key. Type =b4*b23 and then press the DOWN ARROW key. Type =b4*b25 and then press the DOWN ARROW key.

2 With cell B14 selected, click the Sum button on the Home tab on the Ribbon twice. Click cell B16. Type =b6-b14 and then press the ENTER key (Figure 3–30a).

3 Press CTRL+ACCENT MARK (`) to instruct Excel to display the formulas version of the worksheet (Figure 3–30b).

4 When you are finished viewing the formulas version, press CTRL+ACCENT MARK (`) to instruct Excel to display the values version of the worksheet.

Q&A Why should I view the formulas version of the worksheet?

Viewing the formulas version (Figure 3–30b) of the worksheet allows you to check the formulas assigned to the range B5:B16. Recall that formulas were entered in lowercase. You can see that Excel converts all the formulas from lowercase to uppercase.

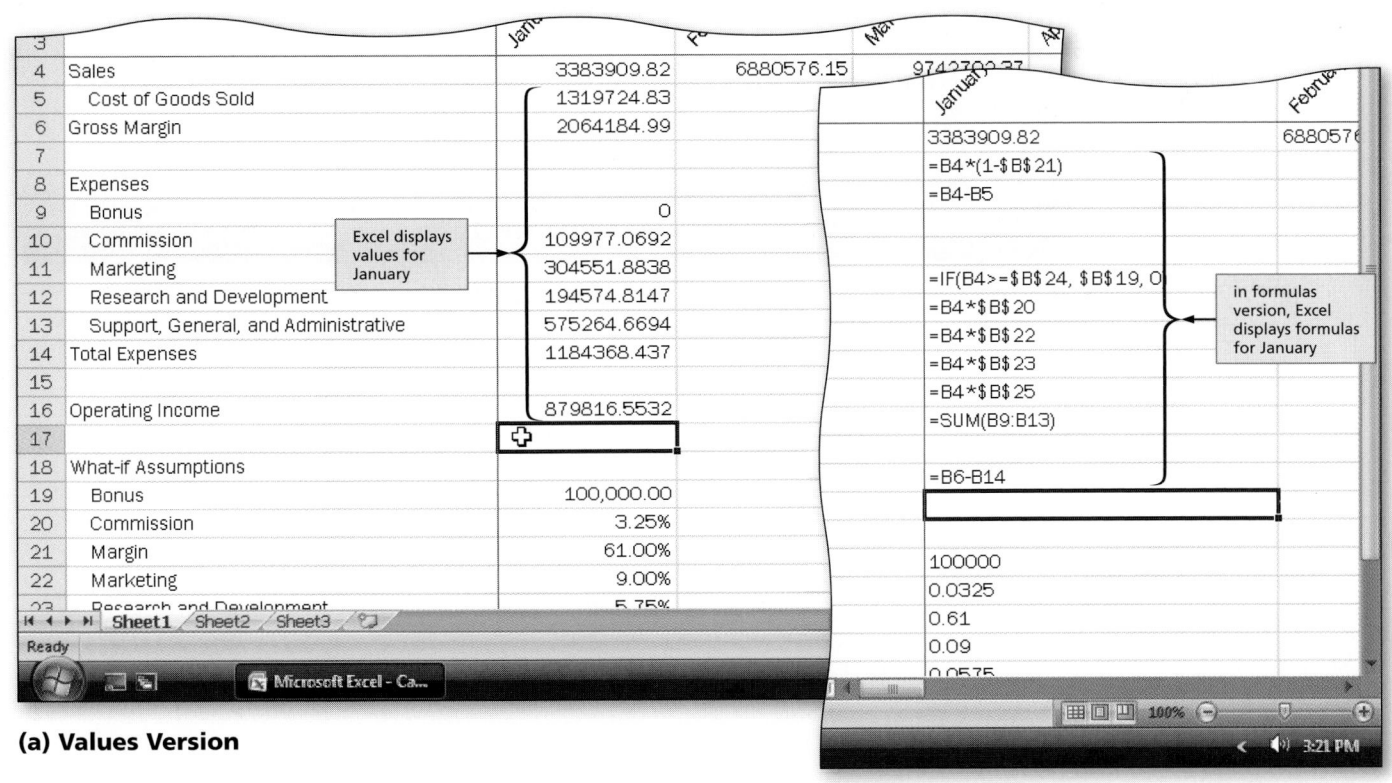

(a) Values Version

(b) Formulas Version

Figure 3–30

To Copy Formulas with Absolute Cell References Using the Fill Handle

The following steps show how to use the fill handle to copy the January formulas in column B to the other five months in columns C through G.

- Select the range B5:B16 and then point to the fill handle in the lower-right corner of cell B16 (Figure 3–31).

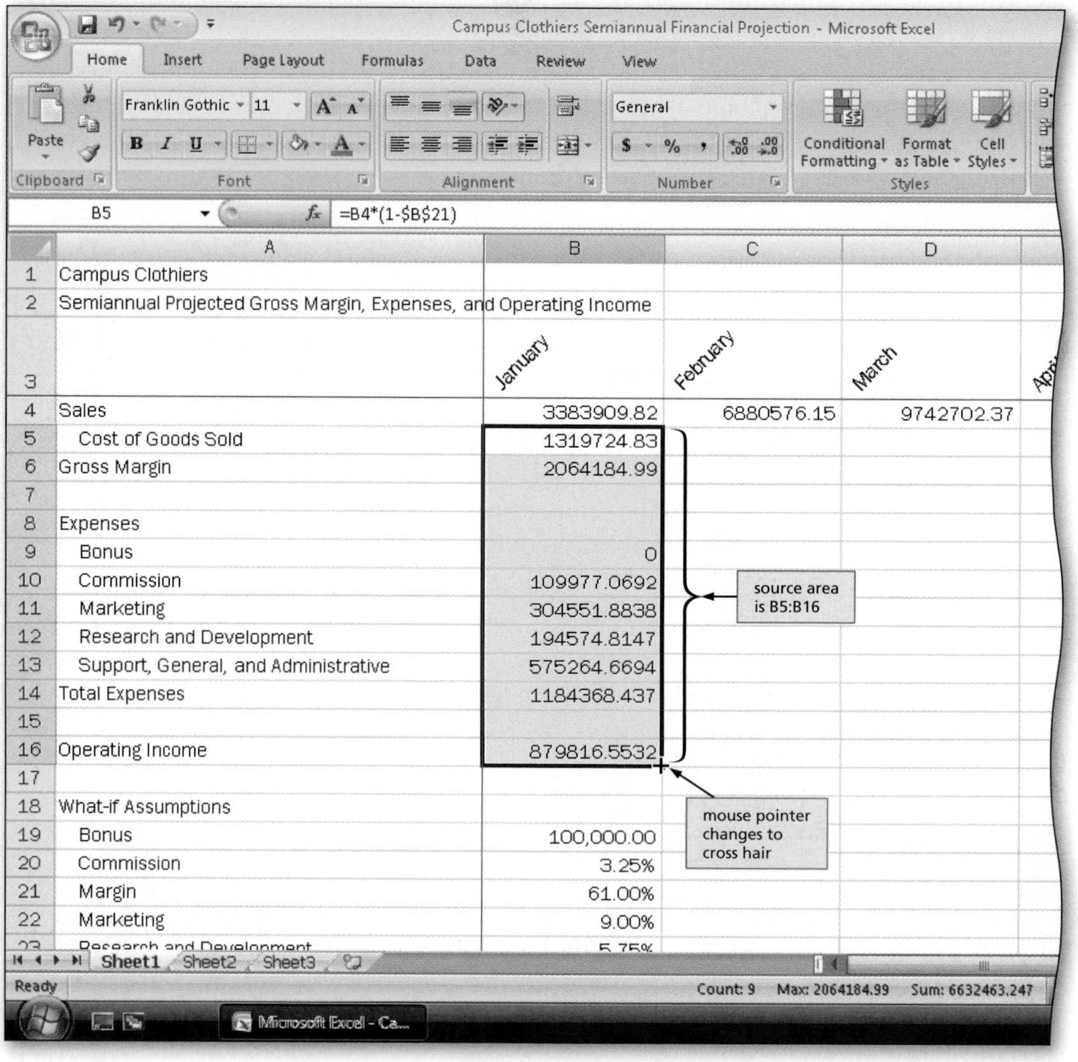

Figure 3–31

2

• Drag the fill handle to the right to select the destination area C5:G16 to copy the formulas from the source area (B5:B16) to the destination area (C5:G16) and display the calculated amounts and Auto Fill Options button (Figure 3–32).

Q&A What happens to the formulas after the copy is made?

Because the formulas in the range B5:B16 use absolute cell references, the formulas still refer to the current values in the Assumptions table when the formulas are copied to the range C5:G16.

Q&A What happened to columns B, C, and D?

As shown in Figure 3–32, as the fill handle is dragged to the right, columns B, C, and D no longer appear on the screen. Column A, however, remains on the screen, because the row titles were frozen earlier in this chapter.

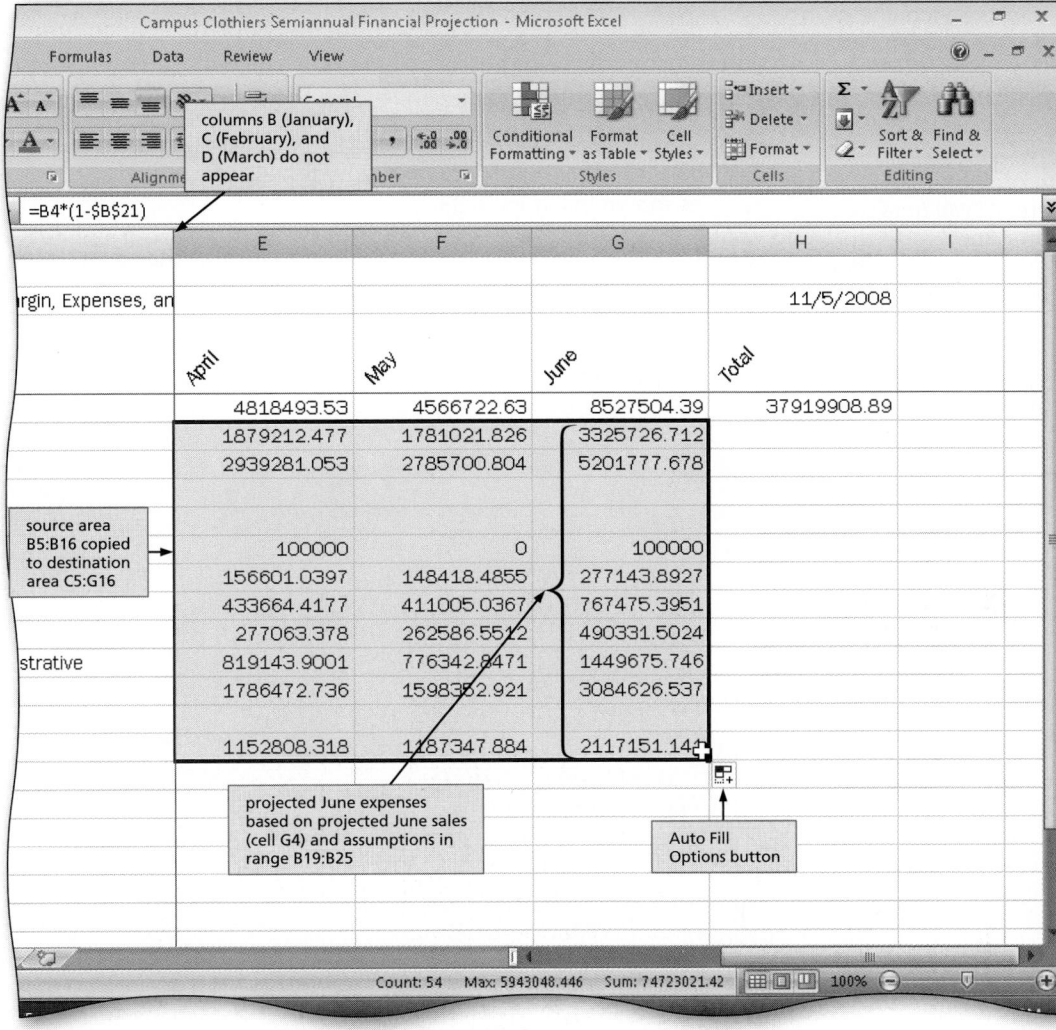

Figure 3–32

BTW

Error Messages
When Excel cannot calculate a formula, it displays an error message in a cell. These error messages always begin with a number sign (#). The more commonly occurring error messages are: #DIV/0! (tries to divide by zero); #NAME? (uses a name Excel does not recognize); #N/A (refers to a value not available); #NULL! (specifies an invalid intersection of two areas); #NUM! (uses a number incorrectly); #REF (refers to a cell that is not valid); #VALUE! (uses an incorrect argument or operand); and ##### (cell not wide enough to display entire entry).

To Determine Row Totals in Nonadjacent Cells

The following steps determine the row totals in column H. To determine the row totals using the Sum button, select only the cells in column H containing numbers in adjacent cells to the left. If, for example, you select the range H5:H16, Excel will display 0s as the sum of empty rows in cells H7, H8, and H15.

1 Select the range H5:H6. Hold down the CTRL key and select the range H9:H14 and cell H16 as shown in Figure 3–33.

2 Click the Sum button on the Ribbon to display the row totals in column H (Figure 3–33).

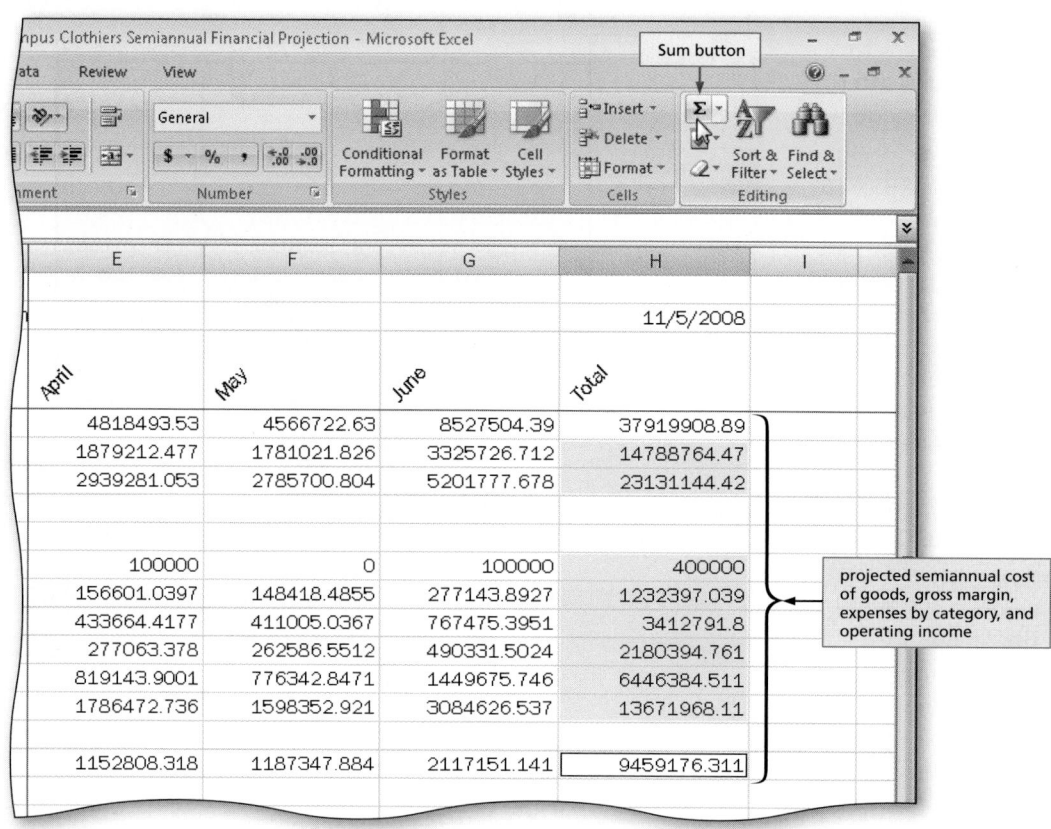

Figure 3–33

BTW

Toggle Commands
Many of the commands on the Ribbon, in the galleries, and the shortcut keys function as a toggle. For example, if you click the Freeze Panes command on the Freeze Panes gallery, the command changes to Unfreeze Panes the next time you view the gallery. These types of commands work like an on-off switch, or toggle.

To Unfreeze the Worksheet Titles and Save the Workbook

All the text, data, and formulas have been entered into the worksheet. The following steps unfreeze the titles and save the workbook using its current file name, Campus Clothiers Semiannual Financial Projection.

1 Press CTRL+HOME to select cell B4 and view the upper-left corner of the screen.

2 Click the View tab on the Ribbon and then click the Freeze Panes button on the Ribbon to display the Freeze Panes gallery (Figure 3–34).

3 Click Unfreeze Panes in the Freeze Panes gallery to unfreeze the titles.

4 Click the Home tab on the Ribbon and then click the Save button on the Quick Access Toolbar.

Q&A Why does pressing CTRL+HOME select cell B4?

When the titles are frozen and you press CTRL+HOME, Excel selects the upper-left cell of the unfrozen section of the worksheet. For example, in Step 1 of the previous steps, Excel selected cell B4. When the titles are unfrozen, then pressing CTRL+HOME selects cell A1.

BTW

Work Days
Assume that you have two dates: one in cell F3 and the other in cell F4. The date in cell F3 is your starting date and the date in cell F4 is the ending date. To calculate the work days between the two dates (excludes weekends), use the following formula: =NETWORKDAYS(F3, F4). For this function to work, make sure the Analysis ToolPak add-in is installed. You can install it on the Add-Ins page of the Excel Options dialog box.

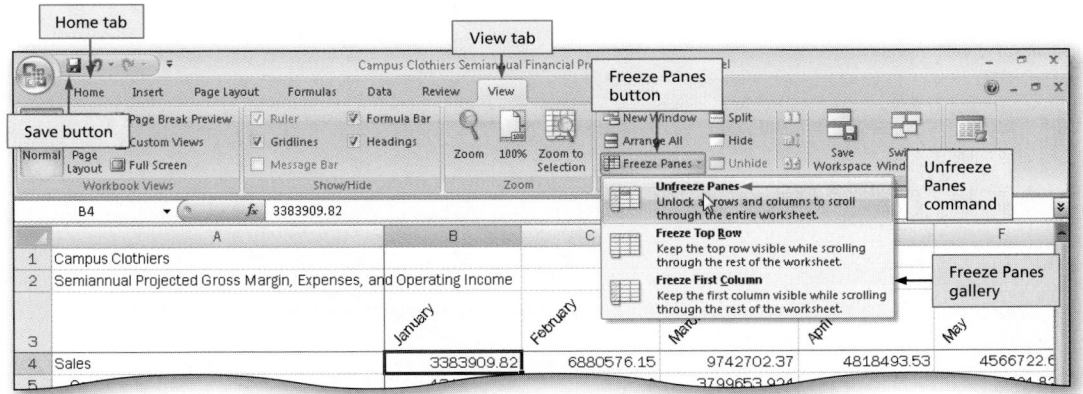

Figure 3–34

Nested Forms of the IF Function

A **nested IF function** is one in which the action to be taken for the true or false case includes yet another IF function. The second IF function is considered to be nested, or layered, within the first. Study the nested IF function below, which determines the eligibility of a person to vote. Assume the following in this example: (1) the nested IF function is assigned to cell K12, which instructs Excel to display one of three messages in the cell; (2) cell H12 contains a person's age; and (3) cell I12 contains a Y or N, based on whether the person is registered to vote.

=IF(H12>=18, IF(I12="Y","Registered","Eligible and Not Registered"),"Not Eligible to Register")

The nested IF function instructs Excel to display one, and only one, of the following three messages in cell K12: (1) Registered; or (2) Eligible and Not Registered; or (3) Not Eligible to Register.

You can nest IF functions as deep as you want, but after you get beyond a nest of three IF functions, the logic becomes difficult to follow and alternative solutions, such as the use of multiple cells and simple IF functions, should be considered.

Formatting the Worksheet

The worksheet created thus far shows the financial projections for the six-month period, from January to June. Its appearance is uninteresting, however, even though some minimal formatting (formatting assumptions numbers, changing the column widths, and formatting the date) was performed earlier. This section will complete the formatting of the worksheet to make the numbers easier to read and to emphasize the titles, assumptions, categories, and totals.

Plan
Ahead

Identify how to format various elements of the worksheet.
The worksheet will be formatted in the following manner so it appears as shown in Figure 3–35: (1) format the numbers; (2) format the worksheet title, column titles, row titles, and operating income row; and (3) format the assumptions table. Numbers in heading rows and total rows should be formatted with a currency symbol. Other dollar amounts should be formatted with a Comma style. The assumptions table should be diminished in its formatting so it does not distract from the main calculations and data in the worksheet. Assigning the data in the assumptions table a font size of 8 point would set it apart from other data formatted with a font size of 11 point.

Selecting Nonadjacent Ranges
One of the more difficult tasks to learn is selecting nonadjacent ranges. To complete this task, do not hold down the CTRL key when you select the first range because Excel will consider the current active cell to be the first selection. Once the first range is selected, hold down the CTRL key and drag through the nonadjacent ranges. If a desired range is not visible in the window, use the scroll arrows to view the range. It is not necessary to hold down the CTRL key while you scroll.

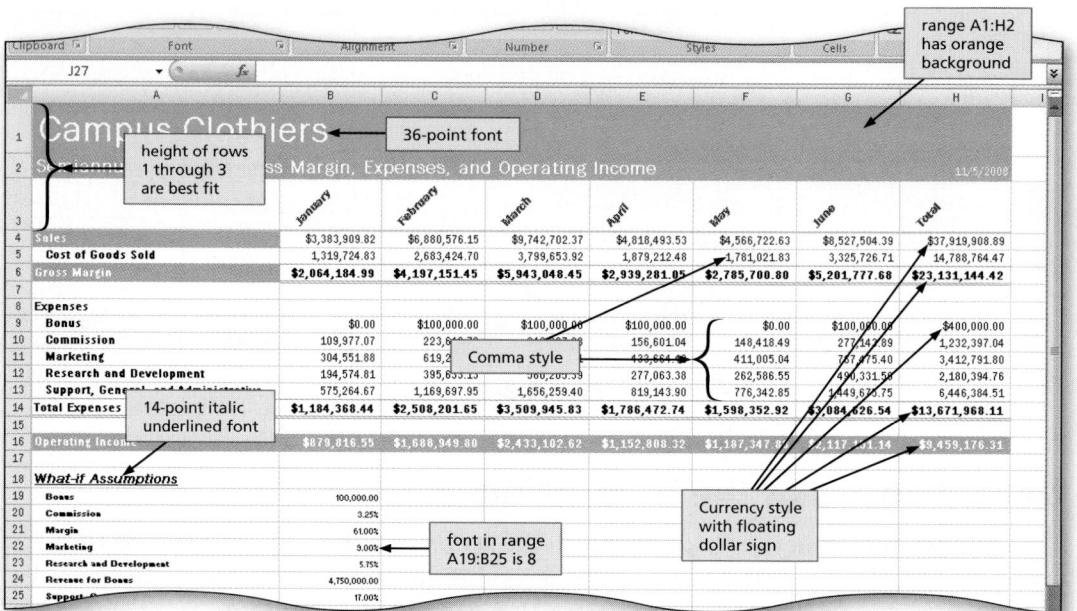

Figure 3–35

To Assign Formats to Nonadjacent Ranges

The numbers in the range B4:H16 are to be formatted as follows:
1. Assign the Currency style with a floating dollar sign to rows 4, 6, 9, 14, and 16.
2. Assign a Comma style to rows 5 and 10 through 13.

To assign a Currency style with a floating dollar sign, use the Format Cells dialog box rather than the Accounting Style button on the Ribbon, which assigns a fixed dollar sign. Also use the Format Cells dialog box to assign the Comma style, because the Comma Style button on the Ribbon assigns a format that displays a dash (-) when a cell has a value of 0. The specifications for this worksheet call for displaying a value of 0 as 0.00 (see cell B9 in Figure 3–35), rather than as a dash. To create a Comma style using the Format Cells dialog box, you can assign a Currency style with no dollar sign. The following steps assign formats to the numbers in rows 4 through 16.

1

- Select the range B4:H4.

- While holding down the CTRL key, select the nonadjacent ranges B6:H6, B9:H9, B14:H14, and B16:H16, and then release the CTRL key.

- Click the Format Cells: Number Dialog Box Launcher on the Ribbon to display the Format Cells dialog box (Figure 3–36).

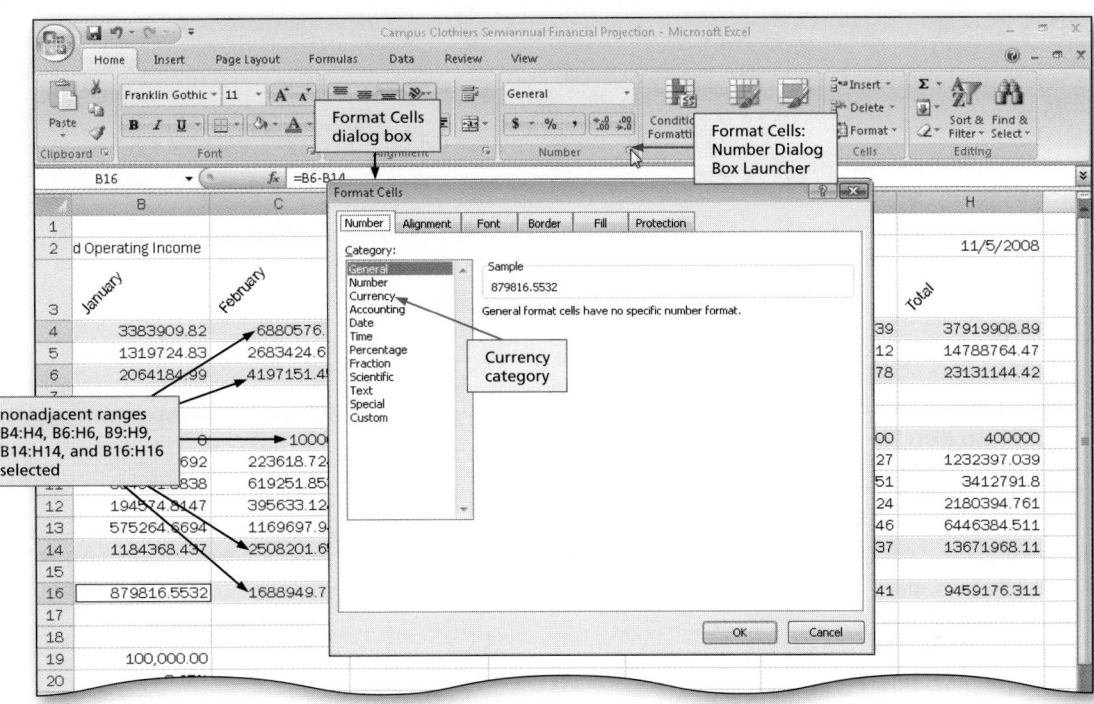

Figure 3–36

2

- Click Currency in the Category list, select 2 in the Decimal places box, click $ in the Symbol list to ensure a dollar sign shows, and click the black font color ($1,234.10) in the Negative numbers list (Figure 3–37).

Q&A

Why was the particular style chosen for the negative numbers?

In accounting, negative numbers often are shown with parentheses surrounding the value rather than with a negative sign preceding the value. Thus, the format (1,234.10) in the

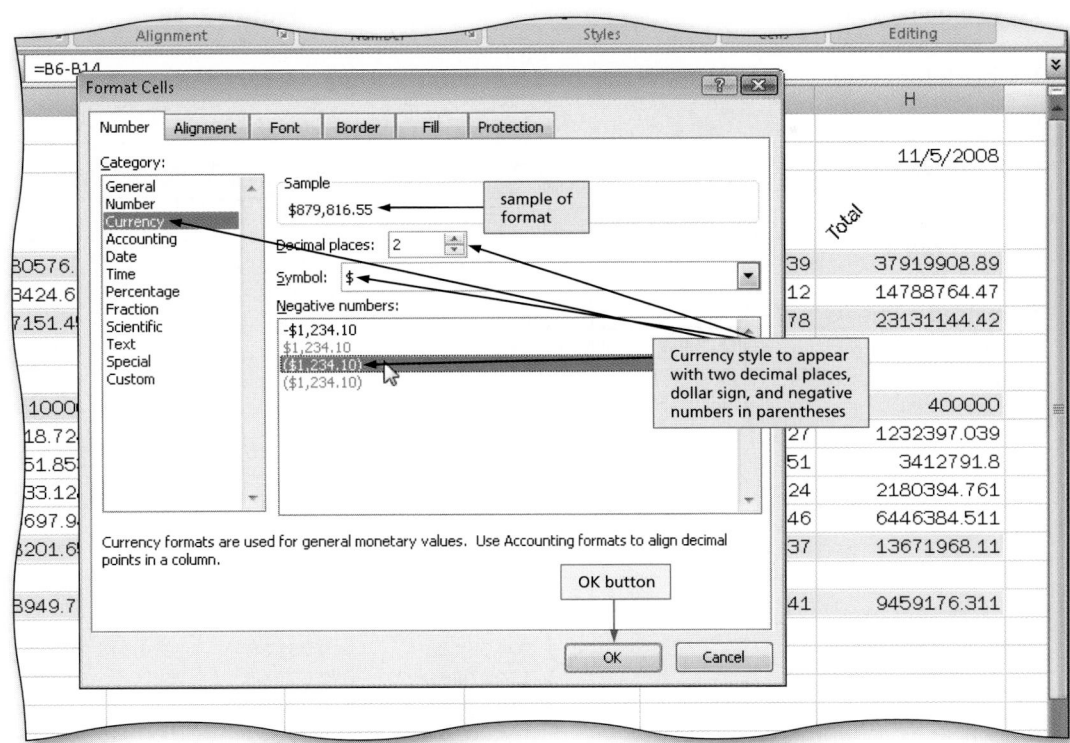

Figure 3–37

Negative numbers list was clicked. The data being used in this chapter contains no negative numbers. However, you must select a format for negative numbers, and you must be consistent if you are choosing different formats in a column, otherwise the decimal points may not line up.

• Click the OK button.

• Select the range B5:H5.

• While holding down the CTRL key, select the range B10:H13, and then release the CTRL key.

• Click the Format Cells: Number Dialog Box Launcher on the Ribbon to display the Format Cells dialog box.

• When Excel displays the Format Cells dialog box, click Currency in the Category list, select 2 in the Decimal places box, click None in the Symbol list so a dollar sign does not show, and click the black font color (1,234.10) in the Negative numbers list (Figure 3–38).

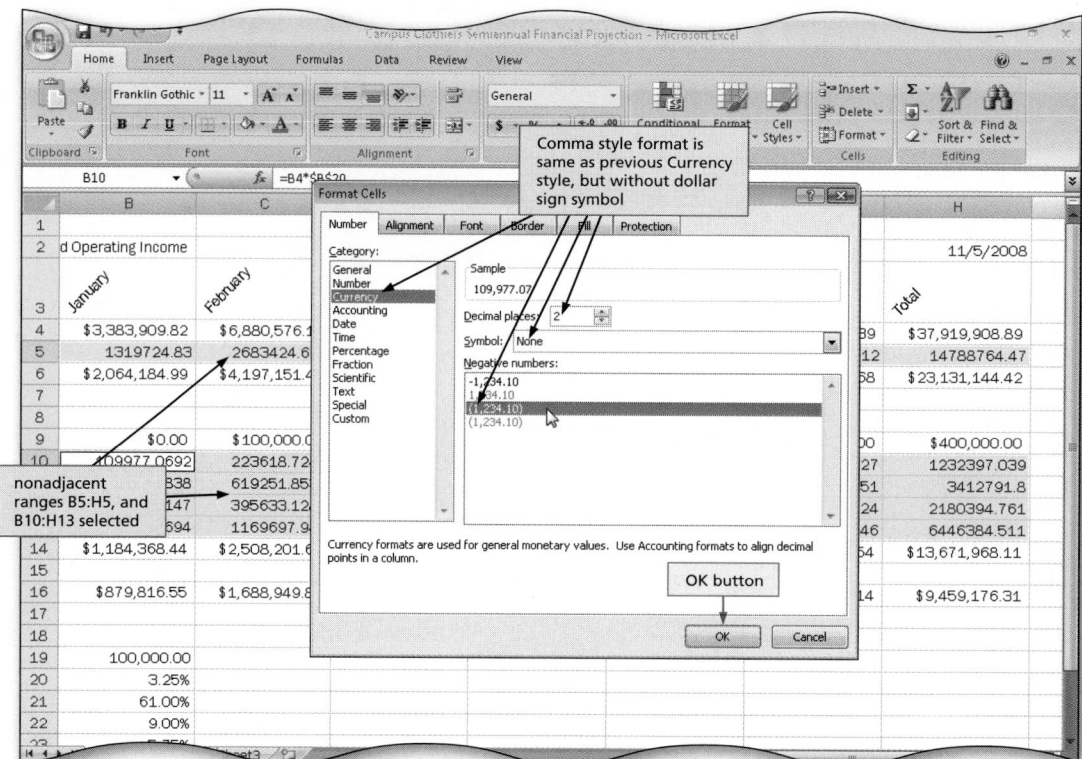

Figure 3–38

• Click the OK button.

• Press CTRL+HOME to select cell A1 to display the formatted numbers as shown in Figure 3–39.

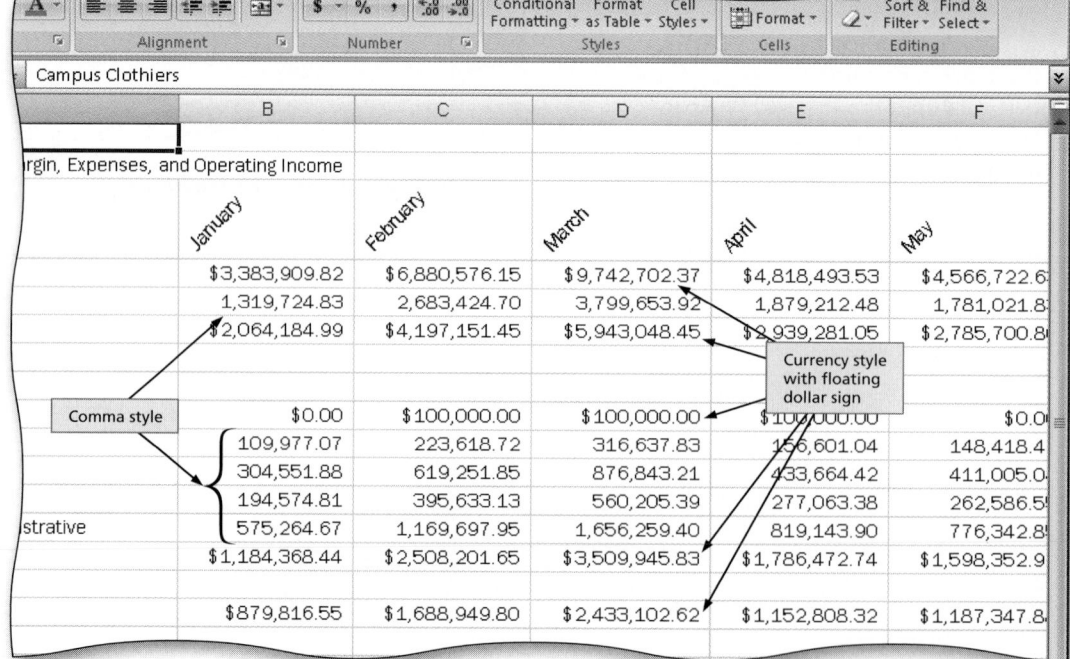

Figure 3–39

Other Ways

1. Right-click range, click Format Cells on shortcut menu, click Number tab, click category in Category list, select format, click OK button

2. Press CTRL+1, click Number tab, click category in Category list, select format, click OK button

To Format the Worksheet Titles

The following steps emphasize the worksheet titles in cells A1 and A2 by changing the font type, size, and color. The steps also format all of the row headers in column A with a Bold font style.

1

- Click the column A heading to select column A.

- Click the Bold button on the Ribbon to bold all of the data in column A (Figure 3–40).

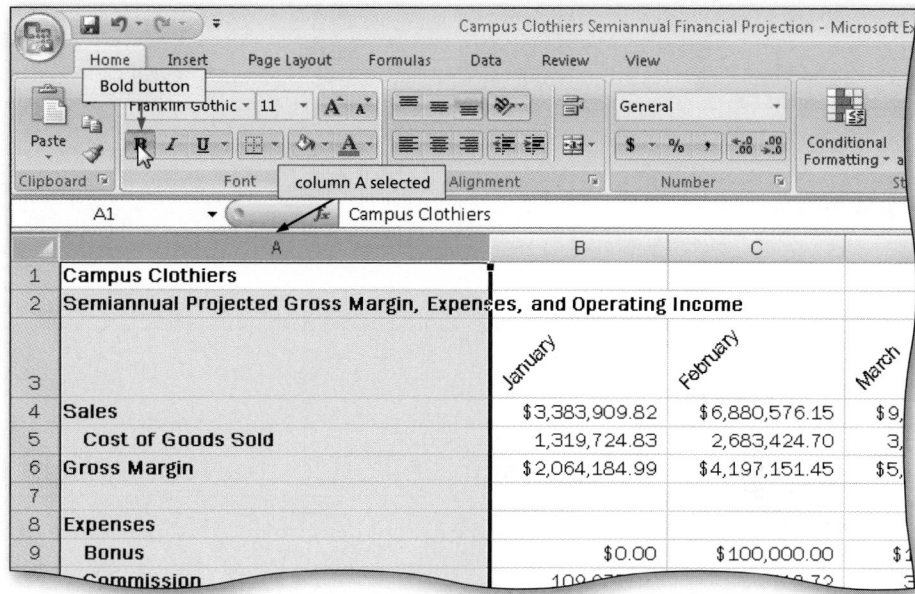

Figure 3–40

2

- Click cell A1 to select it. Click the Font Size box arrow on the Ribbon, and then click 36 in the Font Size list.

- Click cell A2, click the Font Size box arrow, and then click 18 in the Font Size list (Figure 3–41).

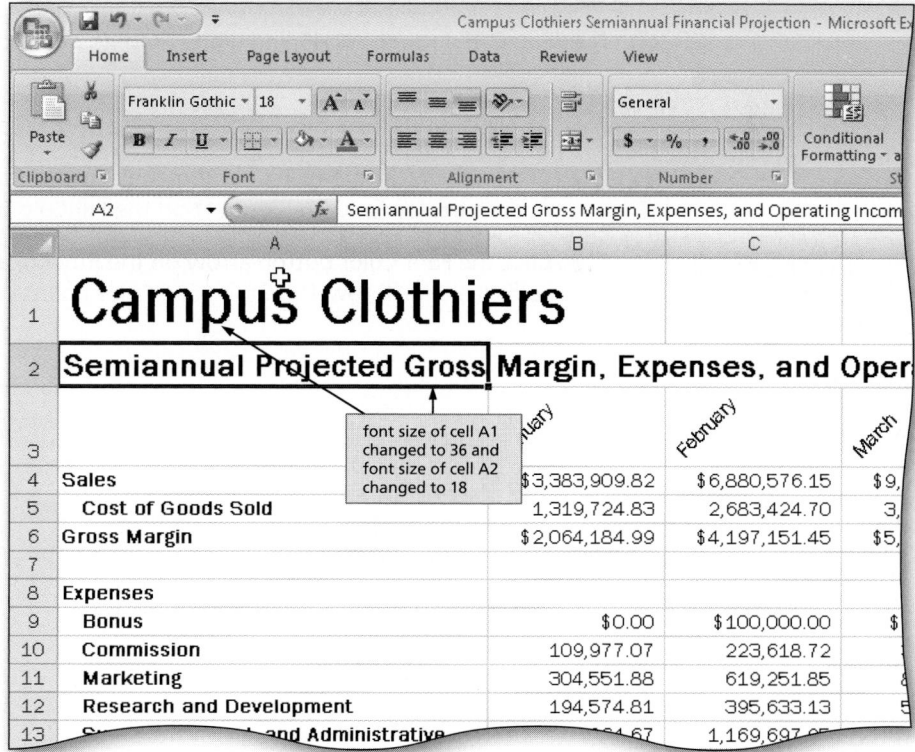

Figure 3–41

3

- Select the range A1:H2 and then click the Fill Color button arrow on the Ribbon.

- Click Orange, Accent 1 (column 5, row 1) on the Fill Color palette.

- Click the Font Color button arrow on the Ribbon and then select White, Background 1 (column 1, row 1) on the Font Color palette (Figure 3–42).

Figure 3–42

Other Ways

1. Right-click range, click Format Cells on shortcut menu, click Fill tab to color background (or click Font tab to color font), click OK button

2. Press CTRL+1, click Fill tab to color background (or click Font tab to color font), click OK button

To Assign Cell Styles to Nonadjacent Rows and Colors to a Cell

The next step to improving the appearance of the worksheet is to format the heading in row 3 and the totals in rows 4, 14, and 16. The following steps format the heading in row 3 with the Heading 3 cell style and the totals in rows 4, 14, and 16 with the Total cell style. Cell A4 also is formatted.

1 Select the range A3:H3 and apply the Heading 3 cell style.

2 Select the range A6:H6 and while holding down the CTRL key, select the ranges A14:H14 and A16:H16.

3 Apply the Total cell style.

4 Click cell A4, click the Fill Color button arrow on the Ribbon, and then click the Orange, Accent 1 color (column 5, row 1) on the Fill Color palette.

5 Click the Font Color button arrow on the Ribbon, and then click the White, Background 1 color (column 1, row 1) on the Font Color palette (Figure 3–43).

The Fill and Font Color Button
You may have noticed that the color bar at the bottom of the Fill Color and Font Color buttons on the Home tab on the Ribbon (Figure 3-42) changes to the most recently selected color. To apply this same color to a cell background or text, select a cell and then click the Fill Color button to use the color as a background or click the Font Color button to use the color as a font color.

		January	Februa	Ma
3				
4	Sales	$3,383,909.82	$6,880,576.15	$9,
5	Cost of Goods Sold	1,319,724.83	2,683,424.70	3,
6	Gross Margin	$2,064,184.99	$4,197,151.45	$5,94
7				
8	Expenses			
9	Bonus	$0.00	$100,000.00	
10	Commission	109,977.07	223,618.72	3
11	Marketing	304,551.88	619,251.85	
12	Research and Development	194,574.81	395,633.13	
13	Support, General, and Administrative	575,264.67	1,168,697.95	1,
14	Total Expenses	$1,184,368.44	$2,508,201.65	$3,5
15				
16	Operating Income	$879,816.55	$1,688,949.80	$2,4
17				

Heading 3 cell style applied

font color and fill color changed

Total cell style applied

Figure 3–43

Copying a Cell's Format Using the Format Painter Button

Using the Format Painter button on the Ribbon, you can format a cell quickly by copying a cell's format to another cell or a range of cells.

To Copy a Cell's Format Using the Format Painter Button

The following steps format cells A6, A14, and the range A16:H16 using the Format Painter button.

- Select cell A4.

- Click the Format Painter button on the Ribbon and then move the mouse pointer onto the worksheet to cause the mouse pointer to change to a block plus sign with a paintbrush (Figure 3–44).

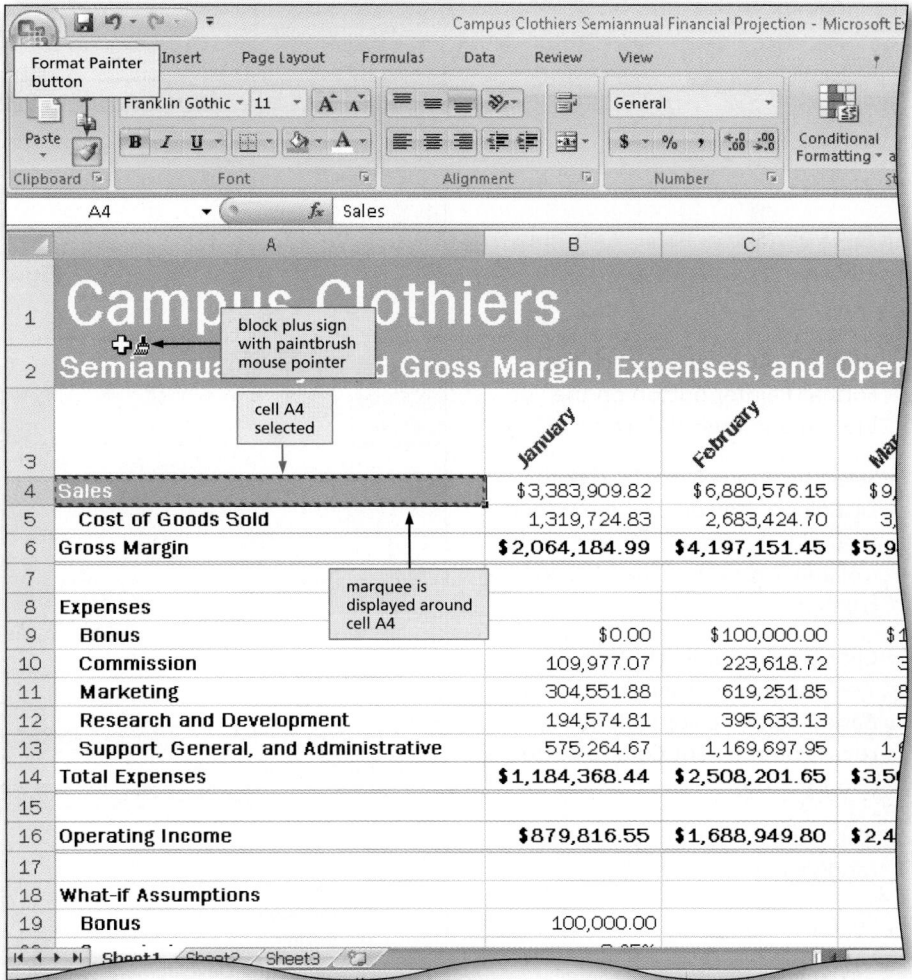

Figure 3–44

- Click cell A6 to assign the format of cell A4 to cell A6 (Figure 3–45).

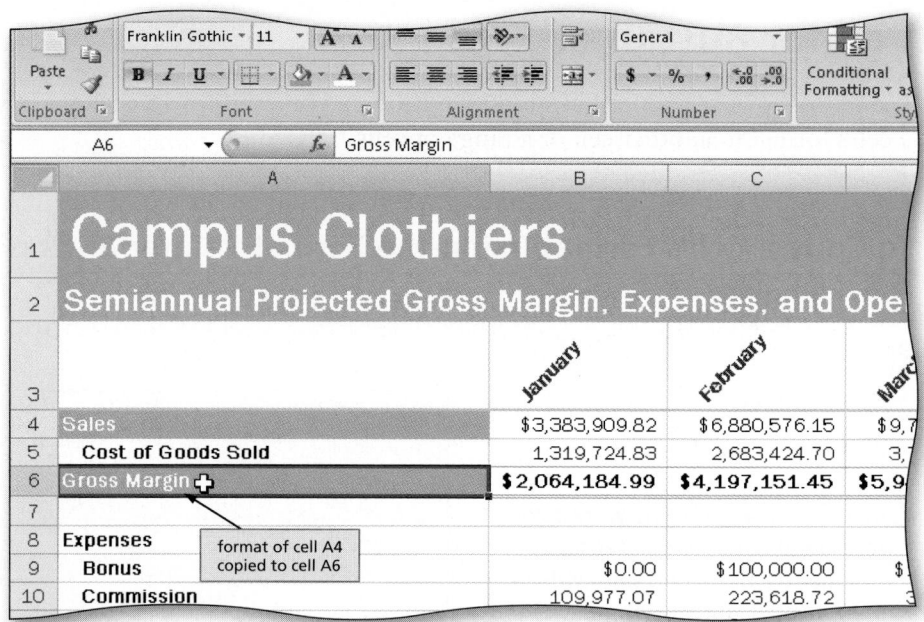

Figure 3–45

- With cell A6 selected, click the Format Painter button on the Ribbon and then click cell A16.

- Select the range B16:H16, click the Fill Color button on the Ribbon, and then click the Orange, Accent 1 color (column 5, row 1) on the Fill Color palette.

- Click the Font Color button on the Ribbon, and then click the Background 1 color (column 1, row 1) on the Font Color palette (Figure 3–46).

- Apply the Currency style to the range B16:G16.

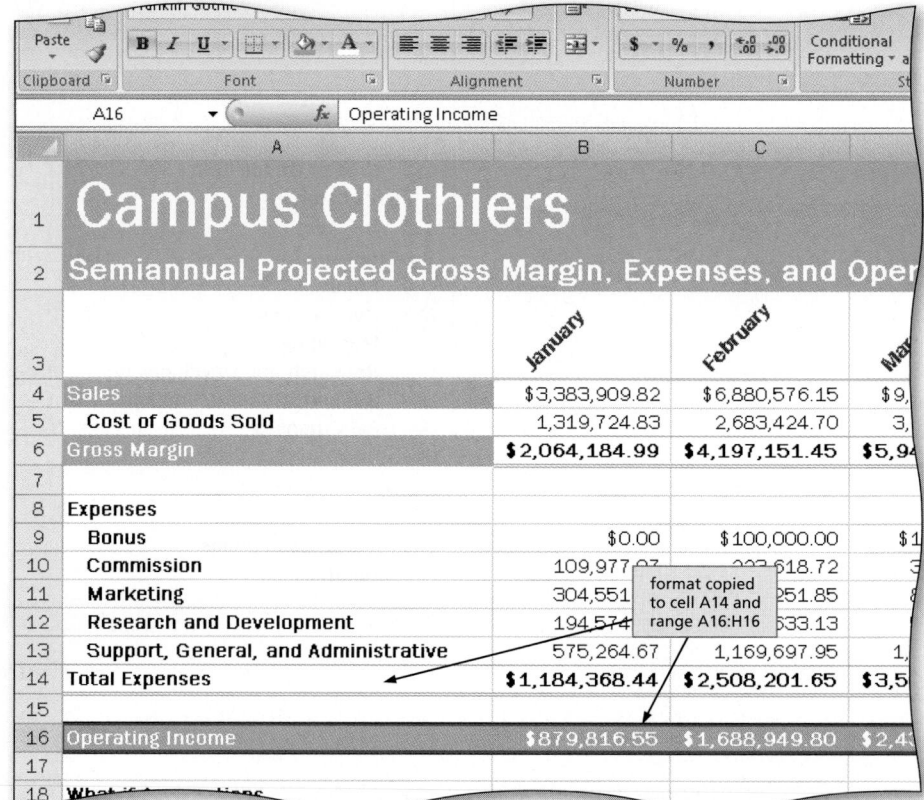

Figure 3–46

Other Ways
1. Click Copy button, select cell, click Paste button, click Paste Special command on Paste menu, click Formats, click OK button 　 2. Double-click Format Painter button

To Format the What-If Assumptions Table and Save the Workbook

The last step to improving the appearance of the worksheet is to format the What-If Assumptions table in the range A18:B25. The specifications in Figure 3–35 on page EX 196 require a 14-point italic underlined font for the title in cell A18 and 8-point font in the range A19:B25. The following steps format the What-If Assumptions table.

1 Scroll down to view rows 18 through 25 and then click cell A18.

2 Click the Font Size box arrow on the Ribbon and then click 14 in the Font Size list. Click the Italic button and then click the Underline button on the Ribbon.

3 Select the range A19:B25, click the Font Size button on the Ribbon, and then click 8 in the Font Size list.

4 Click cell D25 to deselect the range A19:B25 and display the What-If Assumptions table as shown in Figure 3–47.

5 Click the Save button on the Quick Access Toolbar.

Q&A What happens when I click the Italic and Underline buttons?

Recall that when you assign the italic font style to a cell, Excel slants the characters slightly to the right as shown in cell A18 in Figure 3–47. The **underline** format underlines only the characters in the cell, rather than the entire cell, as is the case when you assign a cell a bottom border.

BTW

Painting a Format to Nonadjacent Ranges
Double-click the Format Painter button on the Home tab on the Ribbon and then drag through the nonadjacent ranges to paint the formats to the ranges. Click the Format Painter button to deactivate it.

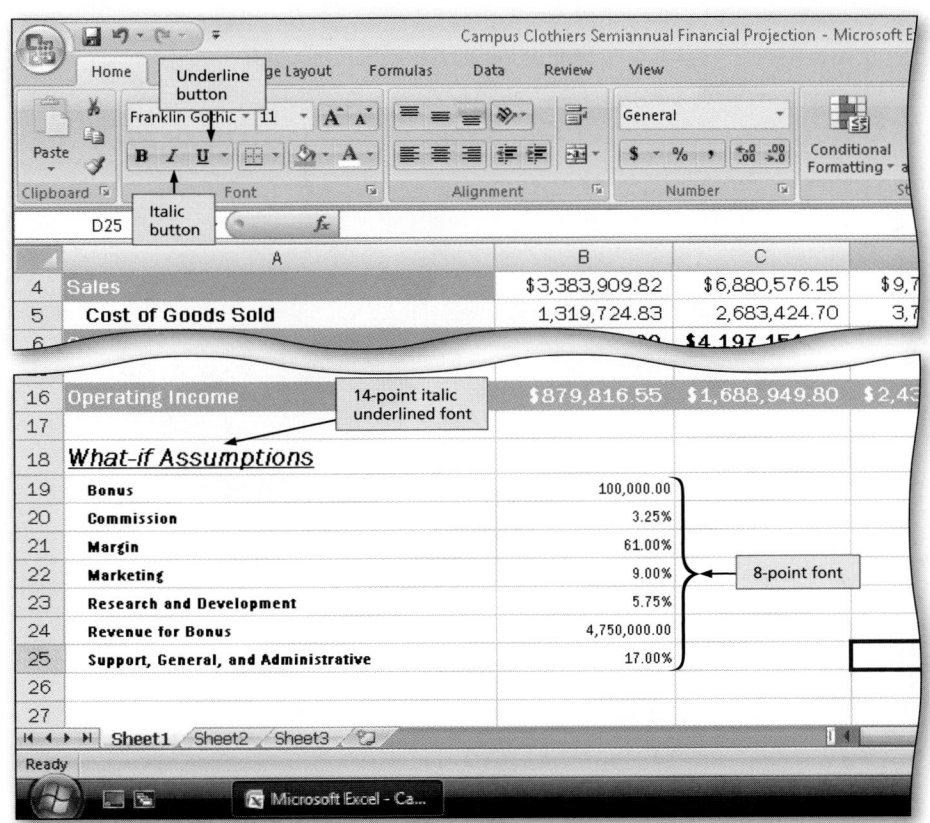

Figure 3–47

Adding a 3-D Pie Chart to the Workbook

The next step in the chapter is to draw the 3-D Pie chart on a separate sheet in the workbook, as shown in Figure 3–48. Use a **Pie chart** to show the relationship or proportion of parts to a whole. Each slice (or wedge) of the pie shows what percent that slice contributes to the total (100%).

Plan Ahead

> **Specify how the chart should convey necessary information.**
> The 3-D Pie chart in Figure 3–48 shows the contribution of each month's projected operating income to the six-month projected operating income. The 3-D Pie chart makes it easy to evaluate the contribution of one month in comparison to the other months.
>
> Unlike the 3-D Column chart created in Chapter 1, the 3-D Pie chart shown in Figure 3–48 is not embedded in the worksheet. Instead, the Pie chart resides on a separate sheet, called a **chart sheet**, which contains only the chart.
>
> In this worksheet, the ranges to chart are the nonadjacent ranges B3:G3 (month names) and B16:G16 (monthly operating incomes). The month names in the range B3:G3 will identify the slices of the Pie chart; these entries are called **category names**. The range B16:G16 contains the data that determines the size of the slices in the pie; these entries are called the **data series**. Because six months are being charted, the 3-D Pie chart contains six slices.
>
> The sketch of the 3-D Pie chart in Figure 3–3b on page EX 166 also calls for emphasizing the month of June by offsetting its slice from the main portion. A Pie chart with one or more slices offset is called an **exploded Pie chart**.

BTW

Charts
You are aware that, when you change a value on which a chart is dependent, Excel immediately redraws the chart based on the new value. Did you know that, with bar charts, you can drag the bar in the chart in one direction or another to change the corresponding value in the worksheet, as well?

BTW

Certification
The Microsoft Certified Application Specialist (MCAS) program provides an opportunity for you to obtain a valuable industry credential – proof that you have the Excel 2007 skills required by employers. For more information, see Appendix G or visit the Excel 2007 Certification Web page (scsite.com/ex2007/cert).

BTW

Chart Items
When you rest the mouse pointer over a chart item, such as a legend, bar, or axis, Excel displays a chart tip containing the name of the item.

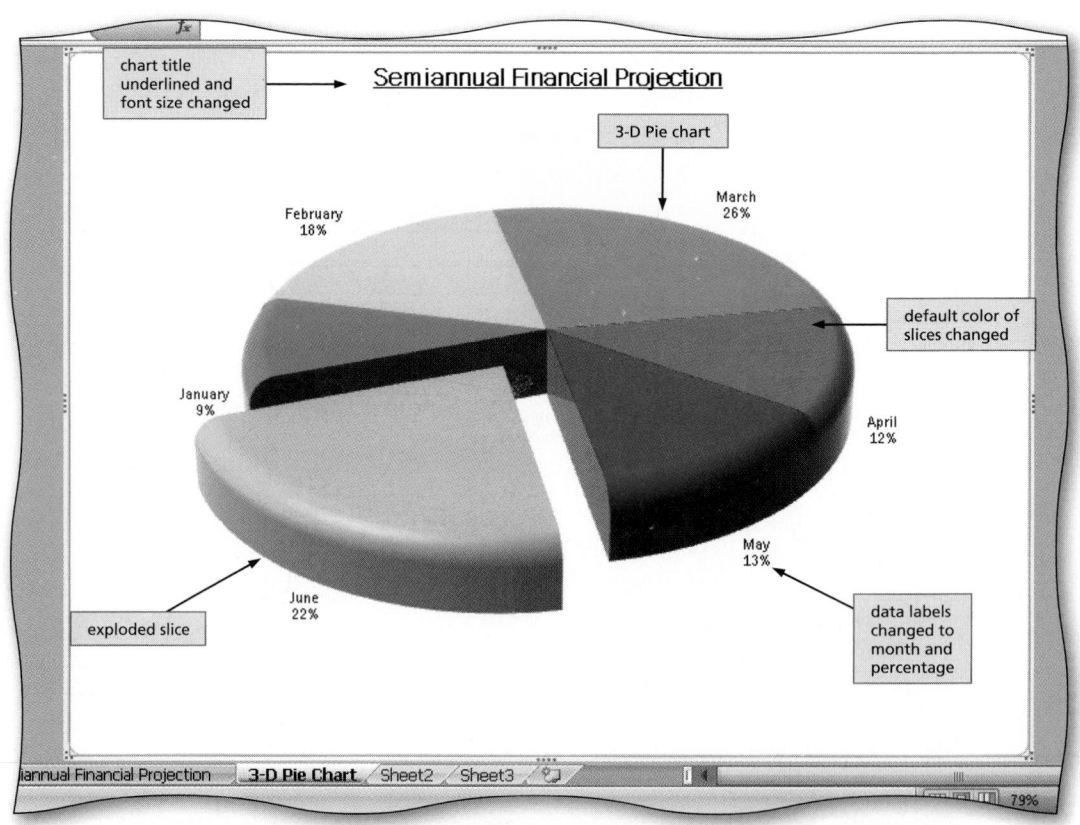

Figure 3–48

As shown in Figure 3–48, the default 3-D Pie chart also has been enhanced by rotating it, changing the colors of the slices, adding a bevel, and modifying the chart title and labels that identify the slices.

To Draw a 3-D Pie Chart on a Separate Chart Sheet

The following steps draw the 3-D Pie chart on a separate chart sheet.

1

- Select the range B3:G3.

- While holding down the CTRL key, select the range B16:G16.

- Click the Insert tab on the Ribbon.

- Click the Pie button on the Ribbon to display the Pie gallery (Figure 3–49).

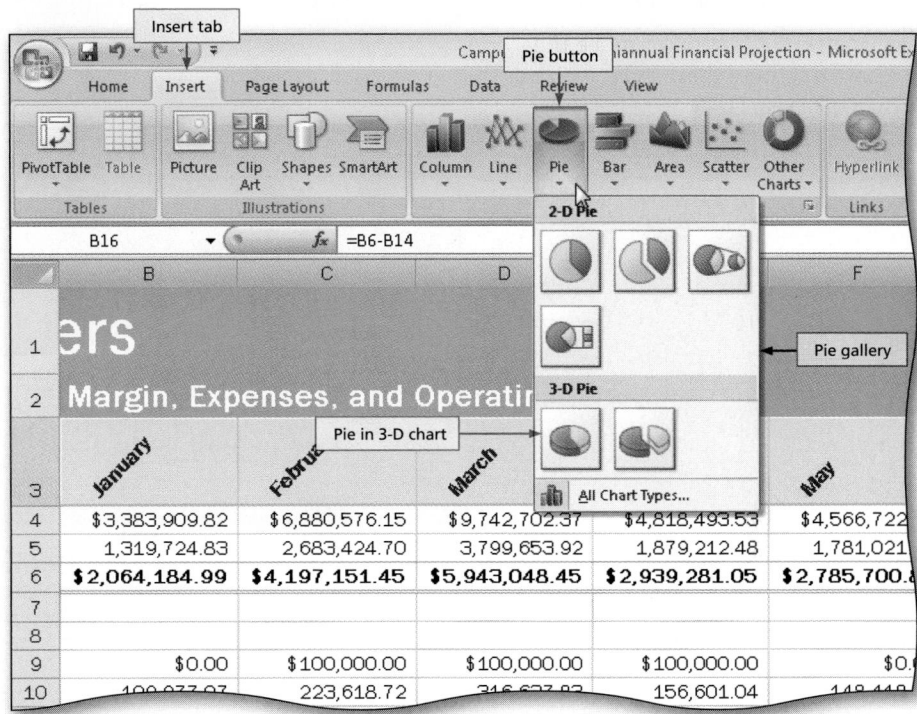

Figure 3–49

- Click Pie in 3-D chart in the Pie gallery.

- When Excel draws the chart, click the Move Chart button on the Ribbon to display the Move Chart dialog box (Figure 3–50).

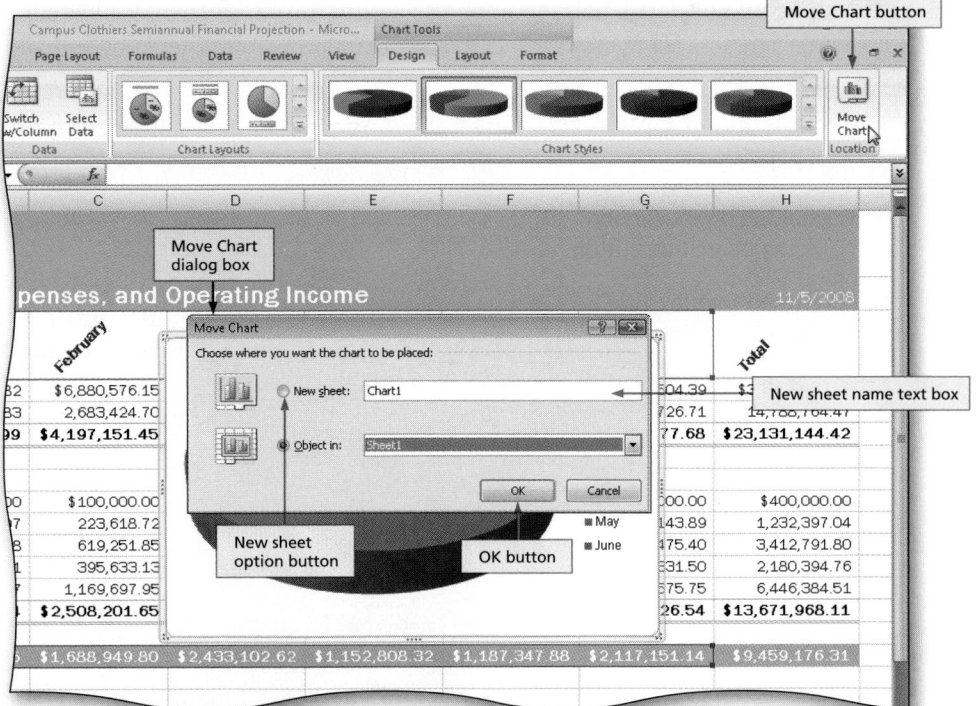

Figure 3–50

- Click the New sheet option button and then type 3-D Pie Chart in the New sheet name text box.

- Click the OK button to move the chart to a new chart sheet with the name 3-D Pie Chart (Figure 3–51).

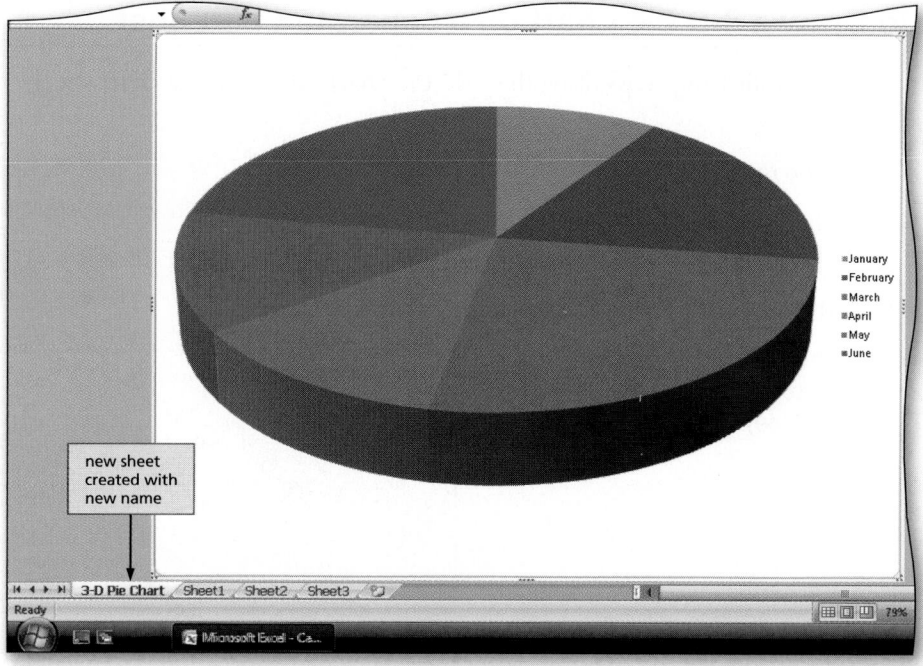

Figure 3–51

Other Ways

1. Select range to chart, press F11

To Insert a Chart Title and Data Labels

The next step is to insert a chart title and labels that identify the slices. Before you can format a chart item, such as the chart title or data labels, you must select it. You can format a selected chart item using the Ribbon or shortcut menu. The following steps insert a chart title, remove the legend, and add data labels.

- Click anywhere in the chart area outside the chart.

- Click the Layout tab on the Ribbon and then click the Chart Title button.

- Click the Centered Overlay Title command in the Chart Title gallery.

- Select the text in the chart title and then type Semiannual Financial Projection as the new chart title (Figure 3–52).

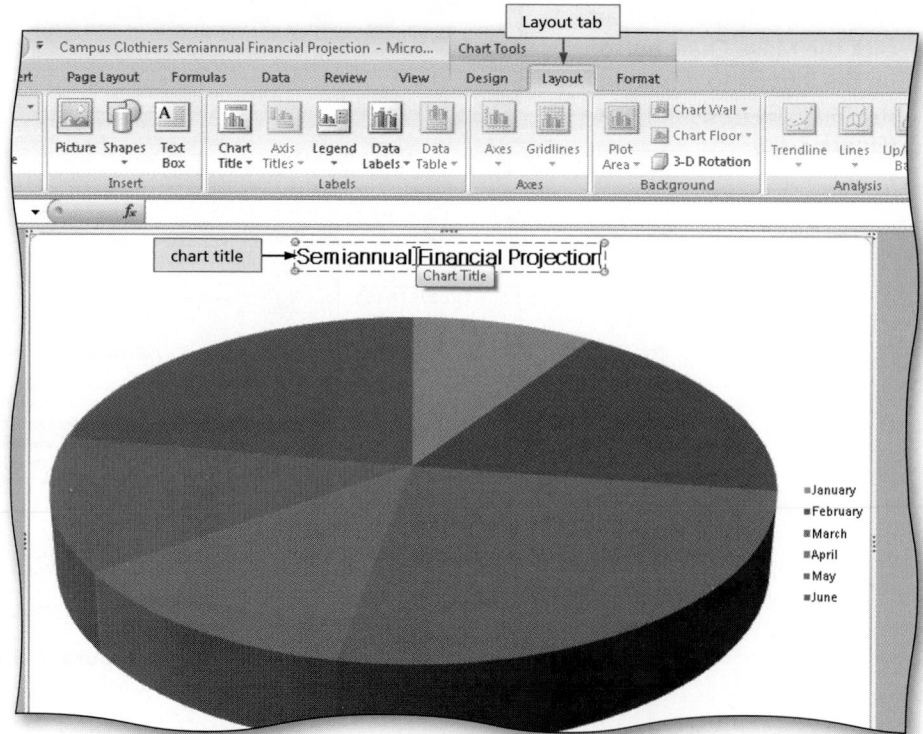

Figure 3–52

2

- Select the text in the new title and then click the Home tab on the Ribbon.

- Click the Underline button to assign an underline font style to the chart title (Figure 3–53).

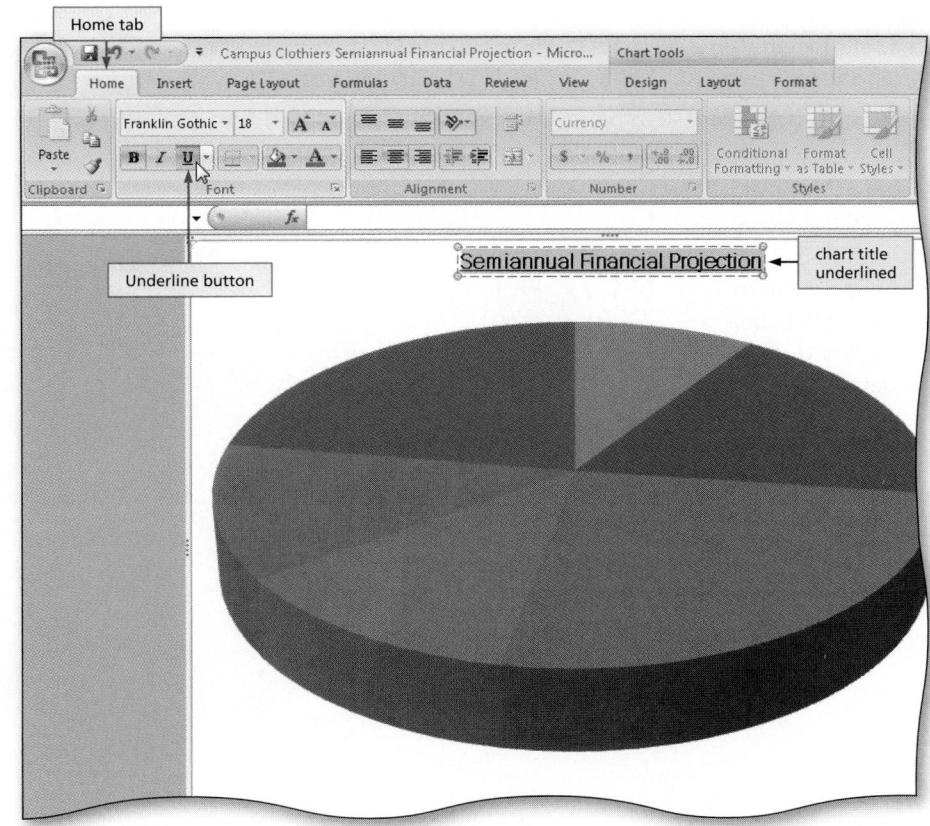

Figure 3–53

3

- Click the Layout tab on the Ribbon and then click the Legend button to display the Legend gallery.

- Point to None in the Legend gallery (Figure 3–54).

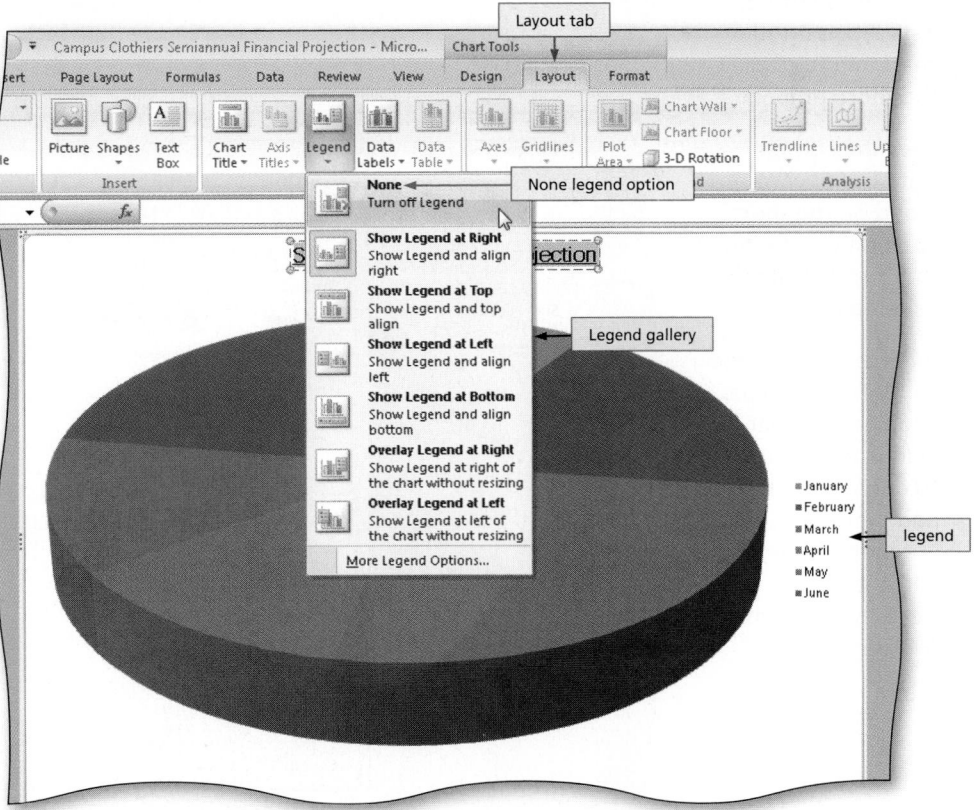

Figure 3–54

4

• Click None to turn off the legend on the chart.

• Click the Data Labels button on the Ribbon and then click Outside End in the Data Labels gallery to display data labels outside the chart at the end of each slice (Figure 3–55).

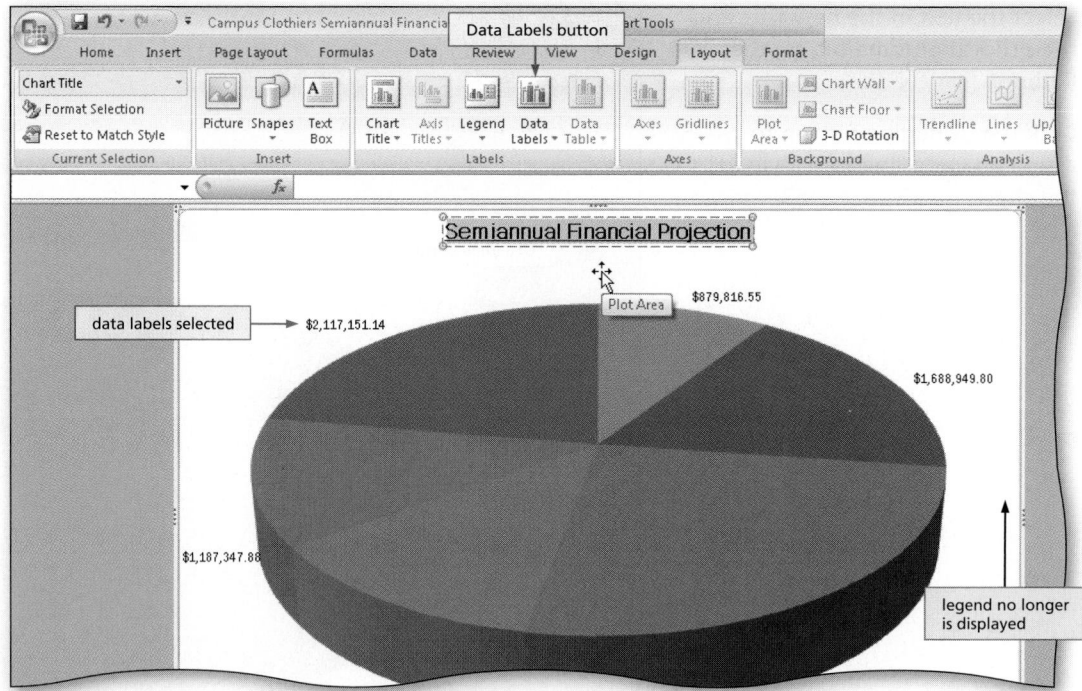

Figure 3–55

5

• If necessary, right-click any data label to select all of the data labels on the chart and to display the shortcut menu.

• Click the Format Data Labels command on the short-cut menu to display the Format Data Labels dialog box.

• If necessary, click the Series Name, Value, and Show Leader Lines check boxes to deselect them and then click the Category Name and Percentage check boxes to select them (Figure 3–56).

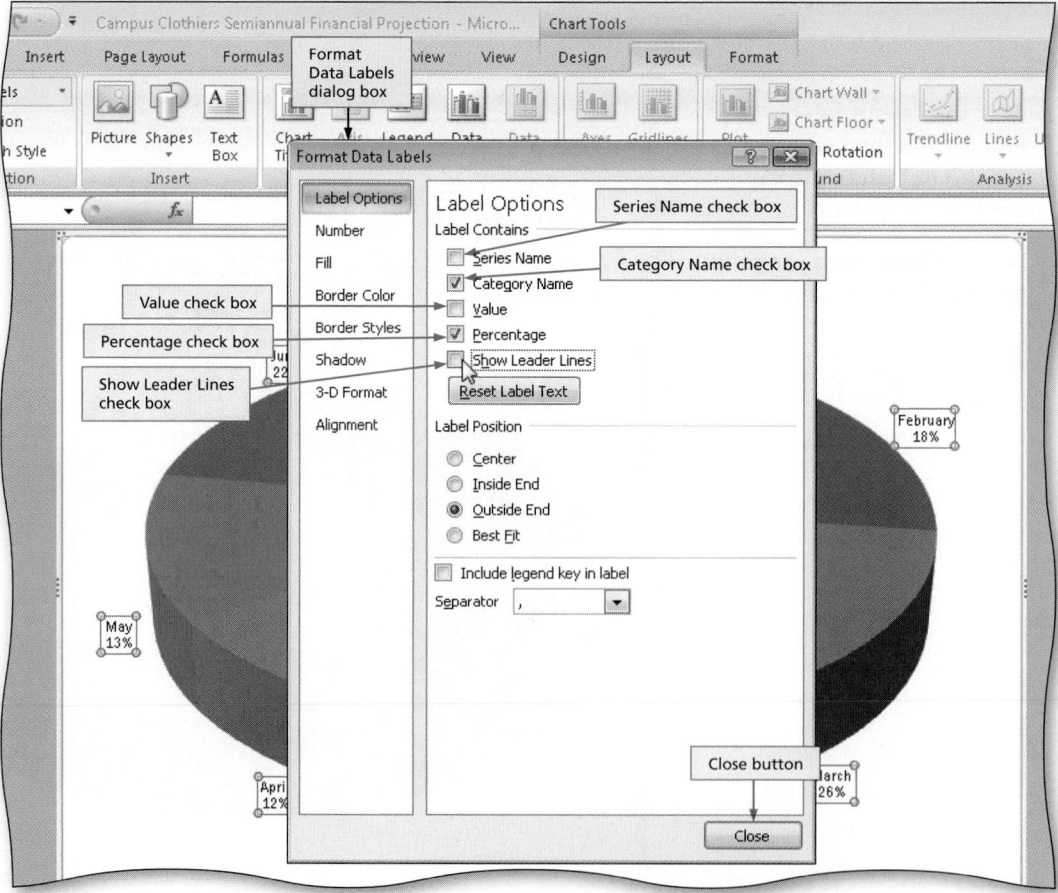

Figure 3–56

6

- Click the Close button to close the Format Data Labels dialog box and display the chart as shown in Figure 3–57.

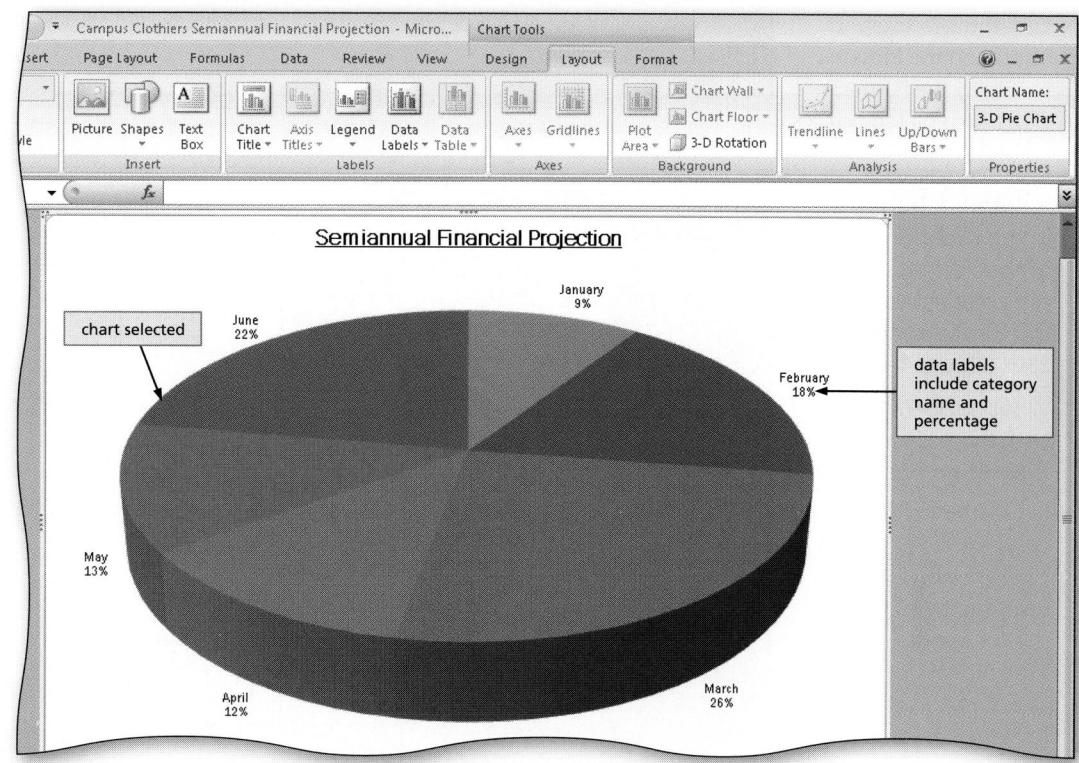

Figure 3–57

To Rotate the 3-D Pie Chart

With a three-dimensional chart, you can change the view to better show the section of the chart you are trying to emphasize. Excel allows you to control the rotation angle, elevation, perspective, height, and angle of the axes by using the Format Chart Area dialog box.

When Excel initially draws a Pie chart, it always positions the chart so that one of the dividing lines between two slices is a straight line pointing to 12 o'clock (or 0°). As shown in Figure 3–57, the line that divides the January and June slices currently is set to 0°. This line defines the rotation angle of the 3-D Pie chart.

To obtain a better view of the offset June slice, the 3-D Pie chart can be rotated 250° to the right. The following steps show how to rotate the 3-D Pie chart.

- Click the 3-D Rotation button on the Ribbon to display the Format Chart Area dialog box.

- Click the Increase X Rotation button in the Rotation area of the Format Chart Area dialog box until the X rotation is at 250° (Figure 3–58).

Q&A

What happens as I click the Increase X Rotation button?

Excel rotates the chart 10° in a clockwise direction each time you click the Increase X Rotation button. The Y box in the Rotation area allows you to control the tilt, or elevation, of the chart. You can tilt the chart towards or away from your view in order to enhance the view of the chart.

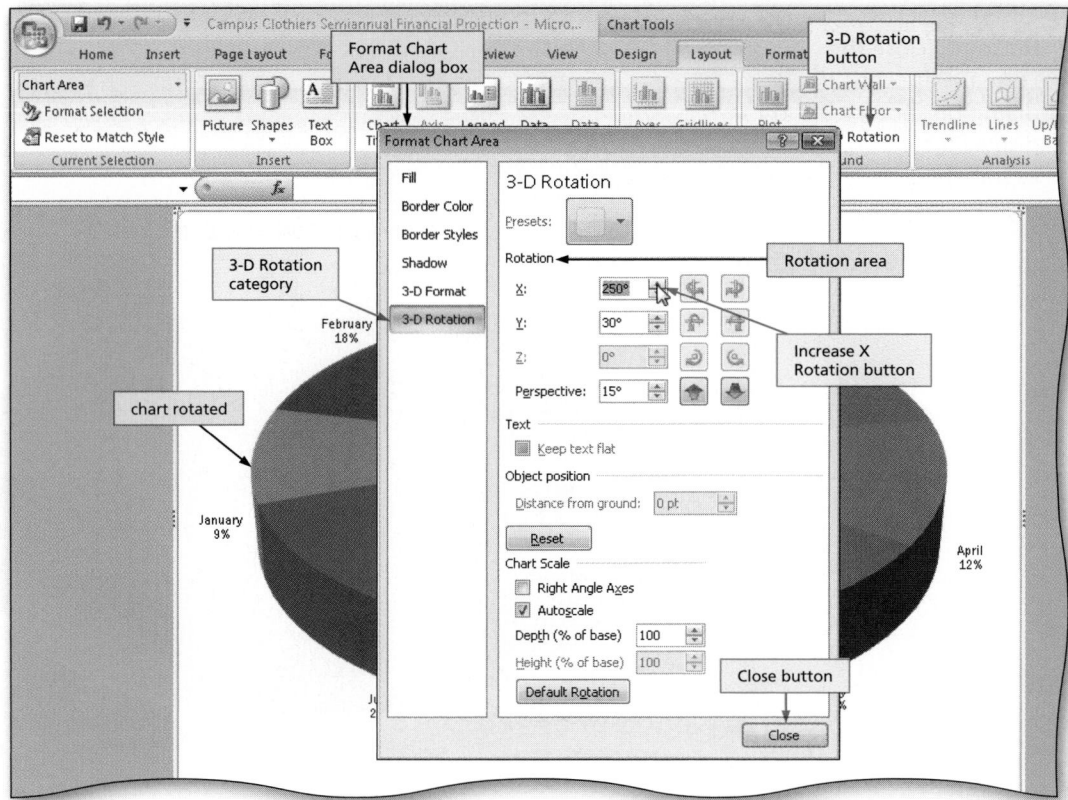

Figure 3–58

- Click the Close button in the Format Chart Area dialog box to display the rotated chart (Figure 3–59).

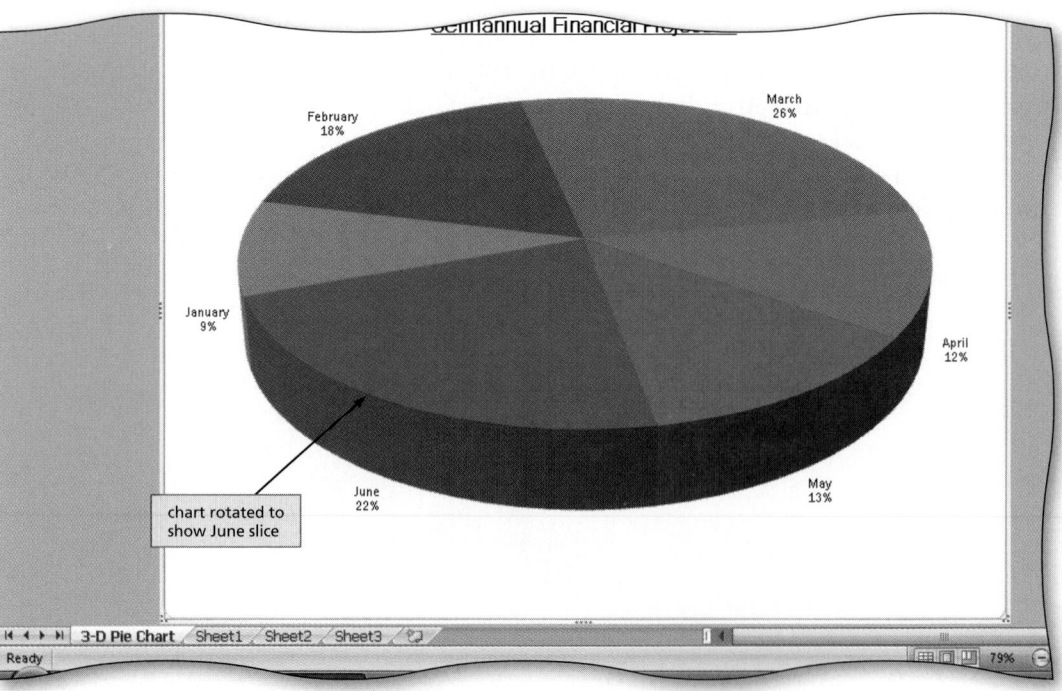

Figure 3–59

To Apply a 3-D Format to the Pie Chart

Excel allows you to apply dramatic 3-D visual effects to charts. The chart shown in Figure 3–59 could be enhanced with a bevel along the top edge. A bevel is a curve that is applied to soften the appearance of a straight edge. Excel also allows you to change the appearance of the material from which the surface of the chart appears to be constructed. The following steps apply a bevel to the chart and change the surface of the chart to a softer-looking material.

1

• Right-click the chart to display the shortcut menu (Figure 3–60).

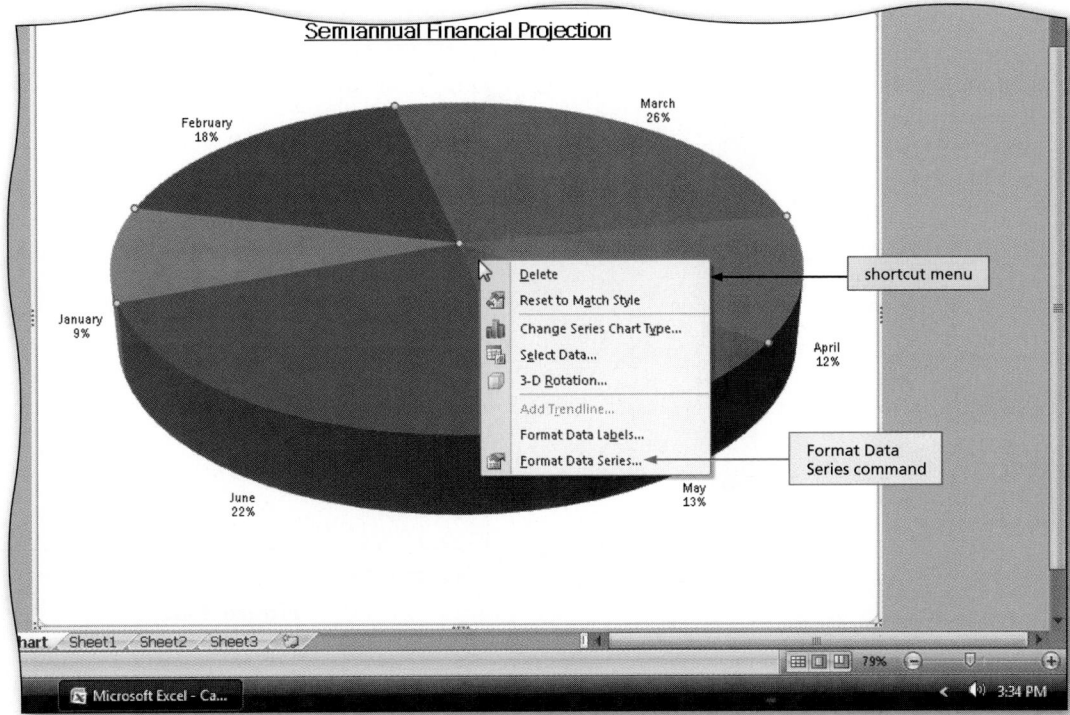

Figure 3–60

2

• Click the Format Data Series command on the shortcut menu to display the Format Data Series dialog box and then click the 3-D Format category on the left side of the dialog box.

• Click the Top button in the Bevel area to display the Bevel gallery (Figure 3–61).

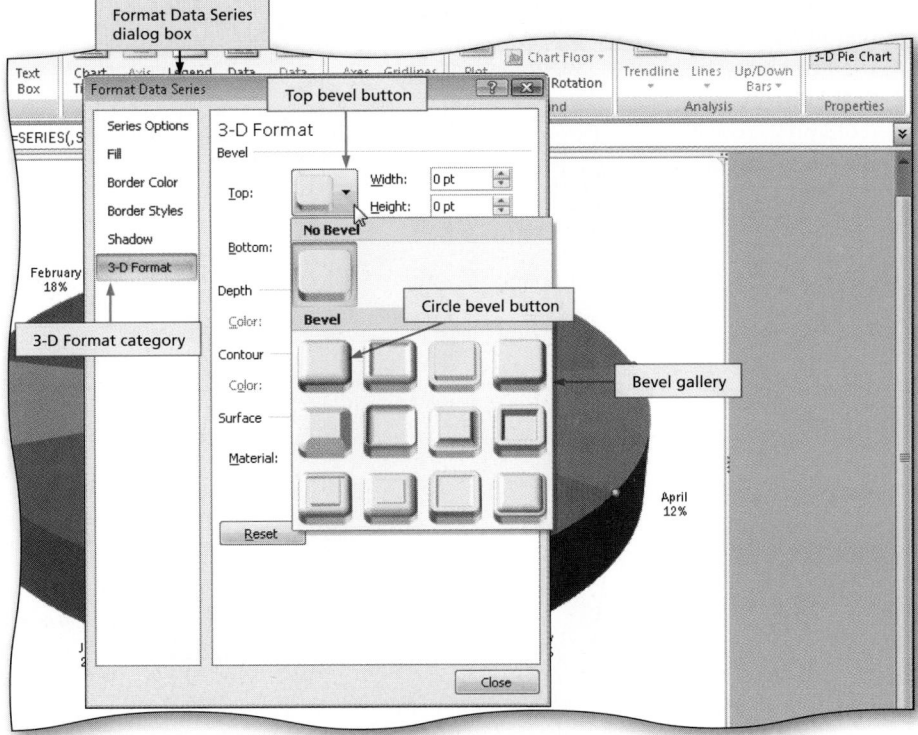

Figure 3–61

- Click the Circle bevel button (column 1, row 1) in the Bevel gallery to add a bevel to the chart.

- Type 50 pt in the top Width box in the Bevel area of the dialog box and then type 50 pt in the uppermost Height box in the Bevel area of the dialog box to increase the width and height of the bevel on the chart (Figure 3–62).

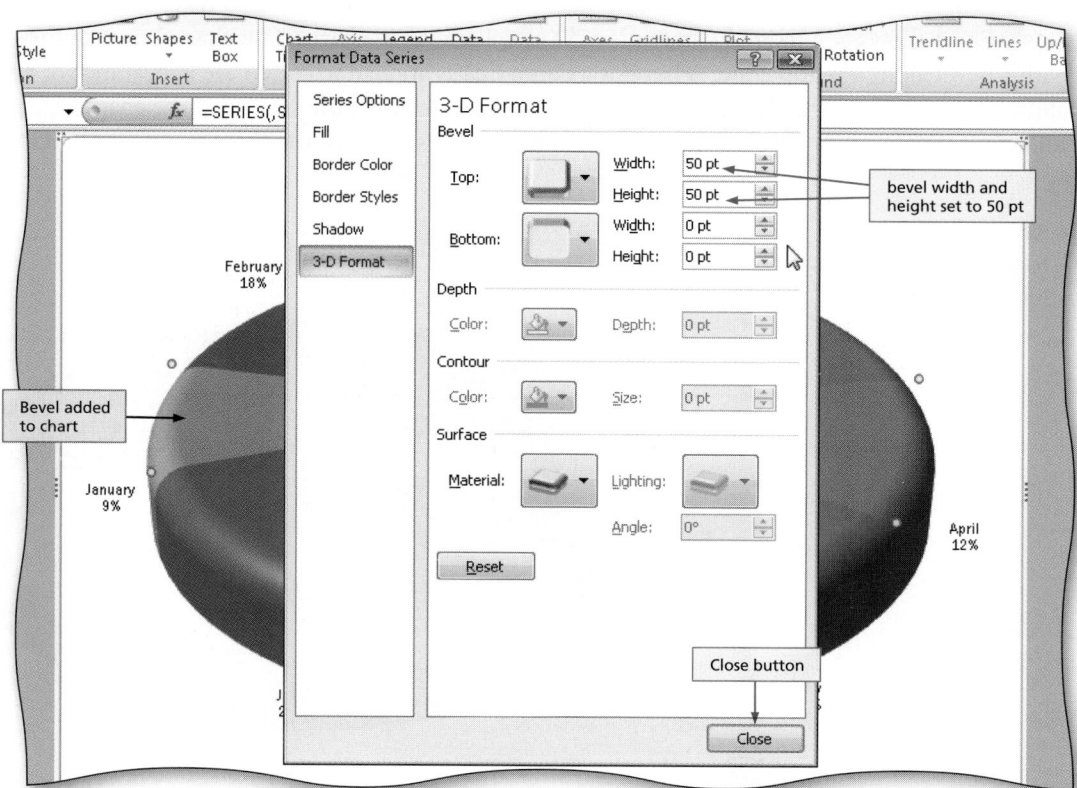

Figure 3–62

- Click the Material button in the Surface area of the Format Data Series dialog box and then point to the Soft Edge button (column 2, row 2) in the Material gallery (Figure 3–63).

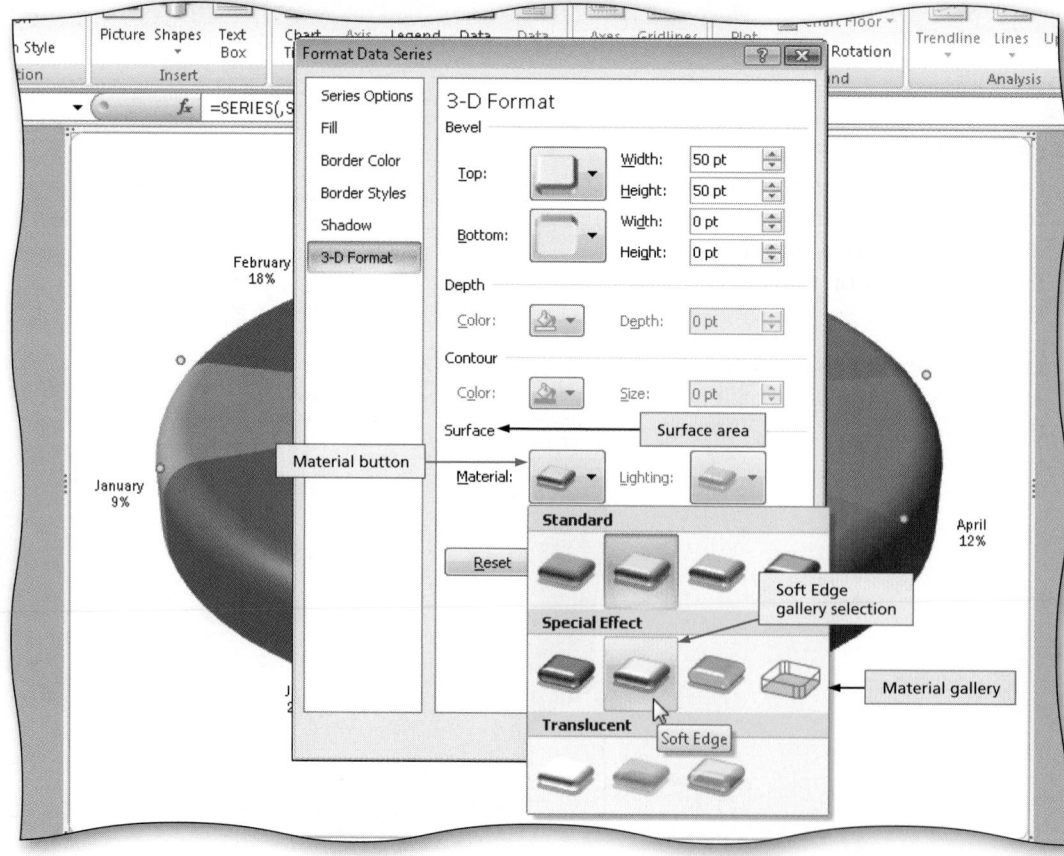

Figure 3–63

5

- Click the Soft Edge button and then click the Close button in the Format Data Series dialog box (Figure 3-64).

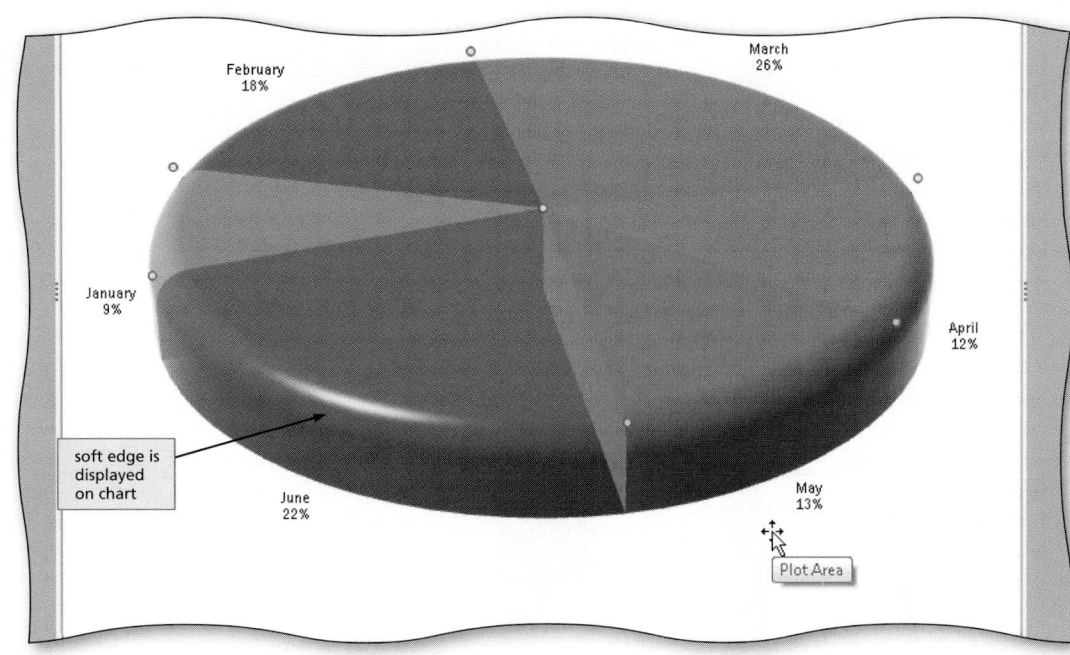

Figure 3–64

To Explode the 3-D Pie Chart and Change the Color of a Slice

The next step is to emphasize the slice representing June by **offsetting**, or exploding, it from the rest of the slices so that it stands out. The following steps explode a slice of the 3-D Pie chart and then change its color.

1

- Click the slice labeled June twice (do not double-click) to select only the June slice.

- Right-click the slice labeled June to display the shortcut menu and then point to Format Data Point (Figure 3–65).

- Click Format Data Point.

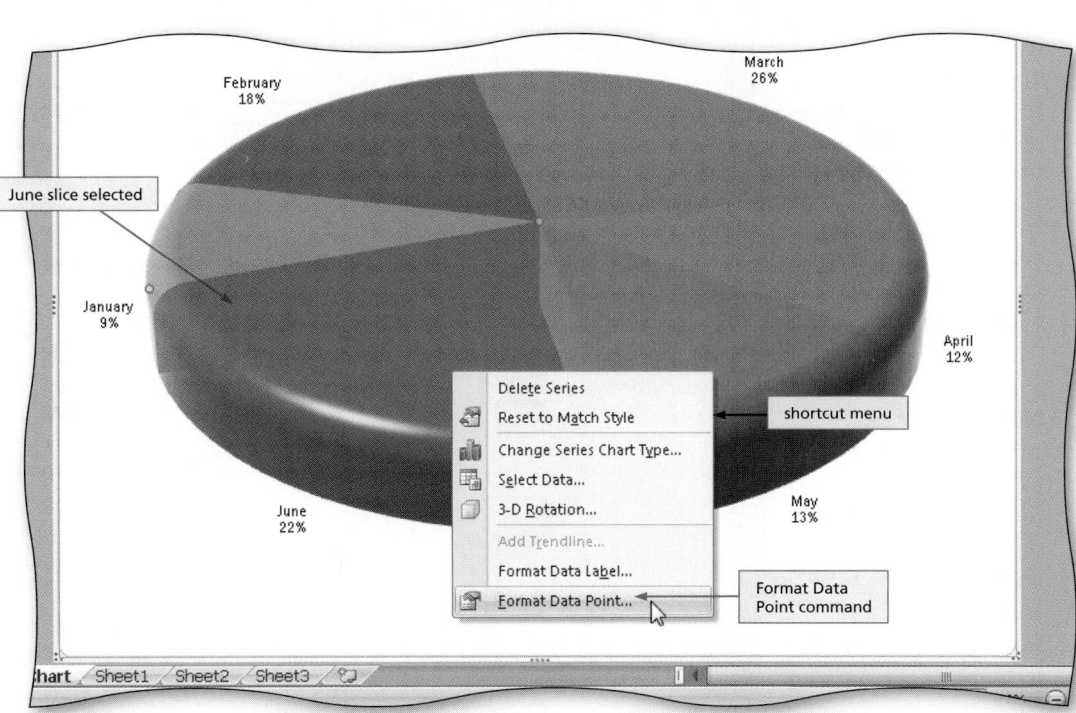

Figure 3–65

2

- When Excel displays the Format Data Point dialog box, drag the Point Explosion slider to the right until the Point Explosion box reads 28% (Figure 3–66).

Should I offset more slices?

You can offset as many slices as you want, but remember that the reason for offsetting a slice is to emphasize it. Offsetting multiple slices tends to reduce the impact on the reader and reduces the overall size of the Pie chart.

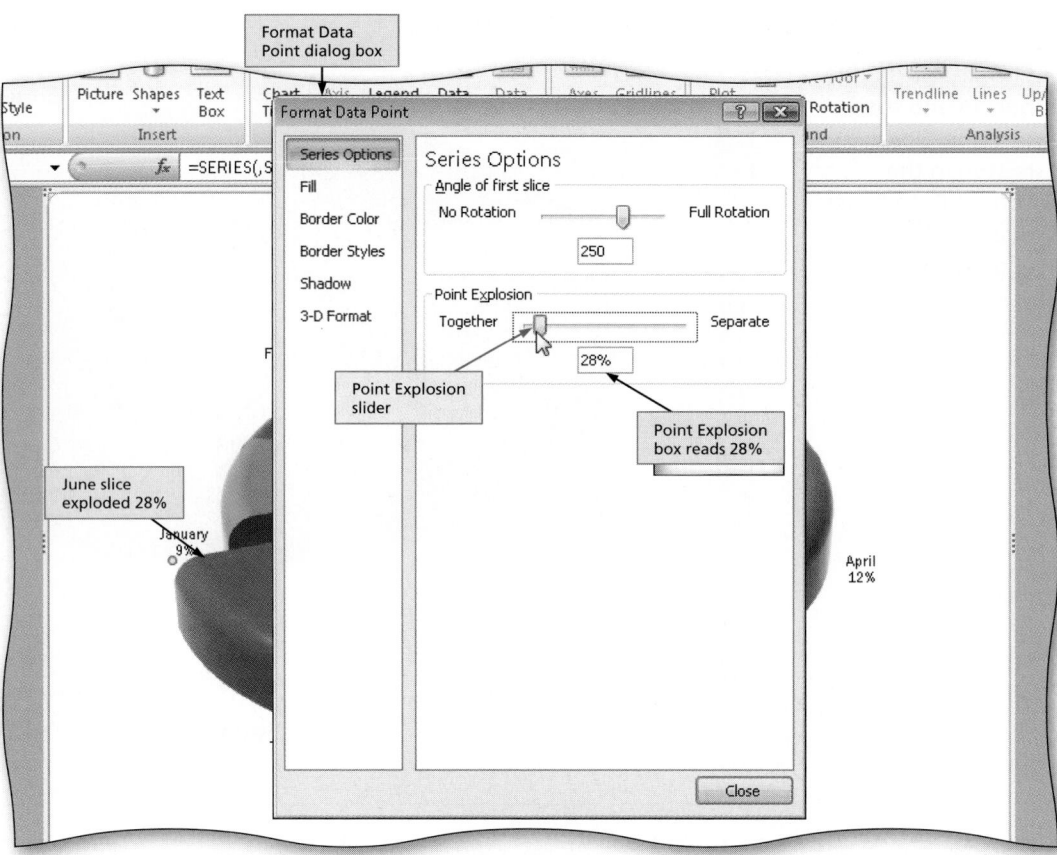

Figure 3–66

3

- Click the Fill category on the left side of the dialog box.

- Click the Solid fill option button and then click the Color button to display the color palette.

- Point to the Orange color in the Standard Colors area (Figure 3–67).

4

- Click the Orange color on the color palette and then click the Close button on the Format Data Point dialog box to change the color of the slice labeled June to orange.

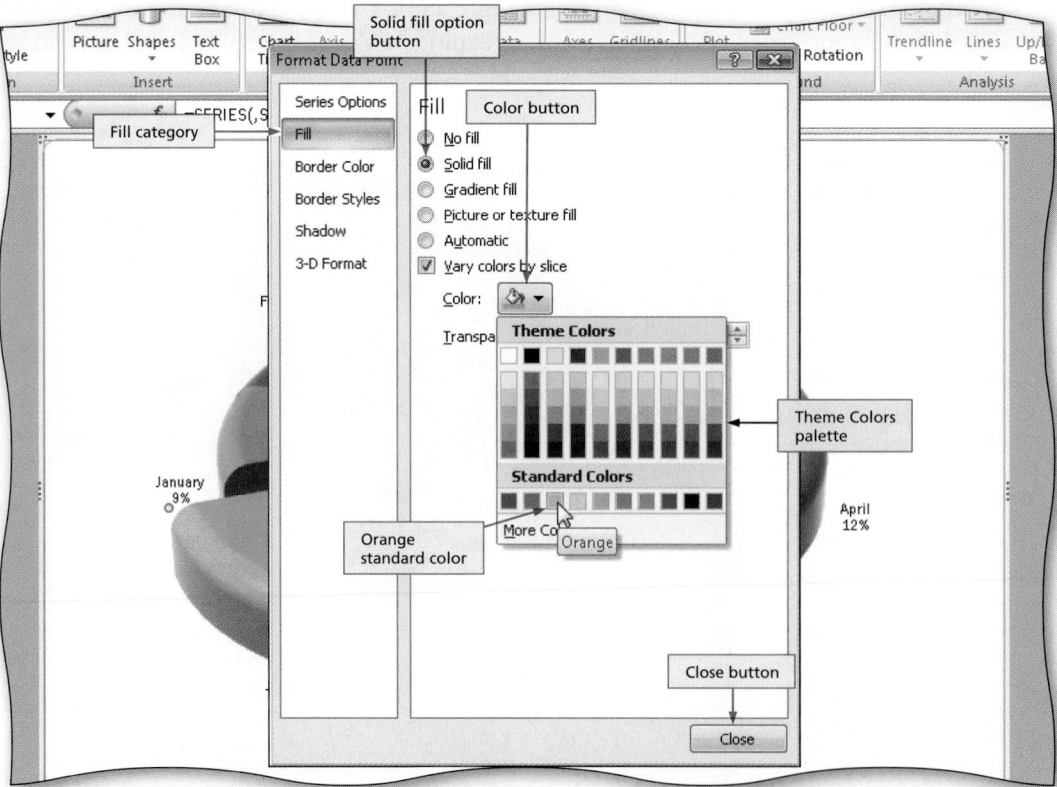

Figure 3–67

To Change the Colors of the Remaining Slices

BTW

Exploding a 3-D Pie Chart
If you click the 3-D Pie chart so that all of the slices are selected, you can drag one of the slices to explode all of the slices.

The colors of the remaining slices also can be changed to enhance the appeal of the chart. The following steps change the color of the remaining five chart slices.

1 Click the slice labeled January twice (do not double-click) to select only the January slice.

2 Right-click the slice labeled January to display the shortcut menu and then click Format Data Point.

3 Click the Fill category on the left side of the dialog box.

4 Click the Solid fill option button and then click the Color button to display the color palette.

5 Click the Green color on the color palette and then click the Close button in the Format Data Point dialog box to change the color of the slice labeled January to green.

6 Repeat steps 1 through 5 for the remaining four slices. Assign the following colors in the Standard Colors area of the color palette to each slice: February – Yellow; March – Light Blue; April – Red; May – Blue. The completed chart appears as shown in Figure 3–68.

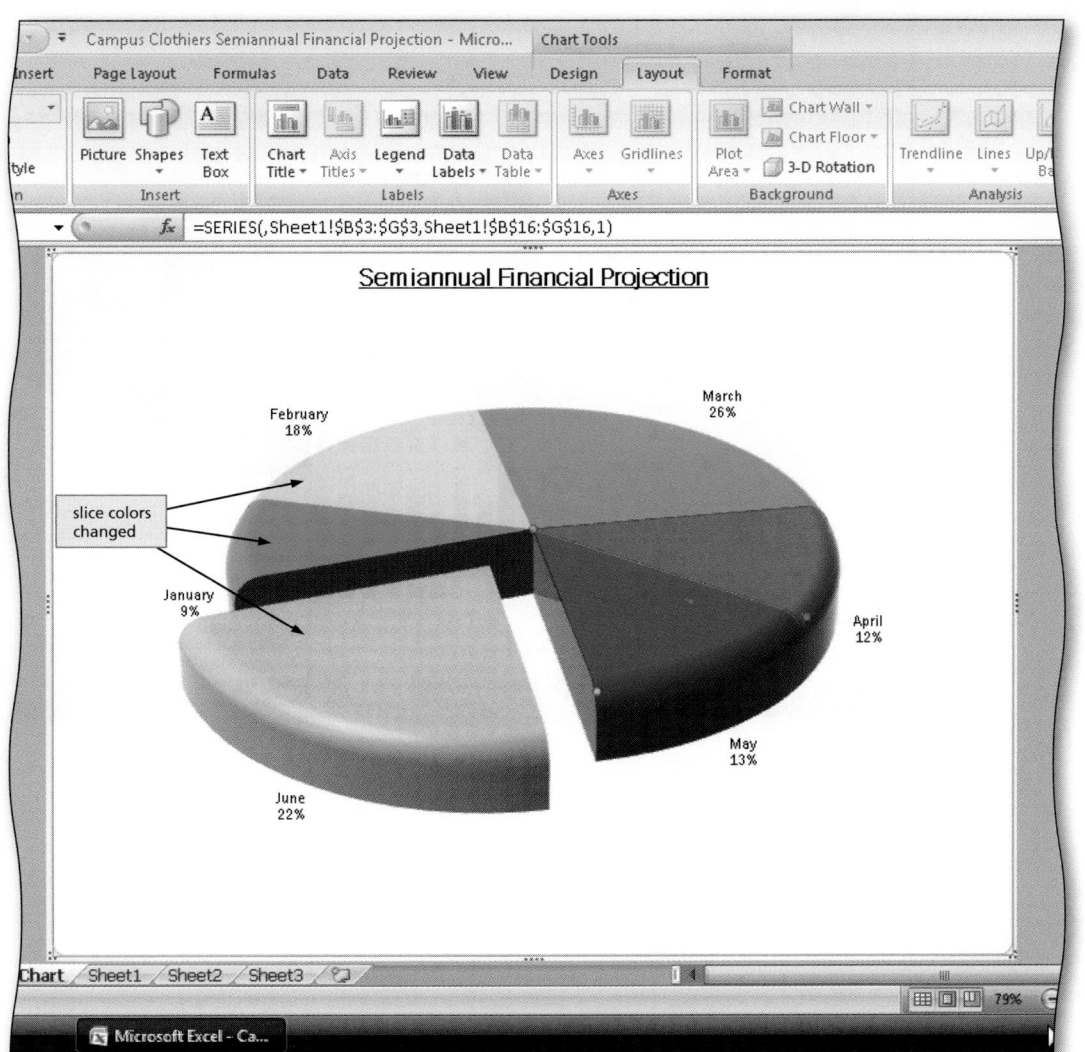

Figure 3–68

Renaming and Reordering the Sheets and Coloring Their Tabs

The final step in creating the workbook is to reorder the sheets and modify the tabs at the bottom of the screen.

To Rename and Reorder the Sheets and Color Their Tabs

The following steps rename the sheets, color the tabs, and reorder the sheets so the worksheet precedes the chart sheet in the workbook.

- Right-click the tab labeled 3-D Pie Chart at the bottom of the screen to display the shortcut menu.
- Point to the Tab Color command to display the color palette (Figure 3–69).

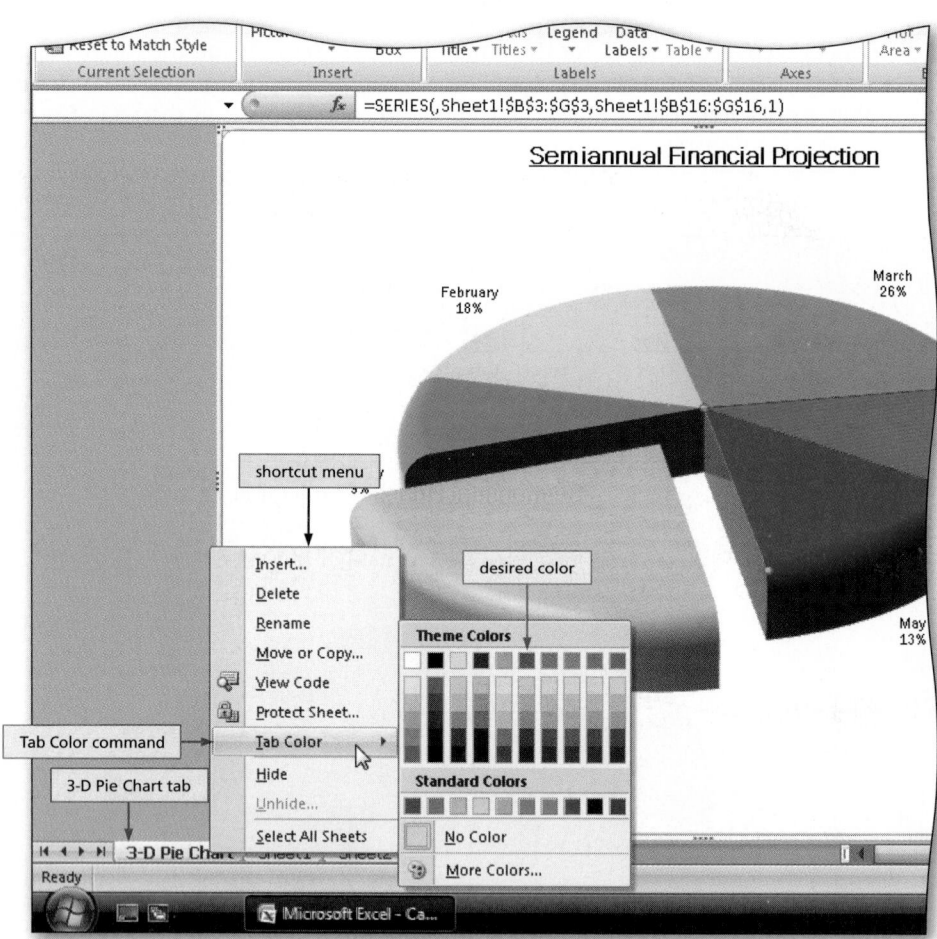

Figure 3–69

- Click Brown, Accent 2 (column 6, row 1) in the Theme Colors area to change the color of the tab to brown.

- Double-click the tab labeled Sheet1 at the bottom of the screen.

- Type Semiannual Financial Projection as the new sheet name and then press the ENTER key.

- Right-click the tab and then click Tab Color on the shortcut menu.

- Point to the Orange, Accent 1 (column 5, row 1) color in the Theme Colors area of the palette (Figure 3–70).

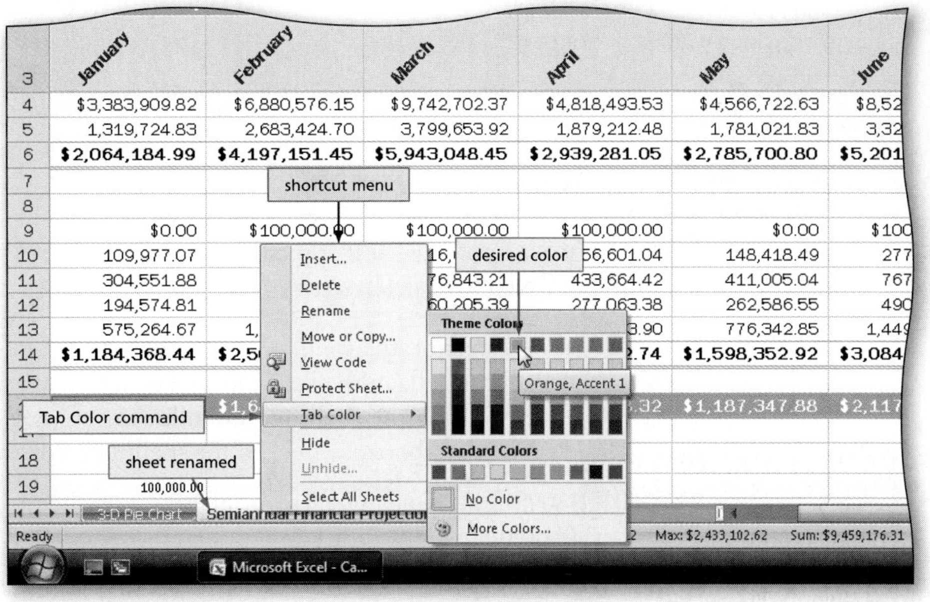

3

- Click Orange, Accent 1 (column 5, row 1) in the Theme Colors area to change the color of the tab to orange.

- Drag the Semiannual Financial Projection tab to the left in front of the 3-D Pie Chart tab to rearrange the sequence of the sheets and then click cell E18 (Figure 3–71).

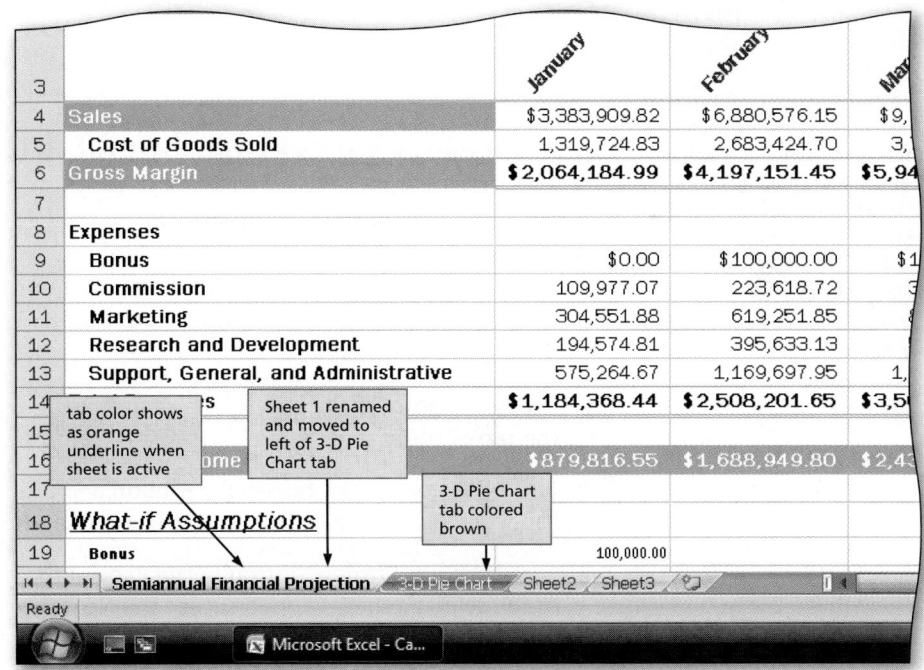

Figure 3–70

Figure 3–71

Other Ways

1. To rename sheet, right-click sheet tab, click Rename on shortcut menu

2. To move sheet, right-click sheet tab, click Move or Copy on shortcut menu

BTW

Checking Spelling
Unless you first select a range of cells or an object before starting the spell checker, Excel checks the selected worksheet, including all cell values, cell comments, embedded charts, text boxes, buttons, and headers and footers.

Checking Spelling, Saving, Previewing, and Printing the Workbook

With the workbook complete, this section checks spelling, saves, previews, and then prints the workbook. Each set of steps concludes with saving the workbook to ensure that the latest changes are saved.

To Check Spelling in Multiple Sheets

By default, the spell checker checks the spelling only in the selected sheets. It will check all the cells in the selected sheets, unless you select a range of two or more cells. Before checking the spelling, the following steps select the 3-D Pie Chart sheet so that the entire workbook is checked for spelling errors.

1 With the Semiannual Financial Projection sheet active, press CTRL+HOME to select cell A1. Hold down the CTRL key and then click the 3-D Pie Chart tab.

2 Click the Review tab on the Ribbon and then click the Spelling button on the Ribbon.

3 Correct any errors and then click the OK button when the spell check is complete.

4 Click the Save button on the Quick Access Toolbar.

BTW

Printing in Black and White
You can speed up the printing process and save ink if you print worksheets with color in black and white. To print a worksheet in black and white on a color printer, do the following: (1) Click the Page Setup Dialog Box Launcher on the Page Layout tab on the Ribbon, click the Sheet tab, and then click 'Black and white' in the Print area. (2) Click the Preview button to see that Excel has removed the colored backgrounds, click the Close button, and then click the OK button. You are now ready to print economically, in black and white.

To Preview and Print the Workbook

After checking the spelling, the next step is to preview and print the sheets. As with spelling, Excel previews and prints only the selected sheets. In addition, because the worksheet is too wide to print in portrait orientation, the orientation must be changed to landscape. The following steps adjust the orientation and scale, preview the workbook, and then print the workbook.

1 Ready the printer. If both sheets are not selected, hold down the CTRL key and then click the tab of the inactive sheet.

2 Click the Page Layout tab on the Ribbon and then click the Page Setup Dialog Box Launcher. Click the Page tab and then click Landscape. Click Fit to in the Scaling area.

3 Click the Print Preview button in the Page Setup dialog box. When the preview of the first of the selected sheets appears, click the Next Page button at the top of the Print Preview window to view the next sheet. Click the Previous Page button to redisplay the first sheet.

4 Click the Print button at the top of the Print Preview window. When Excel displays the Print dialog box, click the OK button to print the worksheet and chart (Figure 3–72).

5 Right-click the Semiannual Financial Projection tab. Click Ungroup Sheets on the shortcut menu to deselect the 3-D Pie Chart tab.

6 Click the Save button on the Quick Access Toolbar.

BTW

Quick Reference
For a table that lists how to complete the tasks covered in this book using the mouse, Ribbon, shortcut menu, and keyboard, see the Quick Reference Summary at the back of this book, or visit the Excel 2007 Quick Reference Web page (scsite.com/ex2007/qr).

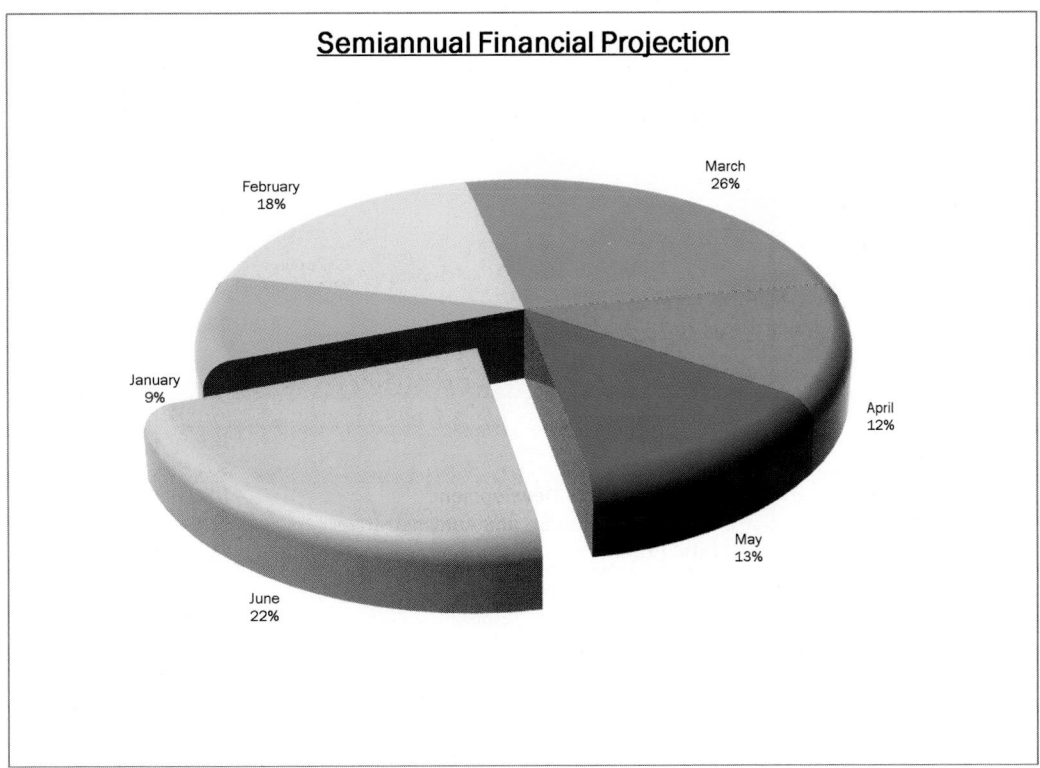

Campus Clothiers
Semiannual Projected Gross Margin, Expenses, and Operating Income   3/21/2007

	January	February	March	April	May	June	Total
Sales	$3,383,909.82	$6,880,576.15	$9,742,702.37	$4,818,493.53	$4,566,722.63	$8,527,504.39	$37,919,908.89
Cost of Goods Sold	1,319,724.83	2,683,424.70	3,799,653.92	1,879,212.48	1,781,021.83	3,325,726.71	14,788,764.47
Gross Margin	$2,064,184.99	$4,197,151.45	$5,943,048.45	$2,939,281.05	$2,785,700.80	$5,201,777.68	$23,131,144.42
Expenses							
Bonus	$0.00	$100,000.00	$100,000.00	$100,000.00	$0.00	$100,000.00	$400,000.00
Commission	109,977.07	223,618.72	316,637.83	156,601.04	148,418.49	277,143.89	1,232,397.04
Marketing	304,551.88	619,251.85	876,843.21	433,664.42	411,005.04	767,475.40	3,412,791.80
Research and Development	194,574.81	395,633.13	560,205.39	277,063.38	262,586.55	490,331.50	2,180,394.76
Support, General, and Administrative	575,264.67	1,169,697.95	1,656,259.40	819,143.90	776,342.85	1,449,675.75	6,446,384.51
Total Expenses	$1,184,368.44	$2,508,201.65	$3,509,945.83	$1,786,472.74	$1,598,352.92	$3,084,626.54	$13,671,968.11
Operating Income	$879,816.55	$1,688,949.80	$2,433,102.62	$1,152,808.32	$1,187,347.88	$2,117,151.14	$9,459,176.31

What-If Assumptions

Bonus	100,000.00
Commission	3.25%
Margin	61.00%
Marketing	9.00%
Research and Development	5.75%
Revenue for Bonus	4,750,000.00
Support, General, and Administrative	17.00%

(a) Worksheet

Semiannual Financial Projection

February 18%
March 26%
January 9%
April 12%
May 13%
June 22%

(b) 3-D Pie Chart

Figure 3–72

BTW

Zooming
You can use the Zoom In and Zoom Out buttons on the status bar to zoom from 10% to 400% to reduce or enlarge the display of the worksheet.

Changing the View of the Worksheet

With Excel, you easily can change the view of the worksheet. For example, you can magnify or shrink the worksheet on the screen. You also can view different parts of the worksheet through window panes.

To Shrink and Magnify the View of a Worksheet or Chart

You can magnify (zoom in) or shrink (zoom out) the appearance of a worksheet or chart by using the Zoom button on the View tab on the Ribbon. When you magnify a worksheet, Excel enlarges the view of the characters on the screen, but displays fewer columns and rows. Alternatively, when you shrink a worksheet, Excel is able to display more columns and rows. Magnifying or shrinking a worksheet affects only the view; it does not change the window size or printout of the worksheet or chart. The following steps shrink and magnify the view of the worksheet.

- If cell A1 is not active, press CTRL+HOME.

- Click the View tab on the Ribbon and then click the Zoom button on the Ribbon to display a list of Magnifications in the Zoom dialog box (Figure 3–73).

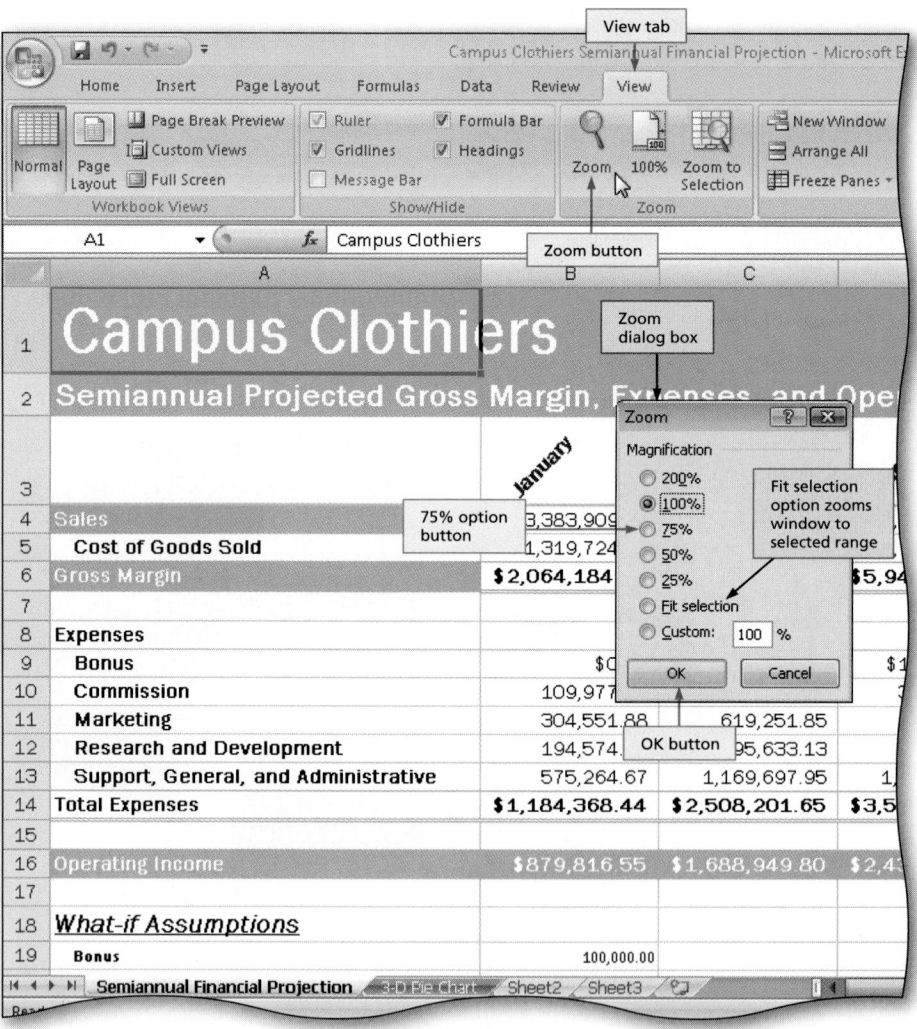

Figure 3–73

2

• Click 75% and then click the OK button to shrink the display of the worksheet to 75% of its normal display (Figure 3–74).

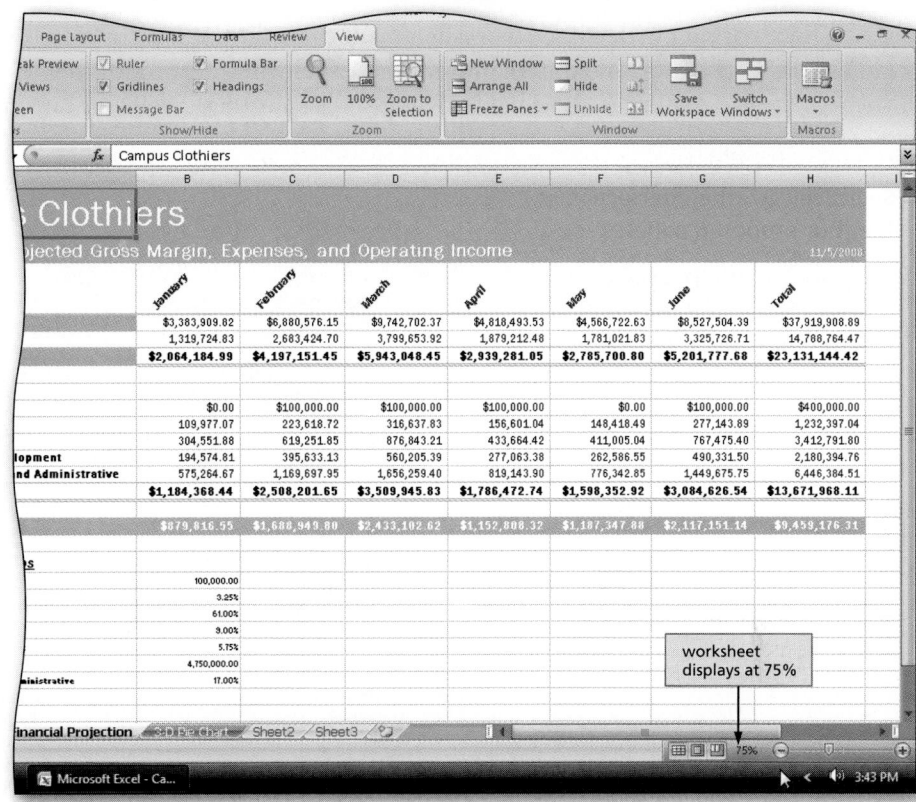

Figure 3–74

3

• Click the Zoom In button on the status bar until the worksheet displays at 100% (Figure 3–75).

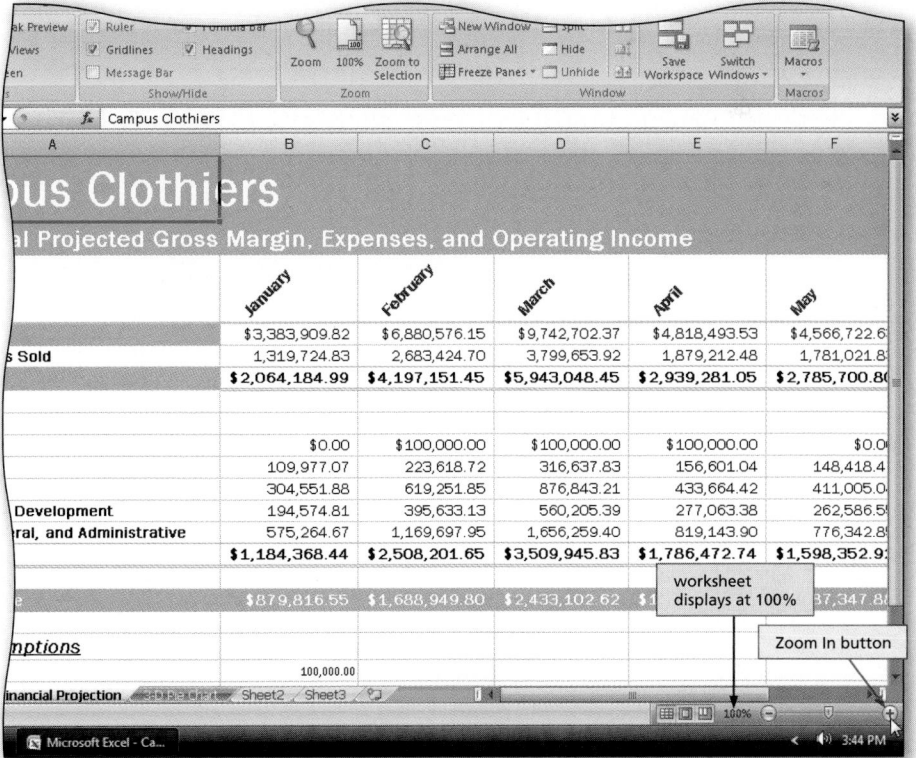

Figure 3–75

To Split a Window into Panes

When working with a large worksheet, you can split the window into two or four panes to view different parts of the worksheet at the same time. Splitting the Excel window into four panes at cell D7 allows you to view all four corners of the worksheet easily. The following steps split the Excel window into four panes.

- Select cell D7, the intersection of the four proposed panes.

- If necessary, click the View tab on the Ribbon and then point to the Split button on the Ribbon (Figure 3–76).

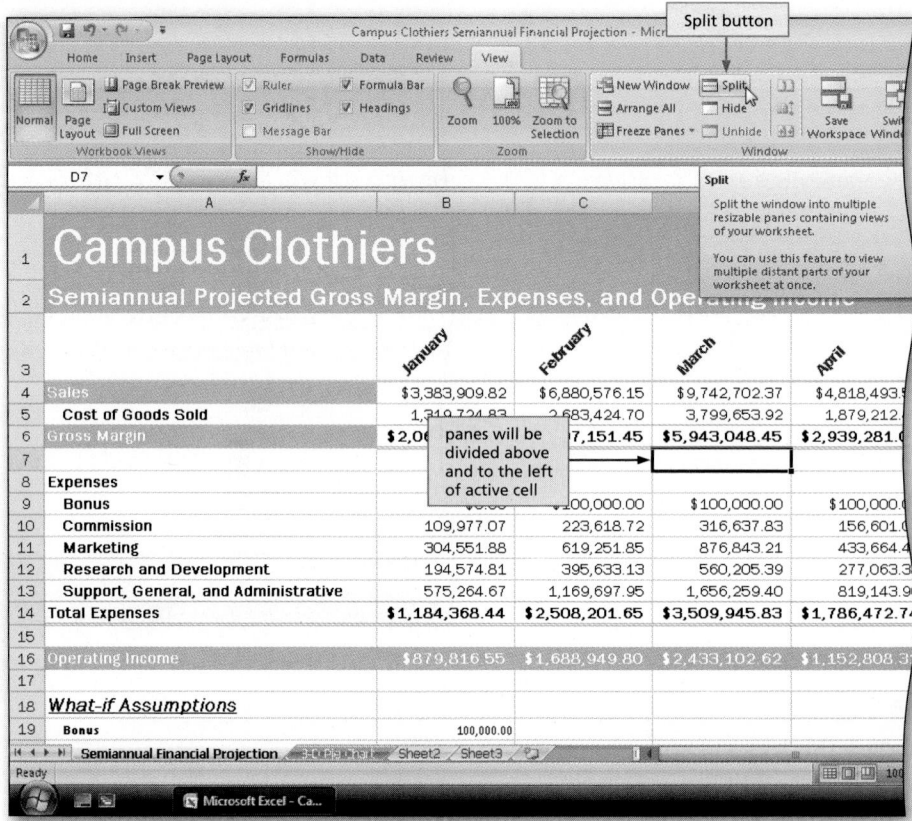

Figure 3–76

- Click the Split button to divide the window into four panes.

- Use the scroll arrows to show the four corners of the worksheet at the same time (Figure 3–77).

Q&A

What is shown in the four panes?

The four panes in Figure 3–77 are used to show the following: (1) range A1:C6 in the upper-left pane; (2) range G1:I6 in the upper-right pane; (3) range A14:C26 in the lower-left pane; and (4) range G14:I26 in the lower-right pane. The vertical split bar is the vertical bar going up and down the middle of the window. The horizontal split bar is the horizontal bar going across the middle of the window. If you use the scroll bars below the window and to the right of the window to scroll the window, you will see that the panes split by the horizontal split bar scroll together vertically. The panes split by the vertical split bar scroll together horizontally. To resize the panes, drag either split bar to the desired location in the window.

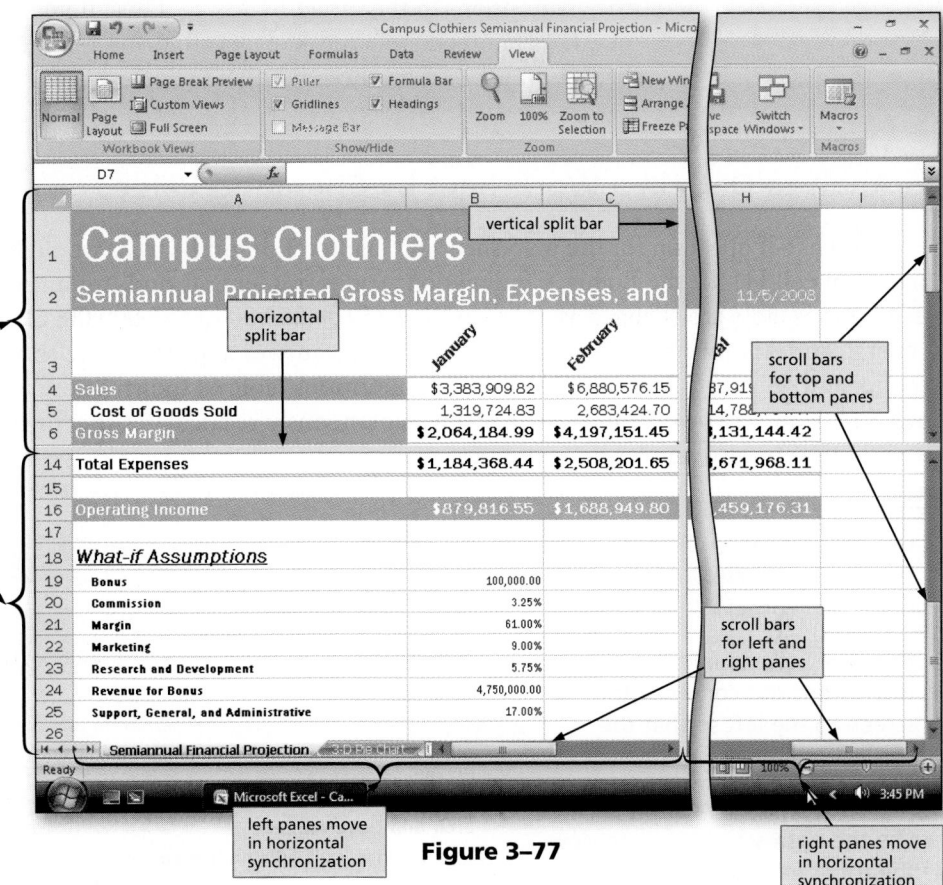

Figure 3–77

Other Ways

1. Drag horizontal split box and vertical split box to desired locations

To Remove the Panes from the Window

1. Position the mouse pointer at the intersection of the horizontal and vertical split bars.

2. When the mouse pointer changes to a four-headed arrow, double-click to remove the four panes from the window.

What-If Analysis

The automatic recalculation feature of Excel is a powerful tool that can be used to analyze worksheet data. Using Excel to scrutinize the impact of changing values in cells that are referenced by a formula in another cell is called **what-if analysis** or **sensitivity analysis**. When new data is entered, Excel not only recalculates all formulas in a worksheet, but also redraws any associated charts.

BTW

Window Panes
If you want to split the window into two panes, rather than four, drag the vertical split box to the far left of the window or horizontal split box to the top of the window (Figure 3–78 on the next page). You also can drag the center of the four panes in any direction to change the size of the panes.

In the workbook created in this chapter, many of the formulas are dependent on the assumptions in the range B19:B25. Thus, if you change any of the assumption values, Excel immediately recalculates all formulas. Excel redraws the 3-D Pie chart as well, because it is based on these numbers.

To Analyze Data in a Worksheet by Changing Values

A what-if question for the worksheet in Chapter 3 might be *what* would happen to the semiannual operating income in cell H16 *if* the Bonus, Commission, Support, General, and Administrative assumptions in the What-If Assumptions table are changed as follows: Bonus $100,000.00 to $75,000.00; Commission 3.25% to 2.25%; Support, General, and Administrative 17.00% to 14.50%? To answer a question like this, you need to change only the first, second, and seventh values in the What-If Assumptions table as shown in the following steps. The steps also divide the window into two vertical panes. Excel instantaneously recalculates the formulas in the worksheet and redraws the 3-D Pie chart to answer the question.

- Use the vertical scroll bar to move the window so cell A6 is in the upper-left corner of the screen.

- Drag the vertical split box from the lower-right corner of the screen to the left so that the vertical split bar is positioned as shown in Figure 3–78.

- Use the right scroll arrow to view the totals in column H in the right pane.

- Enter 75000 in cell B19, 2.25 in cell B20, and 14.50 in cell B25 (Figure 3–78), which causes the semiannual operating income in cell H16 to increase from $9,459,176.31 to $10,886,373.12.

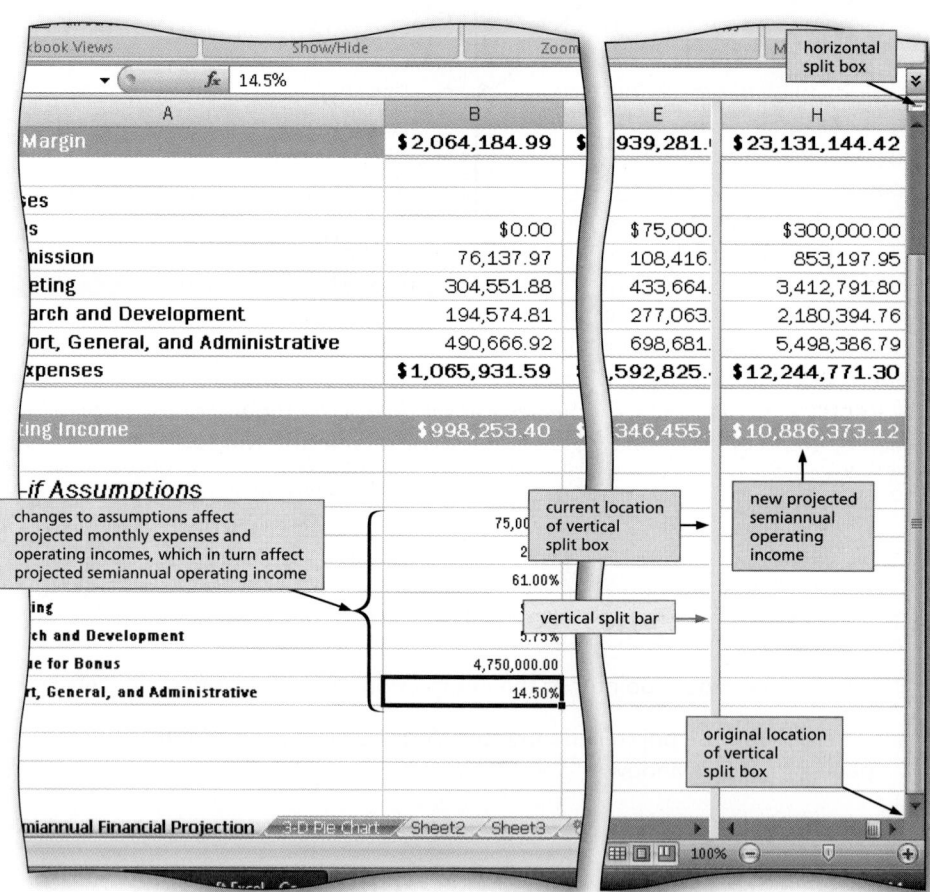

Figure 3–78

To Goal Seek

If you know the result you want a formula to produce, you can use **goal seeking** to determine the value of a cell on which the formula depends. The following steps close and reopen the Campus Clothiers Semiannual Financial Projection workbook. They then show how to use the Goal Seek command on the Data tab on the Ribbon to determine the Support, General, and Administrative percentage in cell B25 that will yield a semiannual operating income of $10,500,000 in cell H16, rather than the original $9,459,176.31.

1

- Close the workbook without saving changes and then reopen it.

- Drag the vertical split box so that the vertical split bar is positioned as shown in Figure 3–79.

- Show column H in the right pane.

- Click cell H16, the cell that contains the semiannual operating income.

- Click the Data tab on the Ribbon and then click the What-If Analysis button on the Ribbon to display the What-If Analysis menu (Figure 3–79).

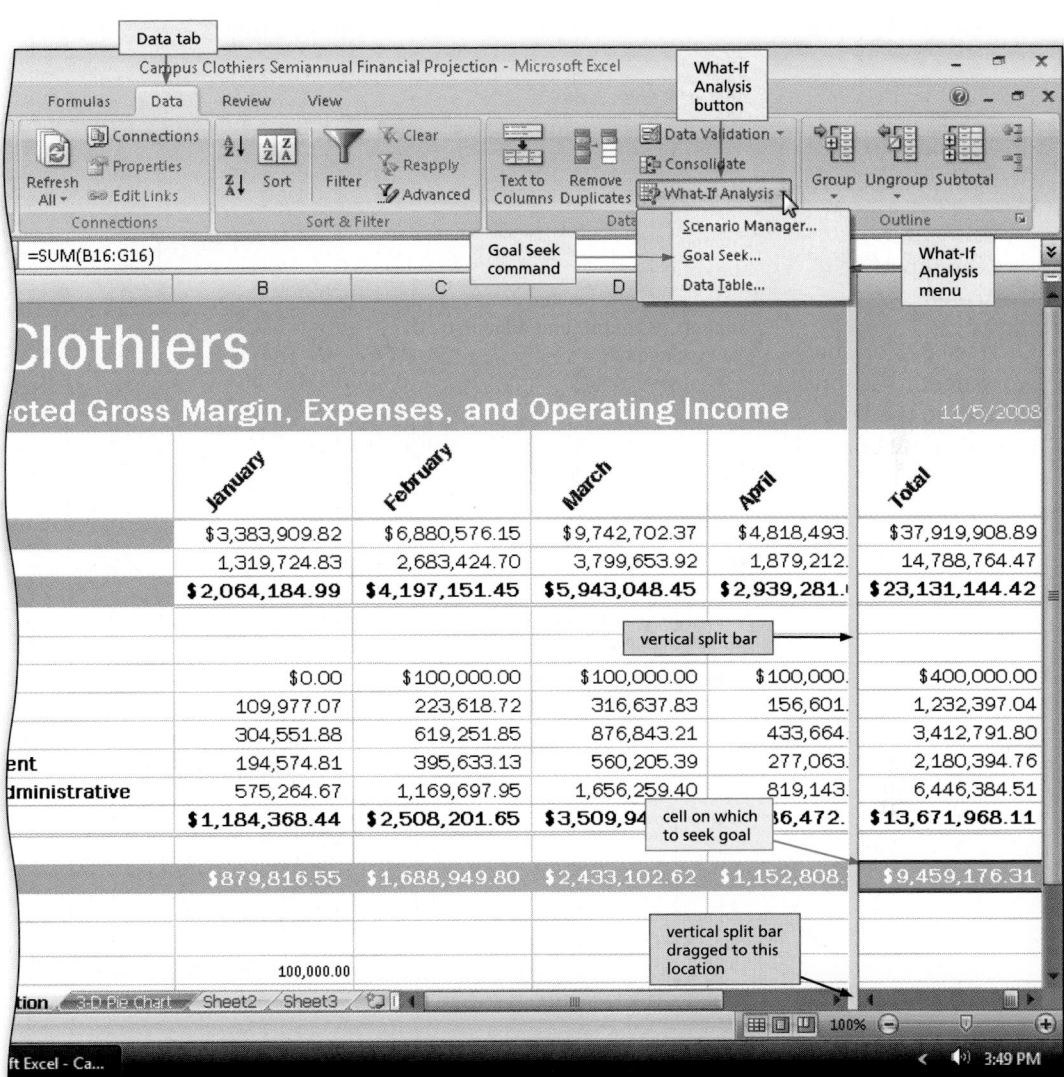

Figure 3–79

● Click Goal Seek to display the Goal Seek dialog box with the Set cell box set to the selected cell, H16.

● When Excel displays the Goal Seek dialog box, click the To value text box, type 10,500,000 and then click the By changing cell box.

● Scroll down so row 4 is at the top of the screen.

● Click cell B25 on the worksheet to assign cell B25 to the By changing cell box (Figure 3–80).

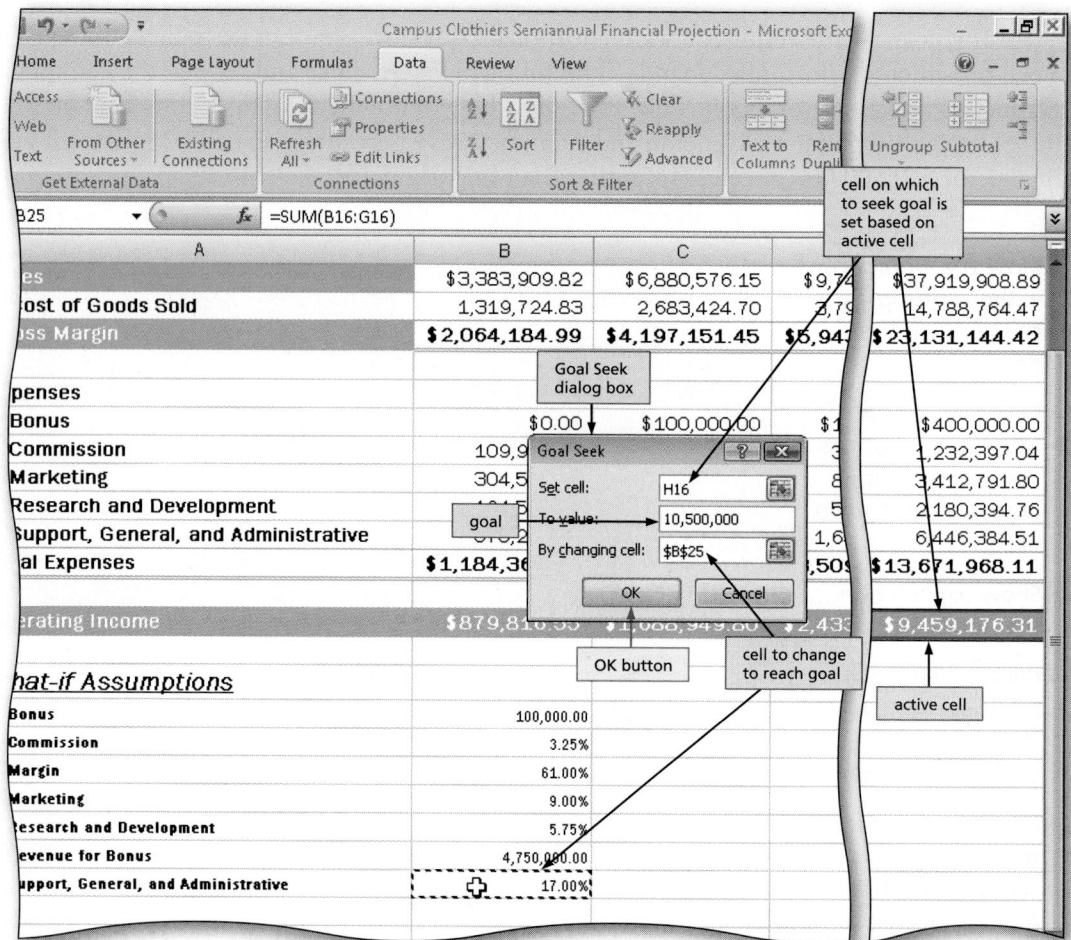

Figure 3–80

3

- Click the OK button to goal seek for the value $10,500,000.00 in cell H16 (Figure 3–81).

What happens when I click the OK button?

Excel immediately changes cell H16 from $9,459,176.31 to the desired value of $10,500,000.00. More importantly, Excel changes the Support, General, and Administrative assumption in cell B25 from 17.00% to 14.26% (Figure 3–81). Excel also displays the Goal Seek Status dialog box. If you click the OK button, Excel keeps the new values in the worksheet. If you click the Cancel button, Excel redisplays the original values.

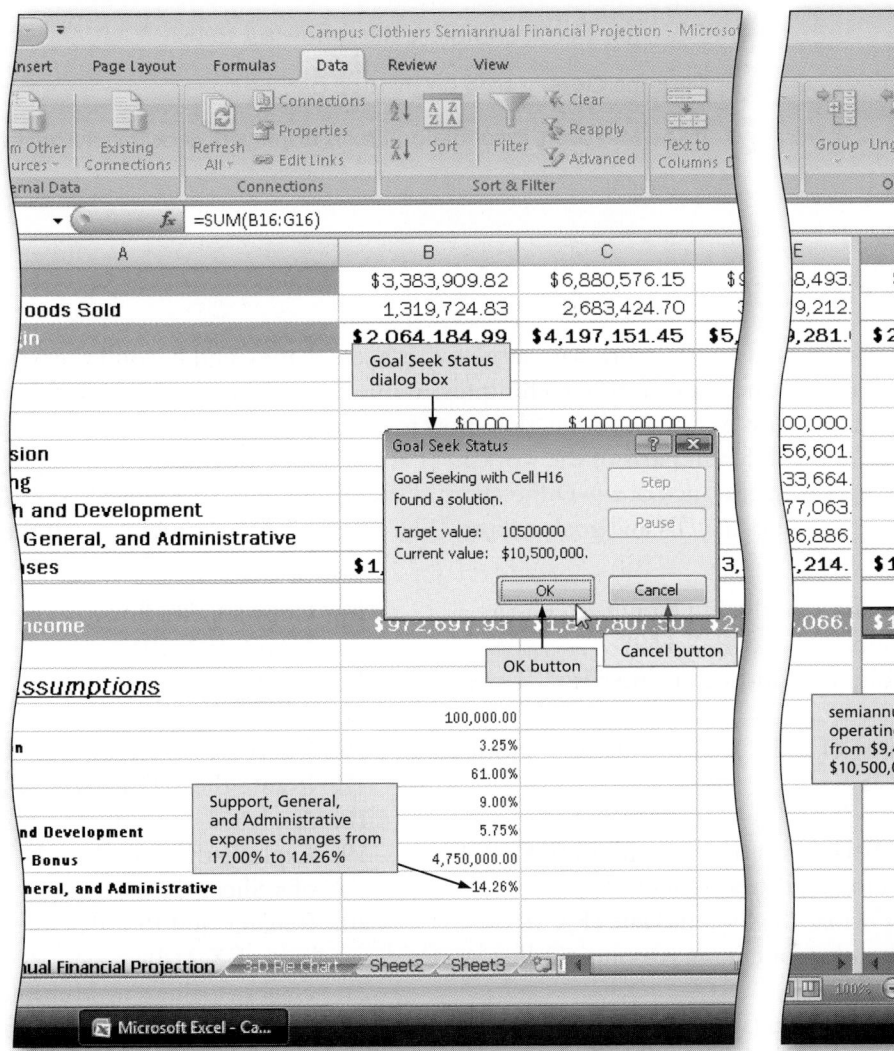

Figure 3–81

4

- Click the Cancel button in the Goal Seek Status dialog box.

Other Ways
1. Press ALT+T, G

Goal Seeking

Goal seeking assumes you can change the value of only one cell referenced directly or indirectly to reach a specific goal for a value in another cell. In this example, to change the semiannual operating income in cell H16 to $10,500,000.00, the Support, General, and Administrative percentage in cell B25 must decrease by 2.74% from 17.00% to 14.26%.

You can see from this goal seeking example that the cell to change (cell B25) does not have to be referenced directly in the formula or function. For example, the semiannual operating income in cell H16 is calculated by the function =SUM(B16:G16). Cell B25 is not referenced in this function. Instead, cell B25 is referenced in the formulas in rows 9 through 13, on which the monthly operating incomes in row 16 are based. Excel thus is capable of goal seeking on the semiannual operating income by varying the value for the Support, General, and Administrative assumption.

Undoing What You Did The Undo button is ideal for returning the worksheet to its original state after you have changed the values in a worksheet to answer a what-if question. To view the original worksheet after answering a what-if question, click the Undo button on the Quick Access Toolbar for each value you changed.

To Quit Excel

To quit Excel, complete the following steps.

1 Click the Close button on the title bar.

2 If the Microsoft Excel dialog box is displayed, click the No button.

Chapter Summary

In this chapter you learned how to work with large worksheets that extend beyond the window, how to use the fill handle to create a series, new formatting techniques, about the difference between absolute cell references and relative cell references, how to use the IF function, how to rotate text in a cell, freeze titles, change the magnification of the worksheet, show different parts of the worksheet at the same time through multiple panes, create a 3-D Pie chart, and improve the appearance of a 3-D Pie chart. This chapter also introduced you to using Excel to do what-if analysis by changing values in cells and goal seeking. The items listed below include all the new Excel skills you have learned in this chapter.

1. Rotate Text and Use the Fill Handle to Create a Series of Month Names (EX 169)
2. Increase Column Widths and Enter Row Titles (EX 173)
3. Copy a Range of Cells to a Nonadjacent Destination Area (EX 175)
4. Insert a Row (EX 177)
5. Enter Numbers with Format Symbols (EX 181)
6. Freeze Column and Row Titles (EX 182)
7. Enter and Format the System Date (EX 184)
8. Enter a Formula Containing Absolute Cell References (EX 187)
9. Enter an IF Function (EX 190)
10. Copy Formulas with Absolute Cell References Using the Fill Handle (EX 192)
11. Unfreeze the Worksheet Titles and Save the Workbook (EX 194)
12. Assign Formats to Nonadjacent Ranges (EX 196)
13. Format the Worksheet Titles (EX 199)
14. Copy a Cell's Format Using the Format Painter Button (EX 201)
15. Draw a 3-D Pie Chart on a Separate Chart Sheet (EX 205)
16. Insert a Chart Title and Data Labels (EX 206)
17. Rotate the 3-D Pie Chart (EX 209)
18. Apply a 3-D Format to the Pie Chart (EX 211)
19. Explode the 3-D Pie Chart and Change the Color of a Slice (EX 213)
20. Rename and Reorder the Sheets and Color Their Tabs (EX 216)
21. Check Spelling in Multiple Sheets (EX 218)
22. Shrink and Magnify the View of a Worksheet or Chart (EX 220)
23. Split a Window into Panes (EX 222)
24. Analyze Data in a Worksheet by Changing Values (EX 224)
25. Goal Seek (EX 225)

 If you have a SAM user profile, you may have access to hands-on instruction, practice, and assessment. Log in to your SAM account (http://sam2007.course.com) to launch any assigned training activities or exams that relate to the skills covered in this chapter.

Learn It Online

Learn It Online is a series of online student exercises that test your knowledge of chapter content and key terms.

Instructions: To complete the Learn It Online exercises, start your browser, click the Address bar, and then enter the Web address `scsite.com/off2007/learn`. When the Office 2007 Learn It Online page is displayed, click the link for the exercise you want to complete and then read the instructions.

Chapter Reinforcement TF, MC, and SA
A series of true/false, multiple choice, and short answer questions that test your knowledge of the chapter content.

Flash Cards
An interactive learning environment where you identify chapter key terms associated with displayed definitions.

Practice Test
A series of multiple choice questions that test your knowledge of chapter content and key terms.

Who Wants To Be a Computer Genius?
An interactive game that challenges your knowledge of chapter content in the style of a television quiz show.

Wheel of Terms
An interactive game that challenges your knowledge of chapter key terms in the style of the television show *Wheel of Fortune*.

Crossword Puzzle Challenge
A crossword puzzle that challenges your knowledge of key terms presented in the chapter.

Apply Your Knowledge

Reinforce the skills and apply the concepts you learned in this chapter.

Understanding Logical Tests and Absolute Cell Referencing

Instructions Part 1: Determine the truth value (true or false) of the following logical tests, given the following cell values: X4 = 25; Y3 = 28; K7 = 110; Z2 = 15; and Q9 = 35. Enter true or false.

a. Y3 < X4   Truth value: _____

b. Q9 = K7   Truth value: _____

c. X4 + 15 * Z2 / 5 <> K7   Truth value: _____

d. K7 / Z2 > X4 − Y3   Truth value: _____

e. Q9 * 2 − 42 < (X4 + Y3 − 8) / 9   Truth value: _____

f. K7 + 300 <= X4 * Z2 + 10   Truth value: _____

g. Q9 + K7 > 2 * (Q9 + 25)   Truth value: _____

h. Y3 = 4 * (Q9 / 5)   Truth value: _____

Instructions Part 2: Write cell K23 as a relative reference, absolute reference, mixed reference with the row varying, and mixed reference with the column varying.

_____ _____ _____ _____

Instructions Part 3: Start Excel. Open the workbook Apply 3-1 Absolute Cell References. See the inside back cover of this book for instructions for downloading the Data Files for Students, or see your instructor for information on accessing the files required in this book. You will recreate the numerical grid pictured in Figure 3–82 on the next page.

Continued >

STUDENT ASSIGNMENTS

Apply Your Knowledge *continued*

Perform the following tasks:

1. Enter a formula in cell C7 that multiplies cell C2 times the sum of cells C3 through C6. Write the formula so that when you copy it to cells D7 and E7, cell C2 remains absolute. Verify your formula by checking it with the values found in cells C7, D7, and E7 in Figure 3–82.

2. Enter a formula in cell F3 that multiplies cell B3 times the sum of cells C3 through E3. Write the formula so that when you copy the formula to cells F4, F5, and F6, cell B3 remains absolute. Verify your formula by checking it with the values found in cells F3, F4, F5, and F6 in Figure 3–82.

3. Enter a formula in cell C8 that multiplies cell C2 times the sum of cells C3 through C6. Write the formula so that when you copy the formula to cells D8 and E8, Excel adjusts all the cell references according to the destination cells. Verify your formula by checking it with the values found in cells C8, D8, and E8 in Figure 3–82.

4. Enter a formula in cell G3 that multiplies cell B3 times the sum of cells C3, D3, and E3. Write the formula so that when you copy the formula to cells G4, G5, and G6, Excel adjusts all the cell references according to the destination cells. Verify your formula by checking it with the values found in cells G3, G4, G5, and G6 in Figure 3–82.

5. Change the document properties, as specified by your instructor. Change the worksheet header with your name, course number, and other information requested by your instructor. Save the workbook using the file name, Apply 3-1 Absolute Cell References Complete, and submit the revised workbook as requested by your instructor.

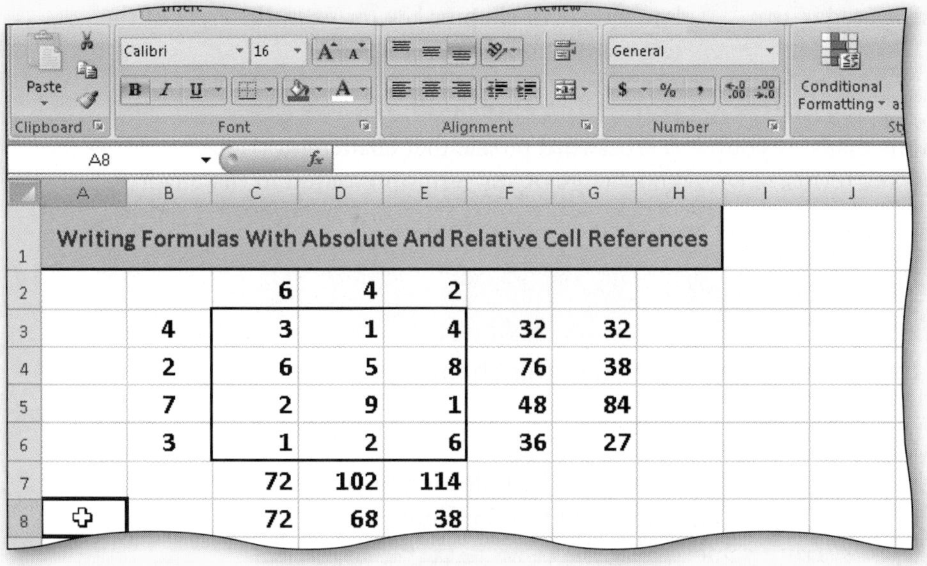

Figure 3–82

Extend Your Knowledge

Extend the skills you learned in this chapter and experiment with new skills. You may need to use Help to complete the assignment.

Nested IF Functions and More About the Fill Handle

Instructions Part 1: Start Excel. You will use nested IF functions to determine values for sets of data.

Perform the following tasks:

1. Enter the following IF function in cell C1:
    =IF(B1="CA","West", IF(B1="NJ","East", IF(B1="IL","Midwest","State Error")))

2. Use the fill handle to copy the nested IF function down through cell C7. Enter the following data in the cells in the range B1:B7 and then write down the results that display in cells C1 through C7 for each set. Set 1: B1 = CA; B2 = NY; B3 = NJ; B4 = MI; B5 = IL; B6 = CA; B7 = IL. Set 2: B1= WI; B2 = NJ; B3 = IL; B4 = CA; B5 = NJ; B6 = NY; B7 = CA.

Set 1 Results: _____

Set 2 Results: _____

Instructions Part 2: Start Excel. Open the workbook Extend 3-1 Create Series. See the inside back cover of this book for instructions for downloading the Data Files for Students, or see your instructor for information on accessing the files required in this book.

Perform the following tasks:

1. Use the fill handle on one column at a time to propagate the fourteen series through row 16 as shown in Figure 3–83. For example, in column A, select cell A2 and drag the fill handle down to cell A16. In column C, hold down the CTRL key to repeat Monday through cell C16. In column D, select the range D2:D3 and drag the fill handle down to cell D16. Likewise, in columns F and I through K, select the two adjacent cells in rows 2 and 3 before dragging the fill handle down to the corresponding cell in row 16.

2. Select cell D21. While holding down the CTRL key, one at a time drag the fill handle three cells to the right, to the left, up, and down to generate four series of numbers beginning with zero and incremented by one.

3. Select cell I21. Point to the cell border so that the mouse pointer changes to a plus sign with four arrows. Drag the mouse pointer down to cell I22 to move the contents of cell I21 to cell I22.

4. Select cell I22. Point to the cell border so that the mouse pointer changes to a plus sign with four arrows. While holding down the CTRL key, drag the mouse pointer to cell M22 to copy the contents of cell I22 to cell M22.

5. Select cell M21. Drag the fill handle in to the center of cell M21 so that the cell is shaded in order to delete the cell contents.

6. Change the document properties, as specified by your instructor. Change the worksheet header with your name,

	B	C	D	E	F	G	H	I	J	K	L	M	N	O	P
1				Using the Magical Fill Handle											
2	Monday	Monday	Mon	January	Jan	1	Version 1	1st Year	-1	1.00%	0.2	2007			
3	Tuesday	Monday	Tue	February	Feb	2	Version 2	2nd Year	-3	3.00%	0.4	2008			
4	Wednesda	Monday	Wed	March	Mar	3	Version 3	3rd Year	-5	5.00%	0.6	2009			
5	Thursday	Monday	Thu	April	Apr	4	Version 4	4th Year	-7	7.00%	0.8	2010			
6	Friday	Monday	Fri	May	May	5	Version 5	5th Year	-9	9.00%	1	2011			
7	Saturday	Monday	Sat	June	Jun	6	Version 6	6th Year	-11	11.00%	1.2	2012			
8	Sunday	Monday	Sun	July	Jul	7	Version 7	7th Year	-13	13.00%	1.4	2013			
9	Monday	Monday	Mon	August	Aug	8	Version 8	8th Year	-15	15.00%	1.6	2014			
10	Tuesday	Monday	Tue	September	Sep	9	Version 9	9th Year	-17	17.00%	1.8	2015			
11	Wednesda	Monday	Wed	October	Oct	10	Version 10	10th Year	-19	19.00%	2	2016			
12	Thursday	Monday	Thu	November	Nov	11	Version 11	11th Year	-21	21.00%	2.2	2017			
13	Friday	Monday	Fri	December	Dec	12	Version 12	12th Year	-23	23.00%	2.4	2018			
14	Saturday	Monday	Sat	January	Jan	13	Version 13	13th Year	-25	25.00%	2.6	2019			
15	Sunday	Monday	Sun	February	Feb	14	Version 14	14th Year	-27	27.00%	2.8	2020			
16	Monday	Monday	Mon	March	Mar	15	Version 15	15th Year	-29	29.00%	3	2021			
17															
18			-3												
19			-2												
20			-1												
21	-2	-1	0		1	2	3								
22			1					Move				Move			
23			2												
24			3												
25															

M21

Sheet1 / Sheet2 / Sheet3

Ready

Extend 3-1 Create Se...

Figure 3–83

course number, and other information requested by your instructor. Save the workbook using the file name, Extend 3-1 Create Series Complete, and submit the revised workbook as requested by your instructor.

Make It Right

Analyze a workbook and correct all errors and/or improve the design.

Inserting Rows, Moving a Range, and Correcting Formulas in a Worksheet
Instructions: Start Excel. Open the workbook Make It Right 3-1 e-MusicPro.com Annual Projected Net Income. See the inside back cover of this book for instructions for downloading the Data Files for Students, or see your instructor for information on accessing the files required for this book. Correct the following design and formula problems (Figure 3–84a) in the worksheet.

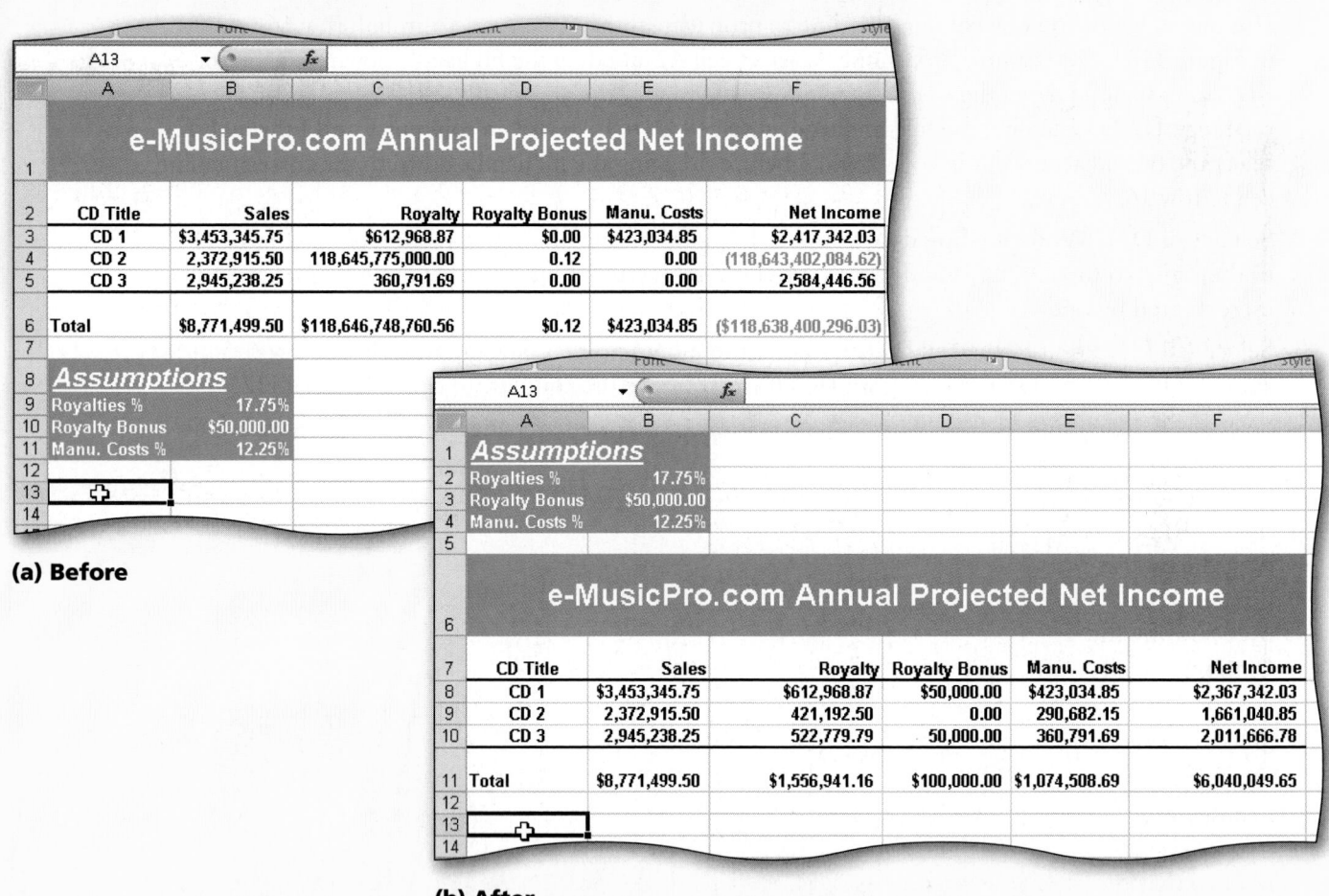

(a) Before

(b) After

Figure 3–84

1. The Royalty in cell C3 is computed using the formula =B9*B3 (Royalties % × Sales). Similar formulas are used in cells C4 and C5. The formula in cell C3 was entered and copied to cells C4 and C5. Although the result in cell C3 is correct, the results in cells C4 and C5 are incorrect. Edit the formula in cell C3 by changing cell B9 to an absolute cell reference. Copy the corrected formula in cell C3 to cells C4 and C5. After completing the copy, click the Auto Fill Options button arrow that displays below and to the right of cell C5 and choose Fill Without Formatting.

2. The Royalty Bonus amounts in cells D3, D4, and D5 are computed using the IF function. The Royalty Bonus should equal the amount in cell B10 ($50,000) if the corresponding Sales in column B is greater than or equal to $2,750,000. If the corresponding Sales in column B is less than $2,750,000, then the Royalty Bonus is zero ($0). The IF function in cell D3 was entered and

copied to cells D4 and D5. The current IF functions in cells D3, D4, and D5 are incorrect. Edit and correct the IF function in cell D3. Copy the corrected formula in cell D3 to cells D4 and D5. After completing the copy, click the Auto Fill Options button arrow that displays below and to the right of cell D5 and choose Fill Without Formatting.

3. The Manufacturing Costs in cell E3 is computed using the formula =B11*B3 (Manu. Costs % x Sales). The formula in cell E3 was entered and copied to cells E4 and E5. Although the result in cell E3 is correct, the results in cells E4 and E5 are incorrect. Edit and correct the formula in cell E3 by changing cell B11 to an absolute cell reference. Copy the corrected formula in cell E3 to cells E4 and E5. After completing the copy, click the Auto Fill Options button arrow that displays below and to the right of cell E5 and choose Fill Without Formatting.

4. Change the design of the worksheet by moving the Assumptions table in the range A8:B11 to the range A1:B4 as shown in Figure 3–84b. To complete the move, insert five rows above row 1 and then drag the Assumptions table to the range A1:B4. Use Figure 3–84b to verify that Excel automatically adjusted the cell references based on the move. Use the Undo button and Redo button on the Quick Access Toolbar to move the Assumptions table back and forth while the results of the formulas remain the same.

5. Change the document properties, as specified by your instructor. Change the worksheet header with your name, course number, and other information requested by your instructor. Save the workbook using the file name, Make It Right 3-1 e-MusicPro.com Annual Projected Net Income Complete, and submit the revised workbook as requested by your instructor.

In the Lab

Create a workbook using the guidelines, concepts, and skills presented in this chapter. Labs are listed in order of increasing difficulty.

Lab 1: Eight-Year Financial Projection

Problem: Your supervisor in the Finance department at Salioto Auto Parts has asked you to create a worksheet that will project the annual gross margin, expenses, total expenses, operating income, income taxes, and net income for the next ten years based on the assumptions in Table 3–9. The desired worksheet is shown in Figure 3–85 on the next page. In Part 1 you will create the worksheet. In Part 2 you will create a chart to present the data, shown in Figure 3–86 on page 236. In Part 3 you will use Goal Seek to analyze three different sales scenarios.

Table 3–9 Salioto Auto Parts Financial Projection Assumptions	
Units Sold in Prior Year	11,459,713
Unit Cost	$13.40
Annual Sales Growth	4.50%
Annual Price Decrease	4.25%
Margin	39.25%

Continued >

In the Lab continued

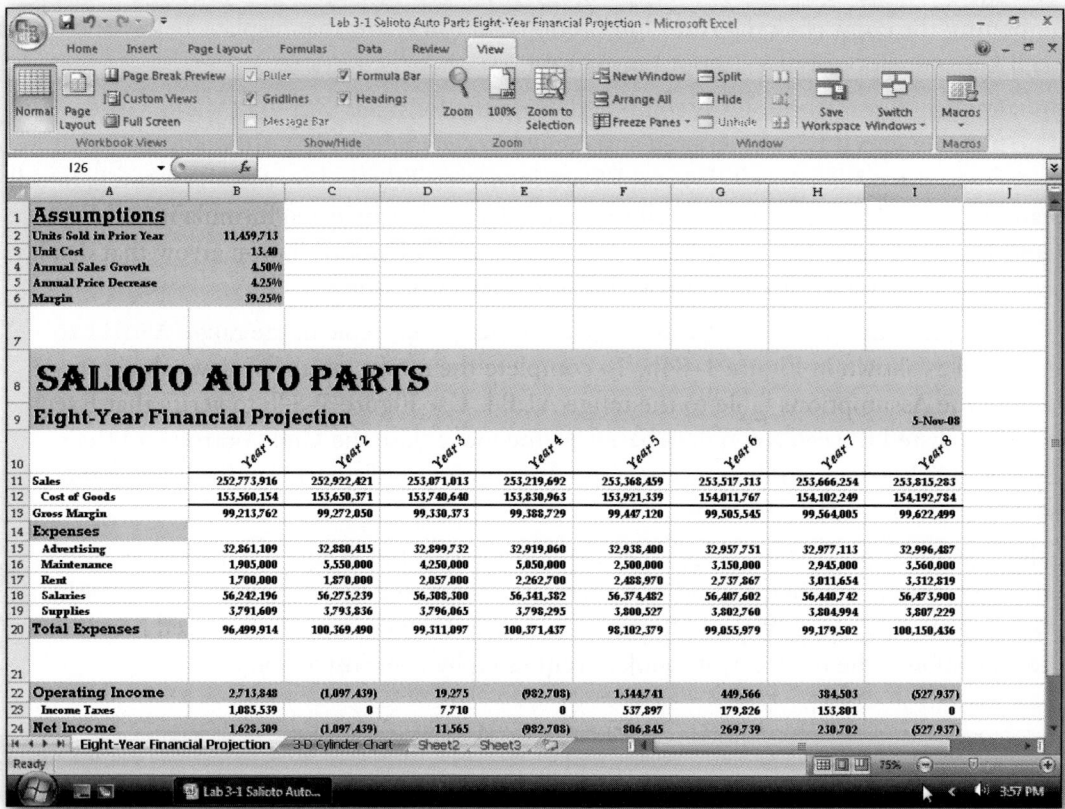

Figure 3-85

Instructions Part 1:

1. Start Excel. Apply the Apex theme to the worksheet by using the Themes button on the Page Layout tab on the Ribbon. Bold the entire worksheet by selecting the entire worksheet and using the Bold button on the Home tab on the Ribbon.

2. Enter the worksheet title Salioto Auto Parts in cell A8 and the subtitle Eight-Year Financial Projection in cell A9. Format the worksheet title in cell A8 to 36-point Algerian (or a similar font). Format the worksheet subtitle in cell A9 to 20-point Rockwell (or a similar font). Enter the system date in cell I9 using the NOW function. Format the date to the 14-Mar-01 style.

3. Change the following column widths: A = 25.00 characters; B through I = 15.00 characters. Change the heights of rows 7, 10, and 21 to 42.00 points.

4. Enter the eight column titles Year 1 through Year 8 in the range B10:I10 by entering Year 1 in cell B10 and then dragging cell B10's fill handle through the range C10:I10. Format cell B10 as follows: (a) increase the font size to 14; (b) center and italicize; and (c) rotate its contents 45°. Use the Format Painter button to copy the format assigned to cell B10 to the range C10:I10.

5. Enter the row titles in the range A11:A24. Change the font in cells A14, A20, A22, and A24 to 14-point Rockwell (or a similar font). Add thick bottom borders to the ranges B10:I10 and B12:I12.

6. Enter the table title Assumptions in cell A1. Enter the assumptions in Table 3-9 in the range A2:B6. Use format symbols when entering the numbers. Change the font size of the table title to 14-point Rockwell and underline it.

7. Select the range B11:I24 and then click the Format Cells: Number Dialog Box Launcher on the Home tab on the Ribbon to display the Format Cells dialog box. Use the Number category in the Format Cells dialog box to assign the Comma style with no decimal places and negative numbers enclosed in parentheses to the range B11:I24.

8. Complete the following entries:
   a. Year 1 Sales (cell B11) = Units Sold in Prior Year * (Unit Cost / (1 − Margin)) or =B2 * (B3 / (1 − B6))
   b. Year 2 Sales (cell C11) = Year 1 Sales * (1 + Annual Sales Growth) * (1 − Annual Price Decrease) or =B11 * (1 + $B$4) * (1 − $B$5)
   c. Copy cell C11 to the range D11:I11.
   d. Year 1 Cost of Goods (cell B12) = Year 1 Sales − (Year 1 Sales * Margin) or =B11 * (1 − $B$6)
   e. Copy cell B12 to the range C12:I12.
   f. Gross Margin (cell B13) = Year 1 Sales − Year 1 Cost of Goods or =B11 − B12
   g. Copy cell B13 to the range C13:I13.
   h. Year 1 Advertising (cell B15) = 500 + 13% * Year 1 Sales or =500 + 13% * B11
   i. Copy cell B15 to the range C15:I15.
   j. Maintenance (row 16): Year 1 = 1,905,000; Year 2 = 5,550,000; Year 3 = 4,250,000; Year 4 = 5,050,000; Year 5 = 2,500,000; Year 6 = 3,150,000; Year 7 = 2,945,000; and Year 8 = 3,560.000.
   k. Year 1 Rent (cell B17) = 1,700,000
   l. Year 2 Rent (cell C17) = Year 1 Rent + 10% * Year 1 Rent or =B17 * (1 + 10%)
   m. Copy cell C17 to the range D17:I17.
   n. Year 1 Salaries (cell B18) = 22.25% * Year 1 Sales or =22.25% * B11
   o. Copy cell B18 to the range C18:I18.
   p. Year 1 Supplies (cell B19) = 1.5% * Year 1 Sales or =1.5% * B11
   q. Copy cell B19 to the range C19:I19.
   r. Year 1 Total Expenses (cell B20) or =SUM(B15:B19)
   s. Copy cell B20 to the range C20:I20.
   t. Year 1 Operating Income (cell B22) = Year 1 Gross Margin − Year 1 Total Expenses or =B13 − B20
   u. Copy cell B22 to the range C22:I22.
   v. Year 1 Income Taxes (cell B23): If Year 1 Operating Income is less than 0, then Year 1 Income Taxes equal 0; otherwise Year 1 Income Taxes equal 40% * Year 1 Operating Income or =IF(B22 < 0, 0, 40% * B22)
   w. Copy cell B23 to the range C23:I23.
   x. Year 1 Net Income (cell B24) = Year 1 Operating Income − Year 1 Income Taxes or =B22 − B23
   y. Copy cell B24 to the range C24:I24.

9. Change the background colors as shown in Figure 3-85. Use Orange (column 3 under Standard Colors) for the background colors.

10. Zoom to: (a) 200%; (b) 75%; (c) 25%; and (d) 100%.

11. Change the document properties, as specified by your instructor. Change the worksheet header with your name, course number, and other information requested by your instructor. Save the workbook using the file name, Lab 3-1 Salioto Auto Parts Eight-Year Financial Projection.

12. Preview the worksheet. Use the Page Setup button to fit the printout on one page in landscape orientation. Preview the formulas version (CTRL+`) of the worksheet in landscape orientation using the Fit to option. Press CTRL+` to instruct Excel to display the values version of the worksheet. Save the workbook again and close the workbook.

13. Submit the workbook as requested by your instructor.

Instructions Part 2:

1. Start Excel. Open the workbook Lab 3-1 Salioto Auto Parts Eight-Year Financial Projection.

2. Use the nonadjacent ranges B10:I10 and B24:I24 to create a 3-D Cylinder chart. Draw the chart by clicking the Column button on the Insert tab on the Ribbon. When the Column gallery is displayed, click the Clustered Cylinder chart type (column 1, row 2). When the chart is displayed, click the Move Chart button on the Ribbon to move the chart to a new sheet.

Continued >

In the Lab *continued*

3. Select the legend on the right side of the chart and delete it. Add the chart title by clicking the Layout tab on the Ribbon, then clicking the Chart Title button. Click Above Chart in the Chart Title gallery. Format the chart title as shown in Figure 3–86.

4. To change the color of the cylinders, click one of the cylinders and use the Shape Fill button on the Format tab on the Ribbon. To change the color of the wall, click the wall behind the cylinders and use the Shape Fill button on the Format tab on the Ribbon. Use the same procedure to change the color of the base of the wall.

5. Rename the sheet tabs Eight-Year Financial Projection and 3-D Cylinder Chart. Rearrange the sheets so that the worksheet is leftmost, and color their tabs as shown in Figure 3–86.

6. Click the Eight-Year Financial Projection tab to display the worksheet. Save the workbook using the same file name (Lab 3-1 Salioto Auto Parts Eight-Year Financial Projection) as defined in Part 1. Submit the workbook as requested by your instructor.

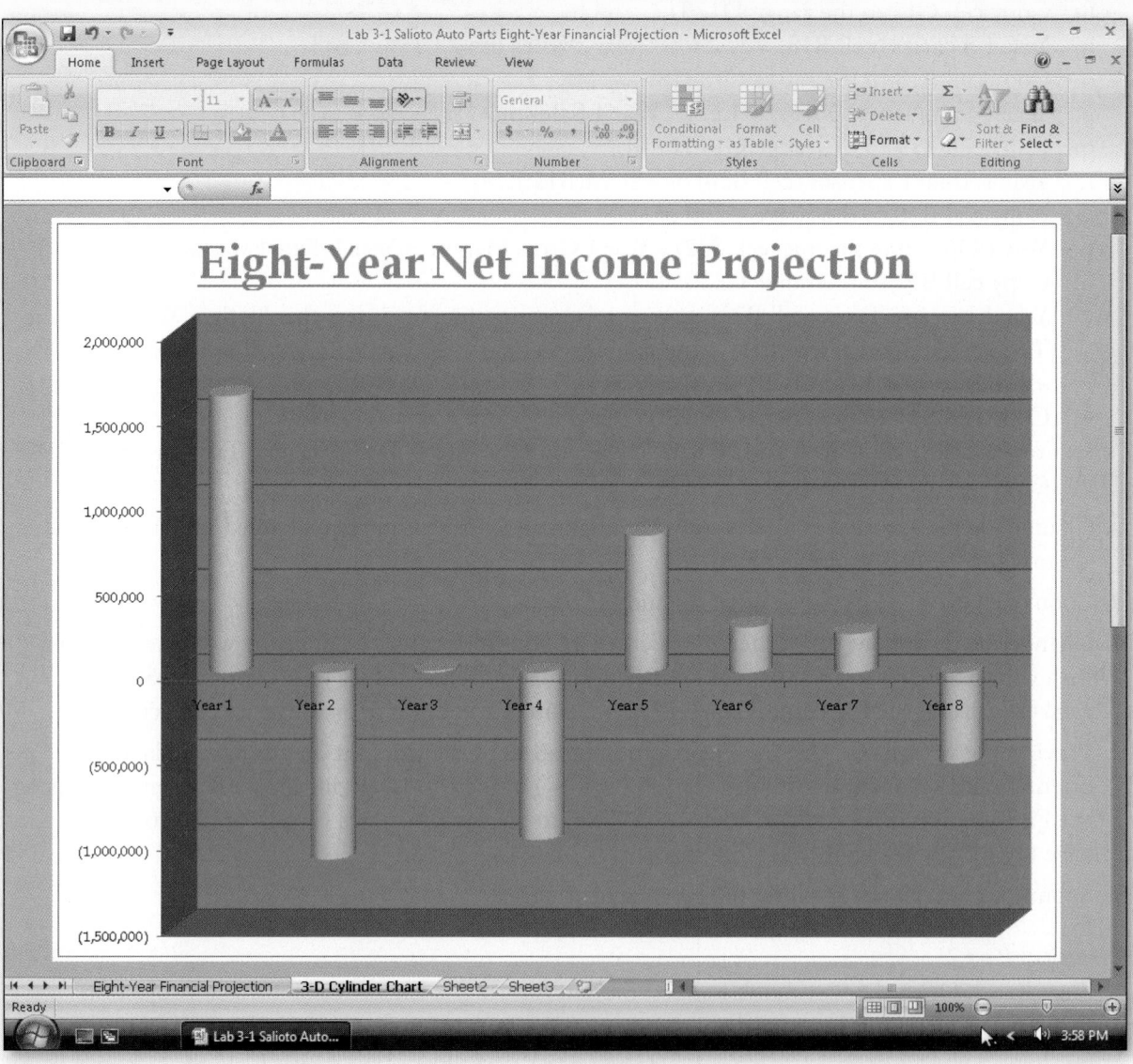

Figure 3–86

Instructions Part 3:

1. Start Excel. Open the workbook Lab 3-1 Salioto Auto Parts Eight-Year Financial Projection. Do not save the workbook in this part. Divide the window into two panes by dragging the horizontal split box between rows 6 and 7. Use the scroll bars to show both the top and bottom of the worksheet. Using the numbers in columns 2 and 3 of Table 3-10, analyze the effect of changing the annual sales growth (cell B4) and annual price decrease (cell B5) on the net incomes in row 24. The resulting answers are in column 4 of Table 3–10. Submit the workbook or results of the what-if analysis for each case as requested by your instructor.

Table 3–10 Salioto Auto Parts Data to Analyze and Results			
Case	Annual Sales Growth	Annual Price Decrease	Year 8 Resulting Net Income in Cell I24
1	7.45%	5.25%	174,568
2	12.75%	−3.00%	6,677,903
3	−7.25%	1.65%	(3,552,156)

2. Close the workbook without saving it, and then reopen it. Use the What-If Analysis button on the Data tab on the Ribbon to goal seek. Determine a margin (cell B6) that would result in a Year 8 net income of $2,000,000 (cell I24). You should end up with a margin of 40.68% in cell B6. Submit the workbook with the new values or the results of the goal seek as requested by your instructor. Do not save the workbook with the latest changes.

In the Lab

Lab 2: Modifying a Weekly Payroll Worksheet

Problem: As a summer intern at Britney's Music Emporium, you have been asked to modify the weekly payroll report shown in Figure 3–87a on the next page. The workbook, Lab 3-2 Britney's Music Emporium Weekly Payroll Report, is included with the Data Files for Students. See the inside back cover of this book for instructions for downloading the Data Files for Students, or see your instructor for information on accessing the files required for this book.

   The major modifications to the payroll report to be made in this exercise include: (1) reformatting the worksheet; (2) adding computations of time-and-a-half for hours worked greater than 40; (3) adding calculations to charge no federal tax in certain situations; (4) adding Social Security and Medicare deductions; (5) adding and deleting employees; and (6) changing employee information. The final payroll report is shown in Figure 3–87b on the next page.

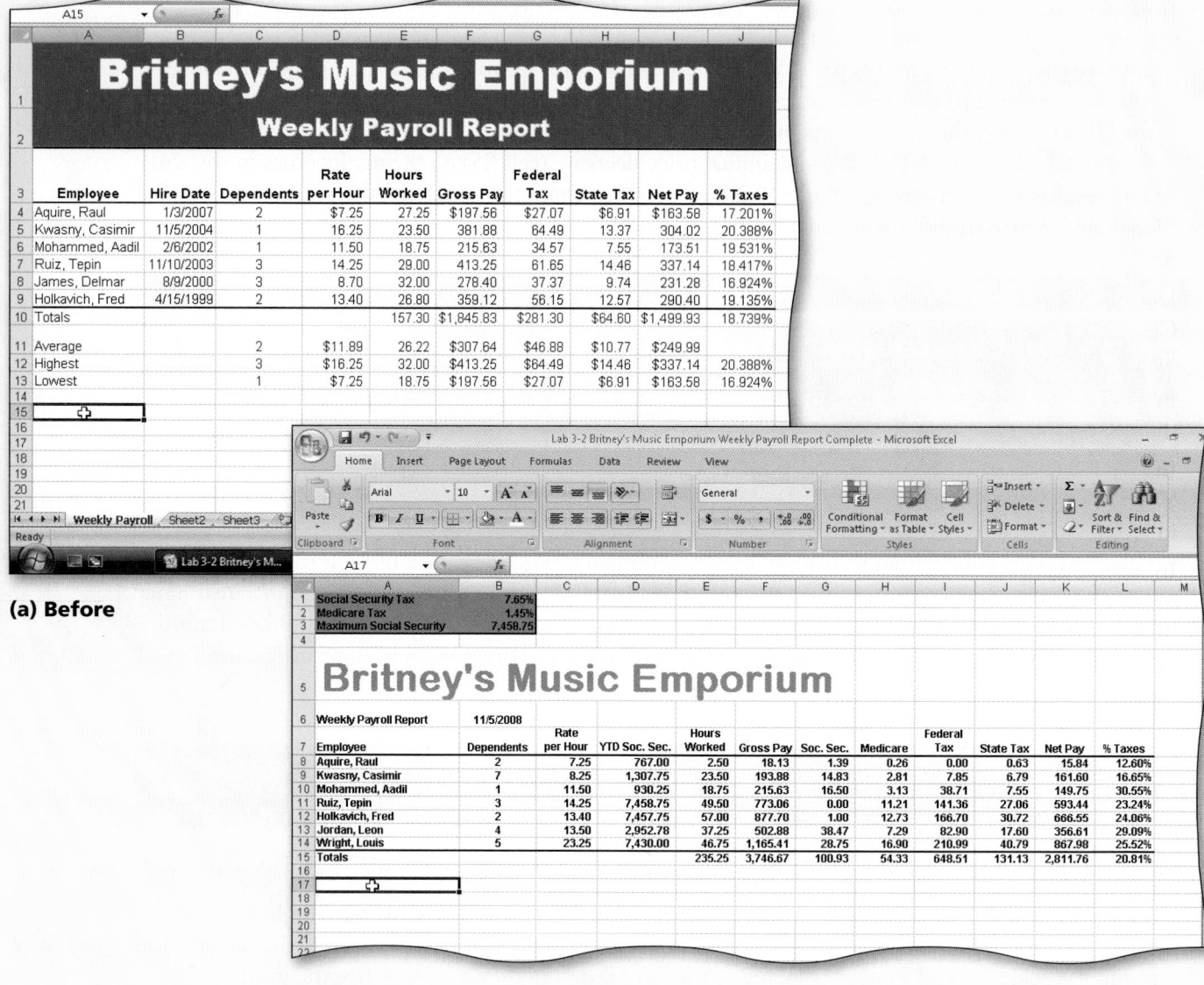

(a) Before

(b) After

Figure 3–87

Instructions Part 1:

1. Start Excel. Open the workbook, Lab 3-2 Britney's Music Emporium Weekly Payroll Report and then save the workbook using the file name Lab 3-2 Britney's Music Emporium Weekly Payroll Report Complete.

2. Select the worksheet by clicking the Select All button. Click the Clear button on the Home tab on the Ribbon and then click Clear Formats on the Clear menu to clear the formatting. Bold the entire worksheet.

3. Delete rows 11 through 13 to remove the statistics below the Totals row. Change all the row heights back to the default height (12.75).

4. Insert four rows above row 1 by selecting rows 1 through 4, right-clicking the selection, and clicking Insert on the shortcut menu.

5. Change the row heights as follows: row 5 = 48.00; rows 6 and 7 = 25.50. One at a time, select cells D7, E7, and G7. For each cell, press the F2 key and then the ENTER key to display the column headings on multiple rows. Center the range B7:J7.

6. Delete column B by right-clicking the column heading and clicking Delete on the shortcut menu.

7. Insert a new column between columns C and D. Change the column widths as follows: A = 25.00; D = 13.00; and E through K = 9.71. Enter the new column D title **YTD Soc. Sec.** in cell D7.

8. Insert two new columns between columns F and G. Enter the new column G title **Soc. Sec.** in cell G7. Enter the new column H title **Medicare** in cell H7.

9. Enhance the worksheet title in cell A5 by using a 36-point light blue Arial Rounded MT Bold (or a similar font) font style as shown in Figure 3–87b.

10. Assign the NOW function to cell B6 and format it to the 3/14/2001 style.

11. Delete employee James, Delmar (row 12). Change Raul Aquire's (row 8) hours worked to 2.5. Change Casimir Kwasny's (row 9) number of dependents to 7 and rate per hour to $8.25. Change Tepin Ruiz's (row 11) hours worked to 49.5 and Fred Holkavich's (row 12) hours worked to 57.

12. Freeze column A and rows 1 through 7 by selecting cell B8, clicking the Freeze Panes button on the View tab on the Ribbon, and then clicking Freeze Panes on the Freeze Panes menu.

13. In column D, enter the YTD Soc. Sec. values listed in Table 3–11.

14. Insert two new rows immediately above the Totals row. Add the new employee data as listed in Table 3–12.

Table 3–11 The Britney Music Emporium's YTD Social Security Values	
Employee	**YTD Soc. Sec.**
Aquire, Raul	767.00
Kwasny, Casimir	1307.75
Mohammed, Aadil	930.25
Ruiz, Tepin	7458.75
Holkavich, Fred	7457.75

Table 3–12 The Britney Music Emporium's New Employee Data				
Employee	**Dependents**	**Rate per Hour**	**YTD Soc. Sec.**	**Hours Worked**
Jordan, Leon	4	13.50	2952.78	37.25
Wright, Louis	5	23.25	7430.00	46.75

15. Center the range B6:B14. Use the Currency category in the Format Cells dialog box to assign a Comma style (no dollar signs) with two decimal places and negative numbers within parentheses to the range C8:K15. Assign a Percent style and two decimal places to the range L8:L15. Draw a thick bottom border in the ranges A7:L7 and A14:L14.

16. As shown in Figure 3–87b, enter and format the Social Security (7.65% with a maximum of $7,458.75) and Medicare tax (1.45%) information in the range A1:B3. Use format symbols where applicable.

17. Change the formulas to determine the gross pay in column F and the federal tax in column I as follows:

   a. In cell F8, enter an IF function that applies the following logic and then copy it to the range F9:F14. If Hours Worked <= 40, then Rate per Hour * Hours Worked, otherwise Rate per Hour * Hours Worked + 0.5 * Rate per Hour * (Hours Worked − 40) or =IF(E8 <= 40, C8 * E8, C8 * E8 + 0.5 * C8 *(E8 − 40))

   b. In cell I8, enter the IF function that applies the following logic and then copy it to the range I9:I14. If (Gross Pay − Dependents * 22.09 > 0, then 20% * (Gross Pay − Dependents * 22.09), otherwise 0 or =IF(F8 − B8 * 22.09 > 0, 20% * (F8 − B8 * 22.09), 0)

Continued >

In the Lab *continued*

18. An employee pays Social Security tax only if his or her YTD Soc. Sec. in column D is less than the Maximum Social Security value in cell B3. Use the following logic to determine the Social Security tax for Raul Aquire in cell G8 and then copy it to the range G9:G14.

Soc. Sec. (cell G8): If Social Security Tax * Gross Pay + YTD Soc. Sec. > Maximum Social Security, then Maximum Social Security − YTD Soc. Sec., otherwise Social Security Tax * Gross Pay or =IF($B$1 * F8 + D8 >= $B$3, $B$3 − D8, $B$1 * F8)

19. In cell H8, enter the following formula and then copy it to the range H9:H14:

Medicare (cell H8) = Medicare Tax * Gross Pay or =$B$2 * F8

20. In cell K8, enter the following formula and copy it to the range K9:K14:

Net Pay (K8) = Gross Pay − (Soc. Sec. + Medicare + Federal Tax + State Tax) or =F8 − (G8 + H8 + I8 + J8)

21. In cell L8, enter the following formula and copy it to the range L9:L14:

% Taxes (cell L8) = (Soc. Sec. + Medicare + Federal Tax + State Tax) / Gross Pay or =(G8 + H8 + I8 + J8) / F8

22. Use the Range Finder (double-click cell) to verify the new totals as shown in row 15 in Figure 3–87b. Unfreeze the worksheet by clicking the Freeze Panes button on the View tab on the Ribbon, and then clicking Unfreeze Panes on the Freeze Panes menu.

23. Preview the worksheet. Use the Page Setup button to change the orientation to landscape and fit the report on one page.

24. Change the document properties, as specified by your instructor. Change the worksheet header with your name, course number, and other information requested by your instructor. Save the workbook.

25. Use the Zoom button on the View tab on the Ribbon to change the view of the worksheet. One by one, select all the percents on the Zoom dialog box. When you are done, return the worksheet to 100% magnification.

26. Preview the formulas version (CTRL+`) in landscape orientation. Close the worksheet without saving the latest changes.

27. Submit the workbook as requested by your instructor.

Instructions Part 2: Start Excel. Open Lab 3-2 Britney's Music Emporium Weekly Payroll Report Complete. Do not save the workbook in this part. Using the numbers in Table 3–13, analyze the effect of changing the Medicare tax in cell B2. The first case should result in a total Medicare tax in cell H15 of $106.78. The second case should result in a total Medicare tax of $166.73. Close the workbook without saving changes. Submit the results of the what-if analysis as requested by your instructor.

Table 3–13 The Britney Music Emporium's Medicare Tax Cases	
Case	**Medicare Tax**
1	2.85%
2	4.45%

Instructions Part 3: Submit results for this part as requested by your instructor.

1. Start Excel. Open Lab 3-2 Britney's Music Emporium Weekly Payroll Report Complete. Select cell F8. Write down the formula that Excel displays in the formula bar. Select the range C8:C14. Point to the border surrounding the range and drag the selection to the range D17:D23. Click cell F8, and write down the formula that Excel displays in the formula bar below the one you wrote down earlier. Compare the two formulas. What can you conclude about how Excel responds when you move cells involved in a formula? Click the Undo button on the Quick Access Toolbar.

2. Right-click the range C8:C14 and then click Delete on the shortcut menu. When Excel displays the Delete dialog box, click Shift cells left and then click the OK button. What does Excel display in cell F8? Click cell F8 and then point to the Trace Error button that is displayed to the left of the cell. Write down the ScreenTip that is displayed. Click the Undo button on the Quick Access Toolbar.
3. Right-click the range C8:C14 and then click Insert on the shortcut menu. When Excel displays the Insert dialog box, click Shift cells right and then click the OK button. What does Excel display in the formula bar when you click cell F8? What does Excel display in the formula bar when you click cell G8? What can you conclude about how Excel responds when you insert cells next to cells involved in a formula? Close the workbook without saving the changes.

In the Lab

Lab 3: Analysis of Indirect Expense Allocations

Problem: Your classmate works part time as a consultant for RockieView Resort and Spa. She has asked you to assist her in creating an indirect expense allocation worksheet (Figure 3–88) that will help the resort and spa administration better evaluate the profit centers described in Table 3–14 on the next page.

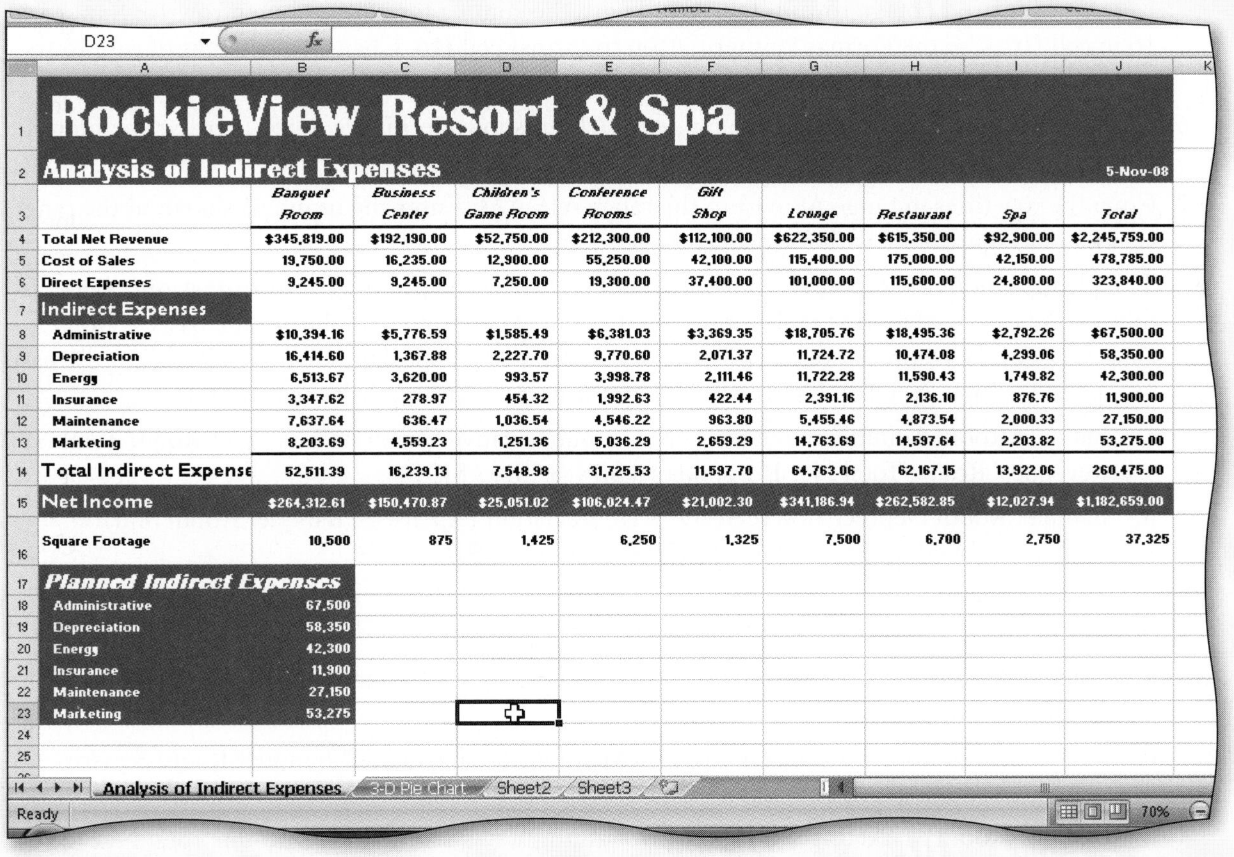

RockieView Resort & Spa

Analysis of Indirect Expenses — 5-Nov-08

	Banquet Room	Business Center	Children's Game Room	Conference Rooms	Gift Shop	Lounge	Restaurant	Spa	Total
Total Net Revenue	$345,819.00	$192,190.00	$52,750.00	$212,300.00	$112,100.00	$622,350.00	$615,350.00	$92,900.00	$2,245,759.00
Cost of Sales	19,750.00	16,235.00	12,900.00	55,250.00	42,100.00	115,400.00	175,000.00	42,150.00	478,785.00
Direct Expenses	9,245.00	9,245.00	7,250.00	19,300.00	37,400.00	101,000.00	115,600.00	24,800.00	323,840.00
Indirect Expenses									
Administrative	$10,394.16	$5,776.59	$1,585.49	$6,381.03	$3,369.35	$18,705.76	$18,495.36	$2,792.26	$67,500.00
Depreciation	16,414.60	1,367.88	2,227.70	9,770.60	2,071.37	11,724.72	10,474.08	4,299.06	58,350.00
Energy	6,513.67	3,620.00	993.57	3,998.78	2,111.46	11,722.28	11,590.43	1,749.82	42,300.00
Insurance	3,347.62	278.97	454.32	1,992.63	422.44	2,391.16	2,136.10	876.76	11,900.00
Maintenance	7,637.64	636.47	1,036.54	4,546.22	963.80	5,455.46	4,873.54	2,000.33	27,150.00
Marketing	8,203.69	4,559.23	1,251.36	5,036.29	2,659.29	14,763.69	14,597.64	2,203.82	53,275.00
Total Indirect Expense	52,511.39	16,239.13	7,548.98	31,725.53	11,597.70	64,763.06	62,167.15	13,922.06	260,475.00
Net Income	$264,312.61	$150,470.87	$25,051.02	$106,024.47	$21,002.30	$341,186.94	$262,582.85	$12,027.94	$1,182,659.00
Square Footage	10,500	875	1,425	6,250	1,325	7,500	6,700	2,750	37,325

Planned Indirect Expenses	
Administrative	67,500
Depreciation	58,350
Energy	42,300
Insurance	11,900
Maintenance	27,150
Marketing	53,275

Figure 3–88

Continued >

In the Lab *continued*

Table 3–14 RockieView Resort and Spa Worksheet Data

	Banquet Room	Business Center	Children's Game Room	Conference Rooms	Gift Shop	Lounge	Restaurant	Spa
Total Net Revenue	345819	192190	52750	212300	112100	622350	615350	92900
Cost of Sales	19750	16235	12900	55250	42100	115400	175000	42150
Direct Expenses	9245	9245	7250	19300	37400	101000	115600	24800
Square Footage	10500	875	1425	6250	1325	7500	6700	2750

Instructions Part 1:   Do the following to create the worksheet shown in Figure 3–88.

1. Apply the Solstice theme to the worksheet. Bold the entire worksheet by selecting the entire worksheet and using the Bold button on the Ribbon.

2. Change the following column widths: A = 28.00; B through I = 13.00; J = 14.00.

3. Enter the worksheet titles in cells A1 and A2 and the system date in cell J2. Format the date to the 14-Mar-01 style.

4. Enter the column titles, row titles, and the first three rows of numbers in Table 3–14 in rows 3 through 6. Center and italicize the column headings in the range B3:J3. Add a thick bottom border to the range B3:J3. Sum the individual rows 4, 5, and 6 in the range J4:J6.

5. Enter the Square Footage row in Table 3–14 with the comma format symbol in row 16. Sum row 16 in cell J16. Use the Format Painter button to format cell J16. Change the height of row 16 to 39.00. Vertically center the range A16:J16 through the use of the Format Cells dialog box.

6. Enter the remaining row titles in the range A7:A17 as shown in Figure 3–88. Increase the font size in cells A7, A14, and A15 to 16 point.

7. Copy the row titles in range A8:A13 to the range A18:A23. Enter the numbers shown in the range B18:B23 of Figure 3–88 with format symbols.

8. The planned indirect expenses in the range B18:B23 are to be prorated across the profit center as follows: Administrative (row 8), Energy (row 10), and Marketing (row 13) on the basis of Total Net Revenue (row 4); Depreciation (row 9), Insurance (row 11), and Maintenance (row 12) on the basis of Square Footage (row 16). Use the following formulas to accomplish the prorating:

   a. Banquet Room Administrative (cell B8) = Administrative Expenses * Banquet Room Total Net Revenue / Resort Total Net Revenue or =$B$18 * B4 / $J$4

   b. Banquet Room Depreciation (cell B9) = Depreciation Expenses * Banquet Room Square Footage / Total Square Footage or =$B$19 * B16 / $J$16

   c. Banquet Room Energy (cell B10) = Energy Expenses * Banquet Room Total Net Revenue / Resort Total Net Revenue or =$B$20 * B4 / $J$4

   d. Banquet Room Insurance (cell B11) = Insurance Expenses * Banquet Room Square Feet / Total Square Footage or =$B$21 * B16 / $J$16

   e. Banquet Room Maintenance (cell B12) = Maintenance Expenses * Banquet Room Square Footage / Total Square Footage or =$B$22 * B16 / $J$16

   f. Banquet Room Marketing (cell B13) = Marketing Expenses * Banquet Room Total Net Revenue / Resort Total Net Revenue or =$B$23 * B4 / $J$4

   g. Banquet Room Total Indirect Expenses (cell B14) = SUM(B8:B13)

   h. Banquet Room Net Income (cell B15) = Total Net Revenue − (Cost of Sales + Direct Expenses + Total Indirect Expenses) or =B4 − (B5 + B6 + B14)

   i. Copy the range B8:B15 to the range C8:I15.

   j. Sum the individual rows 8 through 15 in the range J8:J15.

9. Add a thick bottom border to the range B13:J13. Assign the Currency style with two decimal places and show negative numbers in parentheses to the following ranges: B4:J4; B8:J8; and B14:J15. Assign the Comma style with two decimal places and show negative numbers in parentheses to the following ranges: B5:J6 and B9:J13.

10. Change the font in cell A1 to 48-point Britannic Bold (or a similar font). Change the font in cell A2 to 22-point Britannic Bold (or a similar font). Change the font in cell A17 to 18-point italic Britannic Bold.

11. Use the background color blue and the font color white for the ranges A1:J2; A7; A15:J15; and A17:B23 as shown in Figure 3–88.

12. Rename the Sheet1 sheet, Analysis of Indirect Expenses, and color its tab blue.

13. Update the document properties with your name, course number, and name for the workbook. Change the worksheet header with your name, course number, and other information requested by your instructor. Save the workbook using the file name, Lab 3-3 RockieView Resort and Spa Indirect Expenses Allocations.

14. Preview the worksheet. Use the Page Setup button to change the orientation to landscape and fit the report on one page. Preview the formulas version (CTRL+`) of the worksheet in landscape orientation using the Fit to option button in the Page Setup dialog box. Press CTRL+` to show the values version of the worksheet. Save the workbook again.

15. Divide the window into four panes and show the four corners of the worksheet. Remove the four panes. Close the workbook but do not save the workbook.

Instructions Part 2: Start Excel. Open Lab 3-3 RockieView Resort and Spa Indirect Expenses Allocations. Draw a 3-D Pie chart (Figure 3–89) on a separate sheet that shows the contribution of each category of indirect expense to the total indirect expenses. That is, chart the nonadjacent ranges A8:A13 (category names) and J8:J13 (data series). Show labels that include category names and percentages. Do not show the legend or leader lines. Format the 3-D Pie chart as shown in Figure 3–89. Rename the chart sheet 3-D Pie Chart and color the tab red. Move the chart tab to the right of the worksheet tab. Save the workbook using the file name, Lab 3-3 RockieView Resort and Spa Indirect Expenses Allocations. Submit the workbook as requested by your instructor.

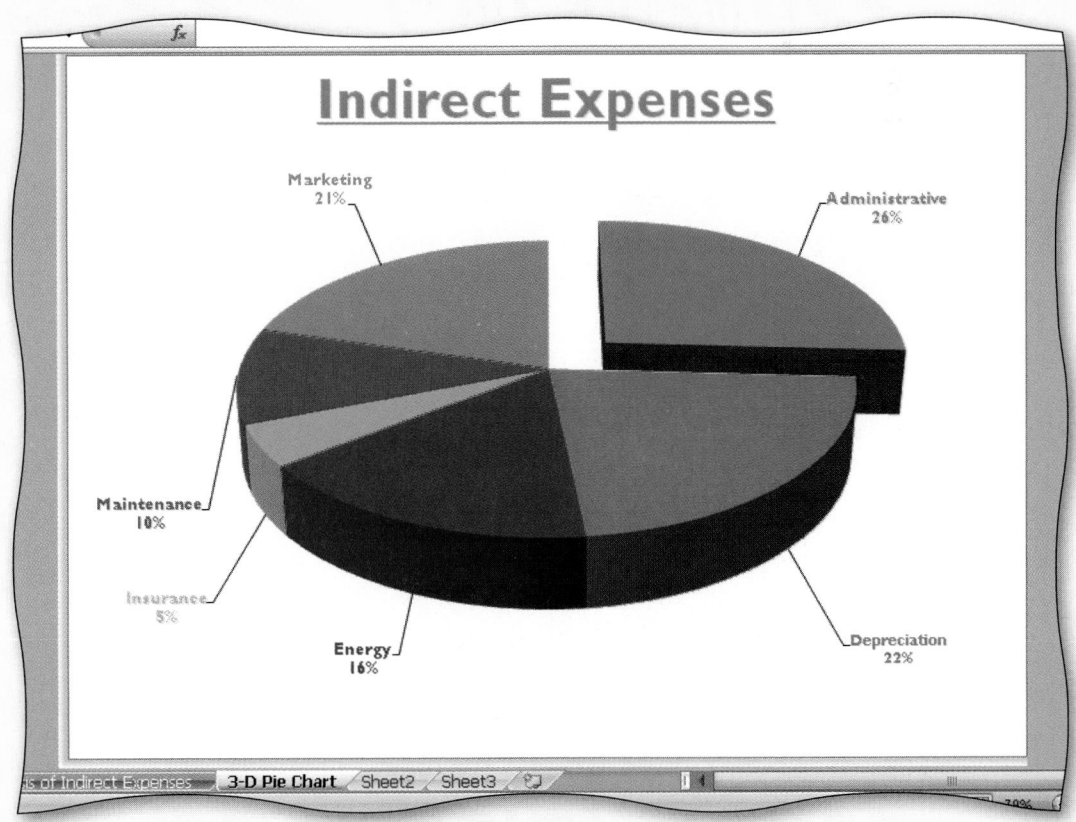

Figure 3–89

Continued >

In the Lab *continued*

Instructions Part 3:   Start Excel. Open Lab 3-3 RockieView Resort and Spa Indirect Expenses Allocations.
1. Using the numbers in Table 3–15, analyze the effect of changing the planned indirect expenses in the range B18:B23 on the net incomes for each profit center. You should end with the following totals in cell J15: Case 1 = $892,684.00 and Case 2 = $869,634.00. Submit the workbook or results for each case as requested by your instructor.
2. Use the What-If Analysis button on the Data tab on the Ribbon to goal seek. Determine a planned indirect Administrative

Table 3–15 RockieView Resort and Spa Indirect Expense Allocations What-If Data		
	Case 1	**Case 2**
Administrative	234000	210000
Depreciation	123500	152000
Energy	67750	48000
Insurance	26200	53000
Maintenance	42000	38000
Marketing	57000	72500

expense (cell B18) that would result in a total net income of $1,200,000 (cell J15). You should end up with a planned indirect Administrative expense of $50,159 in cell B18. Submit the workbook with the new values or the results of the goal seek as requested by your instructor.

Cases and Places

Apply your creative thinking and problem solving skills to design and implement a solution.

● EASIER ●● MORE DIFFICULT

● 1: Five-Year Sales Projections

You have been asked to develop a worksheet for Millennium Steel that shows annual growth for the next five years based on the prior year's sales and growth data. Include an embedded exploded 3-D Pie chart that shows the contribution of each year to the total gross margin. The data and general layout of the worksheet, including the totals, are shown in Table 3–16.

Table 3–16 Millennium Steel Sales Data and General Layout						
	Year 1	**Year 2**	**Year 3**	**Year 4**	**Year 5**	**Total**
Sales	Formula A———————————————————————————→					—
Cost of Goods	Formula B———————————————————————————→					—
Gross Margin	Formula C———————————————————————————→					—
Assumptions						
Prior Year's Sales	35234500					
Annual Growth Rate	−1.75%	12.35%	5.00%	−1.25%	8.75%	
Annual Cost Rate	41.25%	44.00%	33.00%	43.75%	34.25%	
Premium	2.90%	3.10%	4.95%	2.50%	4.50%	

Enter the formulas shown in Table 3–17 in the locations shown in Table 3–16. Copy formulas A, B, and C to the remaining years. The gross margin for the five years should equal $118,986,982.

Table 3–17 Millennium Steel Sales Projection Formulas
Formula A = Prior Year's Sales * (1 + Annual Growth Rate)
Formula B = IF(Annual Growth Rate < 0, Sales * (Annual Cost Rate + Premium), Sales * Annual Cost Rate)
Formula C = Sales − Cost of Goods

Use the concepts and techniques developed in the first three projects to create and format the worksheet and embedded 3-D Pie chart.

Use the Goal Seek command to determine the Year 1 annual growth rate that will generate a total gross margin of $125,000,000. You should end up with a Year 1 annual growth rate of 2.35%. Submit the workbook and results of the goal seek as requested by your instructor.

● 2: Bimonthly Projected Earnings and Expenditures

The *Chesterton Trib* is a small newspaper that publishes stories of local interest. Revenues are earned from subscriptions and the sale of advertising space. A fixed percentage of the Net Revenue is spent on marketing, payroll, commissions (advertising sales only), production costs, and reportorial expenses. The editor has summarized the paper's expenditures over the past year and the anticipated income from subscriptions and advertising on a bimonthly basis as shown in Table 3–18.

With the data, you have been asked to prepare a worksheet for the next shareholder's meeting showing total revenues, total expenditures, and operating incomes for each bimonthly period. Include a 3-D Cylinder chart on a separate sheet that compares the six bimonthly operating incomes. Use the concepts and techniques presented in this project to create and format the worksheet and chart.

Table 3–18 Chesterton Trib Bimonthly Projected Earnings and Expenditures

Revenue	February	April	June	August	October	December
Subscriptions	12178.30	8391.50	15714.50	16340.10	12567.25	12800.15
Advertising	4130.20	6425.00	4123.15	5023.30	7015.75	9273.20

Assumptions						
Marketing	15.60%					
Payroll	21.50%					
Commissions on Advertising	3.25%					
Production Costs	12.50%					
Reportorial Expenses	5.00%					

One shareholder lobbied to reduce marketing expenditures by 3% and payroll costs by 5%. Perform a what-if-analysis reflecting the proposed changes in expenditure assumptions. The reduction in expenditures should result in a total operating income of $59,696.91 or an increase of $9,118.59. Submit the workbook and results of the what-if analysis as requested by your instructor.

•• 3: Projected Used-Truck Savings

Cousin Abe and Aunt Esther own a paint company. Their good friend Billie Bob is retiring after 35 years of delivering the morning newspaper. Billie Bob has offered them the opportunity to take his place next year. The job requires, however, that they own a truck. They need to save enough money over the next six months to buy a $10,000 used truck.

They have job orders at their paint company for the next six months: $22,150 in July, $22,480 in August, $32,900 in September, $31,200 in October, $45,301 in November, and $32,190 in December. Each month, they spend 34.55% of the job order income on material, 3.00% on rollers and brushes, 4.75% on their retirement account, and 39.5% on food and clothing. The remaining profits (orders − total expenses) will be put aside for the used truck. Aunt Esther's retired parents have agreed to provide a bonus of $250 whenever the monthly profit exceeds $2,000. Use the concepts and techniques presented in this project to create and format the worksheet.

Cousin Abe has asked you to create a worksheet that shows orders, expenses, profits, bonuses, and savings for the next six months, and totals for each category. Aunt Esther would like to save for another used truck for $17,000. She has asked you to (a) perform a what-if analysis to determine the effect on the savings by reducing the percentage spent on material to 25% (answer total savings = $16,084.49), and (b) with the original assumptions, goal seek to determine what percentage of profits to spend on food and clothing if $15,000 is needed for the used truck (answer = 29.165%). Submit the workbook and results of the what-if analysis as requested by your instructor.

•• 4: College Expense and Resource Projections

Make It Personal

Attending college with limited resources can be a trying experience. One way to alleviate some of the financial stress is to plan ahead. Develop a worksheet following the general layout in Table 3–19 that shows the projected expenses and resources for four years of college. Use the formulas listed in Table 3–20 and the concepts and techniques presented in this project to create the worksheet.

Table 3–19 College Expense and Resource Projections

Expenses	Freshman	Sophomore	Junior	Senior	Total
Room & Board	$6,125.00	Formula A		⟶	—
Tuition & Books	8,750.00	Formula A		⟶	—
Clothes	750.00	Formula A		⟶	—
Entertainment	1,025.00	Formula A		⟶	—
Miscellaneous	675.00	Formula A		⟶	—
Total Expenses	—	—	—	—	—

Resources	Freshman	Sophomore	Junior	Senior	Total
Savings	Formula B		⟶		—
Parents	Formula B		⟶		—
Job	Formula B		⟶		—
Loans	Formula B		⟶		—
Scholarships	Formula B		⟶		—
Total Resources	—	—	—	—	—

Assumptions	
Savings	10.00%
Parents	20.00%
Job	10.00%
Loans	30.00%
Scholarships	30.00%
Annual Rate Increase	7.50%

After creating the worksheet: (a) perform what-if analysis by changing the percents of the resource assumptions; (b) perform a what-if analysis to determine the effect on the resources by increasing the Annual Rate Increase to 9%; and (c) with the original assumptions, goal seek to determine what the Annual Rate Increase would be for the total expenses to be $100,000. Submit the workbook and results of the what-if analysis as requested by your instructor.

Table 3–20 College Expense and Resource Projections Formulas

Formula A = Prior Year's Expense * (1 + Annual Rate Increase)

Formula B = Total Expenses for Year * Corresponding Assumption

•• 5: Cost of Storing Radio Isotopes

Working Together

A government agency plans to conduct experiments that will result in some radioactive waste. Although the isotopes will break apart into atoms of other elements over time, agency watchdogs are concerned about containment costs while the material still is radioactive. The agency director has asked your group to prepare a worksheet showing the amount of radioactive material remaining, containment costs, estimated agency appropriations, and the percentage of appropriations that will be spent on containment every year for the next decade. The director has outlined the desired worksheet as shown in Table 3–21 on the next page.

Continued >

Cases and Places *continued*

These formulas have been supplied:

Formula A: Amount Remaining = Original Amount × 0.5 (Number of Years Stored / Half-Life)

Formula B: Containment Costs = Containment Cost Per Kilogram × Total Amount Remaining

Formula C: Estimated Appropriations = Appropriations × (1 + Estimated Yearly Increase) (Number of Years Stored / Half-Life)

Formula D: Percentage Spent on Containment = Containment Costs / Estimated Appropriations

The director has asked your group to include a function that prints "Acceptable" below the percentage spent on containment whenever the percentage is less than 1%, otherwise print "Not Acceptable."

Have each member of your team submit a sketch of the proposed worksheet and then implement the best one. Use the concepts and techniques presented in this project to create and format the worksheet. Submit the sketches and workbook as requested by your instructor.

Table 3–21 Cost of Storing Radioactive Isotopes				
	Number of Years Stored			
Number of Years Stored	1	2	3	 10
Amount of Isotope X Remaining (in kg)	Formula A ———————————→			
Amount of Isotope Y Remaining (in kg)	Formula A ———————————→			
Total Remaining (in kg)	—	—	—	.... —
Containment Costs	Formula B ———————————→			
Estimated Appropriations	Formula C ———————————→			
Percentage Spent on Containment	Formula D ———————————→			
	Message ———————————→			

Assumptions	
Original Amount of Isotope X Remaining (in kg)	650
Half-Life of Isotope X (in years)	1
Containment Cost per Kilogram	1000
Estimated Yearly Increase	10.00%
Original Amount of Isotope Y Remaining (in kg)	3000
Half-Life of Isotope Y (in years)	0.45
Appropriations	6000000

Web Feature

Creating Web Pages Using Excel

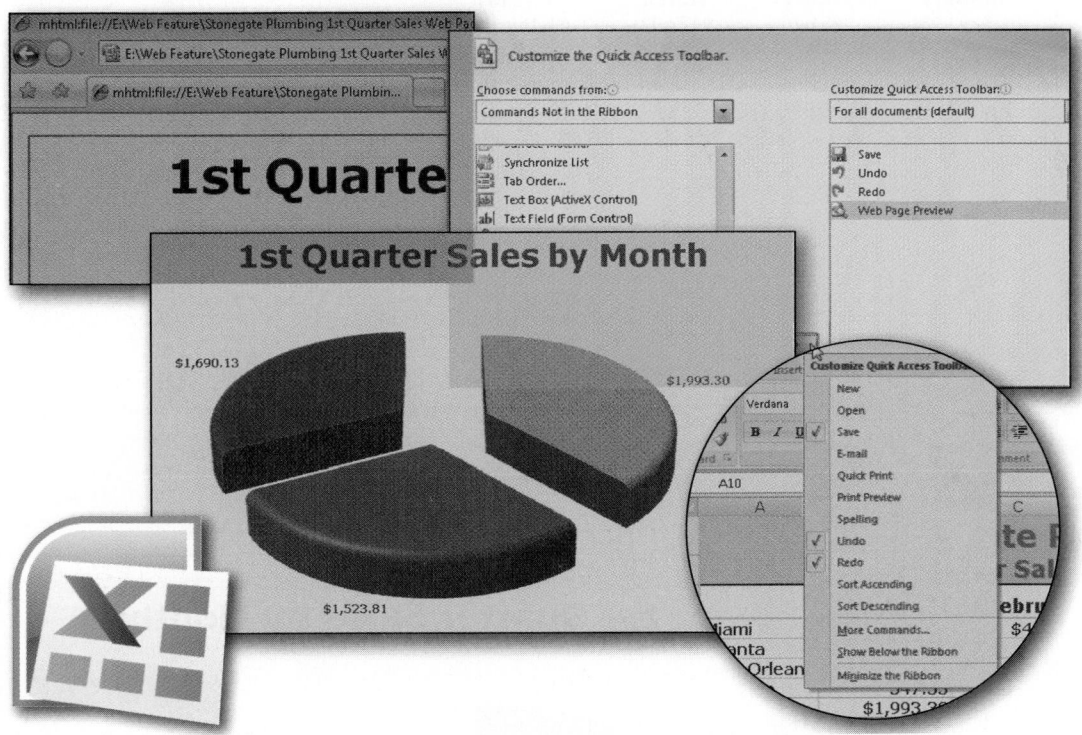

Objectives

You will have mastered the material in this Web feature when you can:

- Customize the Quick Access Toolbar
- Publish a worksheet and chart as a Web page
- Display Web pages published in Excel in a browser
- Complete file management tasks within Excel

Web Feature Introduction

Excel provides fast, easy methods for saving workbooks as Web pages that can be stored on the World Wide Web, a company's intranet, or a local hard disk. A user then can display the workbook using a browser, rather than Excel.

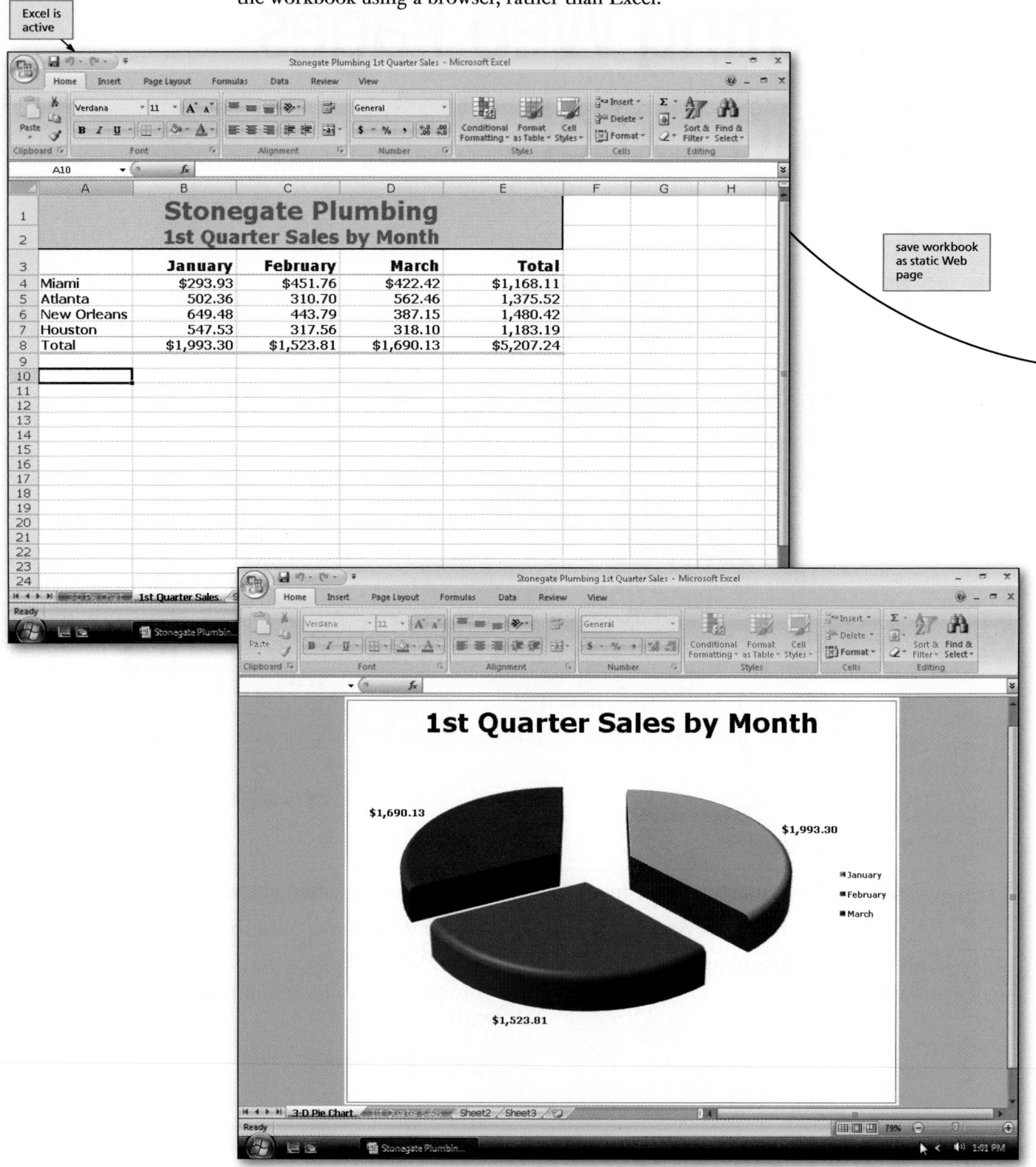

(a) Workbook Viewed in Excel

Figure 1

Project — Workbook with Chart Saved as a Web Page

Figure 1a shows the workbook for Stonegate Plumbing's 1st quarter sales by month. The chief financial officer for the company requests that the information in the worksheet, including the chart, be made available on the company's intranet for others in the company to view. In order to accomplish this task, you must save the workbook as a Web page.

You can save a workbook, or a portion of a workbook, as a Web page. The saved **Web page** is a snapshot of the workbook. It is similar to a printed report in that you can view it, but you cannot modify it. In the browser window, the workbook appears as it would in Microsoft Excel, including sheet tabs that you can click to switch between worksheets. As illustrated in Figure 1, this Web feature shows you how to save a workbook (Figure 1a) as a Web page (Figure 1b) and view it using your browser.

When you use the Save As command on the Office Button menu and choose to save a workbook as a Web page, Excel allows you to **publish workbooks**, which is the process of making a workbook available to others; for example, on the World Wide Web or on a

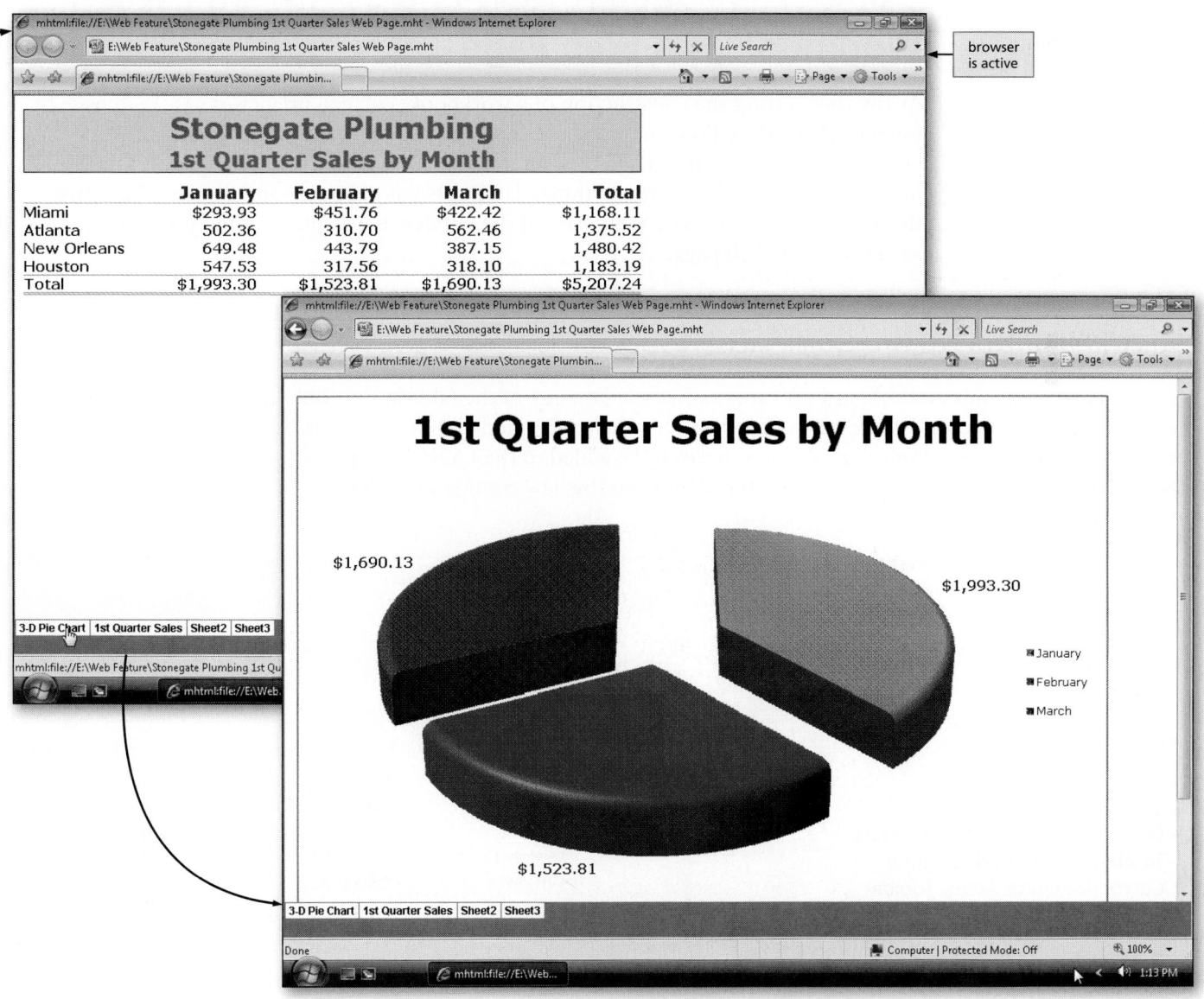

(b) Static Web Page Viewed in Browser

BTW

Web Folders and FTP Locations
You can save any type of file to a Web folder or on an FTP location, just as you would save to a folder on your hard disk. Web folders and FTP locations are particularly useful because they appear as standard folders in Windows Explorer or in the Address bar list. For additional information, see Appendix D.

company's intranet. If you have access to a Web server, you can publish Web pages by saving them on a Web server or on an FTP location. To learn more about publishing Web pages on a Web server or on an FTP location using Microsoft Office applications, refer to Appendix D.

This Web feature illustrates how to create and save the Web pages on a USB flash drive, rather than on a Web server. This feature also demonstrates how to preview a workbook as a Web page and create a new folder using the Save As dialog box.

Overview

As you read through this Web feature, you will learn how to create the worksheet shown in Figure 1 on pages EX 250 and 251 by performing these general tasks:

- Save a Workbook as a Web page
- Preview the Workbook in a Web browser
- Complete file management tasks within Excel

Using Web Page Preview and Saving an Excel Workbook as a Web Page

At any time during the construction of a workbook, you can preview it as a Web page by using the Web Page Preview command. The Web Page Preview command is not available on the Ribbon, but you can add the command to the Quick Access Toolbar. When you invoke the Web Page Preview command, it starts your browser and displays the active sheet in the workbook as a Web page. If the preview is acceptable, then you can save the workbook as a Web page.

To Add a Button to the Quick Access Toolbar

Many commands available in Excel are not included on any of the tabs on the Ribbon. You can, however, add such commands to the Quick Access Toolbar. One such command allows you to preview a document in a Web browser. This command, Web Page Preview, needs to be added to the Quick Access Toolbar so that the Web page can be previewed. The following steps add the Web Page Preview command to the Quick Access Toolbar.

- Connect a USB flash drive with the Data Files for Students on it to one of the computer's USB ports.

- Start Excel and then open the workbook, Stonegate Plumbing 1st Quarter Sales, from the Data Files for Students.

- Click the Customize Quick Access Toolbar button to display the Customize Quick Access Toolbar menu (Figure 2).

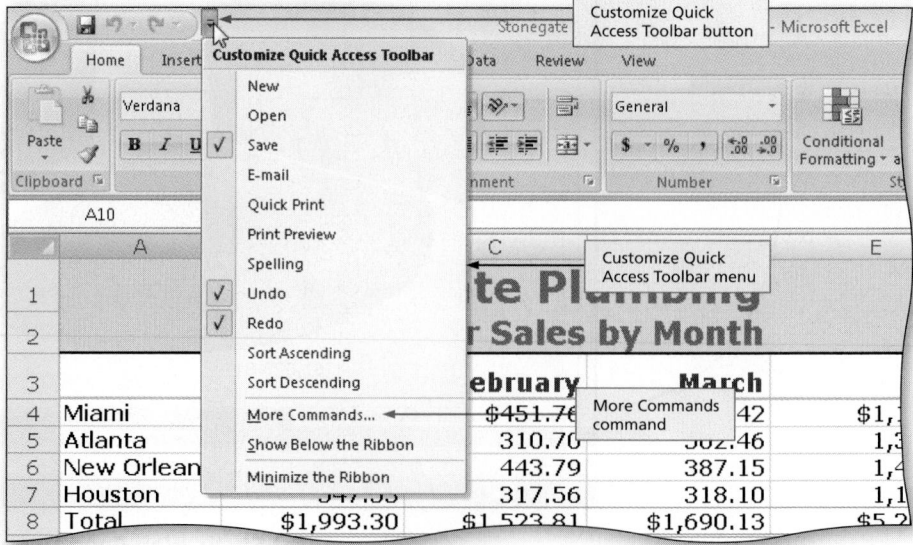

Figure 2

3
- Click the More Commands command on the Customize Quick Access Toolbar menu.

- When the Excel Options dialog box is displayed, click the 'Choose commands from' box arrow to display the 'Choose commands from' list (Figure 3).

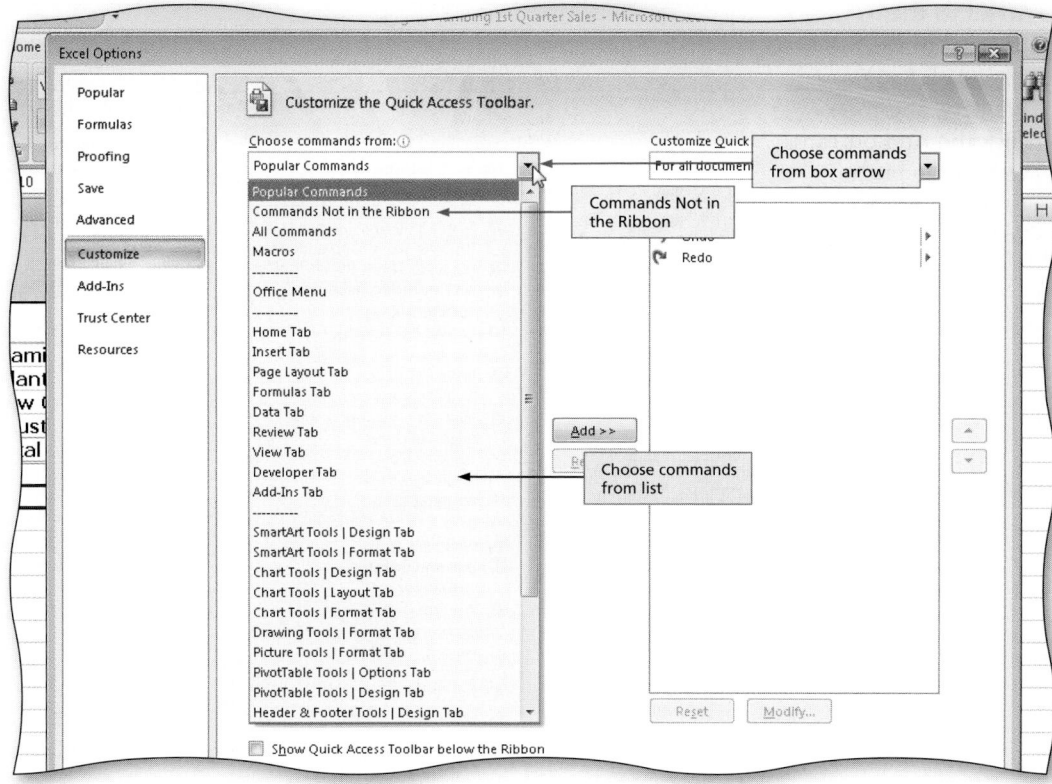

Figure 3

4
- Click Commands Not in the Ribbon in the 'Choose commands from' list to display a list of commands not in the Ribbon (Figure 4).

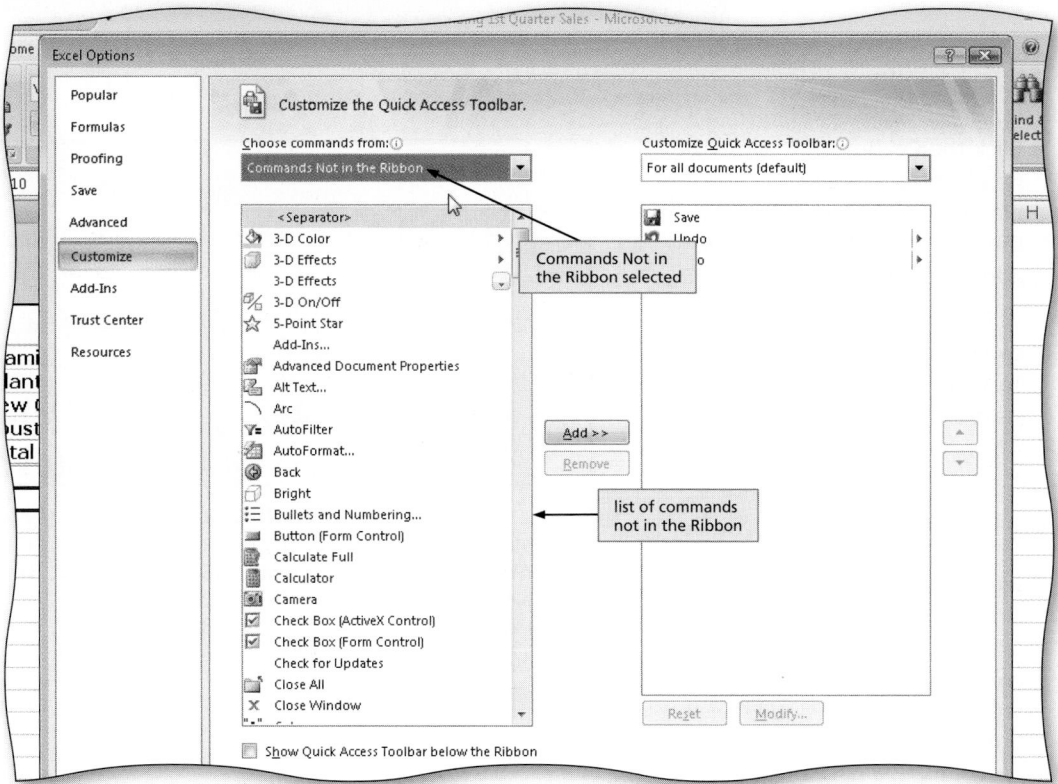

Figure 4

• Scroll to the bottom of the list, click Web Page Preview, and then click the Add button to add the button to the Quick Access Toolbar (Figure 5).

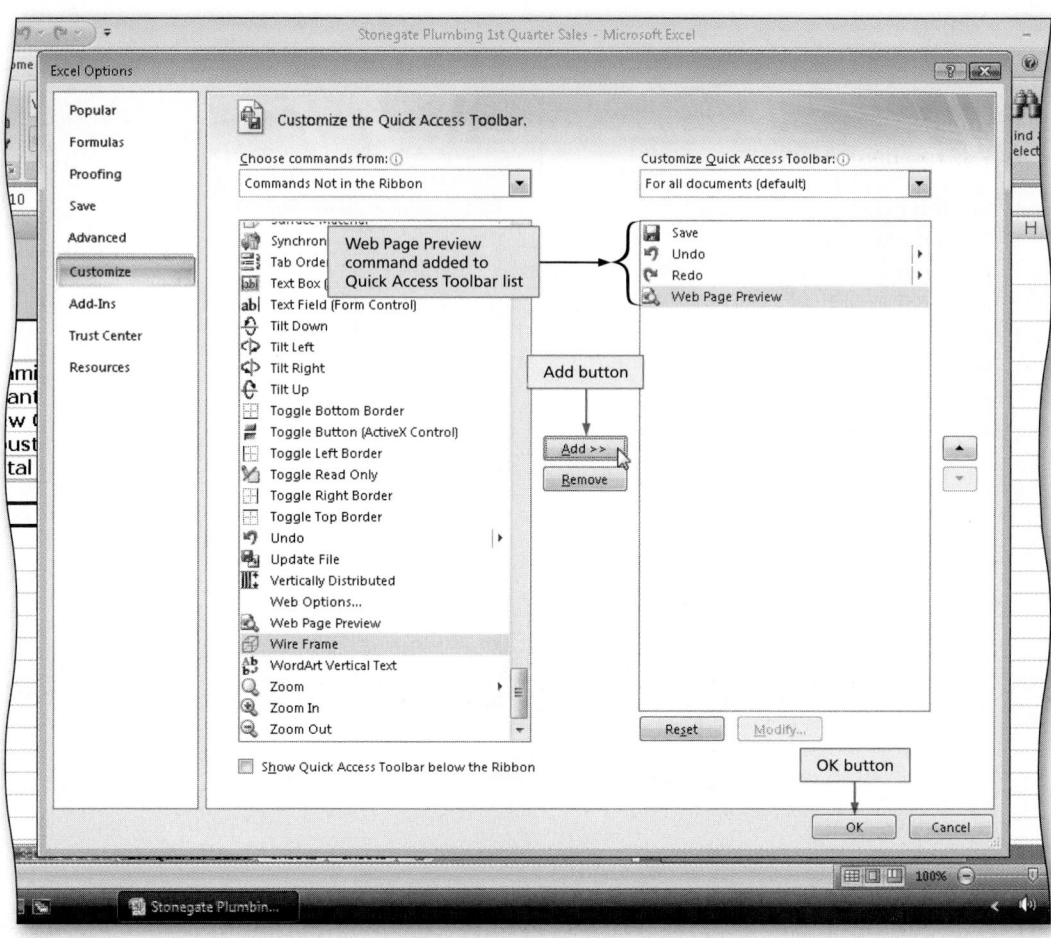

Figure 5

• Click the OK button to close the Excel Options dialog box and display the Quick Access Toolbar with the Web Page Preview button added to it (Figure 6).

Q&A

Will the Web Page Preview command be on the Quick Access Toolbar the next time that I start Excel?

Yes. When you change the Quick Access Toolbar, the changes remain even after you restart Excel. If you share a computer with somebody else or if the Quick Access Toolbar becomes cluttered, Excel allows you to remove commands from the Quick Access Toolbar. The Web Page Preview button is removed from the Quick Access Toolbar later in this Web feature.

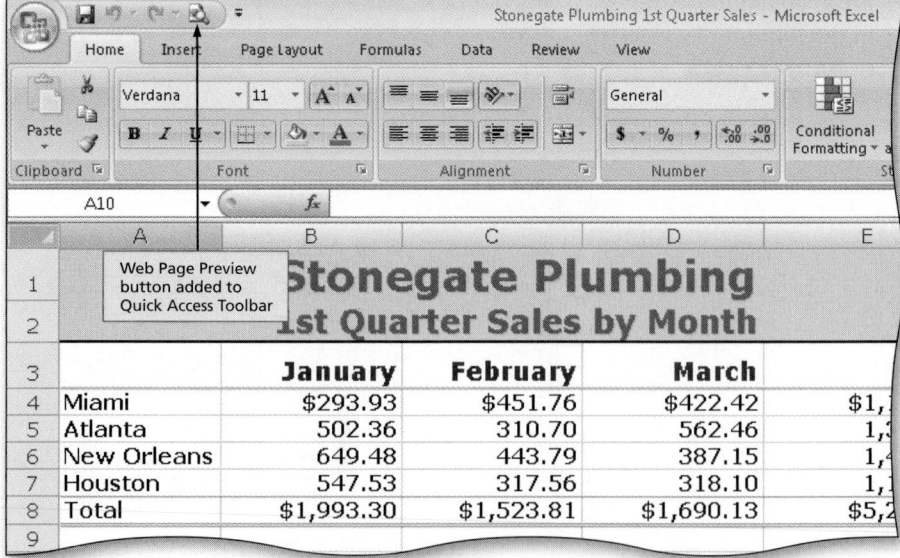

Figure 6

To Preview the Web Page

The following steps preview the Web page version of the workbook in a browser.

1

- Click the Web Page Preview button on the Quick Access Toolbar to display the Web page in your browser. If the security warning appears in the Information bar at the top of the Web page, click its Close button.

- If necessary, click the Maximize button on your browser's title bar (Figure 7).

Q&A

What happens when I click the Web Page Preview button?

Excel starts your browser. The browser displays a preview of how the 1st Quarter Sales sheet will appear as a Web page (Figure 7). The Web page preview in the browser is nearly identical to the display of the worksheet in Excel. A highlighted browser button appears on the Windows Vista taskbar indicating it is active. The Excel button on the Windows Vista taskbar no longer is highlighted.

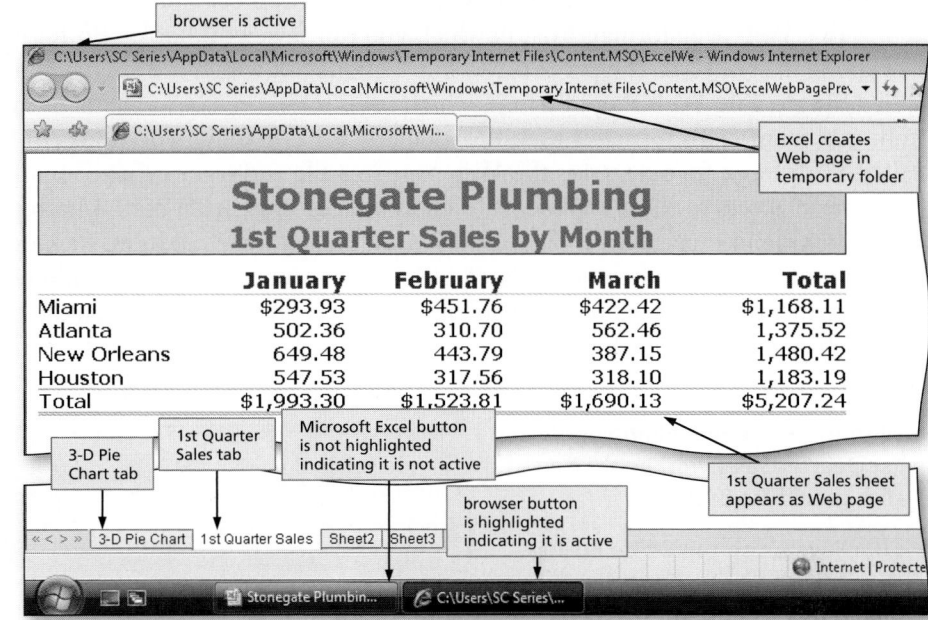

Figure 7

2

- Click the 3-D Pie Chart tab at the bottom of the Web page to display the 3-D Pie chart in the browser (Figure 8).

3

- After viewing the Web page preview of the Stonegate Plumbing 1st Quarter Sales workbook, click the Close button on the right side of the browser title bar to close the browser and make Excel active again.

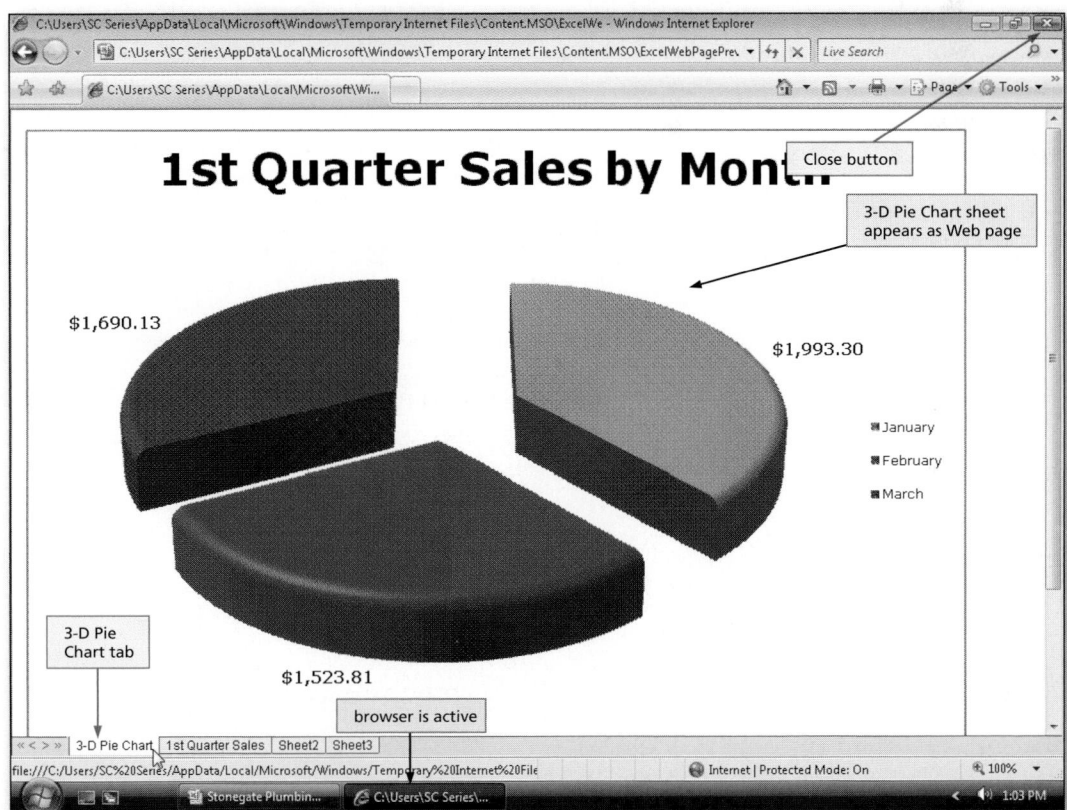

Figure 8

To Save an Excel Workbook as a Web Page in a Newly Created Folder

Once the preview of the workbook as a Web page is acceptable, you can save the workbook as a Web page so that others can view it using a Web browser, such as Internet Explorer or Mozilla Firefox.

Two Web page formats exist in which you can save workbooks. Both formats convert the contents of the workbook into HTML (HyperText Markup Language), which is a language browsers can interpret. One format is called **Single File Web Page format**, which saves all of the components of the Web page in a single file with an .mht extension. This format is useful particularly for e-mailing workbooks in HTML format. The second format, called **Web Page format**, saves the Web page in a file and some of its components in a folder. This format is useful if you need access to the components, such as images, that make up the Web page.

Experienced users organize the files saved on a storage medium, such as a USB flash drive or hard disk, by creating folders. They then save related files in a common folder. Excel allows you to create folders before saving a file using the Save As dialog box. The following steps create a new folder on the USB flash drive and save the workbook as a Web page in the new folder.

- With the Stonegate Plumbing 1st Quarter Sales workbook open, click the Office Button.

- Click Save As on the Office Button menu to display the Save As dialog box (Figure 9).

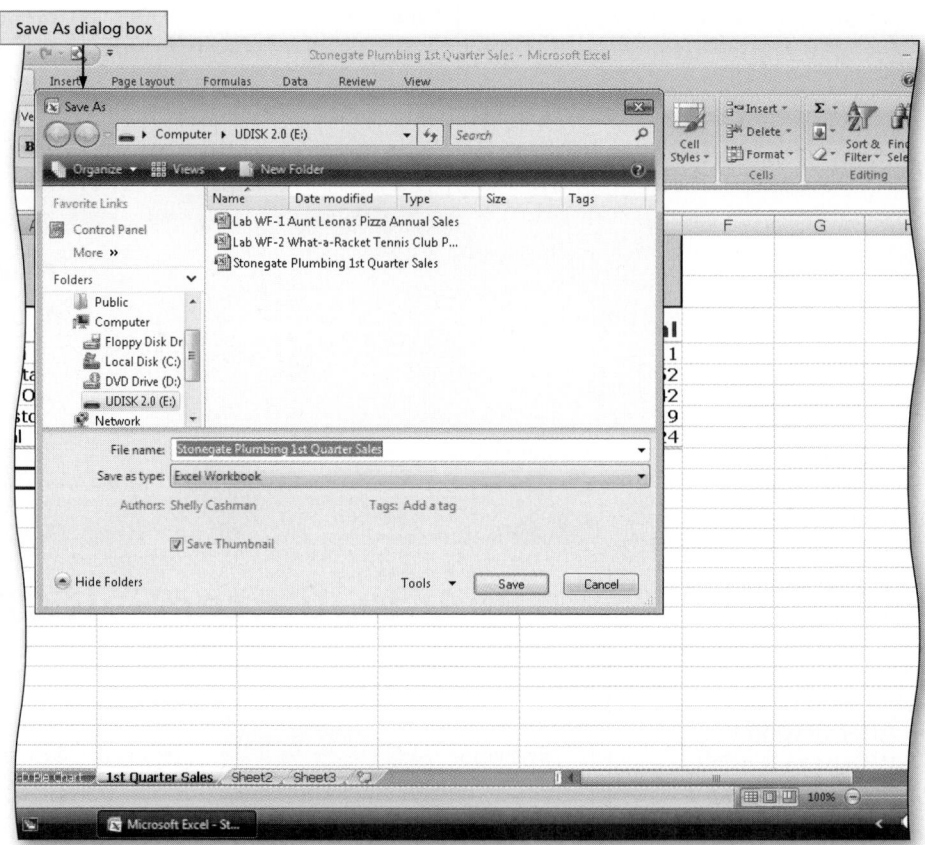

Figure 9

- Type Stonegate Plumbing 1st Quarter Sales Web Page in the File name box.

- Click the 'Save as type' box arrow and then click Single File Web Page.

- Click the Address bar arrow, select UDISK 2.0 (E:) (your USB flash drive name and letter may be different), and then click the New Folder button to create a new folder.

- When Excel displays the new folder with the name New Folder, type Web Feature in the text box (Figure 10).

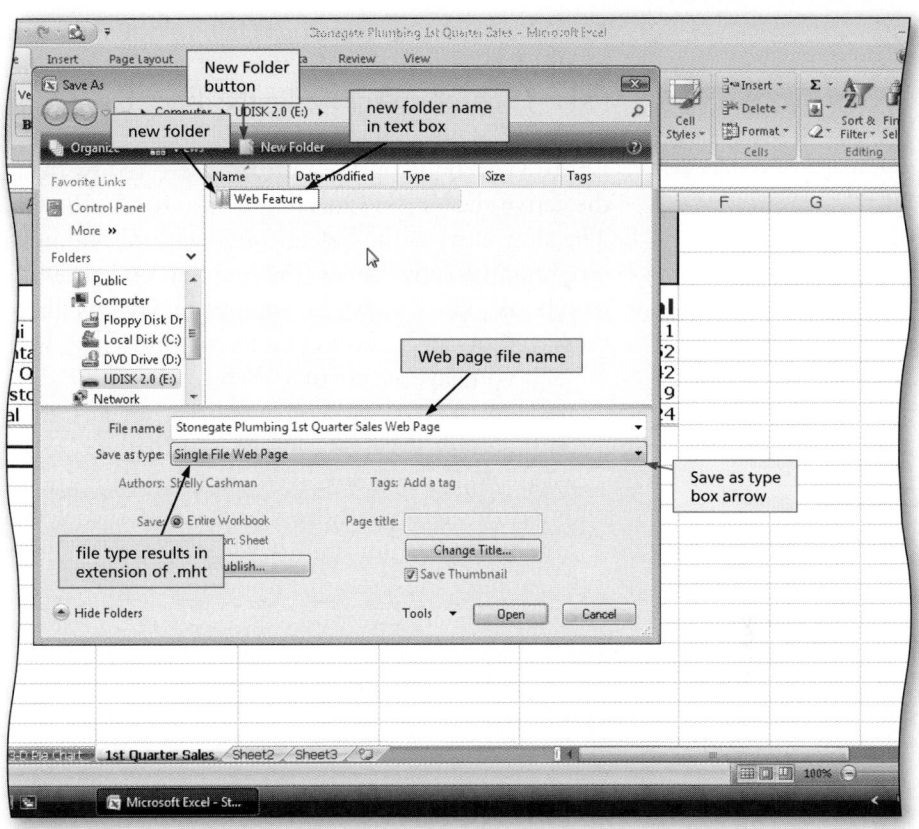

Figure 10

- Press the ENTER key. If the Microsoft Office Excel dialog box appears, click the Yes button.

Q&A
What does Excel do when I press the ENTER key?

Excel automatically selects the new folder named Web Feature in the Address bar (Figure 11). The Entire Workbook option button in the Save area instructs Excel to save all sheets in the workbook as Web pages.

④

- Click the Save button in the Save As dialog box to save the workbook in a single file in HTML format in the Web Feature folder on the USB flash drive.

- If the Microsoft Office Excel dialog box is displayed, click the Yes button.

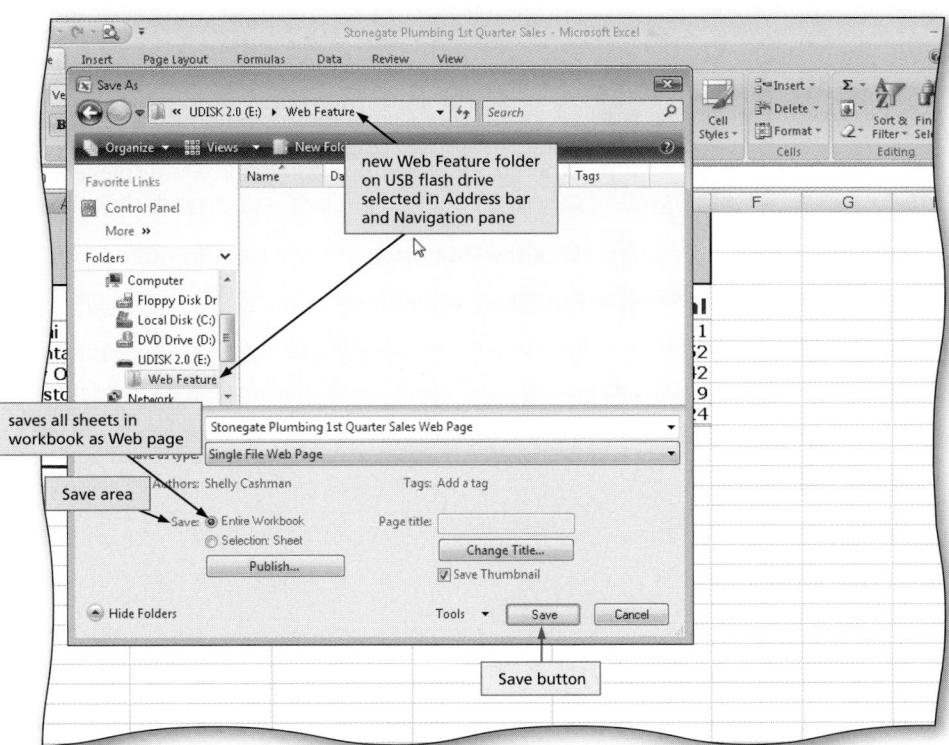

Figure 11

BTW

Creating Links
You can add hyperlinks to an Excel workbook before you save it as a Web page. The hyperlinks in the Excel workbook can link to a Web page, a location in a Web page, or an e-mail address that automatically starts the viewer's e-mail program.

Saving Workbooks as Web Pages

The Save As dialog box changes when you select Single File Web Page, which is in MHTML format, in the 'Save as type' box. When you use the Single File Web Page format, a Save area appears in the dialog box. Within the Save area are two option buttons and a Publish button (Figure 11). You can select only one of the option buttons. The Entire Workbook option button is selected by default. This indicates Excel will save all the active sheets (1st Quarter Sales and 3-D Pie Chart) in the workbook as a Web page. The alternative is the Selection: Sheet option button. If you select this option, Excel will save only the active sheet (the one that currently is displaying in the Excel window) in the workbook. The Publish button in the Save As dialog box in Figure 11 is an alternative to the Save button. It allows you to customize the Web page further.

If you have access to a Web server and it allows you to save files in a Web folder, then you can save the Web page directly on the Web server by clicking the Network icon in the Folders list in the Save As dialog box (Figure 11). If you have access to a Web server that allows you to save on an FTP site, then you can select the FTP site below FTP locations in the Address bar just as you select any folder in which to save a file. To learn more about publishing Web pages in a Web folder or on an FTP location using Office applications, refer to Appendix D.

After Excel saves the workbook in Step 4, it displays the MHTML file in the Excel window. Excel can continue to display the workbook in HTML format, because, within the MHTML file that it created, it also saved the Excel formats that allow it to display the MHTML file in Excel.

BTW

Viewing Source Code
To view the HTML source code for a Web page created in Excel, use your browser to display the Web page, click the Page button and then click View Source.

To Reset the Quick Access Toolbar and Quit Excel

The necessary work with the Excel workbook is complete. The following steps remove the Web Page Preview button from the Quick Access Toolbar and quit Excel.

1 Click the Customize the Quick Access Toolbar button on the Ribbon.

2 Click the More Commands command.

3 When the Excel Options dialog box is displayed, click the Reset button. If the Reset Customizations dialog box is displayed, click the Yes button.

4 Click the OK button in the Excel Options dialog box to close it.

5 Click the Close button on the Microsoft Excel title bar.

Q&A Do I need to remove the button from the Quick Access Toolbar?

No. For consistency, in this book the Quick Access Toolbar is reset after the added buttons no longer are needed. If you share a computer with others, you should reset the Quick Access Toolbar when you are finished using the computer.

File Management Tools in Excel

In the previous set of steps, Excel automatically navigates to the new folder name in the Save in box when you press the ENTER key after typing the new folder name (Figure 11 on page EX 257). It actually was not necessary to create a new folder earlier in this Web feature; the Web page could have been saved on the USB flash drive in the same manner files were saved on the USB flash drive in the previous projects. Creating a new folder, however, allows you to organize your work.

Finally, once you create a folder, you can right-click it while the Save As dialog box is active and perform many file management tasks directly in Excel (Figure 12). For example, once the shortcut menu appears, you can rename the selected folder, delete it, copy it, display its properties, and perform other file management functions.

BTW

Quick Reference
For a table that lists how to complete the tasks covered in this book using the mouse, Ribbon, shortcut menu, and keyboard, see the Quick Reference Summary at the back of this book, or visit the Excel 2007 Quick Reference Web page (scsite.com/ex2007/qr).

BTW

Certification
The Microsoft Certified Application Specialist (MCAS) program provides an opportunity for you to obtain a valuable industry credential – proof that you have the Excel 2007 skills required by employers. For more information, see Appendix G or visit the Excel 2007 Certification Web page (scsite.com/ex2007/cert).

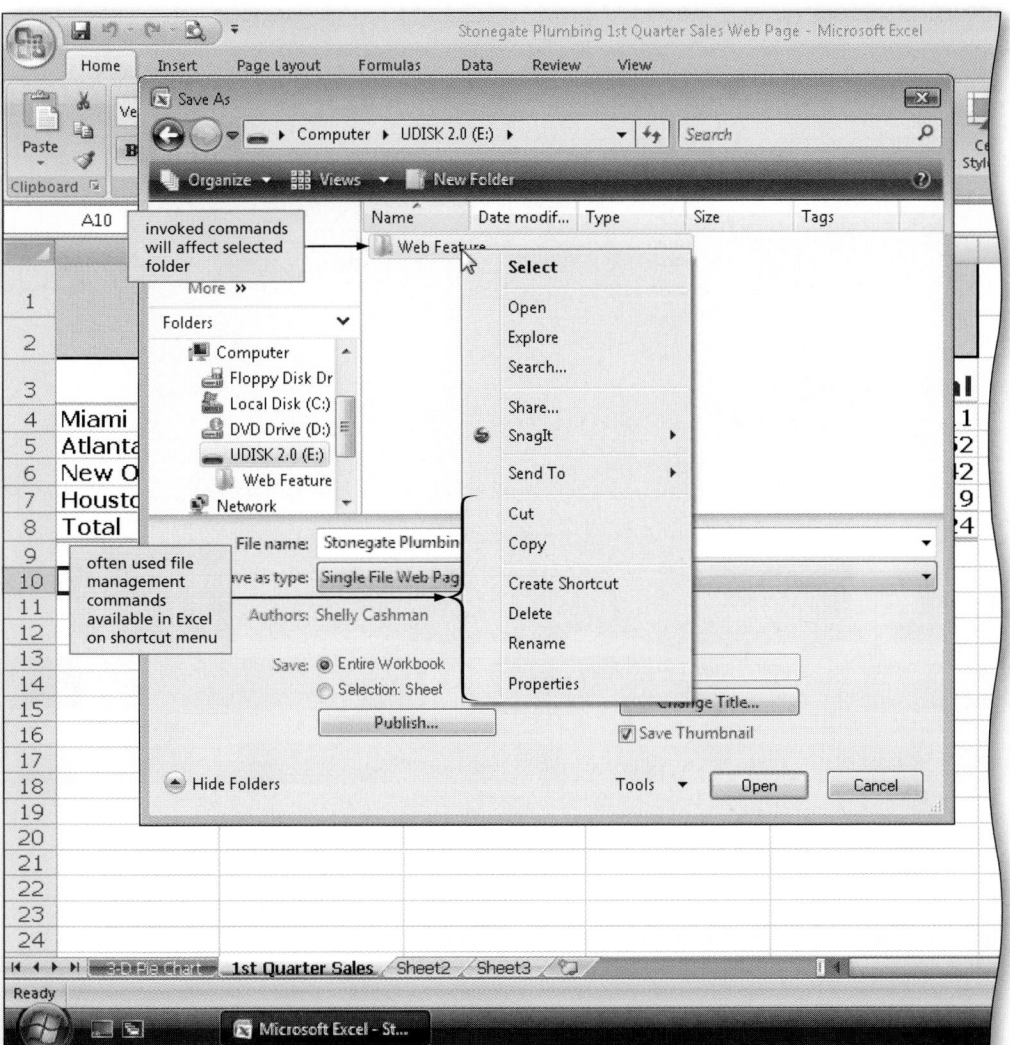

Figure 12

To View and Manipulate the Web Page Using a Browser

With the Web page saved in the Web Feature folder on the USB flash drive, you can now view it using a browser, as shown in the following steps.

- If necessary, connect the USB flash drive with the Data Files for Students to one of the computer's USB ports.

- Click the Start button on the Windows Vista taskbar, click All Programs on the Start menu, and then click Internet Explorer in the All Programs list.

- When the Internet Explorer window opens, type e:\web feature\ stonegate plumbing 1st quarter sales web page.mht in the Address box and then press the ENTER key to display the Web page in your browser (Figure 13). (Your USB flash drive may have a different name and letter.)

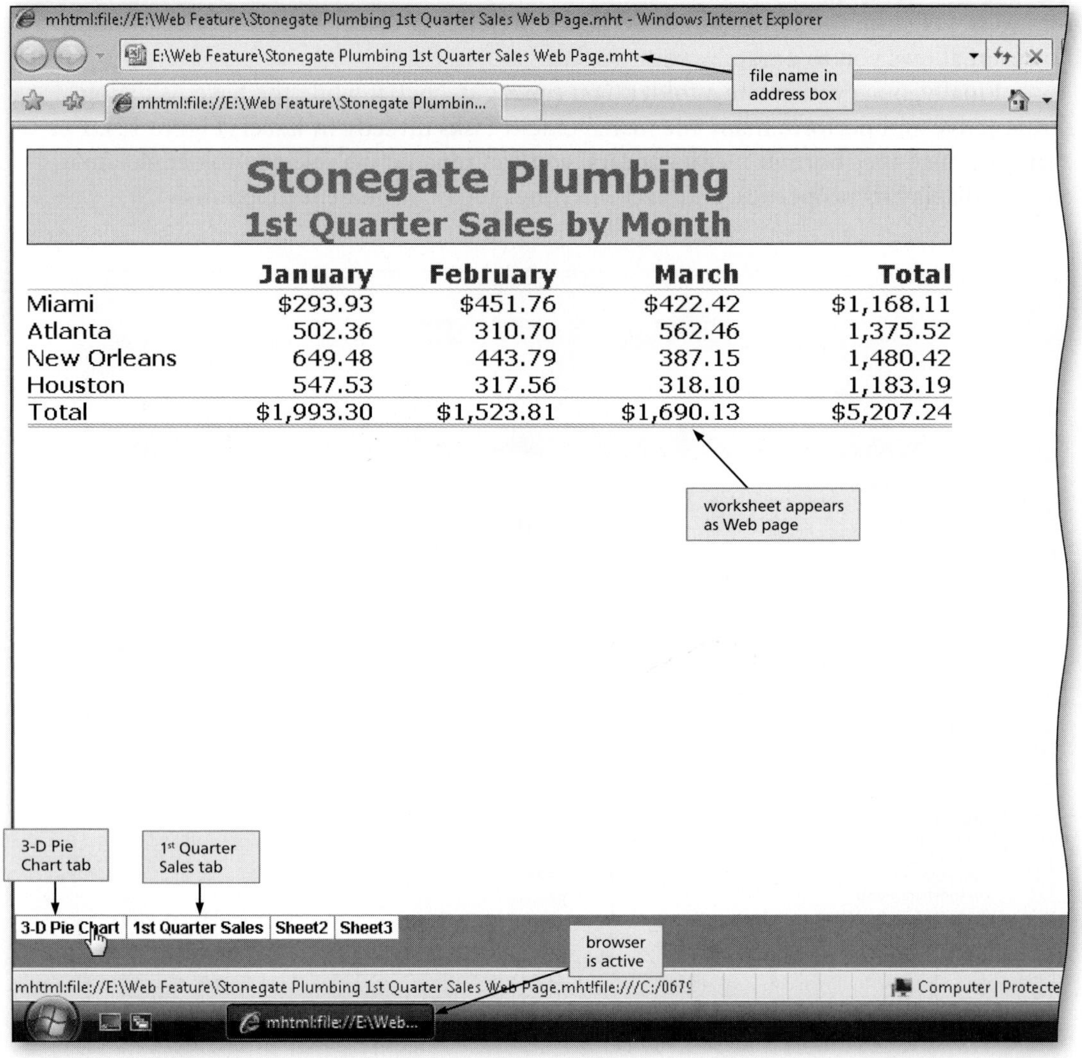

- If the Internet Explorer dialog box appears, click the OK button, right-click the first Internet Explorer button on the Windows Vista taskbar, and then click Close on the shortcut menu. If a security warning appears in the Information bar at the top of the Web page, click its Close button.

Figure 13

Browser window showing:

mhtml:file://E:\Web Feature\Stonegate Plumbing 1st Quarter Sales Web Page.mht - Windows Internet Explorer

E:\Web Feature\Stonegate Plumbing 1st Quarter Sales Web Page.mht — *file name in address box*

mhtml:file://E:\Web Feature\Stonegate Plumbin...

Stonegate Plumbing
1st Quarter Sales by Month

	January	February	March	Total
Miami	$293.93	$451.76	$422.42	$1,168.11
Atlanta	502.36	310.70	562.46	1,375.52
New Orleans	649.48	443.79	387.15	1,480.42
Houston	547.53	317.56	318.10	1,183.19
Total	$1,993.30	$1,523.81	$1,690.13	$5,207.24

worksheet appears as Web page

3-D Pie Chart tab   *1st Quarter Sales tab*

3-D Pie Chart | 1st Quarter Sales | Sheet2 | Sheet3

browser is active

mhtml:file://E:\Web Feature\Stonegate Plumbing 1st Quarter Sales Web Page.mht!file:///C:/0679   Computer | Protecte

mhtml:file://E:\Web...

2

- Click the 3-D Pie Chart sheet tab at the bottom of the window to display the 3-D Pie chart in your browser (Figure 14). If the security warning appears in the Information bar at the top of the Web page, click its Close button.

- Use the scroll arrows to display the lower portion of the chart.

Q&A

What are the benefits of using a browser to view a workbook?

You can see from Figures 13 and 14 that a Web page is an ideal way to distribute information to a large group of people. For example, the Web page could be published on a Web server connected to the Internet and made available to anyone with a computer, browser, and the address of the Web page. It also can be e-mailed easily, because the Web page resides in a single file, rather than in a file and folder. Publishing a workbook as a Web page, therefore, is an excellent alternative to distributing printed copies of the workbook.

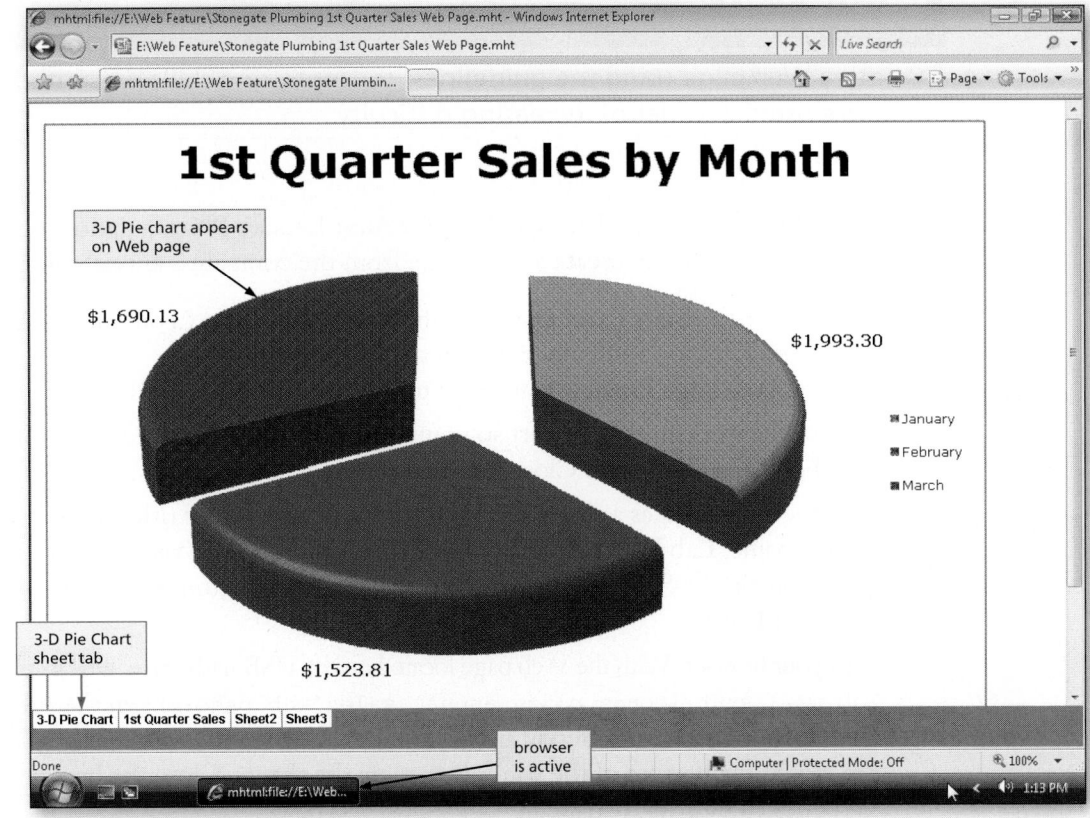

Figure 14

3

- Click the Close button on the right side of the browser title bar to close the browser.

Feature Summary

This Web feature introduced you to customizing the Quick Access Toolbar, previewing a workbook as a Web page, creating a new folder on a USB flash drive, and publishing and viewing a Web page. The items listed below include all the new Office 2007 skills you have learned in this Web feature.

1. Add a Button to the Quick Access Toolbar (EX 252)
2. Preview the Web Page (EX 255)
3. Save an Excel Workbook as a Web Page in a Newly Created Folder (EX 256)
4. View and Manipulate the Web Page Using a Browser (EX 260)

If you have a SAM user profile, you may have access to hands-on instruction, practice, and assessment. Log in to your SAM account (http://sam2007.course.com) to launch any assigned training activities or exams that relate to the skills covered in this feature.

In the Lab

Create a Web page using the guidelines, concepts, and skills presented in this Web feature. Labs are listed in order of increasing difficulty.

1 Creating a Web Page I

Problem: You are a spreadsheet specialist for Aunt Leona's Pizza, a national chain of pizzerias. Your manager has asked you to create a Web page from the company's annual sales workbook.

Instructions Part 1: Start Excel and open the Lab WF-1 Aunt Leonas Pizza Annual Sales workbook from the Data Files for Students. Perform the following tasks:

1. Add the Web Page Preview command to the Quick Access Toolbar.

2. Review the worksheet and chart so you have an idea of what the workbook contains. Preview the workbook as a Web page. Close the browser.

3. Save the workbook as a single file Web page in a new folder titled Web Feature Exercises using the file name, Lab WF-1 Aunt Leonas Pizza Annual Sales Web Page. Make sure you select Entire Workbook in the Save area before you click the Save button. Reset the Quick Access Toolbar and then quit Excel.

4. Start your browser. With the Web page located on the USB flash drive, type e:\web feature exercises\ lab wf-1 aunt leonas pizza annual sales web page.mht in the Address box (your USB flash drive may have a different name and letter). When the browser displays the Web page, click the tabs at the bottom of the window to view the sheets. Close the browser. Submit the assignment as requested by your instructor.

In the Lab

2 Creating a Web Page II

Problem: You work part-time as a spreadsheet analyst for What-a-Racket Tennis Club. You have been asked to create a Web page from the workbook that the company uses to project membership dues and payroll expenses.

Instructions Part 1: Start Excel and open the Lab WF-2 What-a-Racket Tennis Club Projections workbook from the Data Files for Students. Perform the following tasks:

1. Add the Web Page Preview command to the Quick Access Toolbar.

2. Review the 3-D Bar Chart sheet and the Projected Expenses sheet in Excel. Preview the workbook as a Web page. Close the browser.

3. Save the workbook as a Web page (select Web Page in the Save as type box) in the Web Feature Exercises folder using the file name, Lab WF-2 What-a-Racket Tennis Club Projections Web Page. Make sure you select Entire Workbook in the Save area before you click the Save button. Reset the Quick Access Toolbar and then quit Excel. Saving the workbook as a Web page, rather than a single file Web page, will result in an additional folder being added to the Web Feature Exercises folder.

4. Start your browser. Type e:\web feature exercises\lab wf-2 what-a-racket tennis club projections web page.htm in the Address box (your USB flash drive may have a different name and letter). When the browser displays the Web page, click the tabs at the bottom of the window to view the sheets. Close the browser. Submit the assignment as requested by your instructor.

In the Lab

3 File Management within Excel

Problem: Your manager at What-a-Racket Tennis Club has asked you to teach her to complete basic file management tasks from within Excel.

Instructions: Start Excel and click the Open command on the Office Button menu. When Excel displays the Open dialog box, create a new folder called In the Lab 3. Click the Back to button to reselect the drive in the Address bar. Use the shortcut menu to complete the following tasks: (1) rename the In the Lab 3 folder to In the Lab 3A; (2) show the properties of the In the Lab 3A folder; and (3) delete the In the Lab 3A folder.

1 | Creating and Using a Database

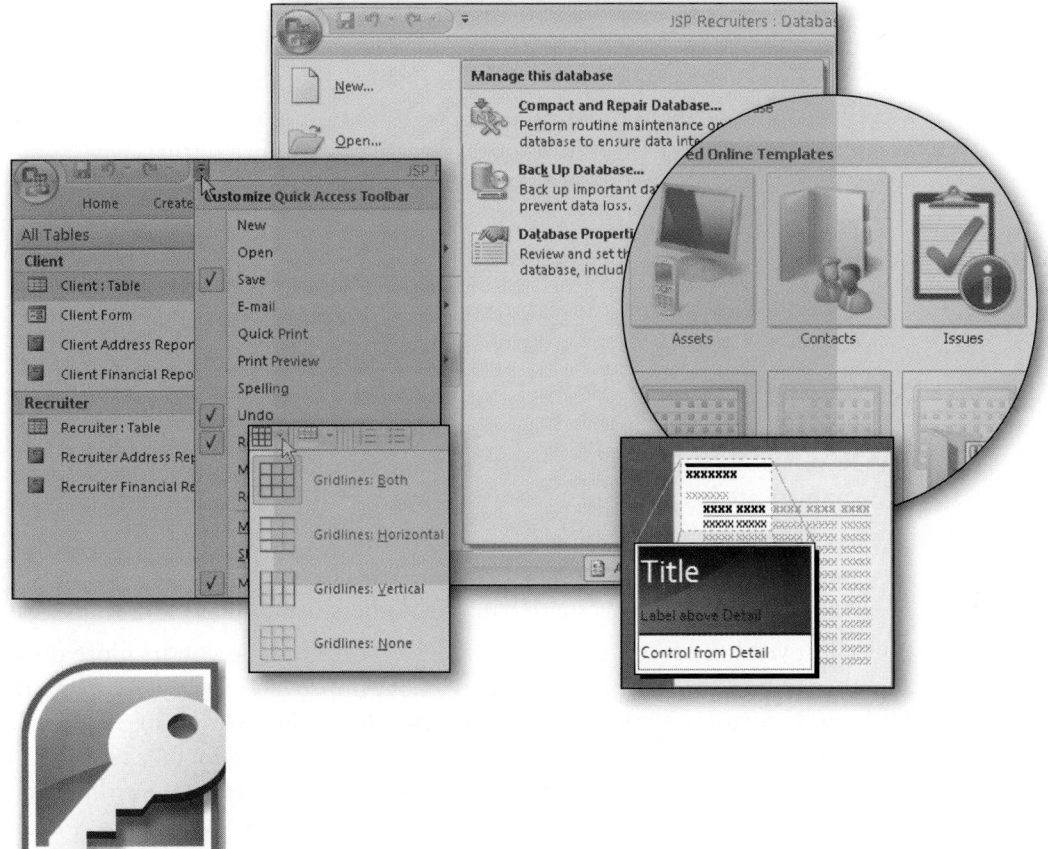

Objectives

You will have mastered the material in this chapter when you can:

- Describe databases and database management systems
- Design a database to satisfy a collection of requirements
- Start Access
- Describe the features of the Access window
- Create a database
- Create a table and add records

- Close a table
- Close a database and quit Access
- Open a database
- Print the contents of a table
- Create and print custom reports
- Create and use a split form
- Use the Access Help system

1 | Creating and Using a Database

What Is Microsoft Office Access 2007?

Microsoft Office Access 2007, usually referred to as simply Access, is a database management system. A database management system, such as Access, is a software tool that allows you to use a computer to create a database; add, change, and delete data in the database; sort the data in the database; retrieve data in the database; and create forms and reports using the data in the database. The term **database** describes a collection of data organized in a manner that allows access, retrieval, and use of that data. Some of the key features in Access are:

- **Data entry and update** Access provides easy mechanisms for adding, changing, and deleting data, including the capability of making mass changes in a single operation.

- **Queries (questions)** Access makes it possible to ask complex questions concerning the data in the database and then receive instant answers.

- **Forms** Access allows the user to produce attractive and useful forms for viewing and updating data.

- **Reports** Access includes report creation tools that make it easy to produce sophisticated reports for presenting data.

- **Web support** Access allows you to save objects, reports, and tables in HTML format so they can be viewed using a browser. You also can import and export documents in XML format as well as share data with others using SharePoint Services.

This latest version of Access has many new features to help you be more productive. Like the other Office applications, it features a new, improved interface utilizing the Ribbon. The new Navigation Pane makes navigating among the various objects in a database easier and more intuitive than in the past. The new version includes several professionally designed templates that you can use to quickly create a database. Sorting and filtering has been enhanced in this version. The new Layout view allows you to make changes to the design of forms and reports at the same time you are browsing the data. Datasheet view also has been enhanced to make creating tables more intuitive. Split form, a new form object, combines both a datasheet and a form as a single unit. Memo fields now support rich text, and there is a new Attachment data type. Using the Attachment data type, a field can contain an attached file, such as a document, image, or spreadsheet.

Project Planning Guidelines

The process of developing a database that communicates specific information requires careful analysis and planning. As a starting point, establish why the database is needed. Once the purpose is determined, analyze the intended users of the database and their unique needs. Then, gather information about the topic and decide what to include in the database. Finally, determine the database design and style that will be most successful at delivering the message. Details of these guidelines are provided in Appendix A. In addition, each project in this book provides practical applications of these planning considerations.

Project — Database Creation

JSP Recruiters is a recruiting firm that specializes in job placement for health care professionals. Because the recruiters at JSP have previous experience in the health care industry, the firm is able to provide quality candidates for employment in hospitals, clinics, medical laboratories, doctors' offices, and other health care facilities.

JSP Recruiters works with clients in need of health care professionals. It assigns each client to a specific recruiter. The recruiter works with the client to determine the necessary qualifications for each job candidate. The recruiter then contacts and does a preliminary review of the qualifications for each candidate before setting up a job interview between the client and the candidate. If the candidate is hired, the client pays a percentage of the new employee's annual salary to the recruiting firm, which then distributes a percentage of that client fee to the recruiter.

To ensure that operations run smoothly, JSP Recruiters organizes data on its clients and recruiters in a database, managed by Access. In this way, JSP keeps its data current and accurate while the firm's management can analyze the data for trends and produce a variety of useful reports.

In Access, a database consists of a collection of tables, each of which contains information on a specific subject. Figure 1–1 shows the database for JSP Recruiters. It consists of two tables. The Client table (Figure 1–1a) contains information about the clients to whom JSP provides services. The Recruiter table (Figure 1–1b) contains information about the recruiters to whom these clients are assigned.

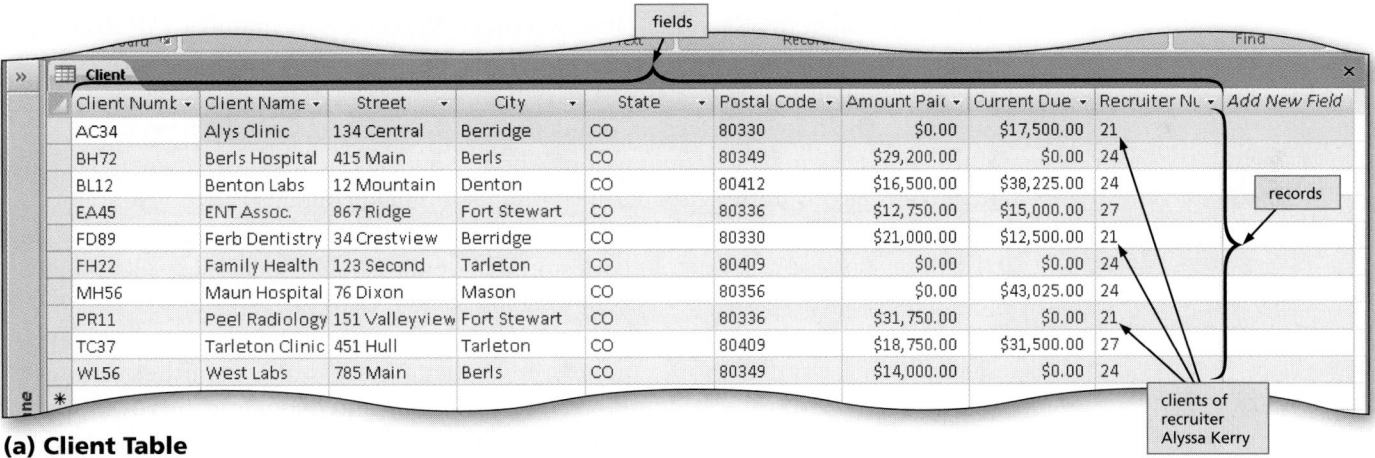

(a) Client Table

(b) Recruiter Table

Figure 1–1

The rows in the tables are called **records**. A record contains information about a given person, product, or event. A row in the Client table, for example, contains information about a specific client.

The columns in the tables are called fields. A **field** contains a specific piece of information within a record. In the Client table, for example, the fourth field, City, contains the city where the client is located.

The first field in the Client table is the Client Number. JSP Recruiters assigns a number to each client. As is common to the way in which many organizations format client numbers, JSP Recruiters calls it a *number*, although it actually contains letters. The JSP client numbers consist of two uppercase letters followed by a two-digit number.

These numbers are unique; that is, no two clients are assigned the same number. Such a field can be used as a **unique identifier**. This simply means that a given client number will appear only in a single record in the table. Only one record exists, for example, in which the client number is BH72. A unique identifier also is called a **primary key**. Thus, the Client Number field is the primary key for the Client table.

The next seven fields in the Client table are Client Name, Street, City, State, Postal Code, Amount Paid, and Current Due. Note that the default width of the columns cuts off the names of some of the columns. The Amount Paid column contains the amount that the client has paid JSP Recruiters year to date (YTD) prior to the current period. The Current Due column contains the amount due to JSP for the current period. For example, client BL12 is Benton Labs. The address is 12 Mountain in Denton, Colorado. The postal code is 80412. The client has paid $16,500 for recruiting services so far this year. The amount due for the current period is $38,225.

JSP assigns each client a single recruiter. The last column in the Client table, Recruiter Number, gives the number of the client's recruiter.

The first field in the Recruiter table, Recruiter Number, is the number JSP Recruiters assigns to the recruiter. These numbers are unique, so Recruiter Number is the primary key of the Recruiter table.

The other fields in the Recruiter table are Last Name, First Name, Street, City, State, Postal Code, Rate, and Commission. The Rate field contains the percentage of the client fee that the recruiter earns, and the Commission field contains the total amount that JSP has paid the recruiter so far this year. For example, Recruiter 27 is Jaime Fernandez. His address is 265 Maxwell in Charleston, Colorado. The Postal Code is 80380. His commission rate is .09 (9%), and his commission is $9,450.

The recruiter number appears in both the Client table and the Recruiter table. It relates clients and recruiters. For example, in the Client table, you see that the recruiter number for client BL12 is 24. To find the name of this recruiter, look for the row in the Recruiter table that contains 24 in the Recruiter Number column. After you have found it, you know the client is assigned to Camden Reeves. To find all the clients assigned to Camden Reeves, you must look through the Client table for all the clients that contain 24 in the Recruiter Number column. His clients are BH72 (Berls Hospital), BL12 (Benton Labs), FH22 (Family Health), MH56 (Maun Hospital), and WL56 (West Labs).

The last recruiter in the Recruiter table, Jan Lee, has not been assigned any clients yet; therefore, her recruiter number, 34, does not appear on any row in the Client table.

Overview

As you read this chapter, you will learn how to create the database shown in Figure 1–1 on the previous page by performing these general tasks:

- Design the database.
- Create a new blank database.

- Create a table and add the records.
- Preview and print the contents of a table.
- Create a second table and add the records.
- Create four reports.
- Create a form.

**Plan
Ahead**

Database design guidelines.

Database design refers to the arrangement of data into tables and fields. In the example in this chapter the design is specified, but in many cases, you will have to determine the design based on what you want the system to accomplish.

When designing a database, the actions you take and the decisions you make will determine the tables and fields that will be included in the database. As you create a database, such as the project shown in Figure 1–1 on page AC 3, you should follow these general guidelines:

1. **Identify the tables.** Examine the requirements for the database in order to identify the main objects that are involved. There will be a table for each object you identified.

   In one database, for example, the main objects might be departments and employees. Thus, there would be two tables: one for departments and the other for employees. In another database, the main objects might be clients and recruiters. In this case, there would also be two tables: one for clients and the other for recruiters. In still another database, the main objects might be books, publishers, and authors. Here there would be three tables: one for books, a second for publishers, and a third for authors.

2. **Determine the primary keys.** Recall that the primary key is the unique identifier for records in the table. For each table, determine the unique identifier, if there is one. For a Department table, for example, the unique identifier might be the Department Code. For a Book table, the unique identifier might be the ISBN number.

3. **Determine the additional fields.** The primary key will be a field or combination of fields in a table. There typically will be many additional fields, each of which contains a type of data. Examine the project requirements to determine these additional fields. For example, in an Employee table, the additional fields might include such fields as Employee Name, Street Address, City, State, Postal Code, Date Hired, Salary, and so on.

4. **Determine relationships among the tables.** Examine the list of tables you have created to see which tables are related. When you determine two tables are related, include matching fields in the two tables. For example, in a database containing employees and departments, there is a relationship between the two tables because one department can have many employees assigned to it. Department Code could be the matching field in the two tables.

5. **Determine data types for the fields.** For each field, determine the type of data the field can contain. One field, for example, might contain only numbers. Another field might contain currency amounts, while a third field might contain only dates. Some fields contain text data, meaning any combination of letters, numbers and special characters (!, ;, ', &, and so on). For example, in an Employee table, the Date Hired field would contain dates, the Salary field would contain currency amounts, and the Hours Worked field would contain numbers. The other fields in the Employee table would contain text data, such as Employee Name and Department Code.

6. **Identify and remove any unwanted redundancy. Redundancy** is the storing of a piece of data in more than one place. Redundancy usually, but not always, causes problems, such as wasted space, difficulties with update, and possible data inconsistency. Examine each table you have created to see if it contains redundancy and, if so, determine whether the redundancy causes these problems. If it does, remove the redundancy by splitting the table into two tables. For example, you may have a single table of employees. In addition to typical employee data (name, address, earnings, and so on), the table might contain Department Number and Department Name. If so, the Department Name could repeat multiple times.

(continued)

(continued)

Every employee whose department number is 12, for example, would have the same department name. It would be better to split the table into two tables, one for Employees and one for Department. In the Department table, the Department Name is stored only once.

7. **Determine a location for the database. The database you have designed will be stored in a single file. You need to determine a location in which to store the file.**

When necessary, more specific details concerning the above guidelines are presented at appropriate points in the chapter. The chapter also will identify the actions performed and decisions made regarding these guidelines during the creation of the database shown in Figure 1–1 on page AC 3.

Designing a Database

This section illustrates the database design process by showing how you would design the database for JSP Recruiters from a set of requirements. In this section, you will use a commonly accepted shorthand to represent the tables and fields that make up the database as well as the primary keys for the tables. For each table, you give the name of the table followed by a set of parentheses. Within the parentheses is a list of the fields in the table separated by columns. You underline the primary key. For example,

Product (Product Code, Description, On Hand, Price)

represents a table called Product. The Product table contains four fields: Product Code, Description, On Hand, and Price. The Product Code field is the primary key.

Database Requirements

JSP Recruiters needs to maintain information on both clients and recruiters. It currently keeps this data in the two Word tables and two Excel workbooks shown in Figure 1–2. They use Word tables for address information and Excel workbooks for financial information.

Client Number	Client Name	Street	City	State	Postal Code
AC34	Alys Clinic	134 Central	Berridge	CO	80330
BH72	Berls Hospital	415 Main	Berls	CO	80349
BL12	Benton Labs	12 Mountain	Denton	CO	80412
EA45	ENT Assoc.	867 Ridge	Fort Stewart	CO	80336
FD89	Ferb Dentistry	34 Crestview	Berridge	CO	80330
FH22	Family Health	123 Second	Tarleton	CO	80409
MH56	Maun Hospital	76 Dixon	Mason	CO	80356
PR11	Peel Radiology	151 Valleyview	Fort Stewart	CO	80336
TC37	Tarleton Clinic	451 Hull	Tarleton	CO	80409
WL56	West Labs	785 Main	Berls	CO	80349

**(a)
Client Address
Information
(Word Table)**

Figure 1–2

**(b)
Client
Financial
Information
(Excel
Workbook)**

	A	B	C	D
1	Client Number	Client Name	Amount Paid	Current Due
2	AC34	Alys Clinic	$0.00	$17,500.00
3	BH72	Berls Hospital	$29,200.00	$0.00
4	BL12	Benton Labs	$16,500.00	$38,225.00
5	EA45	ENT Assoc.	$12,750.00	$15,000.00
6	FD89	Ferb Dentistry	$21,000.00	$12,500.00
7	FH22	Family Health	$0.00	$0.00
8	MH56	Maun Hospital	$0.00	$43,025.00
9	PR11	Peel Radiology	$31,750.00	$0.00
10	TC37	Tarleton Clinic	$18,750.00	$31,500.00
11	WL56	West Labs	$14,000.00	$0.00

**(c)
Recruiter
Address
Information
(Word Table)**

Recruiter Number	Last Name	First Name	Street	City	State	Postal Code
21	Kerry	Alyssa	261 Pointer	Tourin	CO	80416
24	Reeves	Camden	3135 Brill	Denton	CO	80412
27	Fernandez	Jaime	265 Maxwell	Charleston	CO	80380
34	Lee	Jan	1827 Oak	Denton	CO	80413

**(d)
Recruiter
Financial
Information
(Excel
Workbook)**

	A	B	C	D	E
1	Recruiter Number	Last Name	First Name	Rate	Commission
2	21	Kerry	Alyssa	0.10	$17,600.00
3	24	Reeves	Camden	0.10	$19,900.00
4	27	Fernandez	Jaime	0.09	$9,450.00
5	34	Lee	Jan	0.08	$0.00

Figure 1–2 (continued)

For clients, JSP needs to maintain address data. It currently keeps this address data in a Word table (Figure 1–2a). It also maintains financial data for each client. This includes the amount paid and the current due from the client. It keeps these amounts along with the client name and number in the Excel workbook shown in Figure 1–2b.

JSP keeps recruiter address data in a Word table as shown in Figure 1–2c. Just as with clients, it keeps financial data for recruiters, including their rate and commission, in a separate Excel workbook, as shown in Figure 1–2d.

Finally, it keeps track of which clients are assigned to which recruiters. Currently, for example, clients AC34 (Alys Clinic), FD89 (Ferb Dentistry), and PR11 (Peel Radiology) are assigned to recruiter 21 (Alyssa Kerry). Clients BH72 (Berls Hospital), BL12 (Benton Labs), FH22 (Family Health), MH56 (Maun Hospital), and WL56 (West Labs) are assigned to recruiter 24 (Camden Reeves). Clients EA45 (ENT Assoc.) and TC37 (Tarleton Clinic) are assigned to recruiter 27 (Jaime Fernandez). JSP has an additional recruiter, Jan Lee, whose number has been assigned as 34, but who has not yet been assigned any clients.

Naming Tables and Fields

In designing your database, you must name the tables and fields. Thus, before beginning the design process, you must understand the rules for table and field names, which are:

1. Names can be up to 64 characters in length.
2. Names can contain letters, digits, and spaces, as well as most of the punctuation symbols.
3. Names cannot contain periods (.), exclamation points (!), accent graves (`), or square brackets ([ ]).
4. The same name cannot be used for two different fields in the same table.

The approach to naming tables and fields used in this text is to begin the names with an uppercase letter and to use lowercase for the other letters. In multiple-word names, each word begins with an uppercase letter, and there is a space between words (for example, Client Number). You should know that there are other approaches. Some people omit the space (ClientNumber). Still others use an underscore in place of the space (Client_Number). Finally, some use an underscore in place of a space, but use the same case for all letters (CLIENT_NUMBER or client_number).

BTW

Naming Fields
Access 2007 has a number of reserved words, words that have a special meaning to Access. You cannot use these reserved words as field names. For example, Name is a reserved word and could not be used in the Client table to describe a client's name. For a complete list of reserved words in Access 2007, consult Access Help.

Identifying the Tables

Now that you know the rules for naming tables and fields, you are ready to begin the design process. The first step is to identify the main objects involved in the requirements. For the JSP Recruiters database, the main objects are clients and recruiters. This leads to two tables, which you must name. Reasonable names for these two tables are:

Client
Recruiter

Determining the Primary Keys

The next step is to identify the fields that will be the primary keys. Client numbers uniquely identify clients, and recruiter numbers uniquely identify recruiters. Thus, the primary key for the Client table is the client number, and the primary key for the Recruiter table is the recruiter number. Reasonable names for these fields would be Client Number and Recruiter Number, respectively. Adding these primary keys to the tables gives:

Client (<u>Client Number</u>)
Recruiter (<u>Recruiter Number</u>)

BTW

Database Design Language (DBDL)
DBDL is a commonly accepted shorthand representation for showing the structure of a relational database. You write the name of the table and then within parentheses you list all the columns in the table. If the columns continue beyond one line, indent the subsequent lines.

Determining Additional Fields

After identifying the primary keys, you need to determine and name the additional fields. In addition to the client number, the Client Address Information shown in Figure 1–2a on page AC 6 contains the client name, street, city, state, and postal code. These would be fields in the Client table. The Client Financial Information shown in Figure 1–2b also contains the client number and client name, which are already included in the Client table. The financial information also contains the amount paid and the current due. Adding the amount paid and current due fields to those already identified in the Client table and assigning reasonable names gives:

Client (<u>Client Number</u>, Client Name, Street, City, State, Postal Code,
   Amount Paid, Current Due)

Similarly, examining the Recruiter Address Information in Figure 1–2c on page AC 7 adds the last name, first name, street, city, state, and postal code fields to the Recruiter table. In addition to the recruiter number, last name, and first name, the Recruiter Financial Information in Figure 1–2d would add the rate and commission. Adding these fields to the Recruiter table and assigning reasonable names gives:

Recruiter (<u>Recruiter Number</u>, Last Name, First Name, Street, City,
State, Postal Code, Rate, Commission)

Determining and Implementing Relationships Between the Tables

Plan
Ahead

Determine relationships among the tables.
The most common type of relationship you will encounter between tables is the **one-to-many relationship**. This means that each row in the first table may be associated with *many* rows in the second table, but each row in the second table is associated with only *one* row in the first. The first table is called the "one" table and the second is called the "many" table. For example, there may be a relationship between departments and employees, in which each department can have many employees, but each employee is assigned to only one department. In this relationship, there would be two tables, Department and Employee. The Department table would be the "one" table in the relationship. The Employee table would be the "many" table.
    To determine relationships among tables, you can follow these general guidelines:

1. Identify the "one" table.

2. Identify the "many" table.

3. Include the primary key from the "one" table as a field in the "many" table.

According to the requirements, each client has one recruiter, but each recruiter can have many clients. Thus, the Recruiter table is the "one" table, and the Client table is the "many" table. To implement this one-to-many relationship between recruiters and clients, add the Recruiter Number field (the primary key of the Recruiter table) to the Client table. This produces:

Client (<u>Client Number</u>, Client Name, Street, City, State, Postal Code, Amount Paid, Current Due, Recruiter Number)

Recruiter (<u>Recruiter Number</u>, Last Name, First Name, Street, City, State, Postal Code, Rate, Commission)

Determining Data Types for the Fields

Each field has a **data type**. This indicates the type of data that can be stored in the field. Three of the most commonly used data types are:

1. **Text** — The field can contain any characters. A maximum number of 255 characters is allowed in a field whose data type is Text.

2. **Number** — The field can contain only numbers. The numbers either can be positive or negative. Fields are assigned this type so they can be used in arithmetic operations. Fields that contain numbers but will not be used for arithmetic operations usually are assigned a data type of Text.

3. **Currency** — The field can contain only monetary data. The values will appear with currency symbols, such as dollar signs, commas, and decimal points, and with

BTW

Currency Symbols
To show the symbol for the Euro (€) instead of the dollar sign, change the Format property for the field whose data type is currency. To change the default symbols for currency, change the settings in the operating system using the Control Panel.

two digits following the decimal point. Like numeric fields, you can use currency fields in arithmetic operations. Access assigns a size to currency fields automatically. Table 1–1 shows the other data types that are available.

Table 1–1 Additional Data Types	
Data Type	**Description**
Memo	Field can store a variable amount of text or combinations of text and numbers where the total number of characters may exceed 255.
Date/Time	Field can store dates and times.
AutoNumber	Field can store a unique sequential number that Access assigns to a record. Access will increment the number by 1 as each new record is added.
Yes/No	Field can store only one of two values. The choices are Yes/No, True/False, or On/Off.
OLE Object	Field can store an OLE object, which is an object linked to or embedded in the table.
Hyperlink	Field can store text that can be used as a hyperlink address.
Attachment	Field can contain an attached file. Images, spreadsheets, documents, charts, and so on can be attached to this field in a record in the database. You can view and edit the attached file.

In the Client table, because the Client Number, Client Name, Street, City, and State can all contain letters, their data types should be Text. The data type for Postal Code is Text instead of Number, because postal codes are not used in arithmetic operations. You do not add postal codes or find an average postal code, for example. The Amount Paid and Current Due fields both contain monetary data, so their data types should be Currency.

Similarly, in the Recruiter table, the data type for the Recruiter Number, Last Name, First Name, Street, City, State, and Postal Code fields all should be Text. The Commission field contains monetary amounts, so its data type should be Currency. The Rate field contains a number that is not a currency amount, so its data type should be Number.

Identifying and Removing Redundancy

Redundancy means storing the same fact in more than one place. It usually results from placing too many fields in a table — fields that really belong in separate tables — and often causes serious problems. If you had not realized there were two objects, clients and recruiters, for example, you might have placed all the data in a single Client table. Figure 1–3 shows a portion of this table with some sample data. Notice that the data for a given Recruiter (number, name, address, and so on) occurs on more than one record. The data for Camden Reeves is repeated in the figure.

Client Table

clients of recruiter 24

name of recruiter 24 appears more than once

Client Number	Client Name	Street	...	Recruiter Number	Last Name	First Name	...
AC34	Alys Clinic	134 Central	...	21	Kerry	Alyssa	...
BH72	Berls Hospital	415 Main	...	24	Reeves	Camden	...
BL12	Benton Labs	12 Mountain	...	24	Reeves	Camden	...
...	...	...	...	...	...	...	...

Figure 1–3

Storing this data on multiple records is an example of redundancy, which causes several problems, including:

1. Wasted storage space. The name of Recruiter 24 (Camden Reeves), for example, should be stored only once. Storing this fact several times is wasteful.

2. More difficult database updates. If, for example, Camden Reeves's name is spelled wrong and needs to be changed in the database, his name would need to be changed in several different places.

3. A possibility of inconsistent data. There is nothing to prohibit the recruiter's last name from being Reeves on client BH72's record and Reed on client BL12's record. The data would be inconsistent. In both cases, the recruiter number is 24, but the last names are different.

The solution to the problem is to place the redundant data in a separate table, one in which the data no longer will be redundant. If, for example, you place the data for recruiters in a separate table (Figure 1–4), the data for each recruiter will appear only once.

Client Table

Client Number	Client Name	Street	...	Recruiter Number
AC34	Alys Clinic	134 Central	...	21
BH72	Berls Hospital	415 Main	...	24
BL12	Benton Labs	12 Mountain	...	24
...	...	...	...	...

clients of recruiter 24

Recruiter Table

Recruiter Number	Last Name	First Name	...
21	Kerry	Alyssa	...
24	Reeves	Camden	...
...	...	...	...

name of recruiter 24 appears only once

Figure 1–4

Notice that you need to have the recruiter number in both tables. Without it, there would be no way to tell which recruiter is associated with which client. The remaining recruiter data, however, was removed from the Client table and placed in the Recruiter table. This new arrangement corrects the problems of redundancy in the following ways:

1. Because the data for each recruiter is stored only once, space is not wasted.

2. Changing the name of a recruiter is easy. You have only to change one row in the Recruiter table.

3. Because the data for a recruiter is stored only once, inconsistent data cannot occur. Designing to omit redundancy will help you to produce good and valid database designs.

You should always examine your design to see if it contains redundancy. If it does, you should decide whether you need to remove the redundancy by creating a separate table.

BTW

Postal Codes
Some organizations with many customers spread throughout the country will, in fact, have a separate table of postal codes, cities, and states. If you call such an organization to place an order, they typically will ask you for your postal code (or ZIP code), rather than asking for your city, state, and postal code. They then will indicate the city and state that correspond to that postal code and ask you if that is correct.

If you examine your design, you'll see that there is one area of redundancy (see the data in Figure 1–1 on page AC 3). Cities and states are both repeated. Every client whose postal code is 80330, for example, has Berridge as the city and CO as the state. To remove this redundancy, you would create a table whose primary key is Postal Code and that contains City and State as additional fields. City and State would be removed from the Client table. Having City, State, and Postal Code in a table is very common, however, and usually you would not take such action. There is no other redundancy in your tables.

Starting Access

If you are using a computer to step through the project in this chapter, and you want your screen to match the figures in this book, you should change your screen's resolution to 1024 × 768. For information about how to change a computer's resolution, read Appendix E.

Note: If you are using Windows XP, see Appendix F for alternate steps.

To Start Access

The following steps, which assume Windows Vista is running, start Access based on a typical installation. You may need to ask your instructor how to start Access for your computer.

1
- Click the Start button on the Windows Vista taskbar to display the Start menu.

- Click All Programs at the bottom of the left pane on the Start menu to display the All Programs list.

- Click Microsoft Office in the All Programs list to display the Microsoft Office list (Figure 1–5).

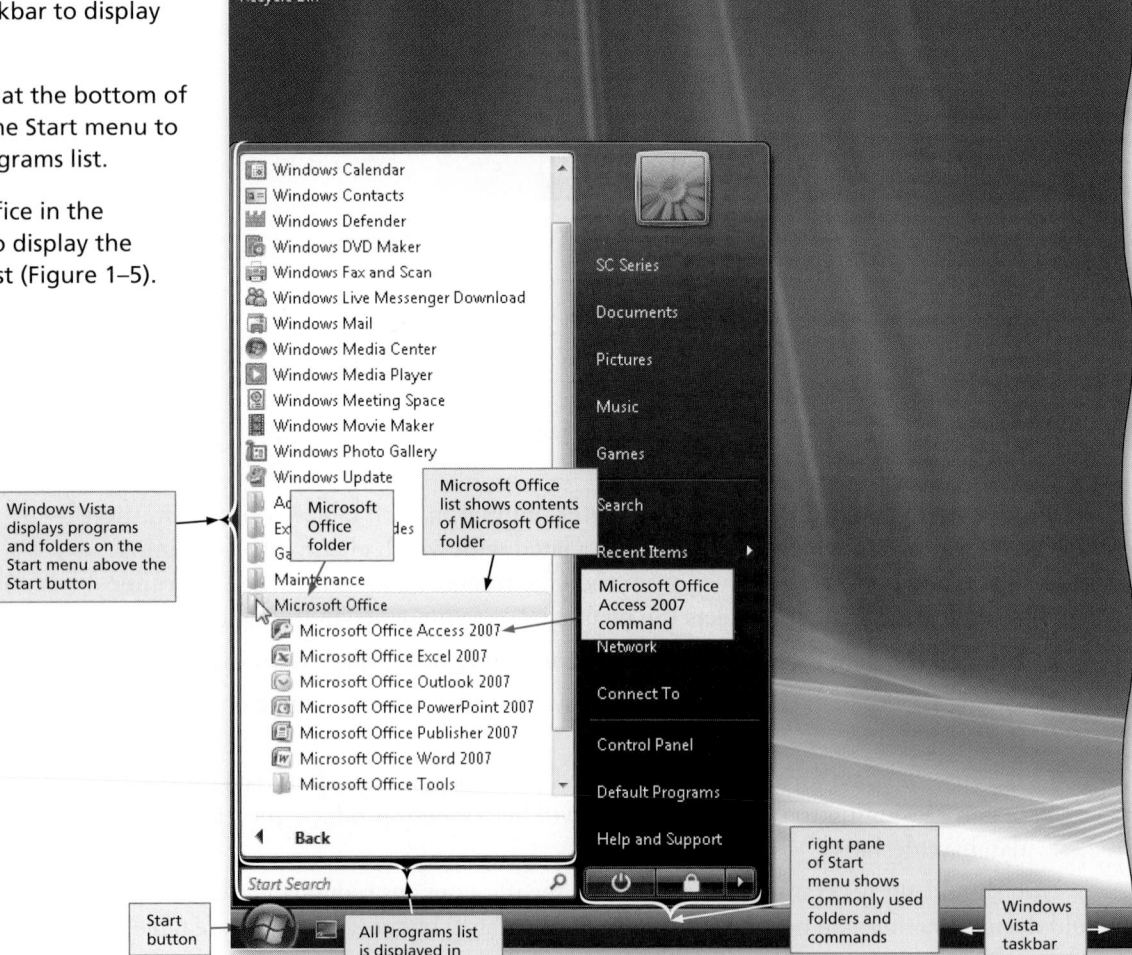

Figure 1–5

2

- Click Microsoft Office Access 2007 to start Access and display the Getting Started with Microsoft Office Access screen (Figure 1–6).

- If the Access window is not maximized, click the Maximize button next to the Close button on its title bar to maximize the window.

Q&A

What is a maximized window?

A maximized window fills the entire screen. When you maximize a window, the Maximize button changes to a Restore Down button.

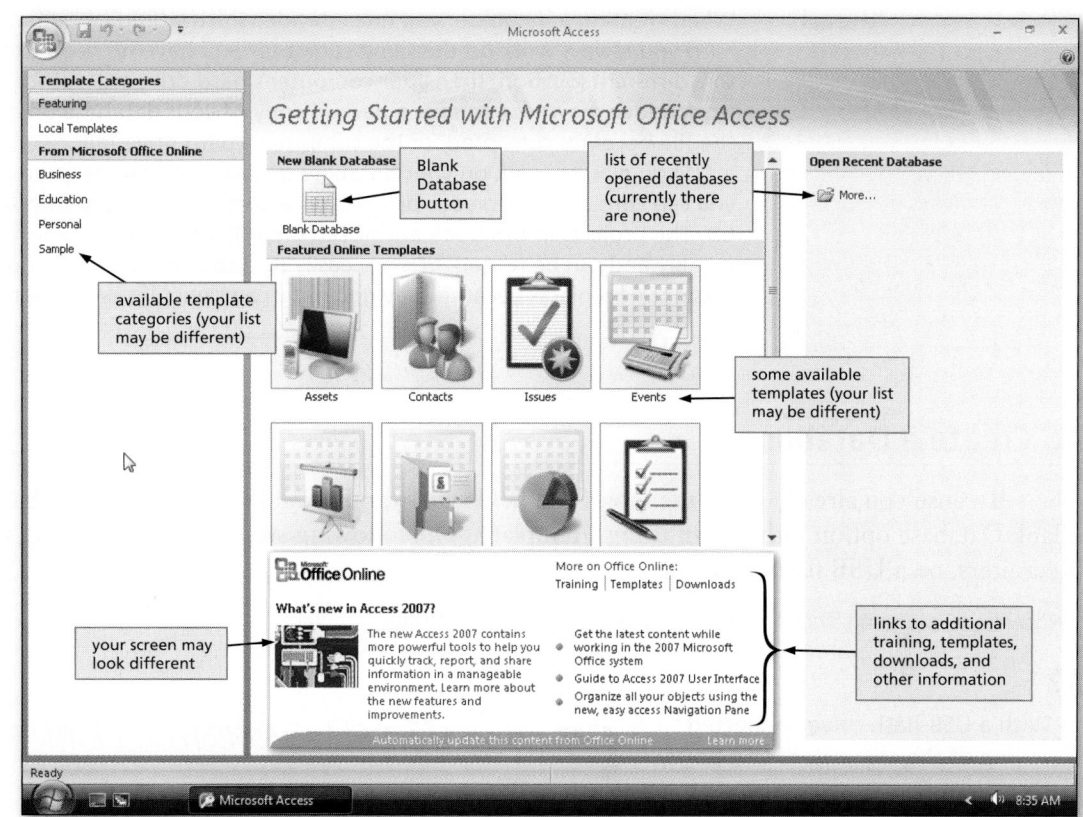

Figure 1–6

Other Ways

1. Double-click Access icon on desktop, if one is present
2. Click Microsoft Office Access 2007 on Start menu

Creating a Database

In Access, all the tables, reports, forms, and queries that you create are stored in a single file called a database. Thus, before creating any of these objects, you first must create the database that will hold them. You can use either the Blank Database option or a template to create a new database. If you already know the tables and fields you want in your database, you would use the Blank Database option. If not, you can use a template. Templates can guide you by suggesting some commonly used databases. If you choose to create a database using a template, you would use the following steps.

TO CREATE A DATABASE USING A TEMPLATE

1. If the template you wish to use is not already visible on the Getting Started with Microsoft Office Access page, double-click the links in the Template Categories pane to display the desired template.

2. Click the template you wish to use.

3. Enter a file name (or accept the suggested file name) and select a location for the database.

4. Click the Create button to create the database or the Download button to download the database and create the database, if necessary.

When you create a database, the computer places it on a storage medium, such as a USB flash drive, CD, or hard disk. A saved database is referred to as a **file**. A **file name** is the name assigned to a file when it is saved.

BTW

Naming Files
File names can be a maximum of 260 characters including the file extension. The file extension for Access 2007 is .accdb. You can use either uppercase or lowercase letters in file names.

<table>
<tr>
<td>Plan
Ahead</td>
<td>

Determine where to create the database.

When creating a database, you must decide which storage medium to use.

If you always work on the same computer and have no need to transport your database to a different location, then your computer's hard drive will suffice as a storage location. It is a good idea, however, to save a backup copy of your database on a separate medium in case the file becomes corrupted, or the computer's hard drive fails.

If you plan to work your database in various locations or on multiple computers, then you can consider saving your projects on a portable medium, such as a USB flash drive or CD. The projects in this book are stored on a USB flash drive, which saves files quickly and reliably and can be reused. CDs are easily portable and serve as good backups for the final versions of projects because they generally can save files only one time.

</td>
</tr>
</table>

To Create a Database

Because you already know the tables and fields you want in the JSP Recruiters database, you would use the Blank Database option rather than using a template. The following steps create a database, using the file name JSP Recruiters, on a USB flash drive.

Note: If you are using Windows XP, see Appendix F for alternate steps.

- With a USB flash drive connected to one of the computer's USB ports, click Blank Database to create a new blank database (Figure 1–7).

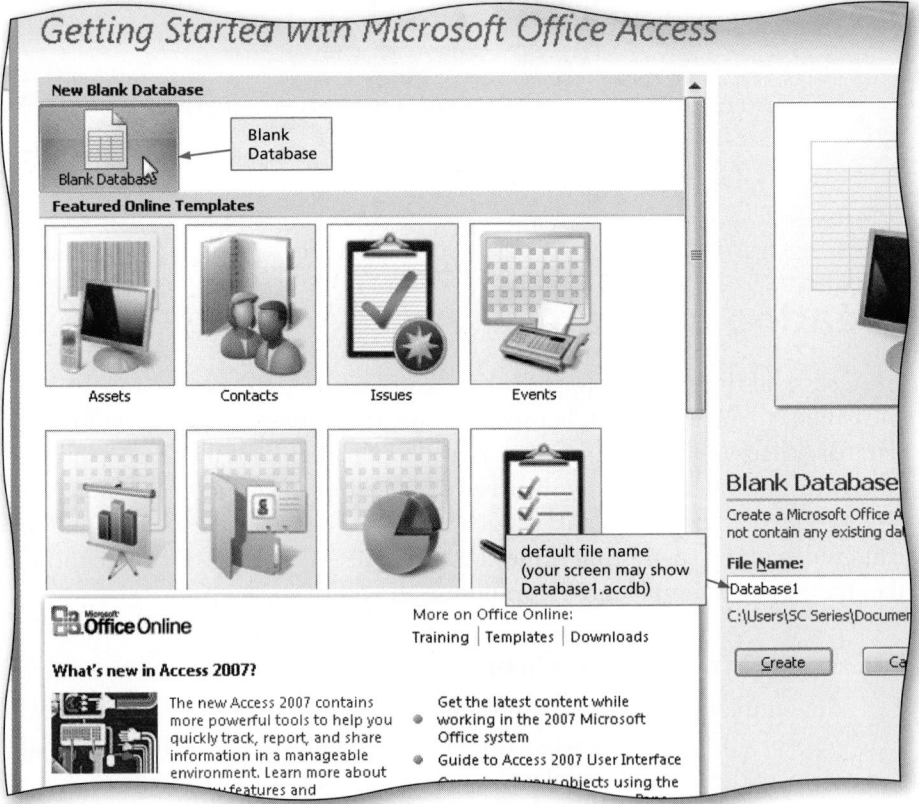

Figure 1–7

2

- Repeatedly press the DELETE key to delete the default name of Database1.

- Type JSP Recruiters in the File Name text box to replace the default file name of Database1 (your screen may show Database1.accdb). Do not press the ENTER key after typing the file name (Figure 1–8).

Q&A What characters can I use in a file name?

A file name can have a maximum of 260 characters, including spaces. The only invalid characters are the back-slash (\\), slash (/), colon (:), asterisk (*), question mark (?), quotation mark ("), less than symbol (<), greater than symbol (>), and vertical bar (|).

3

- Click the 'Browse for a location to put your database' button to display the File New Database dialog box.

- If the Navigation Pane is not displayed in the Save As dialog box, click the Browse Folders button to expand the dialog box.

- If a Folders list is displayed below the Folders button, click the Folders button to remove the Folders list (Figure 1-9).

Q&A Do I have to save to a USB flash drive?

No. You can save to any device or folder. A **folder** is a specific location on a storage medium. You can save to the default folder or a different folder. You also can create your own folders, which is explained later in this book.

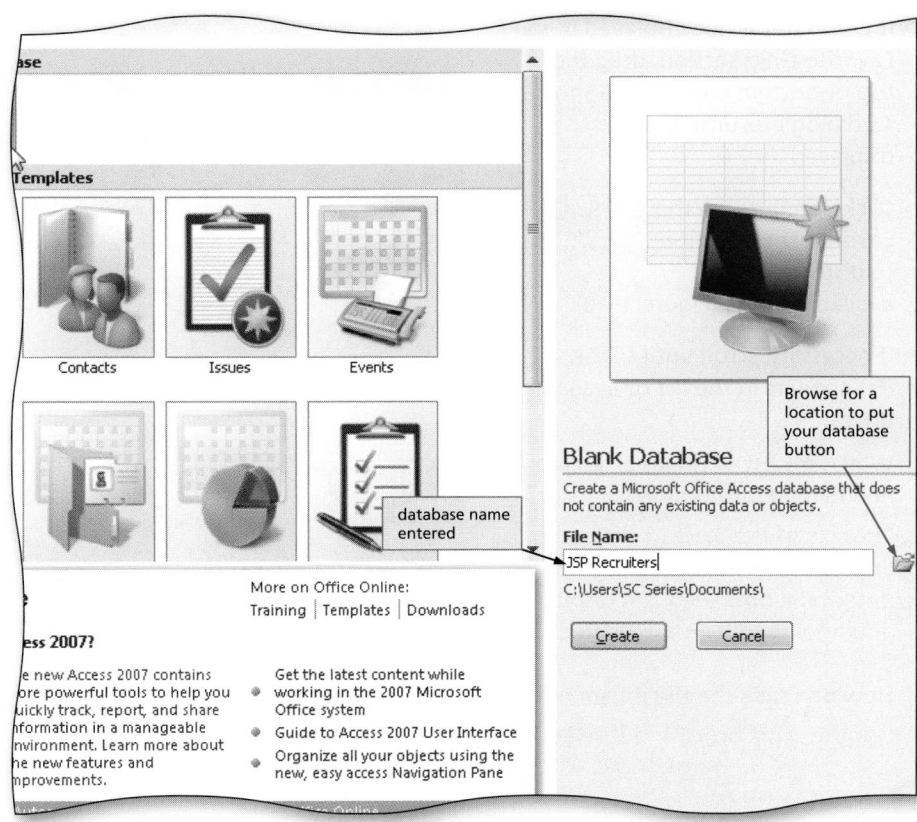

Figure 1–8

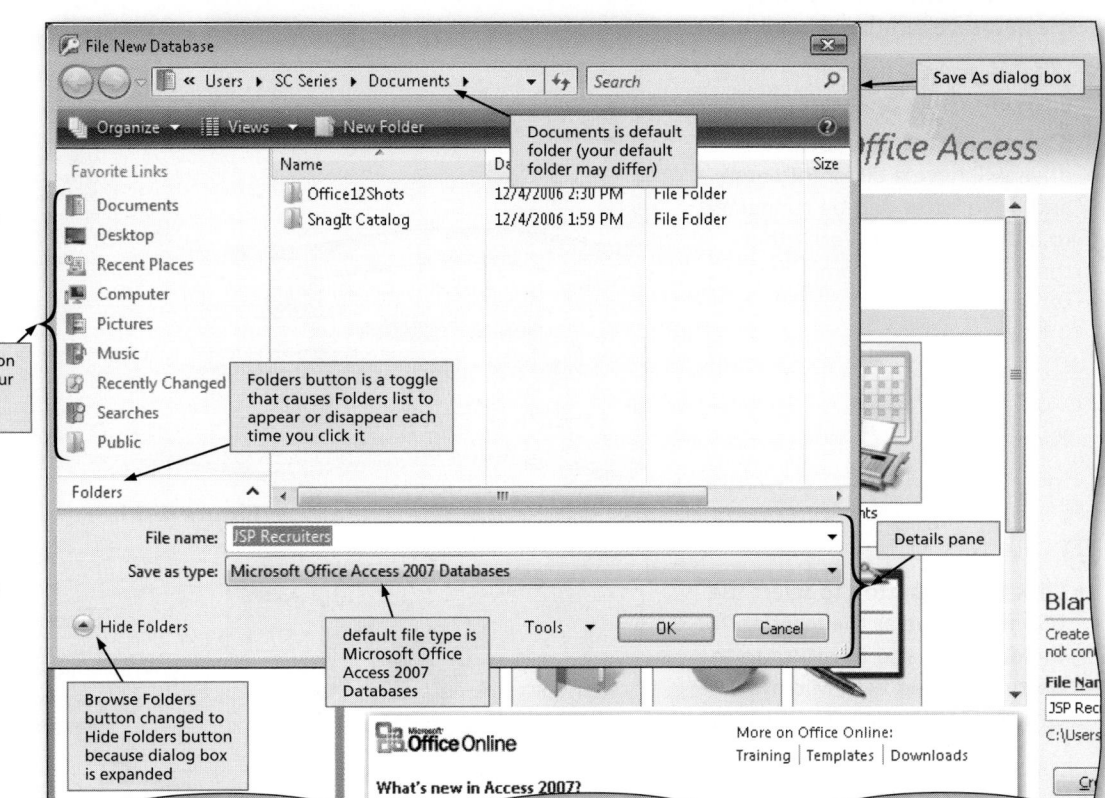

Figure 1–9

- If Computer is not displayed in the Favorite Links section, drag the top or bottom edge of the Save As dialog box until Computer is displayed.

- Click Computer in the Favorite Links section to display a list of available drives (Figure 1–10).

- If necessary, scroll until UDISK 2.0 (E:) appears in the list of available drives.

Q&A
Why is my list of drives arranged and named differently?

The size of the Save As dialog box and your computer's configuration determine how the list is displayed and how the drives are named.

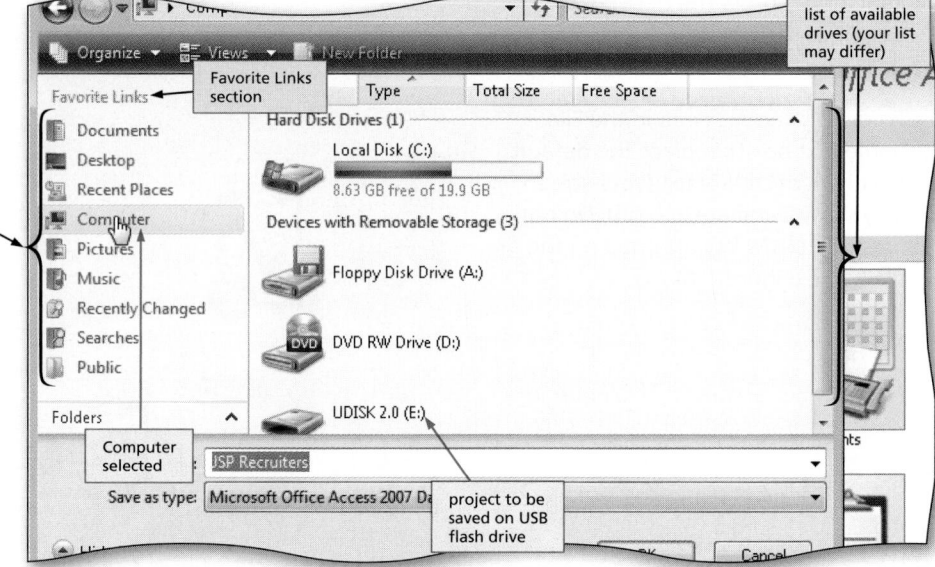

Figure 1–10

Q&A
How do I save the file if I am not using a USB flash drive?

Use the same process, but select your desired save location in the Favorite Links section.

- Double-click UDISK 2.0 (E:) in the Computer list to select the USB flash drive, Drive E in this case, as the new save location (Figure 1–11).

Q&A
What if my USB flash drive has a different name or letter?

It is very likely that your USB flash drive will have a different name and drive letter and be connected to a different port. Verify that the device in your Computer list is correct.

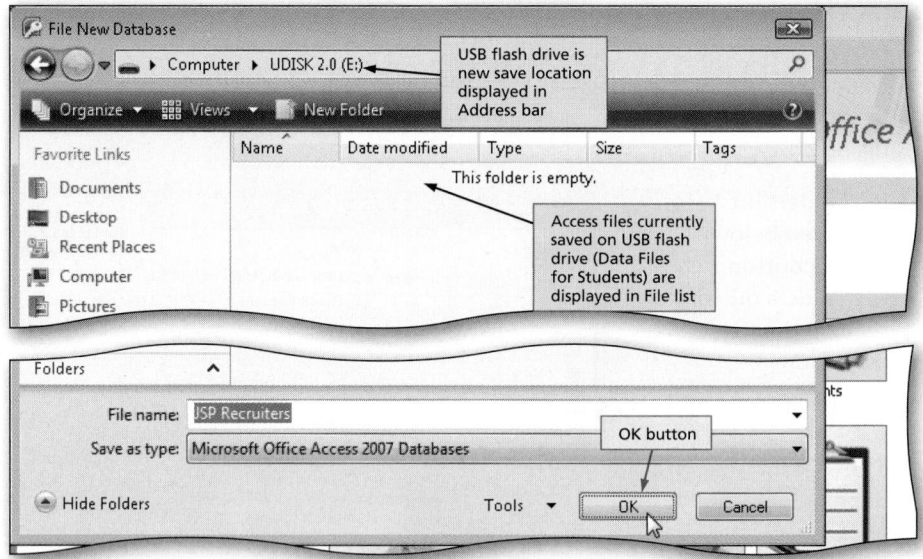

Figure 1–11

- Click the OK button to select the USB flash drive as the location for the database and to return to the Getting Started with Microsoft Office Access screen (Figure 1–12).

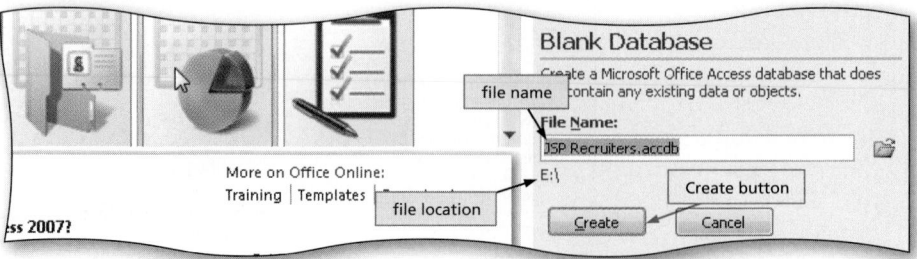

Figure 1–12

7
- Click the Create button to create the database on the USB flash drive with the file name, JSP Recruiters (Figure 1–13).

Q&A

How do I know that the JSP Recruiters database is created?

The name of the database appears in the title bar.

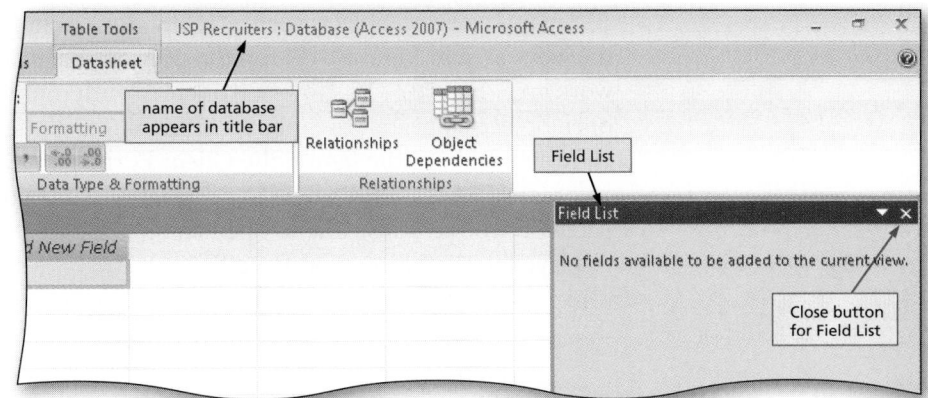

Figure 1–13

8
- If a Field List appears, click its Close button to remove the Field List from the screen (Figure 1–14).

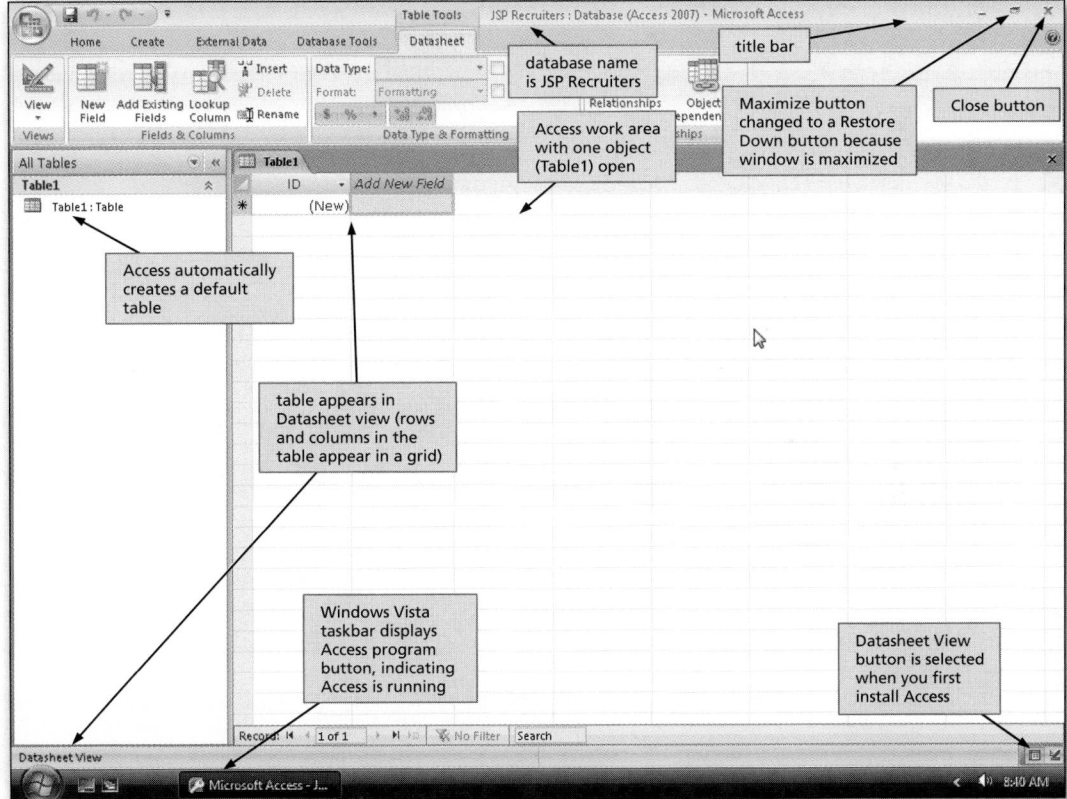

Figure 1–14

The Access Window

The Access window consists of a variety of components to make your work more efficient and documents more professional. These include the Navigation Pane, Access work area, Ribbon, Mini toolbar and shortcut menus, Quick Access Toolbar, and Office Button. Some of these components are common to other Microsoft Office 2007 programs; others are unique to Access.

Other Ways

1. Click Office Button, click Save, type file name, click Computer, select drive or folder, click Save button

2. Press CTRL+S or press SHIFT+F12, type file name, click Computer, select drive or folder, click Save button

Navigation Pane and Access Work Area

You work on objects such as tables, forms, and reports in the **Access work area**. In the work area in Figure 1–14 on the previous page, a single table, Table1, is open in the work area. Figure 1–15 shows a work area with multiple objects open. **Object tabs** for the open objects appear at the top of the work area. You can select one of the open objects by clicking its tab. In the figure, the Client Form is the selected object. To the left of the work area is the Navigation Pane. The Navigation Pane contains a list of all the objects in the database. You use this pane to open an object. You also can customize the way objects are displayed in the Navigation Pane.

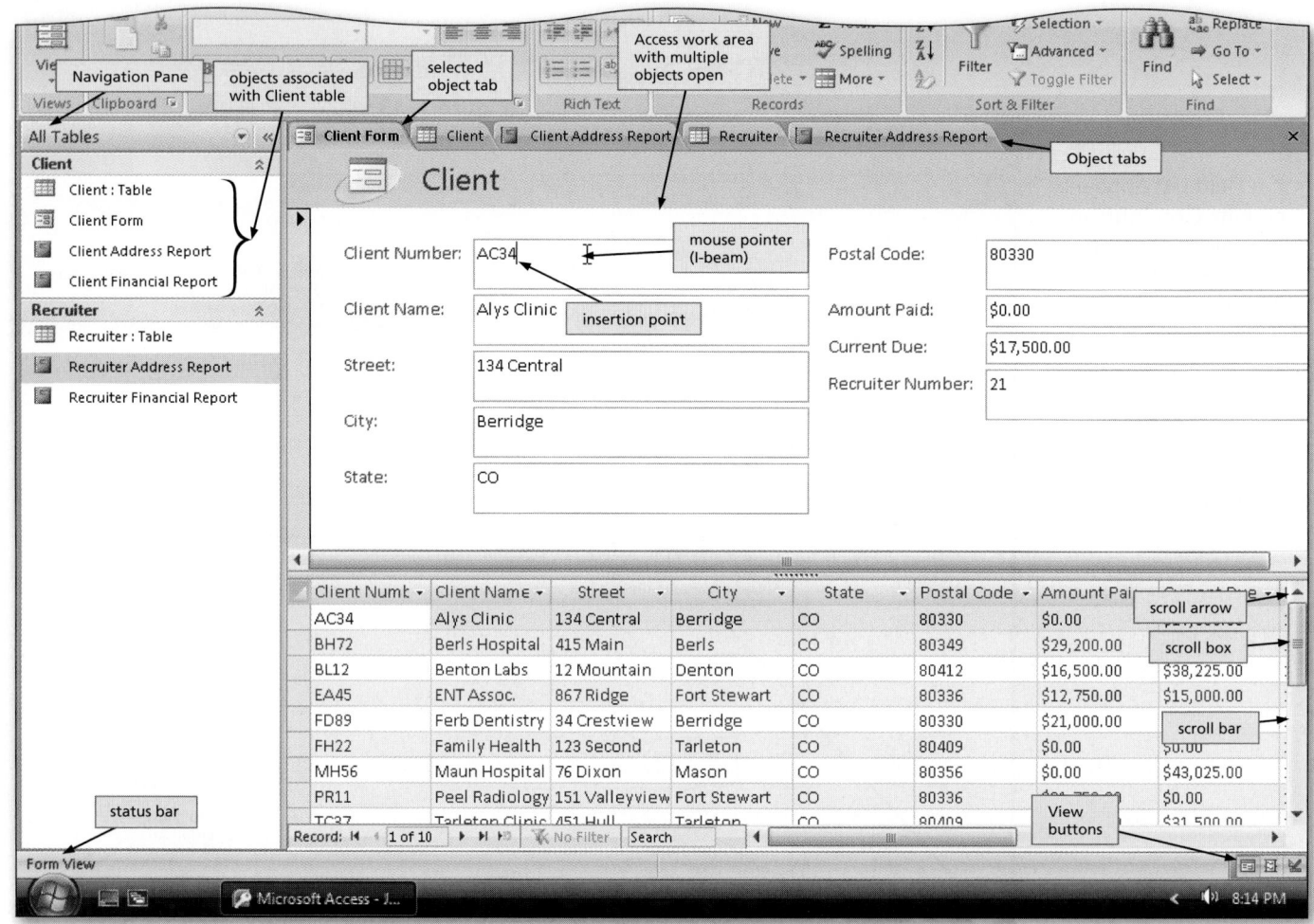

Figure 1–15

The Access work area in Figure 1–15 contains an insertion point, mouse pointer, scroll bar, and status bar. Other elements that may appear in the work area are discussed later in this and subsequent chapters.

Insertion Point The **insertion point** is a blinking vertical bar that indicates where text, graphics, and other items will be inserted. As you type, the insertion point moves to the right.

Mouse Pointer The **mouse pointer** becomes different shapes depending on the task you are performing in Access and the pointer's location on the screen. The mouse pointer in Figure 1–15 is the shape of an I-beam.

Scroll Bar   You use a **scroll bar** to display different portions of a database object in the Access window. At the right edge of the window is a **vertical scroll bar**. If an object is too wide to fit in the Access window, a **horizontal scroll bar** also appears at the bottom of the window. On a scroll bar, the position of the **scroll box** reflects the location of the portion of the database object that is displayed in the Access window. A **scroll arrow** is located at each end of a scroll bar. To scroll through, or display different portions of the object in the Access window, you can click a scroll arrow or drag the scroll box.

Status Bar   The **status bar**, located at the bottom of the Access window above the Windows Vista taskbar, presents information about the database object, the progress of current tasks, and the status of certain commands and keys; it also provides controls for viewing the object. As you type text or perform certain commands, various indicators may appear on the status bar.

   The left edge of the status bar in Figure 1–15 shows that the form object is open in Form view. Toward the right edge are View buttons, which you can use to change the view that is currently displayed.

Ribbon

   The **Ribbon**, located near the top of the Access window, is the control center in Access (Figure 1–16a). The Ribbon provides easy, central access to the tasks you perform while creating a database object. The Ribbon consists of tabs, groups, and commands. Each **tab** surrounds a collection of groups, and each group contains related commands.

   When you start Access, the Ribbon displays four top-level tabs: Home, Create, External Data, and Database Tools. The **Home tab**, called the primary tab, contains the more frequently used commands. To display a different tab on the Ribbon, click the top-level tab. That is, to display the Create tab, click Create on the Ribbon. To return to the Home tab, click Home on the Ribbon. The tab currently displayed is called the **active tab**.

   To allow more space in the Access work area, some users prefer to minimize the Ribbon, which hides the groups on the Ribbon and displays only the top-level tabs (Figure 1–16b). To use commands on a minimized Ribbon, click the top-level tab.

   Each time you start Access, the Ribbon appears the same way it did the last time you used Access. The chapters in this book, however, begin with the Ribbon appearing as it did at the initial installation of the software. If you are stepping through this chapter on a computer and you want your Ribbon to match the figures in this book, read Appendix E.

BTW

Minimizing the Ribbon
If you want to minimize the Ribbon, right-click the Ribbon and then click Minimize the Ribbon on the shortcut menu, double-click the active tab, or press CTRL+F1. To restore a minimized Ribbon, right-click the Ribbon and then click Minimize the Ribbon on the shortcut menu, double-click any top-level tab, or press CTRL+F1. To use commands on a minimized Ribbon, click the top-level tab.

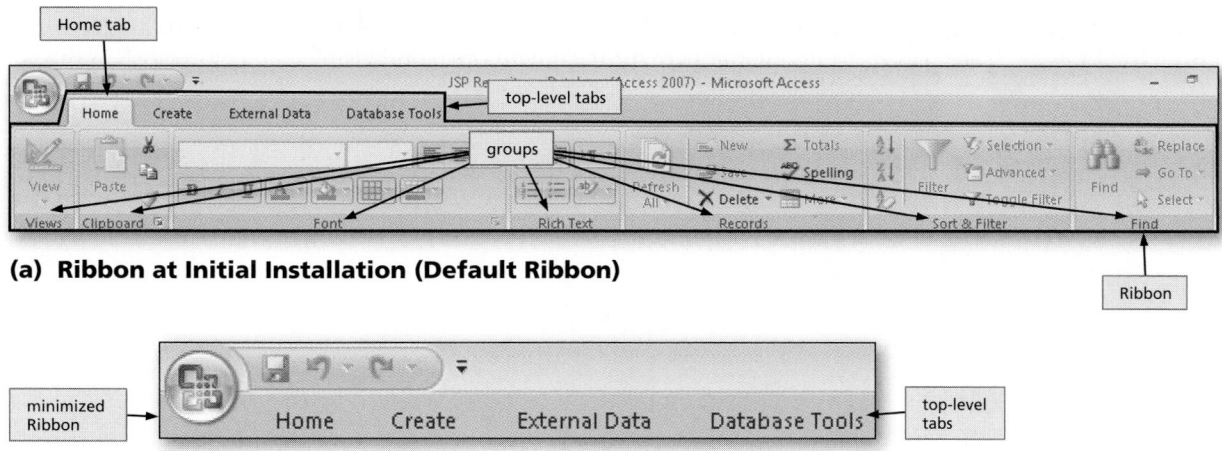

(a) Ribbon at Initial Installation (Default Ribbon)

(b) Minimized Ribbon

Figure 1–16

In addition to the top-level tabs, Access displays other tabs, called **contextual tabs**, when you perform certain tasks or work with objects such as datasheets. If you are working with a table in Datasheet view, for example, the Table Tools tab and its related subordinate Datasheet tab appear (Figure 1–17). When you are finished working with the table, the Table Tools and Datasheet tabs disappear from the Ribbon. Access determines when contextual tabs should appear and disappear based on tasks you perform. Some contextual tabs have more than one related subordinate tab.

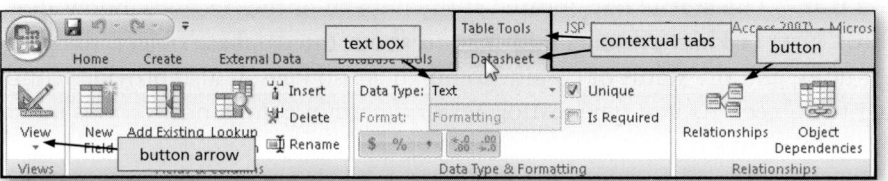

Figure 1–17

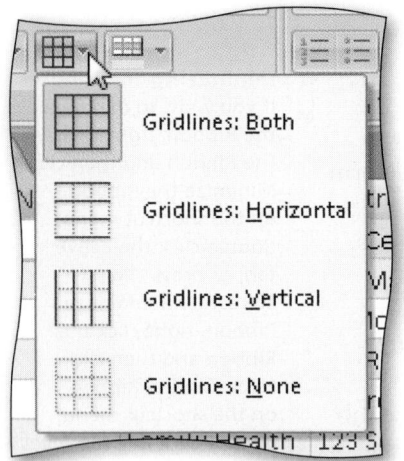

Figure 1–18

Commands on the Ribbon include buttons, boxes (text boxes, check boxes, etc.), and galleries (Figure 1–18). A **gallery** is a set of choices, often graphical, arranged in a grid or in a list. You can scroll through choices on an in-Ribbon gallery by clicking the gallery's scroll arrows. Or, you can click a gallery's More button to view more gallery options on the screen at a time. Some buttons and boxes have arrows that, when clicked, also display a gallery; others always cause a gallery to be displayed when clicked. Many galleries support **live preview**, which is a feature that allows you to point to a gallery choice and see its effect in the database object — without actually selecting the choice.

Some commands on the Ribbon display an image to help you remember their function. When you point to a command on the Ribbon, all or part of the command glows in shades of yellow and orange, and an Enhanced ScreenTip appears on the screen. An **Enhanced ScreenTip** is an on-screen note that provides the name of the command, available keyboard shortcut(s), a description of the command, and sometimes instructions for how to obtain help about the command (Figure 1–19). Enhanced ScreenTips are more detailed than a typical ScreenTip, which usually only displays the name of the command.

The lower-right corner of some groups on the Ribbon has a small arrow, called a **Dialog Box Launcher**, which, when clicked, displays a dialog box or a task pane with additional options for the group (Figure 1–20). When presented with a dialog box, you make selections and must close the dialog box before returning to the database object. A **task pane**, by contrast, is a window that can remain open and visible while you work in the database object.

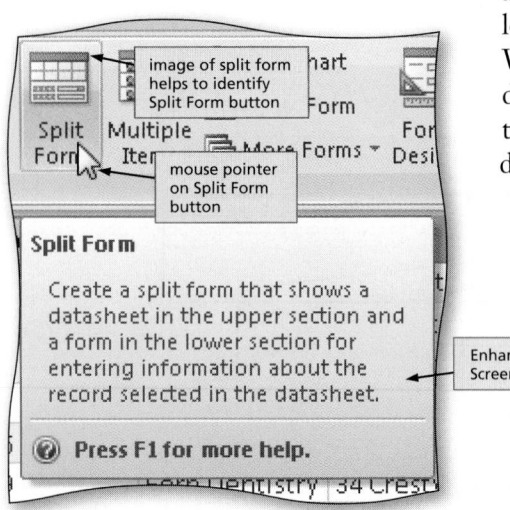

Figure 1–19

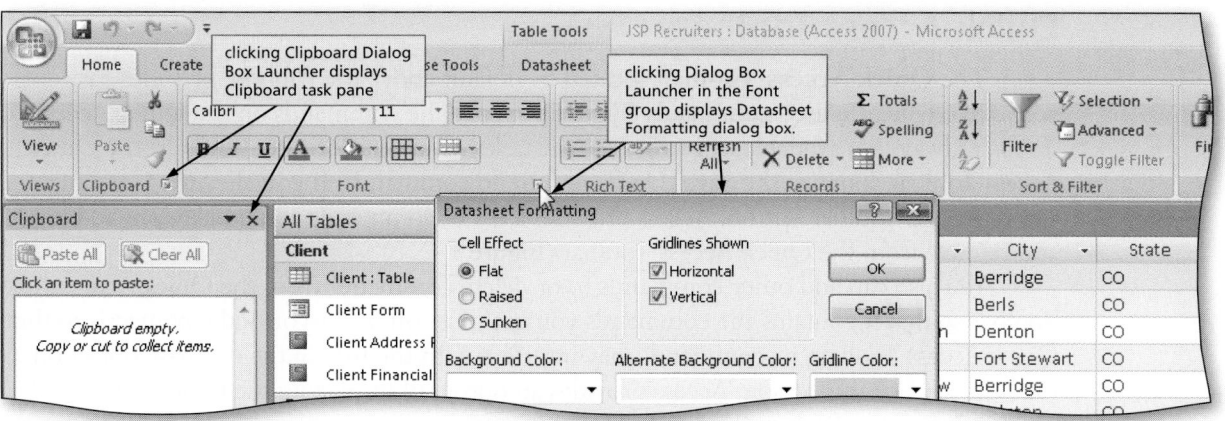

Figure 1–20

Mini Toolbar and Shortcut Menus

The **Mini toolbar**, which appears automatically based on tasks you perform, contains commands related to changing the appearance of text in a database object. All commands on the Mini toolbar also exist on the Ribbon. The purpose of the Mini toolbar is to minimize mouse movement. For example, if you want to use a command that currently is not displayed on the active tab, you can use the command on the Mini toolbar — instead of switching to a different tab to use the command.

When the Mini toolbar appears, it initially is transparent (Figure 1–21a). If you do not use the transparent Mini toolbar, it disappears from the screen. To use the Mini toolbar, move the mouse pointer into the toolbar, which causes the Mini toolbar to change from a transparent to bright appearance (Figure 1–21b).

A **shortcut menu**, which appears when you right-click an object, is a list of frequently used commands that relate to the right-clicked object. When you right-click a table, for example, a shortcut menu appears with commands related to the table (Figure 1–21c).

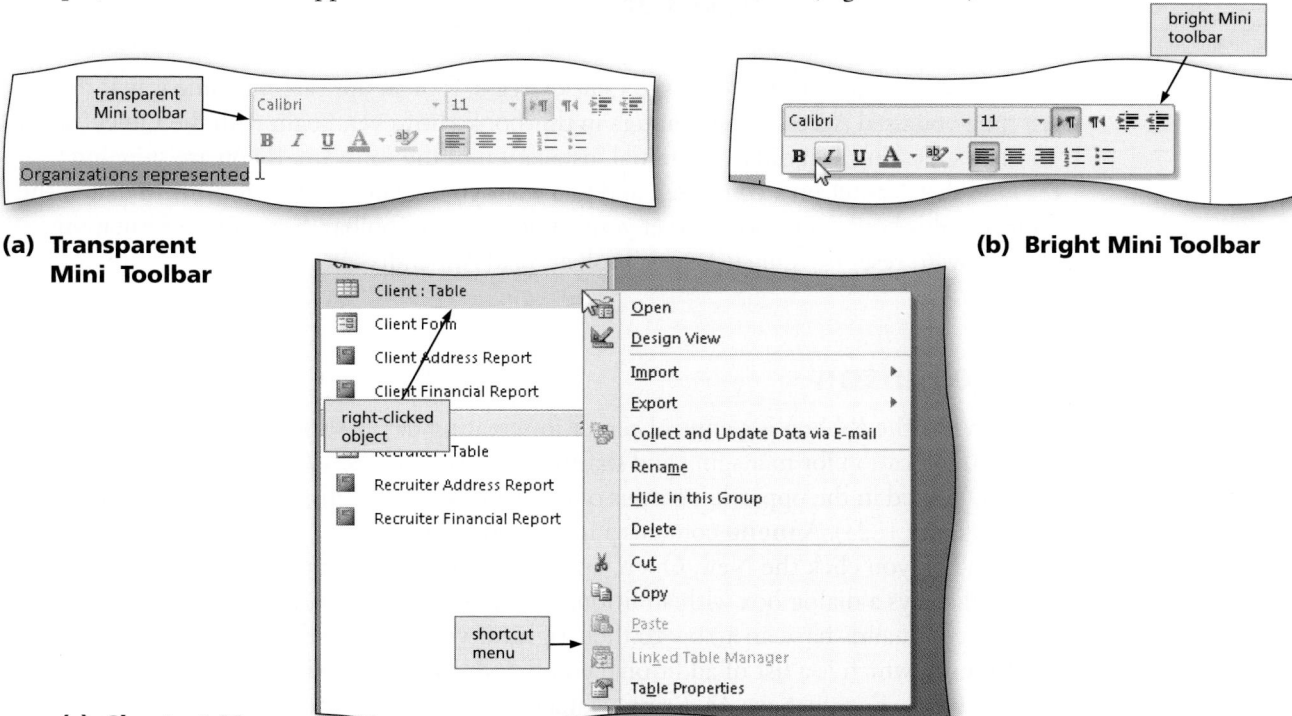

(a) Transparent Mini Toolbar

(b) Bright Mini Toolbar

(c) Shortcut Menu

Figure 1–21

Quick Access Toolbar

The **Quick Access Toolbar**, located by default above the Ribbon, provides easy access to frequently used commands (Figure 1–22a). The commands on the Quick Access Toolbar always are available, regardless of the task you are performing. Initially, the Quick Access Toolbar contains the Save, Undo, and Redo commands. If you click the Customize Quick Access Toolbar button, Access provides a list of commands you quickly can add to and remove from the Quick Access Toolbar (Figure 1–22b).

You also can add other commands to or delete commands from the Quick Access Toolbar so that it contains the commands you use most often. As you add commands to the Quick Access Toolbar, its commands may interfere with the title of the database object on the title bar. For this reason, Access provides an option of displaying the Quick Access Toolbar below the Ribbon (Figure 1–22c).

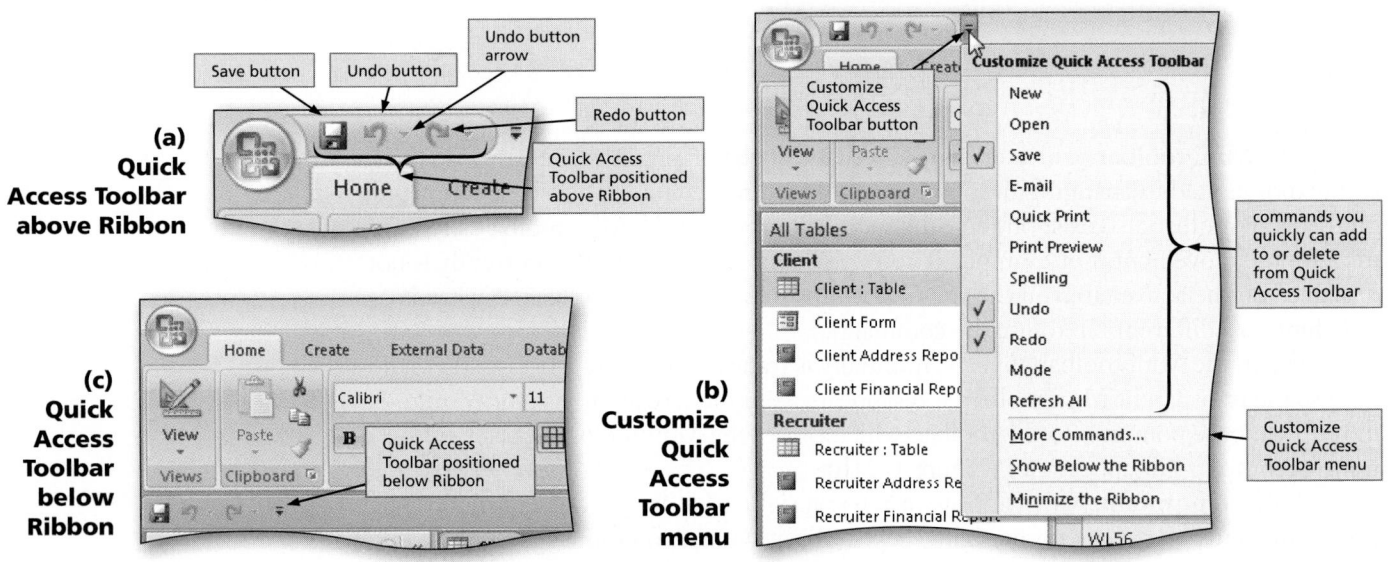

Figure 1–22

Each time you start Access, the Quick Access Toolbar appears the same way it did the last time you used Access. The chapters in this book, however, begin with the Quick Access Toolbar appearing as it did at the initial installation of the software. If you are stepping through this chapter on a computer, and you want your Quick Access Toolbar to match the figures in this book, you should reset your Quick Access Toolbar. For more information about how to reset the Quick Access Toolbar, read Appendix E.

Office Button

While the Ribbon is a control center for creating database objects, the **Office Button** is a central location for managing and sharing database objects. When you click the Office Button, located in the upper-left corner of the window, Access displays the Office Button menu (Figure 1–23). A **menu** contains a list of commands.

When you click the New, Open, and Print commands on the Office Button menu, Access displays a dialog box with additional options. The Save As, Print, Manage, and Publish commands have an arrow to their right. If you point to this arrow, Access displays a **submenu**, which is a list of additional commands associated with the selected command (Figure 1–24). For the Save As, Print, Manage, and Publish commands that do not display a dialog box when clicked, you can point either to the command or the arrow to display the submenu.

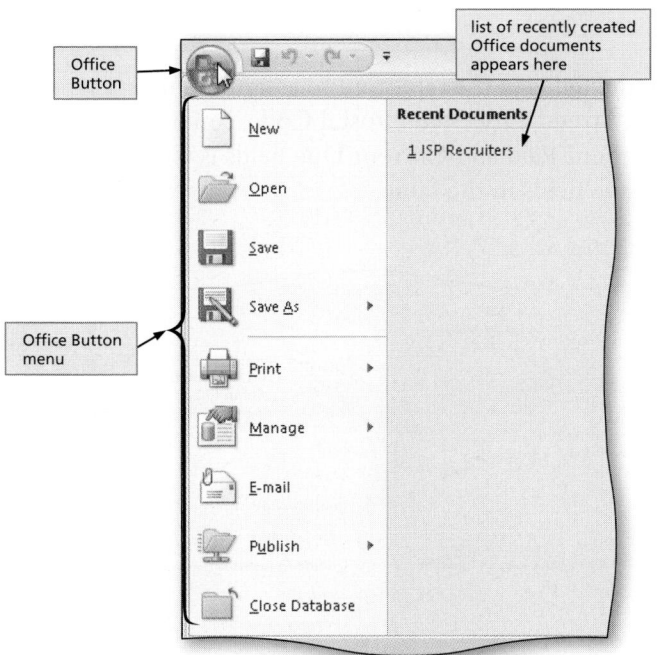

Figure 1–23

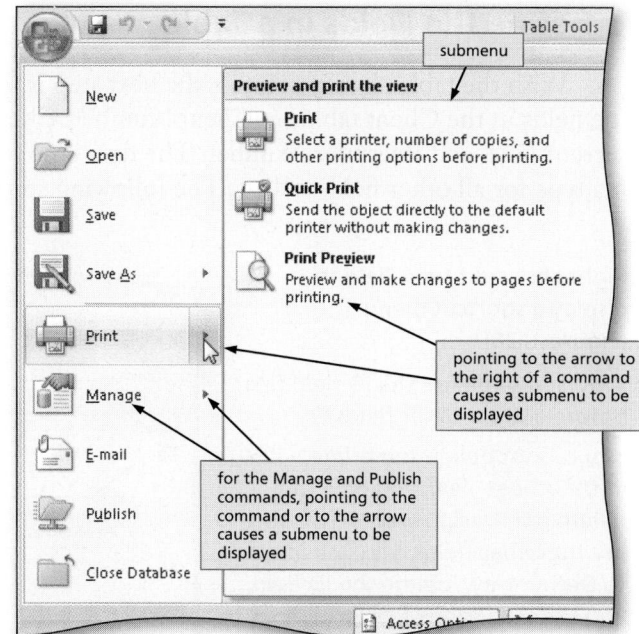

Figure 1–24

Key Tips

If you prefer using the keyboard instead of the mouse, you can press the ALT key on the keyboard to display a **Key Tip badge**, or keyboard code icon, for certain commands (Figure 1–25). To select a command using the keyboard, press its displayed code letter, or **Key Tip**. When you press a Key Tip, additional Key Tips related to the selected command may appear. For example, to select the New command on the Office Button menu, press the ALT key, then press the F key, then press the N key.

To remove the Key Tip badges from the screen, press the ALT key or the ESC key until all Key Tip badges disappear, or click the mouse anywhere in the Access window.

Figure 1–25

Creating a Table

When you first create your database, Access automatically creates a table for you. You can immediately begin defining the fields. If, for whatever reason, you do not have this table or inadvertently delete it, you can create the table by clicking Create on the Ribbon and then clicking the Table button on the Create tab. In either case, you are ready to define the fields.

To Define the Fields in a Table

With the table already created, the next step is to define the fields in the table and to assign them data types. The fields in the Client table are Client Number, Client Name, Street, City, State, Postal Code, Amount Paid, Current Due, and Recruiter Number. The data type for the Amount Paid and Current Due fields is Currency. The data type for all other fields is Text. The following steps define the fields in the table.

- Right-click Add New Field to display a shortcut menu (Figure 1–26).

Q&A

Why don't I delete the ID field first, before adding other fields?

You cannot delete the primary key in Datasheet view; you only can delete it in Design view. After adding the other fields, you will move to Design view, delete the ID field, and then make the Client Number the primary key.

Q&A

Why does my shortcut menu look different?

You right-clicked within the column instead of right-clicking the column heading.

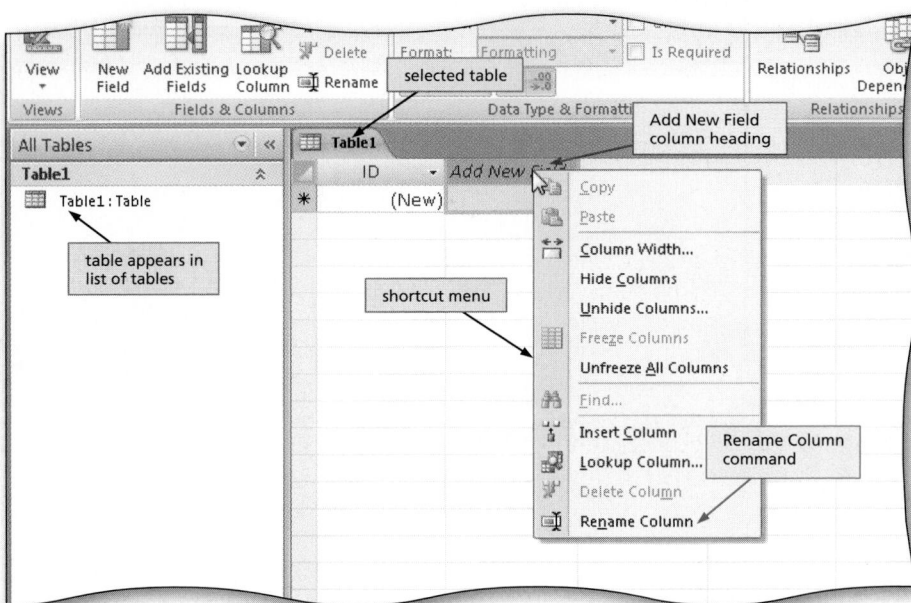

Figure 1–26

- Click Rename Column on the shortcut menu to display an insertion point.

- Type `Client Number` to assign a name to the new field.

- Press the DOWN ARROW key to complete the addition of the field (Figure 1–27).

Q&A

Why doesn't the whole name appear?

The default column size is not large enough for Client Number to appear in its entirety. Later in this book, you will learn how to resize columns so that the entire name can appear.

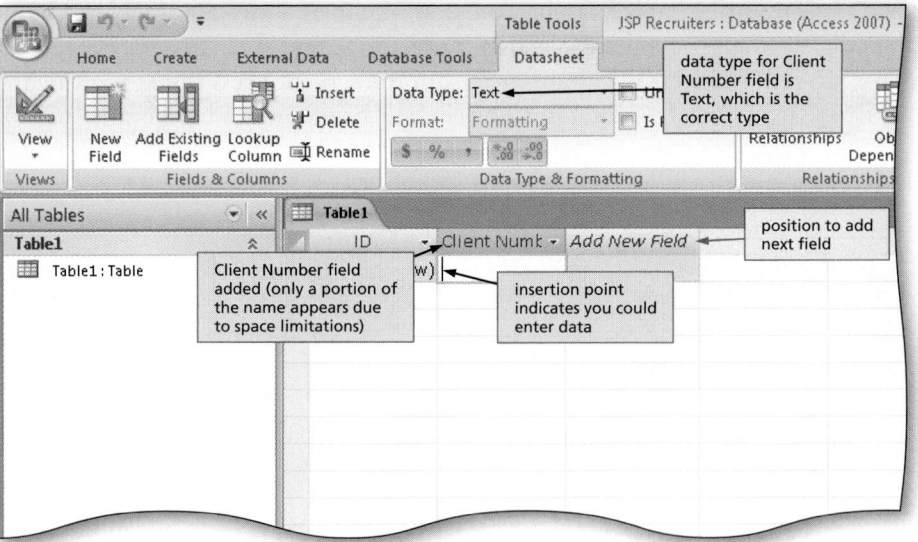

Figure 1–27

3

- Right-click Add New Field to display a shortcut menu, click Rename Column on the shortcut menu to display an insertion point, type `Client Name` to assign a name to the new field, and then press the DOWN ARROW key to complete the addition of the field.

Q&A Did I have to press the DOWN ARROW key? Couldn't I have just moved to the next field or pressed the ENTER key?

You could have pressed the TAB key or the ENTER key to move to the column heading for the

next field. Pressing the DOWN ARROW key, however, completes the entry of the Client Number field and allows you to ensure that the column is assigned the correct data type.

- Using the same technique add the fields in the Client table up through and including the Amount Paid field.

- Click the Data Type box arrow to display the Data Type box menu (Figure 1–28).

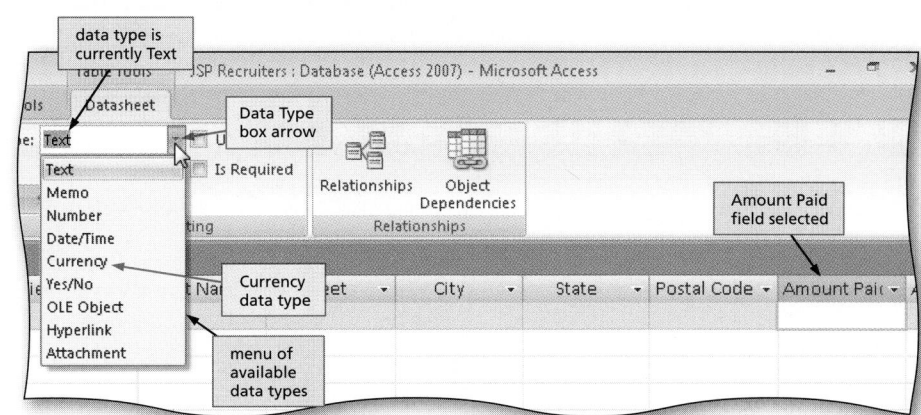

Figure 1–28

4

- Click Currency to select Currency as the data type for the Amount Paid field (Figure 1–29).

Q&A Why does Currency appear twice?

The second Currency is the format, which indicates how the data will be displayed. For the Currency data type, Access automatically sets the format to Currency, which is usually what you would want. You could change it to something else, if desired, by clicking the arrow and selecting the desired format.

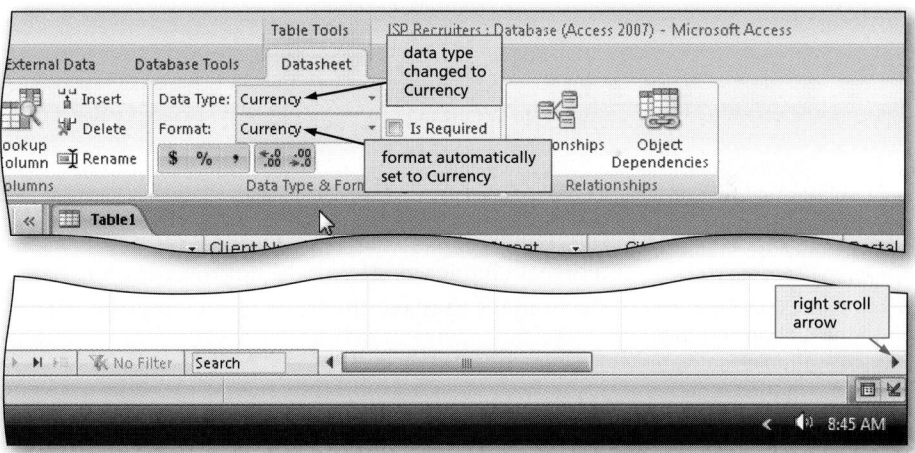

Figure 1–29

5

- Click the right scroll arrow to shift the fields to the left and display the Add New Field column (Figure 1–30).

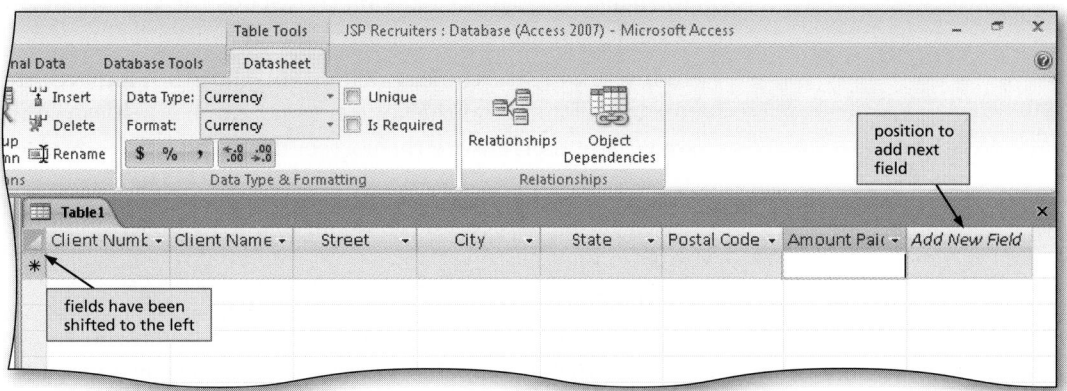

Figure 1–30

6

● Make the remaining entries from the Client table structure shown in Figure 1–31 to complete the structure. Be sure to select Currency as the data type for the Current Due field.

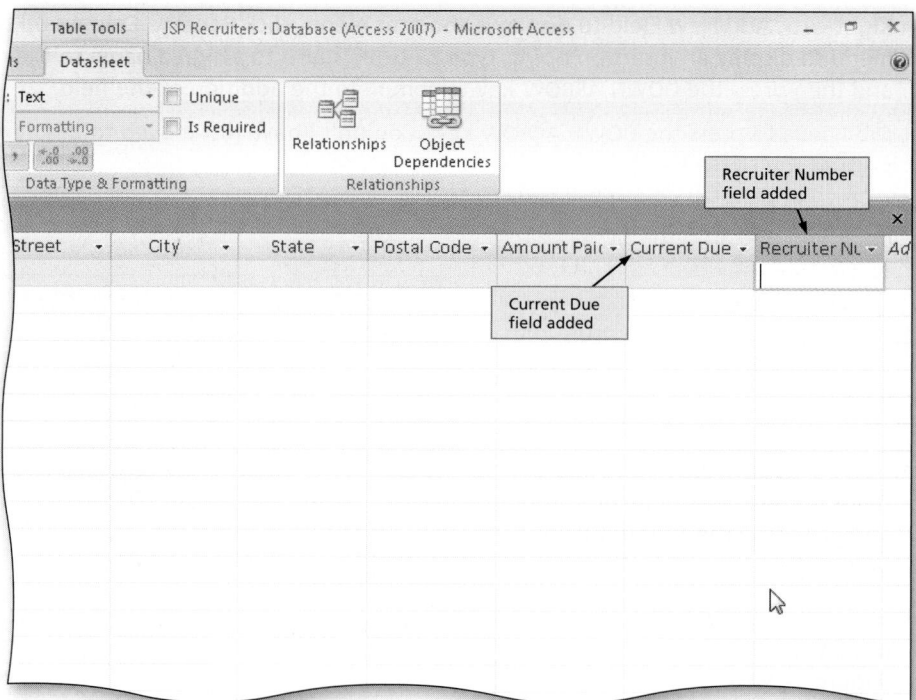

Figure 1–31

BTW

Creating a Table: Table Templates
Access includes table templates that assist you in creating some commonly used tables and fields. To use a template, click Create on the Ribbon and then click the Table Templates button on the Create tab. Click the desired template, make any adjustments you wish to the table that Access creates, and then save the table.

Making Changes to the Structure

When creating a table, check the entries carefully to ensure they are correct. If you discover a mistake while still typing the entry, you can correct the error by repeatedly pressing the BACKSPACE key until the incorrect characters are removed. Then, type the correct characters. If you do not discover a mistake until later, you can use the following techniques to make the necessary changes to the structure:

● To undo your most recent change, click the Undo button on the Quick Access Toolbar. If there is nothing that Access can undo, this button will be dim, and clicking it will have no effect.

● To delete a field, right-click the column heading for the field (the position containing the field name), and then click Delete Column on the shortcut menu.

● To change the name of a field, right-click the column heading for the field, click Rename Column on the shortcut menu, and then type the desired field name.

● To insert a field as the last field, right-click the Add New Field column heading, click Rename Column on the shortcut menu, type the desired field name, click the down arrow, and then ensure the correct data type is already selected.

● To insert a field between existing fields, right-click the column heading for the field that will follow the new field, and then click Insert Column on the shortcut menu. You then proceed just as you do when you insert a field as the last field.

As an alternative to these steps, you may want to start over. To do so, click the Close button for the window containing the table, and then click the No button in the Microsoft Office Access dialog box. Click Create on the Ribbon and then click the Table button to create a table. You then can repeat the process you used earlier to define the fields in the table.

To Save a Table

The Client table structure now is complete. The final step is to save and close the table within the database. At this time, you should give the table a name.

The following steps save the table, giving it the name, Client.

 1

- Click the Save button on the Quick Access Toolbar to save the structure of the table (Figure 1–32).

Q&A

I have an extra row between the row containing the field names and the row that begins with the asterisk. What happened? Is this a problem? If so, how do I fix it?

You inadvertently added a record to the table by pressing some key after you pressed the DOWN ARROW key. Even pressing the Spacebar would add a record. You now have a record you do not want and it will cause problems when you attempt to assign a different primary key. To fix it, you need to delete the record, which you will do in Step 3.

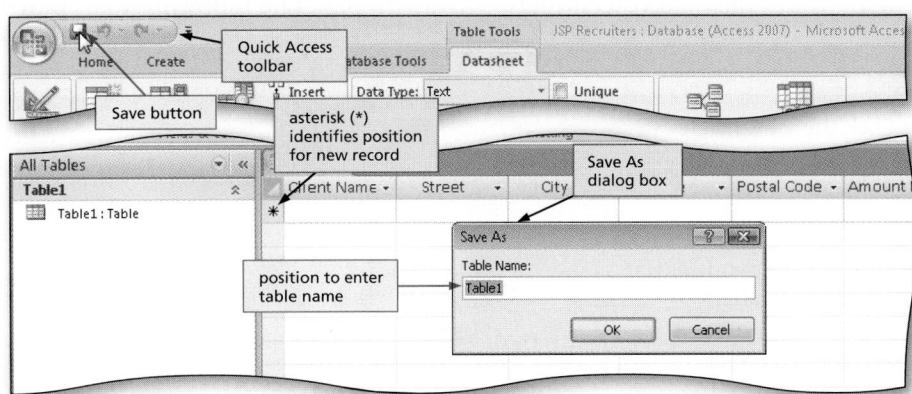

Figure 1–32

 2

- Type `Client` to change the name to be assigned to the table (Figure 1–33).

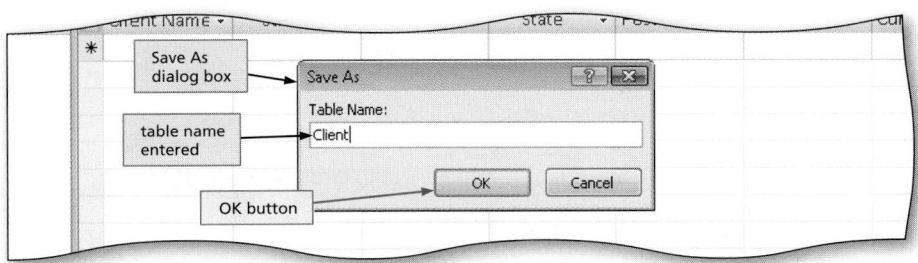

Figure 1–33

 3

- Click the OK button to save the structure with the name, Client (Figure 1–34).

- If you have an additional record between the field names and the asterisk, click the record selector (the box at the beginning of the record), press the DELETE key, and then click the Yes button when Access asks you if you want to delete the record.

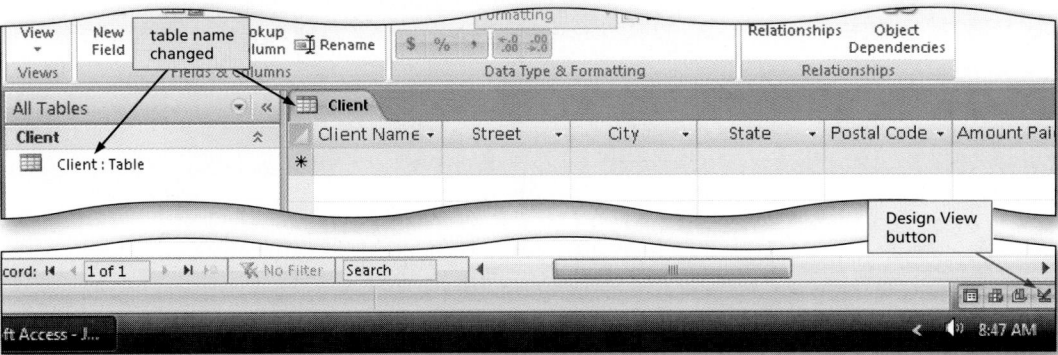

Figure 1–34

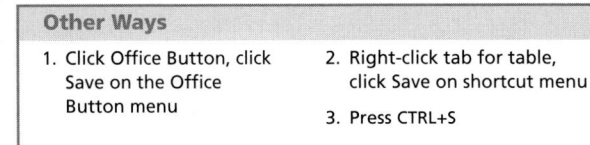

Other Ways

1. Click Office Button, click Save on the Office Button menu
2. Right-click tab for table, click Save on shortcut menu
3. Press CTRL+S

To Change the Primary Key

To change the primary key, you must first delete the ID field that Access created automatically. You then can designate the Client Number field as the primary key. To delete the ID field, the table must appear in Design view rather than Datasheet view. You also can designate the Client Number field as the primary key within Design view. As you define or modify the fields, the **row selector**, the small box or bar that, when you click it, selects the entire row, indicates the field you currently are describing. The following steps move to Design view and then change the primary key.

- Click the Design View button on the status bar to move to Design view.

- Confirm that your data types match those shown in the figure. Make any necessary corrections to the data types (Figure 1-35).

Q&A

Did I have to save the table before moving to Design view?

Yes. If you had not saved it yourself, Access would have asked you to save it.

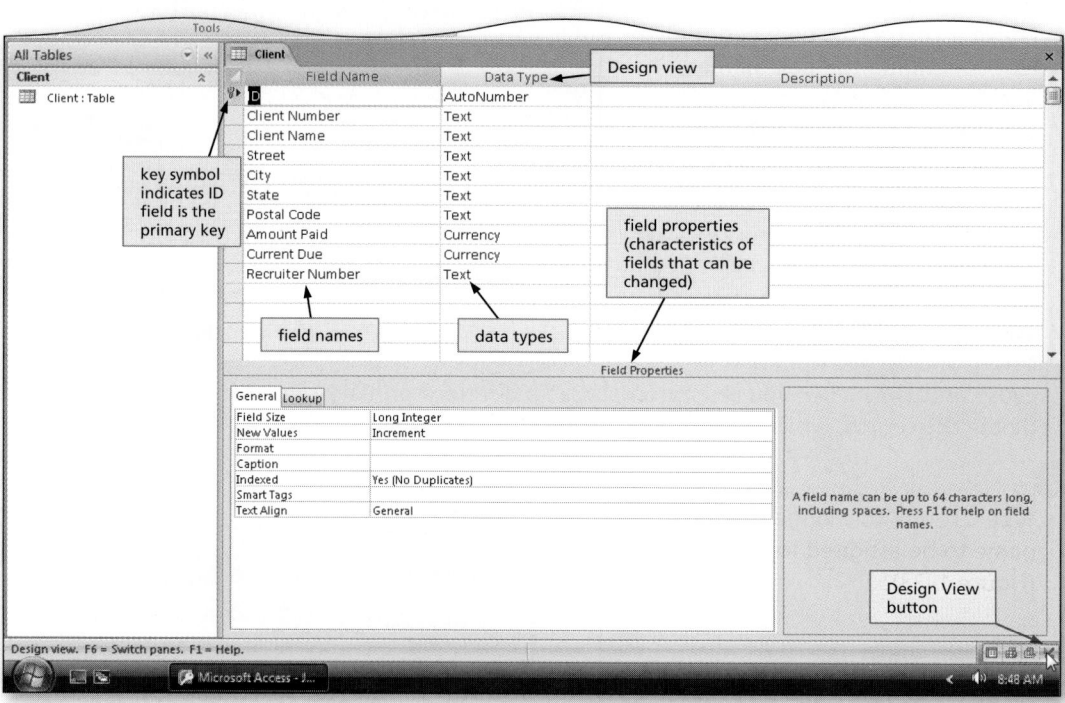

Figure 1–35

- Click the row selector for the ID field to select the field.

- Press the DELETE key to delete the field (Figure 1–36).

Q&A

What if I click the row selector for the wrong field before pressing the DELETE key?

Click the No button in the Microsoft Office Access dialog box. If you inadvertently clicked the Yes button, you have deleted the wrong field. You can fix this by clicking the Close button for the Client table, and then clicking the No button when asked if you want to save your changes.

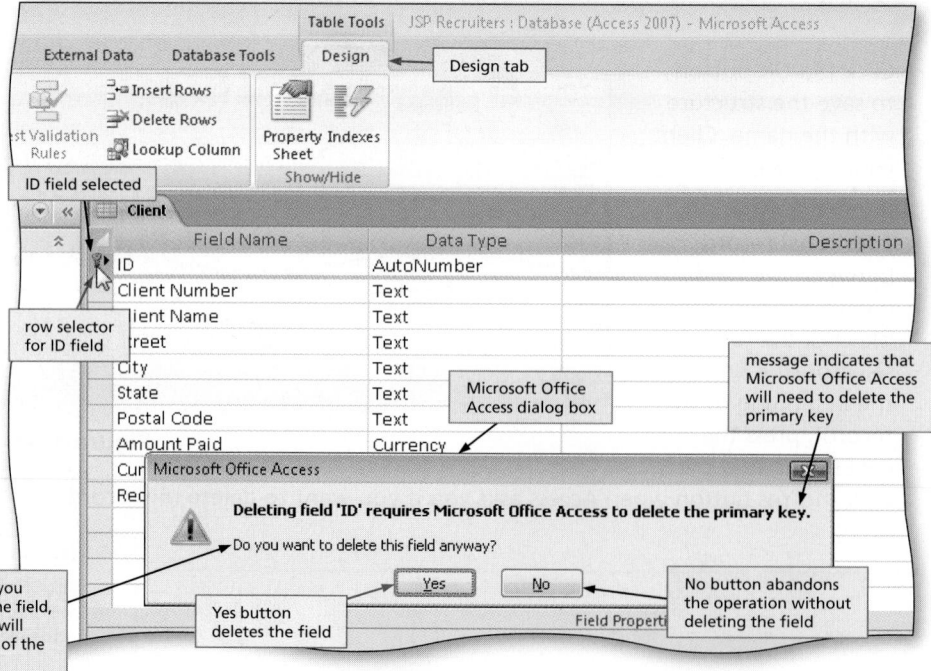

Figure 1–36

3

- Click the Yes button to complete the deletion of the field.

- With the Client Number field selected, click the Primary Key button to designate the Client Number field as the primary key.

- Click the Save button to save the changes (Figure 1–37).

Q&A

When I attempted to save the table I got an error message that indicates index or primary key cannot contain a null value. What did I do wrong and how do I fix it?

You inadvertently added a record to the table by pressing some key after you pressed the DOWN ARROW key. To fix it, click the OK button (you will need to do it twice) and then click the Primary Key button to remove the primary key. Click the Save button to save the table and then click the View button near the upper-left corner of the screen to return to datasheet view. Click the little box immediately to the left of the record you added and press the DELETE key. Click the Yes button when Access asks if it is OK to delete the record. Click the View button again and continue with these steps.

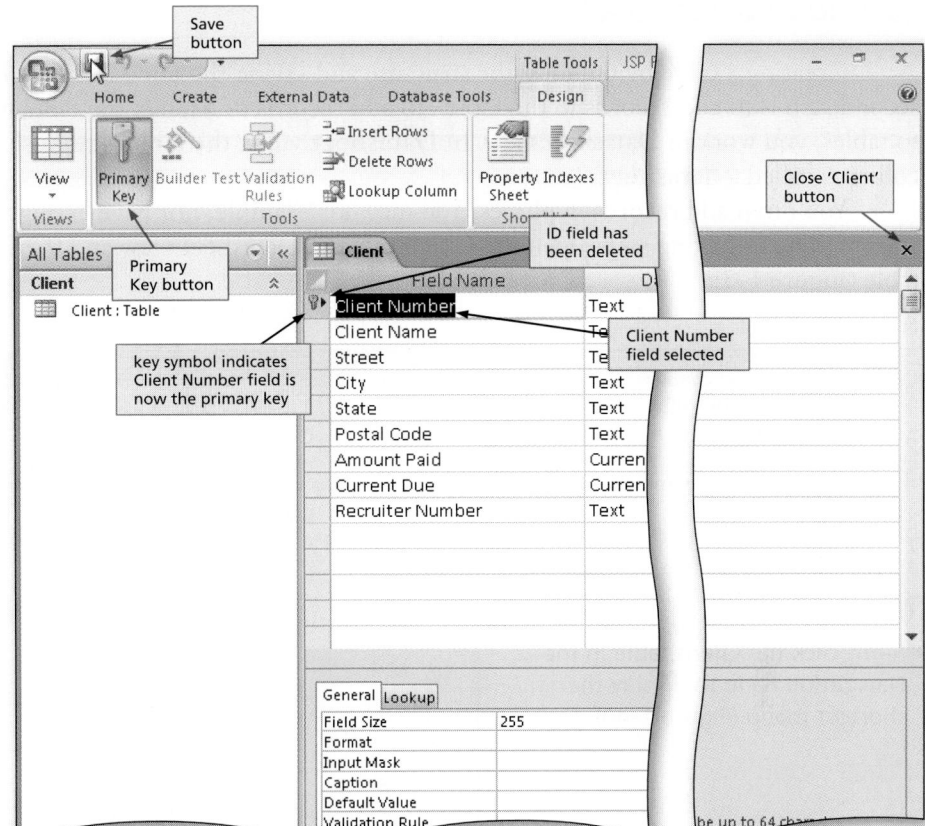

Figure 1–37

4

- Close the Client table by clicking the Close 'Client' button (Figure 1–38).

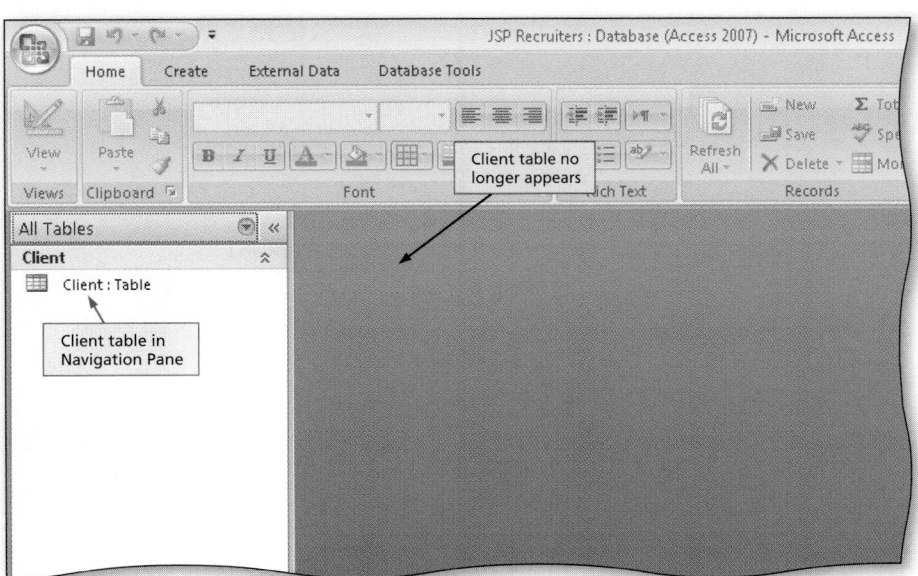

Figure 1–38

To Add Records to a Table

Creating a table by building the structure and saving the table is the first step in a two-step process. The second step is to add records to the table. To add records to a table, the table must be open. When making changes to tables, you work in Datasheet view. In **Datasheet view**, the table is represented as a collection of rows and columns called a **datasheet**.

You often add records in phases. You may, for example, not have enough time to add all the records in one session. The following steps open the Client table in Datasheet view and then add the first two records in the Client table (Figure 1–39).

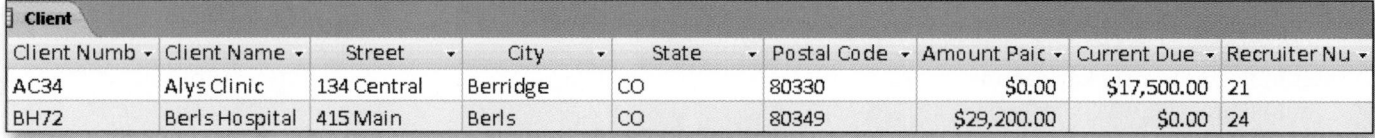

Client Numb ▾	Client Name ▾	Street ▾	City ▾	State ▾	Postal Code ▾	Amount Paic ▾	Current Due ▾	Recruiter Nu ▾
AC34	Alys Clinic	134 Central	Berridge	CO	80330	$0.00	$17,500.00	21
BH72	Berls Hospital	415 Main	Berls	CO	80349	$29,200.00	$0.00	24

Figure 1–39

1

• Right-click the Client table in the Navigation Pane to display the shortcut menu (Figure 1–40).

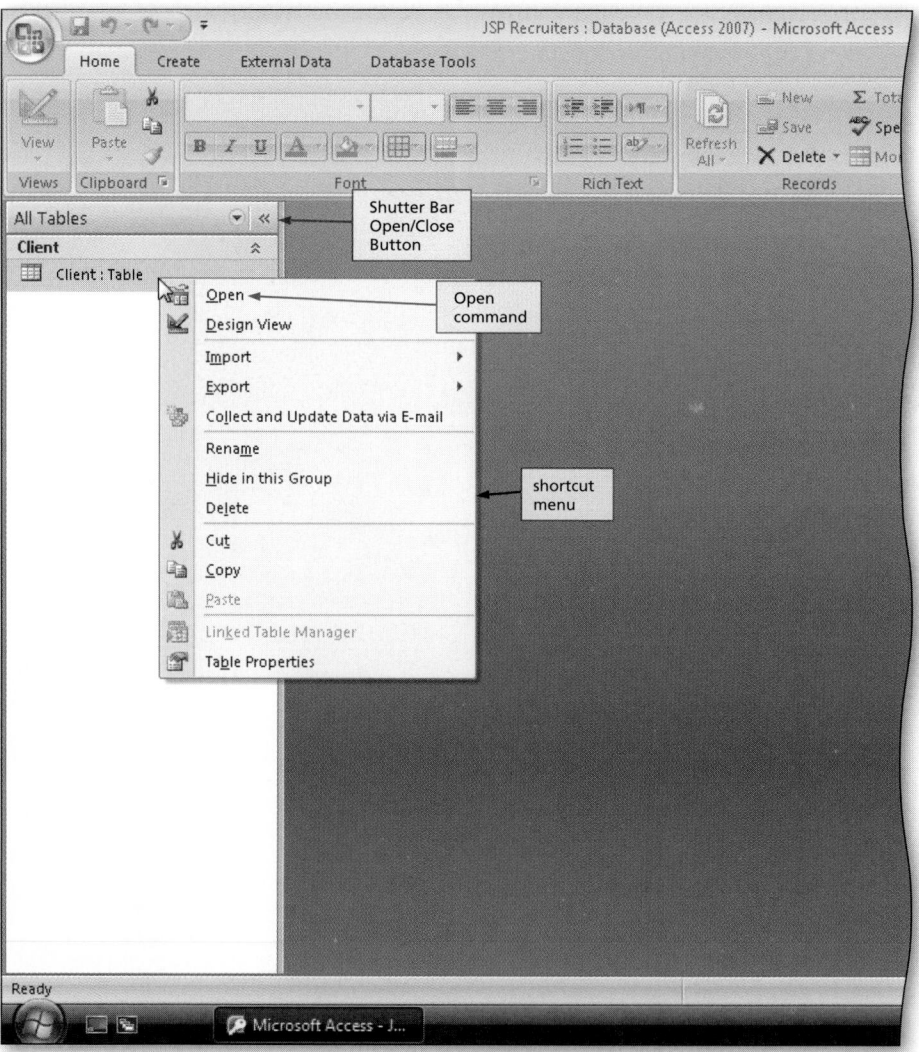

Figure 1–40

• Click Open on the shortcut menu to open the Client table in Datasheet view.

Q&A

What if I want to return to Design view?

There are two ways to get to Design view. You could click Design View on the shortcut menu. Alternatively, you could click Open on the shortcut menu to open the table in Datasheet view and then click the Design View button on the Access status bar.

• Click the Shutter Bar Open/Close Button to hide the Navigation Pane (Figure 1–41).

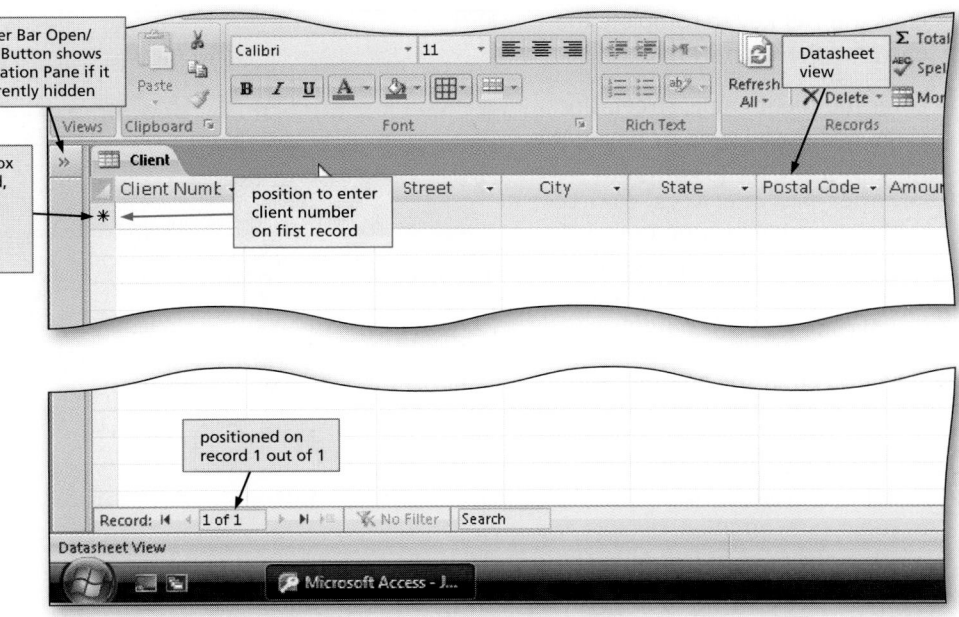

Figure 1–41

• Click in the Client Number field and type AC34 to enter the first client number. Be sure you type the letters in uppercase so they are entered in the database correctly (Figure 1–42).

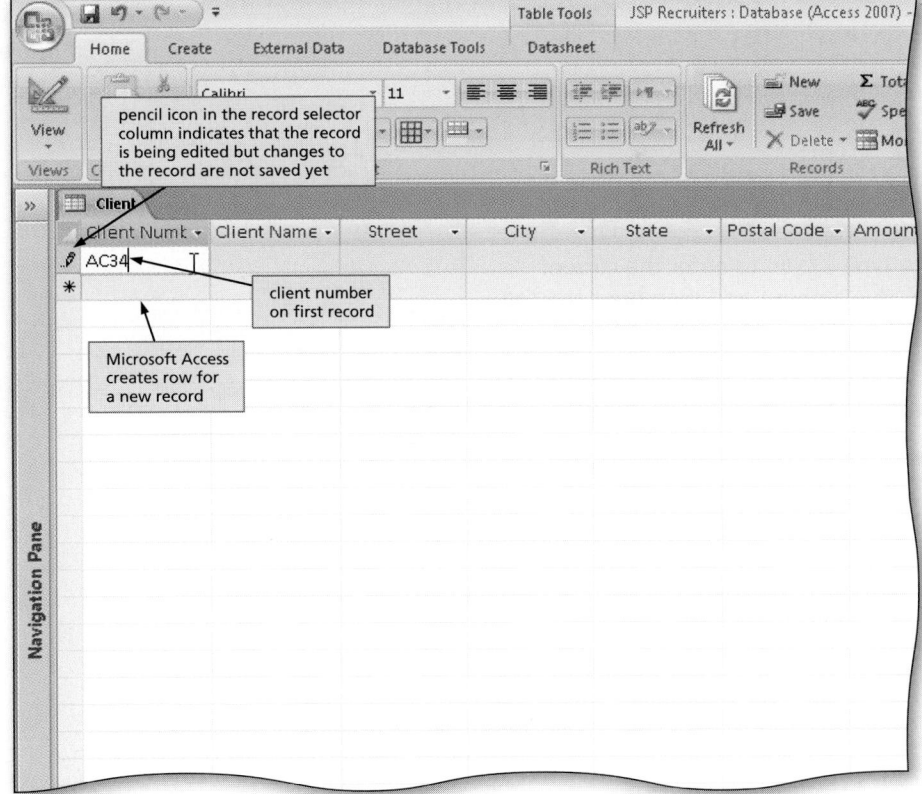

Figure 1–42

4

- Press the TAB key to complete the entry for the Client Number field.

- Enter the client name, street, city, state, and postal code by typing the following entries, pressing the TAB key after each one: `Alys Clinic` as the client name, `134 Central` as the street, `Berridge` as the city, `CO` as the state, and `80330` as the postal code.

- Type `0` to enter the amount paid (Figure 1–43).

Do I need to type a dollar sign?

You do not need to type dollar signs or commas. In addition, because the digits to the right of the decimal point are both zeros, you do not need to type either the decimal point or the zeros.

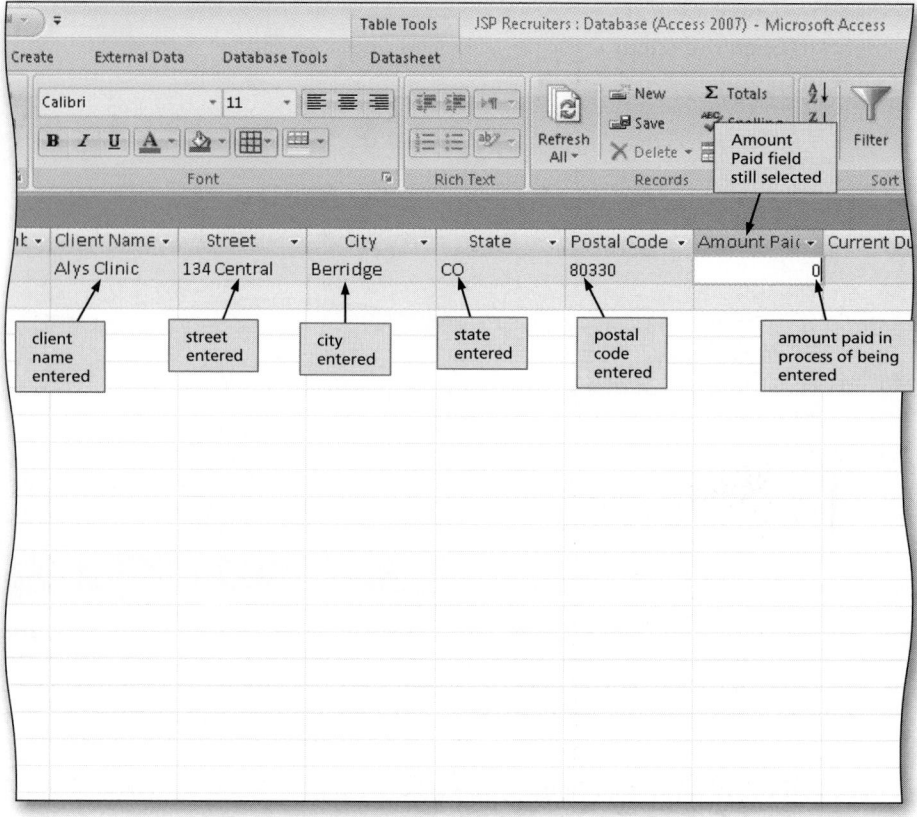

Figure 1–43

5

- Press the TAB key to complete the entry for the Amount Paid field.

- Type `17500` to enter the current due amount and then press the TAB key to move to the next field.

- Type `21` as the Recruiter number to complete data entry for the record (Figure 1–44).

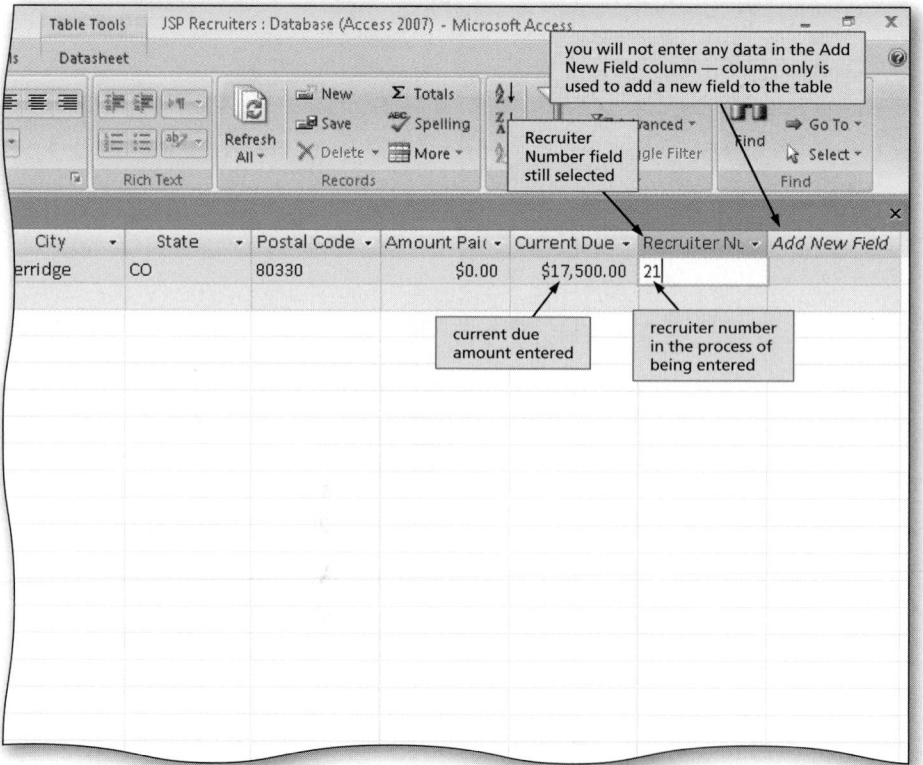

Figure 1–44

6

- Press the TAB key to complete the entry of the first record (Figure 1–45).

Q&A

How and when do I save the record?

As soon as you have entered or modified a record and moved to another record, the original record is saved. This is different from other applications. The rows entered in an Excel worksheet, for example, are not saved until the entire worksheet is saved.

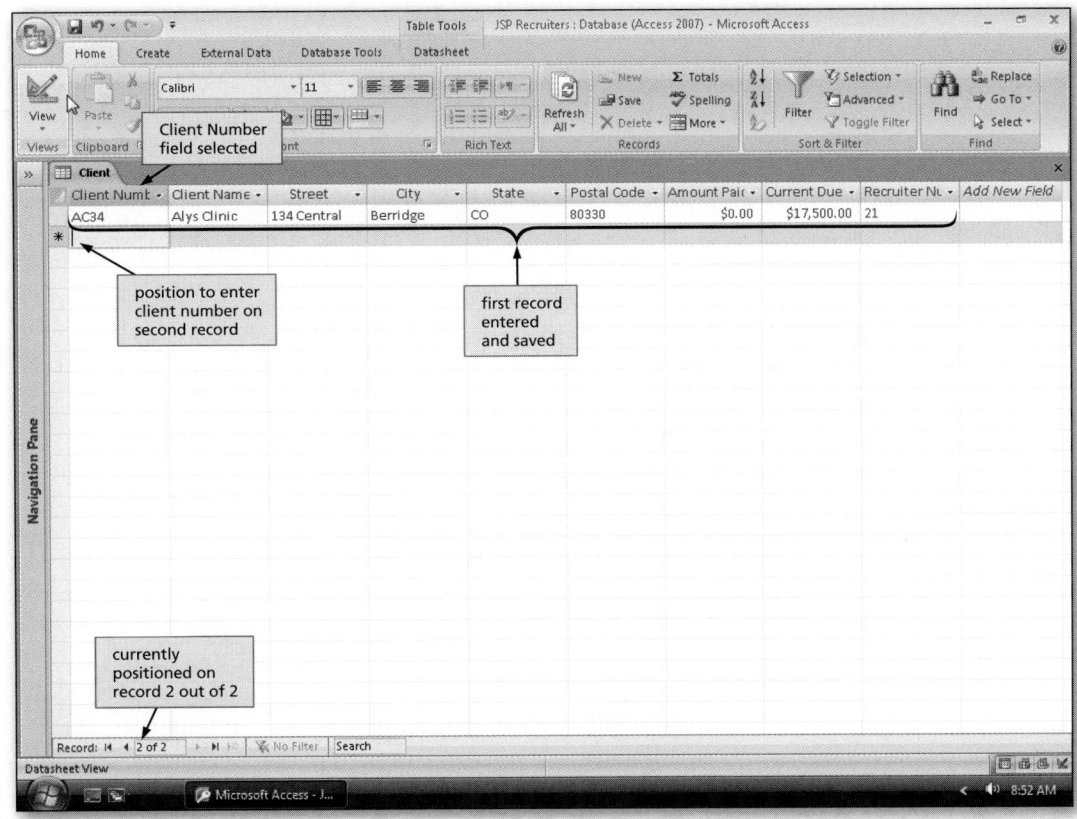

Figure 1–45

7

- Use the techniques shown in Steps 3 through 6 to enter the data for the second record in the Client table (Figure 1–46).

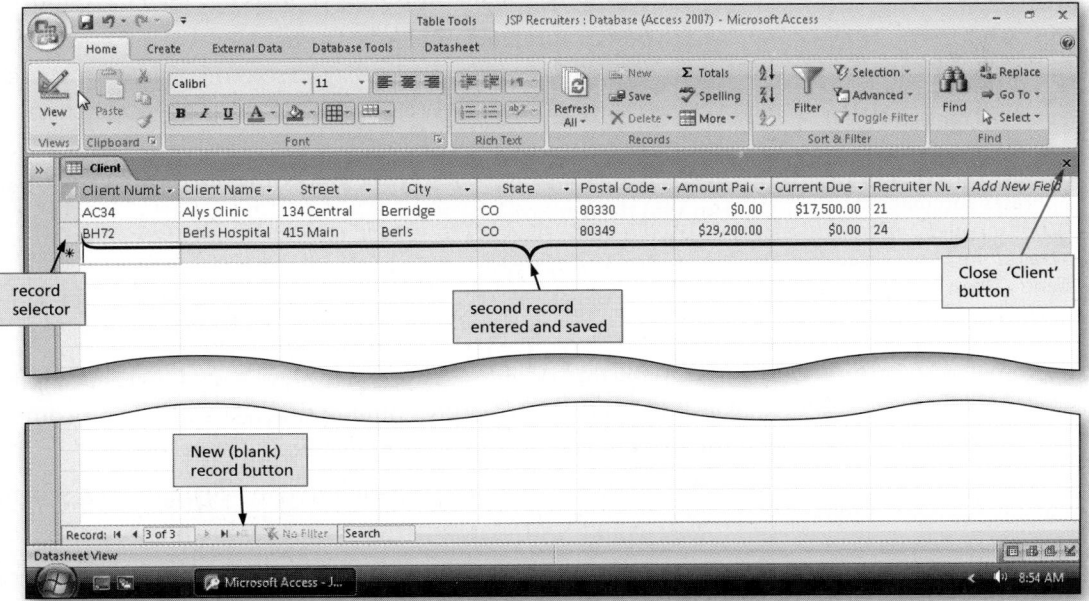

Figure 1–46

BTW

Undo and Redo
You also can undo multiple actions. To see a list of recent actions that you can undo, click the down arrow next to the Undo button on the Quick Access Toolbar. To redo the most recent action, click the Redo button on the Quick Access Toolbar. You also can redo multiple actions by clicking the down arrow next to the button.

BTW

Cut, Copy, and Paste
Just as in other Office applications, you can use buttons in the Clipboard group on the Home tab to cut, copy, and paste data. To cut data, select the data to be cut and click the Cut button. To copy data, select the data and click the Copy button. To paste data, select the desired location and click the Paste button.

BTW

AutoCorrect Options
Using the Office AutoCorrect feature, you can create entries that will replace abbreviations with spelled-out names and phrases automatically. For example, you can create the abbreviated entry *dbms* for *database management system*. Whenever you type dbms followed by a space or punctuation mark, Access automatically replaces dbms with database management system. To specify AutoCorrect rules and exceptions to the rules, click Access Options on the Office Button menu and then click Proofing in the Access Options dialog box.

Making Changes to the Data

Check your entries carefully to ensure they are correct. If you make a mistake and discover it before you press the TAB key, correct it by pressing the BACKSPACE key until the incorrect characters are removed and then typing the correct characters. If you do not discover a mistake until later, you can use the following techniques to make the necessary corrections to the data:

- To undo your most recent change, click the Undo button on the Quick Access Toolbar. If there is nothing that Access can undo, this button will be dim, and clicking it will have no effect.

- To add a record, click the New (blank) record button, shown in Figure 1–46 on the previous page, and then add the record. Do not worry about it being in the correct position in the table. Access will reposition the record based on the primary key, in this case, the Client Number.

- To delete a record, click the Record selector, shown in Figure 1–46, for the record to be deleted. Then press the DELETE key to delete the record, and click the Yes button when Access asks you to verify that you do indeed wish to delete the record.

- To change the contents of one or more fields in a record, the record must be on the screen. If it is not, use any appropriate technique, such as the UP ARROW and DOWN ARROW keys or the vertical scroll bar, to move to it. If the field you want to correct is not visible on the screen, use the horizontal scroll bar along the bottom of the screen to shift all the fields until the one you want appears. If the value in the field is currently highlighted, you can simply type the new value. If you would rather edit the existing value, you must have an insertion point in the field. You can place the insertion point by clicking in the field or by pressing F2. Once you have produced an insertion point, you can use the arrow keys, the DELETE key, and the BACKSPACE key in making the correction. You also can use the INSERT key to switch between Insert and Overtype mode. When you have made the change, press the TAB key to move to the next field.

If you cannot determine how to correct the data, you may find that you are "stuck" on the record. Access neither allows you to move to any other record until you have made the correction, nor allows you to close the table. If you encounter this situation, simply press the ESC key. Pressing the ESC key will remove from the screen the record you are trying to add. You then can move to any other record, close the table, or take any other action you desire.

AutoCorrect

Not visible in the Access window, the **AutoCorrect** feature of Access works behind the scenes, correcting common mistakes when you complete a text entry in a cell. AutoCorrect makes three types of corrections for you:

1. Corrects two initial capital letters by changing the second letter to lowercase.

2. Capitalizes the first letter in the names of days.

3. Replaces commonly misspelled words with their correct spelling. For example, it changes the misspelled word *recieve* to *receive* when you complete the entry. AutoCorrect will correct the spelling automatically of more than 400 commonly misspelled words.

To Close a Table

It is a good idea to close a table as soon as you have finished working with it. It keeps the screen from getting cluttered and prevents you from making accidental changes to the data in the table. The following steps close the Client table.

1

- Click the Close 'Client' button, shown in Figure 1–46 on page AC 33, to close the table (Figure 1–47).

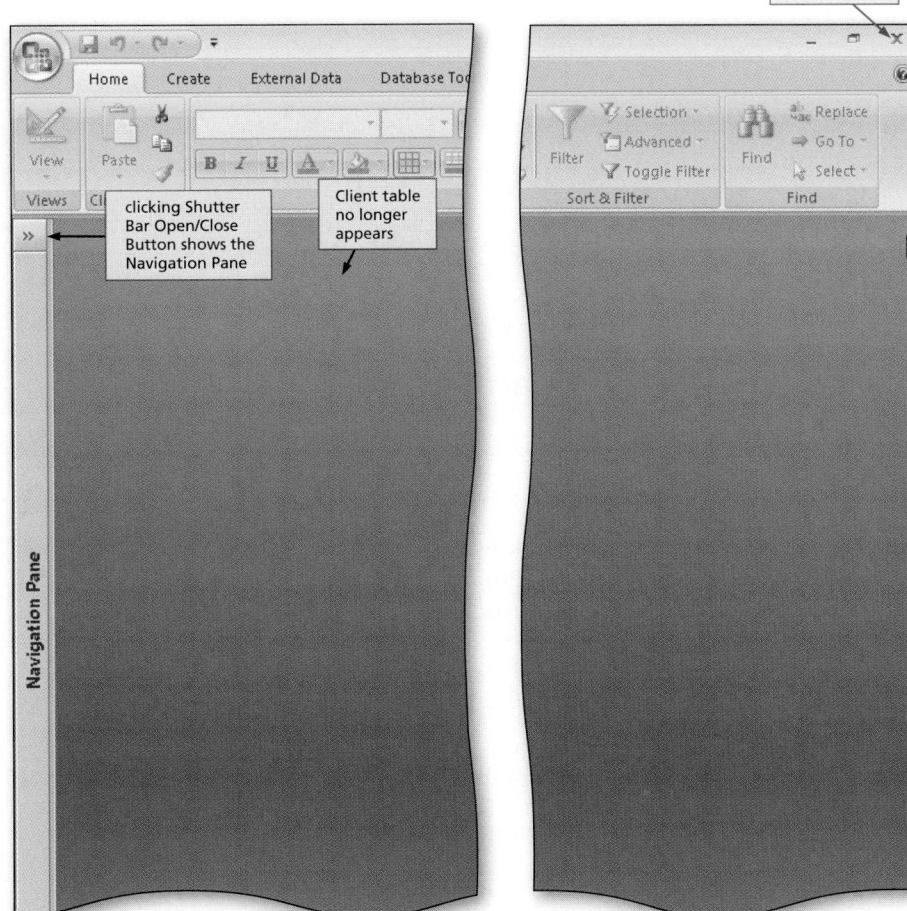

Figure 1–47

Other Ways

1. Right-click tab for table, click Close on shortcut menu

Quitting Access

If you save the object on which you are currently working and then quit Access, all Access windows close. If you have made changes to an object since the last time the object was saved, Access displays a dialog box asking if you want to save the changes you made before it closes that window. The dialog box contains three buttons with these resulting actions:

- Yes button — Saves the changes and then quits Access
- No button — Quits Access without saving changes
- Cancel button — Closes the dialog box and redisplays the database without saving the changes

If no changes have been made to any object since the last time the object was saved, Access will close all windows without displaying any dialog boxes.

To Quit Access

You saved your changes to the table and did not make any additional changes. You are ready to quit Access. The following step quits Access.

1 Click the Close button on the right side of the Access title bar, shown in Figure 1–47 on the previous page, to quit Access.

Starting Access and Opening a Database

Once you have created and later closed a database, you will need to open it in the future in order to use it. Opening a database requires that Access is running on your computer.

Note: If you are using Windows XP, see Appendix F for alternate steps.

To Start Access

The following steps, which assume Windows Vista is running, start Access.

1 Click the Start button on the Windows Vista taskbar to display the Start menu.

2 Click All Programs at the bottom of the left pane on the Start menu to display the All Programs list and then click Microsoft Office in the All Programs list to display the Microsoft Office list.

3 Click Microsoft Office Access 2007 on the Microsoft Office submenu to start Access and display the Getting Started with Microsoft Office Access window (Figure 1–48).

4 If the Access window is not maximized, click the Maximize button on its title bar to maximize the window.

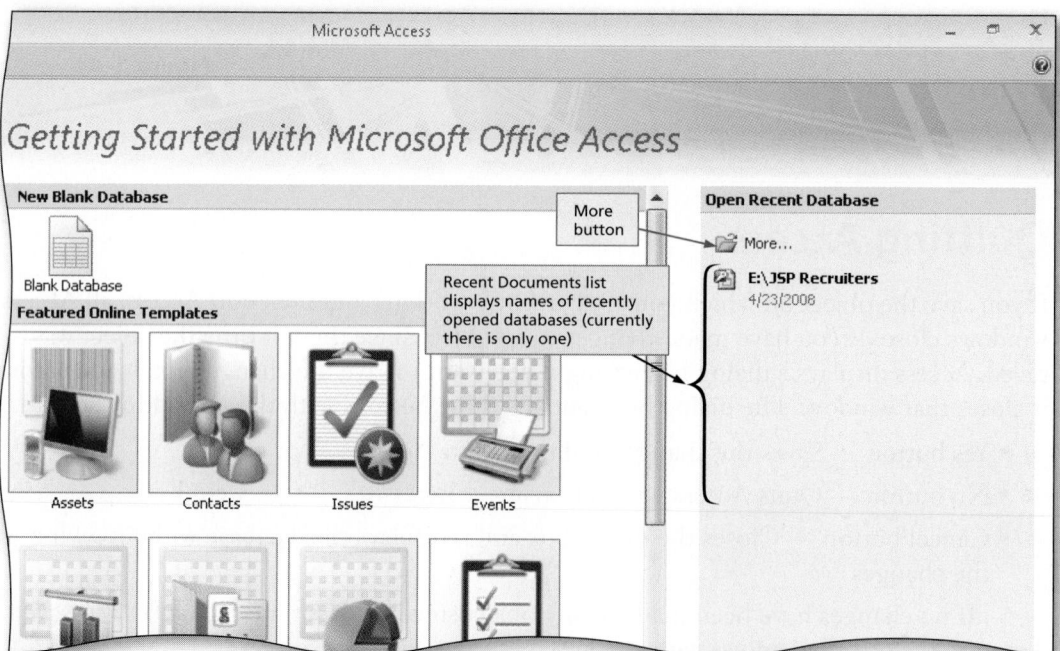

Figure 1–48

To Open a Database from Access

Note: If you are using Windows XP, see Appendix F for alternate steps.

Earlier in this chapter you created your database on a USB flash drive using the file name, JSP Recruiters. There are two ways to open the file containing your database. If the file you created appears in the Recent Documents list, you could click it to open the file. If not, you can use the More button to open the file. The following steps use the More button to open the JSP Recruiters database from the USB flash drive.

1

- With your USB flash drive connected to one of the computer's USB ports, click the More button, shown in Figure 1–48, to display the Open dialog box.

- If the Folders list is displayed below the Folders button, click the Folders button to remove the Folders list.

- If necessary, click Computer in the Favorite Links section.

- Double-click UDISK 2.0 (E:) to select the USB flash drive, Drive E in this case, as the new open location.

- Click JSP Recruiters to select the file name (Figure 1–49).

How do I open the file if I am not using a USB flash drive?

Use the same process, but be certain to select your device in the Look in list. You might need to open multiple folders.

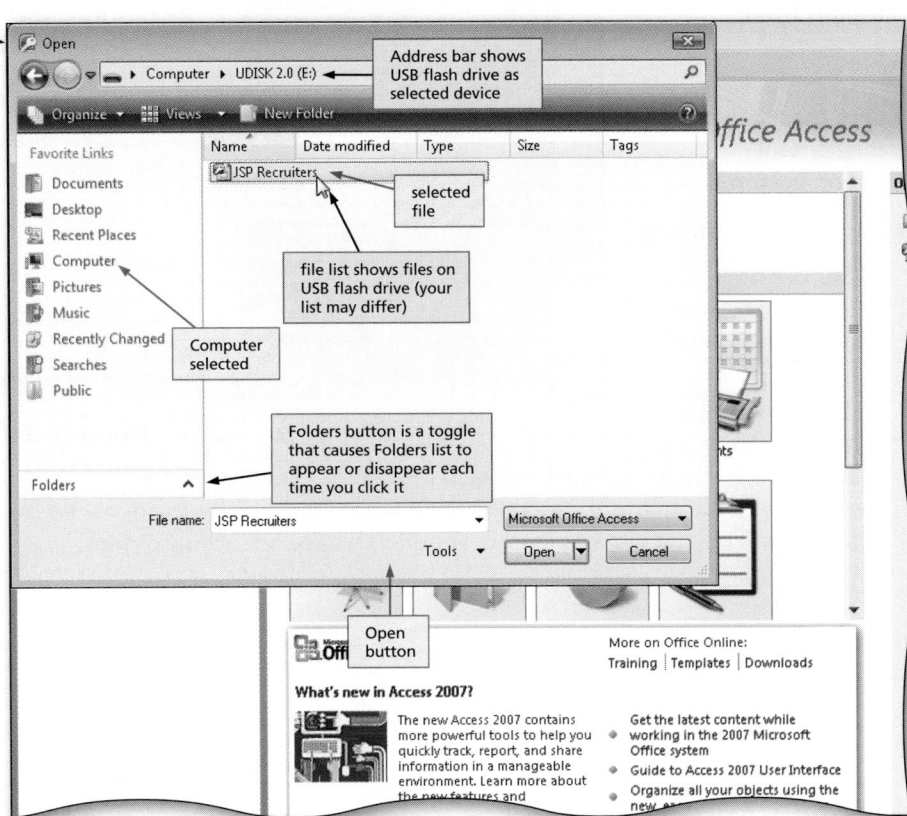

Figure 1–49

2

- Click the Open button to open the database (Figure 1–50).

Why do I see the Access icon and name on the Windows Vista taskbar?

When you open an Access database, an Access program button is displayed on the taskbar. If the contents of a button cannot fit in the allotted button space, an ellipsis appears. If you point to a program button, its entire contents appear in a ScreenTip, which in this case would be the program name followed by the file name.

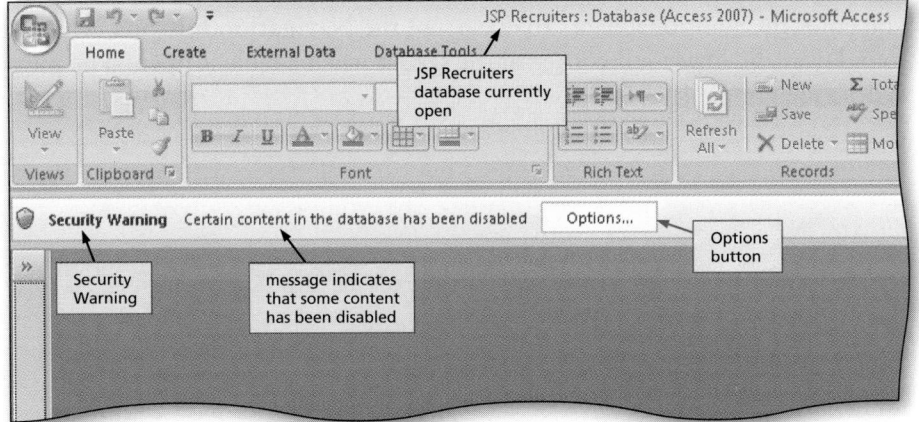

Figure 1–50

- If a Security Warning appears, as shown in Figure 1–50 on the previous page, click the Options button to display the Microsoft Office Security Options dialog box (Figure 1–51).

- Click the 'Enable this content' option button.

- Click the OK button to enable the content.

Q&A When would I want to disable the content?

You would want to disable the content if you suspected that your database might contain harmful content or damaging macros. Because you are the one who created the database and no one else has used it, you should have no such suspicions.

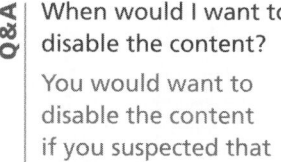

Figure 1–51

Other Ways

1. Click Office Button, double-click file name in Recent Documents list

2. Press CTRL+O, select file name, press ENTER

To Add Additional Records to a Table

You can add records to a table that already contains data using a process almost identical to that used to add records to an empty table. The only difference is that you place the insertion point after the last data record before you enter the additional data. To do so, use the **Navigation buttons**, which are buttons used to move within a table, found near the lower-left corner of the screen when a table is open. The purpose of each of the Navigation buttons is described in Table 1–2.

Table 1–2 Navigation Buttons in Datasheet View	
Button	**Purpose**
First record	Moves to the first record in the table
Previous record	Moves to the previous record
Next record	Moves to the next record
Last record	Moves to the last record in the table
New (blank) record	Moves to the end of the table to a position for entering a new record

The following steps add the remaining records (Figure 1–52) to the Client table.

Client Numb ▾	Client Name ▾	Street ▾	City ▾	State ▾	Postal Code ▾	Amount Paic ▾	Current Due ▾	Recruiter Nu ▾
BL12	Benton Labs	12 Mountain	Denton	CO	80412	$16,500.00	$38,225.00	24
EA45	ENT Assoc.	867 Ridge	Fort Stewart	CO	80336	$12,750.00	$15,000.00	27
FD89	Ferb Dentistry	34 Crestview	Berridge	CO	80330	$21,000.00	$12,500.00	21
FH22	Family Health	123 Second	Tarleton	CO	80409	$0.00	$0.00	24
MH56	Maun Hospital	76 Dixon	Mason	CO	80356	$0.00	$43,025.00	24
PR11	Peel Radiology	151 Valleyview	Fort Stewart	CO	80336	$31,750.00	$0.00	21
TC37	Tarleton Clinic	451 Hull	Tarleton	CO	80409	$18,750.00	$31,500.00	27
WL56	West Labs	785 Main	Berls	CO	80349	$14,000.00	$0.00	24

Figure 1–52

- If the Navigation Pane is hidden, click the Shutter Bar Open/Close Button, shown in Figure 1–51, to show the Navigation Pane (Figure 1–53).

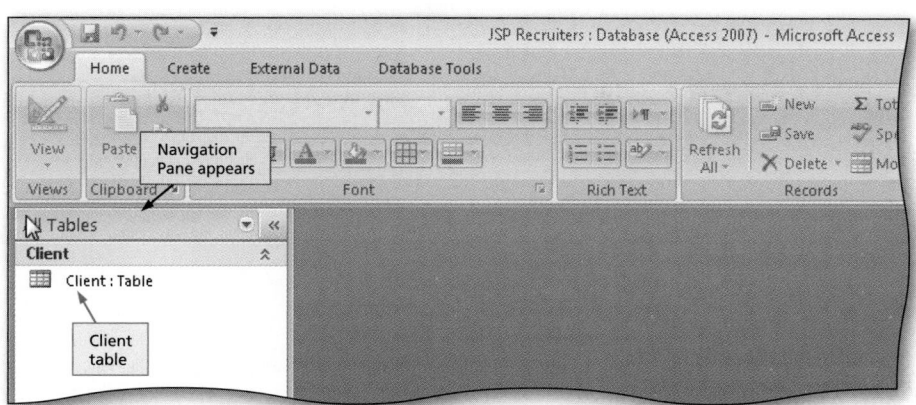

Figure 1–53

- Right-click the Client table in the Navigation Pane to display a shortcut menu.

- Click Open on the shortcut menu to open the Client table in Datasheet view.

- Hide the Navigation Pane by clicking the Shutter Bar Open/Close button (Figure 1–54).

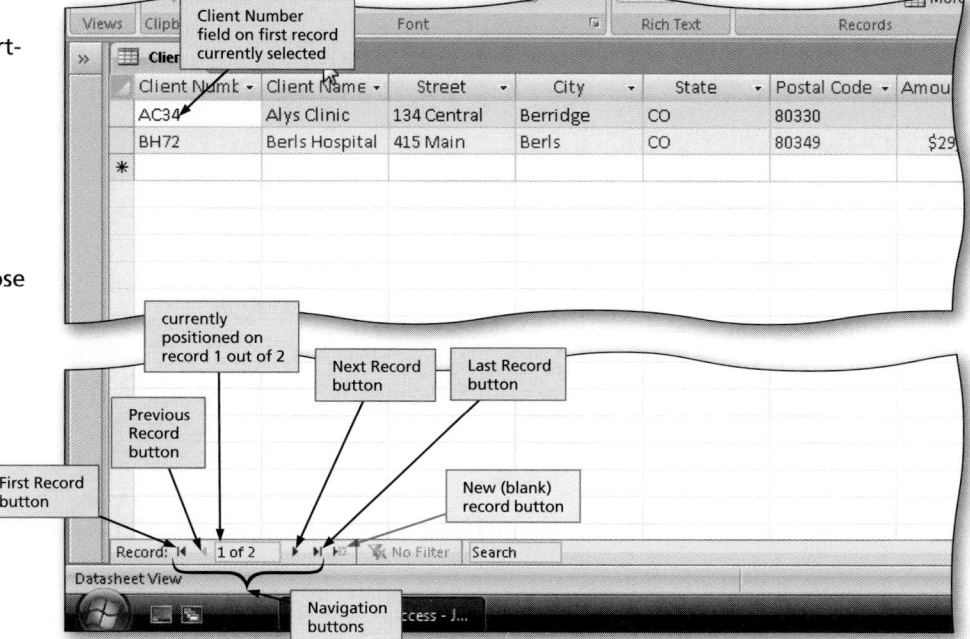

Figure 1–54

- Click the New (blank) record button to move to a position to enter a new record (Figure 1–55).

Why click the New (blank) record button? Could you just click the Client Number on the first open record and then add the record?

You could click the Client Number on the first open record, provided that record appears on the screen. With only two records in the table, this is not a problem. Once a table contains more records than will fit on the screen, it is easier to click the New (blank) record button.

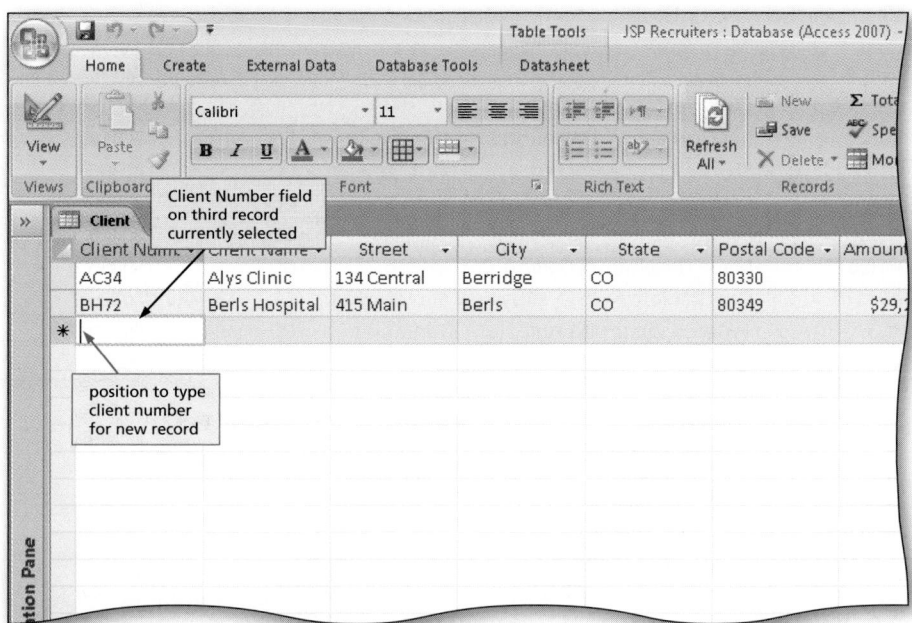

Figure 1–55

- Add the records shown in Figure 1–52 on the previous page, using the same techniques you used to add the first two records (Figure 1–56).

- Click the Close 'Client' button to close the table.

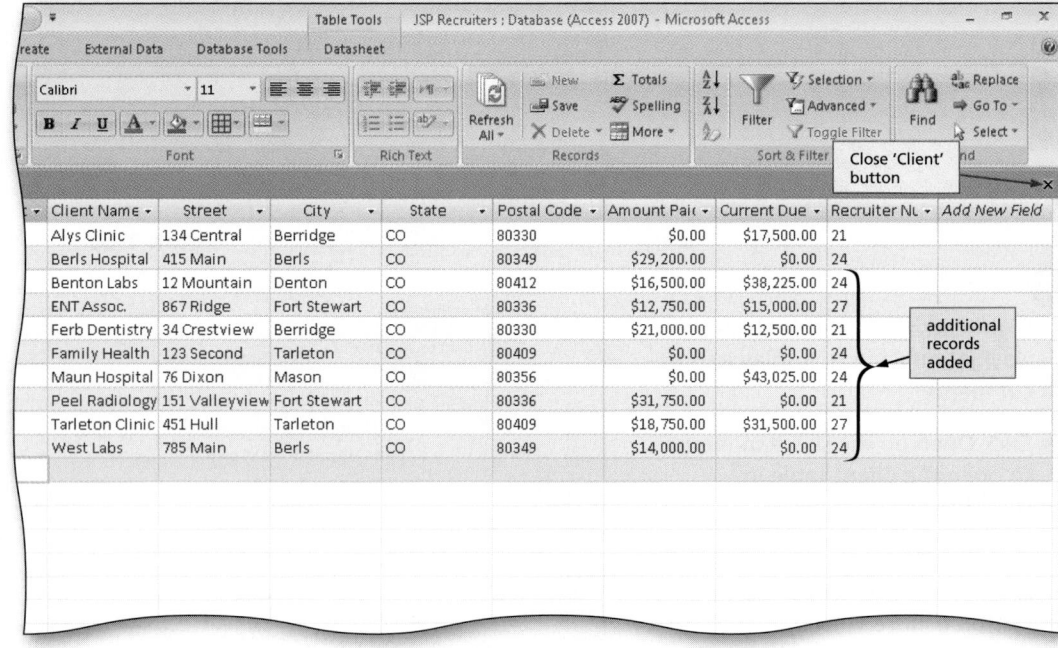

Figure 1–56

Other Ways

1. Click New button in Records group on Ribbon
2. Press CTRL+PLUS SIGN (+)

Previewing and Printing the Contents of a Table

When working with a database, you often will need to print a copy of the table contents. Figure 1–57 shows a printed copy of the contents of the Client table. (Yours may look slightly different, depending on your printer.) Because the Client table is wider substantially than the screen, it also will be wider than the normal printed page in portrait orientation. **Portrait orientation** means the printout is across the width of the page.

Client Number	Client Name	Street	City	State	Postal Code	Amount Paid	Current Due	Recruiter Numb
AC34	Alys Clinic	134 Central	Berridge	CO	80330	$0.00	$17,500.00	21
BH72	Berls Hospital	415 Main	Berls	CO	80349	$29,200.00	$0.00	24
BL12	Benton Labs	12 Mountain	Denton	CO	80412	$16,500.00	$38,225.00	24
EA45	ENT Assoc.	867 Ridge	Fort Stewart	CO	80336	$12,750.00	$15,000.00	27
FD89	Ferb Dentistry	34 Crestview	Berridge	CO	80330	$21,000.00	$12,500.00	21
FH22	Family Health	123 Second	Tarleton	CO	80409	$0.00	$0.00	24
MH56	Maun Hospital	76 Dixon	Mason	CO	80356	$0.00	$43,025.00	24
PR11	Peel Radiology	151 Valleyview	Fort Stewart	CO	80336	$31,750.00	$0.00	21
TC37	Tarleton Clinic	451 Hull	Tarleton	CO	80409	$18,750.00	$31,500.00	27
WL56	West Labs	785 Main	Berls	CO	80349	$14,000.00	$0.00	24

Client   4/23/2008

Figure 1–57

Landscape orientation means the printout is across the length (height) of the page. Thus, to print the wide database table, use landscape orientation. If you are printing the contents of a table that fit on the screen, you will not need landscape orientation. A convenient way to change to landscape orientation is to preview what the printed copy will look like by using Print Preview. This allows you to determine whether landscape orientation is necessary and, if it is, to change the orientation easily to landscape. In addition, you also can use Print Preview to determine whether any adjustments are necessary to the page margins.

To Preview and Print the Contents of a Table

The following steps use Print Preview to preview and then print the Client table.

1
- If the Navigation Pane is hidden, show the Navigation Pane by clicking the Shutter Bar Open/Close Button.

- Be sure the Client table is selected (Figure 1–58).

Q&A
Why do I have to be sure the Client table is selected? It is the only object in the database.

There is no issue when the database contains only one object. Ensuring that the correct object is selected is a good habit to form, however, to make sure that the object you print is the one you want.

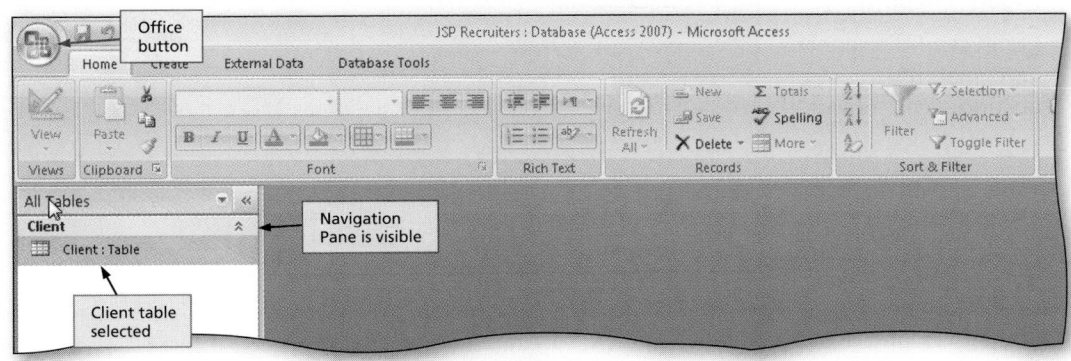

Figure 1–58

2

- Click the Office Button to display the Office Button menu.

- Point to the Print command arrow to display the Print submenu (Figure 1–59).

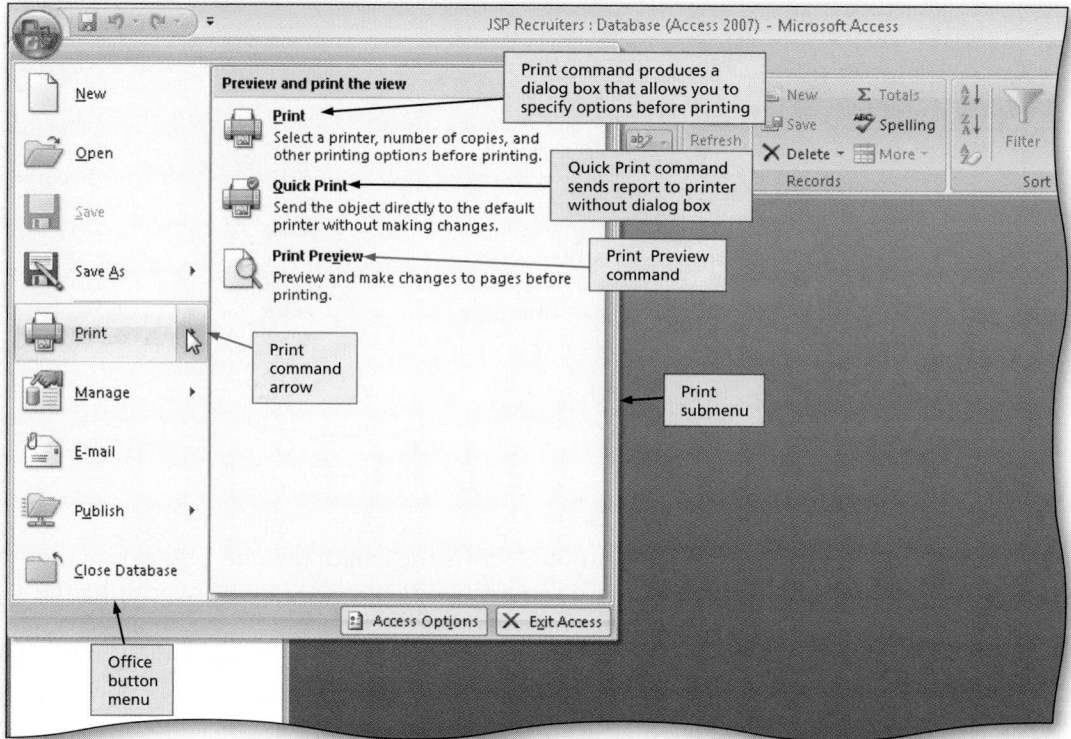

Figure 1–59

3

- Click Print Preview on the Print submenu to display a preview of the report (Figure 1–60).

 Q&A I can't read the report. Can I magnify a portion of the report?

Yes. Point the mouse pointer, whose shape will change to a magnifying glass, at the portion of the report that you wish to magnify, and then click. You can return the view of the report to the one shown in the figure by clicking a second time.

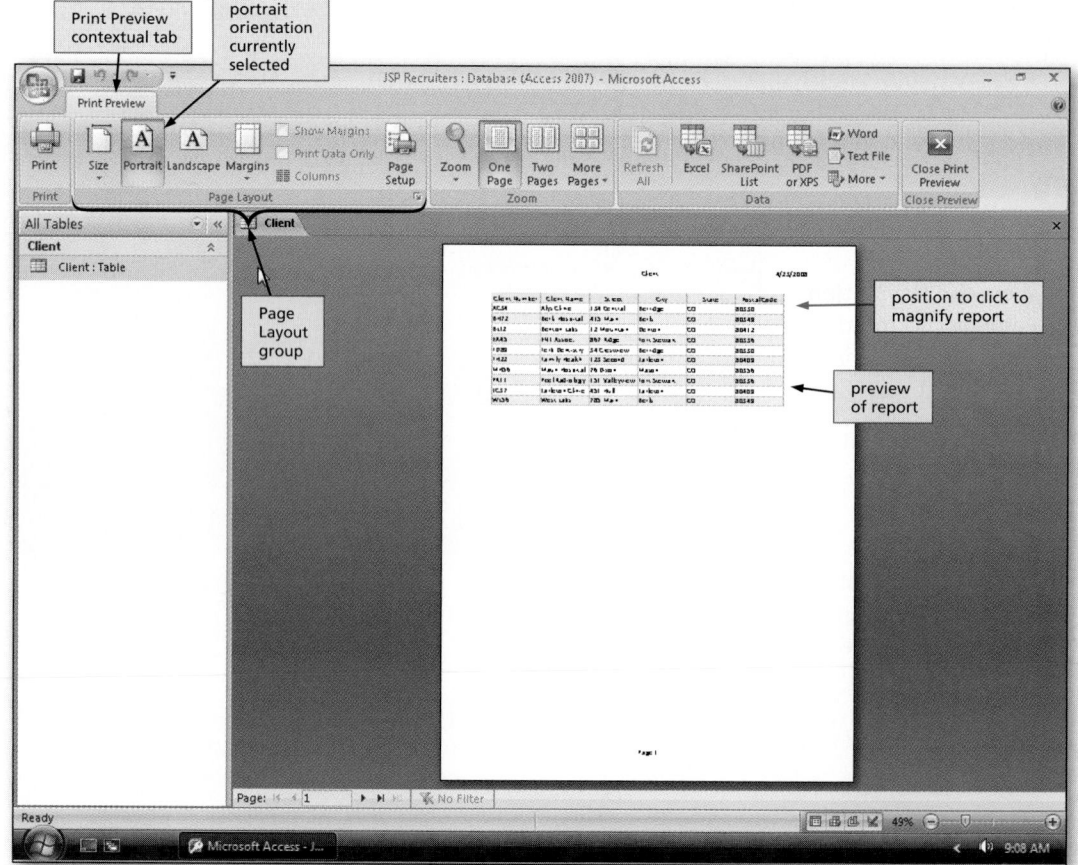

Figure 1–60

4

- Click the mouse pointer in the position shown in Figure 1–60 to magnify the upper-right section of the report (Figure 1–61).

My report was already magnified in a different area. How can I see the area shown in the figure?

There are two ways. You can use the scroll bars to move to the desired portion of the report. You also can click the mouse pointer anywhere in the report to produce a screen like the one in Figure 1–60, and then click in the location shown in the figure.

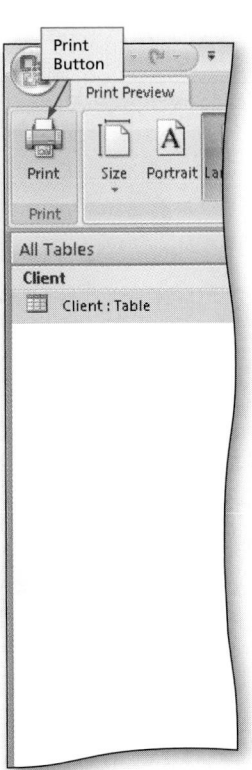

Figure 1–61

5

- Click the Landscape button to change to landscape orientation (Figure 1–62).

6

- Click the Print button on the Print Preview tab to print the report.

- When the printer stops, retrieve the hard copy of the Client table.

- Click the Close 'Client' button to close the Print Preview window.

How can I print multiple copies of my document other than clicking the Print button multiple times?

Click the Office Button, point to the arrow next to Print on the Office Button menu, click Print on the Print submenu, increase the number in the Number of Copies: box, and then click the OK button.

How can I print a range of pages rather than printing the whole report?

Click the Office Button, point to the arrow next to Print on the Office Button menu, click Print on the Print submenu, click the Pages option button in the Print Range box, enter the desired page range, and then click the OK button.

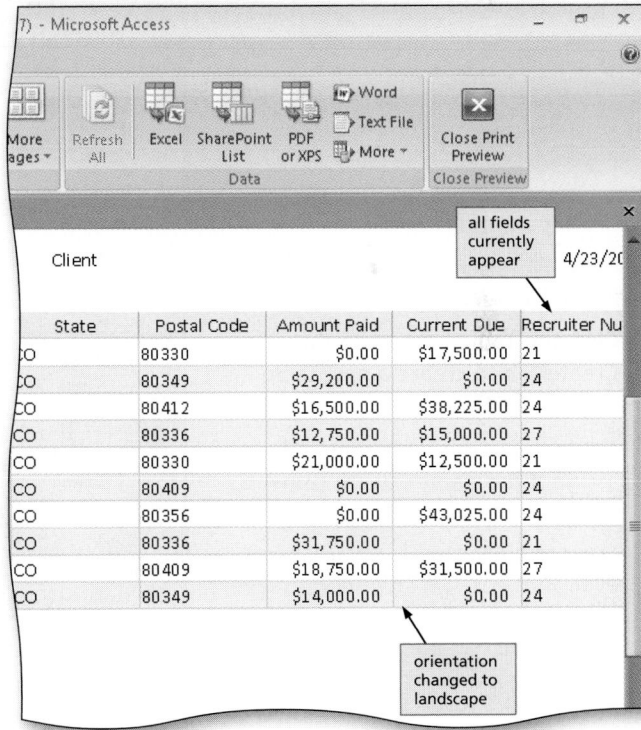

Figure 1–62

Other Ways
1. Press CTRL+P, press ENTER

Creating Additional Tables

The JSP Recruiters database contains two tables, the Client table and the Recruiter table. You need to create the Recruiter table and add records to it. Because you already used the default table that Access created when you created the database, you will need to first create the table. You can then add fields as you did with the Client table.

To Create an Additional Table

The fields to be added are Recruiter Number, Last Name, First Name, Street, City, State, Postal Code, Rate, and Commission. The data type for the Rate field is Number, and the data type for the Commission field is Currency. The data type for all other fields is Text. The following steps create the Recruiter table.

- Click Create on the Ribbon to display the Create tab (Figure 1–63).

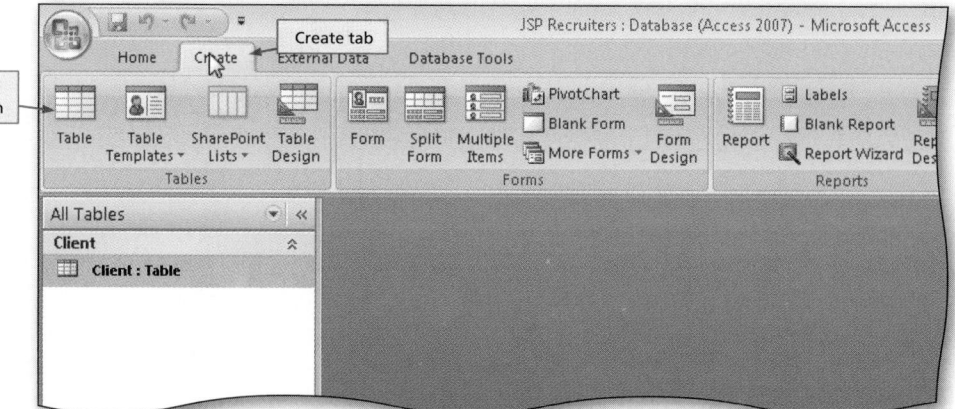

Figure 1–63

- Click the Table button on the Create tab to create a new table (Figure 1–64).

Q&A

Could I save the table now so I can assign it the name I want, rather than Table1?

You certainly can. Be aware, however, that you will still need to save it again once you have added all your fields.

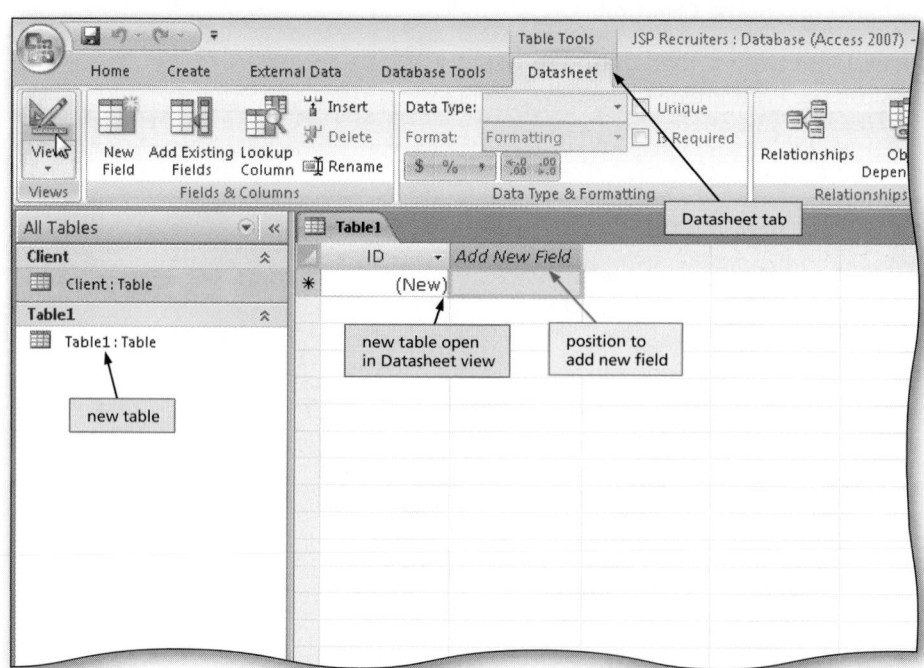

Figure 1–64

- Right-click Add New Field to display a shortcut menu.

- Click Rename Column on the short-cut menu to display an insertion point.

- Type `Recruiter Number` to assign a name to the new field.

- Press the DOWN ARROW key to complete the addition of the field.

- Using the same technique, add the Last Name, First Name, Street, City, State, Postal Code, and Rate fields.

- Click the Data Type box arrow to display the Data Type box menu (Figure 1–65).

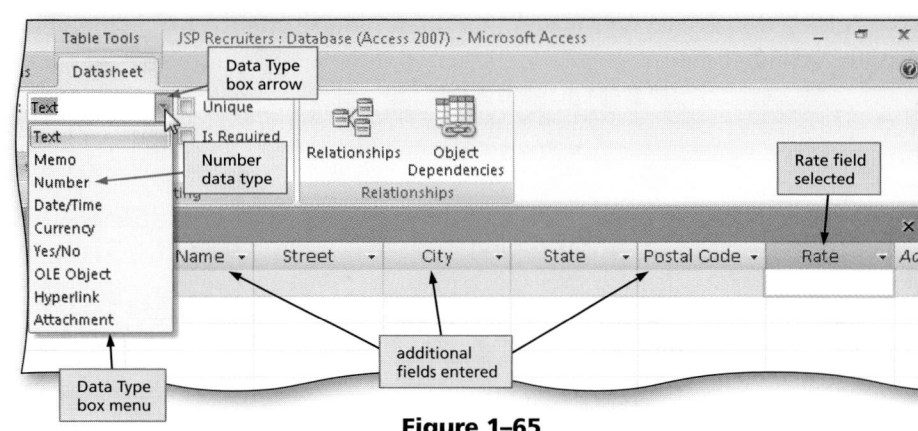

Figure 1–65

- Click Number on the Data Type box menu to select the Number data type and assign the Number data type to the Rate field.

- Add the Commission field and assign it the Currency data type.

- Click the Save button to display the Save As dialog box (Figure 1–66).

Figure 1–66

- Type `Recruiter` to assign a name to the table.

- Click the OK button (Figure 1–67).

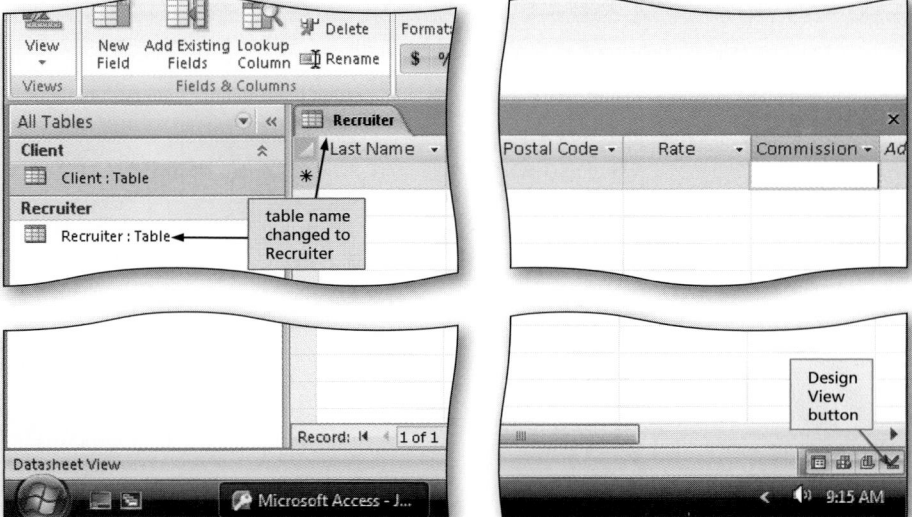

Figure 1–67

To Modify the Primary Key and Field Properties

Fields whose data type is Number often require you to change the field size. Table 1–3 shows the possible field sizes for Number fields.

Table 1–3 Field Sizes for Number Fields	
Field Size	**Description**
Byte	Integer value in the range of 0 to 255.
Integer	Integer value in the range of -32,768 to 32,767.
Long Integer	Integer value in the range of -2,147,483,648 to 2,147,483,647.
Single	Numeric values with decimal places to seven significant digits — requires four bytes of storage.
Double	Numeric values with decimal places to more accuracy than Single — requires eight bytes of storage.
Replication ID	Special identifier required for replication.
Decimal	Numeric values with decimal places to more accuracy than Single — requires 12 bytes of storage.

Because the values in the Rate field have decimal places, only Single, Double, or Decimal would be possible choices. The difference between these choices concerns the amount of accuracy. Double is more accurate than Single, for example, but requires more storage space. Because the rates are only two decimal places, Single is a perfectly acceptable choice.

In addition to changing the field size, you should also change the format to Fixed (a fixed number of decimal places) and the number of decimal places to 2.

The following steps move to Design view, delete the ID field, and make the Recruiter Number field the primary key. They then change the field size of the Rate field to Single, the format to Fixed, and the number of decimal places to 2.

1

- Click the Design View button on the status bar to move to Design view (Figure 1–68).

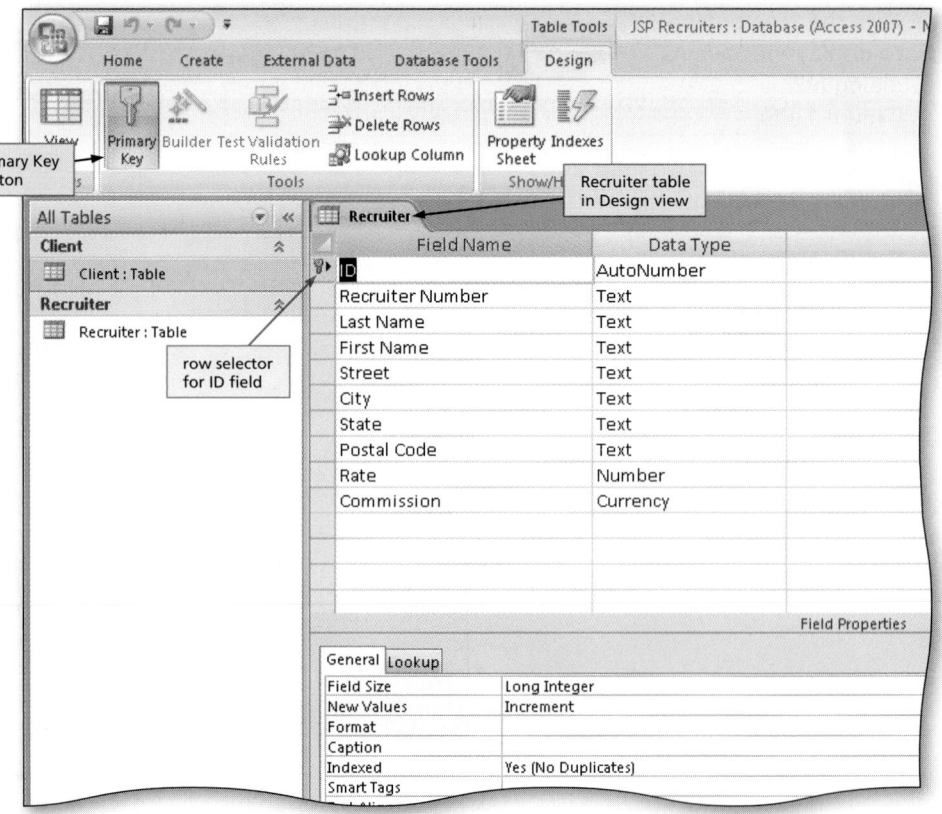

Figure 1–68

2

- Click the row selector for the ID field to select the field.

- Press the DELETE key to delete the field.

- Click the Yes button to complete the deletion of the field.

- With the Recruiter Number field selected, click the Primary Key button to designate the Recruiter Number field as the primary key.

- Click the row selector for the Rate field to select the field (Figure 1–69).

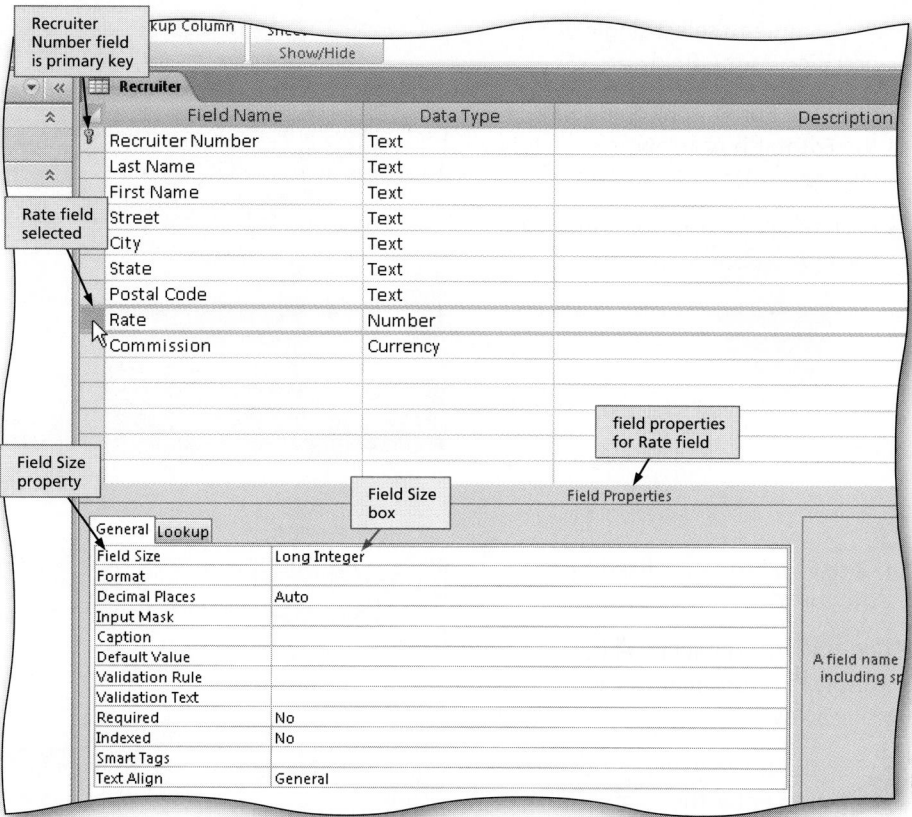

Figure 1–69

3

- Click the Field Size box to display the Field Size box arrow.

- Click the Field Size box arrow to display the Field Size box menu (Figure 1–70).

Q&A

What would happen if I left the field size set to Integer?

If the field size is Integer, no decimal places can be stored. Thus a value of .10 would be stored as 0. If you enter your rates and the values all appear as 0, chances are you did not change the field size.

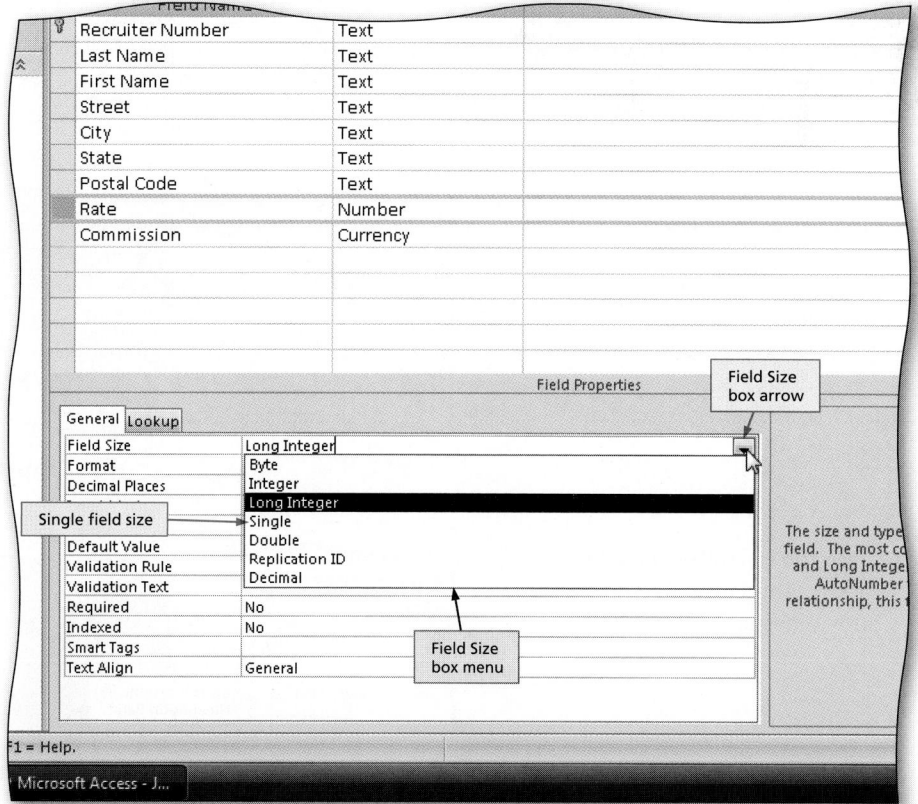

Figure 1–70

4

- Click Single to select single precision as the field size.

- Click the Format box to display the Format box arrow (Figure 1–71).

- Click the Format box arrow to open the Format box menu.

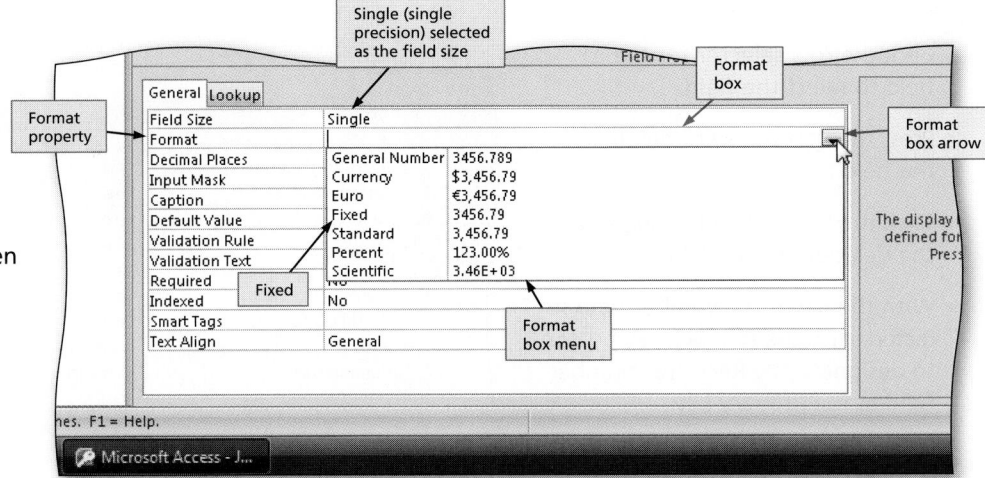

Figure 1–71

5

- Click Fixed to select fixed as the format.

- Click the Decimal Places box to display the Decimal Places box arrow.

- Click the Decimal Places box arrow to enter the number of decimal places.

- Click 2 to select 2 as the number of decimal places.

- Click the Save button to save your changes (Figure 1–72).

Q&A

What is the purpose of the error checking button?

You changed the number of decimal places. The error checking button gives you a quick way of making the same change everywhere Rate appears. So far, you have not added any data, nor have you created any forms or reports that use the Rate field, so no such changes are necessary.

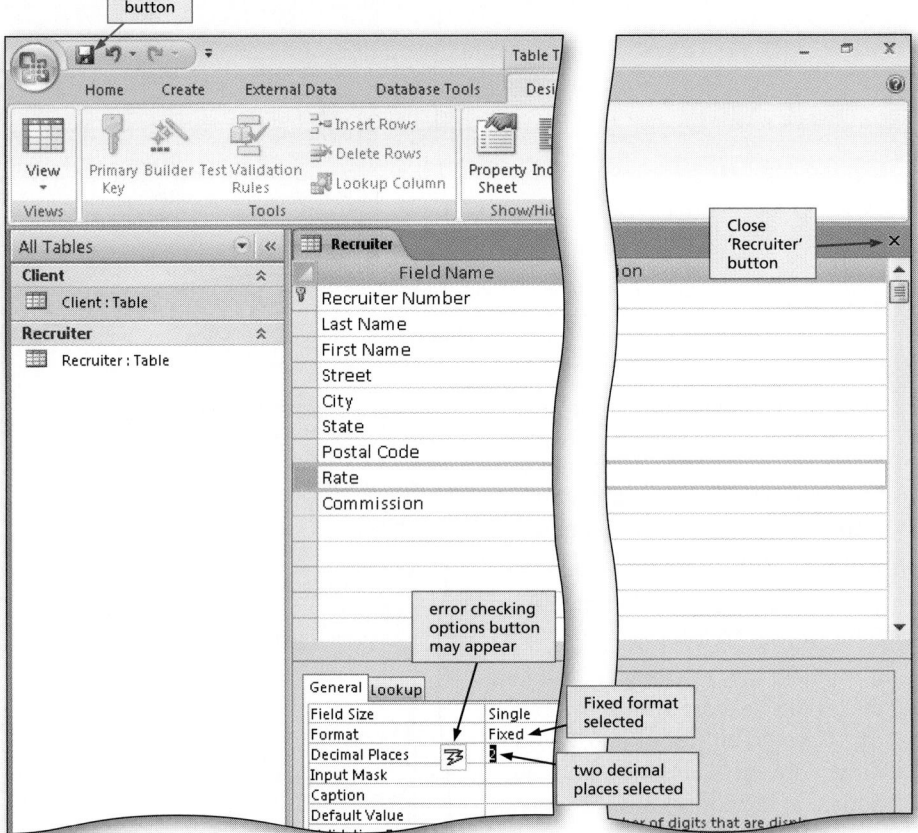

Figure 1–72

6

- Close the Recruiter table by clicking the Close 'Recruiter' button (Figure 1–73).

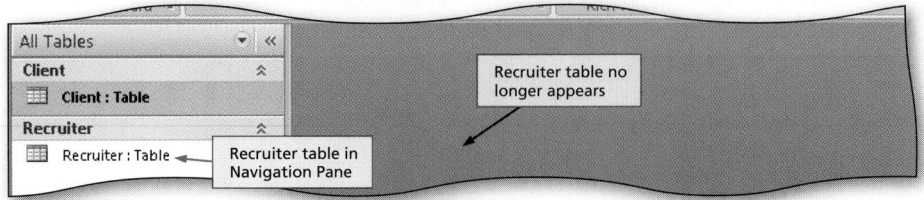

Figure 1–73

To Add Records to an Additional Table

The following steps add the records shown in Figure 1–74 to the Recruiter table.

Recruiter Nu ▾	Last Name ▾	First Name ▾	Street ▾	City ▾	State ▾	Postal Code ▾	Rate ▾	Commission ▾
21	Kerry	Alyssa	261 Pointer	Tourin	CO	80416	0.10	$17,600.00
24	Reeves	Camden	3135 Brill	Denton	CO	80412	0.10	$19,900.00
27	Fernandez	Jaime	265 Maxwell	Charleston	CO	80380	0.09	$9,450.00
34	Lee	Jan	1827 Oak	Denton	CO	80413	0.08	$0.00

Figure 1–74

- Open the Recruiter table in Datasheet view by right-clicking the Recruiter table in the Navigation Pane and then clicking Open on the shortcut menu.

- Enter the Recruiter data from Figure 1–74 (Figure 1–75).

🔎 **Experiment**

- Click in the Rate field on any of the records. Be sure the Datasheet tab is selected. Click the Format box arrow and then click each of the formats in the Format box menu to see the effect on the values in the Rate field. When finished, click Fixed in the Format box menu.

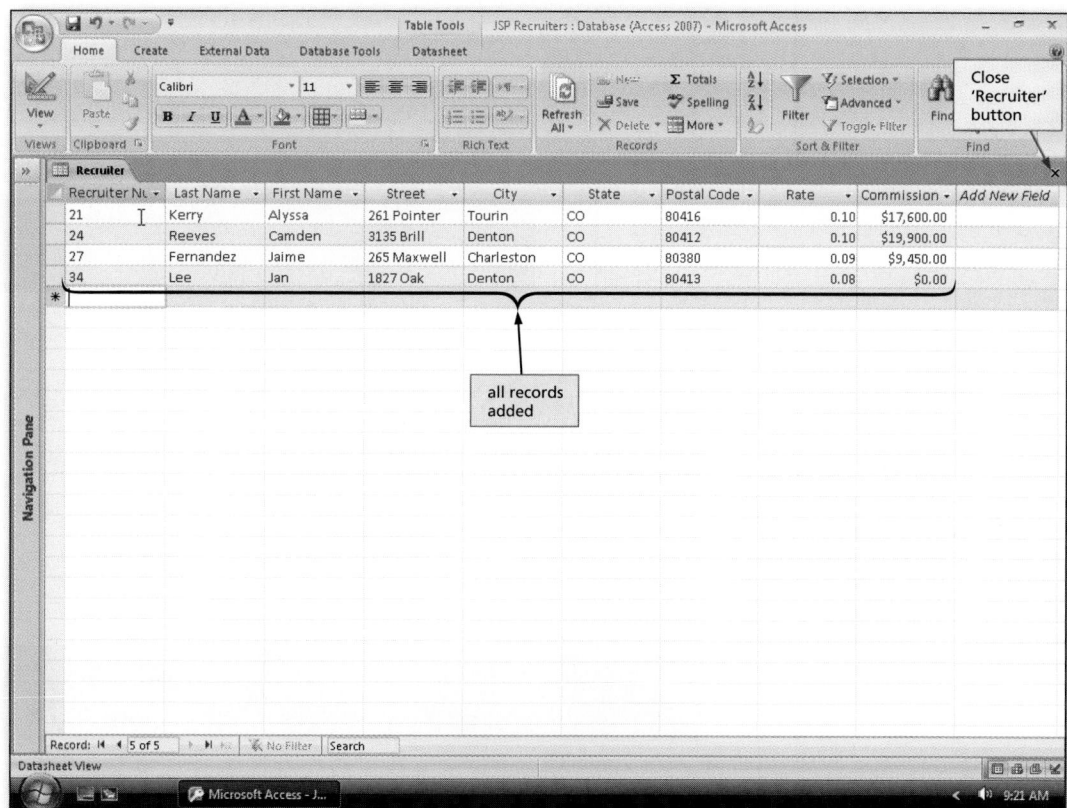

Figure 1–75

- Click the Close 'Recruiter' button to close the table and remove the datasheet from the screen.

Creating a Report

JSP Recruiters needs the following reports. You will create the four reports shown in Figure 1–76 in this section.

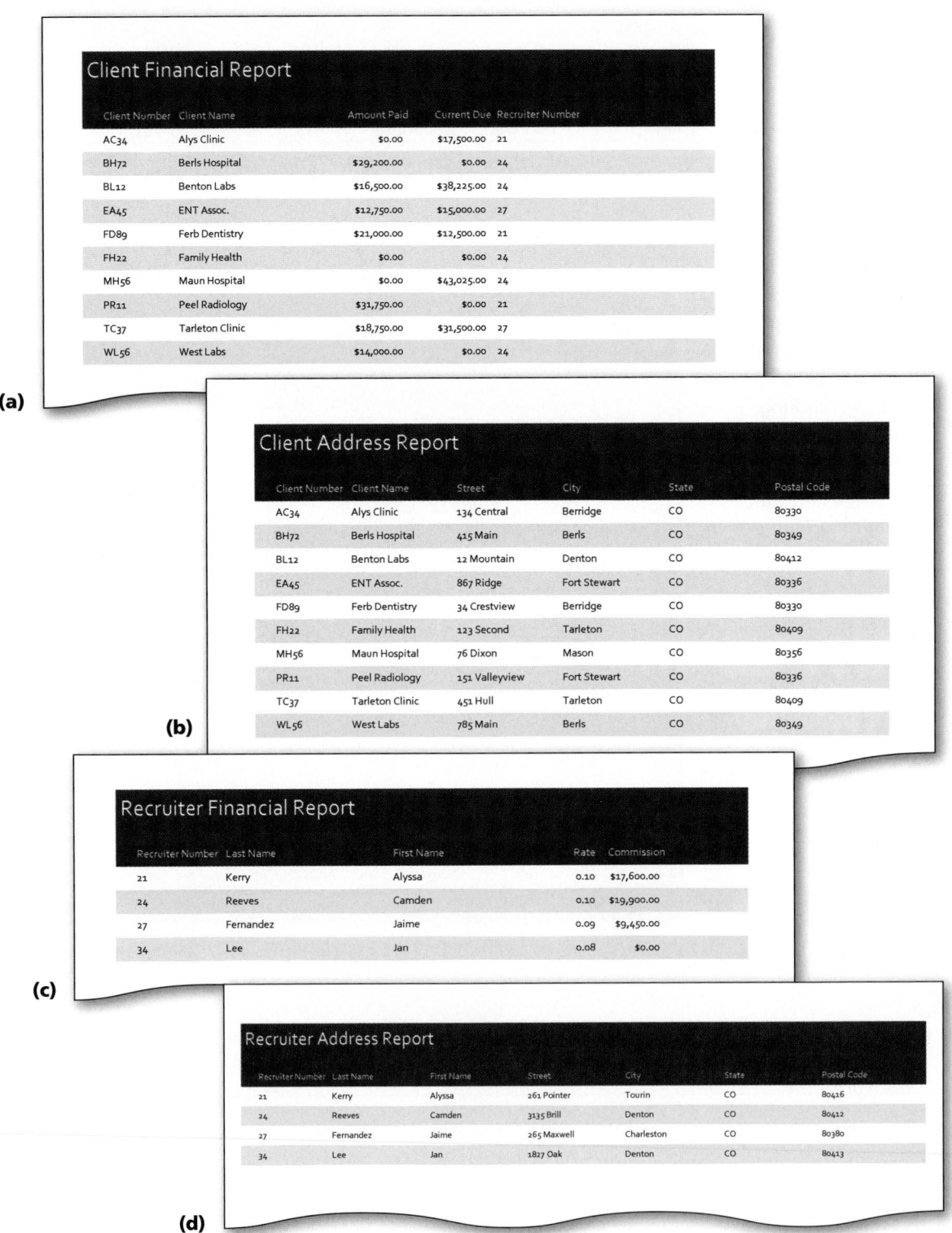

Figure 1–76

To Create a Report

You will first create the report shown in Figure 1–76a. The records in the report are sorted (ordered) by Client Number. To ensure that the records appear in this order, you will specify that the records are to be sorted on the Client Number field. The following steps create the report in Figure 1–76a.

1

- Be sure the Client table is selected in the Navigation Pane.

- Click Create on the Ribbon to display the Create tab.

- Click the Report Wizard button to display the Report Wizard dialog box (Figure 1–77).

Q&A What would have happened if the Recruiter table were selected instead of the Client table?

The list of available fields would have contained fields from the Recruiter table rather than the Client table.

Q&A If the list contained Recruiter table fields, how could I make it contain Client table fields?

Click the arrow in the Tables/ Queries box and then click the Client table in the list that appears.

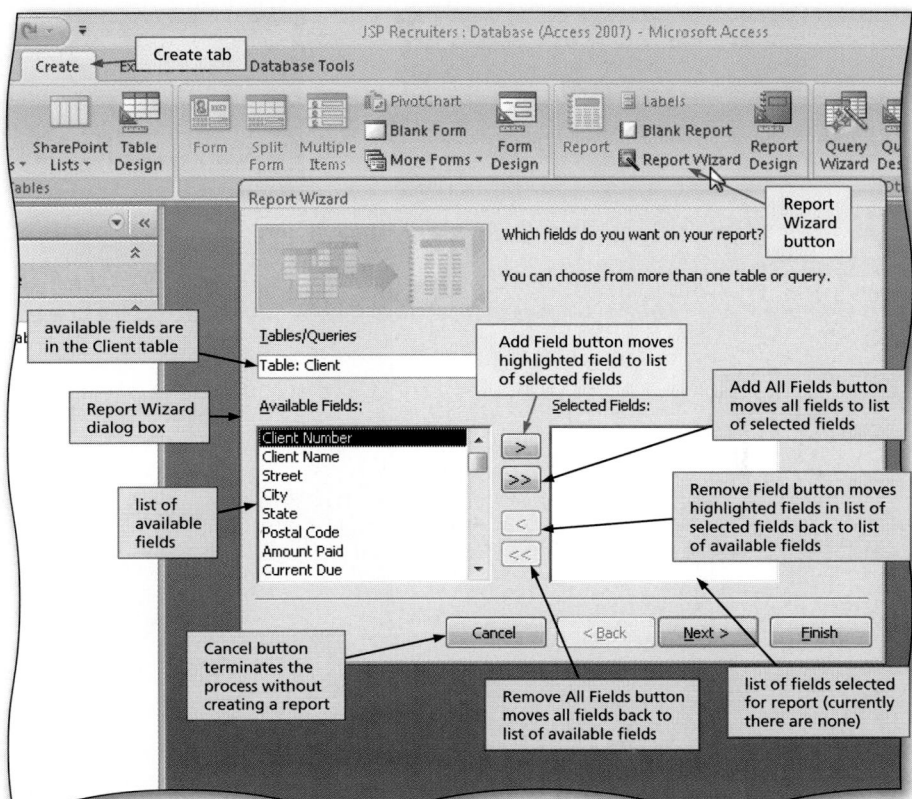

Figure 1–77

2

- Click the Add Field button to add the Client Number field.

- Click the Add Field button to add the Client Name field.

- Click the Amount Paid field, and then click the Add Field button to add the Amount Paid field.

- Click the Add Field button to add the Current Due field.

- Click the Add Field button to add the Recruiter Number field (Figure 1–78).

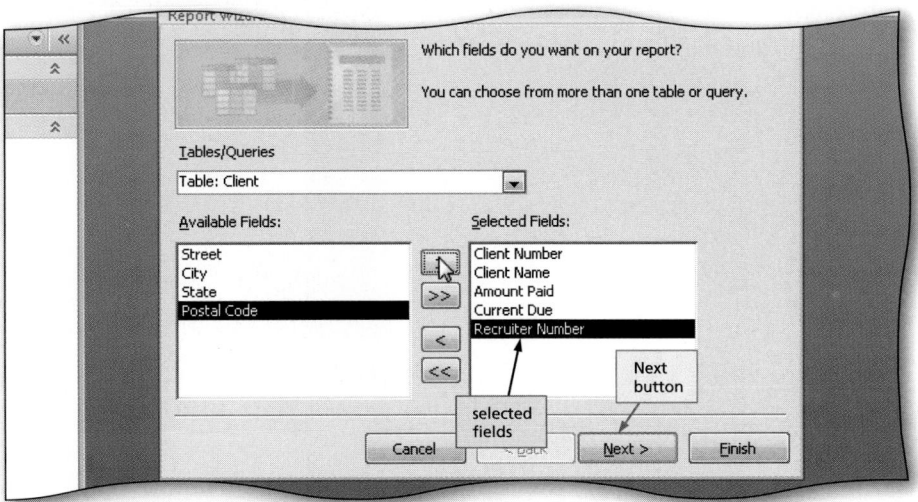

Figure 1–78

● Click the Next button to display the next Report Wizard screen (Figure 1–79).

Q&A What is grouping?

Grouping means creating separate collections of records sharing some common characteristic. For example, you might want to group clients in the same Postal code or that have the same recruiter.

Q&A What if I realize that I have selected the wrong fields?

You can click the Back button to return to the previous screen and then correct the list of fields. You also could click the Cancel button and start over.

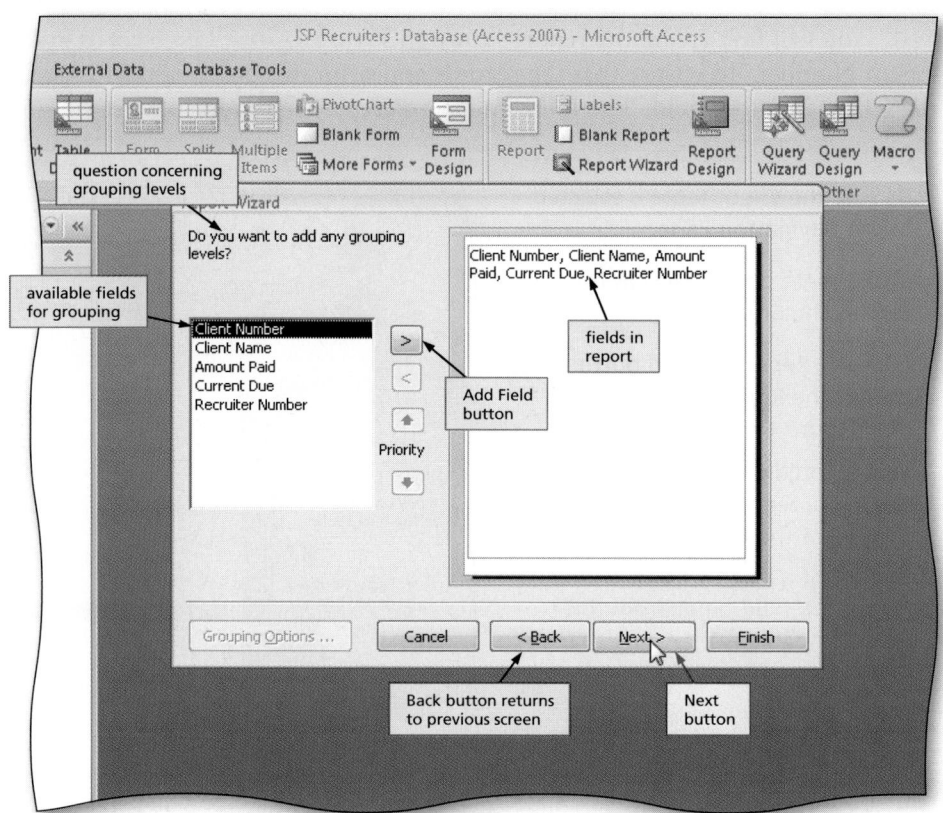

Figure 1–79

● Because you will not specify any grouping, click the Next button in the Report Wizard dialog box to display the next Report Wizard screen.

● Click the box arrow in the text box labeled 1 to display a list of available fields for sorting (Figure 1–80).

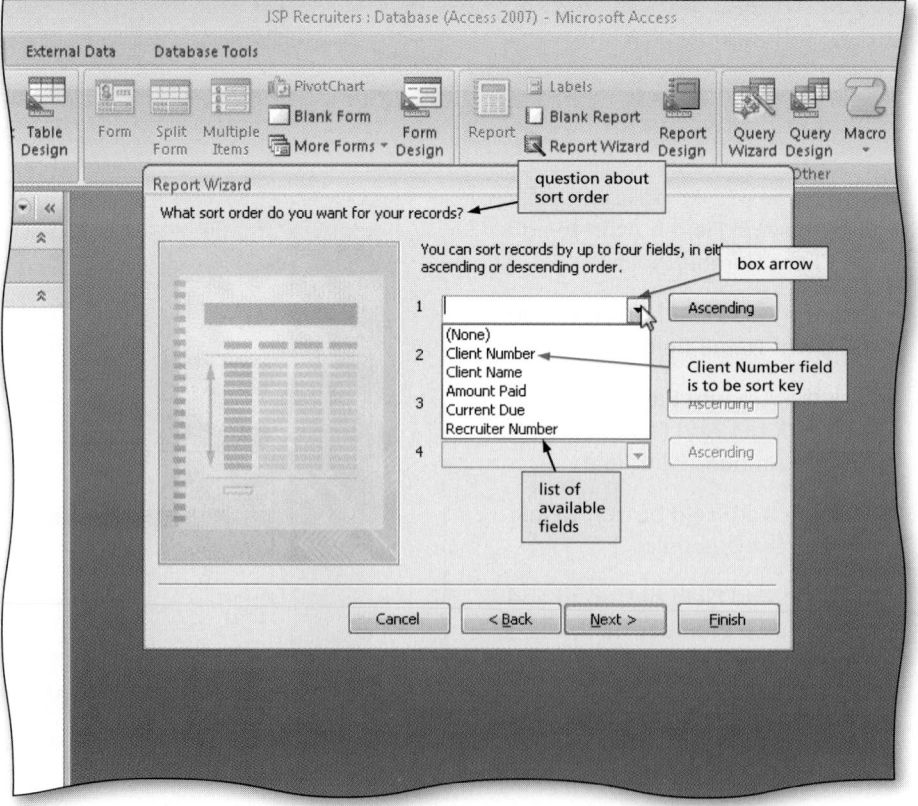

Figure 1–80

5

- Click the Client Number field to select the field as the sort key (Figure 1–81).

Q&A What if I want Descending order?

Click the Ascending button next to the sort key to change Ascending order to Descending. If you decide you want Ascending after all, click the button a second time.

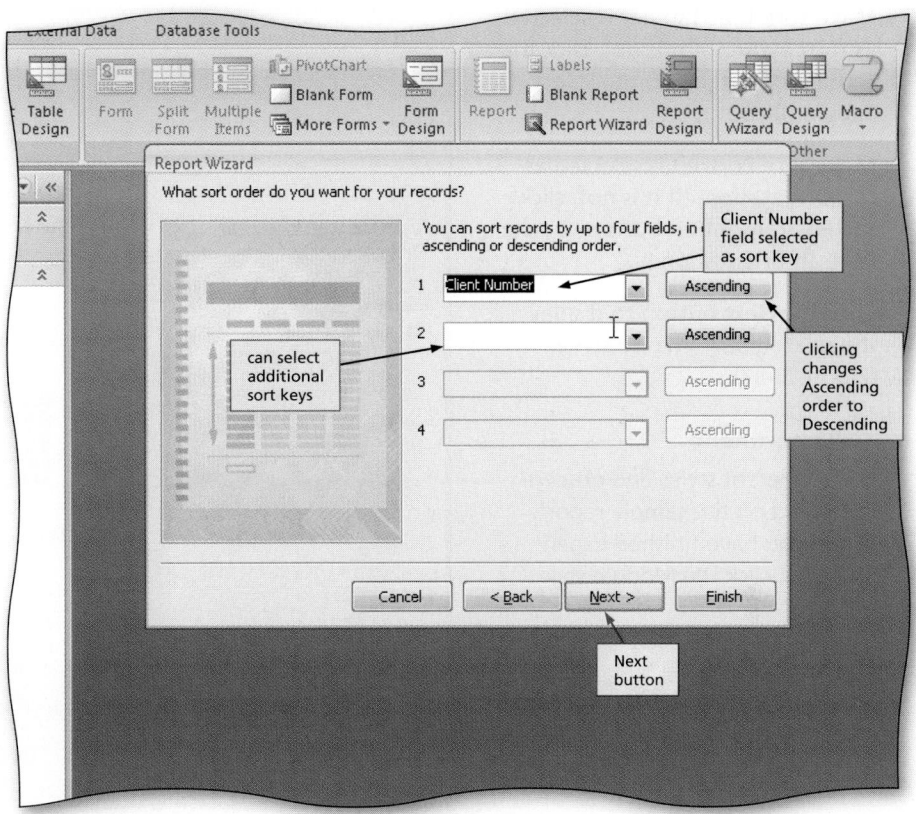

Figure 1–81

6

- Click the Next button to display the next Report Wizard screen (Figure 1–82).

Experiment

- Click different layouts and orientations and observe the effect on the sample report. When you have finished experimenting, click the Tabular option button for the layout and the Portrait option button for the orientation.

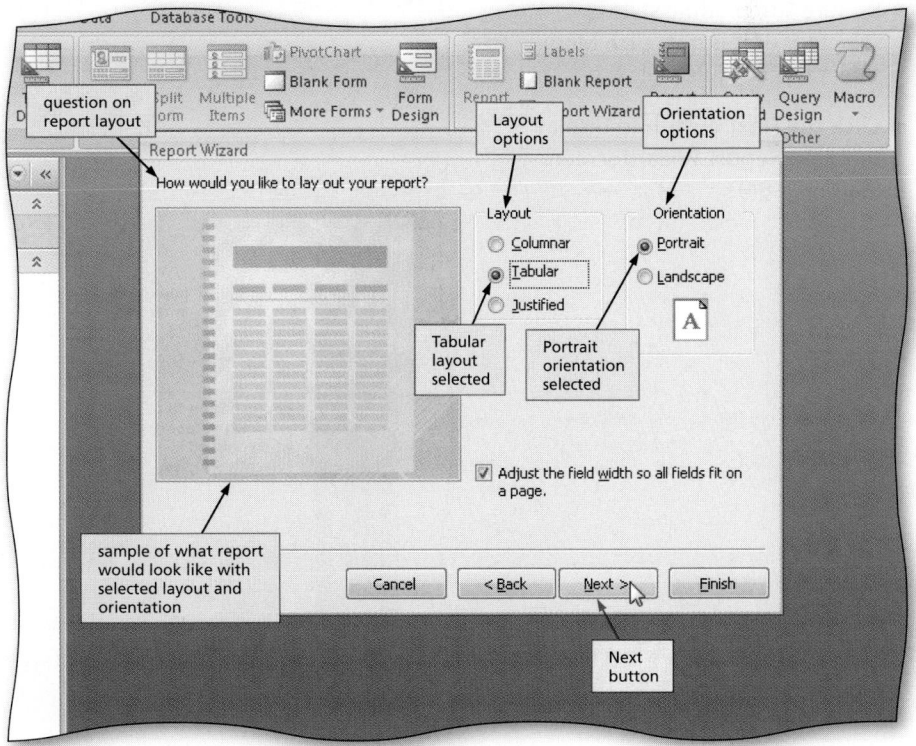

Figure 1–82

7

- Make sure that Tabular is selected as the Layout. (If it is not, click the Tabular option button to select Tabular layout.)

- Make sure Portrait is selected as the Orientation. (If it is not, click the Portrait option button to select Portrait orientation.)

- Click the Next button to display the next Report Wizard screen (Figure 1–83).

Experiment

- Click different styles and observe the effect on the sample report. When you have finished experimenting, click the Module style.

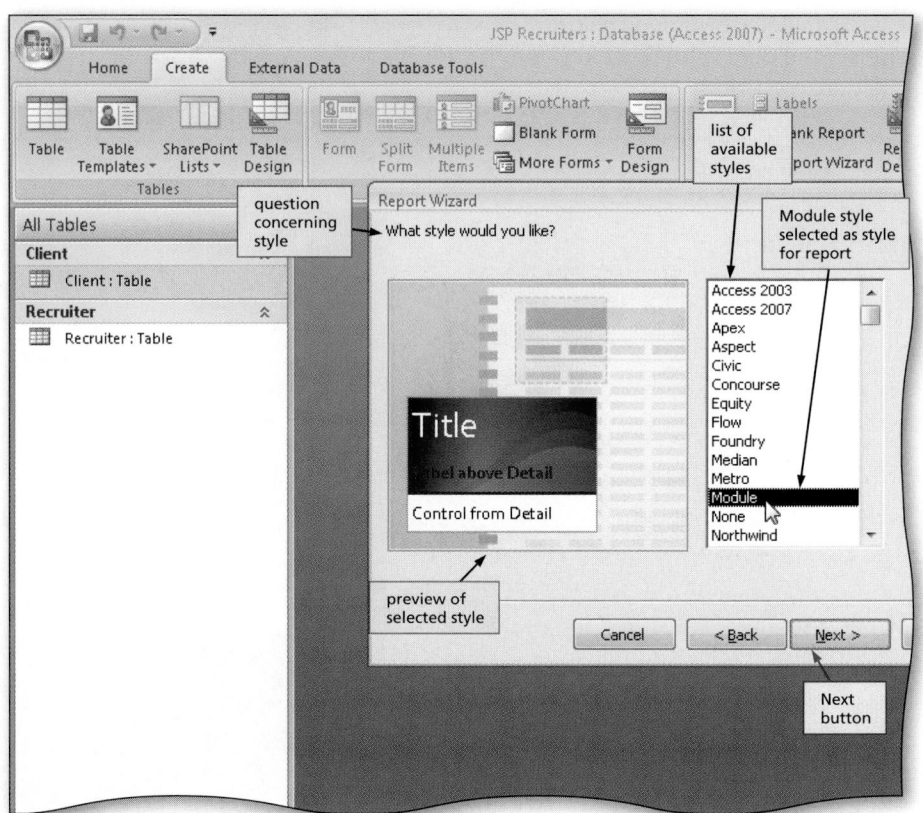

Figure 1–83

8

- Be sure the Module style is selected. (If it is not, click Module to select the Module style.)

- Click the Next button to display the next Report Wizard screen (Figure 1–84).

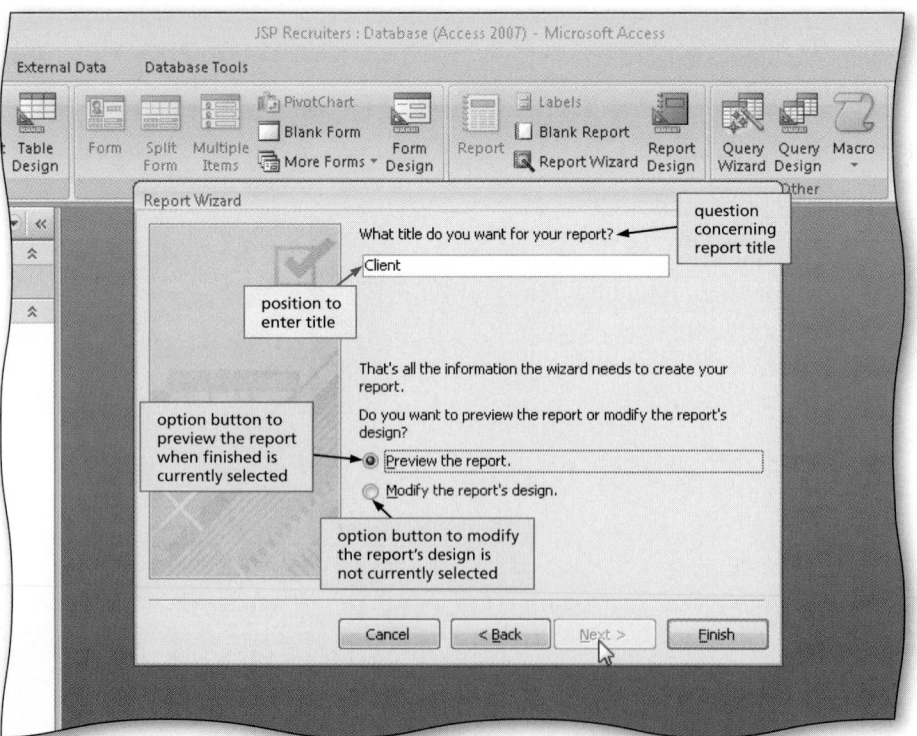

Figure 1–84

9

- Erase the current title, and then type Client Financial Report as the new title (Figure 1–85).

Q&A | How do I erase the title?

You can highlight the existing title and then press the DELETE key. You can click at the end of the title and repeatedly press the BACKSPACE key. You can click at the beginning of the title and repeatedly press the DELETE key.

Q&A | Could I just click after the word, Client, press the Spacebar, and then type Financial Report?

Yes. In general, you can edit the current title to produce the new title using the method with which you are most comfortable.

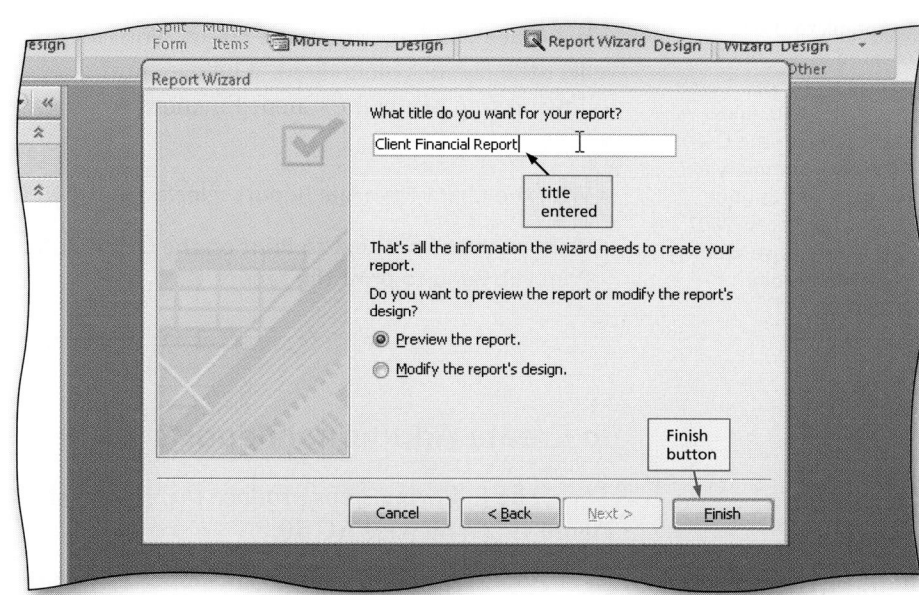

Figure 1–85

- Click the Finish button to produce the report (Figure 1–86).

10

- Click the Close 'Client Financial Report' button to remove the report from the screen.

Q&A | Why didn't I have to save the report?

The Report Wizard saves the report automatically.

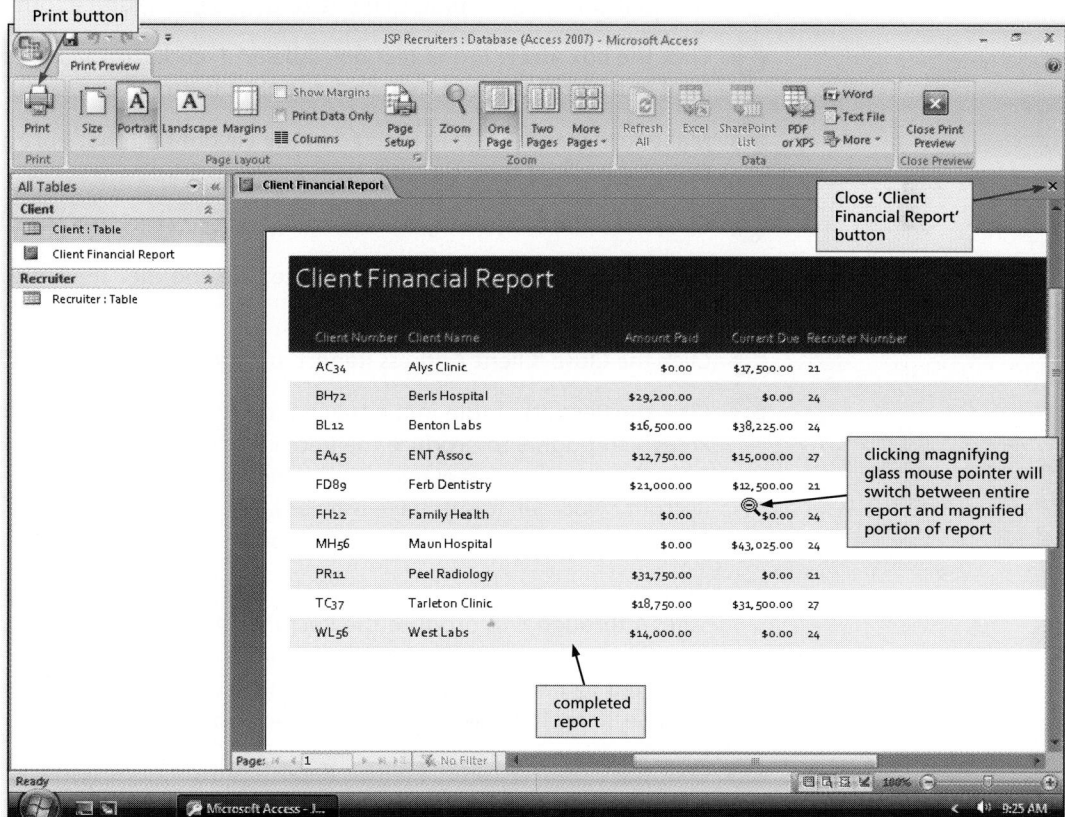

Figure 1–86

To Print a Report

Once you have created a report, you can print it at any time. The printed layout will reflect the layout you created. The data in the report will always reflect current data. The following step prints the Client Financial Report.

- With the Client Financial Report selected in the Navigation Pane, click the Office Button.

- Point to the arrow next to Print on the Office Button menu and then click Quick Print on the Print submenu to print the report.

To Create Additional Reports

The following steps produce the reports shown in Figure 1–76b, Figure 1–76c, and Figure 1–76d on page AC 50.

1 If necessary, click Create on the Ribbon to display the Create tab, and then click the Report Wizard button to display the Report Wizard dialog box.

2 Add the Client Number, Client Name, Street, City, State, and Postal Code fields by clicking each field and then clicking the Add Field button.

3 Click the Next button to move to the screen asking about grouping, and then click the Next button a second time to move to the screen asking about sort order.

4 Click the box arrow in the text box labeled 1, click the Client Number field to select the field as the sort key, and then click the Next button.

5 Make sure that Tabular is selected as the Layout and that Portrait is selected as the Orientation, and then click the Next button.

6 Make sure the Module style is selected, and then click the Next button.

7 Enter `Client Address Report` as the title and click the Finish button to produce the report.

8 Click the Close 'Client Address Report' button to close the Print Preview window.

9 Click the Recruiter table in the Navigation Pane, and then use the techniques shown in Steps 1 through 8 to produce the Recruiter Financial Report. The report is to contain the Recruiter Number, Last Name, First Name, Rate, and Commission fields. It is to be sorted by Recruiter Number. It is to have tabular layout, portrait orientation, and the Module Style. The title is to be Recruiter Financial Report.

10 With the Recruiter table selected in the Navigation Pane, use the techniques shown in Steps 1 through 8 to produce the Recruiter Address Report. The report is to contain the Recruiter Number, Last Name, First Name, Street, City, State, and Postal Code fields. It is to be sorted by Recruiter Number. It is to have tabular layout, landscape orientation, and the Module Style. The title is to be Recruiter Address Report.

11 Click the Close 'Recruiter Address Report' button to close the Print Preview window.

Using a Form to View Data

In Datasheet view, you can view many records at once. If there are many fields, however, only some of the fields in each record might be visible at a time. In **Form view**, where data is displayed in a form on the screen, you usually can see all the fields, but only for one record. To get the advantages from both, many database management systems allow you to easily switch between Datasheet view and Form view while maintaining position within the database. In Access 2007, you can view both a datasheet and a form simultaneously using a split form.

To Create a Split Form

A **split form** combines both a datasheet and a form, thus giving the advantages of both views. The following steps create a split form.

1

- Select the Client table in the Navigation Pane.

- If necessary, click Create on the Ribbon to display the Create tab (Figure 1–87).

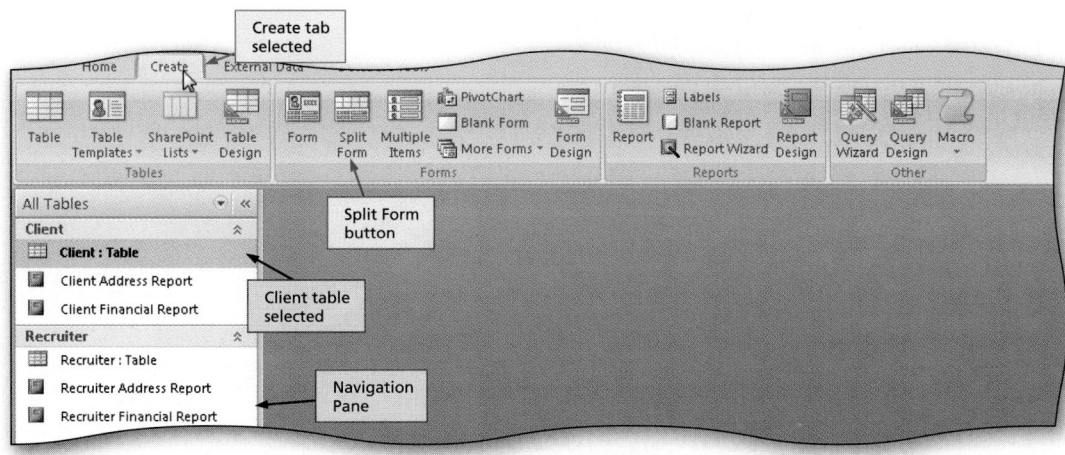

Figure 1–87

2

- Click the Split Form button to create a split form. If a Field List appears, click its Close button to remove the Field List from the screen (Figure 1–88).

Q&A Is the form automatically saved the way the report was created when I used the Report Wizard?

No. You must take specific action if you wish to save the form.

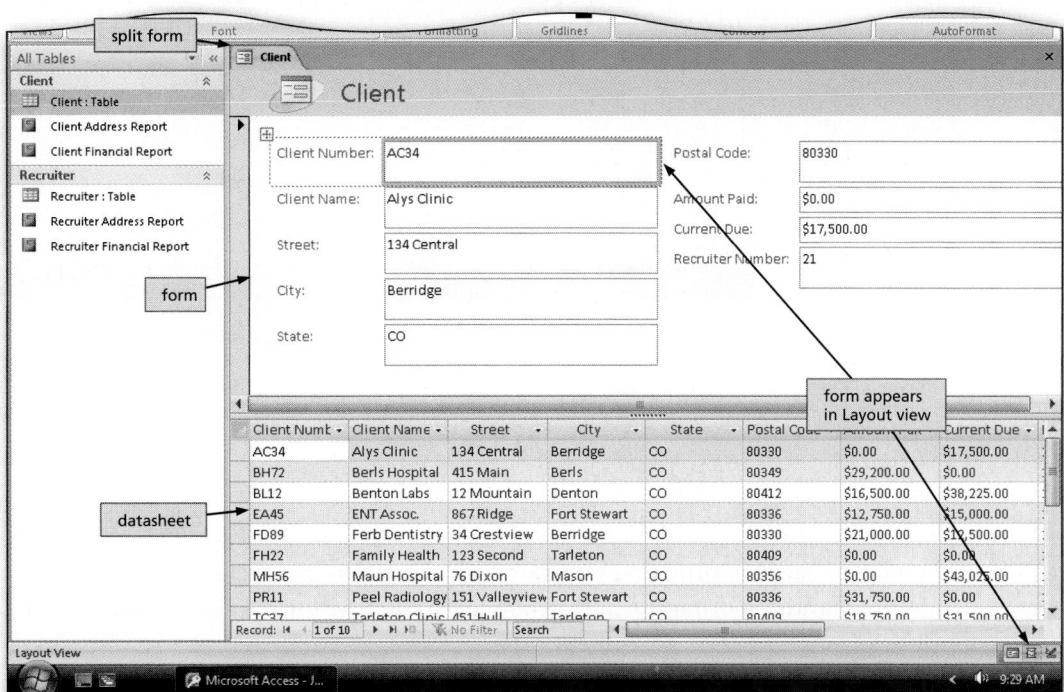

Figure 1–88

3

- Click the Save button to display the Save As dialog box (Figure 1–89).

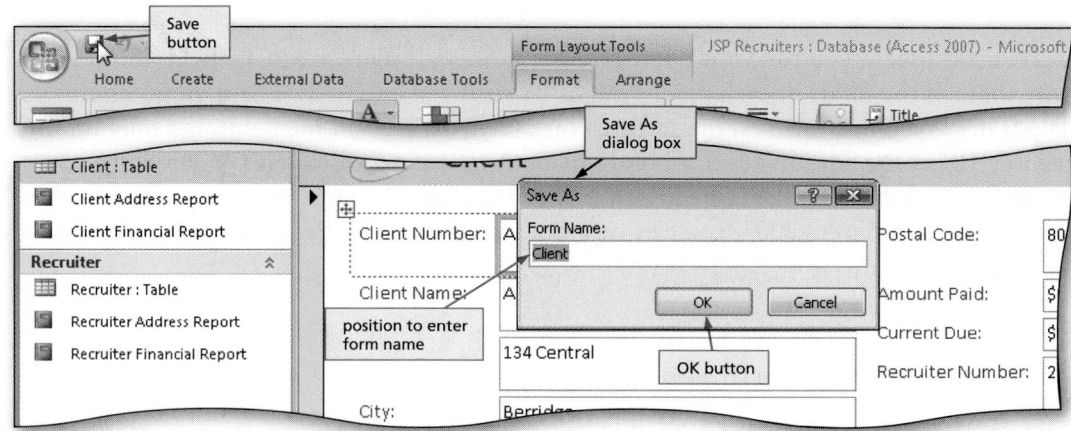

Figure 1–89

4

- Type `Client Form` as the form name, and then click the OK button to save the form.

- If the form appears in Layout view, click the Form View button on the Access status bar to display the form in Form view (Figure 1–90).

Q&A

How can I recognize Layout view?

There are three ways. The left end of the Status bar will contain the words Layout View. There will be shading around the outside of the selected field in the form. The Layout View button will be selected in the right end of the Status bar.

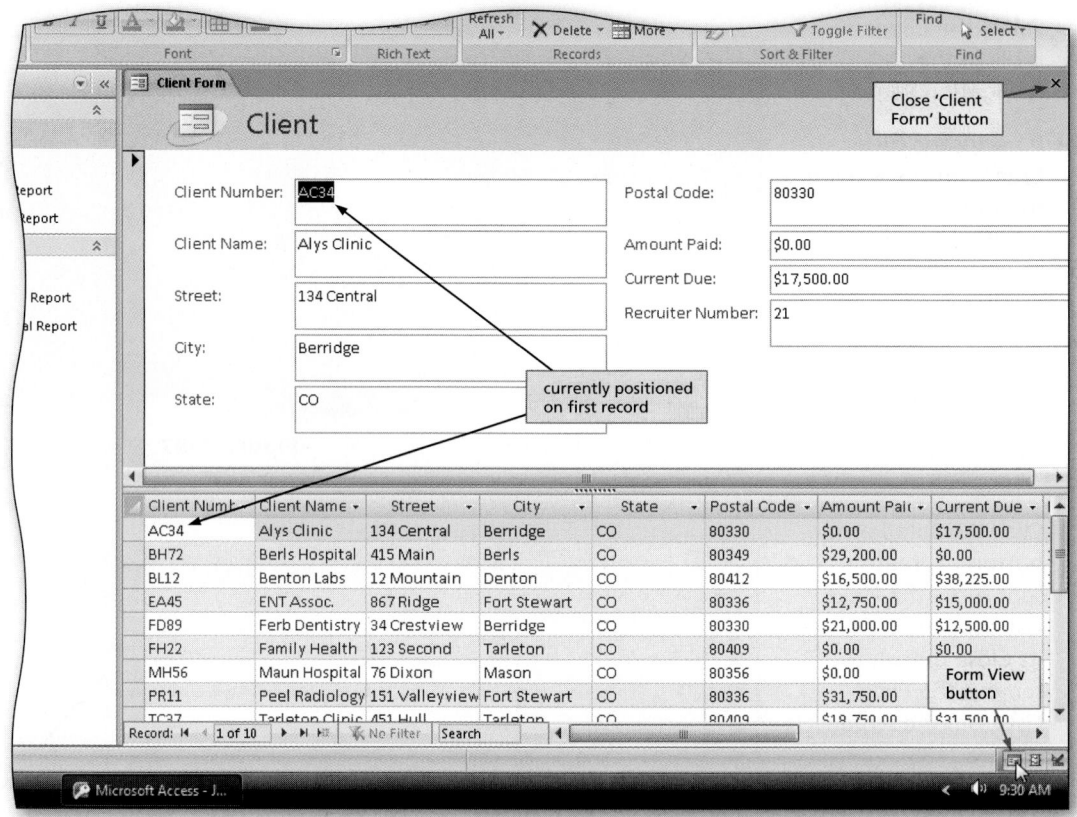

Figure 1–90

To Use a Split Form

After you have saved a form, you can use it at any time by right-clicking the form in the Navigation Pane and then clicking Open in the shortcut menu. If you plan to use the form to enter data, you must ensure you are viewing the form in Form view.

1

- Click the Next Record button four times to move to record 5 (Figure 1–91).

 I inadvertently closed the form at the end of the previous steps. What should I do?

Right-click the form in the Navigation Pane and then click Open on the shortcut menu.

 Do I have to take any special action for the form to be positioned on the same record as the datasheet?

No. The advantage to the split form is that changing the position on either the datasheet or the form automatically changes the position on the other.

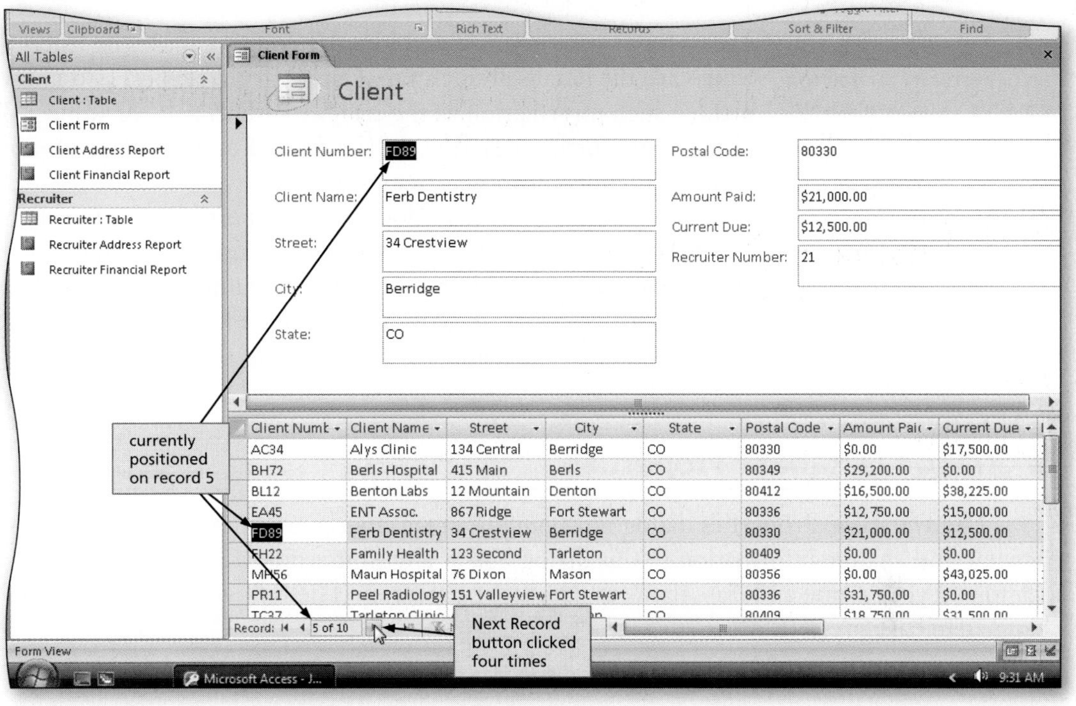

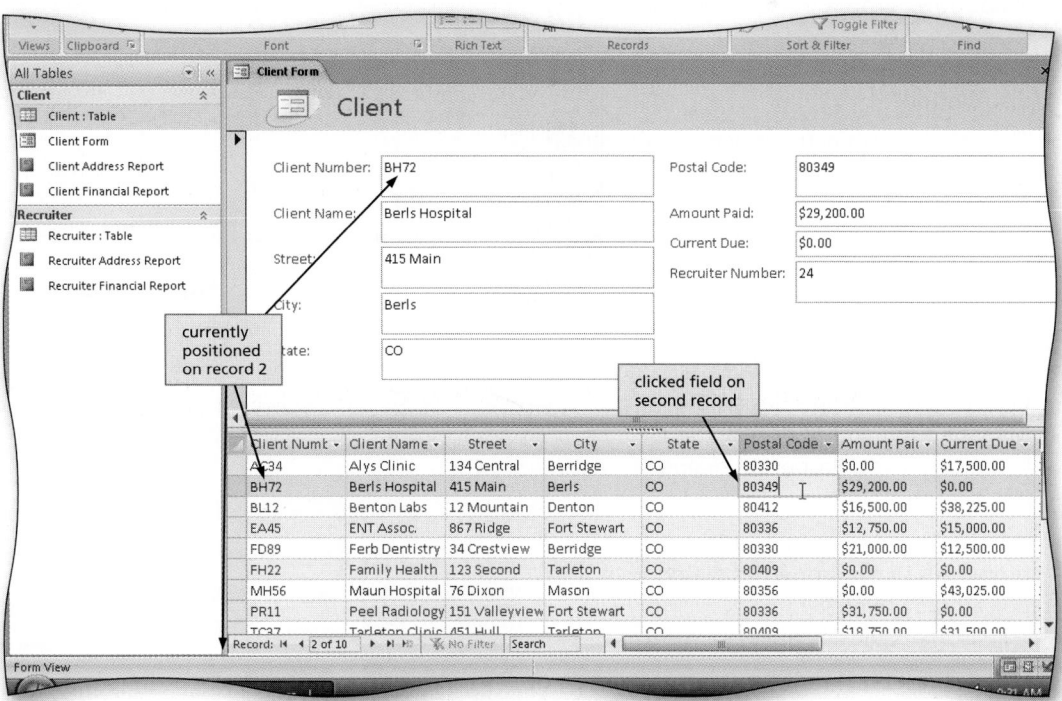

Figure 1–91

2

- Click the Postal Code field on the second record in the datasheet to select the second record in both the datasheet and the form (Figure 1–92).

 Experiment

- Click several fields in various records in the datasheet and observe the effect on the form.

3

- Click the Close 'Client Form' button to remove the form from the screen.

Figure 1–92

BTW

Certification
The Microsoft Certified Application Specialist (MCAS) program provides an opportunity for you to obtain a valuable industry credential — proof that you have the Access 2007 skills required by employers. For more information see Appendix G or visit the Access 2007 Certification Web page (scsite.com/ac2007/cert).

Changing Document Properties

Access helps you organize and identify your databases by using **database properties,** which are the details about a file. Database properties, also known as **metadata,** can include such information as the project author, title, or subject. **Keywords** are words or phrases that further describe the database. For example, a class name or database topic can describe the file's purpose or content.

Five different types of document properties exist, but the more common ones used in this book are standard and automatically updated properties. **Standard properties** are associated with all Microsoft Office documents and include author, title, and subject. **Automatically updated properties** include file system properties, such as the date you create or change a file, and statistics, such as the file size.

To Change Database Properties

The Database Properties dialog box contains areas where you can view and enter document properties. You can view and change information in this dialog box at any time while you are working on your database. It is a good idea to add your name and class name as database properties. The following steps use the Properties dialog box to change database properties.

- Click the Office Button to display the Office Button menu.

- Point to Manage on the Office Button menu to display the Manage submenu (Figure 1–93).

Q&A

What other types of actions besides changing properties can you take to prepare a database for distribution?

The Manage submenu provides commands to compact and repair a database as well as to back up a database.

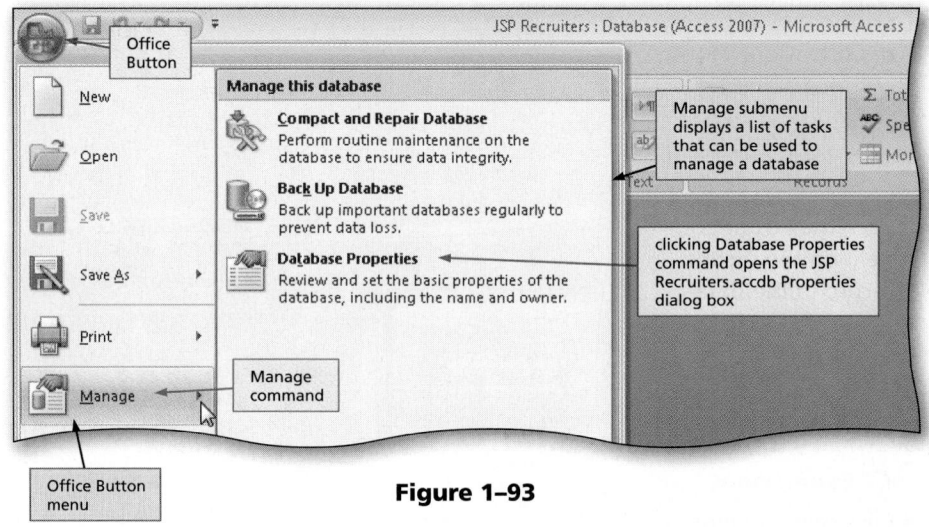

Figure 1–93

- Click Database Properties on the Manage submenu to display the JSP Recruiters.accdb Properties dialog box (Figure 1–94).

Q&A

Why are some of the document properties in my Properties dialog box already filled in?

The person who installed Microsoft Office 2007 on your computer or network may have set or customized the properties.

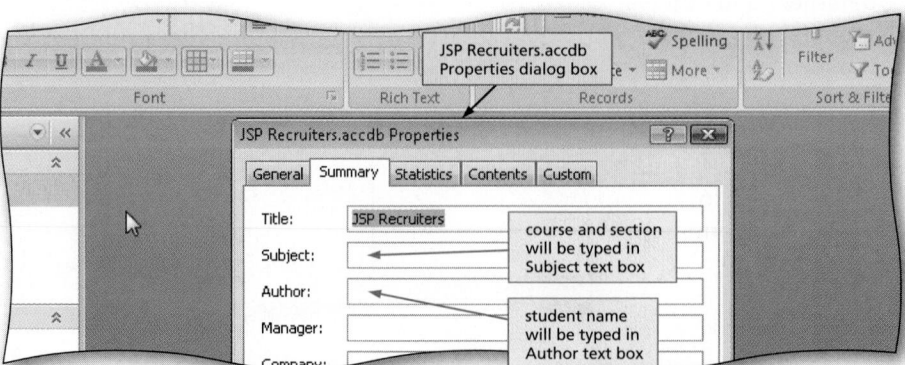

Figure 1–94

❸

- If necessary, click the Summary tab.

- Click the Author text box and then type your name as the Author property. If a name already is displayed in the Author text box, delete it before typing your name.

- Click the Subject text box, if necessary delete any existing text, and then type your course and section as the Subject property.

- Click the Keywords text box, if necessary delete any existing text, and then type Healthcare, Recruiter as the Keywords property (Figure 1–95).

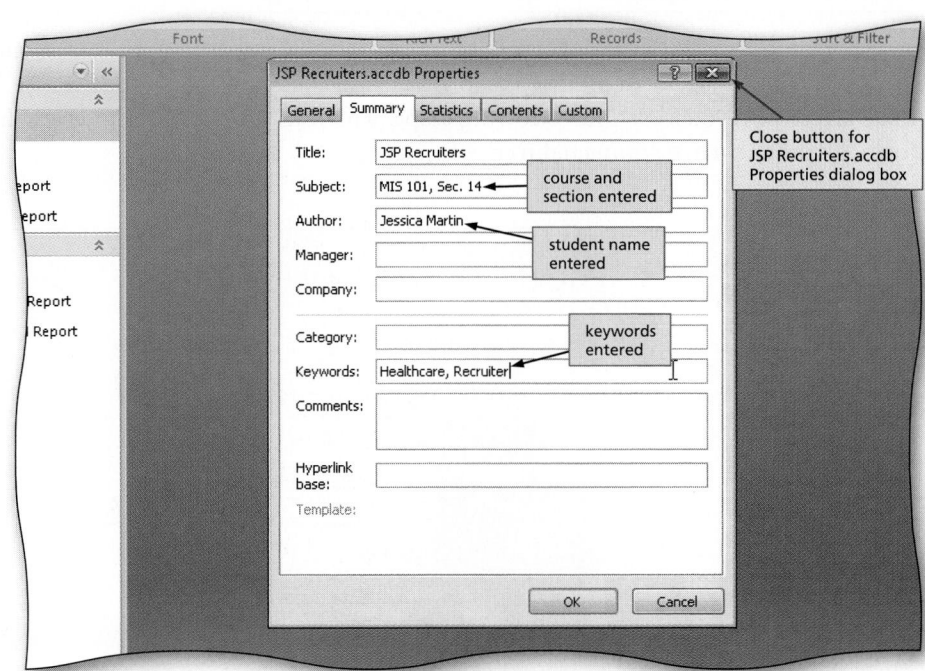

Q&A

What types of properties does Access collect automatically?

Access records such details as when the database was created, when it was last modified, total editing time, and the various objects contained in the database.

Figure 1–95

❹

- Click the OK button to save your changes and remove the JSP Recruiters.accdb Properties dialog box from the screen.

Access Help

At any time while using Access, you can find answers to questions and display information about various topics through **Access Help**. Used properly, this form of assistance can increase your productivity and reduce your frustrations by minimizing the time you spend learning how to use Access.

This section introduces you to Access Help. Additional information about using Access Help is available in Appendix C.

To Search for Access Help

Using Access Help, you can search for information based on phrases, such as create a form or change a data type, or key terms, such as copy, save, or format. Access Help responds with a list of search results displayed as links to a variety of resources. The following steps, which use Access Help to search for information about creating a form, assume you are connected to the Internet.

- Click the Microsoft Office Access Help button near the upper-right corner of the Access window to open the Access Help window.

- Type create a form in the 'Type words to search for' text box at the top of the Access Help window (Figure 1–96).

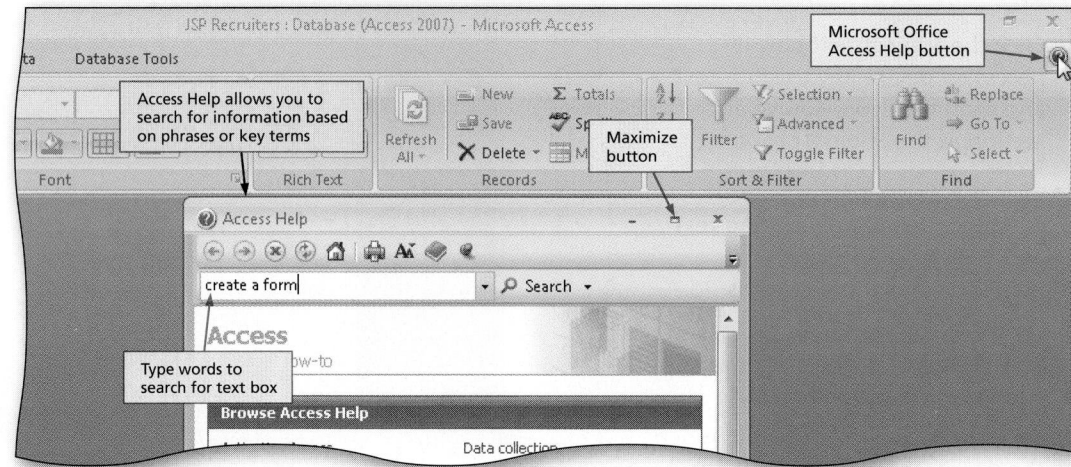

Figure 1–96

- Press the ENTER key to display the search results.

- Click the Maximize button on the Access Help window title bar to maximize the Help window unless it is already maximized (Figure 1–97).

Q&A

Where is the Access window with the JSP Recruiters database?

Access is open in the background, but the Access Help window sits on top of the Microsoft Access window. When the Access Help window is closed, the database will reappear.

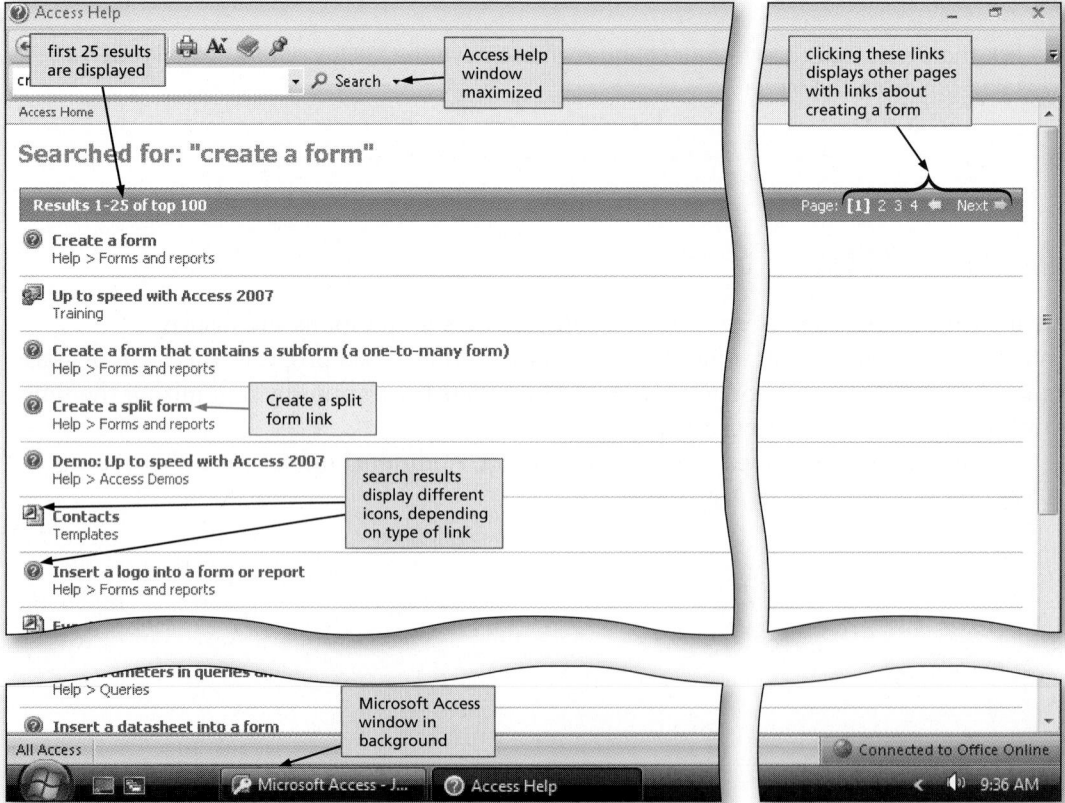

Figure 1–97

3

- Click the 'Create a split form' link to display information regarding creating a split form (Figure 1–98).

 Q&A

What is the purpose of the buttons at the top of the Access Help window?

Use the buttons in the upper-left corner of the Access Help window to navigate through the Help system, change the display, show the Access Help table of contents, and print the contents of the window.

4

- Click the Close button on the Access Help window title bar to close the Access Help window and make the database active.

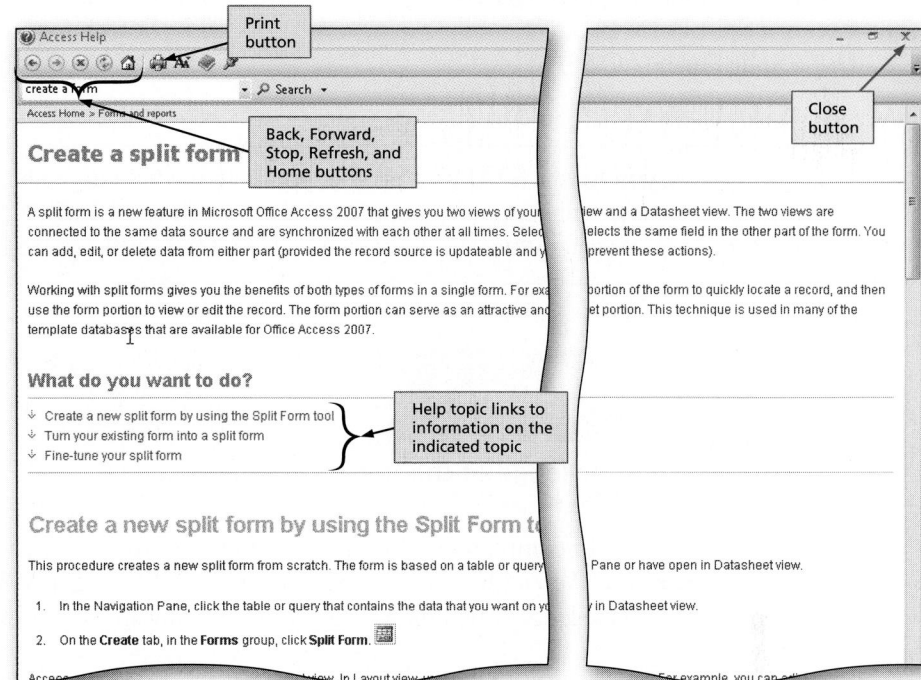

Figure 1–98

Other Ways
1. Press F1

To Quit Access

You saved all your changes and are ready to quit Access. The following step quits Access.

1 Click the Close button on the right side of the Access title bar to quit Access.

Chapter Summary

In this chapter you have learned to design a database, create an Access database, create tables and add records to them, print the contents of tables, create reports, and create forms. The items listed below include all the new Access skills you have learned in this chapter.

1. Start Access (AC 12)
2. Create a Database Using a Template (AC 13)
3. Create a Database (AC 14)
4. Define the Fields in a Table (AC 24)
5. Create a Table Using a Template (AC 26)
6. Save a Table (AC 27)
7. Change the Primary Key (AC 28)
8. Add Records to a Table (AC 30)
9. Close a Table (AC 35)
10. Quit Access (AC 36)
11. Start Access (AC 36)
12. Open a Database from Access (AC 37)
13. Add Additional Records to a Table (AC 38)
14. Preview and Print the Contents of a Table (AC 41)
15. Create an Additional Table (AC 44)
16. Modify the Primary Key and Field Properties (AC 46)
17. Add Records to an Additional Table (AC 49)
18. Create a Report (AC 51)
19. Print a Report (AC 56)

20. Create Additional Reports (AC 56)
21. Create a Split Form (AC 57)
22. Use a Split Form (AC 58)

23. Change Database Properties (AC 60)
24. Search for Access Help (AC 62)
25. Quit Access (AC 63)

 If you have a SAM user profile, you may have access to hands-on instruction, practice, and assessment. Log in to your SAM account (http://sam2007.course.com) to launch any assigned training activities or exams that relate to the skills covered in this chapter.

Learn It Online

Test your knowledge of chapter content and key terms.

Instructions: To complete the Learn It Online exercises, start your browser, click the Address bar, and then enter the Web address scsite.com/ac2007/learn. When the Access 2007 Learn It Online page is displayed, click the link for the exercise you want to complete and then read the instructions.

Chapter Reinforcement TF, MC, and SA
A series of true/false, multiple choice, and short answer questions that test your knowledge of the chapter content.

Flash Cards
An interactive learning environment where you identify chapter key terms associated with displayed definitions.

Practice Test
A series of multiple choice questions that test your knowledge of chapter content and key terms.

Who Wants To Be a Computer Genius?
An interactive game that challenges your knowledge of chapter content in the style of a television quiz show.

Wheel of Terms
An interactive game that challenges your knowledge of chapter key terms in the style of the television show *Wheel of Fortune*.

Crossword Puzzle Challenge
A crossword puzzle that challenges your knowledge of key terms presented in the chapter.

Apply Your Knowledge

Reinforce the skills and apply the concepts you learned in this chapter.

Changing Data, Creating a Form, and Creating a Report
Instructions: Start Access. Open the The Bike Delivers database. See the inside back cover of this book for instructions for downloading the Data Files for Students, or see your instructor for information on accessing the files required in this book.

The Bike Delivers uses motorbikes to provide courier services for local businesses. The Bike Delivers has a database that keeps track of its couriers and customers. The database has two tables. The Customer table (Figure 1–99a) contains data on the customers who use the services of The Bike Delivers. The Courier table (Figure 1–99b) contains data on the individuals employed by The Bike Delivers.

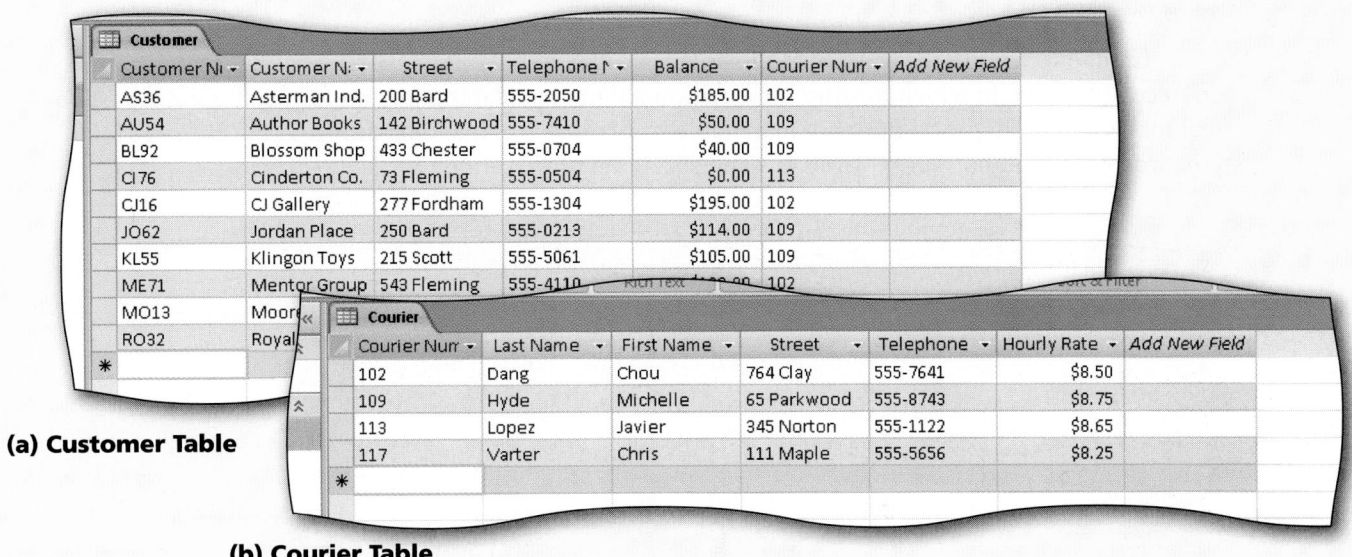

(a) Customer Table

(b) Courier Table

Figure 1–99

Perform the following tasks:

1. Open the Customer table and change the Courier Number for customer KL55 to 113.

2. Close the Customer table.

3. Create a split form for the Courier table. Use the name Courier for the form.

4. Open the form you created and change the street address for Michelle Hyde to 65 Park.

5. Close the Courier form.

6. Create the report shown in Figure 1–100 for the Customer table. The report uses the Module style.

7. Change the database properties, as specified by your instructor. Submit the revised database in the format specified by your instructor.

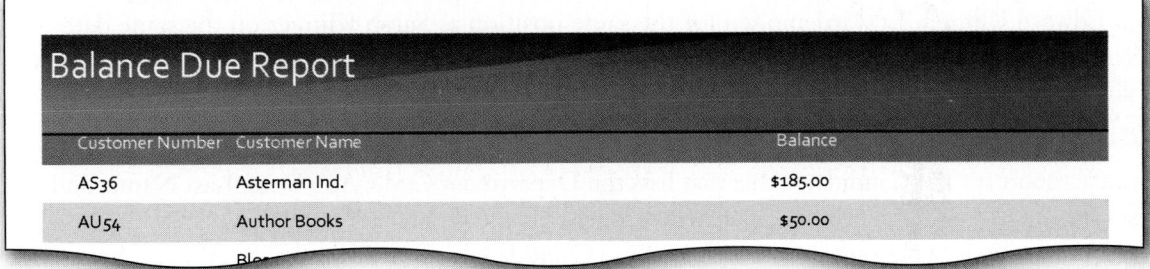

Figure 1–100

Extend Your Knowledge

Extend the skills you learned in this chapter and experiment with new skills. You may need to use Help to complete the assignment.

Changing Formats and Creating Grouped and Sorted Reports

Instructions: Start Access. Open the Camden Scott College database. See the inside back cover of this book for instructions for downloading the Data Files for Students, or see your instructor for information on accessing the files required in this book.

Continued >

Extend Your Knowledge *continued*

Camden Scott College is a small liberal arts college. The Human Resources Director has created an Access database in which to store information about candidates applying for faculty positions. You will make some changes to the Candidate table so that it looks like that shown in Figure 1–101 and create a report that both groups records and sorts them in ascending order.

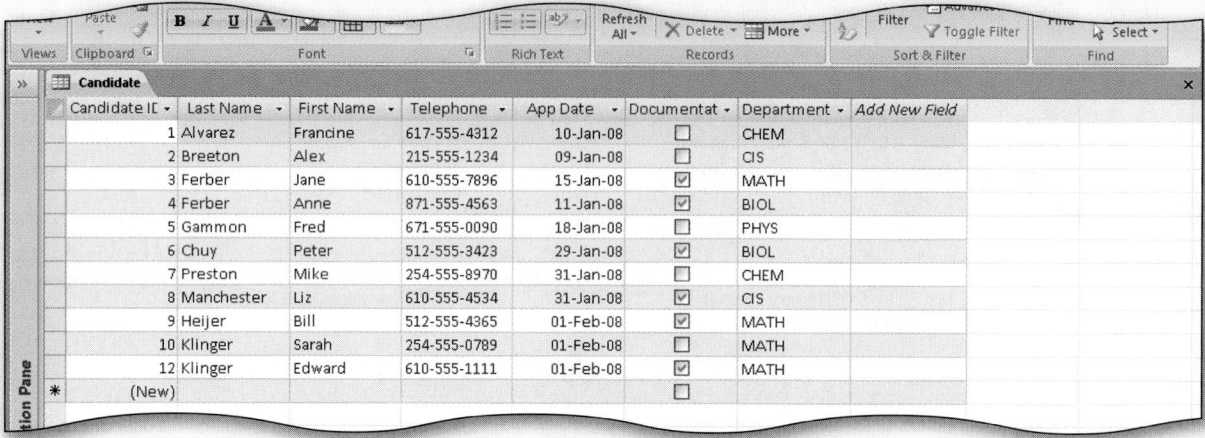

Figure 1–101

Perform the following tasks:

1. Open the Candidate table in Datasheet view and change the column heading for the ID field to Candidate ID.

2. Save the change and open the table in Design view.

3. Select a format for the App Date field that will produce the look shown in Figure 1–101.

4. Change the data type for the Documentation field so that it will match that shown in Figure 1–101.

5. Save the changes.

6. Open the table in Datasheet view. The Human Resources department has received an application from Edward Klinger. Edward applied for the same position as Sarah Klinger on the same date as Sarah. Edward's phone number is 610-555-1111. He did submit all his documentation with his application. Add this record.

7. Add the Quick Print button to the Quick Access Toolbar.

8. Create a report for the Candidate table that lists the Department Code, App Date, Last Name, and First Name. Group the report by Department Code. Sort the report by App Date, Last Name, and then First Name. Choose your own report style and use Candidate by Department as the title of the report.

9. Remove the Quick Print button from the Quick Access Toolbar.

10. Change the database properties, as specified by your instructor. Submit the revised database in the format specified by your instructor.

Make It Right

Analyze a database and correct all errors and/or improve the design.

Correcting Errors in the Table Structure

Instructions: Start Access. Open the SciFi Scene database. See the inside back cover of this book for instructions for downloading the Data Files for Students, or see your instructor for information on accessing the files required in this book.

SciFi Scene is a database containing information on science fiction books. The Book table shown in Figure 1–102 contains a number of errors in the table structure. You are to correct these errors before any additional records can be added to the table. Book Code, not ID, is the primary key for the Book table. The column heading Titel is misspelled. The On Hand field represents the number of books on hand. The field will be used in arithmetic operations. Only whole numbers should be stored in the field. The Price field represents the price of the book. The current data type does not reflect this information.

Change the database properties, as specified by your instructor. Submit the revised database in the format specified by your instructor.

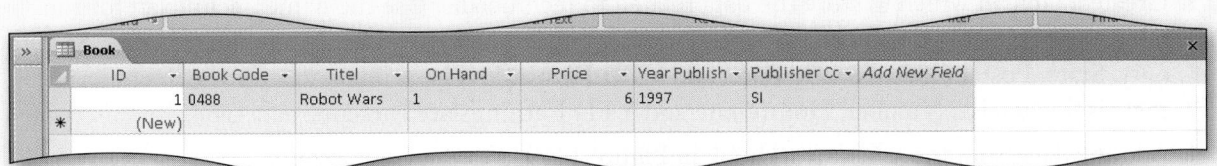

ID	Book Code	Titel	On Hand	Price	Year Publish	Publisher Cc	Add New Field
1	0488	Robot Wars	1		6 1997	SI	
*	(New)						

Figure 1–102

In the Lab

Design, create, modify, and/or use a database using the guidelines, concepts, and skills presented in this chapter. Labs are listed in order of increasing difficulty.

Lab 1: Creating the JMS TechWizards Database

Problem: JMS TechWizards is a local company that provides technical services to several small businesses in the area. The company currently keeps its records in two Excel workbooks. One Excel workbook (Figure 1–103a) contains information on the clients that JMS TechWizards serves. The other Excel workbook (Figure 1–103b) contains information on the technicians that JMS employs. JMS would like to store this data in a database and has asked for your help.

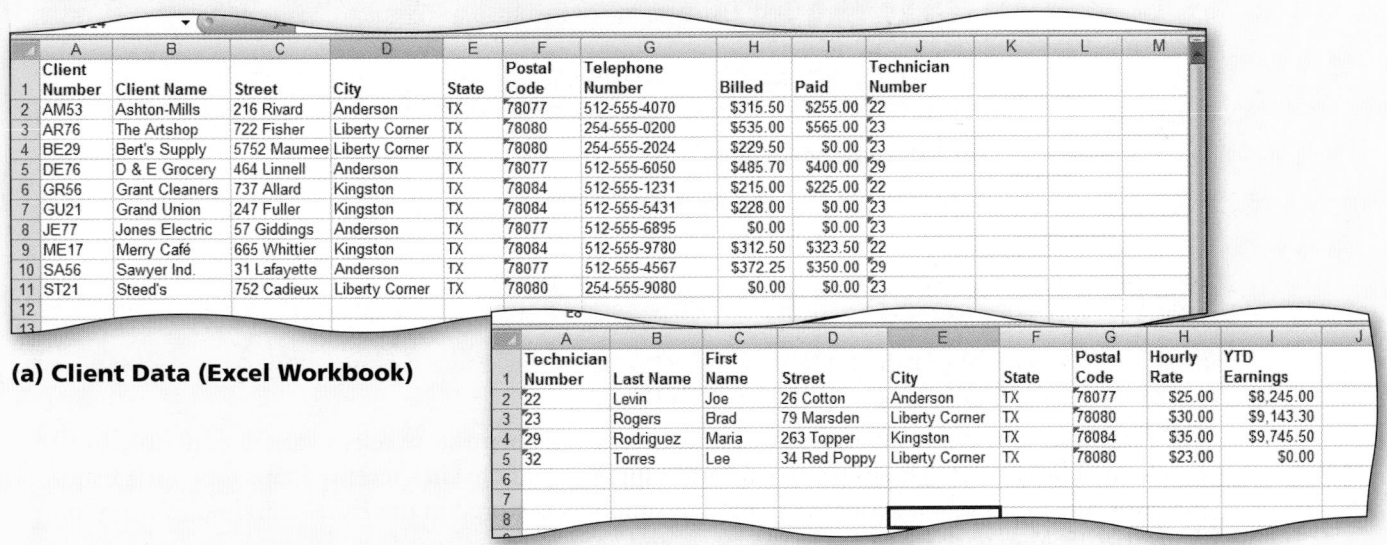

	A	B	C	D	E	F	G	H	I	J	K	L	M
1	Client Number	Client Name	Street	City	State	Postal Code	Telephone Number	Billed	Paid	Technician Number			
2	AM53	Ashton-Mills	216 Rivard	Anderson	TX	78077	512-555-4070	$315.50	$255.00	22			
3	AR76	The Artshop	722 Fisher	Liberty Corner	TX	78080	254-555-0200	$535.00	$565.00	23			
4	BE29	Bert's Supply	5752 Maumee	Liberty Corner	TX	78080	254-555-2024	$229.50	$0.00	23			
5	DE76	D & E Grocery	464 Linnell	Anderson	TX	78077	512-555-6050	$485.70	$400.00	29			
6	GR56	Grant Cleaners	737 Allard	Kingston	TX	78084	512-555-1231	$215.00	$225.00	22			
7	GU21	Grand Union	247 Fuller	Kingston	TX	78084	512-555-5431	$228.00	$0.00	23			
8	JE77	Jones Electric	57 Giddings	Anderson	TX	78077	512-555-6895	$0.00	$0.00	23			
9	ME17	Merry Café	665 Whittier	Kingston	TX	78084	512-555-9780	$312.50	$323.50	22			
10	SA56	Sawyer Ind.	31 Lafayette	Anderson	TX	78077	512-555-4567	$372.25	$350.00	29			
11	ST21	Steed's	752 Cadieux	Liberty Corner	TX	78080	254-555-9080	$0.00	$0.00	23			
12													

(a) Client Data (Excel Workbook)

	A	B	C	D	E	F	G	H	I	J
1	Technician Number	Last Name	First Name	Street	City	State	Postal Code	Hourly Rate	YTD Earnings	
2	22	Levin	Joe	26 Cotton	Anderson	TX	78077	$25.00	$8,245.00	
3	23	Rogers	Brad	79 Marsden	Liberty Corner	TX	78080	$30.00	$9,143.30	
4	29	Rodriguez	Maria	263 Topper	Kingston	TX	78084	$35.00	$9,745.50	
5	32	Torres	Lee	34 Red Poppy	Liberty Corner	TX	78080	$23.00	$0.00	

(b) Technician Data (Excel Workbook)

Figure 1–103

Continued >

In the Lab *continued*

Instructions: Perform the following tasks:

1. Create a new database in which to store all the objects related to the technical services data. Call the database JMS TechWizards.

2. Create a table in which to store the data related to clients. Use the name Client for the table. The fields for the Client table are: Client Number, Client Name, Street, City, State, Postal Code, Telephone Number, Billed, Paid, and Technician Number. Client Number is the primary key. The Billed and Paid fields are currency data type.

3. Create a table in which to store the data related to technicians. Use the name Technician for the table. The fields for the Technician table are: Technician Number, Last Name, First Name, Street, City, State, Postal Code, Hourly Rate, and YTD Earnings. The primary key for the Technician table is Technician Number. Hourly rate and YTD Earnings are currency data type.

4. Add the data from the Client workbook in Figure 1–103a to the Client table.

5. Add the data from the Technician workbook in Figure 1–103b to the Technician table.

6. Create and save the reports shown in Figure 1–104a for the Client table and Figure 1–104b for the Technician table.

7. Change the database properties, as specified by your instructor. Submit the revised database in the format specified by your instructor.

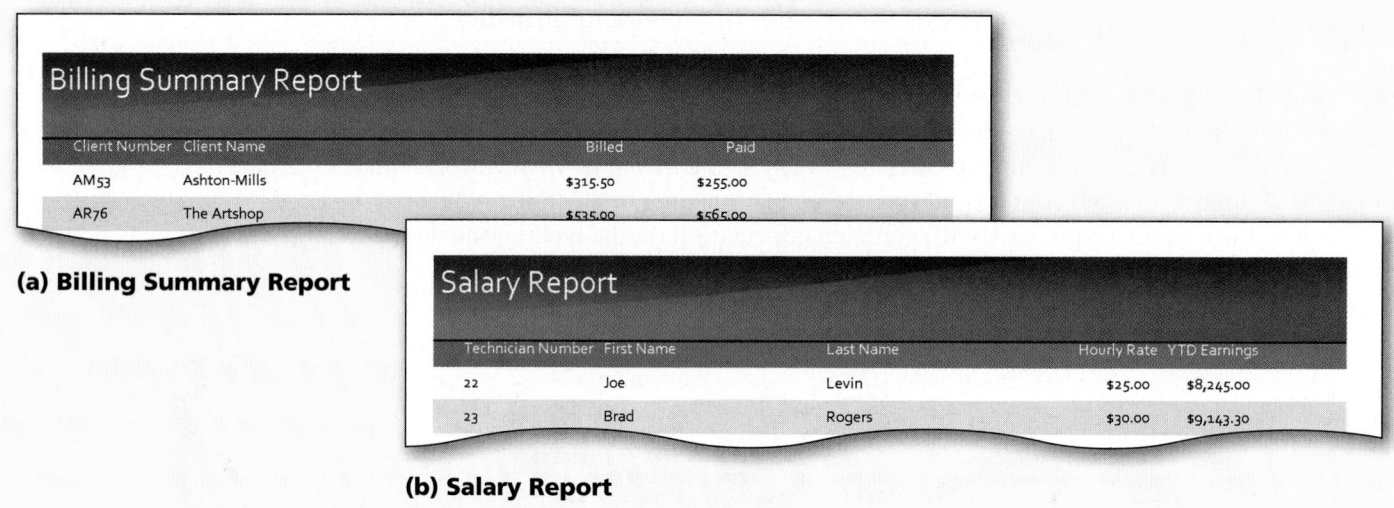

(a) Billing Summary Report

(b) Salary Report

Figure 1–104

In the Lab

Lab 2: Creating the Hockey Fan Zone Database

Problem: Your town has a minor league hockey team. The team store sells a variety of items with the team logo. The store purchases the items from suppliers that deal in specialty items for sports teams. Currently, the information about the items and suppliers is stored in the Excel workbook shown in Figure 1–105. You work part-time at the store, and your boss has asked you to create a database that will store the item and supplier information. You have already determined that you need two tables: an Item table and a Supplier table in which to store the information.

Instructions: Perform the following tasks:

1. Design a new database in which to store all the objects related to the items for sale. Call the database Hockey Fan Zone.

2. Use the information shown in Figure 1–105 to determine the primary keys and determine additional fields. Then, determine the relationships among tables and the data types.

3. Create the Item table using the information shown in Figure 1–105.

4. Create the Supplier table using the information shown in Figure 1–105.

5. Add the appropriate data to the Item table.

6. Add the appropriate data to the Supplier table.

7. Create a split form for the Item table. Use the name Item for the form.

8. Create the report shown in Figure 1–106 for the Item table.

9. Change the database properties, as specified by your instructor. Submit the database in the format specified by your instructor.

	A	B	C	D	E	F	G	H
1	Item Number	Description	On Hand	Cost	Selling Price	Supplier Code	Supplier Name	Telephone Number
2	3663	Ball Cap	30	$11.15	$18.95	LG	Logo Goods	517-555-3853
3	3683	Bumper Sticker	50	$0.95	$1.50	MN	Mary's Novelties	317-555-4747
4	4563	Earrings	10	$4.50	$7.00	LG	Logo Goods	517-555-3853
5	4593	Foam Finger	25	$2.95	$5.00	LG	Logo Goods	517-555-3853
6	5923	Jersey	12	$21.45	$24.75	AC	Ace Clothes	616-555-9228
7	6189	Koozies	35	$2.00	$4.00	MN	Mary's Novelties	317-555-4747
8	6343	Note Cube	7	$5.75	$8.00	MN	Mary's Novelties	317-555-4747
9	7810	Tee Shirt	32	$9.50	$14.95	AC	Ace Clothes	616-555-9228
10	7930	Visor	9	$11.95	$17.00	LG	Logo Goods	517-555-3853
11								

Figure 1–105

Inventory Status Report

Item Number	Description	On Hand	Cost
3663	Ball Cap	30	$11.15
3683	Bumper Sticker	50	$0.95
4563	Earrings	10	$4.50
4593	Foam Finger	25	$2.95
5923	Jersey	12	$21.45
6189	Koozies	35	$2.00
6343	Note Cube	7	$5.75
7810	Tee Shirt	32	$9.50
7930	Visor	9	$11.95

Figure 1–106

In the Lab

Lab 3: Creating the Ada Beauty Supply Database

Problem: A distribution company supplies local beauty salons with items needed in the beauty industry. The distributor employs sales representatives who receive a base salary as well as a commission on sales. Currently, the distributor keeps data on customers and sales reps in two Word documents and two Excel workbooks.

Instructions: Using the data shown in Figure 1–107 on the next page, design the Ada Beauty Supply database. Use the database design guidelines in this chapter to help you in the design process.

Continued >

STUDENT ASSIGNMENTS

In the Lab *continued*

Customer Number	Customer Name	Street	Telephone
AM23	Amy's Salon	223 Johnson	555-2150
BB34	Bob the Barber	1939 Jackson	555-1939
BL15	Blondie's	3294 Devon	555-7510
CM09	Cut Mane	3140 Halsted	555-0604
CS12	Curl n Style	1632 Clark	555-0804
EG07	Elegante	1805 Boardway	555-1404
JS34	Just Cuts	2200 Lawrence	555-0313
LB20	Le Beauty	13 Devon	555-5161
NC25	Nancy's Place	1027 Wells	555-4210
RD03	Rose's Day Spa	787 Monroe	555-7657
TT21	Tan and Tone	1939 Congress	555-6554

(a) Customer Address Information (Word table)

E15

	A	B	C	D	E
1	Customer Number	Customer Name	Balance	Amount Paid	Sales Rep Nur
2	AM23	Amy's Salon	$195.00	$1,695.00	44
3	BB34	Bob the Barber	$150.00	$0.00	51
4	BL15	Blondie's	$555.00	$1,350.00	49
5	CM09	Cut Mane	$295.00	$1,080.00	51
6	CS12	Curl n Style	$145.00	$710.00	49
7	EG07	Elegante	$0.00	$1,700.00	44
8	JS34	Just Cuts	$360.00	$700.00	49
9	LB20	Le Beauty	$200.00	$1,250.00	51
10	NC25	Nancy's Place	$240.00	$550.00	44
11	RD03	Rose's Day Spa	$0.00	$975.00	51
12	TT21	Tan and Tone	$160.00	$725.00	44
13					
14					
15					
16					

(c) Customer Financial Information (Excel Workbook)

Sales Rep Number	Last Name	First Name	Street	City	State	Postal Code
44	Jones	Pat	43 Third	Lawncrest	WA	98084
49	Gupta	Pinn	678 Hillcrest	Manton	WA	98085
51	Ortiz	Gabe	982 Victoria	Lawncrest	WA	98084
55	Sinson	Terry	45 Elm	Manton	WA	98084

(b) Sales Rep Address Information (Word table)

	A	B	C	D	E	F
1	Sales Rep Number	Last Name	First Name	Salary	Comm Rate	Commission
2	44	Jones	Pat	$ 23,000.00	0.05	$613.50
3	49	Gupta	Pinn	$ 24,000.00	0.06	$616.60
4	51	Ortiz	Gabe	$ 22,500.00	0.05	$492.75
5	55	Sinson	Terry	$ 20,000.00	0.05	$0.00
6						

(d) Sales Rep Financial Information (Excel Workbook)

Figure 1–107

When you have completed the database design, create the database, create the tables, and add the data to the appropriate tables. Be sure to determine the correct data types.

Finally, prepare the Customer Status Report shown in Figure 1–108a and the Sales Rep Salary Report shown in Figure 1–108b. Change the database properties, as specified by your instructor. Submit the database in the format specified by your instructor.

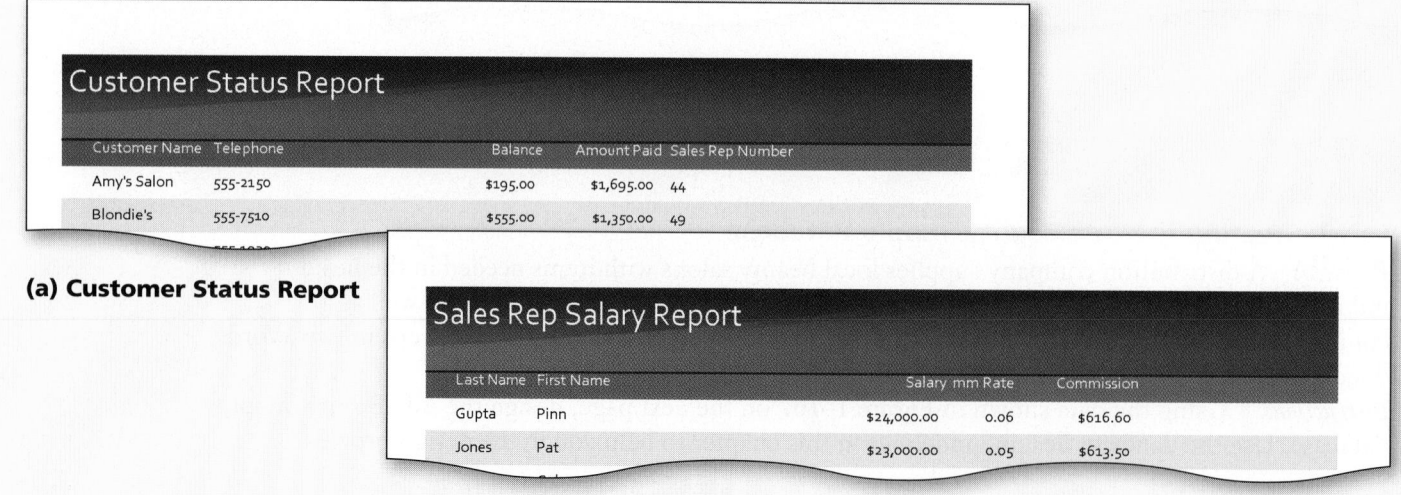

Customer Status Report

Customer Name	Telephone	Balance	Amount Paid	Sales Rep Number
Amy's Salon	555-2150	$195.00	$1,695.00	44
Blondie's	555-7510	$555.00	$1,350.00	49

(a) Customer Status Report

Sales Rep Salary Report

Last Name	First Name	Salary	mm Rate	Commission
Gupta	Pinn	$24,000.00	0.06	$616.60
Jones	Pat	$23,000.00	0.05	$613.50

(b) Sales Rep Salary Report

Figure 1–108

Cases and Places

Apply your creative thinking and problem solving skills to design and implement a solution.

• Easier   •• More Difficult

• 1: Design and Create an E-Commerce Database

Students often have very little money to furnish dorm rooms and apartments. You and two of your friends have decided to use the skills you learned in your e-commerce class to create a Web site specifically for college students to buy and sell used household furnishings.

Design and create a database to store the data that you need to manage this new business. Then create the necessary tables and enter the data from the Case 1-1 Second-Hand Goods document. See the inside back cover of this book for instructions for downloading the Data Files for Students, or see your instructor for information on accessing the files required in this book. Submit your assignment in the format specified by your instructor.

• 2: Design and Create a Rental Database

You are a part-time employee of BeachCondo Rentals. BeachCondo Rentals provides a rental service for condo owners who want to rent their units. The company rents units by the week. Currently, the company keeps information about its rentals in an Excel workbook.

Design and create a database to store the rental data. Then create the necessary tables and enter the data from the Case 1-2 BeachCondo Rentals workbook. See the inside back cover of this book for instructions for downloading the Data Files for Students, or see your instructor for information on accessing the files required in this book. Create an Available Rentals Report that lists the unit number, weekly rate, and owner number. Submit your assignment in the format specified by your instructor.

•• 3: Design and Create a Restaurant Database

Your school is sponsoring a conference that will draw participants from a wide geographical area. The conference director has asked for your help in preparing a database of restaurants that might be of interest to the participants. At a minimum, she needs to know the following: the type of restaurant (vegetarian, fast-food, fine dining, and so on), street address, telephone number, and opening and closing times and days. Because most of the participants will stay on campus, she also would like to know the approximate distance from campus. Additionally, she would like to know about any unique or special features the restaurants may have.

Design and create a database to meet the conference director's needs. Create the necessary tables, determine the necessary fields, enter some sample data, and prepare a sample report to show the director. Submit your assignment in the format specified by your instructor.

•• 4: Design and Create a Database to Help You Find a Job

Make It Personal

Conducting a job search requires careful preparation. In addition to preparing a resume and cover letter, you will need to research the companies for which you are interested in working and contact these companies to let them know of your interest and qualifications.

Microsoft Access includes a Contacts table template that can create a table that will help you keep track of your job contacts. Create a database to keep track of the companies that are of interest to you. Submit your assignment in the format specified by your instructor.

Continued >

Cases and Places *continued*

•• 5: Design a Database that Tracks Student Data

Working Together

Keeping track of students is an enormous task for school administrators. Microsoft Access can help school administrators manage student data. The Database Wizard includes a Students template that can create a database that will maintain many different types of data on students, such as allergies, medications, and emergency contact information.

Have each member of your team explore the features of the Database Wizard and determine individually which tables and fields should be included in a Students database. As a group, review your choices and decide on one common design. Prepare a short paper for your instructor that explains why your team chose the particular database design.

After agreeing on the database design, assign one member to create the database using the Database Wizard. Every other team member should contribute data and add the data to the database. Submit your assignment in the format specified by your instructor.

2 | Querying a Database

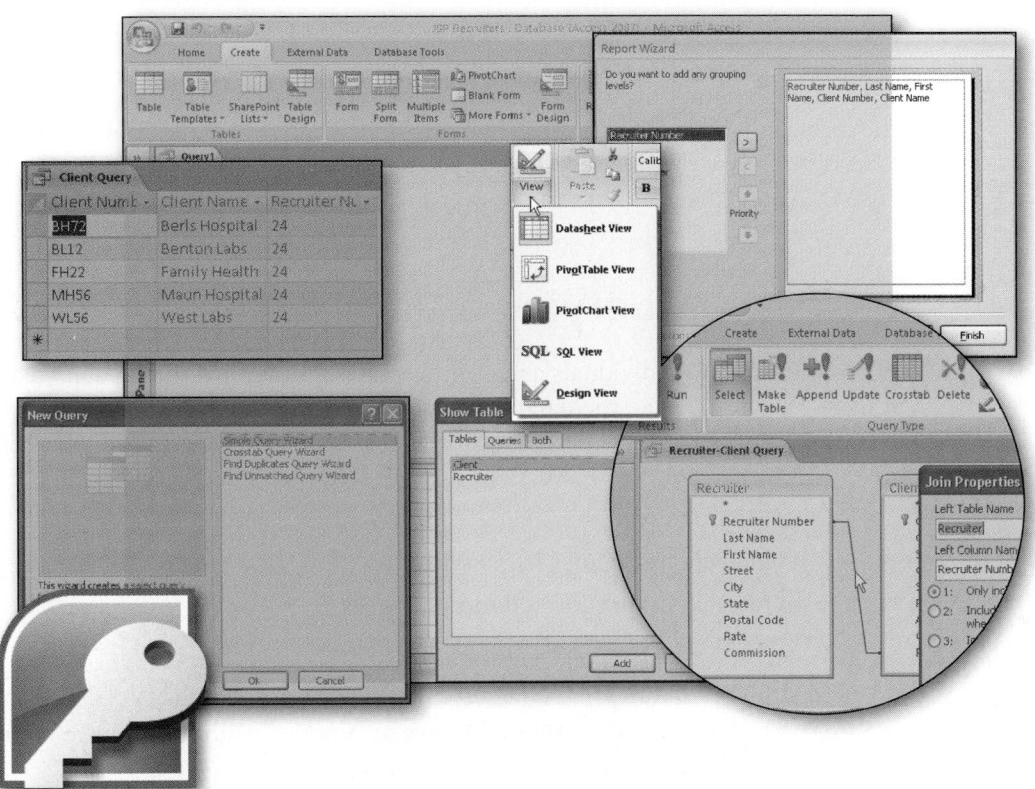

Objectives

You will have mastered the material in this chapter when you can:

- Create queries using the Simple Query Wizard
- Print query results
- Create queries using Design view
- Include fields in the design grid
- Use text and numeric data in criteria
- Create and use parameter queries
- Save a query and use the saved query

- Use compound criteria in queries
- Sort data in queries
- Join tables in queries
- Create a report from a query
- Perform calculations in queries
- Calculate statistics in queries
- Create crosstab queries
- Customize the Navigation Pane

2 | Querying a Database

Introduction

A database management system such as Access offers many useful features, among them the capability of answering questions, the answers to which are found in the database. When you pose a question to Access, or any other database management system, the question is called a query. A **query** is simply a question presented in a way that Access can process.

Thus, to find the answer to a question, you first create a corresponding query using the techniques illustrated in this chapter. After you have created the query, you instruct Access to display the query results; that is, to perform the steps necessary to obtain the answer. Access then displays the answer in Datasheet view.

Project — Querying a Database

Organizations and individuals achieve several benefits from storing data in a database and using Access to manage the database. One of the most important benefits is the capability of easily finding the answers to questions such as those shown in Figure 2-1 and the following, which concern the data in the JSP Recruiters database:

1. What are the number, name, the amount paid, and the current due of client FD89?
2. Which clients' names begin with Be?
3. Which clients are located in Berridge?
4. Which clients have a current due of $0.00?
5. Which clients have an amount paid that is more than $20,000.00?
6. Which clients of recruiter 21 have an amount paid that is more than $20,000.00?
7. In what cities are all the clients located?
8. What is the total amount (amount paid + current due) for each client?
9. What is the client number and name of each client, and what is the number and name of the recruiter to whom each client is assigned?

In addition to these questions, JSP Recruiters needs to find information about clients located in a specific city, but they want to enter a different city each time they ask the question. A parameter query would enable this. The agency also has a special way it wants to summarize data. A crosstab query will present the data in the desired form.

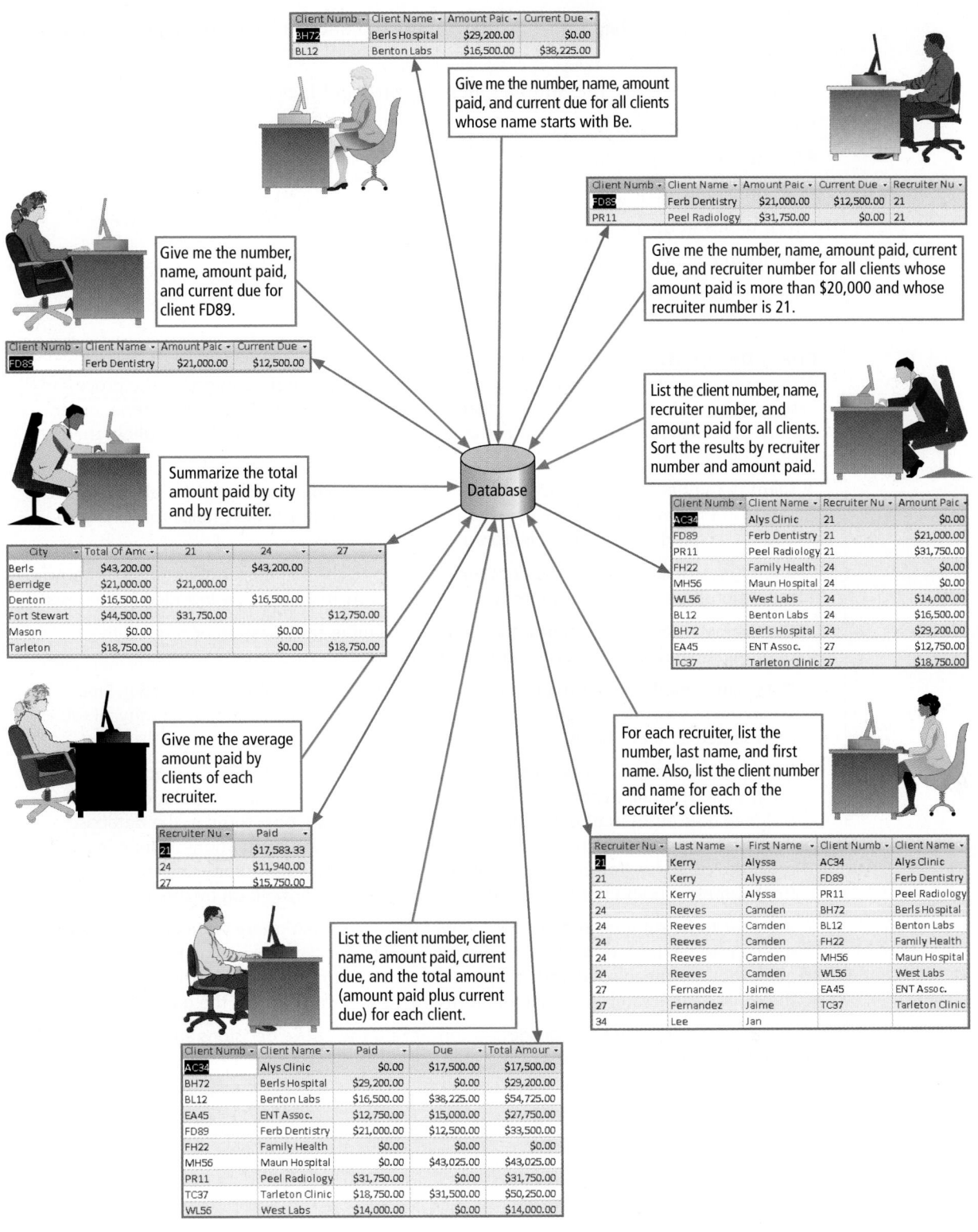

Figure 2–1

Overview

As you read this chapter, you will learn how to query a database by performing these general tasks:

- Create queries using the Simple Query Wizard and Design view
- Use criteria in queries
- Create and use parameter queries
- Sort data in queries
- Join tables in queries
- Perform calculations in queries
- Create crosstab queries

Plan Ahead

> **Query Design Guidelines**
>
> When posing a question to Access, you must design an appropriate query. In the process of designing a query, the decisions you make will determine the fields, tables, criteria, order, and special calculations included in the query. To design a query, you should follow these general guidelines:
>
> 1. **Identify the fields.** Examine the question or request to determine which fields from the tables in the database are involved. Examine the contents of these fields to make sure you understand how the data is stored.
>
> 2. **Identify restrictions.** Unless the question or request calls for all records, determine the restrictions, that is, the conditions records must satisfy in order to be included in the results.
>
> 3. **Determine whether special order is required.** Examine the question or request to determine whether the results must appear in some specific order.
>
> 4. **Determine whether more than one table is required.** If all the fields identified in Step 1 are in the same table, no special action is required. If this is not the case, identify all tables represented by those fields.
>
> 5. **Determine whether calculations are required.** Examine the question or request to determine whether, in addition to the fields determined in Step 1, calculations must be included. Results of mathematical operations typically are not stored in the database because they can be calculated easily when necessary. Such calculations include individual record calculations (for example, adding the values in two fields) or group calculations (for example, finding the total of the values in a particular field on all the records).
>
> 6. **If data is to be summarized, determine whether a crosstab query would be appropriate.** If data is to be grouped by two different types of information, you can use a crosstab query. You will need to identify the two types of information. One of the types will form the row headings and the other will form the column headings in the query results.
>
> When necessary, more specific details concerning the above decisions and/or actions are presented at appropriate points in the chapter.

Starting Access

If you are using a computer to step through the project in this chapter and you want your screen to match the figures in this book, you should change your screen's resolution to 1024 × 768. For information about how to change a computer's resolution, read Appendix E.

To Start Access

The following steps, which assume Windows Vista is running, start Access.

Note: If you are using Windows XP, see Appendix F for alternate steps.

1 Click the Start button on the Windows Vista taskbar to display the Start menu.

2 Click All Programs at the bottom of the left Pane on the Start menu to display the All Programs list and then click Microsoft Office in the All Programs list to display the Microsoft Office list.

3 Click Microsoft Office Access 2007 on the Microsoft Office list to start Access and display the Getting Started with Microsoft Office Access window.

4 If the Access window is not maximized, click the Maximize button on its title bar to maximize the window.

To Open a Database

In Chapter 1, you created your database on a USB flash drive using the file name, JSP Recruiters. There are two ways to open the file containing your database. If the file you created appears in the Recent Documents list, you can click it to open the file. If not, you can use the More button to open the file. The following steps use the More button to open the JSP Recruiters database from the USB flash drive.

Note: If you are using Windows XP, see Appendix F for alternate steps.

1 With your USB flash drive connected to one of the computer's USB ports, click the More button to display the Open dialog box.

2 If the Folders list is displayed below the Folders button, click the Folders button to remove the Folders list.

3 If necessary, click Computer in the Favorite Links section and then double-click UDISK 2.0 (E:) to select the USB flash drive, Drive E in this case, as the new open location. (Your drive letter might be different.)

4 Click JSP Recruiters to select the file name.

5 Click the Open button to open the database.

6 If a Security Warning appears, click the Options button to display the Microsoft Office Security Options dialog box.

7 With the option button to enable this content selected, click the OK button to enable the content.

Creating Queries

Queries are simply questions, the answers to which are in the database. Access contains a powerful query feature. Through the use of this feature, you can find the answers to a wide variety of complex questions.

To Use the Simple Query Wizard to Create a Query

Once you have examined the question you wish to ask to determine the fields involved in the question, you can begin creating the query. If there are no restrictions involved in the query, nor any special order or calculations, you can use the Simple Query wizard. The following steps use the Simple Query wizard to create a query to display the number, name, and recruiter number of all clients.

- If the Navigation Pane is hidden, click the Shutter Bar Open/Close Button to show the Navigation Pane.

- Be sure the Client table is selected.

- Click Create on the Ribbon to display the Create tab.

- Click the Query Wizard button on the Create tab to display the New Query dialog box (Figure 2–2).

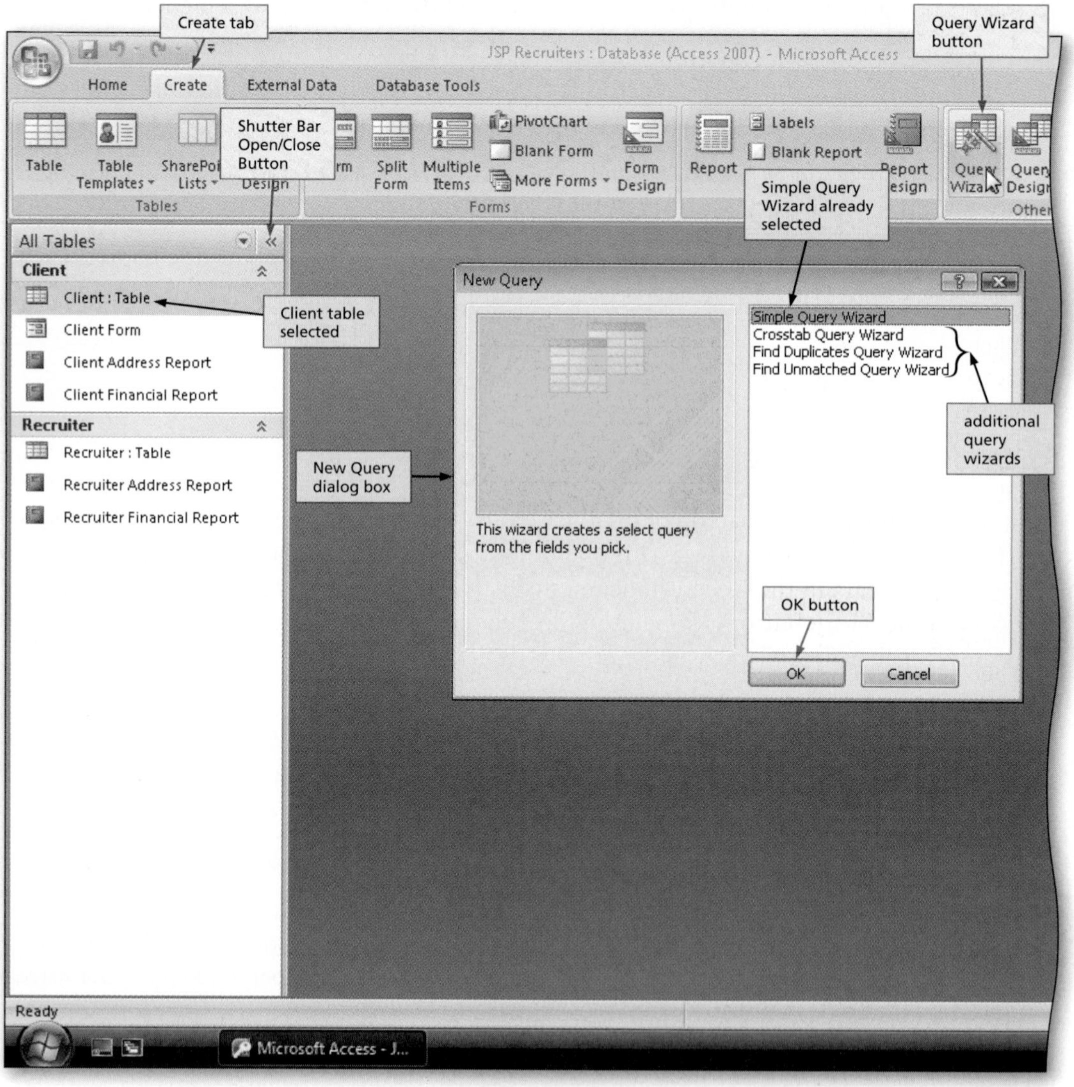

Figure 2–2

- Be sure Simple Query Wizard is selected, and then click the OK button to display the Simple Query Wizard dialog box (Figure 2–3).

Q&A

This looks like the screen I saw in the Report Wizard. Do I select fields in the same way?

Yes. In fact, you will see a similar screen in other wizards and you always select the fields just as you did in the Report Wizard.

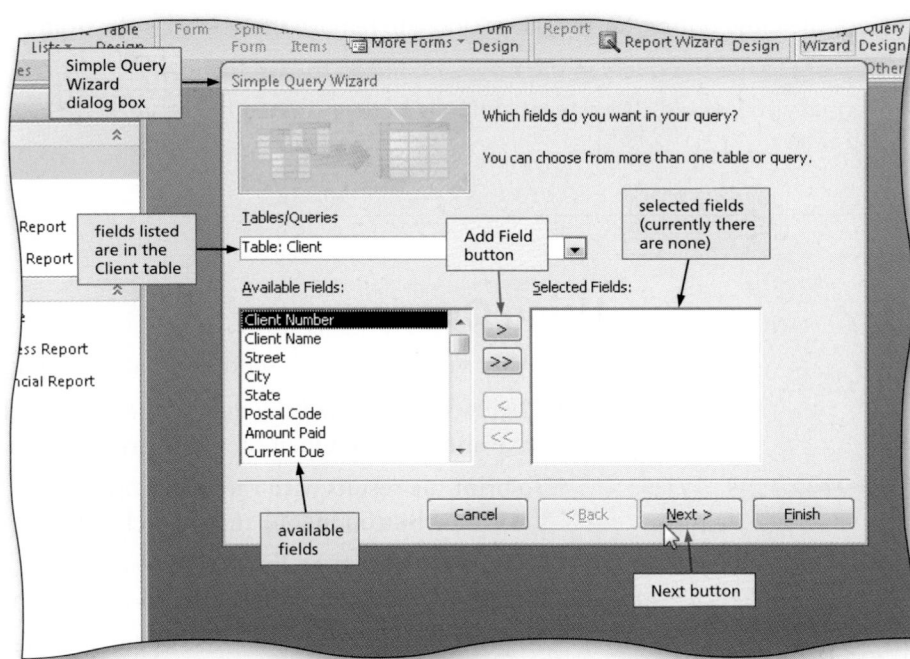

Figure 2–3

- Click the Add Field button to add the Client Number field.

- Click the Add Field button a second time to add the Client Name field.

- Click the Recruiter Number field, and then click the Add Field button to add the Recruiter Number field.

- Click the Next button.

- Be sure the title of the query is Client Query.

- Click the Finish button to create the query (Figure 2–4).

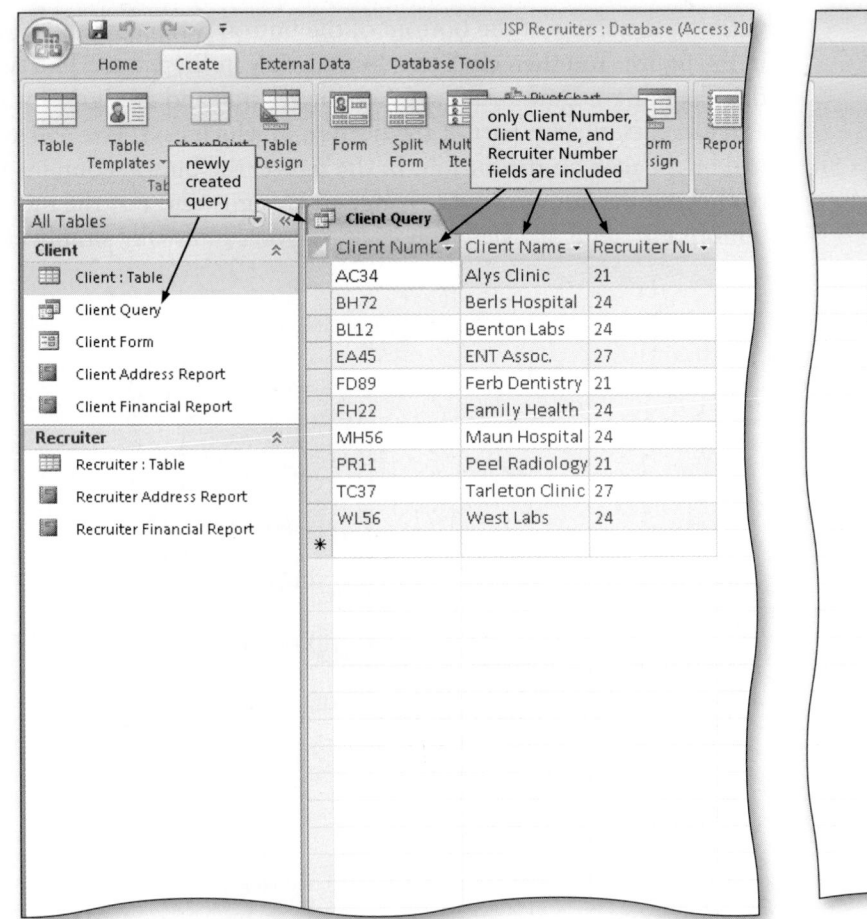
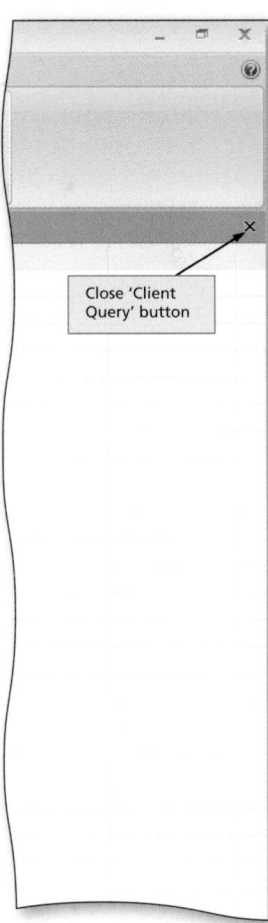

Figure 2–4

4

- Click the Close button for the Client Query to remove the query results from the screen.

Q&A

If I want to use this query in the future, do I need to save the query?

Normally you would. The one exception is a query created by the wizard. The wizard automatically saves the query it creates.

Using Queries

After you have created and saved a query, you can use it in a variety of ways:

- To view the results of the query, open it by right-clicking the query in the Navigation Pane and clicking Open on the shortcut menu.
- To print the results with the query open, click the Office Button, point to Print on the Office Button menu, and then click Quick Print on the Print submenu.
- If you want to change the design of the query, right-click the query and then click Design View on the shortcut menu to open the query in Design view.
- To print the query without first opening it, be sure the query is selected in the Navigation Pane and then click the Office Button, point to Print on the Office Button menu, and then click Quick Print on the Print submenu.

You can switch between views of a query by using the View button (Figure 2–5). Clicking the arrow at the bottom of the button produces the View button menu as shown in the figure. You then click the desired view in the menu. The two views you will use in this chapter are Datasheet view (see the results) and Design view (change the design). You also can click the top part of the button, in which case, you will switch to the view identified by the icon on the button. In the figure, the button contains the icon for Design view, so clicking the button would change to Design view. For the most part, the icon on the button represents the view you want, so you can usually simply click the button.

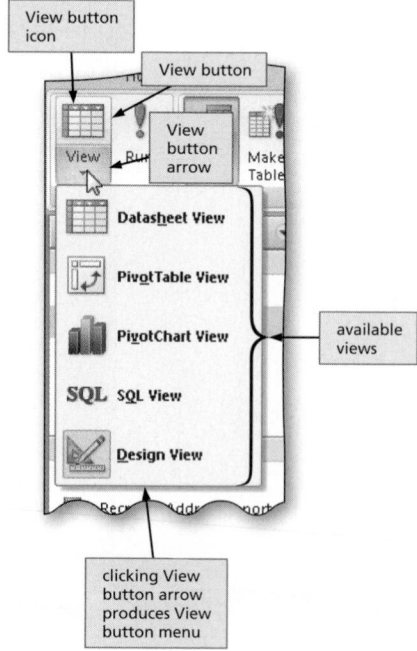

Figure 2–5

To Use a Criterion in a Query

After you have determined the fields to be included in a query, you will determine whether there are any restrictions on the records that are to be included. For example, you might only want to include those clients whose recruiter number is 24. In such a case, you need to enter the 24 as a **criterion**, which is a condition that the records to be included must satisfy. To do so, you will open the query in Design view, enter the criterion below the appropriate field, and then view the results of the query. The following steps enter a criterion to include only the clients of recruiter 24 and then view the query results.

1

- Right-click Client Query to produce a shortcut menu (Figure 2–6).

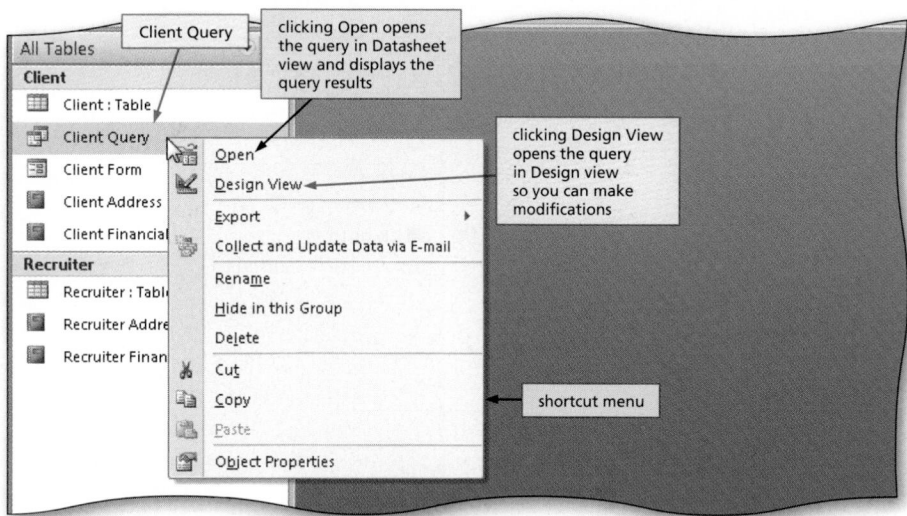

Figure 2–6

2

- Click Design View on the shortcut menu to open the query in Design view (Figure 2–7). (Your field names may be enclosed in brackets.)

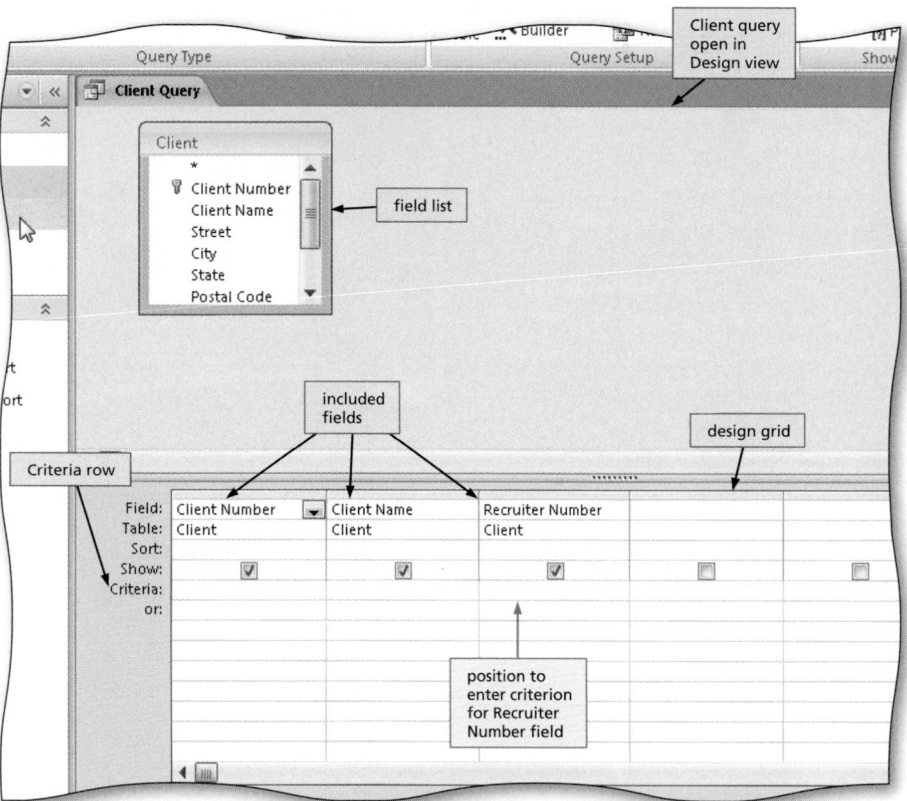

Figure 2–7

● Click the Criteria row in the Recruiter Number column of the grid, and then type 24 as the criterion (Figure 2–8).

Q&A

The Recruiter Number field is a text field. Do I need to enclose the value for a text field in quotation marks?

You could, but it is not necessary, because Access inserts the quotation marks for you automatically.

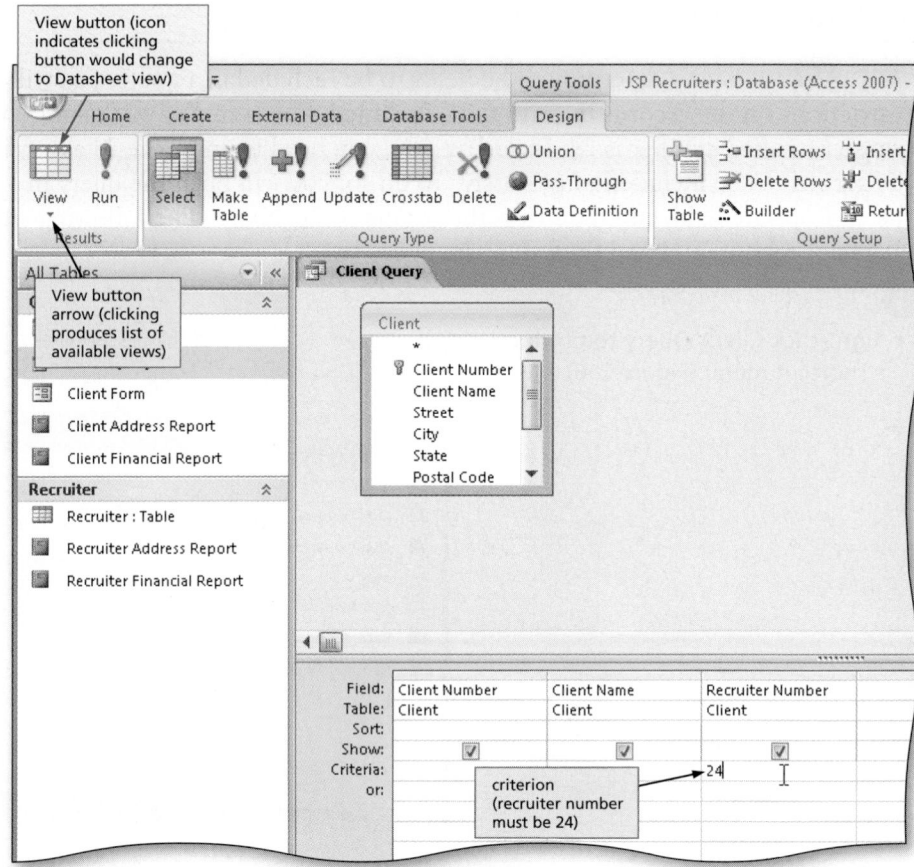

Figure 2–8

● Click the View button to display the results in Datasheet view (Figure 2–9).

Q&A

Could I click the View button arrow and then click Datasheet view?

Yes. If the icon representing the view you want appears on the View button, however, it is easier just to click the button.

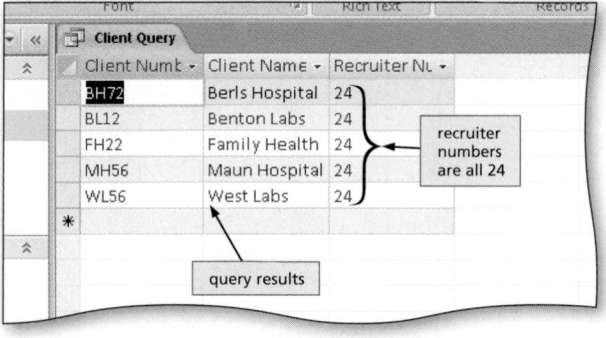

Figure 2–9

● Close the Client Query window by clicking the Close 'Client Query' button.

● When asked if you want to save your changes, click the No button.

Q&A

If I saved the query, what would happen the next time I ran the query?

You would see only clients of recruiter 24.

Other Ways

1. Click Run button on Ribbon
2. Click Datasheet View button on status bar

To Print the Results of a Query

To print the results of a query, use the same techniques you learned in Chapter 1 on pages AC 41 and AC 42 to print the data in the table. The following steps print the current query results.

1 With the Client Query selected in the Navigation Pane, click the Office Button.

2 Point to Print on the Office Button menu.

3 Click Quick Print on the Print submenu.

To Create a Query in Design View

Most of the time you will use Design view to create queries. Once you have created a new query in Design view, you can specify fields, criteria, sorting, calculations, and so on. The following steps create a new query in Design view.

1

- Hide the Navigation Pane.

- Click Create on the Ribbon to display the Create tab.

- Click the Query Design button to create a new query (Figure 2–10).

Q&A

Is it necessary to hide the Navigation Pane?

No. It gives you more room for the query, however, so it is usually a good practice to hide it.

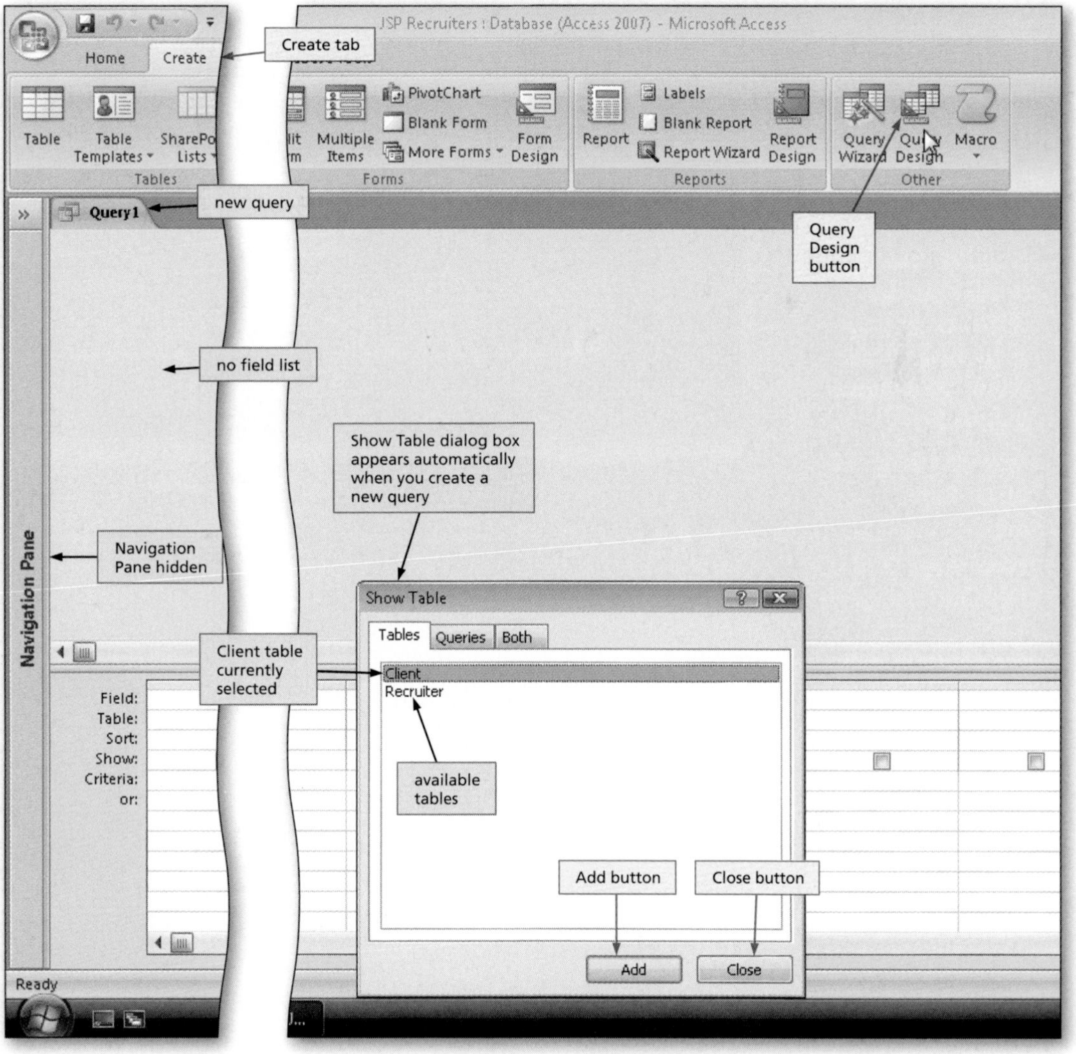

Figure 2–10

2

- With the Client table selected, click the Add button in the Show Table dialog box to add the Client table to the query.

- Click the Close button in the Show Table dialog box to remove the dialog box from the screen.

Q&A What if I inadvertently add the wrong table?

Right-click the table that you added in error and click Remove Table on the shortcut menu. You also can just close the query, indicate that you don't want to save it, and then start over.

- Drag the lower edge of the field box down far enough so all fields in the Client table appear (Figure 2–11).

Q&A How do I drag the lower edge?

Point to the lower edge, press and hold the left mouse button, move the mouse pointer to the new position for the lower edge, and then release the left mouse button. While the mouse pointer points to the lower edge of the field list, its shape changes to a double-headed arrow.

Q&A Is it essential that I resize the field box?

No. You can always scroll through the list of fields using the scroll bar. If you can resize the field box so all fields appear, it is usually more convenient.

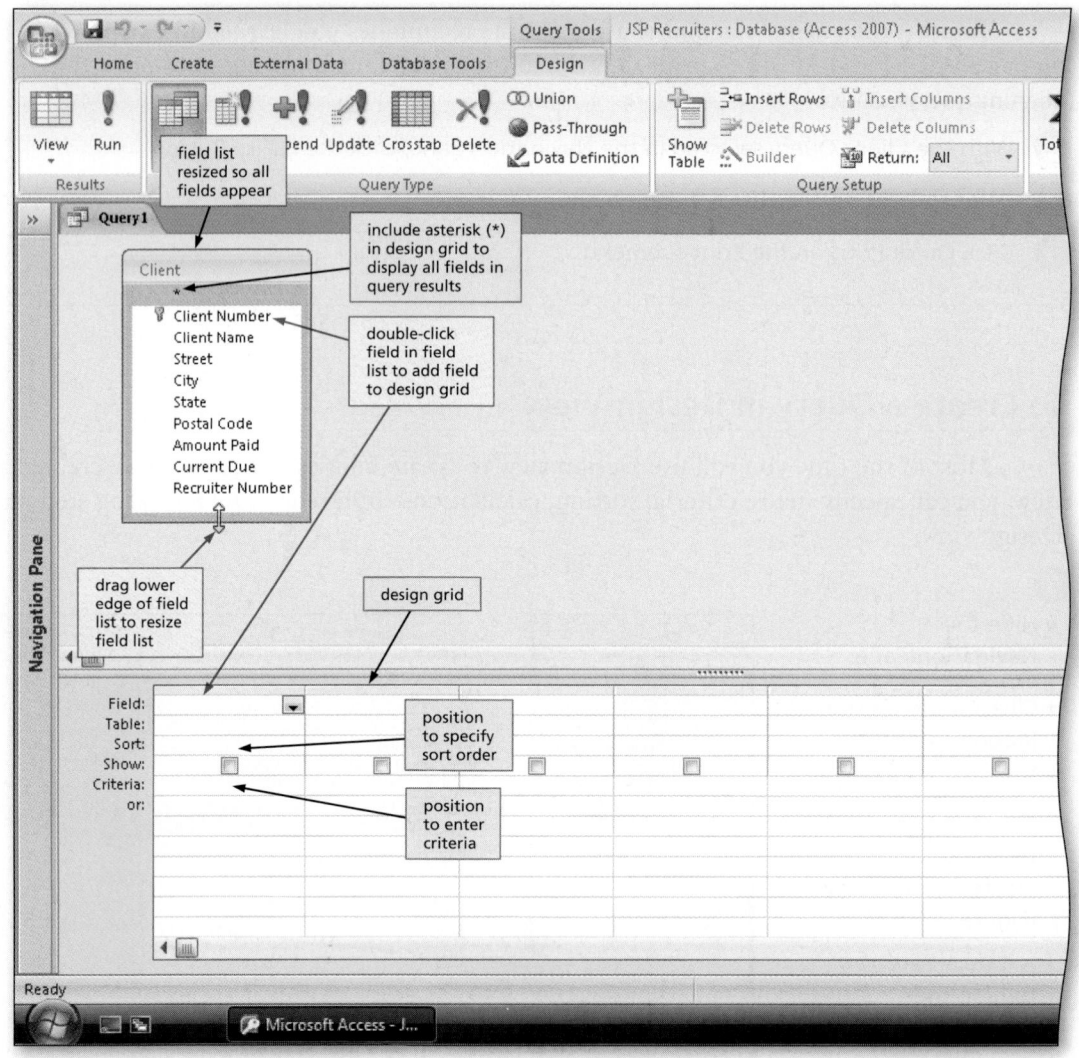

Figure 2–11

To Add Fields to the Design Grid

Once you have a new query displayed in Design view, you are ready to create the query by making entries in the design grid in the lower Pane of the window. You add the fields you want included in the Field row in the grid. Only the fields that appear in the design grid will be included in the results of the query. The following step includes the client number, client name, amount paid, and current due for all clients by adding only those fields in the design grid.

1

- Double-click the Client Number field in the field list to add the Client Number field to the query.

Q&A What if I add the wrong field?

Click just above the field name in the design grid to select the column and then press the DELETE key to remove the field.

- Double-click the Client Name field in the field list to add the Client Name field to the query.

- Add the Amount Paid field to the query by double-clicking the Amount Paid field in the field list.

- Add the Current Due field to the query (Figure 2–12).

Q&A What if I want to include all fields? Do I have to add each field individually?

No. Instead of adding individual fields, you can double-click the asterisk (*) to add the asterisk to the design grid.

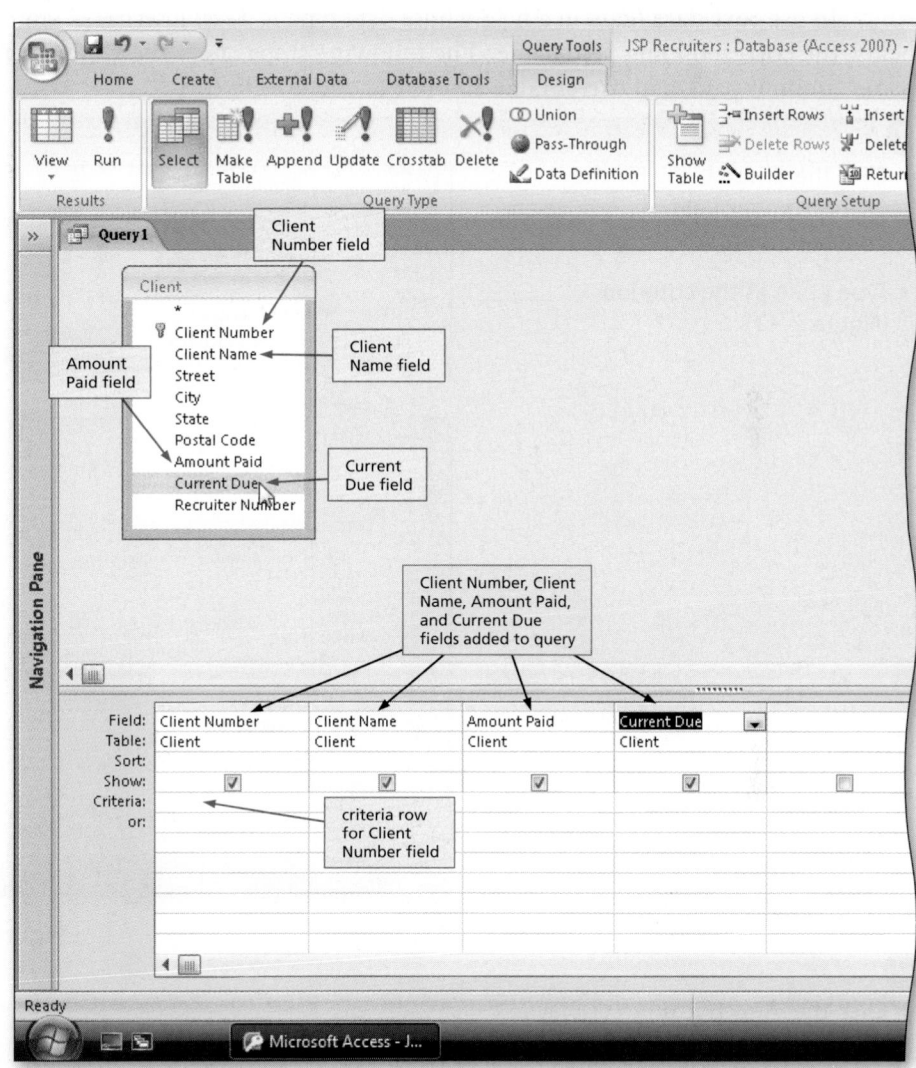

Figure 2–12

Entering Criteria

When you use queries, usually you are looking for those records that satisfy some criterion. In the simple query you created earlier, for example, you entered a criterion to restrict the records that were included to those on which the recruiter number was 24. In another query, you might want the name, amount paid, and current due amounts of the client whose number is FD89, for example, or of those clients whose names start with the letters, Be. You enter criteria in the Criteria row in the design grid below the field name to which the criterion applies. For example, to indicate that the client number must be FD89, you first must add the Client Number field to the design grid. You then would type FD89 in the Criteria row below the Client Number field.

To Use Text Data in a Criterion

To use **text data** (data in a field whose data type is Text) in criteria, simply type the text in the Criteria row below the corresponding field name. The following steps query the Client table and display the client number, client name, amount paid, and current due amount of client FD89.

1

- Click the Criteria row for the Client Number field to produce an insertion point.

- Type FD89 as the criterion (Figure 2–13).

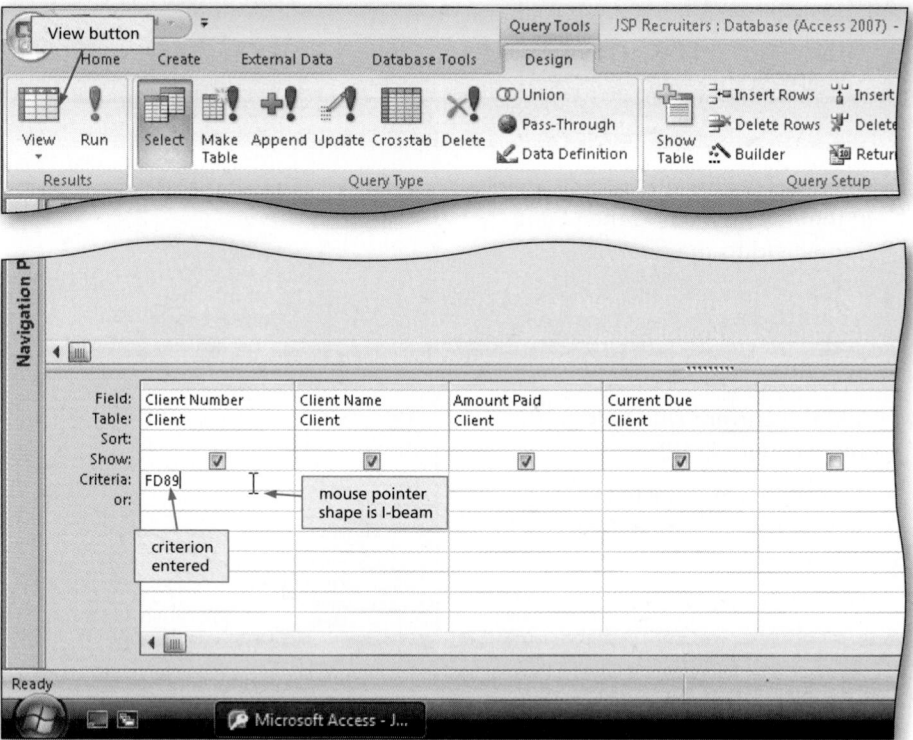

Figure 2–13

2

- Click the View button to display the query results (Figure 2–14).

Q&A

I noticed that there is a View button on both the Home tab and the Design tab. Do they both have the same effect?

Yes. Use whichever one you find most convenient.

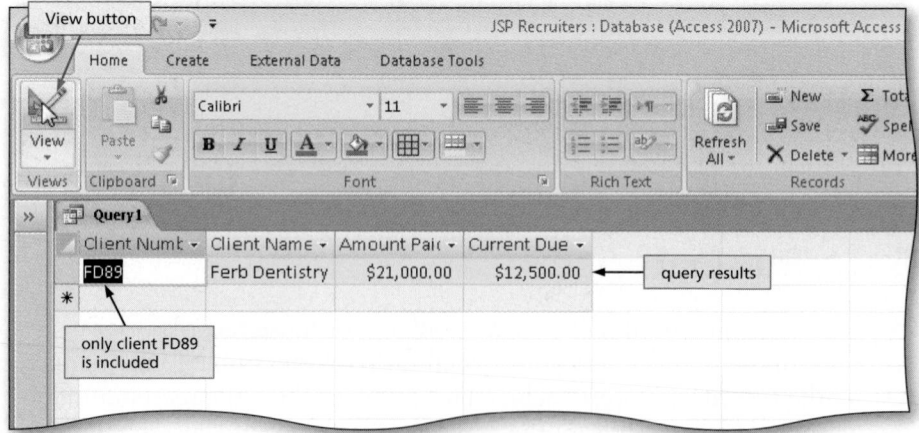

Figure 2–14

To Use a Wildcard

Microsoft Access supports wildcards. **Wildcards** are symbols that represent any character or combination of characters. One common wildcard, the **asterisk** (*), represents any collection of characters. Thus Be* represents the letters, Be, followed by any collection of characters. Another wildcard symbol is the **question mark** (?), which represents any individual character. Thus T?m represents the letter, T, followed by any single character followed by the letter, m, such as Tim or Tom.

The following steps use a wildcard to find the number, name, and address of those clients whose names begin with Be. Because you do not know how many characters will follow the Be, the asterisk is appropriate.

1
- Click the View button to return to Design view.

- If necessary, click the Criteria row below the Client Number field to produce an insertion point.

- Use the DELETE or BACKSPACE key as necessary to delete the current entry.

- Click the Criteria row below the Client Name field to produce an insertion point.

- Type Be* as the criterion (Figure 2–15).

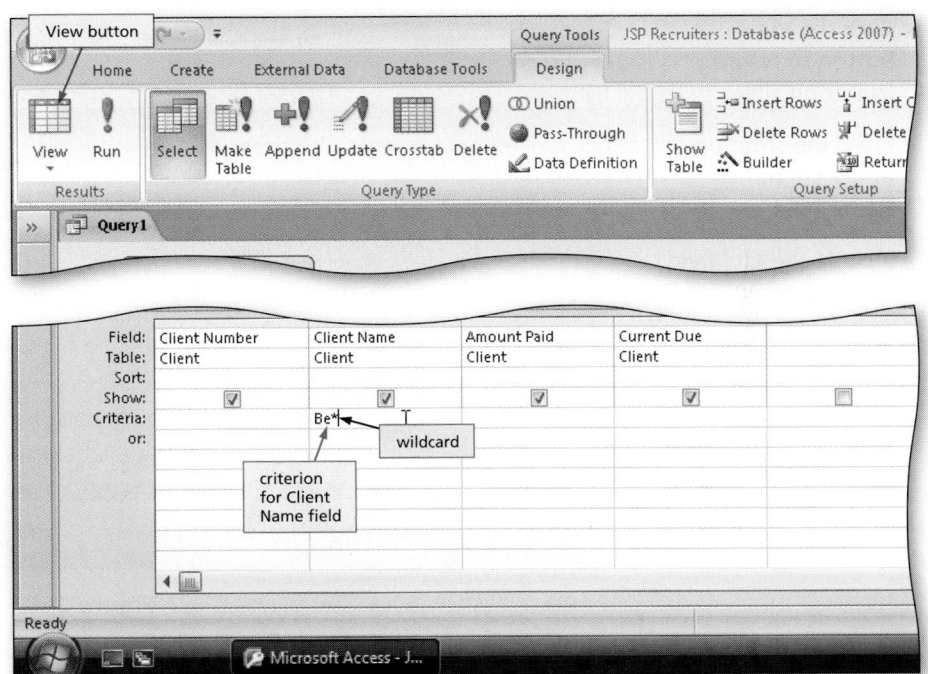

Figure 2–15

2
- View the query results by clicking the View button (Figure 2–16).

 **Experiment**
- Vary the case of the letters in the criteria and view the results to determine whether case makes a difference when entering a wildcard.

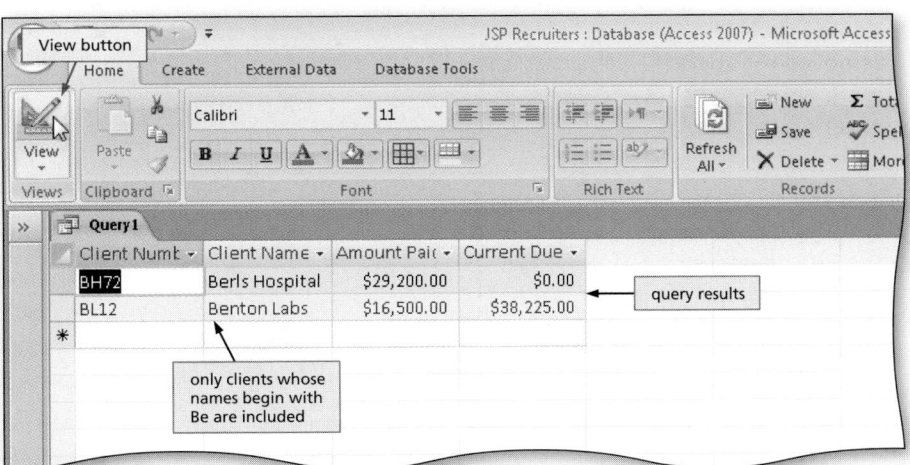

Figure 2–16

To Use Criteria for a Field Not Included in the Results

In some cases, you may have criteria for a particular field that should not appear in the results of the query. For example, you may want to see the client number, client name, address, and amount paid for all clients located in Berridge. The criteria involve the City field, which is not one of the fields to be included in the results.

To enter a criterion for the City field, it must be included in the design grid. Normally, this also would mean it would appear in the results. To prevent this from happening, remove the check mark from its Show check box in the Show row of the grid. The following steps display the client number, client name, amount paid, and current due for clients located in Berridge.

- Click the View button to return to Design view.

- Erase the criterion in the Client Name field.

- Include the City field in the query.

- Type Berridge as the criterion for the City field (Figure 2–17).

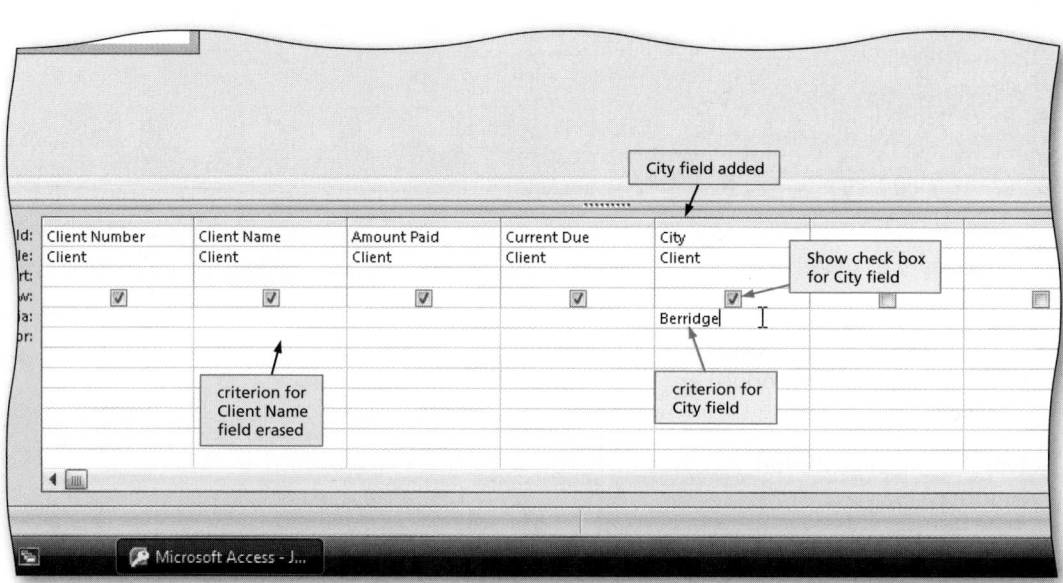

Figure 2–17

- Click the Show check box for the City field to remove the check mark (Figure 2–18).

Q&A Could I have removed the check mark before entering the criterion?

Yes. The order in which you performed the two operations does not matter.

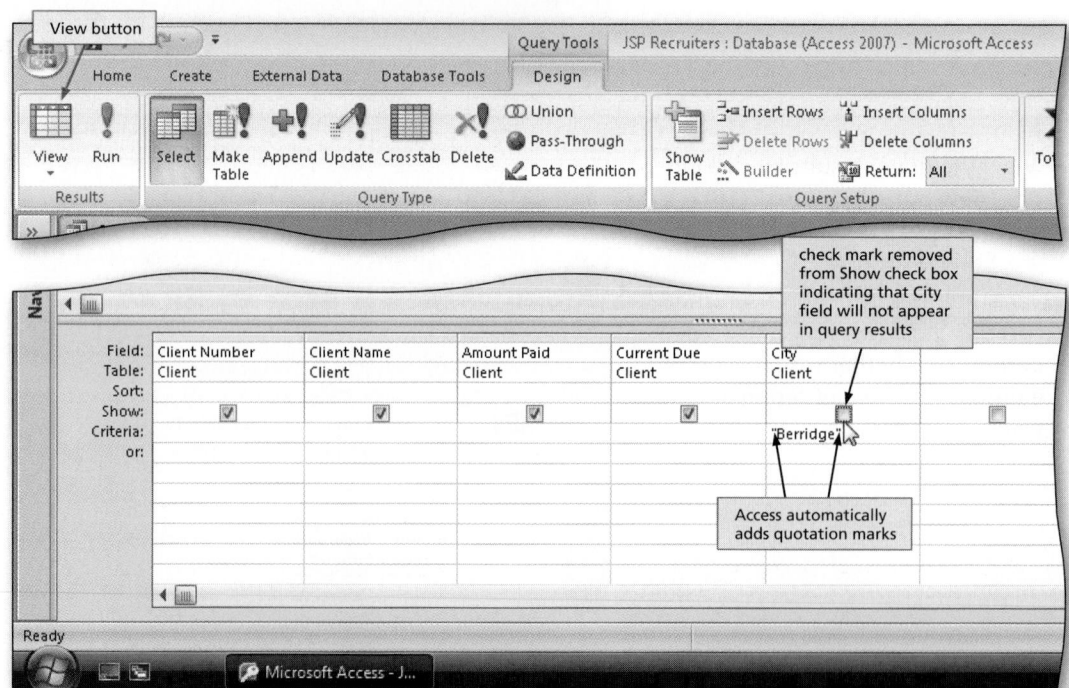

Figure 2–18

3

- View the query results (Figure 2–19).

Experiment

- Click the View button to return to Design view, enter a different city name, and view the results. Repeat this process with a variety of city names, including at least one city name that is not in the database.

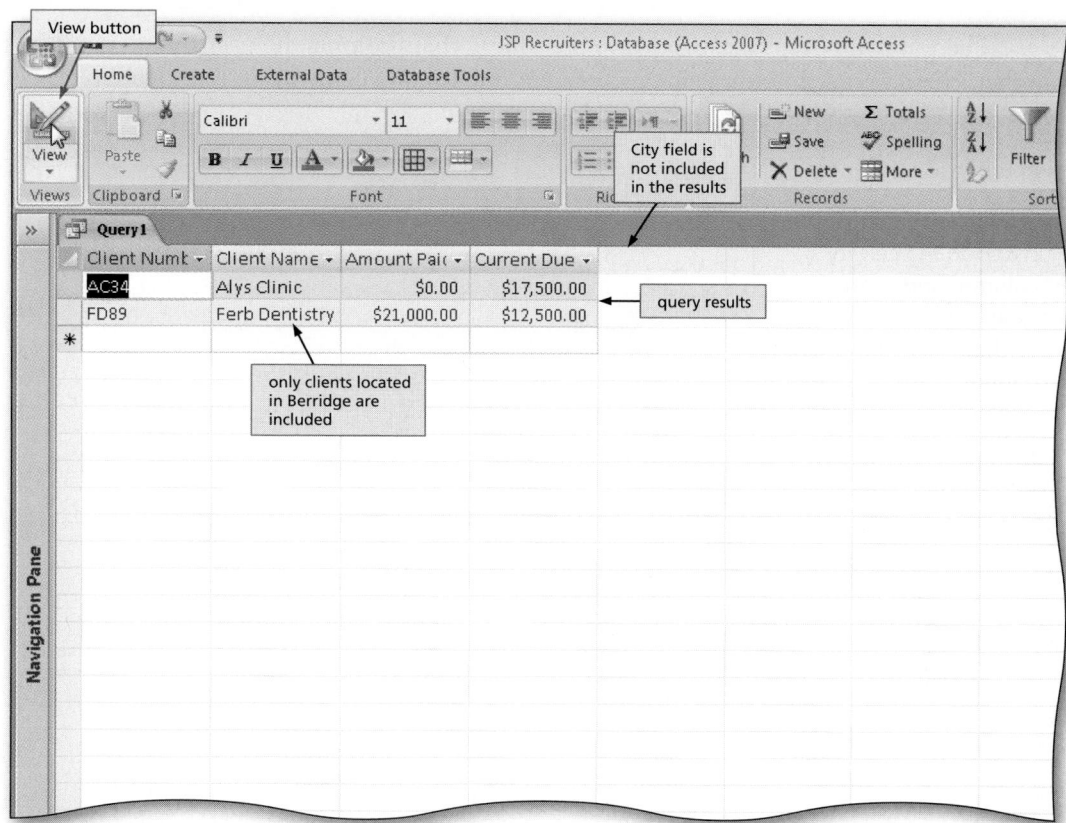

Figure 2–19

Creating a Parameter Query

If you wanted to find clients located in Fort Stewart rather than Berridge, you would either have to create a new query or modify the existing query by replacing Berridge with Fort Stewart as the criterion. Rather than giving a specific criterion when you first create the query, on occasion, you may want to be able to enter part of the criterion when you view the query results and then have the appropriate results appear. For example, to include all the clients located in Berridge, you could enter Berridge as a criterion in the City field. From that point on, every time you ran the query, only the clients in Berridge would appear.

A better way is to allow the user to enter the city at the time the user wants to view the results. Thus a user could view the query results, enter Berridge as the city and then see all the clients in Berridge. Later, the user could use the same query, but enter Fort Stewart as the city, and then see all the clients in Fort Stewart.

To enable this flexibility, you create a **parameter query**, which is a query that prompts for input whenever it is used. You enter a parameter, rather than a specific value, as the criterion. You create a parameter by enclosing a value in a criterion in square brackets. It is important that the value in the brackets does not match the name of any field. If you enter a field name in square brackets, Access assumes you want that particular field and does not prompt the user for input. For example, you could place [Enter City] as the criterion in the City field.

BTW

Removing a Table from a Query
If you add the wrong table to a query or have an extra table in the query, you can remove it by right-clicking the field list for the table and then clicking Remove Table on the shortcut menu.

To Create a Parameter Query

The following steps create a parameter query that prompts the user to enter a city, and then displays the client number, client name, amount paid, and current due for all clients located in that city.

1

● Return to Design view.

● Erase the current criterion in the City column, and then type [Enter City] as the new criterion (Figure 2–20).

Q&A What is the purpose of the square brackets?

The square brackets indicate that the text entered is not text that the value in the column must match. Without the brackets, for example, Access would search for records on which the city is Enter City.

Q&A What if I typed a field name in the square brackets?

Access would simply use the value in that field. In order to create a parameter query, it is essential that the text typed in the square brackets not be a field name.

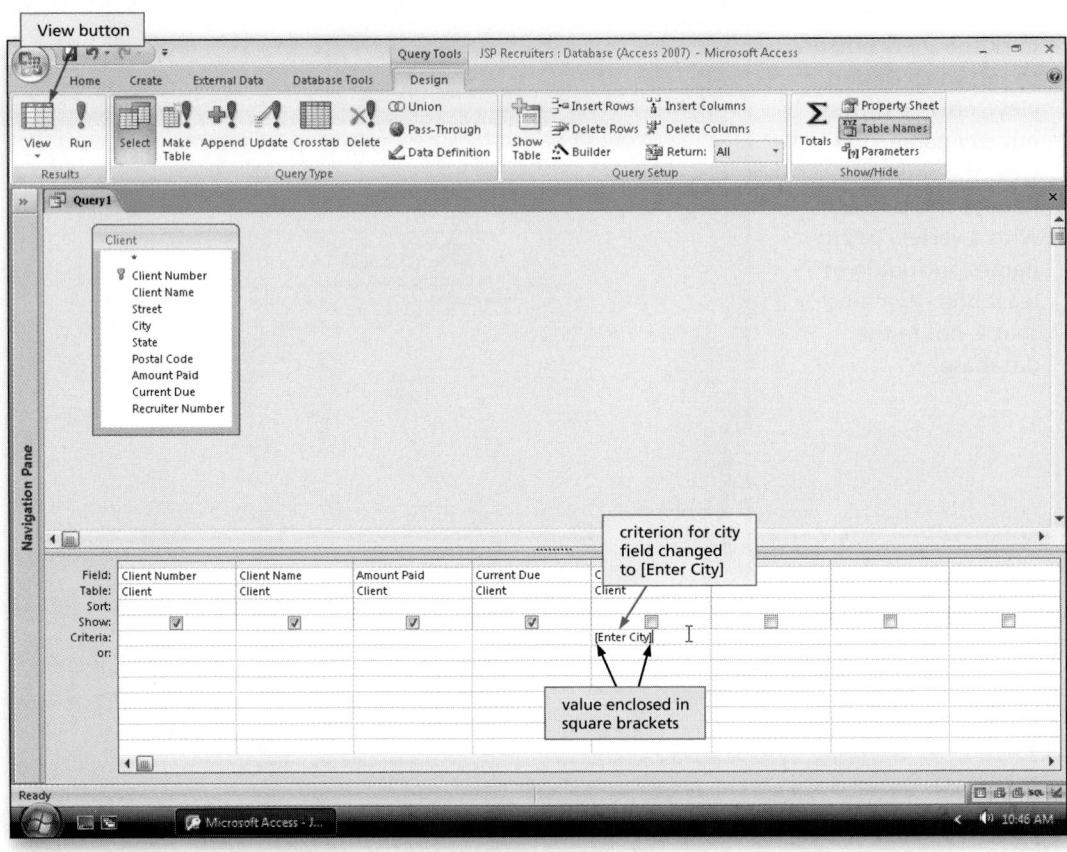

Figure 2–20

2

● Click the View button to display the Enter Parameter Value dialog box (Figure 2–21).

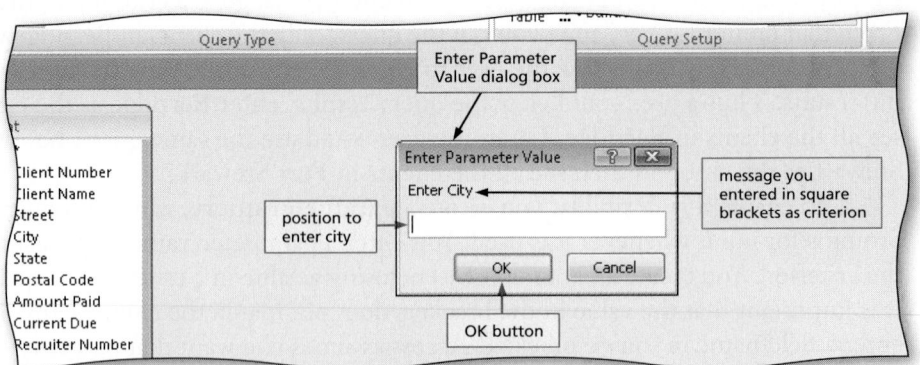

Figure 2–21

3

- Type `Fort Stewart` as the parameter value in the Enter City text box and then click the OK button (Figure 2–22).

🔎 **Experiment**

- Try other characters between the square brackets. In each case, view the results. When finished, change the characters between the square brackets back to Enter City.

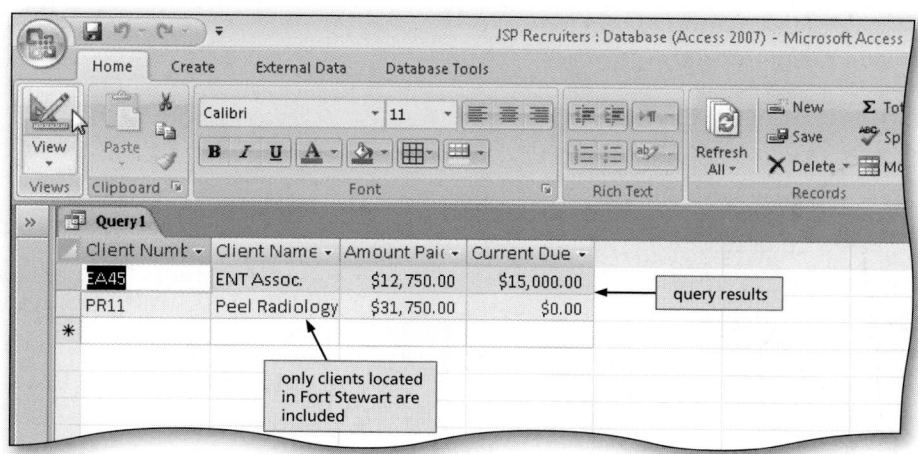

Figure 2–22

Each time you use this query, you will be asked to enter a city. Only clients in the city you enter will be included in the results.

To Save a Query

In many cases, you will want to repeatedly use the queries you construct. By saving the query, you eliminate the need to repeat all your entries. The following steps save the query you just have created and assign it the name Client-City Query.

1

- Click the Save button on the Quick Access Toolbar to open the Save As dialog box.

Q&A

Can I also save from Design view?

Yes. You can save the query when you view it in Design view just as you can save the query when you view the query results in Datasheet view.

- Type `Client-City Query` in the Query Name text box (Figure 2–23).

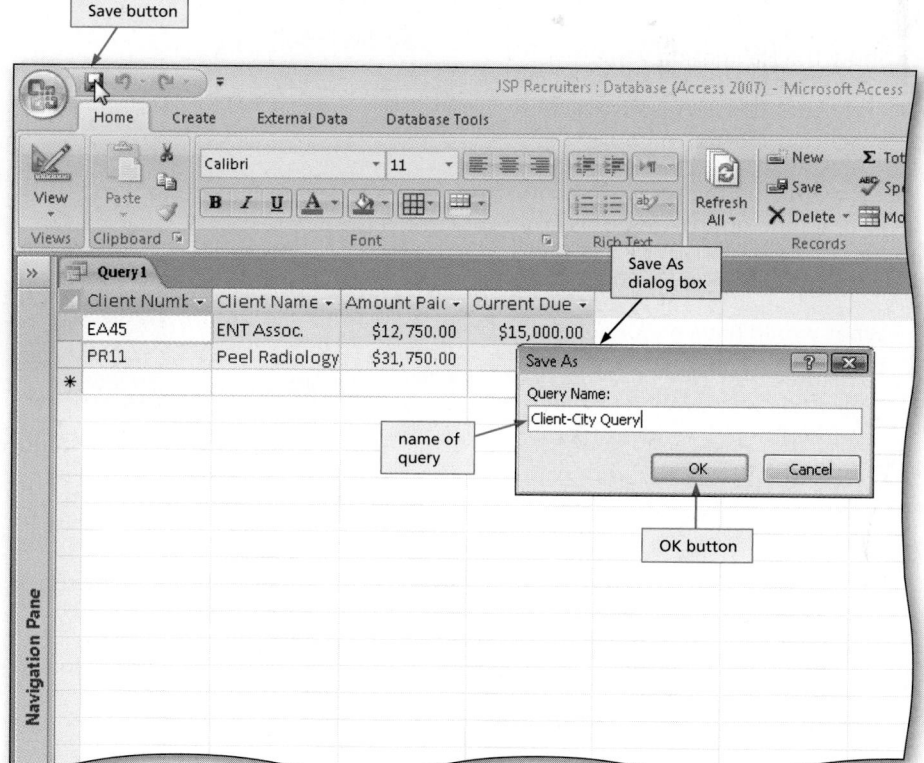

Figure 2–23

- Click the OK button to save the query (Figure 2–24).

- Click the Close 'Client-City Query' button to close the query and remove it from the screen.

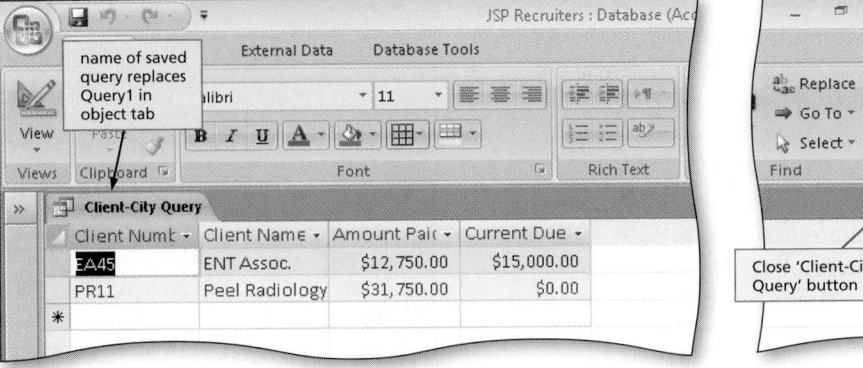

Figure 2–24

Other Ways
1. Right-click tab for query, click Save on shortcut menu
2. Press CTRL+S

To Use a Saved Query

Once you have saved a query, you can use and manipulate it at any time in the future by opening it. When you right-click the query in the Navigation Pane, Access displays a shortcut menu containing commands that allow you to open and change the design of the query. You also can print the results by clicking the Office Button, pointing to Print on the Office button menu, and then clicking Quick Print on the Print submenu.

The query always uses the data that is currently in the table. Thus, if changes have been made to the data since the last time you ran the query, the results of the query may be different. The following steps use the query named Client-City Query.

- Show the Navigation Pane.

- Right-click the Client-City Query to produce a shortcut menu.

- Click Open on the shortcut menu to open the query and display the Enter Parameter Value dialog box (Figure 2–25).

Q&A

What would have happened if there were no parameters?

You would immediately see the results without needing to furnish any additional information.

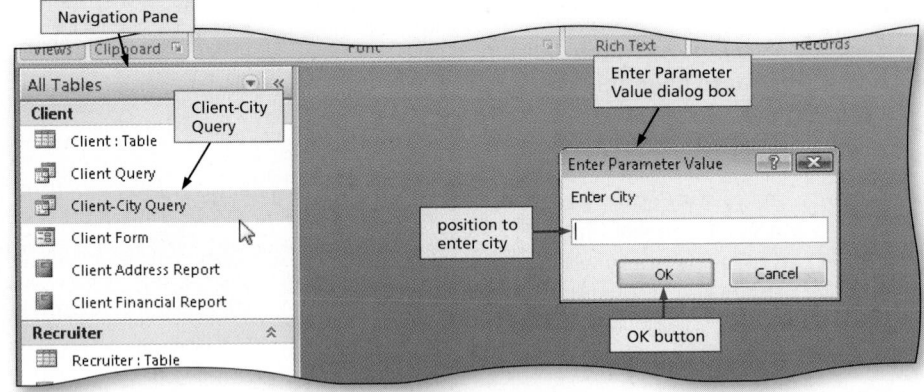

Figure 2–25

- Type `Fort Stewart` in the Enter City text box, and then click the OK button to display the results using Fort Stewart as the city as shown in Figure 2–24.

- Click the Close 'Client-City Query' button, shown in Figure 2–24, to close the query.

To Use a Number in a Criterion

To enter a number in a criterion, type the number without any dollar signs or commas. The following steps display all clients whose current due amount is $0.00.

 1

- Hide the Navigation Pane.

- Click Create on the Ribbon to display the Create tab.

- Click the Query Design button to create a new query.

- With the Client table selected, click the Add button in the Show Table dialog box to add the Client table to the query.

- Click the Close button in the Show Table dialog box to remove the dialog box from the screen.

- Drag the lower edge of the field box down far enough so all fields in the Client table are displayed.

- Include the Client Number, Client Name, Amount Paid, and Current Due fields in the query.

- Type 0 as the criterion for the Current Due field (Figure 2–26).

Q&A Do I need to enter a dollar sign and decimal point?

No. Access will interpret 0 as $0.00, because the data type for the Current Due field is currency.

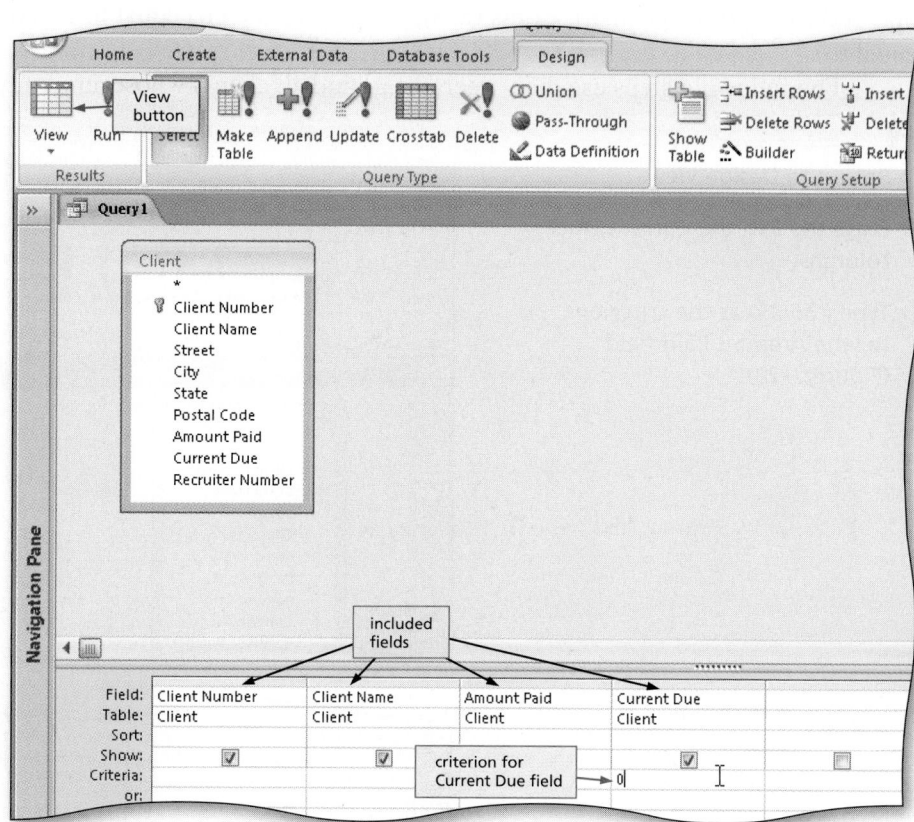

Figure 2–26

 2

- View the query results (Figure 2–27).

Q&A Why did Access display the results as $0.00 when I only entered 0?

Access uses the format for the field to determine how to display the result. In this case the format indicated that Access should include the dollar sign and decimal point.

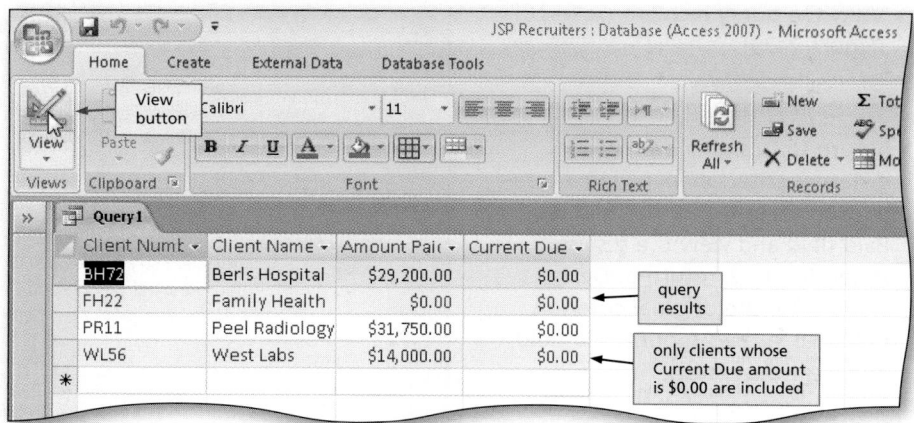

Figure 2–27

To Use a Comparison Operator in a Criterion

Unless you specify otherwise, Access assumes that the criteria you enter involve equality (exact matches). In the last query, for example, you were requesting those clients whose current due amount is equal to 0 (zero). If you want something other than an exact match, you must enter the appropriate **comparison operator**. The comparison operators are > (greater than), < (less than), >= (greater than or equal to), <= (less than or equal to), and NOT (not equal to).

The following steps use the > operator to find all clients whose amount paid is more than $20,000.00.

- Return to Design view.

- Erase the 0 in the Current Due column.

- Type >20000 as the criterion for the Amount Paid field (Figure 2–28).

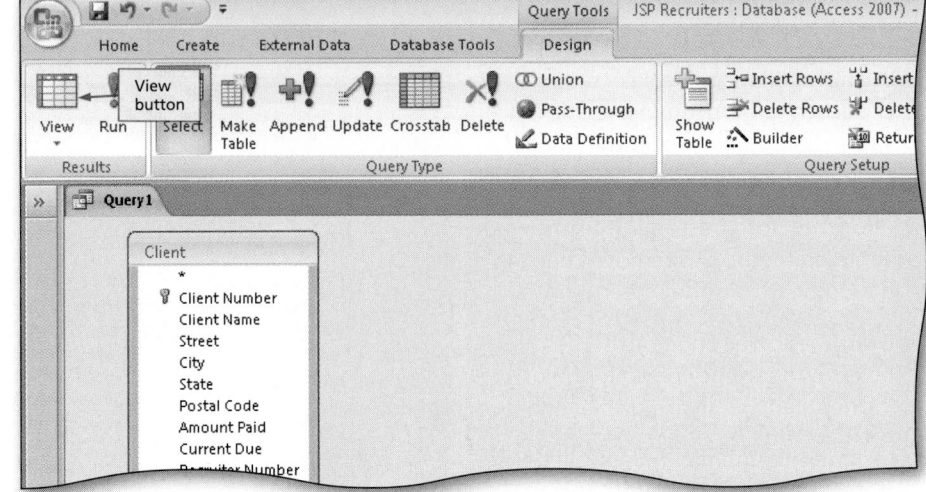

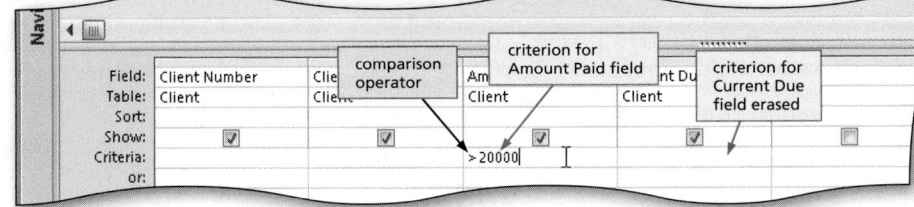

Figure 2–28

- View the query results (Figure 2–29).

Experiment

- Return to Design view. Try a different criterion involving a comparison operator in the Amount Paid field and view the results. When finished, return to Design view, enter the original criterion (>20000) in the Amount Paid field, and view the results.

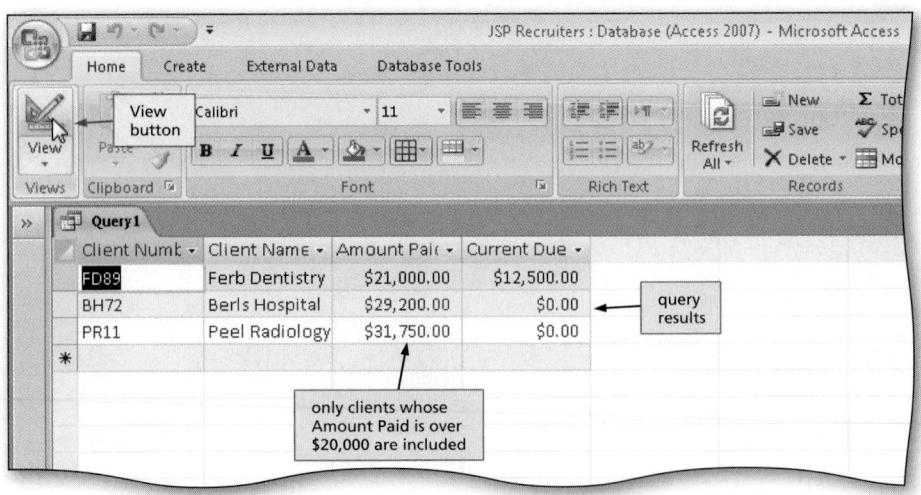

Figure 2–29

Using Compound Criteria

Often you will have more than one criterion that the data for which you are searching must satisfy. This type of criterion is called a **compound criterion**. Two types of compound criteria exist.

In an **AND criterion**, each individual criterion must be true in order for the compound criterion to be true. For example, an AND criterion would allow you to find those clients that have an amount paid greater than $20,000.00 and whose recruiter is recruiter 21.

Conversely, an **OR criterion** is true provided either individual criterion is true. An OR criterion would allow you to find those clients that have an amount paid greater than $20,000.00 or whose recruiter is recruiter 21. In this case, any client whose amount paid is greater than $20,000.00 would be included in the answer, regardless of whether the client's recruiter is recruiter 21. Likewise, any client whose recruiter is recruiter 21 would be included, regardless of whether the client had an amount paid greater than $20,000.00.

BTW

The BETWEEN Operator
The BETWEEN operator allows you to search for a range of values in one field. For example, to find all clients whose amount paid is between $10,000 and $20,000, you would enter Between 10000 and 20000 in the Criteria row for the Amount Paid field.

To Use a Compound Criterion Involving AND

To combine criteria with AND, place the criteria on the same line. The following steps use an AND criterion to find those clients whose amount paid is greater than $20,000.00 and whose recruiter is recruiter 21.

1

- Return to Design view.

- Include the Recruiter Number field in the query.

- Type 21 as the criterion for the Recruiter Number field (Figure 2–30).

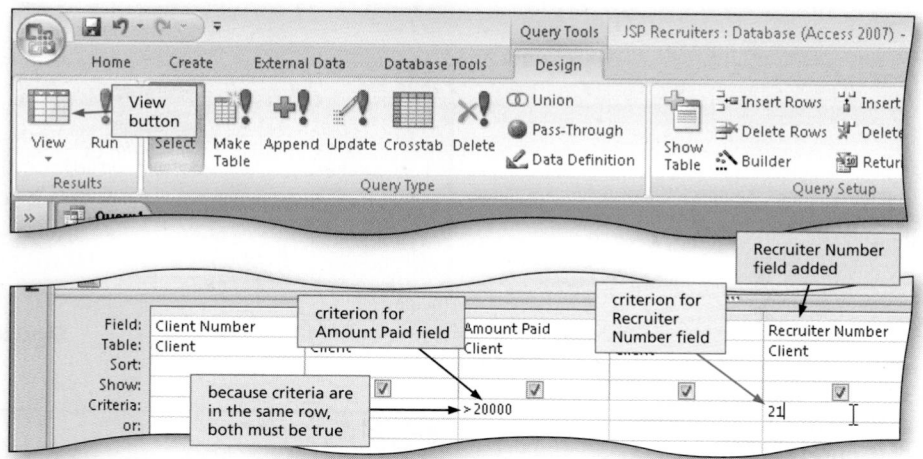

Figure 2–30

- View the query results (Figure 2–31).

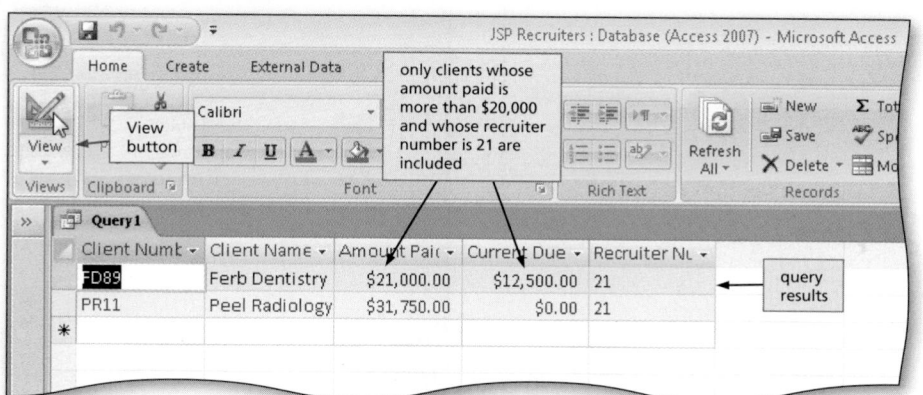

Figure 2–31

To Use a Compound Criterion Involving OR

To combine criteria with OR, the criteria must go on separate lines in the Criteria area of the grid. The following steps use an OR criterion to find those clients whose amount paid is greater than $20,000.00 or whose recruiter is recruiter 21 (or both).

- Return to Design view.

- If necessary, click the Criteria entry for the Recruiter Number field and then use the BACKSPACE key or the DELETE key to erase the entry ("21").

- Click the or: row (the row below the Criteria row) for the Recruiter Number field and then type 21 as the entry (Figure 2–32).

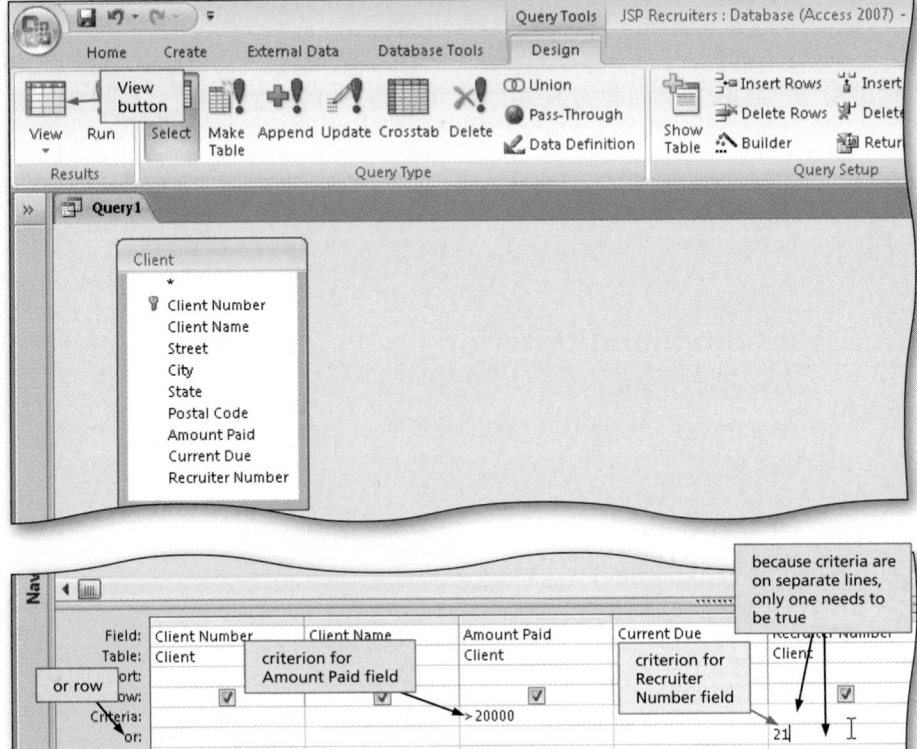

Figure 2–32

- View the query results (Figure 2–33).

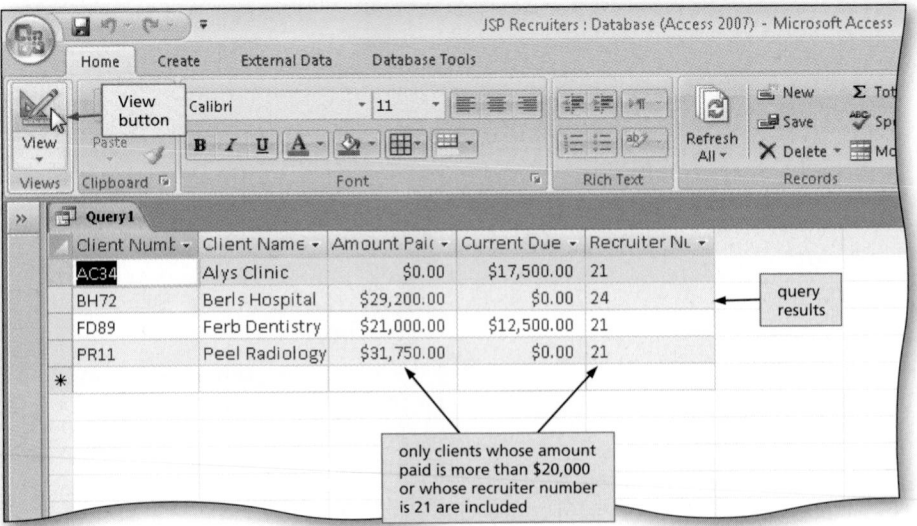

Figure 2–33

Sorting

In some queries, the order in which the records appear really does not matter. All you need to be concerned about are the records that appear in the results. It does not matter which one is first or which one is last.

In other queries, however, the order can be very important. You may want to see the cities in which clients are located and would like them arranged alphabetically. Perhaps you want to see the clients listed by recruiter number. Further, within all the clients of any given recruiter, you might want them to be listed by amount paid from largest amount to smallest.

To order the records in the answer to a query in a particular way, you **sort** the records. The field or fields on which the records are sorted is called the **sort key**. If you are sorting on more than one field (such as sorting by amount paid within recruiter number), the more important field (Recruiter Number) is called the **major key** (also called the **primary sort key**) and the less important field (Amount Paid) is called the **minor key** (also called the **secondary sort key**).

To sort in Microsoft Access, specify the sort order in the Sort row of the design grid below the field that is the sort key. If you specify more than one sort key, the sort key on the left will be the major sort key and the one on the right will be the minor key.

The following are guidelines related to sorting in queries.

BTW

OR Criteria in a Single Field
If you want to combine two criteria with OR in a single field, you can place the criteria on separate lines, or you can place the criteria on the same line with the word OR in between them. For example, to include those records in which the city is Berls or Mason, you could type Berls OR Mason in the Criteria row. You also can use the IN operator, which consists of the word IN followed by the criteria in parentheses. For example, you would type IN (Berls, Mason).

Determine whether special order is required.

1. **Determine whether sorting is required.** Examine the query or request to see if it contains words such as "order" or "sort" that would imply that the order of the query results is important. If so, you need to sort the query.

2. **Determine the sort key(s).** If sorting is required, identify the field or fields on which the results are to be sorted. Look for words such as "ordered by" or "sort the results by," both of which would indicate that the specified field is a sort key.

3. **If using two sort keys, determine major and minor key.** If you are using two sort keys, determine which one is more important. That will be the major key. Look for words such as "sort by amount paid within recruiter number," which imply that the overall order is by recruiter number. Thus, the Recruiter Number field would be the major sort key and the Amount Paid field would be the minor sort key.

4. **Determine sort order.** Words such as "increasing," "ascending," or "low-to-high" imply Ascending order. Words such as "decreasing," "descending," or "high-to-low" imply Descending order. Sorting in alphabetical order implies Ascending order. If there are no words to imply a particular order, you would typically use Ascending.

5. **Determine restrictions.** Examine the query or request to see if there are any special restrictions. One common restriction is to exclude duplicates. Another common restriction is to list only a certain number of records, for example to list only the first five records.

Plan Ahead

To Clear the Design Grid

If the fields you want to include in the next query are different from those in the previous query, it is usually simpler to start with a clear grid, that is, one with no fields already in the design grid. You always can clear the entries in the design grid by closing the query and then starting over. A simpler approach to clearing the entries is to select all the entries and then press the DELETE key. The following steps return to Design view and clear the design grid.

- Return to Design view.

- Click just above the Client Number column heading in the grid to select the column.

Q&A

I clicked above the column heading, but the column is not selected. What should I do?

You didn't point to the correct location. Be sure the mouse pointer turns to a down-pointing arrow and then click again.

- Hold the SHIFT key down and click just above the Recruiter Number column heading to select all the columns (Figure 2–34).

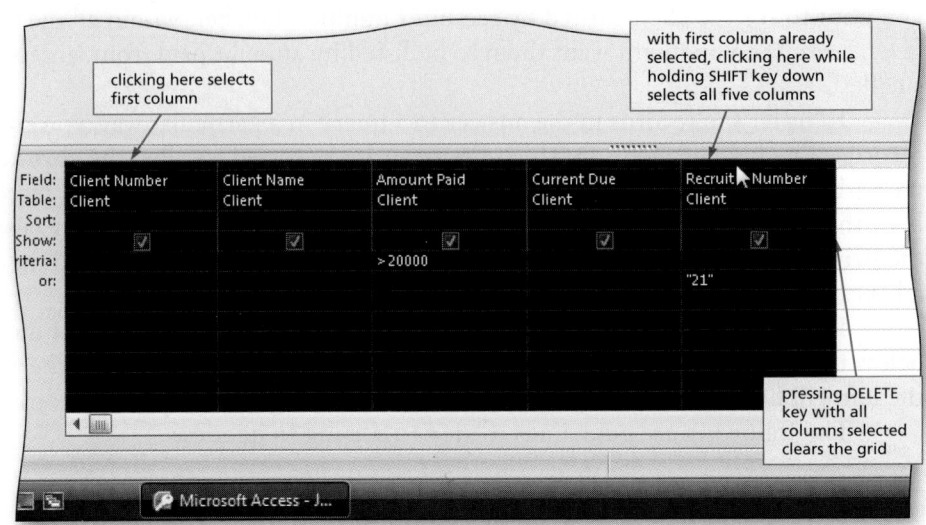

Figure 2–34

- Press the DELETE key to clear the design grid.

To Sort Data in a Query

If you have determined in the design process that a query is to be sorted, you must identify the sort key, that is, the field on which the results are to be sorted. In creating the query, you will need to specify the sort key to Access. The following steps sort the cities in the Client table by indicating that the City field is to be sorted. The steps specify Ascending sort order.

- Include the City field in the design grid.

- Click the Sort row below the City field, and then click the Sort row arrow to display a menu of possible sort orders (Figure 2–35).

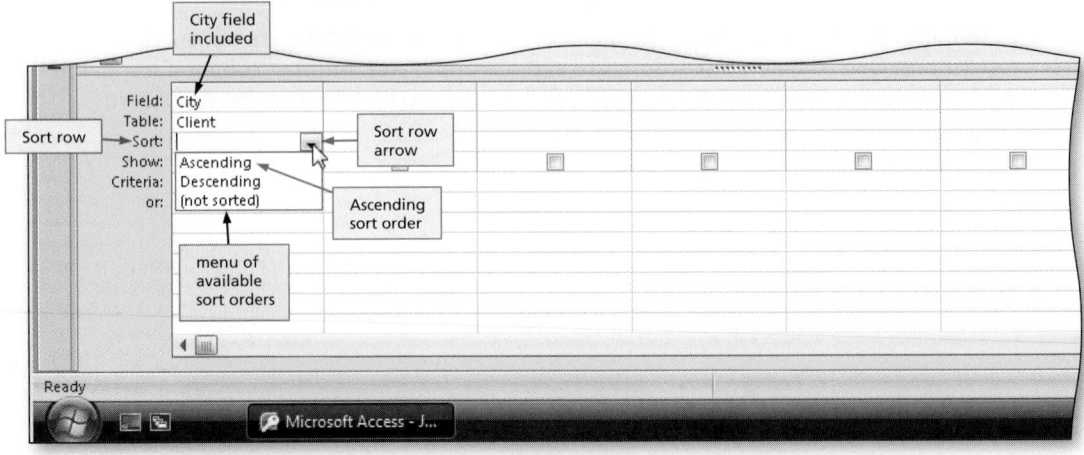

Figure 2–35

2

• Click Ascending to select Ascending sort order (Figure 2–36).

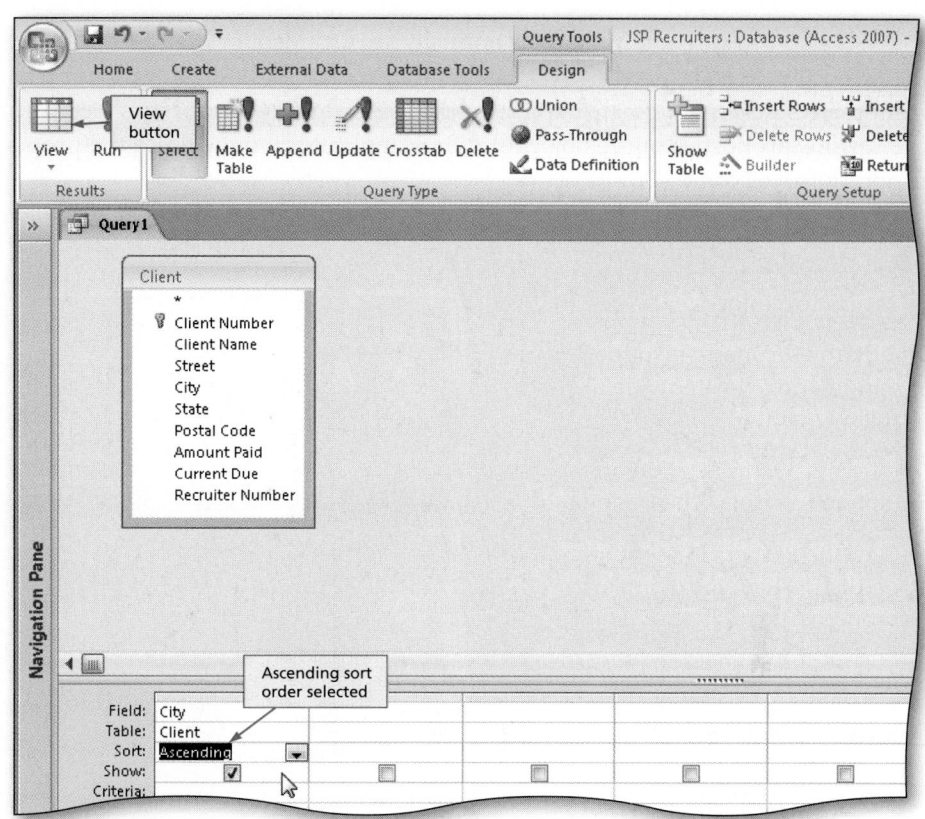

Figure 2–36

3

• View the query results (Figure 2–37).

Experiment

• Return to Design view and change the sort order to Descending. View the results. Return to Design view and change the sort order back to Ascending. View the results.

Q&A

Why do some cities appear more than once?

More than one client is located in those cities.

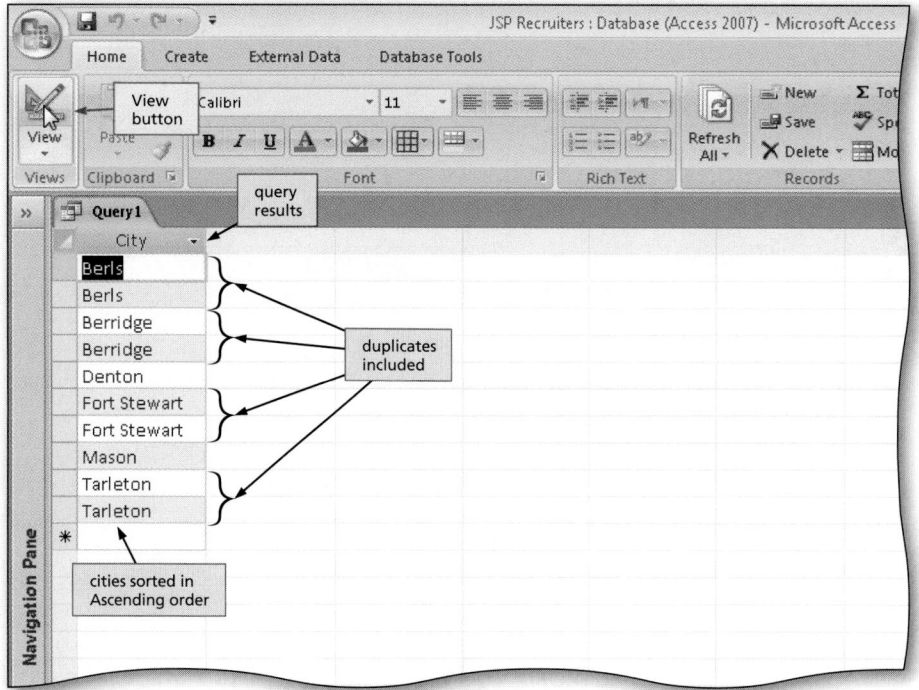

Figure 2–37

To Omit Duplicates

When you sort data, duplicates normally are included. In Figure 2–37 on the previous page, for example, Berridge appeared twice, as did Fort Stewart and Tarleton. These duplicates do not add any value, so you can eliminate them from the results. To eliminate duplicates, display the query's property sheet. A **property sheet** is a window containing the various properties of the object. To omit duplicates, you will use the property sheet to change the Unique Values property from No to Yes.

The following steps produce a sorted list of the cities in the Client table in which each city is listed only once.

- Return to Design view.

- Click the second field in the design grid (the empty field following City).

- If necessary, click Design on the Ribbon to display the Design tab.

- Click the Property Sheet button on the Design tab to display the property sheet (Figure 2–38).

Q&A My property sheet looks different. What should I do?

If your sheet looks different, you clicked the wrong place and will have to close the property sheet and repeat this step.

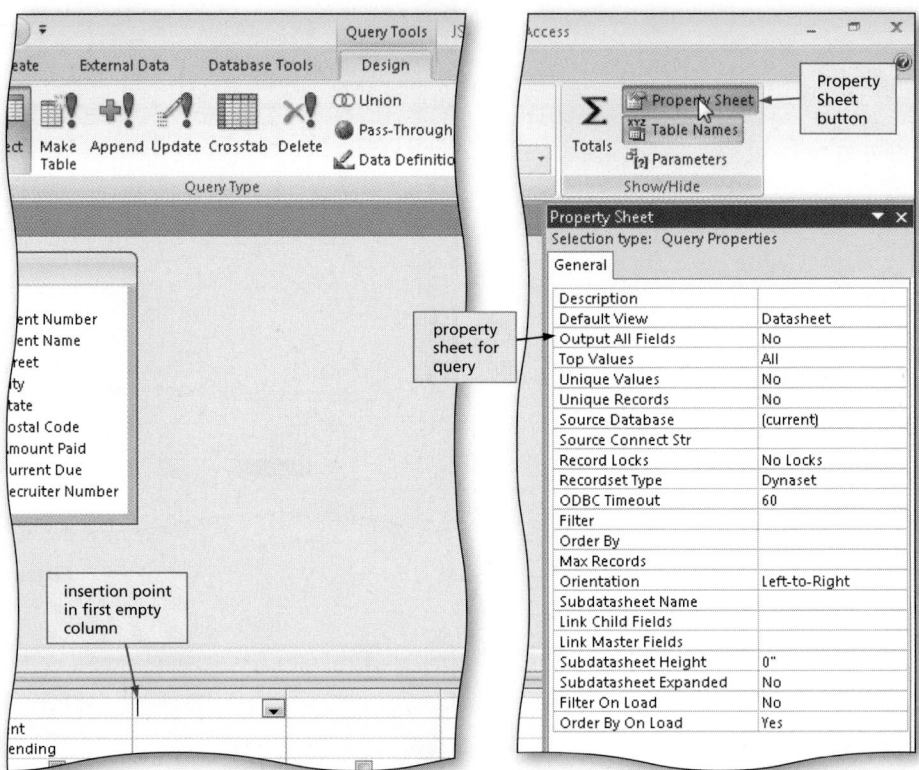

Figure 2–38

- Click the Unique Values property box, and then click the arrow that appears to produce a menu of available choices for Unique Values (Figure 2–39).

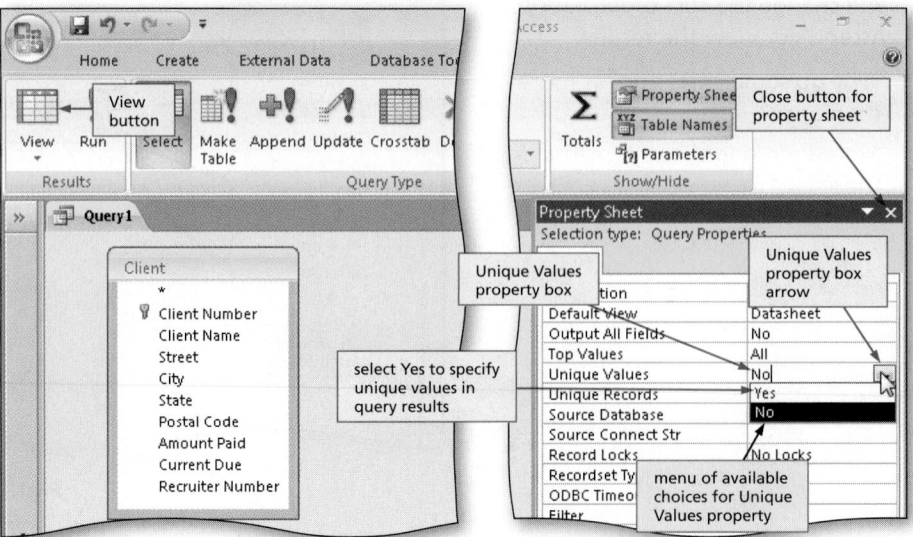

Figure 2–39

- Click Yes and then close the Query Properties sheet by clicking its Close button.

- View the query results (Figure 2–40).

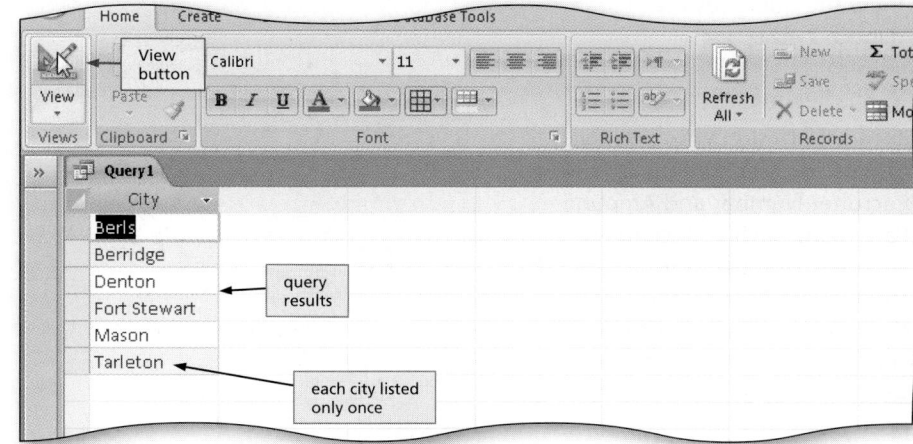

Figure 2–40

To Sort on Multiple Keys

The following steps sort on multiple keys. Specifically, the data is to be sorted by amount paid (low to high) within recruiter number, which means that the Recruiter Number field is the major key and the Amount Paid field is the minor key.

- Return to Design view.

- Clear the design grid.

- Include the Client Number, Client Name, Recruiter Number, and Amount Paid fields in the query in this order.

- Select Ascending as the sort order for both the Recruiter Number field and the Amount Paid field (Figure 2–41).

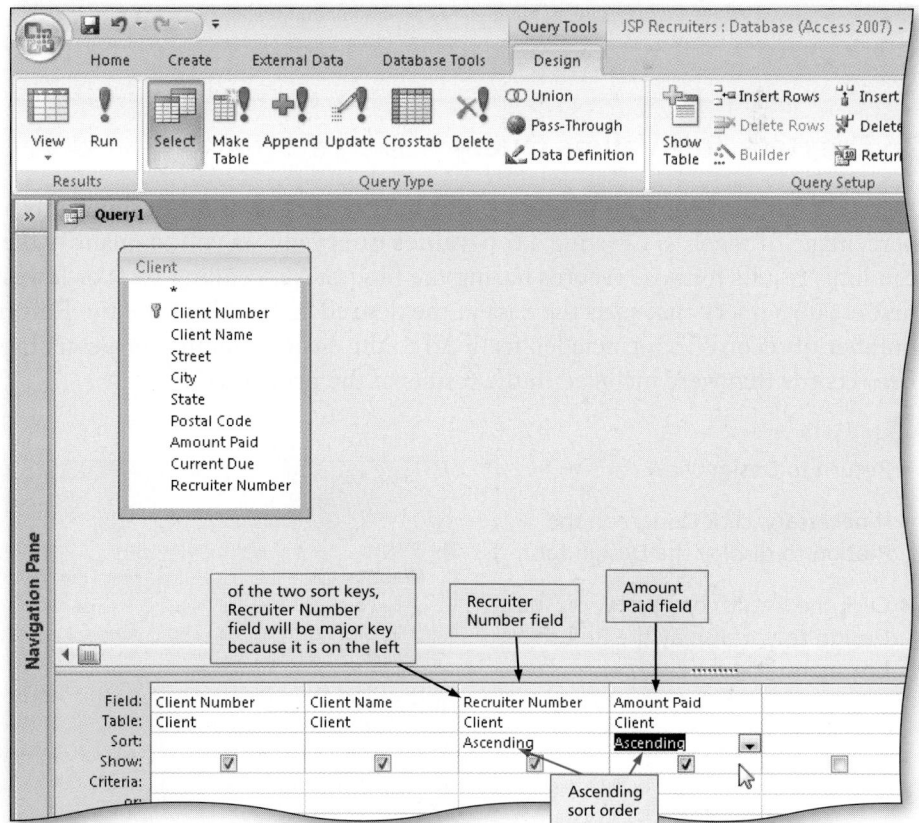

Figure 2–41

2

- View the query results (Figure 2–42).

🔍 **Experiment**

- Return to Design view and try other sort combinations for the Recruiter Number and Amount Paid fields, such as Ascending for Recruiter Number and Descending for Amount Paid. In each case, view the results to see the effect of the changes. When finished, select Ascending as the sort order for both fields.

Q&A

What if the Amount Paid field is to the left of the Recruiter Number?

It is important to remember that the major sort key must appear to the left of the minor sort key in the design grid. If you attempted to sort by amount paid within recruiter number, but placed the Amount Paid field to the left of the Recruiter Number field, your results would be incorrect.

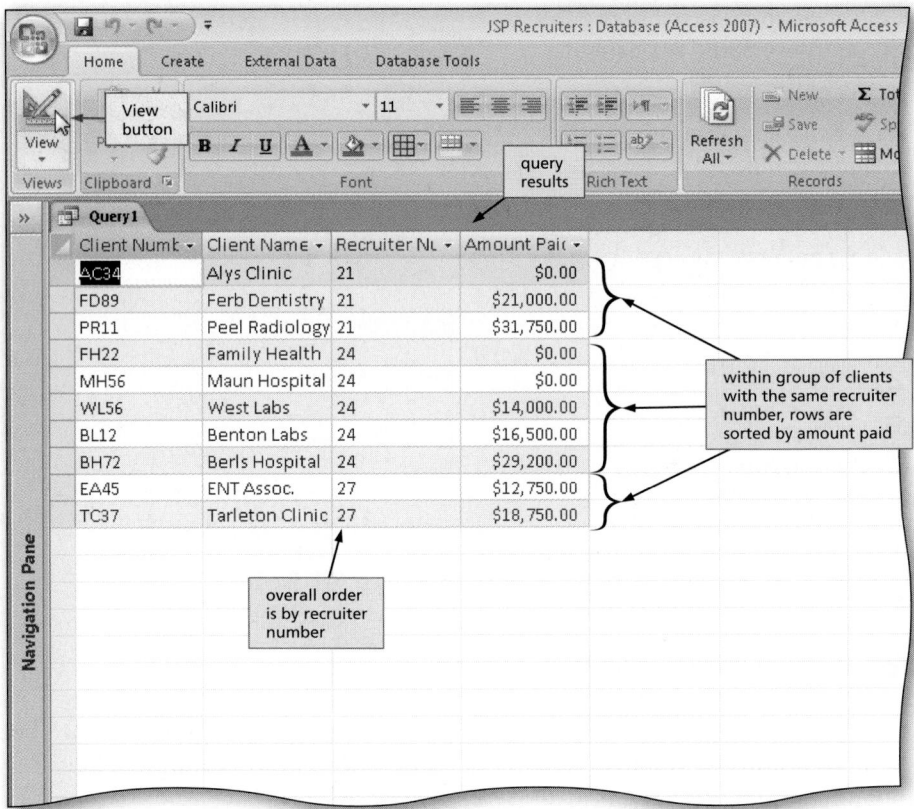

Figure 2–42

To Create a Top-Values Query

Rather than show all the results of a query, you may want to show only a specified number of records or a percentage of records. Creating a **top-values query** allows you to quantify the results. When you sort records, you can limit results to those records having the highest (descending sort) or lowest (ascending sort) values. To do so, first create a query that sorts the data in the desired order. Next, use the Return box on the Design tab to change the number of records to be included from All to the desired number or percentage. The following steps show the first five records that were included in the results of the previous query.

1

- Return to Design view.

- If necessary, click Design on the Ribbon to display the Design tab.

- Click the Return box arrow on the Design tab to display the Return box menu (Figure 2–43).

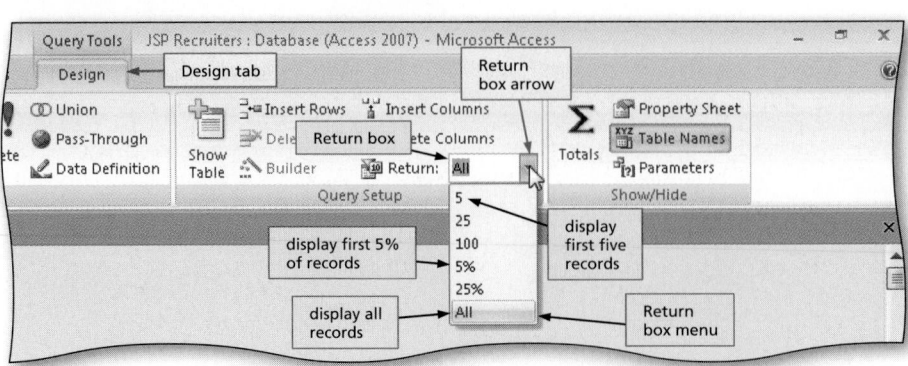

Figure 2–43

2

- Click 5 in the Return box menu to specify that the query results should contain the first five rows.

Q&A Could I have typed the 5? What about other numbers that do not appear in the list?

Yes, you could have typed the 5. For numbers not appearing in the list, you must type the number.

- View the query results (Figure 2–44).

3

- Close the query by clicking the Close 'Query1' button.

- When asked if you want to save your changes, click the No button.

Q&A Do I need to close the query before creating my next query?

Not necessarily. When you use a top-values query, however, it is important to change the value in the Return box back to All. If you do not change the Return value back to All, the previous value will remain in effect. Consequently, you may very well not get all the records you should in the next query. A good practice whenever you use a top-values query is to close the query as soon as you are done. That way, you will begin your next query from scratch, which guarantees that the value is set back to All.

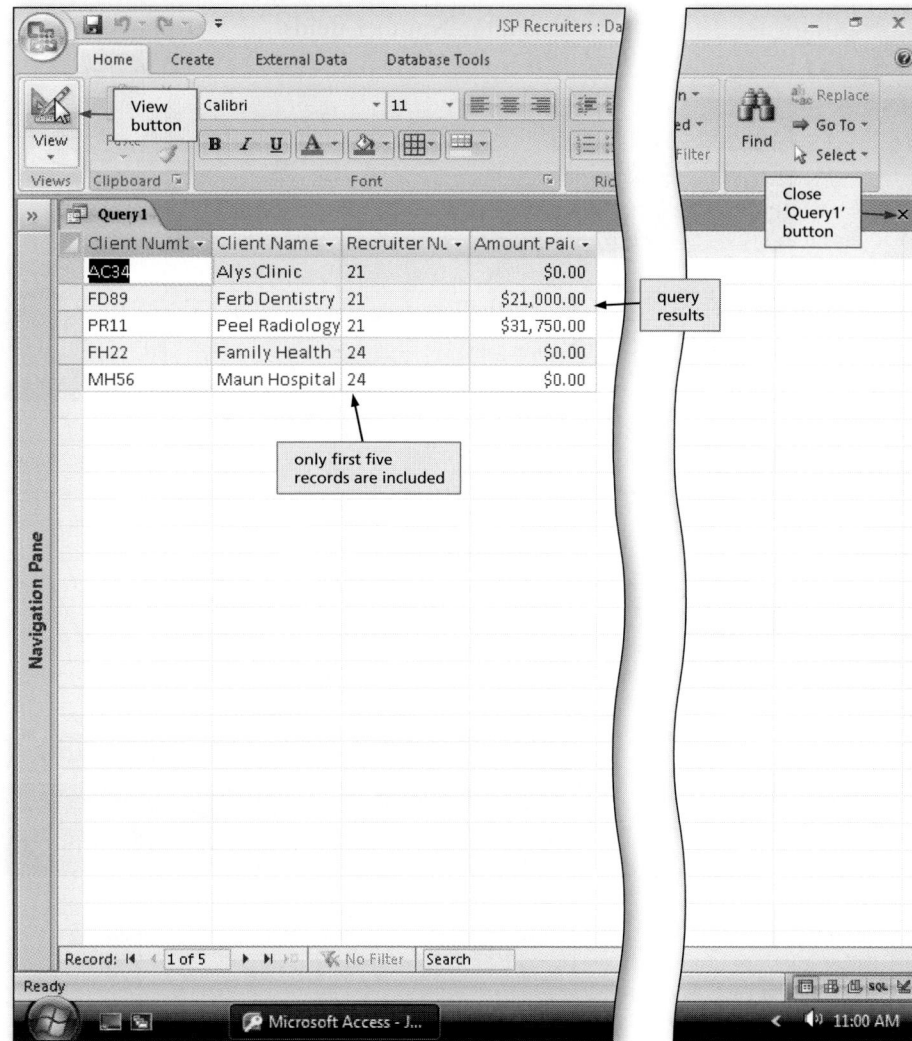

Figure 2–44

Joining Tables

In designing a query, you need to determine whether more than one table is required. If the question being asked involves data from both the Client and Recruiter tables, for example, both tables are required for the query. Such a query may require listing the number and name of each client along with the number and name of the client's recruiter. The client's name is in the Client table, whereas the recruiter's name is in the Recruiter table. Thus, this query cannot be completed using a single table; both the Client and Recruiter tables are required. You need to **join** the tables; that is, to find records in the two tables that have identical values in matching fields (Figure 2–45). In this example, you need to find records in the Client table and the Recruiter table that have the same value in the Recruiter Number fields.

Client table

Client Number	Name	...	Recruiter Number
AC34	Alys Clinic	...	21
BH72	Berls Hospital	...	24
BL12	Benton Labs	...	24
EA45	ENT Assoc.	...	27
FD89	Ferb Dentistry	...	21
FH22	Family Health	...	24
MH56	Maun Hospital	...	24
PR11	Peel Radiology	...	21
TC37	Tarleton Clinic	...	27
WL56	West Labs	...	24

Give me the number and name of each client along with the number and name of each client's recruiter.

Recruiter table

Recruiter Number	Last Name	First Name	...
21	Kerry	Alyssa	...
24	Reeves	Camden	...
27	Fernandez	Jaime	...
34	Lee	Jan	...

Join of Client and Recruiter tables

Client Number	Name	...	Recruiter Number	Last Name	First Name	...
AC34	Alys Clinic	...	21	Kerry	Alyssa	...
BH72	Berls Hospital	...	24	Reeves	Camden	...
BL12	Benton Labs	...	24	Reeves	Camden	...
EA45	ENT Assoc.	...	27	Fernandez	Jaime	...
FD89	Ferb Dentistry	...	21	Kerry	Alyssa	...
FH22	Family Health	...	24	Reeves	Camden	...
MH56	Maun Hospital	...	24	Reeves	Camden	...
PR11	Peel Radiology	...	21	Kerry	Alyssa	...
TC37	Tarleton Clinic	...	27	Fernandez	Jaime	...
WL56	West Labs	...	24	Reeves	Camden	...

Figure 2–45

BTW

Join Types
The type of join that finds records from both tables that have identical values in matching fields is called an inner join. An inner join is the default join in Access. Outer joins are used to show all the records in one table as well as the common records; that is, the records that share the same value in the join field. In a left outer join, all rows from the table on the left are included. In a right outer join, all rows from the table on the right are included.

The following are guidelines related to joining tables.

Plan Ahead

Determine whether more than one table is required.

1. **Determine whether more than one table is required.** Examine the query or request to see if all the fields involved in the request are in one table. If the fields are in two (or more) tables, you need to join the tables.

2. **Determine the matching fields.** If joining is required, identify the matching fields in the two tables that have identical values. Look for the same column name in the two tables or for column names that are similar.

(continued)

(continued)

3. **Determine whether sorting is required**. Queries that join tables often are used as the basis for a report. If this is the case, it may be necessary to sort the results. For example, the Recruiter-Client Report is based on a query that joins the Recruiter and Client tables. The query is sorted by recruiter number and client number.

4. **Determine restrictions**. Examine the query or request to see if there are any special restrictions. For example, the query may only want clients whose current due amount is $0.00.

5. **Determine join properties**. Examine the query or request to see if you only want records from both tables that have identical values in matching fields. If you want to see records in one of the tables that do not have identical values, then you need to change the join properties. When two tables have fields with the same name, you also need to determine which table contains the field to be used in the query. For example, if you want to see all recruiters, even if they have no clients, then you should include the recruiter number from the Recruiter table in the design grid. If you want only records with identical values in matching fields, then it does not matter which matching field you select.

Plan
Ahead

To Join Tables

If you have determined in the design process that you need to join tables, you will first bring field lists for both tables to the upper Pane of the Query window. Access will draw a line, called a **join line**, between matching fields in the two tables indicating that the tables are related. You then can select fields from either table. Access joins the tables automatically.

The first step is to create a new query and add the Recruiter table to the query. Then, add the Client table to the query. A join line will appear connecting the Recruiter Number fields in the two field lists. This join line indicates how the tables are related; that is, linked through these matching fields. (If you fail to give the matching fields the same name, Access will not insert the line. You can insert it manually, however, by clicking one of the two matching fields and dragging the mouse pointer to the other matching field.)

The following steps create a new query, add the Client table, and then select the appropriate fields.

1

● Click Create on the Ribbon to display the Create tab.

● Click the Query Design button to create a new query.

● Click the Recruiter table in the Show Table dialog box to select the table.

● Click the Add button to add a field list for the Recruiter table to the query (Figure 2–46).

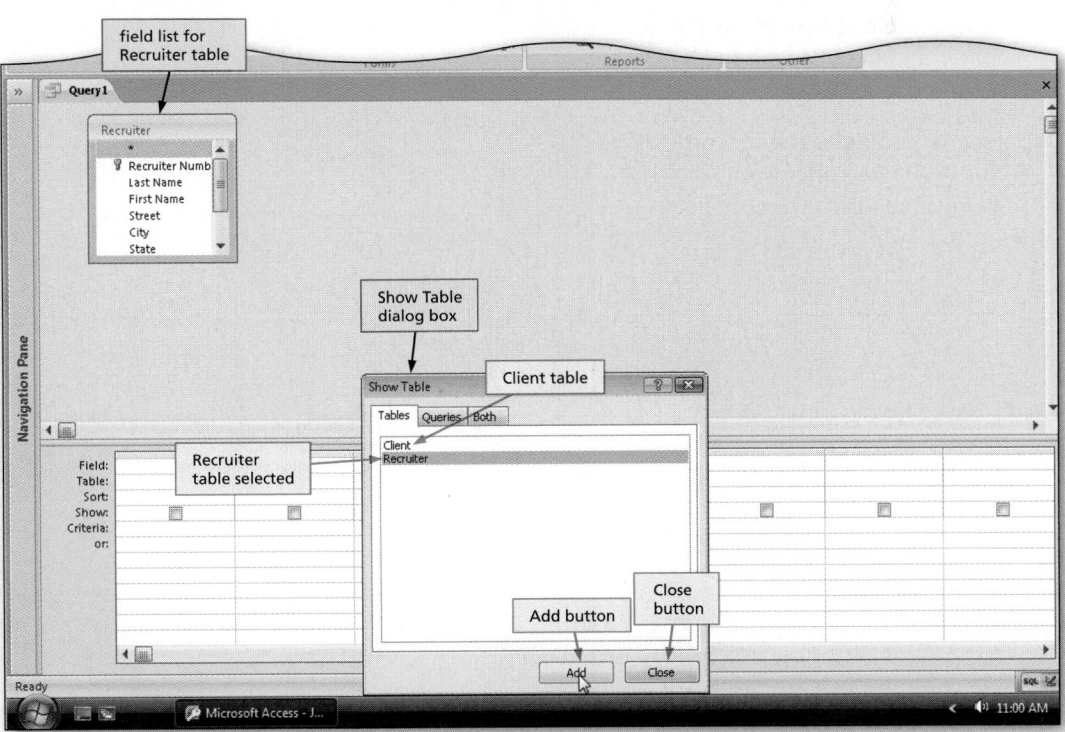

Figure 2–46

2

- Click the Client table in the Show Table dialog box.

- Click the Add button to add a field list for the Client table.

- Close the Show Table dialog box by clicking the Close button.

- Expand the size of the field lists so all the fields in the Recruiter and Client tables appear (Figure 2–47).

Q&A I didn't get a join line. What should I do?

Ensure that the names of the matching fields are exactly the same, the data types are the same, and the matching field is the primary key in one of the two tables. If all of these are true and you still don't have a join line, you can produce one by pointing to one of the matching fields and dragging to the other matching field.

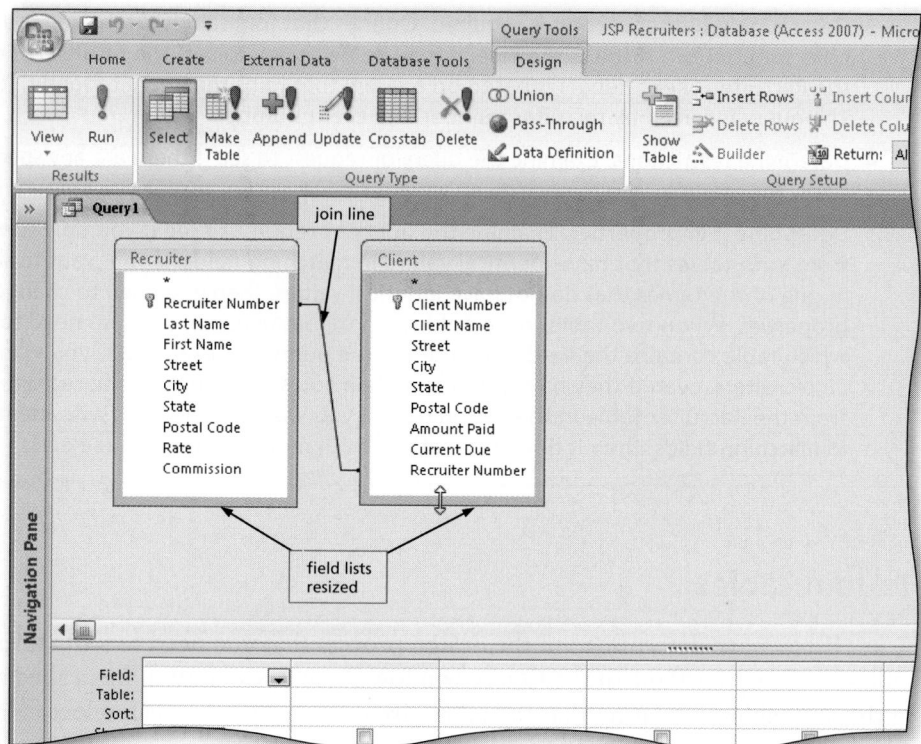

Figure 2–47

3

- In the design grid, include the Recruiter Number, Last Name, and First Name fields from the Recruiter table as well as the Client Number and Client Name fields from the Client table.

- Select Ascending as the sort order for both the Recruiter Number field and the Client Number field (Figure 2–48).

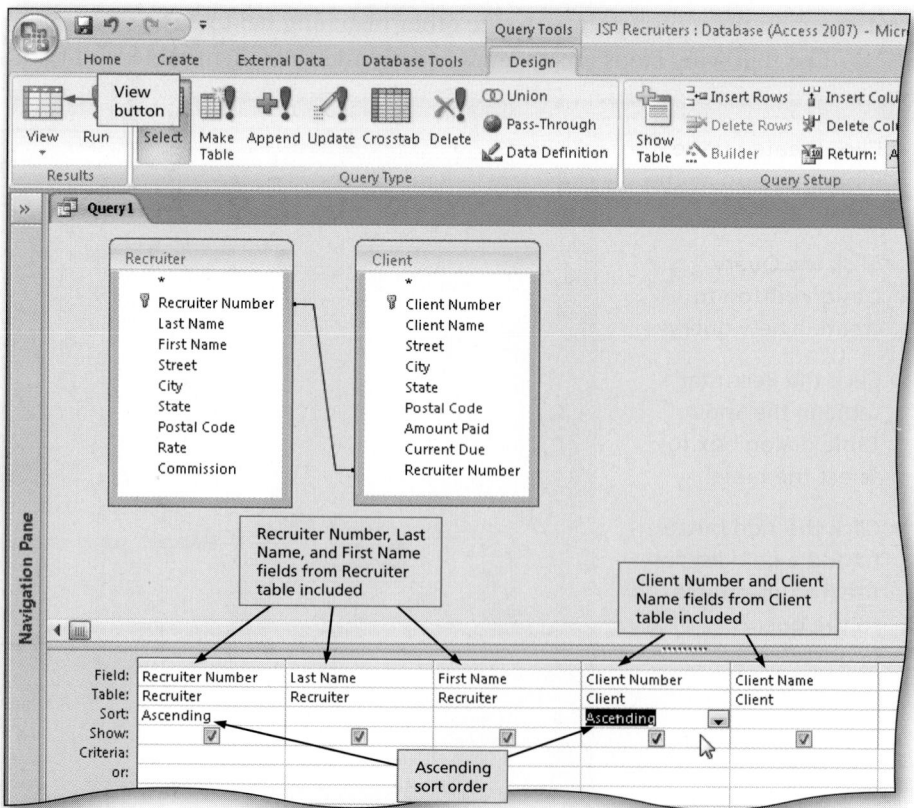

Figure 2–48

4

- View the query results (Figure 2–49).

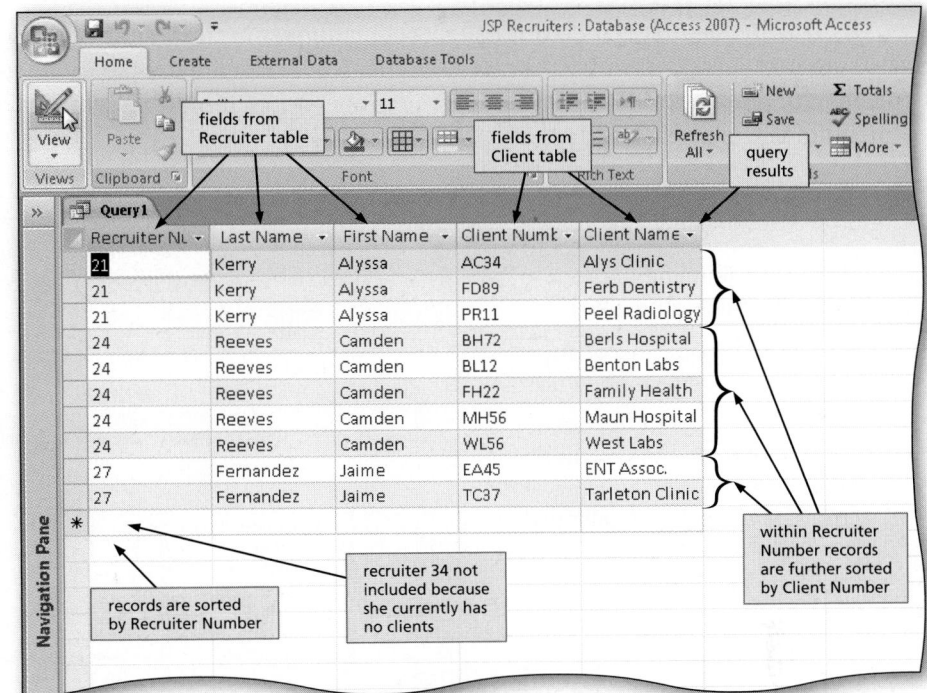

Figure 2–49

To Save the Query

The following steps save the query.

1

- Click the Save button on the Quick Access Toolbar to display the Save As dialog box.

- Type `Recruiter-Client Query` as the query name (Figure 2–50).

2

- Click the OK button to save the query.

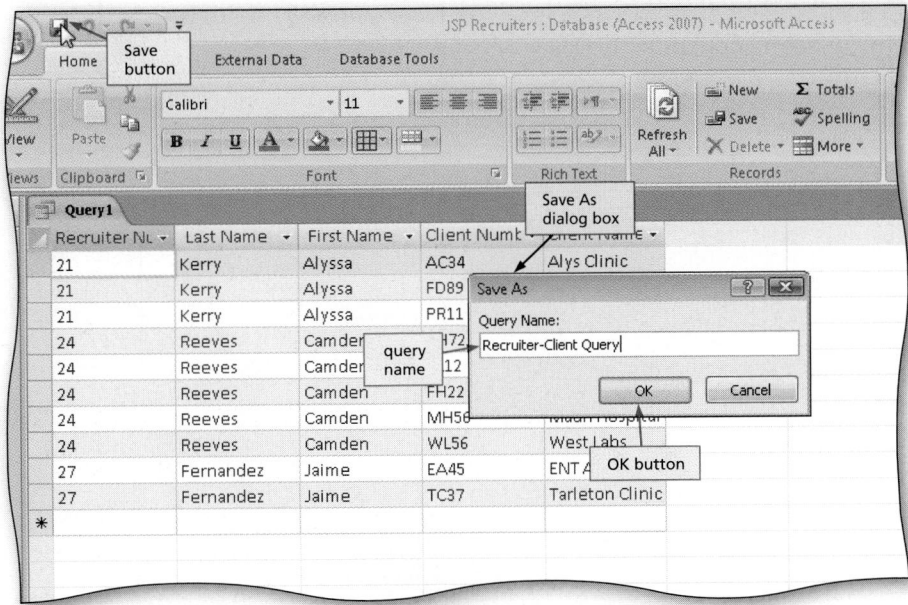

Figure 2–50

To Change Join Properties

Normally records that do not match do not appear in the results of a join query. A recruiter such as Jan Lee, for whom no clients currently exist, for example, would not appear. To cause such a record to be displayed, you need to change the **join properties**, which are the properties that indicate which records appear in a join, of the query, as in the following steps.

 1

• Return to Design view.

• Right-click the join line to produce a shortcut menu (Figure 2–51).

Q&A

I don't see Join Properties on my shortcut menu. What should I do?

If Join Properties does not appear on your shortcut menu, you did not point to the appropriate portion of the join line. You will need to point to the correct portion and right-click again.

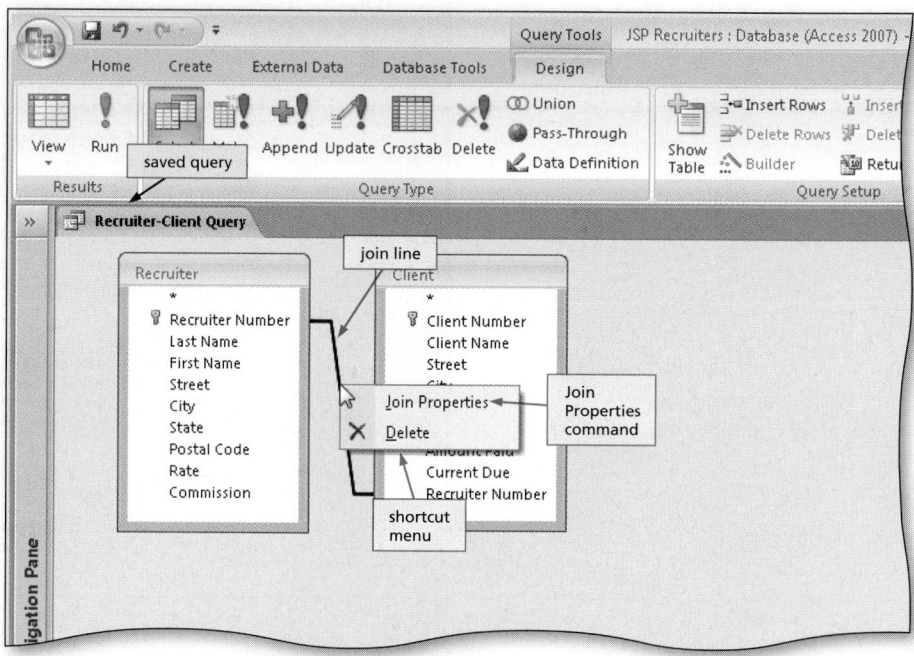

Figure 2–51

2

• Click Join Properties on the shortcut menu to display the Join Properties dialog box (Figure 2–52).

Q&A

How do the options in the Join Properties dialog box match the various types of joins described earlier?

Option button 1 gives an inner join, option button 2 gives a left join, and option button 3 gives a right join.

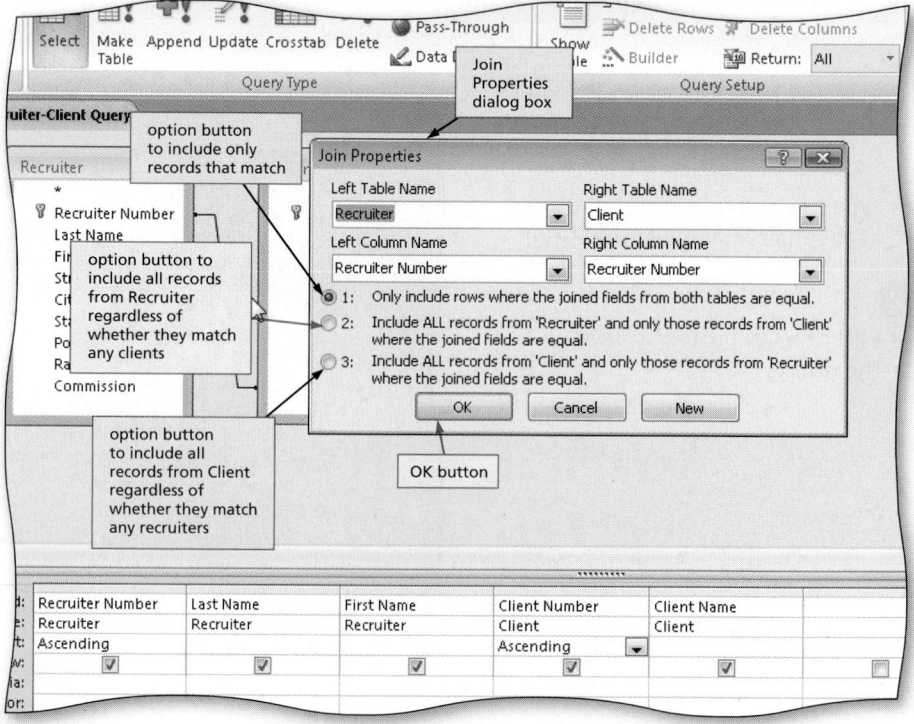

Figure 2–52

3

- Click option button 2 to include all records from the Recruiter table regardless of whether they match any clients.

- Click the OK button.

- View the query results by clicking the View button (Figure 2–53).

- Click the Save button on the Quick Access Toolbar.

Experiment

- Return to Design view, change the Join properties, and select option button 3. View the results to see the effect of this option. When done, return to Design view, change the Join properties, and once again select option button 2.

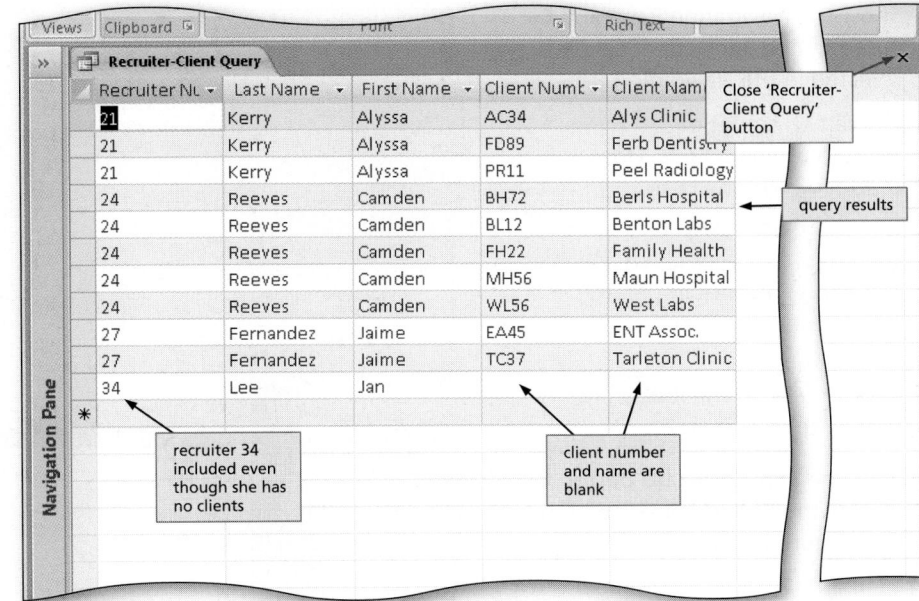

Figure 2–53

4

- Close the Recruiter-Client Query by clicking the Close 'Recruiter-Client Query' button. Click No if asked to save the changes to the query.

To Create a Report Involving a Join

The following steps create the report shown in Figure 2–54. The records in the report are sorted (ordered) by Client Number within Recruiter Number. To ensure that the records appear in this order, the steps specify that the Recruiter Number and Client Number fields are sort keys.

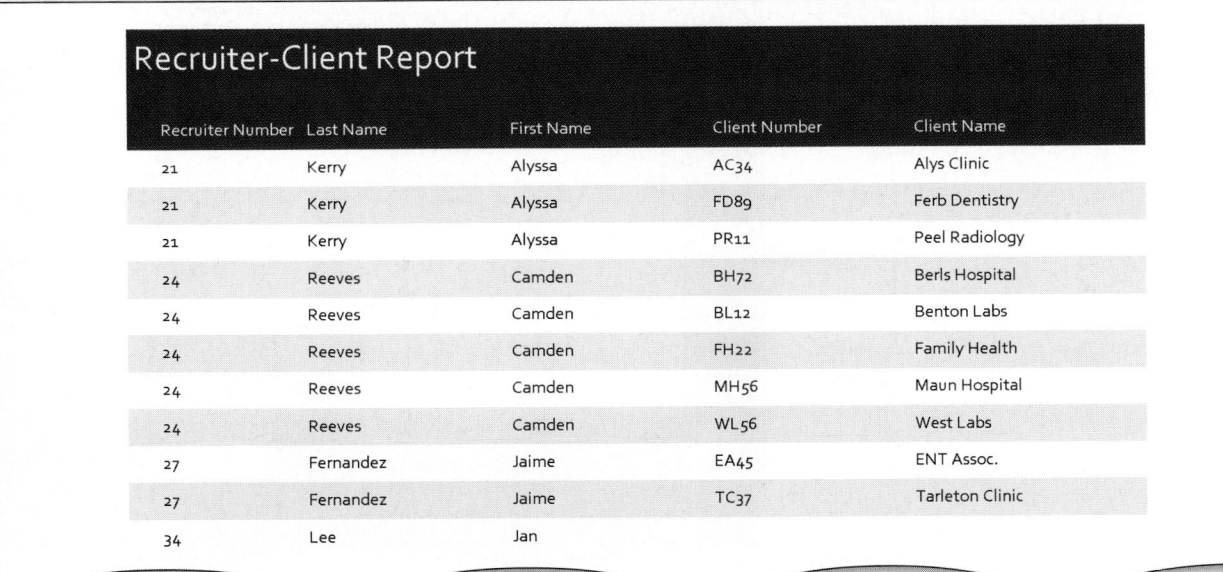

Recruiter Number	Last Name	First Name	Client Number	Client Name
21	Kerry	Alyssa	AC34	Alys Clinic
21	Kerry	Alyssa	FD89	Ferb Dentistry
21	Kerry	Alyssa	PR11	Peel Radiology
24	Reeves	Camden	BH72	Berls Hospital
24	Reeves	Camden	BL12	Benton Labs
24	Reeves	Camden	FH22	Family Health
24	Reeves	Camden	MH56	Maun Hospital
24	Reeves	Camden	WL56	West Labs
27	Fernandez	Jaime	EA45	ENT Assoc.
27	Fernandez	Jaime	TC37	Tarleton Clinic
34	Lee	Jan		

Figure 2–54

1

- Show the Navigation Pane and be sure the Recruiter-Client Query is selected in the Navigation Pane.

Q&A

I have two copies of Recruiter-Client Query. Does it matter which one I use?

No. There are two copies because the recruiter-Client Query involves two tables. It does not matter which one you select.

- Click Create on the Ribbon to display the Create tab.

- Click the Report Wizard button to display the Report Wizard dialog box (Figure 2–55).

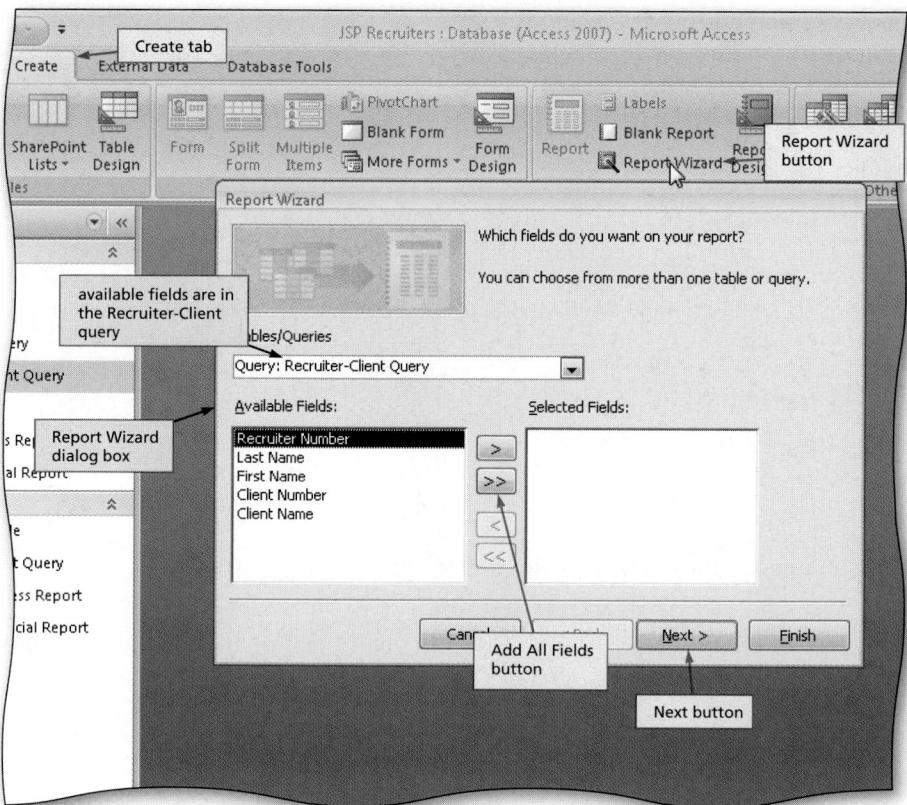

Figure 2–55

2

- Click the Add All Fields button to add all the fields in the Recruiter-Client Query.

- Click the Next button to display the next Report Wizard screen (Figure 2–56).

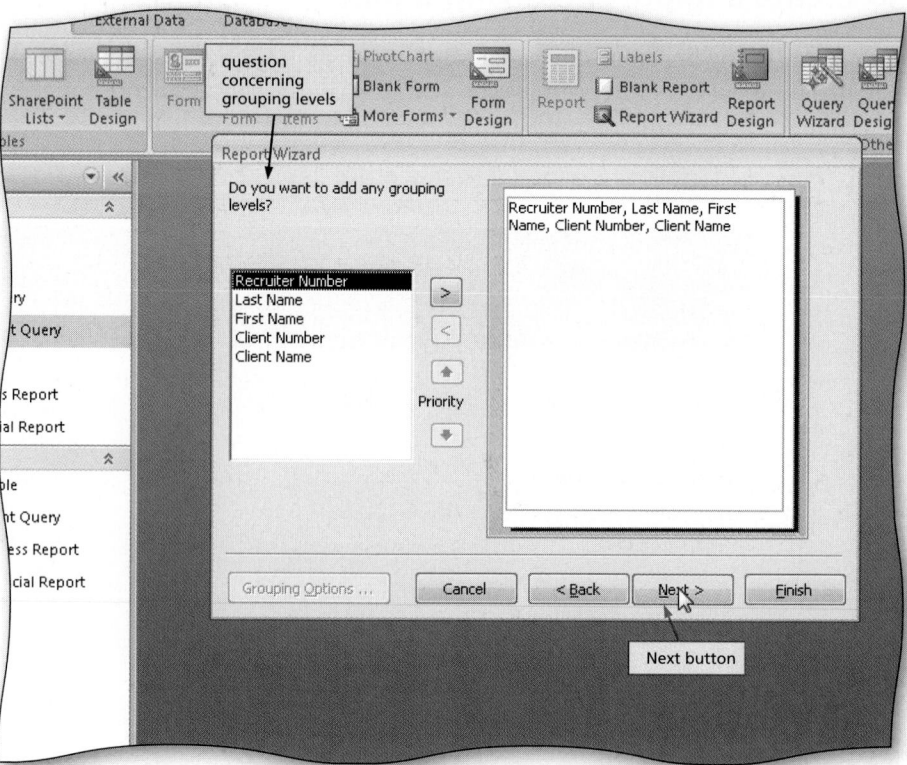

Figure 2–56

- Because you will not specify any grouping, click the Next button in the Report Wizard dialog box to display the next Report Wizard screen.

- Because you already specified the sort order in the query, click the Next button again to display the next Report Wizard screen.

- Make sure that Tabular is selected as the Layout and Portrait is selected as the Orientation.

- Click the Next button to display the next Report Wizard screen.

- Be sure the Module style is selected.

- Click the Next button to display the next Report Wizard screen.

Figure 2–57

- Erase the current title, and then type `Recruiter-Client Report` as the new title.

- Click the Finish button to produce the report (Figure 2–57).

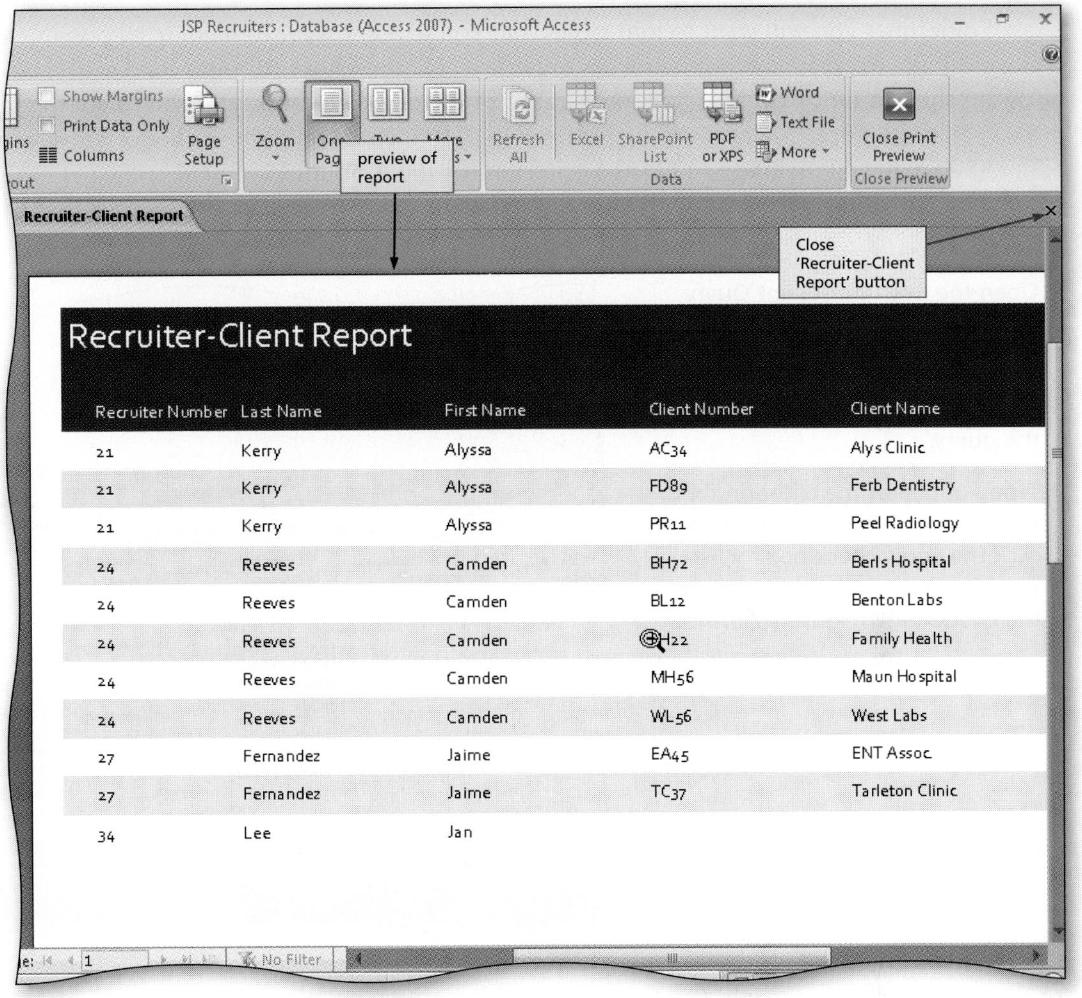

4

- Click the Close button for the Recruiter-Client Report to remove the report from the screen.

To Print a Report

Once you have created a report, you can print it at any time. The layout will reflect the layout you created. The data in the report will always reflect current data. The following step prints the Recruiter-Client Report.

1 With the Recruiter-Client Report selected in the Navigation Pane, click the Office Button, point to Print on the Office button menu, and then click Quick Print on the Print submenu to print the report.

To Restrict the Records in a Join

Sometimes you will want to join tables, but you will not want to include all possible records. For example, you would like to create a report showing only those clients whose Amount Paid is greater than $20,000, but you do not want the Amount Paid field to appear in the results. In such cases, you will relate the tables and include fields just as you did before. You also will include criteria. To include only those clients whose amount paid is more than $20,000.00, you will include >20000 as a criterion for the Amount Paid field.

The following steps modify the Recruiter-Client query to restrict the records that will be included in the join.

- Open the Recruiter-Client Query in Design view and hide the Navigation Pane.

- Add the Amount Paid field to the query.

- Type >20000 as the criterion for the Amount Paid field and then click the Show check box for the Amount Paid field to remove the check mark (Figure 2–58).

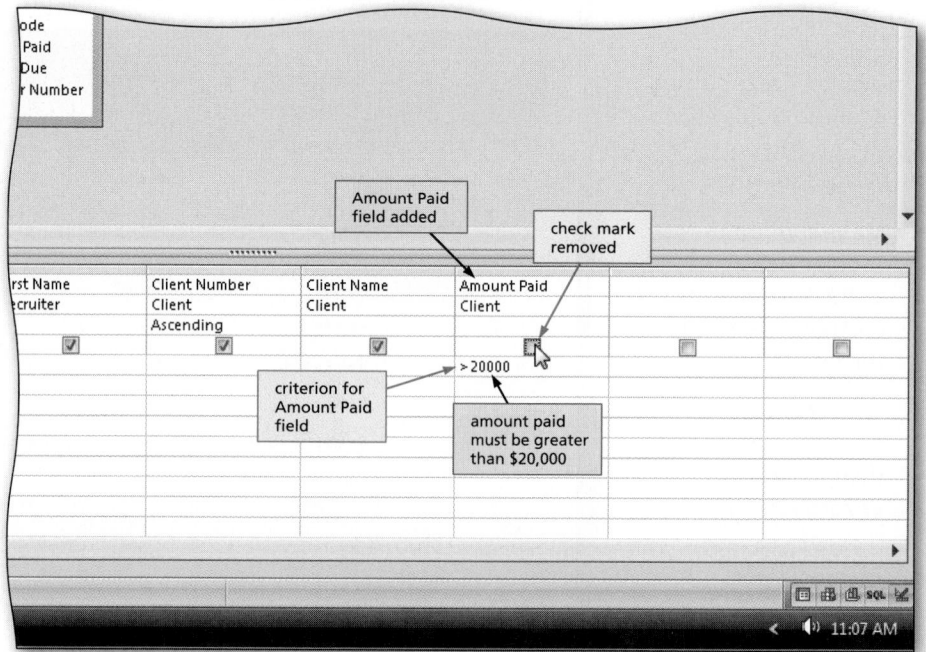

Figure 2–58

- View the query results (Figure 2–59).

- Close the query by clicking the Close 'Recruiter-Client Query' button.

- When asked if you want to save your changes, click the No button.

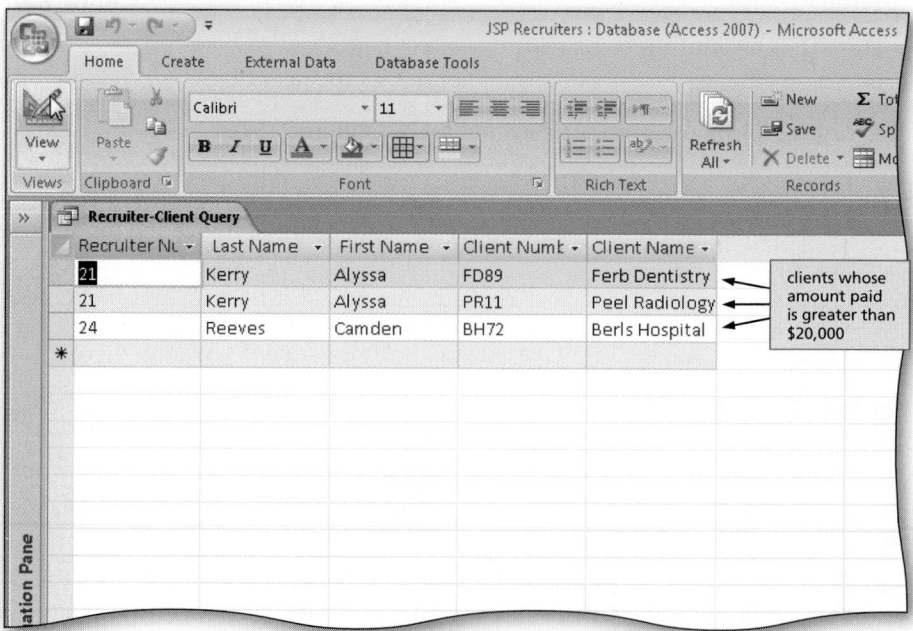

Figure 2–59

Calculations

If you have determined that a special calculation is required for a query, you then need to determine whether the calculation is an individual record calculation (for example, adding the values in two fields) or a group calculation (for example, finding the total of the values in a particular field on all the records).

JSP Recruiters may want to know the total amount (amount paid plus current due) from each client. This would seem to pose a problem because the Client table does not include a field for total amount. You can calculate it, however, because the total amount is equal to the amount paid plus the current due. A field that can be computed from other fields is called a **calculated field**. A calculated field is an individual record calculation.

JSP also may want to calculate the average amount paid for the clients of each recruiter. That is, they want the average for the clients of recruiter 21, the average for the clients of recruiter 24, and so on. This type of calculation is called a group calculation, because it involves groups of records. In this example, the clients of recruiter 21 would form one group, the clients of recruiter 24 would be a second, and the clients of recruiter 27 form a third group.

The following are guidelines related to calculations in queries.

Determine whether calculations are required.

1. **Determine whether calculations are required.** Examine the query or request to see if there are special calculations to be included. Look for words such as "total," "sum," "compute," or "calculate."

2. **Determine a name for the calculated field.** If calculations are required, decide on the name for the field. Assign a name that helps identify the contents of the field. For example, if you are adding the cost of a number of items, the name "Total Cost" would be appropriate. The name, also called an **alias**, becomes the column name when the query is run.

3. **Determine the format for the calculated field.** Determine how the calculated field should appear. If the calculation involves monetary amounts, you would use the currency format. If the calculated value contains decimals, determine how many decimal places to display.

BTW

Expression Builder
Access includes a tool to help you create complex expressions. If you click Build on the shortcut menu (see Figure 2-60 on the next page), Access displays the Expression Builder dialog box. The dialog box includes an expression box, operator buttons, and expression elements. You use the expression box to build the expression. You can type parts of the expression directly and paste operator buttons and expression elements into the box. You also can use functions in expressions.

Plan Ahead

To Use a Calculated Field in a Query

If you have determined that you need a calculated field in a query, you enter a name (alias) for the calculated field, a colon, and then the expression in one of the columns in the Field row. Any fields included in the expression must be enclosed in square brackets [ ]. For the total amount, for example, you will type Total Amount:[Amount Paid]+[Current Due] as the expression.

You can type the expression directly into the Field row. You will not be able to see the entire entry, however, because the Field row is not large enough. The preferred way is to select the column in the Field row and then use the Zoom command on its shortcut menu. When Access displays the Zoom dialog box, you can enter the expression.

You are not restricted to addition in calculations. You can use subtraction (-), multiplication (*), or division (/). You also can include parentheses in your calculations to indicate which calculations should be done first.

The steps on the next page use a calculated field to display the number, name, amount paid, current due, and the total amount for all clients.

- Create a query with a field list for the Client table.

- Add the Client Number, Client Name, Amount Paid, and Current Due fields to the query.

- Right-click the Field row in the first open column in the design grid to display a shortcut menu (Figure 2–60).

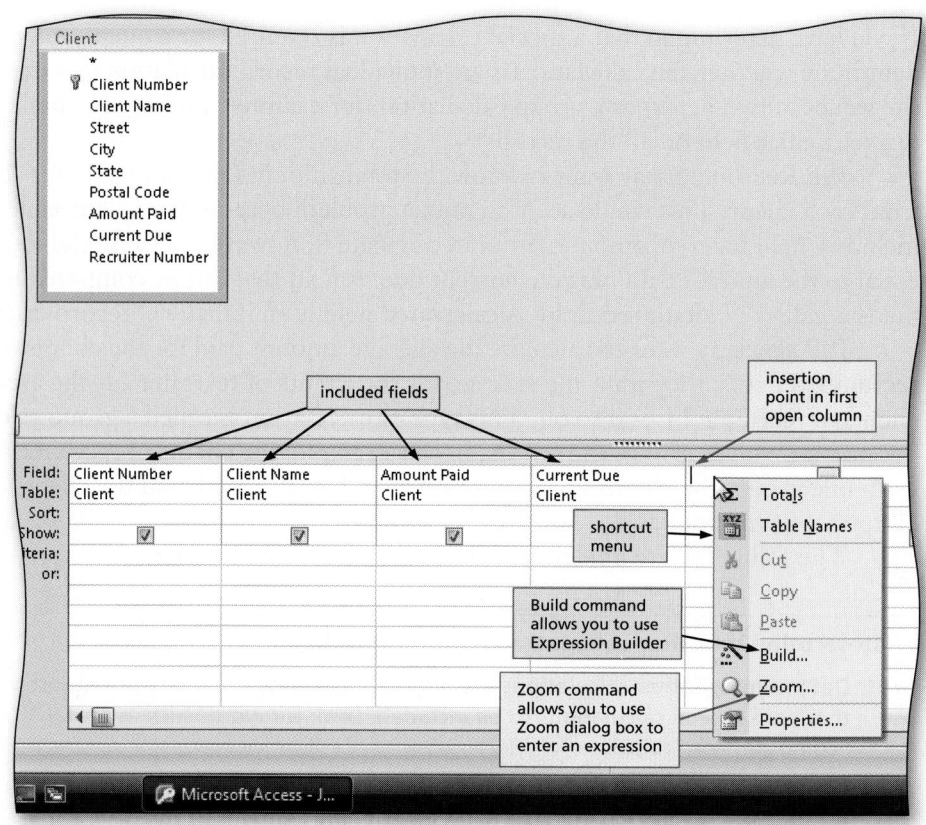

Figure 2–60

- Click Zoom on the shortcut menu to display the Zoom dialog box.

- Type Total Amount:[Amount Paid]+[Current Due] in the Zoom dialog box (Figure 2–61).

Q&A

Do I always need to put square brackets around field names?

If the field name does not contain spaces, square brackets are technically not necessary, although it is still acceptable to use the brackets. It is a good practice, however, to get in the habit of using the brackets.

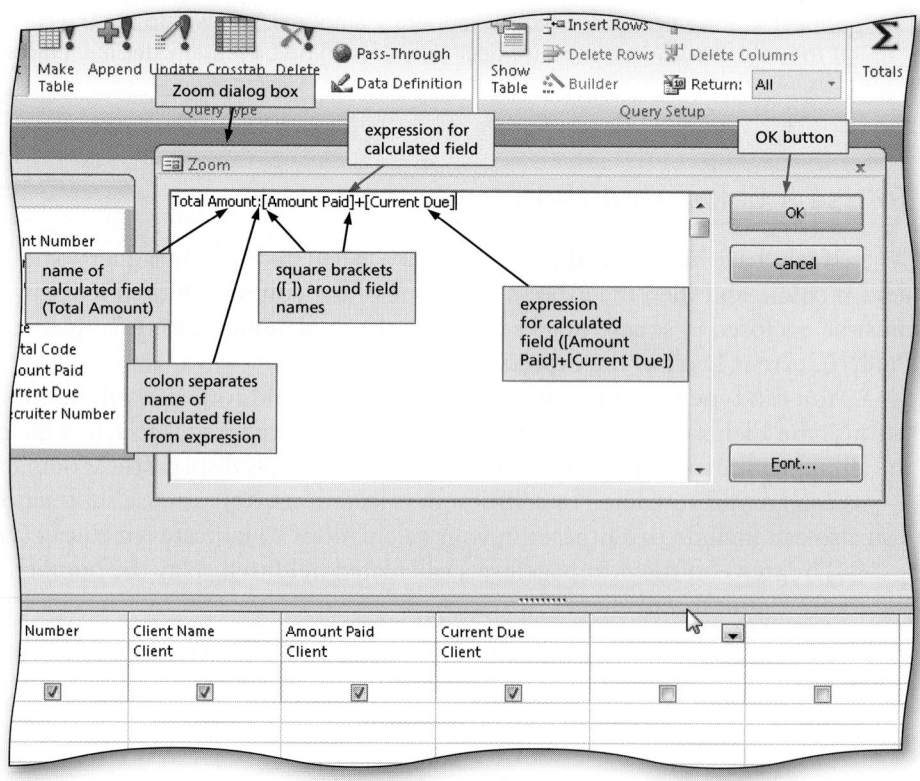

Figure 2–61

3

- Click the OK button to enter the expression (Figure 2–62).

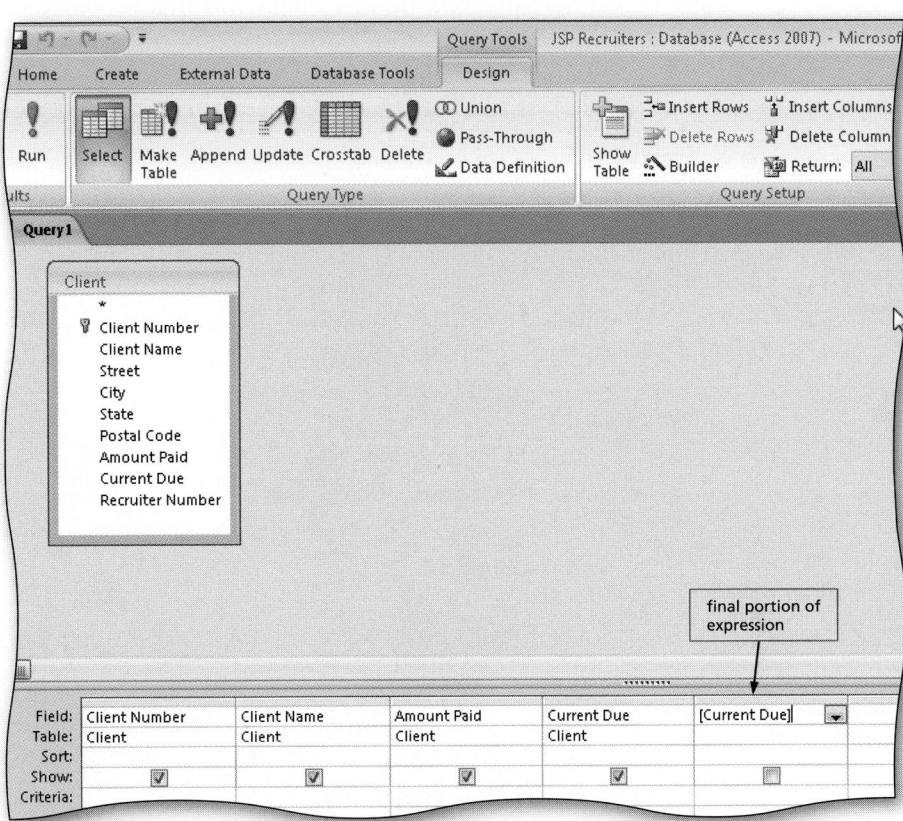

Figure 2–62

4

- View the query results (Figure 2–63).

Experiment

- Return to Design view and try other expressions. In at least one case, omit the Total Amount and the colon. In at least one case, intentionally misspell a field name. In each case, view the results to see the effect of your changes. When finished, re-enter the original expression.

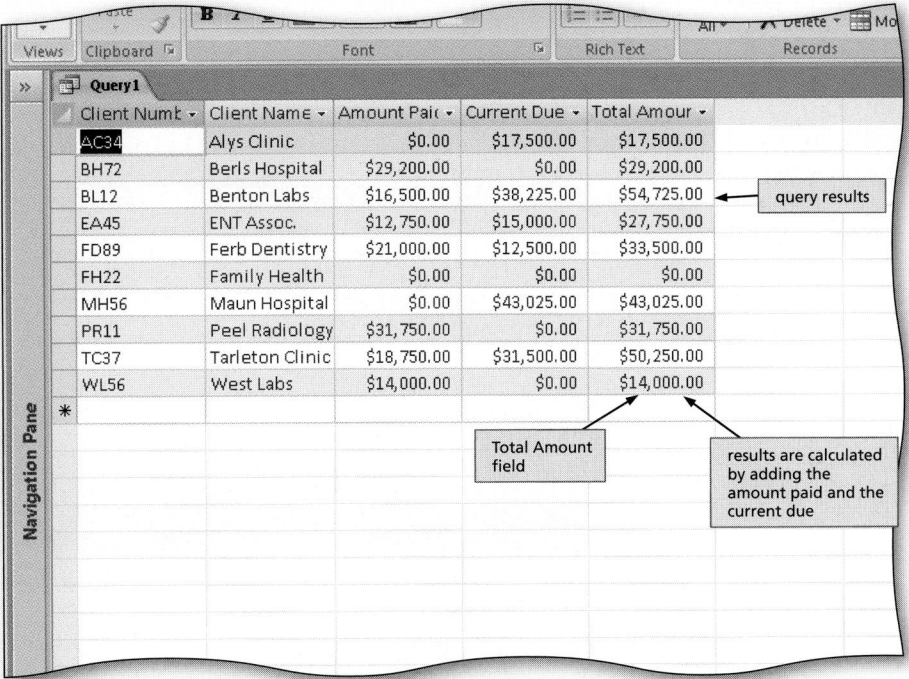

Figure 2–63

Instead of clicking Zoom on the shortcut menu, you can click Build. Access displays the Expression Builder dialog box that provides assistance in creating the expression. If you know the expression you will need, however, it is often easier to enter it using the Zoom command.

To Change a Caption

You can change the way items appear in the results of a query by changing their format. You also can change a query result's heading at the top of a column by changing the caption. Just as when you omitted duplicates, you will make this change by using a property sheet. In the property sheet, you can change the desired property, such as the format, the number of decimal places, or the caption. The following steps change the caption of the Amount Paid field to Paid and the caption of the Current Due field to Due.

- Return to Design view.

- Click Design on the Ribbon to display the Design tab.

- Click the Amount Paid field in the design grid, and then click the Property Sheet button on the Design tab.

- Click the Caption box, and then type Paid as the caption (Figure 2–64).

Q&A

My property sheet looks different. What should I do?

If your sheet looks different, you clicked the wrong place and will have to close the property sheet and repeat this step.

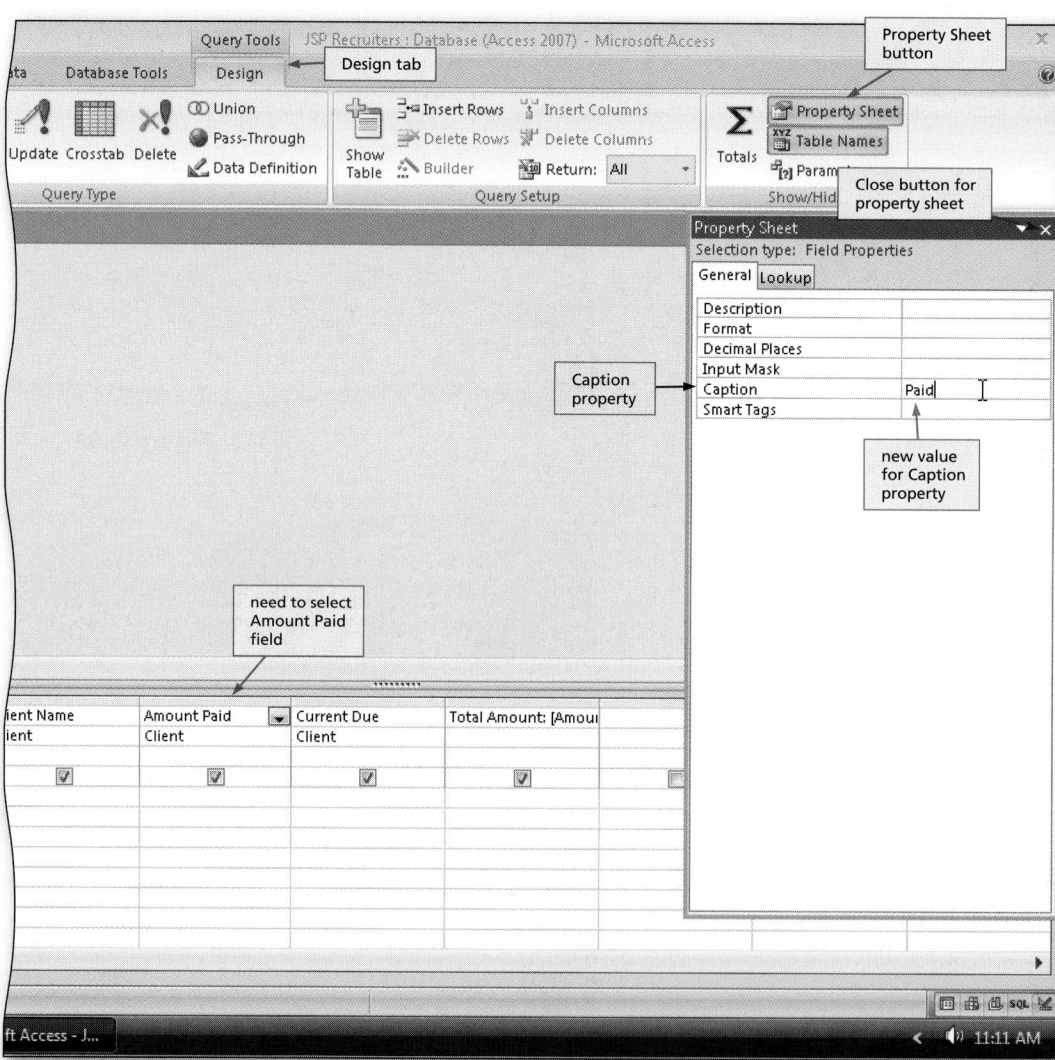

Figure 2–64

- Close the property sheet by clicking its Close button.

- Click the Current Due field in the design grid, and then click the Property Sheet button on the Design tab.

- Click the Caption box, and then type Due as the caption.

- Close the Property Sheet by clicking its Close button.

- View the query results (Figure 2–65).

- Click the Close 'Query1' button to close the query.

- When asked if you want to save your changes, click the No button.

Q&A

What would happen if I clicked the Yes button instead of the No button?

If you had saved the query, the changes you made to the properties would be saved in the database along with the query.

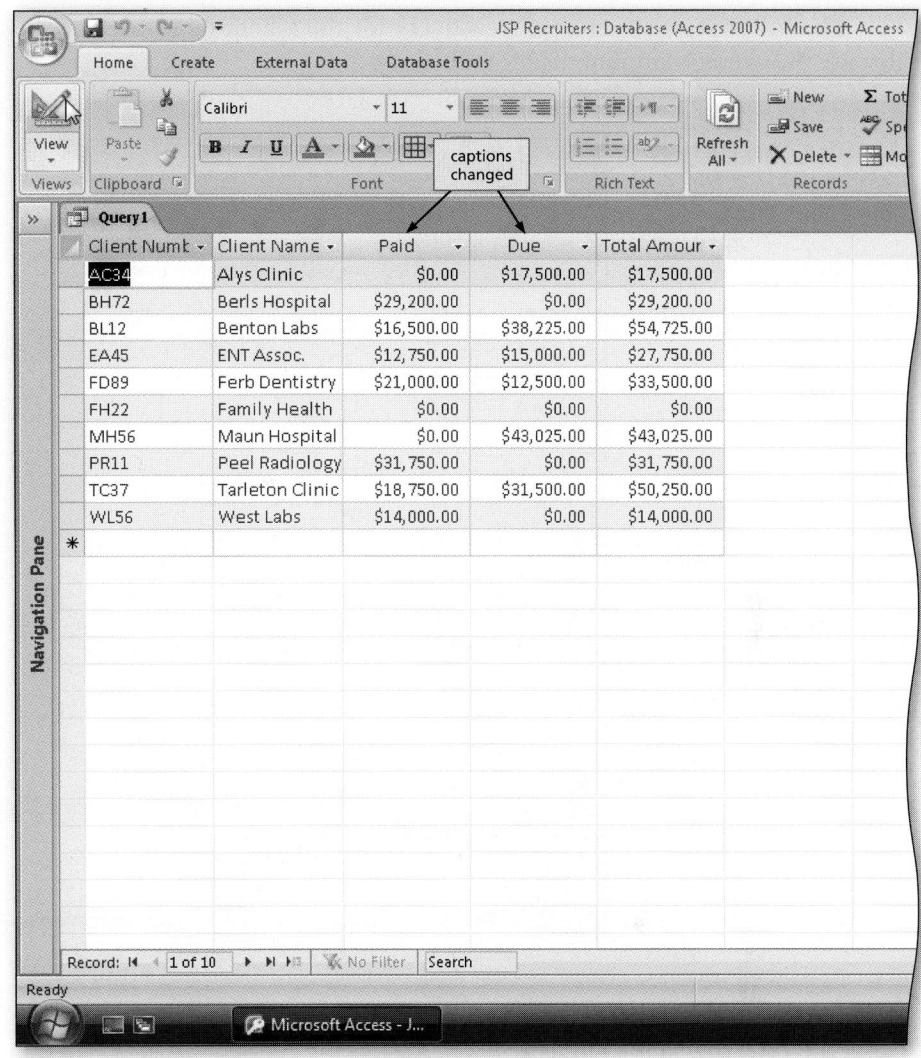

Figure 2–65

Other Ways

1. Right-click field in design grid, click Properties on shortcut menu

Calculating Statistics

For group calculations, Microsoft Access supports several built-in statistics: COUNT (count of the number of records), SUM (total), AVG (average), MAX (largest value), MIN (smallest value), STDEV (standard deviation), VAR (variance), FIRST (first value), and LAST (last value). These statistics are called aggregate functions. An **aggregate function** is a function that performs some mathematical function against a group of records. To use any of these aggregate functions in a query, you include it in the Total row in the design grid. The Total row routinely does not appear in the grid. To include it, click the Totals button on the Design tab.

To Calculate Statistics

The following steps create a new query for the Client table, include the Total row in the design grid, and then calculate the average amount paid for all clients.

1

- Create a new query with a field list for the Client table.

- If necessary, click Design on the Ribbon to display the Design tab.

- Add the Amount Paid field to the query.

- Click the Totals button on the Design tab to include the Total row in the design grid (Figure 2-66).

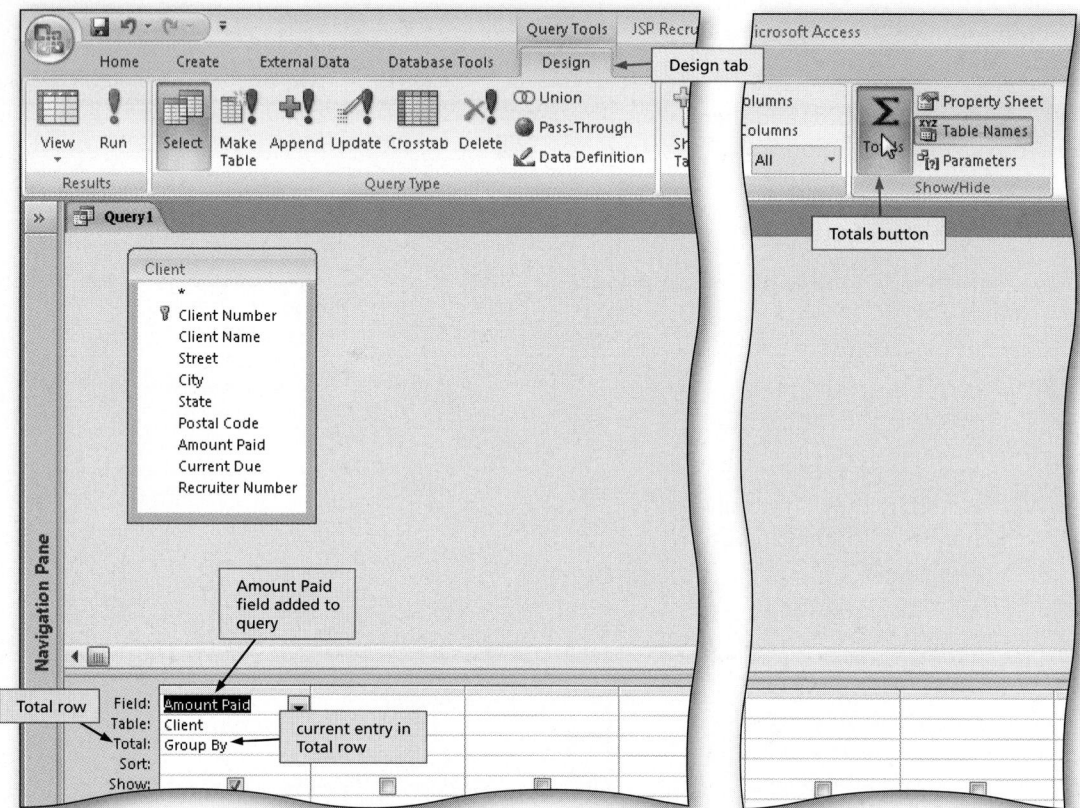

Figure 2–66

2

- Click the Total row in the Amount Paid column to display the Total box arrow.

- Click the Total box arrow to display the Total list (Figure 2–67).

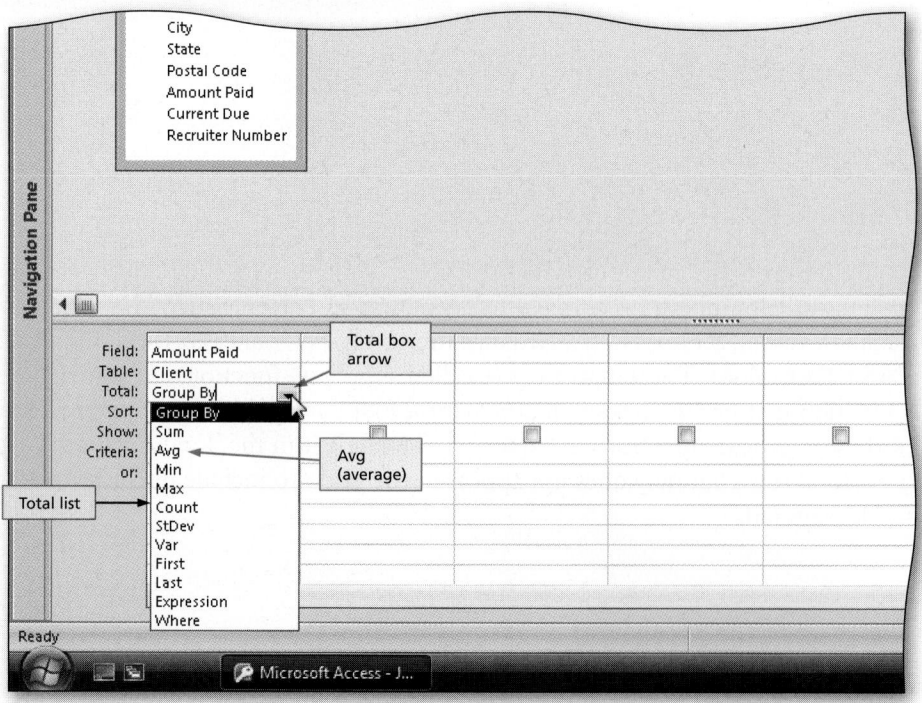

Figure 2–67

3

- Click Avg to indicate that
  Access is to calculate an average
  (Figure 2–68).

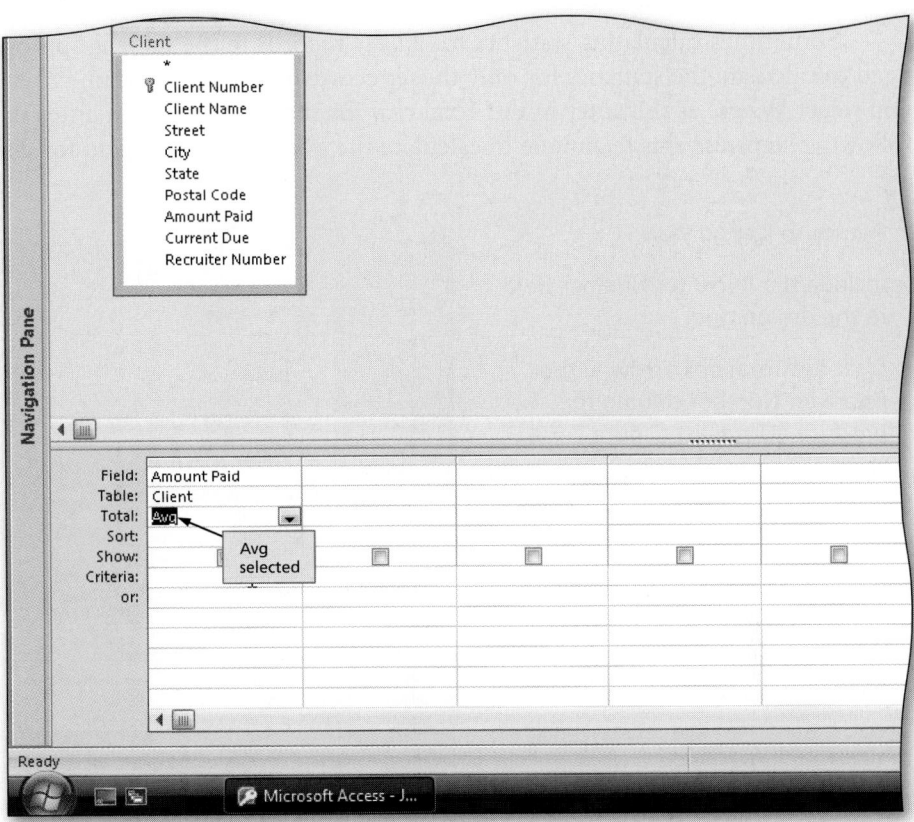

Figure 2–68

4

- View the query
  results (Figure 2–69).

Experiment

- Return to Design view and try
  other aggregate functions. In each
  case, view the results to see the
  effect of your selection. When
  finished, select average
  once again.

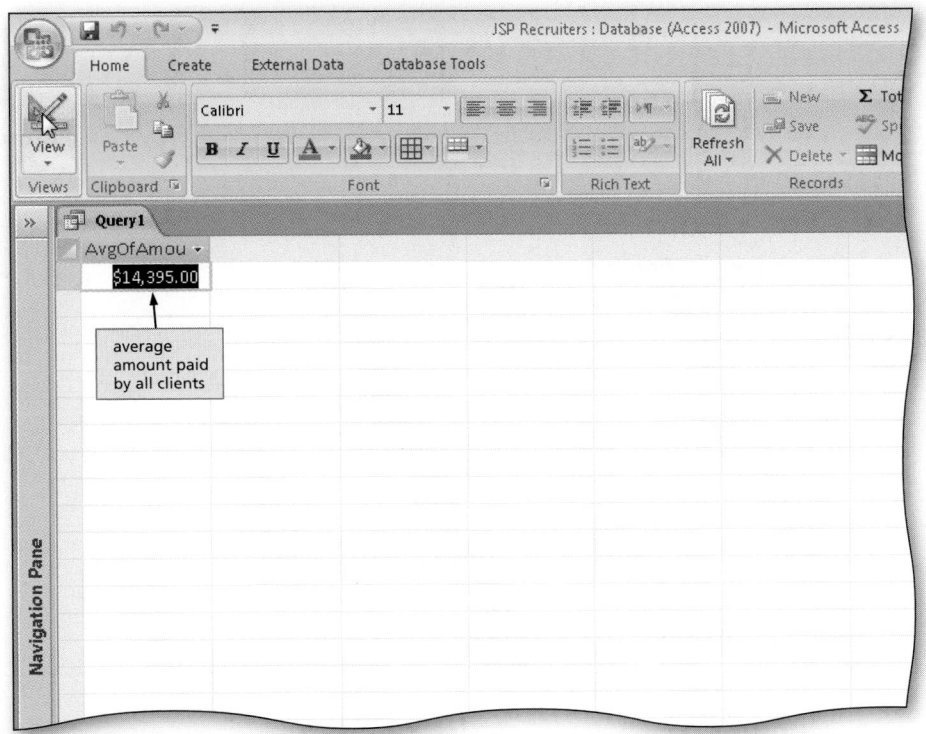

Figure 2–69

To Use Criteria in Calculating Statistics

Sometimes calculating statistics for all the records in the table is appropriate. In other cases, however, you will need to calculate the statistics for only those records that satisfy certain criteria. To enter a criterion in a field, first you select Where as the entry in the Total row for the field, and then enter the criterion in the Criteria row. The following steps use this technique to calculate the average amount paid for clients of recruiter 21.

- Return to Design view.

- Include the Recruiter Number field in the design grid.

- Click the Total box arrow in the Recruiter Number column to produce a Total list (Figure 2–70).

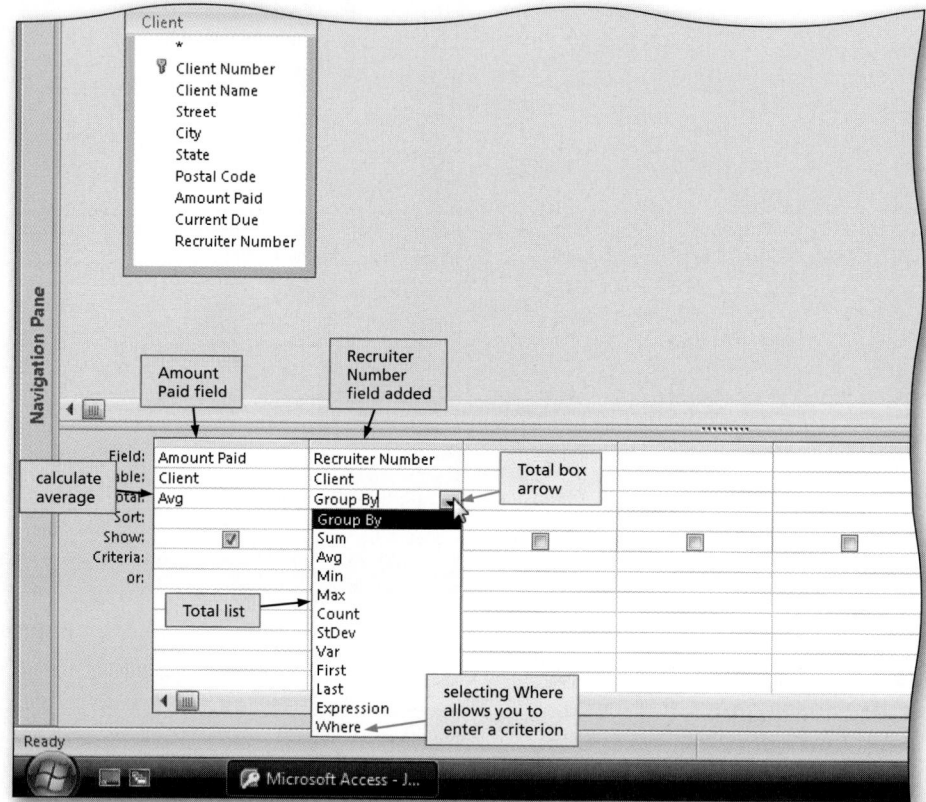

Figure 2–70

- Click Where.

- Type 21 as the criterion for the Recruiter Number field (Figure 2–71).

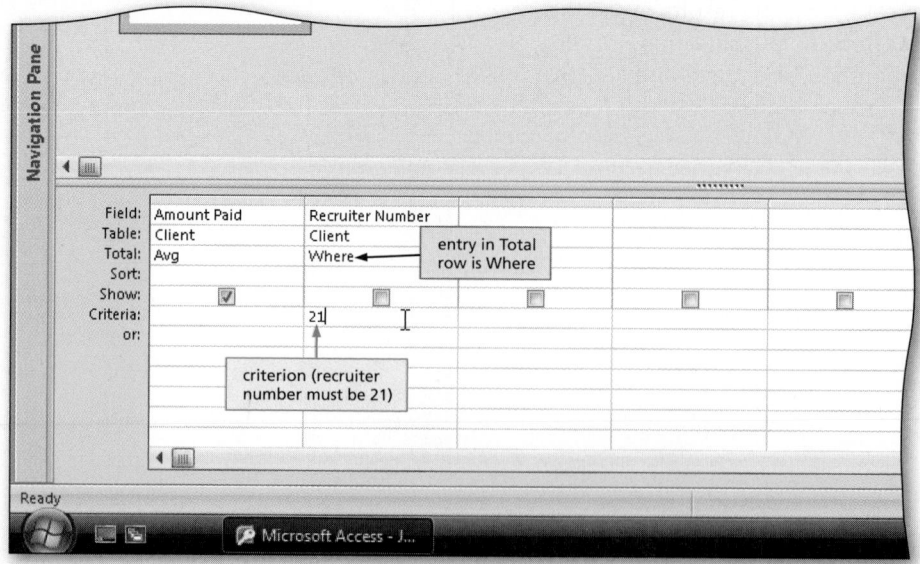

Figure 2–71

- View the query results (Figure 2–72).

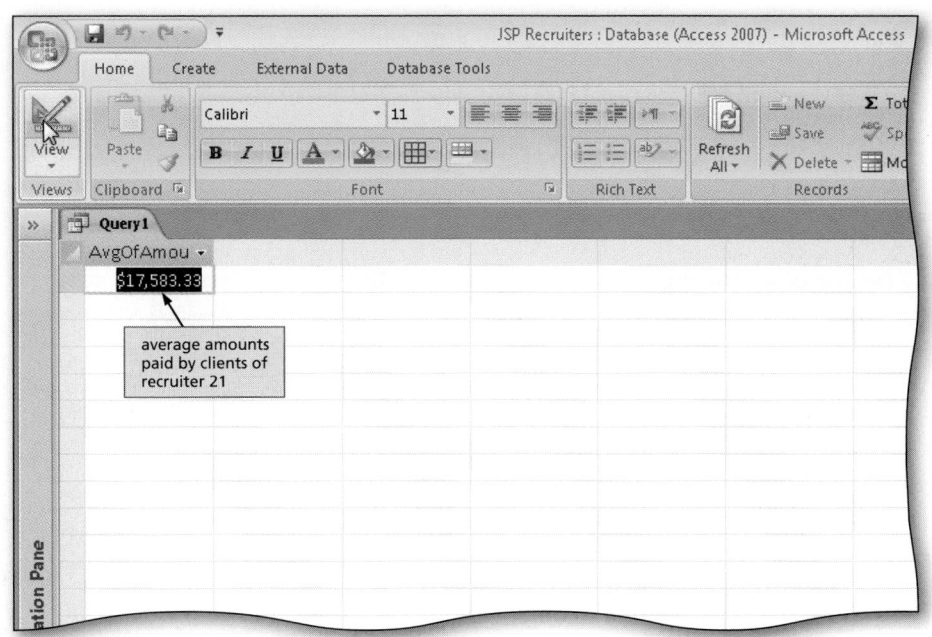

average amounts paid by clients of recruiter 21

Figure 2–72

To Use Grouping

Another way statistics often are used is in combination with grouping; that is, statistics are calculated for groups of records. You may, for example, need to calculate the average amount paid for the clients of each recruiter. You will want the average for the clients of recruiter 21, the average for clients of recruiter 24, and so on.

Grouping means creating groups of records that share some common characteristic. In grouping by Recruiter Number, for example, the clients of recruiter 21 would form one group, the clients of recruiter 24 would form a second, and the clients of recruiter 27 form a third group. The calculations then are made for each group. To indicate grouping in Access, select Group By as the entry in the Total row for the field to be used for grouping.

The following steps calculate the average amount paid for clients of each recruiter.

 1

- Return to Design view and clear the design grid.

- Include the Recruiter Number field in the query.

- Include the Amount Paid field in the query.

- Select Avg as the calculation in the Total row for the Amount Paid field (Figure 2–73).

Q&A

Why didn't I need to change the entry in the Total Row for the Recruiter Number field?

Group By currently is the entry in the Total row for the Recruiter Number field, which is correct; thus, it was not changed.

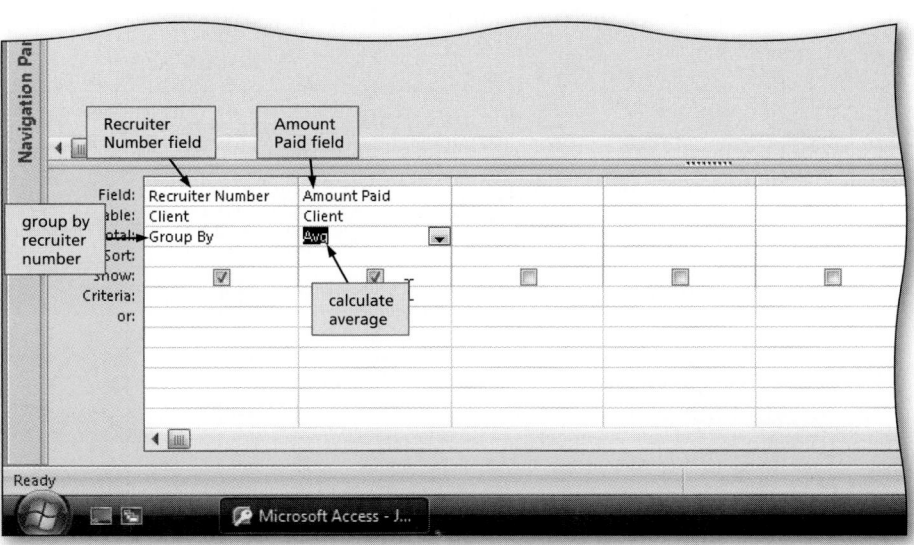

Recruiter Number field

Amount Paid field

group by recruiter number

calculate average

Figure 2–73

2

- View the query results (Figure 2–74).

3

- Close the query.

- Do not save your changes.

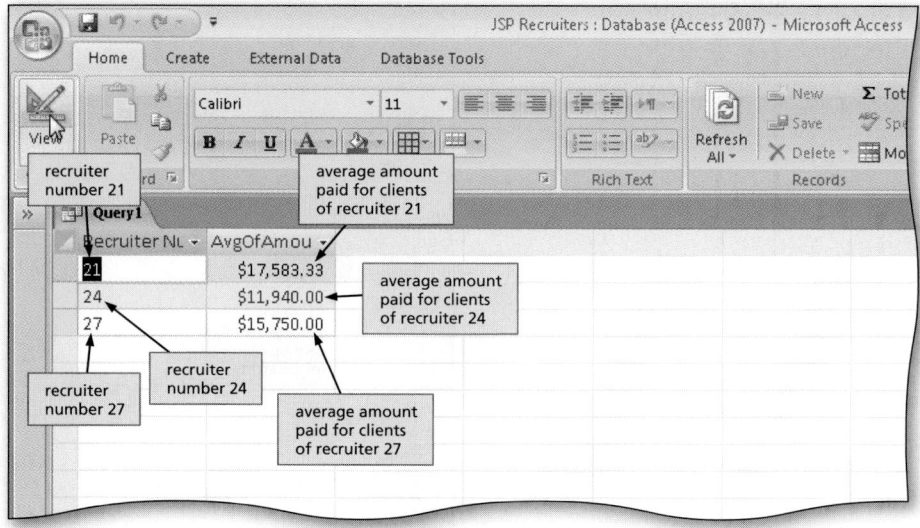

Figure 2–74

Crosstab Queries

Crosstab queries are useful for summarizing data. A crosstab query calculates a statistic (for example, sum, average, or count) for data that is grouped by two different types of information. One of the types will appear down the side of the resulting datasheet, and the other will appear across the top.

For example, if you have determined that a query must summarize the sum of the amounts paid grouped by both city and recruiter number, you could have cities as the row headings, that is, down the side. You could have recruiter numbers as the column headings, that is, across the top. The entries within the data sheet represent the total of the amounts paid. Figure 2–75 shows a crosstab in which the total of amount paid is grouped by both city and recruiter number with cities down the left-hand side and recruiter numbers across the top. For example, the entry in the row labeled Fort Stewart and in the column labeled 21 represents the total of the amount paid by all clients of recruiter 21 who are located in Fort Stewart.

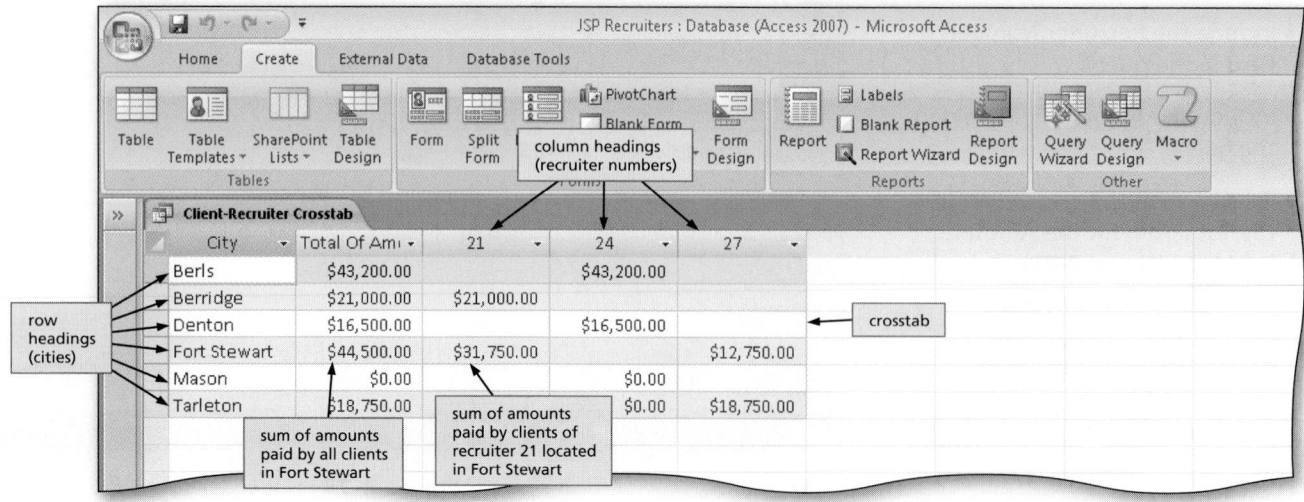

Figure 2–75

To Create a Crosstab Query

The following steps use the Crosstab Query wizard to create a crosstab query.

1

- Click Create on the Ribbon to display the Create tab.

- Click the Query Wizard button to display the New Query dialog box (Figure 2–76).

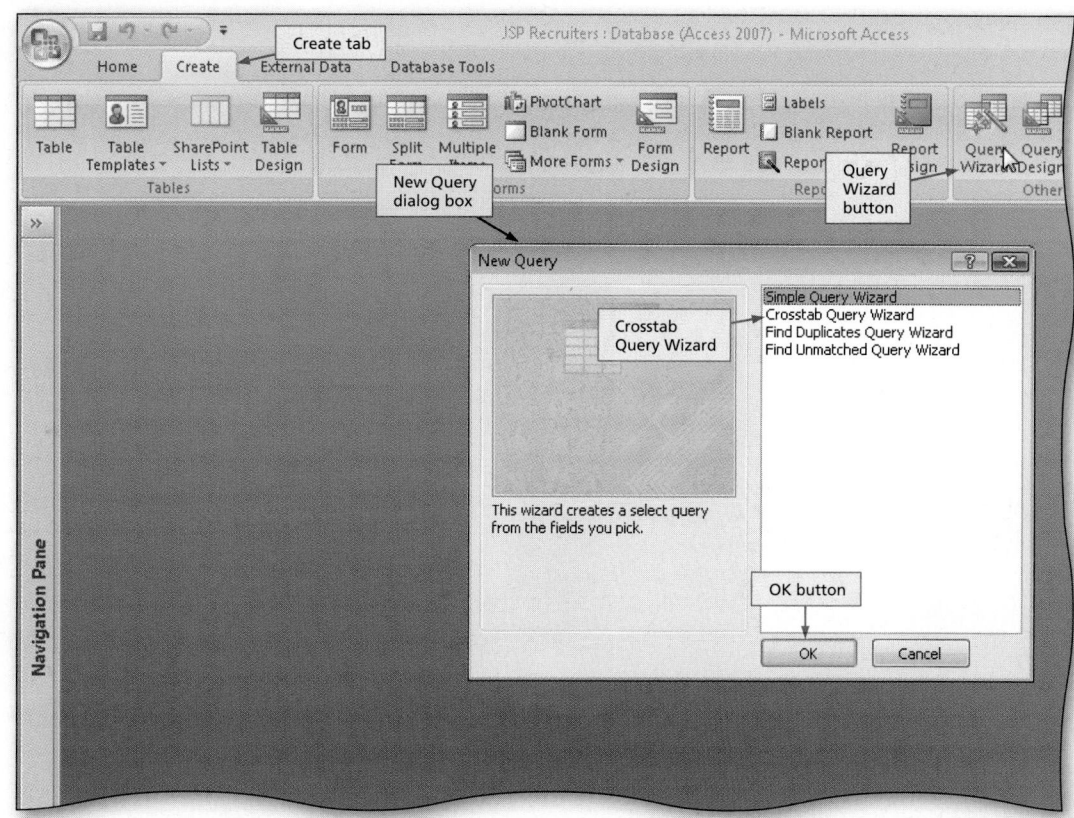

Figure 2–76

2

- Click Crosstab Query Wizard in the New Query dialog box.

- Click the OK button to display the Crosstab Query Wizard (Figure 2–77).

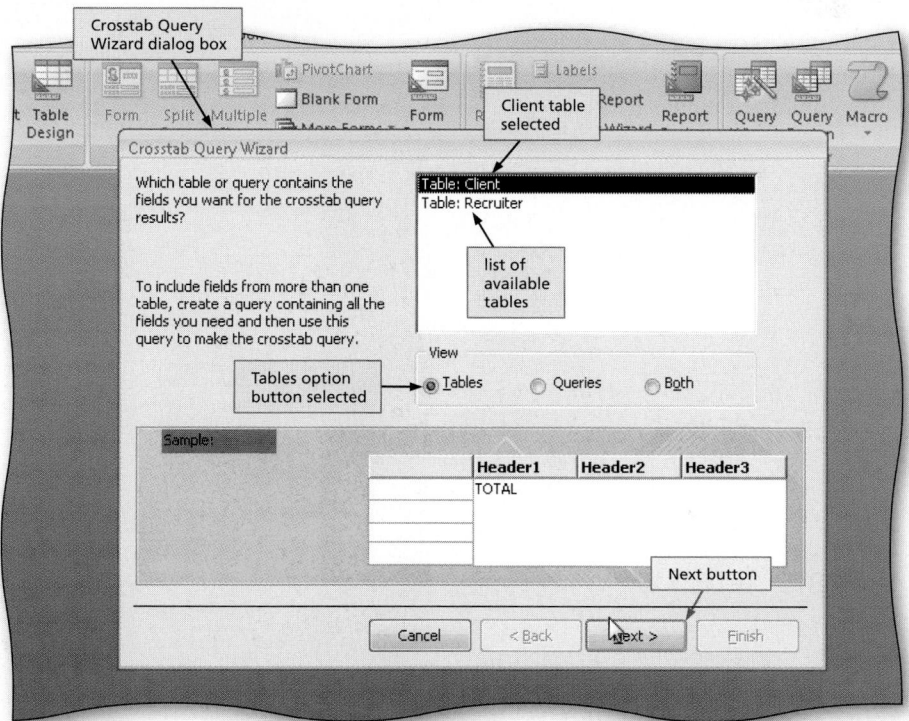

Figure 2–77

3

● With the Tables option button
selected and the Client table
selected, click the Next button to
display the next Crosstab Query
Wizard screen.

● Click the City field, and then click
the Add Field button to select
the City field for row headings
(Figure 2–78).

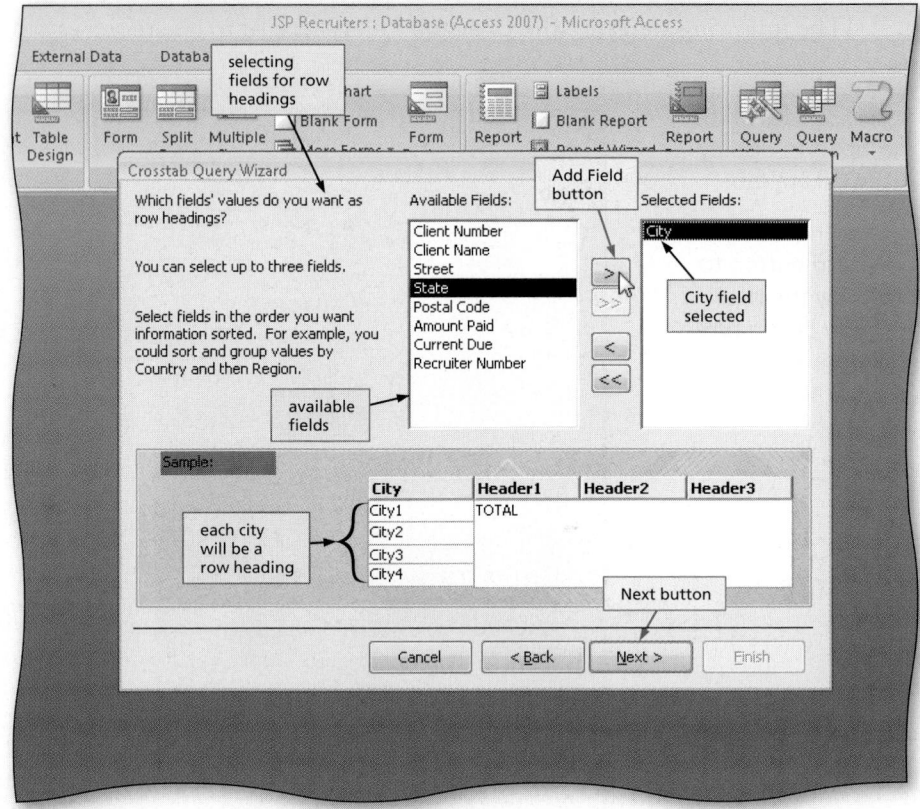

Figure 2–78

4

● Click the Next button to
display the next Crosstab Query
Wizard screen.

● Click the Recruiter Number field to
select the Recruiter Number field
for column headings (Figure 2–79).

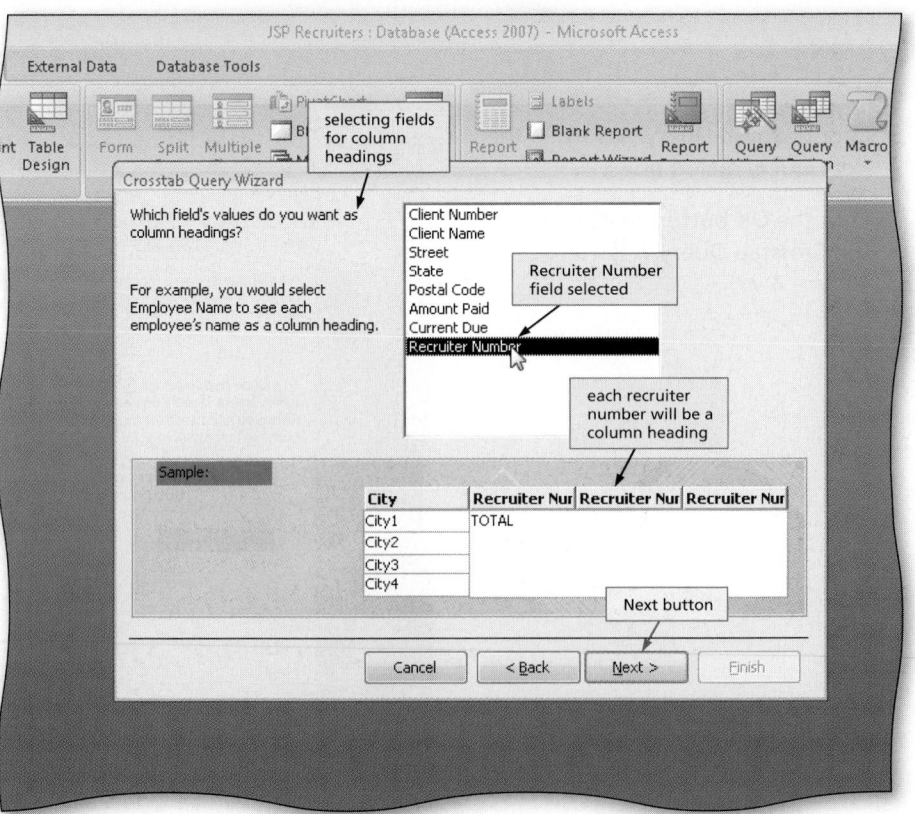

Figure 2–79

5

- Click the Next button to display the next Crosstab Query Wizard screen.

- Click the Amount Paid field to select the Amount Paid field for calculations.

 Experiment

- Click other fields. For each field, examine the list of calculations that are available. When finished, click the Amount Paid field again.

- Click Sum to select Sum as the calculation to be performed (Figure 2–80).

Q&A My list of functions is different. What did I do wrong?

Either you clicked the wrong field, or the Amount Paid field has the wrong data type. If you mistakenly assigned it the Text data type for example, you would not see Sum in the list of available calculations.

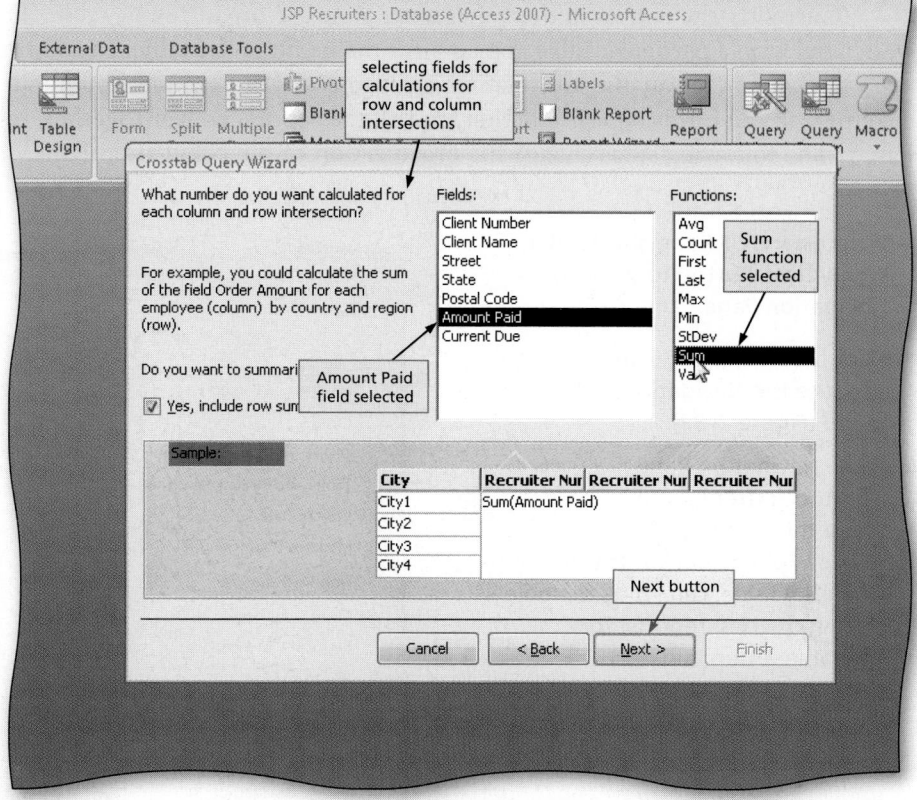

Figure 2–80

6

- Click the Next button to display the next Crosstab Query Wizard screen.

- Type `Client-Recruiter Crosstab` as the name of the query (Figure 2–81).

7

- Click the Finish button to produce the crosstab shown in Figure 2–75 on page AC 122.

- Close the query.

Q&A If I want to view the crosstab at some future date, can I just open the query?

Yes.

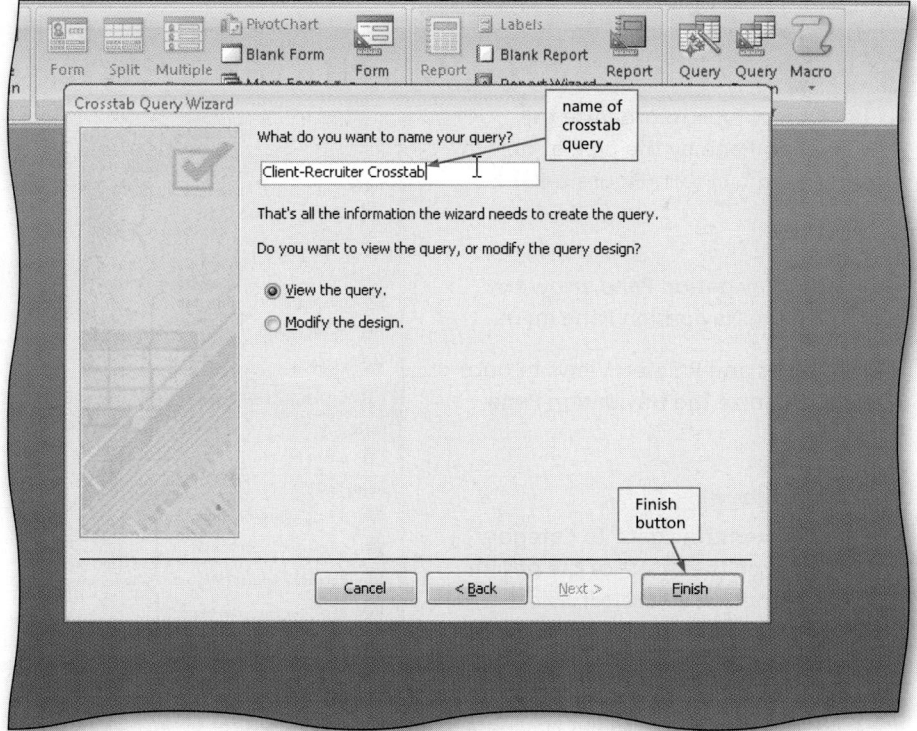

Figure 2–81

To Customize the Navigation Pane

Currently the entries in the Navigation Pane are organized by table. That is, the queries, forms, and reports associated with a particular table appear after the name of the table. In addition, all tables are included. You might want to change the way the information is organized. For example, you might wish to have all the queries appear together, all the forms appear together, and all the reports appear together, regardless of the table on which they are based. The following steps change the organization of the Navigation Pane.

- If necessary, click the Shutter Bar Open/Close Button to show the Navigation Pane.

- Click the Navigation Pane arrow to produce the Navigation Pane menu (Figure 2–82).

Q&A

If the Navigation Pane gets too cluttered, can I hide the objects in a group? For example, if the organization is by table, can I hide the objects (forms, queries, reports) for the table group and only show the table name?

Yes. Click the up arrow on the group bar. The objects under the table group will no longer appear and the up arrow will become a down arrow. To redisplay the objects, click the down arrow.

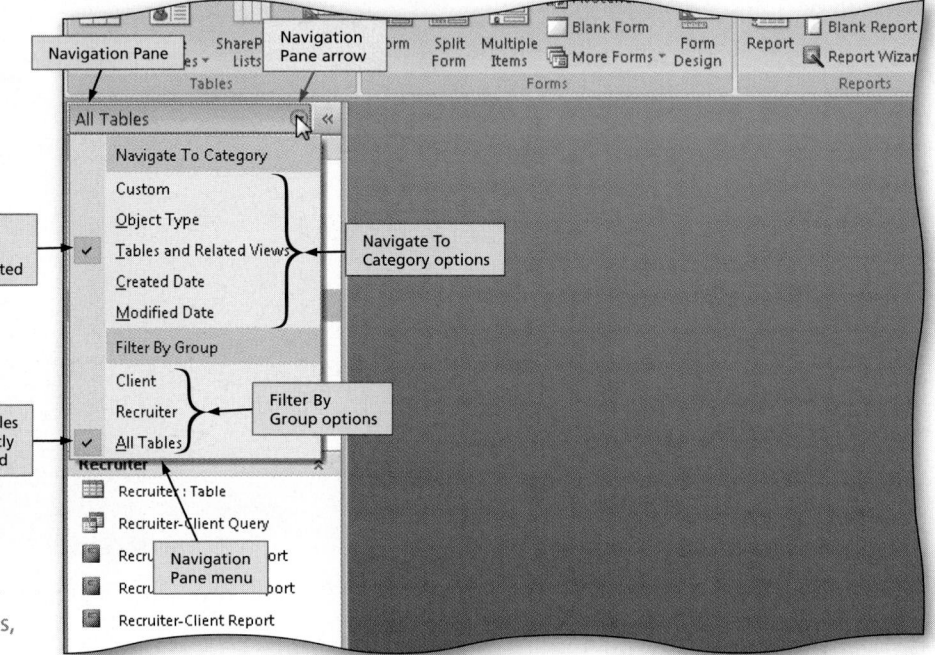

Figure 2–82

- Click Object Type to organize the Navigation Pane by the type of object rather than by table (Figure 2–83).

- Click the Navigation Pane arrow to produce the Navigation Pane menu.

- Click Tables and Related Views to once again organize the Navigation Pane by table.

 **Experiment**

- Select different Navigate To Category options to see the effect of the option. With each option you select, select different Filter By Group options to see the effect of the filtering. When you have finished experimenting, select the Tables and Related Views Navigate To Category option and the All Tables Filter By Group option.

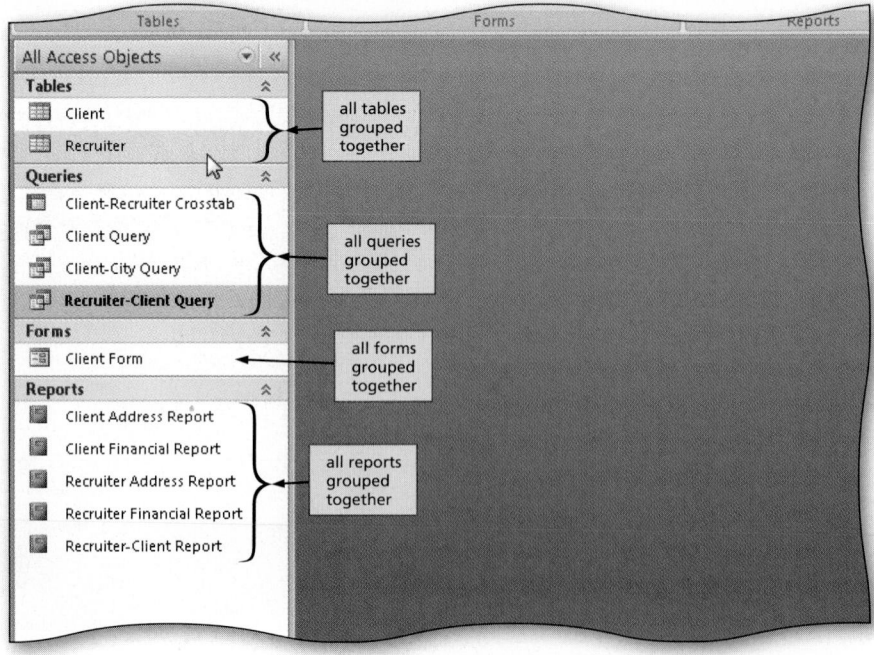

Figure 2–83

To Quit Access

You saved all your changes and are ready to quit Access. The following step quits Access.

1 Click the Close button on the right side of the Access title bar to quit Access.

BTW

Quick Reference
For a table that lists how to complete the tasks covered in this book using the mouse, Ribbon, shortcut menu, and keyboard, see the Quick Reference Summary at the back of this book, or visit the Access 2007 Quick Reference Web page (scsite.com/ac2007/qr).

Chapter Summary

In this chapter you have learned to create queries, enter fields, enter criteria, use text and numeric data in queries, use wildcards, use compound criteria, create parameter queries, sort data in queries, join tables in queries, perform calculations in queries, create crosstab queries, and customize the Navigation Pane. The following list includes all the new Access skills you have learned in this chapter.

1. Use the Simple Query Wizard to Create a Query (AC 78)
2. Use a Criterion in a Query (AC 81)
3. Print the Results of a Query (AC 83)
4. Create a Query in Design View (AC 83)
5. Add Fields to the Design Grid (AC 85)
6. Use Text Data in a Criterion (AC 86)
7. Use a Wildcard (AC 87)
8. Use Criteria for a Field Not Included in the Results (AC 88)
9. Create a Parameter Query (AC 90)
10. Save a Query (AC 91)
11. Use a Saved Query (AC 92)
12. Use a Number in a Criterion (AC 93)
13. Use a Comparison Operator in a Criterion (AC 94)
14. Use a Compound Criterion Involving AND (AC 95)
15. Use a Compound Criterion Involving OR (AC 96)
16. Clear the Design Grid (AC 98)
17. Sort Data in a Query (AC 98)
18. Omit Duplicates (AC 100)
19. Sort on Multiple Keys (AC 101)
20. Create a Top-Values Query (AC 102)
21. Join Tables (AC 105)
22. Save the Query (AC 107)
23. Change Join Properties (AC 108)
24. Create a Report Involving a Join (AC 109)
25. Print a Report (AC 111)
26. Restrict the Records in a Join (AC 112)
27. Use a Calculated Field in a Query (AC 113)
28. Change a Caption (AC 116)
29. Calculate Statistics (AC 118)
30. Use Criteria in Calculating Statistics (AC 120)
31. Use Grouping (AC 121)
32. Create a Crosstab Query (AC 123)
33. Customize the Navigation Pane (AC 126)

Learn It Online

Test your knowledge of chapter content and key terms.

Instructions: To complete the Learn It Online exercises, start your browser, click the Address bar, and then enter the Web address scsite.com/ac2007/learn. When the Access 2007 Learn It Online page is displayed, click the link for the exercise you want to complete and then read the instructions.

Chapter Reinforcement TF, MC, and SA
A series of true/false, multiple choice, and short answer questions that test your knowledge of the chapter content.

Flash Cards
An interactive learning environment where you identify chapter key terms associated with displayed definitions.

Practice Test
A series of multiple choice questions that test your knowledge of chapter content and key terms.

Who Wants To Be a Computer Genius?
An interactive game that challenges your knowledge of chapter content in the style of a television quiz show.

Wheel of Terms
An interactive game that challenges your knowledge of chapter key terms in the style of the television show *Wheel of Fortune*.

Crossword Puzzle Challenge
A crossword puzzle that challenges your knowledge of key terms presented in the chapter.

Apply Your Knowledge

Reinforce the skills and apply the concepts you learned in this chapter.

Using the Query Wizard, Creating a Parameter Query, Joining Tables, and Creating a Report
Instructions: Start Access. Open the The Bike Delivers database that you modified in Apply Your Knowledge in Chapter 1 on page AC 64. (If you did not complete this exercise, see your instructor for a copy of the modified database.)

Perform the following tasks:
1. Use the Simple Query Wizard to create a query for the Customer table. Include the Customer Name, Balance, and Courier Number in the query. Assign the name, Customer Query, to the query.

2. Create a query for the Customer table and add the Customer Number, Customer Name, Courier Number, and Balance fields to the design grid. Sort the records in descending order by Balance. Add a criterion for the Courier Number field that allows the user to enter a different courier each time the query is run. Save the query as Courier Parameter Query.

3. Create a query that joins the Courier and the Customer tables. Add the Courier Number, First Name, and Last Name fields from the Courier table and the Customer Number and Customer Name fields from the Customer table. Sort the records in ascending order by Courier Number and Customer Number. All couriers should appear in the result even if they currently have no customers. Save the query as Courier-Customer Query.

4. Create the report shown in Figure 2–84. The report uses the Courier-Customer Query.

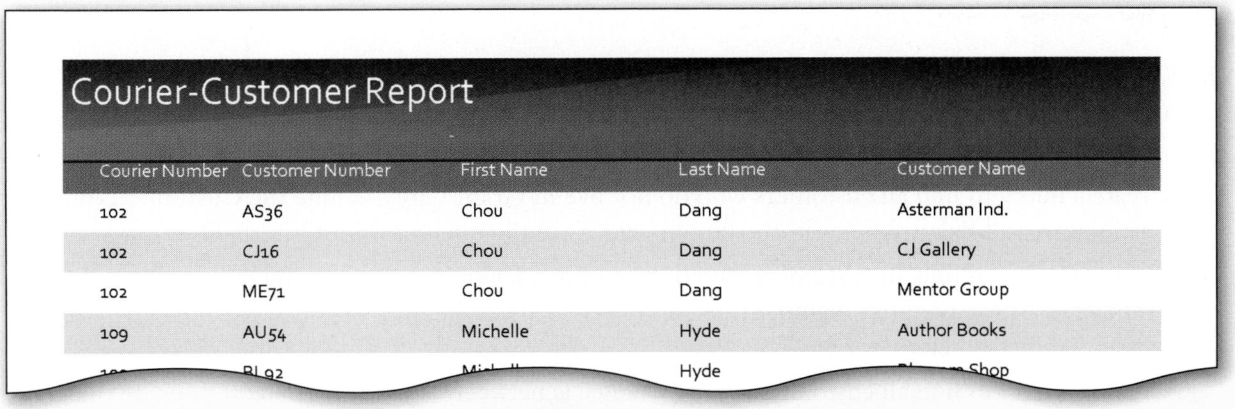

Courier-Customer Report

Courier Number	Customer Number	First Name	Last Name	Customer Name
102	AS36	Chou	Dang	Asterman Ind.
102	CJ16	Chou	Dang	CJ Gallery
102	ME71	Chou	Dang	Mentor Group
109	AU54	Michelle	Hyde	Author Books
	BL92	Mich...	Hyde	...e Shop

Figure 2–84

5. Submit the revised database in the format specified by your instructor.

Extend Your Knowledge

Extend the skills you learned in this chapter and experiment with new skills. You may need to use Help to complete the assignment.

Creating Crosstab Queries, Creating Queries Using Criteria

Instructions: Start Access. Open the Groom n Fluff database. See the inside back cover of this book for instructions for downloading the Data Files for Students, or see your instructor for information on accessing the files required in this book.

Groom n Fluff is a small pet grooming business. The owner has created an Access database in which to store information about the customers she serves and the pet groomers she employs. You will create the crosstab query shown in Figure 2–85. You also will query the database using specified criteria.

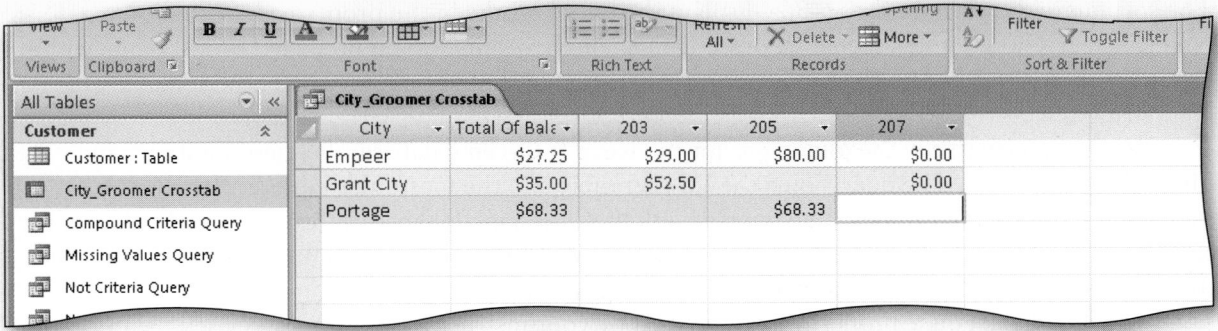

Figure 2–85

Continued >

STUDENT ASSIGNMENTS

Extend Your Knowledge *continued*

Perform the following tasks:

1. Create the crosstab query shown in Figure 2–85 on the previous page. The crosstab groups the average of customers' balances by city and groomer number.

2. Create a query to find all customers who do not live in Grant City. Include the Customer Number, Last Name, and Balance fields in the design grid. Save the query as Not Criteria Query.

3. Create a query to find all customers who do not have a telephone number. Include the Customer Number, Last Name, First Name, Street, and City fields in the query results. Save the query as Missing Values Query.

4. Create a query to find all customers whose balance is between $20.00 and $60.00. Include the Customer Number, Last Name, and Balance fields in the design grid. Save the query as Number Range Query.

5. Create a query to find all customers where the groomer number is 203 or 205 and the balance is greater than $40.00. Include the Customer Number, Last Name, First Name, Balance, and Groomer Number fields in the design grid. Save the query as Compound Criteria Query.

6. Change the database properties, as specified by your instructor. Submit the revised database in the format specified by your instructor.

Make It Right

Analyze a database and correct all errors and/or improve the design.

Correcting Errors in the Query Design

Instructions: Start Access. Open the Keep It Green database. See the inside back cover of this book for instructions for downloading the Data Files for Students, or see your instructor for information on accessing the files required in this book.

Keep It Green is a database maintained by a small landscaping business. The queries shown in Figure 2–86 contain a number of errors that need to be corrected before the queries run properly. The sort query shown in Figure 2–86a displays the query results in the proper order (First Name, Last Name, Street, City) but it is sorted incorrectly. The query results should be sorted by last name within city in ascending order. Also the caption for the Street field should be Address. Save the query with your changes.

When you try to run the join query for the Keep It Green database, the message shown in Figure 2–86b appears. The query joins the Worker table and the Customer table. It also calculates the total amount for each customer. The query should be sorted in alphabetical order by worker last name and customer last name. Correct the error that is causing the message shown in Figure 2–86b and sort the records properly. Save the query with your changes.

Change the database properties, as specified by your instructor. Submit the revised database in the format specified by your instructor.

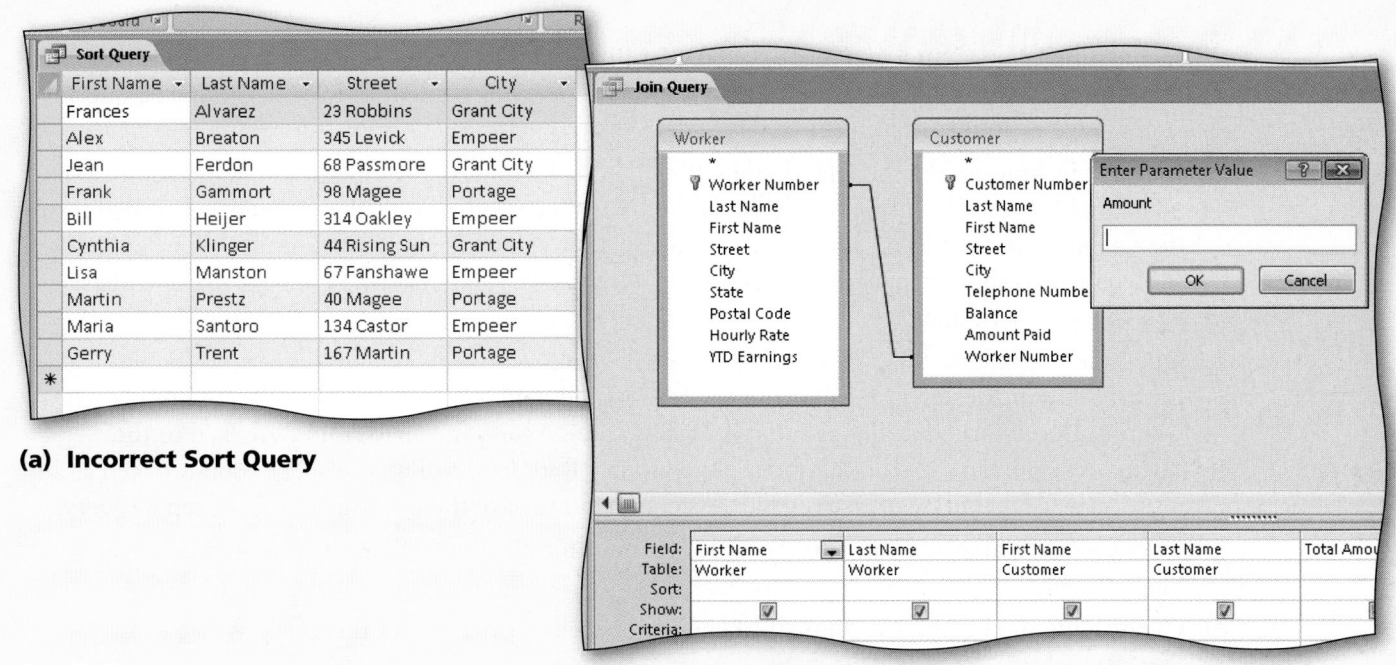

(a) Incorrect Sort Query

(b) Incorrect Join Query

Figure 2–86

In the Lab

Design, create, modify, and/or use a database following the guidelines, concepts, and skills presented in this chapter. Labs are listed in order of increasing difficulty.

Lab 1: Querying the JMS TechWizards Database

Problem: The management of JMS TechWizards has determined a number of questions it wants the database management system to answer. You must obtain answers to the questions posed by management.

Instructions: Use the database created in the In the Lab 1 of Chapter 1 on page AC 67 for this assignment or see your instructor for information on accessing the files required for this book. Perform the following tasks:

1. Open the JMS TechWizards database and create a new query for the Client table that includes the Client Number, Client Name, and Technician Number fields in the design grid for all clients where the technician number is 23. Save the query as Lab 2-1 Step 1 Query.

2. Create a query that includes the Client Number, Client Name, and Paid fields for all clients located in Liberty Corner with a paid amount greater than $500.00. Save the query as Lab2-1 Step 2 Query.

3. Create a query that includes the Client Number, Client Name, Street, and City fields for all clients whose names begin with Gr. Save the query as Lab 2-1 Step 3 Query.

4. Create a query that lists all cities in descending order. Each city should appear only once. Save the query as Lab 2-1 Step 4 Query.

5. Create a query that allows the user to enter the city to search when the query is run. The query results should display the Client Number, Client Name, and Billed. Test the query by searching for those records where the client is located in Anderson. Save the query as Client-City Query.

Continued >

In the Lab *continued*

6. Include the Client Number, Client Name, and Billed fields in the design grid. Sort the records in descending order by the Billed field. Display only the top 25 percent of the records in the query result. Save the query as Lab 2-1 Step 6 Query.

7. Join the Technician and the Client table. Include the Technician Number, First Name, and Last Name fields from the Technician table. Include the Client Number, Client Name, and Billed from the Client table. Sort the records in ascending order by technician's last name and client name. All technicians should appear in the result even if they currently have no clients. Save the query as Technician-Client query.

8. Open the Technician-Client query in Design view and remove the Client table. Add the Hourly Rate field to the design grid following the Last Name field. Calculate the number of hours each technician has worked (YTD Earnings/Hourly Rate). Assign the alias Hours Worked to the calculated field. Change the caption for the Hourly Rate field to Rate. Display hours worked as an integer (0 decimal places). Use the Save As command to save the query as Lab 2-1 Step 8 Query.

9. Create a query to display the average billed amount for all clients. Save the query as Lab 2-1 Step 9 Query.

10. Create a query to count the number of clients for technician 23. Save the query as Lab 2-1 Step 10 Query.

11. Create a query to display the average billed amount for each technician. Save the query as Lab 2-1 Step 11 Query.

12. Create the crosstab shown in Figure 2–87. The crosstab groups total of clients' paid amounts by city and technician number. Save the crosstab as City-Technician Crosstab.

13. Submit the revised database in the format specified by your instructor.

City	Total Of Paid	22	23	29
Anderson	$1,005.00	$255.00	$0.00	$750.00
Kingston	$548.50	$548.50	$0.00	
Liberty Corner	$565.00		$565.00	

Figure 2–87

In the Lab

Lab 2: Querying the Hockey Fan Zone Database
Problem: The management of the Hockey Fan Zone store has determined a number of questions it wants the database management system to answer. You must obtain answers to the questions posed by management.

Instructions: Use the database created in the In the Lab 2 of Chapter 1 on page AC 68 for this assignment, or see your instructor for information on accessing the files required for this book. Perform the following tasks:

1. Open the Hockey Fan Zone database and use the query wizard to create a query that includes the Item Number, Description, On Hand, and Cost fields for all records in the Item table. Name the query Lab 2-2 Step 1 Query.

2. Create a query that includes the Item Number, Description, Cost, and Supplier Code fields for all products where the Supplier Code is LG. Save the query as Lab 2-2 Step 2 Query.

3. Create a query that includes the Item Number and Description fields for all products where the description starts with the letter B. Save the query as Lab 2-2 Step 3 Query.

4. Create a query that includes the Item Number and Description field for all products with a cost less than $5.00. Save the query as Lab 2-2 Step 4 Query.

5. Create a query that includes the Item Number and Description field for all products with a selling price greater than $15.00. Save the query as Lab 2-2 Step 5 Query.

6. Create a query that includes all fields for all products with a selling price greater than $10.00 and where the number on hand is fewer than 10. Save the query as Lab 2-2 Step 6 Query.

7. Create a query that includes all fields for all products that have a selling price greater than $15.00 or a supplier code of AC. Save the query as Lab 2-2 Step 7 Query.

8. Join the Supplier table and the Item table. Include the Supplier Code and Supplier Name fields from the Supplier table and the Item Number, Description, On Hand, and Cost fields from the Item table. Sort the records in ascending order by Supplier Code and Item Number. Save the query as Supplier-Item Query. Note that the Report Wizard limits the size of the On Hand column header because it is a number field.

9. Create the report shown in Figure 2–88. The report uses the Supplier-Item query and the Module style.

Supplier-Item Report

Supplier Code	Item Number	Supplier Name	Description	Hand	Cost
AC	5923	Ace Clothes	Jersey	12	$21.45
AC	7810	Ace Clothes	Tee Shirt	32	$9.50
LG	3663	Logo Goods	Ball Cap	30	$11.15
LG	4563	Logo Goods	Earrings	10	$4.50
LG	4593	Logo Goods	Foam Finger	25	$2.95
LG	7930	Logo Goods	Visor	9	$11.95
MN	3683	Mary's Novelties	Bumper Sticker	50	$0.95
MN	6189	Mary's Novelties	Koozies	35	$2.00
MN	6343	Mary's Novelties	Note Cube	7	$5.75

Figure 2–88

10. Create a query that includes the Item Number, Description, On Hand, and Cost fields. Calculate the inventory value (on hand * cost) for all records in the table. Change the caption for the On Hand column to In Stock. Format inventory value as currency with two decimal places. Sort the records in descending order by inventory value. Save the query as Lab 2-2 Step 10 Query.

11. Create a query that calculates and displays the average cost of all items. Save the query as Lab 2-2 Step 11 Query.

12. Create a query that calculates and displays the average cost of items grouped by supplier code. Save the query as Lab 2-2 Step 12 Query.

13. Submit the revised database in the format specified by your instructor.

In the Lab

Lab 3: Querying the Ada Beauty Supply Database

Problem: The management of Ada Beauty Supply has determined a number of questions it wants the database management system to answer. You must obtain answers to the questions posed by management.

Instructions: Use the database created in the In the Lab 3 of Chapter 1 on page AC 69 for this assignment, or see your instructor for information on accessing the files required for this book. For Part 1 and Part 3, save each query using a format similar to the following: Lab 2-3 Part 1a Query, Lab 2-3 Part 3a Query, and so on. Submit the revised database in the format specified by your instructor.

Instructions Part 1: Create a new query for the Customer table and include the Customer Number, Customer Name, Balance, and Amount Paid fields in the design grid. Answer the following questions: (a) Which customers' names begin with C? (b) Which customers are located on Devon? (c) Which customers have a balance of $0.00? (d) Which customers have a balance greater than $200.00 and have an amount paid less than $800.00? (e) Which two customers have the highest balances? (f) For each customer, what is the total of the balance and amount paid amounts?

Instructions Part 2: Join the Sales Rep and the Customer table. Include the Sales Rep Number, First Name, and Last Name from the Sales Rep table and the Customer Number, Customer Name, and Amount Paid from the Customer table in the design grid. Sort the records in ascending order by Sales Rep Number and Customer Number. All sales reps should appear in the result even if they currently have no customers. Save the query as Sales Rep-Customer Query.

Instructions Part 3: Calculate the following statistics: (a) What is the average balance for customers assigned to sales rep 44? (b) What is the total balance for all customers? (c) What is the total amount paid for each sales rep?

Cases and Places

Apply your creative thinking and problem solving skills to design and implement a solution.

• EASIER   •• MORE DIFFICULT

• 1: Querying the Second Hand Goods Database

Use the Second Hand Goods database you created in Cases and Places 1 in Chapter 1 on page AC 71 for this assignment, or see your instructor for information on accessing the files required for this book. Create queries for the following:

a. Find the number and description of all items that contain the word Table.

b. Find the item number, description, and condition of the item that has the earliest posting date.

c. Find the total price of each item available for sale. Show the item description and total price.

d. Find the seller of each item. Show the seller's first name and last name as well as the item description, price, quantity, and date posted. Sort the results by item description within seller last name.

e. Create a parameter query that will allow the user to enter an item description when the query is run. The user should see all fields in the query result.

f. Find all items posted between April 1, 2008 and April 4, 2008. The user should see all fields in the query result.

Submit the revised database in the format specified by your instructor.

• 2: Querying the BeachCondo Rentals Database

Use the BeachCondo Rentals database you created in Cases and Places 2 in Chapter 1 on page AC 71 for this assignment, or see your instructor for information on accessing the files required for this book. Create queries for the following:

a. Find all units that rent for less than $1,000 per week and have at least two bedrooms. The user should see all fields in the query result.

b. Find all units that are on the fourth floor. (Hint: The first digit of the Unit Number field indicates the floor.) Include the Unit Number and the Weekly Rate fields in the query result.

c. Find all units that have more than one bedroom and more than one bathroom and provide linens. Include the Unit Number, Bedrooms, and Weekly Rate fields in the query result.

d. Owner BE20 offers a 15 percent discount on the weekly rate if renters rent for more than one week. What is the discounted weekly rental rate for his units? Your result should include the unit number, bedrooms, bathrooms, sleeps, and discounted weekly rate in your result. Be sure the discounted rate appears as currency.

e. List the owner's first and last name as well as telephone number. Also include the unit number and the weekly rate. All owners should appear in the result even if they currently have no rental units.

f. Find the highest and lowest weekly rate.

Submit the revised database in the format specified by your instructor.

•• 3: Querying the Restaurant Database

Use the restaurant database you created in Cases and Places 3 in Chapter 1 on page AC 71 for this assignment, or see your instructor for information on accessing the files required for this book. Using the Plan Ahead guidelines presented in this chapter, determine at least five questions the conference director might want to ask the database. Using a word processing program, such as Microsoft Word, write the questions in your own words. Then, design the queries for Access. Run and save each query. Submit the Word document and the revised database in the format specified by your instructor.

Continued >

Cases and Places *continued*

•• 4: Designing Queries to Help in Your Job Search

Make It Personal

Use the contacts database you created in Cases and Places 4 in Chapter 1 on page AC 71 for this assignment, or see your instructor for information on accessing the files required for this book. Consider your own personal job situation. What questions would you want to ask this database? Using a word processing program, such as Microsoft Word, write the questions in your own words. Can your database answer the questions that you listed? If it can, design the queries for Access. Run and save each query. In your Word document, identify which questions were posed to Access and which questions could not be answered. For questions that could not be answered, explain why your database cannot answer the question. Submit the Word document and the revised database in the format specified by your instructor.

•• 5: Creating Queries to Analyze Data

Working Together

Obtain a copy of the weather page of your local newspaper. As a team, choose 30 cities of interest. Create a database that contains one table and has five fields (City, State or Province, High Temp, Low Temp, Sky). Use the newspaper's abbreviations for Sky; for example, c for cloudy, r for rain and so on. Create queries that do the following:

a. Display the five cities with the highest high temperatures.

b. Calculate the difference between the high and low temperatures for each city.

c. Display the average high and low temperature for all cities.

d. List the states or provinces in your table. Each state or province should appear only once.

Write a one-page paper that explains what the team learned from querying the database and any conclusions you can draw about the data — for example, describe the Sky conditions for the cities with the least difference in high and low temperature. Submit the assignment in the format specified by your instructor.

3 Maintaining a Database

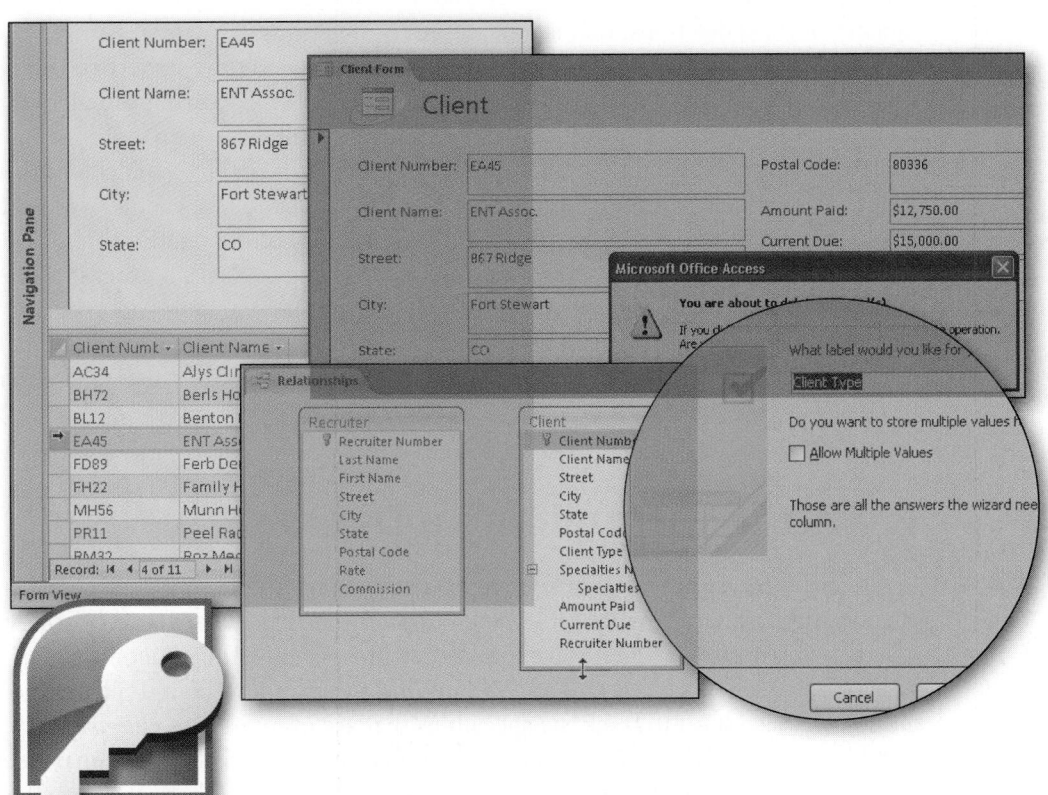

Objectives

You will have mastered the material in this chapter when you can:

- Add, change, and delete records

- Search for records

- Filter records

- Update a table design

- Format a datasheet

- Use action queries to update records

- Specify validation rules, default values, and formats

- Create and use single-valued and multivalued Lookup fields

- Specify referential integrity

- Use a subdatasheet

- Sort records

3 | Maintaining a Database

Introduction

Once a database has been created and loaded with data, it must be maintained. **Maintaining the database** means modifying the data to keep it up-to-date, such as adding new records, changing the data for existing records, and deleting records. Updating can include mass updates or mass deletions; that is, updates to, or deletions of, many records at the same time.

Maintenance of a database can also involve the need to **restructure the database** periodically; that is, to change the database structure. Restructuring can include adding new fields — including both Lookup and multivalued fields — to a table, changing the characteristics of existing fields, and removing existing fields. It also includes the creation of validation rules and referential integrity. Validation rules ensure validity of the data in the database, while referential integrity ensures the validity of the relationships.

Maintaining a database also can include filtering records, a process that ensures that only the records that satisfy some criterion appear when viewing and updating the data in a table. Changing the appearance of a datasheet is a maintenance activity. Finally, backing up the database as well as compacting and repairing a database are database maintenance tasks as well.

Project — Maintaining a Database

JSP Recruiters faces the task of keeping its database up-to-date. As the agency takes on new clients and recruiters, it will need to add new records, make changes to existing records, and delete records. JSP managers have found they must change the structure of the database to categorize the clients by type. They will do this by adding a Client Type field to the Client table. They also want to track the specialties that are of interest to clients. They will do so by adding a Specialties Needed field to the Client table. Because clients may need more than one specialty, this field will be a multivalued field. Along with these changes, JSP staff want to change the appearance of a datasheet when displaying data.

JSP would like the ability to make mass updates, that is, to update or delete many records in a single operation. They want rules that make sure users can enter only valid data into the database, and they want to ensure that it is not possible for the database to contain a client who is not associated with a specific recruiter. Finally, they want to improve the efficiency of certain types of processing, specifically sorting and retrieving data.

Figure 3–1 summarizes some of the various types of activities involved in maintaining the JSP Recruiters database.

Figure 3–1

Overview

As you read through this chapter, you will learn how to maintain a database by performing these general tasks:

- Add, change, and delete records.
- Filter records so that only those records that satisfy some criterion appear in a datasheet or form.
- Change the structure of a table.
- Make mass changes to a table.
- Create validation rules to ensure that the database contains only valid data.
- Change the appearance of a datasheet.
- Enforce relationships by creating referential integrity.
- Order records.
- Perform special database operations such as backing up a database and compacting a database.

Plan
Ahead

Database Maintenance Guidelines

1. **Determine when it is necessary to add, change, or delete records in a database.** Decide when updates are necessary. Also determine whether the updates are to be made to individual records or whether mass updates would be more efficient. For example, if a state changes an area code, a mass update would be more efficient.

2. **Determine whether you should filter records.** For each situation where a user will be working with a table in the database, examine whether it might be desirable to have the records filtered, that is, have only those records that satisfy some criterion appear. For example, if a user only wants to make changes to clients in a particular city, it would be easier to view only those records rather than all the records in the table.

3. **Determine whether additional fields are necessary or whether existing fields should be deleted.** Have there been any changes to the initial requirements that would require the addition of a field (or fields) to one of the tables? If so, you will need to add the field to the appropriate table. Also, now that the database has been in operation for a period of time, determine whether all the fields actually are being used. If some fields are not in use, verify that they are, in fact, no longer needed. If so, you can delete the field from the table.

4. **Determine whether validation rules, default values, and formats are necessary.** Can you improve the accuracy of the data entry process by enforcing data validation? What values are allowed for a particular field? Are there some fields in which one particular value is used more than another? You can control the values that are entered in a field by modifying the table design to include default values, formats, and validation rules.

5. **Determine whether changes to the format of a datasheet are desirable.** Can you improve the appearance of the Datasheet view of your tables? Once you have decided on a particular appearance, it is a good idea to be consistent throughout all your tables except in special circumstances.

6. **Identify related tables in order to implement relationships between the tables.** Examine the database design you created earlier to identify related tables. For each pair of related tables, you will need to make decisions about the implementation of the relationship between the tables.

When necessary, more specific details concerning the above decisions and/or actions are presented at appropriate points in the chapter. The chapter also will identify the use of these guidelines in database maintenance tasks such as those shown in Figure 3–1 on the previous page.

Starting Access

If you are using a computer to step through the project in this chapter and you want your screen to match the figures in this book, you should change your screen's resolution to 1024 × 768. For information about how to change a computer's resolution, read Appendix E.

To Start Access

The following steps, which assume Windows Vista is running, start Access.

1 Click the Start button on the Windows Vista taskbar to display the Start menu.

2 Click All Programs at the bottom of the left Pane on the Start menu to display the All Programs list and then click Microsoft Office in the All Programs list to display the Microsoft Office list.

3 Click Microsoft Office Access 2007 on the Microsoft Office list to start Access and display the Getting Started with Microsoft Office Access window.

4 If the Access window is not maximized, click the Maximize button on its title bar to maximize the window.

Note: If you are using Windows XP, see Appendix F for alternate steps.

To Open a Database

In Chapter 1, you created your database on a USB flash drive using the file name, JSP Recruiters. There are two ways to open the file containing your database. If the file you created appears in the Recent Documents list, you can click it to open the file. If not, you can use the More button to open the file. The following steps use the More button to open the JSP Recruiters database from the USB flash drive.

Note: If you are using Windows XP, see Appendix F for alternate steps.

1 With your USB flash drive connected to one of the computer's USB ports, click the More button to display the Open dialog box.

2 If the Folders list is displayed below the Folders button, click the Folders button to remove the Folders list.

3 If necessary, click Computer in the Favorite Links section and then double-click UDISK 2.0 (E:) to select the USB flash drive, as the new open location. (Your drive letter might be different.)

4 Click JSP Recruiters to select the file name.

5 Click the Open button to open the database.

6 If a Security Warning appears, click the Options button to display the Microsoft Office Security Options dialog box.

7 Click the Enable this content option button.

8 Click the OK button to enable the content.

Updating Records

Keeping the data in a database up-to-date requires updating records in three ways: adding new records, changing the data in existing records, and deleting existing records.

Adding Records

In Chapter 1, you added records to a database using Datasheet view; that is, as you added records, the records appeared on the screen in a datasheet. The data looked like a table. When you need to add additional records, you can use the same techniques.

In Chapter 1, you used a split form to view records. The split form contained both a form and a datasheet. You can use either portion to add records. You also can use a simple form, that is, a form that does not contain a datasheet. Whether you use a simple form or the form portion of a split form, you can use the form to update the table. To add new records, change existing records, or delete records, you use the same techniques you used in Datasheet view. The following steps create a simple form and then add a record to the Client table using the form.

To Create a Simple Form

Rather than using a split form, you may wish just to view the data in a form without also having a datasheet on the screen. If you already have created such a form, you can open it. If not, you can create a simple form to use. The following steps create a simple form.

- Show the Navigation Pane if it is currently hidden.

- If necessary, click the Client table in the Navigation Pane to select it.

- Click Create on the Ribbon to display the Create tab (Figure 3–2).

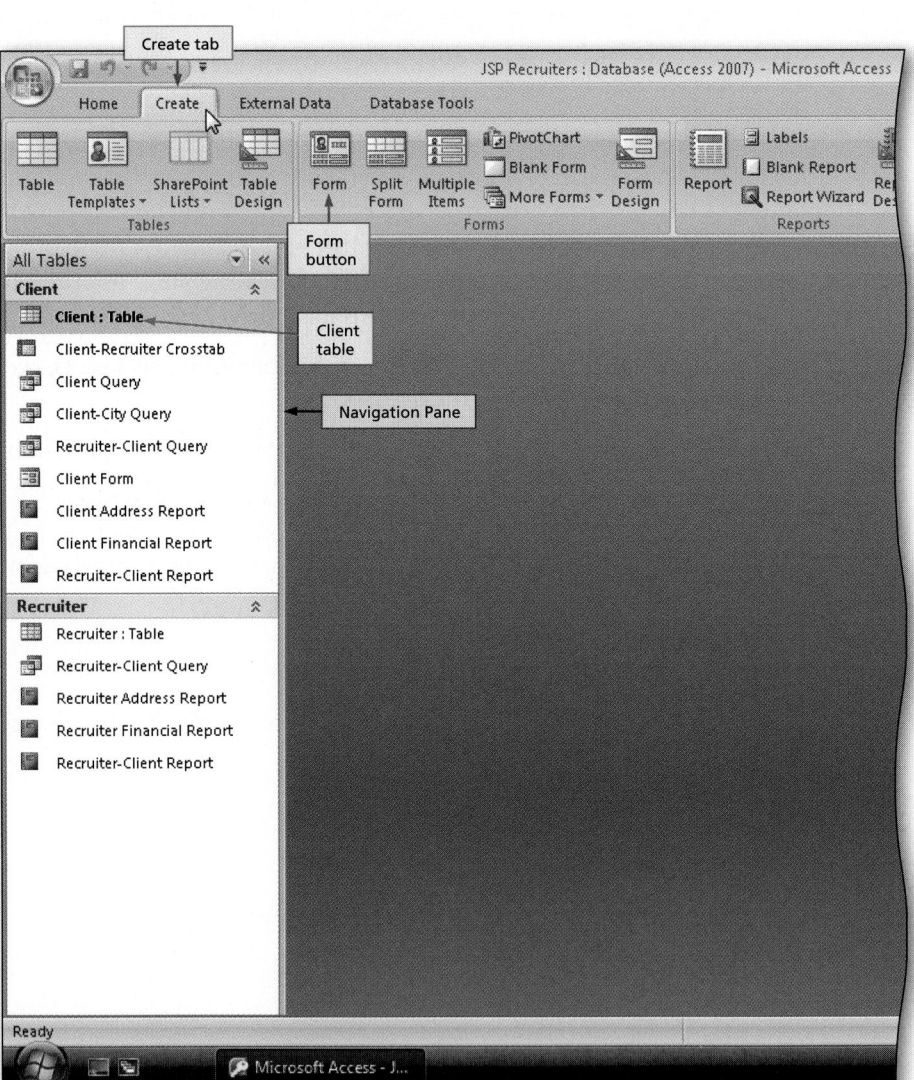

Figure 3–2

2

- Click the Form button on the Create tab to create a simple form (Figure 3–3).

Q&A

How can I tell which view of the form is currently on the screen?

Point to the button that is highlighted in the lower-right corner of the screen. The ScreenTip indicates the current view. At the present time, the form appears in Layout view.

Q&A

Which view should I use if I want to enter records?

Form view.

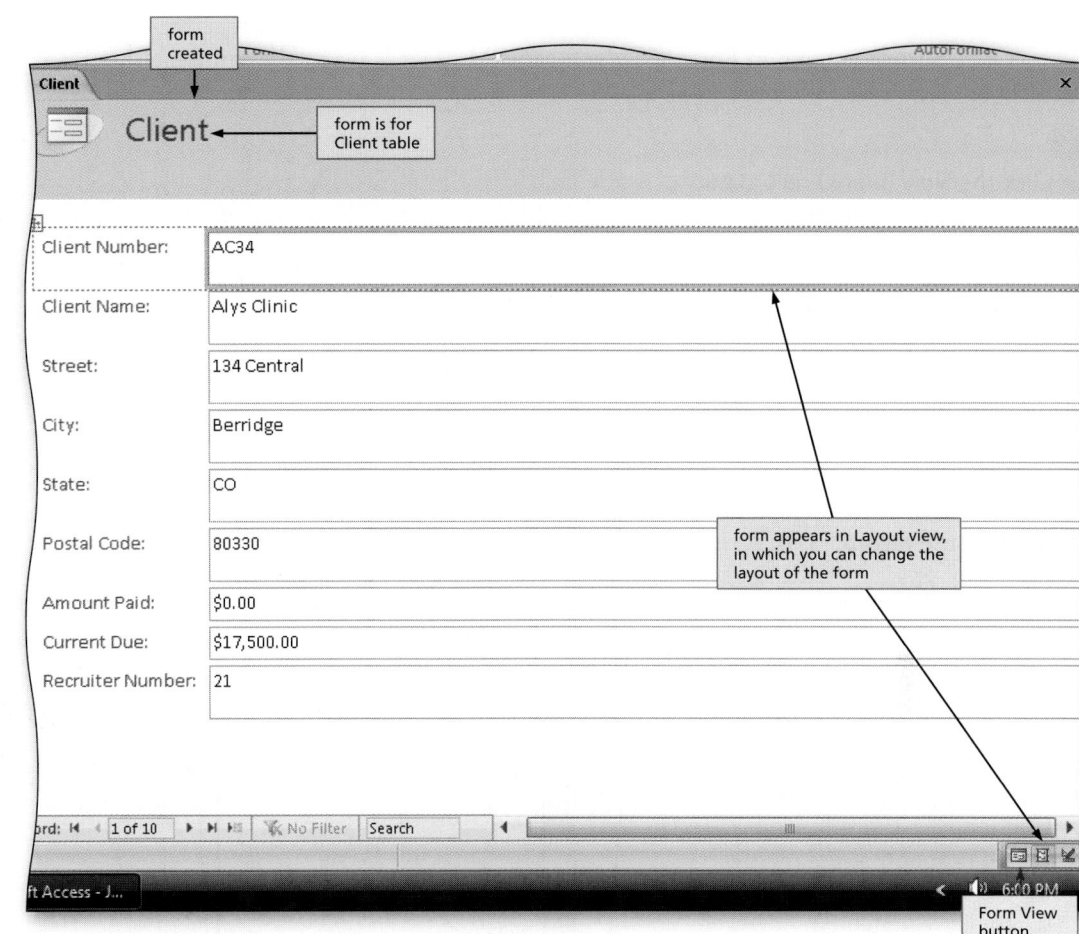

Figure 3–3

3

- Click the Form View button to display the form in Form view (Figure 3–4).

Q&A

Could I use the View button to display the form in Form view?

Yes. Click the arrow at the bottom of the button and then click Form View.

 Experiment

- Click the various navigation buttons (First record, Next record, Previous record, and Last record) to see each button's effect. Click the Current Record box, change the record number, and press the ENTER key to see how to move to a specific record.

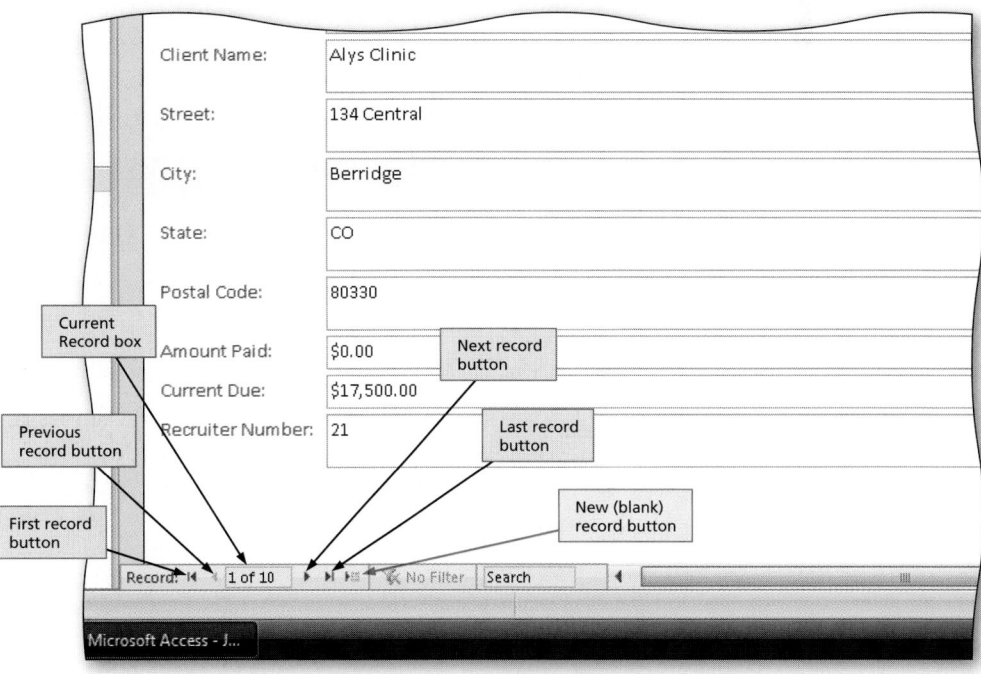

Figure 3–4

To Use a Form to Add Records

Once a form is open in Form view you can add records using the same techniques you used to add records in Datasheet view. The following steps use the form just created to add records.

- Click the New (blank) record button on the Navigation bar to enter a new record, and then type the data for the new record as shown in Figure 3–5. Press the TAB key after typing the data in each field, except after typing the data for the final field (Recruiter Number).

- Press the TAB key to complete the entry of the record.

- Click the Close 'Client' button to close the Client form.

- Click the No button when asked if you want to save your changes.

Q&A

Why not save the form?

If you wish to use this form frequently in the future, you would probably save it. It is very easy to re-create the form whenever you need it, however.

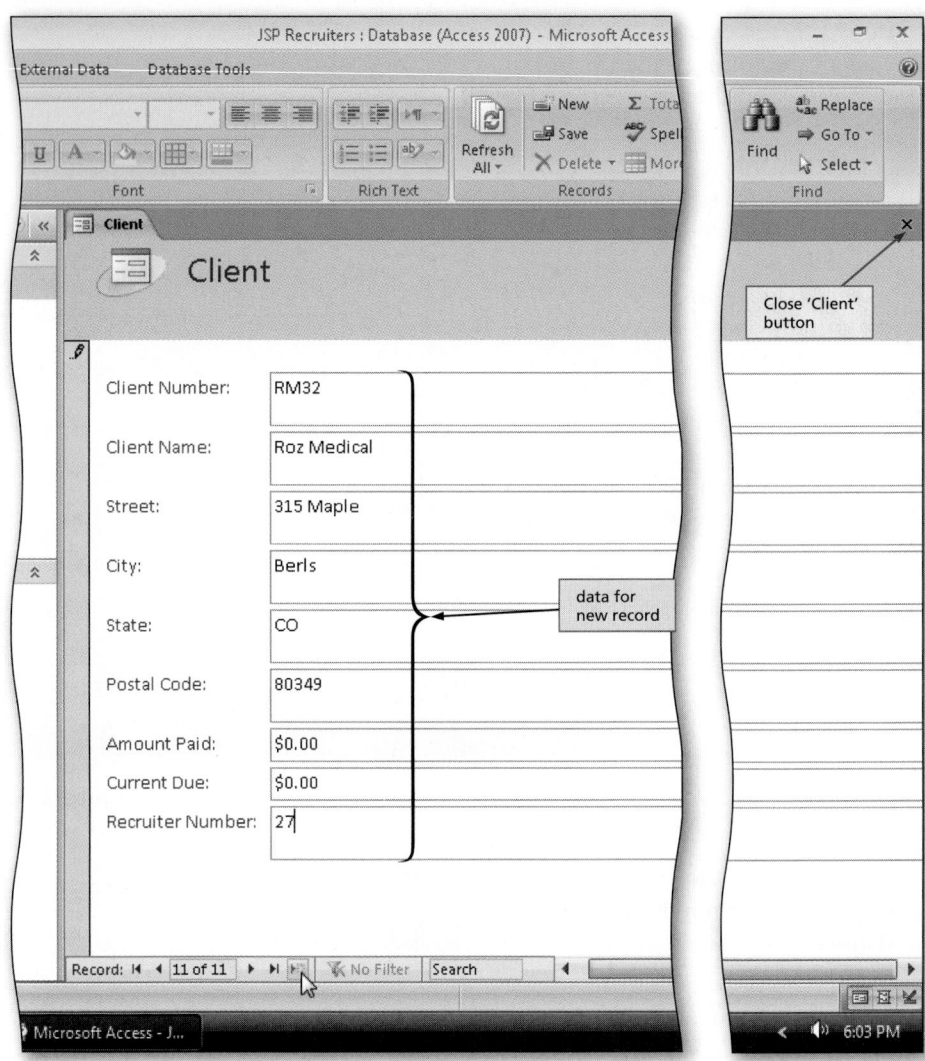

Figure 3–5

Other Ways

1. Click New button on Ribbon
2. Press CTRL+PLUS SIGN (+)

To Search for a Record

In the database environment, **searching** means looking for records that satisfy some criteria. Looking for the client whose number is MH56 is an example of searching. The queries in Chapter 2 also were examples of searching. Access had to locate those records that satisfied the criteria.

A need for searching also exists when using Form view or Datasheet view. To update client MH56, for example, first you need to find the client.

The following steps show how to search for the client whose number is MH56.

①

- Right-click Client Form in the Navigation Pane and click Open on the shortcut menu to open the form in Form view.

- Hide the Navigation Pane (Figure 3–6).

Q&A

Which command on the shortcut menu gives me Form view? I see both Layout view and Design view, but no option for Form view.

The Open command opens the form in Form view.

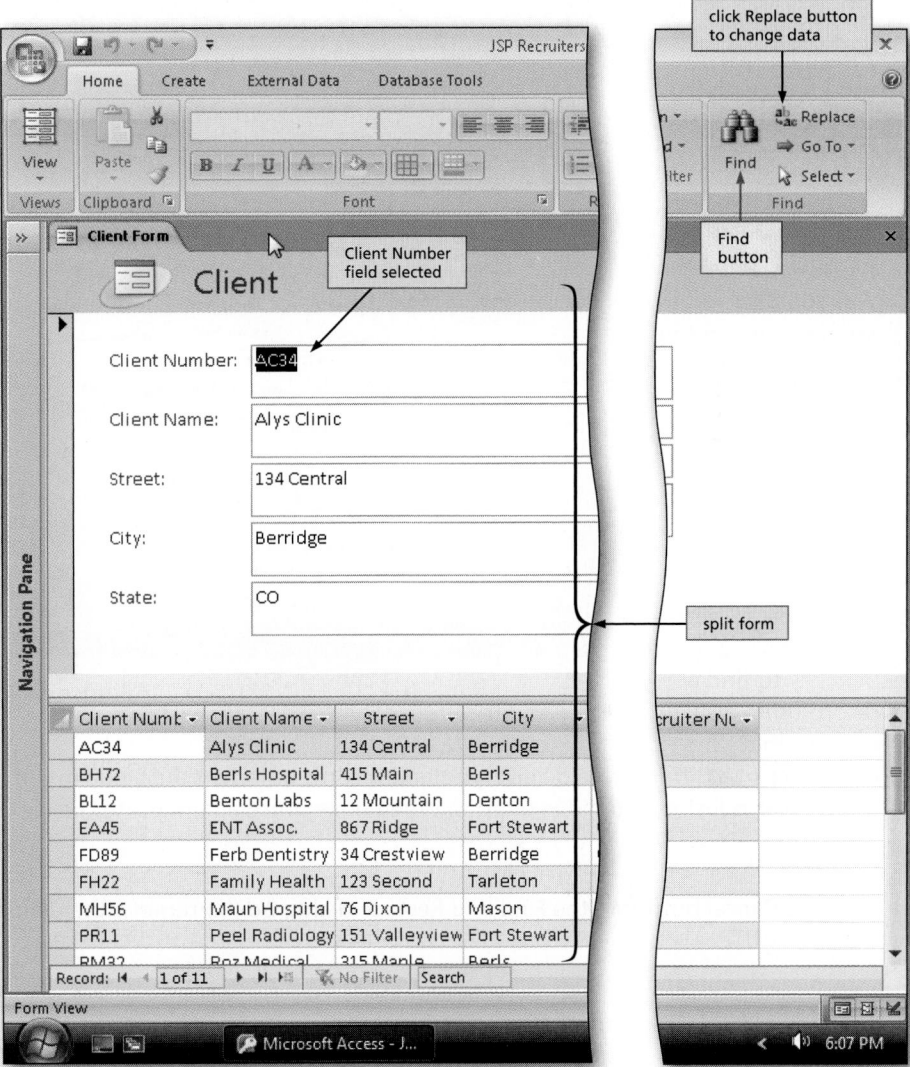

Figure 3–6

2

- Click the Find button on the Home tab to display the Find and Replace dialog box.

- Type MH56 in the Find What text box.

- Click the Find Next button in the Find and Replace dialog box to find client MH56 (Figure 3–7).

Q&A
Can I also find records in Datasheet view or in Form view?

Yes. You use the same process to find records whether you are viewing the data with split form, in Datasheet view, or in Form view.

Experiment

- Find records using other client numbers. Try to find a record using a client number that does not exist. Click in a different field and try to find records based on the value in that field. Try to use wildcards just as you did in queries. When done, once again locate client MH56.

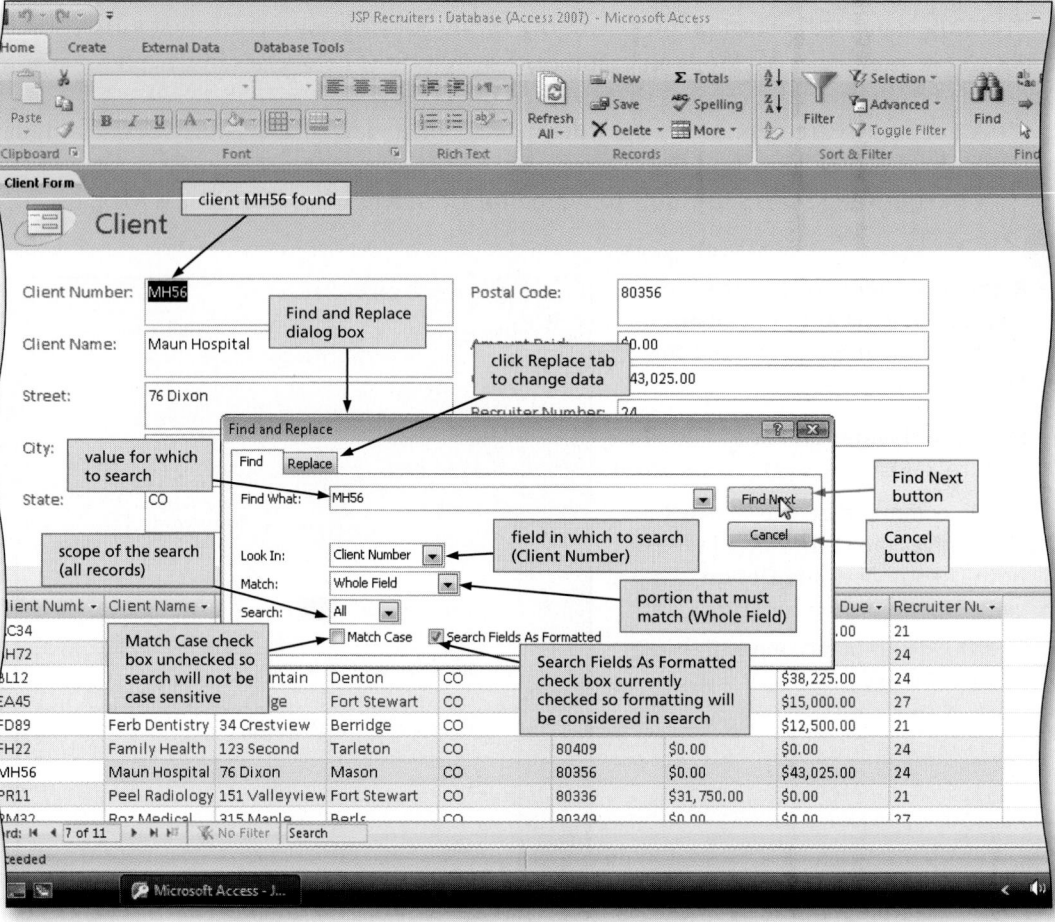

Figure 3–7

3

- Click the Cancel button in the Find and Replace dialog box to remove the dialog box from the screen.

Q&A
Why does the button in the dialog box read Find Next rather than simply Find?

In some cases, after locating a record that satisfies a criterion, you might need to find the next record that satisfies the same criterion. For example, if you just found the first client whose recruiter number is 24, you then may want to find the second such client, then the third, and so on. To do so, click the Find Next button. You will not need to retype the value each time.

Q&A
Can I replace one value with another using this dialog box?

Yes. Either click the Replace button on the Ribbon or the Replace tab in the Find and Replace dialog box. You then can enter both the value to find and the replacement value.

Other Ways

1. Press CTRL+F

To Update the Contents of a Record

After locating the record to be changed, select the field to be changed by clicking the field. You also can press the TAB key repeatedly. Then make the appropriate changes. (Clicking the field automatically produces an insertion point. If you use the TAB key, you will need to press F2 to produce an insertion point.)

The following step uses Form view to change the name of client MH56 from Maun Hospital to Munn Hospital by deleting the letters au and then inserting the letters un after the letter M.

- Click in the Client Name field in the datasheet for client MH56 after the letter M to select the field.

- Press the DELETE key twice to delete the letters au.

- Type the letters un after the letter M.

- Press the TAB key to complete the change and move to the next field (Figure 3–8).

Q&A Could I have changed the contents of the field in the form?

Yes. You first will need to ensure the record to be changed appears in the form. You can then change the value just as in the datasheet.

Q&A Do I need to save my change?

No. Once you move to another record or close this table, the change to the name will become permanent.

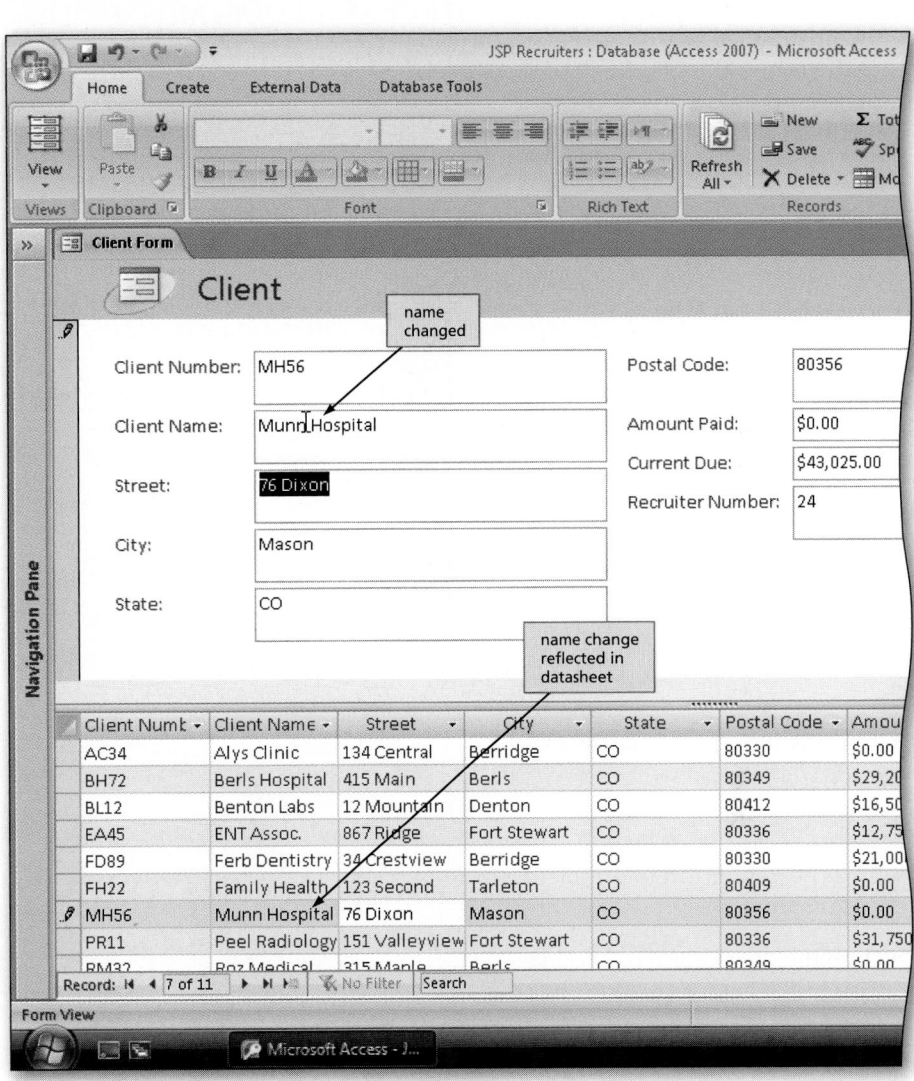

Figure 3–8

To Delete a Record

When records no longer are needed, **delete the records** (remove them) from the table. If client EA45 no longer is served by JSP Recruiters and its final payment is made, the record can be deleted. The following steps delete client EA45.

- With the Client Form open, click the record selector in the data-sheet (the small box that appears to the left of the first field) of the record on which the client number is EA45 (Figure 3–9).

Q&A

That technique works in the data-sheet portion. How do I select the record in the form portion?

With the desired record appearing in the form, click the record selector (the triangle in front of the record) to select the entire record.

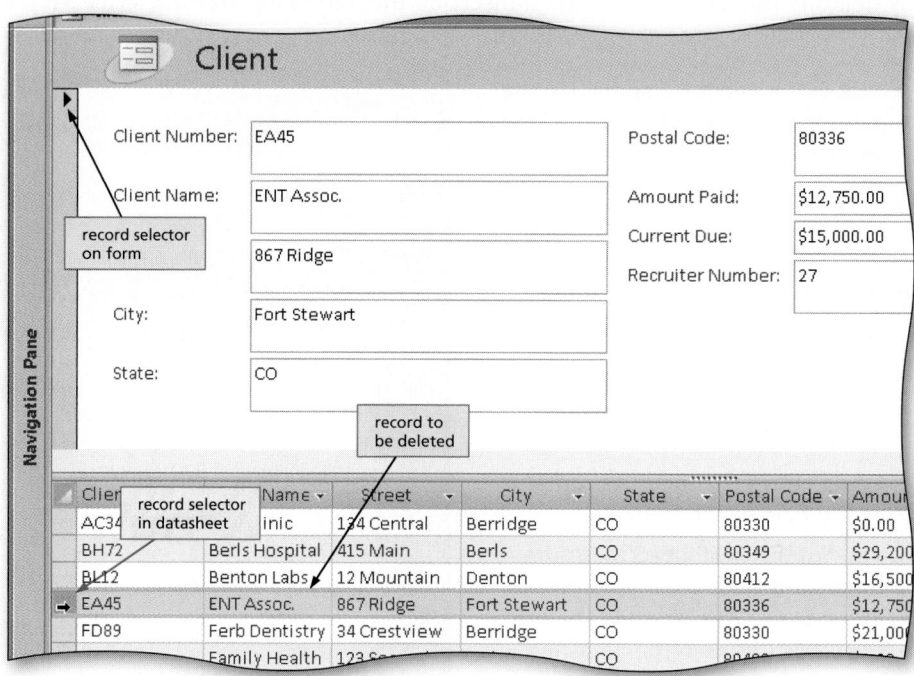

Figure 3–9

- Press the DELETE key to delete the record (Figure 3–10).

- Click the Yes button to complete the deletion.

- Close the Client Form by clicking the Close 'Client Form' button.

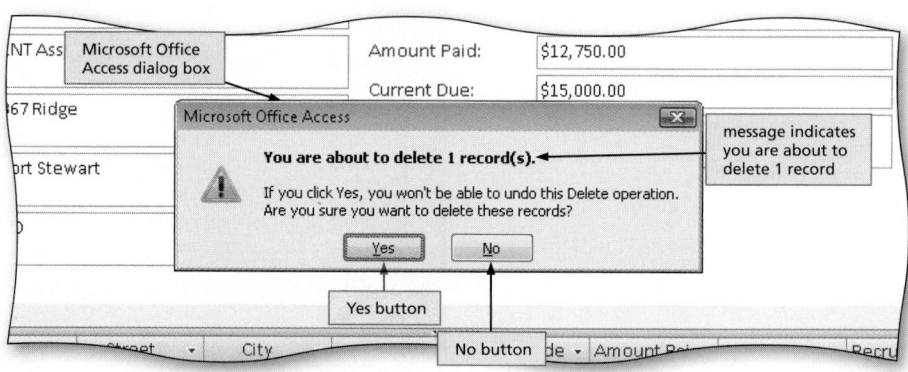

Figure 3–10

Other Ways

1. Click Delete button on Ribbon

Filtering Records

You can use the Find button in either Datasheet view or Form view to locate a record quickly that satisfies some criterion (for example, the client number is MH56). All records appear, however, not just the record or records that satisfy the criterion. To have only the record or records that satisfy the criterion appear, use a **filter**. Four types of filters are available: Filter By Selection, Common Filters, Filter By Form, and Advanced Filter/Sort. You can use a filter in either Datasheet view or Form view.

Plan
Ahead

Determine whether you should filter records.

If you determine that it is desirable to have only those records that satisfy some criterion appear, you have two choices. You can create a query or create a filter. The following guidelines apply to this decision.

1. If you think that you frequently will want to display records that satisfy precisely this same criterion, you should consider creating a query whose results only contain the records that satisfy the criterion. To display those records in the future, simply open the query.

2. If you are viewing data in a datasheet or form and decide you want to restrict the records to be included, it is easier to create a filter than create a query. You can create and use the filter while you are viewing the data.

3. If you have created a filter that you would like to be able to use again in the future, you can save the filter as a query.

If you have decided that it is appropriate to use a filter, you need to decide which type of filter to use.

1. If your criterion for filtering is that the value in a particular field matches or does not match a certain specific value, you can use Filter By Selection.

2. If your criterion only involves a single field but is more complex, for example, that the value in the field begins with a certain collection of letters, you can use a Common Filter.

3. If your criterion involves more than one field, use Filter By Form.

4. If your criterion involves more than a single And or Or, or if it involves sorting, you will probably find it simpler to use Advanced Filter/Sort.

To Use Filter By Selection

The simplest type of filter is called **Filter By Selection**. To use Filter By Selection, you give Access an example of the data you want by selecting the data within the table. You then choose the option you want on the Selection menu. If you have determined that you only want to display those clients located in Berridge, Filter By Selection is appropriate. The following steps use Filter By Selection in Datasheet view to display only the records for clients in Berridge.

- Open the Client Form and hide the Navigation Pane.

- Click the City field on the first record in the datasheet portion of the form to select Berridge as the city (Figure 3–11).

Q&A

Could I have selected the City field on the fourth record, which is also Berridge?

Yes. It does not matter which record you select as long as the city is Berridge.

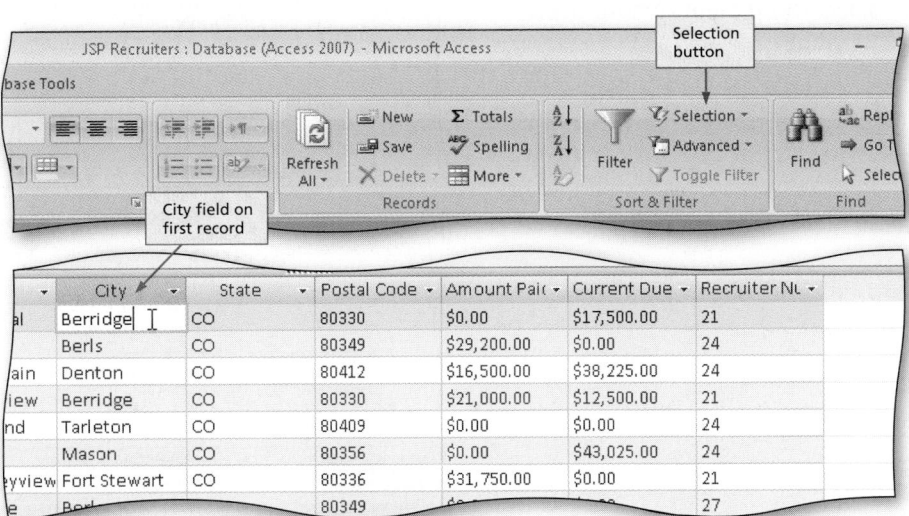

Figure 3–11

2

- Click the Selection button on the Home tab to display the Selection menu (Figure 3–12).

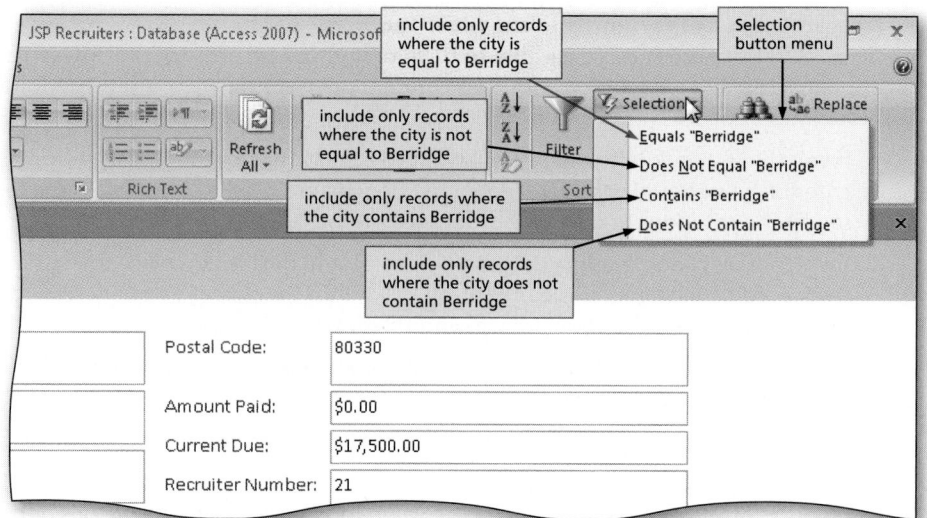

Figure 3–12

3

- Click Equals "Berridge" to select only those clients whose city is Berridge (Figure 3–13).

Q&A Can I also filter in Datasheet view or in Form view?

Yes. Filtering works the same whether you are viewing the data with split form, in Datasheet view, or in Form view.

 Experiment

- Try each of the other values in the Selection menu to see their effect. When done, once again select those clients whose city is Berridge.

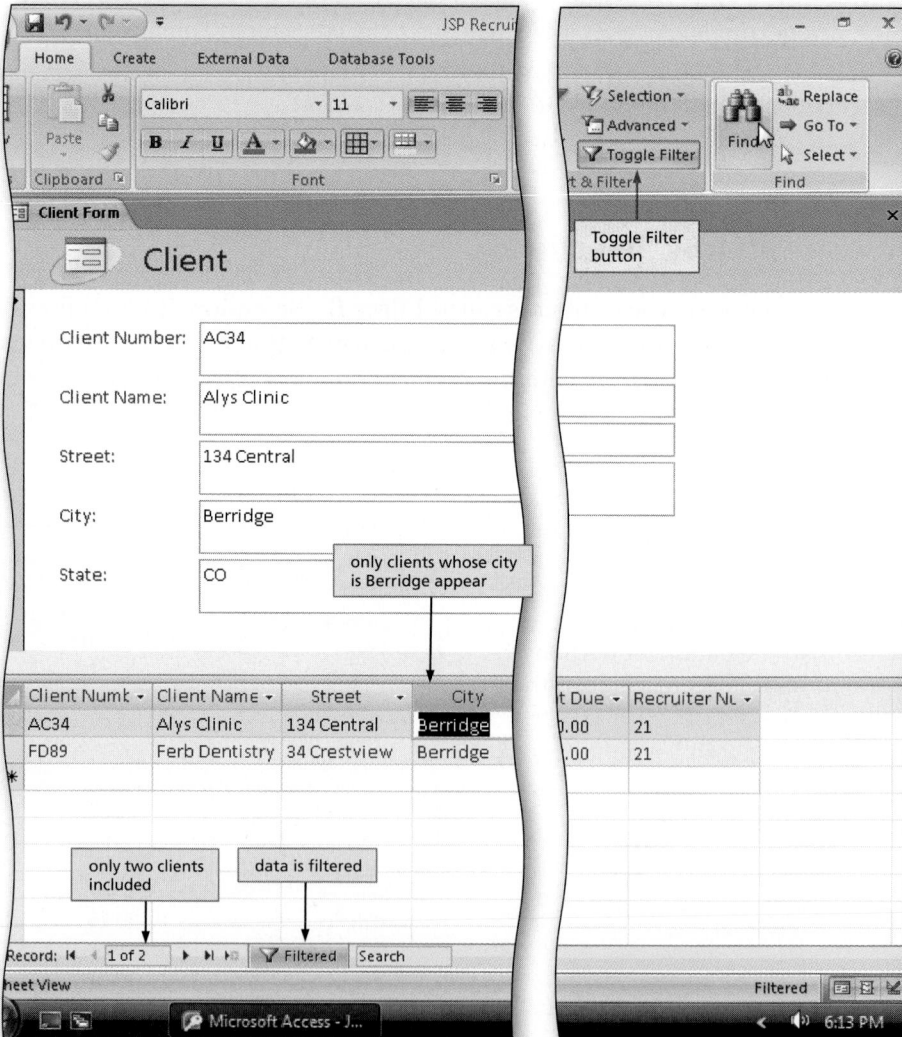

Figure 3–13

To Toggle a Filter

The following step toggles the filter to redisplay all records.

1

- Click the Toggle Filter button on the Home tab to toggle the filter and redisplay all records (Figure 3–14).

Does that action clear the filter?

No. The filter is still in place. If you click the Toggle Filter button a second time, you again will see only the filtered records.

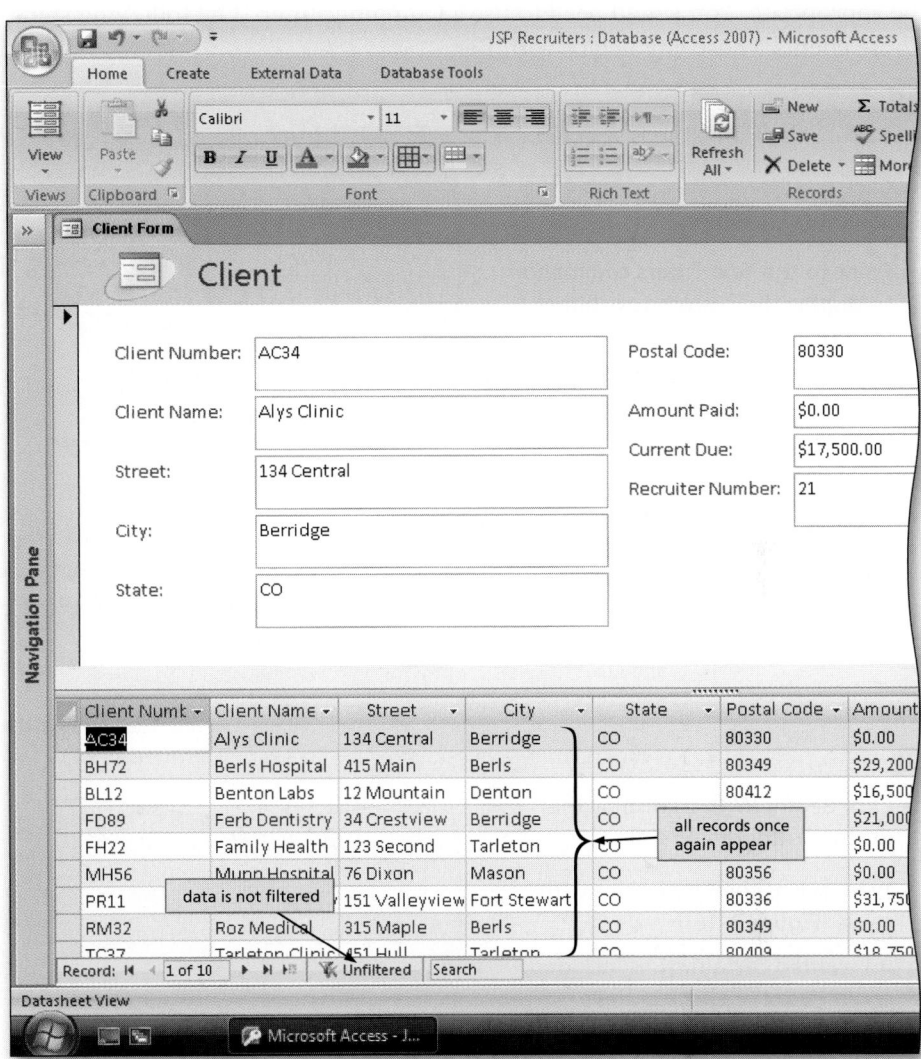

Figure 3–14

To CLEAR A FILTER

Once you have finished using a filter, you can clear the filter. After doing so, you no longer will be able to use the filter by pressing the Toggle Filter button. To clear a filter, you use the following steps.

1. Click the Advanced button on the Home tab.
2. Click Clear All Filters on the Advanced menu.

Using Wildcards in Filters
Both the question mark (?) and the asterisk (*) wildcards can be used in filters created using Advanced Filter/Sort.

To Use a Common Filter

You can filter individual fields by clicking the arrow to the right of the field name and using a Common Filter. If you have determined you want to include those clients whose city begins with Ber, Filter By Selection would not be appropriate. You would need to use a Common Filter. The following steps use a common filter to include only those clients whose city begins with Ber.

 1

- Be sure the Home tab is selected.

- Click the City arrow to display the common filter menu.

- Point to the Text Filters command to display the custom text filters (Figure 3–15).

Q&A
I selected the City field and then clicked the Filter button on the Home tab. My screen looks the same. Is this right?

Yes. That is another legitimate way to display the common filter menu.

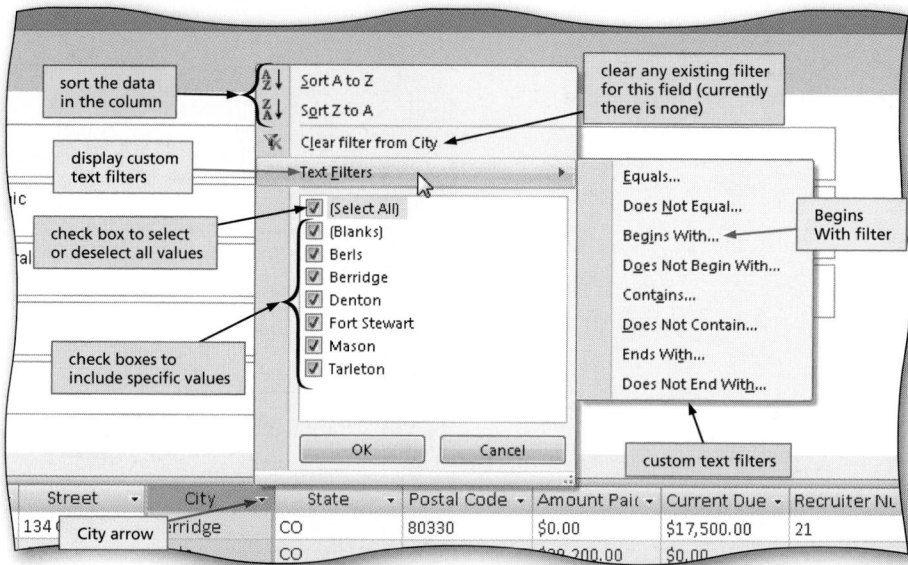

Figure 3–15

 2

- Click Begins With to display the Custom Filter dialog box.

- Type Ber as the City begins with value (Figure 3–16).

Q&A
If I wanted certain cities included, could I use the check boxes?

Yes. Be sure the cities you want are the only ones checked. One way to do this is to click the Select All check box to remove all the check marks and then click the check boxes for the cities you want to include. Another way is to clear the check boxes for the cities you don't want. Use whichever technique you find more convenient.

Experiment

- Try other options in the Common Filter menu to see their effect. When done, once again select those clients whose city begins with Ber.

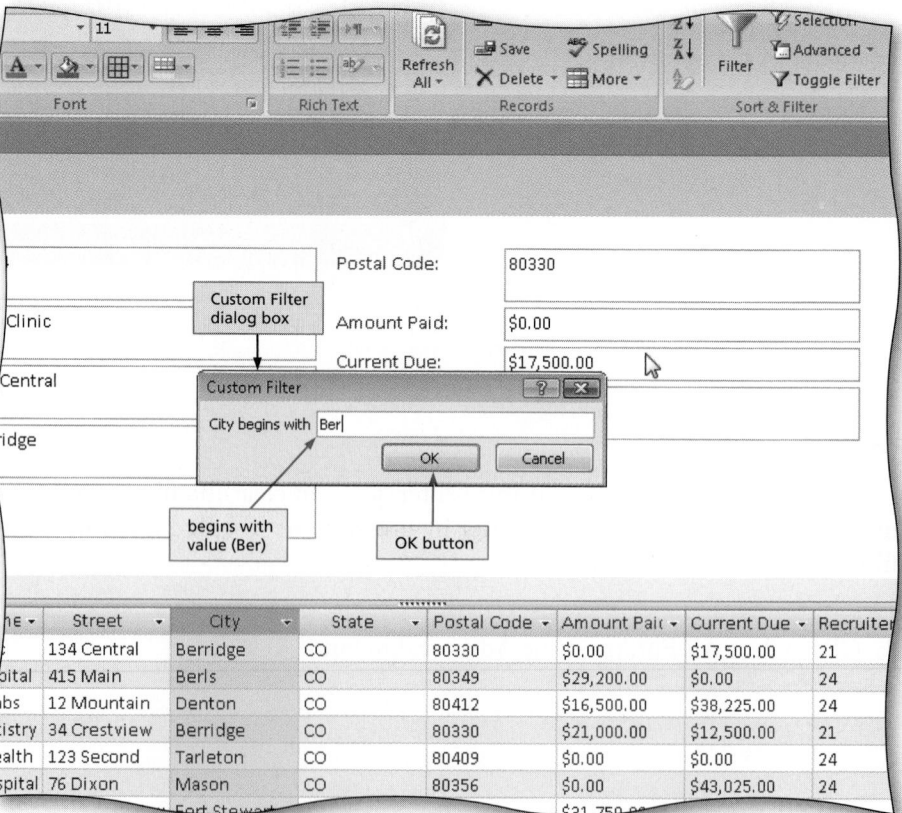

Figure 3–16

3

- Click the OK button to filter the records (Figure 3–17). (Your order may be different.)

Q&A Can I use the same technique in Form view?

In Form view, you would need to click the field and then click the Filter button to display the Common Filter menu. The rest of the process would be the same.

4

- Click the Toggle Filter button on the Home tab to toggle the filter and redisplay all records.

Toggle Filter button

only clients whose city begins with Ber are included

	Street	City	State	Postal Code	Amount Paid	Current Due	Recruiter N
	134 Central	Berridge	CO	80330	$0.00	$17,500.00	21
al	415 Main	Berls	CO	80349	$29,200.00	$0.00	24
try	34 Crestview	Berridge	CO	80330	$21,000.00	$12,500.00	21
	785 Main	Berls	CO	80349	$14,000.00	$0.00	24
	315 Maple	Berls	CO	80349	$0.00	$0.00	27

Figure 3–17

To Use Filter By Form

Filter By Selection is a quick and easy way to filter by the value in a single field. For more complex criteria, however, it is not appropriate. For example, if you determined you only wanted those clients whose postal code is 80330 and whose amount paid is 0, you could not use either the Filter by Selection or the Common Filter processes. Rather, you would use **Filter By Form**. The following steps use Filter By Form to restrict the records that appear.

1

- Click the Advanced button on the Home tab to display the Advanced menu (Figure 3–18).

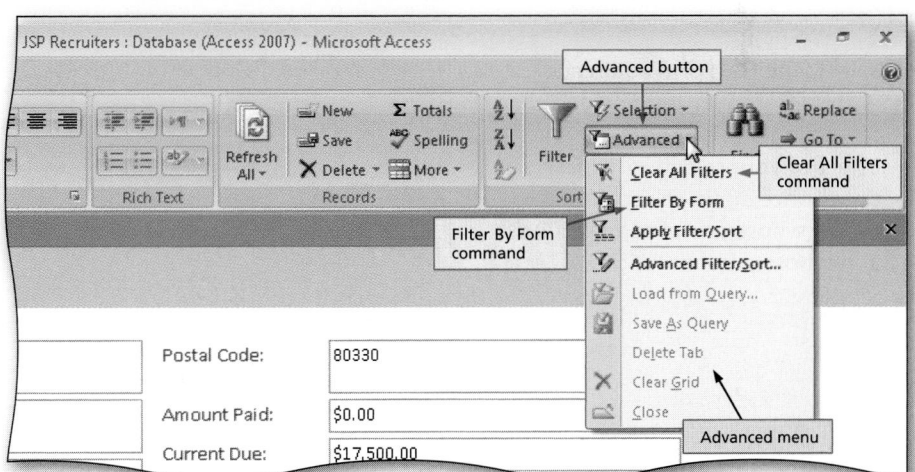

Figure 3–18

2

- Click Clear All Filters on the Advanced menu to clear the existing filter.

- Click the Advanced button on the Home tab to display the Advanced menu a second time.

- Click Filter By Form on the Advanced menu.

- Click the Postal Code field, click the arrow that appears, and then click 80330.

- Click the Amount Paid field, click the arrow that appears, and then click 0 (Figure 3–19).

Is there any difference in the process if I am viewing a table in Datasheet view rather than in Form view or in a split form?

In Datasheet view, you will make your entries in a datasheet rather than a form. Otherwise, the process is the same.

- Click the Toggle Filter button on the Home tab to apply the filter (Figure 3–20).

Experiment

- Select Filter By Form again and enter different criteria. In each case, toggle the filter to see the effect of your selection. When done, once again select those clients whose postal code is 80330 and whose amount paid is 0.

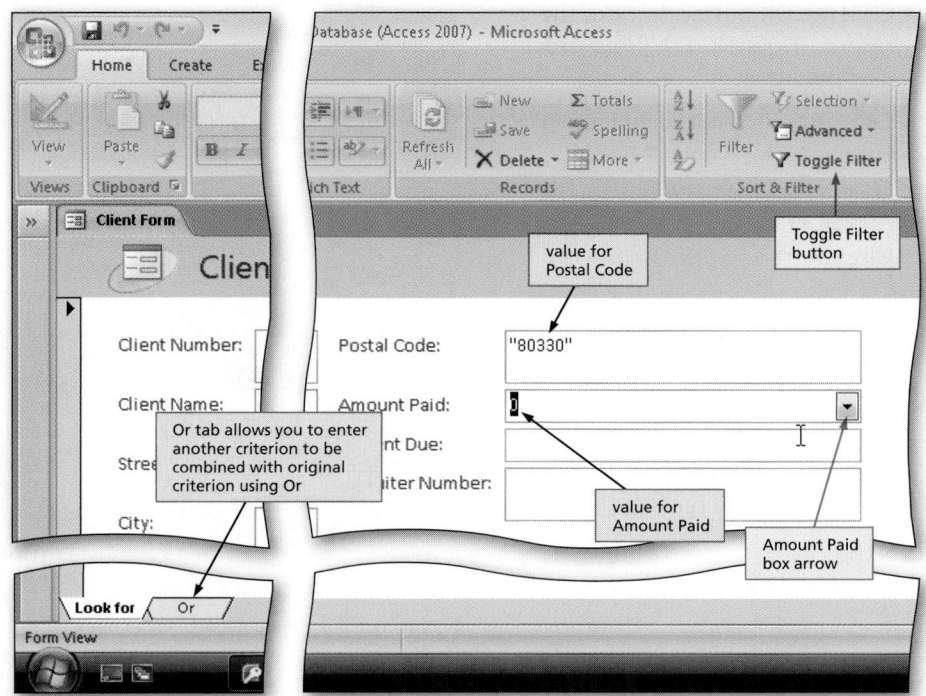

Figure 3–19

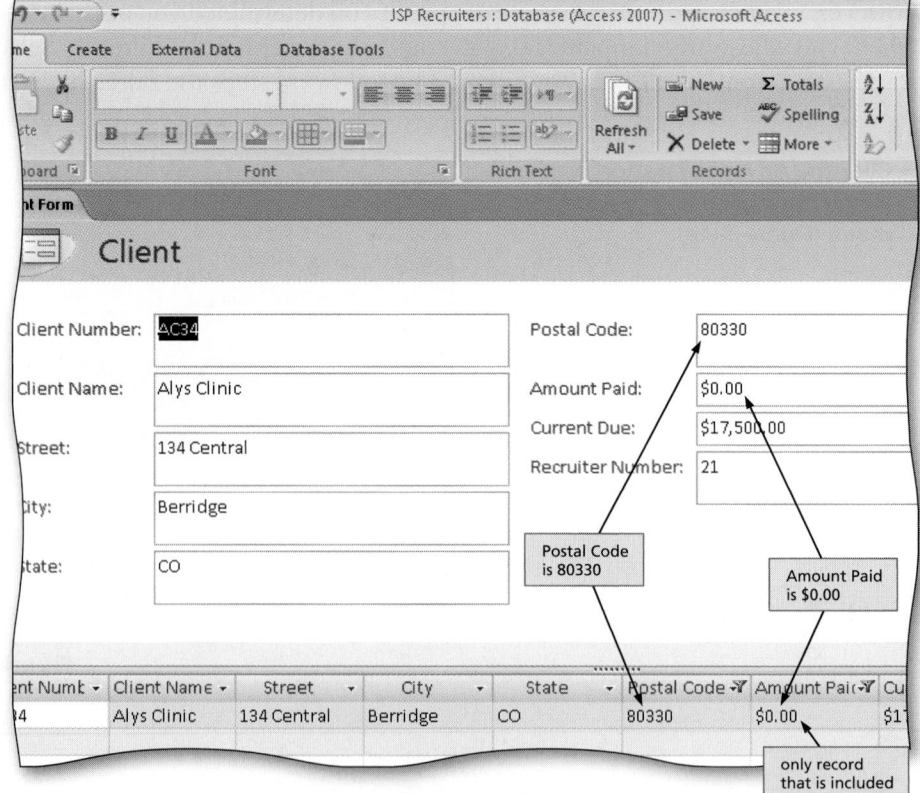

Figure 3–20

To Use Advanced Filter/Sort

In some cases, your criteria may be too complex even for Filter By Form. You might decide you want to include any client for which the postal code is 80330 and the amount paid is $0. You also may want to include any client whose amount paid is greater than $20,000, no matter where the client is located. Further, you might want to have the results sorted by name. To filter records using complex criteria, you need to use Advanced Filter/Sort as in the following steps.

- Click the Advanced button on the Home tab to display the Advanced menu, and then click Clear All Filters on the Advanced menu to clear the existing filter.

- Click the Advanced button on the Home tab to display the Advanced menu a second time.

- Click Advanced Filter/Sort on the Advanced menu.

- Expand the size of the field list so all the fields in the Client Table appear.

- Include the Client Number field and select Ascending as the sort order.

- Include the Postal Code field and enter 80330 as the criterion.

- Include the Amount Paid field and enter 0 as the criterion in the Criteria row and >20000 as the criterion in the Or row (Figure 3–21).

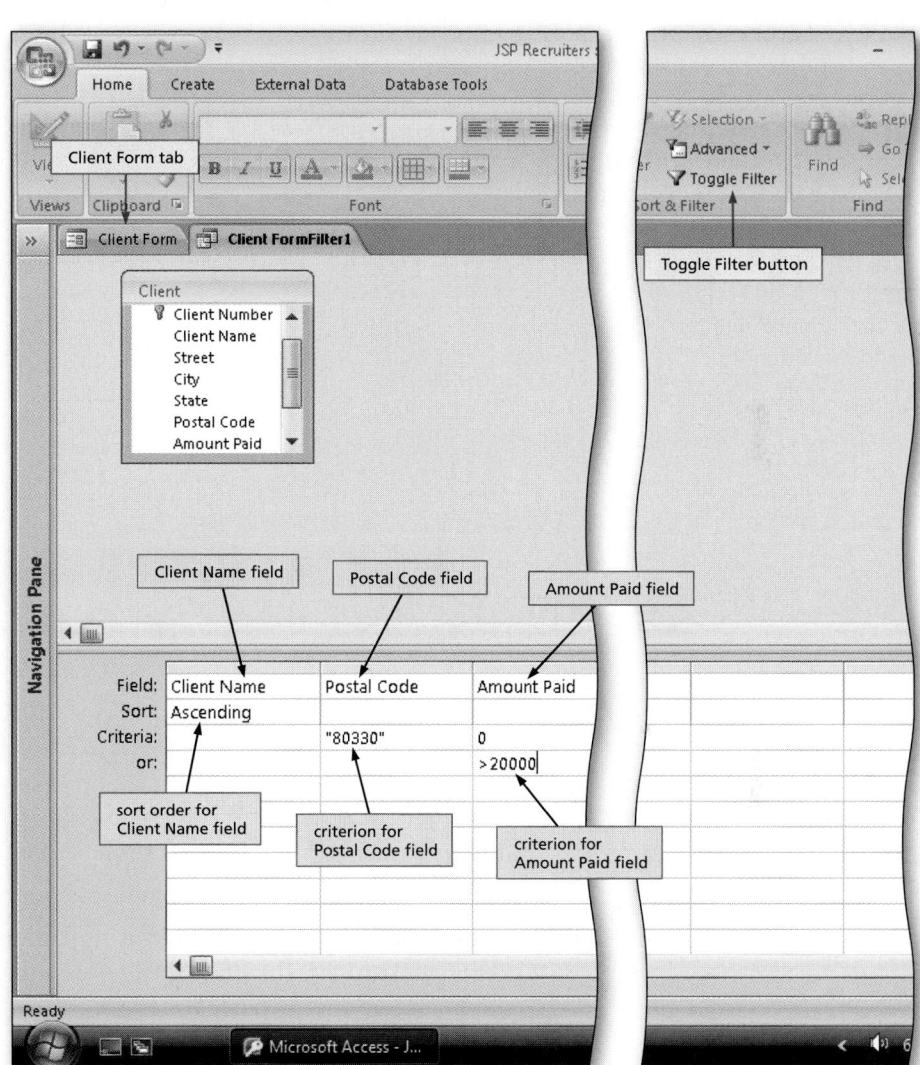

Figure 3–21

2

- Click the Toggle Filter button on the Home tab to toggle the filter and view the results. Click the Client Form tab to view the Client table (Figure 3–22).

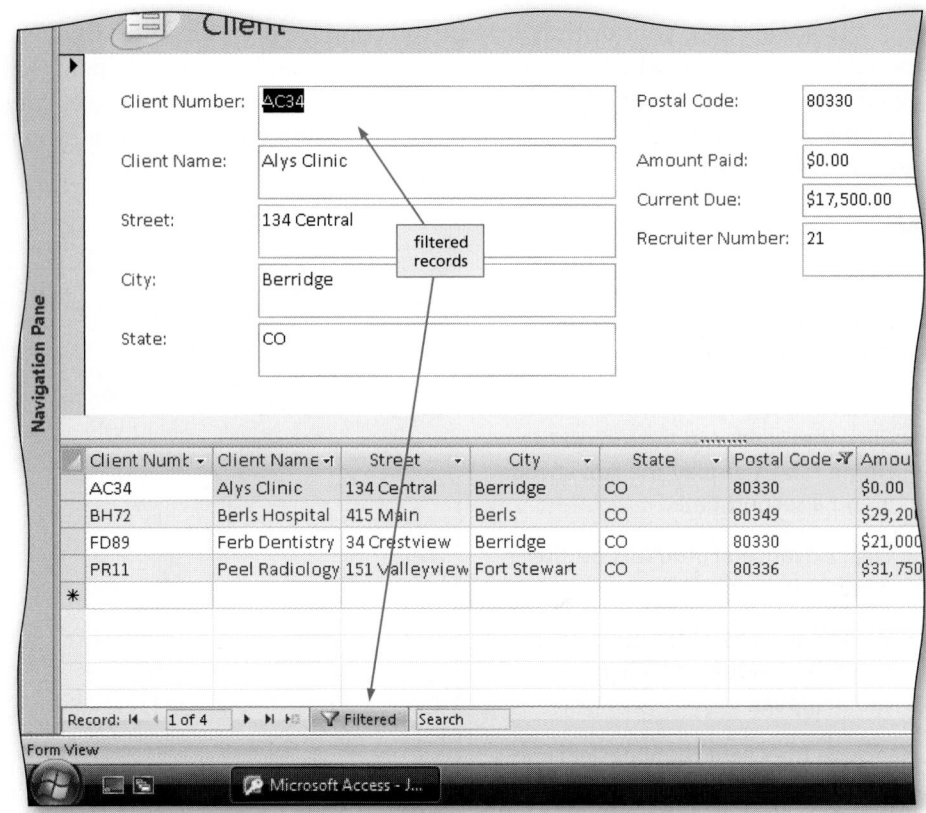

Experiment

- Select Advanced Filter/Sort again and enter different sorting options and criteria. In each case, toggle the filter to see the effect of your selection. When done, change back to the sorting options and criteria you entered in Step 1.

3

- Click Clear All Filters on the Advanced menu.

- Close the Client Form.

Figure 3–22

Filters and Queries

Filters and queries are related in three ways.

1. You can apply a filter to the results of a query just as you can apply a filter to a table.

2. When you have created a filter using either Filter By Form or Advanced Filter/Sort, you can save the filter settings as a query by using the Save As Query command on the Advanced menu.

3. You can restore filter settings that you previously saved in a query by using the Load From Query command on the Advanced menu.

BTW

Moving a Field in a Table Structure
If you add a field to a table and later realize the field is in the wrong location, you can move the field. To do so, click the row selector for the field and then drag the field to the new location.

Changing the Database Structure

When you initially create a database, you define its **structure**; that is, you assign names and types to all the fields. In many cases, the structure you first define will not continue to be appropriate as you use the database.

Perhaps a field currently in the table no longer is necessary. If no one ever uses a particular field, it is not needed in the table. Because it is occupying space and serving no useful purpose, you should remove it from the table. You also would need to delete the field from any forms, reports, or queries that include it.

More commonly, an organization will find that it needs to maintain additional information that was not anticipated at the time the database was first designed. The organization's own requirements may have changed. In addition, outside regulations that the organization must satisfy may change as well. In either case, the organization must add additional fields to an existing table.

To make any of these changes, you first must open the table in Design view.

To DELETE A FIELD

If a field in one of your tables no longer is needed; for example, it serves no useful purpose or it may have been included by mistake, you should delete the field. To delete a field you would use the following steps.

1. Open the table in Design view.
2. Click the row selector for the field to be deleted.
3. Press the DELETE key.
4. When Access displays the dialog box requesting confirmation that you want to delete the field, click the Yes button.

To Add a New Field

You can add fields to a table in a database. JSP Recruiters has decided that it needs to categorize its clients. To do so requires an additional field, Client Type. The possible values for Client Type are MED (which indicates the client is a medical institution), DNT (which indicates the client is a dental organization), or LAB (which indicates the client is a lab). The following steps add the Client Type to the Client table immediately after the Postal Code field.

- Show the Navigation Pane, and then right-click the Client table to display a shortcut menu.
- Click Design View on the shortcut menu to open the Client table in Design view.
- Click the row selector for the Amount Paid field, and then press the INSERT key to insert a blank row above the Amount Paid row (Figure 3–23).

- Click the Field Name column for the new field. If necessary, erase any text that appears.
- Type `Client Type` as the field name and then press the TAB key.

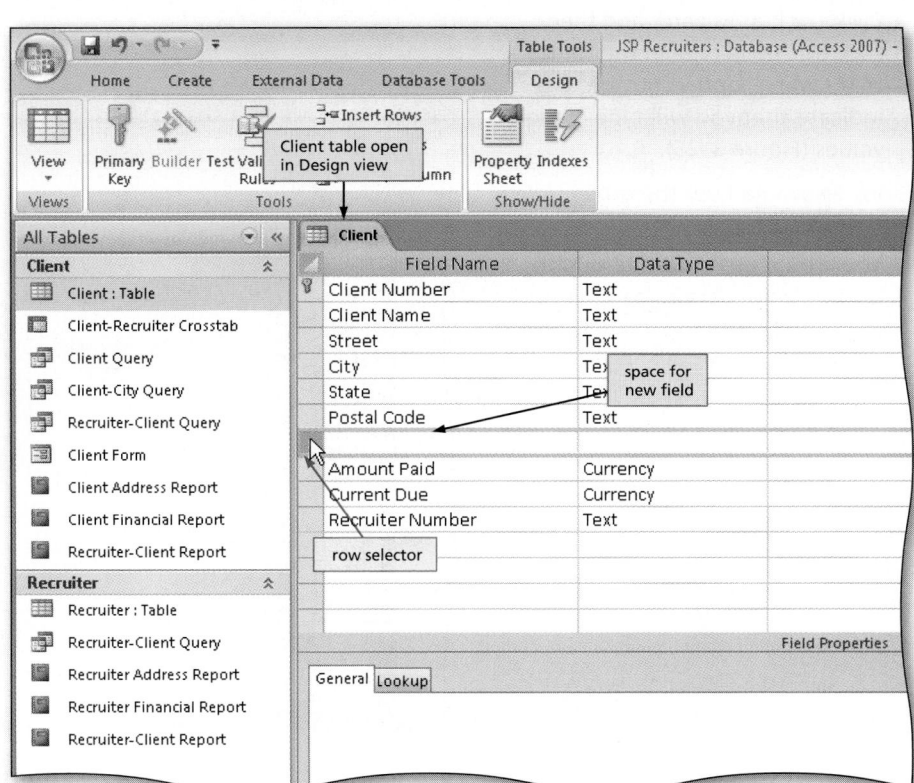

Figure 3–23

Other Ways

1. Click Insert Rows button on Ribbon

To Create a Lookup Field

Because there are only three possible values for the Client Type field, you should make it easy for users to enter the appropriate value. A **Lookup field** allows the user to select from a list of values.

The following steps make the Client Type field a Lookup field.

- If necessary, click the Data Type column for the Client Type field, and then click the arrow to display the menu of available data types (Figure 3–24).

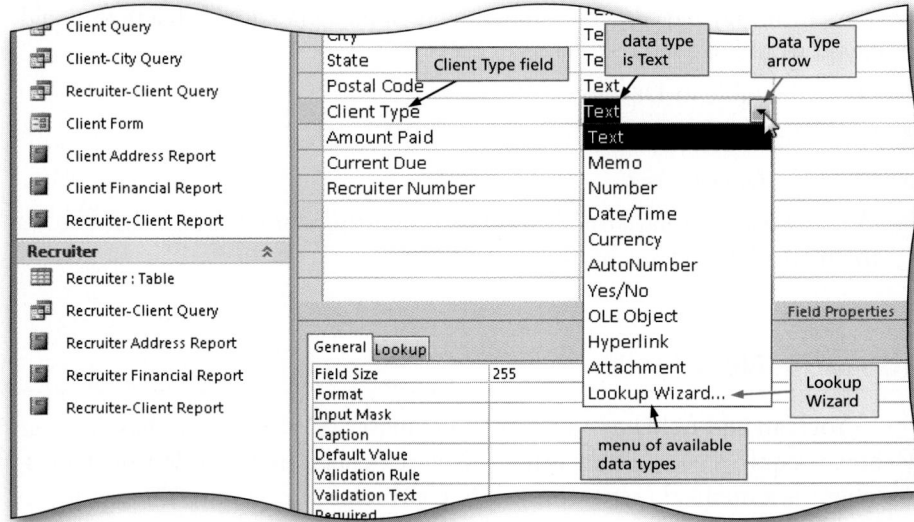

Figure 3–24

- Click Lookup Wizard, and then click the 'I will type in the values that I want.' option button to indicate that you will type in the values (Figure 3–25).

Q&A

When would I use the other option button?

You would use the other option button if the data to be entered in this field is found in another table or query.

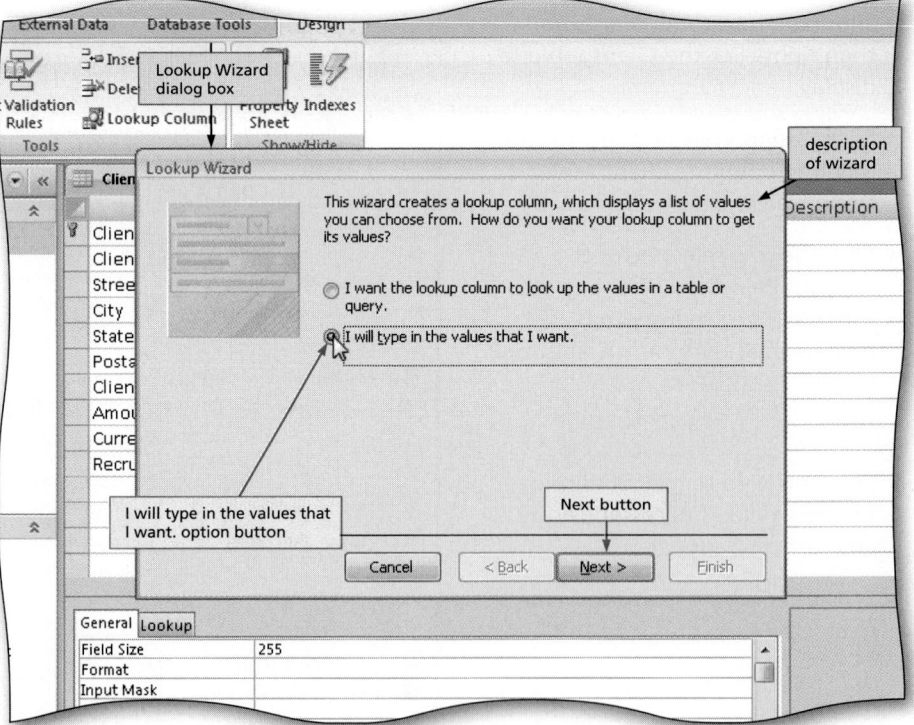

Figure 3–25

3

- Click the Next button to display the next Lookup Wizard screen (Figure 3–26).

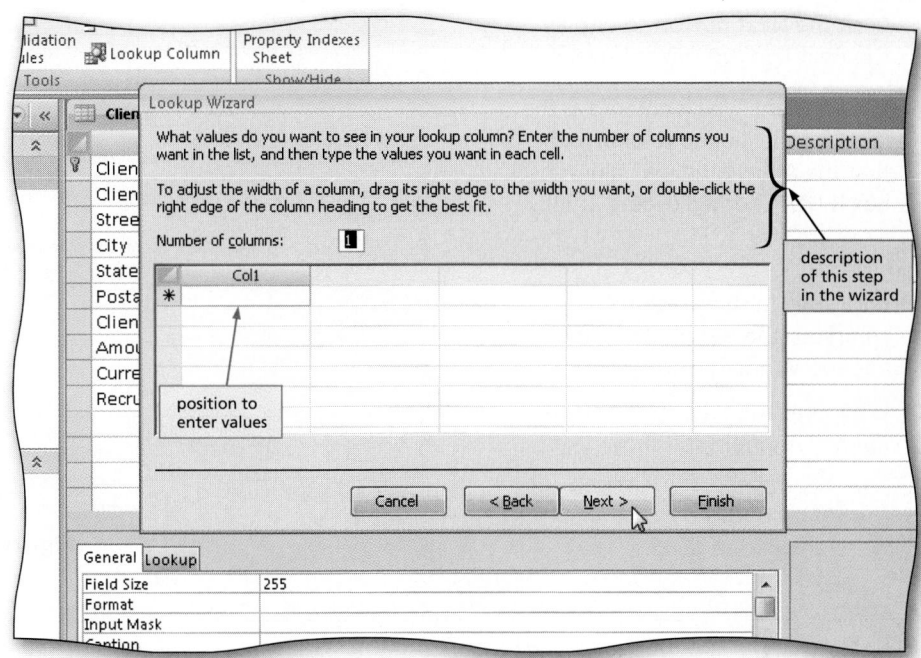

Figure 3–26

4

- Click the first row of the table (below Col1), and then type MED as the value in the first row.

- Press the DOWN ARROW key, and then type DNT as the value in the second row.

- Press the DOWN ARROW key, and then type LAB as the value in the third row (Figure 3–27).

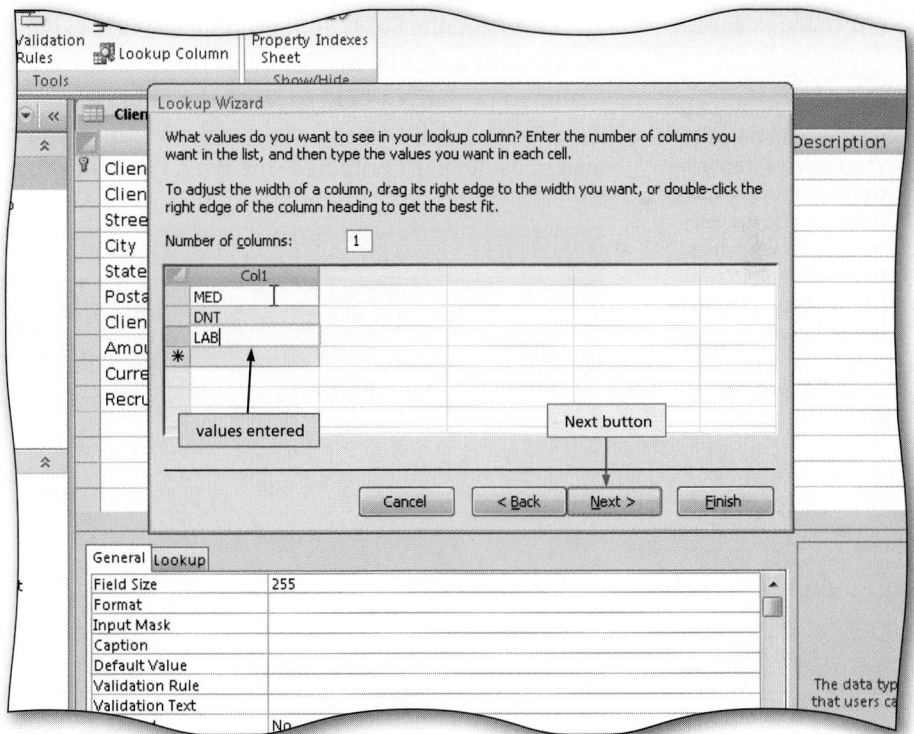

Figure 3–27

● Click the Next button to display the next Lookup Wizard screen.

● Ensure Client Type is entered as the label for the lookup column and that the Allow Multiple Values check box is NOT checked (Figure 3–28).

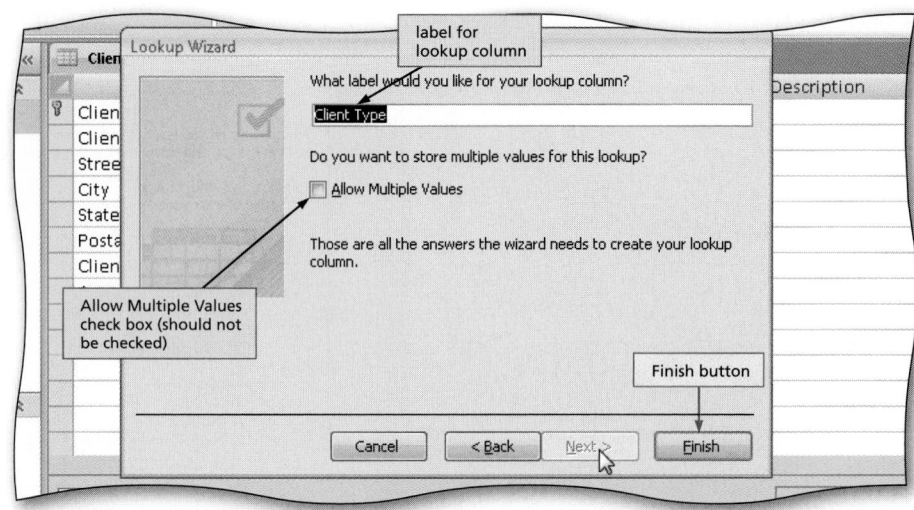

⑥

● Click the Finish button to complete the definition of the Lookup Wizard field.

Q&A

Why does the data type for the Client Type field still show Text?

The data type is still Text because the values entered in the wizard were entered as text.

Figure 3–28

To Add a Multivalued Field

Normally, fields contain only a single value. In Access 2007 it is possible to have **multivalued fields,** that is, fields that can contain more than one value. JSP Recruiters wants to use such a field to store the abbreviations of all the specialties their clients need (see Table 3–1 for the specialty abbreviations and descriptions). Unlike the Client Type, where each client only had one type, clients can require multiple specialty descriptions.

Table 3–1 Specialty Abbreviations and Descriptions	
Specialty Abbreviation	**Description**
CLS	Clinical Laboratory Specialist
CNA	Certified Nursing Assistant
CRNA	Certified Registered Nurse Anesthetist
DH	Dental Hygienist
Dnt	Dentist
EMT	Emergency Medical Technician
NP	Nurse Practitioner
OT	Occupational Therapist
PA	Physician Assistant
Phy	Physician
PT	Physical Therapist
RN	Registered Nurse
RT	Respiratory Therapist

One client might need CNA, PA, Phy, and RN employees (Certified Nursing Assistants, Physician Assistants, Physicians, and Registered Nurses). Another client might only need RTs (Respiratory Therapists).

To create a multivalued field, create a Lookup field being sure to check the Allow Multiple Values check box. The following steps create a multivalued field.

1 Click the row selector for the Amount Paid field, and then press the INSERT key to insert a blank row.

2 Click the Field Name column for the new field, type `Specialties Needed` as the field name, and then press the DOWN ARROW key.

3 Click the Data Type column for the Specialties Needed field, and then click Lookup Wizard in the menu of available data types to start the Lookup Wizard.

4 Click the 'I will type in the values that I want.' option button to indicate that you will type in the values.

5 Click the Next button to display the next Lookup Wizard screen.

6 Click the first row of the table (below Col1), and then type CLS as the value in the first row.

7 Enter the remaining values from the first column in Table 3–1. Before typing each value, press the TAB key to move to a new row.

8 Click the Next button to display the next Lookup Wizard screen.

9 Ensure Specialties Needed is entered as the label for the lookup column.

10 Click the Allow Multiple Values check box to allow multiple values.

11 Click the Finish button to complete the definition of the Lookup Wizard field.

To Save the Changes and Close the Table

The following steps save the changes; that is, it saves the addition of the two new fields and closes the table.

1 Click the Save button on the Quick Access Toolbar to save the changes.

2 Click the Close 'Client' button.

TO MODIFY SINGLE OR MULTIVALUED LOOKUP FIELDS

You may find that you later want to change the list of choices in a Lookup field. If you find you need to modify a single or multivalued Lookup field you have created, you can use the following steps.

1. Open the table in Design view and select the field to be modified.
2. Click the Lookup Tab in the field properties.
3. Change the list in the Row Source property to change the desired list of values.

BTW

Modifying Table Properties
You can change the properties of a table by opening the table in Design view and then clicking the Property Sheet button on the Table Tools tab. Access will display the property sheet for the table. To display the records in a table in an order other than primary key order (the default sort order), use the Order By property. For example, to display the Client table automatically in Client Name order, click the Order By property box, type `Client.Client Name` in the property box, close the property sheet, and save the change to the table design. When you open the Client table in Datasheet view, the records will be sorted in Client Name order.

Mass Changes

In some cases, rather than making individual changes to records, you will want to make mass changes. That is, you will want to add, change, or delete many records in a single operation. You can do this with action queries. An **action query** adds, deletes, or changes data in a table. An **update query** allows you to make the same change to all records satisfying some criterion. If you omit the criterion, you will make the same changes to all records in the table. A **delete query** allows you to delete all the records satisfying some criterion. You can add the results of a query to an existing table by using an **append query**. You also can add the results to a new table by using a **make-table query**.

To Use an Update Query

The Client Type field is blank on every record. One approach to entering the information for the field would be to step through the entire table, assigning each record its appropriate value. If most of the clients have the same type, a simpler approach is available.

In the JSP Recruiters database, for example, most clients are type MED. Initially, you can set all the values to MED. To accomplish this quickly and easily, you can use an update query, which is a query that makes the same change to all the records satisfying a criterion. Later, you can change the type for dental organizations and labs.

The following steps use an update query to change the value in the Client Type field to MED for all the records. Because all records are to be updated, criteria are not required.

1

- Create a new query for the Client table.

- Click the Update button on the Design tab, double-click the Client Type field to select the field, click the Update To row in the first column of the design grid, and then type MED as the new value (Figure 3–29).

Q&A

Don't I have to enter a criterion?

If you only want the change to be made on some of the records, you would need to enter a criterion to identify those records. Without a criterion, the change will be made on all records, which is what you want in this update.

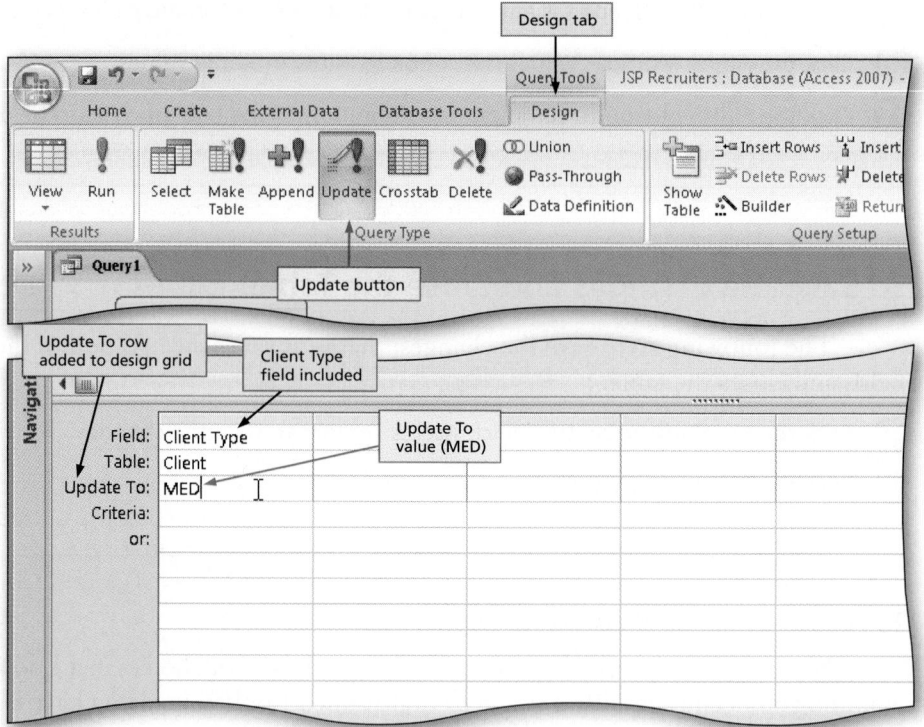

Figure 3–29

2

- Click the Run button on the Design tab to run the query and update the records (Figure 3–30).

Q&A

Why don't I click the View button to update the records?

The purpose of the View button is to simply view results. The Run button causes the updates specified by the query to take place.

Q&A

Why doesn't the dialog box appear on my screen when I click the Run button?

If the dialog box does not appear, it means that you did not choose the Enable this content option button when you first opened the database. Close the database, open it again, and enable the content in the Microsoft Office Security Options dialog box. Then, create and run the query again.

 Experiment

- Create an Update query to change the client type to DNT. Enter a criterion to restrict the records to be updated, and then run the query. Open the table to view your changes. When finished, create and run an Update query to change the client type to MED on all records.

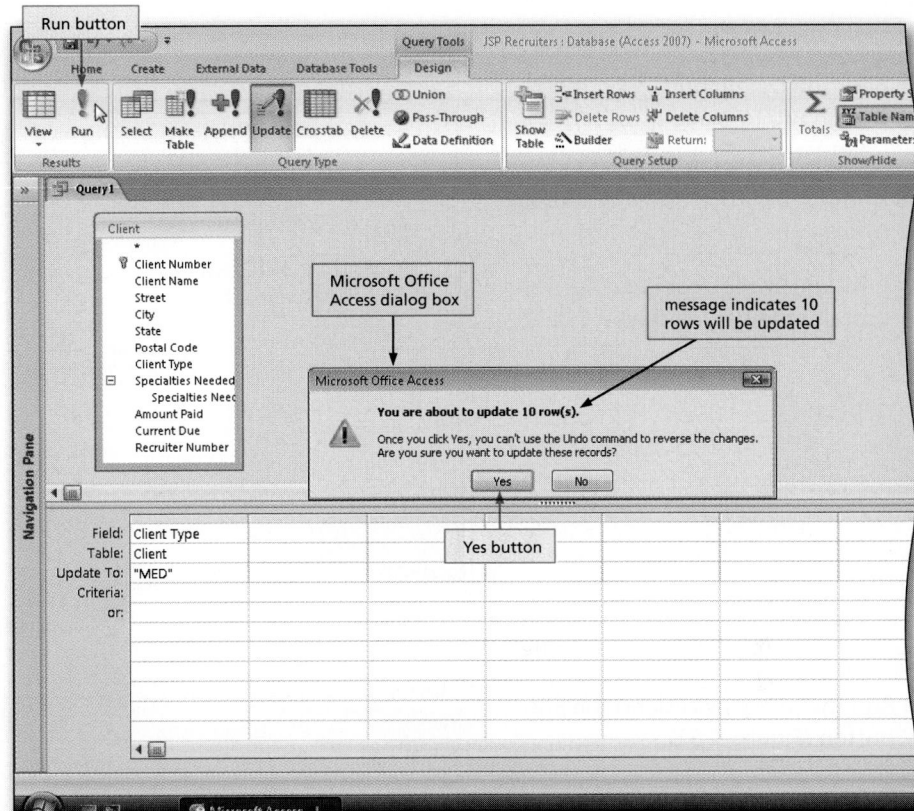

Figure 3–30

3

- Click the Yes button to make the changes.

Other Ways
1. Right-click any open area in upper Pane, point to Query Type on shortcut menu,   click Update Query on Query Type submenu

To Use a Delete Query

In some cases, you may need to delete several records at a time. If, for example, all clients in a particular postal code are to be serviced by another firm, the clients with this postal code can be deleted from the JSP Recruiters database. Instead of deleting these clients individually, which could be very time-consuming in a large database, you can delete them in one operation by using a **delete query**, which is a query that will delete all the records satisfying the criteria entered in the query.

You can preview the data to be deleted in a delete query before actually performing the deletion. To do so, click the View button after you create the query, but before you run it. The records to be deleted then would appear in Datasheet view. To delete the records, click the View button again to change to Design view. Click the Run button, and then click the Yes button in the Microsoft Office Access dialog box when asked if you want to delete the records.

The following steps use a delete query to delete any client whose postal code is 80412 without first previewing the data to be deleted. (Only one such client currently exists in the database.)

- Clear the grid.

- Click the Delete button on the Design tab to make the query a Delete query (Figure 3–31).

- Double-click the Postal Code field to select the field.

- Click the Criteria row for the Postal Code field and type 80412 as the criterion.

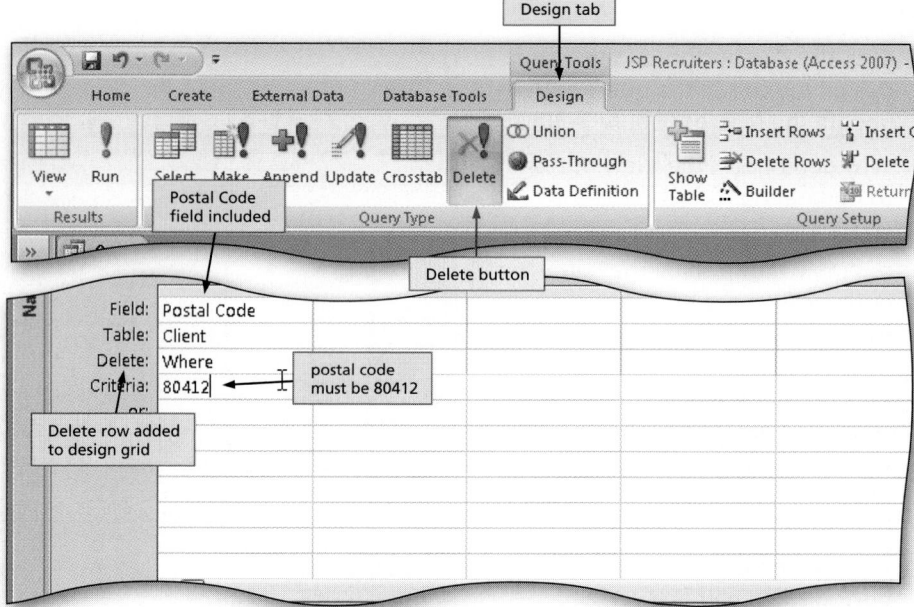

Figure 3–31

- Run the query by clicking the Run button (Figure 3–32).

- Click the Yes button to complete the deletion.

- Close the Query window. Do not save the query.

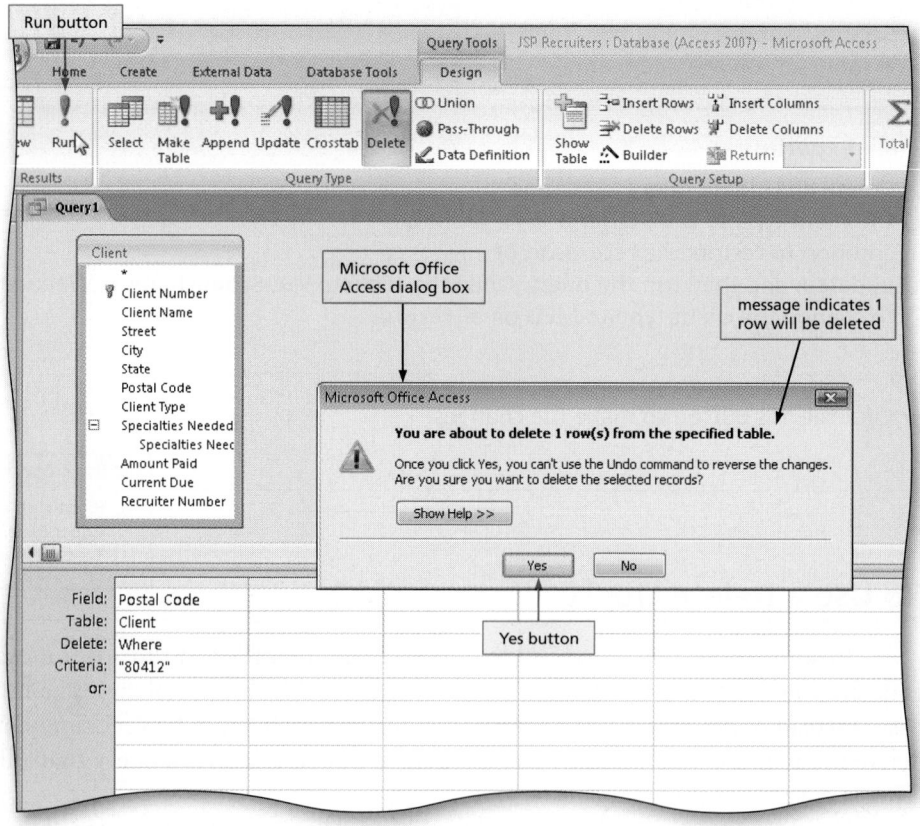

Figure 3–32

Other Ways

1. Right-click any open area in upper Pane, point to Query Type on shortcut menu, click Delete Query on Query Type submenu

TO USE AN APPEND QUERY

An append query adds a group of records from one table to the end of another table. For example, suppose that JSP Recruiters acquires some new clients and a database containing a table with those clients. To avoid entering all this information manually, you can append it to the Client table in the JSP Recruiters database using the append query. To create an append query, you would use the following steps.

1. Create a query for the table containing the records to append.
2. In Design view, indicate the fields to include, and then enter any necessary criteria.
3. View the query results to be sure you have specified the correct data, and then return to Design view.
4. Click the Append button on the Design tab.
5. When Access displays the Append dialog box, specify the name of the table to receive the new records and its location. Run the query by clicking the Run button on the Design tab.
6. When Access indicates the number of records to be appended, click the Yes button.

TO USE A MAKE-TABLE QUERY

In some cases, you might want to add the records from an existing table to a new table, that is, a table that has not yet been created. If so, use a make-table query to add the records to a new table. Access will create this table as part of the process and add the records to it. To create a make-table query, you would use the following steps.

1. Create a query for the table containing the records to add.
2. In Design view, indicate the fields to include, and then enter any necessary criteria.
3. View the query results to be sure you have specified the correct data, and then return to Design view.
4. Click the Make Table button on the Design tab.
5. When Access displays the Make Table dialog box, specify the name of the table to receive the new records and its location. Run the query by clicking the Run button on the Design tab.
6. When Access indicates the number of records to be inserted, click the Yes button.

Validation Rules

You now have created, loaded, queried, and updated a database. Nothing you have done so far, however, makes sure that users enter only valid data. To ensure the entry of valid data, you create **validation rules**; that is, rules that a user must follow when entering the data. As you will see, Access will prevent users from entering data that does not follow the rules. The steps also specify **validation text**, which is the message that will appear if a user violates the validation rule.

Validation rules can indicate a **required field**, a field in which the user actually must enter data. For example, by making the Client Name field a required field, a user actually must enter a name (that is, the field cannot be blank). Validation rules can make sure a user's entry lies within a certain **range of values**; for example, that the values in the Amount Paid field are between $0.00 and $100,000.00. They can specify a **default value**; that is, a value that Access will display on the screen in a particular field before the user begins adding a record. To make data entry of client numbers more convenient, you also can have lowercase letters appear automatically as uppercase letters. Finally, validation rules can specify a collection of acceptable values; for example, that the only legitimate entries for the Client Type field are MED, DNT, and LAB.

BTW

Using Wildcards in Validation Rules
You can include wildcards in validation rules. For example, if you enter the expression, like C?, in the Validation Rule box for the State field, the only valid entries for the field will be CA, CO, and CT.

To Specify a Required Field

To specify that a field is to be required, change the value for the Required property from No to Yes. The following steps specify that the Client Name field is to be a required field.

- Show the Navigation Pane, and then open the Client table in Design view.

- Select the Client Name field by clicking its row selector.

- Click the Required property box in the Field Properties Pane, and then click the down arrow that appears.

- Click Yes in the list (Figure 3–33).

Q&A

What is the effect of this change?

Users cannot leave the Client Name field blank when entering or editing records.

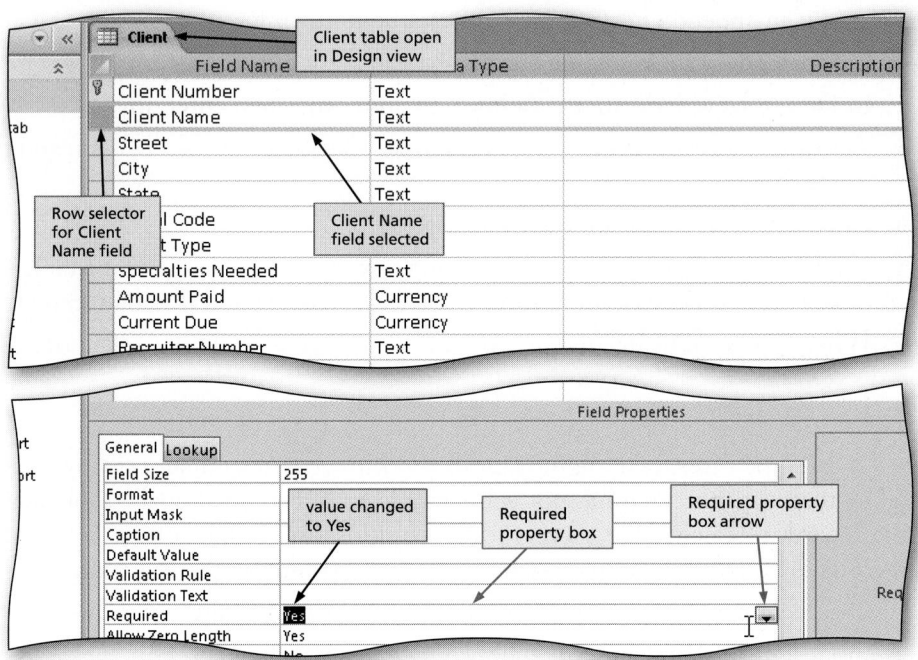

Figure 3–33

To Specify a Range

The following step specifies that entries in the Amount Paid field must be between $0.00 and $100,000.00. To indicate this range, the criterion specifies that the amount paid value must be both >= 0 (greater than or equal to 0) and <= 100000 (less than or equal to 100000).

- Select the Amount Paid field by clicking its row selector, click the Validation Rule property box to produce an insertion point, and then type >=0 and <=100000 as the rule.

- Click the Validation Text property box to produce an insertion point, and then type Must be at least $0.00 and at most $100,000 as the text (Figure 3–34).

Q&A

What is the effect of this change?

Users now will be prohibited from entering an amount paid value that either is less than $0.00 or greater than $100,000.00 when they add records or change the value in the Amount Paid field.

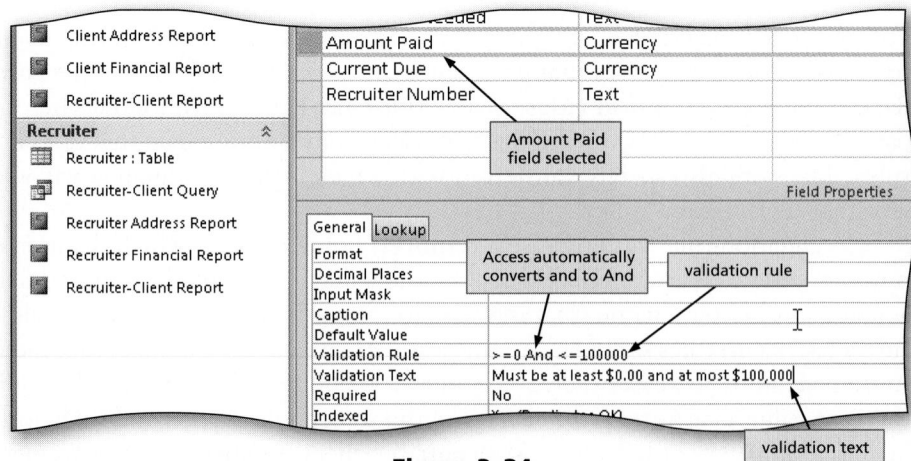

Figure 3–34

To Specify a Default Value

To specify a default value, enter the value in the Default Value property box. The following step specifies MED as the default value for the Client Type field. This simply means that if users do not enter a client type, the type will be MED.

1

- Select the Client Type field. Click the Default Value property box to produce an insertion point, and then type =MED as the value (Figure 3–35).

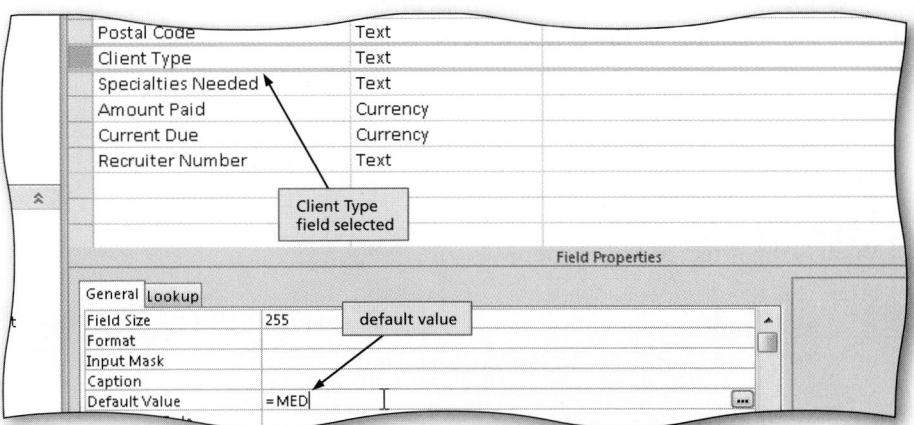

Figure 3–35

To Specify a Collection of Allowable Values

The only allowable values for the Client Type field are MED, DNT, and LAB. An appropriate validation rule for this field prevents Access from accepting any entry other than these three possibilities. The following step specifies the legal values for the Client Type field.

1

- Make sure the Client Type field is selected.

- Click the Validation Rule property box to produce an insertion point and then type =MED Or =DNT Or =LAB as the validation rule.

- Click the Validation Text property box and then type Must be MED, DNT, or LAB as the validation text (Figure 3–36).

Q&A

What is the effect of this change?

Users now will be allowed to enter only MED, DNT, or LAB in the Client Type field when they add records or make changes to this field.

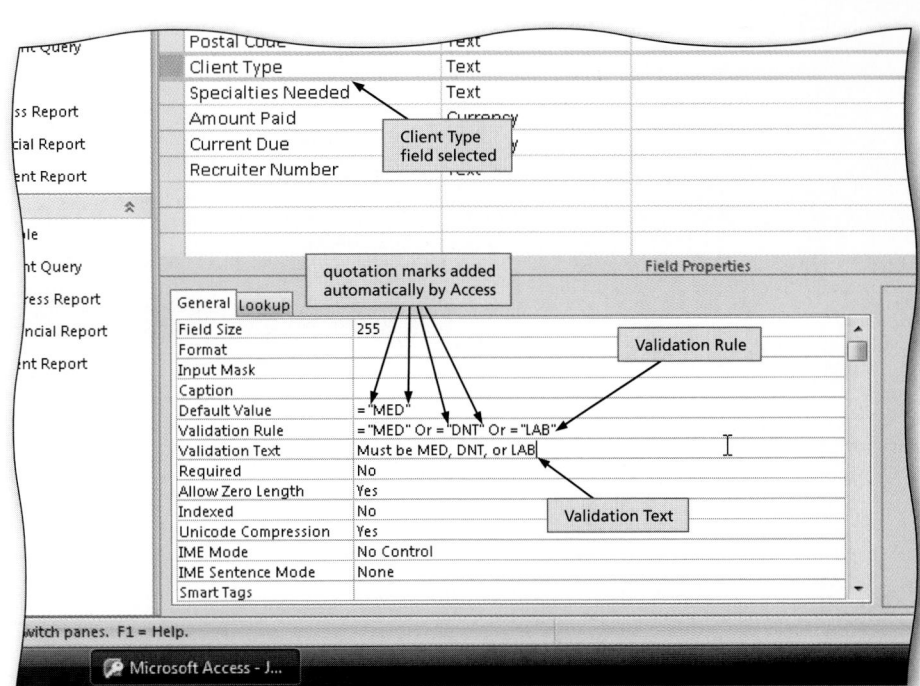

Figure 3–36

To Specify a Format

To affect the way data appears in a field, you can use a **format**. To use a format with a Text field, you enter a special symbol, called a **format symbol**, in the field's Format property box. The Format property uses different settings for different data types. The following step specifies a format for the Client Number field in the Client table and illustrates the way you enter a format. The format symbol used in the example is >, which causes Access to display lowercase letters automatically as uppercase letters. The format symbol < causes Access to display uppercase letters automatically as lowercase letters.

- Select the Client Number field.

- Click the Format property box and then type > (Figure 3–37).

Q&A What is the effect of this change?

From this point on, any lowercase letters will appear automatically as uppercase when users add records or change the value in the Client Number field.

Q&A Client numbers are supposed to be four characters long. Is there a way to ensure users don't type more than four characters?

Yes. The Field Size property dictates how many characters the users can type, so if you wanted to ensure that a maximum of four characters be allowed, you could change the field size from 255 to 4.

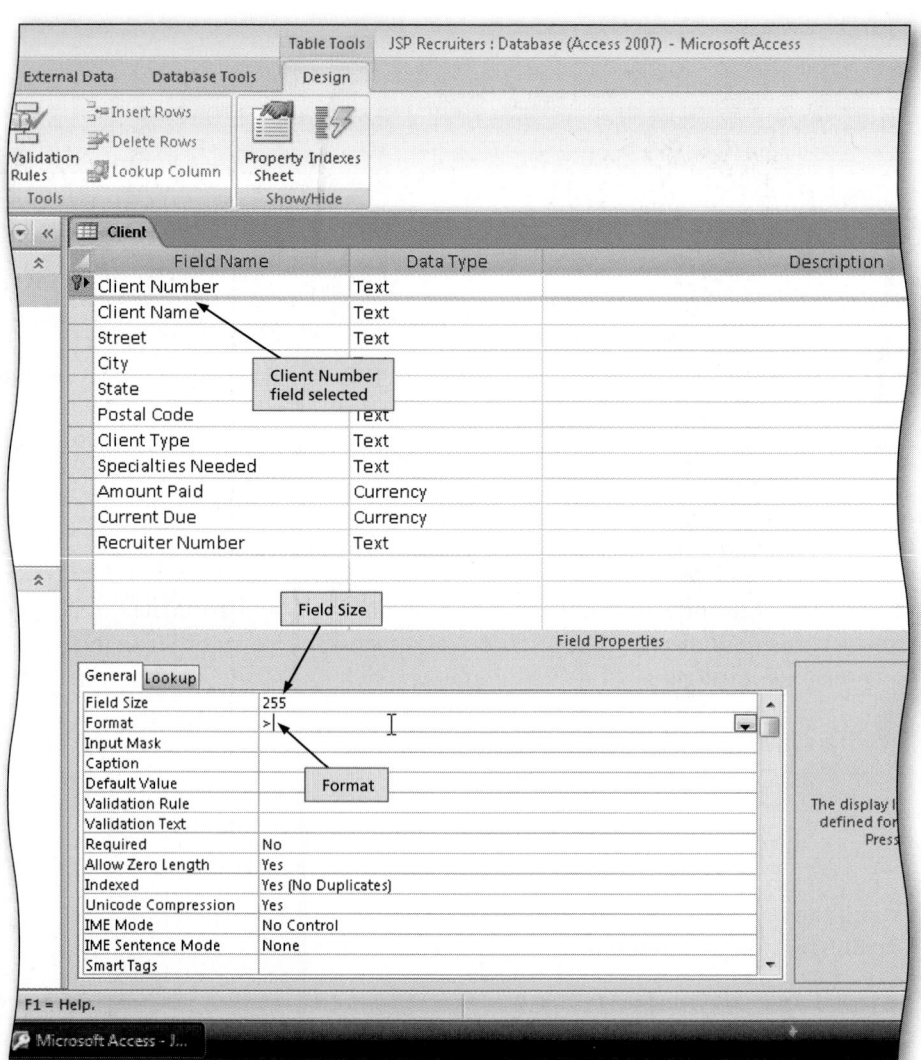

Figure 3–37

To Save the Validation Rules, Default Values, and Formats

The following steps save the validation rules, default values, and formats.

1

- Click the Save button on the Quick Access Toolbar to save the changes (Figure 3–38).

2

- Click the No button to save the changes without testing current data.

- Close the Client table.

Q&A Should I always click the No button when saving validation rules?

If this were a database used to run a business or to solve some other critical need, you would click Yes. You would want to be sure that the data already in the database does not violate the rules.

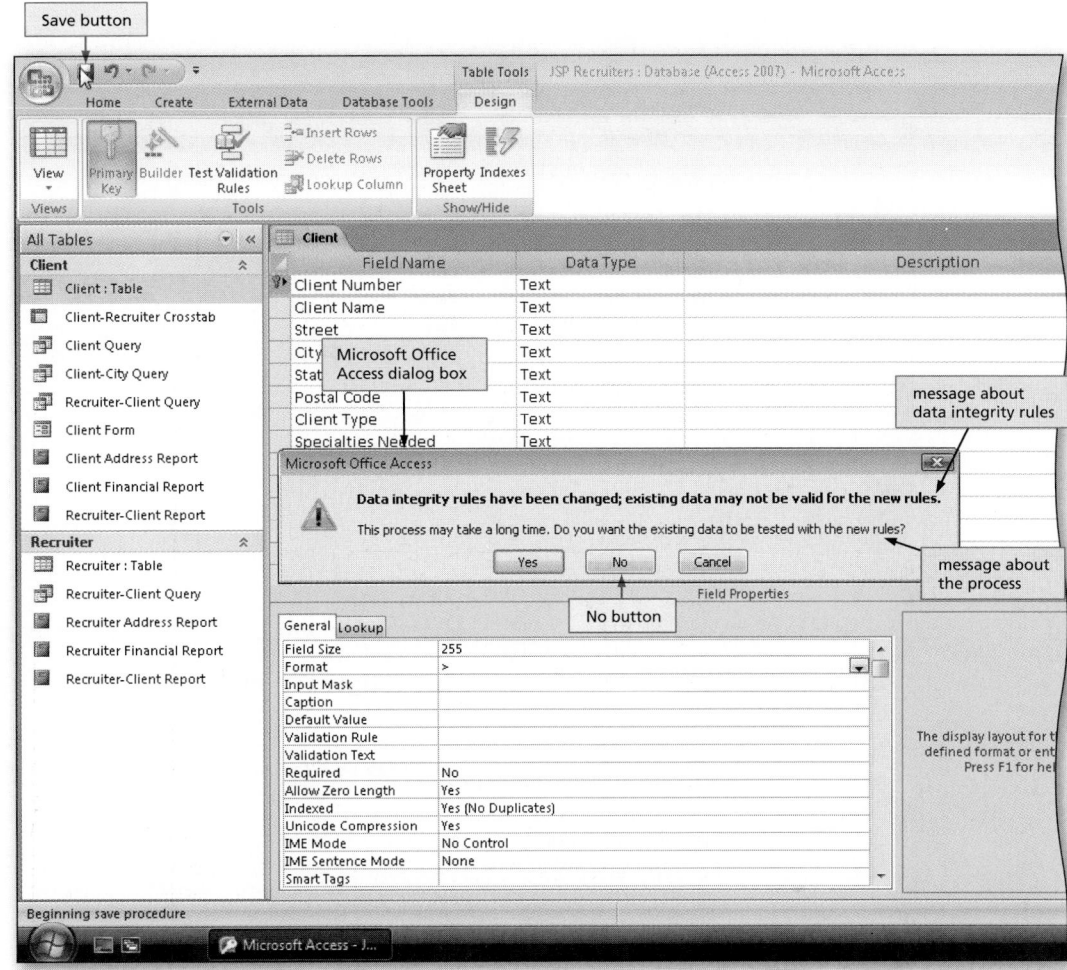

Figure 3–38

Changing Data Types
It is possible to change the data type for a field that already contains data. Before you change a data type, however, you should consider what effect the change will have on other database objects, such as forms, queries, and reports. For example, you could convert a Text field to a Memo field if you find that you do not have enough space to store the data that you need. You also could convert a Number field to a Currency field or vice versa.

Updating a Table that Contains Validation Rules

When updating a table that contains validation rules, Access provides assistance in making sure the data entered is valid. It helps in making sure that data is formatted correctly. Access also will not accept invalid data. Entering a number that is out of the required range, for example, or entering a value that is not one of the possible choices, will produce an error message in the form of a dialog box. The database will not be updated until the error is corrected.

If the client number entered contains lowercase letters, such am49 (Figure 3–39), Access will display the data automatically as AM49 (Figure 3–40).

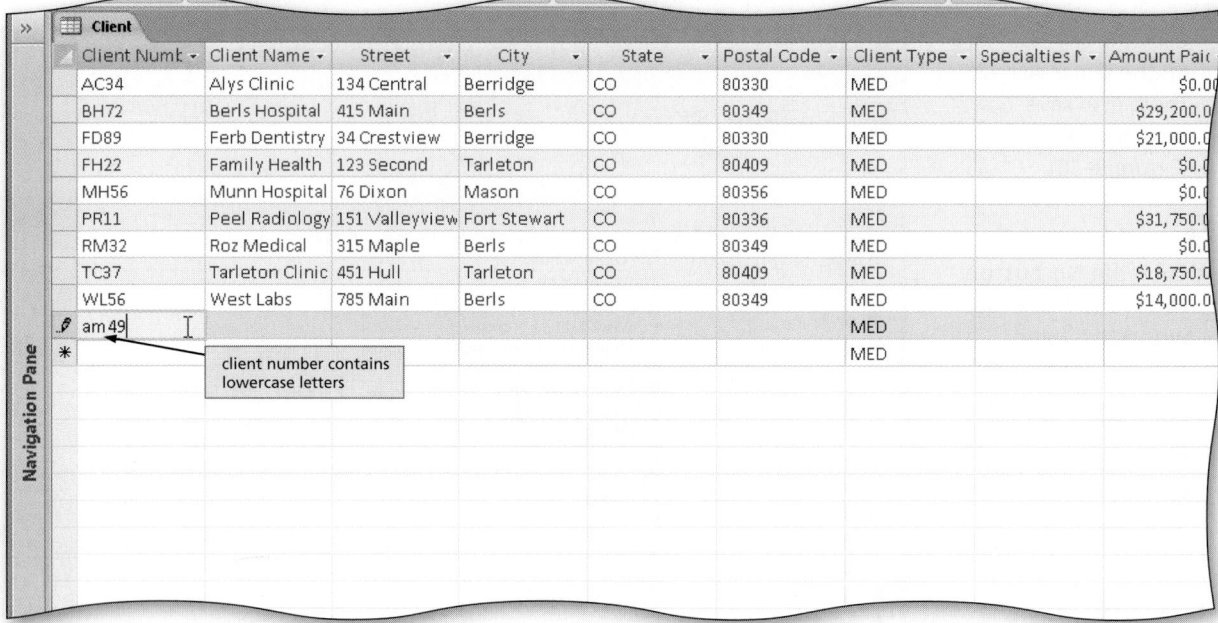

Figure 3–39

Figure 3–40

If the client type is not valid, such as xxx, Access will display the text message you specified (Figure 3–41) and not allow the data to enter the database.

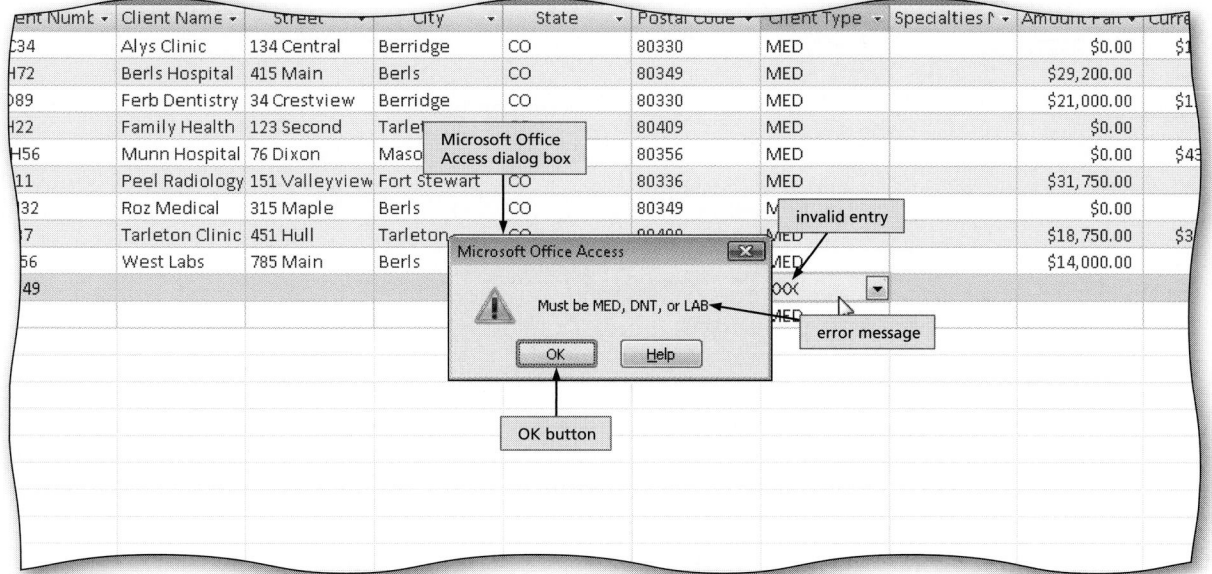

Figure 3–41

If the amount paid value is not valid, such as 125000, which is too large, Access also displays the appropriate message (Figure 3–42) and refuses to accept the data.

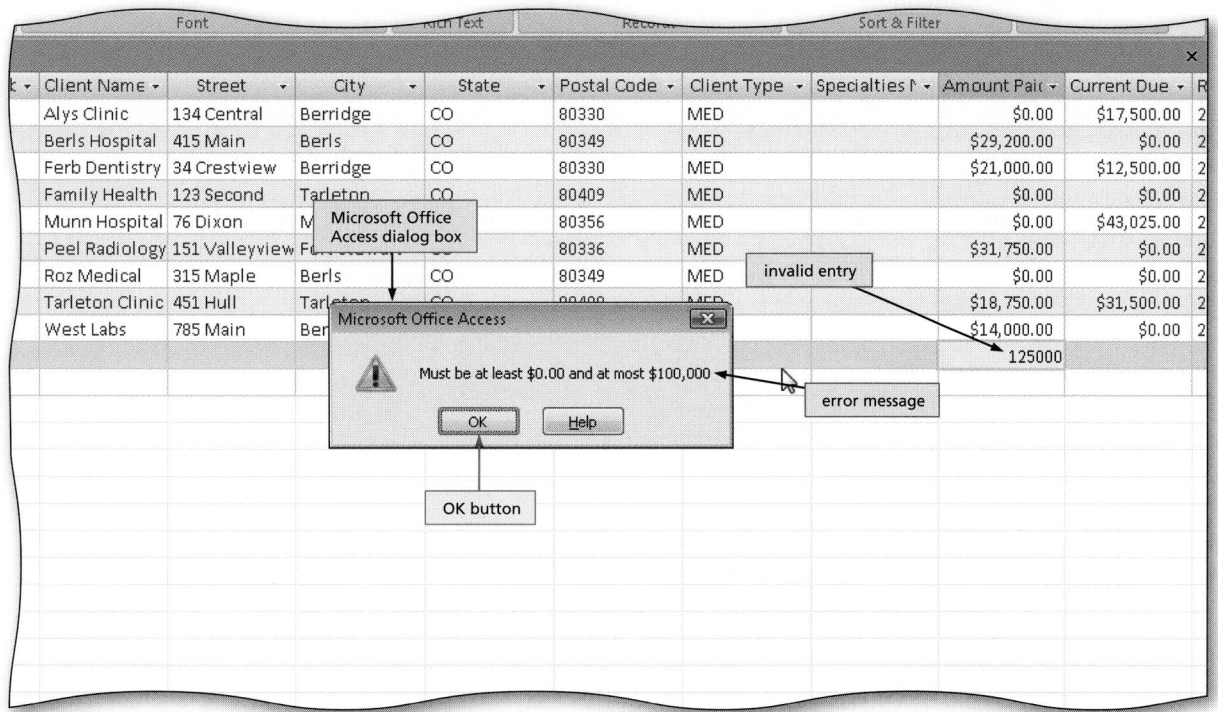

Figure 3–42

If a required field contains no data, Access indicates this by displaying an error message as soon as you attempt to leave the record (Figure 3–43). The field must contain a valid entry before Access will move to a different record.

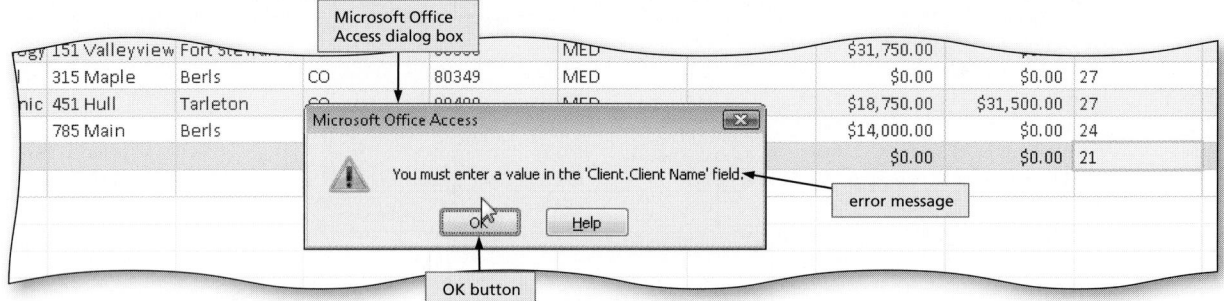

Figure 3–43

When entering data into a field with a validation rule, you may find that Access displays the error message and you are unable to make the necessary correction. It may be that you cannot remember the validation rule you created or it was created incorrectly. In such a case, you neither can leave the field nor close the table because you have entered data into a field that violates the validation rule.

If this happens, first try again to type an acceptable entry. If this does not work, repeatedly press the BACKSPACE key to erase the contents of the field and then try to leave the field. If you are unsuccessful using this procedure, press the ESC key until the record is removed from the screen. The record will not be added to the database.

Should the need arise to take this drastic action, you probably have a faulty validation rule. Use the techniques of the previous sections to correct the existing validation rules for the field.

To Use a Lookup Field

Earlier, you changed all the entries in the Client Type field to MED. Thus, you have created a rule that will ensure that only legitimate values (MED, DNT, or LAB) can be entered in the field. You also made Client Type a Lookup field using a mass change. You can make changes to a Lookup field by clicking the field to be changed, clicking the arrow that appears in the field, and then selecting the desired value from the list.

The following steps change the Client Type value on the third record to DNT and on the ninth record to LAB.

- Open the Client table in Datasheet view and ensure the Navigation Pane is hidden.

- Click in the Client Type field on the third record to display the arrow (Figure 3–44).

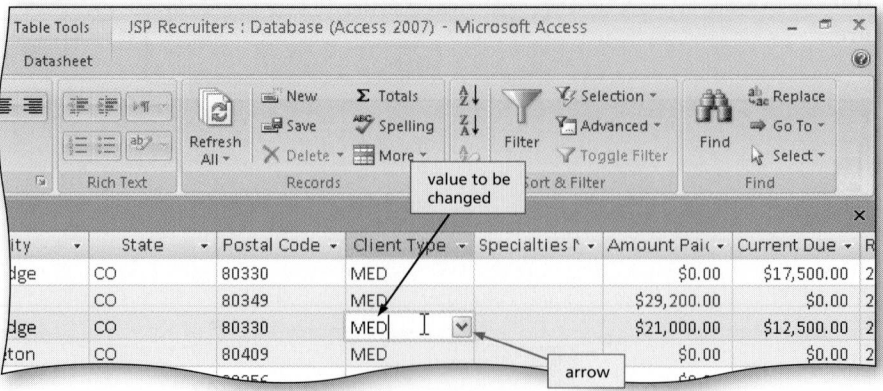

Figure 3–44

2

- Click the down arrow to display the drop-down list of available choices for the Client Type field (Figure 3–45).

Could I type the value instead of selecting it from the list?

Yes. Once you have either deleted the previous value or selected the entire previous value, you can begin typing. You do not have to type the full entry. When you begin with the letter, D, for example, Access will automatically add the NT.

erls	CO	80349	MED			$29,200.00	$0.00	2
erridge	CO	80330	MED ▼		value to	$21,000.00	$12,500.00	2
Tarleton	CO	80409	MED		select (DNT)	$0.00	$0.00	2
Mason	CO	80356	DNT ←			$0.00	$43,025.00	2
ort Stewart	CO	80336	LAB			$31,750.00	$0.00	2
erls	CO	80349	MED			$0.00	$0.00	2
arleton	CO	80409	MED	list of available		$18,750.00	$31,500.00	2
Berls	CO	80349	MED	values		$14,000.00	$0.00	2
			MED					

Figure 3–45

Experiment

- Select the Client Type field on the first record. Try to change the client type by typing various values. Try to type an invalid Client Type (like SPT). When finished, change the value on the record to MED.

3

- Click DNT to change the value.

- In a similar fashion, change MED on the ninth record to LAB (Figure 3–46).

erls	CO	80349	MED			$29,200.00	$0.00	2
erridge	CO	80330	DNT ↖			$21,000.00	$12,500.00	2
arleton	CO	80409	MED			$0.00	$0.00	2
Mason	CO	80356	MED			$0.00	$43,025.00	2
ort Stewart	CO	80336	MED	values changed		$31,750.00	$0.00	2
Berls	CO	80349	MED			$0.00	$0.00	2
Tarleton	CO	80409	MED			$18,750.00	$31,500.00	2
erls	CO	80349	LAB ▼			$14,000.00	$0.00	2
			MED					

Figure 3–46

To Use a Multivalued Lookup Field

Using a multivalued Lookup field is similar to using a regular Lookup field. The difference is that when you drop down the list, the entries all will be preceded by check boxes. You then can check all the entries that you want. The appropriate entries are shown in Figure 3–47. As indicated in the figure, the specialties needed for client AC34 are CNA, PA, Phy, and RN.

Client Number	Client Name	Specialties Needed
AC34	Alys Clinic	CNA, PA, Phy, RN
BH72	Berls Hospital	CLS, OT, PA, Phy, PT, RN
FD89	Ferb Dentistry	DH, Dnt
FH22	Family Health	NP, Phy, RN
MH56	Munn Hospital	CRNA, OT, Phy, PT, RN
PR11	Peel Radiology	RT
RM32	Roz Medical	CNA, NP, PA, Phy, RN
TC37	Tarleton Clinic	NP, PA, Phy, RN
WL56	West Labs	CLS

Figure 3–47

The following steps make the appropriate entries for the Specialties Needed field.

1

- Click the Specialties Needed field on the first record to display the arrow.

- Click the arrow to display the list of available specialties (Figure 3–48).

Q&A

All the specialties currently appear in the box. What if there were too many specialties to fit?

Access would automatically include a scroll bar that you could use to scroll through all the choices.

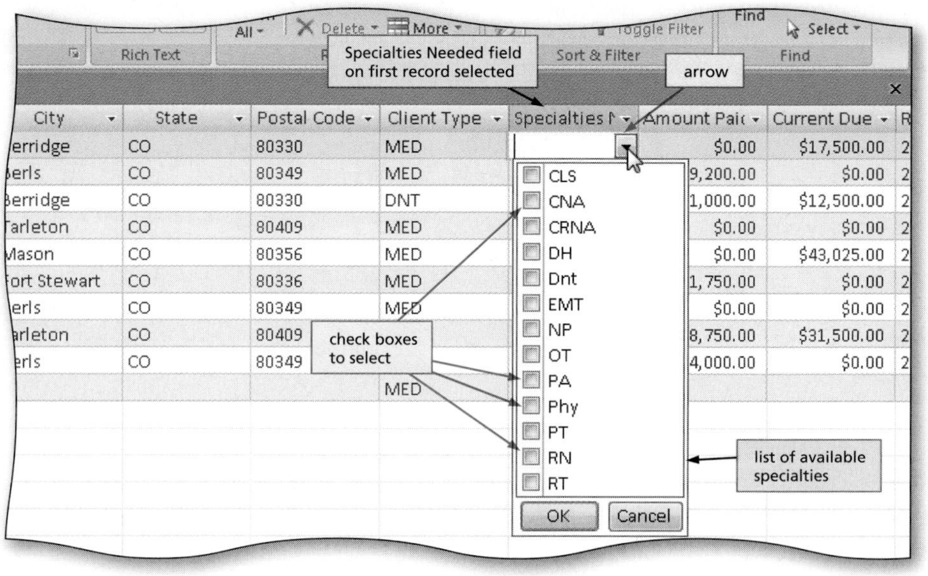

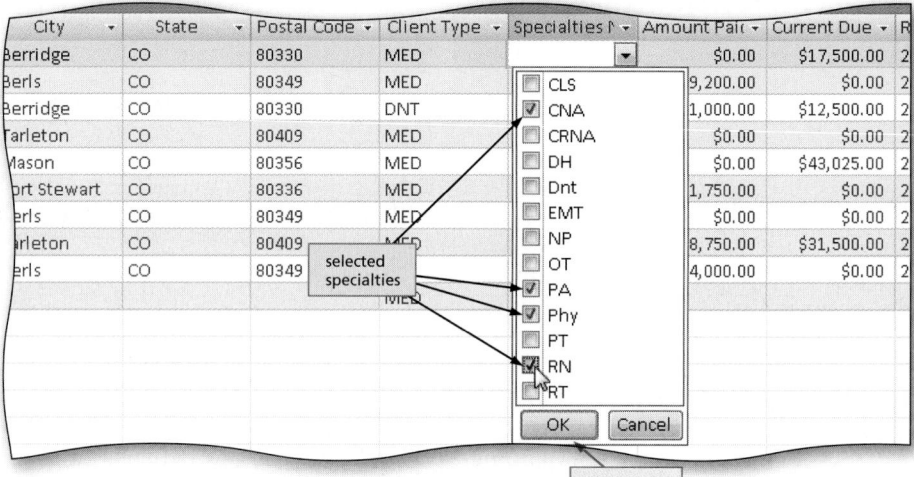

Figure 3–48

2

- Click the CNA, PA, Phy, and RN check boxes to select the specialties for the first client (Figure 3–49).

Figure 3–49

3

- Click the OK button to complete the selection.

- Using the same technique, enter the specialties given in Figure 3–47 on the previous page for the remaining clients (Figure 3–50).

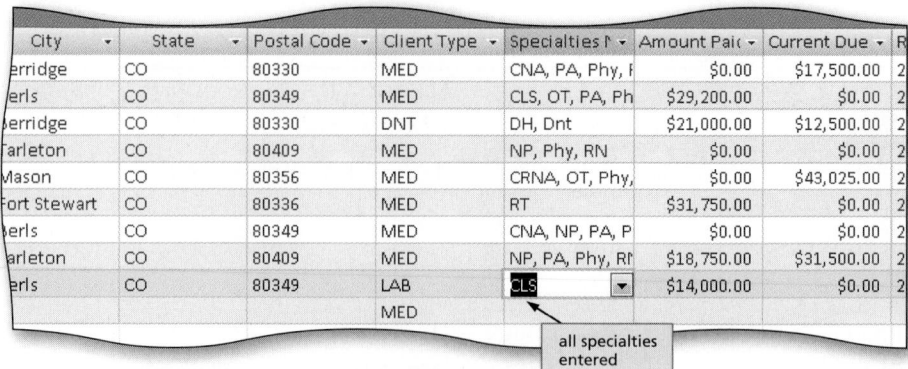

Figure 3–50

To Resize a Column in a Datasheet

The Access default column sizes do not always allow all the data in the field to appear. In some cases, the data may appear, but not the entire field name. You can correct this problem by **resizing** the column (changing its size) in the datasheet. In some instances, you may want to reduce the size of a column. The State field, for example, is short enough that it does not require all the space on the screen that is allotted to it. Changing a column width changes the **layout**, or design, of a table.

The following steps resize the columns in the Client table and save the changes to the layout.

1

• Point to the right boundary of the field selector for the Specialties Needed field (Figure 3–51) so that the mouse pointer becomes a doubled-ended arrow.

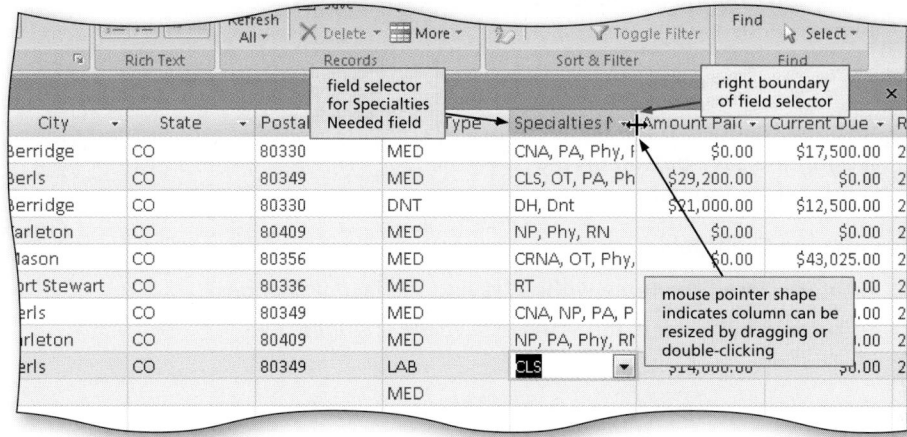

Figure 3–51

2

• Double-click the right boundary of the field selector for the Specialties Needed field to resize the field so that it best fits the data (Figure 3–52).

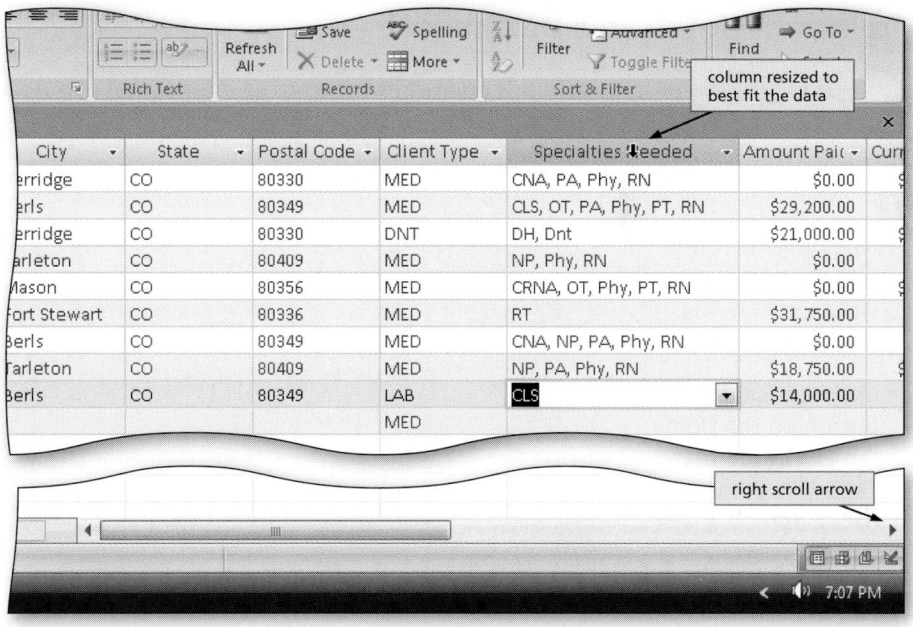

Figure 3–52

3

- Use the same technique to resize all the other fields to best fit the data. To resize the Amount Paid, Current Due, and Recruiter Number fields, you will need to scroll the fields by clicking the right scroll arrow shown in Figure 3–52 on the previous page (Figure 3-53).

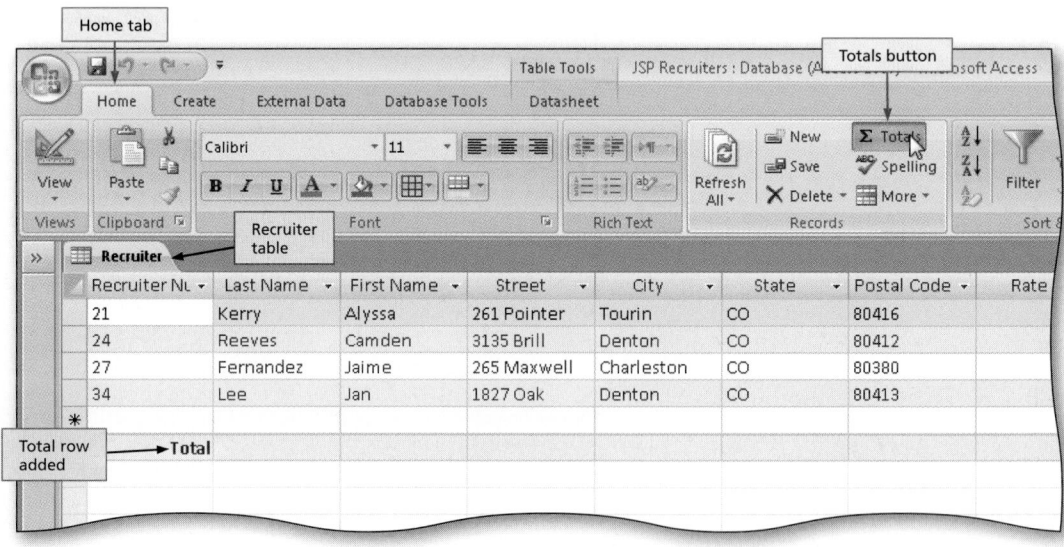

Figure 3–53

4

- Save the changes to the layout by clicking the Save button on the Quick Access Toolbar.

- Close the Client table.

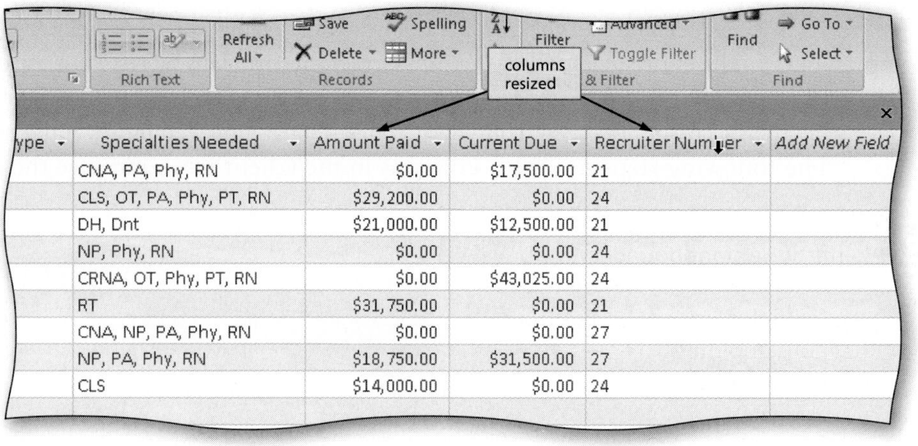

Q&A

What if I closed the table without saving the layout changes?

You would be asked if you want to save the changes.

Other Ways

1. Right-click field name, click Column Width

To Include Totals in a Datasheet

It is possible to include totals and other statistics at the bottom of a datasheet in a special row called the Total row. The following steps display the total of the commissions and the average of the rates for recruiters in the Total row.

1

- Open the Recruiter table in Datasheet view and hide the Navigation Pane.

- Click the Totals button on the Home tab to include the Total row in the datasheet (Figure 3–54).

Figure 3–54

- Click the Total row in the Commission column to display an arrow.

- Click the arrow to display a menu of available computations (Figure 3–55).

Q&A

Will I always get the same list?

No. You only will get the items that make sense for the type of data in the column. You cannot calculate the sum of text data, for example.

- Click Sum to calculate the sum of the commissions.

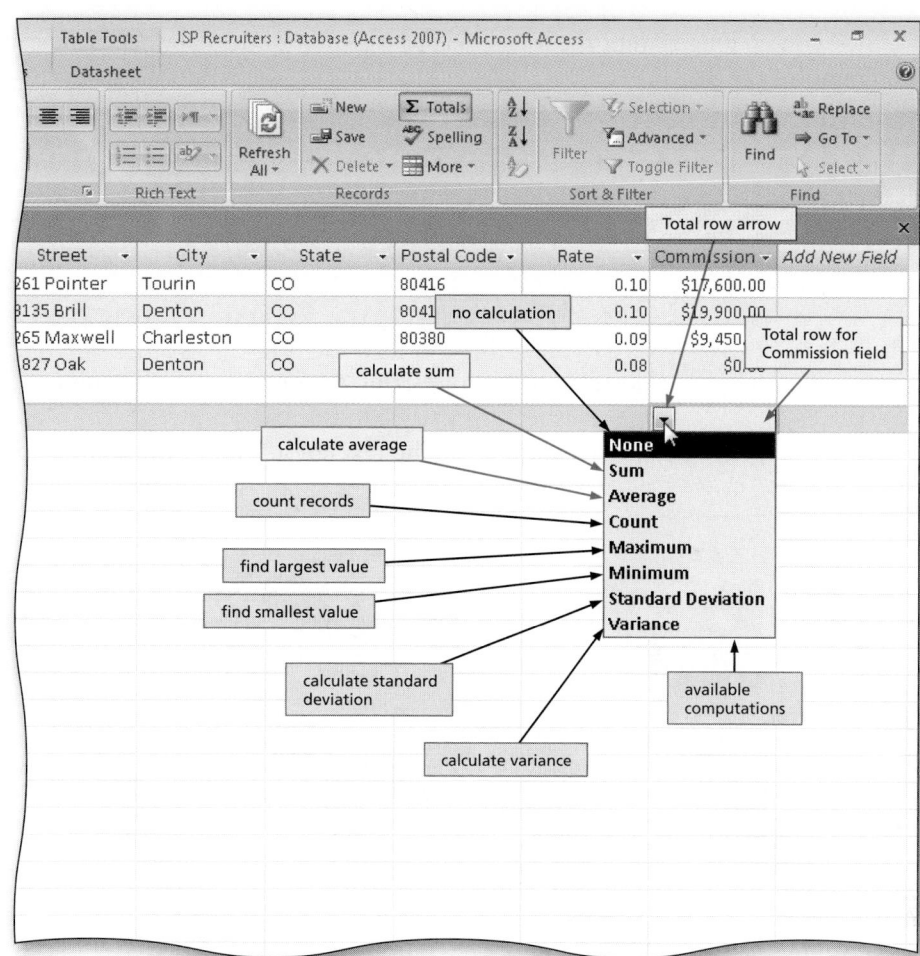

Figure 3–55

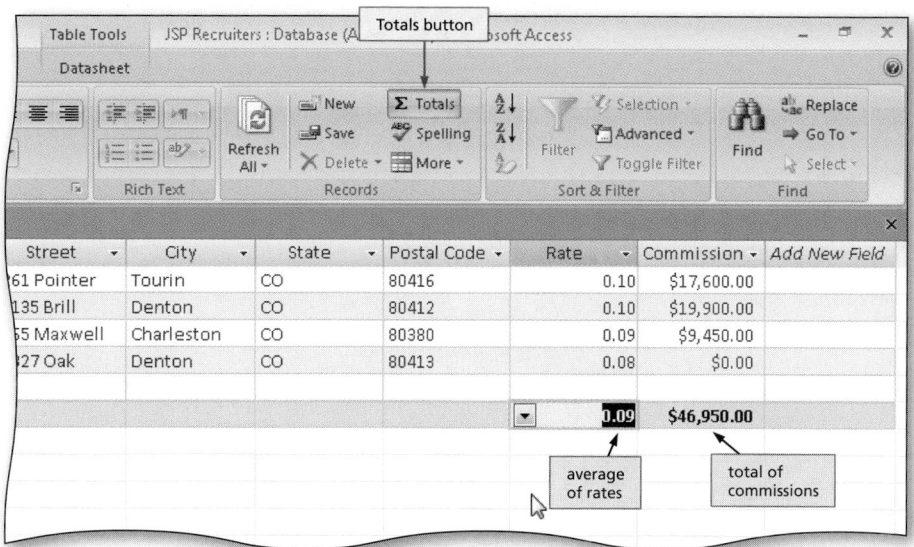

- Click the Total row in the Rate column to display an arrow.

- Click the arrow to display a menu of available computations.

- Click Average to calculate the average of the rates (Figure 3–56).

Experiment

- Experiment with other statistics. When finished, once again select the sum of the commissions and the average of the rates.

Figure 3–56

To Remove Totals from a Datasheet

If you no longer want the totals to appear as part of the datasheet, you can remove the Total row. The following step removes the Total row.

- Click the Totals button on the Home tab to remove the Total row from the datasheet.

Changing the Appearance of a Datasheet

In addition to resizing columns and displaying totals, you can change the appearance of a datasheet in a variety of other ways. For example, you can change the appearance of gridlines or change the text colors and font. Figure 3–57 shows the various buttons, found on the Home tab, that are available to change the Datasheet appearance.

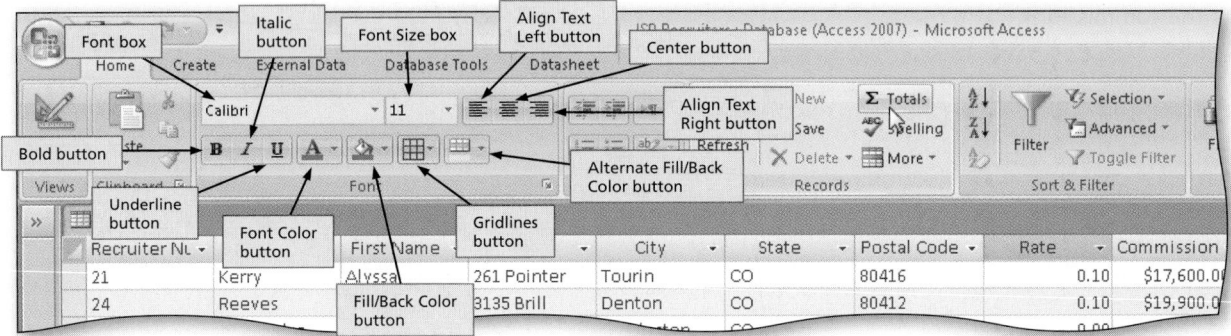

Figure 3–57

The changes to the datasheet will be reflected not only on the screen, but also when you print or preview the datasheet.

Plan Ahead

> **Determine whether changes to the format of a datasheet are desirable.**
> You need to decide if changes to the format of a datasheet would improve its appearance and/or its usefulness. The following are the decisions you would make.
>
> 1. Would totals or other calculations be useful in the datasheet? If so, include the Total row and select the appropriate computations.
>
> 2. Would different gridlines make the datasheet more useful? If so, change to the desired gridlines.
>
> 3. Would alternating colors in the rows make them easier to read? If so, change the alternate fill color.
>
> 4. Would a different font and/or font color make the text stand out better? If so, change the font color and/or the font.
>
> 5. Is the font size appropriate? Can you see enough data at one time on the screen and yet have the data be readable? If not, change the font size to an appropriate value.
>
> 6. Is the column spacing appropriate? Are some columns wider than they need to be? Are there some columns where not all the data is visible? If so, change the column size.
>
> As a general guideline, once you have decided on a particular look for a datasheet, all your datasheets should have the same look, unless there is a compelling reason for one of your datasheets to differ.

To Change Gridlines in a Datasheet

One of the changes you can make to a datasheet is which gridlines appear. You may feel that the appearance would be improved by having only horizontal gridlines. The following steps change the datasheet so that only horizontal gridlines are included.

- Open the Recruiter table in Datasheet view, if it is not already open.
- Click the box in the upper-left corner of the Datasheet selector to select the entire datasheet (Figure 3–58).

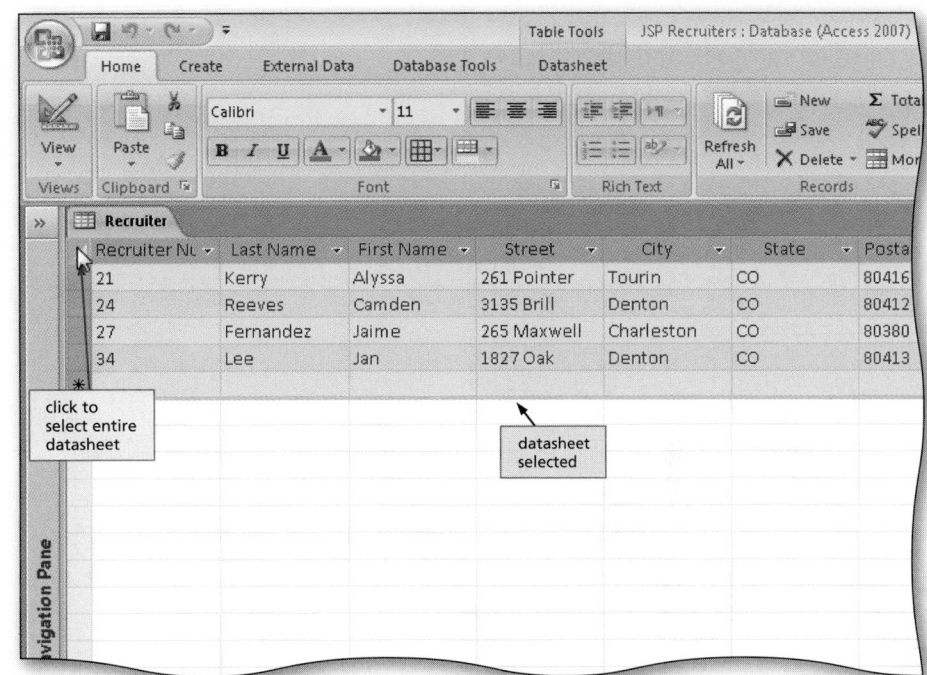

Figure 3–58

- Click the Gridlines button on the Home tab to display the Gridlines gallery (Figure 3–59).

Q&A

Does it matter whether I click the button or the arrow?

In this case, it does not matter. Either one will produce the same result.

- Click the Gridlines: Horizontal command in the Gridlines gallery to include only horizontal gridlines.

 **Experiment**

- Experiment with other gridline options. When finished, once again select horizontal gridlines.

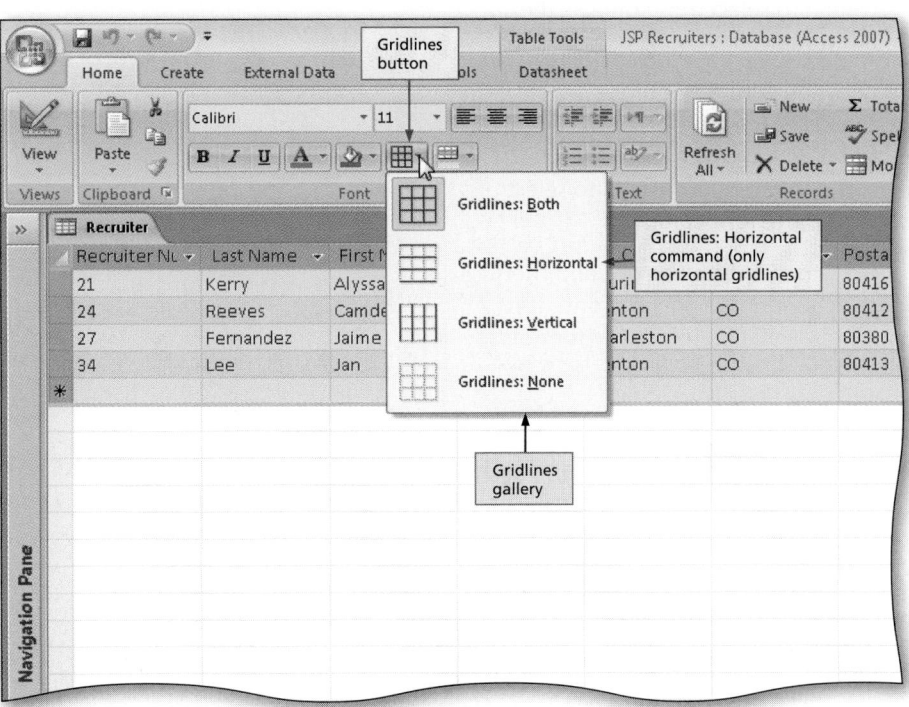

Figure 3–59

To Change the Colors and Font in a Datasheet

You also may decide that you can improve the datasheet by changing the colors and the font. The following steps change the Alternate Fill color, a color that appears on every other row in the datasheet. They also change the font color, the font, and the font size.

- With the datasheet for the Recruiter table selected, click the Alternate Fill/Back Color button arrow to display the color palette (Figure 3–60).

Q&A Does it matter whether I click the button or the arrow?

Yes. Clicking the arrow produces a color palette. Clicking the button applies the currently selected color. When in doubt, you should click the arrow.

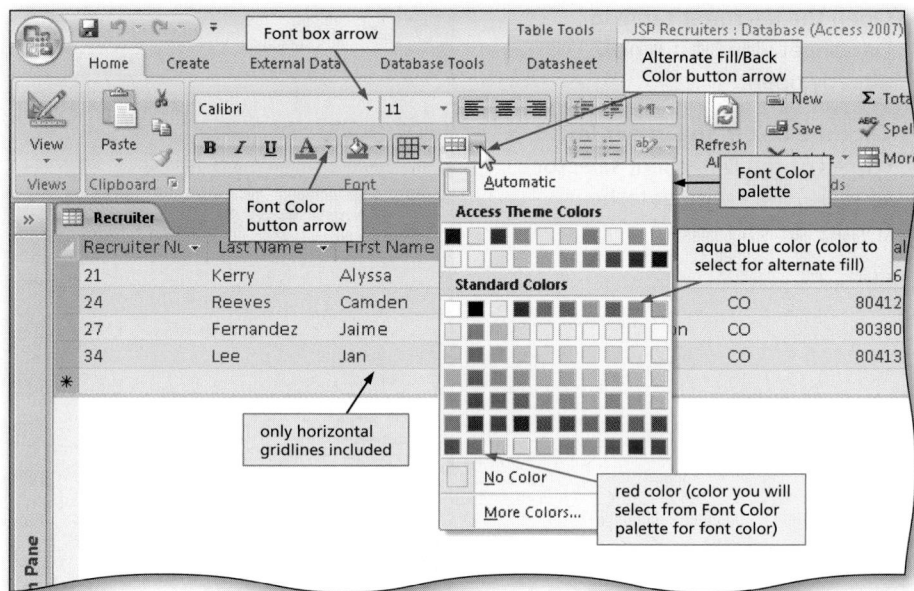

Figure 3–60

- Click Aqua Blue (the second from the right color in the standard colors) to select aqua blue as the alternate color.

- Click the Font Color arrow, and then click Red (the second color in the bottom row) in the lower-left corner of standard colors to select Red as the font color.

- Click the Font box arrow, and then select Bodoni MT as the font. (If it is not available, select any font of your choice.)

- Click the Font Size box arrow, and select 10 as the font size (Figure 3–61).

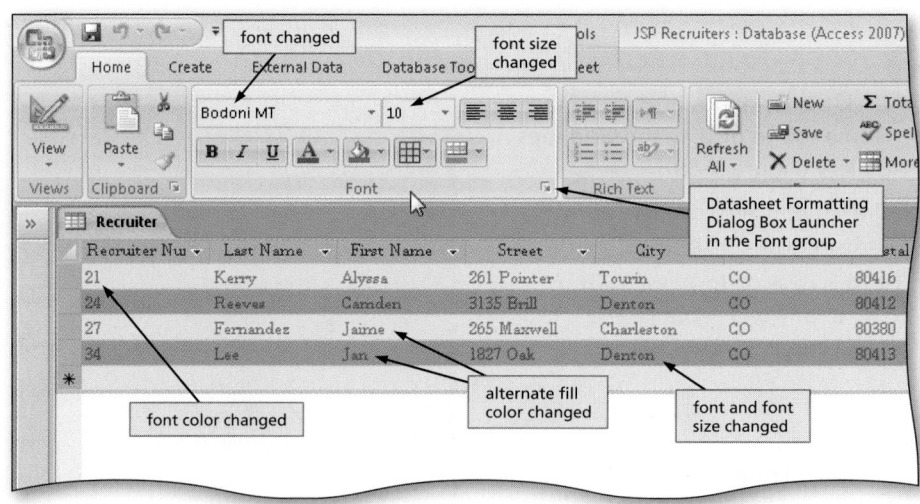

Figure 3–61

Q&A Does the order in which I make these selections make a difference?

No. You could have made these selections in any order.

Experiment

- Experiment with other colors, fonts, and font sizes. When finished, return to the options selected in this step.

Using the Datasheet Formatting Dialog Box

As an alternative to using the individual buttons, you can click the Datasheet Formatting Dialog Box Launcher, shown in Figure 3–61, to display the Datasheet Formatting dialog box (Figure 3–62). You can use the various options in the dialog box to make changes to the datasheet format. Once you are finished, click the OK button to apply your changes.

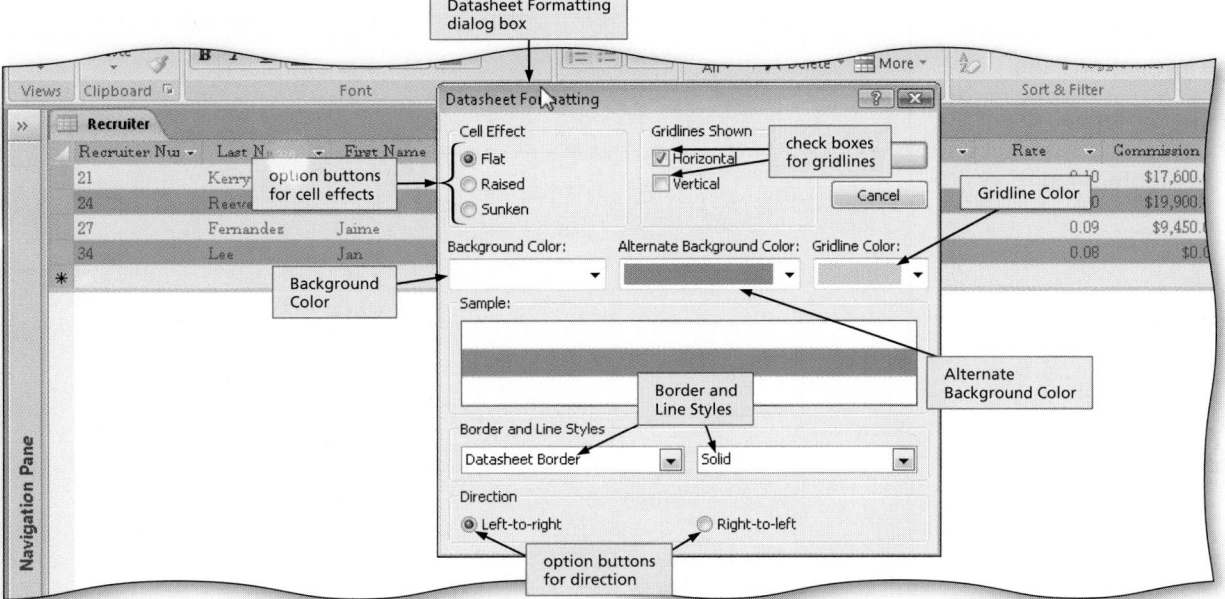

Figure 3–62

To Close the Datasheet Without Saving the Format Changes

The following steps show how to close the datasheet without saving the changes to the format. Because the changes are not saved, the next time you open the Recruiter table it will appear in the original format. If you had saved the changes, the changes would be reflected in its appearance.

1 Click the Close 'Recruiter' button to close the Recruiter table.

2 Click the No button in the Microsoft Office Access dialog box when asked if you want to save your changes.

Multivalued Field in Queries

You can use multivalued fields in queries just as you can use other fields. You have a choice concerning how the multiple values appear. You can choose to have them on a single row or on multiple rows.

To Query a Multivalued Field Showing Multiple Values on a Single Row

To include a multivalued field in the results of a query, place the field in the design grid just like any other field. The results will list all of the values for the multivalued field on a single row, just as in a datasheet. The following steps create a query to display the client number, client name, client type, and specialties needed for all clients.

- Create a query for the Client table and hide the Navigation Pane.

- Include the Client Number, Client Name, Client Type, and Specialties Needed fields (Figure 3–63).

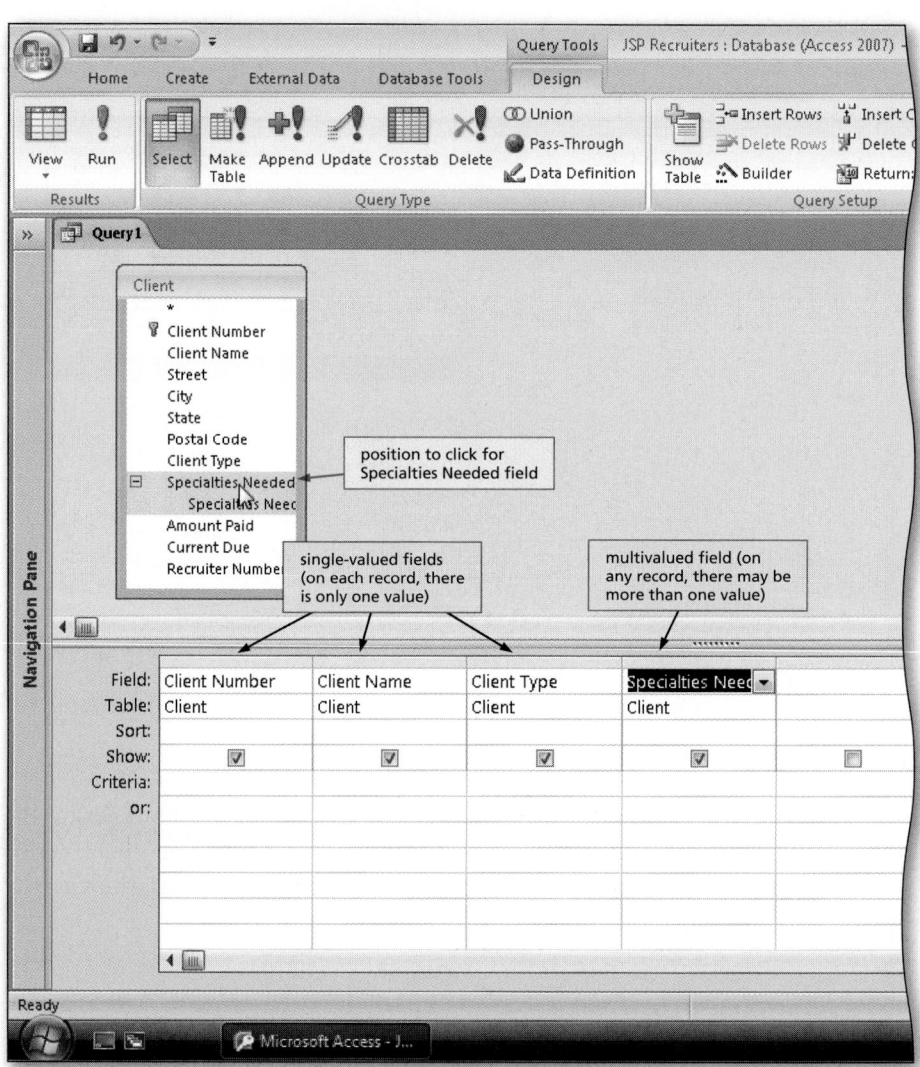

Figure 3–63

2

- View the results (Figure 3–64).

Q&A

Can I include criteria for the multi-valued field?

You can include criteria for the multivalued field when all the entries are displayed on a single row.

Experiment

- Return to Design view and enter various criteria in the Specialties Needed field. Run the queries. When finished, return to the options selected in this step.

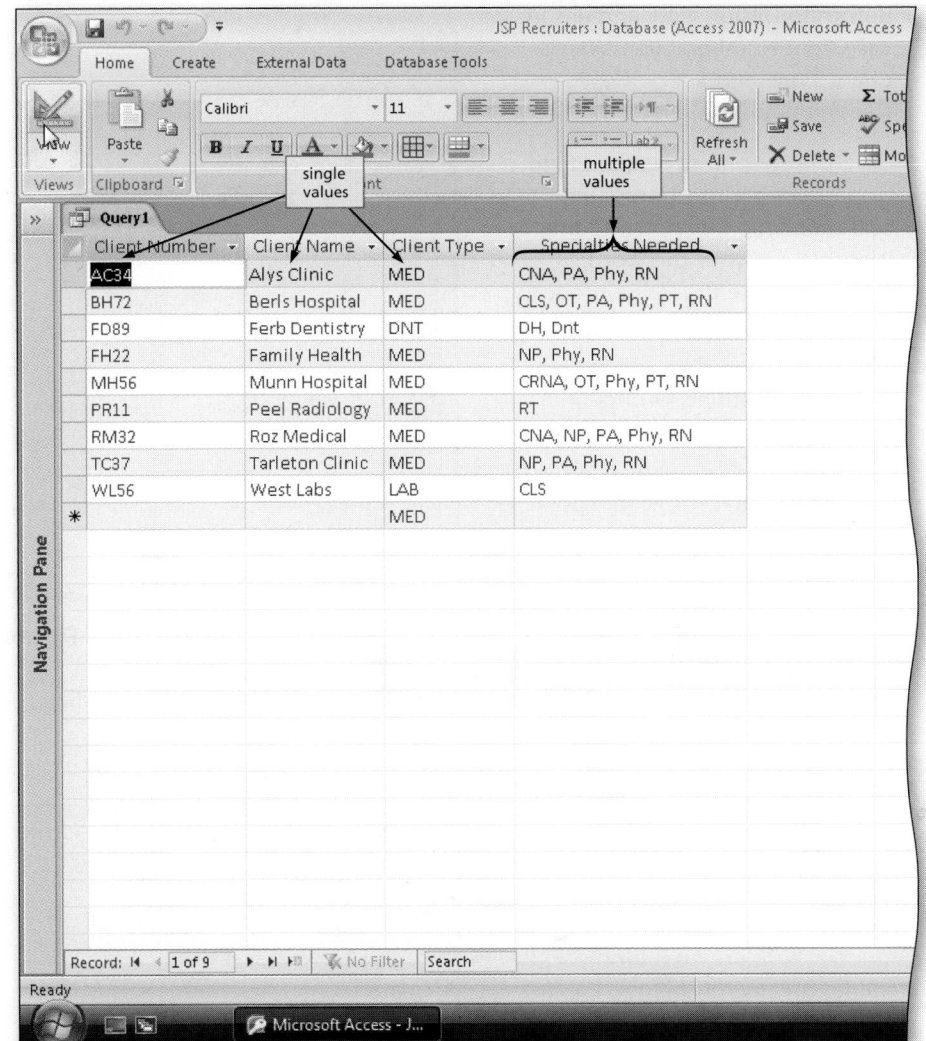

Figure 3–64

To Query a Multivalued Field Showing Multiple Values on Multiple Rows

You may be interested in those clients requiring a particular specialty, for example, those clients needing an RN. Unfortunately, you cannot simply put the desired specialty in the Criteria row just as you would with other fields. Instead you need to change the query so that each specialty occurs on a different row by using the Value property. Once you have done so, you can enter criteria just as you would in any other query.

The following steps use the Value property to display each specialty on a separate row.

1

- Return to Design view and ensure the Client Number, Client Name, Client Type, and Specialties Needed fields are selected.

- Click the Specialties Needed field to produce an insertion point, and then type a period and the word `Value` after the word, Needed, to use the Value property (Figure 3–65).

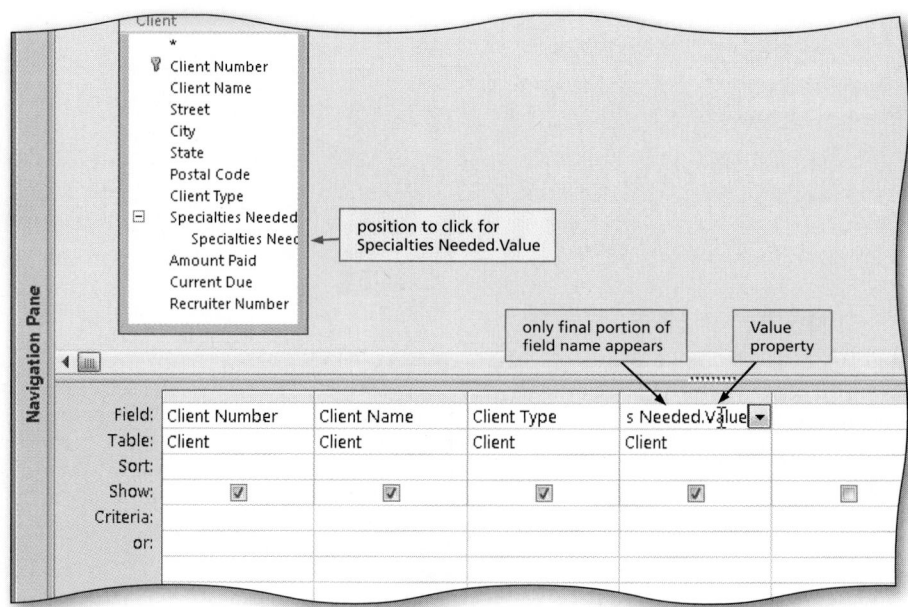

Figure 3–65

Q&A I don't see the word, Specialties. Did I do something wrong?

No. There is not enough room to display the entire name. If you wanted to see it, you could point to the right boundary of the column selector and then either drag or double-click.

Q&A Do I need to type the word Value?

No. You also can double-click the second Specialties Needed entry in the field list.

2

- View the results (Figure 3–66).

Q&A Can I now include criteria for the multivalued field?

Yes. This is now just like any other query. There are no multiple values on any row.

3

- Close the query by clicking the Close 'Query1' button.

- When asked if you want to save the query, click the No button.

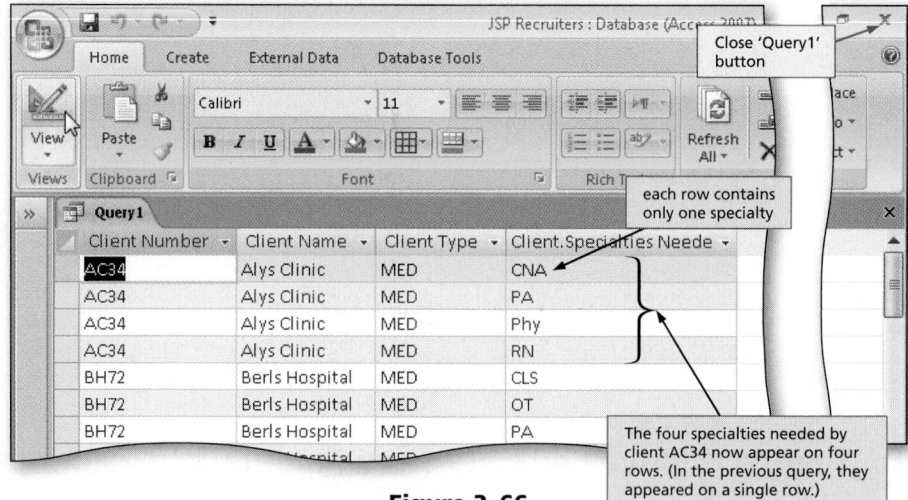

Figure 3–66

Referential Integrity

The property that ensures that the value in a foreign key must match that of another table's primary key is called **referential integrity**. A **foreign key** is a field in one table whose values are required to match the *primary key* of another table. In the Client table, the Recruiter Number field is a foreign key that must match the primary key of the Recruiter table; that is, the Recruiter number for any client must be a recruiter currently in the Recruiter table. A client whose Recruiter number is 92, for example, should not be stored because no such recruiter exists.

In Access, to specify referential integrity, you must define a relationship between the tables by using the Relationships command. Access then prohibits any updates to the database that would violate the referential integrity.

The type of relationship between two tables specified by the Relationships command is referred to as a **one-to-many relationship**. This means that *one* record in the first table is related to (matches) *many* records in the second table, but each record in the second table is related to only *one* record in the first. In the JSP Recruiters database, for example, a one-to-many relationship exists between the Recruiter table and the Client table. *One* recruiter is associated with *many* clients, but each client is associated with only a single recruiter. In general, the table containing the foreign key will be the *many* part of the relationship.

BTW

Relationships
You also can use the Relationships command to specify a one-to-one relationship. In a one-to-one relationship, one record in the first record is related to (matches) one record in the second table. In a one-to-one relationship, the matching fields are both primary keys. For example, if JSP Recruiters maintained a company car for each recruiter, the data concerning the cars might be kept in a Car table, in which the primary key is Recruiter Number—the same primary key as the Recruiter table. Thus, there would be a one-to-one relationship between recruiters and cars. Each recruiter is assigned one car and each car is assigned to one recruiter.

Plan Ahead

Identify related tables in order to implement relationships between the tables.
When specifying referential integrity, you need to decide how to handle deletions. In the relationship between clients and recruiters, for example, deletion of a recruiter for whom clients exist, such as recruiter number 21, would violate referential integrity. Any clients for recruiter 21 no longer would relate to any recruiter in the database. You can handle this in two ways. For each relationship, you need to decide which of the approaches is appropriate.

1. The normal way to avoid this problem is to prohibit such a deletion.

2. The other option is to **cascade the delete.** This means that Access would allow the deletion but then delete all related records. For example, it would allow the deletion of the recruiter but then automatically delete any clients related to the deleted recruiter.

You also need to decide how to handle the update of the primary key. In the relationship between recruiters and clients, for example, changing the recruiter number for recruiter 21 to 12 in the Recruiter table would cause a problem. Clients are in the Client table on which the recruiter number is 21. These clients no longer would relate to any recruiter. You can handle this in two ways. For each relationship, you need to decide which of the approaches is appropriate.

1. The normal way of avoiding the problem is to prohibit this type of update.

2. The other option is to **cascade the update.** This means to allow the change, but make the corresponding change in the foreign key on all related records. In the relationship between clients and recruiters, for example, Access would allow the update but then automatically make the corresponding change for any client whose recruiter number was 21. It now will be 12.

To Specify Referential Integrity

The following steps use the Relationships command to specify referential integrity by specifying a relationship between the Recruiter and Client tables. The steps also ensure that update will cascade, but that delete will not.

1

● Click Database Tools on the Ribbon to display the Database Tools tab (Figure 3–67).

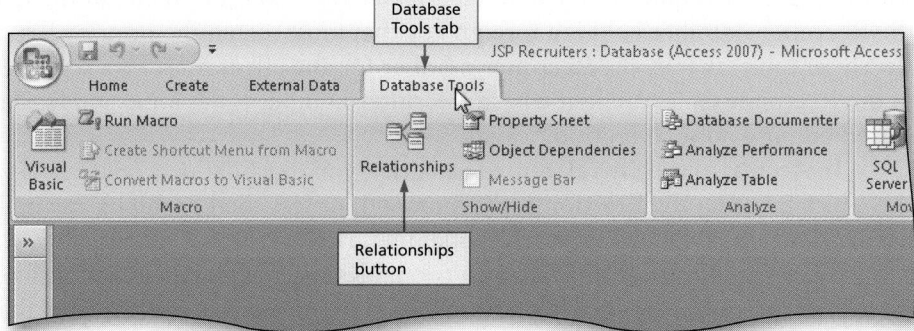

Figure 3–67

2

● Click the Relationships button on the Database Tools tab to open the Relationships window and display the Show Table dialog box (Figure 3–68).

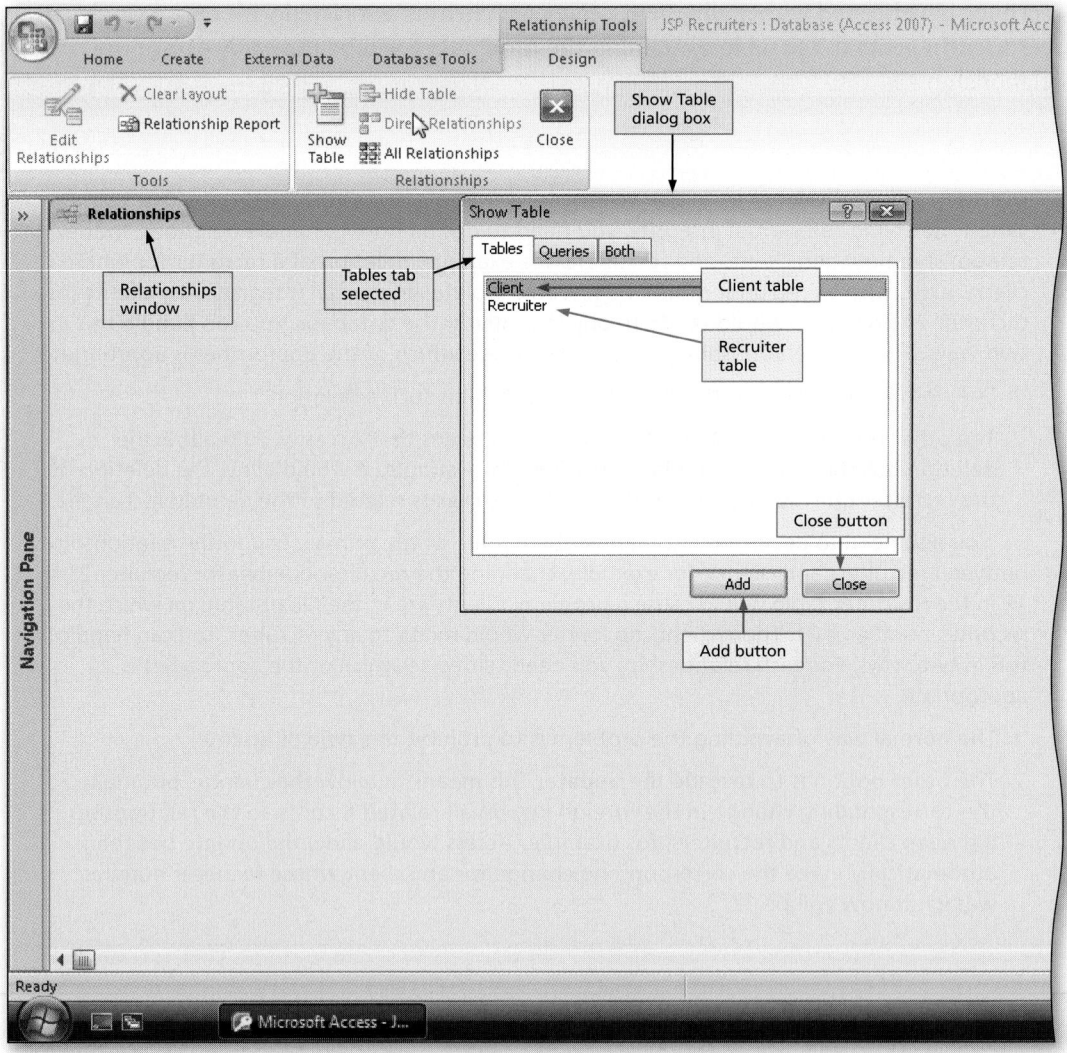

Figure 3–68

- Click the Recruiter table and then click the Add button to add the Recruiter table.

- Click the Client table and then click the Add button to add the Client table.

- Click the Close button in the Show Table dialog box to close the dialog box.

- Resize the field lists that appear so all fields are visible (Figure 3–69).

Q&A Do I need to resize the field lists?

No. You can use the scroll bars. Before completing the next step, however, you would need to make sure the Recruiter Number fields in both tables appear on the screen.

- Drag the Recruiter Number field in the Recruiter table field list to the Recruiter Number field in the Client table field list to open the Edit Relationships dialog box to create a relationship.

Q&A Do I actually move the field from the Recruiter table to the Client table?

No. The mouse pointer will change shape to indicate you are in the process of dragging, but the field does not move.

- Click the Enforce Referential Integrity check box.

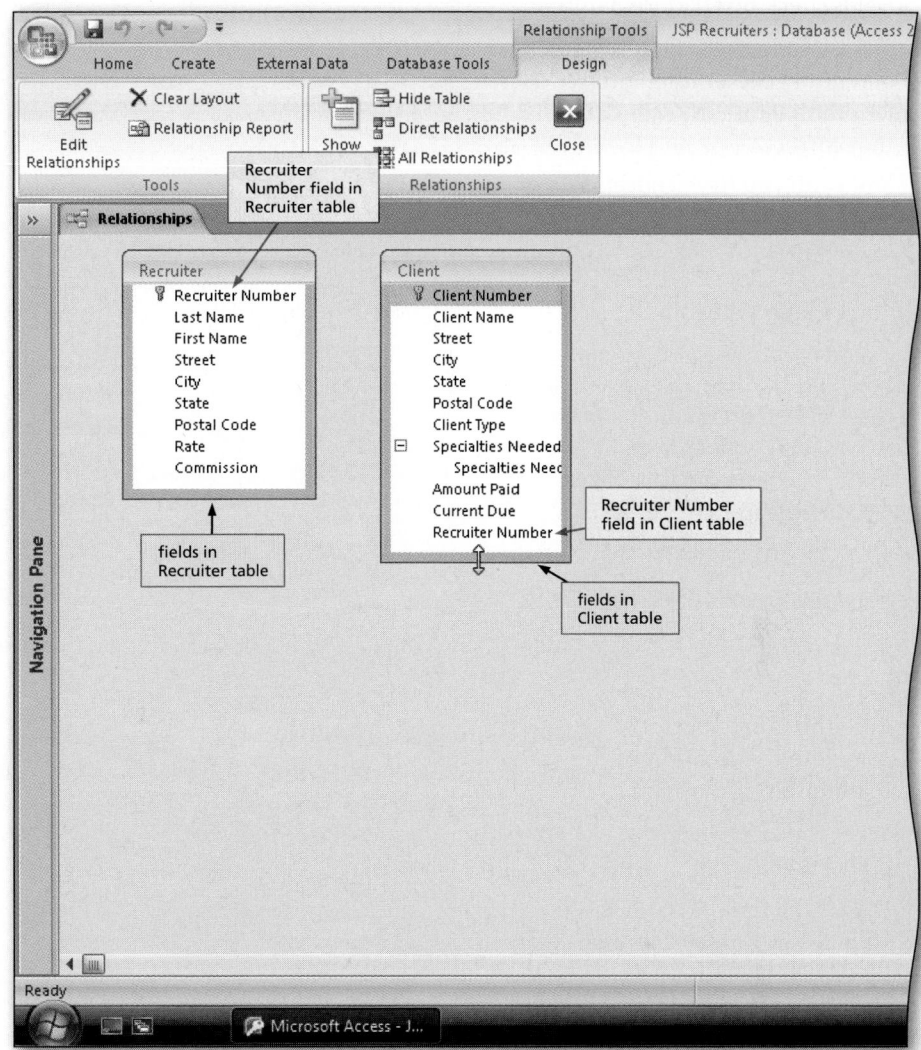

Figure 3–69

● Click the Cascade Update Related Fields check box (Figure 3–70).

 Q&A The Cascade check boxes were dim until I clicked the Enforce Referential Integrity check box. Is that correct?

Yes. Until you have chosen to enforce referential integrity, the cascade options have no meaning.

Q&A Can I change the join type like I can in queries?

Yes. Click the Join Type button in the Edit Relationships dialog box. Just as with queries, option button 1 creates an INNER join, option button 2 creates a LEFT join, and option button 3 creates a RIGHT join.

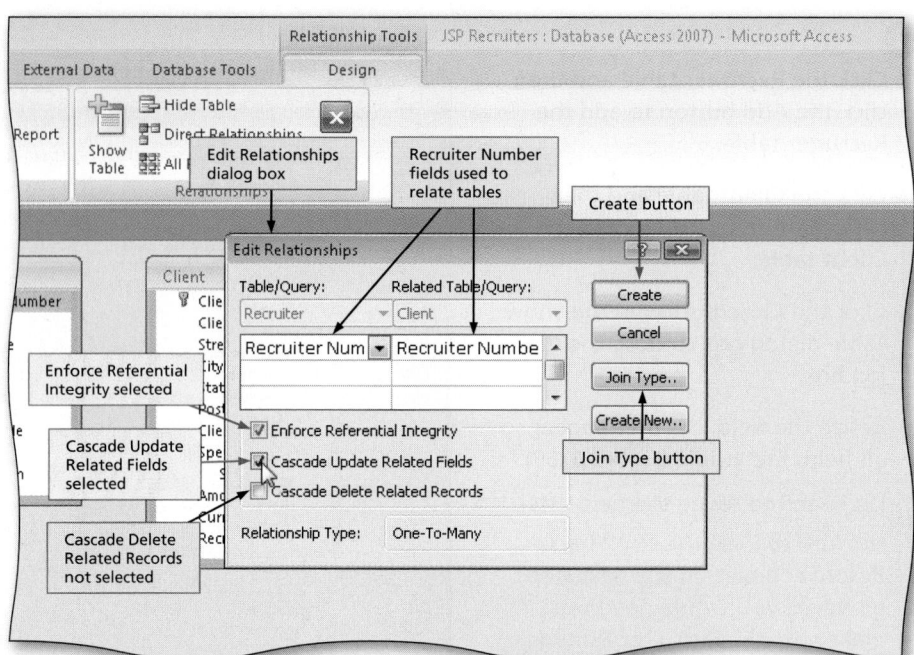

Figure 3–70

❺

● Click the Create button to complete the creation of the relationship (Figure 3–71).

Q&A What is the symbol at the lower end of the join line?

It is the mathematical symbol for infinity. It is used here to denote the "many" end of the relationship.

Q&A Can I print a copy of the relationship?

Yes. Click the Relationship Report button on the Design tab to produce a report of the relationship. You can print the report. You also can save it as a report in the database for future use. If you do not want to save it, close the report after you have printed it and do not save the changes.

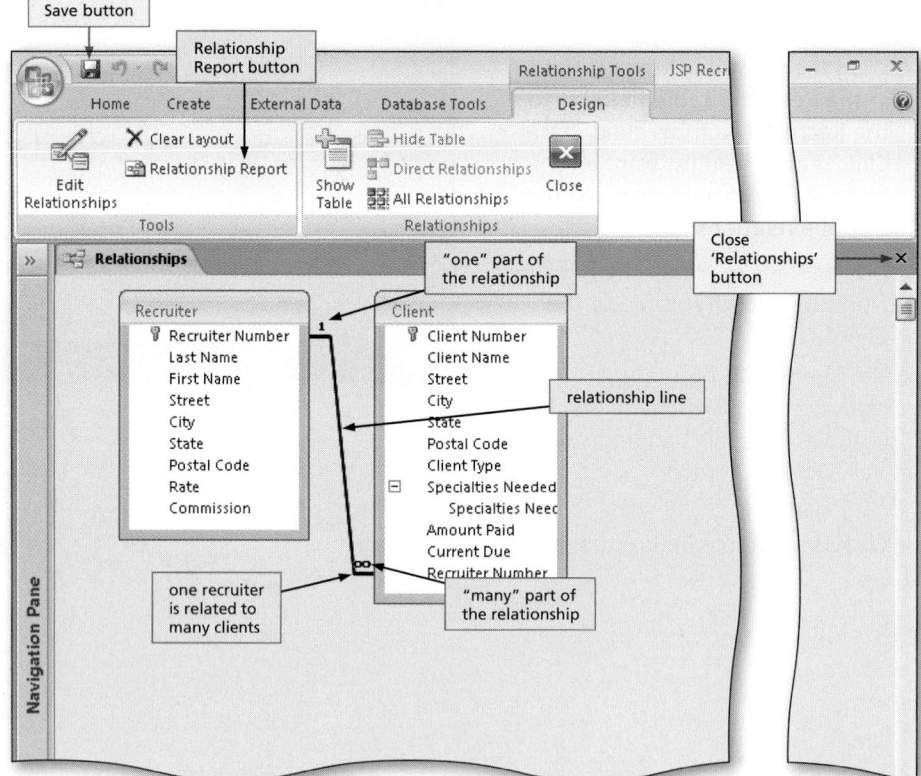

Figure 3–71

6

- Click the Save button on the Quick Access Toolbar to save the relationship you created.

- Close the Relationships window by clicking the Close 'Relationships' button.

Q&A

Can I later modify the relationship if I want to change it in some way?

Yes. Click the Relationships button on the Database Tools tab. To add another table, click the Show Table button on the Design tab. To remove a table, click the Hide table button. To edit a relationship, select the relationship and click the Edit Relationships button.

Effect of Referential Integrity

Referential integrity now exists between the Recruiter and Client tables. Access now will reject any number in the Recruiter Number field in the Client table that does not match a Recruiter number in the Recruiter table. Attempting to change the recruiter number for a client to one that does not match any recruiter in the Recruiter table would result in the error message shown in Figure 3–72. Similarly, attempting to add a client whose recruiter number does not match would lead to the same error message.

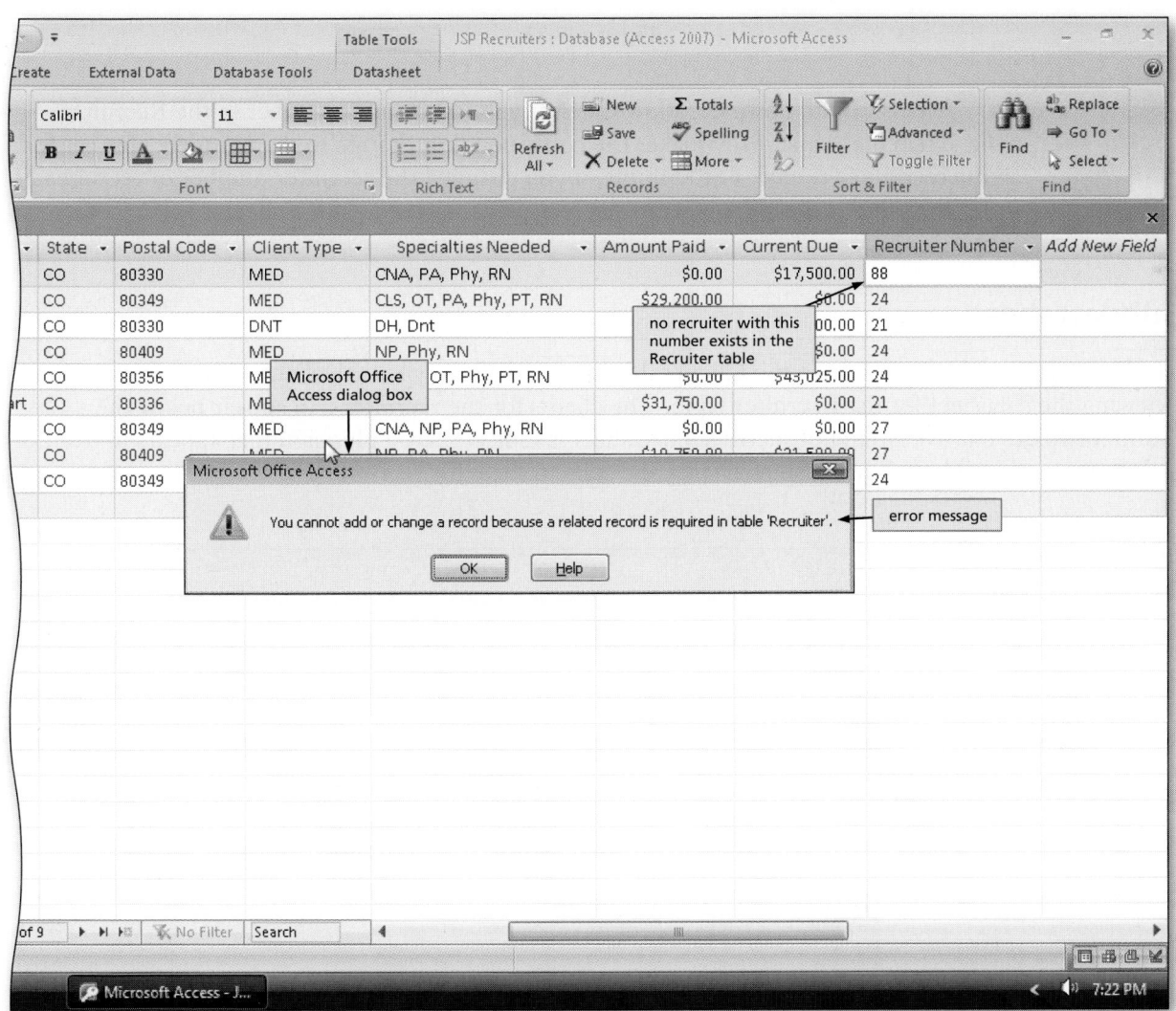

Figure 3–72

Access also will reject the deletion of a recruiter for whom related clients exist. Attempting to delete recruiter 21 from the Recruiter table, for example, would result in the message shown in Figure 3–73.

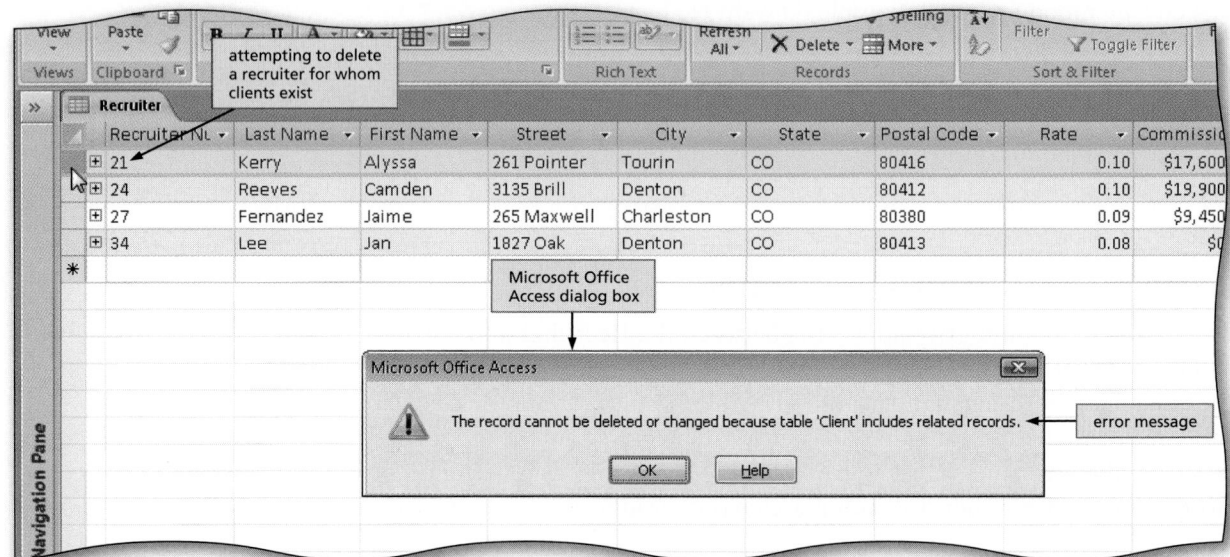

Figure 3–73

Access would, however, allow the change of a recruiter number in the Recruiter table. Then it automatically makes the corresponding change to the recruiter number for all the recruiter's clients. For example, if you changed the recruiter number of recruiter 21 to 12, the same 12 would appear in the recruiter number field for clients.

To Use a Subdatasheet

Now that the Recruiter table is related to the Client table, it is possible to view the clients of a given recruiter when you are viewing the datasheet for the Recruiter table. The clients for the recruiter will appear below the recruiter in a **subdatasheet**. The availability of such a subdatasheet is indicated by a plus sign that appears in front of the rows in the Recruiter table. The following steps display the subdatasheet for recruiter 24.

- Open the Recruiter table and hide the Navigation Pane (Figure 3–74).

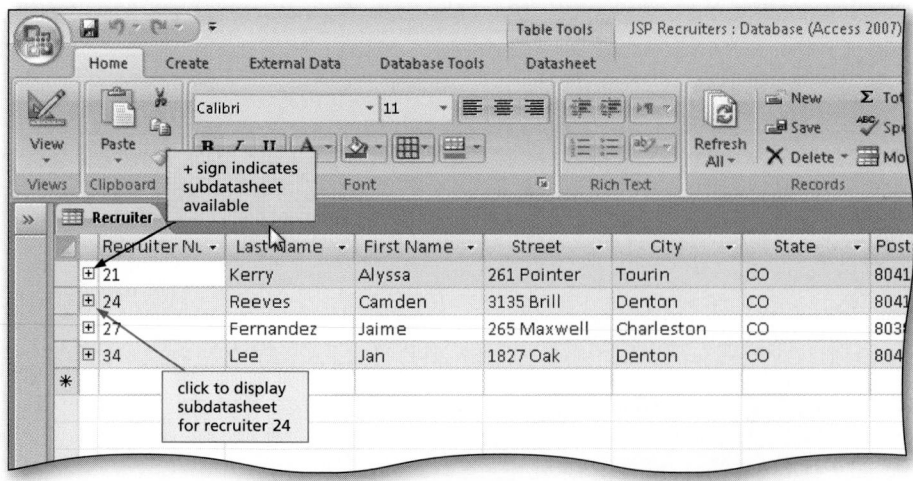

Figure 3–74

2

- Click the plus sign in front of the row for Recruiter 24 to display the subdatasheet (Figure 3–75).

How do I hide the subdatasheet when I no longer want it to appear?

When you clicked the plus sign, it changed to a minus sign. Click the minus sign.

Experiment

- Display subdatasheets for other recruiters. Display more than one subdatasheet at a time. Remove the subdatasheets from the screen.

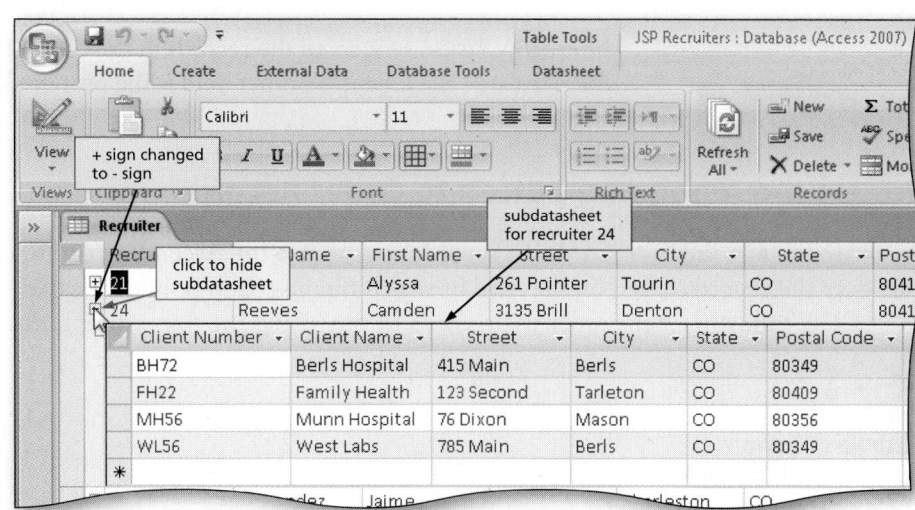

Figure 3–75

3

- Close the datasheet for the Recruiter table.

To Find Duplicate Records

One reason to include a primary key for a table is to eliminate duplicate records. A possibility still exists, however, that duplicate records can get into your database. Perhaps the same client was inadvertently added to the database with a new client number. You can detect this type of redundancy by searching to see if any client's names are duplicated. The **Find Duplicates Query Wizard** allows you to find duplicate records. The following steps illustrate how to use the Find Duplicates Query Wizard to find duplicate records.

1. Click Create on the Ribbon, and then click the Query Wizard button on the Create tab.
2. When Access displays the New Query dialog box, click the Find Duplicates Query Wizard and then click the OK button.
3. Identify the table and field or fields that might contain duplicate information.
4. Indicate any other fields you want displayed.
5. Finish the wizard to see any duplicate records.

To Find Unmatched Records

Occasionally, you may want to find records in one table that have no matching records in another table. For example, you may want to determine which recruiters currently have no clients. The **Find Unmatched Query Wizard** allows you to find unmatched records. The following steps illustrate how to find unmatched records using the Find Unmatched Query Wizard.

1. Click Create on the Ribbon, and then click the Query Wizard button on the Create tab.
2. When Access displays the New Query dialog box, click the Find Unmatched Query Wizard and then click the OK button.
3. Identify the table that may contain unmatched records and then identify the related table.
4. Indicate the fields you want displayed.
5. Finish the wizard to see any duplicate records.

Ordering Records

Normally, Access sequences the records in the Client table by client number whenever listing them because the Client Number field is the primary key. You can change this order, if desired.

To Use the Ascending Button to Order Records

To change the order in which records appear, use the Ascending or Descending buttons. Either button reorders the records based on the field in which the insertion point is located.

The following steps order the records by city using the Ascending button.

- Open the Client table in Datasheet view and hide the Navigation Pane.

- Click the City field on the first record to select the field (Figure 3–76).

Q&A

Did I have to click the field on the first record?

No. Any other record would have worked as well.

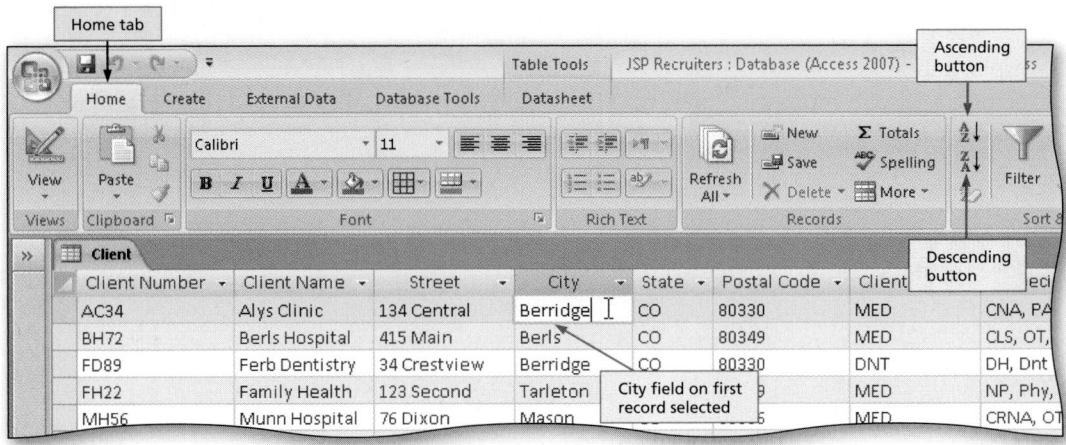

Figure 3–76

- Click the Ascending button on the Home tab to sort the records by City (Figure 3–77).

Q&A

What if I wanted the cities to appear in reverse alphabetical order?

Click the Descending button.

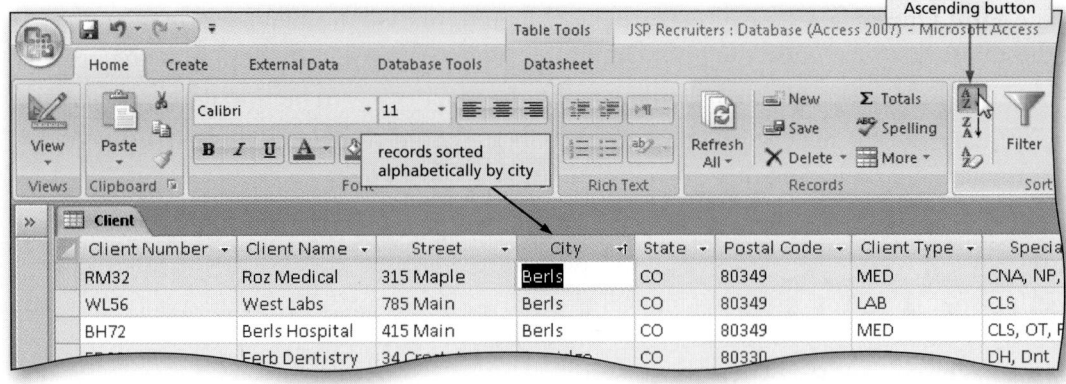

Figure 3–77

Experiment

Sort the records by city in reverse order. When done, sort the records by city in the original order.

- Close the table. When asked if you want to save your changes, click the No button.

Other Ways

1. Right-click field name, click Sort A to Z (for ascending) or Sort Z to A (for descending)

Special Database Operations

The special operations involved in maintaining a database are backup, recovery, compacting a database, and repairing a database.

Backup and Recovery

It is possible to damage or destroy a database. Users can enter data that is incorrect; programs that are updating the database can end abnormally during an update; a hardware problem can occur; and so on. After any such event has occurred, the database may contain invalid data. It even may be totally destroyed.

Obviously, you cannot allow a situation in which data has been damaged or destroyed to go uncorrected. You must somehow return the database to a correct state. This process is called recovery; that is, you **recover** the database.

The simplest approach to recovery involves periodically making a copy of the database (called a **backup copy** or a **save copy**). This is referred to as **backing up** the database. If a problem occurs, you correct the problem by copying this backup copy over the actual database, often referred to as the **live database**.

To backup the database that is currently open, you use the Back Up Database command on the Manage submenu on the Office Button menu. In the process, Access suggests a name that is a combination of the database name and the current date. For example, if you back up the JSP Recruiters database on April 20, 2008, Access will suggest the name JSP Recruiters_2008-04-20. You can change this name if you desire, although it is a good idea to use this name. By doing so, it will be easy to distinguish between all the backup copies you have made to determine which is the most recent. In addition, if you discover that a critical problem occurred on April 18, 2008, you may want to go back to the most recent backup before April 18. If, for example, the database was not backed up on April 17 but was backed up on April 16, you would use JSP Recruiters_2008-04-16.

The following steps back up a database to a file on a hard disk or high-capacity removable disk. You should check with your instructor before completing these steps.

To Back Up a Database

1. Open the database to be backed up.
2. Click the Office Button, and then point to Manage on the Office Button menu.
3. Click Back Up Database on the Manage submenu.
4. Select the desired location in the Save in box. If you do not want the name Access has suggested, enter the desired name in the File name text box.
5. Click the Save button.

Access creates a backup copy with the desired name in the desired location. Should you ever need to recover the database using this backup copy, you can simply copy it over the live version.

Compacting and Repairing a Database

As you add more data to a database, it naturally grows larger. When you delete an object (records, tables, forms, or queries), the space previously occupied by the object does not become available for additional objects. Instead, the additional objects are given new space, that is, space that was not already allocated. To remove this wasted space from the database, you must **compact** the database. The same option that compacts the database also repairs problems that may have occurred in the database.

To Compact and Repair a Database

1. Open the database to be compacted.
2. Click the Office Button, and then point to Manage on the Office Button menu.
3. Click Compact and Repair Database on the Manage submenu.

The database now is the compacted form of the original.

BTW

Certification
The Microsoft Certified Application Specialist (MCAS) program provides an opportunity for you to obtain a valuable industry credential — proof that you have the Access 2007 skills required by employers. For more information, see Appendix G or visit the Access 2007 Certification Web page (scsite.com/ac2007/cert).

BTW

Quick Reference
For a table that lists how to complete the tasks covered in this book using the mouse, Ribbon, shortcut menu, and keyboard, see the Quick Reference Summary at the back of this book, or visit the Access 2007 Quick Reference Web page (scsite.com/ac2007/qr).

BTW

Compacting Error Message on Opening Database
If you open your database and receive a compact error message, you may not be able to view all the objects in your database. You also may not see your tables in tabbed windows. To redisplay all the objects in your database, click the Navigation Pane arrow to display the Navigation Pane menu. Make sure that Tables and Related Views is selected. To make sure that objects appear in tabbed windows, click the Microsoft Office button, click the Access Options button, click Current Database, and make sure the Tabbed Documents option button is selected in the Application Options category.

Additional Operations

Additional special operations include opening another database, closing a database without exiting Access, and saving a database with another name. They also include deleting a table (or other object) as well as renaming an object. Finally, you can change properties of a table or other object, such as the object's description.

When you open another database, Access automatically will close the database that had been open. Before deleting or renaming an object, you should ensure that the object has no dependent objects, that is, other objects that depend on the object you wish to delete.

The following steps describe how you could perform these operations.

TO OPEN ANOTHER DATABASE

1. Click the Office Button.
2. Click Open on the Office Button menu.
3. Select the database to be opened.
4. Click the Open button.

TO CLOSE A DATABASE WITHOUT EXITING ACCESS

1. Click the Office Button.
2. Click Close Database on the Office Button menu.

TO SAVE A DATABASE WITH ANOTHER NAME

1. Click the Office Button.
2. Point to Save As on the Office Button menu.
3. Select the desired format.
4. Enter a name and select a location for the new version.
5. Click the Save button.

TO CHECK FOR DEPENDENT OBJECTS

1. Ensure that the object you wish to check is selected.
2. Click Database Tools on the Ribbon to display the Database Tools tab.
3. Click the Object Dependencies button on the Database Tools tab.
4. Click the 'Objects that depend on me' option button to display any objects that depend on the selected object.

TO DELETE A TABLE OR OTHER OBJECT

1. Right-click the object.
2. Click Delete on the shortcut menu.
3. Click the Yes button in the Microsoft Office Access dialog box.

TO RENAME AN OBJECT

1. Right-click the object.
2. Click Rename on the shortcut menu.
3. Type the new name and press the ENTER key.

TO CHANGE OBJECT PROPERTIES

1. Right-click the object.

2. Click Table Properties (if the object is a table) or Object Properties on the shortcut menu.
3. Change the desired property and click the OK button.

To Quit Access

You saved all your changes and are ready to quit Access. The following step quits Access.

1 Click the Close button on the right side of the Access title bar to quit Access.

Chapter Summary

In this chapter you have learned how to use a form to add records to a table; search for records; delete records; filter records; create and use Lookup fields; create and use multivalued fields; make mass changes; create validation rules; change the appearance of a datasheet; specify referential integrity; and use subdatasheets. The following list includes all the new Access skills you have learned in this chapter.

1. Create a Simple Form (AC 142)
2. Use a Form to Add Records (AC 144)
3. Search for a Record (AC 145)
4. Update the Contents of a Record (AC 147)
5. Delete a Record (AC 148)
6. Use Filter By Selection (AC 149)
7. Toggle a Filter (AC 151)
8. Clear a Filter (AC 151)
9. Use a Common Filter (AC 152)
10. Use Filter By Form (AC 153)
11. Use Advanced Filter/Sort (AC 155)
12. Delete a Field (AC 157)
13. Add a New Field (AC 157)
14. Create a Lookup Field (AC 158)
15. Add a Multivalued Field (AC 160)
16. Save the Changes and Close the Table (AC 161)
17. Modify Single or Multivalued Lookup Fields (AC 161)
18. Use an Update Query (AC 162)
19. Use a Delete Query (AC 163)
20. Use an Append Query (AC 165)
21. Use a Make-Table Query (AC 165)
22. Specify a Required Field (AC 166)
23. Specify a Range (AC 166)
24. Specify a Default Value (AC 167)
25. Specify a Collection of Allowable Values (AC 167)
26. Specify a Format (AC 168)
27. Save the Validation Rules, Default Values, and Formats (AC 169)
28. Use a Lookup Field (AC 172)
29. Use a Multivalued Lookup Field (AC 173)
30. Resize a Column in a Datasheet (AC 175)
31. Include Totals in a Datasheet (AC 176)
32. Remove Totals from a Datasheet (AC 178)
33. Change Gridlines in a Datasheet (AC 179)
34. Change the Colors and Font in a Datasheet (AC 180)
35. Close the Datasheet Without Saving the Format Changes (AC 181)
36. Query a Multivalued Field Showing Multiple Values on a Single Row (AC 182)
37. Query a Multivalued Field Showing Multiple Values on Multiple Rows (AC 183)
38. Specify Referential Integrity (AC 186)
39. Use a Subdatasheet (AC 190)
40. Find Duplicate Records (AC 191)
41. Find Unmatched Records (AC 191)
42. Use the Ascending Button to Order Records (AC 192)
43. Back up a Database (AC 193)
44. Compact and Repair a Database (AC 193)
45. Open Another Database (AC 194)
46. Close a Database Without Exiting Access (AC 194)
47. Save a Database with Another Name (AC 194)
48. Check for Dependent Objects (AC 194)
49. Delete a Table or Other Object (AC 194)
50. Rename an Object (AC 194)
51. Change Object Properties (AC 194)

 If you have a SAM user profile, you may have access to hands-on instruction, practice, and assessment. Log in to your SAM account (http://sam2007.course.com) to launch any assigned training activities or exams that relate to the skills covered in this chapter.

Learn It Online

Test your knowledge of chapter content and key terms.

Instructions: To complete the Learn It Online exercises, start your browser, click the Address bar, and then enter the Web address scsite.com/ac2007/learn. When the Access 2007 Learn It Online page is displayed, click the link for the exercise you want to complete and then read the instructions.

Chapter Reinforcement TF, MC, and SA
A series of true/false, multiple choice, and short answer questions that test your knowledge of the chapter content.

Flash Cards
An interactive learning environment where you identify chapter key terms associated with displayed definitions.

Practice Test
A series of multiple choice questions that test your knowledge of chapter content and key terms.

Who Wants To Be a Computer Genius?
An interactive game that challenges your knowledge of chapter content in the style of a television quiz show.

Wheel of Terms
An interactive game that challenges your knowledge of chapter key terms in the style of the television show *Wheel of Fortune*.

Crossword Puzzle Challenge
A crossword puzzle that challenges your knowledge of key terms presented in the chapter.

Apply Your Knowledge

Reinforce the skills and apply the concepts you learned in this chapter.

Specifying Validation Rules, Updating Records, Formatting a Datasheet, and Creating Relationships

Instructions: Start Access. Open The Bike Delivers database that you modified in Apply Your Knowledge in Chapter 2 on page AC 128. (If you did not complete this exercise, see your instructor for a copy of the modified database.)

Perform the following tasks:
1. Open the Customer table in Design view as shown in Figure 3–78.

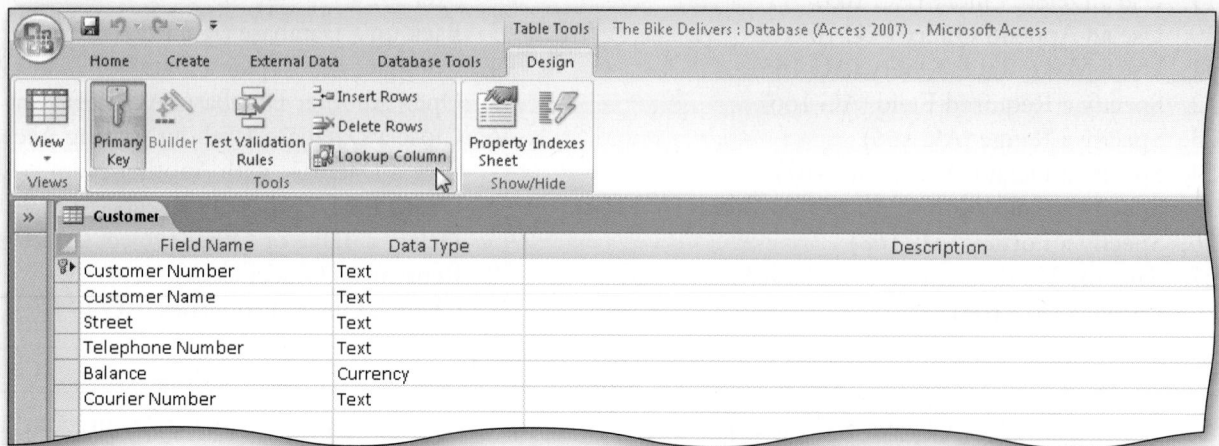

Figure 3–78

2. Format the Customer Number field so any lowercase letters appear in uppercase and make the Customer Name field a required field.

3. Specify that balance amounts must be between $0.0 and $1,000. Include validation text.

4. Save the changes to the Customer table.

5. Create a simple form for the Customer table and find the record for ME71 and change the customer name to Mentor Group Limited. Save the form as Customer Simple Form and close the form.

6. Open the Customer table in Datasheet view and use Filter By Selection to find the record for CI76. Delete the record. Remove the filter.

7. Resize all columns to best fit and remove the gridlines from the datasheet. Save the changes to the layout of the table. Close the Customer table.

8. Establish referential integrity between the Courier table (the one table) and the Customer table (the many table). Cascade the update but do not cascade the delete.

9. Submit the revised database in the format specified by your instructor.

Extend Your Knowledge

Extend the skills you learned in this chapter and experiment with new skills. You may need to use Help to complete the assignment.

Creating Action Queries, Changing Table Properties

Instructions: See the inside back cover of this book for instructions for downloading the Data Files for Students, or see your instructor for information on accessing the files required in this book.

Backyard is a retail business that specializes in products for the outdoors. The owner has created an Access database in which to store information about the products he sells. He recently acquired the inventory of a store that is going out of business. The inventory currently is stored in the Inventory database.

Perform the following tasks:

1. The owner needs to add the items stored in the Product table of the Inventory database to the Item table of the Backyard database. Create and run an append query to create the Item table for the Backyard database shown in Figure 3–79.

Item Code	Description	On Hand	Cost	Selling Price	Add New Field
BA35	Bat House	14	$43.50	$45.50	
BB01	Bird Bath	2	$54.00	$62.00	
BE19	Bee Sculpture	7	$39.80	$42.50	
BL06	Bug Mister	9	$14.35	$15.99	
BO22	Barn Owl Sculp	2	$37.50	$42.99	
BS10	Bunny Sprinkle	4	$41.95	$50.00	
BU24	Butterfly Stake	6	$36.10	$37.75	
FS11	Froggie Sprinkl	5	$41.95	$50.00	
GF12	Globe Feeder	12	$14.80	$16.25	
HF01	Hummingbird F	5	$11.35	$14.25	
LM05	Leaf Mister	3	$29.95	$35.95	
PM05	Purple Martin F	3	$67.10	$69.95	
SF03	Suet Feeder	7	$8.05	$9.95	
WF10	Window feede	10	$14.25	$15.95	

Figure 3–79

Continued >

Extend Your Knowledge *continued*

2. Open the Item table in the Backyard database and change the description for WF10 to Window Bird Feeder. Resize all columns to best fit the data.

3. Sort the datasheet in ascending order by Description.

4. Add a totals row to the datasheet and display the sum of the on hand items, and the average cost and average selling price.

5. Save the changes to the layout of the table. Close the table and rename it Product.

6. Update the table properties for the Product table to include the description, Updated to include items from Inventory database.

7. Using a query, delete all records in the Product table where the description starts with the letter S. Save the query as Delete Query.

8. Change the database properties, as specified by your instructor. Submit the revised database in the format specified by your instructor.

Make It Right

Analyze a database and correct all errors and/or improve the design.

Correcting Table Design Errors

Instructions: Start Access. Open the Care4Pets database. See the inside back cover of this book for instructions for downloading the Data Files for Students, or see your instructor for information on accessing the files required in this book.

Care4Pets provides a variety of services to pet owners. The owner of Care4Pets has decided that she could better manage her business if she added a multivalued field that lists the various types of pets her customers have. She created the field shown in Figure 3–80 but forgot to add Rabbit as one of the pet types. Modify the multivalued Lookup field to include Rabbit as a pet type.

Figure 3–80

Finally, she wanted to add referential integrity between the Groomer table and the Customer table. The relationship shown in Figure 3–81 is not correct and must be fixed. She does not want to cascade the update or the delete. She also wants to create a report for the relationship. Use the name Relationships for Care4Pets for the report.

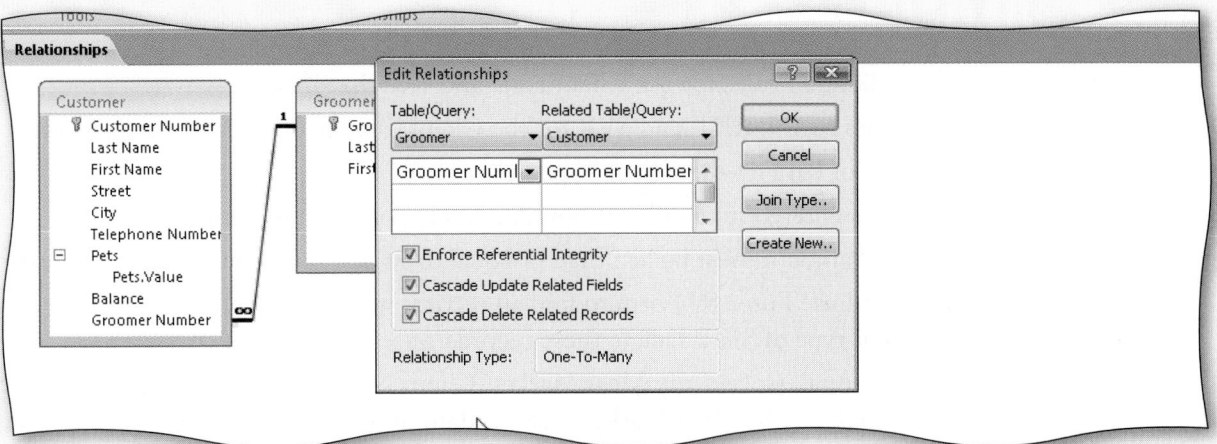

Figure 3–81

Submit the revised database in the format specified by your instructor.

In the Lab

Design, create, modify, and/or use a database following the guidelines, concepts, and skills presented in this chapter. Labs are listed in order of increasing difficulty.

Lab 1: Maintaining the JMS TechWizards Database

Problem: JMS TechWizards is expanding rapidly and needs to make some database changes to handle the expansion. The company needs to know more about its clients, such as the type of business, and it needs to ensure that data that is entered is valid. It also needs to update the records in the database.

Instructions: Use the database created in the In the Lab 1 of Chapter 1 on page AC 67 for this assignment or see your instructor for information on accessing the files required for this book.

Perform the following tasks:
1. Open the JMS TechWizards database and then open the Client table in Design view.
2. Add a Lookup field, Client Type, to the Client table. The field should appear after the Telephone Number field. The field will contain data on the type of client. The client types are MAN (Manufacturing), RET (Retail), and SER (Service). Save these changes to the structure.
3. Using a query, change all the entries in the Client Type column to RET. Save the query as Client Type Update Query.
4. Open the Client table and make the following changes. You can use the Find button, the Replace button, or Filter By Selection to locate the records to change:
   a. Change the client type for clients AM53 and SA56 to MAN.
   b. Change the client type for clients GR56, JE77, and ME17 to SER.
   c. Change the name of client SA56 to Sawyer Industries.
   d. Change the name of client ST21 to Steed's Department Store.
5. Resize all columns to best fit the data and remove the vertical gridlines. Save the changes to the layout of the table.

Continued >

6. Create the following validation rules for the Client table and save the changes.

   a. Specify the legal values MAN, RET, and SER for the Client Type field. Include validation text.

   b. Assign a default value of RET to the Client Type field.

   c. Ensure that any letters entered in the Client Number field appear as uppercase.

   d. Specify that the billed amount must be less than or equal to $1,500.00. Include validation text.

7. Open the Client table and use Filter By Form to find all records where the client is located in Anderson and has a client type of SER. Delete these records.

8. JMS has signed up a new retail store, Cray Meat Market (Client Number CR21) and needs to add the record to the Client table. The Meat Market is at 72 Main in Anderson, TX 78077. The phone number is 512-555-7766. Lee Torres is the technician assigned to the account. To date, they have not been billed for any services. Create a split form for the Client table and use this split form to add the record.

9. Specify referential integrity between the Technician table (the one table) and the Client table (the many table). Cascade the update but not the delete.

10. Compact the database and then back up the database.

11. Submit the revised database in the format specified by your instructor.

In the Lab

Lab 2: Maintaining the Hockey Fan Zone Database

Problem: The management of the Hockey Fan Zone store needs to change the database structure, add validation rules, and update records.

Instructions: Use the database created in the In the Lab 2 of Chapter 1 on page AC 68 for this assignment, or see your instructor for information on accessing the files required for this book.

Perform the following tasks:

1. Open the Hockey Fan Zone database and then open the Item table in Design view.

2. Add a Lookup field, Item Type to the Item table. The field should appear after the Description field. The field will contain data on the type of item for sale. The item types are CAP (caps and hats), CLO (clothing), and NOV (Novelties).

3. Make the following changes to the Item table:

   a. Change the field size for the On Hand field to Integer. The Format should be fixed and the decimal places should be 0.

   b. Make Description a required field.

   c. Specify the legal values CAP, CLO, and NOV for the Item Type field. Include validation text.

   d. Specify that number on hand must be between 0 and 75. Include validation text.

4. Save the changes to the table design. If a dialog box appears indicating that some data may be lost, click the Yes button.

5. Using a query, assign the value NOV to the Item Type field for all records. Save the query as Update Query.

6. Delete the split form for the Item table that you created in Chapter 1. The form does not include the Item Type field. Recreate the split form for the Item table.

7. Use the split form to change the item type for item numbers 3663 and 7930 to CAP. Change the item type for item numbers 5923 and 7810 to CLO.

8. Add the following items to the Item table.

3673	Blanket	NOV	5	$29.90	$34.00	AC
6078	Key Chain	NOV	20	$3.00	$5.00	MN
7550	Sweatshirt	CLO	8	$19.90	$22.95	LG

9. Create an advanced filter for the Item table. The filter should display the item number, item type, description, and number on hand for all items with less than 10 items on hand. Sort the filter by item type and description. Save the filter settings as a query and name the filter Reorder Filter.

10. Resize all columns in the Item table and the Supplier table to best fit.

11. Using a query, delete all records in the Item table where the description starts with the letter F. Save the query as Delete Query.

12. Specify referential integrity between the Supplier table (the one table) and the Item table (the many table). Cascade the update but not the delete.

13. Compact the database.

14. Submit the revised database in the format specified by your instructor.

In the Lab

Lab 3: Maintaining the Ada Beauty Supply Database

Problem: The management of Ada Beauty Supply has determined that some changes must be made to the database structure. A multivalued field must be added. Validation rules need to be added. Finally, some additions and deletions are required to the database.

Instructions: Use the Ada Beauty Supply database created in the In the Lab 3 of Chapter 1 on page AC 69 for this assignment, or see your instructor for information on accessing the files required for this book. Submit the revised database in the format specified by your instructor.

Instructions Part 1: Several changes must be made to the database structure. For example, management would like a multivalued field that lists the type of services each beauty salon offers. This knowledge can help the sales representatives better meet the needs of their customers. Table 3-2 lists the service abbreviations and descriptions that management would like in a Services Offered multivalued field.

Table 3–2 Service Abbreviations and Descriptions	
Service Abbreviation	**Description**
FAC	Facial
HRS	Hair Styling
MNC	Manicure
PED	Pedicure
MST	Massage Therapy
TAN	Tanning

Management wants to ensure that an entry always appears in the Customer Name field and that any letters entered in the Customer Number field appear in uppercase. It also requires that the amount in the Balance field is never less than 0 or greater than $1,000. Make the changes to the database structure. Place the Services Offered field after the Telephone field.

Continued >

In the Lab *continued*

Instructions Part 2: The data for the Services Offered field shown in Figure 3–82 must be added to the database. The address for Elegante is incorrect. It should be 180 Broadway. Le Beauty has changed its name to Le Beauty Day Spa. Nancy's Place has gone out of business. A new salon, PamperMe Day Spa, just opened. The address for the spa is 2125 Lawrence and the phone number is 555-2401. The spa provides all services except hair styling and tanning.

Management wants to use PA10 as the customer number and Terry Sinson is the sales rep. The new spa has purchased $750 worth of supplies but has not paid for them. Format the datasheet to best fit the data.

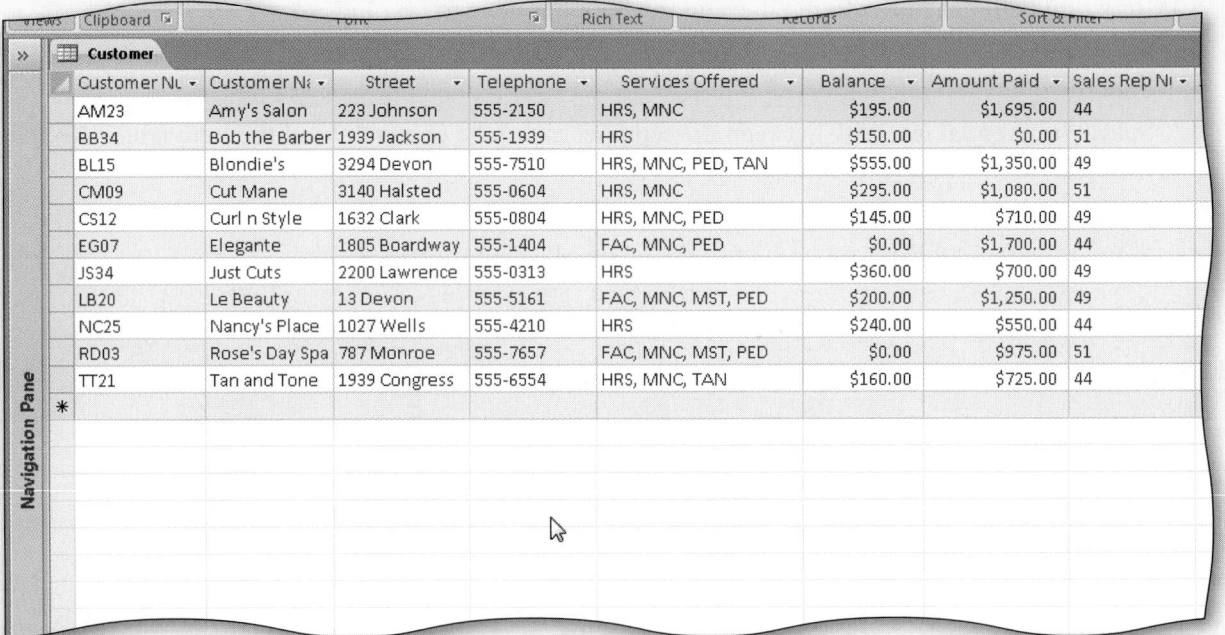

Figure 3–82

Instructions Part 3: Because the sales reps work on commission, management wants to make sure that customers are not assigned to a sales rep who is not in the database. It also wants the ability to change a sales rep number in the Sales Rep table and have the change applied to the Customer table. Create the appropriate relationship that would satisfy management's needs.

Cases and Places

Apply your creative thinking and problem solving skills to design and implement a solution.

• EASIER   •• MORE DIFFICULT

• 1: Maintaining the Second Hand Goods Database

Use the Second-Hand Goods database you created in Cases and Places 1 in Chapter 1 on page AC 71 for this assignment, or see your instructor for information on accessing the files required for this book. Perform each of the following tasks:

a. The Condition field should be a Lookup field. Only the current values in the database should be legal values.

b. A better description for the bookcases is 3-Shelf Bookcase.

c. The duvet has been sold.

d. The minimum price of any item is $2.00.

e. It would be easier to find items for sale if the default sort order for the item table were by description rather than by item number. Also, some of the descriptions are not displayed completely in Datasheet view.

f. Specify referential integrity. Cascade the update and the delete.

Submit the revised database in the format specified by your instructor.

• 2: Maintaining the BeachCondo Rentals database

Use the BeachCondo Rentals database you created in Cases and Places 2 in Chapter 1 on page AC 71 for this assignment, or see your instructor for information on accessing the files required for this book. Perform each of the following tasks:

a. Add the field, For Sale to the Condo Unit table, to indicate whether a condo unit is for sale. The field is a Yes/No field and should appear after the weekly rate.

b. All units owned by Alonso Bonita are for sale.

c. The Bedrooms, Bathrooms, and Sleeps fields always should contain data.

d. Most common condo units have one bedroom, one bathroom, and sleep two people. All condo units should have a minimum of one bedroom, one bathroom, and sleep two people.

e. No unit rents for less than $700 or more than $1,500.

f. Management has just received a new listing from Mark Graty. It is unit 300. The unit sleeps 10, has three bedrooms, has 2.5 bathrooms, and includes linens. The weekly rate is $1,400 and the owner is interested in selling the unit.

g. Specify referential integrity. Do not cascade the update or the delete.

Submit the revised database in the format specified by your instructor.

•• 3: Maintaining the Restaurant Database

Use the restaurant database you created in Cases and Places 3 in Chapter 1 on page AC 71 for this assignment, or see your instructor for information on accessing the files required for this book. Using the Plan Ahead guidelines presented in this chapter, determine what changes need to be made to your database. For example, a multivalued field could be useful to record opening days and times of a restaurant. Another multivalued field could record restaurant specialties. Create any necessary relationships. Examine the relationships to determine if the default join type is appropriate and whether you need to cascade the update and/or delete. Use a word processing program, such as

Continued >

Cases and Places *continued*

Microsoft Word, to explain the changes you need to make to the database. Then, make the changes to the database. Submit the Word document and the revised database in the format specified by your instructor.

•• 4: Updating Your Contacts Database

Make It Personal

Use the contacts database you created in Cases and Places 4 in Chapter 1 on page AC 71 for this assignment, or see your instructor for information on accessing the files required for this book. Consider your own personal job situation. Has the focus of your job search changed? Are there specific jobs within the companies of interest that appeal to you? Have you contacted an individual within a company to express your interest? If so, consider creating another table with a one-to-one relationship between the individual contact and the company. Create a multivalued field to store those specific positions that would interest you. Review the fields in the contacts database. Are there any fields you need to add? Are there any fields you need to delete? Are there any tables that need to be deleted? Are there companies that need to be added to your database? Make any necessary changes to your database structure and update the database. Using a word processing program, such as Microsoft Word, explain what changes you made to your database and why you made the changes. Submit the Word document and the revised database in the format specified by your instructor.

•• 5: Understanding Action Queries, Query Wizards, and Table Design Changes

Working Together

With a make-table query, a user can create a new table from one or more tables in the database. The table can be stored in the same database or a new database. As a team, use the Access Help system to learn more about make-table queries. Then, choose either the Cases and Places 1 database or the Cases and Places 2 database and create a make-table query. For example, for the Hockey Fan Zone, the management could create a table named Supplier Call List that would include the item code, description, and cost of each item as well as the supplier name and telephone number. Write a one-page paper that (1) explains the purpose for which the new table is intended and (2) suggests at least two additional uses for make-table queries. Submit the paper and the database in the format specified by your instructor.

Open the Students database that you created in Chapter 1. As a team, review the data types for each of the fields that are in the database. Do any of these data types need to be changed? For example, is there a field that should store multiple values? Are there any fields that should contain validation rules? Change the data types and add validation rules as necessary. Examine the tables in your database. Delete any tables that you do not need. Determine the relationships among the remaining tables. Are there any one-to-one relationships or one-to-many relationships? Write a one-page paper that explains your reasons for changing (or not changing) the structure of the database. Submit the paper and the database in the format specified by your instructor.

Save the Ada Beauty Supply database as Ada Team Beauty Supply. Research the purpose of the Find Unmatched Query Wizard and the Find Duplicates Query Wizard. Use the Ada Team database and create queries using each of these wizards. Did the queries perform as expected? Open each query in Design view and modify it, for example, add another field to the query. What happened to the query results? Write a one-page paper that explains the purpose of each query wizard and describes the team's experiences with creating and modifying the queries. Submit the paper and database in the format specified by your instructor.

7. Use the split form to change the item type for item numbers 3663 and 7930 to CAP. Change the item type for item numbers 5923 and 7810 to CLO.

8. Add the following items to the Item table.

3673	Blanket	NOV	5	$29.90	$34.00	AC
6078	Key Chain	NOV	20	$3.00	$5.00	MN
7550	Sweatshirt	CLO	8	$19.90	$22.95	LG

9. Create an advanced filter for the Item table. The filter should display the item number, item type, description, and number on hand for all items with less than 10 items on hand. Sort the filter by item type and description. Save the filter settings as a query and name the filter Reorder Filter.

10. Resize all columns in the Item table and the Supplier table to best fit.

11. Using a query, delete all records in the Item table where the description starts with the letter F. Save the query as Delete Query.

12. Specify referential integrity between the Supplier table (the one table) and the Item table (the many table). Cascade the update but not the delete.

13. Compact the database.

14. Submit the revised database in the format specified by your instructor.

In the Lab

Lab 3: Maintaining the Ada Beauty Supply Database

Problem: The management of Ada Beauty Supply has determined that some changes must be made to the database structure. A multivalued field must be added. Validation rules need to be added. Finally, some additions and deletions are required to the database.

Instructions: Use the Ada Beauty Supply database created in the In the Lab 3 of Chapter 1 on page AC 69 for this assignment, or see your instructor for information on accessing the files required for this book. Submit the revised database in the format specified by your instructor.

Instructions Part 1:   Several changes must be made to the database structure. For example, management would like a multivalued field that lists the type of services each beauty salon offers. This knowledge can help the sales representatives better meet the needs of their customers. Table 3-2 lists the service abbreviations and descriptions that management would like in a Services Offered multivalued field.

Table 3–2 Service Abbreviations and Descriptions	
Service Abbreviation	**Description**
FAC	Facial
HRS	Hair Styling
MNC	Manicure
PED	Pedicure
MST	Massage Therapy
TAN	Tanning

Management wants to ensure that an entry always appears in the Customer Name field and that any letters entered in the Customer Number field appear in uppercase. It also requires that the amount in the Balance field is never less than 0 or greater than $1,000. Make the changes to the database structure. Place the Services Offered field after the Telephone field.

Continued >

In the Lab *continued*

Instructions Part 2: The data for the Services Offered field shown in Figure 3–82 must be added to the database. The address for Elegante is incorrect. It should be 180 Broadway. Le Beauty has changed its name to Le Beauty Day Spa. Nancy's Place has gone out of business. A new salon, PamperMe Day Spa, just opened. The address for the spa is 2125 Lawrence and the phone number is 555-2401. The spa provides all services except hair styling and tanning.

Management wants to use PA10 as the customer number and Terry Sinson is the sales rep. The new spa has purchased $750 worth of supplies but has not paid for them. Format the datasheet to best fit the data.

Customer Nu	Customer Na	Street	Telephone	Services Offered	Balance	Amount Paid	Sales Rep N
AM23	Amy's Salon	223 Johnson	555-2150	HRS, MNC	$195.00	$1,695.00	44
BB34	Bob the Barber	1939 Jackson	555-1939	HRS	$150.00	$0.00	51
BL15	Blondie's	3294 Devon	555-7510	HRS, MNC, PED, TAN	$555.00	$1,350.00	49
CM09	Cut Mane	3140 Halsted	555-0604	HRS, MNC	$295.00	$1,080.00	51
CS12	Curl n Style	1632 Clark	555-0804	HRS, MNC, PED	$145.00	$710.00	49
EG07	Elegante	1805 Boardway	555-1404	FAC, MNC, PED	$0.00	$1,700.00	44
JS34	Just Cuts	2200 Lawrence	555-0313	HRS	$360.00	$700.00	49
LB20	Le Beauty	13 Devon	555-5161	FAC, MNC, MST, PED	$200.00	$1,250.00	49
NC25	Nancy's Place	1027 Wells	555-4210	HRS	$240.00	$550.00	44
RD03	Rose's Day Spa	787 Monroe	555-7657	FAC, MNC, MST, PED	$0.00	$975.00	51
TT21	Tan and Tone	1939 Congress	555-6554	HRS, MNC, TAN	$160.00	$725.00	44

Figure 3–82

Instructions Part 3: Because the sales reps work on commission, management wants to make sure that customers are not assigned to a sales rep who is not in the database. It also wants the ability to change a sales rep number in the Sales Rep table and have the change applied to the Customer table. Create the appropriate relationship that would satisfy management's needs.

Microsoft Office **Access 2007**

Integration Feature
Sharing Data Among Applications

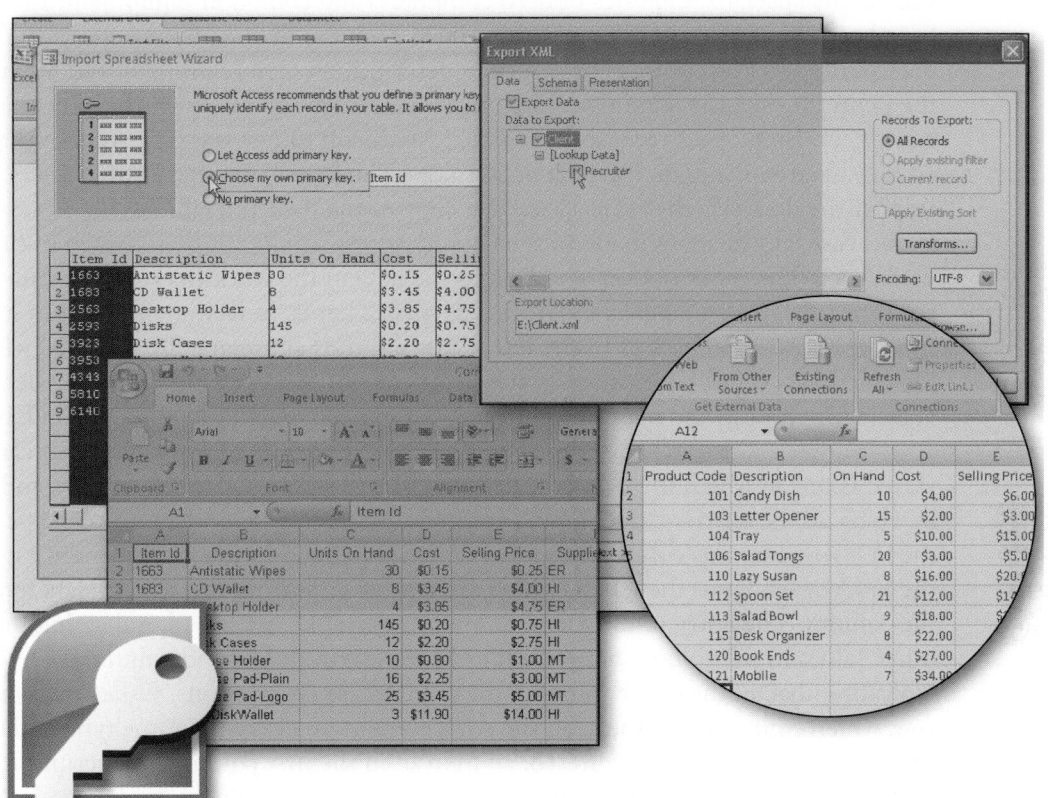

Objectives

You will have mastered the material in this Integration Feature when you can:

- Import from or link to an Excel worksheet
- Import from or link to an Access database
- Import from or link to a text file

- Export data to Excel, Word, and text files
- Publish a report
- Export and import XML data

Integration Feature Introduction

It is not uncommon for people to use an application for some specific purpose, only to find later that another application may be better suited. For example, an organization initially might use Excel to maintain data on inventory only to discover later that the data would be better maintained in an Access database. This feature shows how to use data from other applications in Access. It also shows how to make Access data available to other applications.

Project — Sharing Data Among Applications

Camashaly specializes in sales of used computers and computer equipment. Employees have been using Microsoft Excel to automate a variety of tasks for several years. When determining to keep track of prices, item descriptions, serial numbers, and other data on the items for sale, the administrators originally decided to maintain the data as an Excel worksheet. Employees recently completed Microsoft Office training and now have decided they need to maintain the data in an Access database. They have two choices. They can **import** the data, which means to make a copy of the data as a table in the Access database. In this case, any changes made to the data in Access would not be reflected in the Excel worksheet. The other option is to **link** to the data in the worksheet. When data is linked, the data appears as a table in the Access database, but is, in fact, maintained in its original form in Excel. Any changes to the Excel data are thus automatically reflected when the linked table is viewed in Access. In this arrangement, Access would typically be used as a vehicle for viewing and querying the data, with actual updates being made in Excel.

Figure 1 illustrates the conversion process. The type of worksheet that can be converted is one in which the data is stored as a **list**, that is, a collection of rows and columns in which all the entries in a column represent the same type of data. In this type of list, the first row contains column headings rather than data. In the worksheet in Figure 1a, the first row contains the labels, which are entries indicating the type of data found in the column. The entry in the first column, for example, is Item Id, indicating that all the other values in the column are Item Ids. The entry in the second column is Description, indicating that all the other values in the column are descriptions. Other than the first row, which contains the labels, all the rows contain precisely the same type of data shown in the Access database in Figure 1b: an item Id in the first column, a description in the second column, the number of units on hand in the third column, and so on.

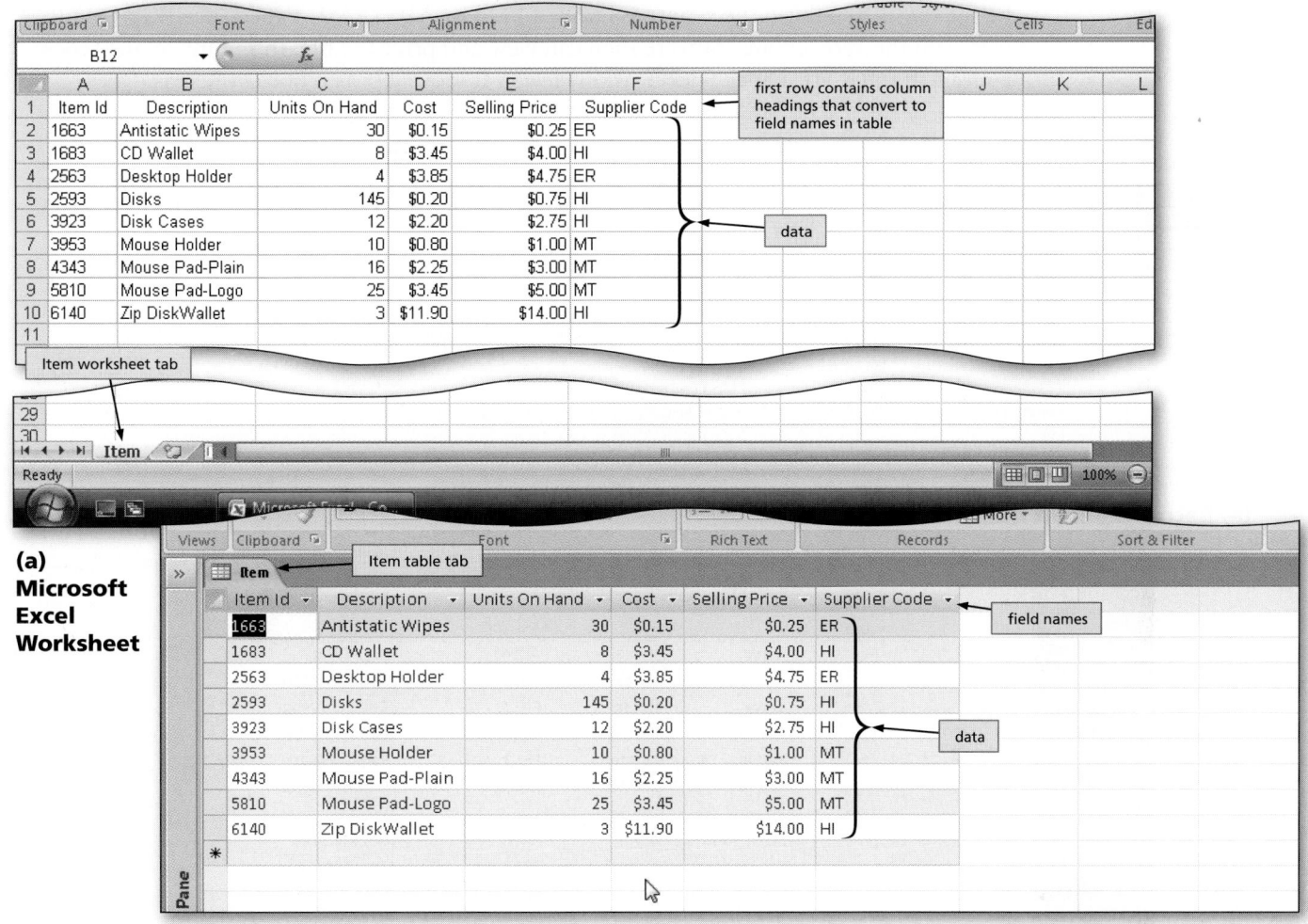

(a) Microsoft Excel Worksheet

(b) Microsoft Access Table

Figure 1

As the figures illustrate, the worksheet, shown in Figure 1a, is copied to an Access table, shown in Figure 1b. The columns in the worksheet become the fields. The column headings in the first row of the worksheet become the field names. The rows of the worksheet, other than the first row, which contains the labels, become the records in the table. In the process, each field will be assigned the data type that seems the most reasonable, given the data currently in the worksheet.

Organizations that currently use Access for their data needs often find that they need to export the data to other applications. JSP Recruiters has determined that it needs to make some of the data in its database available to other applications. Some users need the data in Excel; others want it placed in a Microsoft Word document. Still others want the ability to receive a report by e-mail.

You can **export** (copy) data from an Access database so that another application (for example, Excel) can use the data. Figure 2a on the next page shows the Recruiter-Client query exported to Excel and Figure 2b on the next page shows the same query exported to Word.

At times you may want to send a report to a user by e-mail. It would be prohibitive to send the whole database to the other user, just so the user could print or view the report. In addition, doing so would require the other user to have Microsoft Access installed. A better way is to publish the report as either a PDF or XPS (XML Paper Specification) file. A user with the appropriate software then can view and print the file. In Figure 2c, the report appears in the XML Paper Specification viewer. It looks just as it does in Access.

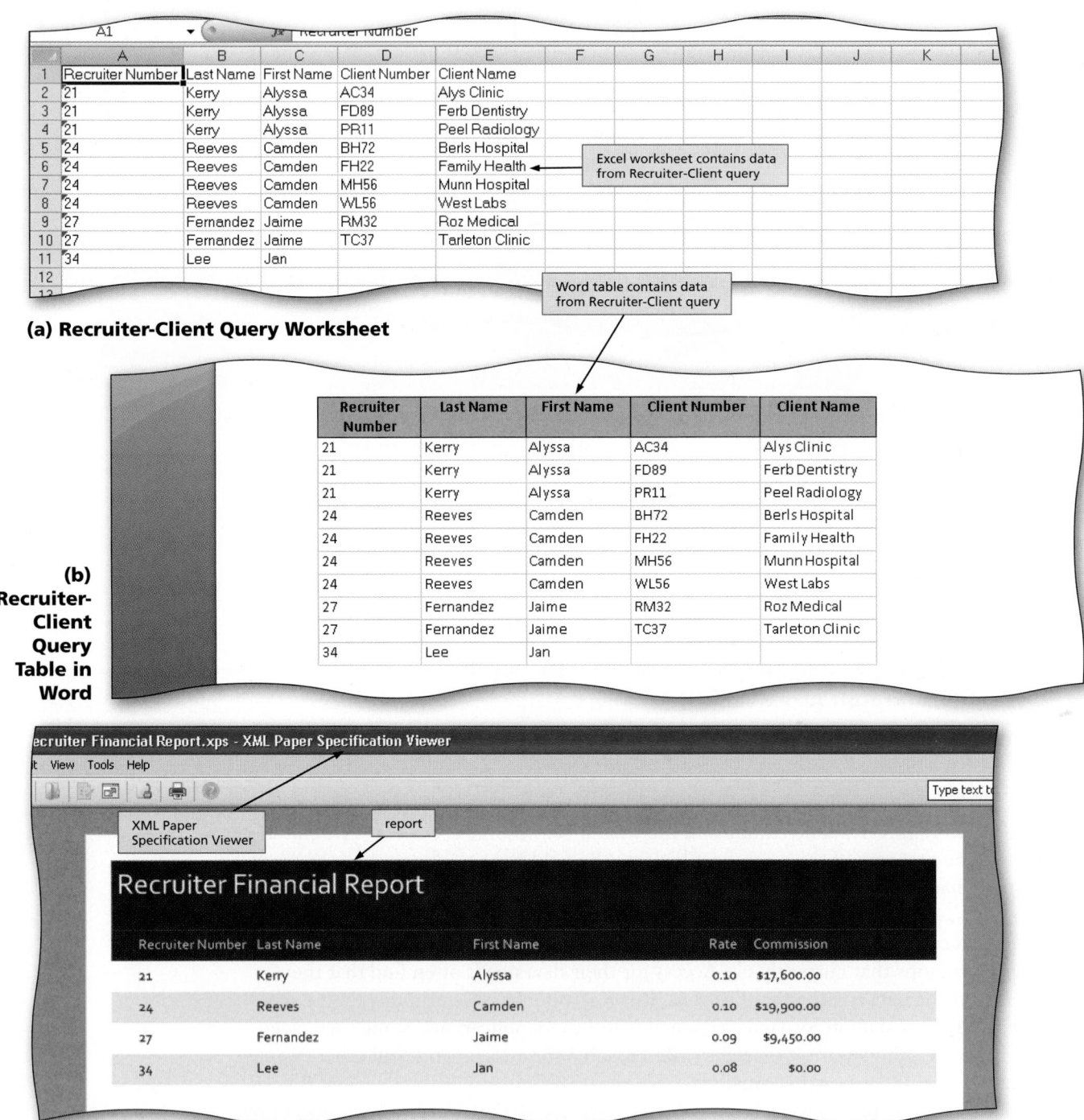

(a) Recruiter-Client Query Worksheet

(b) Recruiter-Client Query Table in Word

(c) XPS Version of Recruiter Financial Report

Figure 2

JSP Recruiters also would like to export the Client and Recruiter tables in such a way that they can be imported easily to a database used by a related organization, JSP Consulting, that handles various accounting functions for JSP Recruiters. The users have learned that the easiest way to do this is to use XML (Extensible Markup Language), which is a language that defines data records on a page, allowing for exchange of data between dissimilar applications. The XML format allows you to export and import both data and structure of multiple related tables in a single operation.

Overview

As you read through this feature, you will learn how to share data among applications by performing these general tasks:

- Import an Excel worksheet into an Access table
- Export a query to Excel
- Export a query to Word
- Publish a report as an XPS file
- Export multiple tables to an XML file
- Import multiple tables from an XML file

BTW

PDF and XPS Formats
Before you export to PDF and XPS formats, check to make sure you have the PDF or XPS button in the Export group on the External Data tab. If not, you must first install a free add-in program. To learn more about installing the add-in, type PDF in the Access Help window and follow the instructions. If you are using a computer in a school or work setting, check with your instructor or IT staff before installing any add-in program.

Plan Ahead

Guidelines for Sharing Data Among Applications

1. **Identify sources of external data for the database.** Does data already exist that you should incorporate into your database? Determine whether the data is in an Excel worksheet, another database, a text file, or some other application.

2. **Determine whether the data you have identified is in an appropriate format.** Is it a collection of rows and columns in which all the entries in a column represent the same type of data? Does the first row contain column headings rather than data? Is the data separated by tabs or by commas?

3. **Determine whether changes made to the data in the original data source should be reflected in the Access table.** If so, linking to the data source is the appropriate action. If not, importing the data would be appropriate.

4. **If the source of data is an Access database, determine whether, in addition to the tables, there are other objects to be imported.** If you import tables, you also can import queries, forms, and reports based on those tables. If, for example, the other database contained a report based on a table you are importing, you can import the report as well, thus saving you the effort of having to recreate the report.

5. **For data in your database that you want to make available to others, determine whether exporting the data is appropriate.** If you export the data, any changes that others make to the data will not be reflected in your database. If it is acceptable that these changes are not reflected, then exporting is appropriate. If not, the data will need to be linked. Linking must take place within the other application.

6. **If data is to be exported, determine the destination application.** The application that will receive the data determines the export process to be used. Common choices are Excel and Word. You also can export to text files in a variety of formats. For applications to which you cannot directly export data, you often can export an appropriately formatted text file that the other application can import. To make reports available to others, rather than exporting the report, you can publish the report, which is the process of making the report available to others on the Web. You can publish the report in either PDF or XPS format, so you would need to determine which is appropriate for the person who wants to be able to view the report.

When necessary, more specific details concerning the above decisions and/or actions are presented at appropriate positions within the feature. The feature also will identify the use of these guidelines in sharing data as shown in Figures 1 and 2.

Starting Access

If you are using a computer to step through the project in this chapter and you want your screen to match the figures in this book, you should change your screen's resolution to 1024 × 768. For information about how to change a computer's resolution, read Appendix E.

To Start Access

The following steps, which assume Windows is running, start Access.

Note: If you are using Windows XP, see Appendix F for alternate steps.

1 Click the Start button on the Windows taskbar to display the Start menu.

2 Click All Programs at the bottom of the left pane on the Start menu to display the All Programs list and then click Microsoft Office in the All Programs list to display the Microsoft Office list.

3 Click Microsoft Office Access 2007 on the Microsoft Office submenu to start Access and display the Getting Started with Microsoft Office Access window.

4 If the Access window is not maximized, click the Maximize button on its title bar to maximize the window.

To Create a New Database

Before importing data from another application to an Access database, you must ensure that a database exists. If there is no database, then you need to create one. The following steps create a database on a USB flash drive that will store the items for Camashaly.

Note: If you are using Windows XP, see Appendix F for alternate steps.

1 With a USB flash drive connected to one of the computer's USB ports, click Blank Database in the Getting Started with Microsoft Office Access screen to create a new blank database.

2 Type Camashaly in the File Name text box and then click the 'Browse for a location to put your database' button to display the File New Database dialog box.

3 Click Computer in the Favorite Links section to display a list of available drives and folders and then double-click UDISK 2.0 (E:) (your letter may be different) in the Computer list to select the USB flash drive as the new save location.

4 Click the OK button to select the USB flash drive as the location for the database and to return to the Getting Started with Microsoft Office Access screen.

5 Click the Create button to create the database on the USB flash drive with the file name, Camashaly.

Importing or Linking Data from Other Applications to Access

The process of importing or linking an Access database uses a wizard. Specifically, if the data is imported from an Excel worksheet, the process will use the **Import Spreadsheet Wizard**; if the data is linked to an Excel worksheet, the process will use the **Link Spreadsheet Wizard**. The wizard takes you through some basic steps, asking a few simple questions. After you have answered the questions, the wizard will import or link the data.

Identify sources of external data for the database: Excel worksheet.
You need to decide whether it is appropriate for data you currently keep in an Excel worksheet to be kept in a database instead. The following are some common reasons for using a database instead of a worksheet:

1. The worksheet contains a great deal of redundant data. As discussed in Chapter 1 on pages AC 10 and AC 12, databases can be designed to eliminate redundant data.

2. The data to be maintained consists of multiple interrelated items. For example, the JSP Recruiters database maintains data on two items, clients and recruiters, and these items are interrelated. A client has a single recruiter and each recruiter is responsible for several clients. The JSP Recruiters database is a very simple one. Databases easily can contain many separate, but interrelated, items.

3. You want to use the powerful query and report capabilities of Microsoft Access.

Plan Ahead

Determine whether the data you have identified is in an appropriate format: Excel worksheet.
Before importing or linking the Excel worksheet you have identified, you need to make sure it is in an appropriate format. The following are some of the actions you should take to ensure correct format:

1. Make sure the data is in the form of a list, a collection of rows and columns in which all the entries in a column represent the same type of data.

2. Make sure that there are no blank rows within the list. If there are, remove them prior to importing or linking.

3. Make sure there are no blank columns within the list. If there are, remove them prior to importing or linking.

4. Determine whether the first row contains column headings that will make appropriate field names in the resulting table. If not, you might consider adding such a row. In general, the process is simpler if the first row in the worksheet contains appropriate column headings.

Plan Ahead

To Import an Excel Worksheet

After Camashaly managers identified that a worksheet named Computer Items contains data that should be in a table in the database, they would import the data. You import a worksheet by using the Import Spreadsheet Wizard. In the process, you will indicate that the first row in the Computer Items worksheet contains the column headings. These column headings then will become the field names in the Access table. In addition, you will indicate the primary key for the table. As part of the process, you could, if appropriate, choose not to include all the fields from the worksheet in the resulting table.

The following steps import the Computer Items Excel worksheet.

Note: If you are using Windows XP, see Appendix F for alternate steps.

1

- Click External Data on the Ribbon to display the External Data tab (Figure 3).

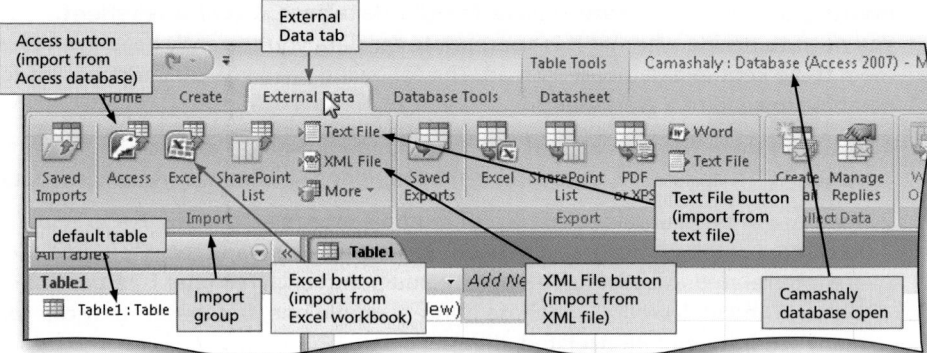

Figure 3

2

- Click the Excel button in the Import group on the External Data tab to display the Get External Data – Excel Spreadsheet dialog box.

- Click the Browse button in the Get External Data – Excel Spreadsheet dialog box.

- If necessary, click the Look in box arrow and then click UDISK 2.0 (E:) to select the USB flash drive in the Look in list as the new open location. (Your drive letter might be different.)

- Click the Computer Items workbook, and then click the Open button to select the workbook (Figure 4).

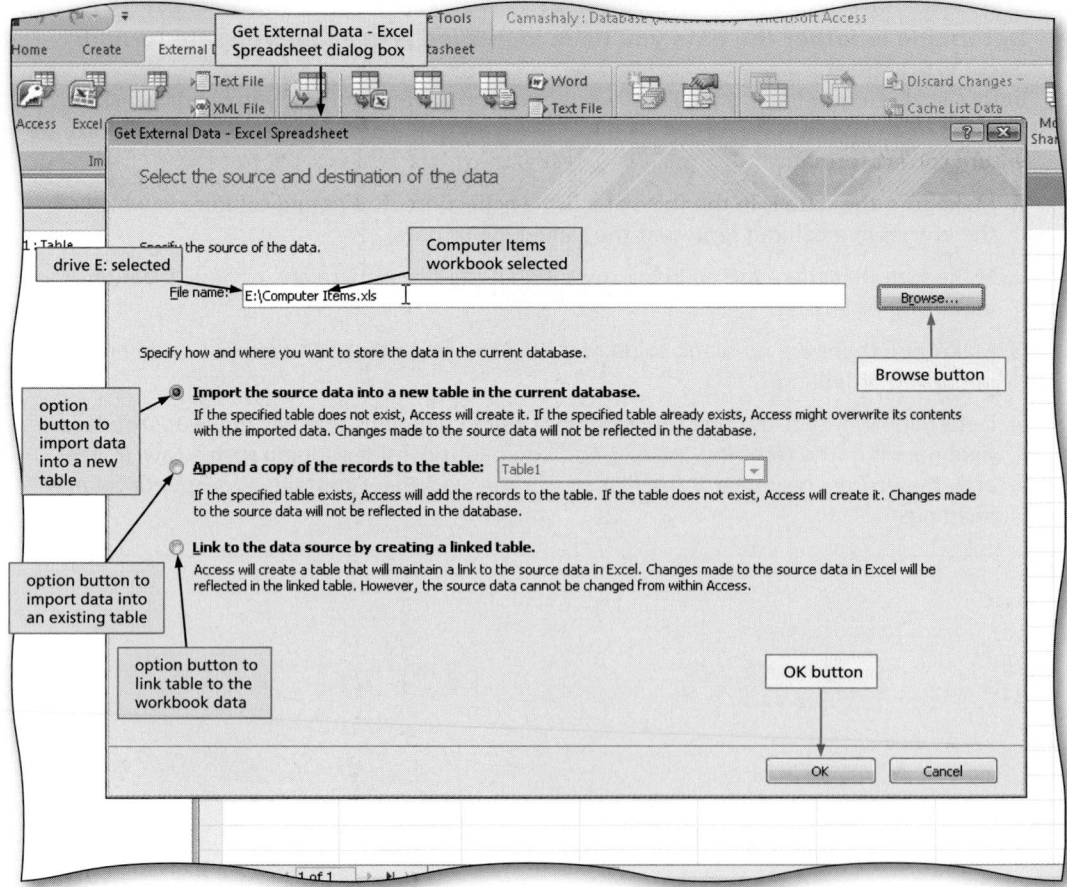

Figure 4

3

- With the option button to import the data to a new table selected, click the OK button to display the Import Spreadsheet Wizard dialog box (Figure 5).

Q&A

What happens if I select the option button to append records to an existing table?

Instead of the records being placed in a new table, they will be added to the existing table, provided the value in the primary key field does not duplicate that on an existing record.

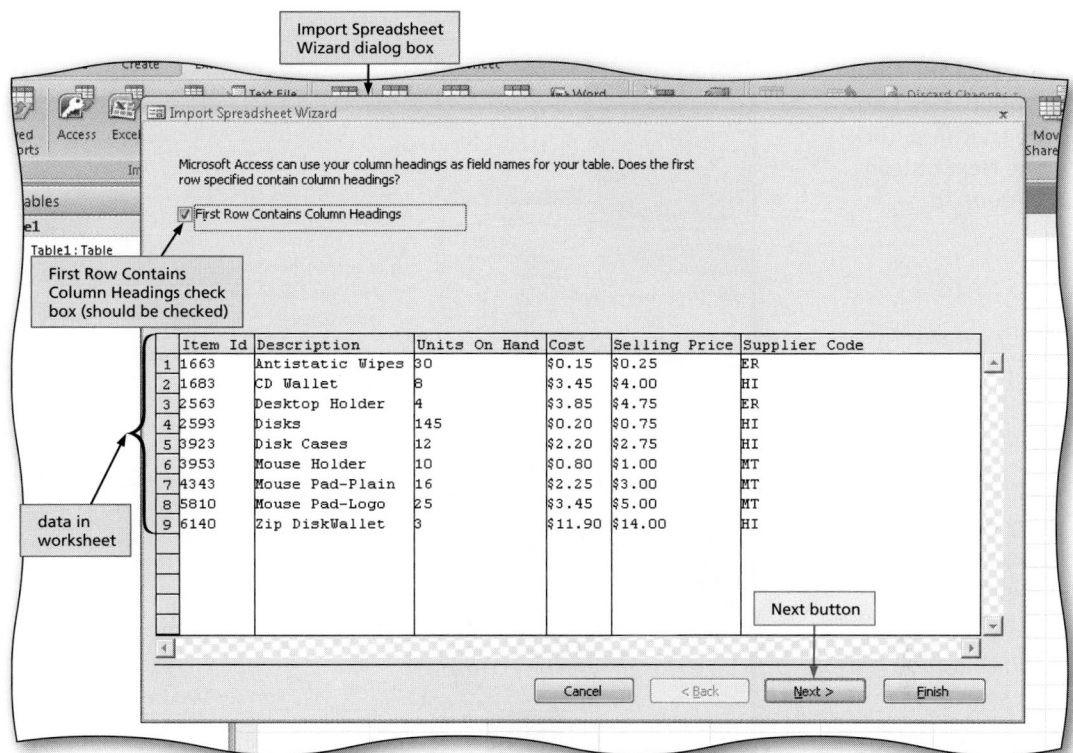

Figure 5

4

- If necessary, click First Row Contains Column Headings to select it.

- Click the Next button (Figure 6).

Q&A

When would I use the options on this screen?

You would use these options if you wanted to change properties for one or more fields. You can change the name, the data type, and whether the field is indexed. You also can indicate that some fields are not to be imported.

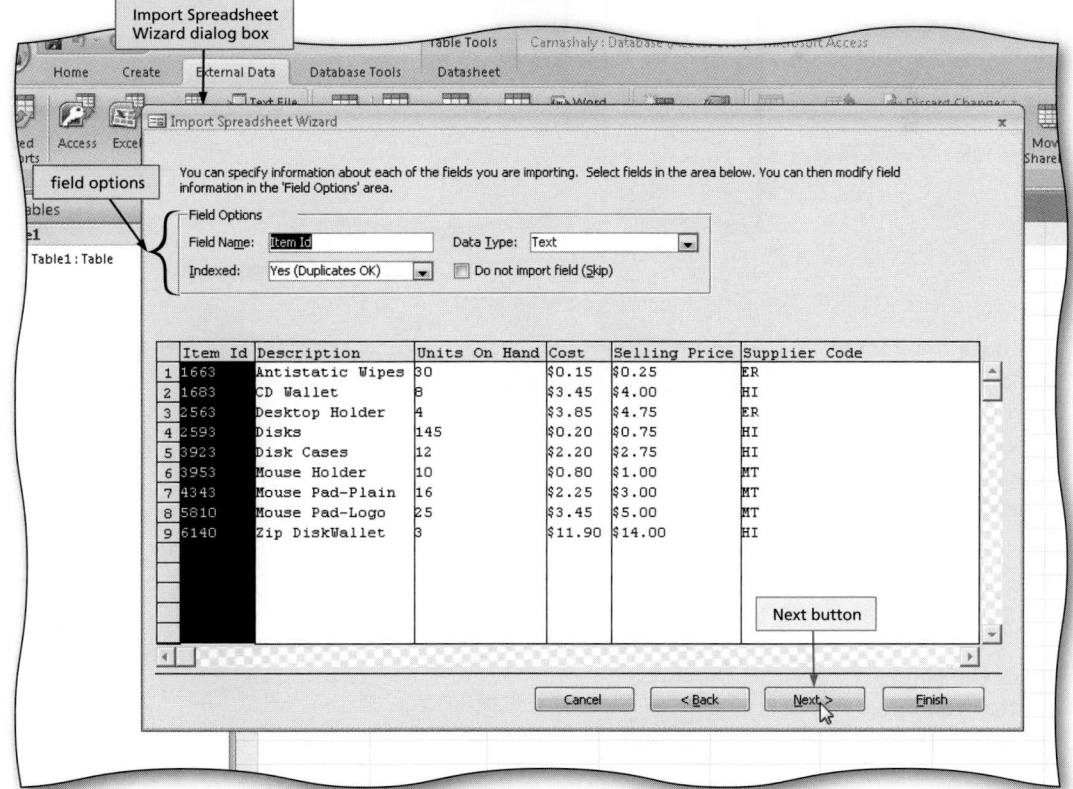

Figure 6

5

- Because the Field Options need not be specified, click the Next button (Figure 7).

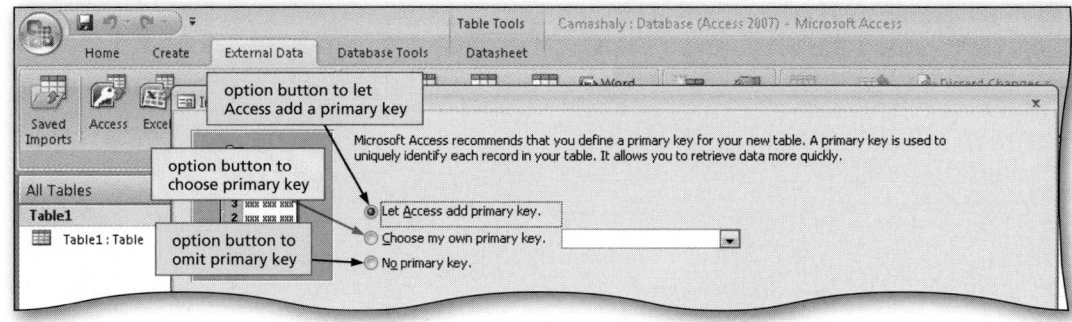

Figure 7

6

- Click the 'Choose my own primary key.' option button (Figure 8).

Q&A

How do I decide which option button to select?

If one of the fields is an appropriate primary key, choose your own primary key from the list of fields. If you are sure you do not want a primary key, choose No primary key. Otherwise, let Access add the primary key.

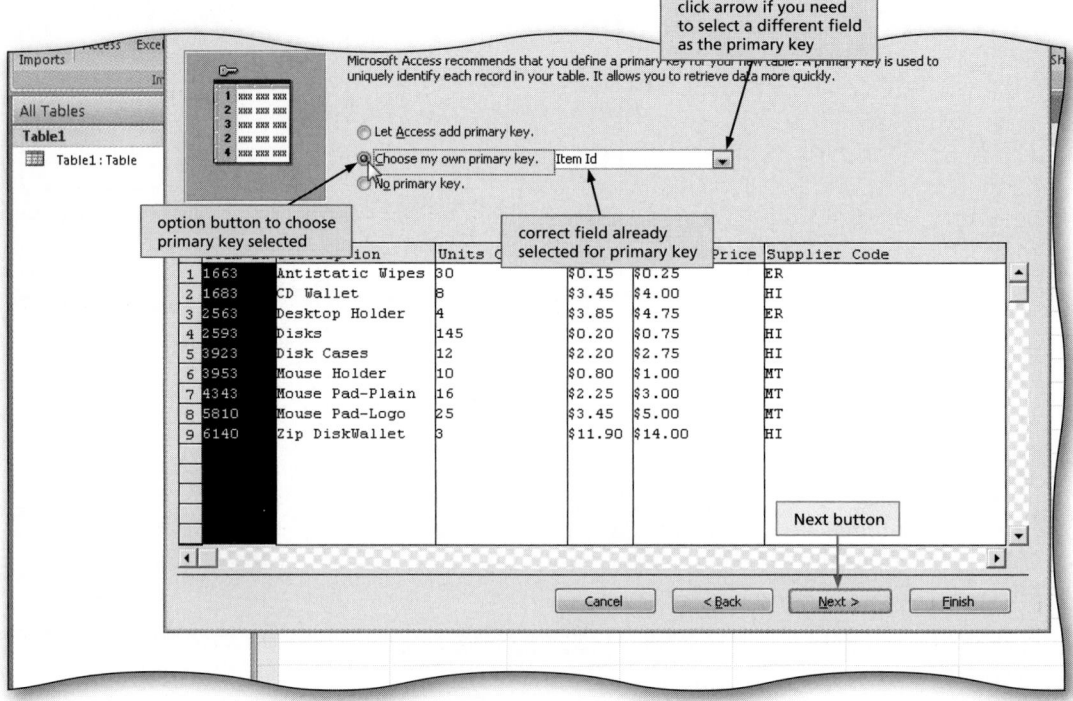

Figure 8

7

- Because the Item Id field, which is the correct field, is already selected as the primary key, click the Next button.

- Be sure Item appears in the Import to Table text box.

- Click the Finish button to import the data (Figure 9).

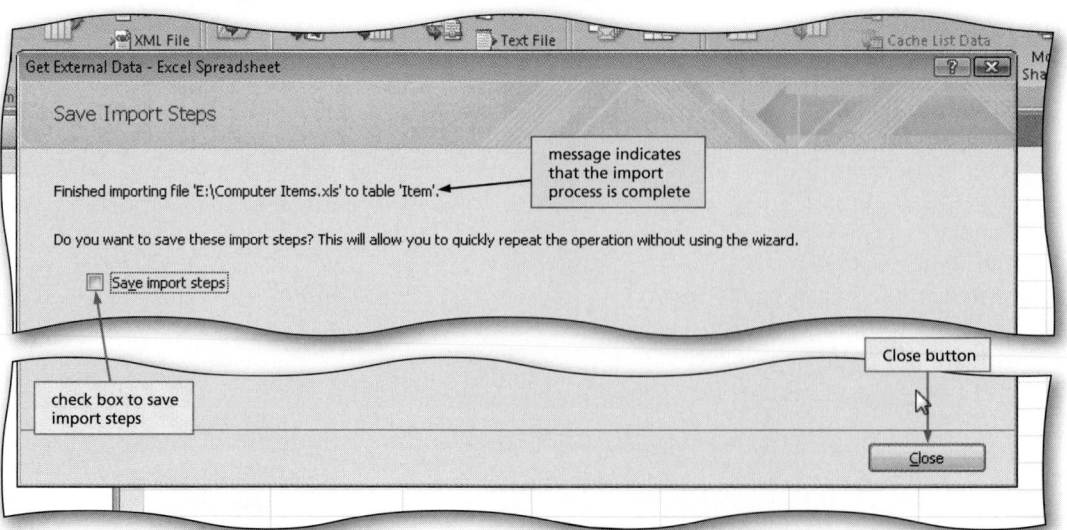

Figure 9

8

- Click the Save import steps check box to display the Save import steps options.

- If necessary, type Import-Computer Items in the Save as text box.

- Type Import data from Computer Items workbook into Item table in the Description text box (Figure 10).

When would I create an Outlook task?

If the import operation is one you will repeat on a regular basis, you can create and schedule the import process just as you can schedule any other Outlook task.

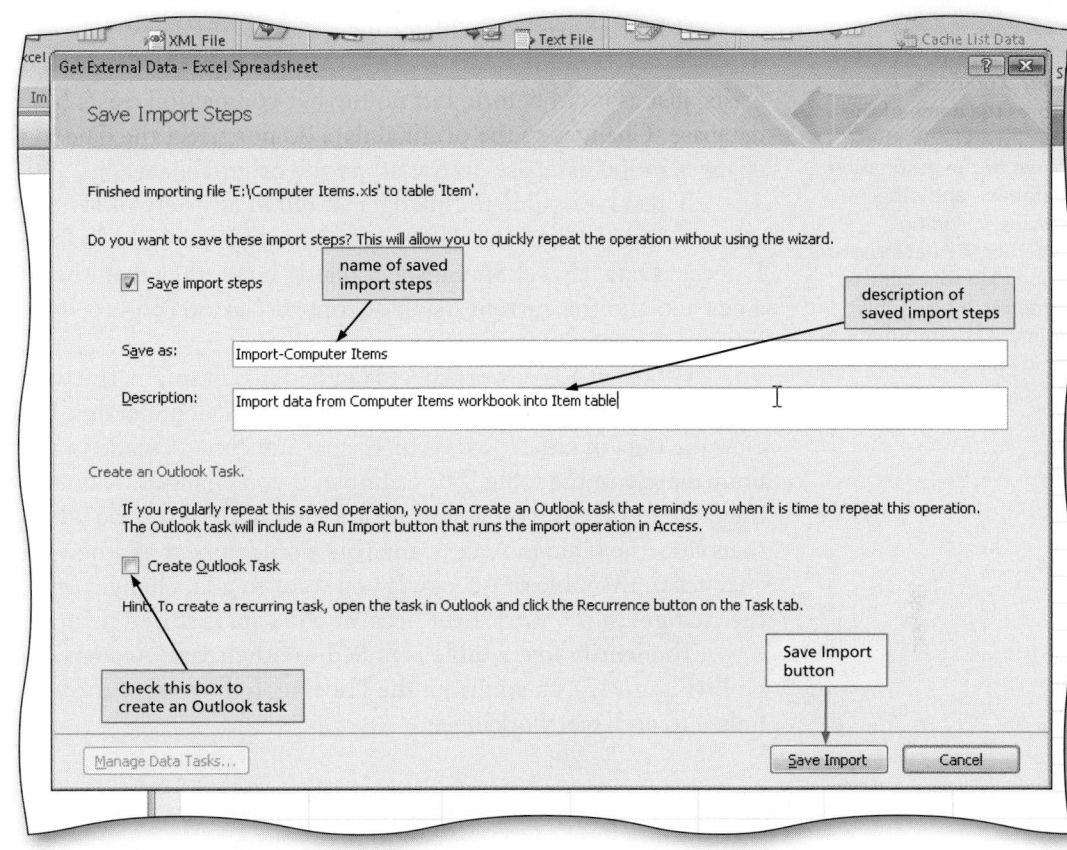

Figure 10

9

- Click the Save Import button to save the import steps (Figure 11).

Figure 11

Other Ways

1. Right-click Table1 : Table in Navigation Pane, point to Import, click appropriate file format

Using the Access Table

After the Access version of the table has been created, you can use it as you would any other table. You can open the table in Datasheet view (Figure 1b on page AC 207). You can make changes to the data. You can create queries or reports that use the data in the table.

By clicking Design View on the table's shortcut menu, you can view the table's structure and make any necessary changes to the structure. The changes may include changing field sizes and types (for those that may not be correct), creating indexes, specifying the primary key, or adding additional fields. If you have imported multiple tables that are to be related, you will need to relate the tables. To accomplish any of these tasks, use the same steps you used in Chapter 3.

BTW

Saving Import Steps
When you save the steps that import data from a Microsoft Office Excel 2007 workbook, Access stores the name of the Excel workbook, the name of the destination database, and other details, including whether the data was appended to a table or added to a new table, primary key information, field names, and so on.

Linking versus Importing

When an external table or worksheet is imported, or converted, into an Access database, a copy of the data is placed as a table in the database. The original data still exists, just as it did before, but no further connection exists between it and the data in the database. Changes to the original data do not affect the data in the database. Likewise, changes in the database do not affect the original data.

It also is possible to link data stored in a variety of formats to Access databases by selecting the 'Link to the data source by creating a linked table' option button on the Get External Data - Excel Spreadsheet dialog box rather than the 'Import the source data into a new table in the current database' option button (Figure 4 on page AC 212). With linking, the connection is maintained.

When an Excel worksheet is linked, for example, the worksheet is not stored in the database. Instead Access simply establishes a connection to the worksheet so you can view the data in either Access or Excel. Any change made in the worksheet will be visible immediately in the table. For example, if you change an address in Excel and then view the table in Access, you would see the new address. If you add a new row in Excel and then view the table in Access, the row would appear as a new record. You cannot make changes to the table in Access. If you want to add, change, or delete data, you must make the changes in the worksheet because the data is stored in an Excel workbook.

To identify that a table is linked to other data, Access places an arrow in front of the table (Figure 12). In addition, the Excel icon in front of the name indicates that the data is linked to an Excel worksheet.

Figure 12

The Linked Table Manager

After you link tables between a worksheet and a database or between two databases, you can modify many of the linked table's features. For example, you can rename the linked table, set view properties, and set links between tables in queries. If you move, rename, or modify linked tables, you can use the **Linked Table Manager** to update the links. To do so, click Database Tools on the Ribbon to display the Database Tools tab. Then click the Linked Table Manager button on the Database Tools tab. The Linked Table Manager dialog box that appears includes instructions on how to update the links.

To Close a Database

The following steps show how to close the database.

1 Click the Office Button to display the Office Button menu.

2 Click Close Database on the Office Button menu.

Importing from or Linking to Data in Another Access Database

Just as you can import data from an Excel worksheet, you can import data from another Access database. Similarly, just as you can link to data in an Excel worksheet, you can link to data in another Access database.

Identify sources of external data for the database: Access database.
You need to decide whether it is appropriate for you to import or link data in another Access database. The following are some common reasons for importing from or linking to another database:

1. You want to combine two databases into one. By importing, you can copy all objects (tables, queries, forms, reports, and so on) from one database to the other.

2. You want to create tables that are similar to tables in another database. When importing, you can choose to copy the table structure without the data. The table created in the process will have all the fields and field properties of the original, but will be empty.

3. You want to copy a collection of related objects from another database. In one operation you could, for example, copy a table along with all queries, forms, and reports that are based on that table.

4. You have several databases, but data in some tables is the same, for example, the Client table must be shared between some of the databases. By linking, any updates to the table in the source database are immediately available to anyone using any of the other databases.

Plan Ahead

TO IMPORT DATA FROM ANOTHER ACCESS DATABASE

The following steps would import data from another Access database into the database that is currently open.

1. Click the Access button in the Import group on the External Data tab.
2. Select the database containing the data to be imported.
3. Be sure the 'Import tables, queries, forms, reports, macros, and modules into the current database' option button is selected and click the OK button.
4. In the Import Objects dialog box, select the tables, queries, forms, reports, macros, and/or modules you wish to import and then click the OK button.
5. Decide if you wish to save the import steps.

TO LINK TO DATA IN ANOTHER ACCESS DATABASE

The following steps would link tables in another Access database into the database that is currently open.

1. Click the Access button in the Import group on the External Data tab.
2. Select the database containing the tables to be linked.
3. Click the 'Link to the data source by creating a linked table' option button to link and then click the OK button.
4. In the Link tables dialog box, select the tables you wish to link and then click the OK button.

Text Files

Text files contain unformatted characters including both readable characters, such as numbers and letters, and some special characters, such as tabs, carriage returns, and line feeds. Typical extensions for text files that can be imported or linked into Access databases are txt, csv, asc, and tab.

To be able to use a text file for importing or linking, it must be organized into records (rows) and fields (columns). Records and fields can be organized in two ways: delimited files and fixed-width files.

In **delimited files**, each record is on a separate line and the fields are separated by a special character, called the **delimiter**. Common delimiters are tabs, semicolons, commas, and spaces. You also can choose any other value that does not appear within the field contents. The csv (comma separated values) file often used in Excel is an example of a delimited file.

In **fixed-width files**, the width of any field is the same on every record. For example, if the width of the first field on the first record is 12 characters, the width of the first field on every other record also must be 12 characters.

Plan Ahead

Identify sources of external data for the database: text file.
You need to decide whether it is appropriate for you to use external data stored in a text file. The following are some common reasons for using a text file for this purpose:

1. Data that you want to import is not available in a format that Access recognizes. You first would export the data from the original application to a text file and then import that text file into Access.

2. You manage data in Access but regularly receive data in text files from other users that needs to be incorporated into your database.

Plan Ahead

Determine whether the data you have identified is in an appropriate format: text file.
Before importing or linking the text file you have identified, you need to make sure it is in an appropriate format. The following are some of the actions you should take to ensure correct format:

1. Make sure the data in the text file consistently follows one of the available formats (delimited or fixed width). If the file is delimited, identify the delimiter and make sure the same one is used throughout. If the file is fixed-width, make sure each field on each record is the same width.

2. Make sure that there are no blank records within the file. If there are, remove them prior to importing or linking.

3. Make sure there are no blank fields within the list. If there are, remove them prior to importing or linking.

4. For each field, make sure the entries in each record represent the same type of data.

5. If it is a delimited file, determine whether the first row contains column headings that will make appropriate field names in the resulting table. If not, you should add such a row. In general, the process is simpler if the first row in a delimited file contains appropriate column headings.

6. Make sure there are no extra paragraph (carriage) returns at the end of the file. If there are, remove them prior to importing or linking.

To Import Data from or Link Data to a Text File

To import data from or link data to a text file, you would use the following steps.

1. Click the Text File button in the Import group on the External Data tab.

2. Select the text file containing the data to be imported.

3. Be sure the 'Import the source into a new table in the current database' option button is selected if you wish to create a new table. Click the 'Append a copy of the records to the table' option button if you wish to add to an existing table, and then select the table. Click the 'Link to the data source by creating a linked table' option button if you wish to link the data. Once you have selected the correct option button, click the OK button.

4. Select the Delimited option button for a delimited file or the Fixed Width option button for a fixed-width file, and then click the Next button.

5a. For a delimited file, select the character that delimits the field values. If you know the file uses a text qualifier, which is a symbol used to enclose character values, select either the double quotation mark (") or the single quotation mark ('). If the first row contains field names, click the First Row contains Field Names check box. Once you have made your selections, click the Next button.

5b. For a fixed-width file, review the structure that Access recommends. If the recommended structure is not appropriate, follow the directions on the screen to add, remove, or adjust the lines. Once you have finished, click the Next button.

6. You can use the next screen if you need to change properties of one or more fields. When finished, click the Next button.

7. If you are importing, select the appropriate primary key, and then click the Next button. If you are linking, you will not have an opportunity to select a primary key.

8. Be sure the table name is correct, and then click the Finish button to import or link the data. Decide if you wish to save the import steps.

Using Saved Import Steps

You can use a set of saved import steps from within Access by clicking the Saved Imports button on the External Data tab. You then will see the Manage Data Tasks dialog box, as shown in Figure 13 on the next page. Select the set of saved import steps you want to repeat. (In this case only the import named Import-Computer Items exists.) Click the Run button to repeat the import steps you saved earlier. If you have created an Outlook task, you can schedule the import operation just as you schedule any other Outlook task.

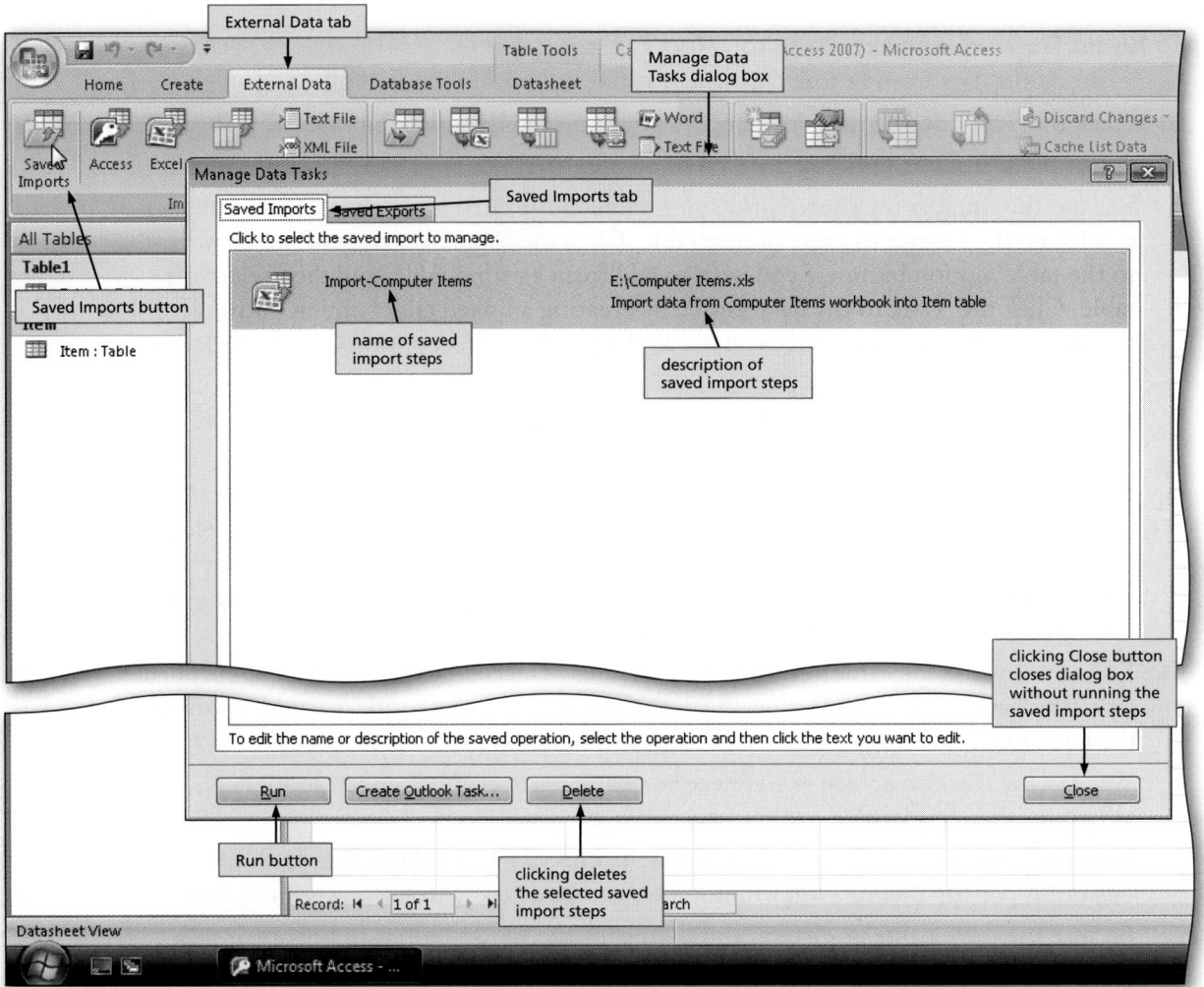

Figure 13

Exporting Data from Access to Other Applications

Exporting is the process of copying database objects to another database, to a worksheet, or to some other format so another application (for example, Excel) can use the data. Businesses need the flexibility of using the same data in different applications. For example, numerical data in a table exported to Excel could be analyzed using Excel's powerful statistical functions. Data also could be exported as an RTF file for use in marketing brochures.

To Open a Database

Before exporting the JSP Recruiters data, you first must open the database. The following steps open the database.

Note: If you are using Windows XP, see Appendix F for alternate steps.

1 With your USB flash drive connected to one of the computer's USB ports, click the More button to display the Open dialog box.

2 If the Folders list is displayed below the Folders button, click the Folders button to remove the Folders list.

3 If necessary, click Computer in the Favorite Links section and then double-click UDISK 2.0 (E:) to select the USB flash drive as the new open location. (Your drive letter might be different.)

4 Click JSP Recruiters to select the file name.

5 Click the Open button to open the database.

6 If a Security Warning appears, click the Options button to display the Microsoft Office Security Options dialog box.

7 Click the 'Enable this content' option button and then click the OK button to enable the content.

To Export Data to Excel

Once JSP Recruiters has decided to make the Recruiter-Client Query available to Excel users, it needs to export the data. To export data to Excel, select the table or query to be exported, and then click the Excel button in the Export group on the External Data tab. The following steps export the Client-Recruiter Query to Excel and save the export steps.

1

- Click the Recruiter-Client Query in the Navigation Pane to select it.

- Click External Data on the Ribbon to display the External Data tab (Figure 14).

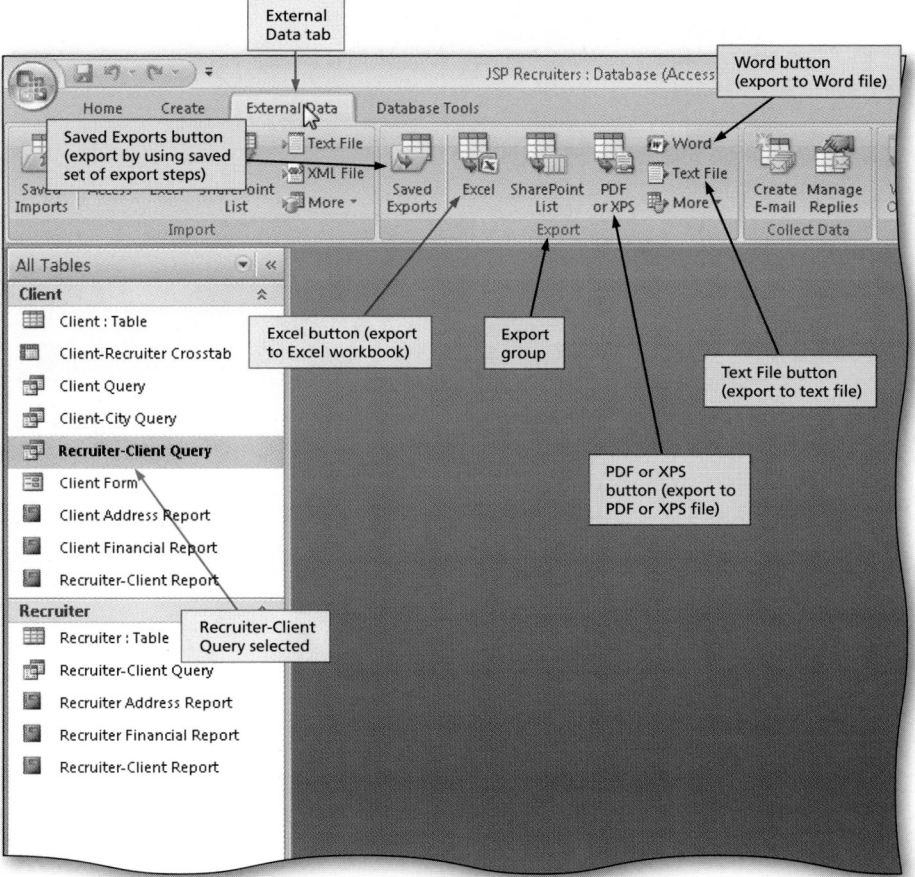

Figure 14

2

- **Click the Excel button in the Export group on the External Data tab to display the Export – Excel Spreadsheet dialog box.**
- **Click the Browse button and select your USB flash drive as the file location.**
- **Be sure the file name is Recruiter-Client Query and then click the Save button (Figure 15).**

Q&A Did I need to browse?

No. You could type the appropriate file location.

Q&A Could I change the name of the file?

You could change it. Simply replace the current file name with the one you want.

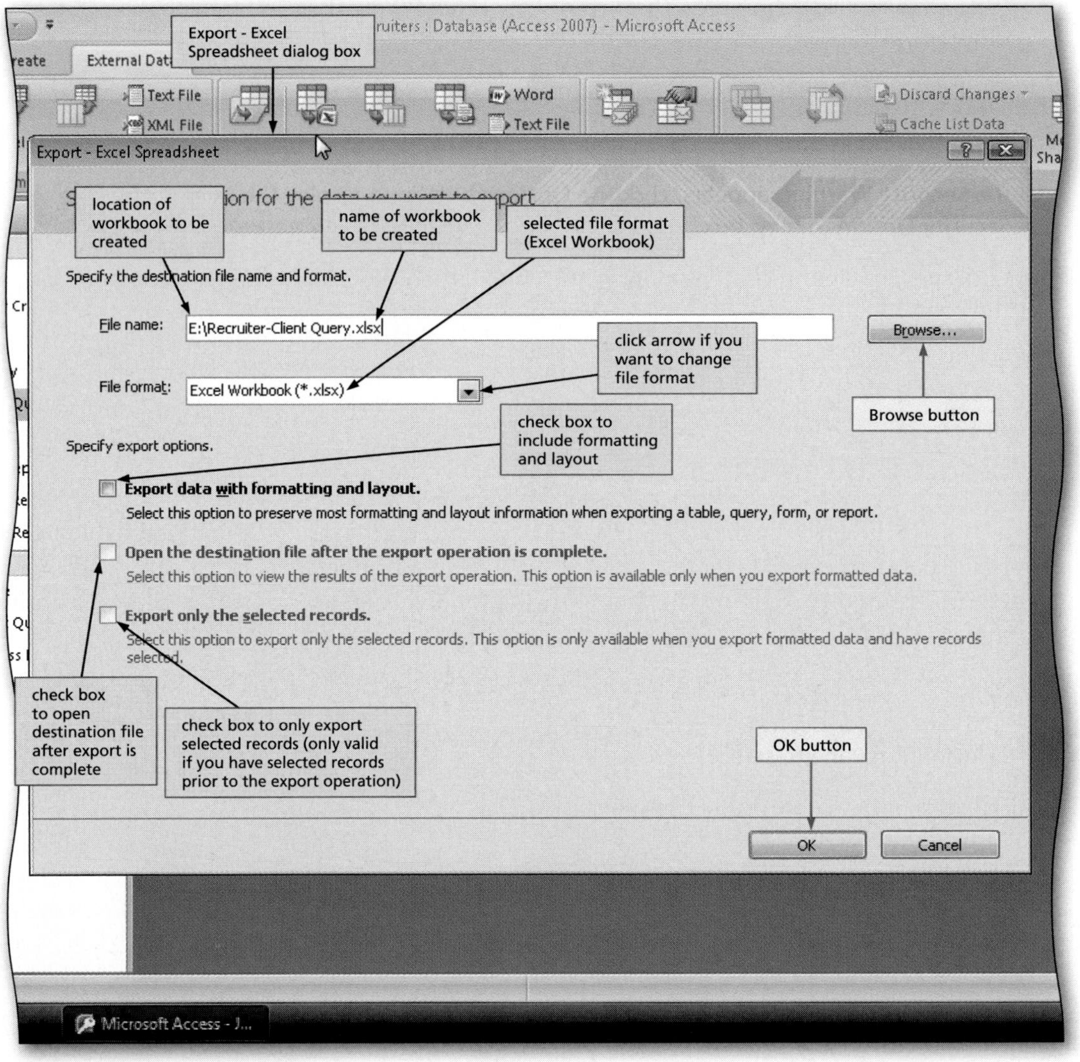
Export - Excel Spreadsheet dialog box
location of workbook to be created
name of workbook to be created
selected file format (Excel Workbook)
click arrow if you want to change file format
Browse button
check box to include formatting and layout
check box to open destination file after export is complete
check box to only export selected records (only valid if you have selected records prior to the export operation)
OK button
Export - Excel Spreadsheet
Specify the destination file name and format.
File name: E:\Recruiter-Client Query.xlsx
File format: Excel Workbook (*.xlsx)
Browse...
Specify export options.
Export data with formatting and layout.
Select this option to preserve most formatting and layout information when exporting a table, query, form, or report.
Open the destination file after the export operation is complete.
Select this option to view the results of the export operation. This option is available only when you export formatted data.
Export only the selected records.
Select this option to export only the selected records. This option is only available when you export formatted data and have records selected.
OK
Cancel

Figure 15

Q&A What if the file I want to export already exists?

Access will indicate that the file already exists and ask if you want to replace it. If you click the Yes button, the file you export will replace the old file. If you click the No button, you must either change the name of the export file or cancel the process.

3

- Click the OK button to export the data (Figure 16).

4

- Click the Save export steps check box to display the Save export steps options.

- If necessary, type Export-Recruiter-Client Query in the Save as text box.

- Type Export the Recruiter-Client Query without formatting in the Description text box.

- Click the Save Export button to save the export steps.

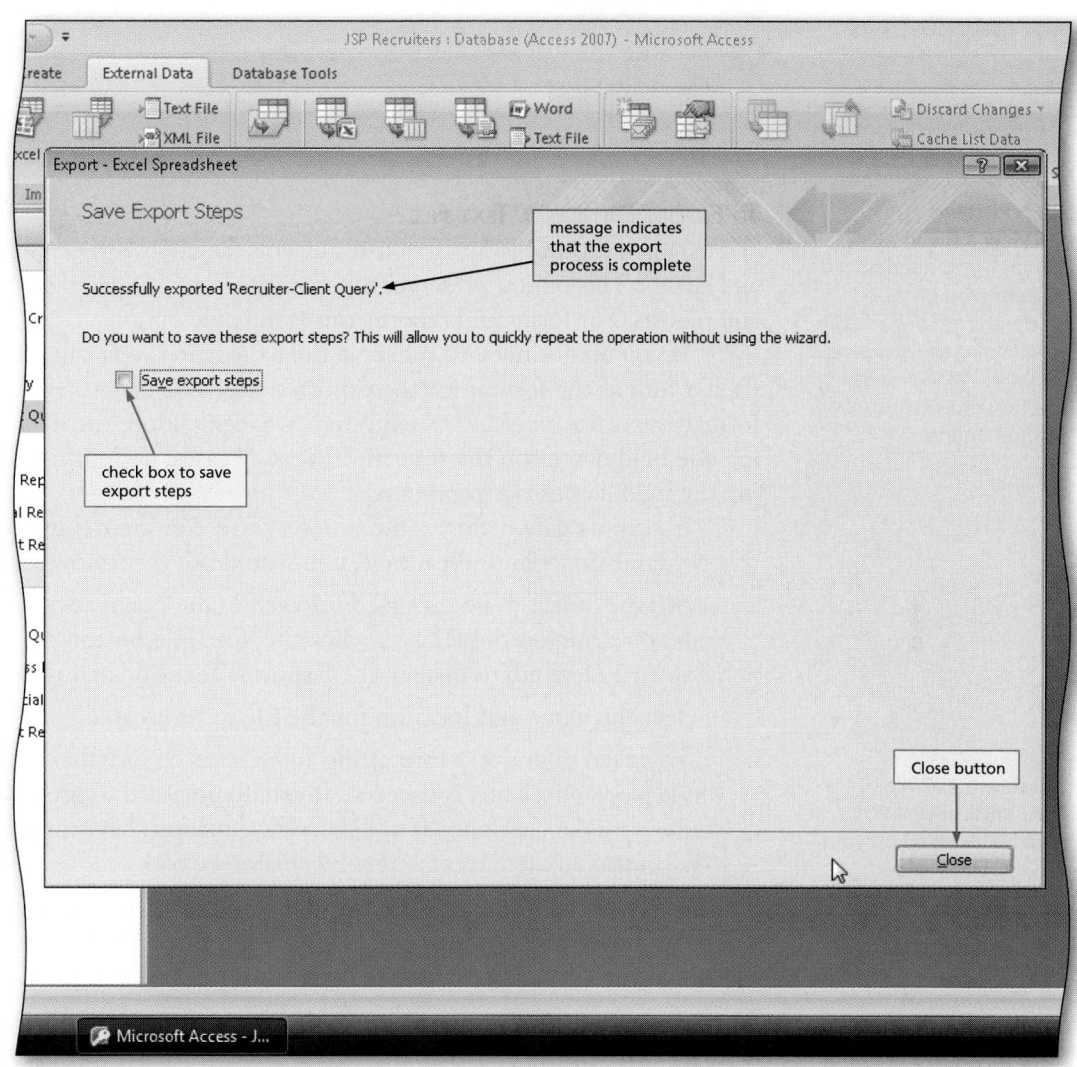

Figure 16

To Export Data to Word

Once JSP Recruiters has decided to also make the Recruiter-Client Query available to Word, it needs to export the data. There is a problem, however. It is not possible to export data to the standard Word format. It is possible, however to export the data as an RTF (rich text file), which Word can access. The following steps export the data to an RTF file. They do not save the export steps.

1 With the Recruiter-Client Query selected in the Navigation Pane and the External Data tab appearing on the screen, click the Word button in the Export group on the External Data tab to display the Export - RTF File dialog box.

2 Select your USB drive as the file location and make sure that Recruiter-Client Query is the file name.

③ If necessary, click the Save button and then click the OK button to export the data.

④ Because you will not save the export steps, click the Close button to close the Export - RTF File dialog box.

TO EXPORT DATA TO A TEXT FILE

When exporting data to a text file, you can choose to export the data with formatting and layout. This option preserves much of the formatting and layout in tables, queries, forms, and reports. For forms and reports, this is the only option.

If you do not need to preserve the formatting, you can choose either delimited or fixed-width as the format for the exported file. The most common option, especially if formatting is not an issue, is delimited. You can choose the delimiter and also whether to include field names on the first row. In many cases, delimiting with a comma and including the field names is a good choice.

To export data from a table or query to a comma-delimited file in which the first row contains the column headings, you would use the following steps.

1. With the object to be exported selected in the Navigation Pane and the External Data tab appearing on the Ribbon, click the Text File button in the Export group on the External Data tab to display the Export - Text File dialog box.

2. Select the name and location for the file to be created.

3. If you need to preserve formatting and layout, be sure the 'Export data with formatting and layout' check box is checked. If you do not need to preserve formatting and layout, make sure the check box is not checked. Once you have made your selection, click the OK button in the Export - Text File dialog box.

4. To create a delimited file, be sure the Delimited option button is selected. To create a fixed-width file, be sure the Fixed Width option button is selected. Once you have made your selection, click the Next button.

5a. If you are exporting to a delimited file, choose the delimiter that you want to separate your fields, such as a comma. Decide whether to include field names on the first row and, if so, click the Include Field Names on First Row check box. If you want to select a text qualifier, select it in the Text Qualifier list. When you have made your selections, click the Next button.

5b. If you are exporting to a fixed-width file, review the position of the vertical lines that separate your fields. If any lines are not positioned correctly, follow the directions on the screen to reposition them. When you have finished, click the Next button.

6. Click the Finish button to export the data.

7. Save the export steps if you wish, or simply click the Close button in the Export - Text File dialog box to close the dialog box without saving the export steps.

To Publish a Report

At JSP Recruiters, the staff would like to make the Recruiter Financial Report available through e-mail, which they can do by publishing the report as either a PDF or XPS file. The following steps publish the Recruiter Financial Report as an XPS file.

Note: If you are using Windows XP, see Appendix F for alternate steps.

- Click the Recruiter Financial Report in the Navigation Pane to select it.

- Click the 'PDF or XPS' button in the Export group on the External Data tab (see Figure 14 on page AC 221) to display the Publish as PDF or XPS dialog box.

- Select your USB drive as the file location. Make sure that Recruiter Financial Report is the file name and that XPS Document is the file type. If necessary, remove the check mark in the 'Open file after publishing' check box.

- Click the 'Standard (publishing online and printing)' option button to create a file that is appropriate for both publishing online and printing (Figure 17).

Q&A
How do I publish as PDF?
Change XPS Document to PDF in the Save as type box.

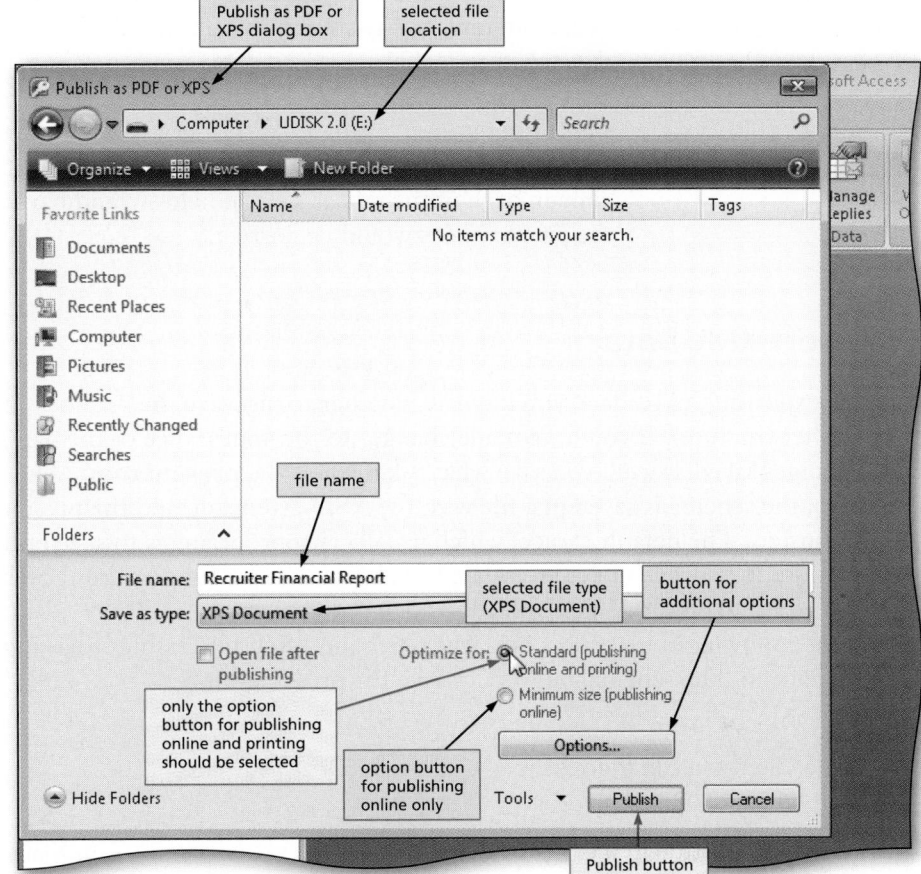

Figure 17

- Click the Publish button to publish the report as an XPS file.

- Because you will not save the export steps, click the Close button to close the Export - XPS dialog box.

Using Saved Export Steps

You can use a set of saved Export steps from within Access by clicking the Saved Exports button on the External Data tab. You then select the set of saved export steps you want to repeat and click the Run button in the Manage Data Tasks dialog box. If you have created an Outlook task, you can schedule the export operation just as you can schedule any other Outlook task.

BTW

Viewing or Printing the Report
To view or print the report stored in the XPS file, use the XML Paper Specification Viewer. If the XML Paper Specification Viewer is not installed on your system, you can obtain it from Microsoft. If you are unable to view or print XPS files, you alternatively can publish the report as a PDF. To do so, change the Save as type from XPS Document to PDF before clicking the Publish button.

BTW

Saving Export Steps
When you save the steps that export formatted data to Microsoft Office Excel or Word 2007, the current filter and column settings of the source object in Access are saved. If the source object (table, query, form, or report) is open when you run the export steps, Access exports only the data that is currently displayed in the view.

XML

Just as Hypertext Markup Language (HTML) is the standard language for creating and displaying Web pages, **Extensible Markup Language (XML)** is the standard language for describing and delivering data on the Web. Another way of viewing the difference is that HTML handles the *appearance* of data within a Web page, whereas XML handles the *meaning* of data. XML is a data interchange standard that allows you to exchange data between dissimilar systems or applications. With XML, you can describe both the data and the structure **(schema)** of the data. You can export tables, queries, forms, or reports.

When exporting XML data, you can choose to export multiple related tables in a single operation to a single XML file. If you later import this XML data to another database, you will import all the tables in a single operation. Thus, the new database would contain each of the tables. All the fields would have the correct data types and sizes and the primary keys would be correct.

To Export XML Data

In exporting XML data, you indicate whether to just save the data or to save both the data and the schema (that is, the structure). If you have made changes to the appearance of the data, such as changing the font, and want these changes saved as well, you save what is known as the **presentation**. The data is saved in a file with the XML extension, the schema is saved in a file with the XSD extension, and the presentation is saved in a file with the XSL extension. The default choice, which usually is appropriate, is to save both the data and schema, but not the presentation. If multiple tables are related, such as the Client and Recruiter tables in the JSP Recruiters data, you can export both tables to a single file.

The following steps export both the Client and Recruiter tables to a single XML file called Client. The steps save the data and the schema, but do not save the presentation.

- Click the Client table in the Navigation Pane to select it.

- Click the More button in the Export group on the External Data tab to display the More button menu with additional export options (Figure 18).

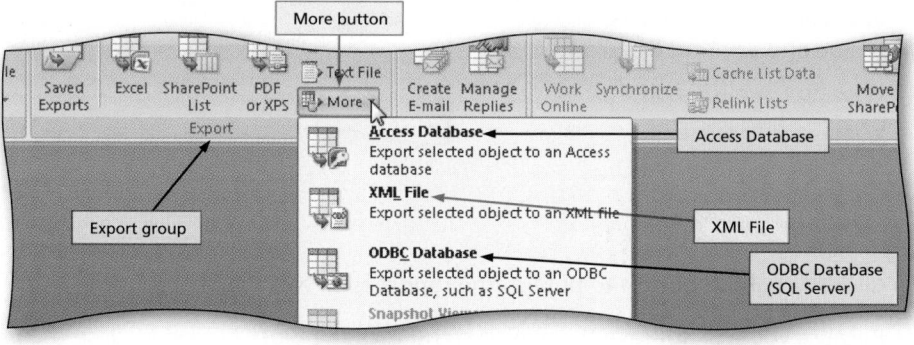

Figure 18

- Click XML File on the More button menu to display the Export - XML File dialog box.

- Select your USB drive as the file location and make sure that Client is the file name (Figure 19).

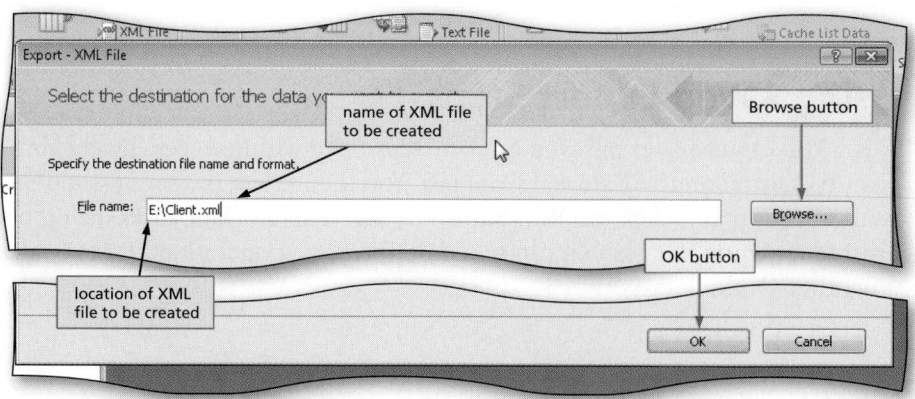

Figure 19

3

- Click the OK button to display the Export XML dialog box (Figure 20).

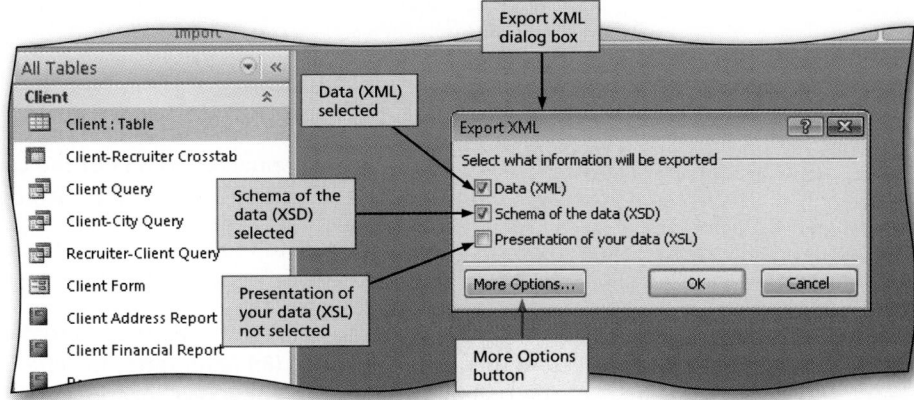

Figure 20

4

- Click the More Options button to specify additional options (Figure 21).

Q&A

What is the purpose of the other tabs in this dialog box?

You can use the Schema tab to indicate whether you want primary key, index information, table properties, and field properties included (normally they are) and whether the schema information is to be stored in a separate file (normally it is). If you want to export the presentation, you can use the Presentation tab to indicate this fact and also specify options concerning how the Presentation will be exported.

Figure 21

5

- Click the expand indicator (the plus sign) to the left of [Lookup Data], and then click the Recruiter check box to select the Recruiter table (Figure 22).

6

- Click the OK button to export the data.

- Because you will not save the export steps, click the Close button to close the Export - XML File dialog box.

- Click the Close Database command on the Office Button menu.

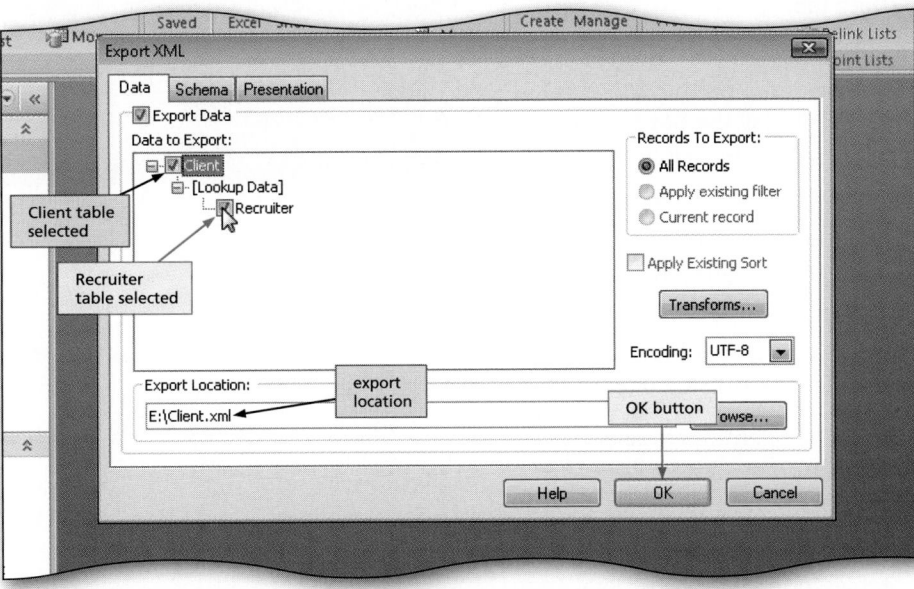

Figure 22

To Create a New Database

Before importing the data from the JSP Recruiters database, you need to create the new JSP Consulting database that will contain the data. The following steps create the JSP Consulting database on a USB flash drive.

1 With a USB flash drive connected to one of the computer's USB ports, click Blank Database in the Getting Started with Microsoft Office Access screen to create a new blank database.

2 Type `JSP Consulting` in the File Name text box and then click the 'Browse for a location to put your database' button to display the File New Database dialog box.

3 Click Computer in the Favorite Links section to display a list of available drives and folders and then click UDISK 2.0 (E:) (your letter may be different) in the Computer list to select the USB flash drive as the new save location.

4 Click the OK button to select the USB flash drive as the location for the database and to return to the Getting Started with Microsoft Office Access screen.

5 Click the Create button to create the database on the USB flash drive with the file name, JSP Consulting.

BTW

Quick Reference
For a table that lists how to complete the tasks covered in this book using the mouse, Ribbon, shortcut menu, and keyboard, see the Quick Reference Summary at the back of this book, or visit the Access 2007 Quick Reference Web page (scsite.com/ac2007/qr).

To Import XML Data

The following steps import both the Client and Recruiter tables stored in the XML file called Client. In addition to having the same data, the fields in both tables will have precisely the same data types and sizes as in the original database. Also, the same fields will have been designated primary keys.

1

• With the JSP Consulting database open, click External Data on the Ribbon to display the External Data tab.

• Click the XML File button in the Import group on the External Data tab to display the Get External Data - XML File dialog box.

• Click the Browse button in the Get External Data - XML File dialog box to display the File Open dialog box.

• Click Computer and then double-click UDISK 2.0 (E:).

• Click the Client file to select it (Figure 23).

Q&A

Should I click the xsd version?

No. If you do, you will import both tables, but none of the data. That is, the tables will be empty.

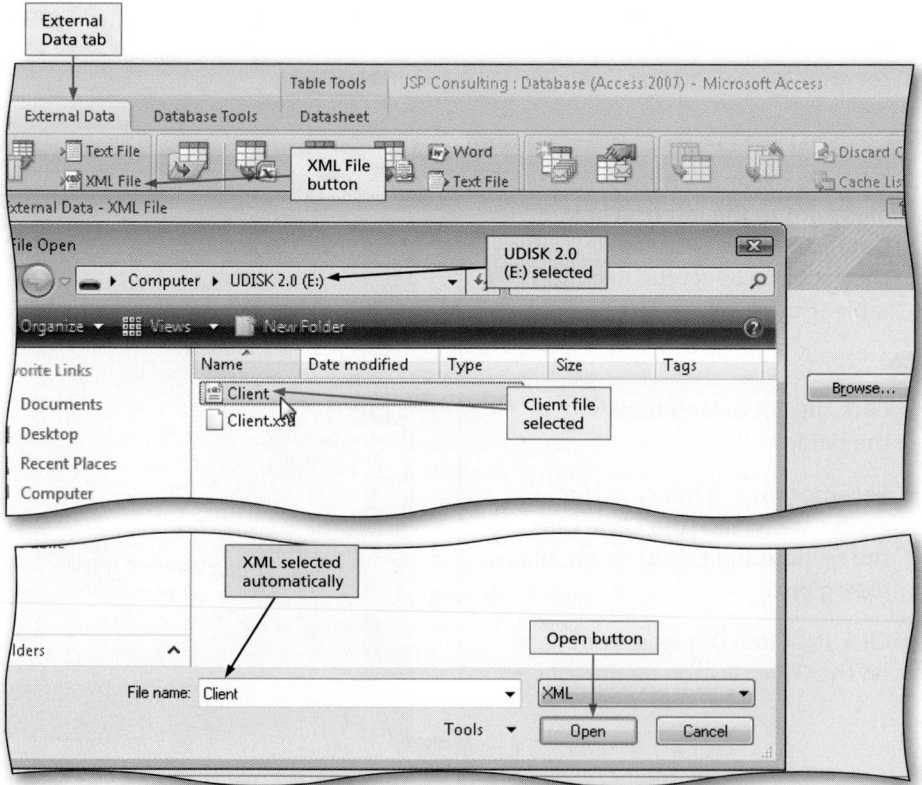

Figure 23

2

- Click the Open button to return to the Get External Data - XML File dialog box (Figure 24).

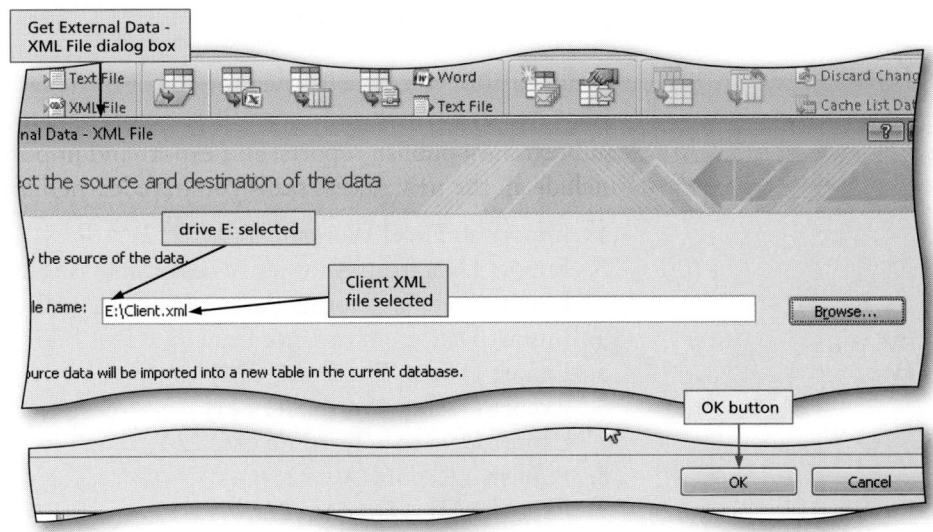

Figure 24

3

- Click the OK button to display the Import XML dialog box (Figure 25).

4

- Be sure the Structure and Data option button is selected and then click the OK button to import the data.

- Because you will not save the import steps, click the Close button to close the Get External Data - XML File dialog box.

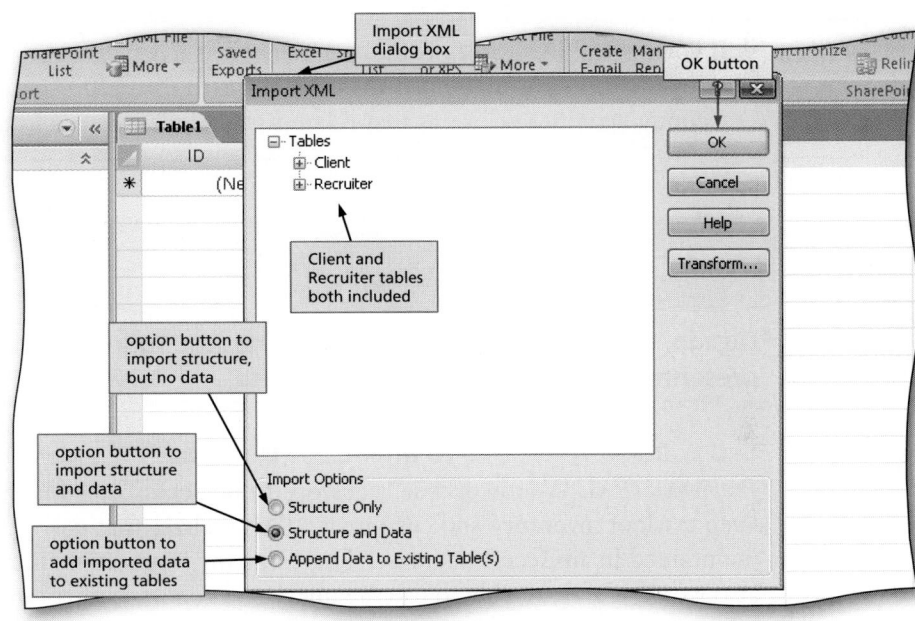

Figure 25

To Quit Access

You are ready to quit Access. The following step quits Access.

1 Click the Close button on the right side of the Access title bar to quit Access.

BTW

Certification
The Microsoft Certified Application Specialist (MCAS) program provides an opportunity for you to obtain a valuable industry credential — proof that you have the Access 2007 skills required by employers. For more information, see Appendix G or visit the Access 2007 Certification Web page (scsite.com/ac2007/cert).

Feature Summary

In this feature you have learned to import from and link to data in Excel worksheets, other Access databases, and text files; export data to Excel worksheets, Word documents, and text files; publish reports; and export and import XML data. The items listed below include all the new Access skills you have learned in this chapter.

1. Import an Excel Worksheet (AC 212)
2. Import Data from Another Access Database (AC 217)
3. Link to Data in Another Access Database (AC 217)
4. Import Data from or Link Data to a Text File (AC 219)
5. Export Data to Excel (AC 221)
6. Export Data to Word (AC 223)
7. Export Data to a Text File (AC 224)
8. Publish a Report (AC 225)
9. Export XML Data (AC 226)
10. Import XML Data (AC 228)

If you have a SAM user profile, you may have access to hands-on instruction, practice, and assessment. Log in to your SAM account (http://sam2007.course.com) to launch any assigned training activities or exams that relate to the skills covered in this feature.

In the Lab

Design, create, modify, and/or use a database following the guidelines, concepts, and skills presented in this feature.

Lab 1: Importing Data to an Access Database

Problem: TAL Woodworks sells custom wood accessories for the home. TAL uses worksheets to keep track of inventory and customers. TAL realizes that customer data would be better handled if maintained in an Access database. The company wants to maintain the products inventory in Excel but also would like to be able to use the query and report features of Access.

Instructions: For this assignment, you will need two files: Customer.csv and Product.xlsx. See the inside back cover of this book for instructions for downloading the Data Files for Students, or see your instructor for information on accessing the files required in this book. Perform the following tasks:

1. Start Access and create a new database in which to store all the objects for TAL Woodworks. Call the database TAL Woodworks.

2. Import the Customer worksheet shown in Figure 26 into Access. The worksheet is saved as a .csv file.

	A	B	C	D	E	F	G	H	I	J	K
1	Customer Number	Name	Address	City	State	Balance					
2	AD23	Adson Gifts	407 Mallory	Tourin	CO	$ 205.00					
3	AR75	Arthur's Interiors	200 Mimberly	Denton	CO	$ 180.00					
4	BE28	Becker Design	224 Harbor Oak	Charleston	CO	$ 170.00					
5	CR66	Casa Grande	506 Mallory	Tourin	CO	$0.00					
6	DL60	Dee's Things	123 Village	Denton	CO	$ 235.00					
7	GR36	Grande Casa	1345 Fern	Charleston	CO	$ 204.00					
8	HA09	Hal's Gifts	568 Denmer	Berridge	CO	$ 245.00					
9	ME17	My House	879 Vinca	Berls	CO	$ 268.00					
10	RO44	Royal Interiors	677 Liatris	Berridge	CO	$0.00					
11	ST22	Steedman's	889 Lantana	Berls	CO	$ 123.00					
12											
13											
14											

Figure 26

3. Use Customer as the name of the table and Customer Number as the primary key.

4. Save the import steps. Be sure to enter a description for the saved steps.

5. Link the Product worksheet shown in Figure 27 to the database.

	A	B	C	D	E	F	G	H	I	J	K	L
1	Product Code	Description	On Hand	Cost	Selling Price							
2	101	Candy Dish	10	$4.00	$6.00							
3	103	Letter Opener	15	$2.00	$3.00							
4	104	Tray	5	$10.00	$15.00							
5	106	Salad Tongs	20	$3.00	$5.00							
6	110	Lazy Susan	8	$16.00	$20.00							
7	112	Spoon Set	21	$12.00	$14.00							
8	113	Salad Bowl	9	$18.00	$25.00							
9	115	Desk Organizer	8	$22.00	$30.00							
10	120	Book Ends	4	$27.00	$34.00							
11	121	Mobile	7	$34.00	$40.00							
12												
13												
14												

Figure 27

6. Rename the linked Product table as Inventory. Then, use the Linked Table Manager to update the link between the Excel worksheet and the Access table.

7. Import the Sales Rep table from the Ada Beauty Supply database that you modified in In the Lab 3 in Chapter 3 on page AC 201. (If you did not complete this exercise, see your instructor for a copy of the modified database.) Sales reps of Ada often sell gift items to salons.

8. Change the database properties, as specified by your instructor. Submit the database in the format specified by your instructor.

In the Lab

Lab 2: Exporting Data to Other Applications

Problem: JMS TechWizards wants to be able to export some of the data in its Access database to other applications. JMS wants to export the City-Technician Crosstab query for further processing in Excel. It also wants to use the Technician table in a Word document as well as e-mail the Salary Report to the company's accounting firm. The company has decided to branch out and offer consulting services. It wants to export the Client and Technician tables as a single XML file and then import it to a new database.

Instructions: Start Access. Open the JMS TechWizards database that you modified in In the Lab 1 in Chapter 3 on page AC 195. (If you did not complete this exercise, see your instructor for a copy of the modified database.) Perform the following tasks:

1. Export the City-Technician Crosstab query to Excel as shown in Figure 28. Save the export steps. Be sure to include a description.

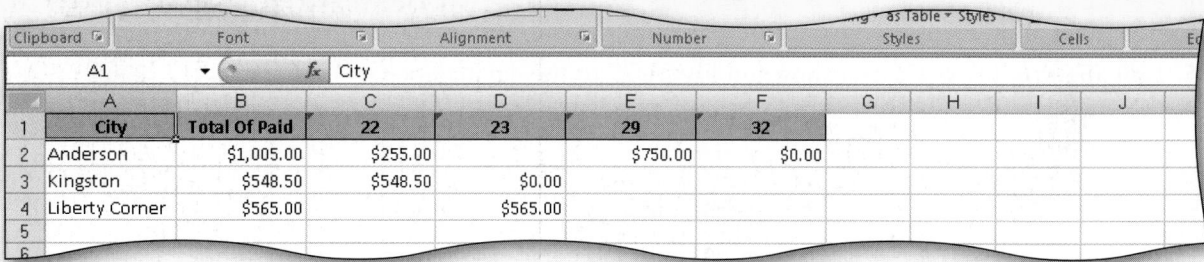

Figure 28

2. Export the Technician table to a Word document. Do not save the export steps.

3. Publish the Salary Report as an XPS file.

4. Export both the Client and Technician tables in XML format. Be sure that both tables are exported to the same file. Do not save the export steps.

5. Create a new database called JMS TechConsultants.

6. Import the Client XML file containing both the Client and Technician tables to the JMS TechConsultants database.

7. Submit the Excel workbook, Word document, XPS file, and JMS TechConsultants database in the format specified by your instructor.

1 | Creating and Editing a Presentation

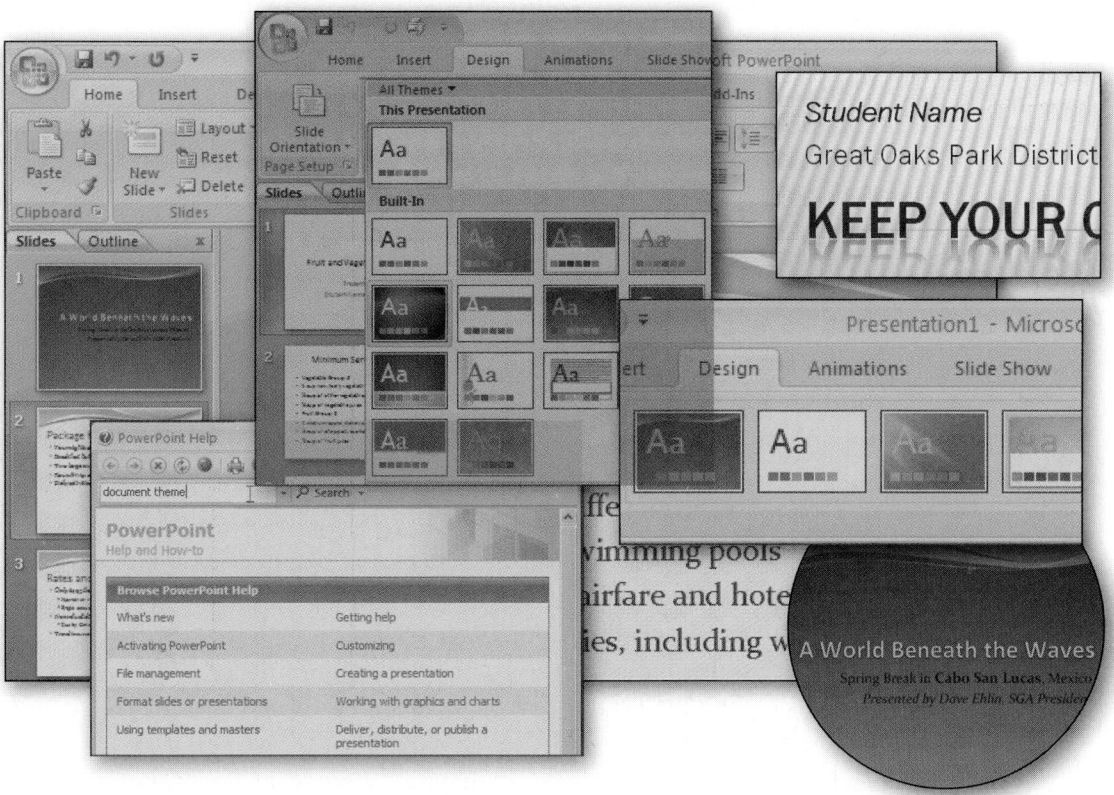

Objectives

You will have mastered the material in this chapter when you can:

- Start and quit PowerPoint
- Describe the PowerPoint window
- Select a document theme
- Create a title slide and text slides with single- and multi-level bulleted lists
- Save a presentation
- Copy elements from one slide to another

- View a presentation in Slide Show view
- Open a presentation
- Display and print a presentation in grayscale
- Check spelling
- Use PowerPoint Help

1 | Creating and Editing a Presentation

What Is Microsoft Office PowerPoint 2007?

Microsoft Office PowerPoint 2007 is a complete presentation graphics program that allows you to produce professional-looking presentations (Figure 1–1). A PowerPoint **presentation** also is called a **slide show**.

PowerPoint contains several features to simplify creating a slide show. For example, the results-oriented user interface can boost productivity by making tasks and options readily accessible. Professionally designed standard layouts help you save time by formatting and creating content. You then can modify these layouts to create custom slides to fit your specific needs. To make your presentation more impressive, you can add diagrams, tables, pictures, video, sound, and animation effects. Additional PowerPoint features include the following:

- **Word processing** — Create bulleted lists, combine words and images, find and replace text, and use multiple fonts and type sizes.
- **Outlining** — Develop your presentation using an outline format. You also can import outlines from Microsoft Word or other word processing programs.
- **Charting** — Create and insert charts into your presentations and then add effects and chart elements.
- **Drawing** — Form and modify diagrams using shapes such as arcs, arrows, cubes, rectangles, stars, and triangles. Then apply Quick Styles to customize and add effects. Arrange these objects by sizing, scaling, and rotating.
- **Inserting multimedia** — Insert artwork and multimedia effects into your slide show. The Microsoft Clip Organizer contains hundreds of media files, including pictures, photos, sounds, and movies.
- **Saving to the Web** — Save presentations or parts of a presentation in HTML format so they can be viewed and manipulated using a browser. You can publish your slide show to the Internet or to an intranet.
- **E-mailing** — Send your entire slide show as an attachment to an e-mail message.
- **Collaborating** — Share your presentation with friends and coworkers. Ask them to review the slides and then insert comments that offer suggestions to enhance the presentation.
- **Preparing delivery** — Rehearse integrating PowerPoint slides into your speech by setting timings, using presentation tools, showing only selected slides in a presentation, and packaging the presentation for a CD.

This latest version of PowerPoint has many new features to increase your productivity. Graphics and other shape effects allow you to add glow, shadowing, 3-D effects, and other appealing visuals. Typography effects enhance the design's impact. PowerPoint themes apply a consistent look to each graphic, font, and table color in an entire presentation. Digital signatures enable you to verify that no one has altered your presentation since you created it, and the Document Inspector removes private data, such as comments and hidden text.

PowerPoint gives you the flexibility to make presentations using a projection device attached to a personal computer or using overhead transparencies. In addition, you can take advantage of the World Wide Web and run virtual presentations on the Internet. PowerPoint also can create paper printouts of the individual slides, outlines, and speaker notes.

Project Planning Guidlines

The process of developing a presentation that communicates specific information requires careful analysis and planning. As a starting point, establish why the presentation is needed. Next, analyze the intended audience for the presentation and their unique needs. Then, gather information about the topic and decide what to include in the presentation. Finally, determine the presentation design and style that will be most successful at delivering the message. Details of these guidelines are provided in Appendix A. In addition, each project in this book provides practical applications of these planning considerations.

Project — Presentation with Bulleted Lists

In Project 1, you will follow proper design guidelines and learn to use PowerPoint to create, save, and print the slides shown in Figures 1–1a through 1–1e on this page and the next. The objective is to produce a presentation, called A World Beneath the Waves, to help the Student Government Association (SGA) President, Dave Ehlin, promote the annual spring break diving and snorkeling trip to Cabo San Lucas, Mexico. This slide show presents the highlights of this trip and promotes the included amenities, tour prices, and the inviting Pacific waters. Some of the text will have formatting and color enhancements. In addition, you will print handouts of your slides to distribute to students.

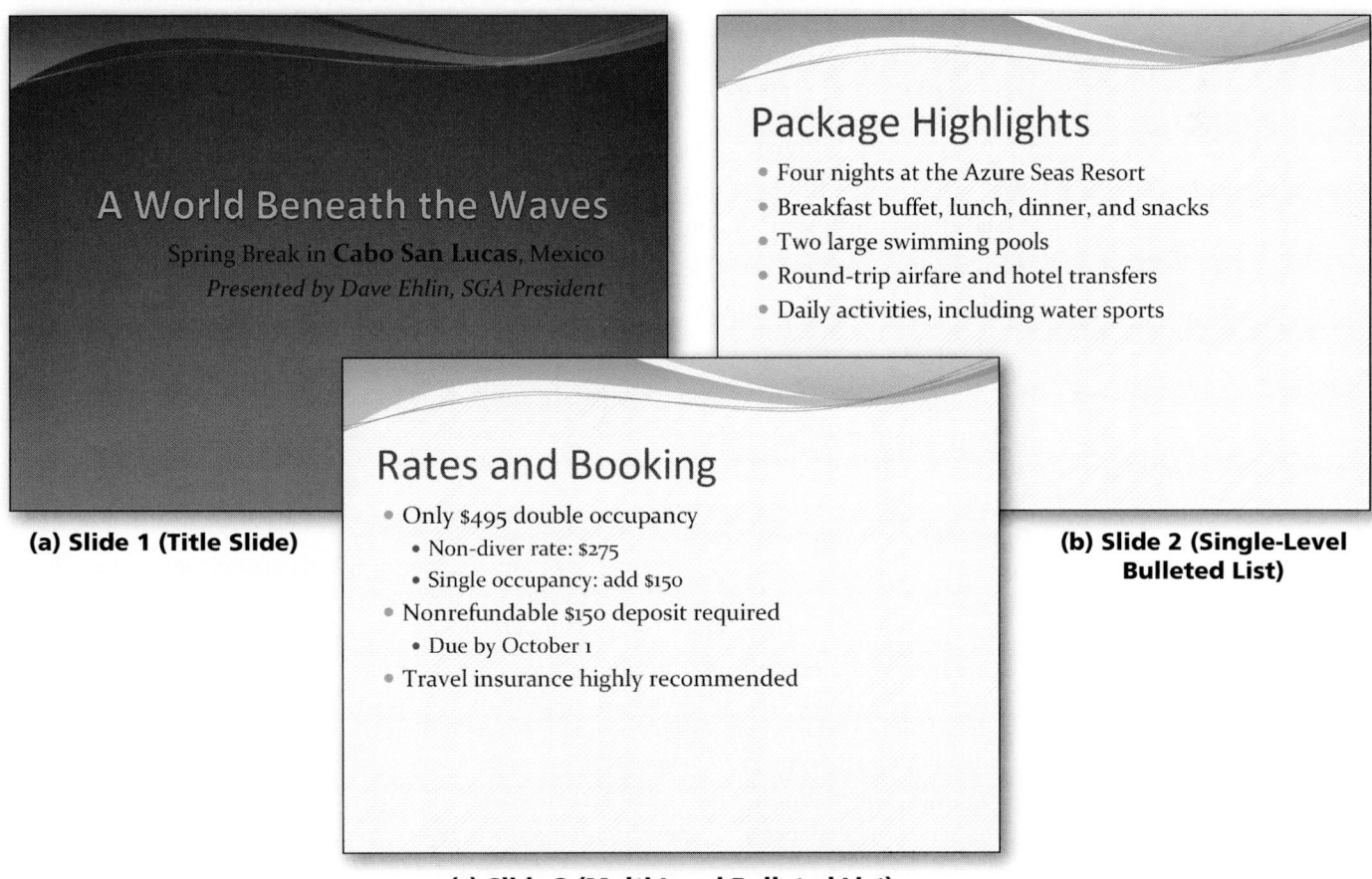

(a) Slide 1 (Title Slide)

(b) Slide 2 (Single-Level Bulleted List)

(c) Slide 3 (Multi-Level Bulleted List)

Figure 1–1

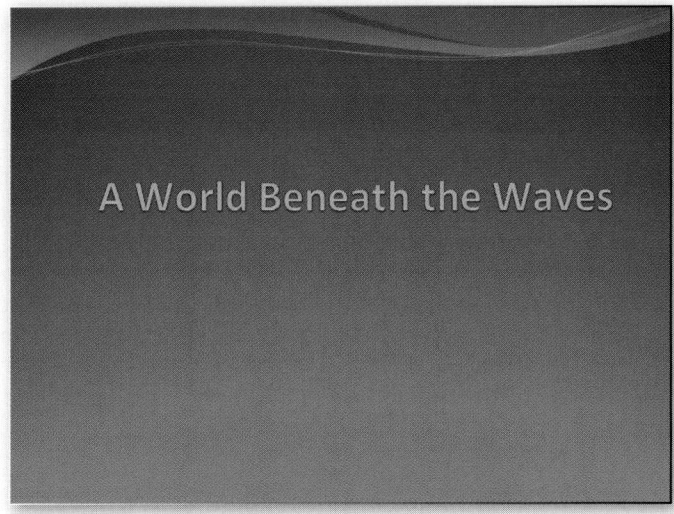

Snorkeling and Diving

- Three days of two-tank boat dives
  - Weights and tanks included
    - Instructors available for beginners
- Various locations based on diving skills
  - Spectacular underwater wildlife and landscapes
    - See squids, sea turtles, snakes, barracudas, and stingrays

(d) Slide 4 (Multi-Level Bulleted List)   **(e) Slide 5 (Closing Slide)**

Figure 1–1 (continued)

PowerPoint allows you to produce slides to use in an academic, business, or other environment. One of the more common uses of these slides is to enhance an oral presentation. A speaker may desire to convey information, such as urging students to participate in a food drive, explaining first aid, or describing the changes in an employee benefit package. The PowerPoint slides should reinforce the speaker's message and help the audience members retain the information presented. An accompanying handout gives audience members reference notes and review material after the presentation's conclusion.

Overview

As you read this chapter, you will learn how to create the presentation shown in Figure 1–1 by performing these general tasks:

- Select an appropriate document theme.
- Enter titles and text on slides.
- Change the size, color, and style of text.
- View the presentation on your computer.
- Save the presentation so you can modify and view it at a later time.
- Print handouts of your slides.

Plan Ahead

General Project Guidelines

When creating a PowerPoint document, the actions you perform and decisions you make will affect the appearance and characteristics of the finished document. As you create a presentation such as the project shown in Figure 1–1, you should follow these general guidelines:

1. **Find the appropriate theme.** The overall appearance of a presentation significantly affects its capability to communicate information clearly. The slides' graphical appearance should support the presentation's overall message. Colors, fonts, and layouts affect how audience members perceive and react to the slide content.

2. **Choose words for each slide.** Use the less is more principle. The less text, the more likely the slides will enhance your speech. Use the fewest words possible to make a point.

(continued)

(continued)

Plan Ahead

3. **Format specific elements of the text.** Examples of how you can modify the appearance, or **format**, of text include changing its shape, size, color, and position on the slide.

4. **Determine where to save the presentation.** You can store a document permanently, or **save** it, on a variety of storage media including a hard disk, USB flash drive, or CD. You also can indicate a specific location on the storage media for saving the document.

   When necessary, more specific details concerning the above guidelines are presented at appropriate points in the chapter. The chapter also will identify the actions performed and decisions made regarding these guidelines during the creation of the slides shown in Figure 1–1.

Starting PowerPoint

If you are using a computer to step through the project in this chapter and you want your screen to match the figures in this book, you should change your screen's resolution to 1024 × 768. For information about how to change a computer's resolution, read Appendix E.

Note: If you are using Windows XP, see Appendix F for alternate steps.

BTW

Decreasing Resolution
You may need to decrease your computer's resolution if you know you are going to run your presentation on another computer that uses a lower resolution, such as 800 × 600 or 640 × 480. This lower resolution, however, may affect the appearance of your slides.

To Start PowerPoint

The following steps, which assume Windows Vista is running, start PowerPoint based on a typical installation. You may need to ask your instructor how to start PowerPoint for your computer.

1
- Click the Start button on the Windows Vista taskbar to display the Start menu.
- Click All Programs at the bottom of the left pane on the Start menu to display the All Programs list.
- Click Microsoft Office in the All Programs list to display the Microsoft Office (Figure 1–2).

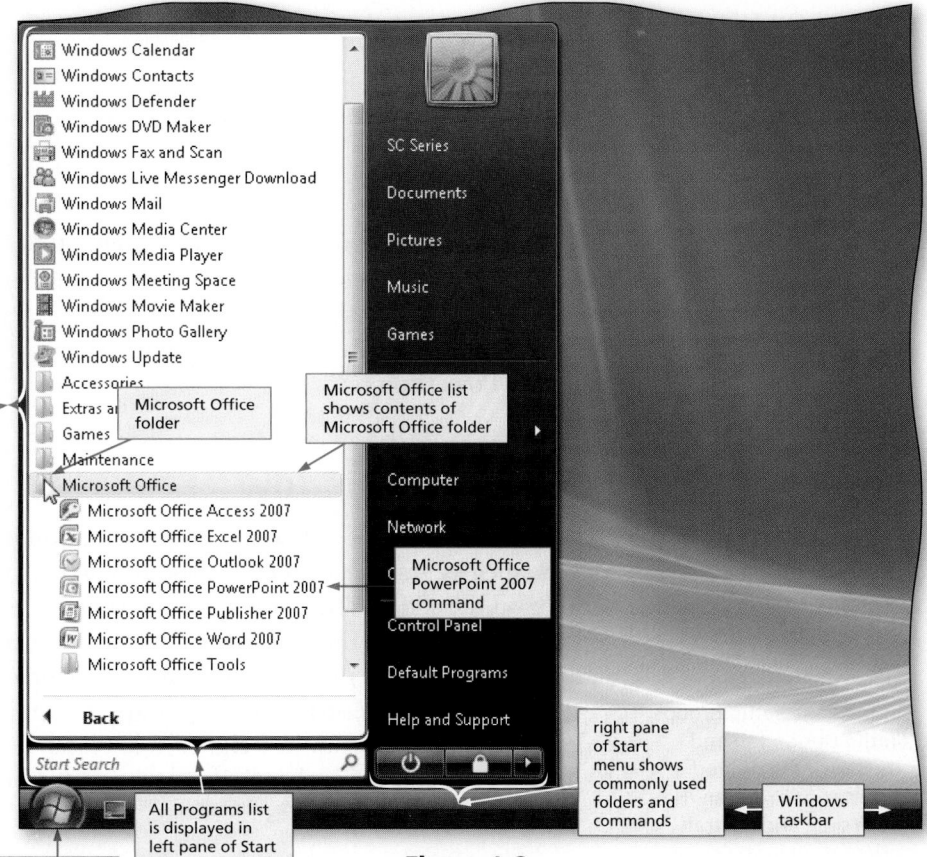

Figure 1–2

2

- Click Microsoft Office PowerPoint 2007 to start PowerPoint and display a new blank document in the PowerPoint window (Figure 1–3).

- If the PowerPoint window is not maximized, click the Maximize button next to the Close button on its title bar to maximize the window.

Q&A

What is a maximized window?

A maximized window fills the entire screen. When you maximize a window, the Maximize button changes to a Restore Down button. When you restore a maximized window, the Restore Down button changes to a Maximize button.

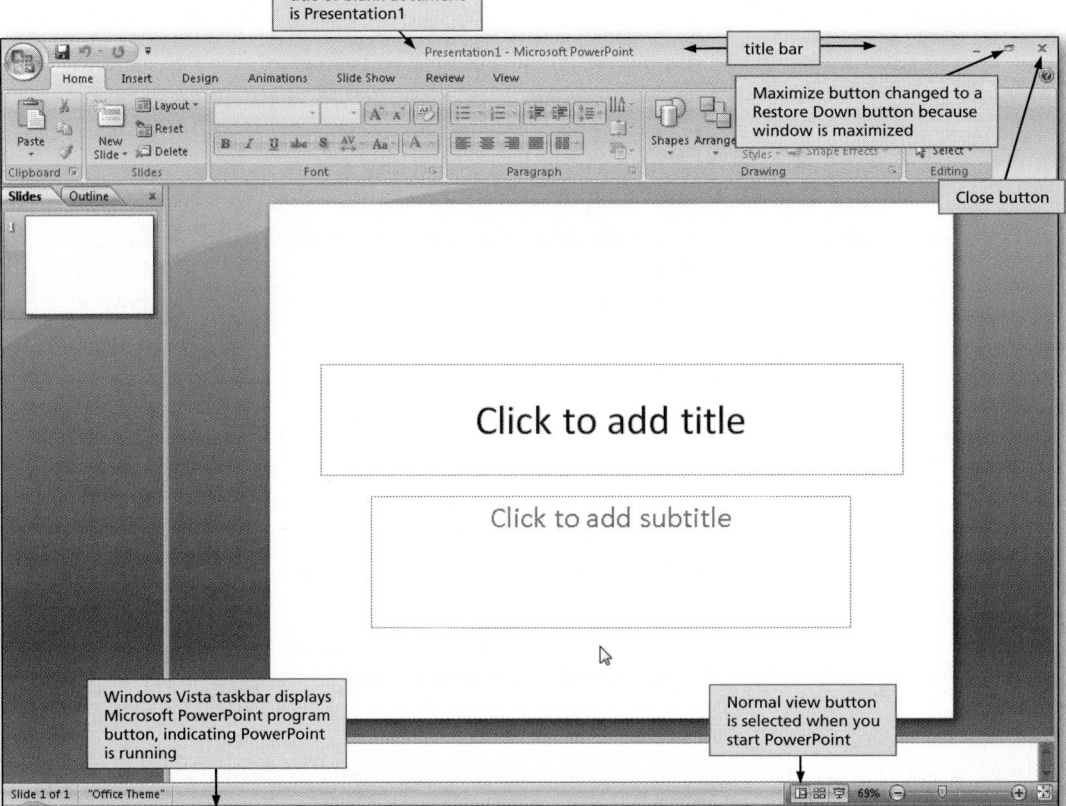

title of blank document is Presentation1

title bar

Maximize button changed to a Restore Down button because window is maximized

Close button

Click to add title

Click to add subtitle

Windows Vista taskbar displays Microsoft PowerPoint program button, indicating PowerPoint is running

Normal view button is selected when you start PowerPoint

Figure 1–3

Other Ways

1. Double-click PowerPoint icon on desktop, if one is present

2. Click Microsoft Office PowerPoint 2007 on Start menu

The PowerPoint Window

The PowerPoint window consists of a variety of components to make your work more efficient and documents more professional. These include the document window, Ribbon, Mini toolbar and shortcut menus, Quick Access Toolbar, and Office Button. Some of these components are common to other Microsoft Office 2007 programs; others are unique to PowerPoint.

PowerPoint Window

The basic unit of a PowerPoint presentation is a **slide**. A slide may contain text and objects, such as graphics, tables, charts, and drawings. **Layouts** are used to position this content on the slide. When you open a new presentation, the default **Title Slide** layout appears (Figure 1–4). The purpose of this layout is to introduce the presentation to the audience. PowerPoint includes eight other built-in standard layouts.

The default (preset) slide layouts are set up in **landscape orientation**, where the slide width is greater than its height. In landscape orientation, the slide size is preset to 10 inches wide and 7.5 inches high when printed on a standard sheet of paper measuring 11 inches wide and 8.5 inches high.

The PowerPoint window in Figure 1–4 contains placeholders, a mouse pointer, and a status bar. Other elements that may appear in the window are discussed later in this and subsequent chapters.

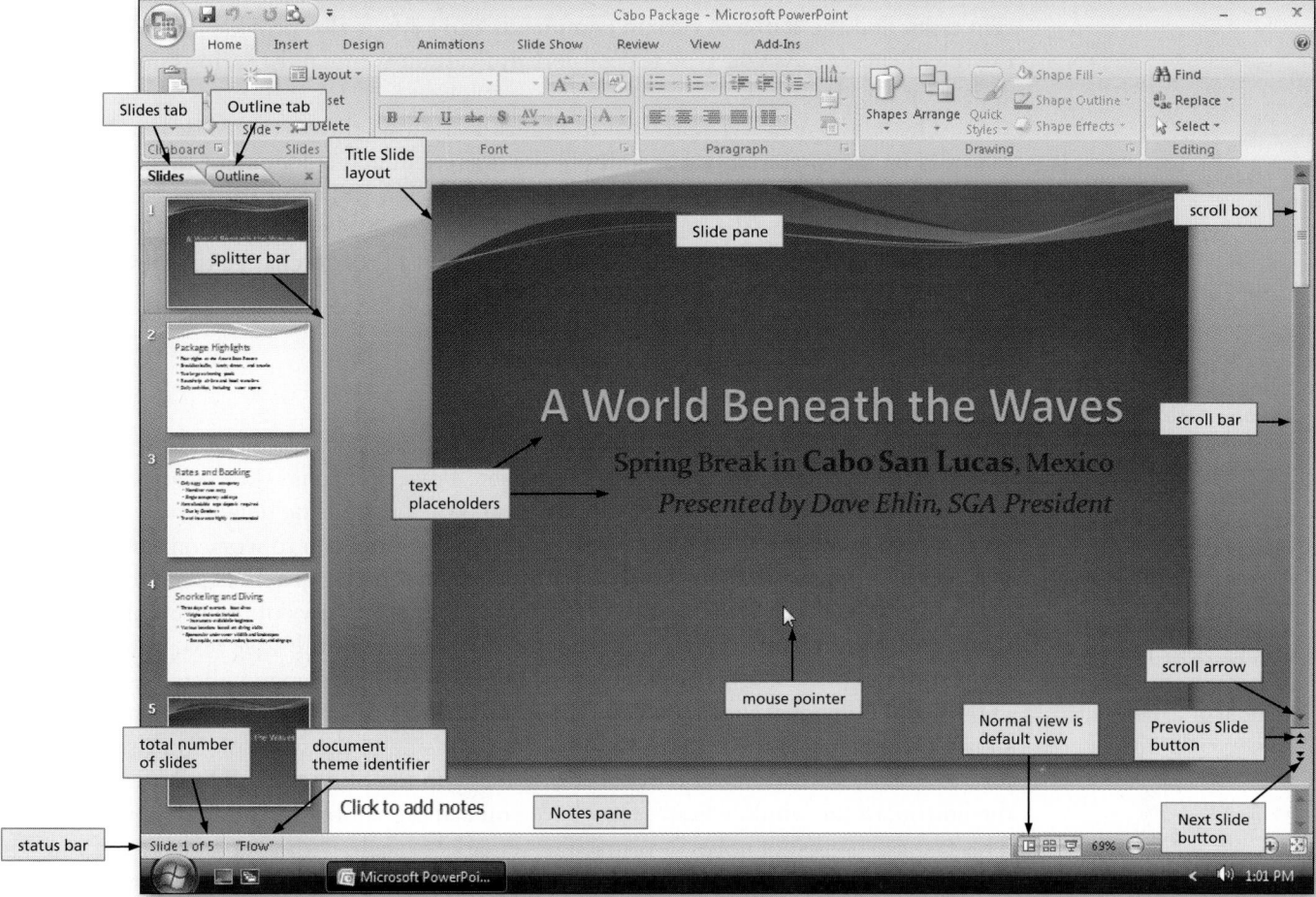

Figure 1–4

PLACEHOLDERS   **Placeholders** are boxes with dotted or hatch-marked borders that are displayed when you create a new slide. All layouts except the Blank slide layout contain placeholders. Depending on the particular slide layout selected, title and subtitle placeholders are displayed for the slide title and subtitle; a content text placeholder is displayed for text, art, or a table, chart, picture, graphic, or movie. The title slide in Figure 1–4 has two text placeholders where you will type the main heading, or title, of a new slide and the subtitle.

MOUSE POINTER   The **mouse pointer** becomes different shapes depending on the task you are performing in PowerPoint and the pointer's location on the screen. The mouse pointer in Figure 1–4 is the shape of a block arrow.

SCROLL BAR   You use the **vertical scroll bar** to display different slides in the document window. When you add a second slide to a presentation, this vertical scroll bar appears on the right side of the Slide pane. On the scroll bar, the position of the **scroll box** reflects the location of the slide in the presentation that is displayed in the document window. A **scroll arrow** is located at each end of a scroll bar. To scroll through, or display different portions of the document in the document window, you can click a scroll arrow or drag the scroll box to move forward or backward through the presentation.

The Previous Slide button and the Next Slide button appear at the bottom of the vertical scroll bar. Click one of these buttons to advance through the slides backwards or forwards.

The **horizontal scroll bar** also may appear. It is located on the bottom of the Slide pane and allows you to display a portion of the slide when the entire slide does not fit on the screen.

STATUS BAR The **status bar**, located at the bottom of the document window above the Windows Vista taskbar, presents information about the document, the progress of current tasks, and the status of certain commands and keys; it also provides controls for viewing the document. As you type text or perform certain commands, various indicators may appear on the status bar.

The left edge of the status bar in Figure 1–4 shows the current slide number followed by the total number of slides in the document and a document theme identifier. A **document theme** provides consistency in design and color throughout the entire presentation by setting the color scheme, font and font size, and layout of a presentation. Toward the right edge are buttons and controls you can use to change the view of a slide and adjust the size of the displayed document.

PowerPoint Views

Using the Notes Pane
As you create your presentation, type comments to yourself in the Notes pane. This material can be used as part of the spoken information you will share with your audience as you give your presentation. You can print these notes for yourself or to distribute to your audience.

The PowerPoint window display varies depending on the view. A **view** is the mode in which the presentation appears on the screen. PowerPoint has three main views: Normal, Slide Sorter, and Slide Show, and also Notes Page. The default view is **Normal view**, which is composed of three working areas that allow you to work on various aspects of a presentation simultaneously. The left side of the screen has a Tabs pane that consists of a **Slides tab** and an **Outline tab** that alternate between views of the presentation in a thumbnail, or miniature, view of the slides and an outline of the slide text. You can type the text of the presentation on the Outline tab and easily rearrange bulleted lists, paragraphs, and individual slides. As you type, you can view this text in the **Slide pane**, which shows a large view of the current slide on the right side of the window. You also can enter text, graphics, animations, and hyperlinks directly in the Slide pane. The **Notes pane** at the bottom of the window is an area where you can type notes and additional information. This text can consist of notes to yourself or remarks to share with your audience. If you want to work with your notes in full page format, you can display them in **Notes Page view**.

In Normal view, you can adjust the width of the Slide pane by dragging the **splitter bar** and the height of the Notes pane by dragging the pane borders. After you have created at least two slides, **scroll bars**, **scroll arrows**, and **scroll boxes** will appear on the right edge of the window.

Ribbon

The **Ribbon**, located near the top of the PowerPoint window, is the control center in PowerPoint (Figure 1–5a). The Ribbon provides easy, central access to the tasks you perform while creating a slide show. The Ribbon consists of tabs, groups, and commands. Each **tab** surrounds a collection of groups, and each group contains related commands.

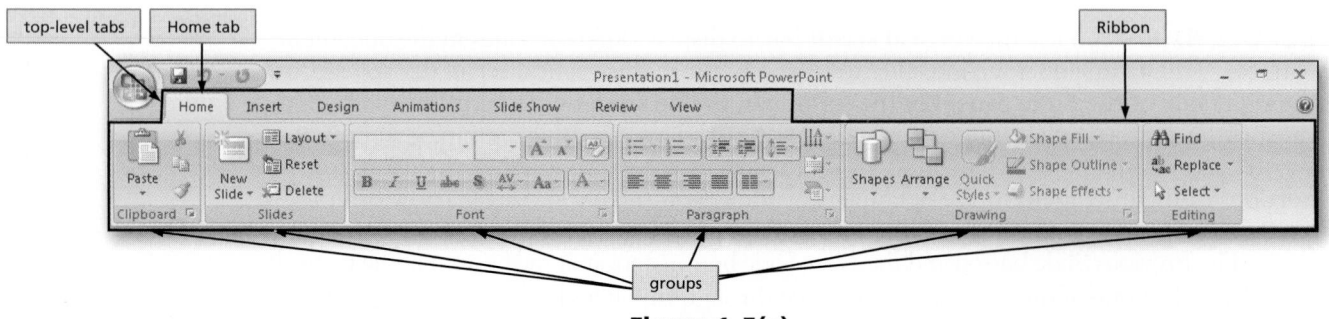

Figure 1–5(a)

When you start PowerPoint, the Ribbon displays seven top-level tabs: Home, Insert, Design, Animations, Slide Show, Review, and View. The **Home tab**, called the primary tab, contains the more frequently used commands. To display a different tab on the Ribbon, click the top-level tab. That is, to display the Insert tab, click Insert on the Ribbon. To return to the Home tab, click Home on the Ribbon. The tab currently displayed is called the **active tab**.

To display more of the document in the document window, some users prefer to minimize the Ribbon, which hides the groups on the Ribbon and displays only the top-level tabs (Figure 1–5b). To use commands on a minimized Ribbon, click the top-level tab.

Each time you start PowerPoint, the Ribbon appears the same way it did the last time you used PowerPoint. The chapters in this book, however, begin with the Ribbon appearing as it did at the initial installation of the software. If you are stepping through this chapter on a computer and you want your Ribbon to match the figures in this book, read Appendix E.

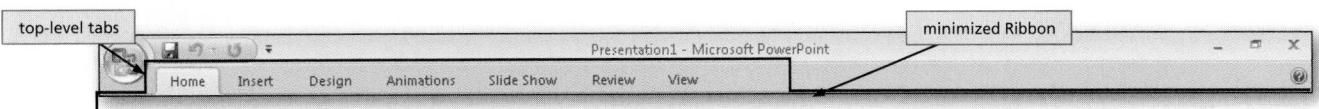

Figure 1–5(b)

In addition to the top-level tabs, PowerPoint displays other tabs, called **contextual tabs**, when you perform certain tasks or work with objects such as pictures or tables. If you insert a picture in a slide, for example, the Picture Tools tab and its related subordinate Format tab appear (Figure 1–6). When you are finished working with the picture, the Picture Tools and Format tabs disappear from the Ribbon. PowerPoint determines when contextual tabs should appear and disappear based on tasks you perform. Some contextual tabs, such as the Chart Tools tab, have more than one related subordinate tab.

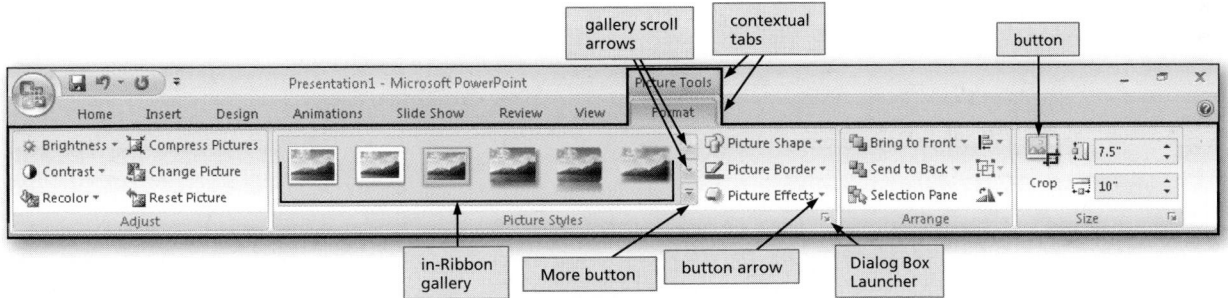

Figure 1–6

Commands on the Ribbon include buttons, boxes (text boxes, check boxes, etc.), and galleries (Figure 1–6). A **gallery** is a set of choices, often graphical, arranged in a grid or in a list. You can scroll through choices on an in-Ribbon gallery by clicking the gallery's scroll arrows. Or, you can click a gallery's More button to view more gallery options on the screen at a time. Some buttons and boxes have arrows that, when clicked, also display a gallery; others always cause a gallery to be displayed when clicked. Most galleries support **live preview**, which is a feature that allows you to point to a gallery choice and see its effect in the document - without actually selecting the choice (Figure 1–7).

BTW

Minimizing the Ribbon
If you want to minimize the Ribbon, right-click the Ribbon and then click Minimize the Ribbon on the shortcut menu, double-click the active tab, or press CTRL+F1. To restore a minimized Ribbon, right-click the Ribbon and then click Minimize the Ribbon on the shortcut menu, double-click any top-level tab, or press CTRL+F1. To use commands on a minimized Ribbon, click the top-level tab.

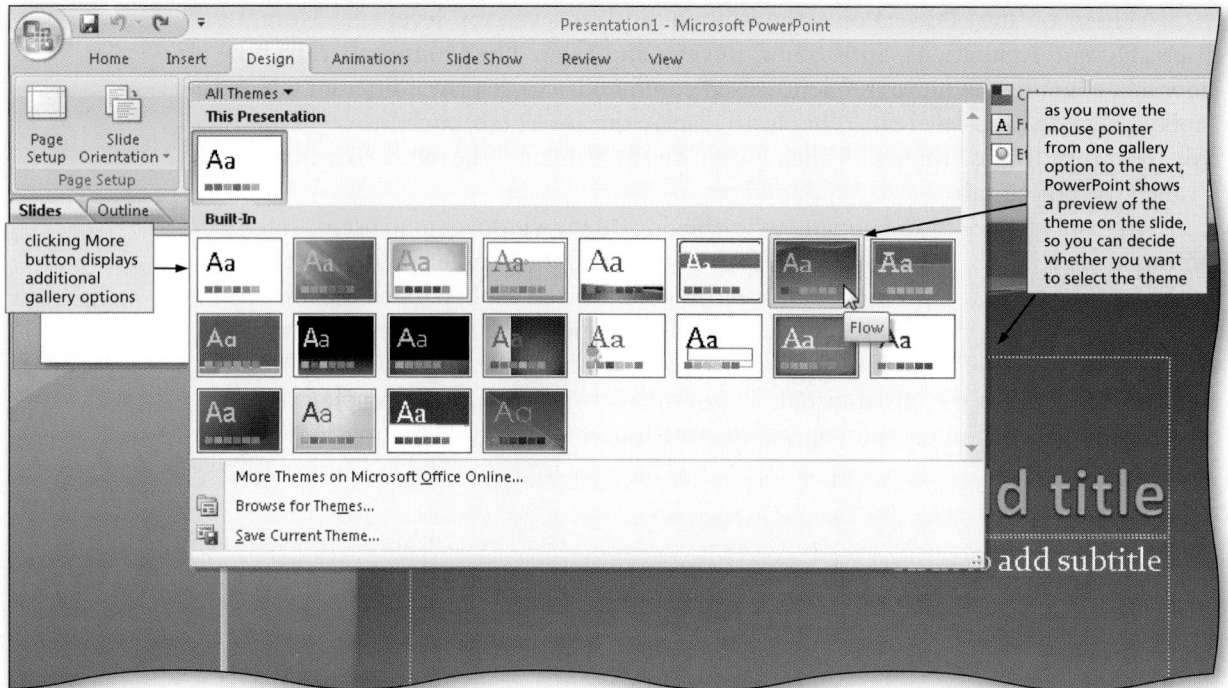

Figure 1–7

Some commands on the Ribbon display an image to help you remember their function. When you point to a command on the Ribbon, all or part of the command glows in shades of yellow and orange, and an Enhanced ScreenTip appears on the screen. An **Enhanced ScreenTip** is an on-screen note that provides the name of the command, available keyboard shortcut(s), a description of the command, and sometimes instructions for how to obtain help about the command (Figure 1–8). Enhanced ScreenTips are more detailed than a typical ScreenTip, which usually only displays the name of the command.

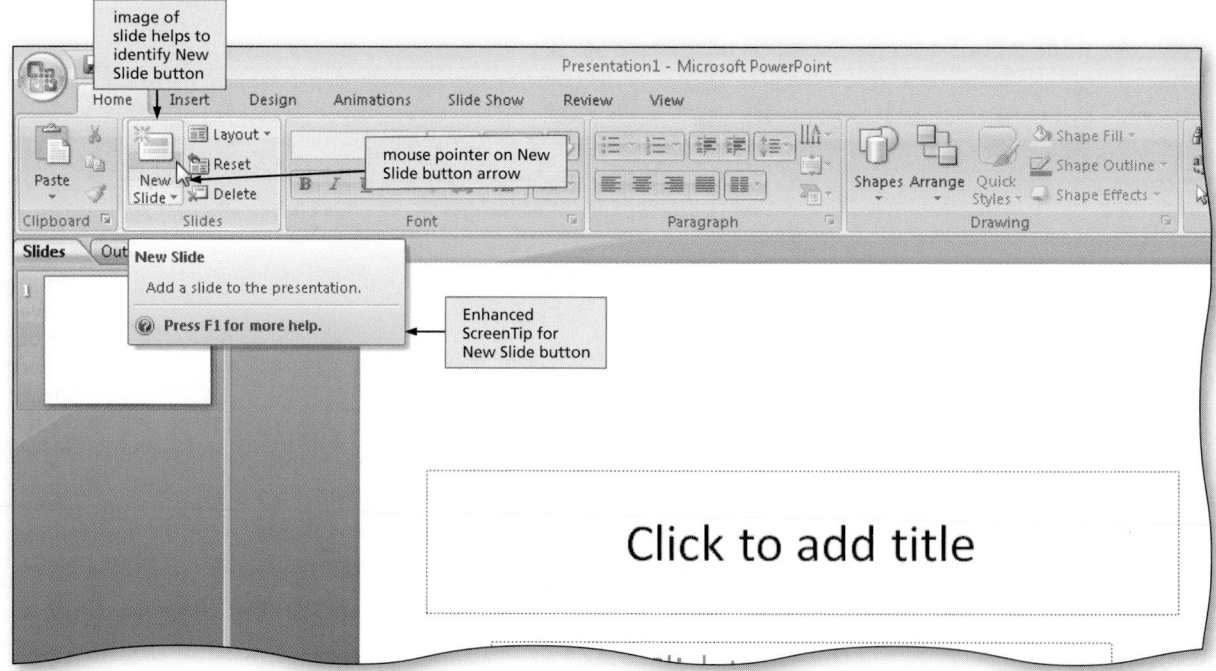

Figure 1–8

The lower-right corner of some groups on the Ribbon has a small arrow, called a **Dialog Box Launcher**, that when clicked displays a dialog box or a task pane with additional options for the group (Figure 1–9). When presented with a dialog box, you make selections and must close the dialog box before returning to the document. A **task pane**, by contrast, is a window that can remain open and visible while you work in the document.

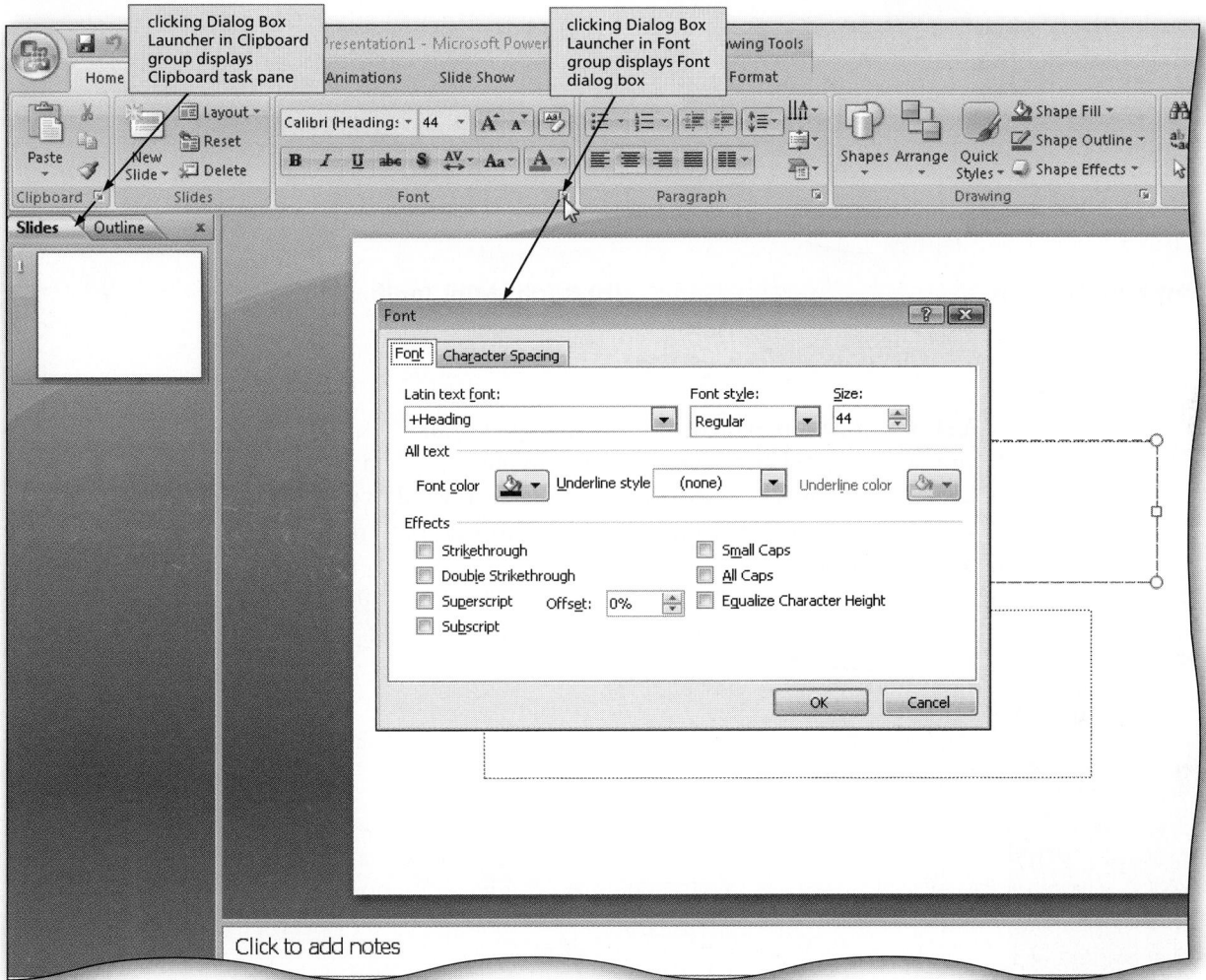

Figure 1–9

Mini Toolbar and Shortcut Menus

The **Mini toolbar**, which appears automatically based on tasks you perform, contains commands related to changing the appearance of text in a slide. All commands on the Mini toolbar also exist on the Ribbon. The purpose of the Mini toolbar is to minimize mouse movement. For example, if you want to use a command that currently is not displayed on the active tab, you can use the command on the Mini toolbar - instead of switching to a different tab to use the command.

When the Mini toolbar appears, it initially is transparent (Figure 1–10a on the next page). If you do not use the transparent Mini toolbar, it disappears from the screen. To use the Mini toolbar, move the mouse pointer into the toolbar, which causes the Mini toolbar to change from a transparent to bright appearance (Figure 1–10b on the next page).

BTW

Turning Off the Mini Toolbar
If you do not want the Mini toolbar to display, click the Office Button, click the PowerPoint Options button on the Office Button menu, and then clear the 'Show Mini Toolbar on selection' check box in the Popular panel.

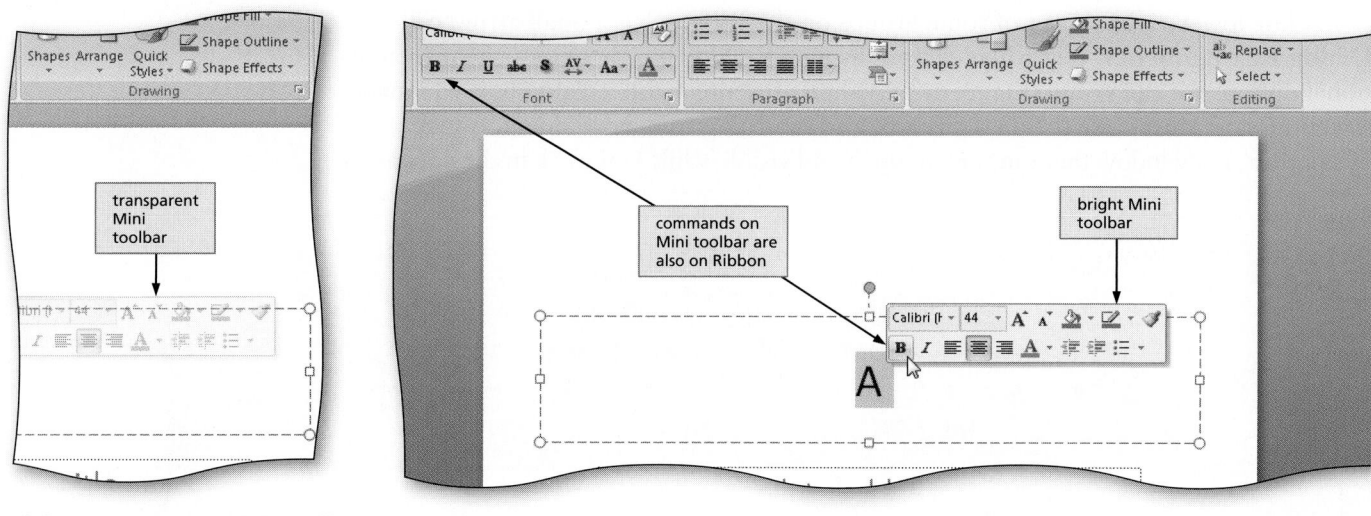

(a) Transparent Mini Toolbar

(b) Bright Mini Toolbar

Figure 1–10

A **shortcut menu**, which appears when you right-click an object, is a list of frequently used commands that relate to the right-clicked object. When you right-click a scroll bar, for example, a shortcut menu appears with commands related to the scroll bar. If you right-click an item in the document window, PowerPoint displays both the Mini toolbar and a shortcut menu (Figure 1–11).

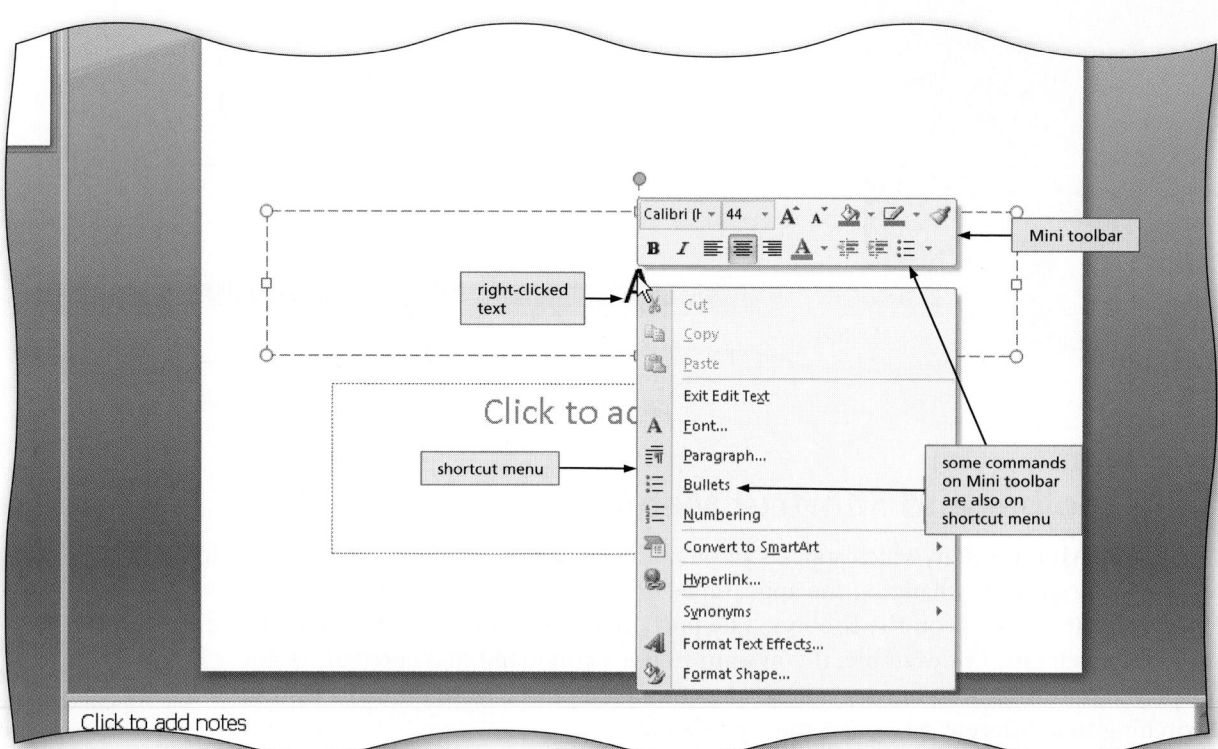

Figure 1–11

Quick Access Toolbar

The **Quick Access Toolbar**, located by default above the Ribbon, provides easy access to frequently used commands (Figure 1–12a). The commands on the Quick Access Toolbar always are available, regardless of the task you are performing. Initially, the Quick Access Toolbar contains the Save, Undo, and Redo commands. If you click the Customize Quick Access Toolbar button, PowerPoint provides a list of commands you quickly can add to and remove from the Quick Access Toolbar (Figure 1–12b).

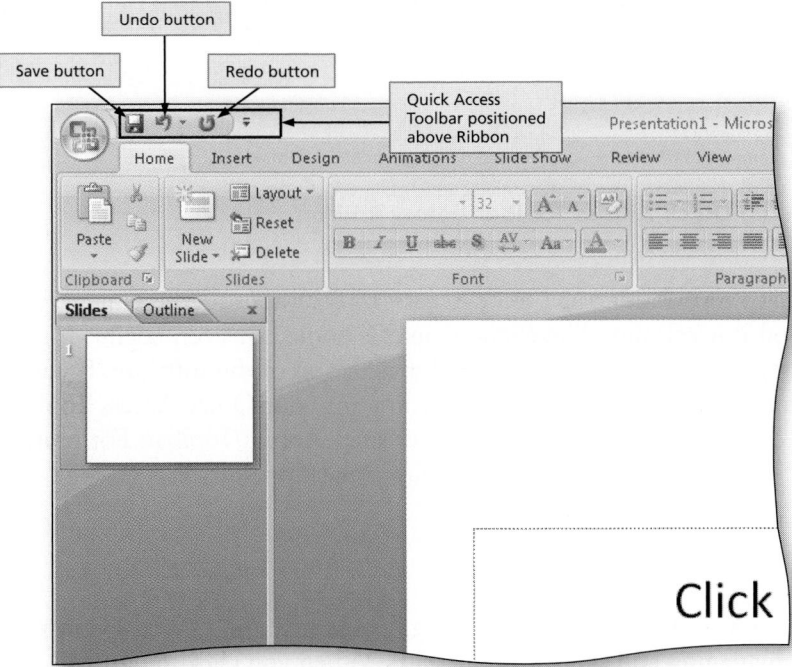

Figure 1–12(a) Quick Access Toolbar above Ribbon

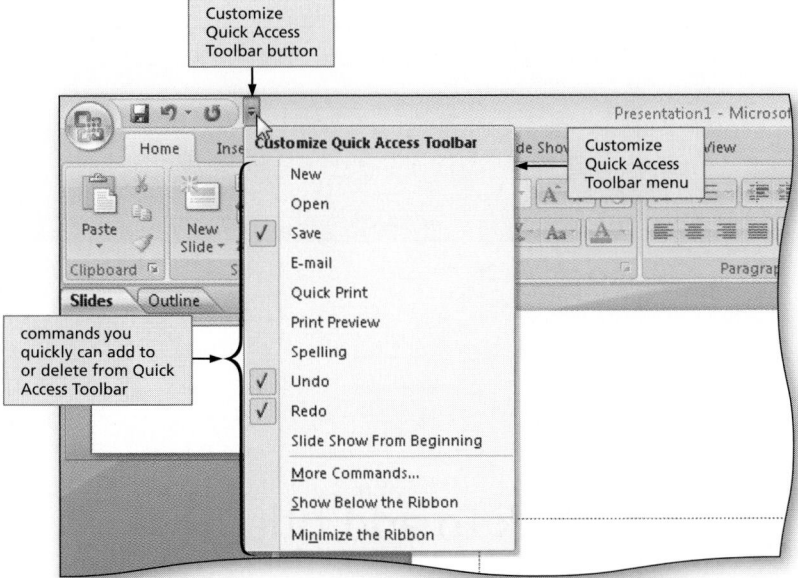

Figure 1–12(b) Customize Quick Access Toolbar

BTW

Quick Access Toolbar Commands
To add a Ribbon command to the Quick Access Toolbar, right-click the command on the Ribbon and then click Add to Quick Access Toolbar on the shortcut menu. To delete a command from the Quick Access Toolbar, right-click the command on the Quick Access Toolbar and then click Remove from Quick Access Toolbar on the shortcut menu. To display the Quick Access Toolbar below the Ribbon, right-click the Quick Access Toolbar and then click Place Quick Access Toolbar below the Ribbon on the shortcut menu.

You also can add other commands to or delete commands from the Quick Access Toolbar so that it contains the commands you use most often. As you add commands to the Quick Access Toolbar, its commands may interfere with the document title on the title bar. For this reason, PowerPoint provides an option of displaying the Quick Access Toolbar below the Ribbon (Figure 1–12c).

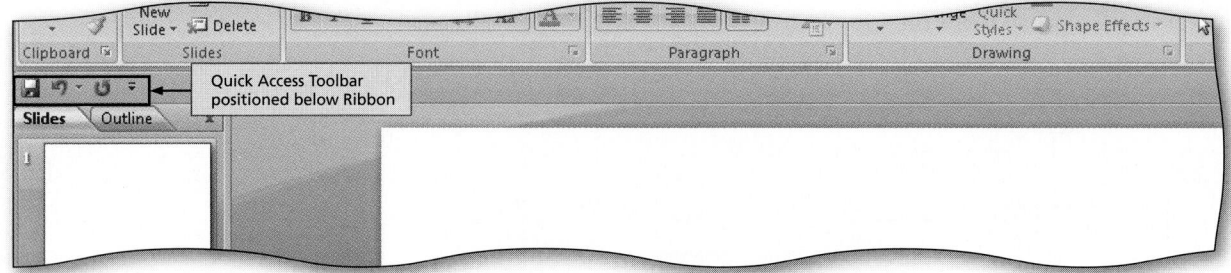

Figure 1–12(c) Quick Access Toolbar below Ribbon

Each time you start PowerPoint, the Quick Access Toolbar appears the same way it did the last time you used PowerPoint. The chapters in this book, however, begin with the Quick Access Toolbar appearing as it did at the initial installation of the software. If you are stepping through this chapter on a computer and you want your Quick Access Toolbar to match the figures in this book, you should reset your Quick Access Toolbar. For more information about how to reset the Quick Access Toolbar, read Appendix E.

Office Button

While the Ribbon is a control center for creating documents, the **Office Button** is a central location for managing and sharing documents. When you click the Office Button, located in the upper-left corner of the window, PowerPoint displays the Office Button menu (Figure 1–13). A **menu** contains a list of commands.

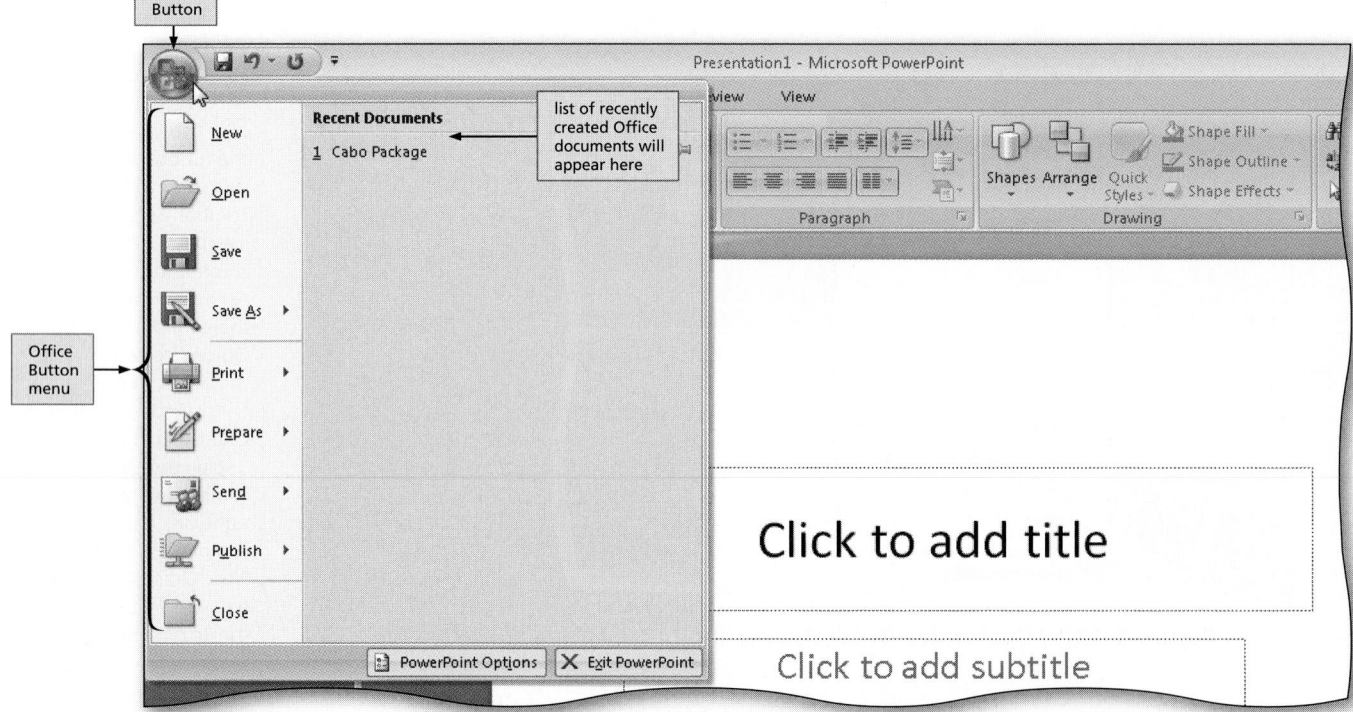

Figure 1–13

When you click the New, Open, Save As, and Print commands on the Office Button menu, PowerPoint displays a dialog box with additional options. The Save As, Print, Prepare, Send, and Publish commands have an arrow to their right. If you point to this arrow, PowerPoint displays a **submenu**, which is a list of additional commands associated with the selected command (Figure 1–14). For the Prepare, Send, and Publish commands that do not display a dialog box when clicked, you can point either to the command or the arrow to display the submenu.

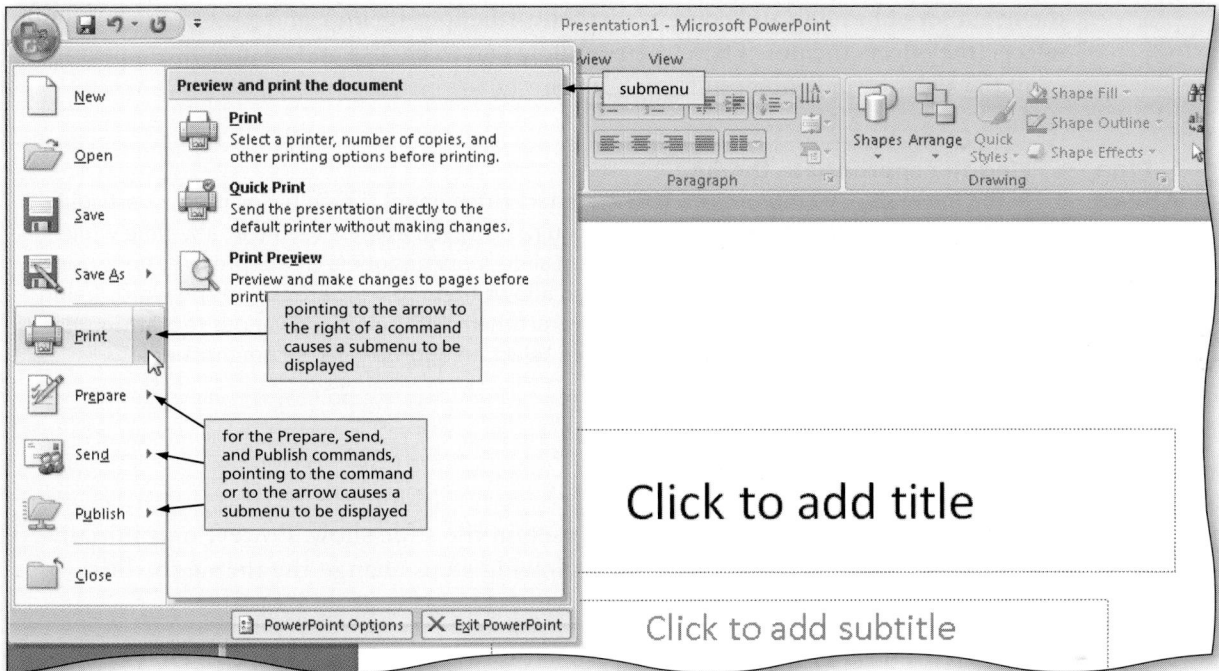

Figure 1–14

Key Tips

If you prefer using the keyboard instead of the mouse, you can press the ALT key on the keyboard to display a **Key Tip badge**, or keyboard code icon, for certain commands (Figure 1–15). To select a command using the keyboard, press its displayed code letter, or **Key Tip**. When you press a Key Tip, additional Key Tips related to the selected command may appear. For example, to select the New command on the Office Button menu, press the ALT key, then press the F key, then press the N key.

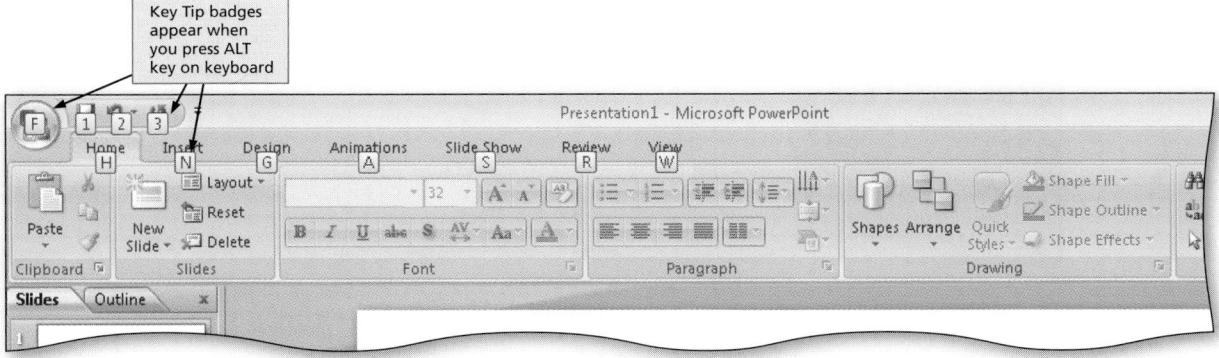

Figure 1–15

To remove the Key Tip badges from the screen, press the ALT key or the ESC key until all Key Tip badges disappear, or click the mouse anywhere in the PowerPoint window.

Choosing a Document Theme

You easily can give a presentation a professional and consistent appearance by using a document theme. This collection of formatting choices includes a set of colors (the color theme), a set of heading and content text fonts (the font theme), and a set of lines and fill effects (the effects theme). These themes allow you to choose and change the appearance of all the slides or individual slides in your presentation.

Plan Ahead

Find the appropriate theme.
In the initial steps of this project, you will select a document theme by locating a particular built-in theme in the Themes group. You could, however, apply a theme at any time while creating the presentation. Some PowerPoint slide show designers create presentations using the default Office Theme. This blank design allows them to concentrate on the words being used to convey the message and does not distract them with colors and various text attributes. Once the text is entered, the designers then select an appropriate document theme.

To Choose a Document Theme

The document theme identifier shows the theme currently used in the slide show. PowerPoint initially uses the **Office Theme** until you select a different theme. The following steps change the theme for this presentation from the Office Theme to the Flow document theme.

- Click Design on the Ribbon to display the Design tab (Figure 1–16).

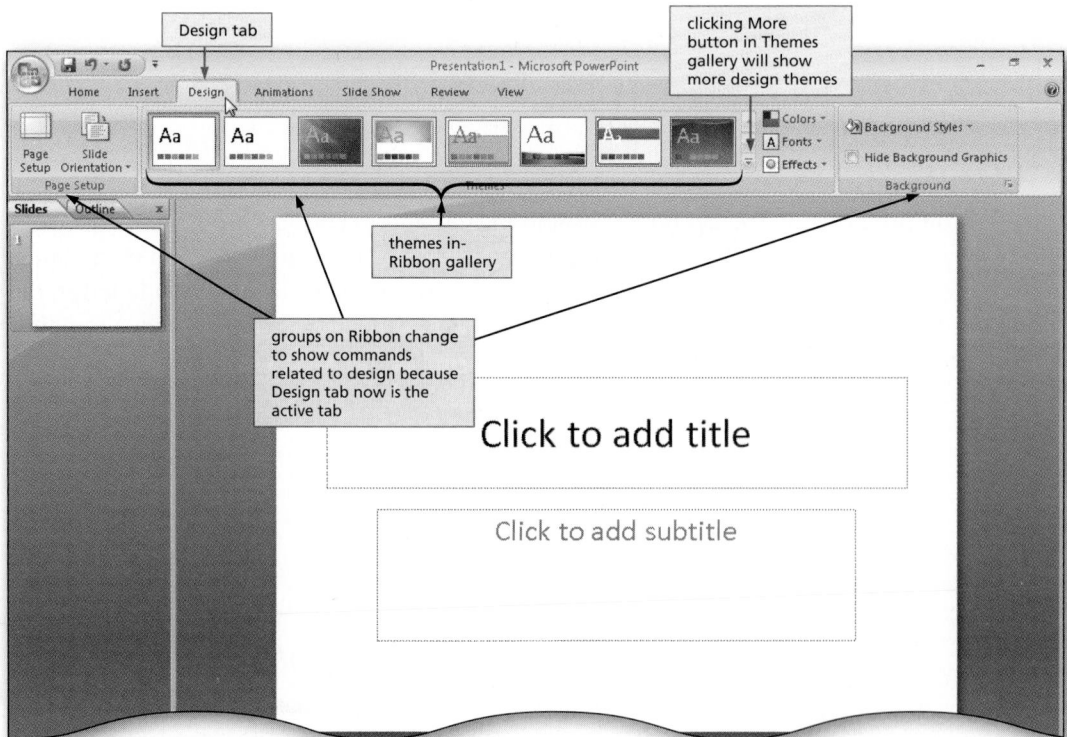

Figure 1–16

2

- Click the More button in the Themes gallery to expand the gallery, which shows more Built-In theme gallery options (Figure 1–17).

 Experiment

- Point to various document themes in the Themes gallery and watch the colors and fonts change on the title slide.

Q&A | Are the themes displayed in a specific order?

Yes. They are arranged in alphabetical order running from left to right. If you point to a theme, a ScreenTip with the design's name appears on the screen.

Q&A | What if I change my mind and do not want to select a new theme?

Click anywhere outside the All Themes gallery to close the gallery.

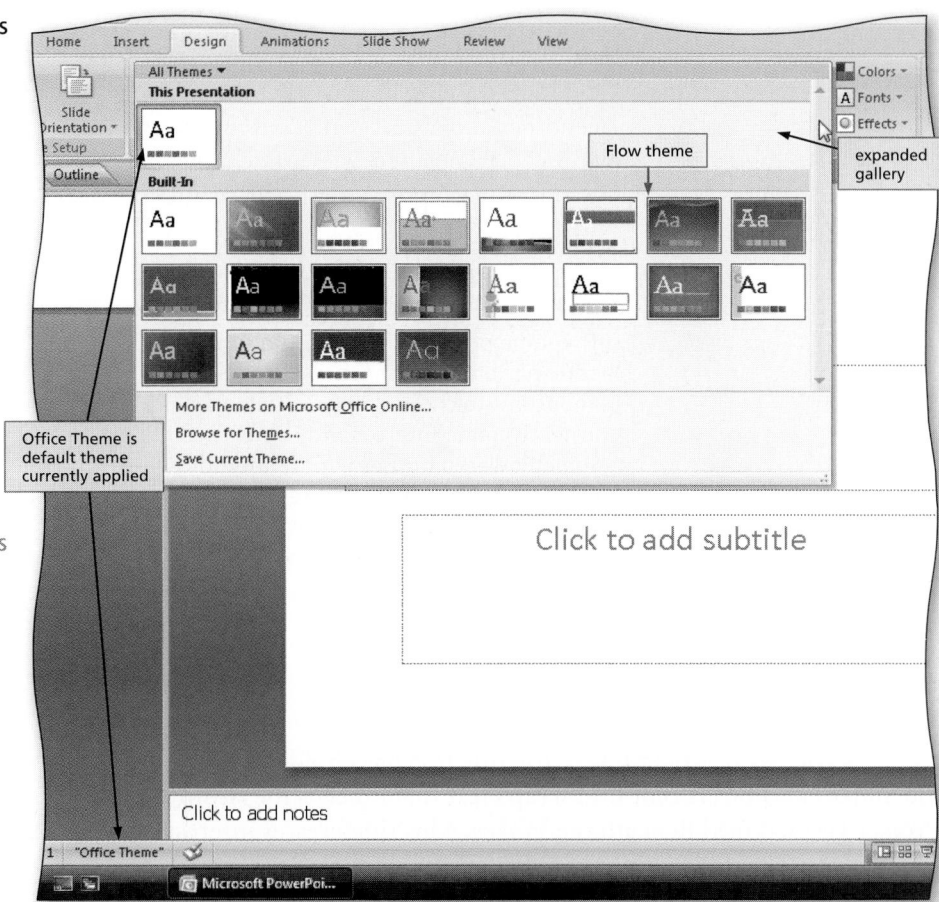

Figure 1–17

3

- Click the Flow theme to apply this theme to Slide 1 (Figure 1–18).

Q&A | If I decide at some future time that this design does not fit the theme of my presentation, can I apply a different design?

Yes. You can repeat these steps at any time while creating your presentation.

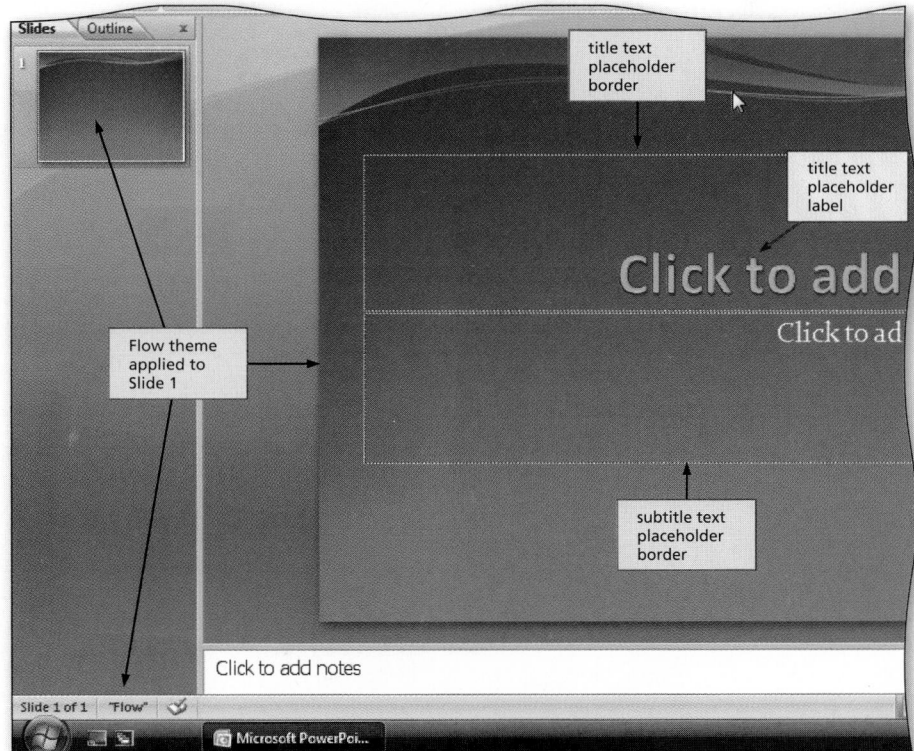

Figure 1–18

Creating a Title Slide

With the exception of a blank slide and a slide with a picture and caption, PowerPoint assumes every new slide has a title. Many of PowerPoint's layouts have both a title text placeholder and at least one content placeholder. To make creating a presentation easier, any text you type after a new slide appears becomes title text in the title text placeholder. The following steps create the title slide for this presentation.

Plan Ahead

Choose the words for the slide.
No doubt you have heard the phrase, "You get only one chance to make a first impression." The same philosophy holds true for a PowerPoint presentation. The title slide gives your audience an initial sense of what they are about to see and hear. It is, therefore, extremely important to choose the text for this slide carefully. Avoid stating the obvious in the title. Instead, create interest and curiosity using key ideas from the presentation.

Some PowerPoint users create the title slide as their last step in the design process so that it reflects the tone of the presentation. They begin by planning the final slide in the presentation so that they know where and how they want to end the slide show. All the slides in the presentation should work toward meeting this final slide.

To Enter the Presentation Title

As you begin typing text in the title text placeholder, the title text also is displayed in the Slide 1 thumbnail in the Slides tab. PowerPoint **line wraps** text that exceeds the width of the placeholder. The presentation title for Project 1 is A World Beneath the Waves. This title creates interest by introducing the concept of exploring the life under water. The following step creates the slide show's title.

- Click the label, Click to add title, located inside the title text placeholder to select the placeholder (Figure 1–19).

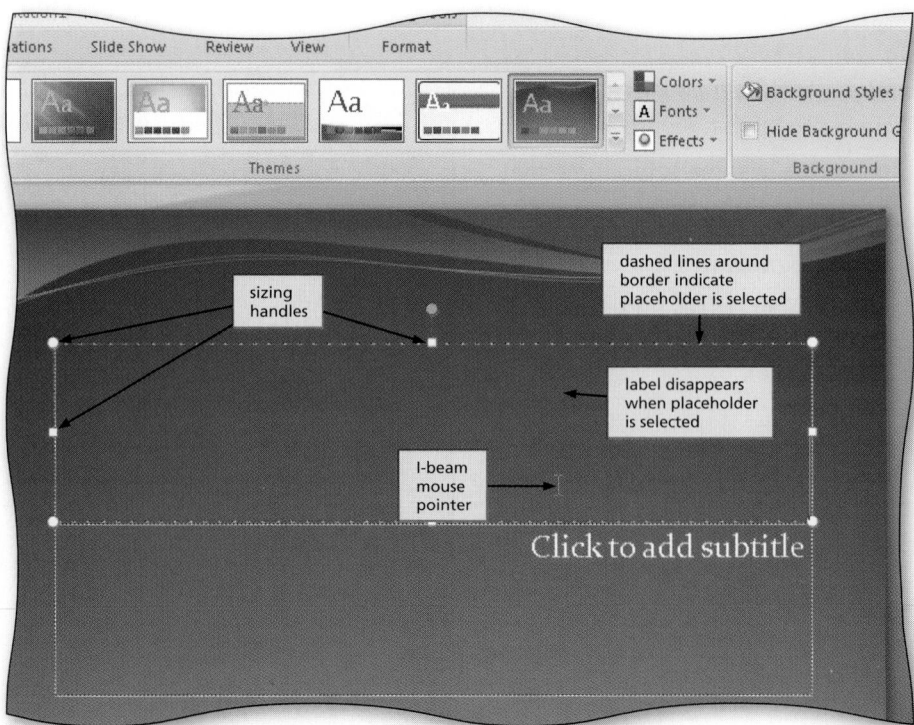

Figure 1–19

2
- Type A World Beneath the
  Waves in the title text placeholder.
  Do not press the ENTER key
  (Figure 1–20).

What if a button with two lines and
two arrows appears on the left side
of the title text placeholder?

The **AutoFit** button displays because
PowerPoint attempts to reduce the
size of the letters when the title text
does not fit on a single line. If you are
creating a slide and need to squeeze
an extra line in the text placeholder,
you can click this button to resize the
existing text in the placeholder so the
spillover text will fit on the slide.

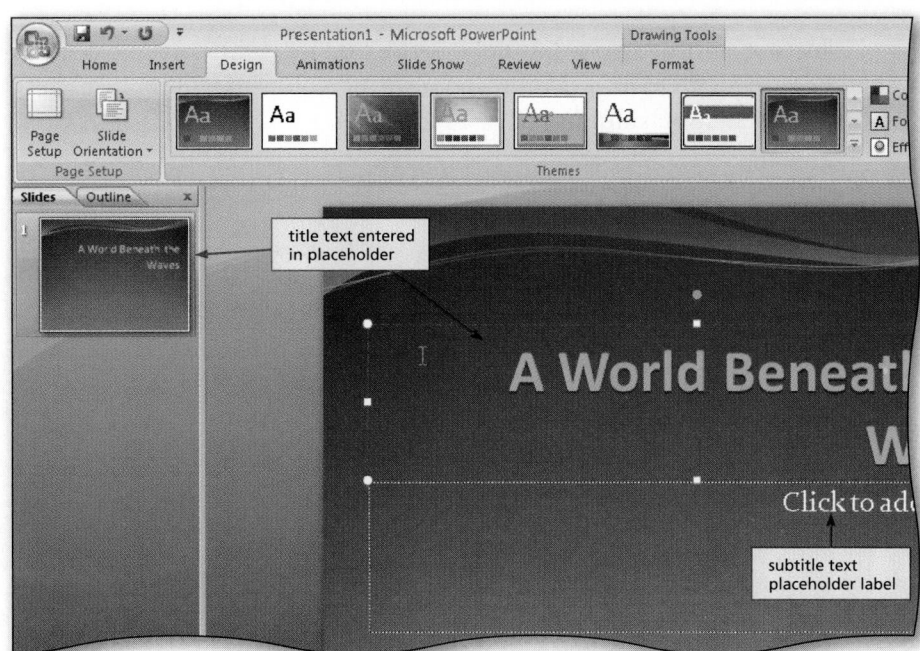

Figure 1–20

Correcting a Mistake When Typing

If you type the wrong letter, press the BACKSPACE key to erase all the characters back
to and including the one that is incorrect. If you mistakenly press the ENTER key after typing the title and the insertion point is on the new line, simply press the BACKSPACE key to
return the insertion point to the right of the letter s in the word Waves.

When you install PowerPoint, the default setting allows you to reverse up to the
last 20 changes by clicking the Undo button on the Quick Access Toolbar. The ScreenTip
that appears when you point to the Undo button changes to indicate the type of change
just made. For example, if you type text in the title text placeholder and then point to the
Undo button, the ScreenTip that appears is Undo Typing. For clarity, when referencing
the Undo button in this project, the name displaying in the ScreenTip is referenced. You
can reapply a change that you reversed with the Undo button by clicking the Redo button
on the Quick Access Toolbar. Clicking the Redo button reverses the last undo action. The
ScreenTip name reflects the type of reversal last performed.

Paragraphs

Subtitle text in the subtitle text placeholder supports the title text. It can appear on
one or more lines in the placeholder. To create more than one subtitle line, you press the
ENTER key after typing some words. PowerPoint creates a new line, which is the second
paragraph in the placeholder. A **paragraph** is a segment of text with the same format that
begins when you press the ENTER key and ends when you press the ENTER key again. This
new paragraph is the same level as the previous paragraph. A **level** is a position within a
structure, such as an outline, that indicates the magnitude of importance. PowerPoint allows
for five paragraph levels.

To Enter the Presentation Subtitle Paragraph

The first subtitle paragraph links to the title by giving specific details about the vacation location, and the second paragraph gives information about the person who will be speaking to the audience. The following steps enter the presentation subtitle.

- Click the label, Click to add subtitle, located inside the subtitle text place-holder to select the placeholder (Figure 1–21).

Figure 1–21

- **Type** Spring Break in Cabo San Lucas, Mexico **and then press the** ENTER **key.**

- **Type** Presented by Dave Ehlin, SGA President **but do not press the** ENTER **key (Figure 1–22).**

Q&A Why do red wavy lines appear below the words, Cabo and Ehlin?

The lines indicate possible spelling errors.

Figure 1–22

Plan Ahead

Identify how to format specific elements of the text.

Most of the time, you use the document theme's text attributes, color scheme, and layout. Occasionally, you may want to change the way a presentation looks, however, and still keep a particular document theme. PowerPoint gives you that flexibility.

Graphic designers use several rules when formatting text.

- Avoid all capital letters, if possible. Audiences have difficulty comprehending sentences typed in all capital letters, especially when the lines exceed seven words. All capital letters leaves no room for emphasis or inflection, so readers get confused about what material deserves particular attention. Some document themes, however, have a default title text style of all capital letters.

- Avoid text with a font size less than 24 point. Audience members generally will sit a maximum of 50 feet from a screen, and at this distance 24-point type is the smallest size text they can read comfortably without straining.

- Make careful color choices. Color evokes emotions, and a careless color choice may elicit the incorrect psychological response. PowerPoint provides a color palette with hundreds of colors. The built-in document themes use complementary colors that work well together. If you stray from these themes and add your own color choices, without a good reason to make the changes, your presentation is apt to become ineffective.

Formatting Characters in a Presentation

Recall that each document theme determines the color scheme, font and font size, and layout of a presentation. You can use a specific document theme and then change the characters' formats any time before, during, or after you type the text.

Fonts and Font Styles

Characters that appear on the screen are a specific shape and size. Examples of how you can modify the appearance, or **format**, of these typed characters on the screen and in print include changing the font, style, size, and color. The **font**, or typeface, defines the appearance and shape of the letters, numbers, punctuation marks, and symbols. **Style** indicates how the characters are formatted. PowerPoint's text font styles include regular, italic, bold, and bold italic. **Size** specifies the height of the characters and is gauged by a measurement system that uses points. A **point** is 1/72 of an inch in height. Thus, a character with a point size of 36 is 36/72 (or 1/2) of an inch in height. **Color** defines the hue of the characters.

This presentation uses the Flow document theme, which uses particular font styles and font sizes. The Flow document theme default title text font is named Calibri. It has a bold style with no special effects, and its size is 56 point. The Flow document theme default subtitle text font is Constantia with a font size of 26 point.

To Select a Paragraph

You can use many techniques to format characters. When you want to apply the same formats to multiple words or paragraphs, it is efficient to select the desired text and then make the desired changes to all the characters simultaneously. The first formatting change you will make will apply to the second paragraph of the title slide subtitle. The following step selects this paragraph.

- Triple-click the paragraph, Presented by Dave Ehlin, SGA President, in the subtitle text placeholder to select the paragraph (Figure 1–23).

Can I select the paragraph using a technique other than triple-clicking?

Yes. You can move your mouse pointer to the left of the first paragraph and then drag it to the end of the line.

Figure 1–23

To Italicize Text

Different font styles often are used on slides to make them more appealing to the reader and to emphasize particular text. Italic type, used sparingly, draws the readers' eyes to these characters. The following step adds emphasis to the second line of the subtitle text by changing regular text to italic text.

 1

- With the subtitle text still selected, click the Italic button on the Mini toolbar to italicize that text on the slide and on the slide thumbnail (Figure 1–24).

Q&A

If I change my mind and decide not to italicize the text, how can I remove this style?

Select the italicized text and then click the Italic button. As a result, the Italic button will not be selected, and the text will not have the italic font style.

Figure 1–24

Other Ways
1. Right-click selected text, click Font on shortcut menu, click Italic in Font style list   2. Click Home tab, click Italic in Font group   3. Press CTRL+I

To Select Multiple Paragraphs

Each of the subtitle lines is a separate paragraph. As previously discussed, PowerPoint creates a new paragraph each time you press the ENTER key. To change the character formatting in both paragraphs, it is efficient to select the desired text and then make the desired changes to all the characters simultaneously.

The next formatting change you will make will apply to both title slide subtitle paragraphs. The following step selects the first paragraph so that you can format both paragraphs concurrently.

 1

- With the second subtitle text paragraph selected, press the CTRL key and then triple-click the first subtitle text paragraph, Spring Break in Cabo San Lucas, Mexico, to select both paragraphs (Figure 1–25).

Q&A

Can I use a different technique to select both subtitle text paragraphs?

Yes. Click the placeholder border so that it appears as a solid line. When the placeholder is selected in this manner, formatting changes will apply to all text in the placeholder.

Figure 1–25

To Change the Text Color

PowerPoint allows you to use one or more text colors in a presentation. To add more emphasis to the title slide subtitle text, you decide to change the color. The following steps add emphasis to both subtitle text paragraphs by changing the font color from white to dark blue.

- With both paragraphs selected, click the Font Color arrow on the Mini toolbar to display the palette of Theme Colors and Standard Colors (Figure 1–26).

Q&A

If the Mini toolbar disappears from the screen, how can I display it once again?

Right-click the text, and the Mini toolbar should appear.

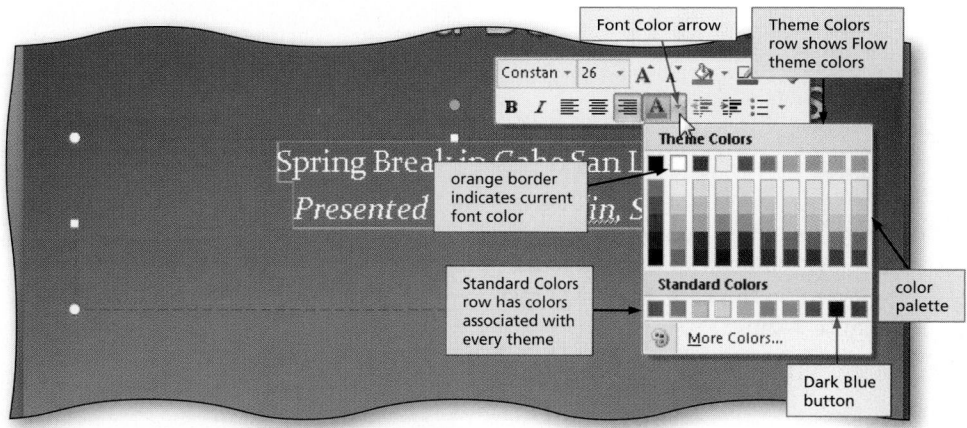

Figure 1–26

- Click the Dark Blue button in the Standard Colors row on the Mini toolbar (row 1, column 9) to change the font color to dark blue (Figure 1–27).

Q&A

Why did I select the color, dark blue?

Dark blue is one of the 10 standard colors associated with every document theme, and it works well with the shades of blue already on the slide. An additional consideration is that dark colors print well.

Figure 1–27

- Click outside the selected area to deselect the two paragraphs.

Other Ways

1. Right-click selected text, click Font on shortcut menu, click Font color button, click Dark Blue in Standard Colors row

2. Click Home tab, click Font Color arrow in Font group, click Dark Blue in Standard Colors row

To Select a Group of Words

PowerPoint designers use many techniques to format characters. To apply the same formats to multiple words or paragraphs, they select the desired text and then make the desired changes to all the characters simultaneously.

To add emphasis to the vacation destination, you want to increase the font size and change the font style to bold for the words, Cabo San Lucas. You could perform these actions separately, but it is more efficient to select this group of words and then change the font attributes. The following steps select a group of words.

- Position the mouse pointer immediately to the left of the first character of the text to be selected (in this case, the C in Cabo) (Figure 1–28).

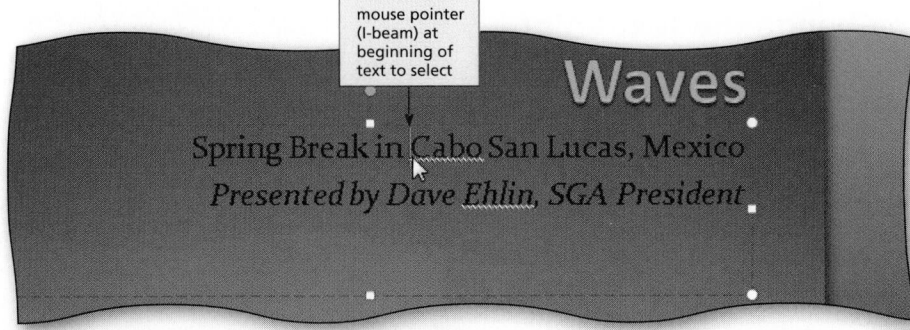

Figure 1–28

- Drag the mouse pointer through the last character of the text to be selected (in this case, the s in Lucas) (Figure 1–29).

Figure 1–29

To Increase Font Size

To add emphasis, you increase the font size for Cabo San Lucas. The Increase Font Size button on the Mini toolbar increases the font size in preset increments. The following step uses this button to increase the font size.

- Click the Increase Font Size button on the Mini toolbar once to increase the font size of the selected text from 26 to 28 point (Figure 1–30).

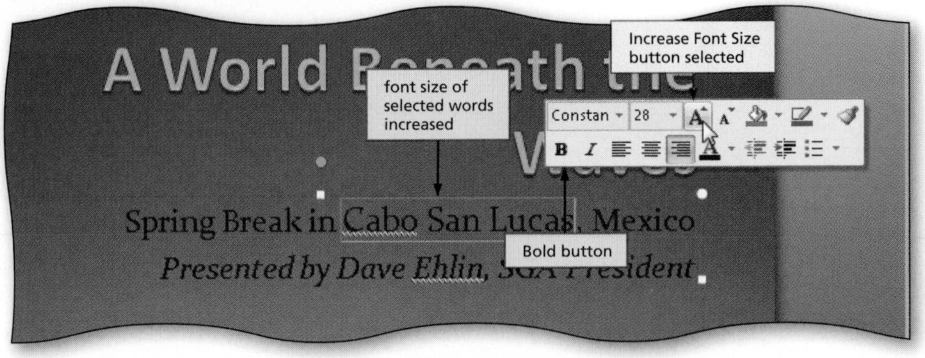

Other Ways

1. Click Home tab, click Increase Font Size button in Font group
2. Click Home tab, click Font Size box arrow, click new font size
3. Press CTRL+SHIFT+>

Figure 1–30

To Bold Text

Bold characters display somewhat thicker and darker than those that display in a regular font style. Clicking the Bold button on the Mini toolbar is an efficient method of bolding text. To add more emphasis to the vacation destination, you want to bold the words, Cabo San Lucas. The following step bolds this text.

- Click the Bold button on the Mini toolbar to bold the three selected words (Figure 1–31).

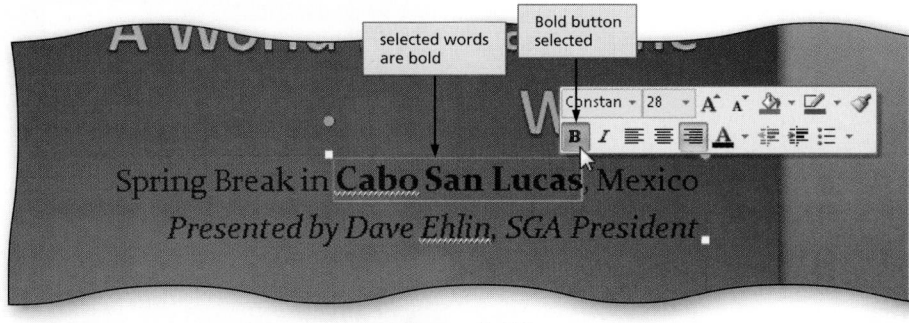

Figure 1–31

Other Ways

1. Click Home tab, click Bold button in Font group
2. Press CTRL+B

Identify how to format specific elements of the text.
Avoid line wraps. Your audience's eyes want to stop at the end of a line. Thus, you must plan your words carefully or adjust the font size so that each point displays on only one line.

Plan Ahead

To Decrease the Title Slide Title Text Font Size

The last word of the title text, Waves, appears on a line by itself. For aesthetic reasons, it is advantageous to have this word appear with the rest of the title on a single line. One way to fit text on one line is to decrease the font size. The process is similar to increasing the font size. Clicking the Decrease Font Size button on the Mini toolbar decreases the size in preset increments. The following steps decrease the font size from 56 to 48 point.

- Select the title slide title text, A World Beneath the Waves (Figure 1–32).

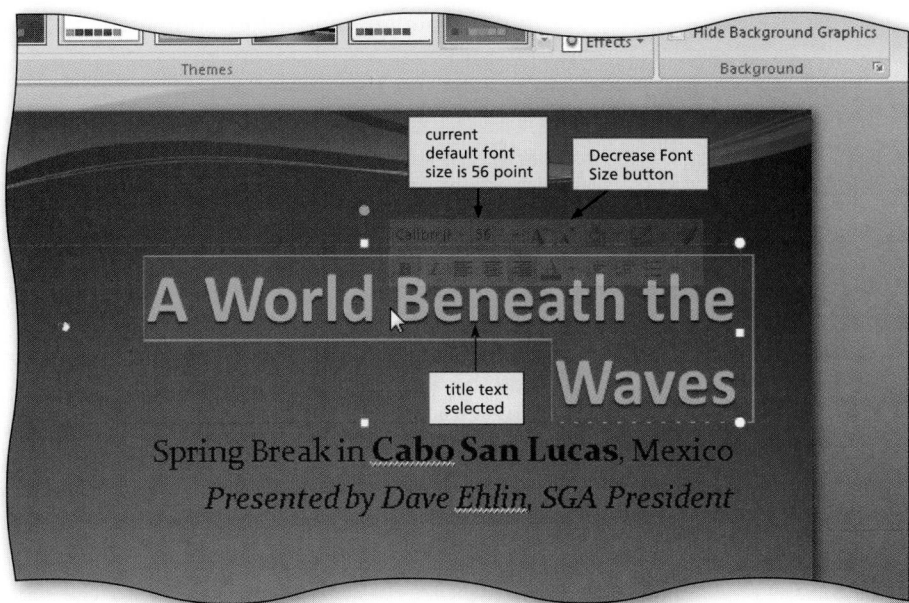

Figure 1–32

2

• Click the Decrease Font Size button on the Mini toolbar twice to decrease the font size from 56 to 48 point (Figure 1–33).

Figure 1–33

Saving the Project

While you are building a presentation, the computer stores it in memory. When you save a presentation, the computer places it on a storage medium such as a USB flash drive, CD, or hard disk. A saved presentation is referred to as a **file**. A **file name** is the name assigned to a file when it is saved.

It is important to save the presentation frequently for the following reasons:

• The presentation in memory will be lost if the computer is turned off or you lose electrical power while PowerPoint is open.

• If you run out of time before completing your project, you may finish your presentation at a future time without starting over.

Plan Ahead

BTW

Saving in a Previous PowerPoint Format
To ensure that your presentation will open in an earlier version of PowerPoint, you must save your file in PowerPoint 97–2003 format. Files saved in this format have the .ppt extension.

Determine where to save the document.
When saving a document, you must decide which storage medium to use.

• If you always work on the same computer and have no need to transport your projects to a different location, then your computer's hard drive will suffice as a storage location. It is a good idea, however, to save a backup copy of your projects on a separate medium in case the file becomes corrupted or the computer's hard drive fails.

• If you plan to work on your projects in various locations or on multiple computers, then you should save your projects on a portable medium, such as a USB flash drive or CD. The projects in this book use a USB flash drive, which saves files quickly and reliably and can be reused. CDs are easily portable and serve as good backups for the final versions of projects because they generally can save files only one time.

To Save a Presentation

You have performed many tasks and do not want to lose the work completed thus far. Thus, you should save the presentation. The following steps save a presentation on a USB flash drive using the file name, Cabo Package.

Note: If you are using Windows XP, see Appendix F for alternate steps.

1
- With a USB flash drive connected to one of the computer's USB ports, click the Save button on the Quick Access Toolbar to display the Save As dialog box. (Figure 1–34).

- If the Navigation pane is not displayed in the Save As dialog box, click the Browse Folders button to expand the dialog box.

- If a Folders list is displayed below the Folders button, click the Folders button to remove the Folders list.

Q&A Do I have to save to a USB flash drive?

No. You can save to any device or folder. A **folder** is a specific location on a storage medium. You can save to the default folder or a different folder. You also can create your own folders, which is explained later in this book.

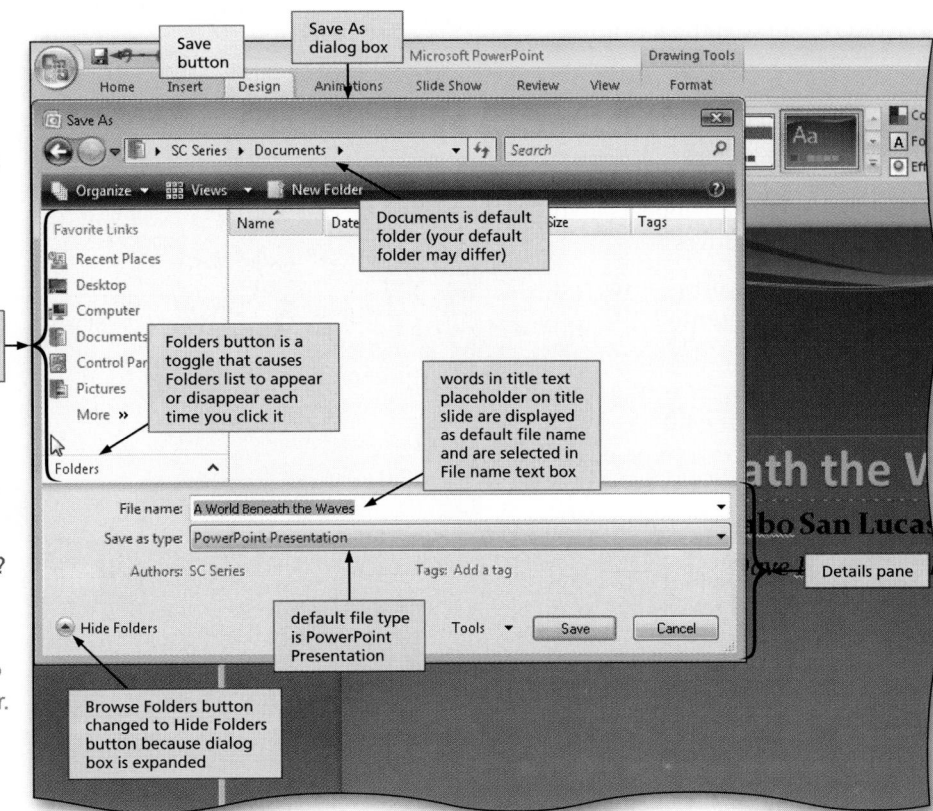

Figure 1–34

2
- Type Cabo Package in the File name box to change the file name. Do not press the ENTER key after typing the file name (Figure 1–35).

Q&A What characters can I use in a file name?

A file name can have a maximum of 260 characters, including spaces. The only invalid characters are the backslash (\), slash (/), colon (:), asterisk (*), question mark (?), quotation mark ("), less than symbol (<), greater than symbol (>), and vertical bar (|).

Q&A What are file properties and tags?

File properties contain information about a file such as the file name, author name, date the file was modified, and tags. A tag is a file property that contains a word or phrase about a file. You can organize and locate files based on their file properties.

Figure 1–35

- If Computer is not displayed in the Favorite Links section, drag the top or bottom edge of the Save As dialog box until Computer is displayed.

- Click Computer in the Favorite Links section to display a list of available drives (Figure 1–36).

- If necessary, scroll until UDISK 2.0 (E:) appears in the list of available drives.

Q&A Why is my list of drives arranged and named differently?

The size of the Save As dialog box and your computer's configuration determine how the list is displayed and how the drives are named.

Q&A How do I save the file if I am not using a USB flash drive?

Use the same process, but select your desired save location in the Favorite Links section.

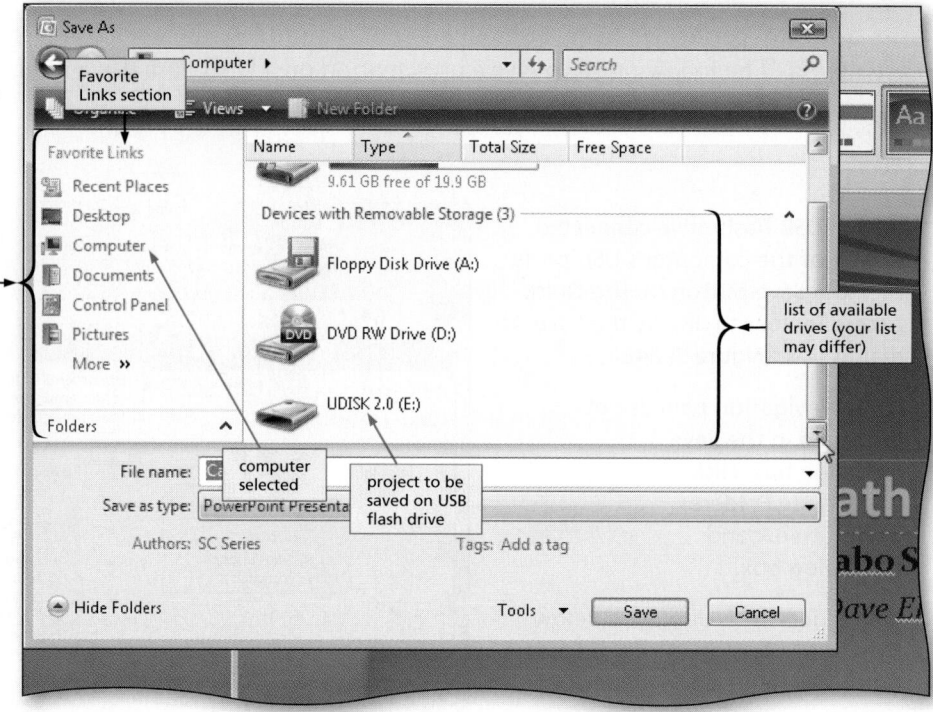

Figure 1–36

- Double-click UDISK 2.0 (E:) in the Computer list to select the USB flash drive, Drive E in this case, as the new save location (Figure 1–37).

Q&A What if my USB flash drive has a different name or letter?

It is very likely that your USB flash drive will have a different name and drive letter and be connected to a different port. Verify the device in your Computer list is correct.

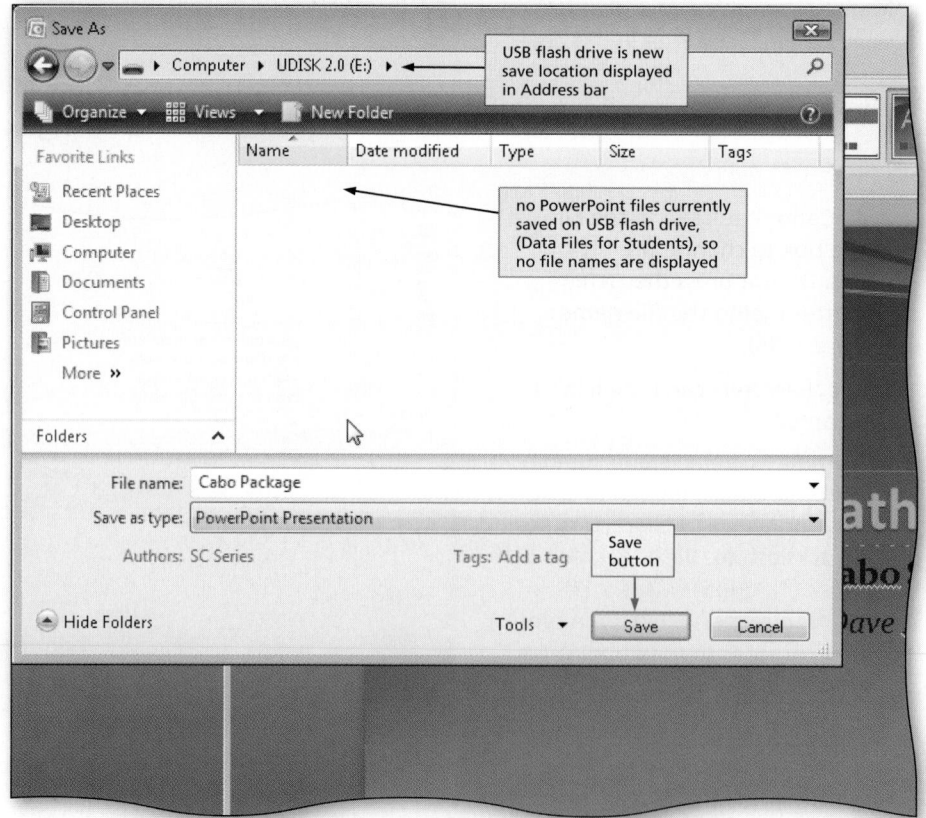

Figure 1–37

5

- Click the Save button in the Save As dialog box to save the presentation on the USB flash drive with the file name, Cabo Package (Figure 1–38).

Q&A How do I know that the project is saved?

While PowerPoint is saving your file, it briefly displays a message on the status bar indicating the amount of the file saved. In addition, your USB drive may have a light that flashes during the save process.

Q&A Why is .pptx displayed immediately to the right of the file name?

Depending on your Windows Vista settings, .pptx may be displayed after you save the file. The file type .pptx is a PowerPoint 2007 document. Previous versions of PowerPoint had a file type of .ppt.

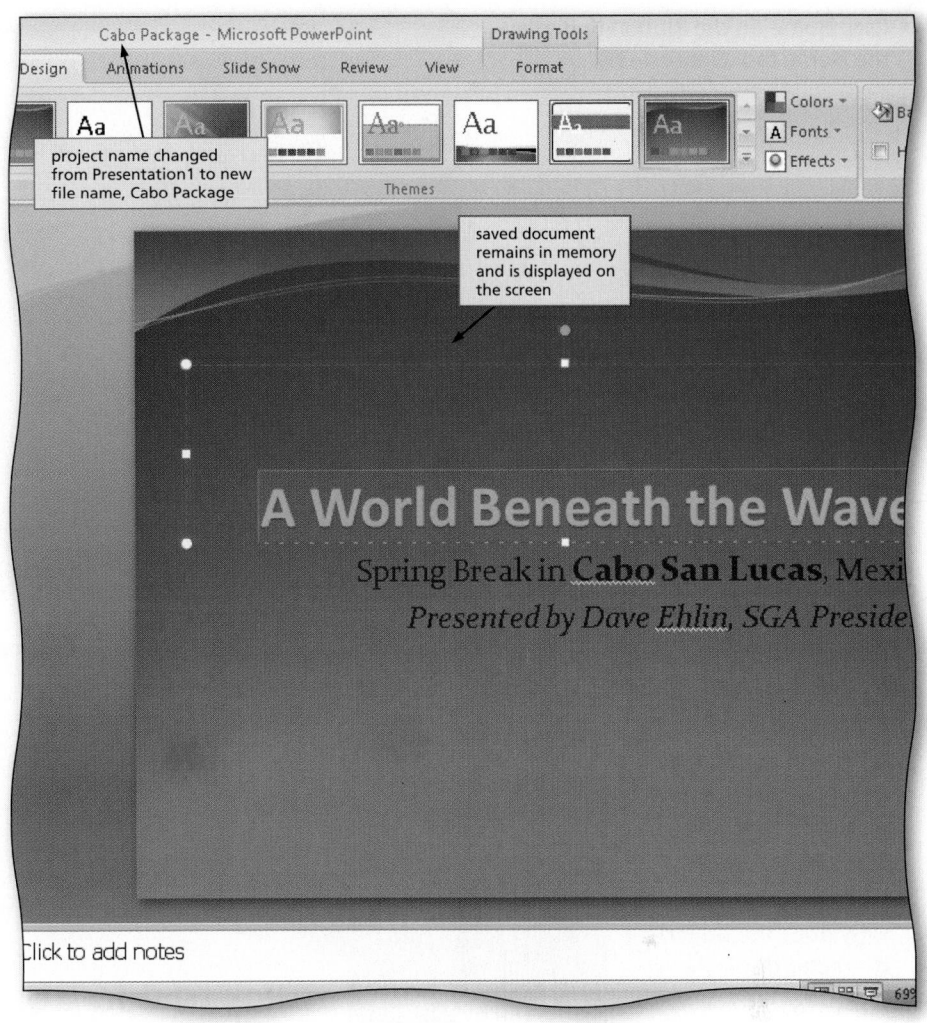

Figure 1–38

Adding a New Slide to a Presentation

With the title slide for the presentation created, the next step is to add the first text slide immediately after the title slide. Usually, when you create a presentation, you add slides with text, graphics, or charts. Some placeholders allow you to double-click the placeholder and then access other objects, such as media clips, charts, diagrams, and organization charts. You can change the layout for a slide at any time during the creation of a presentation.

Other Ways

1. Click Office Button, click Save, type file name, click Computer, select drive or folder, click Save button

2. Press CTRL+S or press SHIFT+F12, type file name, click Computer, select drive or folder, click Save button

To Add a New Text Slide with a Bulleted List

When you add a new slide, PowerPoint uses the Title and Content slide layout. This layout provides a title placeholder and a content area for text, art, charts, and other graphics. A vertical scroll bar appears in the Slide pane when you add the second slide so that you can move from slide to slide easily. A thumbnail of this slide also appears in the Slides tab. The following steps add a new slide with the Title and Content slide layout.

- Click Home on the Ribbon to display the Home tab (Figure 1–39).

Figure 1–39

- Click the New Slide button in the Slides group to insert a new slide with the Title and Content layout (Figure 1–40).

Q&A Why does the bullet character display a blue dot?

The Flow document theme determines the bullet characters. Each paragraph level has an associated bullet character.

Q&A I clicked the New Slide arrow instead of the New Slide button. What should I do?

Click the Title and Content slide thumbnail in the layout gallery.

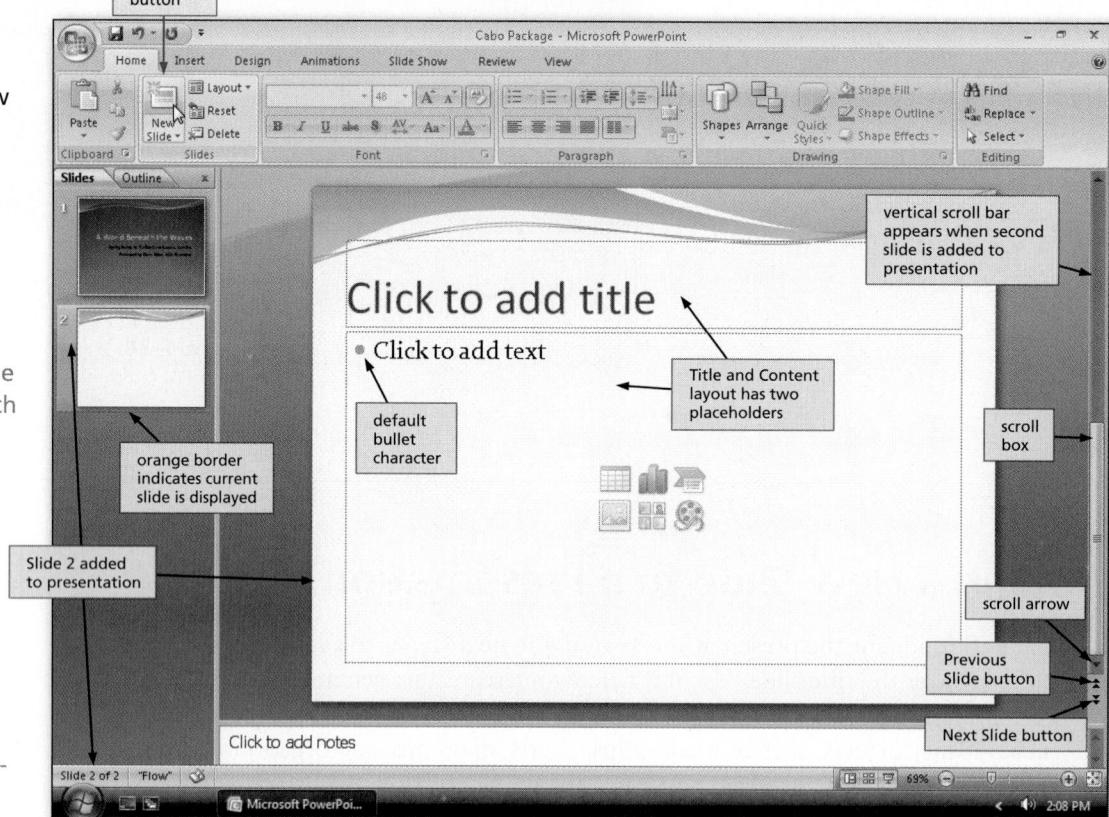

Figure 1–40

Other Ways

1. Press CTRL+M

**Plan
Ahead**

> **Choose the words for the slide.**
> All presentations should follow the 7 × 7 rule which states that each slide should have a maximum of seven lines, and each line should have a maximum of seven words. PowerPoint designers must choose their words carefully and, in turn, help viewers read the slides easily.

Creating a Text Slide with a Single-Level Bulleted List

The information in the Slide 2 text placeholder is presented in a bulleted list. All the bullets appear at the same paragraph level, called the first level.

To Enter a Slide Title

PowerPoint assumes every new slide has a title. The title for Slide 2 is Package Highlights. The following step enters this title.

- Click the label, Click to add title, to select it and then type Package Highlights in the placeholder. Do not press the ENTER key (Figure 1–41).

Q&A What are those six icons grouped in the middle of the slide?

You can click one of the icons to insert a specific type of content: table, chart, SmartArt graphic, picture, clip art, or media clip.

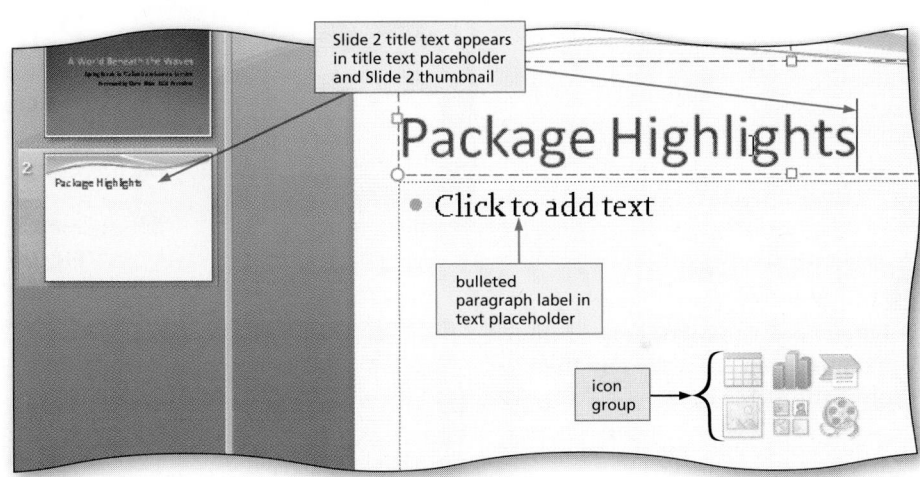

Figure 1–41

To Select a Text Placeholder

Before you can type text into the text placeholder, you first must select it. The following step selects the text placeholder on Slide 2.

- Click the label, Click to add text, to select the text placeholder (Figure 1–42).

Q&A Why does my mouse pointer have a different shape?

If you move the mouse pointer away from the bullet, it will change shape.

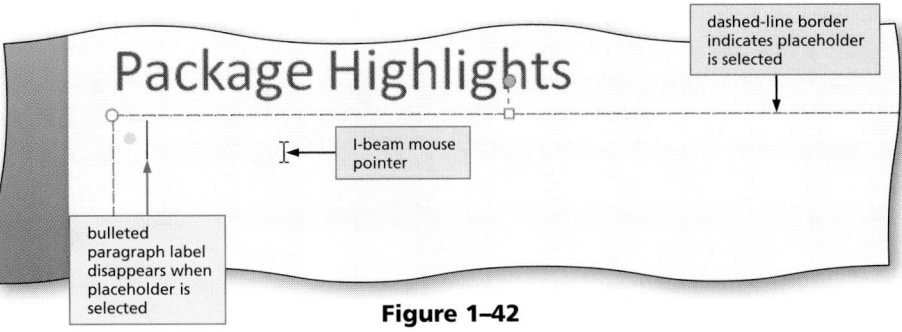

Figure 1–42

Other Ways
1. Press CTRL+ENTER

To Type a Single-Level Bulleted List

The content placeholder provides an area for the text characters. When you click inside a placeholder, you then can type or paste text. If your text exceeds the size of the placeholder, PowerPoint will attempt to make the text fit by reducing the text size and line spacing. **Line spacing** is the amount of vertical space between the lines of text.

As discussed previously, a bulleted list is a list of paragraphs, each of which is preceded by a bullet. A paragraph is a segment of text ended by pressing the ENTER key. The next step is to type the single-level bulleted list, which consists of five paragraphs (Figure 1–1b on page PPT 3). The following steps create a single-level bulleted list.

1

- Type `Four nights at the Azure Seas Resort` and then press the ENTER key to begin a new bulleted first-level paragraph (Figure 1–43).

Q&A Can I delete bullets on a slide?

Yes. If you do not want bullets to display on a particular paragraph, click the Bullets button in the Paragraph group on the Home tab or right-click the paragraph and then click the Bullets button on the Mini toolbar.

Figure 1–43

2

- Type `Breakfast buffet, lunch, dinner, and snacks` and then press the ENTER key.

- Type `Two large swimming pools` and then press the ENTER key.

- Type `Round-trip airfare and hotel transfers` and then press the ENTER key.

- Type `Daily activities, including water sports` but do not press the ENTER key (Figure 1–44).

Q&A I pressed the ENTER key in error, and now a new bullet appears after the last entry on this slide. How can I remove this extra bullet?

Press the BACKSPACE key.

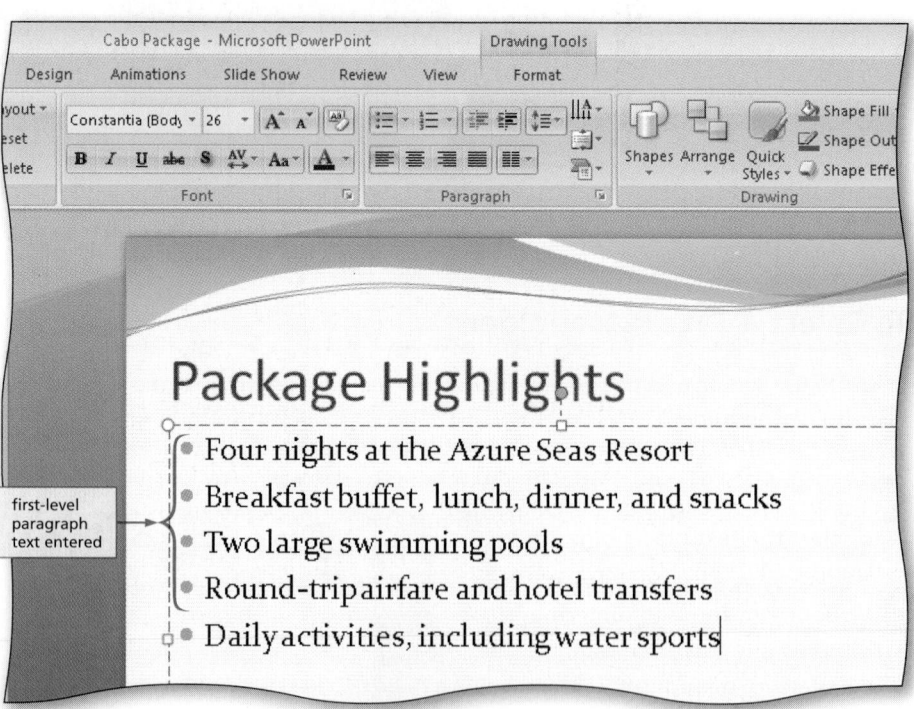

Figure 1–44

Creating a Text Slide with a Multi-Level Bulleted List

Slides 3 and 4 in Figure 1–1 on pages PPT 3–4 contain more than one level of bulleted text. A slide that consists of more than one level of bulleted text is called a **multi-level bulleted list slide**. Beginning with the second level, each paragraph indents to the right of the preceding level and is pushed down to a lower level. For example, if you increase the indent of a first-level paragraph, it becomes a second-level paragraph.

Creating a text slide with a multi-level bulleted list requires several steps. Initially, you enter a slide title in the title text placeholder. Next, you select the content text placeholder. Then, you type the text for the multi-level bulleted list, increasing and decreasing the indents as needed. The next several sections add a slide with a multi-level bulleted list.

To Add a New Slide and Enter a Slide Title

When you add a new slide to a presentation, PowerPoint keeps the same layout used on the previous slide. PowerPoint assumes every new slide has a title. The title for Slide 3 is Rates and Booking. The following steps add a new slide (Slide 3) and enter a title.

1

- Click the New Slide button in the Slides group on the Home tab to insert a new slide with the Title and Content layout (Figure 1–45).

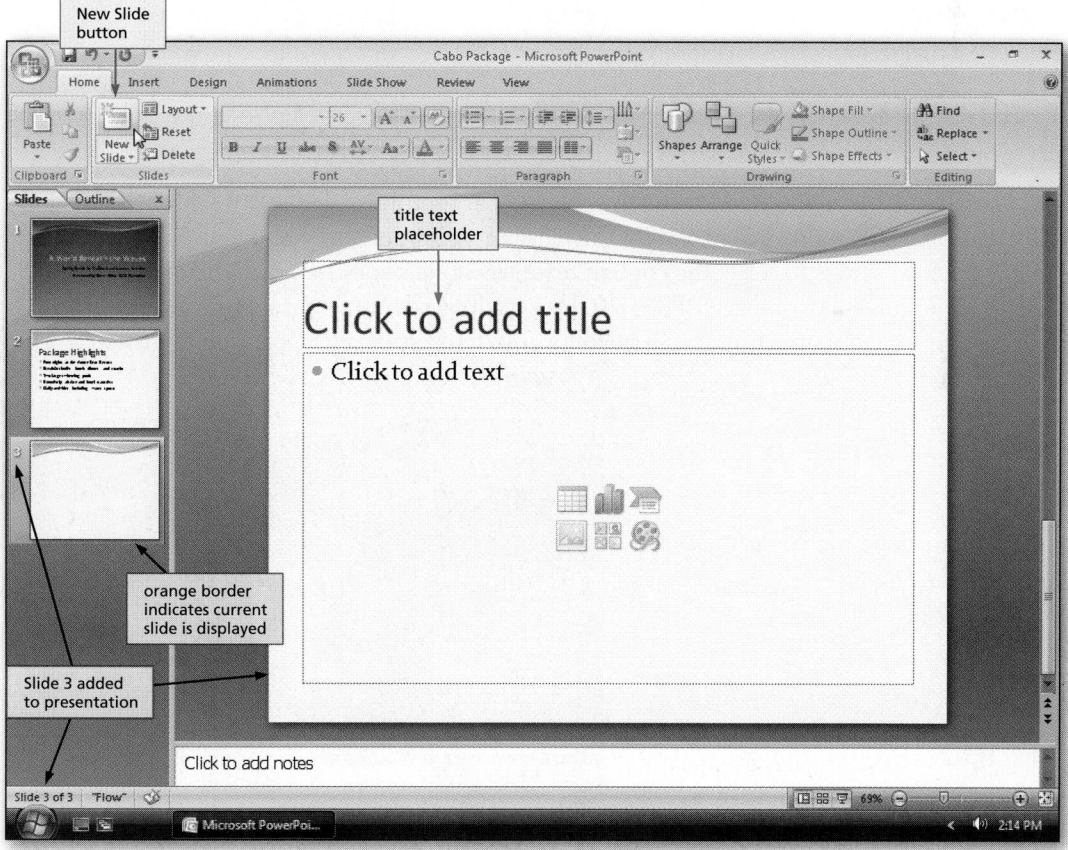

Figure 1–45

• Click the title text placeholder and then type Rates and Booking in this placeholder. Do not press the ENTER key (Figure 1–46).

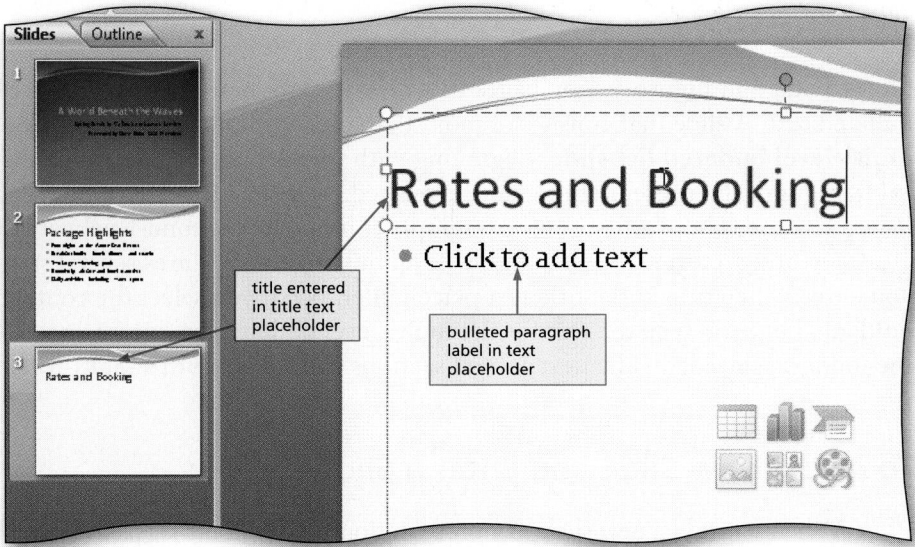

Figure 1–46

To Type a Multi-Level Bulleted List

In a multi-level bulleted list, a lower-level paragraph is a subset of a higher-level paragraph. It usually contains information that supports the topic in the paragraph immediately above it.

The next step is to select the content text placeholder and then type the multi-level bulleted list, which consists of six entries (Figure 1–1c on page PPT 3). Creating a lower-level paragraph is called **demoting** text; creating a higher-level paragraph is called **promoting** text. The following steps create a list consisting of three levels.

• Click the bulleted paragraph text placeholder.

• Type Only $495 double occupancy and then press the ENTER key (Figure 1–47).

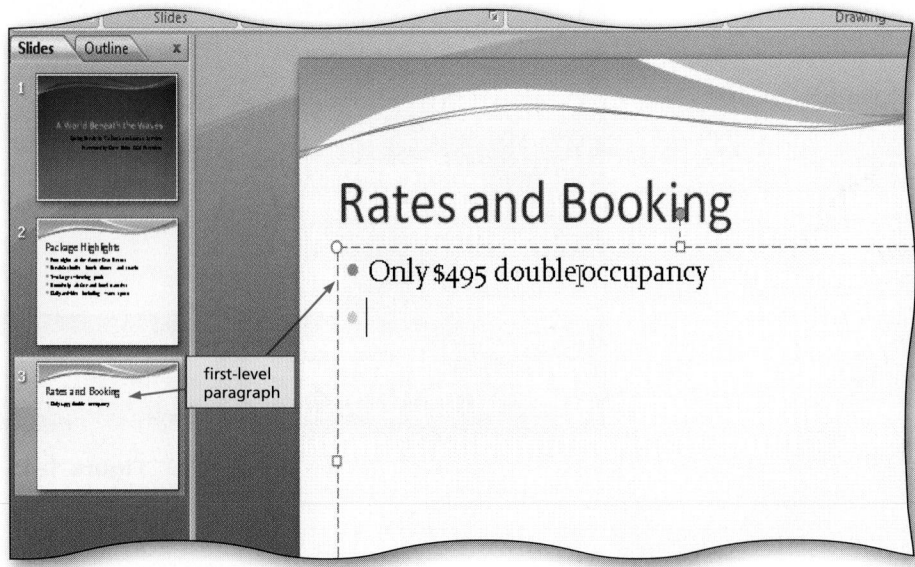

Figure 1–47

2

- Click the Increase List Level button in the Paragraph group to indent the second paragraph below the first and create a second-level paragraph (Figure 1–48).

Q&A

Why does the bullet for this paragraph have a different size and color?

A different bullet is assigned to each paragraph level.

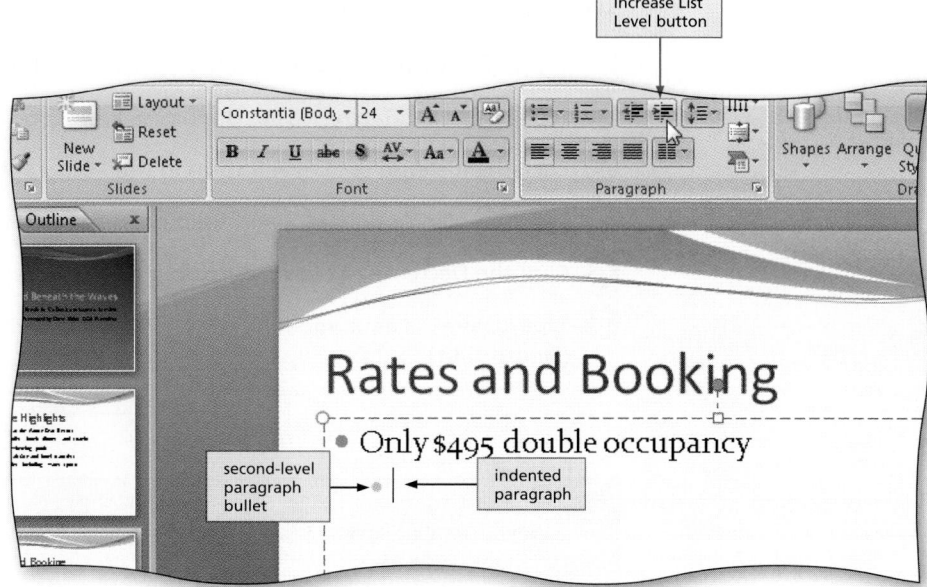

Figure 1–48

3

- Type Non-diver rate: $275 and then press the ENTER key to add a new paragraph at the same level as the previous paragraph.

- Type Single occupancy: add $150 and then press the ENTER key (Figure 1–49).

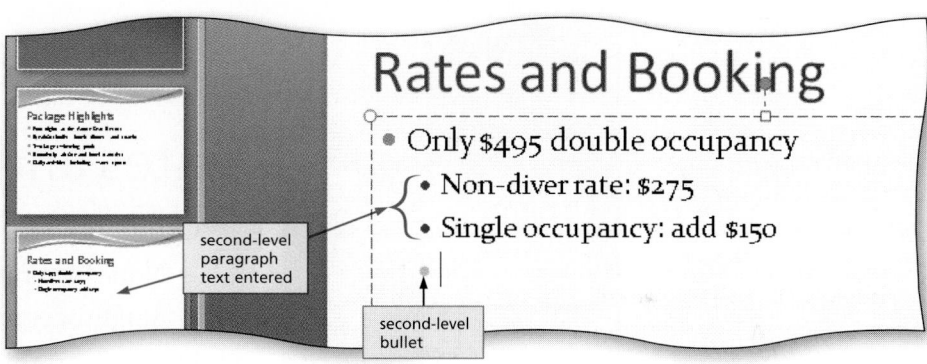

Figure 1–49

4

- Click the Decrease List Level button in the Paragraph group so that the second-level paragraph becomes a first-level paragraph (Figure 1–50).

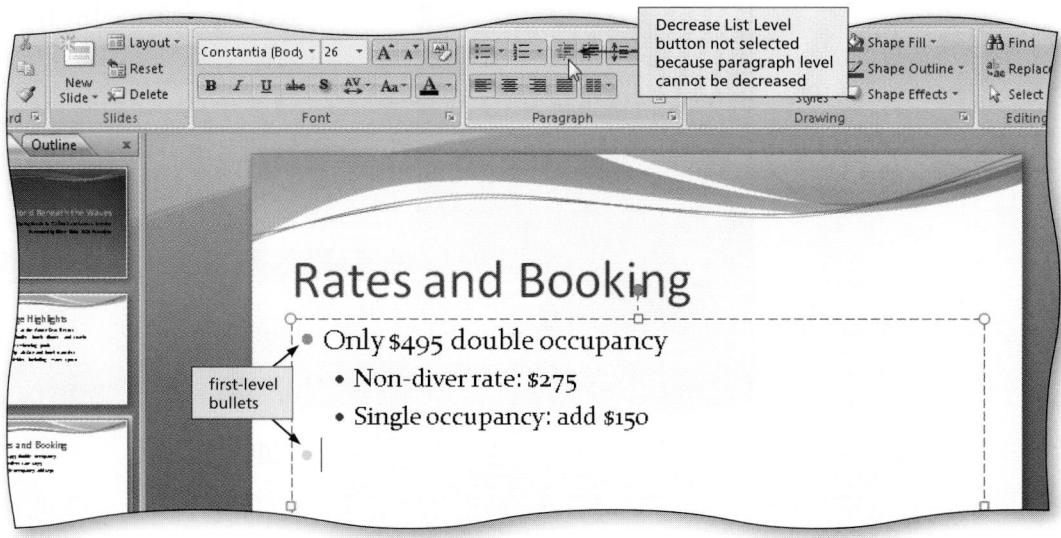

Other Ways

1. Press TAB to promote paragraph; press SHIFT+TAB to demote paragraph

Figure 1–50

To Type the Remaining Text for Slide 3

The following steps complete the text for Slide 3.

1 Type `Nonrefundable $150 deposit required` and then press the ENTER key.

2 Click the Increase List Level button in the Paragraph group to demote the paragraph.

3 Type `Due by October 1` and then press the ENTER key.

4 Click the Decrease List Level button in the Paragraph group to promote the paragraph.

5 Type `Travel insurance highly recommended` but do not press the ENTER key (Figure 1–51).

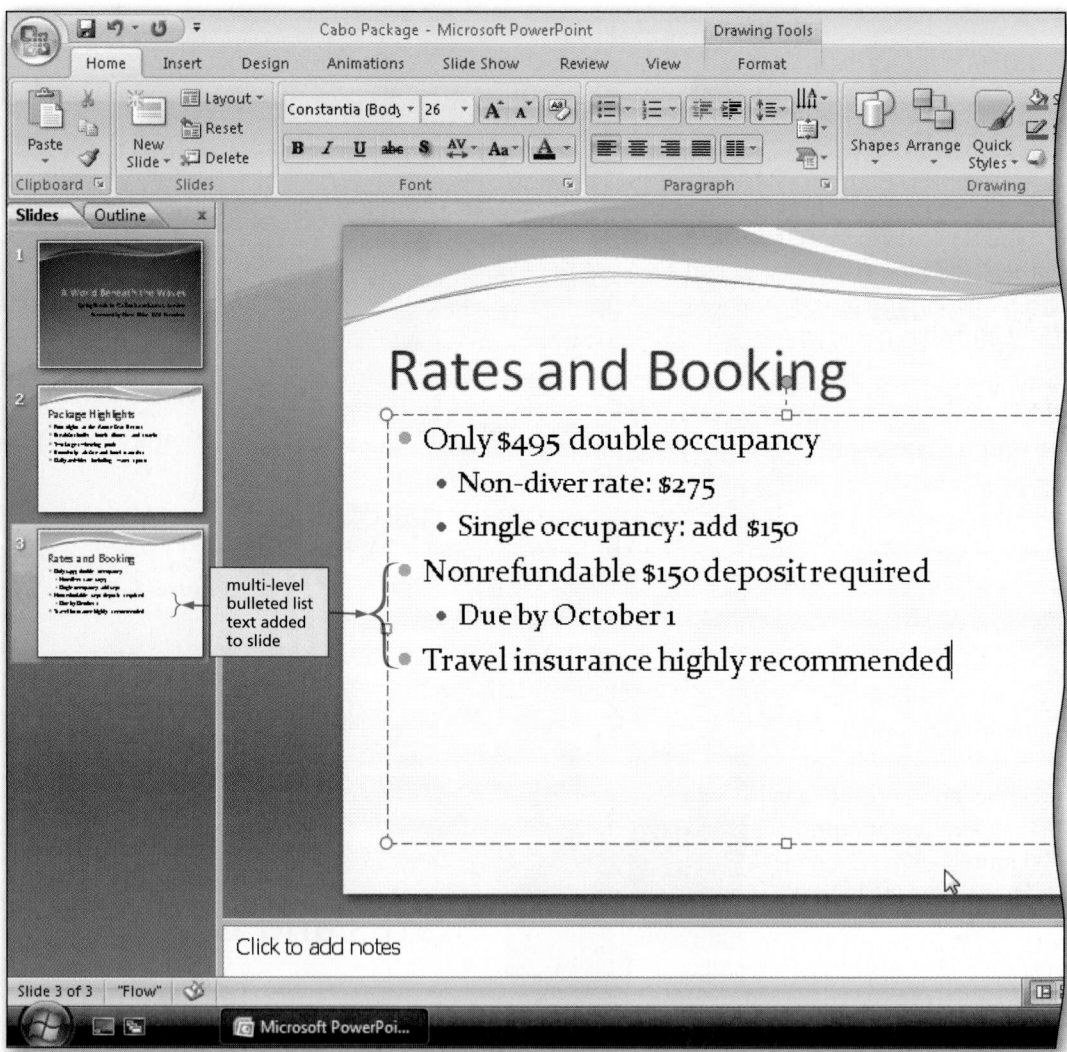

Figure 1–51

To Create Slide 4

Slide 4 is the final multi-level bulleted text slide in this presentation. It has three levels. The following steps create Slide 4.

1 Click the New Slide button in the Slides group.

2 Type Snorkeling and Diving in the title text placeholder.

3 Press CTRL+ENTER to move the insertion point to the text placeholder.

4 Type Three days of two-tank boat dives and then press the ENTER key.

5 Click the Increase List Level button. Type Weights and tanks included and then press the ENTER key (Figure 1–52).

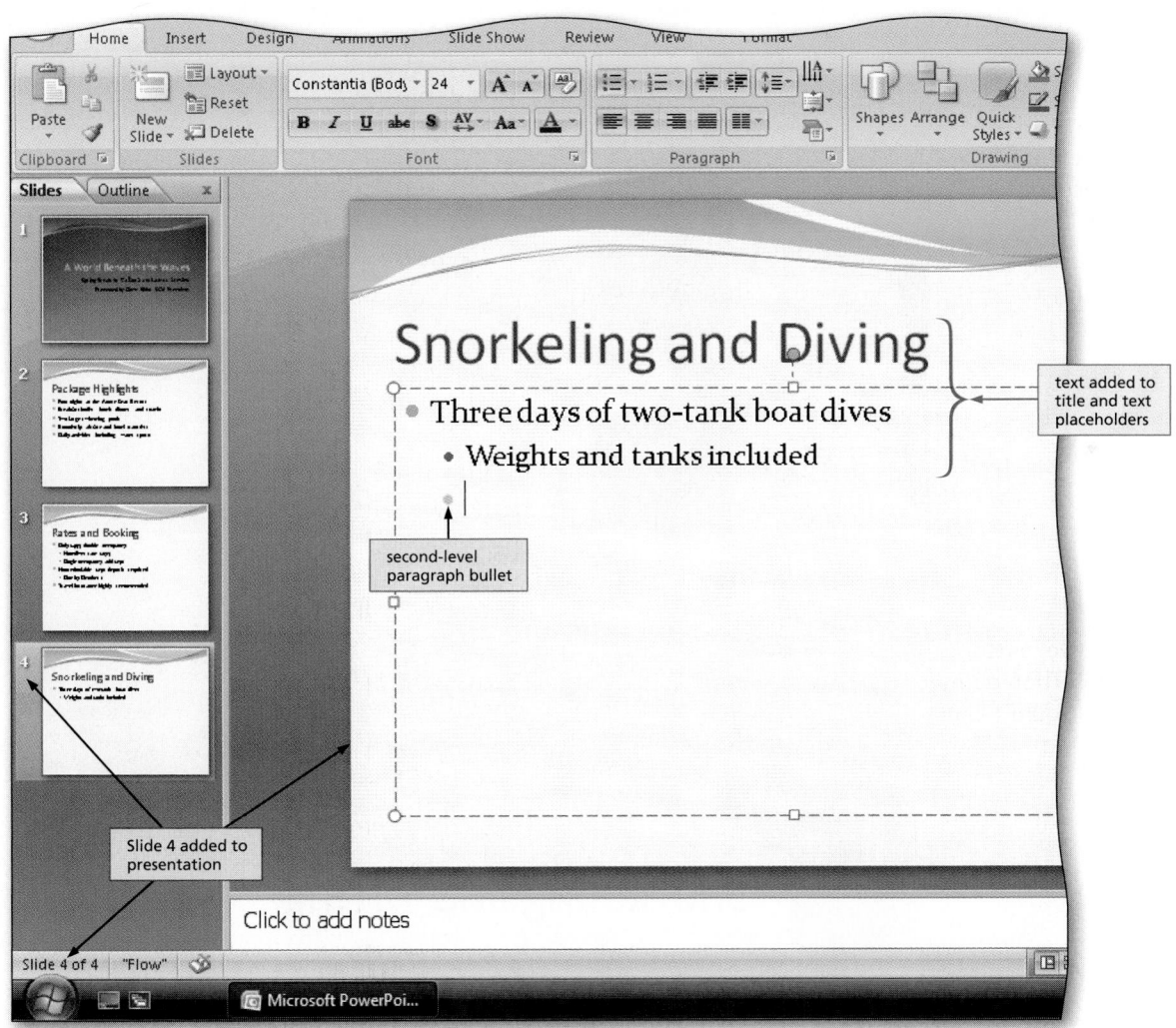

Figure 1–52

To Create a Third-Level Paragraph

Slide 4 contains detailed information about the particular dives. Each additional paragraph becomes more specific and supports the information in the paragraph above it.

The next line in Slide 4 is indented an additional level, to the third level. The following steps demote the text to a third-level paragraph.

1
- Click the Increase List Level button so that the second-level paragraph becomes a third-level paragraph (Figure 1–53).

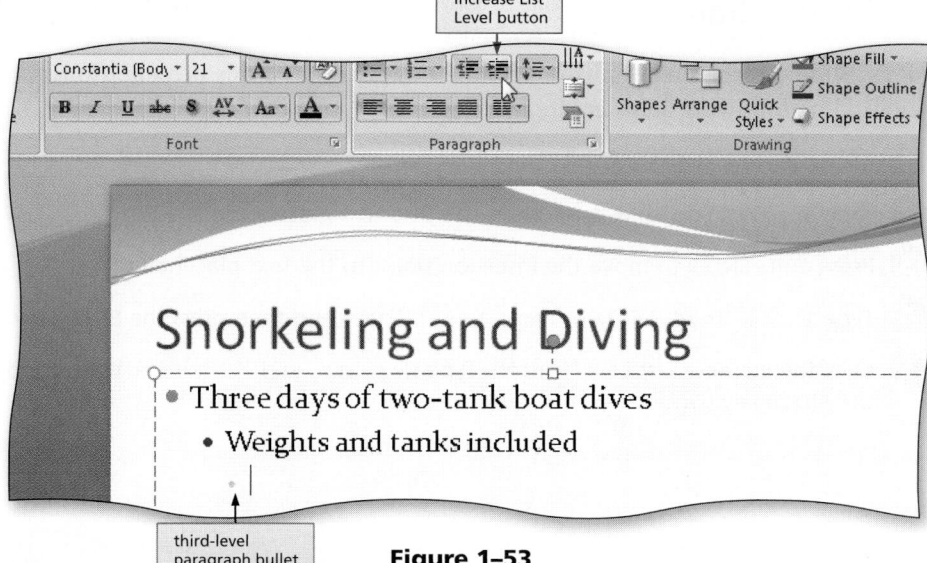

Figure 1–53

2
- Type Instructors available for beginners and then press the ENTER key to create a second third-level paragraph (Figure 1–54).

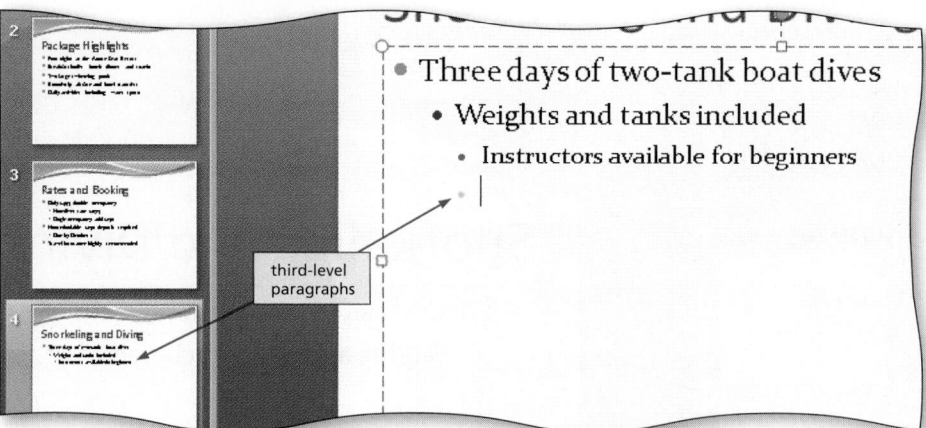

Figure 1–54

3
- Click the Decrease List Level button two times so that the insertion point appears at the first level (Figure 1–55).

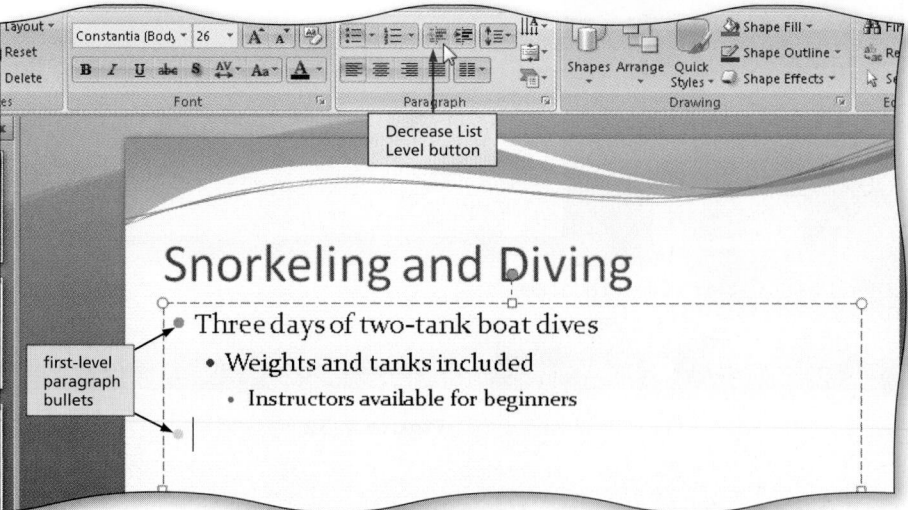

Figure 1–55

To Type the Remaining Text for Slide 4

The next three paragraphs concern what divers and snorkelers will view. The following steps type the remaining text for Slide 4.

1 Type Various locations based on diving skills and then press the ENTER key.

2 Press the TAB key to increase the indent to the second level.

3 Type Spectacular underwater wildlife and landscapes and then press the ENTER key.

4 Press the TAB key to increase the indent to the third level.

5 Type See squids, sea turtles, snakes, barracudas, and stingrays but do not press the ENTER key (Figure 1–56).

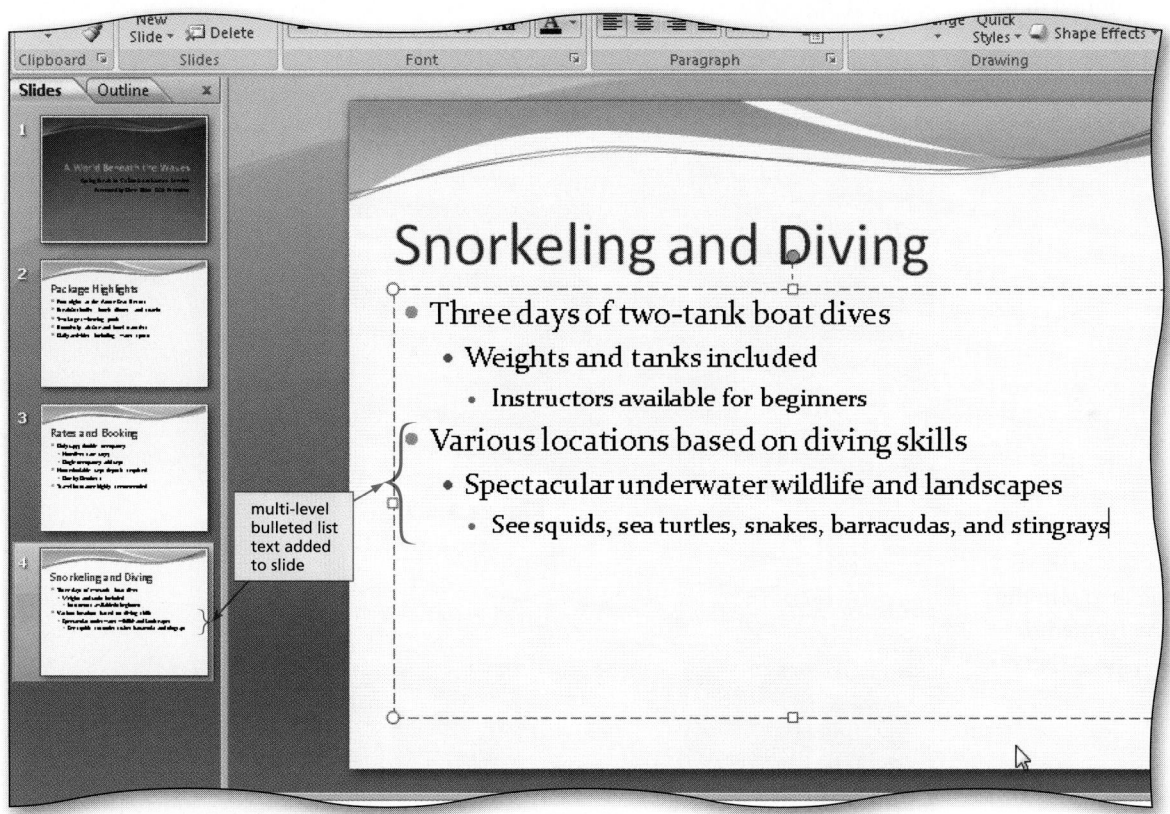

Figure 1–56

Choose the words for the slide.
After the last bulleted list slide in the slide show appears during a slide show, the default PowerPoint setting is to end the presentation with a **black slide**. This black slide appears only when the slide show is running and concludes the slide show, so your audience never sees the PowerPoint window. It is a good idea, however, to end the presentation with a final, closing slide to display at the end of the presentation. This slide ends the presentation gracefully and should be an exact copy, or a very similar copy, of your title slide. The audience will recognize that the presentation is drawing to a close when this slide appears. It can remain on the screen when the audience asks questions, approaches the speaker for further information, or exits the room.

Plan Ahead

Ending a Slide Show with a Closing Slide

All the text slides are created for the Cabo Package slide show. This presentation thus far consists of a title slide, one text slide with a single-level bulleted list, and two text slides with a multi-level bulleted list. A closing slide that resembles the title slide is the final slide to create.

To Duplicate a Slide

When two slides contain similar information and have the same format, duplicating one slide and then making minor modifications to the new slide saves time and increases consistency.

Slide 5 will have the same layout and design as Slide 1. The most expedient method of creating this slide is to copy Slide 1 and then make minor modifications to the new slide. The following steps duplicate the title slide.

- Click the Slide 1 thumbnail in the Slides tab to display Slide 1 (Figure 1–57).

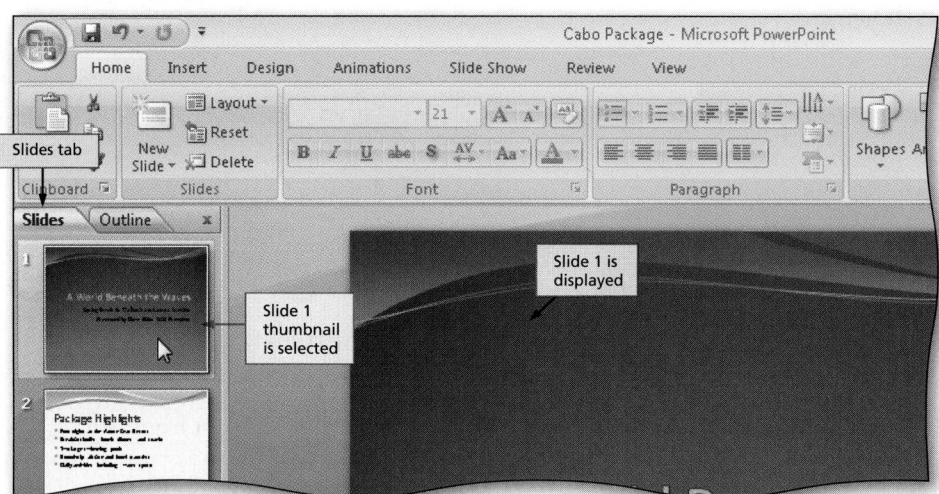

Figure 1–57

- Click the New Slide arrow in the Slides group on the Home tab to display the Flow layout gallery (Figure 1–58).

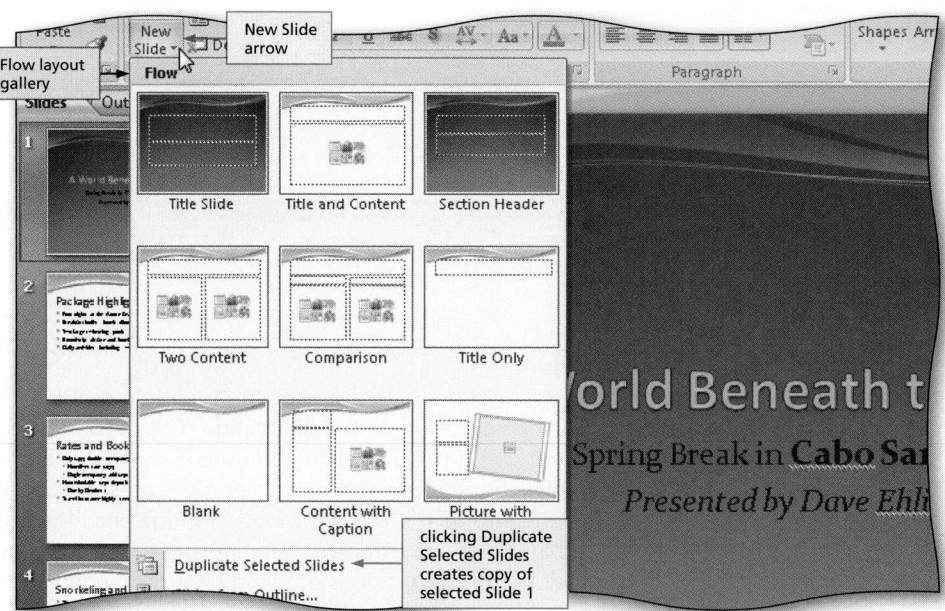

Figure 1–58

3

- Click Duplicate Selected Slides in the Flow layout gallery to create a new Slide 2, which is a duplicate of Slide 1 (Figure 1–59).

Figure 1–59

To Arrange a Slide

The new Slide 2 was inserted directly below Slide 1 because Slide 1 was the selected slide. This duplicate slide needs to display at the end of the presentation directly after the final title and content slide.

Changing slide order is an easy process and is best performed in the Tabs pane. When you click the slide thumbnail and begin to drag it to a new location, a line indicates the new location of the selected slide. When you release the mouse button, the slide drops into the desired location. Hence, this process of dragging and then dropping the thumbnail in a new location is called **drag and drop**. You can use the drag-and-drop method to move any selected item, including text and graphics. The following step moves the new Slide 2 to the end of the presentation so that it becomes a closing slide.

- With Slide 2 selected, drag the Slide 2 slide thumbnail in the Slides pane below the last slide thumbnail (Figure 1–60).

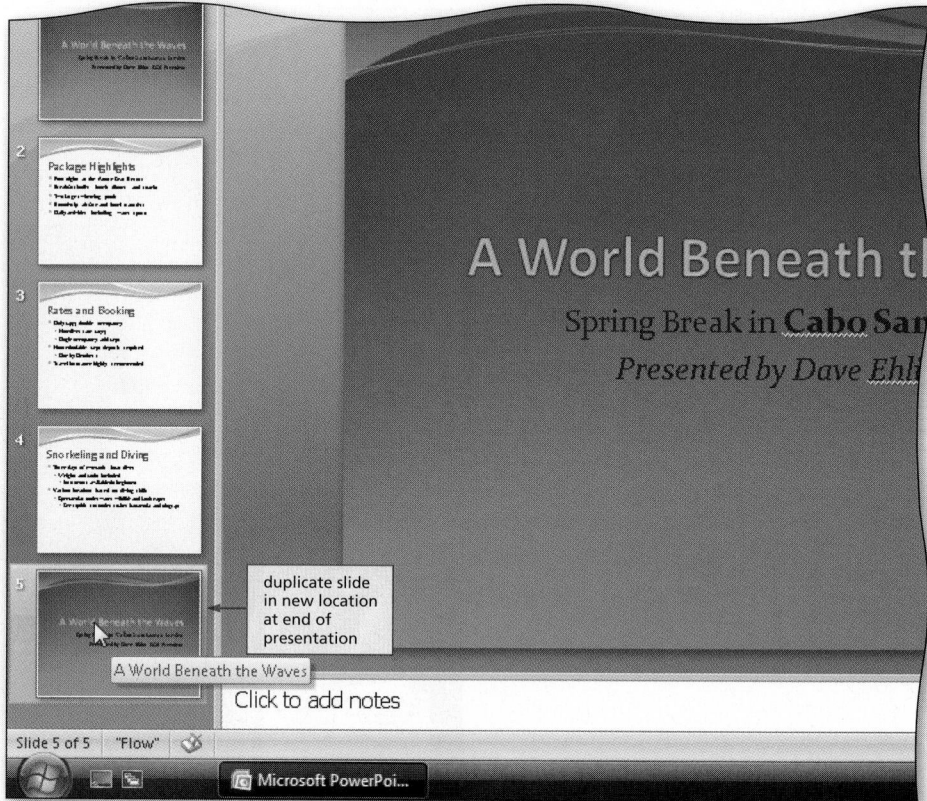

Figure 1–60

Other Ways

1. Click slide icon on Outline tab, drag icon to new location
2. In Slide Sorter view click slide thumbnail, drag thumbnail to new location

To Delete All Text in a Placeholder

To keep the ending slide clean and simple, you want only the slide show title, A World Beneath the Waves, to display on Slide 5. The following steps delete both paragraphs in the subtitle placeholder.

- With Slide 5 selected, click the subtitle text placeholder to select it (Figure 1–61).

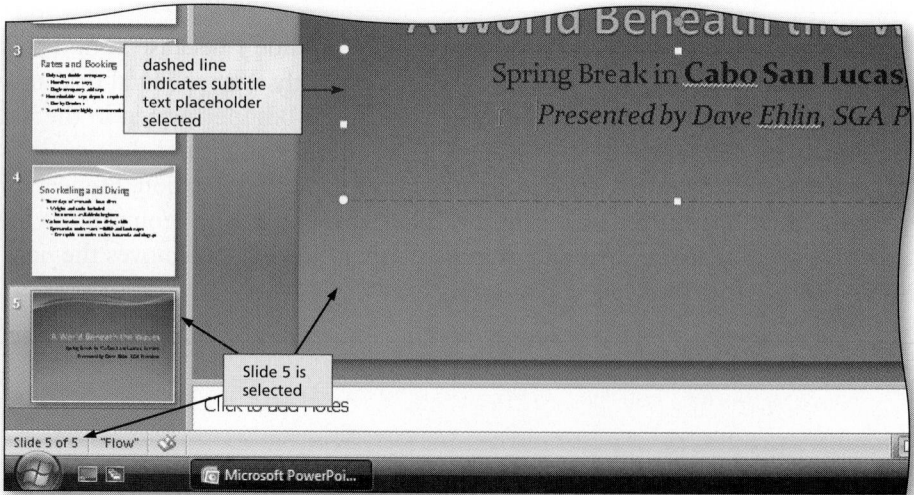

Figure 1–61

2

• Click the subtitle text placeholder border to change the border from a dashed line to a solid line (Figure 1–62).

Figure 1–62

3

• Click the Cut button in the Clipboard group on the Home tab to delete all the text in the subtitle text placeholder (Figure 1–63).

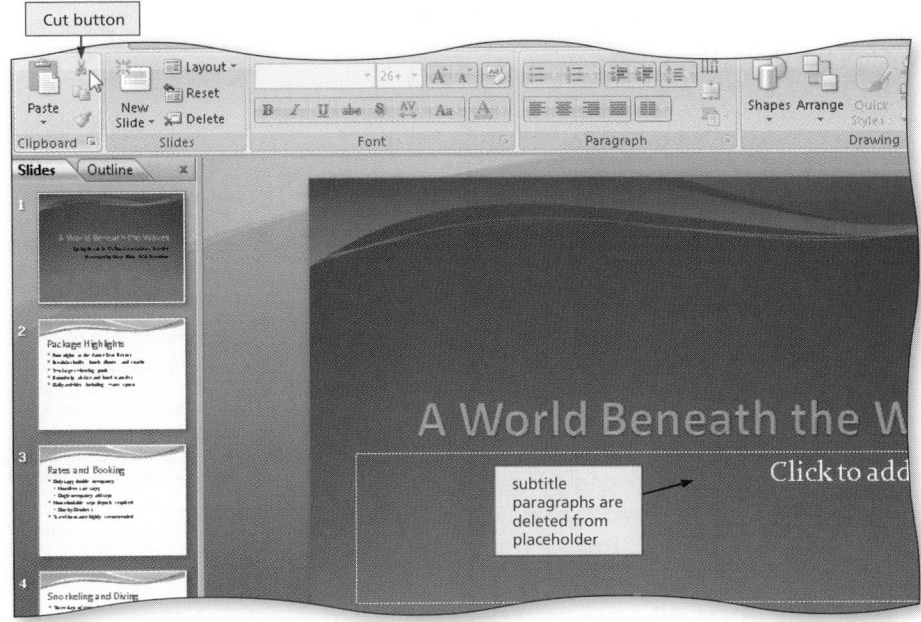

Figure 1–63

Changing Document Properties and Saving Again

PowerPoint helps you organize and identify your files by using document properties, which are the details about a file. **Document properties**, also known as **metadata**, can include such information as the project author, title, or subject. **Keywords** are words or phrases that further describe the document. For example, a class name or document topic can describe the file's purpose or content.

Document properties are valuable for a variety of reasons:

• Users can save time locating a particular file because they can view a document's properties without opening the document.

• By creating consistent properties for files having similar content, users can better organize their documents.

• Some organizations require PowerPoint users to add document properties so that other employees can view details about these files.

Five different types of document properties exist, but the more common ones used in this book are standard and automatically updated properties. **Standard properties**

BTW

Converters for Earlier PowerPoint Versions
The Microsoft Web site has updates and converters if you are using earlier versions of PowerPoint. The Microsoft Office Compatibility Pack for Word, Excel and PowerPoint 2007 File Format will allow you to open, edit, and save Office 2007 documents that you receive without saving them in the earlier version's file format.

are associated with all Microsoft Office documents and include author, title, and subject. **Automatically updated properties** include file system properties, such as the date you create or change a file, and statistics, such as the file size.

To Change Document Properties

The **Document Information Panel** contains areas where you can view and enter document properties. You can view and change information in this panel at any time while you are creating a document. Before saving the presentation again, you want to add your name and class name as document properties. The following steps use the Document Information Panel to change document properties.

1
- Click the Office Button to display the Office Button menu.

- Point to Prepare on the Office Button menu to display the Prepare submenu (Figure 1–64).

Q&A

What other types of actions besides changing properties can you take to set up a document for distribution?

The Prepare submenu provides commands related to sharing a document with others, such as allowing or restricting people to view and modify your document, checking to see if your presentation will run in earlier versions of PowerPoint, and searching for hidden personal information.

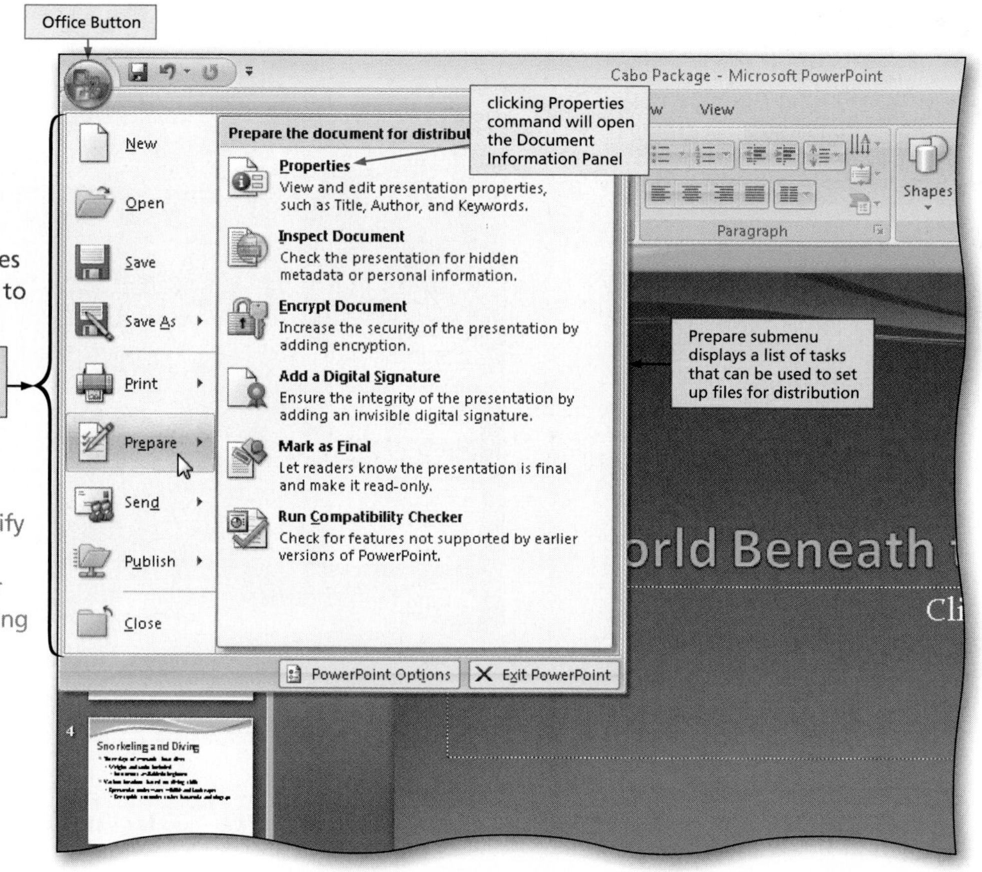

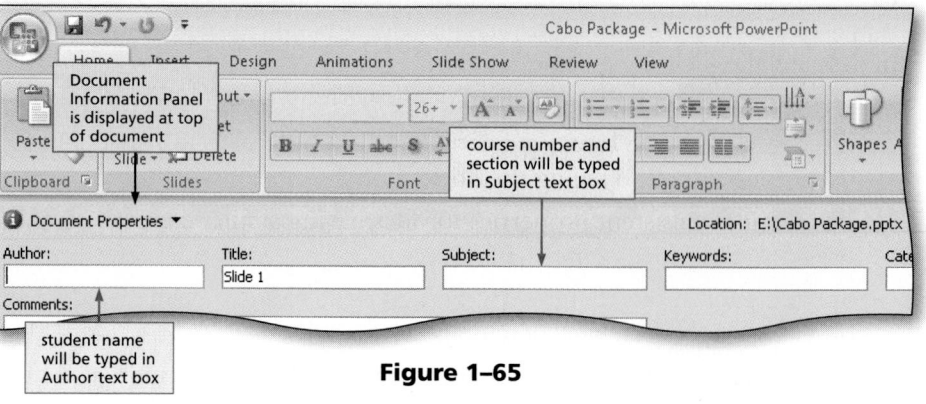

Figure 1–64

2
- Click Properties on the Prepare submenu to display the Document Information Panel (Figure 1–65).

Q&A

Why are some of the document properties in my Document Information Panel already filled in?

The person who installed Microsoft Office 2007 on your computer or network may have set or customized the properties.

Figure 1–65

3

• Click the Author text box, if necessary, and then type your name as the Author property. If a name already is displayed in the Author text box, delete it before typing your name.

• Click the Subject text box, if necessary delete any existing text, and then type your course number and section as the Subject property (Figure 1–66).

 Q&A

What types of document properties does PowerPoint collect automatically?

PowerPoint records such details as how long you worked at creating your project, how many times you revised the document, and what fonts and themes are used.

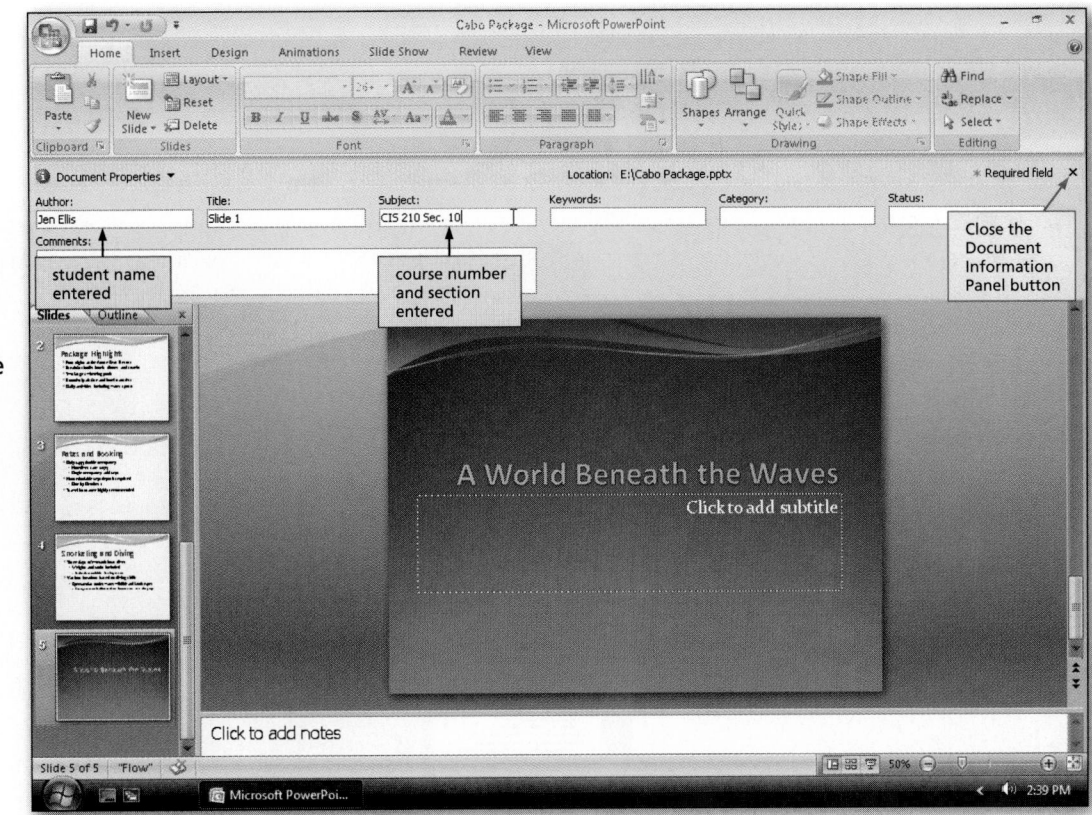

Figure 1–66

4

• Click the Close the Document Information Panel button so that the Document Information Panel no longer is displayed.

To Save an Existing Presentation with the Same File Name

Saving frequently cannot be overemphasized. You have made several modifications to the presentation since you saved it earlier in the chapter. When you first saved the document, you clicked the Save button on the Quick Access Toolbar, the Save As dialog box appeared, and you entered the file name, Cabo Package. If you want to use the same file name to save the changes made to the document, you again click the Save button on the Quick Access Toolbar. The following step saves the presentation again.

1

- Click the Save button on the Quick Access Toolbar to overwrite the previous Cabo Package file on the USB flash drive (Figure 1–67).

Q&A

Why did the Save As dialog box not appear?

PowerPoint overwrites the document using the settings specified the first time you saved the document. To save the file with a different file name or on different media, display the Save As dialog box by clicking the Office Button and then clicking Save As on the Office Button menu. Then, fill in the Save As dialog box as described in Steps 2 through 5 on pages PPT 27 through PPT 29.

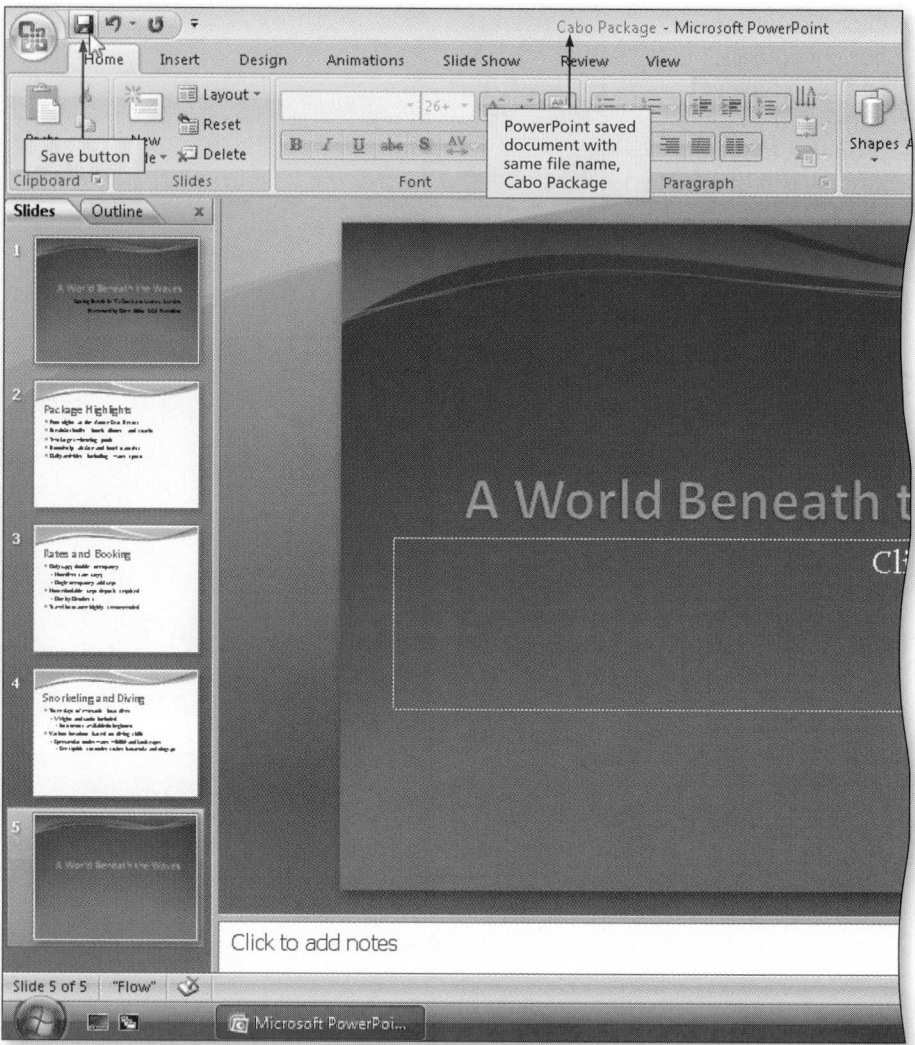

Figure 1–67

Other Ways

1. Press CTRL+S or press SHIFT+F12, press ENTER

Moving to Another Slide in Normal View

When creating or editing a presentation in Normal view, you often want to display a slide other than the current one. You can move to another slide using several methods.

- Drag the scroll box on the vertical scroll bar up or down to move through the slides in the presentation.
- Click the Next Slide or Previous Slide button on the vertical scroll bar. Clicking the Next Slide button advances to the next slide in the presentation. Clicking the Previous Slide button backs up to the slide preceding the current slide.
- On the Slides tab, click a particular slide to display that slide in the Slide pane.

To Use the Scroll Box on the Slide Pane to Move to Another Slide

Before continuing with developing this project, you want to display the title slide by dragging the scroll box on the vertical scroll bar. When you drag the scroll box, the **slide indicator** shows the number and title of the slide you are about to display. Releasing the mouse button shows the slide. The following steps move from Slide 5 to Slide 1 using the scroll box on the Slide pane.

- Position the mouse pointer on the scroll box.

- Press and hold down the mouse button so that Slide: 5 of 5 A World Beneath the Waves appears in the slide indicator (Figure 1–68).

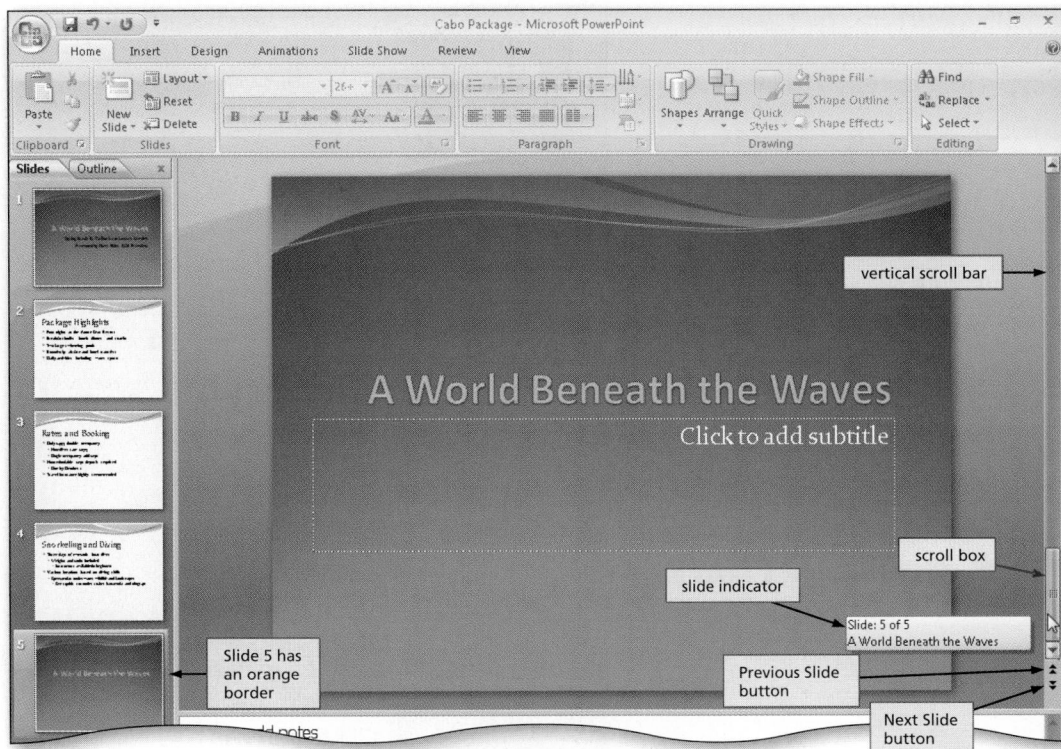

Figure 1–68

- Drag the scroll box up the vertical scroll bar until Slide: 1 of 5 A World Beneath the Waves appears in the slide indicator (Figure 1–69).

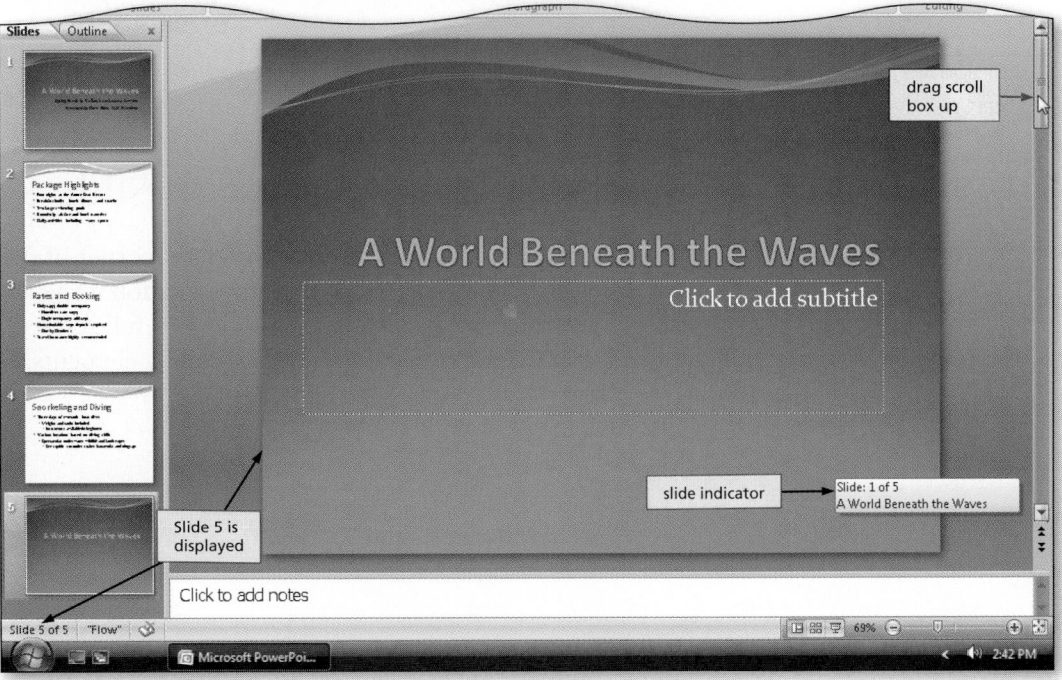

Figure 1–69

3

- Release the mouse button so that Slide 1 appears in the Slide pane and the Slide 1 thumbnail has an orange border in the Slides tab (Figure 1–70).

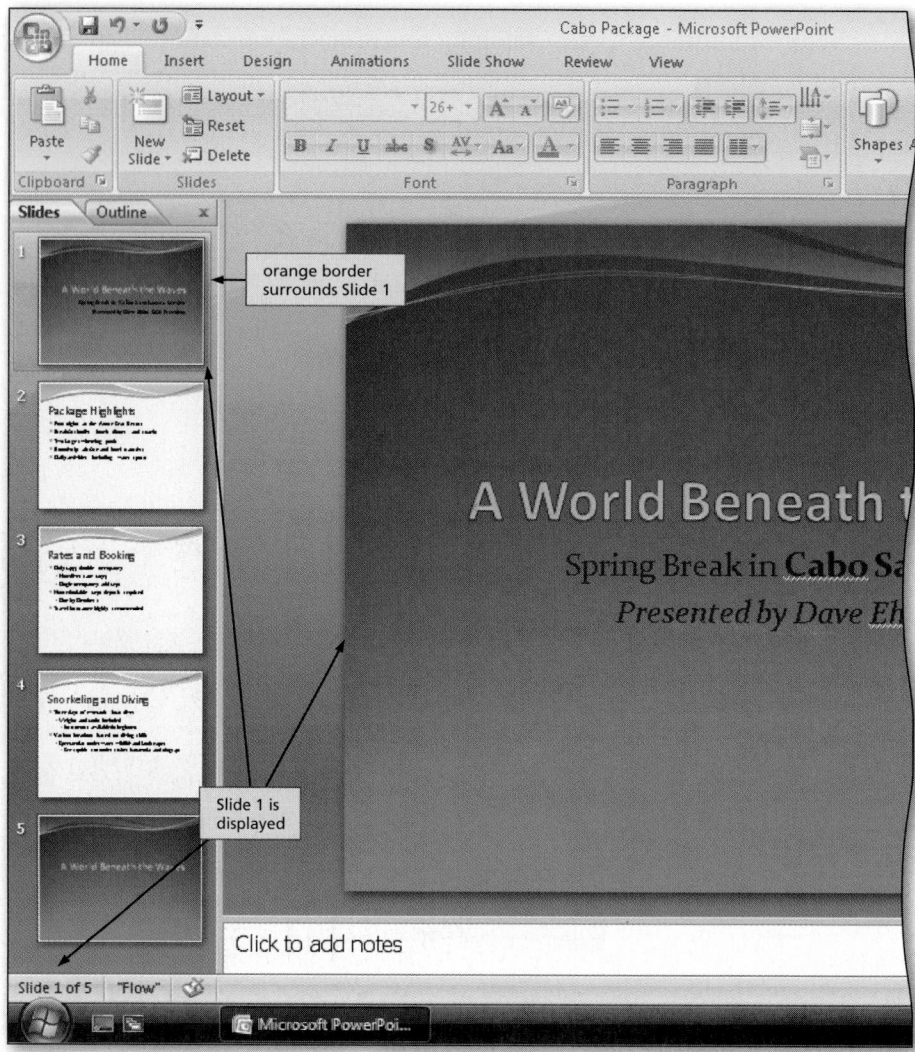

Figure 1–70

Viewing the Presentation in Slide Show View

The Slide Show button, located in the lower-right corner of the PowerPoint window above the status bar, allows you to show a presentation using a computer. The computer acts like a slide projector, displaying each slide on a full screen. The full-screen slide hides the toolbars, menus, and other PowerPoint window elements.

To Start Slide Show View

When making a presentation, you use **Slide Show view**. You can start Slide Show view from Normal view or Slide Sorter view. Slide Show view begins when you click the Slide Show button in the lower-right corner of the PowerPoint window on the status bar. PowerPoint then shows the current slide on the full screen without any of the PowerPoint window objects, such as the menu bar or toolbars. The following steps start Slide Show view.

 1

• Point to the Slide Show button in the lower-right corner of the PowerPoint window on the status bar (Figure 1–71).

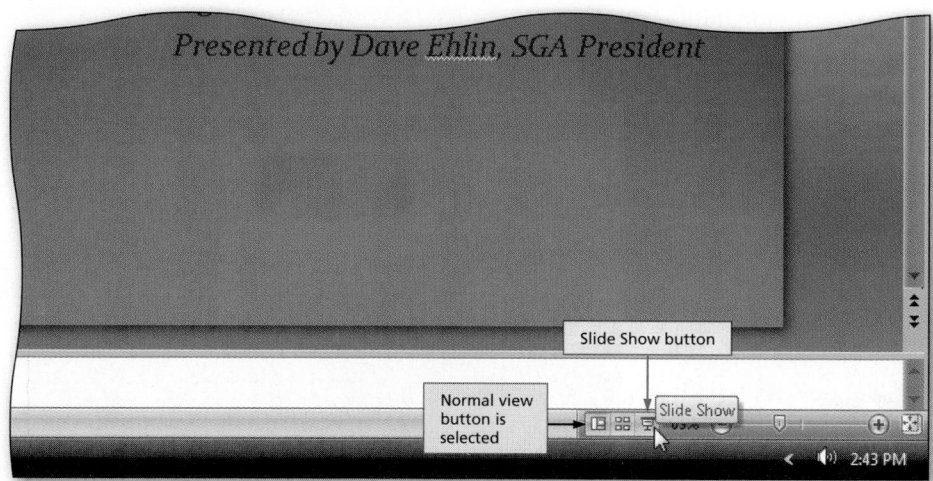

Figure 1–71

 2

• Click the Slide Show button to display the title slide (Figure 1–72).

Q&A Where is the PowerPoint window?

When you run a slide show, the PowerPoint window is hidden. It will reappear once you end your slide show.

Figure 1–72

Other Ways

1. Click Slide Show tab, click From Beginning button in Start Slide Show group
2. Press F5

To Move Manually through Slides in a Slide Show

After you begin Slide Show view, you can move forward or backward through the slides. PowerPoint allows you to advance through the slides manually or automatically. During a slide show, each slide in the presentation shows on the screen, one slide at a time. Each time you click the mouse button, the next slide appears. The following steps move manually through the slides.

- Click each slide until Slide 5 (A World Beneath the Waves) is displayed (Figure 1–73).

Q&A
I see a small toolbar in the lower-left corner of my slide. What is this toolbar?

The Slide Show toolbar appears when you begin running a slide show and then move the mouse pointer. The buttons on this toolbar allow you to navigate to the next slide, the previous slide, to mark up the current slide, or to change the current display.

Slide 5 is displayed in Slide Show view

Figure 1–73

- Click Slide 5 so that the black slide appears with a message announcing the end of the slide show (Figure 1–74).

Q&A
How can I end the presentation at this point?

Click the black slide to return to Normal view in the PowerPoint window or press the ESC key.

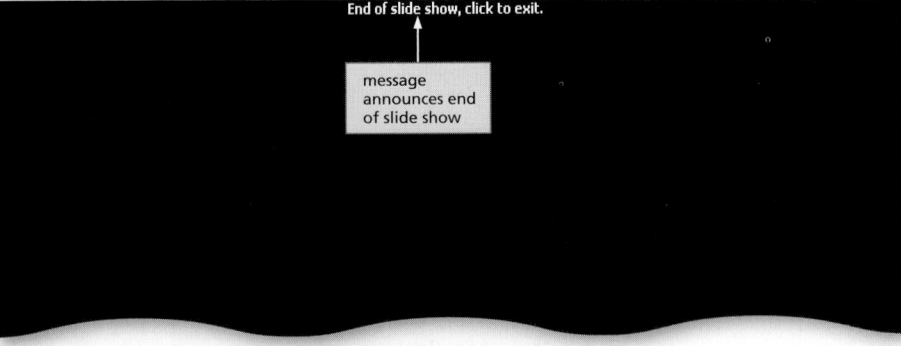

End of slide show, click to exit.

message announces end of slide show

Figure 1–74

Other Ways

1. Press PAGE DOWN to advance one slide at a time, or press PAGE UP to go back one slide at a time

2. Press RIGHT ARROW or DOWN ARROW to advance one slide at a time, or press LEFT ARROW or UP ARROW to go back one slide at a time

3. If Slide Show toolbar is displayed, click Next Slide or Previous Slide button on toolbar

To Display the Pop-Up Menu and Go to a Specific Slide

Slide Show view has a shortcut menu, called a **pop-up menu**, that appears when you right-click a slide in Slide Show view. This menu contains commands to assist you during a slide show.

When the pop-up menu appears, clicking the Next command moves to the next slide. Clicking the Previous command moves to the previous slide. Pointing to the Go to Slide command and then clicking the desired slide allows you to move to any slide in the presentation. The Go to Slide submenu contains a list of the slides in the presentation. You can go to the requested slide by clicking the name of that slide. Additional pop-up menu commands allow you to change the mouse pointer to a ballpoint or felt tip pen or highlighter that draws in various colors, make the screen black or white, create speaker notes, and end the slide show. The following steps go to the title slide (Slide 1) in the Cabo Package presentation.

1

- With the black slide displaying in Slide Show view, right-click the slide to display the pop-up menu.

2

- Point to Go to Slide on the pop-up menu, and then point to 2 Package Highlights in the Go to Slide submenu (Figure 1–75).

Q&A

Why does my pop-up menu appear in a different location on my screen?

The pop-up menu appears near the location of the mouse pointer at the time you right-click.

3

- Click 2 Package Highlights to display Slide 2.

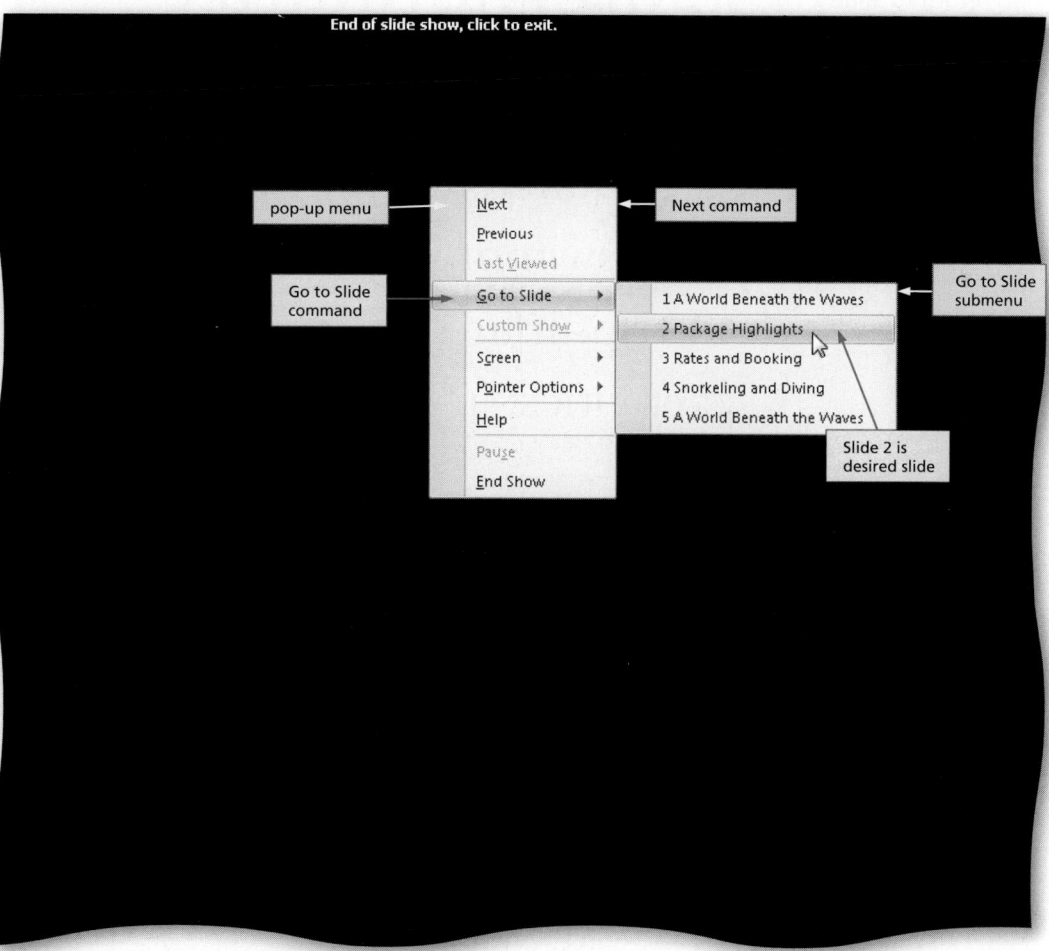

Figure 1–75

To Use the Pop-Up Menu to End a Slide Show

The End Show command on the pop-up menu ends Slide Show view and returns to the same view as when you clicked the Slide Show button. The following steps end Slide Show view and return to Normal view.

- Right-click Slide 2 and then point to End Show on the pop-up menu (Figure 1–76).

- Click End Show to return to Slide 2 in the Slide pane in Normal view.

- If the Microsoft Office PowerPoint dialog box appears, click the Yes button.

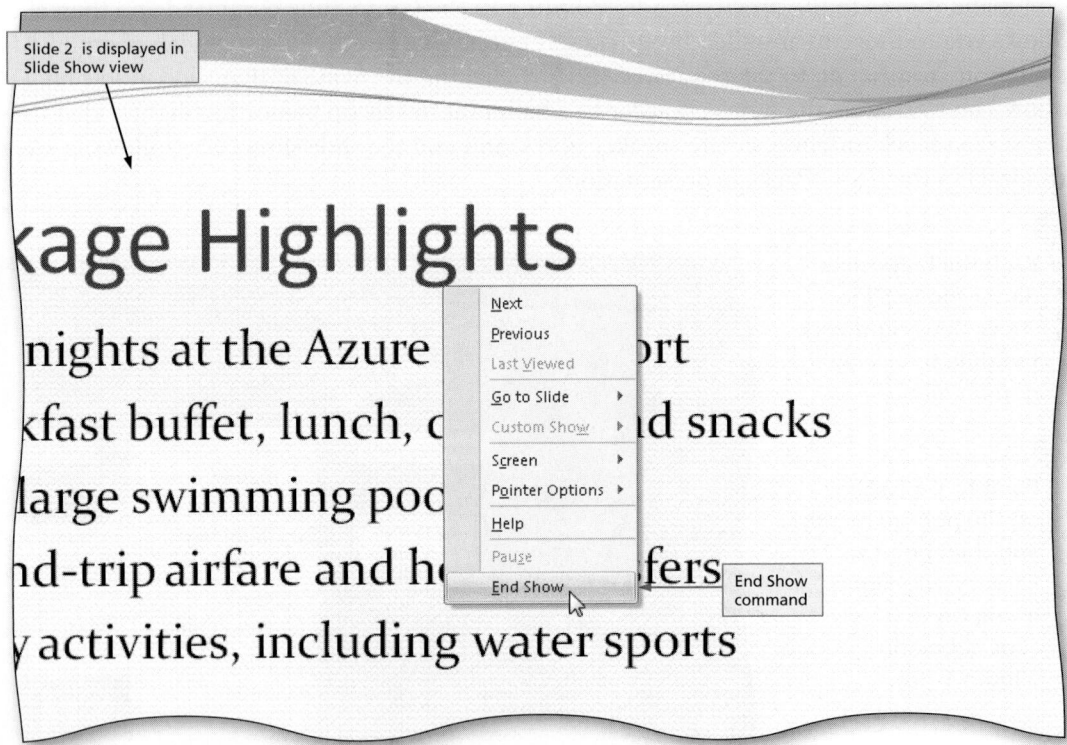

Figure 1–76

Other Ways

1. Press ESC (shows slide last viewed in Slide Show view)

Quitting PowerPoint

When you quit PowerPoint, if you have made changes to a presentation since the last time the file was saved, PowerPoint displays a dialog box asking if you want to save the changes you made to the file before it closes that window. The dialog box contains three buttons with these resulting actions:

- Yes button — Saves the changes and then quits PowerPoint
- No button — Quits PowerPoint without saving changes
- Cancel button — Closes the dialog box and redisplays the presentation without saving the changes

If no changes have been made to an open presentation since the last time the file was saved, PowerPoint will close the window without displaying a dialog box.

To Quit PowerPoint with One Document Open

You saved the presentation prior to running the slide show and did not make any changes to the project. The presentation now is complete, and you are ready to quit PowerPoint. When you have one document open, the following steps quit PowerPoint.

1

Point to the Close button on the right side of the PowerPoint title bar (Figure 1–77).

2

- Click the Close button to quit PowerPoint.

Q&A What if I have more than one PowerPoint document open?

You would click the Close button for each open document. When you click the last open document's Close button, PowerPoint also quits. As an alternative, you could click the Office Button and then click the Exit PowerPoint button on the Office Button menu, which closes all open PowerPoint documents and then quits PowerPoint.

Figure 1–77

Other Ways
1. With one document open, double-click Office Button   PowerPoint button on Windows Vista taskbar, click Close on shortcut menu
2. Click Office Button, click Exit PowerPoint on Office Button menu   4. With one document open, press ALT+F4
3. With one document open, right-click Microsoft

Starting PowerPoint and Opening a Presentation

Once you have created and saved a presentation, you may need to retrieve it from your storage medium. For example, you might want to revise the document or print it. Opening a presentation requires that PowerPoint is running on your computer.

To Start PowerPoint

Note: If you are using Windows XP, see Appendix F for alternate steps.

The following steps, which assume Windows Vista is running, start PowerPoint.

1 Click the Start button on the Windows Vista taskbar to display the Start menu.

2 Click All Programs at the bottom of the left pane on the Start menu to display the All Programs list and then click Microsoft Office in the All Programs list to display the Microsoft Office list.

3 Click Microsoft Office PowerPoint 2007 on the Microsoft Office list to start PowerPoint and display a new blank presentation in the PowerPoint window.

4 If the PowerPoint window is not maximized, click the Maximize button on its title bar to maximize the window.

To Open a Presentation from PowerPoint

Earlier in this chapter you saved your project on a USB flash drive using the file name, Cabo Package. The following steps open the Cabo Package file from the USB flash drive.

- With your USB flash drive connected to one of the computer's USB ports, click the Office Button to display the Office Button menu (Figure 1–78).

Q&A

What files are shown in the Recent Documents list?

PowerPoint displays the most recently opened document file names in this list. If the name of the file you want to open appears in the Recent Documents list, you could click it to open the file.

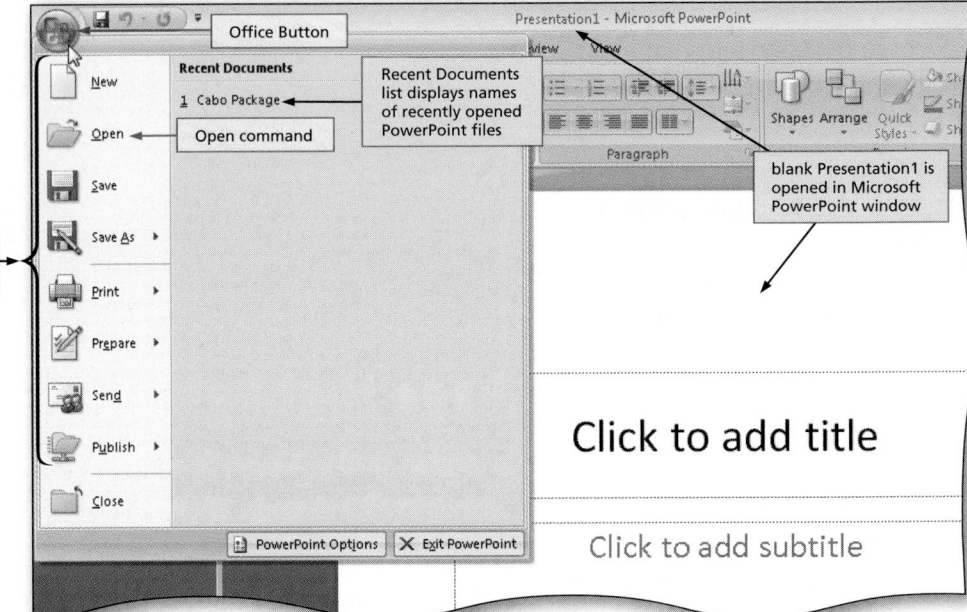

Figure 1–78

- Click Open on the Office Button menu to display the Open dialog box.

- If the Folders list is displayed below the Folders button, click the Folders button to remove the Folders list.

- If necessary, click Computer in the Favorite Links section and then scroll until UDISK 2.0 (E:) appears in the list of available drives.

- Double-click UDISK 2.0 (E:) to select the USB flash drive, Drive E in this case, as the new open location.

- Click Cabo Package to select the file name (Figure 1–79).

Q&A

How do I open the file if I am not using a USB flash drive?

Use the same process, but be certain to select your device in the Computer list.

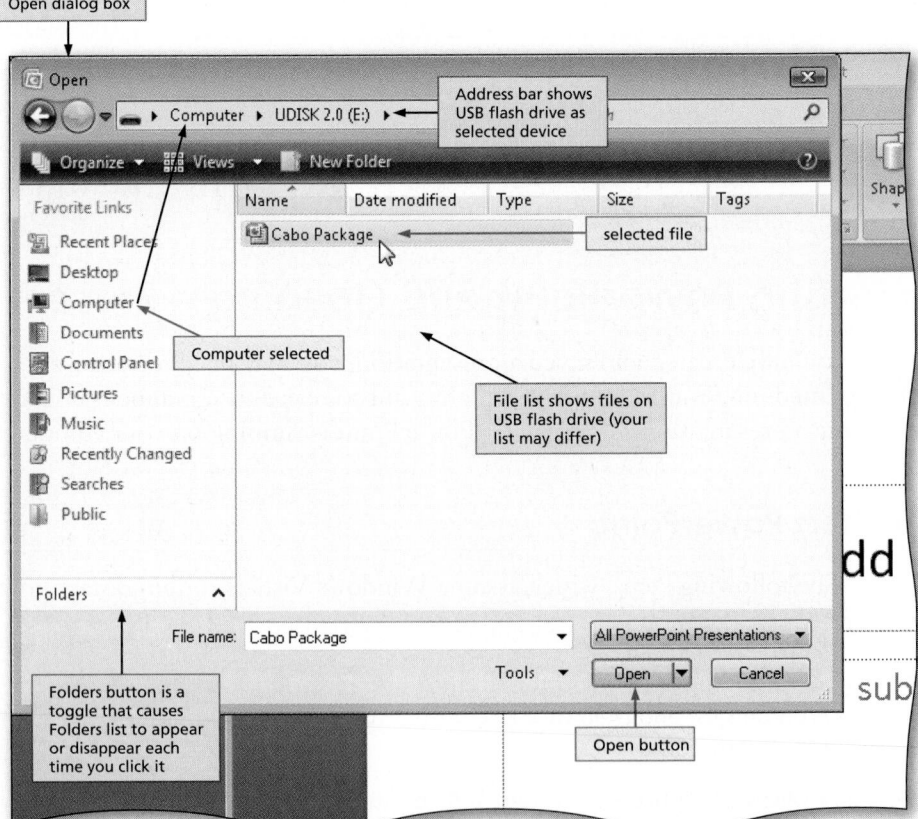

Figure 1–79

3

● Click the Open button to open the selected file and display Slide 1 in the PowerPoint window (Figure 1–80).

Q&A

Why are the PowerPoint icon and name on the Windows Vista taskbar?

When you open a PowerPoint file, a PowerPoint program button is displayed on the taskbar. The button contains an ellipsis because some of its contents do not fit in the allotted button space. If you point to a program button, its entire contents appear in a ScreenTip, which in this case would be the program name followed by the file name.

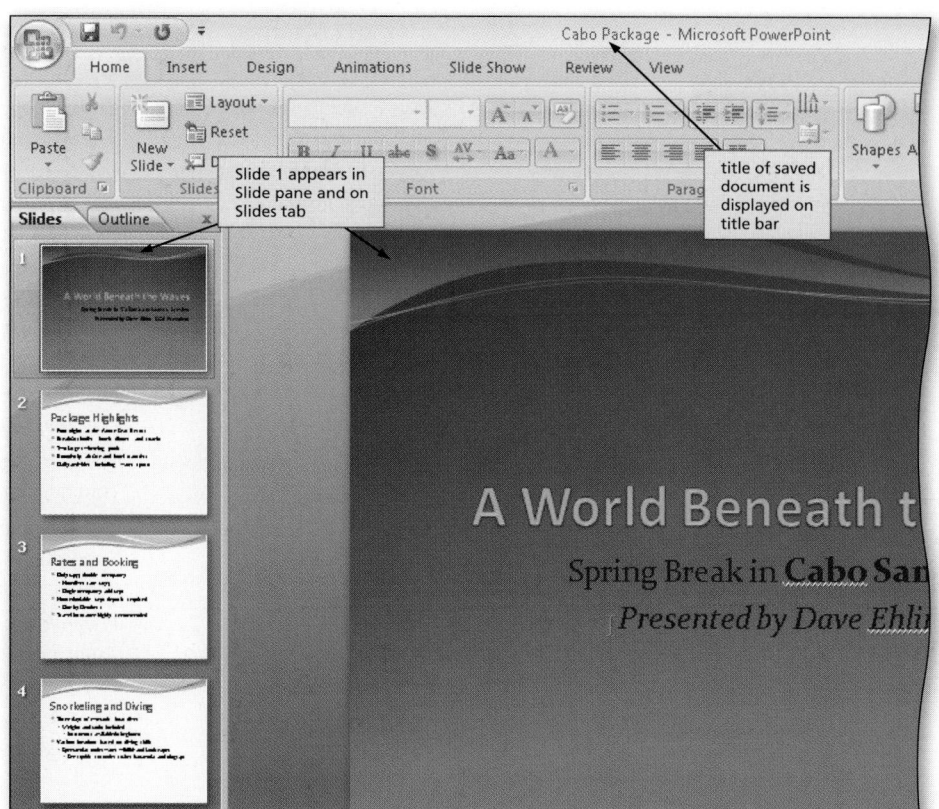

Figure 1–80

Other Ways

1. Click Office Button, double-click file name in Recent Documents list
2. Press CTRL+O, select file name, press ENTER

Checking a Presentation for Spelling Errors

After you create a presentation, you should check it visually for spelling errors and style consistency. In addition, you use PowerPoint's Spelling tool to identify possible misspellings. Do not rely on the spelling checker to catch all your mistakes. While PowerPoint's spelling checker is a valuable tool, it is not infallible. You should proofread your presentation carefully by pointing to each word and saying it aloud as you point to it. Be mindful of commonly misused words such as its and it's, through and though, and to and too.

PowerPoint checks the entire presentation for spelling mistakes using a standard dictionary contained in the Microsoft Office group. This dictionary is shared with the other Microsoft Office applications such as Word and Excel. A **custom dictionary** is available if you want to add special words such as proper names, cities, and acronyms. When checking a presentation for spelling errors, PowerPoint opens the standard dictionary and the custom dictionary file, if one exists. When a word appears in the Spelling dialog box, you can perform one of several actions.

Table 1–1 Spelling Dialog Box Buttons and Actions

Button Name	When To Use	Action
Ignore	Word is spelled correctly but not found in dictionaries	Continues checking rest of the presentation but will flag that word again if it appears later in document
Ignore All	Word is spelled correctly but not found in dictionaries	Ignores all occurrences of the word and continues checking rest of presentation
Change	Word is misspelled	Click proper spelling of the word in Suggestions list. PowerPoint corrects word, continues checking rest of presentation, but will flag that word again if it appears later in document.
Change All	Word is misspelled	Click proper spelling of word in Suggestions list. PowerPoint changes all occurrences of misspelled word and continues checking rest of presentation.
Add	Add word to custom dictionary	PowerPoint opens custom dictionary, adds word, and continues checking rest of presentation.
Suggest	Correct spelling is uncertain	Lists alternative spellings. Click the correct word from the Suggestions box or type the proper spelling. Corrects the word and continues checking the rest of the presentation.
AutoCorrect	Add spelling error to AutoCorrect list	PowerPoint adds spelling error and its correction to AutoCorrect list. Any future misspelling of word is corrected automatically as you type.
Close	Stop spelling checker	PowerPoint closes spelling checker and returns to PowerPoint window.

To Check Spelling

The standard dictionary contains commonly used English words. It does not, however, contain many proper names, abbreviations, technical terms, poetic contractions, or antiquated terms. PowerPoint treats words not found in the dictionaries as misspellings. The following steps check the spelling on all slides in the Cabo Package presentation.

- Click Review on the Ribbon to display the Review tab (Figure 1–81).

Figure 1–81

2

- Click the Spelling button in the Proofing group to start the spelling checker and display the Spelling dialog box (Figure 1–82).

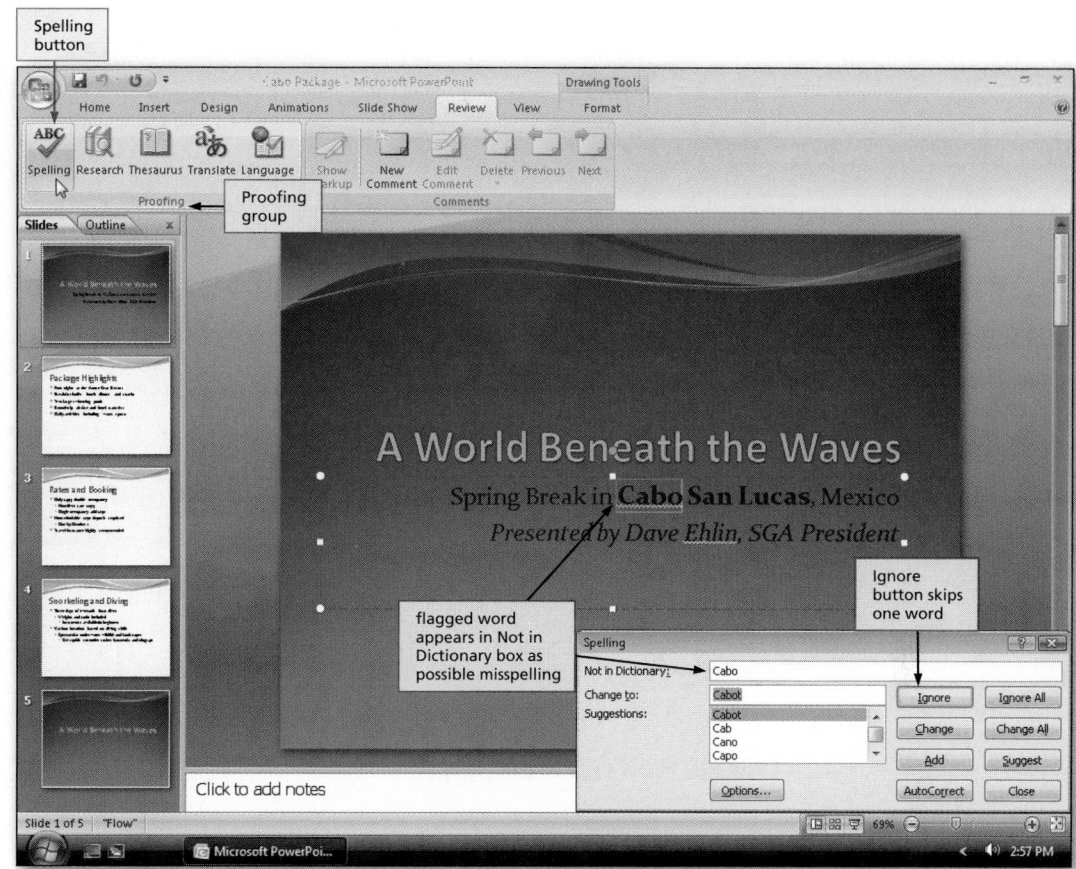

Figure 1–82

3

- Click the Ignore button to skip the word, Cabo (Figure 1–83).

Q&A

Cabo is not flagged as a possible misspelled word. Why not?

Your custom dictionary contains the word, so it is recognized as a correct word.

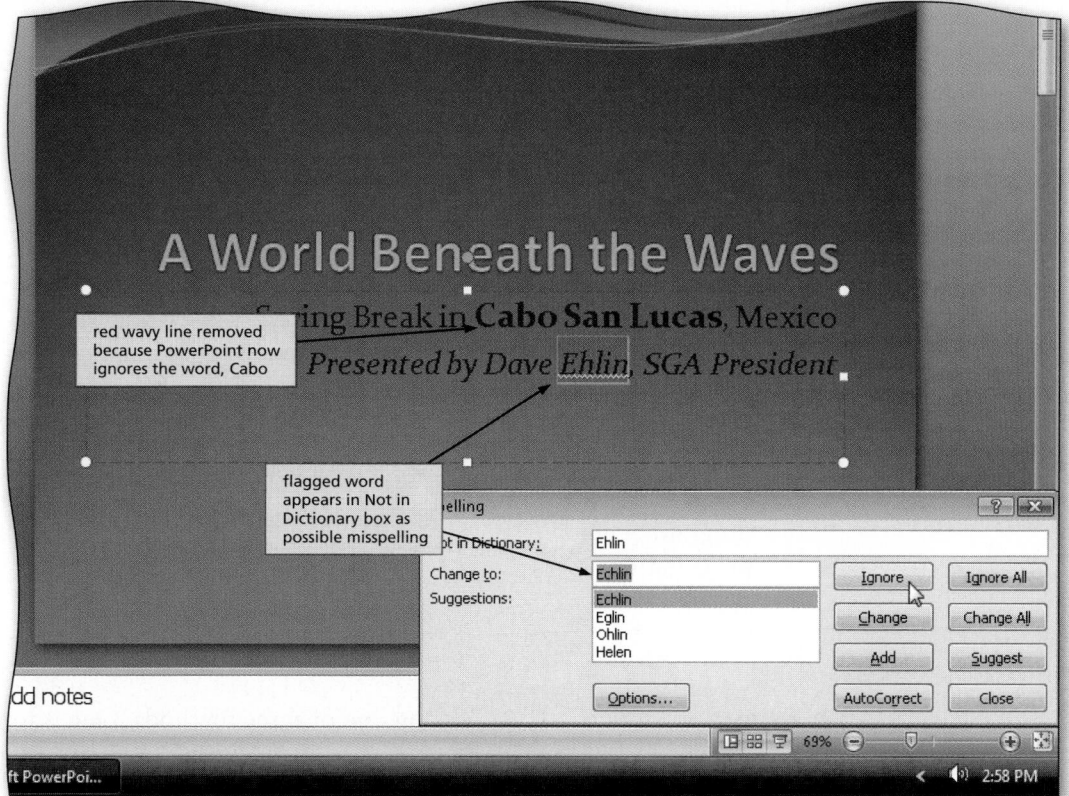

Figure 1–83

4
- Click the Ignore button to skip the word, Ehlin.

- When the Microsoft Office PowerPoint dialog box appears, click the OK button to close the spelling checker and return to the current slide, Slide 1, or to the slide where a possible misspelled word appeared.

- Click the slide to remove the box from the word, Ehlin (Figure 1–84).

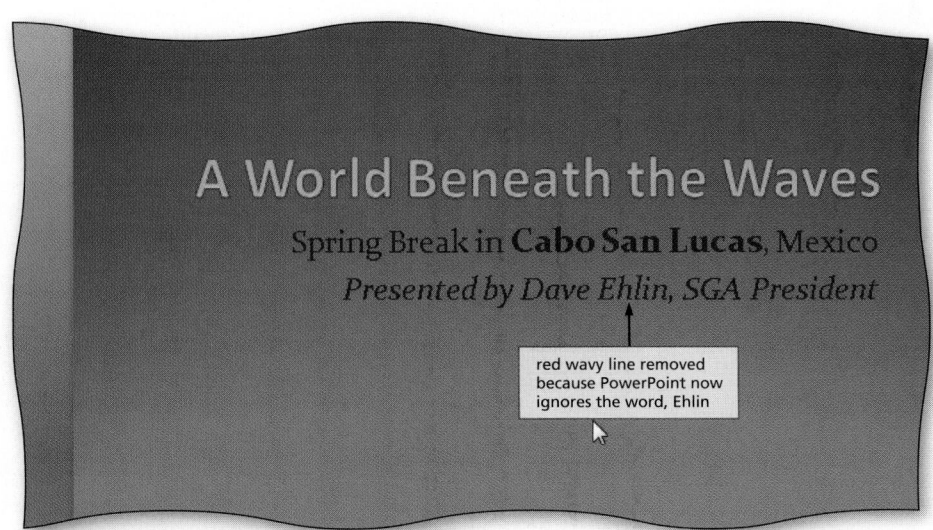

Figure 1–84

Correcting Errors

After creating a presentation and running the spelling checker, you may find that you must make changes. Changes may be required because a slide contains an error, the scope of the presentation shifts, or the style is inconsistent. This section explains the types of errors that commonly occur when creating a presentation.

Types of Corrections Made to Presentations

BTW

Certification
The Microsoft Certified Application Specialist (MCAS) program provides an opportunity for you to obtain a valuable industry credential – proof that you have the PowerPoint 2007 skills required by employers. For more information see Appendix G or visit the PowerPoint 2007 Certification Web page (scsite.com/ppt2007/cert).

You generally make three types of corrections to text in a presentation: additions, deletions, and replacements.

- Additions are necessary when you omit text from a slide and need to add it later. You may need to insert text in the form of a sentence, word, or single character. For example, you may want to add the presenter's middle name on the title slide.

- Deletions are required when text on a slide is incorrect or no longer is relevant to the presentation. For example, a slide may look cluttered. Therefore, you may want to remove one of the bulleted paragraphs to add more space.

- Replacements are needed when you want to revise the text in a presentation. For example, you may want to substitute the word, their, for the word, there.

Editing text in PowerPoint basically is the same as editing text in a word processing program. The following sections illustrate the most common changes made to text in a presentation.

Deleting Text

You can delete text using one of three methods. One is to use the BACKSPACE key to remove text just typed. The second is to position the insertion point to the left of the text you wish to delete and then press the DELETE key. The third method is to drag through the text you wish to delete and then press the DELETE key. Use the third method when deleting large sections of text.

Replacing Text in an Existing Slide

When you need to correct a word or phrase, you can replace the text by selecting the text to be replaced and then typing the new text. As soon as you press any key on the keyboard, the selected text is deleted and the new text is displayed.

PowerPoint inserts text to the left of the insertion point. The text to the right of the insertion point moves to the right (and shifts downward if necessary) to accommodate the added text.

Displaying a Presentation in Grayscale

Printing handouts of a presentation allows you to use them to make overhead transparencies. The Color/Grayscale button on the Color/Grayscale group on the View tab shows the presentation in black and white before you print. Pure Black and White alters the slides' appearance so that black lines display on a white background. Shadows and other graphical effects are hidden. Grayscale shows varying degrees of gray.

To Display a Presentation in Grayscale

The Color/Grayscale button on the Color/Grayscale group on the View tab changes from color bars to shades of black, called grayscale, and white. After you view the text objects in the presentation in grayscale, you can make any changes that will enhance printouts produced from a black and white printer or photocopier. The following steps display the presentation in grayscale.

1
- Click View on the Ribbon to display the View tab (Figure 1–85).

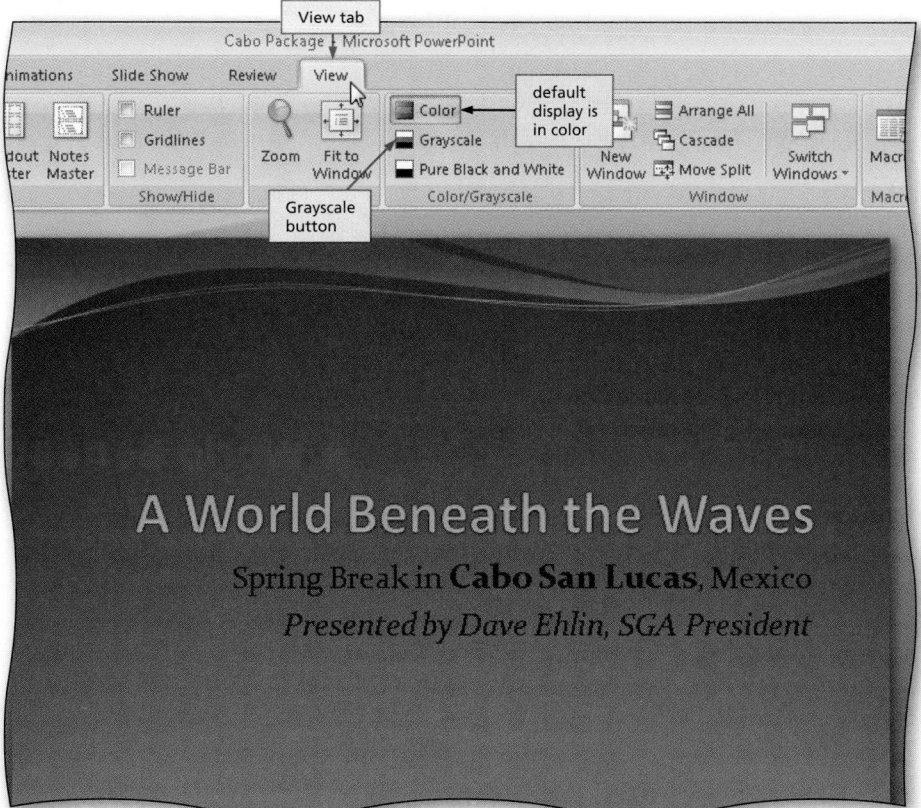

Figure 1–85

2
- Click Grayscale in the Color/Grayscale group to display Slide 1 in grayscale in the Slide pane (Figure 1–86).

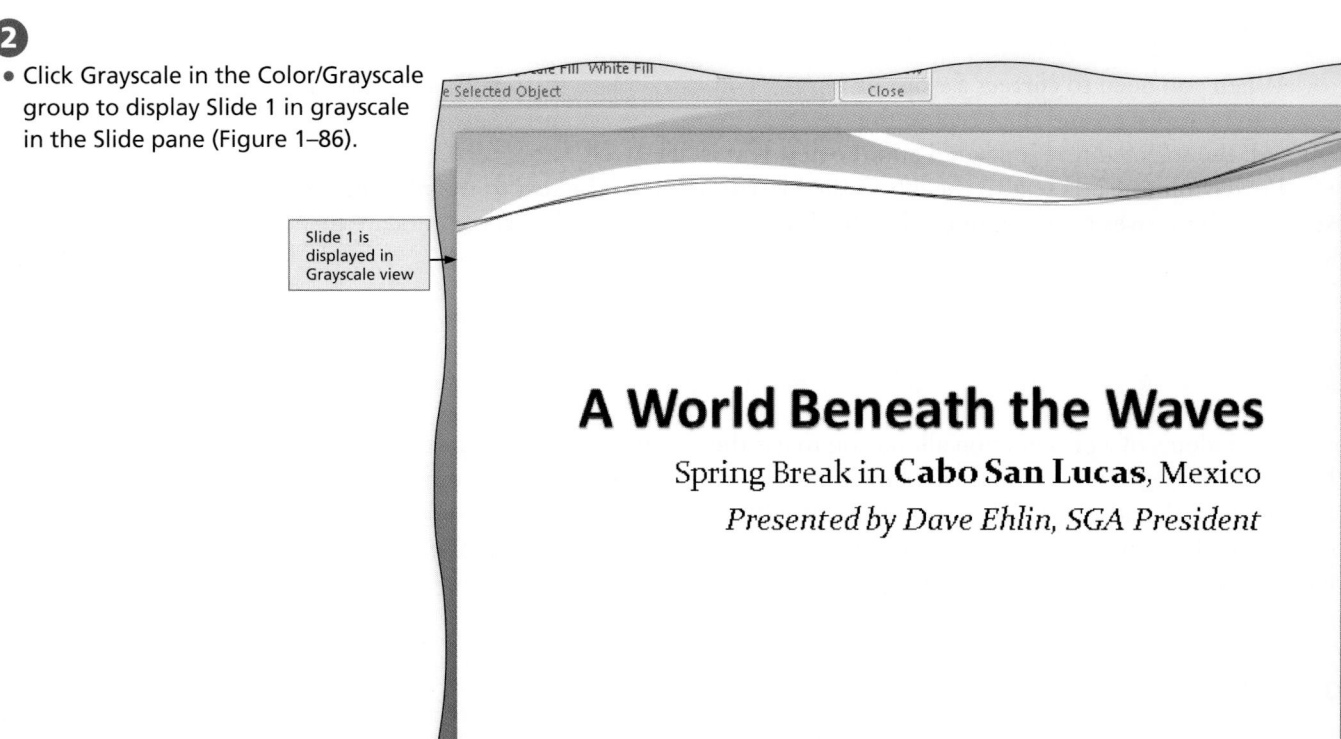

Figure 1–86

3
- Click the Next Slide button four times to view all slides in the presentation in grayscale (Figure 1–87).

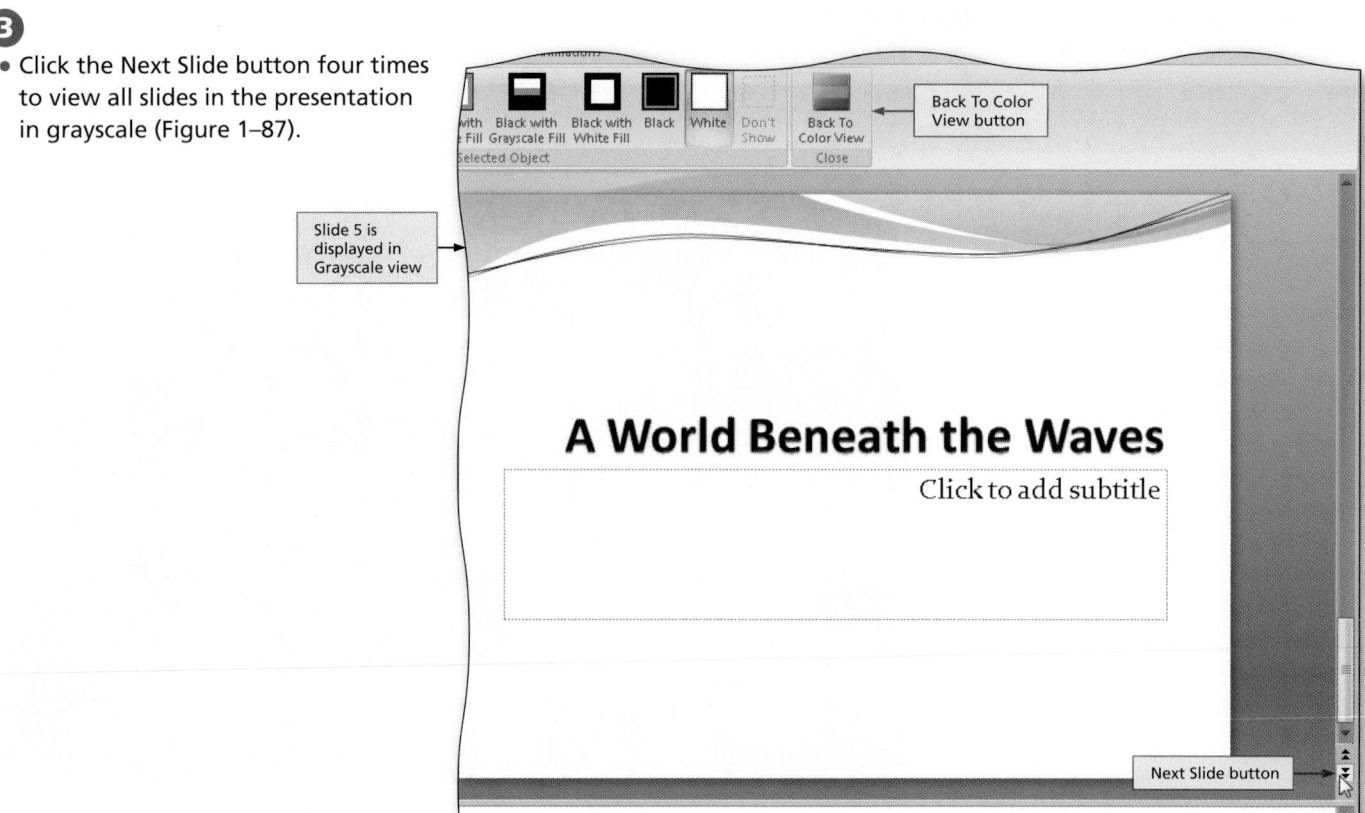

Figure 1–87

4
- Click the Back To Color View button in the Close group to return to the previous tab and display Slide 5 with the default Flow color scheme (Figure 1–88).

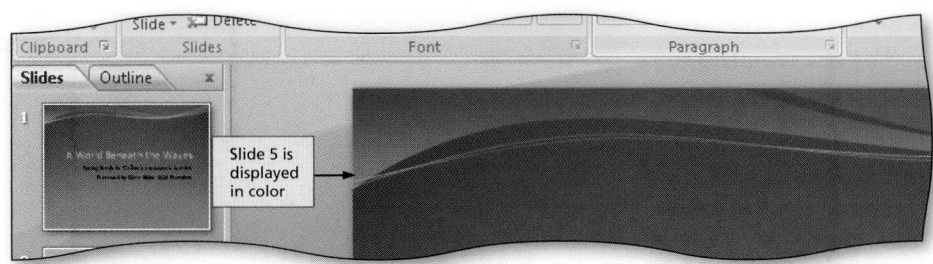

Slide 5 is displayed in color

Figure 1–88

Printing a Presentation

After you create a presentation, you often want to print it. A printed version of the presentation is called a **hard copy** or **printout**.

Printed copies of your presentation can be useful for the following reasons:

- Many people prefer proofreading a hard copy of the presentation rather than viewing the slides on the screen to check for errors and readability.

- Someone without computer access or who could not attend your live presentation can view the slides' content.

- Copies can be distributed as handouts to people viewing your presentation.

- Hard copies can serve as reference material if your storage medium is lost or becomes corrupted and you need to re-create the presentation.

It is a good practice to save a presentation before printing it, in the event you experience difficulties with the printer.

To Print a Presentation

With the completed presentation saved, you may want to print it. The following steps print all five completed presentation slides in the saved Cabo Package project.

1
- Click the Office Button to display the Office Button menu.

- Point to Print on the Office Button menu to display the Print submenu (Figure 1–89).

Q&A

Can I print my presentation in black and white to conserve ink or toner?

Yes. Click the Office Button, point to the arrow next to Print on the Office Button menu, and then click Print Preview on the Print submenu. Click the Options button on the Print Preview tab, point to Color/Grayscale on the Options button menu, and then click Pure Black and White on the Color/Grayscale submenu. Click the Print button on the Print submenu.

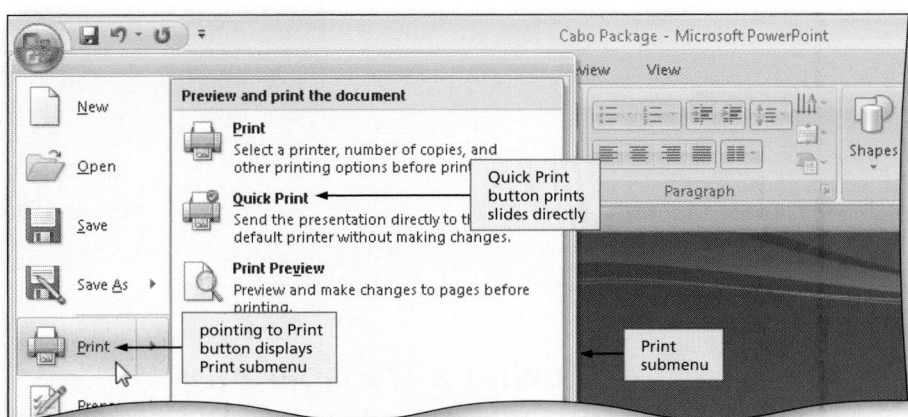

Quick Print button prints slides directly

pointing to Print button displays Print submenu

Print submenu

Figure 1–89

2

- Click Quick Print on the Print submenu to print the slides.

- When the printer stops, retrieve the hard copy of the five Cabo Package slides (Figures 1–90a through 1–90e).

Q&A

How can I print multiple copies of my document other than clicking the Print button twice?

Click the Office Button, point to Print on the Office Button menu, click Print on the Print submenu, increase the number in the Number of copies box, and then click the OK button.

Q&A

Do I have to wait until my presentation is complete to print it?

No, you can follow these steps to print your slides at any time while you are creating your presentation.

(a) Slide 1

(b) Slide 2

(c) Slide 3

(d) Slide 4

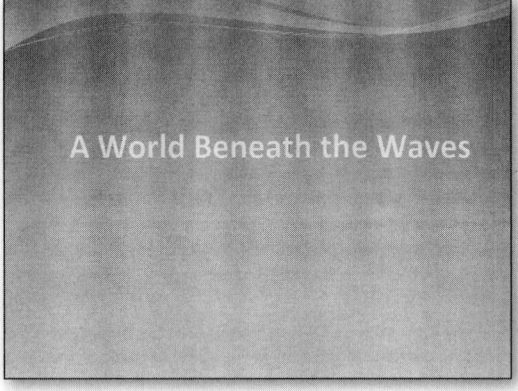

(e) Slide 5

Figure 1–90

Other Ways

1. Press CTRL+P

BTW

Quick Reference
For a table that lists how to complete the tasks covered in this book using the mouse, Ribbon, shortcut menu, and keyboard, see the Quick Reference Summary at the back of this book, or visit the PowerPoint 2007 Quick Reference Web page (scsite.com/ppt2007/qr).

Making a Transparency

With the handouts printed, you now can make overhead transparencies using one of several devices. One device is a printer attached to your computer, such as an inkjet printer or a laser printer. Transparencies produced on a printer may be in black and white or color, depending on the printer. Another device is a photocopier. Because each of these devices requires a special transparency film, check the user's manual for the film requirement of your specific device, or ask your instructor.

PowerPoint Help

At any time while using PowerPoint, you can find answers to questions and display information about various topics through **PowerPoint Help**. Used properly, this form of assistance can increase your productivity and reduce your frustrations by minimizing the time you spend learning how to use PowerPoint.

This section introduces you to PowerPoint Help. Additional information about using PowerPoint Help is available in Appendix C.

BTW

PowerPoint Help
The best way to become familiar with PowerPoint Help is to use it. Appendix C includes detailed information about PowerPoint Help and exercises that will help you gain confidence in using it.

To Search for PowerPoint Help

Using PowerPoint Help, you can search for information based on phrases such as save a presentation or format a chart, or key terms such as copy, save, or format. PowerPoint Help responds with a list of search results displayed as links to a variety of resources. The following steps, which use PowerPoint Help to search for information about using document themes, assume you are connected to the Internet.

1

- Click the Microsoft Office PowerPoint Help button near the upper-right corner of the PowerPoint window to open the PowerPoint Help window.

- Type document theme in the Type words to search for text box at the top of the PowerPoint Help window (Figure 1–91).

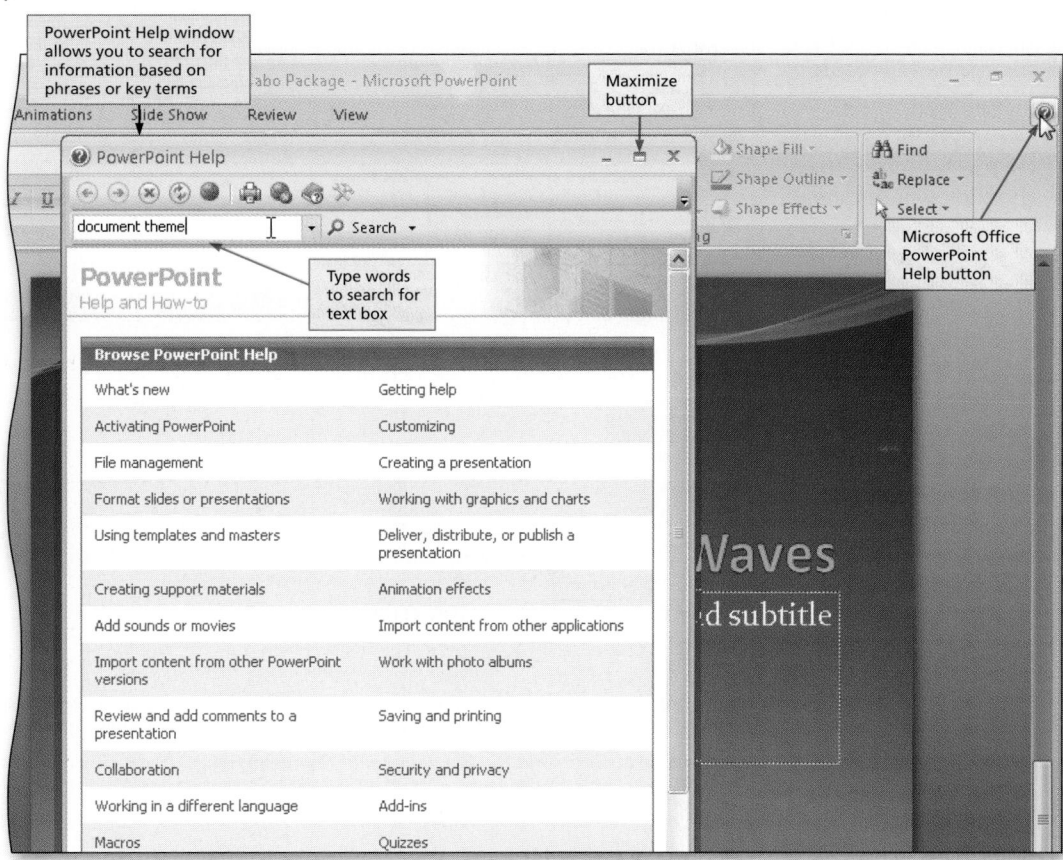

Figure 1–91

2

- Press the ENTER key to display the search results.

- Click the Maximize button on the PowerPoint Help window title bar to maximize the Help window (Figure 1–92).

Q&A

Where is the PowerPoint window with Slide 1?

PowerPoint is open in the background, but the PowerPoint Help window is overlaid on top of the Microsoft PowerPoint window. When the PowerPoint Help window is closed, the slide will reappear.

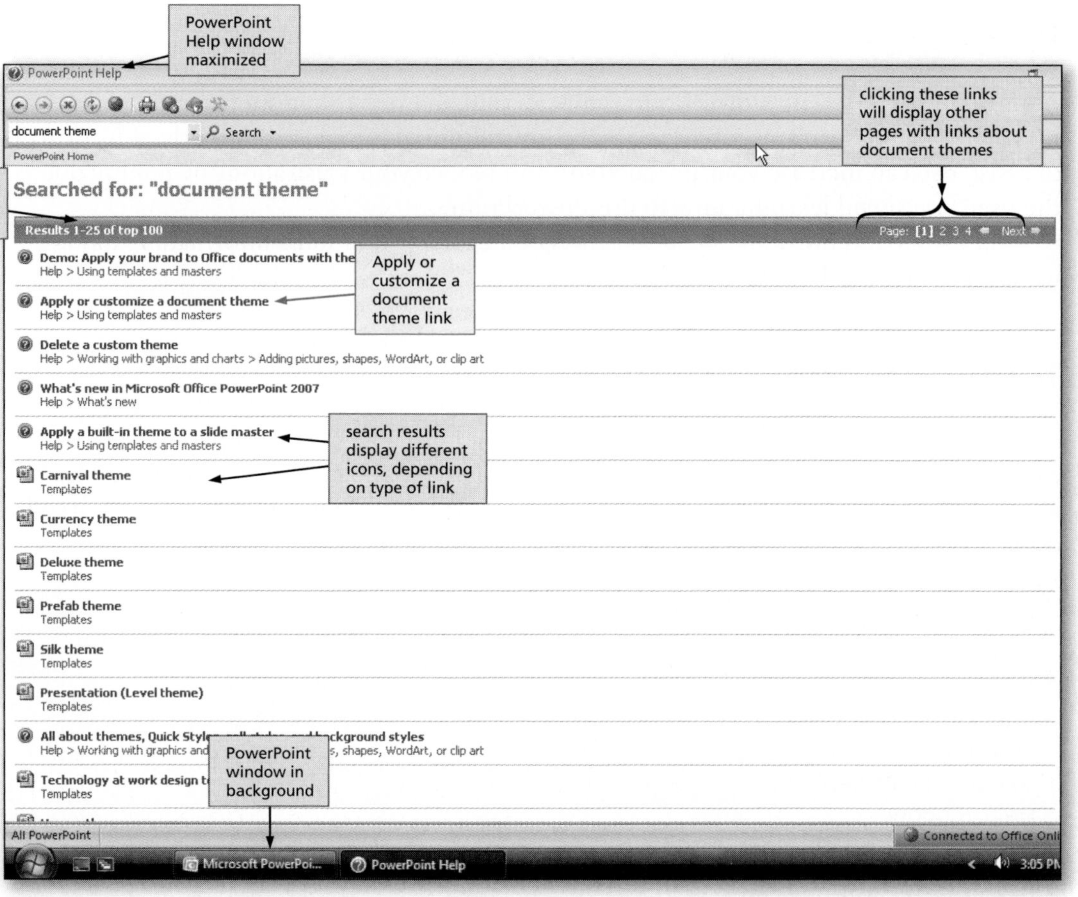

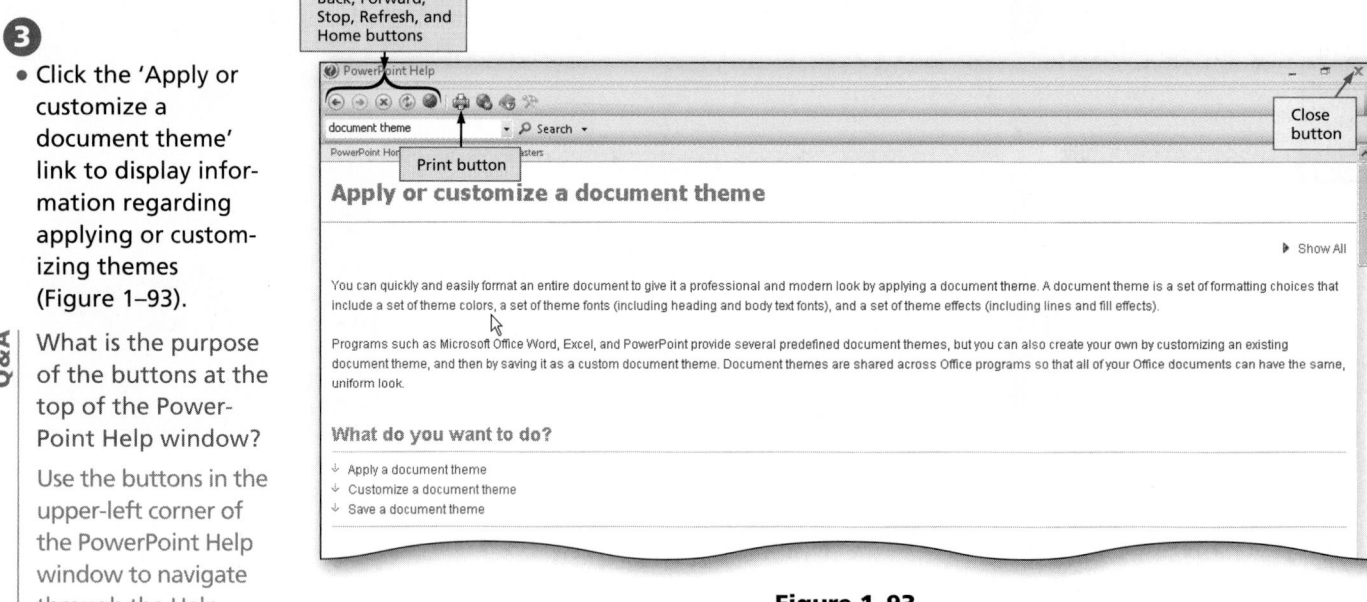

Figure 1–92

3

- Click the 'Apply or customize a document theme' link to display information regarding applying or customizing themes (Figure 1–93).

Q&A

What is the purpose of the buttons at the top of the Power-Point Help window?

Use the buttons in the upper-left corner of the PowerPoint Help window to navigate through the Help system, change the display, show the PowerPoint Help table of contents, and print the contents of the window.

Figure 1–93

4

- Click the Close button on the PowerPoint Help window title bar to close the PowerPoint Help window and display Slide 5.

Other Ways
1. Press F1

To Quit PowerPoint

The following steps quit PowerPoint.

1 Click the Close button on the right side of the title bar to quit PowerPoint; or, if you have multiple PowerPoint documents open, click the Office Button and then click the Exit PowerPoint button on the Office Button menu to close all open documents and quit PowerPoint.

2 If necessary, click the No button in the Microsoft Office PowerPoint dialog box so that any changes you have made are not saved.

Chapter Summary

In this chapter you have learned how to apply a document theme, create a title slide and text slides with bulleted lists, format text, view the presentation in Slide Show view, and print slides as handouts. The items listed below include all the new PowerPoint skills you have learned in this chapter.

1. Start PowerPoint (PPT 5)
2. Choose a Document Theme (PPT 16)
3. Enter the Presentation Title (PPT 18)
4. Enter the Presentation Subtitle Paragraph (PPT 20)
5. Select a Paragraph (PPT 21)
6. Italicize Text (PPT 22)
7. Select Multiple Paragraphs (PPT 22)
8. Change the Text Color (PPT 23)
9. Select a Group of Words (PPT 24)
10. Increase Font Size (PPT 24)
11. Bold Text (PPT 25)
12. Decrease the Title Slide Title Text Font Size (PPT 25)
13. Save a Presentation (PPT 27)
14. Add a New Text Slide with a Bulleted List (PPT 29)
15. Enter a Slide Title (PPT 31)
16. Select a Text Placeholder (PPT 31)
17. Type a Single-Level Bulleted List (PPT 32)
18. Add a New Slide and Enter a Slide Title (PPT 33)
19. Type a Multi-Level Bulleted List (PPT 34)
20. Create a Third-Level Paragraph (PPT 37)
21. Duplicate a Slide (PPT 40)
22. Arrange a Slide (PPT 41)
23. Delete All Text in a Placeholder (PPT 42)
24. Change Document Properties (PPT 44)
25. Save an Existing Presentation with the Same File Name (PPT 45)
26. Use the Scroll Box on the Slide Pane to Move to Another Slide (PPT 47)
27. Start Slide Show View (PPT 49)
28. Move Manually through Slides in a Slide Show (PPT 50)
29. Display the Pop-Up Menu and Go to a Specific Slide (PPT 51)
30. Use the Pop-Up Menu to End a Slide Show (PPT 52)
31. Quit PowerPoint with One Document Open (PPT 53)
32. Open a Presentation from PowerPoint (PPT 54)
33. Check Spelling (PPT 55)
34. Display a Presentation in Grayscale (PPT 59)
35. Print a Presentation (PPT 61)
36. Search for PowerPoint Help (PPT 63)

 If you have a SAM user profile, you may have access to hands-on instruction, practice, and assessment. Log in to your SAM account (http://sam2007.course.com) to launch any assigned training activities or exams that relate to the skills covered in this chapter.

Learn It Online

Test your knowledge of chapter content and key terms.

Instructions: To complete the Learn It Online exercises, start your browser, click the Address bar, and then enter the Web address `scsite.com/ppt2007/learn`. When the Office 2007 Learn It Online page is displayed, click the link for the exercise you want to complete and then read the instructions.

Chapter Reinforcement TF, MC, and SA
A series of true/false, multiple choice, and short answer questions that test your knowledge of the chapter content.

Flash Cards
An interactive learning environment where you identify chapter key terms associated with displayed definitions.

Practice Test
A series of multiple choice questions that test your knowledge of chapter content and key terms.

Who Wants To Be a Computer Genius?
An interactive game that challenges your knowledge of chapter content in the style of a television quiz show.

Wheel of Terms
An interactive game that challenges your knowledge of chapter key terms in the style of the television show *Wheel of Fortune*.

Crossword Puzzle Challenge
A crossword puzzle that challenges your knowledge of key terms presented in the chapter.

Apply Your Knowledge

Reinforce the skills and apply the concepts you learned in this chapter.

Modifying Character Formats and Paragraph Levels
Instructions: Start PowerPoint. Open the presentation, Apply 1-1 Keep Your Cool, from the Data Files for Students. See the inside back cover of this book for instructions on downloading the Data Files for Students, or contact your instructor for more information about accessing the required files.

The two slides in the presentation stress the importance of drinking plenty of water on hot days. The document you open is an unformatted presentation. You are to modify the document theme and text, indent the paragraphs, and format the text so the slides look like Figure 1–94.

Perform the following tasks:
1. Change the document theme to Trek. Note that the Trek theme uses all capital letters for the title text. On the title slide, use your name in place of Student Name and bold and italicize your name. Increase the title text font size to 44 point.

(a) **Slide 1 (Title Slide)**
Figure 1–94

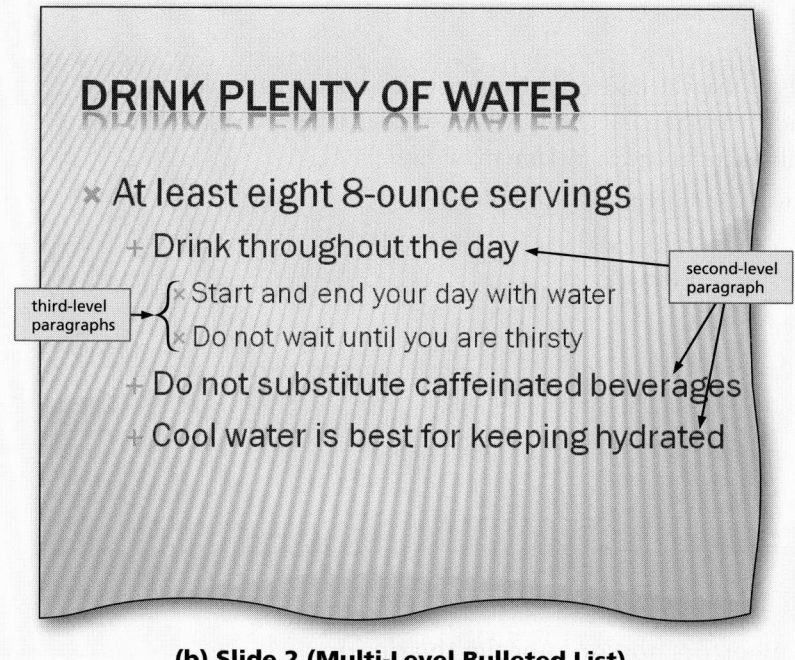

(b) Slide 2 (Multi-Level Bulleted List)
Figure 1–94 (continued)

2. On Slide 2, increase the indent of the second, fifth, and sixth paragraphs (Drink throughout the day; Do not substitute caffeinated beverages; Cool water is best for keeping hydrated) to second-level paragraphs. Then change paragraphs three and four (Start and end your day with water; Do not wait until you are thirsty) to third-level paragraphs.

3. Check the spelling, and then display the revised presentation in grayscale.

4. Change the document properties, as specified by your instructor. Save the presentation using the file name, Apply 1-1 Drink Water. Submit the revised document in the format specified by your instructor.

Extend Your Knowledge

Extend the skills you learned in this chapter and experiment with new skills. You may need to use Help to complete the assignment.

Changing Slide Theme and Text

Instructions: Start PowerPoint. Open the presentation, Extend 1-1 Nutrition, from the Data Files for Students. See the inside back cover of this book for instructions on downloading the Data Files for Students, or contact your instructor for more information about accessing the required files.

You will choose a theme (Figure 1–95), format slides, and create a closing slide.

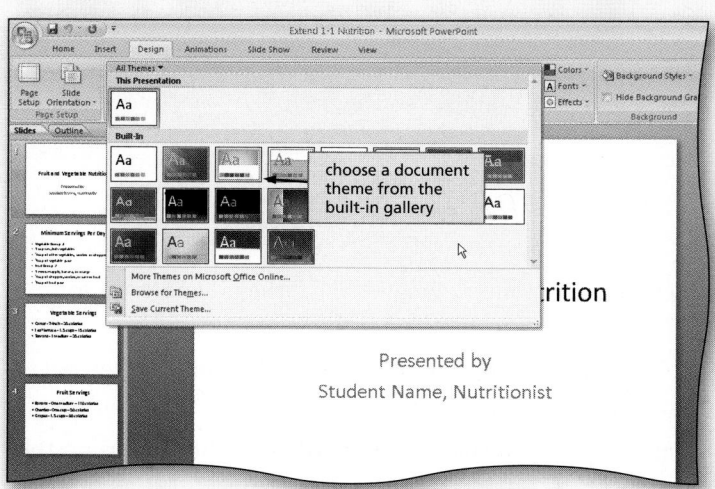

Perform the following tasks:

1. Apply an appropriate document theme.

2. On Slide 1, use your name in place of Student Name. Format the text using techniques you learned in this chapter, such as changing the font size and color and also bolding and italicizing words.

Figure 1–95

Continued >

Extend Your Knowledge *continued*

3. On Slide 2, adjust the paragraph levels so that the lines of text are arranged under vegetable and fruit categories. Edit the text so that the slide meets the 7 × 7 rule, which states that each line should have a maximum of seven words, and each slide should have a maximum of seven lines.

4. On Slides 3 and 4, create paragraphs and adjust the paragraph levels.

5. Create an appropriate closing slide using the title slide as a guide.

6. Change the document properties, as specified by your instructor. Save the presentation using the file name, Extend 1-1 Fruit and Vegetables.

7. Add the Print button to the Quick Access Toolbar and then click this button to print the slides.

8. Delete the Print button from the Quick Access Toolbar.

9. Submit the revised document in the format specified by your instructor.

Make It Right

Analyze a presentation and correct all errors and/or improve the design.

Correcting Formatting and List Levels

Instructions: Start PowerPoint. Open the presentation, Make It Right 1-1 Indulge, from the Data Files for Students. See the inside back cover of this book for instructions on downloading the Data Files for Students, or contact your instructor for more information about accessing the required files.

Correct the formatting problems and errors in the presentation while keeping in mind the guidelines presented in this chapter.

Perform the following tasks:

1. Change the document theme from Metro, shown in Figure 1–96, to Opulent.

2. On Slide 1, replace the words, Fall Semester, with your name. Format your name so that it displays prominently on the slide.

3. Move Slide 2 to the end of the presentation so that it becomes the new Slide 4.

4. Use the spell checker to correct the misspellings. Analyze the slides for other word usage errors that the spell checker did not find.

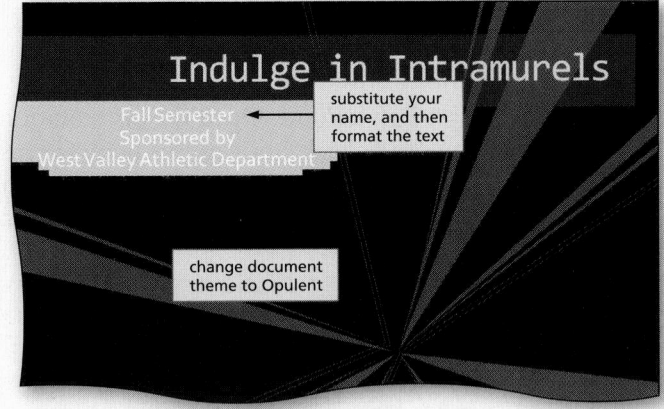

Figure 1–96

5. On Slide 2, increase the Slide 2 title (Athletic Events) font size to 40. Make the indent levels for paragraphs 2, 4, and 6 the same level.

6. On Slide 3, change the title text (Awards Ceremony) font size to 40. Make the indent levels for paragraphs 3 and 5 the same level.

7. Change the document properties, as specified by your instructor. Save the presentation using the file name, Make It Right 1-1 Intramurals.

8. Submit the revised document in the format specified by your instructor.

In the Lab

Design and/or create a presentation using the guidelines, concepts, and skills presented in this chapter. Labs 1, 2, and 3 are listed in order of increasing difficulty.

Lab 1: Creating a Presentation with Bulleted Lists

Problem: Many of the important steps you will take in your life are influenced by your credit report. Buying a car, renting an apartment, and even applying for a job often require a credit check. Your credit score can make or break your ability to obtain the goods you truly want and need. One of your assignments in your economics class is to give a speech about establishing credit. You develop the outline shown in Figure 1–97 and then prepare the PowerPoint presentation shown in Figures 1–98a through 1–98d.

Instructions: Perform the following tasks.

1. Create a new presentation using the Aspect document theme.

2. Using the typed notes illustrated in Figure 1–97, create the title slide shown in Figure 1–98a using your name in place of Marc Kantlon. Italicize your name. Decrease the font size of the title paragraph, Give Yourself Some Credit, to 40. Increase the font size of the first paragraph of the subtitle text, Understanding Your Credit Report, to 28.

3. Using the typed notes in Figure 1–97, create the three text slides with bulleted lists shown in Figures 1–98b through 1–98d.

Give Yourself Some Credit
  Understanding Your Credit Report
  Marc Kantlon
  Economics 101

Credit Report Fundamentals
  Generated by three companies
          Experian, Equifax, TransUnion
  Factors
          How much you owe to each company
          Payment history for each company
                  Includes utilities, medical expenses, rent

How FICO Is Calculated
  Range - 760 (excellent) to 620 (poor)
          35% - Payment history
          30% - Amounts owed
          15% - Credit history length
          10% - New credit
          10% - Credit types

Improve Your FICO Score
  Pay bills on time
  Avoid opening many new accounts
          Open only if you intend to use
  Keep balances low
          Less than 25% of credit limit
  Review credit report yearly

Figure 1–97

Continued >

In the Lab *continued*

4. On Slide 3, change the font color of the number, 760, to green and the number, 620, to red.

5. Check the spelling and correct any errors.

6. Drag the scroll box to display Slide 1. Click the Slide Show button to start Slide Show view. Then click to display each slide.

7. Change the document properties, as specified by your instructor. Save the presentation using the file name, Lab 1-1 Credit.

8. Submit the document in the format specified by your instructor.

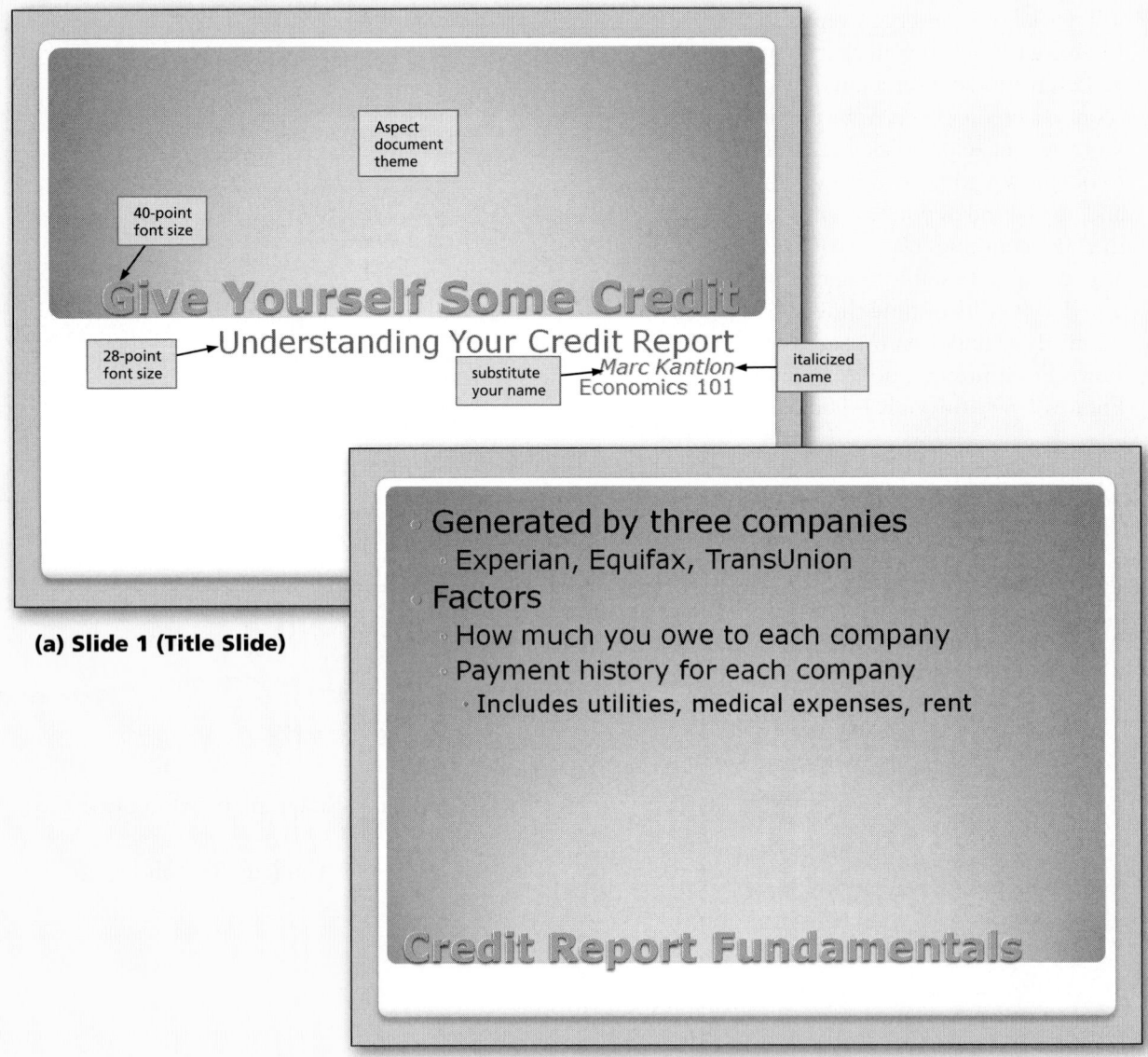

(a) Slide 1 (Title Slide)

(b) Slide 2

Figure 1–98

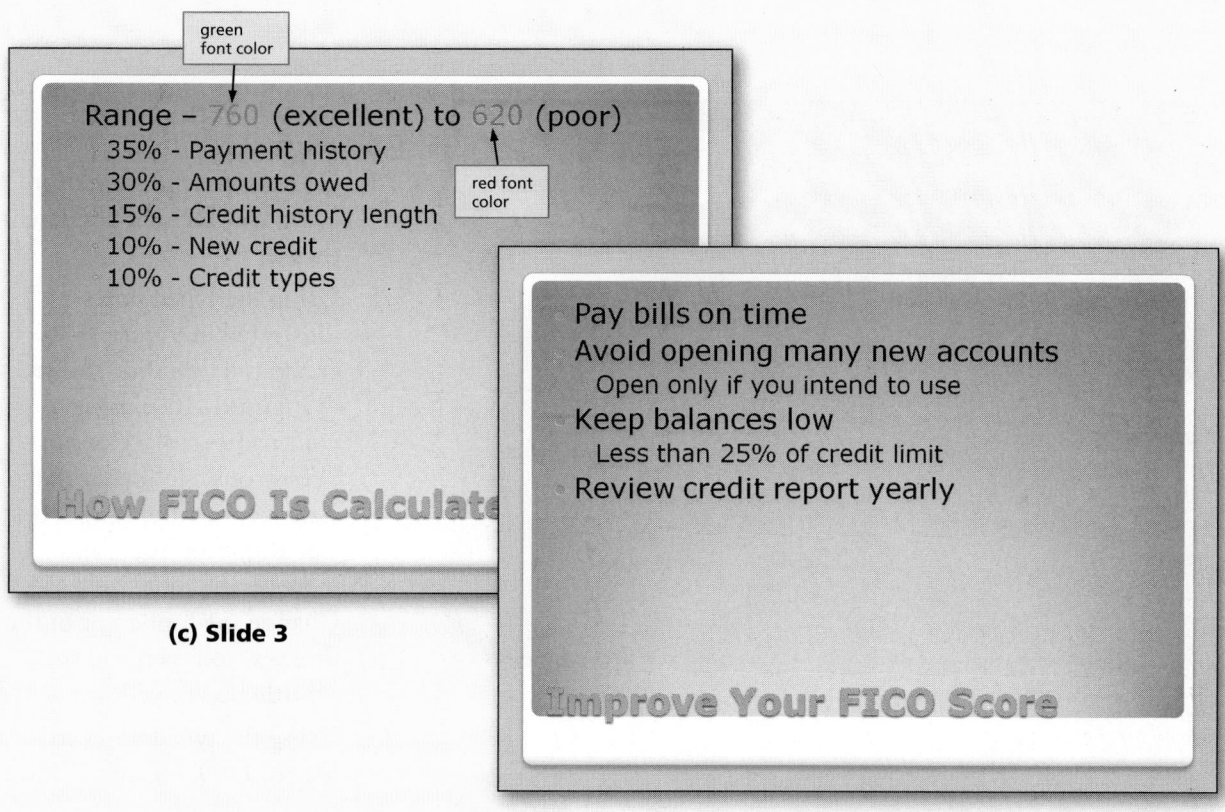

(c) Slide 3

(d) Slide 4

Figure 1–98 (continued)

In the Lab

Lab 2: Creating a Presentation with Bulleted Lists and a Closing Slide

Problem: Hybrid vehicles have received much attention in recent years. Everyone from environmentalists to movie stars are driving them, and potential buyers wait for months until the vehicles arrive in dealers' showrooms. You work part-time at Midwest State Bank, and the loan department manager, Jen Westbrook, has asked you to develop a PowerPoint presentation to accompany her upcoming speech. She hands you the outline shown in Figure 1–99 and asks you to create the presentation shown in Figures 1–100a through 1–100e.

Is a Hybrid Car Right for You?
Jen Westbrook, Midwest State Bank Loan Department Manager

Are They a Good Value?
Depends upon your driving habits
Government offers tax credits
Excellent resale value
Efficient gas consumption

What Is Their Gas Mileage?
Depends upon make and size
City: Ranges from 18 to 60 mpg
Highway: Ranges from 21 to 66 mpg
Actual mileage affected by driving patterns

What Makes Them Work?
Use two motors
Gas
Smaller, more efficient than traditional vehicle
Electric
Gives gas engine extra power boost
May power car entirely

See me for your next car purchase
Jen Westbrook, Midwest State Bank Loan Department Manager

Figure 1–99

Continued >

In the Lab *continued*

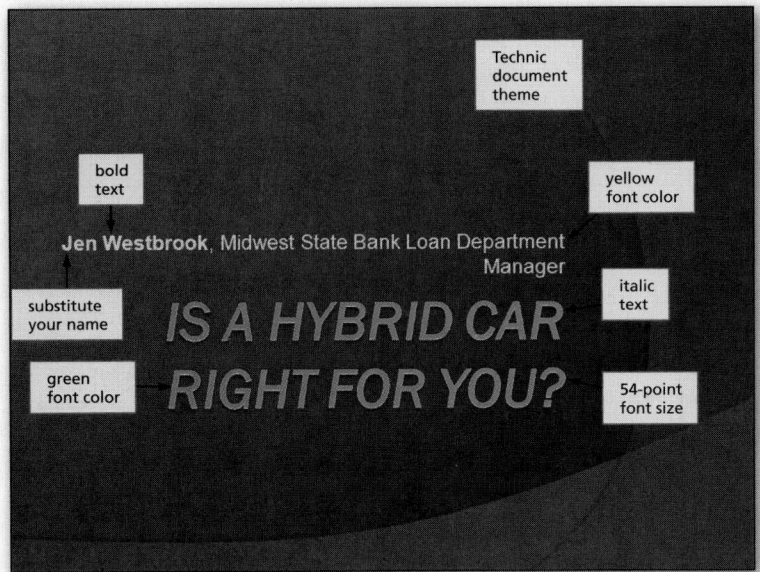

(a) Slide 1 (Title Slide)

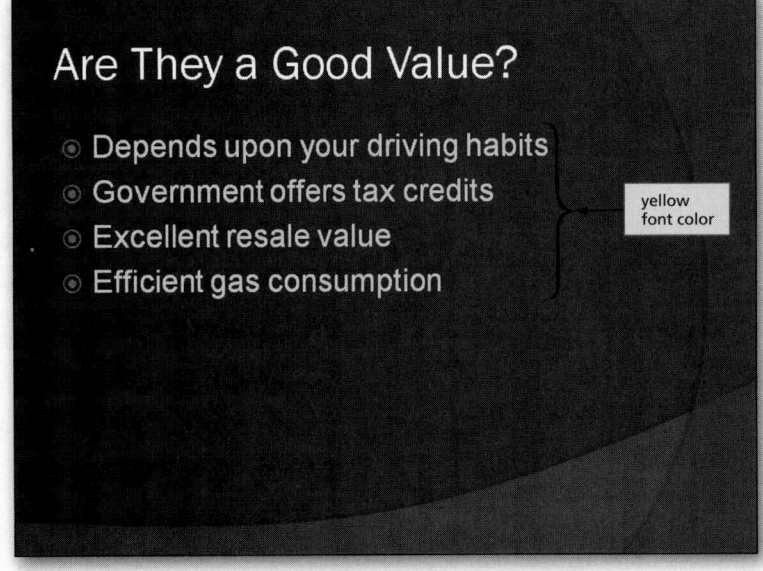

(b) Slide 2

Figure 1–100

Instructions: Perform the following tasks.

1. Create a new presentation using the Technic document theme.

2. Using the typed notes illustrated in Figure 1–99, create the title slide shown in Figure 1–100a using your name in place of Jan Westbrook. Bold your name. Italicize the title, Is a Hybrid Car Right for You?, and increase the font size to 54. Change the font color of the title text to green and the subtitle text to yellow.

3. Using the typed notes in Figure 1–99, create the three text slides with bulleted lists shown in Figures 1–100b through 1–100d. Change the color of all the bulleted list paragraph text to yellow.

4. Duplicate the title slide and then move the new closing slide to the end of the presentation. Change the Slide 5 title text, increase the font size to 66, and remove the italics.

5. Check the spelling and correct any errors.

6. Drag the scroll box to display Slide 1. Click the Slide Show button to start Slide Show view. Then click to display each slide.

7. Change the document properties, as specified by your instructor. Save the presentation using the file name, Lab 1-2 Hybrids.

8. Submit the revised document in the format specified by your instructor.

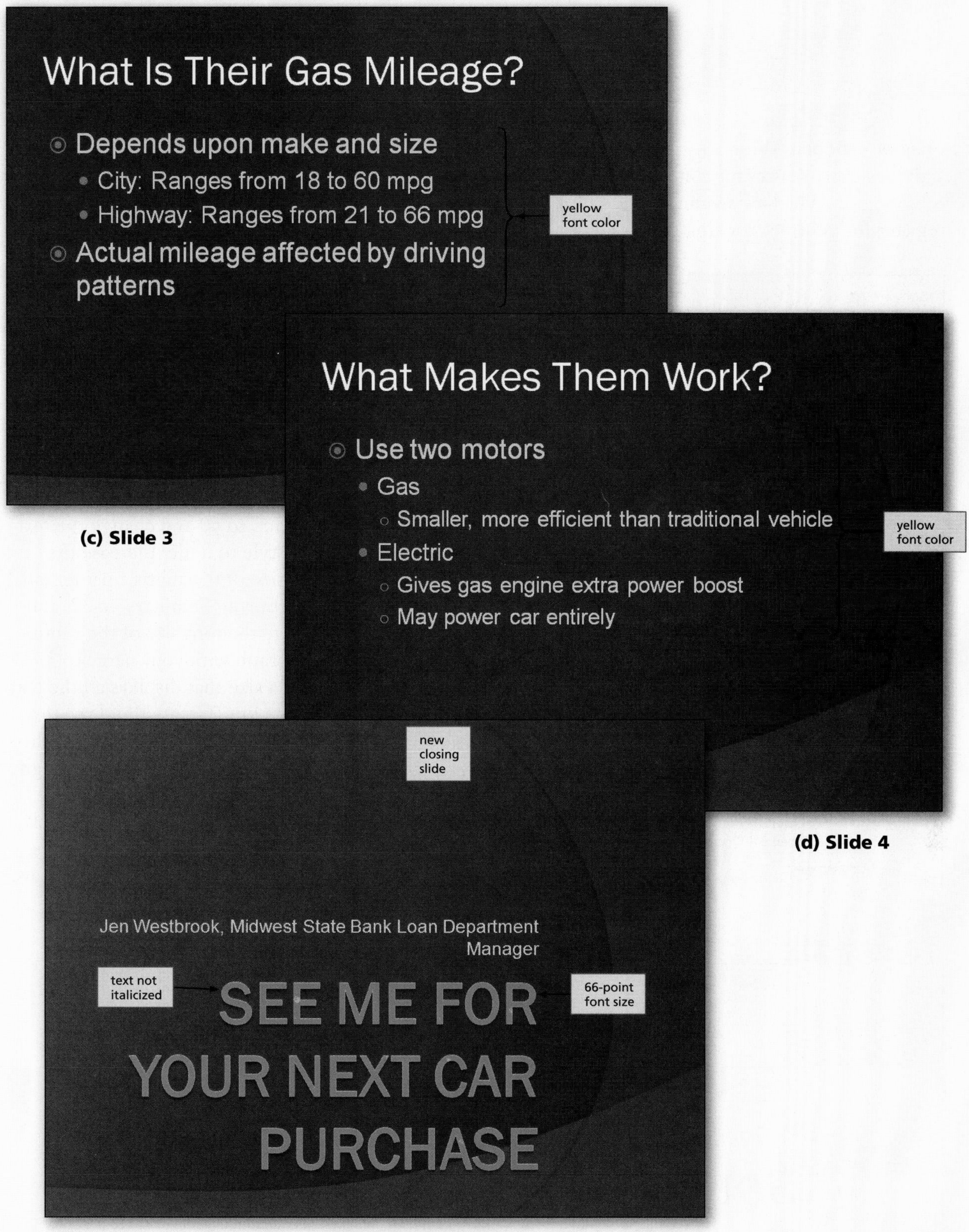

(c) Slide 3

(d) Slide 4

(e) Slide 5 (Closing Slide)

Figure 1–100 (continued)

In the Lab

Lab 3: Creating and Updating Presentations

Problem: Bobbie Willis, the public relations director for the South Haven Park District, plans activities every season for community residents and promotes the offerings using a PowerPoint presentation. The new seminars for senior citizens this spring are quilting and t'ai chi. Adults can register for gourmet cooking lessons and kickball. Teens can enroll in sailing and fencing lessons.

South Haven Park District
New Spring Seminars
Bobbie Willis, Director

Seniors' Seminars
    Quilting
        Quilts made from donated fabrics
        Sewing machines provided
    T'ai Chi
        Gentle warm-ups
        12 slow, continuous movements
        Easy cool-down exercises

Adults' Seminars
    Almost Gourmet
        Learn techniques from a professional chef
            Everyone prepares and enjoys the dinners
                Come hungry!
    Kickball
        Learn techniques and rules

Teens' Seminars
    Sailing
        Sail a 30-foot sailboat at your first class
    Fencing
        Three levels
            Level 1 – Beginning Foil
            Level 2 – Foil, Epee, and Saber
            Level 3 – Open Strip Fencing

Figure 1–101

Instructions Part 1: Using the outline in Figure 1–101, create the presentation shown in Figure 1–102. Use the Oriel document theme. On the title slide shown in Figure 1–102a, type your name in place of Bobbie Willis, increase the font size of the title paragraph, South Haven Park District, to 60 and change the text font style to italic. Increase the font size of the subtitle paragraph, New Spring Seminars, to 32, and change the font size of the subtitle paragraph with your name to 37 or to a size that displays all the text on one line. Create the three text slides with multi-level bulleted lists shown in Figures 1–102b through 1–102d.

Correct any spelling mistakes. Change the document properties, as specified by your instructor. Save the presentation using the file name, Lab 1-3 Part One Spring Seminars. Display the presentation in grayscale.

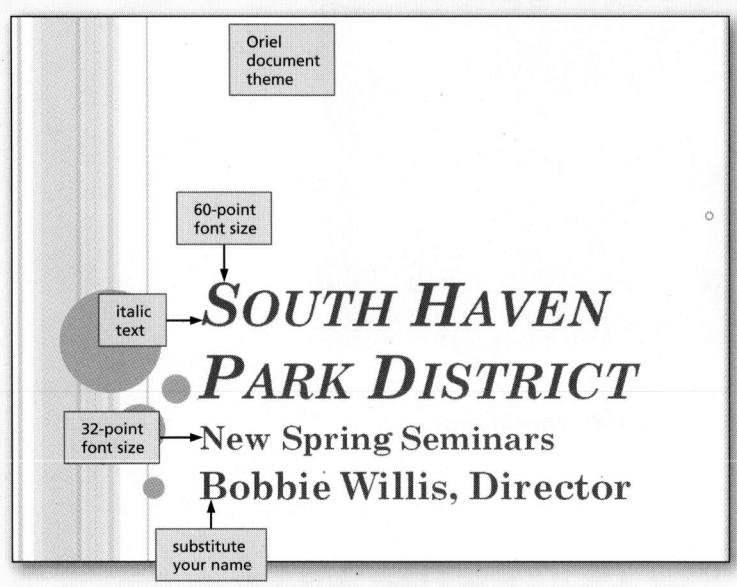

(a) Slide 1 (Title Slide)
Figure 1–102

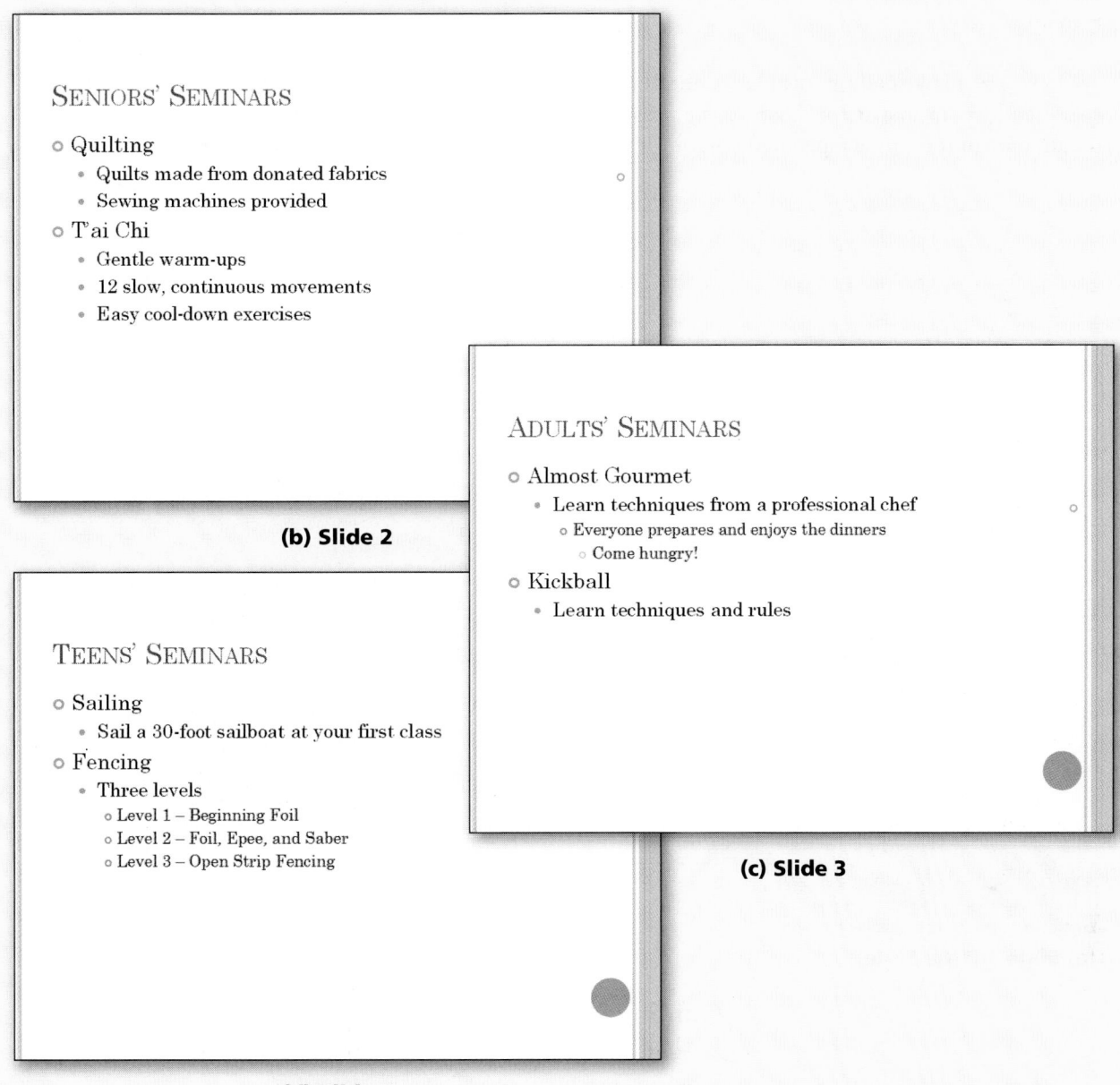

(b) Slide 2

(c) Slide 3

(d) Slide 4

Figure 1–102 (continued)

Instructions Part 2: The South Haven Park District staff members want to update this presentation to promote the new Fall seminars. Modify the presentation created in Part 1 to create the presentation shown in Figure 1–103. To begin, save the current presentation with the new file name, Lab 1-3 Part Two Fall Seminars. Change the document theme to Civic. On the title slide, remove the italics from the title paragraph, South Haven Park District, decrease the font size to 44, and bold the text. Change the first subtitle paragraph to New Fall Seminars. Then change your title in the second subtitle paragraph to Executive Director and change the font size of the entire paragraph to 28.

On Slide 2, change the first first-level paragraph, Quilting, to Quilting for the Holidays. Change the first second-level paragraph, Quilts made from donated fabrics, to Quilts will be raffled at Annual Bazaar. Change the title of the second seminar to Intermediate T'ai Chi.

On Slide 3, change the first second-level paragraph under Almost Gourmet to Holiday feasts and parties. Then change the second-level paragraph under Kickball to Seminar concludes with single elimination tournament.

On Slide 4, change the first class from Sailing to Climbing and then change the course description second-level paragraph to Covers verbal signals, rope, knots, harnesses, belaying.

Continued >

In the Lab *continued*

Correct any spelling mistakes, and then view the slide show. Change the document properties, as specified by your instructor. Display the presentation in grayscale. Submit both Part One and Part Two documents in the format specified by your instructor.

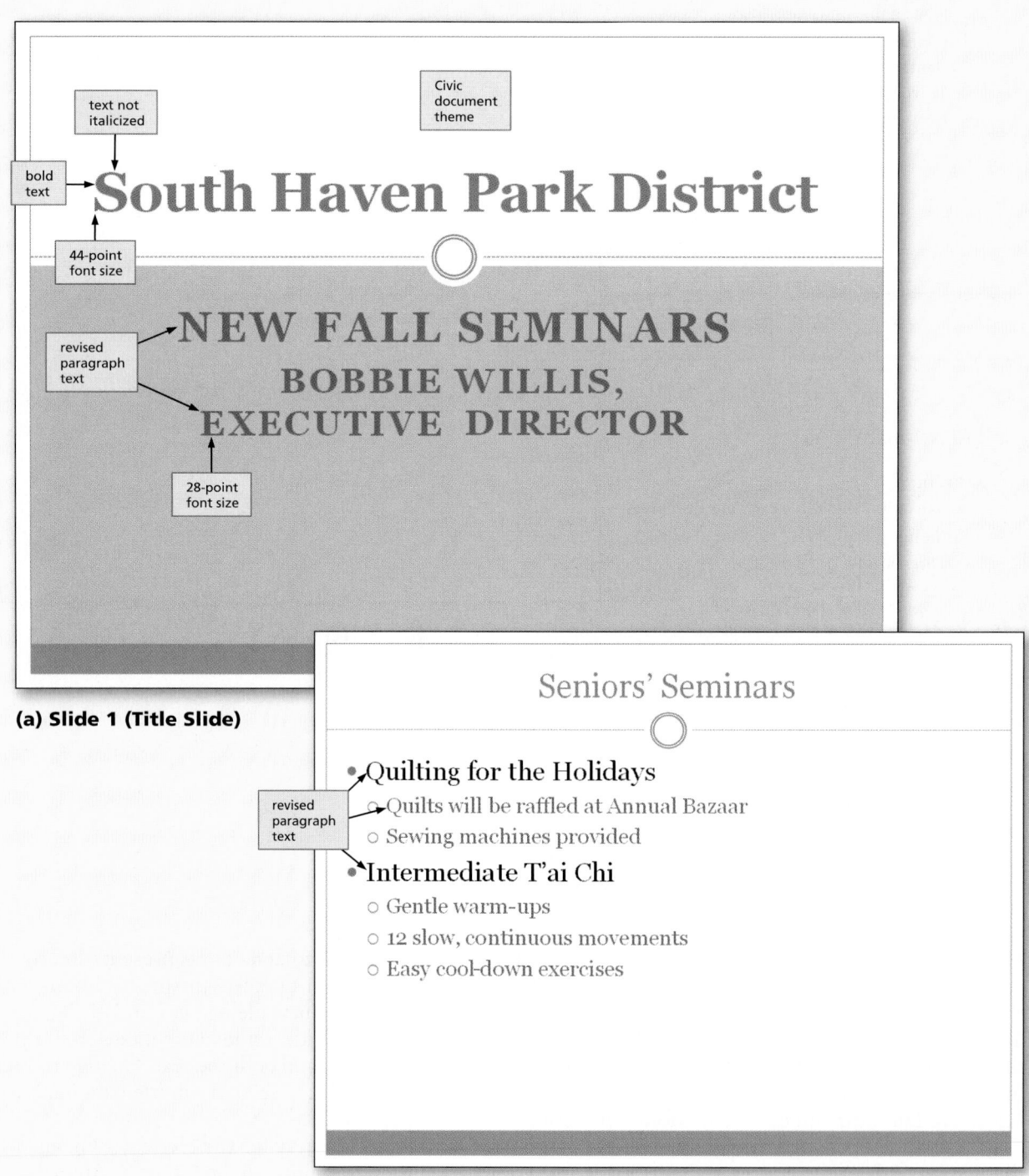

(a) Slide 1 (Title Slide)

(b) Slide 2

Figure 1–103

(c) Slide 3

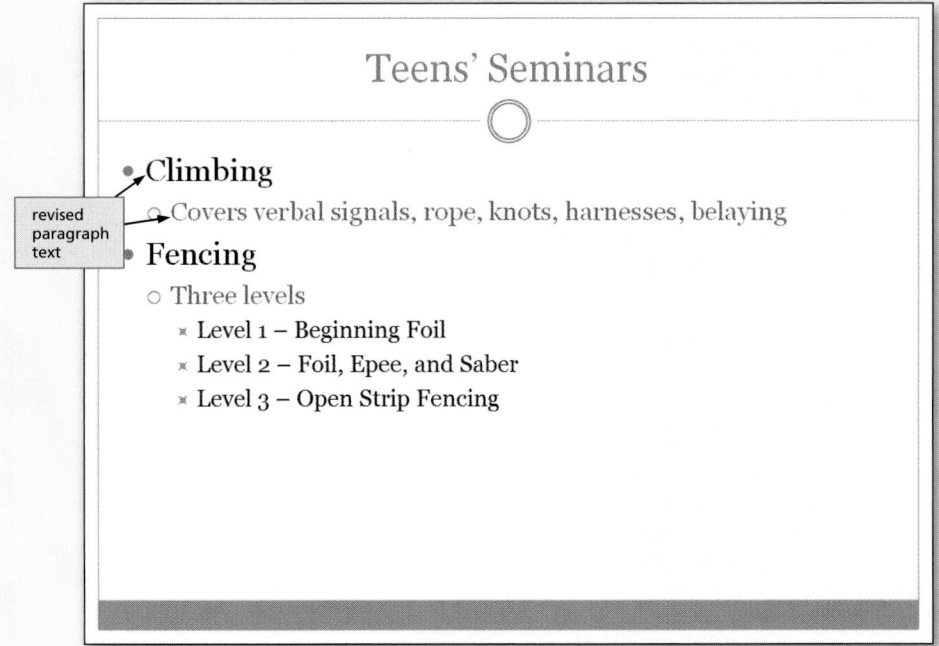

(d) Slide 4

Figure 1–103 (continued)

Cases and Places

Apply your creative thinking and problem solving skills to design and implement a solution.

● Easier   ●● More Difficult

Note: Remember to use the 7 × 7 rule as you design the presentations: a maximum of seven words on a line and a maximum of seven lines on one slide.

● 1: Design and Create an Ocean and Seas Presentation

Salt water covers more than two-thirds of the Earth's surface. This water flows freely between the Earth's five oceans and seas, which all are connected. In preparation for your next snorkeling and diving adventure, you have been reading about the oceans and seas. You decide to prepare a PowerPoint presentation to accompany a speech that is required in your Earth Science class. You create the outline shown in Figure 1–104 about these waters. Use this outline along with the concepts and techniques presented in this chapter to develop and format a slide show with a title slide and three text slides with bulleted lists. Be sure to check spelling.

Water, Water, Everywhere
The Earth's Oceans and Seas
Jamel Thomas
Earth Science 203

Major Bodies of Water
    Four oceans: Pacific, Atlantic, Indian, and Arctic
        Pacific is largest and deepest
            64,186,300 square miles
            12,925 feet average depth
    Fifth ocean delimited in 2000
            Southern Ocean north of Antarctica

Coral Reefs
    Form in shallow, warm seas
    Made of coral polyps' skeletons
        Grow on top of old skeletons
    Spend adult lives fixed to same spot
    Coral diseases increasing dramatically past 10 years
        Responding to onset of bacteria, fungi, viruses

Ocean Zones
        Sunlit (down to 650 feet)
                Sea plants and many animals
        Twilight (down to 3,300 feet)
            Many different fish
        Sunless (down to 13,100 feet)
                Animals feed on dead food from above

Figure 1–104

• 2: Design and Create an Industrial Revolution Presentation

The Industrial Revolution changed the way people worked and lived in many parts of the world. With its roots in Britain in the 18th century, the Industrial Revolution introduced new machines, steam power, and trains. As part of your World History homework assignments, you develop the outline shown in Figure 1–105 about the Industrial Revolution and then create an accompanying PowerPoint presentation. Use the concepts and techniques presented in this chapter to develop and format this slide show with a title slide, three text slides with bulleted lists, and a closing slide. Be sure to check spelling.

The Industrial Revolution
1700 - 1850
Sonia Banks
World History 108

British Inventors
   First machines spun and wove cloth quickly
      Wealthy businessmen built factories
         Spinning Jenny machine spun 16 threads simultaneously
   Angered people who made cloth at home
      Luddites protested by smashing machines
         Led by Ned Ludd

Steam Power
   James Watt invented first steam engine in 1782
      Hundreds of his engines used throughout Britain
   George Stephenson designed steam train, The Rocket
      Peak speed: 30 mph
      Used to transport goods in 1829

Coal Mining
   Coal needed to boil water to create steam
   Mining towns boomed
      Deep mines dug
      Men, women, and children worked long hours
         Many people killed and injured

Figure 1–105

Continued >

Cases and Places *continued*

•• 3: Design and Create a Recycling Presentation

Many communities require recycling of household waste. Residents are required to separate paper, plastics, and glass and put each material in special bins or bags. Electronic equipment also can be recycled. Your community has developed a special program for broken or obsolete computers and peripherals, office equipment and products, small home appliances, and entertainment equipment. These items include personal computers, printers, cellular telephones, toasters, televisions, DVD players, and video game consoles. Community officials will be collecting these items during the next two Fridays at your local police station and a nearby shopping center. They will not accept air conditioners, humidifiers, and hazardous wastes. Using the concepts and techniques presented in this chapter, develop a short PowerPoint presentation to show at various businesses and offices in your community. Emphasize that recycling is important because electronic products have very short useful lives. They produce waste and may contain hazardous materials, but many components can be salvaged. Include one slide with acceptable products and another with unacceptable products.

•• 4 Design and Create Your Favorite or Dream Car Presentation

Make It Personal

Ever since Henry Ford rolled the first Model T off his assembly line in 1908, people have been obsessed with cars. From the sporty Corvette to the environmentally friendly Prius, everyone has a favorite car or dream car. Use the concepts and techniques presented in this chapter to create a slide show promoting a particular vehicle. Include a title slide, at least three text slides with bulleted lists, and a closing slide. Format the text using colors, bolding, and italics where needed for emphasis. Be sure to check spelling.

•• 5: Design and Create a Financial Institutions Presentation

Working Together

Financial institutions such as banks, savings and loans, and credit unions offer a variety of products. Have each member of your team visit, telephone, or view Web sites of three local financial institutions. Gather data about:

1) Savings accounts

2) Checking accounts

3) Mortgages

4) Certificates of deposit

After coordinating the data, create a presentation with at least one slide showcasing each financial institution. As a group, critique each slide. Submit your assignment in the format specified by your instructor.

2 | Creating a Presentation with Illustrations and Shapes

Objectives

You will have mastered the material in this chapter when you can:

- Create slides from a blank presentation
- Change views to review a presentation
- Change slide layouts
- Add a background style
- Insert, move, and size clip art
- Insert a photograph from a file
- Delete a placeholder

- Change font color
- Format text using the Format Painter
- Add and size a shape
- Apply Quick Styles to placeholders and shapes
- Select slide transitions
- Preview and print an outline and handout

2 | Creating a Presentation with Illustrations and Shapes

Introduction

In our visual culture, audience members enjoy viewing effective graphics. Whether reading a document or viewing a PowerPoint presentation, people increasingly want to see photographs, artwork, graphics, and a variety of type. Researchers have known for decades that documents with visual elements are more effective than those that consist of only text because the illustrations motivate audiences to study the material. People remember at least one-third more information when the document they are seeing or reading contains visual elements. These graphics help clarify and emphasize details, so they appeal to audience members with differing backgrounds, reading levels, attention spans, and motivations.

BTW

Delivery Skills
While illustrations and shapes help audience members retain important points in a slide show, keep in mind that a speaker's presentation skills are the most effective part of a presentation. The presenter's posture, eye contact, volume, gestures, and rate establish the tone and tempo of the presentation. A good presentation rarely overcomes poor delivery skills.

Project — Presentation with Illustrations and a Shape

The project in this chapter follows graphical guidelines and uses PowerPoint to create the presentation shown in Figure 2–1. This slide show, which discusses identity theft, has a variety of illustrations and visual elements inserted on a gray background. Clip art and photographs add interest. Transitions help one slide flow gracefully into the next during a slide show. Slide titles have a style that blends well with the background and illustrations. The slide handouts include an outline of the slides and print all four slides on one page.

This presentation uses Quick Styles, which are collections of formatting options for objects and documents. The Quick Styles, like the document themes introduced in Chapter 1, are created by Microsoft's visual designers and give your presentation a professional look. When you rest your mouse pointer on a Quick Style thumbnail in the Quick Style gallery, you will see how the various colors, fonts, and effects are combined, and you can select the image that best fits the impression you want to present in your slide show.

Overview

As you read through this chapter, you will learn how to create the presentation shown in Figure 2–1 by performing these general tasks:

- Create a new presentation from a blank presentation.
- Review presentation in a variety of views.
- Insert and format shapes.
- Insert photographs and clips.
- Print an outline and a handout.

Protect Your Good Name

Reduce Your Risk of
Identity Theft

(a)

Reduce Access to Personal Data

- Shred credit card offers
- Use a locked mailbox
- Mail envelopes *inside* the post office
- Remove listing from telephone directory

(b)

Internet and Security Safeguards

- Install a firewall
- Install and update virus protection software
- Never respond to phishing e-mail
- Use credit, not debit, cards when shopping

(c)

Beware of 'Shoulder Surfers'
Shield your hand when entering your PIN
Thieves may be watching with binoculars

(d)

Figure 2–1

<table>
<tr>
<td>

**Plan
Ahead**

</td>
<td>

General Project Guidelines

When creating a PowerPoint presentation, the actions you perform and decisions you make will affect the appearance and characteristics of the finished document. As you create a presentation with illustrations, such as the project shown in Figure 2–1, you should follow these general guidelines:

1. **Focus on slide text content.** Give some careful thought to the words you choose to use. Some graphic designers advise starting with a blank screen so that the document theme does not distract from or influence the words.

2. **Use single quotation marks.** PowerPoint slides generally use a single quotation mark in several instances.

   • The introduction of an unfamiliar term

   • A quotation

   • Nicknames

   • Composition titles

3. **Adhere to copyright regulations.** Copyright laws apply to printed and Web-based materials. You can copy an existing photograph or artwork if it is in the public domain, if your company owns the graphic, or if you have obtained permission to use it. Be certain you have the legal right to use a desired graphic in your presentation.

4. **Use color effectively.** Your audience's eyes are drawn to color on a slide. Used appropriately, color can create interest by emphasizing material and promoting understanding. Be aware of symbolic meanings attached to colors, such as red generally representing danger, electricity, and heat.

5. **Use serif fonts for titles and sans serif fonts for body text.** Typefaces are divided into two categories: serif and sans serif. A serif letter generally has thin and thick areas, with the thin areas at the end of the lines. A sans serif letter generally is the same thickness. The letters in this box are sans serif.

6. **Choose graphics that serve a purpose.** Illustrations and art should help your audience remember and understand information. They should be uncluttered and visually appealing. Determine why you need each graphic and the kind of information it communicates.

7. **Consider graphics for multicultural audiences.** In today's intercultural society, your presentation might be viewed by people whose first language is different from yours. Some graphics have meanings specific to a culture, so be certain to learn about your intended audience and their views.

   When necessary, more specific details concerning the above guidelines are presented at appropriate points in the chapter. The chapter also will identify the actions you perform and decisions made regarding these guidelines during the creation of the presentation shown in Figure 2–1.

</td>
</tr>
</table>

Starting PowerPoint

Chapter 1 introduced you to starting PowerPoint, selecting a document theme, creating slides with bulleted lists, and printing a presentation. The following steps summarize starting a new presentation. To start PowerPoint, Windows Vista must be running. If you are using a computer to step through the project in this chapter and you want your screen to match the figures in this book, you should change your computer's resolution to 1024 × 768. For more information about how to change a computer's resolution, see Appendix E.

To Start PowerPoint

Note: If you are using Windows XP, see Appendix F for alternate steps.

1 Click the Start button on the Windows Vista taskbar to display the Start menu.

2 Click All Programs at the bottom of the left pane on the Start menu to display the All Programs list and then click Microsoft Office in the All Programs list.

3 Click Microsoft Office PowerPoint 2007 to start PowerPoint and display a new blank presentation in the PowerPoint window.

4 If the PowerPoint window is not maximized, click the Maximize button next to the Close button on its title bar to maximize the window.

Focus on slide text content.

Once you have researched your presentation topic, many methods exist to begin developing slide content.

- Select a document theme and then enter text, illustration, and tables.

- Open an existing presentation and modify the slides and theme.

- Import an outline created in Microsoft Word.

- Start with a blank presentation that uses the default Office Theme. Consider this practice similar to an artist who begins creating a painting with a blank, white canvas.

Experiment using different methods of developing the initial content for slides. Experienced PowerPoint users sometimes find one technique works better than another to stimulate creativity or help them organize their ideas in a particular circumstance.

Plan Ahead

Creating Slides from a Blank Presentation

In Chapter 1, you selected a document theme and then typed the content for the title and text slides using single- and multi-level bulleted lists. In this chapter, you will type the slide content for the title and text slides, select a background, and then format the text.

BTW

Introducing the Presentation
Before your audience enters the room, start the presentation and display Slide 1. This slide should be visually appealing and provide general interest in the presentation. An effective title slide gives a good first impression.

To Create a Title Slide

Recall from Chapter 1 that the title slide introduces the presentation to the audience. In addition to introducing the presentation, this project uses the title slide to capture the audience's attention by using title text and a shape, which is a movable, resizable graphical element. You will add this shape after you have typed the text for all four slides. The following step creates the slide show's title.

1 Type `Protect Your Good Name` in the title text placeholder (Figure 2–2 on the next page).

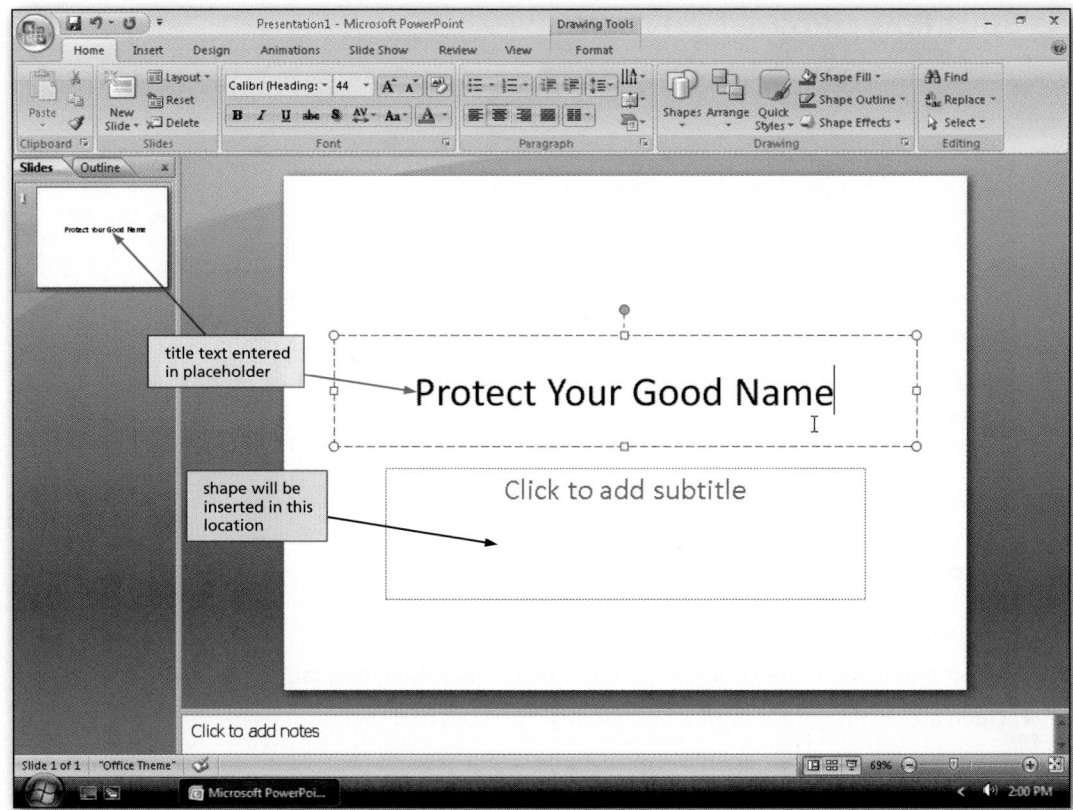

Figure 2–2

<table>
<tr><td>Plan
Ahead</td><td>**Use sans serif fonts for content text.**
When a new slide is displayed during your presentation, your audience members focus on the title and then read the words in the content placeholder. Generally more words appear in the content placeholder, so designers use sans serif typefaces to decrease reading time.</td></tr>
</table>

To Create the First Text Slide with a Single-Level Bulleted List

The first text slide you create in Chapter 2 describes tips for helping prevent thieves from accessing personal information. The four suggestions are displayed as second-level paragraphs. The following steps add a new slide (Slide 2) and then create a text slide with a single-level bulleted list.

1 Click the New Slide button in the Slides group.

2 Type `Reduce Access to Personal Data` in the title text placeholder.

3 Press CTRL+ENTER, type `Shred credit card offers` in the content text placeholder, and then press the ENTER key.

4 Type `Use a locked mailbox` and then press the ENTER key.

5 Type `Mail envelopes inside the post office` and then press the ENTER key.

6 Type `Remove listing from telephone directory` but do not press the ENTER key.

7 Italicize the word, inside, in the third bulleted paragraph (Figure 2–3).

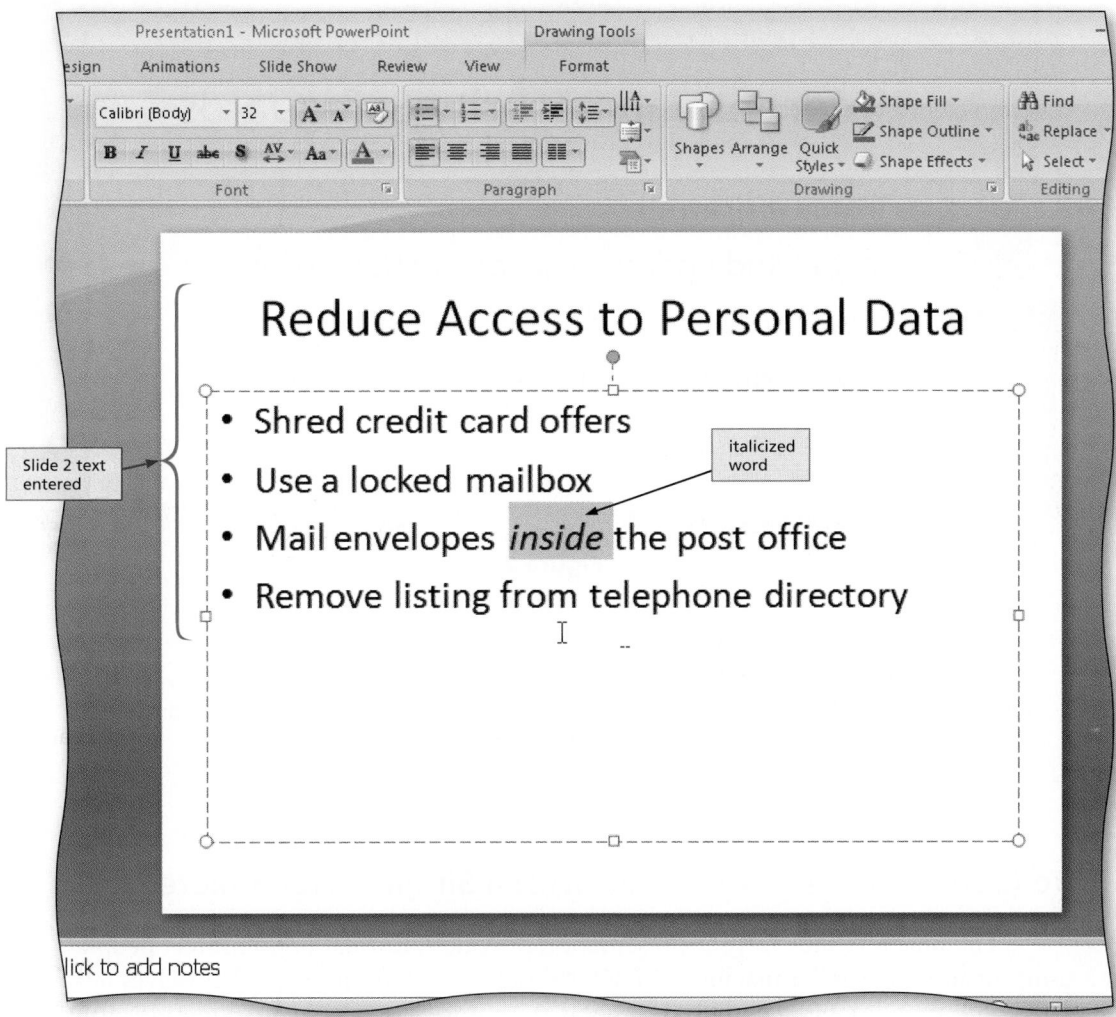

Figure 2–3

To Create the Second Text Slide with a Single-Level Bulleted List

The second text slide contains suggestions to help computer users protect their sensitive electronic files from cyber-intruders. The following steps add a new slide (Slide 3) and then create a text slide with a single-level bulleted list.

1 Click the New Slide button in the Slides group.

2 Type `Internet and Security Safeguards` in the title text placeholder.

3 Press CTRL+ENTER, type `Install a firewall` in the content text placeholder, and then press the ENTER key.

4 Type `Install and update virus protection software` and then press the ENTER key.

5 Type Never respond to phishing e-mail and then press the ENTER key.

6 Type Use credit, not debit, cards when shopping but do not press the ENTER key (Figure 2–4).

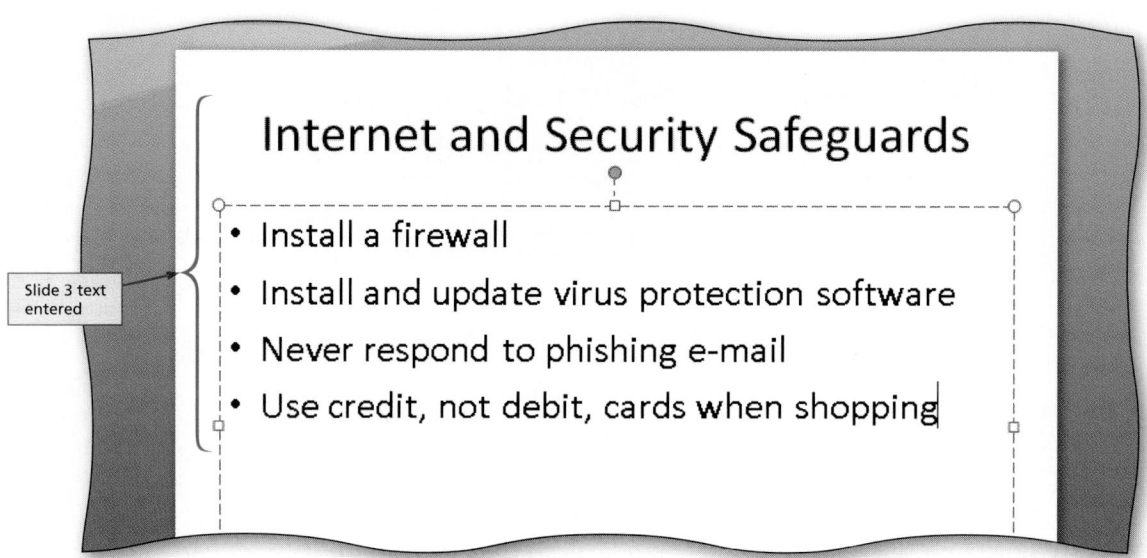

Figure 2–4

Use single quotation marks.
Type an apostrophe for the single quotation mark. PowerPoint generally will invert the first single quotation mark, making it an open-quotation mark, after you type a second single quotation mark, which then becomes a close-quotation mark.

To Create the Third Text Slide with a Single-Level Bulleted List

The final text slide in your presentation provides information to protect people using an automatic teller machine (ATM). "Shoulder surfers" position themselves near an ATM and often use binoculars and cameras to capture a user's personal identification number (PIN). The following steps add a new slide (Slide 4) and then create a text slide with two second-level bulleted paragraphs.

1 Click the New Slide button in the Slides group.

2 Type Beware of 'Shoulder Surfers' in the title text placeholder.

3 Press CTRL+ENTER, type Shield your hand when entering your PIN in the content text placeholder, and then press the ENTER key.

4 Type Thieves may be watching with binoculars but do not press the ENTER key (Figure 2–5).

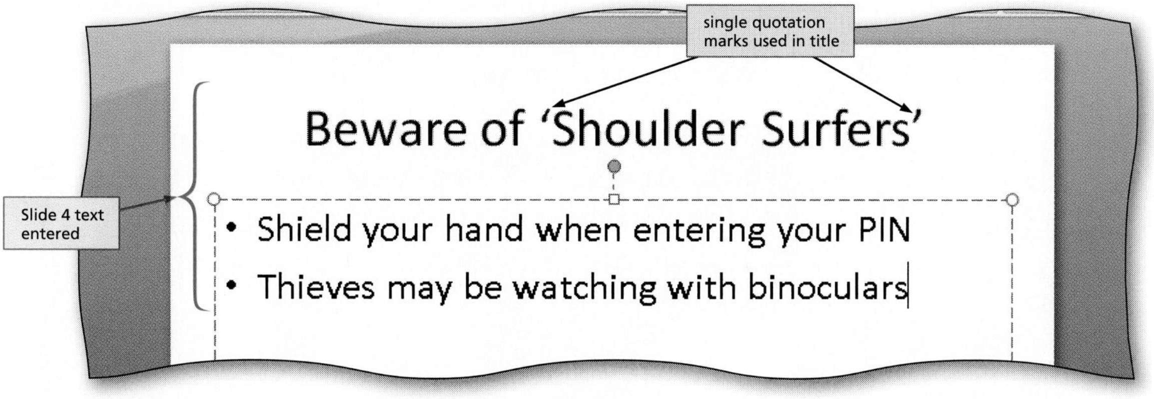

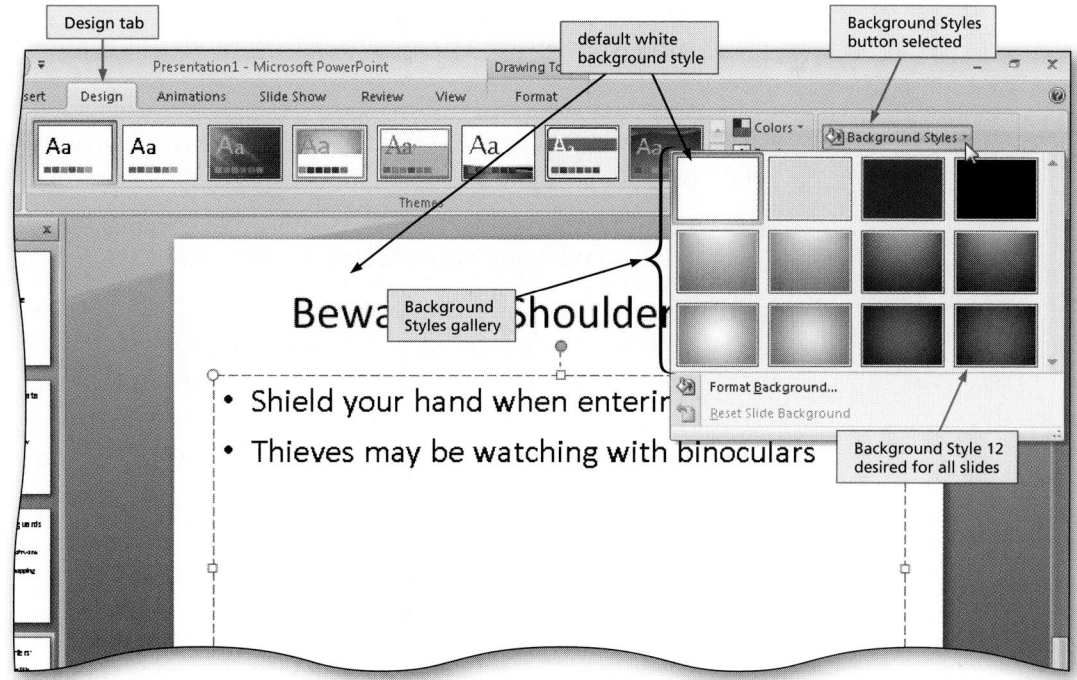

Figure 2–5

To Choose a Background Style

Now that the basic text paragraphs for the title and three text slides have been entered, you need to make design decisions. In creating Project 1, you chose a theme that determined the colors, fonts, and effects. You also can select these elements individually without choosing a theme. In Project 2, you will choose a background that fits the tone of your presentation and then choose fonts and effects. PowerPoint provides 12 white, ivory, blue, and black **background styles**. Background styles have designs that may include color, shading, patterns, and textures. **Fill effects** add pattern and texture to a background, which add depth to a slide. The following steps add a background style to all slides in the presentation.

1

- Click Design on the Ribbon to display the Design tab.

- Click the Background Styles button in the Background group to display the Background Styles gallery (Figure 2–6).

 Experiment

- Point to various styles themes in the Background Styles gallery and watch the backgrounds changes on the slide.

 Are the backgrounds displayed in a specific order?

Yes. They are arranged in order from white to black running from left to right. The first row has solid backgrounds; the middle row has darker fills at the bottom; the bottom row has darker fills on the sides. If you point to a background, a ScreenTip with the background's name appears on the screen.

Figure 2–6

2

- Click Background Style 12 to apply this background to all the slides (Figure 2–7).

If I decide later that this background style does not fit the theme of my presentation, can I apply a different background?

Yes. You can repeat these steps at any time while creating your presentation.

What if I want to apply this background style to only one slide?

When the gallery is displaying, right-click the desired style and then click Apply to Selected Slides.

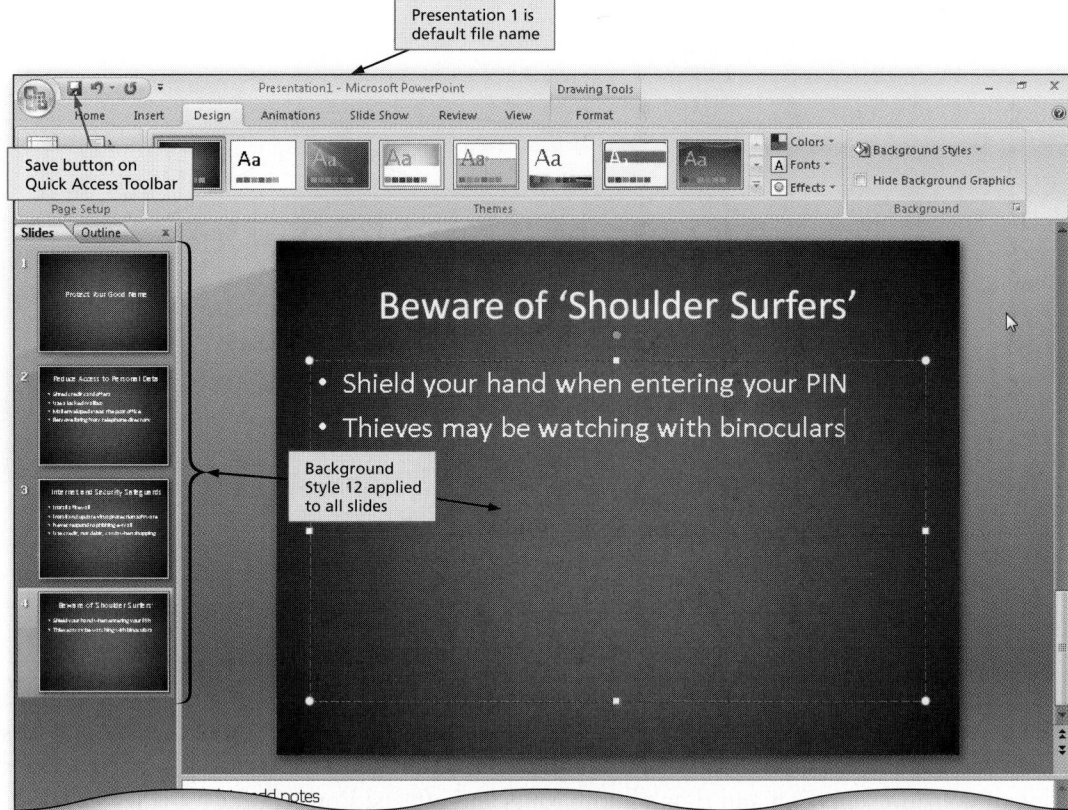

Figure 2–7

To Save a Presentation

You have performed many tasks to create the slide show and do not want to risk losing the work completed thus far. Accordingly, you should save the presentation. For a detailed example of the procedure summarized below, refer to pages PPT 27 through PPT 29 in Chapter 1.

1 With a USB flash drive connected to one of the computer's USB ports, click the Save button on the Quick Access Toolbar to display the Save As dialog box.

2 Type Identity Theft in the File name text box to change the file name. Do not press the ENTER key after typing the file name. If Computer is not displayed in the Favorite Links section, drag the top or bottom edge of the Save As dialog box until Computer is displayed. Click Computer in the Favorite Links section.

3 Double-click your USB flash drive in the list of available drives.

4 Click the Save button in the Save As dialog box to save the presentation on the USB flash drive with the file name, Identity Theft.

Changing Views to Review a Presentation

In Chapter 1, you displayed slides in Slide Show view to evaluate the presentation. Slide Show view, however, restricts your evaluation to one slide at a time. Recall from Chapter 1 that Slide Sorter view allows you to look at several slides at one time, which is why it is the best view to use to evaluate a presentation for content, organization, and overall appearance. After reviewing the slides, you can change the view to Normal view to continue working on the presentation.

To Change the View to Slide Sorter View

You can review the four slides in this presentation all in one window. The following step changes the view from Normal view to Slide Sorter view.

- Click the Slide Sorter button at the lower right of the PowerPoint window to display the presentation in Slide Sorter view (Figure 2–8).

Q&A

Why is Slide 4 selected?

It is the current slide in the slide pane.

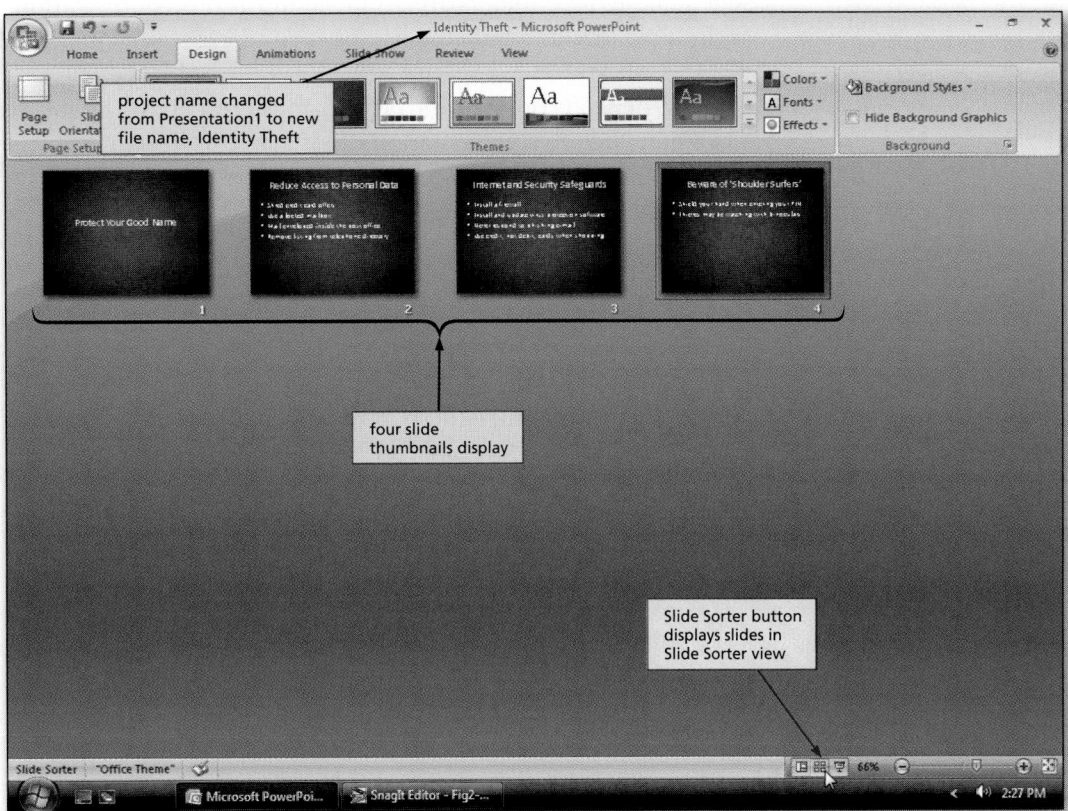

Figure 2–8

To Change the View to Normal View

You can make changes to text in Normal view and on the Outline tab. It is best, however, to change the view to Normal view when altering the slide layouts and formats so you can see the results of your changes. Switching between Slide Sorter view and Normal view helps you review your presentation, assess whether the slides have an attractive design and adequate content, and are organized for the most impact. The following steps change the view from Slide Sorter view to Normal view.

- Click the Normal button at the lower right of the PowerPoint window to display the presentation in Normal view (Figure 2–9).

Figure 2–9

BTW

Using the Find Command
Rather than viewing all the slides in your presentation to look for a particular word or phrase you typed, use the Find command to locate this text. Click the Home tab, click the Find button in the Editing group, type the text in the Find what text box, and then click the Find Next button.

Changing Layouts

When you developed this presentation, PowerPoint applied the Title Slide layout for Slide 1 and the Title and Content layout for the other three slides in the presentation. These layouts are the default styles. A **layout** specifies the arrangement of placeholders on a slide. These placeholders are arranged in various configurations and can contain text, such as the slide title or a bulleted list, or they can contain content, such as SmartArt graphics, pictures, charts, tables, shapes, and clip art. The placement of the text, in relationship to content, depends on the slide layout. You can specify a particular slide layout when you add a new slide to a presentation or after you have created the slide.

Using the **Layout gallery**, you can choose a slide layout. The nine layouts in this gallery have a variety of placeholders to define text and content positioning and formatting. Three layouts are for text: Title Slide, Section Header, and Title Only. Five are for text and content: Title and Content, Two Content, Comparison, Content with Caption, and Picture with Caption. The Blank layout has no placeholders. If none of these standard layouts meets your design needs, you can create a **custom layout**. A custom layout specifies the number, size, and location of placeholders, background content, and optional slide and placeholder-level properties.

When you change the layout of a slide, PowerPoint retains the text and objects and repositions them into the appropriate placeholders. Using slide layouts eliminates the need to resize objects and the font size because PowerPoint automatically sizes the objects and text to fit the placeholders.

To Change the Slide Layout to Two Content

Notice the slides have a significant amount of space and look plain. These observations indicate a need to add visual interest to the slides. The next several sections improve the presentation by changing layouts and adding clip art and photos. Before you add these graphical elements, you must change the slide layouts.

Adding clip art and a photograph to Slides 2, 3, and 4 requires two steps. First, change the slide layouts and then insert the clip or photo into the content placeholders. The following steps change the slide layout on Slide 2 from Title and Content to Two Content.

1
- Click the Previous Slide button on the vertical scroll bar twice to display Slide 2.

- Click Home on the Ribbon to display the Home tab.

- Click the Layout button in the Slides group on the Home tab to display the Layout gallery (Figure 2–10).

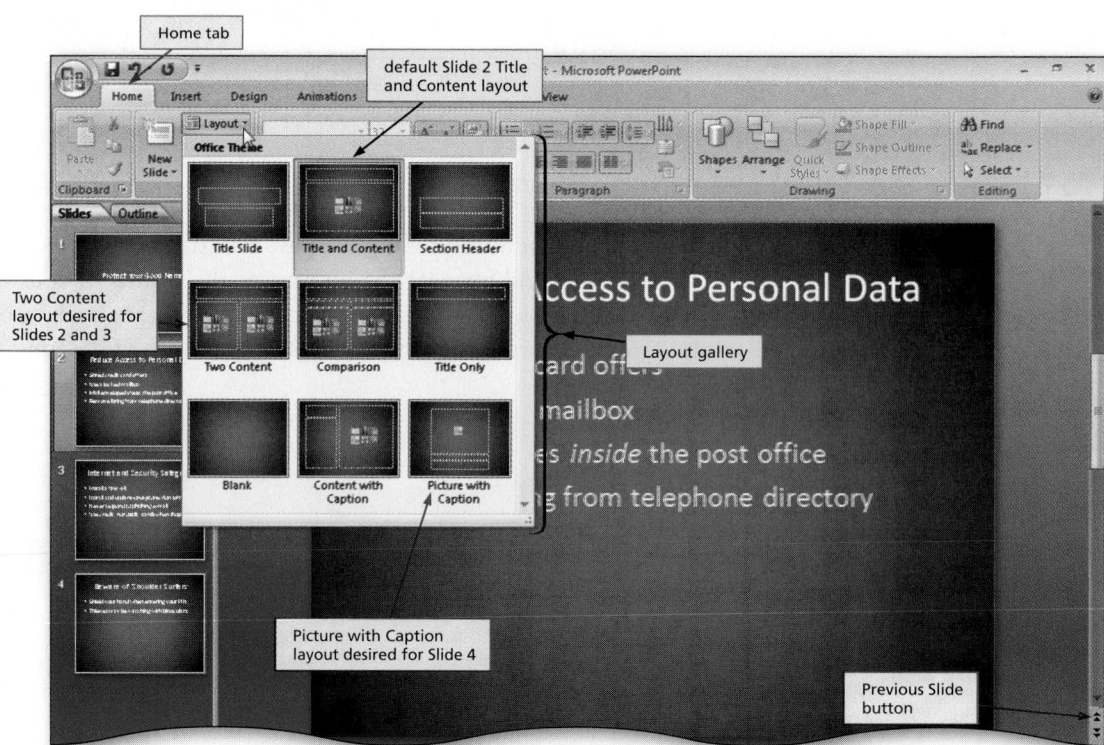

Figure 2–10

- Click Two Content to apply that layout to Slide 2 (Figure 2–11).

Q&A

Why did the bulleted list move to the left placeholder?

PowerPoint assumes you want your bulleted list to display on the left side of your slide. If you want the list to display on the right side, you will need to move the placeholders on the slide.

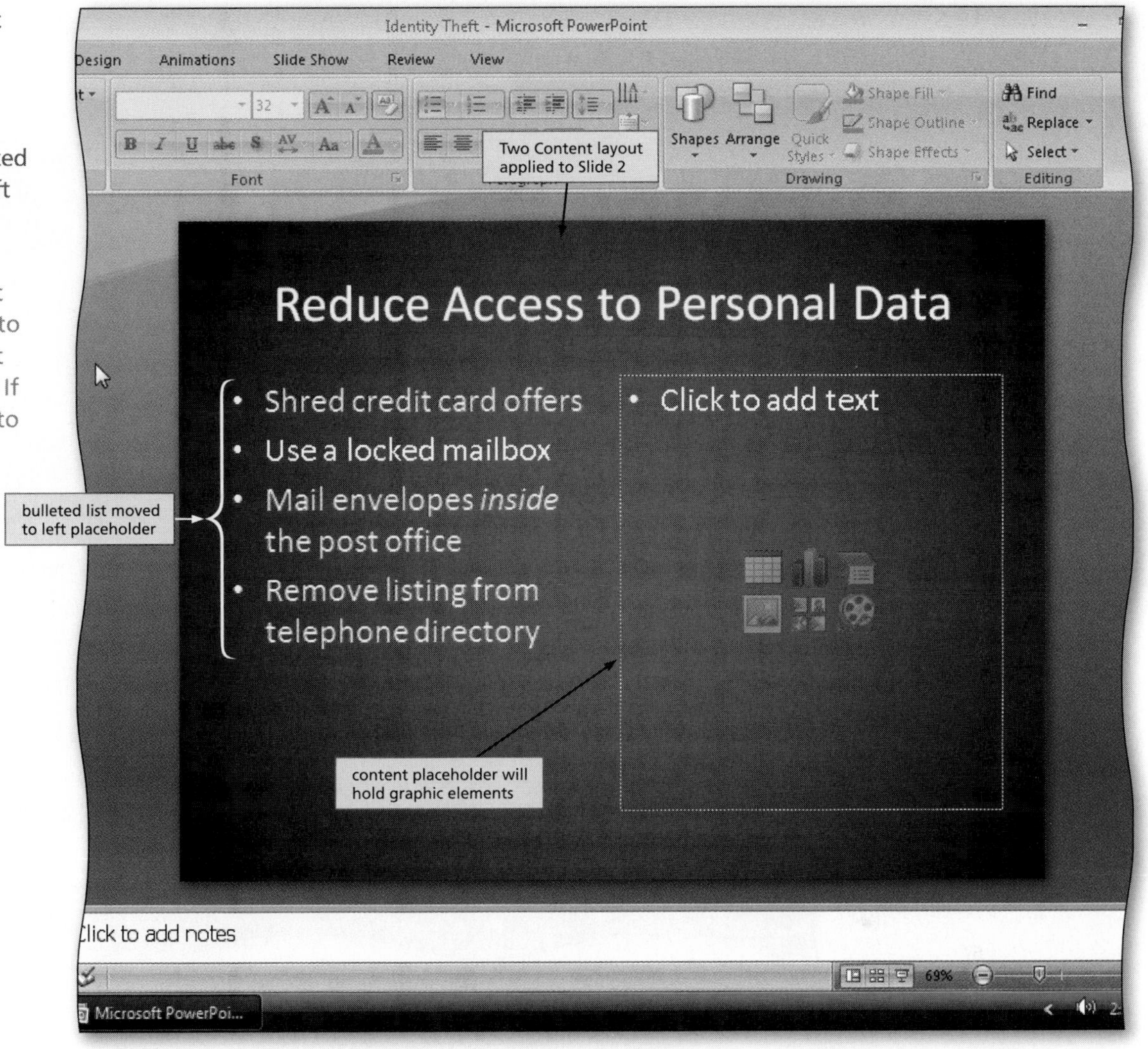

Figure 2–11

To Change the Slide Layout to Two Content

Slide 3 also will have a bulleted list and a graphic element, so the layout needs to change to accommodate this slide content. The following steps change the Slide 3 layout to Two Content.

1. Click the Next Slide button.

2. Click the Layout button in the Slides group on the Home tab to display the Layout gallery.

3. Click Two Content to apply the layout to Slide 3 (Figure 2–12).

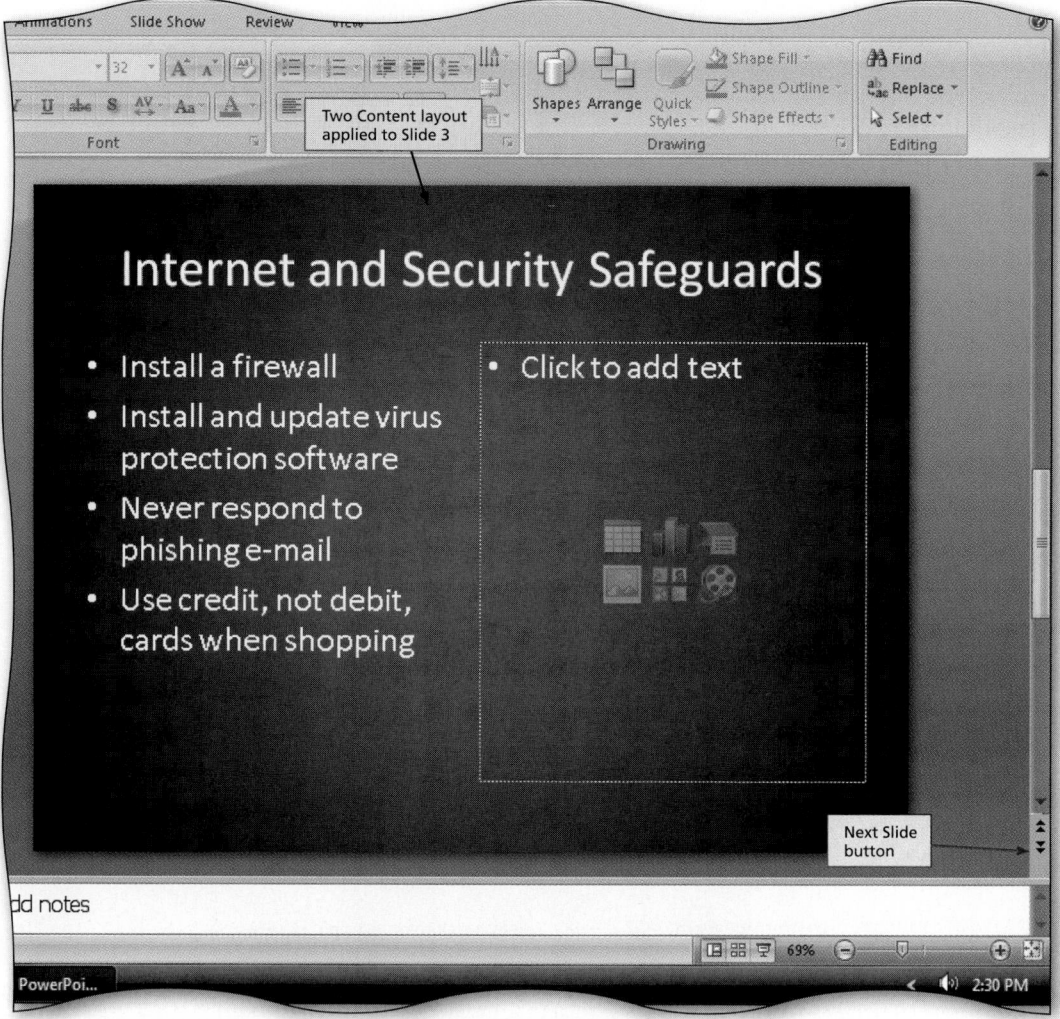

Figure 2-12

To Change the Slide Layout to Picture with Caption

The Slide 4 text discusses exercising caution while using an automatic teller machine (ATM). You have a photograph of a person using an ATM, and you want to display this graphic prominently on the slide. The Picture with Caption layout serves this purpose well, so the layout needs to change to accommodate this slide content. The following steps change the Slide 4 layout to Picture with Caption.

1 Click the Next Slide button.

2 Click the Layout button in the Slides group.

3 Click Picture with Caption to apply the layout to Slide 4 (Figure 2–13).

Q&A Why did the font size of the title and bulleted list text decrease?

PowerPoint reduced the font size to make room for the large upper content placeholder. You can increase the font size of this text if you desire.

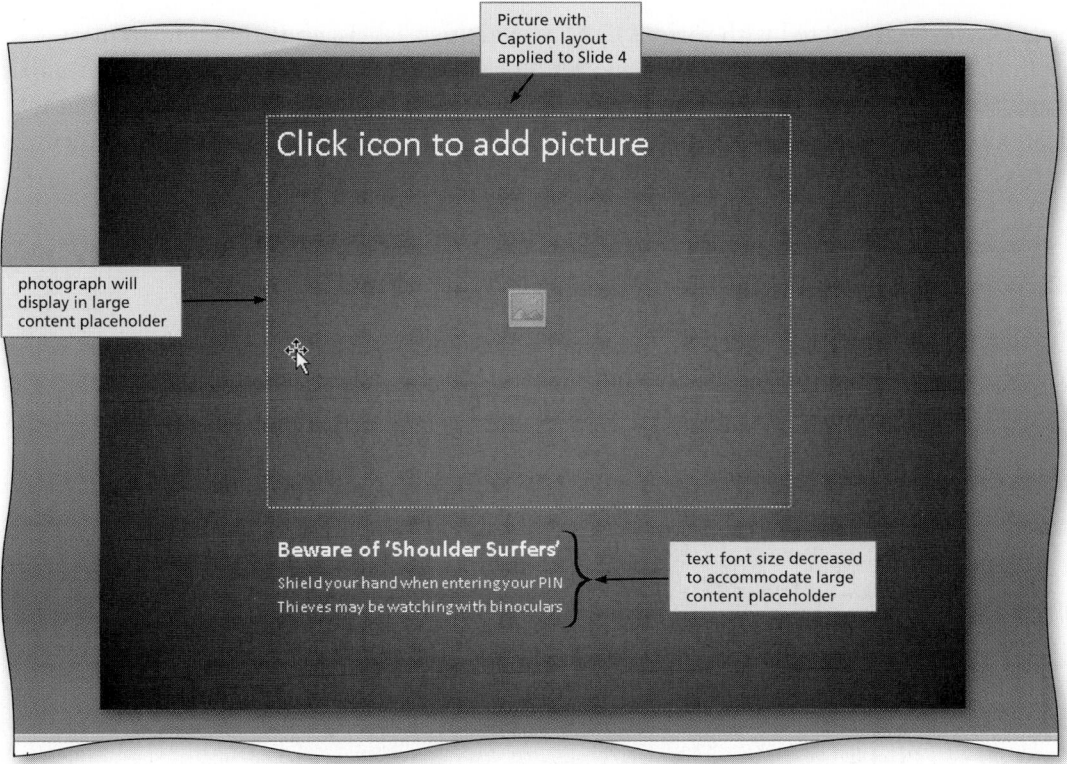

Figure 2–13

Inserting Clip Art and Photographs into Slides

A **clip** is a single media file, including art, sound, animation, and movies. Adding a clip can help increase the visual appeal of many slides and can offer a quick way to add professional-looking graphic images and sounds to a presentation without creating these files yourself. This art is contained in the **Microsoft Clip Organizer**, a collection of drawings, photographs, sounds, videos, and other media files shared with Microsoft Office applications. The **Office Collections** contains all these media files included with Microsoft Office.

You also can add your own clips to slides. You can insert these files directly from a storage medium, such as a USB flash drive. In addition, you can add them to the other files in the Clip Organizer so that you can search for and reuse these images, sounds, animations, and movies. When you create these media files, they are stored on your hard disk in **My Collections**. The Clip Organizer will find these files and create a new collection with these files. Two other locations for clips are Shared Collections and Web Collections. Files in the **Shared Collections** typically reside on a shared network file server and are accessed by multiple users. The **Web Collections** clips reside on the Microsoft Clip Art and Media Home page on the Microsoft Office Online Web site. They are available only if you have an active Internet connection.

BTW

Importing Clips
Previous versions of PowerPoint imported clips automatically the first time a user desired to insert clips. PowerPoint 2007 requires the user to import the clips on first use by clicking the Organize clips link in the Clip Art task pane, clicking the File menu in the Favorites – Microsoft Clip Organizer dialog box, pointing to Add Clips to Organizer in the File menu, and then clicking Automatically.

The Clip Art Task Pane

You can add clips to your presentation in two ways. One way is by selecting one of the slide layouts that includes a content placeholder with a Clip Art button. A second method is by clicking the Clip Art button in the Illustrations area on the Insert tab. Clicking the Clip Art button opens the Clip Art task pane. The **Clip Art task pane** allows you to search for clips by using descriptive keywords, file names, media file formats, and clip collections. Specific file formats could be for clip art, photographs, movies, and sounds. Clips are organized in hierarchical **clip collections**, which combine topic-related clips into categories, such as Academic, Business, and Technology.

Clips have one or more keywords associated with various entities, activities, labels, and emotions. In most instances, the keywords give the name of the clip and related categories. For example, an image of a cow in the Animals category has the keywords animals, cattle, cows, dairies, farms, and Holsteins. You can enter these keywords in the Search for text box to find clips when you know one of the words associated with the image. Otherwise, you may find it necessary to scroll through several categories to find an appropriate clip.

To Insert a Clip from the Clip Organizer into a Content Placeholder

Depending on the installation of the Microsoft Clip Organizer on your computer, you may not have the clip art used in this chapter. Contact your instructor if you are missing clips used in the following steps. If you have an open connection to the Internet, clips from the Microsoft Office Online Web site will display automatically as the result of your search results.

With the Two Content layout applied to Slide 2, you insert clip art into the right content placeholder. The following steps insert clip art of a shredder into the content placeholder on Slide 2.

- Click the Previous Slide button twice to display Slide 2.

- Click the Clip Art button in the content placeholder to display the Clip Art task pane.

- Click the Search for text box in the Clip Art task pane, delete any letters that are present, and then type shredder in the Search for text box (Figure 2–14).

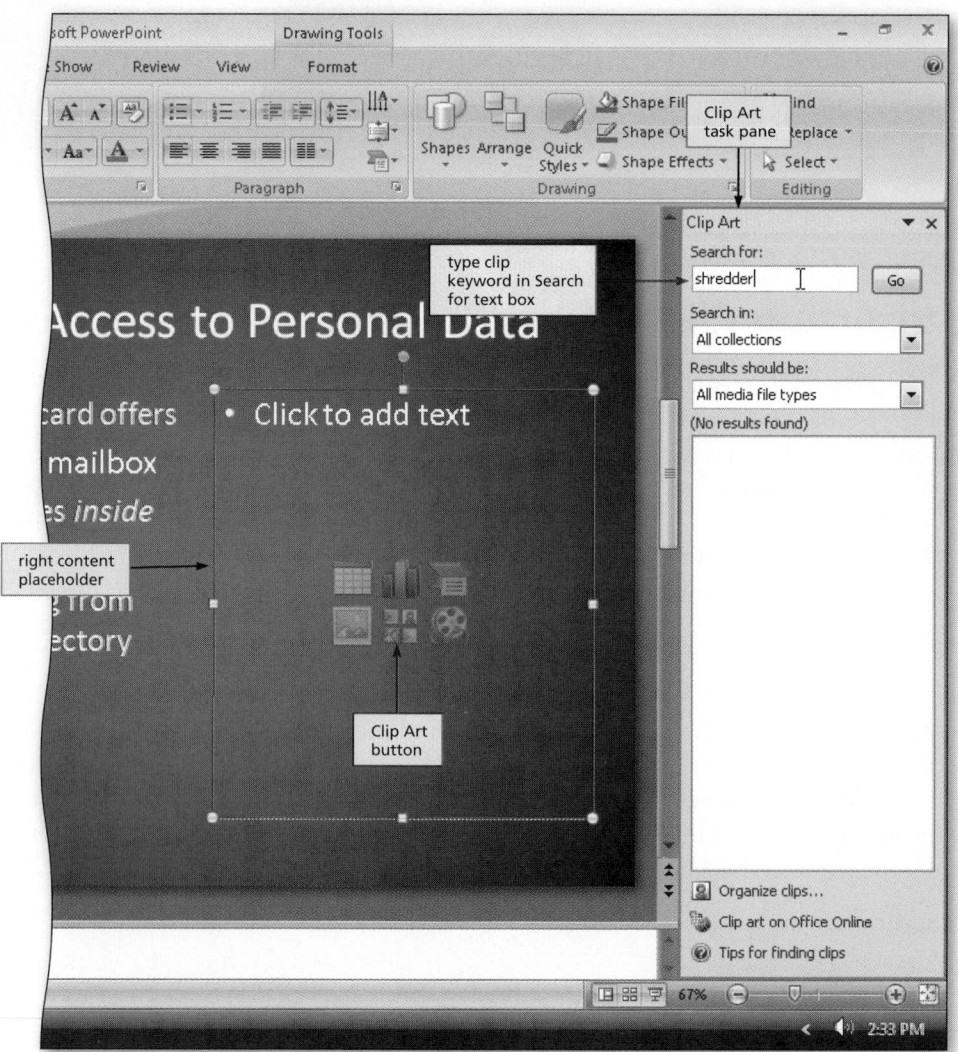

Figure 2–14

2

- Click the Go button so that the Microsoft Clip Organizer will search for and display all pictures having the keyword, shredder.

- If necessary, click the Yes button if a Microsoft Clip Organizer dialog box appears asking if you want to include additional clip art images from Microsoft Office Online.

- If necessary, scroll down the list to display the shredder clip shown in Figure 2–15

- Click the clip to insert it into the right content placeholder (Figure 2–15).

Q&A What if the shredder image displayed in Figure 2–15 is not shown in my Clip Art task pane?

Select a similar clip. Your clips may be different depending on the clips installed on your computer and if you have an open connection to the Internet.

Q&A What is the blue globe image that displays in the lower-left corner of the clips in the Clip Art task pane?

The globe indicates that the image was obtained from the Microsoft Office Online Web site.

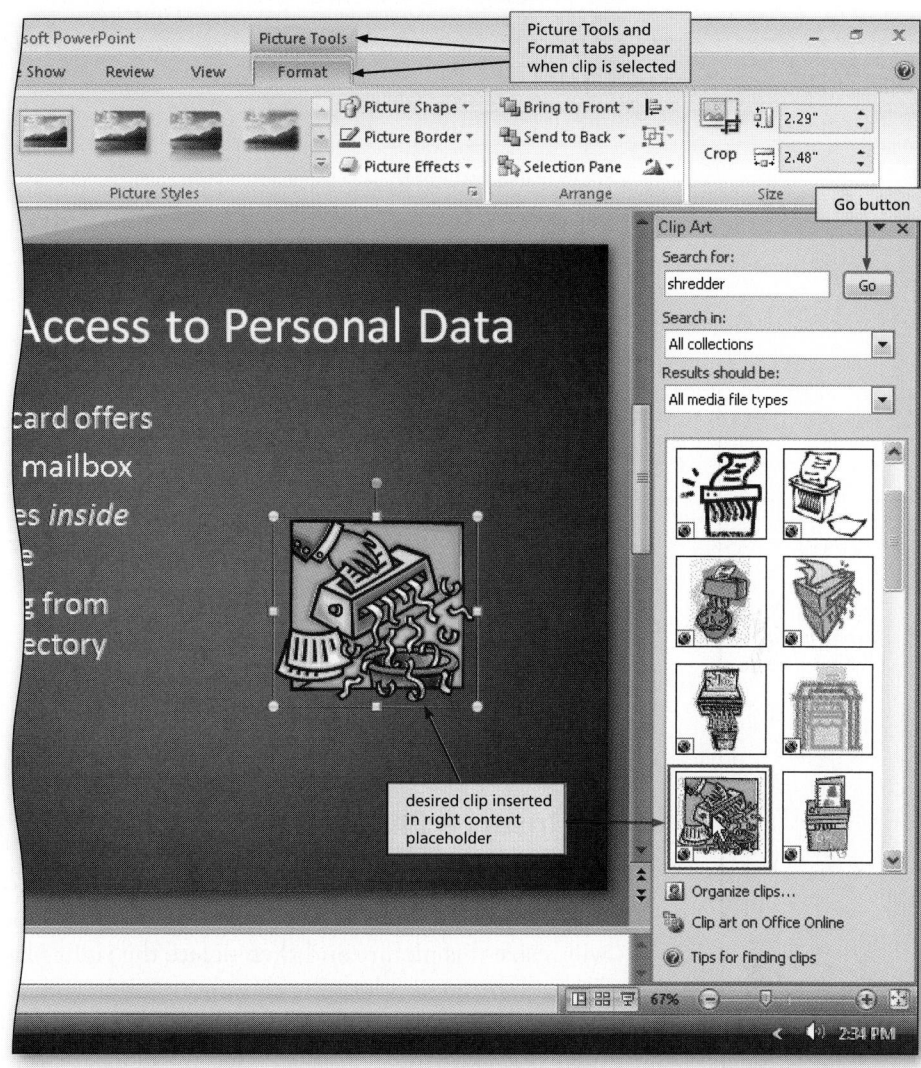

Figure 2–15

Adhere to copyright regulations.
You have permission to use the clips from the Microsoft Clip Organizer. If you want to use a clip from another source, be certain you have the legal right to insert this file in your presentation. Read the copyright notices that accompany the clip and are posted on the Web site. The owners of these images and files often ask you to give them credit for using their work, which may be satisfied by stating where you obtained the images.

Plan Ahead

Photographs and the Clip Organizer

In addition to clip art, you can insert pictures into a presentation. These may include scanned photographs, line art, and artwork from compact discs. To insert a picture into a presentation, the picture must be saved in a format that PowerPoint can recognize. Table 2–1 identifies some of the formats PowerPoint recognizes.

You can import files saved with the .emf, .gif, .jpg, .png, .bmp, .rle, .dib, and .wmf formats directly into PowerPoint presentations. All other file formats require separate filters that are shipped with the PowerPoint installation software and must be installed. You can download additional filters from the Microsoft Office Online Web site.

Table 2–1 Primary File Formats PowerPoint Recognizes	
Format	**File Extension**
Computer Graphics Metafile	.cgm
CorelDRAW	.cdr, .cdt, .cmx, and .pat
Encapsulated PostScript	.eps
Enhanced Metafile	.emf
FlashPix	.fpx
Graphics Interchange Format	.gif
Hanako	.jsh, .jah, and .jbh
Joint Photographic Experts Group (JPEG)	.jpg
Kodak PhotoCD	.pcd
Macintosh PICT	.pct
PC Paintbrush	.pcx
Portable Network Graphics	.png
Tagged Image File Format	.tif
Windows Bitmap	.bmp, .rle, .dib
Microsoft Windows Metafile	.wmf
WordPerfect Graphics	.wpg

To Insert a Photograph from the Clip Organizer into a Slide

Next you will add a photograph to Slide 3. You will not insert this picture into a content placeholder, so it will display in the center of the slide. Later in this chapter you will resize this picture and then delete the right placeholder because it is not being used. To start the process locating this photograph, you do not need to click the Clip Art button icon in the content placeholder because the Clip Art task pane already is displayed. The following steps add a photograph to Slide 3.

1 Click the Next Slide button to display Slide 3.

2 Click the Search for text box in the Clip Art task pane and then delete the letters in the text box.

3 Type credit card and then click the Go button.

4 If necessary, scroll down the list to display the picture of a credit card shown in Figure 2–16 and then click the photograph to insert it into Slide 3 (Figure 2–16).

Q&A Why is my photograph so large on the slide?

The photograph was inserted into the slide and not into a content placeholder. You will resize the picture later in this chapter.

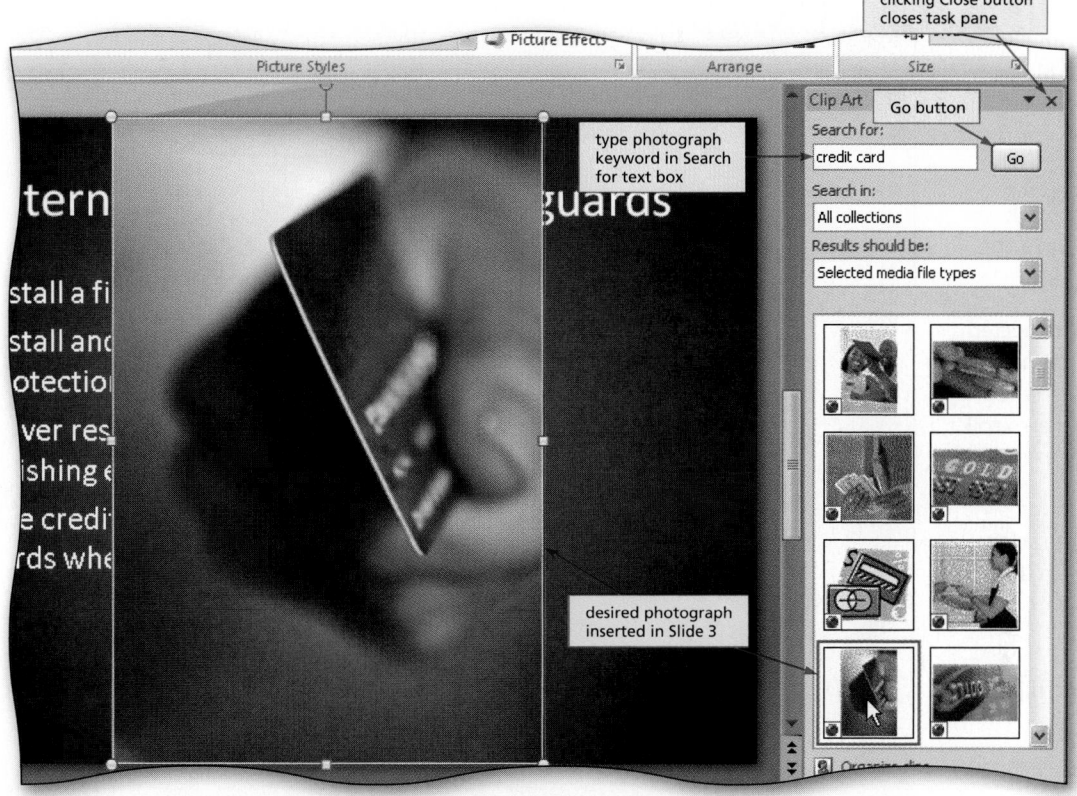

Figure 2–16

To Insert a Photograph from a File into a Slide

The final image to insert in the presentation is a photograph on Slide 4. This slide uses the Picture with Caption layout, so the picture will display in the top placeholder. The following steps add a picture from the Data Files for Students. See the inside back cover of this book for instructions on downloading the Data Files for Students, or contact your instructor for more information on accessing the required files. The following steps insert a photograph of a student using an automatic teller machine (ATM).

Note: If you are using Windows XP, see Appendix F for alternate steps.

1
- Click the Next Slide button to display Slide 4.

- Click the Close button in the Clip Art task pane so that it no longer is displayed (Figure 2–17).

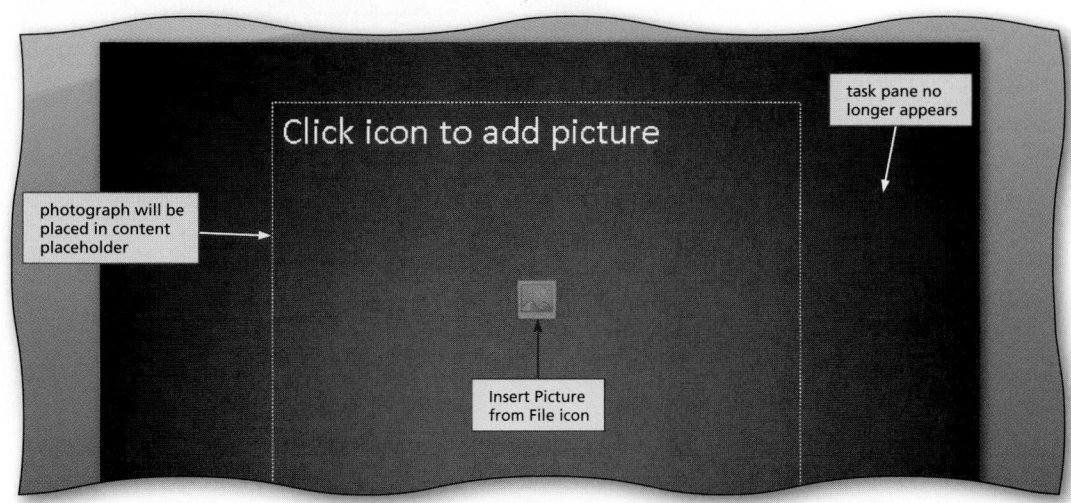

Figure 2–17

2

- Click the Insert Picture from File icon in the content placeholder to display the Insert Picture dialog box.

- If the Folders list is displayed below the Folders button, click the Folders button to remove the Folders list.

- With your USB flash drive connected to one of the computer's USB ports, if necessary, click Computer in the Favorite Links section and then scroll until UDISK 2.0 (E:) appears in the list of available drives.

- Double-click UDISK 2.0 (E:) to select the USB flash drive, Drive E in this case, as the device that contains the picture.

- Click ATM to select the file name (Figure 2–18).

Q&A

What if the photograph is not on a USB flash drive?

Use the same process, but select the device containing the photograph in the Favorite Links section.

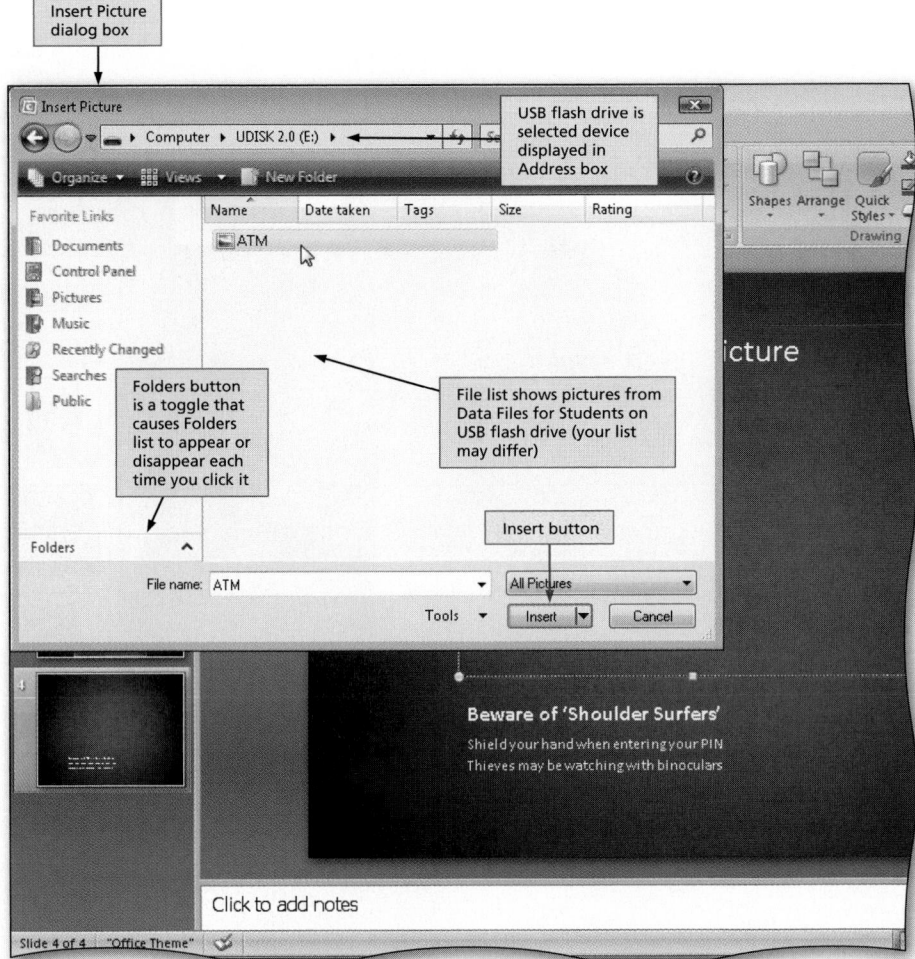

Figure 2–18

3

- Click the Insert button in the dialog box to insert the picture into Slide 4 (Figure 2–19).

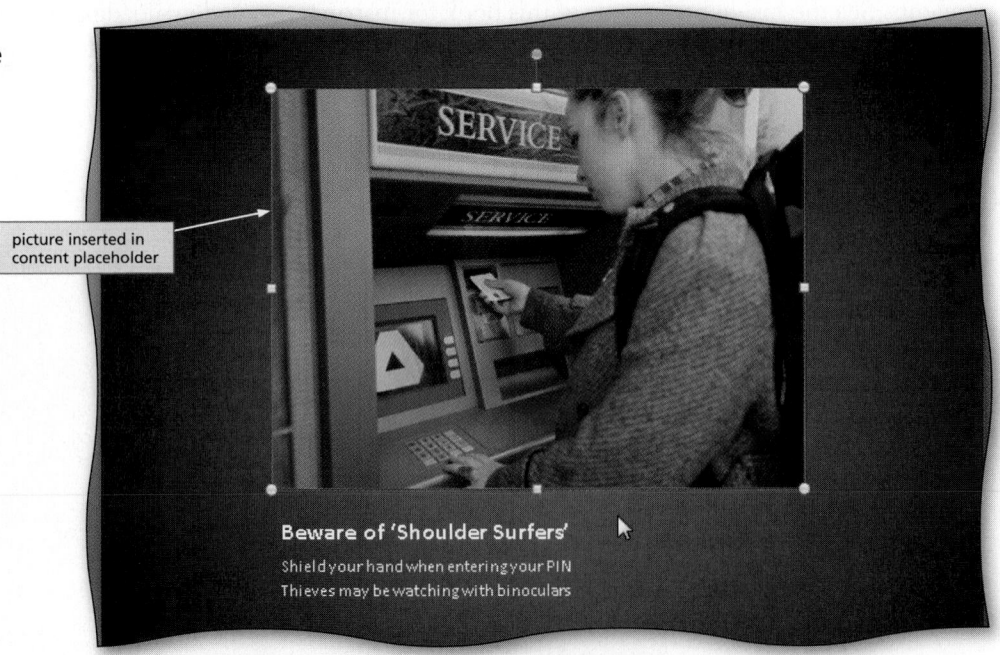

picture inserted in content placeholder

Figure 2–19

Resizing Clip Art and Photographs

Sometimes it is necessary to change the size of clip art. **Resizing** includes both enlarging and reducing the size of a clip art graphic. You can resize clip art using a variety of techniques. One method involves changing the size of a clip by specifying exact dimensions in a dialog box. Another method involves dragging one of the graphic's sizing handles to the desired location. A selected graphic appears surrounded by a **selection rectangle**, which has small squares and circles, called **sizing handles** or move handles, at each corner and middle location.

To Resize Clip Art

On Slide 2, much space appears around the clip, so you can increase its size. The photograph on Slide 3 is too large for the slide, so you should reduce its size. To change the size, drag the corner sizing handles to view how the clip will look on the slide. Using these corner handles maintains the graphic's original proportions. Dragging the square sizing handles alters the proportions so that the graphic becomes more or less high or more or less wide. The following steps increase the size of the Slide 2 clip using a corner sizing handle.

- Click the Previous Slide button two times to display Slide 2.

- Click the shredder clip to select it and display the selection rectangle.

- Point to the upper-left corner sizing handle on the clip so that the mouse pointer shape changes to a two-headed arrow (Figure 2–20).

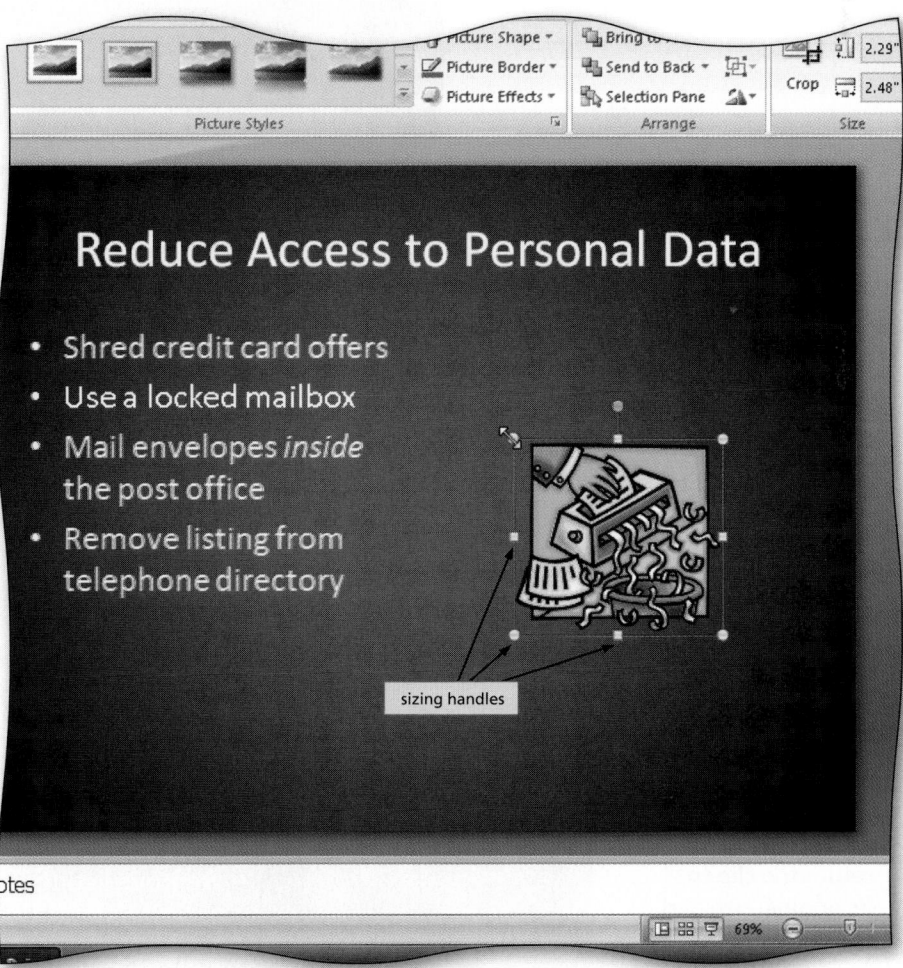

Figure 2–20

2

- Drag the sizing handle diagonally toward the center of the slide until the mouse pointer is positioned approximately as shown in Figure 2–21.

Q&A What if the clip is not the same size shown in Figure 2–21?

Repeat Steps 1 and 2.

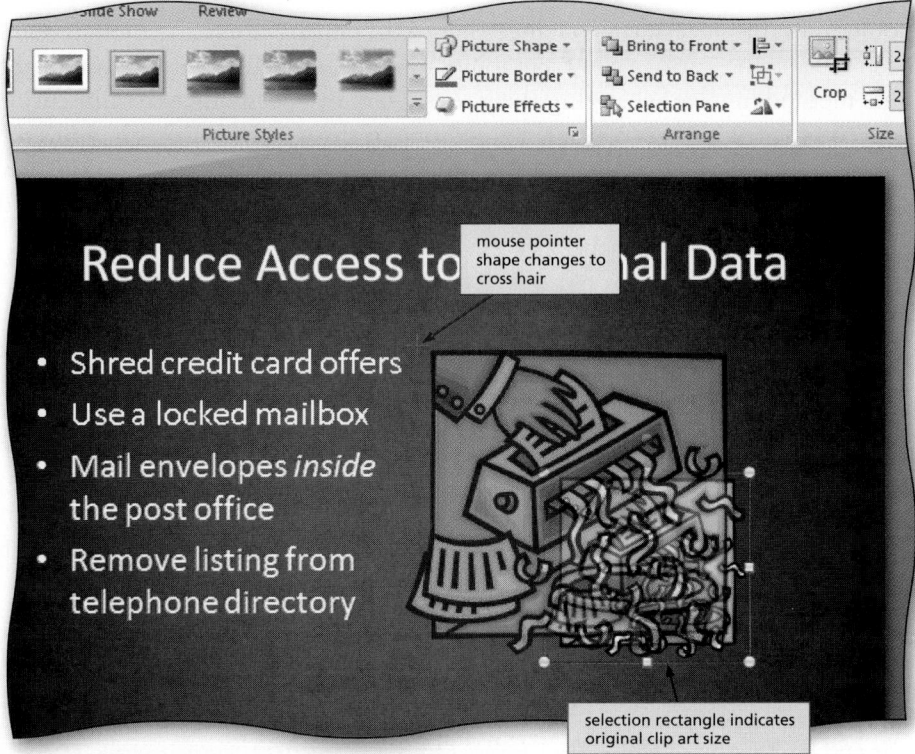

Figure 2–21

3

- Release the mouse button to resize the clip. If necessary, select the clip and then use the ARROW keys to position the clip as shown in Figure 2–21.

4

- Click outside the clip to deselect it (Figure 2–22).

Q&A What happened to the Picture Tools and Format tabs?

When you click outside the clip, PowerPoint deselects the clip and removes the Picture Tools and Format tabs from the screen.

Q&A What if I want to return the clip to its original size and start again?

With the graphic selected, click the Reset button in the Slides group on the Home tab.

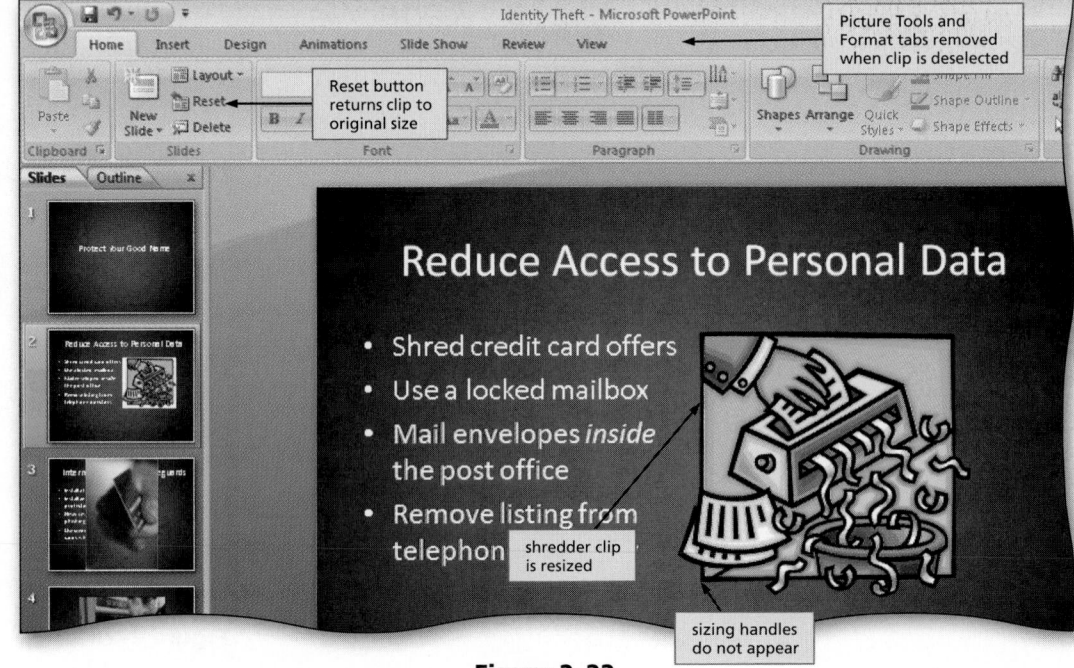

Figure 2–22

To Resize a Photograph

The credit card picture in Slide 3 fills the middle of the slide and covers some text, so you should reduce its size. The following steps resize this photograph using a sizing handle.

1 Click the Next Slide button to display Slide 3.

2 Click the credit card photograph to select it.

3 Drag the upper-left corner sizing handle on the photograph diagonally inward until the photograph is resized approximately as shown in Figure 2–23.

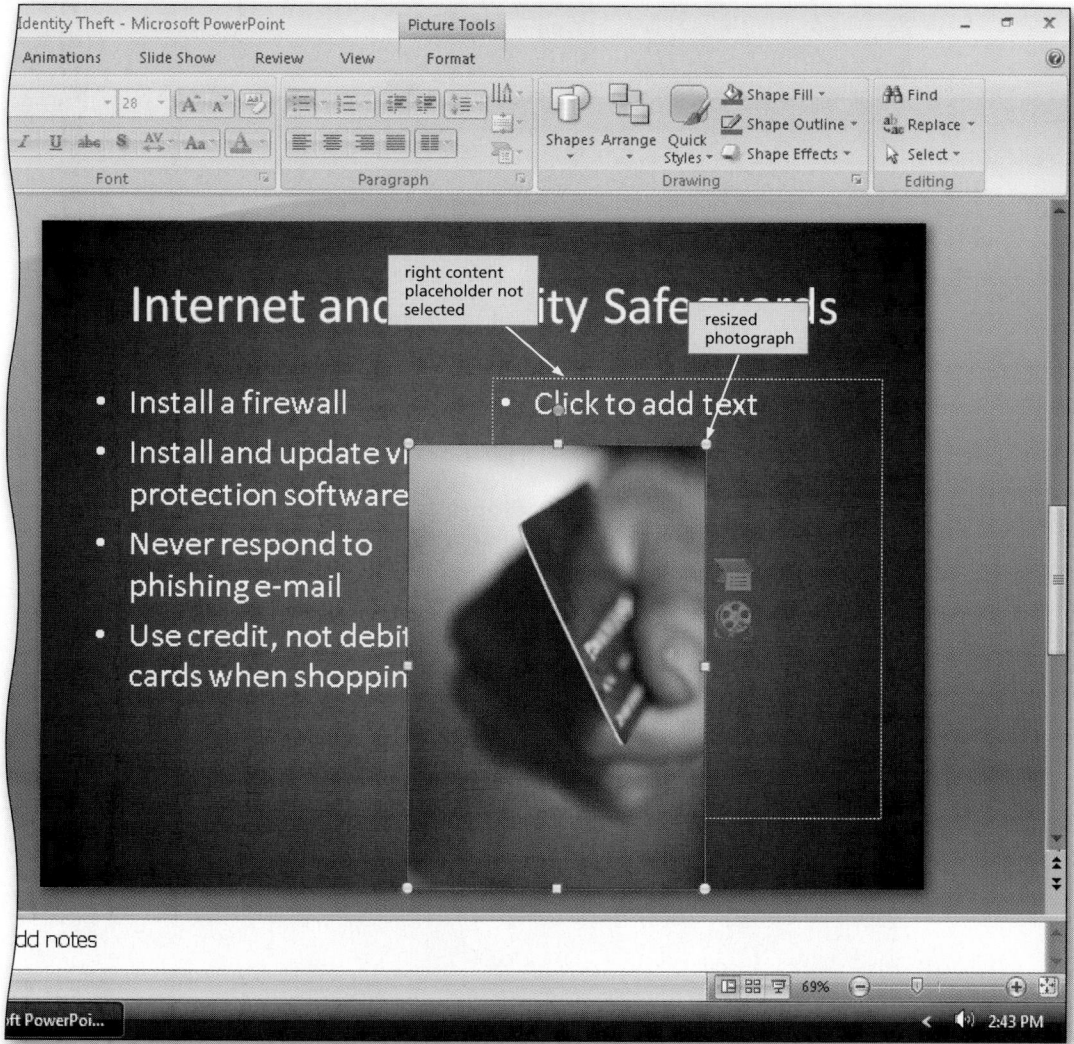

Figure 2–23

To Delete a Placeholder

The credit card photograph was inserted into the slide and not into a content placeholder. The right content placeholder, therefore, is not needed, so you can delete it from the slide. The following steps delete this placeholder.

- Click the right content placeholder to select it.

- Click the edge of the placeholder so the border is displayed as a solid line (Figure 2–24).

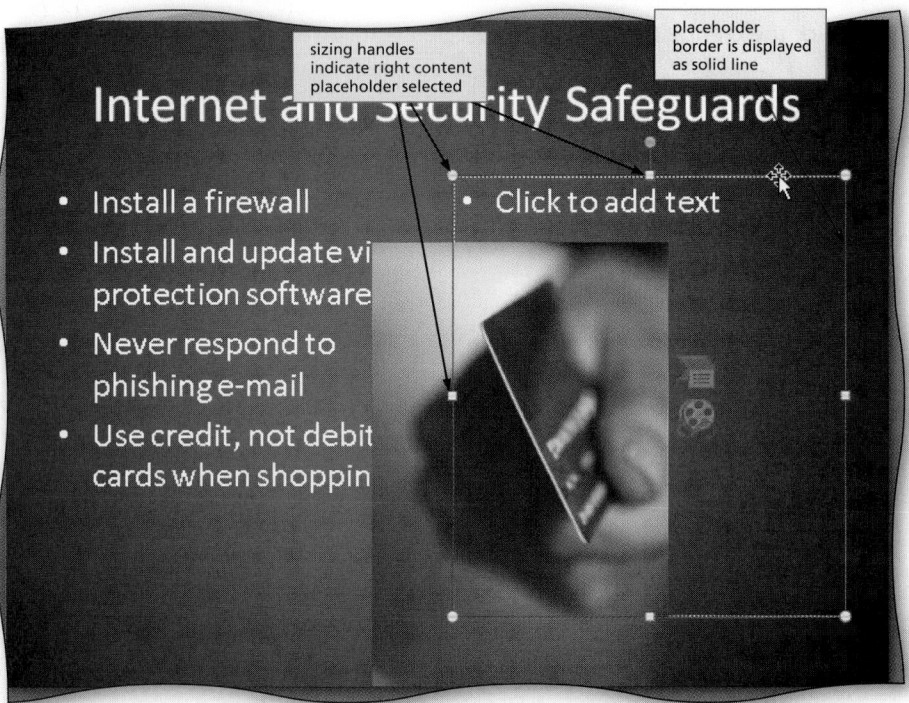

Figure 2–24

- Press the DELETE key to delete the placeholder from Slide 2 (Figure 2–25).

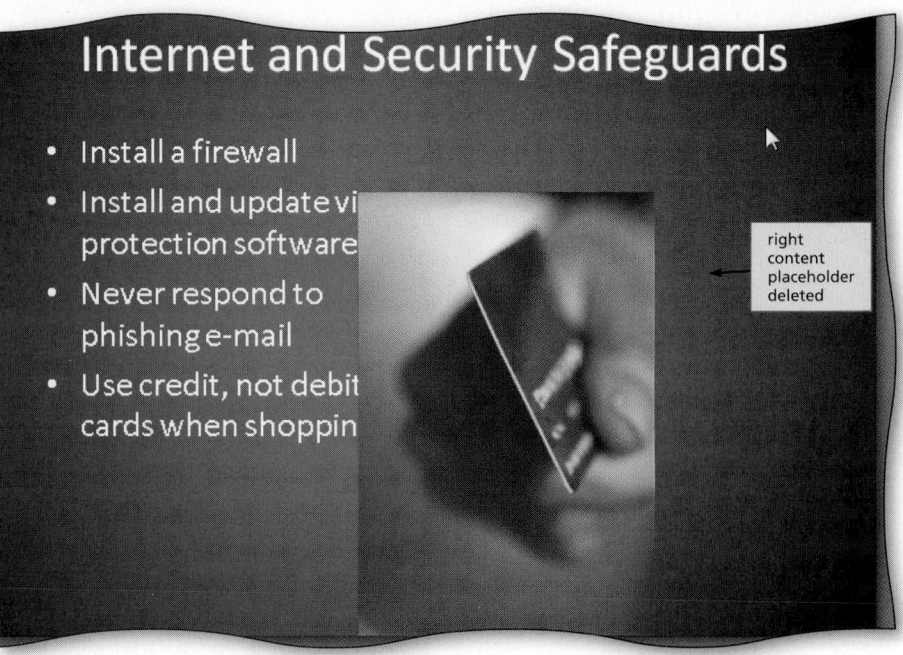

Figure 2–25

To Move Clips

After you insert clip art or a picture on a slide, you may want to reposition it. The credit card photograph on Slide 3 and the shredder clip on Slide 2 could be centered in the spaces between the bulleted text and the right edge of the slide. The following steps move these graphics.

- Click the credit card photograph on Slide 3 to select it and then press and hold down the mouse button.

- Drag the photograph diagonally upward toward the word, Safeguards (Figure 2–26).

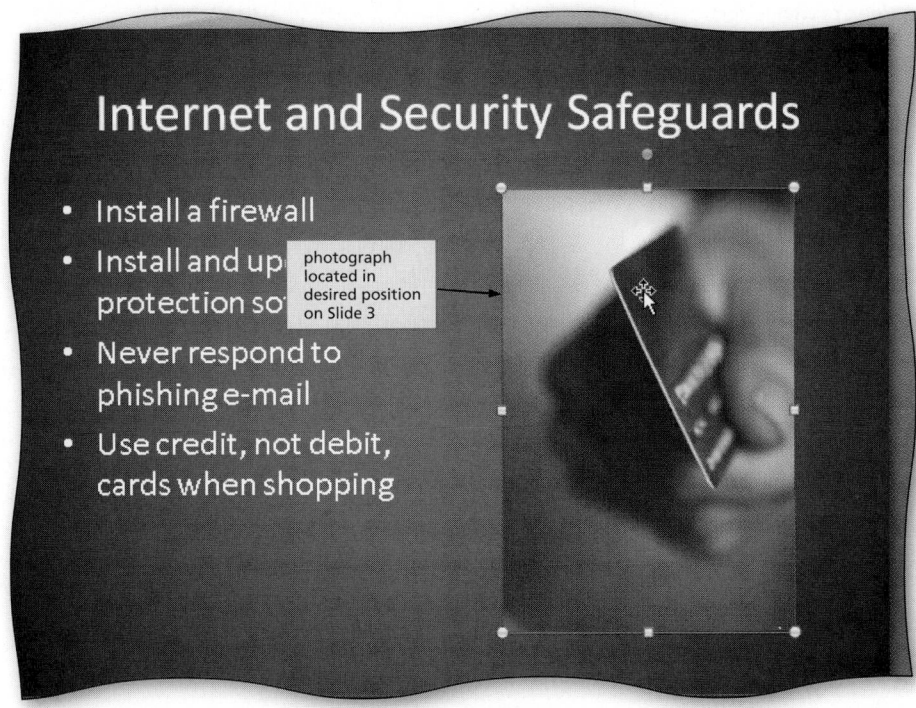

Figure 2–26

2

- Click the Previous Slide button to display Slide 2.

- Click the shredder clip to select it, press and hold down the mouse button, and then drag the photograph toward the right side of the slide (Figure 2–27).

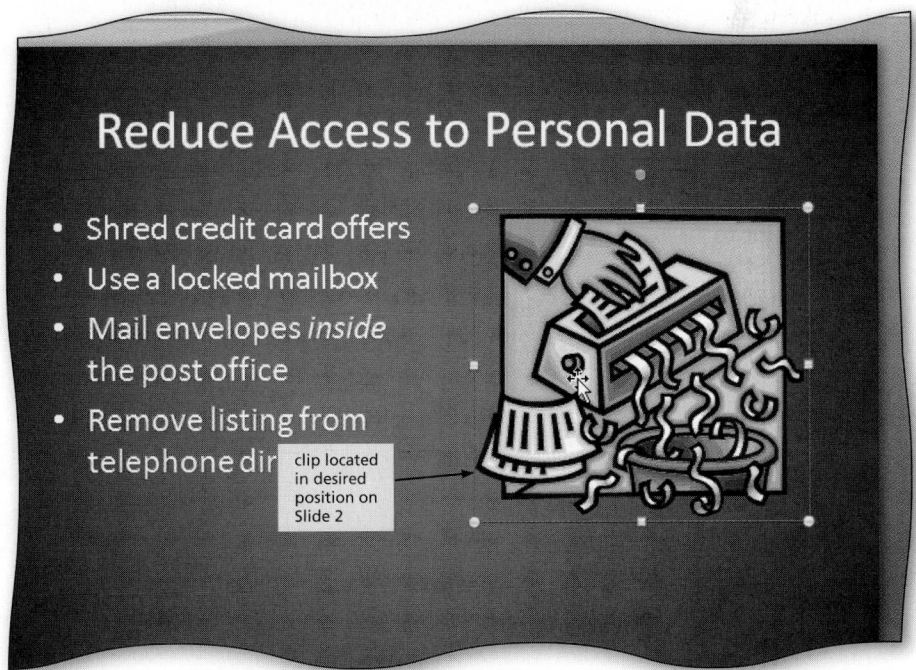

Figure 2–27

BTW

Inserting Special Characters
You can insert characters not found on your keyboard, such as the Euro sign (€), the copyright sign (©), and Greek capital letters (e.g., Δ, E, Θ). To insert these characters, click the Insert tab on the Ribbon, and then click the Symbol button in the Text group. When the Symbol dialog box is displayed, you can use the same font you currently are using in your presentation, or you can select another font. The Webdings, Webdings 2, and Webdings 3 fonts have a variety of symbols.

To Save an Existing Presentation with the Same File Name

You have made several changes to your presentation since you last saved it. Thus, you should save it again. The following step saves the presentation again.

 Click the Save button on the Quick Access Toolbar to overwrite the previous Identity Theft file on the USB flash drive.

Formatting Title and Content Text

Choosing well-coordinated colors and styles for text and objects in a presentation is possible by using **Quick Styles**, which are defined combinations of formatting options. The styles in the Quick Styles Gallery have a wide variety of font, background, and border colors. You even can create a custom Quick Style and give it a unique name. Once you select a particular Quick Style and make any other font changes, you then can copy these changes to other text using the **Format Painter**. The Format Painter allows you to copy all formatting changes from one object to another.

To Format Title Text Using Quick Styles

The 42 Quick Styles are displayed in thumbnails in the Quick Style gallery. When you place your mouse pointer over a Quick Style thumbnail, PowerPoint changes the text and shows how the Quick Style affects the formatting. The title text in this presentation will have a light orange background, a dark orange border, and black letters. The following steps apply a Quick Style to the title text.

- Click the Slide 2 title text placeholder to select it.

- Click the Quick Styles button in the Drawing group on the Home tab to display the Quick Styles gallery. Point to the Subtle Effect – Accent 6 Quick Style (row 4, column 7) to display a live preview of the style (Figure 2–28).

🔎 **Experiment**
- Point to various styles in the Quick Styles gallery and watch the format of the text, backgrounds, and borders change in the placeholder.

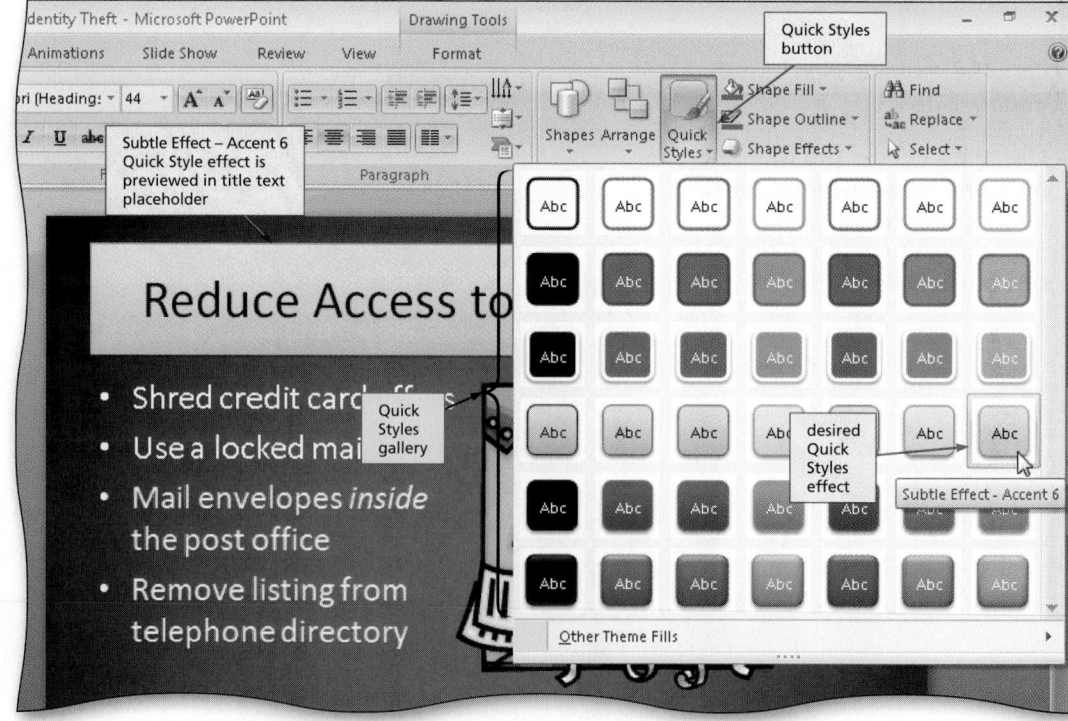

Figure 2–28

2

- Click the Subtle Effect – Accent 6 Quick Style (row 4, column 7) to apply this format to the title text placeholder (Figure 2–29).

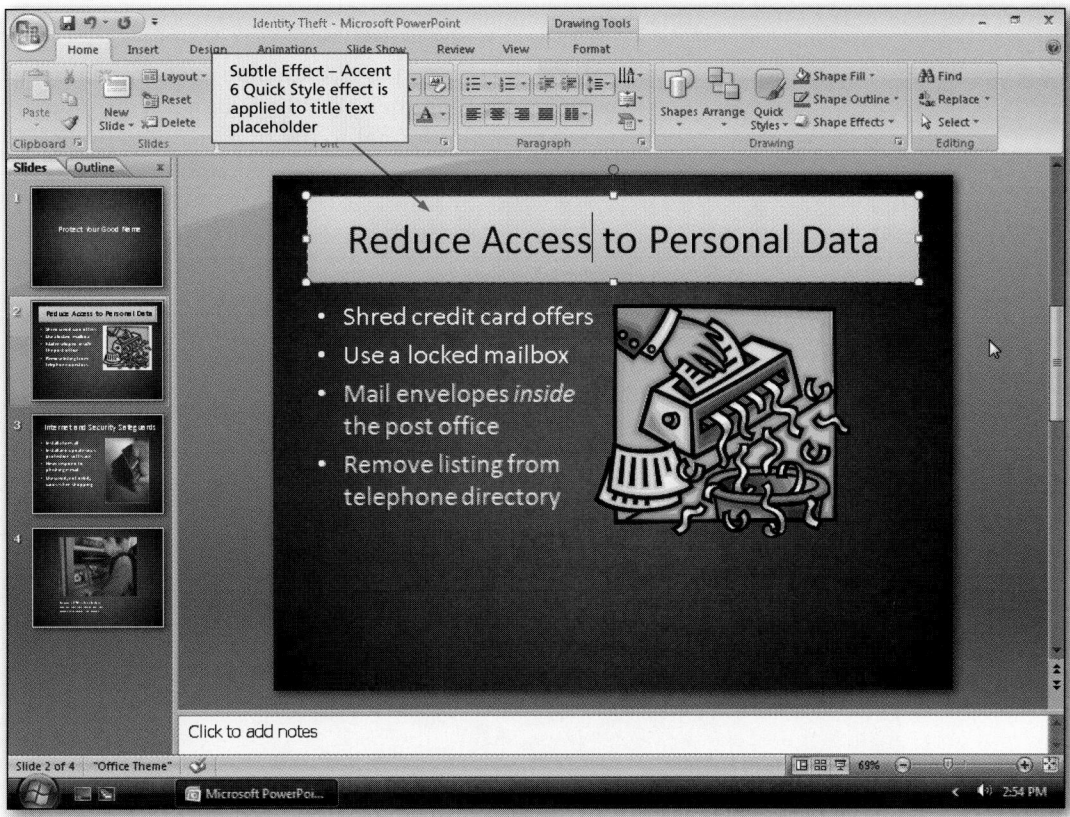

Figure 2–29

To Format Remaining Title Text Using Quick Styles

Once you have applied a Quick Style to one title text placeholder, it is a good idea to use the same style for consistency. The following steps apply the Subtle Effect – Accent 6 Quick Style to the title text placeholder on Slides 3 and 4.

1 Click the Next Slide button to display Slide 3. Click the title text placeholder and then click the Quick Styles button in the Drawing group to display the Quick Styles gallery.

2 Click the Subtle Effect – Accent 6 Quick Style (row 4, column 7) to apply this format to the title text placeholder.

3 Click the Next Slide button to display Slide 4. Click the title text placeholder, click the Quick Styles button, and then click the Subtle Effect – Accent 6 Quick Style (row 4, column 7) to apply this format to the title text placeholder (Figure 2–30).

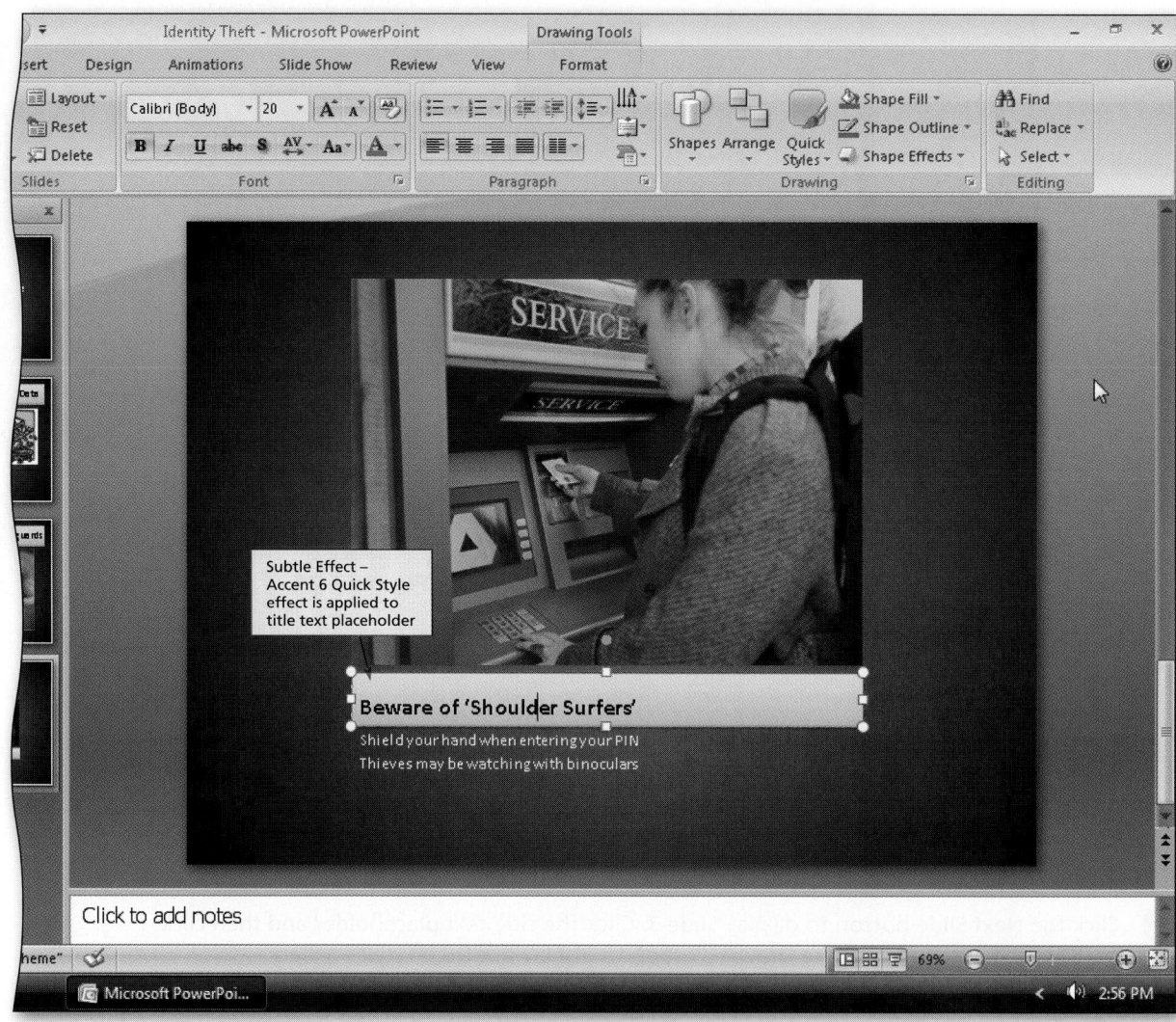

Figure 2–30

Plan
Ahead

Use serif fonts for titles.
The design guidelines for title text differ from the guidelines for content body text. You would like your audience members to remember the main points of your presentation, and you can help their retention by having them read the title text more slowly than they read the words in the content text placeholder. The uneven lines in serif typefaces cause eye movement to slow down. Designers, therefore, often use serif fonts for the slide title text.

To Change the Heading Font

The default Office Theme heading and body text font is Calibri with a font size of 28 point. Calibri is a sans serif font, and designers recommend using a serif font to draw more attention to the slide title text. The following steps change the font from Calibri to Cambria.

- Click the Previous Slide button two times to display Slide 2. Triple-click the title text paragraph. With the text selected, click the Font box arrow in the Font group on the Home tab to display the Font gallery (Figure 2–31).

Q&A

Will the fonts in my Font gallery be the same as those in Figure 2–31?

Your list of available fonts may differ, depending on the type of printer you are using.

- Scroll through the Font gallery, if necessary, and then point to Cambria (or a similar font) to display a live preview of the title text in Cambria font.

ⓟ Experiment

- Point to various fonts in the Font gallery and watch the font of the title text change in the document window.

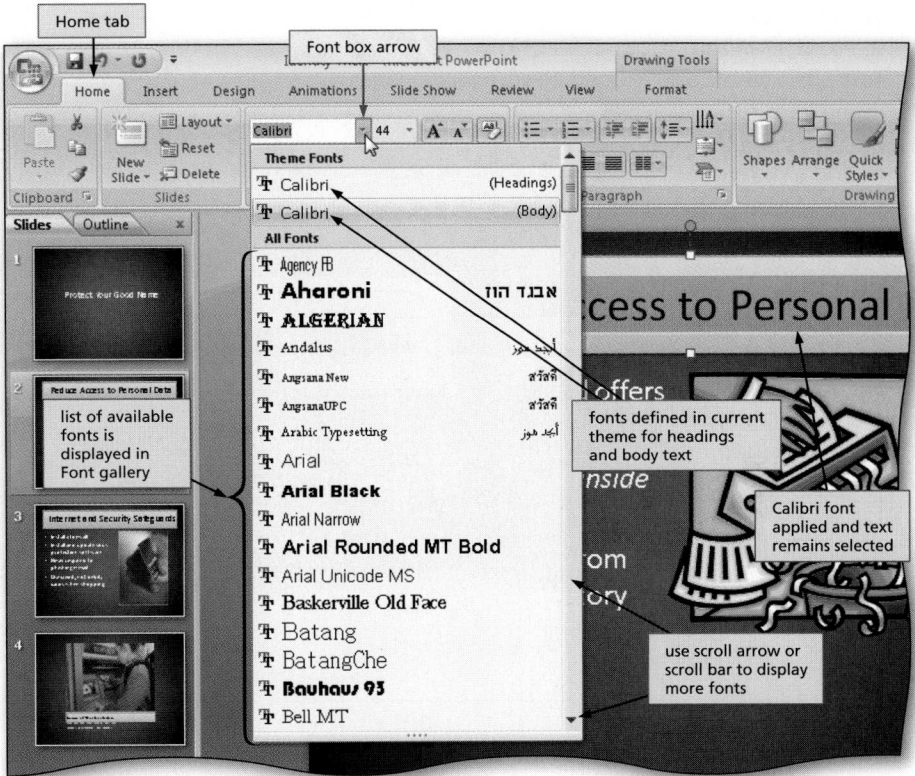

Figure 2–31

❸

- Click Cambria (or a similar font) to change the font of the selected text to Cambria (Figure 2–32).

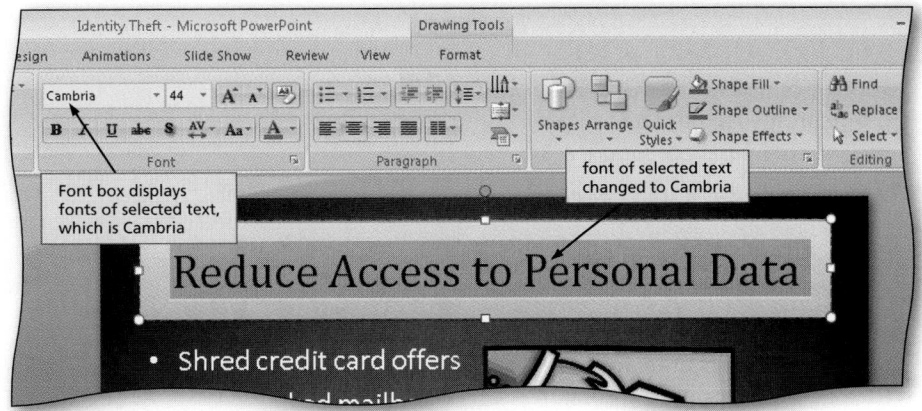

Figure 2–32

Other Ways

1. Click Font box arrow on Mini toolbar, click desired font in Font gallery

2. Right-click selected text, click Font on shortcut menu, click Font tab, select desired font

in Font list or type a font in Font box, click OK button

3. Click Dialog Box Launcher in Font group, click Font tab, select desired font in Font

list or type a font in Font box, click OK button

4. Press CTRL+SHIFT+F, click Font tab, select desired font in the Font list, click OK button

To Shadow Text

A **shadow** helps the letters display prominently by adding a shadow behind the text. The following step adds a shadow to the selected title text, Reduce Access to Personal Data.

- With the text selected, click the Text Shadow button in the Font group on the Home tab to add a shadow to the selected text (Figure 2–33).

Q&A

How would I remove a shadow?

You would click the Shadow button a second time, or you immediately could click the Undo button on the Quick Access Toolbar.

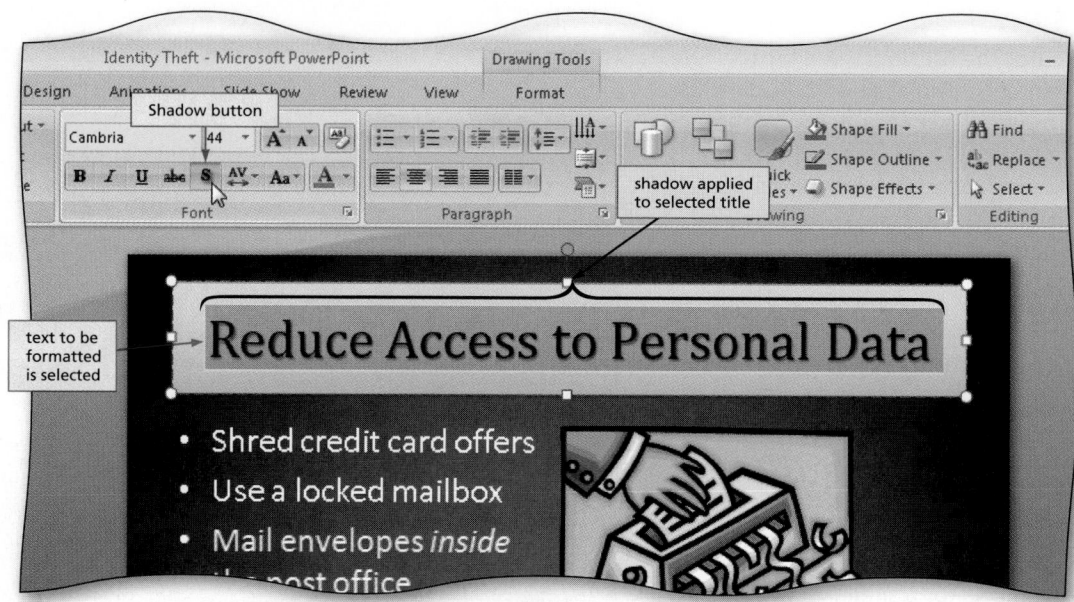

Figure 2–33

To Change Font Color

Color is used to emphasize or draw attention to specific text. The following step changes the title text font color from black to dark red.

- With the text selected, click the Font Color box arrow in the Font group on the Home tab to display the Font Color gallery (Figure 2–34).

Q&A

What is the difference between the colors shown in the Theme Colors area and the Standard Colors?

The ten colors in the top row of the Theme Colors area are two text, two background, and six accent colors in the Office Theme; the five colors in each column under the top row display different transparencies. The ten standard colors are available in every document theme.

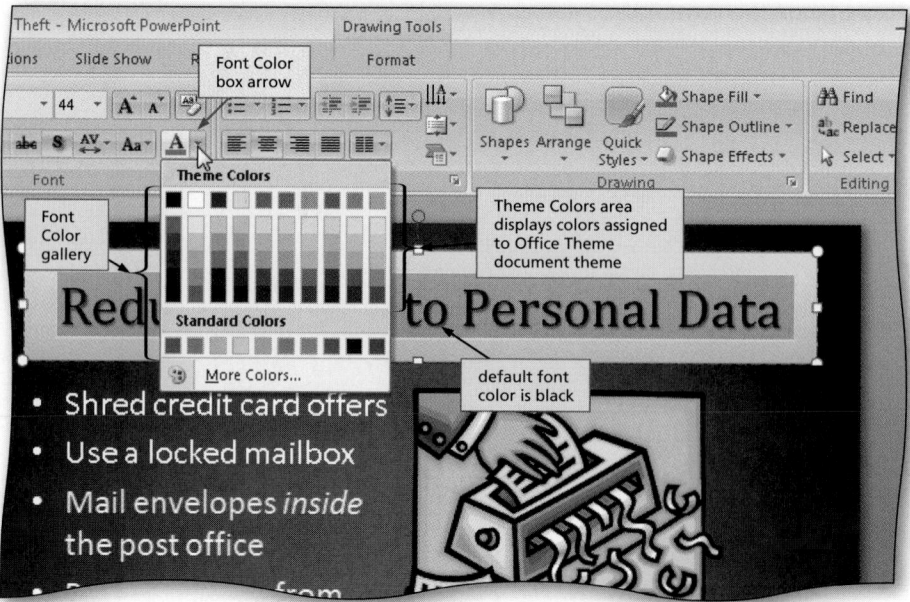

Figure 2–34

2

- Point to the Dark Red color in the Standard Colors row to display a live preview of the title text in a Dark Red color (Figure 2–35).

Experiment

- Point to various colors in the Font Color gallery and watch the title text color change in the slide.

3

- Click Dark Red to change the title text font color.

Q&A

How would I change a color?

You would click the Font Color box arrow and then select another color in the Font Color gallery.

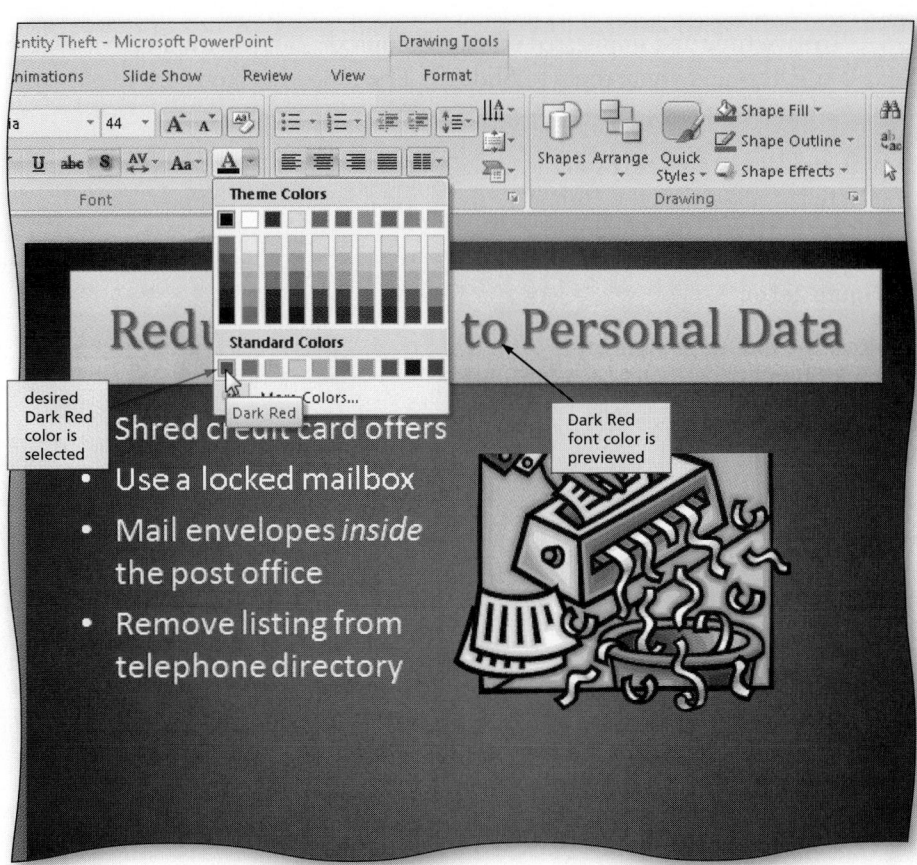

Figure 2–35

Other Ways	
1. Click Font color box arrow on Mini toolbar, click desired color in Font Color gallery 2. Right-click selected text, click Font on shortcut menu, click Font tab, select desired color in Font color list, click OK button	3. Click Dialog Box Launcher in Font group, click Font tab, select desired color in Font color list, click OK button 4. Press CTRL+SHIFT+F, click Font tab, select desired color in Font color list, click OK button

Format Painter

To save time and avoid formatting errors, you can use the Format Painter to apply custom formatting to other places in your presentation quickly and easily. You can use this feature in three ways:

- To copy only character attributes, such as font and font effects, select text that has these qualities.
- To copy both paragraph attributes, such as alignment and indentation and character attributes, select the entire paragraph.
- To apply the same formatting to multiple words, phrases, or paragraphs, double-click the Format Painter button and then select each item you want to format. You then can press the ESC key or click the Format Painter button to turn off this feature.

BTW

Deleting WordArt
If you decide you no longer want the WordArt text to display on your slide, select this text, click the Format tab on the Ribbon, click the Quick Styles button, and then click Clear WordArt.

To Format Slide 3 Text Using the Format Painter

To save time and duplicated effort, you quickly can use the Format Painter to copy formatting attributes from the Slide 2 title text and apply them to Slides 3. The following steps use the Format Painter to copy formatting features.

- With the Slide 2 title text still selected, double-click the Format Painter button in the Clipboard group in the Home tab (Figure 2–36).

- Move the mouse pointer off the Ribbon.

Q&A Why did my mouse pointer change shape?

The mouse pointer changed shape by adding a paint brush to indicate that the Format Painter function is active.

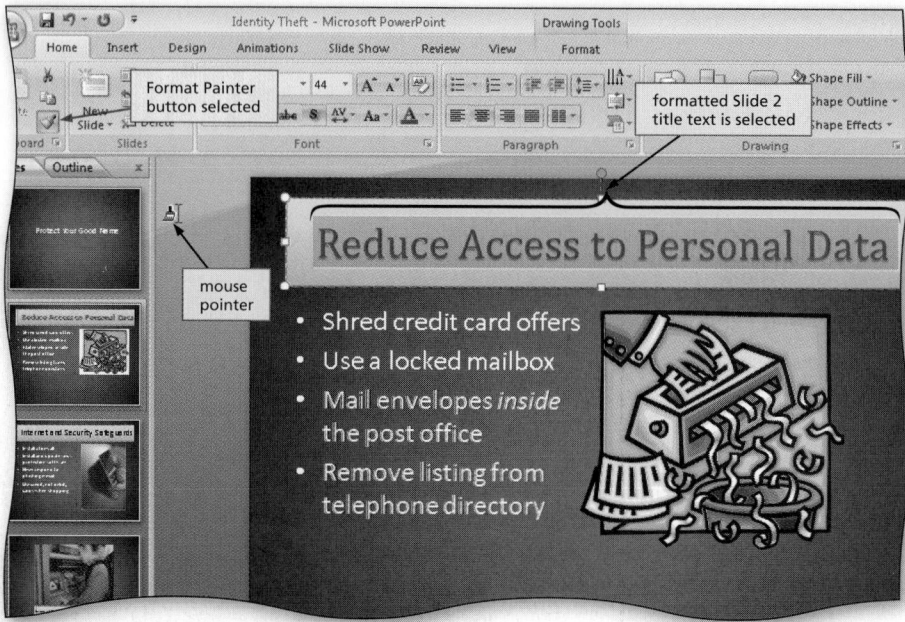

Figure 2–36

- Click the Next Slide button to display Slide 3. Triple-click the title text placeholder to apply the format to all the title text (Figure 2–37).

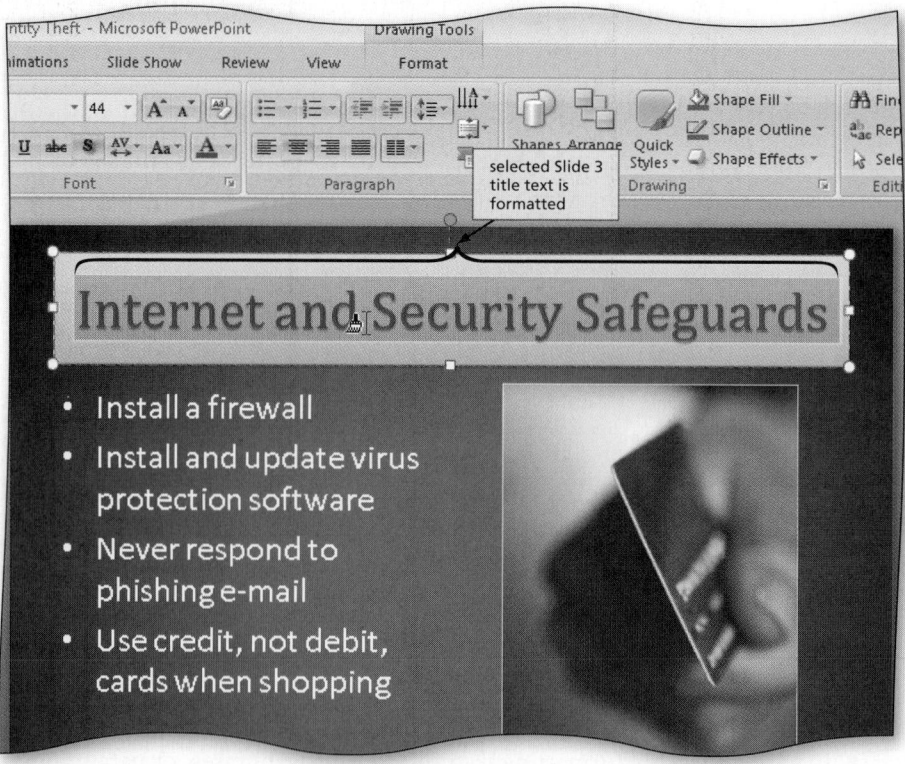

Figure 2–37

To Format Remaining Title Text

Once you have applied formatting characteristics to one text placeholder, you should maintain consistency and apply the same formats to the other title text characters. The following steps use the Format Painter to change the font and font color and apply a shadow to the Slide 4 and Slide 1 title text.

1 Click the Next Slide button to display Slide 4. Triple-click the title text placeholder to apply the format to all title text characters.

Q&A What happened to all the letters in my title?

The Format Painter applied a style that does not fit in the current placeholder. You will adjust the font size so that all the words are displayed.

2 Click the Previous Slide button three times to display Slide 1. Triple-click the title text placeholder to apply the format to all title text characters.

3 Press the ESC key to turn off the Format Painter feature (Figure 2–38).

Other Ways

1. Click Format Painter button on Mini toolbar

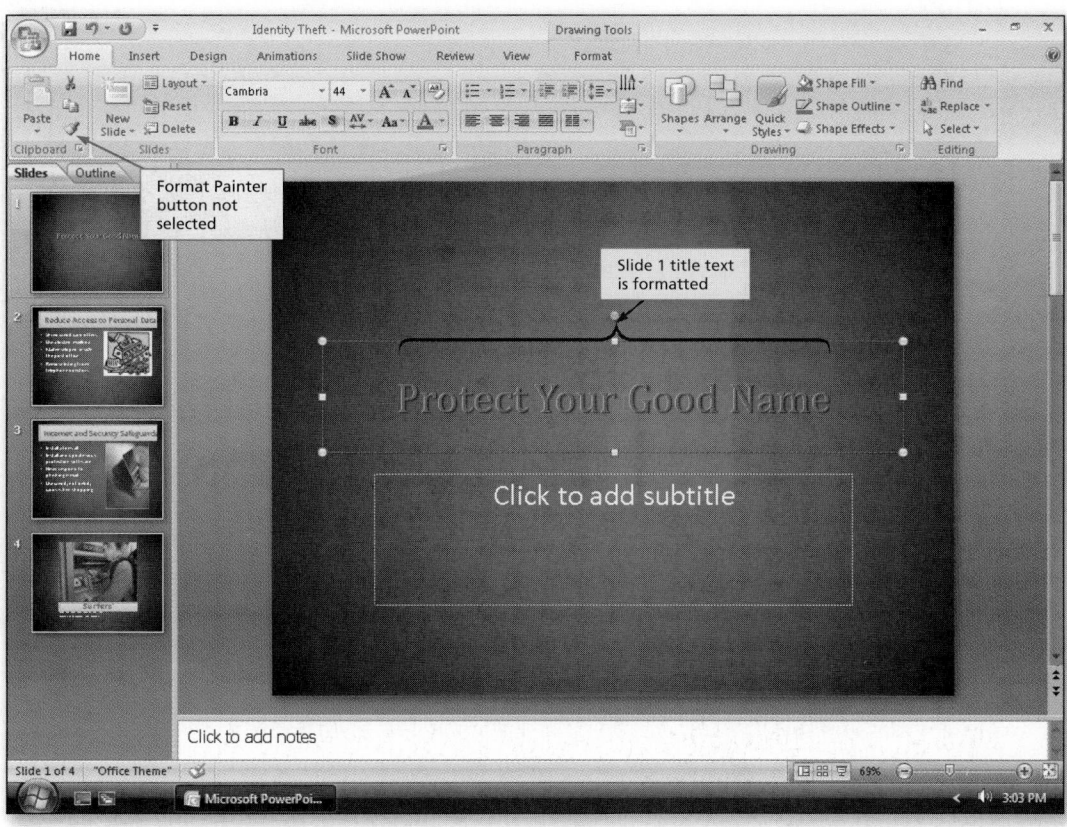

Figure 2–38

To Size Slide 4 Text

The Slide 4 title text placeholder is too small to accommodate the formatting characteristics you applied to the text. The text will fit if you reduce the font size. In addition, the body text should be enlarged for readability. The following steps adjust the size of the Slide 4 title and body text.

1 Click the Next Slide button three times to display Slide 4.

2 Select both body text paragraphs in the content text placeholder and then click the Increase Font Size button on the Mini toolbar four times to increase the font size to 24 point.

3 Triple-click the title text placeholder and then click the Decrease Font Size button on the Mini toolbar three times to reduce the font size to 32 point.

4 Click the slide anywhere outside the placeholders to deselect it (Figure 2–39).

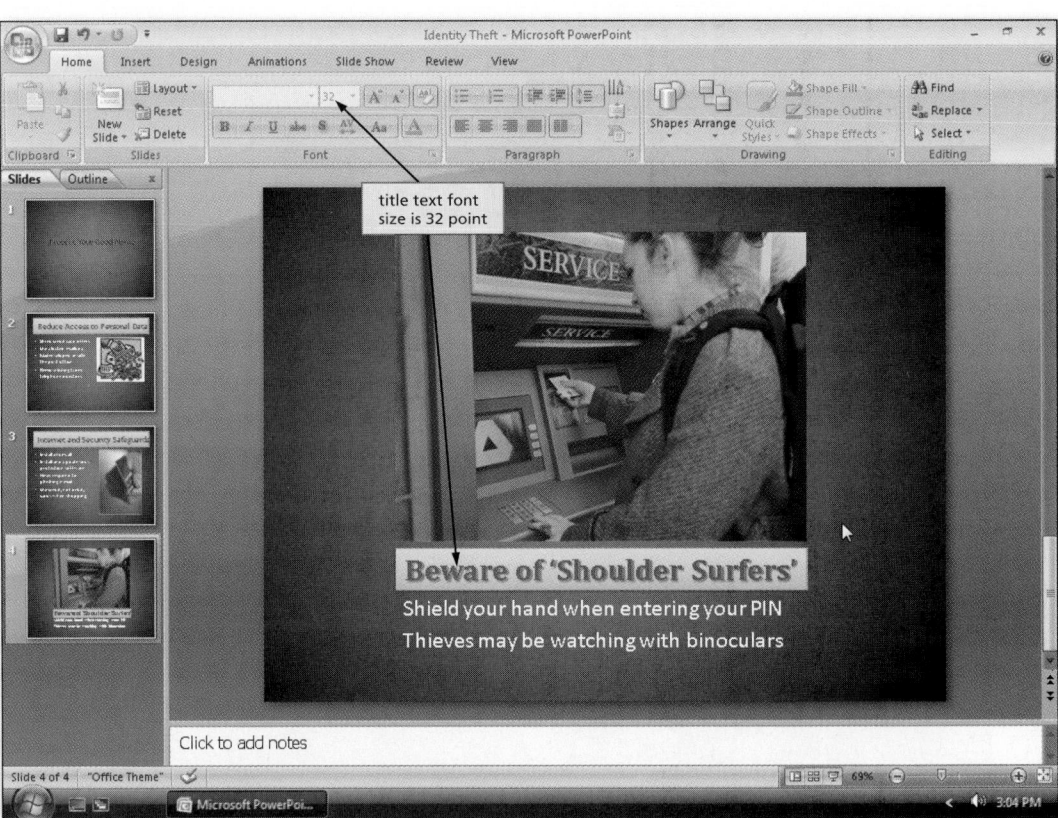

Figure 2–39

Adding and Formatting a Shape

One method of getting the audience's attention at the start of a slide show is to have graphical elements on the title slide. PowerPoint provides a wide variety of shapes that can add visual interest to a slide. Shape elements include lines, basic geometrical shapes, arrows, equation shapes, flowchart symbols, stars, banners, and callouts.

Slide 1 in this presentation is enhanced in a variety of ways. First, the title text font size is increased to aid readability and to catch the audience's attention. Then a shape is inserted below the title text with additional formatted text. Finally, the subtitle text placeholder is deleted because it no longer is needed.

To Increase Title Slide Font Size

The title on a slide should be large enough to stimulate the audience's interest and announce the topic of the presentation. The following steps increase the Slide 1 title text.

1 Click the Previous Slide button three times to display Slide 1.

2 Select the Slide 1 title text, Protect Your Good Name. Click the Increase Font Size button on the Mini toolbar six times until the font size is 80 point (Figure 2–40).

3 Click the slide anywhere outside the title text placeholder to deselect it.

Figure 2–40

To Add a Shape

After adding a shape to a slide, you can change its default characteristics by adding text, bullets, numbers, and Quick Styles. You also can combine multiple shapes to create a more complex graphic. The following steps add a banner shape to Slide 1.

- Click the Shapes button in the Drawing group on the Home tab to display the Shapes gallery. Point to the Wave banner shape in the Stars and Banners area (Figure 2–41).

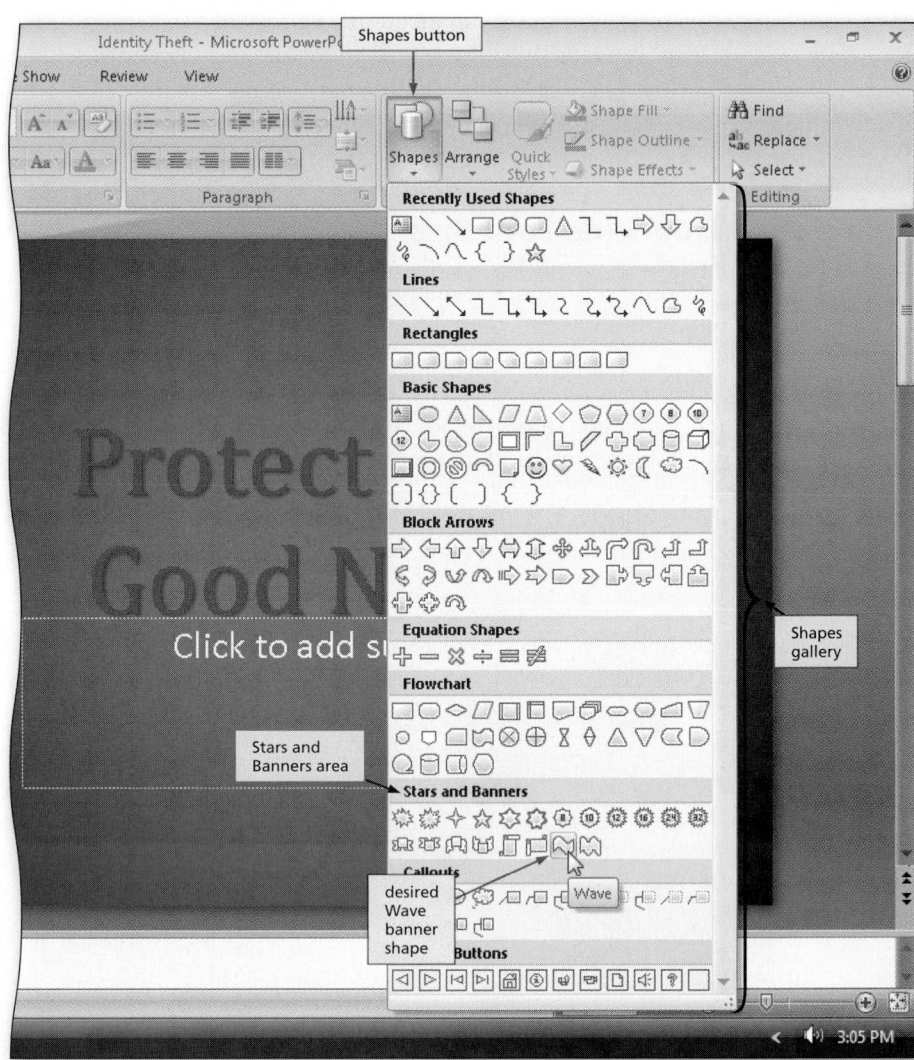

Figure 2–41

- Click the Wave shape (Figure 2–42).

Q&A Why did my pointer change shape?

The pointer changed to a plus shape to indicate the Wave shape has been added to the Clipboard.

Figure 2–42

3

- Click Slide 1 anywhere below the title text to insert the Wave shape (Figure 2–43).

Figure 2–43

Other Ways

1. Click More button in Insert Shapes group on Format tab in Drawing Tools tab

To Resize a Shape

The next step is to resize the Wave shape. The shape should be enlarged so that it appears prominently on the slide and can hold the subtitle text. The following steps resize the selected Wave shape.

1

- With the Wave shape still selected, point to the lower-right corner sizing handle on the picture so that the mouse pointer shape changes to a two-headed arrow (Figure 2–44).

What if my shape is not selected?

To select a shape, click it.

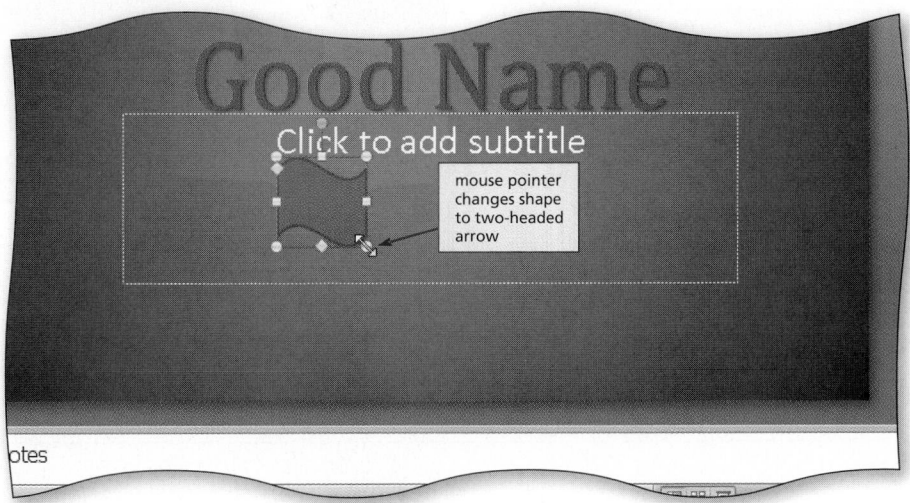

Figure 2–44

• Drag the sizing handle diagonally outward and downward until the Wave shape is the approximate size of the one shown in Figure 2–45.

Figure 2–45

• Release the mouse button to resize the shape (Figure 2–46).

Q&A What if the shape is the wrong size?

Repeat Steps 1 and 2.

Q&A What if I want to move the shape to a different location on the slide?

With the shape selected, press the ARROW keys or drag the shape to the desired location.

Other Ways

1. Enter shape height and width in Height and Width text boxes in Size group on Format tab in Drawing Tools contextual tabs

2. Click Dialog Box Launcher in Size group on Format tab in Drawing Tools contextual tabs, click Size tab, enter desired height and width values in text boxes, click Close button

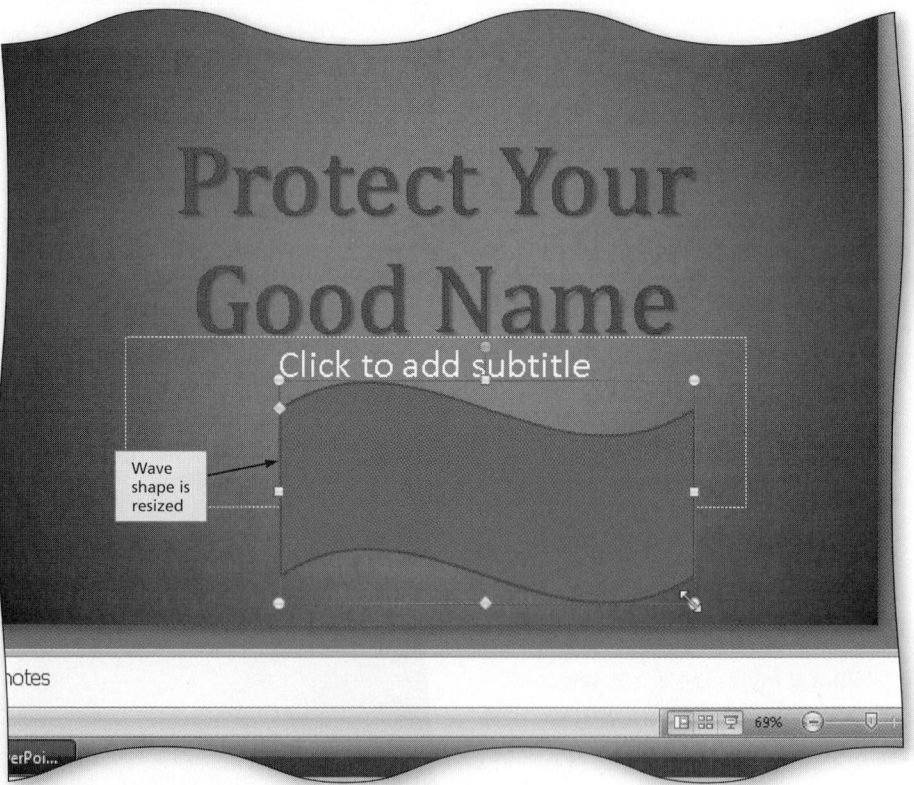

Figure 2–46

To Add Text to a Shape

The banner shape is displayed on Slide 1 in the correct location. The next step is to add text stating that the presentation will cover strategies to help prevent identity theft. The following step describes how to add this information to the shape.

- With the Wave banner shape selected, type Reduce Your Risk of Identity Theft in the shape (Figure 2–47).

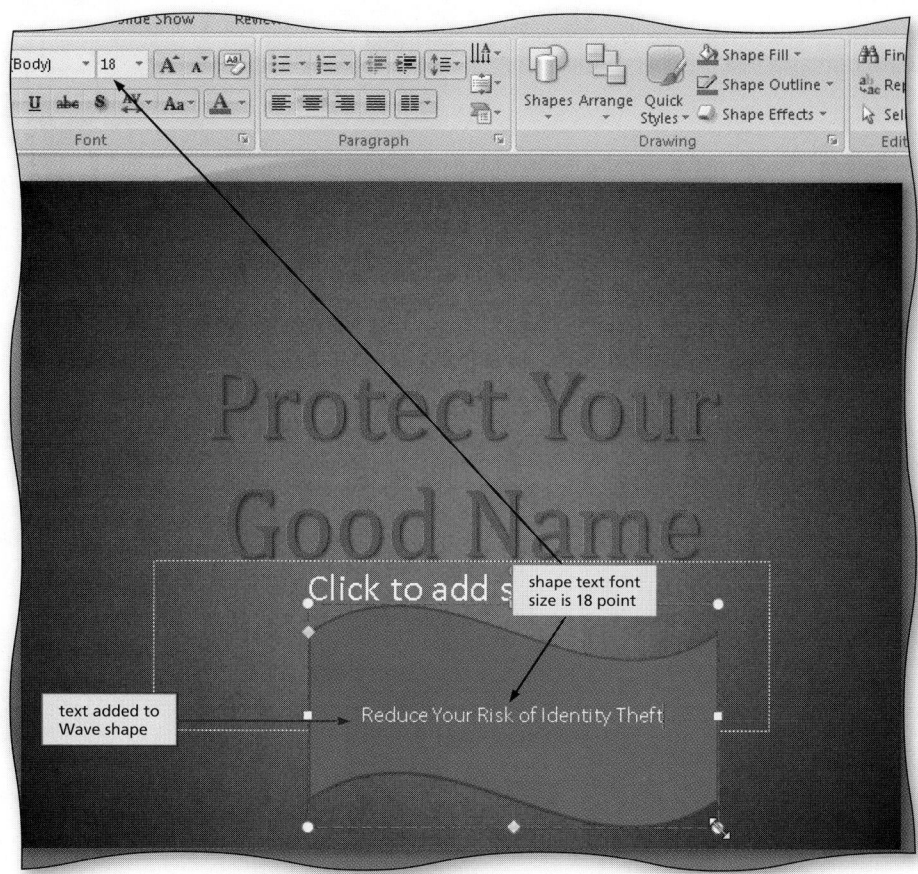

Figure 2–47

To Format Shape Text and Add a Shape Quick Style

Formatting text in a shape follows the same techniques as formatting text in a placeholder. You can change font, font color and size, and alignment, and you also can apply a Shape Quick Style. The following steps describe how to format the shape text by increasing the font size and adding a Shape Quick Style.

- Triple-click the Wave shape text to select it and then click the Increase Font Size button on the Mini toolbar five times until the font size is 36 point (Figure 2–48).

Figure 2–48

- Click the Shape Quick Styles button in the Drawing group on the Home tab to display the Quick Styles gallery (Figure 2–49).

- Point to the Subtle Effect – Accent 6 Shape Quick Style (row 4, column 7) to display a live preview of the style.

Experiment

- Point to various styles in the Quick Styles gallery and watch the format of the text, backgrounds, and borders change in the Wave shape.

- Click the Subtle Effect – Accent 6 Shape Quick Style (row 4, column 7) to apply this format to the shape.

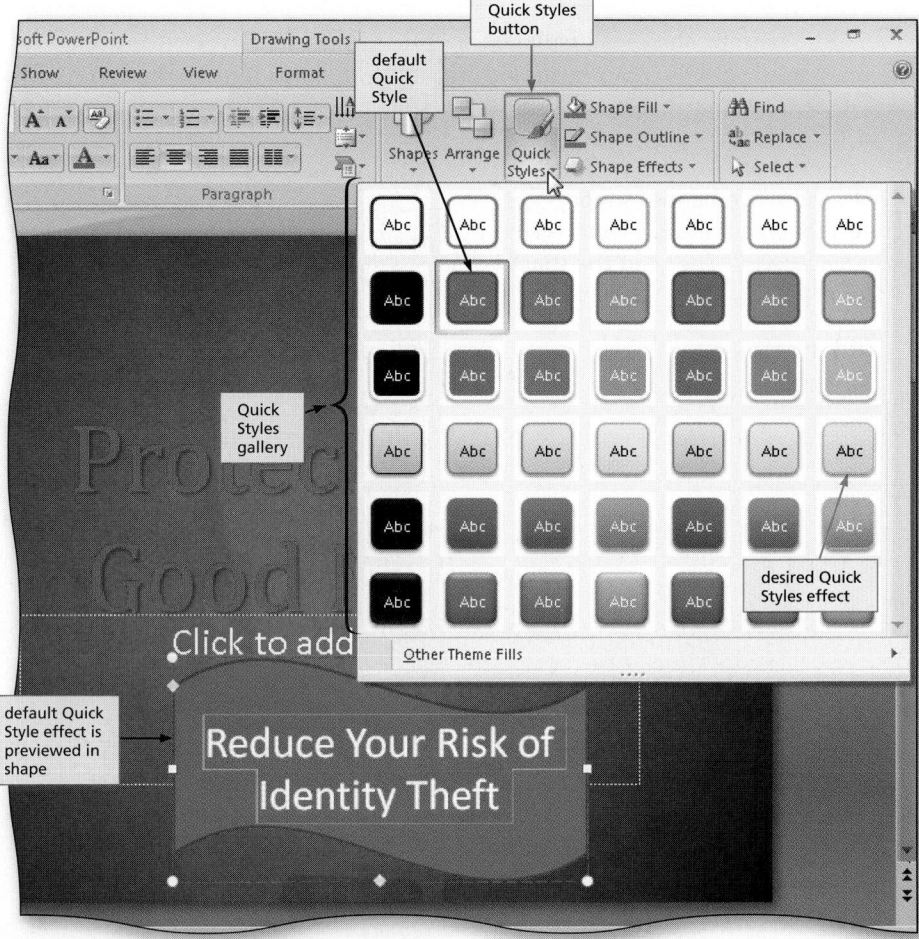

Figure 2–49

- Click outside the shape to deselect it (Figure 2–50).

Figure 2–50

To Delete a Placeholder

The subtitle placeholder no longer is necessary on Slide 1 because the shape fills the area below the title text. The following steps delete the Slide 1 subtitle placeholder.

1

- Click the subtitle text placeholder border two times to change the border to a solid line (Figure 2–51).

Figure 2–51

2

- Press the DELETE key to delete the placeholder. If necessary, select the shape and then use the ARROW keys to center the shape under the title text (Figure 2–52).

Figure 2–52

> **Use simple transitions.**
> Transitions help segue one slide into the next seamlessly. They should not be used decoratively or be something on which an audience member focuses. For consistency, use the same transition throughout the presentation unless you have a special circumstance that warrants a different effect.

Adding a Transition

PowerPoint provides many animation effects to add interest and make a slide show presentation look professional. **Animation** includes special visual and sound effects applied to text or content. A **slide transition** is a special animation effect used to progress from one slide to the next in a slide show. You can control the speed of the transition effect and add a sound.

PowerPoint provides more than 50 different transitions in the Quick Styles group. They are arranged into five categories that describe the types of effects:

- Fades and Dissolves - Blend one slide seamlessly into the next slide
- Wipes - Gently uncover one slide to reveal the next
- Push and Cover - Appear to move one slide off the screen
- Stripes and Bars – Use blinds and checkerboard patterns
- Random – Use vertical and horizontal bars or an arbitrary pattern that changes each time you run the presentation.

To Add a Transition between Slides

In this presentation, you apply the Uncover Right transition in the Wipes category to all slides and change the transition speed to Medium. The following steps apply this transition to the presentation.

1
- Click the Animations tab on the Ribbon and then point to the More button in the Transition to This Slide group (Figure 2–53).

Q&A
Is a transition applied now?

No. The first slide icon in the Transitions group has an orange border, which indicates no transition has been applied.

Figure 2–53

2

- Click the More button to expand the Transitions gallery.

- Point to the Uncover Right transition (row 2, column 2) in the Wipes category in the Transitions gallery to display a live preview of this transition (Figure 2–54).

Experiment

- Point to various styles in the Transitions gallery and watch the transitions on the slide.

Figure 2–54

3

- Click Uncover Right in the Wipes category in the Transitions gallery to apply the Uncover Right transition to the title slide.

Q&A Why does a star appear next to Slide 1 in the Slides tab?

The star indicates that a transition animation effect is applied to that slide.

- Click the Transition Speed arrow in the Transition to This Slide group on the Animations tab to display three possible speeds: Slow, Medium, and Fast (Figure 2–55).

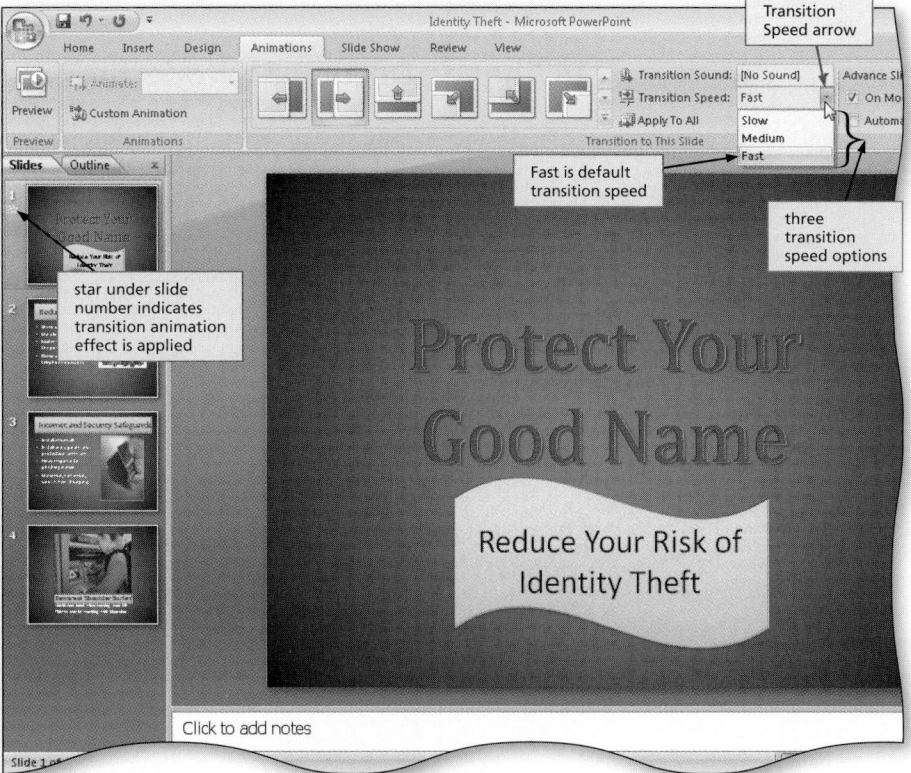

Figure 2–55

- Click Medium to change the transition speed for Slide 1 to Medium.

- Click the Apply to All button in the Transition to This Slide group on the Animations tab to apply the Uncover Right transition and Medium speed to all four slides in the presentation (Figure 2–56).

Q&A

What if I want to apply a different transition and speed to each slide in the presentation?

Repeat Steps 2 through 5 for each slide individually.

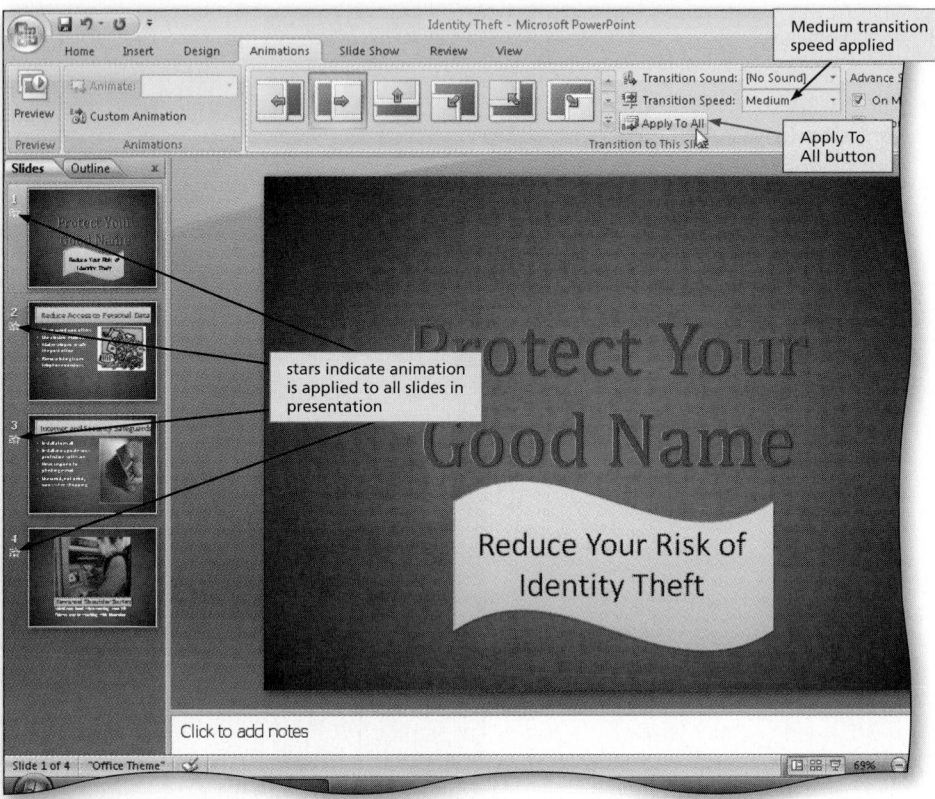

Figure 2–56

To Change Document Properties

Before saving the presentation again, you want to add your name, class name, and some keywords as document properties. The following steps use the Document Information Panel to change document properties.

1 Click the Office Button to display the Office Button menu, point to Prepare on the Office Button menu, and then click Properties on the Prepare submenu to display the Document Information Panel.

2 Click the Author text box, if necessary, and then type your name as the Author property. If a name already is displayed in the Author text box, delete it before typing your name.

3 Click the Subject text box, if necessary delete any existing text, and then type your course and section as the Subject property.

4 Click the Keywords text box, if necessary delete any existing text, and then type identity theft, Internet safeguards, PIN as the Keywords properties.

5 Click the Close the Document Information Panel button so that the Document Information Panel no longer is displayed.

To Save an Existing Presentation with the Same File Name

You have made several changes to the presentation since you last saved it. Thus, you should save it again. The following step saves the document again.

Note: If you are using Windows XP, see Appendix F for alternate steps.

1 Click the Save button on the Quick Access Toolbar to overwrite the previous Identity Theft file on the USB flash drive.

To Run an Animated Slide Show

All changes are complete, and the presentation is saved. You now can view the Identity Theft presentation. The following step starts Slide Show view.

1 Click the Slide Show button to display the title slide (Figure 2–57).

2 Click each slide and view the transition effect and slides.

Figure 2–57

Quick Reference
For a table that lists how to complete the tasks covered in this book using the mouse, Ribbon, shortcut menu, and keyboard, see the Quick Reference Summary at the back of this book, or visit the PowerPoint 2007 Quick Reference Web page (scsite.com/ppt2007/qr).

Printing a Presentation as an Outline and Handouts

During the development of a lengthy presentation, it often is easier to review an outline in print rather than on the screen. Printing an outline also is useful for audience handouts or when your supervisor or instructor wants to review your subject matter before you develop the presentation fully. In addition, printing two or more slides on one page helps audience members see relationships between slides and also conserves paper. You can preview your print selections to see how your printout will look.

The **Print What list** in the Page Setup group or in the Print dialog box contains options for printing slides, handouts, notes, and an outline. If you want to print handouts, you can specify whether you want one, two, three, four, six, or nine slide images to display on each page. The next two sections preview and then print the presentation outline and the presentation slides as a handout.

To Preview and Print an Outline

Recall that in Chapter 1 each slide printed on a separate page when you clicked Quick Print on the Print submenu. When you want to print other materials, such as an outline, notes, or handouts, you click Print on the Print submenu and select what form of output you desire. The following steps preview and print an outline.

1
- Click the Office Button to display the Office Button menu.

- Point to Print on the Office Button menu to display the Print submenu (Figure 2–58).

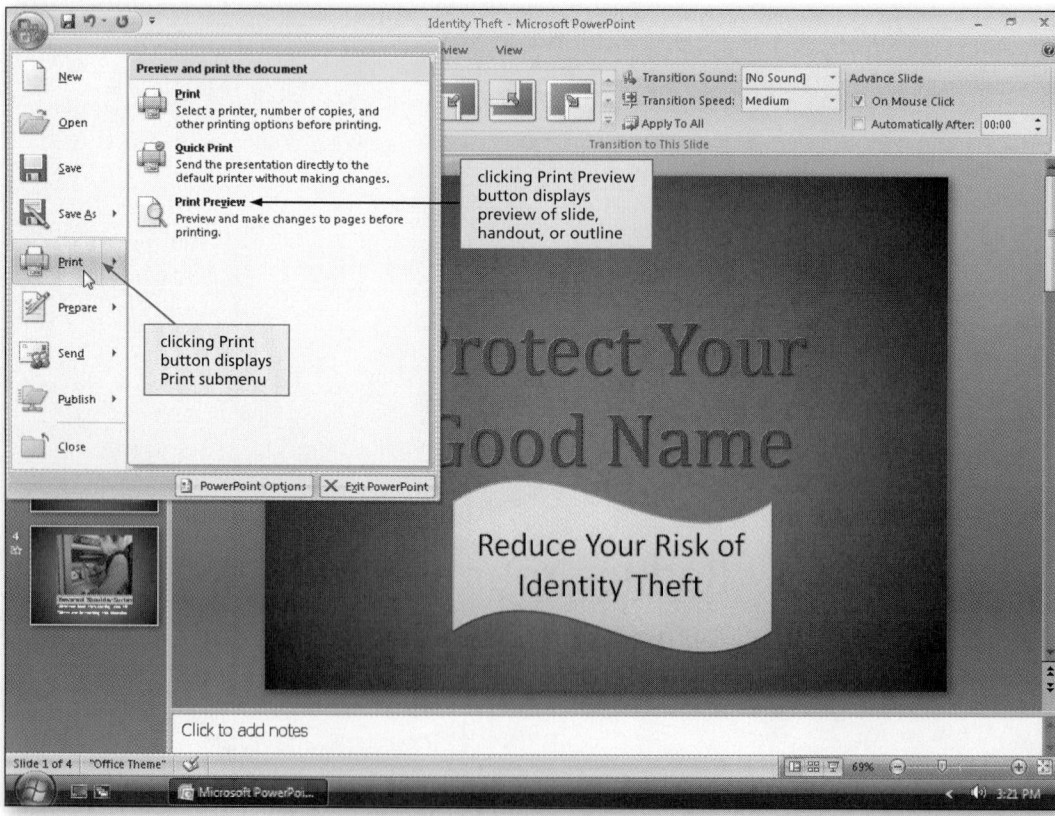

Figure 2–58

2

- Click Print Preview on the Print submenu to display a preview of a slide, handout, or outline of the presentation.

Q&A

Why does the slide preview image vary among slides, handouts, and outlines?

PowerPoint retains the settings last specified for previewing and printing. If, for example, you last specified to print in Grayscale, the current document will print in Grayscale unless you change the setting.

- If an outline is not previewed, click the Print What box arrow in the Page Setup group on the Print Preview tab to display a list of output types in the Print What list (Figure 2–59).

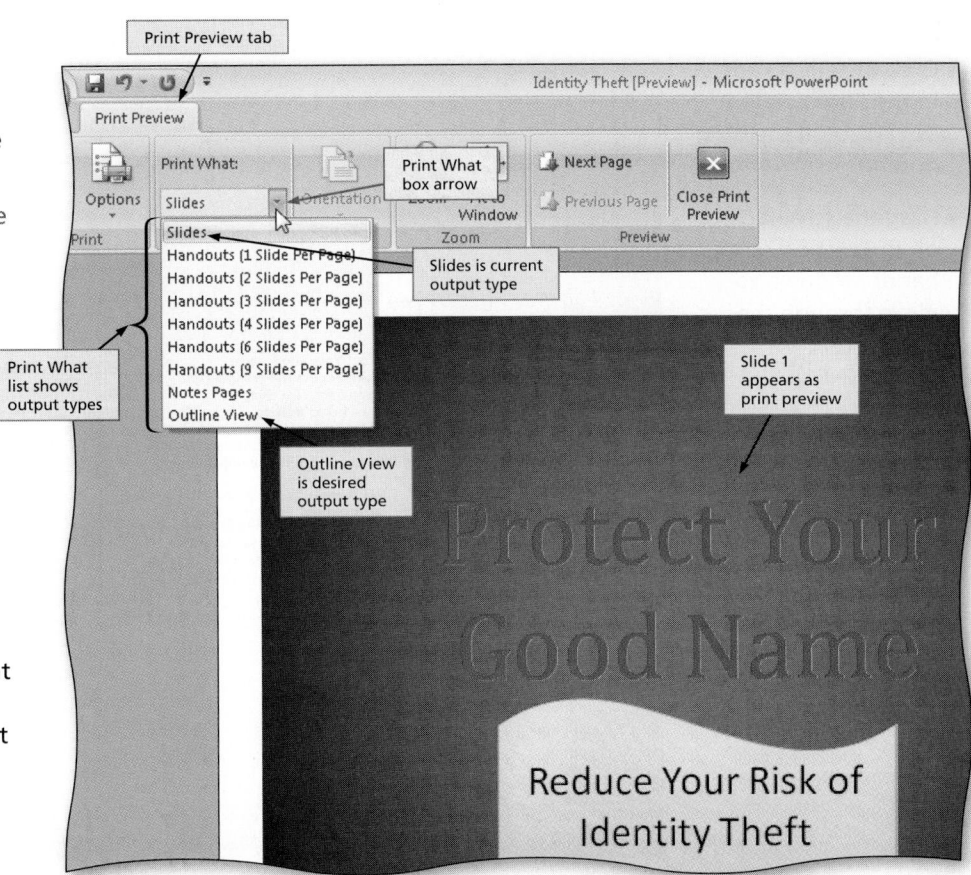

Figure 2–59

3

- Click Outline View in the Print What list if this choice is not already selected.

- Click the Zoom button in the Zoom group on the Print Preview tab to open the Zoom dialog box.

- Click 100% in the Zoom dialog box to change the zoom so that you can read the outline easily on the screen (Figure 2–60).

Q&A

If I change the zoom percentage, will the document print differently?

Changing the zoom has no effect on the printed document.

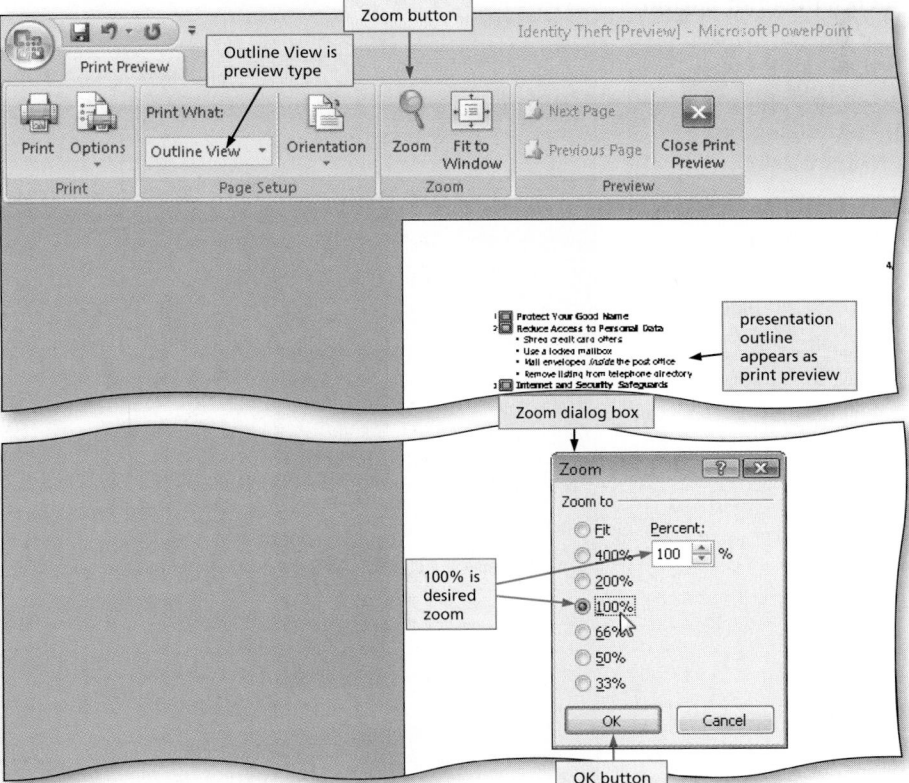

Figure 2–60

4

- Click the OK button in the Zoom dialog box to zoom the outline.

- Drag the scroll box on the vertical scroll bar up or down to move through the outline text (Figure 2–61).

Q&A

If I do not want to print my outline now, can I cancel this print request?

Yes. Click the Close Print Preview button in the Print Preview window to return to Normal view.

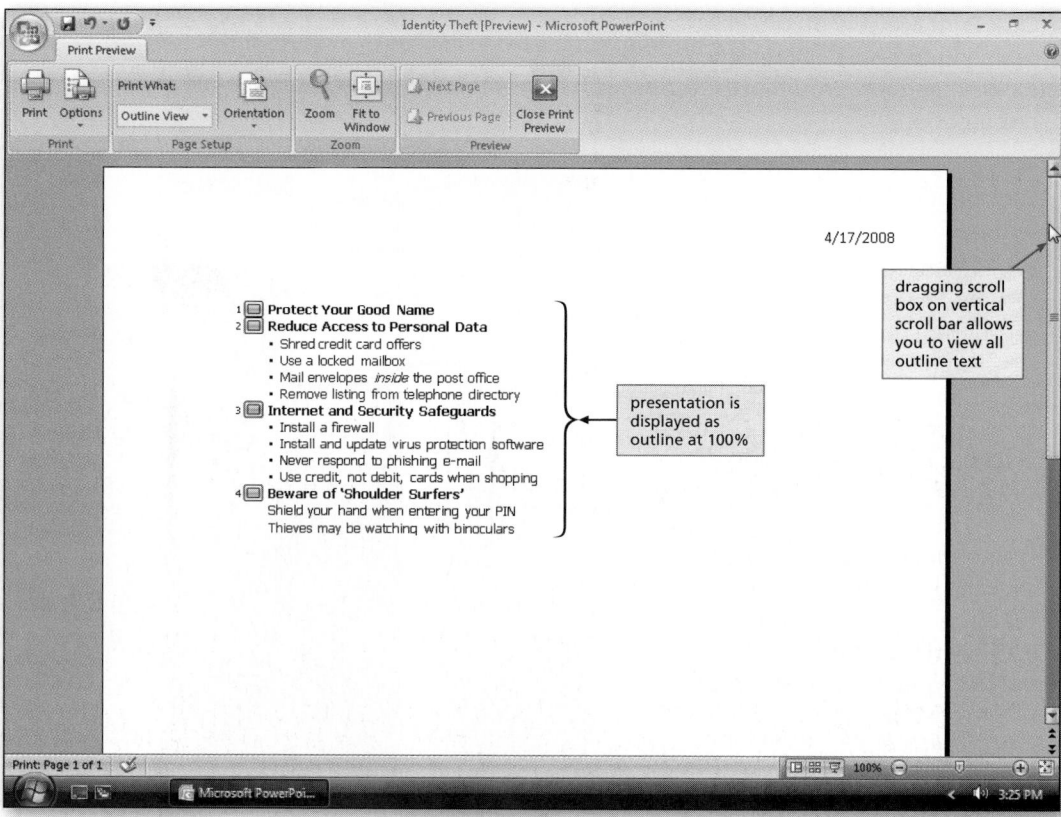

Figure 2–61

5

- Click the Print button in the Print group on the Print Preview tab to display the Print dialog box (Figure 2–62).

Q&A

What if my Print dialog box displays a different printer name?

It is likely a different printer name will display. Just ensure that the printer listed is the correct device you want to use to print your outline.

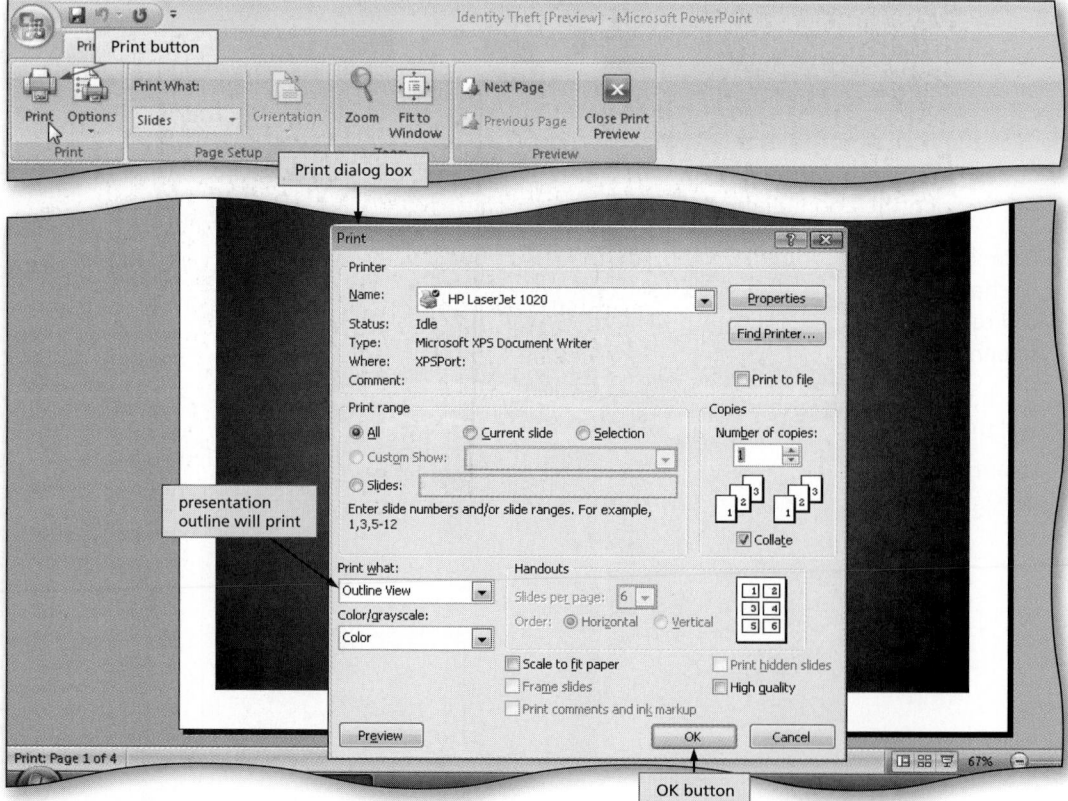

Figure 2–62

6
- Click the OK button to print the outline (Figure 2–63).

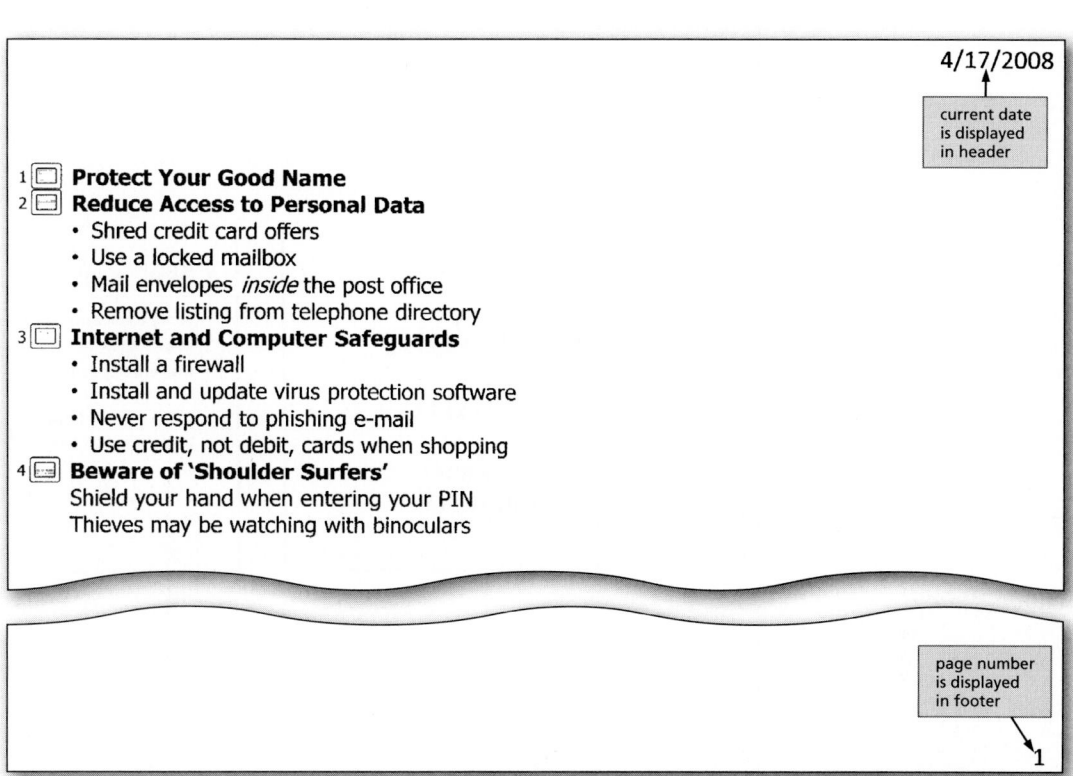

4/17/2008

current date is displayed in header

1. **Protect Your Good Name**
2. **Reduce Access to Personal Data**
   - Shred credit card offers
   - Use a locked mailbox
   - Mail envelopes *inside* the post office
   - Remove listing from telephone directory
3. **Internet and Computer Safeguards**
   - Install a firewall
   - Install and update virus protection software
   - Never respond to phishing e-mail
   - Use credit, not debit, cards when shopping
4. **Beware of 'Shoulder Surfers'**
   Shield your hand when entering your PIN
   Thieves may be watching with binoculars

page number is displayed in footer

1

Figure 2–63

Other Ways

1. Drag Zoom slider on status bar
2. Click Zoom button on status bar, select desired zoom percent or type, click OK button

To Preview and Print Handouts

Printing handouts is useful for reviewing a presentation because you can analyze several slides displayed simultaneously on one page. Additionally, many businesses distribute handouts of the slide show before a presentation so the attendees can refer to a copy.

The default slide print order is Horizontal so that Slides 1 and 2, and 3 and 4 are adjacent to each other. You can change this order to Vertical, which shows Slides 1 and 4, and 2 and 3 adjacent to each other, by clicking Options in the Print group on the Print Preview tab and then changing the printing order.

The following steps preview and print presentation handouts.

1 Click the Print What box arrow in the Page Setup group.

2 Click Handouts (4 Slides Per Page) in the Print What list. Drag the scroll box on the vertical scroll bar up or down to move through the page.

3 Click the Print button in the Print group.

4 Click the OK button in the Print dialog box to print the handout (Figure 2–64).

5 Click the Close Print Preview button in the Preview group on the Print Preview tab to return to Normal view.

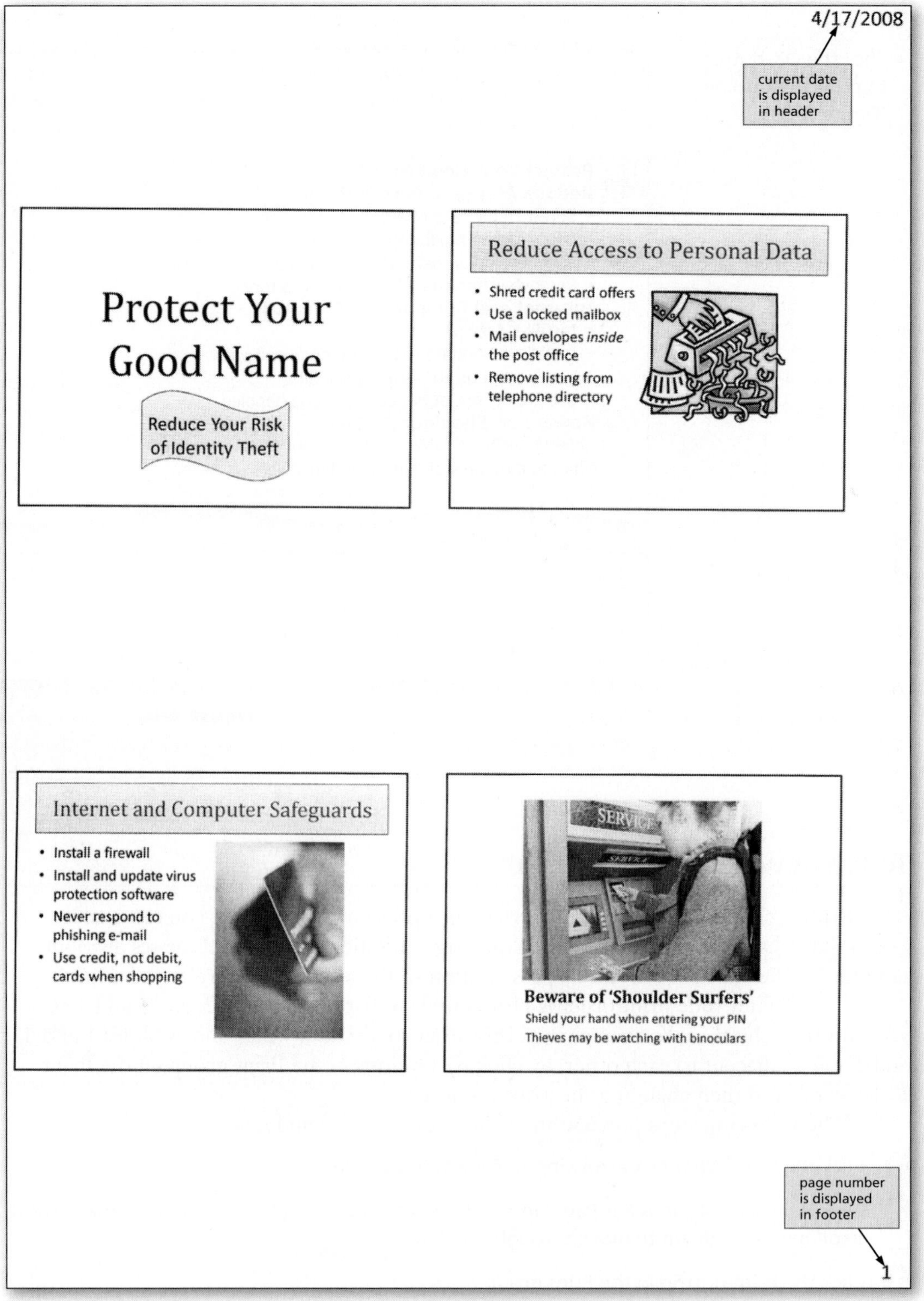

Figure 2–64

Saving and Quitting PowerPoint

If you made any changes to your presentation since your last save, you should save it again before quitting PowerPoint. The following steps save changes to the presentation and quit PowerPoint.

To Quit PowerPoint

This project is complete. The following steps quit PowerPoint.

1 Click the Office Button and then click the Exit PowerPoint button.

2 If necessary, click the Yes button in the Microsoft Office PowerPoint dialog box so that any changes you have made are saved.

Chapter Summary

In this chapter you have learned how to create slides from a blank presentation, change slide layouts, add a background style, insert clip art and pictures, size graphic elements, apply Quick Styles, select slide transitions, and preview and print an outline and handout. The items listed below include all the new PowerPoint skills you have learned in this chapter.

1. Choose a Background Style (PPT 89)
2. Change the View to Slide Sorter View (PPT 91)
3. Change the View to Normal View (PPT 91)
4. Change the Slide Layout to Two Content (PPT 92)
5. Change the Slide Layout to Picture with Caption (PPT 94)
6. Insert a Clip from the Clip Organizer into a Content Placeholder (PPT 96)
7. Insert a Photograph from the Clip Organizer into a Slide (PPT 98)
8. Insert a Photograph from a File into a Slide (PPT 99)
9. Resize Clip Art (PPT 100)
10. Resize a Photograph (PPT 103)
11. Delete a Placeholder (PPT 104)
12. Move Clips (PPT 105)
13. Format Title Text Using Quick Styles (PPT 106)
14. Format Remaining Title Text Using Quick Styles (PPT 107)
15. Change the Heading Font (PPT 109)
16. Shadow Text (PPT 110)
17. Change Font Color (PPT 110)
18. Format Text Using the Format Painter (PPT 112)
19. Format Remaining Title Text (PPT 113)
20. Add a Shape (PPT 116)
21. Resize a Shape (PPT 117)
22. Add Text to a Shape (PPT 119)
23. Format Shape Text and Add a Shape Quick Style (PPT 119)
24. Add a Transition between Slides (PPT 122)
25. Preview and Print an Outline (PPT 122)
26. Preview and Print Handouts (PPT 129)

 If you have a SAM user profile, you may have access to hands-on instruction, practice, and assessment. Log in to your SAM account (http://sam2007.course.com) to launch any assigned training activities or exams that relate to the skills covered in this chapter.

Learn It Online

Test your knowledge of chapter content and key terms.

Instructions: To complete the Learn It Online exercises, start your browser, click the Address bar, and then enter the Web address scsite.com/ppt2007/learn. When the Office 2007 Learn It Online page is displayed, click the link for the exercise you want to complete and then read the instructions.

Chapter Reinforcement TF, MC, and SA
A series of true/false, multiple choice, and short answer questions that test your knowledge of the chapter content.

Flash Cards
An interactive learning environment where you identify chapter key terms associated with displayed definitions.

Practice Test
A series of multiple choice questions that test your knowledge of chapter content and key terms.

Who Wants To Be a Computer Genius?
An interactive game that challenges your knowledge of chapter content in the style of a television quiz show.

Wheel of Terms
An interactive game that challenges your knowledge of chapter key terms in the style of the television show *Wheel of Fortune*.

Crossword Puzzle Challenge
A crossword puzzle that challenges your knowledge of key terms presented in the chapter.

Apply Your Knowledge

Reinforce the skills and apply the concepts you learned in this chapter.

Changing the Background and Adding Photographs and a Quick Style
Instructions: Start PowerPoint. Open the presentation, Apply 2-1 Lifestyle, from the Data Files for Students. See the inside back cover of this book for instructions on downloading the Data Files for Students, or contact your instructor for more information about accessing the required files.

The four slides in the presentation present basic guidelines for maintaining a healthy lifestyle and focus on proper weight, exercise, and food choices. The document you open is an unformatted presentation. You are to add and size photographs, change the background style, change slide layouts, apply a transition, and use the Format Painter so the slides look like Figure 2-65.

Perform the following tasks:
1. Change the background style to Style 11 (row 3, column 3). On the title slide, use your name in place of Student Name and bold and italicize your name and change the font color to orange. Increase the title text font size to 72 point, change the font to Baskerville Old Face, and change the font color to Dark Blue.

2. On Slides 2 and 4, change the layout to Two Content and then insert the photographs shown in Figure 2-65b and 2-65d from the Microsoft Clip Organizer.

3. On Slide 3, change the layout to Picture with Caption and then insert the picture shown in Figure 2-65c from the Microsoft Clip Organizer. Delete the text placeholder. Change the title text font size to 44 point, center this text, and then add the italic font style and shadow effect. Use the Format Painter to format the title text on Slides 2 and 4.

4. Apply the Subtle Effect – Accent 1 Quick Style (row 4, column 2) to the Slides 2, 3, and 4 title text placeholders. Apply the Uncover Left wipe transition (row 2, column 1) to all slides.

5. Check the spelling, and then display the revised presentation in Slide Sorter view.

6. Change the document properties, as specified by your instructor. Save the presentation using the file name, Apply 2–1 Healthy Lifestyle. Submit the revised document in the format specified by your instructor.

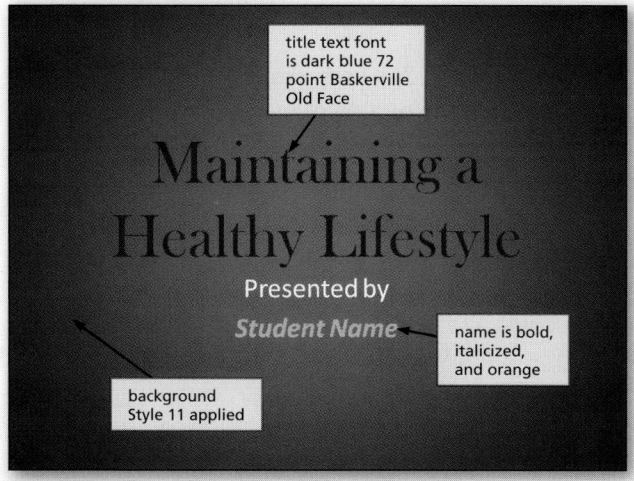

(a)

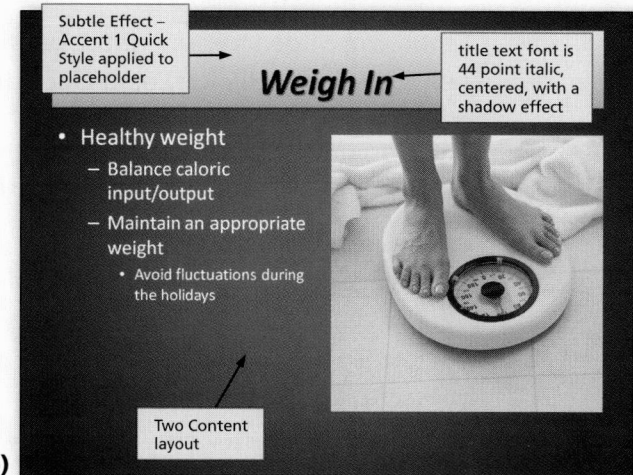

(b)

(c)

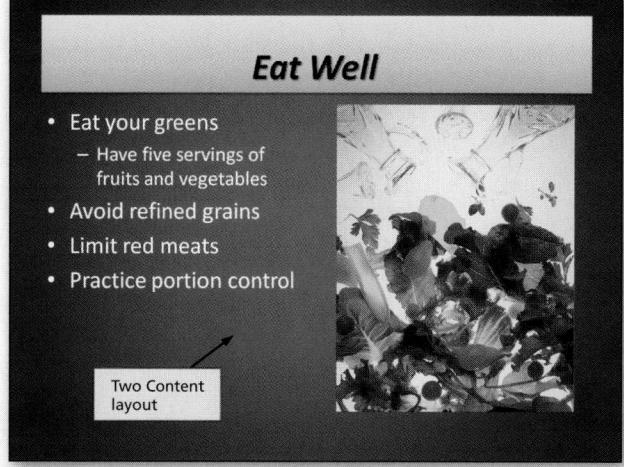

(d)

Figure 2–65

Extend Your Knowledge

Extend the skills you learned in this chapter and experiment with new skills. You may need to use Help to complete the assignment.

Changing Slide Layouts and Moving Clips

Instructions: Start PowerPoint. Open the presentation, Extend 2-1 Fats, from the Data Files for Students. See the inside back cover of this book for instructions on downloading the Data Files for Students, or contact your instructor for more information on accessing the required files.

You will choose a background, format slides, and copy clips (Figure 2–66).

Perform the following tasks:

1. Add an appropriate background style.

2. On Slide 1, use your name in place of Student Name. Format the text using techniques you learned and applied in this chapter, such as changing the font size and color and also bolding and italicizing words.

3. Slide 7 contains a variety of clips downloaded from the Microsoft Clip Organizer. Review the slides in the presentation and then move clips from Slide 7 to the appropriate slides. You do not need to use all the clips. Delete Slide 7 when you have finished moving the desired clips to the slides.

4. Change the slide layouts to accommodate the clips. Size the clips when necessary. Edit the text so that each slide meets the 7 × 7 rule, which states that each line should have a maximum of seven words, and each slide should have a maximum of seven lines.

5. Apply an appropriate transition to all slides.

6. Change the document properties, as specified by your instructor. Save the presentation using the file name, Extend 2-1 Enhanced Fats.

7. Submit the revised document in the format specified by your instructor.

variety of clips to consider moving to previous slides in presentation

Figure 2–66

Make It Right

Analyze a presentation and correct all errors and/or improve the design.

Applying Background and Quick Styles

Instructions: Start PowerPoint. Open the presentation, Make It Right 2-1 Safety, from the Data Files for Students. See the back inside cover of this book for instructions on downloading the Data Files for Students, or contact your instructor for more information on accessing the required files.

Correct the formatting problems and errors in the presentation while keeping in mind the guidelines presented in this chapter.

Perform the following tasks:

1. Change the document theme from Verve, shown in Figure 2–67, to Paper. Apply the Style 7 background style (row 2, column 3).

2. On Slide 1, replace the words, Student Name, with your name. Apply a Quick Style to your name and the title text so that they display prominently on the slide.

3. Move Slide 2 to the end of the presentation so that it becomes the new Slide 5.

4. Use the spell checker to correct the misspellings. Analyze the slides for other word usage errors that the spell checker did not find.

5. Adjust the clip art sizes so they do not overlap text and are the appropriate dimensions for the slide content.

6. Select a Quick Style to apply to the Slides 2 through 5 title text. Center the title text and apply a shadow.

7. Apply an appropriate transition to all slides. Change the speed to Slow.

8. Change the document properties, as specified by your instructor. Save the presentation using the file name, Make It Right 2-1 Home Safety.

9. Submit the revised document in the format specified by your instructor.

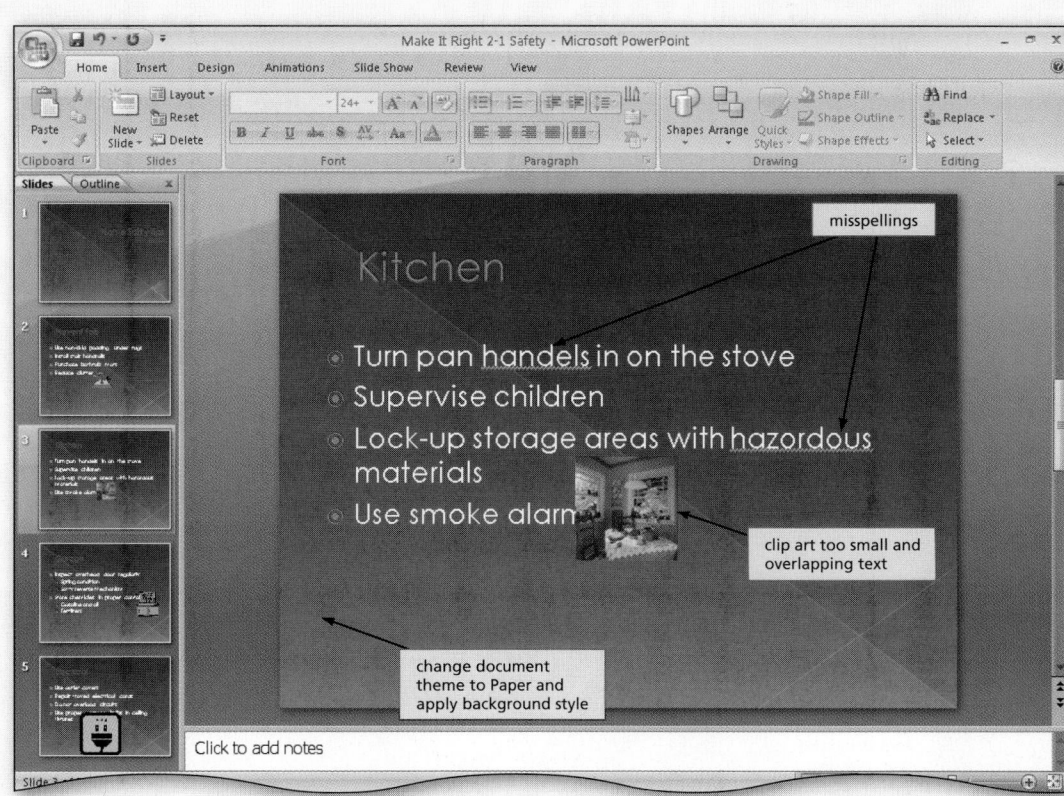

Figure 2–67

In the Lab

Design and/or create a presentation using the guidelines, concepts, and skills presented in this chapter. Labs 1, 2, and 3 are listed in order of increasing difficulty.

Lab 1: Creating a Presentation with a Clip and Shapes

Problem: The ear affects balance while it enables us to hear. This organ can be divided into three parts for analysis: outer, middle, and inner. The outer ear is composed of a flap and the auditory canal. The middle ear has three tiny bones called the auditory ossicles and the eustachian tube, which links the ear to the nose. The inner ear contains the spiral-shaped cochlea and also the semicircular canals and the vestibule, which control balance. You are studying the ear as a unit in your health class, so you decide to develop a PowerPoint slide that names these parts to help you study for a quiz. Create the slide shown in Figure 2–68 from a blank presentation.

Instructions: Perform the following tasks.

1. Apply the Style 6 background style (row 2, column 2) to the slide. Change the layout to Content with Caption. Import the ear diagram clip from the Microsoft Clip Organizer.

2. Type the slide title and caption body text shown in Figure 2–68. Use your name in place of Bill Tracy, and then italicize this text and change the font color to Blue (color 8 in the Standard Colors row). Change the color of the title text to Dark Red (color 1 in the Standard Colors row) and increase the font size to 24.

3. Use the Right Arrow, Left Arrow, Up Arrow, and Down Arrow shapes in the Block Arrow section to point to the parts of the ear shown in Figure 2–68. Add the number to each arrow. Apply the Subtle Effect – Accent 3 Quick Style (row 4, column 4) to each arrow. Change the font size of each arrow text to 24 point and bold these numbers.

4. Check the spelling and correct any errors.

5. Change the document properties, as specified by your instructor. Save the presentation using the file name, Lab 2-1 Ear.

6. Submit the revised document in the format specified by your instructor.

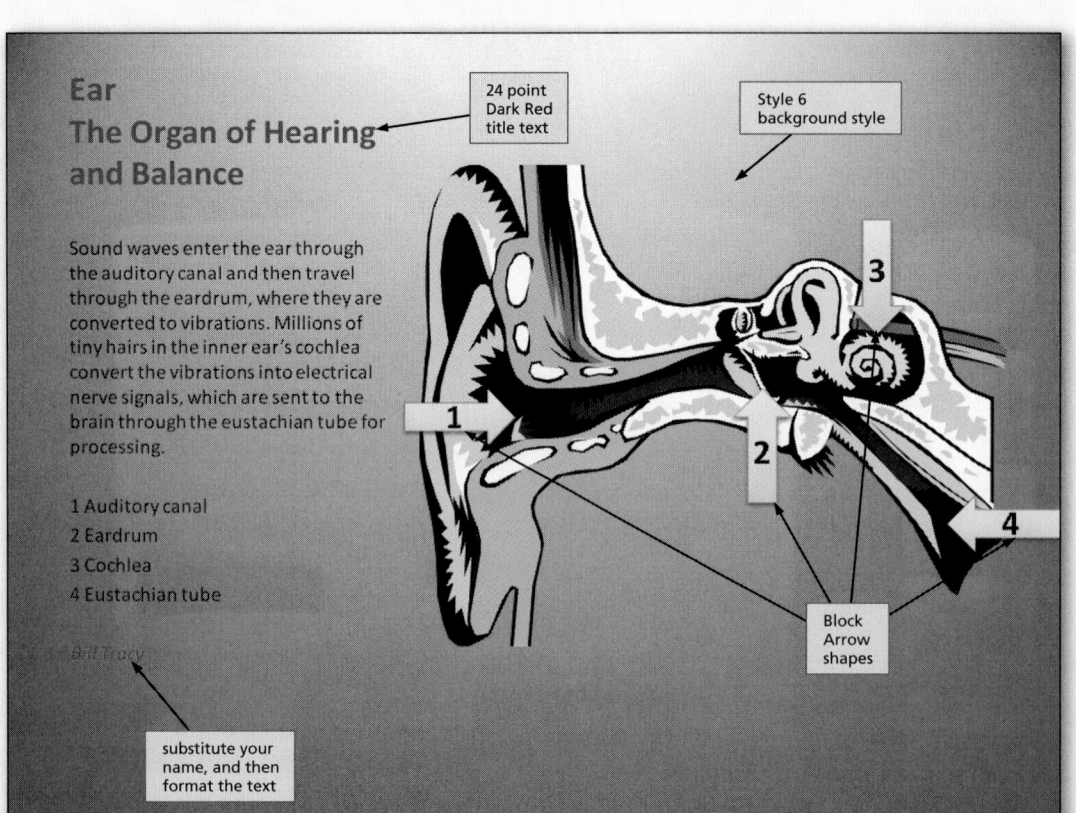

Figure 2–68

In the Lab

Lab 2: Creating a Presentation with Photographs Inserted from a File

Problem: Destructive insects damage specific species of trees throughout the world. You have learned in your Botany 202 class that the Asian Longhorn Beetle, the Emerald Ash Borer, the Gypsy Moth, and the Western Pine Beetle are among trees' biggest pests. One of your assignments in your botany class is to give a speech about common tree pests. You develop the outline shown in Figure 2–69 and then prepare the PowerPoint presentation shown in Figures 2–70a through 2–70f. You have obtained permission from the U.S. Forestry Department to copy photographs from its Web site to your slide show; these photographs are on your Data Files for Students.

Tree Pests
Creatures That Bug Our Trees
Jim DeYoung
Botany 202

Asian Longhorn Beetle
- Native to China
- Transported to United States in infested packing material

Emerald Ash Borer
- Killed 20 million trees in Michigan, Ohio, and Indiana
- Firewood quarantines to prevent new infestations

Gypsy Moth
- Spread to U.S. in 1870
- Oaks and Aspens are most common hosts
- Larva defoliate trees
- Small mammals and birds are predators

Western Pine Beetle
- Infest Ponderosa and Coulter pine trees
  - Mainly Western states
- Tree loss considered normal ecological process

Acknowledgements
- Photos and information courtesy of the USDA Forest Service
  - forestry.about.com

Figure 2–69

Continued >

In the Lab *continued*

Instructions: *Perform the following tasks.*

1. Create a new presentation using the Foundry document theme. Apply the Style 7 background style (row 2, column 3).

2. Using the typed notes illustrated in Figure 2–69, create the title slide shown in Figure 2–70a using your name in place of Jim DeYoung. Bold your name and apply a shadow.

3. Insert the Isosceles Triangle shape (row 1, column 3 in the Basic Shapes category) in the top center of Slide 1. Size the shape so that the top and bottom align with the edges of the brown area of the slide, as shown in Figure 2–70a.

4. Using the typed notes in Figure 2–69, create the five text slides with bulleted lists shown in Figures 2–70b through 2–70f. Use the Two Content slide layout for Slides 2 through 5 and the Title and Content slide layout for Slide 6.

5. Insert the appropriate pictures from your Data Files for Students on Slides 2 through 5.

6. Apply the Wedge transition (row 1, column 5 in the Wipes category) to all slides. Change the speed to Medium. Check the spelling and correct any errors.

7. Review the slides in Slide Sorter view to check for consistency, and then change the view to Normal.

8. Drag the scroll box to display Slide 1. Click the Slide Show button to start Slide Show view. Then click to display each slide.

9. Change the document properties, as specified by your instructor. Save the presentation using the file name, Lab 2-2 Tree Pests.

10. Submit the document in the format specified by your instructor.

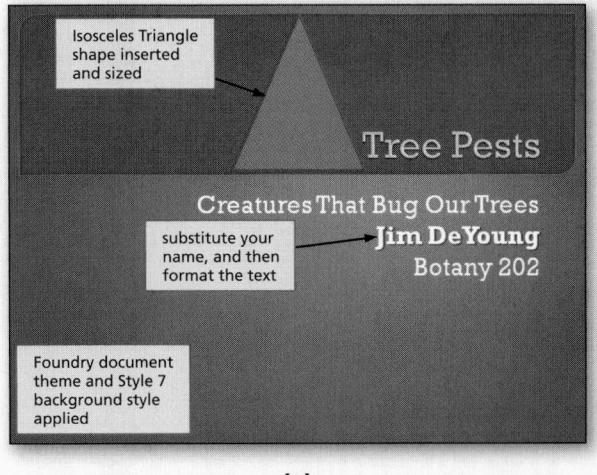

(a)

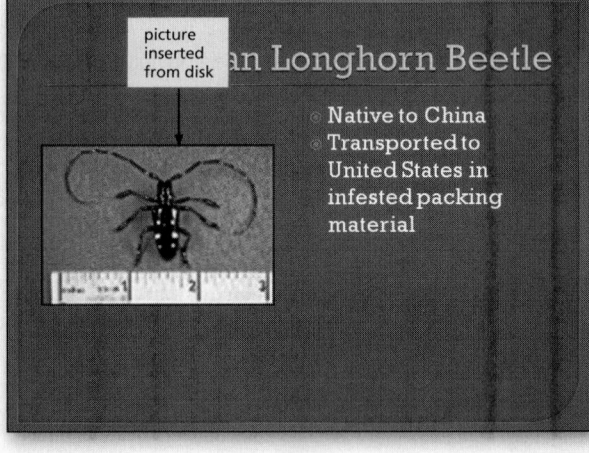

(b)

Figure 2–70

(c)

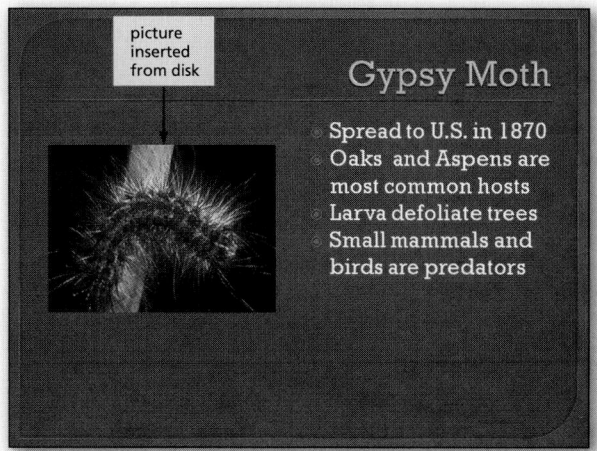

(d)

(e)

(f)

Figure 2–70

In the Lab

Lab 3: Creating a Presentation with Clips and Shapes

Problem: Snowboarding's popularity has soared in recent years; even Cameron Diaz and Space Shuttle astronauts have a passion for the sport. But with this increase in snowboarders has come a corresponding increase in injuries. The most common injuries are caused by a failure to follow common sense precautions. In order to maximize the time on the slopes, snowboarders need to prepare for the sport by wearing proper equipment, getting into condition, and snowboarding under control. Bryan Howell owns a local ski and snowboard shop in your town and has asked you to prepare a PowerPoint presentation that he can share with equipment buyers and renters. He hands you the outline shown in Figure 2–71 and asks you to create the presentation shown in Figures 2–72a through 2–72d.

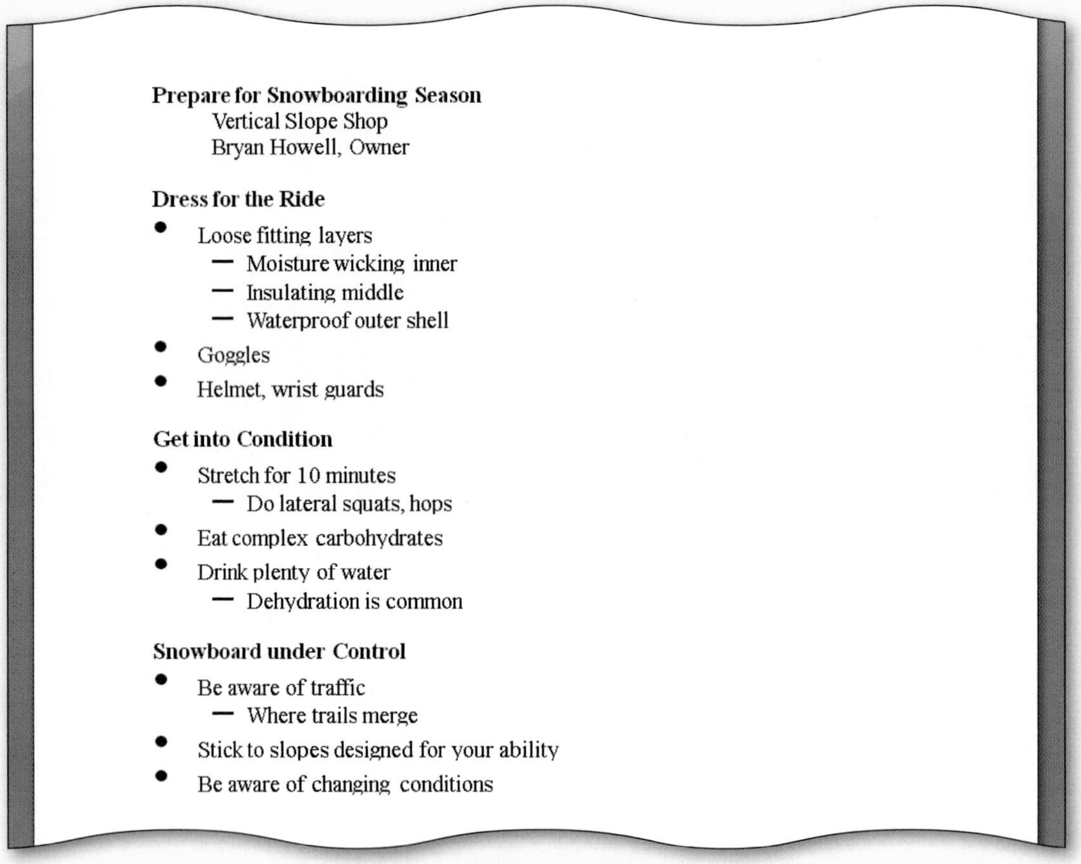

Prepare for Snowboarding Season
Vertical Slope Shop
Bryan Howell, Owner

Dress for the Ride
- Loose fitting layers
  - Moisture wicking inner
  - Insulating middle
  - Waterproof outer shell
- Goggles
- Helmet, wrist guards

Get into Condition
- Stretch for 10 minutes
  - Do lateral squats, hops
- Eat complex carbohydrates
- Drink plenty of water
  - Dehydration is common

Snowboard under Control
- Be aware of traffic
  - Where trails merge
- Stick to slopes designed for your ability
- Be aware of changing conditions

Figure 2–71

Instructions: Perform the following tasks.

1. Use the typed notes illustrated in Figure 2–71 to create four slides shown in Figures 2–72a through 2–72d from a blank presentation. Apply the Style 7 background style (row 2, column 3). Use your name in place of Bryan Howell on the title slide shown in Figure 2–72a. Bold your name.

2. Insert the Right Triangle shape (row 1, column 4 in the Basic Shapes category) on Slide 1. With the shape selected, click the Arrange button in the Drawing group on the Home tab, point to Rotate in the Position Objects group, and then click Flip Horizontal to turn the triangle shape. Drag the shape to the lower-right corner of the slide, increase the size to that shown in Figure 2–72a, and apply the Colored Outline - Accent 3 Quick Style (row 1, column 4).

3. Italicize the Slide 1 title text, Prepare for Snowboarding Season, align the text left, and change the font color to Black. Align the subtitle text left and change the font color to Green (color 6 in the Standard Colors row).

4. Add the photographs and clip art shown in Figures 2–72a through 2–72d from the Microsoft Clip Organizer. Adjust the clip sizes when necessary.

5. Change the Slide 2 title text font size to 54 point, change the font to Forte, and then change the color to Green. Use the Format Painter to format the title text on Slides 3 and 4 with the same features as on Slide 2.

6. Apply the Newsflash transition (row 6, column 2 in the Wipes category) to all slides. Change the speed to Medium. Check the spelling and correct any errors.

7. Click the Slide Sorter button, view the slides for consistency, and then click the Normal button.

8. Change the document properties, as specified by your instructor. Save the presentation using the file name, Lab 2-3 Snowboarding.

9. Submit the revised document in the format specified by your instructor.

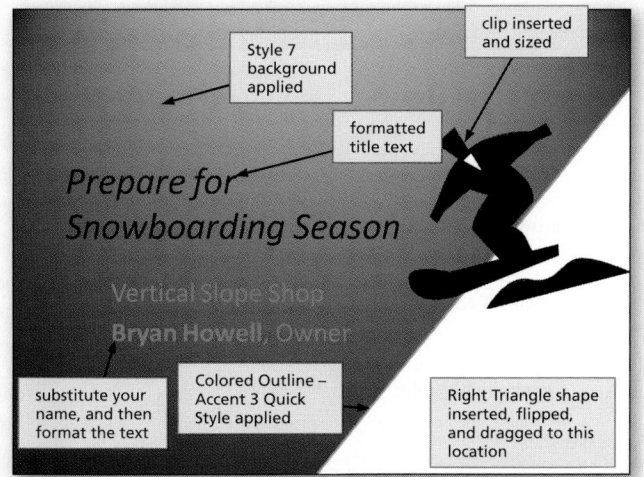

(a)

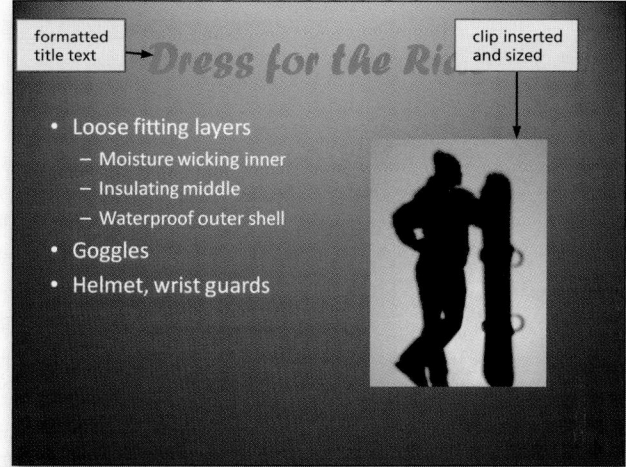

(b)

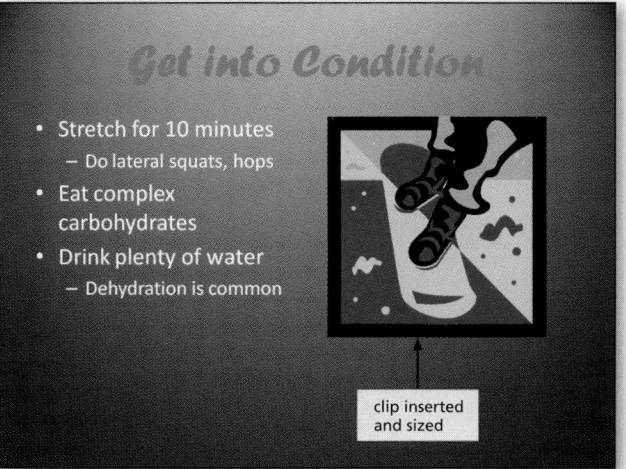

(c)

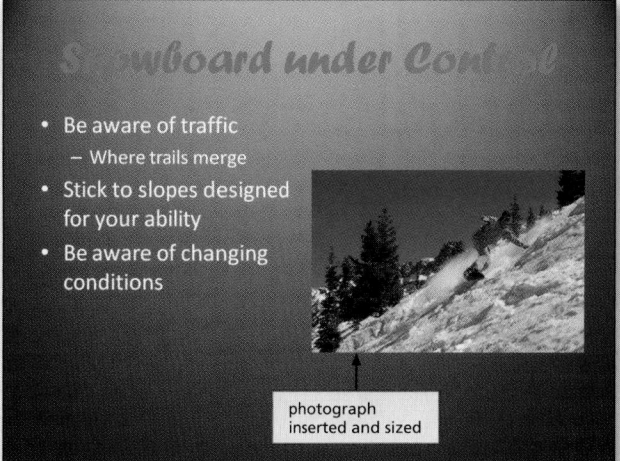

(d)

Figure 2–72

Cases and Places

Apply your creative thinking and problem solving skills to design and implement a solution.

● EASIER ●● MORE DIFFICULT

Note: Remember to use the 7 × 7 rule as you design the presentations: a maximum of seven words on a line and a maximum of seven lines on one slide.

● 1: Design and Create an Energy Efficiency Presentation

Global demand, industry deregulation, and regional conflicts have increased energy prices. The United States Department of Energy predicts energy use will grow 33 percent by 2030. Despite these staggering numbers, homeowners can undertake relatively simple measures to be energy efficient. Create a presentation using the outline in Figure 2–73. Apply at least three objectives found at the beginning of this chapter to develop the presentation. Add a title slide with a shape and a closing slide that cites your references. Be sure to check spelling.

Home Energy Savings Tips

Save Money While You Help the Environment

Bright Ideas
- Lighting accounts for more than 10 percent of electric bill
- Change to compact florescent lights (CFLs)
  - Use 50-75 percent less energy
  - Last up to ten times longer than conventional bulbs

Keep It Clean
- Wash only *full* loads of clothes and dishes
- Keep dryer vents clean
- Air dry dishes when possible
- Use ENERGY STAR products

Stay Out of Hot Water
- Heating water accounts for 13 percent of energy bill
- Use low-flow fixtures
- Repair leaks
- Lower thermostat
- Insulate heater

References
- www1.eere.energy.gov/consumer/tips/save_energy.html
- www.exeloncorp.com/comedcare/
- www.energystar.gov/]

Figure 2–73

• 2: Design and Create a Hypertension Presentation

According to the National Heart, Lung, and Blood Institute, nearly one-third of American adults are inflicted by the "silent killer," high blood pressure. This disease affects people of all ages and ethnicities. Use the concepts and techniques presented in this chapter to create a presentation following the outline in Figure 2–74, which includes the definition of hypertension and hypertension categories, has tips on controlling high blood pressure, and lists Web sites to view for further information. Insert photographs and clips, and apply a subtle slide transition to all slides. Be sure to check spelling.

Blood Pressure 101
Taking Control of the Silent Killer

Blood Pressure Definition
- Force of blood on vein walls
  - Pressure units: milligrams of mercury (mgHg)
- Defined by two numbers
  - Systolic: Pressure during beats
  - Diastolic: Pressure between beats
- Read as the systolic over diastolic level
  - Example: 125 over 74

Adult Blood Pressure Categories
- Normal
  - Systolic < 120
  - Diastolic < 80
- Prehypertension
  - Systolic 120 – 139
  - Diastolic 80 – 89
- Hypertension
  - Systolic > 140
  - Diastolic > 90

Detection
- No symptoms
- Person must be tested
  - Sphygmomanometer and stethoscope used

Hypertension Prevention Tips
- Eat healthy
  - Fruits, vegetables
  - Low fat diet
- Maintain weight
- Exercise regularly

References
- National Heart, Lung, and Blood Institute
  www.nhlbi.nih.gov
- American Heart Association
  www.americanheart.org/presenter.jhtml

Figure 2–74

Continued >

Cases and Places *continued*

•• 3: Design and Create a Portable Media Player Presentation

Video tape recorders were immensely popular more than three decades ago with several competing standards introduced in the market. Each technology touted different features. Today, the situation is similar with portable media players and cellular telephones that can download music from the Internet or rip files from your computer. Your supervisor at NextPhase Electronics recognizes buyers need assistance learning about these devices. She has asked you to prepare a presentation summarizing one of these players for next month's Saturday Seminar Series at the store. Research a specific portable media player and create a slide for each of the following attributes: featured model, user interface, and finding and loading songs. Select art and photographs from the Microsoft Clip Organizer, and add a title slide and summary slide to complete your presentation. Format the title slide with a shape and the text with colors and bolding where needed for emphasis.

•• 4: Design and Create a Campus Orientation Presentation

Make It Personal

Feedback from new students at your school cites difficulties navigating your campus. Incoming students mention the library, registrar, and health services as locations most often sought. To address these concerns, you volunteered as a member of the New Student Orientation Team to create a presentation and distribute a handout showing frequently accessed areas of the school. Use the concepts and techniques presented in this chapter to develop and format a slide show with a title slide and at least three text slides with bulleted lists. Create a slide for each landmark that briefly describes its location, and use clips and text to annotate it. Obtain a map of your campus and import it as a picture into your presentation. Select slide layouts that permit both the map and a bulleted list to appear on each slide. Use the arrow shapes to indicate the location of the landmark on the map. Add a background style and slide transitions. Be sure to check spelling. Print a handout with two slides on each page to distribute to new students on campus.

•• 5: Design and Create a Wellness Program Presentation

Working Together

Health care costs continue to rise at nearly double the inflation rate. Many health insurance companies are becoming proactive in containing those costs by offering reimbursement for wellness programs. Have each member of your team visit, telephone, or view Web sites of three health insurance companies. Gather information about:

1) Health screenings

2) Fitness center amenities

3) Self-Improvement classes

4) Wellness program benefits

After coordinating the data, create a presentation with a least one slide showcasing each topic. As a group, critique each slide. Submit your assignment in the format specified by your instructor.

Web Feature

Creating Web Pages Using PowerPoint

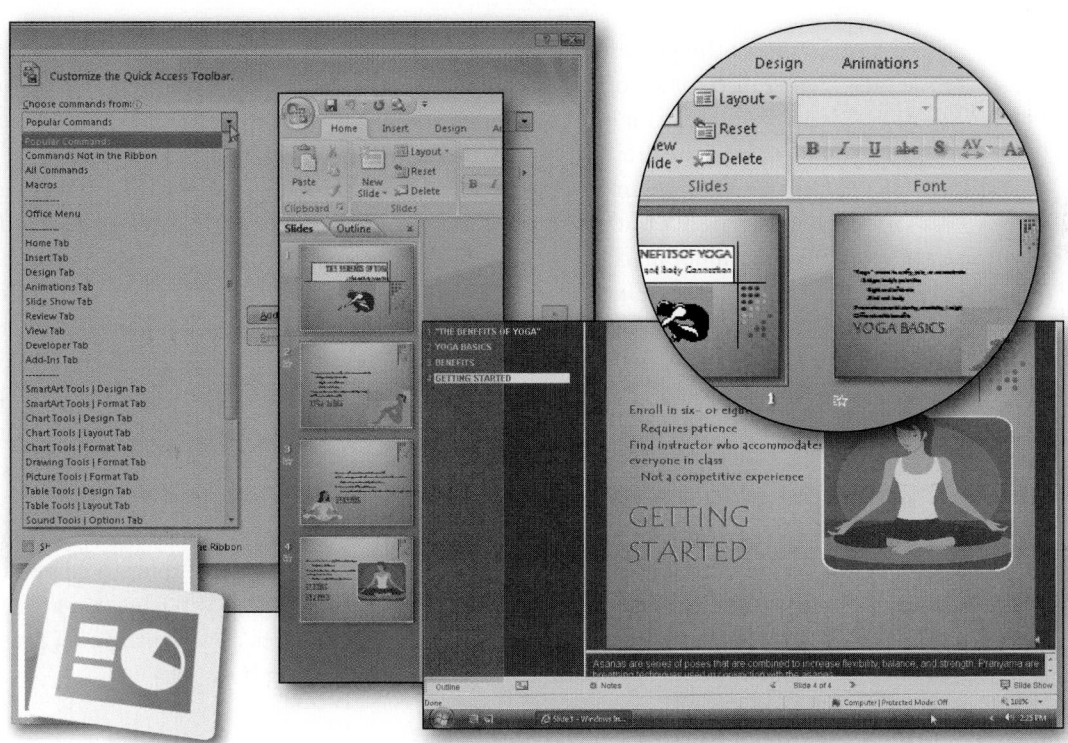

Objectives

You will have mastered the material in this Web feature when you can:

- Preview and save a presentation as a Web page
- Customize the Quick Access Toolbar
- Display Web pages created in PowerPoint in a browser
- Complete file management tasks within PowerPoint

Web Feature Introduction

The graphic design power of PowerPoint allows you to create vibrant presentations that convey information in a clear, interesting manner. Some of these presentations are created for small, specific audiences, such as student club members planning a fundraising activity. In this case, the presentation may be shown in an office. Other presentations are designed for large, general audiences, such as potential students planning a campus visit. These students can view the presentation on their school's **intranet**, which is an internal network that uses Internet technologies. On a grand scale, you can inform the entire world about the contents of your presentation by posting your slide show to the World Wide Web.

Project — Web Page

Figure 1a shows the presentation describing yoga fundamentals in Slide Sorter view. The Fitness Center director at your school requests that the information in the slide be made available on the school's intranet for employees and student workers to view. In order to accomplish this task, you must save the presentation as a Web page.

You can save a presentation, or a portion of a presentation as a Web page. The saved **Web page** is a snapshot of the presentation. It is similar to a running slide show in that you can view it, but you cannot modify it. In the browser window, the presentation appears as it would in Microsoft PowerPoint, including a Next Slide button you can click to advance the slides. As illustrated in Figure 1, this Web feature shows you how to save a presentation (Figure 1a) as a Web page (Figures 1b through 1e) and view it using your browser.

PowerPoint allows you to **publish presentations**, which is the process of making existing presentations available to others on the World Wide Web or on a company's intranet, when you use the Save As command on the Office Button menu and choose to save a presentation as a Web page. If you have access to a Web server, you can publish Web pages by saving them on a Web server or on an FTP location. To learn more about publishing Web pages on a Web server or on an FTP location using Microsoft Office applications, refer to Appendix D.

This Web feature illustrates how to create and save the Web pages on a USB flash drive, rather than on a Web server. This feature also demonstrates how to preview a presentation as a Web page and create a new folder using the Save As dialog box.

Overview

As you read through this feature, you will learn how to create the yoga Web pages shown in Figures 1b, 1c, 1d, and 1e by performing these general tasks:

- Preview and save PowerPoint presentations as Web pages.
- Add a button to the Quick Access Toolbar.
- Use Windows Explorer to view Web pages.

Using Web Page Preview and Saving a PowerPoint Presentation as a Web Page

At any time during the construction of a presentation, PowerPoint makes it easy to preview how it will display on an intranet or on the World Wide Web by using the Web Page Preview command. When you invoke the Web Page Preview command, it starts your browser and displays the active slide in the presentation as a Web page without saving files. By previewing your slide show, you can decide which features look good and which need modification. The left side of the window includes the navigation frame, which is the outline of the presentation. The outline contains a table of contents consisting of each slide's title text. You can click the Expand/Collapse Outline button below the navigation frame to view the complete slide text. The right side of the window shows the complete slide in the slide frame. The speaker notes, if present, are displayed in the notes frame below the slide frame. Once the preview is acceptable, you then can save the presentation as a Web page. The Web Page Preview command is not available on the Ribbon, but you can add the command to the Quick Access Toolbar.

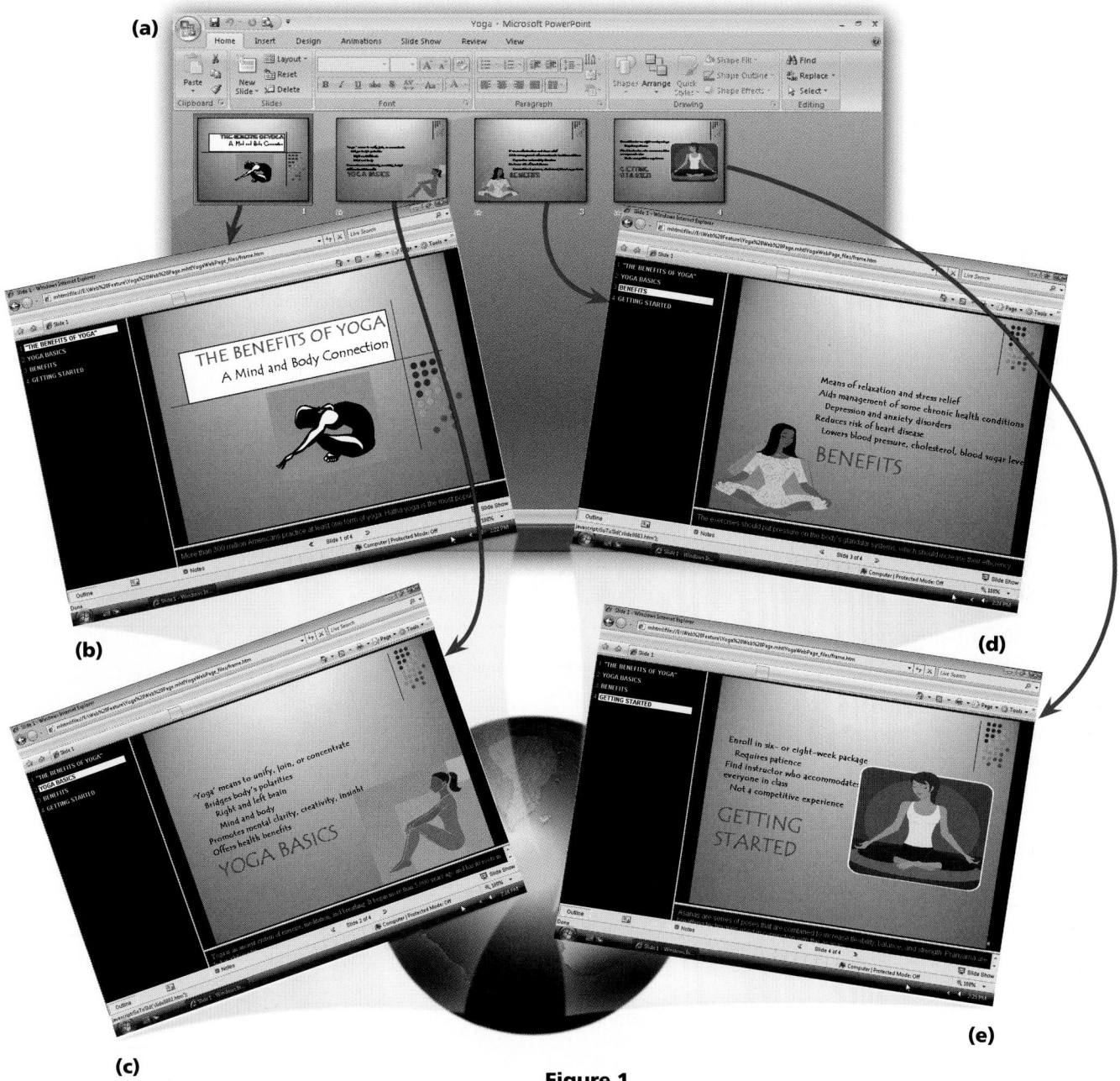

Figure 1

<table>
<tr><td>Plan
Ahead</td><td>

General Project Guidelines

When creating the yoga Web pages, the actions you perform and decisions you make will affect the appearance and characteristics of the finished presentation. As you create Web pages, such as the project shown in Figure 1, you should follow these general guidelines:

1. **Develop an effective presentation.** Your slide show should provide essential information to a specific audience. Text should be succinct and meaningful. Graphics, such as illustrations, and color should add visual appeal and promote understanding. Ask someone else to view your presentation and give you suggestions for improvements.

2. **Preview and review the Web pages created from your PowerPoint presentation.** Preview the Web page to assess readability and visual interest. Be certain to test your finished Web page document in at least one browser program to check if it looks and works as you intended.

3. **Publish your Web page.** Once you have created a Web page, you can publish it, which makes it available to others on a network, such as the World Wide Web or a company's intranet. Many Internet service providers offer storage space on their Web servers at no cost to their subscribers. The procedures for using Microsoft Office to publish a Web page are discussed in Appendix D.

This Web Feature focuses on the second guideline, identifying the actions you perform and the decisions you make during the creation of the Web pages shown in Figure 1. Chapters 1 and 2 presented details about how to accomplish the goals of the first guideline listed above, and Appendix D presents details about how to achieve the goals of the last guideline.

</td></tr>
</table>

To Add a Button to the Quick Access Toolbar

Many commands available in PowerPoint are not included on any of the tabs on the Ribbon. You can, however, add such commands to the Quick Access Toolbar. One such command allows you to preview a document in a Web browser. This command, Web Page Preview, needs to be added to the Quick Access Toolbar so that the Web page can be previewed. The following steps add the Web Page Preview command to the Quick Access Toolbar.

- Connect a USB flash drive to one of the computer's USB ports.

- Start PowerPoint and then open the presentation, Yoga, from the Data Files for Students.

- Click the Customize Quick Access Toolbar button to display the Customize Quick Access Toolbar menu (Figure 2).

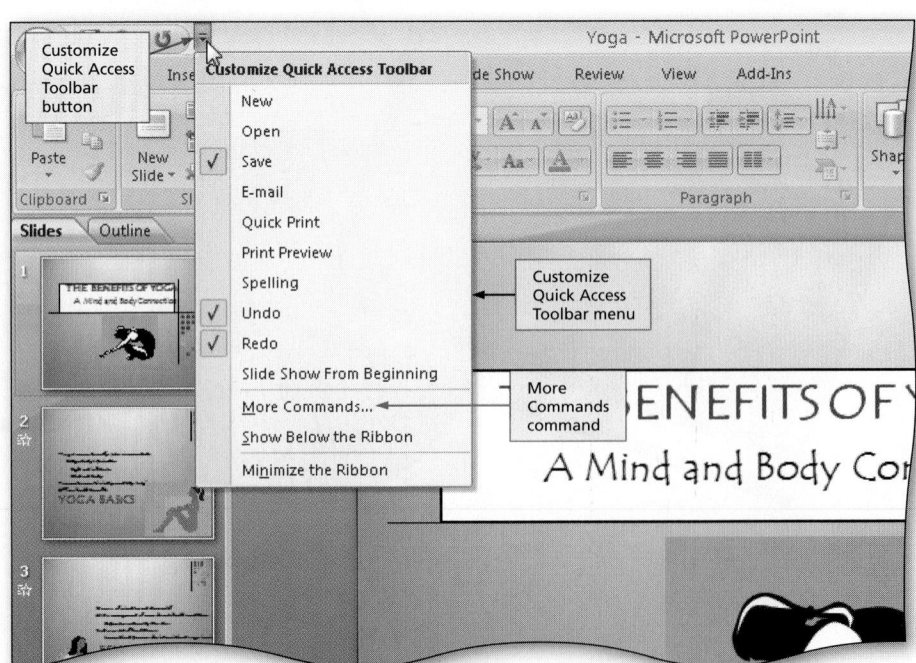

Figure 2

3

- Click the More Commands command on the Customize Quick Access Toolbar menu.

- When the PowerPoint Options dialog box is displayed, click the 'Choose commands from' box arrow to display the 'Choose commands from' list (Figure 3).

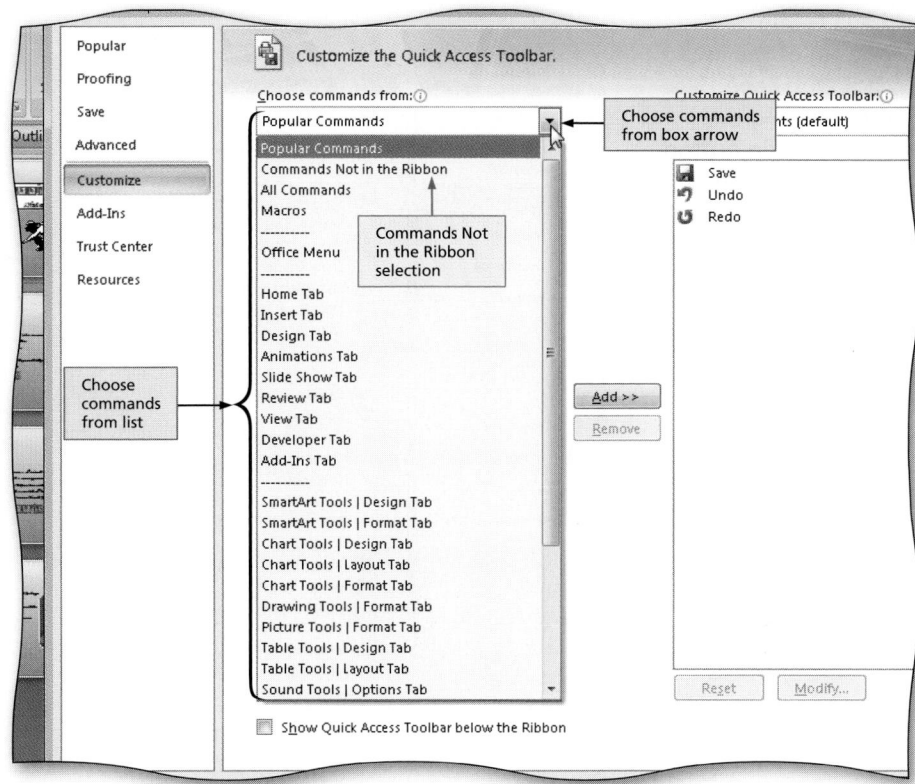

Figure 3

4

- Click Commands Not in the Ribbon in the 'Choose commands from' list to display a list of commands not in the Ribbon (Figure 4).

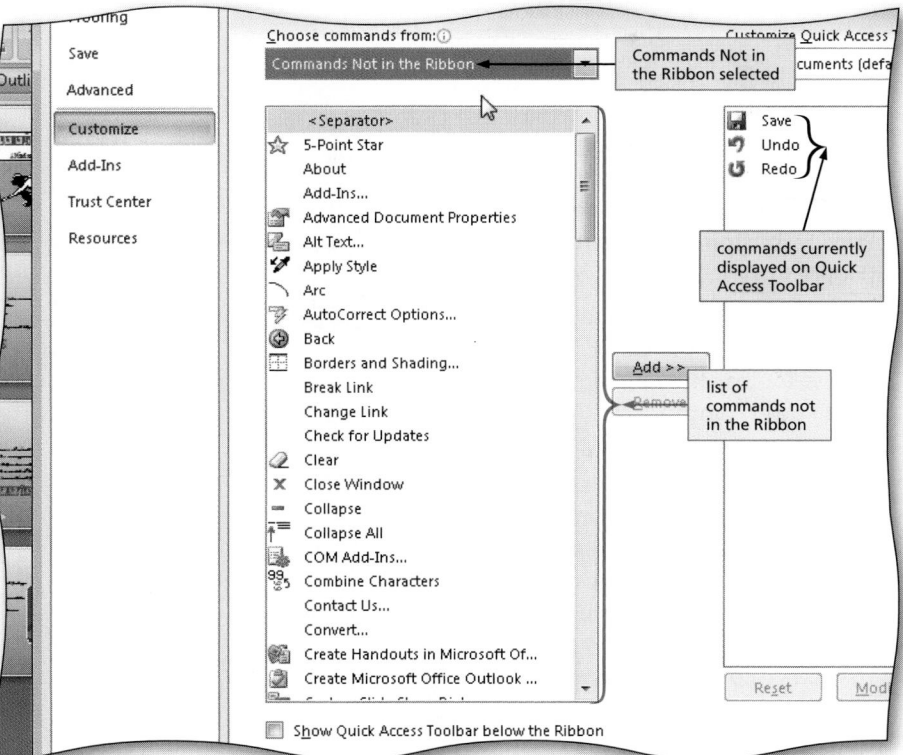

Figure 4

- Scroll to the bottom of the list, click Web Page Preview, and then click the Add button to add the button to the Quick Access Toolbar (Figure 5).

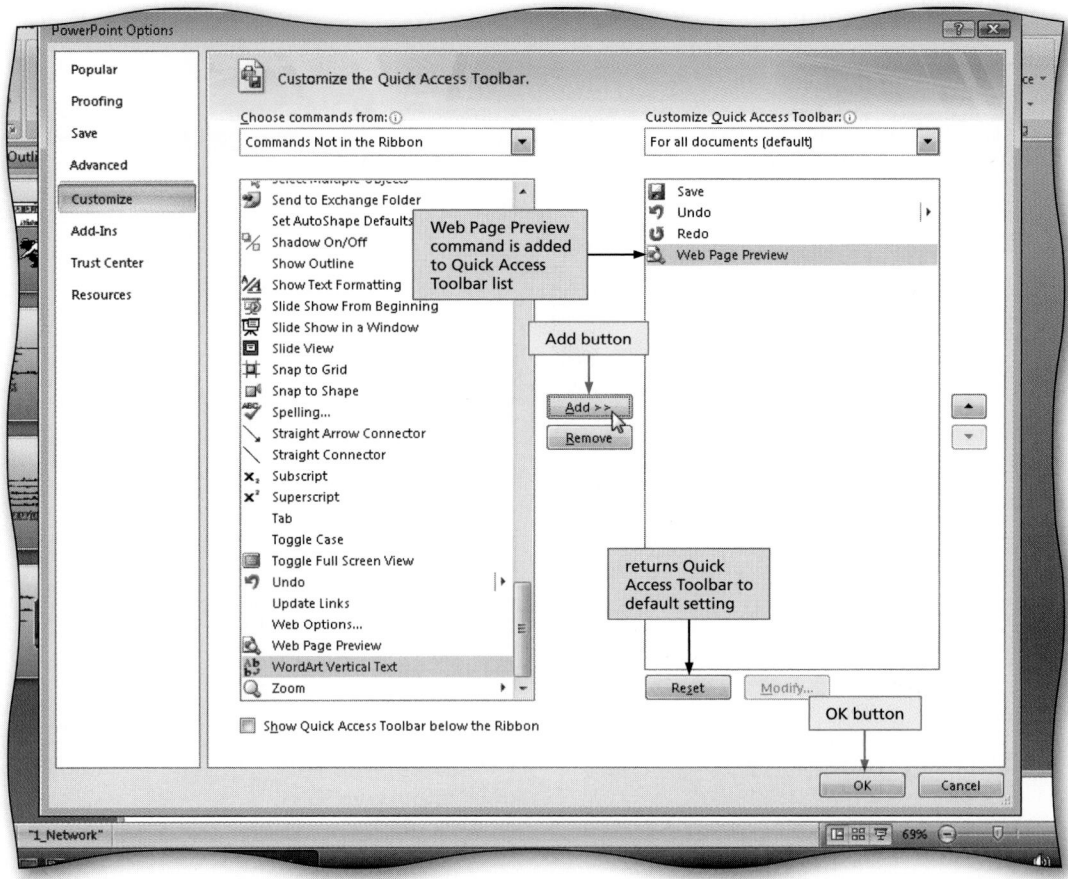

Figure 5

- Click the OK button to close the PowerPoint Options dialog box and display the Quick Access Toolbar with the Web Page Preview button added to it (Figure 6).

Q&A

Will the Web Page Preview command be in the Quick Access Toolbar the next time I start PowerPoint?

Yes. When you change the Quick Access Toolbar, the changes remain even after you restart PowerPoint. If you share a computer with somebody else or if the Quick Access Toolbar becomes cluttered, PowerPoint allows you to remove commands from the Quick Access Toolbar. You will remove the Web Page Preview button from the Quick Access Toolbar later in this Web feature.

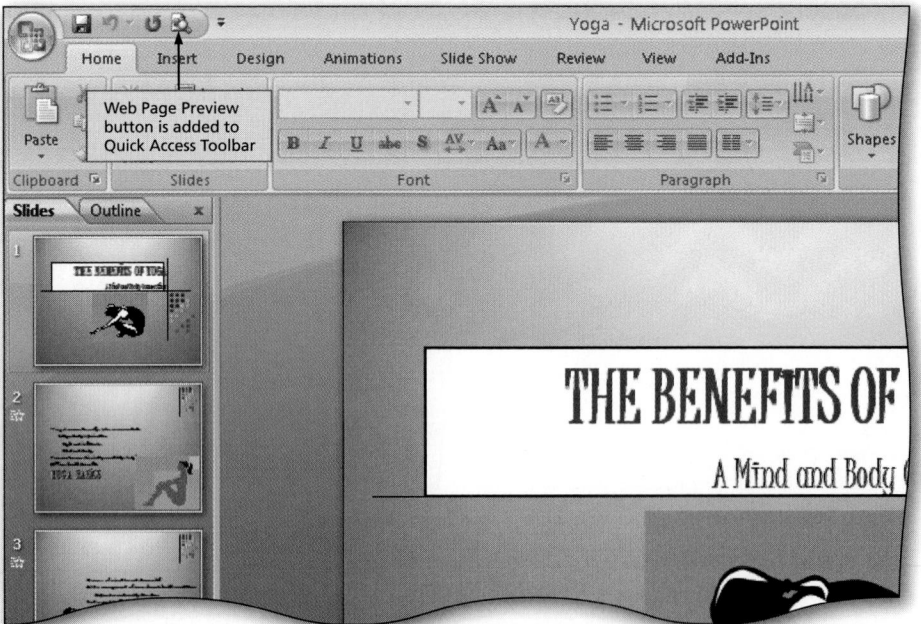

Figure 6

To Preview the Web Page

The following steps preview the presentation in a browser.

1

- Click the Web Page Preview button on the Quick Access Toolbar to display the Web page in your browser. If the Information Bar dialog box appears, click the Close button. If the security warning appears in the Information bar at the top of the Web page, click it and then click 'Allow Blocked Content' to run the ActiveX controls. If the Information Bar appears asking for an add-on from Microsoft, see your instructor.

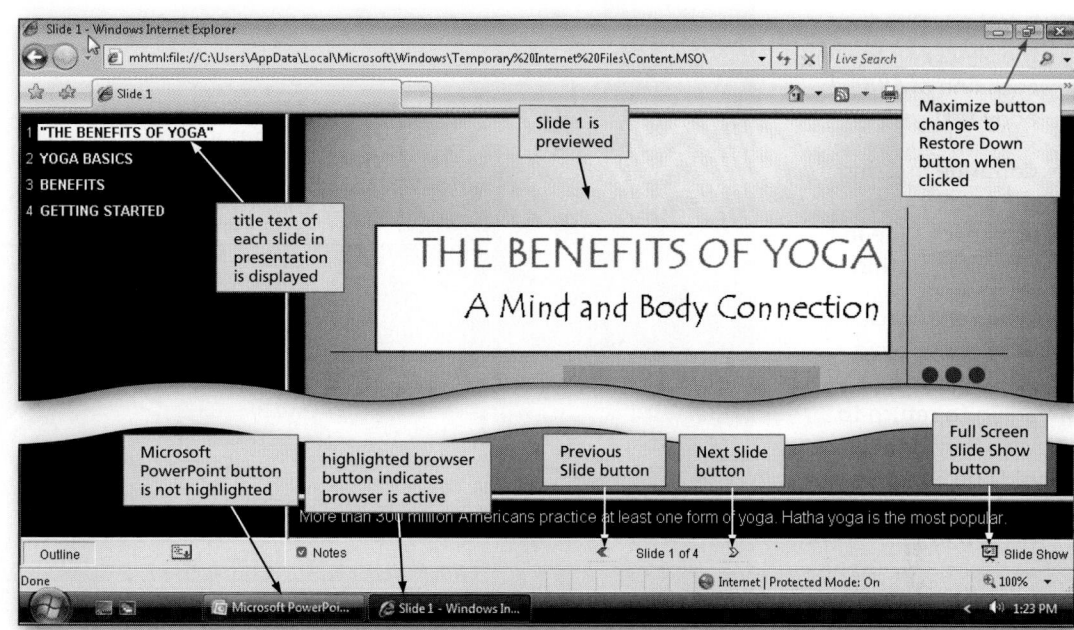

Figure 7

- If necessary, click the Maximize button on your browser's title bar (Figure 7).

Q&A What happens when I click the Web Page Preview button?

PowerPoint starts your browser and it displays a preview of how Slide 1 will appear as a Web page (Figure 7). The Web page preview is nearly identical to the display of the slide in PowerPoint.

2

- Click the Full Screen Slide Show button to have Slide 1 fill the entire screen (Figure 8).

Must I always view the full screen of each slide?

Q&A No. Viewing the slides in a full screen helps you review their style and spelling easily and allows you to see how the slides will be displayed when viewed in a browser.

Figure 8

3

- Press the SPACEBAR to display the Slide 2 title text. Continue pressing the SPACEBAR to view each line of Slide 2 body text.

- Continue pressing the SPACEBAR to view each slide in the presentation.

- When the black slide is displayed, press the SPACEBAR again to return to Web Page preview of Slide 1 in the browser window (Figure 9).

- Click the Close button on the right side of the browser title bar to close the browser and make PowerPoint active again.

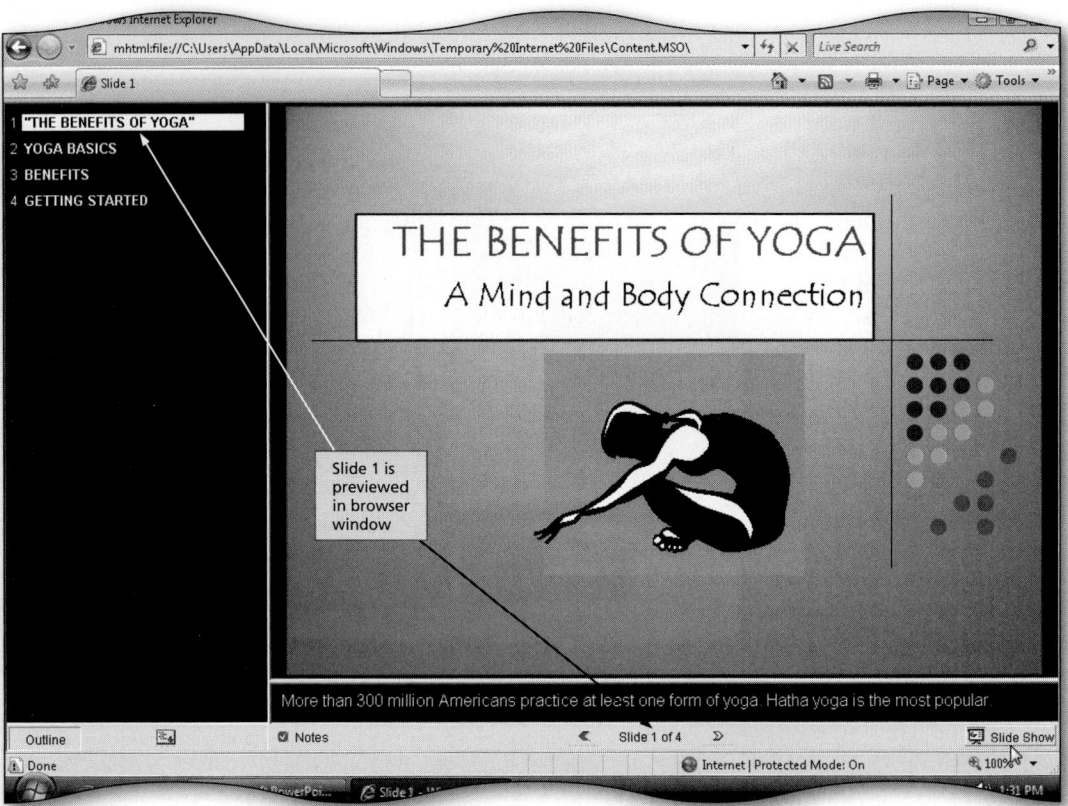

Figure 9

BTW

Viewing Transitions
If slide transitions do not appear when you are previewing your Web Page, you should check your Web Options settings. To do this, click the Office Button, click the PowerPoint Options button, click Advanced, scroll down and then click the Web Options button in the PowerPoint Options dialog box, if necessary click the General tab in the Web Options dialog box, and then click Show slide animation while browsing if it is not selected already.

Web Page Format Options

Once the preview of the presentation as a Web page is acceptable, you can save the presentation as a Web page so that others can view it using a Web browser, such as Internet Explorer or Mozilla Firefox.

You can save the presentation in one of two Web page formats. Both formats convert the contents of the presentation into HTML (HyperText Markup Language), which is a language browsers can interpret. One format is called **Single File Web Page format**, which saves all of the components of the Web page in a single file with an .mht extension. This format is useful particularly for e-mailing presentations in HTML format. The second format, called **Web Page format**, saves the Web page in a file and some of its components in a folder. This format is useful if you need access to the components, such as illustrations, that comprise the Web page.

To Save a PowerPoint Presentation as a Web Page in a Newly Created Folder

Experienced users organize the files saved on a storage medium, such as a USB flash drive or hard disk, by creating folders. They then save related files in a common folder. PowerPoint allows you to create folders before saving a file using the Save As dialog box. The following steps create a new folder on the USB flash drive and then save the Yoga presentation as a Web page in the new folder.

1

- With the Yoga presentation open, click the Office Button.

- Click Save As on the Office Button menu to display the Save As dialog box (Figure 10).

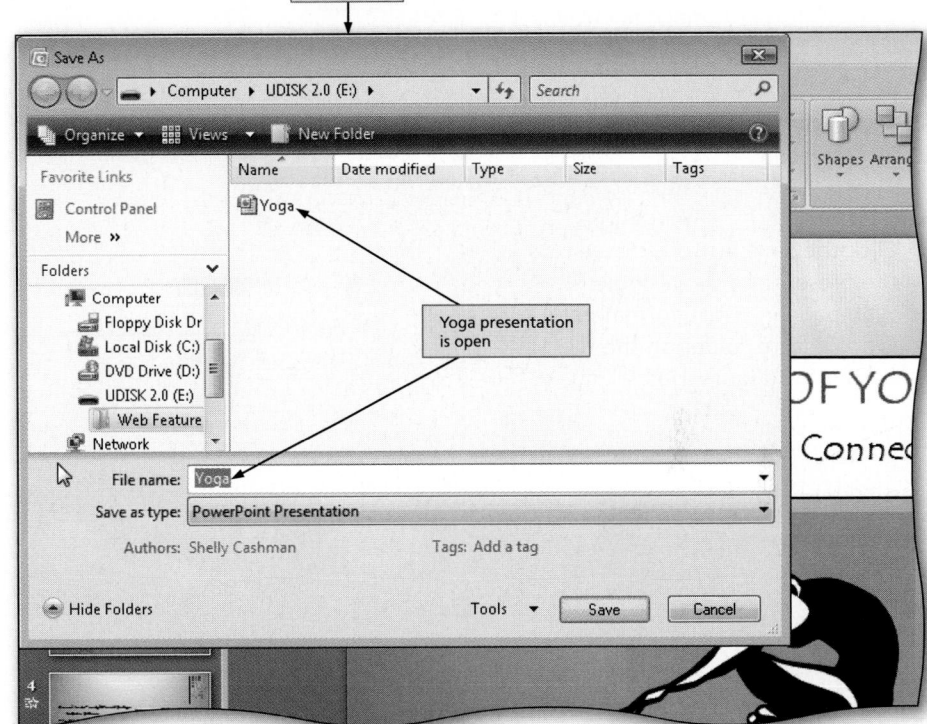

Figure 10

2

- Type `Yoga Web Page` in the File name text box.

- Click the 'Save as type' box arrow and then scroll down and click Single File Web Page.

- If the name of your USB flash drive does not appear in the Favorite Links section, click Computer in the Favorite Links section and then double-click UDISK 2.0 (E:) (your USB flash drive name and letter may be different).

- Click the New Folder button to create a new folder.

- When PowerPoint displays the new folder named New Folder, type `Web Feature` in the text box (Figure 11).

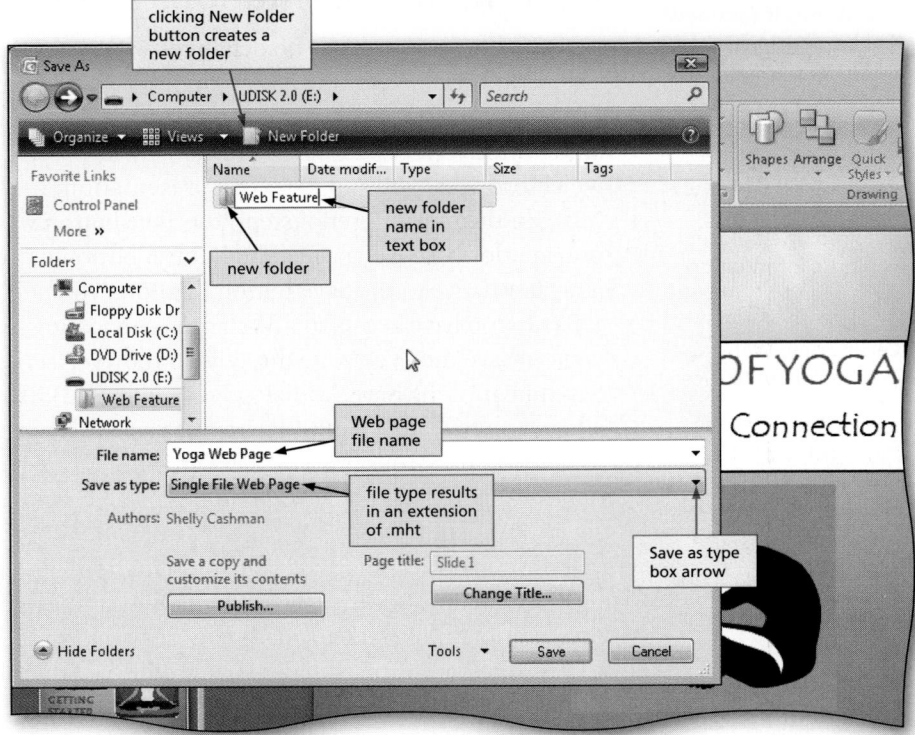

Figure 11

3

- Press the ENTER key. If the Microsoft Office PowerPoint dialog box appears, click the Yes button.

What does PowerPoint do when I press the ENTER key?

PowerPoint automatically selects the new folder Web Feature in the Address bar. PowerPoint saves all slides in the presentation as Web pages.

4

- Click the Save button to save the presentation in a single file Web page in HTML format in the Web Feature folder on the USB flash drive (Figure 12).

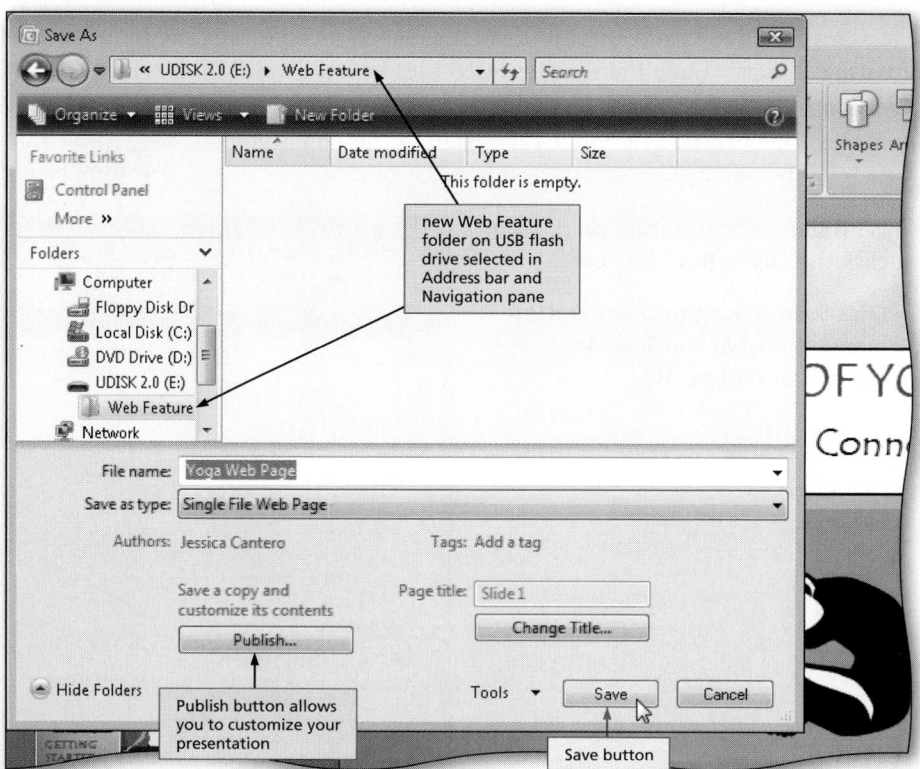

Figure 12

BTW

Certification
The Microsoft Certified Application Specialist (MCAS) program provides an opportunity for you to obtain a valuable industry credential – proof that you have the PowerPoint 2007 skills required by employers. For more information see Appendix G or visit the PowerPoint 2007 Certification Web page (scsite.com/ppt2007/cert).

Publishing Presentations as Web Pages

The Save As dialog box changes when you select Single File Web Page in the 'Save as type' box. When you use the Single File Web Page format, a Save area appears in the dialog box. Within the Save area is a Publish button (Figure 12). Some publishing options allow you to select particular slides for your presentation, display speaker notes, and select which browsers will support your presentation.

In the previous set of steps, the Save button was used to save the PowerPoint presentation as a Web page. The Publish button in the Save As dialog box shown in Figure 12 is an alternative to the Save button. It allows you to customize the Web page further.

If you have access to a Web server that allows you to save files in a Web folder, then you can save the Web page directly on the Web server by clicking the Network folder in the Save in bar of the Save As dialog box (Figure 12). If you have access to a Web server that allows you to save on an FTP site, then you can select the FTP site below FTP locations in the Save in box just as you select any folder on which to save a file. To learn more about publishing Web pages in a Web folder or on an FTP location using Office applications, refer to Appendix D.

After PowerPoint saves the presentation in Step 4, it displays the MHTML file – not the presentation – in the PowerPoint window. PowerPoint can continue to display the presentation in HTML format, because within the MHTML file that it created, it also saved the PowerPoint formats that allow it to display the MHTML file in PowerPoint. This is referred to as **round tripping** the MHTML file back to the application in which it was created.

To Reset the Quick Access Toolbar and Quit PowerPoint

Your work with the PowerPoint presentation is complete. The following steps remove the Web Page Preview button from the Quick Access Toolbar and quit PowerPoint.

1 Click the Customize the Quick Access Toolbar button on the Ribbon.

2 Click the More Commands command.

3 When the PowerPoint Options dialog box is displayed, click the Reset button. If the Reset Customizations dialog box is displayed, click the Yes button.

4 Click the OK button on the PowerPoint Options dialog box to close it.

5 Click the Close button on the Microsoft PowerPoint title bar.

Q&A Do I need to remove the button from the Quick Access Toolbar?

No. For consistency, the Quick Access Toolbar is reset after the added buttons are no longer needed. If you share a computer with others, you should reset the Quick Access Toolbar.

File Management Tools in PowerPoint

In the previous set of steps, PowerPoint automatically navigates to the new folder name in the Save in box when you press the ENTER key after typing the new folder name (Figure 12). It was not necessary to create a new folder earlier in this Web feature. You nevertheless could have saved the Web page on the USB flash drive in the same manner in which you saved files on the USB flash drive in the previous projects. Creating a new folder, however, allows you to organize your work.

Finally, once you create a folder, you can right-click it while the Save As dialog box is active and perform many file management tasks directly in PowerPoint (Figure 13). For example, once the shortcut menu appears, you can rename the selected folder, delete it, copy it, display its properties, and perform other file management functions.

BTW

Quick Reference
For a table that lists how to complete the tasks covered in this book using the mouse, Ribbon, shortcut menu, and keyboard, see the Quick Reference Summary at the back of this book, or visit the PowerPoint 2007 Quick Reference Web page (scsite.com/ppt2007/qr).

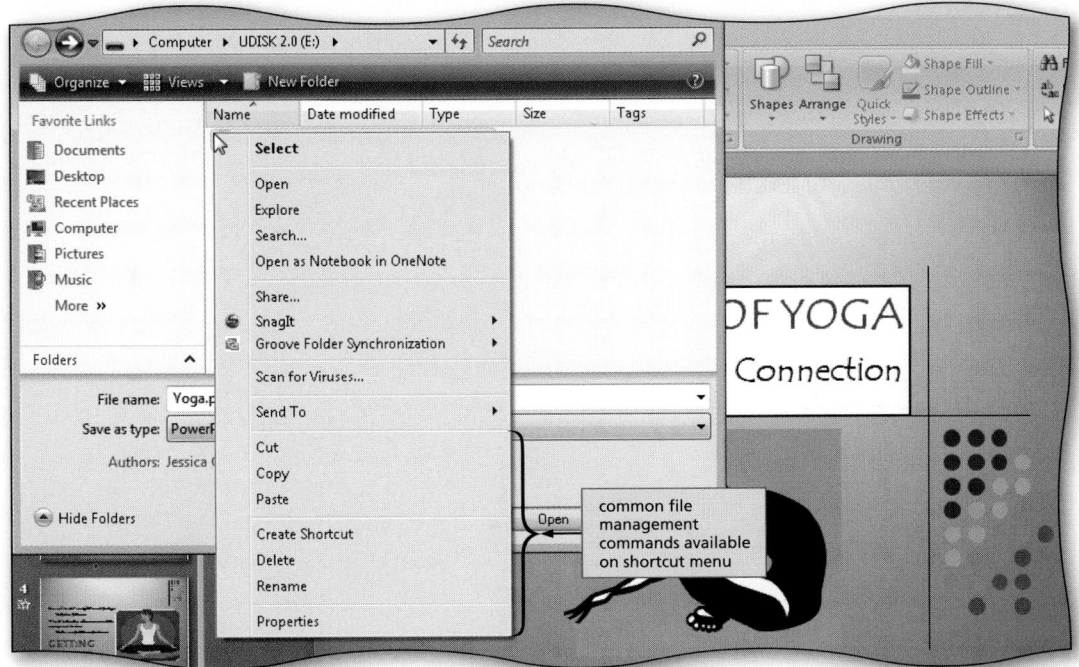

common file management commands available on shortcut menu

Figure 13

To View the Web Page Using a Browser

With the Web page saved in the Web Feature folder on the USB flash drive, you now can view it using a browser. If you want to display or hide the navigation frame, click the Show/Hide Outline button below the outline. Later, if you want to redisplay the navigation frame, click the Show/Hide Outline button again. Similarly, the Show/Hide Notes button below the slide frame allows you to display or conceal the speaker notes, if present, on a particular slide. To review a slide you have seen already, click the Previous Slide button. The following steps view the Yoga Web page using your browser.

- If necessary, connect the USB flash drive to one of the computer's USB ports.

- Click the Start button on the Windows Vista taskbar, click All Programs on the Start menu, and then click Internet Explorer on the All Programs list.

- When the Internet Explorer window appears, type `E:\Web Feature\ Yoga Web Page.mht` in the Address bar and then press the ENTER key to display the Web page in your browser (Figure 14). (Your USB flash drive may have a different name and letter).

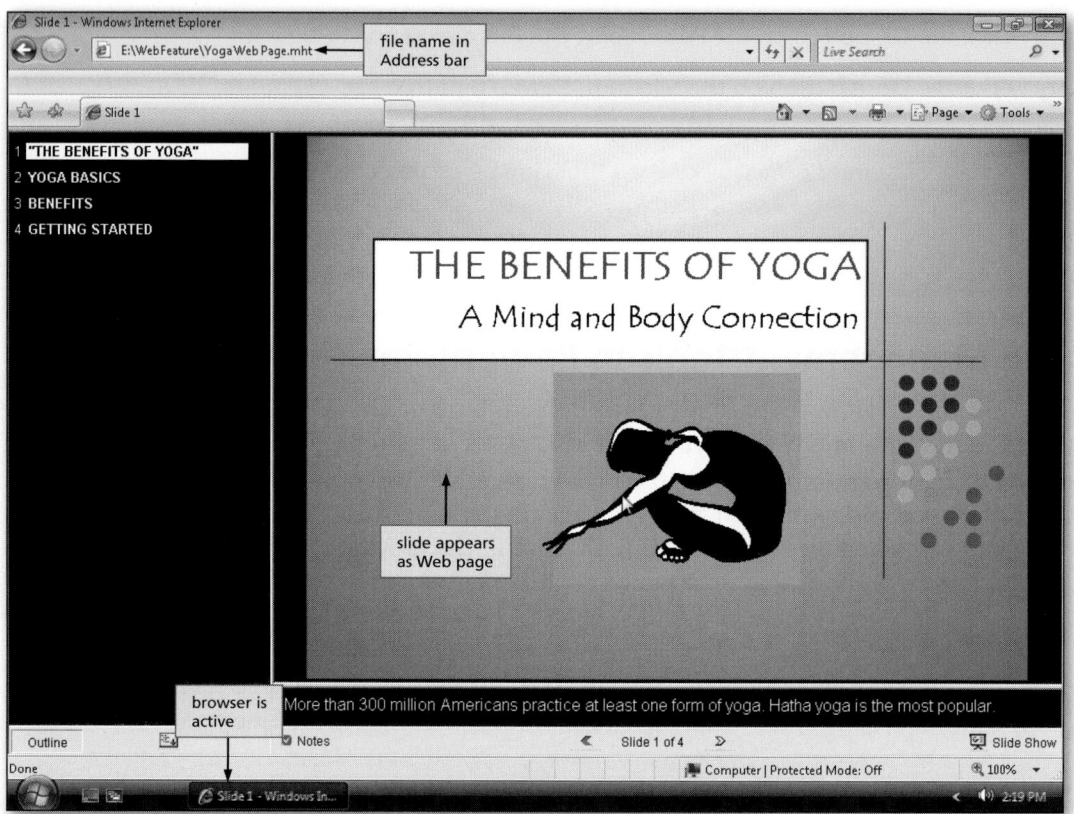

Figure 14

- If the Internet Explorer dialog box appears, click the OK button, right-click the first Internet Explorer button on the Windows Vista taskbar, and then click Close on the shortcut menu. If a security warning appears in the Information Bar, click it to view the options and then click Allow Blocked Content on the shortcut menu.

- If the Security Warning dialog box is displayed, click the Yes button.

Q&A What are the benefits of using a browser to view a presentation?

You can see from Figures 14 and 15 that a Web page is an ideal way to distribute information to a large group of people. For example, the Web page could be published on a Web server connected to the Internet and made available to anyone with a computer, browser, and the address of the Web page. It also can be e-mailed easily, because the Web page resides in a single file, rather than in a file and folder. Publishing a Web page of a presentation, thus, is an excellent alternative to distributing printed copies of the presentation.

Q&A Can I review a slide I have seen already?

Yes. Click the Previous Slide button.

- Click the Expand/
  Collapse Outline but-
  ton at the bottom
  of the window to
  display the text of
  each slide in outline
  form in the naviga-
  tion frame.

- Click the Next Slide
  button three times
  to view all four slides
  in your browser
  (Figure 15).

Q&A

What if I want to
display or hide the
navigation and notes
frames?

To hide the naviga-
tion frame, click the
Show/Hide Outline
button below the
outline. Later, if
you want to redis-
play the navigation
frame, click the
Show/Hide Outline
button again. Similarly,
the Show/Hide Notes button below the slide frame allows you to display or conceal the speaker notes, if present, on a
particular slide.

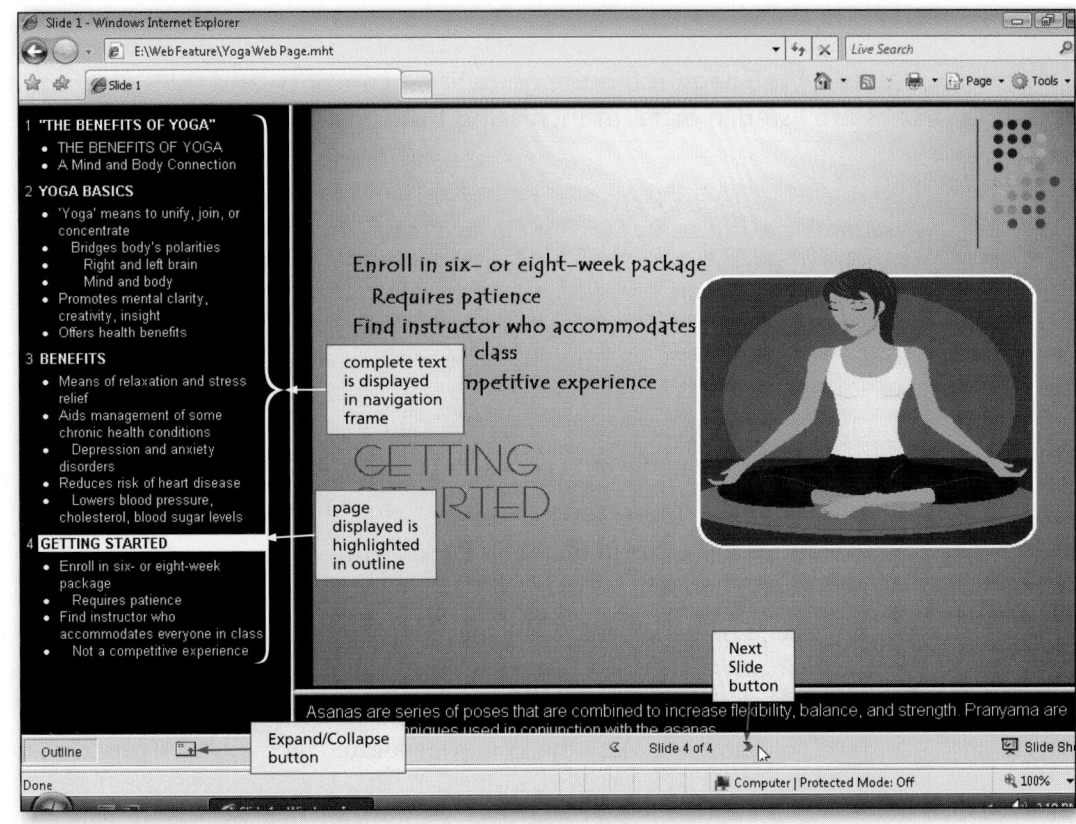

Figure 15

❸

- Click the Close button on the right side of the browser title bar to close the browser.

Feature Summary

This Web feature introduced you to customizing the Quick Access Toolbar, previewing a presentation as a Web page, creating a new folder on a USB flash drive, and viewing a Web page. The items listed below include all the new Office 2007 skills you have learned in this Web feature.

1. Add a Button to the Quick Access Toolbar (PPT 148)
2. Preview the Web Page (PPT 151)
3. Save a PowerPoint Presentation as a Web Page in a Newly Created Folder (PPT 153)

4. Reset the Quick Access Toolbar and Quit Power Point (PPT 155)
5. View the Web Page Using a Browser (PPT 156)

In the Lab

Create a Web page using the guidelines, concepts, and skills presented in this Web feature. Labs are listed in order of increasing difficulty.

Lab 1: Creating a Web Page from the A World Beneath the Waves Presentation

Problem: Dave Ehlin, the Student Government Association (SGA) president, wants to expand the visibility of the A World Beneath the Waves presentation you created in Chapter 1. He believes a Web page would be an excellent vehicle to help promote the spring break trip to Cabo San Lucas, Mexico and has asked you to help transfer the presentation to the Internet.

Instructions:

1. Open the Cabo Package presentation shown in Figure 1–1 on page PPT 5 that you created in Chapter 1. (If you did not create this presentation, see your instructor for a copy.)

2. Add the Web Page Preview command to the Quick Access Toolbar.

3. Review the five slides in the Cabo Package presentation, and then preview the presentation as a Web page. Close the browser.

4. Save the presentation as a single file Web page in a new folder titled Web Feature Exercises using the file name, Lab WF-1 Cabo Package Web Page. Reset the Quick Access Toolbar and then quit PowerPoint.

5. Start your browser. With the Web page located on the USB flash drive, type `E:\Web Feature Exercises\Lab WF-1 Cabo Package Web Page.mht` in the Address bar (your USB flash drive may have a different name and letter). When the browser displays the Web page, click the Expand/Collapse Outline button at the bottom of the window to display the text of each slide in outline form.

6. Click the Next Slide button at the bottom of the window to view the slides. Close the browser. Submit the assignment as requested by your instructor.

In the Lab

Lab 2: Creating and Printing a Web Page from the Identity Theft Presentation

Problem: The Identity Theft presentation you developed in Chapter 2 could provide useful information for consumers, so you want to save this presentation as a Web page and post it to the Internet.

Instructions:

1. Open the Identity Theft presentation shown in Figure 2–1 on page PPT 83 that you created in Chapter 2. (If you did not create this presentation, see your instructor for a copy.)

2. Add the Web Page Preview command to the Quick Access Toolbar.

3. Review the four slides in the Identity Theft presentation, and then preview the presentation as a Web page. Close the browser.

4. Save the presentation as a Web page (select Web Page in the Save as type box) in the Web Feature Exercises folder using the file name, Lab WF-2 Identity Theft Web Page. Reset the Quick Access Toolbar and then quit PowerPoint. Saving the presentation as a Web page, rather than a single file Web page, will result in an additional folder being added to the Web Feature Exercises folder.

5. Start your browser. With the Web page located on the USB flash drive, type `E:\Web Feature Exercises\Lab WF-2 Identity Theft Web Page.mht` in the Address bar (your USB flash drive may have a different name and letter). When the browser displays the Web page, click the Next Slide button at the bottom of the window to view the slides.

6. Print the Web page by clicking the Print button on the Toolbar.

7. Close the browser. Submit the assignment as requested by your instructor.

Continued >

In the Lab

Lab 3: File Management within PowerPoint

Problem: One of your classmates has asked you to teach him how to perform basic file management tasks from within PowerPoint.

Instructions:

1. Start PowerPoint and then click the Open command on the Office Button menu. When PowerPoint displays the Open dialog box, create a new folder called In the Lab 3 on your USB flash drive.

2. Use the shortcut menu to complete the following tasks: (1) rename the In the Lab 3 folder to In the Lab 3A; (2) show the properties of the In the Lab 3A folder; and (3) delete the In the Lab 3A folder.

1 Managing E-Mail and Contacts with Outlook

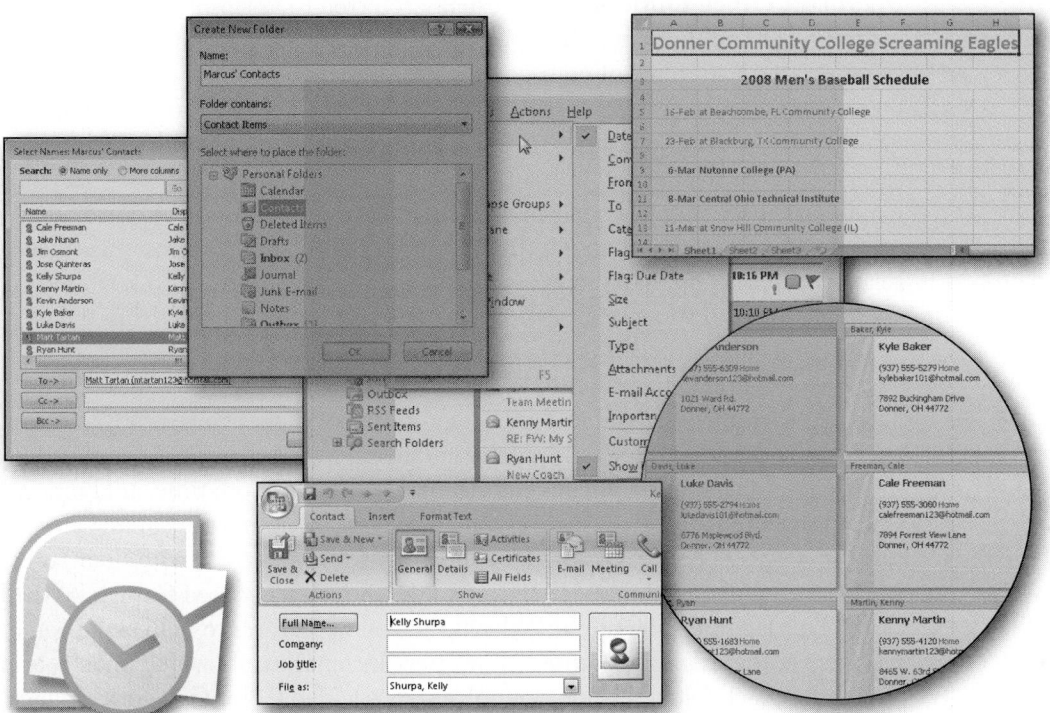

Objectives

You will have mastered the material in this chapter when you can:

- Start and quit Outlook
- Open, read, print, reply to, and delete electronic mail messages
- View a file attachment
- Create and insert an e-mail signature
- Compose, format, and send e-mail messages
- Insert a file attachment in an e-mail message
- Flag, categorize, sort, and filter e-mail messages

- Set e-mail importance, sensitivity, and delivery options
- Create a personal folder
- Create and print a contact list
- Use the Find a Contact feature
- Organize the contact list
- Track activities of a contact
- Use Outlook's Help

1 | Managing E-Mail and Contacts with Outlook

What Is Microsoft Office Outlook 2007?

Microsoft Office Outlook 2007, usually referred to as simply Outlook, is a powerful communications and scheduling program that helps you communicate with others (Figure 1–1), keep track of your contacts, and organize your calendar. Personal information management (PIM) programs such as Outlook provide a way for individuals and work-groups to organize, find, view, and share information easily. Outlook allows you to send and receive electronic mail (e-mail) and permits you to engage in real-time messaging with family, friends, or coworkers using instant messaging. Outlook also provides you with the means to organize your contacts. Users can track e-mail messages, meetings, and notes related to a particular contact. Outlook's Calendar, Contacts, Tasks, and Notes components aid in this organization. Contact information readily is available from the Outlook Calendar, Mail, Contacts, and Task components by accessing the Find a Contact feature.

Electronic mail (e-mail) is the transmission of messages and files over a computer network. E-mail has become an important means of exchanging information and files between business associates, classmates and instructors, friends, and family. Businesses find that using e-mail to send documents electronically saves both time and money. Parents with students away at college or relatives who are scattered across the country find that communicating by e-mail is an inexpensive and easy way to stay in touch with their family members. In fact, exchanging e-mail messages is one of the more widely used features of the Internet.

This latest version of Outlook has many new features to help make you more productive. For example, Outlook now offers Instant Search, which finds your information, no matter which folder it is in. Outlook also has added Color Categories, which let you apply the same color category to e-mail, calendar, and task items so you can visually locate all associated items. Outlook has added flags you can use to create and mark a follow-up item for tracking. The new To-Do Bar is a feature that integrates tasks, e-mail messages flagged for follow up, and calendar information in a toolbar located adjacent to the Reading pane.

To illustrate the features of Outlook, this book presents a series of projects that use Outlook to create and send e-mail messages and create and manage a contact list.

Project Planning Guidelines

> The process of composing an e-mail message that communicates specific information requires careful analysis and planning. As a starting point, establish why the message is needed. Once the purpose is determined, analyze the intended readers of the message and their unique needs. Then, gather information about the topic and decide what to include in the message. Finally, determine the document design and style that will be most successful at delivering the message. Creating a contact list is simply a matter of who you want to add to the list. The contact list can be used to store people you have frequent contact with via e-mail, telephone, or fax. The contact list can also be used as a mailing list. Each project in this book provides practical applications of these planning considerations.

Project — Communicating Over the Internet

The project in this chapter follows general guidelines and uses Outlook to create the contacts and messages shown in Figure 1–1. To communicate with individuals and groups, you typically send or deliver some kind of message. Telephone calls, faxes, and letters are examples of messages. E-mail is a convenient way to send information to multiple recipients simultaneously, instantly, and inexpensively.

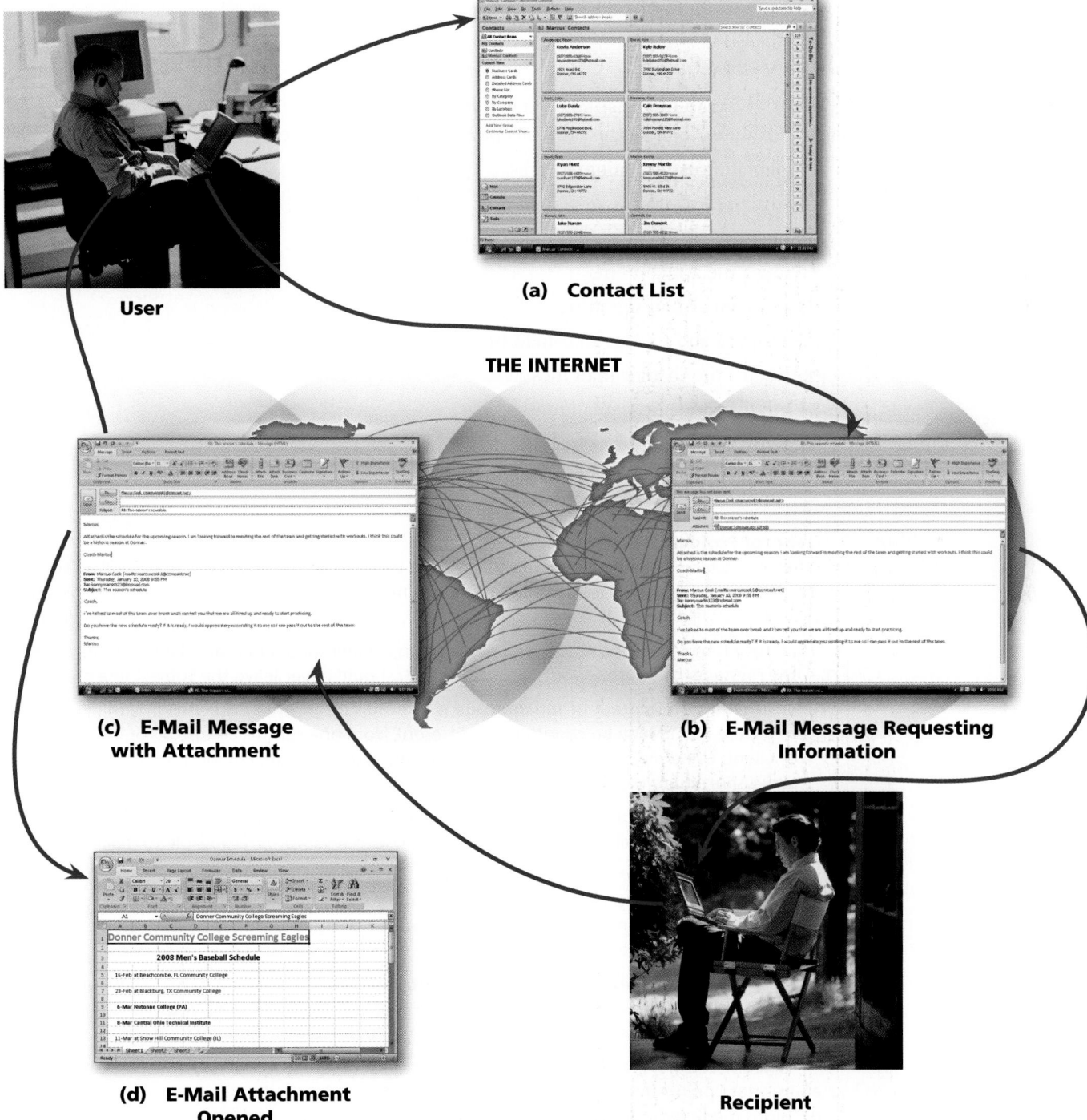

User

(a) Contact List

THE INTERNET

(c) E-Mail Message with Attachment

(b) E-Mail Message Requesting Information

(d) E-Mail Attachment Opened

Recipient

Figure 1–1

As the captain of the Donner Community College baseball team, you use Outlook to keep the players up to date with team information using your school e-mail system. You also use the contact list to store addresses and phone numbers of each member of the team. The project uses the communications features of Outlook to compose, send, and read e-mail messages. In addition to using Outlook's communication tools, this project shows you how to create and organize a contact list. Using the contact list (Figure 1–1a on the previous page), a user selects a recipient for an e-mail message and then sends an e-mail message requesting information from the recipient (Figure 1–1b). The recipient replies by sending an e-mail message (Figure 1–1c) and includes the requested information as an attachment (Figure 1–1d), or a file included with the e-mail message, that the recipient can open.

Overview

As you read this chapter, you will learn how to communicate over the Internet as shown in Figure 1–1 on the previous page by performing these general tasks:

- Open and read e-mail messages.
- Print an e-mail message.
- Reply to and forward an e-mail message.
- View a file attachment.
- Create an e-mail signature.
- Compose and format an e-mail message.
- Attach a file to an e-mail message.
- Organize and sort e-mail messages.
- Create and organize a contact list.
- Print a contact list.

Plan Ahead

General Project Guidelines

When creating an e-mail message, the actions you perform and decisions you make will affect the appearance and characteristics of the finished message. As you create an e-mail message such as those shown in Figure 1–1 on the previous page, you should follow these general guidelines:

1. **Choose the words for the Subject line.** The Subject line should indicate the main subject of the message. Use as few words as possible. You should never leave the Subject line blank.

2. **Ensure that the content of the message is appropriate for the recipient.** An e-mail sent to a close friend may be considerably different from one sent to an instructor, coworker, or client. Use e-mail etiquette when composing your message. For work related e-mails, avoid shortening words or using abbreviations (i.e., u for you, r for are, 2 for to, etc.).

3. **Choose the words for the text.** Follow the *less is more* guideline. The less text, the more likely the message will be read to completion. Use as few words as possible to make a point.

4. **Identify how to format various elements of the text.** The overall appearance of a message significantly affects its ability to communicate clearly. Examples of how you can modify the appearance, or format, of text include changing its shape, size, color, and position on the page.

5. **Alert the recipient when sending large file attachments.** Some e-mail servers allow file attachments up to a certain size. If possible, compress large files using WinZip or comparable software. If several attachments are required, you may have to send multiple e-mails.

When necessary, more specific details concerning the above guidelines are presented at appropriate points in the chapter. The chapter also will identify the actions performed and decisions made regarding these guidelines during the creation of the messages shown in Figure 1–1 on the previous page.

Starting and Customizing Outlook

If you are using a computer to step through the project in this chapter and you want your screen to match the figures in this book, you should change your screen's resolution to 1024 × 768. For information about how to change a computer's resolution, read Appendix E.

To Start and Customize Outlook

The following steps, which assume Windows Vista is running, start Outlook based on a typical installation. You may need to ask your instructor how to start Outlook for your computer.

Note: If you are using Windows XP, see Appendix F for alternate steps.

1

- Click the Start button on the Windows Vista taskbar to display the Start menu.

- Click All Programs at the bottom of the left pane on the Start menu to display the All Programs list.

- Click Microsoft Office in the All Programs list to display the Microsoft Office list (Figure 1–2).

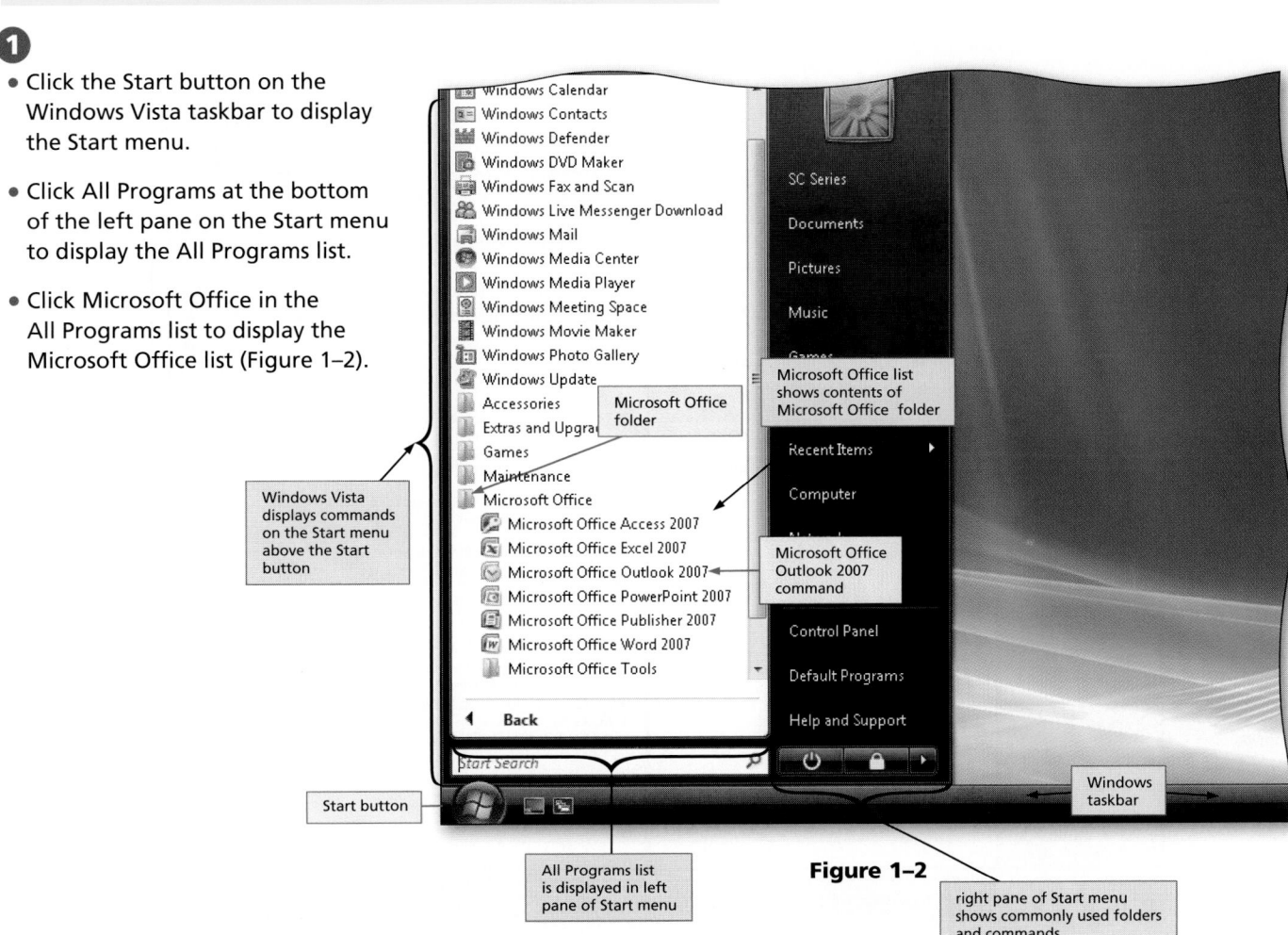

Figure 1–2

● Click Microsoft Office Outlook 2007 to start Outlook. If necessary, click the Mail button in the Navigation Pane and then click the Inbox folder in the Mail Folders pane to display the Inbox message pane (Figure 1–3).

● If the Inbox – Microsoft Office Outlook window is not maximized, click the Maximize button next to the Close button on its title bar to maximize the window.

Q&A

What is a maximized window?

A maximized window fills the entire screen. When you maximize a window, the Maximize button changes to a Restore Down button.

● Drag the right border of the Inbox message pane to the right so that the Inbox message pane and the Reading pane have the same width.

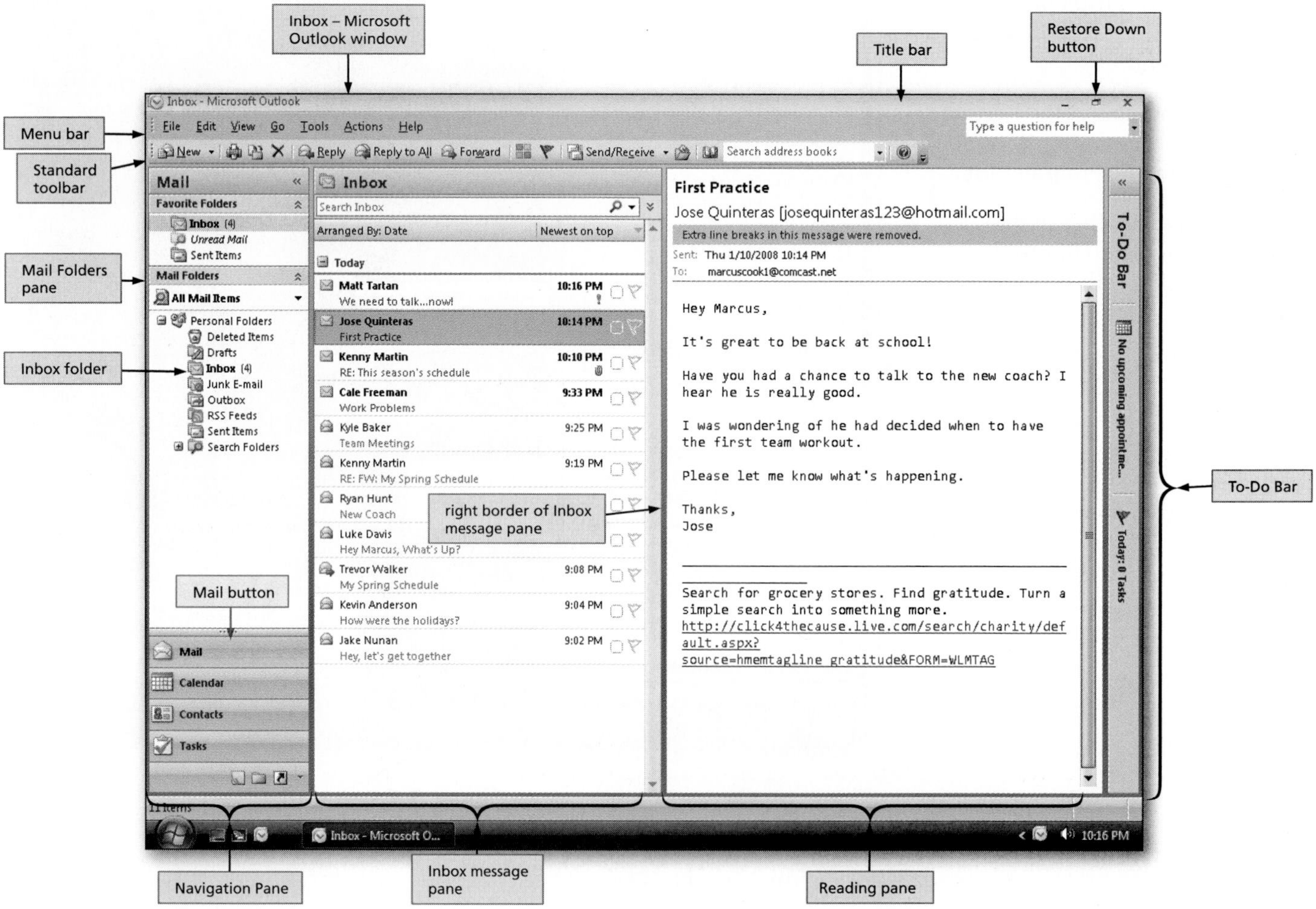

Figure 1–3

Other Ways

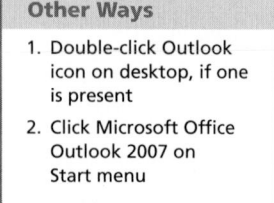

1. Double-click Outlook icon on desktop, if one is present
2. Click Microsoft Office Outlook 2007 on Start menu

The Inbox — Microsoft Outlook Window

The Inbox – Microsoft Outlook window shown in Figure 1–3 comprises a number of elements that you will use consistently as you work in the Outlook environment. Figure 1–4 illustrates the Standard toolbar, located below the title bar and the menu bar. The Standard toolbar contains buttons specific to Outlook. The button names indicate their functions. Each button can be clicked to perform a frequently used task, such as creating a new mail message, printing, or sending and receiving mail.

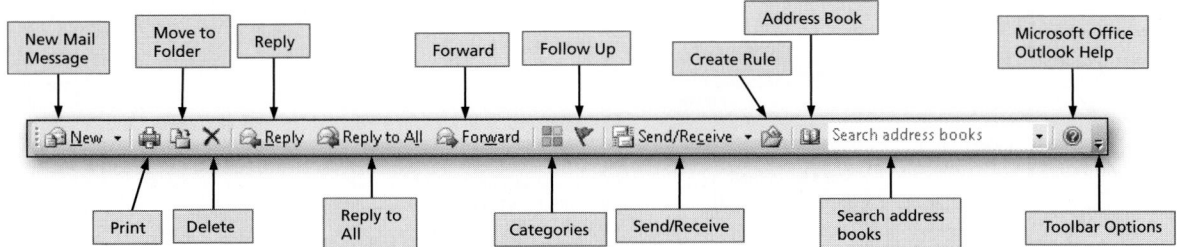

Figure 1–4

The Inbox – Microsoft Outlook window is divided into four panes: the Navigation Pane on the left side of the window, the Inbox message pane to the left of center, the Reading pane to the right of center, and the To-Do Bar on the far right side of the window (Figure 1–5 on the next page).

Navigation Pane The **Navigation Pane** (Figure 1–5) is set up to help you navigate Microsoft Outlook while using any of the program's components (Mail, Calendar, Contacts, or Tasks). It comprises one or more panes and two sets of buttons. Although the two sets of buttons remain constant, the area of the Navigation Pane above the buttons changes depending on the active Outlook component. When you click the Mail button, Outlook displays Mail in the title bar of the Navigation Pane. When using Mail, the Navigation Pane includes two panes: Favorite Folders and Mail Folders. The **Favorite Folders** pane contains duplicate names of your favorite folders in the Mail Folders pane. To add a folder in the Mail Folders pane to the list of favorite folders, right-click the folder and then click the Add to Favorite Folders.

Below the Favorite Folders pane, the **Mail Folders** pane contains a set of folders associated with the communications tools of Outlook Mail (Deleted Items, Drafts, Inbox, Junk E-mail, Outbox, RSS Feeds, Sent Items, and Search Folders).

The **Deleted Items folder** holds messages that you have deleted. As a safety precaution, you can retrieve deleted messages from the Deleted Items folder if you later decide to keep them. Deleting messages from the Deleted Items folder permanently removes the messages from Outlook. The **Drafts folder** retains copies of messages that you are not yet ready to send. The **Inbox folder** is the destination for incoming mail. The **Junk E-mail folder** is the destination folder for unwanted messages or messages of an unknown origin. You can customize the settings for Outlook to direct only messages that meet certain criteria to the Inbox folder. Messages not meeting those criteria are sent to the Junk E-mail folder. The **Outbox folder** temporarily holds messages you send until Outlook delivers the messages. The **RSS Feeds folder** is new to Outlook. **Really Simple Syndication (RSS)** feeds allow you to receive current information from sources that are updated frequently, such as news headlines or blogs, without having to visit the various Web sites. The **Sent Items folder** retains copies of messages that you have sent. The **Search Folders folder** is actually a group of folders that allows you to group your messages easily in one of three ways – messages for follow up, large messages, or unread messages.

BTW

The Inbox Window
The screen in Figure 1–3 on the previous page shows how the Inbox window looks after you have received several e-mail messages. Your screen may look different depending on your screen resolution and Outlook settings.

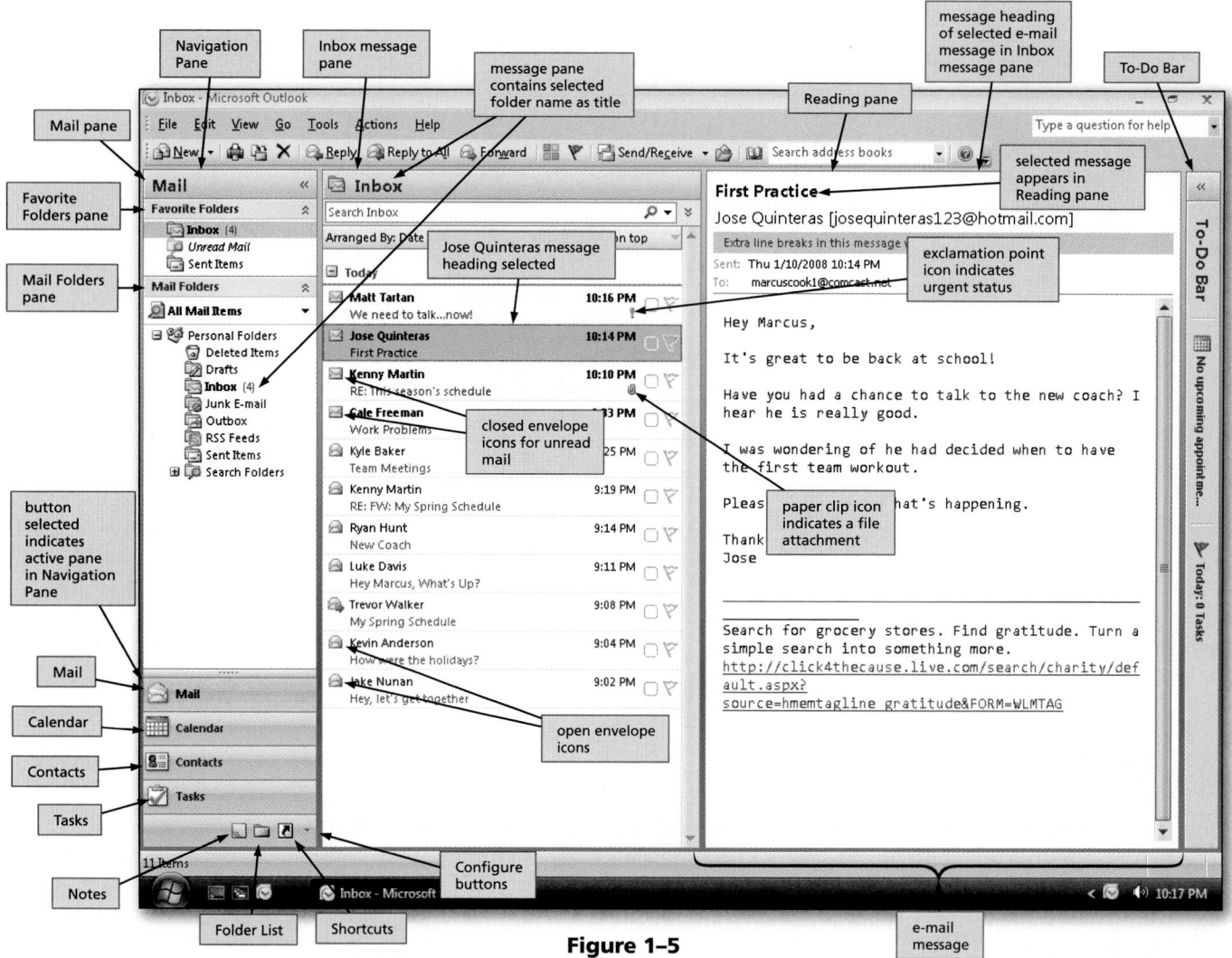

Figure 1–5

Folders can contain e-mail messages, faxes, and files created in other Windows applications. Folders in bold type followed by a number in parentheses, such as **Inbox** (4), indicate the number of messages in the folder that are unopened. Other folders may appear on your computer instead of or in addition to the folders shown in Figure 1–5.

The two sets of buttons at the bottom of the Navigation Pane contain shortcuts to the major components of Outlook (Mail, Calendar, Contacts, Tasks, Notes, Folder List, Shortcuts, and Configure buttons).

Message Pane The Inbox **message pane** (shown in Figure 1–5) lists the contents of the folder selected in the Mail Folders pane. In Figure 1–5, the Inbox folder is selected. Thus, the message pane lists the e-mails received.

Figure 1–6 shows the Arranged By shortcut menu that appears when you click or right-click the Arranged By column header in the Inbox message pane. The command you choose on the Arranged By shortcut menu causes Outlook to display a column header to the right indicating the sort order within the Arranged By grouping. In Figure 1–5, the Arranged By option is Date. This predefined pairing of a grouping and a sort (Arranged By: Date/Newest on top) is called an **arrangement**. Predefined arrangements allow you to sort your messages in various ways.

Several small icons may appear to the right of a message: an **exclamation point icon** indicates that the message is high priority and should be read immediately, a **paper clip icon** indicates that the message contains an attachment. A message heading that appears in bold

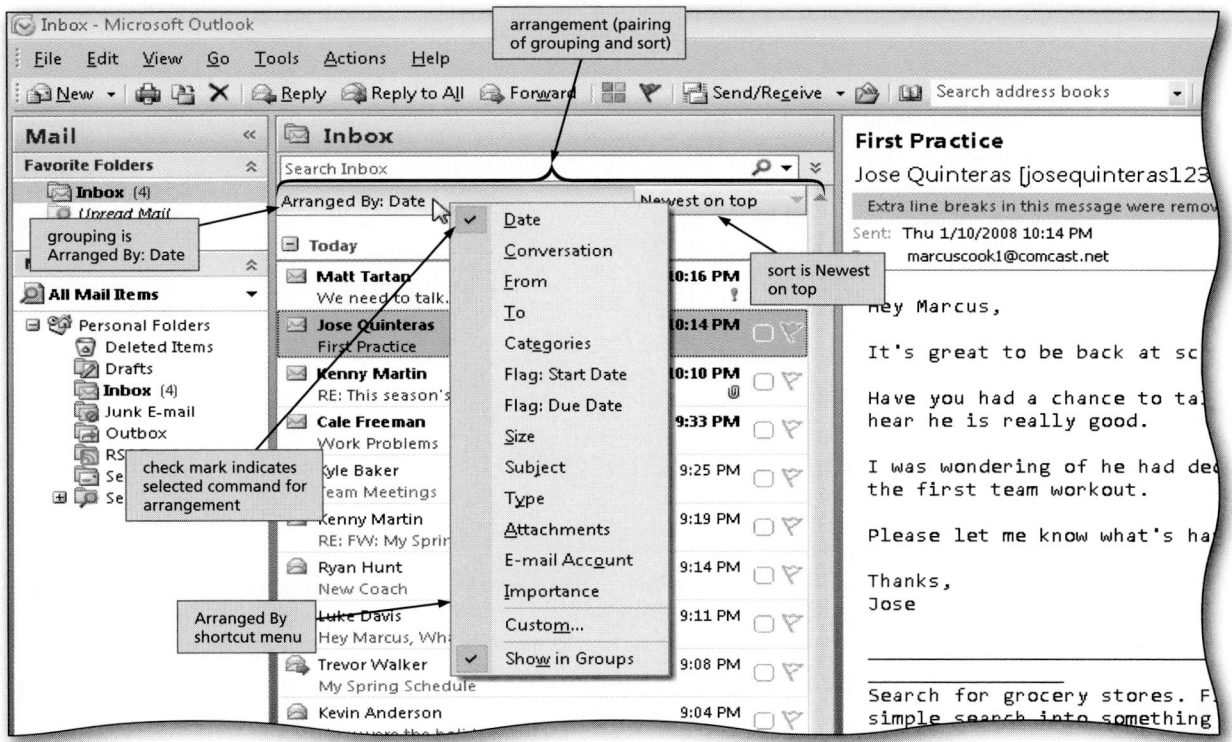

Figure 1–6

type with a **closed envelope icon** to the left identifies an unread e-mail message. An **open envelope icon** indicates a read message. In Figure 1–5, the second e-mail message is highlighted and therefore is displayed in the Reading pane on the right. The closed envelope icon and bold message heading indicate the e-mail message has not been read. The e-mail messages on your computer may be different.

The closed envelope icon is one of several icons called **message list icons**, which appear to the left of the message heading. Message list icons indicate the status of the message. The icon may indicate an action that was performed by the sender or one that was performed by the recipient. The actions may include reading, replying to, forwarding, digitally signing, or encrypting a message. Table 1–1 contains a partial list of message list icons and the action performed on the e-mail message.

Table 1–1 Message List Icons and Actions			
Message List Icon	**Action**	**Message List Icon**	**Action**
	The message has been opened.		The message is in progress in the Drafts folder.
	The message has not been opened.		The message is digitally signed and unopened.
	The message has been replied to.		The message is digitally signed and opened.
	The message has been forwarded.		

Reading Pane   The Reading pane (Figure 1–5) contains the text of the selected e-mail message. The message header appears at the top of the Reading pane and contains the e-mail subject (First Practice), the sender's name and/or e-mail address (Jose Quinteras [josequinteras123@hotmail.com]), and the recipient's e-mail address (marcuscook1@ comcast.net). Outlook displays the text of the selected message below the message header. Using the View menu, you can display the Reading pane to the right of the message pane (vertically), as shown in Figure 1–5 on page OUT 8, or you can display it at the bottom of the message pane (horizontally) according to your personal preference.

To-Do Bar The To-Do Bar is a new feature in Outlook 2007. The To-Do Bar keeps e-mail messages flagged for follow up, tasks, appointments, and other calendar information in one place. When displayed, the To-Do Bar contains a Date Navigator, an appointment list, and a task list. The To-Do Bar is displayed by clicking the double arrow button at the top of the To-Do Bar (Figure 1–5).

BTW

Reading E-Mail Messages
If Outlook is not the active window on your screen, it still provides a mail notification alert informing you when you receive a new message. Outlook displays a semitransparent ScreenTip momentarily by the Outlook icon in the notification area, showing the sender's name, subject of the message, and the first few words of the message body.

Working with Incoming Messages

Note: If you are stepping through this project on a computer and you want your screen to appear the same as in the figures in the Mail component section of this project, then you should ask your instructor to help you (or see page OUT 67) to import Marcus' Inbox from the Data Files for Students. Once you have imported Marcus' Inbox, click the plus sign (+) next to the Inbox folder in the Mail Folders list, and then select Marcus' Inbox folder. See the inside back cover of this book for instructions for downloading the Data Files for Students or see your instructor for information about accessing files for this book.

To Open (Read) an E-Mail Message

To view the complete message in its own window, it must be opened. The following step opens the e-mail message from Jose Quinteras.

- Double-click the Jose Quinteras message heading in the Inbox message pane to display the First Practice window (Figure 1–7).

- If necessary, maximize the window.

Q&A What happens to the message heading in the message pane after the message is opened?

When you double-click the message heading in the message pane, Outlook changes the closed envelope icon to an opened envelope icon, and no longer displays the message heading in bold type.

Other Ways

1. Right-click message heading, click Open on shortcut menu
2. Click message heading, on File menu point to Open, click Selected Items on Open submenu
3. Select message heading, press CTRL+O

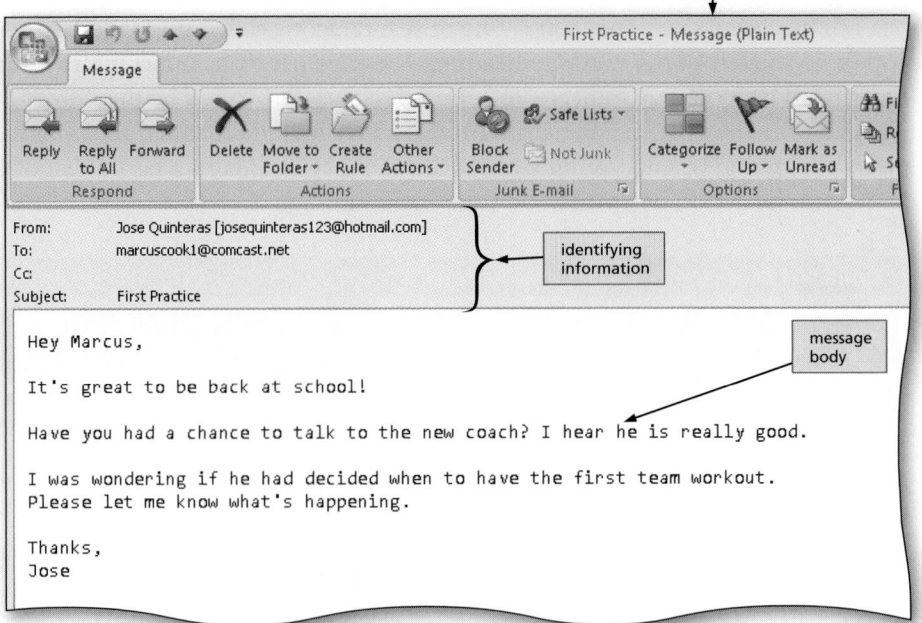

Figure 1–7

Ribbon

The **Ribbon**, located near the top of the Outlook window, is the control center in Outlook (Figure 1–8a). The Ribbon provides easy, central access to the tasks you perform while creating or working with a message, contact, calendar item, or task. The Ribbon consists of tabs, groups, and commands. Each **tab** surrounds a collection of groups, and each group contains related commands. Figure 1–8a illustrates the Ribbon for the Message window.

When you open a message, the Message window Ribbon displays the Message tab. The Message tab contains the more frequently used commands.

To display more of the document in the document window, some users prefer to minimize the Ribbon, which hides the groups on the Ribbon and displays only the Message tab (Figure 1–8b). To use commands on a minimized Ribbon, click the top-level tab.

Each time you open a message, the Ribbon appears the same way it did the last time you used Outlook. The chapters in this book, however, begin with the Ribbon appearing as it did at the initial installation of the software. If you are stepping through this chapter on a computer and you want your Ribbon to match the figures in this book, read Appendix E.

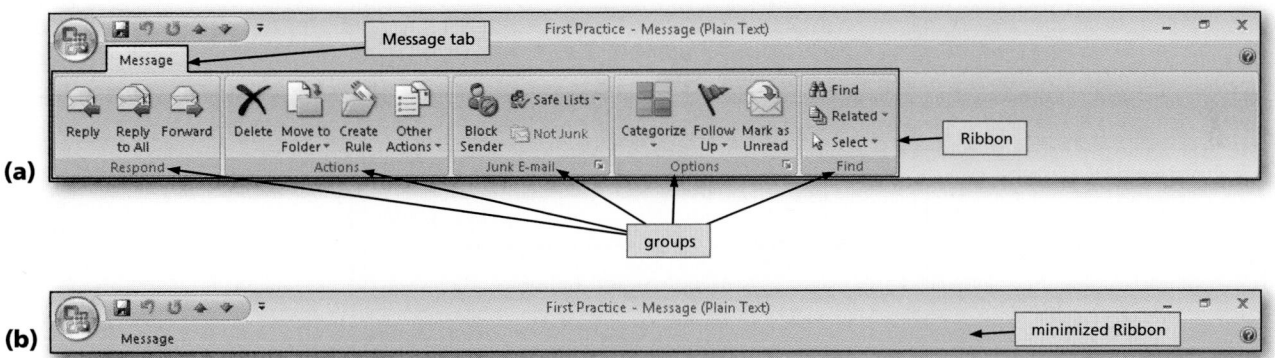

Figure 1–8

Some commands on the Ribbon display an image to help you remember their function. When you point to a command on the Ribbon, all or part of the command glows in shades of yellow and orange, and an **Enhanced ScreenTip** appears on the screen. An Enhanced ScreenTip is an on-screen note that provides the name of the command, available keyboard shortcut(s), a description of the command, and, sometimes, instructions for how to obtain help about the command (Figure 1–9). Enhanced ScreenTips are more detailed than a typical ScreenTip, which usually only displays the name of the command.

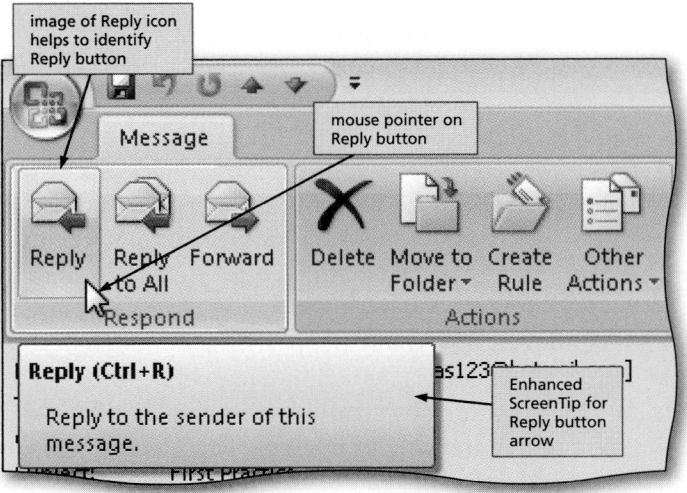

Figure 1–9

The lower-right corner of some groups on the Ribbon has a small arrow, called a **Dialog Box Launcher**, that when clicked displays a dialog box or a task pane with additional options for the group (Figure 1–10). When presented with a dialog box, you make selections and must close the dialog box before returning to the document. A **task pane**, by contrast, is a window that can remain open and visible while you work in the document.

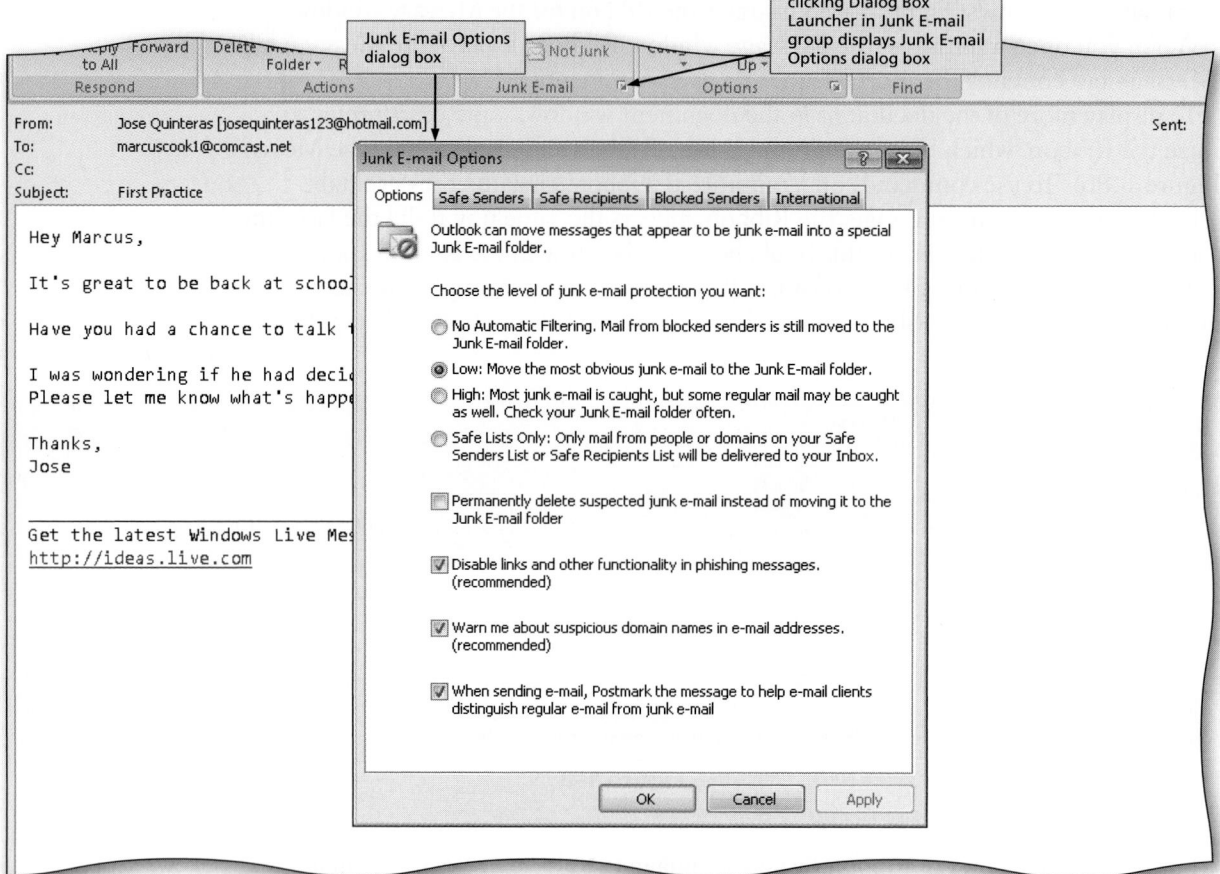

Figure 1–10

Quick Access Toolbar

The **Quick Access Toolbar**, located by default above the Ribbon, provides easy access to frequently used commands (Figure 1–11a). The commands on the Quick Access Toolbar always are available, regardless of the task you are performing. Initially, the Quick Access Toolbar contains the Save, Undo, and Redo commands. If you click the Customize Quick Access Toolbar button, Outlook provides a list of commands you quickly can add to and remove from the Quick Access Toolbar (Figure 1–11b).

You also can add other commands to or delete commands from the Quick Access Toolbar so that it contains the commands you use most often. As you add commands to the Quick Access Toolbar, its commands may interfere with the document title on the title bar. For this reason, Outlook provides an option of displaying the Quick Access Toolbar below the Ribbon (Figure 1–11c).

Each time you start Outlook, the Quick Access Toolbar appears the same way it did the last time you used Outlook. The chapters in this book, however, begin with the Quick Access Toolbar appearing as it did at the initial installation of the software. If you are stepping through this chapter on a computer and you want your Quick Access Toolbar to match the figures in this book, you should reset your Quick Access Toolbar. For more information about how to reset the Quick Access Toolbar, read Appendix E.

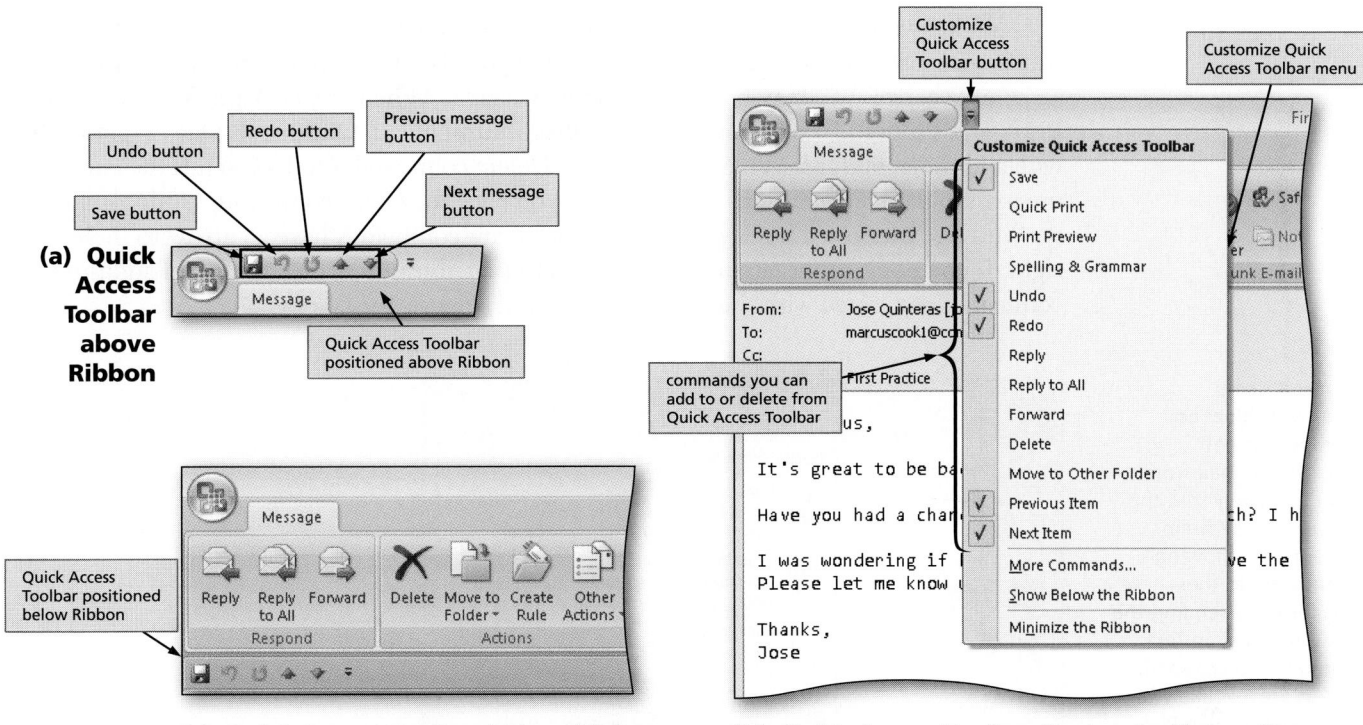

(a) **Quick Access Toolbar above Ribbon**

(c) **Quick Access Toolbar below Ribbon**

(b) **Quick Access Toolbar Customization options**

Figure 1–11

Office Button

While the Ribbon is a control center for creating documents, the **Office Button** is a central location for managing Outlook items. When you click the Office Button, located in the upper-left corner of the window, Outlook displays the Office Button menu (Figure 1–12). A **menu** contains a list of commands.

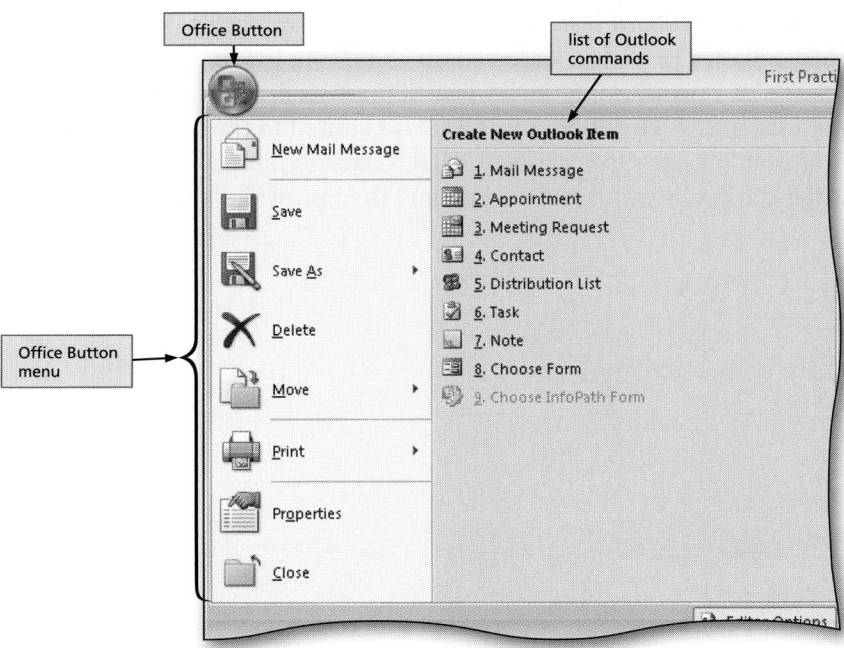

Figure 1–12

BTW

Quick Access Toolbar Commands
To add a Ribbon command to the Quick Access Toolbar, right-click the command on the Ribbon and then click Add to Quick Access Toolbar on the shortcut menu. To delete a command from the Quick Access Toolbar, right-click the command on the Quick Access Toolbar and then click Remove from Quick Access Toolbar on the shortcut menu. To display the Quick Access Toolbar below the Ribbon, right-click the Quick Access Toolbar and then click Show Quick Access Toolbar below the Ribbon on the shortcut menu.

When you click the New Mail Message command, Outlook opens the message window to compose a new mail message. When you click the Save command, Outlook saves any changes you may have made to the message. When you click the Save As, Move, Print, and Properties commands on the Office Button menu, Outlook displays a dialog box with additional options. When you click the Delete command, Outlook sends the current message to the Deleted Items folder. When you click the Close command, Outlook closes the Message window. The Save As, Move, and Print commands have an arrow to their right. If you point to this arrow, Outlook displays a **submenu**, which is a list of additional commands associated with the selected command (Figure 1–13).

BTW

Spam Filters
If an individual or company is not receiving e-mail from you, it is likely that the recipient's ISP spam filter is not allowing it through to their mailbox. Try sending the message in Plain Text format, because spam filters are less likely to drop an e-mail in Plain Text format.

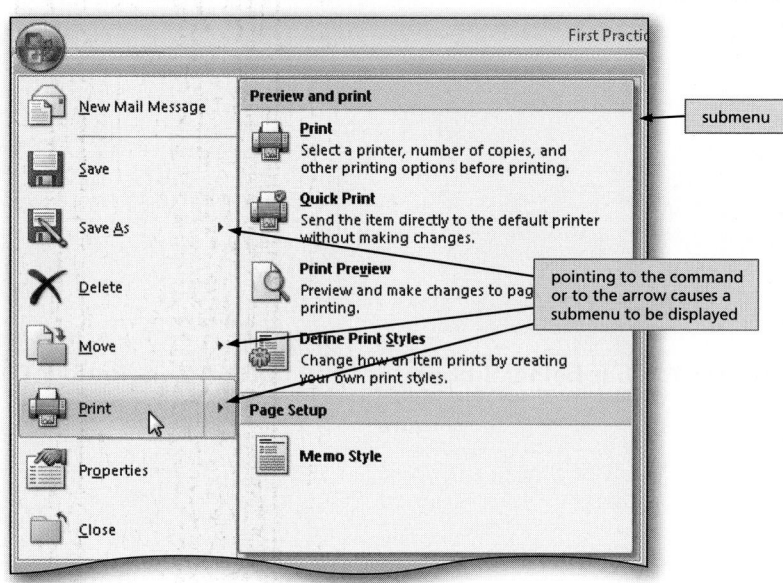

Figure 1–13

Key Tips

If you prefer using the keyboard instead of the mouse, you can press the ALT key on the keyboard to display a **Key Tip badge**, or keyboard code icon, for certain commands (Figure 1–14). To select a command using the keyboard, press its displayed code letter, or **Key Tip**. When you press a Key Tip, additional Key Tips related to the selected command may appear. For example, to select the New Mail Message command on the Office Button menu, press the ALT key, then press the F key, and then press the N key.

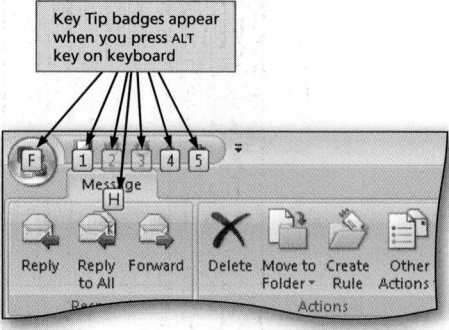

Figure 1–14

To remove the Key Tip badges from the screen, press the ALT key or the ESC key until all Key Tip badges disappear, or click the mouse anywhere in the Message window.

To Close an E-Mail Message

After reading the message from Jose, Marcus closes it. The following step closes the Message window.

- Click the Close button on the title bar (Figure 1–15) to close the Message window

Q&A

Why did the number next to the Inbox folder change from 4 to 3?

When you close the Message window, the Jose Quinteras message heading in the message pane no longer appears in bold type and the closed envelope icon changes to an open envelope icon to indicate the message has been opened. In addition, the Inbox folder in the Mail Folders pane indicates three messages remain unopened.

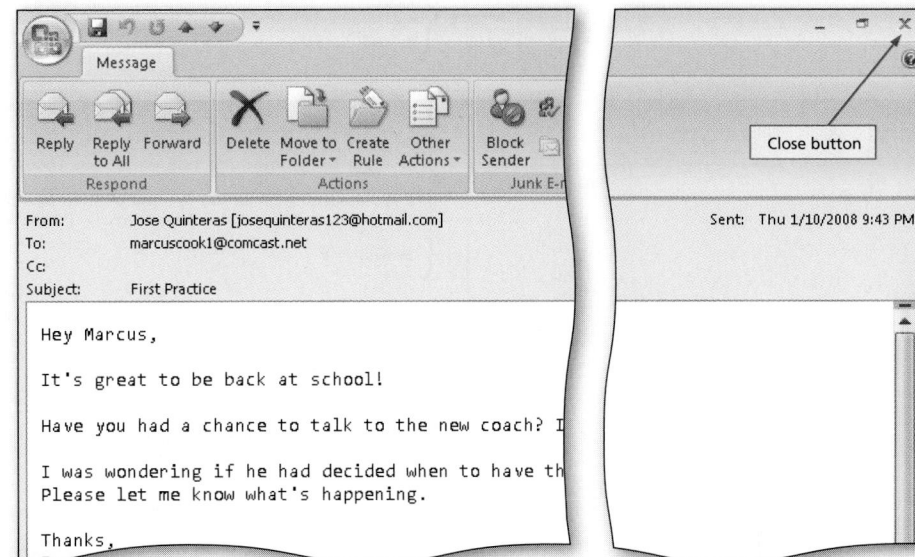

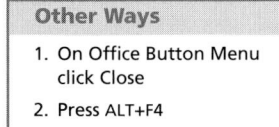
Close button

From: Jose Quinteras [josequinteras123@hotmail.com]   Sent: Thu 1/10/2008 9:43 PM
To: marcuscook1@comcast.net
Cc:
Subject: First Practice

Hey Marcus,

It's great to be back at school!

Have you had a chance to talk to the new coach? I

I was wondering if he had decided when to have th
Please let me know what's happening.

Thanks,

Figure 1–15

Other Ways
1. On Office Button Menu click Close
2. Press ALT+F4

To Print an E-Mail Message

Often, you will want to have a hard copy of your e-mail messages. You print the contents of an e-mail message from the Inbox window. The following steps print the e-mail message from Jose Quinteras.

- Point to the Print button on the Standard toolbar (Figure 1–16).

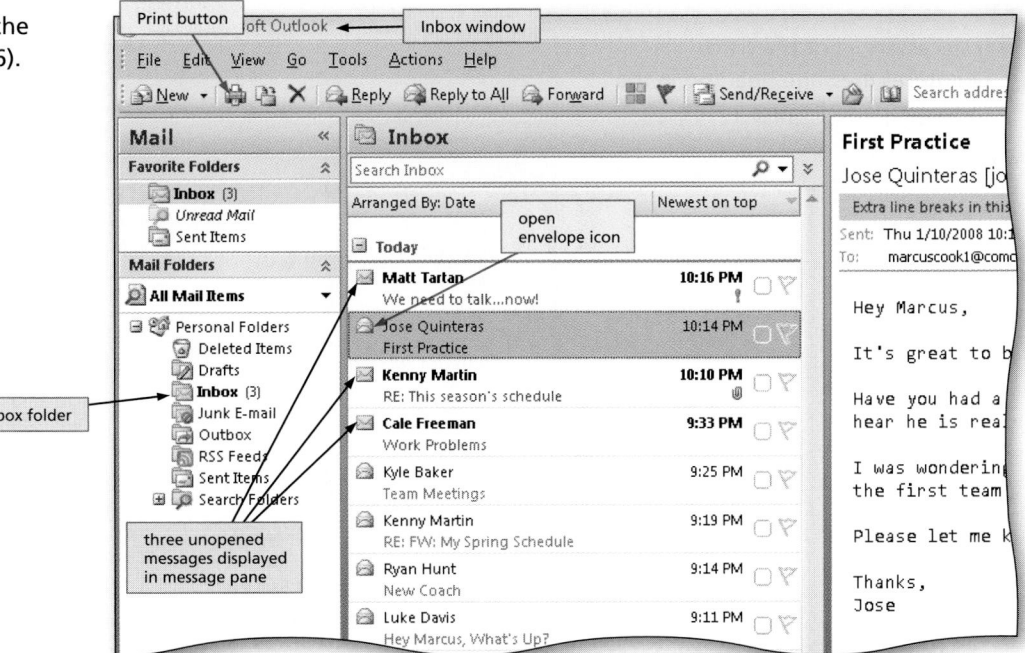

Print button ...oft Outlook   Inbox window

| File | Edit | View | Go | Tools | Actions | Help |

New   X   Reply   Reply to All   Forward   Send/Receive   Search addre

Mail

Favorite Folders
- Inbox (3)
- Unread Mail
- Sent Items

Mail Folders
- All Mail Items
  - Personal Folders
    - Deleted Items
    - Drafts
    - Inbox (3)   ← Inbox folder
    - Junk E-mail
    - Outbox
    - RSS Feeds
    - Sent Items
    - Search Folders

three unopened messages displayed in message pane

Inbox

Search Inbox

Arranged By: Date   Newest on top

Today   open envelope icon

Matt Tartan   10:16 PM
We need to talk...now!

Jose Quinteras   10:14 PM
First Practice

Kenny Martin   10:10 PM
RE: This season's schedule

Cale Freeman   9:33 PM
Work Problems

Kyle Baker   9:25 PM
Team Meetings

Kenny Martin   9:19 PM
RE: FW: My Spring Schedule

Ryan Hunt   9:14 PM
New Coach

Luke Davis   9:11 PM
Hey Marcus, What's Up?

First Practice

Jose Quinteras [jo

Extra line breaks in this

Sent: Thu 1/10/2008 10:1
To: marcuscook1@comc

Hey Marcus,

It's great to b

Have you had a
hear he is rea

I was wondering
the first team

Please let me k

Thanks,
Jose

Figure 1–16

2

● Click the Print button to print the message shown in Figure 1–17.

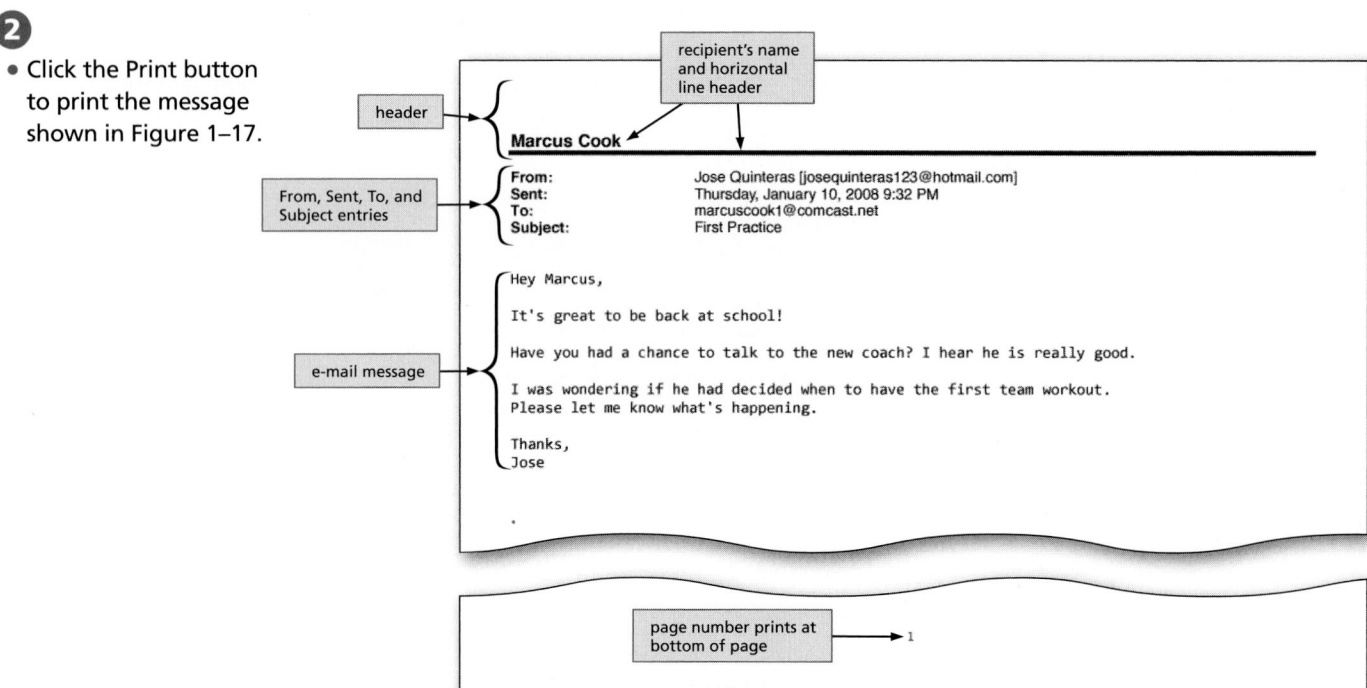

Figure 1–17

Other Ways		
1. On File Menu click Print, click OK button	2. Press ALT+F, press P, press ENTER	3. Press CTRL+P, press ENTER

To Reply to an E-Mail Message

The Reply button allows you to reply quickly to an e-mail message using the sender's e-mail address. The following steps reply to the e-mail message from Jose Quinteras.

1

● If necessary, click the Jose Quinteras message heading in the message pane (Figure 1–18).

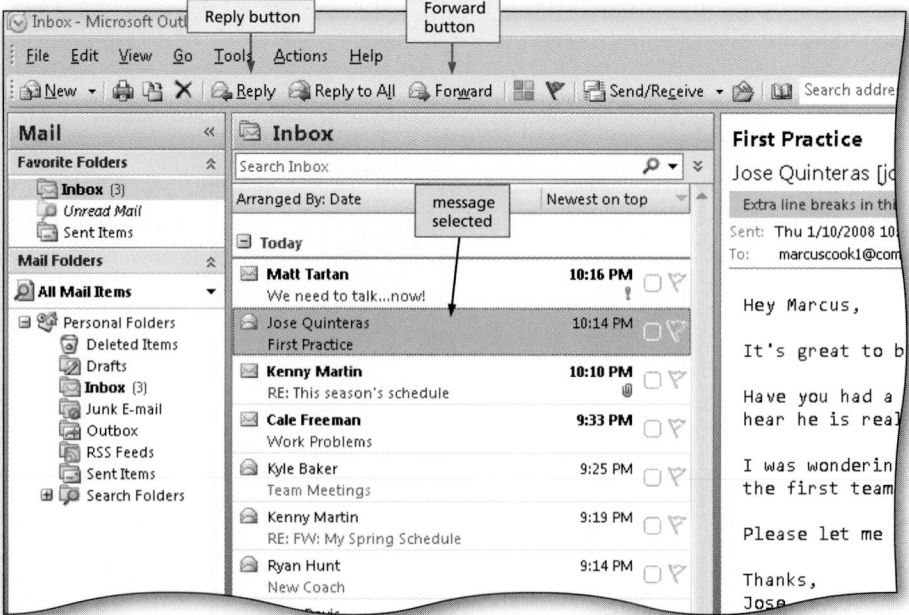

Figure 1–18

2

- Click the Reply button on the Standard toolbar to open the RE: First Practice - Message window.

- When Outlook displays the Message window for the reply, if necessary, double-click the title bar to maximize the window.

- Type the e-mail reply (Figure 1–19).

Q&A Why is there RE: at the beginning of the Subject line and in the Title bar?

The RE: indicates it is the reply, the subject of the message identifies the title of the window, and Message indicates it is the Message window.

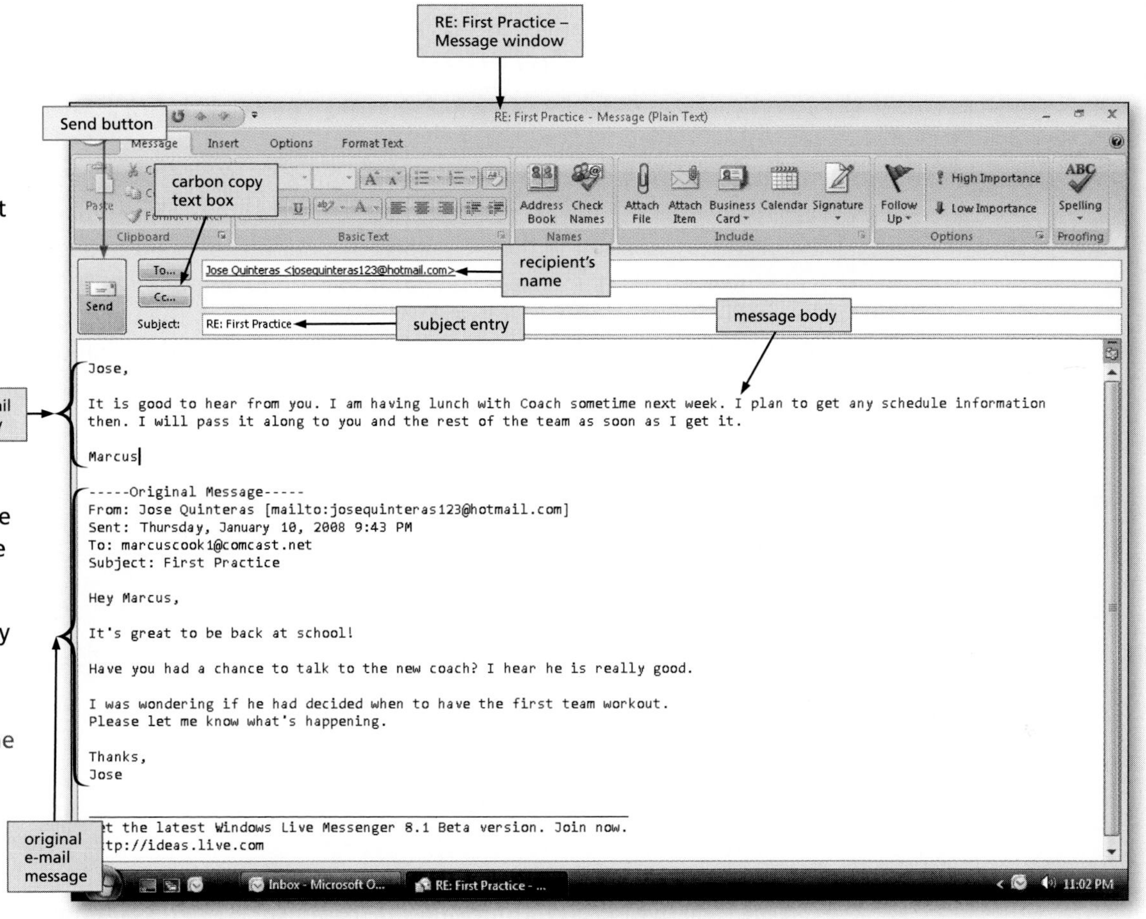

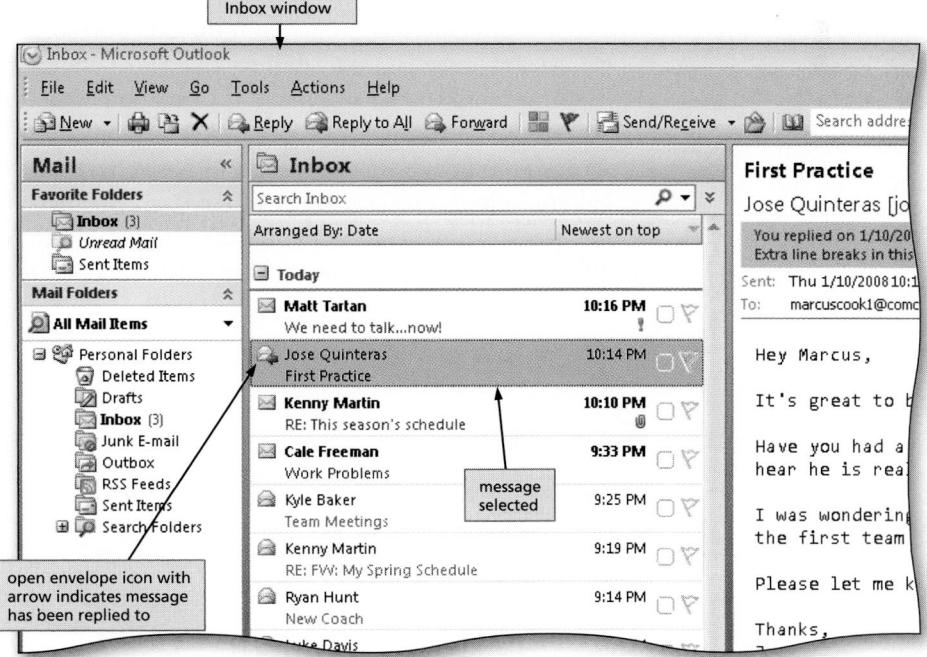

Figure 1–19

3

- Click the Send button to send the message and return to the Inbox window (Figure 1–20).

Q&A What happened to the sent message?

Outlook closed the Message window and stores the reply e-mail in the Outbox folder while it sends the message. Outlook then moves the message to the Sent Items folder. The original message in the message pane now shows an open envelope icon with an arrow to indicate a reply has been sent.

Figure 1–20

New Message Ribbon

The Ribbon for a reply message, new message, or forwarded message is similar to the Ribbon for a Word window (Figure 1–21). The Ribbon provides easy, central access to the tasks you perform while creating a message. The New Message Ribbon, in comparison to the Ribbon discussed earlier, consists of multiple tabs, groups, and commands. As in the previous Ribbon, each tab surrounds a collection of groups, and each group contains related commands. Many of the Ribbon commands will be inactive if the message format is Plain Text. To activate all of the commands, the message must be in HTML or Rich Text format. These formats are discussed later in this chapter.

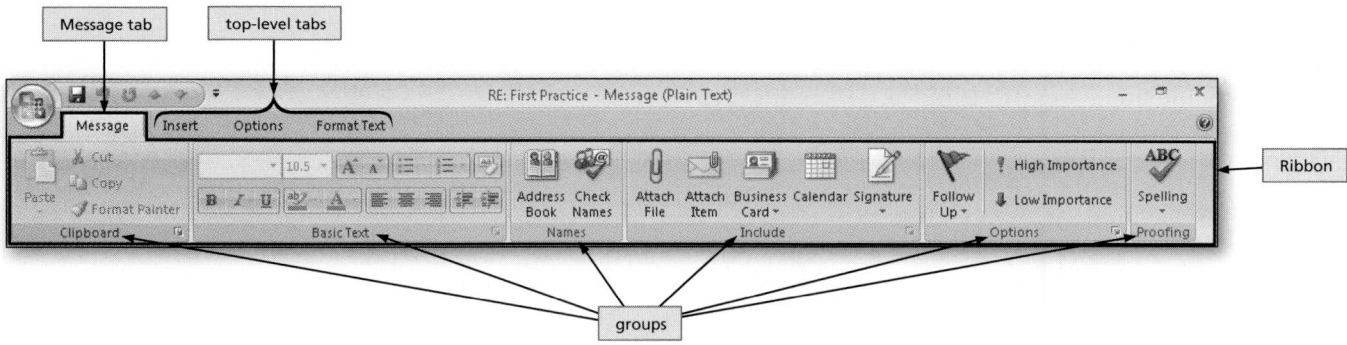

Figure 1–21

When you open a new mail Message window, the Ribbon displays four top-level tabs: Message, Insert, Options, and Format Text. The **Message tab**, called the primary tab, contains the more frequently used commands. To display a different tab on the Ribbon, click the top-level tab. That is, to display the Insert tab, click Insert on the Ribbon. To return to the Message tab, click Message on the Ribbon. The tab currently displayed is called the **active tab**.

Commands on the Ribbon include buttons, boxes (text boxes, check boxes, etc.), and galleries (Figure 1–22). A **gallery** is a set of choices, often graphical, arranged in a grid or list. You can scroll through choices on an in-Ribbon gallery by clicking the gallery's scroll arrows. Or, you can click a gallery's More button to view more gallery options on the screen at a time. Some buttons and boxes have arrows that, when clicked, also display a gallery; others always cause a gallery to be displayed when clicked. Most galleries support **live preview**, which is a feature that allows you to point to a gallery choice and see its effect in the document — without actually selecting the choice.

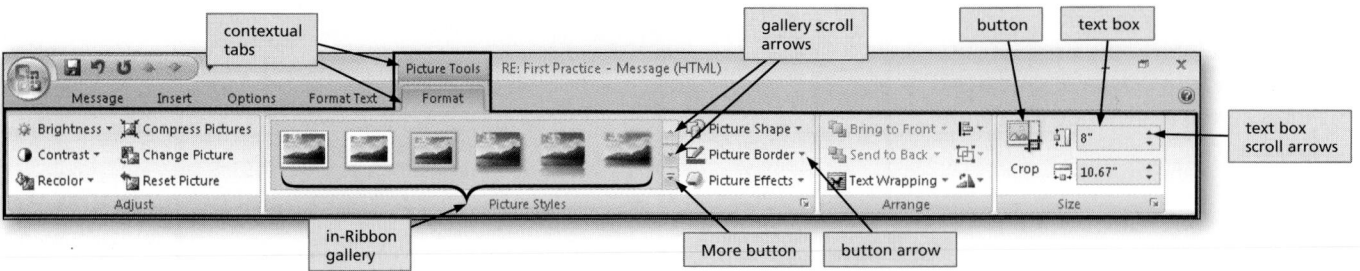

Figure 1–22

In addition to the top-level tabs, Outlook displays other tabs, called **contextual tabs**, when you perform certain tasks or work with objects such as pictures or tables. If you insert a picture in the message, for example, the Picture Tools tab and its related subordinate Format tab appear (Figure 1–22).

Message Formats

Outlook offers three message formats: Plain Text, HTML, and Rich Text, summarized in Table 1–2.

Table 1–2 Message Formats

Message Format	Description
HTML	HTML format is the default format used when you create a message in Outlook. HTML supports the inclusion of pictures and basic formatting, such as text formatting, numbering, bullets, and alignment. HTML is the recommended format for Internet mail because the most popular e-mail programs use it.
Plain Text	Plain Text format is understood by all e-mail programs and is the most likely format to make it through a company's virus-filtering program. Plain text does not support basic formatting, such as bold, italic, colored fonts, or other text formatting. It also does not support pictures displayed directly in the message.
Rich Text	Rich Text Format (RTF) is a Microsoft format that only the latest versions of Microsoft Exchange and Outlook understand. RTF supports more formats than HTML or Plain Text, as well as linked objects and pictures.

To Change Message Formats

The following steps change the message format.

1
- With a Message window active, click the Options tab (Figure 1–23).

2
- Click the appropriate command (Plain Text, HTML, or Rich Text) in the Format group.

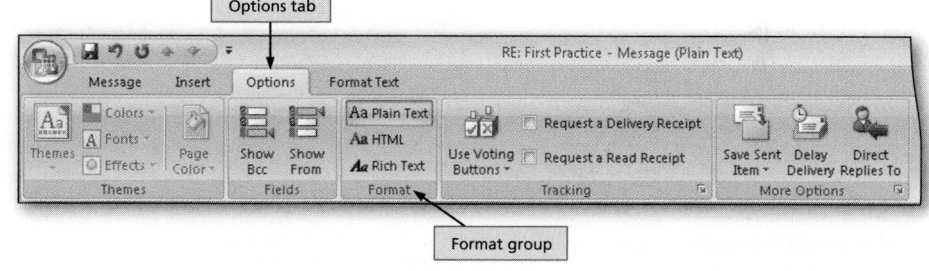

Options tab

Format group

Figure 1–23

BTW

Replying to an E-Mail Message
Many e-mail users prefer to reply to a message without including the original e-mail message along with their response. To remove the original message from all e-mail replies, click Tools on the menu bar, click Options, and then click the E-mail Options button in the Preferences sheet of the Options dialog box. In the E-mail Options dialog box, select 'Do not include original message text' in the 'When replying to a message' list.

BTW

Message Formatting
Changing the format of an e-mail message also can help prevent the possibility of virus infection. Many viruses are found in HTML formatted messages. To help protect against viruses, you can configure Outlook to display opened messages automatically in plain text. Click Trust Center on the Tools menu and then click E-mail Security in the Trust Center dialog box and select Read all standard mail in plain text in the Read as Plain Text area.

To Forward an E-Mail Message

You can forward an e-mail message to additional recipients. The following steps forward the Jose Quinteras e-mail message to the team's coach.

 1

- With the Inbox window active, click the Jose Quinteras message header in the message pane.

- Click the Forward button on the Standard toolbar (Figure 1–24).

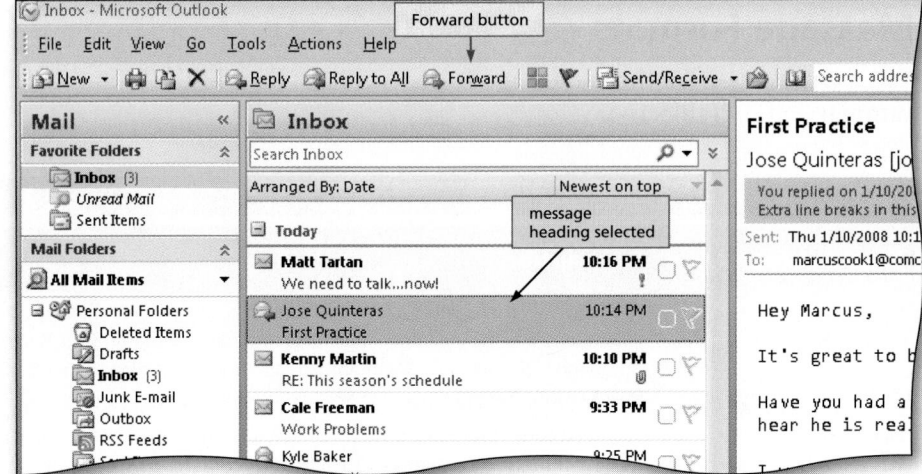

Figure 1–24

 2

- When Outlook displays the Message window for the forwarded message, type kennymartin123@hotmail.com in the To text box as the recipient's e-mail address. (If you are stepping through this task, use an actual e-mail address in the To text box.)

- Enter the forwarding message in the message body (Figure 1–25).

 3

- Click the Send button to forward the original message along with the new message to Kenny.

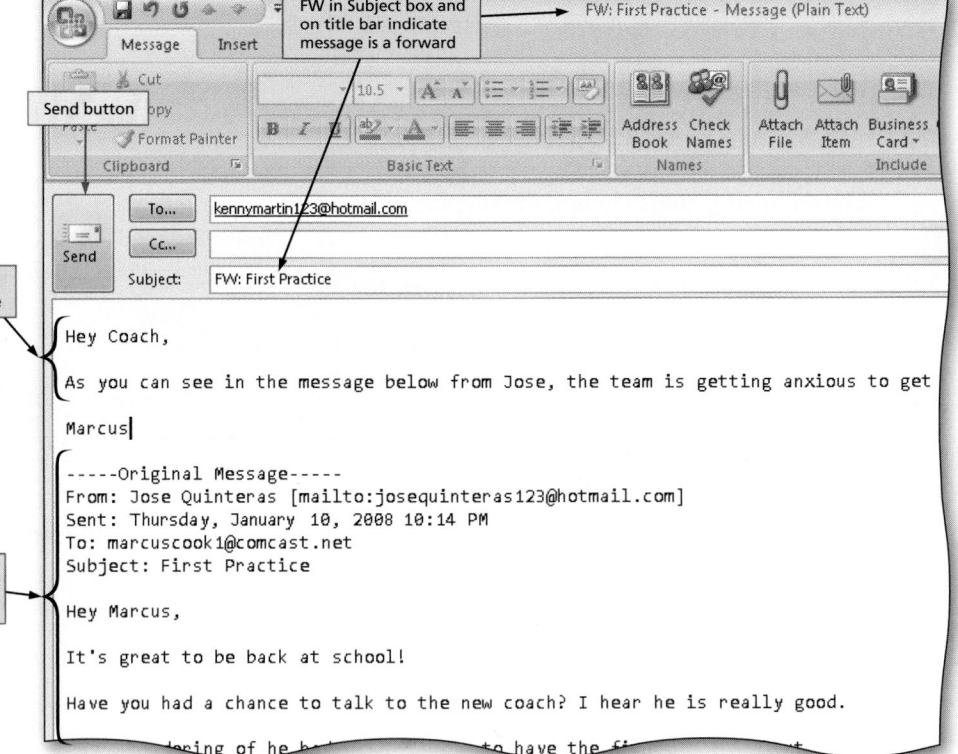

Figure 1–25

Other Ways

1. Right-click message heading, click Forward on shortcut menu

2. Press CTRL+F

To Delete an E-Mail Message

Deleting a message removes the e-mail message from the Inbox folder, saving disk space and making new messages easier to find. The following steps delete the e-mail message from Jose Quinteras.

1

- With the Inbox window active, click the Jose Quinteras message heading in the message pane to select the message (Figure 1–26).

Q&A Why did the envelope icon for this message change to an open envelope with a forward pointing blue arrow instead of the backward pointing purple arrow?

The backward pointing purple arrow indicated that you replied to the message. The forward pointing blue arrow indicates that you have forwarded the message. The status of the envelope icon represents your last action with the message.

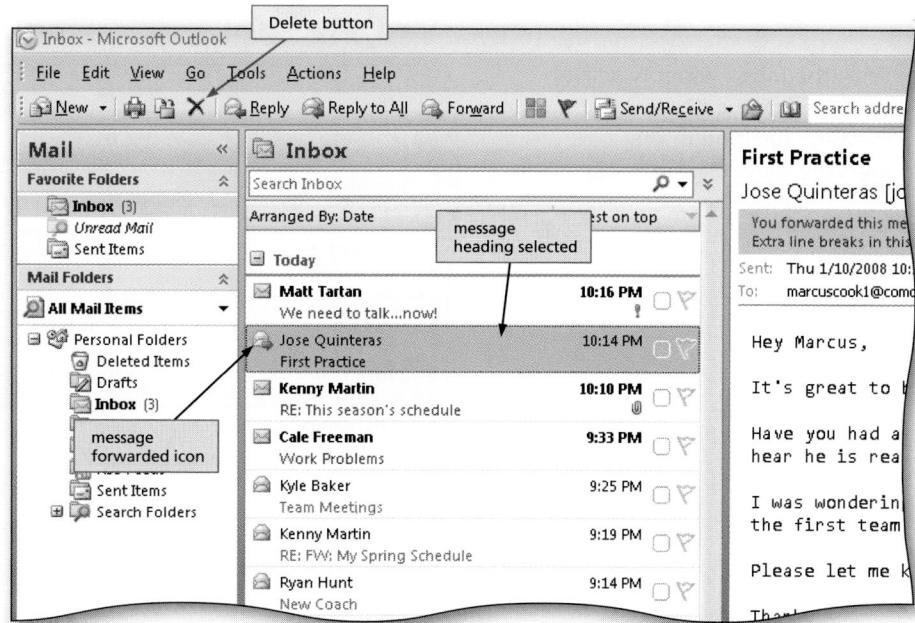

Figure 1–26

2

- Click the Delete button on the Standard toolbar to remove the message from your Inbox (Figure 1–27).

Q&A Is the message permanently deleted?

Outlook moves the message to the Deleted Items folder. To permanently delete an e-mail message from the Deleted Items folder, click the Deleted Items folder icon in the Mail Folders pane, select the message in the Deleted Items message pane, click the Delete button, and then click the Yes button in the Microsoft Office Outlook dialog box.

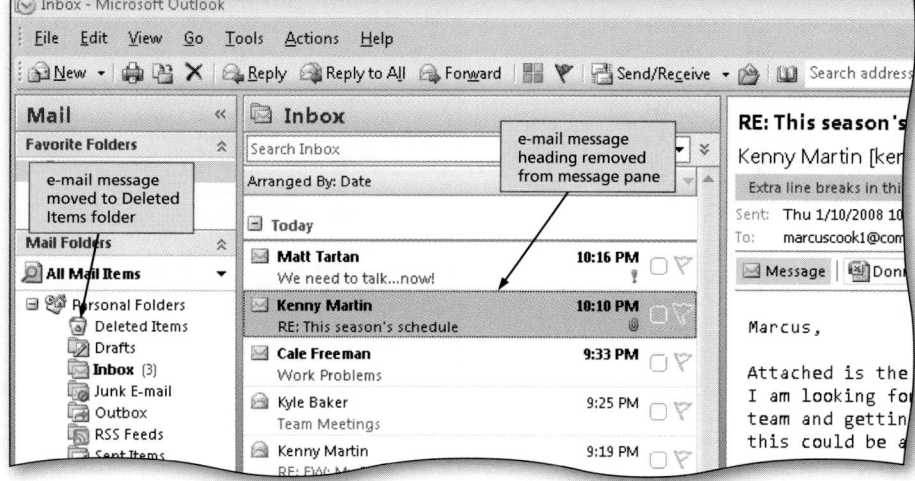

Figure 1–27

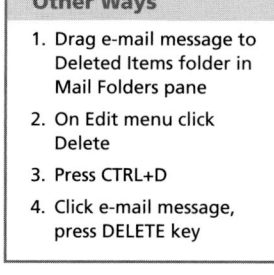

Other Ways

1. Drag e-mail message to Deleted Items folder in Mail Folders pane
2. On Edit menu click Delete
3. Press CTRL+D
4. Click e-mail message, press DELETE key

To View a File Attachment

A paper clip icon in a message heading indicates that the message contains a file attachment. The message from Kenny Martin (see Figure 1–28) contains an attachment — in this case, a schedule for the team. The following steps open the message and view the contents of the file attachment.

- With the Inbox window active, double-click the Kenny Martin message heading in the message pane (Figure 1–28).

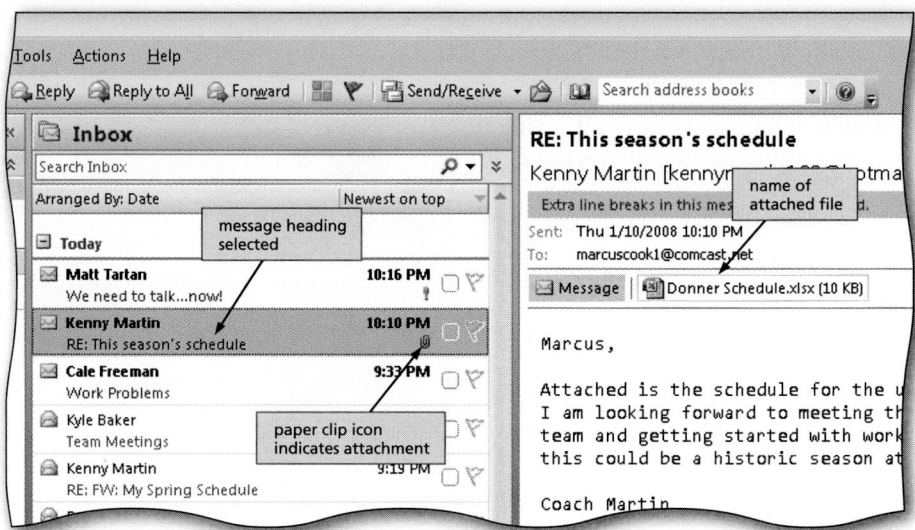

Figure 1–28

- If necessary, maximize the RE: This season's schedule – Message window (Figure 1–29).

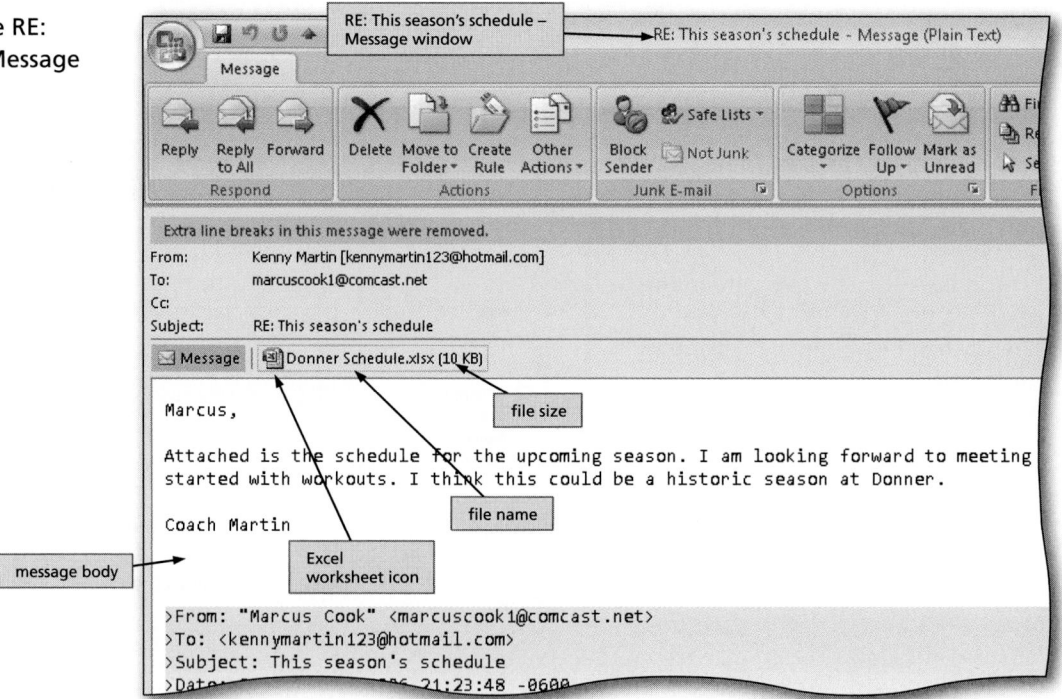

Figure 1–29

3

- Double-click the Donner Schedule icon in the Attachments area to open the Donner Schedule Microsoft Excel file (Figure 1–30).

- If Outlook displays the Opening Mail Attachment dialog box, click the Open button.

Q&A

What type of files can I open?

File attachments can be any type of file; however, files can be viewed only if your computer has the appropriate software. For example, if your computer does not have Excel installed, then you cannot view an Excel file attachment.

4

- After viewing the worksheet, click the Close button on the right side of the title bar in the Excel window to close the attachment and Excel.

- Click the Close button in the Message window.

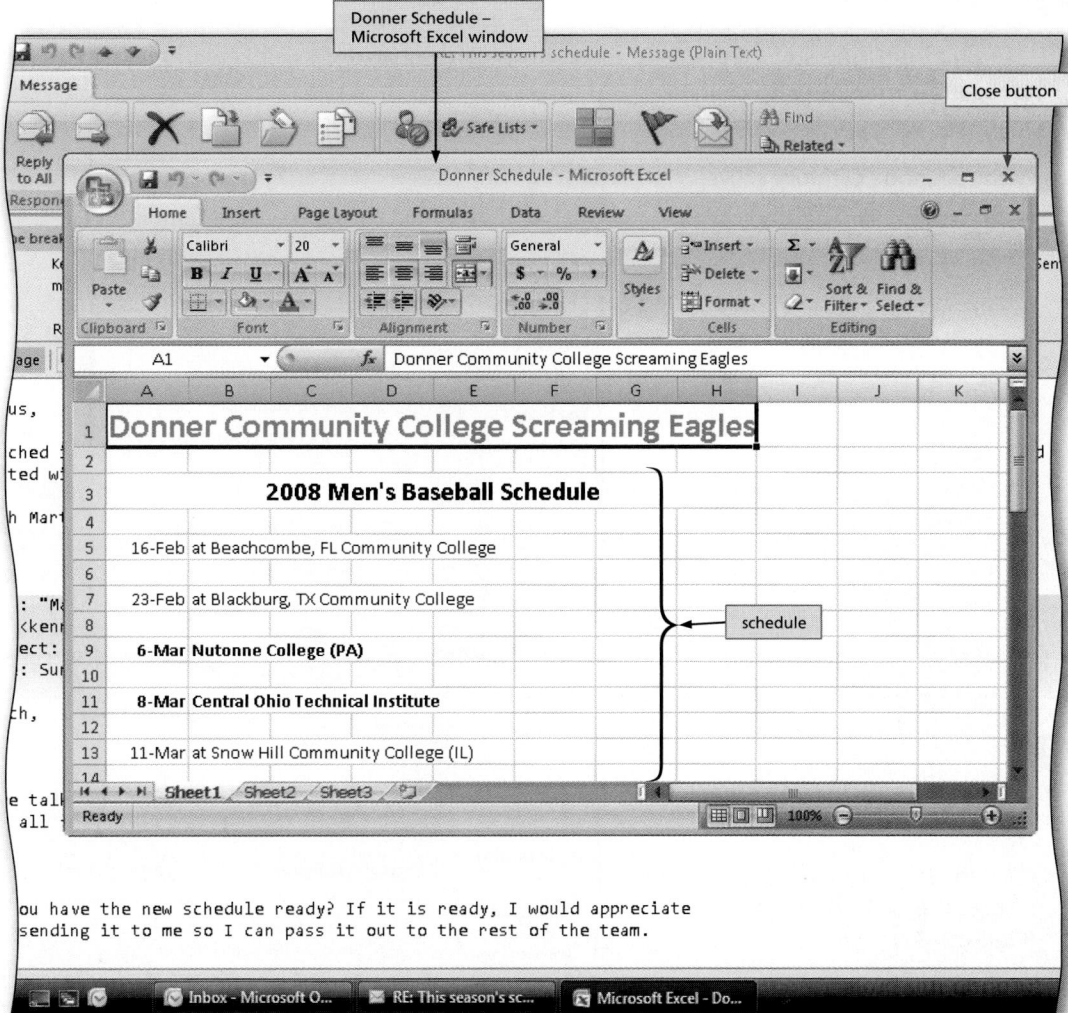

Figure 1–30

Other Ways

1. Double-click file attachment name in Reading pane
2. Click Save button in Opening Mail Attachments dialog box to save attachment to hard drive or portable storage device
3. On File menu point to Save Attachments to save attachment to hard drive or portable storage device

Working with Outgoing Messages

Before composing a new mail message, you should create an e-mail signature to save time when sending messages.

An **e-mail signature** is a unique message automatically added to the end of an outgoing e-mail message. It can consist of text and/or pictures. The type of signature you add may depend on the recipient of the message. For messages to family and friends, a first name may be sufficient, while messages to business contacts may include your full name, address, telephone number, and other business information. Outlook allows you to create a different signature for each e-mail account created in Outlook.

To Create and Insert an E-Mail Signature

The following steps create and insert an e-mail signature in an e-mail message. The signature will be used by Marcus in his role as team captain.

- With the Inbox window active, click Tools on the menu bar to display the Tools menu (Figure 1–31).

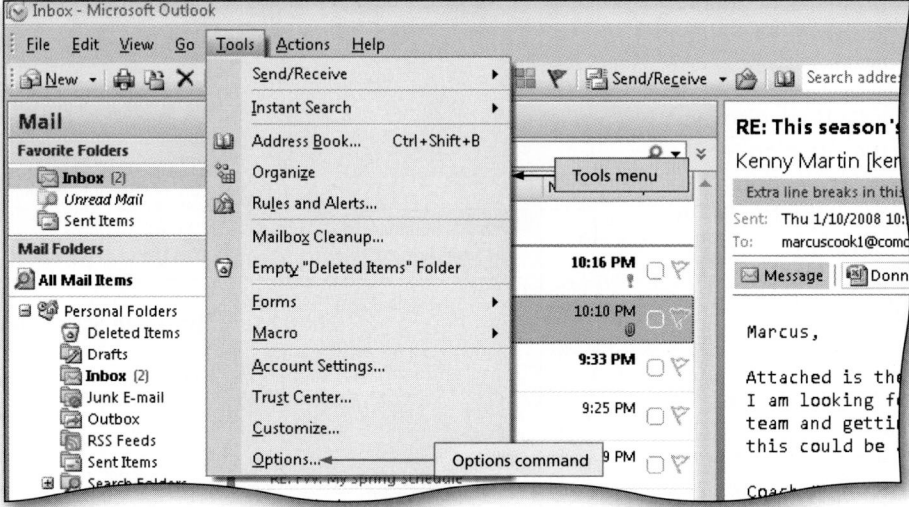

Figure 1–31

2

- Click Options on the Tools menu to display the Options dialog box.

- Click the Mail Format tab to display the Mail Format sheet (Figure 1–32).

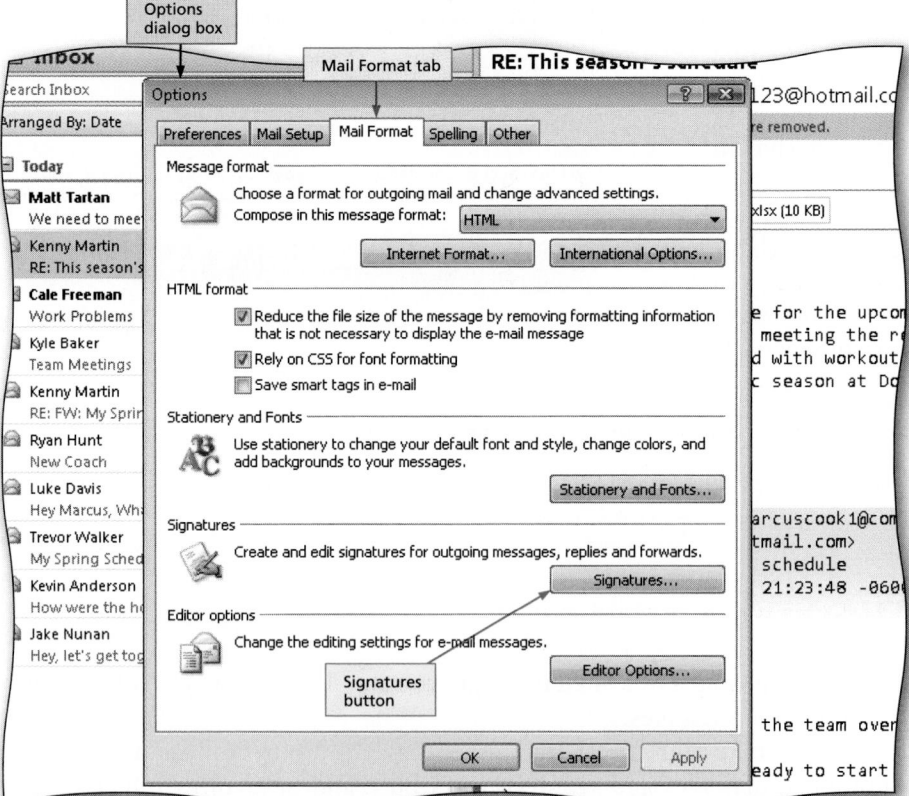

Figure 1–32

3

- Click the Signatures button to display the Signatures and Stationery dialog box (Figure 1–33).

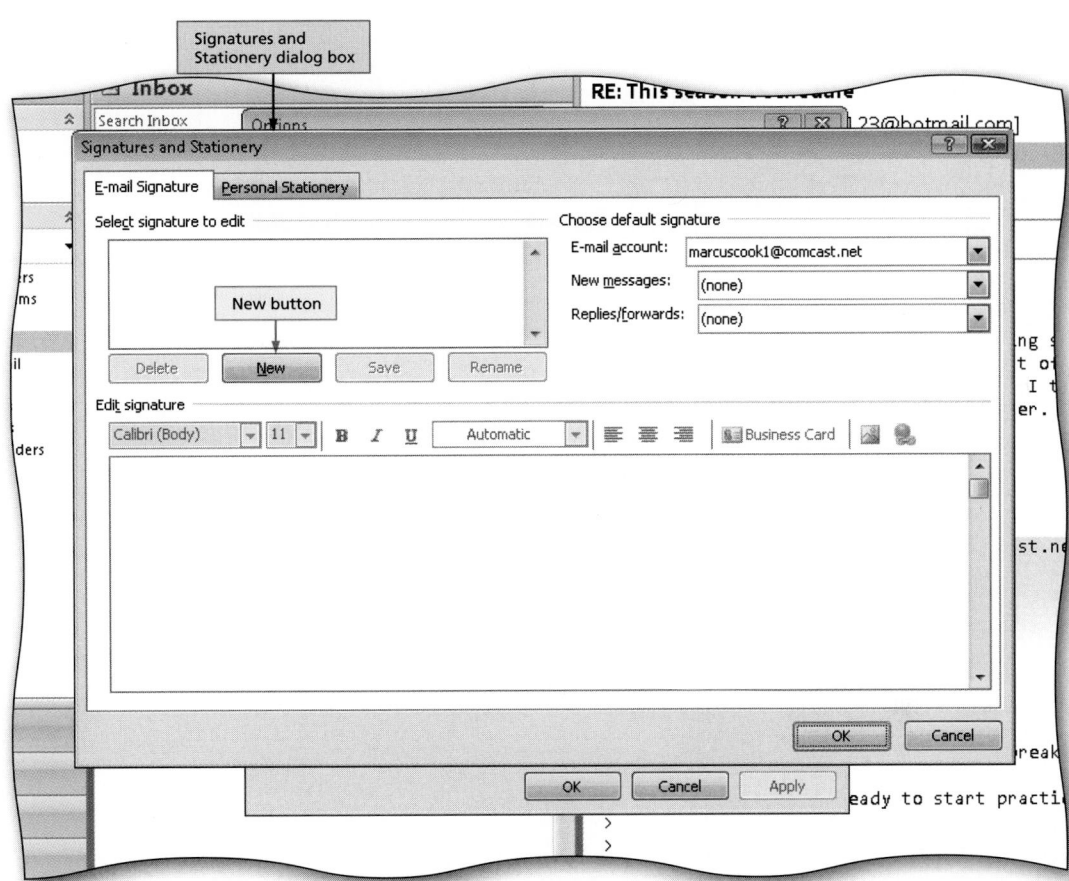

Figure 1–33

4

- Click the New button to display the New Signature dialog box.

- When Outlook displays the New Signature dialog box, type Team in the 'Type a name for this signature' text box (Figure 1–34).

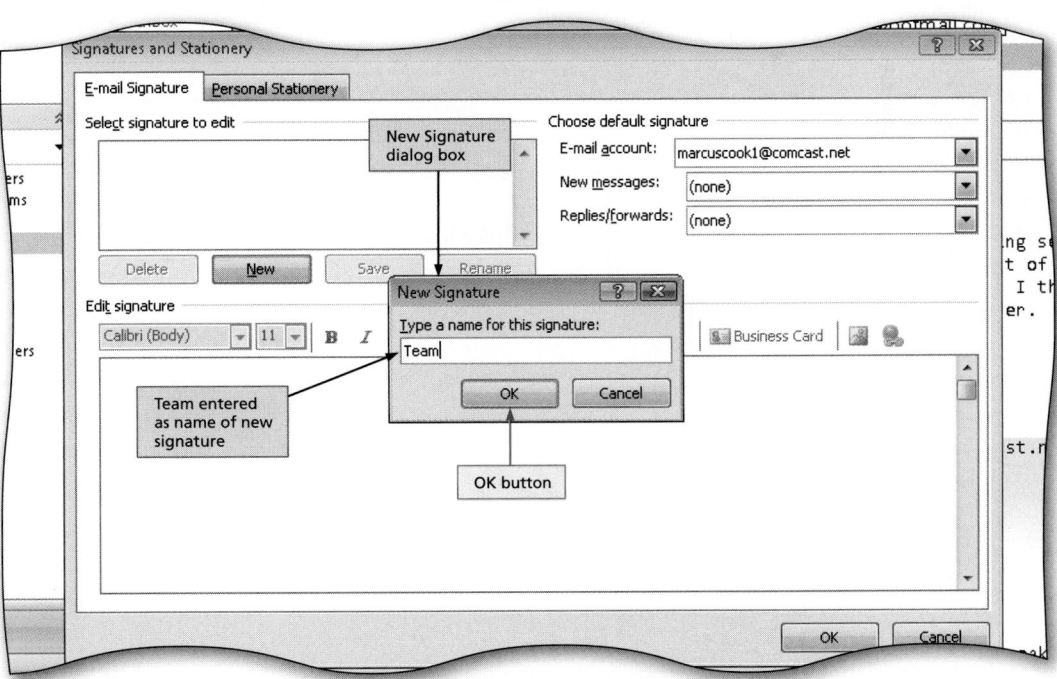

Figure 1–34

- Click the OK button.

- Click in the Edit signature area of the Signatures and Stationery dialog box and type `Marcus Cook – Team Captain` as the signature (Figure 1–35).

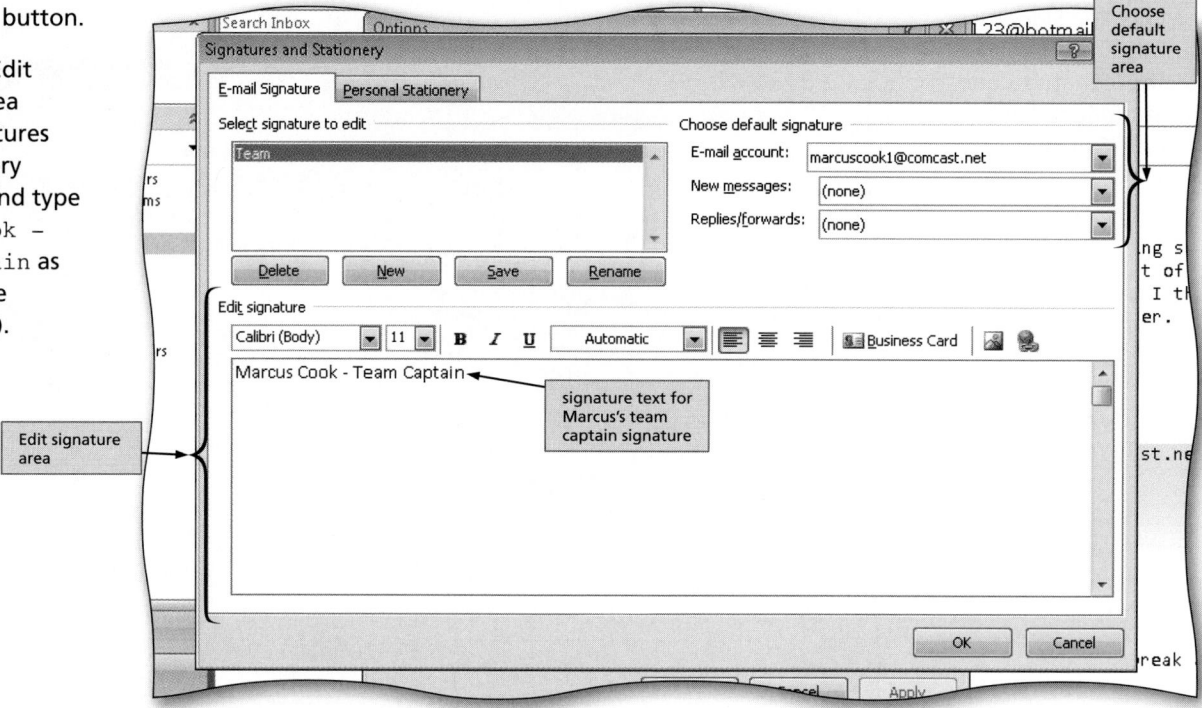

Figure 1–35

- In the Choose default signature area of the Signatures and Stationery dialog box, select the appropriate e-mail account (if you are stepping through this project, ask your instructor for the appropriate e-mail account).

- If necessary, select Team in the New messages box and the Replies/forwards box to select it as the default signature (Figure 1–36).

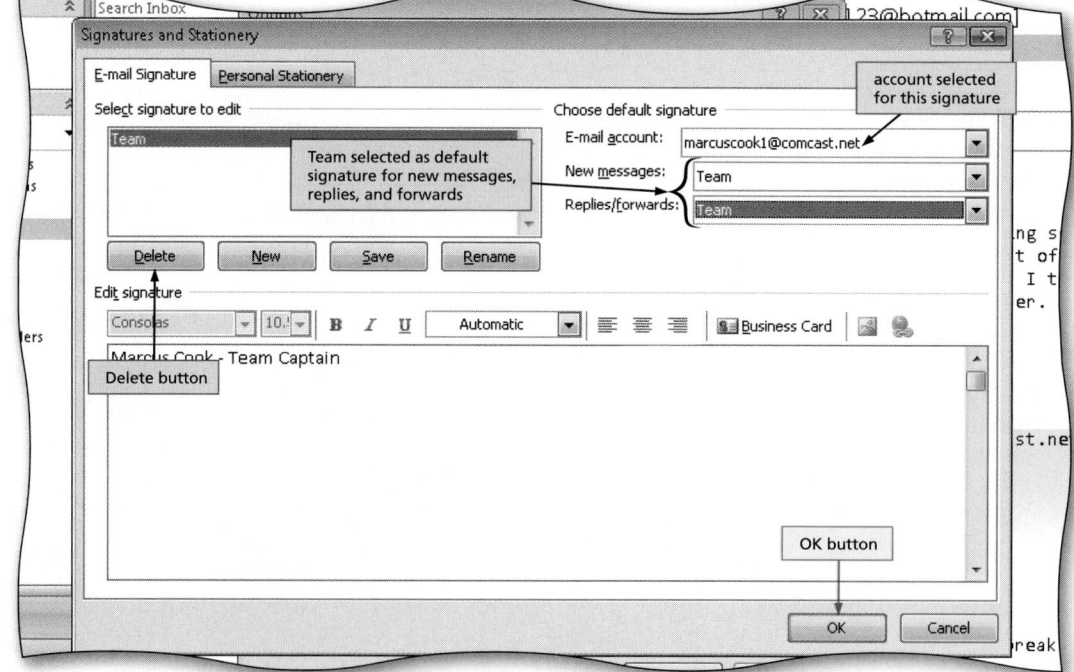

Figure 1–36

- Click the OK button to close the Signatures and Stationery dialog box. Click OK in the Options dialog box to close the dialog box.

Q&A

What do I do with my signature now that it is created?

Your signature will be inserted automatically in all new messages as well as reply and forward messages. You also can modify or remove your signatures at any time using the Signatures and Stationery dialog box.

Other Ways

1. Press ALT+T, press O

E-Mail Signatures for Multiple Accounts

You can create unique signatures for different accounts by adding new signatures and selecting a different account in the Choose default signature area of the Signatures and Stationary dialog box (Figure 1–36).

New Mail Messages

In addition to opening and reading, replying to, forwarding, and deleting e-mail messages, you will have many occasions to compose and send original e-mail messages. When you compose an e-mail message, you must know the e-mail address of the recipient of the message, enter a brief one-line subject that identifies the purpose or contents of the message, and then type the message in the message body.

You also can **format** an e-mail message to enhance the appearance of the message. Formatting refers to changing the style, size, and color of the text document.

BTW

E-Mail Signatures
Outlook allows you to add signatures to your e-mail messages that you create in Word 2007. Some of the advantages to creating them in Word is the ability to insert pictures and hyperlinks into the signature.

To Compose an E-Mail Message

The following steps compose a formatted e-mail message to Kenny Martin with an attachment.

1

• With the Inbox window active, point to the New Mail Message button on the Standard toolbar (Figure 1–37).

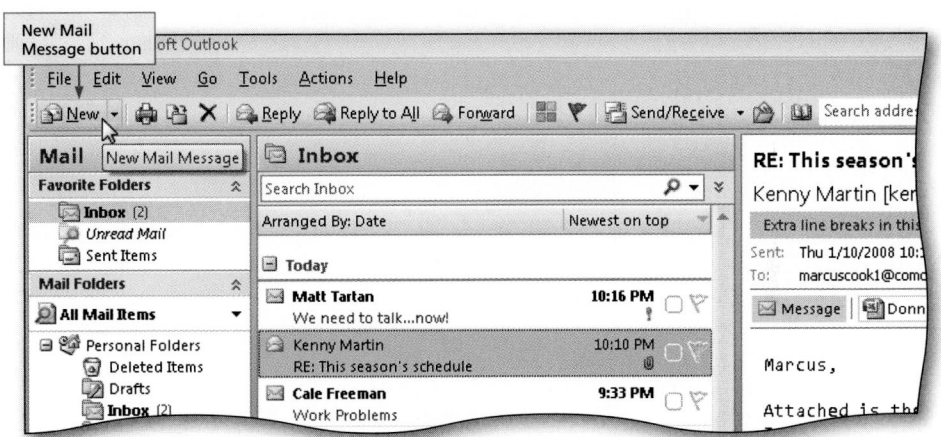

Figure 1–37

2

• Click the New Mail Message button to open the Untitled – Message window (Figure 1–38).

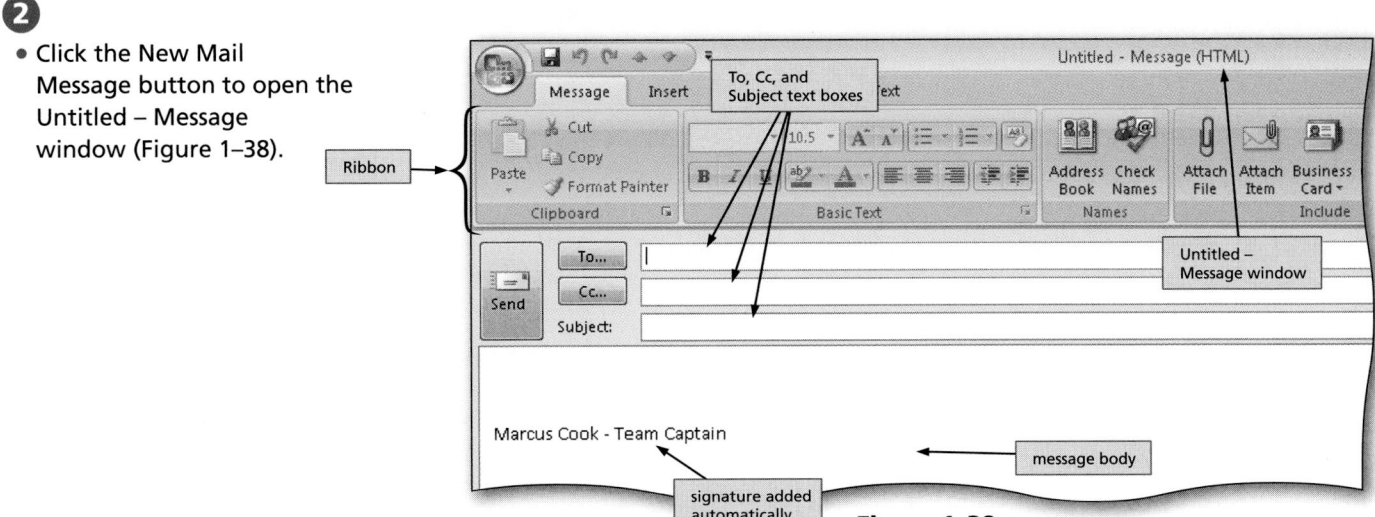

Figure 1–38

3

- Type kennymartin123@
hotmail.com in the To text box,
click the Subject text box, and then
type Draft Practice Schedule
in the Subject text box
(Figure 1–39).

- Press the TAB key to move the
insertion point into the message
body area.

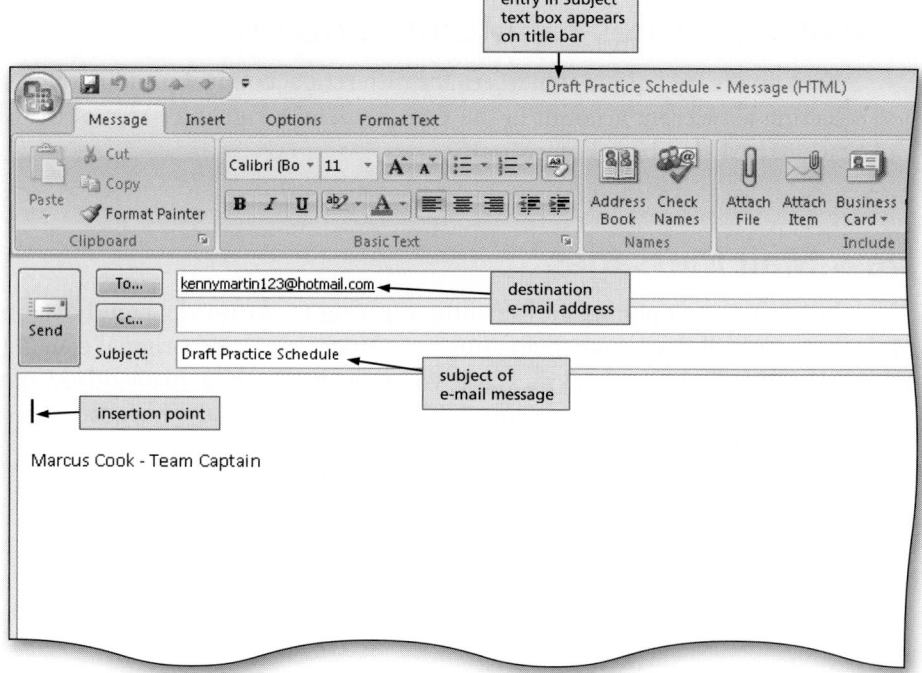

Figure 1–39

4

- Type the e-mail
message (Figure 1–40).

Q&A

What if I make a
mistake while typing
a message?

When you enter a
message, you can use
the DELETE key and
BACKSPACE key to
correct errors.
If you are using
Microsoft Word as
your e-mail editor
and you have the
appropriate Spelling
options selected, then
the spell checker will
flag the misspelled words
with a red wavy line. Furthermore, the message will be spell checked before it is sent.

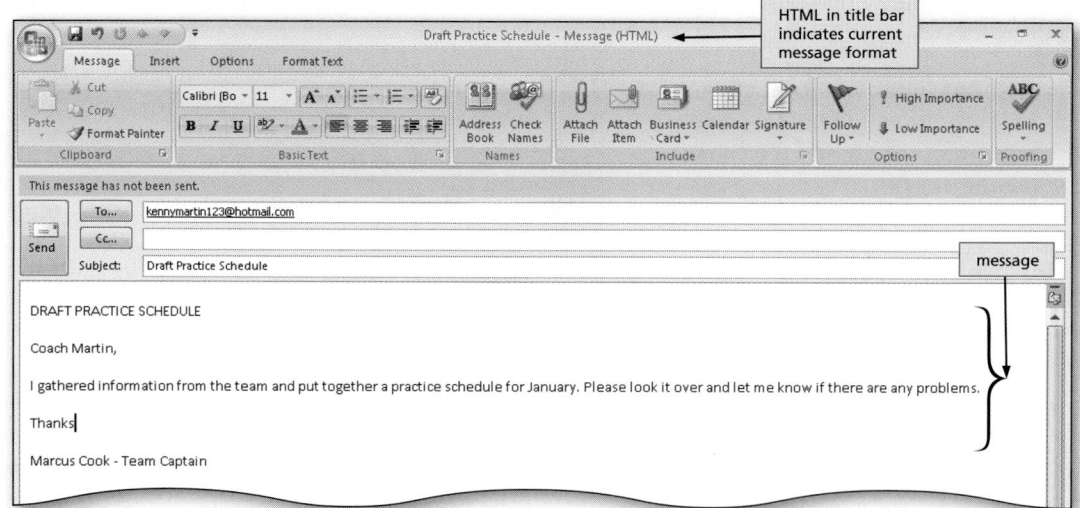

Figure 1–40

To Format an E-Mail Message

Outlook's default message format is HTML, which allows you to customize text with numbering, bullets, alignment, signatures, and linking to Web pages. The following steps center the text, DRAFT PRACTICE SCHEDULE, change the font size to 36-point, and change the color of the text to red. A **font size** is measured in points. A **point** is equal to 1/72 of one inch in height. Thus a font size of 36 points is approximately one-half inch in height.

1

- Highlight the text, DRAFT PRACTICE SCHEDULE, in the message body and then click the Format Text tab (Figure 1–41).

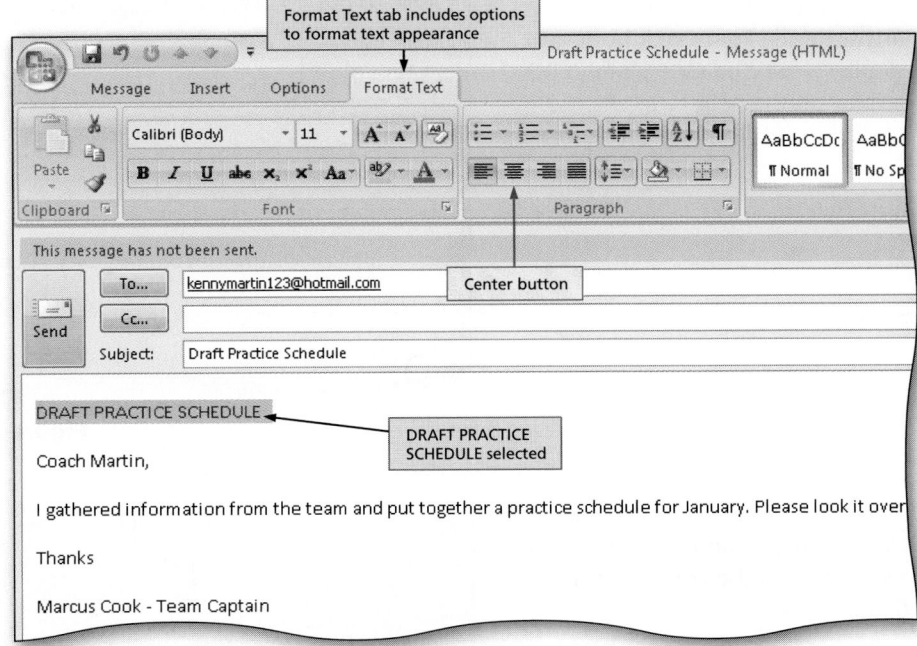

Figure 1–41

2

- Click the Center button in the Paragraph group on the Format Text tab to center the selected text (Figure 1–42).

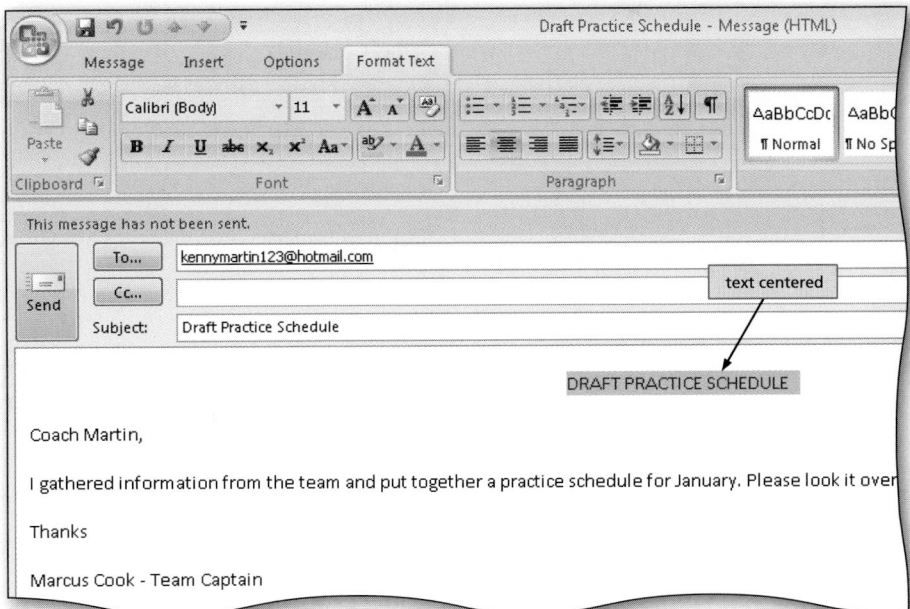

Figure 1–42

- Click the Font Color button in the Font group on the Format Text tab to change the color of the selected text to red (Figure 1–43).

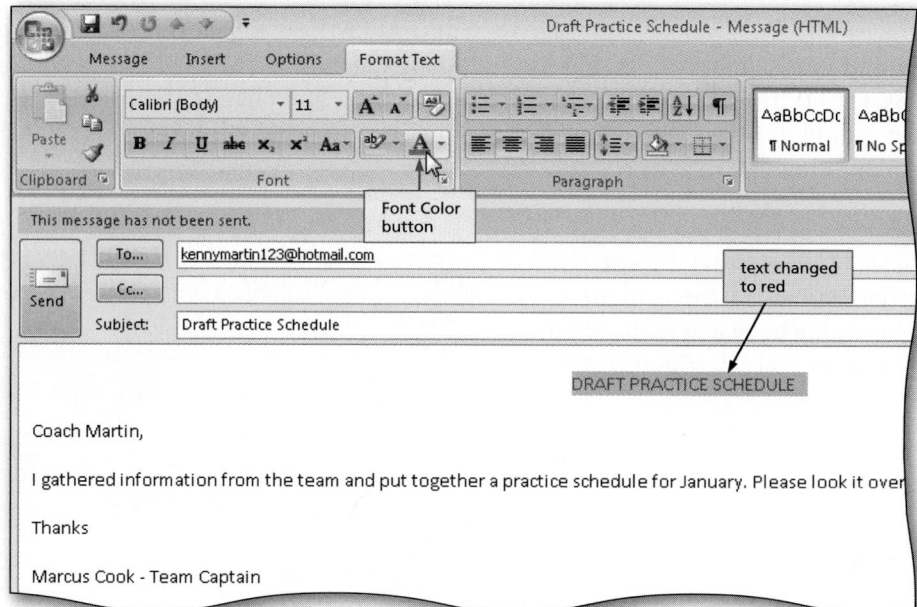**Q&A**

How do I pick a color other than red?

To select a font color, click the box arrow on the Font Color button to display a color palette. Simply click a color on the palette to change the color of the text.

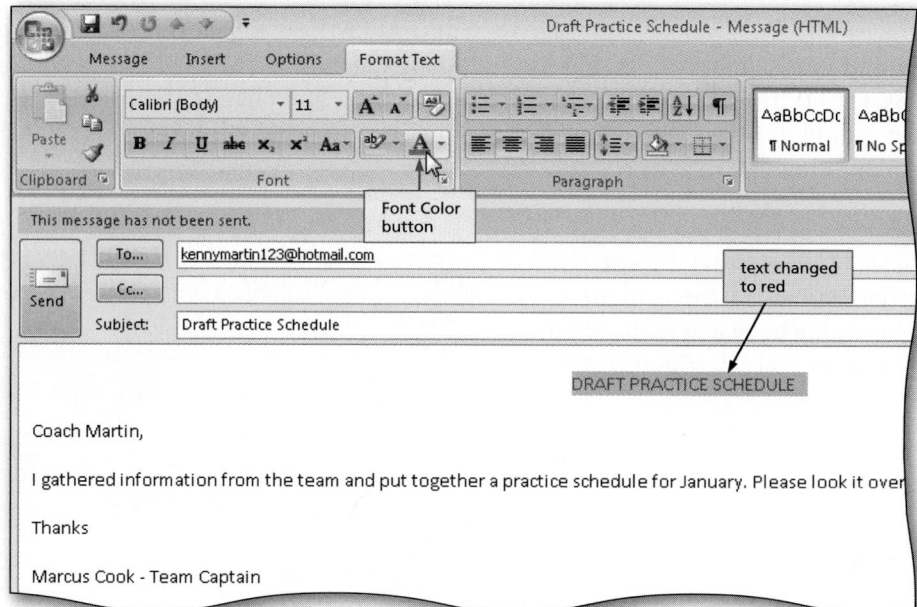

Figure 1–43

- Click the Font Size box arrow in the Font group on the Format Text tab to display the Font Size list (Figure 1–44).

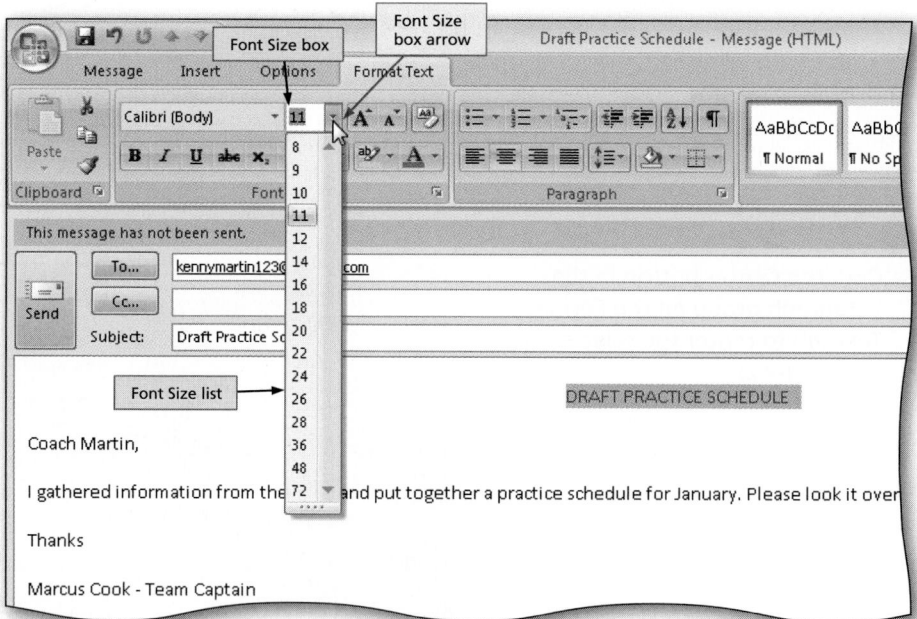

Figure 1–44

5

- Scroll down the Font Size list, click 36, and then click the selected text to remove the selection (Figure 1–45).

Q&A

Why do I have to select the entire text to change the format?

Because centering is a paragraph format, you can simply click within the text, and then click the Center button. Font size, however, is a character format, so you must select the characters in the entire text before you select a new font size.

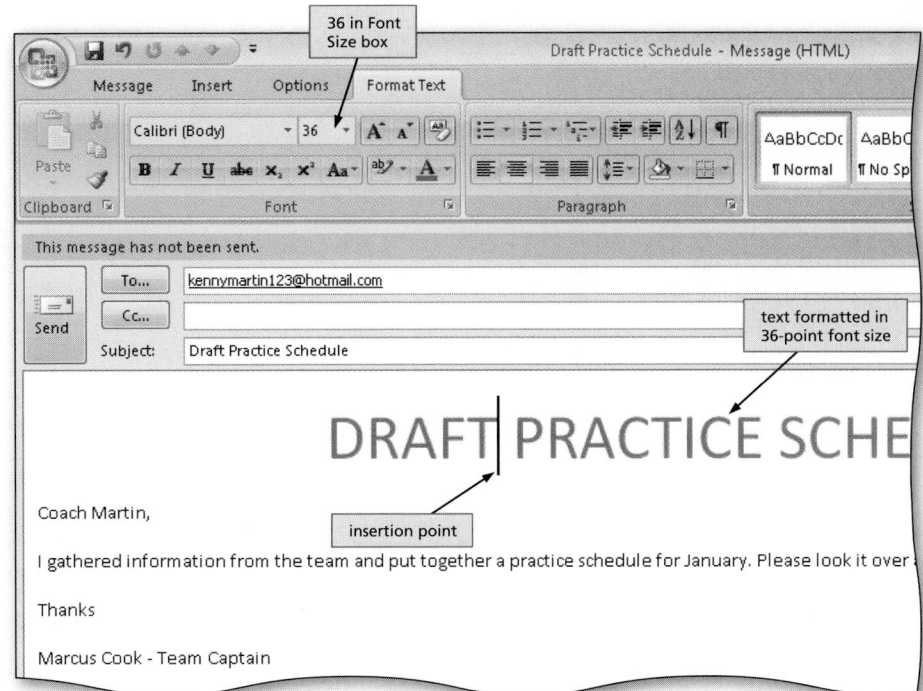

Figure 1–45

To Attach a File to an E-Mail Message and Send the Message

Outlook allows you to attach almost any kind of file to your message. You may need to send a Word document, an Excel worksheet, a picture, or other type of file. The following steps attach the Draft Practice Schedule.xlsx file to the e-mail message.

Note: If you are using Windows XP, see Appendix F for alternate steps.

- Click the Insert tab on the Ribbon and then click the Attach File button in the Include group to display the Insert File dialog box (Figure 1–46).

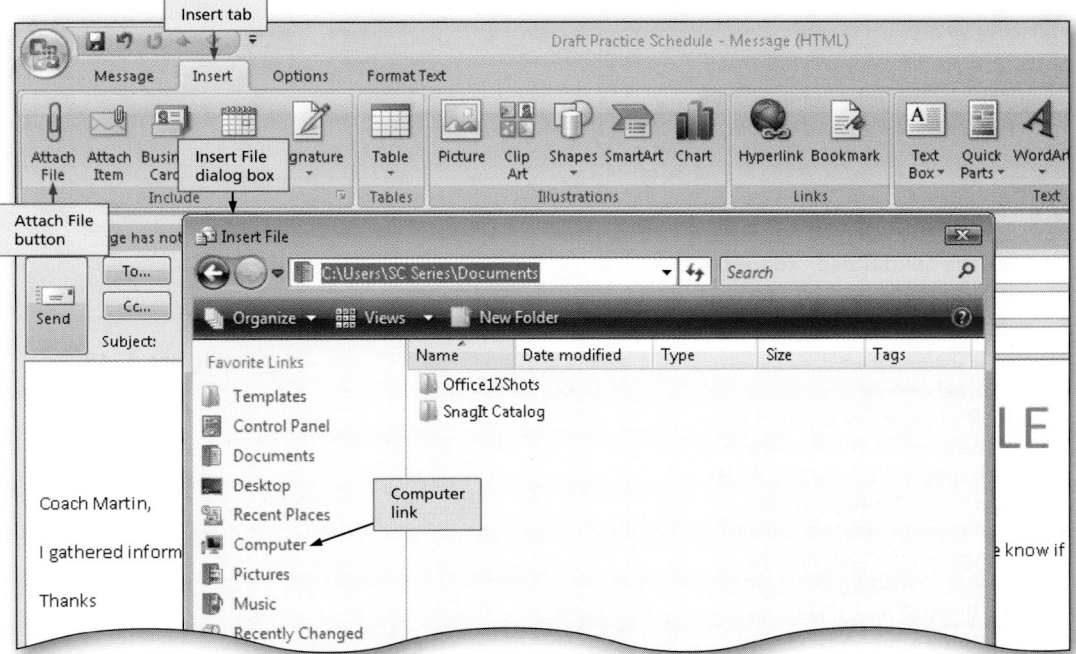

Figure 1–46

2

- With your USB flash drive connected to one of the computer's USB ports, if necessary, click Computer in the Favorite Links section and then scroll until UDISK 2.0 (E:) appears in the list of available drives.

- Double-click UDISK 2.0 (E:) to select the USB flash drive, drive E in this case, in the Look in list as the new open location.

- Click Draft Practice Schedule in the Insert File dialog box (Figure 1–47).

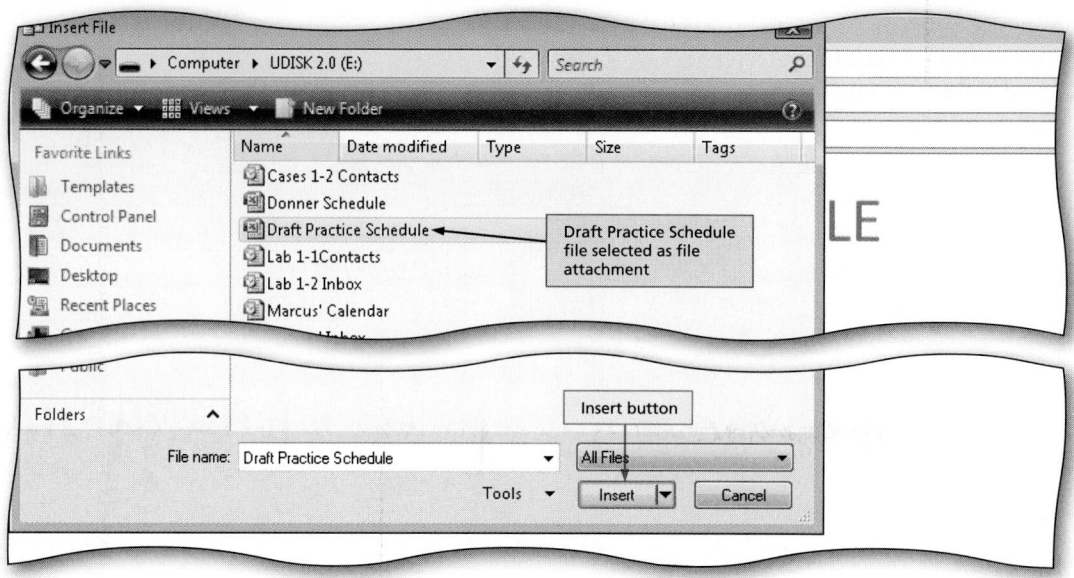

Figure 1–47

- Click the Insert button in the Insert File dialog box to insert the file into the message (Figure 1–48).

Q&A What if I have more than one file to send?

You can attach multiple documents to the same e-mail message. Simply perform the previous steps for each attachment. Keep in mind, however, that some Internet service providers limit the total size of e-mail messages you can attach. You should keep the sum of the file sizes attached to an e-mail message to less than 1 MB.

3

- Click the Send button to send the message and close the Message window (Figure 1–48).

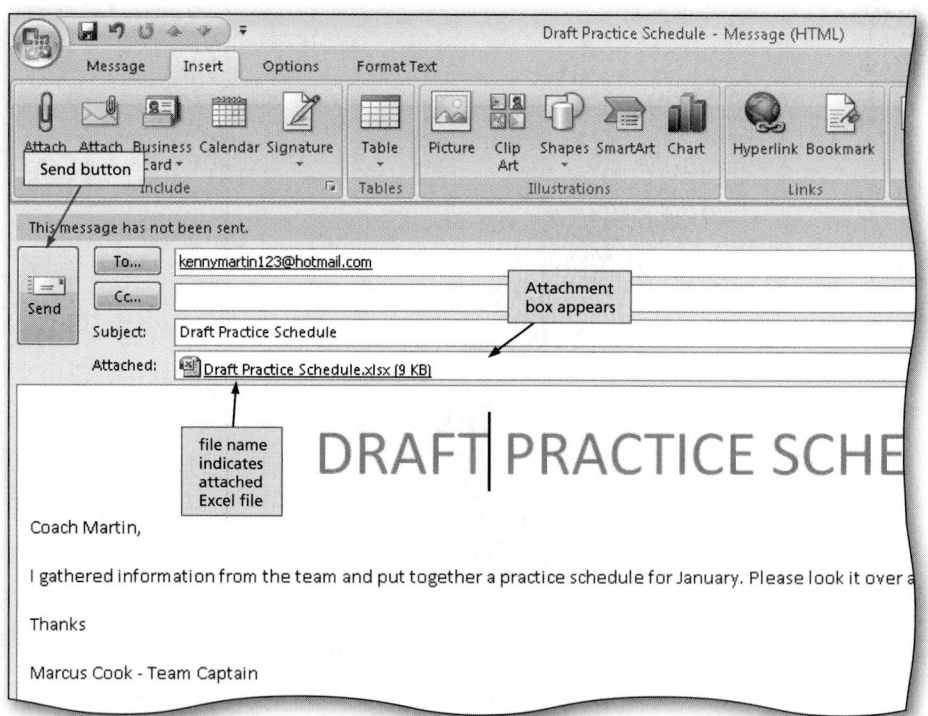

Figure 1–48

BTW
File Attachments
Outlook allows other ways for a file to be inserted into a message. You can drag a file from any folder on your computer to a message, or you can copy and paste a file into a message as an attachment by right-clicking the file, clicking Copy on the shortcut menu, and then in the Outlook message, clicking Paste on the Edit menu.

Organizing E-Mail Messages

Keeping track of your incoming messages can be a challenge, especially if you receive a lot of mail. Two features that can help you organize your messages are the Category box and Follow Up flag, located to the right of the message headings. The **Category box** option on an e-mail message can be assigned one of six different default colors, or you can create your own categories with different colors. Color selection and the meaning of each color are entirely at the discretion of the user. For example, you could assign red to indicate a message from your boss, yellow could mean a message from your best friend, and purple may be a message from your parents.

The **Follow Up flag** option on an e-mail message can be assigned one of five different flags, or you can customize your own Follow Up flag. These flags are used to remind you to follow up on an issue. When you select a flag, Outlook adds a reminder message in the Reading pane. Outlook also adds a task to the To-Do Bar.

To Categorize E-Mail Messages

Marcus would like to organize his messages. The following steps categorize, flag, and sort e-mail messages.

1

- With the Inbox window active, right-click the Kenny Martin message heading to display the message shortcut menu.

- Point to Categorize to display the Categories submenu (Figure 1–49).

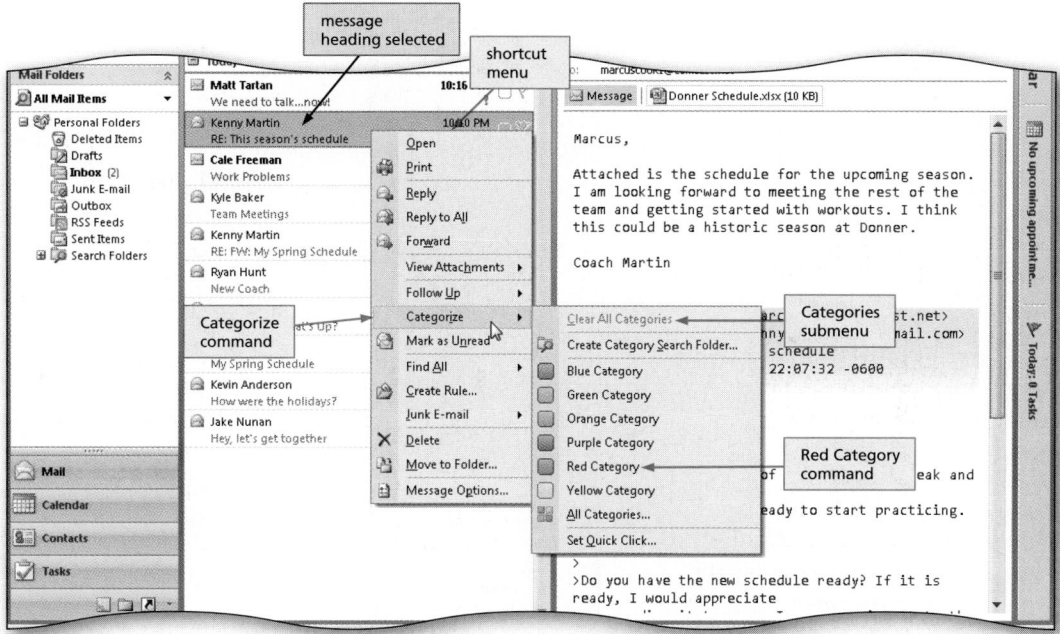

Figure 1–49

BTW

Junk E-Mail Filters
A useful feature in Outlook is the Junk E-mail Filter. The filter is on by default. It automatically evaluates whether an unread message should be sent to the Junk E-mail folder. While you can configure the Junk E-mail Filter to your own personal settings, the default settings evaluate several factors, such as content, time the message was sent, and who sent the message. To change junk e-mail settings, click Options on the Tools menu, and then click the Junk E-mail button in the Preferences sheet of the Options dialog box. Make the preferred changes in the Junk E-mail Options dialog box. Note that the Junk E-mail folder may not be available if you use an Exchange Server e-mail account.

- Click the Red Category command on the Categories submenu. If the Rename Category dialog box appears, click No.

- Repeat Steps 1 and 2 to categorize the remaining messages in the message pane (Figure 1–50).

Other Ways

1. Right-click Categorize box, click appropriate category color
2. On Actions menu point to Categorize, click appropriate category color
3. Click the Category button on the Standard toolbar, click appropriate category color
4. Press ALT+A, press I

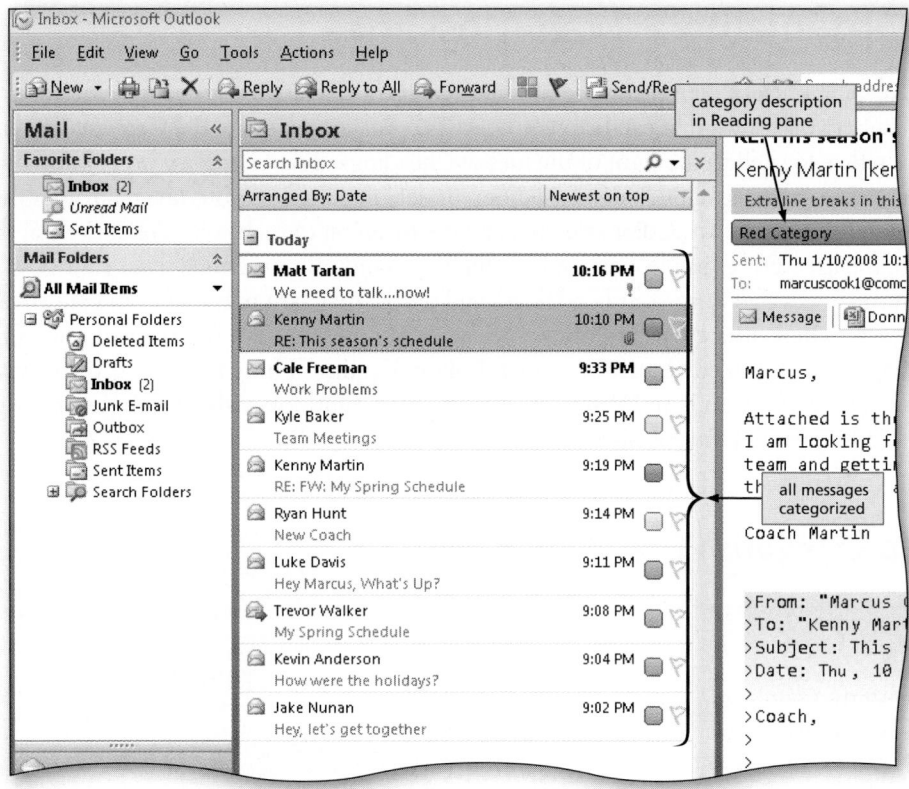

Figure 1–50

To Flag E-Mail Messages

The following steps mark a message with a flag that indicates the message needs to be dealt with today.

- With the Inbox window active, right-click the Kenny Martin message heading to display the message shortcut menu (Figure 1–51).

- Point to Follow Up to display the Follow Up submenu (Figure 1–51).

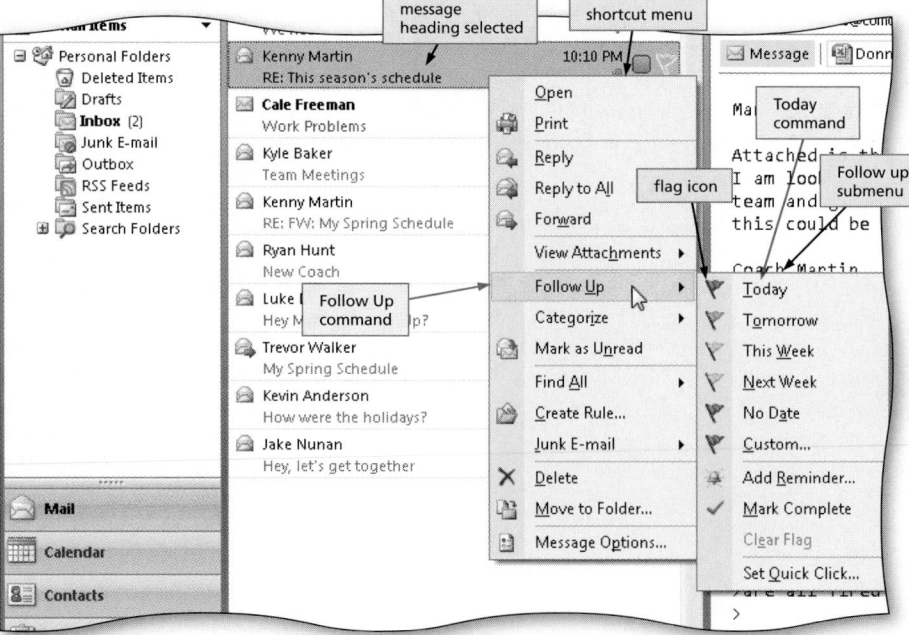

Figure 1–51

②

- Click the Today command on the Follow Up submenu to assign a Follow Up flag with today as the due date.

- Repeat Steps 1 and 2 to add Follow Up flags to the remaining messages in the message pane (Figure 1–52).

- Select different flags as necessary.

Q&A

What does the Follow Up message in the Reading pane mean?

You can select from five default Follow Up flags. The message in the Reading pane corresponds to that selection and assigns a Start date and Due date to the selection (today, tomorrow, this week, and next week).

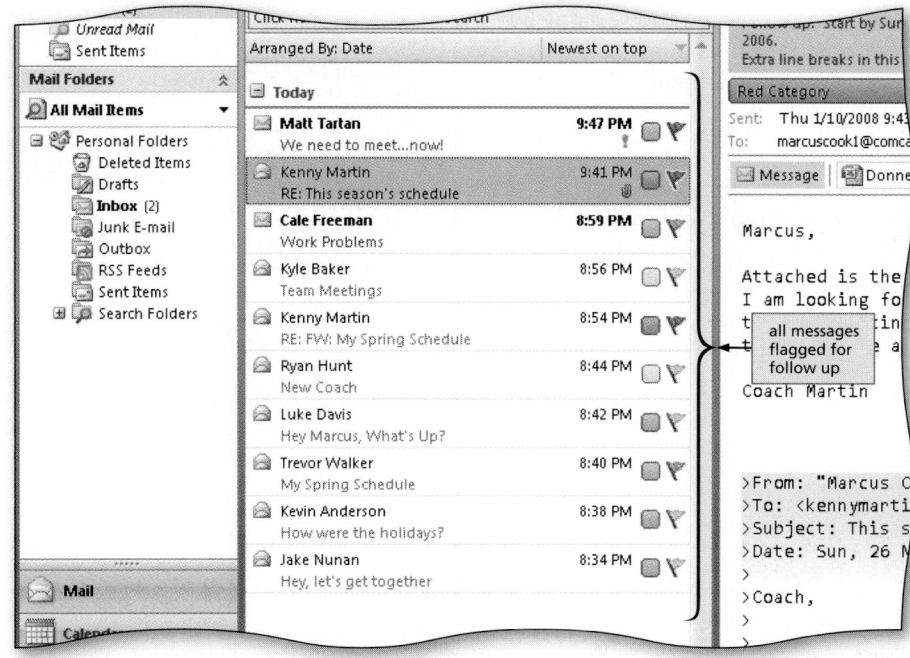

Figure 1–52

Other Ways

1. Right-click Follow Up flag, click appropriate flag

2. On Actions menu point to Follow Up, click appropriate flag

3. Click the Follow Up button on the Standard toolbar, click appropriate flag

4. Press ALT+A, press U

To Sort E-Mail Messages by Category Color

After categorizing and flagging the appropriate messages, you can sort the messages by category color. The following steps sort the messages by category color.

①

- With the Inbox window active, click View on the menu bar to open the View menu. Point to Arrange By to display the Arrange By submenu (Figure 1–53).

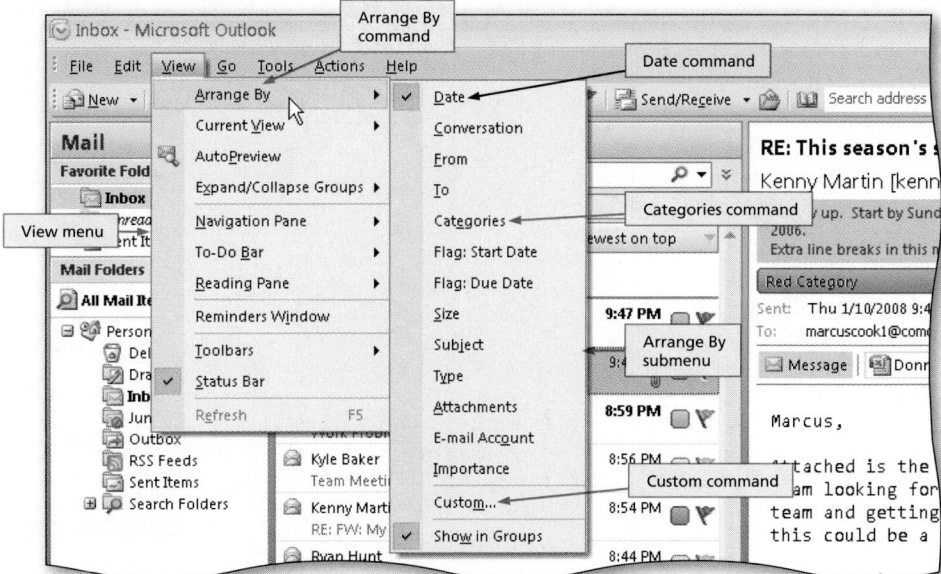

Figure 1–53

• Click Categories on the Arrange By submenu to sort the messages by Category (Figure 1–54).

• Return to the previous view by repeating Step 1 and then clicking Date on the Arrange By submenu.

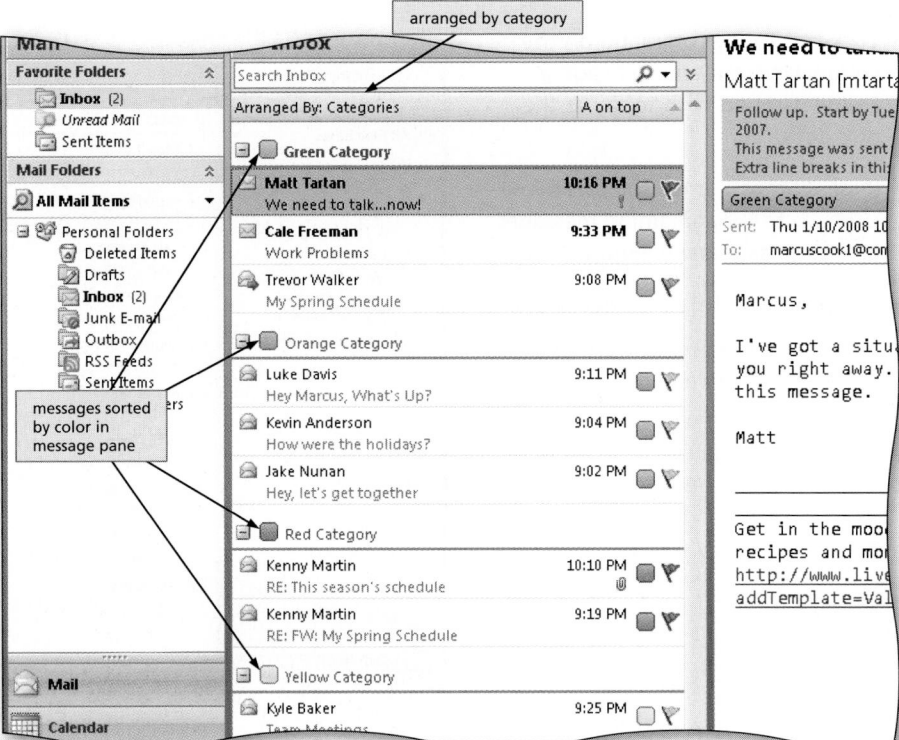

Figure 1–54

Other Ways

1. Press ALT+V, press A, press E

To Create and Apply a View Filter

The following steps create and apply a view filter to show only messages from Kenny Martin.

• With the Inbox window active, click View on the menu bar.

• Point to Arrange By on the View menu and then click Custom on the Arrange By submenu to display the Customize View: Messages dialog box (Figure 1–55).

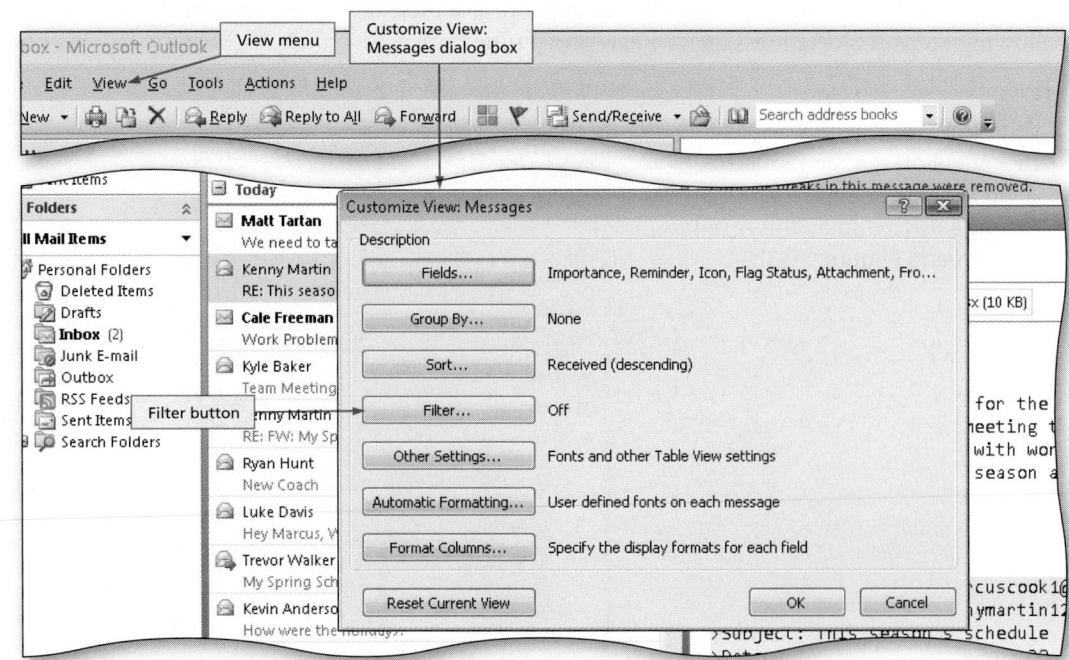

Figure 1–55

• Click the Filter button to display the Filter dialog box.

• Click the From text box (Figure 1–56).

• Type `Kenny Martin` in the From text box to specify that only e-mail messages from Kenny Martin are to appear.

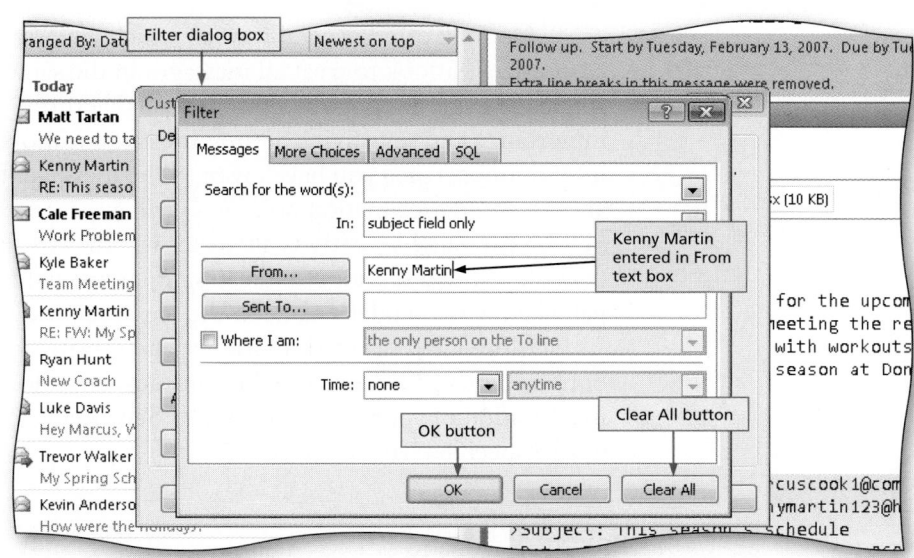

Figure 1–56

• Click the OK button in the Filter dialog box and the Customize View: Message dialog box to close both boxes and apply the view filter (Figure 1–57).

Q&A

How do I know that my other messages have not been deleted?

Outlook displays a message on the status bar and the Inbox pane title bar when a view filter is applied to a selected folder. It also shows the total number of messages remaining in the Inbox folder on the status bar.

4

• Repeat Steps 1 and 2 to display the Filter dialog box.

• Click the Clear All button in the Filter dialog box to remove the view filter.

• Close the Filter and Customize View: Message dialog boxes by clicking the OK button in each dialog box.

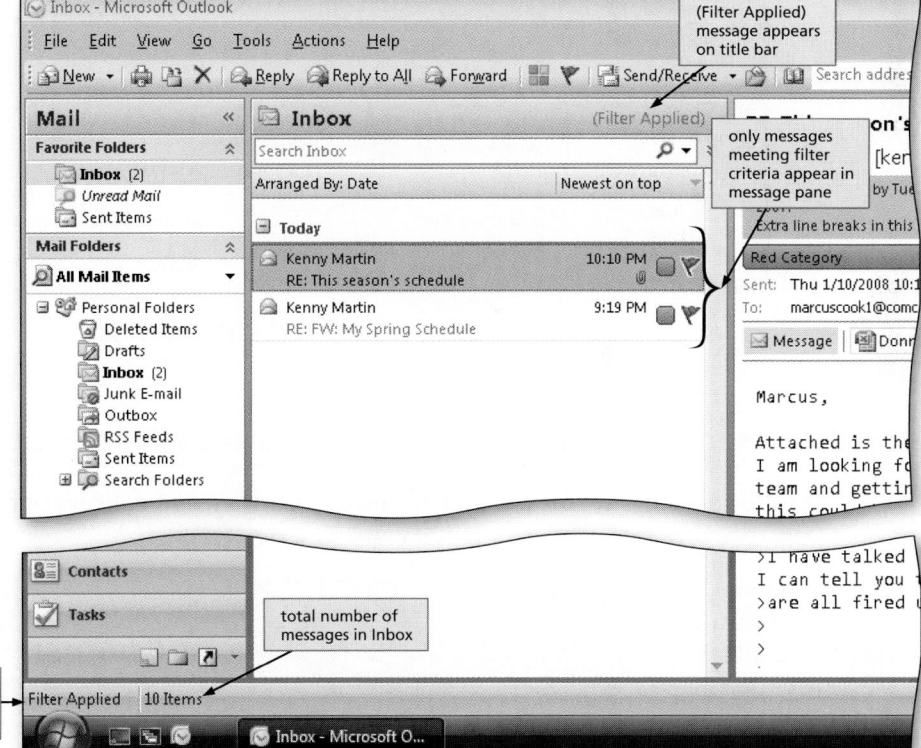

Figure 1–57

E-Mail Message Options

Outlook offers several ways in which you can customize your e-mail. You can either customize Outlook to treat all messages in the same manner, or you can customize a single message. Among the options available through Outlook are setting e-mail message importance and sensitivity. Setting **message importance** will indicate to the recipient the level of importance you have given to the message. For example, if you set the importance at high, a red exclamation point icon will appear with the message heading (Figure 1–58). Setting **message sensitivity** indicates whether the message is personal, private, or confidential. A message banner indicating the sensitivity of the message appears in the Reading pane below the sender's name in the message header, as shown in Figure 1–58.

Along with setting importance and sensitivity, Outlook also offers several delivery options. You can have replies to your message automatically forwarded, save sent messages in a location of your choice (default is Sent Items folder), or delay delivering a message until a specified date and time.

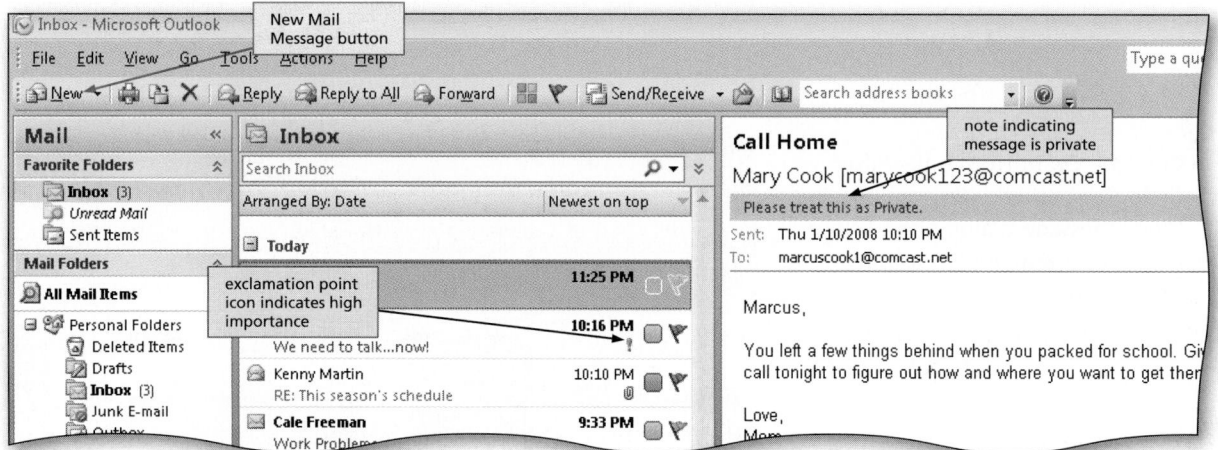

Figure 1–58

To Set Message Importance, Sensitivity, and Delivery Options in a Single Message

The following steps set message importance, sensitivity, and delivery options in a single message.

1

- With the Inbox window active, click the New Mail Message button on the Standard toolbar.

- Enter the message information (Figure 1–59).

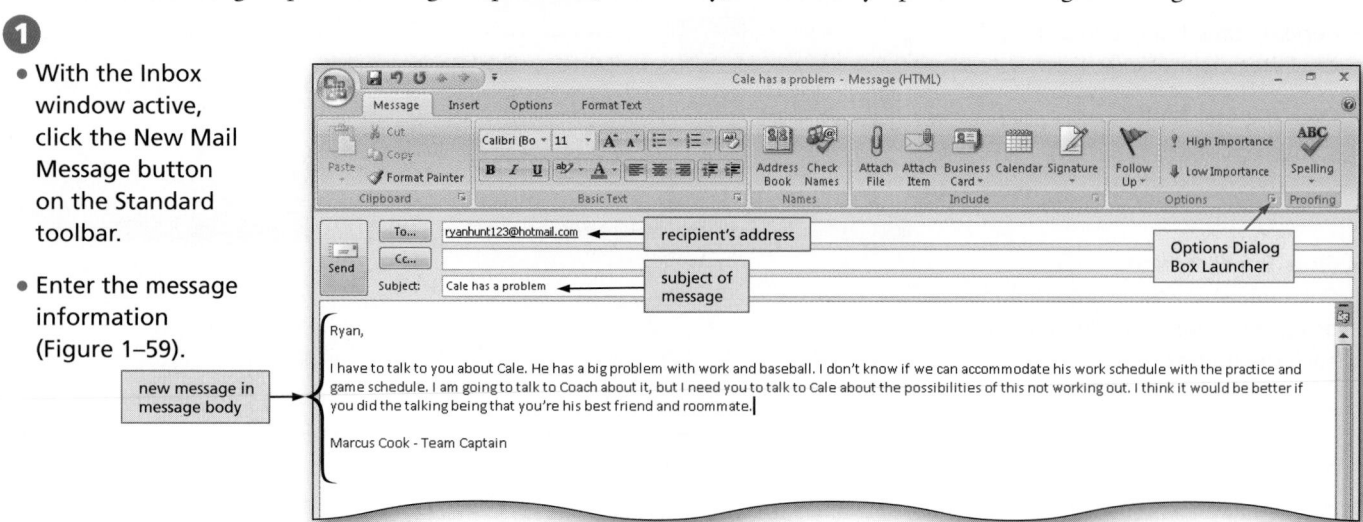

Figure 1–59

2

- Click the Options Dialog Box Launcher on the Ribbon to display the Message Options dialog box (Figure 1–60).

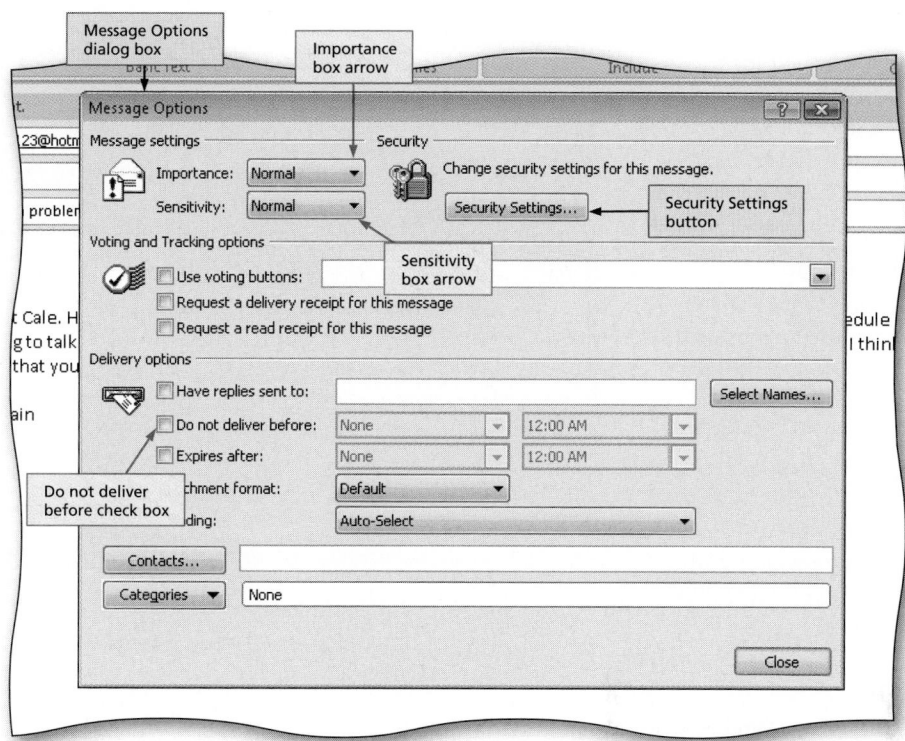

Figure 1–60

3

- Click the Importance box arrow and then select High in the Importance list.

- Click the Sensitivity box arrow and then select Private in the Sensitivity list.

- Click the 'Do not deliver before' check box in the Delivery options area to select it.

- Select January 14, 2008 in the calendar and 12:00 PM as the time in the respective delivery boxes (Figure 1–61).

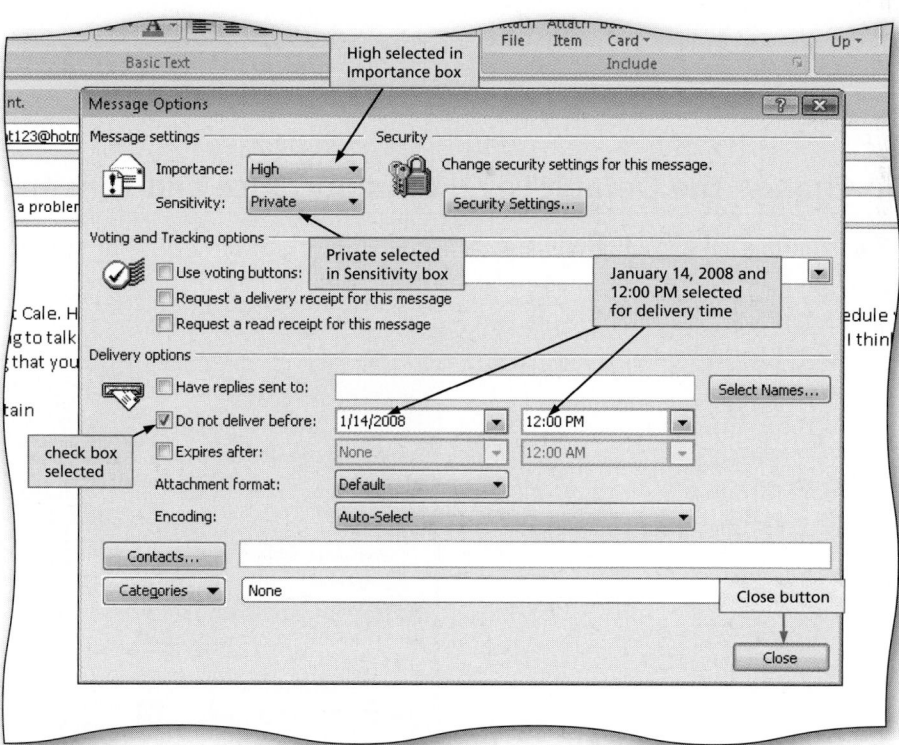

Figure 1–61

• Click the Close button to close the dialog box.

Q&A

How do I know that my settings have been applied to this message?

Notice that the High Importance button on the Ribbon is highlighted (Figure 1–62). While you cannot see it, the recipient of the message will receive the message with a red exclamation

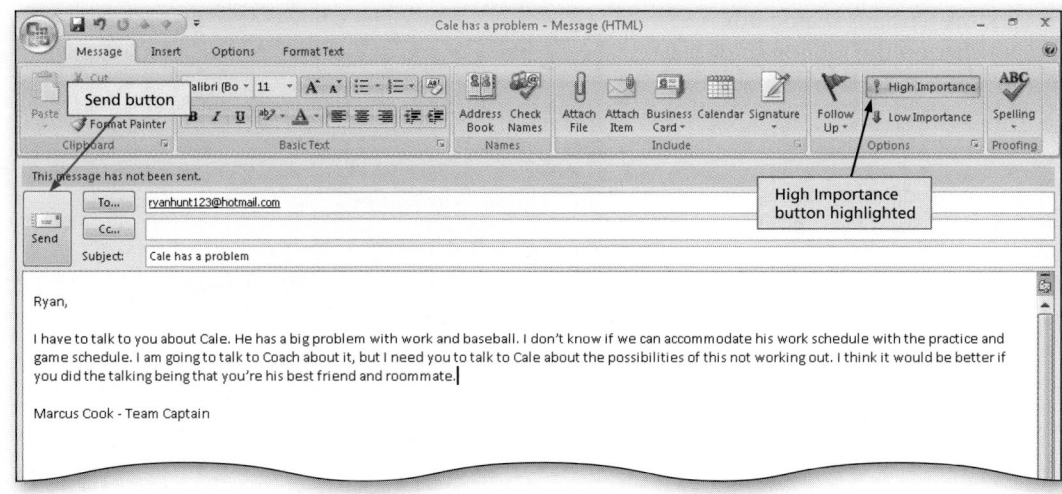

Figure 1–62

point icon and the message heading indicating the e-mail is private, like the one shown in Figure 1–58 on page OUT 38.

• Click the Send button to send the message.

Q&A

What does Outlook do with the message while it is waiting for the specified date and time to send the message?

Outlook stores the message in the Outbox folder until the specified date and time arrive. At that time, the message will be sent.

To Change the Default Level of Importance and Sensitivity

Outlook allows you to change the default level for either or both of these options. The following steps change the default level of importance and sensitivity for all outgoing messages.

• With the Inbox window active, click Tools on the menu bar and then click Options on the Tools menu to display the Options dialog box (Figure 1–63).

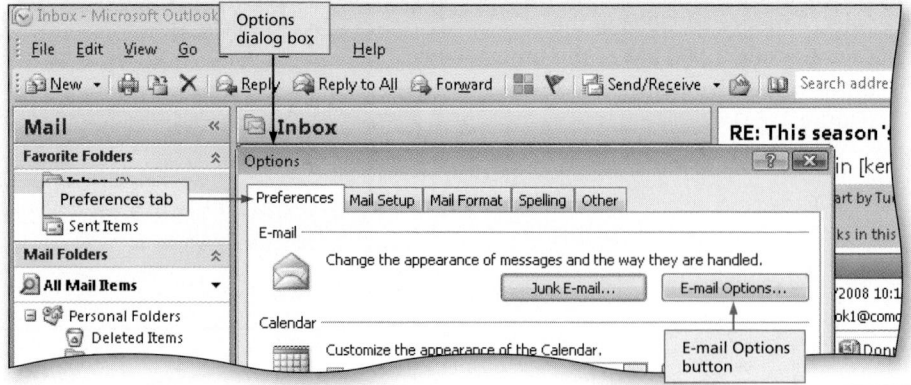

Figure 1–63

2

- In the Preferences sheet, click the E-mail Options button to display the E-mail Options dialog box (Figure 1–64).

- Click the Advanced E-mail Options button to open the Advanced E-mail Options dialog box.

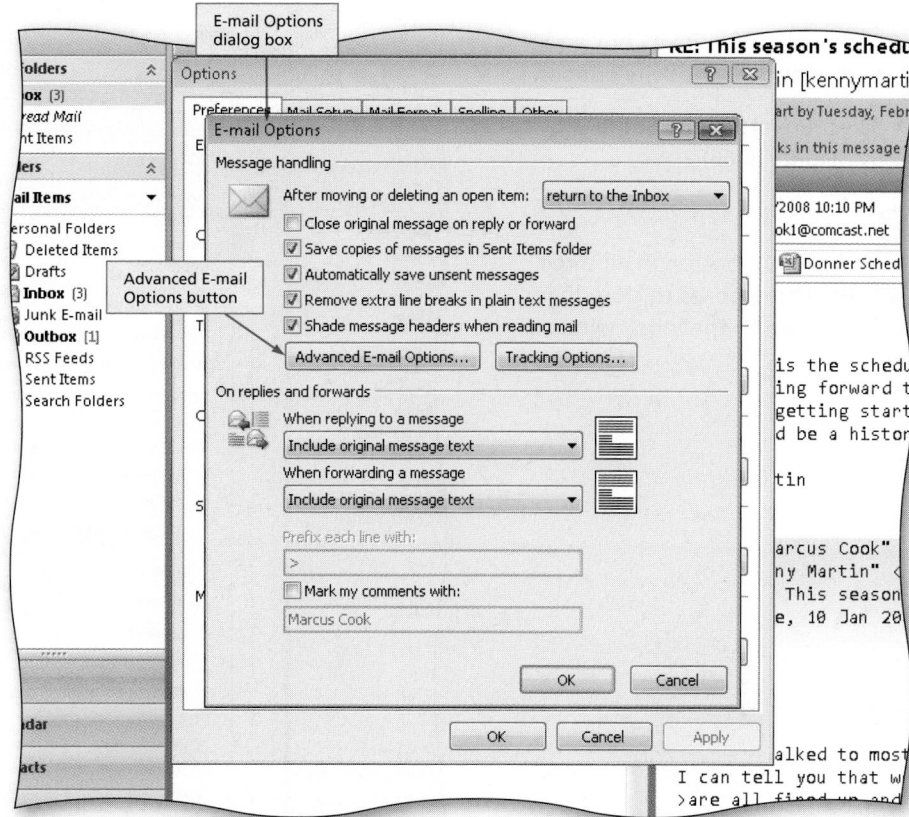

Figure 1–64

3

- Click the Set importance box arrow to display the importance options (Figure 1–65).

- Select High in the Set importance list.

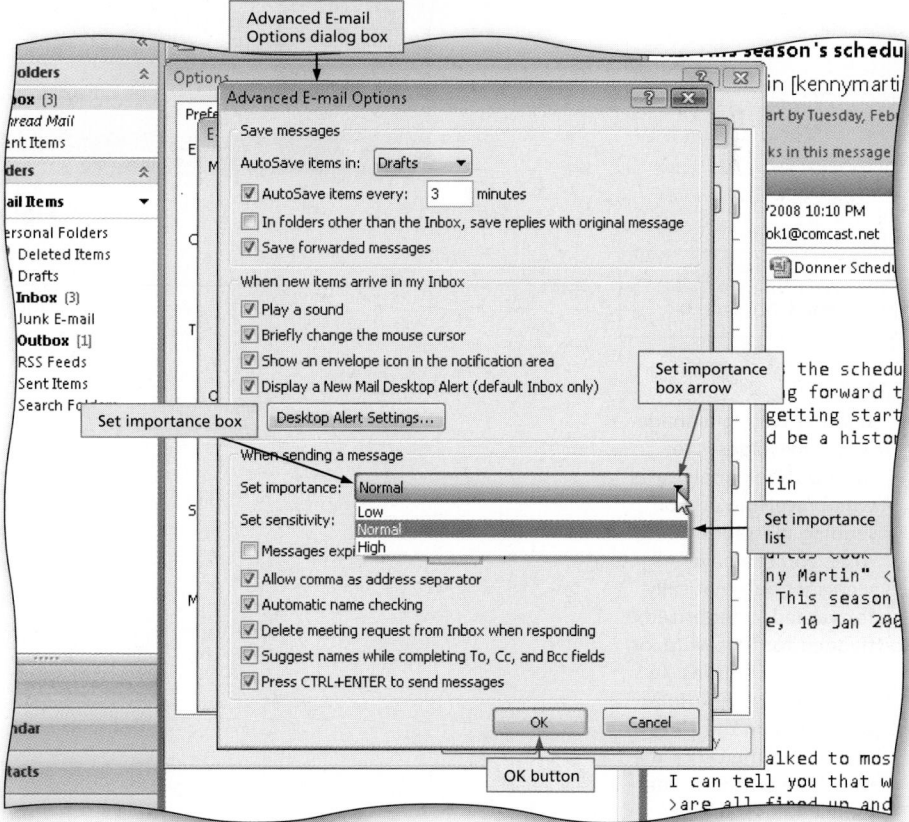

Figure 1–65

- Click the Set sensitivity box arrow to display the sensitivity options.

- Select Private in the Set sensitivity list (Figure 1–66).

- Click the OK button in all three open dialog boxes to close them and return to the Inbox window.

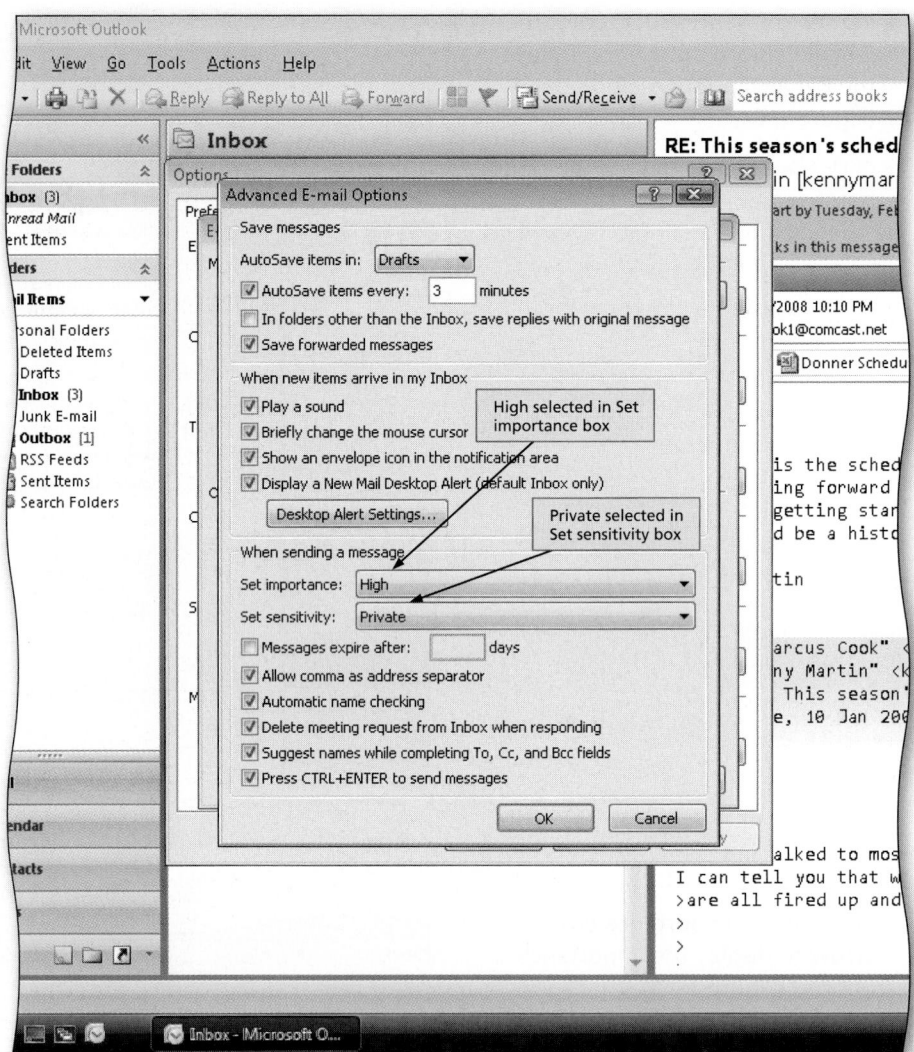

Figure 1–66

BTW

Rules
Another way to manage e-mail messages is to have Outlook apply rules when receiving and/or sending messages. Using rules, you can have messages automatically forwarded, categorized, flagged for follow up, or apply other options. To create a rule, click Rules and Alerts on the Tools menu, and then click the New Rule button in the E-mail Rules sheet of the Rules and Alerts dialog box.

Search Folders

Outlook offers a feature called the Search Folders folder in the Mail Folders pane (Figure 1–67). The **Search Folders folder** includes a group of folders that allows you to group and view your messages quickly in one of three ways: (1) Categorized Mail, (2) Large Mail, and (3) Unread Mail. **Categorized Mail** messages are messages to which you have assigned a category. These messages are sorted by color. **Large Mail** messages are messages containing very large file attachments. These messages are grouped by size: Large (100 to 500 KB), Very Large (500 KB to 1 MB), and Huge (1 to 5 MB). **Unread Mail** comprises messages that have not been opened or have not been marked as read even though you may have read them in the Reading pane. Figure 1–67 shows messages in the Categorized Mail folder.

BTW

Security Settings
Clicking the Security Settings button (Figure 1–60 on page OUT 39) opens a dialog box that allows you to apply certain security restrictions on a message, such as encrypting the message or adding a digital signature.

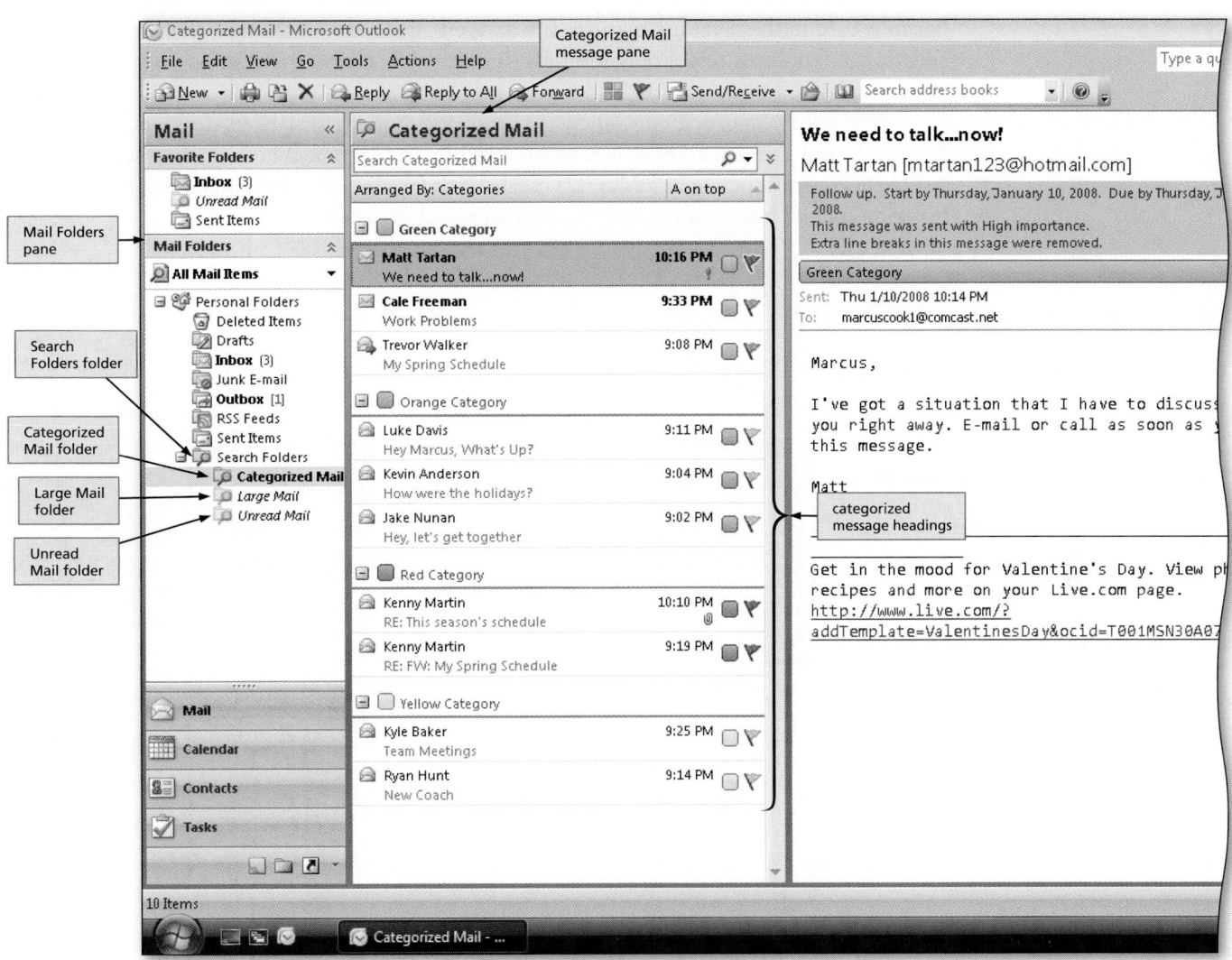

Figure 1–67

Using Contacts

The **Contacts component** of Outlook allows you to store information about individuals and companies. People with whom you communicate for school, business, or personal reasons are your **contacts**. To help organize information about personal contacts, some people keep names, addresses, and telephone numbers in business card files and address books. With the Outlook Contacts component, you can create and maintain important contact information in a **contact list**, which is stored in the Contacts folder. Your contact list is like an electronic address book that allows you to store names, addresses, e-mail addresses, and more. Once you have entered the information, you can retrieve, sort, edit, organize, or print your contact list. Outlook also includes a **Find option** that lets you search for a contact name in your address book while you are using the Calendar, Inbox, or other Outlook components.

When the Contacts folder is open, information about each contact appears on a business card in the default **Business Cards view**. Each card includes fields for name, address, and multiple telephone numbers (home, work, cellular, and so on), e-mail, and Web page addresses. You can choose which fields are displayed on the cards using the View menu.

Previously, an e-mail message was composed, signed, formatted, and sent to Kenny Martin. Kenny's e-mail address was typed into the To text box. The following sections show how to (1) create a personal folder; (2) create a contact list; (3) edit contact information; (4) print contact information; and (5) send an e-mail to a contact.

To Create a Personal Folder

The following steps create a personal folder for Marcus Cook.

1

- Click the Contacts button in the Navigation Pane to open the Contacts window.

- When Outlook displays the Contacts window, right-click Contacts in the My Contacts pane to display the Contacts shortcut menu (Figure 1–68).

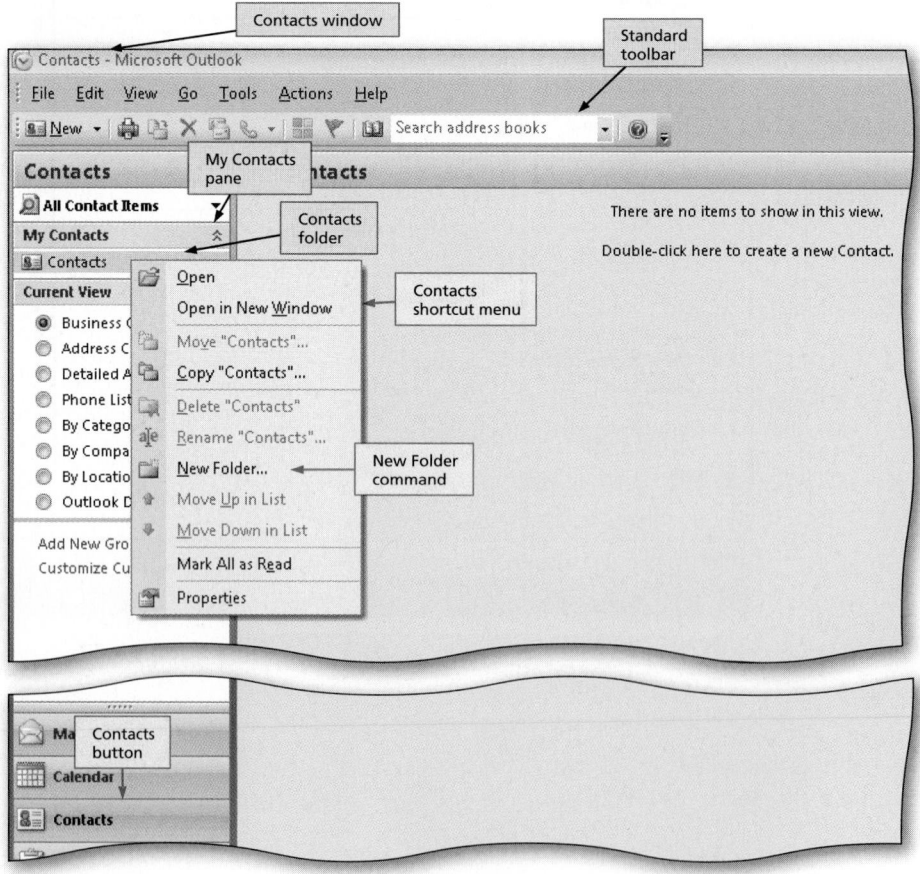

Figure 1–68

2

- Click New Folder on the Contacts shortcut menu to display the Create New Folder dialog box. Type `Marcus' Contacts` in the Name text box (Figure 1–69).

- If necessary, select Contact Items in the Folder contains list.

- Click Contacts in the Select where to place the folder list.

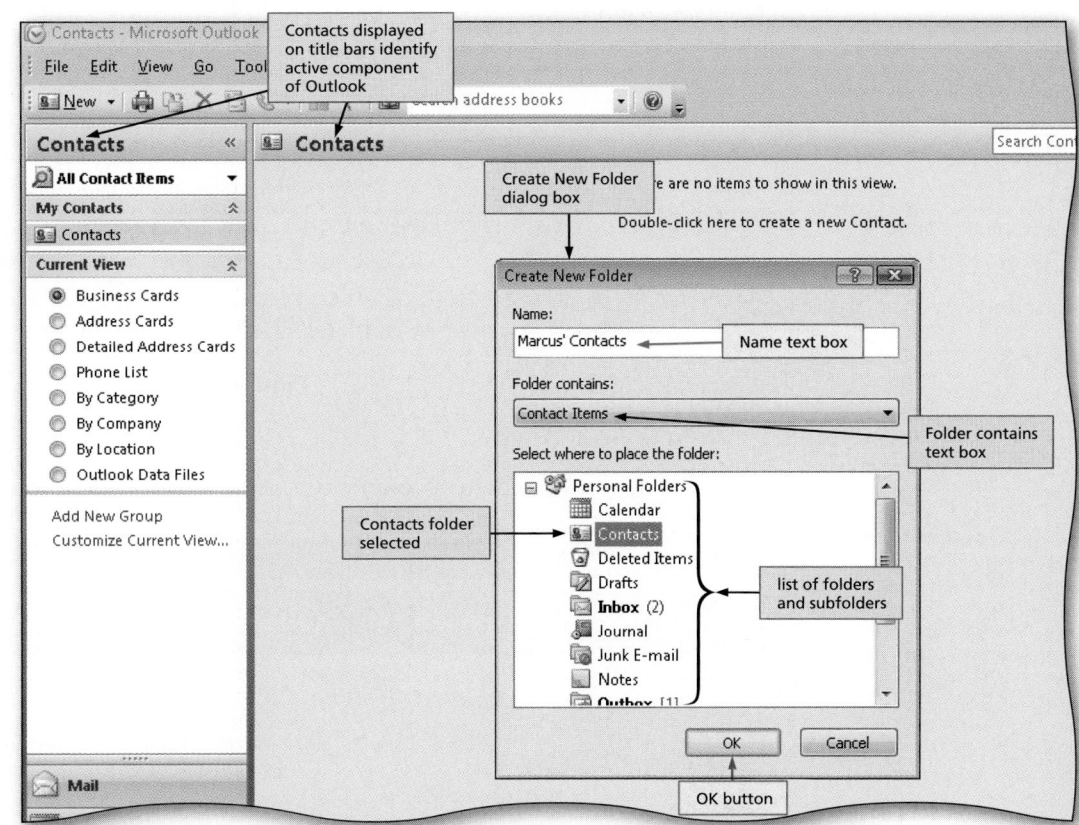

Figure 1–69

3

- Click the OK button to close the Create New Folder dialog box.

- In the Contacts window, click Marcus' Contacts in the My Contacts list (Figure 1–70).

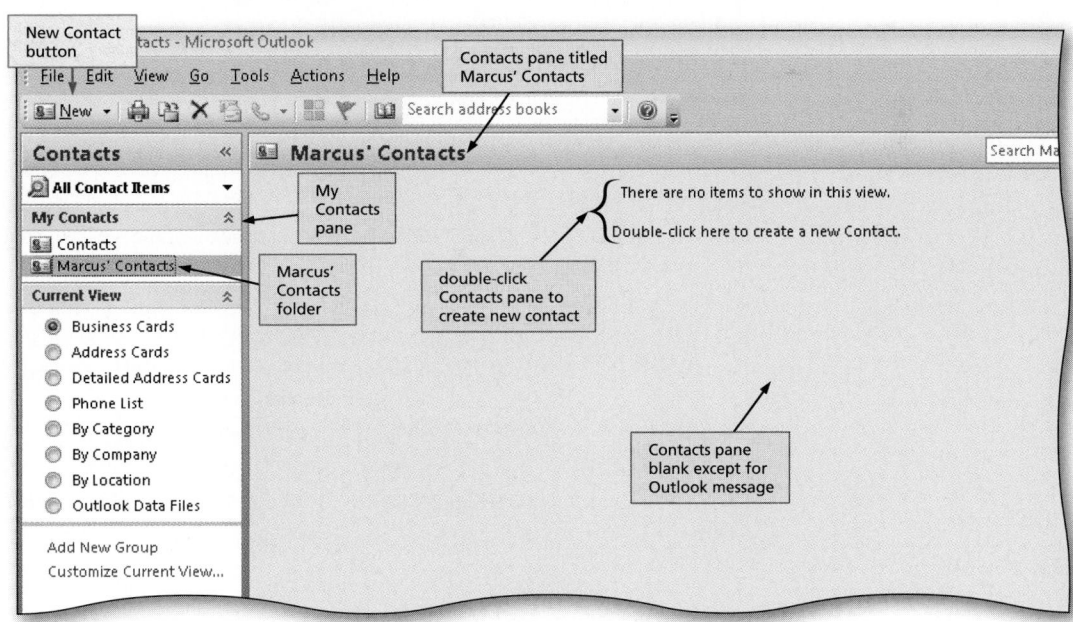

Figure 1–70

Other Ways		
1. On File menu point to New, click Folder on New submenu	2. On File menu point to Folder, click New Folder on Folder submenu	
	3. Press CTRL+SHIFT+E	

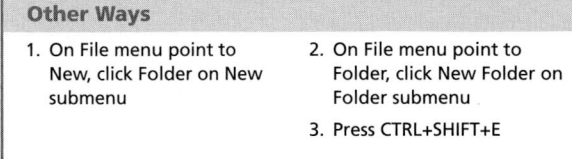

Figure 1–71 illustrates the Standard toolbar located below the menu bar in the Contacts window.

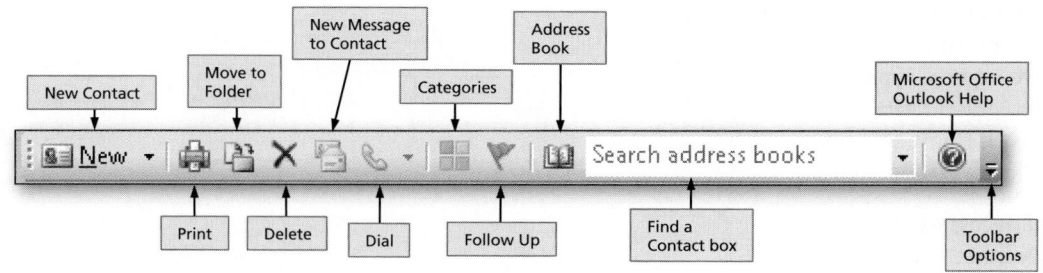

Figure 1–71

Next, you will create a contact list using the information included in Table 1–3.

Table 1–3 Contact Information			
Name	**Telephone**	**Address**	**E-Mail Address**
Kenny Martin	(937) 555-4120	8465 W. 63rd St. Donner, OH 44772	kennymartin123@hotmail.com
Jose Quinteras	(937) 555-7539	8868 Ashwood Lane Donner, OH 44772	josequinteras123@hotmail.com
Kelly Shurpa	(937) 555-9823	214 W. Lincoln Ave. Donner, OH 44772	kshurpa123@hotmail.com
Matt Tartan	(937) 555-0258	5246 Brookfield Ct. Donner, OH 44772	mtartan123@hotmail.com
Jim Osmont	(937) 555-6211	9812 River Rd. Donner, OH 44772	josmont123@hotmail.com
Cale Freeman	(937) 555-3080	7894 Forrest View Lane Donner, OH 44772	calefreeman123@hotmail.com
Kyle Baker	(937) 555-5279	7892 Buckingham Drive Donner, OH 44772	kylebaker101@hotmail.com
Ryan Hunt	(937) 555-1683	8792 Edgewater Lane Donner, OH 44772	ryanhunt123@hotmail.com
Luke Davis	(937) 555-2794	6776 Maplewood Blvd. Donner, OH 44772	lukedavis101@hotmail.com
Trevor Walker	(937) 555-8805	4476 Maplewood Blvd. Donner, OH 44772	trevwalker123@hotmail.com
Kevin Anderson	(937) 555-6309	1021 Ward Rd. Donner, OH 44772	kevanderson123@hotmail.com
Jake Nunan	(937) 555-2148	8924 65th Street Donner, OH 4477	jakenunan123@hotmail.com

To Create a Contact List

The following steps create a contact list.

● With the Contacts window active and Marcus' Contacts folder selected, click the New Contact button on the Standard toolbar (Figure 1–70 on page OUT 45) to open the Untitled-Contact window. If necessary, maximize the window.

● Type Kenny Martin in the Full Name text box (Figure 1–72).

● Click the Home text box in the Phone numbers area.

● Type 9375554120 as the home telephone number.

● Click the Addresses box arrow and select Home. (If the Location Information dialog box appears, enter your local area code and click the OK button to close the dialog box.)

● Click the text box in the Addresses area, type 8465 W. 63rd St. and then press the ENTER key.

● Type Donner, OH 44772 to complete the address entry.

● Click the E-mail text box.

● Type kennymartin123 @hotmail.com as the e-mail address and then press the TAB key to complete the contact information for Kenny Martin (Figure 1–73).

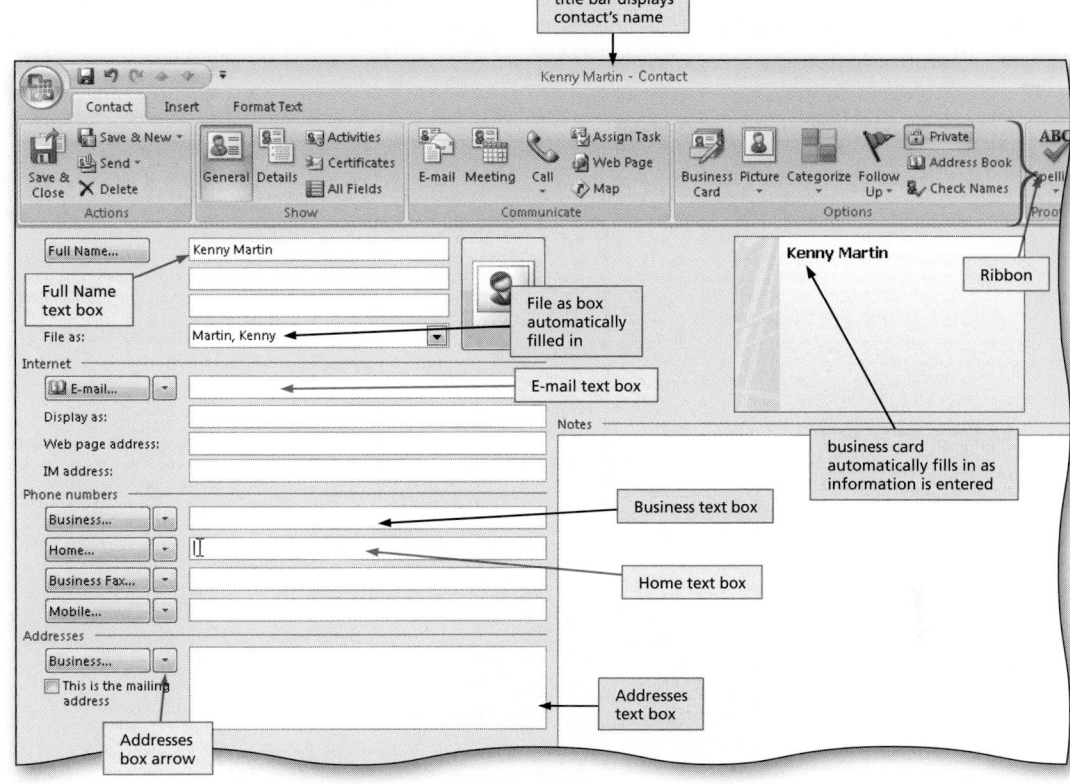

Figure 1–72

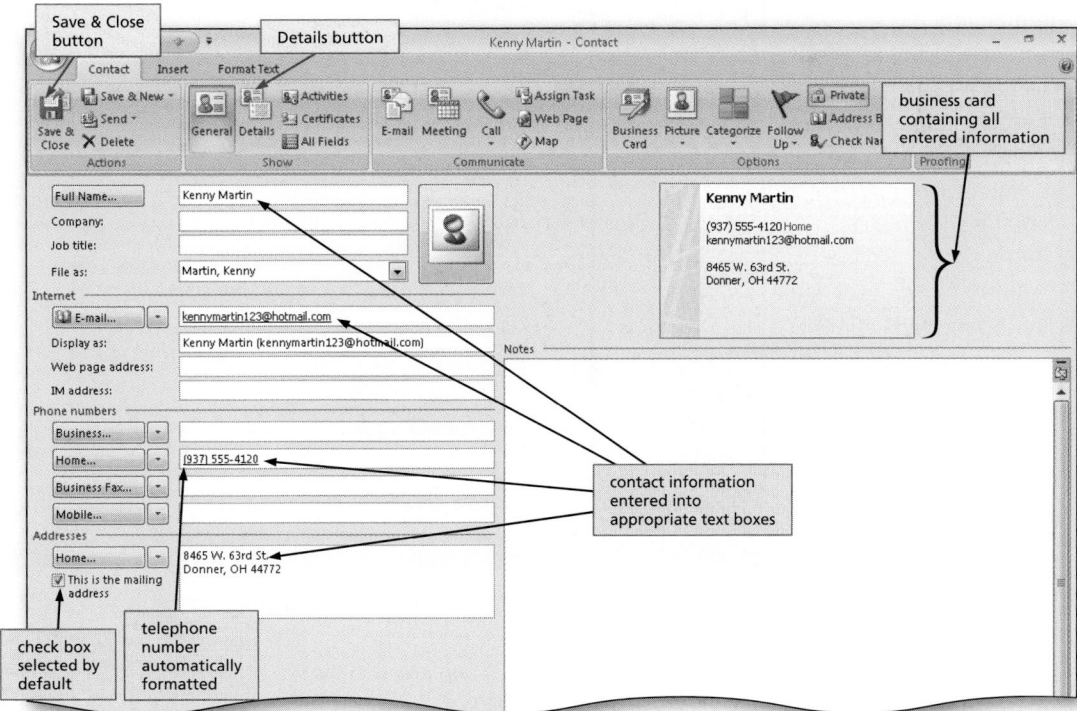

Figure 1–73

3

• Click the Save & Close button on the Ribbon to display the Marcus' Contacts window with the Kenny Martin business card in the Marcus' Contacts pane (Figure 1–74).

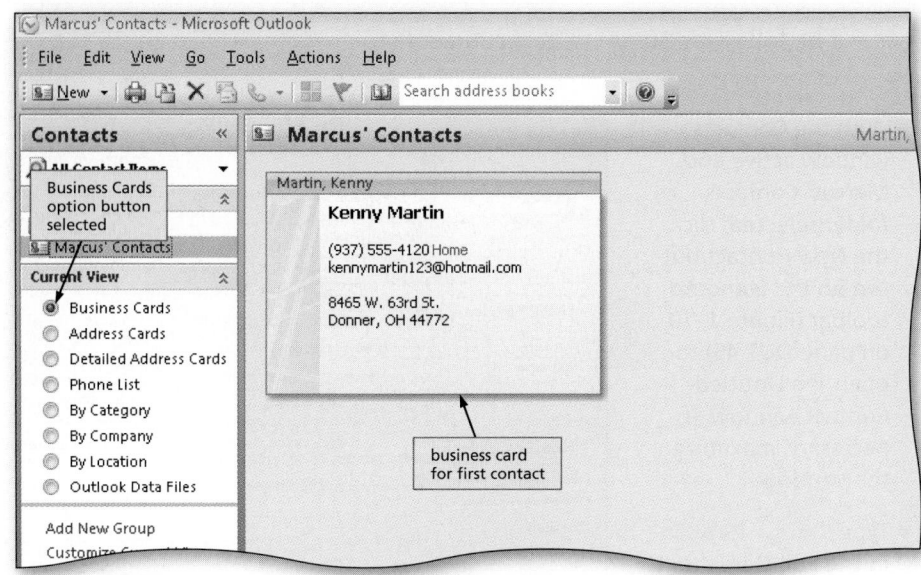

Figure 1–74

4

• Click the New Contact button on the Standard toolbar.

• Repeat Steps 2 through 4 to enter the 11 remaining contacts in Table 1–3 (Figure 1–75).

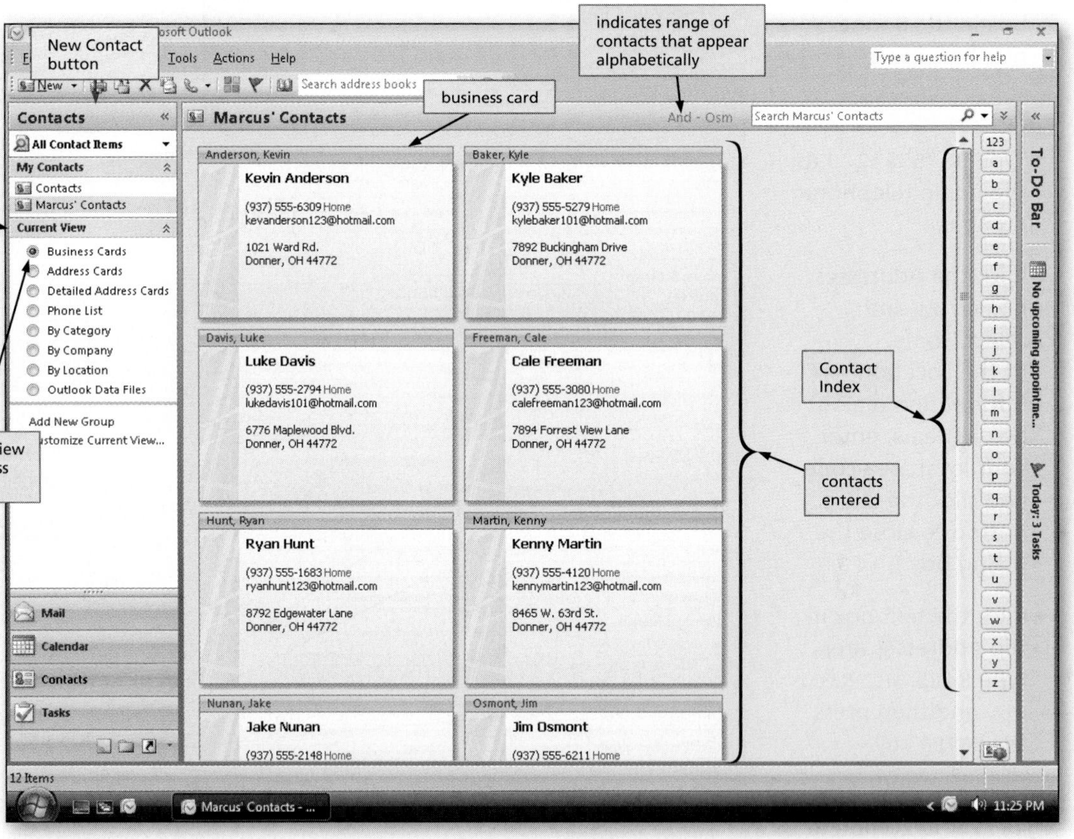

Q&A

Is it possible to store information different from what is shown in the Contact window?

By clicking the Details command in the Show group on the Ribbon (Figure 1–73 on page OUT 47), you can enter a contact's department, manager's name, nickname, and birthday information.

Figure 1–75

Other Ways	
1. On File menu point to New, click Contact on New submenu	2. On Actions menu click New Contact
	3. Press CTRL+SHIFT+C

To Change the View and Sort the Contact List

The following steps change the view from Business Cards to Phone List, sort the contact list in descending sequence, and then change back to Business Cards view.

1

- With the Marcus' Contacts – Microsoft Outlook window active, click Phone List in the Current View pane of the Navigation Pane.

- With the Phone List in ascending sequence by the File As field, click the File As column heading in the Contacts pane to display the contact list in descending sequence by last name (Figure 1–76).

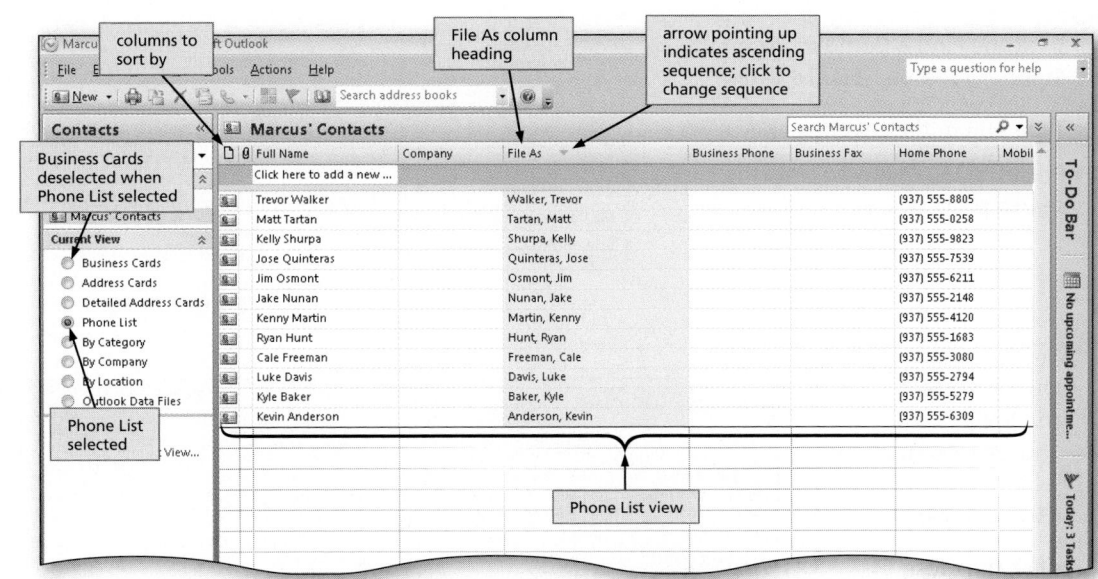

Figure 1–76

2

- After reviewing the contact list in Phone List view, click Business Cards in the Current View pane in the Navigation Pane to return to Business Cards view.

Q&A

Are there other ways to sort Outlook information?

If you right-click a column heading in any Outlook component and point to the Arrange By command on the shortcut menu (Figure 1–77), you can see the Arrange By commands.

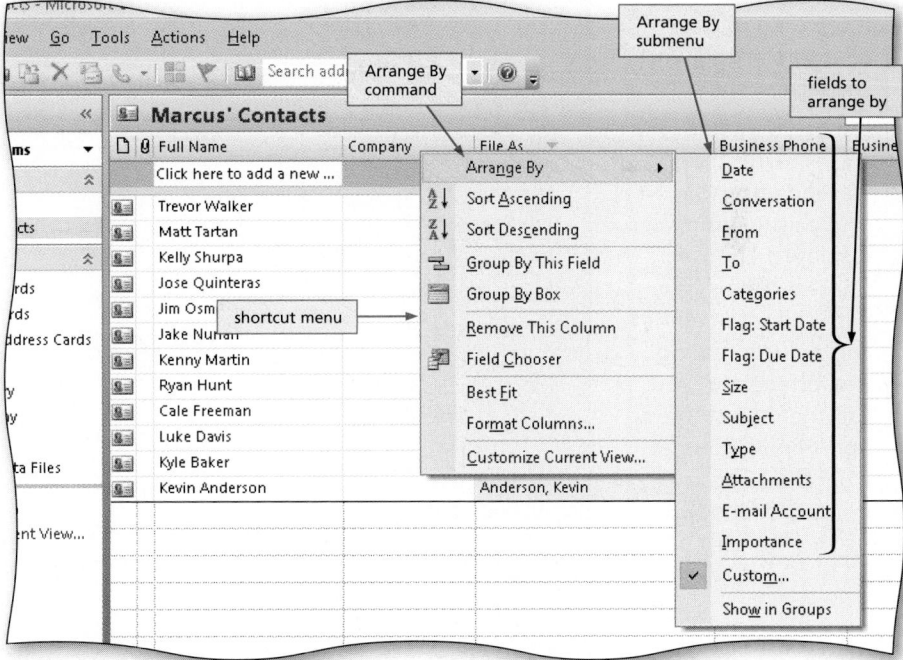

Figure 1–77

To Find a Contact

A contact record was created for Kelly Shurpa. This record can be found easily by using the Find a Contact box to type a part of the contact name as shown in the following steps.

1

- Click the Find a Contact box on the Standard toolbar (Figure 1–78).

- Type shu in the text box.

- Press the ENTER key to start the search process.

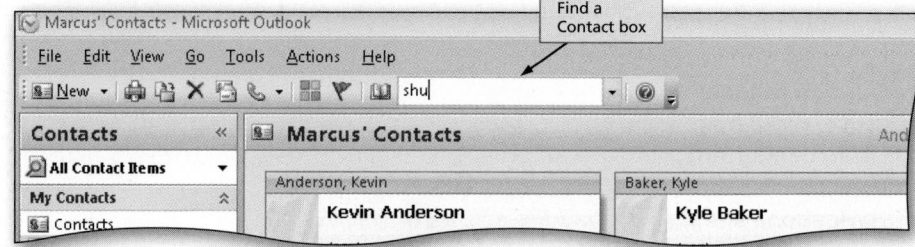

Figure 1–78

2

- Outlook opens the Kelly Shurpa – Contact window (Figure 1–79).

- Click the Close button to return to Business Card view.

Q&A

What if there is more than one contact starting with the letters, shu?

If more than one contact with the starting letters, shu, exists, Outlook displays a Choose Contact dialog box with the list of all contacts containing the letters, shu. You can then select the appropriate contact from the Choose Contact dialog box.

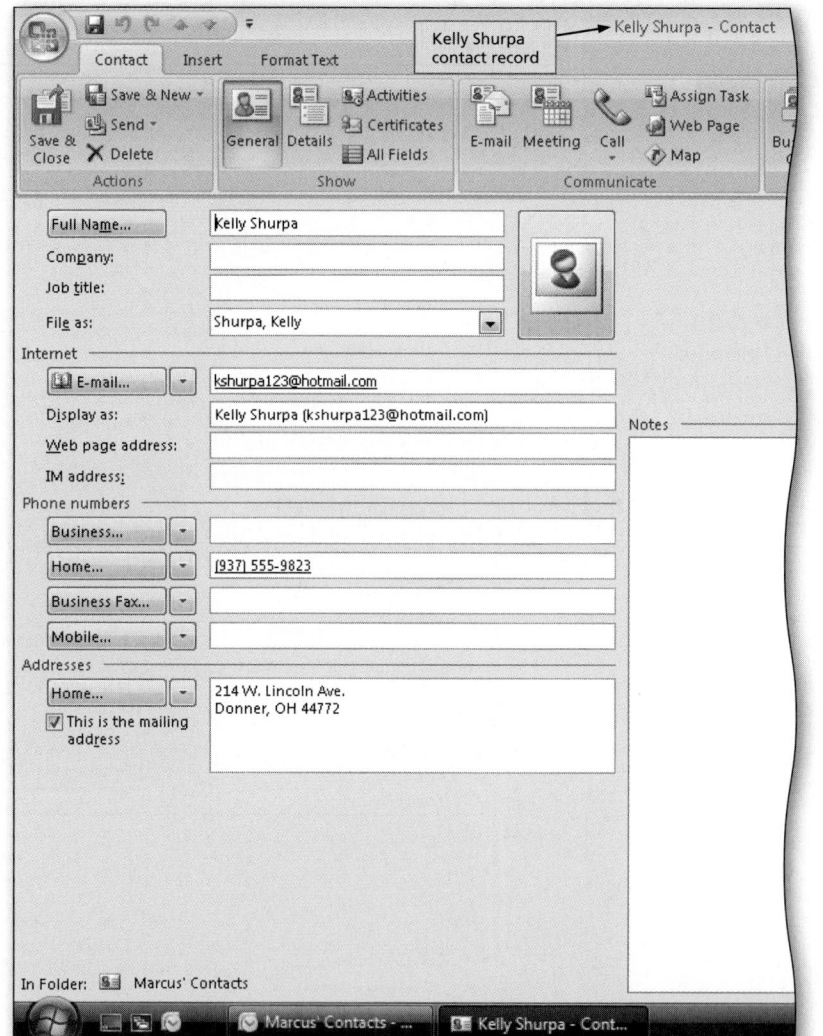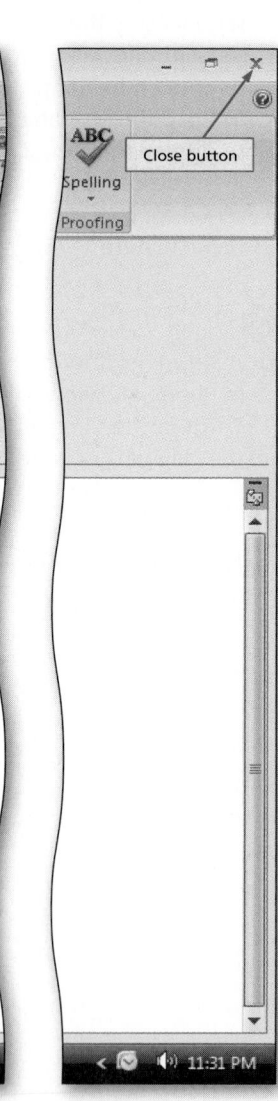

Figure 1–79

Other Ways

1. On Tools menu point to Instant Search, click Instant Search on Instant Search submenu

2. Press CTRL+SHIFT+F

To Organize Contacts

To help manage your contacts further, the contact list can be categorized and sorted using Outlook's default color categories, or using your own categories to group contacts by company, department, a particular project, a specific class, and so on. You also can sort by any part of the address; for example, you can sort by postal code for bulk mailings. The following steps assign the baseball players as a contact category with a color designation.

- Click Tools on the menu bar and then click Organize on the Tools menu.

- Click the name bar of the Kevin Anderson contact record.

- Hold down the CTRL key and then click the name bars of Cale Freeman and Ryan Hunt.

- Release the CTRL key.

- Click the 'Add contacts selected below to' box arrow to display a list of categories (Figure 1–80).

- Click Blue Category in the list.

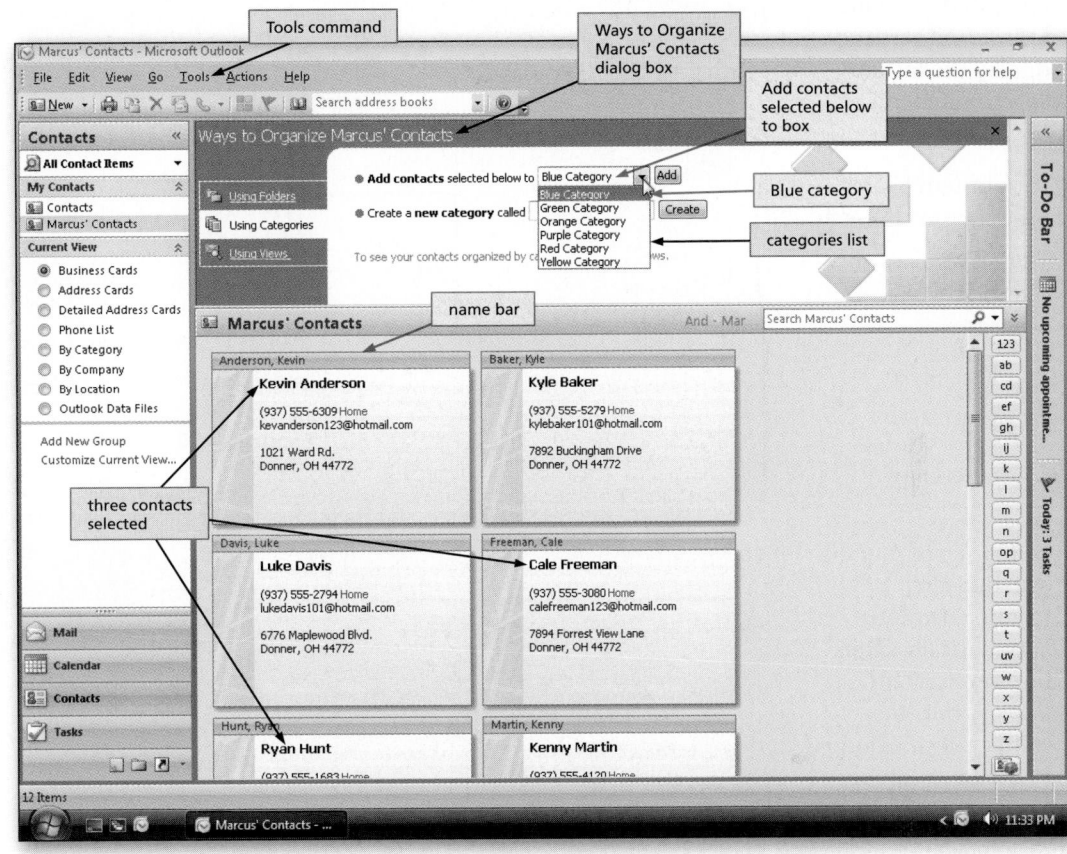

Figure 1–80

- Click the Add button to add the selected records to the Blue Category (Figure 1–81).

- Click the Close button in the Ways to Organize Marcus' Contacts dialog box to close it.

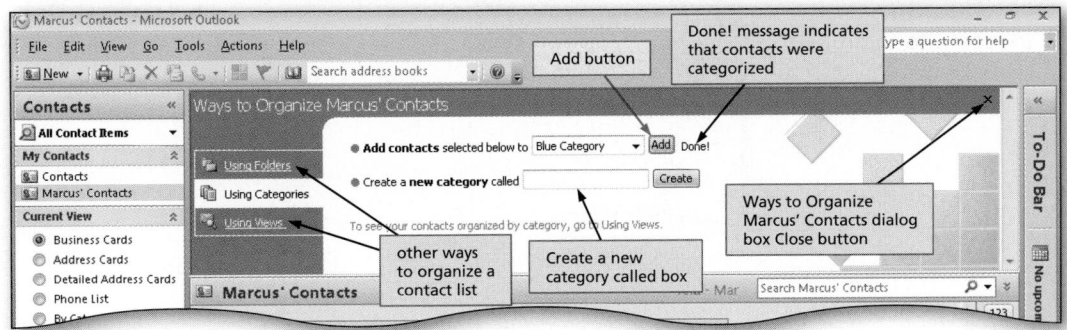

Figure 1–81

Other Ways

1. Press ALT+T, press Z

To Display the Contacts in a Category

The following steps use the Instant Search command to display contacts within a certain category.

1

- With the Contacts window active, click Tools on the menu bar and then point to Instant Search to display the Instant Search submenu (Figure 1–82).

- Click Instant Search on the Instant Search submenu.

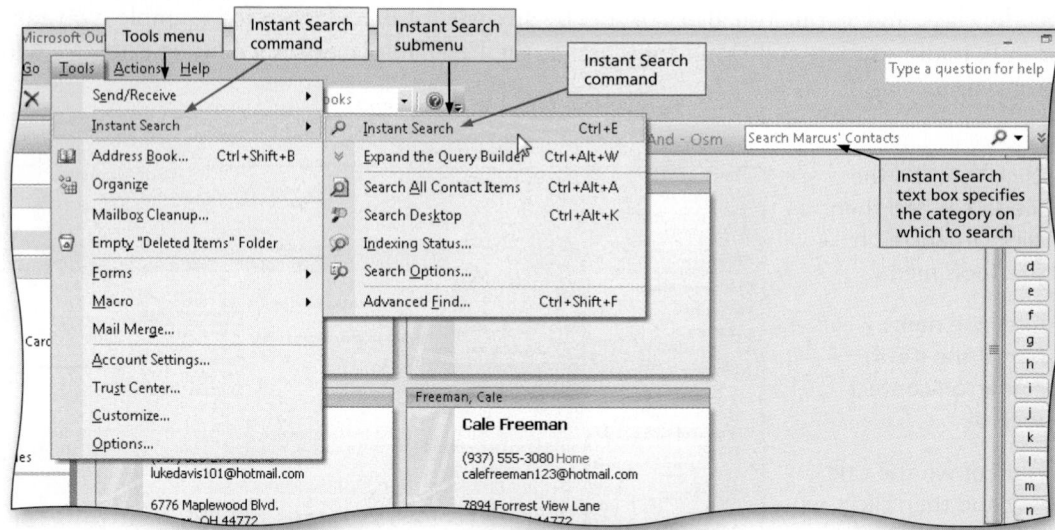

Figure 1–82

2

- Type Blue Category in the Instant Search text box. Outlook automatically filters the contacts and displays only the contacts that belong to the Blue Category (Figure 1–83).

- After viewing the contacts in the Blue Category, click the Clear Search button to return to the full Contacts window.

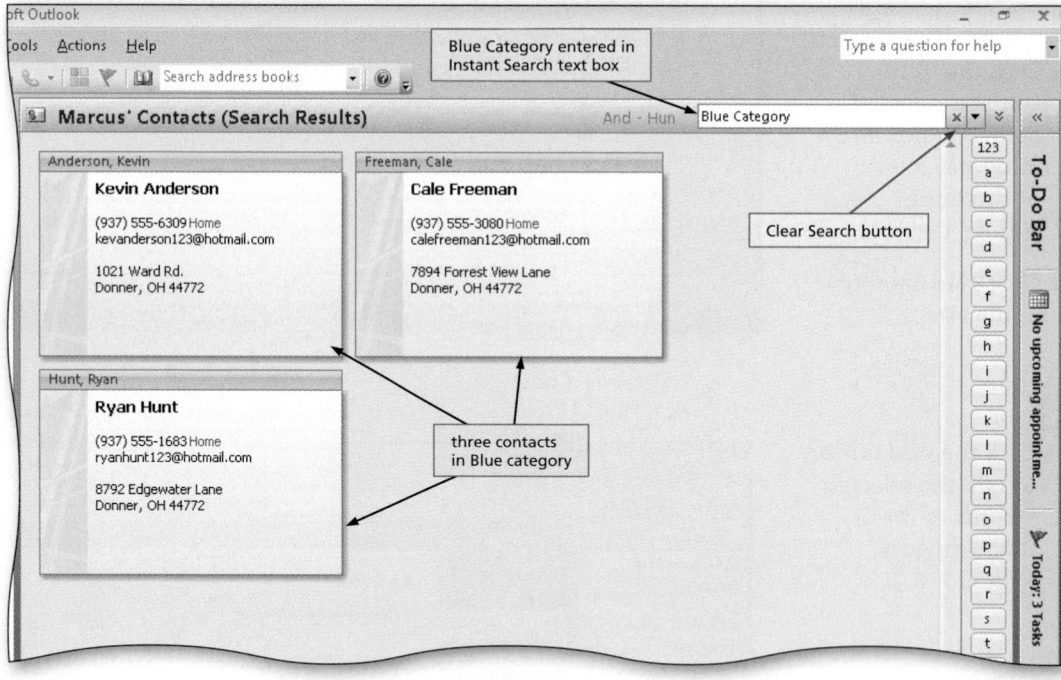

Figure 1–83

Other Ways

1. Press CTRL+E
2. Press ALT+T, press I

To Preview and Print the Contact List

The following steps preview and print the entire contact list.

1

● With the Contacts window active, click the Print button on the Standard toolbar to display the Print dialog box (Figure 1–84).

● Click the Preview button to display a preview of the printout (Figure 1–85 on the next page).

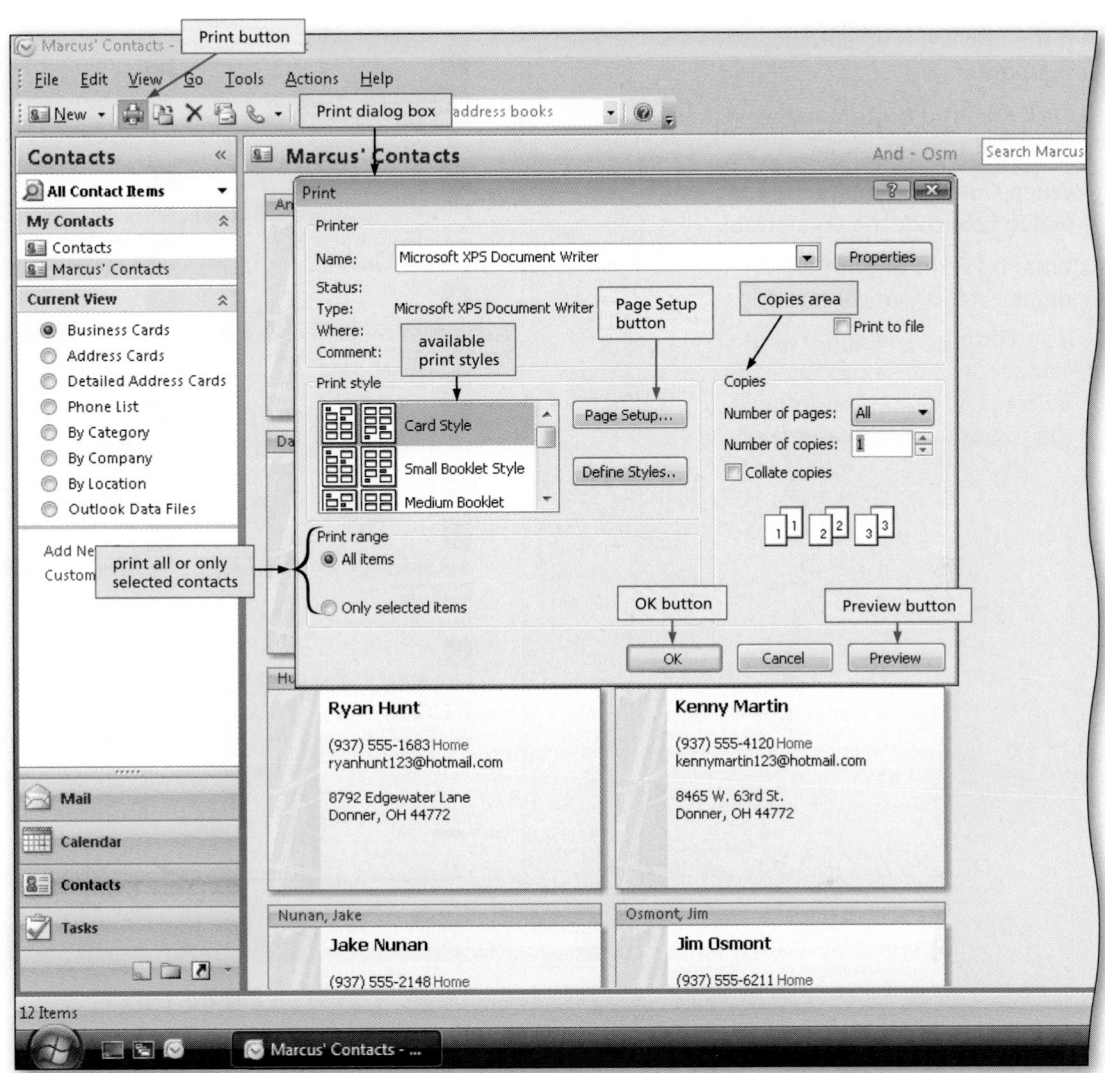

Figure 1–84

BTW

Contacts
You can organize contacts from one or more Contacts folders in a personal distribution list. Outlook also detects duplicates and provides the option to merge the new information with the existing contact entry. You also can filter your contact list and then use the filtered list to begin a mail merge from Outlook.

2

- After viewing the preview of the printed contacts list, click the Close button.

- If the preview is acceptable, ready the printer.

- Click the Print button on the Standard toolbar.

- When Outlook displays the Print dialog box, click the OK button.

Q&A

What if I want to print just a single category of contacts?

If you display a category of contacts and then click the Print button, Outlook will print only the contacts in that category.

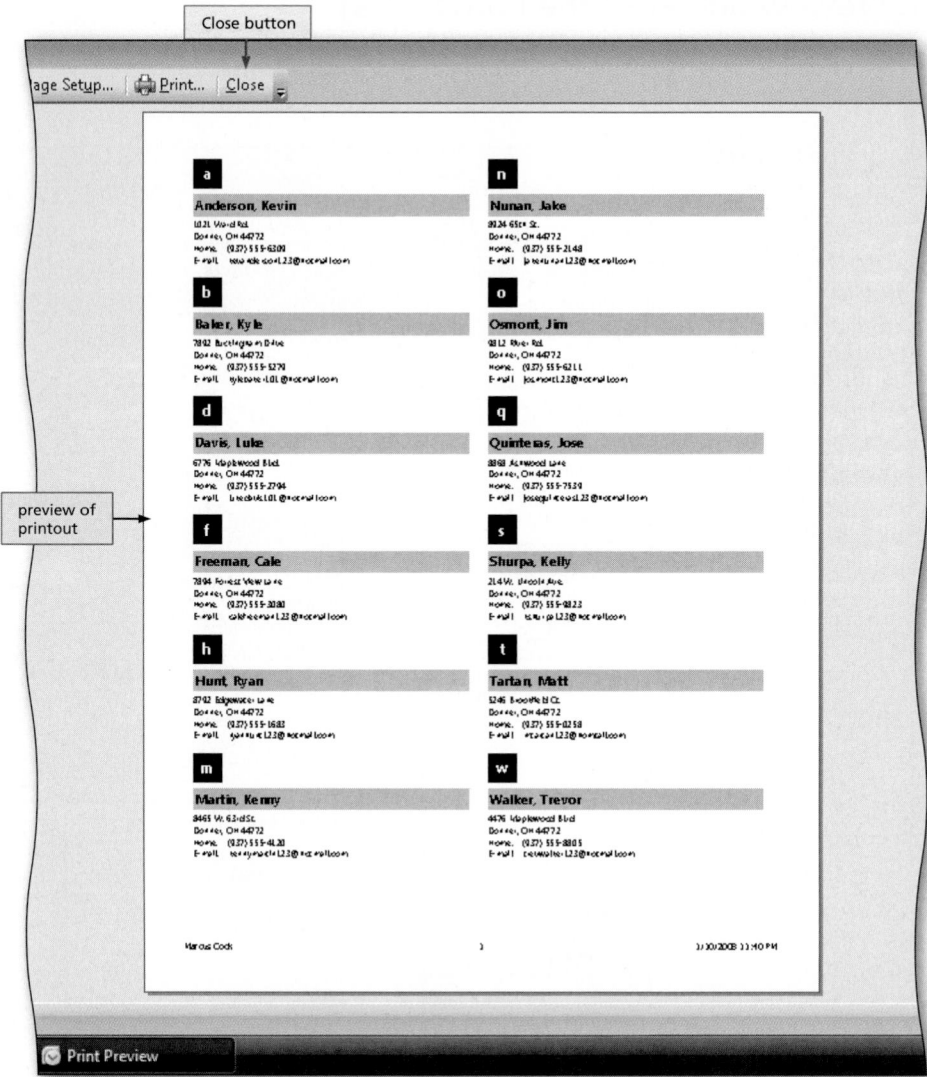

Figure 1–85

Other Ways

1. On File menu click Print
2. On File menu click Print Preview, click Print button in Print Preview window
3. Press CTRL+P

BTW

Business Contact Manager

Outlook 2007 with Business Contact Manager offers complete small business contact management capabilities to Outlook 2007. It allows you to organize customer and prospect information, manage sales and marketing activities, develop and track marketing activities, and centralize project information in one location. Among the capabilities of Business Contact Manager are tools for creating targeted mailing lists, personalizing and distributing print and e-mail marketing materials, and tracking results.

To Use the Contact List to Address an E-Mail Message

The following steps use the contact list to address an e-mail message to Matt Tartan.

1

- Click the Mail button in the Navigation Pane to display the Inbox window.

- Click the New Mail Message button on the Standard toolbar to display the Untitled – Message window (Figure 1–86).

- When Outlook displays the Untitled – Message window, if necessary, double-click its title bar to maximize it.

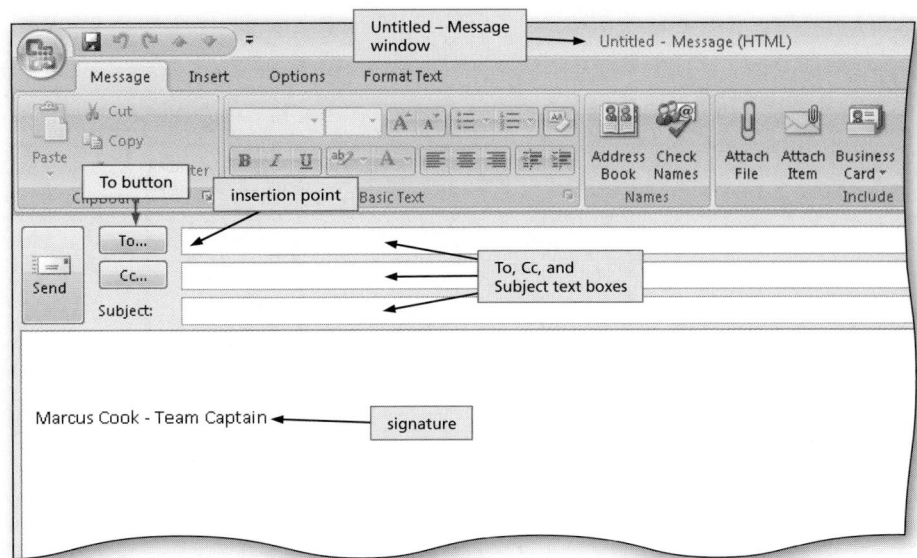

Figure 1–86

2

- Click the To button to display the Select Names dialog box (Figure 1–87).

- Click the Address Book box arrow.

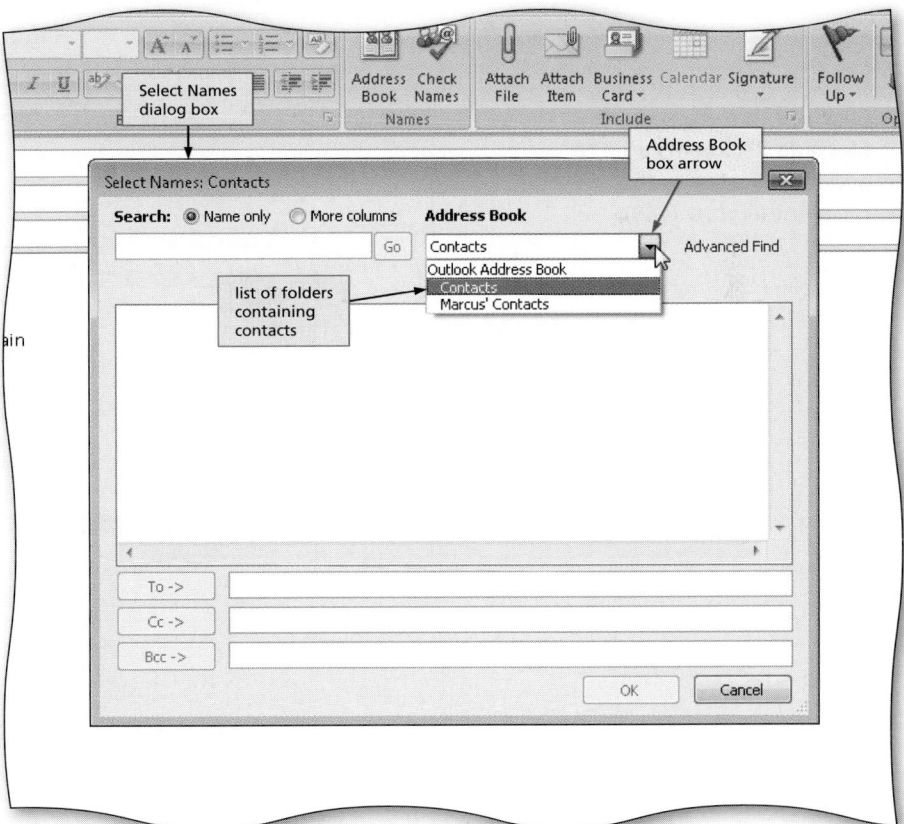

Figure 1–87

- Click Marcus' Contacts in the list.

- Click the Matt Tartan entry in the contact list (Figure 1–88).

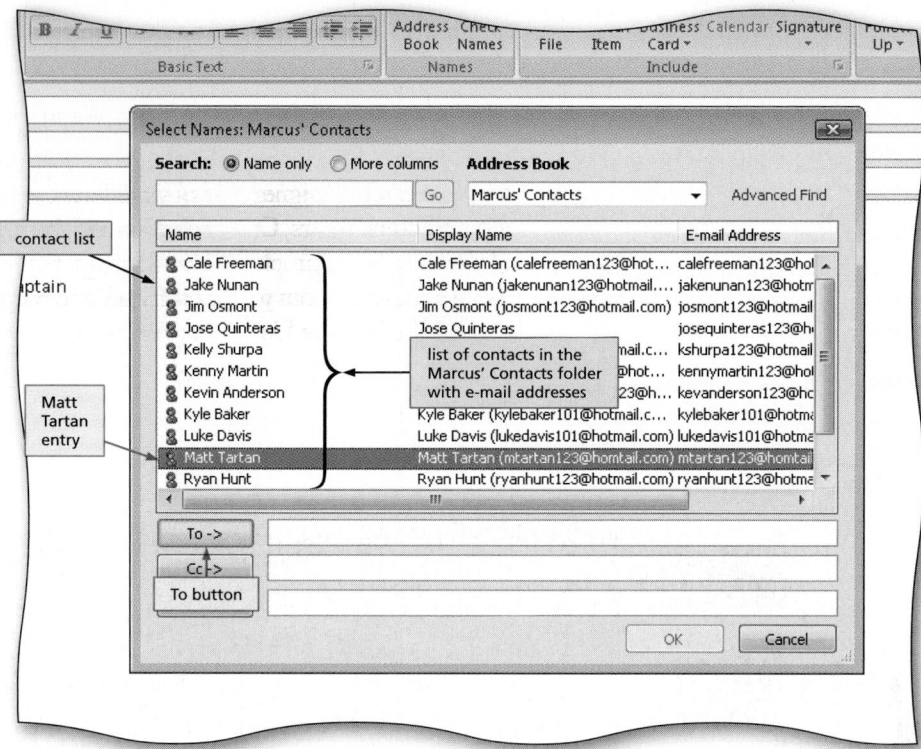

Figure 1–88

- Click the To button in the Message Recipients area to add Matt Tartan as the message recipient (Figure 1–89).

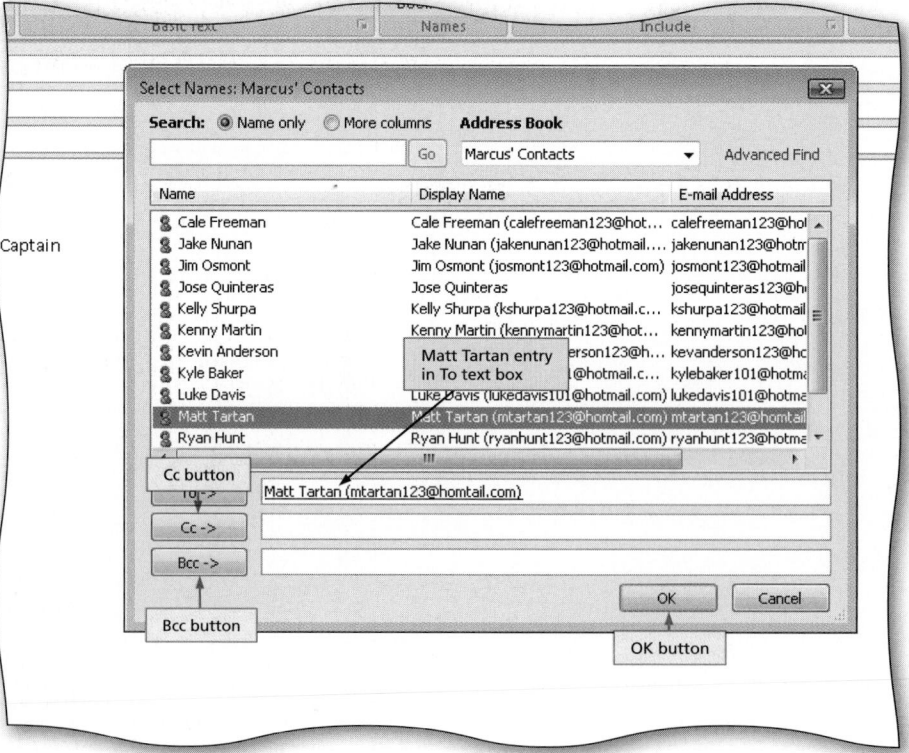

Figure 1–89

- Click the OK button to close the Select Names dialog box.

- Click the Subject text box and then type `Carwash Fund-raiser` as the entry (Figure 1–90).

- Press the TAB key to move the cursor to the message area.

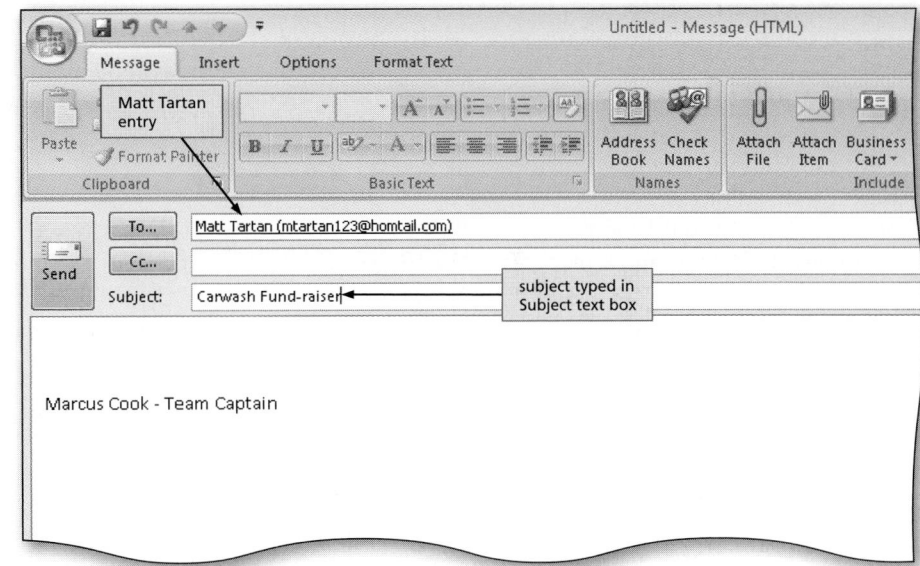

Figure 1–90

6

- Type the message (Figure 1–91).

- Click the Send button to send the message and close the Message window.

Q&A Can I add more than one name to the To text box?

You can add as many names as you want to the To text box. You also can add names to the Cc text box. If you do not want those listed in the To text box or Cc text box to know you sent a copy to someone else, send a blind copy by adding the name to the Bcc text box.

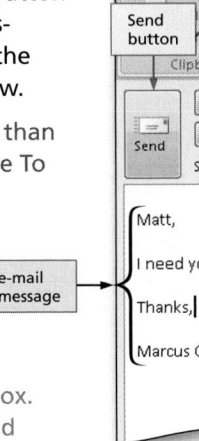

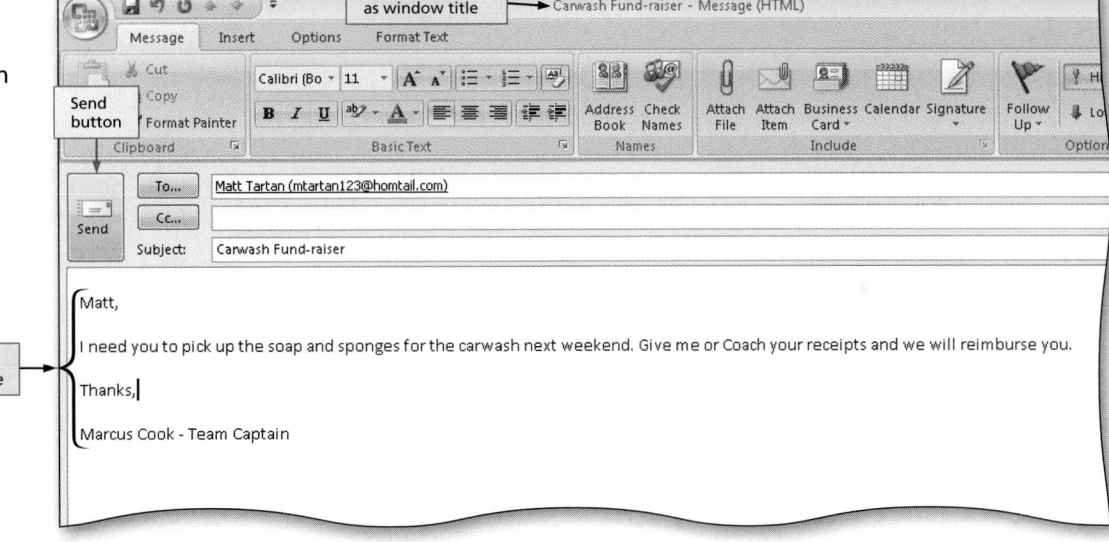

Figure 1–91

Other Ways

1. Click Address Book command on Message window Ribbon

To Create a Distribution List

Outlook can send the same message to a group of recipients using a distribution list. The following steps create a distribution list titled Chemistry Lab Group that includes four members from Marcus' Contacts list.

 1

• With the Contacts window active, click the New Contact button arrow on the Standard toolbar to display the New Contact menu (Figure 1–92).

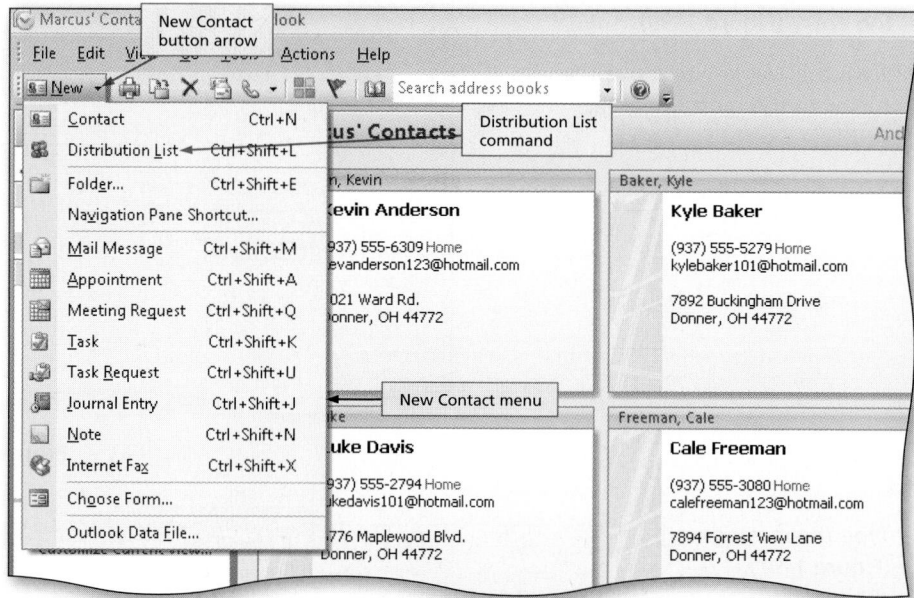

Figure 1–92

 2

• Click Distribution List to display the Untitled – Distribution List window. Type Chemistry Lab Group in the Name text box, and then click the Select Members button on the Ribbon to display the Select Members dialog box.

• Click the Address Book box arrow and click Marcus' Contacts.

• Select Jake Nunan and then click the Members button to add Jake to the Chemistry Lab Group distribution list.

• Add Kyle Baker and Trevor Walker to the list in the same manner (Figure 1–93).

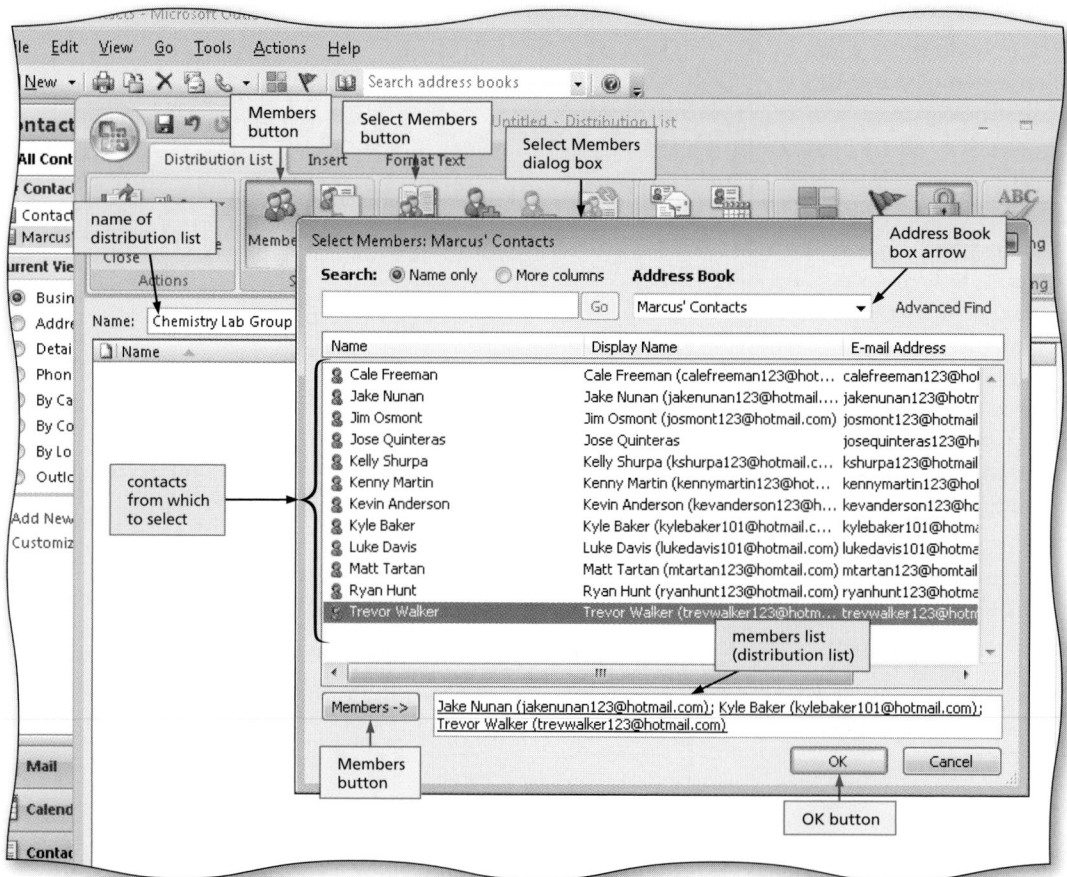

Figure 1–93

• Click the OK button to close the Select Members dialog box and display the Chemistry Lab Group – Distribution List window showing the members of the Chemistry Lab Group distribution list (Figure 1–94).

• Click the Save & Close command on the Ribbon to close the Chemistry Lab Group – Distribution List window and activate the Contacts window.

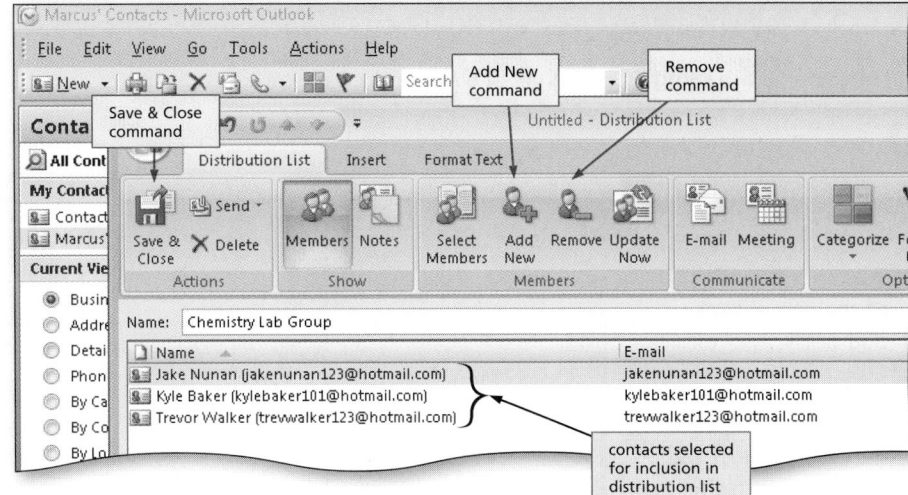

Figure 1–94

• Click the Address Book button on the Standard toolbar to display the Address Book dialog box.

• Select Marcus' Contacts in the Address Book list to display the contact list, which now includes the Chemistry Lab Group distribution list (Figure 1–95).

• Click the Close button to close the the Address Book window.

Q&A

Can I edit or add to a distribution list after it is saved?

Yes. The Chemistry Lab Group – Distribution List window in Figure 1–94 includes two commands in the Members group on the Ribbon that are useful for modifying a distribution list. The Add New command lets you add a contact that is not already in the distribution list. The Remove command lets you delete names from the distribution list, although they remain in your Outlook contact list.

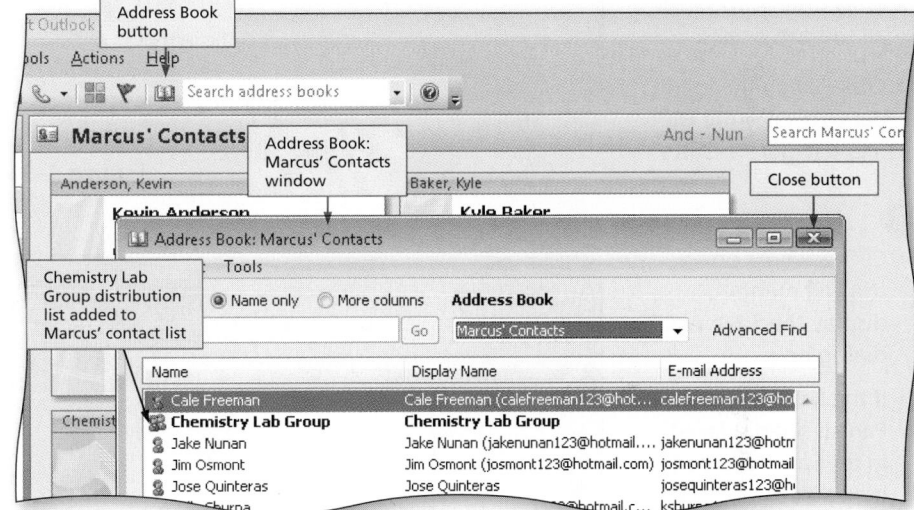

Figure 1–95

Saving Outlook Information in Different Formats

You can save Outlook files on external storage devices in several formats. For example, you can save messages and contact lists in text format, which can be read or copied into other applications.

To Save a Contact List as a Text File and Display it in WordPad

The following steps save a contact list on a USB flash drive as a text file and display it in WordPad.

Note: If you are using Windows XP, see Appendix F for alternate steps.

- Connect the USB flash drive containing the Data Files for Students to one of the computer's USB ports.

- With the Contacts window active, click the name bar of the first contact in the contact list.

- Press CTRL+A to select all the contacts.

- Click File on the menu bar to display the File menu (Figure 1–96).

Figure 1–96

- Click Save As on the File menu to display the Save As dialog box.

- If the Navigation Pane is not displayed in the Save As dialog box, click the Browse Folders button to expand the dialog box.

- If a Folders list is displayed below the Folders button, click the Folders button to remove the Folders list.

- Type `Marcus' Contacts` in the File name text box.

- If necessary, select Text Only in the Save as type box.

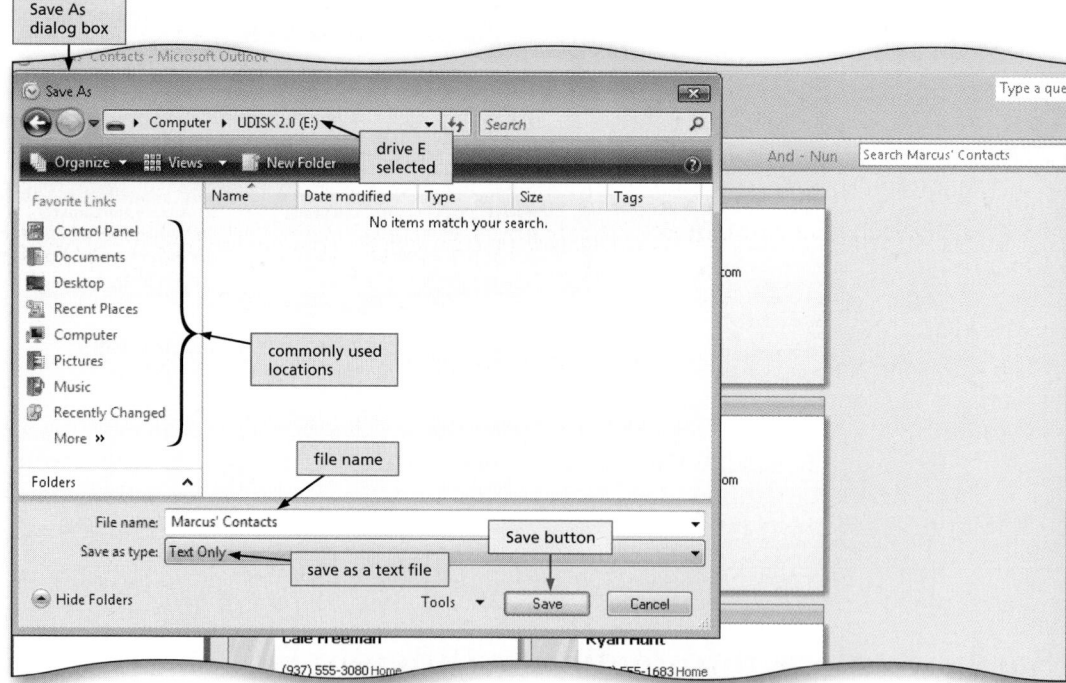

Figure 1–97

- If Computer is not displayed in the Favorite Links section, drag the top or bottom edge of the Save As dialog box until Computer is displayed.

- Click Computer in the Favorite Links section to display a list of available drives. If necessary, scroll until UDISK 2.0 (E:) appears in the list of available drives. Double-click UDISK 2.0 (E:) in the Computer list to select the USB flash drive, Drive E in this case, as the new save location. (Figure 1–97).

3

- Click the Save button in the Save As dialog box to save the file on the USB flash drive with the file name, Marcus' Contacts.

- Click the Start button on the Windows Vista taskbar to display the Start menu.

- Click All Programs at the bottom of the left pane on the Start menu to display the All Programs list. Click Accessories on the All Programs list, and then click WordPad on the Accessories list to open the WordPad text editor.

- When WordPad starts, click the Maximize button on the title bar, click File on the menu bar, and then click Open.

- When WordPad displays the Open dialog box, click the Files of type box arrow, select All Documents, click Computer in the Favorite Links section to display a list of available drives.

- If necessary, scroll until UDISK 2.0 (E:) appears in the list of available drives, and then double-click UDISK 2.0 (E:) in the Computer list to select the USB flash drive, Drive E in this case, as the new save location.

- Double-click Marcus' Contacts to display Marcus' Contacts as a text file (Figure 1–98).

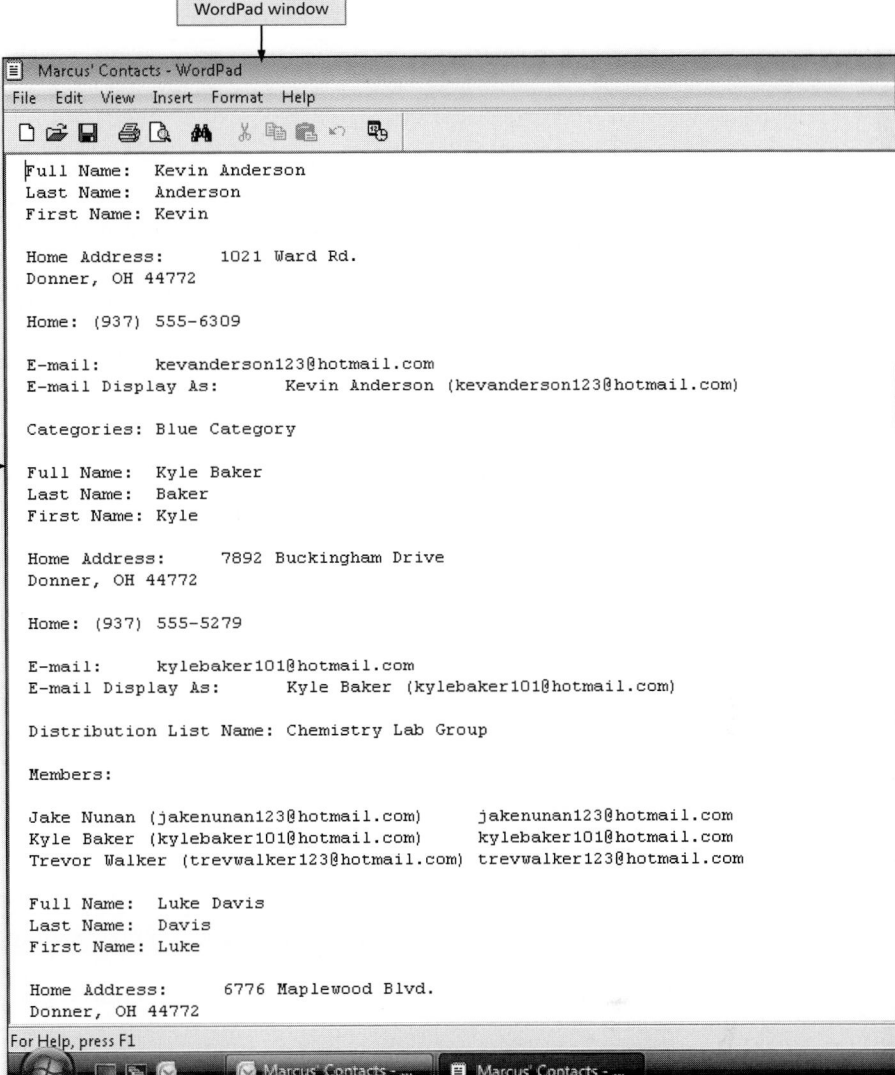

Figure 1–98

4

- After viewing the text file, click the WordPad Close button.

Tracking Activities

When you are dealing with several contacts, it can be useful to have all associated e-mails, documents, or other items related to a contact available quickly. Outlook makes these items accessible through the Activities command in the Show group, located on the Contact window Ribbon. Clicking this command for a contact opens a list of all items related to that contact. Outlook searches for items linked only to the contact in the main Outlook folders (Contacts, Calendar, etc.); however, you can create and add new folders to be searched.

To Track Activities for a Contact

The following steps track the activities of Kenny Martin.

1

- With the Contacts window active, double-click the Kenny Martin contact heading.

- Click the Activities command on the Ribbon to display the Activities sheet showing a list of items related to Kenny Martin (Figure 1–99).

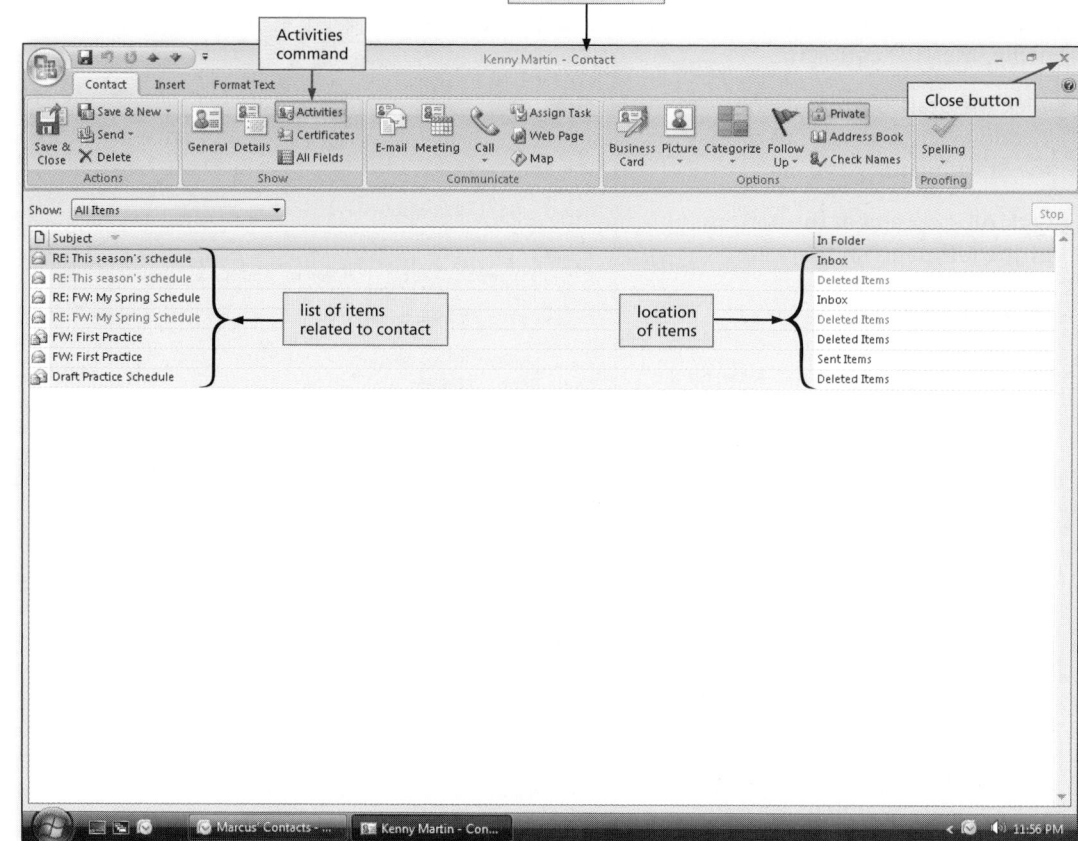

Figure 1–99

Outlook Help

At any time while using Outlook, you can find answers to questions and display information about various topics through **Outlook Help**. The Help features can increase your productivity and reduce your frustrations by minimizing the time you spend learning how to use Outlook.

This section introduces you to Outlook Help. Additional information about using Outlook Help is available in Appendix C.

To Search for Outlook Help

Using Outlook Help, you can search for information based on phrases such as "send an e-mail message" or "format text," or key terms such as "copy," "save," or "format." Outlook Help responds with a list of search results displayed as links to a variety of resources. The following steps, which use Outlook Help to search for information about selecting text, assume you are connected to the Internet.

1

- Click the Microsoft Office Outlook Help button on the Standard toolbar to open the Outlook Help window.

- Type format text in the 'Type words to search for' text box at the top of the Outlook Help window (Figure 1–100).

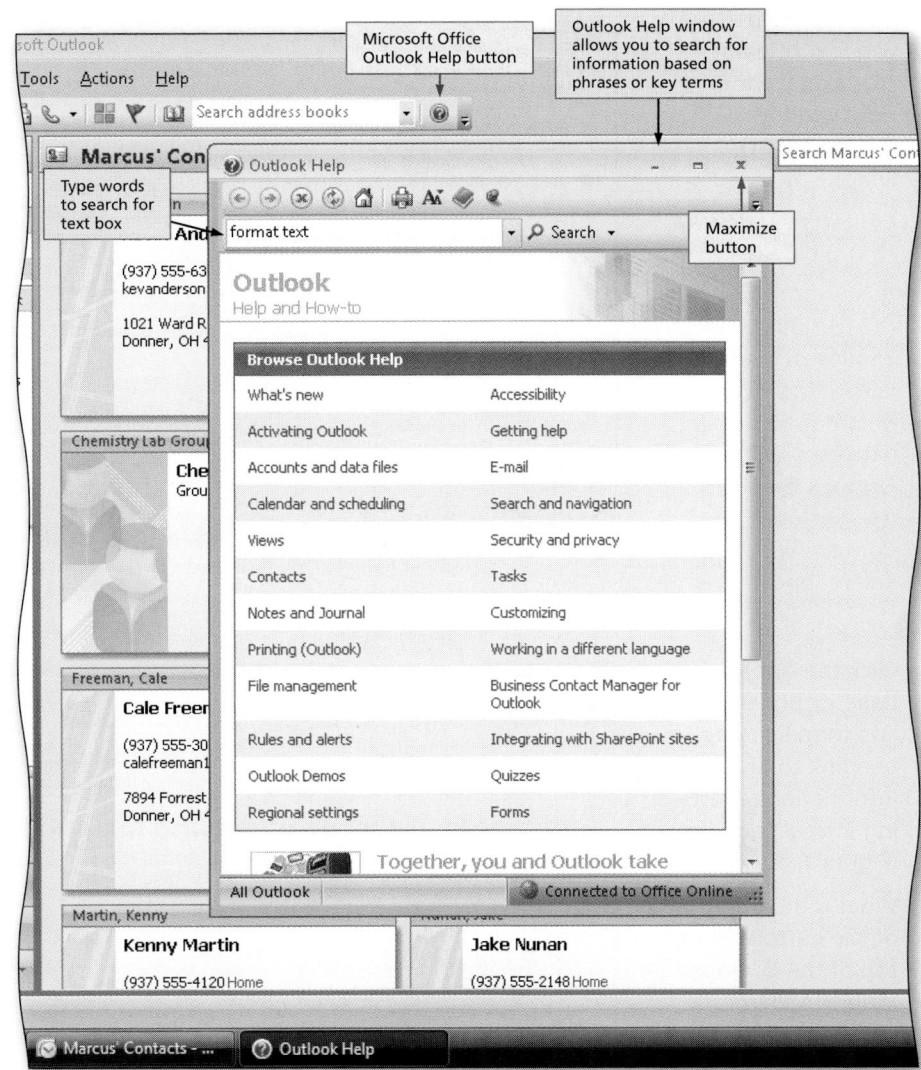

Figure 1–100

2

- Press the ENTER key to display the search results.

- Click the Maximize button on the Outlook Help window title bar to maximize the Help window (Figure 1–101).

Q&A

Where is the Contacts window?

Outlook is open in the background, but the Outlook Help window is overlaid on top of the Microsoft Outlook window. When the Outlook Help window is closed, the Contacts window will reappear.

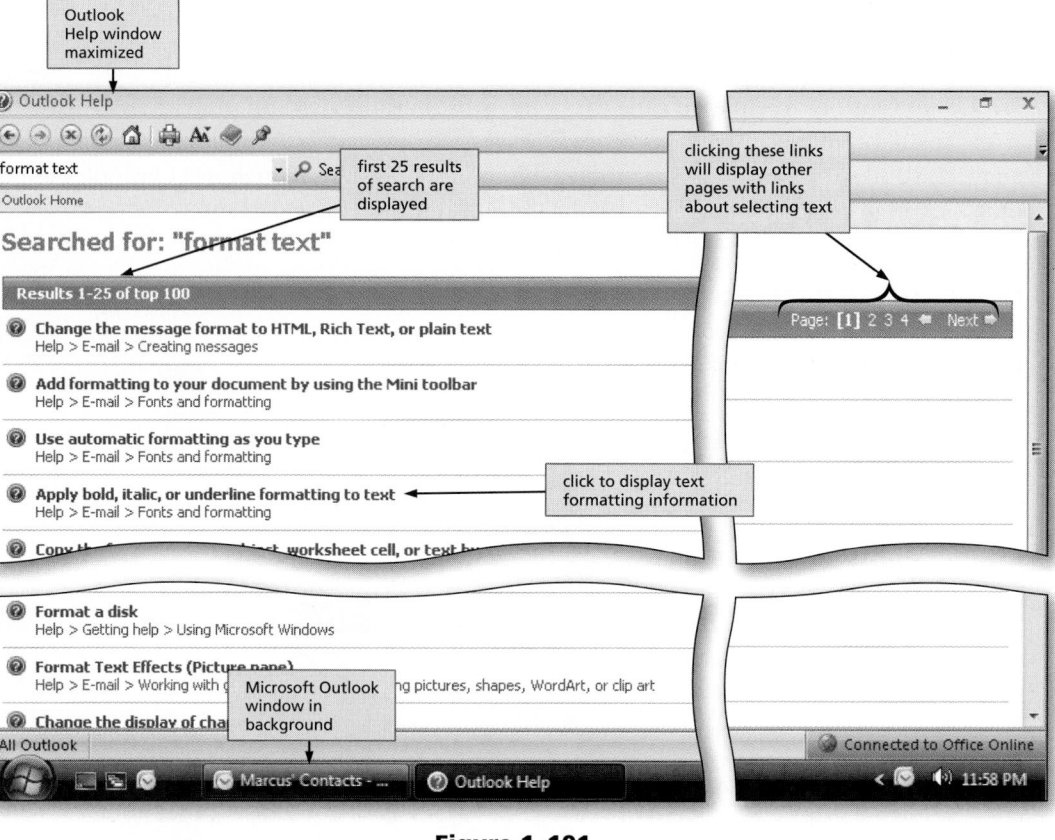

Figure 1–101

3

- Click the Apply bold, italic, or underline formatting to text link to display information regarding formatting text (Figure 1–102).

Q&A

What is the purpose of the buttons at the top of the Outlook Help window?

Use the buttons in the upper-left corner of the Outlook Help window to navigate through the Help system, change the display, show the Outlook Help table of contents, and print the contents of the window.

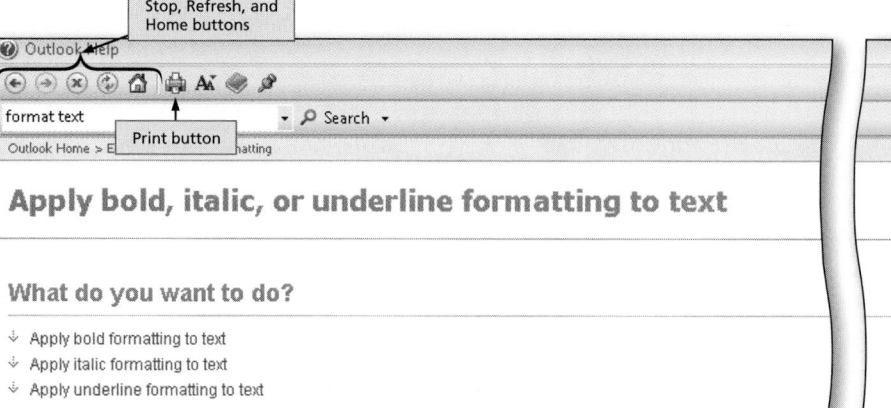

Figure 1–102

4

- Click the Close button on the Outlook Help window title bar to close the Outlook Help window and redisplay the Contacts window.

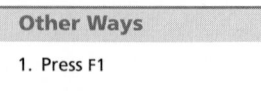

Other Ways

1. Press F1

To Quit Outlook

The following steps quit Outlook.

1 Click the Close button on the right side of the title bar to quit Outlook.

2 If necessary, click the Exit Without Sending button in the Microsoft Office Outlook dialog box so that any messages saved in your Outbox are not sent.

BTW **Certification**
The Microsoft Certified Application Specialist (MCAS) program provides an opportunity for you to obtain a valuable industry credential – proof that you have the Outlook 2007 skills required by employers. For more information see Appendix G or visit the Outlook 2007 Certification Web page (scsite.com/out2007/cert).

Chapter Summary

In this chapter you have learned how to use Outlook to open, read, print, reply to, forward, delete, sign, compose, format, and send e-mail messages. You opened and viewed file attachments as well as attached a file to an e-mail message. You learned how to categorize, flag, sort, and set importance and delivery options to e-mail messages. You added and deleted contacts to a contact list. Finally, you used the contact list to create a distribution list and track activities of a contact. The items listed below include all the new Outlook skills you have learned in this chapter.

1. Start and Customize Outlook (OUT 5)
2. Open (Read) an E-Mail Message (OUT 10)
3. Close an E-Mail Message (OUT 15)
4. Print an E-Mail Message (OUT 15)
5. Reply to an E-Mail Message (OUT 16)
6. Change Message Formats (OUT 19)
7. Forward an E-Mail Message (OUT 20)
8. Delete an E-Mail Message (OUT 21)
9. View a File Attachment (OUT 22)
10. Create and Insert an E-Mail Signature (OUT 24)
11. Compose an E-Mail Message (OUT 27)
12. Format an E-Mail Message (OUT 29)
13. Attach a File to an E-Mail Message and Send the Message (OUT 31)
14. Categorize E-Mail Messages (OUT 33)
15. Flag E-Mail Messages (OUT 34)
16. Sort E-Mail Messages by Category Color (OUT 35)
17. Create and Apply a View Filter (OUT 36)
18. Set Message Importance, Sensitivity, and Delivery Options in a Single Message (OUT 38)
19. Change the Default Level of Importance and Sensitivity (OUT 40)
20. Create a Personal Folder (OUT 44)
21. Create a Contact List (OUT 47)
22. Change the View and Sort the Contact List (OUT 49)
23. Find a Contact (OUT 50)
24. Organize Contacts (OUT 51)
25. Display the Contacts in a Category (OUT 52)
26. Preview and Print the Contact List (OUT 53)
27. Use the Contact List to Address an E-Mail Message (OUT 55)
28. Create a Distribution List (OUT 58)
29. Save a Contact List as a Text File and Display it in WordPad (OUT 60)
30. Track Activities for a Contact (OUT 62)
31. Search for Outlook Help (OUT 63)
32. Quit Outlook (OUT 65)

 If you have a SAM user profile, you may have access to hands-on instruction, practice, and assessment. Log in to your SAM account (http://sam2007.course.com) to launch any assigned training activities or exams that relate to the skills covered in this chapter.

BTW **Quick Reference**
For a table that lists how to complete the tasks covered in this book using the mouse, Ribbon, shortcut menu, and keyboard, see the Quick Reference Summary at the back of this book, or visit the Outlook 2007 Quick Reference Web page (scsite.com/out2007/qr).

Learn It Online

Test your knowledge of chapter content and key terms.

Instructions: To complete the Learn It Online exercises, start your browser, click the Address bar, and then enter the Web address scsite.com/out2007/learn. When the Outlook 2007 Learn It Online page is displayed, click the link for the exercise you want to complete and then read the instructions.

Chapter Reinforcement TF, MC, and SA
A series of true/false, multiple choice, and short answer questions that test your knowledge of the chapter content.

Flash Cards
An interactive learning environment where you identify chapter key terms associated with displayed definitions.

Practice Test
A series of multiple choice questions that test your knowledge of chapter content and key terms.

Who Wants To Be a Computer Genius?
An interactive game that challenges your knowledge of chapter content in the style of the television quiz show.

Wheel of Terms
An interactive game that challenges your knowledge of chapter key terms in the style of the television show *Wheel of Fortune*.

Crossword Puzzle Challenge
A crossword puzzle that challenges your knowledge of key terms presented in the chapter.

Apply Your Knowledge

Reinforce the skills and apply the concepts you learned in this chapter.

Creating a Contact List
Instructions: Start Outlook. Create a Contacts folder using your name as the name of the new folder. Create a contact list using the people listed in Table 1–4. Sort the list by last name in descending sequence. When the list is complete, print the list in Card Style view and submit to your instructor.

Name	Telephone	Address	E-mail Address	Grade Level
Greg Sanders	(937) 555-4120	8465 W. 63rd St. Donner, OH 44772	gsanders@isp.com	Junior
Dan Gilbert	(937) 555-7539	8868 Ashwood Lane Donner, OH 44772	dgilbert@isp.com	Freshman
Heather Nichols	(937) 555-9823	214 W. Lincoln Ave. Donner, OH 44772	hnichols@isp.com	Freshman
Valerie Prince	(937) 555-0258	5246 Brookfield Ct. Donner, OH 44772	vprince@isp.com	Junior
Rafael Perez	(937) 555-6211	9812 River Rd. Donner, OH 44772	rperez@isp.com	Sophomore
Keith Lee	(937) 555-3080	7894 Forrest View Lane Donner, OH 44772	klee@isp.com	Sophomore

Table 1–4 Contact Information

Extend Your Knowledge

Extend the skills you learned in this chapter and experiment with new skills. You may need to use Help to complete the assignment.

Categorizing Contacts and Creating a Distribution List

Instructions: Start Outlook. Using the contact list created in Apply Your Knowledge, create a category for each grade level (freshman, sophomore, junior, and senior) and categorize each student as follows: Greg Sanders – Junior, Dan Gilbert – Freshman, Heather Nichols – Freshman, Valerie Prince – Junior, Rafael Perez – Sophomore, Keith Lee – Sophomore.

Create a distribution list consisting of juniors and seniors. When the list is complete, print the list in Card Style view and submit to your instructor.

Make It Right

Analyze a document and correct all errors and/or improve the design.

Importing Subfolders for the In the Lab Exercises

Follow these steps to import subfolders for the following Make it Right and In the Lab exercises:

1. Connect the USB flash drive containing the Data Files for Students to your computer.
2. Click File on the Outlook menu bar and then click Import and Export.
3. In the Import and Export Wizard dialog box, click Import from another program or file and then click the Next button.
4. In the Import a File dialog box, click Personal Folder File (.pst) and then click the Next button.
5. In the Import Personal Folders dialog box, click the Browse button to access drive E (your USB flash drive letter may be different), select the appropriate subfolder, click Open, and then click the Next button.
6. In the Import Personal Folders dialog box, select the appropriate folder from which to import and then click the Finish button.

Continued >

Make It Right *continued*

Editing a Contact List

Instructions: Start Outlook. Import the MIR 1-1 Contacts folder (Figure 1–103) into Outlook. See the inside back cover of this book for instructions for downloading the Data Files for Students, or see your instructor for information on accessing the files required in this book.

The contact list contains 20 contacts. The five contacts in Table 1–5 need to have their information updated. Locate each contact using the Find a Contact box and change the applicable fields.

Print the revised contact list and submit it to your instructor.

Table 1–5 Revised Contact Information				
Name	**Telephone**	**Address**	**E-mail Address**	**Category**
Jennifer Craig	(916) 555-5686	354 Rutledge St. Condor, CA 95702	jcraig@isp.com	Blue
Andrew Brinckman	(916) 555-4565	8453 Whitcomb St. Condor, CA 95702	abrinckman@isp.com	Blue
Courtney Croel	(916) 555-2348	7456 Brummitt Rd. Condor, CA 95702	ccroel@isp.com	Blue
Ryan Bachman	(916) 555-7410	4654 Ashford Ct. Condor, CA 95702	rbachman@isp.com	Blue
Kris Davids	(916) 555-3647	678 E. 7th Ave. Condor, CA 95702	kdavids@isp.com	Blue

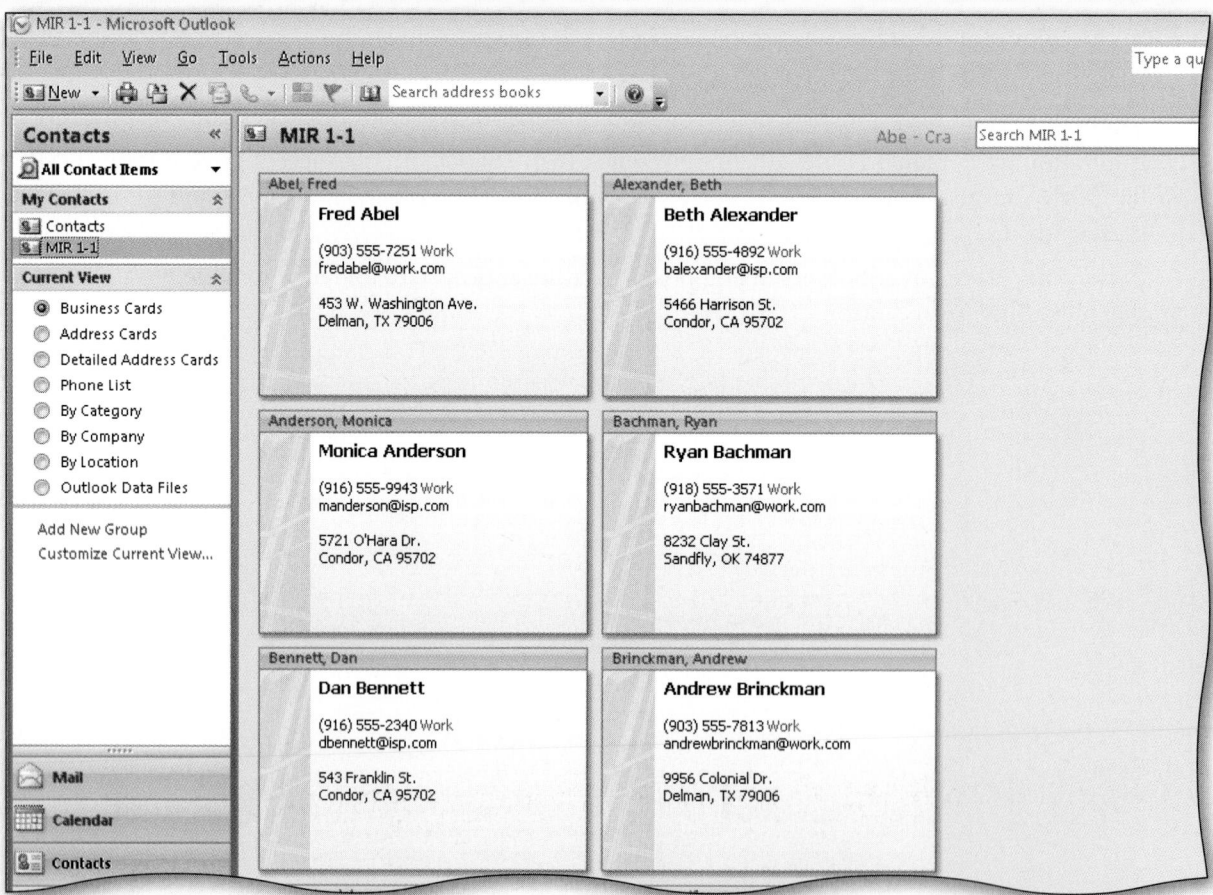

Figure 1–103

In the Lab

Design and/or create Outlook items using the guidelines, concepts, and skills presented in this chapter. Labs are listed in order of increasing difficulty.

Lab 1: Creating a Distribution List and Sending E-Mail

Problem: You are the campaign manager of your mother's campaign for a city council seat. Besides coordinating appearances and advertising, your responsibilities also include soliciting and organizing campaign donations.

Instructions Part 1: Perform the following tasks:

1. Import the Lab 1-1 Contacts folder (Figure 1–104) into Outlook.

2. Create two distribution lists: one consisting of monetary donors, the other consisting of non-monetary donors. Each contact is categorized by type of donation.

3. Print each distribution list and submit to your instructor.

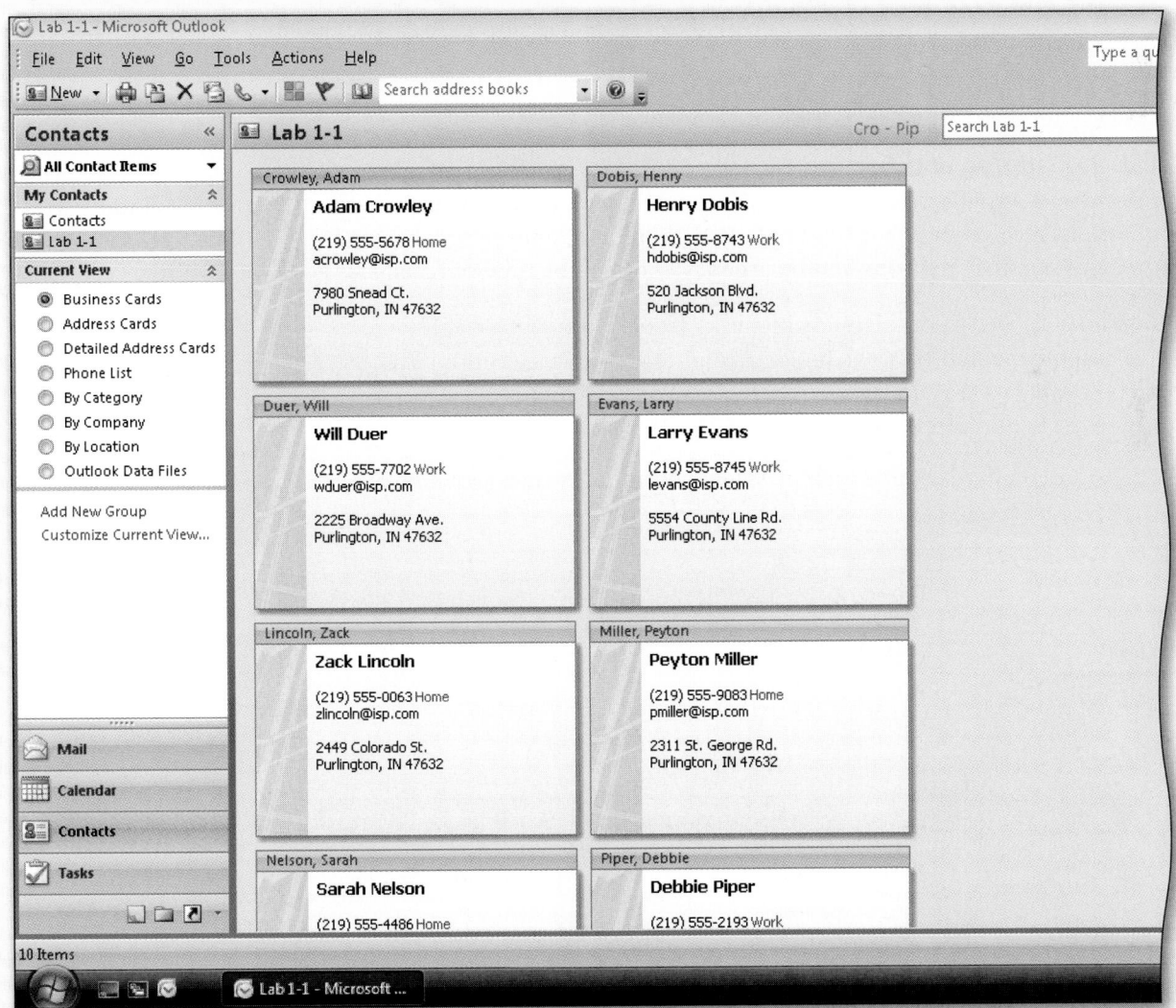

Figure 1–104

Continued >

In the Lab *continued*

Instructions Part 2: Perform the following tasks:

1. Compose a message to each group created in Part 1. The message to monetary donors should thank them for their past support and request donations for this year's campaign. The message to non-monetary donors should thank them for their past support and include a request for the same contribution to this year's campaign.

2. Set the sensitivity for each message as confidential.

3. Using Microsoft Word, create a document called Campaign Platform, and include this file as an attachment with your e-mail messages.

4. Set the delivery for each message to March 1, 2008 at 10:00 a.m.

5. Format your messages to monetary donors as Plain Text and your messages to non-monetary donors as HTML.

6. Print each message and submit to your instructor.

Instructions Part 3: Save the Lab 1-1 contact list as a text file. Open the file using WordPad. Print the contact list from WordPad and submit to your instructor.

In the Lab

Lab 2: Flagging and Sorting Messages

Problem: As student director of the Computer Help Center, you are responsible for responding to questions received by e-mail. Some questions require a more timely response than others, so you need a way to sort the questions first by urgency and then by time of receipt.

Instructions: Perform the following tasks:

1. Import the Lab 1-2 Inbox folder (Figure 1–105) into Outlook.

2. Read through each message and apply the appropriate Follow Up flag to each message (Today, Tomorrow, or This Week).

3. After you have flagged each message, sort the messages based on the Follow Up flag.

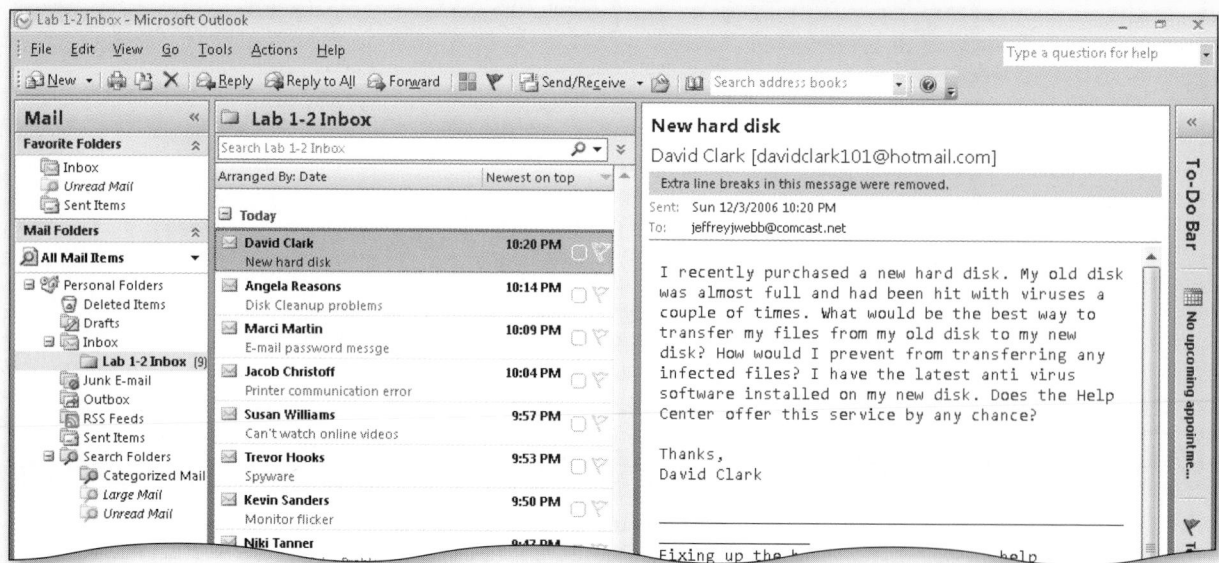

Figure 1–105

In the Lab

Lab 3: Creating an E-Mail Signature, Replying To, and Forwarding Messages

Problem: With all the Computer Help Center messages sorted and flagged, you now have to respond to the messages. You need to perform this task in an efficient manner, as it is the Computer Help Center's policy to respond to questions within three working days. Policy also requires that the name of the person responding, the Computer Help Center's telephone number, and its hours of operation appear on every reply.

Instructions Part 1:   Perform the following tasks:

1. Create an e-mail signature consisting of your name, title (Student Director), a telephone number (555-1234), and hours of operation (8:00 a.m. – 8:00 p.m., Closed Sundays).

2. Click the New Message button on the Standard toolbar. Print the blank message containing the signature and submit to your instructor.

Instructions Part 2:   Perform the following tasks:

1. Send a reply with the importance set at high to the messages flagged for follow up Today.

2. Forward the messages flagged for follow up Tomorrow. You may use fictitious e-mail addresses for this exercise, because the messages will not actually be sent.

3. Submit printouts of the replies to your instructor.

Instructions Part 3:   Perform the following tasks:

1. Clear all the This Week Follow Up flags from the appropriate messages. Use Search Folders to display only the messages flagged for follow up. Make a list of the sender's name, subject, and Follow Up flag type and submit to your instructor.

2. Using information from Microsoft Outlook Help, create a unique signature for a separate e-mail account. See your instructor about setting up a separate e-mail account.

3. Print a blank message containing the signature and submit to your instructor.

Cases and Places

Apply your creative thinking and problem solving skills to design and implement a solution.

• Easier   •• More Difficult

• 1: Create a Personal Contact List

Create a contact list of your family, friends, and colleagues. Include their names, addresses, telephone numbers, e-mail addresses, and IM addresses (if any). Enter the employer for each contact if appropriate. For family members, use the Detail sheet to list birthdays and wedding anniversaries (if any). Print the contact list and submit to your instructor.

• 2: Modify a Contact List

Import the Cases 1-2 Contacts folder into Outlook. You are the manager of the Personnel Department for a large automobile dealership. Your responsibilities include updating the company contact list whenever someone changes positions, receives a promotion, or other changes occur. Byron Taylor has received a promotion to Parts Manager and was rewarded with a private office (Room 3A), private telephone ((812) 555-1278), and his own e-mail address (btaylor@autodealer.com). The information in his current record contains the general telephone number and dealership's e-mail. Make the appropriate changes to Byron Taylor's contact record. Submit a printout to your instructor.

•• 3: Apply a View Filter and Track Contact Activities

Import the Cases 1-3 Inbox folder into Outlook. You work in the IT department of a large company. Every day you receive several e-mail messages about various computer problems within the company. A coworker, Bailey Smithers, has sent several e-mail messages to the IT department complaining that her problem has yet to be solved. You have been told to immediately solve her problem. Apply a filter to the Cases 1-3 Inbox folder to display only the messages from Bailey Smithers. Respond to her latest e-mail message while sending a copy to your supervisor to show that you have found a resolution to the problem. Submit a printout of your reply to your instructor. Add Bailey Smithers to your contact list. Track the activities of Bailey Smithers. List the first five entries from the Activities list and submit to your instructor. After printing your reply message, delete all the messages from Bailey Smithers and remove the filter.

•• 4: Compose and Format an E-Mail Message

Make It Personal

Being involved with your studies, extracurricular activities, and college life in general, can prevent you from keeping in touch with family and friends. Compose an e-mail message to a close relative or friend. Your message should contain information on your class schedule, activities, and new friends that you have made. Compose the message in HTML format. Format the text of your message to enhance its appearance. Use Outlook Help to insert a picture of the campus or your school's logo into the message body. Print the e-mail and submit to your instructor.

•• 5: Compile Contact Information

Working Together

Have each member of your team submit a design of a form for collecting contact information. Have them base the form on available fields in the General and Detail sheets in the Contact window. Have the team select the best form design. After selecting a form, make photocopies for the entire class. Have your classmates fill out the form. Collect the forms and create a contact list from the collected information. Print the final contact list and submit to your instructor.

1 Integrating Office 2007 Applications and the World Wide Web

Objectives

You will have mastered the material in this chapter when you can:

- Integrate the Office 2007 applications to create a Web site

- Add hyperlinks to a Word document

- Embed an Excel chart into a Word document

- Add a hyperlink to a PowerPoint slide

- Create Web pages from a PowerPoint presentation

- Add a hyperlink to an Access report

- Create a Web page from an Access report

- Test a Web site in a browser

1 | Integrating Office 2007 Applications and the World Wide Web

Introduction

Integration means joining parts so they work together or form a whole. In information technology, common usages can include the following:

1. Integration during product development combines activities, programs, or hardware components into a functional unit.
2. Integration in manufacturing can bring different companies' products together into an efficiently working system.
3. Integration in marketing combines products or components to meet objectives such as sharing a common purpose or creating demand. It includes such matters as consistent product pricing and packaging, advertising, and sales campaigns.
4. Integration in product design allows a unifying purpose and/or architecture, such as the Microsoft Office System. (The products also are sold individually, but they are designed with the same larger objectives and/or architecture.)

This Integration chapter will show you how you can use the functionality and productivity tools of the Microsoft Office System.

Project — Integrating Office 2007 Applications and the World Wide Web

Many businesses advertise their products and services on the Internet. Companies find it easy to create Web pages using information already saved in word processing, spreadsheet, database, or presentation software formats. The Web pages shown in Figure 1–1 include information about the Makin-It Real Estate Company. This small business specializes in selling homes near the local college campus to first-time homebuyers. The owners of the business want to advertise their services and homes for sale on an attractive Web page.

The project in the chapter follows proper design guidelines and uses Office 2007 applications to create the Web pages and other documents shown in Figure 1–1. The Web page creation capabilities of Microsoft Office 2007 make it simple for you to create an entire Web site using the information available. Word allows you to create and save a document as a Web page. Word also allows you to embed an Excel chart in a document, which can be included in a Web page. PowerPoint provides the same capability and adds a navigation structure for browsing. In addition, an Access report can be saved as a Web page so that users can view database contents online. Several sources of information already exist that can be beneficial to creating a Web page. The following four files of information are supplied to help you get started:

1. A Word document that contains the company letterhead, including logo images, company name, and company address (Figure 1–1a on page INT 4).

2. An Excel workbook with a Bar chart graphically illustrating the company's breakdown of home sales per year (Figure 1–1b on page INT 4).

3. A PowerPoint presentation that contains general information about the company's services (Figure 1–1g on page INT 5).

4. An Access database containing information about homes that currently are for sale through the company (Figure 1–1c on page INT 4).

The Makin-It Real Estate Web site should include the following:

1. A home page with a Bar chart that contains the homes sold by the company per year (Figure 1–1e on page INT 5). Three hypertext links also are included on the home page: Company Services, Homes for Sale, and E-mail for Information.

2. The Homes for Sale Web page (Figure 1–1d on page INT 4) is created from the Access file. Clicking the Homes for Sale link on the home page accesses this Web page. On this Web page, visitors can view the homes for sale from the company, categorized by the type of home.

3. The PowerPoint Web page (Figure 1–1g on page INT 5) displays information about services provided by the company. Clicking the Company Services link on the home page accesses this Web page.

4. Using the E-mail for Information hyperlink, you can create an e-mail message (Figure 1–1f on page INT 5). E-mail is sent to the e-mail address manager@isp.com.

Overview

As you read this chapter, you will learn how to create the Web pages shown in Figure 1–1 by performing these general tasks:

- Insert hyperlinks in the Word document
- Embed the Excel chart in the Word document
- Save the Word document as a Web page
- Add a hyperlink to the PowerPoint presentation
- Save the PowerPoint presentation as a Web page
- Create the Access report
- Add a hyperlink to the Access report
- Save the Access report as a Web page
- Test the Web site

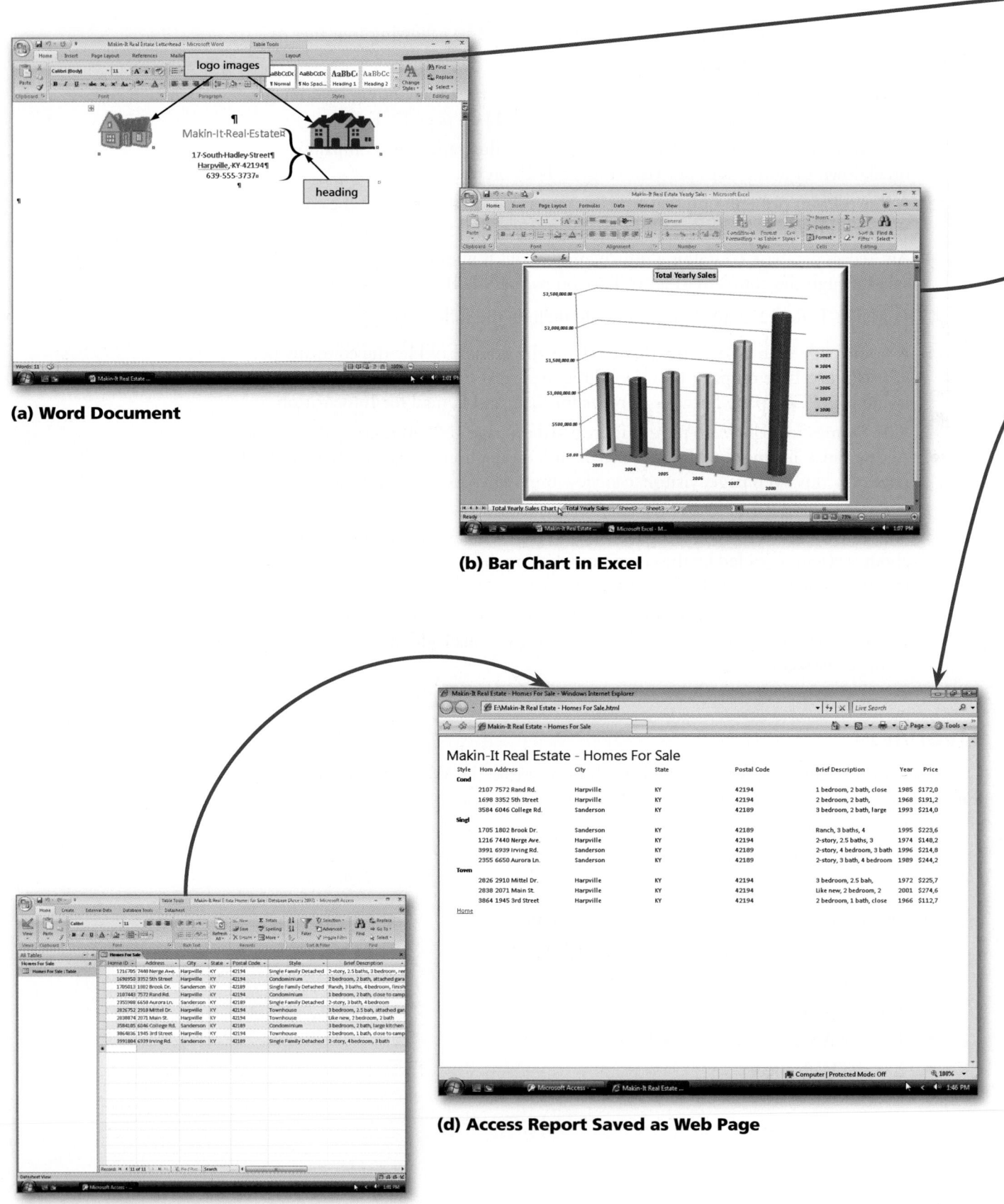

(a) Word Document

(b) Bar Chart in Excel

(c) Access Table

(d) Access Report Saved as Web Page

Figure 1–1

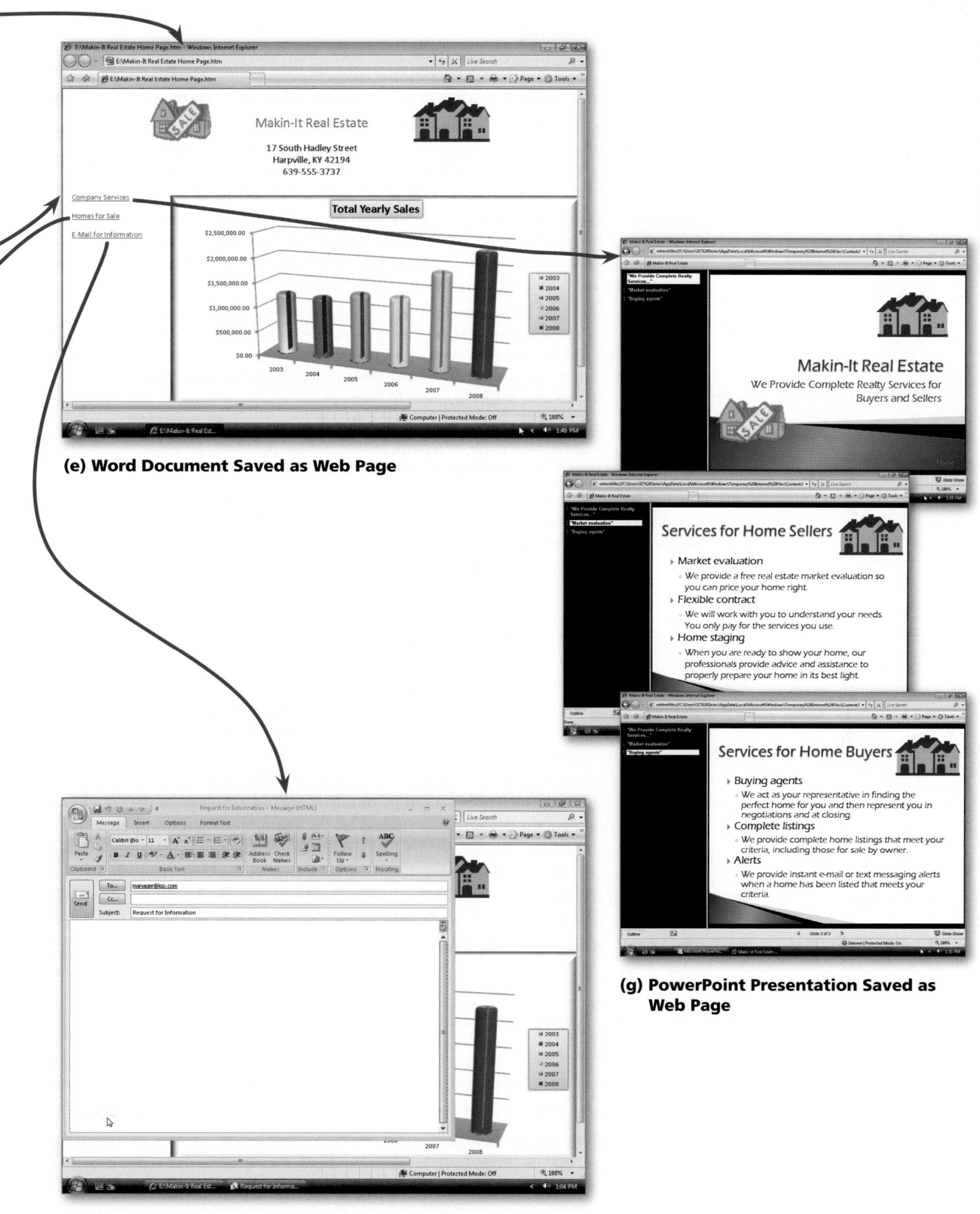

(e) Word Document Saved as Web Page

(f) New E-Mail Message Created from Hyperlink

(g) PowerPoint Presentation Saved as Web Page

Plan Ahead

General Project Decisions

When creating Web pages from many Office 2007 documents, you need to make several decisions that will determine the appearance and characteristics of the finished Web pages. As you create the Web pages shown in Figure 1–1, you should follow these general guidelines:

1. **Choose hyperlink names and locations.** Decide upon the names of the various Web pages and their location on media before creating the Web pages. For example, the first two hyperlinks in Figure 1–1e open Web pages named Company Services and Homes for Sale. The third hyperlink, E-Mail for Information, is easily understood by a Web page visitor.

2. **Ascertain the navigational structure of the Web pages.** The arrows shown between the Web pages in Figure 1–1 are an example of a navigational structure. Determine which pages link to other pages before the Web pages are created. The navigational structure shown in Figure 1–1 is appropriate for a small Web site.

3. **Determine appropriate file names for Web pages.** File names used for each of the Web pages shown in Figure 1–1 need to be determined when planning the pages because the file names are used to create the hyperlinks that are needed to navigate the Web pages. When naming these files, appropriate file names should be used. Save all Web pages to the same location so that they are easier to manage.

4. **Organize the layout of the home page.** Follow good design and visual layout principles to create an inviting home page. The page should not be cluttered, and the user should know what to do without the need for instructions.

5. **Plan the layout of the Access report.** Follow good Access report design guidelines to create the Access report. The fact that the report is to be used as a Web page requires additional thought and planning.

BTW

Web Pages
Making information available on the Internet is a key aspect of business today. To facilitate this trend, the Office 2007 applications easily allow you to generate Web pages from existing files. An entire Web site can be created with files from Word, Excel, PowerPoint, or Access by selecting the Web Page file type in the Save As dialog box.

Adding Hyperlinks to a Word Document

The Web site created for Makin-It Real Estate consists of an initial Web page, called the **home page**, (Figure 1–1e on the previous page) with two hyperlinks to other Web pages, an e-mail link, and a Bar chart. Clicking a **hyperlink**, which can be text or an image, allows you to jump to another location. Text is used (Company Services, Homes for Sale, E-Mail for Information) for the three hyperlinks on the Makin-It Real Estate home page. The first hyperlink (Company Services) jumps to a PowerPoint Web page that contains three Web pages that explain the services offered by the company. A second hyperlink (Homes for Sale) jumps to an Access report that provides a list of homes for sale extracted from Makin-It Real Estate's Homes for Sale Access database. This Web page allows inquiries only; updating the database is prohibited. The third hyperlink (E-Mail for Information) creates an e-mail message. In order to place the three hyperlinks to the left of the Bar chart, a table will be created in the Word document.

To Start Word, Open an Existing Document, and Save the Document with Another Name

The first step in this chapter is to open the Word document, Makin-It Real Estate Letterhead, and save it with the new file name, Makin-It Real Estate Home Page.

Note: If you are using Windows XP, see Appendix F for alternate steps.

1 Connect the USB flash drive containing the Data Files for Students to an available USB port on your computer. See the inside back cover of this book for instructions for downloading the Data Files for Students or see your instructor for information on accessing the files required in this book.

2 Start Word. Click the Office Button and then click Open on the Office Button menu.

3 If necessary, click Computer in the Favorite Links section of the Navigation pane and then double-click UDISK 2.0 (E:) to select the USB flash drive as the new open location. (Your USB drive may have a different name and letter.)

4 Double-click Makin-It Real Estate Letterhead to open the Makin-It Real Estate Letterhead document.

5 Click the Office Button and then click Save As on the Office Button menu. Type Makin-It Real Estate Home Page in the File name text box and then click the Save button in the Save As dialog box to save the document as Makin-It Real Estate Home Page.

6 Click the Web Layout button on the status bar to view the document in Web Layout view (Figure 1–2).

7 Click the Show/Hide ¶ button on the Ribbon to show hidden formatting symbols.

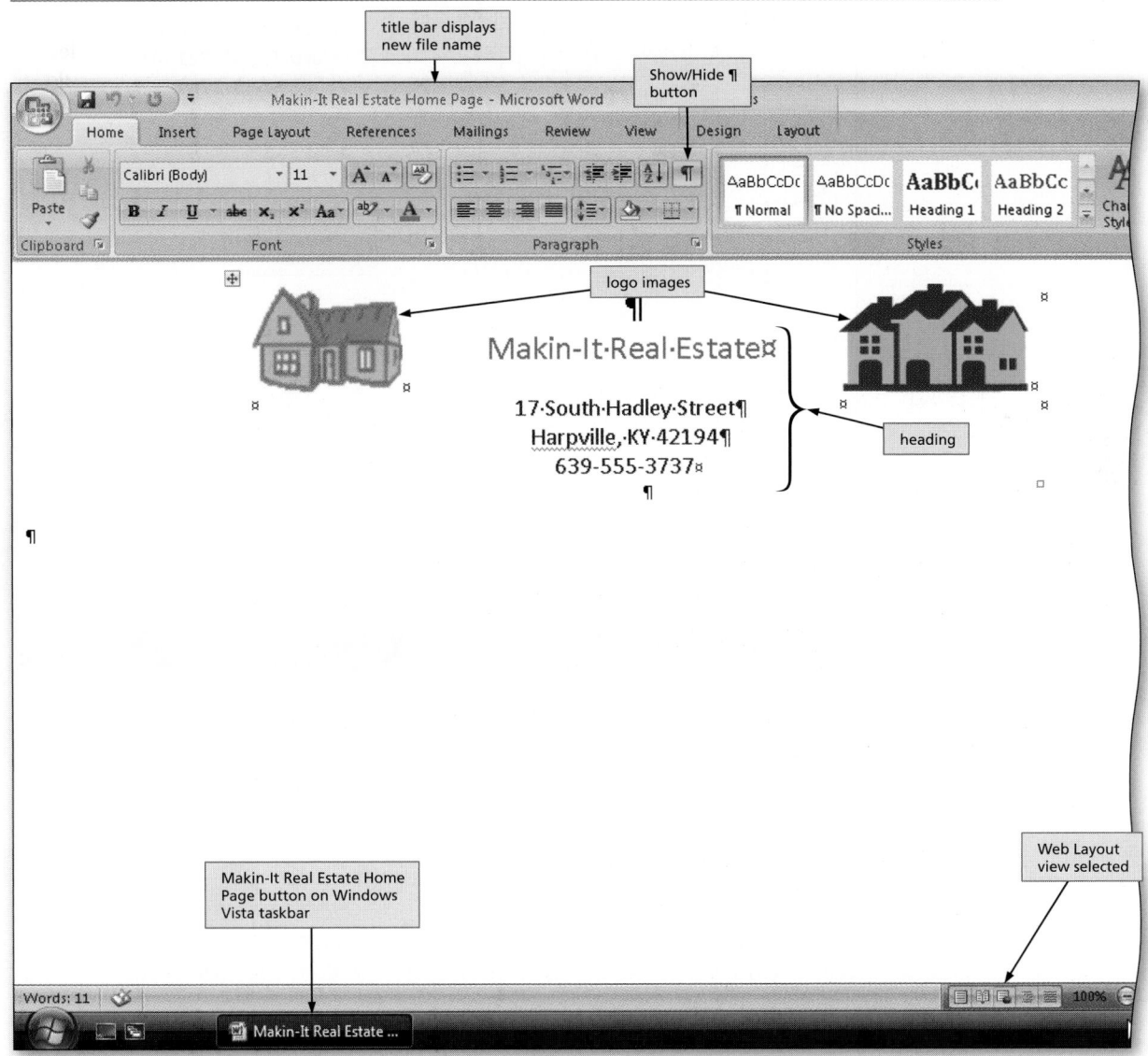

Figure 1–2

To Insert a Table into a Word Document

The next task is to insert a table with two columns and one row. The left column will contain three hyperlinks. The right column will contain the Bar chart.

The following steps add a table to the Makin-It Real Estate Home Page document.

- Position the insertion point on the second paragraph mark below the company telephone number.

- Click the Insert tab on the Ribbon and then click the Table button on the Ribbon.

- Drag the mouse pointer through the first two cells in the Table gallery and do not release the mouse button (Figure 1–3).

- Release the mouse button to insert the table and close the Table gallery.

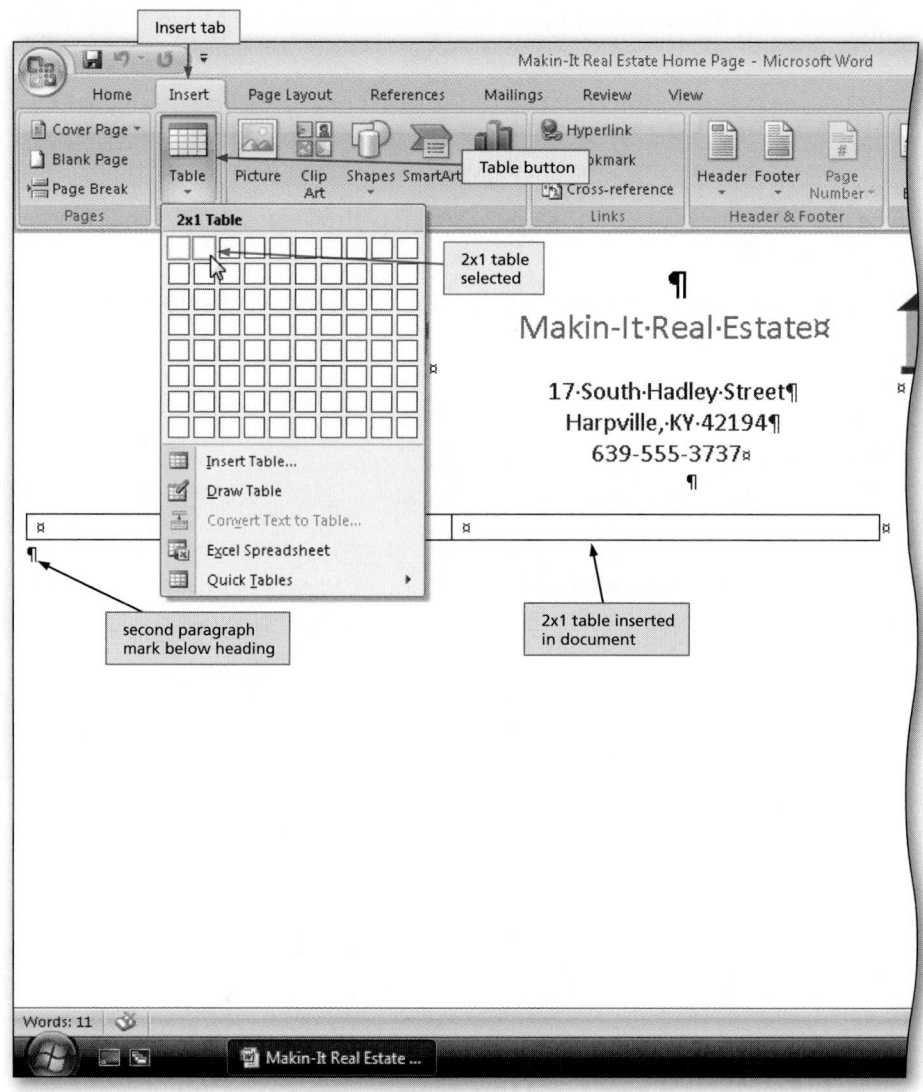

Figure 1–3

Other Ways
1. Press ALT+N, T

To Remove the Table Border, View Gridlines, and AutoFit the Table Contents

The table border for the new table is not necessary for the Web page. In order to place the contents in the document properly, however, gridlines should be displayed to serve as a guide for inserting the hyperlinks and chart. The cells in the table also should be formatted to adjust their size automatically to accommodate the data inserted in the table. The AutoFit to Contents option allows you to make the columns in a table automatically adjust to the contents. The following steps remove the border of the table, display gridlines in the tables in the document, and set the AutoFit to Contents option for the table. The heading in the document, including the clip art images, is already included in a table.

- Select both cells in the new table.

- If necessary, click the Design tab on the Ribbon.

- Click the Borders button arrow on the Ribbon to display the Borders gallery (Figure 1–4).

- Click No Border in the Borders gallery to remove the borders from the table.

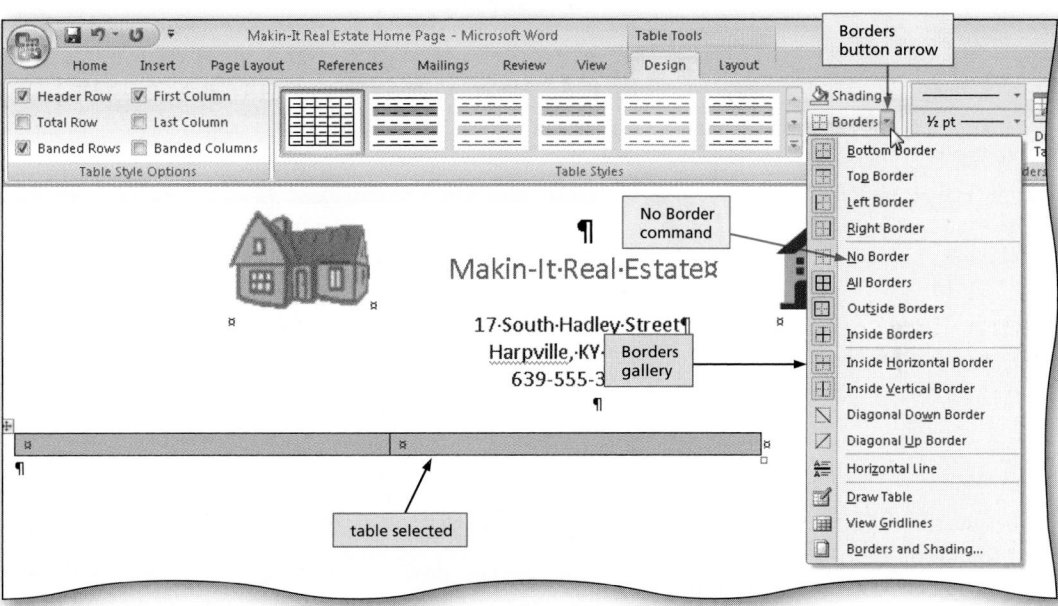

Figure 1–4

❸

- Click the Layout tab on the Ribbon.

- Click the View Gridlines button on the Ribbon to display gridlines in both tables in the document (Figure 1–5).

Q&A

When should I use gridlines?

Gridlines can be used as a guide when entering text or images. When the document is viewed in your browser or printed, the gridlines do not display or print.

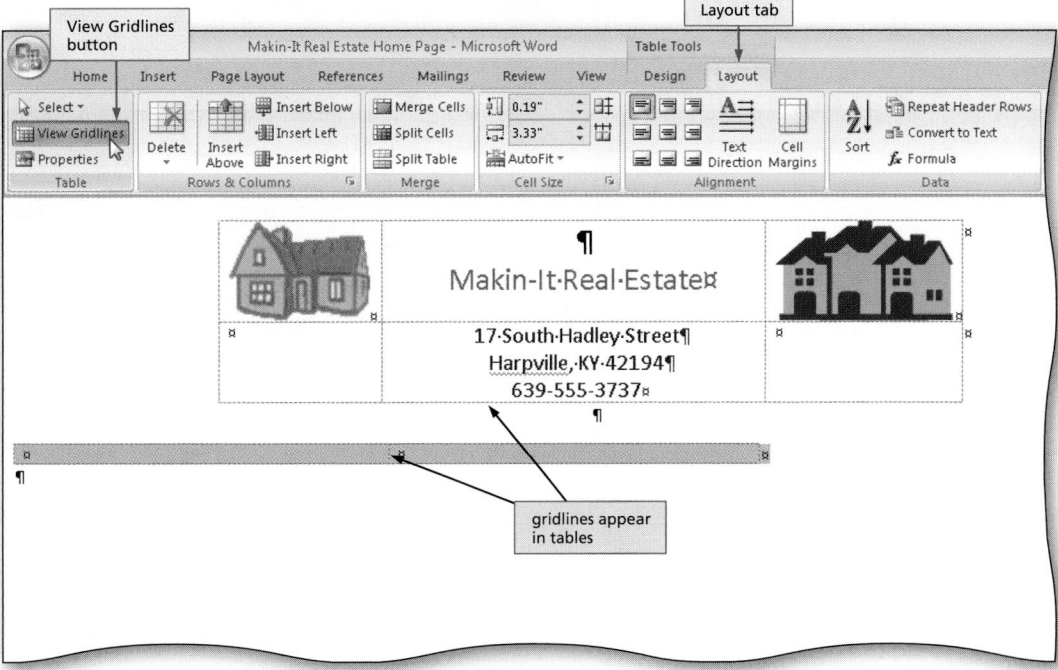

Figure 1–5

- Click the AutoFit button arrow on the Ribbon to display the AutoFit gallery (Figure 1–6).

Figure 1–6

- Click AutoFit Contents in the AutoFit gallery to shrink the selected cells to fit their contents (Figure 1–7).

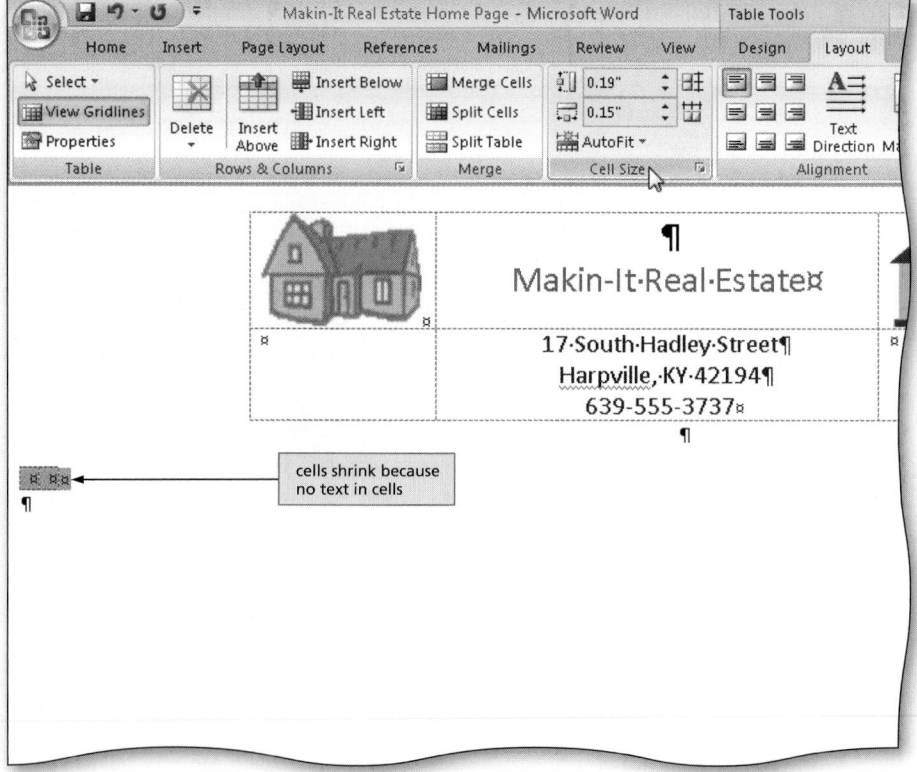

Figure 1–7

To Insert Text for Hyperlinks

After creating the borderless table, you must insert the three text phrases that will be used as hyperlinks on the home page. These phrases (Company Services, Homes for Sale, and E-Mail for Information) allow the Web page visitor to jump to two other Web pages and create an e-mail message. The following steps add the text phrases that are used as hyperlinks.

- If necessary, click the leftmost cell in the table to place the insertion point in the cell.

- Type Company Services and then press the ENTER key twice.

- Type Homes for Sale and then press the ENTER key twice.

- Type E-Mail for Information but do not press the ENTER key to complete the entry of the three text phrases that will be used as hyperlinks (Figure 1–8).

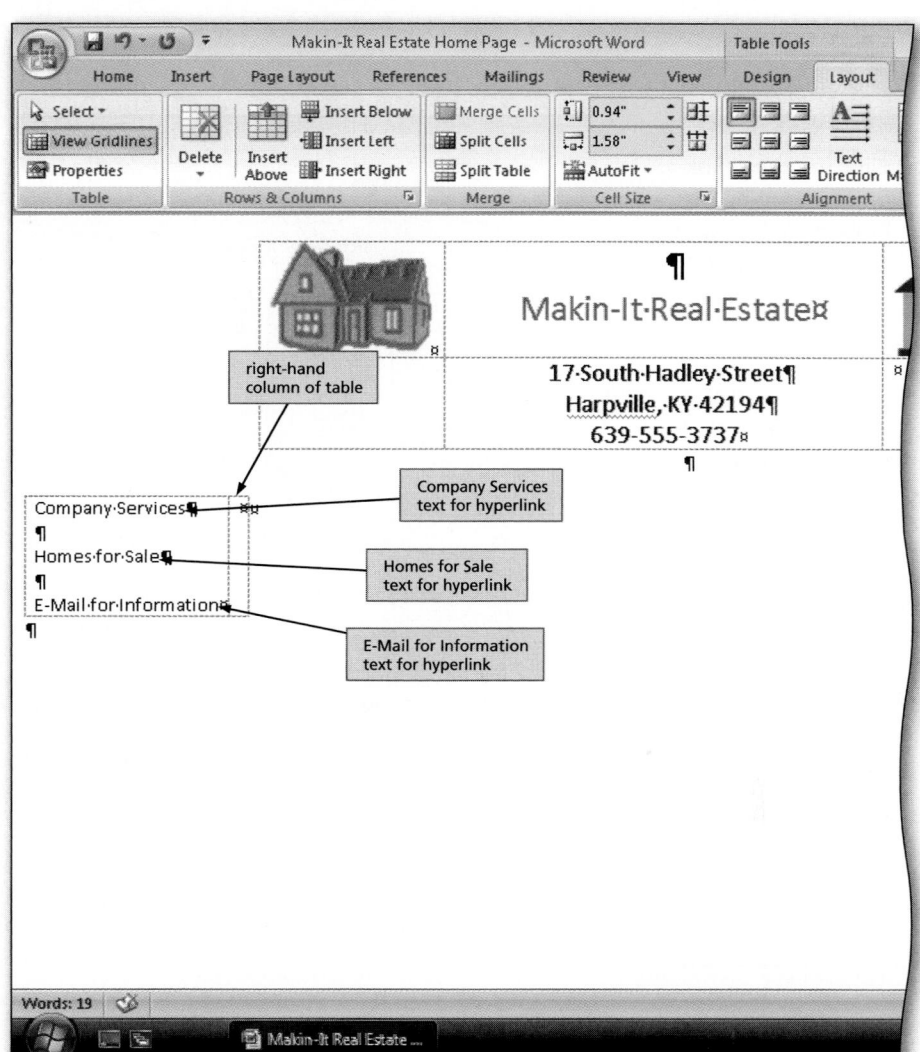

Figure 1–8

To Create a Hyperlink to PowerPoint Web Pages

The **Insert Hyperlink feature** provides the capability of linking to an existing file or Web page, to a place within the current document, to a newly created document, or to an e-mail address. In this chapter, two hyperlinks (Company Services and Homes for Sale) will be created that link to Web pages. The Company Services hyperlink will jump to a PowerPoint presentation that is saved as a Web page using the Web page name, CompanyServices. htm. The Homes for Sale hyperlink jumps to an Access report page using the Web page name, Homes for Sale.htm.

You will create the report later from an existing Access database. The third text phrase (E-Mail for Information) links to an e-mail address, allowing the Web page visitor to send an e-mail message to the company's manager.

The following steps create a hyperlink for the first text phrase.

1

- Drag through the text, Company Services, in the table to select the text.

- Click the Insert tab on the Ribbon.

- Click the Hyperlink button on the Ribbon to display the Insert Hyperlink dialog box.

2

- If necessary, click the Existing File or Web Page button on the Link to bar.

- Type CompanyServices. htm in the Address text box (Figure 1–9).

3

- Click the OK button to assign the hyperlink to the Company Services phrase.

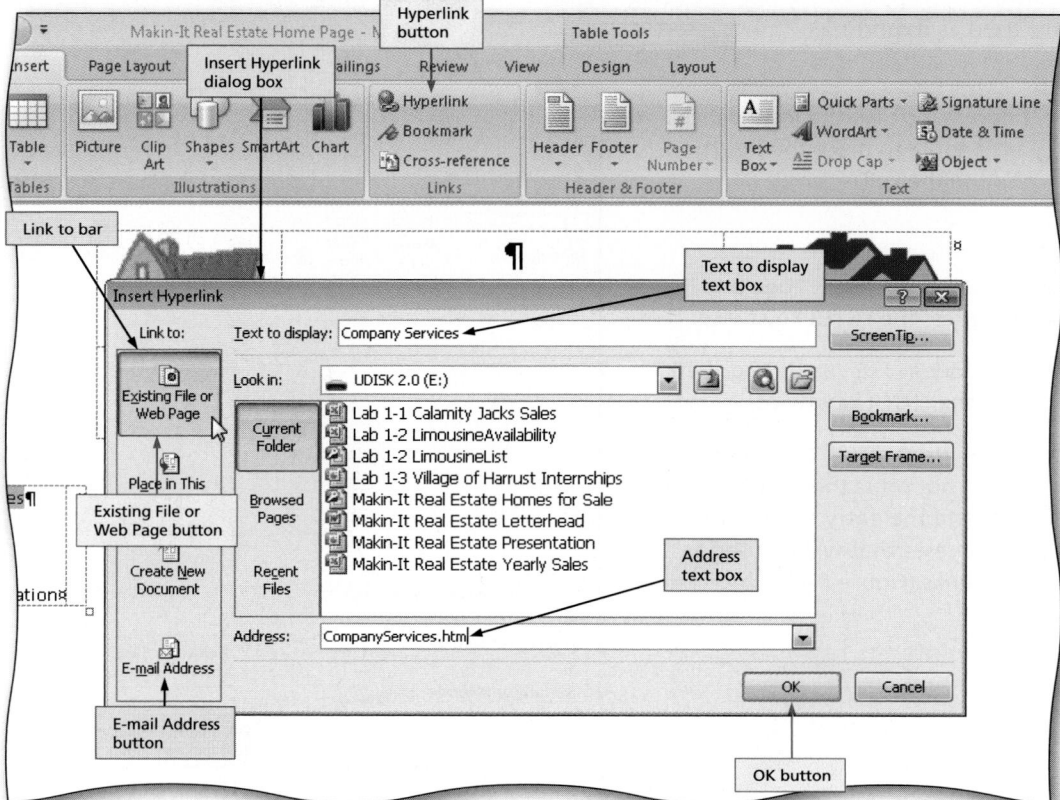

Figure 1–9

 Q&A How does the hyperlink function?

After saving the Word document as a Web page, the visitor clicks the text, Company Services, and the CompanyServices.htm file on the USB flash drive is displayed.

Other Ways

1. Right-click selected words, click Hyperlink on shortcut menu
2. Press CTRL+K

To Insert the Remaining Hyperlinks

The following steps add the remaining two hyperlinks.

1 Drag through the text, Homes for Sale, in the table. Click the Hyperlink button on the Ribbon.

2 Type Makin-It Real Estate - Homes for Sale.htm in the Address text box and then click the OK button.

3 Drag through the text, E-Mail for Information. Click the Hyperlink button on the Ribbon and then click the E-mail Address button on the Link to bar.

4 Type manager@isp.com in the E-mail address text box.

5 Type Request for Information in the Subject box and then click the OK button (Figure 1–10).

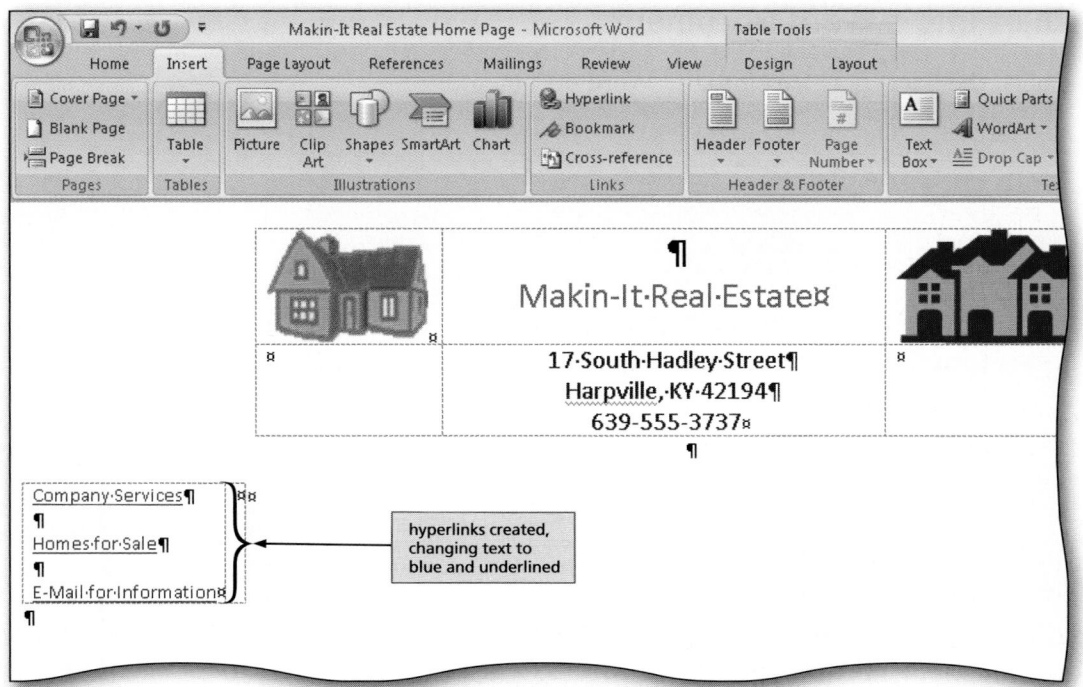

Figure 1–10

Embedding an Excel Chart into a Word Document

This chapter uses the **Object Linking and Embedding (OLE)** feature of Microsoft Office 2007 to insert the Excel chart into a Word document. OLE allows you to incorporate parts of a document or entire documents from one application into another. The Bar chart in Excel is called a **source object** (Figure 1–1b on page INT 4) and the Makin-It Real Estate Home Page document is the **destination document**. An embedded object becomes part of the destination document. This chapter illustrates using the Paste Special command to embed the Excel object. **Paste Special** inserts an object into Word, but still recognizes the **source program**, the program used to create the object. When you double-click an embedded object, such as the Total Yearly Sales chart, the source program opens within the destination document and allows you to make changes. In this example, Excel is the source program.

To Start Excel and Open an Existing Workbook

The following steps open the Excel workbook in preparation for copying the chart from the workbook.

Note: If you are using Windows XP, see Appendix F for alternate steps.

1 Start Excel. Click the Office Button and then click Open on the Office Button menu.

2 If necessary, click Computer in the Favorite Links section of the Navigation pane and then double-click UDISK 2.0 (E:) to select the USB flash drive as the new open location. (Your USB drive may have a different name and letter.)

3 Double-click Makin-It Real Estate Yearly Sales to open the Makin-It Real Estate Yearly Sales workbook.

BTW

Hyperlinks
Hyperlinks can link to both external locations and internal locations within the current document. To link to a location inside the current document, select the Place in This Document option in the Link to bar in the Insert Hyperlink dialog box. The Microsoft Office 2007 application then will provide a list of locations within the current document to which you can link.

BTW

Embedded Objects
The advantage of using an integrated set of applications, such as Microsoft Office 2007, is the capability of sharing information among applications. The Object Linking and Embedding (OLE) features of Office 2007 make the integration process more efficient. A chart created in Excel can be included in a Word document using OLE. To edit the embedded object, double-click it. The source program then starts and opens the source object for editing.

To Embed an Excel Chart into a Word Document

The following steps embed the Excel Bar chart into the Word document.

1
• If necessary, click the Total Yearly Sales Chart tab to make the sheet tab active (Figure 1–11).

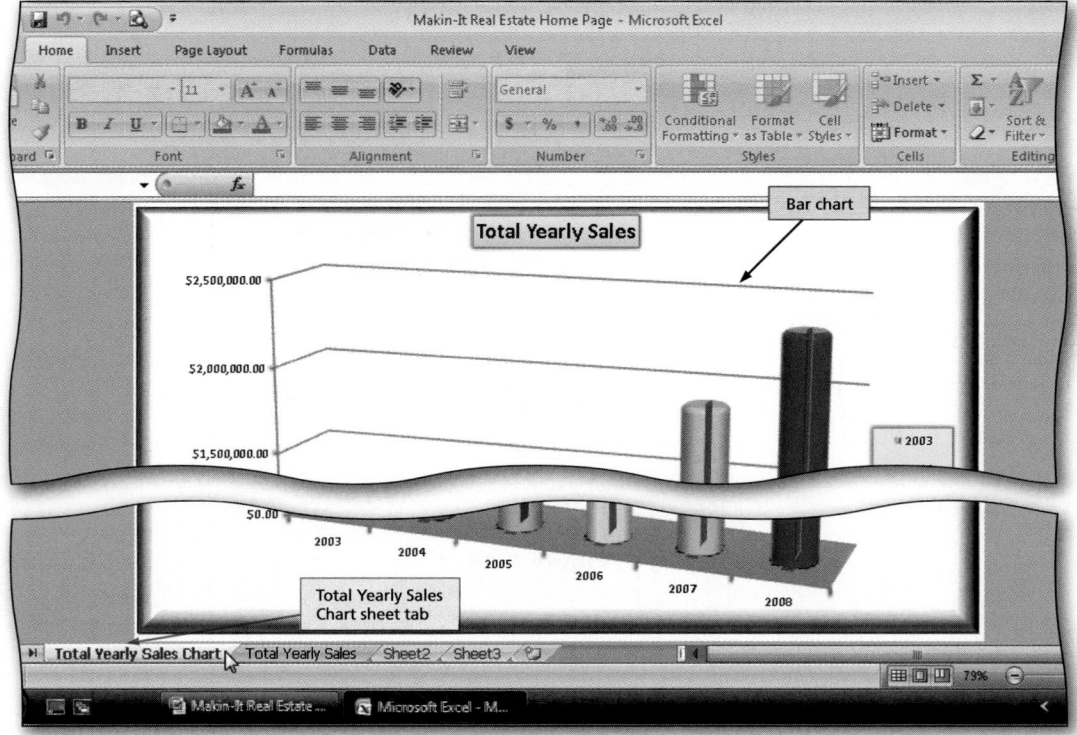

Figure 1–11

2
• Click the white area around the chart area to select the chart and then click the Copy button on the Ribbon to place a copy of the Bar chart on the Office Clipboard (Figure 1–12).

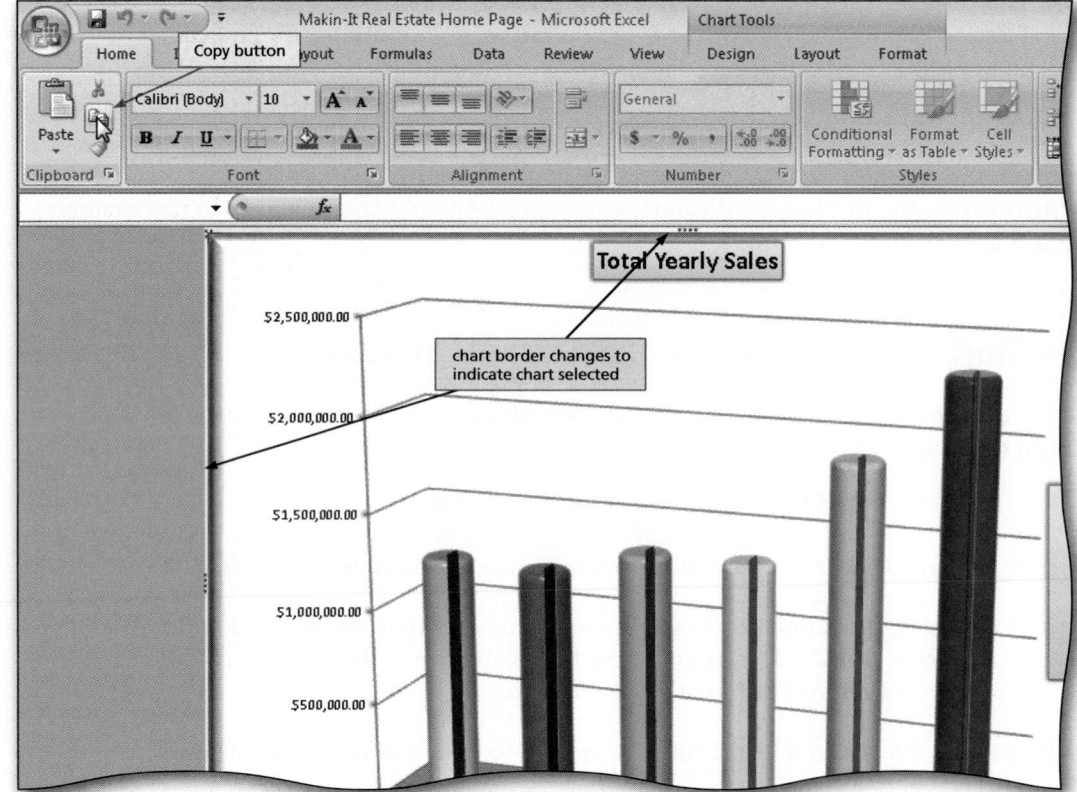

Figure 1–12

3

- Click the Makin-It Real Estate Home Page button on the Windows Vista taskbar.

- If necessary, click the right cell of the lower table to place the insertion point in the right cell of the table.

- Click the Home tab on the Ribbon.

- Click the Paste button arrow on the Ribbon to display the Paste gallery (Figure 1–13).

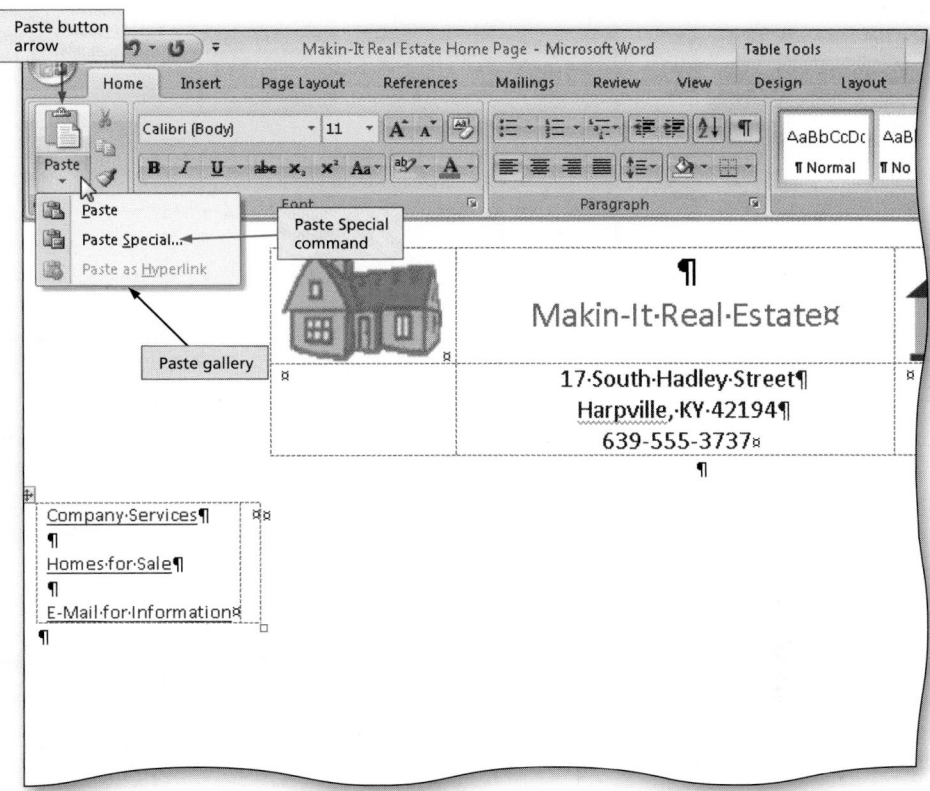

Figure 1–13

4

- Click Paste Special to display the Paste Special dialog box.

- If necessary, click Microsoft Office Excel Chart Object in the As list (Figure 1–14).

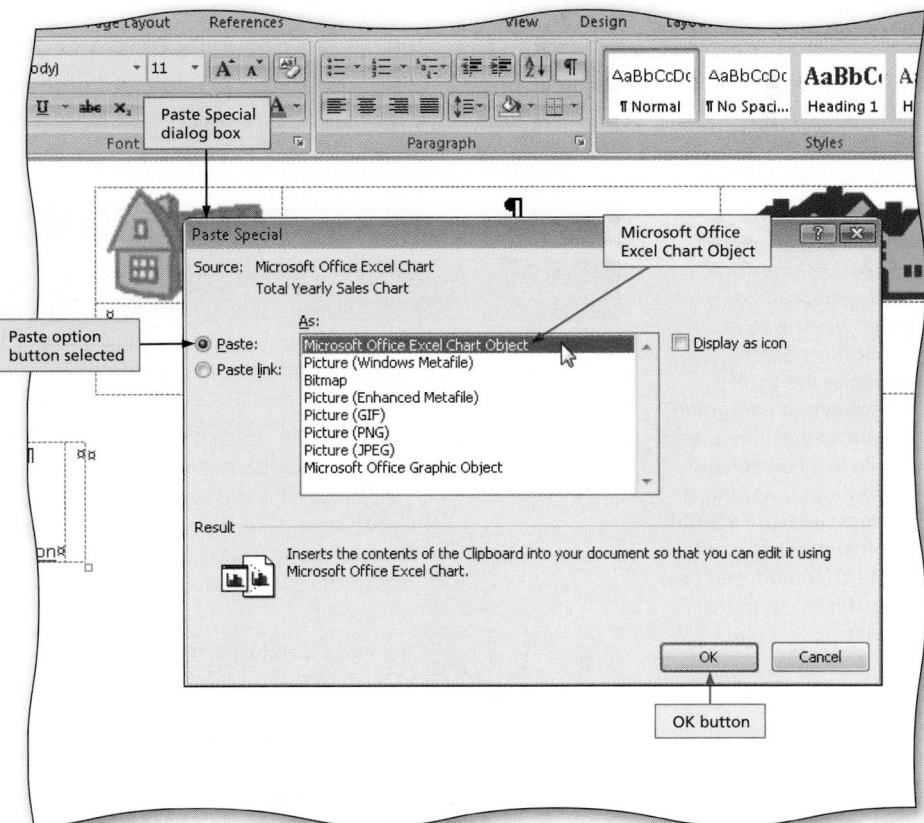

Figure 1–14

5

- Click the OK button to embed the Bar chart into the document (Figure 1–15).

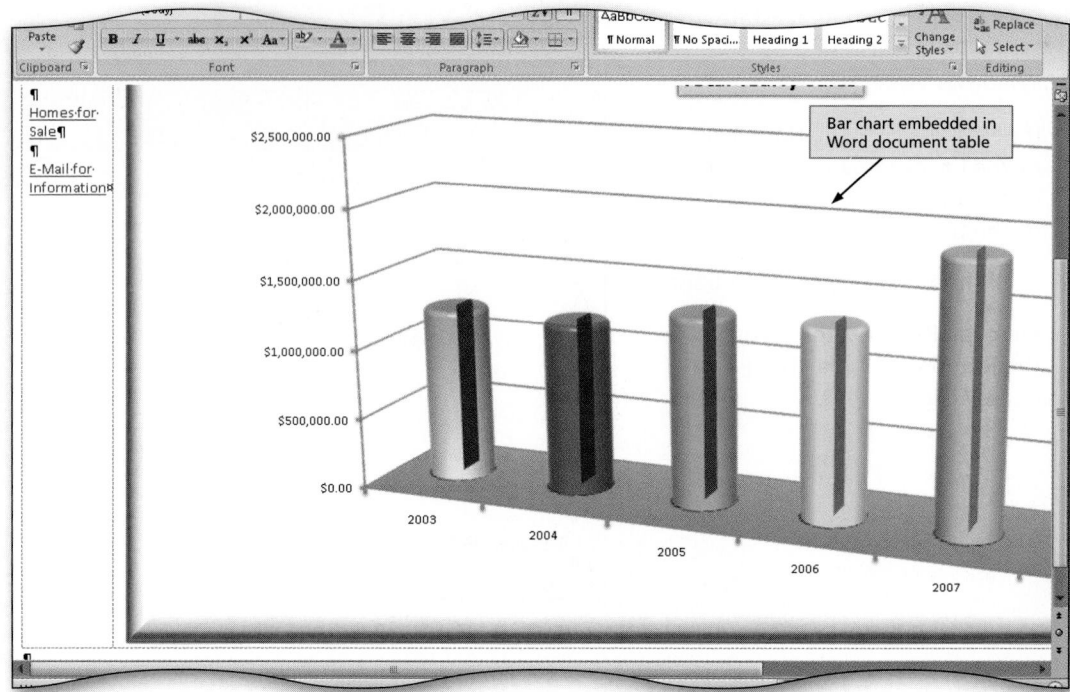

Bar chart embedded in Word document table

Figure 1–15

Copy Methods

All Office 2007 applications allow you to use three methods to copy objects among applications: (1) copy and paste; (2) copy and embed; and (3) copy and link. The first method uses the Copy and Paste buttons. The latter two use the Copy button and the Paste Special command. Table 1–1 summarizes the differences among the three methods.

BTW

Objects
Objects can be nearly any part of an Office 2007 application or other Windows Vista application. Some examples are Excel worksheets, a paragraph in a Word document, and a slide in a PowerPoint presentation. As long as you use the Paste Special command to paste data in the Clipboard, you can keep data in its native format.

Table 1–1 Copy Methods	
Method	**Characteristics**
Copy and paste	The source object becomes part of the destination document. An object may be edited, but the editing features are limited to those of the destination application. An Excel worksheet becomes a Word table. If changes are made to values in the Word table, any original Excel formulas are not recalculated.
Copy and embed	The source object becomes part of the destination document. An object may be edited in the destination document using source editing features. The Excel worksheet remains a worksheet in Word. If you make changes to values in the worksheet with Word active, Excel formulas will be recalculated. If you change the worksheet in Excel without the document open in Word, however, these changes will not display in the Word document the next time you open it.
Copy and link	The source object does not become part of the destination document, even though it appears to be. Instead, a link is established between the two documents, so that when you open the Word document, the worksheet displays within the document, as though it were a part of it. When you attempt to edit a linked worksheet in Word, the system activates Excel. If you change the worksheet in Excel, the changes also will display in the Word document the next time you open it.

To Change the Size of an Embedded Object

    The embedded Bar chart slightly exceeds the margins of the Makin-It Real Estate Home Page document. Reducing the size of the Bar chart will improve the layout of the document. When an Office 2007 document includes an embedded object from another Office 2007 document, you can edit the object in place. When you edit an object in place, the destination document's application displays commands on the Ribbon from the source document's application. For example, when you edit the Total Yearly Sales chart in the Makin-It Real Estate Home Page, the Ribbon changes so that you can use commands from Excel even though you are working in Word.

    The following steps reduce the size of the chart by editing the object in place.

- Click the View Ruler button above the vertical scroll box.

- If necessary, use the vertical scroll bar on the right side of the Word window to scroll to the top of the document.

- Drag the Move Table Column slider to the right so the border aligns with the left border of the upper table.

- Right-click the Bar chart to display the shortcut menu.

- Click Worksheet Object on the short-cut menu to display the Worksheet Object shortcut menu and then point to the Edit command (Figure 1–16).

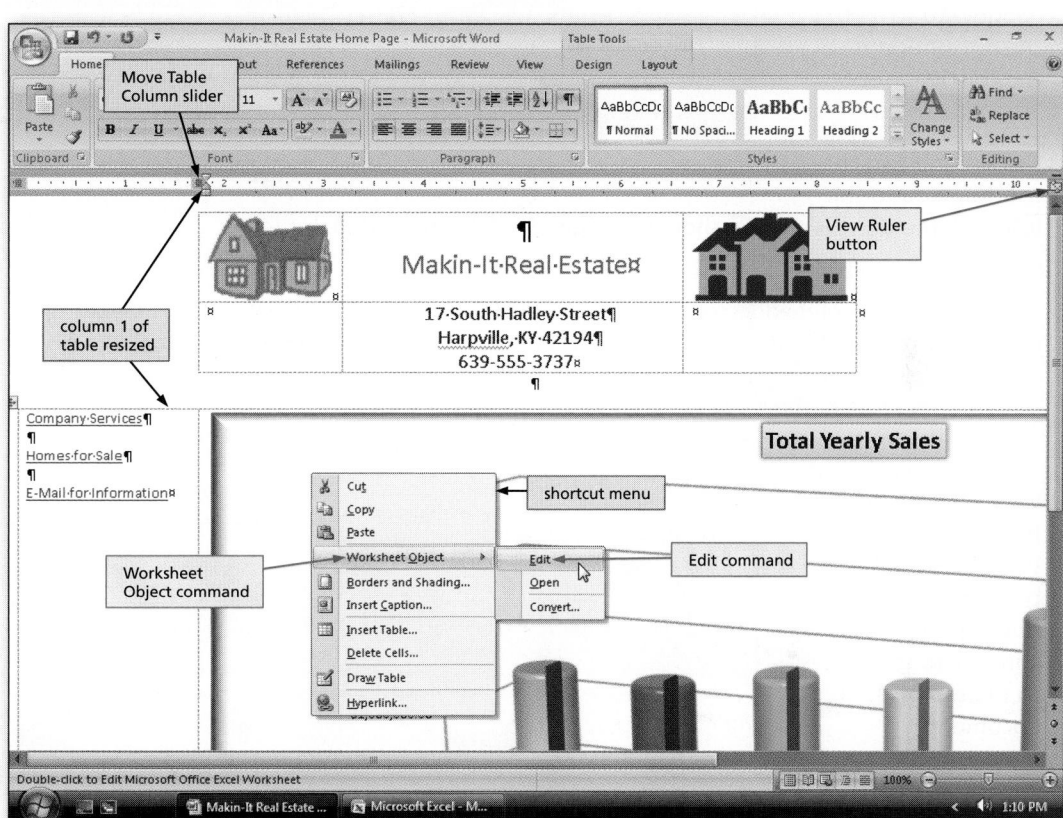

Figure 1–16

- Click Edit to begin editing the chart in place.

- Click anywhere in the chart to select it.

- Use the scroll bars on the bottom and right sides of the Word window to scroll to the bottom-right of the chart.

- Drag the lower-right sizing handle of the chart up and to the left until the chart is sized as shown in Figure 1–18 (Figure 1–17).

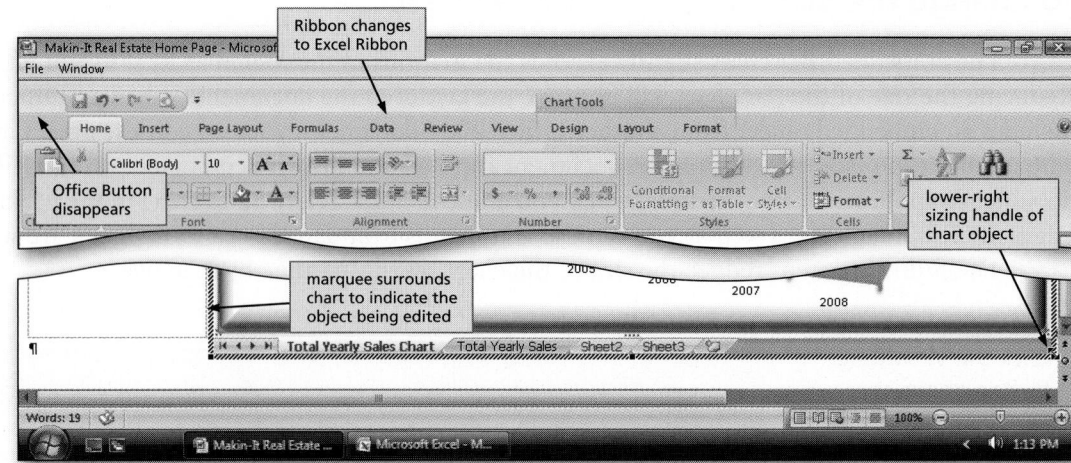

Figure 1–17

Q&A

What happened to the Ribbon?

When you edit an embedded object in place, the destination application, which is Word in this case, displays contextual commands in the Ribbon for the application in which the embedded object was created. You now can edit the Excel chart as though you are working in Excel. This method of editing is much simpler than the entire Excel application opening in order for you to edit the chart.

- If necessary, use the scroll bars on the bottom and right sides of the Word window to scroll to the top of the document.

- Click next to the E-Mail for Information hyperlink in the first column of the table to display the Word Ribbon (Figure 1–18).

Q&A

Why did the Word Ribbon appear?

When you are finished editing an embedded object in place, you can click anywhere outside the embedded object in the destination document to reactivate the destination document's Ribbon commands.

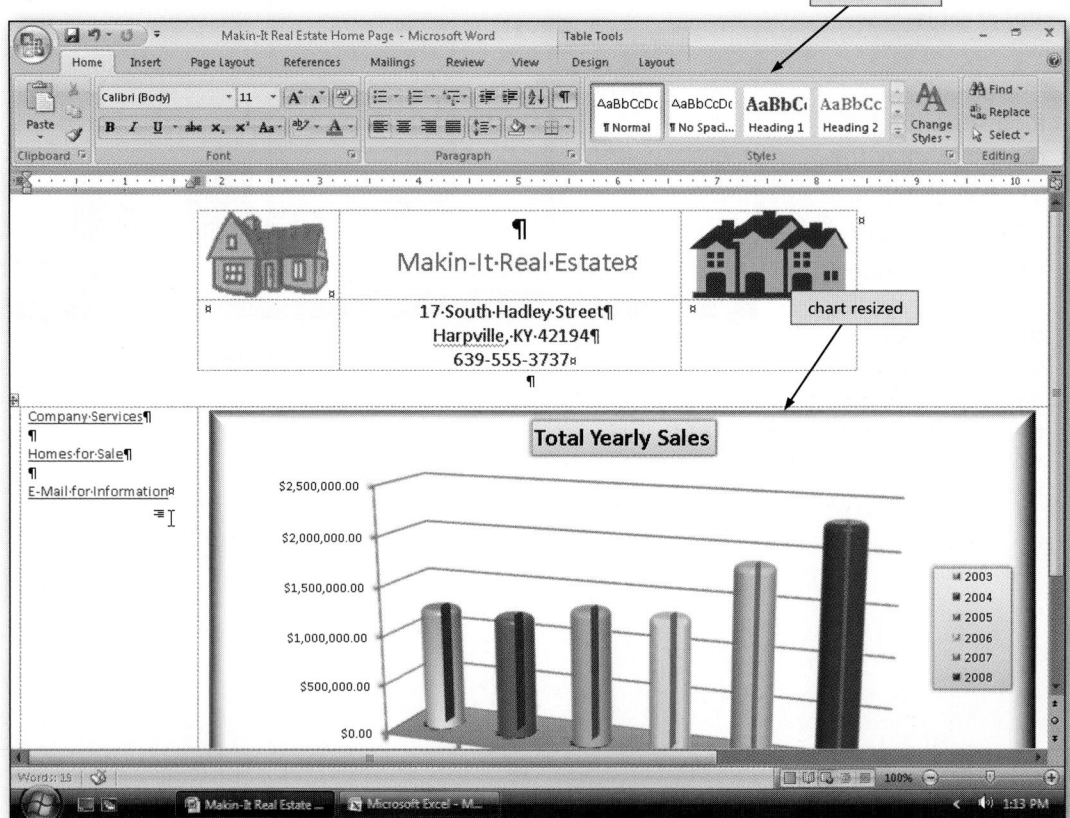

Figure 1–18

To Quit Excel

With the Bar chart embedded in the Word document, you no longer need the Makin-It Real Estate Yearly Sales workbook open. The following steps quit Excel.

1 Right-click the Microsoft Excel - Makin-It Real Estate Yearly Sales button on the Windows Vista taskbar. Click Close on the shortcut menu. If prompted to save changes, click the No button.

2 If the Microsoft Excel dialog box displays regarding saving the large amount of information on the Clipboard, click the No button.

BTW

Resizing
To resize an image proportionally from a corner, you can press and hold down the SHIFT key while dragging a corner sizing handle. To resize vertically, horizontally, or diagonally from the center outward, press and hold down the CTRL key while dragging a sizing handle. To resize proportionally from the center outward, press and hold down the CTRL+SHIFT keys and drag a corner sizing handle.

Viewing the Word Document in Your Browser and Saving It as a Web Page

The next task is to view the Word document in your browser to verify that all information and links in the document are accurate. After verifying its accuracy, you then can save the Word document as an HTML file. Saving the Word document as an HTML file makes it possible for it to be viewed using a browser, such as Internet Explorer.

To Add a Button to the Quick Access Toolbar

Many commands available in Word are not included on any of the tabs on the Ribbon. You can, however, add such commands to the Quick Access Toolbar. One such command allows you to preview a document in a Web browser. This command, Web Page Preview, needs to be added to the Quick Access Toolbar so that the Web page can be previewed. The following steps add the Web Page Preview command to the Quick Access Toolbar.

1

- Click the Customize Quick Access Toolbar button arrow to display the Customize Quick Access Toolbar menu (Figure 1–19).

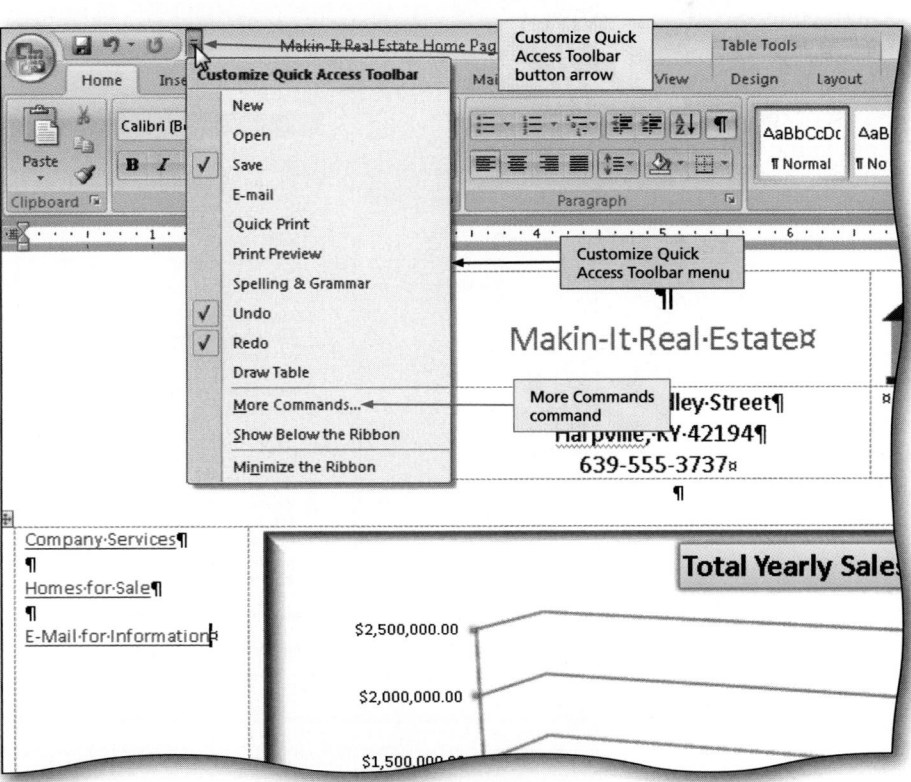

Figure 1–19

- Click the More Commands command on the Customize Quick Access Toolbar menu.

- When the Word Options dialog box is displayed, click the 'Choose commands from' box arrow to display the Choose commands from list (Figure 1–20).

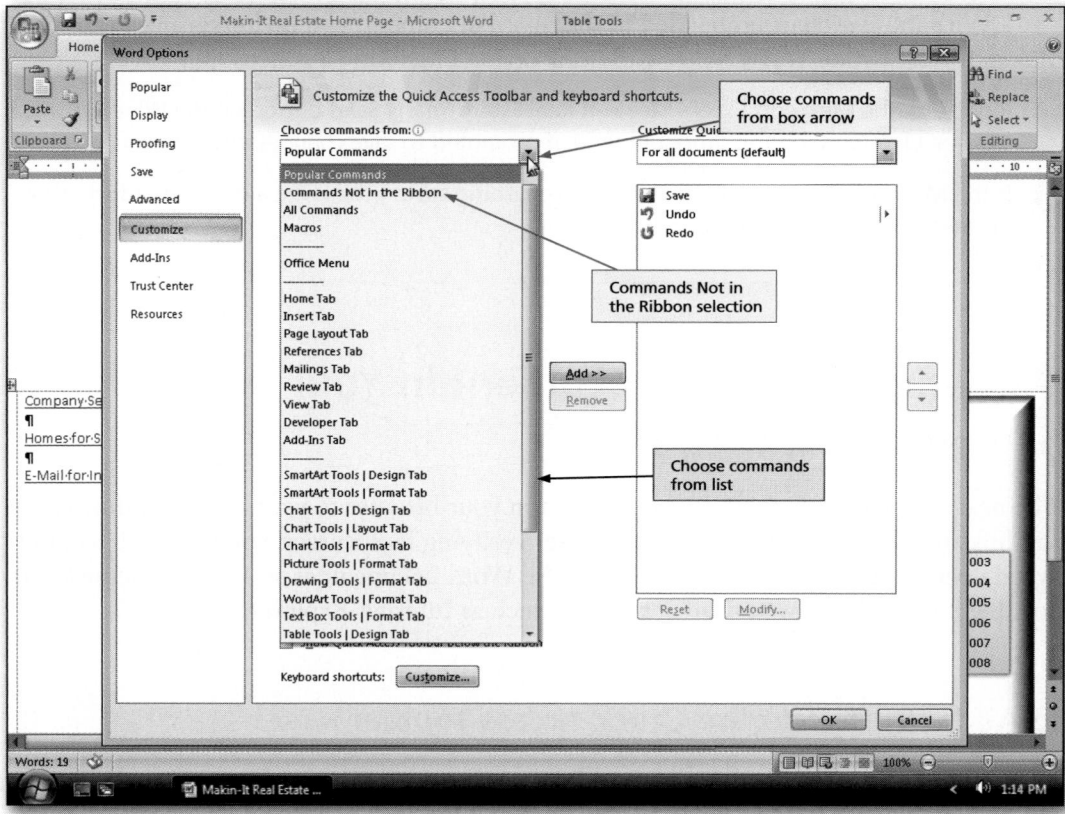

Figure 1–20

- Click Commands Not in the Ribbon in the 'Choose commands from' list to display a list of commands not in the Ribbon (Figure 1–21).

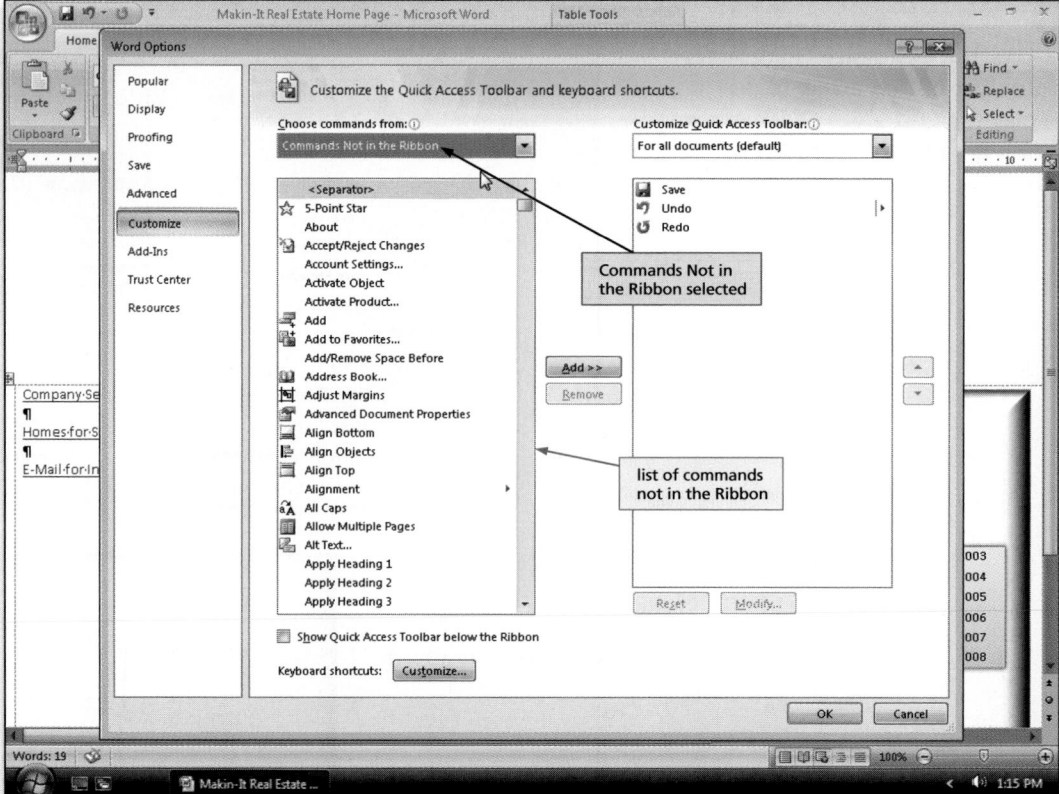

Figure 1–21

4

● Scroll to the bottom of the list, click Web Page Preview, and then click the Add button to add the button to the Quick Access Toolbar (Figure 1–22).

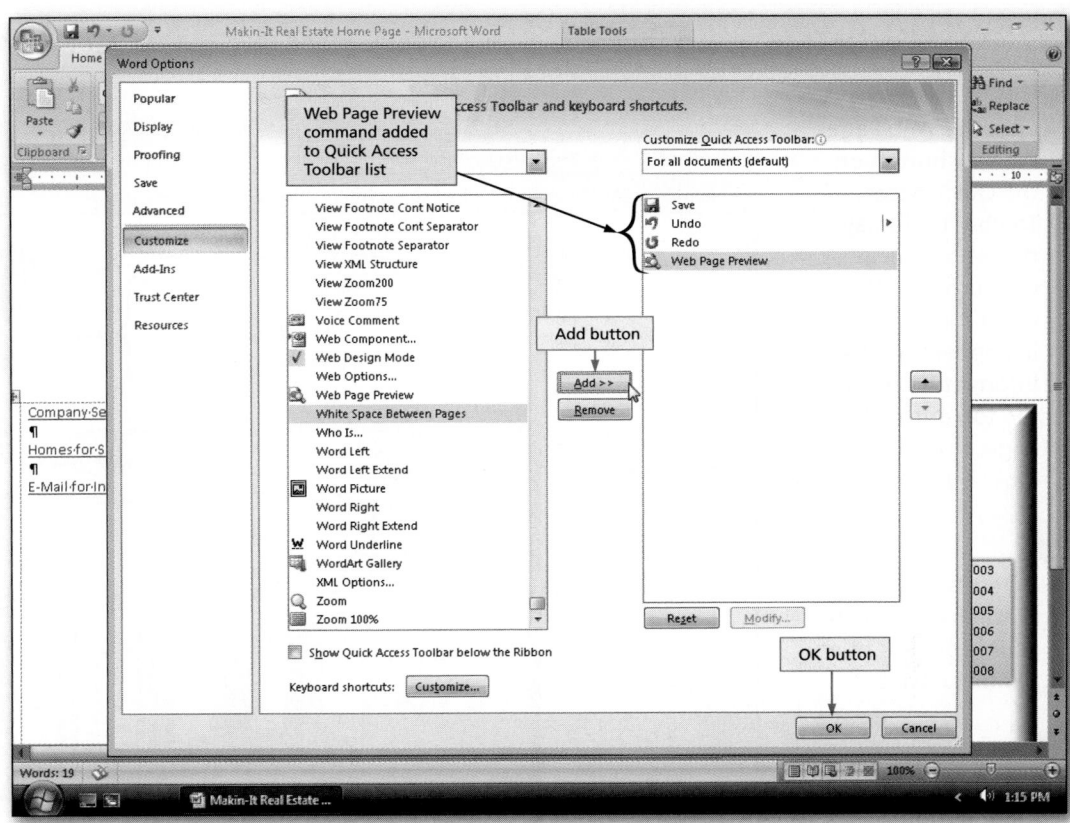

Figure 1–22

5

● Click the OK button to close the Word Options dialog box (Figure 1–23).

Q&A

Will the Web Page Preview command be on the Quick Access Toolbar the next time that I start Word?

Yes. When you change the Quick Access Toolbar, the changes remain even after you restart Word. If you share a computer with somebody else or if the Quick Access Toolbar becomes cluttered, Word allows you to remove commands from the Quick Access Toolbar. The Web Page Preview button is removed from the Quick Access Toolbar later in this chapter.

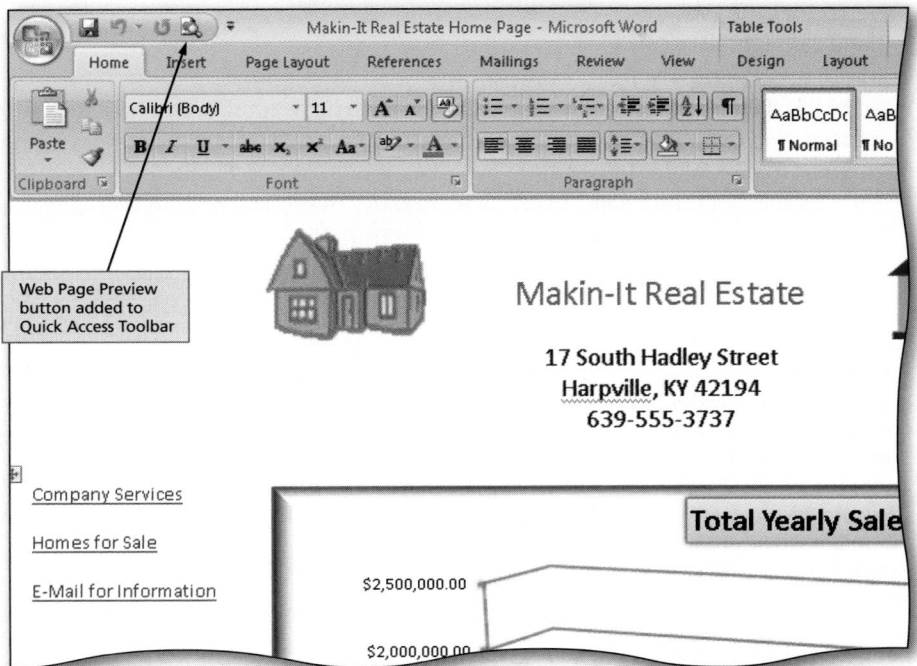

Figure 1–23

To Preview the Web Page

The following steps preview the document in the browser and then save the Word document as an HTML file.

- Click the Web Page Preview button on the Quick Access Toolbar to display the Web page in your browser. If the security warning appears in the Information bar at the top of the Web page, then click its Close button.

- If necessary, click the Maximize button on your browser's title bar (Figure 1–24).

3
- Click the browser's Close button.

Q&A

How should I verify the Web page?

Verify that the Web page contains all information necessary

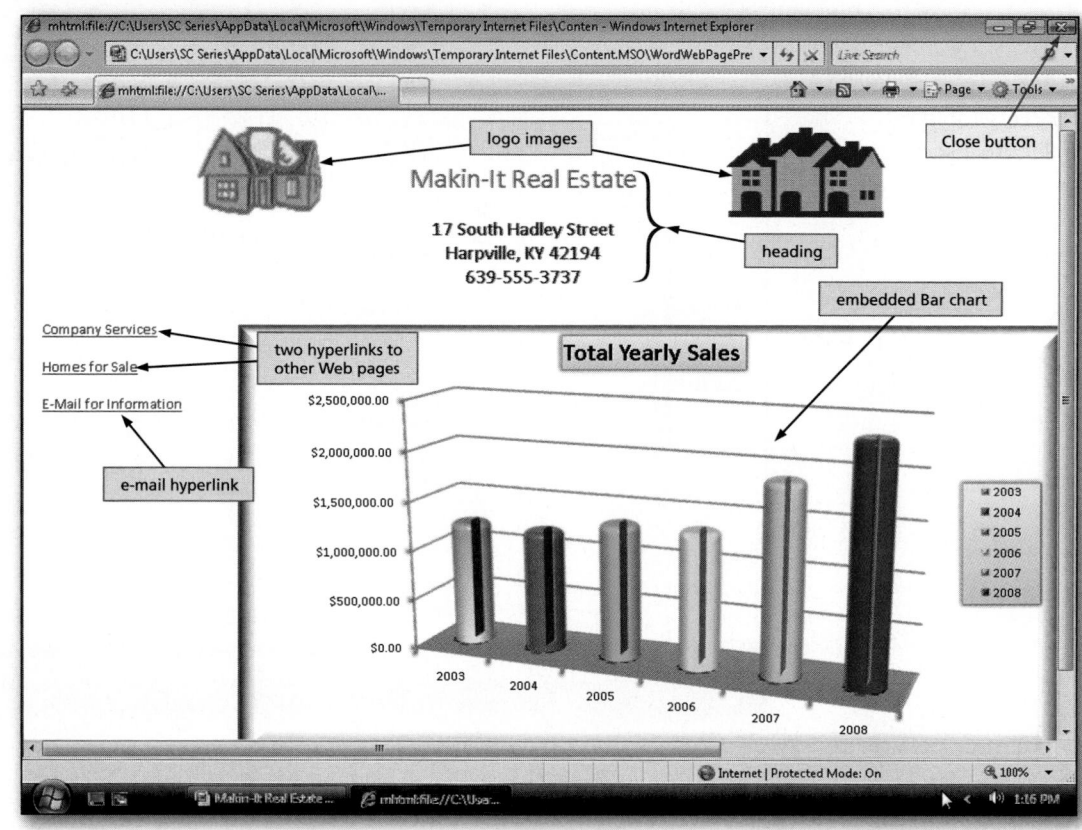

Figure 1–24

and is displayed as shown in Figure 1–24. The Web page consists of a heading with logo images and the company name, address, and telephone number. A borderless table displays three hyperlinks in the left column and a Bar chart in the right column. The E-Mail for Information hyperlink should display a new message when you click it. The other two links, Company Services and Homes for Sale, do not work because the corresponding Web pages are not available until later in this chapter.

To Save a Document with a New File Name

If the Web page is correct, save it on the USB flash drive as an HTML file. If changes need to be made to the Web page, return to the Word document and correct it. The following steps save the document as a Web page.

1 Click the Office Button and then click the Save As command.

2 Type `Makin-It Real Estate Home Page` in the File name text box if necessary.

3 Select Web Page in the Save as type box.

4 If necessary, click Computer in the Favorite Links section of the Navigation pane and then double-click UDISK 2.0 (E:) to select the USB flash drive as the new open location. (Your USB flash drive may have a different name and letter.)

5 Click the Save button in the Save As dialog box. If the Microsoft Office Word dialog box displays, click the Continue button.

Q&A Why should I save the document as a Web page?

Saving an existing Word document as a Web page allows you quickly to get a Word document ready for copying to the Web or to an intranet. One alternative to this is to write the Hypertext Markup Language (HTML) to develop the Web pages. **HTML** is a programming language used for Web page creation. The home page created earlier in this chapter could be created by writing HTML tags (code). For documents that already are in Word format, the easier method is to use the Word Save as Web Page command. This essentially creates the HTML code for you and saves it in a file. While the HTML code is in the file, you do not need to understand HTML code.

To Reset the Quick Access Toolbar and Quit Word

The necessary work with the Word document is complete. The following steps remove the Web Page Preview button from the Quick Access Toolbar and quit Word.

1 Click the Customize the Quick Access Toolbar button arrow on the Ribbon.

2 Click the More Commands command.

3 When the Word Options dialog box is displayed, click the Reset button. If the Reset Customizations dialog box is displayed, click the OK button.

4 Click the OK button on the Word Options dialog box to close it.

5 Click the View Ruler button to close the ruler.

6 Click the Close button on the Microsoft Word title bar.

Q&A Do I need to remove the button from the Quick Access Toolbar?

No. For consistency with this book, reset the Quick Access Toolbar after the added buttons are no longer needed. If you share a computer with others, you should reset the Quick Access Toolbar when you are finished using the computer.

BTW

Web Programming Languages
A number of programming languages can be used to create Web pages. Web pages created using the Save as Web Page command on the File menu can be enhanced with other Web programming languages, such as ASP, DHTML, and JavaScript.

Creating a PowerPoint Presentation Web Page

PowerPoint 2007 allows you to create Web pages from an existing PowerPoint presentation, using the same method used earlier in this chapter to save a Word document as a Web page. The presentation then can be viewed using your browser.

To Start PowerPoint and Open an Existing Presentation

The PowerPoint presentation used in this chapter consists of three slides (Figure 1–1g on page INT 5). The first slide is a title slide, containing the company name and graphics. Slide 2 consists of information about services for home sellers. Slide 3 includes information about services for home buyers. This information can be used in its present format to enhance a presentation about the company's services. As Web pages, you can use this presentation to address a much wider, global audience on the World Wide Web.

The following steps open an existing PowerPoint presentation.

Note: If you are using Windows XP, see Appendix F for alternate steps.

1 Start PowerPoint. Click the Office Button and then click Open on the Office Button menu.

2 If necessary, click Computer in the Favorite Links section of the Navigation pane and then double-click UDISK 2.0 (E:) to select the USB flash drive as the new open location. (Your USB drive may have a different name and letter.)

3 Double-click Makin-It Real Estate Presentation to open the Makin-It Real Estate Presentation presentation (Figure 1–25).

Figure 1–25

BTW

Keeping Links Fresh
When you create a Web page, it is important to make sure that all of your hyperlinks are functional as time goes on. Links to other pages can become stale, or nonfunctional, if another Web page creator or an external site takes a page offline. Automated tools can help you identify when pages to which you are hyperlinking no longer are available.

To Add Text for a Hyperlink into a PowerPoint Presentation

One of the more important features of Web sites is their capability of linking from one Web page to another using hyperlinks. In earlier steps in this chapter, you added three hyperlinks to the Makin-It Real Estate home page. Once Web page visitors link to the PowerPoint Web pages, however, they cannot return to the home page without using the Back button on the browser's toolbar. This is not a convenient way for Web page visitors to navigate through the Web site. The following steps add a Home link to the first slide of the PowerPoint presentation (Figure 1–1e on page INT 5).

1 Click the Insert tab on the Ribbon.

2 Click Text Box on the Ribbon.

3 Draw the outline of the text box in the location shown on the slide in Figure 1–26.

4 If necessary, click inside the text box.

5 Type Home as the hyperlink text (Figure 1–26).

Other Ways

1. Press ALT+N, press X

Figure 1–26

To Insert a Hyperlink into a PowerPoint Presentation

After you enter the text for the hyperlink, you can create the hyperlink itself. When clicked, the hyperlink jumps to the Makin-It Real Estate home page created previously in this chapter and saved on the USB flash drive. To create the hyperlink, you will use the Hyperlink button on the Insert tab on the Ribbon.

The following steps create the PowerPoint hyperlink.

1
- Double-click the word, Home, inside the text box you just inserted.

2
- If necessary, click the Insert tab on the Ribbon.

- Click the Hyperlink button on the Ribbon to display the Insert Hyperlink dialog box.

3
- If necessary, click the Existing File or Web Page button on the Link to bar.

- Type e:\Makin-It Real Estate Home Page.htm in the Address text box. (Your USB drive may have a different name and letter.) Click the OK button to add the hyperlink to the text in the text box (Figure 1–27).

Figure 1–27

Other Ways

1. Right-click highlighted word, click Hyperlink on shortcut menu
2. Press CTRL+K

To Add a Button to the Quick Access Toolbar and View the Web Page in Your Browser

Just as in the previous section of this chapter, the following steps display the Web page before saving it. It is important to verify all of the Web page navigation features before saving the file. Because the Web Page Preview button is not available on the Ribbon, the button must first be added to the Quick Access Toolbar.

1 Click the Customize Quick Access Toolbar button arrow to display the Customize Quick Access Toolbar menu.

2 Click the More Commands command on the Customize Quick Access Toolbar menu.

3 When the PowerPoint Options dialog box is displayed, click the 'Choose commands from' box arrow to display the Choose commands from list.

4 Click Commands Not in the Ribbon in the Choose commands from list to display a list of commands not in the Ribbon. Scroll to the bottom of the list, click Web Page Preview, and then click the Add button to add the button to the Quick Access Toolbar.

5 Click the OK button to close the PowerPoint Options dialog box.

6 Click the Web Page Preview button on the Quick Access Toolbar to display the Web page in your browser. If the security warning appears in the Information bar at the top of the Web page, then click its Close button.

7 If necessary, click the Maximize button on your browser's title bar (Figure 1–28).

Figure 1–28

Using Hyperlinks in PowerPoint

Slide 1 of the PowerPoint presentation Web page contains a hyperlink to the home page of the Makin-It Real Estate Web site. Although you created this hyperlink by adding a text box to the first slide, you also can create hyperlinks from existing text or images in a PowerPoint presentation. For example, one of the logo images on slide 1 could be used as a hyperlink to the home page of the Web site. Using one of those images, however, does not give the Web page visitor a clear idea of where the hyperlink will lead. It is more appropriate to create a hyperlink to the home page from text — for example, Home — that makes sense to the visitor.

In addition to any hyperlinks that are added to the presentation, PowerPoint automatically creates hyperlinks in the left column of the Web page, called the **outline**. Using the Expand/Collapse Outline button below the outline pane, you can expand or collapse the outline and navigate through the Web page presentation (Figure 1–28). The text in the heading of each slide is used as the phrases for these hyperlinks. When you click a link, you jump to that particular slide within the presentation. The ease of navigation within a PowerPoint Web page is valuable to the Web page visitor.

BTW

Web Page Publishing
The Web pages created in this project all are stored locally on your computer. Typically, a Web page must be published to a server inside the organization or at your ISP. Microsoft offers a Web Page Publishing Wizard to assist in moving all of the related files and directories that comprise a Web site.

To Save the PowerPoint Presentation as a Web Page

The next step is to save the PowerPoint presentation as a Web page. When you save a PowerPoint presentation as a Web page, the Web page is saved in a default folder. All supporting files, such as backgrounds and images, are organized in this folder automatically. The name of the PowerPoint slide show opened in this section is Makin-It Real Estate Presentation. To simplify the naming of the Web page, the Web page will be saved with the name CompanyServices.htm. PowerPoint uses the name of the saved Web page and adds the string, _files, for the name of the new folder. When saving the current presentation as a Web page, the folder name that PowerPoint Web creates is CompanyServices_files. The default name for the first slide in the presentation is frame.htm. The structure used in the folder organization makes Web page publishing easier because you can keep track of all of the files associated with the Web page. You also can edit the files manually, rather than using PowerPoint.

The steps below save the PowerPoint presentation as a Web page.

BTW

Outline
The outline pane is displayed by default when you view a presentation in a browser. To hide this pane, click the Outline button while in the browser. Click the Outline button again to redisplay the outline pane.

1 Click the Microsoft PowerPoint button on the Windows Vista taskbar.

2 Click the Office Button and then click the Save As command.

3 If necessary, type CompanyServices in the File name text box.

4 Select Web Page in the 'Save as type' box.

5 If necessary, click Computer in the Favorite Links section of the Navigation pane and then double-click UDISK 2.0 (E:) to select the USB flash drive as the new open location. (Your USB flash drive may have a different name and letter.)

6 Click the Save button in the Save As dialog box to save the PowerPoint presentation as a Web page.

To Remove a Button from the Quick Access Toolbar, Quit PowerPoint, and Close Your Browser

After saving the PowerPoint presentation as a Web page, you can remove the Web Page Preview button from the Quick Access Toolbar, quit PowerPoint, and close your browser, as shown in the following steps.

1 Click the Customize the Quick Access Toolbar button arrow on the Ribbon.

2 Click the More Commands command.

3 When the PowerPoint Options dialog box is displayed, click the Reset button. If the Reset Customizations dialog box is displayed, click the OK button.

4 Click the OK button on the PowerPoint Options dialog box to close it.

5 Click the Close button on the PowerPoint title bar.

6 Click the Close button on the browser title bar.

BTW

Viewing Web Pages
In addition to Microsoft Windows Vista environments, many environments exist for viewing Web pages. When creating a Web page with special features, such as data access pages, it is important to make sure that the special features are supported within the environment in which the Web page viewers operate. For example, users who view Web pages on Apple Macintosh computers may have a different Web page viewing experience.

Creating a Web Page from an Access Report

The next task in the Makin-It Real Estate Web site creation is to use an Access database to create a report and save it as a Web page. One of the more common purposes of reports is for viewing records in a database via a company's intranet or the World Wide Web. Reports provide a method to make inquiries of large amounts of data in a selective way.

To Start Access and Open an Existing Database

The following steps open an Access database.

Note: If you are using Windows XP, see Appendix F for alternate steps.

1 Start Access. Click the Office Button and then click Open on the Office Button menu.

2 If necessary, click Computer in the Favorite Links section of the Navigation pane and then double-click UDISK 2.0 (E:) to select the USB flash drive as the new open location. (Your USB drive may have a different name and letter.)

3 Double-click Makin-It Real Estate Homes for Sale to open the Makin-It Real Homes for Sale database (Figure 1–29).

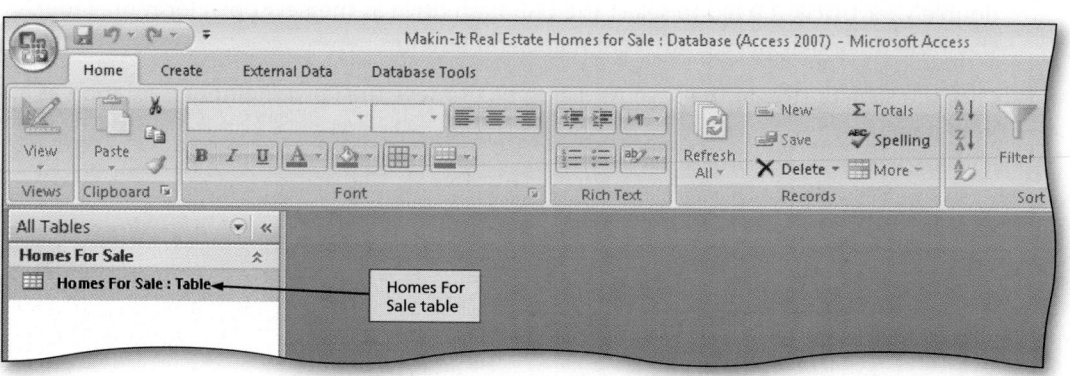

Figure 1–29

To Create a Report Using the Report Wizard

For the Makin-It Real Estate Web site, you do not want the database to be altered by the Web page visitor in any way. The visitors should be allowed to view only the data. Creating an Access report and then publishing the report as a Web page will achieve this goal. The Web page visitors can view all data, but they cannot change the data itself.

The following steps create a new Access report.

1

- Click the Create tab on the Ribbon.

- Click the Report Wizard button on the Ribbon.

- When the Report Wizard dialog box is displayed, click the Add All Fields button to move all the fields in the table to the Selected Fields list (Figure 1–30).

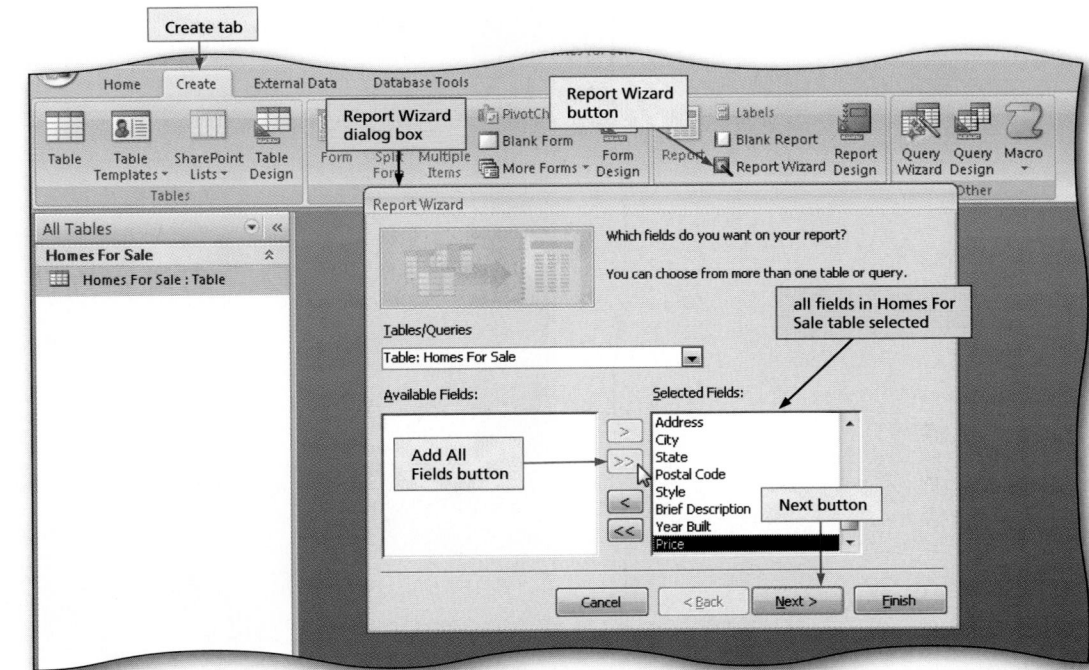

Figure 1–30

2

- Click the Next button.

- Click Style in the box on the left and then click the Add button to group the report by Style (Figure 1–31).

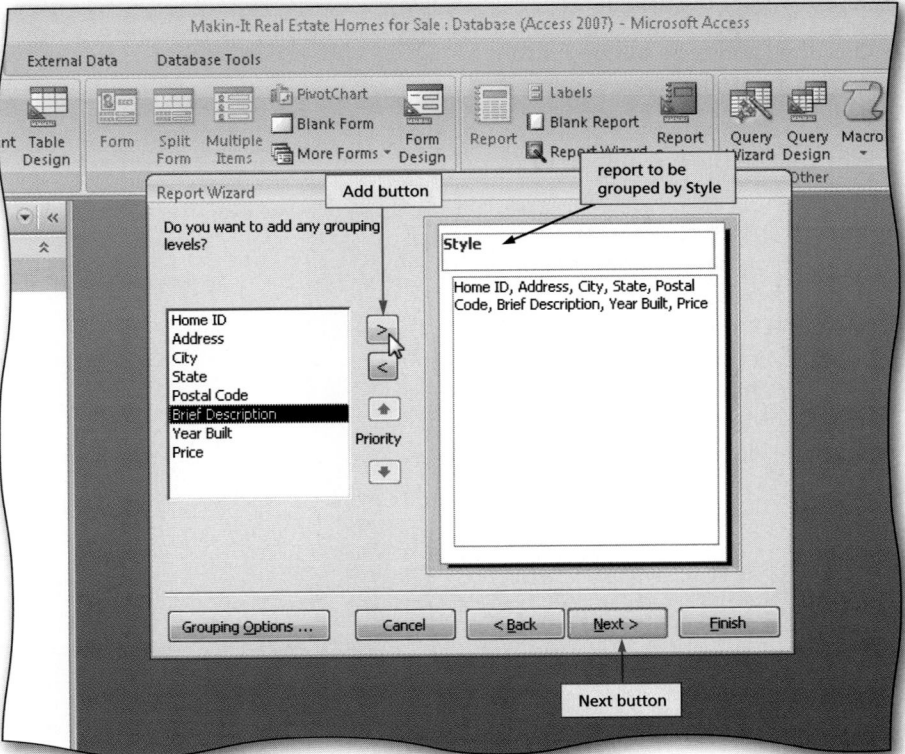

Figure 1–31

- Click the Next button to display options for sorting records (Figure 1–32).

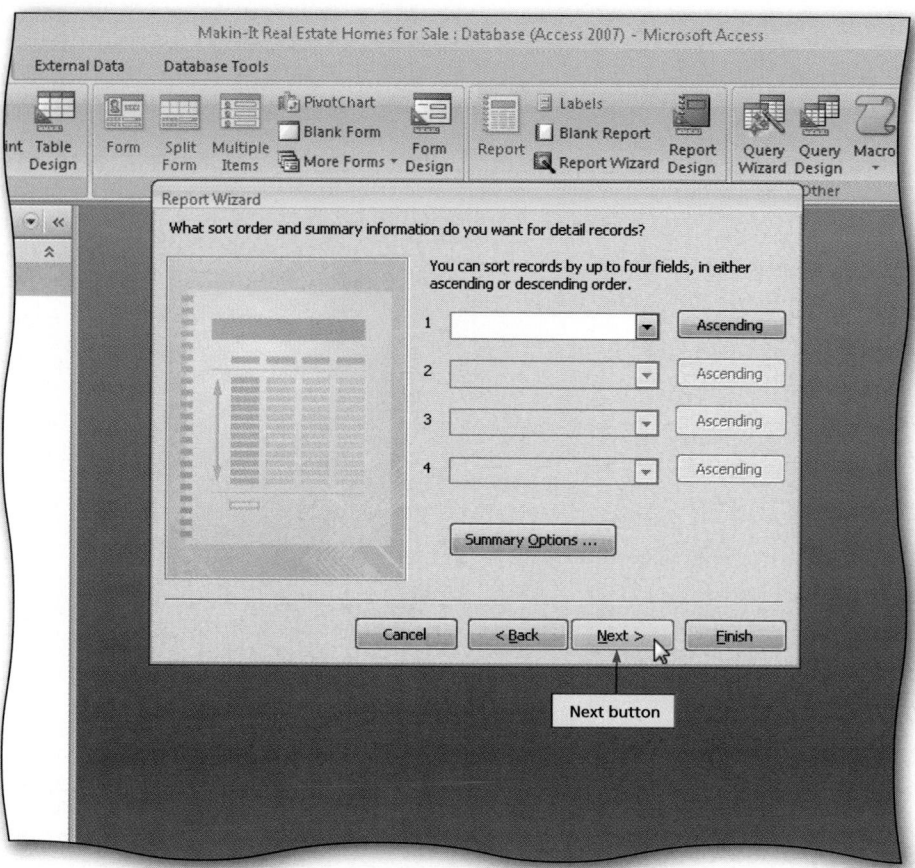

Figure 1–32

- Click the Next button.

- Click the Landscape option button in the Orientation area to select it (Figure 1–33).

Q&A

Why change the orientation to landscape?

When you plan to use a report as a Web page, set the orientation to landscape so that the report takes up as much horizontal space as possible. If portrait is selected, then the Web page visitor might see a large empty margin on the right side of the page.

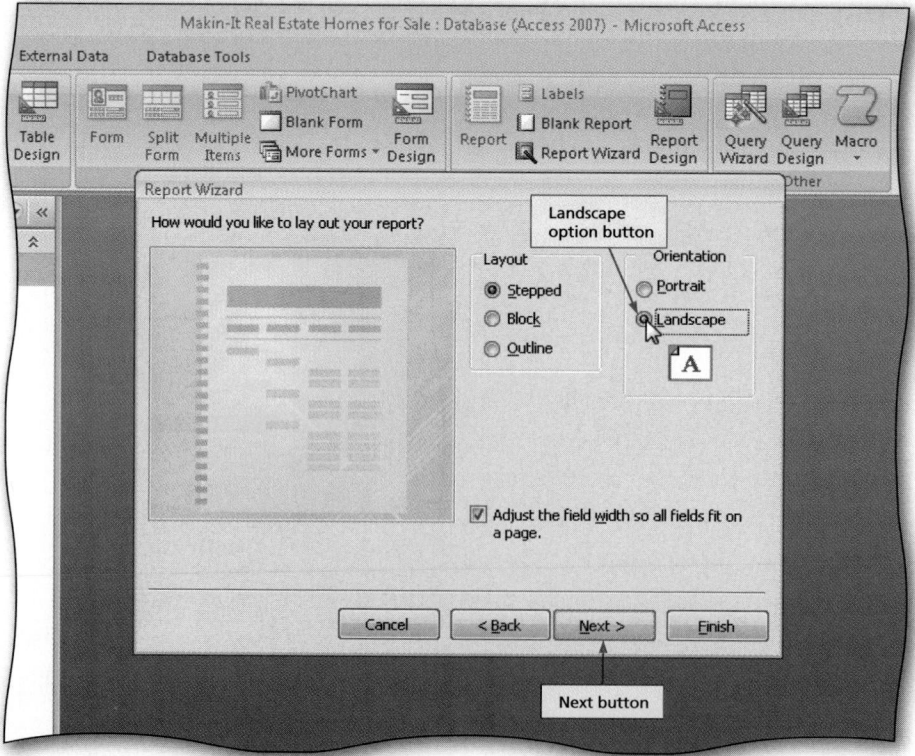

Figure 1–33

- Click the Next button.

- If necessary, click the Access 2007 style in the list on the right (Figure 1–34).

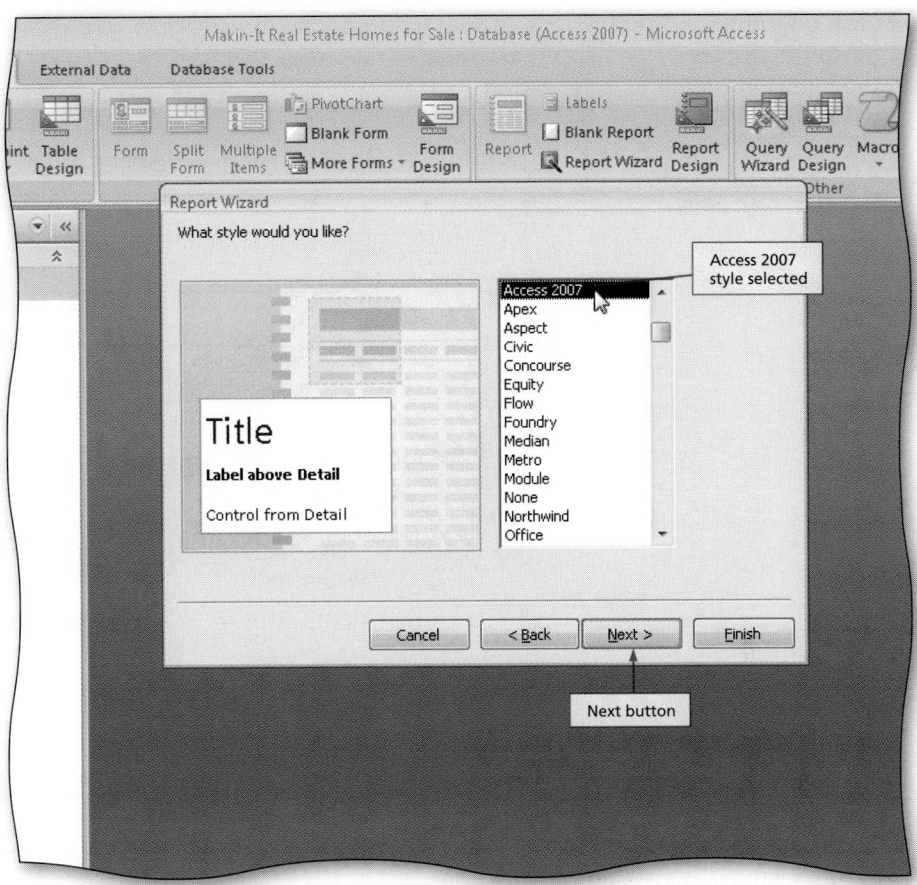

Figure 1–34

- Click the Next button and then type Makin-It Real Estate - Homes For Sale in the 'What title do you want for your report?' text box.

- If necessary, click the 'Modify the report's design' option button to select it (Figure 1–35).

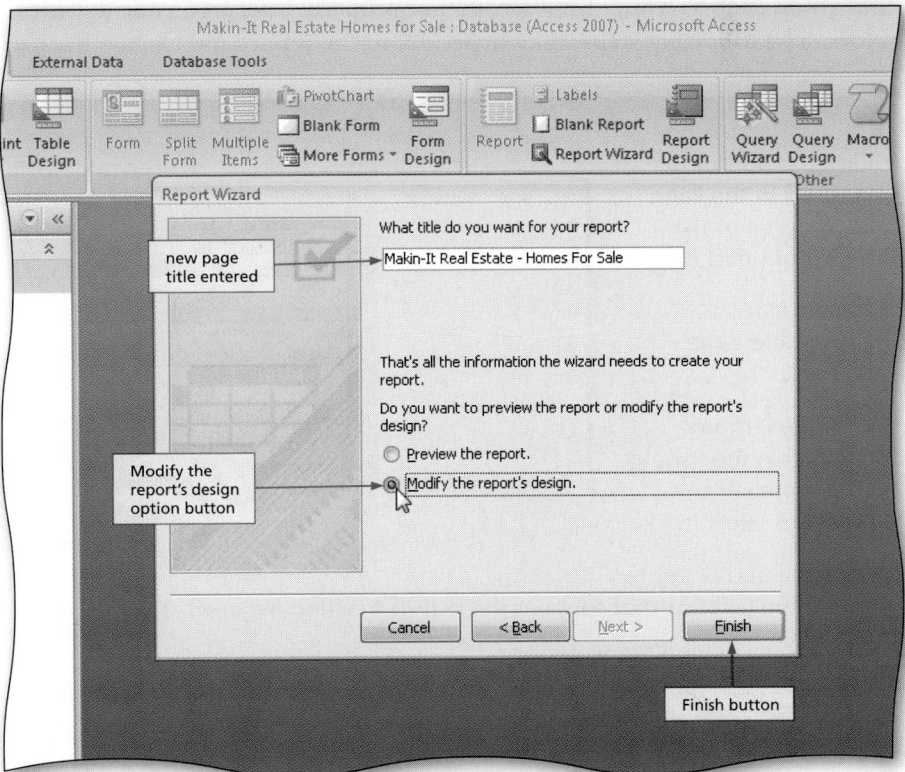

Figure 1–35

- Click the Finish button to display the report in Design view (Figure 1–36).

- If necessary, close the Field List task pane.

Figure 1–36

To Add a Hyperlink to a Report and Change the Text Background Color

Just as you did on the PowerPoint Web page, you should add a hyperlink on the report that links to the home page. This allows the Web page visitor to return to the Makin-It Real Estate home page without having to click the Back button on the browser's toolbar repeatedly. When you plan to save a report as a Web page, the background color of the elements of the Web page – such as the report title, column titles, and rows – should be changed to a light color, such as white. Browsers do not properly interpret some default colors used by Access for the background colors. The following steps add a hyperlink to the report and change the background colors of the elements in the report to white.

- Click the rightmost text box in the Page Footer area of the report to select it.

- Press the DELETE key to delete the text box.

- Click the leftmost text box in the Page Footer area of the report to select it.

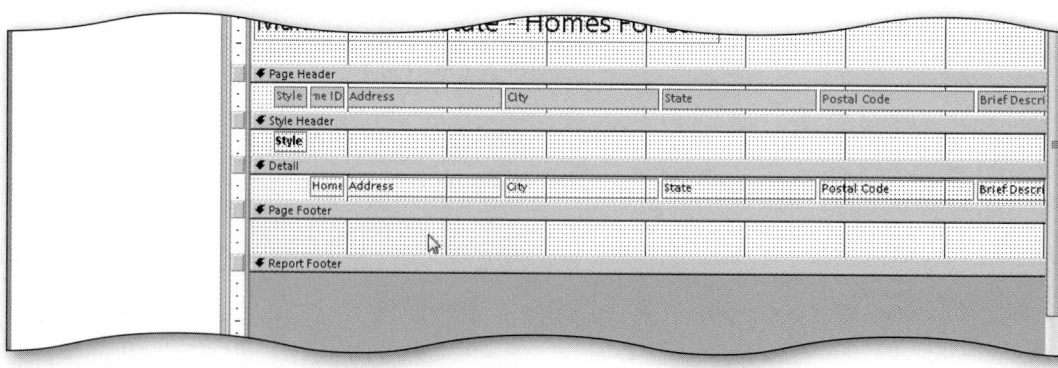

Figure 1–37

- Press the DELETE key to delete the text box that contains the NOW() function (Figure 1–37).

Q&A

Why should I delete these items?

The report will be saved as a Web page. Web pages should not include page footer items such as page numbers because when the report is displayed in a Web browser, it will display as one long continuous page in the browser. There will never be a second page in the Web browser. A report footer, therefore, would be a good design choice, but not a page footer.

• Click the Insert Hyperlink button on the Ribbon to display the Insert Hyperlink dialog box.

• If necessary, click the Existing File or Web Page button in the Link to bar.

• Click the 'Text to display' text box and then type Home as the text to display for the hyperlink.

• Click the Address box and then type e:\Makin-It Real Estate Home Page.htm (Figure 1–38).

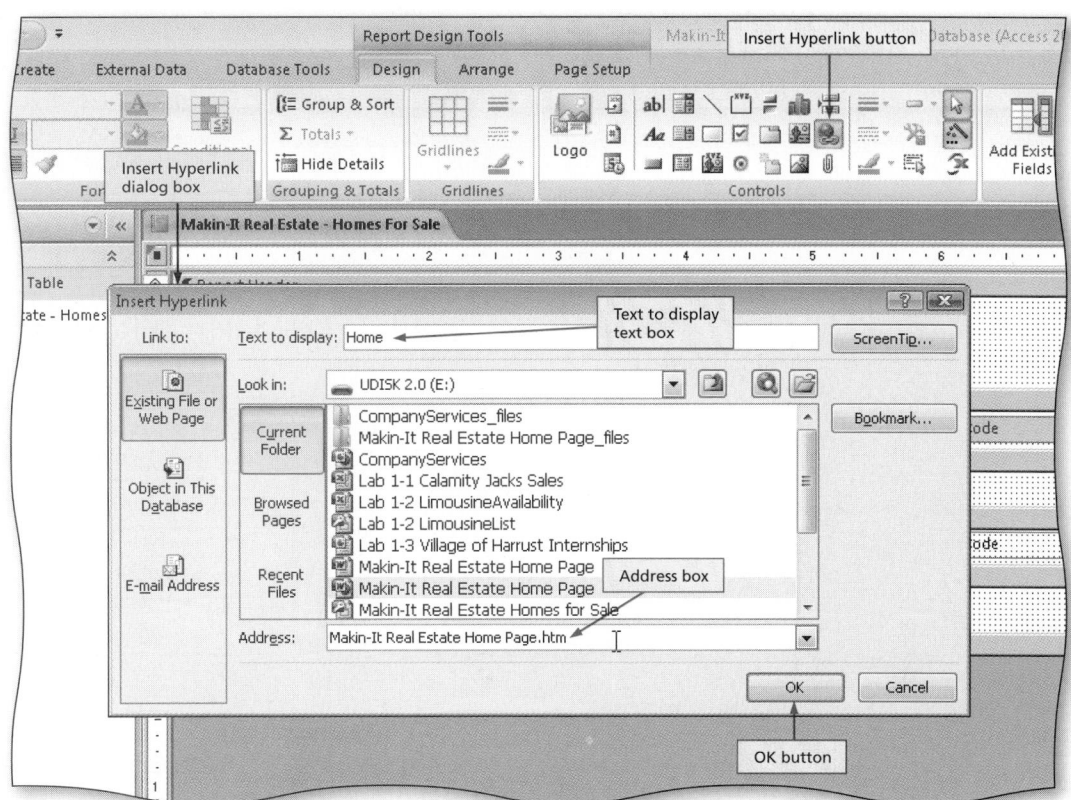

Figure 1–38

• Click the OK button to insert the hyperlink (Figure 1–39).

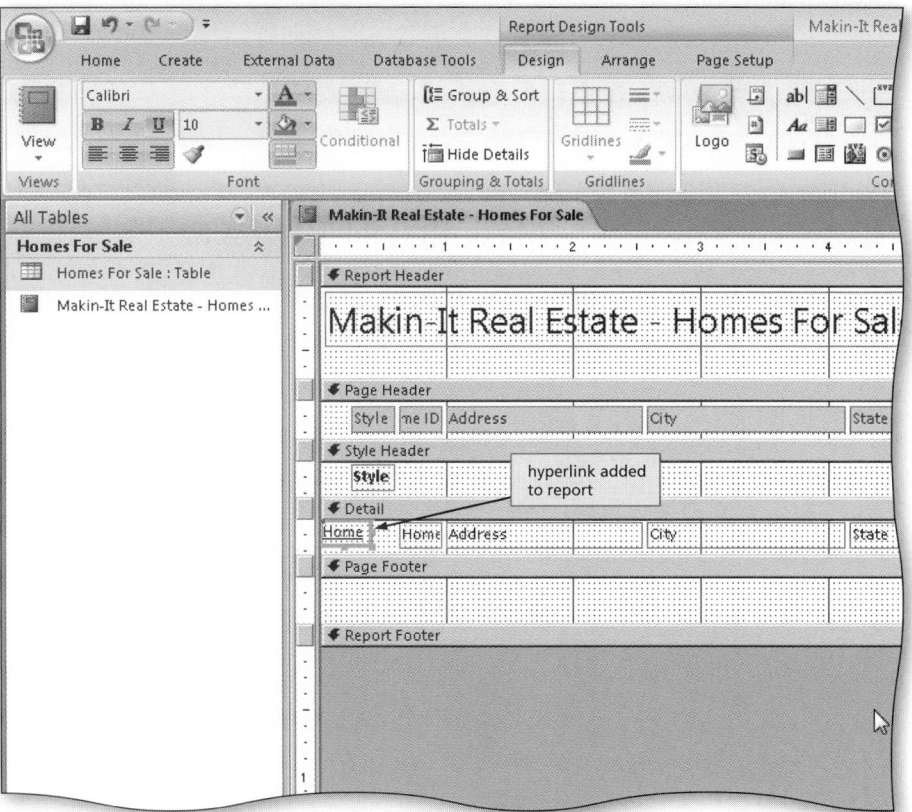

Figure 1–39

- Drag the hyperlink to the lower-left corner of the Page Footer area of the report (Figure 1–40).

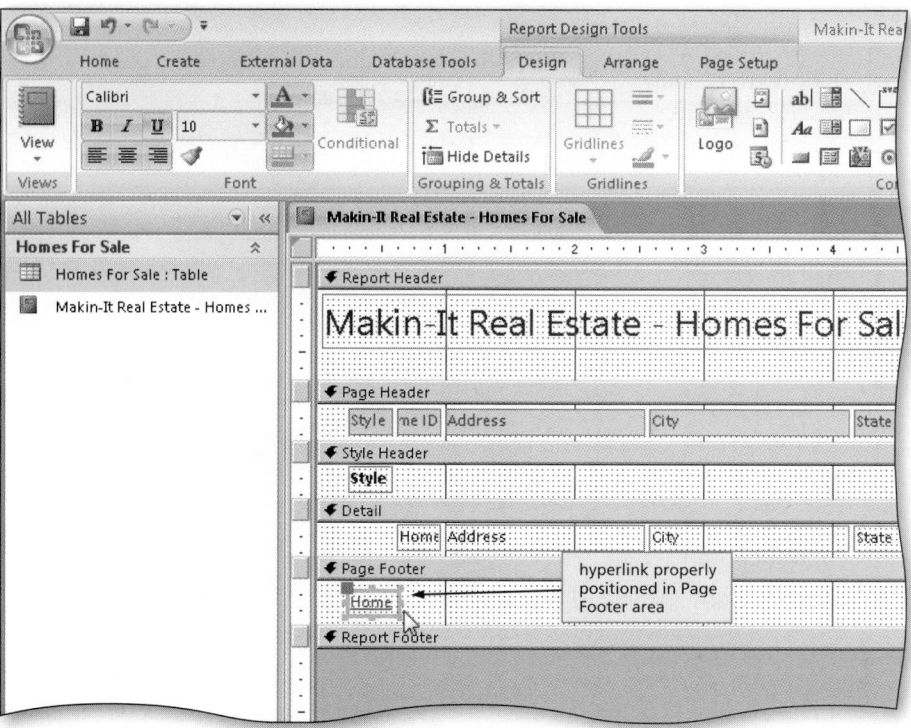

Figure 1–40

- Click anywhere in the Style header in the Page header area to select it.

- Click the Plus icon in the upper-left corner of the Style header to select all items in the body of the report (Figure 1–41).

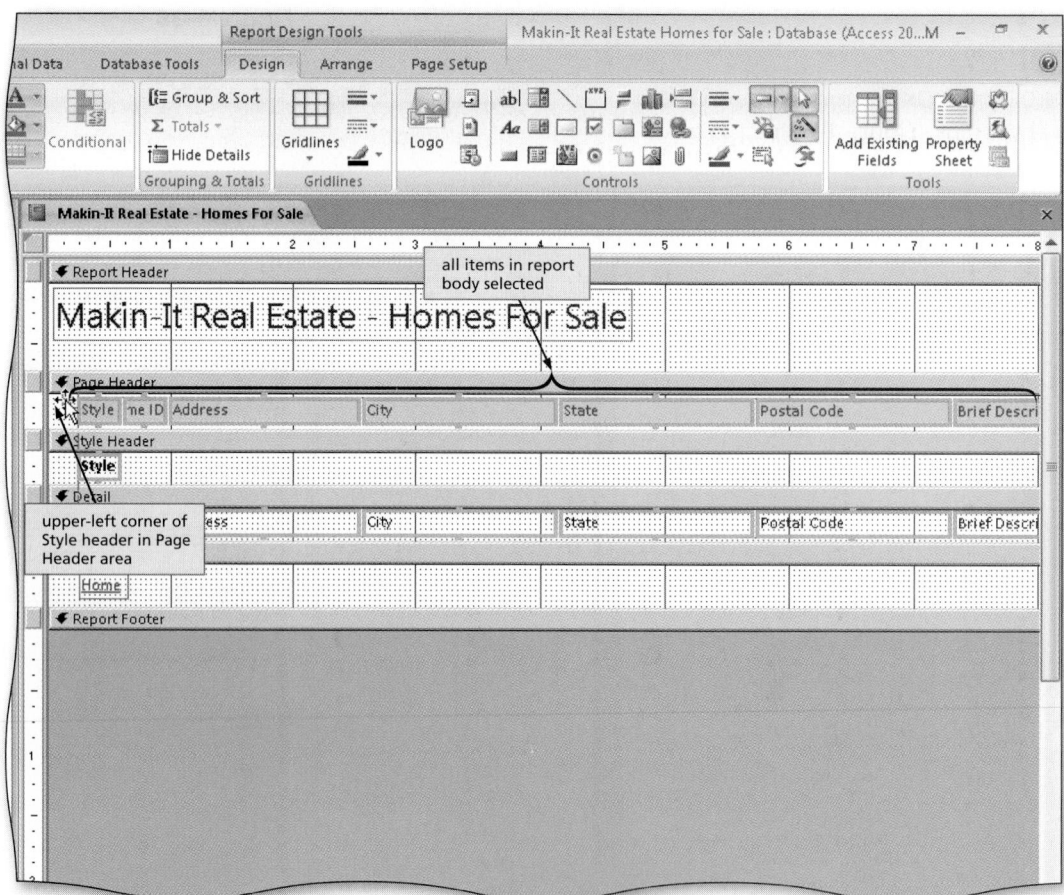

Figure 1–41

6

- Click the Fill/Back Color button arrow on the Ribbon and then click the White color (column 1, row 1) in the Standard Colors area of the Fill/Back Color palette to change the background color of the selected items to white.

- Click the report title in the Report Header area.

- While holding down the SHIFT key, click the Home hyperlink in the Page Footer area to select it.

- Click the Fill/Back Color button on the Ribbon to change the background color of the selected items to white (Figure 1–42).

Q&A

Why should I change the background color of these items?

Some items do not properly display when a Microsoft Access report is saved as a Web page. These items were transparent by default. The Web browser cannot understand transparency. By assigning a background color, you avoid this problem.

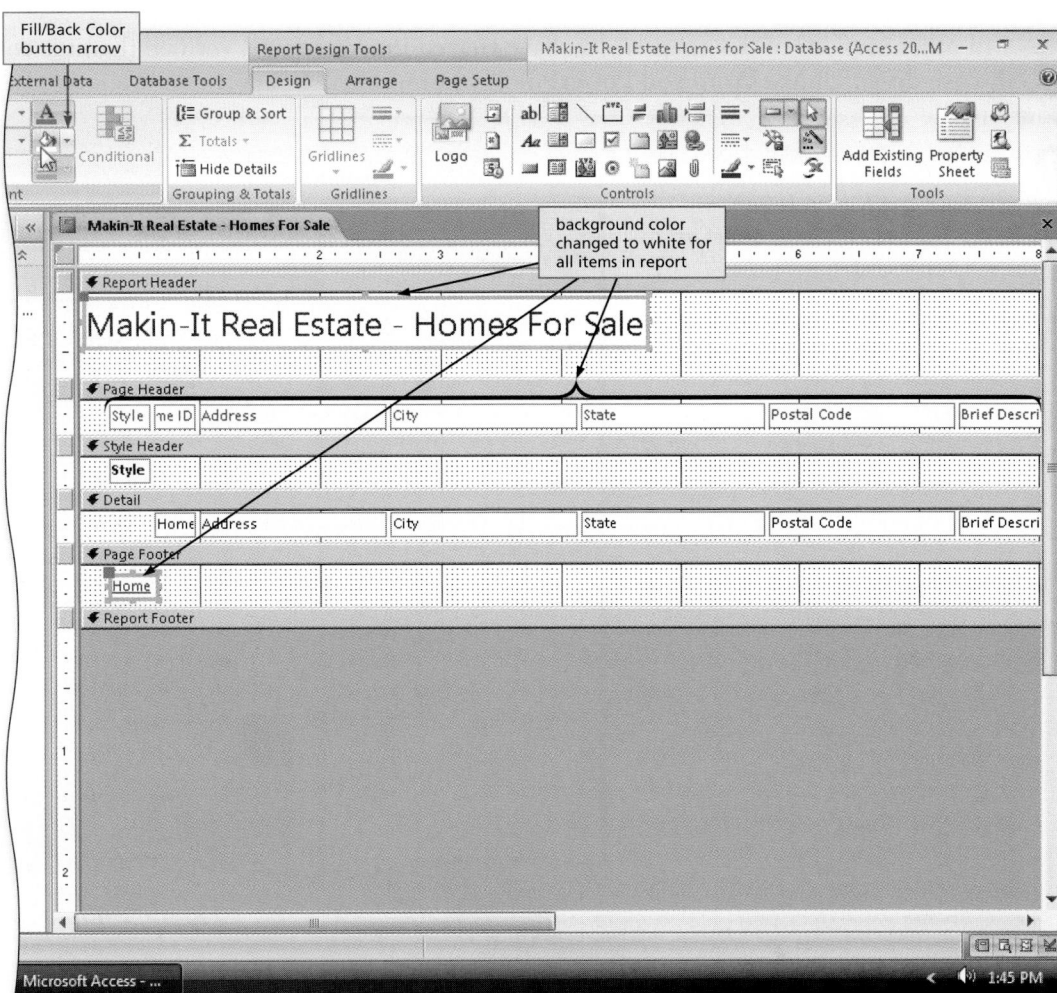

Figure 1–42

To Save the Report and View It in Your Browser

In other sections of this chapter, you have viewed the Web page, verified that it is correct, and then saved it on a USB flash drive. Unlike Word and PowerPoint, you must save a report as a Web page before you can preview it in your browser.

- Right-click the Makin-It Real Estate - Homes For Sale report in the All Tables list.

- Point to the Export command on the shortcut menu (Figure 1–43).

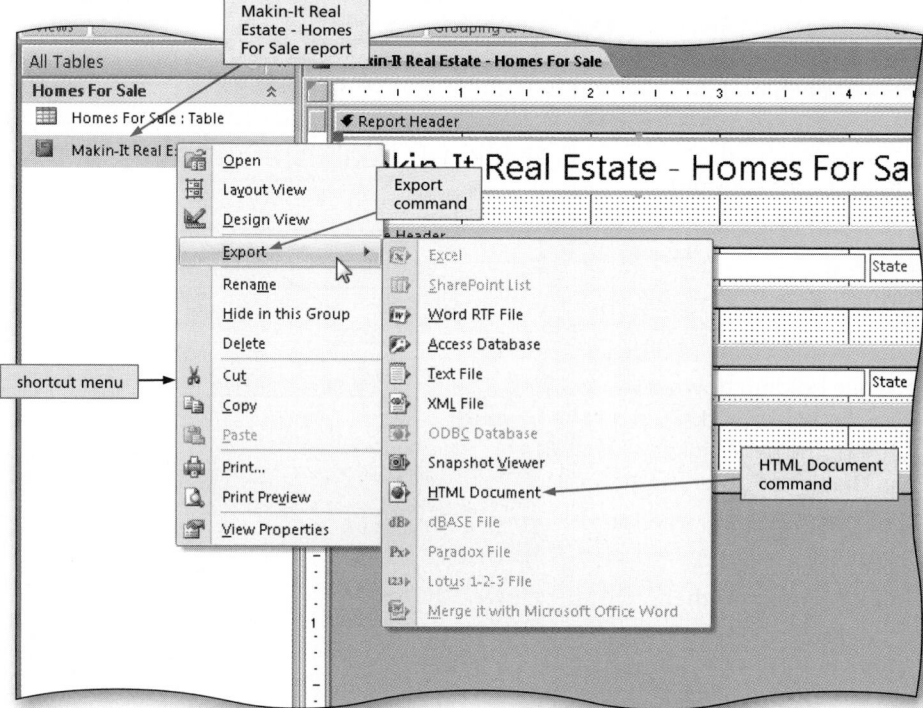

Figure 1–43

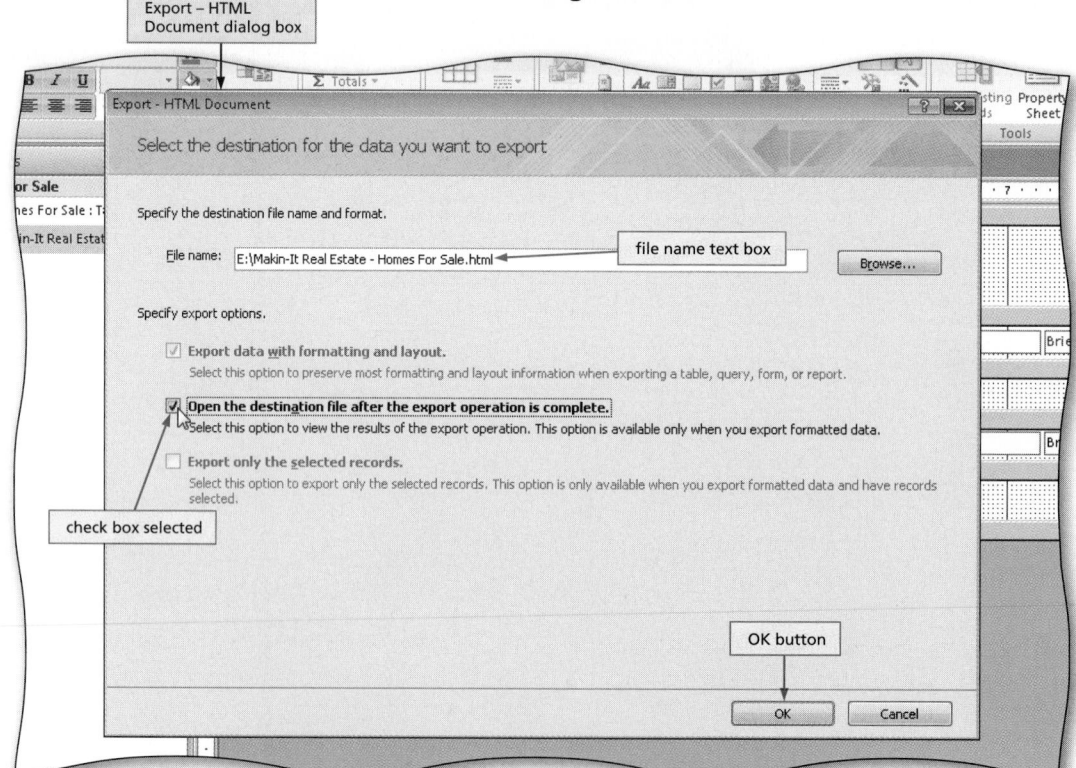

- If necessary, click Export, then click HTML Document.

- When the Export - HTML Document dialog box is displayed, double-click the File name text box and then type `E:\Makin-It Real Estate - Homes For Sale.html` as the file name.

- Click the 'Open the destination file after the export operation is complete' check box to select it (Figure 1–44).

Figure 1–44

③

• Click the OK button.

• When the HTML Output Options dialog box is displayed, click the OK button to open the report in your browser (Figure 1–45). If the security warning appears in the Information bar at the top of the Web page, click its Close button.

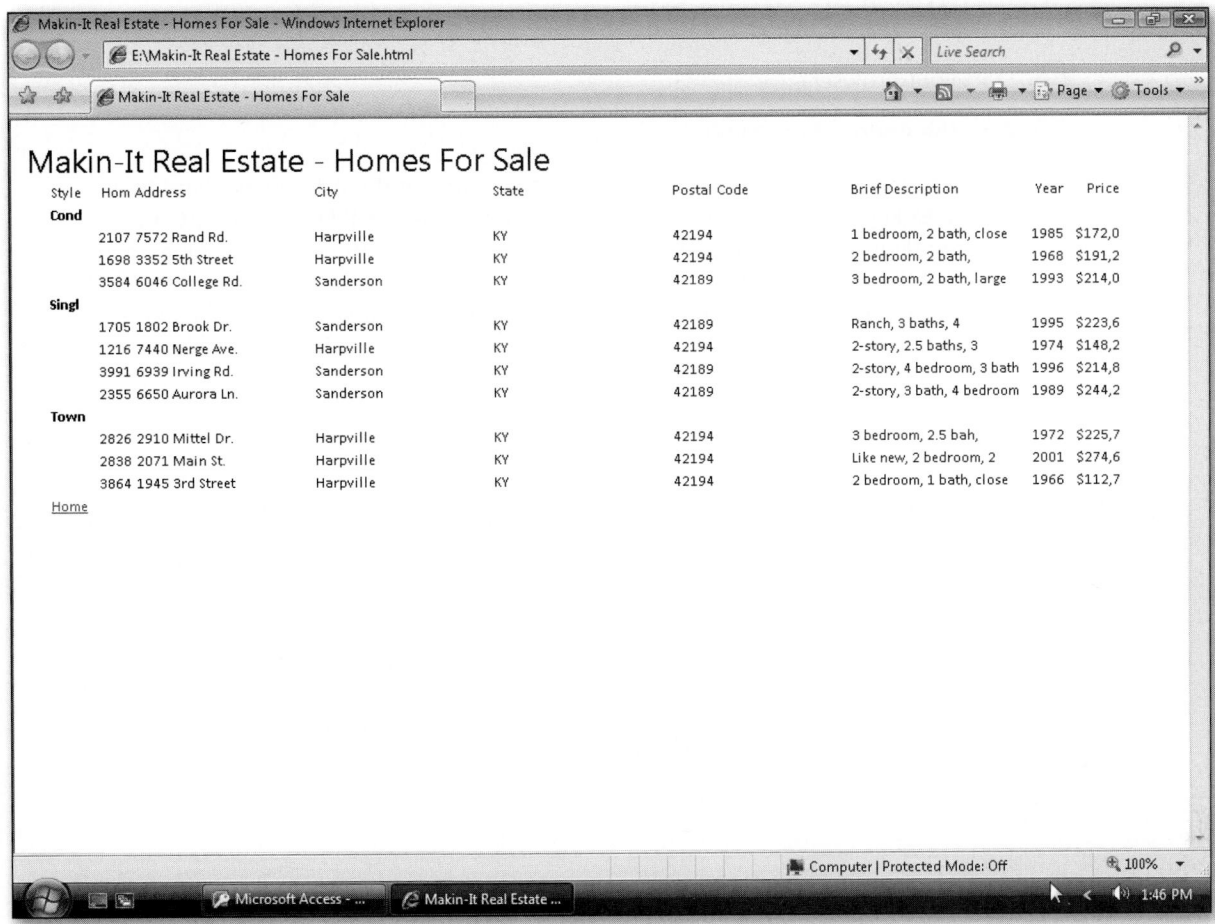

Figure 1–45

To Close Your Browser and Quit Access

After you preview the report in your browser, you can close your browser and quit Access, as shown in the following steps.

1 Click your browser's Close button.

2 If the Export – HTML Document dialog box is displayed, click the Close button.

3 Click the Close button on the Access title bar to quit Access. Save changes to the report if you are prompted to save the changes.

Testing the Web Site

The Makin-It Real Estate Web site is complete. To ensure that all the links in the Web site are viable, the following steps open the home page and then thoroughly test the entire Web site.

To Test the Web Site

① Start your browser.

② Click the Address bar of your browser.

③ Type `e:\Makin-It Real Estate Home Page.htm` in the Address bar, and then press the ENTER key to display the home page of the Makin-It Real Estate Web site in your browser (Figure 1–46). (Your USB flash drive may have a different drive name and letter.) If the Internet Explorer dialog box appears, click the OK button, right-click the first Internet Explorer button on the Windows Vista taskbar, and then click Close on the shortcut menu. If a security warning appears in the Information bar at the top of the Web page, click its Close button.

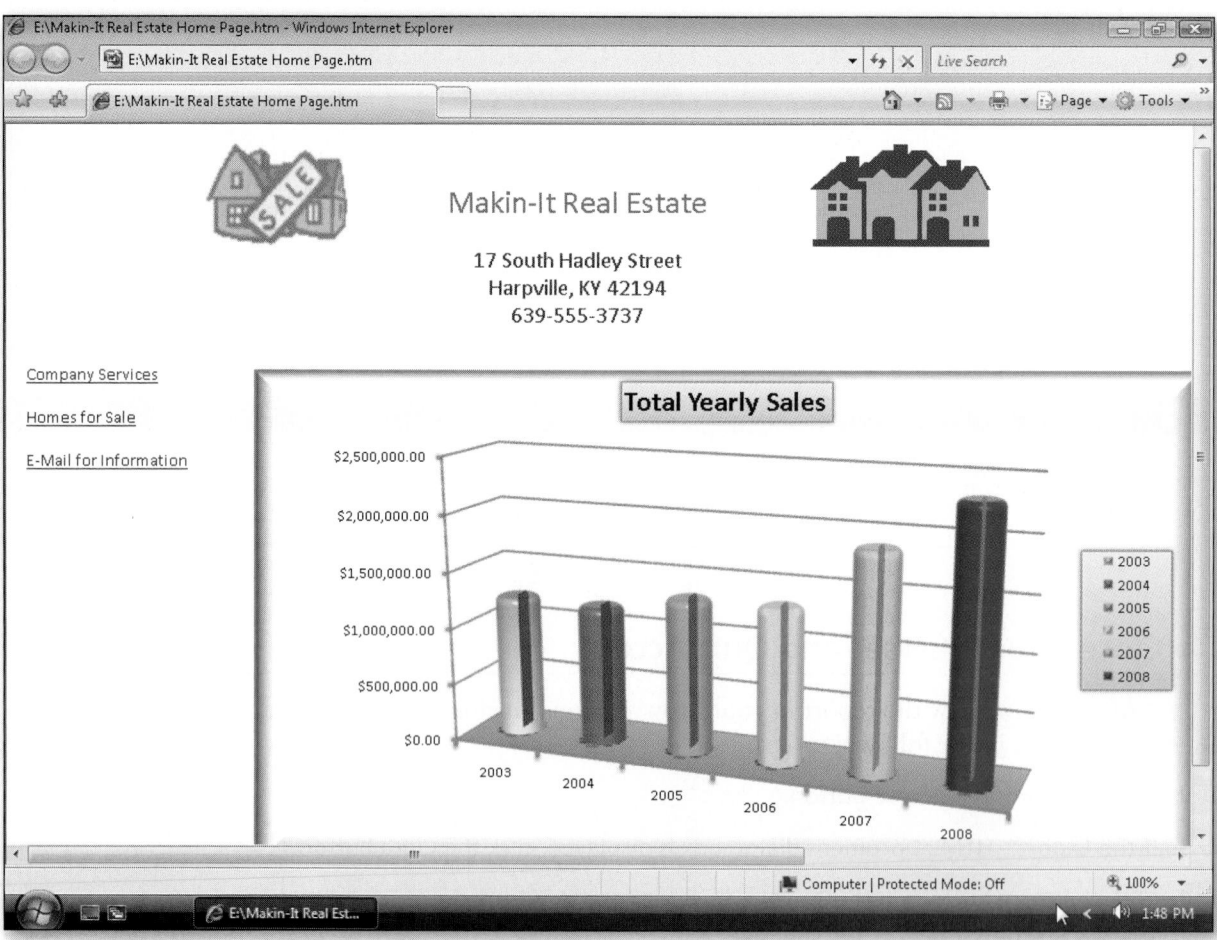

Figure 1–46

To Verify the Hyperlinks

All hyperlinks should be tested by clicking them and verifying that they jump to the correct Web page. Three hyperlinks are on the home page: Company Services, Homes for Sale, and E-Mail for Information. The following steps test the links.

1 Click the Company Services hyperlink.

2 Click the navigation buttons to view all slides on the Web page.

3 On the first slide on the PowerPoint Web page, click the Home hyperlink.

4 Click the Homes for Sale hyperlink.

5 On the Access report page, click the Home hyperlink.

6 Click the E-Mail for Information hyperlink to display a new e-mail message with manager@isp.com in the To text box.

To Quit E-Mail and Close Your Browser

With the hyperlinks verified, the steps on the next page quit the e-mail program and the browser.

1 Click the Close button on your e-mail program's title bar. Click No if asked to save changes.

2 Click the Close button on your browser's title bar.

Chapter Summary

This chapter introduced you to integrating Microsoft Office 2007 applications. You opened an existing Word document and created a two-column, one-row, borderless table. You then inserted three hyperlinks, embedded a Bar chart from an existing Excel worksheet, and saved that document as an HTML file. You then opened an existing PowerPoint presentation, added a hyperlink to the first slide, and saved this presentation as a Web page. Finally, you opened an existing Access database and created a report, which you saved as a Web page. You saved that report and viewed and tested all Web pages and hyperlinks. The items listed below include all the new Office 2007 skills you have learned in this chapter.

1. Insert a Table into a Word Document (INT 8)
2. Remove the Table Border, View Gridlines, and AutoFit the Table Contents (INT 9)
3. Insert Text for Hyperlinks (INT 11)
4. Create a Hyperlink to PowerPoint Web Pages (INT 11)
5. Embed an Excel Chart into a Word Document (INT 14)
6. Change the Size of an Embedded Object (INT 17)
7. Add a Button to the Quick Access Toolbar (INT 19)
8. Preview the Web Page (INT 22)
9. Insert a Hyperlink into a PowerPoint Presentation (INT 25)
10. Create a Report Using the Report Wizard (INT 29)
11. Add a Hyperlink to a Report and Change the Text Background Color (INT 32)
12. Save the Report and View It in Your Browser (INT 36)

Learn It Online

Learn It Online is a series of online student exercises that test your knowledge of chapter content and key terms.

Instructions: To complete the Learn It Online exercises, start your browser, click the Address bar, and then enter the Web address `scsite.com/int2007/learn`. When the Integration 2007 Learn It Online page is displayed, click the link for the exercise you want to complete and then read the instructions.

Chapter Reinforcement TF, MC, and SA
A series of true/false, multiple choice, and short answer questions that test your knowledge of the chapter content.

Flash Cards
An interactive learning environment where you identify chapter key terms associated with displayed definitions.

Practice Test
A series of multiple choice questions that test your knowledge of chapter content and key terms.

Who Wants To Be a Computer Genius?
An interactive game that challenges your knowledge of chapter content in the style of a television quiz show.

Wheel of Terms
An interactive game that challenges your knowledge of chapter key terms in the style of the television show *Wheel of Fortune*.

Crossword Puzzle Challenge
A crossword puzzle that challenges your knowledge of key terms presented in the chapter.

In the Lab

Create a workbook using the guidelines, concepts, and skills presented in this chapter. Labs are listed in order of increasing difficulty.

Lab 1: Creating a Web Page in Word with an Embedded Excel Chart

Problem: As vice president of Calamity Jack's Home Disaster Recovery Service, you have created a worksheet and chart in Excel to analyze the sales for the past year. Create a Web page in Word and embed the chart from the Calamity Jack's Sales workbook on the home page. Add a link to a second Web page and an e-mail link to calamityjacks@isp.com below the chart. Create a second Web page in Word by embedding the Calamity Jack's Sales worksheet.

Instructions: Perform the following tasks.

1. Start Excel by opening the Lab 1-1 Calamity Jack's Sales workbook.

2. Start Word and create a new document in Web Layout view. Add a title and subtitle as shown in the Web page preview of the document in Figure 1–47. Select the chart in Excel from the Yearly Sales Chart worksheet, copy it, and use the Paste Special dialog box in Word to embed the Microsoft Office Excel Chart Object. Resize the chart so that it fits in the Word window without the need to scroll to see the right edge of the chart.

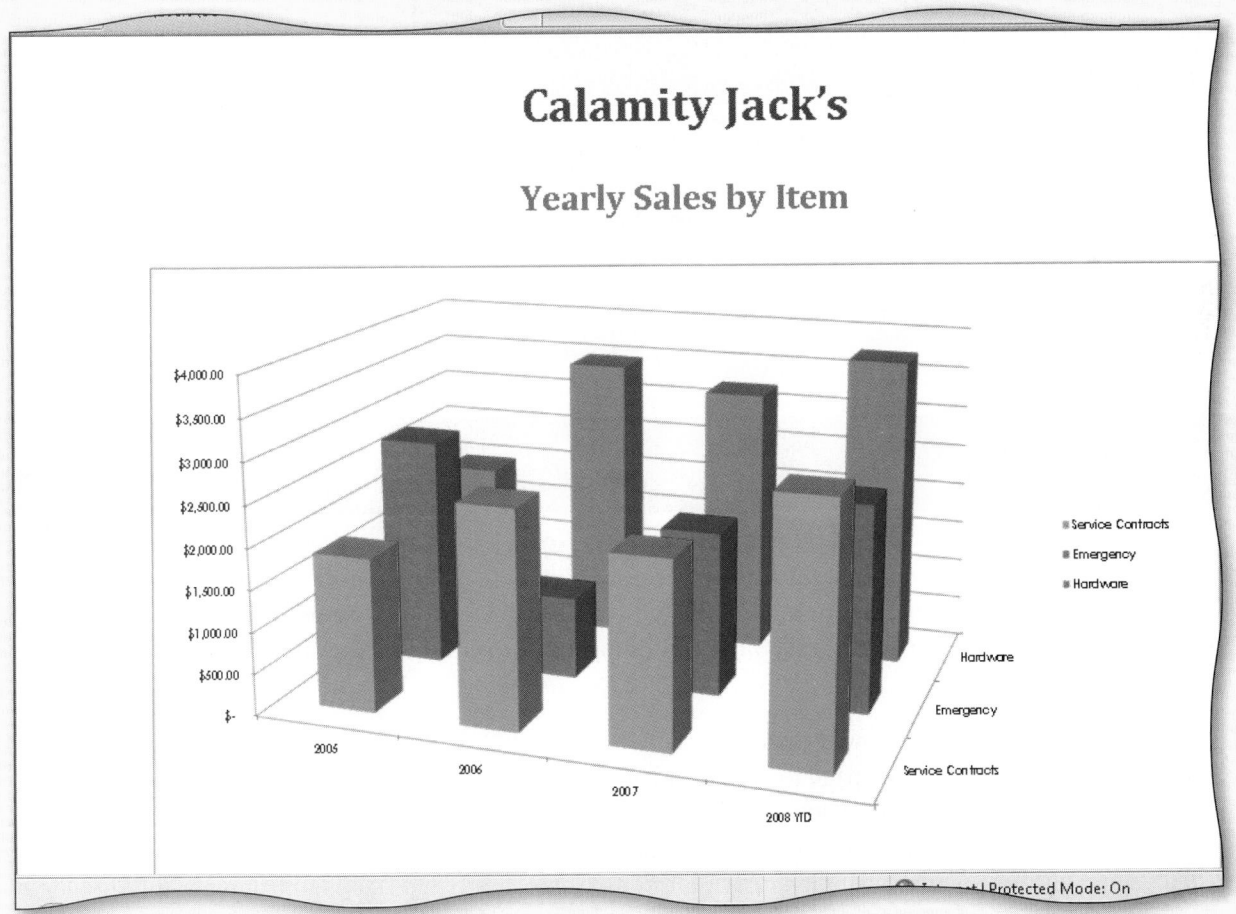

Figure 1–47

Continued >

In the Lab *continued*

3. Add two hyperlinks to the bottom of the page in a centered table as shown in Figure 1–47. The first hyperlink should jump to the Web page Lab_1-1_CalamityJacksSales.htm, which is created next. The second hyperlink creates an e-mail message to calamityjacks@isp.com with the subject About Our Company.

4. Save this file as a Web page named Lab_1-1_CalamityJacks.htm.

5. Create a new document in Word in Web Layout view.

6. Embed the Excel worksheet into the Word page. That is, switch to Excel, select the worksheet named Yearly Sales Analysis, select and copy the worksheet to the Clipboard, switch to Word, and use the Paste Special command in the Paste gallery in Word to embed the Excel Worksheet Object.

7. Save this file as a Web page with the name Lab_1-1_CalamityJacksSales.htm.

8. View the Lab_1-1_CalamityJacks.htm file in your browser (Figure 1–47). Print the Web page. Click the Yearly Sales link to navigate to the Lab_1-1_CalamityJacksSales.htm page (Figure 1–48).

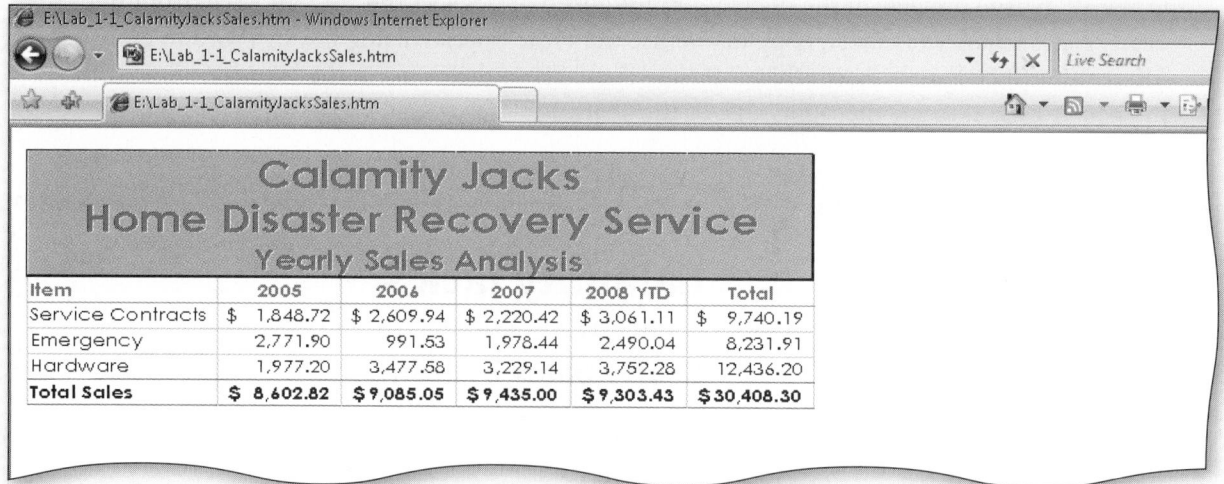

Figure 1–48

In the Lab

Lab 2: Posh Limousine Rental Web Site with an Access Report and an Excel Worksheet

Problem: As the assistant manager of Posh Limousine Services, Matt Ruginis is responsible for keeping track of limousines that are rented on a per-day basis. He would like you to design a site that allows customers to view the availability of limousines for rent. He also wants an e-mail link for customer questions.

Instructions: Perform the following tasks.

1. Start Word. Create a home page for the Post Limousine Availability Web site (Figure 1–49). Add a title and a borderless table below the title. In the left column, insert three hyperlinks. The first hyperlink should go to Lab_1-2_LimousineList.htm (Figure 1–50). The second hyperlink should go to Lab_1-2_LimousineAvailability.htm (Figure 1–51 on page INT 44). The third hyperlink should start an e-mail message to assistantmanager@isp.com. Type the text in the right column. Save the Web page as Lab_1-2_PoshLimousineServices.htm.

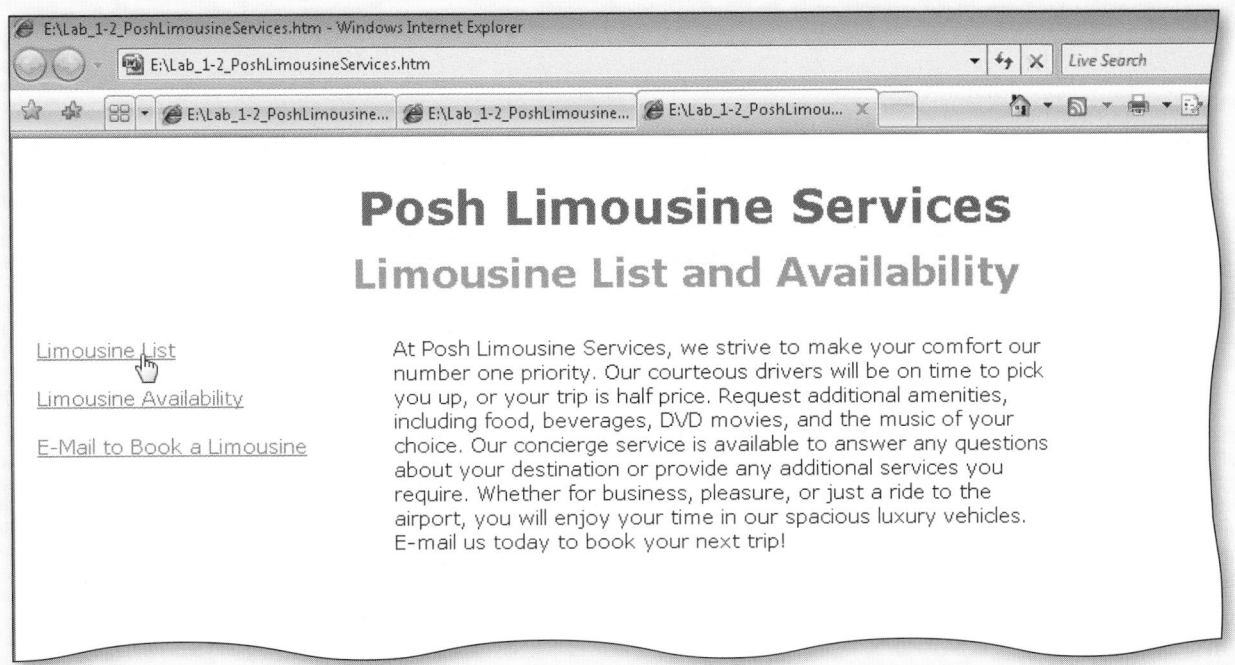

Figure 1–49

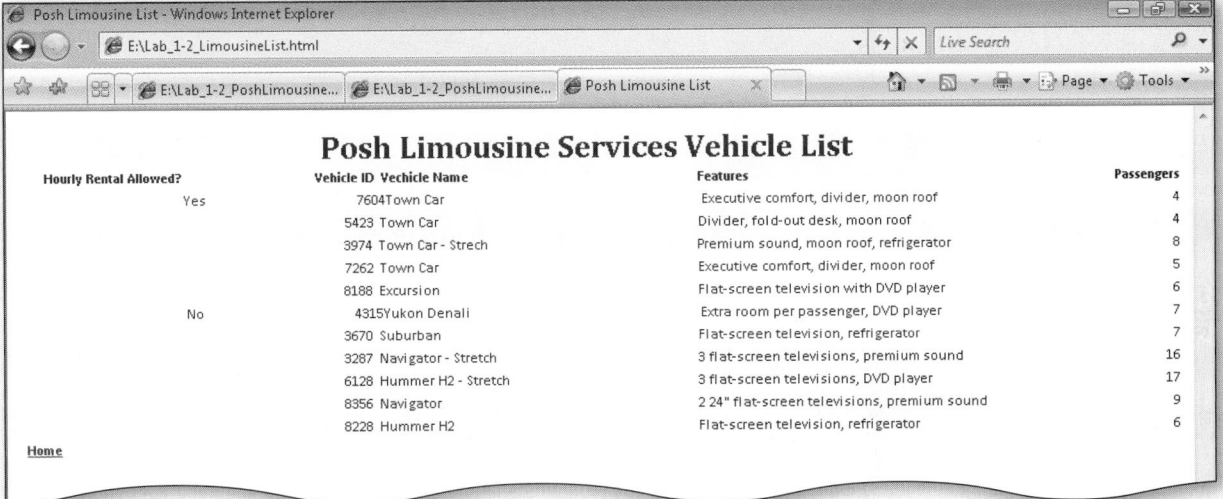

Figure 1–50

2. Start Access by opening the Lab 1-2 LimousineList.mdb database on the Integration Data Disk. Create an Access Report saved as a Web page from the LimousineList table. Create a grouping level using the Hourly Rental Allowed field. Add a title as shown in Figure 1–50. Add a link named Home that links to the Lab_1-2_PoshLimousineServices.htm home page at the bottom of the Access Report Web page. Save the Access Report Web page as Lab_1-2_LimousineList.

3. Start Excel by opening the Lab 1-2 LimousineAvailability workbook on the Integration Data Disk. Create a Web page from the workbook by using the Save As command on the Office Button menu and choosing Web Page as the file type. Use the file name, Lab_1-2_LimousineAvailability.htm.

4. View the Lab_1-2_PoshLimousineServices.htm Web page in your browser. Verify that all links operate properly by clicking each one.

Continued >

In the Lab *continued*

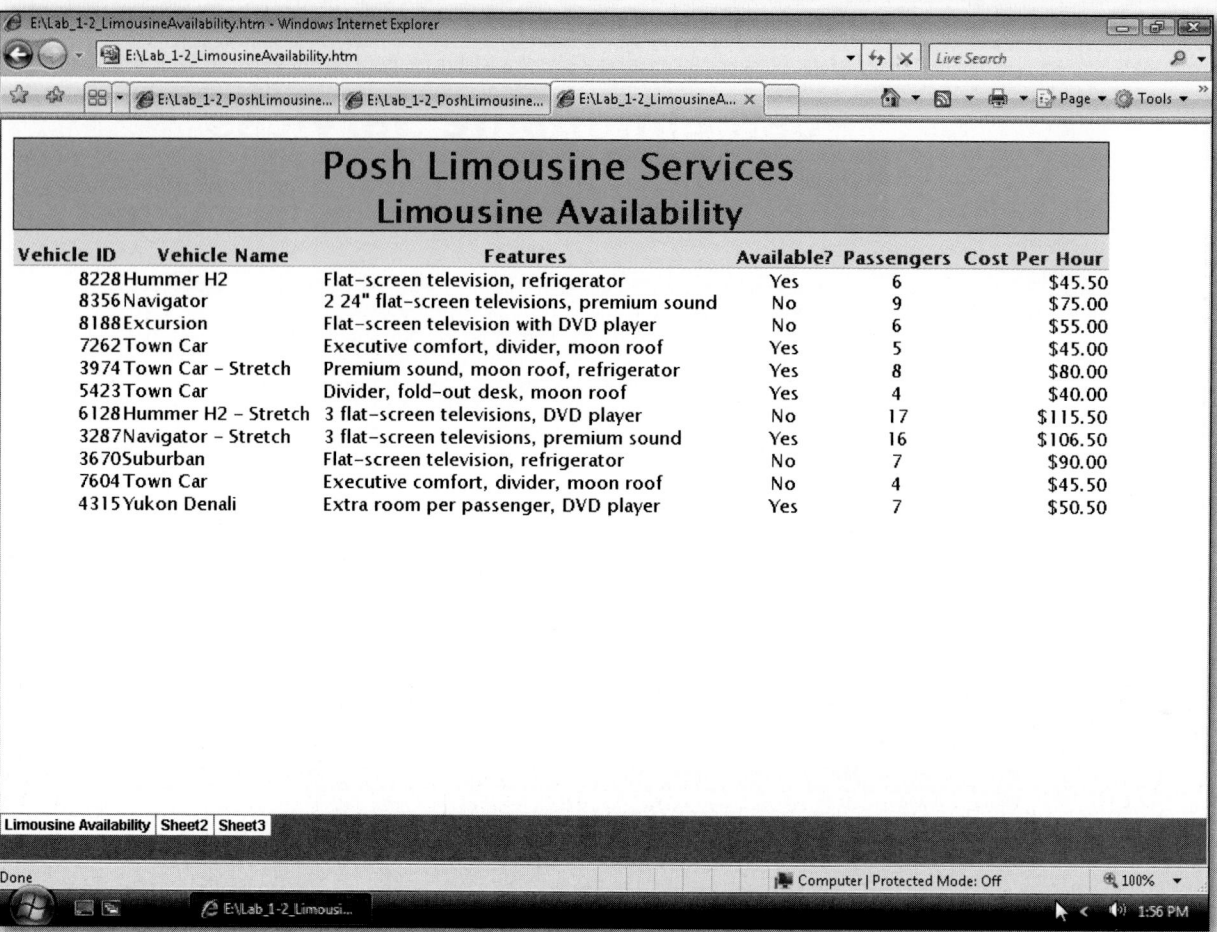

Figure 1–51

In the Lab

Lab 3: Web Site Incorporating PowerPoint Web Pages

Problem: As a part-time employee with the Village of Harrust, you have been asked to create a Web page that publicizes the village's summer intern program (Figures 1–52 and 1–53). The specific information for the internships is located in a PowerPoint presentation, which has four pages.

Instructions: Perform the following tasks.

Start Word. Create the Web page as shown in Figure 1–52. Insert two hyperlinks. The first hyperlink should link to Lab 1-3 Village of Harrust Internships.htm, and the second should link to an e-mail address at manager@vilharrust.gov. Use clip art to insert the picture of a municipal building. Save this Web page as Lab_1-3_VillageofHarrustHomePage.htm.

Figure 1–52

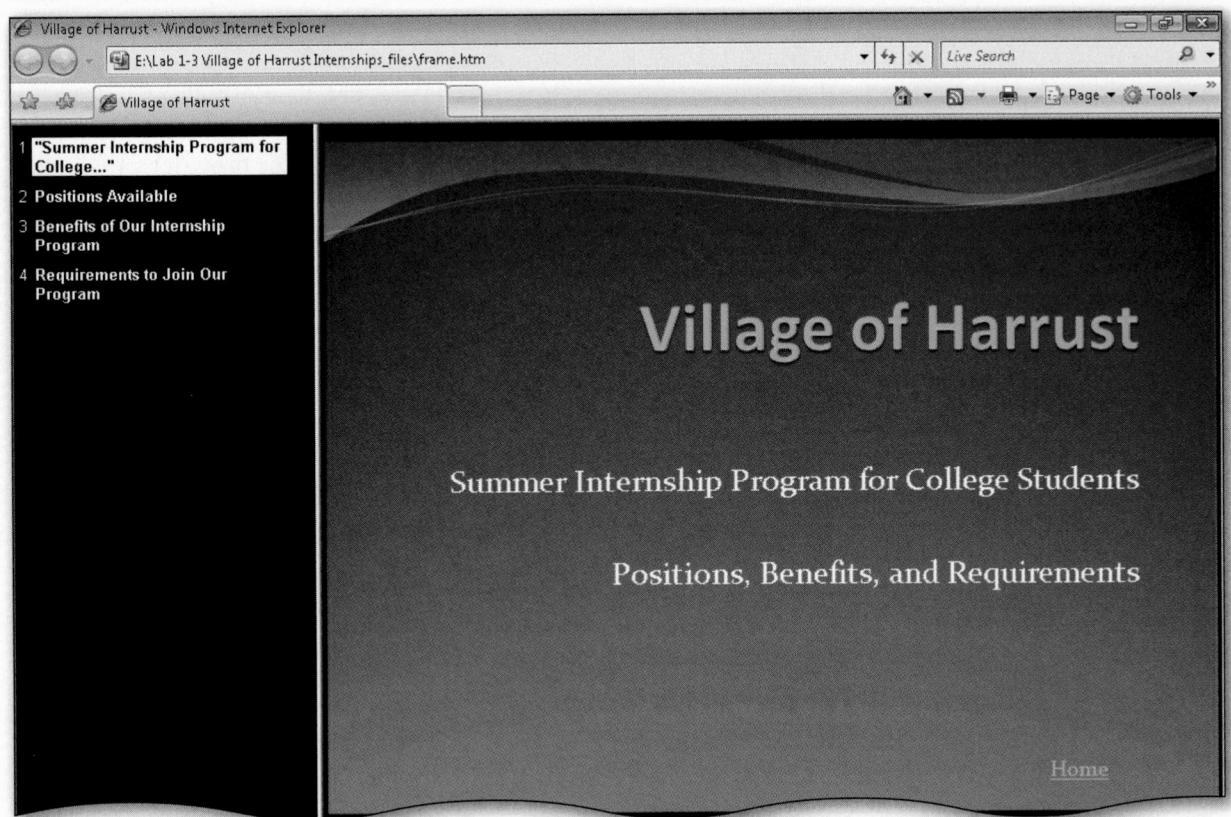

Figure 1–53

Open the Lab 1-3 PowerPoint presentation Lab 1-3 Village of Harrust Internships. Add a link named Home at the bottom of the first page of the presentation that jumps to the Lab_1-3_ VillageofHarrustHomePage.htm Web page. Save the PowerPoint presentation as Web pages on the Integration Data Disk. Name the Web pages Lab 1-3 Village of Harrust Internships.htm. View the Web pages in your browser.

Cases and Places

Apply your creative thinking and problem solving skills to design and implement a solution.

● Easier ●● More Difficult

● 1: Design and Create a Lawn Care Service Web Site

During your summer break, you and your friends decide to get your exercise by providing lawn care services for local residents and businesses. You plan to offer four services, each at a different rate. To mow a small yard with push mowers, you will charge $15 per week for each quarter acre. To mow a large yard with riding mowers, you will charge $22 per week for each quarter acre. To provide weeding and tree pruning, you will charge $20 per week. Additional lawn care service, including dethatching and fertilizing, will cost $50 for the summer per quarter acre. Create a worksheet in Excel that summarizes each of these plans. Create a Web page using Word that embeds the Excel worksheet; the goal of the Web site is to inform new customers of the services provided. Make sure to include an e-mail address on the Web page.

● 2: Analyze the Cost of Internet Access in a Web Page

You have been asked to research the cost of various types of Internet access for local small businesses. Research the different types of Internet access available to small businesses in your area, and determine the following for each: service provider name, service level, speed, contact name, contact telephone number, contract restrictions, and costs. Create an Excel worksheet and charts summarizing your data and graphing the speed and costs for each service provider. Using Word, create a Web page and embed the worksheet on the home page of the Web site. Create another Web page, and embed the chart(s) from Excel. Create a link to the Excel chart(s) Web page and a link to each service provider's Web page.

●● 3: Design and Create a Customer Complaint Web Page

Your housing association has asked you to help to organize and evaluate complaints from residents. Create an Access database and add eight items to it with the following information for each complaint: complaint number, resident ID number, type of complaint, description, date of complaint, resolution date of the complaint, name of staff member who resolved the complaint, and how the complaint was resolved. From this table, create an Access report saved as a Web page using the type of complaint as the grouping level. Include all of the items in the Access database in the Web page. Use a search engine to find relevant links about each type of complaint – such as drainage, landscaping, and noise – that are relevant to housing associations, and create links to one Web page each for each category at the bottom of the Access report Web page.

●● 4: Design and Create a Summer Internship Web Site

Make It Personal

As an intern for your school's placement program, you have been asked to create a Web page on which students can view information about summer internships available in the local area. Using your own field of interest as a guide, create an Access database and add information to the database about prospective summer internships regarding your area of interest. Include the following fields: organization name, preferred major, type of job, job description, number of positions available, and whether the organization has participated in an internship program in the past. From this table, create an Access report and save it as a Web page using the preferred major as the grouping level. Create a Web page using Word that will act as the Web page for the organization list and create a link to the Access report Web page. Be sure to include a link to your e-mail address on the Web page.

•• 5: Design and Create an Informational Web Site about a Foreign Country

Working Together

Gather basic statistical data about a foreign country, including population, important business and industry, and other demographic data. Have one member of your team create an Excel 3-D Pie chart to summarize the demographic information that you find. Have another member create a PowerPoint presentation that contains at least four major points regarding the country that may make the country interesting to potential visitors, including information about business and industry. A third member should create an Access report saved as a Web page that includes information about popular tourist destinations in the country. Embed the Excel chart into one of the PowerPoint slides. Create a link from one of the PowerPoint pages to the Access report Web page. Save the PowerPoint presentation as Web pages. Include relevant links to Web pages regarding the country.

Appendix A
Project Planning Guidelines

Using Project Planning Guidelines

The process of communicating specific information to others is a learned, rational skill. Computers and software, especially Microsoft Office 2007, can help you develop ideas and present detailed information to a particular audience.

Using Microsoft Office 2007, you can create projects such as Word documents, Excel spreadsheets, Access databases, and PowerPoint presentations. Computer hardware and productivity software such as Microsoft Office 2007 minimizes much of the laborious work of drafting and revising projects. Some communicators handwrite ideas in notebooks, others compose directly on the computer, and others have developed unique strategies that work for their own particular thinking and writing styles.

No matter what method you use to plan a project, follow specific guidelines to arrive at a final product that presents information correctly and effectively (Figure A–1). Use some aspects of these guidelines every time you undertake a project, and others as needed in specific instances. For example, in determining content for a project, you may decide that a bar chart communicates trends more effectively than a paragraph of text. If so, you would create this graphical element and insert it in an Excel spreadsheet, a Word document, or a PowerPoint slide.

Determine the Project's Purpose

Begin by clearly defining why you are undertaking this assignment. For example, you may want to track monetary donations collected for your club's fundraising drive. Alternatively, you may be urging students to vote for a particular candidate in the next election. Once you clearly understand the purpose of your task, begin to draft ideas of how best to communicate this information.

Analyze Your Audience

Learn about the people who will read, analyze, or view your work. Where are they employed? What are their educational backgrounds? What are their expectations? What questions do they have?

PROJECT PLANNING GUIDELINES

1. DETERMINE THE PROJECT'S PURPOSE
Why are you undertaking the project?

2. ANALYZE YOUR AUDIENCE
Who are the people who will use your work?

3. GATHER POSSIBLE CONTENT
What information exists, and in what forms?

4. DETERMINE WHAT CONTENT TO PRESENT TO YOUR AUDIENCE
What information will best communicate the project's purpose to your audience?

Figure A–1

Design experts suggest drawing a mental picture of these people or finding photographs of people who fit this profile so that you can develop a project with the audience in mind.

By knowing your audience members, you can tailor a project to meet their interests and needs. You will not present them with information they already possess, and you will not omit the information they need to know.

Example: Your assignment is to raise the profile of your college's nursing program in the community. How much do they know about your college and the nursing curriculum? What are the admission requirements? How many of the applicants admitted complete the program? What percent pass the state Boards?

Gather Possible Content

Rarely are you in a position to develop all the material for a project. Typically, you would begin by gathering existing information that may reside in spreadsheets or databases. Web sites, pamphlets, magazine and newspaper articles, and books could provide insights of how others have approached your topic. Personal interviews often provide perspectives not available by any other means. Consider video and audio clips as potential sources for material that might complement or support the factual data you uncover.

Determine What Content to Present to Your Audience

Experienced designers recommend writing three or four major ideas you want an audience member to remember after reading or viewing your project. It also is helpful to envision your project's endpoint, the key fact you wish to emphasize. All project elements should lead to this ending point.

As you make content decisions, you also need to think about other factors. Presentation of the project content is an important consideration. For example, will your brochure be printed on thick, colored paper or transparencies? Will your PowerPoint presentation be viewed in a classroom with excellent lighting and a bright projector, or will it be viewed on a notebook computer monitor? Determine relevant time factors, such as the length of time to develop the project, how long readers will spend reviewing your project, or the amount of time allocated for your speaking engagement. Your project will need to accommodate all of these constraints.

Decide whether a graph, photograph, or artistic element can express or emphasize a particular concept. The right hemisphere of the brain processes images by attaching an emotion to them, so audience members are more apt to recall these graphics long term rather than just reading text.

As you select content, be mindful of the order in which you plan to present information. Readers and audience members generally remember the first and last pieces of information they see and hear, so you should put the most important information at the top or bottom of the page.

Summary

When creating a project, it is beneficial to follow some basic guidelines from the outset. By taking some time at the beginning of the process to determine the project's purpose, analyze the audience, gather possible content, and determine what content to present to the audience, you can produce a project that is informative, relevant, and effective.

Appendix B
Introduction to Microsoft Office 2007

What Is Microsoft Office 2007?

Microsoft Office 2007 is a collection of the more popular Microsoft application software. It is available in Basic, Home and Student, Standard, Small Business, Professional, Ultimate, Professional Plus, and Enterprise editions. Each edition consists of a group of programs, collectively called a suite. Table B-1 lists the suites and their components.
Microsoft Office Professional Edition 2007 includes these six programs: Microsoft Office Word 2007, Microsoft Office Excel 2007, Microsoft Office Access 2007, Microsoft Office PowerPoint 2007, Microsoft Office Publisher 2007, and Microsoft Office Outlook 2007. The programs in the Office suite allow you to work efficiently, communicate effectively, and improve the appearance of the projects you create.

Table B-1

	Microsoft Office Basic 2007	Microsoft Office Home & Student 2007	Microsoft Office Standard 2007	Microsoft Office Small Business 2007	Microsoft Office Professional 2007	Microsoft Office Ultimate 2007	Microsoft Office Professional Plus 2007	Microsoft Office Enterprise 2007
Microsoft Office Word 2007	✓	✓	✓	✓	✓	✓	✓	✓
Microsoft Office Excel 2007	✓	✓	✓	✓	✓	✓	✓	✓
Microsoft Office Access 2007					✓	✓	✓	✓
Microsoft Office PowerPoint 2007		✓	✓	✓	✓	✓	✓	✓
Microsoft Office Publisher 2007				✓	✓	✓	✓	✓
Microsoft Office Outlook 2007	✓		✓				✓	✓
Microsoft Office OneNote 2007		✓				✓		
Microsoft Office Outlook 2007 with Business Contact Manager				✓	✓	✓		
Microsoft Office InfoPath 2007						✓	✓	✓
Integrated Enterprise Content Management						✓	✓	✓
Electronic Forms						✓	✓	✓
Advanced Information Rights Management and Policy Capabilities						✓	✓	✓
Microsoft Office Communicator 2007							✓	✓
Microsoft Office Groove 2007						✓		✓

Microsoft has bundled additional programs in some versions of Office 2007, in addition to the main group of Office programs. Table B–1 on the previous page lists the components of the various Office suites.

In addition to the Office 2007 programs noted previously, Office 2007 suites can contain other programs. Microsoft Office OneNote 2007 is a digital notebook program that allows you to gather and share various types of media, such as text, graphics, video, audio, and digital handwriting. Microsoft Office InfoPath 2007 is a program that allows you to create and use electronic forms to gather information. Microsoft Office Groove 2007 provides collaborative workspaces in real time. Additional services that are oriented toward the enterprise solution also are available.

Office 2007 and the Internet, World Wide Web, and Intranets

Office 2007 allows you to take advantage of the Internet, the World Wide Web, and intranets. The Microsoft Windows operating system includes a **browser**, which is a program that allows you to locate and view a Web page. The Windows browser is called Internet Explorer.

One method of viewing a Web page is to use the browser to enter the Web address for the Web page. Another method of viewing a Web page is clicking a hyperlink. A **hyperlink** is colored or underlined text or a graphic that, when clicked, connects to another Web page. Hyperlinks placed in Office 2007 documents allow for direct access to a Web site of interest.

An **intranet** is a private network, such as a network used within a company or organization for internal communication. Like the Internet, hyperlinks are used within an intranet to access documents, pages, and other destinations on the intranet. Unlike the Internet, the materials on the network are available only for those who are part of the private network.

Online Collaboration Using Office

Organizations that, in the past, were able to make important information available only to a select few, now can make their information accessible to a wider range of individuals who use programs such as Office 2007 and Internet Explorer. Office 2007 allows colleagues to use the Internet or an intranet as a central location to view documents, manage files, and work together.

Each of the Office 2007 programs makes publishing documents on a Web server as simple as saving a file on a hard disk. Once placed on the Web server, users can view and edit the documents and conduct Web discussions and live online meetings.

Using Microsoft Office 2007

The various Microsoft Office 2007 programs each specialize in a particular task. This section describes the general functions of the more widely used Office 2007 programs, along with how they are used to access the Internet or an intranet.

Microsoft Office Word 2007

Microsoft Office Word 2007 is a full-featured word processing program that allows you to create many types of personal and business documents, including flyers, letters, resumes, business documents, and academic reports.

Word's AutoCorrect, spelling, and grammar features help you proofread documents for errors in spelling and grammar by identifying the errors and offering suggestions for corrections as you type. The live word count feature provides you with a constantly updating word count as you enter and edit text. To assist with creating specific documents, such as a business letter or resume, Word provides templates, which provide a formatted document before you type the text of the document. Quick Styles provide a live preview of styles from the Style gallery, allowing you to preview styles in the document before actually applying them.

Word automates many often-used tasks and provides you with powerful desktop publishing tools to use as you create professional looking brochures, advertisements, and newsletters. SmartArt allows you to insert interpretive graphics based on document content.

Word makes it easier for you to share documents for collaboration. The Send feature opens an e-mail window with the active document attached. The Compare Documents feature allows you easily to identify changes when comparing different document versions.

Word 2007 and the Internet   Word makes it possible to design and publish Web pages on the Internet or an intranet, insert a hyperlink to a Web page in a word processing document, as well as access and search the content of other Web pages.

Microsoft Office Excel 2007

Microsoft Office Excel 2007 is a spreadsheet program that allows you to organize data, complete calculations, graph data, develop professional looking reports, publish organized data to the Web, and access real-time data from Web sites.

In addition to its mathematical functionality, Excel 2007 provides tools for visually comparing data. For instance, when comparing a group of values in cells, you can set cell backgrounds with bars proportional to the value of the data in the cell. You can also set cell backgrounds with full-color backgrounds, or use a color scale to facilitate interpretation of data values.

Excel 2007 provides strong formatting support for tables with the new Style Preview gallery.

Excel 2007 and the Internet   Using Excel 2007, you can create hyperlinks within a worksheet to access other Office documents on the network or on the Internet. Worksheets saved as static, or unchanging Web pages can be viewed using a browser. The person viewing static Web pages cannot change them.

In addition, you can create and run queries that retrieve information from a Web page and insert the information directly into a worksheet.

Microsoft Office Access 2007

Microsoft Office Access 2007 is a comprehensive database management system (DBMS). A **database** is a collection of data organized in a manner that allows access, retrieval, and use of that data. Access 2007 allows you to create a database; add, change, and delete data in the database; sort data in the database; retrieve data from the database; and create forms and reports using the data in the database.

Access 2007 and the Internet   Access 2007 lets you generate reports, which are summaries that show only certain data from the database, based on user requirements.

Microsoft Office PowerPoint 2007

Microsoft Office PowerPoint 2007 is a complete presentation graphics program that allows you to produce professional looking presentations. With PowerPoint 2007, you can create informal presentations using overhead transparencies, electronic presentations using a projection device attached to a personal computer, formal presentations using 35mm slides or a CD, or you can run virtual presentations on the Internet.

PowerPoint 2007 and the Internet   PowerPoint 2007 allows you to publish presentations on the Internet or other networks.

Microsoft Office Publisher 2007

Microsoft Office Publisher 2007 is a desktop publishing program (DTP) that allows you to design and produce professional quality documents (newsletters, flyers, brochures, business cards, Web sites, and so on) that combine text, graphics, and photographs. Desktop publishing software provides a variety of tools, including design templates, graphic manipulation tools, color schemes or libraries, and various page wizards and templates. For large jobs, businesses use desktop publishing software to design publications that are **camera ready**, which means the files are suitable for production by outside commercial printers. Publisher 2007 also allows you to locate commercial printers, service bureaus, and copy shops willing to accept customer files created in Publisher.

Publisher 2007 allows you to design a unique image, or logo, using one of more than 45 master design sets. This, in turn, permits you to use the same design for all your printed documents (letters, business cards, brochures, and advertisements) and Web pages. Publisher includes 70 coordinated color schemes; 30 font schemes; more than 10,000 high-quality clip art images; 1,500 photographs; 1,000 Web-art graphics; 340 animated graphics; and hundreds of unique Design Gallery elements (quotations, sidebars, and so on). If you wish, you also can download additional images from the Microsoft Office Online Web page on the Microsoft Web site.

Publisher 2007 and the Internet   Publisher 2007 allows you easily to create a multipage Web site with custom color schemes, photographic images, animated images, and sounds.

Microsoft Office Outlook 2007

Microsoft Office Outlook 2007 is a powerful communications and scheduling program that helps you communicate with others, keep track of your contacts, and organize your schedule. Outlook 2007 allows you to view a To-Do bar containing tasks and appointments from your Outlook calendar. Outlook 2007 allows you to send and receive electronic mail (e-mail) and permits you to engage in real-time communication with family, friends, or coworkers using instant messaging. Outlook 2007 also provides you with the means to organize your contacts, and you can track e-mail messages, meetings, and notes with a particular contact. Outlook's Calendar, Contacts, Tasks, and Notes components aid in this organization. Contact information is available from the Outlook Calendar, Mail, Contacts, and Task components by accessing the Find a Contact feature. **Personal information management (PIM)** programs such as Outlook provide a way for individuals and workgroups to organize, find, view, and share information easily.

Microsoft Office 2007 Help

At any time while you are using one of the Office programs, you can interact with **Microsoft Office 2007 Help** for that program and display information about any topic associated with the program. Several categories of help are available. In all programs, you can access Help by pressing the F1 key on the keyboard. In Publisher 2007 and Outlook 2007, the Help window can be opened by clicking the Help menu and then selecting Microsoft Office Publisher or Outlook Help command, or by entering search text in the 'Type a question for help' text box in the upper-right corner of the program window. In the other Office programs, clicking the Microsoft Office Help button near the upper-right corner of the program window opens the program Help window.

The Help window in all programs provides several methods for accessing help about a particular topic, and has tools for navigating around Help. Appendix C contains detailed instructions for using Help.

Collaboration and SharePoint

While not part of the Microsoft Office 2007 suites, SharePoint is a Microsoft tool that allows Office 2007 users to share data using collaborative tools that are integrated into the main Office programs. SharePoint consists of Windows SharePoint Services, Office SharePoint Server 2007, and, optionally, Office SharePoint Designer 2007.

Windows SharePoint Services provides the platform for collaboration programs and services. Office SharePoint Server 2007 is built on top of Windows SharePoint Services. The result of these two products is the ability to create SharePoint sites. A SharePoint site is a Web site that provides users with a virtual place for collaborating and communicating with their colleagues while working together on projects, documents, ideas, and information. Each member of a group with access to the SharePoint site has the ability to contribute to the material stored there. The basic building blocks of SharePoint sites are lists and libraries. Lists contain collections of information, such as calendar items, discussion points, contacts, and links. Lists can be edited to add or delete information. Libraries are similar to lists, but include both files and information about files. Types of libraries include document, picture, and forms libraries.

The most basic type of SharePoint site is called a Workspace, which is used primarily for collaboration. Different types of Workspaces can be created using SharePoint to suit different needs. SharePoint provides templates, or outlines of these Workspaces, that can be filled in to create the Workspace. Each of the different types of Workspace templates contain a different collection of lists and libraries, reflecting the purpose of the Workspace. You can create a Document Workspace to facilitate collaboration on documents. A Document Workspace contains a document library for documents and supporting files, a Links list that allows you to maintain relevant resource links for the document, a Tasks list for listing and assigning To-Do items to team members, and other links as needed. Meeting Workspaces allow users to plan and organize a meeting, with components such as Attendees, Agenda, and a Document Library. Social Meeting Workspaces provide a place to plan social events, with lists and libraries such as Attendees, Directions, Image/Logo, Things To Bring, Discussions, and Picture Library. A Decision Meeting Workspace is a Meeting Workspace with a focus on review and decision-making, with lists and libraries such as Objectives, Attendees, Agenda, Document Library, Tasks, and Decisions.

Users also can create a SharePoint site called a WebParts page, which is built from modules called WebParts. WebParts are modular units of information that contain a title bar and content that reflects the type of WebPart. For instance, an image WebPart would contain a title bar and an image. WebParts allow you quickly to create and modify a SharePoint site, and allow for the creation of a unique site that can allow users to access and make changes to information stored on the site.

Large SharePoint sites that include multiple pages can be created using templates as well. Groups needing more refined and targeted sharing options than those available with SharePoint Server 2007 and Windows SharePoint Services can add SharePoint Designer 2007 to create a site that meets their specific needs.

Depending on which components have been selected for inclusion on the site, users can view a team calendar, view links, read announcements, and view and edit group documents and projects. SharePoint sites can be set up so that documents are checked in and out, much like a library, to prevent multiple users from making changes simultaneously. Once a SharePoint site is set up, Office programs are used to perform maintenance of the site. For example, changes in the team calendar are updated using Outlook 2007, and changes that users make in Outlook 2007 are reflected on the SharePoint site. Office 2007 programs include a Publish feature that allows users easily to save file updates to a SharePoint site. Team members can be notified about changes made to material on the site either by e-mail or by a news feed, meaning that users do not have to go to the site to check to see if anything has been updated since they last viewed or worked on it. The search feature in SharePoint allows users quickly to find information on a large site.

Appendix C
Microsoft
Office 2007 Help

Using Microsoft Office Help

This appendix shows how to use Microsoft Office Help. At any time while you are using one of the Microsoft Office 2007 programs, you can use Office Help to display information about all topics associated with the program. To illustrate the use of Office Help, this appendix uses Microsoft Office Word 2007. Help in other Office 2007 programs responds in a similar fashion.

In Office 2007, Help is presented in a window that has Web browser-style navigation buttons. Each Office 2007 program has its own Help home page, which is the starting Help page that is displayed in the Help window. If your computer is connected to the Internet, the contents of the Help page reflect both the local help files installed on the computer and material from Microsoft's Web site. As shown in Figure C–1, two methods for accessing Word's Help are available:

1. Microsoft Office Word Help button near the upper-right corner of the Word window

2. Function key F1 on the keyboard

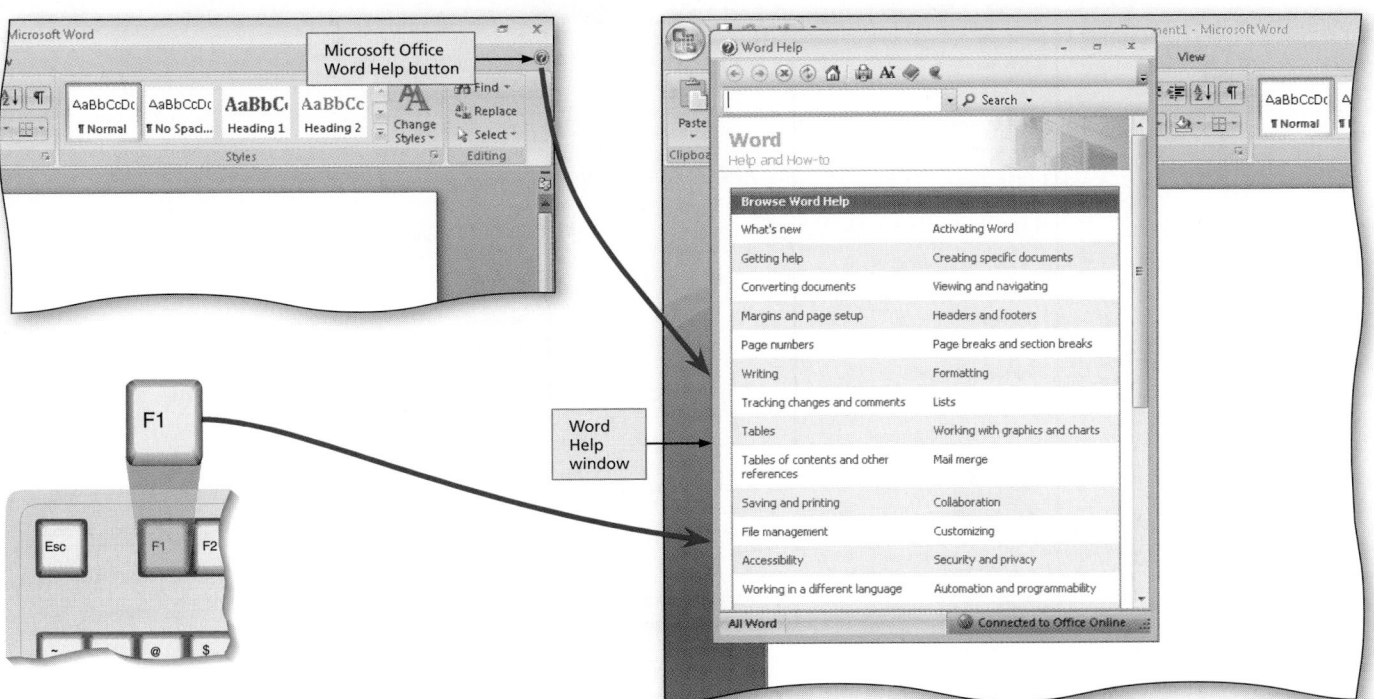

Figure C–1

To Open the Word Help Window

The following steps open the Word Help window and maximize the window.

1

- Start Microsoft Word, if necessary. Click the Microsoft Office Word Help button near the upper-right corner of the Word window to open the Word Help window (Figure C–2).

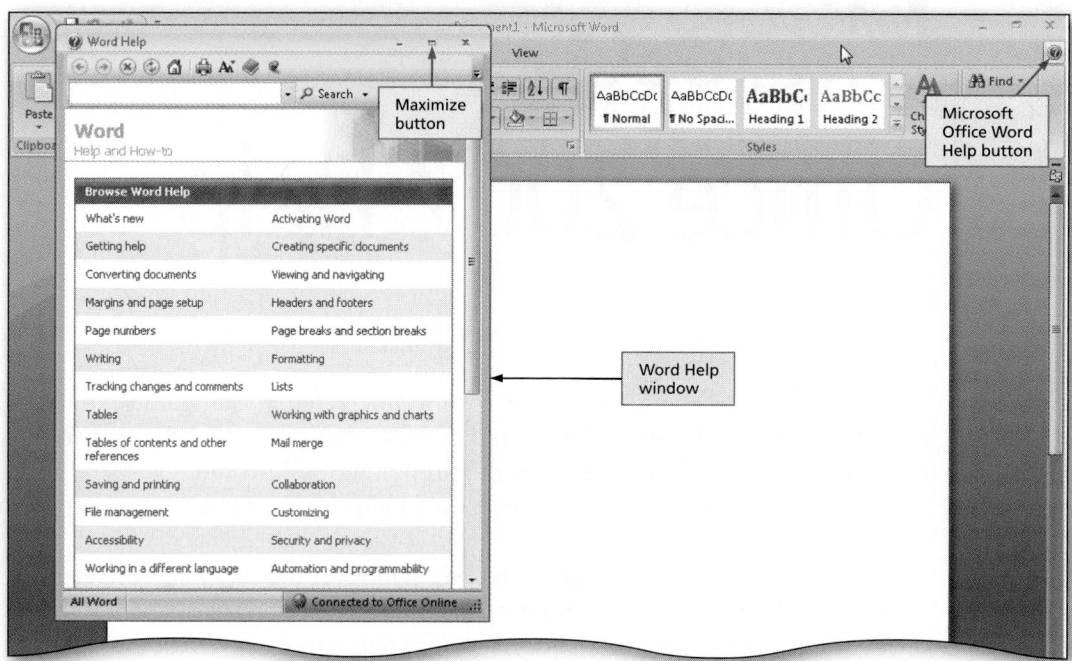

Figure C–2

2

- Click the Maximize button on the Help title bar to maximize the Help window (Figure C–3).

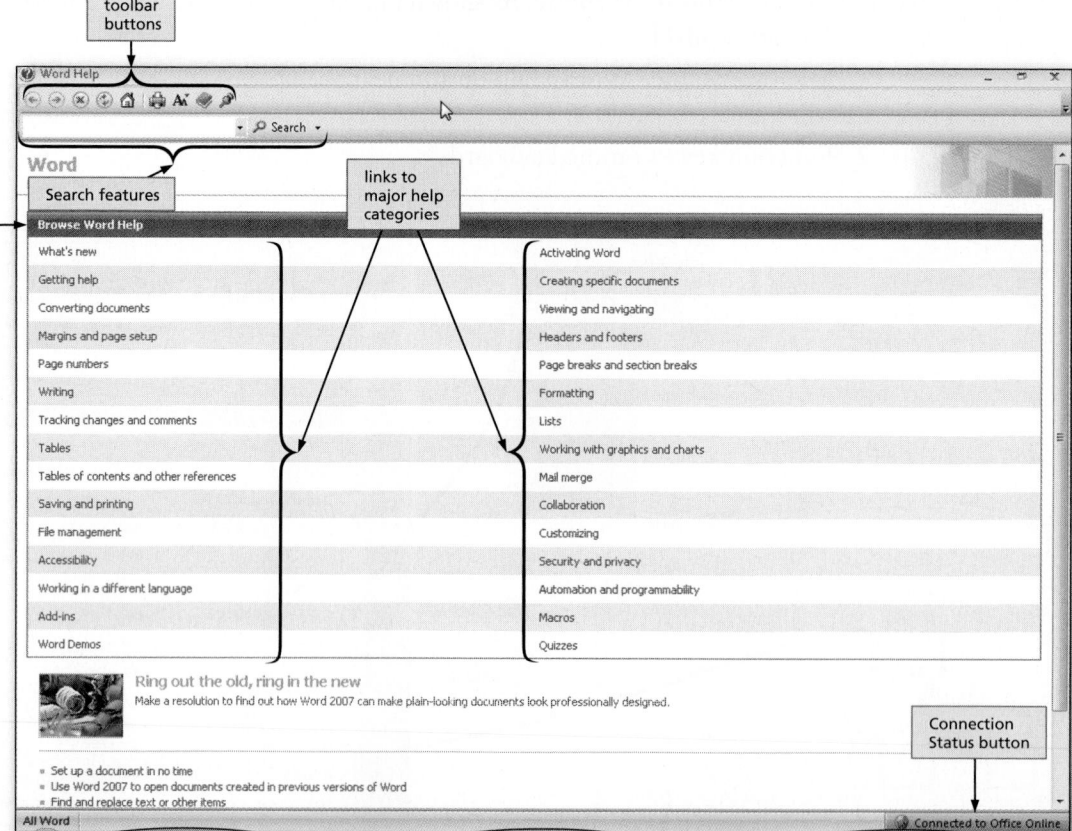

Figure C–3

The Word Help Window

The Word Help window provides several methods for accessing help about a particular topic, and also has tools for navigating around Help. Methods for accessing Help include searching the help content installed with Word, or searching the online Office content maintained by Microsoft.

Figure C–3 shows the main Word Help window. To navigate Help, the Word Help window includes search features that allow you to search on a word or phrase about which you want help; the Connection Status button, which allows you to control where Word Help searches for content; toolbar buttons; and links to major Help categories.

Search Features

You can perform Help searches on words or phrases to find information about any Word feature using the 'Type words to search for' text box and the Search button (Figure C–4a). Click the 'Type words to search for' text box and then click the Search button or press the ENTER key to initiate a search of Word Help.

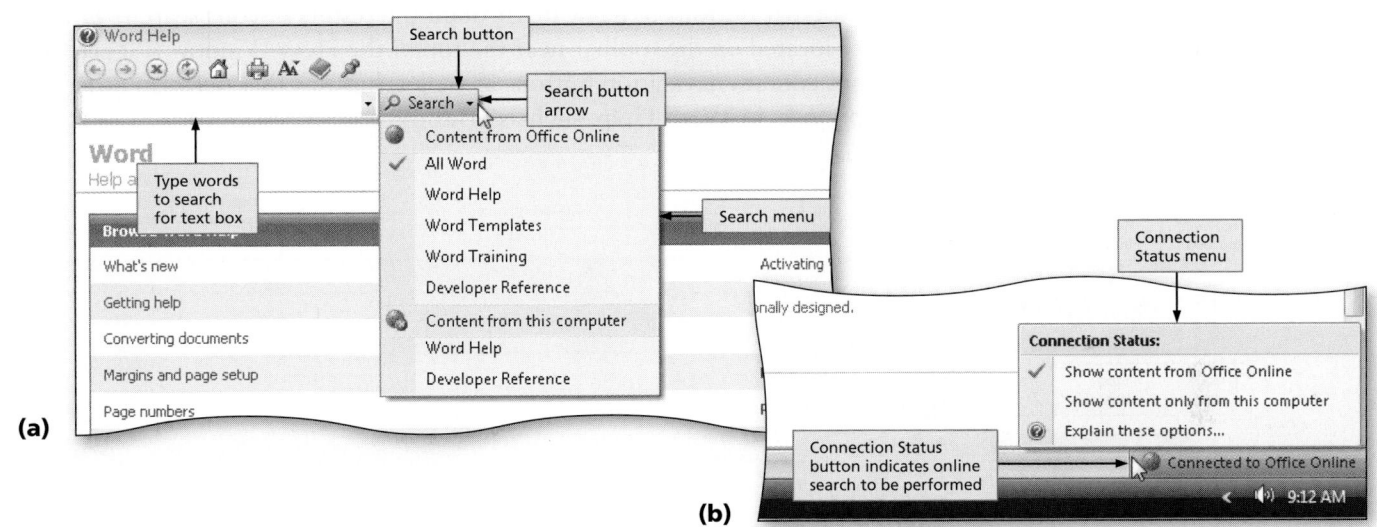

(a)

(b)

Figure C–4

Word Help offers the user the option of searching the online Help Web pages maintained by Microsoft or the offline Help files placed on your computer when you install Word. You can specify whether Word Help should search online or offline from two places: the Connection Status button on the status bar of the Word Help window, or the Search button arrow on the toolbar. The Connection Status button indicates whether Help currently is set up to work with online or offline information sources. Clicking the Connection Status button provides a menu with commands for selecting online or offline searches (Figure C–4b). The Connection Status menu allows the user to select whether Help searches will return content only from the computer (offline), or content from the computer and from Office Online (online).

Clicking the Search button arrow also provides a menu with commands for an online or offline search (Figure C–4a). These commands determine the source of information that Help searches for during the current Help session only. For example, assume that your preferred search is an offline search because you often do not have Internet access. You would set Connection Status to 'Show content only from this computer'. When you have Internet access, you can select an online search from the Search menu to search Office Online for information for your current search session only. Your search will use the Office Online resources until you quit Help. The next time you start Help, the Connection Status once again will be offline. In addition to setting the source of information that Help searches for during the current Help session, you can use the Search menu to further target the current search to one of four subcategories of online Help: Word Help, Word Templates, Word Training, and Developer Reference. The local search further can target one subcategory, Developer Reference.

In addition to searching for a word or string of text, you can use the links provided on the Browse Word Help area (Figure C–3 on page APP 10) to search for help on a topic. These links direct you to major help categories. From each major category, subcategories are available to further refine your search.

Finally, you can use the Table of Contents for Word Help to search for a topic the same way you would in a hard copy book. The Table of Contents is accessed via a toolbar button.

Toolbar Buttons

You can use toolbar buttons to navigate through the results of your search. The toolbar buttons are located on the toolbar near the top of the Help Window (Figure C–5). The toolbar buttons contain navigation buttons as well as buttons that perform other useful and common tasks in Word Help, such as printing.

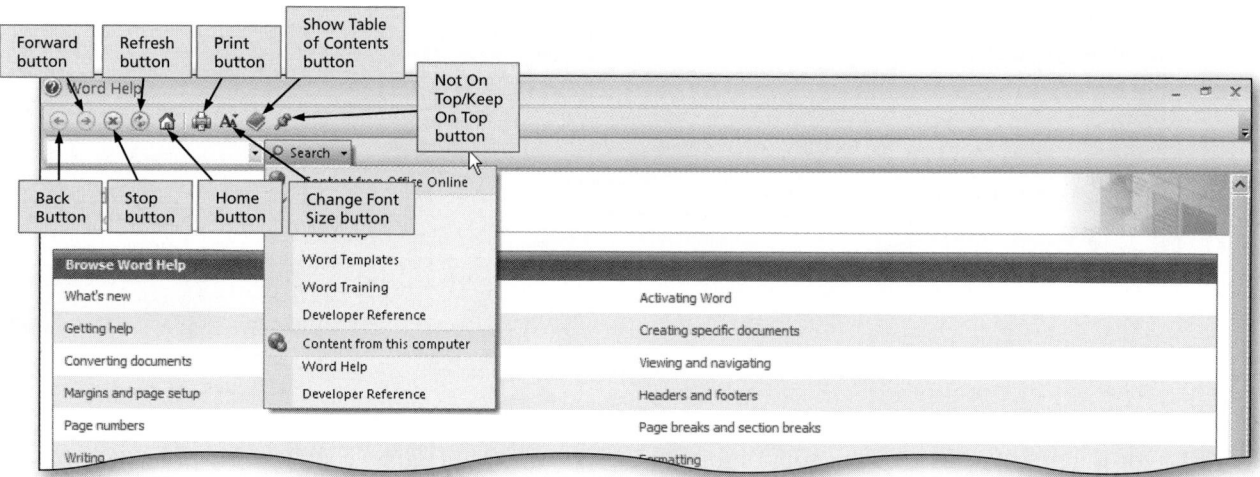

Figure C–5

The Word Help navigation buttons are the Back, Forward, Stop, Refresh, and Home buttons. These five buttons behave like the navigation buttons in a Web browser window. You can use the Back button to go back one window, the Forward button to go forward one window, the Stop button to stop loading the current page, and the Home button to redisplay the Help home page in the Help window. Use the Refresh button to reload the information requested into the Help window from its original source. When getting Help information online, this button provides the most current information from the Microsoft Help Web site.

The buttons located to the right of the navigation buttons — Print, Change Font Size, Show Table of Contents, and Not on Top — provide you with access to useful and common commands. The Print button prints the contents of the open Help window. The Change Font Size button customizes the Help window by increasing or decreasing the size of its text. The Show Table of Contents button opens a pane on the left side of the Help window that shows the Table of Contents for Word Help. You can use the Table of Contents for Word Help to navigate through the contents of Word Help much as you would use the Table of Contents in a book to search for a topic. The Not On Top button is an example of a toggle button, which is a button that can be switched back and forth between two states. It determines how the Word Help window behaves relative to other windows. When clicked, the Not On Top button changes to Keep On Top. In this state, it does not allow other windows from Word or other programs to cover the Word Help window when those windows are the active windows. When in the Not On Top state, the button allows other windows to be opened or moved on top of the Word Help window.

You can customize the size and placement of the Help window. Resize the window using the Maximize and Restore buttons, or by dragging the window to a desired size. Relocate the Help window by dragging the title bar to a new location on the screen.

Searching Word Help

Once the Word Help window is open, several methods exist for navigating Word Help. You can search for help by using any of the three following methods from the Help window:

1. Enter search text in the 'Type words to search for' text box
2. Click the links in the Help window
3. Use the Table of Contents

To Obtain Help Using the Type words to search for Text Box

Assume for the following example that you want to know more about watermarks. The following steps use the 'Type words to search for' text box to obtain useful information about watermarks by entering the word, watermark, as search text. The steps also navigate in the Word Help window.

1

- Type watermark in the 'Type words to search for' text box at the top of the Word Help window.

- Click the Search button arrow to display the Search menu (Figure C-6).

- If it is not selected already, click All Word on the Search menu to select the command. If All Word is already selected, click the Search button arrow again to close the Search menu.

Q&A Why select All Word on the Search menu?

Selecting All Word on the Search menu ensures that Word Help will search all possible sources for information on your search term. It will produce the most complete search results.

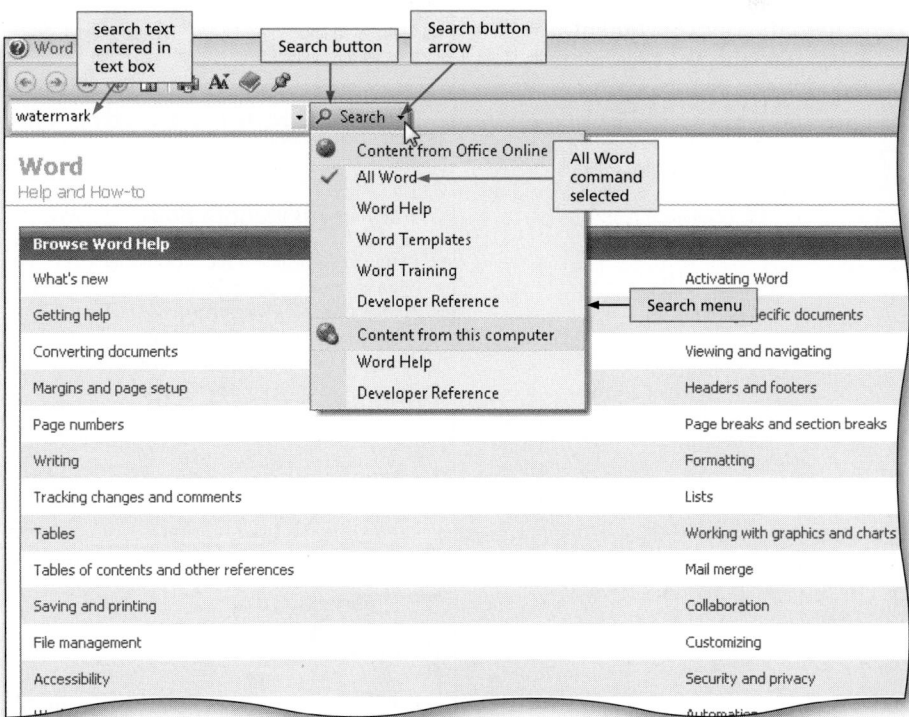

Figure C–6

- Click the Search button to display the search results (Figure C–7).

Q&A

Why do my results differ?

If you do not have an Internet connection, your results will reflect only the content of the Help files on your computer. When searching for help online, results also can change as material is added, deleted, and updated on the online Help Web pages maintained by Microsoft.

Q&A

Why were my search results not very helpful?

When initiating a search, keep in mind to check the spelling of the search text; and to keep your search very specific, with fewer than seven words, to return the most accurate results.

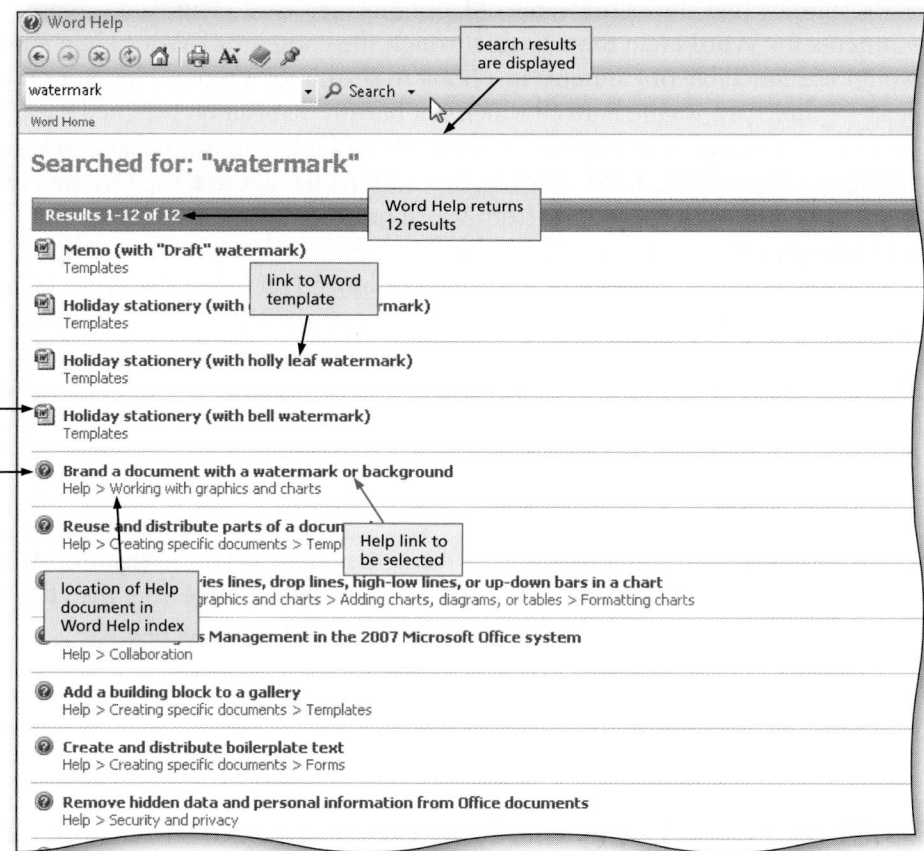

Figure C–7

- Click the 'Brand a document with a watermark or background' link to open the Help document associated with the link in the Help window (Figure C–8).

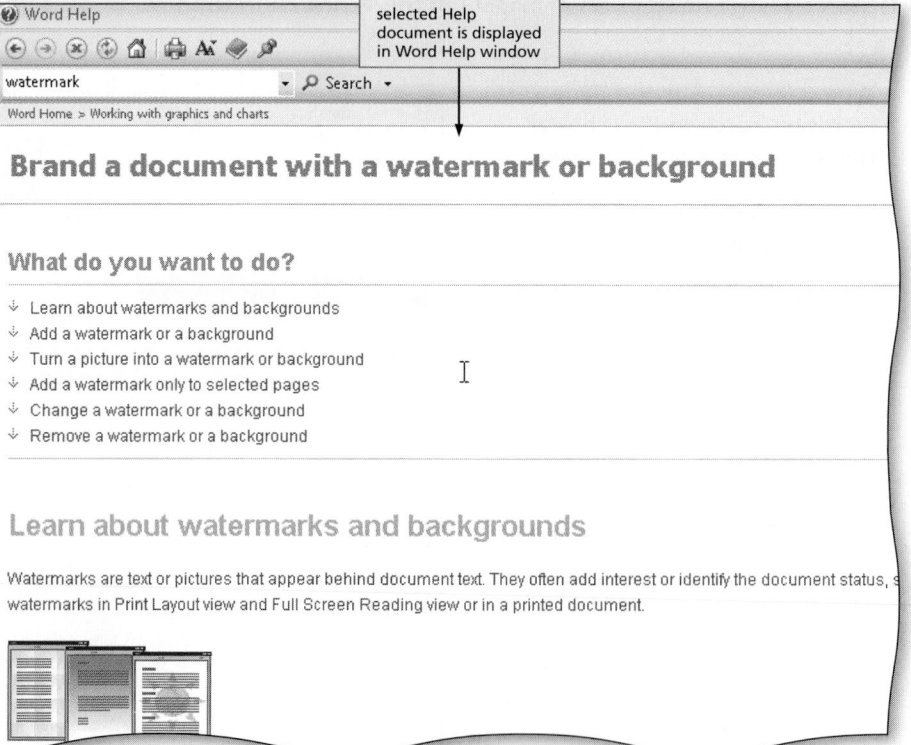

Figure C–8

4

- Click the Home button on the taskbar to clear the search results and redisplay the Word Help home page (Figure C–9).

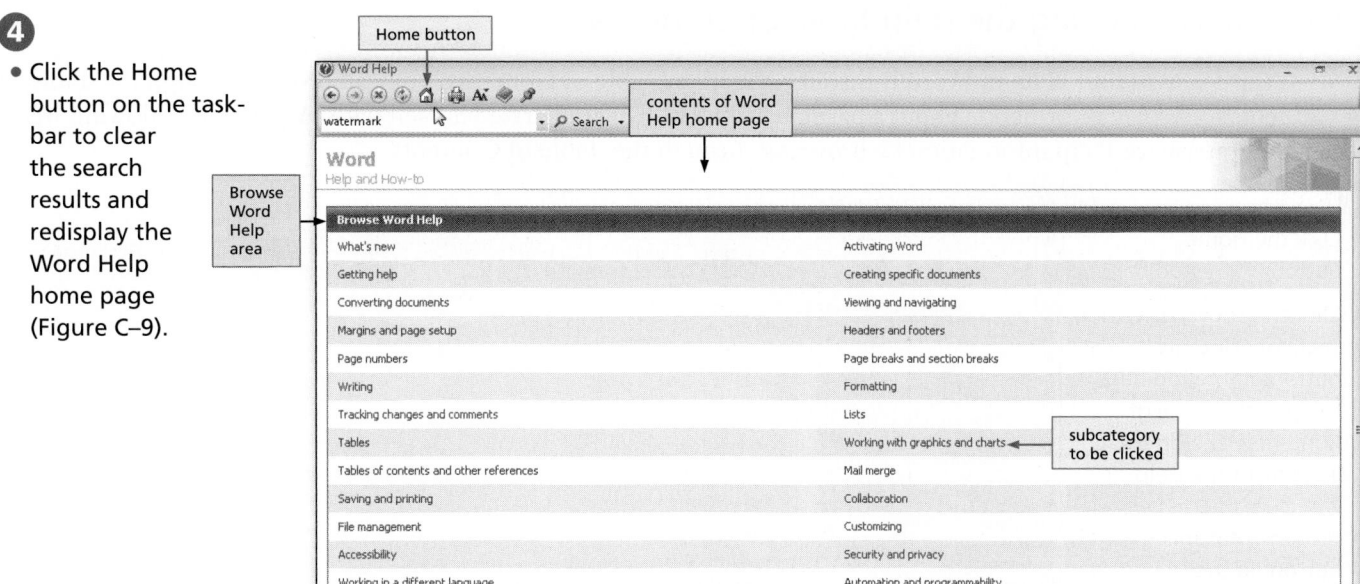

Figure C–9

To Obtain Help Using the Help Links

If your topic of interest is listed in the Browse Word Help area, you can click the link to begin browsing Word Help categories instead of entering search text. You browse Word Help just like you would browse a Web site. If you know in which category to find your Help information, you may wish to use these links. The following steps find the watermark Help information using the category links from the Word Help home page.

1

- Click the 'Working with graphics and charts' link to open the 'Working with graphics and charts' page.

- Click the 'Brand a document with a watermark or background' link to open the Help document associated with the link (Figure C–10).

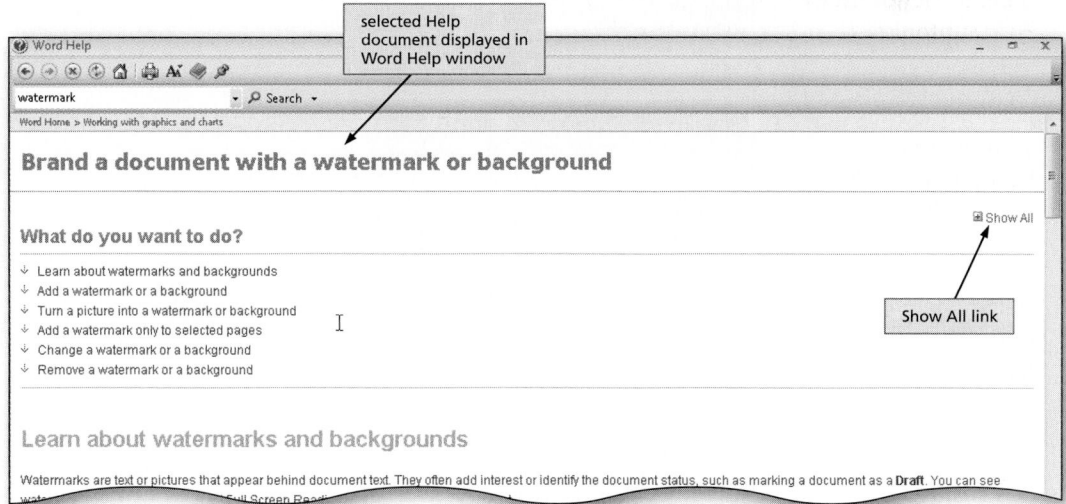

Figure C–10

Q&A What does the Show All link do?

In many Help documents, additional information about terms and features is available by clicking a link in the document to display additional information in the Help document. Clicking the Show All link opens all the links in the Help document that expand to additional text.

To Obtain Help Using the Help Table of Contents

A third way to find Help in Word is through the Help Table of Contents. You can browse through the Table of Contents to display information about a particular topic or to familiarize yourself with Word. The following steps access the watermark Help information by browsing through the Table of Contents.

1

- Click the Home button on the toolbar.

- Click the Show Table of Contents button on the toolbar to open the Table of Contents pane on the left side of the Help window. If necessary, click the Maximize button on the Help title bar to maximize the window (Figure C–11).

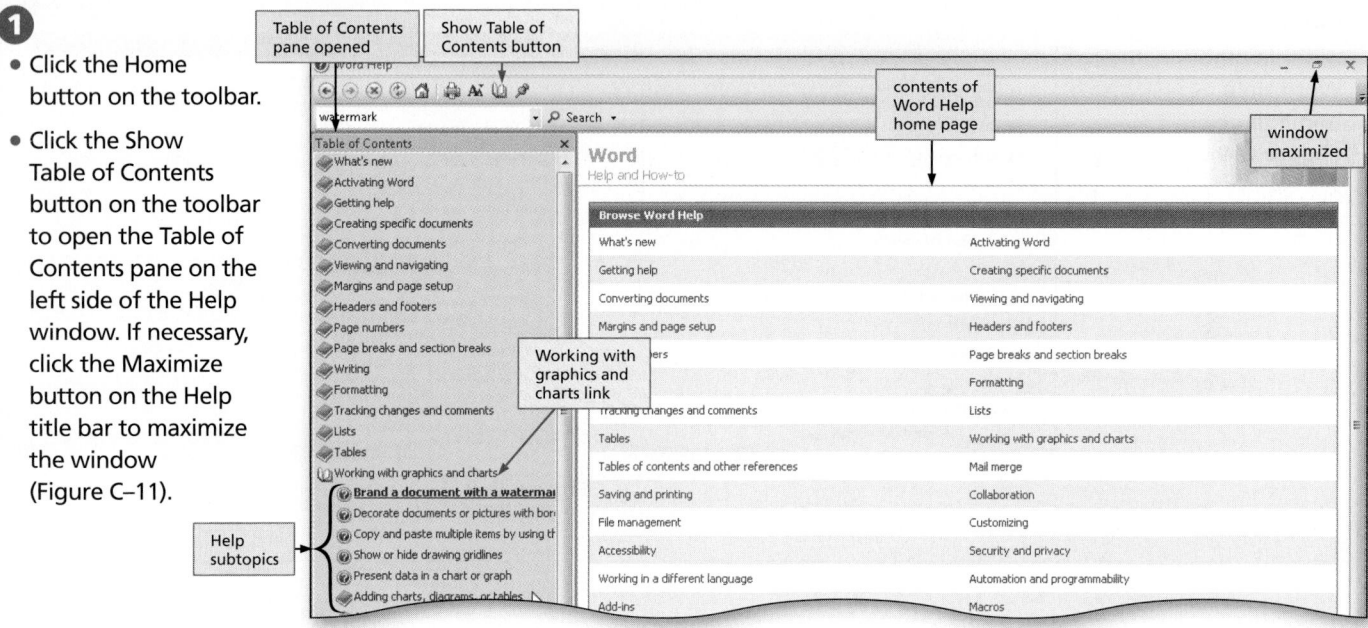

Figure C–11

2

- Click the 'Working with graphics and charts' link in the Table of Contents pane to view a list of Help subtopics.

- Click the 'Brand a document with a watermark or background' link in the Table of Contents pane to view the selected Help document in the right pane (Figure C–12).

Q&A

How do I remove the Table of Contents pane when I am finished with it?

The Show Table of Contents button acts as a toggle switch. When the Table of Contents pane is visible, the button changes to Hide Table of Contents. Clicking it hides the Table of Contents pane and changes the button to Show Table of Contents.

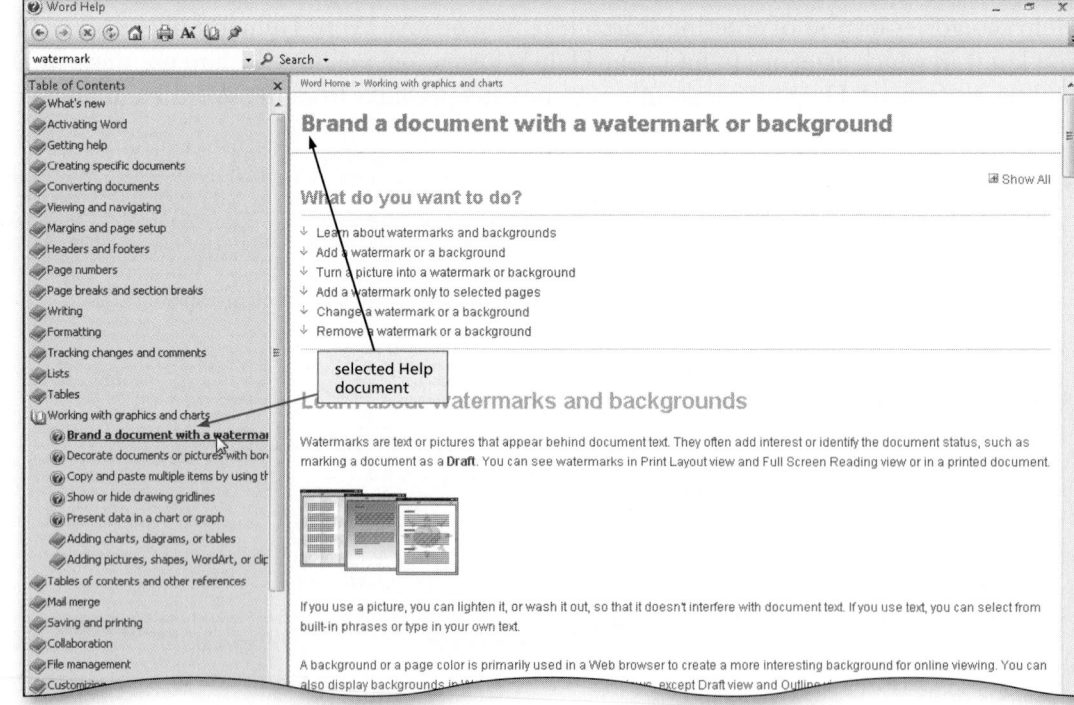

Figure C–12

Obtaining Help while Working in Word

Often you may need help while working on a document without already having the Help window open. For example, you may be unsure about how a particular command works, or you may be presented with a dialog box that you are not sure how to use. Rather than opening the Help window and initiating a search, Word Help provides you with the ability to search directly for help.

Figure C–13 shows one option for obtaining help while working in Word. If you want to learn more about a command, point to the command button and wait for the Enhanced ScreenTip to appear. If the Help icon appears in the Enhanced ScreenTip, press the F1 key while pointing to the command to open the Help window associated with that command.

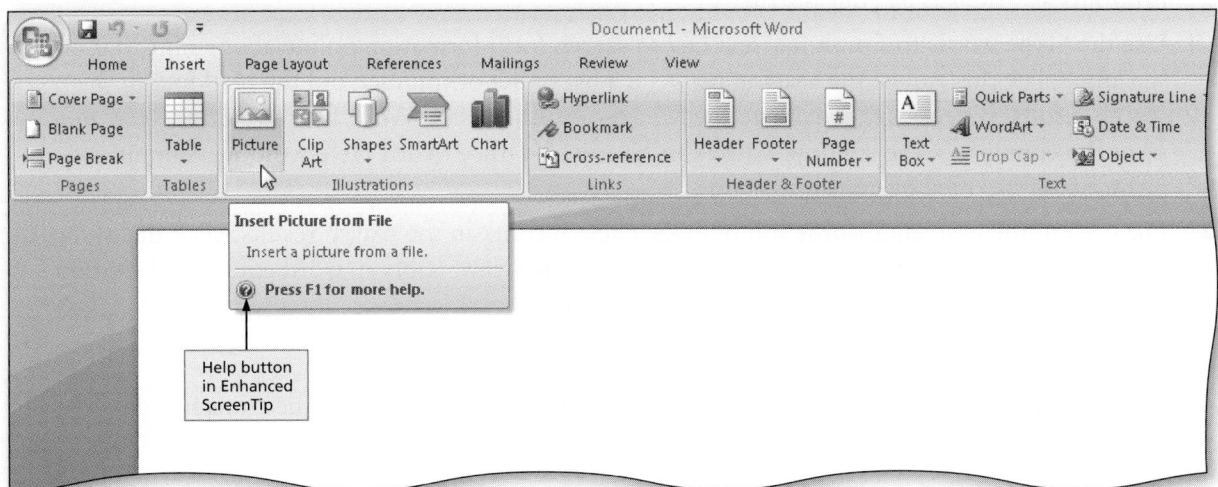

Figure C–13

Figure C–14 shows a dialog box with a Get help button in it. Pressing the F1 key while the dialog box is displayed opens a Help window. The Help window contains help about that dialog box, if available. If no help file is available for that particular dialog box, then the main Help window opens.

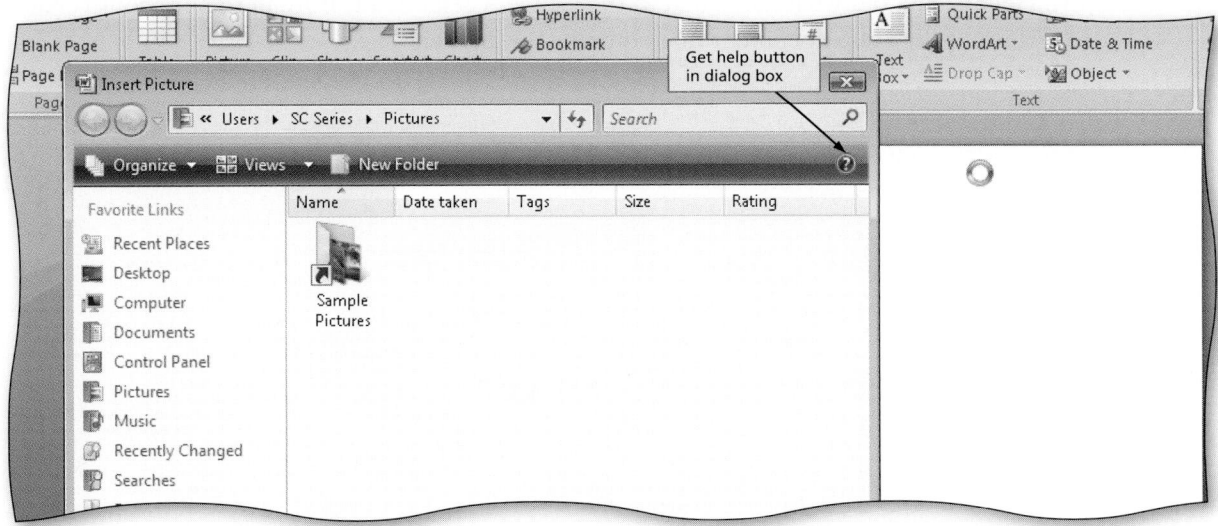

Figure C–14

Use Help

1 Obtaining Help Using Search Text

Instructions: Perform the following tasks using Word Help.

1. Use the 'Type words to search for' text box to obtain help about landscape printing. Use the Connection Status menu to search online help if you have an Internet connection.

2. Click Select page orientation in the list of links in the search results. Double-click the Microsoft Office Word Help window title bar to maximize it. Read and print the information. At the top of the printout, write down the number of links Word Help found.

3. Use the Search menu to search for help offline. Repeat the search from Step 1. At the top of the printout, write down the number of links that Word Help found searching offline. Submit the printouts as specified by your instructor.

4. Use the 'Type words to search for' text box to search for information online about adjusting line spacing. Click the 'Adjust the spacing between a list bullet or number and the text' link in the search results. If necessary, maximize the Microsoft Office 2007 Word Help window. Read and print the contents of the window. Close the Microsoft Office Word Help window. Submit the printouts as specified by your instructor.

5. For each of the following words and phrases, click one link in the search results, click the Show All link, and then print the page: page zoom; date; print preview; Ribbon; word count; and citation. Submit the printouts as specified by your instructor.

2 Expanding on Word Help Basics

Instructions: Use Word Help to better understand its features and answer the questions listed below. Answer the questions on your own paper, or submit the printed Help information as specified by your instructor.

1. Use Help to find out how to customize the Help window. Change the font size to the smallest option and then print the contents of the Microsoft Office Word Help window. Change the font size back to its original setting. Close the window.

2. Press the F1 key. Search for information about tables, restricting the search results to Word Templates. Print the first page of the Search results.

3. Search for information about tables, restricting the search results to Word Help files. Print the first page of the Search results.

4. Use Word Help to find out what happened to the Office Assistant, a feature in the previous version of Word. Print out the Help document that contains the answer.

Appendix D
Publishing Office 2007 Web Pages to a Web Server

With the Office 2007 programs, you use the Save As command on the Office Button menu to save a Web page to a Web server using one of two techniques: Web folders or File Transfer Protocol. A **Web folder** is an Office shortcut to a Web server. **File Transfer Protocol (FTP)** is an Internet standard that allows computers to exchange files with other computers on the Internet.

You should contact your network system administrator or technical support staff at your Internet access provider to determine if their Web server supports Web folders, FTP, or both, and to obtain necessary permissions to access the Web server. If you decide to publish Web pages using a Web folder, you must have the Office Server Extensions (OSE) installed on your computer.

Using Web Folders to Publish Office 2007 Web Pages

When publishing to a Web folder, someone first must create the Web folder before you can save to it. If you are granted permission to create a Web folder, you must obtain the Web address of the Web server, a user name, and possibly a password that allows you to access the Web server. You also must decide on a name for the Web folder. Table D–1 explains how to create a Web folder.

Office 2007 adds the name of the Web folder to the list of current Web folders. You can save to this folder, open files in the folder, rename the folder, or perform any operations you would to a folder on your hard disk. You can use your Office 2007 program or Windows Explorer to access this folder. Table D–2 explains how to save to a Web folder.

Table D–1 Creating a Web Folder

1. Click the Office Button and then click Save As or Open.

2. When the Save As dialog box (or Open dialog box) appears, click the Tools button arrow, and then click Map Network Drive... When the Map Network Drive dialog box is displayed, click the 'Connect to a Web site that you can use to store your documents and pictures' link.

3. When the Add Network Location Wizard dialog box appears, click the Next button. If necessary, click Choose a custom network location. Click the Next button. Click the View examples link, type the Internet or network address, and then click the Next button. Click 'Log on anonymously' to deselect the check box, type your user name in the User name text box, and then click the Next button. Enter the name you want to call this network place and then click the Next button. Click to deselect the 'Open this network location when I click Finish' check box, and then click the Finish button.

Table D–2 Saving to a Web Folder

1. Click the Office Button, click Save As.

2. When the Save As dialog box is displayed, type the Web page file name in the File name text box. Do not press the ENTER key.

3. Click the Save as type box arrow and then click Web Page to select the Web Page format.

4. Click Computer in the Navigation pane.

5. Double-click the Web folder name in the Network Location list.

6. If the Enter Network Password dialog box appears, type the user name and password in the respective text boxes and then click the OK button.

7. Click the Save button in the Save As dialog box.

Using FTP to Publish Office 2007 Web Pages

When publishing a Web page using FTP, you first must add the FTP location to your computer before you can save to it. An FTP location, also called an **FTP site**, is a collection of files that reside on an FTP server. In this case, the FTP server is the Web server.

To add an FTP location, you must obtain the name of the FTP site, which usually is the address (URL) of the FTP server, and a user name and a password that allows you to access the FTP server. You save and open the Web pages on the FTP server using the name of the FTP site. Table D–3 explains how to add an FTP site.

Office 2007 adds the name of the FTP site to the FTP locations list in the Save As and Open dialog boxes. You can open and save files using this list. Table D–4 explains how to save to an FTP location.

Table D–3 Adding an FTP Location
1. Click the Office Button and then click Save As or Open.
2. When the Save As dialog box (or Open dialog box) appears, click the Tools button arrow, and then click Map Network Drive... When the Map Network Drive dialog box is displayed, click the 'Connect to a Web site that you can use to store your documents and pictures' link.
3. When the Add Network Location Wizard dialog box appears, click the Next button. If necessary, click Choose a custom network location. Click the Next button. Click the View examples link, type the Internet or network address, and then click the Next button. If you have a user name for the site, click to deselect 'Log on anonymously' and type your user name in the User name text box, and then click Next. If the site allows anonymous logon, click Next. Type a name for the location, click Next, click to deselect the 'Open this network location when I click Finish' check box, and click Finish. Click the OK button.
4. Close the Save As or the Open dialog box.

Table D–4 Saving to an FTP Location
1. Click the Office Button and then click Save As.
2. When the Save As dialog box is displayed, type the Web page file name in the File name text box. Do not press the ENTER key.
3. Click the Save as type box arrow and then click Web Page to select the Web Page format.
4. Click Computer in the Navigation pane.
5. Double-click the name of the FTP site in the Network Location list.
6. When the FTP Log On dialog box appears, enter your user name and password and then click the OK button.
7. Click the Save button in the Save As dialog box.

Appendix E
Customizing Microsoft Office 2007

This appendix explains how to change the screen resolution in Windows Vista to the resolution used in this book. It also describes how to customize the Word window by changing the Ribbon, Quick Access Toolbar, and the color scheme.

Changing Screen Resolution

Screen resolution indicates the number of pixels (dots) that the computer uses to display the letters, numbers, graphics, and background you see on the screen. When you increase the screen resolution, Windows displays more information on the screen, but the information decreases in size. The reverse also is true: as you decrease the screen resolution, Windows displays less information on the screen, but the information increases in size.

The screen resolution usually is stated as the product of two numbers, such as 1024×768 (pronounced "ten twenty-four by seven sixty-eight"). A 1024×768 screen resolution results in a display of 1,024 distinct pixels on each of 768 lines, or about 786,432 pixels. The figures in this book were created using a screen resolution of 1024×768.

The screen resolutions most commonly used today are 800×600 and 1024×768, although some Office specialists set their computers at a much higher screen resolution, such as 2048×1536.

To Change the Screen Resolution

The following steps change the screen resolution from 1280×1024 to 1024×768. Your computer already may be set to 1024×768 or some other resolution.

- If necessary, minimize all programs so that the Windows Vista desktop appears.

- Right-click the Windows Vista desktop to display the Windows Vista desktop shortcut menu (Figure E–1).

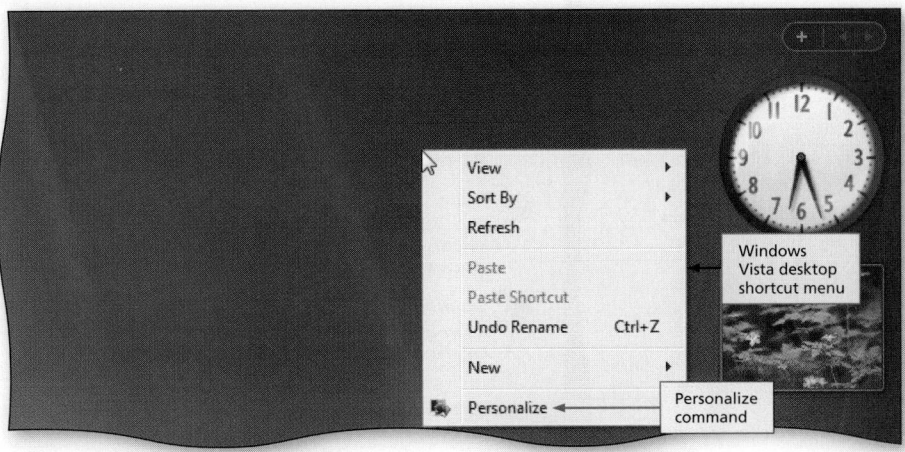

Figure E–1

2

• Click Personalize on the shortcut menu to open the Personalization window.

• Click Display Settings in the Personalization window to display the Display Settings dialog box (Figure E–2).

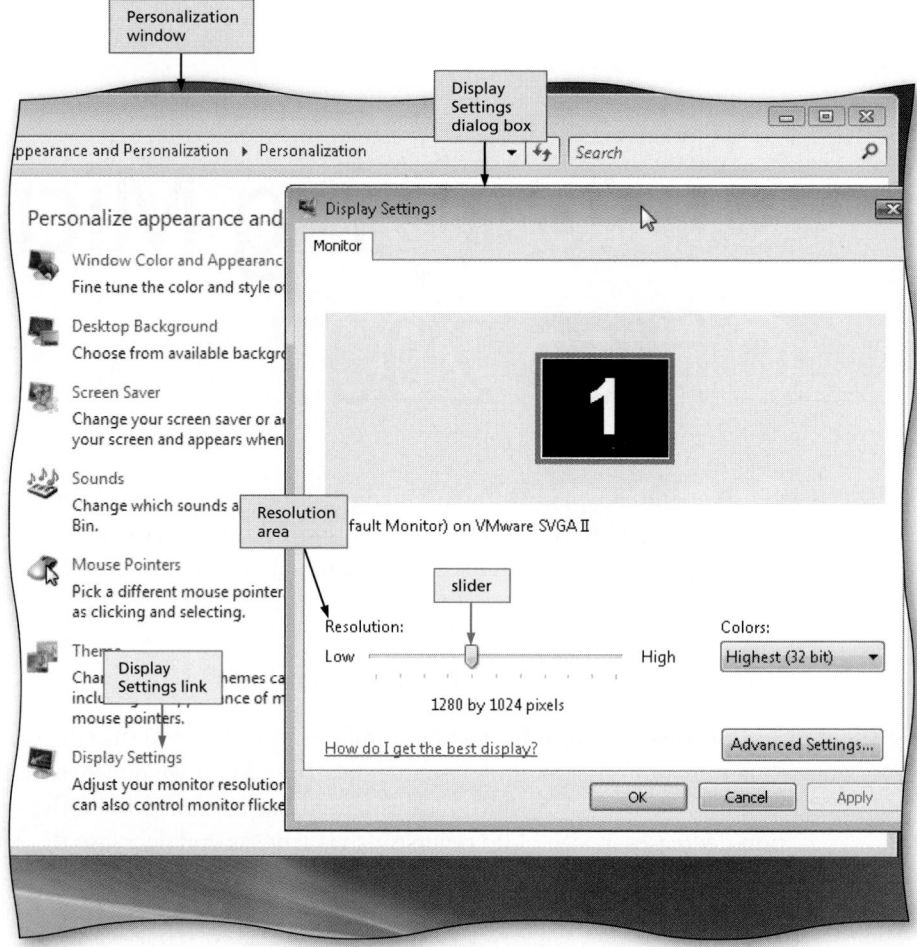

Figure E–2

3

• Drag the slider in the Resolution area so that the screen resolution changes to 1024 × 768 (Figure E–3).

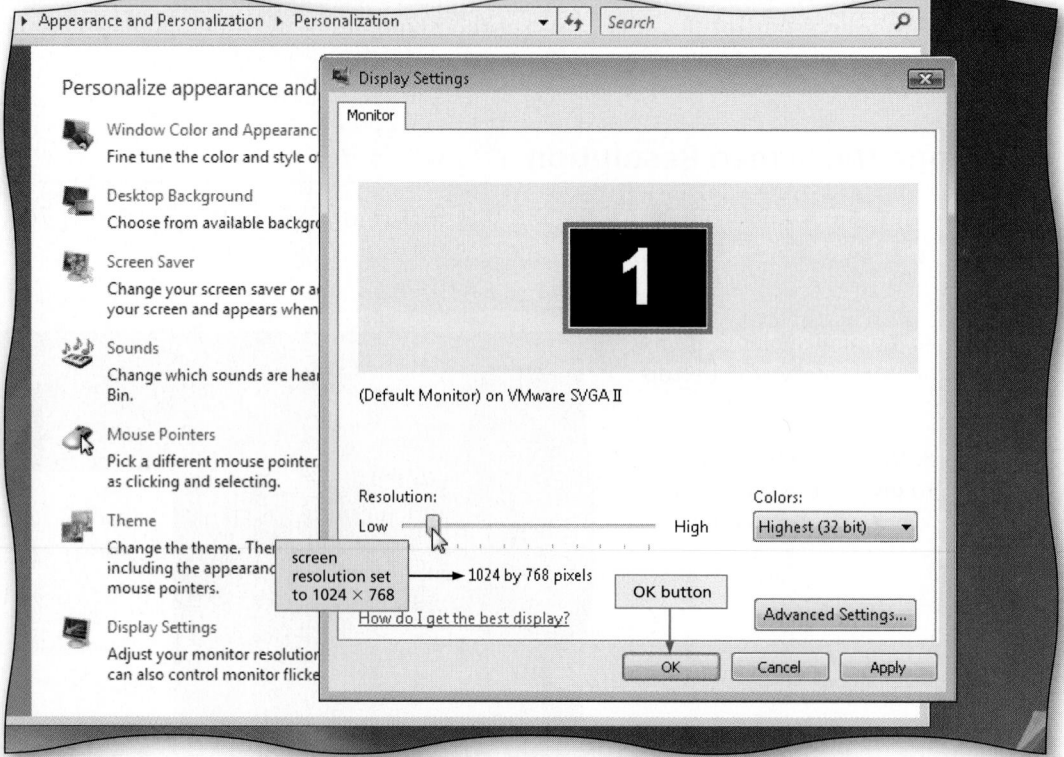

Figure E–3

4
- Click the OK button to change the screen resolution from 1280 × 1024 to 1024 × 768 (Figure E–4).

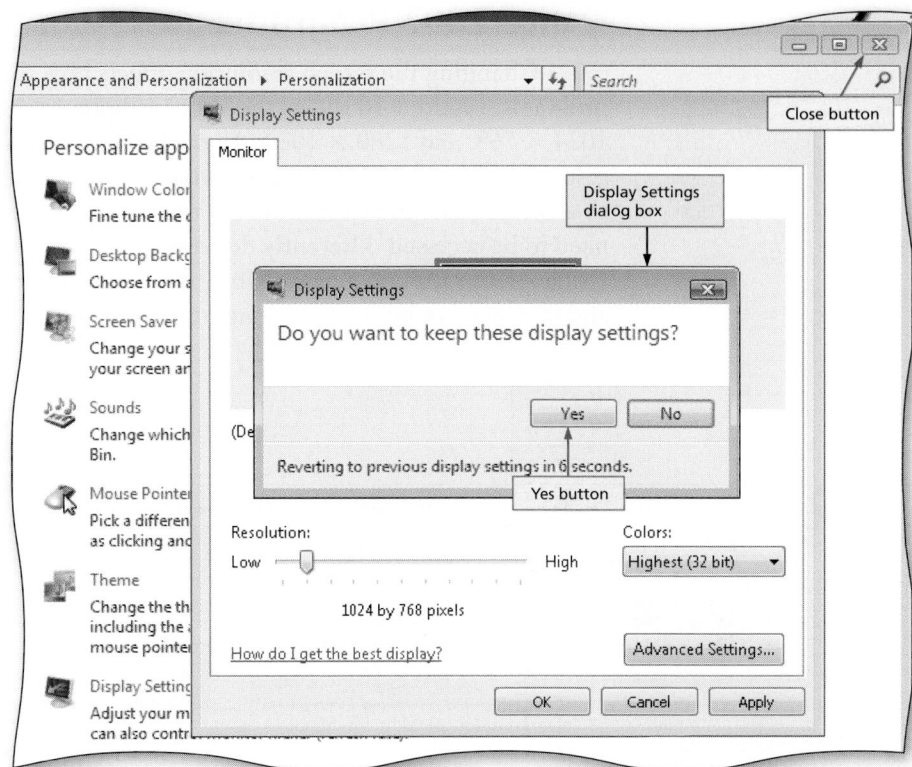

Figure E–4

5
- Click the Yes button in the Display Settings dialog box to accept the new screen resolution (Figure E–5).

 What if I do not want to change the screen resolution after seeing it applied after I click the OK button?

You either can click the No button in the inner Display Settings dialog box, or wait for the timer to run out, at which point Windows Vista will revert to the original screen resolution.

- Click the Close button to close the Personalization Window.

Figure E–5

Screen Resolution and the Appearance of the Ribbon in Office 2007 Programs

Changing the screen resolution affects how the Ribbon appears in Office 2007 programs. Figure E–6 shows the Word Ribbon at the screen resolutions of 800 × 600, 1024 × 768, and 1280 × 1024. All of the same commands are available regardless of screen resolution. Word, however, makes changes to the groups and the buttons within the groups to accommodate the various screen resolutions. The result is that certain commands may need to be accessed differently depending on the resolution chosen. A command that is visible on the Ribbon and available by clicking a button at one resolution may not be visible and may need to be accessed using its group button at a different resolution.

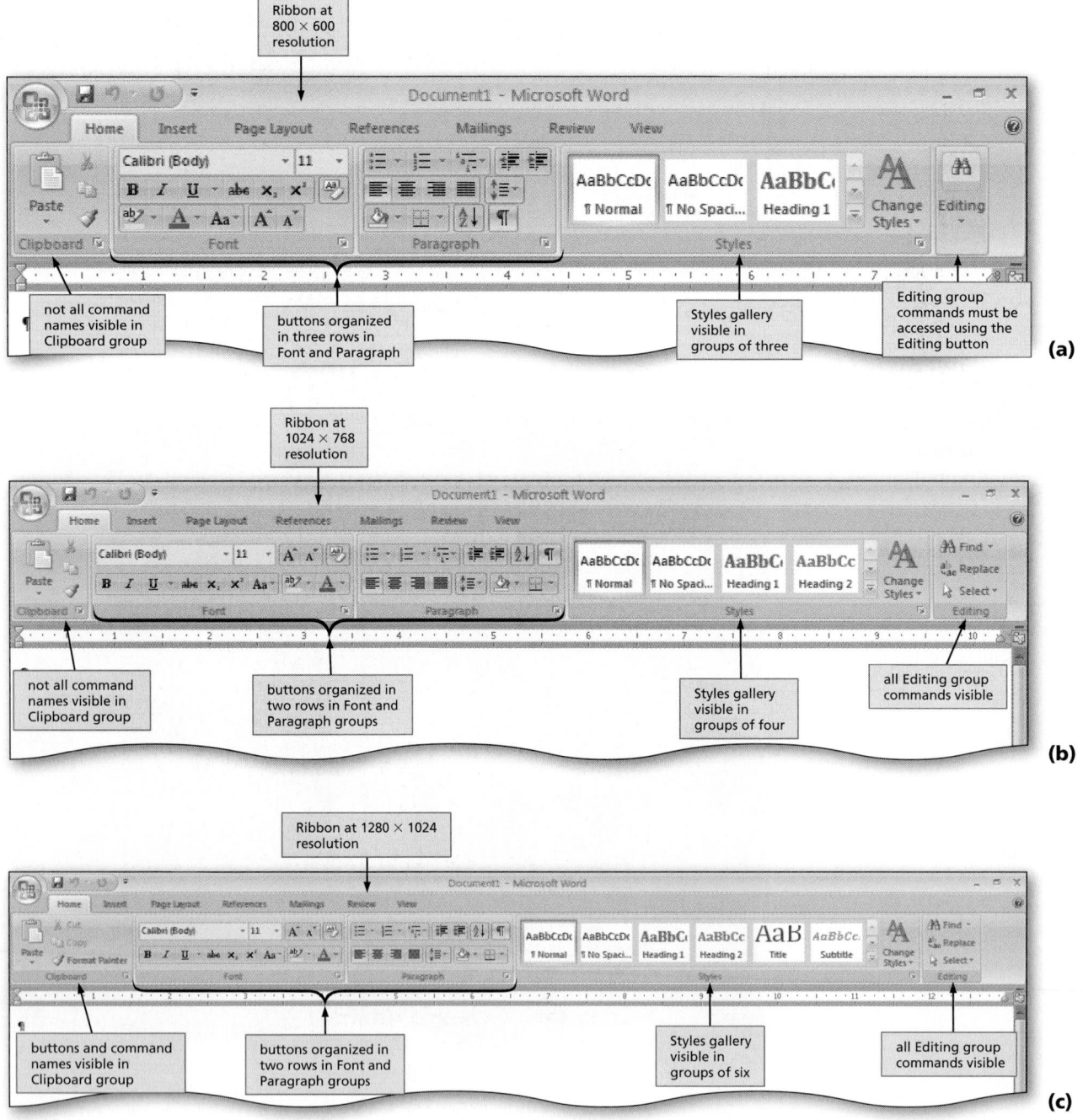

Figure E–6

Comparing the three Ribbons, notice changes in content and layout of the groups and galleries. In some cases, the content of a group is the same in each resolution, but the layout of the group differs. For example, the same buttons appear in the Font and Paragraph groups in the three resolutions, but the layouts differ. The buttons are displayed in three rows at the 800 × 600 resolution, and in two rows in the 1024 × 768 and 1280 × 1024 resolutions. In other cases, the content and layout are the same across the resolution, but the level of detail differs with the resolution. In the Clipboard group, when the resolution increases to 1280 × 1024, the names of all the buttons in the group appear in addition to the buttons themselves. At the lower resolution, only the buttons appear.

Changing resolutions also can result in fewer commands being visible in a group. Comparing the Editing groups, notice that the group at the 800 × 600 resolution consists of an Editing button, while at the higher resolutions, the group has three buttons visible. The commands that are available on the Ribbon at the higher resolutions must be accessed using the Editing button at the 800 × 600 resolution.

Changing resolutions results in different amounts of detail being available at one time in the galleries on the Ribbon. The Styles gallery in the three resolutions presented show different numbers of styles. At 800 × 600, you can scroll through the gallery three styles at a time, at 1024 × 768, you can scroll through the gallery four styles at a time, and at 1280 × 1024, you can scroll through the gallery six styles at a time.

Customizing the Word Window

When working in Word, you may want to make your working area as large as possible. One option is to minimize the Ribbon. You also can modify the characteristics of the Quick Access Toolbar, customizing the toolbar's commands and location to better suit your needs.

To Minimize the Ribbon in Word

The following steps minimize the Ribbon.

 1

- Start Word.
- Maximize the Word window, if necessary.
- Click the Customize Quick Access Toolbar button on the Quick Access Toolbar to display the Customize Quick Access Toolbar menu (Figure E–7).

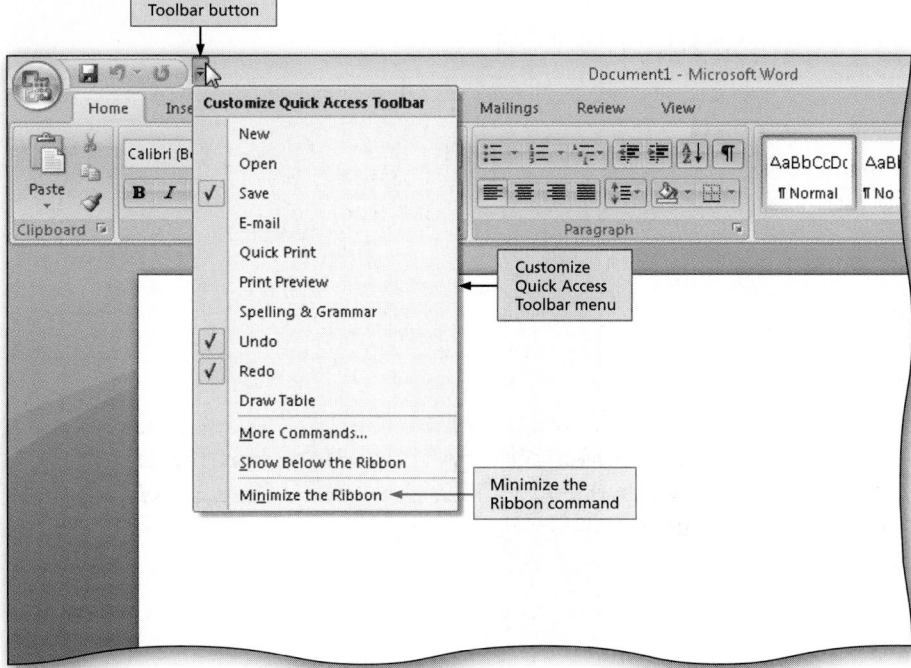

Figure E–7

2

● Click Minimize the Ribbon on the Quick Access Toolbar to reduce the Ribbon display to just the tabs (Figure E–8).

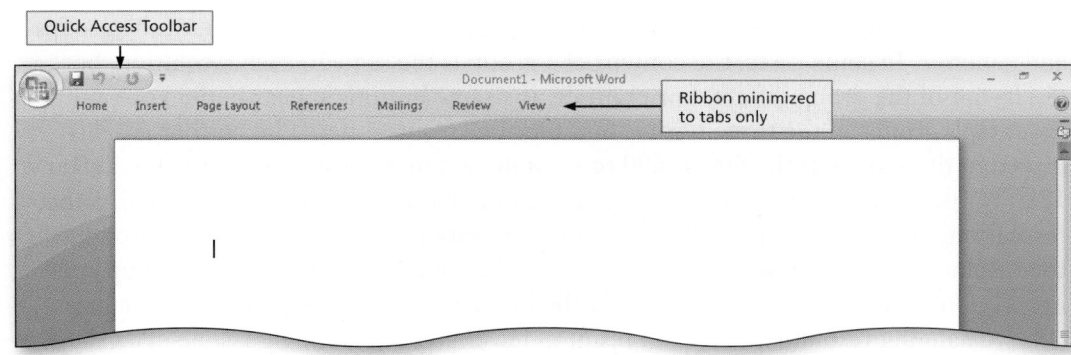

Figure E–8

Customizing and Resetting the Quick Access Toolbar

The Quick Access Toolbar, located to the right of the Microsoft Office Button by default, provides easy access to some of the more frequently used commands in Word (Figure E–7). By default, the Quick Access Toolbar contains buttons for the Save, Undo, and Redo commands. Customize the Quick Access Toolbar by changing its location in the window and by adding additional buttons to reflect which commands you would like to be able to access easily.

To Change the Location of the Quick Access Toolbar

The following steps move the Quick Access Toolbar to below the Ribbon.

1

● Double-click the Home tab to redisplay the Ribbon.

● Click the Customize Quick Access Toolbar button on the Quick Access Toolbar menu to display the Customize Quick Access Toolbar menu (Figure E–9).

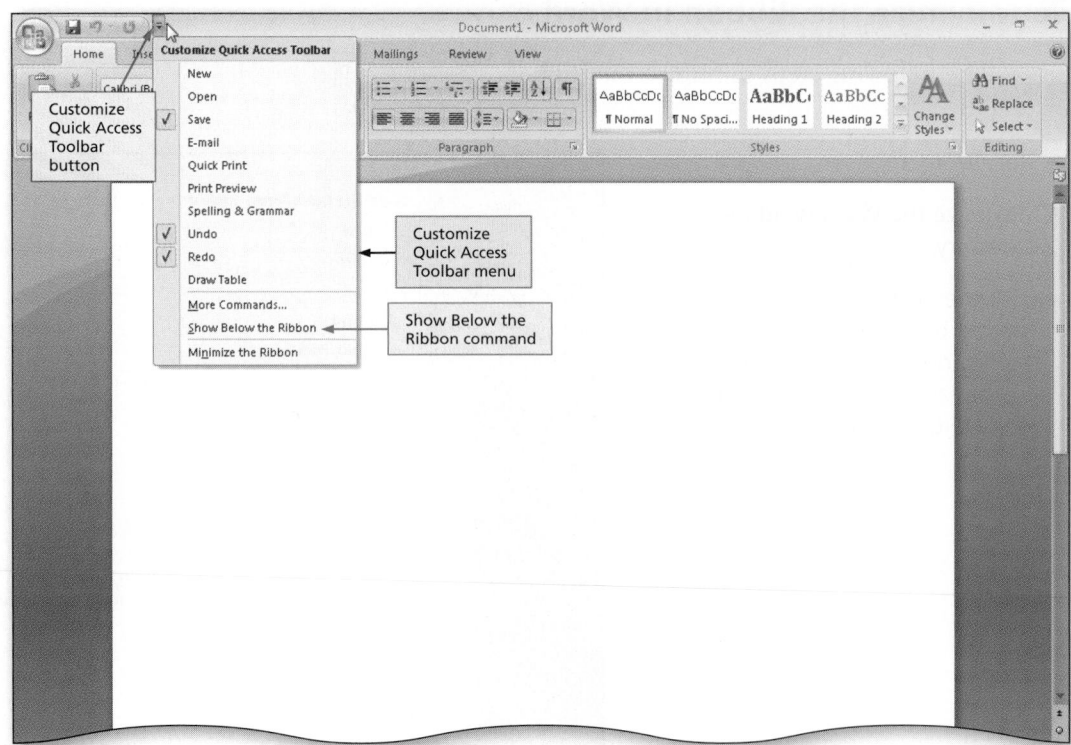

Figure E–9

- Click Show Below the Ribbon on the Quick Access Toolbar menu to move the Quick Access Toolbar below the Ribbon (Figure E–10).

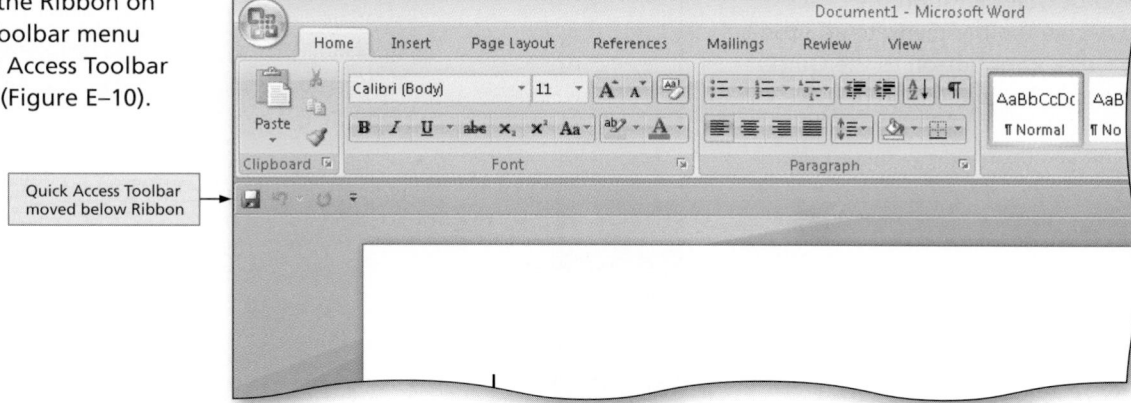

Quick Access Toolbar moved below Ribbon

Figure E–10

To Add Commands to the Quick Access Toolbar Using the Customize Quick Access Toolbar Menu

Some of the more commonly added commands are available for selection from the Customize Quick Access Toolbar menu. The following steps add the Quick Print button to the Quick Access Toolbar.

- Click the Customize Quick Access Toolbar button to display the Customize Quick Access Toolbar menu (Figure E–11).

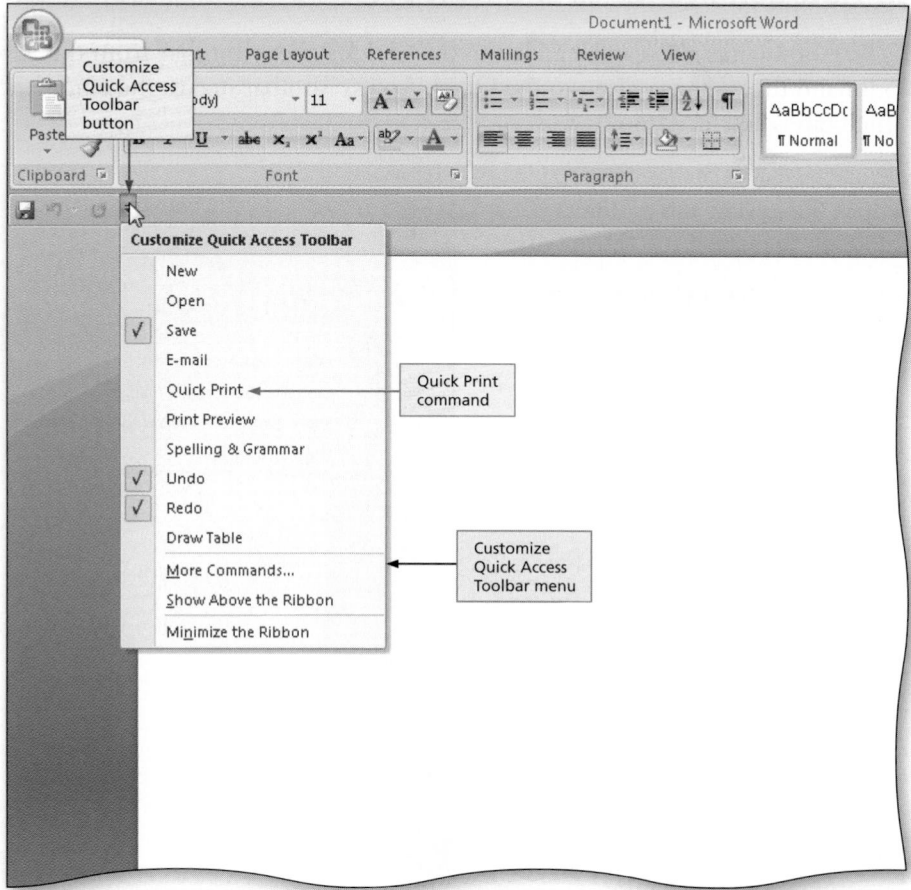

Customize Quick Access Toolbar button

Quick Print command

Customize Quick Access Toolbar menu

Figure E–11

- Click Quick Print on the Quick Access Toolbar menu to add the Quick Print button to the Quick Access Toolbar (Figure E–12).

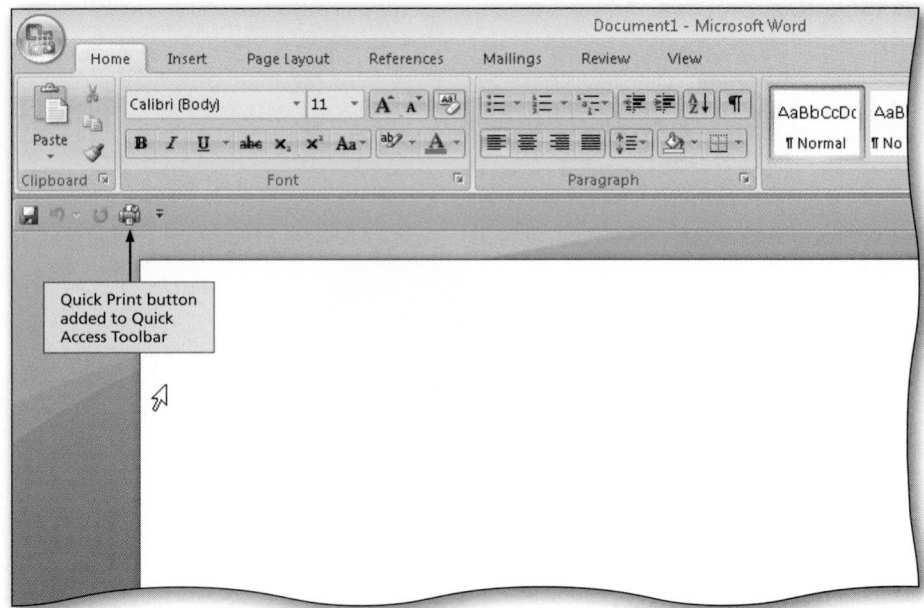

Figure E–12

To Add Commands to the Quick Access Toolbar Using the Shortcut Menu

Commands also can be added to the Quick Access Toolbar from the Ribbon. Adding an existing Ribbon command that you use often to the Quick Access Toolbar makes the command immediately available, regardless of which tab is active.

- Click the Review tab on the Ribbon to make it the active tab.

- Right-click the Spelling & Grammar button on the Review tab to display a shortcut menu (Figure E–13).

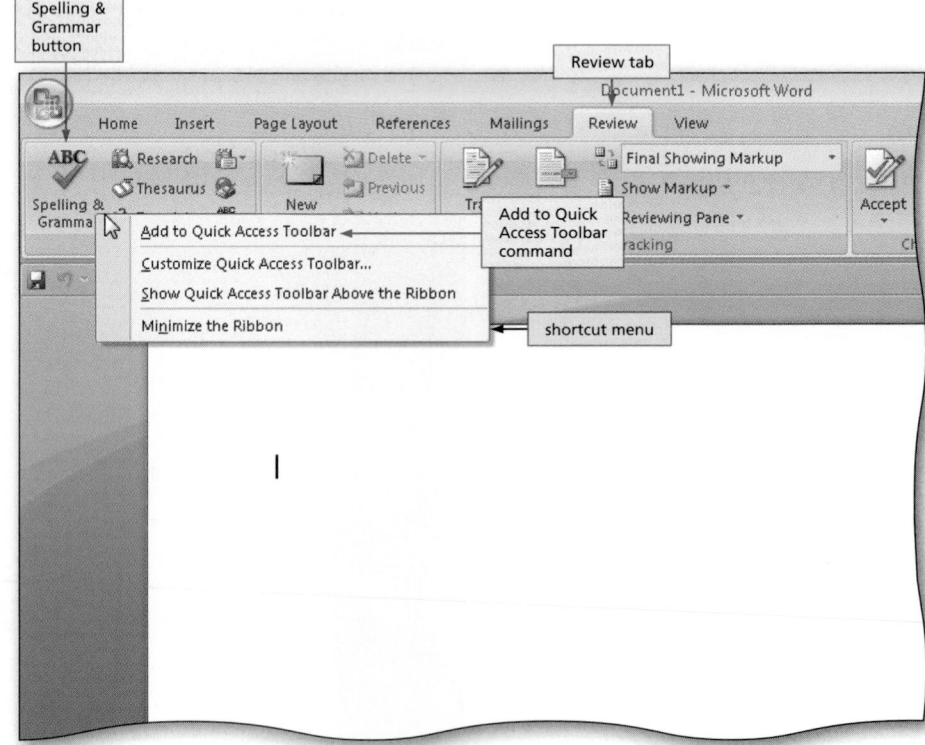

Figure E–13

2

● Click Add to Quick Access Toolbar on the shortcut menu to add the Spelling & Grammar button to the Quick Access Toolbar (Figure E–14).

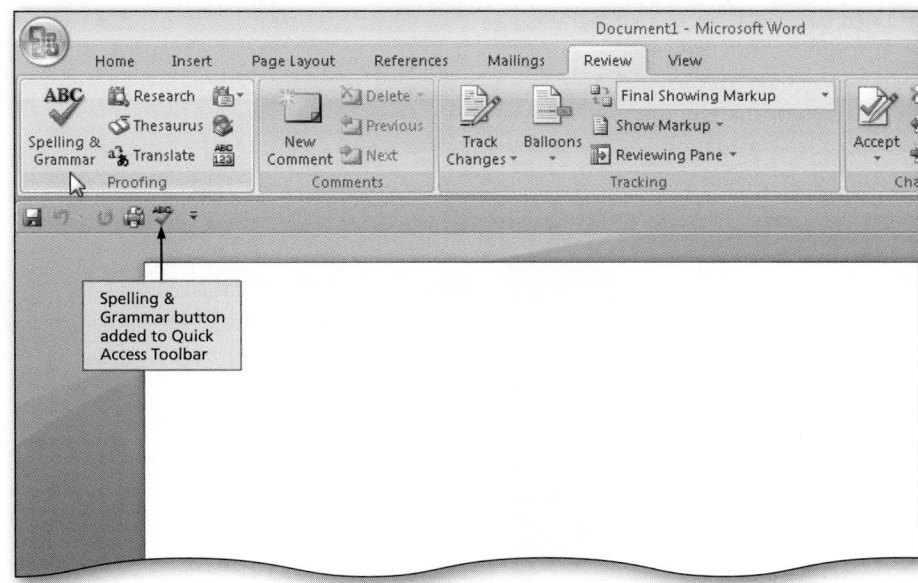

Figure E–14

To Add Commands to the Quick Access Toolbar Using Word Options

Some commands do not appear on the Ribbon. They can be added to the Quick Access Toolbar using the Word Options dialog box.

1

● Click the Office Button to display the Office Button menu (Figure E–15).

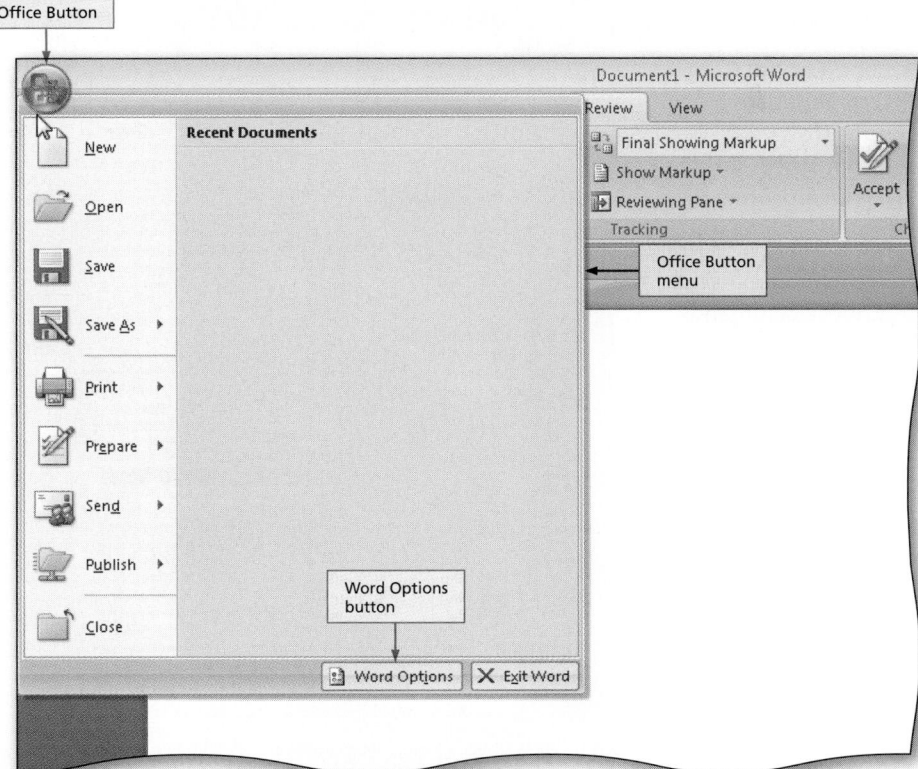

Figure E–15

- Click the Word Options button on the Office Button menu to display the Word Options dialog box (Figure E–16).

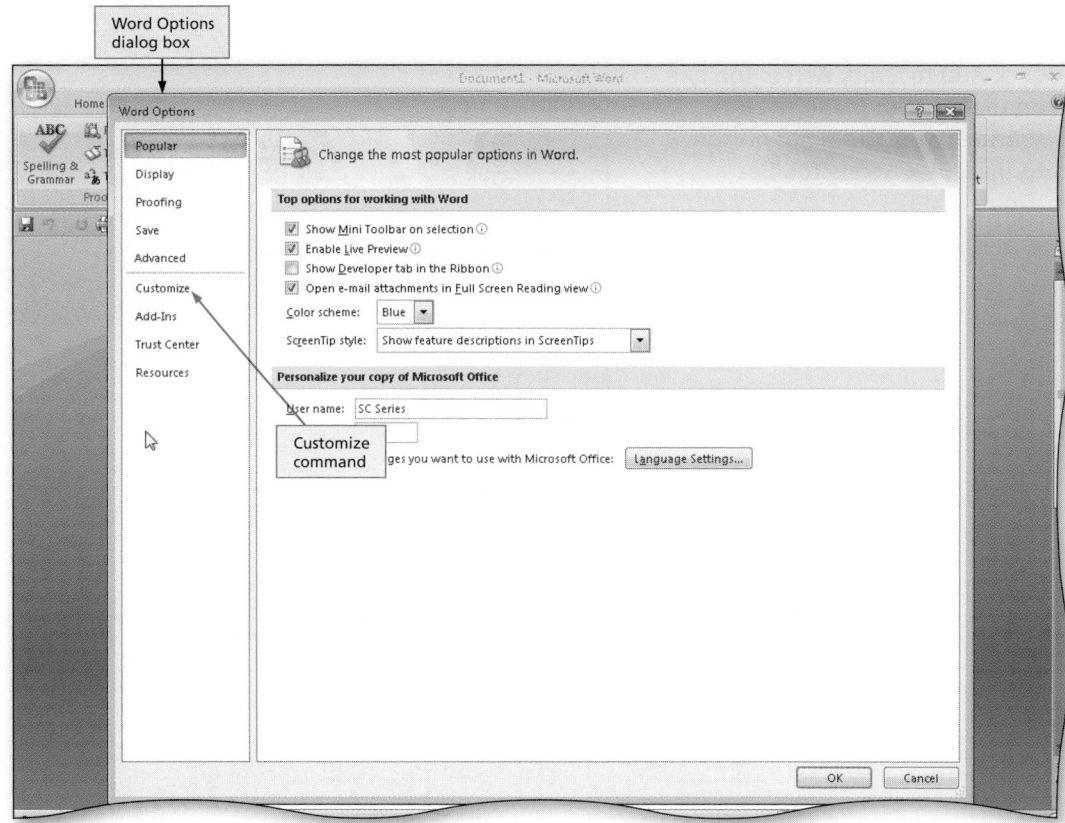

Figure E–16

- Click Customize in the left pane.

- Click 'Choose commands from' box arrow to display the 'Choose commands from' list.

- Click Commands Not in the Ribbon in the 'Choose commands from' list.

- Scroll to display the Web Page Preview command.

- Click Web Page Preview to select it (Figure E–17).

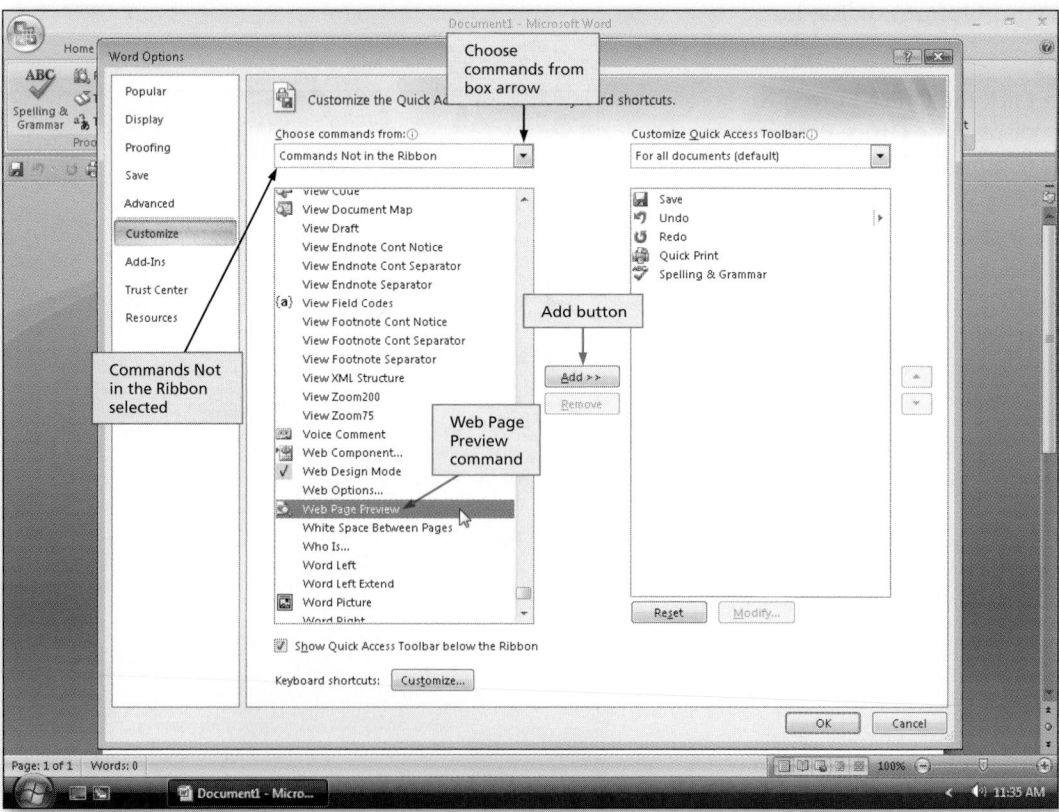

Figure E–17

4

- Click the Add button to add the Web Page Preview button to the list of buttons on the Quick Access Toolbar (Figure E–18).

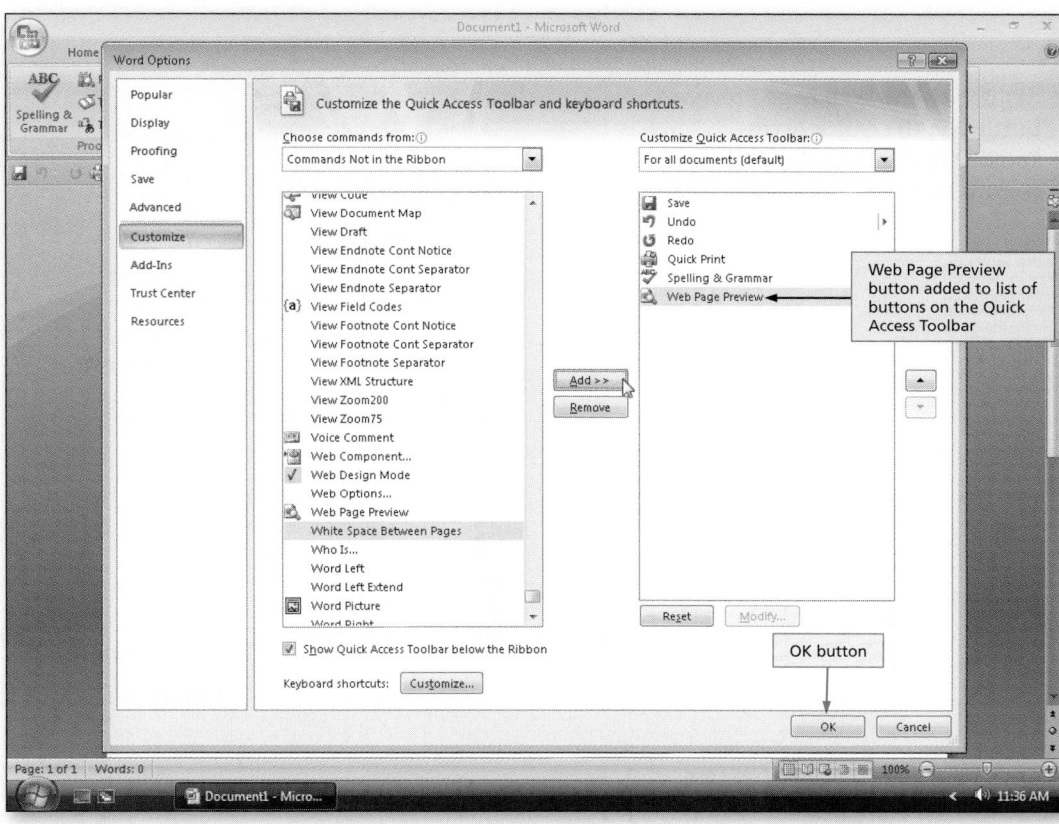

Figure E–18

5

- Click the OK button to add the Web Page Preview button to the Quick Access Toolbar (Figure E–19).

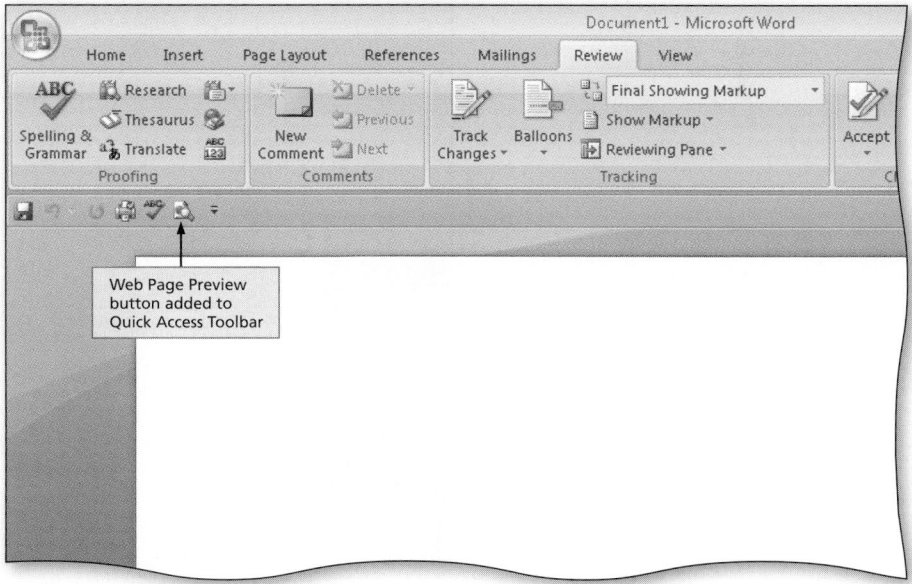

Figure E–19

Other Ways
1. Click Customize Quick Access Toolbar button, click More Commands, select commands to add, click Add button, click OK button

To Remove a Command from the Quick Access Toolbar

1

• Right-click the Web Page Preview button on the Quick Access Toolbar to display a shortcut menu (Figure E–20).

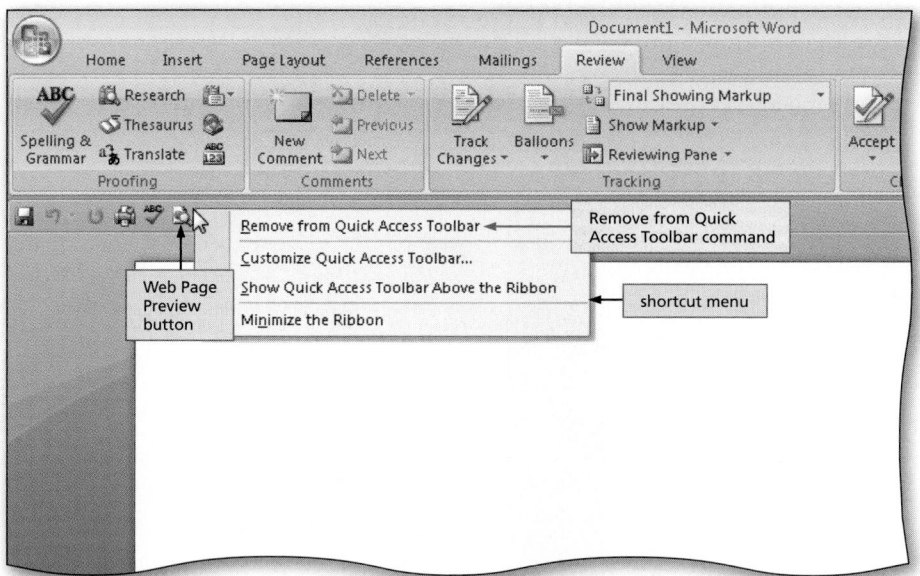

Figure E–20

2

• Click Remove from Quick Access Toolbar on the shortcut menu to remove the button from the Quick Access Toolbar (Figure E–21).

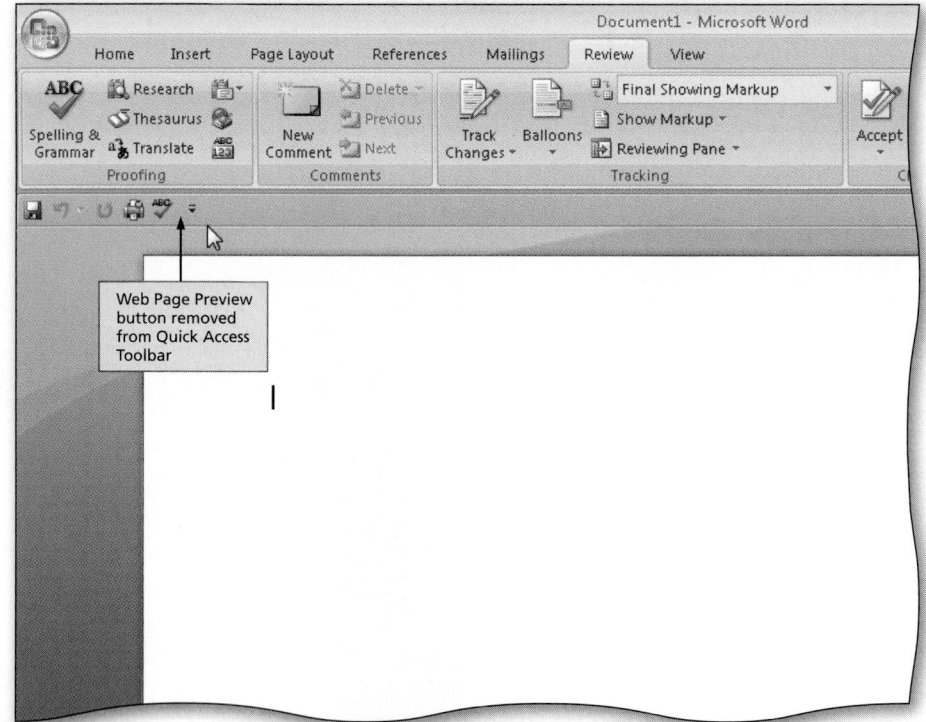

Figure E–21

Other Ways

1. Click Customize Quick Access Toolbar button, click More Commands, click the command you wish to remove in the Customize Quick Access Toolbar list, click Remove button, click OK button

2. If the command appears on the Customize Quick Access Toolbar menu, click the Customize Quick Access Toolbar button, click the command you wish to remove

To Reset the Quick Access Toolbar

1

- Click the Customize Quick Access Toolbar button on the Quick Access Toolbar.

- Click More Commands on the Quick Access Toolbar menu to display the Word Options Dialog box.

- Click the Show Quick Access Toolbar below the Ribbon check box to deselect it (Figure E–22).

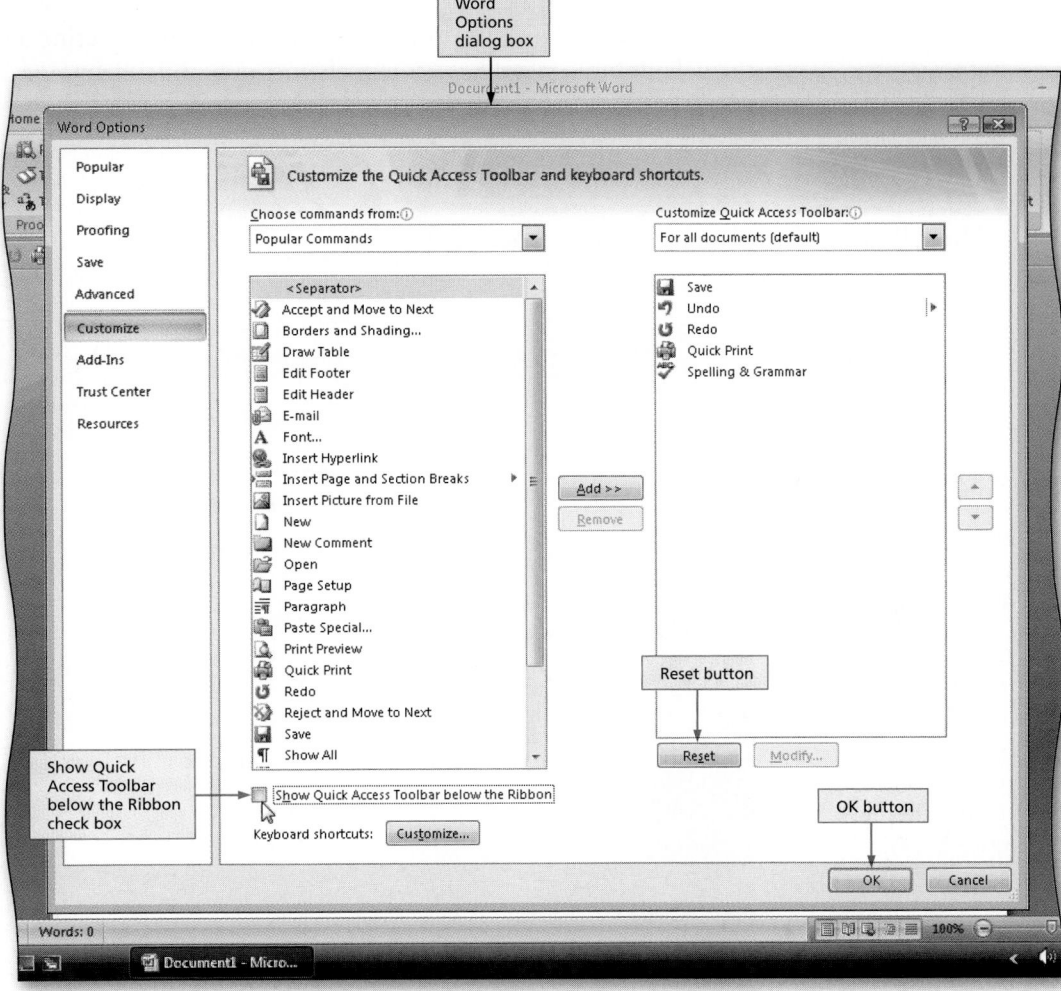

Figure E–22

- Click the Reset button, click the Yes button in the dialog box that appears, and then click the OK button in the Word Options dialog box, to reset the Quick Access Toolbar to its original position to the right of the Office Button, with the original three buttons (Figure E–23).

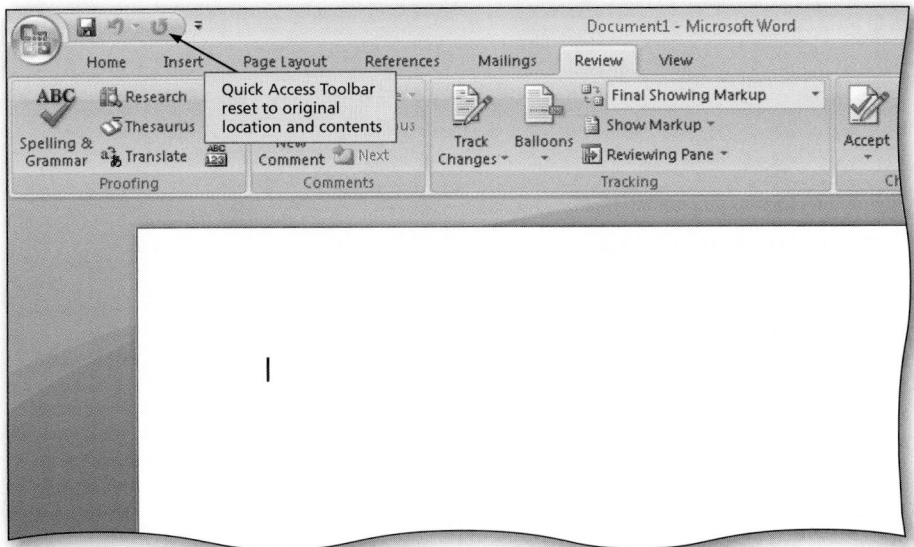

Figure E–23

Changing the Word Color Scheme

The Microsoft Word window can be customized by selecting a color scheme other than the default blue one. Three color schemes are available in Word.

To Change the Word Color Scheme

The following steps change the color scheme.

1
- Click the Office Button to display the Office Button menu.

- Click the Word Options button on the Office Button menu to display the Word Options dialog box.

- If necessary, click Popular in the left pane. Click the Color scheme box arrow to display a list of color schemes (Figure E–24).

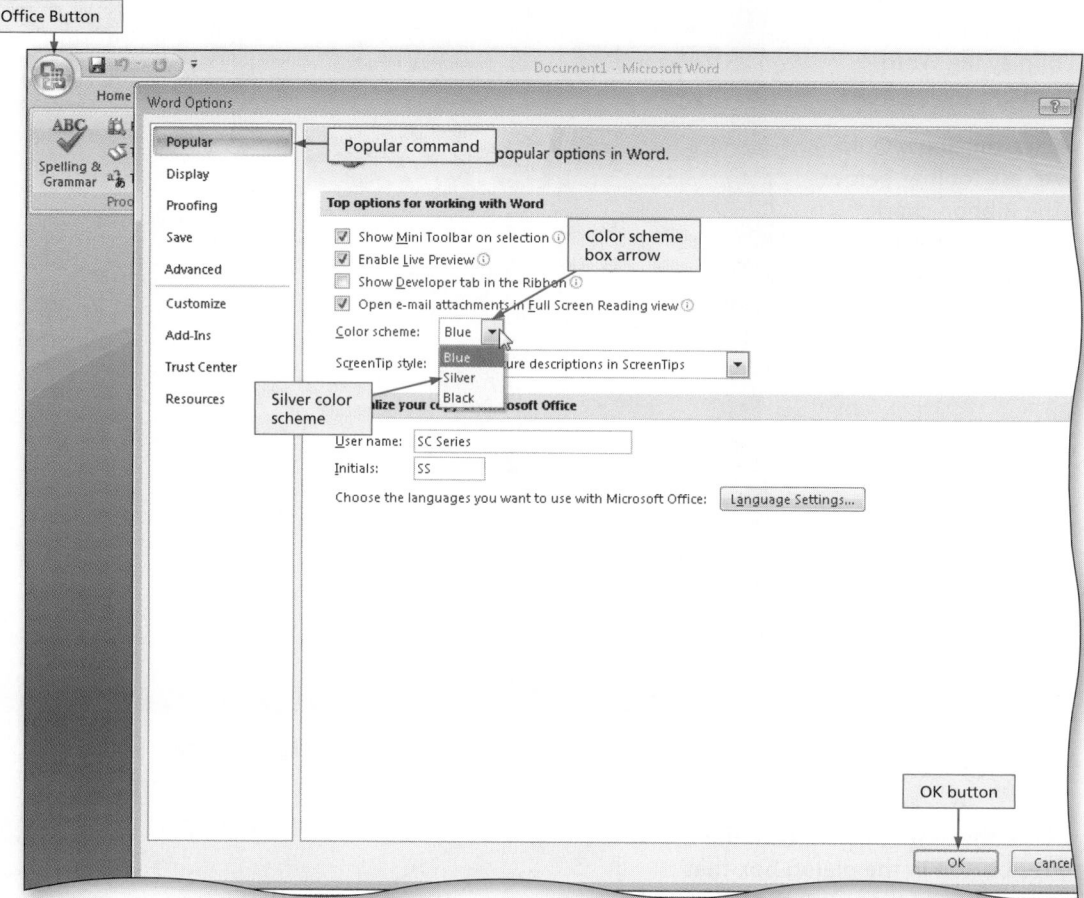

Figure E–24

2
- Click Silver in the list.

- Click the OK button to change the color scheme to silver (Figure E–25).

 How do I switch back to the default color scheme?

Follow the steps for changing the Word color scheme, and select Blue from the list of color schemes.

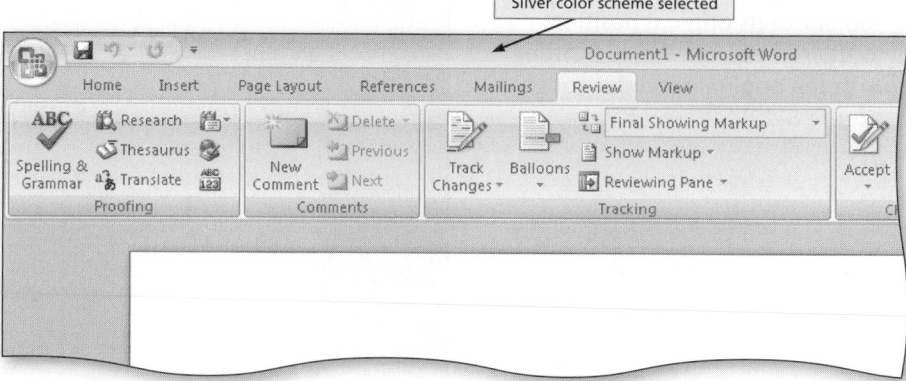

Figure E–25

Appendix F

Steps for the Windows XP User

For the XP User of this Book

For most tasks, no differences exist between using Office 2007 under the Windows Vista operating system and using an Office 2007 program under the Windows XP operating system. With some tasks, however, you will see some differences, or need to complete the tasks using different steps. This appendix shows how to Start an Application, Save a Document, Open a Document, Insert a Picture, and Insert Text from a File while using Microsoft Office under Windows XP. To illustrate these tasks, this appendix uses Microsoft Word. The tasks can be accomplished in other Office programs in a similar fashion.

To Start Word

The following steps, which assume Windows is running, start Word based on a typical installation. You may need to ask your instructor how to start Word for your computer.

1

- Click the Start button on the Windows taskbar to display the Start menu.

- Point to All Programs on the Start menu to display the All Programs submenu.

- Point to Microsoft Office on the All Programs submenu to display the Microsoft Office submenu (Figure F–1).

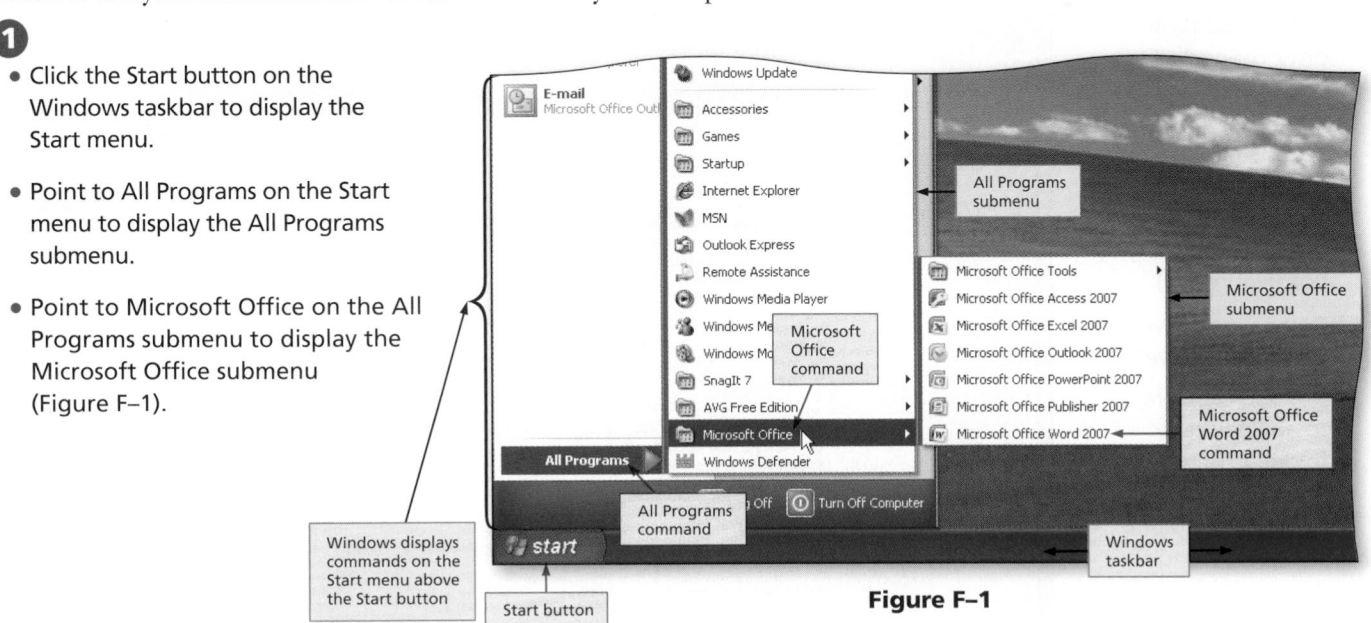

Figure F–1

- Click Microsoft Office Word 2007 to start Word and display a new blank document in the Word window (Figure F–2).

- If the Word window is not maximized, click the Maximize button next to the Close button on its title bar to maximize the window.

- If the Print Layout button is not selected, click it so that your screen layout matches Figure F–2.

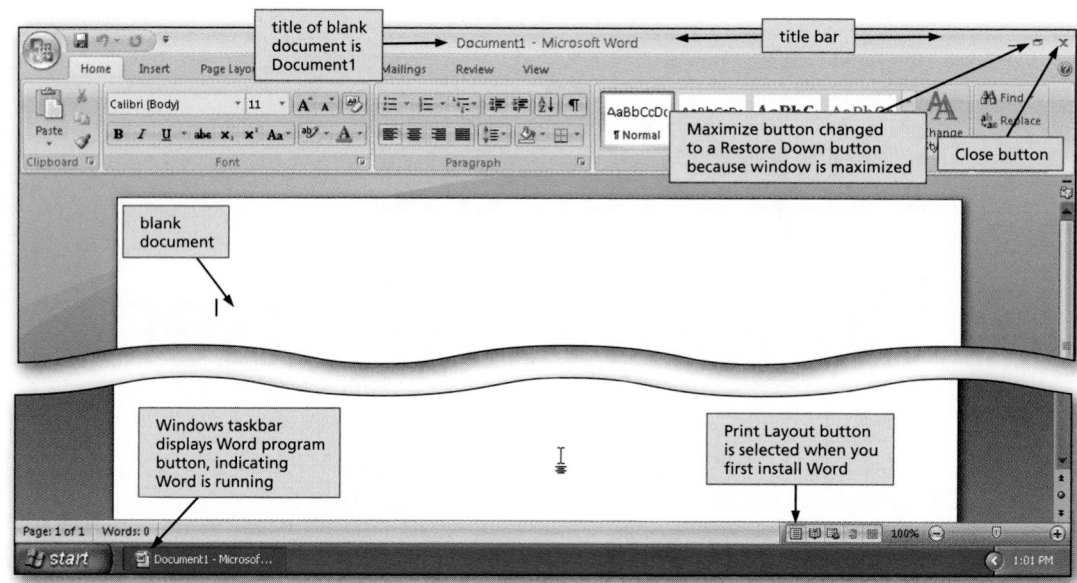

Figure F–2

Other Ways

1. Double-click Word icon on desktop, if one is present
2. Click Microsoft Office Word 2007 on Start menu

To Save a Document

After editing, you should save the document. The following steps save a document on a USB flash drive using the file name, Horseback Riding Lessons Flyer.

- With a USB flash drive connected to one of the computer's USB ports, click the Save button on the Quick Access Toolbar to display the Save As dialog box (Figure F–3).

Q&A

Do I have to save to a USB flash drive?

No. You can save to any device or folder. A **folder** is a specific location on a storage medium. You can save to the default folder or a different folder. You also can create your own folders, which is explained later in this book.

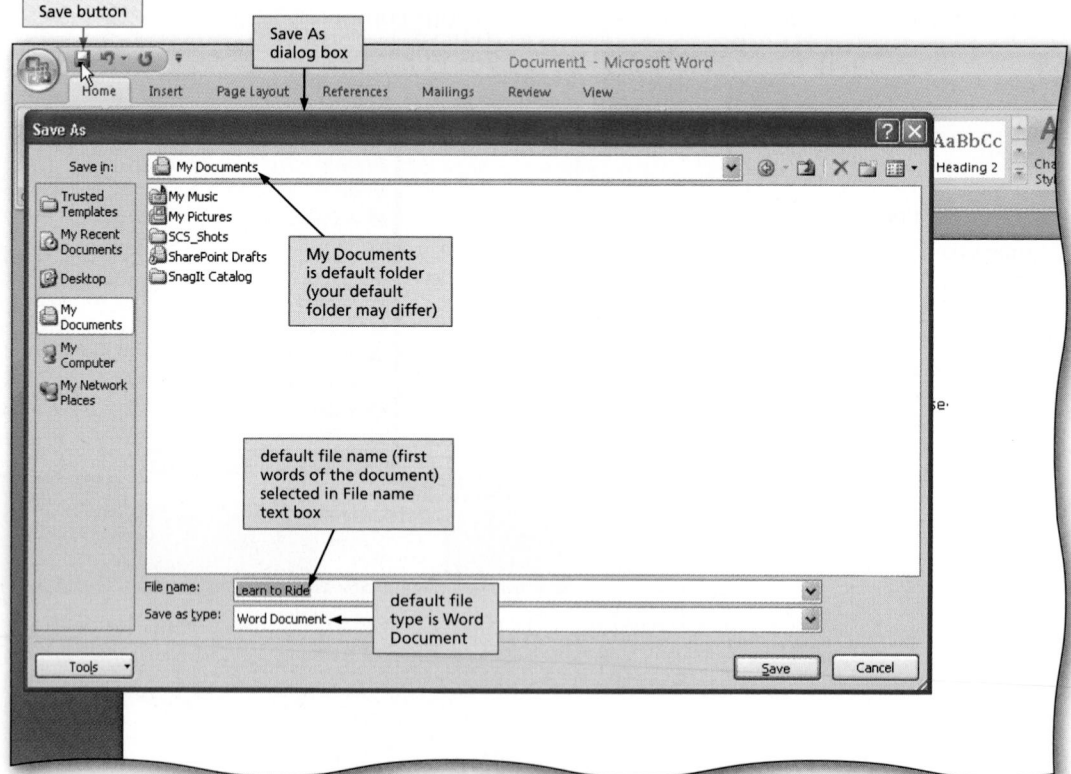

Figure F–3

2

- Type the name of your file (Horseback Riding Lessons Flyer in this example) in the File name text box to change the file name. Do not press the ENTER key after typing the file name (Figure F–4).

Q&A What characters can I use in a file name?

A file name can have a maximum of 255 characters, including spaces. The only invalid characters are the backslash (\), slash (/), colon (:), asterisk (*), question mark (?), quotation mark ("), less than symbol (<), greater than symbol (>), and vertical bar (|).

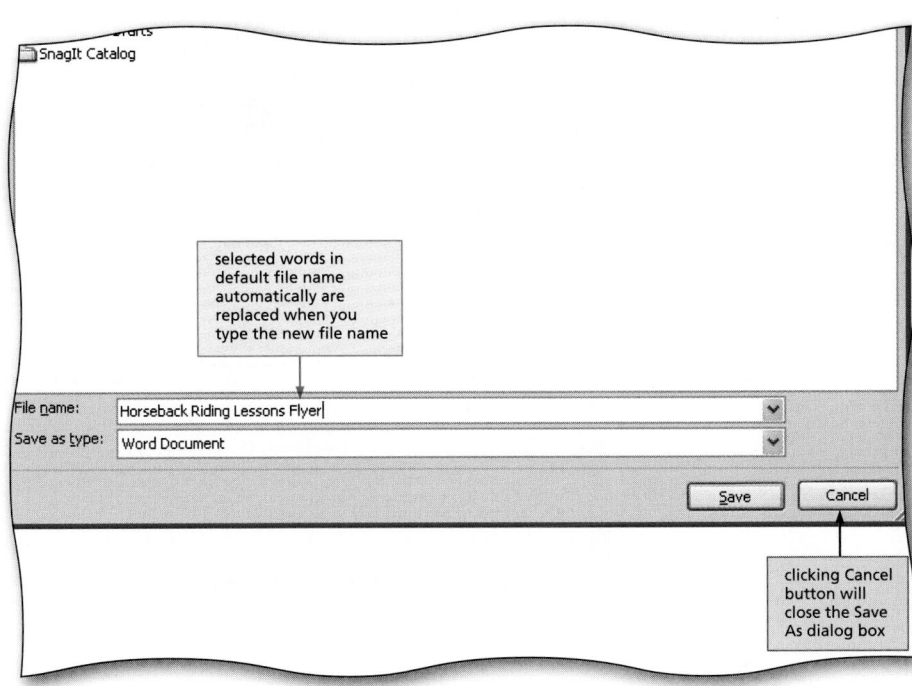

Figure F–4

3

- Click the Save in box arrow to display a list of available drives and folders (Figure F–5).

 Q&A Why is my list of files, folders, and drives arranged and named differently from those shown in the figure?

Your computer's configuration determines how the list of files and folders is displayed and how drives are named. You can change the save location by clicking shortcuts on the **My Places bar**.

Q&A How do I save the file if I am using a USB flash drive?

Use the same process, but be certain to select your device in the Save in list.

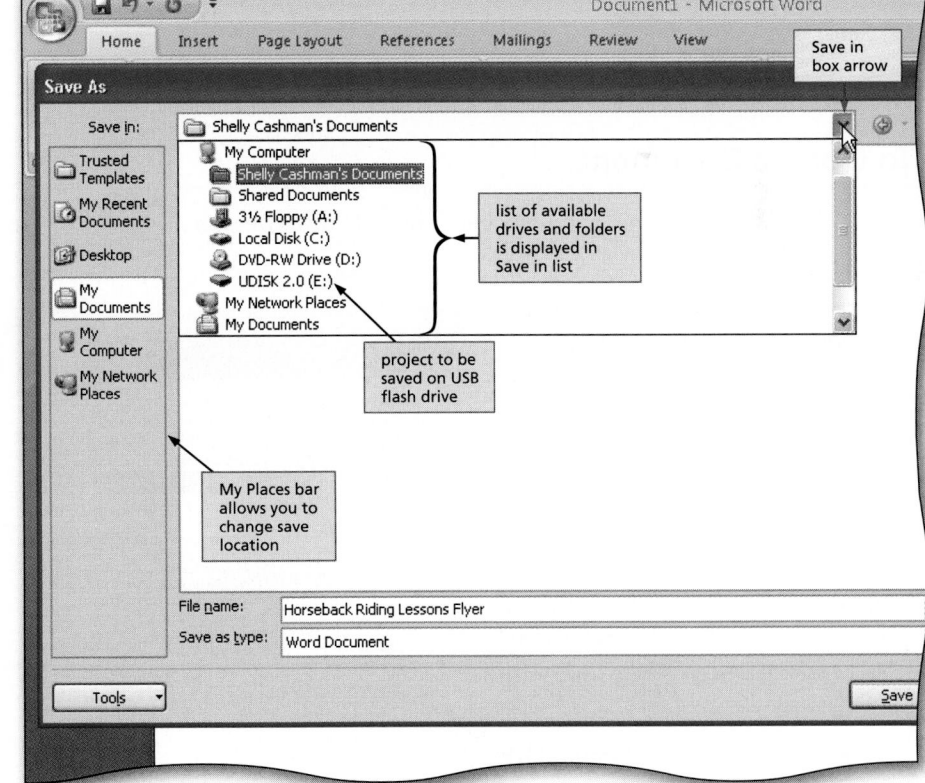

Figure F–5

- Click UDISK 2.0 (E:) in the Save in list to select the USB flash drive, Drive E in this case, as the new save location (Figure F–6).

- Click the Save button to save the document.

Q&A

What if my USB flash drive has a different name or letter?

It is very likely that your USB flash drive will have a different name and drive letter and be connected to a different port. Verify the device in your Save in list is correct.

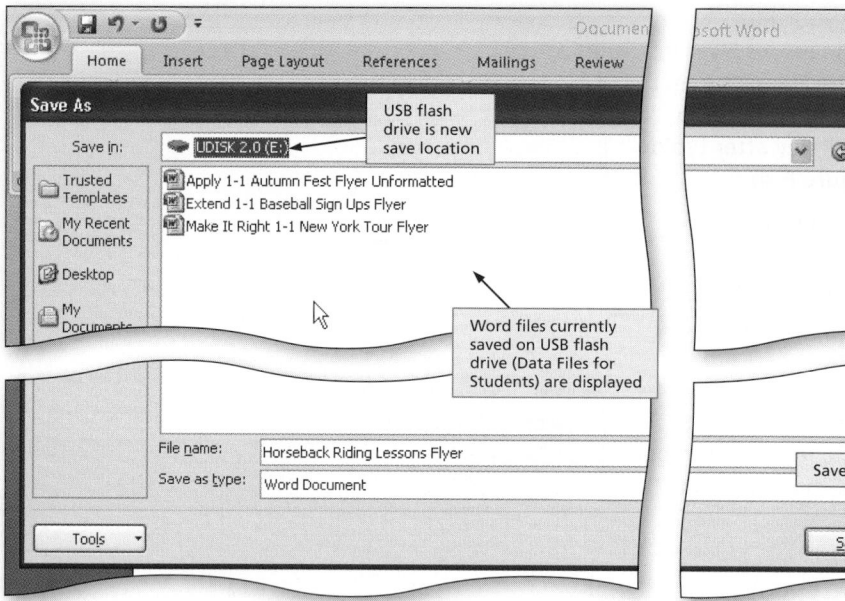

Figure F–6

Other Ways

1. Click Office Button, click Save, type file name, select drive or folder, click Save button

2. Press CTRL+S or press SHIFT+F12, type file name, select drive or folder, click Save button

To Open a Document

The following steps open the Horseback Riding Lessons Flyer file from the USB flash drive.

- With your USB flash drive connected to one of the computer's USB ports, click the Office Button to display the Office Button menu.

- Click Open on the Office Button menu to display the Open dialog box.

- If necessary, click the Look in box arrow and then click UDISK 2.0 (E:) to select the USB flash drive, Drive E in this case, in the Look in list as the new open location.

- Click Horseback Riding Lessons Flyer to select the file name (Figure F–7).

- Click the Open button to open the document.

Q&A

How do I open the file if I am not using a USB flash drive?

Use the same process, but be certain to select your device in the Look in list.

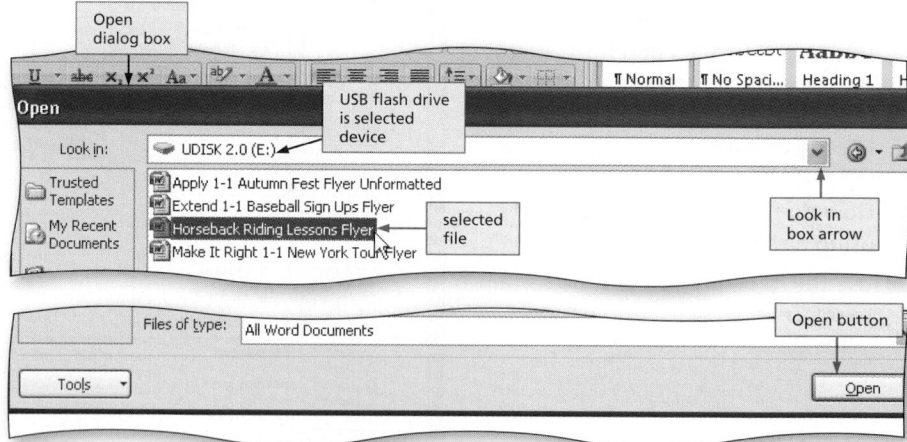

Figure F–7

Other Ways

1. Click Office Button, double-click file name in Recent Documents list

2. Press CTRL+O, select file name, press ENTER

To Insert a Picture

The following steps insert a centered picture, which, in this example, is located on a USB flash drive.

1 Position the insertion point where you want the picture to be located. Click Insert on the Ribbon to display the Insert tab. Click the Insert Picture from File button on the Insert tab to display the Insert Picture dialog box.

2 With your USB flash drive connected to one of the computer's USB ports, if necessary, click the Look in box arrow and then click UDISK 2.0 (E:) to select the USB flash drive, Drive E in this case, in the Look in list as the device that contains the picture. Select the file name of the picture file.

3 Click the Insert button in the dialog box to insert the picture at the location of the insertion point in the document.

To Insert Text from a File

The following steps insert text from a file located on the USB flash drive.

1 Click where you want to insert the text. Click Insert on the Ribbon to display the Insert tab. Click the Object button arrow in the Text group to display the Object menu. Click Text from File to display the Insert File dialog box.

2 With your USB flash drive connected to one of the computer's USB ports, if necessary, click the Look in box arrow and then click UDISK 2.0 (E:) to select the USB flash drive, Drive E in this case, in the Look in list as the device that contains the file. Click to select the file name.

3 Click the Insert button in the dialog box to insert the file at the location of the insertion point in the document.

To Create a New Database

The following steps create a database on a USB flash drive.

1 With a USB flash drive connected to one of the computer's USB ports, click Blank Database in the Getting Started with Microsoft Office Access screen to create a new blank database.

2 Type the name of your database in the File Name text box and then click the 'Browse for a location to put your database' button to display the File New Database dialog box.

3 Click the Save in box arrow to display a list of available drives and folders and then click UDISK 2.0 (E:) (your letter may be different) in the Save in list to select the USB flash drive as the new save location.

4 Click the OK button to select the USB flash drive as the location for the database and to return to the Getting Started with Microsoft Office Access screen.

5 Click the Create button to create the database on the USB flash drive with the file name you selected.

To Open a Database

The following steps use the More button to open a database from the USB flash drive.

1 With your USB flash drive connected to one of the computer's USB ports, click the More button to display the Open dialog box.

2 If necessary, click the Look in box arrow and then click UDISK 2.0 (E:) to select the USB flash drive in the Look in list as the new open location. (Your drive letter might be different.)

3 Select the file name. Click the Open button to open the database.

4 If a Security Warning appears, click the Options button to display the Microsoft Office Security Options dialog box. With the option button to enable this content selected, click the OK button to enable the content.

Appendix G
Microsoft Business Certification Program

What Is the Microsoft Business Certification Program?

The Microsoft Business Certification Program enables candidates to show that they have something exceptional to offer – proved expertise in Microsoft Office 2007 programs. The two certification tracks allow candidates to choose how they want to exhibit their skills, either through validating skills within a specific Microsoft product or taking their knowledge to the next level and combining Microsoft programs to show that they can apply multiple skill sets to complete more complex office tasks. Recognized by businesses and schools around the world, more than 3 million certifications have been obtained in more than 100 different countries. The Microsoft Business Certification Program is the only Microsoft-approved certification program of its kind.

What Is the Microsoft Certified Application Specialist Certification?

The Microsoft Certified Application Specialist certification exams focus on validating specific skill sets within each of the Microsoft Office system programs. Candidates can choose which exam(s) they want to take according to which skills they want to validate. The available Application Specialist exams include:

- Using Microsoft® Windows Vista™
- Using Microsoft® Office Word 2007
- Using Microsoft® Office Excel® 2007
- Using Microsoft® Office PowerPoint® 2007
- Using Microsoft® Office Access 2007
- Using Microsoft® Office Outlook® 2007

> For more information and details on how Shelly Cashman Series textbooks map to Microsoft Certified Application Specialist certification, visit scsite.com/off2007/cert.

What Is the Microsoft Certified Application Professional Certification?

The Microsoft Certified Application Professional certification exams focus on a candidate's ability to use the 2007 Microsoft® Office system to accomplish industry-agnostic functions, for example Budget Analysis and Forecasting, or Content Management and Collaboration. The available Application Professional exams currently include:

- Organizational Support
- Creating and Managing Presentations
- Content Management and Collaboration
- Budget Analysis and Forecasting

Index

3-D
  clustered column worksheet,
    EX 49–54
  pie charts, adding to workbooks,
    EX 204–216
  pie charts, displaying in browser,
    EX 255

A

.accdb files, AC 13
Access
  See also databases
  described, AC 2
  exporting to other applications,
    AC 220–224
  Help, obtaining, AC 61–63
  Navigation pane, AC 126
  program described, APP 5
  quitting, AC 35–36, AC 63, AC 127
  referential integrity, specifying,
    AC 185–191
  reports, creating and printing,
    AC 50–56
  reports, creating Web pages from,
    INT 28–32
  sharing data among applications,
    AC 206–229
  starting, AC 12–13, AC 36–38,
    AC 77
  window, using, AC 17–23
Accessories programs, WIN 14
Accounting Number Format,
    EX 114–116
accounts, obtaining e-mail, EX 142
activities, tracking for e-mail
    contacts, OUT 61–62
add-ins, installing, AC 209
adding
  See also inserting
  3-D pie chart to workbook,
    EX 204–216
  background colors to Web pages,
    WD 221
  borders to Word pages, WD 48–50
  buttons to Quick Access Toolbar,
    PPT 148–150
  commands to Quick Access
    Toolbar, APP 27–31
  fields to database tables, AC 157
  gadgets to Windows Sidebar,
    WIN 10–11

icons to desktop, WIN 16–17
  records to database tables,
    AC 30–33, AC 49, AC 141–148
  shapes, PPT 115–122
  slide transitions, PPT 122–124
  Word table rows, WD 180
Address bar, Windows Explorer,
    WIN 18, WIN 29–30
address, inside, WD 169
addresses, hyperlink, WD 220
addressing, absolute vs. relative,
    EX 186–189
addressing envelopes, WD 203–204
aggregate functions, AC 117–119
aligning text using tab stops,
    WD 158–160
AND criterion, AC 95–96
animated slide shows, PPT 125
append queries, AC 165
application programs
  See also specific program
  described, WIN 4
  integrating with the Web, INT 2–6
  starting, WIN 27–28
applying
  Quick Style, WD 150
  Word table styles, WD 24–25,
    WD 176–177
arguments
  in functions, EX 98, EX 105
  Function Arguments dialog box,
    EX 101
arithmetic operations, EX 92
arrangements, OUT 8
arrows, scroll, WIN 15
art, clip. *See* clip art
Art gallery, WD 49
ascending order, AC 53, AC 192
asterisk (*), Access wildcard, AC 87,
    AC 151
attachments
  adding to e-mail messages,
    OUT 31–32
  viewing e-mail, OUT 22–23
Auto Fill Options, EX 28,
    EX 171–172
AutoCalculate, EX 62–63
AutoCorrect
  in worksheets, EX 19, EX 96,
    EX 129
  vs. building blocks, WD 172–173
  as you type, WD 91–94

AutoFit
  applying to Word tables, INT 9–10,
    WD 178
  using in presentations, PPT 19
AutoFormat, WD 162–163,
    WD 181
AVERAGE function, EX 98–100

B

background colors
  text, on Web page report,
    INT 32–37
  on Web pages, WD 221, WD 222
  on worksheets, EX 110–112
background repagination, WD 107
background styles for presentations,
    PPT 89–90
backing up databases, AC 193
bar charts, INT 14–16
Basic interface, Windows Vista,
    WIN 5–6
best fit, worksheet column width,
    EX 122
BETWEEN operator, AC 95–96
bibliographical lists, creating and
    updating, WD 113, WD 117
bibliography style, changing,
    WD 95
black slides, PPT 39
blank lines, inserting into
    documents, WD 15
bold
  characters in documents, WD 34
  text in presentations, PPT 25
  worksheet cell entries, EX 38
book, steps for Windows XP users of
    this, APP 35–39
borders
  applying to worksheet titles,
    EX 110–112
  around pictures in documents,
    WD 45
  bottom bordering paragraphs,
    WD 161
  page, adding to documents,
    WD 48–50, WD 55
  removing table, INT 7
box borders, applying to worksheet
    titles, EX 110–112
brackets. *See* square brackets

browser
  Internet Explorer. *See* Internet
    Explorer
  Office 2007, Windows Explorer,
    APP 4
  testing Web pages in, WD 223
  viewing and manipulating Web
    pages, EX 260–261, PPT 156–157
  Web, WIN 27
browsing
  Help and Support topics,
    WIN 60–63
  World Wide Web, WIN 29–33
building blocks, creating and
    inserting, WD 170, WD 172–173,
    WD 200
bulleted lists
  in documents, WD 32,
    WD 180–181
  in presentations, PPT 3–5, PPT 29,
    PPT 31–33, PPT 86–89
Business Contact Manager, OUT 54
Business Edition, Windows Vista,
    WIN 5
business letters, WD 166
buttons
  See also specific button
  adding to Quick Access Toolbar,
    INT 19–21, PPT 148–150,
    EX 252–254

C

calculated fields, AC 113
calculating
  sums, AC 117, EX 24–26
  using AutoCalculate, EX 62
calculations
  absolute vs. relative addressing,
    EX 186–189
  formula, EX 90–91
  functions, EX 104
  using in queries, AC 113–116
camera ready publications, APP 6
captions, changing query,
    AC 116–117
cascading deletes, AC 185, AC 188
Category box, Outlook, OUT 33
cells, Word table, WD 173
cells, worksheet
  applying styles to, EX 112
  copying and pasting, EX 174–177

copying using fill handles,
    EX 26–28
correcting errors on, EX 63–66
entering column, row titles,
    EX 19–22
entering text into, EX 18–19
formatting, EX 34–47
inserting and deleting, EX 177–179
moving vs. copying, EX 177
nonadjacent, determining row
    totals in, EX 194
rotating and shrinking entries in,
    EX 114
rotating text in, EX 168–171
selecting, EX 15, EX 47
values, and charting, EX 49
centering
  data in worksheet cells, EX 113
  page contents vertically, WD 50
  paragraphs in documents, WD 26
  Word tables, WD 179
  works cited page title, WD 112
  worksheet cells, EX 40–41
certification
  Microsoft Business Certification
    Program, APP 40
  Microsoft Certified Application
    Specialist, APP 40, AC 60
changing
  color schemes, APP 34
  colors in presentations, PPT 21
  database primary keys, AC 28,
    AC 46
  database properties, AC 60–61
  database structure, AC 26–30,
    AC 156–161
  datasheet appearance, AC 178–180
  document properties, WD 50–52,
    WD 130, WD 182
  document properties in
    presentations, PPT 43–45
  document settings, WD 77–78
  e-mail message formats, OUT 19
  font colors, WD 193
  presentation layouts, PPT 92–95
  screen resolution, APP 21–25
  theme colors in documents, WD 39
  workbook themes, EX 109
  worksheet cells, EX 49
  worksheet column appearance,
    EX 122–124
  worksheet fonts, EX 36–37

worksheet names, EX 140–141
worksheet views, EX 220–223
characters
  formatting in presentations,
    PPT 21–26
  formatting in documents generally,
    WD 22, WD 34
  leader, WD 158
  line break, WD 195
  nonprinting, WD 14, WD 25
  special, inserting, PPT 106
  tab, in documents WD 159–160,
    WD 178
  width in documents, WD 18
charts
  adding 3-D clustered column, to
    worksheet, EX 48–54
  adding 3-D pie chart to workbook,
    EX 204–216
  embedding into documents,
    INT 13–16
  Excel types, EX 48
  inserting titles, data labels,
    EX 206–209
citations
  documentation styles for,
    WD 94–98
  editing, WD 98, WD 104–105,
    WD 109, WD 110
  inserting, WD 96–97
  inserting placeholder, WD 108
  in research papers, WD 76–77
clearing
  paragraph formatting, WD 162
  worksheet cells, ranges of cells,
    EX 66–67
Click and Type feature, WD 85
clicking with mouse, WIN 4
client computers, WIN 4
clip art
  inserting into slides, PPT 95–97
  inserting into documents,
    WD 153–154
  resizing, PPT 101–104
Clip Art task pane, PPT 95–96
Clip Organizer, clip collections,
    PPT 95–99, WD 153
Clipboard
  See also Office Clipboard
  copying and pasting text using,
    WD 119–122

clips
  copyright regulations, Microsoft
    Clip Organizer, PPT 97
  importing, moving, PPT 95,
    PPT 105
closing
  database tables, AC 35
  e-mail messages, OUT 15
  expanded folders, WIN 57
  Help and Support, WIN 63
  tabs on tabbed Web pages, WIN 33
  windows, WIN 21, WIN 24
  Word documents, WD 59–60
code, viewing Web page source,
    EX 258
collaboration
  online, using Office 2007, APP 4
  and SharePoint, APP 7–8
collapsing drives and folders,
    WIN 24, WIN 43
color schemes in documents,
    APP 34, WD 37
coloring
  graphics, WD 156
  text, WD 152–153
  worksheet tabs, EX 216–217
colors
  background, on worksheets,
    EX 110–112
  changing font, PPT 110–111,
    WD 193
  changing in datasheets, AC 179
  changing in presentations, PPT 21
  changing picture border, WD 45
  changing pie chart, EX 213–215
  changing theme, WD 150
  conserving ink, toner, EX 57
  documents, WD 37
  Fill and Font Color buttons,
    EX 200
  font, EX 34, WD 160
  page borders, to documents,
    WD 48–50
  presentations, PPT 20, PPT 21
  themes, EX 107
  transparent, setting in graphics,
    WD 157
  worksheets, workbooks, EX 108
column headers, Windows Explorer,
    WIN 19
columns, Word table, WD 177–178
columns, worksheet
  adjusting, EX 46
  changing width, height,
    EX 122–126

deleting, EX 180
entering titles, EX 19–21
entering titles into, EX 87–89
formatting, EX 114
freezing titles, EX 181–182
hiding, unhiding, changing width,
    EX 122–124
increasing width of, EX 173–174
inserting, EX 179
planning, EX 16
Comma Style format, EX 45,
    EX 114–115, EX 196
Command Bar, Windows Explorer,
    WIN 19
command-line, starting Excel using,
    EX 87
commands
  See also specific command
  Quick Access Toolbar, APP 27–32,
    EX 254, OUT 12–13, PPT 13–14,
    WD 10
  toggling Ribbon, EX 194
compacting databases, AC 193
comparison operators, using in
    criterion queries, AC 94
composing
  See also creating
  e-mail messages, OUT 27–28
compound criteria in queries,
    AC 95–96
computers
  logging on, off, WIN 7–9,
    WIN 64–66
  resolution. *See* resolution
Concourse theme, using, EX 109
conditional formatting operators,
    EX 121–124
conditions in conditional formatting,
    EX 118
constants, replacing formulas with,
    EX 191
contact lists
  creating, OUT 47–48
  saving, displaying, OUT 60–61
  using to address e-mail messages,
    OUT 55–57
contacts
  tracking activities, OUT 61–62
  using, OUT 44–62
content controls
  entering and formatting text in,
    WD 197
  entering more text in, WD 194
  and templates, WD 185–186

contextual tabs, EX 10, PPT 9,
    WD 8
converting
  hyperlinks to text, WD 163–164
  slides from previous PowerPoint
    version, PPT 43
copying
  backing up. *See* backing up
  formulas using fill handles,
    EX 95–96, EX 192–193
  files by right-dragging, WIN 52–54
  items to Office Clipboard, WD 189
  between Office 2007 applications,
    INT 16
  and pasting text, WD 188–192
  slides, PPT 40–41
  worksheet cell formats, EX 201–202
  worksheet cells, EX 26–28, EX
    169–171, EX 174–177
copyright regulations on Microsoft
    Clip Organizer clips, PPT 97
correcting
  errors on worksheets, EX 63–67
  mistakes using AutoCorrect, ,
    AC 34, EX 19–21, WD 91–94
  mistakes while typing, PPT 19
  spelling in worksheets, EX 127–129
  worksheet errors, EX 164
COUNT aggregate function,
    AC 117
cover letters
  creating, WD 146, WD 165–182
  planning effective, WD 149
creating
  contact lists, OUT 47–48
  cover letters, WD 165–182
  database forms, AC 57–58
  database queries, AC 74–103
  database tables, AC 23–26,
    AC 44–49
  databases, AC 13–17, AC 210
  distribution lists, OUT 58–59
  documents using WordPad,
    WIN 44–47
  e-mail messages, OUT 14
  e-mail signature, OUT 23–27
  e-mail view filters, OUT 36–37
  folder on removable drive,
    WIN 39–40
  folders in Outlook, OUT 44–46
  letterhead, WD 149–151
  queries, parameter, AC 89–92
  queries, simple, AC 78–80
  Quick Style, WD 90–91

research papers, WD 74
resumes using templates,
WD 183–186
Web pages from Access reports,
INT 28–32
Web pages from PowerPoint
presentations, INT 23–27
Web pages using Excel,
EX 250–261
Web pages using Word,
WD 216–223
worksheets, EX 3–4
criterion
adding fields to design grid,
AC 85–86
and update queries, AC 162
using comparison operators in,
AC 94
using compound, AC 95–96
using in calculating statistics,
AC 120–121
using in field not included in
results, AC 88–89
using in queries, AC 81–82
using numbers in, AC 93
crosstab queries, AC 122–125
Crosstab Query Wizard,
AC 123–125
currency
format, setting, AC 25
symbols and database data types,
AC 9–10
Currency style, EX 117
current date, inserting, WD 168–169
custom dictionaries for spell-
checking, PPT 55–58, WD 127
customizing
Access Navigation pane, AC 126
Office 2007, APP 21–34
Outlook, OUT 5–6
Quick Access Toolbar, APP 26–33,
OUT 12–13
Word window, APP 25–26
cutting and pasting. *See* copying,
pasting

D

data
centering in worksheet cells,
EX 113
entering into Word tables,
WD 174–175

data types
changing in database fields, AC 169
and database design, AC 5, AC 9–10
Database Design Language
(DBDL), AC 8
database fields
deleting, AC 156
moving in table structure, AC 156
multivalued, adding, AC 160–161
using calculated, AC 113–116
database forms, creating, AC 57–58
database management systems, AC–2
database records
adding to tables, AC 30–33,
AC 38–40, AC 49
deleting, AC 148, AC 163–164
described, AC 4
duplicates, finding, AC 191
filtering, AC 148–156
grouping, AC 52, AC 121–122
ordering, AC 192–195
restricting in joins, AC 112
saving, AC 33
sorting, AC 97–103
unmatched, finding, AC 191
updating, AC 141–147
database tables
adding records to, AC 30–33,
AC 38–40, AC 49
closing, AC 35
creating, AC 23–26, AC 44–49
joining, AC 103–107
and make-table queries, AC 165
naming, AC 8
previewing and printing, AC 40–43
removing from queries, AC 89
saving, AC 27
with validation rules, updating,
AC 169–178
databases
See also Access
backup, recovery, repair, compact,
AC 193
changing structure of, AC 26–30,
AC 156–161
creating, AC 13–17, AC 210
datasheets. *See* datasheets
described, AC 2
designing, AC 6–12
exporting to other applications,
AC 220–224
importing worksheets into,
AC 212–215

maintenance generally, AC 138,
AC 140
mass changes, making, AC 162–164
naming tables, fields, AC 8
opening, AC 36–38, AC 77
properties, changing, AC 60–61
querying. *See* queries, querying
records. *See* database records
resizing datasheet columns,
AC 175–176
sharing data between Access,
AC 217
tables. *See* database tables
undoing changes, AC 34
validation rules, using, AC 165–178
Datasheet Formatting dialog box,
AC 181–184
Datasheet view, AC 30, AC 82,
AC 146
datasheets
changing appearance of,
AC 178–180
resizing columns in, AC 175–176
and subdatasheeets, AC 190–191
totals in, AC 176–178
dates
formatting of, EX 183–185
inserting current, WD 168–169
MLA documentation style, WD 84
DBDL (Database Design
Language), AC 8
debugging described, EX 135–136
decimal places
in Access, AC 47–48
in Excel, EX 23
decisions
making with IF function,
EX 189–190
what-if analysis. *See* what-if analysis
default value, and validation rules,
AC 165, AC 167
defining database tables, AC 24–26
delete queries, AC 163–164
Deleted Items folder, OUT 7,
OUT 21
deleting
See also removing
database fields, AC 156
database records, AC 148
desktop icons, WIN 25
e-mail messages, OUT 21, OUT 37
embedded charts, EX 67
files, WIN 56–57

placeholders, PPT 104
text and lines, WD 193
text from existing documents,
    WD 59
text from presentations, PPT 58
text in presentation placeholder,
    PPT 42–43
text with BACKSPACE key, WD 13
Word table rows, WD 180,
    WD 186–187
WordArt, PPT 111
worksheet cells, EX 177–179
worksheet columns, rows, EX 180
deletions from documents, WD 58
delimited files, AC 218
demoting text in presentations,
    PPT 34
descending sort order, AC 53,
    AC 99, AC 192
Design view
  clearing design grid, sorting
    records, AC 98–103
  creating queries in, AC 82
  described, AC 31
designing
  See also planning
  database queries, AC 76
  databases, AC 5–6, AC 6–12
  letterheads, WD 149–150
desktop
  features and navigation of,
    WIN 10–18
  icons, deleting, opening windows
    using, WIN 18, WIN 25
  Windows Explorer, using,
    WIN 18–21
  windows, opening, closing, sizing,
    WIN 21–24
destination
  area, copying to in, EX 27
  drives, folders, copying files,
    WIN 52
Dialog Box Launcher
  Access, AC 20
  Excel, EX 11, EX 198
  Outlook, OUT 12
  PowerPoint, PPT 11
  Word, WD 9
dialog boxes
  See also specific dialog box
  described, WIN 25
dictionaries
  main, custom, WD 127
  spell-checking, PPT 55–58

disabling database content, AC 38
displaying
  e-mail contacts, OUT 52
  folder contents, WIN 44, WIN 54
  formatting marks in documents,
    WD 14, WD 77
  presentations in grayscale,
    PPT 59–61
  rulers in documents, WD 87
  system date on worksheets,
    EX 183–185
distribution lists, creating,
    OUT 58–59
Document Information Panel,
    PPT 44, WD 51–53
document properties
  changing in documents, WD 50–52,
    WD 130–131, WD 182, WD 202
  changing in worksheets, EX 54–57
  changing in presentations,
    PPT 43–45
documents
  See also specific products
  attaching to e-mail messages,
    OUT 31–32
  creating, saving in WordPad,
    WIN 44–52
  requirements, described, EX 3–5
  Word. *See* Word documents
dollar signs ($) in Excel, EX 23,
    EX 114, EX 116–117, EX 187
domain names in URLs, WIN 28–29
.dotm files, WD 150
double-clicking mouse, WIN 10,
    WIN 18
double-spacing, WD 78
down scroll arrow, WIN 15
downloading hierarchy of folders,
    WIN 40–41
draft quality printing, WD 53,
    WD 130
Drafts folder, OUT 7
drag-and-drop editing, WD 119,
    WD 121
dragging
  described, WIN 15
  right-. *See* right-dragging
  windows to move, resize,
    WIN 22–23
  worksheet cells, EX 179
dragging with dropping
  arranging slides, PPT 41–42
  moving worksheet cells, EX 177
Draw Table feature, WD 179

drives, AC 13
  expanding, collapsing, WIN 42–43
  network, WIN 37
  path names and (table), WIN 37
  USB flash. *See* USB flash drives
duplicating. *See* copying

E

e-mail
  account, obtaining, EX 142
  described, OUT 2
  E-mail Filter feature, OUT 33
  spam filter, OUT 14
E-mail Filter feature, OUT 33
e-mail messages
  attachments, adding to,
    OUT 31–32
  closing, printing, OUT 15–16
  composing, formatting,
    OUT 27–31
  contact lists, using to address,
    OUT 55–57
  deleting, OUT 21, OUT 37
  flagging, OUT 33–35
  forwarding, OUT 20
  importance, sensitivity, delivery
    options, OUT 38–42
  opening, OUT 10
  outgoing, working with,
    OUT 23–32
  replying to, OUT 16–17
  rules, applying, OUT 42
  saving in different formats,
    OUT 60–61
  signatures, creating and inserting,
    OUT 23–27
  sorting, OUT 35–36
  view filters, applying, OUT 36–37
  viewing attachments, OUT 22–23
e-mailing workbooks, EX 142–143
Ease of Access icon, WIN 7
editing
  citation sources, WD 104–105
  citations, WD 98, WD 110
  drag-and-drop, WD 119, WD 121
  embedded objects, INT 13
  in-cell, on worksheets, EX 64–65
  Word table cells, WD 175
editions of Windows Vista, WIN 5
electronic mail. *See* e-mail
embedded charts in worksheets,
    EX 49, EX 67

endnotes, WD 100, WD 106
Enhanced Screen Tips
 Access, AC 20
 Excel, EX 11
 Outlook, OUT 11
 PowerPoint, PPT 10
 Word, WD 9
Enterprise edition, Windows Vista,
 WIN 5
envelope icon on e-mail message,
 OUT 9, OUT 21
envelopes, addressing, printing,
 WD 203–204
equal sign (=) and formulas, EX 91,
 EX 92, EX 99
error checking worksheets, EX 129
error messages
 database compacting error, AC 193
 #REF!, EX 180
errors, correcting, EX 63–67,
 PPT 58, WD 57–60
Excel
 See also spreadsheets, worksheets
 adding to startup submenu, EX 167
 Auto Fill Options, EX 28,
  EX 171–172
 calculating sums, EX 24–26
 charts, EX 48–53
 charts, embedding into documents,
  INT 13–16
 creating Web pages using,
  EX 250–261
 described, EX 2–3
 e-mailing workbook within,
  EX 142–143
 Edit mode, EX 63–64
 exporting Access data to,
  AC 221–222
 exporting data from Web sites,
  EX 137–140
 file management tools, EX 259–261
 font type, style, size, color,
  EX 34–47
 functions in, EX 82, EX 104,
  EX 99–105
 Help, EX 7, EX 67–68
 importing into Access database,
  AC 212–215
 numeric limitations of, EX 22
 Office Button, EX 14
 program described, APP 5
 quitting, EX 59

selecting cells, EX 15, EX 47
smart tags, option buttons,
 EX 96–97
spell checking worksheets,
 EX 127–129, EX 218
starting, EX 6–7, EX 87
what-if analysis, using, EX 162,
 EX 164, EX 223–227
workbooks, EX 7
worksheet window, using, EX 9–15
exclamation point icon on e-mail
 message, OUT 8
expanding folders, drives, WIN 23,
 WIN 42
exploding (offsetting) pie charts,
 EX 213–215
exporting
 data from Access, AC 207, AC 209,
  AC 220–224
 XML data, AC 226–227

F

Favorite Folders pane, OUT 7
Favorites Links list, Windows
 Explorer, WIN 19
fields, database
 adding to design grid, AC 85
 changing, AC 46–48
 defining, AC 24–26
 described, AC 4
 naming, AC 8
file attachments, viewing,
 OUT 22–23
file management
 methods for, WIN 52–58
 tools , EX 259–261, PPT 155–157
file names, WD 18, WD 53
file specifications, WIN 29
File Transfer Protocol (FTP),
 publishing Web pages via,
 APP 19–20
files
 attaching to e-mail messages,
  OUT 31–32
 copying by right-dragging,
  WIN 52–54
 deleting by right-clicking,
  WIN 56–57
 e-mail view, OUT 36–37
 naming database, AC 13, AC 15
 naming presentation, PPT 27

organizing using hierarchical
 format, WIN 36–37
renaming, WIN 55
text. *See* text files
Word, WD 18
Fill and Font Color buttons, EX 200
fill effects
 adding to presentations, PPT 89–90
 adding to Web page background,
  WD 222
fill handles
 copying formulas using, EX 95–96,
  EX 192–193
 copying range of cells using,
  EX 104–105
 copying worksheet cells using,
  EX 26–28, EX 169–171
Filter By Form, AC 153–154
Filter By Selection, AC 149
filtered Web Page format, WD 218
filtering database records,
 AC 148–156
filters
 clearing database record, AC 151
 E-mail Filter feature, OUT 33
 e-mail spam, OUT 14
Find and Replace dialog box,
 WD 124
Find command, locating text using,
 PPT 90
finding
 See also searching
 Outlook contacts, OUT 44,
  OUT 50
FIRST aggregate function, AC 117
First Line Indent marker, WD 88
first-line indents in documents,
 WD 88–89
fixed-width files, AC 218
flags, e-mail, OUT 33–35
flash drives, WIN 37
floating dollar signs, formatting in
 worksheets, EX 114, EX 116–117
folders
 See also specific folder
 closing expanded, WIN 57
 collapsing, WIN 24
 creating, OUT 44–46
 creating on removable drives,
  WIN 39–40
 creating using WordPad,
  WIN 47–52

displaying contents of, WIN 44, WIN 54

downloading hierarchy of, WIN 40–41

expanding, WIN 23

naming, WIN 38

organizing using hierarchical format, WIN 36–37

Outlook, OUT 7–8

path names and (table), WIN 37

saving to, AC 15

saving WordPad document in new, WIN 47–52

source and destination, when copying files, WIN 52–54

Web. *See* Web folders

working with, WIN 34–35

Follow Up submenu, OUT 34–35

Font gallery, PPT 109

font sets, WD 37

fonts

changing color, EX 39, PPT 110–111, WD 193

changing in datasheets, AC 179

changing in worksheets, EX 36–38

changing size in documents, WD 28

changing theme, WD 39–40

coloring, WD 160

increasing size, WD 151–152

sans serif, PPT 94

sizing, WD 23

using, EX 34

using in presentations, PPT 20, PPT 25–26

footers in documents, WD 79–83

footnotes in documents, WD 99–106

foreign keys, and referential integrity, AC 185

Form view, AC 57, AC 143, AC 146

Format Painter, PPT 106, PPT 111–113

Format Painter button, EX 201–203

format symbols, EX 180

formats

See also specific format

datasheet, changing, AC 178–180

e-mail message, OUT 19

hierarchical, organizing files and folders, WIN 36

import support, PPT 98

saving presentations, PPT 26

specifying data field, AC 168–169

undoing on worksheets, EX 66

verifying using Range Finder, EX 106–107

Web page, PPT 152, EX 256–257

Word documents, WD 36–40

formatting

AutoFormat, WD 162–163

characters in presentations, PPT 21–26

clearing, WD 162

conditional, in worksheets, EX 118–121

dates in worksheets, EX 114

e-mail messages, OUT 27–31

numbers in worksheets, EX 44–45, EX 114–118

pictures in documents, WD 40–42

pie charts, EX 204–216

shapes, PPT 115–122

single vs. multiple paragraphs in documents, WD 26–32

system date, EX 183–185

text as hyperlinks, WD 220–221

text in content controls, WD 197

text using Quick Styles, PPT 106–108

text using shortcut keys, WD 86

Web pages, WD 220–223

What-If Assumptions table, EX 203

Word documents generally, WD 22

worksheet cells, EX 34–47

worksheet column titles, EX 42–43

worksheet titles, EX 110, EX 199–200

worksheets, EX 107–114

worksheets generally, EX 33–34

formatting marks in documents, WD 14, WD 77, WD 150

forms

creating database, AC 2, AC 57–60

updating databases using, AC 141–148

Formula AutoComplete, EX 99

formula bar, EX 12

formulas

absolute vs. relative addressing, EX 186–189

copying using fill handles, EX 95–96, EX 192–193

copying worksheet, EX 201–202

determining values using goal

seeking, EX 225–228

entering using Point mode, EX 93–94

entering IF functions in worksheets, EX 189–190

entering into worksheets, EX 90–91

replacing with constants, EX 191

version of worksheet, printing, EX 135–136, EX 191

forwarding e-mail messages, OUT 20

freezing worksheet titles, EX 181–182

FTP locations, and Web folders, EX 252

Function Wizard, EX 26

functions

See also specific function

absolute vs. relative addressing, EX 186–189

entering into worksheets, EX 98

generally, EX 82

G

Gadget Gallery, WIN 10–11

gadgets, adding, removing from Windows Sidebar, WIN 10–12

galleries

See also specific gallery

Access, AC 20

Excel, EX 112

Outlook, OUT 18

PowerPoint, PPT 9–10

Word, WD 8

Goal Seek command, using for formula values, EX 225–228

grammar checking in documents, WD 16–17, WD 125–126

graphical user interfaces (GUIs)

Basic, and Windows Aero, WIN 5–6

described, WIN 3

graphics

See also pictures

coloring, WD 156

described, WD 153

resizing, WD 155

setting transparent color in, WD 157

sizing handles on, PPT 101

grayscale
  displaying presentation in,
    PPT 59–61
  printing in, EX 57
greater than (>) operator, AC 94
greater than or equal to (>=)
    operator, AC 94
gridlines
  changing in datasheets, AC 179
  viewing, INT 9
  worksheet, EX 7
grids, adding fields to, AC 85
grouping
  database records, AC 52
  using with statistics, AC 121–122
groups on Excel Ribbon, EX 9
Grow Font button, WD 151–152
guidelines for planning, APP 1–2

H

handouts, printing presentations as,
    PPT 125–130
hanging indents in documents,
    WD 116
hard copies of worksheets, EX 57
hard page breaks, WD 112
headers in documents, WD 79–83
headings
  e-mail message, OUT 10
  formatting worksheet, EX 200
  in worksheets, EX 7–8, EX 43
Help
  Access, AC 61–63
  Excel, EX 7, EX 67–68
  Office 2007, APP 7, APP 9–10,
    WIN 58–63
  Outlook, OUT 62–64
  PowerPoint, PPT 63–64
  Word, WD 60–61
hiding
  formatting marks in documents,
    INT 7, WD 14
  worksheet columns, rows, EX 122,
    EX 126–127
hierarchical format, organizing files
    and folders using, WIN 36
Home Basic edition, Windows Vista,
    WIN 5
home pages, INT 6, WIN 28
Home tab
  Excel Ribbon, EX 9–10

PowerPoint Ribbon, PPT 9
horizontal ruler in documents,
    WD 87
HTML (Hypertext Markup
    Language)
  e-mail message format, OUT 19
  saving documents in HTML
    format, WD 218–219
  viewing Web page source code,
    EX 258
HTTP (Hypertext Transfer
    Protocol), Web pages and,
    WIN 28
hyperlinks
  See also links
  adding to reports, INT 32–34
  converting to text, WD 163–164
  formatting text as, WD 220–221
  inserting into PowerPoint Web
    pages, INT 11–13
  inserting into documents, INT 6–7
  inserting text for, INT 11
  testing, INT 24
  using, verifying, APP 4, INT 27,
    INT 39
Hypertext Transfer Protocol
    (HTTP), WIN 28
hyphen, nonbreaking, WD 171

I

icons
  See also specific icon
  Access, AC 37
  adding to desktop, WIN 16–17
IF function
  making decisions using,
    EX 189–190
  nesting, EX 195
images. *See* graphics, photographs,
    pictures
Import Spreadsheet Wizard,
    AC 211–215
importance, e-mail setting,
    OUT 38–42
importing
  clips, PPT 95
  data between databases, AC 217
  data from Access generally, AC 206,
    AC 209, AC 211
  data into Excel using Web query,
    EX 137–140

files into Clip Organizer,
    PPT 97–98
  vs. linking data, AC 216
  worksheets into databases,
    AC 212–215
in-Ribbon gallery, EX 10
Inbox, Outlook, OUT 7–10
indenting paragraphs, WD 196
infinity symbol, and referential
    integrity, AC 188
inner joins, AC 104
Insert function dialog box, EX 98,
    EX 101, EX 104
Insert Hyperlink feature,
    INT 11–13, INT 33
Insert mode, EX 64–65, WD 58
inserting
  See also adding
  blank lines in documents, WD 15
  building blocks, WD 172
  citation placeholders, WD 101
  citations and sources, WD 96–97
  clip art into documents,
    WD 153–154
  clip art into slides, PPT 95
  clips into content placeholders,
    PPT 96–97
  current date, WD 168–169
  e-mail signatures into e-mail
    messages, OUT 23–27
  footnotes reference marks, WD 100
  hyperlinks into PowerPoint Web
    pages, INT 11–13
  hyperlinks into documents,
    INT 6–7
  leader characters, WD 158
  nonbreaking space, WD 171
  page numbers in documents,
    WD 82
  photographs into slides,
    PPT 106–107
  pictures in documents, WD 40–42
  special characters, PPT 106
  synonyms in text, WD 124–125
  tables into documents, INT 7–8
  text into existing documents,
    WD 58
  Word tables, WD 173–174
  worksheet cells, columns,
    EX 177–179
insertion point
  in Access work area, AC 18

in documents, WD 6
in worksheets, EX 17
inside address and salutation,
   WD 169
installing add-ins, AC 209
Instant Search boxes, WIN 31
integrating Office 2007 applications
   and Web, INT 2–6
integrity, referential. *See* referential
   integrity
Internet
   Access and, APP 5
   e-mail contact links, OUT 59
   Excel and, APP 5
   Office 2007 and, APP 4
   PowerPoint and, APP 6
   Publisher 2007 and, APP 6
   Word and, APP 5
Internet Explorer described,
   WIN 27–28
intranets, and Office 2007, APP 4
italicizing text
   in presentations, PPT 21
   in documents, WD 36

J

joining
   changing join properties,
      AC 108–109
   database tables, AC 103–107,
      AC 112
junk e-mail, E-mail Filter feature,
   OUT 33
Junk E-mail folder, OUT 7

K

Key Tips
   Access, AC 23–26
   Excel, EX 15
   Outlook, OUT 14
   PowerPoint, PPT 15–16
   Word, WD 12
keyboard
   described, WIN 3
   indicators, status bar, EX 9
   as input device, WIN 26
   scrolling in documents, WD 43
   selecting range using, EX 97
   shortcuts, notation for, WIN 26
   worksheet formulas, entering using,
      EX 91

keychain drives, WIN 37–38
keys
   See also specific key
   primary. *See* primary keys
   shortcut, WD 86
   sorting, AC 98–103
keywords
   database properties, AC 60–61
   in presentation document
      properties, PPT 43
   in document properties, WD 50

L

labels
   chart data, EX 204
   mailing, WD 204
landscape orientation
   printing datasheets, AC 40–41
   printing worksheets, EX 129–132
   for slide shows, PPT 6
LAST aggregate function, AC 117
Layout gallery, PPT 92
layouts
   home pages, INT 6
   presentation, PPT 6, PPT 92–95
   resizing datasheet columns,
      AC 175–176
leader characters, inserting, WD 158
left-aligned text in worksheet cells,
   EX 18, EX 22, EX 168
Left Indent marker, WD 88
less than (<) operator, AC 94
less than or equal to (<=) operator,
   AC 94
letterhead
   creating, WD 149–151
   saving, WD 164
levels, paragraph, PPT 19, PPT 38
line breaks, inserting, WD 194–195
line spacing in documents,
   WD 78–79
line wraps in presentations, PPT 18
lines
   deleting, WD 193
   join, AC 105–106
   selecting, WD 27
Link Spreadsheet Wizard, AC 211
Linked Table Manager, updating
   query links with, AC 216
linking data to Access databases,
   AC 211, AC 216, AC 217

links
   See also hyperlinks
   bulleted. *See* bulleted lists
   creating in workbooks, EX 258
   Excel worksheet to Access data,
      AC 206
   updating using Linked Table
      Manager, AC 216
lists
   bibliographical, creating, WD 113
   bulleted. *See* bulleted lists
   and data conversion, AC 206
   research paper sources, WD 111
live preview, AC 20, EX 10,
   OUT 18, PPT 9, WD 8
logging on, off your computer,
   WIN 7–9, WIN 64–66
logical operators in IF functions,
   EX 189
Lookup fields
   creating, AC 158–160
   multivalued, AC 173–174
   using in queries, AC 172–175
Lookup Wizard, AC 158–160

M

magnifying. *See* zooming
mail, electronic. *See* e-mail
Mail Folders, OUT 7
mailing labels, creating and printing,
   WD 204
major sort keys, A 97, AC 102
make-table queries, AC 165
managing files. *See* file management
margins, changing worksheet's,
   EX 130–132
mathematical operations
   using, AC 113
   using AutoCalculate, EX 62–63
MAX function, EX 98, EX 101–102
MAX (largest value) aggregate
   function, AC 117
maximizing
   windows, AC 13, WIN 20
   Word Help, WD 61
maximums, determining using
   AutoCalculate, EX 62–63
MCAS (Microsoft Certified
   Application Specialist), AC 60,
   AC 122

menus
See also specific menu
described, WIN 13
shortcut. *See* shortcut menus
merging worksheet cells, EX 40–41
message pane, OUT 8–9
messages
e-mail. *See* e-mail messages
error. *See* error messages
metadata
database properties, AC 60–61
worksheet, workbook properties,
EX 54
presentation document properties,
PPT 43
MHTML file format, PPT 154
Microsoft Business Certification
Program, APP 40
Microsoft Certified Application
Professional, APP 40
Microsoft Certified Application
Specialist, APP 40, AC 60,
AC 122
Microsoft Clip Organizer, PPT 95
Microsoft Office 2007. *See*
Office 2007
Microsoft Office Access 2007.
See Access
Microsoft Office Excel 2007.
See Excel
Microsoft Office Outlook 2007.
See Outlook
Microsoft Office PowerPoint 2007.
See PowerPoint
Microsoft Office Professional
Edition 2007, APP 3
Microsoft Office Publisher 2007,
APP 6
Microsoft Office Word 2007.
See Word
Microsoft SharePoint, APP 7–8
Microsoft Windows Vista. *See* Vista
Microsoft Windows XP.
See Windows XP
MIN function, EX 98, EX 102–104
MIN (smallest value) aggregate
function, AC 117
Mini toolbar
Access, AC 21
Excel, EX 12
PowerPoint, PPT 11–12
Word, WD 9–10, WD 151

minimizing
Access Ribbon, AC 19
Excel Ribbon, EX 10
Outlook Ribbon, OUT 11
PowerPoint Ribbon, PPT 9
windows, WIN 19
Word Ribbon, WD 7
minor sort keys, AC 97, AC 102
mistakes
See also AutoCorrect
correcting while typing in
worksheets, EX 19
correcting while typing in
documents, WD 91–94
MLA documentation style
applying, WD 95
date format, WD 84
described, WD 76–77
headers, WD 80
works cited page, WD 111
Mode indicators, status bar, EX 9
modifications to documents, WD 58
modifying. *See* changing
money, currency symbols, and
database design, AC 9–10
monitors
changing screen resolution,
APP 21–25
described, WIN 3
mouse
described, WIN 3
operations, WIN 26
pointer in Access, AC 18
pointer in PowerPoint window,
PPT 7
pointer in Word, WD 7
pointing, clicking with, WIN 4
scrolling in documents, WD 43
moving
to another slide in presentation,
PPT 46–48
clips, PPT 105
text, WD 119–122
vs. copying worksheet cells, EX 177
windows by dragging, WIN 22
Mozilla Firefox, WIN 27
MSN MoneyCentral Investor Stock
Quotes, EX 139
multi-level bulleted lists, PPT 33
multivalued database fields,
AC 160–161, AC 181–184

multivalued Lookup fields,
AC 173–174
My Collections, PPT 95

N

Name box, using, EX 47
names
changing worksheet, EX 140–141
file, WD 18
user. *See* user names
naming
database files, AC 13, AC 15
database tables, fields, AC 8
folders, WIN 38
PowerPoint files, PPT 27
Web pages, INT 6
Word documents, WD 20
workbooks, EX 29, EX 31
worksheets, workbook files, EX 29,
EX 86, EX 216–217
Navigation buttons, AC 38–39
Navigation pane
Access, AC 18–19, AC 126
Outlook, OUT 7–8
Windows Explorer, WIN 19
negative numbers, handling, EX 197
nesting IF functions, EX 195
network drives, WIN 37
networks described, WIN 37
New Message Ribbon, OUT 18
nonbreaking spaces, hyphens,
inserting, WD 171
nonprinting characters, WD 14,
WD 25
Normal style, WD 23, WD 150
Normal view, EX 129, PPT 46,
PPT 91, PPT 92
NOT (not equal to) operator, AC 94
Notes Page view, PPT 8
Notes pane, PPT 8
NOW function, displaying system
date on worksheets, EX 183–185
numbers
calculating. *See* calculating,
calculations
entering as text into worksheets,
EX 24
entering into range of worksheet
cells, EX 90

entering into worksheets,
EX 22–24, EX 180–181
formatting in worksheets, EX 44–45
formatting using Ribbon,
EX 114–118
negative, EX 197

O

Object Linking and Embedding
(OLE) feature, INT 13
objects
on desktop, WIN 10
sizing embedded, INT 17–18
source and destination (OLE),
INT 13
Office 2007
applications, copying between,
INT 16
customizing, APP 21–34
Help, APP 7, APP 9–10
online collaboration using, APP 4
programs in, APP 3–6
Office Button
Access, AC 22–23
Excel workbook control, EX 14
Outlook, OUT 13–14
Word, WD 10
Office Clipboard
copying and pasting text,
WD 188–192
copying graphics using, WD 190
copying worksheet cells using,
EX 174–175
pasting from, WD 191–192
Office Collections, PPT 95
Office Theme, PPT 16, PPT 109
offsetting charts, EX 213–214
OLE (Object Linking and
Embedding) feature, INT 13
one-to-many relationships, and
referential integrity, AC 185
online collaboration using
Office 2007, APP 4
opening
databases, AC 36–38, AC 77
documents, WD 56–57
link in tabbed Web page,
WIN 31–32
presentations, PPT 54–55
Start Menu, WIN 13–15
windows, WIN 18, WIN 21–22
workbooks, EX 60–61

operating systems, WIN 2
operations, arithmetic, EX 92
operators
comparison. *See* comparison
operators
conditional formatting, EX 121–124
logical, in IF functions, EX 189
OR criterion, AC 95–96
ordering
database records, AC 192–195
descending, ascending,, AC 53
organizations, and domain name
extensions (table), WIN 29
organizing
arranging slides, PPT 41–42
e-mail contacts, OUT 51, OUT 53
e-mail messages, OUT 33–37
files and folders, WIN 36–37
Outbox folder, OUT 7, OUT 17
outer joins, AC 104
Outline tab, PowerPoint window,
PPT 8
outlines, viewing presentation as,
INT 27
outlines, printing presentations as,
PPT 125–130
Outlook
Contacts, using, OUT 44–62
described, OUT 2
e-mail message options,
OUT 38–43
Help, using, OUT 62–65
Inbox panes, OUT 7–10
incoming messages, working with,
OUT 10–23
organizing e-mail messages,
OUT 33–37
outgoing messages, working with,
OUT 23–32
program described, APP 6
quitting, OUT 65
starting and customizing, OUT 5–6
overtype mode, EX 64–65, WD 58

P

page breaks
automatic, WD 107–108
manual, WD 112
Page Layout View, EX 129–132
page numbers, inserting in
documents, WD 82

page setup, EX 136
pages
Web. *See* Web pages
Word documents. *See* Word
documents
panes
See also specific pane
splitting windows into, EX 222–223
paper clip icon on e-mail message,
OUT 8
Paragraph Dialog Launcher,
WD 158
paragraph mark (¶), WD 14
paragraphs
bottom borders, WD 161
centering in documents, WD 26
changing spacing above, below,
WD 50–51, WD 195
first-line indent, WD 88–89
formatting, WD 22, WD 26–32
indenting, WD 196
right-aligned, WD 81
spacing in documents, WD 78–79
tab stops, WD 159–160
parameter queries, AC 89–92
parentheses (( ))
in calculated fields in queries,
AC 113
in functions, EX 100
overriding formula order of
operations, EX 92
parenthetical citations, WD 76
passwords, determining your, WIN 8
paste area, EX 27
Paste Options button, WD 122,
WD 192
Paste Special, INT 13, INT 16
pasting
and copying text, WD 188–192
from Office Clipboard,
WD 191–192
text, WD 119
worksheet cells, EX 175–177
path names, drives, folders (table),
WIN 37
paths described, WIN 29
PDF format
exporting to, AC 209
saving documents in, WD 183
viewing, AC 224
Percent style format, EX 118

Personal information management (PIM) programs, APP 6
photographs
  See also pictures
  inserting into slides, PPT 98–99
  resizing, PPT 103
pictures
  applying styles in documents, WD 44
  inserting in documents, WD 40–42
  photographs and Clip Organizer, PPT 97–98
Pictures folder, WIN 21
pie charts
  adding 3-D, to workbook, EX 204–216
  exploding (offsetting), EX 213–214
PIM (personal information management) programs, APP 6
pixels described, EX 122
placeholders
  deleting, PPT 104
  deleting text in presentation, PPT 42–43
  inserting citation, WD 101, WD 108
  inserting clips from Clip Organizer, PPT 96–97
  in presentations, PPT 7, PPT 19, PPT 34
plain text, e-mail message format, OUT 19
planning
  See also designing
  calculations, EX 24
  cover letter and resume, WD 149
  cover letters, WD 165
  charts, EX 48
  flyers, WD 12
  graphics in documents, WD 41
  pie charts, EX 204
  presentations, PPT 3, PPT 16, PPT 18, PPT 20, PPT 84
  projects, guidelines for, APP 1–2
  research papers, WD 76, WD 83–84
  resume Web page, WD 216
  slide content development, PPT 86
  Web pages, PPT 148
  Word documents, WD 4, WD 23
  worksheets, EX 16, EX 85, EX 90, EX 108, EX 165–166, EX 196

plus sign (+)
  mouse pointer, EX 8
  in Inbox folder, OUT 10
Point mode, entering formulas using, EX 93–94, EX 101
point size
  in presentations, PPT 21
  in worksheet cells, EX 34, EX 38
pointing with mouse, WIN 4
pop-up menus, Slide Show view, PPT 51–52
portrait orientation
  printing datasheets, AC 40–41
  printing worksheets, EX 129
  for slide shows, PPT 6
positioning
  graphics on slides, PPT 105
  paper orientation, printing, AC 40–41
  Quick Access Toolbar, APP 26–27
postal codes, AC 12
PowerPoint
  See also presentations
  creating hyperlinks in, INT 27–29
  creating Web pages using, PPT 146–157
  described, PPT 2–3
  document themes, PPT 16–17
  file management tools, PPT 155–157
  files, naming, PPT 27
  Help, PPT 63–64
  Key Tips, PPT 15–16
  Mini toolbar, shortcut menus, PPT 11–12
  Office Button, PPT 14–15
  program described, APP 6
  Quick Access Toolbar, PPT 13–14
  quitting, PPT 52–53, PPT 65
  Ribbon, PPT 8–10
  saving, PPT 26
  starting, PPT 5–6, PPT 53, PPT 84–85
  window, using, PPT 6–8
presentations
  See also PowerPoint; slides
  adding new slide to, PPT 29–31
  animated slide shows, PPT 125
  background styles, choosing, PPT 89–90
  with bulleted lists, PPT 86–89

  changing document properties, PPT 43–45
  changing layouts, PPT 92–95
  changing views to review, PPT 90–91
  correcting errors in, PPT 58
  creating text slide with, PPT 31–32
  creating title slide, PPT 85–86
  creating Web pages from, INT 23–27
  creating with illustrations and shapes, PPT 82–100
  deleting text from, PPT 58
  ending, PPT 39–40
  exporting XML data, AC 226–227
  formatting characters in, PPT 21–26
  opening, PPT 54–55
  planning, PPT 3, PPT 84
  printing, PPT 61–62
  printing as outlines and handouts, PPT 125–130
  saving, PPT 26–29, PPT 45–46
  saving as Web pages, PPT 153–154
  speaker's delivery skills, PPT 82
  spell checking, PPT 55–58
  transparencies in, PPT 62
  viewing in Slide Show view, PPT 48–52
previewing
  database tables, AC 40–43
  e-mail contacts, OUT 53–54
  gallery choices, Outlook, OUT 18
  presentations, PPT 126–128
  printouts, EX 60
  Web pages, PPT 151–152, EX 252–255
  worksheets before printing, EX 132–124
Previous Location button, Windows Explorer, WIN 18
primary keys
  changing, AC 28, AC 46
  in database fields, AC 4, AC 5, AC 8
  and referential integrity, AC 185
Print dialog box, EX 133
Print Layout view, WD 6
print preview
  Word, WD 57, WD 201–202
  Excel, EX 60
Print Scaling option, EX 137

Print What list, PPT 126
printers, selecting, PPT 128
printing
  Access reports, AC 56, AC 111
  in black and white, EX 218
  conserving ink, toner, WD 53,
    EX 57, EX 57–58
  database table relationship, AC 188
  documents, WD 53–55,
    WD 130–131
  e-mail contacts, OUT 53
  e-mail messages, OUT 15–16
  envelopes, WD 203–204
  handouts, PPT 129–130
  mailing labels, WD 204
  presentations, PPT 61–62,
    PPT 128–129
  presentations as outline and
    handouts, PPT 125–130
  queries, AC 83
  range of pages, AC 43
  resumes, WD 185
  worksheets, EX 129–135
printouts, EX 57
Professional Edition, Office 2007,
  APP 3
programs
  See also specific program
  in Microsoft Office 2007, APP 3–6
  PIM (personal information
    management), APP 6
projects
  Access, AC 2–6
  cover letter and resume,
    WD 146–149
  creating Web pages using
    PowerPoint, PPT 146–148
  creating Web pages using Word,
    WD 216–217
  financial projection worksheet,
    EX 162–167
  maintaining databases, AC 138–139
  Office 2007 application integration,
    INT 2–6
  Outlook, OUT 3–4
  planning guidelines, APP 1–2
  presentation with bulleted lists,
    PPT 3–5
  presentations with illustrations and
    shapes, PPT 82–84
  querying databases, AC 74–76
  research paper creation, WD 74–76

saving workbook, EX 29–32
sharing data among applications,
  AC 206–209
Word document with picture,
  WD 2–4
workbook with chart saved as Web
  page, EX 251–252
worksheet with embedded chart,
  EX 2–5
worksheet with formulas, functions,
  queries, EX 82–86
promoting text in presentations,
  PPT 34
proofreading, WD 76, WD 118
properties
  automatically updated, PPT 44,
    WD 51
  database, changing, AC 60–61
  database table join, AC 108–109
  document. *See* document properties
protocols. *See also specific protocol*
Publisher 2007, and PowerPoint,
  APP 6
publishing
  Access reports, AC 225
  resumes as Web pages,
    WD 216–217
  Web pages, PPT 148
  Web pages to Web servers,
    APP 19–20
  workbooks, EX 252
punctuation, spacing after, WD 106

Q

queries
  append, make-table, AC 165
  calculating statistics, AC 117–122
  calculations, using, AC 113–116
  changing captions, AC 116–117
  creating, using, printing, AC 80–85
  criteria, using in, AC 81–82,
    AC 85–86
  crosstab, AC 122–125
  delete, AC 163–164
  designing database, AC 76
  lookup fields, using, AC 172–175
  omitting duplicates, AC 100–101
  parameter, AC 89–92
  printing, AC 83
  saved, using, AC 92
  saving, AC 91

sorting records, AC 97–103
table joins, AC 103–107
top-values, creating, AC 102–103
update, AC 162–163
using compound criteria in,
  AC 95–96
using criterion in calculating
  statistics, AC 120–121
using multivalued fields in,
  AC 181–184
Web. *See* Web queries
wildcards, using, AC 87
querying
  databases generally, AC 74
  multivalued fields on, AC 182–184
question mark (?), Access wildcard,
  AC 87, AC 151
Quick Access Toolbar
  Access, AC 22
  adding button to, PPT 148–150,
    EX 252–254
  adding commands to, INT 19–21
  customizing, resetting, APP 26–33
  Excel, EX 13, EX 65
  Outlook, OUT 12–13
  PowerPoint, PPT 13–14
  removing commands, APP 32
  resetting, APP 33, EX 258
  Word, WD 10–11
Quick Parks gallery, WD 198
Quick Styles
  applying, WD 150
  creating, WD 90–91
  in documents, WD 36
  formatting text using, PPT 106–108
quitting
  Access, AC 35–36, AC 63, AC 127
  Excel, EX 59
  Outlook, OUT 65
  PowerPoint, PPT 52–53, PPT 65
  Word, WD 55, WD 62, WD 132
quotation marks ("") in Access text
  fields, AC 82

R

Range Finder, using, EX 106–107,
  EX 164
range of values, AC 165, AC 166
RE:, in e-mail messages, OUT 17
reading e-mail messages, OUT 10
Reading pane, OUT 9–10

Really Simple Syndication, RSS Feeds folder, OUT 7
records, database, AC 4
recovering databases, AC 193
redoing and undoing changes, AC 34
redundancy, removing from databases, AC 5, AC 10–12
#REF! error message, EX 180
referencing, absolute vs. relative, EX 186–189
referential integrity, specifying, AC 185–191
Refresh button, Windows Explorer, WIN 18
refreshing worksheet data, EX 139
relational operators, conditional formatting, EX 121
relationships, database
  determining, implementing, AC 9
  and referential integrity, AC 185–191
relative vs. absolute addressing, EX 186–189
removable media
  creating folder on, WIN 39–40
  types of, WIN 37–38
removing
  See also deleting
  commands from Quick Access Toolbar, APP 32, EX 254
  gadgets from Windows Sidebar, WIN 12
  panes from windows, EX 223
  redundancy from databases, AC 10–12
renaming
  files, WIN 55
  worksheets, EX 216–217
repagination, background, WD 107
repairing databases, AC 193
replying to e-mail messages, OUT 16–17, OUT 19
Report Wizard, AC 52–55, AC 111, INT 29–32
reports
  Access, creating and printing, AC 50–56, AC 225
  adding hyperlinks on Web page report, INT 32–34
  changing text background color, INT 32–37

creating from database table joins, AC 108–111
creating Web pages from Access, INT 28–32
required fields, AC 165
requirements documents and planning worksheets, EX 3–5
research papers
  creating, WD 74
  proofreading, WD 118
Research task pane, WD 128–130
reserved words, symbols
  for database creation, AC 15
  in worksheets, workbooks, EX 31
  folder names, WIN 38
  in Word window, WD 20
resizing
  charts, EX 53
  clip art and photographs, PPT 101–104
  database fields, AC 84
  datasheet columns, AC 175–176
  graphics using Size dialog box, WD 155
  images proportionately, INT 19
  shapes, PPT 117–118
  windows, WIN 19
  Word table columns, WD 177–178
resizing graphics in documents, WD 46–47
resizing handles, Word tables, WD 178
resolution
  changing screen, APP 21–25
  decreasing monitor's, PPT 5
  optimizing screen, WIN 8
Restart command, WIN 7
restoring windows, WIN 20
restructuring databases, AC 138
resumes
  creating using template, WD 183–186
  described, WD 146
  planning, WD 149
  printing, WD 185
Ribbon
  Access, AC 19–21
  Excel, EX 9–11, EX 114–118, EX 194
  Outlook, OUT 11–12, OUT 18, OUT 48

PowerPoint, PPT 8–9
screen resolution and, APP 24–25
Word, APP 25–26, WD 7–9, WD 86
rich text, e-mail message format, OUT 19
right-aligning
  paragraphs, WD 81
  text in worksheet cells, EX 168
right-clicking
  deleting files by, WIN 56–57
  mouse, WIN 12
right-dragging
  to copy files, WIN 52–54
  to delete desktop icon, WIN 25
rotating
  pie charts, EX 209–210
  text in worksheet cells, EX 168–171
  worksheet cell entries, EX 114
round tripping MHTML files, PPT 154
row selector, AC 28
rows, Word table
  adding, deleting, WD 180
  deleting, WD 186–187
  resizing, WD 178
rows, worksheet
  changing height, EX 126
  deleting, EX 180
  entering titles, EX 21–22, EX 88
  freezing titles, EX 181–182
  hiding, EX 126, EX 127
  inserting, EX 177–179
  planning, EX 16
RSS Feeds folder, OUT 7
ruler
  displaying, WD 158
  setting custom tab stops using, WD 167
rulers in documents, WD 87
rules
  database validation, AC 165–178
  e-mail, OUT 42

S

salutation of cover letter, WD 169
sans serif, fonts, using for titles, PPT 108
Save as Web Page command, INT 22

Saved Exports feature, AC 225
Saved Imports feature, AC 219–220
saved queries, using, AC 92
saving
  Access reports, AC 55
  database files, AC 16–17
  database queries, AC 91, AC 107
  database records, AC 33
  database tables, AC 27, AC 44
  documents in PDF, XPS formats,
    WD 183
  Outlook information in different
    formats, OUT 60–61
  presentations, PPT 26–29,
    PPT 45–46
  presentations as Web pages,
    PPT 153–154
  templates, WD 164
  Word documents, WD 18–21,
    WD 87
  Word documents as Web pages,
    INT 19–22, WD 218–219
  Word documents to Web servers,
    WD 219
  Word documents with same file
    name, WD 53
  workbooks as Web pages,
    EX 256–257
  WordPad documents, WIN 47–52
  workbooks, EX 29–32, EX 106
scaling prints, EX 137
schemas
  exporting XML, AC 226–227
  Word color, APP 34
screen resolution, APP 21–25,
  PPT 5, WIN 8
Screen Tips
  Access, AC 20
  Outlook, OUT 10–11
scroll bar
  in Access window, AC 19
  in PowerPoint window, PPT 7
  in Word window, WD 7
  in worksheet window, EX 9
scroll bars, box, WIN 15
scrolling in documents, WD 43
Search box, Windows Explorer,
  WIN 18
Search Folders folder, OUT 7,
  OUT 43
searching
  Access Help, AC 61–63

for database records, AC 145–146
  Excel Help, EX 67–68
  information using Research task
    pane, WD 128–130
  Outlook Help, OUT 63–64
  Word Help, APP 11–15,
    WD 60–61
secondary sort keys, AC 97
security
  e-mail settings, OUT 43
  untrusted content warning, Access,
    AC 38
Select Browse Object menu,
  WD 118–119
selecting text, techniques for,
  WD 120
selection rectangle, and resizing
  graphics, PPT 101
sensitivity analysis. *See* what-if
  analysis
sensitivity, e-mail setting,
  OUT 38–42
Sent Items folder, OUT 7
servers
  described, WIN 4, WIN 37
  publishing Web pages on, WD 219,
    EX 252
  Web. *See* Web servers
services, Office SharePoint
  Server 2007, APP 7–8
shadowing text, PPT 110
Shape Quick Style, PPT 119–120
shapes, adding formatting,
  PPT 115–122
Shared Collections, PPT 95
SharePoint services, and
  collaboration, APP 7–8
sharing
  Access data among applications,
    AC 206–229
  workbooks, EX 14
shortcut keys, WD 86
shortcut menus
  in Access, AC 21
  described, WIN 17
  in Excel, EX 12
  in PowerPoint, PPT 12
  using, WIN 25
  in Word, WD 9–10, WD 102–103
shortcuts
  keyboard. *See* keyboard shortcuts
  menu. *See* menu shortcuts

shoulder surfing, PPT 88
shrinking
  worksheet cell entries, EX 114
  worksheet, chart appearance,
    EX 220–223
Shut Down command, WIN 7
signatures, e-mail, OUT 23–27
Simple Query Wizard, AC 78–80
Single File Web page format,
  PPT 152, EX 256
Size dialog box, WD 155
sizing
  fonts in documents, WD 23,
    WD 28, WD 151–152
  objected embedded in documents,
    INT 17–18
  windows by dragging, WIN 23
  worksheet columns using best fit,
    EX 122
  worksheets, EX 9, EX 135–136
sizing handles on graphics, PPT 101
Sleep command, WIN 8
slide indicator, PPT 47–48
Slide pane, PowerPoint window,
  PPT 8
slide shows
  See also presentations
  described, PPT 2
Slide Sorter view, reviewing
  presentations in, PPT 91
slides
  adding to presentation, PPT 29–31
  adding transitions, PPT 122–124
  animated shows, PPT 125
  arranging, PPT 41–42
  changing layouts, PPT 92–95
  creating title, PPT 85–86
  described, PPT 6
  inserting clip art into, PPT 95
  inserting photographs into,
    PPT 98–99
  replacing text in, PPT 59
  using bulleted lists, PPT 86–89
Slides tab, PowerPoint window,
  PPT 8
soft page breaks, WD 107
sorting
  contact lists, OUT 49
  e-mail messages, OUT 35–36
  query records, AC 97–103
source code, viewing Web page,
  EX 258

source drives, folders, copying files, WIN 52–54

sources, citation, WD 96–97, WD 99, WD 109

spaces, inserting nonbreaking, WD 171

spacing, paragraph, WD 195

spam, e-mail filter, OUT 14

special characters, inserting, PPT 106

specifications, file, WIN 29

spell checking
  documents, WD 16–17, WD 125–126
  presentations, PPT 55–58
  workbooks, worksheets, EX 127–129, EX 218

split forms, AC 57–59, AC 63

splitter bar in PowerPoint window, PPT 8

splitting
  merged worksheet cells, EX 41
  windows into panes, EX 222–223

spreadsheets. *See* worksheets

SQL Server and multivalued database fields, AC 160

square brackets ([]), use in parameter queries, AC 89, AC 90

standard deviation aggregate function, AC 117

Standard toolbar, OUT 7–10

Start menu
  opening, WIN 13–15
  opening window using, WIN 21–22
  starting application programs, WIN 27–28

start pages, WIN 28

Start Search box, Start Menu, WIN 44–47

starting
  Access, AC 12–13, AC 36–38, AC 77
  application programs, WIN 27–28
  Excel, EX 6–7
  Outlook, OUT 5–6
  PowerPoint, PPT 5–6, PPT 53, PPT 84–85
  Windows Vista, WIN 7
  Word, WD 4–5

Startup submenu, adding programs to, EX 167

statistical functions, EX 98

statistics
  calculating in queries, AC 117–122
  word count in documents, WD 107

status bar
  Access, AC 19
  Excel, EX 9
  PowerPoint, PPT 8
  Word window, WD 7

STDEV (standard deviation) aggregate function, AC 117

stock quotes, MSN MoneyCentral Investor Stock Quotes, EX 139

storage media for databases, AC 14

style formats in documents, WD 38

style sets in documents, WD 36–38

styles
  See also specific style
  applying picture in documents, WD 44
  applying Word, WD 24–26
  background, for presentations, PPT 89–90
  bibliography, WD 95
  business letter, WD 166
  changing worksheet cell, EX 35–38, EX 42–43
  footnote text, WD 102–105
  MLA documentation style, WD 76–77
  modifying using Styles task pane, WD 114–115
  using in presentations, PPT 21
  Word document, WD 24–26
  Word table, WD 176–177
  worksheet cell, applying, EX 112

subdatasheets, AC 190–191

submenus
  Access, AC 22–23
  described, OUT 14
  Excel, EX 14
  PowerPoint, PPT 15
  Word, WD 10

subtitles, selecting for worksheets, EX 16

Sum button, using, EX 97, EX 102

SUM (total) aggregate function, AC 117

sums, calculating, EX 24–26, EX 28–29

support. *See* Help and Support

symbols
  format, AC 168, EX 180

infinity, for many- relationship, AC 188

reserved words. *See* reserved words, symbols

synonyms, finding and inserting, WD 124–125

system date, displaying on worksheets, EX 183–185

T

tab characters
  in documents, WD 159–160
  in Word tables, WD 178

tab stops
  aligning text using, WD 158–160
  setting custom, using ruler, WD 167

tabbed Web pages, WIN 31–32

Table of Contents, Help and Support, WIN 62–63

tables, database. *See* database tables

tables, Word. *See* Word tables

tabs
  See also specific tab
  Access Ribbon, AC 19–20
  coloring worksheet, EX 216–217
  New Message Ribbon, OUT 18
  PowerPoint, PPT 8–9
  in Ribbon feature, OUT 11
  on tabbed Web pages, WIN 33
  worksheet, EX 7, EX 141
  worksheet window, EX 9–10

tag names, citations, WD 101

tags, smart, EX 96–97

task pane
  Access, AC 20
  Clip Art, PPT 95–96
  Clipboard, WD 191–192
  Excel, EX 11
  Outlook, OUT 12
  PowerPoint, PPT 11
  Research, WD 128–130
  Word, WD 9

templates
  creating databases using, AC 13–14
  creating resume using, WD 183–186
  database table, AC 26
  saving, WD 164
  Word document, WD 146

testing
  hyperlinks, INT 24, WD 221
  Web pages in Web browser,
    WD 223
  Web sites, INT 38–39
text
  adding to shapes, PPT 119
  aligning using tab stops,
    WD 158–160
  bold in documents, WD 34
  coloring, WD 152–153
  converting hypertext to,
    WD 163–164
  copying and pasting, WD 188–192
  data, using in criterion queries,
    AC 86–87
  deleting, WD 193
  deleting from presentations,
    PPT 58
  entering into documents,
    WD 12–15
  entering into WordPad documents,
    WIN 47
  entering into worksheets, EX 15–19
  entering more in content controls,
    WD 194
  finding and replacing, WD 123–125
  formatting using Format Painter,
    PPT 111–113
  formatting using Quick Styles,
    PPT 106–108
  inserting special characters,
    PPT 106
  italicizing in documents, WD 36
  modifying in content control,
    WD 187–188
  moving, WD 119–122
  promoting, demoting, PPT 34
  rotating in worksheet cells,
    EX 168–171
  shadowing, PPT 110
  underlining in documents, WD 35
  wrapping, EX 87–89, WD 14–15
text files
  exporting Access data to, AC 224
  importing into, linking to database,
    AC 218–219
theme colors, changing, WD 201
themes
  PowerPoint document, PPT 8,
    PPT 16–17
  in Excel, EX 34, EX 37, EX 107,
    EX 109
  in Word, WD 23, WD 150

thesaurus, WD 124, WD 125–126
time, updating system, EX 183
tips. See Key Tips, ToolTips
title slides, PPT 18–20, PPT 85–86
titles
  centering works cited page,
    WD 112
  creating title slide, PPT 18–20
  entering into worksheets, EX 87–89
  entering worksheet, EX 17–18,
    EX 21–22
  formatting worksheet, EX 199–200
  freezing worksheet, EX 181–182
  inserting chart, EX 206–209
  using sans serif font for, PPT 108
  worksheet rows, columns, EX 19–22
To-Do bar, OUT 10
toggling database record filters,
    AC 151
toolbars. See specific toolbar
top-values queries, AC 102–103
transitions, adding slide,
    PPT 122–124
transparencies, using in
    presentations, PPT 62
transparent colors, setting in
    graphic, WD 157
turning off
  computers, WIN 66
  Mini toolbar, PPT 11
type. See fonts

U

Ultimate Edition, Windows Vista,
    WIN 5
underlining
  text in documents, WD 35
  wavy, for misspelled words, WD 16
undoing
  actions in documents, WD 32–33
  database changes, AC 26, AC 34
  typing, PPT 19
  worksheet changes, EX 65, EX 180,
    EX 227
unhiding. See displaying
Uniform Resource Locators.
    See URLs
unique identifiers in database fields,
    AC 4
up scroll arrow, WIN 15
update queries, AC 162–163

updating
  bibliographical lists, WD 117
  database records, AC 141–147
  database tables containing
    validation rules, AC 169–178
  PowerPoint slide from previous
    version, PPT 43
  system date, time, EX 183
URLs (Uniform Resource Locators)
  browsing Web using, WIN 30
  described, WIN 28–29
USB flash drives
  creating databases using, AC 14–17
  described, WIN 37–38
  opening database on, AC 37
  opening documents, WD 56–57
  removing from port after work,
    EX 69
  saving documents to, WD 21
  saving worksheets to, EX 30–32
USB ports, WIN 37–38
user-friendly, WIN 3
user interface described, WIN 3
user names, choosing, WIN 8

V

validation rules, database,
    AC 165–178
value axis in charts, EX 50
values
  formula, determining using Goal
    Seek command, EX 225–228
  and validation rules, AC 165–167
  version of worksheet, printing,
    EX 135–136
VAR (variance) aggregate function,
    AC 117
verifying
  formulas, EX 106–107, EX 164
  Web page navigation features,
    INT 26, INT 39
versions of Microsoft Office 2007,
    APP 3–4
vertical ruler in documents, WD 87
viewing
  database records through forms,
    AC 57–58
  file attachments, OUT 22–23
  gridlines, INT 9
  multiple Web pages, WIN 31–32

PDF, XPS files, AC 224
presentations in Slide Show view, PPT 48–52
views
  Outlook, changing, OUT 49
  PowerPoint, PPT 8, PPT 90–91
  Slide Show, PPT 48–52
  worksheet, EX 220–223
Vista. *See* Windows Vista

W

warning of untrusted database content, AC 38
Web
  browsing, WIN 29–33
  Office 2007 and, APP 4, INT 2–6
Web browsers, WIN 27
Web Collections, PPT 95
Web folders
  and FTP locations, EX 252
  publishing Web pages using, APP 19–20
Web Layout view in Word, INT 22
Web Page format, PPT 152, EX 256
Web Page Publishing Wizard, INT 27
Web pages
  adding background colors to, WD 221
  adding pattern fill effect to background, WD 222
  creating from Access report, INT 28–32
  creating using Excel, EX 250–261
  creating using PowerPoint, INT 23–27, PPT 146–157
  creating using Word, WD 216–223
  described, WIN 28
  formatting, WD 220–223
  inserting hyperlinks into PowerPoint, INT 11–13
  previewing, PPT 151–152, EX 255
  publishing to Web servers, APP 19–20
  saving workbook as, EX 256–257
  saving presentations as, INT 27, PPT 153–154
  saving Word documents as, INT 19–22, WD 218–219
  testing in Web browser, WD 223

viewing, manipulating using browser, EX 260–261
Web queries, importing data into Excel using, EX 137–140
Web servers
  publishing Web pages to, APP 19–20
  publishing Word documents on, WD 219
Web sites
  described, WIN 28
  SharePoint, APP 7–8
  testing, INT 38–39
Welcome Center, WIN 10
Welcome screen, Windows Vista, WIN 7
what-if analysis, using in worksheets, EX 162, EX 164, EX 223–227
What-If Assumptions table, EX 181, EX 203
width
  changing worksheet column, EX 173–174
  Word table rows and columns, WD 180
wildcards, Access, AC 87, AC 151, AC 165
windows
  See also specific window
  closing, WIN 21
  minimizing, maximizing, AC 13, WIN 19, WIN 20
  moving, sizing, resizing, WIN 22, WIN 23
  opening using desktop icon, WIN 18
  Outlook, customizing, OUT 6
  PowerPoint, using, PPT 6–8
  splitting into panes, EX 222–223
  Word, using, APP 25–26, WD 4–12
  worksheet, EX 9–15
Windows Aero GUI, WIN 5
Windows Explorer, using, WIN 18–21
Windows Help and Support, using, WIN 58–63
Windows Sidebar, adding and removing gadgets, WIN 10–12
Windows Taskbar, WD 188
Windows Vista
  described, overview, WIN 2–6

desktop features, icons, gadgets, WIN 10–18
editions of, WIN 5
Help and Support, using, WIN 60–63
logging on, WIN 8–9
starting, WIN 7
Windows Explorer, WIN 18–21
Windows XP users, and this book, APP 35–40
wizards. *See specific wizard*
Word
  color schemes, changing, APP 34
  creating Web pages using, WD 216–223
  described, WD 2
  documents. *See* Word documents
  entering text, WD 12–15
  exporting Access data to, AC 223–224
  fonts, font sizes, styles and themes, WD 23
  Help, APP 9–17, WD 60–61
  insert and overtype mode, WD 58
  and the Internet, APP 5
  Key Tips, WD 12
  Mini toolbar, shortcut menus, WD 9–10
  program described, APP 4–5
  Quick Access Toolbar, Office Button, WD 10–11
  quitting, WD 55, WD 62, WD 132
  Ribbon, WD 7–9, INT 16
  starting, WD 4–5
  Web Layout view, INT 22
  window, customizing, APP 25–26
  window, using, WD 4–12
  Windows XP users, steps for, APP 35–40
Word documents
  adding hyperlinks to, INT 6–7
  adding page borders, WD 48–50
  applying picture styles, WD 44
  automatic page breaks, WD 107–108
  bibliographical lists, creating, WD 113
  bold characters, WD 34
  building blocks, using, WD 170
  bulleted lists, WD 32

changing spacing around paragraphs, WD 50

changing document settings, WD 77–78

citations, WD 94–98

Click and Type feature, WD 85

closing, WD 59–60

copying and pasting text, WD 188–192

correcting errors in, WD 57–60

counting words in, WD 107

displaying formatting marks, WD 14

documentation styles, WD 76

embedding Excel chart into, INT 13–16

entering text into, WD 12–14

finding and replacing text, WD 123–125

fonts, font sizes, WD 23

footnotes, endnotes, WD 99–106

formatting marks in, WD 77, WD 150

formatting paragraphs, characters generally, WD 22

formatting single vs. multiple paragraphs, characters, WD 26–31

grammar checking, WD 125–126

hanging indents, WD 116

hiding formatting marks in, INT 7

inserting clip art into, WD 153–154

inserting current date, WD 168–169

inserting tables into, INT 7–8

inserting text into existing, WD 58

italicizing text in, WD 36

line and paragraph spacing, WD 78–79

opening, WD 56–57

page borders, WD 48–50, WD 55

page numbers, inserting in header, WD 82

pictures, inserting, WD 40–42

print preview, WD 201–202

printing, WD 53–55

proofreading, WD 76

Research task pane, looking up information using, WD 128–130

resizing graphics, WD 46–47

rulers in, WD 87

saving, WD 18–21

saving as Web pages, INT 19–23, WD 218–219

saving with same name, WD 165

scrolling around, WD 43

selecting groups of words, WD 33

sizing embedded objects in, INT 17–18

spell checking, WD 16–17, WD 125–126

spelling and grammar check, WD 16–17

styles, applying, WD 24–25

switching between, WD 189

underlining characters, WD 35

undoing, redoing, WD 32–33

using styles in, WD 36–40

wordwrap, WD 14–15

Word tables

adding, deleting rows, WD 180

applying table styles, WD 176–177

borders, gridlines, AutoFitting contents, INT 9–10

described, WD 173

entering data into, WD 174–175

inserting empty, WD 173–174

resizing columns in, WD 177–178

selecting, centering, WD 179

selecting contents, WD 178

WordArt, PPT 111

WordPad

creating document and folder using, WIN 44–52

viewing contact lists in, OUT 61–62

words

counting in documents, WD 107

finding and inserting synonyms, WD 124

wordwrap feature, WD 14–15, WD 174–175

work area, Access, AC 18–19

work days, EX 195

workbooks

adding 3-D pie chart to, EX 204–216

changing themes, EX 109

creating hyperlinks in, EX 258

e-mailing within Excel, EX 142–143

naming, EX 29, EX 31

opening, EX 60–61

saving, EX 29–32, EX 106

saving as Web pages, EX 256–257

works cited, in research papers, WD 77, WD 111

worksheets

adding 3-D clustered column to, EX 49–54

adjusting column width, EX 46, EX 173–174

aesthetics vs. function, EX 84

Auto Fill Options, EX 28, EX 169–171

cells. *See* cells, worksheet

changing column width, height, EX 122–126

changing margins, headers, orientation, EX 130–132

changing views, EX 220–223

changing names of, EX 140–141

conditional formatting, EX 118–121

copying and pasting cells, EX 175–177

copying cell formulas, EX 201–202

copying cells using fill handle, EX 26–28

correcting errors on, EX 63–67

creating, methodology for, EX 3–5

debugging, EX 135–136

determining multiple totals, EX 28–29

entering column, row titles, EX 19–22

entering numbers into, EX 22–24, EX 180–181

entering text into, EX 15–19

entering titles, EX 87–89

error checking, EX 129

fitting entries to cells, EX 174–175

font type, style, size, color, EX 34–47

formatting, EX 88, EX 107–114

formatting column titles, total row, EX 42–43

formatting generally, EX 33–34

formatting numbers in, EX 44–45

formatting titles, EX 110, EX 199–200

formulas, entering into, EX 90–91

freezing titles, EX 181–182

gridlines, EX 8

hiding, unhiding columns, EX 122

in-cell editing, EX 64–65

inserting cells, EX 177–179

inserting columns, EX 179
merging cells, EX 40–41
naming, renaming, EX 216–217
planning, EX 16, EX 108
printing, EX 57–58, EX 129–135
printing formulas or values version
  of, EX 135–136
selecting cells, EX 47–48
spell checking, EX 127–129,
  EX 218
splitting merged cells, EX 41
system date, displaying,
  EX 183–185
working with cells, EX 7–8
Workspaces, SharePoint, APP 7–8
World Wide Web. *See* Web

wrapping, text
  in Excel, EX 87–89
  in PowerPoint, PPT 18
  in Word, WD 14–15

X

XML (Extensible Markup
  Language)
  exporting data, AC 226–227
  importing data into Access,
    AC 228–229
XPS format
  exporting to, AC 209
  publishing Access report in, AC 225
  saving documents in, WD 183
  viewing files in, AC 224

Y

y-axis in charts, EX 50

Z

Zip codes, AC 12
zooming
  in datasheets, AC 42–43
  in print preview, WD 202
  in documents, WD 12, WD 45–46,
    WD 50, WD 193
  worksheet, chart appearance,
    EX 220–223

Quick Reference Summary

In the Microsoft Office 2007 programs, you can accomplish a task in a number of ways. The following five tables (one each for Microsoft Office Word 2007, Microsoft Office Excel 2007, Microsoft Office Access 2007, Microsoft Office PowerPoint 2007, and Microsoft Office Outlook 2007) provide a quick reference to each task presented in this textbook. The first column identifies the task. The second column indicates the page number on which the task is discussed in the book. The subsequent four columns list the different ways the task in column one can be carried out.

Table 1 Microsoft Office Word 2007 Quick Reference Summary

Task	Page Number	Mouse	Ribbon	Shortcut Menu	Keyboard Shortcut
1.5 Line Spacing	WD 86		Line spacing button on Home tab	Paragraph	Indents and Spacing tab	CTRL+5
AutoCorrect Entry, Create	WD 93	Office Button	Word Options button	Proofing	AutoCorrect Options button			
AutoCorrect Options Menu, Display	WD 92	Point to text automatically corrected, point to small blue box, click AutoCorrect Options button			
Background Color, Add	WD 221		Page Color button on Page Layout tab		
Bibliographical List, Create	WD 113		Bibliography button on References tab	Insert Bibliography		
Bibliographical List, Modify Source and Update List	WD 117		Manage Sources button on References tab	select source	Edit button		
Bibliography Style, Change	WD 95		Bibliography Style box arrow on References tab		
Bold	WD 34	Bold button on Mini toolbar	Bold button on Home tab	Font	Font tab	Bold in Font style list	CTRL+B
Border, Paragraph	WD 161		Page Borders on Page Layout tab	Borders tab		

Table 1 Microsoft Office Word 2007 Quick Reference Summary *(continued)*

Task	Page Number	Mouse	Ribbon	Shortcut Menu	Keyboard Shortcut
Building Block, Create	WD 170		Quick Parts button on Insert tab | Save Selection to Quick Part Gallery		ALT+F3
Building Block, Insert	WD 172		Quick Parts button on Insert tab | building block name		F3
Bullets, Apply	WD 32	Bullets button on Mini toolbar	Bullets button on Home tab	Bullets	ASTERISK KEY | SPACEBAR
Capital Letters	WD 86		Change Case button on Home tab | UPPERCASE	Font	CTRL+SHIFT+A
Case of Letters, Change	WD 86		Change Case button on Home tab	Font | Font tab	SHIFT+F3
Center	WD 26	Center button on Mini toolbar	Center button on Home tab	Paragraph | Indents and Spacing tab	CTRL+E
Citation Placeholder, Insert	WD 101		Insert Citation button on References tab | Add New Placeholder		
Citation, Insert and Create Source	WD 96		Insert Citation button on References tab | Add New Source		
Citation, Edit	WD 98	Click citation, Citation Options box arrow | Edit Citation			
Close Document	WD 60	Office Button | Close			
Count Words	WD 107	Word Count indicator on status bar	Word Count button on Review tab		CTRL+SHIFT+G
Color Text	WD 152	Font Color button arrow on Mini toolbar	Font Color button arrow on Home tab		
Content Control, Change Text	WD 187	Triple-click content control, change text			
Copy	WD 189		Clipboard Dialog Box Launcher on Home tab	Copy	CTRL+C
Cut	WD 121		Cut button on Home tab	Cut	CTRL+X
Date, Insert	WD 168		Insert Date and Time button on Insert tab		
Delete Text	WD 59				DELETE
Dictionary, Custom, View or Modify Entries	WD 127	Office Button | Word Options button | Proofing | Custom Dictionaries button			
Dictionary, Set Custom	WD 127	Office Button | Word Options button | Proofing | Custom Dictionaries button | select desired dictionary name | Change Default button			
Document Properties, Set or View	WD 51	Office Button | Prepare | Properties			

Table 1 Microsoft Office Word 2007 Quick Reference Summary *(continued)*

Task	Page Number	Mouse	Ribbon	Shortcut Menu	Keyboard Shortcut
Documents, Switch Between	WD 189	Program button on Windows taskbar	Switch Windows button on View tab		ALT+TAB
Double-Space Text	WD 87		Line spacing button on Home tab	Paragraph | Indents and Spacing	CTRL+2
Double-Underline	WD 35		Font Dialog Box Launcher on Home tab	Font | Font tab	CTRL+SHIFT+D
Envelope, Address and Print	WD 203		Envelopes button on Mailings tab | Envelopes tab | Print button		
File, Create from Existing File	WD 165	Office Button | New | New from existing			
Find Text	WD 124	Select Browse Object button on vertical scroll bar | Find icon	Find button on Home tab		CTRL+F
Find and Replace Text	WD 123	Select Browse Object button on vertical scroll bar | Find icon | Replace tab	Replace button on Home tab		CTRL+H
First-Line Indent Paragraphs	WD 88	Drag First Line Indent marker on ruler	Paragraph Dialog Box Launcher on Home tab | Indents and Spacing tab	Paragraph | Indents and Spacing tab	TAB
Font Size, Change	WD 28	Font Size box arrow on Mini toolbar	Font Size box arrow on Home tab	Font | Font tab	CTRL+SHIFT+P
Font Size, Decrease	WD 152	Shrink Font button on Mini toolbar	Shrink Font button on Home tab	Font | Font tab	CTRL+SHIFT+<
Font Size, Decrease 1 Point	WD 86			Font | Font tab	CTRL+ [
Font Size, Increase	WD 151	Grow Font button on Mini toolbar	Grow Font button on Home tab		CTRL+SHIFT+>
Font Size, Increase 1 Point	WD 86			Font | Font tab	CTRL+]
Font, Change	WD 29	Font box arrow on Mini toolbar	Font box arrow on Home tab	Font | Font tab	CTRL+SHIFT+F
Footnote Reference Mark, Insert	WD 100		Insert Footnote button on References tab		CTRL+ALT+F
Footnote, Delete	WD 106	Delete note reference mark in document window	Cut button Home tab		BACKSPACE | BACKSPACE
Footnote, Edit	WD 106	Double-click note reference mark in document window	Show Notes button on References tab		
Footnote, Move	WD 106	Drag note reference mark in document window	Cut button on Home tab | Paste button on Home tab		
Footnote Style, Modify	WD 102		Click footnote text | Styles Dialog Box Launcher | Manage Styles button | Modify button	Style | Footnote Text | Modify button	

Table 1 Microsoft Office Word 2007 Quick Reference Summary *(continued)*

Task	Page Number	Mouse	Ribbon	Shortcut Menu	Keyboard Shortcut
Formatting Marks	WD 14		Show/Hide ¶ button on Home tab		CTRL+SHIFT+*
Formatting, Clear	WD 162		Clear Formatting button on Home tab		CTRL+ SPACEBAR
Graphic, Insert	WD 153		Clip Art button on Insert tab		
Graphic, Recolor	WD 156		Recolor button on Format tab	Format Picture | Picture | Recolor button	
Graphic, Resize	WD 46	Drag sizing handle	Format tab in Picture Tools tab or Size Dialog Box Launcher on Format tab	Size | Size tab	
Graphic, Set Transparent Color	WD 157		Recolor button on Format tab | Set Transparent Color		
Hanging Indent, Create	WD 116	Drag Hanging Indent marker on ruler	Paragraph Dialog Box Launcher on Home tab | Indents and Spacing tab	Paragraph | Indents and Spacing tab	CTRL+T
Hanging Indent, Remove	WD 86		Paragraph Dialog Box Launcher on Home tab | Indents and Spacing tab	Paragraph | Indents and Spacing tab	CTRL+SHIFT+T
Header & Footer, Close	WD 83	Double-click dimmed document text	Close Header and Footer button on Design tab		
Header, Display	WD 80	Double-click dimmed header	Header button on Insert tab | Edit Header		
Help	WD 60		Office Word Help button		F1
Hyperlink, Format Text As	WD 220		Insert Hyperlink button on Insert tab	Hyperlink	CTRL+K
Hyperlink, Remove	WD 163		Hyperlink button on Insert tab | Remove Link button	Remove Hyperlink	
Indent Paragraph	WD 196	Drag Left Indent marker on ruler	Increase Indent button on Home tab	Paragraph | Indents and Spacing sheet	CTRL+M
Insertion Point, Move to Beginning of Document	WD 24	Scroll to top of document, click			CTRL+HOME
Insertion Point, Move to End of Document	WD 25	Scroll to bottom of document, click			CTRL+END
Italicize	WD 36	Italic button on Mini toolbar	Italic button on Home tab	Font | Font tab	CTRL+I
Justify Paragraph	WD 86		Justify button on Home tab	Paragraph | Indents and Spacing tab	CTRL+J
Left-Align	WD 86		Align Text Left button on Home tab	Paragraph | Indents and Spacing tab	CTRL+L
Line Break, Enter	WD 194				SHIFT+ENTER

Table 1 Microsoft Office Word 2007 Quick Reference Summary *(continued)*

Task	Page Number	Mouse	Ribbon	Shortcut Menu	Keyboard Shortcut
Move Selected Text	WD 121	Drag and drop selected text	Cut button on Home tab | Paste button on Home tab	Cut | Paste	CTRL+X; CTRL+V
Nonbreaking Space, Insert	WD 171		Symbol button on Insert tab | More Symbols | Special Characters tab		CTRL+SHIFT+SPACEBAR
Open Document	WD 56	Office Button | Open			CTRL+O
Page Border, Add	WD 48		Page Borders button on Page Layout tab		
Page Break, Manual	WD 112		Page Break button on Insert tab		CTRL+ENTER
Page Number, Insert	WD 82		Insert Page Number button on Design tab		
Paragraph, Add Space Above	WD 79		Line spacing button on Home tab | Add Space Before (After) Paragraph	Paragraph | Indents and Spacing tab	CTRL+0 (zero)
Paragraph, Decrease Indent	WD 196	Decrease Indent button on Mini toolbar	Decrease Indent button on Home tab	Paragraph | Indents and Spacing tab	CTRL+SHIFT+M
Paragraph, Remove Space After	WD 195		Line spacing button on Home tab | Remove Space After Paragraph	Paragraph | Indents and Spacing tab	
Paragraphs, Change Spacing Above and Below	WD 50		Spacing Before box arrow on Page Layout tab	Paragraph | Indents and Spacing tab	
Paste	WD 191		Clipboard Dialog Box Launcher on Home tab	Paste	CTRL+V
Pattern Fill Effect for Background, Add	WD 222		Page Color button on Page Layout tab | Fill Effects | Pattern tab		
Picture Border, Change	WD 45		Picture Border button on Format tab		
Picture Style, Apply	WD 44		Picture Tools and Format tabs | More button in Picture Styles gallery		
Picture, Insert	WD 41		Picture button on Insert tab		
Print Document	WD 54	Office Button | Print | Print			CTRL+P
Print Document Properties	WD 130	Office Button | Print | Print | Print what box arrow			
Print Preview	WD 201	Office Button | Print | Print Preview			
Quick Style, Create	WD 90		More button in Styles gallery | Save Selection as a New Quick Style	Styles | Save Selection as a New Quick Style	
Quit Word	WD 55	Close button on right side of Word title bar			ALT+F4
Remove character formatting (plain text)	WD 87		Font Dialog Box Launcher on Home tab | Font tab	Font | Font tab	CTRL+SPACEBAR

Table 1 Microsoft Office Word 2007 Quick Reference Summary *(continued)*

Task	Page Number	Mouse	Ribbon	Shortcut Menu	Keyboard Shortcut
Remove paragraph formatting	WD 87		Font Dialog Box Launcher on Home tab	Font | Font tab	CTRL+Q
Research Task Pane, Use	WD 128	Hold down ALT key, click word to look up			
Right-Align Paragraph	WD 81		Align Text Right button on Home tab	Paragraph | Indents and Spacing tab	CTRL+R
Rulers, Display	WD 87	View Ruler button on vertical scroll bar	View Ruler on View tab		
Save Document as Web Page	WD 218	Office Button | Save As | Other Formats			F12
Save Document, Same Name	WD 53	Save button on Quick Access Toolbar			CTRL+S
Save New Document	WD 19	Save button on Quick Access Toolbar			CTRL+S
Select Block of Text	WD 33	Click at beginning of text, hold down SHIFT key and click at end of text to select; or drag through text			CTRL+SHIFT+RIGHT ARROW and/or DOWN ARROW
Select Browse Object Menu, Use	WD 118	Select Browse Object button on vertical scroll bar			ALT+CTRL+HOME
Select Character(s)	WD 120	Drag through character(s)			CTRL+SHIFT+RIGHT ARROW
Select Entire Document	WD 120	Point to left of text and triple-click			CTRL+A
Select Graphic	WD 46	Click graphic			
Select Line	WD 27	Point to left of line and click			SHIFT+DOWN ARROW
Select Lines	WD 30	Point to left of first line and drag up or down			CTRL+SHIFT+DOWN ARROW
Select Paragraph	WD 90	Triple-click paragraph			SHIFT+DOWN ARROW
Select Paragraphs	WD 30	Point to left of first paragraph, double-click, and drag up or down			
Select Sentence	WD 120	Press and hold down CTRL key and click sentence			CTRL+SHIFT+RIGHT ARROW
Select Word	WD 59	Double-click word			CTRL+SHIFT+RIGHT ARROW
Select Words	WD 33	Drag through words			CTRL+SHIFT+RIGHT ARROW
Single-Space Lines	WD 86		Line spacing button on the Home tab	Paragraph | Indents and Spacing tab	CTRL+1
Small uppercase letters	WD 86		Font Dialog Box Launcher on Home tab | Font tab	Font | Font tab	CTRL+SHIFT+K
Sort Paragraphs	WD 200		Sort button on Home tab		
Source, Edit	WD 104	Click citation, Citation Options box arrow | Edit Source			

Table 1 Microsoft Office Word 2007 Quick Reference Summary *(continued)*

Task	Page Number	Mouse	Ribbon	Shortcut Menu	Keyboard Shortcut
Spelling and Grammar	WD 125	Spelling and Grammar Check icon on status bar | Spelling	Spelling & Grammar button on Review tab	Right-click flagged text | Spelling	F7
Spelling and Grammar Check as You Type	WD 16	Spelling and Grammar Check icon on status bar		Correct word on shortcut menu	
Style Set, Change	WD 37		Change Styles button on Home tab | Style Set on Change Styles menu		
Styles Task Pane, Open	WD 25		Styles Dialog Box Launcher		ALT+CTRL+SHIFT+S
Styles, Apply	WD 24		Styles gallery		
Styles, Modify	WD 90		Styles Dialog Box Launcher		
Subscript	WD 86		Font Dialog Box Launcher on Home tab	Font | Font tab	CTRL+EQUAL SIGN
Superscript	WD 86		Font Dialog Box Launcher on Home tab	Font | Font tab	CTRL+SHIFT+PLUS SIGN
Synonym, Find	WD 124		Thesaurus on Review tab	Synonyms | desired word	SHIFT+F7
Tab Stops, Set	WD 158, WD 167	Click tab selector, click ruler on desired location	Paragraph Dialog Box Launcher | Tabs button	Paragraph | Tabs button	
Table Columns, Resize	WD 177	Double-click column boundary	AutoFit button on Layout tab	AutoFit | AutoFit to Contents	
Table Style, Apply	WD 176		More button in Table Styles gallery		
Table, Delete Rows	WD 186		Delete button on Layout tab | Delete Rows		
Table, Insert	WD 173		Table button on Insert tab		
Table, Select	WD 179	Click table move handle	Select button on Layout tab | Select Table on Select menu		
Table, Select Cell	WD 178	Click left edge of cell			
Table, Select Column	WD 178	Click border at top of column			
Table, Select Multiple Adjacent Cells, Rows, or Columns	WD 178	Drag through cells, rows, or columns			
Table, Select Multiple Nonadjacent Cells, Rows, or Columns	WD 178	Select first cell, row, or column, hold down CTRL key while selecting next cell, row, or column			
Table, Select Next Cell	WD 178	Drag through cell			TAB
Table, Select Previous Cell	WD 178	Drag through cell			SHIFT+TAB
Table, Select Row	WD 178	Click to left of row			
Theme Colors, Change	WD 39		Change Styles button on Home tab | Colors on Change Styles menu		

Table 1 Microsoft Office Word 2007 Quick Reference Summary *(continued)*

Task	Page Number	Mouse	Ribbon	Shortcut Menu	Keyboard Shortcut
Theme Fonts, Change	WD 40		Change Styles button on Home tab | Fonts on Change Styles menu		
Underline	WD 35		Underline button on Home tab	Font | Font tab	CTRL+U
Underline words, not spaces	WD 86				CTRL+SHIFT+W
Zoom	WD 46	Zoom Out and Zoom In buttons on status bar	Zoom button on View tab		

Table 2 Microsoft Office Excel 2007 Quick Reference Summary

Task	Page Number	Mouse	Ribbon	Shortcut Menu	Keyboard Shortcut
AutoCalculate	EX 62	Select range | right-click AutoCalculate area | click calculation			
Bold	EX 38	Bold button on Mini toolbar	Bold button on Home tab or Font Dialog Box Launcher on Home tab | Font tab	Format Cells | Font tab | Bold in Font style list	CTRL+B
Borders	EX 111	Borders button on Mini toolbar	Borders button on Home tab or Alignment Dialog Box Launcher on Home tab | Border tab	Format Cells | Border tab	CTRL+1 | B
Cell Style, change	EX 35		Cell Styles button on Home tab		
Center	EX 113	Right-click cell | Center button on Mini toolbar	Center button on Home tab or Alignment Dialog Box Launcher on Home tab	Format Cells | Alignment tab	CTRL+1 | A
Center Across Columns	EX 40	Right-click selection | Merge & Center button on Mini toolbar	Merge & Center button on Home tab or Alignment Dialog Box Launcher on Home tab	Format Cells | Alignment tab	CTRL+1 | A
Chart, Add	EX 50, 205		Dialog Box Launcher in Charts group on Insert tab		F11
Clear Cell	EX 66	Drag fill handle back	Clear button on Home tab	Clear Contents	DELETE
Clear Worksheet	EX 66		Select All button on worksheet | Clear button on Home tab		
Close Workbook	EX 59		Close button on Ribbon or Office Button | Close		CTRL+W
Color Background	EX 110		Fill Color button on Home tab or Font Dialog Box Launcher on Home tab | Fill tab	Format Cells | Fill tab	CTRL+1 | F

Table 2 Microsoft Office Excel 2007 Quick Reference Summary *(continued)*

Task	Page Number	Mouse	Ribbon	Shortcut Menu	Keyboard Shortcut
Color Tab	EX 216			Tab Color	
Column Width	EX 46, 122	Drag column heading boundary	Home tab | Format button | Column Width	Column Width	ALT+O | C | W
Comma Style Format	EX 44		Comma Style button on Home tab or Number Dialog Box Launcher on Home tab | Accounting	Format Cells | Number tab | Accounting	CTRL+1 | N
Conditional Formatting	EX 119		Conditional Formatting button on Home tab		ALT+O | D
Copy and Paste	EX 175		Copy button and Paste button on Home tab	Copy to copy; Paste to paste	CTRL+C; CTRL+V
Copy to adjacent cells	EX 27	Select source area | drag fill handle through destination cells	Select source area | click Copy button on Home tab | select destination area | click Paste button on Home tab	Right-click source area | click Copy | right-click destination area | click Paste	
Currency Style Format	EX 116		Currency Style button on Home tab or Format Cells | Number | Currency	Format Cells | Number | Currency	CTRL+1 | N
Cut	EX 64		Cut button on Home tab	Cut	CTRL+X
Date	EX 184	Insert Function button in formula bar | Date & Time | NOW	Date & Time button on Formulas tab | NOW		CTRL+SEMICOLON
Date, Format	EX 113		Font Dialog Box Launcher on Home tab | Number tab | Date	Format Cells | Number tab | Date	
Decimal Place, Decrease	EX 115		Decrease Decimal button on Home tab or Number Dialog Box Launcher on Home tab | Number tab | Currency	Format Cells | Number tab | Currency	CTRL+1 | N
Decimal Place, Increase	EX 118		Increase Decimal button on Home tab or Number Dialog Box Launcher on Home tab | Number tab | Currency	Format Cells | Number tab | Currency	CTRL+1 | N
Delete Rows or Columns	EX 180		Home tab | Delete button arrow | Delete Sheet Rows or Home tab | Delete button arrow | Delete Sheet Columns	Delete | Entire row or Delete | Entire column	
Document Properties, Set or View	EX 55	Office Button | Prepare | Properties			ALT+F | E | P
E-Mail from Excel	EX 142	Office Button | Send | E-Mail			ALT+F | D | E
Embedded Chart, Delete	EX 67				Select chart, press DELETE
File Management	EX 259		Office Button | Save As | right-click file name		ALT+F | A | right-click file name

Table 2 Microsoft Office Excel 2007 Quick Reference Summary *(continued)*

Task	Page Number	Mouse	Ribbon	Shortcut Menu	Keyboard Shortcut
Fit to Print	EX 156		Page Setup Dialog Box Launcher on Page Layout tab		ALT+P | SP
Folder, New	EX 259		Office Button | Save As | Create New Folder button		ALT+F | A
Font Color	EX 39	Font Color box arrow on Mini toolbar	Font Color button arrow on Home tab or Font Dialog Box Launcher on Home tab	Format Cells | Font tab	CTRL+1 | F
Font Size, Change	EX 38	Font Size box arrow on Mini toolbar	Font Size box arrow on Home tab or Font Dialog Box Launcher on Home tab	Format Cells | Font tab	CTRL+1 | F
Font Size, Increase	EX 39	Increase Font Size button on Mini toolbar	Increase Font Size button on Home tab		
Font Type	EX 36	Font box arrow on Mini toolbar	Font box arrow on Home tab or Font Dialog Box Launcher in Font group on Home tab	Format Cells | Font tab	CTRL+1 | F
Formula Assistance	EX 101	Insert Function button in formula bar	Insert Function button on Formulas tab		CTRL+A after you type function name
Formulas Version	EX 136				CTRL+ACCENT MARK
Freeze Worksheet Titles	EX 182		Freeze Panes button on the View tab | Freeze Panes		ALT+W | F
Full Screen	EX 9		Full Screen button on View tab		ALT+V | U
Function	EX 101	Insert Function button in formula bar	Insert Function button on Formulas tab		SHIFT+F3
Go To	EX 48	Click cell	Find & Select button on Home tab		F5
Goal Seek	EX 225		What-If Analysis button on Data tab | Goal Seek		ALT+T | G
Help	EX 67 and Appendix C		Microsoft Office Excel Help button on Ribbon		F1
Hide Column	EX 122	Drag column heading boundary	Format button on Home tab | Hide & Unhide or Hide & Unhide button on View tab	Hide	CTRL+0 (zero) to hide CTRL+SHIFT+) to display
Hide Row	EX 126	Drag row heading boundary		Hide	CTRL+9 to hide CTRL+SHIFT+(to display
In-Cell Editing	EX 63	Double-click cell			F2
Insert Rows or Columns	EX 178		Home tab | Insert button arrow | Insert Sheet Rows or Home tab | Insert button arrow | Insert Sheet Columns	Insert	ALT+I | R or C
Insert Single Cell or Range of Cells	EX 179		Home | Insert button arrow | Insert Cells		

Table 2 Microsoft Office Excel 2007 Quick Reference Summary *(continued)*

Task	Page Number	Mouse	Ribbon	Shortcut Menu	Keyboard Shortcut
Italicize	EX 203		Italic button on Home tab or Font Dialog Box Launcher on Home tab | Font tab	Format Cells | Font tab	CTRL+I
Margins, Change	EX 130		Margins button on Page Layout tab		
Merge Cells	EX 41		Merge & Center button on Home tab or Alignment Dialog Box Launcher on Home tab	Format Cells | Alignment tab	ALT+O | E | A
Move Cells	EX 177	Point to border and drag	Cut button on Home tab; Paste button on Home tab	Cut; Paste	CTRL+X; CTRL+V
Move Sheet	EX 217	Drag sheet tab to desired location		Move or Copy	
Name Cells	EX XXX	Click Name box in formula bar, type name	Define Name button on Formulas tab		ALT+I | N | D
New Workbook	EX 67	Office Button | New			CTRL+N
Open Workbook	EX 61	Office Button | Open			CTRL+O
Paste Options	EX 176		Paste button arrow on Home tab		
Percent Style Format	EX 118		Percent Style button on Home tab or Number Dialog Box Launcher on Home tab | Percentage	Format Cells | Number tab | Percentage	CTRL+1 | N or CTRL+SHIFT+%
Preview Worksheet	EX 132	Office Button | Print | Print Preview			ALT+F | W | V
Print Worksheet	EX 132	Office Button | Print			CTRL+P
Quit Excel	EX 59	Close button on title bar Office Button | Exit Excel			ALT+F4
Range Finder	EX 106	Double-click cell			
Redo	EX 65	Redo button on Quick Access Toolbar			ALT+3 or CTRL+Y
Remove Splits	EX 223	Double-click split bar	Split button on View tab		ALT+W | S
Rename Sheet tab	EX 217	Double-click sheet tab | type sheet name		Rename	
Rotate Text	EX 169		Alignment Dialog Box Launcher on Home tab	Format Cells | Alignment tab	ALT+O | E | A
Row Height	EX 125	Drag row heading boundary	Format button on Home tab | Row Height	Row Height	ALT+O | R | E
Save Workbook, New Name	EX 57		Office Button | Save As		ALT+F | A
Save Workbook, Same Name	EX 57	Save button on Quick Access Toolbar	Office Button | Save		CTRL+S
Select All of Worksheet	EX 67	Select All button on worksheet			CTRL+A

Table 2 Microsoft Office Excel 2007 Quick Reference Summary *(continued)*

Task	Page Number	Mouse	Ribbon	Shortcut Menu	Keyboard Shortcut
Select Cell	EX 15	Click cell or click Name box, type cell reference, press ENTER			Use arrow keys
Select Multiple Sheets	EX 218	CTRL+click tab or SHIFT+click tab		Select All Sheets	
Series	EX 169	Drag fill handle			ALT+E | I | S
Shortcut Menu	EX 12	Right-click object			SHIFT+F10
Spell Check	EX 127		Spelling button on Review tab		F7
Split Cell	EX 41		Merge & Center button on Home tab or Alignment Dialog Box Launcher on Home tab | click Merge cells to deselect	Format Cells | Alignment tab | click Merge cells to deselect	ALT+O | E | A
Split Window into Panes	EX 222	Drag vertical or horizontal split box	Split button on View tab		ALT+W | S
Stock Quotes	EX 138		Existing Connections button on Data tab		ALT+D | D | D
Sum	EX 25	Function Wizard button in formula bar | SUM	Sum button on Home tab	Insert Function button on Formulas tab	ALT+=
Underline	EX 203		Underline button on Home tab or Font Dialog Box Launcher on Home tab	Format Cells | Font tab	CTRL+U
Undo	EX 65	Undo button on Quick Access Toolbar			ALT+2, CTRL+Z
Unfreeze Worksheet Titles	EX 194		Freeze Panes button on View tab | Unfreeze Panes		ALT+W | F
Unhide Column	EX 122	Drag hidden column heading boundary to right	Unhide button on View tab	Unhide	ALT+O | C | U
Unhide Row	EX 127	Drag hidden row heading boundary down	Unhide button on View tab	Unhide	ALT+O | R | U
Web Page, Save Workbook As	EX 256	Office button | Save As | Save as type: arrow | Single File Web Page or Office button | Save As | Save as type: arrow | Web Page			
Worksheet Name, Change	EX 141	Double-click sheet tab, type new name		Rename	
Workbook Theme, Change	EX 109		Themes button on Page Layout tab		
Zoom	EX 220	Zoom box on status bar or Zoom In and Zoom Out buttons on status bar	Zoom button on View tab		ALT+V | Z

Table 3 Microsoft Office Access 2007 Quick Reference Summary

Task	Page Number	Mouse	Ribbon	Shortcut Menu	Keyboard Shortcut
Add New Field	AC 24	Right-click Add New Field in Datasheet	Insert Rows button on Design Tab	Design View | INSERT	
Add Record	AC 30, 38	New (blank) record button	New button on Home tab	Open | Click in field	CTRL+PLUS SIGN (+)
Calculate Statistics	AC 118		Totals button on Design tab		
Change Colors and Font	AC 180		Alternate Fill/Back Color button arrow or Font Color button arrow or Font box arrow on Home tab		
Change Database Properties	AC 60	Office button | Manage | Database Properties			
Change Gridlines	AC 179		Gridlines button on Home tab		
Change Primary Key	AC 28	Delete field | Primary Key button	Design View button on Design tab | select field | Primary Key button		
Clear Query	AC 98				Select all entries | DELETE
Close Object	AC 35	Close button for object		Right-click item | Close	
Create Calculated Field	AC 113			Zoom	SHIFT+F2
Create Crosstab Query	AC 123		Query Wizard button on Create tab | Crosstab Query Wizard		
Create Database	AC 14	Blank Database button or Office Button | Save			CTRL+S or SHIFT+F12 or ALT+I
Create Form	AC 142		Form button on Create tab		
Create Query	AC 78		Query Design button on Create tab		
Create Report	AC 51		Report Wizard button on Create tab		
Create Table	AC 23	Office Button | Save button	Table button on Create tab		CTRL+S or SHIFT+F12
Customize Navigation Pane	AC 126	Navigation Pane arrow | Object Type			
Delete Record	AC 148	Click Record Selector | DELETE	DELETE button		
Define Fields in a Table	AC 24		Right-click Add New Field on Datasheet tab | Rename Column	Right-click Add New Field | Rename Column	
Exclude Field from Query Results	AC 112	Show check box			
Export Query	AC 221		Select query | desired application button in Export group on External Data tab		

Table 3 Microsoft Office Access 2007 Quick Reference Summary (continued)

Task	Page Number	Mouse	Ribbon	Shortcut Menu	Keyboard Shortcut
Field Size	AC 46		Design View button on Design tab | select field | Field Size box		
Filter by Selection	AC 149		Selection button on Home tab | select criterion		
Format a Calculated Field	AC 116		Property Sheet button on Design tab		
Format a Field	AC 168	Select field | Format property box			
Group in Query	AC 121	Total row or include multiple fields in query			
Import Data	AC 212		Desired application in Import group on External Data tab		
Include All Fields in Query	AC 85	Double-click asterisk in field list	Query Design button on Create tab | Add All Fields button		
Include Field in Query	AC 85		Query Design button on Create tab | select field | Add Field button		
Join Tables	AC 105		Query Design button on Create tab | bring field lists for tables into upper pane		
Link Tables	AC 217		Access button on External Data tab | select database | OK button		
Lookup Field	AC 172	Data Type column for field | Lookup Wizard			
Move to First Record	AC 39	First Record button			
Move to Last Record	AC 39	Last Record button			
Move to Next Record	AC 39	Next Record button			
Move to Previous Record	AC 39	Previous Record button			
New Item	various	Office button | Open			
Omit Duplicates	AC 100	Open Property Sheet, set Unique Values to Yes	Property Sheet button on Design tab | Unique Values	Properties | Unique Values	
Open Database	AC 37	More button | Open button or Office button | double-click file name			CTRL+O
Open Table	AC 26	Open button		Open	
Preview Table	AC 41	Office button | Print | Print Preview			ALT+F, W, V
Print Object	AC 41, 56	Office button | Print | Quick Print or Print			CTRL+P
Quit Access	AC 36	Close button			

Table 3 Microsoft Office Access 2007 Quick Reference Summary *(continued)*

Task	Page Number	Mouse	Ribbon	Shortcut Menu	Keyboard Shortcut
Referential Integrity	AC 186		Relationships button on Database Tools tab		
Resize a Column	AC 175	In Datasheet view, double-click right boundary of the field selector		Right-click field name | Column Width	
Save Form	AC 58	Office button | Save			CTRL+S
Save Query	AC 91	Save button or Office button | Save			CTRL+S
Save Table	AC 27	Save button	Office button | Save	Save	CTRL+S
Search for Access Help	AC 62	Microsoft Office Access Help button			F1
Search for Record	AC 145		Find button on Home tab		CTRL+F
Select Fields for Report	AC 51		Report Wizard button on Create tab | Add Field button		
Simple Query Wizard	AC 78		Query Wizard button on Create tab		
Sort Data in Query	AC 98		Select field in Design grid | Ascending		
Sort on Multiple Keys	AC 101	Assign two sort keys			
Split Form	AC 57		Split Form button on Create tab		
Start Access	AC 12	Start button | All Programs | Microsoft Office | Microsoft Office Access 2007			
Switch Between Form and Datasheet Views	AC 57	Form View or Datasheet View button			
Update Query	AC 162		Update button on Design tab | select field, Update To row, enter new value	Query Type | Update Query	
Use Advanced Filter/Sort	AC 155		Advanced button on Home tab | Advanced/ Filter Sort		
Use AND Criterion	AC 95				Place criteria on same line
Use Criterion	AC 81	Right-click query | Design View | Criteria row			
Use OR Criterion	AC 96				Place criteria on separate lines

Table 4 Microsoft Office PowerPoint 2007 Quick Reference Summary

Task	Page Number	Mouse	Ribbon	Shortcut Menu	Keyboard Shortcut
Add Shapes	PPT 119		Shapes button on Home tab | select shape		
Add Transition	PPT 122		Transition effect on Animations tab or More button in Transition to This Slide group on Animations tab | select transition		ALT+A | T
Change Size, Clip Art, Photo, or Shape	PPT 101, 103, 117	Drag sizing handles	Dialog Box Launcher in Size group of Format tab | Size tab | enter height and width values or Size group of Format tab | enter height and width values		
Clip Art, Insert	PPT 96	Clip Art icon in slide	Clip Art button on Insert tab		
Demote a Paragraph	PPT 34	Increase List Level button on Mini toolbar	Increase List Level button on Home tab		TAB or ALT+SHIFT+ RIGHT ARROW
Display a Presentation in Grayscale	PPT 59		Grayscale button on View tab		ALT+V | C | U
Document Properties	PPT 44	Office Button | Prepare | Properties			
Document Theme, Choose	PPT 16		More button on Design tab | theme		
End Slide Show	PPT 54			End Show	ESC or HYPHEN
Font, Change	PPT 109	Font button or Font box arrow on Mini toolbar	Font button on Home tab or Font arrow on Home tab | select font or Font Dialog Box Launcher on Home tab | Latin text font arrow on Font tab	Font | Latin text font arrow on Font tab	CTRL+SHIFT+F | Font tab | Latin text font arrow
Font Color	PPT 23, 110	Font Color button or Font Color arrow on Mini toolbar	Font Color button on Home tab or Font Color arrow on Home tab | select color or Font Dialog Box Launcher on Home tab | Font color button on Font tab | select color	Font | Font color button on Font tab | select color	CTRL+SHIFT+F | Font tab | Font color button | select color
Font Size, Decrease	PPT 25	Decrease Font Size button or Font Size arrow on Mini toolbar	Decrease Font Size button on Home tab or Font Size arrow on Home tab | size	Font Size arrow | Size	CTRL+SHIFT+LEFT CARET (<)
Font Size, Increase	PPT 24	Increase Font Size button or Font Size arrow on Mini toolbar	Increase Font Size button on Home tab or Font Size arrow on Home tab | size	Font size arrow | Size	CTRL+SHIFT+RIGHT CARET (>)
Help	PPT 63 and Appendix A		Office PowerPoint Help button		F1

Table 4 Microsoft Office PowerPoint 2007 Quick Reference Summary *(continued)*

Task	Page Number	Mouse	Ribbon	Shortcut Menu	Keyboard Shortcut
Insert Photograph	PPT 98, 99	Insert Picture from File icon on slide	Picture button on Insert tab		
Move Clip Art or Photo	PPT 105	Drag			
Next Slide	PPT 47	Next Slide button on vertical scroll bar			PAGE DOWN
Normal View	PPT 91	Normal View button at lower-right PowerPoint window	Normal button on View tab		ALT+V | N
Open Presentation	PPT 54	Office Button | Open | select file			CTRL+O
Preview Presentation as Web Page	PPT 151	[Assumes Web Page Preview button has been added to Quick Access toolbar] Web Page Preview button			
Previous Slide	PPT 50, 51	Previous Slide button on vertical scroll bar			PAGE UP
Print a Presentation	PPT 61	Office Button | Print			CTRL+P
Print an Outline	PPT 122	Office Button | point to Print | Print Preview | Print What arrow | Outline View			
Promote a Paragraph	PPT 34	Decrease List Level button on Mini toolbar	Decrease List Level button on Home tab		SHIFT+TAB or ALT+SHIFT+ LEFT ARROW
Quick Access Toolbar, Add Buttons	PPT 148	Customize Quick Access Toolbar button | select from command options			
Quick Access Toolbar, Reset	PPT 154	Customize Quick Access Toolbar button | More Commands | Reset button			
Quit PowerPoint	PPT 53	Double-click Office Button or Close button on title bar or Office Button | Exit PowerPoint		Right-click Microsoft PowerPoint button on taskbar | Close	ALT+F4 or CTRL+Q
Save a Presentation	PPT 27	Save button on Quick Access toolbar or Office Button | Save			CTRL+S or SHIFT+F12
Save as Web Page	PPT 152	Office Button | Save As | add File name | change Save as type to Single File Web Page | Save button			ALT+F | G or F12
Slide, Add	PPT 29		New Slide button on Home tab or New Slide arrow on Home tab | choose slide type		CTRL+M
Slide, Arrange	PPT 41	Drag slide in Slides tab to new position or in Slide Sorter View drag slide to new position			

Table 4 Microsoft Office PowerPoint 2007 Quick Reference Summary *(continued)*

Task	Page Number	Mouse	Ribbon	Shortcut Menu	Keyboard Shortcut
Slide, Background	PPT 89		Background Styles button on Design tab | select style	Format Background	
Slide, Duplicate	PPT 40		New Slide arrow on Home tab | Duplicate Selected Slides		
Slide Layout	PPT 92, 94		Layout button on Home tab		
Slide Show View	PPT 49	Slide Show button at lower-right PowerPoint window	Slide Show button on View tab or From Beginning button on Slide Show tab		F5 or ALT+V | W
Slide Sorter View	PPT 91	Slide Sorter View button at lower-right in PowerPoint window	Slide Sorter button on View tab		ALT+V | D
Spelling Check	PPT 55		Spelling button on Review tab		F7
Text, Add Shadow	PPT 110		Text Shadow button on Home tab		
Text, Bold	PPT 25	Bold button on Mini toolbar	Bold button on Home tab		CTRL+B
Text, Change Color	PPT 23	Font Color button or Font Color arrow on Mini toolbar	Font color arrow on Home tab | choose color	Font | Font color button | choose color	
Text, Delete	PPT 42		Cut button on Home tab	Cut	DELETE or CTRL+X or BACKSPACE
Text, Formatting with Quick Styles	PPT 119		Quick Styles button on Home tab | select style		
Text, Italicize	PPT 22	Italic button on Mini toolbar	Italic button on Home tab	Font | Font style arrow | Italics	CTRL+I
Text, Select	PPT 21	Drag to select | double-click to select word | triple-click to select paragraph			SHIFT+DOWN ARROW or SHIFT+RIGHT ARROW
Use Format Painter	PPT 112	Format Painter button on Mini toolbar	Double-click Format Painter button on Home tab | select text with a format you want to copy | select other text to apply previously selected format | press ESC to turn off Format Painter		
Zoom for Printing	PPT 128	Drag Zoom slider on status bar or Office Button | point to Print | Print Preview |	Zoom button on View tab | select zoom		
Zoom for Viewing Slides	PPT 127	Drag Zoom slider on status bar	Zoom button on View tab | select zoom		

Table 5 Microsoft Office Outlook 2007 Quick Reference Summary

Task	Page Number	Mouse	Ribbon	Shortcut Menu	Keyboard Shortcut
Address E-Mail Message	OUT 27	Mail button in Inbox window	New Mail Message button on Message tab | To button		
Attach File to E-Mail Message	OUT 31	Attach File button on Standard toolbar in Message window	Attach File button on Insert tab		
Close an E-Mail Message	OUT 15	Click Close button on title bar in Message window			ALT+F, C
Compose E-Mail Message	OUT 27	New button on Standard toolbar	New | Mail Message*		CTRL+N
Create Contact List	OUT 47	New button on Standard toolbar	Actions | New Contact*	New Contact	CTRL+SHIFT+C
Create Distribution List	OUT 58	New Contact button on Standard toolbar	New Contact button | Distribution List*		CTRL+SHIFT+L
Create E-Mail Signature	OUT 24		Tools | Options | Mail Format tab | Signatures button*		ALT+T, O
Create Personal Folder	OUT 44	Contacts button in Navigation pane	File | New | Folder*	New Contacts | New Folder	CTRL+SHIFT+E
Create View Filter	OUT 36		View | Arrange By*	Custom	
Delete E-Mail Message	OUT 21	Delete button on Standard toolbar	Select message | Delete*		CTRL+D or DELETE
Display Contacts	OUT 52	Find a Contact box on Standard toolbar	Tools | Instant Search*		CTRL+E or ALT+T, I
Find a Contact	OUT 50	Find a Contact box on Standard toolbar	Tools | Instant Search | Advanced Find*		CTRL+SHIFT+F
Flag E-Mail Messages	OUT 34	Follow Up button on Standard toolbar	Actions | Follow Up*	Follow Up	ALT+A, U
Forward E-Mail Message	OUT 20	Forward button on Standard toolbar		Forward	CTRL+F
Open E-Mail Message	OUT 10	Double-click message	File | Open*	Open	CTRL+O
Print Contact List	OUT 53	Print button on Standard toolbar	File | Print* or File | Print Preview | Print*		CTRL+P
Print E-Mail Message	OUT 15	Print button on Standard toolbar	File | Print | OK button*		CTRL+P, ENTER
Reply to E-Mail Message	OUT 16	Reply button on Standard toolbar	Reply button on Message tab		CTRL+R
Save Contact List as Text File	OUT 60	Select name bar of contact | CTRL+A | File | Save As	File | Save As*		
Send E-Mail Message	OUT 31	Send button in Message window	Send button on Insert tab		
Set Message Importance, Sensitivity, and Delivery Options	OUT 38	New Mail Message button on Standard toolbar in Message window	Options dialog box launcher in the Options group on the Message tab		
Sort E-Mail Messages	OUT 35	Arrange By Command on View menu			ALT+V, A, E

indicates a task handled by the Outlook Standard menu instead of the Ribbon